First published 1998
by Routledge
11 New Fetter Lane, London EC4P 4EE
Simultaneously published in the USA and Canada
by Routledge
29 West 35th Street, New York, NY 10001

©1998 Routledge

Typeset in Monotype Times New Roman by
Routledge

Printed in England by
T J International Ltd, Padstow, Cornwall, England

Printed on acid-free paper which conforms to ANS1.Z39, 48-1992 and ISO 9706 standards

British Library Cataloguing-in-Publication Data
A catalogue record for this book is available from the British Library

The Library of Congress Cataloguing-in-Publication data is given in volume 10.

ISBN: 0415-07310-3 (10-volume set)
ISBN: 0415-18706-0 (volume 1)
ISBN: 0415-18707-9 (volume 2)
ISBN: 0415-18708-7 (volume 3)
ISBN: 0415-18709-5 (volume 4)
ISBN: 0415-18710-9 (volume 5)
ISBN: 0415-18711-7 (volume 6)
ISBN: 0415-18712-5 (volume 7)
ISBN: 0415-18713-3 (volume 8)
ISBN: 0415-18714-1 (volume 9)
ISBN: 0415-18715-X (volume 10)

ISBN: 0415-16916-X (CD-ROM)
ISBN: 0415-16917-8 (10-volume set and CD-ROM)

Routledge
Encyclopedia of
PHILOSOPHY

General Editor
EDWARD CRAIG

London and New York

Contents

Using the *Encyclopedia*
List of entries

Using the *Encyclopedia*

The *Routledge Encyclopedia of Philosophy* is designed for ease of use. The following notes outline its organization and editorial approach and explain the ways of locating material. This will help readers make the most of the *Encyclopedia*.

SEQUENCE OF ENTRIES

The *Encyclopedia* contains 2,054 entries (from 500 to 19,000 words in length) arranged in nine volumes with a tenth volume for the index. Volumes 1–9 are arranged in a single alphabetical sequence, as follows:

Volume 1: A posteriori *to* Bradwardine, Thomas

Volume 2: Brahman *to* Derrida, Jacques

Volume 3: Descartes, René *to* Gender and science

Volume 4: Genealogy *to* Iqbal, Muhammad

Volume 5: Irigaray, Luce *to* Lushi chunqiu

Volume 6: Luther, Martin *to* Nifo, Agostino

Volume 7: Nihilism *to* Quantum mechanics, interpretation of

Volume 8: Questions *to* Sociobiology

Volume 9: Sociology of knowledge *to* Zoroastrianism

Alphabetical order

Entries are listed in alphabetical order by word rather than by letter with all words including *and*, *in*, *of* and *the* being given equal status. The exceptions to this rule are as follows:

- biographies: where the forenames and surname of a philosopher are inverted, the entry takes priority in the sequence, for example:

Alexander, Samuel (1859–1938)
Alexander of Aphrodisias (*c.* AD 200)
Alexander of Hales (*c.* 1185–1245)

- names with prefixes, which follow conventional alphabetical placing (see Transliteration and naming conventions below).

A complete alphabetical list of entries is given in each of the Volumes 1 to 9.

Inverted titles

Titles of entries consisting of more than one word are often inverted so that the key term (in a thematic or signpost entry) or the surname (in a biographical entry) determines the place of the entry in the alphabetical sequence, for example:

Law, philosophy of *or*
Market, ethics of the *or*
Hart, Herbert Lionel Adolphus (1907–93)

Conceptual organization

Several concerns have had a bearing on the sequence of entries where there is more than one key term.

In deciding on the sequence of entries we have tried, wherever possible, to integrate philosophy as it is known and studied in the USA and Europe with philosophy from around the world. This means that the reader will frequently find entries from different philosophical traditions or approaches to the same topic close to each other, for example, in the sequence:

Political philosophy [signpost entry]
Political philosophy, history of
Political philosophy in classical Islam
Political philosophy, Indian

Similarly, in entries where a philosophical tradition or approach is surveyed we have tried, whenever appropriate, to keep philosophical traditions from different countries together. An example is the sequence:

Confucian philosophy, Chinese
Confucian philosophy, Japanese
Confucian philosophy, Korean
Confucius (551–479 BC)

Finally, historical entries are usually placed with contemporary entries under the topic rather than the historical period. For example, in the sequence:

Language, ancient philosophy of
Language and gender
Language, conventionality of
Language, early modern philosophy of
Language, Indian theories of
Language, innateness of

DUMMY TITLES

The *Encyclopedia* has been extensively cross-referenced in order to help the reader locate their topic of interest. Dummy titles are placed throughout the alphabetical sequence of entries to direct the reader to the actual title of the entry where a topic is discussed. This may be under a different entry title, a synonym or as part of a larger entry. Wherever useful we have included the numbers of the sections (§§) in which a particular topic or subject is discussed. Examples of this type of cross-reference are:

AFRICAN AESTHETICS *see*
AESTHETICS, AFRICAN

CANGUILHEM, GEORGES *see*
FRENCH PHILOSOPHY OF SCIENCE §§3–4

TAO *see* DAO

GLOSSARY OF LOGICAL AND MATHEMATICAL TERMS

A glossary of logical and mathematical terms is provided to help users with terms from formal logic and mathematics. 'See also' cross-references to the glossary are provided at the end of entries where the user might benefit from help with unfamiliar terms. The glossary can be found in Volume 5 under L (LOGICAL AND MATHEMATICAL TERMS, GLOSSARY OF).

THE INDEX VOLUME

Volume 10 is devoted to a comprehensive index of key terms, concepts and names covered in Volumes 1–9, allowing readers to reap maximum benefit from the *Encyclopedia*. A guide to the index can be found at the beginning of the index. The index volume includes a full listing of contributors, their affiliations and the entries they have written. It also includes permission acknowledgements, listed in publisher order.

STRUCTURE OF ENTRIES

The *Routledge Encyclopedia of Philosophy* contains three types of entry:

- 'signpost' entries, for example, METAPHYSICS; SCIENCE, PHILOSOPHY OF; EAST ASIAN PHILOSOPHY. These entries provide an accessible overview of the sub-disciplines or regional coverage within the *Encyclopedia*; they provide a 'map' which directs the reader towards and around the many entries relating to each topic;
- thematic entries, ranging from general entries such as KNOWLEDGE, CONCEPT OF, to specialized topics such as VIRTUE EPISTEMOLOGY;
- biographical entries, devoted to individual philosophers, emphasizing the work rather than the life of the subject and with a list of the subject's major works.

Overview

All thematic and biographical entries begin with an overview which provides a concise and accessible summary of the topic or subject. This can be referred to on its own if the reader does not require the depth and detail of the main part of the entry.

Table of contents

All thematic and biographical entries over 1000 words in length are divided into sections and have a numbered table of contents following the overview. This gives the headings of each of the sections of the entry, enabling the reader to see the scope and structure of the entry at a glance. For example, the table of contents in the entry on HERACLITUS:

1 Life and work
2 Methodology
3 Unity of opposites and perspectivism
4 Cosmology
5 Psychology, ethics and religion
6 Influence

Cross-references within an entry

Entries in the *Encyclopedia* have been extensively cross-referenced in order to indicate other entries that may be of interest to the reader. There are two types of cross-reference in the *Encyclopedia*:

1. 'See' cross-references

Cross-references within the text of an entry direct the reader to other entries on or closely related to the topic under discussion. For example, a reader may be directed from a conceptual entry to a biography of the philosopher whose work is under discussion or vice versa. These internal cross-references appear in small capital letters, either in parentheses, for example:

Opponents of naturalism before and since Wittgenstein have been animated by the notion that the aims of social science are not causal explanation and improving prediction, but uncovering rules that make social life intelligible to its participants (see EXPLANATION IN HISTORY AND SOCIAL SCIENCE).

or sometimes, when the reference is to a person who

has a biographical entry, as small capitals in the text itself, for example:

> Thomas NAGEL emphasizes the discrepancy between the objective insignificance of our lives and projects and the seriousness and energy we devote to them.

For entries over 1,000 words in length we have included the numbers of the sections (§) in which a topic is discussed, wherever useful, for example:

> In *Nicomachean Ethics*, Aristotle criticizes Plato's account for not telling us anything about particular kinds of goodness (see ARISTOTLE §§ 21–6).

2. 'See also' cross-references

At the end of the text of each entry, 'See also' cross-references guide the reader to other entries of related interest, such as more specialized entries, biographical entries, historical entries, geographical entries and so on. These cross-references appear in small capitals in alphabetical order.

References

References in the text are given in the Harvard style, for example, Kant (1788), Rawls (1971). Exceptions to this rule are made when presenting works with established conventions, for example, with some major works in ancient philosophy. Full bibliographical details are given in the 'List of works' and 'References and further reading'.

Bibliography

List of works

Biographical entries are followed by a list of works which gives full bibliographical details of the major works of the philosopher. This is in chronological order and includes items cited in the text, significant editions, dates of composition for pre-modern works (where known), preferred English-language translations and English translations for the titles of untranslated foreign-language works.

References and further reading

Both biographical and thematic entries have a list of references and further reading. Items are listed alphabetically by author's name. (Publications with joint authors are listed under the name of the first author and after any individual publications by that author). References cited in the text are preceded by an asterisk (*). Further reading which the reader may find particularly useful is also included.

The authors and editors have attempted to provide the fullest possible bibliographical information for every item.

Annotations

Publications in the 'List of works' and the 'References and further reading' have been annotated with a brief description of the content so that their relevance to readers' interests can be quickly assessed.

EDITORIAL STYLE

Spelling and punctuation in the *Encyclopedia* have been standardized to follow British English usage.

Transliteration and naming conventions

All names and terms from non-roman alphabets have been romanized in the *Encyclopedia*. Foreign names have been given according to the conventions within the particular language.

Arabic

Arabic has been transliterated in a simplified form, that is, without macrons or subscripts. Names of philosophers are given in their Arabic form rather than their Latinate form, for example, IBN RUSHD rather than AVERROES. Arabic names beginning with the prefix 'al-' are alphabetized under the substantive part of the name and not the prefix, for example:

> KILWARDBY, ROBERT (d. 1279)
> AL-KINDI, ABU YUSUF YAQUB IBN ISHAQ (d. *c*.866–73)
> KNOWLEDGE AND JUSTIFICATION, COHERENCE THEORY OF

Arabic names beginning with the prefix 'Ibn' are alphabetized under 'I'.

Chinese, Korean and Japanese

Chinese has been transliterated using the Pinyin system. Dummy titles in the older Wade–Giles system are given for names and key terms; these direct the reader to the Pinyin titles.

Japanese has been transliterated using a modified version of the Hepburn system.

Chinese, Japanese and Korean names are given in Asian form, that is, surname preceding forenames, for example:

> WANG FUZHI
> NISHITANI KEIJI

The exception is where an author has chosen to present their own name in conventional Western form.

Hebrew

Hebrew has been transliterated in a simplified form, that is, without macrons or subscripts.

Russian

Cyrillic characters have been transliterated using the Library of Congress system. Russian names are usually given with their patronymic, for example, BAKUNIN, MIKHAIL ALEKSANDROVICH.

Sanskrit

A guide to the pronunciation of Sanskrit can be found in the INDIAN AND TIBETAN PHILOSOPHY signpost entry.

Tibetan

Tibetan has been transliterated using the Wylie system. Dummy titles in the Virginia system are given for names and key terms. A guide to Tibetan pronunciation can be found in the INDIAN AND TIBETAN PHILOSOPHY signpost entry.

European names

Names beginning with the prefixes 'de', 'von' or 'van' are usually alphabetized under the substantive part of the name. For example:

BEAUVOIR, SIMONE DE
HUMBOLDT, WILHELM VON

The exception to this rule is when the person is either a national of or has spent some time living or working in an English-speaking country. For example:

DE MORGAN, AUGUSTUS
VON WRIGHT, GEORG HENRIK

Names beginning with the prefix 'de la' or 'le' are alphabetized under the prefix 'la' or 'le'. For example:

LA FORGE, LOUIS DE
LE DOEUFF, MICHÈLE

Names beginning with 'Mc' or 'Mac' are treated as 'Mac' and appear before Ma.

Historical names

Medieval and Renaissance names where a person is not usually known by a surname are alphabetized under the forename, for example:

GILES OF ROME
JOHN OF SALISBURY

List of entries

Below is a complete list of entries in the order in which they appear in the *Routledge Encyclopedia of Philosophy.*

Artistic style
Artistic taste
Artist's intention
Arya Samaj
Asceticism
Ash'ariyya and Mu'tazila
Asmus, Valentin Ferdinandovich
Astell, Mary
Atheism
Atomism, ancient
Atonement
Augustine
Augustinianism
Aureol, Peter
Aurobindo Ghose
Austin, John
Austin, John Langshaw
Australia, philosophy in
Authority
Autonomy, ethical
Avenarius, Richard
Averroism
Averroism, Jewish
Awakening of Faith in Mahāyāna
Awareness in Indian thought
Axiology
Axiom of choice
Ayer, Alfred Jules
Bachelard, Gaston
Bacon, Francis
Bacon, Roger
al-Baghdadi, Abu'l-Barakat
Bakhtin, Mikhail Mikhailovich
Bakunin, Mikhail Aleksandrovich
Báñez, Domingo
Bar Hayya, Abraham
Barth, Karl
Barthes, Roland
Bartolus of Sassoferrato (or Saxoferrato)
Bataille, Georges
Baudrillard, Jean
Bauer, Bruno
Baumgardt, David
Baumgarten, Alexander Gottlieb
Bayle, Pierre
Beattie, James
Beauty
Beauvoir, Simone de
Beck, Jacob Sigismund
Behaviourism, analytic
Behaviourism in the social sciences
Behaviourism, methodological and scientific
Being

Belief
Belief and knowledge
Belinskii, Vissarion Grigorievich
Bell's theorem
Benjamin, Walter
Bentham, Jeremy
Bentley, Richard
Berdiaev, Nikolai Aleksandrovich
Bergson, Henri-Louis
Berkeley, George
Berlin, Isaiah
Bernard of Clairvaux
Bernard of Tours
Bernier, François
Bernstein, Eduard
Beth's theorem and Craig's theorem
Bhartṛhari
Bible, Hebrew
Biel, Gabriel
Bioethics
Bioethics, Jewish
Blackstone, William
Blair, Hugh
Blanchot, Maurice
Blasius of Parma
Bloch, Ernst Simon
Bobbio, Norberto
Bodily sensations
Bodin, Jean
Boehme, Jakob
Boethius, Anicius Manlius Severinus
Boethius of Dacia
Bogdanov, Aleksandr Aleksandrovich
Bohr, Niels
Bold, Samuel
Bolzano, Bernard
Bonaventure
Bonhoeffer, Dietrich
Bonnet, Charles
Boole, George
Boolean algebra
Bosanquet, Bernard
Bourdieu, Pierre
Boutroux, Emile
Bowne, Borden Parker
Boyle, Robert
Bradley, Francis Herbert
Bradwardine, Thomas
Brahman
Brahmo Samaj
Brazil, philosophy in
Brentano, Franz Clemens
Bridgman, Percy William
Brinkley, Richard

Brito, Radulphus
Broad, Charlie Dunbar
Brown, Thomas
Browne, Peter
Brunner, Emil
Bruno, Giordano
Brunschvicg, Léon
Bryce, James
Buber, Martin
Büchner, Friedrich Karl Christian Ludwig (Louis)
Buddha
Buddhism, Ābhidharmika schools of
Buddhism, Mādhyamika: India and Tibet
Buddhism, Yogācāra school of
Buddhist concept of emptiness
Buddhist philosophy, Chinese
Buddhist philosophy, Indian
Buddhist philosophy, Japanese
Buddhist philosophy, Korean
Buffier, Claude
Buffon, Georges Louis Leclerc, Comte de
Bulgakov, Sergei Nikolaevich
Bultmann, Rudolf
Buridan, John
Burke, Edmund
Burley, Walter
Burthogge, Richard
Bushi philosophy
Business ethics
Butler, Joseph
Byzantine philosophy
Cabanis, Pierre-Jean
Cabral, Amílcar
Cajetan (Thomas de Vio)
Calcidius
Callicles
Calvin, John
Cambridge Platonism
Campanella, Tommaso
Campbell, George
Campbell, Norman Robert
Camus, Albert
Cantor, Georg
Cantor's theorem
Capreolus, Johannes
Cardano, Girolamo
Carlyle, Thomas
Carmichael, Gershom
Carnap, Rudolf
Carneades
Carolingian renaissance
Cassirer, Ernst

An alphabetical list of contributors, their affiliations and the entries they have written can be found in the index volume (Volume 10).

BRAHMAN

The Sanskrit word brahman *(neuter) emerged in late Vedic literature and Upaniṣads (900–300 BC) as the name (never pluralized) of the divine reality pervading the universe, knowledge or experience of which is a person's supreme good. The word's earliest usage (often pluralized) is to refer to the verses of the oldest work in Sanskrit (and in any Indo-European language), the* Ṛg Veda *(c.1200 BC), which is a compilation of poems and hymns to Indo-European gods. The individual verses of the poems are mantras (*brahmāṇi*), whose proper enunciation in the course of ritual and sacrifice was thought to secure various aims. Thematically, the* Ṛg Veda *and other early Indian literature presents a sense of pervasive divinity. Apparently through an assimilation of the idea of the magic of mantras to the divine immanence theme the word* brahman *assumed its later meaning. In any case, Brahman – the Absolute, the supremely real – became the focus of Indian spirituality and the centre of much metaphysics for almost three thousand years, down to the present day. In the Upaniṣads, which are mystic treatises containing speculation about Brahman's nature and relation to ourselves and the world, the central positions of Vedānta schools emerge, all of which are philosophies of Brahman. But not even in the narrow set of the earliest and most universally accepted Upaniṣads (numbering twelve or thirteen) is there expressed a consistent worldview. Important themes about Brahman may be identified, but there is no overall unity of conception, despite what later exegetes claim. The unity of the early Upaniṣads concerns the premier importance of mystical knowledge or awareness of Brahman (*brahma-vidyā*), not precisely what it is that is to be mystically known. The classical Indian philosophical schools of Vedānta systematized the thought of early Upaniṣads.*

1 The Vedas and Vedic literature
2 Upaniṣads
3 Advaita Vedānta
4 Post-Upaniṣadic Indian theism

1 The Vedas and Vedic literature

The poems of the *Ṛg Veda*, most but not all of which address gods of an Indo-European pantheon, were transmitted until modern times through the care of a priestly caste. A Vedic (later, Hindu) priest is known as a *brāhmaṇa* or even a *brahmán* (masculine, as opposed to *bráhman*, neuter). The apparent etymological connection between the word for the Absolute and that for the caste has provoked no little consternation and speculation in a sociological vein among modern scholars. The solution to the mystery appears to lie in the shamanic role of the poet-cum-priest in early Indo-European society. According to Vedic scholars, the poems of the *Ṛg Veda* seem the results of competitions in eloquence among seers (*kavis*) or shamans over generations, each poem conceived as inspired by a shaman's sense of 'occult correspondences between the sacred and profane' (Renou 1953: 10). As Vedic society became more settled in its practices, rituals and sacrifices became fixed, with shamans assuming the offices of priests and keepers (that is, memorizers) of the sacred hymns. Original composition ceased, and the *Ṛg* and three other Vedas assumed their canonical forms. Individual verses of the poems, referred to in the Vedas themselves as *bráhman* (neuter), became central to ritual performances, and the importance of the overall content – stories of the gods, identifications of correspondences among spheres of life, and so on – waned. The verses, known as 'mantras', were considered invested with magical power.

Vedic themes were not forgotten, however. Throughout the *Ṛg Veda*, a sense of pervasive divinity is expressed. Gods correspond to, or inhere in, natural forces, and there is a divine structure and rhythm to the universe as a whole. Moreover, although the gods hymned are plural, each when addressed is said to be supreme. At places, a kind of monotheism is evident: 'They have styled Him Indra [the Chief of the gods], Mitra [the Friend], Varuṇa [the Venerable], Agni [Fire], also the celestial, great-winged Garutmā; for although one, poets speak of Him diversely; they say Agni, Yama [Death]), and Mātariśvan [Lord of breath]' (*Ṛg Veda* 1.164.46). This verse has been interpreted as an early expression of Indian henotheism: one God, that is, Brahman, takes various divine forms, and is worshipped in various forms by people according to personal proclivities. Thematically, the Vedas express a multifarious divinity and unitive spirituality important to most subsequent Indian religion.

In later Vedic literature – prose appendages called *brāhmaṇa* and *āraṇyaka* – the supreme force moving the gods and operative throughout the universe is designated for the first time *brahman* (neuter). The term conveys a sense of mystery, and distinct proposals are made about just what Brahman is (for example, wind, breath, the sun). Brahman is said to be *svayam-bhū*, 'self-existent', and is identified with Prajāpati, 'Father of Creatures'. The *Śatapatha Brāhmaṇa* (*c.*900 BC) declares at 10.2.3: 'In the beginning this universe was just Brahman; Brahman created these gods.'

2 Upaniṣads

Early Upaniṣads (from 800 to 300 BC) represent a break with the ritualism of later Vedic literature, and speculation about Brahman becomes decidedly more pronounced. Debates on metaphysical topics called *brahmôdya*, 'discourses on Brahman', held in the courts of kings and princes, are recorded. (A *brahmôdya* was apparently only a riddle contest in the earlier period.) In particular, the reasonings of the 'Brahman-knower' Yājñavalkya against various opponents in the court of King Janaka, as reported in the Bṛhadāraṇyaka Upaniṣad (*c.*800 BC), may be taken to usher in a new era of Indian thought, marked by abstraction and self-conscious argument.

However, the early Upaniṣads present at best variations on central views. No single coherent worldview is expressed, but rather arguments and proposals centred on Brahman and Brahman's relation to ourselves and the universe. Despite what later exegetes claim, there is no unity of theory. Later proponents of Upaniṣadic philosophies (called Vedāntins) look for an overall unity because they view the Upaniṣads as revealed texts.

Many Upaniṣadic passages are exploratory, playfully spinning stories with rather abstruse morals, or etymologies, usually false, of words with psychological meanings. Brahman is usually approached psychologically; the early Upaniṣads are predominantly mystical texts. The self as known in meditation is the medium for knowing the Absolute, the self's mysterious ground, which turns out to be the ground of the entire universe. As though announcing a discovery, some Upaniṣads proclaim the identity of the self and Brahman. Several rich psychological conceptions are worked out and asserted with a tone of confidence that contrasts with the tentativeness of statements about Brahman.

Nevertheless, there are at least ten themes about Brahman that reverberate throughout both early Upaniṣads themselves and later Vedāntic philosophy: (1) Brahman is self (*ātman*) and consciousness; (2) Brahman is world ground; (3) Brahman is transcendent of 'names and forms' (*nāma-rūpa*), that is, transcendent of finite individuality; (4) Brahman is unitary, the coincidence of opposites, and omnipresent; (5) Brahman has 'nondual' (*advaita*) self-awareness; (6) Brahman is the essence or finest part of everything; (7) Brahman is the locus of value, with awareness of Brahman as the 'supreme personal good' (*parama-puruṣārtha*) and 'liberation' (*mukti*) from fear and evil; (8) Brahman is mystically discoverable; (9) Brahman is beyond the power of thought; (10) Brahman is the creator and inner controller of all things.

It would be difficult, if not strictly impossible, to read the Upaniṣads uninfluenced by the centuries of later commentary and interpretation. The great debate among classical Vedāntins concerns the question of the theism of early Upaniṣads, or, more broadly, how Brahman relates to the world. The theistic interpretation – of Brahman as God creating a world of real particulars – is eschewed by the Advaita (Non-Dualist) school. Theistic Vedāntins cite Upaniṣadic passages stating that Brahman determines individual names and forms, *nāma-rūpa*. In their view, Brahman is a primordial Will and Controller – that is, 'God', *īśvara*. The dispute is irresolvable in the Upaniṣads themselves. Theme (10) is as pronounced as any, textually speaking. But Advaitin exegetes find a way of subordinating it to other themes. Conversely, Vedāntic theists interpret Upaniṣadic monism as underscoring their understanding of creation as emanation. Brahman as God looses forth (or manifests, *sṛjate*) the world out of God's own substance, as a spider's web is spun out of its own body.

The Advaita interpretation emphasizes themes (4) and (5), the unity and self-awareness of Brahman. At Bṛhadāraṇyaka 4.1.7, Yājñavalkya says, 'With only an awareness of *ātman*, self, should one meditate, for here [in the self] all these things become one.' The prominence of monism here – a spiritual monism in accordance with the idea (theme (1)) that Brahman is self or consciousness – provides grounds for interpreting individuality ('names and forms') as *mere* names and forms, as Advaita would do. The logic of the reasoning is not complex: if there is just one thing, how can there be many?

Moreover, in other Upaniṣadic passages, Brahman is explained through an analogy with dreaming, an analogy that fuels an Advaita assimilation of the theistic doctrine of creation to the idea of the One. Bṛhadāraṇyaka 4.3.9–10: '[Sleeping,] one takes along the stuff of this all-embracing universe [and] tears it apart himself [and] shapes it himself. . . . He is the all-maker, for he is the maker of everything.' Advaitins understand the 'He' as Brahman identical with *ātman*, who enjoys various states of himself – specifically, waking, dreaming and a state transcending both where the soul is 'aware only of its own light' (see also the Māṇḍūkya Upaniṣad). In the dream state, emanationism seems valid, and waking, says the Upaniṣad, is like dreaming. But states involving awareness of objects other than the self are expressly declared to be less valuable than self-illumination. Thus a subordination of theist emanationist cosmology to an illusionism about diversity seems to be called for, too: this is the Advaita reading.

Vedāntic theists, for their part, propose a stratified view of reality, of Brahman, ranging from an essential Divine to material things. Passages such as Taittirīya Upaniṣad 2.1–, with its theory of five sheaths progressively manifesting an essential soul, and Chāndogya Upaniṣad 6.8.7–, with its proclamations that Brahman is an indwelling essence (theme (6)) can be read as supporting the stratified reading: there is an essential Brahman, both transcendent and dwelling in the heart of everything, who progressively manifests in this world. Physical things may be furthest from what God is in God's own nature, but, as Taittirīya 3.1.2 says, 'matter [too] is Brahman'. Perhaps the most significant theistic passage comes from the Bṛhadāraṇyaka (3.7.1–23): 'He who, dwelling in the earth, is other than the earth, whom the earth does not know, whose body the earth is, who controls the earth from within – is the Self, the Inner Controller, the Immortal' (this last refrain – verse 3 – is then repeated with substitutions). Finally, the Sanskrit word for God, īśvara and cognates (such as īś), appear in early Upaniṣads dozens of times as apparent synonyms of brahman.

3 Advaita Vedānta

The classical Indian philosophical schools of Vedānta systematized the thought of early Upaniṣads. These schools divide broadly into the psychological monism of Advaita Vedānta and theistic views of Brahman championed by non-Advaitins. According to Advaita, the central Upaniṣadic teaching is that Brahman is the self. The world, and God, are illusions of false consciousness. According to Indian theism, in contrast, Brahman is God, the real creator of a real universe. Despite this opposition, concessions regarding Brahman can be discerned in each camp.

Developments in thought about Brahman continue long past the early Upaniṣads to such modern philosophers as AUROBINDO GHOSE and Sarvepalli RADHAKRISHNAN. Most contributions occur under the banner of the Advaita Vedānta school or a confederation of Indian theists. There is also speculation about Brahman as Speech (śabda-brahman) in the writings of BHARTṚHARI. Both Advaita and Indian theism are intellectually long and complex movements, and we shall confine ourselves exclusively to the the most significant developments in the thought about Brahman.

Advaitins devote special attention to Brahman's nature and how it is possible for us to conceive of that nature on the one hand, and to the relation, or nonrelation, of Brahman to the world on the other. In the first case, the concern is principally to shore up a sense of the value of liberation. In the second, it is to defend a view of Brahman as an absolute unity admitting no differentiation whatsoever.

Advaitin thought about Brahman's nature appears to be soteriologically motivated; that is to say, a view of experience or realization of oneself as Brahman, considered the supreme goal of life, dictates the direction of its elaborations. Classical Advaita also asserts that nothing positive can be predicated of Brahman (themes (3) and (9)), since positive characterization is confined to differentiating finite things. But inasmuch as this view stands in tension with elaborations of Brahman's nature, it is usually conveniently ignored or muted through speculation, not very successful, about the power of metaphor and indirect indication (upalakṣaṇa). The soteriological need is overriding.

A stock characterization of Brahman as saccidānanda emerges at the centre of this project: Brahman as existent or existence (sat), as awareness (cit) and as bliss (ānanda: the compound saccidānanda is formed by euphonic combination). Brahman is in fact said to be the sole existent, the single reality; the sole consciousness, a single self of everyone; and a supreme bliss. Who would not want to realize this?

There is controversy in particular concerning how Brahman is bliss. Some insist that this is said only to indicate that Brahman is not subject to the hedonic content of our normal experience; others that this underscores the supreme value of personal realization of Brahman. In either case, a soteriological context is key. The spirit of the elaboration is not to spell out how Brahman underpins our everyday experience, how Brahman as existent underlies the existence of everything, how Brahman as conscious sustains consciousness, and the like. Advaitins when confronted with such interpretation typically retreat to their stance about metaphor and indirect indication, though some do say that the bliss of Brahman is (distantly) reflected in our finest moments of worldly pleasure and happiness.

Exegetically, conflict with theistic Vedāntins seems to have inspired the notion of nirguṇa brahman contrasting with saguṇa brahman, Brahman as 'without' and 'with qualities', though the distinction also dovetails with the Advaita type of negative theology. Brahman-without-qualities is supremely real; Brahman-with-qualities is talked about in scripture as a concession to obtuse minds. Scripture is like a patient teacher (guru), and it is difficult to appreciate that Brahman as supremely real has no qualities. Scripture talks about God – Brahman-with-qualities – as a preparation for the austere truth.

Advaitins face obvious difficulties in upholding the view that Brahman is an absolute unity admitting no differentiation. Since Brahman is the only reality, diversity has to be illusory. But how can what is illusory even appear? And how did our spiritual ignorance – or awareness of diversity (and not of Brahman) – originate? How could it possibly originate, given that Brahman, as understood by Advaita, is the sole reality? Much reflection is devoted throughout the long history of Advaita to everyday perceptual illusion, since this is the analogy used for Brahman's relation, or nonrelation, to the world. One Advaita camp also maintains that the world of appearance has structure, that it can be studied and explained in its own terms, though not in relation to Brahman, which is a reality of an entirely different order. Another, dialectical, camp eschews such a two-tiered view, arguing that the reality of Brahman means that no sense can be made of the appearance of diversity, even in its own terms. This camp presents a barrage of arguments against all known pluralist ontologies, particularly that of Nyāya-Vaiśeṣika.

4   Post-Upaniṣadic Indian theism

The understanding of Brahman as God – the Creator and Sustainer of the universe as both its stuff and a will that fundamentally shapes things – is developed in devotional texts of popular religion, such as the *Bhagavad Gītā* (Song of God, *c.*200 BC), as well as in polemical treatises by theistic philosophers. The philosophers are much occupied with explaining precisely how the individual soul is distinct from Brahman, and the sense, if any, in which the two may be said to be identical. RĀMĀNUJA (eleventh century) works an analogy between a substance as quality-bearer and the qualities it bears: God bears souls as accidental qualities, and is the necessary support of their appearance. Other theists use other metaphors; that of the ocean (God) and waves (souls) is common. The question is shaped by the controversy with Advaita and the Advaita insistence that the soul and Brahman are one.

Theistic philosophers also tend to stress God's love for the soul, teaching, in accord with the *Bhagavad Gītā*, that the best way to mystical knowledge of Brahman is not meditation or asceticism (associated with Advaita, Yoga and Buddhism), but rather a corresponding *bhakti*, or love of God. The whole world is God's play (*līlā*), say theistic Vedāntins; and through love of God, and worship and devotion, we are eventually to realize this and find in every experience the embrace of the Divine (see MADHVA). Indian theists from the classical age into the modern conceive of a supreme personal good as a spiritual act of love-making.

The *Bhagavad Gītā* uses a Vedic motif, developed by later theists, to explain the process of emanation:

sacrifice. Brahman sacrifices its infinity in becoming finite, and thereby creates the world. Several theists trace a process of contraction through gods and goddesses and earthly incarnations (*avatāra*) of God, through humans and animals and down to rocks and dust. Through sacrifice, Brahman emanates the world as its body. The *Bhagavad Gītā* teaches that through a reverse sacrifice of offering of the finite, a soul finds Brahman transcendent, the supreme good.

See also: COSMOLOGY AND COSMOGONY, INDIAN THEORIES OF §1; GOD, INDIAN CONCEPTIONS OF; MONISM, INDIAN; PANTHEISM §§1–3; ŚAṄKARA; SELF, INDIAN THEORIES OF §§1–2, 7; VEDĀNTA

References and further reading

* *Bhagavad Gītā* (200 BC–AD 200, disputed), trans. F. Edgerton, Harvard Oriental Series 38–9, Cambridge, MA: Harvard University Press, 1944, paperback repr. 1972. (Though Edgerton's interpretive essay – orginally volume 39 in the HOS – too much reflects outworn assumptions of nineteenth-century indologists, his translation is excellent, faithful and elegant. There are, however, dozens of acceptable translations into English and other modern languages.)

Dasgupta, S. (1922–55) *A History of Indian Philosophy*, Cambridge: Cambridge University Press, 5 vols. (The latter volumes trace the history of Indian theism; volume 1 presents the core of Advaita as well as views of the early Upaniṣads and the Vedas; volume 2 presents Advaita in greater detail and much of its history.)

Phillips, S.H. (1995) *Classical Indian Metaphysics: Refutations of Realism and the Emergence of 'New Logic'*, La Salle, IL: Open Court. (Contains a section on the early Upaniṣads that is the model for the discussion of Upaniṣadic views of Brahman here.)

Potter, K.H. (ed.) (1981) *Encyclopedia of Indian Philosophies*, vol. 3, *Advaita Vedānta*, Princeton, NJ: Princeton University Press. (Contains an excellent introduction to Advaita philosophy, as well as summaries of works in the early Advaita school.)

* Renou, L. (1953) *Religions of Ancient India*, New York: Schocken. (A study of Vedic religion and society written by the great Vedic scholar for nonspecialists.)

* Ṛg Veda (*c.*1200 BC), trans. K.F. Geldner, *Der Rig-Veda*, Harvard Oriental Series 33–6, Cambridge, MA: Harvard University Press, 1951. (A translation commonly cited by scholars.)

Thieme, P. (1952) 'Brahman', *Zeitschrift der*

Deutschen Morgenländischen Gesellschaft 102: 91–129. (A watershed study of the semantic development of the word *brahman*, a topic with which much late nineteenth- and early twentieth-century scholarship was preoccupied.)

* Upaniṣads (800–300 BC), trans. P. Olivelle, *Upaniṣads*, Oxford: Oxford University Press, 1996. (A new translation that may well be the best; readable and accurate. The translations in the present entry are by Stephen Phillips.)

Warrier, A.G.K. (1977) *God in Advaita*, Simla: Indian Institute of Advanced Study. (Shows that Śaṅkara, the great Advaitin, takes seriously the Upaniṣadic teaching of *saguṇa brahman* – that is, God.)

STEPHEN H. PHILLIPS

BRAHMO SAMAJ

The Brahmo (or Brahma) Samaj ('Society of Brahma') is the name of a theistic society founded by Raja Rammohun Roy in Calcutta in 1828. It advocated reform, and eventually abolition, of the traditional caste system, as well as legislation aimed at improving the social status of women and greater protection of children. Also dedicated to Hindu religious reform, the Brahmo Samaj stressed a monotheistic doctrine with a policy of tolerance and respect for all major religions of the world. The society split into two factions in 1866, largely over the issue of the speed of reform. Another split occurred in 1878 over whether the society's constitution was to be fully democratic. The democratic wing, called the Sadhāraṇ Brahmo Samaj ('Universal Brahma Society'), is still active in India.

1　**Rammohun Roy**
2　**Debendranath Tagore and Keshub Chunder Sen**

1　Rammohun Roy

The early history of the Brahmo (or Brahma) Samaj is closely tied to the life of its founder, Rammohun Roy. Born in the village of Radhanagar in the Hoogly district of Bengal on May 22, 1772 into an orthodox Brahmanical family, Rammohun Roy (Rāmamohan Raya) worked for the East India Company from 1803 to 1814. He received in his boyhood the traditional education of the country and soon attained remarkable proficiency in Arabic, Persian and Sanskrit. Later in life he learned Greek, Latin and Hebrew. The study of Islamic theology shook his faith in the popular polytheistic and idolatrous forms of Hindu worship, and made him a lifelong admirer of the uncompromising monotheism of Islam. His subsequent acquaintance with the Upaniṣads, the *Brahmasūtra* and the *Bhagavad Gītā* convinced him that the concept of the unity of the Godhead constitutes the essence of Hinduism. He also came to have profound respect for the moral precepts of Jesus Christ.

Like many of his contemporaries, Rammohun Roy saw Indian society in the nineteenth century as caught in a vicious web created by religious superstition and social obscurantism. Hinduism, as Max Weber observed in his celebrated sociological study of Indian religion (1916), had become a compound of magic, animism and superstition. One of the features of society that Roy found most distressing was the socially inferior position of women. The birth of a girl was usually unwelcome; her marriage became a financial burden for her parents, who customarily had to pay the husband's family a dowry; and, if her husband died before her, her widowhood was seen as inauspicious. Because of these attitudes, attempts to kill girl infants at birth were not unusual. At the other end of life, it was also not unusual for widows to burn themselves alive on the funeral pyres of their deceased husbands, a practice known as *satī*, which literally means 'good woman'. Roy described this as 'murder according to every religious text'.

Another debilitating factor in Hindu society was the system of hereditary caste, which sought to maintain hierarchical social segregation on the basis of ritual status. Rammohun Roy came to be convinced that the rules and regulations of caste hampered social mobility, fostered social divisions and sapped individual initiative. Above all other injustices of the caste system was the humiliation of untouchability, which militated against human dignity. There were innumerable other practices in the Hindu society of his day that Roy saw as marked by arbitrary constraints, credulity, uncritical acceptance of authority, bigotry and blind fatalism. Rejecting them as features of a decadent society, Roy's Brahmo Samaj ('Society of Brahma'), established in Calcutta in 1828, sought to create a social climate for modernization.

Rammohun Roy was fully alive to the challenge that had come to India in the form of Western civilization and felt strongly the need for a new philosophy which would, without sacrificing the genuine spiritual heritage of India, absorb and assimilate the modernism imported from the West. He warmly advocated the introduction of Western science and technology in the educational curriculum and became a pioneer of English education and socially progressive journalism in India.

Rammohun Roy and his Brahmo Samaj advocated the emancipation of women. They opposed polygamy, indentured servitude and the custom of *satī*. It was due to Roy's efforts that William Bentinck, then Governor General of India, passed the famous regulation number XVII declaring *satī* a criminal offence. The Brahmo Samaj also opposed child marriage and the rigidity of the caste system, and it supported the remarriage of widows, equal rights for men and women, and the right of daughters to inherit property.

The creed of the Brahmo Samaj was declared to be universal monotheism. Its worship could be joined by anyone irrespective of their religious affiliations. Hence, according to Brahmo Samaj doctrine, there is no divine incarnation and no priestly mediation. Nature, earth and heaven were all said to have been created by a single God. Since there was no need for the mediation of priests, there was to be no hereditary priestly class and no performance of sacrifices. The Brahmo Samaj laid an emphasis on universal love for all human beings, irrespective of race or creed. Despite the universalistic features of the Brahmo Samaj, Roy gave a decidedly Hindu character to the form of worship within it. Worship at this early stage consisted of readings from the Vedas and the Upaniṣads, a sermon and devotional music.

2 Debendranath Tagore and Keshub Chunder Sen

Next to give organizational machinery to the Brahmo Samaj was Debendranath Tagore (Devendranatha Thakura, 1817–1905). He established the Tattvabodhini Sabha in 1839 with the objective of propagating Brahmo *dharma*. Until 1866 he remained the accredited leader of the Calcutta Brahmo Samaj and carried forward the best tradition of the days of Rammohun Roy. A doctrinal change that occurred in Brahmoism during this time was the abandonment of the belief in the infallibility of Hindu scriptures. Tagore laid more pronounced emphasis on *bhakti*, or devotion, in his exposition of religious texts. Under his inspiring leadership the Brahmo Samaj played a distinguished role in sponsoring social reforms such as the remarriage of widows, spreading education and vigorously opposing the efforts of Christian missionaries to gain converts from the ranks of Hindus.

The next phase of the Brahmo movement is dominated by Keshub Chunder Sen (Keśavacandra Sena, 1838–84), who joined the Samaj in 1857 and became Tagore's right-hand man. Having imbibed more of Western culture and Christian influence, Sen advocated a much more aggressive programme than Tagore, the latter favouring a slow and cautious approach to social reform. The two radically different temperaments led to a parting of the ways and paved the way for the first schism in the society. In 1866 Sen established the Brahmo Samaj of India (Akhila-Bhārata Brahma-samāja, 'Pan-Indian Brahma Society'), after withdrawing along with his supporters from the parent body, which henceforth came to be known as Ādi Brahmo Samaj ('The Original Brahmo Samaj').

Sen's Brahmo Samaj of India adopted a much more radical and comprehensive scheme of social reform than before, including programmes for female education and emancipation, and the complete abolition of caste distinction. Its activities led to the formation of the Indian Reform Association in 1870 and the enactment of the Native Marriage Act of 1872, which fixed the marriageable age of girls and boys at 14 and 18 respectively.

Probably owing to Christian influence, the doctrine of the Brahmo Samaj of India placed much more emphasis on the sense of sin, the spirit of repentance and the efficacy of prayer. The scriptures of Hinduism, Islam, Christianity and Buddhism were studied with great respect. An infusion of devotional fervour into Brahmoism made it a practical religious culture. Sen had a sympathetic and respectful attitude towards all religions and proclaimed a comprehensive synthesis of religions under the title of the Nava Vidhāna ('New Dispensation') in 1880. The New Dispensation called for faith in a living God, and explained that the several religions of the world are but varying interpretations of this one God. Though diverse and fragmentary, the religions of the world were seen as mutually complementary rather than exclusive.

The second schism of the Brahmo Samaj occurred in 1878, when a band of Sen's followers demanded the introduction of a democratic constitution for the Samaj, which was not conceded. To make matters more complicated, Sen's daughter had been married in violation of the provisions of the Native Marriage Act of 1872. The dissenters formed the Sadhāraṇ Brahmo Samaj ('Universal Brahma Society'), which took shape under the leadership of Anand Mohan Bose (Ānandamohan Basu) and framed a democratic constitution based on a universal adult franchise. It declared in 1882 that it was about to establish a worldwide republic. This new body has proved up until now the most powerful and active branch of the Brahmo Samaj of India.

See also: ARYA SAMAJ; VEDĀNTA §4

References and further reading

Chakrabarti, S.K. (1991) *Role of Brahmo Samaj in the History of Bengal*, Calcutta: Barnali. (Describes the historical background of the origin of the Brahmo Samaj movement in Bengal.)

Dasgupta, B.N. (1980) *The Life and Times of Rajah Rammohun Roy*, New Delhi: Ambika. (A good biography of Raja Rammohun Roy, the founder of the Brahmo Samaj.)

Kopf, D. (1979) *The Brahmo Samaj and the Shaping of the Modern Indian Mind*, Princeton, NJ: Princeton University Press. (Illustrates the impact of the Brahmo Samaj on the people of India after independence.)

Roy, Raja Rammohun (1906) *The English Works of Raja Rammohun Roy*, ed. J.C. Ghose, Allahabad: Panini Office, 4 vols. (A collection of some of Roy's administrative, political, religious and philosophical writing.)

—— (1977) *Selected works of Raja Rammohun Roy*, New Delhi: Government of India Ministry of Information and Broadcasting. (A collection of articles by Roy.)

Sen, K.C. (1980) *Keshub Chunder Sen in England: Diaries, Sermons, Addresses and Epistles*, Calcutta: Writers Workshop. (A monograph containing the diary kept by the founder of the Brahmo Samaj of India during a visit to England, along with some of his public addresses.)

* Weber, M. (1916) *The Religion of India: The Sociology of Hinduism and Buddhism*, trans. and ed. H.H. Gerth and D. Martindale, Glencoe, IL: Free Press, 1958. (One of a series of works dealing with the economic ethics of the world's religions.)

K.S. KUMAR

BRAZIL, PHILOSOPHY IN

It is possible to distinguish between European philosophy in Brazil and Brazilian philosophy. The former refers to Brazilians who participate in discussions of issues occurring in the European philosophic tradition without any reference to Brazilian reality and its problems; the latter to those Brazilian intellectuals who respond to the problems growing out of situations which have confronted the nation historically whether their philosophical orientations have originated in Europe or elsewhere. This entry focuses on the latter and generally follows a historical progression. This progression spans from the precabralian Tupi-Guarani speaking societies of eastern South America to the healthy development of Brazilian philosophy since 1950 after the founding of the Institute of Brazilian Philosophy.

1 **Precabralian Tupi-Guarani worldview**
2 **Philosophy in sixteenth-century Portugal**
3 **Colonial Brazil: philosophical problems**
4 **Adaptations of African ideas and values**
5 **Enlightenment thought in eighteenth-century Brazil**
6 **Philosophical ambiance at Independence**
7 **Philosophy during the Empire: eclecticism and positivism**
8 **Reactions to positivism: School of Recife, spiritualism and modernism**
9 **Brazilian philosophy since 1950**

1 Precabralian Tupi-Guarani worldview

Pedro Álvarez Cabral was a Portuguese navigator who accidentally discovered the Brazilian coast in 1500. A nascent precabralian civilization extended along eastern South America which still exists in so far as a common set of assumptions, attitudes and values is operative among extant Tupi-Guarani speaking societies. When the Portuguese arrived they found a lingua franca uniting these people. A comparative study of myths of creation and destruction of the earth reveals a creative spirit, in the very act of creativity, emerging out of fundamental chaos in which irrational forces of annihilation struggle against any emergent deity with the capability to dispel darkness and nihility – 'he-who-creates-his-own-body-out-of-primeval-darkness' (Gillette Sturm 1991) – sustaining himself in the process, while simultaneously creating the heavens and the earth through creative wisdom. The creative process is intentionally dialectic, a dynamic struggle between opposites, involving feminine–masculine collaboration. The view of temporality is neither cyclical nor linear, but helical. Creation of language, love and sacred song lays the foundation for humanity, but the temporal process is marked by a tendency toward deterioration: tiring, aging, dying. An annual ceremony at planting time is performed to drive away malevolent forces which threaten the germination of seeds and growth of plants with death and destruction. From the earliest records there are reports of groups who have followed leaders who have predicted catastrophes and the end of the world, marching towards the Atlantic and serving as models for other messianic movements in the Brazilian interior.

2 Philosophy in sixteenth-century Portugal

The sixteenth century witnessed the most exciting period in Portuguese intellectual history marking a golden age of Portuguese philosophy. It was the time of the voyages of discovery when the tiny nation of Portugal established commercial outposts on the shores and islands of four continents and briefly became a world power in trade and commerce.

Portuguese philosophers and intellectuals reflected the latest developments in European thought and also contributed actively to the formation of the mind of modern Europe.

Early in the century the Dutch humanist Desiderius ERASMUS attracted a group of Portuguese disciples. In 1547 the king founded the Royal College of Humanities at the University of Coimbra and entrusted it to humanists, although within eight years its control was transferred to the Jesuits (see COLLEGIUM CONIMBRICENSE). None the less, northern European and Italian humanism made their impact on sixteenth-century Portugal, even in formulations of scholastic resurgence later in the century at Coimbra. Among leading Portuguese humanists during the sixteenth century were João de Barros, Damião de Gois, Francisco de Holanda, André de Resende and Francisco de Sá de Miranda.

The famous School of Sagres in southern Portugal, which provided training in navigational skills and the use of new navigational instruments, cannot be considered a research centre for experimental science. However, the publications of several Portuguese involved in navigation, or who had the opportunity for travel to foreign lands, point to a decided change in orientation concerning the study of natural science, as well as to the beginnings of experimental methodology in the effort to understand natural phenomena. Among the experientialists were Duarte Pacheco Pereira and Garcia de Orta. The experimentalists include Pedro Nunes and José de Castro. Worthy of mention also is the sceptic and forerunner of Cartesian methodology Francisco SANCHES.

The instruments of the Counter-Reformation, including Inquisition and Index, became operative during the sixteenth century and the Society of Jesus was given responsibility for the direction of Portuguese educational curricula in 1555. However, the resurgence of Scholasticism, which had one of its points of origin at the University of Coimbra, was not a retrenchment to earlier orthodoxy, but an advance in the great tradition. Those who moulded the Second Scholasticism at Coimbra hailed from both Portugal and Spain. These were Pedro da FONSECA, the 'Portuguese Aristotle', Luis de MOLINA and Francisco SUÁREZ. They produced a new philosophy curriculum referred to as *Cursus Conimbricensis*.

3 Colonial Brazil: philosophical problems

Portugal never established a university in Brazil. Students were expected to matriculate at the Universities of Coimbra or Évora. Several monastic orders founded colleges and seminaries where prospective university students could pursue an undergraduate curriculum based on the approved model at Coimbra.

The presence of indigenous people posed several unique problems. Questions were posed regarding whether these people were human, what kind of humans they were and what rights they had to land and liberty. In 1548 when Portugal sent the first governor-general to consolidate its territories in Brazil the crown made clear that priority was to be given to Christian missions among the indigenous. Eleven years earlier a papal bull had declared the Indians to be fully human and proscribed deprivations of their freedom or possessions. In the light of royal regulation and the papal bull the question of the humanity of the Indians and their rights under natural law should not have been raised. Yet by 1557 Manuel da Nóbrega, director of Jesuit missions, published his *Dialogue concerning the Conversion of the Gentiles*, in which the central question was 'Do these have a soul like us?' It also dealt with issues of slavery, land sovereignty, nomadism, cannibalism, differences in 'nations' of Indians, social institutions and ethics. Both sides of the debate are represented equally with standard arguments taken from scripture and classic Greek and Roman philosophy. In the end the equality of all persons is declared. The nature/nurture distinction is emphasized: Indians do not differ essentially from other humans; the differences lie in the social milieu. Other Jesuits who concerned themselves with new issues were José de Anchieta and Antônio Vieira.

4 Adaptations of African ideas and values

In their defence of the Brazilian Indians the Jesuits recommended the use of African slaves. This led to the introduction of cultural traditions differing from both the indigenous and the European. Traditional societies in subSaharan Africa are characterized by a strong sense of integrated community extended to elements in the nonhuman environment. The soil upon which the society was established by the ancestors becomes a focal point uniting the generations as both burial-place and source of fertility which sustains the living and guarantees continuity of community. The slave trade forced Africans into permanent exile from their homeland and alienated them from their communities. This threatened human survival through a rootlessness which made existence impossible unless a process of transplantation to new soil and re-establishment of community occurred which again made possible contact with one's ancestral homeland and historical social heritage. The achievement of this end included large-scale slave revolts and the founding of *quilombos*, autonomous communities of runaway slaves in the interior, coronation ceremonies for African chieftains in which historic traditions were incorporated with reaffirmation of allegiance to a sovereign representing the continuity of community; the invocation of nature and ancestral spirits in possession ceremonies.

After 1950 a body of literature emerged giving intellectual articulation to the worldview implicit in the practices of the African-Brazilian community. An important issue is the extent to which the African past remains essential to the community. José Ribeiro de Souza speaks for the 're-Africanization' movement and works through the Institute for Afro-Brazilian Studies for the preservation in Brazil of west African languages. Alfred Costa Moura calls for total de-Africanization. W.W. da Matta-Silva takes a middle position in which African roots constitute an essential base for a universal intellectual and religious position.

5   Enlightenment thought in eighteenth-century Brazil

Academies, arcadias and literary societies based on Graeco-Roman models and encouraging revival of classical Arcadian literary style appeared in southern Europe during the Renaissance. Early in the eighteenth century they were transformed from centres of debate on literary questions articulated in the baroque style of Gongorism into conduits for reception, diffusion and discussion of Enlightenment ideas. They were private associations selecting their own members and determining their own objectives and procedures. In 1724 the Brazilian Academy of the 'forgotten ones' was founded to produce an interdisciplinary history of Brazil based on observation and primary documentation. The Scientific Academy of Rio de Janeiro discussed questions of physics, chemistry, botany, medicine, surgery and agriculture, in addition to maintaining a botanical garden and carrying on active correspondence with the Swedish Royal Academy of Sciences. Many similar societies appeared throughout Brazil which gradually added sociopolitical topics to the agenda.

Agitation for educational reform began in Portugal early in the century, leading to the decision to change the Coimbra curriculum drastically, giving responsibility for Portuguese education to the Order of the Oratory instead of the Society of Jesus. Philosophy was no longer handmaid to theology; physics was liberated from Aristotelian philosophy; natural science was divided into autonomous scientific disciplines stressing laboratory research. Students returning to Brazil from studies in Europe brought these new ideas and procedures with them, leading to radical changes in secondary and collegiate education.

Brazilian authors addressing Enlightenment issues included Matias Aires Ramos da Silva (1700–63), whose book *Problems of Civil Architecture* (*c.*1740) was an exposition of the latest developments in the natural sciences of physics and chemistry; Tomaz Antônio Gonzaga (1744–1810), whose *Treatise on Natural Law* (*c.*1790) was a critical exposition of new directions in natural law theory; Nino Marques Pereira (1652–1735), whose novel depicting a journey from Salvador to São Paulo ridicules the professors of the Second Scholasticism; José Joaquim de Cunha de Azeredo Coutinho (1742–1821), economic theorist who argued for physiocrat principles and was founder of a model college focusing on scientific studies and experimentation emphasizing practical application to the Brazilian situation and Francisco Luís Leal (1740–1820), author of the first history of philosophy in Portuguese which distinguished between the 'ancients' and the 'illustrious moderns'.

6   Philosophical ambiance at Independence

The first articulate stirrings towards independence from Portugal began with the Minas conspiracy of 1789, the 1798 revolt of the tailors in Bahia and the Pernambuco Insurrection of 1817. Ideological roots are found in the literary and scientific academies, the curricular reform at Coimbra and the lodges of freemasonry. Five intellectuals, alive at the time of the declaration of independence by Pedro I, are representative of the philosophical spectrum.

José da Silva Lisboa, Viscount of Cairu (1756–1835) was a political conservative, out of sympathy with the French Revolution, who favoured retaining the United Kingdom of Portugal and Brazil, which had been instituted in 1815. He was a disciple of Adam Smith and advocated the lifting of all restrictions imposed by policies of feudalism and mercantilism in favour of the *laissez-faire* principle of British economic liberalism.

José Bonifacio de Andrada e Silva (1763–1835), known as the Patriarch of Independence, returned to Brazil in 1819 as a member of the leading scientific academies of the European continent after spending thirty-six years there as a geologist and metallurgist. The first grand master of the Grand Orient of Brazilian Freemasons, he believed in the rational structure of the universe and the guarantee of rights of all humans by natural law. However, his insistence that Brazil was not yet ready for complete social transformation did not endear him to the republicans.

Silvestre Pinheiro Ferreira (1769–1846) supported the United Kingdom of Portugal and Brazil, which had been established in 1815 and the moderative power of the monarch. Fundamentally a Lockean, he was disturbed none the less by the failure of the empiricists to provide a complete system to support scientific and political theory and attempted to derive such a system through a reinterpretation of Aristotelian categories (see ARISTOTLE §7; LOCKE, J.).

Frei Joaquim do Amor Divino e Caneca (1774–1825) was a Mason imbued with the spirit of French encyclopedism (see DIDEROT, D. §1.). He spoke for the nascent social revolutionary movement and was concerned especially with guaranteeing rights for the lower classes of Brazilian society.

Diogo Antônio Feijó (1784–1843) was a priest-philosopher and politician. He was also the leader of a small group of Kantians in São Paulo who broke with the stale ideas of French encyclopedism and the sensualism of Condillac, aware that Kant provided a radically new direction in philosophy (see CONDILLAC, E.B. DE; KANT, I.).

7 Philosophy during the Empire: eclecticism and positivism

Diverse motives had impelled the leaders of movements for independence. Some favoured a new economic order, but with a continuation of political ties with Portugal. Others urged political independence without changing the monarchical form of government. Voices were heard favouring republicanism. Some called for transformation of the socioeconomic order. This diversity of viewpoints, combined with Brazil's geographical immensity and a partial slave economy, caused some to predict that Brazil would become fragmented into several autonomous states. Leadership concerned with maintaining unity called for conciliation in the face of the divisiveness existing during the first decades of the empire.

Francisco José de Carvalho Mont'Alverne (1784–1858) is credited with directing Brazilian thought during the Regency and the period of 'conciliation' along the lines of Victor Cousin's eclectic spiritualism (see COUSIN, V.). As H.-A. Taine put it, eclecticism proposed a peace treaty to all systems, just as representative government provided a forum to satisfy all elements of society. Its popularity in Brazil introduced intellectuals to the European philosophic scene in a panoramic, if vague, view. The political realm was also well served, because eclecticism provided an ideological basis for moderates. Eclecticism appealed especially to medical scientists concerned with issues of physiological psychology, such as Eduardo Ferreira Franca (1809–57), professor of medical chemistry in Bahia and José Maria de Morais Valle (1824–86), professor of medicine in Rio de Janeiro. In that vein are the works of Domingos

José Gonçalves de Magalhães (1811–82), *Facts of the Human Spirit* (1858) and *Soul and Brain* (1876).

By the mid-nineteenth century Brazilian students of mathematics, physics and medicine were encountering AUGUSTE COMTE in France and Comtean positivism began to replace eclecticism in scientific circles. A series of doctoral dissertations began to appear in the 1850s written from a Comtean perspective. In 1876 Benjamin Constant (1833–91), professor of mathematics at the Military School and Luís Pereira Barreto (1840–1923), author of *As Três Filosofias* (1874) founded the Brazilian Positivist Association. The association was committed to realizing Comtean sociopolitical values. Two years later when Miguel Lemos (1854–1917) and Raimundo Teixeira Mendes (1855–1927) returned from France, the positivist Apostolate of Brazil was established. Comtean positivism had profound influence on the Brazilian intelligentsia, but was fragmented into scientific, political and religious factions (see POSITIVIST THOUGHT IN LATIN AMERICA §5).

8 Reactions to positivism: School of Recife, spiritualism and modernism

The first reaction against Comtean positivism took the form of a polemic between Comteans in Rio and adherents of Spencerian evolutionary naturalism in Recife (see SPENCER, H.). Silvio Romero (1851–1914), historian of Brazilian philosophy and literature, recounted the polemic in *Doctrine Against Doctrine: Evolutionism and Positivism in the Republic* (1894). Along with Clovis Bevilaqua (1859–1944), Fausto Cardoso (1864–1906), Tito Lívio de Castro (1864–90) and Artur Orlando (1858–1916), he is identified with the School of Recife, centred in the Law School of Recife and headed by Tobias Barreto de Meneses (1849–89). Tobias Barreto had abandoned eclecticism because of its vagueness and Comtean positivism because of its rejection of metaphysics. Spencerianism was followed by an enthusiastic espousal of 'Germanism' and the development of a naturalistic monism inspired by Noiré.

Two of Tobias's students broke with him as they moved in different directions, but both strongly influenced the birth of Brazilian modernism. José Pereira da Graça Aranha (1868–1931) articulated a unique metaphysical position of monism based on aesthetics and mysticism. Raimundo de Farias Brito (1862–1917), impelled by a sense of bankruptcy in European culture, spent much time critically examining the development of modern philosophic and scientific thought, and formulating a 'philosophy of spirit' (see ANTI-POSITIVIST THOUGHT IN LATIN AMERICA).

9 Brazilian philosophy since 1950

Philosophic activity has been especially productive since the 1950s. Much credit goes to the founding in 1950 of the Institute of Brazilian Philosophy, a truly inclusive national association, and the *Revista Brasileira de Filosofia* (Review of Brazilian Philosophy), which began publication in 1951, founded by Miguel Reale. Through national and regional congresses and an active programme of adult education the Institute of Brazilian Philosophy has fostered much philosophical dialogue. Reale has been a controversial figure and a firm believer in intellectual and political pluralism. He is known especially for his tridimensional theory of law and his philosophical position of 'ontognosiology'. He is also one of the founders of the Interamerican Society of Philosophy and the International Association for Philosophy of Law and Social Philosophy.

A concern for study of Brazilian philosophy is seen in the work of João Cruz Costa (1962) and Antônio Paim (1967; 1983) and several series of publications of the classic texts of the tradition. Official interest in the utility of philosophy in determining national policy was evident in President Juscelino Kubitshek's establishment of the Advanced Institute of Brazilian Studies (ISEB) as part of his administration. Under the direction of the philosopher Roland Cavalcanti de Albuquerque Corbisier, one of the divisions was concerned with philosophical issues and involved collaboration with Álvaro Vieira Pinto and Hélio Jaguaribe.

Brazilian philosophers who have established an international reputation in their fields include Leônidas Hegenberg and Newton Carneiro Alfonso da Costa who have been associated with the Centre for Logic, Epistemology and History of Science at the Federal University of Campinas, Romano Galeffi, founder of the Brazilian Centre for Studies in Aesthetics, Henrique C. de Lima Vaz, Leonardo and Clovis Boff, Hugo Assman, Dom Helder Câmara, Rubem Alves, theologians of liberation (see LIBERATION THEOLOGY), Paulo Freire, educational theorist, Leôncio Basbaum, Caio Prado Junior, J. Chasin, Marxists, Stanislavs Ladusãns, Catholic philosopher and Gerd Bornheim, phenomenologist.

Antônio Paim (1983) has pointed to a group of Brazilian philosophers whose concerns are similar enough to constitute a movement with roots in Brazil's intellectual past and a commitment to a pluralistic, dialogic approach to philosophical issues with a concern for cultural context. Paim calls this the Culturalist School and mentions as prime movers, *inter alia*, Miguel Reale, Djacir Menezes and Luís Washington Vita.

See also: LATIN AMERICA, COLONIAL THOUGHT IN; CULTURAL IDENTITY

References and further reading

Crippa, A. (ed.) (1978) *As idéias filosóficas no Brasil* (Philosophical Ideas in Brazil), São Paulo: Convívio, 3 vols. (A survey of philosophical history in Brazil from the perspective of a leading Catholic thinker. Vol. 1 covers the eighteenth and nineteenth centuries; vols 2 and 3 deal with the twentieth century, the former covering Marxists and Catholics, Farias Brito and Vicente Ferreira da Silva and the Culturalist movement, the latter dealing with natural law theorists, philosophy of education, aesthetics, logic and philosophy of science.)

* Cruz Costa, J. (1962) *Panorama of the History of Philosophy in Brazil*, Washington, DC: Pan American Union. (A condensed version of the *History of Ideas in Brazil* (1964) commissioned as part of a series of brief introductions to philosophy in the Americas.)

—— (1964) A *History of Ideas in Brazil: the Development of Philosophy in Brazil and the Evolution of National History*, Berkeley, CA: University of California Press. (The leading historian of Brazilian philosophy relates national and societal development, covering colonial formation and its basis in Portuguese philosophy and culture.)

* Gonçalves de Magalhães, D.S. (1858) *Facts of the Human Spirit*, Paris: Garnier. (Deals with eclecticism and concerns itself with issues of physiological psychology.)

* —— (1876) *Soul and Brain*, Rio de Janeiro: Garnier. (This book also hinges on eclecticism and provides an ideological basis for moderates.)

* Gonzaga, T.A. (*c.*1790) *Treatise on Natural Law*, Rio de Janeiro: National Library of Lisbon, 1953. (An exposition of changing directions in natural law.)

* Nóbrega, da M. (1557) *Dialogue concerning the Conversion of the Gentiles*, Lisbon: Comissão do IV Centenário da Fundação de São Paulo, 1954. (Important issues, such as slavery, land sovereignty and differences between 'nations' of Indians are dealt with.)

* Paim, A. (1967) *História das idéias filosóficas no Brasil* (History of Philosophical Ideas in Brazil), São Paulo: Editora Convívium, 3rd edn, 1984. (Paim addresses the relation between the history of philosophy in general and national philosophic traditions and considers the unique problematic confronting Brazilian philosophers.)

* —— (1983) *Bibliografia filosófica brasileira, 1808–1985* (Bibliography of Brazilian Philosophy, 1808–1985), Salvador: Centro de documentação do

pensamento brasileiro, 3 vols. (An account of all philosophical books published in Brazil from 1808 to 1985, including translations into Portuguese.)

* Pereira Barreto, L. (1874) *As Três Filosofias* (The Three Philosophies), part 1, *Theological Philosophy*, Rio de Janeiro: Laemmert; part 2, *Metaphysical Philosophy*, Jacaret: Comercial, 1876. (Published in two parts.)

* *Revista Brasileira de Filosofia* (Review of Brazilian Philosophy) (1951–), São Paulo: Instituto Brasileira de Filosofia. (A quarterly journal.)

* Romero, S. (1894) *Doctrine Against Doctrine: Evolutionism and Positivism in the Republic*, Rio de Janeiro: Tipografia de J.B. Nunes. (The polemic between Comteans in Rio and adherents of Spencerian evolutionary naturalism in Recife is recounted in this book.)

* Sturm Gillette, F. (1991) 'Ontological Categories Implicit in the Mbyá-Guaraní Creation Myth', in M.H. Preuss (ed.) *Past, Present and Future: Selected Papers on Latin American Indian Literatures*, Culver City, CA: Labyrinthos, 117–22. (León Cadigen also transcribed the myth in *Guaraní en Ayvu Rapyta: míticos de los Mbyá-Guaraní del Guaira*, 1959.)

FRED GILLETTE STURM

BRENTANO, FRANZ CLEMENS (1838–1917)

Brentano was a philosopher and psychologist who taught at the Universities of Würzburg and Vienna. He made significant contributions to almost every branch of philosophy, notably psychology and philosophy of mind, ontology, ethics and the philosophy of language. He also published several books on the history of philosophy, especially Aristotle, and contended that philosophy proceeds in cycles of advance and decline. He is best known for reintroducing the scholastic concept of intentionality into philosophy and proclaiming it as the characteristic mark of the mental. His teachings, especially those on what he called descriptive psychology, influenced the phenomenological movement in the twentieth century, but because of his concern for precise statement and his sensitivity to the dangers of the undisciplined use of philosophical language, his work also bears affinities to analytic philosophy. His anti-speculative conception of philosophy as a rigorous discipline was furthered by his many brilliant students. Late in life Brentano's philosophy radically changed: he advocated a sparse ontology of physical and mental things (reism), coupled with a linguistic fictionalism stating that all language purportedly referring to non-things can be replaced by language referring only to things.

1 **Life and intellectual development**
2 **Psychology**
3 **Intentionality**
4 **Types of being: substance, accident and boundary**
5 **Truth**
6 **Ethics and the theory of value**
7 **Philosophical theology**
8 **Historiography of philosophy**

1 Life and intellectual development

Franz Brentano came from a talented family. He mastered ancient and scholastic philosophy as well as the works of COMTE and the British empiricists. He always prized ARISTOTLE above other philosophers, and regarded German Idealism as the nadir of philosophy. Brentano's vision of philosophy as an exact discipline sharing its true method with natural science inspired his many famous students, who included such noted philosophers as Anton Marty, Carl Stumpf, Alexius MEINONG, Christian von Ehrenfels, Edmund HUSSERL , and Kazimierz TWARDOWSKI, as well as later political leaders German Chancellor Georg Hertling and the first President of Czechoslovakia, Thomas G. Masaryk.

Brentano's life was one of controversy and disappointment. In 1864 he became a Roman Catholic priest and played an important role in the discussion of the proposed doctrine of papal infallibility. In a position paper commissioned by the Bishops of Germany he recommended that they reject the doctrine. When the doctrine was officially proclaimed, Brentano felt justified in giving in to other doubts that had been tormenting him, concluding, for example, that the doctrine of the Trinity was contradictory. In 1873 he resigned from the priesthood, the church, and his position in Würzburg. His career as a Professor in Vienna was short-lived. A legal controversy surrounding the question whether ex-priests could marry led him to resign his Professorship in 1880, a position to which, in a *cause célèbre*, he was never reinstated, remaining an instructor (*Privatdozent*) until he left Austria for Italy in 1895. In later years he became blind and was estranged from several of his older students. Brentano did not relish publication: apart from the uncompleted *Psychology* he published mainly short papers, lectures, and monographs on the history of philosophy. His views underwent continuous revision, but a major change occurred during the first decade of the twentieth century, when his ontological views went through a

'Copernican revolution' whose results even his closest followers found difficulty in accepting. Large quantities of letters, lecture notes and dictated pieces remained unpublished at his death. Many of these were edited from Prague between the wars, with support from Masaryk.

2 Psychology

Brentano's interest in psychology dated from his early occupation with the work of Aristotle and the British empiricists. *Psychologie vom empirischen Standpunkt* (*Psychology from an Empirical Standpoint*) (1874) helped establish psychology as an independent discipline. Following Comte in deliberately eschewing metaphysical controversy, Brentano, though believing in the soul, determined psychology as the science not of the soul but of mental *phenomena*. He writes: 'All the data of our consciousness are divided into two great classes: the class of physical and the class of mental phenomena.' Brentano initially restricted scientific investigation to phenomena or appearances and regarded the assumption that there are things in themselves as very uncertain. Physical phenomena are those sense-objects (for example, colours, sounds, odours) that we experience whenever we have a sensation or an imagined or dreamed counterpart of a sensation.

Comte had held inner observation to be impossible, since it would require us to split ourselves mentally in two. Brentano countered that inner perception is possible, because every mental act is accompanied by a secondary awareness of itself. Inner perception and memory form the solid experiential basis of psychology. Brentano was concerned in the *Psychology* to establish a proper taxonomy of mental acts. Following Descartes, he divides them into three classes: ideas (*Vorstellungen*), judgments and a third class comprising emotions, feelings, desires and acts of will, variously called interests or phenomena of love and hate. Ideas merely present something, judgments accept as existent or reject as nonexistent something presented, while interests take a pro- or con-attitude to something judged. Thus interests presuppose judgments and these in their turn presuppose ideas. So all mental phenomena are either ideas or are founded on ideas. Brentano's classification has not been widely accepted.

From the late 1880s Brentano divided psychology into descriptive psychology, which he also sometimes called 'phenomenology' (see PHENOMENOLOGICAL MOVEMENT), and genetic psychology. The former is an a priori, philosophical discipline concerned with the basic elements of consciousness and their modes of structural combination, resting on the certain evidence of inner perception. The latter is a posteriori, empirical and probabilistic, concerned with the causal laws governing how mental phenomena arise and perish and the connections between the mental and the physiological.

3 Intentionality

In the search for a positive criterion marking off mental from physical phenomena Brentano revived the Aristotelian-Thomistic conception of intentional inexistence in the *Psychology*. Every mental phenomenon is intentional, contains an object in itself, or no physical phenomenon does. In seeing something is seen, in judging something is accepted or rejected, in hoping something is hoped for and so on. Hence psychology cannot be reduced to or replaced by a physical science. Brentano maintained this demarcation principle but modified his conception of intentionality in a more epistemologically realist direction. A middle phase finds him rejecting the immanent conception of objects, accepting that the object of intentionality may be outside consciousness, and may be real, or an *ens rationis*, like a state of affairs, or even nonexistent. This middle view was most influential among his students.

Brentano's student Twardowski went on to distinguish the mental acts themselves from their subjects, from their objects and their contents. Your seeing Jones would be, according to Twardowski's account, a mental act that has you as its subject, Jones as its object and a visual image as its content. Every mental act then has an object, but not all such objects exist or are real. This view influenced Meinong's theory of objects (see MEINONG, A. §§2–4; TWARDOWSKI, K. §3).

However, Brentano himself later rejected all non-real and nonexistent objects (see §4 below). Since someone who judges (correctly) that unicorns do not exist seems to stand in a rejecting relation to something nonexistent, Brentano came to regard intentionality as not a relation but as merely relation-like, the similarity being that we think of relations in a similar way. In thinking of John touching Mary, we think directly of John and indirectly of Mary, but she too exists. In thinking of Mary rejecting unicorns we think directly of the unicorn-rejecting subject Mary and only indirectly of what she rejects. There are no non-real objects; they are fictions engendered by a careless use of language.

Brentano emphasizes that, in knowing that one is in a mental state, one knows directly and immediately that there is a certain individual thing – namely, the one who is in that state. And *you*, of course, are the one who is in your mental state. We may single out

13

three different phases of this situation: (1) I can know that I hope for rain; (2) as a rational being, I can conceive what it is to hope for rain; and (3) that the only type of entity that can have the property of hoping for rain is an individual thing or substance.

Following Leibniz, Brentano distinguishes two types of certainty: the certainty we can have with respect to the existence of our conscious states, and the a priori certainty that may be directed upon axioms and other necessary truths. These two types may be combined in a significant way. At a given moment, I may be certain, on the basis of inner perception, that there is believing, desiring, hoping and fearing; and I may also be certain a priori that there cannot be believing, desiring, hoping and fearing unless there is a substance that believes, desires, hopes and fears. In such a case, it will be certain for me (Brentano says that I 'perceive') that there is a substance that believes, desires, hopes and fears. It is also axiomatic, Brentano says, that if one is certain that a given substance exists, then one is identical with that substance.

4 Types of being: substance, accident and boundary

In Brentano's earlier writings he assumed that in addition to concrete individual things or *entia realia*, there are also 'non-things' or *entia irrealia*, falling into several different categories. They include: (1) 'intentionally inexistent' objects, such as that devil that is supposed to 'exist in mind' when one thinks about a devil; (2) those objects, often called 'propositions', thought to be designated by 'that'-clauses or sentential gerundives (as in 'that there are living beings on Venus', or 'there being living things on Venus'); (3) properties or universals, such as redness and being-both-round-and-square; and (4) states and events.

Brentano's rejection of such 'non-things' was based upon two general principles. First, the only objects that we can think about, strictly speaking, are concrete individual things. We do think of concrete things; 'think of' is univocal; therefore whatever we think of is a concrete thing. 'Concrete' does not here imply materiality. God and the soul, according to Brentano, are concrete but non-material. Second, an adequate understanding of language will show us that any plausible statement that ostensibly refers to such non-things may be construed as pertaining only to concrete things. Brentano defends the second principle with considerable ingenuity.

The theory of 'concrete predication' tells us that all of our thoughts may be adequately expressed by using concrete terms in place of predicates. We may best understand this theory if we imagine that all predicates in our language have been replaced by

terms, and consider a view of the world which might naturally suggest itself to us if our language were in fact of such a sort, as it very well could have been. 'Concrete predication' may recall what Aristotle had said of simple judgments: 'An "affirmation" is a statement affirming something of something; a "negation" is a statement denying something of something'. In simple affirmative judgments, Aristotle said, we combine things; and in simple negative judgments we separate them. Since such statements as 'Mary is thinking' are for us a natural way of describing people, one might suppose that, when a person is thinking, they stand in a certain relation to the property of thinking. But if we say 'Some persons are *thinkers*' (Brentano uses '*ein Denkendes*', which one might translate more literally as 'a thinking-thing') then it may be more natural to suppose that we are describing not a relation between an individual thing and a property, but a relation between those individual things that are persons and those individual things that are thinkers. What, then, is the relevant relation between persons and thinkers?

Brentano uses Aristotle's term and says that the thinker is an 'accident' of its subject. Aristotle had said, however, that accidents are 'in' their subjects. Brentano saw that there was a reason for reversing this, claiming that accidents *contain* their subjects. The relation of substance to accident is similar in fundamental respects to that of part to whole. Brentano tells us what may seem surprising at first, that a substance is a part of its accidents. An accidental determination of a substance is a larger whole which is not necessary to its substance. If I happen to be thinking at the moment, I am a substance which, for now, is a thinker. The thinker is, at the moment, an accident of that substance which is identical with me. An accident is something containing its substance but not necessary to the substance.

A substance is *necessary to* its accidents. The accidents could not exist unless the subject exists – just as, according to the principle of 'mereological essentialism', every whole is ontologically dependent upon its parts. But no accident is necessary to its subject; hence the use of the word 'accident'. The expression 'X is an accident of Y' does not then introduce any unfamiliar concept into ontology, but refers only to a more generalized version of the part–whole concept.

In addition to distinguishing those individuals that are accidents from those that are substances, Brentano points out that there are individuals of still another sort. These include the points, lines and surfaces that constitute the inner and outer 'boundaries' of spatial objects. Boundaries exhibit a unique type of ontological dependence. Every boundary is necessarily such that it is a boundary of some constituent of the thing of which it *is* a boundary; but this is not to say that, for any thing of which it is a boundary, the boundary is necessarily such that it is a constituent of it. The point is of fundamental importance to ontology and the theory of categories, and may be put more precisely. Every boundary x is necessarily such that it is a boundary of (and therefore a constituent of) some constituent y of the entity z of which it happens to be a boundary. But from this fact, it does not follow that there is a constituent w of z which is such that x is necessarily a constituent of w. For example, a spatial point P is necessarily such that it is a constituent of a constituent C of the line L of which P happens to be a constituent. But, for any constituent C of L that you might mention, P need not be a constituent of C; some smaller constituent of C would do just as well. Analogously, this holds for the relation of lines to surfaces and for the relation of surfaces to three-dimensional bodies.

By contemplating the concept of a boundary in this way, Brentano claimed, we acquire the concept of infinite divisibility by means of which we can then understand what it is for an entity to be 'continuous'. The general problem of the continuum occupied Brentano throughout his philosophical career.

5   Truth

Like Aristotle, Brentano holds that the primary sense of 'true' is its application to beliefs or judgments; a secondary sense is its application to sentences. This theory of truth is properly called a 'doxastic theory'. Brentano originally upheld a version of the correspondence theory of truth, but since his mature ontology has no place for such entities as facts or propositions, his final theory is not a correspondence theory as it is usually understood (see TRUTH, CORRESPONDENCE THEORY OF §§1–2).

By reflecting upon judgments that are certain, according to Brentano, we obtain the concept of the 'correctness' of judgment. Once we have this concept, we are able to extend it beyond the sphere of the certain and thereby derive the broader concept of truth. We may speak, then, of a strict sense and of an extended sense of 'correct'. In its strict sense, 'correct' will mean the same as 'certain'. (Actually, Brentano uses 'evident' in place of 'certain'; but he uses it in the way in which most epistemologists now use 'certain'.) If, however, we use 'correct' in its extended sense, then we may also say that a judgment is correct if it agrees with a judgment that is certain – that is, if it accepts what a judge who has certainty would accept or rejects what such a judge would reject. In *Wahrheit und Evidenz* (The True and the Evident), Brentano defines truth thus:

> Truth pertains to the judgment of one who judges correctly – one who judges about a thing in the way in which a person who judged with evidence would judge about it; it pertains to the judgment of one who asserts what the person who judges with evidence would assert.
>
> (1930, 139; 1966, 122)

The concept of correctness also plays an essential role in Brentano's moral philosophy and general theory of value.

6   Ethics and the theory of value

Brentano's moral philosophy is based upon his theory of value. His theory of value, in turn, is a theory of 'intrinsic value', about what is good in itself, or good as an end, about what is bad in itself, or bad as an end, and more generally about the relation of intrinsic preferability. Brentano's theory of intrinsic value is based upon the analogy he believes to hold between intellectual and emotive phenomena. One may take an intellectual stand towards an object of thought, thereby having a positive belief or a negative belief about that object; one may 'affirm' the object or 'deny' it. One may also take an emotive stand with respect to the object, in which case one 'loves' the object or one 'hates' it. Brentano uses 'love' and 'hate' somewhat broadly to cover what we might call, respectively, 'pro-feelings' and 'anti-feelings'.

What does it mean to say that a thing is intrinsically good or intrinsically bad? Brentano appeals again to the concept of correctness which is central to his theory of knowledge and truth. To say that a thing is intrinsically good, according to Brentano, is to say that it is 'correct to love' that thing as an end; and to say that a thing is intrinsically bad is to say that it is 'correct to hate' it as an end. Brentano believed that we can be immediately aware of the correctness of certain of our emotive attitudes, just as we can be immediately aware of the correctness (that is, the truth) of certain of our intellectual attitudes. In each case, the correctness consists in a relation of appropriateness or fittingness between the attitude and its object.

Brentano constructs a hierarchy of values in which pleasure plays a subordinate role. The principal bearers of intrinsic value, he claims, are conscious states. Some but not all conscious states are intrinsically good. And every conscious state *as* a conscious state contains some part that is intrinsically good. Every correct judgment is intrinsically good; so too is every correct emotion and every enrichment of our intellectual life. Since every intrinsic evil is itself a conscious state, there can be no intrinsic evil that does not include some intrinsic good. Among the things that are 'predominantly bad' are error, pain, every unjustified act of hate (especially the hatred of that which is good), and every unjustified act of love (especially of that which is bad). Sensory pleasure is, as such, intrinsically good.

A complete account of Brentano's value theory would take into consideration a detailed analysis of aesthetic value, and also Brentano's views on instrumental or practical value, which are broadly utilitarian.

7 Philosophical theology

Brentano's philosophical theology depends upon a combination of the traditional arguments from motion and from contingency (see GOD, ARGUMENTS FOR THE EXISTENCE OF §1). He attempts to show that there can be no uncaused events and that the hypothesis according to which there is just one necessary substance, upon which all contingent things depend, has a probability approaching certainty. He combines this proof with an appeal to the evidence for design that we find when we contemplate ourselves and other living beings. Any sound epistemology, Brentano believes, will concede that there is such evidence. He then argues that the necessary substance is personal in that it is an intelligent being having both intellectual and emotive consciousness. It is also an immaterial being and is not a subject of accidents.

What distinguishes Brentano's conception of God from that of most theologians is the thesis that God, like everything else, is a temporal being. Brentano describes an instance of God's temporal consciousness this way:

'He now knows, for example, that I am writing down these thoughts. Yesterday, however, he did not know this, but rather that I will write them down later. And similarly he will know tomorrow that I have written them down'

(1976: 105; 1988: 87).

8 Historiography of philosophy

Brentano published five monographs on Aristotle, and several of his works on the history of philosophy have been published posthumously. His most characteristic view is that philosophy goes through cycles of advance and decline in four phases: a constructive theoretical phase, then in successively greater decline a practical phase, a sceptical phase and finally a mystical phase. The cycle then repeats itself. Brentano

discerned three such cycles from the pre-Socratics to the German idealists, one each in ancient, medieval and modern philosophy. He clearly saw himself as ushering in a fourth constructive phase, a view to which one may give assent. Despite its obvious simplifications, the model is better than most others in accommodating philosophy's uncertain progress.

See also: INTENTIONALITY; PSYCHOLOGY, THEORIES OF §§1–2

List of works

Brentano, F. (1862) *Von der mannigfachen Bedeutung des Seienden nach Aristoteles*, Freiburg im Breisgau: Herder; repr. Darmstadt, Wissenschaftliche Buchgesellschaft, 1960; trans. and ed. R. George, *On the Several Senses of Being in Aristotle*, Berkeley, CA: University of California Press, 1975. (Brentano's Berlin doctoral dissertation: a catalogue of the ways Aristotle says something may be said to be; includes a classification and justification of the categories.)

—— (1874) *Psychologie vom empirischen Standpunkte*, Leipzig: Duncker & Humblot; 2nd edn, ed. O. Kraus, Leipzig, Meiner, 1924; repr. Hamburg, Meiner, 1973; trans. A.C. Rancurello, D.B. Terrell and L.L. McAlister and ed. L.L. McAlister, *Psychology from an Empirical Standpoint*, London, Routledge, 1969; 2nd edn, 1995. (Brentano's best-known and most influential work, though incomplete. Contains a defence of psychology as an autonomous discipline, the famous delimitation of its subject matter, mental phenomena, via intentional existence, and a threefold classification of mental phenomena into ideas, judgments, and phenomena of love and hate (interests), which include both feeling and will.)

—— (1889) *Vom Ursprung sittlicher Erkenntnis*, Leipzig: Duncker & Humblot; 4th edn, ed. O. Kraus, Hamburg: Meiner, 1955; trans. R.M. Chisholm and E.H. Schneewind, *The Origin of our Knowledge of Right and Wrong*, London: Routledge, 1969. (Brentano's ethics in a small compass, based on a theory of intrinsic value defined in terms of correct interests and preferences, supplemented by a utilitarian account of instrumental value.)

—— (1926) *Die vier Phasen der Philosophie und ihr augenblicklicher Stand* (The Four Phases of Philosophy and Its Present Status), Leipzig: Meiner; repr. Hamburg: Meiner, 1968. (Brentano's theory of the cyclical rise and decline of philosophy.)

—— (1929) *Vom Dasein Gottes*, ed. A. Kastil, Leipzig: Meiner; repr. Hamburg, Meiner, 1968; trans. S. Krantz, *On the Existence of God*, Dordrecht,

Nijhoff, 1987. (Posthumously published treatise setting out Brentano's probabilistic proof for the existence of God.)
—— (1930) *Wahrheit und Evidenz*, ed. O. Kraus, Leipzig: Meiner; repr. Hamburg, Meiner, 1974; trans. R.M. Chisholm, I. Politzer and K.R. Fischer, and ed. R.M. Chisholm, *The True and the Evident*, London, Routledge, 1966. (A chronologically arranged series of writings on truth, beginning with Brentano's somewhat half-hearted espousal of a correspondence theory and ending with its rejection in favour of the view that a true (correct) judgment is one which someone judging with evidence would accept.)
—— (1933) *Kategorienlehre*, ed. A. Kastil, Leipzig: Meiner; repr. Hamburg, Meiner, 1974; trans. R.M. Chisholm and N. Guterman, *The Theory of Categories*, Dordrecht: Nijhoff, 1981. (A miscellaneous collection of late writings on categories and ontology, setting out Brentano's opposition to Aristotle and his economical ontology of reism. Discusses meanings of 'be', substance and accident, relations and linguistic fictions.)
—— (1952) *Grundlegung und Aufbau der Ethik*, Hamburg: Meiner; ed. F. Mayer-Hillebrand, trans. E.H. Schneewind, *The Foundation and Construction of Ethics*, London: Routledge & Kegan Paul, 1973. (Compiled from the notes Brentano made for his enormously popular lectures on practical philosophy in Vienna, 1876–94.)
—— (1976) *Philosophische Untersuchungen zu Raum, Zeit und Kontinuum*, selected from the unpublished papers by A. Kastil, ed. S. Körner and R.M. Chisholm, Hamburg: Meiner; trans. B. Smith, *Philosophical Investigations on Space, Time, and the Continuum*, London: Croom Helm, 1988. (Subject matter as the title describes: contains Brentano's account of time-consciousness, his anti-Cantorian theory of the continuum and his unorthodox views on boundaries.)
—— (1982) *Deskriptive Psychologie*, ed. R.M. Chisholm and W. Baumgartner, Hamburg: Meiner; trans. B. Müller, *Descriptive Psychology*, London: Routledge, 1995. (Edited from Vienna lecture notes: psychology from Brentano's influential middle period, when he had distinguished descriptive psychology (phenomenology) from genetic psychology.)

References and further reading

Baumgartner, W., Burkard, F.-P. and Wiedman, F. (eds) (1988–) *Brentano Studien*, Dettelbach: Röll. (An international yearbook devoted to Brentano. Essays in English and German.)

Chisholm, R.M. (1982) *Brentano and Meinong Studies*, Amsterdam: Rodopi. (Contains essays on several aspects of Brentano's philosophy.)
—— (1986) *Brentano and Intrinsic Value*, Cambridge: Cambridge University Press. (Introductory account of Brentano's views, with discussion of hierarchy of values, organic unities and evil.)
Chisholm, R.M. and Haller, R. (eds) (1978) *Die Philosophie Franz Brentanos* (The Philosophy of Franz Brentano), Amsterdam: Rodopi; also in *Grazer Philosophische Studien* 5. (Nineteen essays on various aspects of Brentano's philosophy.)
—— (eds) (1987) *The Descriptive Psychology of the Brentano School*, special issue of *Topoi* 6 (1). (Seven essays on Brentano's philosophy.)
Kastil, A. (1951) *Die Philosophie Franz Brentanos, Eine Einführung in seine Lehre* (The Philosophy of Franz Brentano, An Introduction to his Teaching), Munich: Lehnen. (A paraphrase of Brentano's opinions by the person who probably knew them best, still a useful all-round introduction, but lacking scholarly apparatus.)
McAlister, L.L. (ed.) (1976) *The Philosophy of Brentano*, London: Duckworth. (An informative collection including personal reminiscences by Stumpf and Husserl.)

RODERICK M. CHISHOLM
PETER SIMONS

BRETHREN OF PURITY
see IKHWAN AL-SAFA'

BRIDGMAN, PERCY WILLIAM (1882–1961)

Bridgman founded high-pressure experimental physics and was committed to a classical empiricist view of science – a view challenged by twentieth-century developments in relativistic and quantum mechanics. He argued that developments in special relativity showed the experimental operations scientists performed were suitable substitutes for basic constituents of matter, thus founding operationalism, a methodological position which influenced logical positivism and, transformed beyond his recognition, was expropriated by the behaviourist school in the social sciences. As Bridgman grappled with the challenges of general relativity and quantum mechanics, he increasingly parted company with his positivistic and behaviourist followers by moving more towards subjectivist views of science and knowledge. These later views led him to see and explore intimate connections between foundations of scientific knowledge and human freedom.

Bridgman developed a leak-proof seal for pressure-pistons which enabled him to obtain far higher pressures than his predecessors. He discovered allotropic forms such as 'hot ice' – solid water at 80° – and abrupt phase transitions wherein materials went from solid to liquid without an intermediary plastic stage. Existing theory neither predicted nor explained such phenomena, and so experimental work proceeded in a theoretical vacuum. This reinforced Bridgman's classical empiricist belief that observation of, and experimentation on, reality was the basis of all science, not theorizing.

Bridgman construed Einstein's 1905 special relativity theory (see EINSTEIN, A. §2; RELATIVITY THEORY, PHILOSOPHICAL SIGNIFICANCE OF; SPACETIME), as showing that Newtonian space and time had no objective standing, thereby abolishing the absolute dichotomy between matter and motion and calling into question the ontological status of the quantities experimental science measured. He wrestled with the relativistic challenge in the 1914–26 'dimensional analysis' disputes over the ontological status of measured quantities in physics, coming to the following conclusions: the quantities of physics are the products measurement produces according to a particular set of operations. Primary qualities are merely those regarded as fundamental. The dimensions of a primary quantity have no absolute significance, being merely reflections of the rules of operation in measurement. Since equations express equality of measured numbers, they too have no absolute physical significance.

Bridgman's operational philosophy, introduced in 1927, essentially generalizes his dimensional analysis position and is strongly conditioned by his highly successful experimental discoveries done in an area where existing theory provided little guidance. His philosophical concern was making sense of experimentation and its place in an increasingly theoretical physics if absolute qualities did not exist. He concluded that special relativity also undercut such absolute principles as the uniformity of nature. The focal issue became how to make sense of truth without lapsing into irrationalism if an absolute or transcendental reality is rejected.

Bridgman interpreted Einstein's special relativity theory as showing that objectivity is to be found in what the physicist *does*. What is real *is* what is meaningful and 'we mean by any concept nothing more than a set of operations; the concept is synonymous with the corresponding set of operations'. Each operation thus defines a separate concept. For Bridgman the measuring operations were the *only* permanent physical entities. Bridgman saw operationalism as a method for analysis – for sorting out what was and was not real among scientific assertions – and not a criterion for regimenting or demarcating the scientific from the unscientific as others interpreted it (see OPERATIONALISM).

Bridgman later moved from the idea that meanings of scientific claims were the operations the scientist performed to the view that knowledge is the product of human activity and rests on acts of the understanding – an essential private knowledge component that is not to be compromised by externally imposed demands for consistency. Critics accused Bridgman of flirting with solipsism, a charge he steadfastly denied.

Bridgman interpreted general relativity theory as reintroducing absolutes to science. Since he had come to reject all absolutes, Bridgman rejected general relativity theory. His attempts to reconcile quantum theory and thermodynamics focused on what they showed about the limits of human subjectivity, reinforcing his rejection of all absolutes as unknowable. Metaphysical and other absolutes including absolute ethical principles thus were illegitimate vehicles for imposing conformity of intellect on others.

In subjectivity of knowledge Bridgman found the source of cognitive freedom: to be scientific is to rely on the intellect, accepting only what is operationally knowable, and thus is the paradigm of intellectual integrity. Intellectual integrity is the essence of freedom. In social, moral and political realms, the path to freedom is to be scientific. What was real socially and what was morally binding were what was true. To assess truth one relied on operational analysis. In *The Intelligent Individual and Society* (1938) he subjected social and moral concepts to operational analysis, arguing that 'duty', 'responsibility', the idea of a 'right', and 'justice' all fail to have operational meaning and thus have only coercive utility. So, too, the state fails to exist as an entity in its own right. Bridgman rejected the idea that 'the best and deepest interests of the individual are coincident with those of society'. Rather than embracing solipsism he found that the key to individual freedom from authority is one's isolation and subjectivity. Freedom is the only ultimate.

See also: GENERAL RELATIVITY, PHILOSOPHICAL RESPONSES TO; LOGICAL POSITIVISM; MEASUREMENT, THEORY OF

List of works

Bridgman, P.W. (1922) *Dimensional Analysis*, New Haven, CT: Yale University Press. (His position here lays the basis for his operationalist philosophy.)

—— (1927) *The Logic of Modern Physics*, New York: Macmillan; repr. Salem, NH: Ayer Co., 1993. (Original statement of his operationalism.)

—— (1931) *The Physics of High Pressure*, London: G. Bell & Sons. (Based on his high pressure scientific experiments.)

—— (1936) *The Nature of Physical Theory*, Princeton, NJ: Princeton University Press; repr. in *Philosophical Writings of Percy Williams Bridgman*, New York: Arno Press, 1980. (In this work Bridgman pursues the subjectivist tendencies in his operationalism.)

—— (1938) *The Intelligent Individual and Society*, New York: Macmillan. (Basic articulation of his extension of operational method to social and moral philosophy with an emphasis on issues of individual freedom.)

—— (1941) *The Nature of Thermodynamics*, Cambridge, MA: Harvard University Press. (This summarizes Bridgman's attempts to deal with the epistemological implications of nature having indeterministic stochastic properties.)

—— (1952) *The Nature of Some of Our Physical Concepts*, New York: Philosophical Library; repr. in *Philosophical Writings of Percy Williams Bridgman*, New York: Arno Press, 1980. (Later restatement of his operationalist philosophy similar to his 1936 work.)

—— (1955) *Reflections of a Physicist*, New York: Philosophical Library, 2nd edn; repr. New York: Arno Press, 1980. (This contains reprints of nearly all his philosophical and nontechnical papers.)

—— (1959) *The Way Things Are*, Cambridge, MA: Harvard University Press. (A reiteration of his 1938 views on society and freedom.)

—— (1962) *A Sophisticate's Primer of Relativity*, Middletown, CT: Wesleyan University Press; 2nd edn, 1983. (First edition contains a critical commentary by A. Grünbaum, the second an introduction by A. Miller, unpublished notes of Bridgman's from the 1920s, and drafts.)

—— (1964) *Collected Experimental Papers*, Cambridge, MA: Harvard University Press, 7 vols. (Contains a complete bibliography of his scientific writings.)

References and further reading

Moyer, A.E. (1991) 'P.W. Bridgman's Operational Perspective on Physics. Part I: Origins and Development' and 'Part II: Refinements, Publications, and Receptions', *Studies in the History and Philosophy of Science* 22: 237–58, 373–97. (Historical account of development of his ideas.)

Walter, M.L. (1990) *Science and Cultural Crisis: An Intellectual Bibliography of Percy Williams Bridgman (1882–1961)*, Stanford, CA: Stanford University Press. (An invaluable, detailed biography based on archival and published sources. Does an excellent job of relating how Bridgman's scientific work informs his philosophical views. Contains comprehensive bibliography.)

FREDERICK SUPPE

BRINKLEY, RICHARD
(*fl.* 1350–73)

Richard Brinkley was a Franciscan theologian at the University of Oxford in the latter half of the fourteenth century. Probably at the request of his superiors, he undertook an attack on nominalism and conceptualism, resulting in his best-known work, Summa logicae (Synopsis of Logic). Other works include a commentary on Peter Lombard's Sentences, which survives only fragmentarily and in a student's shortened version. Brinkley had a significant influence on several generations of Oxford logicians and Parisian theologians.

Brinkley was active at Oxford University sometime between 1350 and 1373. His successors called him *Doctor Bonus* or *Doctor Valens* (the 'Good Doctor' or 'Capable Doctor'). His principal surviving philosophical work is the lengthy *Summa logicae* (Synopsis of Logic) comprising over one hundred manuscript folia (roughly equivalent to 500 ordinary printed pages). Brinkley's extant theological works include fragments of his *Commentum super Sententias*, a commentary on the *Sentences* of Peter LOMBARD, which also survives in a shortened version (*abbreviatio*) by Stephen Gaudet, who delivered his own commentary on the *Sentences* in 1361–2 (see Kaluza 1989: 181–88). The same manuscript in which Gaudet's *abbreviatio* is found also contains *Quaestiones magnae* and *Quaestiones breves* (Long Questions and Short Questions) on various philosophical issues in theological contexts, probably also by Brinkley. Lost works by Brinkley include a *Distinctiones scholasticae* (Scholastic Distinctions) listed by John Bale in the sixteenth century, and a *Quaestiones theologicales Biligam et Brinkel* (Theological Questions of Brinkley and [Richard] Billingham, probably a student's compilation), mentioned in an old Prague University library catalogue. The *Lectura super Sententias* (Lecture on the *Sentences*) mentioned by Bale is very likely identical with the *Commentum*. Bale also mentions a *Determinationes* (Determinations), but this work is probably by William of Foville, a Franciscan of Cambridge University.

Brinkley's *Summa logicae* seems to date from between 1360 and 1373 (see Gál and Wood 1980: 77–8), perhaps after his theological works. It was unusual but not unheard of for a medieval thinker to produce purely philosophical works after entering the faculty of theology. In Brinkley's case, this unusual sequence might have resulted from his having been ordered by his superiors to write a logical work against the predominant nominalism and conceptualism of his time. The *Summa logicae* advertises itself as a manual for young students, but primarily it is a polemical defence of the realist position regarding universals. It consists of seven parts: 'On Terms', 'On Universals', 'On the Categories', 'On the Supposition of Terms', 'On Propositions', 'On Insolubles' and 'On Obligations'.

Brinkley advances his position with sophisticated theories, some of which are of contemporary interest. For instance, in Part V of the *Summa logicae*, continuing a debate between Adam WODEHAM and Walter CHATTON, Brinkley argues against Richard Billingham (Regent Master at Oxford in 1349), William of Bermingham (a Doctor of Theology by 1362) and Richard Feribrigge (Rector of Shelton in 1361), who hold, respectively, that what a proposition signifies is a mode of a thing, a mental act or simply the significate of the subject term. Brinkley rejects the need for any intensional semantic entity, and holds the extentionalist position that the primary significate of any proposition is the coordinated things in the world signified by the terms of the proposition. Brinkley's views may have been known to Henry Hopton, ALBERT OF SAXONY and John WYCLIF.

Brinkley's theory of supposition is thoroughly informed by his realist views. For instance, for Brinkley simple supposition occurs whenever a term designates an independent, extra-mental universal, as does the term 'man' in the proposition 'Man is a species'. Even compared to other realists, Brinkley adopted some unusual positions, such as his rejection of the usual interpretation of material supposition, associated with a term's standing for itself (as does the term 'man' in the proposition 'Man is monosyllabic'). All supposition, Brinkley says, requires a relation, and nothing can be related to itself.

Brinkley's theological writings are dated between 1350 and 1360. Like most ostensibly theological works of his day, his writings are an amalgam of physics, moral philosophy, epistemology and metaphysics, as well as pure theological speculation. It is difficult to assess the full range of Brinkley's thought definitively, given the fragmentary state of his literary remains. Much of what we know of him depends on allusions to his writings in the works of other authors. While Brinkley never achieved the status of an authority, he prompted both assent and dissent among several generations of Parisian theologians. In the fourteenth century alone, authors whom he influenced include Angelus of Dobelin, Dionysius of Montina, Galerand of Pendref, Henry Totting of Oyta, Jacob of Eltville, John Bramarth, John Hiltalingen of Basel (and his associate Paul de Fonte), Peter of Candia, Stephen Gaudet and William Centueri of Cremona.

See also: LANGUAGE, MEDIEVAL THEORIES OF; NOMINALISM; REALISM AND ANTIREALISM

List of works

Brinkley, Richard (c.1350–60) *Commentum super Sententias* (Commentary on the *Sentences*), selection edited in Z. Kaluza, 'L'oeuvre théologique de Richard Brinkley, OFM', *Archives d'histoire doctrinale et littéraire du Moyen-âge* 56, 1989: 169–273. (Only fragments of this work survive. For a manuscript, see Bibl. Nazionale (Florence), conv. soppr. B 6 910 (*sine fol.*).)

—— (c.1350–60) *Quaestiones magnae* and *Quaestiones breves* (Long Questions and Short Questions), selection edited in Z. Kaluza, 'L'oeuvre théologique de Richard Brinkley, OFM', *Archives d'histoire doctrinale et littéraire du Moyen-âge* 56, 1989: 169–273. (Original manuscript in Paris (Bibl. Nat., lat. 16535, ff. 128r–129r) also contains Stephen Gaudet's *abbreviatio*.)

—— (c.1360–73) *Summa logicae* (Synopsis of Logic), Part V ed. in M.J. Fitzgerald, *Richard Brinkley's Theory of Sentential Reference: 'De significato propositionis' from Part V of His Summa nova de logica*, Studien und Texte zur Geistesgeschichte des Mittelalters XVIII, Leiden: Brill, 1987; Part VI ed. in P.V. Spade, *An Anonymous Fourteenth Century Treatise on 'Insolubles': Text and Study*, Toronto, Ont.: The Pontifical Institute of Mediaeval Studies, 1969; Part VII ed. P.V. Spade and G. Wilson, *Richard Brinkley's Obligationes: A Late Fourteenth Century Treatise on the Logic of Disputation*, Münster: Aschendorff, 1995; five various chapters ed. in G. Gál and R. Wood, 'Richard Brinkley and His *Summa logicae*', *Franciscan Studies* 40, 1980: 59–101.

References and further reading

Fitzgerald, M.J. (ed.) (1987) *Richard Brinkley's Theory of Sentential Reference: 'De significato propositionis' from Part V of His Summa nova de logica*, Studien und Texte zur Geistesgeschichte des Mittelalters XVIII, Leiden: Brill. (Edition and English translation (by M.J. Fitzgerald) of Part V of the *Summa logicae*, with a discussion of Brinkley's semantic theory and its influence.)

* Gál, G. and Wood, R. (1980) 'Richard Brinkley and His *Summa logicae*', *Franciscan Studies* 40: 59–101. (An introduction to the *Summa logicae*, with an edition of five scattered chapters from Parts I–IV.)

* Kaluza, Z. (1989) 'L'oeuvre théologique de Richard Brinkley, OFM' (The Theological Work of Richard Brinkely, OFM), *Archives d'histoire doctrinale et littéraire du Moyen-âge*: 169–273. (The most thorough discussion of Brinkley's theological work, with a complete edition of Stephen Gaudet's *Abbreviatio* of the *Commentum super Sententias*, a surviving fragment of the *Commentum*, question 3, and a selection from the *Quaestiones magnae*.)

Spade, P.V. (1969) *An Anonymous Fourteenth Century Treatise on 'Insolubles': Text and Study*, Toronto, Ont.: The Pontifical Institute of Mediaeval Studies. (A transcription of Part VI of the *Summa logicae*.)

—— (1991) 'Richard Brinkley's *De insolubilibus*: A Preliminary Assessment', *Rivista di storia della filosofia* 46: 245–56. (A critical analysis of Brinkley's theory of obligationes.)

—— (1993) 'Opposing and Responding: A New Look at "Positio"', *Medioevo* 19: 233–70. (Edition of selected passages of Part VI of the *Summa logicae*, the *Insolubilia*.)

Spade, P.V. and Wilson, G. (eds) (1995) *Richard Brinkley's Obligationes: A Late Fourteenth Century Treatise on the Logic of Disputation*, Beiträge zur Geschichte der Philosophie und Theologie des Mittelalters, NF 43, Münster: Aschendorff. (Edition, with an introduction and some comments, of Part VII of the *Summa logicae*.)

ROBERT ANDREWS

BRITISH EMPIRICISTS

see HUME, DAVID; LOCKE, JOHN

BRITO, RADULPHUS (*c*.1270–*c*.1320)

Radulphus Brito was a prominent master of arts at the University of Paris around 1300. In order to secure the foundation of concepts in extramental reality, he devised a system of four types of 'intentions', first and second, abstract and concrete. As a philosopher of language, similar concerns made him claim a formal identity between the modes of signifying (of words) and the modes of being signified (of things).

Probably a native of Brittany, Radulphus Brito (Ralph the Breton) must have been born about 1270, as he became a master of arts in Paris no later than 1296 and doctor of theology, also in Paris, about 1311–2. He died in 1320 or later.

The extant body of Radulphus' work is mainly unedited. Most of it relates to his activity as a master of arts, and comprises questions on the Aristotelian Organon, including Porphyry's *Isagōgē*, the anonymous *Six Principles* and Boethius' *De differentiis topicis* (On Topical Differences), and on Aristotle's *De anima*, *Physics*, *Meteorology* and *Metaphysics*, as well as on some mathematical and astronomical textbooks. There are also *sophismata* (investigations of particular logical problems), and a work on grammatical theory, *Quaestiones super Priscianum Minorem* (Questions on Priscian Minor), also called *Modi significandi* (Modes of Signifying). From Radulphus' career in theology we have questions on Peter Lombard's *Sentences*, a *Quodlibet* and *Quaestiones in Vesperis* (Evening Questions).

Radulphus became quickly famous, and younger contemporaries such as Bartholomew of Bruges attempted to dispute his views. The logical works continued to be read until some time in the fifteenth century, especially in Italy, and in the 1430s some parts were translated into Greek by Georgios (Gennadios) Scholarios (see BYZANTINE PHILOSOPHY).

Radulphus' fame rests on his epistemology, and in particular his distinction between concrete and abstract first and second intentions, the conceptual counterparts of such series of nouns as 'man, humanity; universal, universality'. Traditionally, first intentions such as 'horse' were distinguished from second intentions such as *species*, which presuppose the first ones. Radulphus divided both first and second intentions into abstract and concrete ones. The abstract first intention is a formal concept, such as 'humanity'. It is based on the features or manifestations (modes of being, *apparentia*) of some essence (or 'nature'). Reasoning, for example, is a manifestation of human nature. This abstract first intention is a thought (*cognitio*) whose object is man, but it does not include its object. The concrete first intention is the object of the abstract one, but it is not purely extramental. It is the thing (for example, man) considered simply as thought of by means of the formal concept (humanity). Alternatively, it is described as an aggregate of the thing and the thought by which we grasp it. This ontological duplicity was often criticised in later times, but what Brito wanted was to secure the lifeline between concepts and their objects without moving the objects into the mind.

Likewise for the second intentions, the modes of being form the basis of concept formation, but this time the modes in question are not proper to some nature but common to natures. The abstract second intention, (for example, universality), is a concept derived from the common feature of being capable of occurring in several individuals or types. This feature is shared by, for example, 'man' and 'donkey', both of which can occur in several individuals, and also by 'animal', which can occur in several species. Our intellect need perform no comparison to construct a Porphyrian tree; sensory acquaintance with a single individual suffices to recognize, for instance, that sensing (which characterizes animals) is a trait apt to be shared by more beings than reason (which is reserved for humans). The corresponding concrete second intention (universal) is the thing (man) considered simply as conceived of by means of the formal concept of universality.

Earlier thinkers had held that second intentions arise from inspection and comparison of things already grasped by the mind. Brito wanted to generate them through direct inspection of the entities that gave rise to the first intentions. His aim was clearly to strengthen the link of the second intentions to reality by making them thoughts of things rather than of thoughts.

The linguistic theory (modism) prevalent in Radulphus' days took grammatical categories to be features (modes of signifying) of significative words but derived from features (modes of being) of things (see LANGUAGE, MEDIEVAL THEORIES OF). Some decades of discussion had revealed weaknesses of the theory, and Brito fought an uphill battle to save it. Thus, to avoid difficulties arising from the existence of equivocal words, modes of signifying had been split into active modes, residing in words, and passive ones (modes of being signified), residing in things, such that one active mode could correspond to several passive ones. Seeing that this compromised the basic modistic idea of deriving features of thought and of language from features of reality, Radulphus claimed that the active modes are

formally, but not materially, identical with passive modes, which in turn are materially identical with passive modes of being and of understanding. This view was taken over by the influential grammarian Thomas of Erfurt.

See also LANGUAGE, MEDIEVAL THEORIES OF; LOGIC, MEDIEVAL

List of works

Brito, Radulphus (*c.*1270–*c.*1320) *Quaestiones super librum De anima* (Commentary on Aristotle's *On the Soul*), ed. W. Fauser, *Der Kommentar des Radulphus Brito zu Buch III De anima*, Beiträge zur Geschichte der Philosophie und Theologie des Mittelalters NF 12, Münster: Aschendorff, 1974.

—— (*c.*1270–*c.*1320) *Quaestiones super libra Topicarum Boethii* (Questions on Boethius' *Topics*), ed. N.J. Green-Pedersen and J. Pinborg, Radulphus Brito: Commentary on Boethius' De differentiis topicis and the Sophism 'Omnis homo est omnis homo', *Cahiers de l'Institut du Moyen-Age Grec et Latin* 26, 1978.

—— (*c.*1270–*c.*1320) *Sophisma 'Omnis homo est omnis homo'* (Sophism: 'Every Man is Every Man'), eds N.J. Green-Pedersen and J. Pinborg, 'Commentary on Boethius' De differentiis topicis and the Sophism 'Omnis homo est omnis homo', *Cahiers de l'Institut du Moyen-Age Grec et Latin* 26, 1978.

—— (*c.*1270–*c.*1320) *Quaestiones super Priscianum Minorem* (Questions on Priscian Minor), eds H.W. Enders and J. Pinborg, *Grammatica Speculativa* 3.1–2, Stuttgart–Bad Cannstatt: Fromman-Holzboog, 1980. (On pages 15–19 there is a complete list of extant works by Radulphus of Brito, and of published extracts. Supplements to this list can be found in Ebbesen and Pinborg (1981–2): 318, n.3–5.)

—— (*c.*1270–*c.*1320) *Quaestiones super Artem Veterem* (Questions on the Old Logic), ed. S. Ebbesen and J. Pinborg, 'Gennadios and Western Scholasticism. Radulphus Brito's *Ars Vetus* in Greek Translation', *Classica et Mediaevalia* 33, 1981–2: 263–319. (This is an edition of the prologue of the question.)

—— (*c.*1270–*c.*1320) *Quaestiones super librum Elenchorum* (Questions on the *Sophistical Refutations*), ed. S. Ebbesen and J. Pinborg, 'Gennadios and Western Scholasticism. Radulphus Brito's *Ars Vetus* in Greek Translation', *Classica et Mediaevalia* 33, 1981–2: 263–319. (This is an edition of the prologue of the question.)

—— (*c.*1270–*c.*1320) *Sophisma 'Aliquis homo est species'* (Sophism: 'Some Man is a Species'), ed. J. Pinborg, 'Radulphus Brito's Sophism on Second

Intentions', *Vivarium* 13, 1975: 119–52. (Edition of the sophism.)

—— (*c.*1270–*c.*1320) *Quaestiones super librum Porphyrii* (Questions on Porphyry's *Isagōgē*), ed. J. Pinborg, 'Radulphus Brito on Universals', *Cahiers de l'Institut du Moyen-Age Grec et Latin* 35, 1980: 56–142. (Edits long section from the questions on Porphyry. An extract from this work also appears in H. Roos, 'Zur Begriffsgeschichte des Terminus "apparens" in den logischen Schriften des ausgehenden 13. Jahrhunderts', in J. Moller and H. Kohlenberger (eds) *Virtus politica. Festgabe zum 75. Geburtstag von Alfons Hufnagel*, Stuttgart-Bad Cannstatt: Frommann-Holzboog, 1974, 323–34.)

References and further reading

Ebbesen, S. (1980) 'Is 'canis currit' ungrammatical? Grammar in Elenchi commentaries', *Historiographia Linguistica* 7 (1/2): 53–68. (Inter alia, on the problem of active and passive modes of signifying.)

Marmo, C. (1994) *Semiotica e linguaggio nella scolastica: Parigi, Bologna, Erfurt 1270– 1330* (Semiotics and Language in Scholasticism: Paris, Bologna, Erfurt, 1270–1330), Rome: Istituto Storico Italiano per il Medio Evo. (A large-scale study of modism, based on both grammatical and logical texts.)

Pinborg, J. (1967) *Die Entwicklung der Sprachtheorie im Mittelalter* (The Development of the Theory of Language in the Middle Ages), Beiträge dur Geschichte der Philosophie und Theologie des Mittelalters, Texte und Untersuchungen 42.2, Münster: Ashendorff, and Copenhagen: Frost-Hansen. (The foundation of all later work on modism.)

—— (1972) *Logik und Semantik im Mittelalter. Ein Überblick* (Logic and Semantics in the Middle Ages: A Survey), Stuttgart–Bad Cannstatt: Frommann-Holzboog. (Pays special attention to Brito.)

—— (1984) *Medieval Semantics, Selected Studies on Medieval Logic and Grammar*, ed. S. Ebbesen, London: Variorum. (Several relevant papers, including one on the reception of Brito's theory of intentions.)

STEN EBBESEN

BROAD, CHARLIE DUNBAR (1887–1971)

A Cambridge contemporary of Russell, Moore and Wittgenstein, C.D. Broad wrote on an exceptional range of topics, including causation, perception, the philosophy of space and time, probability and induction, mind and body, ethics and the history of philosophy. He typically set out a number of received positions on a topic, explored their consequences with great clarity, and then came to a cautious estimate of where the truth probably lay. However, Broad made some notable contributions of his own, especially on perception (he defended a representative theory), induction (he argued that our inductive practices require the existence of natural kinds), and time (he argued that tensed facts cannot be analysed away). Although his talents lay in very careful analysis, Broad insisted that there was a proper place in philosophy for metaphysical speculation; he particularly admired McTaggart, and his monumental Examination of McTaggart's Philosophy *(1933, 1938) contains some of Broad's best work.*

1 **Conception of philosophy**
2 **Perception**
3 **Induction**
4 **Time**
5 **Ethics**

1 Conception of philosophy

Broad was born near London and educated at Dulwich College and Trinity College, Cambridge, initially as a natural scientist. He then switched to philosophy, winning a prize fellowship at Trinity in 1911: his revised dissertation was published as *Perception, Physics and Reality* (1914). After teaching at St Andrews, Broad became professor of philosophy at Bristol University in 1920, then succeeded McTaggart as Fellow in Moral Science at Trinity College in 1923. Broad's return to Cambridge coincided with the publication of *Scientific Thought* (1923). *The Mind and Its Place in Nature* (1925) and *Five Types of Ethical Theory* (1930) quickly followed, and the first volume of his *Examination of McTaggart's Philosophy* appeared in 1933. The same year, Broad became Knightbridge Professor of Moral Philosophy in Cambridge. For most of the tenure of the professorship he was, at least by his own account, an 'unbelieving Pope' who 'no longer believed in the importance of philosophy' – though he continued to publish a steady flow of articles, and after retiring in 1953 he wrote a vigorous 'Reply to My Critics'. He also wrote extensively on psychical research, in which he had a lifelong interest.

Broad's later disaffection lay, more precisely, with the style of philosophy practised in a Cambridge that was increasingly under the spell of Ludwig Wittgenstein. In *Perception, Physics And Reality*, Broad had written that the only way of assessing a fundamental philosophical thesis is to see 'what would follow if it were true and then try to judge whether these results make that which implies them probable or improbable'. And he continued to regard philosophy as similar in this way to science: in his 'Reply', Broad still maintained that 'the philosophy of the physical world and of our perception of it [is] analogous in certain respects (though profoundly dissimilar in certain others) to the making and testing of a far-reaching scientific hypothesis' (Schilpp 1959). This conception of philosophy (now widely shared by many philosophers influenced, for example, by Quine) put him profoundly at odds with the 'Wittgersnappers', who saw thinkers such as Broad as conceptual delinquents in the grip of pseudo-problems, and recommended close attention to our ordinary language as appropriate therapy. But for Broad, 'in philosophy it is equally silly to be a slave to common speech or to neglect it'. And he always insisted that there is a proper place not just for Critical Philosophy – 'the analysis and definition of our fundamental concepts, and the clear statement and resolute criticism of our fundamental beliefs' – but also for Speculative Philosophy which hopes 'to reach some general conclusions as to the nature of the Universe, and as to our position and prospects in it'.

Much of his writing directly reflects Broad's conception of philosophy: like a judicious scientist, he weighs up the evidence for and against various theories, and then comes to a guarded verdict about their relative acceptability. The final chapter of *Mind and Its Place in Nature* is an extreme example, where he defines seventeen possible accounts of the relation between the mental and the physical, gradually whittles these down to a short list of three, finally judging one of them – 'emergent materialism' – as 'on all the evidence which is available to me…the most likely view'. In other hands this approach could make for tedium, but Broad writes with model clarity, and often with admirable elegance enlivened by flashes of mordant wit.

2 Perception

Broad discussed perception more often than any other topic. In particular, *Scientific Thought* contains a classic development of the sense-datum theory. When perceiving a stick half immersed in water, it looks bent; and 'the most obvious analysis of the facts is that, when we judge that a straight stick *looks* bent, we are aware of an object [a 'sensum', to use Broad's preferred term] which really *is* bent, and which is related in a peculiarly intimate way to the physically straight stick'. Broad stresses that there are promising alternatives to this analysis of perceptual experience

in terms of the apprehension of some special kind of transitory object. Still, in *Scientific Thought* he assumes that the sensum analysis is basically correct, and then explores how it should be developed in detail.

This approach has fallen into considerable disfavour since Austin's classic assault on sense-data theories, for example (see AUSTIN, J.L. §2); but it would be wrong to conclude that there can now be nothing of interest in Broad's investigations. As he remarks in *Mind and Its Place in Nature*, 'a perceptual situation [such as seeing a cat] is "intuitive", while a thought-situation with the same kind of epistemological object [such as thinking of a cat] is "discursive"'. Judging *my cat is ginger* involves thinking of something as being a cat; but one can see a ginger cat without having the concept of a cat at all – the perceptual experience has, to use a later idiom, a nonconceptual content. And much of Broad's discussion of sensa can be read as an examination of such nonconceptual contents in a framework which need not presuppose that sensa are genuine 'objects'. For example, he revealingly investigates how our visual experiences interlock with our experiences of bodily movement and touch as we explore the world so as simultaneously to determine the rather different spatial characters of our visual and tactual perceptual contents.

Broad defends a refined version of Locke's account of our knowledge of the physical world (our experiences are caused by a world which, in certain respects, they resemble). But in *Scientific Thought*, Broad suggests that there is no conclusive proof to be had here. Rather, we can only indicate those facts about our sense experience 'which would give a high final probability to the belief in a physical world, provided it had a finite [non-zero] antecedent probability'. This probabilistic realism sharply distinguishes Broad from Russell, who at the time was aiming to 'construct' the external world from sense-data, rather than riskily infer it – and also from G.E. Moore, who was a realist but not a probabilist (see PERCEPTION §2; SENSE-DATA §§1–3).

3 Induction

Another pregnant suggestion involving probability appears in Broad's early account of causality. In *Perception, Physics and Reality*, he examines some alleged difficulties about causation raised by idealist philosophers such as Bradley, and suggests that the way out is to hold that the proper form of a causal law is 'the occurrence of X at any moment increases the probability of Y's occurrence at a moment τ later over what it would have been if X had not happened'.

But this novel proposal is not further explored (although in *Examination of McTaggart's Philosophy* Broad continues to make room for indeterministic causation). What Broad does concentrate on, in his many discussions related to probability, is the question of the character and justification of inductive reasoning. His long paper, 'The Relation Between Induction and Probability' ([1918] 1968), is noteworthy. Broad argues that inferences such as 'All observed *S*'s have been *P*: hence the next *S* will be *P*' are irreducibly probabilistic. However, he also argues that we cannot immediately apply to scientific inductions the results from probability theory that govern artificial situations like predicting the colour of a ball drawn from a bag. On certain assumptions we can show that if a random sample of *m* balls has proved to be all red, then the probability that the next ball out of the bag is red is $(m+1)/(m+2)$, so almost 1 when *m* is large. But we cannot carry over such a result in order to guarantee a high probability to the prediction that the next swan will be white, having observed many white swans, because the assumptions that apply in the artificial case do not apply in nature.

If an appeal to probability theory is not enough to warrant our induction here, what more is needed? Our most confident inductions are just those which deal with things that 'are believed to belong to what Mill would call a Natural Kind' (such as 'swan'): taking his cue from this, Broad argues that it is the real existence of natural kinds with characteristic causal powers which is required to underpin our inductive practices – and equally, is bound up with the very idea of a world containing 'continuants', that is, particular things that persist through time.

4 Time

Broad's *Examination of McTaggart's Philosophy* is a very detailed commentary on McTaggart's *Nature of Existence* (it concludes that 'none of McTaggart's more characteristic conclusions have been established by his arguments', a persuasive verdict that still leaves Broad rating McTaggart alongside Leibniz as a speculative metaphysician). But it also contains a series of interwoven discussions in which Broad offers his own independent treatment of various issues. Perhaps the most impressive of these is 'The "Nature" of a Continuant', where Broad extends his work on kinds, arguing, for example, that the only way of making sense of counterfactual claims about what a given thing would have done if its circumstances had been different 'presupposes constancy of nature in individuals and the existence of natural kinds'.

However, the best-known part of *Examination of McTaggart's Philosophy* deals with time. We think of

time as essentially involving change, and change as involving events that were still in the future becoming present, and then receding into the past – yet McTaggart famously argues that this conception leads to contradiction. Broad's analysis of McTaggart's reasoning here is definitive. 'He assumes that what is meant by a sentence with a *temporal copula* [such as 'is now', 'was', 'will be'] must be completely...expressible by a sentence or combination of sentences in which there is no temporal copula, but only temporal predicates and non-temporal copulas.' Thus, the truth that event *E will* occur consists in *E*'s having (timelessly!) the property of futurity. But eventually, the truth will be that *E is now* happening, so – on the same assumption – that different truth consists in *E*'s timelessly having the incompatible property of presentness. Contradiction ensues: hence, Broad concludes, we must reject McTaggart's tacit assumption that temporal copulas can be replaced by temporal predicates.

Broad also criticizes Russell's very different attempt to analyse away temporal copulas by treating, for instance, '*E* will occur' as meaning '*E* is later than this utterance' – where the 'is' is timeless. Broad argues that this theory requires us to conceive of past, present and future events as timelessly 'coexisting' in a way that it is impossible for us to render intelligible, or at least not compatibly with 'the fact that at any moment [certain events] are marked out from all the rest by the quality of presentness'. He concludes that tensed facts (as expressed using temporal copulas) are fundamental; or, in other words, 'Absolute Becoming' is an irreducible feature of the world. Broad's reasoning here is debatable – but his discussion remains a paradigm presentation of the 'tensed' view of time (see TENSE AND TEMPORAL LOGIC).

5 Ethics

At the end of his widely read *Five Types of Ethical Theory*, Broad favours a mild form of ethical intuitionism; but later articles are non-committal. Indeed, in his 'Reply', when asked to commit himself on meta-ethical questions such as 'Do moral claims express *judgments* which are true or false?' or 'Are moral characteristics non-natural?', Broad confesses that he has 'no decided opinion'. On first-order questions, such as the merits of utilitarianism, Broad's usual philosophical caution is compounded by the belief that no single criterion of right action is likely to do justice to the complexity of our ethical lives. But lacking an axe to grind, his ethical discussions (if not especially original) are exceptionally careful and judicious, and remain valuable – where more recent writers have overlooked his writings, such as those on moral-sense theories, it has often been at the cost of labouring to rediscover distinctions already elegantly made by Broad.

List of works

Broad, C.D. (1914) *Perception, Physics and Reality*, Cambridge: Cambridge University Press. (Defends a Lockean causal theory of perception.)

—— (1923) *Scientific Thought*, London: Kegan Paul, Trench, Trubner & Co. (Part I – on space, time and motion – includes an excellent early treatment of the significance of the theory of relativity. Part II further develops the sensum analysis of perception.)

—— (1925) *The Mind and Its Place in Nature*, London: Kegan Paul, Trench, Trubner & Co. (Extended treatments of the unconscious and 'The Alleged Evidence for Human Survival of Bodily Death' are sandwiched between illuminating and influential discussions of the mind–body problem.)

—— (1930) *Five Types of Ethical Theory*, London: Kegan Paul, Trench, Trubner & Co. (Discusses Spinoza, Butler, Hume, Kant and Sidgwick: a textbook from before the era of textbooks, deservedly very widely used for many years.)

—— (1933, 1938) *Examination of McTaggart's Philosophy*, Cambridge: Cambridge University Press. (Over 1,250 pages, the 'mausoleum' in which Broad inters his admired teacher's philosophy contains some of his own most impressive work.)

—— (1952) *Ethics and the History of Philosophy*, London: Routledge & Kegan Paul. (Mostly reprinted historical papers; but includes his influential inaugural lecture 'Determinism, Indeterminism and Libertarianism'.)

—— (1953) *Religion, Philosophy and Psychical Research*, London: Routledge & Kegan Paul. (Further reprinted papers; 'The Relevance of Psychical Research to Philosophy' usefully sums up Broad's stance on the topic – he is far from credulous, but insists that it behoves philosophers to examine the evidence carefully, and not merely dismiss the possibility of psychic phenomena on shaky a priori grounds.)

—— (1962) *Lectures on Psychical Research*, London: Routledge & Kegan Paul.

—— (1968) *Induction, Probability and Causation*, ed. J. Hintikka, Dordrecht: Reidel. (Reprints Broad's important papers on these topics, including 'The Relation Between Induction and Probability' from *Mind* 1918, 1920.)

—— (1971) *Broad's Critical Essays in Moral Philosophy*, ed. D. Cheney, London: Allen & Unwin. (A comprehensive collection – includes the fine 'Some Reflections on Moral-Sense Theories in Ethics'.)

—— (1975) *Leibniz, An Introduction*, ed. C. Lewy, Cambridge: Cambridge University Press. (Edited from undergraduate lectures given in 1949–50: a useful student text, with a particularly good treatment of Leibniz's theory of corporeal substances.)

—— (1978) *Kant, An Introduction*, ed. C. Lewy, Cambridge: Cambridge University Press. (Edited by Lewy from lectures given in 1951–2: again, a very accessible and reliable student text.)

—— (1985) *Ethics*, ed. C. Lewy, Dordrecht: Nijhoff. (Broad lectured on ethics almost every year from 1933–4 to 1952–3, the evolving course providing the setting from which a number of his papers were excerpted: this book is edited from his final set of lectures.)

References and further reading

Britton, K. (1978) 'Charlie Dunbar Broad, 1887–1971', *Proceedings of the British Academy* 64: 289–310. (An accessible review of the man and his work.)

* McTaggart, J.M.E. (1921, 1927) *The Nature of Existence*, Cambridge: Cambridge University Press, 2 vols. (Broad edited the second, posthumously published volume of McTaggart's *magnum opus*.)

* Schilpp, P.A. (ed.) (1959) *The Philosophy of C.D. Broad*, New York: Tudor. (Contains Broad's 'Autobiography', twenty-one critical essays – still overall the most useful discussions of his philosophy – and Broad's 'Reply to My Critics'. It also contains a detailed bibliography of Broad's publications up to 1959.)

PETER SMITH

BROWN, THOMAS (1778–1820)

Thomas Brown was the last prominent figure in the Scottish philosophical tradition deriving from David Hume and Thomas Reid. Like Reid, he took the mind's knowledge about itself to be a datum it is pointless to challenge or try to justify, since no other grounds can be more certain for us. But he defended Hume's account of causation as nothing more than invariable succession. The mind, therefore, is a simple substance, whose successive states are affected by and affect the states of physical objects: the laws according to which these changes take place are no harder to grasp than the effects of gravitation. Brown's lectures, published as delivered daily to Edinburgh students, seek to classify the laws of the mind so that we can conveniently understand ourselves, and direct our lives accordingly; the last quarter of his course draws conclusions for ethics and natural religion.

1 Life
2 Writings
3 Philosophical outlook

1 Life

Son of the minister of Kilmabreck, Thomas Brown was a precocious child who entered Edinburgh University in 1793 at 15, and after hearing Dugald Stewart's lectures in the following year submitted searching criticisms of them in writing (see STEWART, D.). He soon made a name in Edinburgh literary circles, and after abortive legal studies qualified as a medical doctor in 1803, submitting a thesis in Latin (which he was said to speak as fluently as English; his knowledge of modern European languages was also considerable). He entered medical practice, but kept up his philosophical interests, and when Stewart's health failed in 1809 Brown was made first his assistant and then his 'colleague' in the Edinburgh Chair of Moral Philosophy, in fact discharging all its duties until he himself fell ill in 1819. He died in the following year. His lectures, mostly written during the day before their first delivery, were highly thought of. They were published unrevised after his death, and throw an interesting light on his youthful student audience, being written in a powerful and complex Ciceronian style and peppered with quotations from a wide range of authors in Latin, French and Italian: Juvenal, Horace, Cicero and particularly Seneca are assumed to be familiar and are often not translated. He also quotes extensively from his favourite English poets, Alexander Pope and Mark Akenside. He published several volumes of his own ponderous poetry, in a similar style, which made little impact, but his lectures continued to be in demand (21st edition, 1851) until William Hamilton and idealism eclipsed the Scottish school; he has scarcely been remarked since.

2 Writings

Brown was one of the last notable exponents of the Scottish COMMON SENSE SCHOOL of philosophy, owing much to David HUME and Thomas REID, but more to the former. His mature position is a substance dualism, in which Hume's 'theatre of the mind' has become a simple substance, the successive states of which – a series of 'feelings' – constitute its subject's mental life. His first publication, *Observa-tions on the Zoonomia of Erasmus Darwin* (1798), an attack on the Zoonomia, was of little philosophical interest, but in his *Short Inquiry into the Nature of the Relation of Cause and Effect* (1803, much extended by the 3rd edition, 1818) he clarifies and purges Hume's view of causation. He defends Hume's account of causation as nothing but invariable succession, mounting a powerful attack on the notion of power, particularly that of unexercised power, as wielded by Reid. However, he also uses tools furnished by Reid: the world consists of substances; general terms are essentially abbreviations of lists of substances, suiting our own practical purposes, and descriptions are abstractions from states of those substances; we have by virtue of our nature some beliefs about the world that are not optional and are in no need of justification, and indeed could not be justified by anything more certain. Brown maintains, against Hume, that our belief that like antecedents are always followed by like consequences is just one such fundamental and pervasive belief; thus Hume's explanation of the effects of custom is out of place (experiments explore what the true causes of an effect are; we already believe there is some cause or other). He also mounts a vigorous demolition of Hume's whole impression/idea distinction, so as to detach belief from 'vivacity'; as a consequence Brown is able to combine bare Humean causal laws with complete absence of scepticism about both matter and God.

3 Philosophical outlook

Brown's philosophical acumen is better displayed in criticism of rival theories, through careful analysis and telling use of concrete examples, than in supporting his own. He was inclined (perhaps as a result of his scientific training, which he puts to good use as a source of examples) to apply Ockham's razor where possible, though not at the expense of convenience – for example, he does not recommend that we should abandon speaking of powers, merely that we should be careful not to be taken in by the language which reifies them. Although he shares Reid's reliance on consciousness as our only evidence for the mind's operations, as well as Reid's use of first principles, he scoffs at multiplying 'powers' of the mind. Rather, the philosophical ambition should be to seek out and systematize the kinds of changes it invariably displays in various kinds of situation. His lectures, published under the title *Lectures on the Philosophy of the Human Mind* (1820), also promise practical benefits, since understanding the mind and its operations (and its limitations) will give us a better picture of our divinely appointed nature and destiny. The extensive range of rhetorical aids which so recommended him to his audiences is consciously deployed to this exhortatory purpose, particularly in the later lectures on ethics and natural theology.

For Brown, then, the mind is a simple substance, changes in which (throughout called 'feelings') follow changes in the bodily organs of sense, and vice versa. Its simplicity, and hence distinctness, enables him to fend off materialism: the bodily organs are mere aggregates of particles which our senses are too weak to distinguish and the physiological unity of which is a mere matter of descriptive convenience; but there cannot be half a thought at the northwest corner of the mind; therefore the mind is not the physical lump. Its distinctness also affords him an argument for immortality. The particles of the body are all conserved at death, being merely redistributed: why therefore, in the face of the obvious presumptions, should God see fit to single out the separate mental substance for destruction? Problems about how we can understand a causal relation between the physiological and the mental are put firmly aside: there is no a priori grasp of any causal relation (nothing about the look of gunpowder can tell you what will happen if you put a match to it), and so we must just observe what correlations actually obtain, as in any other science (gravitation's influence at a distance is at first sight equally problematic). It may well seem that this picture of the mind is open to Reid's criticisms of the theory of ideas (see REID, T.§1); but Brown characteristically meets this doubt head on, arguing that Reid misguidedly took as literal what for most theorists since the collapse of Aristotelian real universals was merely convenient metaphor, and that, for such as Hume, 'ideas' in the proper sense were not the *object* of mental attention but its vehicle.

However, like Reid, Brown claims that our knowledge of things is through their properties, that is, how they behave. So the mind can be considered as effect and cause of contemporary states of other substances and as itself a succession of states. Although at any given moment its state is simple, this can be analysed, like a chemical substance, into the result of simpler inputs. 'Consciousness' does not name a separate power, but is a generic name for every kind of feeling – that is, mental awareness; nor is perception distinct from sensation. Abandoning previous ways of classifying mental operations, Brown deals first with changes in the mind which we discover to depend on outside causes (in our organs) and then with those which the mind itself produces. It emerges that though belief in a 'permanent external system of things' is for adults not optional, it may be explainable in terms of early experience. He speculates at length about the way in which kinaesthetic sensations may provide the associations with vision which can account for how

the infant solves George Berkeley's problem of deriving spatial information from colours (see BERKELEY, G.).

The affections of the mind caused by its own internal states Brown describes in terms of ingeniously various laws of 'suggestion': the extensive and detailed discussions of particular emotions are full of interest. Like Reid, Brown takes care to avoid regressive accounts: the mind cannot aim at producing a volition without circularity, and so desires and 'volitions' differ only as long-term and short-term states, causing effects in muscular action. The resulting ethics is a moral-sense account reminiscent of Francis Hutcheson's, classifying moral feelings towards human agents separately from the other emotions (see HUTCHESON, F. §2). This requires, and delivers, criticism of Adam Smith's rival account (see SMITH, A.), but Brown is really more interested in classifying our duties and reminding us at full oratorical stretch of the powerful motives in human nature for fulfilling them.

List of works

Brown, T. (1798) *Observations on the Zoonomia of Erasmus Darwin*, Edinburgh: Mundell. (Academic infighting, of no enduring interest.)

—— (1803) *A Short Inquiry into the Nature of the Relation of Cause and Effect, with Observations on the Nature and Tendency of the Doctrine of Mr Hume*, Edinburgh: Walker & Greig; enlarged 3rd edn Edinburgh: Constable, 1818. (Study of Hume's constant-conjunction theory, detached from Hume's metaphysics and defended against Reid's criticisms. Clear statement of problems of evidence and experimental research in science.)

—— (1820) *Lectures on the Philosophy of the Human Mind*, Edinburgh: Tait, 4 vols. (Brown's lecture course as delivered to Edinburgh undergraduates day by day. A broadly associationist psychology which seeks to classify and analyse mental operations of all kinds – perception, judgment, thought, desire, value.)

References and further reading

Davie, G. (1961) *The Democratic Intellect*, Edinburgh: Edinburgh University Press. (General work on Scottish culture in Edinburgh at the Enlightenment period.)

Dictionary of National Biography (1886) vol. 7: 31, article on Thomas Brown, London: Smith Elder. (Full biography, but not very helpful about philosophical views.)

Laurie, H. (1902) *Scottish Philosophy in its National*

Development, Glasgow: Maclehose. (Now somewhat dated in approach.)

McCosh, J. (1875) *The Scottish Philosophy: Biographical, Expository, Critical*, New York: Carter; repr. Bristol: Thoemmes, 1990. (Probably still the most useful general work on the Scottish Common Sense School. Several pages devoted to each individual figure, including biography and summary of philosophical positions.)

Robinson, D.S. (1961) *The Story of Scottish Philosophy*, New York: Exposition Press.

CHRISTOPHER BRYANT

BROWNE, PETER (1666–1735)

Peter Browne, an Irish bishop, was a critic of Locke's theory of ideas. His chief philosophical concern was to explain how human beings can conceive of God. He proposed that God's existence and attributes can be understood analogically, by their real – though inevitably partial – resemblance to human things. He distinguished between analogy, which turns on a 'real resemblance', and metaphor, which turns on a merely imagined one.

Browne entered Trinity College Dublin in 1682 and became a fellow in 1692. He served as provost of Trinity from 1699 until 1710, when he became Bishop of Cork and Ross in the south of Ireland. George Berkeley was a student and fellow at the college during Browne's tenure as provost. Years later, in the Fourth Dialogue of *Alciphron*, Berkeley, without naming Browne, attacked his analogical theology (see BERKELEY, G. §11). He took Browne to be denying that we have any notion at all of God's attributes. Browne's angry reply occupies the long final chapter of his *Things Divine and Supernatural* (1733).

Browne's first publication of philosophical interest was his *Letter* (1697) on John Toland's *Christianity Not Mysterious* (1696) (see TOLAND, J.). Relying on a simple version of the doctrine of analogy elaborated in his later works, Browne argues that although religious mysteries can be understood only in part, they *can* be understood and can therefore be believed. He also argues that they can be believed with good reason. It is perfectly legitimate to trust informants we know to be truthful and able, even if we cannot fully comprehend what they relate. And if their authority is confirmed by miracles our 'evidence or degree of knowledge' will mount even higher.

Browne's main philosophical work, *The Procedure, Extent, and Limits of Human Understanding* (1728), is in part a logic textbook meant to correct 'the false and Pernicious principles in some of our modern Writers of Logic and Metaphysics' (1728: 34). John Locke is the foremost example (see LOCKE, J. §§3–6). Like John SERGEANT, Browne rejects Locke's definition of knowledge as perception of the agreement or disagreement of ideas. 'The Word *Idea*,' he writes, 'should be limited and confined to our simple Sensations only', and to the 'various Alterations and Combinations of them' which he calls 'compounded ideas' (1728: 63). Compounded ideas differ from 'complex notions' or 'conceptions', in which ideas are combined with an immediate consciousness of the mind's operations and affections. Locke's over-broad use of the word 'idea' is, Browne suggests, one sign of his tendency to overestimate the mind's passivity. Another is Locke's denial, in his assault on the syllogism, of 'all true *Illation*, or the *Actual* infering one thing from another' (1728: 422). Instead Locke gives us 'a mere naked *juxta-Position* of Ideas' (1728: 422).

Browne's mature doctrine of analogy is presented in the *Procedure*, but it is spelled out more fully in *Things Divine and Supernatural* (1733). The doctrine rests on a distinction between analogy and metaphor. In each case we use one idea or conception to stand for another. But in analogy there is a 'real resemblance' or 'true correspondence' between the terms; in metaphor the resemblance is merely imagined. In what Browne calls 'human' analogy, each term is known – or knowable – directly; it follows that 'human' analogy can, at least in principle, be paraphrased away. In 'divine' analogy, the second, divine term cannot be known directly. Divine analogy is therefore 'necessary' or inescapable, if things divine are to be understood at all. 'Thus we contemplate things *Supernatural*', as he had written in the *Procedure*, 'not by looking directly *Upward* for any *Immediate View* of them; but as we behold the heavenly Bodies, by casting our Eyes *Downward* to the *Water*' (1728: 425).

List of works

Browne, P. (1697) *A letter in answer to a book entitled Christianity Not Mysterious; as also to all those who set up for reason and evidence in opposition to revelation & mysteries*, Dublin. (A reply to John Toland's *Christianity Not Mysterious*.)

—— (1728) *The procedure, extent, and limits of human understanding*, London; repr. New York: Garland, 1976. (Browne's main work, develops an anti-Lockean theory of knowledge.)

—— (1733) *Things divine and supernatural conceived by analogy with things natural and human*, London;

repr. New York: Garland, 1976. (The fullest statement of Browne's doctrine of analogy and metaphor.)

References and further reading

* Berkeley, G. (1732) *Alciphron*, in A.A. Luce and T.E. Jessop (eds) *The Works of George Berkeley, Bishop of Cloyne*, vol. 3, London: Thomas Nelson, 1950. (Berkeley criticizes Browne's doctrine in the Fourth Dialogue, §§17–18, and presents his own account of analogical predication in §21.)

Berman, D. (1982) 'Enlightenment and Counter-Enlightenment in Irish Philosophy', *Archiv für Geschichte der Philosophie* 64: 148–65. (Assesses Browne's place in the history of Irish philosophy in the early eighteenth century.)

—— (ed.) (1993) *Alciphron in Focus*, London: Routledge. (A convenient edition of selections from Berkeley's *Alciphron* with critical commentary. Includes the Fourth Dialogue and a brief excerpt from Browne's reply.)

KENNETH P. WINKLER

BRUNNER, EMIL (1889–1966)

Emil Brunner was one of the most influential Protestant theologians of the twentieth century. He was a minister of the Swiss Reformed Church, a professor at the University of Zurich, and held distinguished lectureships in England, the USA and Japan. He joined the 'dialectical school' early in his career, but tried to rehabilitate natural theology, which led to a rift with Barth. His works were widely read and often served as basic texts in Reformed and Presbyterian seminaries. He rejected the historicist reduction of Christ to a wise teacher figure that was characteristic of neo-Protestantism. He was also critical of modern philosophical anthropologies – as propounded by Marx or Nietzsche, for example – because he felt that they reduced human essence to a single dimension. Only theological anthropology can fully interpret human essence; and of central importance here is the 'I–Thou encounter', whereby the fulfilment of the human 'I' is achieved through a relationship with the divine 'Thou'. Brunner also unfolded an original view on the relation of theology to philosophy. Reason, he argued, is essential for the elucidation and communication of faith. Philosophy, in so far as it indicates the limitations of reason, can serve to prepare us for the revelation of the Absolute.

1 Theology of crisis
2 Eristic and natural theology
3 Theology of encounter
4 Faith and reason

1 Theology of crisis

Emil Brunner was born in Winterthur in Switzerland. His religious and theological education was marked by three main influences: a socio-eschatological, a historico-critical and a phenomenological. The first of these was mediated through his father, who was acquainted with religious socialism and especially enthralled by Christoph Blumhardt's eschatological message. He also read Hermann Kutter and Leonhard Ragaz and studied Herknew's and Sombart's socio-economic works. At the University of Zurich, Brunner received a solid training in the historico-critical method. His teachers were liberals, and one of them, Walter Köhler, was a disciple of Ernst TROELTSCH. In 1911, he spent a semester in Berlin, where he attended Adolf von Harnack's lectures. The phenomenological influence manifested itself when Brunner, searching for a rigorous formulation of Christian belief, read first Kant, and then discovered Edmund Husserl.

After a year in England (1913–14), where he frequented the Christian Labour Movement and the Brotherhood Movement, he received his doctorate in theology in Zurich. His dissertation examined the use of symbol in religious knowledge. Brunner took his theme from Kant and Bergson and his method from HUSSERL (§§2, 6). As knowledge of a higher world, religious knowledge is inherent in the consciousness of ethical norms. In the wake of KANT (§11), Brunner's theologizing process proceeded from ethics to faith.

The First World War destroyed Brunner's hopes for a better world. Blumhardt's belief in the imminent coming of the kingdom of God, to which Brunner had held, was shattered dramatically. Like Karl Barth, Brunner turned back to the foundations of Christian doctrine and action. He spent a year of research at Union Theological Seminary in New York (1919–20), then, in 1921, defended his *Habilitationsschrift* at the University of Zurich, which led to his appointment there the following year; in 1924, he took the chair of systematic and practical theology. It was at this time that Brunner discovered Barth's *Der Römerbrief* (*The Epistle to the Romans*) (1919) and joined the 'theologians of crisis' contributing regularly to the journal *Zwischen den Zeiten* (Between the Times) (see BARTH, K. §§1–2). He subsequently became a major exponent of 'the theology of crisis'. Like Barth, Brunner found inspiration in Kierkegaard's warning against the accommodation of Christian faith to human culture (see KIERKEGAARD, S.A. §§4–5). His main concern was to restore the sovereignty of God. Thus he centred theology on the gospel of sin and grace while emphasizing the infinite qualitative distinction between God – the Wholly-Other – and human beings. Brunner denied human beings any natural knowledge of God, whether by reason, feeling or will; the knowledge of God is exclusively supernatural. Faith in revelation is the sole medium for our knowledge of God. Brunner insisted on the primacy of biblical revelation.

Having returned to the supernaturalism of the sixteenth-century Protestant Reformation, Brunner launched a spectacular offensive against neo-Protestantism, or liberalism. *Die Mystik und das Wort* (Mysticism and the Word) (1924) distinguishes Christian faith from the modern understanding of religion, as exemplified by Friedrich SCHLEIERMACHER (§7); *Der Mittler* (The Mediator) (1927) claims allegiance to Nicene and Chalcedonian Christology. Brunner defended the divinity of Christ the Mediator against the lives of Jesus presented by the historicizing and psychologizing schools of the nineteenth century. What he most disapproved of in neo-Protestantism was the reduction of Christ to a wise teacher or a heroic figure, the identification of progress with divine providence, and uncritical confidence in human nature.

2 Eristic and natural theology

In 1929, Brunner published a programmatic article, 'Die andere Aufgabe der Theologie' (The Other Task of Theology), which presaged the coming break with Barth. Responding to an epistemological, a missionary and an ethical motive, Brunner's theology was shifting from the content of revelation (the 'what') to the appropriation of revelation (the 'how'). Whereas expounding God's revelation in Christ through Scripture defines the first theological task, the second one consists in clearing the path for its appropriation by human beings. Brunner called 'eristic' the type of apologetics that stresses the delusion of reason; he claimed to have borrowed this theology from Pascal, Hamann and Kierkegaard. An article entitled 'Die Frage nach den "Anknüfungspunkt" als Problem der Theologie' (The Question of the 'Point of Contact' as a Theological Problem) (1932) argues in favour of an innate human disposition to the divine. In it, Brunner contends that the Word of God does not encounter a passive, unresponsive being, but a thinking subject, a responsive and responsible person. Brunner called the 'point of contact' that which corresponds in episte-

mology to the human ability to hear and respond to God's revelation, in anthropology to the infralapsarian image of God, and in ethics to evil conscience.

The rehabilitation of natural theology, though of a different kind, came in 1934. Brunner's essay 'Natur und Gnade' (Nature and Grace) prompted Barth's uncompromising censure (1935). The dispute culminated in a rupture between the two, though Brunner did not advocate a Roman Catholic type of natural theology. For Brunner, natural theology serves a threefold purpose: to ground personal and social ethics; to provide a philosophical substructure to dogmatics; and to enable Christian preaching and education. It lays the foundation for expositions of revelation. Brunner drew a distinction between subjective natural theology (Roman Catholic) and objective natural theology (Scripture and Calvin). Whereas the former implies the natural knowability of God, the latter consists only in a gnoseologically inoperable general revelation. Sin has disconnected the knowledge of God from general revelation. Hence Brunner argued that God's special revelation in Christ constitutes the source of knowledge for God's general revelation in nature, history and human consciousness. Contrary to Roman Catholic natural theology, Brunner's so-called 'Christian natural theology' claims to preserve a Christocentric gnoseology. Notwithstanding this, Barth felt that Brunner's call for a rehabilitation of natural theology in Christian theology disrupted the post-Reformation emphasis on faith.

3 Theology of encounter

Brunner made ample use of the psychological-anthropological 'I–Thou' relationship in all his major works, including *Das Gebot und die Ordnungen* (The Divine Imperative) (1932), *Der Menschen im Widerspruch* (Man in Revolt) (1937), *Wahrheit als Begegnung* (Truth as Encounter) (1938), *Offenbarung und Vernunft* (Revelation and Reason) (1941) and the three-volume *Dogmatik* (1946–60), which unfolds a liberal, modernized version of Reformed theology. The I–Thou relationship was borrowed from the personalist philosophy of existence that Martin BUBER (§4) and Ferdinand Ebner professed. In *Man in Revolt*, Brunner argues that all philosophical anthropologies, whether realist (Aristotle), idealist (Plato), pantheist (Stoics) or naturalist (Darwin), provide a distorted image of the human being because of their false interpretation of human essence. The leading philosophical anthropologies of our time, namely those of Darwin, Nietzsche, Marx and Freud, reduce human essence to a single principle and thus fail to account for human reality as a whole. Only theological anthropology, which is biblical, Christo-centric and based on faith, correctly explains human essence. Theological anthropology deals with human responsibility. The Word of God is the source of theological anthropology and also makes it knowable by us. Thus a human being is not only a sensitive and thinking subject, but also an 'I' whose fulfilment depends on a relationship to the human-divine 'Thou'. For Brunner, this scheme offers an escape from the traditional alternatives of objective or subjective anthropology. For the truth of faith is neither an objective nor a subjective truth but 'truth as encounter'. Likewise, revelation is not the disclosure of supernatural facts or truths, but God's self-revelation. The truth of revelation is thus also 'truth as encounter'. The knowledge of faith is understood as a synthetic theory that removes the contradictions of human thought and life. Life without Christ is life in contradiction.

4 Faith and reason

From the vantage point of Christian theology, the relationship between faith and reason concerns three things: the use of philosophical terminology, the auxiliary function of philosophical analysis, and the legitimacy of the philosophical endeavour (see FAITH §§4–5). Like Barth, Brunner occasionally used philosophical concepts. Divine revelation cannot avoid human reason nor is it fundamentally opposed to reason. For reason is the quintessence of a human being's natural ability to know: it is the capacity to conceive and to formulate ideas. Thus faith needs reason for its rational elucidation; it is a matter of understanding and communication. Consequently, the employment of reason is essential to Christian education. Brunner viewed reason (*Vernunft*) not merely as understanding (*Verstand*) but also as part of the image of God. Whereas understanding is limited to finite and objective knowledge, reason is the power to transcend, to relate to the beyond. The use of philosophical terminology is necessary and legitimate, and may go as far as a partial or global appropriation of a philosophical scheme; an example is the 'I–Thou' relationship, which enables theological discourse to avoid dualism without falling into monism.

The issue of whether philosophy should be regarded as the handmaid of theology was much debated among the 'theologians of crisis'. Rudolf BULTMANN (§§2–3) favoured this type of relationship, whereas Barth disapproved of it. In *Erlebnis, Erkenntnis und Glaube* (Experience, Insight and Belief 1921), his *Habilitationsschrift* for Zurich, Brunner advocated a constructive relationship between theol-

ogy and a type of philosophy that he labelled 'philosophy of origin' (*Philosophie des Ursprungs*). Critical and deconstructive, the 'philosophy of origin', as developed by Plato, Descartes and Kant, emphasizes and respects the finitude of human nature. It is an inverted science, which postulates the idea of a world beyond, an original and absolute other world, but acknowledges the limitations of this idea. Thus, the 'philosophy of origin' can be a valuable auxiliary to Christian faith. By stressing the inadequate outcome of all rational endeavour, the 'philosophy of origin' prepares human beings to receive the Absolute as ultimate principle and meaning, and thereby clears the path for the 'miracle' of God's Word, namely for revelation and faith. As a preparation for faith, the 'philosophy of origin' functions as a handmaid to theology.

Regarding the legitimacy of philosophical endeavour, Brunner justified and restricted it. In *Revelation and Reason*, he enunciated a law of contiguity which allows for a Christian philosophy. The choice is no longer between theology and philosophy but between existential faith and philosophical and theological reflection. In faith as encounter, faith restores reason's original purpose. Whereas reason provides access to an objective, impersonal, universally valuable truth, faith, as encounter with the divine 'Thou', is given a valid and life-transforming truth. In faith as encounter, the believing/knowing subject does not acquire the knowledge of an objective and objectifiable truth, but becomes God's possession. Finally, faith and reason together build a dialectical relationship similar to the dialectic of Law and Gospel.

List of works

Brunner, E. (1979–) *Emil Brunner: Werke* (Collected Works), ed. R. Wehrli, Zurich: Theologischer Verlag. (Multiple volumes, still being produced.)

—— (1921) *Erlebnis, Erkenntnis und Glaube* (Experience, Insight and Belief), Tübingen: Mohr. (Brunner's *Habilitationsschrift*, in which he advocates the 'Philosophy of Origin', which can do justice to human finitude and thus fit with theology.)

—— (1924) *Die Mystik und das Wort: der Gegensatz zwischen moderner Religionsauffassung und christlichen Glauben, dargestellt an der Theologie Schleiermachers* (Mysticism and the Word: The Conflict between Modern Religious Belief and Christian Faith, with Reference to the Theology of Schleiermacher), Tübingen: Mohr. (Like Karl Barth, Brunner defined himself to some extent over against Schleiermacher, particularly in this work.)

—— (1927) *Der Mittler: Zur Besinnung über den Christusglauben*, Tübingen: Mohr; trans. O. Wyon,

The Mediator: A Study of the Central Doctrine of the Christian Faith, London: Lutterworth, 1934. (A lengthy presentation of Brunner's broadly orthodox Christology.)

—— (1929) 'Die andere Aufgabe der Theologie' (The Other Task of Theology), *Zwischen den Zeiten* 7. (Theology must, *pace* Barth, ask how revelation is humanly appropriated – this is its other task.)

—— (1932a) 'Die Frage nach den "Anknüfungspunkt" als Problem der Theologie' (The Question of the 'Point of Contact' as a Theological Problem), *Zwischen den Zeiten* 7. (The question of the human reception of revelation led Brunner to a break with Barth through positing a fundamental human receptivity: the *Anknüfungspunkt* of the title.)

—— (1932b) *Das Gebot und die Ordnungen: Entwurf einer protestantisch-theologischen Ethik* (The Law and the Rules: Outline of a Protestant Theological Ethics), Zurich: Zwingli-Verlag, 4th edn, 1939; 2nd edn trans. O. Wyon, *The Divine Imperative: A Study in Christian Ethics*, London: Lutterworth, 1937. (An ethics consonant with Brunner's focus on the encounter between God and fallen humanity, and Protestant ambiguity about 'law'.)

—— (1934) 'Natur und Gnade: zum Gespräch mit Karl Barth', *Theological Existenz heute* 14; trans. P. Fraenkel, 'Nature and Grace', in K. Barth and E. Brunner, *Natural Theology*, London: Geoffrey Bles, 1946. (Brunner suggests a rehabilitation of natural theology as preparatory work for theology. The article prompted, and in English is printed with, Barth's famous published reply, 'Nein!')

—— (1935) *Unser Glaube: Eine Christliche Unterweisung*, Bern and Leipzig: Gotthelf Verlag; trans. J.W. Rilling, *Our Faith*, London: SCM, 1949. (A brief and simple guide to Brunner's understanding of credal Christian faith.)

—— (1937) *Der Menschen im Widerspruch: die christliche Lehre von wahrem und von wirklichen Menschen* (Man in Revolt: The Christian Doctrine of True Man and of Man as He Appears in the World), Berlin: Furche-Verlag; trans. O. Wyon, *Man in Revolt: A Christian Anthropology*, London: Lutterworth, 1939. (Despite his strong natural theology, Brunner retained a deeply Protestant view of fallen humanity, best seen in this book.)

—— (1938) *Wahrheit als Begegnung*, Zurich: Zwingli-Verlag; trans A.W. Loos, *Truth as Encounter*, London: SCM, 1964. (An earlier, incomplete translation was published as *The Divine–Human Encounter* (London: SCM, 1944), but the original German title captures the 'paradoxical' subject-matter best.)

—— (1941) *Offenbarung und Vernunft: die Lehre von der christlichen Glaubenserkenntnis*, Zurich: Zwingli-Verlag; trans. O. Wyon, *Revelation and Reason: The Christian Doctrine of Faith and Knowledge*, London: SCM, 1947. (Deals with broadly epistemological issues, and the foundation of faith in revelation.)

—— (1943) *Gerechtigkeit: eine Lehre von den Grundgesetzen der Gesellschaftsordnung* (Justice: A Study of the Foundations of the Social Order), Zurich: Zwingli-Verlag; trans. M. Hattiger, *Justice and the Social Order*, London: Lutterworth, 1945. (Brunner's constant social-ethical emphasis is most explicit in this work on the nature of society and the justice which must lie at its heart.)

—— (1946–60) *Dogmatik*, Zurich: Zwingli-Verlag, 3 vols; trans. O. Wyon (vols 1 and 2) and D. Cairns (vol. 3), London: Lutterworth, 1949–62. (Volume 1: the doctrine of God; volume 2: the doctrines of creation and redemption; volume 3: the doctrines of Church, faith and 'the consummation'.)

—— (1947–8) *Christianity and Civilization*, London: Nisbet, 2 vols. (Brunner's Gifford Lectures, originally published in English.)

References and further reading

* Barth, K. (1919) *Der Römerbrief*, Bern: Bäschlin; 2nd edn, much changed, Munich: Chr. Kaiser Verlag, 1922; 6th edn trans. E.C. Hoskyns, *The Epistle to the Romans*, Oxford: Oxford University Press, 1968. (Brunner was one of those theologians inspired by Barth's seminal work.)

* —— (1934) 'Nein! Antwort an Emil Brunner', *Theological Existenz heute* 14; trans. P. Fraenkel, 'No! Answer to Emil Brunner', in K. Barth and E. Brunner, *Natural Theology*, London: Geoffrey Bles, 1946. (A famous and blunt rejection of Brunner's natural theology.)

Brunner, H.H. (1986) *Mein Vater und sein Altester: Emil Brunner in seiner und meiner Zeit* (My Father and his Oldest Son: Emil Brunner in His and My Time), Zurich: Theologischer Verlag. (One of the only biographical works available.)

Buber, M. (1958) *I and Thou*, trans. R. Gregor Smith, New York: Scribner. (Perhaps the central philosophical influence on Brunner, this book proposes the centrality of I–Thou rather than I–It relationships.)

Ebner, F. (1921) *Das Wort und die geistigen Realitäten*. (A personalist influence on Brunner's early development, although less important than Buber.)

Kegley, C.W. (ed.) (1962) *The Theology of Emil Brunner*, New York: Macmillan. (Contains essays by prominent theologians, autobiographical material and a reponse from Brunner, and a bibliography complete to 1962.)

Kutter, H. (1904) *Sie Müssen! Ein Offenes Wort an die*

christliche Gesellschaft (You Must! An Open Word to Christian Society), Berlin: Hermann Walther Verlagsbuchhandlung. (This initiated the religious socialist movement which so influenced Brunner.)

Hesselink, J. (1989) 'Emil Brunner: A Centennial Perspective', *The Christian Century*, Dec. 13. (Discusses the state of Brunner scholarship and the possibilities for a Brunner revival.)

JEAN-LOUP SEBAN

BRUNO, GIORDANO (1548–1600)

Giordano Bruno was an Italian philosopher of nature and proponent of artificial memory systems who abandoned the Dominican Order and, after a turbulent career in many parts of Europe, was burned to death as a heretic in 1600. Because of his unhappy end, his support for the Copernican heliocentric hypothesis, and his pronounced anti-Aristotelianism, Bruno has often been hailed as the proponent of a scientific worldview against supposed medieval obscurantism. In fact, he is better interpreted in terms of Neoplatonism and, to a lesser extent, Hermeticism (also called Hermetism). Several of Bruno's later works were devoted to magic; and magic may play some role in his many books on the art of memory. His best-known works are the Italian dialogues he wrote while in England. In these Bruno describes the universe as an animate and infinitely extended unity containing innumerable worlds, each like a great animal with a life of its own. His support of Copernicus in La Cena de le ceneri *(The Ash Wednesday Supper) was related to his belief that a living earth must move, and he specifically rejected any appeal to mere mathematics to prove cosmological hypotheses. His view that the physical world was a union of two substances, Matter and Form, had the consequence that apparent individuals were merely collections of accidents. He identified Form with the World-Soul, but although he saw the universe as permeated by divinity, he also believed in a transcendent God, inaccessible to the human mind. Despite some obvious parallels with both Spinoza and Leibniz, Bruno seems not to have had much direct influence on seventeenth-century thinkers.*

1   Life
2   Works
3   Memory and magic
4   Cosmology
5   Metaphysics
6   Influence

1   Life

Giordano Bruno was born in Nola, near Naples, and frequently called himself 'the Nolan'. His baptismal name was Filippo, and he adopted the name 'Giordano' on entering the Dominican Order in 1565. He fled from the Dominicans in 1576 on learning that he was to be accused of heterodox views, and wandered in Italy for a while, supporting himself by private teaching and tutoring. By 1579 he was in Geneva, where the municipal records show that he petitioned against a denial of participation in the Calvinist sacraments. This denial was apparently the result of Bruno's attack on a leading philosopher, which also led to brief imprisonment. Next he went to France, finally settling in Toulouse, where he lectured on Aristotle's *On the Soul*. He was in Paris 1581–3, where his lectures attracted the attention of Henri III. From 1583 to 1585 he was in London, staying at the house of the French ambassador, Michel de Castelnau. Unknown to Castelnau, Bruno was probably a spy, reporting to Sir Francis Walsingham, Elizabeth I's secretary, about the plots of the English Catholics (see Bossy 1991). He had an unfortunate experience in Oxford in 1583, being forced to abandon a series of lectures when a member of the audience pointed out that he was plagiarizing the works of FICINO. When Michel de Castelnau was recalled to Paris at the end of 1585, Bruno went with him. After some problems there, including opposition roused by a disputation in which his view of the universe was defended by a pupil, he turned to the German Protestant universities. In 1586 he went to Marburg, and matriculated at the university there but (as the Rector has recorded) angrily withdrew his name when denied the right to teach philosophy publicly. He then went to Lutheran Wittenberg, where he was allowed to lecture. In 1588 he visited the court of Rudolph II in Prague, and then went to Helmstadt, where he seems to have been excommunicated by the Protestants. In 1590 he was resident in the Carmelite monastery in Frankfurt. At this point he was invited by a Venetian nobleman, Zuan (a form of 'Giovanni') Mocenigo, to go to Venice and teach him the art of memory, and he took up the invitation in the autumn of 1591. In May 1592 Mocenigo, perhaps disappointed at what he had learned, handed Bruno over to the Venetian Inquisition. The following year they handed Bruno over to the Roman Inquisition. A long sequence of interrogations followed. In the end he refused to recant, though the list of final charges is not known. Despite the fact that heretics were normally strangled in prison and burned only in effigy, Bruno was burned to death on February 17, 1600, in the Campo dei Fiori in Rome.

2 Works

Bruno was an extremely prolific writer who wrote more than fifty works and opuscula, of which nearly forty, all from the period 1582–91, are now available in print. He wrote one comedy, *Il Candelaio* (The Torch-Bearer) (1582a), which influenced Molière, and several didactic and critical works. His works on magic, probably written in Helmstadt, were all unpublished during his lifetime. His most significant works include those on the art of memory and Ramon Llull's combinatory method. His first surviving work on these (or any other) issues is *De umbris idearum* (On the Shadows of Ideas) (1582b), published with *Ars memoriae* (On the Art of Memory). In 1583 there followed four works in one volume: *Ars reminiscendi* (On the Art of Remembering), *Explicatio triginta sigillorum* (The Explanation of the Thirty Seals), *Sigillus sigillorum* (The Seal of Seals), and a letter to Oxford setting out his claims to be heard. Another work in the same series is *Lampas triginta statuarum* (The Lamp of Thirty Statues) (*c.*1587).

Much of Bruno's fame rests on his six Italian dialogues. The cosmological dialogues are: *La Cena de le ceneri* (*The Ash Wednesday Supper*) (1584a); *De la causa, principio et uno* (*Cause, Principle and Unity*) (1584b); *De l'infinito universo et mondi* (*On the Infinite Universe and Worlds*) (1584c). The moral dialogues are: *Spaccio della bestia trionfante* (*The Expulsion of the Triumphant Beast*) (1584d), modelled on the satirist Lucian; *Cabala del cavallo Pegaseo con l'aggiunta de l'Asino cillenico* (The Kabbalah of the Pegasean Horse with an Appendix on the Cillenican Ass) (1585a); *De gl'Heroici Furori* (*The Heroic Frenzies*) (1585b), a sonnet sequence with prose commentaries.

The final version of Bruno's philosophical and cosmological speculations is found in three Latin poems with prose accompaniment, published in 1591: *De triplici minimo et mensura* (On the Threefold Minimum and Measure); *De monade, numero et figura* (On the Monad, Number and Figure); *De innumerabilibus, immenso et infigurabili* (On the Innumerables, the Immense and the Infigurable).

Bruno was never a professional philosopher with a permanent university post, a fact which helps explain both his chaotic style of writing and his exploration of various literary forms. He did not write organized textbooks, and there is little close argumentation or precise definition in his works. On the other hand, particularly in his dialogues, he is witty, bawdy, disputatious and hostile. Women are 'a chaos of irrationality' ([1584b] 1964: 118); his contemporary PATRIZI is that 'excrement of pedantry, who has soiled many quires with his Peripatetic Discussions'

([1584b] 1964: 99); Oxford doctors, who know beer better than Greek, are characterized by 'discourteous impoliteness and brazen ignorance' ([1584a] 1975: 142). His invective is balanced by elaborate praise of 'the Nolan', who has 'set free the human spirit and cognition' ([1584a] 1975: 60).

One feature of Bruno's style that seems particularly strange to modern readers, is his elaborate, extravagant, use of verbal descriptions of images, seals and emblems (symbolic devices representing abstract qualities, astral powers and so on). These devices are often arranged in groups of thirty, though *The Expulsion of the Triumphant Beast* is organized around forty-eight constellations, each linked to a vice which is to be expelled and replaced by the contrary virtue.

The influences on Bruno's work are manifold. As a Dominican, he had studied Thomas AQUINAS, whom he greatly admired, and Thomistic distinctions and categories still pervade his works. Obviously he knew ARISTOTLE well, though he is generally opposed to his views. He frequently refers to the Presocratics (see PRESOCRATIC PHILOSOPHY), and also to LUCRETIUS, but his general framework is Neoplatonic. PLATO and PLOTINUS are of particular importance, along with the *Corpus Hermeticum*, IBN GABIROL and NICHOLAS OF CUSA. Bruno also made much use of Ramon Llull, Marsilio Ficino and AGRIPPA VON NETTESHEIM (§5), especially Agrippa's *De occulta philosophia* (1533).

3 Memory and magic

The art of memory, which grew out of rhetoric, had a long history (see MEMORY §1). It developed rules for the cultivation of so-called artificial memory. These rules focused on places and images. First, one should imagine a place, such as a house with several rooms; then one should place images in each room. Later, by wandering in thought through the rooms, one would be enabled to remember the topics or things associated with each image. Bruno was trained in this tradition, but when he went to Paris, he became acquainted with Ramon Llull's combinatory art, which involved using letters and figures to represent basic concepts, and writing them on moving wheels in order to make new combinations (see LLULL, R. §2). Bruno adapted Llull's technique by employing images and emblems in place of mere letters. On turning the concentric wheels, one could relate the images in various ways and multiply the triggers of memory, as well as the complexity of what was represented.

Bruno's use of images has been linked to magic and Hermeticism (or Hermetism) as well as to the privileging of the imagination in epistemology. On the traditional view, the imagination was taken to be one of the inner senses, and had two functions, the forming of images which help us to retain sense impressions in memory, and the manipulation of images to form images of things never experienced, such as a golden mountain. Given a realist epistemology, images both reflected the outer world and formed a basis for the operations of the intellect. Bruno seems not to have departed from this account, and while he naturally emphasized the imagination when speaking of artificial memory, his other accounts of the human search for knowledge always subordinate the imagination to the intellect. The noetic process is triggered by sense perception, and involves an ascent beyond the imagination to as much understanding as the human mind can achieve. In *The Heroic Frenzies* Bruno emphasizes that love is the stimulus, and that the final ascent to union with God through understanding is unattainable in this life. There are difficulties with Bruno's epistemology, in that it is not always clear how much room is assigned to illumination from above, or how it is that human notions (the 'shadows of ideas') reflect the divine ideas that structure the world without being innate, but it is not the case that his account of cognition is reducible to his account of the imagination.

The link between magic and the art of memory can be explained by appeal to Bruno's realist framework, together with the premises that symbols and reality are linked and that knowledge as such has operative force. If external symbols and internal images represent not just the world but the natural forces which pervade it, the magician can achieve mastery of these natural forces by increasing his ability to represent them. Not only that, he can even influence others by projecting images into their minds. While Bruno's works on magic were all written at the end of his literary activity, he does speak of natural magic (as opposed to black magic) approvingly in *The Expulsion of the Triumphant Beast*. He describes the cult of the ancient Egyptians as 'magic and divine' ([1584d] 1964: 239), and says that their 'magic and divine rites' provide a way of ascent 'to the Divinity by means of the same ladder of Nature by which Divinity descends even to the lowest things in order to communicate herself' ([1584d] 1964: 236).

Frances Yates links both these references to magic and Bruno's praise of the ancient Egyptian religion to the *Corpus Hermeticum*, a group of writings dating from AD 100 to AD 300, and attributed to the mythical Egyptian sage Hermes Trismegistus. She argues that Bruno's main aim in all his writings was to preach Hermeticism, and to establish it as the one true religion. Although her thesis is overstated, it does provide a way of reconciling Bruno's works on magic with his more directly philosophical works (see HERMETISM).

4 Cosmology

Bruno is best known for his championship of Copernicus in *The Ash Wednesday Supper*. In *De Revolutionibus Orbium Coelestium* (On the Revolutions of the Heavenly Spheres) (1543), Copernicus had argued both that the earth had its own daily rotation, and that it rotated around the sun (see COPERNICUS, N.). These theses challenged Aristotelian cosmology, but the force of the challenge was recognized only gradually. It was not until 1616 that *De Revolutionibus* was put on the Index of books forbidden by the Roman Catholic Church, and ironically, it may have been in part Bruno's defence of Copernicus that led to this result, for he pointed out that Copernicus' theory was inconsistent with the standard ways of interpreting the Bible at that time. Bruno took Copernican cosmology more seriously and less metaphorically than Yates suggests when she writes 'The sun-centred universe was the symbol of Bruno's vision of universal magical religion, inspired by the works of "Hermes Trismegistus"' (Yates 1982: 219). Nonetheless, it is true that Bruno showed little interest in the mathematical basis of Copernicus' work. He criticized Copernicus for 'being more intent on the study of mathematics than of nature' ([1584a] 1975: 57), a point which ties in with his other attacks on mathematics, and his emphasis on numerology in such writings as *De monade*. Moreover, Bruno got some of the technical details wrong, perhaps because he was drawing on the writings of a French bishop, Pontus de Tyard, who was favourable to Copernicus, but muddled.

In both *The Ash Wednesday Supper* and *On the Infinite Universe and Worlds* Bruno makes a series of cosmological claims that owe much to LUCRETIUS and Nicholas of Cusa. First, the universe is infinite, which means that it can have no centre, though there are many world-systems each of which may have its own centre. Second, these worlds may be inhabited. Third, the stars can be regarded as suns, that is, as self-luminous bodies, and they should not be seen as fixed on spheres. Fourth, the earth is made of the same stuff as the other worlds: there is no difference of kind between the sublunar realm and the heavenly realms, as Aristotelians argued. Finally, the celestial bodies that constitute the universe are 'intelligent animals' ([1584a] 1975: 46). Indeed, it is because the earth is animate that it must rotate. It has an 'innate animal instinct' ([1584c] 1950: 266), and there is no need to postulate extrinsic movers.

5 Metaphysics

Bruno's main argument for the infinity of the world relied on his view of God as infinite in power and goodness. Goodness diffuses itself, and the only appropriate product of infinite power must itself be infinite. He went on to give an account of the created world in largely Neoplatonic terms. In *De umbris idearum* he claims that all things are ordered and connected, and he presents a fairly standard account of the 'ladder of nature' (*scala naturae*, or the Great Chain of Being), with pure act or infinite unity at the top and matter or infinite number at the bottom. The intelligences or pure spirits come below God, followed by the corporeal world, with soul as an intermediary.

The theme of the ladder of nature goes together with two other themes, the division into three worlds (found in the *Corpus Hermeticum*), and the Neoplatonic scheme of *exitus* and *reditus*, or going out and coming back, ascending and descending. The three worlds are described in *Sigillus sigillorum*. The first world is the *fons idearum* (the fount of ideas) which is God himself as containing the divine Ideas by which the created world is structured; the second is the *mundus ideatus*, the created world; and the third is the human mind which reflects the created world. Just as God's power flows down the ladder of nature, creating the third world through the second, so human contemplation ascends the ladder, knowing the first world through the second.

This Neoplatonic schema was considerably complicated by Bruno's account of matter in *Cause, Principle and Unity*. While he retained Aristotle's account of physical reality in terms of form and matter, he attacked Aristotle's view of prime matter as purely receptive and devoid of form. Rather, matter contains all things within itself, and 'unfolds what it holds folded-up' ([1584b] 1964: 131). Forms both desire and need matter. In language very reminiscent of IBN GABIROL (§2), Bruno developed his theory by claiming that there are just two substances (apart from the transcendent God, who is the only genuine substance), namely Matter and Form, and these are united. Universal Form is identified with the World-Soul, which through its faculty of intellect serves as efficient cause of the world, and through its status as form, animates and informs the world. As a result, it is both a part of the universe (as form) and not a part (as efficient cause). It was this part of Bruno's theory that led to mistaken accusations of pantheism.

His view of matter has two consequences. First, he rejected the Neoplatonic hierarchy in relation to the created world. One can no longer think of matter as at the bottom of the ladder, for it is indivisible from form and indeed from life: 'there is not the least corpuscle that doesn't contain internally some portion that may become alive' ([1584b] 1964: 87). Second, he abandoned the Aristotelian account of individuals as substances belonging to a species. Neither *humanitas* ('humanity') nor *Socrateitas* ('Socrateity') are substantial forms, that is forms which by union with matter constitute a substance capable of receiving accidents. Instead, Socrates is himself an accident of the one material substance, and so what we take to be an individual is a collection of fleeting accidents.

Bruno also believed in atomism (see ATOMISM), but his account in *De triplici minimo et mensura* seems to retain the dualism of form and matter. Atoms are the smallest parts of things, and are indivisible, but there are different types of atom. Some atoms are the constituents of material things, other atoms are soul, while a third simple element, the monad, is found rationally in numbers and essentially in all things ([1582–1600] 1962 vol. I, part 3: 140). Indeed, Bruno even calls God the monad of monads (*monadum monas*) ([1582–1600] 1962 vol. I, part 3: 146) because he is one in the fullest sense.

6 Influence

At first, Bruno had little influence, partly because his works were placed on the Index in 1603, but also because some of them were in Italian, while Latin remained the language of science and scholarship well into the seventeenth century. KEPLER cites him a number of times, and there seem to be hints of his thought in SPINOZA and in LEIBNIZ, but it is difficult to tell whether there was any direct influence. He became popular in Germany in the late eighteenth and early nineteenth centuries, when such thinkers as Schelling and Jacobi praised him for his supposed pantheism. In the later nineteenth century he became an Italian national hero, and was regarded as a martyr for freedom of thought and modern science.

See also: COPERNICUS, N.; HERMETISM; IBN GABIROL; NEOPLATONISM; NICHOLAS OF CUSA

List of works

Bruno, G. (1582–1600) *Opera latine conscripta* (Collected Works in Latin), ed. F. Fiorentino, F. Tocco, H. Vitelli, V. Imbriani and C.M. Tallarigo, Naples: Dom. Morano, Florence: Le Monnier, 1879–91, 3 vols in 8 parts; repr. Stuttgart and Bad Cannstatt: Frommann-Holzboog, 1962. (This edition has only a few textual notes and no indexes.)

—— (1582–1600) *Opere italiane* (Works in Italian), ed. G. Gentile and B. Spampanato, Bari: Laterza, 1907–9, 3 vols; 2nd revised edn, 1925–7; 3rd edn of first 2 vols, *Dialoghi italiani* (Dialogues in Italian), ed. G. Aquilecchia, Florence: Sansoni, 1958; repr. 1985.

—— (1582a) *Il Candelaio* (The Torch-Bearer), ed. G. Barberi Squarotti, Turin: Giulio Einaudi, 1964.

—— (1582b) *Le opere latine. Edizione storico-critica vol. I: De umbris idearum* (Works in Latin: Historical-Critical Edition. Vol. I: On the Shadows of Ideas), ed. R. Sturlese, Florence: Olschki, 1991. (The first of a proposed full critical edition of Bruno's Latin works.)

—— (1582c) *Ars memoriae* (On the Art of Memory), in F. Fiorentino, F. Tocco, H. Vitelli, V. Imbriani and C.M. Tallarigo (eds) *Opera latine conscripta*, vol. 2, part 1, Stuttgart and Bad Cannstatt: Frommann-Holzboog, 1962.

—— (1583a) *Ars reminiscendi* (On the Art of Remembering), in F. Fiorentino, F. Tocco, H. Vitelli, V. Imbriani and C.M. Tallarigo (eds) *Opera latine conscripta*, vol. 2, part 2, Stuttgart and Bad Cannstatt: Frommann-Holzboog, 1962.

—— (1583b) *Explicatio triginta sigillorum* (The Explanation of the Thirty Seals), in F. Fiorentino, F. Tocco, H. Vitelli, V. Imbriani and C.M. Tallarigo (eds) *Opera latine conscripta*, vol. 2, part 2, Stuttgart and Bad Cannstatt: Frommann-Holzboog, 1962.

—— (1583c) *Sigillus sigillorum* (The Seal of Seals), in F. Fiorentino, F. Tocco, H. Vitelli, V. Imbriani and C.M. Tallarigo (eds) *Opera latine conscripta*, vol. 2, part 2, Stuttgart and Bad Cannstatt: Frommann-Holzboog, 1962.

—— (1584a) *La Cena de le ceneri*, ed. G. Aquilecchia, Turin: Giulio Einaudi, 1955; trans. S.L. Jaki, *The Ash Wednesday Supper. La Cena de le Ceneri*, The Hague and Paris: Mouton, 1975; trans. E. Gosselin and L. Lerner, *The Ash Wednesday Supper: La cena de le ceneri*, Hamden, CT: Archon Books, 1977.

—— (1584b) *De la causa, principio et uno*, ed. G. Aquilecchia, Turin: Giulio Einaudi, 1973; trans. J. Lindsay, *Five Dialogues by Giordano Bruno: Cause, Principle and Unity*, New York: International Publishers, 1964; trans. S.T. Greenburg, *The Infinite in Giordano Bruno with a Translation of his Dialogue 'Concerning the Cause, Principle, and One'*, New York: Octagon Books, 1978.

—— (1584c) 'De l'infinito universo et mondi', trans. D.W. Singer, 'On the Infinite Universe and Worlds', in *Giordano Bruno: His Life and Thought*, New York: Henry Schuman, 1950. (Singer's work also contains valuable secondary material: see Singer 1950 for details.)

—— (1584d) *Spaccio della bestia trionfante*, ed. M. Ciliberto, Milan: Biblioteca Universale Rizzoli, 1985; English trans. A.D. Imerti, *The Expulsion of the Triumphant Beast*, New Brunswick, NJ: Rutgers University Press, 1964; repr. London and Lincoln, NB: University of Nebraska Press, 1992.

—— (1585a) *Cabala del cavallo Pegaseo con l'aggiunta de l'Asino cillenico* (The Kabbalah of the Pegasean Horse with an Appendix on the Cillenican Ass), in *Opere italiane*, ed. G. Gentile and B. Spampanato, Bari: Laterza, 2nd edn, 1925–7.

—— (1585b) *Des fureurs héroïques (De gl'Heroici Furori)*, ed. and trans. P.-H. Michel, Paris: Les Belles Lettres, 1954; English trans. P.E. Memmo, *Giordano Bruno's 'The Heroic Frenzies'*, Chapel Hill, NC: University of North Carolina Press, 1964.

—— (*c.*1587) *Lampas triginta statuarum* (The Lamp of Thirty Statues), in F. Fiorentino, F. Tocco, H. Vitelli, V. Imbriani and C.M. Tallarigo (eds) *Opera latine conscripta*, vol. 3, Stuttgart and Bad Cannstatt: Frommann-Holzboog, 1962.

—— (1591a) *De triplici minimo et mensura* (On the Threefold Minimum and Measure), in F. Fiorentino, F. Tocco, H. Vitelli, V. Imbriani and C.M. Tallarigo (eds) *Opera latine conscripta*, vol. 1, part 3, Stuttgart and Bad Cannstatt: Frommann-Holzboog, 1962.

—— (1591b) *De monade, numero et figura* (On the Monad, Number and Figure), in F. Fiorentino, F. Tocco, H. Vitelli, V. Imbriani and C.M. Tallarigo (eds) *Opera latine conscripta*, vol. 1, part 2, Stuttgart and Bad Cannstatt: Frommann-Holzboog, 1962.

—— (1591c) *De innumerabilibus, immenso et infigurabili* (On the Innumerables, the Immense and the Infigurable), in F. Fiorentino, F. Tocco, H. Vitelli, V. Imbriani and C.M. Tallarigo (eds) *Opera latine conscripta*, vol. 1, parts 1–2, Stuttgart and Bad Cannstatt: Frommann-Holzboog, 1962.

References and further reading

* Bossy, J. (1991) *Giordano Bruno and the Embassy Affair*, New Haven, CT, and London: Yale University Press. (Referred to in §1. Lively discussion of Bruno's supposed career as a spy, his life and personality.)

Ciliberto, M. (1990) *Giordano Bruno*, Bari: Laterza. (General discussion of Bruno's philosophy, most useful for its chronology of life and works and its full, topically organized bibliography. This work is written in Italian.)

Feingold, M. (1984) 'The Occult Tradition in the English Universities of the Renaissance: A Reassessment', in B. Vickers (ed.) *Occult and Scientific Mentalities in the Renaissance*, Cambridge: Cambridge University Press, 73–94. (A re-evaluation of Bruno at Oxford.)

Gosselin, E.A. (1988) 'Bruno's "French Connection": A Historiographical Debate', in I. Merkel and A.G. Debus (eds) *Hermeticism and the Renaissance: Intellectual History and the Occult in Early Modern Europe*, Washington, DC: The Folger Shakespeare Library, London and Toronto, Ont.: Associated University Presses, 166–81. (Llullism and Copernicanism in France and Bruno's intellectual development.)

Kristeller, P.O. (1964) *Eight Philosophers of the Italian Renaissance*, Stanford, CA: Stanford University Press. (Contains a readable introduction to Bruno's thought.)

Michel, P.-H. (1973) *The Cosmology of Giordano Bruno*, trans. R.E.W. Maddison, London: Methuen. (A reliable account which complements Védrine 1967.)

Singer, D.W. (1950) *Giordano Bruno: His Life and Thought With Annotated Translation of His Work 'On the Infinite Universe and Worlds'*, New York: Henry Schuman. (Good biography, with a useful chronological bibliography of Bruno's writings.)

Spruit, L. (1988) *Il problema della conoscenza in Giordano Bruno* (The Problem of Knowledge in Giordano Bruno), Naples: Bibliopolis. (A helpful study of Bruno's epistemology in relation to his other doctrines.)

Védrine, H. (1967) *La conception de la nature chez Giordano Bruno* (Giordano Bruno's Understanding of Nature), Paris: Vrin. (A reliable account which complements Michel 1973.)

* Yates, F. (1964) *Giordano Bruno and the Hermetic Tradition*, Chicago, IL, and London: University of Chicago Press. (Referred to in §3. The classic account of Bruno's Hermeticism.)

—— (1966) *The Art of Memory*, Chicago, IL: University of Chicago Press, London: Routledge & Kegan Paul. (A rich discussion of the art of memory in the medieval and Renaissance periods, with much material on Bruno and on his relation to Ramon Llull.)

* —— (1982) *Lull and Bruno: Collected Essays, Volume I*, London: Routledge & Kegan Paul. (Referred to in §4. A useful spectrum of Yates' views.)

E. J. ASHWORTH

BRUNSCHVICG, LÉON (1869–1944)

Brunschvicg occupied a central place in French philosophy during the first part of the twentieth century. In 1909 he became a professor at the Sorbonne, teaching there and at the École Normale Supérieure for the next thirty years. His indefatigable activity, wide curiosity and erudition made him a leading figure of French philosophy. His influence is manifest in the work of Bachelard, Piaget, Guéroult, Nabert, Koyré and Sartre. His most important work lay in the field of the philosophy of mathematics, where (among other things) he introduced French philosophers to the work of Frege and Russell.

1 Life
2 *Les étapes de la philosophie mathématique* (The Stages in the Philosophy of Mathematics) (1912)
3 Other works

1 Life

Léon Brunschvicg was born in Paris in 1869, and educated alongside Louis Couturat at the Lycée Condorcet and the École Normale Supérieure. In 1893 he helped to found the *Revue de Métaphysique et de Morale*, which remains one of the most distinguished French journals. In 1897 he received his doctorate for his dissertation, *La modalité du jugement* (The Modality of Judgment). He wrote here that 'the proof of a single theorem is sufficient to give us the joy and security of certainty, since it implies truth' (1897: 237), which is the starting-point for his philosophy of mathematics. His subsequent teaching career was spent in Paris; but he died at Aix-les-Bains, where he had taken refuge during the war.

2 *Les étapes de la philosophie mathématique* (The Stages in the Philosophy of Mathematics) (1912)

In his most important work, *Les étapes de la philosophie mathématique* (The Stages in the Philosophy of Mathematics) (1912), Brunschvicg sets out the principal stages of philosophical reflection on mathematics. What fundamentally concerns him here is the problem of truth: he writes in the preface (unfortunately omitted from the 1972 edition) that he aims to resolve this problem by 'a meditation on the discipline which has employed the greatest scrupulousness and subtlety in its search for the truth' (1912: xi). Brunschvicg's concern to elucidate the underlying commitment within mathematics to a conception of truth can be contrasted with the conventionalism of his older contemporary Henri POINCARÉ who looked primarily to the practical achievements of mathematics (see CONVENTIONALISM §1).

Brunschvicg undertakes a massive survey of the evolution of mathematical thought, from the first attempts of primitive peoples to develop a number system to the most advanced results of the modern age. Among the most important discussions are those devoted to classical antiquity (which deal with the number theories of Pythagoras and Plato and with Aristotle's logic, and that of the work of Descartes (concerning his analytic geometry and his conception of a universal mathematics). Brunschvicg also sets out the philosophical account of mathematics to be found at the start of the modern period in the works of Kant and Comte, who both believed that mathematics was a completed science. This account was overturned during the nineteenth century, however, when profound changes in mathematical techniques were introduced, and new lines for research opened up in all directions. In discussing this, Brunschvicg devotes a long chapter to the development of modern logical theory – to Boole, Peano, Frege and, above all, Russell.

The final chapters are devoted to drawing the moral of this long historical inquiry. Brunschvicg here clarifies his own point of view, and presents a qualified form of 'intellectualism' in his final chapter on 'The reaction against "mathematism": the sense of intellectualism in mathematics'. Up to now, he claims, the philosophy of mathematics has lacked a proper appreciation of the nature of truth in mathematics. In accepting that the logical order of exposition reverses the direction of the psychological order of discovery, philosophers of mathematics admit implicitly that the concern for rigour that is characteristic of reasoning is foreign to, indeed opposed to, the discovery of mathematical truth. Thus their conclusion should be that the logical formalization of mathematics makes no difference to its truth. So even in mathematics one should bear in mind the two distinctive marks of the intellect – 'an indefinite capacity for progress' joined with 'a perpetual disquiet about verification'. As such, mathematics represents one of the most powerful and lasting achievements of the human genius; it reveals to us the capacities of the human intellect, and should be as much a foundation for our knowledge of the mind as it is for the natural sciences. 'The activity of the mind has been free and productive only since the epoch when mathematics brought to mankind the true standard of truth' ([1912] 1972: 577).

3 Other works

Brunschvicg's numerous writings are diverse. One area of interest was the history of philosophy, especially seventeenth-century French philosophy. He produced the standard edition of Pascal's *Pensées et opuscules* (1897); wrote *Spinoza et ses contemporains* (Spinoza and His Contemporaries) (1923); and in 1942 completed *Descartes et Pascal: lecteurs de Montaigne* (Descartes and Pascal: Readers

of Montaigne) (1944). In an earlier work on a much grander historical scale, entitled *Le Progrés de la conscience dans la philosophie occidentale* (The Progress of Consciousness in Western Philosophy) (1927), he had opened up wider and bolder lines of thought.

Brunschvicg also wrote on the philosophy of science. He took the view that the development of science was not autonomous: philosophy is not to be separated from science and should not pretend to a superior or distinctive kind of truth. This line of thought, which continues that of *Les étapes de la philosophie mathématique*, is presented in *L'expérience humaine et la causalité physique* (Human Experience and Physical Causality) (1922) and *La physique du vingtième siècle et la philosophie* (Philosophy and Twentieth-Century Physics) (1936). For Brunschvicg, the development of science reveals the work of the human intellect and shows reason at work; as Plato held, the philosopher or the scientist should be able to concern himself with truth in a completely disinterested spirit, following to the limit the movement of commitment which, from Copernicus to Einstein, has manifested the character of the human intellect. In the same spirit, the philosopher and scientist should seek to bring together the pursuit of truth with that of beauty and the good. Grasped in its essence, science should aim to be what it was for Plato, Descartes and Kant: our way of gaining access to the truths of the human spirit.

See also: FRENCH PHILOSOPHY OF SCIENCE

List of works

None of these works have been translated into English.

Brunschvicg, L. (1897) *La modalité du jugement* (The Modality of Judgment), Paris: Alcan. (Thesis defended at the Sorbonne on 29 March 1897. Outlines the programmes of subsequent books.)

—— (1897) *Pensées et opuscules de Blaise Pascal*, intro. L. Brunschvig, Paris: Hachette; repr. 1945. (Highly commended by the Académie française.)

—— (1912) *Les étapes de la philosophie mathématique* (The Stages in the Philosophy of Mathematics), Paris: Alcan; revised edn, Paris: Blanchard, 1972. (A description of the different stages in the mathematical philosophical process.)

—— (1922) *L'expérience humaine et la causalité physique* (Human Experience and Physical Causality), Paris: Alcan. (A description of contemporary science. Book XV deals with theories of relativity.)

—— (1923) *Spinoza et ses contemporains* (Spinoza and

His Contemporaries), Paris: Alcan. (Biographical and comparative.)

—— (1924) *Le génie de Pascal* (The Genius of Pascal), Paris: Hachette. (Deals more thoroughly with certain aspects of Pascal's work already discussed in earlier works.)

—— (1927) *Le progrés de la conscience dans la philosophie occidentale* (The Progress of Consciousness in Western Philosophy), Paris: Alcan. (Gives an account of the development of consciousness.)

—— (1931) *De la connaissance de soi* (On Self-Conciousness), Paris: Alcan. (A description of the necessity for self-knowlede.)

—— (1936) *La physique du vingtième siècle et la philosophie* (Philosophy and Twentieth Century Physics), Paris: Hermann. (A complement to *L'expérience humaine et la causalité physique.*)

—— (1944) *Descartes et Pascal, lecteurs de Montaigne* (Descartes and Pascal: Readers of Montaigne), New York: Brentano's. (Places an emphasis on the literary aspects of Descartes and Pascal.)

References and further reading

Boirel, R. (1964) *Brunschvicg*, Paris: Presses Universitaires de France. (An account of Brunschvicg's life and works, with an exposition of his philosophy.)

MAURICE LOI

BRYCE, JAMES (1838–1922)

James Bryce, British statesman and writer, combined a distinguished public life with scholarship in history, politics and law. As a jurist his interest lay in historical jurisprudence, but he is best remembered for his comparative politics. He contributed significantly to democratic political theory and to a liberal-historicist approach in philosophy of law.

Bryce was born in Belfast in 1838, of Ulster Scottish descent. He was educated at Glasgow University and Oxford University. Although called to the Bar in 1867, he preferred scholarship, travel and public service. As Regius Professor of Civil Law at Oxford (1870–93), he reinvigorated the study of Roman law in Britain and helped to reform legal education. He entered Parliament as a Liberal MP in 1880 and held several ministerial offices between 1886 and 1906. He was Ambassador to the USA (1907–13), was elevated to the peerage as Viscount Bryce of Dechmont in 1914, and remained active in public life until his death.

Bryce diffused his energies widely and was a prolific writer and scholar as well as a man of affairs. In *The Holy Roman Empire* (1864) he propounded a thesis of historical unity stretching from ancient Rome to nineteenth-century Germany. In other works he portrayed England's legal system as emulating, in the modern world, Roman law in the ancient, and emphasized an Anglo-American affinity. His *The American Commonwealth* (1888) was a monumental treatise designed to supersede Tocqueville's more impressionistic account, and incidentally testified to the success of democracy and of federalism. It was an instant classic. Bryce wrote influentially on the classification and characteristics of constitutions and on comparative politics, for example in *Modern Democracies* (1921). His studies of political systems were determinedly empiricist and his research was invariably supplemented by contacts, conversation and travel: one modern critic suggested that his 'genius largely consisted of an infinite capacity for taking trains'.

Studies in History and Jurisprudence (1901) was perhaps his most representative work. As a typical nineteenth-century liberal, he espoused *laissez-faire* economics, favoured religious and political liberty, distrusted state intervention, but was not free from apprehensions concerning majoritarian democracy. As a historian, he implied biological laws of development, and cannot be acquitted of what Popper was to term historicism (see POPPER, K.R. §4). In his philosophy of law, he dismissed natural law theories as a priori and speculative, but faulted aspects of the analytical jurisprudence of Austin and Bentham as being not only historically indefensible but also inapplicable to contemporary societies (see AUSTIN, J.; BENTHAM, J.). In juristic interests and endeavour he was closer to the comparative method and historical jurisprudence of Maine.

However, he lacked Maine's inclination to theorize. Harold Laski's observation on Bryce's 'insatiable appetite for facts and grotesque inability to weigh them' was unkind but not entirely unfair. In a changing world which he struggled to comprehend, the public servant was garlanded with honours, but the scholar restricted himself to fact-gathering and classification or lofty pronouncements on public affairs.

See also: COMMON LAW; JURISPRUDENCE, HISTORICAL; LAW, PHILOSOPHY OF; RULE OF LAW

List of works

Bryce, J. (1864) *The Holy Roman Empire*, London: Macmillan, 4th edn, 1875. (A history of the

Romano-Germanic Empire as the centrepiece of European civilization.)

—— (1888) *The American Commonwealth*, London and New York: Macmillan, 4th edn, 1914. (An account of, and reflections on, the US constitutional and political system as it had developed by the mid-nineteenth century.)

—— (1901) *Studies in History and Jurisprudence*, Oxford: Oxford University Press. (Essays on history, Roman law, English law, constitutional theory, ancient and modern political systems, and jurisprudential concepts.)

—— (1921) *Modern Democracies*, London: Macmillan. (Comparative treatise on democratic theory and institutions, with studies of some systems.)

References and further reading

Fisher, H.A.L. (1927) *James Bryce*, London: Macmillan. (This is the standard biography, readily accessible to the general reader.)

Tulloch, H. (1988) *James Bryce's 'American Commonwealth'*, Woodbridge: The Royal Historical Society/The Boydell Press. (Gives an account of Bryce's political thought in the context of his intellectual biography.)

COLIN MUNRO

BSAM-YAS *see* TIBETAN

PHILOSOPHY

BUBER, MARTIN (1878–1965)

Martin Buber covered a range of fields in his writings, from Jewish folklore and fiction, to biblical scholarship and translation, to philosophical anthropology and theology. Above all, however, Buber was a philosopher, in the lay-person's sense of the term sense: someone who devoted his intellectual energies to contemplating the meaning of life.

Buber's passionate interest in mysticism was reflected in his early philosophical work. However, he later rejected the view that mystical union is the ultimate goal of relation, and developed a philosophy of relation. In the short but enormously influential work, Ich und Du *(I and Thou), Buber argued that the I emerges only through encountering others, and that the very nature of the I depends on the quality of the relationship with the Other. He described two fundamentally different ways of relating to others: the*

common mode of 'I–It', in which people and things are experienced as objects, or, in Kantian terms, as 'means to an end'; and the 'I–Thou' mode, in which I do not 'experience' the Other, rather, the Other and I enter into a mutually affirming relation, which is simultaneously a relation with another and a relation with God, the 'eternal Thou'.

Buber acknowledged that necessity of I–It, even in the interpersonal sphere, but lamented its predominance in modern life. Through his scholarly work in philosophy, theology and biblical exegesis, as well as his translation of Scripture and adaptations of Hasidic tales, he sought to reawaken our capacity for I–Thou relations.

1 Life
2 Early writings
3 *Ich und Du*
4 Relationship with Jewish philosophy
5 Theology and hermeneutics

1 Life

Martin Mordechai Buber was born in Vienna. Following the divorce of his parents when he was three years old, he spent most of his childhood in Lemberg, Galicia, with his grandparents Solomon and Adele Buber. This separation from his parents, particularly his mother, had a profound effect on the subsequent development of Buber's philosophy of relation. His abiding childhood memory was not of his mother leaving him – he expected her to come for him any day – but of being told at the age of four by a baby-sitter that his mother would never return. 'I suspect,' he later wrote, 'that everything I experienced of genuine encounter during the course of my life had its origin in that moment on the balcony' (1972: 18–19).

At the age of fourteen, Buber returned to his father's house, where he lived with his father and stepmother. He rejected the traditional Judaism of his father and grandparents, and became increasingly interested in philosophy, particularly the works of Kant and Nietzsche. In 1896 Buber enrolled as a student of philosophy at the University of Vienna. Two years later he moved to the University of Leipzig and joined the Zionist movement (see ZIONISM). Buber was still not interested in the religious tradition he had rejected as an adolescent, but he devoted his energies to the renewal of Jewish culture.

As a delegate to the Third Zionist Congress in 1899, Buber spoke on behalf of the Propaganda Committee, but he used the platform to emphasize the importance of education rather than propaganda. In 1901 he was appointed editor of the weekly Zionist publication *Die Welt*, in which he again stressed the need for a Jewish cultural renaissance. Later in the same year he became a member of the Zionist Democratic Fraction which was opposed to the programme of Theodor Herzl and, at the Fifth Zionist Congress, he resigned as editor of *Die Welt*. Shortly after the Congress, Buber withdrew from political affairs. From about 1903 onwards, he immersed himself in the study of Hasidism. Although initially attracted to the literary qualities of the Hasidic tales, he gradually developed an appreciation of their spiritual content and took it upon himself to communicate the message of Hasidism to the assimilated Jews of western Europe, and to humanity at large.

During the years 1906 to 1911, Buber attended lectures at the University of Berlin, especially those given by Wilhelm DILTHEY. Dilthey's hermeneutic theory was an important influence on Buber's approach to interpretation, as manifested both in his Hasidic writings and in his later work of biblical translation and commentary (see HERMENEUTICS). Buber resumed public life in 1909. He exerted a profound influence on Jewish youth in central Europe through his lectures and publications. In 1916 he founded *Der Jude*, a monthly publication which promoted the Jewish cultural renaissance. Buber's Zionism continued to diverge from the mainstream. He sought complete equality and cooperation between Jews and Arabs and believed that Palestine could become the shared homeland of two autonomous peoples. His political philosophy also diverged from the dominant conception of socialism. He believed that a socialist society could never come about through the mechanism of the state; rather, it depended on a renewal of relationships among individuals.

Buber's reflections on the relations between people developed into his most famous work, *Ich und Du*, which was published in 1923. Although he continued to write for over forty years, *Ich und Du* is unquestionably his masterpiece. 'It is the vessel into which he pours the learning and wisdom acquired over the years' and 'everything that he wrote afterwards can be traced back to it' (Vermes 1994: 27). In 1925, Buber took on a project that would occupy him for decades: a new German translation of the Hebrew Bible. Begun in collaboration with Franz Rosenzweig, the work was continued by Buber on his own after Rosenzweig's premature death in 1929. The final volume of *Die Schrift* was published in 1961. Buber did not actively work on the translation between 1932 and 1949, but he continued to reflect on the Hebrew Bible, publishing works of biblical criticism and theology, including *Königtum Gottes* (Kingship of God) (1932), 'Die Frage an den Einzelnen' (Question to the Single One) (1936), *Torat ha-Neviim* (The Prophetic Faith) (1940), and *Moshe* (Moses) (1946).

In 1930, Buber was appointed professor of religion at the University of Frankfurt. He retained this position until 1933, when, following the Nazi rise to power, he was forced to leave the university. In the same year he became director of the Central Office for Jewish Education and head of the Jüdisches Lehrhaus in Frankfurt. He travelled throughout Germany, lecturing and teaching, until 1935, when he was prohibited from speaking at Jewish gatherings. Buber moved to Jerusalem in 1938, when he was appointed to the newly created chair of social philosophy at the Hebrew University. He taught there until his retirement in 1951. After retiring Buber continued to write, and he lectured extensively abroad. In his later works he wrestled with the themes of good and evil and the suffering of the innocent, publishing *Bilder von Gut und Böse* (Good and Evil) (1952) and *Gottsfinsternis* (Eclipse of God) (1953).

2 Early writings

Buber's period of intense research into Hasidism resulted in two books of Hasidic legends: *Die Geschichten des Rabbi Nachman* (The Tales of Rabbi Nachman) (1906) and *Die Legende des Baalschem* (The Legends of the Baal-Shem) (1908). Influenced by both Nietzsche and Dilthey, Buber did not simply translate the Hasidic tales, but retold them, attempting to renew the old stories for his generation. Although determined to retain the original spirit of the tales, he believed, following Dilthey's hermeneutics, that his empathy with the Hasidic masters gave him licence to edit and embellish their stories. Buber's interpretation of Hasidism was criticized by scholars, notably Gershom Scholem.

Buber's early enthusiasm for mysticism is also evident in *Daniel: Gespräche von der Verwirklichung* (Daniel: Dialogues on Realization) (1913), the main theme of which is the quest for meaning in human life. Although many of the observations in *Daniel* prefigure the more mature *Ich und Du*, the earlier work specifies a form of mystical union as the ultimate aim of relation. The eponymous Daniel urges his companion to come to know a tree not by observing it, but by identifying with it, to the extent that she feels its bark to be her own skin.

3 *Ich und Du*

In *Ich und Du*, the mystical ideal of union is replaced by a dialogical notion of relation. The relation between a person and a tree is again presented as an example, but this time the aim is not to identify with the tree, but to encounter it, entering into dialogue with it. Dialogue with a tree? Many readers find this notion mysterious, if not mystical. Yet it is essential to note that, according to Buber, dialogical relation is not limited to the interpersonal sphere. The thesis of *Ich und Du* is that there are two fundamental modes of relating to others. Buber names these two fundamental attitudes 'I–Thou' and 'I–It':

To man the world is twofold, in accordance with his twofold attitude.

The attitude of man is twofold, in accordance with the twofold nature of the primary words which he speaks.

The primary words are not isolated words, but combined words.

The one primary word is the combination *I–Thou*.

The other primary word is the combination *I–It*; wherein, without a change in the primary word, one of the words *He* and *She* can replace *It*.

Hence the *I* of man is also twofold.

For the *I* of the primary word *I–Thou* is a different *I* from that of the primary word *I–It*.

(1923: 3)

Buber explores the dual nature of human existence through the pronouns that a person speaks. He insists that the 'I' does not exist independently of the others it addresses; 'there is no *I* taken in itself, but only the *I* of the primary word *I–Thou* and the *I* of the primary word *I–It*' (1923: 4). The world of It is the world of discrete objects; the corresponding I is the self who experiences something, and this 'something' can as easily be a person as a thing. In a clear departure from his earlier mysticism, Buber also insists that there is no fundamental difference between 'inner' and 'outer' experiences – both belong to the world of It.

The I–Thou, by contrast, is a reciprocal relation in which there is no experience of the Other but, rather, a mutual encounter, in which each party affects and affirms the Other. It can only take place if 'the primary word I–Thou' is spoken 'with the whole being'. The relation to the Thou is direct, not mediated by the I's concepts, preconceptions, or intentions. The encounter is lived as a discovery of the uniqueness and concrete presence of the Other *qua* Other and, in a sense, as revelation, for Buber insists that 'in each *Thou* we address the eternal *Thou*' (1923: 6).

Buber discusses three spheres in which the I–Thou relation is possible: life with nature, life with people, and life with 'spiritual beings' (*geistige Wesenheiten* or, as Wood translates it, 'forms of spirit' (1969: 43)). Buber is not concerned here with mystical beings, but

with aesthetic inspiration. He asserts that the true artist does not express himself, but responds to an encounter with a 'form which desires to be made through him into a work' (1923: 9).

Of the three spheres, only that of inter-human relations permits a literal dialogue of I with Thou. However, Buber employs the linguistic metaphor of 'saying Thou' to discuss relations in all three spheres. He notes that when we address creatures as Thou, 'our words cling to the threshold of speech' and that, in addressing forms of spirit as Thou, we speak with our being, not with our lips (1923: 6). Linguistic terms in *Ich und Du*, including 'word', 'language', 'dialogue' and 'speech', are primarily used metaphorically to convey the qualities of presence, dynamism and reciprocity which characterize the I–Thou relation (Kepnes 1992: 31); indeed, according to Kohanski's reading of Buber, 'the very act of turning to another in relation is an act of speaking, even when not a word is uttered between them' (1982: 268).

I–Thou is clearly the privileged mode of existence. For Buber, 'all real living is meeting [the *Thou*]' (1923: 11). But he also recognizes that I–It, the ordinary mode of existence, is indispensable. In *Ich und Du* he does not call for the abandonment of I–It, which would be impossible, but aims rather to re-awaken the reader's potential for true relation.

4 Relationship with Jewish philosophy

Ich und Du is not a work of Jewish philosophy in the sense of 'philosophy of Judaism'; it deals with universal philosophical themes and is intended for a broad audience. Nevertheless, the philosophy expounded in its pages shares many key features with those of other twentieth-century Jewish philosophers, notably Hermann Cohen, Franz Rosenzweig and Emmanuel Levinas. The conception of the 'I–Other' relationship within these Jewish thinkers' writings differs markedly from the dominant view in modern western philosophy – epitomized by Sartre's exclamation 'Hell is the Other!' – that this relationship is fundamentally antagonistic. Buber, Cohen, Rosenzweig and Levinas all reject this view of the I–Other relationship. They see a positive, welcoming response to the Other as the *sine qua non* of authentic selfhood.

According to these thinkers, the 'I' emerges from addressing the 'you' (or 'thou'). For each of them, in different ways, the interpersonal relationship is also the site of transcendence. In Buber's terms, 'in each *Thou* we address the eternal *Thou*'; in Levinas', the Other's face 'is the manifestation of the height in which God is revealed' (1961: 79).

Nevertheless, despite the resemblances between these thinkers, both Rosenzweig and Levinas criticized *Ich und Du*. Levinas took issue with Buber's characterization of the I–Thou. One of his major criticisms was that Buber 'understood the Thou primarily as partner and friend and thus gave primacy to a relationship of reciprocity' (see Bernasconi 1988: 105), in contrast with Levinas's own emphasis on the asymmetry of the 'Je–Vous', or 'face-to-face' relation, through which I become aware of my inescapable responsibility for the Other, without regard to the Other's responsibility for me.

Commenting upon the galley proofs of *Ich und Du*, Rosenzweig wrote to Buber: 'In your setting up the I–It, you give the I–Thou a cripple for an opponent. True, this cripple rules the modern world: however, this does not change the fact that it is a cripple' (see Horwitz 1988: 227).

5 Theology and hermeneutics

Although Buber did not alter *Ich und Du* in response to Rosenzweig's criticism, Rosenzweig's 'New Thinking' was a major influence on the development of Buber's subsequent work, particularly in the areas of hermeneutics and theology. Steven Kepnes (1992) has traced the development of Buber's hermeneutics and theology from his early pantheistic, romantic period, through the dialogical thought of *Ich und Du*, to Buber's later version of narrative theology, which both transcends and incorporates the insights of *Ich und Du*. Buber's later work on the Bible continued to emphasize moments of encounter, both with God and between human beings, but his equally strong interest in the Bible as a source for the common memory of the Jewish people reveals the influence of Rosenzweig's notions of creation, revelation and redemption. In Buber's later thought, a Jew reads the Bible not simply to facilitate an I–Thou encounter with the text, but to discover in the biblical narratives resources for addressing the reader's own situation.

From the early 1940s, Buber's reflections on the Bible centred, unsurprisingly, on the theme of innocent suffering. He drew upon Job, Deutero-Isaiah and the Psalms in his attempt to express the suffering and fragile hope of his generation, describing the Holocaust era as a time of the 'eclipse of God'. Buber attempted no theodicy. He sought rather to express the Job-like faith of those who await the end of the eclipse:

> Do we stand overcome before the hidden face of God like the tragic hero of the Greeks before faceless fate? No, rather even now we contend... with God.... In such a state we await His voice, whether it comes out of the storm or out of a stillness that follows it. Though his coming

appearance resemble no earlier one, we shall recognize again our cruel and merciful Lord.
>
> (1952b: 225)

See also: HOLOCAUST, THE; JEWISH PHILOSOPHY, CONTEMPORARY; HASIDISM

List of works

Buber, M. (1962–4) *Werke*, vol. 1, Munich and Heidelberg: Kosel-Verlag and Verlag Lambert Schneider. (Contains all of Buber's major philosophical works.)

—— (1906) *Die Geschichten des Rabbi Nachman; Ihm nacherzählt von Martin Buber*, Frankfurt: Rütten und Loening; trans. M. Friedman, *The Tales of Rabbi Nachman*, Atlantic Highlands, NJ: Humanities Press International, 1988. (The first fruit of a five-year period of research into Hasidism, this book is not a simple anthology of tales and legends which Rabbi Nachman of Bratslav taught to his disciples, but Buber's own retelling of the stories. It opens with 'Jewish Mysticism', an essay on Hasidism.)

—— (1908) *Die Legende des Baalschem*, Frankfurt: Rütten und Loening; trans. M. Friedman, *The Legends of the Baal-Shem*, New York: Schocken, 1969. (This work established Buber's reputation as a first-class German writer. It is a free retelling of the legendary life of Rabbi Israel ben Eliezer (1700–60), the founder of the Hasidic movement, with an introductory essay on 'The Life of the Hasidim', in which Buber outlines his interpretation of Hasidic thought.)

—— (1913) *Daniel: Gespräche von der Verwirklichung*, Leipzig: Insel-Verlag; trans. M. Friedman, *Daniel: Dialogues on Realization*, New York: Holt, 1964. (This collection of five dialogues on the themes of direction, reality, meaning, polarity and unity is Buber's first work of general philosophy. Since Buber later rejected some of its teachings, the work is primarily of importance for readers interested in the development of his thought.)

—— (1923) *Ich und Du*, Leipzig: Insel Verlag; trans. R.G. Smith, *I and Thou*, New York: Charles Scribner's Sons, 2nd edn, 1958; trans. W. Kaufman, *I and Thou*, New York: Charles Scribner's Sons, 1970. (The page numbers used in references to the work in this entry are those from the Smith translation; Kaufman's translation substitutes 'you' for 'thou' everywhere except the title. *Ich und Du* is Buber's most famous and influential work, in which he describes two modes of relating to others: 'I–Thou' and 'I–It'. The first is a reciprocal, mutually affirming encounter between self and Other; it is the route to authentic selfhood. The second designates the commonplace attitude of using or experiencing an object. While recognizing that the I–It mode of relation is indispensable, even in the realm of interpersonal relations, Buber argues that a renewal of society can take place only through a reawakening of our potential for I–Thou encounters.)

—— (1932) *Königtum Gottes*, Berlin: Schocken; trans. R. Scheimann, *The Kingship of God*, Atlantic Highlands, NJ: Humanities Press International, 1988. (The first of Buber's purely scholarly studies of the Hebrew Bible, which are mainly concerned with the theme of messianism. Buber interprets the covenant between God and Israel as the means by which the kingship of God is to be actualized in communal life.)

—— (1936) 'Die Frage an den Einzelnen', trans. R.G. Smith, 'The Question to the Single One', in M. Friedman (ed.) *Between Man and Man*, New York: Macmillan, 1965. (Here, Buber responds sensitively yet critically to Kierkegaard's attempt to prepare himself for a true relation with God by renouncing both marriage and the body politic. Buber himself rejects the path of renunciation, and holds that 'the man who loves God and his companion in one... receives God for his companion'.)

—— (1942) *Torat ha-Neviim*, Tel Aviv: Bialik; trans. C. Witten-Davis, *The Prophetic Faith*, New York: Harper & Row, 1960. (Considered by many scholars to be Buber's finest work of biblical exegesis, this study examines the role of God's 'servants' – Job, Abraham, Moses, David and Isaiah – as partners in the revelation of the God of history. Buber rejects traditional interpretations which identify the suffering servant of Deutero-Isaiah with either corporate Israel or Christ. Instead, he sees the servant as a perfected human being whose task is to bring Israel back to the service of God, thus heralding the beginning of God's kingdom on earth.)

—— (1945) *Moshe*, Jerusalem: Schocken; trans. *Moses: The Revelation and the Covenant*, New York: Harper & Row, 1958; repr. Atlantic Highlands, NJ: Humanities Press International, 1988. (In this work Buber continues the exposition of Hebrew messianism begun in *Königtum Gottes*, and develops his approach to the Bible as a historical account of a particular people's response to moments of I–Thou encounter with God.)

—— (1946, 1947) *Or ha-Ganuz – Sippurey Hasidim*, Jerusalem and Tel Aviv: Schocken, 2 vols; trans. O. Marx, *Tales of the Hasidim: The Early Masters and Tales of the Hasidim: The Later Masters*, New York: Schocken, 1995. (These two collections of legendary anecdotes about the great Hasidic masters are of

importance for tracing the development of Buber's hermeneutics. In the introduction to the first volume, Buber criticizes his earlier collections of Hasidic legends for being too free. The anecdotes in these two volumes are related without embellishment or imaginative additions.)

—— (1947) *Netivot be-Utopia*, Tel Aviv: Am Oved; German translation, *Pfade in Utopia*, Heidelberg: L. Schneider, 1950; English trans. R.F.C. Hull, *Paths in Utopia*, New York: Macmillan, 1988. (An important contribution to both social philosophy and the history of socialism, this work includes chapters on Proudhon, Marx, Lenin and other utopian thinkers. Buber also discusses a variety of experiments in collective living, including the Israeli *kibbutz*, which he describes as 'an experiment that did not fail'.)

—— (1950) *Zwei Glaubenweisen*, Zurich: Manesse; trans. N. Goldhawk, *Two Types of Faith*, New York: Macmillan, 1986. (In this controversial study of Jesus and Paul, Buber presents Jesus' conception of faith as *emunah*, a Hebrew term which, Buber notes, implies both 'fidelity' and 'trust'. For Paul, by contrast, faith is cognitive and entails belief in a proposition.)

—— (1951) 'Distance and Relation', *Hibbert Journal* 49; trans. R.G. Smith, in M. Friedman (ed.) *The Knowledge of Man: A Philosophy of the Interhuman*, Atlantic Highlands, NJ: Humanities Press International, 1988. (This essay is the most important exposition of Buber's mature social anthropology. Buber analyses the movements of 'setting at a distance' and 'entering into relation' which underlie both the 'I–It' and 'I–Thou' relations.)

—— (1952a) *Bilder von Gut und Böse*, Cologne: Hegner; trans. R.G. Smith, *Good and Evil*, New York: Charles Scribner's Sons, 1952. (Buber develops an anthropological analysis of evil based on both biblical texts and Zoroastrian myths.)

—— (1952b) *An Der Wende*, Cologne: Hegner; English translation ed. N. Glatzer, *On Judaism*, New York: Schocken, 1972. (A collection of Buber's speeches on Jewish themes, delivered in Germany and central Europe from 1909 to 1918, and the four lectures he gave in America in 1951–2. It includes 'Der Dialog zwischen Himmel und Erde', translated in the Glatzer edition by E. Jospe as 'The Dialogue Between Heaven and Earth', which is of particular importance for readers interested in Buber's response to the Holocaust.)

—— (1953) *Gottsfinsternis*, trans. M. Friedman, E. Kamenka, N. Guterman and I.M. Lask, *Eclipse of God: Studies in the Relation Between Religion and Philosophy*, New York: Harper & Row; repr. with introduction by R. Seltzer, Atlantic Highlands, NJ:

Humanities Press International, 1988. (In this collection of nine essays on religion and philosophy, Buber criticizes contemporary thinkers, including Nietzsche, Bergson, Heidegger, Sartre and Jung, who have denied transcendence and thus contributed to the 'eclipse of God'.)

—— (1954) 'Elemente des Zwischenmenschlichen', in *Die Schriften über das dialogische Prinzip*, Heidelberg: L. Schneider; trans. R.G. Smith, 'Elements of the Interhuman', in M. Friedman (ed.) *The Knowledge of Man: A Philosophy of the Interhuman*, Atlantic Highlands, NJ: Humanities Press International, 1988. (Buber argues for distinguishing between the realm of the 'interhuman' and that of the 'social'. The former refers to the sphere of direct dialogical relation, the latter describes impersonal group relations.)

—— (1955) 'Der Mensch und sein Gebild', Heidelberg: Lambert Schneider; trans. M. Friedman, 'Man and His Image-Work', in M. Friedman (ed.) *The Knowledge of Man: A Philosophy of the Interhuman*, Atlantic Highlands, NJ: Humanities Press International, 1988. (An important statement of Buber's aesthetics, based on his epistemological theory that 'I–It' knowledge is derived from the 'I–Thou' relation.)

—— (1956) 'Dem Gemeinschaftlichen folgen', *Die Neue Rundschau* 67 (4): 582–600; trans. M. Friedman, 'What is Common to All', in M. Friedman (ed.) *The Knowledge of Man: A Philosophy of the Interhuman*, Atlantic Highlands, NJ: Humanities Press International, 1988. (Buber draws upon Heraclitus to analyse the emergence of a common world, and thus a 'We', through meaningful human speech.)

—— (1957) 'Guilt and Guilt Feelings', *Psychiatry* 20 (2); trans. M. Friedman, in M. Friedman (ed.) *The Knowledge of Man: A Philosophy of the Interhuman*, Atlantic Highlands, NJ: Humanities Press International, 1988. (Contra Freud and other thinkers, Buber argues that guilt is not always reducible to neurosis or social convention. The possiblity of real guilt is implicit in a philosophy of personal responsibility.)

—— (1960a) 'Das Wort, das gesprochen wird', in R. Oldenbourg (ed.) *Wort und Wirklichkeit*, Munich: Bayerische Akademie der Schönen Künste; trans. M. Friedman, 'The Word that is Spoken in Word and Reality', in M. Friedman (ed.) *The Knowledge of Man: A Philosophy of the Interhuman*, Atlantic Highlands, NJ: Humanities Press International, 1988. (Buber analyses the importance of lived speech for human existence, arguing that it is ambiguity that constitutes the tension and fruitfulness of living language.)

—— (1960b) *Begegnung: Autobiographische Fragmente*, Stuttgart: W. Kohlhammer; trans. and ed. M. Friedman, *Meetings*, La Salle, IL: Open Court, 1972. (A collection of twenty autobiographical anecdotes, some of which appear in Buber's earlier work, which Buber assembled in place of a conventional autobiography for *The Philosophy of Martin Buber*. Each fragment relates an event, meeting or 'mismeeting' which had an important influence on the development of his thought.)

Buber, M. and Rogers, C.R. (1960) 'Dialogue between Martin Buber and Carl R. Rogers', *Psychologia – An International Journal of Psychology in the Orient* 3 (4); repr. in M. Friedman (ed.) *The Knowledge of Man: A Philosophy of the Interhuman*, Atlantic Highlands, NJ: Humanities Press International, 1988. (Transcript of a 1957 discussion between Buber and the American psychologist Carl Rogers. The dialogue brings out differences between their approaches to psychology, and elaborates the significance of Buber's thought for psychotherapy.)

Buber, M. (1965) *Between Man and Man*, ed. M. Friedman, New York: Macmillan. (Collection of essays including 'Die Frage an den Einzelnen', 'Dialogue', 'Education', 'Education and Character' and 'What is Man?'.)

—— (1967) *The Philosophy of Martin Buber*, trans. M. Friedman *et al.*, ed. M. Friedman and P.A. Schilpp, Library of Living Philosophers, Cambridge: Cambridge University Press. (Includes Buber's 'Autobiographical Fragments' and 'Replies to Critics', as well as essays on Buber's thought by Gabriel Marcel, Emmanuel Levinas, Emil Fackenheim and Ernst Simon, among others.)

References and further reading

* Bernasconi, R. (1988) '"Failure of Communication" as a Surplus: Dialogue and Lack of Dialogue Between Buber and Levinas', in R. Bernasconi and D. Wood (eds) *The Provocation of Levinas: Rethinking the Other*, London: Routledge. (Bernasconi analyses Levinas' various criticisms of Buber and Buber's responses to them.)

Friedman, M. (1991) *Encounter on the Narrow Ridge: A Life of Martin Buber*, New York: Paragon House. (An accessible intellectual biography of Buber which includes an annotated bibliography of Buber's most important works in English translation.)

* Gibbs, R. (1992) *Correlations in Rosenzweig and Levinas*, Princeton, NJ: Princeton University Press, ch. 7. (Comprises a brief comparative study of the I–Thou relation in Cohen, Buber, Rosenzweig and

Levinas, which is useful for students and scholars alike.)

* Horwitz, R. (1988) *Buber's Way to 'I and Thou': The Development of Martin Buber's Thought and His 'Religion as Presence' Lectures*, New York: The Jewish Publication Society. (An accessible account of the development of Buber's thought up to the publication of *Ich und Du* which includes Horwitz's translation of Buber's 1922 lectures on 'Religion as Presence' and a selection of letters from the Buber–Rosenzweig correspondence.)

* Kepnes, S. (1992) *The Text as Thou: Martin Buber's Dialogical Hermeneutics and Narrative Theology*, Bloomington, IN: Indiana University Press. (A scholarly but accessible analysis of the development of Buber's hermeneutics and theology.)

* Kohanski, A. (1982) *Martin Buber's Philosophy of Interhuman Relation*, London: Associated University Presses. (An introduction to Buber's philosophy which includes a helpful 'Index of Terminology'.)

* Levinas, E. (1961) *Totalité et infini*, The Hague: Martinus Nijhoff; trans. A. Lingis, *Totality and Infinity: An Essay on Exteriority*, Pittsburgh, PA: Duquesne University Press. (Develops a quasi-phenomenological account of the ethical relationship between self and Other which is in many ways similar to Buber's I–Thou. Levinas, however, insists on the asymmetry of the 'face-to-face' relation, in which I become aware of my inescapable responsibility for the Other, without thinking about the Other's responsibility for me.)

Theunissen, M. (1984) *The Other: Studies in the Social Ontology of Husserl, Heidegger, Sartre and Buber*, trans. C. Macann, London: MIT Press. (Scholarly study of the phenomenology of the I–Other relation.)

* Vermes, P. (1994) *Buber on God and the Perfect Man*, London: Littman Library of Jewish Civilization. (An introduction to Buber's life and thought which includes a précis of *Ich und Du*.)

* Wood, R. (1969) *Martin Buber's Ontology*, Evanston, IL: Northwestern University Press. (A study of Buber's thought, grounded in a systematic analysis of the form and content of *Ich und Du*.)

TAMRA WRIGHT

BÜCHNER, FRIEDRICH KARL CHRISTIAN LUDWIG (LOUIS) (1824–99)

Ludwig Büchner wrote one of the most popular and polemical books of the strong materialist movement in later nineteenth century Germany, his Kraft und Stoff *(Force and Matter) (1855). He tried to develop a comprehensive worldview, which was based solely on the findings of empirical science and did not take refuge in religion or any other transcendent categories in explaining nature and its development, including human beings. When Büchner tried to expose the backwardness of traditional philosophical and religious views in scientific matters, his arguments had some force, but the positive part of his programme was not free of superficiality and naivety. Büchner's writings helped to strengthen progressive and rational traditions inside and outside philosophy, but they can also serve as the prime example of the uncritical nineteenth-century belief in science's capacity to redeem humankind from all evil.*

Büchner is commonly grouped together with Karl Vogt and Jacob Moleschott as one of the classical triumvirate of materialist philosophers in nineteenth-century Germany. Their special variant of materialism is often distinguished from other brands as 'mechanical', 'bourgeois', 'scientific' or 'vulgar' (see MATERIALISM §3). Büchner's *Kraft und Stoff* (Force and Matter) became the most popular and enduring work of the materialist movement. Up to the First World War, it went through twenty-one editions and was translated into seventeen foreign languages, where it often saw numerous editions of its own.

Ludwig Büchner was born in Darmstadt, Germany. Like his brothers and sisters, he had a predilection for literary and journalistic activity and was engaged in republican and revolutionary opposition against the oppression of the *Vormärz* era. Büchner took up medicine at the university of Gießen in 1843 and became active in the revolutionary democratic movement of the time. In 1848 he entered his father's medical practice. In 1852 he became lecturer in medicine at the university of Tübingen, but soon lost his post when *Kraft und Stoff* appeared. He returned to Darmstadt where he stayed for the rest of his life, practising medicine, popularizing science and writing on materialist philosophy, political and social issues.

In *Kraft und Stoff*, Büchner set out to formulate the philosophical consequences which he saw in the science of his day. He propagated a thorough empiricism, rejected metaphysics and speculative philosophy and every aprioristic tendency. No supranaturalism or idealism was to be allowed in the explanation of natural events and processes.

The arguments of the book are more or less all derived from its central claim, taken from Moleschott, that there is 'no matter without force and no force without matter'. Force is inseparably bound to a material substrate and thus cannot be regarded as a kind of supernatural, transcendent entity. All changes and events follow mechanical laws. These laws are not imposed on nature from outside, but are built into matter itself. Matter is eternal and has no bounds, neither on a microscopic nor on a macroscopic scale. It is ruled by rigid and universal laws which do not allow for miracles. Soul or mind, as well as organic life, are the product of specially combined materials that are endowed with special mechanical forces. There is neither an immaterial spiritual substance, nor a vital force, nor an externally set purpose of nature.

Neither Büchner's claims nor his supportive arguments can be said to be original. *Kraft und Stoff* was less an elaborated philosophical essay than a racily written summary of the materialistic trends of his time which did not mince its words and was intelligible to the layperson. At the same time, it carried a strong political significance. The flourishing of research in the natural sciences and technology was seen as a new and effective form of opposition against the reactionary political powers which had defeated all liberal-republican and national aspirations by suppressing the revolution of 1848. The growing labour movement took Büchner's materialism as a refutation and exposure of the ideology of the ruling classes and devoured his book. This sort of writing also quenched the thirst for knowledge of several generations of students at the *Gymnasium*. By appealing to the impartiality and the common sense of the autonomous reader and leaving the intricacies and obscurities of German speculative philosophy behind, Büchner's work gave rise to a new genre of popularizing literature in which a rational and empiricist *Weltanschauung* is developed on the basis of natural science. Ernst Haeckel, Wilhelm Ostwald, Wilhelm Bölsche, the early Vienna Circle and to a certain extent even Ludwig Wittgenstein in his *Tractatus* all continued this tradition. As Büchner put it: 'Philosophical elaborations not accessible to every educated person are not worth the printer's ink used for them. What is thought out clearly can be said clearly and plainly' (1855).

In the course of time Büchner enlarged the topics of his writings mainly in two respects. After the rise of Darwinism he emphasized its intimate relation to or even virtual identity with materialism and tried to show its positive implications for a general theory of progress. The other attempt at expanding the realm of his philosophy was to erect a humanistic and rational sociopolitical theory on his materialism which still owed very much to his liberal ideas of 1848. After the foundation of the new *Reich* he did not succumb to the temptations of nationalism, although his social and political ideals started to become obsolete and did not find a large number of supporters. His considerations included a far-sighted condemnation of the anti-Semitism of his time.

Büchner's work met with harsh opposition from many different quarters. From a philosophical point of view, the most important and momentous criticism was expressed by Friedrich Albert Lange (§2) in his *Geschichte des Materialismus und Kritik seiner Bedeutung in der Gegenwart* (History of Materialism and Criticism of its Present Importance) (1866). While standing up for Büchner against the accusation that materialism leads to immorality, and conceding a materialist methodology as even a necessity for the working scientist, Lange gave a penetrating analysis of the internal difficulties, weaknesses and inconsistencies of the philosophy of Büchner and other materialists.

This kind of criticism formed a crucial motive for rising Neo-Kantianism and led to a general recovery of philosophy's standing in Germany. Even among those who admitted the centrality of science for modern society and saw much truth in materialism, the conviction arose that philosophy had more to say than is contained in *Kraft und Stoff* and that it had not lost the right of autonomy *vis-à-vis* science.

List of works

Büchner, L. (1848) *Beiträge zur Hall'schen Lehre von einem excito-motorischen Nerven-System* (Contributions to Hall's theory of an excito-motorous nervous system), Gießen: Schild. (Büchner's medical dissertation from 9 September 1848.)

—— (1855) *Kraft und Stoff. Empirisch-naturphilosophische Studien. In allgemein-verständlicher Darstellung*, Frankfurt am Main: Meidinger; trans. J.F. Collingwood, *Force and Matter, or Principles of the Natural Order of the Universe*, London: Trübner, 1864. (Subtitle is changed in later editions. 5th German edn, 1858, 21st German edn, Leipzig: Thomas 1904. The 4th English edn of 1884 was much reprinted.)

—— (1857) *Natur und Geist. Gespräche zweier Freunde über den Materialismus und über die real-philosophischen Fragen der Gegenwart. In allgemeinverständlicher Form* (Nature and mind. Conversations of two friends on materialism and the real philosophical questions of the present), Frankfurt am Main: Meidinger.

—— (1861, 1875) *Physiologische Bilder* (Physiological images), Leipzig: Thomas, 2 vols. (On physiological topics.)

—— (1862, 1884) *Aus Natur und Wissenschaft. Studien, Kritiken und Abhandlungen* (About nature and science. Studies, critiques and treatises), Leipzig: Thomas, 2 vols. (A collection of essays on different subjects.)

—— (1863) *Herr Lasalle und die Arbeiter. Bericht und Vortrag über das Lasalle'sche Arbeiterprogramm, erstattet auf dem Arbeitertag in Rödelheim am 19. April 1863, im Auftrag des Central-Comités der Arbeiter des Maingaus* (Herr Lasalle and the workers. Report and address on Lasalle's Worker-programme), Frankfurt am Main: Baist. (A discussion and criticism of the views of Ferdinand Lasalle, an early proponent of the social-democratic movement in Germany.)

—— (1868) *Sechs Vorlesungen über die Darwin'sche Theorie von der Verwandlung der Arten und die erste Entstehung der Organismenwelt* (Six Lectures on Darwin's theory of the transformation of species and the origin of the organic world), Leipzig: Thomas. (Lectures on Darwin's theory of evolution.)

—— (1869) *Die Stellung des Menschen in der Natur, in Vergangenheit, Gegenwart und Zukunft. Oder: Woher kommen wir? Wer sind wir? Wohin gehen wir?*, Leipzig: Thomas; trans. W.S. Dallas, *Man in the Past, Present and Future*, London: Asher, 1872. (A popular account of the results of recent scientific research as regards the origin and prospects of the human race.)

—— (1884) *Der Fortschritt in Natur und Geschichte im Lichte der Darwin'schen Theorie* (Progress in nature and history in the light of Darwin's theory), Stuttgart: Schweizerbart.

—— (1885) *Der neue Hamlet. Poesie und Prosa aus den Papieren eines verstorbenen Pessimisten* (The new Hamlet. Poetry and prose from the papers of a deceased pessimist), Zürich: Verlags-Magazin, J. Schabelitz. (This is a collection of early literary work by Büchner which includes an interesting autobiographical fragment on 189–196. It appeared under the pseudonym Carl Ludwig. A second edition appeared under the author's real name in Gießen, E. Roth, 1901.)

—— (1889) *Das künftige Leben und die moderne Wissenschaft. Zehn Briefe an eine Freundin* (Life beyond death and modern science. Letters to a female friend), Leipzig: Spohr.

—— (1890) *Fremdes und Eignes aus dem geistigen Leben der Gegenwart* (Notes from myself and others on the spiritual life of the present), Leipzig: Spohr. (A collection of essays on different subjects.)

—— (1894) *Darwinismus und Sozialismus, oder: Der Kampf ums Dasein und die moderne Gesellschaft* (Darwinism and Socialism, or: the struggle for existence and modern society), Leipzig: Günther.

—— (1894) *Meine Begegnung mit Ferdinand Lasalle. Ein Beitrag zur Geschichte der sozialdemokratischen Bewegung in Deutschland. Nebst fünf Briefen Lasalles* (My encounter with Ferdinand Lasalle. A contribution to the history of the Social-Democratic movement in Germany. With five letters by Lasalle), Berlin: Hertz & Süßenguth. (Recollection of his encounter with Lasalle, the founder of the German social-democratic party.)

—— (1898) *Am Sterbelager des Jahrhunderts. Blicke eines freien Denkers aus der Zeit in die Zeit*, Gießen: Roth; partly trans. J. MacCabe, *Last Words on Materialism*, London: Watts, 1901. (A collection of essays on different subjects; chapter 12 is on the Jewish question.)

—— (1900) *Im Dienste der Wahrheit. Ausgewählte Aufsätze aus Natur und Wissenschaft* (In the service of truth. Selected papers on nature and science), Gießen: Roth. (Again a collection of essays. Contains a biography of Ludwig Büchner by his younger brother Alex.)

—— (1901) *Kaleidoskop. Skizzen und Aufsätze aus Natur und Menschenleben* (Kaleidoscope. Sketches and essays from nature and human life), Gießen: Roth. (This collection contains an appreciation of Büchner's work by Wilhelm Bölsche: 'Zur Geschichte der volkstümlichen Naturforschung' (On the history of popular research of nature).)

Wittich, D. (ed.) (1971) *Vogt, Moleschott, Büchner: Schriften zum kleinbürgerlichen Materialismus in Deutschland* (Vogt, Moleschott, Büchner: writings of vulgar materialism), Berlin: Akademie, 2 vols. (This reprint of the important writings of materialists includes also a reprint of the 1855 edition of *Kraft und Stoff*. The editor gives a useful 82-page introduction.)

References and further reading

Berglar, P. (1976) 'Der neue Hamlet – Ludwig Büchner in seiner Zeit' (The new Hamlet – Ludwig Büchner in his time), *Archiv für Kulturgeschichte* 58 (1): 204–26. (An account of Büchner's development.)

Büchner, A. (1963) *Die Familie Büchner. Georg Büchners Vorfahren, Eltern und Geschwister* (The Büchner family: Georg Büchner's ancestors, parents, brothers and sister), Hessische Beiträge zur deutschen Literatur, Darmstadt: Roether. (On the background of Büchner's family. Pages 64–81 give an account of Büchner's life by his grand-nephew and a reprint of Büchner's autobiographical fragment.)

Gregory, F. (1977) *Scientific Materialism in Nineteenth-Century Germany*, Dordrecht: Reidel. (Standard account, comprehensive and very readable.)

—— (1977) 'Scientific versus Dialectical Materialism: a Clash of Ideologies in Nineteenth-Century German Radicalism', *Isis* 68: 206–23. (Deals with the relation of Büchner's brand of materialism with that of Marx and Engels.)

Janet, P. (1864) *Le Matérialisme contemporain en Allemagne, examen du système du docteur Büchner*, Paris: Baillière; trans. G. Masson, *The Materialism of the Present Day. A Critique on Dr. Büchner's System*, London, 1865. (Criticism of Büchner's work by a French philosopher which was also influential in its German translation.)

* Lange, F.A. (1866) *Geschichte des Materialismus und Kritik seiner Bedeutung in der Gegenwart*, Iserlohn: Baedeker; augmented and altered 2nd edn, 2 vols, 1873–75; trans. E.C. Thomas, *The History of Materialism and Criticism of its Present Importance*, London: The English & Foreign Philosophical Library, 1877–9, 3 vols; repr. with intro. by B. Russell, London: Kegan Paul, 1925, 1 vol. (The second edition was particularly influential in its criticism of mechanical materialism. Lange's account of the relation of science and philosophy after Kant is still extremely valuable today.)

Lübbe, H. (1963) *Politische Philosophie in Deutschland. Studien zu ihrer Geschichte* (Political philosophy in Germany: studies of its history), Basel: Schwabe; repr. München: Deutscher Taschenbuch Verlag, 1974. (The 3rd part deals with the intimate relation of scientific materialism with politics/political philosophy and its transformation into the movement of 'scientific monism' in Germany in later years.)

* Moleschott, J. (1852) *Der Kreislauf des Lebens. Physiologische Antworten auf Liebig's Chemische Briefe* (The circulation of life: physiological answers to Liebig's chemical letters), Mainz: Zabern. (Response to a book by the chemist J. von Liebig. This book of a fellow materialist was of particular influence on Büchner.)

Negri, A. (1981) *Trittico materialistico: Georg Büchner, Jakob Moleschott, Ludwig Büchner* (A materialist tryptich: Georg Büchner, Jakob Moleschott, Ludwig Büchner), Roma: Cadmo. (Valuable information on Marx's and Engel's comments on Büchner and on the concept of death in nineteenth-century materialism.)

Schnädelbach, H. (1983) *Philosophie in Deutschland 1831–1933*, Frankfurt: Suhrkamp; trans. E.

Matthews, *Philosophy in Germany 1831–1933*, Cambridge: Cambridge University Press, 1984. (A useful introductory text which puts the materialistic movement in nineteenth-century German philosophy in a wider context. See 66–108 on science.)

Schreiner, K. (1977) 'Der Fall Büchner. Studien zur Geschichte der akademischen Lehrfreiheit an der Universität Tübingen im 19. Jahrhundert' (Büchner's case: studies in the history of academic freedom at the University of Tübingen in the nineteenth century), *Beiträge zur Geschichte der Universität Tübingen 1477–1977*, ed. H. Decker-Hauff, Tübingen: Attempto, 307–46. (An account of Büchner's time at Tübingen, his dismissal from his academic position and its influence on the general political development. Based on extensive archival sources that give a vivid account of the circumstances.)

Ziegler, T. (1899) *Die geistigen und sozialen Strömungen des neunzehnten Jahrhunderts* (The intellectual and social movements of the nineteenth century), Berlin: Bondi. (Chapter 11, 'Naturwissenschaft und Philosophie um die Mitte des Jahrhunderts', gives a vivid, still readable and valid account.)

MICHAEL HEIDELBERGER

BUDDHA (6th–5th century BC)

The title of Buddha is usually given to the historical founder of the Buddhist religion, Siddhārtha Gautama, although it has been applied to other historical figures, Buddhist and non-Buddhist, and to many who may be mythological. The religion which he founded was enormously successful and for a long period was probably the most widespread world religion. It is sometimes argued that it is not so much a religion as a kind of philosophy. Indeed, Buddhism bears close comparison with some of the philosophical schools of the Hellenistic world in this respect. The Buddha himself does not seem to have known the concept of a transcendent God and most schools of Buddhism have repudiated it on the grounds, among others, that it undermines personal responsibility for action. Buddhism could be considered as a kind of 'metareligion', open to many religious practices and tolerating others, but not identifiable with religious activity as such – more a kind of philosophical structuring of religion together with a methodology for self-development. Associated with this latter is an elaborate and sophisticated account of mental states and the functioning of consciousness. Characteristic of earlier Buddhist thought is a positive emphasis upon balanced states and a strong rejection of any form of underlying substance and most types of changelessness.

The date when the Buddha, or Siddhārtha Gautama, lived is not certain. For some time most scholars thought that the main period of his activity was in the late sixth century BC, but many believe it more likely that he died close to the end of the fifth century BC, making him a near contemporary of Socrates. Varied information about his life has been preserved, although it is difficult to differentiate between accurate biography and later legend. Scholars are divided on this issue.

It is known that he was born in a noble family among a people called the Sākyas who dwelt near the present-day borders of India and Nepal. After marriage and the birth of a son he experienced some kind of existential crisis. Extant literature presents him as perceptive to the sickness, old age and mortality inherent in life and perceiving the possibility of a solution to such problems. So he went forth ultimately 'for the welfare and benefit of the many-folk' (as many early Buddhist texts put it) and took up the wandering lifestyle of a homeless religious mendicant. He studied under various spiritual teachers and then, seeking to go beyond what he had learned from them, he adopted, together with a group of companions, the common Indian practice of severe asceticism for around six years. He rejected this method as ineffectual and returned to more moderate practices at which point he achieved the spiritual breakthrough that made him a *buddha*. The remainder of his life was spent teaching the way he had found, or rather rediscovered, to his disciples.

This way is often characterized as the 'Middle Way' between the extremes of pursuing sensual pleasures and suffering torment as a means of self-purification and applies both to spiritual praxis and intellectual understanding. The Middle Way also seeks to avoid the extremes of 'eternalism' and 'annihilationism'. These are terms for commitment as a result of a psychological bias – either towards the belief that there is an unchanging immortal soul that survives death or that death is the final end and there is no continuity after the destruction of the body. Similarly any suggestion that the soul or life principle (*jīva*) is identical to, or completely distinct from the body is avoided. Preferences with regard to the universe were also considered to be the result of psychological bias, for example, whether or not it is eternal in time, and whether it is finite or infinite in space.

With regard to practice, the Buddha especially advocated the development of the meditation states known as *jhānas* (*dhyāna*). Since these were characterized by a pleasant state of mind, they contrasted with the painful methods of practice widespread in the Indian religion of the day. These states also placed a stress on clarity and conscious awareness, as distinct from the apparent valuation of unconscious trance-like states in pre-Buddhist Indian religion. This emphasis led to the development of methods of study and practice which strongly asserted the importance of insight and understanding (*prajñā*). For most later forms of Buddhism and probably for the Buddha himself, the actual goal of Buddhist meditation represented an awakening which permanently integrated both the meditative states of the *jhānas* and a high development of understanding. It is this which is referred to in the early texts as acquiring the 'vision of truth' or '*dhamma* eye' and is seen as the basis for the awakening or *bodhi*, taught by the Buddha, or Awakened One.

According to early Buddhists, the Buddha presented his teaching on two levels. At an introductory stage he put forward a simple model of the good life, advocating both the practice of generosity and moral restraint. This was probably linked to a picture of the world as one where living beings were reborn in a series of after-death destinies, including rebirth as a human being or animal (see KARMA AND REBIRTH, INDIAN CONCEPTIONS OF). Such a view appears to have been already widely known, even by the Greeks of that time. Living such a life was seen as creating conditions for a better mental state, capable of understanding more profound truths. For the Buddha these more advanced truths were his higher teaching and were referred to as the Four Noble Truths.

The Buddha probably rejected monism. Early on his followers developed a type of process philosophy which emphasized the universality of change in ordinary experience and rejected the idea that there was any kind of fixed essence behind things. This applied both to the world at large and to the individual. Thus, notions of a world-soul, or ground of being and a permanent, unchanging individual nature were repudiated. The picture they adopted saw life in terms of harmonious interaction of multiple processes. Fundamental to this was the notion of *dhamma* (Sanskrit *dharma*) – the lawful and harmonious nature of things. This *dhamma* was rediscovered by the Buddha and his teaching was understood as the presentation of a universal law which exists in some sense, whether or not it is known about.

Our knowledge of the Buddha's teachings and of early Buddhism in general derives primarily from the collection of texts known as the *tipiṭaka*, or 'three baskets': the canonical writings of early Buddhism. The earliest extant version of these is that preserved in the Pāli language by the southern Buddhists. At first it was preserved within the oral tradition, but was written down in Sri Lanka, formerly Ceylon in the first century BC. Translations of similar texts of diverse origins and dates are preserved in the Chinese Buddhist Canon. Undoubtedly some of this material is as old as the corresponding (and often similar) sources in the Pāli Canon, but it is mixed with material of later origin. Some texts in Sanskrit were discovered in libraries (mostly in Nepal) in the nineteenth century and more recently in the monastic libraries of Tibet, in a ruined library at Gilgit in Kashmir and (often fragmentary) in various desert locations in central Asia. However, most of these appear to be slightly later than the equivalent texts in Pāli. Most recent of all is the acquisition by the British Museum in 1995 of a number of fragments of a version of the Canon in the Gāndhārī language, apparently dating from the first century AD or earlier.

See also: BUDDHIST PHILOSOPHY, INDIAN; BUDDHIST PHILOSOPHY, CHINESE; BUDDHIST PHILOSOPHY, JAPANESE; BUDDHIST PHILOSOPHY, KOREAN

References and further reading

Carrithers, M. (1983) *The Buddha*, Oxford and New York: Oxford University Press. (A succinct account.)

Gombrich, R. (1988) *Theravāda Buddhism: a Social History from Ancient Benares to Modern Columbo*, London and New York: Routledge & Kegan Paul. (Chapters 3–5 include a valuable account of the ancient Indian background to early Buddhism.)

Harvey, P. (1990) *An Introduction to Buddhism: Teachings, History and Practices*, Cambridge and New York: Cambridge University Press. (A good introduction to Buddhism.)

Lamotte, É. (1958) *History of Indian Buddhism: from the Origins to the Śaka Era*, Louvain: Peeters Press, 1988. (The standard history. Magisterial, although a little dated since its first publication in French.)

Ñāṇamoli, B. (1972) *The Life of the Buddha as it Appears in the Pali Canon: the Oldest Authentic Record*, Kandy, Sri Lanka: Buddhist Publication Society. (A useful collection of many of the original texts in translation.)

Pye, M. (1979) *The Buddha*, London: Duckworth. (An interesting attempt to distinguish myth, legend and history.)

Thomas, E.J. (1927) *The Life of Buddha*, London: Routledge & Kegan Paul, 1975. (A classic, but still useful account.)

L.S. COUSINS

BUDDHISM, ĀBHIDHARMIKA SCHOOLS OF

During the first centuries after the Buddha, with the development of a settled life of scholarly study and religious practice, distinct schools began to emerge within the Buddhist community. In their efforts to organize and understand the Buddha's traditional teachings, these schools developed a new genre of text, called 'Abhidharma', to express their doctrinal interpretations. More importantly, the term 'Abhidharma' was also used to refer to the discriminating insight that was not only requisite for the elucidation of doctrine but also indispensable for religious practice: only insight allows one to isolate and remove the causes of suffering.

Abhidharma analysis is innovative in both form and content. While earlier Buddhist discourses were colloquial, using simile and anecdotes, Abhidharma texts were in a highly regimented style, using technical language, intricate definitions and complex classifications. The Abhidharma genre also promoted a method of textual exegesis combining scriptural citation and reasoned arguments.

In content, the hallmark of Abhidharma is its exhaustive classification of all factors that were thought to constitute experience. Different schools proposed different classifications; for example, one school proposed a system of seventy-five distinct factors classified into five groups, including material form, the mind, mental factors, factors dissociated from material form and mind, and unconditioned factors. These differences led to heated doctrinal debates, the most serious of which concerned the manner of existence of the individual factors and the modes of their conditioning interaction. For example, do the factors actually exist as real entities or do they exist merely as provisional designations? Is conditioning interaction always successive or can cause and effect be simultaneous in the same moment? Other major topics of debate included differing models for mental processes, especially perception.

1 Abhidharma
2 Philosophical significance: methods of exegesis and argument
3 Philosophical significance: nature of reality and conditioning relations
4 Philosophical significance: perception and insight

1 Abhidharma

By about the first century BC, about 200 to 300 years after the death of the Buddha, the community of his followers had changed significantly. From a loose grouping of itinerant mendicants, practising largely as individuals, there emerged communities with a settled life of scholarly study and religious discipline. In this more organized setting, Buddhist monks began to re-examine the received teaching, to extend it to new areas, and to elaborate and refine techniques designed to ensure its preservation. Eventually, this new scholastic enterprise became not only the medium for transmitting and understanding the traditional teaching but also tradition in its own right and, for the various schools that were soon to emerge, the source of multiple, even rival traditions.

The Buddhist community developed into separate schools for many reasons: geographic dispersion and isolation; selective patronage; contact with non-Buddhists; disagreements over disciplinary codes; the absence of a single institutional authority; the divergent views of influential teachers; specialization in segments of Buddhist scripture; and, finally, doctrinal disagreements. Among these, disputes about doctrine, or rather the elaboration and analysis of doctrine in the context of disputation with rivals, became a defining activity of the emergent schools. This analysis was called 'Abhidharma'. Although its original meaning is not certain, most interpretations agree that it refers to its purpose of supplementing (abhi-) or clarifying the teaching (dharma). Abhidharma is not only a genre of texts but also, more importantly, the analytic method and the insight through which one correctly comprehends the Buddhist teaching. For Abhidharma is not an end in itself; the scholastic enterprise, like the original teaching, serves a soteriological goal. Abhidharma enables the practitioner to discriminate those aspects of experience that are defiling and so lead to suffering from those that are virtuous; through this discriminating insight, one can remove the defilements, cultivate virtue, and thereby emulate the Buddha and attain enlightenment (see SUFFERING, BUDDHIST VIEWS OF ORIGINATION OF).

According to the self-understanding of the later Buddhist schools, the Abhidharma simply organizes and explicates the often implicit and embryonic teaching preserved in the collections of discourses on doctrine (sūtra) that are attributed to the Buddha. But while the tradition did not consider Abhidharma as innovative – indeed, most schools attributed the content, if not the very words, of the Abhidharma to the Buddha himself – it is none the less clear that the Abhidharma treatises record doctrinal debate that stimulated new doctrines and new methods of exegesis.

Though evidence suggests that each of the early Buddhist schools preserved and transmitted its own complete set of texts, which would have included an Abhidharma collection, only two are extant: that of the Theravāda school, which became predominant in Sri Lanka and spread to southeast Asia; and that of the Sarvāstivāda school, which became predominant in north, especially northwest, India and spread to central Asia. Although at opposite ends of the geographical and doctrinal range of schools, these two have Abhidharma collections that are similar in number (seven base texts with commentaries, despite no direct correspondence between the texts of the two collections) and, more significantly, in style and doctrinal subjects. Also, each collection fortunately has a text (the *Kathāvatthu* and its commentary among the Theravādin texts, and the *Mahāvibhāṣā* among the Sarvāstivādin) that, by extensively citing the views of other schools lacking extant Abhidharma works, completes our picture of early Buddhist sectarian views.

2 Philosophical significance: methods of exegesis and argument

With the Abhidharma emphasis on discriminating analysis as the proper mode of religious praxis, Buddhist thought becomes 'philosophical'. However, the philosophical contribution of Abhidharma cannot be understood apart from its specific sectarian and doctrinal context. Only later, with the appearance of Buddhist logicians (see DIGNĀGA; DHARMAKĪRTI), do familiar, abstract philosophical problems become central, and pragmatic soteriological concerns recede somewhat into the background.

In structure and style of presentation, even more than in subject matter, Abhidharma is radically innovative. The colloquial, earlier discourses that persuaded with simile, metaphor and anecdote are replaced by a precise, regimented style and technical terminology that demonstrates by definition, exegesis, catechesis and taxonomy. Despite its technical character, Abhidharma was not a sterile tangent in the development of Buddhist thought, but was the representative core of the Buddhist monastic worldview.

As is to be expected in a strongly traditional culture, the innovative character of Abhidharma did not spring up in an abrupt or discontinuous way; instead, it grew over centuries, with roots in two tendencies that can be traced to the earlier Buddhist discourses. The first of these tendencies was a penchant for analysis pursued with the goal of encompassing in an intricate classificatory system all the factors (dharma) thought to constitute experience. This included topical lists of factors distinguished by numeric and qualitative criteria as well as complex combinations of sets of categories yielding matrices (*mātṛkā*). In this exhaustive listing, all factors of experience would be strictly defined and their relation to all other factors would be clearly indicated by their placement within the various categories; guided by this exhaustive enumeration, the religious practitioner could then distinguish those factors to be cultivated from those to be removed. The second tendency was more expository than analytic and evolved from dialogues about doctrine conducted in the early Buddhist community. Such discussions would often begin with a quotation from earlier discourses or a doctrinal point to be defined and would then proceed using a pedagogical technique of question and answer.

Abhidharma texts also document the concurrent development of organized methods of exegesis and argument. While similar due to shared beginnings, the canons of Buddhist schools became widely divergent; contradictions occur even within the texts of a single school. In order to judge the authenticity and authority of different passages and texts, to interpret them accurately and to mediate conflicting positions, the schools began to elaborate a systematic hermeneutics. In general, the interpretative principles applied were inclusive and harmonizing: any statement deemed in conformity with the teaching of the Buddha or with his enlightenment experience was accepted as genuine; hierarchies were created that incorporated divergent passages by valuing them differently; contradictory passages in the discourses or within Abhidharma texts were said to represent the variant perspectives from which the Buddhist teaching could be presented. Notable for its parallel with later Buddhist ontology and epistemology was the hermeneutic technique whereby certain passages or texts were judged to express absolute truth or reality explicitly, while others, apparently expressing mere conventional truth, nevertheless were judged to have implicit meaning. For the Ābhidharmika schools, accordingly, the Abhidharma texts were considered explicit, whereas the collections of discourses were merely implicit and thus in need of further interpretation.

More formal methods of argumentation begin to appear in Abhidharma texts of the middle period (first centuries AD), which record doctrinal disagreements and debates among rival schools. These texts exhibit a stylized pattern using both supporting scriptural references and reasoned investigations, both of which were considered equally effective in argument. In the earliest examples of such arguments, the reasoned investigations did not yet possess the power of independent proof and were considered valid only in conjunction with supportive scriptural citations. However, in texts of the later period, supporting scriptural references became decontextualized com-

monplaces – cited simply to validate the occurrence of terms – and reasoned investigations began to be appraised by independent nonscriptural criteria such as internal consistency and the absence of fallacious causal justification and other logical faults.

3 Philosophical significance: nature of reality and conditioning relations

The exhaustive Abhidharma analysis of experience occasioned doctrinal controversies that could be termed ontological: namely, the manner of existence of the different factors constituting experience; the nature of the reality that they represent; and the dynamics of their interaction, or conditioning. Simple enumerations of factors representing various analytical perspectives are found even in the earlier discourses. Abhidharma texts preserve these earlier analyses, but elaborate more comprehensive and complex intersecting classifications that attempt to clarify the unique identity of each factor as well as all possible modes of interaction among factors. Virtually every early Buddhist school proposed some method of classification, but the lists of specific factors varied greatly. For example, the Sarvāstivādins enumerated seventy-five factors (*dharma*) categorized in five groups: material form (eleven); mind (one); mental factors (forty-six); factors dissociated from material form and mind (fourteen); and unconditioned factors (three). The forty-six mental factors were then subcategorized into groups reflecting their moral quality, a determination essential for correct practice.

The variant lists proposed by other schools often reflect differences of opinion on major issues. Implicit in the Sarvāstivādin categorization of factors is a model of mental processes whereby each moment is characterized by the occurrence of a single instance of mind (*citta*), which serves as a focal point necessarily arising together with ten mental factors that perform specific psychological functions: for example, such factors as feelings, volition, concepts, insight and mindfulness. In addition to these omnipresent and necessary mental factors, mind may also arise with other factors of either a virtuous or unvirtuous moral quality. Other schools, among them the Dārṣṭāntikas, rejected this model and claimed that more than one mental activity could not occur simultaneously in the same moment, but rather could arise only sequentially in successive moments. Indeed, some sources suggest that certain Dārṣṭāntika masters recognized the existence of only three such mental factors – feelings, concepts and volition – which were thought to arise in successive moments.

Perhaps the most significant controversy debated in

55

the context of these lists concerns modes of existence, specifically, the manner of existence of the individual factors and their conditioning interaction. Within the earlier discourses, the enumerating of factors was motivated not simply by a need to organize the teaching to meet the demands of oral transmission, but rather had a doctrinal function. The fundamental Buddhist teaching of nonself (see BUDDHIST PHILOSOPHY, INDIAN §1) was thought to be validated by demonstrating that no perduring, unchanging, independent 'self' (ātman) could be found in an entity as a whole, in any of the constituents that the entity comprises, or outside the entity. All entities were thus proven to be impermanent, that is, arising and passing away without any constant essence. In Abhidharma treatises, the increasingly detailed enumerations of factors were intended to demonstrate this fundamental truth of existence as essenceless and impermanent; nevertheless, they led to markedly different ontological models.

A distinctive ontology was constructed by the Sarvāstivādins ('those who profess that everything exists'), who offered a radical interpretation of impermanence as momentariness, where all factors constituting experience exist separately, arising and passing away within the span of a single moment. In a reality that is an array of radically momentary factors, continuity as commonly experienced and indeed any interaction among the discrete factors would seem to be a logical impossibility. A factor arising in one moment could not act as a condition for an as yet nonexistent future factor, and that subsequent factor could not be said to be conditioned by a past and nonexistent factor of the previous moment. To safeguard ordinary experience, the Sarvāstivādins suggested a novel reinterpretation of existence: each factor, they claimed, is characterized by both an intrinsic nature, which exists unchanged in the past, present and future, and an activity, which, arising and passing away due to the influence of conditions, exists only in the present moment. Only factors that are thus both defined by intrinsic nature and characterized by activity can be considered to exist as real entities; composite objects, consisting of factors and constituting ordinary experience, exist only provisionally. The Sarvāstivādins saw this as the only model that would preserve the Buddhist doctrine of impermanence, since each factor's activity is conditioned. Conditioning interaction in the past, present and future would still be possible given an existing intrinsic nature. Later Sarvāstivādins, in an effort to clarify this causal functioning and maintain temporal distinctions, claimed that a factor's present functioning should be distinguished from its functioning in the past or future. Present functioning, or 'activity', refers

to homogeneous causation through which a factor conditions the arising of a similar factor in the subsequent moment. Past and future functioning, or 'capability', would include various causal functions, such as serving as an object of cognition in the case of memory, or acting as an immediately prior cause in the arising of a subsequent effect.

The Sarvāstivādin ontological model became the subject of heated debate and was rejected by other Ābhidharmika schools such as the Dārṣṭāntikas, who claimed that factors exist only in the present and not in the past and future. Factors do not exist as isolated units of intrinsic nature that manifest a particular activity through the influence of other isolated conditions. Instead, their activity is to be equated with their very existence. The process of causal activity, the Dārṣṭāntikas argued, is experience itself; the fragmentation of this process into discrete factors possessed of individual existence and unique efficacy is nothing but a mental fabrication.

These ontological investigations generated complex theories of conditioning and intricate typologies of causes and conditions. There is evidence of several rival classifications: the Theravādins proposed a set of twenty-four conditions; the Sarvāstivādins, separate sets either of four conditions or of six causes; and the school represented by the *Śāriputrābhidharmaśāstra, ten conditions. Each of these individual causes and conditions accounts for a specific mode of conditioning interaction: for example, one cause explains the association among mental factors; another, the maturation of efficacious action; still another, the reciprocal influence of simultaneous factors; and yet another, the arising of a similar subsequent factor. Besides establishing different typologies of causes and conditions, the schools also disagreed on the causal modality exercised by these specific types. The Sarvāstivādins acknowledged that certain of these causes and conditions arise prior to their effects, while others, which exert a supportive conditioning efficacy, arise simultaneously with them. The Dārṣṭāntikas, however, allowed only successive causation; a cause must always precede its effect. In these debates about causality, the nature of animate or personal causation – that is, efficacious action, or karman – and the theory of dependent origination intended to account for its activity were, naturally, central issues because of their fundamental role in all Buddhist teaching (see CAUSATION, INDIAN THEORIES OF §§1, 6).

4 Philosophical significance: perception and insight

Abhidharma investigations also extended into the field of epistemology, not for its own sake, but rather for an understanding of how the liberating insight that annuls ignorance and the suffering it causes can arise. To this end, Abhidharma texts carried out a thorough analysis of mental processes, which were all interpreted as varieties of perception. In general, every instance of consciousness, which includes five externally directed varieties of consciousness, and mental consciousness as a sixth, was understood as intentional, occurring only in dependence upon three conditions: a sense organ; a suitable sense object; and the previous moment of consciousness. However, schools disagreed about the specific roles of the sense object, sense organ and consciousness, and about the distinctive character of mental consciousness.

For the Sarvāstivādins, the sense organ grasps the object and consciousness apprehends the general character of the object as grasped by the sense organ: that is, its character as visual form, sound, odour, and so on. The various mental factors simultaneous with that moment of consciousness grasp the particular characteristics of the object. When apprehended in the present moment by consciousness and its associated mental factors, the object becomes internalized as an 'object-support'. In this model of consciousness, erroneous cognition is possible, but such cognition is grounded in an existent object, despite being erroneously grasped by the sense organ or erroneously apprehended by consciousness. Error thus lies in the internal object-support, not in the external object.

In the case of the five externally directed sense organs, the object exists as a real entity and is apprehended only when it is present; indeed, its function as an object verifies its existence as a real entity. The object and sense organ condition the arising of a simultaneous apprehending consciousness. Thus, perception assumes a model of simultaneous conditioning. Mental consciousness also functions according to the model of external perception. The previous moment of consciousness, whatever the type, serves as the mental sense organ for the arising of the subsequent moment of mental consciousness. Any object, whether past, present or future, can be apprehended by mental consciousness. This includes really existent objects – for example, mental factors such as feelings and concepts or any object of the other five varieties of consciousness – or the composite entities of ordinary experience, which exist only provisionally. Both the organ and object then condition the arising of a present moment of mental consciousness.

The Dārṣṭāntikas consider this Sarvāstivādin model a mere provisional description of perception; no experience, they maintain, including perception, can be analysed into components that actually exist as discrete factors possessing individual activities. The sense organ, sense object, and consciousness are

simply provisionally discriminated in the midst of an experienced causal stream. Further, they claim that one cannot establish a relationship of cause and effect within the same moment; as a result, one cannot look to an object in one moment producing consciousness in that very moment. If that were the case, perception would become a successive causal process whereby the sense organ and object in one moment condition the arising of consciousness in a subsequent moment; in effect, perception would always involve apprehension of a past and – for the Dārṣṭāntikas, who reject the existence of past factors – nonexistent object.

Building upon the Abhidharma texts, later Buddhist thought would continue to refine both its dialectical method and its examination of core philosophical issues in the context of debates largely conducted with a variety of extra-Buddhist traditions. But with the passing of the Ābhidharmika schools and the historical conditions that stimulated their particular intersectarian mode of disputation, with its interweaving of hermeneutical and logical argument, there passed also a unique creative phase in the history of Indian thought. Only some of their unique legacy of subtle analyses remains, never fully subsumed into the later tradition and relatively unstudied to this day.

See also: BUDDHIST PHILOSOPHY, JAPANESE; SENSE PERCEPTION, INDIAN VIEWS OF

References and further reading

Bareau, A. (1947–50) 'Les Sectes bouddhiques du Petit Véhicule et leurs Abhidharmapiṭaka' (Lesser-Vehicle Buddhist Sects and their Abhidharmapiṭaka), *Bulletin de l'École Française d'Extrême-Orient* 44, fasc. 1: 1–11. (Review of Abhidharma collections of early Indian Buddhist schools.)

—— (1955) *Les Sectes bouddhiques du Petit Véhicule* (Lesser-Vehicle Buddhist Sects), Saigon: École Française d'Extrême-Orient. (Extensive collection of the doctrinal positions of early Indian Buddhist schools.)

Buddhaghosa (5th century AD) *Visuddhimagga*, trans. Bhikkhu Ñāṇamoli, *The Path of Purification*, Colombo: A. Senage, 1956. (Later compendium of virtually the entirety of Theravādin Abhidhamma analysis.)

Cox, C. (1995) *Disputed Dharmas: Early Buddhist Theories on Existence. An Annotated Translation of the Section on Factors Dissociated from Thought from Saṅghabhadra's Nyāyānusāra*, Studia Philologica Buddhica Monograph Series, Tokyo: The International Institute for Buddhist Studies. (Study of later Sarvāstivādin *dharma* classification and ontology.)

Dhammasaṅgaṇi (3rd–1st centuries BC) , trans. C.A.F. Rhys Davids, *A Buddhist Manual of Psychological Ethics*, London: Pali Text Society, 1974, reprint of 1900 edn. (Theravādin Abhidhamma work employing elaborate matrices to specify types of mind (*citta*).)

Frauwallner, E. (1995) *Studies in Abhidharma Literature and the Origins of Buddhist Philosophical Systems*, trans. S.F. Kidd, Albany, NY: State University of New York Press. (Studies of northern Indian Abhidharma texts.)

Hirakawa, A. (1990) *A History of Indian Buddhism*, trans. P. Groner, Honolulu, HI: University of Hawaii Press. (History of early Indian Buddhism, focusing on doctrine.)

* *Kathāvatthu* (3rd–1st centuries BC) trans. S.Z. Aung and C.A.F. Rhys Davids, London: Pali Text Society, 1969, reprint of 1915 edn. (Theravādin Abhidhamma work detailing contending positions on key doctrinal points.)

Lamotte, É. (1988) *History of Indian Buddhism*, trans. S. Webb-Boin, Louvain and Paris: Peeters Press. (Thorough history of all aspects of early Indian Buddhism.)

La Vallée Poussin, L. de (ed.) (1925) 'La Controverse du temps et du *pudgala* dans le *Vijñānakāya*' (The Controversy over Time and *pudgala* in the *Vijñānakāya*), *Études asiatiques* 1: 343–76. (Sections from the Sarvāstivādin Abhidharma text, the *Vijñānakāya* (3rd–1st centuries BC).)

—— (ed.) (1930) 'Documents d'Abhidharma: Textes relatifs au *nirvāṇa* et aux *asaṃskṛtas* en général I – II' (Abhidharma Documents: Texts Concerning *nirvāṇa* and *asaṃskṛtas* in General, I – II), *Bulletin de l'École Française d'Extrême-Orient* 30: 1–28, 247–98. (Sections from Sarvāstivādin Abhidharma texts of the 2nd–5th centuries AD.)

—— (ed.) (1936–1937a) 'Documents d'Abhidharma: la controverse du temps' (Abhidharma Documents: The Controversy over Time), *Mélanges chinois et bouddhiques* 5: 7–158. (Sections from Sarvāstivādin Abhidharma texts of the 2nd–5th centuries AD.)

—— (ed.) (1936–1937b) 'Documents d'Abhidharma: les deux, les quatre, les trois vérités' (Abhidharma Document: The Two Truths, the Four Truths and the Three Truths), *Mélanges chinois et bouddhiques* 5: 159–87. (Sections from Sarvāstivādin Abhidharma texts of the 2nd–5th centuries AD.)

Stcherbatsky, T. (1923) *The Central Conception of Buddhism and the Meaning of the Word 'Dharma'*, Delhi: Motilal Banarsidass, 1970. (Brief study of Abhidharma classifications.)

Vasubandhu (5th century AD) *Abhidharmakośa*, trans.

L. de la Vallée Poussin, *L'Abhidharmakośa de Vasubandhu*, Paris: Librairie Orientaliste Paul Geuthner, 1923–31, 6 vols; trans. (of La Vallée Poussin edn) L. Pruden, Berkeley, CA: Asian Humanities Press, 1988–90, 4 vols. (Later digest of northern Indian Abhidharma teachings, including also polemical arguments on doctrinal points.)

Williams, P. (1981) 'On the Abhidharma Ontology', *Journal of Indian Philosophy* 9: 227–57. (Study of Sarvāstivādin ontology.)

COLLETT COX

BUDDHISM, MĀDHYAMIKA: INDIA AND TIBET

Madhyamaka ('the Middle Doctrine') Buddhism was one of two Mahāyāna Buddhist schools, the other being Yogācāra, that developed in India between the first and fourth centuries AD. The Mādhyamikas derived the name of their school from the Middle Path (madhya-madhyamapratipad) doctrine expounded by the historical Siddhārtha, prince of the Śākya clan, when he gained the status of a buddha, enlightenment. *The Madhyamaka, developed by the second-century philosopher Nāgārjuna on the basis of a class of* sūtras *known as the* Prajñāpāramitā *('Perfection of Wisdom'), can be seen in his foundational* Mūlamadhyamakakārikā *(Fundamental Central Way Verses). Therein he expounds the central Buddhist doctrines of the Middle Path in terms of interdependent origination (pratītyasamutpāda), conventional language (prajñapti), no-self nature (niḥsvabhāva) and voidness (śūnyatā). He grants that the* dharma *taught by the enlightened ones is dependent upon two realities (dve satye samupāśritya) – the conventional reality of the world (lokasaṃvṛtisatyam) and reality as the ultimate (satyam paramārthataḥ). Although voidness is central to Madhyamaka, we are warned against converting* śūnyatā *into yet another 'ism'.*

Historically, Madhyamaka in India comprises three periods – the early period (second to fifth century), represented by the activities of Nāgārjuna, Āryadeva and Rāhulabhadra; the middle period (fifth to seventh century) exemplified by Buddhapālita and Bhāvaviveka (founders respectively of the *Prāsaṅgika and *Svātantrika schools of Madhyamaka), and Candrakīrti; and the later period (eighth to eleventh century), which includes Śāntarakṣita and Kamalaśīla, who fused the ideas found in the Madhyamaka and Yogācāra systems. Many of the Indian Madhyamaka scholars of the later period contributed to Madhyamaka developments in Tibet.

1   The early period (second to fifth century)

Nāgārjuna (c. AD 150–200). Nāgārjuna's life story can be seen in such writings as Xuanzang's *Travels in the Western World* and Kumārajīva's *History of the Bodhisattva Nāgārjuna* (both in Chinese), and the histories of Buddhism by Bu-ston and Tāranātha (in Tibetan). Most of the accounts found in these works, however, are fictions and there are discrepancies between the Chinese and Tibetan traditions. But since Kumārajīva (AD 350–409) lived relatively close to the period attributed to NĀGĀRJUNA and was a great scholar of *Prajñāpāramitā* ('Perfection of Wisdom') literature, certain information given in his account can be trusted from certain perspectives.

Both archeological records and textual evidences point to Nāgārjuna as a historical person. For example, in southern India, near the river Kushnara, there remains a cave named Nāgārjunakoṇḍa, and Nāgārjuna's association with such kings as the King of Satavana is recorded in the *Suhṛllekha* (A Letter to a Friend) and the *Ratnāvali* (Garland of Jewels).

Many works are attributed to Nāgārjuna, among which the following are considered by scholars to be genuine: *Mūlamadhyamakakārikā* (Fundamental Central Way Verses), *Yuktiṣaṣṭikā* (Sixty Verses on Reasoning), *Śūnyatāsaptati* (Seventy-Verse Commentary on Emptiness), *Vigrahavyāvartani* (Refutation of Objections), *Vaidalyasūtra* (Teaching of Vaidalya), *Ratnāvali*, *Suhṛllekha* and *Pratītyasamutpāda-hṛdayakārikā* (Verses on the Heart of Interdependent Origination).

Nāgārjuna developed his philosophy of *śūnyatā* (voidness) as a critical response to views held by Indian Realists such as Sāṅkhya and Vaiśeṣika, the Indian schools of logic such as the Nyaiyāyika, and such Hīnayāna Buddhists as the Sarvāstivādas and other Abhidharma philosophers. Although the Abhidharma ideas that Nāgārjuna criticized did not coincide totally with those found in Sarvāstivāda, the idea of existence developed by the Realists did (see BUDDHISM, ĀBHIDHARMIKA SCHOOLS OF). Nāgārjuna also aimed to refute non-Buddhist schools such as Sāṅkhya and Vaiśeṣika. It was the idea that the objects of perception possess substantive qualities in the external world – the common thread among these Realist schools – that Nāgārjuna attacked.

The Indian system of logic was both the mother and opponent of Nāgārjuna's system of logic. Without doubt, tenets such as *chala* (quibble), *jāti* (analogue), *nigrahasthana* (defeat), and so on, found in the *Nyāyasūtra* (Teaching on Logical Arguments), were forerunners of Nāgārjuna's system of critique. Also his use of *prasaṅga* (*reductio ad absurdum*) is an application of the *tarka* (reasoning) method found in the *Nyāyasūtra* (see NYĀYA-VAIŚEṢIKA §6).

Āryadeva (c. AD 170–270). It is said that Āryadeva was born in southern India or perhaps Sri Lanka and was a disciple of Nāgārjuna. His life story can be seen in such writings as Xuanzang's *Travels in the Western World*, Kumārajīva's *History of the Bodhisattva Āryadeva* and Candrakīrti's commentary, *Catuḥśatakavṛtti*.

Three works are attributed to Āryadeva: *[Bodhi-sattvayogācāra-]Catuḥśataka* (Text of Four Hundred Verses) (Sanskrit, Chinese translation and Tibetan), *Śataśāstra* (A Hundred Verses) (Chinese translation only) and *Akṣaraśataka* (Tibetan and Chinese translation). Kumārajīva's Chinese translation of the *Śataśāstra* is a popular text with the Sanlun school of Chinese and Japanese (Sanron) Buddhism. With regard to the *[Bodhisattvayogācāra-]Catuḥśataka*, there remain Candrakīrti's commentary in Tibetan translation and Dharmapāla's (530–61) commentary in Chinese translation; however, in each case, only the last nine chapters of the text appear. Only about one-third of the Sanskrit original remains. Although the whole work can be found in Tibetan translation, the difficulties of the first half of the Tibetan text mean that very little work has been done on this part.

Rāhulabhadra (c. AD 200–300). Little is known of Rāhulabhadra other than that he was Āryadeva's disciple. Of his compositions, two Sanskrit works remain: *Prajñāpāramitāstotra* (Stotra on the Perfection of Wisdom), attributed in Tibetan Tripiṭaka to Nāgārjuna, and *Saddharmapuṇḍarīkastava* (Stava on the Lotus of the Wonderful Law). Other works seem to have been attributed to him, as some of his verses are quoted by Asaṅga and Paramārtha in their works.

2   The middle period (fifth to seventh century)

In the first chapter of Avalokitavrata's (seventh century?) commentary on the *Prajñāpradīpa* (Lamp of Wisdom) and in the postscript found in Nāgārjuna's own work, the *Akutobhayā* (Nāgārjuna's Auto Commentary), it is said there were eight commentaries on the *Mūlamadhyamakakārikā*; however, only those by Buddhapālita, Bhāvaviveka, and Candrakīrti are renowned, as the remainder are either not very useful, or are not extant at present. Along with Avalokitavrata, Śāntideva (c.650–700) and Prajñākaramati (c.950–1030) were active during this period.

Avalokitavrata's *Prajñāpradīpaṭīkā* (Lamp of Wisdom Commentary), extant in Tibetan translation, is a huge text and a very erudite commentary on the various Indian and Buddhist schools; consequently, it serves as a very important source book. Avalokita-vrata knew about Candrakīrti and Dharmakīrti (c. 600–60), but because he did not utilize their logic, we can surmise that he was their contemporary.

In the histories of Buddhism by Bu-ston and Tāranātha, Śāntideva is credited as the author of the *Śikṣāsamuccaya* (A Compendium of Buddhist Doctrine), the *Sūtrasamuccaya* (A Compendium of Buddhist Sutras) and the *Bodhicaryāvatāra* (Entering the Path of Enlightenment). The *Sūtrasamuccaya*, extant in the Tibetan canon, purports to be by Nāgārjuna, but because some of the sixty or so *sūtras* quoted in it were composed after Nāgārjuna's death, this attribution is difficult as the text stands.

Although commentaries on Śāntideva's *Bodhicaryāvatāra* abound, it is Prajñākaramati's *Bodhicaryāvatārapañjika* (Entering the Path of Enlightenment Commentary) which is the most famous. It comments on the first nine chapters, but not the tenth. Prajñākaramati probably began it as a commentary on the ninth chapter, and then added commentary on the first eight chapters later. Judging from his criticism of Sautrāntika and Yogācāra, we can assume that Prajñākaramati was a Mādhyamika, but it is difficult to determine to which school he belonged. Although in terms of his dates Prajñākaramati falls into the later period, he is discussed here as a commentator on Śāntideva's work.

According to later Tibetan doxographies, the Middle Period is also characterized by Madhyamaka splitting into the *Prāsaṅgika and *Svātantrika schools.

Buddhapālita (c. 470–540). Buddhapālita's *Mūlamadhyamakavṛtti* (Fundamental Central Way Verses Commentary), a commentary in twenty-seven chapters, exists only in Tibetan translation. Although from the seventh *kārikā* of chapter twenty-three the content of the text is identical with Nāgārjuna's *Akutobhayā*, its importance can be inferred from Bhāvaviveka's vehement criticism of it and Candrakīrti's concerted defence. The text's distinctive character lies in Buddhapālita's presentation of Nāgārjuna's use of dilemma and tetralemma from the standpoint of plural *prasaṅgas* – that is, he divides the tetralemma into two or four different *prasaṅga* (*reductio ad absurdum*) arguments. It is probably for this reason that Buddhapālita is seen as the founder of the *Prāsaṅgika school and was criticized by Bhāvaviveka.

Bhāvaviveka (c. 500–70). Bhāvaviveka, or Bhavya, is known by many different names, but because Candrakīrti, in his *Prasannapāda* (Lucid Exposition), calls him Bhāvaviveka, he is known generally by that name. He is said to have written four works: *Prajñāpradīpa[-mūlamadhyamakavṛtti]*, *Madhyamakahṛdayakārikā*, *Tarkajvālā* (Blaze of Argument) (*Madhyamakahṛdayavṛtti*) and *Dashengzhangzhenlun* (extant in Chinese only). In the Tibetan canon there is another work, the *Nikāyabhedavibhaṅga-vyākhyāna*, attributed to Bhāvaviveka, but its content corresponds to the discussion of the Hīnayāna found in fourth chapter of the *Tarkajvālā*. The authenticity of two other works ascribed to him, the *Madhyamakaratnapradīpa* (Jewel of the Central Way Lamp) and the *Madhyamakārtha-saṃgraha*, is doubtful.

The *Prajñāpradīpa[-mūlamadhyamakavṛtti]* is the first full-scale commentary on the *Mūlamadhyamakakārikā* and is important in two respects. First, Bhāvaviveka's interpretation of the various arguments presented by Nāgārjuna was strongly influenced by Dignāga's logic. Bhāvaviveka established many categorical syllogisms, the so-called *svatantra-anumāna* (independent inference), and hence his system is known as the *Svātantrika school. Second, he criticized Buddhapālita's version of *prasaṅga* as being merely *prasaṅga* without the minor and major premises.

The *Madhyamakahṛdayakārikā* (Verses on the Heart of the Central Way) consists of eleven chapters, but it is only the first three that discuss Madhyamaka philosophy. In the rest, Bhāvaviveka discusses the doctrines of Hīnayāna Buddhism, Yogācāra, Sāṅkhya, Vaiśeṣika, Vedānta and other schools. In this manner, he establishes the Madhyamaka on the one hand, and on the other he criticizes other schools and thus develops his work around the system of doctrinal classification that was further developed by scholars such as Śāntarakṣita. The Sanskrit manuscript of this text was discovered circa 1938.

The *Tarkajvālā*, extant only in Tibetan translation, is Bhāvaviveka's auto-commentary on the *Prajñāpradīpa*. Because within this text, reference to Bhāvaviveka is made by the title *ācarya*, there is some doubt as to whether Bhāvaviveka is the author. The *Dashengzhangzhenlun* has been translated into French by Louis de la Vallée Poussin, but because the text is difficult and its contents differ from the *Prajñāpradīpa* and the *Madhyamakahṛdayakārikā*, research on it has been slow and laborious.

Candrakīrti (c. 600–50). Candrakīrti's *Prasannapāda* is not only the sole extant Sanskrit commentary on Nāgārjuna's *Mūlamadhyamakakārikā* but is also the one from which the Sanskrit *kārikās* are derived. His *Madhyamakāvatāra* discusses the essentials of the Madhyamaka in accordance with the stages of the ten perfections found in the *Daśabhūmikasūtra* (Teaching on the Ten Stages). Other works attributed to Candrakīrti, in Tibetan translations, are the *Pañcaskandhaprakaraṇa* (Five Aggregates Commentary), and commentaries on the *Śūnyatāsaptati*, the *Yuktiṣaṣṭika* and the *Catuḥśataka*.

*Svātantrika and *Prāsaṅgika. The fact that Bhāvaviveka criticized and Candrakīrti defended Buddhapālita indicates a two-way split in the Madhyamaka school, although the terms 'Prāsaṅgika' and 'Svātantrika' are not to be found in any of the extant Sanskrit texts. They are probably derived from translating into Sanskrit the Tibetan terms *thal 'gyur ba* and *rang rgyud pa* respectively. Although these terms are found in Tibetan Buddhist literature prior to Tsong kha pa, it is he who can be credited with giving them prominence, after which they began to be utilized in the Tibetan *Grub-mtha'* texts. To understand the manner in which the *Prāsaṅgikas and the *Svātantrikas develop their respective theses requires a comprehensive background in the development of logic in India. The controversy between the two was not settled by Candrakīrti; its development is closely aligned with the logical proofs for *reductio ad absurdum* arguments produced after the eighth century and with the idea of *antarvyāpti* (intrinsic determination of universal concomitance) introduced by eleventh-century Buddhist logicians. Thus, in discussing the controversy between the two, one must take into consideration the developments in logic that occured after Candrakīrti.

3 The later period (eighth to eleventh century)

The special characteristics of the later period, which began with Śāntarakṣita, were: (1) the influence of Dharmakīrti's logico-epistemological school (although there was still dependence on Nāgārjuna's thought); (2) the fact that most philosophers belonged to the Svātantrika school (an exception is Prajñākaramati); and (3) the incorporation of tenets of the Yogācāra tradition. Madhyamaka of this period can be seen as a rendezvous between Madhyamaka and Yogācāra (see DHARMAKĪRTI; BUDDHISM, YOGĀCĀRA SCHOOL OF). As well as the thinkers described below, there were others, such as Jitari, Bodhibhadra and Advayavajra (eleventh century), who wrote expositions of the doctrines of the various Buddhist schools, while others still – for example, Kambala (*c.*700), Ratnākaraśanti (*c.*eleventh century) and Atīśa (982–1055) – were actively engaged in the synthesis of Madhyamaka and Yogācāra in India and in the development of Madhyamaka Buddhism in Tibet.

Jñānagarbha (eighth century). Very little is known about Jñānagarbha, except that he was Śāntarakṣita's teacher and the author of the *Satyadvayavibhaṅga*

(Analysis of the Two Realities), the *Satyadvayavibhaṅgavṛtti* (Analysis of the Two Realities Commentary) and the *Yogabhāvanāmārga* (Path to the Practice of Yoga), all extant in Tibetan only. He translated texts on Madhyamaka and epistemology into Tibetan and consequently may have entered Tibet before Śāntarakṣita.

Śāntarakṣita (*c.*725–84). Śāntarakṣita was a scholar-monk in Nālandā who composed the *Tattvasaṃgraha*, the *Madhyamakālaṃkāra*, and his own commentary on it, the *Madhyamakālaṃkāravṛtti*, and a commentary on Jñānagarbha's *Satyadvayavibhaṅga*. With the exception of the first, which can also be found in Sanskrit, all are extant in Tibetan only. In criticizing the Indian philosophical traditions, both Buddhist and non-Buddhist, Śāntarakṣita gives a wealth of information regarding the philosophical status of the time. The reason for his critical analysis was of course to establish Madhyamaka as the highest doctrine of all. Although he considered *śūnyatā* as the highest truth, he claimed that from the worldly level one should accept the Yogācāra claim of *vijñaptimātra* (information-only), and thus he can be seen as an adherent of the Yogācāra-Madhyamaka. In so far as he respected the system of inference, he can be seen as an adherent of the *Svātantrika position. In 763, he entered Tibet and then returned to India. He returned again to Tibet in 771 and worked together with Padmasaṃbhava to establish the bSam-yas temple. He also initiated the first six monks of Tibet and devoted the rest of his life to the development of Buddhism there.

Kamalaśīla (*c.*740–97). A student of Śāntarakṣita, Kamalaśīla wrote brilliant commentaries on his teacher's works, the *Tattvasaṃgrhapañjika* (Compendium of Principles Commentary) and the *Madhyamakālaṃkārapañjika* (Central Way Ornament Commentary). Besides these, he wrote the *Madhyamakāloka* (Light of Central Way), the *Tattvāloka* (Light of Reality) and the *Sarvadharmaniḥsvabhāvasiddhi* (Establishment of the No-Self-Nature of all Dharmas). Invited by King Khri srong lde brtsan, Kamalaśīla entered Tibet in 794. It is said that he defeated the Chinese monk, Hva-shang Ma-he-yan, in a debate held in bSam-yas (Samyay) monastery. The Madhyamaka tradition is supposed to have become firmly established in Tibet as a result. For the Tibetan Buddhists he composed a trilogy known as the First, Second and Third *Bhāvanākrama* (Steps of Religious Meditative Practices), in which he denounced the 'sudden enlightenment' view held by Chinese Chan Buddhists (see BUDDHIST PHILOSOPHY, CHINESE §9).

Vimuktisena (eighth century). Vimuktisena, teacher of Haribhadra, was a well-known figure in the

Tibetan tradition, but his biography is not clear. His *Abhisamayālaṃkāravṛtti* (Ornament of Realizations Commentary) is a commentary on the *Abhisamayālaṃkāra* (Ornament of Realizations) attributed to the teacher Maitreyanātha, who expounded the foundational doctrine of Yogācāra. As not much is known about this text, it is difficult to determine the extent of Vimuktisena's dedication to Madhyamaka thought. According to the Tibetan tradition, he belongs to the same lineage as Śāntarakṣita and Kamalaśīla.

Haribhadra (c.800). Haribhadra composed a huge treatise called *Aṣṭasāhasrikāprajñāpāramitāvyākhyā Abhisamayālaṃkārāloka*, a commentary on the *Aṣṭasāhasrikāprajñāpāramitāsūtra* (Teaching of the Perfection of Wisdom in 8,000 Verses) in accordance with the divisions of the *Abhisamayālaṃkāra* attributed to Maitreyanātha. In this treatise, he criticized the Sarvāstivāda, the Sautrāntika, the Alīkākāravāda Yogācāra (who hold the theory of the unreal image of cognition) and the Satyākāravāda Yogācāra (who hold the theory of the real image of cognition) by following the method of critique in Śāntarakṣita's *Madhyamālaṃkāra*. He also explained the basic Madhyamaka teaching of no self-nature (*niḥsvabhāva*) for all entities and having classified the causal principle into four types (many causes, one effect; many causes, many effects; one cause, many effects; one cause, one effect) he disproved all of them.

4 Madhyamaka in Tibet

Buddhism was first introduced into Tibet during the reign of King Khri srong lde brtsan (741–97). At that time, Śāntarakṣita was invited to inaugurate the bSam-yas monastery and initiated the first six monks (*Sad Mi Drug*) of Tibetan origin. Later, Kamalaśīla was invited. Buddhist texts were translated and Buddhist studies advanced, but because both Śāntarakṣita and Kamalaśīla were adherents of Madhyamaka thought (*dBu-ma-pa*), Madhyamaka had a great influence on Tibetan Buddhism.

However, influence was not exerted from India alone, for Chinese Chan was also making its presence felt in Tibet. This interaction led to the famous debate between the Chinese Chan master Hva-shang (also Ho-shang) Ma-he-yan and Kamalaśīla in the latter part of the eighth century. The outcome established the superiority of Kamalaśīla and the Indian tradition, and resulted in Khri srong lde brtsan requesting Kamalaśīla to explain what the nonsubstantive view of phenomena meant in the context of the three learnings of listening, thinking and practice; as a response, Kamalaśīla proceeded to compose the First *Bhāvanākrama* (Stages of Practice) (*sGom-rim dang-*

po). When asked how to put into practice such a teaching, he composed the Second *Bhāvanākrama* (*sGom-rim bar-pa*), and finally, when asked what the result would be, he composed the Third and last *Bhāvanākrama* (*sGom-rim tha-ma*). In this text, he criticized the mistake made by Hva-shang Mahāyāna. He presented this to the king, who was overjoyed with it. Consequently, Kamalaśīla composed a commentary (*Don-'grel*), the *Madhyamakāloka* (*dBu-ma snang-ba*), in which he synthesized the correct teaching and the correct principle.

Although Śāntarakṣita and Kamalaśīla are seen as Yogācāra-Mādhyamikans, their activities are more representative of an Indian Madhyamaka tradition in Tibet rather than an indigenous Tibetan Madhyamaka. Unlike the case of the Indian subcontinent, Madhyamaka ideas in Tibet are found within the various doctrines of Tibetan Buddhist orders rather than constituting an independent Madhyamaka Buddhist school. The Tibetan *Grub-mtha'* texts discuss Madhyamaka as a single system, but what these texts explain are the tenets of Madhyamaka with respect to a general classification of doctrine rather than with respect to the Madhyamaka school in particular. Consequently, a unique feature of Tibetan Buddhism is that the indigenous schools incorporate tenets of several Indian Buddhist traditions, such as Sarvāstivāda, Sautrāntika, Yogācāra and Madhyamaka, and therefore it is difficult to discuss Madhyamaka as an indigenous school in Tibet. This means that to investigate Madhyamaka in Tibet is to examine how the Tibetan Buddhist schools, such as the dGe-lugs-pa (Gelukba), the Sa-skya-pa (Sagyaba), the rNying-ma-pa (Nyingmaba), and the bKa'-brgyud-pa (Gagyuba), incorporate the foundational Indian Madhyamaka tenets of *śūnyatā*, *saṃvṛtisatya*, *paramārthasatya*, and so on, within their own systems.

Among the various schools, it is with respect to the dGe-lugs-pa school that we find the most comprehensive discussion of the Madhyamaka system. The dGe-lugs-pa was founded by TSONG KHA PA BLO BZANG GRAGS PA (Dzongkaba Losang dragba, 1357–1419), who at the age of nineteen heard a lecture on the *Prajñāpāramitā* from Kun-dga'-dpal, who belonged to the Sa-skya-pa school, and also heard lectures on the *Madhyamakāvatāra* and *Abhidharmakośa* (Treasury of Higher Dharma) from Red mda' ba (Rendawa, 1349–1412). He wrote the *gSer-phreng*, a commentary on the *Abhisamayālaṃkāra*, when he was thirty-one years old, but we cannot see Tsong kha pa's own thinking appearing yet. At thirty-three he began to study under dBu-ma-pa (Umaba), to whom he addressed questions regarding the *Svatāntrika (Rang-rgyud-pa, ranggyüba) and the *Prāsaṅgika (Thal-'gyur-ba, talgyurwa). When he was forty-six he wrote the *Lam-rim-chen-mo* (The Great Stages of the Path), a text which was modelled on Atīśa's *Bodhipathapradīpa* and finally established Tsong kha pa's original thinking regarding Madhyamaka. He severely criticized the normative interpretation in Tibet that *śūnyatā* referred to the view of neither existence nor nonexistence held by the mTha'-bral dbu-ma'i lugs ('school of Madhyamaka free of extremes'). Instead, he stressed that *śūnyatā* was absolutely beyond any claim that, for example, the absolute is freed from the two extreme views and also from conventional language, which resembles the view held by Hva-shang Mahāyāna that Buddhahood is attained when one is freed from all discriminations.

Tsong kha pa's understanding of Madhyamaka is expressed again and again in his works, for example, the *Legs-bshad snying-po* (Essence of Good Explanations), the *Rigs-pa'i rgya-mtsho* (Ocean of Reasoning) and the *gDongs-pa rab-gsal* (Exposition of Intention). He was severely criticized by Śā-kya mchog-ldan (1428–1507) in his *dBu ma rnam nges* (Determination of the Middle) and by such mTha'-bral dbu-ma'i lugs scholars as Śā-skya sTag-tshang-pa (1405–?) in his *Grub-mtha' kun-shes* (All-knowing Tenets) and Go ram pa (Goramba, 1429–89) in his *lTa ba'i shan 'byed*. In response to these criticisms, Se-ra rJe-tsun-pa Chos-kyi rgyal-mtshan (1469–1546) and his disciple bDe legs nyi ma attacked Śā-skya sTag-tshang-pa and Go ram pa in their *lTa-ngan-mun-sel* (Light Within Views) and the great scholar Jam dbyangs bzhad pa (Jamyang shayba, 1648–1722) attacked Śā-kya mchog-ldan in his *Grub-mtha' chen-mo* (Great Tenets).

See also: BUDDHIST CONCEPT OF EMPTINESS; BUDDHIST PHILOSOPHY, INDIAN; BUDDHIST PHILOSOPHY, JAPANESE; SENG ZHAO; TIBETAN PHILOSOPHY

References and further reading

* Āryadeva (*c.* AD 170–270) *Catuḥśataka* (Text of Four Hundred Verses), trans. K. Lang, *Āryadeva's Catuḥśataka, On the Bodhisattva's Cultivation of Merit and Knowledge*, Indiske Studier 7, Copenhagen: Akademisk Forlag, 1986. (A useful English translation with which to gain insight into Āryadeva's thoughts.)

Harada, S. (1982) 'Chibetto Bukkyō no Chūkan Shisō' (Madhyamaka Thought of Tibetan Buddhism), in A. Hirakawa, Y. Kajiyama and J. Takazaki (eds) *Kōza Daijō Bukkyō* (Lectures on Mahāyāna Buddhism), Tokyo: Shunjusha, vol. 7: 284–314. (An important source for the present entry.)

Kajiyama, Y. (1982) 'Chūkan Shisō no Rekishi to Bunken' (The History and Literature of Madhyamaka Thought), in A. Hirakawa, Y. Kajiyama and J. Takazaki (eds) *Kōza Daijō Bukkyō*, Tokyo: Shunjusha, vol. 7: 1–83. (An important source for the present entry.)

—— (1989) *Studies in Buddhist Philosophy*, ed. K. Mimaki, Kyoto: Rinsen Book Co. (An important source for the present entry; see especially the article on Madhyamaka, pages 21–7.)

Kalupahana, D.J. (trans.) (1986) *Nāgārjuna: The Philosophy of the Middle Way*, Albany, NY: State University of New York Press. (An English translation of the *Mūlamadhyamakakārikā*.)

Lindtner, C. (trans.) (1982) *Nagarjuniana: Studies in the Writing and Philosophy of Nāgārjuna*, Copenhagen: Akademisk Forlag. (A translation, with explanatory text, of Nāgārjuna's major works. A must for Nāgārjunian study.)

Matsumoto, S. (1989) 'Tsonkapa to gelukupa' (Tsong kha pa and dGe-lugs-pa) in G. Nagao *et al.* (eds) *Chibeto Bukkyō* (Tibetan Buddhism), Tokyo: Iwanami Shoten, 224–62. (An important source for the present entry.)

Mimaki, K. (ed.) (1977) 'Le *Grub mtha' rnam bźag rin chen phreṅ ba* de dKon mchog 'jigs med dbaṅ po (1718–91): Texte tibétain édité, avec une introduction', in *Zinbun* 14: 55–112, Memoirs of the Research Institute for Humanistic Studies, Kyoto University. (Useful reference for Tibetan Buddhist Schools.)

—— (ed. and trans.) (1982) *Blo gsal grub mtha'. Chapitres IX (Vaibhāṣika) et XI (Yogācāra) édités et Chapitre XII (Mādhyamika) édité et traduit*, Kyoto: Zinbun Kagaku Kenkyūsho. (An informative exposition on Madhyamaka in India and Tibet.)

* Nāgārjuna (*c.* AD 150–200) *Mūlamadhyamakakārikā* (Fundamental Central Way Verses), trans. K.K. Inaba, *Nāgārjuna, A Translation of his Mūlamadhyamakakārikā with an Introductory Essay*, Tokyo: The Hokuseido Press, 1970. (English translation of the verses with Sanskrit text.)

* —— (*c.* AD 150–200) *Ratnāvalī* (Garland of Jewels), ed. M. Hahn, Bonn: Indica et Tibetica Verlag, 1982. (Sanskrit, Tibetan and Chinese text.)

Ramanan, K.V. (trans.) (1971) *Nāgārjuna's Philosophy as Presented in the Mahā-Prajñāpāramitā-Śāstra*, Varanasi: Bharatiya Vidya Prakashan. (An English translation with a commentary by the author on a Chinese Madhyamaka text.)

Ruegg, D.S. (1981) *The Literature of the Madhyamaka School of Philosophy in India*, Wiesbaden: Otto Harrasowitz. (A must for further research in the field.)

Ruegg, D.S. and Schmithausen, L. (eds) (1990)

Earliest Buddhism and Madhyamaka, Leiden: Brill. (Five outstanding articles on Madhyamaka by leading writers in the field.)

Sprung, M. (trans.) (1979) *Lucid Exposition of the Middle Way*, Boulder, CO: Prajñā Press. (A useful translation of the *Mūlamadhyamakakārikā*.)

Streng, F.J. (trans.) (1967) *Emptiness: A Study in Religious Meaning*, New York: Abington Press. (A readable English translation of the *Mūlamadhyamakakārikā* interpreted from a philosophical view.)

LESLIE S. KAWAMURA

BUDDHISM, YOGĀCĀRA SCHOOL OF

Yogācāra is one of the two schools of Indian Mahāyāna Buddhism. Its founding is ascribed to two brothers, Asaṅga and Vasubandhu, but its basic tenets and doctrines were already in circulation for at least a century before the brothers lived. In order to overcome the ignorance that prevented one from attaining liberation from the karmic rounds of birth and death, Yogācāra focused on the processes involved in cognition. Their sustained attention to issues such as cognition, consciousness, perception and epistemology, coupled with claims such as 'external objects do not exist' has led some to misinterpret Yogācāra as a form of metaphysical idealism. They did not focus on consciousness to assert it as ultimately real (Yogācāra claims consciousness is only conventionally real), but rather because it is the cause of the karmic problem they are seeking to eliminate.

Yogācāra introduced several important new doctrines to Buddhism, including vijñaptimātra, three self-natures, three turnings of the dharma-wheel and a system of eight consciousnesses. Their close scrutiny of cognition spawned two important developments: an elaborate psychological therapeutic system mapping out the problems in cognition with antidotes to correct them and an earnest epistemological endeavour that led to some of the most sophisticated work on perception and logic ever engaged in by Buddhists or Indians.

Although the founding of Yogācāra is traditionally ascribed to two half-brothers, Asaṅga and Vasubandhu (fourth–fifth century BC), most of its fundamental doctrines had already appeared in a number of scriptures a century or more earlier, most notably the Saṃdhinirmocanasūtra *(Elucidating the Hidden Connections) (third–fourth century BC). Among the key Yogācāra concepts introduced in the* Saṃdhinirmocanasūtra *are the notions of 'only-cognition' (*vijñaptimātra*), three self-natures (*trisvabhāva*), warehouse consciousness (*ālayavijñāna*), overturning the basis (*āśrayaparāvtti*) and the theory of eight consciousnesses.*

The Saṃdhinirmocanasūtra *proclaimed its teachings to be the third turning of the wheel of* dharma. *Buddha lived around sixth–fifth century BC, but* Mahāyāna Sūtra *did not begin to appear probably until five hundred years later. New Mahāyāna Sūtra continued to be composed for many centuries. Indian Mahāyānists treated these Sūtras as documents which recorded actual discourses of the Buddha. By the third or fourth century a wide and sometimes incommensurate range of Buddhist doctrines had emerged, but whichever doctrines appeared in Sūtras could be ascribed to the authority of Buddha himself. According to the earliest Pāli Sutta, when Buddha became enlightened he turned the wheel of dharma, that is, began to teach the path to enlightenment. While Buddhists had always maintained that Buddha had geared specific teachings to the specific capacities of specific audiences, the Saṃdhinirmocanasūtra established the idea that Buddha had taught significantly different doctrines to different audiences according to their levels of understanding; and that these different doctrines led from provisional antidotes (pratipakṣa) for certain wrong views up to a comprehensive teaching that finally made explicit what was only implicit in the earlier teachings. In its view, the first two turnings of the wheel – the teachings of the Four Noble Truths in Nikāya and Abhidharma Buddhism and the teachings of the Madhyamaka school, respectively – had expressed the dharma through incomplete formulations that required further elucidation (neyārtha) to be properly understood and thus effective. The first turning, by emphasizing entities (such as dharmas and aggregates) while 'hiding' emptiness, might lead one to hold a substantialistic view; the second turning, by emphasizing negation while 'hiding' the positive qualities of the dharma, might be misconstrued as nihilism. The third turning was a middle way between these extremes that finally made everything explicit and definitive (nīthartha). In order to leave nothing hidden, the Yogācārins embarked on a massive, systematic synthesis of all the Buddhist teachings that had preceded them, scrutinizing and evaluating them down to the most trivial details in an attempt to formulate the definitive Buddhist teaching. Stated another way, to be effective all of Buddhism required a Yogācārin reinterpretation. Innovations in abhidharma analysis, logic, cosmology, meditation methods, psychology, philosophy and ethics are among their most important contributions. Asaṅga's magnum opus, the* Yogācārabhūmiśāstra *(Treatise on the Stages of Yoga Practice), is a comprehensive encyclopedia of Buddhist terms and models, mapped out according to his Yogācārin view of how one progresses along the stages of the path to enlightenment.*

1 **Historical survey**
2 **Yogācāra contrasted with metaphysical idealism**
3 **The role of epistemology**
4 **Primacy of epistemology**
5 **Karma**
6 **The storage and ripening of karma**
7 **Matter and cognitive appropriation**
8 **Eight types of consciousnesses**
9 **Three self-natures**
10 **Five stages**

1 Historical survey

Asaṅga and Vasubandhu became the first identifiable Yogācārins, each having initially been devoted to other schools of Buddhism. Both were prolific authors, although Asaṅga attributed a portion of his writings to Maitreya, the future Buddha living in Tuṣita heaven. Some modern scholars, such as H. Ui (1929) have argued that this Maitreya was an actual human teacher, not the future Buddha, but the tradition is fairly clear. After Asaṅga has spent twelve years of fruitless meditation alone in a cave, in a moment of utter despair Maitreya appears to him and transports him to Tuṣita heaven where he instructs him in previously unknown Yogācārin works. These works Asaṅga then introduces to his fellow Buddhists. Precisely which texts these are is less clear since the Chinese and Tibetan traditions assign different works to Maitreya.

According to tradition, Vasubandhu first studied Vaibhāṣika Buddhist teachings, writing an encyclopedic summary of those teachings, the *Abhidharmakośa* (Treasury of Abhidharma), that has become a standard work throughout the Buddhist world. As he grew critical of Vaibhāṣika teachings, he wrote a commentary on that work refuting many of its tenets. Intellectually restless for a while, Vasubandhu composed a variety of works that chart his journey to Yogācāra, the best known of these being the *Karmasiddhiprakaraṇa* (Investigation Establishing Karma) and *Pañcaskandhakaprakaraṇa* (Investigation into the Five Aggregates). These works show a deep familiarity with the Abhidharmic categories discussed in the *Abhidharmakośa* and attempts to rethink them; the philosophical and scholastic disputes of the day are also explored and the new positions Vasubandhu formulates in these texts bring him closer to Yogācārin conclusions. On the basis of some conflicting accounts in old biographies of Vasubandhu, a few modern scholars have argued that these texts along

with the *Abhidharmakośa* were the work of another author. However, as the progression and development of his thought is so strikingly evident in these works and the similarity of vocabulary and style of argument so apparent across the texts, the theory of the existence of two Vasubandhus has little merit.

The writings of Asaṅga (and/or Maitreya) and Vasubandhu ranged from vast encyclopedic compendia of Buddhist doctrine (for example, *Yogācārabhūmiśāstra, Mahāyānasaṃgraha, Abhidharmasamuccaya*), to terse versified encapsulations of Yogācāra praxis (for example, *Triṃśikā, Trisvabhāvanirdeśa*), to focused systematic treatises on Yogācāra themes (for example, *Viṃśatika, Madhyāntavibhāga*), to commentaries on well-known Mahāyānic scriptures and treatises, such as the *Saddharmapuṇḍarīka* (Lotus) and the *Vajracchedika* (Diamond-cutter) *Sūtras*.

As the *Saṃdhinirmocanasūtra* offers highly sophisticated doctrines, it is reasonable to assume that these ideas had been under development for some time, possibly centuries, before this scripture emerged. Since Asaṅga and Vasubandhu lived a century or more after the *Saṃdhinirmocana* appeared, it is also reasonable to assume that these ideas had been further refined by others in the interim. Thus the traditional claim that the two brothers are the founders of Yogācāra at best could be considered to be a half-truth. According to tradition Asaṅga converted Vasubandhu to Yogācāra after having been taught by Maitreya; he is not known to have had any other notable disciples. Tradition does assign two major disciples to Vasubandhu: DIGNĀGA, the great logician and epistemologist, and Sthiramati, an important early Yogācāra commentator. It is unclear whether either ever actually met Vasubandhu (current scholarship deems it unlikely). They may have been disciples of his thought, acquired exclusively from his writings or through some forgotten intermediary teachers. These two disciples exemplify the two major directions into which Vasubandhu's teachings split.

After Vasubandhu Yogācāra developed into two distinct directions or branches: a logico-epistemic tradition exemplified by such thinkers as Dignāga, DHARMAKĪRTI, Śāntarakṣita and Ratnakīrti; an Abhidharmic psychology, exemplified by such thinkers as Sthiramati, Dharmapāla, Xuanzang (Hsüan-tsang (*c*.659 BC)) and (again) Ratnakīrti (see BUDDHISM, ĀBHIDHARMIKA SCHOOLS OF). While the first branch focused on questions of epistemology and logic, the other wing refined and elaborated the Abhidharma analysis developed by Asaṅga and Vasubandhu. These branches were not entirely separate, and many Buddhists wrote works that contributed to both. Dignāga, for instance, besides works on epistemology and logic also wrote a commentary on Vasubandhu's *Abhidharmakośa*. What united both branches was a deep concern with the process of cognition, that is, analyses of how we perceive and think. The former wing approached that epistemologically, while the latter wing approached it psychologically and therapeutically. Both identified the root of all human problems as cognitive errors that needed correction.

Several Yogācāra notions basic to the Abhidharma wing came under severe attack by other Buddhists, especially the notion of *ālayavijñāna*, which was denounced as something akin to the Hindu notions of *ātman* (permanent, invariant self) and *prakṛti* (primordial substrative nature from which all mental, emotional and physical things evolve) (see SĀṄKHYA). Eventually the critiques became so entrenched that the Abhidharma wing atrophied. By the end of the eighth century it was eclipsed by the logico-epistemic tradition and by a hybrid school that combined basic Yogācāra doctrines with Tathāgatagarbha thought. The logico-epistemological wing sidestepped much of the critique by using the term *cittasantāna*, or mindstream, instead of *ālayavijñāna*, for what amounted to roughly the same idea. It was easier to deny that a stream represented a reified self. The Tathāgatagarbha hybrid school was no stranger to the charge of smuggling notions of selfhood into its doctrines, as for example, it explicitly defined *tathāgatagarbha* as 'permanent, pleasant, *self* and pure'. Many Tathāgatagarbha texts argue for the acceptance of selfhood (*ātman*) as a sign of higher accomplishment. The hybrid school attempted to conflate *tathāgatagarbha* with the *ālayavijñāna*. Key works of the hybrid school include the *Laṅkāvatārasūtra*, *Ratnagotravibhāga* (Uttaratantra) and in China the *Awakening of Faith*.

In China during the sixth and seventh centuries, Buddhism was dominated by several competing forms of Yogācāra (see BUDDHIST PHILOSOPHY, CHINESE). A major schism between orthodox versions of Yogācāra and Tathāgatagarbha hybrid versions was finally settled in the eighth century in favour of a hybrid version, which became definitive for all subsequent forms of East Asian Buddhism. Yogācāra ideas were also studied and classified in Tibet. The Nyingma and Dzog Chen schools settled on a hybrid version similar to the Chinese Tathāgatagarbha hybrid; the Gelugpas subdivided Yogācāra into a number of different types and considered them preparatory teachings for studying Prāsaṅgika Madhyamaka, which Gelugpas ranked as the highest Buddhist teaching. The Tibetans, however, tended to view the logico-epistemological tradition as distinct from Yogācāra proper, frequently labelling them Sautrāntika instead.

2 Yogācāra contrasted with metaphysical idealism

The school was called Yogācāra (Yoga practice) because it provided a comprehensive, therapeutic framework for engaging in the practices that lead to the goal of the *bodhisattva* path, namely enlightened cognition. Meditation served as the laboratory in which one could study how the mind operated. Yogācāra focused on the question of consciousness from a variety of approaches, including meditation, psychological analysis, epistemology (how we know what we know, how perception operates, what validates knowledge), scholastic categorization and karmic analysis.

Yogācāra doctrine is summarized in the term *vijñaptimātra*, 'nothing-but-cognition' (often rendered as 'consciousness-only' or 'mind-only'), which has sometimes been interpreted as indicating a type of metaphysical idealism, that is, the claim that the mind alone is real and everything else is created by the mind. However, the Yogācārin writings themselves argue something very different. Consciousness (*vijñāna*) is not the ultimate reality or solution, but rather the root problem. This problem emerges in ordinary mental operations and it can only be solved by bringing those operations to an end.

Yogācāra tends to be misinterpreted as a form of metaphysical idealism primarily because its teachings are taken for ontological propositions rather than as epistemological warnings about karmic problems. The Yogācāra focus on cognition and consciousness grew out of its analysis of karma and not for the sake of metaphysical speculation. Two things should be clarified in order to explain why Yogācāra is not metaphysical idealism: the meaning of the term 'idealism' and the important difference between the way Indian and Western philosophers regard philosophy.

The term 'idealism' came into vogue roughly during the time of I. KANT (although it was used earlier by others, such as G.W. LEIBNIZ) for one of two trends that had emerged in reaction to Cartesian philosophy. R. DESCARTES had argued that there were two basic yet separate substances in the universe: extension (the material world of things in space) and thought (the world of mind and ideas) (see GERMAN IDEALISM). Subsequently, opposing camps took one or the other substance as their metaphysical foundation, treating it as the primary substance, while reducing the remaining substance to a derivative status. Materialists argued that only matter was ultimately real so that thought and consciousness derived from physical entities (such as chemistry, brain states). Idealists countered that the mind and its ideas were ultimately real and that the physical world derived from the mind (for example, the mind of God, G. Berkeley's *esse est percipi* (to be is to be perceived), or from ideal prototypes) (see BERKELEY, G.). Materialists gravitated toward mechanical, physical explanations for why and how things existed, while Idealists tended to look for purposes – moral as well as rational – to explain existence. Idealism meant 'idea-ism', frequently in the sense of Plato's notion of 'ideas' (*eidos*), denoting ideal types that transcended the physical, sensory world and provided the form (*eidos*) that gave matter meaning and purpose. As materialism buttressed by advances in materialistic science gained wider acceptance, those inclined towards spiritual and theological aims turned increasingly toward idealism as a countermeasure. Before long there were many types of materialism and idealism.

Idealism in its broadest sense came to encompass everything that was not materialism, which included so many different types of positions that the term lost any hope of univocality. Most forms of theistic and theological thought were, by this definition, types of idealism, even if they accepted matter as real, since they also asserted something as more real than matter, either as the creator of matter (in monotheism) or as the reality behind matter (in pantheism) (see PANTHE-ISM). Extreme empiricists who only accepted their own experience and sensations as real were also idealists. Thus, 'idealism' united monotheists, panthe-ists and atheists. At one extreme were various forms of metaphysical idealism which posited the mind as the only ultimate reality. The physical world was either an unreal illusion, or not as real as the mind that created it. To avoid solipsism (which is a subjectivized version of metaphysical idealism), meta-physical idealists posited an overarching mind that envisages and creates the universe.

A more limited type of idealism is epistemological, which argues that since knowledge of the world only exists in the mental realm we cannot know actual physical objects as they truly are, but only as they appear in our mental representations of them. Epistemological idealists could be ontological materi-alists, accepting that matter exists substantially; they could even accept that mental states derived at least in part from material processes. What they denied was that matter could be known in itself directly without the mediation of mental representations. Although unknowable in itself, the existence of matter and its properties could be known through inference based on certain consistencies in the way material things are represented in perception.

Transcendental idealism contends that not only matter, but also the self remains transcendental in an act of cognition. Kant and HUSSERL, who were both transcendental idealists, defined 'transcendental' as that which constitutes experience but is not itself given in experience. A mundane example would be the eye, which is the condition for seeing even though the eye does not see itself. By applying vision and drawing inferences from it, one can come to know the role eyes play in seeing, although one never sees one's own eyes. Similarly, things in themselves and the transcendental self could be known if the proper methods were applied for uncovering the conditions that constitute experience, although such conditions do not them-selves appear in experience. Even when epistemologi-cal issues are at the forefront, it is ontological concerns, such as the status of self and objects, that are really at stake. Western philosophy rarely escapes this ontological slant. Those who accepted that both the self and its objects were unknowable except through reason and that such reason was their cause and purpose for existing – thus epistemologically and ontologically grounding everything in the mind and its ideas – were called absolute Idealists, such as F.W.J. von SCHELLING, G.W.F. HEGEL and F.H. BRADLEY, since only such ideas are absolute while all else is relative to them (see ABSOLUTE, THE).

With the exception of some epistemological ideal-ists, what unites all the positions described thus far, including the materialists, is that they are ontological. They are concerned with the ontological status of the objects of sense and thought, as well as the ontological nature of the self who knows. Mainstream Western philosophy since PLATO and ARISTOTLE has treated ontology and metaphysics as the ultimate philosophic pursuit, with epistemology's role being little more than to provide access and justification for one's ontological pursuits and commitments. Since many of what are decried as philosophy's excesses – such as scepticism, solipsism and sophistry – have been accused of deriving from overactive epistemolo-gical questioning, epistemology has often been held to be suspect and in some theological formulations, considered entirely dispensable in favour of faith. Ontology is primary and epistemology is either secondary or expendable.

3 The role of epistemology

In Indian philosophy one finds the reverse of the positions described. Epistemology (*pramāṇavāda*) is primary both in the sense that it must be engaged in prior to attempting any other philosophical endea-vour and that the limits of one's metaphysical claims are always inviolably set by the parameters established by one's epistemology. Before one can make claims, one must establish the basis on which such claims can be proven and justified. The Indians went so far as to concede that if one wishes to debate with an opponent, one must first find a common epistemological ground upon which to argue. Failing that, no meaningful debate can take place.

Since one's ontology (*prameya*) depends on what one's epistemology makes allowable, many Indian schools tried to include things in their list of valid means of knowledge (*pramāṇa*) that would facilitate their claims. Hindus, for instance, considered their Scriptures to be valid means of knowledge, but other Indians, such as Buddhists and Jains, rejected the authority of the Hindu Scriptures. Therefore, if a Hindu debated with a Buddhist or Jain, he or she could not appeal to the authority of Hindu Scriptures, but had to find common epistemological ground. In the case of Buddhism that would be perception and inference; in the case of Jainism, it would only be inference. All schools except Jains accepted perception as a valid means of knowledge, meaning that sensory knowledge is valid (if qualified as nonerroneous or nonhallucinatory). What is not presently observed but is in principle observable can be known by inference. Without actually seeing the fire, one knows it must exist on a hill when one sees smoke in that location because both fire and smoke are in principle observable entities and an observed necessary relation (*vyāpti*) exists between smoke and fire (think of the expression, there is no smoke without fire). If one were close to the fire on the hill, the fire could be observed. One cannot make valid inferences about things impossible to perceive, such as unicorns, since no necessary observable relation is obtainable so one cannot infer that a unicorn is on the hill. Perceptibility therefore is an indispensable component of both perception and inference, and thus for Buddhists, of all valid knowledge. In order to be considered 'real' (*dravya*) by the standards of Buddhist logic, a thing must produce an observable effect. Buddhists argued among themselves whether something was real only while it was producing this observable effect (the Sautrāntika position), or whether something could be considered real if it produced an observable effect at some moment during its existence (the Sarvāstivāda position). However, it was generally agreed that a thing must have observable causal efficacy (*kāraṇa*) in order to be considered real. This helps explain the centrality of perception and consciousness for Yogācāra theory.

The logico-epistemological branch of Yogācāra drew a sharp distinction between perception and inference. Perception involves sensory cognitions of unique, momentary, discrete particulars. Inference involves linguistic, conceptual universals, since words are meaningful and communicative only to the extent they designate and participate in universal classes commonly shared and understood by users of the language. Inferences are true or false depending on how accurately they approximate sensory particulars, but even when linguistically true, they are only still true relative (*saṃvṛti*) to the sensations they approximate. Conversely, sensation (and only sensation) is beyond language. Sensory cognition devoid of linguistic overlay or theoretical assertions (*samāropa*) is correct cognition and precisely, not approximately, true (*paramārtha*). While this seems to involve metaphysical claims about categories such as particulars and universals, sensation and language, in fact it is a request that we should cognize things as they are without imposing any metaphysical assertions or conceptual framework whatsoever. The cognitive and epistemic, not the metaphysical, is at stake. What is the case is beyond description, not because it is something ineffable residing outside or behind human experience, but because it is the very sensory stuff of human experience whose momentary unique actuality cannot be reduced to universalistic, eternalistic language or concepts. To interpret this position itself as a metaphysics of particularity is to miss its point.

4 Primacy of epistemology

Epistemological concerns pervade Indian philosophy. This is especially true of Buddhist philosophy. Many Buddhist texts assert that higher understanding has nothing to do with ontology, that focusing on the existence or nonexistence of something (*astināsti, bhāvābhāva*) is a misleading category error. They typically remove important items – such as emptiness and *nirvāṇa* – from ontological consideration by explicitly declaring that these have nothing to do with existence or nonexistence, or being and nonbeing. They further warn that this is not a licence to imagine a higher sense of existence or being into which such items are then subsumed or sublated. The Buddhist goal is not the construction of a more perfect ontology. Instead its primary target is always the removal of ignorance. Hence, while Buddhists frequently suspend ontological and metaphysical speculation (*tarka*), denouncing it as useless or dangerous, correct cognition (*samyagjñāna*) is invariably lauded. Even Madhyamakas, who question the feasibility of much of Buddhist epistemology, insist that we should understand where the errors lie and correct the way we cognize accordingly. Stated bluntly, Buddhism is concerned with seeing, not being, that is, epistemology rather than ontology.

Tellingly, no Indian Yogācāra text ever claims that the world is created by the mind. What they do claim is that we mistake our projected interpretations of the world for the world itself, that is, we take our own mental constructions to be the world. Their vocabulary for this is as rich as their analysis: *kalpanā* (projective conceptual construction), *parikalpa* and *parikalpita* (ubiquitous imaginary constructions), *abhūtaparikalpa* (imagining something in a locus in which it does not exist), *prapañca* (proliferation of conceptual constructions), to mention a few. Correct cognition is defined as the removal of those obstacles which prevent us from seeing dependent causal conditions in the manner they actually become (*yathābhūtam*). For Yogācāra these causal conditions are cognitive, not metaphysical; they are the mental and perceptual conditions by which sensations and thoughts occur, not the metaphysical machinations of a Creator or an imperceptible domain. What is known through correct cognition is euphemistically called *tathatā*, or 'suchness', which the texts are quick to point out is not an actual thing, but only a word (*prajñaptimātra*).

What is crucial in the foregoing for understanding Yogācāra is that its attention to perceptual and cognitive issues is in line with basic Buddhist thinking and that this attention is epistemological rather than metaphysical. When Yogācārins discuss 'objects' they are talking about cognitive objects, not metaphysical entities. Rather than offer one more ontology, they attempt to uncover and eliminate the predilections and proclivities (*āśrava*, *anuśaya*) that compel people to generate and cling to such theoretical constructions. According to Yogācāra, all ontologies are epistemological constructions. Therefore, to understand how cognition operates is to understand how and why people construct the ontologies to which they cling. Ontological attachment is a symptom of cognitive projection (*pratibimba*, *parikalpita*). Careful examination of Yogācāra texts reveals that they make no ontological claims, except to question the validity of making those ontological claims. Such ontological silence derives from the fact that, were they to offer a metaphysical description, that description would be appropriated by its interpreters whose proclivities would project onto it what they wish reality to be, thereby reducing the description to their own presupposed theory of reality. Such projective reductionism is the problem and is the definition of *vijñaptimātra*: to mistake one's projections for that onto which one is projecting. Vasubandhu's *Triṃśikā* (Thirty Verses) states that if one clings to one's projection of the idea of *vijñaptimātra*, then one fails to dwell truly in the understanding of *vijñaptimātra* (verse 27 [1984]). Enlightened cognition free of all cognitive errors is defined as *nirvikalpajñāna*, or 'cognition without imaginative construction', that is, without conceptual overlay. Ironically, Yogācāra's interpreters and opponents could not resist reductively projecting metaphysical theories onto what Yogācārins did say, at once proving Yogācāra was right and making actual Yogācāra teachings that much harder to understand. Interpreting their epistemological analyses as metaphysical pronouncements fundamentally misconstrues their project.

The arguments Yogācāra deploys frequently resemble those made by epistemological idealists. Recognizing those affinities, early twentieth-century Western scholars compared Yogācāra to Kant. More recently scholars have begun to think that Husserl's phenomenology comes even closer. Indeed, there are intriguing similarities, for instance, between Husserl's description of noesis (consciousness projecting its cognitive field) and noema (the constructed cognitive object) on the one hand, and Yogācāra's analysis of the (cognitive) grasper and the grasped (*grāhaka* and *grāhya*) on the other hand. However, there are also important differences between the ideas of those Western philosophers and Yogācāra, most markedly that Kant and Husserl play down notions of causality, while Yogācāra developed complex systematic causal theories it deemed to be of the greatest importance; there is no counterpart to either karma or enlightenment in the Western theories, while these are the very *raison d'être* for all of Yogācāra theory and practice; finally, Western philosophies are produced to afford the best possible access to an ontological realm (at least sufficient to acknowledge its existence), while Yogācāra is critical of that motive in all its manifestations. To the extent that epistemological idealists can also be critical realists, Yogācāra may be deemed a type of epistemological idealism with the proviso that the purpose of its arguments was not to engender an improved ontological theory or commitment, but rather an insistence that we shift our attention to the epistemological and psychological conditions that compel us to construct and attach to ontological theories (see EPISTEMOLOGY, INDIAN SCHOOLS OF; ONTOLOGY IN INDIAN PHILOSOPHY).

5 Karma

The key to Yogācāra theory lies in the Buddhist notions of karma which they inherited and rigorously reinterpreted (see KARMA AND REBIRTH, INDIAN CONCEPTIONS OF). As earlier Buddhist texts explained, karma is responsible for suffering and ignorance and consists of any intentional activity of body, language, or mind. Since the crucial factor is intent and intent is a cognitive condition, whatever is noncognitive must necessarily lack intent and be nonkarmic. Hence, by definition, whatever is noncognitive can have no karmic influence or consequences. Since Buddhism aims at overcoming ignorance and suffering through the elimination of karmic conditioning, Buddhism, they reasoned, is only concerned with the analysis and correction of whatever falls within the domain of cognitive conditions. Hence questions about the ultimate reality of that which is noncognitive are irrelevant for solving the problem of karma. Further, Yogācārins emphasize that categories such as materiality (*rūpa*) are cognitive. Materiality is an abstract classification of the colours, textures and sounds experienced in acts of perception and it is only to the extent that they are experienced, perceived and ideologically grasped, thereby becoming objects of attachment, that they have karmic significance. Intentional acts also have moral motives and consequences. Since effects are shaped by their causes, an act with a wholesome intent would tend to yield wholesome fruits, while unwholesome intentions produce unwholesome effects.

In contrast to the cognitive karmic dimension, Buddhism considered material elements (*rūpa*) to be karmically neutral. The problem with material things is not their materiality, but the psychology of appropriation (*upādāna*) – desiring, grasping, clinging, attachment – that infests our ideas and perceptions of such things. It is not the materiality of gold that leads to problems, but rather our *ideas* about the value of gold and the attitudes and actions we engage in as a result of those ideas. Those ideas were acquired through previous experiences. By repeated exposure to certain ideas and cognitive conditions, one is conditioned to respond habitually in a similar manner to similar circumstances. Eventually these habits are embodied, becoming reflexive and presuppositional. For Buddhists this process of embodied conditioning (*saṃskāra*) is not confined to a single lifetime, but accrues over many. *Saṃsāra* (the continuous cycle of birth and death) is the karmic enactment of this repetition, the reoccurrence of cognitive embodied habits in new life situations and life forms.

For all Buddhists this follows a simple sensory calculus by which we are conditioned: pleasurable feelings we wish to retain, or repeat; painful feelings we wish to cut off, or avoid; pleasure and pain, reward and punishment, approval and disapproval. Our karmic habits (*vāsanā*) are constructed this way. Since nothing is permanent, pleasurable feelings cannot be maintained or repeated permanently; painful things (such as sickness and death) cannot be avoided permanently. However, we do imagine all sort of permanent things, from God to souls to essences, in an effort to avoid facing the fact that none of us has a permanent self. We believe that if we can prove something is permanent then we too have a chance for permanence. The greater the dissonance between our actual impermanent experience and our expectations

for permanent desired ends, the more we suffer and the greater tendency (*anuśaya*) towards projecting our desires onto the world. The anxiety about our lack of self and all the cognitive and karmic mischief it generates is called several things by Yogācāra, including *jñeyāvaraṇa* (obstruction of the knowable, that is, our self-obsessions which prevent us from seeing things as they are) and *abhūtaparikalpa* (imagining something, such as permanence or a self, to exist in a locus in which it is absent).

6 The storage and ripening of karma

Previous Buddhists, especially in the Abhidharma schools, had developed a sophisticated metaphoric vocabulary to describe and analyse the causes and conditions of karma in terms of seeds (*bīja*). Just as a plant develops from its roots unseen underground, so do previous karmic experiences fester unseen in the mind; just as a plant sprouts from the ground when nourished by proper conditions, so karmic habits under the right causes and conditions reassert themselves as new experiences; just as plants reach fruition by producing new seeds that re-enter the ground to take root and begin regrowing a similar plant of the same kind, so karmic actions produce wholesome or unwholesome fruit that become latent seeds for a later, similar type of action or cognition. Just as plants reproduce only their own kind, so do wholesome or unwholesome karmic acts produce effects after their own kind. This cycle served as a metaphor for the process of cognitive conditioning, as well as the recurrent cycle of birth and death (*saṃsāra*). Since Yogācāra accepts the Buddhist doctrine of momentariness, seeds are said to perdure for only a moment during which time they become the cause of a similar seed that succeeds them. Momentary seeds are causally linked in sequential chains, each momentary seed a link in a chain of karmic causes and effects (see MOMENTARINESS, BUDDHIST DOCTRINE OF).

Seeds are basically divided into two types: wholesome and unwholesome. Unwholesome seeds are the acquired cognitive habits preventing one from reaching enlightenment. Wholesome, or pure, unpolluted seeds give rise to more pure seeds, which bring one closer to enlightenment. In general Yogācāra differentiates inner seeds (personal conditioning) from external seeds (being conditioned by others). One's own seeds can be modified or affected by exposure to external conditions (external seeds), which can be beneficial or detrimental. Exposure to polluting conditions intensifies one's unwholesome seeds, while contact with pure conditions, such as hearing the correct teaching (*Saddharma*), can stimulate one's wholesome seeds to increase, thereby diminishing and ultimately eradicating one's unwholesome seeds.

Another metaphor for karmic conditioning that accompanies the seed metaphor is 'perfuming' (*vāsanā*). A cloth exposed to the smell of perfume acquires its scent. Similarly one is mentally and behaviourally conditioned by what one experiences. This conditioning produces karmic habits, but just as the odour can be removed from the cloth so can one's conditioning be purified of perfumed habits. Typically three types of perfuming are discussed: linguistic and conceptual habits; habits of self-interest and 'grasping self' (*ātmagrāha*), that is, the belief in self and what belongs to self; and habits leading to subsequent life situations (*bhāvāṅgavāsanā*), that is, the long-term karmic consequences of specific karmic activities.

Yogācāra literature debates the relation between seeds and perfuming. Some claim that seeds and perfuming are really two terms for the same thing, that is, acquired karmic habits. Others claim that seeds are simply the effects of perfuming, so that all conditioning is acquired through experience. Still others contend that 'seed' refers to the chains of conditioned habits one already has (whether acquired in this life, in some previous life, or even 'beginninglessly'), while 'perfuming' denotes the experiences one has that modify or affect the development of one's seeds. 'Beginningless' might be understood as a corollary to Husserl's term 'transcendental', that is, a causal sequence constituting a present experience whose own original cause remains undisclosed in this experience. Some claimed that one's possibilities for enlightenment depended entirely on the sort of seeds one already possessed; perfuming merely acted as a catalyst, but could not provide wholesome seeds if one did not already possess them. Beings utterly devoid of wholesome seeds were called *icchantikas* (incorrigibles); such beings could never reach enlightenment. Some other Mahāyāna Buddhists, feeling that this violated the Mahāyāna dictum of universal salvation, attacked the incorrigibility doctrine.

The karmic cause of the fundamental disease (*duḥkha*) is desire expressed through body, speech, or mind. Therefore Yogācāra focused exclusively on cognitive and mental activities in relation to their intentions, that is, the operations of consciousness, since the problem was located there. Buddhism had always identified ignorance and desire as the primary causes of suffering and rebirth. Yogācārins mapped these mental functions in order to dismantle them. Because maps of this sort were also creations of the mind they too would ultimately have to be abandoned in the course of the dismantling, but their therapeutic value would have been served in bringing about enlightenment. This view of the provisional expediency of Buddhism can be traced back to Buddha himself. Yogācārins describe enlightenment as resulting from overturning the cognitive basis (*āśrayaparavṛtti*), that is, overturning the conceptual projections and imaginings which act as the base of our cognitive actions. This overturning transforms the basic mode of cognition from consciousness (*vi-jñāna*, discernment) into *jñāna* (direct knowing). The *vi-* prefix is equivalent to *dis-* in English (dis-criminate, distinguish) meaning to bifurcate or separate from. Direct knowing was defined as nonconceptual (*nirvikalpa*), that is, devoid of interpretive overlay.

7 Matter and cognitive appropriation

The case of material elements is important for understanding one reason why Yogācāra is not metaphysical idealism. No Yogācāra text denies materiality (*rūpa*) as a valid Buddhist category. On the contrary, Yogācārins include materiality in their analysis. Their approach to materiality is well rooted in Buddhist precedents. Frequently Buddhist texts substitute the term 'sensory contact' (Pāli: *phassa*, Sanskrit: *sparśa*) for the term 'materiality'. This substitution is a reminder that physical forms are sensory, that they are known to be what they are through sensation. Even the earliest Buddhist texts explain that the four primary material elements are the sensory qualities solidity, fluidity, temperature and mobility; their characterization as earth, water, fire, and air, respectively, is declared an abstraction. Instead of concentrating on the fact of material existence, one observes how a physical thing is sensed, felt, perceived. Yogācāra never denies that there are sense-objects (*viṣaya*, *artha*, *ālambana*, etc.), but it denies that it makes any sense to speak of cognitive objects occurring outside an act of cognition. Imagining such an occurrence is itself a cognitive act. Yogācāra is interested in why we feel compelled to so imagine.

Everything we know, conceive, imagine, or are aware of, we know through cognition, including the notion that entities might exist independent of our cognition. The mind does not create the physical world, but it produces the interpretive categories through which we know and classify the physical world. It does this so seamlessly that we mistake our interpretations for the world itself. Those interpretations which are projections of our desires and anxieties become obstructions (*āvaraṇa*) preventing us from seeing what is actually the case. In simple terms we are blinded by our own self-interests, prejudices (which means what is already prejudged) and desires. Unenlightened cognition is an appropriative act in which cognitive objects are apprehended (*upalabdhi*). Yogācāra does not speak about subjects and objects; instead it analyses perception in terms of graspers (*grāhaka*) and what is grasped (*grāhya*).

Yogācāra at times resembles epistemological idealism, which does not claim that this or any world is constructed by mind, but rather that we are usually incapable of distinguishing our mental constructions and interpretations of the world from the world itself. This narcissism of consciousness Yogācāra calls *vijñaptimātra*, 'nothing but conscious construction'. A deceptive trick is built into the way consciousness operates at every moment. Consciousness projects and constructs a cognitive object in such a way that it disowns its own creation, pretending the object is 'out there' in order to render that object capable of being appropriated. Even while what we cognize is occurring within our act of cognition, we cognize it *as if* it were external to our consciousness. Realization of *vijñaptimātra* exposes this trick intrinsic to consciousness's workings, thereby eliminating it. When that deception is removed one's mode of cognition is no longer termed *vijñāna* (consciousness); it has become direct cognition, *jñāna*. Consciousness engages in this deceptive game of projection, dissociation and appropriation because there is no 'self'. According to Buddhism, the deepest, most pernicious erroneous view held by sentient beings is that a permanent, eternal, immutable, independent self exists. There is no such self and deep down we know that. This makes us anxious as it indicates that no self or identity endures forever. To assuage that anxiety, we attempt to construct a self, to fill the anxious void, to do something enduring. The projection of cognitive objects for appropriation is consciousness's main tool for this construction. If I own things (ideas, theories, identities, material objects), then 'I am'. If there are eternal objects that I can possess, then I too must be eternal. To undermine this desperate and erroneous appropriative grasping, Yogācāra texts such as the *Madhyāntavibhāga* say: 'Negate the object, and the self is also negated' (1: 4, 8).

Yogācārins deny the existence of external objects in two senses. In terms of conventional experience they do not deny the existence of objects such as chairs, colours and trees, but rather reject the claim that such things appear anywhere other than in consciousness. It is externality, not objects *per se*, that they challenge. They believe moreover that while such objects are admissible as conventions, in more precise terms there are no chairs, or trees. These are merely words and concepts by which we gather and interpret discrete sensations that arise moment by moment in a causal flux. These words and concepts are mental projections. The point is not to elevate consciousness, but to warn us not to be fooled by our own cognitive narcissism. Enlightened cognition is likened to a great mirror that impartially and fully reflects everything before it without attachment to what has passed nor in expectation of what might arrive. Yogācārins refuse to provide answers to the question of what sorts of objects enlightened ones cognize, apart from saying it is purified of karmic pollution (*anāsrava*), since whatever description they might offer would only be appropriated and reduced to the habitual cognitive categories that are already preventing us from seeing properly.

8 Eight types of consciousnesses

The most famous innovation of the Yogācāra school was the doctrine of eight types of consciousness. Standard Buddhism described six types of consciousness, each produced by the contact between its specific sense organ and a corresponding sense object. When a functioning eye comes into contact with a colour or shape, visual consciousness is produced. When a functioning ear comes into contact with a sound, auditory consciousness is produced. Consciousness does not create the sensory sphere, but is an effect of the interaction of a sense organ and its proper object. If an eye does not function but an object is present, visual consciousness does not arise. The same is true if a functional eye fails to encounter a visual object. Consciousness depends on sensation. There are a total of six sense organs (eye, ear, nose, mouth, body and mind) which interact with their respective sensory object domains (visual, auditory, olfactory, gustatory, tactile and mental spheres). These domains in turn amount to six distinct types of consciousness. It is worthy of note that the mind is considered another sense as it functions like the other senses with the activity of a sense organ (*manas*), its domain (*manodhātu*) and the consciousness (*manovijñāna*) resulting from the contact of organ and object. Each domain is discrete so that vision, audition and each of the remaining spheres function apart from each other. Hence the deaf can see and the blind can hear. Objects, too, are entirely specific to their domain and the same is true of consciousnesses. Visual consciousness is entirely distinct from auditory conscioussness, and so on. These eighteen components of experience, that is, six sense organs, six sense object domains and six resulting consciousnesses, were called the eighteen *dhātus*. According to standard Buddhist doctrine these eighteen exhaust the full extent of everything in the universe, or more accurately, the sensorium.

Early Buddhist Abhidhamma, focusing on the mental and cognitive aspects of karma, expanded the three components of the mental level – mind (*manas*), mental objects (*manodhātu*) and mental consciousness (*manovijñāna*) – into a complex system of categories. The apperceptive vector in any cognitive moment was called *citta*. The objects, textures, emotional, moral and psychological tones of *citta*'s cognitions were called *caittas* (literally, 'associated with *citta*'). *Caittas* were subdivided into numerous categories that varied in different Buddhist schools. Some *caittas* are universal, that is, they are components of every cognition (for example, sensory contact, hedonic tone, attention); some are specialized, that is, they only occur in some, not all, cognitions (for example, resolve, mindfulness, meditative clarity). Some *caittas* are wholesome (for example, faith, tranquillity, lack of greed, hatred, or misconception), some unwholesome; some are mental disturbances (*kleśa*) (appropriational intent, aversion, arrogance), or secondary mental disturbances (anger, envy, guile, shamelessness) and some are karmically indeterminate (torpor, remorse).

As Abhidharma grew more complex, disputes intensified between different Buddhist schools across a range of issues. For Yogācāra the most important problems revolved around questions of causality and consciousness. To avoid the idea of a permanent self, Buddhists claimed *citta* was momentary. Since a new *citta* apperceived a new cognitive field each moment, the apparent continuity of mental states was explained by claiming each *citta*, in the moment it ceased, also caused its successor. This was fine for continuous perceptions and thought processes, but difficulties arose since Buddhists identified a number of situations in which no *citta* at all was present or operative, including certain meditative conditions explicitly defined as devoid of *citta*. If a preceding *citta* had to be temporally contiguous with its successor, how could one explain the sudden restarting of *citta* after a period of time had elapsed since the prior *citta* had ceased? Where had *citta* or its causes been residing in the interim? Analogous questions arose, such as, from where does consciousness re-emerge after deep sleep? How does consciousness begin in a new life? The various Buddhist attempts to answer these questions led to more difficulties and disputes.

Yogācārins responded by rearranging the tripartite structure of the mental level of the eighteen *dhātus* into three novel types of consciousnesses. *Manovijñāna* (empirical consciousness) became the sixth consciousness (and operated as the sixth sense organ, which previously had been the role of *manas*), surveying the cognitive content of the five senses as well as mental objects. *Manas* became the seventh consciousness, redefined as primarily obsessed with various aspects and notions of self and thus called

'defiled *manas*' (*kliṣṭamanas*). The eighth consciousness, *ālayavijñāna* (warehouse consciousness) was novel. Warehouse consciousness was defined in several ways. It is the receptacle of all seeds, storing experiences as they 'enter' until they are sent back out as new experiences, like a warehouse handles goods. It was also called *vipāka* consciousness, meaning the maturing of karmic seeds when the consequences of previous karmic actions have matured sufficiently to actualize in present experience. Seeds gradually matured in the repository consciousness until karmically ripe, when they reassert themselves as karmic consequences. *Ālayavijñāna* was also called the basic consciousness (*mūlavijñāna*) as it retains and deploys the karmic seeds that both influence and are influenced by the other seven modes of consciousness. When, for instance, the sixth consciousness is dormant (while one sleeps, or is unconscious), its seeds reside in the eighth consciousness and they restart when the conditions for their arising are present. The eighth consciousness is largely a mechanism for storing and deploying seeds of which by and large it remains unaware. *Cittas* occur as a stream in *ālayavijñāna*, but they mostly cognize the activities of the other consciousnesses, not their own seeds. In those states devoid of *citta*, the flow of *cittas* are repressed, but their seeds continue to regenerate without being noticed until they reassert a new stream of *cittas*. Warehouse consciousness acts as the pivotal karmic mechanism, but is itself karmically neutral. Each individual has its own warehouse consciousness which perdures from moment to moment and life to life. Although it is nothing more than a collection of everchanging 'seeds', it is continually changing and therefore not a permanent self. There is no universal collective mind in Yogācāra.

Enlightenment consists in bringing the eight consciousness to an end, replacing them with enlightened cognitive abilities (*jñāna*). Overturning the basis transforms the five sense consciousnesses into immediate cognitions that accomplish what needs to be done (*kṛtyānuṣṭhānajñāna*). The sixth consciousness becomes immediate cognitive mastery (*pratyavekṣaṇajñāna*), in which the general and particular characteristics of things are discerned just as they are. This discernment is considered nonconceptual (*nirvikalpajñāna*). *Manas* becomes the immediate cognition of equality (*samatājñāna*), equalizing self and other. When the warehouse consciousness finally ceases it is replaced by the great mirror cognition (*Mahādarśajñān*) that sees and reflects things just as they are, impartially, without exclusion, prejudice, anticipation, attachment, or distortion. The grasper–grasped relation has ceased. It should be noted that all of these 'purified' cognitions engage the world in immediate and effective ways by removing the self-bias, prejudice and obstructions that previously had prevented one from perceiving beyond one's own narcissistic consciousness. When consciousness ends, true knowledge begins. One more Yogācāra innovation was the notion that a special type of cognition emerged and developed *after* enlightenment. This post-enlightenment cognition was called *pṛṣṭhalabdhajñāna*. Since enlightened cognition is nonconceptual its objects cannot be described.

9 Three self-natures

The three self-nature theory (*trisvabhāva*), which is explained in many Yogācāra texts including an independent treatise by Vasubandhu, maintains that there are three 'natures' or cognitive realms at work: the conceptually constructed realm (*parikalpitasvabhāva*) ubiquitously imputes unreal conceptions, especially permanent 'selves', into whatever it experiences, including oneself; the realm of causal dependency (*paratantrasvabhāva*), when mixed with the constructed realm, leads one to mistake impermanent occurrences in the flux of causes and conditions for fixed, permanent entities. It can be purified of these delusions by the third element, the perfectional realm (*pariniṣpannasvabhāva*), which, like the Madhyamaka notion of emptiness on which it is based, acts as an antidote (*pratipakṣa*) that 'purifies' all delusional constructions out of the causal realm. When the causally dependent realm is cleansed of all defilements it becomes 'enlightened'. These self-natures are also called the three non-self-natures, as they lack fixed, independent, true, permanent identities and therefore should not be hypostatized. The first is unreal by definition; the third is intrinsically 'empty' of self-nature. The second (which is the only 'real' one) is of an unfixed nature as it can be 'mixed' with either of the other two. Understanding the purified second nature is equivalent to understanding dependent origination (*pratītyasamutpāda*), which all schools of Buddhism accept as Buddhism's core doctrine and which tradition claims Buddha came to realize under the Bodhi tree on the night of his enlightenment (see SELF, INDIAN THEORIES OF).

10 Five stages

Yogācāra literature is so vast that one should not be surprised to find that many of the attempts to provide detailed systems run into conflict with each other. Since it was a self-critical scholastic tradition, it was not uncommon for Yogācāra texts to discuss and criticize the positions of other Yogācāra works, as well

as their more obvious opponents. Yogācāra positions on the stages of the path are diverse. The *Daśabhūmikasūtraśāstra*, a commentary on the *Ten Stages Scripture* attributed to Vasubandhu, describes the progress of the Bodhisattva path to Mahāyānic liberation in ten stages, comparable to the ten stages implicit in the Mahāyānic formulation of the ten perfections of wisdom. Asaṅga's *Yogācārabhūmiśāstra* describes a series of seventeen stages. There are other formulations, such as the five-stage path that offers a useful survey of the other formulations.

The first stage is called 'provisioning' (*sambhārāvasthā*) since this is the stage at which one collects and stocks up on provisions for the journey. These provisions primarily consist of orienting oneself toward the pursuit of the path and developing the proper character, attitude and resolve to accomplish it. It begins the moment the aspiration for enlightenment arises (*bodhicitta*). The next stage is the 'experimental' stage (*prayogāvasthā*), in which one begins to experiment with correct Buddhist theories and practices, learning which of them work and which are true. One begins to suppress the grasper–grasped relation and begins to study carefully the relation between things, language and cognition. After honing one's discipline, one eventually enters the third stage, 'deepening understanding' (*prativedhāvasthā*). Some texts refer to this as the path of corrective vision (*darśanamārga*). This stage ends once one has acquired some insight into nonconceptual cognition.

Nonconceptual cognition deepens in the next stage, the path of cultivation (*bhāvanāmārga*). The grasper–grasped relation is utterly eliminated as are all cognitive obstructions. This path culminates in the overturning of the basis, or enlightenment. In the final stage (*niṣṭhāvasthā*), one abides in unexcelled complete enlightenment and engages the world through the five immediate cognitions. All one's activities and cognitions at this stage are 'postrealization'. As a Mahāyānist, from the first stage one has been devoting oneself not only to one's own attainment of enlightenment, but to the attainment of enlightenment by all sentient beings. In this stage such a pursuit becomes one's sole concern.

See also: BUDDHIST PHILOSOPHY, INDIAN; BUDDHIST PHILOSOPHY, JAPANESE; WÔNCH'ŬK

References and further reading

Anacker, S. (1984) *Seven Works of Vasubandhu*, Delhi: Motilal Banarsidass. (Important translation and discussion of key works by Vasubandhu, including some of his pre-Yogācāra treatises and the *Triṃśikā* (Thirty Verses), 183–90.)

Buswell, R.E. (1989) *The Formation of Ch'an Ideology in China and Korea: The Vajrasamādhisūtra, a Buddhist Apocryphon*, Princeton, NJ: Princeton University Press. (The introductory essay contains the most thorough published account in English of the debate between Chinese Yogācāra and Tathāgatagarbha schools. However, its presentation represents the latter's viewpoint which substantially distorts actual Yogācāra positions.)

Griffiths, P. (1986) *On Being Mindless: Buddhist Meditation and the Mind–Body Problem*, La Salle, IL: Open Court. (Analytic philosophical discussion of the 'mindless' cessation meditations, translating and examining some relevant sections of Theravāda, Vaibhāṣika and Yogācāra texts. Helpful for understanding how Yogācārin positions relate to Buddhism at large.)

Griffiths, P., Hakamaya, N., Keenan, J. and Swanson, P. (1989) *The Realm of Awakening: Chapter Ten of Asaṅga's Mahāyānasaṃgraha*, New York and Oxford: Oxford University Press. (Collective effort from a class taught by Hakamaya at the University of Wisconsin. Compares and translates Chinese and Tibetan versions of the root text as well as major commentaries. A good presentation of the scholastically dense style of some Yogācāra texts.)

Hayes, R.P. (1988) *Dignāga on the Interpretation of Signs, Studies of Classical India*, vol. 9, Dordrecht: Kluwer Academic Publishers. (A superb and challenging examination of Buddhism's most famous logician.)

Kochumuttom, T. (1982) *A Buddhist Doctrine of Experience*, Delhi: Motilal Banarsidass. (Translation and critical analysis of Vasubandhu's major Yogācāra texts, including the *Triṃsikā* (Thirty Verses), 127–63. It argues that Vasubandhu's texts should be interpreted as critical realism rather than idealism.)

* *Laṅkāvatārasūtra* (*c*.5th–6th century), trans. D.T. Suzuki, Boulder, CO: Prajña Press, 2nd edn, 1978. (Claims to be based on the Sanskrit, but more closely follows the Chinese editions.)

Lusthaus, D. (forthcoming) *Buddhist Phenomenology: The Cheng Weishilun in Philosophic Context*, Albany, NY: State University of New York Press. (An investigation of the transmission of Yogācāra philosophy from India to China.)

Nagao, G. (1991) *Mādhyamika and Yogācāra*, trans. L. Kawamura, Albany, NY: State University of New York Press. (Fine collection of essays by one of Japan's leading Yogācāra scholars.)

Powers, J. (1991) *The Yogācāra School of Buddhism: A Bibliography*, Metuchen, NJ: Scarecrow Press. (A fairly comprehensive bibliography, listing virtually all known Yogācāra works in Sanskrit and Tibetan and most standard Western language works. Its coverage of East Asian Yogācāra is less complete.)

—— (1995) *Wisdom of the Buddha: The Saṃdhinirmocana Mahāyāna Sūtra*, Berkeley, CA: Dharma Publishing. (Based on one of the Tibetan versions, this is the only complete English translation. It draws on Lamotte's work, but is not as extensive.)

Rahula, W. (trans.) (1971) *Le Compendium de la Super-Doctrine d'Asaṅga* (Abhidharmasamuccaya), Paris: Publications de l'École Française d'Extrême Orient. (The only Western language translation of this important Asaṅga text.)

Sparham, G. (trans.) (1993) *Ocean of Eloquence: Tsong-kha-pa's Commentary on the Yogācāra Doctrine of Mind*, Albany, NY: State University of New York Press. (Translation of an interesting work by the great Tibetan Gelugpa reformer from his early days.)

Takasaki, J. (1966) *A Study of the Ratnagotravibhāga*, Rome: Serie Orientale Roma 33, Instituto Italiano per il Medio ed Estremo Oreinte. (Contains translations of the text and a critical study of its history and contents.)

Tatz, M. (1986) *Asaṅga's Chapter on Ethics with the commentary of Tsong-kha-pa*, Lewiston, NY: Edwin Mellen Press. (Translation and discussion of the section on ethics from the Bodhisattvabhūmi chapter of the *Yogācārabhūmi*.)

* Ui, H. (1929) 'Maitreya as an Historical Personage', in *Indian Studies in Honor of Charles Rockwell Lanman*, Cambridge, MA: Harvard University Press. (A discussion of Maitreya as an actual human teacher.)

* Vasubandhu (4th or 5th century AD) *Abhidharmakośa*, ed. and trans. L. de la Vallée Poussin, *L'abhidharmakośa de Vasubandhu*, Paris/Louvain: Paul Geuthner, 1923–31, 6 vols; repr. Brussels: Institut belge des hautes études chinoises, 1971, 6 vols; trans. L.M. Pruden, Berkeley, CA: Asian Humanities Press, 1988. (La Vallée Poussin's is still the best translation available of this key work from Vasubandhu's phase as an Abhidharma scholar; Pruden's translation, from La Vallée Poussin's French, is to be used with great caution, but is the only one available in English.)

* —— (4th or 5th century AD) *Karmasiddhiprakaraṇa*, trans. S. Anacker, 'Discussion for the Demonstration of Action', in Anacker 1984; trans. E. Lamotte, 'Le Traité de l'acte de Vasubandhu. *Karmasiddhiprakaraṇa*', *Mélanges chinois et bouddiques* 4: 151–288, 1936. (A work in which Vasubandhu criticizes Sarvāstivādin views of the mechanics of ethically charged actions and their fruitions.)

75

* —— (4th or 5th century AD) *Madhyāntavibhāgaśāstra*, trans. S. Anacker, 'Commentary on the Separation of the Middle from Extremes', in Anacker 1984; trans. T. Kochumuttom, 'Discrimination Between Middle and Extremes', in Kochumuttom 1982. (An important Yogācāra work.)

* —— (4th or 5th century AD) *Pañcaskandhaprakaraṇa*, trans. S. Anacker, 'A Discussion of the Five Aggregates', in Anacker 1984. (An analysis of the classes of characteristics that constitute the physical body and the mentality of human beings.)

* —— (4th or 5th century AD) *Saṃdhinirmocanasūtra*, trans. É. Lamotte, Louvain and Paris: Université de Louvain and Adrian Maisonneuve, 1935. (Richly annotated French translation drawing on Tibetan and Chinese versions.)

* —— (4th or 5th century AD) *Trisvabhāvanirdeśa*, trans. S. Anacker, 'The Teaching of the Three Own-Beings', in Anacker 1984; trans. T. Kochumuttom, 'A Treatise on the Three Natures', in Kochumuttom 1982; trans. F. Tola and C. Cragonetti, 'The *Trisvabhāvakārikā* of Vasubandhu', *Journal of Indian Philosophy* 11: 225–66, 1983. (An important work in early Yogācāra theory.)

* —— (4th or 5th century AD) *Trimśikākārikāvṛtti*, trans. L. de la Vallée Poussin, along with the *Vimśatikākārikāvṛtti* and a Chinese commentary by Xuanzang as *La Siddhi de Hsuan-tsang*, Paris, 1928–48, 3 vols; trans. S. Anacker, 'The Thirty Verses', in Anacker 1984; trans. T. Kochumuttom, 'A Treatise in Thirty Stanzas', in Kochumuttom 1982. (An important Yogācāra treatise.)

* Xuanzang (Hsüan-tsang) (*c*.659 BC) *Cheng weishilun* (Treatise Establishing Vijñaptimātra), Taishō Shinshū Daizokyō, 1585, 1–59; 1st edn trans. L. de La Vallée Poussin, *Vijñaptimātrāsiddhi*, Paris: Librairie Orientaliste Paul Geuthner, 2 vols, 1928; 3rd edn trans. W. Tat, *Ch'eng Wei-Shih Lun: The Doctrine of Mere Consciousness*, Hong Kong, 1973; partial English translation by S. Ganguly, *Treatise in Thirty Verses on Mere-Consciousness*, Delhi: Motilal Banarsidass. (Xuanzang's seventh-century Chinese work, a commentary on Vasubandhu's *Trimśikā* that drew on Sanskrit commentaries, became one of the standard expositions of Yogācāra doctrine in East Asia. La Vallée Poussin's rendition is loose, drawing on old Japanese scholarship and Chinese commentaries. He interprets the text idealistically. Tat's version is an English rendition of La Vallée Poussin's French text, minus the latter's extensive annotations. Ganguly's abridgement is convenient but frequently mistaken.)

DAN LUSTHAUS

BUDDHIST CONCEPT OF EMPTINESS

'Emptiness' or 'voidness' is an expression used in Buddhist thought primarily to mark a distinction between the way things appear to be and the way they actually are, together with attendant attitudes which are held to be spiritually beneficial. It indicates a distinction between appearance and reality, where the paradigm for that distinction is 'x is empty (śūnya) of y', and emptiness (śūnyatā) is either the fact of x's being empty of y or the actual absence itself as a quality of x. It thus becomes an expression for the ultimate truth, the final way of things. Śūnya is also a term which can be used in the nontechnical contexts of, for example, 'The pot is empty of water'. These terms, however, are not univocal in Buddhist thought. If x is empty of y, what this means will depend upon what is substituted for 'x' and 'y'. In particular, any simplistic understanding of 'emptiness' as the Buddhist term for the Absolute, approached through a sort of via negativa, would be quite misleading. We should distinguish here perhaps four main uses of 'empty' and 'emptiness': (1) all sentient beings are empty of a Self or anything pertaining to a Self; (2) all things, no matter what, are empty of their own inherent or intrinsic existence because they are all relative to causes and conditions, a view particularly associated with Nāgārjuna and the Mādhyamika school of Buddhism; (3) the flow of nondual consciousness is empty of hypostasized subject–object duality, the Yogācāra view; (4) the Buddha-nature which is within all sentient beings is intrinsically and primevally empty of all defilements, a notion much debated in Tibetan Buddhism.

1 **Empty of Self or anything pertaining to Self**
2 **Emptiness in Vaibhāṣika Abhidharma**
3 **Madhyamaka critique and development**
4 **Emptiness of subject–object duality in Yogācāra**
5 **Intrinsic purity of the innate Buddha-nature**

1 Empty of Self or anything pertaining to Self

Conceptually and probably chronologically, one of the earliest uses of 'emptiness' (*śūnyatā*, also translated as 'voidness') in Buddhist thought is to refer to an absence specifically of an immutable and permanent 'Self' (*ātman*), a constant referent for the term 'I', the Self postulated by non-Buddhist teachers and presupposed at least implicitly even by 'the person in the street'. Grasping after 'me and mine' is held to generate an impetus towards continued rebirth and therefore suffering. Discovery of emptiness, the fact that really there is no such thing as a Self and therefore no coherent real basis for the destructive patterns of 'me and mine', leads to a letting-go of grasping which finally issues in *nirvāṇa*, the cessation of rebirth and suffering, a state sometimes itself spoken of as 'the empty'. This *nirvāṇa* is said to be 'seeing things the way they really are', that is, seeing emptiness, the absence of Self (see NIRVĀṆA). Already, therefore, we can detect the use of 'emptiness' to designate the ultimate truth, that is, what is ultimately the case, how things really are. This analysis was clarified by the claim that all sentient beings are empty (*śūnya*) of a Self or anything pertaining to a Self, and really consist of ever-changing patterns of physical form, sensations, conceptions, other mental factors such as volitions, and the flow of consciousness. This list of five ever-changing 'aggregates' (*skandhas*) which are what is really there, contrasted with a Self which is really not there (that is, the aggregates are empty of a Self), was elaborated even further in the development of Abhidharma thought and eventually issued in a clear distinction between conventional truth (or reality, *satya*) and ultimate truth.

2 Emptiness in Vaibhāṣika Abhidharma

In the classical Vaibhāṣika (Sarvāstivāda) Abhidharma, all things (not just sentient beings) can be divided into primary existents (*dravyasat*) and secondary existents, conceptual constructs (*prajñaptisat*) (see BUDDHISM, ĀBHIDHARMIKA SCHOOLS OF). Conceptual constructs – such as a forest, a table, a pot, the mind or a sentient being – are presented linguistically and cognitively, but are thought to be conventionalities and not ultimate realities since they are constructs out of primary existents (also known as *dharmas*), those data (such as sense-data) which are immediately presented and could not be further analysed away for fear of infinite regress and/or complete destruction. Most of these primary existents are the results of causes and are radically impermanent, indeed almost instantaneous; they form a series, a flow. They are the ultimate truths/realities. Thus from this Abhidharma perspective, although tables and sentient beings appear to be realities in their own right, really they are conceptual constructs out of more basic and ineliminable data into which they can be analysed. On the level of what is really there – 'really' in the sense of primary, ineliminable, unconstructed and therefore 'simple' reality, in other words, on the final, ultimate level, the 'ultimate truth' – there are no tables and sentient beings, for they are conceptual constructs and therefore only 'conventional truths'. Reality is empty of conceptually constructed and reified entities. The soteriological

correlate of this is renunciation (an emptying), the letting-go of attachment to conceptual constructs, which as constructs are sure to perish when their causes cease to operate. Attachment to things which by nature are perishable leads to suffering and continued rebirth. These conceptual constructs are empty of any ultimate significance, are ultimately valueless and are not worthy of attachment. In this letting-go lies liberation, final immutable freedom from suffering.

In this Vaibhāṣika distinction between primary and secondary existence there is an essential ontological aspect with axiological implications which is thought to be fundamental to enlightenment. It is arguable that this aspect, while implicit, is less central in some other Abhidharma traditions. The ontological distinction is marked by the concept of *svabhāva* ('own' or 'inherent' existence). While most primary existents are radically impermanent, the results of causes, they still exist in a different sort of way from conceptual constructs. Primary existents have 'own-existence', in contrast to secondary existents, which are simply constructs. Secondary existents are *niḥsvabhāva* – they lack (or are empty of) own-existence. If x is the result of the particular type of causation associated with conceptual construction then x is a secondary existent (*prajñaptisat*) and is empty of own-existence. If, on the other hand, x exists but is not the result of this particular sort of causation then it has own-existence; secondary existents are constructed out of these primary existents (*dharmas*) – primary existents inasmuch as they are not empty of own-existence.

We have seen already a move from the idea that all things are empty of a Self – that is, no matter where one looks, one cannot find anything which could be called one's Self (*ātman*), and therefore there is also nothing which is truly 'mine' – to an idea by no means identical that certain things are empty of own-existence. By an understandable but stretched sense of the word 'Self' to mean something like 'essence' ('self-identity') one could say that conceptual constructs are also empty of a Self, not just because I cannot find my Self in them but also because *qua* conceptual constructs they lack an essence. The problem here is that this could lead to an ambiguity in the term 'Self'. From the earliest Buddhist sources we have the statement that all things are empty of a Self. From a Vaibhāṣika point of view, however, while this is true it could not mean that all things are empty of own-existence, that is, that all things are secondary existents, conceptual constructs (*niḥsvabhāva*), for that would be to deny the distinction between primary and secondary existents and produce the absurdity that all things are constructs with nothing left for them to be constructed out of. That could only mean that nothing exists at all.

3 Madhyamaka critique and development

It is precisely in the claim that *all* things absolutely and without exception, no matter what, are empty that the concept of emptiness really comes to the fore in Buddhist thought. This claim is most frequently associated with the Perfection of Wisdom (*Prajñāpāramitā*) literature and its philosophical clarification and development in the Madhyamaka school, particularly the work of Nāgārjuna (*c.*150–200 AD) and his commentators, such as Candrakīrti (*c.*600–50) (see BUDDHISM, MĀDHYAMIKA: INDIA AND TIBET). Here emptiness indeed means that for all *x*, *x* is empty of own-existence (*y*). The key to understanding this lies in the relationship between emptiness and causation. If *x* is the result of causes then *x* is not nonexistent, but also *x* does not have own-existence, that is, the existence of *x* is given to it by its causes, its existence is contingent and not intrinsic to it. *X* as contingent is arguably ontologically simply the intersection point of a set of causal forces – pure relativity. *X* does not have inherent existence, and the concept of *svabhāva* slides from that of own-existence in contrast to the sort of existence possessed by conceptual constructs such as forests and tables to that of inherent, noncontingent and therefore uncaused existence. Nothing which is the result of causes can have its existence inherent in itself. If something were inherently existent it would be permanently (that is, necessarily) existent. There is therefore a contradiction between causation and inherent existence. Thus in these terms even the Vaibhāṣika primary existents which are part of a causal flow become empty of inherent existence. While there may be a relative distinction between primary and secondary existents (clearly tables and suchlike can still be analysed into parts), this distinction, the follower of Madhyamaka wants to argue, ceases to have any ontological significance. In fact in the last analysis all things, no matter what, are secondary existents – they are all conceptual constructs.

For Madhyamaka, emptiness, that very absence – a complete and total absence of something which simply does not exist anywhere, a simple nonexistence (*abhāvamātra*) – of inherent existence in any *x* (because *x* is always in some sense the result of causal conditioning) is the ultimate truth in that if one analyses in order to find the fundamental simples (primary existents) out of which all things are constructed, nothing will ever be found. Analysis can dissolve away *everything* into secondary existence. Thus if we ask what exists ultimately, that is, what has

the type of existence called ultimate or primary, it is found (it can be shown through analysis, commonly a sort of *reductio ad absurdum*, Nāgārjuna would say) that nothing has that sort of existence. On the level of ultimate existence there is nothing. That absence of ultimate existence (that is, that emptiness) applied to everything (including emptiness itself) is the ultimate truth, what is found if one searches for any ultimate status for *x*. Therefore it follows not only that if *x* is causally conditioned it is empty (of inherent existence), but also that emptiness must be the very absence of inherent existence in something or other (an *x*). In terms of actuality, emptiness (the ultimate truth) requires causally conditioned existence (the conventional truth). In fact, emptiness is precisely what makes conditioned conventional reality what it is – conventional (and not ultimate) truth. If emptiness is the absence of *y* in *x* then it can be argued that there has to be an *x* – an *x* which turns out to lack *y* – in order for it to be empty of inherent existence. *X* therefore indeed exists, but as a noninherently existing, conventional entity, a conceptual construct. In order for causally conditioned existence to be causally conditioned existence it must be empty of inherent existence, that is, empty. Thus Nāgārjuna and Candrakīrti want to argue that holding all things to be empty (all things as secondary existents) does not imply the existence of nothing at all (that is, nihilism, *pace* the follower of Vaibhāṣika Abhidharma, who is unpersuaded and still finds something very strange in all of this). Rather, since emptiness is the result of causal conditioning emptiness must imply the existence of things in the causally conditioned way they actually are and must be (a point made strongly – for his opponents rather too strongly – in fifteenth-century Tibet by TSONG KHA PA BLO BZANG GRAGS PA).

Emptiness, Nāgārjuna says, far from being nihilism and destroying all things (Buddhism included), is the very condition for their being. It is his opponent, who holds to a static world of inherent existences, who destroys all things. Any understanding of emptiness which does not see or show how emptiness implies existence as it actually is, Nāgārjuna would want to say, is not the correct understanding of emptiness. This includes any understanding of emptiness as itself an inherently existent Ultimate Reality. If emptiness is the pure absence of inherent existence in *x*, then without *x* there could be no emptiness. Thus just as *x* is contingent, causally conditioned, so in some sense must be its emptiness. Therefore emptiness too is empty of inherent existence. Madhyamaka here is emphatically not a form of *via negativa* leading to a pure, nonconceptual Absolute. Emptiness is empty, the Buddha is empty, enlightenment is empty – not in the sense that they are Realities beyond all mundane conceptualizing, but inasmuch as they result from some form of causal conditioning. Nevertheless, it does not follow that enlightenment, for example, ceases to be positively important (is empty in *that* sense). For Nāgārjuna, as a follower of Mahāyāna Buddhism, the welfare of sentient beings is supremely (one might say absolutely) important, but sentient beings and their welfare are still empty of inherent existence. It is because they and their welfare are empty that they can be helped. One could not change an inherently existent misery.

4 Emptiness of subject–object duality in Yogācāra

The claim that all things without exception are conceptual constructs, secondary existents (*prajñapti-sat*, that is, *niḥsvabhāva*, empty of inherent existence) is a characteristically Madhyamaka claim. For the follower of Vaibhāṣika it is a patent contradiction which must make Madhyamaka an ontological nihilism, notwithstanding any protest to the contrary. To make the counterclaim that something must exist as a foundation for conceptual construction in order to avoid nihilism is to posit that at least one thing must have primary existence (*dravyasat*). To make this claim is to differ from Madhyamaka in ontologically the strongest possible way. It seems that we have this radical disagreement not only in Vaibhāṣika thought but also in a different way in Yogācāra. Yogācāra texts too ridicule as nihilism the claim that all things are conceptual constructs. Thus Yogācāra texts *must* postulate at least one thing as a primary existent, not a conceptual construct. In fact in Yogācāra thought that thing is the flow of nondual consciousness. It is a flow of consciousness which serves as the actual substratum for an erroneous bifurcation into the polarized (and linguistically reified) subjects and objects of unenlightened duality, and also as the necessary substratum for realizing that actually the flow is empty of hypostasized, reified and polarized subjects and objects. Thus from this perspective the ultimate, enlightening truth is also said to be emptiness, but here the ultimate truth is that something which really exists in the strongest possible sense – the flow of consciousness – is empty of projected subjects and objects, which do not really exist at all. As in Vaibhāṣika, we have here at least an implicit denial of an equation between causal conditioning and absence of own-existence. Since for Yogācāra too it would appear that all things, including the flow of consciousness, are in some sense causally conditioned, the alternative to the denial of this equation is to hold (with Madhyamaka) the absurdity that all things are secondary existents, that

is, putative nihilism (see BUDDHISM, YOGĀCĀRA SCHOOL OF §§1–4).

5 Intrinsic purity of the innate Buddha-nature

There is also in Buddhist thought a teaching of the Buddha-nature (*tathāgatagarbha*), which asserts the presence within each sentient being of something which enables that being to become a *buddha* ('awakened one'). Commonly that thing is spoken of as intrinsically pure, primevally present, and sometimes as primevally enlightened. The terms 'Mind' and even 'Self' (*ātman*) are sometimes used of it, but the Buddha-nature is also said to be empty. Often this is taken as meaning that the Buddha-nature is intrinsically and primevally empty of all the defilements of unenlightenment, which never really taint its nature. They are adventitious or contingent, which is why they can be removed. One can become enlightened because there is a sense in and a level at which there is no unenlightenment. Yet this Buddha-nature is also spoken of as not-empty, for it is not empty of all the attributes and qualities of enlightenment which are intrinsic (that is, necessary) to it and therefore never cease. The great question much debated in Tibet was whether in accepting the Buddha-nature, it should nevertheless be taken as empty of its own inherent existence (on the Madhyamaka model) or not. In one common Tibetan view (widespread also in East Asian Buddhism, but strongly opposed by others, particularly in Tibet) the Buddha-nature really does inherently and immutably exist in all sentient beings, primevally pure and enlightened, an emptiness (Mind) empty of all defilements, including the defilements of conceptuality. As nonconceptual, this emptiness cannot even be said to be 'emptiness', certainly not in the sense of '*x* is empty of *y*', which is just a relative, mundane emptiness. It can be approached only through nonconceptual gnosis (see MI BSKYOD RDO RJE). It is just possible that here we reach something akin to emptiness seen as an Absolute approached through a *via negativa*.

It is perhaps necessary to distinguish the foregoing philosophical discussions of emptiness in Indo-Tibetan thought from the use of 'emptiness' within the practical context of descriptions of meditation practice (for example, as an 'empty mind'). In Tibetan meditation it is common for the practitioner to reduce everything to emptiness and then generate out of that emptiness the forms of *buddhas*, or oneself in the form of a *buddha*, and so on. It would be interesting to explore further the relationship between the preceding conceptual discussions of Buddhist philosophy and purported 'nonconceptual' mental states, 'blank-minds', and so on.

See also: BUDDHIST PHILOSOPHY, INDIAN; BUDDHIST PHILOSOPHY, CHINESE §12; CAUSATION, INDIAN THEORIES OF §6; ERROR AND ILLUSION, INDIAN CONCEPTIONS OF §1; FAZANG; HASIDISM §2; LINJI; NOMINALISM, BUDDHIST DOCTRINE OF

References and further reading

Buddhadāsa Bhikkhu (1994) *Heartwood of the Bodhi Tree: The Buddha's Teaching on Voidness*, trans. Dhammavicayo, ed. Santikaro Bhikkhu, Boston, MA: Wisdom Publications. (Very clear oral teachings by an eminent Thai Theravāda meditation master on 'empty of Self and pertaining to Self'.)

Cabezón, J.I. (1994) *Buddhism and Language: A Study of Indo-Tibetan Scholasticism*, Albany, NY: State University of New York Press. (An excellent and not too technical introduction to Madhyamaka and language within the context of Tibetan scholasticism.)

Hookham, S.K. (1990) *The Buddha Within: Tathāgatagarbha Doctrine According to the Shen-tong Interpretation of the Ratnagotravibhāga*, Albany, NY: State University of New York Press. (A detailed, sympathetic exposition of the teachings of an inherently existent Buddha-nature and their relationship to other Buddhist traditions.)

Nagao, G. (1991) *Mādhyamika and Yogācāra: A Study of Mahāyāna Philosophies*, ed. and trans. L.S. Kawamura, Albany, NY: State University of New York Press, ch. 5. (An important paper on the Yogācāra approach to emptiness in relation to that of Madhyamaka.)

Napper, E. (1989) *Dependent Arising and Emptiness*, Boston, MA: Wisdom Publications. (Probably the best introduction to Tsong kha pa's influential approach to emptiness. Some material, particularly the translations, is technical and difficult, but the earlier chapters, which include a critique of contemporary approaches in the light of Tsong kha pa are very accessible and contain all the important points.)

Ruegg, D.S. (1981) *The Literature of the Madhyamaka School of Philosophy in India*, vol. 7, fasc. 1 of J. Gonda (ed.) *A History of Indian Literature*, Wiesbaden: Otto Harrassowitz. (Rather like a detailed annotated bibliography at times, but a standard work on Indian Madhyamaka by its leading authority. Highly recommended, with many insights.)

Streng, F. (1967) *Emptiness: A Study in Religious Meaning*, Nashville, TN and New York: Abingdon Press. (Dated but extremely readable introduction to Madhyamaka, with some translated texts. Places Madhyamaka within the context of Religious Studies and the history of Buddhism. An excellent bibliography up to its date of publication.)

Williams, P. (1981) 'On the Abhidharma Ontology', *Journal of Indian Philosophy* 9: 227–57. (Very technical study of Vaibhāṣika Abhidharma, particularly the *svabhāva* and primary/secondary distinction of existents.)

—— (1989) *Mahāyāna Buddhism: The Doctrinal Foundations*, London: Routledge, chaps 2–5. (Accessible introductions to Perfection of Wisdom, Madhyamaka, Yogācāra and Buddha-nature teachings within the context of Mahāyāna Buddhism.)

—— (1992) 'Non-Conceptuality, Critical Reasoning and Religious Experience: Some Tibetan Buddhist discussions', in M. McGhee (ed.) *Philosophy, Religion and the Spiritual Life*, Cambridge: Cambridge University Press. (A paper aimed at philosophers with no background in Buddhist Studies, introducing Tibetan Madhyamaka and the role of reasoning within it, with a discussion of some problems concerning nonconceptual states and 'empty minds'.)

PAUL WILLIAMS

BUDDHIST DOCTRINE OF MOMENTARINESS *see* MOMENTARINESS, BUDDHIST DOCTRINE OF

BUDDHIST DOCTRINE OF NOMINALISM *see* NOMINALISM, BUDDHIST DOCTRINE OF

BUDDHIST PHILOSOPHY, CHINESE

When Buddhism first entered China from India and Central Asia two thousand years ago, Chinese favourably disposed towards it tended to view it as a part or companion school of the native Chinese Huang–Lao Daoist tradition, a form of Daoism rooted in texts and practices attributed to Huangdi (the Yellow Emperor) and Laozi. Others, less accepting of this 'foreign' incursion from the 'barbarous' Western Countries, viewed Buddhism as an exotic and dangerous challenge to the social and ethical Chinese civil order. For several centuries, these two attitudes formed the crucible within which the Chinese understanding of Buddhism was fashioned, even as more and more missionaries arrived (predominantly from Central Asia) bringing additional texts, concepts, rituals, meditative disciplines and other practices. Buddhists and Daoists borrowed ideas, terminology, disciplines, cosmologies, institutional structures, literary genres and soteric models from each other, sometimes so profusely that today it can be difficult if not impossible at times to determine who was first to introduce a certain idea. Simultaneously, polemical and political attacks from hostile Chinese quarters forced Buddhists to respond with apologia and ultimately reshape Buddhism into something the Chinese would find not only inoffensive, but attractive.

In the fifth century AD, Buddhism began to extricate itself from its quasi-Daoist pigeonhole by clarifying definitive differences between Buddhist and Daoist thought, shedding Daoist vocabulary and literary styles while developing new distinctively Buddhist terminology and genres. Curiously, despite the fact that Mahāyāna Buddhism had few adherents in Central Asia and was outnumbered by other Buddhist schools in India as well, in China Mahāyāna became the dominant form of Buddhism, so much so that few pejoratives were as stinging to a fellow Buddhist as labelling him 'Hīnayāna' (literally 'Little Vehicle,' a polemical term for non-Mahāyānic forms of Buddhism). By the sixth century, the Chinese had been introduced to a vast array of Buddhist theories and practices representing a wide range of Indian Buddhist schools. As the Chinese struggled to master these doctrines it became evident that, despite the fact that these schools were all supposed to express the One Dharma (Buddha's Teaching), their teachings were not homogenous, and were frequently incommensurate.

By the end of the sixth century, the most pressing issue facing Chinese Buddhists was how to harmonize the disparities between the various teachings. Responses to this issue produced the Sinitic Mahāyāna schools, that is, Buddhist schools that originated in China rather than India. The four Sinitic schools are Tiantai, Huayan, Chan and Pure Land (Jingtu). Issues these schools share in common include Buddha-nature, mind, emptiness, tathāgatagarbha, *expedient means (*upāya*), overcoming birth and death (*saṃsāra*), and enlightenment.*

1   Historical overview

The development of Chinese Buddhist philosophy can be divided roughly into four periods: (1) the early introduction of Indian and Central Asian Buddhism (first–fourth centuries AD); (2) the formative development of Chinese versions of Indian and Central Asian Schools (fifth–seventh centuries); (3) the emergence of distinctively Sinitic Buddhist schools (seventh–twelfth centuries); and (4) the continuance of Chinese Buddhism into the present day (thirteenth century onwards).

From the fourth through the seventh centuries, Buddhists periodically realized that the positions being engendered in China were at variance with their Indian antecedents, and attempted to correct the problem, either through the introduction of additional translations or by clarifying differences between Buddhist and native Chinese ideas. By the eighth century, the Chinese had apparently become satisfied with the types of Buddhism they had developed, since from then on they lost interest in Indian commentaries and treatises and instead turned their attention toward Chinese commentaries on the Buddhist scriptures – such as the *Lotus Sutra* and *Huayan Sutra* – that had assumed importance for Chinese Buddhist traditions. Moreover, even though missionaries continued to arrive in China and new translations continued to be produced through the thirteenth century, none of the significant developments in Indian Buddhism (such as Buddhist syllogistic logic) from the seventh century onwards had any lasting impact on Chinese Buddhism, and many important texts and thinkers (for example, Dharmakīrti, Candrakīrti, Śāntarakṣita) remained virtually unknown in East Asia until modern times (see BUDDHIST PHILOSOPHY, INDIAN).

2   Earliest developments

The first undisputed reference to Buddhism in China is an edict by Emperor Ming to Liu Ying, king of Qu, in the year AD 65, which mentions sacrifices performed by the king to Buddha as well as favourable treatment for Buddhist monks and laymen; the edict also identifies King Liu Ying as a follower of Huang–Lao Daoism. For the next few centuries, the Chinese continued to view Buddhist texts and practices as a part of or supplement to Daoism. Buddhism seemed to share important issues with the types of Daoism practised in this period, including the metaphysical primacy of emptiness, meditation techniques, dietary and behavioural disciplines, afterlife theories connected to moral and behavioural discipline, expansive pantheons and cosmologies, striving for the soteriological transformation of the ordinary human condition, rigorous and subtle intellectual traditions, and magical and yogic powers. These affinities, however, were more apparent than real, since the Buddhist approaches to these issues usually differed sharply from their Daoist counterparts, though Buddhists did not assert their distinctiveness until the fifth century.

Buddhist monks and businessmen representing a variety of Buddhist schools and disciplines continued to arrive in China, establishing Buddhist communities in Loyang and elsewhere. It took several centuries for the Chinese to notice how disparate the various forms of Buddhism really were. Initially the Chinese were most interested in Buddhist meditation techniques, including chanting and visualizations, which they adopted as supplements to Daoistic techniques. Daoism held out the promise that one could become a sage or perfected person, or even an immortal, but the exact details of how to accomplish this transformation remained elusive and vague. In comparison to many of the Daoist texts which were esoteric, hard to find, and frequently obscure in presentation, Buddhist texts seemed systematic and detailed, providing step-by-step procedures for practitioners.

Along with meditation manuals, the earliest Buddhist texts to become popular in China were Āvadana materials (legends of the Buddha and Buddhist heroes) and the Perfection of Wisdom Scriptures (*Prajñāpāramitā Sutras*). About half a dozen schools formed around varying interpretations of the Perfection of Wisdom Scriptures, mixing ideas found in these and other Buddhist texts with concepts prominent among Chinese intelligentsia. One Prajñā school, called the Original Nothingness school (*Benwu*), adopted a neo-Daoist cosmology: everything has emerged from a primordial, original emptiness, and everything returns to that void. This was a thorough misconstrual of Buddhist emptiness (see BUDDHIST CONCEPT OF EMPTINESS). Another school, called the Mind Empty school (*Xinwu*), equated the primordial Nothing with the nature of mind (see ZHI DUN). Each of the Prajñā schools managed either to promote a metaphysical substantialized emptiness which they opposed to form, or smuggle an eternal self or spirit into their formulations, despite Buddhism's emphatic rejection of the notion of permanent selfhood.

Dao'an (AD 312–85) criticized the Prajñā schools, challenging their faithfulness to authentic Buddhist positions as well as the translation methodologies behind the texts they and other Chinese Buddhists had come to rely on. In particular, he criticized the practice of 'matching the meanings' (*geyi*), by which translators seeking Chinese equivalents for Indian Buddhist technical terms and concepts borrowed heavily from Daoist literature. This 'matching of meanings' was a mixed blessing. Packaging Buddhist ideas in familiar terms made them amenable and understandable, but the 'matches' were often less than perfect, distorting or misrepresenting Buddhism. For instance, early translators chose a well-known Daoist and Confucian term, *wuwei* (nondeliberative activity), to translate *nirvāṇa*. Arguably, *wuwei* and *nirvāṇa* represent the teloi of Daoism and Buddhism, respectively, but it is not obvious that they denote the same telos (see DAOIST PHILOSOPHY §6; NIRVĀA). Later, to emphasize the uniqueness of Buddhist *nirvāṇa*, translators dropped *wuwei* in favour of a transliteration, *niepan*. *Wuwei* was retained to render another important Buddhist notion, *asaṃskṛta* (unconditioned). The semantic connotations of Daoist *wuwei* and Buddhist *wuwei*, while possibly overlapping in some senses, were nonetheless quite distinct: for Daoists it meant a mode of interacting effortlessly and naturally with the world, while for Buddhists it denoted something unaffected by causes and conditions, that neither arose nor ceased. Chinese readers inevitably came to conflate the semantic ranges of such terms, which over the centuries led to some distinctively Chinese Buddhist concepts. After Dao'an, Chinese Buddhism asserted its distinctiveness from native Chinese traditions and Buddhists adopted increasingly critical hermeneutic approaches to translation.

3 Indian transplants: Madhyamaka and *icchantikas*

In the critical environment that followed Dao'an, two sets of events moved Chinese Buddhism in new directions. First, Kumārajīva, a Mahāyāna Buddhist from Kucha in Central Asia, was brought to Changan, the Chinese capital, in 401. Under the auspices of the ruler, he began translating numerous important works with the help of hundreds of assistants, including some of the brightest minds of his day. Some works, such as the *Lotus Sutra*, *Vimalakīrti Sutra* and *Diamond Sutra*, quickly became popular classics. He also introduced the emptiness philosophy of Nāgārjuna's Madhyamaka thought (see BUDDHISM, MĀDHYAMIKA: INDIA AND TIBET; NĀGĀRJUNA), which in China came to be called the Three Treatise School (Sanlun) after the three Madhyamaka texts he translated: the *Madhyamaka-kārikās*, the *Twelve Gate Treatise* and Āryadeva's *One Hundred Verse Treatise*. In a series of famous letters exchanged with a disciple of Dao'an, Huiyuan (344–416), who had mastered most of the Buddhist theory and practice known in China up to that time, Kumārajīva attacked the shortcomings of the current Chinese Buddhist theories and argued persuasively for the preeminence of Madhyamaka in matters of both theory and practice. His leading disciple, SENG ZHAO (384–414), further popularized Madhyamaka thought by packaging it in an exquisite adoption of the literary style of Laozi (see DAODEJING) and ZHUANGZI, both of whom were extremely popular amongst literati at that time. Sanlun thought continued to spread through the fifth through seventh centuries, greatly influencing other Buddhist schools. After Jizang (549–623), who attempted to synthesize Madhyamakan emptiness with the Buddha-nature and *tathāgatagarbha* thought gaining prominence at his time, the Sanlun school declined, its most important ideas absorbed by other schools.

Second, in 418 Faxian (the first Chinese monk successfully to return to China with scriptures from pilgrimage to India) and Buddhabhadra produced a partial translation of the Mahāyāna *Nirvāṇa Sutra*. One of the topics it discusses is the *icchantika*, incorrigible beings lacking the requisites for achieving enlightenment. Daosheng (*c.*360–434), a disciple of Huiyuan, convinced that all beings, including *icchantikas*, must possess Buddha-nature and hence are capable of enlightenment, insisted that the *Nirvāṇa Sutra* be understood in that light. Since that violated the obvious meaning of the text, Daosheng was unanimously rebuked, whereupon he left the capital in disgrace. In AD 421, a new translation by Dharmakṣema of the *Nirvāṇa Sutra* based on a Central Asian original appeared containing sections absent from the previous version. The twenty-third chapter of Dharmakṣema's version contained passages declaring that Buddha-nature was indeed universal, and that even *icchantikas* possessed it and could thus reach the goal. Daosheng's detractors in the capital were humbled, suddenly impressed at his prescience. The lesson was never forgotten, so that two centuries later, when Xuan Zang (600–64) translated Indian texts that once again declared that *icchantikas* lacked the requisite qualities to attain enlightenment, his school was attacked from all quarters as promoting a less than 'Mahāyānic' doctrine. However, it should be noted that there is no clear precedent or term in Indian Buddhism for 'Buddha-nature'; the notion probably either arose in China through a certain degree of license taken by translators when rendering terms like *buddhatva* ('Buddhahood', an accomplishment, not a primordial ontological ground), or it developed from nascent forms of the theory possibly constructed in Central Asia. However, from this moment on, Buddha-nature become one of the foundational tenets of virtually all forms of East Asian Buddhism.

4 Indian transplants: *tathāgatagarbha* and Yogācāra

A dispute at the start of the sixth century presaged a conflict that would take the Chinese Buddhists more than two centuries to settle. Two Indian monks collaborated on a translation of Vasubandhu's *Daśabhūmikasūutra śāstra* (Treatise on the Ten Stages Sutra; in Chinese, *Shidijing lun*, or *Dilun* for short). The *Dilun* described the ten stages through which a *bodhisattva* proceeded on the way to *nirvāṇa*, and Vasubandhu's exposition of it highlighted aspects most in accord with the tenets of the Yogācāra school (see BUDDHISM, YOGĀCĀRA SCHOOL OF; VASUBANDHU). While translating, an irreconcilable difference of interpretation broke out between the two translators, Bodhiruci and Ratnamati. Bodhiruci's reading followed a relatively orthodox Yogācāra line, while Ratnamati's interpretation leaned heavily toward a Buddhist ideology only beginning to receive attention in China, *tathāgatagarbha* thought. Bodhiruci went on to translate roughly forty additional texts, and was later embraced by both the Huayan and Pure Land traditions as one of their early influences (see §§8, 10). Ratnamati later collaborated with several other translators on a number of other texts. Both sides attempted to ground their positions on interpretations of key texts, especially the *Dilun*. The Yogācāra versus Yogācāra-*tathāgatagarbha* conflict became one of the critical debates amongst sixth and seventh century Chinese Buddhists.

Yogācāra focused on the mind and distinguished eight types of consciousness: five sensory consciousnesses; an empirical organizer of sensory data (*mano-vijñāna*); a self-absorbed, appropriative consciousness (*manas*); and the eighth, a warehouse consciousness (*ālaya-vijñāna*) that retained the karmic impressions of past experiences and coloured new experiences on the basis of that previous conditioning. The eighth consciousness was also the fundamental consciousness. Each individual is constituted by the karmic stream of one's own *ālaya-vijñāna*, that is, one's karmic conditioning. Since, like a stream, the *ālaya-vijñāna* is reconfigured each moment in response to constantly changing conditions, it is not a permanent self, although, being nothing more than a sequential chain of causes and effects, it provides sufficient stability for an individual to maintain a sense of continuity. According to classical Yogācāra texts, the mind (that is, *ālaya-vijñāna* and the mental events associated with it) is the problem, and enlightenment results from bringing this consciousness to an end, replacing it with the Great Mirror Cognition (*ādarśa-jñāna*); instead of discriminating consciousness, one has direct immediate cognition of things just as they are, as impartially and comprehensively as a mirror.

This type of enlightenment occurs during the eighth stage according to the *Dilun* and other texts.

The term *tathāgatagarbha* (in Chinese, *rulaizang*) derives from two words: *tathāgata* (Chinese, *rulai*) is an epithet of the Buddha, meaning either 'thus come' or 'thus gone'; *garbha* means embryo, womb or matrix, and was translated into Chinese as *zang*, meaning 'repository'. In its earliest appearances in Buddhist texts, *tathāgatagarbha* (repository of buddhahood) signified the inherent capacity of humans (and sometimes other sentient beings) to achieve buddhahood. Over time the concept expanded and came to signify the original pristine pure ontological Buddha-ness intrinsic in all things, a pure nature that is obscured or covered over by defilements (Sanskrit, *kleśa*; Chinese *fannao*), that is, mental, cognitive, psychological, moral and emotional obstructions. It was treated as a synonym for Buddha-nature, though Buddha-nature dynamically understood as engaged in a struggle against defilements and impurities. In Chinese Buddhism especially, the soteriological goal consisted in a return to or recovering of that original nature by overcoming or eliminating the defilements. The battle between the pure and impure, light and dark, enlightenment and ignorance, good and evil and so on, took on such epic proportions in Chinese Buddhist literature that some scholars have compared it to Zoroastrian or Manichean themes, though evidence for the influence of those religions on Buddhist thought has been more suggestive than definitive (see MANICHEISM; ZOROASTRIANISM).

In their classical formulations the *ālaya-vijñāna* and *tathāgatagarbha* were distinct items differing from each other in important ways – for instance, enlightenment entailed bringing the *ālaya-vijñāna* to an end, while it meant actualizing the *tathāgatagarbha*; the *ālaya-vijñāna* functioned as the karmic mechanism *par excellence*, while *tathāgatagarbha* was considered the antipode to all karmic defilements. Nonetheless some Buddhist texts, such as the *Laṅkāvatāra Sūtra*, conflated the two. Those identifying the two argued that the *ālaya-vijñāna*, like *tathāgatagarbha*, was pure and its purity became permanently established after enlightenment. Those opposing the conflation countered that the *ālaya-vijñāna* was itself defiled and needed to be eliminated in order to reach enlightenment. For the conflators, *tathāgatagarbha* was identified with Buddha-nature and with mind (*xin*) (see XIN). Mind was considered pure, eternal, and the ontological ground of reality (*Dharma-dhātu*), while defiled thought-instants (*nian*) that engaged in delusionary false discriminations had to be eliminated. Once *nian* were eliminated, the true, pure nature of the mind would brilliantly shine forth, like the sun coming out from behind the clouds.

A third view was added when Paramārtha, another Indian translator with his own unique interpretation of Yogācāra, arrived in the middle of the sixth century. For his followers the most important of his translations was the *She dasheng lun* (Sanskrit title, *Mahāyānasaṃgraha*), or *Shelun*, a quasi-systematic exposition of Yogācāra theory by one its founders, Asaṅga. In some of his translations he added a ninth consciousness beyond the usual eight, a 'pure consciousness' that would pervade unhindered once the defiled *ālaya-vijñāna* was destroyed. His translations, which sometimes took liberties with the Sanskrit originals, offered a more sophisticated version of the conflation theory.

5 The *Awakening of Faith in Mahāyāna*

These debates and their ramifications dominated Chinese Buddhist thought in the sixth century. On one side was a substantialistic nondual metaphysic whose eternalistic ground was variously called Buddha-nature, mind, *tathāgatagarbha*, *Dharma-dhātu* and suchness (*tathatā*; in Chinese, *rulai*). On the other side was an anti-substantialist critique that eschewed any form of metaphysical reification, emphasizing emptiness as the absence of permanent selfhood or independent essence in anything. To the anti-substantialists the *tathāgatagarbha* position sounded dangerously close to the notion of eternalistic, reified selfhood that Buddha had rejected. Mahāyāna texts had declared that there were four conceptual perversions or reversals behind human delusion: (1) seeing a self in what lacks self; (2) seeing permanence in the impermanent; (3) seeing happiness in what is suffering; and (4) seeing purity in the impure. Yet starting with the earliest *tathāgatagarbha* texts – such as *The Lion's Roar of Queen Śrīmālā* – *tathāgatagarbha* was brazenly defined as 'self, eternal, happiness and pure'. In the face of these and other disparities, the Chinese asked how, if there is only one *dharma* (teaching), there can be such incommensurate variety.

The *Awakening of Faith in Mahāyāna*, a Chinese composition purporting to be a translation by Paramārtha of an Indian text, became an instant classic by offering a masterly synthesis of Buddhist teachings that seemed to resolve many of the disparities (see AWAKENING OF FAITH IN MAHĀYĀNA). Its central tenet is that there is one Mind that has two aspects. One aspect is suchness and the other is *saṃsāra*, the cycle of birth and death, arising and ceasing. Suchness also has two aspects, emptiness and non-empty. Emptiness in this text means suchness is beyond predication, neither one nor many, neither the same nor different. Non-empty means it is endowed with all the marvellous qualities and merits of a Buddha, 'as numerous as the sands along the banks of the Ganges'. The link between suchness and the realm of arising and ceasing is *tathāgatagarbha* in association with the *ālaya-vijñāna*. Ignorance, enlightenment and pursuit of the Path are all on the arising and ceasing side.

In a pivotal passage that would become foundational for most forms of Chinese, Korean and Japanese Buddhism, the *Awakening of Faith in Mahāyāna* states that on the basis of Original Enlightenment there is non-enlightenment; on the basis of non-enlightenment there is initial enlightenment; and on the basis of initial enlightenment there is final enlightenment, which is the full realization of original enlightenment. Beyond the problem of theodicy that it raises (the text does not offer a clear explanation for why or how non-enlightenment arises), several issues emerge. First, suddenly there is no longer simply one enlightenment that is achieved at the culmination of a spiritual path, but instead several enlightenments, one of which (original enlightenment) precedes even entering the path. What the text calls initial enlightenment had been termed *bodhicitta* or *cittotpāda* (arousing the aspiration for enlightenment) in previous Buddhist literature. Arousing this aspiration is what the title *Awakening of Faith in Mahāyāna* signifies. Now, rather than marking a singular, ultimate achievement, the term 'enlightenment' referred to several things: an atemporal originary ground upon which everything else plays out, including non-enlightenment; one's initial resolve or insight that leads one to begin pursuing the path; the final achievement at the end of the path, an achievement that is not only anticlimactic, but is little more than an unravelling of the intersection of original and initial enlightenment. This reinforced the conviction of Chinese Buddhists that the conflationist approach, with its emphasis on Buddha-nature or mind as ground, was the correct view.

One of the first to recognize the importance of the *Awakening of Faith in Mahāyāna* was a Korean monk named WŎNHYO. He wrote a commentary on the text that reached China, where it influenced FAZANG, a foundational thinker of the Huayan school, who used its ideas as a major cornerstone for his thinking. Since the *Dilun*, originally an independent text, had eventually been incorporated into the *Huayan Sutra* as one of its chapters, and that scripture became the basic text of the Huayan school, many of the issues that had emerged from the debates on the *Dilun* were absorbed and reconfigured by the Huayan thinkers. In a sense, it was ultimately Ratnamati's interpretation that prevailed after two centuries of debate. The *Awakening of Faith in Mahāyāna* became pivotal for

Chinese Buddhism, is still one of the foundations of Korean Buddhism and, though it has been eclipsed in Japan by other texts such as the *Lotus Sutra*, many of its ideas, such as the idea of original enlightenment (*hongaku*), still exert a profound influence. This text set the stage for the development of distinctively East Asian forms of Buddhism.

6 The Chinese Buddhist Schools

Although the ideas and literature of many different forms of Buddhism reached China – including Sarvāstivāda, Mahīśāsika, Saṃmitīya, Dharmaguptaka, Sautrāntika and others – only Madhyamaka and Yogācāra developed Chinese schools and lineages. Madhyamaka disappeared as an independent school after Jizang, but its influence and the preeminence of Nāgārjuna never abated. The sixth century was basically a battleground of competing Yogācāric theories.

In the seventh century the famous Chinese pilgrim Xuanzang (600–64) spent sixteen years travelling in Central Asia and India. He returned to China in 645 and translated seventy-four works. Due in part to his accomplishments as a traveller and translator, and in part to the eminent favour bestowed on him by the Chinese emperor upon his return, Xuanzang became the most prominent East Asian Buddhist of his generation. He promoted an orthodox form of Yogācāra as it was then being practised in India, and students flocked to him from Japan and Korea as well as China. Not everyone was enamoured of the Buddhist ideology he had brought back. Zhiyan (602–68), who would later be considered one of the patriarchs of the Huayan school, was openly critical of Xuanzang's teachings, and FAZANG had joined Xuanzang's translation committee late in Xuanzang's life, only to quit in disgust at Xuanzang's 'distorted' views. While in India, Xuanzang had discovered how far Chinese Buddhism had deviated from its Indian source, and his translations and teachings were deliberate attempts to bring Chinese Buddhism back in line with Indian teachings. The ideas he opposed (primarily but not exclusively those that had been promoted by Paramārtha's school) were already deeply entrenched in Chinese Buddhist thinking. While he was alive his pre-eminence made him unassailable, but once he died his detractors attacked his successor, Kuiji (632–82), and successfully returned Chinese and East Asian Buddhism to the trajectory established by the conflationists. (WŎNCH'ŬK, a Korean student of Xuanzang, was a rival of Kuiji who fared better with the revivalists since he attempted to harmonize the teachings of Paramārtha and Xuanzang.) The underlying ideology of this resurgence, which reached its intellectual apex over the course of the Tang and Song Dynasties (sixth–twelfth centuries), was neatly summarized by the label '*dharma*-nature' (*faxing*), that is, the metaphysical ground of Buddha-nature *qua dharma-dhātu qua* mind-nature *qua tathāgatagarbha*. Fazang argued that orthodox Yogācāra only understood *dharma* characteristics (*faxiang*), that is, phenomenal appearances, but not the deeper underlying metaphysical reality, '*dharma*-nature'. After Fazang, all the Sinitic Buddhist schools considered themselves *dharma*-nature schools; Yogācāra and sometimes Sanlun were considered merely *dharma* characteristics schools.

Four *dharma*-nature schools emerged. Each school eventually compiled a list of its patriarchs through whom its teachings were believed to have been transmitted. Modern scholarship in Japan and the West has shown that these lineages were usually forged long after the fact, and frequently were erroneous or distorted the actual historical events. For instance, while Huiyuan was an active promoter of the Sarvāstivādin teachings introduced during his time by Sanghadeva and Buddhabhadra, the later Pure Land schools dubbed him their initial Chinese patriarch on the basis of his alleged participation in Amitābha rituals, allegations that were probably first concocted during the Tang Dynasty. Similarly, the lineage of six Chan patriarchs from Bodhidharma to Huineng is unlikely; the Huayan lineage (Du Shun to Zhiyan to Fazang to Chengguan) was largely an invention of the 'fourth' patriarch, Chengguan: his predecessors were unaware that they were starting a new lineage and rather thought that they were reviving the true old-time religion of Paramārtha. It was also during the Tang dynasty that Tantra briefly passed through China, from whence it was brought to Japan and became firmly established as the Shingon school.

7 The Chinese Buddhist Schools: Tiantai

Though considered its third patriarch, the intellectual founder of the Tiantai school was ZHIYI (538–97). Responding to the proliferation of different Buddhist theories and practices, he proposed a masterly, detailed synthesis that definitively set Chinese Buddhism in its own direction. To the question of why there was an abundance of incommensurate teachings despite the fact that there could only be one *dharma*, Zhiyi replied that all the different vehicles of Buddhism were ultimately one vehicle (*eka-yāna*), an idea championed by the *Lotus Sutra*. More specifically, he offered a *panjiao*, or classificatory scheme of teachings, to explain the discrepancies. His *panjiao* was complex and brilliant (and further refined much

later by Chegwan, a Korean Tiantai monk in China), but in simple form it can be summarized as follows.

Buddha offered different teachings to different audiences based on the differing capacities of audiences to comprehend what he preached. According to the basic narrative, which became the way all Chinese Buddhists thought of Buddha's teaching career, upon reaching enlightenment under the Bodhi Tree, Buddha, enraptured by his new vision, began to describe that vision in immediate and exuberant terms. This became the *Huayan Sutra*. (In reality, this 'sutra' is a collection of disparate texts – none probably composed earlier than the third century AD – that were gradually compiled together over several more centuries.) When he finished (it took two or three weeks) he realized that no one had understood the sublime meaning of his words, and immediately began to teach a simplified, preparatory teaching which became the Hīnayāna teachings. After twenty years of preparatory teachings, he introduced the next level, beginners' Mahāyāna (basically Yogācāra and Madhyamaka). In the next period he introduced advanced Mahāyāna (the *Vaipūlya Sutras*), and finally in his last days, having now trained many advanced students, he preached the *Lotus Sutra* and the *Nirvāṇa Sutra*. In effect this *panjiao* asserts that the two highest sutras offered by Buddha were the *Huayan* and *Lotus*; but whereas the *Huayan* was too sublime to be understood by any save the most advanced or enlightened students, the *Lotus* represented Buddha's most comprehensive, cumulative, mature and accessible teaching, every bit as sublime as the *Huayan*, but now presented in a pedagogically effective manner. For that reason, Zhiyi made the *Lotus Sutra* the foundational text of Tiantai. As for the remaining teachings, as the *Lotus* itself explains, different 'truths' can be superseded once they have served their task of raising one to a higher level where a different 'truth' holds sway. Buddhism, according to the *Lotus* and Tiantai, is a system of expedient means (*upāya*) leading one with partial truths to ever greater, more comprehensive truths. Tiantai teachings are 'Round Teachings', meaning that they encircle or encompass everything and, lacking sharp edges, are therefore Perfect. Other forms of Buddhism are not 'wrong', but are only partial visions of the One Vehicle that Tiantai most perfectly and completely embodies.

Zhiyi, based on an exhaustive exposition of a verse from Nāgārjuna's *Madhyamaka-kārikās* (24: 18), devised a theory of three truths: provisional, empty and middle. The first two are mirror images of each other, two ways of speaking about causes and conditions. A table can provisionally be called a table, since its perceptible form has arisen through causes and conditions, and it only exists provisionally on the basis of those temporary conditions. The table is empty because, being the product of causes and conditions, it lacks its own intrinsic, independent nature. It is 'middle' because neither the provisional nor the empty truth about the table fully captures its reality. It is both provisional and empty, and simultaneously neither provisional nor empty. As Zhiyi put it, 'wondrous being is identical to true emptiness'. Zhiyi sought many ways to express the nondual middle truth. For instance, rejecting the obvious dualism of the distinction most of his contemporaries made between pure mind (*xin*) and deluded thought-instants (*nian*), Zhiyi declared that every deluded thought-instant was identical to three thousand chilicosms. The details of the formulas he used to arrive at the number three thousand is less important than fact that it is meant to encompass the full extent of Buddhist cosmological metaphysics. The whole universe in all its dimensions is entailed in every moment of thought. Rather than attempt to eliminate deluded thinking to reach a purified mind, Zhiyi claimed each moment of deluded thinking was already identical to enlightenment. One merely has to see the mind and its operations as they are. This idea was later taken over by the Chan (Zen) school, which expressed it in sayings such as 'Zen mind is everyday mind'.

The middle approach is also evident in the Tiantai notion of three gates, or three methods of access to enlightened vision: the Buddha-gate, the gate of sentient beings and the mind-gate. The Buddha-gate was considered too difficult, too abstruse, too remote; one had to be a Buddha already to fully comprehend it. The sentient-being gate (the various methods taught and practised by any sort of being) was also too difficult because there are too many different types of sentient beings all with their own types of delusions, so that this gate is a confusing cacophony of disparate methods, some which may not be appropriate for some beings. The easiest and hence preferable gate was the mind-gate. It is no more remote than this very moment of cognition, its diversity can be observed in every thought-instant, and nothing could ever be more appropriately suited for an individual than to observe one's own mind. Tiantai cultivated many types of meditation for that purpose.

8 The Chinese Buddhist Schools: Huayan

Drawing on a *panjiao* similar to that of Zhiyi, the Huayan school chose the *Huayan Sutra* (Sanskrit title *Avataṃsaka Sutra*, Chinese *Huayan jing*) for its foundational scripture. What immediately differentiates Huayan from typically Indian approaches is that instead of concentrating on a diagnosis of the human problem, and exhorting and prescribing solutions for it, Huayan immediately begins from the point of view of enlightenment. In other words, its discourse represents a nirvanic perspective rather than a samsaric perspective. Instead of detailing the steps that would lead one from ignorance to enlightenment, Huayan immediately endeavours to describe how everything looks through enlightened eyes.

Like Tiantai, Huayan offers a totalistic, encompassing 'round' view. A lived world as constituted through a form of life experience is called a *dharmadhātu*. Chengguan, the 'fourth' Huayan patriarch, described four types of *dharma-dhātus*, each successively encompassing its predecessors. The first is *shi*, which means 'event', 'affair' or 'thing'. This is the realm where things are experienced as discrete individual items. The second is called *li* (principle), which in Chinese usage usually implies the principal metaphysical order that subtends events as well as the rational principles that explicate that order. Often *li* is used by Buddhists as a synonym for emptiness. The first sustained analysis based on the relation of *li* and *shi* was undertaken by the Korean monk WŎNHYO in his commentary on the *Awakening of Faith in Mahāyāna*, which influenced early Huayan thinkers like FAZANG. The *li–shi* model went on to become an important analytic tool for all sorts of East Asian philosophers, not just Buddhists. In the realm of *li*, one clearly sees the principles that relate *shi* to each other, but the principles are more important than the individual events. In the third realm, one sees the mutual interpenetration or 'non-obstruction' of *li* and *shi* (*lishi wu'ai*). Rather than seeing events while being oblivious to principle, or concentrating on principle while ignoring events, in this realm events are seen as instantiations of principle, and principle is nothing more than the order by which events relate to each other.

In the fourth and culminating *dharma-dhātu*, one sees the mutual interpenetration and non-obstruction of all events (*shishi wu'ai*). In this realm, everything is causally related to everything else. Huayan illustrates this with the image of Indra's net, a vast net that encompasses the universe. A special jewel is found at the intersection of every horizontal and vertical weave in the net, special because each jewel reflects every other jewel in the net, so that looking into any one jewel, one sees them all. Every event or thing can disclose the whole universe because all mutually interpenetrate each other without barriers or obstruction.

This form of nondualism is not monistic because *shishi wu'ai* does not obliterate the distinctions between things, but rather insists that everything is connected to everything else *without* losing distinctiveness. Identity and difference, in this view, are merely two sides of the same coin, which, though a single coin, still has two distinct sides that should not be confused for each other. Mutual interpenetration is temporal as well as spatial; past, present and future mutually interpenetrate. Hence according to Huayan, to enter the path towards final enlightenment is, in an important sense, to have already arrived at that destination.

9 The Chinese Buddhist Schools: Chan

Better known in the West by its Japanese pronunciation, Zen, Chan emerged as a reaction against the increasing scholastic complexities of the Tiantai and Huayan schools and their voluminous, hairsplitting literature, which, some Chan practitioners believed, could be more of an obstacle than an aid to enlightenment. The Pāli term for meditative absorption, *jhāna* (Sanskrit, *dhyāna*), was transliterated into Chinese as *Channa*, and then shortened to *Chan*. Until the early Tang Dynasty, *chanshi* (Chan master) meant a monk adept at meditation, though it did not specify what sorts of meditation he was practising. Some monks were called *dharma* masters (*fashi*), some were called scriptural masters (*zangshi*), some were called disciplinary masters (*lushi*) and some were meditation masters. These titles could be applied to a monk (or nun) of any school, since they denoted one's methodological focus rather than one's ideological leanings.

Chan begins to denote a specific doctrinal and meditative ideology around the time of Huineng (638–713). Although Chan tradition describes a transmission by five patriarchs culminating in Huineng as the sixth patriarch, as noted above, that transmission is more fiction than fact. Huineng's followers established the Southern School of Chan, which unleashed a polemical tirade against the Northern School. Since the Northern School disappeared about a thousand years ago, our only source of information on these schools was the prejudiced accounts of the Southern School, until the discovery at Dunhuang early this century of Northern School documents. We now know that many different versions of lineage histories were circulated, and, more importantly, that the positions attributed to the Northerners by their Southern rivals were grossly inaccurate and unfair. In fact, the Northern School had initially been the more successful of the two, but its success led to its ultimate ruin, since its growing dependence on Imperial patronage made it a vulnerable target during times of Imperial persecution of Buddhism. The Southern School, because it had

taken root in remote areas less affected by actions of the Central government, survived the persecutions relatively intact.

Huineng is depicted in the *Platform Sutra* (authored by his leading follower and promoter, Shenhui) as an illiterate seller of firewood who experiences sudden enlightenment while overhearing someone reciting the *Diamond Sutra*. He joins a monastery where, without any official training in scriptures or meditation, he demonstrates that his enlightenment is more profound than all the monks who had been practising for years. Hence sudden enlightenment is one of the main tenets of the *Platform Sutra* (and subsequently for all forms of Chan). Another is 'direct pointing at mind', which, similar to the Tiantai approach, means that what is important is to observe one's own mind, to recognize that the nature of one's mind is Buddha-nature itself (see PLATFORM SUTRA).

While some Buddhists had argued that the goal was wisdom, and meditation was merely a means to that goal, Huineng argued for the inseparability of meditation and wisdom. Using an analytic device probably introduced by the so-called neo-Daoist Wang Bi (226–49), the *tiyong* model (see TI AND YONG), Huineng claimed that meditation is the essence (*ti*) of wisdom, and wisdom is the function (*yong*) of meditation. Wisdom does not produce meditation, nor does meditation produce wisdom; nor are meditation and wisdom different from each other. He drew an analogy to a lamp: the lamp is the *ti*, while its light is the *yong*. Wherever there is a (lit) lamp, there is light; wherever there is lamplight, there is a lamp. Lamp and light are different in name but identical in substance (*ti*), hence nondual.

Huineng's style of Chan was still sober, calm, rational, and rooted in commonly accepted Buddhist tenets. New and more radical elements were soon incorporated into Chan, some iconoclastically renouncing meditation and practice as well as scholasticism, and others trying earnestly to work out a rational system by which Chan could be syncretized with the other schools. ZONGMI (780–841) considered a patriarch of both the Chan and Huayan schools, attempted just such a synthesis, but his sober approach was soon overshadowed in China by more abrupt, startling forms of Chan.

Of the 'Five Houses of Chan', only the Linji school survives today in China, Taiwan and Korea. Based on the teachings of LINJI (d. 867), this school possibly provided Buddhism with its most 'Chinese' voice. Chan literature of the Linji and related schools were among the first texts ever written in vernacular as opposed to classical Chinese. Daoist elements also began to appear prominently. Zhuangzi's 'true man' becomes Linji's 'true man of no rank' who is going in and out of each person's face this very moment, and is always right here before one. The anecdotal humour associated with Zhuangzi's stories and the irreverent exploits of the Bamboo Sages of the Six Dynasties period clearly infused the style of Chan anecdotes. Rather than indulge in elaborate, complicated theoretical abstractions, Chan focused on experience as lived, in terms familiar to anyone immersed in Chinese culture (though often exotic to Western students, which has led to the common misconception that Chan is nonsensical or obscurantist).

Teaching techniques began to overshadow doctrinal content. At the heart of Chan training are the exchanges between teacher and student. Records, called *gongan*, were compiled of classic encounters, and even these eventually became part of the teaching techniques, as they were presented to students as riddles to concentrate on during meditation. To disrupt the sort of idle or pernicious speculation that could prove a hindrance to enlightenment, abrupt and shocking techniques were employed, from radical statements such as, 'If you meet Buddha on the road, kill him!', to exchanges punctuated by blows and shouts (all the more startling in the subdued monastic atmosphere in which they would unexpectedly occur). Linji's methods were designed to make students confront and overcome their mental and emotional habits and crutches, so as to become truly free and independent. Even dependency on Buddhism could be such a crutch. Linji summarized his teaching with the phrase: 'Don't be deceived.'

10 The Chinese Buddhist Schools: Pure Land

All forms of Chinese Buddhism, including Chan, contain devotional elements and rituals, but for Pure Land Buddhists devotionalism is the essence. The origins of Pure Land Buddhism are somewhat unclear. While undoubtedly devotional practices were imported to China by monks and laity (and these were blended with native Chinese forms of devotionalism), there does not seem to be a distinct school in India devoted to rebirth in Amitābha's Pure Land. As noted earlier, the traditional lineages are not very helpful for reconstructing the school's history. According to tradition, early contributors to Pure Land thought and practice include Tanluan (476–542), Dao Chuo (562–645) and his student Shandao (613–81). The term 'Pure Land' (*jingtu*) may itself be largely a product of certain license taken by translators. The term *jingtu* appears in Kumārajīva's translation of the *Vimalakīrti Sutra* where the Tibetan version simply has 'Buddha lands' (the Sanskrit version is no longer extant). Apparently, Xuanzang was the first explicitly

to associate Sukhāvatī (Amitābha's Paradise) with the term 'pure land'. The main scriptures for Pure Land practice were the Larger and Smaller *Sukhāvatī-vyuha Sutras* and the *Guan Wuliangshoufo jing*.

At the beginning of the Tang Dynasty, several forms of Buddhist devotionalism were popular, including cults devoted to Mañjuśrī (Bodhisattva of Wisdom), Guanyin (Bodhisattva of Compassion, at that time particularly popular as a patron saint and protector of travellers), Maitreya (the future Buddha) and Amita (a conflation of Amitābha and Amitāyus whose names mean 'Infinite Light' and 'Infinite Life' respectively, and are possibly deities of Central Asian origin). Arguably the most popular form of devotionalism was the Maitreya cult. The Empress Wu (r. 683–705), a great patron of Buddhism but generally reviled in Chinese history as an unscrupulous usurper, considered herself an incarnation of Maitreya. Due to her unpopularity once dethroned, people wanted to distance themselves from her and anything associated with her. Unfortunately this effectively extinguished Maitreya worship in China. Worshippers of Amita filled the void.

Pure Land theology maintained that people were living in the age of degenerate *dharma*, when study and personal effort were insufficient for making progress on the path to liberation. Relying on one's own efforts was in fact deemed a form of self-theory, or the selfishness and arrogance that comes from erroneous views of self. Rather than indulge in egoistic fantasies, one ought to rely on the power and grace of Amita. Amita was a *buddha* (whether he was an earlier incarnation of the historical Buddha or another person altogether is answered differently by different Pure Land sources) who, while still a *bodhisattva*, vowed to help sentient beings once he became a *buddha*. He has the power to transfer to anyone he deems worthy sufficient merit to enable them to be born in his Pure Land, the Western Paradise. In the earliest forms of Pure Land devotionalism a variety of practices were cultivated, but these were eventually pared down to chanting the *nianfo*, literally 'remembrance of Buddhas' (in Sanskrit, *buddhānusmṛti*), which in Chinese is 'Na-mu A-mi-to Fo' (Hail Amita Buddha).

11 Sinicizing Buddhist concepts

Since the time of MENCIUS, the ultimate ontological issue in China was the question of human nature and mind (which Mencius and most Chinese thinkers treated as synonyms). Pre-Han Chinese philosophers had debated whether human nature was originally good, bad or neutral. The written Chinese character for 'nature', *xing*, consists of two parts: the left side means 'mind' and the right side means 'birth', which led Chinese thinkers to debate whether human nature was determined by what one is born with, namely appetites and desires, or whether it reflects the nature of one's mind, which in Chinese thought invariably carried an onto-ethical rather than strictly cognitive connotation. The word *xin* literally means 'heart', indicating that – unlike Western conceptions that draw a sharp line between the head and the heart – for the Chinese, thinking and feeling originated in the same bodily locus. Feeling empathy or compassion as well as rationally abstracting principles and formulating ethical codes were all activities of *xin*, heart-and-mind (see XIN; XING).

Indian Buddhism had little to say about human nature, with many forms of Buddhism rejecting the very concept of essential nature. Some of the early polemics against Buddhism in China explicitly attacked it for neglecting to address the question of human nature. The notion of Buddha-nature was developed, in part, to redress that failing. Since Indian Buddhists were deeply interested in the mind in terms of cognitive processes such as perception, thinking, attention and so on (see MIND, INDIAN PHILOSOPHY OF; SENSE PERCEPTION, INDIAN VIEWS OF), it was a natural step for the Chinese to read these initially in the light of the Chinese discourse on mind, and to further develop interpretations of this material in line with Chinese concerns. Hence passages that in Sanskrit dealt primarily with epistemology or cognitive conditions often became, in their Chinese renderings, psycho-moral descriptions. The Sanskrit term *ekacitta*, a mind with singular focus (but literally meaning 'one mind') becomes the metaphysical one mind of the *Awakening of Faith in Mahāyāna*. Similarly, Indian and Chinese philosophers had developed very different types of causal theories. Indian Buddhists accepted only efficient causes as real, while Chinese Buddhists tended to interpret Buddhist causal theories as examples of formal causes.

12 Sinicizing Buddhist concepts: emptiness

Before Buddhism entered China Daoists had already embraced a notion of emptiness which it took Buddhists several centuries to realize was significantly different from their own (see DAOIST PHILOSOPHY). Laozi had contrasted the empty or open (*xu*) with the solid. What made a wheel functional was its empty hub; what made a vessel or room functional was its open space. Hence emptiness (or openness) is not worthless but rather the key to functionality and usefulness (see DAODEJING). Later Daoists contrasted existents (*you*) with nonexistence (*wu*), and claimed

that all existence emerges from nonexistence and ultimately returns to nonexistence (see YOU-WU). Some Chinese metaphysicians, such as Wang Bi, wrote about primordial nonexistence (*yuan wu, benwu*) as the metaphysical source, destination and substratum for all existent things. Thus form and emptiness were opposed, contrasting poles, and emptiness had primacy.

Some early Chinese Buddhists interpreted Buddhist emptiness in the same fashion, especially in the Prajñā schools. Eventually Buddhists realized, as the *Heart Sutra* says, that form and emptiness are not opposed to each other, but that 'form itself is emptiness, emptiness itself *is* form, form is not different from emptiness, emptiness is not different from form.' In other words, Buddhist 'emptiness' did not mean 'open' or 'nonexistence'. Emptiness (*śūnyatā*) signified the absence of an eternal, independent, self-causing, invariant, essential self-nature (*svabhāva*) or selfhood (*ātman*) in any thing or person. Whatever existed did so by virtue of a perpetually changing web of causes and conditions that themselves were products of other causes and conditions. Stated simplistically, emptiness does not mean that a table is unreal or nonexistent, or that its solid texture or colour are unreal; it does mean that the concept of tableness is unreal, and that the abstractions 'solidity' and 'colour' are unreal apart from the discrete and particular sensations one has at specific moments due to specific causes and conditions. Buddhist emptiness is not a primal void, but the absence of self-essence (see BUDDHIST CONCEPT OF EMPTINESS). To avoid being confused with Daoist concepts of emptiness, the Buddhists eventually chose a new term, *kong*, to render their 'emptiness'.

Emptiness is neither the origin nor terminus for forms; forms themselves at any moment are emptiness. Since everything is causally connected with everything else, and there are no independent identities beyond or behind such causes and conditions, everything, according to Huayan, mutually interpenetrates and conditions everything else. Every thing defines and is defined by every other thing.

13 Sinicizing Buddhist concepts: suffering and ignorance

For all forms of Indian Buddhism, the fundamental fact with which Buddhism begins, and the problem it attempts to solve, is the problem of suffering (*duḥkha*). The first of the Four Noble Truths is: 'All is suffering.' Suffering does not mean simply pain. Buddhism does not deny joy, pleasure, delight and so on; but it claims that all is impermanent, so that whatever the source of a particular pleasure, that pleasure can never be permanent. The more pleasure one feels, the greater becomes one's attachment to the presumed source. The greater the attachment, the greater the pain at the loss of that pleasure. Since everything is impermanent, such loss is inevitable. So, ironically, pleasure itself is 'suffering'. Suffering is the affective reaction to impermanence. According to general Buddhist causal analysis, the causes of suffering are desire and ignorance. We desire permanent pleasures because we are ignorant of the fact that all is impermanent, empty of eternal selfhood. As the Four Noble Truths state, these causes of suffering can be eliminated, and Buddhism is the method or path for eliminating those causes. The purpose of Buddhism, then, is the elimination of suffering.

Chinese Buddhist texts do occasionally mention suffering, but usually in passing. Instead the root problem became ignorance. Discussions of the dialectical conflict between ignorance and enlightenment grew so pervasive that suffering was all but forgotten. This shift helped reinforce the emphasis on mind and mind-nature. Enlightenment was no longer defined as awakening to the causes of suffering, but instead denoted seeing the nature of the mind itself (see SUFFERING, BUDDHIST VIEWS OF ORIGINATION OF).

14 Sinicizing Buddhist concepts: is Buddha-nature good or evil?

The pre-Han debate about whether human nature is good, evil or neutral was echoed in debates between Chinese Buddhists about Buddha-nature. Huayan contended that Buddha-nature and *tathāgatagarbha* were pristinely pure and good, filled with infinite good merits and qualities. In the fully realized perfection of Buddha-nature all evil, impurities and delusions have been eradicated.

This position was opposed by Tiantai, which argued that some evil (that is, some ignorance) remains in Buddha-nature. Following the Daoist sense of nonduality, in which good and evil or pure and impure are complimentary opposites as impossible to separate from each other as East from West, Tiantai accused Huayan of dualistic extremism. From the Tiantai perspective, Huayan's 'obsession' with purity and goodness was one-sided and dualistic. Moreover, Tiantai insisted that it is necessary for Buddha-nature to retain some traces of evil and delusion in order to understand and empathize with the plight of ordinary sentient beings. If one becomes too rarefied, too transcendent, one loses touch with the everyday reality in which people wander deludedly, and thus one becomes incapable of effectively saving such people. Buddhahood, for Tiantai, was not simply a matter of correctly seeing or understanding

in a 'pure' way, but was at its core salvific; Buddhahood is the active liberation of sentient beings from ignorance.

The debate on Buddha-nature heated up during the Song Dynasty. Heterodox forms of Tiantai tinged with Huayan's 'purity obsession' appeared, and these were challenged sharply by the orthodox Tiantai thinkers from their headquarters on Tiantai mountain (from which the school took its name). The heterodox schools were labeled the Off-Mountain groups, while the orthodoxy styled itself the On-Mountain group. Zhili (959–1028), one of the On-Mountain leaders, had a keen intellect alert to the subtlest hints of Huayan-like thinking lurking in the rhetoric of Off-Mountain thinkers; his writings systematically ferret out and refute those implications with a logical sophistication rarely equalled amongst Chinese Buddhist philosophers.

These debates gain additional importance when viewed in the larger context of Chinese intellectual history. In the pre-Han period, Mencius' contention that human nature is originally good did not prove persuasive. Others argued that human nature was essentially neutral and subject to the influence of external conditions. Another early Confucian, XUNZI, had argued that human nature was basically selfish and greedy, which is why human society needs sages such as CONFUCIUS to guide them beyond the baseness of their own nature (see XING). Han Confucians sided with Xunzi rather Mencius. The Tiantai position, by insisting that some evil and ignorance exists even in Buddha-nature, was close to some readings of Xunzi's position, while the idealistic optimism of the Huayan view clearly showed parallels with Mencius. Between the Han and Song Dynasties (third through tenth centuries), Confucianism was by and large intellectually stagnant. It found new vitality in the Song in part by reabsorbing back into itself the elements it had 'lent' to the Buddhists (and to some extent Daoists as well). The elements they took back had been modified and expanded by the Buddhists, and given metaphysical foundations that the neo-Confucians retained and continued to rework. Neo-Confucian thinkers, especially after ZHU XI (1130–1200), rediscovered Mencius and unanimously embraced his view of the original goodness of human nature. Looked at another way, neo-Confucianism adopted Huayan's metaphysics of nature. Zhu Xi's famous dialectic of principle (*li*) and 'material-energy' (*qi*) owed more than a little to Huayan's *li* and *shi* metaphysics (see LI; QI).

See also: AWAKENING OF FAITH IN MAHĀYĀNA; BUDDHIST PHILOSOPHY, INDIAN; BUDDHIST PHILOSOPHY, JAPANESE; BUDDHIST PHILOSOPHY,

KOREAN; CHINESE PHILOSOPHY; DAOIST PHILOSOPHY; FAZANG; LINJI; NEO-CONFUCIAN PHILOSOPHY; PLATFORM SUTRA; SENG ZHAO; ÛISANG; WÔNCH'ǓK; WÔNHYO; ZHI DUN; ZHIYI; ZONGMI

References and further reading

Buswell, R. (ed.) (1990) *Chinese Buddhist Apocrypha*, Honolulu, HI: University of Hawaii Press. (An important collection of essays detailing the impact of apocryphal texts – Chinese creations purporting to represent Indian originals – on the development of Chinese Buddhism.)

Ch'en, K. (1964) *Buddhism in China*, Princeton, NJ: Princeton University Press. (Though somewhat dated, still a classic overview of the early history of Buddhism in China.)

—— (1973) *The Chinese Transformation of Buddhism*, Princeton, NJ: Princeton University Press. (Another dated classic.)

Cook, F. (1977) *Hua-yen Buddhism: The Jewel Net of Indra*, University Park, PA: Pennsylvania State University Press. (A good introduction to basic Huayan doctrine.)

Gimello, R. (1976) 'Chih-yen (602–668) and the Foundations of Hua-yen Buddhism', Ph.D. dissertation, Columbia University. (Though unpublished, this remains the best historical analysis available in English of Chinese Buddhism in the sixth and seventh centuries.)

Gregory, P. (1995) *Inquiry Into the Origin of Humanity: An Annotated Translation of Tsung-mi's Yüan-jen lun with a Modern Commentary*, Honolulu, HI: Kuroda Institute and University of Hawaii Press. (A translation of an important Chinese text, richly annotated by Gregory, who intends this book as a survey and primer of Chinese Buddhist thought for intermediate students.)

Hurvitz, L. (1960–2) *Chih-I (538–597): An Introduction to the Life and Ideas of a Chinese Buddhist Monk*, Mélanges chinois et bouddhiques vol. 12. (A thorough overview of the foundational Tiantai thinker, Zhiyi.)

Liu Ming-wood (1994) *Madhyamaka Thought in China*, Leiden: Brill. (Useful discussion of the key developments in Chinese Madhyamaka, especially Liu's treatment of Jizang.)

Robinson, R. (1967) *Early Mādhyamika in India and China*, Madison, WI: University of Wisconsin Press. (Classic work, detailing the efforts of Kumārajīva and his contemporaries.)

Swanson, P. (1989) *The Philosophy of T'ien-t'ai*, Berkeley, CA: Asian Humanities Press. (Important historical overview of the texts and issues that lead to Zhiyi's distinctive philosophy, with a partial translation of one of Zhiyi's discussions of the *Lotus Sutra* that serves as a good example of the dense textual style of this form of Buddhism.)

Wright, A. (1990) *Studies in Chinese Buddhism*, ed. R. Somers, New Haven, CT: Yale University Press. (Essays dealing with important people and issues during the formative years of Buddhism in China.)

Yampolsky, P. (1967) *The Platform Sutra of the Sixth Patriarch*, New York: Columbia University Press. (Yampolsky's translation of this Chan sutra is somewhat problematic, but his introductory essays demonstrate the importance of critical historical methods for approaching this material.)

Zürcher, E. (1959) *The Buddhist Conquest of China*, Leiden: Brill, 2 vols. (Another classic, dealing with the formative periods of Chinese Buddhism.)

DAN LUSTHAUS

BUDDHIST PHILOSOPHY IN TIBET *see* TIBETAN PHILOSOPHY

BUDDHIST PHILOSOPHY, INDIAN

Buddhism was an important ingredient in the philosophical melange of the Indian subcontinent for over a millennium. From an inconspicuous beginning a few centuries before Christ, Buddhist scholasticism gained in strength until it reached a peak of influence and originality in the latter half of the first millennium. Beginning in the eleventh century, Buddhism gradually declined and eventually disappeared from northern India. Although different individual thinkers placed emphasis on different issues, the tendency was for most writers to offer an integrated philosophical system that incorporated ethics, epistemology and metaphysics. Most of the issues addressed by Buddhist philosophers in India stem directly from the teachings attributed to Siddhārtha Gautama, known better through his honorific title, the Buddha.

The central concern of the Buddha was the elimination of unnecessary discontent. His principal insight into this problem was that all dissatisfaction arises because people (and other forms of life as well) foster desires and aversions, which are in turn the consequence of certain misunderstandings about their identity. Discontent can be understood as frustration, or a failure to achieve what one wishes; if one's wishes are generally unrealistic and therefore unattainable, then one will naturally be generally dissatisfied. Since the Buddha saw human frustration as an effect of misunderstandings concerning human nature, it was natural for Buddhist philosophers to attend to questions concerning the true nature of a human being. Since the Buddha himself was held as the paradigm of moral excellence, it was also left to later philosophers to determine what kind of being the Buddha had been. A typical question was whether his example was one that ordinary people could hope to follow, or whether his role was in some way more than that of a teacher who showed other people how to improve themselves.

The Buddha offered criticisms of many views on human nature and virtue and duty held by the teachers of his age. Several of the views that he opposed were based, at least indirectly, on notions incorporated in the Veda, a body of liturgical literature used by the Brahmans in the performance of rituals. Later generations of Buddhists spent much energy in criticizing Brahmanical claims of the supremacy of the Veda; at the same time, Buddhists tended to place their confidence in a combination of experience and reason. The interest in arriving at correct understanding through correct methods of reasoning led to a preoccupation with questions of logic and epistemology, which tended to overshadow all other philosophical concerns during the last five centuries during which Buddhism was an important factor in Indian philosophy.

Since the Buddha saw human frustration as an effect that could be eliminated if its cause were eliminated, it was natural for Buddhist philosophers to focus their attention on a variety of questions concerning causality. How many kinds of cause are there? Can a multiplicity of effects have a single cause? Can a single thing have a multiplicity of causes? How is a potentiality triggered into an actuality? Questions concerning simplicity and complexity, or unity and plurality, figured prominently in Buddhist discussions of what kinds of things in the world are ultimately real. In a tradition that emphasized the principle that all unnecessary human pain and conflict can ultimately be traced to a failure to understand what things in the world are real, it was natural to seek criteria by which one discerns real things from fictions.

1 **Human nature**
2 **Ethics**
3 **Buddha-nature**
4 **Epistemology**
5 **Metaphysics**

1 **Human nature**

A key tenet of Buddhist doctrine is that discontent is an outcome of desires grounded in false beliefs. The most important of these false beliefs are that (1) one's own individual existence is more important than those of other individuals, and that (2) fulfilment can be achieved by acquiring and owning property. If these misunderstandings can be replaced by an accurate view of human nature, suggested the Buddha, then unrealistic craving and ambition will cease, and so will frustration. Happiness, in other words, can be achieved by learning to recognize that (1) no one is more important than anyone else, since all beings ultimately have the same nature, and that (2) the very idea of ownership is at the root of all conflicts among living beings. The methods by which one achieves contentment, according to the Buddha, are both intellectual and practical. One can gradually become free of the kinds of beliefs that cause unnecessary pain to oneself and others by carefully observing one's own feelings and thoughts, and how one's own words and actions affect others. To counter the view that one's own individual existence is more important than the existence of other beings, Buddhist philosophers adopted the radical strategy of trying to show that in fact human beings do not have selves or individual identities. That is, an attempt was made to show that there is nothing about a person that remains fixed throughout a lifetime, and also that there is nothing over which one ultimately has real control. Failure to accept the instability, fragmentation and uncontrollability of one's body and mind is seen as a key cause of frustration of the sort that one could avoid by accepting things as they really are. On the other hand, realizing that all beings of all kinds are liable to change and ultimately to die enables one to see that all beings have the same fundamental destiny. This, combined with the recognition that all living beings strive for happiness and wellbeing, is an important stage on the way to realizing that no individual's needs, including one's own, are more worthy of consideration than any other's.

The notion that one does not have an enduring self has two aspects, one personal and the other social. At the personal level, the person is portrayed in Buddhist philosophy as a complex of many dozens of physical and mental events, rather than as a single feature of some kind that remains constant while all peripheral features undergo change. Since these constituent events are incessantly undergoing change, it follows that the whole that is made up of these constituents is always taking on at least some difference in nature. Whereas people might tend to see themselves as having fixed personalities and characters, the Buddha argued it is always possible for people either to improve their character through mindful striving, or to let it worsen through negligence and obliviousness.

Looking at the social aspects of personal identity, the Buddha maintained, in contrast to other views prevalent in his day, that a person's station in human society need not be determined by birth. According to the view prevalent in ancient and classical Indian society, a person's duties, responsibilities and social rank were determined by levels of ritual purity; these were in turn influenced by pedigree and gender and various other factors that remained constant throughout a person's lifetime. In criticizing this view, Buddhist philosophers redefined the notions of purity and nobility, replacing the concept of purity by birth with that of purity by action (karma) (see KARMA AND REBIRTH, INDIAN CONCEPTIONS OF §5). Thus the truly noble person, according to Buddhist standards, was not one who had a pure and revered ancestry, but rather one who habitually performed pure and benevolent actions.

Given these basic ideas of human nature as a starting point, later generations of Buddhist thinkers were left with the task of explaining the mechanisms by which all the components of a person work together; this also involved trying to explain how human beings can gradually change their character. While there was general agreement on the principle that the intentions behind one's actions led eventually to resultant mental states, that benevolent actions resulted in a sense of wellbeing, while malevolent actions resulted in uneasiness and vexation, the precise details of how karmic causality took place were a matter of much dispute. Especially difficult was the question of how actions committed in one lifetime could influence the character of a person in a different lifetime, for Buddhists accepted the notion of rebirth that was common in Indian systems of thought. Discussions of how people could improve their character presuppose that the people in question have not become irreversibly depraved. One controversy that arose among Buddhist thinkers was whether there are beings who become so habitually perverse that they can no longer even aspire to improve their character; if so, then such beings would apparently be heir to an unending cycle of rebirths.

The view of the person as a set of interconnected modules, the precise contents of which were always changing, was characterized by Buddhists as avoiding the untenability of two other hypotheses that one might form about human nature. One hypothesis is that a person has some essential core that remains unchanged through all circumstances. This core survives the death of the physical body and goes on to acquire a new body through a process of reincarnation. According to this view, the unchanging essential part of a person is eternal. The second hypothesis is that a person takes on an identity at birth and carries it through life but loses the identity altogether at death. The Buddhist view, characterized as a middle way between these two extremes, is that a person's character is always in flux, and that the factors that determine the particular changes in a person's mentality continue to operate even after the body housing that mentality dies. So Buddhists tended to claim that what goes from one living body to another is not an unchanging essence, but rather a set of tendencies to behave in certain ways.

2 Ethics

The strongest motivation for accepting the doctrine of rebirth was to support the notion that people are accountable for their actions to the very end of their lives; the doctrine thus plays a central role in Buddhist ethical theory. It was noted in the preceding section that the Buddhist view of the person was described as a middle path between two equally untenable extremes. In the realm of conduct also, the Buddhists described theirs as a middle path or a moderate position that avoided extreme views of human conduct. In order to understand the various positions against which the Buddhists defined their views on appropriate conduct, it should be borne in mind that the central question being asked by the Buddha and his contemporaries was how to achieve contentment. The strategies recommended by different thinkers were closely related to their views of life after death. Those who held that a person has only one life tended to argue that one's life should be spent in the pursuit of as much pleasure as is possible without bringing pain and injury to oneself. Restraint in the pursuit of pleasure was seen as necessary only to the extent that excessive indulgence might shorten one's life and decrease one's opportunities for future pleasure seeking.

Philosophers who accepted the doctrine of rebirth, on the other hand, tended to argue that the only kind of happiness worth pursuing was lasting freedom from the pains and turmoil of life; this could be won only by bringing rebirth to an end. After death, they said, all living beings are eventually reborn in a form of life determined by the accumulated effects of deeds done in previous lives. Although some forms of life might be very pleasant and offer a temporary reward for previous good actions, every form of life involves some amount of pain and suffering, even if it is only an anxiety that one's present peace and happiness will eventually come to an end and be replaced by more direct forms of physical and mental pain. Therefore, the only hope of any lasting freedom from the pains of existence is to remove oneself from the cycle of birth and death altogether. Exactly how this was to be achieved was a matter of much controversy, but some drastic methods involved undergoing extreme forms of austerity and even self-inflicted pain. The Buddhist middle path, therefore, was one that avoided two extremes: one extreme was the self-indulgence of those who denied life after death altogether, and the other was the self-torture recommended by some ascetics as the only way to gain freedom.

Buddhist philosophers tended to agree that a person's mentality at any given moment is either virtuous, vicious or neutral. This means that all of one's mental characteristics in a given moment have the same orientation, which is either towards a state of happiness, the natural consequence of virtue, or towards a state of discontent, the natural consequence of vice. The principal virtues that were said to cooperate in a healthy mentality were correct understanding, which manifested itself as a sense of shame, and a sense of decency, usually interpreted as respect for oneself and respect for others. Thus if one has the virtue of having a sense of shame, then while that sense of shame is functioning, one will also have the virtues of being generous, free of malice and open-minded; having these virtues makes one likely to behave in ways that conduce to the health of oneself and others. If, on the other hand, one has the vice of being shameless, then one will also have the vices of being deluded and agitated and therefore prone to behave in ways likely to bring harm to oneself and others. While virtuous and vicious mental qualities cannot be present in the same mentality at the same moment, it could very well be that a person vacillates between virtuous and vicious frames of mind. Indeed, this is said to be the condition of the vast majority of living beings (see DUTY AND VIRTUE, INDIAN CONCEPTIONS OF §3; VIRTUES AND VICES).

Despite a tendency to agree on these basic matters, Buddhist philosophers disagreed with one another over several other questions. There was, for example, controversy over whether people could arrive at stages of attainment from which they could never backslide. Some argued that once people gained certain insights into reality, then they could no longer be deluded in the ways that result in acting on self-centred motivations. Others argued that, even if backsliding might be unlikely for some people, it is in principle always possible, and therefore a person can never afford to be complacent. Another controversy arose over whether a vicious person could be fully aware of a virtuous person's virtues, some Buddhists holding the view that only a virtuous person can recognize that another person is also virtuous. Yet another matter of controversy had to do with whether the merit of being virtuous could be transferred to others. Some argued that each person is strictly accountable for their own actions and that no one can escape the ill effects of their intentionally harmful actions. Others claimed that merit can be transferred to others, enabling them to experience levels of happiness that they could never have deserved on the merit of their own actions. Closely tied to this controversy was the question mentioned above, concerning whether some beings fall into such states of depravity that they can no longer even aspire to be good. Those philosophers who accepted that beings could become depraved to this extent but denied that merit can be transferred had to conclude that some beings would never attain *nirvāṇa* (see NIRVĀṆA). Other philosophers, for whom the prospect of eternal suffering in the cycle of birth seemed unjust, favoured the doctrine that merit could be transferred, thus enabling these thoroughly depraved beings to undergo the change of mentality necessary to begin leading a life of virtue.

3 Buddha-nature

Even in the earliest strata of Buddhist literature that has survived to the present, the Buddha is portrayed in a variety of ways. Some passages depict him as a man who skilfully answers questions that have been put to him, either by answering the questions or by showing why the question as asked cannot be answered. The passages were clearly designed to portray the Buddha as a paragon of wisdom, whose careful and analytic thinking could be used as a model for those seeking to arrive at correct understanding. The Buddha is also portrayed as a model of virtue, a man who has mastered the art of living in the world without bringing harm to other living beings and whose concern for the welfare of all living things around him is unsurpassed. Interspersed with these passages that focus on the Buddha as a remarkable man, there are other passages that portray the Buddha as a superhuman miracle worker whose mastery of yogic technique has given him the power to travel hundreds of kilometres in the blink of an eye, transport himself and his followers through the air, know the precise thoughts of other people, see into the past and future, heal serious wounds merely by looking at them, and soothe wild and dangerous animals by merely speaking gently to them. Some texts show him inviting his followers to question everything he says and to accept nothing on his authority; in other passages, he is portrayed as a man to whom even the wisest and most knowledgeable gods come so that the profound mysteries of the universe can be explained to them in clear words. Given the diversity of things said about the Buddha in the texts that Buddhists regarded as authoritative, it is no wonder that among the points about which there was considerable controversy was the nature of the Buddha himself. Discussions about the nature of the Buddha were as important to some Buddhist philosophers as discussions about the nature of God were to the theologians of theistic traditions (see BUDDHA).

The earliest extant record of controversies concerning the nature of the Buddha is a work known as *Kathāvatthu* (Points of Controversy), supposed to have been written around 246 BC by an elder monk known as Tissa Moggalīputta. This treatise mentions over two hundred topics over which there was controversy among Buddhists, of which several pertain to the nature of the Buddha. According to this text, some Buddhists held to the view that the Buddha pervades all regions of space at all times and has the power to suspend all the laws of nature at will; others argued that the Buddha exists only where his human body is located and that he is bound by all the natural laws by which other living beings are bound. Those who accepted the Buddha as a ubiquitous and eternal entity tended to claim that the human Buddha was merely a manifestation in human form that appeared for the sake of guiding human beings. This apparition, they claimed, had no real need for food and shelter or other material requirements of life, but it accepted such gifts from devotees so that they might learn the benefits of generosity. Moreover, this apparition was said to be wholly lacking any of the unpleasant physical or mental traits of a human being and never had any thoughts that were not directed at teaching people how to cultivate virtue and attain *nirvāṇa*. Other Buddhists rejected this view of the Buddha altogether and argued that he was a mortal just like all other mortals, except that among the limited range of topics about which he had knowledge was the important matter of how to achieve lasting peace and happiness. This issue was controverted for over a millennium in India, with Dharmakīrti and some of his followers taking up the view of the Buddha as an ordinary mortal, while some members of the Yogācāra movement took up the position that the Buddha was more of a cosmic principle; the eleventh-century Buddhist Ratnakīrti eventually argued that all particular acts of individual awareness are merely parts of a single, universal consciousness, which he identified as the mind of the Buddha (see BUDDHISM, YOGĀCĀRA SCHOOL OF).

The position taken by Ratnakīrti may be the logical conclusion of an idea first mentioned in the *Kathāvatthu*, namely, that one becomes an Awakened One (*buddha*) by acquiring a quality known as awakening (*bodhi*). Tissa Moggalīputta himself rejected this idea, arguing that if awakening were something that one could attain, it would also be something that one could lose, in which case a *buddha* could cease to be a *buddha*; his view, therefore, was that awakening is not a positive trait but merely the absence of delusions. Dissenting from this view, other Buddhists (and especially members of the Yogācāra school) argued that *buddhas* become *buddhas* as a result of realizing an innate potential to become awakened. This innate potential, called the embryo of the knower of truth (*tathāgata-garbha*), was said by some to exist in all living beings, thereby making all living beings *buddhas*, or at least *buddhas* in the making. From this view that every sentient being has the essential quality of a *buddha*, even if this essence is somehow obscured from view by others, it was a short step to the view that all sentient beings are identical in their essence and therefore not really different from one another. Closely related to this controversy over the nature of the Buddha's essence was the issue of whether there are degrees of buddhahood or different ranks of *buddhas*. Tissa Moggalīputta had argued that being a *buddha* is a matter of being free of delusion, and either one is free or one is not; there can be no degrees of freedom. Other thinkers took the view that although all beings are essentially *buddhas* in their nature, they manifest their essences to a different extent, and therefore one may speak of degrees of buddhahood.

4 Epistemology

Siddhārtha Gautama the Buddha is portrayed in Buddhist literature as ridiculing the sacrificial rituals of the Brahmans and accusing the priests of fabricating them for no better reason than to make money from the wealthy and to manipulate the powerful. Attacking the sacrificial practices of the Brahman priests in this way eventually led to challenging the authority of the Vedic literature that the priests considered sacred. An early Buddhist philosopher who challenged the authority of sacred texts was NĀGĀRJUNA, whose arguments called into question the very possibility of justified belief. In a text called *Vigrahavyāvartanī* (Averting Disputes), Nāgārjuna argued that all opinions are warranted by an appeal to experience, or to various forms of reasoning, or to the authority of tradition. Now among the opinions that one may hold, said Nāgārjuna, is the opinion that all opinions are warranted in one of those ways. Nothing, however, seems to warrant that opinion. If one should claim that that opinion is self-warranting, then why not grant that all other opinions are also self-warranting? On the other hand, if that opinion requires substantiation, the result will be an infinite regress. Therefore, concluded Nāgārjuna, no opinion can be grounded. Realizing that one can never arrive at certainty thus becomes for Nāgārjuna the most reliable way of freeing oneself from the various delusions that cause unhappiness in the world. Dispelling delusions is therefore not a matter of discovering truth, but a matter of realizing that all opinions that pass as knowledge are not really knowledge at all.

Although Nāgārjuna's scepticism managed to capture the spirit of some passages of Buddhist literature that depict the Buddha as questioning the authoritarianism of other teachers, it did not leave adequate room for distinguishing truth from error. Most Buddhist philosophers who came after Nāgārjuna, therefore, placed an emphasis on both eliminating error and securing positive knowledge. DIGNĀGA, modifying theories of knowledge that Brahmanical thinkers had developed, argued that there are just two types of knowledge, each having a distinct subject matter unavailable to the other: through the senses one gains knowledge of particulars that are physically present, while the intellect enables one to form concepts that take past and future experiences into consideration.

In an important work called *Ālambanaparīkṣa* (Examining the Support of Awareness) Dignāga developed an argument that his predecessor VASUBANDHU had made. Here Dignāga argued that a cognition is accurate only if the subject matter of the cognition is identical to that which causes the awareness to arise. So, for example, if one sees a dead tree in the dark and takes it to be a man, then the subject matter of the cognition is a man, which is not identical to the dead tree that is causing the cognition; the cognition is therefore inaccurate. Given this principle, said Dignāga, it follows that none of our sensory cognitions is accurate, because each of them is really caused by atoms massed together; nevertheless, we are never aware of anything as a mass of atoms. Instead, what we are aware of is such things as human beings, elephants and trees. These notions of things as human beings or elephants, however, are purely conceptual in nature and are not in accord with the realities that exist in the external world. Therefore, he concluded, the only objects of our awareness are concepts; we are never directly aware of realities as they occur outside the mind.

Dignāga's essays rekindled an interest in epistemological questions among Buddhist philosophers that lasted for several centuries. As influential as his theories in logic and the sources of knowledge were, there was little in them that explicitly referred to previous Buddhist doctrine. It was left to the systematic philosopher DHARMAKĪRTI to draw out the implications that questions of logic and epistemology had for people interested in the traditional Buddhist preoccupation with eliminating delusions concerning the nature of the self in order to win freedom from discontent.

Dharmakīrti's system of epistemology was centred around his criticism of the Brahmanical doctrine of the special authority of the Veda, which the Brahmans supposed had been revealed to humanity by God. He combined this criticism with a defence of the doctrine that the Buddha was a source of knowledge. The Brahmanical claim of authority for their scriptures is based upon the notion that God is omniscient and compassionate; this idea, said Dharmakīrti, is extravagant and laughable. The Buddhist claim for the authority of the Buddha, on the other hand, is based on the modest claim that the Buddha was an ordinary man who could see the root cause of discontent, knew how to eliminate the cause, and took time to teach other human beings what he had discovered. Moreover, argued Dharmakīrti, the Buddha taught nothing but principles that every human being could confirm. Full confirmation of the Buddha's teachings was said to be impossible for a person whose vision was still clouded by delusions. On the other hand, to a person who had learned to listen to wise counsel, reflect on it and then put it into practice, all the teachings of the Buddha on the question of winning *nirvāṇa* would be confirmed.

The form of reflection that Dharmakīrti recommended was based upon a systematic study of the principles of legitimate inference; most delusions, he contended, stem from forming hasty generalizations from limited experience. Most doctrinal matters about which philosophers dispute, he said, cannot be decided with certainty. In this respect, Dharmakīrti adopted the cautious attitude of the Buddha and Nāgārjuna towards unwarranted opinions and assumptions. At the same time, he tried to show that the extreme scepticism that had characterized the work of such thinkers as Nāgārjuna was also unwarranted. This epistemological 'middle path', consisting of modest claims about the extent of the Buddha's knowledge and yet insisting that the Buddha's doctrines were true and distinguishable from falsehoods, set the tone for most of the Buddhist philosophy that evolved in India until the time that Buddhism stopped being an important factor in the philosophical milieu of the Indian subcontinent. The focus on epistemological issues enabled Buddhists to set aside the sometimes bitter disputes over the question of which Buddhist scriptures were authentic (see EPISTEMOLOGY, INDIAN SCHOOLS OF §1).

5 Metaphysics

Given the emphasis in Buddhist teachings on the role of erroneous belief as a cause of unhappiness, it was natural that Buddhist philosophers should focus on questions of ontology and the theory of causation. Ontology was important, since a kind of intellectual error that was supposed to lead to unhappiness was being mistaken about what exists. The theory of causation was important, since the eradication of the cause of unhappiness was supposed to result in the removal of unhappiness itself.

The earliest attempts to systematize the teachings of Buddhism were in the genre of literature known as 'Abhidharma', in which all the factors of human experience were classified according to a variety of schemata (see BUDDHISM, ABHIDHARMIKA SCHOOLS OF). The study of the relationships among these classes of factors eventually evolved into a detailed theory of causality, in which several types of causal relationship were enumerated. There were many schools of Abhidharma, and each had its own set of schemata for the classification and enumeration of the factors of experience. Indeed, each had its own interpretation of what the very word 'Abhidharma' means; among the possible interpretations of the word, a common one is that it means a higher or more advanced doctrine, or a doctrine that leads to a higher form of wisdom. The variety of approaches taken in Abhidharma literature makes it difficult to discuss this literature in any but the most general way. Among most schools of Abhidharma, there was a commitment to the idea that the best strategy for coming to an understanding of any complex being is to analyse that being into its ultimate parts. An ultimate part is that which cannot be analysed into anything more simple. Most Buddhist systematists held to the principle that the ultimately simple building blocks out of which things are made are ultimately real, while complex things that are made up of more simple parts are not ultimately real; they are held to be real only through the consensus of a community. As was seen above in the section on human nature (§1), for example, there was a strong tendency for Buddhists to accept that a person's character is the product of many components; these components were held to be real, but the person was held to be ultimately unreal. The idea of a person may be a fiction, but it is one that makes the running of society more manageable, and therefore it can be regarded as a consensual reality, in contrast to an ultimate reality.

The philosopher Nāgārjuna questioned the whole attempt to make a distinction between consensual and ultimate truths. One interpretation of his philosophical writings is that he was trying to show that every attempt to understand the world can only be an approximation on which there may be some degree of consensus; there is, however, no understanding that can claim to have arrived at an adequate description of things as they really are. Along with this radical criticism of the very enterprise of trying to discern ultimate from consensual realities, Nāgārjuna criticized the doctrine that the simple constituents that serve as causes of more complex beings are more real than the complex beings themselves. This principle had rested on the assumption that the more simple a being is, the closer it is to being independent. In fact, he argued, the apparently simple constituents are no less dependent than their apparently complex effects. To this fact of being dependent upon other things, Nāgārjuna gave the name emptiness; since all beings are dependent for their existence on other beings, he said, all beings are empty.

Later Buddhist philosophers, beginning especially with Dharmakīrti, devoted their energy increasingly to refuting the claims, advanced by some Brahmanical thinkers, that the whole universe can be traced back to a single cause. Dharmakīrti argued that if all things in the history of the world had a single cause, such as God or some type of primordial matter, then there would be no way to account for all the formal variety in the world at any given time, nor would it be possible to account for the fact that events unfold in sequences. If all the formal and temporal diversity are already inherent in the cause, he argued, then the cause is not a single thing after all. One might argue that the diversity exists in the single cause only as a potential of some kind; this, however, only raises the problem of explaining how that potential is actualized. If the potential is activated by something outside the cause that possesses it, then the outside agency must be counted among the causal factors along with the primary cause, in which case there is no longer a single cause. Besides general arguments directed against the view that all things could have any single cause, Dharmakīrti also gave arguments against the existence of a creator God in particular. The universe, he observed, shows no signs of having been designed by anyone intelligent. Even if it were conceded for the sake of argument that the world might have been made by some intelligent being, there is still no sign that this being had any concern for any living beings. Later generations of Buddhist philosophers expanded upon Dharmakīrti's arguments against the existence of a single intelligent creator, but most of these expansions took the form of replying to the objections of opponents rather than formulating new arguments (see CAUSATION, INDIAN THEORIES OF §6).

During the last five hundred years that Buddhism was an important factor in Indian philosophy (600–1100), criticism of Buddhist doctrines by Brahmanical and Jaina religious philosophers, as well as from anti-religious materialists, forced Buddhist thinkers to refine some of their arguments and even to abandon some of their doctrinal positions. Arguments among Buddhists became much less a feature of Buddhist philosophy than arguments against non-Buddhist opponents. Within Buddhism itself, there was a tendency to try to reconcile differences that in earlier centuries had divided Buddhists against each other, at least doctrinally. This new spirit of overcoming sectarianism resulted in several ingenious attempts to fuse the old Abhidharma schools, the Mādhyamika schools, the Yogācāra schools and the Buddhist epistemologists. Few new issues were raised in this last five-hundred-year period, and not many new arguments were discovered to defend old positions. Careful scholarship tended to replace philosophical innovation as the principal preoccupation of later Buddhist intellectuals, such as Śāntarakṣita, Kamalaśīla, Jñānaśrīmitra and Ratnakīrti. It was during this period of the decline of Buddhism in India that Buddhist philosophy was introduced into Tibet. Once established there, it received a new impetus from a range of Tibetan intellectuals who were able to study many of these doctrines with a fresh perspective.

See also: BUDDHISM, MĀDHYAMIKA: INDIA AND TIBET; BUDDHIST CONCEPT OF EMPTINESS; BUDDHIST PHILOSOPHY, CHINESE; BUDDHIST PHILOSOPHY, JAPANESE; BUDDHIST PHILOSOPHY, KOREAN; HINDU PHILOSOPHY; JAINA PHILOSOPHY; MOMENTARINESS, BUDDHIST DOCTRINE OF; NOMINALISM, BUDDHIST DOCTRINE OF; SUFFERING, BUDDHIST VIEWS OF ORIGINATION OF; TIBETAN PHILOSOPHY

References and further reading

Conze, E. (1967) *Buddhist Thought in India*, Ann Arbor, MI: University of Michigan Press. (A good survey of the issues and the schools of Indian Buddhism.)

Frauwallner, E. (trans.) (1956) *Die Philosophie des Buddhismus*, ed. W. Ruben, Berlin: Akademie-Verlag, 3rd revised edn, 1969. (A collection of important Indian Buddhist philosophical texts translated into German.)

Griffiths, P.J. (1994) *On Being Buddha*, Albany, NY: State University of New York Press. (The first two chapters present a cogent general account of the place of doctrine and philosophy within Indian Buddhism.)

Kalupahana, D.J. (1976) *Buddhist Philosophy: A Historical Analysis*, Honolulu, HI: University of Hawaii Press. (Informative, though biased to a view of Buddhism as 'empirical' and 'anti-metaphysical'.)

Mookerjee, S. (1980) *The Buddhist Philosophy of Universal Flux*, Delhi: Motilal Banarsidass. (Excellent account of the doctrines held and arguments advanced in the later scholastic period.)

* Nāgārjuna (*c.* AD 150–200) *Vigrahavyāvartanī* (Averting Disputes), trans. K. Bhattacharya, 'The Dialectical Method of Nāgārjuna', *Journal of Indian Philosophy* 1: 217–61, 1971. (A superb study, including a translation from the original Sanskrit with introduction and notes; see §4.)

* Tissa Moggalīputta (*c.*246 BC) *Kathāvatthu* (Points of Controversy), trans. Shwe Zan Aung and C.A.F. Rhys Davids, London: The Pali Text Society, 1979. (The standard English translation of the earliest collection of points disputed by Buddhists during the first two centuries after the Buddha's career, part of the *abhidhamma* section of the Pāli canon; see §3.)

Warder, A.K. (1970) *Indian Buddhism*, Delhi: Motilal Banarsidass. (This thorough study of the history of Buddhism in India contains several chapters on the history and principal schools of its philosophy.)

Williams, P. (1989) *Mahāyāna Buddhism: The Doctrinal Foundations*, London: Routledge. (The first six chapters of this excellent and readable study deal mostly with Buddhist philosophy in India. Also contains discussions of Tibetan and Chinese developments.)

RICHARD P. HAYES

BUDDHIST PHILOSOPHY, JAPANESE

Buddhism transformed Japanese culture and in turn was transformed in Japan. Mahāyāna Buddhist thought entered Japan from the East Asian continent as part of a cultural complex that included written language, political institutions, formal iconography and Confucian literature. From its introduction in the sixth century through to the sixteenth century, Japanese Buddhism developed largely by incorporating Chinese Buddhism, accommodating indigenous beliefs and reconciling intersectarian disputes. During the isolationist Tokugawa Period (1600–1868), neo-Confucian philosophy and Dutch science challenged the virtual hegemony of Buddhist ways of thinking, but served more often as alternative and sometimes complementary models than as incompatible paradigms. Only since the reopening of Japan in 1868 has Japanese Buddhist thought seriously attempted to come to terms with early Indian Buddhism, Western thought and Christianity.

Through the centuries, Buddhism gave the Japanese people a way to make sense of life and death, to explain the world and to seek liberation from suffering. When it engaged in theorizing, it did so in pursuit of religious fulfilment rather than of knowledge for its own sake. As an extension of its practical bent, Japanese Buddhist thought often tended to collapse differences between Buddhism and other forms of Japanese religiosity, between this phenomenal world and any absolute realm, and between the means and end of enlightenment. These tendencies are not Japanese in origin, but they extended further in Japan than in other Buddhist countries and partially define the character of Japanese Buddhist philosophy.

In fact, the identity of 'Japanese Buddhist philosophy' blends with almost everything with which we would contrast it. As a development and modification of Chinese traditions, there is no one thing that is uniquely Japanese about it; as a Buddhist tradition, it is characteristically syncretistic, often assimilating Shintō and Confucian philosophy in both its doctrines and practices. Rituals, social practices, political institutions and artistic or literary expressions are as essential as philosophical ideas to Japanese Buddhism.

Disputes about ideas often arose but were seldom settled by force of logical argument. One reason for this is that language was used not predominately in the service of logic but for the direct expression and actualization of reality. Disputants appealed to the authority of Buddhist sūtras because these scriptures were thought to manifest a direct understanding of reality. Further, as reality was thought to be all-inclusive, the better position in the dispute would be that which was more comprehensive rather than that which was more consistent but exclusive. Politics and practical consequences did play a role in the settling of disputes, but the ideal of harmony or conformity often prevailed.

The development of Japanese Buddhist philosophy can thus be seen as the unfolding of major themes rather than a series of philosophical positions in dispute. These themes include the role of language in expressing truth; the non-dual nature of absolute and relative, universal and particular; the actualization of liberation in this world, life or body; the equality of beings; and the transcendent non-duality of good and evil.

1   Language
2   Doctrine and truth
3–5 Universal and particular
6   Theodicy and ethics

1   Language

The practical, soteriological nature of Buddhism makes it wary of what Wittgenstein called the bewitchment of the mind by language. Yet the view that Buddhism disregards language is an oversimplification, especially in Japan. Japanese Buddhism has a positive appreciation of language, particularly of its non-referential usage. Buddhist thought first came to Japan in the form of *sūtras* and commentaries written in Chinese characters. Written language was still so novel, and categories of thought so limited, that the content of these texts could be read as manifestations of new realities rather than as ideas referring to Buddhism. Some of the earliest literature composed in Japan, such as the poetry collection *Man'yōshū*, mentions *kotodama*, the spiritual power of words that makes things present. Although scholars articulated this theory of language only much later and aligned it with Shintō (see MOTOORI NORINAGA), it may apply to the early understanding of Chinese Buddhist as well as indigenous words. Words had the power not only to manifest things in the world but also to change them; before Buddhist texts represented a doctrinal and ethical system, they provided incantations to heal illness and bring prosperity to the land.

The ritualistic use of language continued through the centuries and was often central to the expression of doctrine. Practitioners often used single words or phrases as the condensed form of a doctrine or lengthy *sūtra*. KŪKAI, for example, recited the Sanskrit formulas for the Womb and Diamond Mandalas to better envision these pictorial representations of the cosmic order. He proposed that intoning mantras could make the basic sounds of the cosmos audible. He used *dhāranī* or magical formulae not only as a means of purifying body and mind and allowing him to understand the point of every Buddhist scripture, but also as the means by which his patron bodhisattva could fulfill all wishes. Even when later Pure Land School teachers such as Shinran suspected discursive language and discouraged belief in worldly benefit through magical transformation, they taught that the sincere invocation of Amida Buddha's name has the power to actualize the salvation of all sentient beings. Buddhists of the Nichiren schools chanted the name of the *Wondrous Lotus Sutra*, *namu myōhō renge kyō*, as a condensation and realization of all doctrines contained in it. Rinzai Zen teachers advocated the practice of *kanna* or 'contemplating the [crucial] phrase' of a dialogue, or of compressing the already condensed *Heart Sutra* into a single word. As long as the words are 'live' and not dead repetitions, Zen teachers conceived such practices as shortcuts to enlightenment that immediately put the practitioner in a frame of mind to realize the point of Buddhist doctrines.

The transformative as well as expressive nature of

language is evident in perhaps the most important collection of premodern Japanese philosophical literature, the *Shōbōgenzō* (Treasury of the True Dharma Eye), by the thirteenth-century Zen master DŌGEN. One chapter begins: 'As for the Buddha Way, not to voice it is impossible.' This statement does not command one to proclaim the teachings of Buddhism, but rather connects one's attainment of truth with its expression in the world. Such expression includes but is not limited to language. Another chapter of the *Shōbōgenzō* states, 'All buddhas and patriarchs are able to voice the Way', that is, to express truth in all their words and actions. By virtue of their realization of non-duality or no ultimate opposition, they can directly express the Way and not merely refer to it. They can also experience as the words of the Buddha 'the preaching of non-sentient beings', the 'sounds of the valley streams and the forms of the mountains'. This idea, explained further below (see §5), seems to collapse any ultimate distinction between sign and signified. Words express themselves, as do valley streams and the forms of mountains. This 'expressing' or 'voicing of the Way' does not stand for or represent something other than itself, and language used representationally is not privileged to express reality. The limitation placed on the power of representational language here is accompanied by an expanded meaning of 'expression' or 'voicing of the Way' that includes both linguistic and nonlinguistic forms.

2 Doctrine and truth

When early readers began to understand Buddhist texts as expressions of doctrines, and implicitly to grasp written language as signs signifying ideas, they came to understand the world in terms of formerly unseen relations. The Buddhist categories they applied were Chinese translations of Sanskrit terms, and this usage remained predominant even after modern Japanese scholars turned to Indian sources. The categories included names for the basic factors or elements of existence and the relations of cause and effect, conditioned and unconditioned, part and whole, relative and absolute.

The first systematic study of these categories and relations occurred in the so-called six schools of Nara, during the historical period of the same name (710–81). These 'schools' were more bodies of doctrine than independent sects with their own adherents. Often the doctrines were studied together in the same locale, such as the great temple Tōdaiji. The Japanese version of the Indian Abhidharmakośa school stressed the analysis of some seventy five conditioned and unconditioned constituents (*dhar-*

mas) of existence and some ten types of direct and indirect causes that give rise to the conditioned factors.

As abstract as it appears, this analysis was intended as a kind of psychological examination to remove obstacles on the path to liberation. The Jōjitsu (Establishment of Truth) school proceeded to show the emptiness, or lack of substantial reality, of all constituents. The Ritsu (Precept) school conveyed very specific ethical and administrative rules to regulate the ordination and life of monks and nuns, and taught that the observance of precepts was one purification necessary for enlightenment. As discussed below, however, it did not provide an ethical theory or general principles for determining good and evil (see §6).

The Sanron (Three Treatises) school derived from Indian Mādhyamika philosophy (see BUDDHISM, MĀDHYAMIKA: INDIA AND TIBET). It practiced the refutation of all claims of the existence or non-existence, truth or falsity, of separate elements and doctrines. The discursive language used to refute all views ultimately pointed to its own limit, beyond which lay absolute truth. The Hossō school formed the scholastic counterpart to Indian Yogācāra or 'consciousness-only' philosophy (see BUDDHISM, YOGĀCĀRA SCHOOL OF). It criticized the Mādhyamika tendency to absolutize emptiness, explained the role of consciousness in the appearance of self and world, and taught that enlightenment requires a conversion of the deep unconsciousness, called the 'storehouse' consciousness. It rejected the teaching that enlightenment is equally attainable by all. The sixth school, the Kegon (Flower Garland), was historically no more influential than these last two, but introduced a principle crucial to an understanding of the treatment of doctrines and truth in subsequent Japanese Buddhism.

The Nara schools took over doctrines and analyses from their Chinese counterparts virtually without change. These doctrines were partially incompatible with each other, but the discrepancies seemed little cause for dispute. Various doctrines and categories show up in later Japanese Buddhist philosophy, often as a foil for more innovative ideas. An example is the way the Abhidharma breakdown of reality and time forms the springboard of one chapter of Dōgen's *Shōbōgenzō*, 'Ocean Reflecting Samādhi'. This work first accepts the Abhidharma analysis of the causal arising of all elements but then disrupts it to proclaim the totality and sufficiency of each moment. In general, the failure of scholastic doctrines to challenge later generations of Japanese Buddhist thinkers is a sign that the latter have been more at home with practical reasoning and reconciliation than with formal argumentation and adjudication of claims. Indeed, until its introduction from the West there was in Japan no formal logic, where the rules of validity are separable from the content of the argument (see LOGIC IN JAPAN). This lack does not necessarily point to a deficiency in the ability to reason, however, but may have to do with a way of relating absolute and relative, universal and particular. The philosophy of the Kegon school best epitomizes that way.

The Kegon school accounted for the variety of doctrines by placing them in a scheme of increasing difficulty and comprehensiveness. The level of the teachings matches the hearer's capacity to understand. Partial teachings, in other words, are 'skillful means' designed to lead one to more difficult and comprehensive teachings. The Kegon school typifies the inclusion characteristic of much of Japanese and Chinese Buddhist thought. One Buddhist school would incorporate rather than exclude the doctrines of rival schools, but would regard them as incomplete and place them on a lower level. To be sure, the hermeneutic of inclusion was often politically motivated, intended to increase a power base by incorporating and not alienating other groups; but it also followed the dialectical principle that rival or alternative beliefs were partial truths that fit into a larger scheme.

The Kegon scriptural hermeneutic privileged its own source *sūtras* and was rivaled by a similar scheme offered in the tremendously influential *Lotus Sutra*, but it developed a philosophy of totality and interrelation crucial for understanding most Japanese Buddhist thinking. According to this philosophy, each part or constituent of reality perfectly reflects the whole, and the whole depends upon each and every constituent part. All individual parts are therefore equivalent as conditions of the whole, and at the same time they are distinct and interdependent. The implications of this philosophy of nature for a theory of truth are the key to approaching Japanese Buddhist thought. There is no whole, universal or absolute, without its manifestation in concrete, distinct and relative particulars. In the twentieth century, NISHIDA KITARŌ reformulated this principle paradoxically: the more relative a truth is – that is, the more deeply embedded or embodied in particulars – the more absolute it is. The absolute must encompass the relative, not stand in opposition to it. In general, Japanese Buddhist philosophy developed through a kind of synecdochic argumentation that appealed not to *a priori* reasons or empirical evidence, nor simply to scriptural sources of authority, but to this mutual accommodation of relative and absolute.

3 Universal and particular

Three interrelated themes display the mutual accommodation of relative and absolute, universal and particular: the locus of liberation, its actuality and the equality of beings.

Indian Mahāyāna *sūtras* introduced the idea that liberation does not lead to a transcendent realm different from this world, but they often spoke of the 'three immeasurable eons' required for its attainment. In contrast, many seminal Buddhist thinkers in Japan developed one Chinese view of the locus of liberation: the idea of becoming a buddha in this very body (*sokushin jōbutsu*). For Saichō (767–822), the founder of the Tendai school, it meant only a partial realization of buddhahood; but by the time of Tendai scholar Annen (841–89?) it referred to buddhahood attained in this very life. KŪKAI (774–835), founder of the rival Shingon school, taught that yogic practices involving body (*mudra*s or symbolic hand gestures), speech (*mantras*) and mind (mental concentration and visualizations) could unify the practitioner with the Buddha Mahāvairocana. Such practices made it possible to attain buddhahood in this very body. This doctrine, popularized by Kūkai, provided a theoretical basis for the bodily aspects of practice and the enactment of rituals that were important especially in the esoteric traditions of Tendai and Shingon Buddhism.

In summary, the idea of becoming a buddha in this very body or life involved a temporal and a metaphysical reduction. First, it collapsed the various stages of the path to enlightenment that were so important in various Buddhist traditions, and reduced the 'three immeasurable eons' to one lifetime. Second, it collapsed any remnant of a difference between the physical reality of life on earth and a transcendent realm, between the transient human body and the transcendent *dharma*-body. The body we are born with is the site of realization and symbolically embodies the entire universe, the 'truth-body' of the Buddha. DŌGEN modified the idea further and proclaimed that 'this very mind is buddha' (*sokushin zebutsu*) when the discursive mind was disengaged. Although Dōgen speaks of 'mind' and not body, no psychophysical dualism is implied here.

Other Buddhist reformers of the Kamakura period (1192–1333) qualified the idea that liberation was possible in this world or life. Hōnen and SHINRAN placed this possibility in the Pure Land, which they usually considered as immediately accessible if intermediate between this world and the realm of final enlightenment. Even where it was imagined as a different world, this Pure Land was not nearly so remote a goal as Indian views of *nirvāna*, and was sometimes in effect made immanent in this world. Ippen explicitly stated that the Pure Land was indeed identical with this world. NICHIREN too emphasized this world as the locus of salvation.

The affirmation of this world in Japanese thought is often called phenomenalism (see PHENOMENAL-ISM), but this description neglects the principle or absolute said to interpenetrate all phenomena. One tenet of Kegon philosophy was that 'principles are not impeded by things' (rijimuge). Tendai Buddhism stressed the Mahāyāna doctrine of the 'identity of the phenomenal and the real' (genshō zoku jissō), and proposed that the phenomena of the world are aspects of Buddha. Dōgen wrote that the 'true reality' (jissō) is in fact all things, and that birth and death (impermanence) (see MUJŌ) is Buddha or nirvāṇa. To understand these developments in Japanese Buddhism, however, one needs to consider the question of the actuality of liberation.

4 Universal and particular (cont.)

Many Indian Mahāyāna sūtras teach that all sentient beings possess the nature of Buddha. The Lotus Sutra proclaims further that the historical Buddha is not a man who attained awakening but rather is a manifestation of the universal buddhahood that is available to all. It rejected schemes that differentiated levels of potential in beings and that excluded the lowest level from eventual enlightenment. Saichō advocated universal buddhahood, based on the language of the Lotus Sutra. Universal buddhahood and 'becoming Buddha in this very body' are ideas based on the notion of hongaku, the Chinese doctrine that all beings are 'originally or inherently awakened'. Inherent enlightenment, in contrast to 'acquired enlightenment', is timeless and independent of spiritual development. For some contemporary scholars such as Tamura Yoshirō, the hongaku idea is definitive not only of Buddhism in medieval Japan but of Japanese culture in general, since it underlies the ideals of equality, harmony and conformity (Tamura 1987).

The ideas of inherent and acquired enlightenment do not form logical contraries, since both depend upon the buddha-nature in all beings, but rather pose a practical question: how is this innate enlightenment related to practice? Legend has it that DŌGEN encountered this question in his boyhood Tendai training and made it an existential problem: why undergo rigorous practice when we are endowed with 'dharma nature' by birth? Dōgen's answer is thought to be a criticism of the hongaku idea, but can also be seen as its limit. He proposed 'the unity of practice and realization': 'The dharma [truth] is not manifested unless one practices; it is not attained unless there is

realization' (Shōbōgenzō bendōwa). The practice of concentrated mind–body, epitomized in zazen or seated meditation, is a way to actualize our inherent nature. In §1 above, Dōgen's words were quoted: 'As for the Buddha Way, not to voice it is impossible...' and this sentence concludes: 'not to study [practice] it is remote.' Dōgen thus collapses the distinction between practice as means and enlightenment as end. Instead, zazen, the practice of awakening, becomes the manifestation of enlightenment.

Like Dōgen, other Kamakura Period Buddhist reformers reacted against the complacency encouraged by the idea of original enlightenment, but modified rather than rejected it. For Hōnen and Shinran the only 'practice' that counts is the nembutsu or invocation of the Buddha Amida. In his form as the Bodhisattva Dharmakara, Amida enunciated a primal vow that made his enlightenment contingent on that of all sentient beings. Those with sincere faith in Amida's vow were assured of rebirth in the Pure Land, where final enlightenment will be possible. In the original story, countless lifetimes elapse before Dharmakara becomes Amida Buddha, but the logic of the conditions may suggest a non-dual, timeless relation: since Amida Buddha is indeed here to save us, our liberation need only be actualized in this moment. Some writings of Shinran explicitly suggest that to recollect Amida Buddha with a believing mind (shinjin) is already to actualize buddhahood, without waiting to be reborn in the Pure Land. Moreover, this entrusting invocation is strictly speaking not a practice at all; that is, it is not accomplished through one own efforts or 'self-power' but rather is a gift of Amida, a result of Amida's 'other-power'. Ippen stated that 'the nembutsu is what recites the nembutsu'. Although faith in personal effort is considered futile, as in some interpretations of inherent enlightenment, true reality must be activated by personal faith. This again is a variation on the theme of the actualization of reality (see FAITH; SALVATION).

5 Universal and particular (cont.)

The idea of universal buddhahood supported both syncretistic tendencies in Japanese Buddhism and the equality of all beings. The first undermined any ultimate difference between Buddhist and Shintō objects of veneration, and the second any difference between the human and natural worlds, or what we today call culture and nature.

Syncretistic tendencies were formalized in the theory of honji suijaku. This theory regarded indigenous Shintō deities (kami) as trace manifestations (suijaku) of buddhas and bodhisattvas, who were their original ground or true nature (honji). The theory appears to establish a hierarchical relationship, with the *bodhisattva*s as more basic and important than the *kami*, and thus Buddhism as more fundamental than Shintō. This interpretation implies that the Shintō gods cannot exist without the Buddhist ideal beings. It not only reverses the historical order of their appearance in Japan; it misplaces the emphasis. In fact, the *honj–suijaku* theory often worked to set the two realms and their objects of veneration on a par with one another. If a *kami* functioned as a trace or attribute of a bodhisattva, the particular *bodhisattva* was best manifested in the *kami*. The reality of the one depended upon that of the other. This interdependence was explicit in a Tendai version of *honji suijaku* theory according to which the true nature could only be perceived in its manifestations. A fourteenth-century Shintō school simply reversed the order of *bodhisattva* and *kami*. Moreover, specific Buddhist and Shintō ideal beings are sometimes identified with one another and then contrasted with other pairs. In the twentieth century, a 'new religion' called Gedatsukai in effect identifies the Buddha Mahāvairocana and the Shintō deity Tenjinchigi as *honji*, and gives other Buddhist-Shintō deities the status of *suijaku*. These examples illustrate that the accessibility of ideal beings was more important than any rank order, which was historically variable (see SHINTŌ).

The theory of original ground and trace manifestation was developed in the late Heian Period (794–1185), contemporaneous with the idea of inherent enlightenment. Yet the underlying association of Shintō and Buddhism is evident much earlier and lasted until much later. At the very beginning of Japanese Buddhism, the *Nihon shoki* (Chronicles of Japan) report that the Emperor Yōmei (d. 587) 'believed in the Law of the Buddha and reverenced the Way of the Gods'. Yet the name 'Way of the Gods' (Shintō) was a Chinese, quasi-Buddhist concept. In effect, Buddhism prevailed and was established as the state religion, at least temporarily, through the efforts of Yōmei's sister, Empress Suiko, and especially of his son, Prince Shōtoku, who wrote commentaries on *sūtras* and built temples (see SHŌTOKU CONSTITUTION). In the Nara Period (710–81), Shintō shrines were incorporated into Buddhist temples in order to protect land interests, and Buddhist altars built near shrines ensured the protection of Shintō. At one locale the god of war, Hachiman, was named the Bodhisattva Daijizaiten in 783; at others he was associated with different *bodhisattva*s. In the ninth century, KŪKAI proposed a 'dual aspect' theory that, for example, identified the sun goddess Amaterasu with Mahāvairocana, the Buddha of Great Illumination, whom Kūkai further identified with the *dharmakāya* or truth-body of Buddha. Although

Tokugawa Period (1600–1868) nativists such as MOTOORI NORINAGA reasserted the superiority of indigenous Shintō, the Buddhist inclusion of Shintō was not effectively challenged on a national scale until the early Meiji government's policies (in the 1870s) of 'separating gods and buddhas', persecuting Buddhism and establishing State Shintō. Religion and state have had separate legal status since the Second World War, but Buddhist and Shintō teachings and customs still coexist in Japanese family life.

Japanese Buddhist thought extended the idea of universal buddhahood to the equality of all beings. In particular, the idea of inherent enlightenment lent support to the doctrine of the Buddha-nature of non-sentient beings that is often alluded to in medieval Japanese literature. It was both Tendai and Nichiren doctrine that the grass and trees – in other words, beings not possessed of a sensitive mind – can become buddhas: 'Grasses, trees, mountains and rivers all attain buddhahood' became a frequent saying in medieval Buddhist texts. A chapter of Dōgen's *Shōbōgenzō* quotes the enlightenment verse of Chinese poet Su Dongpo:

> The sounds of the valley streams are His long, broad tongue;
> The forms of the mountains are His pure body.
> At night I heard the myriad *sūtra*-verses uttered
> How can I relate to others what they say?
>
> (Cook 1989: vii)

For Dōgen, this verse provides one answer to the questions, 'where is buddha?', 'what is buddha?' and 'how does he preach?' The preaching of nonsentient beings, a frequent theme in Dōgen, is echoed earlier in the poetry of Saigyō. It expands Dōgen's view of 'expression' (discussed in §1) to the world of nature. Whether the traditional Japanese love of nature preceded or succeeded the absolute significance accorded to the phenomenal world cannot be determined.

6 Theodicy and ethics

Japanese Buddhist treatments of theodicy and ethics also reveal ways in which Buddhism was transformed in Japan. Theodicy is meant here in Max Weber's general sense of an explanation that make the injustices of life intelligible and accounts for evil in the world (see WEBER, M.). In classical Indian thought, the notion of *karma* answers the problem of both moral and natural evil. Karmic retribution means that every deed or action has consequences and evil deeds bring about suffering. Suffering is not punishment by a God who is free to punish or not, but rather is an inevitable consequence of evil actions.

There are accordingly practical reasons to avoid evil and do good. In early Indian thought the notion of *karma* entailed that of transmigration. *Karma* is, as it were, the momentum of our actions that propels us through *saṃsāra*, the continuous cycles of birth and death. This transmigration occurs through various lifetimes and life forms, mythologized as the six realms of hell, hungry ghosts, animals, fighting demons, humans and gods. The Buddha taught a way of liberation that is a release from transmigration and its cause, *karma*, whether good or evil (see KARMA AND REBIRTH, INDIAN CONCEPTIONS OF). In later Japanese Buddhist philosophy, attachment to self and the concomitant ignorance of the reality of no-self were stressed as the root cause of *saṃsāra*.

After Buddhism was introduced to Japan, people easily accepted the notion of karmic retribution but not the literal belief of rebirth as animals or lower life forms. Transmigration through the six realms of *saṃsāra* played a larger role in Japanese literature and theatre than in philosophical discussions, which focused more on the practical path to liberation. Good deeds were not the means to liberation; they did not, for example, ensure rebirth in the Pure Land, whether taken as the physical abode or spiritual state wherein final liberation is possible. Hōnen, and later SHINRAN in his *Tannishō* (Lamenting the Deviations) went so far as to state that: 'If a good person attains birth in the Pure Land, how much more so the evil person'.

The apparent incompatibility between any notion of rebirth and the Indian Buddhist doctrine of no-self or no-soul was not an issue in traditional Japanese Buddhist thought. Moreover, even after the Japanese understood this doctrine they, like the Chinese, continued to believe in the spirits of ancestors who remain somehow present among the living. That folk belief has played a stronger role in everyday life and religious practices than has Buddhist doctrine. Logically, the disassociation of good deeds and liberation would seem to compromise the theodicy offered by the notion of karmic retribution, and ancestor veneration to compromise the doctrine of no substantial self which is the basis of compassion with all living beings. In effect, however, the compromises have meant little more than finding a middle course, or superimposing the two metaphysically incompatible beliefs. Belief in karmic retribution has encouraged the avoidance of deeds conventionally deemed evil, and thus supported conventional ethics; but karmic retribution does not entail any final resolution to misery. Only religious practice, whether conceived as self-power or other-power, holds out the prospect of final liberation, or at least the actualization of one's inherent enlightenment. In the meantime, one is to do good and avoid evil; more specifically, one is to adhere to conventional Buddhist precepts such as not killing, stealing, lying and so on. Similarly, veneration of ancestral spirits, including Buddhist patriarchs, has encouraged a respect for tradition and social order, while non-ego has been extolled as the basis of right action in both Japanese Buddhism and Confucianism. If we seek in Japanese Buddhist philosophy a coherent theory of ethics as a separate branch of philosophy, we find instead a variety of practical reasons; for a moral theory, we would have to refer to Confucianism (see CONFUCIAN PHILOSOPHY, JAPANESE).

This general description receives closer definition in the views of Shinran and DŌGEN. Dōgen's ethical views reflect both the penchant to practical reasoning and the transcendence of ethics in the realization of enlightenment. Dōgen's sermons to monks training under him admonish them to keep the precepts while recognizing that their content is relative to the situation. Ultimately, the practice of keeping precepts is subsumed into *zazen* or the practice of realization. Dōgen's more philosophical writings transform practical admonitions such as 'do good' and 'do no evil' into proclamations of the realized state: 'the non-production of evil, the performance of good'. Ultimately, both Dōgen and Shinran would have us transcend the duality of good and evil to manifest, through uncontrived actions, absolute non-dual reality or 'suchness', which is perfect as it is. There is no cause–effect relation between morality and enlightenment, and so the issue is not the situational relativity of morality but, once again, the problem that the absolute is not complete without its manifestation in the phenomenal. Here ethical issues would give way to the problem of inherent enlightenment. The contemporary interpreter D.T. Suzuki advocated Zen enlightenment as the solution and simply proclaimed it to be 'beyond good and evil' (Suzuki 1964). On the other hand, the idea of inherent enlightenment has come under attack in the 1990s as perpetuating the status quo of society and blinding Japanese Buddhism to the need for reform guided by a social ethics.

See also: AESTHETICS, JAPANESE; BUDDHIST PHILOSOPHY, CHINESE; BUDDHIST PHILOSOPHY, INDIAN; CONFUCIAN PHILOSOPHY, JAPANESE; DŌGEN; KŪKAI; KYOTO SCHOOL; MUJŌ; NICHIREN; SHINRAN; SHINTŌ

References and further reading

* Cook, F. (1989) *Sounds of Valley Streams*, Albany, NY: State University of New York Press. (An

introduction to enlightenment in Dōgen's Zen, with a translation of nine essays from the *Shōbōgenzō*.)

Dobbins. J. (1989) *Jōdo Shinshū: Shin Buddhism in Medieval Japan*, Bloomington, IN: Indiana University Press. (A systematic treatment of the doctrines and major figures, such as Hōnen and Shinran, of the Pure Land school.)

Groner, P. (1984) *Saichō: The Establishment of the Japanese Tendai School*, Berkeley, CA: Berkeley Buddhist Studies Series. (A systematic study of the founder and teachings of the Tendai school, including the doctrine of attaining Buddhahood in this very existence.)

Hubbard, J. and Swanson, P. (eds) (1997) *Pruning the Bodhi Tree: The Storm Over Critical Buddhism*, Honolulu, HI: University of Hawaii Press. (Translations of articles by two major critics of the legacy of inherent enlightenment, N. Hakayama and S. Matsumoto, with responses from differing perspectives.)

Hakeda, Y. (1972) *Kūkai: Major Works*, New York: Columbia University Press. (An introduction to and translations of the seminal writings of Kūkai, the founder of the Shingon or 'Truth–word' school of esoteric Buddhism.)

Kitagawa, J. (1987) *On Understanding Japanese Religion*, Princeton, NJ: Princeton University Press. (A collection of essays by a historian of religions that treats both specific topics and the general character of Japanese Buddhism in a manner accessible to the general reader.)

Kiyota, M. (ed.) (1987) *Japanese Buddhism: Its Tradition, New Religions and Interaction with Christianity*, Los Angeles, CA and Tokyo: Buddhist Books International. (Essays in the first section elaborate the doctrines of the universal and the particular, and of rebirth and transmigration.)

LaFleur, W. (1983) *The Karma of Words: Buddhism and the Literary Arts in Medieval Japan*, Berkeley, CA: University of California Press. (Presents the Buddhist philosophical background to Japanese literary works, often in contrast to Western, especially Platonic thinking.)

Matsunaga, A. (1969) *The Buddhist Philosophy of Assimilation*, Tokyo: Sophia University and Charles Tuttle Co. (Presents the *honji suijaku* theory.)

Matsunaga, D. and Matsunaga, A. (1974) *Foundations of Japanese Buddhism*, Los Angeles, CA and Tokyo: Buddhist Books International, 2 vols. (A detailed historical survey from the beginnings through the Muromachi Period, 1338–1573.)

Nakamura, H. (1964) *Ways of Thinking of Eastern Peoples*, Honolulu, HI: University of Hawaii Press. (Expounds the acceptance of the phenomenal world as absolute, the social matrix of values and the emphasis of symbolic expression over logical thinking.)

* Suzuki, D.T. (1964) *An Introduction to Zen Buddhism*, New York: Grove Press. (Essays by the most influential advocate of the distinctiveness of Zen Buddhism.)

* Tamura Yoshirō (1987) 'Japanese Culture and the Tendai Concept of Original Enlightenment', *Japanese Journal of Religious Studies* 14: 203–10. (A brief argument for the positive cultural significance of the *hongaku* idea of inherent enlightenment.)

Unno, T. (trans.) (1984) *Tannisho: A Shin Buddhist Classic*, Honolulu, HI: Buddhist Study Center Press. (A translation of Shinran's most influential writing, 'Lamenting the Deviations [from the true teaching]', and an essay on the central doctrines of the True Pure Land school.)

Watanabe, S. (1970) *Japanese Buddhism: A Critical Appraisal*, Tokyo: Kokusai Bunka Shinkokai. (A realistic and detailed but non-technical treatment of the characteristics of Japanese Buddhism.)

JOHN C. MARALDO

BUDDHIST PHILOSOPHY, KOREAN

Buddhism was transmitted to the Korean peninsula from China in the middle of the fourth century AD. Korea at this time was divided into three kingdoms: Kokuryô, Paekche and Silla. Both Kokuryô and Paekche accepted Buddhism as a state religion immediately after it was introduced, to Kokuryô in 372 AD and to Paekche in 384 AD. However, it was not until two centuries later that Silla accepted Buddhism as a state religion. This was because Silla was the last of the three kingdoms to become established as a centralized power under the authority of one king.

It is not coincidental that Buddhism was accepted by these three states at the very same time that a strong kingship, independent of the aristocracy, was created. These newly established kingships needed a new ideology with which to rule, separate from the age-old shamanistic tradition which had been honored among the previous loose confederations of tribes. Buddhism fulfilled this need. It became a highly valued tool which kings used shrewdly, not only to provide their societies with a political ideology but to give them a foundation from which to build a viable system of ethics and philosophical thinking. Given this historical legacy, Korean Buddhism came to possess a feature which set it apart from the other East Asian traditions: it became 'state-protection' Buddhism. Although this was not a particularly sophisticated phenomenon on a philosophical level, this feature had a lasting influence on all aspects of Buddhist thought in Korea. In general, Korean Buddhism has followed a course of development more or less parallel to that of the greater East Asian context, although with notably closer ties to China than to Japan. There is no historical evidence which indicates any direct intellectual transmission from India, Buddhism's birthplace; rather, most of the philosophical development of Buddhism in Korea occurred as Korean monks travelled to China to study and obtain Buddhist texts which had either been written in or translated into Chinese. Despite such close ties to China, however, Korean Buddhism has developed its own identity, distinct from that of its progenitor.

Compared to Indian and Central Asian Buddhism, which developed along clear historical lines, the development of Buddhism in China was largely dependent on the personalities of individual monks, and was thus affected by such factors as their region of origination and the particular texts which they emphasized. Thus, in the process of assimilating Indian Buddhism, the Chinese created and developed a number of widely varying schools of Buddhist thought. In Korea, however, such a diverse number of philosophical traditions was never established. Rather, one of the distinct features of Korean Buddhism has been its preference for incorporating many different perspectives into a single, cohesive body of thought.

1   Three Kingdoms period (372–668 AD)

When Buddhism arrived on the Korean peninsula, Korea was in a period of transition, changing from loose tribal societies to states ruled by centralized kingships. Buddhism was strongly patronized by the kings, as it provided them with a valuable political ideology, but nevertheless it had to face the challenge of countering the indigenous belief system based firmly on shamanistic ritualism. In response to this challenge, certain Buddhist doctrines which tended to undermine animistic beliefs received special emphasis in Korea. An example of these is the doctrine of *karma*, which asserts the importance of ethical action by humans and denies the power of gods and spirits in shaping human destiny. However, Buddhism also resorted to the tactic of assimilation. The heavenly being Hanunim, a shamanistic deity, was absorbed into the Buddhist conception of heaven. Similarly, the

indigenous shamanistic worship of mountains, earth deities and dragons all became integrated into the Buddhist religious system.

Only fragmentary bits of information are available concerning Buddhist philosophy during its early existence in Korea. As previously discussed, the development of Buddhist studies in Korea ran almost parallel to that in China. Both Mahāyāna schools, such as Tientai, Huayan and Dilun, as well as Hīnayāna schools, including Abhidharma and the Sarvāstivāda and Vinaya traditions, were introduced. However, it seems that Mādhyamika philosophy formed the mainstream of Buddhist doctrinal thought during this period. Names of Korean monks from the Kokuryô and Paekche kingdoms are often mentioned, particularly in Japanese records, as masters of Mādhyamika theory or as founders of the Sanron (in Chinese, Sanlun) school in Japan (the Sanlun school was based on the sinicized interpretation of the Indian Mādhyamika).

We can learn much about the Korean interpretation of Mādhyamika theory by investigating the contributions of Sûngnang, an eminent Korean monk. Although we have no exact record of his date of birth, according to the Biography of Fadu in the *Liang Gaosengzhuan* (The Liang Biographies of the Eminent Monks), Sûngnang succeeded to the lineage after the Master Fadu passed away in 500 AD. Sûngnang's unique interpretations represented a turning point not only for Sanlun studies but for Chinese Buddhist studies as a whole. Through the decisive contributions of Sûngnang, Sanlun was established by Jizang (549–623 AD) as one of the major schools in Chinese Buddhist history. Sûngnang's own works have not been transmitted, but his philosophical ideas are cited throughout Jizang's writings.

During Sûngnang's time, Chinese Buddhist studies were divided into Northern/Abhidharma and Southern/Satyasiddhi. Sanlun was considered part of the Satyasiddhi school, whose doctrine was based on Abhidharma theory and centered around the Hīnayāna concept of the Four Noble Truths. Sûngnang, however, made a distinction between Satyasiddhi and Sanlun, and he demarcated a boundary between the Old and New Sanlun. He is best known for his two-truth theory, in which he distinguished between conventional and ultimate truth. In his view, these are not ontological truths, but represent rather a convenient pedagogical device for teachers. In discussions concerning truth, some say that it is existence, some say that it is nonexistence, others say that it is either existence or nonexistence, while still others say that it is neither existence nor nonexistence. Sûngnang claimed, however, that none of these statements represent the complete truth, but merely indicate one aspect of it. Thus, in his view, the two truths represent different expressions of the excellent teaching of the Middle Path.

For Sûngnang, the Middle Path was not a state situated between existence and nonexistence, or duality and non-duality. Rather, he saw it as consisting of three levels: on the first level, the existence of all beings is considered as conventional truth, and the emptiness of all things is regarded as ultimate truth. Here, emptiness is called ultimate truth in response to the followers of Abhidharma who advocated the existence of *dharmas*. On the second level, the existence and emptiness of the first level are both viewed as conventional truth while the denial of both is seen as ultimate truth. This is Sûngnang's rebuttal to the Satyasiddhi school, which admits the dualism of existence and emptiness, positing emptiness as ultimate truth. Finally, on the third and last level, it is recognized that both truths as well as all three levels, are merely teaching devices. Thus, the three gates or three levels are expounded only in order to realize the truth of not three. This non-acquisition of, and non-abiding in, one level or one truth is initially named the ultimate.

The structure of Sûngnang's theory indicates a process of continuing dialectics to a level of infinity. As such, it negates any fixed concepts which regard the ultimate as a state arrived at through progression. For Sûngnang and his followers, a highest level does not exist; rather, this dialectic method of denial continues endlessly. The ultimate truth, then, cannot be the ultimate; it is not an absolute reality. This is why Sûngnang asserted that the two-truth theory was not a principle but only a pedagogical tool. He showed clearly that it is not possible to verbalize or conceptualize about ultimate truth. Any attempt to do so will only bring one back to the level of conventional truth. This unique philosophy marked the beginning of the New Sanlun school and was elaborated on first by Zhouyong and then by Jizang, who finalized its ideas in the latter half of the sixth century.

2 Unified Silla period (668-935 AD)

This period was one of religious maturity and innovation; as such, it represented the culmination of Buddhist influence in Korea, both culturally and doctrinally. Buddhism fully blossomed and flourished at this time, reaching heights that it would never see again. On the one hand, influences from China were still felt, as new schools of thought were introduced by Silla monks returning from the Tang dynasty. On the other hand, Korean Buddhist scholarship by such eminent monks as Wônhyo (617–86) played an important role in the development of Chinese Buddhist thought as well. However, unlike the Tang tendency towards sectarianism, Unified Silla leaned towards a synthesis of various aspects of Buddhist thought into a type of interdenominational philosophy, the so-called *t'ong pulgyo*, or Buddhism of total interpenetration. The syncretic approach of Korean Buddhist philosophy can be best understood under the following headings: the reconciliation of doctrinal disputes, the Silla Hwaom School, the Silla Vijñānavāda School, and the introduction of Sôn (Chan) Buddhism from China.

3 Unified Silla period: reconciliation of doctrinal disputes

One of the most important proponents of this syncretic approach was the noted monk and scholar WÔNHYO. In his view, the various disputes which arose among Buddhist scholars were similar to the story of the blind men's description of an elephant: each man was only defining one aspect of the animal. In one sense, they were all wrong, because each failed to fully describe the elephant. In another sense, however, they were not entirely wrong, as what they were describing was not something other than the elephant.

Wônhyo was not interested in merely partial or incomplete understandings, however; rather, he focused on integrating a variety of doctrines into one complete view, as seen from a higher perspective. This view has been termed *hwajaeng*, or the 'reconciliation of doctrinal controversy'. The hermeneutical device used in this doctrinal reconciliation is well represented in his unique genre of Buddhist commentarial work, *chong-yo*, as well as in his concepts of *kae* (unfolding or opening) and *hap* (folding or sealing) the truth. Wônhyo is believed to have composed approximately seventeen of these *chong-yo*, of which only five are extant. *Chong* translates as doctrine or theme, and *yo* means essence. Thus, for example, one of his works, the *Yolban'gyong chongyo*, translates as the 'Doctrinal Essentials of the Nirvāṇa Sutra'. Here, 'doctrine' refers to the various ideas which are discussed, and 'essentials' integrates them into one primary framework of thought. Similarly, by his usage of the word 'unfolding' (*kae*), Wônhyo indicates a variety of ideas and analyses, while through 'folding' (*hap*) he denotes how these themes may be synthesized into one cohesive unit of understanding. Doctrine, then, reflects the unfolding of the one into the many, whereas essence refers to the folding of the many back into the one.

Another device which Wônhyo used in order to reconcile opposites and thus denote their non-duality was his theory of essence-function (Korean: *ch'e-yong*) (see TI AND YONG). In his *Taesung kisillon so* (Treatise on Awakening Mahāyāna Faith) he asserts that Mahāyāna is a synonym for One-Mind. This One-Mind represents essence, or *ch'e*, while the variety of mental and physical states, or the arising of *dharmas*, represents function, or *yong*. In terms of its internal logic, essence-function is no different from the *kae-hap* (folding and unfolding) formulation. According to Wônhyo, when the essence of Mahāyāna, or One-Mind, is unfolded, immeasurable and limitless meaning can be found in its doctrine. Conversely, when the doctrine is folded, it returns to its essence, which consists of two aspects: the absolute and the phenomenal. The limitless meanings of One-Mind are identical to this essence and are completely amalgamated within it. Therefore, One-Mind unfolds and folds freely, and establishes and refutes without restrictions.

In this way, the myriads of sensory impressions are brought to a permanent end and return to the source of One-Mind. Thus, there is nothing that is not advocated and nothing that is not refuted. Wônhyo calls the advocacy concession or acceptance (*hwanho*), and he labels the refutation variously as deprivation (*t'al*), negation (*kyon*), return (*wang*) or prohibition (*purho*).

Wônhyo was particularly concerned with using his hermeneutic tools to reconcile the Mādhyamika and Yogācāra doctrines. In his view, Nāgārjuna's *Mūla-madhyamakaśāstra* and *Dvādaśanikāyaśāstra* offer a thorough dialectic critique of all views which a person might advocate, to the extent that they abolish both the views refuted and the act of refutation (see NĀGĀRJUNA). However, because Mādhyamika dialectics do not affirmatively acknowledge both the subject and object of this refutation, the approach is purely negative, and thus nothing is established. On the other hand, the Yogācāra school accomplishes a thorough analysis of all mental states and accordingly establishes both the shallow and profound teachings. However, because the Yogācārins do not continue on to refute what they have established, theirs is a purely positive approach, and thus, nothing is refuted. Doctrinal controversy arose between the two schools due to the fact that the Mādhyamikas attached to refutation and deprivation, whereas the Yogācārins attached to establishment and acceptance. Each recognized only a part of the truth; although neither was entirely wrong, at the same time neither was altogether correct.

Wônhyo was able, based on his unique usage of unfolding and folding, to reconcile these differences by including them into a single Buddhist teaching, that of One-Mind, which allows for both affirmation and negation. According to Wônhyo, the *Taesung kisillon*, a noted Mahāyāna text upon which he based his well-known commentary, is a syncretic work which embraces the positions of both Mādhyamika and Yogācāra (see AWAKENING OF FAITH IN MAHĀYĀNA). He asserts that while it refutes all relative views (as represented by the two above-mentioned schools), it also embraces them comprehensively within the all-encompassing One-Mind.

4 Unified Silla period: Silla Hwaôm school

Another vital contribution to Korean Buddhist thought was made by ÛISANG (625–702), who was a contemporary of Wônhyo and is known as the founder of the Korean Hwaôm school (Huayan in Chinese) based on the Avatāmsaka Sūtra. Unlike Wônhyo, who had never been to China, Ûisang spent almost ten years there and studied under Zhiyan (602–68), the second patriarch of the Chinese Huayan school. The *Hwaôm ilsung popke to* (Diagram of the Dharmadhātu of the One Vehicle of Hwaôm) is Ûisang's only major extant work, and is comprised of his *Haein sammae to* (Diagram of Ocean Seal Samādhi) and an autocommentary.

The *Ocean Seal*, as it is commonly known, written while Ûisang was in China, is a poem consisting of 210 characters. It opens with the word *pop* (*dharma*) and closes with *pul* (Buddha), thus signifying the cause-and-effect relationship between the two. By placing both of these characters in the centre of a diagram in the form of a maze, Ûisang articulated the basic theme of Hwaom philosophy which asserts that beginning and end, or cause and effect, occupy the same position while still retaining their own distinctive characteristics. In this way, he depicted Hwaôm philosophy as a mystery of simultaneous mutual penetration. In addition, he pointed to the Hwaôm soteriological position that within the fifty-two stages of a *bodhisattva*'s career, the first stage of initial faith itself embodies all fifty-two stages, including the final stage of marvellous enlightenment. Of this position, a well-known Hwaôm aphorism states, 'The moment one arouses an enlightenment thought (*bodhicitta*), instantly perfect enlightenment is attained.'

Although Ûisang's expression of Hwaôm theory in the *Ocean Seal* was not his own creation, it succeeded in ably representing the main ideas of the school, both symbolically and graphically. The *Ocean Seal* is traditionally presented to monks upon completion of their course of study, a mark of how highly esteemed it is in the Korean Buddhist tradition. It is also chanted in Korean Buddhist ceremonies as a *dhāranī*, having been endowed with a special mantric power. Along with Wônhyo's philosophy of the reconciliation of opposites, Ûisang's contributions to Hwaôm theory helped to create the Korean tradition of *t'ong pulgyo* and provided the foundation for the synthesis of the doctrinal or scriptural schools (Kyo) and the meditational schools (Sôn) by Chinul in the following Koryô dynasty.

5 Unified Silla period: Silla Vijñānavāda school

There were actually three different systems of Yogācāra (or Mind-Only) philosophy which were transmitted into Korea from China during the Unified Silla period. The first can actually be traced back to the Three Kingdoms period, when Won'gwang (d. 630) returned to Korea after studying the *Mahāyānasanùgraha* (in Chinese, *Shelun*) in China. However, it was not until WÔNCH'ŪK (612–96) arrived on the scene that any significant study of Yogācāra was undertaken in Korea. Wônch'ūk is considered the major figure among Silla monks studying Yogācāra doctrine. His system is classified as the Old Yogācāra, founded by the Indian monk Paramārtha (499–569). This is in order to distinguish it from the New Yogācāra, which was founded by the Chinese monk Xuanzang (602–64). Xuanzang translated Dharmapāla's *Vijñāptimātratāsiddhi* into Chinese and his new school, which was established on the basis of this text, became known as the Faxiang (Dharma Characteristics) school.

The two Yogācāra schools, Old and New, differed in their theoretical approaches and there were conflicts between them. Wônch'ūk and his disciples eventually established their own school, called the Ximing school. This was followed by the Silla Vijñānavāda school, which included such noted monks as Tojung and T'aehyon. Vijñānavāda theory in Silla developed its own unique characteristics quite distinct from those of Xuanzang's school in China. The Silla school not only effected a synthesis of the various Vijñānavāda schools in China, but it also adopted theories from other Chinese schools, such as Tientai and Huayan. It achieved this synthesis through its understanding of the term 'One Vehicle', an approach made possible by the work of Wônhyo. Like Wônhyo, the Silla Vijñānavāda school attempted to reconcile the teaching of Mādhyamika with that of Yogācāra, but by using the concept of one sound as its reference point. Here, Wônch'ūk was referring to the Buddha's teaching, which has one meaning but is given different explanations depending on one's level of understanding. Wônch'ūk's concept of 'one sound' is, of course, comparable to the concept of the One Vehicle, as both are nothing but teaching devices used to comprehend various understandings from a higher vantage point.

6 Unified Silla period: introduction of Sôn

A new epoch occurred in Korean Buddhism upon the transmission of Sôn (Chan) Buddhism from China. This new movement, with its strong emphasis on meditational practice, entered Korea not long after it was introduced into China. According to traditional accounts, it was Pômnang (*fl.* 632–46) who first introduced Chan Buddhism to Korea, following his study under Daoxin (580–651), the fourth patriarch of the Chinese Chan school. His lineage was passed down through Sinhaeng, Chunbôm and Hyeûn until it reached Chisôn Tohon (824–82), who founded the Mount Huiyang school, the oldest Sôn lineage in Korea, in 879. Within a hundred-year period, from the eighth to the ninth centuries, eight other mountain schools were founded. From this time onwards, the term Nine Mountains has come to represent Korean Sôn schools in general, and this number remained unchanged during the early Koryô period.

In contrast to the Chinese Chan schools, which were categorized as the Five Schools and Seven Orders and which maintained sharp sectarian distinctions, the Korean Nine Mountain schools were classified according to the identities of their founders. Only a monk who had originally studied in China was entitled to be the founder of a new school. Furthermore, in the Korean tradition, the relation between teacher and disciple was considered more important than the philosophical doctrine espoused. This differed sharply from the Chinese Chan tradition, in which lineage affiliation was based directly on doctrine. The Korean approach was to regard what they called the Five Schools and Seven Orders not as different schools, but rather as different families of the same school. For this reason, the Nine Mountain schools, regardless of their founders, were all considered to belong to the Chogye order. The name Chogye (in Chinese, Zaoxi) was taken from the mountain associated with Huineng, who was regard as the progenitor of Chan before its division into five schools and seven orders.

Eight of Korea's nine mountain schools (the exception was the Mount Sumi school) were derived from or related to the Chinese Hongzhou school. As noted by Zongmi (780–841), the noted Chinese Buddhist commentator and philosopher, the Hongzhou school had a close doctrinal affiliation with Huayan. Most of the Korean monks who came to China to study Buddhism were already familiar with Hwaôm philosophy, as it was the predominant school in Korea at that time. Therefore it is not surprising that they were attracted to the Hongzhou school. However, the fundamental difference between Huayan and Chan must not be overlooked: while the former emphasizes scriptural study, the latter rejects it, choosing rather to espouse 'a separate transmission outside the scriptures'. This crucial difference may also have attracted the Silla monks, who were perhaps frustrated with the philosophically elaborate and priest-centred Hwaôm school.

Immediately upon Sôn's introduction to Unified Silla, an antagonistic tension was created between the new Sôn and the old doctrinal schools, particularly Hwaôm. Sôn masters perceived the scripture-based Hwaôm school as antithetical to their practice-oriented mission. Later, however, they altered their approach in an effort to synthesize the messages of the two schools.

7 Koryô period (918–1392): parallel cultivation of doctrinal study and contemplation

Upon the collapse of the Silla dynasty, the Korean peninsula reverted back to three kingdoms, until King T'aejo unified the country and subsequently founded the Koryô dynasty. Under the Koryô, Buddhism was fully supported not only by the royal family but by the entire apparatus of the Korean government. The price, however, was tight government control.

Despite these controls, discord between the radical Sôn schools and the more conservative doctrinal proponents continued, and it was not till Ûich'ôn (1055–1101) that a serious attempt was made to reconcile these conflicts. Although his background was in Hwaôm, Ûich'ôn studied various schools of Buddhist thought throughout his career. Most notably, he travelled to China in 1085 and studied with renowned teachers of the Huayan, Tientai, Pure Land, Vinaya and Chan sects there. Upon returning to Korea, he attempted to incorporate Sôn into the system of Tientai (in Korean, Ch'ônt'ae). He felt that meditation was essential not only for followers of Sôn but for members of all Buddhist schools, and he criticized the polarization of the two approaches, doctrinal and meditational. From his perspective, which favoured scriptural study yet also emphasized meditational practice, although *dharma* is devoid of words and appearances, it is not separate from them. Similarly, doctrinal study and meditation do not oppose each other but should be seen as complements; each is a requisite tool for the attainment of awakening.

Yet Ûich'ôn was unable to accept the radical doctrine of the Sôn of his time. He acknowledged the validity of Sôn only on the condition that it remained based on scriptural teachings. For him, the Sôn dictum of 'transmission outside the scriptures' was not acceptable as a valid Buddhist teaching. He believed that the practitioners of his time, by

abandoning the scriptures, were veering dangerously towards heresy. He felt that his own *kyogwan kyomsu*, or 'parallel cultivation of doctrinal study and contemplation', was the correct approach. Viewing the system of Ch'ônt'ae as one which harmonized Sôn and scriptural study, Ûich'ôn attempted to consolidate the Sôn school into the Ch'ônt'ae order. However, he was unable to accomplish this, thanks not only to his early death, but also to of his narrow understanding of Sôn.

It was CHINUL (1158–1210) who effectively assimilated Sôn into the mainstream Korean Buddhist tradition, if not in its entirety, at least in the area of doctrine. Chinul lived during one of the most difficult times in the history of Koryô Buddhism. Having become dependent on the support of the government, Koryô Buddhism had lost most, if not all, of its earlier spiritual vitality; corruption was at its peak and discipline in the monasteries was increasingly lax. Chinul perceived the Buddhism of his day as subject to 'ten kinds of disease', and his endeavours to effect a rapprochement between the Sôn and doctrinal schools were founded on his deep concern about this decline.

If Wônhyo's philosophy of harmonization was aimed at ending the doctrinal disputes among the various schools, Chinul's intent was to provide a theoretical scheme for harmonizing Sôn with the scriptural schools, and to offer a radical approach to the issue of final enlightenment based on the doctrinal teachings of Mahāyāna. He attempted ultimately to provide a systematic, theoretical framework which would incorporate both theory and experience. Being a Sôn monk, he was deeply aware that only through one's own experience can one attain final, ultimate liberation. The primary value of his theory, then, was that it clearly displayed an understanding of the necessity of practice.

Unlike Ûich'ôn, whose viewpoint was rooted in the doctrinal teachings, Chinul's foundation was in Sôn. His syncretic vision was therefore to establish a new Sôn school which would incorporate not only various teachings of the traditional Chan schools in China, but various doctrinal teachings as well. His primary intent was to systematize a comprehensive soteriological scheme for Sôn which would be pertinent to practitioners of various levels of capacity. He was inspired in this task by the great Chinese Buddhist thinker ZONGMI, a patriarch of both the Huayan and the Heze school of Chan. Chinul, deeply frustrated with the deterioration of Sôn in his time, was especially attracted by the balanced approach of the Heze school, which encompassed both the intellectual understanding of the scriptural teachings and the radical, anti-intellectual spirit of Chan. Chinul's soteriological scheme of sudden enlightenment followed by gradual self-cultivation reflects the Heze approach.

In an inscription written by Kunsu Kim (*fl.* 1216–20), it is said that Chinul established three main approaches to Sôn practice, directly reflecting his own enlightenment experiences: the balanced practice of meditation and wisdom, inspired by the *Platform Sutra* (see PLATFORM SUTRA); faith and understanding according to the complete and sudden teachings, inspired by the Li Tongxuan's *Exposition of the Huayanjing* (*Avatamsaka Sūtra*); and finally, the shortcut approach of *hwadu* (in Chinese, *huatou*) investigation. We can elucidate Chinul's philosophical system by examining these three approaches.

8 Koryô period: balanced cultivation of meditation and wisdom

In his *Susim kyol* (Secrets on Cultivating the Mind), Chinul elucidates a method for cultivating the mind after a sudden, initial enlightenment experience. According to him, sudden enlightenment represents a realization of the nature of true mind as having two aspects: voidness and calmness in its essence, and numinous awareness in its function. These in turn correspond to the two aspects of *dharma*, immutability and adaptability. Mind is in its essence originally void and calm, and yet at the same time it adapts freely in infinite ways, depending on one's level of consciousness. Thus if one's consciousness is deluded, Mind appears ignorant, while if it is awakened, Mind manifests a numinous awareness.

In Chinul's system, gradual practice should follow after the sudden, initial awakening to the nature of True Mind. Chinul correlates the essence and function of Mind with meditation (*samādhi*) and wisdom (*prajñā*), respectively: in the task of cultivation, meditation is the essence and wisdom is the function of Mind; they are inseparable, nondual aspects of the same thing. This dynamic concept of the interrelationship of meditation and wisdom further entails that in cultivating Mind one should be alert in the void and calm mental state, and calm in the state of numinous awareness: calm and alertness represent meditation and wisdom, which are inseparable and nondual, and thus must be practiced simultaneously in cultivation.

Even if one attains a sudden awakening to the nature of Mind and thus realizes the identity of meditation and wisdom, the balanced cultivation of meditation and wisdom is still important: due to the residue of defilements and the karmic force deriving from long-standing habits, one's mind-nature does not always have its original harmony. The two

nondual, inseparable aspects of mind, essence and function, can become bifurcated, as if they were two different, separate entities. An excess of essence can produce too much calmness, which in turn leads to dullness, while an excess of function can produce over-alertness, thereby easily causing distraction.

Since Chinul follows the sudden approach to enlightenment, in which enlightenment precedes cultivation, his interpretation of meditation and *samādhi* as essence and function differs from that of the gradual school of Sôn. In the latter, where practices are centred on the gradual removal of defilements in order to achieve perfect Buddhahood, meditation is used to counter the defilements in the conditioned realm, and wisdom is used thereafter to counter discriminative thinking. These two different methods are intended to ultimately achieve a penetrating insight into the nature of reality. However, although Chinul does not exclude the possibility that the gradual approach to meditation and wisdom may be used as an expedient means for counteracting defilements, he felt it should be allowed only after the experience of sudden awakening. In fact, Chinul urges that at all levels of practice, as well as at all stages of a practitioner's development, both meditation and wisdom should be combined, just as the principle of balance, that is, of calmness and alertness, must be maintained in order to access the enlightenment experience.

9 Koryô period: faith and understanding according to the complete and sudden teaching

More often than not, the doctrinal teachings based on scriptures were considered by Sôn masters as a grave fallacy, an impediment to attaining final enlightenment. From their perspective, this is especially true because the conceptual or discriminatory nature of doctrinal teachings cannot invoke the Absolute, which is ineffable. On the other hand, Hwaôm, as one of the doctrinal schools, considered Sôn as merely representing the sudden teaching, which they considered a lesser teaching than the final, complete doctrine of Hwaôm. These two main branches of Mahāyāna Buddhism thus seemed to contradict each other, not only in terms of doctrinal framework, but also in their soteriological schemes.

Chinul believed that Sôn and Hwaôm were not necessarily contradictory, but could serve to complement each other. He felt that the conceptual framework of Hwaôm could help to enhance practitioners' understanding, especially those with a lesser capacity, of the mind-to-mind transmission of the esoteric teachings of Sôn. He was especially concerned about the Sôn practitioners of his time, whom he felt had strayed from correct practice due to their lack of a proper understanding of scriptural teachings. He feared that they were meditating in a state of ignorance and thus in vain. Chinul felt that proper guidance in the scriptural teachings was necessary for them to achieve final enlightenment

However, it was not an easy task to synthesize the two, thanks to their different orientations. Hwaôm philosophy systemized the path to enlightenment into fifty-two stages, beginning with the ten levels of faith and ending with the stage of Buddhahood. Often a temporal scheme was assumed, such as a period of three incalculable aeons, or more than several lives, from the initial stage of faith to the final attainment of Buddhahood. Within this progressive scheme, Hwaôm soteriology postulated a process of learning, practice and realization, in which each stage proceeds sequentially in a causal relationship. Chinul thus incorporated the soteriology of Hwaôm, which assumes a progressive development within a temporal scheme, into the sudden teaching approach of Sôn. It was in Li Tongxuan's *Exposition of the Avatamsaka Sutra* that he found a means of incorporating the two systems into a viable soteriological scheme.

Inspired by Li Tongxuan's unique interpretation of the Huayan soteriological structure, and recapitulating the latter's essential message, Chinul was able to propose, as another possible approach to Sôn practice, the method of faith and understanding as detailed in his *Wondon Songbullon* (Complete and Sudden Attainment of Buddhahood). Chinul noted that unmoving wisdom, or the wisdom of universal brightness, is essentially identical with the deluded mind. Through a sudden awakening to this essential identity, one can enter directly the initial abiding stage, the stage of the arising of *bodhicitta*, in which one may directly experience the fact that one is a Buddha. From this stage onward, the subsequent stages of the *bodhisattva* path can be instantly achieved because of the functioning of inherent Buddhahood. Such a soteriological structure is possible due to the fact that unmoving wisdom is not merely a fruit to be attained at the final stage, but also a cause for the final attainment of buddhahood. Moreover, from the initial stage of faith to the final attainment of buddhahood, it is the unmoving wisdom of Buddha which operates unceasingly.

10 Koryô period: shortcut approach of *hwadu* investigation

Although Chinul incorporated the theoretical framework of Hwaôm into Sôn practice, he did not forget to indicate that theories and conceptual frameworks need to be abandoned at a certain stage. In their place,

Chinul proposed his method of *hwadu* investigation, which is like a finger pointing to the moon.

Chinul never lost sight of the fact that the goal of Sôn practice is to transcend conceptual understanding, thus leaving behind all discriminatory thoughts. As a means of achieving this goal Chinul found the investigation of *hwadu* most effective, a method, which in his words, cuts through iron and split nails.

Hwadu is often considered a synonym for *kongan* (in Chinese, *gongan*). More precisely, however, the *hwadu* is the essential point of the *kongan*, which is used as a topic of meditation in the Sôn school. The purpose of *hwadu* investigation is to help practitioners break through views based on their conceptual understanding of the *dharma* and to ultimately return them to the source of all discriminative thought. Thus, Chinul referred to the function of the *hwadu* as one of cleansing knowledge and understanding.

The *hwadu* method is also called the shortcut approach, as it involves no conceptual descriptions but rather points one directly to the truth right from the inception of practice. In his *Kanhwa Kyorui Ron* (Resolving Doubts About Observing the *Hwadu*), Chinul discusses the three mystery gates, or three different methods, differentiated according to one's capacity for attaining the ultimate teaching of the Sôn school: (1) the mystery of essence, which involves the conceptual understanding of the Buddha-*dharma*, such as the doctrine of the unimpeded interpenetration of all phenomena of the Hwaôm school; (2) the mystery of the word, which helps one eliminate the defects of conceptual understanding and ultimately destroy it; and (3) the mystery of mystery, in which practitioners abandon the interpretive analytical approach altogether and investigate the word itself. This method transcends any trace of a sign which a word may signify and finally results in the awareness of the noumenal state, that is, the void and calm state of mind.

In making *hwadu* the cardinal approach of Sôn practice, Chinul was influenced by Dahui Zonggao (1089–1163), a disciple of Yuanwu Gejin of the Linji school in China. Inspired by the *Dahui yulu* (The Records of Dahui), Chinul was the first Korean Sôn master to introduce the *hwadu* into Korean Sôn practice. *Hwadu* became a hallmark of Korean Sôn and, combined with the concurrent cultivation of meditation and wisdom, and the doctrine of sudden awakening and gradual practice, represents the essence of Korean Sôn.

In summary, Chinul systematized a Korean approach to Sôn practice which stood apart from all other schemes. Its uniqueness lay in the fact that it synthesized the doctrinal teachings into Sôn practice, provided a theoretical framework for Sôn practice, and maintained the fundamental spirit of Sôn teaching by postulating *hwadu* investigation as a shortcut to the final attainment of enlightenment. With only slight variations through the ages, this structure has been maintained by Korean Sôn practitioners ever since.

After Chinul's time, Koryô Buddhism began to gradually decline. This was primarily due to the political instability of the Koryô court after the Mongol invasion, but it was caused in part by the corruption of the Buddhist monasteries and monks. However, there were still contributions made by such monks as Kyônghan Paegun (1290–1374), T'aego Pou (1301–82) and Naong Hyegûn (1320–76), who tried to restore the strength of Buddhism in the latter Koryô. All three had returned from Yuan China after studying under the Linji (in Korean, Imje) school, which places a strong emphasis on *hwadu* practice. The most radical and confrontational methods of the Linji school became very popular in Korea and had a great impact on Korean Sôn practice. However, due to the general social instability of the times, there was insufficient support for a sustained reinvigoration of Buddhism.

In this period of decline the Korean literati, whose official education was grounded in neo-Confucian philosophy, succeeded in supplanting Buddhism as a state-sponsored ideology (see CONFUCIAN PHILO-SOPHY, KOREAN). Chinese philosophies, such as Daoism and neo-Confucianism, became increasingly influential, and monks like Kyônghan and Naong began to study these schools of thought. This represents the beginning of another unique trend in Korean Buddhism, as monks began to emphasize the study of non-Buddhist philosophies. Korea became more and more Confucianized, first in a political sense and later throughout society as a whole. This move toward Confucianism began gradually in the latter period of Koryô and accelerated with the beginning of the Chosôn dynasty, which was founded in 1392.

11 Chosôn period (1392–1910)

The Chosôn dynasty was founded on the basis of neo-Confucianism, which combined a strong political ideology with a practical ethics emphasizing the importance of the family. Neo-Confucianism was strongly antagonistic towards Buddhism, as Buddhist monks left their families and maintained strict celibacy. During the Chosôn dynasty Buddhism was not only suppressed by those in political power but also largely ignored by intellectuals. In terms of social stratification, monks were ranked in the same class as the servants and were not allowed to enter the capital city. Amidst such harsh circumstances, Buddhism became completely marginalized.

The Buddhists of this period used their adverse circumstances as an opportunity to systematize a harmonized perspective which reconciled the philosophical conflicts among neo-Confucianism, Buddhism and Daoism (the three systems were often called *samgyo* or the Three Religions.) This synthesis in turn served once again to set Korean Buddhism apart as a unique system of thought.

Kihwa (1376–1433), otherwise known as Hamhô Tûkt'ong, continued the syncretic view of Korean Sôn systematized by Chinul, and was also the first Buddhist monk to advocate Buddhism against the neo-Confucian attack. He was also the first Buddhist monk to assert the intrinsic unity of the three religions, Buddhism, Confucianism and Daoism. Kihwa's life and times are reflected in his philosophical system. He was a prolific writer of Buddhist exegeses, in which he freely used Confucian concepts as well as citations from Confucian texts in order to clarify Buddhist ideas: he saw Buddhism and Confucianism as supplementary and not contradictory systems. He objected not only to the exclusivist attitude of Sôn practitioners toward the doctrinal schools, but also of Confucianism toward Buddhism. Before he studied Buddhism he was educated, like most sons from upperclass families, in the Confucian classics. He often used poetry, both from his own pen and from the classics, as a means of elucidating Buddhist texts (see CHINESE CLASSICS).

His syncretic approach is well demonstrated in his *Hyônjông non* (Treatise on Manifesting Righteousness). In this apologetic essay on the unity of Buddhism and Confucianism, he not only defends Buddhism using the language of Confucians, but he goes one step further and advocates Buddhism using scriptural evidence from the Confucian classics. In this treatise, Kihwa identifies the various mental functions, which he termed usually as the arising of *dharma*, with emotions, often described as the obstruction of the true nature of mind in neo-Confucianism. In so doing, he is pointing out the similarities between Buddhism and Confucianism in the sense that both attempt to eliminate the arising of *dharma* or obstructions of the mind so that the true nature will be manifested. Buddhists call this the 'enlightened state', while Confucians call it 'being a saint'. Kihwa stressed that in terms of the final goal there is no discrepancy between them, and in fact there exists an intrinsic unity between the two. Further, as the title *Treatise on Manifesting Righteousness* implies, Kihwa saw that both ultimately reveal the truth. He also demonstrated that Buddhist cultivation does not differ from the Confucian principle of cultivating the mind, step by step, beginning with cultivation of the personal life, continuing with regulation of the family and national order, and finally ending with world peace (see DAXUE). Moreover, he claimed that the Buddhist teaching allowed people to pursue different levels of practice according to their capacity, from the *bodhisattva* path to the merit-making of ordinary people. With this, Kihwa intended to demonstrate the superiority of the Buddhist teaching, which in his view embraces a universality that includes all kinds of people, in contrast to the soteriology of Confucianism, which is often limited to the highly educated.

Regarding the social aspect of the two systems, Confucianism was often considered to be superior to Buddhism. Kihwa believed otherwise. He felt that the Confucian system, by using tactics of reward and punishment in governing the people, enforced a mere superficial obedience. In contrast, as Buddhism based its teachings on the law of cause and effect, and as it further propagated the value of silence through meditation, it promoted a more spontaneous response.

Kihwa also developed the issue of social ethics, including filial piety, the most important aspect of Confucian ethics, into the greater context of truth itself, which he termed *to* (in Chinese, *dao*), or the Way. He defined the Buddhist perspective of the truth, the Way, as consisting of two aspects, the unchangeable principle and temporary expediency. According to him, only by both maintaining principle and adapting to change through the use of expedients can one achieve completion of the Way. However, the formalistic and family-centred ethics of Confucianism cannot achieve both of these goals. Similarly, he felt that one who is still subject to passions is not able to be loyal to the state and, at same time, to be filial at home. Only when one becomes free from one's own passions and conceptual boundaries can one extend oneself to universal altruism, as represented in the Confucian concept of humanity, *in* (in Chinese, *ren*), or the great compassion of Buddhism. Residing in the mountains away from home is neither unfilial nor disloyal, but is a greater form of filial piety and loyalty to the state, unimpeded by any particular phenonema. The Buddhist aim of achieving an unimpeded state between principle and phenomena, as well as among phenomena, was focused not on leaving society or the world, but rather on realizing the perfection of society.

Unlike the fourth and fifth century Chinese apologetic defenses of Buddhism, Kihwa defended Buddhism more positively and often advocated its superiority. However, before he became a Buddhist he was well known as a promising young Confucian scholar. One of his biographical accounts tells us that his interest in Buddhism was motivated by the sudden death of a friend, and also by a monk who questioned him about the Confucian practice of encouraging people to serve their parents meat, yet espousing universal affection toward all living beings. As this account illustrates, his spiritual and intellectual quest was more concerned with ontological and soteriological issues. Although he seems to have found some insight through Sôn meditation, his quest did not stop there, but further impelled him to discern an intrinsic unity among the various philosophical and religious teachings of his time. His pseudonym was Tûkt'ong, which means attainment of interpenetration; it is an apt title, as he diligently pursued this goal not merely in regard to Sôn and the Buddhist doctrinal teachings, but also in connection to all the existing teachings of his time. Dismissing the question as to which of the three teachings, Confucianism, Buddhism or Daoism, was superior, he instead felt that they were intrinsically identical. For Kihwa, the Daoist teachings of non-action and the Confucian teachings of being responsive but always calm were no different from the teaching of Sôn Buddhism, which espouses being: 'Calm but always illuminating; illuminating but always calm.'

Wônhyo's synthesis of the various doctrinal disputes was succeeded and developed by Chinul's syncretic view attesting to the unity of Sôn and scriptural teaching; this in turn was followed by Kihwa's harmonization of the three religious teachings. This tradition of the syncretic perspective in Korean Buddhism was further developed by Hyujông (1520–1604), known as Sôsan Taesa (Great Master of the Western Mountain) (see SÔSAN HYUJÔNG).

Hyujông was not only the central Buddhist figure during the Chosôn period, but also one of the most influential figures in the entire history of Korean Buddhism. He not only continued to propagate the syncretic perspective of the unity of Sôn and doctrinal teachings as formulated by Chinul, but he also attempted to reconcile the three teachings in terms of their ultimate message of truth.

By Hyujông's time, the various doctrinal schools had been reconfigured into one unified school, called Kyo, or scriptural teaching, while the Sôn schools were categorized under the single, unified name of Sôn. The conflict between Sôn and the doctrinal teachings still existed as an active point of controversy among Korean monks. As the titles of his major works, such as *Sôn'ga kwigam* (The Mirror of the Sôn school), *Sôn'gyo sôk* (An Interpretation of Sôn and Kyo) and *Sôn'gyo kyôl* (The Secret on Sôn and Kyo), illustrate, Hyujông's major concern was to reconcile Sôn and the scriptural teachings by incorporating the doctrinal schools into Sôn. While generally agreeing with Chinul's syncretic teachings, Hyujông contrasted Sôn practice more sharply with Kyo and ultimately espoused Sôn's supremacy. He felt that since the intrinsic unity of Sôn and Kyo had already been clarified by the efforts of Chinul, his mission was not to reassert this point, but rather to establish a correct relationship between the two in terms of the means of attaining ultimate enlightenment.

According to Hyujông, the source of both Sôn and Kyo are the Buddha, but one refers to his mind and the other to his words. Regarding the relation between Sôn and Kyo, he asserted that Kyo is what reaches wordlessness from the word, while Sôn is what reaches wordlessness from wordlessness itself. Wordlessness means here the true nature of mind or the enlightenment state which cannot be reached through any verbal, logical description. By saying that both Kyo and Sôn reach wordlessness, however, Hyujông did not mean that one can reach the ultimate state through Kyo. Rather, he meant that Kyo, beginning with the word (that is, scriptural teaching), should be applied and then continued ultimately for the purpose of attaining the state of wordlessness. In other words, one may begin practice by studying Kyo, but in the process of attaining enlightenment, Kyo must be discarded and Sôn must be practised. This relation between Sôn and Kyo is well elaborated in his theory of *sagyo ipson*, the principle of abandoning Kyo and entering Sôn, which is still followed in present day Korean Buddhism. In this way, Hyujông acknowledged the efficacy of Kyo as a part of Buddhist practice, yet he also asserted the supremacy of Sôn practice by postulating the limitations of intellectual understanding. Thus, he refused to recognize the possibility of attaining enlightenment through the use of Kyo alone. Of course, not every practitioner needs to follow both Kyo and Sôn practices successively. According to Hyujông, the person of high capacity may not find it necessary to follow both practices, but the person of middle or low capacity cannot omit doctrinal study, Kyo.

In his other work, *Samga Kwigam* (Mirror of the Three Teachings), Hyujông's purpose was to demonstrate that all of the three East Asian intellectual traditions, Confucianism, Buddhism and Daoism, ultimately lead to the truth, *to*, or the Way. The intrinsic unity of the three teachings was first expostulated by his predecessor, Kihwa. However, while Kihwa's approach can be said to incorporate Confucianism and Daoism into Buddhism, especially Sôn Buddhism, and thus ultimately to advocate the superior position of the Buddhist teaching, Hyujông's approach was different. He shows us the core or the essentials of the three teachings, and by doing so he reveals the similarities among the three, although he does not ignore their differences. He felt that to espouse the superiority of one teaching over another was to be guilty of sectarianism. In interpreting each teaching of the three religions, he used a higher perspective to reconcile their minor differences into the greater context of their intrinsic unity. His approach, the synthesis of discrepancies into a higher perspective, immediately reminds one of Wônhyo's method of *kae* (unfolding) and *hap* (folding): by unfolding discrepancies, the various functions of the truth are displayed, and by folding them, the discrepancies are reconciled into the essence of the truth itself. In the epilogue of the *Samga Kwigam*, he mentions that his intention is to provide a communication channel while overcoming the limits of sectarian views. He called the three teachings 'three gates', indicating his perception of them as different means of attaining the ultimate goal. This goal, which is the realization of the ultimate truth, has often been termed *to*, or the Way, in the East Asian tradition, and carries no sectarian connotation. To realize this *to*, one's mind-eye, or wisdom, is the key. Hyujông's all-inclusive spirit, which perpetuates the long syncretic tradition of Korean religious thought, continues to have a great impact on contemporary Korean Buddhism.

12 Conclusion

Since Buddhism was introduced into the Korean peninsula during the latter half of the fourth century, Korean Buddhism has undergone three major paradigm shifts. The first occurred as a response to Korea's indigenous belief system, which may be characterized as shamanistic animism; this period extends from Buddhism's incipient stage to the Three Kingdoms period. The second shift represents the Korean effort to understand various doctrines and corresponds to the Unified Silla and Koryô periods. The third shift involved the defense of Buddhism from the criticisms of neo-Confucianism during the Chosôn period. Each paradigm shift represented a Buddhist response to challenges from either within or outside itself; in this way, Korean Buddhist philosophy developed continually. The new understandings which occurred at each shift did not disappear with the next shift, but rather remained as integral aspects of the Korean Buddhist tradition.

Buddhism's first challenge came from the indigenous shamanistic beliefs which had helped to consolidate the various tribes of the peninsula into unified kingdoms. The Korean Buddhist response was *hoguk pulgyo*, or state-protection Buddhism. Lectures on Buddhist *sūtras* as well as ceremonies to ensure national security were held regularly during the Koryô period. Even during the Chosôn period, when Buddhism was suppressed, the tradition of *hoguk pulgyo* continued in modified form as armed monks organized into armies to resist the Japanese invasion. Although the concept of *hoguk pulgyo* was never elaborated into a sophisticated philosophy, it is nevertheless a pervasive element in the development of Korean Buddhism.

In the second shift characterizing the Koreanization of Buddhism, both Wônhyo and Chinul played pivotal roles. By Wônhyo's time, the major Buddhist texts, as well as the doctrines of the numerous Chinese Buddhist schools, had been introduced to Korea. Wônhyo, using his own hermeneutics of *kae* (unfolding) and *hap* (folding), and his *hwajaeng* (reconciliation of disputes) theory, attempted to reconcile the various doctrinal disputes. In doing so, he neither accepted nor denied any one sectarian perspective. While refusing to accept any one particular doctrine as the whole truth, he recognized all doctrines as the unfolding of one mind, or the Buddha-nature. On the other hand, by 'folding' the various disputes, he synthesized them into a higher perspective of the truth. This approach reflected the fundamental spirit of Korean Buddhism, which preferred to emphasize the similarities rather than the discrepancies among Buddhist schools and among other religions. Thus the primary characteristic of Korean Buddhism, *t'ong pulgyo*, the Buddhism of total interpenetration, began with Wônhyo. It was Chinul, during the Koryô period, who attempted to reconcile the disputes between Sôn and Hwaôm, the latter representing the scriptural tradition in Korean Buddhism. To establish a new approach to Sôn, he assimilated the theoretical framework of Hwaôm, long considered to be the anithesis of the Sôn approach.

The third shift came from the challenge of neo-Confuciansm, which became the new state ideology of the Chosôn dynasty. Kihwa, and later Hyujông, attempted to maintain the tradition of Chinul's syncretic approach to Sôn while at the same time creating the theoretical framework for the intrinsic unity of the three major intellectual traditions of Korea and all East Asia: Confucianism, Buddhism and Daoism. Continuing the approach, begun by Wônhyo and Chinul, of reconciling disputes by way of a higher perspective, Hyujông suggested that each of the three teachings is a gate leading to the same goal, that is, the *to*, or Way.

In the early twentieth century Korean Buddhists, together with the rest of their countrymen, suffered from colonization by Japan. During this time, from 1910 to 1945, many Korean Buddhist monks such as Master Yongsông (1864–1940), Master Hanyông (1870–1948) and, most notably, Master Manhae (1879–1944) became engaged in a variety of political activities. These worldly involvements, which pulled them away from their practice in the mountains, were undertaken in the *bodhisattva* spirit, that is, as a means of helping to directly alleviate the suffering of others. Due to their participation in these activities, philosophical study was also undermined. Those monks who wished to study Buddhism on a scholarly level travelled to Japan and enrolled in universities there. Japanese Buddhists in turn left their own country for Europe and absorbed the Western perspective from such countries as England, Germany and France. They gradually incorporated this new knowledge into their previous systems of understanding, and in the process Japanese Buddhist philosophy was significantly altered. The Korean monks who visited Japan were exposed to this new perspective and dutifully introduced it to their fellow Buddhists upon returning to Korea. From this time also, Buddhism began to be taught in the universities. This period marks the beginning of a bifurcation between monks and scholars, the significance of which became increasingly reflected in Buddhist scholarship.

In the 1970s and 1980s the philosophical study of Buddhism began to re-appear with renewed interest and energy. This was due to both external and internal factors: externally, Korean Buddhism faced new challenges from the West, primarily in the forms of Christianity and Western philosophy, while internally, the division between monks and scholars had become even more pronounced. In the 1980s a debate arose among monks and scholars over the issue of 'sudden' versus 'gradual'. Although this debate centred around the age-old conflict between direct experience and intellectual understanding, and thus between Sôn and doctrinal schools, due to the above-mentioned influences the conflict has become a new focus for modern Korean Buddhist thought. The debate itself has become well known not only throughout Korea but internationally as well. Yet to this day, no satisfactory resolution has been reached: some emphasize the importance of direct experience while others stress the necessity of intellectual understanding. Perhaps the conflict cannot be resolved, and this may be a reflection of our modern times. Yet what seems to be called for is a new methodology with which to consider the problem. The *t'ong pulgyo*'s perspective is unique to Korea and has served well in the past. Can Korean Buddhists find another way to embrace the understanding which it signifies, or do they need to discover an altogether different means of confronting the issue, one that stands outside of *t'ong pulgyo*? The times are unique; certainly any approach towards resolving the difficulties must be unique as well.

See also: AWAKENING OF FAITH IN MAHĀYĀNA;
BUDDHIST PHILOSOPHY, CHINESE; CHINUL;
PLATFORM SUTRA; SÔSAN HYUJÔNG; ÛISANG;
WÔNCH'ŬK; WÔNHYO

References and further reading

Buswell, R. (1983) *The Korean Approach to Zen: The Collected Works of Chinul*, Honolulu, HI: University of Hawaii Press. (This work includes a brief outline of Korean Buddhism before Sôn, but mainly deals with Chinul's life and works. It includes an English translation of most of the major works of Chinul, and a bibliography of works on Korean Buddhism written in Asian languages.)

Ha Tae-hung and Mintz, G. (1972) *Samguk Yusa: Legend and History of the Three Kingdoms of Ancient Korea*, Seoul: Yonsei University Press. (This is a translation of the *Samguk Yusa*, one of the most important historical sources for studying Korean Buddhist history during the Three Kingdoms period and the Unified Silla period. The original work in classical Chinese was written by monk Iryon in the thirteenth century.)

Han'guk Pulgyo Chônsô (Complete Collection of Korean Buddhist Works) (1979–89), Seoul: Dongguk University Press. (This complete collection of Korean Buddhist works is the most recent critical edition of Korean Buddhist works from the Silla period to the Chosôn period.)

Kamstra, J.H. (1967) *Encounter or Syncretism: The Early Growth of Japanese Buddhism*, Leiden: Brill. (Part 3 includes a very useful survey of Korean Buddhism from its beginnings to the period of its introduction into Japan in the sixth century.)

Keel Hee-sung (1977) 'Chinul: The Founder of Korean Son (Zen)', Ph.D. dissertation, Harvard University. (Discusses Chinul's contribution to Korean Sôn and the uniqueness of the Korean Sôn tradition.)

Korean Buddhist Research Institute (ed.) (1993) *The History and Culture of Buddhism in Korea*, Seoul: Dongguk University Press. (This edited translation of works on Korean Buddhism covers the Three Kingdoms period to modern times.)

Lancaster, L. and Yu Chai-shin (eds) (1989) *Introduction of Buddhism to Korea*, Studies in Korean Religions and Culture vol. 3, Berkeley, CA: Asian Humanities Press. (This edited English translation of articles on Korean Buddhism, originally written in Korean or Japanese, is a very useful guide for studying Korean Buddhism during the Three Kingdoms period and has a comprehensive bibliography.)

—— (eds) (1991) *Assimilation of Buddhism in Korea: Religious Maturity and Innovation in the Silla Dynasty*, Studies in Korean Religions and Culture vol. 4, Berkeley, CA: Asian Humanities Press. (This volume covers Korean Buddhism during the Unified Silla period.)

Lancaster, L. and Sung Bae-park (1979) *The Korean Buddhist Canon: A Descriptive Catalogue*, Berkeley, CA: University of California Press. (This compiles all basic bibliographical information concerning Buddhist classical texts in Chinese.)

Lee, P. (ed.) (1993) *Sourcebook of Korean Civilization: From Early Times to the Sixteenth Century*, New York: Columbia University Press. (This includes various excerpts from classical works, originally in classical Chinese. It includes an English translation of important Buddhist philosophical exegeses.)

—— (1969) *Lives of Eminent Korean Monks: The Haedong Kosung Chon*, Cambridge, MA: Harvard University Press. (This is a translation of the biographies of eminent monks of the Three Kingdoms period. The original work in classical Chinese was written by Kakhun during the Koryô period.)

Odin, S. (1982) *Process Metaphysics and Hua-Yen Buddhism: A Critical Study of Cumulative Penetration Vs. Interpenetration*, Albany, NY: State University of New York. (This comparative study of Huayan Buddhism and Whitehead's process philosophy includes in its appendix a translation of Ûisang's autocommentary on the *Ocean Seal Samādhi*.)

Park Sung-bae (1983) *Buddhist Faith and Sudden Enlightenment*, Albany, NY: State University of New York. (This is a most provocative discussion of Korean Sôn practice, presenting the spirit of Buddhist meditation in the East Asian tradition and also ably depicting the uniqueness of Korean Sôn practice.)

Shim Jae-ryong (1979) 'The Philosophical Foundation of Korean Zen Buddhism: The Integration of Son and Kyo by Chinul', Ph.D. dissertation, University of Hawaii. (Discusses Chinul's contribution to Korean Sôn and the uniqueness of the Korean Sôn tradition.)

SUNGTAEK CHO

BUFFIER, CLAUDE (1661–1737)

A French Jesuit who flourished in the early eighteenth century, Buffier developed an outlook that he referred to as common-sense philosophy. While deeply influenced by the philosophies of Descartes and Locke, he saw their reliance on the testimony of inner experience to be conducive to scepticism concerning the external world. In reaction to this, he sought to establish the irrevocable claims of various 'first truths', which pointed towards external reality and qualified it in various respects. His work anticipates certain themes that surfaced later in the common-sense philosophy of Thomas Reid.

Buffier was born in Poland to French parents. He pursued his studies in the Jesuit college at Rouen, and entered there as a novitiate at the age of 18. His career was spent almost entirely at the college of Louis-le-Grand in Paris, first as a teacher then, after 1699, as 'scriptor', a position that enabled him to devote all his energies to writing. He wrote extensively on philosophy, geography, history, and grammar (often in verse, to facilitate memorization) and made important contributions to the Dictionnaire de Trévoux and the Mémoires de Trévoux.

Buffier's philosophical writings provide little indication of his Jesuit commitments – perhaps it was this that led Voltaire to refer to him as 'the only Jesuit to have put forward a reasonable philosophy in his works'. It is DESCARTES and LOCKE who emerge as principal sources of Buffier's thinking, though he was no slavish disciple of either. To both of these thinkers he owed the belief that inner experience (*le sentiment intime*) provides the strongest possible certification for truth, and that any logically correct inferences based on such experience are equally incontrovertible. Yet he realized that if we take such evidence to be the only philosophically legitimate evidence, solipsism and scepticism follow immediately. And these positions he regarded as absurd.

Rather than call into question the Cartesian premises, as some later thinkers were to do, Buffier sought to establish that various propositions pointing towards the external world and indicating something of its nature are every bit as acceptable, philosophically, as the claims of immediate experience. These propositions he termed the first truths of common sense (*le sens commun*), and he held that they reflect certain dispositions that nature has placed in us all in order to bring unity to what would otherwise be a heterogeneous mass of idiosyncratic judgments springing from the immediate experience of each of us.

First truths are not established by any straightforwardly deductive process, for they are only to be reasoned *from*. They reveal themselves instead through their clarity and universality: no propositions offered to support or supplant them could be formulated more clearly than they are; and they show themselves either to be explicitly acceptable to all sane persons who have reached the age of reason, or to be embedded in the conduct of all, even of those who might indulge in their denial. Some examples of these

first truths are: Bodies exist; There are other beings and other people than myself in the world; I possess something I call intelligence and something independent of this intelligence that I call my body; The presence of design, such as we find in a watch, requires an intelligent designer; The self or soul is absolutely one; I possess a free will.

While Buffier does recognize certain differences between the claims of outer and inner experience, he refuses simply to place them on the same scale and declare the former to be weaker than the latter. Instead, he will say that both are equally 'certain', although through inner experience we grasp truths with greater 'vividness'; or that to deny inner experience would take one out of 'oneself', while to deny our outer experience would place one outside 'reason' (by leaving one with no ultimate premises to reason from); or that denial of the former might lead to contradiction, but denial of the latter would indicate some form of madness (taking one outside the domain of reasonability). The exigencies of life, in short, require us to accept and live in accord with the dictates of common sense.

Buffier accepts calling such truths innate ideas, if we mean by this that they constitute certain dispositions by which the mind grasps reality. However, he rejects any belief in innate ideas (see INNATE KNOWLEDGE) if these are construed as particular items standing permanently before the mind for contemplation. In fact Buffier rejects the very conception of ideas as 'things' that stand before the mind, regarding them instead purely as modifications of our soul in so far as it is thinking, which suggests that the mind, when it receives an idea, is no more distinguishable from that idea than a ball set in motion is distinguishable from the motion it receives. This point, touched upon but lightly by Buffier, was to become the very focus of Reid's critique of the 'ideal system' (see REID, T.).

Noticeably absent from Buffier's list of first truths is any that makes mention of God's existence. He believed, rather, that this particular truth followed reasonably from the first truth by which we infer the existence of an intelligent designer from the observation of design in an object. Quite generally, where philosophical and scientific questions are concerned, Buffier maintains an empiricist's reserve, deploring such speculative excesses as one finds in Descartes' physics or Malebranche's metaphysics. And while his principal philosophical priority involves overcoming the hyperbolic scepticism associated with solipsism, he freely affirms our ignorance of the ultimate causal forces at work in the universe. The essences of things that we can know are but nominal essences, while real essences stand beyond our reach – real essences being understood by Buffier not as those that ground the qualities of a given substance, but as those that render an individual truly unique. Out of this ignorance, however, emerges an emphasis on the important position occupied by probability (*vraisemblance*) in forming sound opinions and making judicious decisions.

See also: COMMON SENSE SCHOOL

List of works

Buffier, C. (1843) *Œuvres philosophiques du Père Buffier* (Philosophical Works of Father Buffier), ed. Bouillier, F., Paris: Charpentier. (Contains the *Traité*, the *Eléments*, the *Examen*; preceded by a substantial and insightful introduction.)

—— (1704) *Examen des préjugez vulgaires, pour disposer l'esprit à juger sainement de tout* (Examination of common prejudices), Paris: Chez Mariette. (A dialogue aiming to resolve twelve commonly disputed issues; showing, for example, that two people can disagree yet be both in the right and that women can be adept in all the sciences.)

—— (1714) *Les principes du raisonnement exposez en deux logiques nouvèles* (Principles of Reasoning Expounded in Two New Logics), Paris: Chez Pierre Witte. (An examination of the many different senses in which the notion of truth is employed, leading to the recommendation that we should broaden our criteria of this concept.)

—— (1724) *Traité des premières véritez et de la source de nos jugements, où l'on examine le sentiment des philosophes sur les premières notions des choses*, Paris: Veuve Mongé; trans. anon. *First Truths, and the Origin of Our Opinions Explained, with an inquiry into the sentiments of moral philosophers relative to our primary notions of things to which is prefixed a detection of the Plagarism, Concealment and Ingratitude of Doctors Reid, Beattie, Oswald*, London: Johnson, 1780. (The work in which the central tenets of Buffier's doctrine of common sense are most clearly and systematically exposed.)

—— (1725) *Eléments de métaphisique à la portée de tout le monde* (Elements of Metaphysics, Accessible to Everyone), Paris: Pierre François Giffart. (An examination, presented in dialogue form, of the nature, significance, and utility of metaphysical reflection.)

References and further reading

Aguilar, J.A.V. (1957) *El Sentido Común en las Obras Filosóficas del P. Claude Buffier, S.I.* (Common Sense in the Philosophical Works of Father Claude Buffier, S.J.), Barcelona: Seminario Conciliar.

Marcil-Lacoste, L. (1982) *Claude Buffier and Thomas Reid: Two Common-Sense Philosophers*, Kingston and Montreal: McGill-Queen's University Press. (Good comparison between Buffier and Reid, requiring some philosophical sophistication; good bibliography of secondary literature.)

Montgomery, F.K. (1930) *La vie et l'œuvre du Père Buffier* (The Life and Work of Father Buffier), Paris: Association du Doctorat. (Brief biography and general look at the whole corpus of Buffier's work, not just the philosophical items. Contains a complete enumeration of Buffier's writings.)

Sortais, G. (1928) 'Le Cartésianisme chez les Jésuites français aux dix-septième et dix-huitième siècles' (Cartesianism among the French Jesuits of the Seventeenth and Eighteenth Centuries), *Archives de Philosophie* 6 (3): 1–93.

Wilkins, K.S. (1969) 'A Study of the Works of Claude Buffier', *Studies on Voltaire and the Eighteenth Century* 66, Geneva: Bestermann. (Good biography, including detailed treatment of Buffier as an educator. Views him generally from the philosophical perspective. Good secondary bibliography.)

JAMES W. MANNS

BUFFON, GEORGES LOUIS LECLERC, COMTE DE (1707–88)

Both as a scientist and as a writer, Buffon was one of the most highly esteemed figures of the European Enlightenment. In depicting the perpetual flux of the dynamic forces of Nature, he portrayed the varieties of animal and vegetable species as subject to continual change, in contrast with Linnaeus, whose system of classification based on physical descriptions alone appeared timeless. But Buffon's definition of a species in terms of procreative power excluded the evolutionary hypothesis that any species could become transformed into another. Hybrids, as imperfect copies of their prototypes, were in his scheme ultimately destined to become sterile rather than to generate fresh species. By virtue of the same definition, he judged that the different races of mankind formed family members of a single species, since the mating of humans of all varieties was equally fertile.

1   **Career**
2   **His *Histoire naturelle***
3   **His notion of a species**
4   **His anthropology**

1 Career

In his own lifetime among the most highly esteemed of all the *philosophes* of the age of Enlightenment, Buffon achieved eminence within the intellectual and political establishments of his day rather than, like either Diderot or Voltaire, as an independent writer outspokenly critical of prevalent orthodoxies. Born in Montbard, he first gained distinction and early admission to both the Académie des Sciences and the Royal Society for his work on mathematics. By 1739 his writings on organic nature had won him sufficient renown to secure his appointment as keeper of the Jardin du Roi in Paris, which formed both a botanical garden and a zoological museum. From that base until his death, he became one of the most celebrated men of science and letters in France. On account of its being published by the Imprimerie Royale, his massive *Histoire naturelle* (Natural History, 1749–88) largely escaped the clutches of censorship and official criticism which befell so many of his prominent contemporaries. In 1753 he was elected a member of the Académie Française, and he was to become a corresponding member of more scientific and learned societies than perhaps any other figure of the eighteenth century. Hume remarked of him that he seemed less like a writer than a marshal of France.

2 His *Histoire naturelle*

Buffon conceived his *Histoire naturelle* principally as an account of the generative and degenerative properties of Nature, along lines which contrasted with the descriptive taxonomy of Linnaeus, and it was set within an even wider cosmology opposed to the mechanistic philosophy of Newton. As distinct from the Linnaean system of classification based upon observable similarities of organic structure, Buffon's causal and developmental scheme of Nature addressed its procreative powers and variable manifestations through time and space. Through his reading of such works as Madame Du Châtelet's *Institutions de physique* (Instruction in Physics) of 1740, he was persuaded that Christian Wolff's conception of Nature as a set of dynamic forces of impulsion which engendered the life-forms of matter was more plausible than Newton's notion of inert Nature framed by absolute time and space (see WOLFF, C.; NEWTON, I.).

Supposing that the planets had been formed from the impact of comets with the sun, he argued that the topography of the earth was attributable to the effects of erosion. Just as civil history records the epochs of the revolutions of human affairs and the occurrence of moral events, so does natural history record the physical development and transformations of the world, he claimed. In his creation of heaven and earth, God had made only the matter of the universe. The earth's consolidation, with the introduction of water, the birth of volcanoes, the separation of continents, the generation of animals and the emergence of the human race, constituted the history of all organic substance, which Buffon was to term *les époques de la nature* in the most celebrated volume of his work, bearing that title, published in 1778. From his manuscripts it appears that he supposed the earth might be 3 million years old, but in print he allowed only a total of around 75,000 years.

3 His notion of a species

Buffon's early interest in mathematics had included research in infinitesimal calculus, a subject which accorded well with the ancient doctrine to which he subscribed, of a natural chain of being, or *scala naturae*, linking all vegetables and animals by a series of gradations of their physical form. In part because he accepted that Nature's ladder consisted of unbroken steps, each in its place from the start, Buffon doubted the central premise of what would become evolutionary or Darwinian biology, according to which one species generates another. Along lines corresponding to Plato's theory of Forms, he even maintained that, because species are perpetual and permanent, they comprise the only true beings in Nature. Each individual organism, or what is now termed a 'phenotype', he thought, was patterned by the *molécule organique* or *moule intérieur* of its prototype – which today would be termed the 'genotype' of its species as a whole.

But Buffon's conception of each species' form was more dynamic than that of any philosopher of nature before him. The most striking difference between the world's animal and vegetable matter, he claimed, is the power of movement possessed by animals alone, allowing for the fact that some animals, such as oysters, lack that power as well. Buffon noted that individual members of species may be altered or improved by climate or nourishment, and he therefore stressed that the phenotypes of organisms were marked by their differences or variability. Permanence or fixity, however, was generically inherent in every species, he insisted. Contending that Nature is in continual flux, he perceived the diverse instantiations of species as either improving or degenerating according to their circumstances, a point which he illustrated most strikingly with respect to the flora and fauna of the New World as contrasted with the Old, in so far as he deemed the North American puma to be a diminutive lion and the South American llama just a small camel.

The crucial factor which determined the nature of a species, according to Buffon, was not physical resemblance of bodily parts, as in Linnaeus' taxonomy, but procreative ability – a species being defined as a constant succession of similar individuals that can reproduce together. The sterility of hybrids – such as a mule interbred from the horse and ass – made it difficult for Buffon to lend credence to any ideas of descent with modification or the transformation of one species into another, as had been mooted by his contemporary, Maupertuis (see SPECIES).

4 His anthropology

Buffon's definition of a 'species' in terms of its power of procreation led him to view the whole of humanity as forming only one species, whose populations were differentially tinged by the sun in higher and lower latitudes. There could be other determinants of race, he allowed, such as bile or blood, but in general he supposed that skin colour was an acquired characteristic shaped essentially by climate, thus following Montesquieu's conjectures on the climatological determinants of men's moral traits (see MONTESQUIEU). Believing that the progenitors of the human race must have been white, Buffon held that the skin colour of blacks was merely a deformation of the archetype of humanity. This proposition excludes the evolution of mankind from the ape, since a white archetype would scarcely have arisen from a black animal without a soul, he thought. But it did permit a proposition that others would pursue to a racist conclusion – that apes might be degenerate blacks.

Buffon himself categorically rejected that hypothesis, both because he thought the human faculty of reason established an unbridgeable gulf between mankind and the rest of Nature, and because there was no evidence of viable offspring from matings between apes and humans such as were produced from the racial interbreeding of blacks and whites. Stressing that animation – or life – is a property of matter, while thought is a property of spirit alone, he was convinced that the entire human race sprang from the same family and formed only one species. A disciple, Cornelius De Pauw, nevertheless contended in his *Recherches philosophiques sur les américains* that the native inhabitants of America had degenerated to the level of orang-utans, a proposition rejected by Henry HOME, Lord Kames, in the polygenist theory of multiple races which he set out in his *Sketches of the History of Man* of 1774, largely as a refutation of the monogenetic anthropology of Buffon.

See also: DARWIN, C.; ENLIGHTENMENT, CONTINENTAL; EVOLUTION, THEORY OF; SPECIES

List of works

Buffon, G.L.L. (1749–88) *Histoire naturelle, générale et particulière* (General and particular natural history), Paris: Imprimerie Royale.

References and further reading

Blanckaert, C. (1993) 'Buffon and the Natural History of Man: Writing History and the "Foundational Myth" of Anthropology', *History of Human Sciences*, 6: 13–50. (Addresses diverse interpretations of Buffon's pioneering contribution to the history of anthropology, with a substantial bibliography.)

Duchet, M. (1971) *De l'homme* (On Man), Paris: François Maspero. (Includes an introductory essay on Buffon's anthropology.)

Farber, P.L. (1972) 'Buffon and the Concept of Species', *Journal of the History of Biology*, 5: 259–4. (Traces the changes and development of Buffon's philosophy of nature.)

Fellows, O. and Milliken, S.F. (1972) *Buffon*, in *World Authors Series*, vol. 243, New York: Twayne. (A synoptic treatment of Buffon's life, the nature of his theory of evolution and his style.)

Gerbi, A. (1973) *The Dispute of the New World: The History of a Polemic, 1750–1900.* (A comprehensive account of the influence of Buffon's denigration of the natural species of America, originally published in Italian in 1955.)

Lovejoy, A.O. (1959) 'Buffon and the Problem of Species', in B. Glass, O. Temkin and W. Strauss, Jr. (eds), *Forerunners of Darwin, 1745-1859*, Baltimore, MD: Johns Hopkins University Press, 84–113. (Originally published in 1911 in *Popular Science Monthly*, a wide-ranging assessment of Buffon's steps towards evolutionism.)

Roger, J. (1993) *Les sciences de la vie dans la pensée française du XVIIIe siècle*, Paris: Michel, 3rd edn. (The third edition of a text first published in 1963, which comprehensively locates Buffon's natural history within its scientific and philosophical context.)

Sloan, P. (1995) 'The Gaze of Natural History', in C. Fox, R. Porter and R. Wokler (eds), *Inventing Human Science: Eighteenth-Century Domains*, Berkeley, CA and Los Angeles: University of California Press, 112–51. (Addresses Buffon's contributions to eighteenth-century natural history and anthropology, by contrast with those of Linnaeus).

Wilkie, J.S. (1956–7) 'The Idea of Evolution in the Writings of Buffon', *Annals of Science* 12: 48–62, 212–27 and 255–66. (Offers various explanations of Buffon's failure to produce a fully generalized theory of evolution.).

Wokler, R. (1976) 'Tyson and Buffon on the Orangutan', *Studies on Voltaire and the Eighteenth Century*, 155: 1–19. (Assesses Buffon's account of the animal limits of humanity in terms of a scheme of comparative anatomy.)

ROBERT WOKLER

BULGAKOV, SERGEI NIKOLAEVICH (1871–1944)

A luminary of the Russian Religious-Philosophical Renaissance, Bulgakov moved from Marxism, to idealism, to Christianity in the early twentieth century. He rejected historical determinism, class struggle and all theories of progress that accept the suffering of one generation as a bridge to the happiness of another. He regarded the abolition of poverty as a moral imperative, insisted that Christianity mandates political and social reform, and wanted to create a new culture in which Orthodox Christianity would permeate every area of Russian life. His most important philosophical works, Filosofiia khoziaistva, chast' pervaia (The Philosophy of the Economy, Part I) (1912) and Svet nevechernyi (Unfading Light) (1917), reflect his turn to a Solov'ëvian mysticism which apotheosized transfiguration, Sophia and Godmanhood (Bogochelovechestvo). Bulgakov saw the cosmos as an organic whole, animated and structured by a World Soul, an entelechy that he called Sophia, Divine Wisdom. Sophia mediates between God and his creation, working mysteriously through human beings. In emigration, Bulgakov developed new interpretations of Orthodox dogmatics and participated in the ecumenical movement. His lifelong concerns were the Church in the world and the interconnection of religion and life. His writings on contemporary political, social and cultural issues helped inspire the Russian Religious-Philosophical Renaissance.

1   Life and early writings
2   The Philosophy of the Economy and Unfading Light
3   From Orthodox philosopher to dogmatic theologian

1   Life and early writings

Bulgakov was born in Livny, Orel province, a descendant of six generations of priests. He started out to be one, but left the seminary in 1888, studied in a secular gymnasium and then entered Moscow University's juridical faculty, graduating in 1894. He had advanced training in economics and statistics and taught these subjects at the Moscow Technical Institute. A 'legal Marxist' in the mid-1990s, Bulgakov contributed to left-leaning journals and was a progenitor of the 'back to Kant' movement, which tried to supplement Marxism with an autonomous ethic. His book, *O rynkakh pri kapitalisticheskom proizvodstve* (On Markets in Capitalist Production) (1897), which argued that Russia could achieve capitalism on the basis of its domestic market alone, brought him a national reputation. Between 1898 and 1900 Bulgakov did research for his doctoral dissertation in Western Europe, mostly in Germany. His chance discovery of Raphael's Sistine Madonna at an art gallery in Dresden made him realize, though not immediately, that he needed 'not a philosophical idea but a living faith in God, Christ, and the Church'. In 1898 he married Elena Tokmatova. They had two sons and a daughter; a mystical experience at the funeral of a third son, who died in 1909 at the age of 3, deepened Bulgakov's religiousness.

After returning to Russia, Bulgakov taught political economy at the Kiev Polytechnical Institute and Kiev University. In *Kapitalizm i zemledelie* (Capitalism and Agriculture) (1900) he argued that small farms are more productive and stable than large ones, contradicting the Marxist view. His essay, 'Basic Problems of the Theory of Progress' appeared in the symposium *Problemy idealizma* (Problems of Idealism) (1902) and in his own collection, *Ot Marksizma k idealizmu* (From Marxism to Idealism) (1903). One essay asked the question 'What does the philosophy of Solov'ëv give to the contemporary consciousness?' 'Positive all unity' and fusion of Christian theory and Christian practice (see SOLOV'ËV, V.S.) was Bulgakov's answer. Already critical of abstract German Idealism, he believed that philosophy must encompass 'living experience'. In 1904 he became a co-editor of Merezhkovskii's journal *Novyi Put'* (New Path) and, in 1905, of its successor *Voprosy zhizni* (Problems of Life). During the Revolution of 1905 Bulgakov advocated a Union of Christian Politics, and helped found the Christian Brotherhood of Struggle and the Moscow branch of the Religious Philosophical Society. In 1906 he left Kiev to become Professor of Political Economy at the Moscow Commercial Institute and to teach at Moscow University. The same year, he was elected to the second Duma as a non-Party Christian Socialist on the Kadet slate. Bulgakov regarded the popularity of socialism as a punishment for the sins of historical Christianity and a call to repent for ignoring poverty and injustice. In 1908 he returned to the Russian Orthodox Church. Around the same time Bulgakov began a second intensive reading of Solov'ëv and became close friends with the philosopher-priest Pavel FLORENSKII. In 1909, Bulgakov attacked the revolutionary intelligentsia as egoistic and destructive in 'Geroizm i podvizhnichestvo' (Heroism and Selfless Devotion), his contribution to *Signposts* (see SIGNPOSTS MOVEMENT). The same year, he called for an Orthodox work ethic as part of a larger attempt to create a distinctive Orthodox culture that would permeate every area of Russian life from the most exalted to the most prosaic. In 1910, Bulgakov helped found the Orthodox publishing house Put'. In 1911, he resigned from Moscow University in protest against the suspension of university autonomy, but resumed teaching there in 1917. As a delegate to the All Russian Council of the Orthodox Church (1917–18), he worked to restore the Patriarchate.

In June 1918 Bulgakov was ordained as a priest, losing his professorship as a result. He taught at the University of Simferopol, in the Crimea, until 1921. After being expelled from Russia on 30 December 1922, he lived in Prague for two years and then settled in Paris. He helped found the Russian Student Christian movement and the Orthodox Theological Institute, serving as its Dean and as Professor of Dogmatic Theology. In 1939, Bulgakov lost his voice almost completely as a result of surgery for throat cancer, but he continued to celebrate the liturgy and to conduct his classes.

2 The Philosophy of the Economy and Unfading Light

These works represent Bulgakov's attempt to create an Orthodox philosophy. In *Filosofiia khoziaistva, chast' pervaia* (The Philosophy of the Economy, Part I), he discussed the meaning and significance of the economy, including its epistemology, ontology and phenomenology, and promised to discuss ethics and eschatology in Part II. His purpose was to reveal an inherent cosmic meaning in the most prosaic human actions – production and consumption – as well as the intrinsic kinship of man and the cosmos and their basis in God and in Sophia, the mediator between God and the world. Interpreting 'Marx in the spirit of Boehme and Boehme in the spirit of Marx', Bulgakov stressed the centrality of labour, the need to increase production, and the Hegelian and Marxist concepts of freedom and necessity, mingling these ideas with

Boehme's concept of the World Soul (see BOEHME, J.). Bulgakov taught that human labour, physical and mental, has metaphysical and cosmic significance because through it, Sophia permeates and transfigures the world. All human activity contains elements of freedom and necessity, of Sophia and anti-Sophia respectively. Explaining economic activity (activity conducted out of necessity) in terms of the Fall, Bulgakov maintained that before it, labour was disinterested and loving, but then 'nature, damned by God, became a hostile force, armed with the powers of hunger and death'. Economic activity became a struggle for survival, concealing the Sophianic significance of labour and engendering the materialistic ideology of economism, the view of life as only or primarily an economic process. Science arose as part of man's attempt to subjugate 'Tsar Nature', and therefore also contains Sophianic and anti-Sophianic elements, as does art – the most Sophian human activity. Creative activity is of divine origin, by way of Sophia, for only God can create. But God allows man to participate in his salvation and to be a co-creator. Labour is humankind's means of redemption.

Objecting to the Kantian bifurcation of subject and object, Bulgakov maintained that man is the subject *and* the object of the economy, and stressed the former, the active subject, the proprietor (*khoziain*) of a farm or a business. He described economic creativity as a primarily psychological phenomenon, 'a phenomenon of [internal or] spiritual life', and associated creativity with individuality and freedom. An Orthodox economy would be characterized by *sobornost'*, unity in love and freedom, not impersonal collectivism or egoistic individualism. Egoism was a result of the Fall, which shattered the wholeness of the cosmos, and separated people from one another.

Bulgakov looked forward to a new era when the tyranny of nature would be overcome, when man would rule the economy instead of being ruled by it. Labour would again be voluntary and joyful, and would merge with artistic creativity. This 'leap from necessity to freedom' was not foreordained, he insisted, because the principle of Sophia is freedom. But elsewhere in the book, Bulgakov explained the apparent discord and chaos of economic life as the workings of a superpersonal force, a mystical version of Hegel's 'cunning of reason' and suspiciously akin to 'necessity'.

Bulgakov never wrote Part II. He considered *Svet nevechernyi* (Unfading Light) the continuation of Part I, but it was more theological in nature. Bulgakov argued that God created the world out of nothing as an emanation of his own nature, not as something alien or external to him, and then pronounced his creation 'very good' (Genesis 1.31). This means that Christians must not reject the world, or nature, or 'the flesh'. Bulgakov also argued that God created the world as dynamic becoming, not as eternal being. Therefore, the world is not evil but incomplete. In the section titled 'The Sophianicity of the Creature', Bulgakov described Sophia as the living link between God and the creature, as a kind of fourth hypostasis outside and different from the Trinity, and as the object of God's love. He was ambiguous on whether Sophia is a person or a force, but he did say that Sophia is revealed to the world as beauty. In later works, Bulgakov distinguished between the 'divine Sophia' and the 'created' or 'creaturely Sophia', but he continued to emphasize their ultimate metaphysical identity and hence the consubstantiality of God and the cosmos. In *Svet nevechernyi*, Bulgakov attacked Boehme's mysticism as pantheism or 'immanentism' and declared that this 'heresy' became the basis of subsequent German thought. But Bulgakov also argued that pantheism contains a grain of religious truth and must be absorbed into an Orthodox cosmology which does not negate the world. In later works he distinguished panentheism from pantheism. Apropos of the promised treatment of ethics and eschatology, Bulgakov attributed evil to the nothingness or non-being that is the substratum of the cosmos and that erupts in human wilfulness, but he provided no guidelines for conduct except to condemn egoism and individualism and praise humility and love. Bulgakov's eschatology featured the transfiguration of the world through art, which he called 'Sofiiurgy', not 'theurgy', as the Symbolists did, and the divinization of all humankind, that is, Godmanhood. Resurrection would be a universal phenomenon, for man is 'one Adam' and the cosmos is 'one corporeality and one body'.

3 From Orthodox philosopher to dogmatic theologian

Svet nevechernyi, *Die Tragödie der Philosophie* (The Tragedy of Philosophy) and *Filosifiia imeni* (The Philosophy of the Name), the latter two written between 1919 and 1921, mark Bulgakov's transition from Orthodox philosophy to dogmatic theology, and his rejection of philosophic idealism. In *Die Tragödie der Philosophie*, Bulgakov declared that philosophy must be the handmaiden of religion, not just of theology; that is, philosophy must encompass religious experience, ritual, and personal revelation. He criticized Kant, Fichte, Hegel and Spinoza extensively, partly because they dichotomized consciousness into 'I–not I'. Bulgakov posited a dialogic consciousness – 'I am thou, he, you, and we' –

relating this conception to a triune theory of human relations which he in turn related to the Holy Trinity. *Filosofiia imeni* was Bulgakov's response to a dispute in the Orthodox Monastery of Mount Athos about whether the name of God was itself divine and also to Symbolist writers' debates on the nature of the Word. Bulgakov argued that the name of God was inseparable from the divinity but not identifiable with it, and that the very act of naming connects God and man. Words are living symbols that connect the empirical and the invisible worlds.

In emigration Bulgakov turned to patristics as part of a heightened emphasis on Orthodox tradition and on the Church as an institution. He described the Church as a living body, the Body of Christ, and maintained that tradition, including dogma, encompasses 'the new in the old and the old in the new'. Bulgakov interpreted Orthodox dogmatics in this spirit. Sophiology, treated somewhat differently, remained his central theological concept. The émigré Church in Karlovtsi, Serbia, and the Moscow Patriarchate alike accused him of heresy. Underlying their attack was hostility to any reinterpretation of dogma at all. Bulgakov's dogmatic works are not available in English. To date, they have not been reprinted in Russia, but his earlier writings are available and are attracting a great deal of attention.

See also: RUSSIAN RELIGIOUS-PHILOSOPHICAL RENAISSANCE

List of works

Bulgakov, S. (1897) *O rynkakh pri kapitalisticheskom proizvodstve* (On Markets in Capitalist Production), Moscow: A.G. Kolchugin. (Argues that Russia could achieve capitalism on the basis of its domestic market alone.)

—— (1900) *Kapitalizm i zemledelie* (Capitalism and Agriculture), St Petersburg: V.A. Tikhonov. (Argues that small farms are more productive and stable.)

—— (1903) *Ot Marksizma k idealizmu* (From Marxism to Idealism), St Petersburg: Obshchestvennaia Pol'za. (Collection including 'Basic Problems of the Theory of Progress'.)

—— (1909, 1911) *Dva grada* (Two Cities), Moscow: Put', 2 vols. (Articles written between 1904 and 1909.)

—— (1912) *Filosofiia khoziaistva chast' pervaia* (The Philosophy of the Economy, Part I), Moscow: Put'. (Discusses the meaning and significance of the economy, including its epistemology, ontology and phenomenology.)

—— (1917) *Svet nevechernyi* (Unfading Light), Moscow: Put'. (Bulgakov considered this a continuation of *Filosofiia khoziaistva chast' pervaia*, though more theological in nature.)

—— (1918) *Tikhie dumy* (Quiet Thoughts), Moscow: Leman & Sakharov.

—— (1926) *Sv. Pëtr i Ioann* (Saints Peter and John), Paris: YMCA-Press.

—— (1927a) *Die Tragödie der Philosophie* (The Tragedy of Philosophy), Darmstadt: Otto Reichl. (Marks Bulgakov's transition from Orthodox to dogmatic theology.)

—— (1927b) *Kupina neopalimaia* (The Burning Bush), Paris: YMCA-Press. (This volume about the Virgin Mary, and the following two, constitute Bulgakov's 'small trilogy'.)

—— (1927c) *Drug zhenikha* (Friend of the Bridegroom), Paris: YMCA-Press. (St John the Baptist is the subject of this book.)

—— (1929) *Lestnitsa Iakovlia: Ob angelakh* (Jacob's Ladder: About Angels), Paris: YMCA-Press. (This volume is about angels and higher states of being.)

—— (1933) *O bogochelovechestve I, agnets Bozhii* (On Divine Humanity I, The Lamb of God), Paris: YMCA-Press. (This volume about Jesus, and the following two, constitute Bulgakov's 'great trilogy'.)

—— (1936) *O bogochelovechestve II, uteshitel* (On Divine Humanity II, The Comforter), Paris: YMCA-Press. (This volume is about the Holy Spirit.)

—— (1937) *Sophia, The Wisdom of God*, London; revised edn, Hudson, NY: Lindesfarne, 1993. (An outline of Sophiology, from an unpublished Russian manuscript.)

—— (1945) *O bogochelovechestve III, nevesta agnetsa* (On Divine Humanity III, The Bride of the Lamb), Paris: YMCA-Press. (This work concerns the Church.)

—— (1946) *Avtobiograficheskie zametki* (Autobiographical Notes), ed. L.A. Zander, Paris: YMCA-Press.

—— (1948) *Apokalipsis Ioanna* (The Apocalypse of John), Paris: YMCA-Press.

—— (1953) *Filosofiia imeni* (The Philosophy of the Name), Paris: YMCA-Press. (Concerns the name of God, and the nature of the Word.)

—— (date unknown) *Pravoslavie*, Paris: YMCA-Press; repr., Moscow: Terra, 1991; abridged trans. The Russian Orthodox Church, London, 1935; repr. Crestwood, NY: St Vladimir's Seminary, 1988.

—— (1993) *S.N. Bulgakov, Sochineniia v dvukh tomakh* (S.N. Bulgakov, Selected Works in Two Volumes), ed. S. Khoruzhi (vol. 1) and I. Rodianskaia (vol. 2), Moscow: Nauka. (Volume 1 includes Khoruzhi's introductory article 'Vekhi filosofskogo tvorchestva o. Sergeia Bulgakova' (Landmarks of the Philosophical Work of Father Sergei Bulgakov), Bulga-

kov's *Tragediia filosofii*, and selected articles. Volume 2, contains Rodianskaia's introductory essay, 'S.N. Bulgakov – Publitsist i obshchestvennyi deiatel'' (S.N. Bulgakov – Writer and Public Figure) and selected articles, mostly from *Dva grada*.)

—— (1976) *A Bulgakov Anthology*, eds N. Zernov and J. Pain, Philadelphia, PA: Westminster. (Brief excerpts from Bulgakov's works.)

For additional bibliography see Evtuhov (1996) and Zander (1948).

References and further reading

Evtuhov, C. (1996) *The Cross and the Sickle: Sergei Bulgakov and the Fate of Russian Religious Philosophy*, Ithaca, NY: Cornell University Press (Bulgakov's thought in the context of the Russian Silver Age.)

Kornblatt J.D. and Gustafon, R. (eds) (1996) *Russian Religious Thought, Contexts and New Perspectives*, Madison, WI: University of Wisconsin Press. (Contains three articles on Bulgakov: B.G. Rosenthal, 'The Nature and Function of Sophia in Bulgakov's Prerevolutionary Thought'; M.A. Meerson, 'Sergei Bulgakov's Philosophy of Personality'; and P. Valliere, 'Sophiology as the Dialogue of Orthodoxy with Modern Civilization'.)

Rosenthal, B.G. (1991) 'The Search for a Russian Orthodox Work Ethic', in E. Clowes, S. Kassow and J.L. West (eds) *Between Tsar and People*, Princeton, NJ: Princeton University Press, 57–74. (Bulgakov's search for an ethic based on labour that is creative and loving.)

Zander, L. (1948) *Bog i mir* (God and the World), Paris: YMCA-Press, 2 vols. (A respectful study of Bulgakov's worldview.)

BERNICE GLATZER ROSENTHAL

BULTMANN, RUDOLF (1884–1976)

Rudolf Bultmann was one of the most influential Protestant theologians of the period that immediately followed the Second World War. A founding member of the school of dialectical theology in the 1920s, he was a major New Testament scholar, who refined the method of form criticism. He argued that the Synoptic Gospels reveal not the historical Jesus, but the Christ of faith, the Christ-myth developed by the early church. The existentialist philosophy of Martin Heidegger was a major influence, and he adapted it to the needs of Christian theology, devising an existential access to faith. He contrasted Historie *– objective, factual accounts of historical events – with* Geschichte *– the meaning that people choose to give to those events. One must demythologize the New Testament – strip it of its prescientific imagery – before one can interpret its significance for oneself. Bultmann defined biblical hermeneutics as an inquiry into the reality of human existence and proposed a new understanding of the person and teaching of Christ. Central to this is the concept of the* kerygma, *the proclamation of the salvation-event focused on Christ. It is in response to the* kerygma *that a human being can actively opt for faith. Bultmann reinterpreted the Lutheran doctrine of justification and the theology of the cross in the light of this.*

1   Life
2   History and myth
3   Existential interpretation
4   *Kerygma* and eschatology

1   Life

Rudolf Bultmann was the son of a minister of the German Evangelical Lutheran Church. At Oldenburg he attended the same gymnasium as Karl Jaspers. He read theology at Tübingen, Berlin and Marburg. Karl Müller (Church history), Adolf von Harnack (history of dogma), Hermann Gunkel (Old Testament), Adolf Jülicher and Johannes Weiss (New Testament), and Wilhelm Herrmann (systematic theology) were among his teachers. He graduated in New Testament studies in 1912. His teaching activity began at the University of Marburg, where he spent a lot of time in the company of Martin Rade, whose theological journal *Die christliche Welt* had a wide audience. In 1916 he was invited to teach at Breslau and received a call to a chair at Giessen in 1920. A year later, he was offered a chair at the university of Marburg. Meanwhile he had released *Die Geschichte der synoptischen Tradition* (*The History of the Synoptic Tradition*) (1921).

At Marburg, Bultmann taught New Testament for thirty years. There he became acquainted with Rudolf Otto and Martin Heidegger. During the National Socialist dictatorship, he courageously joined the Confessing Church and spoke openly against the 'Aryan Paragraph'. In 1941, he delivered a highly influential lecture to a circle of ministers: 'New Testament and Mythology: The Problem of Demythologizing the New Testament Revelation'. Bultmann's demythologizing programme aroused ecclesiastical indignation which resulted in its official rejection at the General Synod of the German Evangelical Church in 1952. His years at Marburg were among his most creative: *Jesus* (1926), *Das*

Evangelium des Johannes (*The Gospel of John*) (1941), *Theologie des Neuen Testaments* (*Theology of the New Testament*) (1948–51), *Das Urchristentum in Rahmen der antiken Religionem* (*Primitive Christianity in its Contemporary Setting*) (1949) and *History and Eschatology* (1957) were among the works he wrote. Most of his articles were collectively published in *Glauben und Verstehen* (*Faith and Understanding*) (1933–65). Bultmann retired in 1951.

2   History and myth

As a member of the school of dialectical theology that Karl BARTH (§§1–2), Eduard Thurneysen and Emil BRUNNER (§1) had started in the early 1920s, Bultmann rejected the liberal way of treating Christian faith as a phenomenon of the history of religion. However, unlike Barth, he carried forward the tradition of biblical criticism. In spite of the acknowledgement of the paradoxical nature of revelation and faith in Barth's *Der Römerbrief* (*The Epistle to the Romans*) (1919), Bultmann did not surrender the method of history of religion that he had successfully applied in his doctoral dissertation. He was interested in understanding early Christianity within the wider religious and cultural context of its time, and endeavoured to retrace the influence of pre-Christian Gnosticism, Jewish apocalyptic and Manicheism on the New Testament writings. This orientation led to the later theory of demythologization. Like David Friedrich STRAUSS (§1) and the School of Marburg, Bultmann had a modern worldview and wanted to cleanse the New Testament of its naïve prescientific one. His exegetical research primarily concerned the pre-literary traditions of the New Testament. He investigated the internal development of the text, its 'setting in life' (*Sitz im Leben*) and its literary genres. In this way, he made significant contributions to form criticism.

What are the results of Bultmann's historical investigations? *The History of the Synoptic Tradition* (1921) provides an analysis of the origin and the redactorial process of the traditions underlying the narrative of Jesus' life. In the Synoptic Gospels, the original proclaimer, Jesus, has become the Christ, the one proclaimed as God's decisive act for human beings. The Synoptic Gospels offer an extended picture of the faith of the early Church in Jesus the Christ. They do not proclaim the historical Jesus but the Christ of faith (*der Christus des Glaubens*), the *kerygma*, the Christ-myth. Bultmann unveiled a process in Christology whereby Jesus the historical being developed into the mythical idea of a celestial being, a God-elected king of the eschaton, the pre-existing *logos* and co-begetter of the universe. In a famous monograph (1926), Bultmann characterized this process as a transformation of the Gospel of Christ into the Gospel about Christ. He claimed that the supernatural events in Jesus' life, including the miracles attributed to him, were legendary, mythical accounts. Jesus probably was a disciple of John the Baptist, an eschatological prophet. He created his own community of followers which rivalled that of the Baptist. But unlike the Baptist, Jesus was both a rabbi who taught the Law of God and a prophet who proclaimed the imminent end of the world. Jesus died as a messianic prophet.

Throughout his work, Bultmann thoroughly respected the principles of positivist historiography. In his view, there is only one historical method, common to both the believer and the unbeliever. Against Nietzsche, who claimed that there are only interpretations, he maintained that historical events are knowable objectively. He was aware of the historian's subjectivity, but subjectivity is not subjectivism. In this respect, the most subjective history is the most objective. Bultmann, however, did not confine himself to the quest for the historical Jesus. The meaning of the Christ-event for the believer, its significance for the individual, was of crucial importance to him. Owing to the adoption of Heidegger's existential analysis, Bultmann was able to draw an all-important distinction between *Historie* and *Geschichte*. *Historie* concerns objective, factual accounts of past events, whereas *Geschichte* points to the intentionality or the meaning of events for the people who encounter them. Historical facts are neutral, but *geschichtliche* events concern people's existence and prompt a for-or-against decision on their part. In order to discover the response of Christian faith to the Christ-event, one must divest the New Testament of the prescientific imagery in which it has been cast; one must 'demythologize' its message. This was the purpose of Bultmann's demythologizing programme.

3   Existential interpretation

Once demythologized, theological doctrines such as virgin birth, pre-existence, resurrection, ascension, original sin, miracles, angels, demons, and so on must be interpreted in order to attain their significance for the individual. In accordance with the early Martin HEIDEGGER (§§2–3), Bultmann put forth an existential interpretation. Heidegger's *Sein und Zeit* (*Being and Time*) (1927) phenomenologically describes the existential structure of the human being. In this analysis of the ontological constitution of *Dasein* (being-in-the-world), existence is understood as a special mode of being independent of natural determination. Fundamental ontology is related to, but not identical

with, anthropology. As Bultmann retained from Barth a trans-subjective understanding of revelation and faith, so he borrowed an existentialist ontology from Heidegger. Bultmann's concern for existence derived from a need to secure a realm of freedom in a world of causality and necessity. Contrary to the rational being, who is confined to objectivity, the free and volitional being exists in and through their decisions. For, by its essence, will is intentionality, project and decision; freedom is openness to the future. According to Bultmann, a human being's existence is realized in life acts, in the intentionality of decisions which are made ever anew and involve the whole being. A human being may exist either authentically or inauthentically. Inauthentic existence is the search for satisfaction and security in tangible reality, whereas authentic existence is life based on intangible realities, in free and responsible openness to the future, in faith.

Bultmann repeatedly claimed that Heidegger's fundamental ontology was neutral. It therefore can profitably be used to interpret any biblical text, and does not imply a subordination of the Bible to a philosophical framework. For the historian cannot investigate *for me* what that text means about God and his action, nor answer the question of the meaning of a given biblical text *for me*. For any understanding presupposes a prior understanding of the subject. A prior understanding or prior knowledge of the possibilities of one's life is the presupposition for the understanding of any biblical text. Bultmann also adopted Heidegger's idea of a hermeneutical circle. But he further drew a distinction between the existentialist understanding of philosophical analysis, which he called *das Existentiale*, and the pre-philosophical, concrete and ontic self-understanding that he labelled *das Existentielle*. Only the latter clears the way for the understanding and the appropriation of the revelatory action of God.

Consequently, biblical interpretation involves more than linguistic, grammatical and historical research. It implies both an ontology and an anthropology. The connection of text and interpreter, which is founded on the relationship of the interpreter to life, is a further presupposition for the understanding of any biblical text. I can recognize God's action only if I already have an existential (*existentiell*) knowledge of God. I can understand the *kerygma* when it speaks to me of God because I have an existential self-understanding. Thus biblical hermeneutics is understood as an inquiry into the reality of human existence. However, Bultmann did not substitute the existential-eschatological for the historical-objective, but established an authentic relationship instead of the perversion of objectivization or mythologization.

4 *Kerygma* and eschatology

In his early writings, Bultmann established a relationship between theology and anthropology. Theology is a discourse based on divine revelation. However, such a discourse is only possible if it concomitantly speaks about human beings. Thus theology is dialectic on two accounts: the dialectic of the hidden god and the dialectic of human existence. According to Bultmann, theology is the conceptual description of the existence of human beings as being determined by God. God should not be objectified or mythologized; God is the *eschaton*. Revelation is not the disclosure of a set of objective or objectifiable truths, but is God's judgment on the world; it concerns human existence at its deepest. As anthropology is existential (*existentiell*), so theology is eschatological.

The *kerygma*, or proclamation of the salvation-event, is the focal concept of Christian theology. According to the New Testament, Jesus Christ, the Crucified and Risen One, is the eschatological event, the action by which God has set an end to the old world (see ESCHATOLOGY §1). The *kerygma* is message, testimony and proclamation; preaching is part of the essence of the Word. As eschatological event, the proclaimed *kerygma* is not only the occasion for the decision as to faith, but also the condition for faith. Jesus Christ is present in the *kerygma* and encounters human beings through the *kerygma*. Preaching is in itself an eschatological event prompting an eschatological decision on the part of the hearer.

Bultmann was a Lutheran. The doctrine of justification and the theology of the cross receive a special emphasis in his eschatological theology. The God that human beings encounter through justification by faith is no object of knowledge and thought; it is the acting, transcendent and hidden God. Thus, to have faith is to believe in spite of experience. In faith, a human being surrenders all human securities and overcomes the predicament of human existence, the despair in which human existence is thrown, by choosing freely in favour of authentic existence. Under God's grace, a human being acknowledges a new self-understanding, embraces a new life and accepts a new responsible mode of action born of love. Through the human response to the *kerygma* the 'old man', torn by sin and anxiety, is transformed into a 'new man', freed from this world and rooted in the world beyond. The demythologizing programme that Bultmann launched in the 1950s is fundamentally related to the Lutheran doctrine of justification (see JUSTIFICATION, RELIGIOUS §4). The programme was a radical implementation of the doctrine of justification by faith in the field of knowledge and thought.

The cross of Christ is the salvation-event proclaimed by the New Testament. By the cross, Bultmann does not mean the historical-objective (*historisch*) fact of the crucifixion, but the historical-personal (*geschichtlich*) faith-event that the early Church experienced in relation to the crucifixion. The cross is God's liberating judgment on the world. Because Christ was crucified *for us*, the cross creates a new situation between God and human beings. The cross is not a mere event in the past which can be objectively contemplated. The cross is an occurrence of faith. To the believer, it is an ever-present and repeatable reality, in the sacraments as well as in daily life. Regarding the resurrection, which is inseparable from the cross, Bultmann taught that it was a further proclamation of the eschatological meaning of the cross. The resurrection is no historical fact, but an occurrence of faith. The Easter faith of the early Church was a faith in the glorified Christ. The resurrection is the main eschatological event, the salvation-event that signifies the believer's newness of life. The preached word renders the cross and the resurrection, or the *kerygma*, repeatedly present for all to hear.

In Bultmann's theology, ecclesiology is not less important than Christology. Because God and the Word are eschatological, God's revelation in Christ is not merely a past occurrence to be historically traced. The Word is an ever-living reality which is encountered where it is preached, and among those in which it is alive. Since justification by faith is not only freedom from sin but also freedom for obedience, Christians are called to an exemplary ethical life and to responsible action in political life. The living Christ reveals himself to the world through the work of salvation that is constantly operating in and through the Church. The end of the world and the coming of the kingdom of God are proclaimed to the world only through the Church. From there the Word calls today's humanity to experience crucifixion and resurrection; the eschatological event is continued in the Church. The Church is the eschatological community, and, like Jesus Christ, the incognito of God.

See also: EXISTENTIALIST THEOLOGY; HERMENEUTICS, BIBLICAL §4

List of works

Bultmann, R. (1921) *Die Geschichte der synoptischen Tradition*, Göttingen: Vandenhoeck & Ruprecht; trans. J. Marsh, *The History of the Synoptic Tradition*, New York: Harper & Row, 1963. (A classic work on the process of redaction which led to the Synoptic Gospels as we know them.)

—— (1926) *Jesus*, Berlin: Deutsche Bibliothek; trans. L.P. Smith and E. Huntress Lantero, *Jesus and the Word*, New York: Scribner, 1934. (Bultmann's Christology, based on the Jesus preached by the early Church.)

—— (1933–65) *Glauben und Verstehen*, Tübingen: Mohr, 4 vols; vol. 1 trans. L.P. Smith, *Faith and Understanding*, Philadelphia, PA: Fortress Press, 1987; vol. 2 trans. J.C.G. Greig, *Essays Philosophical and Theological*, London: SCM, 1955. (Bultmann's collected essays, on any and every topic.)

—— (1941) *Das Evangelium des Johannes*, Göttingen: Vandenhoeck & Ruprecht; trans. G.R. Beasley-Murray, R.W.N. Hoare and J.K. Riches, *The Gospel of John: A Commentary*, Oxford: Blackwell, 1971. (A very detailed and innovative form-critical commentary.)

—— (1948–51) *Theologie des Neuen Testaments*, Tübingen: Mohr, 2 vols; trans. K. Grobel, *Theology of the New Testament*, New York: Scribner, 1951–5. (Material on Johannine theology, the rise of the early Church, and the development of doctrine.)

Bultmann, R. *et al.* (1948–55) *Kerygma und Mythos: ein theologisches Gesprach*, ed. H.W Bartsch, Hamburg: Reich & Heidrich, 5 vols; trans. R.H. Fuller, *Kerygma and Myth: A Theological Debate*, London: SCM Press, 2 vols, 1953, 1962. (Selections from the first two German volumes are in the first English volume, and selections from the last three are in the second. This is the definitive guide to the theological debate on demythologization.)

Bultmann, R. (1949) *Das Urchristentum in Rahmen der antiken Religionem*, Zurich: Artemis-Verlag; trans. R.H. Fuller, *Primitive Christianity in its Contemporary Setting*, New York: Meridian, 1957. (Sections on the Old Testament, Jewish, Greek and Hellenistic backgrounds to primitive Christianity. It is particularly dated in its treatment of Judaism.)

—— (1957) *History and Eschatology*, Edinburgh: Edinburgh University Press. (Bultmann's Gifford Lectures, demythologizing eschatological claims.)

—— (1958) *Jesus Christ and Mythology*, New York: Scribner. (Bultmann's 1951 Yale Shaffer Lectures, once again stating the demythologizing programme.)

—— (1961) *Existence and Faith: Shorter Writings of Rudolf Bultmann*, ed. S. Ogden, London: Hodder & Stoughton. (Some overlap with the *Glauben und Verstehen* volumes mentioned, but a good collection with a strong introduction.)

Bultmann, R. and Barth, K. (1971) *Karl Barth – Rudolf Bultmann Briefwechsel 1922–1966*, ed. B. Jaspert, Zurich: Theologischer Verlag; trans. and ed. G.W. Bromiley, *Karl Barth – Rudolf Bultmann Letters 1922 – 1966*, Edinburgh: T. & T. Clark,
1982. (Useful both for the controversy between Barth and Bultmann, and for their autobiographical content.)

Bultmann, R. (1985) *New Testament and Mythology*, ed. S. Ogden, London: SCM. (Some overlap with the *Glauben und Verstehen* volumes. Contains the important 1941 article on demythologizing, 'New Testament and Theology'.)

References and further reading

* Barth, K. (1919) *Der Römerbrief*, Bern: Bäschlin; 2nd edn, much changed, Munich: Chr. Kaiser Verlag, 1922; 6th edn trans. E.C. Hoskyns, *The Epistle to the Romans*, Oxford: Oxford University Press, 1968. (Bultmann was deeply influenced by this initator of 'dialectical theology'.)

Braaten, C.E. and Harrisville, R. (eds) (1962) *Kerygma and History: A Symposium on the Theology of Rudolf Bultmann*, New York: Abingdon, 1962. (An important collection of essays by prominent theologians.)

Evang, M. (1988) *Rudolf Bultmann in seiner Frühzeit* (Rudolf Bultmman's Early Years), Tübingen. (A meticulous survey of Bultmann's development and the influences that shaped him.)

Fergusson, D. (1992) *Bultmann*, London: Chapman. (A short but helpful volume in the Outstanding Christian Thinkers series.)

* Heidegger, M. (1927) *Sein und Zeit*, Tübingen: Neomarius Verlag, 10th edn, 1963; trans. J. Macquarrie and E. Robinson, *Being and Time*, London: SCM, 1962. (The main philosophical influence on Bultmann.)

Jaspert, B. (ed.) (1989) *Rudolf Bultmanns Werk und Wirkung*, Darmstadt: Wissenschaftliche Buchgesellschaft. (Thirty essays from prominent scholars, covering the state of the field in Bultmann studies. Five are in English.)

Johnson, R.A. (1987) 'Introduction', in R.A. Johnson (ed.) *Rudolf Bultmann: Interpreting Faith for the Modern Era*, London: Collins. (A good short introduction to the main issues.)

Jones, G. (1991) *Bultmann: Towards a Critical Theology*, Cambridge: Polity Press. (Good on the philosophical background and political implications of Bultmann's work.)

Kegley, C.W. (ed) (1967) *The Theology of Rudolf Bultmann*, New York: Harper & Row. (Biographical material and a response by Bultmann, several good essays, and a bibliography complete to 1967.)

Morgan, R. (1989) 'Rudolf Bultmann', in D. Ford (ed.) *The Modern Theologians*, Oxford: Blackwell. (Helpful, particularly on Bultmann's relationship to his theological forebears.)

Painter, J. (1987) *Theology as Hermeneutics: Rudolf Bultmann's Interpretation of the History of Jesus*, Sheffield: Almond Press. (Concentrates on the extent to which Bultmann's whole position is intended as an interpretation of the New Testament.)

JEAN-LOUP SEBAN

BUNDLE THEORY OF MIND
see MIND, BUNDLE THEORY OF

BURGERSDIJK, F.
see ARISTOTELIANISM IN THE 17TH CENTURY

BURIDAN, JOHN
(*c*.1300–after 1358)

Unlike most other important philosophers of the scholastic period, John Buridan never entered the theology faculty but spent his entire career as an arts master at the University of Paris. There he distinguished himself primarily as a logician who made numerous additions and refinements to the Parisian tradition of propositional logic. These included the development of a genuinely nominalist semantics, as well as techniques for analyzing propositions containing intentional verbs and paradoxes of self-reference. Even in his writings on metaphysics and natural philosophy, logic is Buridan's preferred vehicle for his nominalistic and naturalistic vision.

Buridan's nominalism is concerned not merely with denying the existence of real universals, but with a commitment to economize on entities, of which real universals are but one superfluous type. Likewise, his representationalist epistemology accounts for the difference between universal and singular cognition by focusing on how the intellect cognizes its object, rather than by looking for some difference in the objects themselves. He differs from other nominalists of the period, however, in his willingness to embrace realism about modes of things to explain certain kinds of physical change.

Underlying Buridan's natural philosophy is his confidence that the world is knowable by us (although not with absolute certainty). His approach to natural science is empirical in the sense that it emphasizes the

evidentness of appearances, the reliability of a posteriori modes of reasoning and the application of certain naturalistic models of explanation to a wide range of phenomena. In similar fashion, he locates the will's freedom in our evident ability to defer choice in the face of alternatives whose goodness appears dubious or uncertain.

1 **Life and works**
2 **Logic**
3 **Metaphysics and epistemology**
4 **Natural philosophy**
5 **Ethics**

1 Life and work

It is testimony to Buridan's stature and influence that many of the events traditionally associated with his life are the stuff of legend. The stories that the King of France ordered that he be thrown into the Seine in a sack because of a scandalous affair with the Queen, or that, after being driven from Paris for his nominalist teachings, he went on to found the University of Vienna, cannot be verified. What we do know of his life is derived from the facts of his academic career (Faral 1950; Michael 1985). From these it can be inferred that Buridan was born shortly before 1300, probably in Béthune in northwestern France. He served as rector of the University of Paris in 1328, and again in 1340. University documents indicate that he received several benefices to support his work, and that he was much esteemed by his colleagues. He is last mentioned in a document of 1358, and probably died a short time after.

Buridan's academic career was unusual in two respects. First, he spent his entire career as a Master of Arts, without ever seeking an advanced degree in theology. He accordingly produced no commentary on the *Sentences* of Peter LOMBARD, one of the main genres of philosophical writing in the fourteenth century. Almost all of his written work is based on the Parisian arts curriculum, and reflects his pedagogical concerns as a member of the arts faculty. Second, he remained a secular cleric rather than joining an order such as the Dominicans or Franciscans. This freed him from the doctrinal disputes which often arose between religious orders, something which can be seen in the eclectic character of his work.

Buridan's logical writings are in the form of handbooks and commentaries intended for use by students of logic. Most of his non-logical works appear as short commentaries (*expositiones*) or longer critical studies (*quaestiones*), usually in several versions, based on his lectures on the works of ARISTOTLE. In addition to the entire Organon, these

131

included lectures on the *Metaphysics, Physics, On the Heavens, On the Soul, Parva naturalia, Nicomachean Ethics* and *Politics*. Only a few of these works are available in modern editions, and none can be dated precisely. However, copies and early printed versions were distributed throughout European universities, where they often served as primary texts for courses in logic and Aristotelian philosophy. As a result, Buridan's teachings continued to shape European thought well into the Renaissance.

2 Logic

Buridan belongs to the 'terminist' tradition of medieval logic, so called because its practitioners regarded terms as the primary unit of logical analysis. He wrote his most comprehensive logical work, the *Summulae de dialectica* (Summary of Dialectic), as a commentary on the *Tractatus* or *Summulae logicales* (Summary of Logic), a terminist textbook composed by PETER OF SPAIN almost a century earlier. However, because Buridan charged himself with 'analyzing and supplementing' Peter's rather elementary remarks 'sometimes differently' than Peter himself had expressed them, his comments served as a forum for his own innovative ideas in logic (see Pinborg 1975).

One section of Peter's text rewritten entirely by Buridan is the treatise on supposition, which deals with the referential function of significative terms in propositional contexts. In this section, Buridan presents a revised account of the divisions of supposition that better expresses his nominalist ontology. He rejects in particular the notion of 'simple supposition', by which some logicians held that common terms such as 'man' could refer to 'universal natures... distinct from singulars outside the soul' (*Summulae* IV, 3). In Buridan's view, terms refer only to particulars, although they can do so in different ways depending upon their semantic function. Buridan also rejects as superfluous the idea of his Parisian contemporary GREGORY OF RIMINI that what propositions signify, or 'make known', is an abstract object that is 'complexly signifiable'. Further expression of Buridan's nominalism can be found in the *Tractatus de consequentiis* (Treatise on Consequences), an advanced study of the theory of inference, in which he argues that one need posit no additional cause for the falsity of a sentence beyond what makes its corresponding negation true.

Buridan moved the Parisian tradition in new directions by developing and then systematically applying semantic theory to solve philosophical problems (Klima 1991, 1992). As well as characterizing his revision of the doctrine of supposition, this emerges in his analysis of the meaning of propositions containing intentional verbs (for example, 'you know the one approaching'), in which he appeals to the counterpart doctrine of appellation to show how we can 'understand the same thing in many different ways' (*Sophismata* IV, seventh remark) without altering the particular denotation of the concept or term used to signify it. Buridan has also achieved some notoriety among modern logicians for his solution to the liar paradox, in part because it preserves bivalence (see SEMANTIC PARADOXES AND THEORIES OF TRUTH). This turns on his suggestion that a proposition *P* is true if and only if (1) it signifies things as they are, and (2) it entails, in conjunction with a proposition asserting that *P* actually exists, another proposition asserting that *P* is true. Buridan then argues that self-referentially paradoxical propositions (for example, 'every proposition is false') are false because they cannot consistently satisfy both conditions. Even if we assume that they signify things as they are, the propositions they entail are false because the subject and predicate of the entailed propositions do not 'stand for the same' (if *P* is 'every proposition is false', then *P* itself must be false, not true), thus failing the second condition (*Sophismata* VIII, seventh sophism) (for discussion see Spade 1978; Hughes 1982) (see LANGUAGE, MEDIEVAL THEORIES OF; LOGIC, MEDIEVAL).

3 Metaphysics and epistemology

Like most medieval nominalists, Buridan argues that commonality is not a real feature of the world. 'Universals,' he says, 'do not exist outside the soul, but are only concepts of the soul by which it conceives of many things indifferently' (*Summulae* IV, 3). Medieval nominalism, however, was a complex and evolving doctrine whose adherents were not merely interested in the question of universals. The distinctiveness of Buridan's nominalism consists in the way he implements the more general nominalist aim to economize on entities, of which real universals are but one superfluous type (see NOMINALISM; UNIVERSALS).

Buridan's contribution to the nominalist theory of universals was to develop the semantics for an intentionalist account of common concepts. In a discussion influenced by his Parisian predecessor Peter ABELARD, Buridan argues that concepts such as 'humanity' and 'rationality' are best understood as ways of conceiving individual human beings, rather than as mirroring abstract entities (de Rijk 1992). Although Buridan, like WILLIAM OF OCKHAM, accepts only substances and qualities in his basic ontology, his explanation of certain kinds of physical change reflects this tendency to multiply modes or 'ways' of being, rather than things. Thus he regards changes in the shape or position of a physical substance as changes in the mode(s) of its qualities, that is, in *how* it is, whereas the unadorned substance–quality view would be forced to posit the generation of new qualities. Medieval nominalists also disagreed about where (and how) to use the razor, or principle of parsimony, a fact which distinguishes Buridan's nominalism from other versions. Buridan differs from his older English contemporary William of Ockham, for example, in his willingness to embrace quantitative forms to explain the impenetrability of bodies.

In epistemology, Buridan is a representationalist who rejects the idea that human knowers possess any intuitive modes of cognition, that is, those which (following William of Ockham and John DUNS SCOTUS) involve the direct and unmediated awareness of some present object (Zupko 1993a) (see PERCEP-TION, EPISTEMIC ISSUES IN). Buridan maintains that on the contrary, all cognition, including singular cognition, occurs when the intellect apprehends an object by means of a particular species or concept representing it. How we use the concept in our act of apprehension determines whether we cognize singu-larly or universally: singularly, if its object appears to us 'in the manner of something existing in the presence of the person cognizing it'; universally, if we focus on certain features of the concept to the exclusion of others, for example, if we use Socrates's humanity to understand 'all human beings, indiffer-ently' (*Quaestiones super De anima*, third redaction, III, q.8).

Buridan touches on the issue of epistemic justifica-tion in the course of rebutting certain sceptical objections to the possibility of scientific knowledge (some of which are associated with his Parisian contemporary, NICHOLAS OF AUTRECOURT) with naturalistic arguments based on the reliability of human cognitive processes. Thus, he contends that induction and sense perception are justified on the a posteriori grounds that both tend to produce beliefs that are free from doubt and error (although not infallible), and have verifiable results (Zupko 1993a). In general, however, Buridan is much more interested in explaining how we come to have knowledge than he is in exploring the grounds for knowledge claims, an orientation his work shares with most pre-Cartesian epistemology.

4 Natural philosophy

Historians of science have long recognized Buridan's contributions to the field of mechanics, most notably his development of the theory of impetus, or impressed force, to explain projectile motion (Grant

1977). Rejecting the discredited Aristotelian notion of antiperistasis, according to which the tendency of projectiles to continue moving is due to a proximate but external moving cause (such as the air), Buridan thought that only an internal motive force, trans-mitted from the original mover to the projectile, could explain its continued motion. His account of im-pressed force differs from others in that he did not see it as self-dissipating: '[this] *impetus*,' he says, 'would be of infinite duration, were it not diminished and corrupted by a contrary which resists it, or by something inclining it to a contrary [motion]' (*In Metaphysicam Aristotelis quaestiones* XII, q.9). He also views impetus as a variable quality whose strength is determined by the speed of and the quantity of matter in its moving subject, so that the acceleration of a falling body is understood in terms of its accumulation of successive increments of impetus. Buridan did not himself use the concept of impetus to revolutionize mechanics, however, since he remained an Aristotelian in other respects, for example in his assumptions that motion and rest are contrary states of bodies, and that the world is finite in extent.

Buridan's explanation of motion is a product of his approach to natural science, which is empirical in the sense that it emphasizes the evidentness of appear-ances, the reliability of a posteriori modes of reason-ing and the application of certain naturalistic models of explanation to a wide range of phenomena. Against the notion that scientific knowledge must be demonstrative and its truths absolutely certain, Buridan argues that natural science, at least, concerns only what happens assuming the common course of nature. This stems from his theological assumption that it is always possible for an omnipotent deity to deceive us in ways we could never detect, tempered by his confidence (for which he often cites empirical evidence) that our powers of perceptual judgment and inductive inference are reliable enough to make 'the comprehension of truth with certitude possible for us' (*In Metaphysicam Aristotelis quaestiones* II, q.1). Likewise, Buridan is confident that certain models of explanation can be used to grasp a whole range of natural phenomena. Thus, the concept of impetus re-emerges in his psychology to explain the difference between occurrent and dispositional modes of intel-lectual cognition, as well as in his ethics where it is used to account for the relative ease with which virtuous people are able to perform good actions.

Buridan also made an important contribution to the fourteenth-century debate on infinity and con-tinuity, arguing for the divisibilist view that contin-uous magnitudes are composed not of indivisible atoms but of parts divisible without end, and that the parts of a continuum constitute a potentially infinite set. Again, what is distinctive about Buridan's divisibilism is the way he defends it, by using semantic theory to explain the truth conditions of propositions containing (apparently non-referring) terms such as 'point', the meaning of the term 'infinite' in categorematic and syncategorematic contexts, and the use of the term 'possible' as a modal operator to express the notion of potential infinity (Thijssen 1985; Knuuttila 1992; Zupko 1993b). The mathematical and physical considerations prominent in other medieval discussions of continua occur secondarily for Buridan, almost as an afterthought (see NATURAL PHILOSOPHY, MEDIEVAL).

5 Ethics

Among the most influential of Buridan's commentaries on Aristotle was his *Quaestiones super decem libros ethicorum Aristotelis ad Nicomachum* (Questions on the Ten Books of the *Nicomachean Ethics*), a work containing sophisticated accounts of the structure of the will, the nature of human freedom and the phenomenon of *akrasia*, or weakness of the will (see AKRASIA). In moral psychology, Buridan appears to effect a compromise between the 'intellectualist' or 'naturalist' tradition associated with ARISTOTLE (§§21–5) and Thomas AQUINAS (§13), and the 'voluntarist' tradition of AUGUSTINE (§§12–14) and Franciscan thinkers such as DUNS SCOTUS (§14) and WILLIAM OF OCKHAM (§10). Thus he contends (with the former) that human happiness ultimately consists in an intellectual act, 'the perfect comprehension of God', rather than in a volitional act such as willing or loving, although (with the latter) he emphasizes the role of the will as a self-determining power in achieving that end. The compromise appears to turn on Buridan's innovative concept of free choice, which builds upon Albert the Great's notion that moral certainty admits of degrees (Saarinen 1993) (see ALBERT THE GREAT §5). Buridan's idea is that even if the will cannot choose evil as such, it still has the power to defer its choice whenever the goodness of the alternatives presented to it remains doubtful or uncertain: a move which, given our poor epistemic position in this life, seems to guarantee the will a certain amount of freedom in practice. The compromise is only apparent, however, because Buridan also insists that deferment is possible only if 'the intellect would judge it to be good to consider the matter further' (*Quaestiones super decem libros ethicorum* III, q.5), a claim which, together with his assumption that the will can choose non-optimally only through ignorance or impediment (q.3–5; 9), places deferment squarely in the province of the intellect, which weighs the relative goodness and badness of possible courses of action, including deferment. The voluntarist language Buridan appropriates to describe the will's freedom is thus used in an intellectualist sense, perhaps to dispel the cloud of heterodoxy that had surrounded several of the main principles of intellectualist moral psychology since the condemnations of 1277 (Zupko 1995).

Buridan's peculiar conception of freedom also provides the most plausible explanation of the use of his name in the example traditionally known as 'Buridan's ass', in which a donkey starves to death because it is unable to choose between two equidistant and equally tempting piles of hay. This particular example is unknown in Buridan's writings, although there are similar cases. The example probably originated as a parody of Buridan's theory introduced by later authors, who perhaps found absurd the idea that the will's freedom could consist in inaction, that is, in its ability to defer the act of either accepting or rejecting some proposed course of action (see FREE WILL).

See also: ARISTOTELIANISM, MEDIEVAL; BURLEY, W.; GERARD OF ODO; LANGUAGE, MEDIEVAL THEORIES OF; MARSILIUS OF INGHEN; NOMINALISM; UNIVERSALS; WILLIAM OF OCKHAM

List of works

Buridan, John (c.1300–58) *Summulae de dialectica* (Summary of Dialectic), *Perutile compendium totius logicae Ioannis Buridani cum praeclarissima solertissimi viri Ioannis Dorp expositione*, Venice, 1499; repr. Frankfurt: Minerva, 1965. (Incunabular edition of the *Summulae de dialectica*, with a commentary by John Dorp of Leiden.)

—— (c.1300–58) *Quaestiones super octo physicorum libros Aristotelis* (Questions on Aristotle's *Physics*), *Ioannis Buridani subtilissime quaestiones super octo physicorum libros Aristotelis*, Paris, 1509; repr. as *Kommentar zur Aristotelischen Physik*, Frankfurt: Minerva, 1964. (Incunabular edition of the questions on Aristotle's *Physics*.)

—— (c.1300–58) *Quaestiones super decem libros ethicorum Aristotelis ad Nicomachum* (Question's on Aristotle's *Nicomachean Ethics*), *Quaestiones Ioannis Buridani super decem libros ethicorum Aristotelis ad Nicomachum*, Paris, 1513; repr. as *Super decem libros ethicorum*, Frankfurt: Minerva, 1968. (Incunabular edition of the questions on Aristotle's *Nicomachean Ethics*.)

—— (c.1300–58) *Quaestiones super octo libros politicorum Aristotelis* (Questions on Aristotle's *Politics*), Paris, 1513; repr. Frankfurt: Minerva, 1969. (Incunabular edition of the questions on Aristotle's *Politics*.)

—— (*c.* 1300–58) *In Metaphysicam Aristotelis quaestiones* (Questions on Aristotle's *Metaphysics*), *In Metaphysicen Aristotelis quaestiones argutissimae magistri Joannis Buridani*, Paris, 1588 (actually 1518); repr. as *Kommentar zur Aristotelischen Metaphysik*, Frankfurt: Minerva, 1964. (Incunabular edition of the questions on Aristotle's *Metaphysics*.)

—— (*c.*1300–58) *Quaestiones super libris quattuor De caelo et mundo* (Questions on Aristotle's *On the Heavens*), ed. E.A. Moody, *Iohannis Buridani Quaestiones super libris quattuor De caelo et mundo*, Cambridge, MA: Medieval Academy of America, 1942. (Edition of the questions on Aristotle's *On the Heavens*.)

—— (*c.*1300–58) *Tractactus de consequentiis* (Treatise on Consequences), ed. H. Hubien, *Iohannis Buridani Tractatus de consequentiis*, Louvain: Publications Universitaires de Louvain, 1976; trans. P. King, *Jean Buridan's Logic: The Treatise on Supposition; the Treatise on Consequences*, Boston: Reidel, 1985. (Edition and English translation of Buridan's study on inference.)

—— (*c.*1300–58) *Sophismata* (Sophisms), ed. T.K. Scott, Jr, *Iohannis Buridani Sophismata*, Stuttgart: Frommann, 1977. (Translations include that of T.K. Scott, Jr., *John Buridan: Sophisms on Meaning and Truth*, New York: Appleton-Century-Crofts, 1966, and that in G.E. Hughes, *John Buridan on Self-Reference*, Cambridge: Cambridge University Press, 1982, Chapter 8.)

—— (*c.*1300–58) *Quaestiones in Praedicamenta* (Questions on Aristotle's *Categories*), ed. J. Schneider, *Iohannes Buridanus: Quaestiones in Praedicamenta*, Munich: Beck, 1983. (Edition of the questions on Aristotle's *Categories*.)

—— (*c.*1300–58) *Quaestiones longe super librum Perihermeneias* (Questions on Aristotle's *De interpretatione*), ed R. van der Lecq, *Johannes Buridanus: Questiones longe super librum Perihermeneias*, Nijmegen: Ingenium, 1983. (Edition of the questions on Aristotle's *De interpretatione*.)

—— (*c.*1300–58) *Quaestiones in Aristotelis De anima* (Questions on Aristotle's *On the Soul*), first redaction, ed. B. Patar, *Le Traité de l'âme de Jean Buridan [de prima lectura]*, Louvain-la-Neuve: Éditions de l'Institut Supérieur de Philosophie, 1991. (Edition of the first version of Buridan's questions on Aristotle's *On the Soul*. The reference in the text of this entry is to the as yet unpublished third redaction.)

—— (*c.*1300–58) *Tractatus de infinito* (Treatise on Infinity), ed. J. M. Thijssen, *John Buridan's Tracta-*

tus de infinito, Nijmegen: Ingenium, 1991. (Edition of this quasi-independent treatise, contained in Book III of the final version of *Quaestiones super octo physicorum libros Aristotelis*.)

—— (*c.*1300–58) *Tractatus de suppositionibus* (Treatise on Supposition), ed. M.E. Reina, 'Giovanni Buridano: *Tractatus de suppositionibus*', *Rivista critica di storia della filosofia* 12, 1957: 175–208; 323–52; trans. P. King, *Jean Buridan's Logic: The Treatise on Supposition; the Treatise on Consequences*, Boston: Reidel, 1985. (Reina is anedition of Treatise IV of *Summulae de dialectica*; King is an English translation.)

—— (*c.*1300–58) *Quaestio de puncto* (Question on Points), ed. V. Zoubov, 'Jean Buridan et les concepts du point au quatorzième siècle', *Mediaeval and Renaissance Studies* 5, 1961: 43–95. (Edition of Buridan's independent treatise on points.)

References and further reading

* de Rijk, L.M. (1992) 'John Buridan on Universals', *Revue de Métaphysique et de Morale* 97 (1): 35–59. (Explains Buridan's semantic approach to the question of universals, as well as its similarities to that of Peter Abelard.)

* Faral, E. (1950) *Jean Buridan: Maître dès Arts de l'Université de Paris* (Jean Burdian: Master of Arts of the University of Paris), Extrait de l'Histoire littéraire de la France, Tome XXVIII, 2e partie, Paris: Imprimerie Nationale. (Still the best account of the many sources on Buridan's life and times.)

Grant, E. (1977) *Physical Science in the Middle Ages*, Cambridge: Cambridge University Press, 50–5. (Clear explanation of the application of Buridan's theory of impetus to the case of projectile motion.)

* Hughes, G.E. (1982) *John Buridan on Self-Reference: Chapter Eight of Buridan's Sophismata with a Translation, an Introduction, and a Philosophical Commentary*, New York: Cambridge University Press. (Discusses Buridan's treatment of self-referential paradoxes.)

* Klima, G. (1991) 'Latin as a Formal Language: Outlines of a Buridanian Semantics', *Cahiers de l'Institut du Moyen-Âge Grec et Latin* 61: 78–106. (Offers a model-theoretic construction of key elements in Buridan's semantic theory.)

* —— (1992) '"*Debeo tibi equum*": A Reconstruction of the Theoretical Framework of Buridan's Treatment of the Sophisma', *S – European Journal for Semiotic Studies* 4: 141–59. (Formalizes the role of the doctrine of appellation in Buridan's analysis of intentional verbs.)

* Knuuttila, S. (1989) 'Natural Necessity in John Buridan', in S. Caroti (ed.) *Studies in Medieval*

Natural Philosophy, Florence: Olschki. (Investigates Buridan's application of the statistical interpretation of modality to natural possibilities and nomic natural necessities.)

* Michael, B. (1985) 'Johannes Buridan: Studien zu seinem Leben, seinen Werken und zur Rezeption seiner Theorien im Europa des späten Mittelalters' (John Buridan: Studies on His Life, His Work and the Reception of His Theories in the Later Middle Ages), Ph.D. dissertation, University of Berlin. (Authoritative inventory and overview of the complicated textual tradition surrounding Buridan's writings.)

Normore, C. (1985) 'Buridan's Ontology', in J. Bogen and J.E. McGuire (eds) *How Things Are: Studies in Predication and the History and Philosophy of Science*, Dordrecht: Reidel, 189–203. (Discusses the motivation for Buridan's realism about modes.)

* Pinborg, J. (ed.) (1975) *The Logic of John Buridan*, Acts of the Third European Symposium on Medieval Logic and Semantics, Copenhagen: Museum Tusculanum. (Contains ten studies on different aspects of Buridan's logic.)

* Saarinen, R. (1993) 'John Buridan and Donald Davidson on *Akrasia*', *Synthese* 96 (1): 133–54. (Discusses Buridan's explanation of the phenomenon of weakness of will, including his indebtedness to Albert the Great.)

* Spade, P.V. (1978) 'John Buridan on the Liar: A Study and Reconstruction', *Notre Dame Journal of Formal Logic* 19 (4): 579–90. (Formalizes Buridan's solution to the liar paradox in a way that is sensitive to interpretive difficulties in the relevant texts.)

* Thijssen, J.M. (1985) 'Buridan on Mathematics', *Vivarium* 23 (1): 55–77. (Explains and illustrates Buridan's logico-semantic approach to mathematics.)

Walsh, J.J. (1980) 'Teleology in the Ethics of Buridan', *Journal of the History of Philosophy* 18 (3): 265–86. (Examines the intellectualist and voluntarist aspects of Buridan's moral teleology.)

* Zupko, J. (1993a) 'Buridan and Skepticism', *Journal of the History of Philosophy* 31 (2): 191–221. (Explains Buridan's response to scepticism as a consequence of his naturalistic epistemology.)

* —— (1993b) 'Nominalism Meets Indivisibilism', *Medieval Philosophy and Theology* 3: 158–85. (Compares Buridan's divisibilist account of continuous magnitudes with those of Ockham and Adam Wodeham in the context of their replies to the indivisibilist argument that a sphere coming into contact with a plane surface must touch it at an indivisible point.)

* —— (1995) 'Freedom of Choice in Buridan's Moral Psychology', *Mediaeval Studies* 57: 75–99. (Argues that the novel Buridanian act of deferment does not represent a voluntarist departure from what would otherwise be a straightforwardly intellectualist theory of volition, because as Buridan presents it, deferment does not make the will any more autonomous or free.)

JACK ZUPKO

BURKE, EDMUND (1729–97)

Edmund Burke's philosophical importance lies in two fields, aesthetics and political theory. His early work on aesthetics, the Philosophical Enquiry into the Origin of our Ideas of the Sublime and Beautiful *(1757), explored the experiential sources of these two, as he claimed, fundamental responses, relating them respectively to terror at the fear of death and to the love of society.*

Active in politics from 1759, and Member of Parliament from 1765, he wrote and delivered a number of famous political pamphlets and speeches, on party in politics – Thoughts on the Causes of the Present Discontents *(1770), on the crisis with the American colonies –* On Conciliation with America *(1775), on financial reform and on the reform of British India –* Speech on Mr Fox's East India Bill *(1783). While clearly informed by a reflective political mind, these are, however,* pièces d'occasion, *not political philosophy, and their party political provenance has rendered them suspect to many commentators.*

His most powerful and philosophically influential works were written in opposition to the ideas of the French Revolution, in particular Reflections on the Revolution in France *(1790), which has come to be seen as a definitive articulation of anglophone political conservatism. Here Burke considered the sources and desirability of social continuity, locating these in a suspicion of abstract reason, a disposition to follow custom, and certain institutions – hereditary monarchy, inheritance of property, and social corporations such as an established Church. His* Appeal from the New to the Old Whigs *(1791) insisted on the distinction between the French and Britain's revolution of 1688; while his final works,* Letters on a Regicide Peace *(1795), urged an uncompromising crusade on behalf of European Christian civilization against its atheist, Jacobin antithesis.*

1   **Early work**
2   **The party-political pamphleteer**
3   **Philosophical orientation**

1   Early work

Edmund Burke was born on 12 January 1729, of Anglo-Catholic parents, in Dublin. As a young man at Trinity College his early aspirations were literary. He produced a periodical – *The Reformer* – devoted, in the manner of Addison and Steele's *Spectator*, to the reformation of taste as part of a self-conscious moral and political programme, and he retained a concern with the role of manners and taste in sustaining a viable and stable political society. Leaving Dublin to read law at the Temple Inn, he settled in London. There he published a philosophical satire, *A Vindication of Natural Society* (1756), followed a year later by *A Philosophical Enquiry into the Origin of our Ideas of the Sublime and Beautiful*. This achieved prominence for him both in London society, where he moved in the literary and artistic coterie of Samuel Johnson, David Garrick and Joshua Reynolds, and abroad. He was contracted to edit the *Annual Register* from 1758, for which he also wrote an annual political survey and the book reviews.

Burke's conservatism was founded on a deep and often explicit mistrust of metaphysics and abstraction, which for some commentators has rendered doubtful his status as a true political theorist, and even more so as a philosopher. The description of his writings as philosophical is further called into question by their occasional, polemical and often party-political character. However, these early mature writings – and a surviving notebook – reveal a pervasive sceptical epistemological position which is entirely consistent with, and arguably underpins his later political theory. In *A Vindication of Natural Society* Burke satirized the confident rationalism which the First Viscount Bolingbroke, in his posthumously published *Philosophical Works* (1755), had applied critically to religion. The *Vindication* was an ironic 'defence' of the state of nature, exercised through a hyperbolically rationalist critique of existing society, in a kind of *reductio ad absurdum* of Deist arguments (see DEISM). A preface to the second edition clarified his concern to warn against the terrible consequences of applying human reason to areas beyond its very limited competence.

A year later his *Philosophical Enquiry* was published; seventeen English editions were produced in Burke's lifetime and the work was an important influence on European aesthetics. It was translated and discussed by Gotthold Ephraim Lessing in his *Bemerkungen über Burkes philosophische Untersuchungen* (Remarks on Burke's philosophical enquiries) (1758), absorbed by Denis Diderot, and was a significant influence on Immanuel Kant (see BEAUTY; SUBLIME, THE). French and German translations were published in 1765 and 1773 respectively. The work was a resolutely empiricist enquiry into the experiential sources of our responses to the sublime and the beautiful rooted in Lockean sensationist psychology (see LOCKE, J.). Burke rejected the Third Earl of Shaftesbury's claim to be able to derive moral or aesthetic standards from empirical observation, and implicitly criticized Francis Hutcheson in rejecting the ascription of a new 'sense' for each dimension of human response (see SHAFTESBURY, THIRD EARL OF; HUTCHESON, F.). He allied himself methodologically to Isaac Newton in seeking only to describe the phenomena actually observed or experience gained through introspection, and not going beyond that to hazard underlying general principles or forces at work.

Burke saw the sources of the beautiful in the social and pleasurable, those of the sublime in a vicarious appreciation of that which threatens self-preservation, and pain. It was thus, in an important sense, as Burke claimed, a 'theory of the passions' rather than a narrowly aesthetic work, and he stressed its relevance for all persons concerned with 'affecting the passions'. Burke was critical of a number of contemporary theories of beauty, including those neoclassical, utilitarian or Platonic theories which related it to 'proportion', 'fitness' or 'goodness'. Beauty was evoked by the soft, the smooth, and the delicate, and its affective power was by far the weaker of the two responses. Unsurprisingly, as has been pointed out by critics since Dugald Stewart, 'the idea of female beauty was uppermost in Mr Burke's mind when he wrote', and a particular conception of female beauty too: Burke's aesthetic is heavily gendered, a source of comment both for the modern psychobiographer and for feminist critics.

Burke's greater originality lay in his account of the much stronger principle of the sublime. Here, controverting established neoclassicism, Burke stresses the greater power of ideas that are obscure, indistinct and infinite. He anticipates romanticism in stressing the more intense emotional effects produced by imprecise images – and therefore by words, rather than painting, which suggest without delineating. He explains this power through the sublime's capacity to 'over-take our reason', which in turn derives from the inability of reason, on a Lockean account conceived of as the comparison of ideas, to operate where ideas are not (as the sublime never is) 'clear and distinct'. The power of the sublime is linked to religion and politics. Burke follows Hutcheson in drawing attention to the sublime effects produced by the obscurity of 'heathen temples' and the social distancing of political leaders, but goes beyond him in developing a distinction between the social virtues, which are associated with the beautiful response, and the political virtues, linked to austerity, power and the sublime.

2 The party-political pamphleteer

Burke's commitment to a political career began when he entered the service of Lord Rockingham, the opposition Whig leader, in 1765 and took a seat in Parliament later that same year. His most famous political pamphlets and speeches from that period include *Thoughts on the Causes of the Present Discontents* (1770) on party in politics; *On Conciliation with America* (1775) on the crisis with the American colonies; and *Speech on Mr Fox's East India Bill* (1783) on financial reform and on the reform of British India.

The political pamphlets are extremely issue-oriented, and invoke, rather than articulate, a conception of politics. Joining a century-long debate, Burke defends embryonic party association – 'when bad men combine, the good must associate' – on the basis of principled opposition, against the ministerial view that opposition parties were at the least 'factious', and possibly disloyal. His defence of party grouping *within* Parliament contrasts with his deprecation of it outside. In a famous speech to his Bristol constituents he rejected their right to organize so as to 'instruct' MPs, articulating a famous distinction between a representative and a delegate. Here as elsewhere Burke is looked back on as a founder or contributor to a Whiggish developmental account of constitutional practice, which it is not clear the historical record will sustain. In his speeches and writings on America he pursued a policy of reconciliation that stressed the futility of making stands on issues of principle which might never emerge, and could in any case never be enforced. His Economical Reform Bill of 1780, on the other hand, did pursue a principled distinction – between the King's private household finances and those of the Exchequer – seeking, for reasons widely urged, to extinguish the public financial sources of the Crown's influence and patronage threatening parliamentary independence.

These works fit broadly within an ideological position which derives in part from moderate oppositionist thought and Court Whig sentiments. Burke accepted the institutions of political and economic modernization, the importance of safeguarding credit and the moral and political role of a state Church – more especially in times of crisis. However, like opposition Whigs he wanted to limit the Crown's control of patronage through places and supply beyond parliamentary control, and he was anxious about the moral and political effects of Empire – especially where, as in the case of India, through enabling the creation of large fortunes which could be used to buy political influence, and providing the experience of unconstitutionally restrained power, it threatened liberty at home. Another source of political destabilization in this political orthodoxy was insecurity of property. Despite Burke's acceptance of modernizing Whig institutions – the Bank of England, a national debt and a market in stock and bonds – he was acutely aware of the potentially destabilizing effects of property speculation. The image of gambling as destructive of both individual rationality and social coherence haunted the eighteenth century since at least the South Sea Bubble, and Burke draws on all these resources when he comes to denounce in *Reflections on the Revolution in France* (1790) the Revolutionaries' political economy and for their having reduced France to 'one great play table' and produced a people whose 'impulses, passions, and superstitions [are] of those who live on chance'.

Despite their congruities with well-established patterns of argument, neither these, nor the works of his later, French revolutionary period, are in any sense works of systematic philosophy, as the *Philosophical Enquiry* is. Burke's wider political position emerges episodically in parenthetical observations, epigrams and observations, which engage and resonate with a number of important political languages and issues of his time, and which only contentiously, and with some effort at reconstruction, constitute a political philosophy. One consequence of this is a considerable diversity of interpretation about Burke's precise – or even general – theoretical location. Within the last hundred years Burke has been characterized as a utilitarian, a radical Lockean, a Court Whig, a natural law theorist, a common law theorist, and a proto-romantic.

3 Philosophical orientation

Even in the more theoretically-oriented political works is a series of issues of philosophical significance and in the treatment of which a broad continuity can be seen with Burke's earlier works. Central among these are his fear of atheism; his conception of the political order as resting on an 'opinion' which is potentially unstable and a product of cultural and practical experiences; and a defence of tradition, both in substance, and on grounds sceptical of other sources of knowledge. In each of these cases it is an abstract 'reason' which Burke sees as the threat. Pride in the power of abstract reason fuelled the deist attacks on Christianity both in his youth and in Jacobin France. Philosophical speculation, especially when taken up by the politically inexperienced, detached people from valuable socialized dispositions and created political expectations and opinions which were not only unrealistic, in the sense of being cut adrift from the empirically validated institutions, practices and customs of the society, but positively harmful. For such abstract principles seemed to justify not merely the adjustment of institutions and practices to circumstance – a necessary condition, he recognized, for a tradition to incorporate and accumulate experience – but their reconstruction *de novo*. Such rationalist appraisal of tradition undermined the presumption in its favour necessary for its preservation, for although tradition provided real benefits in terms of social continuity and stable expectations, Burke believed that such a defence could be articulated with only the greatest of difficulty to the enthusiastic rationalist mind.

Burke's response to the French Revolution (1790) was directed in particular at the language of radical natural rights, and the fear of its being imported to England. But the occasion of that fear was the Unitarian Richard Price's sermon 'On the Love of our Country', in which PRICE compared the deficiencies of Britain's Glorious Revolution of 1688 to what the French were succeeding in achieving. Price's religious rationalism was of the stamp Burke had attacked in his early *Vindication of Natural Society*. Radical deists (which Burke judged Unitarians to be) were now applying in earnest to politics those very arguments of religious rationalists which Burke had attacked in his youth when he had applied them ironically to politics. Natural right, far from providing a continuing standard of probity in political society, was inconsistent, Burke urged in Hobbesian fashion (see HOBBES, T.), with its very existence – the inconsistency being amply demonstrated by the fact that it is only in virtue of surrendering our natural rights that we can enjoy our civil rights. Conversely, in reasserting the former we effectively dissolve the social bonds. While this account seems to entail some version of social contract theory, Burke's conception of the emergence of society is so historicized that such a contract cannot be the act of any one set of natural agents, but is rather a partnership across time and between generations. The corollaries drawn are that no one generation has the right to abrogate the contract, and exclude future generations from benefiting thereby, and moreover, that if such an abrogation were to occur, the re-establishment of society would be not an act, but a long and hazardous historical process.

Burke's response to Price's invitation to imitate France comprised, as well as an attack on radical natural rights doctrine, a more general attack on abstract theory in politics, and an argument about

English historiography and the status of 1688 – continued at some length a year later in his *Appeal from the New to the Old Whigs* (1791). To natural right, Burke opposed tradition; to rationalism, sentiment; and to the interpretation of 1688 as a failed revolution, the view of it as a desperate bid to sustain continuity – 'a revolution not made but prevented'.

Burke had a complex conception of tradition owing much to Edward Coke, Hale and the English common law tradition. Custom – and even 'prejudice' – comprising the accumulated adjustment to circumstance of many generations, represented a kind of collective rationality which individuals cannot create. There was also, for Burke a sense in which, rational or not, the sustenance of such collective practices over time – or even the belief that they have been so sustained – constitutes the identity of the society.

Burke's more general arguments against attempts to use rational criteria for social criticism focus on a number of deficiencies he had long identified in rationalism. A major feature was the indeterminacy of reason when not embedded in social practice. This insistence on social embeddedness has been a feature of much recent political debate, not only about values and principles but about personality itself. Burke here presages Hegel, as well as modern communitarians such as Ernest Mandel and Alasdair MacIntyre (see COMMUNITY AND COMMUNITARIANISM). For Burke, assessing the consequences of any social institution apart from an actual practice in its historical context is extremely hazardous, since its consequences and those of its fit with other institutions are unpredictable. The presumption in favour of natural right over positively existing institutions is a recipe for anarchy, for it represents an attempt to dissociate individuals from those shared beliefs and conventions which alone make social life possible. Even the assumption of majority decision-making, Burke points out, so far from being natural is a 'violent fiction of positive law'. The indeterminacy of rationalism was psychological as well as logical: at an individual level moral rationalism left the individual perplexed as to how to apply a rule, whereas 'prejudice renders a man's virtue his habit' and so provides an unhesitating and culturally appropriate response.

A second deficiency in reason – already famously stressed by Hume – was its ineffectual properties as a motivator. To replace traditional institutions and beliefs with rationalist schemes, however good, risked the failure of a people to adhere to them. The prejudicial partiality for one's immediate family and locality, for known and accepted patterns of life, was the basis of any moral or political reality, both psychologically and in extent. The love of family and the 'little platoon' was the affective basis of ever-widening social circles through which we ultimately conceived affection for our country. By contrast, Price's conditional patriotism, and the internationalism of the revolutionaries, Burke characterized as cold and ultimately ineffectual, leading to a love of humankind but not of any individuals. Moreover, the political consequences of abandoning custom and the motivating sentimental attachments to it would, Burke thought, be the increasing need to resort to coercion.

Burke identified British political culture as peculiarly suited to avoiding the intrusion of a-prioristic reasoning; it is praised as comprising a proper and continuing predisposition to conserve. The events of 1688 thus represented the successful avoidance of constitutional discontinuity at the price of some minor deviation in the line of descent. The principle of inheritance – in the monarchy and the Lords, as well as in the private property of family estates – links an important natural process – that is, reproduction – and natural sentiments – that is, family affection – to social practices conducive to continuity, and so to the epistemological collective benefits outlined above. Religion plays an important role in underpinning respect for these institutions, which might not otherwise be forthcoming, or might otherwise be undermined by a variety of processes at work in society, including moral or religious scepticism.

The French Revolution thus not only promulgated a political doctrine which Burke believed to be fundamentally flawed, but its actions – in undermining the Church and destabilizing property and even the currency – were destroying those institutions participation in which sustained shared patterns of belief and knowledge that comprised the community. Burke successfully predicted that a dictatorship would emerge from the atomized, institutionally dislocated or uprooted society.

Crucial to Burke's pessimism is an Augustinian sense of humankind's fallen and imperfect nature, from which we are preserved only by the painfully acquired veneer of civilization, which can be very quickly lost. Rejecting the Rousseauean art–nature polarity (see ROUSSEAU, J.-J.), Burke affirms that 'art is man's nature'. It is nevertheless a second nature that is only acquired with care over a long time, and failure to acquire or sustain it reveals a savage and violent nature of a Hobbesian kind, which, Burke insists, will result from the reassertion of natural right. Throughout the mid twentieth century Burke's thought was regularly appealed to by practising conservative politicians in Britain, and by American Cold-War ideologues. While much recent conservative thought has been so organized around the role of the market, as, in Burke's terms, to be the application of 'abstract'

principle, a thinker such as Michael OAKESHOTT can be seen as operating in a recognisably Burkean intellectual environment.

See also: CONSERVATISM; CONTRACTARIANISM; REVOLUTION; RIGHTS; TRADITION AND TRADITIONALISM

List of works

Burke, E. (1886) *The Works of the Right Honorable Edmund Burke*, London: Bell.

—— (1981–) *The Writings and Speeches of Edmund Burke*, ed. P. Langford, Oxford: Oxford University Press. (In preparation.)

—— (1757) *A Philosophical Enquiry into the Origin our Ideas of the Sublime and Beautiful*, ed. J.T. Boulton, London and New York: Routledge & Kegan Paul; Columbia University Press, 1958. (This contains an excellent historical and critical introduction.)

References and further reading

Furniss, T. (1993) *Edmund Burke's Aesthetic Ideology*. Cambridge: Cambridge University Press.

Kramnick, I., (1977) *The Rage of Edmund Burke*, New York: Basic Books. (Explores the gender dimension of Burke's personality and political theorising.)

* Lessing, G.E. (1758) *Bemerkungen über Burkes philosophische Untersuchungen* (Remarks on Burke's philosophical enquiries) (Discussion of Burke's *Philosophical Enquiry.*)

O'Brien, C.C. (1992) *The Great Melody*, London: Sinclair-Stevenson. (A very full and reflective biography.)

Pocock, J.G.A. (1960) 'Burke and the Ancient Constitution', *Historical Journal*, 3 (2).

Pocock, J.G.A. (1982) 'The Political Economy of Burke's Analysis of the French Revolution', *Historical Journal*, 25 (2); repr. in J.G.A. Pocock, *Virtue Commerce and History*, Cambridge: Cambridge University Press, 1985.

Wilkins, B.T. (1967) *The Problem of Burke's Political Philosophy*, Oxford: Oxford University Press. (The most cautious of the 'natural law' interpretations of Burke.)

IAN HAMPSHER-MONK

BURLEY, WALTER
(*c.*1275–*c.*1345)

*Active in the first half of the fourteenth century, Burley
received his arts degree from Oxford before 1301 and
his doctorate in theology from Paris before 1324. At
one time a fellow of Merton College, he – along with
Thomas Bradwardine, Richard Kilvington and others –
became a member of the household of Richard de Bury,
Bishop of Durham and served several times as envoy of
the King of England to the papal court. Despite his
extra-university activities, Burley continued to compose
Aristotelian commentaries and to engage in disputations to the end of his life. A clear and prolific writer,
Burley has been labelled an 'Averroist' and a 'realist'
because of his arguments against Ockham, but it would
perhaps be more accurate to see him as a middle-of-the-
road Aristotelian whose intellectual activity coincided
with the transition between the approaches of Thomas
Aquinas and Duns Scotus on the one hand and those of
William of Ockham and the Oxford Calculators on the
other.*

Born around 1275, Walter Burley became an Oxford
Master of Arts sometime before 1301. He was a fellow
of Merton College, Oxford in 1305, but by 1310 he
was a student of theology at Paris. A colophon dated
1324 cites Burley as a doctor of theology. In 1327
Burley was appointed King Edward's envoy to the
papal court, where he was again in 1343. In between,
he was a member of the household of Richard Bury,
Bishop of Durham, and conducted a disputation in
Bologna in 1341. He probably died soon after 1344,
when he is last mentioned.

Although Burley became a doctor of theology, he
continued to write philosophical works throughout
his life, commenting on all of Aristotle's logical works
and on many of his other works as well, sometimes
more than once. He also wrote independent treatises
on philosophical subjects. Of his commentary on
Peter Lombard's *Sentences* there is no known copy,
nor are other explicitly theological works ascribed to
him (although the *Tractatus primus* probably resulted
from Burley's 'Principium' on the *Sentences*). His *De
puritate artis logicae* (On the Purity of the Art of
Logic) exists in a shorter version written about 1324
and a longer version written in 1325–8, responding to
Ockham's *Summa logicae* of 1324. His commentary
on Aristotle's *Physics* survives in manuscript in a
version written before 1316; revised versions were
printed many times, no doubt because of the
commentary's completeness and clarity. Accurate,
extensive quotations from earlier commentators are
included.

In natural philosophy, Burley is best known for
having held the 'succession of forms' theory of
intension and remission, which treats qualitative
forms, such as whiteness or heat, as similar to
substantial forms, such as humanity. Each form is
thought of as corresponding to one degree of quality.
As a body is heated, at each instant it loses the degree
of heat it had and acquires a greater degree. There are
infinitely many indivisible degrees of heat, and
between any two degrees there are other degrees.
GODFREY OF FONTAINES had held a similar theory in
explaining augmentation and diminution. In the later
fourteenth century, most natural philosophers followed not Godfrey and Burley, but DUNS SCOTUS,
who had developed the so-called 'addition theory' of
intension and remission: when a quality is intensified
new parts are added, which produce a higher degree.
Thus the previous degree of quality is not lost, as in
the succession theory, but becomes part of the new
degree. However, as long as the issue of how to
explain the intension and remission of forms continued to be discussed, the succession theory was
nearly always taken seriously.

Burley's treatise on first and last instants represents
a standard view. For Burley, as for most other
fourteenth-century authors, 'permanent' entities –
that is, those that are wholly existent at once, unlike
motion – have a first instant of being but no last
instant. When water is heated and becomes air, there
is a first instant at which the air exists but no last
instant of the water. On the other hand, for
'successive' entities such as motions, there is neither
a first instant at which the motion exists, nor a last
instant of motion before the body comes to rest.
Combining his ideas of first and last instants and his
ideas of intension and remission, Burley argued in the
Tractatus primus that all degrees of heat must be of
the same species, rejecting such separate, contrary
species as hotness, temperateness and coldness.

WILLIAM OF OCKHAM and other fourteenth-century nominalists such as John BURIDAN developed
physical theories that minimized the types of entities
in the world, maintaining that there are only
substances and qualities unless there are special
reasons for relaxing this rule. Burley, on the other
hand, seems not to have been motivated by any
preference for ontological parsimony. Thus, for
Ockham, motion cannot exist separately from the
moving body. Alteration as a kind of motion is simply
the body altered and the degrees of quality (*forma
fluens*) that it successively takes on. Burley adhered
to Ockham's view for alteration, but relaxed it for
local motion. If local motion were not something
more than the body and the places it successively
takes on, Buridan argued, then if God rotated the

cosmos as a whole and there was nothing at rest to act as a reference point, it would be impossible to distinguish the cosmos in rotation from the cosmos at rest. Finding this conclusion unacceptable, Buridan concluded that in local motion there must be a flux (*fluxus formae*) as well as the places occupied. Burley, when confronted with similar questions, did not even try to develop a theory of motion that did not involve a *fluxus formae* as well as a *forma fluens*, but instead easily accepted the assumption that there is a *fluxus formae*. Likewise, while the nominalists emphasized that distances can exist and be measured only on bodies, so that when bodies move, the distances measured on them must likewise change, Burley took it as unproblematic that when two bodies are at rest, the distance between them remains the same, whether or not there is an unchanging body on which to measure the distance.

Because Burley belonged to no religious order, he has had no modern confrères interested in perpetuating a knowledge of his views. In the current state of scholarship, Burley appears more often as someone holding views contrasting with those of the nominalists than as someone whose theories are of interest for their own sake. Yet Burley's works were widely used, even after the advent of printing, probably more because of their thoroughness and clarity than because of the unique positions that Burley upheld. Burley's work would repay further study as a source of information about the views that were typical of early fourteenth-century scholasticism.

See also: BURIDAN, J.; LANGUAGE, MEDIEVAL THEORIES OF; NATURAL PHILOSOPHY, MEDIEVAL; WILLIAM OF OCKHAM

List of works

For a more complete list, see Weisheipl (1969) or Wood (1988b). Wood lists 50 surviving authentic works plus 17 lost, doubtful or spurious works. Included here are longer works and works that have received modern editions. For many more details on manuscripts and early printed editions of Burley's Aristotelian commentaries, including many works not listed here, see C. Lohr (1988) 'Medieval Latin Aristotle Commentaries', *Traditio* 24: 171–87.

Burley, Walter (1301) *Quaestiones in Librum Perihermeneias* (Questions on the *Perihermeneias*), ed. S. Brown, 'Walter Burley's Quaestiones in Librum Perihermeneias', *Franciscan Studies* 34, 1974: 200–95. (Twenty years later, Burley composed his so-called Middle Commentary on the *Perihermeneias* (ed. S. Brown, 'Walter Burley's Middle

Commentary on Aristotle's Perihermeneias', *Franciscan Studies* 33, 1973: 42–134).)

—— (*c.*1302) *Obligationes* (Obligations), part trans. in N. Kretzmann and E. Stump, *Logic and Philosophy of Language*, The Cambridge Translations of Medieval Philosophical Texts vol. I, Cambridge: Cambridge University Press, 1988, 370–412. (Burley's treatment of the common scholastic disputational exercise called 'obligations').)

—— (*c.*1302) *Insolubilia* (Insolubles), ed. M.L. Roure, 'La Problématique des propositions insolubiles au XIIIe siècle et au début de XIVe, suivie de l'édition des traités de W. Shyreswood, W. Burley and Th. Bradwardine', *Archives d'histoire doctrinale et littéraire du moyen âge* 37, 1971: 262–84. (Related to the previous work and perhaps composed at about the same time, this work treats those propositions that seem to falsify themselves, such as 'I am telling a lie.')

—— (early version pre-1316; later versions 1324–7 and 1334–7) *In Physicas Aristotelis. Expositio et Questiones* (On Aristotle's *Physics*: Exposition and Questions (various revisions and titles)), Pavia, 1488; Venice, 1482, 1491, 1501 (repr. Hildesheim: Olms, 1972), 1508; Bologna, 1589. (Existing in several versions, Burley's exposition of and questions on Aristotle's *Physics* combined a detailed passage-by-passage explanation of Aristotle's text, and often of Averroes' commentary on it, with occasional digressions to answer questions or doubts.)

—— (before *c.*1316?) *Tractatus expositorius super libros posteriorum Aristotelis* (Expository Treatise on the Books of Aristotle's *Posterior Analytics*), Venice, 1497, 1504; Oxford, 1517; repr. of edition with Robert Grosseteste's *In Aristotelis Posteriorum analyticorum libros*, Frankfurt: Minerva, 1966. (Burley's commentary on the *Posterior Analytics*.)

—— (before 1320?) *Tractatus de suppositionibus* (Treatise on Supposition), ed. S. Brown, 'Walter Burleigh's Treatise *De Suppositionibus* and its influence on William of Ockham', *Franciscan Studies* 32, 1972: 15–64. (Burley's work on a central concept of the new logic.)

—— (1320–3) *Tractatus de formis* (Treatise on Forms), ed. F.J.D. Scott, Veröffentlichungen der Kommission für die Herausgabe ungedruckter Texte aux der mittelalterlichen Geisteswelt, Bd. 4, Munich: Verlag der Bayerischen Akademie der Wissenschaften, 1970. (One of Burley's shorter works that has received a modern edition, this provides a general overview of Burley's theory of forms. Various other short, mostly logical works have been edited by H. Shapiro and various collaborators; see Murdoch and Sylla (1970) for details.)

—— (1320–7) *Tractatus primus* or *Tractatus de activitate, unitate et augmento formarum activarum habaentium contraria et suscipientium magis et minus* (First Treatise, or Treatise on the Activity, Unity and Augmentation of Active Forms Having Contraries and Undergoing More or Less), MSS Bruges, Stadsbibl. 501, 70r–105r; Vat. lat. 817, ff. 203–223r. (Exists only in manuscript form. Contains Burley's theory of the succession of forms in its formative stages.)

—— (after 1327?) *Tractatus secundus* or *Tractatus de intensione et remissione formarum* (Second Treatise, or Treatise on the Intension and Remission of Forms), Venice, 1496. (The mature statement of Burley's succession of forms theory and of its justifications. For a discussion, see Maier (1968).)

—— (1320s?) *Utrum contradicto sit maxima oppositio* (Whether Contradiction is the Maximum Opposition), ed. R. Palacz, 'Gualterii Burleii Quaestio: Utrum contradicto sit maxima oppositio (MS. Vat. Ottob. 318, f. 141va–145vb)', *Mediaevalia Philosophica Polonorum* XI, 1968, 128–39, 152–6; ed. L.M. de Rijk, 'Burley's So-called *Tractatus Primus*, with an Edition of the Additional Quaestio "Utrum contradicto sit maxima oppositio"', *Vivarium* 34, 1996: 161–91. (Brief logical work.)

—— (1320s?) *De exclusivis* (On Exclusions), ed. L.M. de Rijk, 'Walter Burley's Tract *De exclusivis*: An Edition', *Vivarium* 23, 1984: 23–54. (Brief logical work.)

—— (1320s?) *De exceptivis* (On Exceptions), ed. L.M. de Rijk, 'Walter Burley's *De exceptivis*, an Edition', *Vivarium* 24, 1986: 22–49. (Brief logical work.)

—— (shorter version before 1324; longer version 1325–8) *De puritate artis logicae* (On the Purity of the Art of Logic), ed. P. Boehner, St. Bonaventure, NY: Franciscan Institute, 1955; section on consequences trans. in N. Kretzmann and E. Stump, *Logic and the Philosophy of Language*, The Cambridge Translations of Medieval Philosophical Texts vol. I, Cambridge: Cambridge University Press, 284–311. (A typical fourteenth-century textbook of new logic, which may be compared to Ockham's logical works to see the points on which fourteenth-century logicians tended to agree or disagree with each other.)

—— (before 1327) *De primo et ultimo instanti* (On the First and the Last Instant), ed. H. Shapiro and C. Shapiro, *Archiv für Geschichte der Philosophie* 47, 1965: 157–73. (This is a working rather than critical edition of Burley's ideas concerning first and last instants.)

—— (c. 1333–41) *Exposition super libros Ethicorum Aristotelis* (Exposition of the Books of Aristotle's *Ethics*), Venice, 1481, 1500. (Towards the end of his life, Burley continued to compose commentaries on the major works of the Aristotelian corpus.)

—— (final version 1337) *Expositio super artem veterem Porphyrii et Aristotelis* (Exposition of the Old Art of Porphyry and Aristotle), Venice, 1481, 1497 (repr. Frankfurt: Minerva, 1967), 1519 and many others. (A commentary on the old logic.)

—— (1340–3) *Expositio super librum Politicorum* (Exposition on the book of *Politics*). (Exists in many manuscripts, though relatively neglected by recent scholars.)

pseudo-Burley (?) *De vita et moribus philosophorum* (The Lives and Customs of the Philosophers). (Previously thought to be by Burley; see J. Prelog (1990) 'De Pictagora phylosopho. Die Biographie des Pythagoras in dem Walter Burley zugeschriebenen Liber de vita et moribus philosophorum,' *Medioevo. Rivista di storia della filosofia medievale* 16: 191–251.)

References and further reading

Jung-Palczewska, E. (1986) 'Le problème d'averroïsme de Walter Burley dans son Commentaire sur la "Physique"' (The Problem of the Averroism of Walter Burley in his Commentary on the *Physics*), *Studia Mediewistyczne* 24: 101–9. (Argues that Burley was not an Averroist, but rather tried to expound Aristotle's meaning, Averroes' meaning where relevant, and then in some cases to give his own opinion, which was likely to follow Catholic views when these diverged from Aristotle (for instance, on the eternity of the world or on free will).)

Kitchel, M.J. (1971) 'The *De Potentiis Animae* of Walter Burley', *Medieval Studies* 33: 85–113. (See for Burley's views on the human intellect and soul.)

Maier, A. (1955) 'Ein unbeachteter "Averroist" des XIV Jahrhunderts: Walter Burley', (An Unnoticed 'Averroist' of the Fourteenth Century: Walter Burley), *Medioevo e Rinascimento: Studi in onore di Bruno Nardi*, Florence; reprinted in A. Maier, *Ausgehendes Mittelalter: Gesammelte Aufsätze zur Geistesgeschichte des 14. Jahrhunderts*, 2 vols, Rome: Edizioni di Storia e Letteratura, 1964–7. (Puts Burley's work in its fourteenth-century context.)

—— (1968) *Zwei Grundprobleme der scholastischen Naturphilosophie* (Two Fundamental Problems of Scholastic Natural Philosophy), Rome: Edizioni di Storia e Letteratura, 3rd edn. (See the chapter 'Nachträge zu Walter Burleys Traktat De intensione et remissione formarum'. As always for fourteenth-century natural philosophy, Maier's work is fundamental.)

Martin, C. (1964) 'Walter Burley', in *Oxford Studies*

Presented to Daniel Callus, Oxford: Clarendon Press, 194–230. (Comprehensive collection of the biographical information available about Burley.)

Murdoch, J.E. and Sylla, E.D. (1970) 'Burley, Walter', in *Dictionary of Scientific Biography*, New York: Charles Scribner's Sons, vol. 2, 608–12. (Provides more detail about Burley's work insofar as it is relevant to the history of science.)

Sylla, E.D. (1988) 'Walter Burley's *Tractatus Primus*: Evidence Concerning the Relations of Disputations and Written Works', *Franciscan Studies* 44: 257–74. (Deals with Burley's *Tractatus primus* and the various opponents whose opinions are considered in that work.)

Una Juarez, A. (1978) *La Filosofia del Siglo XIV. Contexto Cultural de Walter Burley* (The Philosophy of the Fourteenth Century. The Cultural Context of Walter Burley), Madrid: Biblioteca 'La Cuidad de Dios' Real Monasterio de el Escorial. (A survey of fourteenth-century philosophy as relevant to the work of Burley.)

Weisheipl, J.A. (1969) 'Repertorium Mertonense' (Mertonian Inventory), *Mediaeval Studies* 31: 174–224. (Includes a list of Burley's known works together with manuscript locations.)

Wood, R. (1988a) 'Walter Burley's *Physics* Commentaries', *Franciscan Studies* 43: 275–327. (Distinguishes several editions, and shows that the commentaries ascribed to Burley in Erfurt manuscripts are not in fact authentic.)

—— (1988b) 'Studies on Walter Burley 1968–1988', *Bulletin de philosophie médiévale* 30: 233–50. (Lists facsimile editions, modern editions and articles on Burley.)

—— (1989–90) 'Walter Burley on Motion in A Vacuum', *Traditio* 45: 191–217. (As Wood explains, Burley suggest there could be a quantitative extension without a substance present (as occurs in the Eucharist), and if so, motion might occur in it.)

EDITH DUDLEY SYLLA

BURNET, GILBERT

see CAMBRIDGE PLATONISM

BURNETT, JAMES

see MONBODDO, LORD (JAMES BURNETT)

BURTHOGGE, RICHARD (*c.*1638–*c.*1704)

Richard Burthogge, perhaps the first but certainly not the least interesting modern idealist, was a minor philosopher who responded to a variety of English and Dutch influences. His epistemology, constructed as an undogmatic framework within which to debate theological and metaphysical issues, contains remarkable resemblances to later, even recent idealism. He argued that, since our faculties help to shape their objects, we never know things as they are in themselves: all the immediate objects of thought are appearances. 'Metaphysical truth' is therefore beyond us, but we approach 'logical truth' in so far as our notions harmonize or cohere with one another and with experience. In this spirit, Burthogge advocated a tolerant reasonableness in religion, while in metaphysics he postulated a universal mind, united with matter, of which individual minds are local manifestations.

1 Life
2 Theory of knowledge
3 Theory of mind

1 Life

Richard Burthogge was born in Plymouth, England, and educated at Exeter Grammar School, at Oxford (B.A. 1658) and at Leiden in Holland (M.D. 1662). He returned to his native Devon and became a prosperous medical practitioner. His first theological works, *Divine goodness* (1672) and *Causa Dei* (1675), wrestled with the problems of evil, grace and divine justice. *Organum Vetus et Novum* (1678) was Burthogge's epistemological response to the 'Proud *Ignorance*, Ignorant *Zeal*, and Impertinent Reasoning' of his critics. It rested on an anti-dogmatic probabilism characteristic of such advocates of toleration as William CHILLINGWORTH and the Cambridge Platonists (see CAMBRIDGE PLATONISM), together with a thesis which Burthogge could have heard expounded in Leiden by GEULINCX, that the objects of logic and knowledge are shaped by the forms of our understanding. Between 1684 and 1691 further works called for 'a general toleration', and attempted to settle religious disputes by 'harmonious' interpretation of scripture and historical evidence. In 1694 *An Essay upon Reason, and the Nature of Spirits* set out Burthogge's theory of knowledge as prolegomenon to a theory of mind which, although dualistic, owed something to Spinoza. This work was also influenced by Locke, to whom it was dedicated and with whom a correspondence ensued. *Of the Soul of the World, and of Particular Souls* (1699), again addressed to Locke, gave further arguments for Burthogge's hypothesis. The Calvinist doctrine of predestined salvation was attacked once more in *Christianity a Revealed Mystery* (1702), an unorthodox exegesis of *Romans* VIII.28–30. In 1703 this argument was pursued in letters to Locke, who then offered the same interpretation in his *Paraphrase* of St Paul. It seems not to be known when Burthogge died.

2 Theory of knowledge

Burthogge's fundamental epistemological principle, expounded in both *Organum* and *An Essay*, is that things are known by us only as they are in our faculties (that is sense, imagination and understanding), and that 'Every Faculty hath a hand, though not the sole hand, in making its immediate Object'. Philosophers recognize that 'Colours are [not] without the Eye...although they seem so to Sense' (1678: 13–14). Yet the understanding equally 'doth *Pinn* its Notions upon Objects' (1694: 58): substance, accidents, powers, similitude, whole, part, cause, effect and so on 'own no other kind of Existence than...an Objective [that is, intentional] one'. Yet it does not follow that nothing is real, since intentional or 'cogitable' beings are characteristically grounded in realities: 'Notions of the Minde are *bottomed* on *Sentiments* of Sense; so that as Realities are Grounds to Sentiments, so Sentiments are Grounds to Notions' (1678: 15–16). The hinge here is our awareness in sensation that external realities are acting on us – just that awareness which masks the contribution of the faculty itself. Voluntary fictions obviously lack such grounding, while, although sensory illusions and dreams are both 'real' in having causes outside the mind, in the former case the causes are unusual, and in the latter they are 'Causes only, and not Objects as well as Causes' (1694: 78).

Understanding, it is explained in *An Essay*, arises from sense by means of language. Words are images which aid thought either by calling other images or notions to mind or by standing in place of them. Indeed, ideas of the understanding are nothing but definitions, both 'of words' and 'made by words'. This allows for notions of things 'perfectly intelligible and mental', but such notions are necessarily shaped by language and even further from reality than the images or sensations on which they are based (1694: 27–34).

Burthogge recurs to the traditional point that to apprehend something through an attribute is to apprehend it imperfectly under a notion or aspect or *modus concipiendi*, and yet we can only apprehend things through their attributes. In *An Essay* this thought is developed on Lockean lines: our experience is only of qualities, but we conceive 'that other things are under them, which do uphold and support them, and consequently, that are *subjects*, or substances' (1694: 98) (see LOCKE, J. §§4–5). In *Organum*, Burthogge had emphasized a comparison with our imperfect knowledge of God. As to know God through his attributes is to know him only by analogy, so in general 'to us men *things* are nothing but as they stand in our *Analogie*' (1678: 12). There is, however, a difference between the Light of Faith and the Light of Reason. Revelation supplies analogies for spiritual, rather than natural things. They should be employed as such, and reason should endeavour to harmonize them, but none should be insisted on 'as if it were adequate, or just'. Still less should they be used in opposition to natural reason (1678: 26–34).

Organum also contains what is perhaps the clearest and most forthright statement of a coherence theory of truth in the seventeenth century (see TRUTH, COHERENCE THEORY OF). Because we cannot get behind our notions, 'metaphysical truth' is of no concern to us. 'Logical truth', however, when 'rightly shewn', is naturally distinguished by the understanding. The criterion of logical truth cannot be the Stoic or Cartesian clear and distinct perception, since any criterion must lie in the object, not in the way in which we perceive it. Nor does it lie in innate tendencies or principles. Truth, as the ground of assent, is the objective harmony, congruity and coherence of things 'in the Frame and Scheme of them in our Mindes'. Natural reasoning assumes a harmonious world as the object of a unified science: in 'science as it is in Arch-work, the Parts uphold one another'. To prove something is to fit it into 'a Scheme and Frame of Notions bottomed on things'. Any hypothesis is in principle vulnerable to a more coherent hypothesis, but to doubt without reason is 'unreasonable and contradictious' (1678: 47–60).

3 Theory of mind

In contrast to Locke, Burthogge argues in *An Essay* that, despite our ignorance of their real natures, we cannot suppose that mind is a power of matter; nor can we, with Spinoza, suppose them identical (see LOCKE, J. §5; SPINOZA, B. DE. §§5–6). Since the attributes through which we distinguish them, extension and thought (and, with thought, agency), are mutually irreducible by us, we simply have to abide by our 'Refracted, Inadequate, *Real-Notional* way of conceiving' (1694: 107). Pure matter appears as passive; pure mind, which is God, as active. Mind as we know it in ourselves and in animals, however, appears inextricably 'concreted' with matter. Experience shows that reason itself requires a properly working organ. The best hypothesis is that everything in nature is a combination of matter with a universal spirit which activates and controls it. The species of living, sensitive and rational things are produced according to the 'Texture and Quality' of their material structure. The organs of perception and thought 'catch and retain' specific forms of cogitation as a mirror catches an image from motions in the medium, or a glass catches the vibrations of a lute-string. Without matter so in harmony with mind, there would be no individuation of thoughts or, indeed, of souls, which are 'portions' of 'the Soul of the World'. This panpsychist hypothesis allows that human souls are generated in the same general way as animal souls, a piece of common sense doubted only by the Cartesians.

List of works

Burthogge, R. (1921) *The Philosophical Writings of Richard Burthogge*, ed. M.W. Landes, Chicago, IL, and London: Open Court. (Contains the *Organum Vetus et Novum, Of the Soul of the World*, with selections from *An Essay upon Reason*. Introduction presents Burthogge as precursor of Kant.)

—— (1672) *TAΓAΘON, or, Divine Goodness Explicated and Vindicated from the Exceptions of the Atheist*, London. (Attempts to reconcile the existence of evil, and the doctrines of grace and of salvation by faith, with divine goodness and justice.)

—— (1675) *Causa Dei, or an Apology for God*, London. (As above, allowing means of salvation to heathens, since God cannot require impossibilities.)

—— (1678) *Organum Vetus et Novum: or, A Discourse of Reason and Truth*, London; repr. in *The Philosophical Writings of Richard Burthogge*, ed. M.W. Landes, Chicago, IL, and London: Open Court, 1921. (Bases an anti-dogmatic epistemology and coherence theory of truth on the principle that the objects of knowledge are shaped by our faculties and notions.)

—— (1683) *An argument for infants baptisme, deduced from the analogy of faith, and harmony of the scriptures*, London; 2nd edn, 1684. (Typical of Burthogge's theological arguments, this one finds analogical and biblical grounds in favour of infant baptism.)

—— (1687) *Prudential reasons for repealing the penal laws against all recusants, and for a general toleration*, London. (An appeal for religious toleration, published anonymously.)

—— (1690) *The Nature of Church-government, freely discussed and set out*. (Anonymously published

argument that the form of church government is a practical matter, not determined by scriptural authority.)

—— (1694) *An Essay upon Reason, and the Nature of Spirits*, London; repr. in *British philosophers and theologians of the 17th and 18th centuries*, 10, New York and London: Garland, 1976. (Restates the theory of *Organum* as a methodological framework for a speculative, panpsychic theory of the relation between mind and body.)

—— (1699) *Of the Soul of the World; and of Particular Souls: in a Letter to Mr. Lock*, London; repr. in *The Philosophical Writings of Richard Burthogge*, ed. M.W. Landes, Chicago, IL, and London: Open Court, 1921. (Further argument, from the coherence of scripture, various authorities and purported facts, for panpsychism.)

—— (1702) *Christianity a Revealed Mystery: or, the gracious purpose of God toward the gentiles*, London. (An attack on the Calvinist doctrine of the elect which apparently influenced Locke.)

—— (1979–82) *The Correspondence of John Locke*, vols 5, 6 and 7, ed. E. S. de Beer, Oxford: Oxford University Press. (Contains letters from Burthogge, some on predestination.)

References and further reading

Gruenbaum, J. (1939) *Die Philosophie Richard Burthogges*, Bern: J. Kleiner. (This doctoral dissertation is the only modern monograph.)

Lennon, T.M. (1993) *The Battle of the Gods and Giants*, Princeton, NJ: Princeton University Press. (Chapter 3, §11, discusses Burthogge's 'tendency' to idealism in the context of debates about 'enthusiasm', toleration and analogy.)

Nuchelmans, G. (1983) *Judgement and Proposition from Descartes to Kant*, Amsterdam: North Holland. (Chapter 6 contains a discussion of Burthogge's relation to Geulincx.)

Yolton, J.W. (1968) *John Locke and the Way of Ideas*, Oxford: Oxford University Press. (Contains discussions of Burthogge's relation to Locke.)

MICHAEL AYERS

BUSHI PHILOSOPHY

Bushi is one of several terms for the warrior of premodern Japan; samurai is another. The 'way of the warrior' – that is, the beliefs, attitudes and patterns of behaviour of the premodern Japanese warrior – is commonly called bushidō *(literally, the 'way of the bushi'). However,* bushidō *is actually a phrase of rather late derivation, and in premodern times was never exclusively used to describe the warrior way.*

Two of the earliest and most enduring phrases for the way of the warriors who rose in the provinces of Japan in the late ninth and tenth centuries were the 'way of the bow and arrow' and the 'way of the bow and horse'. These phrases, however, referred to little more than prowess in the military arts, the most important of which, as the second phrase clearly specifies, were horse riding and archery. For many centuries no one in Japan undertook to define systematically what the way of the warrior in a larger sense was or should be. Warrior beliefs, ideals and aspirations – including loyalty, courage, the yearning for battlefield fame, fear of shame and an acute sense of honour and 'face' – were widely recognized, but neither warriors nor others apparently felt the need to codify them in writing.

*Not until the establishment of the Tokugawa military government (shogunate) in 1600, which brought two and a half centuries of nearly uninterrupted peace to Japan, did philosophers begin to study and write about the warrior way (*bushidō*). Concerned about the meaning and proper role of a ruling warrior class during an age of peace, philosophers posited that warriors should not only maintain military preparedness to deal with fighting that might occur, but should also develop themselves, through education based primarily on Confucianism, to serve as models and moral exemplars for all classes of Japanese society.*

1 **Early beliefs**
2 **The warrior way in the age of the country at war**
3 **The Tokugawa period and the concept of** *bushidō*

1 Early beliefs

A warrior class emerged in the provinces of Japan in the late ninth and tenth centuries because the court government in Kyoto, headed by an emperor but administered mainly by regents of the Fujiwara family, left local governance largely to local families. In the absence of firm control from the court, men of locally powerful families, holding offices in provincial and district governments, took up arms to maintain the peace and deal with disputes over land and other issues.

However, with few exceptions, these warriors did not seek to assert their independence from the Kyoto court. On the contrary, they often turned to the court for support in conflicts with other warriors or officials. They also greatly respected and admired court society and culture. In ensuing centuries, warriors repeatedly sought to obtain court ranks and offices, even though these might be purely

ornamental, and to acquire knowledge of court culture. A distinctive feature of the warrior way as it evolved over the ages was the steady acquisition by warriors of courtly ways. As the records put it, warriors combined the *bun* (the courtly and cultural) with the *bu* (the military).

As warrior bands formed and contended for local and regional power in the middle and late Heian period (794–1185), they evolved feudal institutions very similar to the feudalism of western Europe in its medieval age. Chief among these institutions was the lord–vassal relationship. Chronicles known as war tales, records of the lives and battles of warriors, depict the intimate personal attachments that bound lords and vassals, telling of vassals prepared to give their lives for their lords at a moment's notice and of lords who bestowed upon vassals the kind of love normally given by fathers to their sons. Of course, not all warriors behaved like the idealized characters of the war tales; but the tales presented models for ages to come of how warriors ought to conduct themselves, especially in their roles as lords and as vassals.

As noted above, warriors fought primarily on horseback with the bow as their principal weapon. In battles between armies, warriors usually paired off to contend one-against-one, using their swords when they entered into close combat. Since it was difficult to kill an enemy with a sword from horseback, the warrior tried to unseat his foe, then leap down and stab him to death. Although in later centuries the sword came to be looked upon as the soul of the warrior, in this early age the warrior's great pride lay in his skill with the bow, wielded while riding a horse.

From earliest times the warrior displayed great pride in *na* (name), a term that connoted not only a sense of pride in family but also a determination to uphold personal honour and to achieve fame on the battlefield. Concern about *na*, however, had the potential to conflict with the warrior's obligation of loyal service to his lord. The warrior anticipated reward for victory in battle; and indeed usually received from his lord a portion of the lands and other wealth seized from defeated enemies. However, if the warrior pursued his own interests too aggressively in a battle – not only in the quest for material reward but also to achieve personal fame and glory – he could be difficult to command and could even undermine his lord's battle strategy.

The converse of the warrior's pride in name and thirst for fame was his fear of shame. The warrior was of course shamed if he was perceived to be timid or cowardly, but shame could also be experienced simply by defeat in battle, no matter how well a warrior had fought. The war tales often speak of warriors driven by the single-minded desire to expiate shame, suggesting that shame was a major factor in the frequent undertakings of revenge that we find in warrior history. In later centuries, the pursuit of revenge became institutionalized in the vendetta.

2 The warrior way in the age of the country at war

One of the most important periods in the shaping of the warrior way was the *sengoku jidai*, the 'age of the country at war' (1478–1573). The Ōnin War, fought largely in Kyoto during the decade 1467–77, destroyed Kyoto and plunged Japan into a state of disunion and conflict that lasted nearly a century. Beginning about 1500, territorial domains were established by warrior chieftains whom historians call *daimyō*, and through much of the early and middle sixteenth century these *daimyō* fought fiercely among themselves. Finally, one of the *daimyō*, Oda Nobunaga, emerged as a unifier. Entering Kyoto in 1568, Nobunaga began a process of national unification that was completed in 1590 by his vassal and successor, Toyotomi Hideyoshi.

So intense and widespread was the fighting in the *sengoku* age that there were real fears it would tear apart the social fabric of Japan. Warrior values were sorely tested; indeed, some were openly abandoned. If the lord–vassal relationship, based on the vassal's loyalty to his lord and the lord's loving care of his vassal, was the essence of Japanese feudalism, then feudalism fared poorly in the *sengoku* age. This was a time of frequent, outright treachery, which witnessed *daimyō* violating treaties with impunity and vassals betraying their lords or simply abandoning them in favour of those who offered richer rewards.

It is instructive to note that, in the legal codes they compiled for their domains, the *daimyō* of the *sengoku* age said little about loyalty but a great deal about disloyalty. Hereditary (*fudai*) vassals – that is, vassals whose families had served a *daimyō* house for generations – were expected to be loyal. Non-hereditary (*tozama*) vassals, on the other hand, were not only not held to high standards of commitment and loyalty, they were scarcely criticized if they shifted from one *daimyō* to another, seeking a better (more powerful and more generous) lord.

The *daimyō* especially feared fighting between vassals, which could cause serious ruptures in both their armies and their governments. To prevent such fighting, they included in their domainal codes what can be called 'no questions asked' laws. These laws specified that, if two vassals began to fight, both would be punished without any inquiry into the cause of the clash. The more powerful *daimyō* decreed that the punishment for fighting between vassals was death. The vassal of one prominent *daimyō*, however, charged that the 'no questions asked' law went against

the warrior's 'manly way' (*otoko no michi*), since it encouraged the warrior to restrain himself even if insulted or otherwise provoked. The vassal said that warriors worthy of being called warriors had to be aggressive, ready to fight whenever challenged, and predicted that the 'no questions asked' law would nurture meek, if not cowardly, vassals.

A major event during the *sengoku* age was the appearance of Europeans in Japan for the first time. The first Europeans to set foot on Japanese soil were Portuguese traders who arrived in 1543 in a Chinese junk. Soliciting trade, the Portuguese introduced the Japanese to Christianity and guns (muzzle-loading muskets); during the ensuing century, trade, Christianity and guns became the main staples of intercourse with Europeans. Japanese warriors had been exposed to the use of gunpowder during the two unsuccessful invasions of Japan by Mongol troops in 1274 and 1281. However, this exposure had not led to any significant experimentation with gunpowder by the Japanese themselves during the next three centuries. Hence, we may suppose that the Japanese were utterly astonished when they first observed the firing of guns by the Portuguese. Immediately recognizing the extraordinary value of guns for warfare, the *daimyō* of the *sengoku* age eagerly sought to acquire them. However, guns were not readily obtainable; the Portuguese could only import so many, and establishing gun foundries in Japan was expensive. Some important battles were won with guns in the late sixteenth century, but by the time guns became widely available around 1600, the fighting had ceased. Thus guns did not revolutionize warfare in Japan during this period. Had they done so, they would surely also have undermined if not destroyed the special status of the warrior or *samurai* class. As it was, the 'way of the warrior' remained the way of elite fighters specially trained in the complex military arts of horsemanship, archery and use of the sword.

3 The Tokugawa period and the concept of *bushidō*

With the establishment of the Tokugawa shogunate in 1600, Japan's ruling warrior class lost its principal *raison d'être*, which was fighting. No one could have known at the time that peace would prevail, with few exceptions, for more than two and a half centuries. Hence, throughout the seventeenth century at least, the rulers of the shogunate were absorbed first and foremost with security, taking measures to prevent a reversion to the bloodshed and chaos of the *sengoku* age.

One of the most important steps that had been taken to end the warfare, unify the country and make unification lasting was the separation of peasants and warriors. In the late sixteenth century, those warriors who had not already done so were obliged to move from the countryside into the castle towns of their *daimyō*; simultaneously the peasants, who were ordered to remain in their villages, were disarmed in a national 'sword hunt' that deprived them of their swords and other weapons.

Removed from the land and transformed into urban residents, warriors became stipendiaries, the recipients of regular stipends based on the revenue derived from agricultural fiefs held by them or their ancestors during the *sengoku* age. High-ranking warriors received, for the most part, generous stipends and were employed by their *daimyō* in the domainal governments. Those on the lower end of the warrior scale were usually not so employed and were obliged to get along on meagre stipends.

The existence of a large number of idle stipendiaries among the warriors troubled philosophers. Yamaga Sokō (1622–85), a Confucian scholar whose name is closely associated with the formulation of *bushidō* during the Tokugawa period (although he himself used the abbreviated term *shidō*), observed: '...the *samurai* eats food without growing it, uses utensils without manufacturing them, and profits without buying or selling. What is the justification for this?' (Tsunoda *et al.* 1958: 398). Sokō's answer was that the function of the *samurai* in society was to serve his lord loyally and to stand as an exemplar of high moral standards to the lower classes, peasants, artisans and merchants. The acquisition of high moral standards – that is, Confucian moral standards – was premised on the acquisition of education (see CONFUCIAN PHILOSOPHY, JAPANESE).

Strongly influenced by the thought of Yamaga Sokō, *bushidō* came to comprise two parts. The first part was military preparedness and a romantic looking back to the great fighting traditions of the past. Countless editions of the war tales and other records of ancient and medieval battles, biographies of the great warrior heroes of the past and the like were published during the Tokugawa period. In addition, many schools in military tactics and the martial arts were founded, including one by Yamaga Sokō.

The second part of *bushidō* concerned the ethical training urged by Sokō. This not only resulted in the articulation of an ethical code for warriors of a kind that we do not find prior to the Tokugawa period, but also greatly stimulated education in general among warriors. Hence, *bushidō* contributed importantly to the evolution of the warrior class as an intellectual as well as ruling elite.

If the *bushidō* just described was based primarily on Confucian rationalism, there was another *bushidō* nurtured by a different, powerfully 'irrational' school of thought. This school derived from the belief, adumbrated above in the discussion of the feudal lord–vassal relationship, that vassals ought to serve their lords in a spirit of absolute self-sacrifice: vassals should, indeed, be prepared to relinquish their lives in a moment's notice for their lords. The war tales, for example, speak of vassals who considered their lives as no more important than a 'speck of dust' or a 'goose feather' in the service of their lords.

The bible of this irrational school of *bushidō* was the *Hagakure*, an early eighteenth-century compilation of the views of Yamamoto Tsunetomo, vassal to the *daimyō* of a western domain. In one of the most famous proclamations in all of Japanese literature, Tsunetomo asserts in the *Hagakure* that: 'The way of the warrior (*bushidō*) is found in death' (trans. Wilson 1979: 17). But, as Tsunetomo explains, it is not sufficient for the warrior to be resigned to the fact that he may be killed. He must be prepared at all times to face death at a moment's notice, and when confronted with a situation in which he must decide between living or dying, he should unhesitatingly choose to die. In such a situation there can be no calculating or 'rationalizing'. The warrior must fight like a madman to his death, even though aware that others may later judge his actions to have been wrong or foolish. Utterly unconcerned about 'achieving' anything, the true warrior devotes himself single-mindedly to acting in a death-defying – or more precisely, a death-attaining – way.

The *Hagakure*, with its extreme views about proper warrior behaviour, was written after the passage of a century of Tokugawa peace and during a time (the Genroku cultural epoch) that celebrated the lives of merchants and artisans, whose chief goals in life were to earn money and enjoy the luxuries it could buy. Genroku culture was totally antithetical to traditional warrior values, at least as those values were idealized in writings like the war tales. A *cri de coeur* against what Yamamoto Tsunetomo viewed as the moral deterioration of the times, the *Hagakure* was an anachronistic attempt to rally the spirit of the warrior class, most of whose members could only have been bewildered at the prospect of rushing to their deaths in an age when warfare had been suspended for so long that no one had any experience of it.

But in fact, an incident had occurred just a few years before the publication of the *Hagakure* that seemed to suggest that the traditional warrior values centred on the selfless service of vassals to their lords, which Yamamoto Tsunetomo so admired and so yearned to revive, were still alive. One of the most famous events in all of Japanese history, this incident was the sensational revenge of the forty-seven *rōnin* (masterless *samurai*). In 1701, a *daimyō* in attendance at the shogun's castle in Edo (modern Tokyo) assaulted and wounded one of the shogun's officials. For having drawn his sword in the castle the *daimyō* was condemned to death, and that same day he disembowelled himself – that is, he committed *seppuku*, the warrior's way of suicide. Two years later, a group of the *daimyō*'s vassals, who had become *rōnin* because of their lord's death, fulfilled a secret pact by attacking the residence of and killing the official the *daimyō* had assaulted (the exact reason for the assault is not known). Seven weeks later the *rōnin*, condemned to death for violating shogunate law, themselves committed *seppuku*.

Although this act of revenge – this carrying out of a vendetta (*katakiuchi*) – has stirred the spirits of many Japanese over the years, it was in fact an isolated incident and not in any sense illustrative of the way warriors behaved or were expected to behave. Yamamoto Tsunetomo in fact criticized the *rōnin* because they did not spring into action immediately against the enemy of their lord but instead calculated and schemed for two years. More fundamentally, this vendetta was unusual because nearly all the other vendettas by warriors during the Tokugawa period were based on avenging kin rather than feudal lords.

Nevertheless, the revenge of the forty-seven *rōnin* was important in the history of *bushidō* because it drew attention to the special character of the lord–vassal relationship among warriors, reaffirming the ideal of vassals acting selflessly, even to the point of forfeiting their lives, in the service of their lord. In the modern age, after the dissolution of the *samurai* class and the establishment of a conscript army, this spirit was still held to set Japanese soldiers apart from those of other countries. Even as late as the Second World War the spirit of the Japanese soldier, prepared to die if necessary for his emperor, was exalted and accorded special consideration in the strategic planning of many Japanese commanders.

See also: CONFUCIAN PHILOSOPHY, JAPANESE; HONOUR; JAPANESE PHILOSOPHY; POLITICAL PHILOSOPHY, HISTORY OF; WAR AND PEACE, PHILOSOPHY OF

References and further reading

Mills, D.E. (1976) '*Kataki-uchi*: The Practice of Blood-Revenge in Pre-Modern Japan', *Modern Asian Studies* 10 (4): 525–42. (Article on the practice of vendetta.)

* Tsunoda Ryusaku *et al.* (eds) (1958) *Sources of Japanese Tradition*, New York: Columbia University Press. (Includes the work by Yamaga quoted in this entry.)

Varley, P. (1994) *Warriors of Japan, As Portrayed in the War Tales*, Honolulu, HI: University of Hawaii Press. (Description of the *samurai* class.)

* Yamamoto Tsunetomo (1716) *Hagakure* (In the Shadow of the Leaves), trans. W.S. Wilson, Tokyo: Kodansha, 1979. (One of the most prominent works of *bushi* philosophy.)

PAUL VARLEY

BUSINESS ETHICS

Business ethics is the application of theories of right and wrong to activity within and between commercial enterprises, and between commercial enterprises and their broader environment. It is a wide range of activity, and no brief list can be made of the issues it raises. The safety of working practices; the fairness of recruitment; the transparency of financial accounting; the promptness of payments to suppliers; the degree of permissible aggression between competitors: all come within the range of the subject. So do relations between businesses and consumers, local communities, national governments and ecosystems. Many, but not all, of these issues can be understood to bear on distinct, recognized groups with their own stakes in a business: employees, shareholders, consumers, and so on. The literature of business ethics tends to concentrate on 'stakeholders' – anyone who occupies a role within the business or who belongs to a recognized group outside the business that is affected by its activity – but not in every sort of business. Corporations are often discussed to the exclusion of medium-sized and small enterprises.

Theories of right and wrong in business ethics come from a number of sources. Academic moral philosophy has contributed utilitarianism, Kantianism and Aristotelianism, as well as egoism and social contract theory. There are also theories that originate in organized religion, in the manifestos of political activists, in the thoughts of certain tycoons with an interest in social engineering, and in the writings of management 'gurus'. Recently, business ethics has been affected by the ending of the Cold War, and the breakdown of what were once command economies. These developments have encouraged enthusiasts for the market economy to advocate moral and political ideas consistent with capitalism, and the handing over to private companies of activity in certain countries that has long been reserved for the state.

1 Stakeholders and the range of business ethics

The concept of the stakeholder – someone who occupies a role within the business or who belongs to a recognized group outside the business that is affected by its activity – lies at the centre of business ethics. The literature tends to concentrate on stakeholders in bigger companies on the American model: companies quoted on stock exchanges, with impressive turnovers, large numbers of employees, and several layers of management. Such companies are involved with a wide range of stakeholders, both internal and external to the organization. The 'internal' stakeholders include directors, managers, ordinary shopfloor or 'blue-collar' employees, and shareholders. Outside the company there are customers, suppliers, competitors, local communities, and one or more levels of government. Business ethics as a whole may be regarded as a unified understanding of the obligations of those who run a business – directors or top managers – to the rest of a business' stakeholders. Alternatively it may be seen as a unified understanding of the typical ethical risks or problems facing the internal stakeholders in their dealings with one another and outsiders. Both conceptions are well represented in the literature, and both accommodate the central issues of business ethics.

2 Internal stakeholders: the case of employees

Perhaps the leading 'internal' stakeholders of a firm are its employees, whose fortunes depend on those of the firm in the most direct way. The firm may be the only source of income for each of its employees, and the income may be used to support many others. Employees may depend on their job for a considerable proportion of their social life and their most rewarding activity. Having a particular job, or having a job at all, may be an important source of self-esteem (see WORK, PHILOSOPHY OF). With so many connections to the good things in life, the role of employee cannot fail to matter morally. Equal opportunity and employment protection legislation reflect the importance of having and keeping a job. In many industrialized countries discrimination in recruitment on the grounds of race or sex or religion is against the law. In western Europe dismissal from a full-time job can be legally challenged, and redundancy can be accompanied by significant financial compensation.

Different types of employee have different sorts of stake in different businesses, and businesses have different stakes in different employees. A worker on the factory floor and the manager above him are both employees, but their roles in the firm are likely to make different moral demands on them and their employers. It may fall to the manager to sack factory workers for some offence or to make them redundant during a recession. It may fall to a worker to make known a costly production defect or to complain of harassment by someone higher up in the organization. The manager may strongly disagree with the decision to sack the workers, and yet be responsible for carrying it out. The worker may wonder whether making known the defect will indirectly cost them their job: putting right the defect may be expensive, and redundancies may be the firm's way of covering its losses. On the other hand, if the defect is not made known, perhaps the safety of a very large number of consumers will be threatened. Serious consequences may also attend the report of harassment. The complainant risks not being believed, and probably the embarrassing details will be made the subject of gossip. Perhaps the person complained about will retaliate in some way. And the firm may be forced to decide between two employees, neither of whose talents it can afford to lose.

Not every moral theory is suited to weighing what is at stake in such cases, and several different theories may be required to do justice to all stakeholders in business ethics. Utilitarianism and Aristotelianism have resources for capturing the value of employment in general, since each works with a concept of wellbeing or welfare which embraces many different goods, including those associated with having a job (see UTILITARIANISM; ARISTOTLE §21). Kantianism is able to give weight to the way in which consumers are put at risk by not publicizing the production defect, and the way in which the wellbeing of employees can be sacrificed for a short-term reduction in the costs of a business (see KANTIAN ETHICS). Kantianism is also able to make sense of the wrong of harassment, and therefore to justify a decision to press a complaint against harassment. In all of these cases, albeit in different ways, persons are treated as means, and Kantianism highlights such treatment as a kind of immorality. Aristotelianism is sometimes thought to be able to coordinate the moral demands that fall on people in their role as manager or worker with the moral demands that fall upon them in the rest of their lives. The manager who is uncomfortable with sacking people may be someone who tries to pursue a policy of benevolence or charity whenever possible. The worker who balks at overlooking the production defect in the factory may be in the habit of being honest and open away from work.

Aristotelianism prescribes the cultivation of patterns of behaviour that serve one in one's private as well as in one's public life, and that cannot be abandoned without a morally significant loss to the agent. Utilitarianism and Kantianism, on the other hand, sometimes diagnose the reluctance to depart from characteristic patterns of behaviour as a kind of squeamishness or self-indulgence. Sacking the workers may be unpleasant, according to these theories, but it may be best on balance for everyone, or necessary if one is to honour promises to shareholders or creditors.

3 External stakeholders: social responsibility

It is not only Kantianism, utilitarianism and Aristotelianism which are invoked to deal with the obligations of a firm to the wider world. Sometimes the firm is said to be party to a social contract which confers a duty to transfer profits or services to the communities in which it operates, in return for the good will or custom or labour of members of those communities (see CONTRACTARIANISM). Sometimes it is said to be in the firm's self-interest to benefit communities. These things are said, at any rate, by those who think that businesses have obligations to external stakeholders at all. There are well-known advocates of the view that company philanthropy within a host community violates a prior and overriding obligation of a firm to its shareholders. The more profit or employee time is diverted to noncommercial and non-profit-making activity, so it is argued, the less there is to redistribute to shareholders, who after all own the company and invest in it usually on the understanding that the company will maximize returns to them.

The view that firms have no business helping the community is now widely contradicted by the behaviour of large commercial enterprises themselves. The directors of such enterprises accept that philanthropy is often expected by local communities and shareholders alike, and sometimes endorsed by consumers in the form of greater approval for, and loyalty to, firms that go in for it. In the UK retail sector, for example, market research has confirmed the commercial benefits of a caring public image.

If it is in the interest of firms to give money or time to helping the community, and if they give the help because of the commercial benefits, is the help morally creditable? Much depends on whether the help is given only for the commercial benefits. If it is only for the commercial benefits, then probably only egoism – the theory that something is right if and only if it serves one's own interest – makes the act moral, and egoism is strongly counterintuitive as a moral theory (see EGOISM AND ALTRUISM). On the other hand, although business people see the value of self-interest, it is uncharacteristic for them to say or think that acts of corporate charity serve only self-interest. Perhaps they would not go in for donations of money or time if they were not going to pay the firm in some way; this does not mean that nothing else matters. The motivation can be mixed, as it is when directors of enterprises themselves have strong philanthropic impulses, but can also see that the philanthropy will be good for public relations. In the case where the motivation is mixed and the benefits to the community are real, then several theories assign moral credit to corporate giving, including utilitarianism, different versions of theories that say that businesses are parties to a social contract, and Aristotelianism. Even a Kantian theory can assign considerable positive value to company philanthropy with a mixed motivation, so long as it is the right sort of mix. The action that is in accordance with duty but motivated by extra-moral forces can still be honourable, beautiful, and so on according to Kant.

What are the appropriate forms of corporate philanthropy or 'social responsibility'? The question has an edge in places where the private sector is increasingly expected by government to pay directly for, or sponsor programmes in, schools and hospitals, and when businesses are partners with the state in big transportation and housing projects. Does a firm go beyond what can reasonably be demanded of it when it takes over responsibility in one place for a service or institution that the state is responsible for elsewhere? Should it help only with public services or institutions, refraining from taking a leading role? And if it gives help, should the help have some relation to its business activity? Should a construction firm donate construction advice or labour for a public housing scheme; or should it lend the scheme one of its accountants? Should a supermarket take charge of recycling packaging on the goods it sells rather than lending its property-buying expertise to the public sector? Here a version of social contract theory, according to which business has an obligation to fulfil the expectations it creates in society, provides a clue to the answer. The closer a firm's philanthropy to its public business activity, the less the risk of creating new, perhaps over-demanding, expectations among the public and confusion among internal stakeholders.

Many questions about the obligations of businesses to the wider world are less tractable than those we have been pursuing. For example, what are the obligations of transnational firms in societies with very different levels of prosperity? In what special circumstances are the assets of firms open to expropriation in the name of the public interest? To what extent is the law rather than corporate policy the best medium for stipulating the limits of corporate obligation?

4 Conflicts between obligations to stakeholders

Fulfilling obligations to one set of stakeholders can involve a firm in conflicts with another set. A policy of reducing costs may be pursued to maximize returns to shareholders, and yet it may involve the dismissal of productive and loyal employees. Recalling faulty goods for the sake of consumer safety may similarly conflict with the duty to maximize returns. Keeping suppliers waiting for their money may be justified by a duty to manage the liquid assets of a firm as profitably as possible, but it may drive the supplier into bankruptcy; and so on. The existence of these conflicts does not show, as might be thought, that it is unprofitable to gear obligations in business ethics to stakeholders. But it does raise the question of whether there is a pecking order among stakeholders, so that obligations to one group typically outweigh obligations to another. The literature sometimes suggests that one or another group of internal stakeholders is pre-eminent: sometimes it is employees and sometimes it is shareholders. Neither group is uncontroversially the pre-eminent one, and much depends on facts about the firm with the conflicting obligations. It may be that for some firms at some times meeting obligations to employees makes the difference between staying in business and bankruptcy; for other firms it may be shareholders. Either way, considerations about the requirements of staying in business at a given time seem relevant to the pecking order; and when the survival of the business is not in question, it may be considerations about which group is the more important to the growth of the business.

5 Further questions

Not all questions in business ethics can be resolved into questions of what a business owes to its stakeholders. Questions can be asked about the morality of the market economy or of pursuing profit in general (see MARKET, ETHICS OF THE). Capitalism as an economic system, or democratic capitalism as a politico-economic system, can be subjected to moral appraisal. Occasionally the large question of the morality of capitalism is pursued in the literature without an enthusiastic audience among business people. Yet the relevance of the question has increased with the collapse of the command economy and the communist state. A market economy may be a condition for membership in the community of nations for countries once within the orbit of the Soviet Union, just as it has become the unquestioned condition for aid to the developing countries of Africa and Asia. On the other hand, it may be that a bias in some places towards a 'social market' and in others towards a purer form of the market will simulate the old rivalry between capitalism and socialism.

The collapse of the Soviet bloc has put one sort of gloss on the question of the desirability of capitalism; the Green movement is responsible for another (see GREEN POLITICAL PHILOSOPHY; ENVIRONMENTAL ETHICS). An economic system predicated on the possibility of indefinite growth, and the satisfaction, no questions asked, of a very wide variety of consumer demands, seems to many to be immoral in its profligacy and its relentless draining of natural resources. The Green complaint against capitalism goes far deeper than a protest against pollution and the loss of wilderness. It is a protest against the picture of technological and economic progress that both market and command economies have in common. More generally, it is a protest against the idea that nature is an economic resource, and that the human ability to produce by transforming nature is a good thing. Perhaps more fundamentally still, it is a protest against the identification of the good with the satisfaction of human desire. Business ethics has yet to confront these protests.

See also: APPLIED ETHICS; DEVELOPMENT ETHICS; ECONOMICS AND ETHICS; PROFESSIONAL ETHICS

References and further reading

Beauchamp,T. and Bowie, N. (eds) (1988) *Ethical Theory and Business*, Englewood Cliffs, NJ: Prentice Hall; 5th edn, 1997. (Collection of essays and cases prefaced by a discussion of the bearing on business ethics of utilitarianism and deontological theories.)

Hoffman, W.M. (1989) 'The Cost of a Corporate Conscience', *Business and Society Review* Spring 1989. (Acknowledges that social responsibility can be a burden to business.)

Schmidheiny, S. and Business Council for Sustainable Development (1992) *Changing Course: A Global Business Perspective on Business and the Environment*, Boston, MA: MIT Press. (Articles on 'Green' business initiatives throughout the world.)

Solomon, R. (1992) *Ethics and excellence: Co-operation and Integrity in Business*, New York: Oxford University Press. (Adapts the Aristotelian concept of virtue to the demands of business ethics; works out virtues for managers.)

Sorell, T. and Hendry, J. (1994) *Business Ethics.*

Oxford: Heinemann. (A review of the subject from a British and western European perspective.)

TOM SORELL

BUTLER, JOSEPH (1692–1752)

Joseph Butler the moral philosopher is in that long line of eighteenth-century thinkers who sought to answer Thomas Hobbes on human nature and moral motivation. Following the Third Earl of Shaftesbury, he rejects any purely egoistic conception of these. Instead, he analyses human nature into parts, of which he notices in detail appetites, affections, and passions on the one hand and the principles of self-love, benevolence, and conscience on the other. His ethics consists in the main in showing the relation of these parts to each other. They form a hierarchy, ordered in terms of their natural authority, and while such authority can be usurped, as when the particular passions overwhelm self-love and conscience, the system that they constitute, or human nature, is rightly proportioned when each part occupies its rightful place in the ordered hierarchy. Virtue consists in acting in accordance with that ordered, rightly proportioned nature.

As a philosopher of religion, Butler addresses himself critically to the eighteenth-century flowering of deism in Britain. On the whole, the deists allowed that God the Creator existed but rejected the doctrines of natural and, especially, revealed religion. Butler's central tactic against them is to argue, first, that the central theses associated with natural religion, such as a future life, are probable; and second, that the central theses associated with revealed religion, such as miracles, are as probable as those of natural religion. Much turns, therefore, on the success of Butler's case in appealing to what is present in this world as evidence for a future life.

1 Life
2–4 Moral philosophy
5 Philosophy of religion
6 Personal identity

1 Life

For more than a century following the death of Thomas Hobbes in 1679, philosophers, theologians, and thinking men generally felt obliged to address his alleged reduction of morality to self-interest and his alleged banishment of God from the universe. Both views represent misreadings of Hobbes, but both quickly settled into received interpretations of him. The first view provoked an outpouring of moral

philosophy that today, still, we associate with the work of the Cambridge Platonists, the Third Earl of Shaftesbury, Bernard Mandeville, Francis Hutcheson, and, eventually, David Hume and Adam Smith. The second became allied with the claims of the British deists and so with the writings of men such as Herbert of Cherbury, John Toland, Anthony Collins, Matthew Tindal, Thomas Chubb, and, later, Hume, Edward Gibbon, and Thomas Paine. The two views were connected, since religious scepticism was widely thought to be destructive of morality.

No figure is more central to these intellectual currents of the period than Joseph Butler. With *The Analogy of Religion, Natural and Revealed, to the Constitution and Course of Nature* (1736), he dealt DEISM a serious blow. Though one of the chief monuments of English philosophical theology, the *Analogy* was a topical work, directed against Tindal and the deists, and today, since the disputes to which it is a response have died out, it is little read. With Butler's other major work, matters are quite different. His *Fifteen Sermons Preached at the Rolls Chapel* (1726) is one of the enduring classics of British moral philosophy, and parts of it, such as the refutation of psychological egoism, are widely celebrated. To the *Analogy*, Butler appended two indices – one on ethics, the other on personal identity, which mounts a lasting criticism of John Locke on the subject.

Butler was born in May 1692, in Wantage, Berkshire. The son of a dissenter, he was sent to Samuel Jones' academy in Tewkesbury, from where he corresponded with Samuel Clarke about several matters arising out of Clarke's Boyle Lectures (1704–5) on the being and attributes of God (see CLARKE, S.). (Today, this exchange is little read.) Butler impressed Clarke and subsequently enjoyed his support. At Tewkesbury, Butler converted to the established Church and so was able to enter Oriel College, Oxford, in 1714, where he again made important and powerful friends. Upon his taking his degree in 1718, Butler's supporters secured his appointment as Preacher at the Rolls Chapel in London, and his rise in the Church began. In time, he would become Bishop of Bristol, Dean of St. Paul's, and Bishop of Durham. That he enjoyed royal favour was obvious from his appointment as Clerk of the Closet, first to Queen Caroline in 1736, then to George II himself in 1747. Shortly after his assumption of the See of Durham in 1750, Butler fell ill and eventually took himself away to Bristol and then Bath, where he died in June 1752.

2 Moral philosophy

In the *Sermons* (preface: 8), Butler's aim is to explain

'what is meant by the nature of man, when it is said that virtue consists in following, and vice in deviating from it' and to show that this claim about virtue or morality 'is true' (1765: 8). Everything turns, therefore, upon what this nature is taken to be. Over this matter, however, commentators do not agree.

According to Butler, human nature is a system of parts – these are the particular passions, benevolence, self-love, and conscience – and of the relations of these parts. In this last regard, Butler makes several points. Some parts of human nature are superior to others in terms of natural authority, which in turn orders the system; natural authority is to be distinguished from actual strength; and all cases of the usurpation of authority by strength are violations of human nature. The usual interpretation of Butler can now be stated. Virtue consists in acting in accordance with the nature of man, when the parts of that nature and system are in right proportion. These parts are in right proportion when our inward principles (whereby he means general principles of action or motives) exhibit their ordered authority, and these principles exhibit their ordered authority when the particular passions are controlled and regulated by benevolence and self-love and when conscience or the principle of reflection controls and regulates benevolence and self-love, as well as the particular passions, and so reigns supreme over the system. Human nature is thus a three-level affair: the particular passions; the principles of benevolence and self-love; and conscience.

A more radical interpretation is possible. This takes seriously passages in which Butler marks off the authority of self-love from that of benevolence, as when he remarks that 'reasonable self-love and conscience are the chief or superior principles in the nature of man' (Sermons, III: 13) as well as the fact that his examples of benevolence almost invariably involve particular passions. It also takes seriously Butler's claim about self-love and conscience that 'an action may be suitable to this nature, though all other principles are violated; but becomes unsuitable if either of those are' (Sermons, III: 13). Accordingly, human nature can appear to be a two-level affair, with the particular passions and benevolence on one level and self-love and conscience, now reigning jointly over the system, on another. Plainly, on this interpretation, the role of self-love in Butler's ethics is much more enhanced than on the usual interpretation.

When the inward principles in man exhibit their ordered authority, the system of human nature is in harmony, balance, and right proportion. Acts may be proportionate or disproportionate to man's nature; when they are proportionate, they are natural, when disproportionate, unnatural. An act is unnatural or disproportionate, not because it fails to be in accordance with the strongest principle in one at the time, but because it involves the usurpation of authority by strength. If hatred overwhelms self-love, then even though hatred is as much a part of our nature as self-love, the resultant action is unnatural. Thus, virtue consists in acting in accordance with the constitution of man, when the parts of this constitution are in right proportion; the act in question, natural and proportionate to human nature, is right. Vice consists in allowing a lower part of our constitution in terms of authority to predominate over a higher one and acting accordingly; the act, unnatural and disproportionate, is wrong. Thus, rightness and wrongness are matters of proportion, and the disproportion that a wrong or unnatural act involves is determined, not by its consequences, but by comparison of it with the nature of the agent, with, that is, whether it is suitable to the ordered system that is our nature. Thus, Butler is no consequentialist.

Particular passions. We have all manner of appetites, affections, and passions, from hunger, thirst, and bodily needs generally to compassion, love, and hate. Butler normally lumps all these together in order to contrast them with self-love and conscience, so that he usually writes as if the passions formed a single principle of action or motive. With regard to the particular passions, Butler emphasizes three points. First, we have all kinds of such passions or desires, and every one of them is 'a real part of our nature' (*Sermons*, III: 1). Second, some of our passions seem 'to respect self, or tend to private good'; others seem 'to respect others, or tend to public good' (*Sermons*, I: 6). That we have other-regarding passions, such as love, pity, and compassion, Butler never doubts, and he castigates Hobbes for holding otherwise. These other-regarding passions are as much a part of our nature as our self-regarding ones. Third, our self-regarding and other-regarding passions are not to be identified with self-love and benevolence, respectively. For example, we cannot equate satisfied desire with self-love; for the gratification of a particular desire is often at the expense of self-interest.

Self-love. Self-love is a general desire for one's happiness, and it is 'inseparable' from any creature 'who can reflect upon themselves and their own interest or happiness, so as to have that interest an object to their minds' (*Sermons*, XI: 3). It is thus, unlike passion, a reflective or rational principle. As such, it provides us a measure of control and regulation of the passions, in which task it is assisted by conscience, and it is a calculative principle, ranging over the likely consequences of acts to determine which are likely to be in our (long-term) interest. Butler's emphasis is always on restraining the passions, else they usurp the authority of self-love and conscience and so motivate us at the expense of our interest and judgment. Significantly, too, whereas the passions are occurrent – particular desires for this or that thing – self-love is an abiding, general desire for our own happiness.

Benevolence. If benevolence were a general principle of action on a par with self-love, we should expect Butler to maintain that it is an abiding desire for the happiness of others and so is an independent and reflective principle that aims at their happiness and restrains and regulates the passions. But he nowhere asserts that we have any such abiding desire, especially a general desire aimed at others indiscriminately or at humanity in general. His examples of benevolence are more limited – typically, confined to family and friends – and thus appear to be particular passions. He does insist that benevolence is not contrary to self-love, but this only makes the point, dubious if taken too far, that being benevolent can make us happy and serve private ends.

Happiness. Though self-love aims at happiness, it is not the same thing as happiness. Happiness consists in 'the enjoyment of those objects, which are by nature suited to our passions'; self-love simply 'helps us to gain or make use of' those objects (*Sermons*, XI: 6). We do not make things suitable to our passions; nature does this. We simply find that we take delight in certain things as a result of their engaging our passions, and self-love helps put us in the way of securing them. Without particular passions, then, happiness could not exist, since it 'consists in the gratification of particular passions' (*Sermons*, XI: 6). Thus, to aim at happiness makes no sense; one needs to aim at securing the objects of some of one's particular passions.

3 Moral philosophy (cont.)

Butler now adds an important point. Particular passions are particular desires for particular objects, and we individuate these desires by means of their objects. One is a desire for food, another for revenge, and what satisfies these desires is obtaining their particular objects. This feature of desires is quite independent of whether the desire, or its satisfaction, is to our interest or happiness. A desire for heroin is aimed at having the drug, and an injection of heroin satisfies this desire; this is true even if such a desire, or its satisfaction, is not to our interest.

Psychological egoism. The refutation of psychological egoism applies the content of the preceding discussion. For example, psychological hedonism is the view that each of us pursues exclusively our own pleasure. Were this view true, all of our desires would

have the same object, pleasure, and this is plainly false. As a doctor who desires to cure my patient, I do not desire pleasure; I desire that my patient be made better. In other words, as a doctor, not all my particular desires have as their object some facet of myself; my desire for the well-being of my patient does not aim at alteration in myself but in another. My desire is *other*-regarding; its object is *external* to myself.

Of course, pleasure may arise from my satisfied desire in such cases, though equally it may not; but my desire is not aimed at my own pleasure. The same is true of happiness or interest: my satisfied desire may make me happy or further my interest, but these are not the objects of my desire. Here, Butler simply notices that desires have possessors – those whose desires they are – and if satisfied desires produce happiness, their possessors experience it. The object of a desire can thus be distinguished from the possessor of the desire: if, as a doctor, my desire is satisfied, I may be made happy as a result; but neither happiness nor any other state of myself is the object of my desire. That object is other-regarding, my patient's well-being. Without some more sophisticated account, psychological egoism is false.

Conscience. Conscience is a principle of reflection that judges acts right or wrong and characters and motives virtuous or vicious. It also, however, approves or disapproves of what it finds. Thus, in the dissertation *Of the Nature of Virtue*, an appendix to the *Analogy*, conscience is described both as a 'sentiment of the understanding' and 'a perception of the heart', and in the *Sermons*, Butler maintains that it is in virtue of conscience that man 'is a moral agent'. Thus, he gives every evidence of rejecting the view that morals are either a matter of reason or a matter of sentiment, an option upon which Hume was subsequently to insist.

As a reflective principle, conscience reflects in the case of acts upon whether they are natural and proportionate to our nature, and this brings in the authority of parts. To say of conscience that it possesses 'supreme' authority is to say that no act may violate or usurp it and remain proportionate to the system that is our nature. But this Butler says of self-love as well, and the implication seems to be that self-love and conscience are the 'chief or superior principles' in man. Exactly in what the supremacy of principles consists is a matter of controversy, particularly as regards conscience; but naturalness and unnaturalness are crucial to its understanding.

The pronouncements by conscience of naturalness or unnaturalness are not calculative, for example, based on consequences, but immediate and, presumably, infallible. We have 'the rule of right within', and we have only to attend to it, to appreciate its authority, if not its strength, to see our way, morally (*Sermons*, III: 3). Much is unclear here, both because Butler does not give particular examples of how determinations of rightness are arrived at by appeals to naturalness and because the kind of intuitionism that seems implied by his remarks is simply assumed in its results to be uniform throughout all 'plain' and 'honest' men (*Sermons*, III: 4).

4   Moral philosophy (cont.)

If benevolence does not conflict with self-love, neither does conscience; indeed, conscience and self-love are 'perfectly coincident', if not here, then in the hereafter. They always, Butler says, 'lead us in the same way' (*Sermons*, III: 13). Apart from the invocation of God and the hereafter, there is no warrant for this claim in Butler's account of human nature, which poses a problem. If duty and interest pull us sometimes in different directions, and if we cannot violate either and remain true to our ordered nature, what do we do? A virtual guarantee of the coincidence of duty and interest seems required to avoid this impasse, and an appeal to the goodness of God is supposed to provide it.

Revelation. Curiously, this invocation of the goodness of God strikes an odd note. For Butler stresses that, exclusive of any belief in revealed religion, man is 'a law to himself' (*Sermons*, III: 3) and that one's obligation to obey this law flows from 'its being the law of your nature' (*Sermons*, III: 6). This obligation remains in force, even if 'the prospect of a future life were ever so uncertain'. But if we assume that a future life is uncertain, how can we use the hereafter to guarantee that we will not have to face a choice between duty and happiness? And if we do face that choice, Butler says that, when we 'sit down in a cool hour', we cannot justify the pursuit of virtue to ourselves 'till we are convinced that it will be for our happiness or at least not contrary to it' (*Sermons*, XI: 21). What if we are not convinced? Even treating the 'cool hour' passage as aberrant, the problem of a choice between duty and interest remains.

Strength and motivation. One of the most pronounced features of the *Sermons*, namely, Butler's repeated insistence that benevolence, conscience, and virtue are not opposed to self-love, can now be understood. Human nature may be hierarchical, based on the authority of parts, but the strength of self-love, prudence, and the self-regarding passions is great. Even if we have other-regarding passions and benevolent affections, will they be strong enough to motivate us at the expense of interest? If it could be shown that they were not at the expense of interest

but actually served it, then one could hitch, for example, self-love to the cause of benevolence, and so perhaps increase the latter's chances of motivating us. Otherwise, we have to contend with the facts that (i) our other-regarding passions are rarely as strong as our self-regarding ones; (ii) we have no general desire for the happiness of others; (iii) our particular passions for the happiness of certain others typically do not carry us beyond the persons whose happiness is the object of those passions; and (iv) prudence and self-love are powerful driving forces of our nature. What reason have we to think that we will choose benevolence over self-love?

Nor does conscience come off any better. For even if we allow it a motivational element and so regard it as more than judgment or reflection, that is, even if we allow that it can generate a desire in opposition to the desires in which the self-regarding particular passions, prudence, and self-love flow, Butler laments that its 'strength' and 'power' may be inappropriate to its authority. In fact, then, we may not be sufficiently motivated either to act benevolently or to pursue virtue. What Butler needs is a policy of insurance in these regards. That policy in both cases is to bring happiness and self-love to the rescue; hence, the repeated insistence that benevolence, conscience, and virtue are not 'contrary' to happiness or interest.

In the case of conscience and virtue, then, the motivational problem can be acute. Butler never says of actual individuals that they will come to love to be virtuous for its own sake; accordingly, it matters to his position that duty and interest or happiness coincide. But if they imperfectly coincide in this world, and if I am powerfully driven to seek my own happiness, then exactly how is the knowledge that God will rectify matters in the hereafter supposed to motivate me sufficiently powerfully to forego my happiness in this world? And even if we assume this knowledge about God gives rise to or is accompanied by a desire to forego my happiness in this world, why is this desire assumed to be more powerful than my desire for my happiness, unless I do in fact love virtue for its own sake? An answer is required, if conscience is to be the 'guide' of our moral lives.

5   Philosophy of religion

By the time the *Analogy* was published, deism was rampant. It consisted not so much in a positive body of doctrine as in doubts about the Christian stories and the Church, and the sowing of such doubts, even when belief in God remained, was worrisome to the orthodox. For mere belief in God's existence, obviously, would not validate the specific claims of the Christian revelation. To validate these, Butler's effort is in two parts. First, he tries to show that, if the deists accept the existence of an intelligent Creator of the natural world, then when they examine God's handiwork, in order to find out what it contains and how it operates, they will find probable: (i) that there is a future life, in which 'our capacity of happiness and misery' persists; (ii) that 'our happiness and misery Hereafter' depend 'upon our actions Here', in terms of God's rewards and punishments; and (iii) that 'our present life is a state of probation for a future one', in that our present life exposes us to temptations that we must resist, if we have a concern for our future happiness. This material occupies Part I of the *Analogy*. Second, Butler turns in Part II to parts of the Christian revelation, and tries to show that when we look at what we find in this life, it is probable not only that there would be such a revelation, parts of which are 'imperfectly comprehended' by us and so about which we are doomed to 'ignorance', but also that many of the distinctive doctrines of Christianity, such as the coming of the Messiah and miracles by a divine personage, pass muster. His aim in this latter regard is to show that 'there is no presumption against a revelation as miraculous' and that 'the general scheme of Christianity, and the principal parts of it, are conformable to the experienced constitution of things, and the whole perfectly credible'.

While, doubtless, there are individuals who regard Part II of the *Analogy* as an integral part of their defence of Christianity, most modern readers will find Part I the more intriguing. It is there that Butler displays his argument form – analogical or inductive reasoning from what we find here in this life to what is probable in the life to come – and shows us what he is going to regard as evidence here for the probability of a claim about the hereafter. On both counts, the modern temper is likely to register deep scepticism, on the one hand about the usefulness of inductive reasoning from here to the hereafter, on the other about exactly what we will take as evidence for the probability of claims about the hereafter, for example, that God will reward and punish us for what we do here. Of course, to some extent, this scepticism and talk of evidence for claims about the hereafter get wrapped up in all the discussion since Hume's *Dialogues concerning Natural Religion* (1779) about design and purpose in the natural world, and there is no doubt that, as far as the Christian revelation is concerned, Butler must achieve rather impressive feats with the evidence to make probable that God has 'by external revelation, given us an account of himself and his moral government over the world' (*Analogy*, II, vii: 31) (see HUME, D. §6). Then, too, general worries about induction and what it can establish are

never far from the surface here, as Butler meticulously marshals his evidence in favour of the truth of natural and revealed religion.

Butler certainly believes that the evidence for natural and revealed religion is considerable and their probable truth high. But what if the deist does not go along with this, as, indeed, he might not, given that at the time what passed as evidence was being increasingly called into question? Every fresh attack on or alternative explanation of it lowered the probable truth of natural and revealed religion. Here, in a way, is the test Butler must meet. He tries to meet it with two claims. First, even if the probability of Christianity is low or slight, it does not follow that it is false. Second, even if its probability is low or slight, if we act, then we must act 'upon that presumption or low probability, though it be so low as to leave the mind in very great doubt which is the truth'. In life, probability must be our guide, and this is true even when the probability in question is slight. Put differently, if we have any regard for our own happiness, we must act on the basis of what is more probable, though this probability be extraordinarily small. This is true in the case of Christianity: if its truth be ever so slightly more probable than its falsity, then we should act on it. In *A Charge to the Clergy of the Diocese of Durham* (1751), Butler turns this into something akin to Pascal's wager when he remarks of Christianity that, even if it were only slightly probable, 'it ought in all reason, considering its infinite importance, to have nearly the same influence upon practice, as if it were thoroughly believed' (see PASCAL, B.). In the *Analogy*, Butler puts this point about conduct very emphatically: whether Christianity is true or may be true, whether it is certain or doubtful 'in the highest supposable degree', makes no practical difference. Doubting, he says, 'necessarily implies some degree of evidence for that, of which we doubt', and some, even slight evidence for Christianity 'does as really lay men under obligations, as a full conviction that it is true'.

This argument for Christianity can appear a modest one, far removed from the ringing endorsements to which the orthodox were accustomed; in fact, this very modesty – few assumptions, few grand claims, no a priori reasoning, reliance upon evidence – would appear to be part of Butler's appeal. Yet, the argument itself seems to point the way to a beginning of criticism of it. If slight evidence in favour of Christianity should induce us (to believe it or) to act in accordance with it, should slight evidence against it induce us (to disbelieve it or) to act contrarily? If probability is the guide of life, what if there is slight probability against an afterlife, miracles, and so on? If Butler responds that there can never be such evidence or probability, this seems implausible; after all, Hume adduces at least some evidence for rejecting miracles. If Butler responds that such evidence or probability is never at a level to be compelling, then, even if this is true, why are his opponents forced to a level of compelling evidence, in order to have evidence enough to act upon? And if Butler responds that we have to weigh and balance the evidence in order to decide where the balance of evidence falls, then we need to be told what the principles are by which we weigh and balance. No such principles are set out, and weighing and balancing evidence is not a process on display in the *Analogy*. In short, at least one reading of Butler is that he holds that there is nothing in the natural world (and the claims of natural and revealed religion) that could give one even the slightest evidence against belief in an afterlife or miracles, so that such things can be held by him to be probable because those who oppose them are bereft, not of compelling evidence, but of evidence altogether. As it were, religion wins because there is in effect nothing to oppose it. The deists would not have accepted this, nor today, perhaps, would anyone not already religious, either in the natural or, more realistically, the revealed sense.

6 Personal identity

In the Dissertation *Of Personal Identity* Butler turns to an issue of central importance to the *Analogy* – an afterlife, and whether we shall be the same person then as we are now. This leads him directly into a discussion of in what sameness of person consists, and on this score he makes (at least) four points, which in the main are with respect to Locke's discussion of personal identity in his *Essay Concerning Human Understanding* (1689).

First, 'upon comparing the consciousnesses of one's self, or one's own existence, in any two moments', there 'immediately arises to the mind the idea of personal identity'. Such a comparison shows that one is the same self from moment to moment.

Second, though this consciousness now of what is past shows our identity to ourselves, it does not constitute our identity. As Butler puts it, 'consciousness of personal identity presupposes, and therefore cannot constitute, personal identity; any more than knowledge, in any other case, can constitute truth, which it presupposes'. Trying to analyse personal identity in terms of memory, therefore, as Locke at one point is taken to have done, will not work; memory presupposes personal identity.

Third, in response to Locke's question of whether the same self is the same substance, a question that arises because consciousness of one's existence at two different times are two successive consciousnesses, Butler observes that such successive consciousnesses, while numerically different, are 'consciousnesses of one and the same thing or object; of the same person, self, or living agent'. Consciousness that one is the same person or self is consciousness that one is the same thing, which, if this thing is called substance, as in Locke, is consciousness that one is the same substance. Butler notices that Locke defines person as 'a thinking intelligent being' and personal identity as 'the sameness of rational being', and he maintains, accordingly, that the same rational being is the same substance, since being and substance here 'stand for the same idea'.

Fourth, we may distinguish between loose and strict senses of 'sameness'. In the loose sense, a tree remains the same over time even though it loses or gains parts or properties; indeed, over time, all of its parts or properties may change and it remain the same tree. In the strict sense, however, this is impossible; that is, it is a contradiction to say of the tree then and now that it is the same 'when no part of their substance, and no one of their properties is the same'. Sameness of persons refers to this second sense, so that sameness in this regard 'cannot subsist with diversity of substance'.

All four of these points have figured prominently in discussions of personal identity, and theorists even today often develop elaborate accounts of sameness of person either around or with them. *Of Personal Identity* remains very much alive (see PERSONAL IDENTITY).

See also CONSCIENCE; SHAFTESBURY, THIRD EARL OF

List of works

Butler, J. (1896) *Collected Works*, ed. W.E. Gladstone, Oxford: Clarendon Press, 2 vols. (Volume 1 contains *The Analogy*, the dissertations *Of Personal Identity, Of the Nature of Virtue* and the *Correspondence with Samuel Clarke*. Volume 2 contains Butler's various sermons and the *Charge to the Durham Clergy*.)

—— (1804) *The Works of Joseph Butler*, Edinburgh: Constable. (This includes a life of Butler by Dr. Kippis.)

—— (1900) *Collected Works*, ed. J.H. Bernard, London: Macmillan. (This edition of Butler's collected works is more difficult to find and employs a different division of the texts from Gladstone's division.)

—— (1716) *Several Letters to the Reverend Dr. Clarke, from a Gentleman in Gloucestershire*, London. (A discussion of some points in Clarke on the being and attributes of God.)

—— (1726) *Fifteen Sermons Preached at the Rolls Chapel*, London. (One of the classics of British moral philosophy.)

—— (1736) *The Analogy of Religion Natural and Revealed, to the Constitution and Course of Nature*, Dublin: Ewing. (One of the great achievements of British theology.)

—— (1751) *A Charge to the Clergy of the Diocese of Durham*, London. (An exhortation to the Clergy of Durham to look to the well-being of their flock.)

—— (1765) *Fifteen Sermons to which are added Six Sermons Preached on Public[k] Occasions*, London: Horsfield. (Six sermons on topics of interest in the period, including charity schools and liberty.)

References and further reading

Broad, C. D. (1923) 'Butler as a Theologian', *The Hibbert Journal* 21: 637–56. (Analysis of the main argument lines of the *Analogy*).

—— (1930) *Five Types of Ethical Theory*, London, Routledge & Kegan Paul. (Survey of Butler's ethics.)

Cunliffe, C. (ed.) (1992) *Joseph Butler's Moral and Religious Thought*, Oxford: Clarendon Press. (Collection of original articles on Butler's ethics and philosophy of religion.)

Duncan-Jones, A. (1952) *Butler's Moral Philosophy* Harmondsworth: Penguin. (Overview of Butler's ethics, from an ordinary language perspective.)

Frey, R.G. (forthcoming) *Joseph Butler*, Oxford: Oxford University Press. (Overview of Butler's ethics primarily, with chapters on his philosophy of religion and his views on personal identity.)

* Hume, D. (1779) *Dialogues Concerning Natural Religion*, ed. N Kemp Smith, London: Collier Macmillan Publishers; New York: Macmillan Publishing Company, 1947.

Jeffner, A. (1966) *Butler and Hume on Religion*, Stockholm: Diakonistyrelsens Bokforlag. (Compares and contrasts the two thinkers.)

* Locke, J. (1689) *An Essay concerning Human Understanding*, ed. P.H. Nidditch, Oxford: Oxford University Press, 1975. (A classic work in British empiricism and epistemology.)

Mossner, E. C. (1990) *Bishop Butler and the Age of Reason*, Bristol: Thoemmes. (Primarily sketches Butler's place in the deist controversies of the eighteenth century.)

* Pascal, B. (1670) *Pensées and Other Writings*, New York: Oxford University Press, 1995, 152. (Jottings and aphorisms on God, religion and religious scepticism.)

Penelhum, T. (1959) 'Personal Identity, Memory and Survival', *Journal of Philosophy*, 56: 82–903. (Discusses and makes use of Butler on personal identity.)

—— (1985) *Butler*, London, Routledge & Kegan Paul. (Analyses the main arguments of Butler's ethics and philosophy of religion.)

Perry, J. (ed.) (1975) *Personal Identity*, Berkeley, CA: University of California Press. (Collection on personal identity, including remarks on Butler.)

Shoemaker, S. (1959) 'Personal Identity and Memory', *Journal of Philosophy*, 56: 868–82. (Refers to and builds upon Butler's discussion of personal identity.)

Stephen, L. (1962) *A History of English Thought in the Eighteenth Century*, London: Rupert Hart-Davis, 2 vols. (Discusses both Butler's ethics and philosophy of religion and places him in both respects amongst the thinkers of his age.)

Sturgeon, N. (1976) 'Nature and Convention in Butler's Ethics', *Philosophical Review*, 85: 316–56. (Discussion of what it means 'to follow' in Butler's ethics.)

White, A. R. (1952) 'Conscience and Self-love in Butler's Sermons', *Philosophy*, 27: 329–44. (Assesses the relation between conscience and self-love in Butler's ethics.)

R.G. FREY

BYZANTINE PHILOSOPHY

In Byzantium from the ninth century through to the fifteenth century, philosophy as a discipline remained the science of fundamental truths concerning human beings and the world. Philosophy, the 'wisdom from without', was invariably contrasted with the 'philosophy from within', namely theology. The view that philosophy is 'the handmaiden of theology', which the Greek Church Fathers derived from Philo and the Alexandrian school of theology, was not the dominant position in Byzantium as it was in the West; philosophy, and logic in particular, was never treated as a mere background to, or tool of, theology. By the same token, theology in Byzantium never developed into a systematic method of dialectical inquiry into Christian truths, or a science. Thus the initial distinction between philosophy and theology remained intact.

In terms of institutional practice, theological schools and studies did not exist in Byzantium and the main purpose of higher studies was to train state functionaries. This instruction, based on philosophy and the quadrivium, was mainly private, but it received support from the emperor and the church and we do hear of occasional interference by the secular or ecclesiastical authorities, perhaps because of professional or personal rivalries among the philosophy teachers. Furthermore, Byzantium had no independent universities or centers of study instituted by monastic orders as there were in the West, where social and political conditions were different.

Philosophy in Byzantium also steered clear of involvement in the theological controversies that arose from time to time. The prevalent model of the thinker in Byzantium was a sort of encyclopedic teacher of philosophy, an erudite scholar who kept in touch with the sciences of the quadrivium (arithmetic, geometry, astronomy and music) and other disciplines and set the philosophical tone of the scientific curricula. The development of philosophy in Byzantium was thus very different from that of Western scholasticism.

1 **Historical outline**
2 **The basic tenets of philosophical thought in Byzantium**
3 **General characteristics of Byzantine philosophy**
4 **The study of Byzantine philosophy**

1 **Historical outline**

Although early Christian writers on the ascetic theory of life had adopted the term *philosophia*, the earliest manifestations of autonomous philosophical thought in Byzantium appeared in the ninth and tenth centuries with the 'Christian humanists' such as Photios, Patriarch of Constantinople, Arethas of Patras, Bishop of Caesarea, and Leo the Mathematician (or Philosopher). Photios elaborated the doctrine of the Trinity in the dispute over the procession of the Holy Spirit (the *filioque* dispute) using the armoury of Aristotle's theory of substances (the distinction between 'first substance' and 'second substance'). He was keenly interested in Aristotelian logic, rejecting Plato's self-existent 'ideas', and he collected works by many ancient writers. Arethas copied and commented on works by Plato and Aristotle and wrote critical notes on logic, ontology and psychology.

In the late eleventh and twelfth centuries, the growing study of philosophy reflects the great boost given to higher education and learning by the foundation in 1045 of the 'University' of Constantinople. Among the teachers known as *hypatoi tōn philosophōn* (first among philosophers) were Michael Psellos, undoubtedly the most important and most prolific of the Byzantine polymaths, Ioannes Italos, Theodoros of Smyrna, Eustratios of Nicaea and Michael of Ephesos. The last two are better known as

commentators on Aristotle. The general outlook of the pre-eminent philosophers of this period, and the particular tendencies in their work, display the basic characteristics of Byzantine philosophy but with some distinctive features, such as an even stronger leaning towards the classical models of Greek philosophy and attempts to pursue a more autonomous line of inquiry into problems of knowledge, the natural world and human nature.

The temporary conquest of the Byzantine Empire by the Latin crusaders in 1204 shifted the centre of Byzantine intellectual life away from Constantinople. The flowering of literature and learning in at Nicaea, in Asia Minor, and the presence there of excellent teachers and writers of philosophy such as Nikephoros Blemmydes and Theodoros II Laskaris led to the emergence of generations of scholars well versed in philosophy and science. These men produced an impressive body of original work, especially in astronomy, during the politically troubled but culturally brilliant Paleologan period (1261–1453), the final two centuries of the Byzantine Empire. Outstanding among this group were Theodoros Metochites, Nikephoros Gregoras, Theodoros Choumnos, Georgios Pachymeres, Maximos Planoudes, Gennadios-Scholarios and Bessarion.

This splendid renaissance which coincided with the end of the empire also spread from the capital to other centres such as Thessalonika and Mystras. Thessalonika was associated with the fourteenth-century Hesychast movement of Gregorios Palamas and his followers, a movement that had a considerable impact on Byzantine philosophy and also, more importantly, on the survival of Orthodoxy as a source and driving force of spirituality in the ensuing centuries of Turkish supremacy throughout the Balkans. Mystras, in the Peloponnese, was the home of the last great philosopher and perhaps the most original thinker of Byzantium, Georgios Gemistos-Plethon.

The awareness of Greek national identity had been cultivated, to a greater or lesser extent in earlier centuries but especially in the Palaeologan period, along with the development of Byzantine humanism. This movement had many features in common with the Italian humanism of the Renaissance. In particular, they shared a belief in the value and utility of the ancient Greek civilization with all its achievements, in the sciences no less than in other fields (see HUMANISM, RENAISSANCE). There was a great surge of interest in the sciences, particularly mathematics and astronomy, and a number of major writers on these subjects emerged. Many works were also written on natural phenomena and cosmology.

2 The basic tenets of philosophical thought in Byzantium

The basic tenets that consistently characterized Byzantine philosophical thought throughout its history are first, the personal hypostasis of God as the principle not only of substance but also of being; second, the creation of the world by God and the temporal finitude of the universe; third, the continuous process of creation and the purpose behind it; and fourth, the character of the perceptible world as 'the realization in time of that which is perceptible to the mind', having its eternal hypostasis in the divine intellect (*nous*), the *Logos* (see CREATION AND CONSERVATION, RELIGIOUS DOCTRINE OF).

Phenomena, in Byzantine philosophy, are real hypostases to which the creator has given material existence by uniting them with the matter already created. Matter has no eternal existence: the ancient doctrine of uncreated, incorruptible matter is rejected utterly. Ideas have no self-existent hypostasis but are conceived by God and are instruments of God's creative will and omnipotence. The general characteristics of sensible things (*universalia*) can be apprehended by the process of abstractive recognition; here the conceptual realism of the Alexandrian commentators on Aristotle is adopted and nominalism is rejected (see ARISTOTLE COMMENTATORS; NOMINALISM).

Both the world and the human race are subject to divine providence, which is personal in character. Human self-determination does not conflict with the manifestation of divine providence, and Byzantine thinking on the subject presents a full affirmation of human free will. The soul as a spiritual substance, being by its very nature immortal, always belongs to one particular body. This personal soul is directly connected with the human being's intellectual powers, which help him or her to achieve happiness by means of the freedom of decision. The relationship between God and human beings is based on love, which explains the central place of the human race in creation. Comparing Byzantine with ancient ontology, one can say in general that where the latter has 'being' the former has the doctrine of 'existence'. The doctrines of the personal relationship between soul and body and the immortality of the personal soul are elaborated much more lucidly than in ancient philosophy (see SOUL, NATURE AND IMMORTALITY OF THE).

3 General characteristics of Byzantine philosophy

The most important general characteristic of Byzantine philosophy, apparent in every period, is the absence of philosophical systems with real originality or independence. Instead, we find individual philosophers with an excellent classical education, extremely well versed in the writings of the ancient philosophers and with a discerning eye for subtleties of meaning. As far as Byzantine philosophers were concerned, the world view was fixed and crystalized and the study of philosophy was always regarded as a preparatory means to the ultimate end, which transcends the bounds of nature and cognition and consists in closer communion with God. Thus inquiry into such problems as the relation of faith to opinion and to knowledge – issues to which Christianity gave a new dimension with its concept of the individual – are the main areas in which philosophy is brought face to face with theology, and also Christianity with Hellenism.

On the one hand, therefore, Byzantine philosophers were quite familiar with the doctrines of the ancient Greek philosophers and had no difficulty in assimilating their ideas. It helped, of course, that they had a better knowledge of the language in which those texts were written than did those living outside the Greek-speaking world. A close attunement to the Greek spirit led Byzantine philosophers to preserve the ancient philosophical texts, and to produce a fine set of commentaries on the most important of them (especially the Aristotelian and Neoplatonic writings) in the early post-classical period. In time this also generated an authentic (if unsystematic) philosophical tradition in the Byzantine world and produced some fine philosophers. Their main sources of inspiration were twofold: patristic theology (though with many of the ideas and methods of ancient Greek philosophy grafted on to it, after suitable modification) and first-hand study of Greek philosophical writings. The main purpose of studying these texts was to provide training in philosophical methods without regard to the 'rightness' or 'wrongness' of the views expressed in them, with the additional aim of resolving difficulties or rebutting theses that conflicted with the new (Christian) world view.

On the other hand, ancient Greek and Christian thought remained basically opposed to one another, despite the ever-increasing use of the ideas and methods of ancient philosophy which had helped to shape Christian doctrine in its final form. This antithesis was not all-embracing: some principles of pagan teaching in specific areas, chiefly ontology and cosmology, were rejected while others, especially in the realm of logical reasoning (for example, the apodictic syllogism, but not the dialectic method) and the natural sciences, were accepted. Moreover, the study of the ancient philosophers was not limited to commentary and interpretation but sometimes prompted critical discussion or even original elaboration of problems and the formulation of solutions.

Thus for example, theological difficulties led to the clarification of philosophical concepts relating to the distinction between the essence (*ousia*) and activity (*energeia*) of God in the Hesychast controversy, where the debate was conducted using the armoury of classical metaphysics. The Byzantines always remained genuinely interested in grafting the teaching of the Scriptures and the Church Fathers onto ancient Greek wisdom, and in 'capturing concepts in Christ' and the eventual synthesis of 'philosophy' and 'knowledge of God'. This explains the ever-present influence of the great philosophers of antiquity throughout the Christian Middle Ages.

As regards the more specific and controversial question of the Byzantines' Platonism, Aristotelianism or Neoplatonism, the trends outlined above explain the frequent transformations undergone by many of the Platonic, Aristotelian and even Neoplatonic elements adopted by Byzantine thinkers, especially on such great issues as the concept of God, the relationship of the perceptible world to the absolute and the generation and essential nature of the soul. This has to be taken into account for an understanding of the so-called Platonism or Aristotelianism of the Byzantines and of their affinity with the thinking of the Neoplatonists. The affinity with any of these schools is largely external, inasmuch as the elements borrowed from them are chiefly methodological and logical, and the same language and terminology are used. This is particularly true of Neoplatonism, the phase of ancient Greek philosophy closest chronologically to the Byzantine period (see NEOPLATONISM). As regards the relationship of the most typical Byzantine philosophers with PLATO and ARISTOTLE, we find a balanced synthesis of logical and intuitive tendencies, with Aristotle on the side of logic and Plato on the side of intuition (see ARISTOTELIANISM, MEDIEVAL; PLATONISM, MEDIEVAL).

Leaving aside certain specific cases of accurate interpretation of the classical philosophers by Byzantine philosophers of the first rank, this attitude to both Plato and Aristotle gives Byzantine thought a typical manner of interpretation which leads away from the historical (that is, authentic) Plato and Aristotle. Furthermore, the preoccupation with the two great ancients ranges from pure study and interpretation for educational purposes to the fierce wrangling between rival schools that characterized the final centuries of the Byzantine Empire. In the former category we have the long line of Byzantine commentators on Aristotle, whose work established an authoritative and textually reliable Byzantine hermeneutic tradition which followed in the footsteps of the Alexandrian commentators, whose work they knew well and made good use of (see ARISTOTLE COMMENTATORS). Thus they were instrumental in rehabilitating Aristotle's philosophy in the West after the Renaissance and ending the dominance of scholasticism and Averroism (see AVERROISM; MEDIEVAL PHILOSOPHY; RENAISSANCE PHILOSOPHY).

The 'Platonism' of the Byzantines was the Platonic system which, having undergone many transformations, had been handed down to them from the Early Christian period and was often invoked for the defence of Orthodoxy against heresies. In the strife between the Hesychast movement of Gregorios Palamas and its opponents, many of the points at issue were Platonic concepts which had often exercised the minds of theologians and Christian philosophers in the past. In the fifteenth century, shortly before and immediately after the fall of Constantinople, individual interpretations of Plato and Aristotle led to the fierce philosophical dispute over the superiority of one or the other among the Greek scholars who had fled to Italy and were working as teachers or translators.

The interest taken in Neoplatonism by philosophers from Psellos to Plethon was manifested in a similar way, but it provoked a strong reaction, not only in terms of opposition to individual Neoplatonists such as IAMBLICHUS and especially PROCLUS, but also in more general opposition on the part of the 'Aristotelians' to Orthodox theology and Western scholasticism in the dispute of the fourteenth and fifteenth centuries. The most obvious case in point is mystical theology, which is at once an ally and an adversary of Neoplatonism, especially in its attitudes to both Byzantine scholarship and Latin rationalism. During these two centuries mysticism was again the arena in which many philosophical concepts continued to exist not only externally but in personal practice. Here in mysticism, as also in Byzantine art, are to be found genuine metaphysical riches and experiential philosophical participation, which owes much to its contact with Neoplatonism. This explains the opposition of the church (or at least the official church) to this particular form of Byzantine spirituality, and it also accounts for Plethon's conflict with the church. Plethon had turned philosophy into a stirring experience and was fighting to resuscitate the Greeks' awareness of their national identity through philosophy.

The relationship between the Greek Orthodox East and the Catholic West (leaving aside the keen interest of both in Aristotle's philosophy) is of interest in connection with the conflict between the philosophical approaches of the two cultures. Despite attempts to improve mutual understanding in the Palaeologan period, when pro-Latin theologians and philosophers were active in the East, and despite the existence of numerous translations of Latin works (mostly by Thomas AQUINAS) in the East, Byzantium remained closed to Western scholasticism right to the end. On the other hand, it is now known that Byzantium exerted a fertile influence on the West even before the forced migration of Greek scholars following the collapse of the Byzantine Empire in 1453 (see ARISTOTELIANISM, RENAISSANCE; GEORGE OF TREBIZOND; PLATONISM, RENAISSANCE).

4 The study of Byzantine philosophy

Byzantine philosophy began attracting keen interest among scholars after the Second World War, long after most other periods and regions in the history of philosophy. A great deal of historical material is now available concerning the writings and teachings of major Byzantine philosophers and, more generally, concerning the cultivation of ideas and the trends of philosophical thought during those six hundred years.

Scholars now generally accept such fundamental premises as the unbroken continuity of Greek philosophy throughout the Greek-speaking world from classical times through late antiquity to Neoplatonism, recognizable in many tenets of the Church Fathers and in Christian Byzantium. In particular, the importance of linguistic continuity, which meant that ancient writings were widely used and understood in Byzantium, should not be underrated. Also, the accepted view of the relationship between theology and philosophy in Byzantium has been revised, with a more correct assessment of the dependence of Byzantine philosophy on patristic theology. Lastly, new facts have emerged and received opinions have been revised with regard to the relations and interaction between the Greek East and the Latin West in the realm of philosophy.

In conclusion, some methodological observations are called for concerning the background of Byzantine philosophy and the possibility of its systematic presentation. The philosophical output of this period, of which we have only fragmentary knowledge, is extremely varied and is spread over a wide variety of writings. Moreover, many important works are still unpublished or are available only in old and imperfect editions. Although many useful specialized books and papers have been written in recent years, the Byzantines' indebtedness to ancient philosophy has not been sufficiently studied or definitively assessed. Consequently any survey of the period could only be more or less schematic, though it can and must show the vigour and vitality of ancient Greek philosophy throughout the long era of Christian Byzantium.

See also: ARISTOTLE COMMENTATORS; GREEK PHILOSOPHY: IMPACT ON ISLAMIC PHILOSOPHY; ISLAMIC PHILOSOPHY; MEDIEVAL PHILOSOPHY; NEOPLATONISM; PATRISTIC PHILOSOPHY; PLATONISM, EARLY AND MIDDLE; RENAISSANCE PHILOSOPHY

References and further reading

Anastos, M. and Benakis, L.G. (1979–80) 'Philosophy in Byzantium', in *History of the Greek Nation*, Athens: Ekdotike Athinon, vol. 8, 266–73 (Anastos); 9, 348–71 (Benakis). (In Greek.)

Benakis, L.G. (1971) 'Byzantine Philosophy. Forschungsbericht 1949–1971' (Byzantine Philosophy: Report on Research 1949–71), *Philosophia* 1: 390–433. (In Greek with German summary.)

—— (1982) 'The Problem of General Concepts in Neoplatonism and Byzantine Thought', in D.J. O'Meara (ed.) *Neoplatonism and Christian Thought*, Norfolk: International Society for Neoplatonic Studies, 75–86. (Includes discussion of Neoplatonist elements in Byzantine philosophy.)

—— (1986) 'Die Stellung des Menschen im Kosmos in der byzantinischen Philosophie' (The Position of Man in the Cosmos in Byzantine Philosophy), in *L'homme et son univers au Moyen Age, Actes du VIIème Congrès Internationale de philosophie médiévale (Man and His Universe in the Middle Ages, Transactions of the VIIth International Congress on Medieval Philosophy)*, Louvain-la-Neuve, vol. I, 56–75. (Cosmology in Byzantine philosophy.)

—— (1987) 'Grundbibliographie zum Aristoteles-Studium in Byzanz' (Basic Bibliography of the Study of Aristotle in Byzantium), *Aristoteles. Werk und Wirkung, Paul Moraux gewidmet*, Berlin: de Gruyter, 352–79. (Bibliography of Aristotelian works from Byzantium.)

—— (1988) 'Commentaries and Commentators on the Logical Works of Aristotle in Byzantium', *Gedankenzeichen. Festschrift für Klaus Oehler*, Tübingen: Stauffenburg, 3–12. (Byzantine commentators on the Organon.)

—— (1991a) 'Commentaries and Commentators on the Works of Aristotle (except the Logical Ones) in Byzantium', *Historia Philosophiae Medii Aevi. Festschrift für Kurt Flasch*, Amsterdam: Grüner, 45–54. (Byzantine commentators on Aristotle's other works.)

—— (1991b) 'Bibliographie internationale sur la Philosophie Byzantine (1949–1990)' (International Bibliography of Byzantine Philosophy (1949–90)), *Bibliographie Byzantine publié à l'occasion du XVIIIe Congrès Internationale d'Études Byzantines* (Byzantine Bibliography Published on the Occasion of the XVIIIth International Congress on Byzantine Studies), Athens: Comité Hellénique des Études Byzantines, 319–77. (Includes more than 400 titles in systematic and chronological order, plus bibliography on the Church Fathers and philosophy.)

CPhMA – Philosophi Byzantini (1984–92), Athens: The Academy of Athens. (The first critical editions of works by Nicholas of Methone, Nikephoros Blemmydes, Gorgios Gemistos-Plethon, Georgios Pachymeres and others. Each work presents the full Greek text, accompanied by a critical apparatus, an introduction, a translation into English (Pachymeres), French (Plethon) or German (Blemmydes) and full indexes. Further volumes are in preparation. Works of philosophical interest by Michael Psellos and Plethon have also been published in recent years in editions by L.G. Benakis, U. Criscuolo, J. Duffy, P. Gautier, D. O'Meara and G. Weiss; see Benakis (1991b).)

Hunger, H. (1978–91) 'Philosophie', in *Die hochsprachliche profane Literatur der Byzantiner*, vol. I, Munich: Beck, 3–62; Greek translation with new bibliography by L.G. Benakis, Athens: Cultural Foundation of the National Bank of Greece , 1991, 39–122. (Summary of Byzantine philosophical writings.)

—— (1993) 'Philosophie. B. Byzanz', *Lexikon des Mittelalters* (Dictionary of the Middle Ages), vol. VI, Munich: Artemis & Winkler, col. 2092–100. (The most recent survey, taking into consideration many new editions and relevant studies.)

Lemerle, P. (1971) *Le premier humanisme byzantin. L'enseignement et la culture à Byzance des origines au Xe siècle* (The First Byzantine: Education and Culture in Byzantium from the Beginning to the Tenth Century), Paris: Presses Universitaires de France, Bibliotheque Byzantine. (Discusses humanism in Byzantium during the so-called Macedonian Renaissance.)

Meyendorff, J. (1973) *Défence des saints hésychastes. Grégoire Palamas* (Gregory Palamas and the Defence of the Hesychast Saints), Leuven: Spicilegium Sacrum Louvaniense. (On the fourteenth-century mystical movement, the Hesychasts, and their most prominent member, Gregory Palamas.)

Oehler, K. (1969) *Antike Philosophie und byzantinisches Mittelalter* (Ancient Philosophy and Medieval Byzantium), Munich: Beck. (On the inheritance of ancient philosophy in Byzantium.)

—— (1990) 'Die Byzantinische Philosophie' (Byzantine Philosophy), in *Contemporary Philosophy: A New Survey*, vol. 6/2, Philosophy and Science in the Middle Ages, Dordrecht: Kluwer, 639–49.

Podskalsky, G. (1977) *Theologie und Philosophie in Byzanz. Der Streit um die theologische Methodik in der spätbyzantinischen Geistesgeschichte (14/15. Jh.)* (Theology and Philosophy: The Debate About Historical Method in Late Byzantium (14th–15th Centuries)), Munich: Beck. (Relations between theology and philosophy at the end of the Byzantine period.)

Tatakis, B.N. (1949) *La Philosophie byzantine* (Byzantine Philosophy), Paris: Presses Universitaires de France. (The first systematic survey of the subject, now somewhat out of date.)

—— (1969) 'La philosophie grecque patristique et byzantine' (Greek Patristic and Byzantine Philosophy), in *Histoire de la Philosophie*, vol. I, *Orient-Antiquité-Moyen âge*, Encyclopedie de la Pléiade, Paris: Gallimard, 936–1005. (Survey of late Greek, patristic and Byzantine philosophy.)

Woodhouse, C.M. (1986) *Gemistos Plethon: The Last of the Hellenes*, Oxford: Clarendon Press. (The life of Gemistos-Plethon, perhaps the most original thinker in Byzantium.)

PHIL LINOS BENAKIS

C

CABALA **CABALA** *see* KABBALAH

CABANIS, PIERRE-JEAN (1757–1808)

Cabanis believed in the possibility of a 'science of man', having its basis in medicine. He tried to show how a materialist conception of the human organism can throw light on our mental and moral life. The properties of living matter were derived from physical laws, but had their own peculiarities. In particular, the property of sensibility (being able to have sensations) and the property of motility (involving the experience of effort and of resistance to it) were the keys to understanding human nature.

Though the thrust of Cabanis' thought is materialistic, his emphasis on medical science distinguishes him both from the mechanistic tradition as represented by La Mettrie, and from the intellectualist tradition represented by Condillac, in which sensations are taken as given mental items, from which the rest of our mental life is constructed by operations of reasoning or association.

1 Life and works
2 Thought

1 Life and works

Cabanis was born in Cosnac in the Limousin. He was registered as a medical doctor in Reims in 1784, after seven years' study in Paris (during which he had already become a protégé of Mme d'Helvétius, encountering Condillac, Condorcet, Benjamin Franklin, Mirabeau and Theodore Roosevelt in her circle). His radical ideas about the reform of medical practice and education would perhaps have made it difficult for him to be accepted by the medical establishment in Paris at the time. However, he did not make his profession as a doctor (though he treated Mirabeau, and published an account of Mirabeau's illness and death in 1791). Instead, he put his medical knowledge to political and philosophical use. In 1790, he wrote his *Observations sur les hôpitaux* (Observations on Hospitals) and this led

to public office, including membership of the Commission on Hospitals, under the revolutionary régime. He also took an active interest in educational reform.

Like many members of the salon of Mme d'Helvétius at Auteuil, he withdrew from the public scene during the Reign of Terror, for fear of Robespierre. When he re-emerged, it was to stand for the ideals of reason, the perfectibility of the human species, and freedom. He was made Professor of Hygiene, and Professor of Clinical Medicine at the École de Médecine in Paris, and was elected to the Conseil des Cinq-Cents. On the creation of the Institut de France, he became a member of the short-lived 'Class of Moral and Political Sciences', where he delivered the series of memoirs which formed his major work, published in 1802: the *Rapports du physique et du moral de l'homme (Relations between the Physical and the Mental in Man)*. He became a senator in 1797, having supported Bonaparte's *coup d'état* of 18 Brumaire. However, he overtly opposed Bonaparte's growing authoritarianism. He belonged to a group of thinkers devoted to *idéologie* (the 'science of ideas'). The word was coined by Destutt de Tracy, a leader of that group, which included figures like Condorcet, Laplace and Lavoisier. But Napoleon soon adopted a repressive approach, and the appellation *idéologue* came to connote intellectual, social and political subversiveness. In about 1807, Cabanis seems to have composed a letter to Fauriel on first causes, in which he made concessions to the religious revival. The letter was published only in 1824, but we may surmise that Cabanis felt the need to seek some accommodation with the Imperial authority, as did other thinkers in the first decade of nineteenth-century Paris.

2 Thought

Cabanis was among those figures of the Enlightenment and post-Enlightenment period who believed passionately in the possibility and importance of a 'science of man'. The systematic understanding of brute matter which the mechanical philosophy had made possible should be matched in our understanding of the human species. This was not, of course, a new ideal, but what was distinctive in Cabanis' pursuit of it was his view that this understanding must be rooted in medical science, broadly conceived.

The memoirs which make up his *Relations between the Physical and the Mental in Man*, though materialist in cast, are concerned primarily with the special properties of living matter, especially in the human species. However, this was not necessarily a vitalist position. Indeed, Cabanis places his study of these properties in the context of a much more general principle, that of *attraction*, illustrated by gravity in physics, and by 'affinities' in chemistry and biology. Nevertheless, it is clear that he gives a certain autonomy to our understanding of living matter. Cabanis began this work by insisting that the moral and medical sciences must deal with human beings as whole creatures. Like DESCARTES, he insisted on the union of mind and body, but unlike Descartes he was no dualist, adopting a broadly materialist approach, which gave a central role to sensation. The property of being able to have sensations, though peculiar to living matter, was derived from more general physical laws, and could give rise to unconscious as well as conscious psychological phenomena. The physiological underlayers of sensation could be seen at work in differences between the sexes, and other mental differences between people arising from their inherited physical constitution in interaction with environmental factors. Cabanis had no account of how life arose, and thought that we should not speculate about causes whose existence could not (as he thought) be experimentally verified, but he believed that one source of the development of life was the inheritance of acquired characteristics. This led him to argue for selective breeding of humans.

This summary of a diverse and wide-ranging set of memoirs is very incomplete, but it shows how Cabanis held a position which already had a substantial background, for instance, in the work of Boerhaave, Stahl, Bonnet, Haller, La Mettrie and others, authors whose importance he fully acknowledged. But these thinkers were divided. Could our understanding of living matter be a simple derivation from our understanding of matter in general? Or were there special types of explanation at play in the case of living matter? Some maintained that a single principle was at work in living matter, others, like Haller, made a radical distinction between a physical property of 'irritability' responsible for lower and unconscious functions not involving sensation, and a sensitive property which was responsible for sensation and other mental functions which were derived from it.

Cabanis, as we have already indicated, preferred a monistic position. Indeed, he was particularly known for his claim that just as the stomach digests food, so the brain is a device for digesting sense impressions:

he said that it carried out 'the secretion of thought'. Some of his contemporaries, such as Maine de Biran, strongly rejected this claim. Nevertheless, Cabanis' systematic treatment of the physiological underlayer of our mental existence, with its exploration of internal factors such as sex, health, bodily chemistry, inherited dispositions, habituation, as well as external ones such as nutrition and climate, marked a distinct break with the intellectualist analyses of eighteenth-century sensualism, typified by CONDILLAC. Like BONNET, whom he admired, Cabanis could be seen as attempting to 'naturalize' sensualism. *Relations* is a wide-ranging work which also gives an important role to language, envisages 'transformism' (a precursor of evolutionary theory) and emphasizes the importance of motility: Cabanis claims that the consciousness of self requires the experience of effort, and of resistance to it (this view influenced Maine de Biran, who made it a main element in his own philosophy).

There is significant disagreement about how to read Cabanis' position. Some, including some modern commentators, have regarded him simply as a materialist. Others have viewed his work as endorsing some version of vitalism. The situation is further complicated by the posthumously published letter to Fauriel on first causes (*Lettre à Fauriel sur les causes premières*, 1824). Although called a 'letter', this is in fact a book-length opus. Some commentators have gone so far as to ignore it; others have viewed it as a recantation of Cabanis' former robust materialism; others again consider that it raises questions of method which were Cabanis' concern all along. On the latter interpretation, we should point out how, all along, Cabanis abjured the search for 'essences', 'occult powers' or 'first causes', a commonplace at the time. We should be empiricists, neither postulating nor speculating about the unobservable, but confining ourselves to what can be established by observation. The letter to Fauriel, however, distinguishes between what can be 'demonstrated' in this way, and what can be argued for only by calculating probabilities. The latter may, according to this 'letter', re-admit a religious world-view as something with a certain probability, even though it cannot be demonstrated by scientific methods. In the background were Châteaubriand's *Le Génie du Christianisme* (1802), and the influence of the Illuminati, and the many other factors which were bringing the end of the Enlightenment (see ILLUMINATI).

Whether or not we regard this posthumously published 'letter' as a recantation, Cabanis' principal work had a substantial and fruitful impact on the early development of psychology and its connections with physiology, being reprinted several times up to the middle of the nineteenth century.

See also: HUMAN NATURE, EIGHTEENTH-CENTURY SCIENCE OF; LA METTRIE, J.O. DE

List of works

Cabanis, P.-J.G. (1956) *Œuvres philosophiques* (Philosophical works), ed. J. Cazeneuve and C. Lehec, Paris: Presses Universitaires de France. (Cabanis' collected philosophical works.)

—— (1790) *Observations sur les hôpitaux* (Observations on Hospitals). (Included in Cabanis (1798).)

—— (1791) *Journal de la maladie et de la mort d'Honoré-Gabriel-Victor Riquetti de Mirabeau* (Journal of the Illness and Death of Mirabeau). (Included in Cabanis (1798).)

—— (1798) *Du degré de certitude de la médecine* (On the Degree of Certainty of Medicine), Paris: Firmin Didot; 2nd edn, 1803. (Second edition included *Observations on Hospitals* and *Journal of the Illness and Death of Mirabeau*.)

—— (1798) *Rapport fait au Conseil des Cinq-Cents sur l'organisation des Ecoles de Médecine* (Report to the Council of Five Hundred on the Organization of Medical Schools) ; photographic repr. Paris: Éditions de la Cité des sciences et de l'industrie, 1989. (Works of Cabanis about the administration and practice of medicine.)

—— (1802) *Rapports du physique et du moral de l'homme* (Relations between the Physical and the Mental in Man), Paris; 2nd edn, Paris: Crapelet, 1805; photographic repr., Paris: Slatkine, 1980. (Distinctive views on the mind–body question. The 1980 reprint is of an 1844 edition.)

—— (1804) *Coup d'œil sur les révolutions et sur la réforme de la médecine*, Paris: Crapart; trans. A. Henderson, *Sketch of the Revolutions of Medical Science, and Views relating to its Reform*, London: Johnson, 1806. (Proposals for medicine.)

—— (1807a) *Observations sur les affections catarrhales en général: et particulièrement sur celles connues sous les noms de rhumes de cerveau et rhumes de poitrine* (Observations on Catarrhal Infections Generally: In Particular on Those Known as Head Colds and Chest Colds), Paris: Crapart. (On catarrhal infections.)

—— (1807b) *Lettre à Fauriel sur les causes premières* (Letter to Fauriel on First Causes), ed. F. Bérard, Paris: Gabon, 1824. (On first causes; published posthumously.)

References and further reading

Azouvi, F. (1992) *L'Institution de la raison: la révolution culturelle des idéologues* (The Institution of Reason: the Cultural Revolution of the 'Idéologues'), Paris: Éditions de l'École des hautes études en sciences sociales, Vrin. (A collection of articles on the ideals and activities of Cabanis' intellectual circle.)

Cailliet, É. (1943) *La Tradition littéraire des idéologues* (The Literary Tradition of the Idéologues), Philadephia, PA: American Philosophical Society. (A thorough study of the immediate intellectual milieu to which Cabanis belonged.)

Colonna d'Istria, F. (1911–7) Five articles in *Revue de métaphysique et de morale*, vols. 19–21, 24–5. (These articles constitute an effective overview of some main aspects of Cabanis' work.)

Moravia, S. (1974) *Il pensiero degli 'idéologues': scienza e filosofia in Francia 1780–1815* (The Thought of the Idéologues: Science and Philosophy in France 1780–1815), Florence: La Nuova Italia. (Another authoritative account of 'ideology'.)

Poyer, G. (ed.) (1910) *Cabanis: choix de textes et introduction* (Cabanis: Selected texts and introduction), Paris: Louis Michaud. (Contains a brief but useful biography.)

Staum, M.S. (1980) *Cabanis: enlightenment and medical philosophy in the French revolution*, Princeton, NJ: Princeton University Press. (A very useful study.)

Tissot, C. J. (1843) *Anthropologie spéculative générale*, (Speculative General Anthropology), Paris. (A valuable document showing the impact of the work of Cabanis and Maine de Biran on the early stages of empirical psychology.)

F.C.T. MOORE

CABRAL, AMÍLCAR (1924–73)

Amílcar Cabral was founder and leader of the African Party for the Independence of Guinea and Cape Verde (PAIGC), which led a war of liberation in the Portuguese colonies of Guinea Bissau and Cape Verde that ended with the recognition of their joint independence by the Portuguese government in October 1974. Cabral was assassinated in 1973, the victim of an attempted coup aimed at taking over the PAIGC leadership. Thus he did not live to see the independence for which he had struggled. Cabral's importance for African political philosophy lies in his having developed an undogmatic left-wing analysis of the situation of the Guinean peasantry. While familiar with Marxist analysis, Cabral was always willing to adapt it to the empirical realities of the Guinean situation. His writings on the role of culture in the nationalist struggle, which have important affinities with Gramsci, combine theoretical ingenuity with detailed local knowledge.

1 Life
2 Political philosophy

1 Life

Amílcar Lopes Cabral was born on the Guinean mainland in Bafatá. Later he moved to the island of São Tiago in the Cape Verde islands. He began primary education only at the age of twelve, but by twenty he had completed in eight years an education that normally took eleven. During this period, Cabral participated in the literary current that grew up around the journal *Claridade* (1936–60). He wrote poetry that was nationalist but not explicitly anti-colonial, like much of the work of this group.

In 1945 he won a prestigious scholarship to the Higher Institute of Agronomy in Lisbon. He gained his degree in March 1952. While in Portugal he met other students from Portuguese Africa. He came to know a number of those who later became leaders in the independence struggles in Portugal's African colonies, among them Agostinho Neto, Angola's first president and Mario de Andrade, later head of the Popular Movement for the Liberation of Angola (MPLA); but unlike many of them, Cabral never joined the Portuguese Communist Party.

During this period Cabral was also engaged with what he called the 're-Africanization of the spirit'. He argued that this was a necessary step for 'assimilated' Africans like himself if they were to play a positive role in the nationalist struggle. Cabral's work at that time was strongly influenced by his reading of the *négritude* poets and of *Présence Africaine*, the major journal of that movement (see AFRICAN PHILOSOPHY, FRANCOPHONE §4). Cabral returned to Guinea in 1952 to direct the research of a government experimental station near Bissau, the colony's capital. In 1953 he was asked by the authorities to conduct an agricultural survey of the colony. This experience played a crucial role in the development of his ideas. It provided him with first-hand knowledge of peasant life throughout the country and allowed him to 're-Africanize' himself by cultural immersion. In 1955 he returned to Portugal.

On returning to Guinea for a short visit in 1956 he helped found the African Party for the Independence of Guinea and Cape Verde (PAIGC). For the next four years Cabral worked as an agronomist in Portugal and Angola, where he was involved with the foundation of Angola's Marxist liberation movement (MPLA) through contacts from his student days.

In 1959 Cabral returned to Guinea to take part in a momentous meeting of the PAIGC at which some crucial decisions were taken. These included shifting the focus of the struggle from urban to rural areas, moving their political headquarters out of the country and promoting the idea of armed struggle against colonial rule. Moving their headquarters was possible because Guinée, the neighbouring French colony, had recently become independent. For the remainder of his life Cabral had a home in Guinée and the PAIGC conducted its programme of decolonization from a base there. From 1960 Cabral primary focus was on the political education of the party's core membership. Over the next decade the political mobilization of the Guinean peasantry played a central role in the work of the PAIGC.

From 1962 the PAIGC developed a guerrilla army trained to work with the peasantry. The group also built support from village chiefs and elders. Cabral was involved in the organization of both the war and the party's diplomacy as it sought to gain international support. He also organized the elections in 1972 which saw the creation of the National Assembly that declared independence eight months after his assassination in January 1973. The overthrow of the fascist regime in Portugal in the spring of 1974 led to Portugal's recognition of the independence of Guinea and Cape Verde in October of that year.

2 Political theory

In 'The Weapon of Theory' (1966), probably his most widely-cited work, Cabral makes a number of quite specific criticisms and modifications of the Marxist tradition, as he understood it. For example, it cannot be the case that history begins only after the development of classes, as many European Marxists in the post-war period had argued. He claimed that there were no classes in the Marxist sense in much of Africa, Asia and Latin America before colonialism, or in early European history. His analysis of Guinean (and other) societies taught him there was not always class struggle throughout history, therefore, something else must have been the 'motive force of history' ([1966] 1980: 123) before the existence of class systems. This force is the mode of production, which means 'the level of the productive forces and the system of ownership' ([1966] 1980: 123). Class struggle did not exist in earlier forms of society in which there was a low level of development of the productive forces, such as technology and no private ownership of land. Cabral maintained that there was still historical development and offered an analysis of three stages of development of the mode of production, communal, agrarian and then socialist.

Within this analysis Cabral thought that European colonialism in Africa and elsewhere interfered with the historical development of African societies. He saw national liberation as 'the regaining of the historical personality' ([1966] 1980: 130) of a people. Foreign domination of the productive forces of an agrarian colony by a capitalist metropolis drives the history of a people according to a logic inappropriate to the level of productive forces in their society. Cabral went on to analyse the forms of stratification and the relations of production that imperialism imposed upon colonies.

Cabral's political theory was developed in the context of his experience as a colonial subject and as the leader of a war of national liberation. Like all successful twentieth-century revolutionaries he succeeded in a context where there was almost no proletariat. He had to develop an account of his struggle which faced the reality that the PAIGC consisted of a petty-bourgeois leadership mobilizing a peasantry.

The key to national liberation, he thought, lay in the sphere of culture, but the role of culture depended on which class you were addressing. This was because of the 'class-character' of culture in the struggle for liberation. He resolutely opposed the notion implicit in *négritude* that the 're-Africanization of the spirit', or 'return to the source' ([1966] 1980: 63) he had experienced as a member of the petty bourgeoisie was relevant to the situation of the rural peasantry. He felt this was because imperialism had had little effect on peasant culture. He also rejected *négritude*'s notion that there was a single African culture.

Cabral argued instead that it was necessary to nurture the popular culture of the indigenous peoples as the basis for a developing nationalist consciousness. With a critical approach to this aim a humanism that transcended nationality could be achieved. He also believed, perhaps because of his training in agronomy, that it was important to develop a scientific culture that would support the technology required for economic development.

The greatest challenge for national liberation was that the petty bourgeoisie would be tempted to become more bourgeois and ally itself with international capital. This is what happened to those societies that became neocolonial states after formal independence. (In Cabral's view this would have included most of the states of Francophone Africa, except for Guinea.) The result was that the task of the revolutionary party was to shape the consciousness of the petty bourgeoisie before independence in such a way that they would become 'capable of committing suicide as a class' because they were 'completely identified with the deepest aspirations of the people'

([1966] 1980: 136). Cabral placed a great deal of emphasis on the cultural and ideological work of shaping the consciousness of the petty bourgeoisie, just as he had insisted on shaping the national consciousness of the peasantry. It is this aspect that bears a resemblance to Gramsci. This view is substantially at odds with much Marxist thinking which has denied the possibility that there can be a revolutionary petty bourgeoisie. Subsequent African history suggests that it is Cabral who is mistaken on this issue.

Cabral's detailed analysis of the role of the popular culture of the peasantry as a basis for the development of national consciousness has had a great influence on cultural thought among intellectuals in Africa since the 1980s.

See also: FANON, F.; GRAMSCI, A.; MARX. K.

List of works

Cabral, A. (1969) *Revolution in Guinea*, London: Stage One. (Speeches and writings in which Cabral discusses the conduct of the war of liberation in Guinea.)
—— (1973) *Return to the Source*, New York: Monthly Review Press. (Selected speeches, including 'The Weapon of Theory' and an important essay on 'Identity and Dignity in the Context of National Liberation', which discusses the idea of a 'return to the source' quite extensively.)
—— (1966) 'Weapon of Theory', in *Unity and Struggle*, London: Heinemann, 1980. (Translates most of the major essays including 'The Weapon of Theory' and an important essay on 'National Liberation and Culture'.)

References and further reading

Chabal, P. (1983) *Amilcar Cabral: Revolutionary Leadership and People's War*, Cambridge: Cambridge University Press. (The first scholarly biography with a substantial chapter devoted to Cabral's social and political thought. Also contains a thorough bibliography of Cabral's writings.)
Chilcote, R.L. (1991) *Amílcar Cabral's Revolutionary Theory and Practice: A Critical Guide*, Boulder, CO: Lynne Rienner. (Contains an annotated bibliography of work on and by Cabral.)
* *Claridade* (1936–60), repr. in *Claridade: revista de arte e letras*, Linda-a-Velha, Portugal: Africa, Literatura, Arte e Cultura, 1986.
* *Présence Africaine* (African Presence) (1947–), Paris. (This quarterly is the major journal of the *négritude* movement. It is published by the publishing house

of the same name that has also produced many influential journals.)

K. ANTHONY APPIAH

CAITANYA *see* GAUDĪYA VAISNAVISM

CAJETAN (THOMAS DE VIO) (1468–1534)

Thomas de Vio, better known as Cajetan, has long been considered to be the outstanding commentator on the philosophical thought of Thomas Aquinas. He has had a great influence not only on discussions about Aquinas' theory of analogical predication regarding God and creatures but also on discussions about Aquinas' fundamental notions of essence and existence. On both counts his interpretations are at variance with Aquinas himself. He also set himself in opposition to Aquinas when he denied in his later writings that the immortality of the human soul could be demonstrated, arguing that it is a doctrine that must be accepted simply on faith, like the doctrines of the Trinity and the Incarnation. His explication of Aquinas' cognitive psychology is an interesting development that goes beyond Aquinas.

1 Life
2 Logic and analogy
3 Natural philosophy
4 Psychology
5 Metaphysics

1 Life

Thomas de Vio was born at Gaeta. Entering the Dominican Order there in 1484, he first studied at Naples. In 1491 he was sent to Padua where he studied theology and metaphysics. Valentino da Camerino, a Dominican, had been appointed to the university's chair of Thomistic metaphysics in 1489. After Valentino was elected in 1494 to be provincial of the Roman province, he resigned his posts as professor of Thomistic metaphysics and as regent master in the Dominican *studium generale*. This was done before the 1494–5 academic year began. Despite his youth, Cajetan was called upon to fill Valentino's two posts temporarily. At the end of that academic year, he left Padua. Subsequently he taught theology at Pavia from 1497 to 1499. By 1501 he was in Rome as the procurator of the Dominican Order. He was named vicar general in 1507 and the following year he was elected master general – the head of the Dominican Order. In 1517 he was named a cardinal by Pope Leo X. The following year, while on a diplomatic mission for Leo in Germany, he had discussions with Martin LUTHER. He later wrote treatises defending the papal position. During the 1520s Cajetan turned his attention to biblical exegesis and he published commentaries on almost all the books of the Bible.

2 Logic and analogy

Although Cajetan wrote commentaries on Aristotle's *Categories* and *Posterior Analytics* and on Porphyry's *Isagōgē*, he is better known for his views on analogy, which supposedly explicate the position of Thomas AQUINAS (§9). He begins his *De Nominum Analogia* (*The Analogy of Names*), which was finished at Pavia in 1498, by lamenting that contemporary explanations of analogy are badly mistaken and lead astray those who study metaphysics. He is thereby attacking the views of fellow Dominicans, some of whom are his contemporaries. Cajetan takes 'analogy' to mean proportion or proportionality, and he claims to derive this account of the word from the Greeks, that is, from ARISTOTLE (§7). According to Cajetan, there are three types of analogy to which all other analogies can be reduced. They are (1) the analogy of inequality, (2) the analogy of attribution or proportion, and (3) the analogy of proportionality. According to the first, the analogy of inequality, there is a common term or word for the analogous things and the notion connected to the common term is wholly the same. However, the analogous things share unequally in the nature involved, for example, 'body' as found in corruptible bodies on the surface of the earth and 'body' as found in the heavenly bodies, which Cajetan (following Aristotelian tradition) takes to be incorruptible. Since the notion of body is wholly the same, namely a substance subject to three dimensions, the logician considers the analogous things to be univocal. On the other hand, the philosopher studies the actual natures of the analogous things and therefore takes the analogous things to be equivocal (different in kind). The second type of analogy, analogy according to attribution, involves things of which there is a common name and also a notion that is the same. The distinguishing feature of this type of analogy is that there are different notions involved, according to the different relationships between the analogous things and that common name. An example is the term 'healthy', when it is applied to an animal, a medicine and urine. Only the first of the analogous things actually has the perfection, namely health as pertaining to the animal, whereas the perfection is said of medicine and other things by an extrinsic denomination, that is, by a term denoting an external relationship such as 'cause of' or 'sign of'.

Finally there is analogy of proportionality, which Cajetan considers to be analogy properly so-called. The name or term and the notion are the same only proportionally. What is involved in proportionality is a comparison of proportions; for example, eight is to four as six is to three. Cajetan explains that philosophers have extended the term 'proportionality' to any similarity of proportions, so that one can say substance is to its existence as accident is to its existence. He believes that only this type of analogy enables us to know the intrinsic being, goodness and truth of things. Accordingly, he ranks analogy of proportionality above the other two types of analogy. Indeed, he judges that those who do not know and accept it are incapable of successfully studying metaphysics. Cajetan's position in fact stands in opposition to that of Thomas Aquinas, who held to analogy of proportionality only in his *Quaestiones disputatae de veritate* (Disputed Questions on Truth). Otherwise Aquinas only maintained the analogy of proportion based on attribution or reference to one First Being, namely God, and on all things other than God participating in an existence given them directly by God (see LANGUAGE, RENAISSANCE PHILOSOPHY OF).

3 Natural philosophy

In an early question entitled 'Whether Mobile Being is the Subject in Natural Philosophy', finished at Milan in 1499, Cajetan states that the limits of natural philosophy extend to and include the human soul, which is partly separated from and partly joined to matter. Neither the Intelligences that cause the motion of the heavenly bodies nor the angels are studied in natural philosophy. However, philosophers disagree as to whether their subject-matter is mobile being, mobile body, natural body or sensible substance. Cajetan takes the followers of Thomas Aquinas to hold that mobile being (which includes more than mobile body) is the true subject of natural philosophy. Accordingly, things are studied in natural philosophy from the formal aspect of their mobility (see VERNIA, N. §3).

Another key topic treated by Cajetan concerns the principle of individuation, the basis for there being a multiplicity of material individuals in the same species or kind. In his early commentary *In De Ente et Essentia divi Thomae Aquinatis* (*Commentary on 'Being and Essence'*), which was finished at Padua in 1495, Cajetan took prime matter and its capacity for a particular quantity – this quantity rather than that

quantity – to be the principle of individuation. He calls it 'designated matter' (*materia signata*) and attributes the notion to Aquinas. He later rejected this position on the grounds that the individual unity of Socrates would then be based on something accidental to him, namely quantity. Cajetan thus holds in his *Commentaria in Summa Theologiae divi Thomae Aquinatis* (Commentary on Aquinas' *Summa theologiae*) that prime matter, which is the root and cause of quantity, is prior to quantity, and of itself numerically distinct. Matter somehow pre-contains quantity.

4 Psychology

Cajetan's position on the immortality of the human soul underwent an evolution. In a sermon on immortality preached before Pope Julius II in 1503, Cajetan gave three arguments for the immortality of the human soul: that the soul knows all bodies and stands above them in judgment; that the soul has a natural desire to live forever; and that human beings enjoy a freedom of action that radically distinguishes them from the animals and can be explained only by immortality. He again maintained that human immortality was demonstrable in his *Commentaria in Primam Partem Summae Theologiae* (Commentary on the First Part of Aquinas' *Summa theologiae*), finished in 1507. He accepts Aquinas' argument that the soul must be immaterial and subsistent (that is, able to exist on its own), since it knows all material objects and therefore has an operation which it does not share with the body. He also accepts Aquinas' idea that even though the intellect depends on the phantasm for the object of cognition it is independent of the body in its very act of cognition (see AQUINAS, T. §10). Subsequently in his *Commentaria in De anima Aristotelis* (Commentary on Aristotle's *On the Soul*), finished in 1509, he points out that learned men have given opposing interpretations of Aristotle's words. He himself takes Aristotle to deny human immortality, emphasizing that for Aristotle all human cognition requires the presence of a phantasm. On the other hand, he emphasizes that he rejects the false position that, according to the principles of philosophy, the possible intellect (as opposed to the agent intellect) is corruptible. Indeed, he offers arguments for immortality on his own account. Nonetheless Cajetan was attacked for his interpretation of Aristotle by such fellow Dominicans as his former teacher, Valentino da Camerino, as well as by Francesco SILVESTRI, Bartolomeo de Spina and Crisostomo Javelli.

Some years later Cajetan came to reject any rational demonstration of immortality. In his commentary on the Epistle to the Romans, finished at Gaeta in 1528, he lists immortality with the Trinity and the Incarnation as mysteries that he accepted on faith. And in his commentary on Ecclesiastes, finished at Rome in 1534, he takes Chapter 3 to place immortality in doubt, since humans and animals are made from dust and return to dust. He then states explicitly that no philosopher has ever demonstrated immortality, that there is no demonstrative argument for immortality, and that immortality is believed on faith or is accepted on the basis of arguments that are only probable (see SOUL, NATURE AND IMMORTALITY OF THE).

In *Commentaria in De anima Aristotelis*, Cajetan observes that the human soul is treated by the natural philosopher as if it is joined to the body, but by the metaphysician as if it can be considered in abstraction from the body. Of special interest is Cajetan's interpretation of Aquinas' cognitive psychology found in his *Commentaria in Summa Theologiae*. Following Aquinas, he states that knowledge is gained by way of assimilation through a similitude (*similitudo*) of the thing known, namely an intelligible species that precedes the act of cognition. He rejects a view that had been defended by Agostino NIFO (§3) and other contemporaries, namely that an intelligible species is unnecessary since the act of cognition itself serves as the similitude. Cajetan explains that the light of the agent intellect enables the nature or quiddity that is present in the phantasm to shine forth without there also shining forth the individuality (*singularitas*) of the thing. The intelligible species is thus jointly produced in the possible intellect by a phantasm so-illuminated and by the agent intellect. Considered formally (*formaliter*), the intelligible in act is the intelligible species. But considered objectively (*obiective*), that is, from the point of view of the object known, the intelligible in act is the quiddity that the light of the agent intellect causes to shine forth in the phantasm.

5 Metaphysics

Some of Cajetan's basic metaphysical ideas differ notably from those of Aquinas, his supposed master. In his early commentary on the *Sentences* of Peter Lombard (which was never published), Cajetan closely follows Johannes CAPREOLUS, an earlier Thomist, when he speaks of essence and existence as really distinct. He adopts from Capreolus the terminology of 'the being of essence' (*esse essentiae*) and 'the being of actual existence' (*esse existentiae actualis*). The same dependence on Capreolus is found in Cajetan's *Commentary on 'Being and Essence'*, where he again characterizes the 'being of essence'

and the 'being of actual existence' as really distinct. They are 'things' (*res*) from which each creature is composed. Cajetan makes the surprising and questionable claim that this is the position of AQUINAS (§9). It should be noted that in fact while Aquinas maintains as a basic doctrine that being (*esse*) is the first actuality of all and the source of all other actualities in an individual thing, Cajetan holds that being is the last or ultimate actuality (*ultima actualitas*) in an individual thing. Indeed, it is added to essence, which appears to possess in some way a being of its own for Cajetan.

See also: AQUINAS, T. §§9, 10; ARISTOTELIANISM, RENAISSANCE; THOMISM

List of works

Cajetan [Vio, T. de] (1495) *In De Ente et Essentia divi Thomae Aquinatis*, ed. M.-H. Laurent, Turin: Marietti, 1934; trans. L.H. Kendzierski and F.C. Wade, *Cajetan: Commentary on 'Being and Essence'*, Mediaeval Philosophical Texts in Translation 14, Milwaukee, WI: Marquette University Press, 1964. (*In De Ente* was finished at Padua in 1495 and first published at Venice in 1496. While commenting on Aquinas' text, Cajetan develops metaphysical ideas of his own.)

—— (1496) *Aristotle: On Interpretation. Commentary by Saint Thomas and Cajetan (Peri Hermeneias)*, trans. J.T. Oesterle, Mediaeval Philosophical Texts in Translation 11, Milwaukee, WI: Marquette University Press, 1962. (Cajetan here completes Aquinas' commentary on the *De interpretatione*, which stopped after Book II, Lesson 2. The text of Cajetan's addition to the commentary was first published at Venice in 1496 in Aquinas' *Expositio in Libros Posteriorum et in De Interpretatione*.)

—— (1496) *In libros Posteriorum analyticorum Aristotelis additamenta* (Additions on Aristotle's *Posterior Analytics*), Venice: Simon de Luere, 1505. (This is Cajetan's own commentary on the *Posterior Analytics*, completed at Brescia in 1496.)

—— (1497) *Commentaria in Porphyrii Isagogen ad Praedicamenta Aristotelis* (Commentary on Porphyry's *Isagōgē* regarding Aristotle's *Praedicamenta*), ed. I.M. Marega, Rome: Angelicum, 1934. (Completed around 1497; first published in 1505. Contains references to Albert the Great, Aquinas and Averroes.)

—— (1498) *Scripta philosophica: Commentaria in Praedicamenta Aristotelis* (Commentary on Aristotle's *Praedicamenta*), ed. M.-H. Laurent, Rome: Angelicum, 1934. (Completed at Pavia in 1498 and first published at Venice in 1505. Cajetan thought that this work should hold first place among Aristotle's logical writings and therefore be studied even before Porphyry's *Isagōgē*.)

—— (1498) *De Nominum Analogia*, in P.H. Hering (ed.) *Scripta philosophica: De nominum analogia. De conceptu entis*, Rome: Angelicum, 1952; trans. A. Bushinski and H.J. Koren, *The Analogy of Names and the Concept of Being*, Pittsburgh, PA: Duquesne University Press, 1953. (The *De Nominum Analogia* was completed in Pavia in 1498 and published at Venice in 1506. In it Cajetan presents his views on predications about God.)

—— (1499) *Quaestio de subiecto naturalis philosophiae* (Question on the Subject of Natural Philosophy), in *Opuscula omnia*, Lyons: Juntas, 1587; repr. Hildesheim: Olms, 1995, 207–11. (Finished at Milan in 1499; first published at Venice in 1506. Cajetan defends as the position of Thomas Aquinas and his followers, the Thomists, that mobile being is the subject of natural philosophy.)

—— (1499) *Quaestio de infinitate Dei* (Question on the Infinity of God), in *Opuscula omnia*, Lyons: Juntas, 1587; repr. Hildesheim: Olms, 1995, 192–206. (Finished at Pavia in 1499 and first published at Venice in 1506. Drawing on Aquinas, Cajetan argues that God's creative power is intensively infinite since it requires no passive potency on which to operate.)

—— (1503) *Oratio habita coram Julio secundo pontifice de immortalitate animorum* (Oration before Pope Julius II on the Immortality of Souls), in *Opuscula omnia*, Lyons: Juntas, 1587; repr. Hildesheim: Olms, 1995, 186–8; trans. J.K. Sheridan, *On the Immortality of Minds*, in L.A. Kennedy (ed.) *Renaissance Philosophy: New Translations*, The Hague: Mouton, 1973, 46–54. (In this sermon delivered in 1503, Cajetan maintains that immortality can be proven and offers various arguments for it.)

—— (1507) *Commentaria in Primam Partem Summae Theologiae* (Commentary on the First Part of *Summa theologiae*), in T. Aquinas, *Opera omnia*, vol. 5, Rome: Typographia Polyglotta, 1889. (This commentary was finished at Rome in 1507 and first published in 1508.)

—— (1509) *Commentaria in De anima Aristotelis* (Commentary on Aristotle's *On the Soul*), ed. P.I. Coquelle, Rome: Angelicum, 1938–9, 2 vols; G. Picard and G. Pelland (eds) *Commentaria in libros Aristotelis De anima liber III*, Bruges: Desclée de Brouwer, 1965. (Cajetan's original *In De anima Aristotelis* was completed at Rome in February 1509 and published that same year at Florence; the first two books of the commentary appear in Coquelle, the third in Picard and Pelland.)

—— (1509) *De conceptu entis* (On the Concept of Being), in P.H. Hering (ed.) *Scripta philosophica: De nominum analogia. De conceptu entis*, Rome: Angelicum, 1952, 97–102; trans. A. Bushinski and H.J. Koren, *The Analogy of Names and the Concept of Being*, Pittsburgh, PA: Duquesne University Press, 1953, 79–83. (Finished at Rome in 1509 and published in 1511.)

—— (1978) *Cajetan Responds: A Reader in Reformation Controversy*, trans. J. Wicks, Washington, DC: The Catholic University of America Press. (Translation of various short works written against the Lutherans: introductory essays on Cajetan's biography and on Cajetan and the Reformation.)

References and further reading

Ashworth, E.J. (1992) 'Analogical Concepts: The Fourteenth-Century Background to Cajetan', *Dialogue* 21: 399–413. (Identifies the sources of three views attacked by Cajetan.)

Bobik, J. (1956) 'The *Materia Signata* of Cajetan', *The New Scholasticism* 30: 127–53. (On Cajetan's discussion of the principle of individuation.)

Gilson, E. (1953) 'Cajetan et l'existence', *Tijdschrift voor Philosophie* 15: 267–87. (Gilson poses the question: what did Cajetan think of the distinction between, or rather the composition of, essence and existence or act of being?)

—— (1955) 'Cajetan et l'humanisme théologique', *Archives d'histoire doctrinale et littéraire du moyen âge* 22: 113–36. (On Cajetan's response to Aristotle and Aquinas on the immortality of the soul.)

Gunten, A.F. von (1997) 'Cajetan et Capreolus', in G. Bedouelle, R. Cessario and K. White (eds) *Jean Capreolus et son Temps 1380–1444*, special issue of *Mémoire Dominicaine* 1: 213–38. (Shows both that Cajetan depended on Capreolus for information regarding critics of Aquinas and also that he frequently studied those critics' writings. The author also compares Cajetan's and Capreolus' positions on individuation and other topics.)

Hegyi, J. (1959) *Die Bedeutung des Seins bei den klassischen Kommentatoren des heiligen Thomas von Aquin: Capreolus, Silvester von Ferrara, Cajetan* (The Meaning of Being in the Classic Commentators on Aquinas: Capreolus, Silvestri and Cajetan), Pullacher Philosophische Forschungen 4, Pullach bei München: Berchmanskolleg, 109–48. (Full examination of Cajetan's teaching about being, beings and analogy.)

Klubertanz, G. (1960) *St Thomas Aquinas on Analogy: A Textual Analysis and Systematic Synthesis*, Chicago, IL: Loyola University Press, 5–17, 118–23,

136–7. (Some discussion of Cajetan in relation to the texts of Aquinas.)

Marc, A. (1933) 'L'idée de l'être chez Saint Thomas et dans la scolastique postérieure' (The Idea of Being in Aquinas and the Later Scholastics), in *Archives de philosophie*, Paris: Beauchesne, vol. 10, cahier 1. (Pages 50–66 of this monograph discuss Cajetan on the idea of being, including abstraction and proportional unity.)

Maurer, A. (1966) 'Cajetan's Notion of Being in his Commentary on the *Sentences*', *Mediaeval Studies* 28: 268–78. (Cajetan's position on essence and existence, as found in the unedited manuscript of his commentary on the *Sentences* of Peter Lombard. Strong dependence on Johannes Capreolus noted.)

Montagnes, B. (1963) *La doctrine de l'analogie de l'être d'après Saint Thomas d'Aquin* (The Doctrine of the Analogy of Being according to Aquinas), Philosophes médiévaux 6, Louvain: Publications Universitaires and Paris: Béatrice-Nauwelaerts, 126–58. (Discussion of Cajetan on analogy. Montagnes makes it clear that Cajetan is not a trustworthy guide to Aquinas.)

Pinchard, B. and Ricci, S. (eds) (1993) *Rationalisme analogique et humanisme théologique. La culture de Thomas de Vio 'Il Gaetano'* (Analogical Rationalism and Theological Humanism. The Culture of Cajetan), Naples: Vivarium. (A collection of fifteen essays on Cajetan's philosophy and theology.)

Poppi, A. (1966) *Causalità e infinità nella scuola padovana dal 1480 al 1513* (Causality and Infinity in the Paduan School from 1480 to 1513), Padua: Antenore, 170–85. (Discusses Cajetan on God's intensive infinity, and how this relates to God's efficient causality.)

Schwartz, H. (1954) 'Analogy in St Thomas and Cajetan', *The New Scholasticism* 28: 127–44. (Argues that Cajetan misunderstood Aquinas.)

Stöve, E. (1991) 'De Vio, Tommaso (Tommaso, Gaetano, Caetano)', *Dizionario biografico degli italiani* 39: 567–78. (Full biographical details and full bibliography of both primary and secondary sources.)

Tavuzzi, M. (1993) 'Some Renaissance Thomist Divisions of Analogy', *Angelicum* 70: 93–121. (Discussion of Cajetan's contemporaries on analogy.)

—— (1994) 'Valentino Da Camerino, O.P. (1438–1515): Teacher and Critic of Cajetan', *Traditio* 49: 287–386. (Discusses Valentino's possible influence on Cajetan; gives useful details of Cajetan's early career.)

Wells, N.J. (1968) 'On Last Looking into Cajetan's Metaphysics: A Rejoinder', *The New Scholasticism*

42: 112–7. (Relates Cajetan's position on the real distinction between essence and existence to that of Albert the Great.)

EDWARD P. MAHONEY

CALCIDIUS (*c.* 4th century AD)

The Platonist Calcidius (sometimes less correctly spelt Chalcidius) was the author of a Latin work containing a partial translation of, and partial commentary on, Plato's Timaeus. *Although of uncertain date, the doctrinal content of his commentary reflects the thought of the Middle Platonist era (c.50 BC–AD 200).*

Calcidius' date and place of operation are uncertain, the only clue residing in his dedication of his work to one Osius, who has been taken, following identifications in a number of manuscripts, to be the Bishop of Corduba (AD 256–357) and spiritual advisor of Constantine. This identification has been challenged, mainly on the grounds that Isidore of Seville makes no mention of Calcidius in his enumeration of all the Spanish writers that he knows, but this is not conclusive. It is also true that his language is more consistent with a fifth-century than a fourth-century date, but even this is not conclusive when weighed against considerations of content. The main issue is whether Calcidius is to be regarded as exclusively dependent on Middle Platonist sources or as influenced also by the *Timaeus* commentary of Porphyry. In fact, there are sufficient indications that, unless Calcidius was being very selective (which does not seem to be his method), he knows nothing of Porphyry. His work seems primarily to be a translation of a number of Middle Platonist or Peripatetic Greek sources (or even of a single such source). Identifiable sources include the second century Peripatetic Adrastus of Aphrodisias, who wrote a commentary on the *Timaeus* concentrating on the mathematical and 'scientific' aspects, and the Neo-Pythagorean NUMENIUS.

What we have is a translation of the dialogue as far as 53c, followed by a detailed commentary, beginning with *Timaeus* 31c (Calcidius ignores the introductory portion) and breaking off also at 53c (although a translation of, and commentary on, the whole seems to have been envisaged). It is hardly suitable in the case of Calcidius to speak of a distinct philosophical stance, since it is doubtful that he is putting much of himself into the commentary, but he reflects various interesting Middle Platonic positions. In chapter 176, for example, he presents a sequence of supreme god, intellect and world-soul which accords well with the systems of Numenius and ALCINOUS. The supreme god is identified with the Good of Plato's *Republic*, but there is no need to take it as a Neoplatonic One. At the other end of the scale, his doctrine that matter is neither corporeal nor incorporeal, but potentially both (chaps 319–20), agrees with that of Alcinous, APULEIUS and Hippolytus.

See also: NEOPLATONISM; NEO-PYTHAGOREANISM; PERIPATETICS; PLATONISM, EARLY AND MIDDLE

List of works

Calcidius (*c.* 4th century AD) *Timaeus a Calcidio translatus*, ed. J.H. Waszink, London: Warburg Institute, 1962; trans. J.C.M. van Winden, *Calcidius on Matter: His Doctrine and Sources*, Leiden: Brill, 1965, chaps 268–354; trans. J. den Boeft, *Calcidius on Fate: His Doctrine and Sources*, Leiden: Brill, 1970, chaps 142–90; trans. J. den Boeft, *Calcidius on Daemons*, Leiden: Brill, 1977, chaps 127–36. (Waszink is an excellent edition, with introduction, but the text is in Latin. Van Winden and den Boeft provide translations of selected chapters, with commentary.)

References and further reading

Dillon, J. (1977) *The Middle Platonists*, London: Duckworth, 401–8. (Introductory account of Calcidius.)
Gersh, S. (1986) *Middle Platonism and Neoplatonism, The Latin Tradition*, Notre Dame, IN: University of Notre Dame Press, vol. 2, 421–92.
Waszink, J.H. (1964) *Studien zum Timaioskommentar des Calcidius* (Studies on Calcidius' Commentary on Timaeus), vol. 1, Leiden: Brill. (Essays on various topics arising in the first half of the commentary; the second volume was never published.)

JOHN DILLON

CALLICLES (late 5th century BC)

Callicles, although known only as a character in Plato's Gorgias (the dramatic date of which is somewhere between 430 and 405 BC), was probably an actual historical person. Employing a distinction between nature (physis) and convention (nomos), he argues eloquently that the naturally superior should seize both political power and a greater share of material goods: it is only a convention of the weak majority which labels such behaviour unjust. In private life the superior should indulge their desires freely: excess and licence are true virtue and happiness.

Callicles is a wealthy and aristocratic young Athenian with ambitions to be a democratic leader, and the detail that Plato bestows on his portrait strongly suggests that he did in fact exist. Plato may have deliberately selected someone whose youthful promise was known to have come to nothing, as a warning against moral and intellectual indiscipline (there is a hint that Callicles was later arrested). Despite his proclaimed contempt for Sophists, his views appear indebted to those of GORGIAS and may consequently be distorted by Plato's anti-Sophistic bias (see PLATO; SOPHISTS).

Callicles attacks Socrates' claim that doing wrong is more shameful than being wronged (see SOCRATES §4). This, he argues, is simply the conventional notion of justice, which is nothing but a craven invention of the weak majority to restrain the stronger few: the weak proclaim that equality of both power and wealth is 'just' because equality is the most they can expect. In nature, however, might is right, as is clear from both the animal kingdom and interstate relations. This is not simply brute fact, but a prescription: it is true justice, the 'law of nature'. It is thus naturally more shameful to suffer wrong than to do it, as the former shows that one is too weak to protect oneself and one's own. Natural justice decrees that those who are superior in courage, manliness and practical competence should appropriate both political control and the greater share of goods, and it is similarly a natural imperative that the superman should freely indulge his physical desires; the convention that praises self-restraint again results from a conspiracy of the weak majority who lack the natural force to satisfy their own urges. Breaking free from convention is the mark of nature's lions, and such 'real men' are in sharp contrast to the feeble, impractical philosopher.

By appealing to an alternative 'natural justice', Callicles is more radical than contemporary supporters of *physis* over *nomos*, such as ANTIPHON and THRASYMACHUS, who employ 'justice' solely in its conventional sense. He implies an antithesis between reason and desire, the latter being the true self. Any restraint on the desires, whether from society or from one's reason, is thus an unacceptable infringement of personal liberty. He is adamant that it is he, not Socrates, who truly understands human nature.

Callicles' defence of natural force is open to challenge, particularly for its appeal to the animal world. His notion of 'natural justice', being based on nothing more than description of the existing order, would be accused by some philosophers of committing the 'naturalistic fallacy' (see NATURALISM IN ETHICS §3). Furthermore, it is debatable whether his depiction of animal predators is correct. Do they really pursue individual interests to the total exclusion of group conventions? And if such apparent 'conventions' are simply a manifestation of their 'nature', does this not dissolve the antithesis on which Callicles relies?

It is also unclear whether human aggression is as natural as Callicles claims (he implies that everyone would imitate the superman if they could). Some would argue that, although we all possess egoistic drives, they only develop into ruthlessly competitive behaviour when encouraged by society. The only 'natural' aspect of the aggressive superman might be that it is natural to absorb social conventions, for good or ill. This, however, would only demonstrate again that Callicles' required antithesis between nature and culture is false.

Nor does he appear to have thought through what a society run by supermen would be like. How would they behave towards each other? Or would a single superman emerge from each community? And presumably the laws made by such supermen would have to command Callicles' respect. In disparaging manmade *nomoi*, he simply assumes a democratic framework. (The relation between Callicles' contemptuous dismissal of the majority and his democratic aspirations is an intriguing question in itself.)

Despite these and other inconsistencies and philosophic shortcomings, Callicles is an important figure. There is evidence that he was a strong influence on NIETZSCHE and it is not difficult to see why. He challenges us to reconsider the origins and nature of social 'morality' and makes a vigorous bid for the possibility of self-directed virtues. He raises pertinent questions about the nature of 'manliness' and the relative merits of the active and the contemplative life. Above all, he forces us to reflect on the issues of personal identity and freedom, on which all his arguments depend.

See also: PHYSIS AND NOMOS

References and further reading

Berman, S. (1991) 'Socrates and Callicles on Pleasure', *Phronesis* 36: 117–40. (A lucid and lively discussion.)

Guthrie, W.K.C. (1969) *A History of Greek Philosophy*, vol. 3, Cambridge: Cambridge University Press; part of vol. 3 repr. as *The Sophists*, Cambridge: Cambridge University Press, 1971. (Helpful discussions of Callicles, especially pages 101–7.)

Kerferd, G.B. (1981) *The Sophistic Movement*, Cambridge: Cambridge University Press. (The best introductory handbook to the Sophists in general.)

* Plato (c.395–387 BC) *Gorgias*, ed. E.R. Dodds, Oxford: Clarendon Press, 1959; trans. T. Irwin, Oxford: Clarendon Press, 1979. (The earlier edition is scholarly and sensitive; it includes Greek text, with introduction and commentary and contains a useful appendix on Callicles and Nietzsche; the translation, with introduction and notes, contains a crisp and rigorous appraisal of Callicles' philosophical position.)

ANGELA HOBBS

CALVIN, JOHN (1509–64)

John Calvin, French Protestant reformer and theologian, was a minister among Reformed Christians in Geneva and Strasbourg. His Institutes of the Christian Religion *(first edition 1536) – which follows the broad outline of the Apostles' Creed and is shaped by biblical and patristic thought – is the cornerstone of Reformed theology.*

Calvin's religious epistemology links self-knowledge and knowledge of God. He identifies in humans an innate awareness of God, which is supported by the general revelation of God in creation and providence. Because sin has corrupted this innate awareness, Scripture – confirmed by the Holy Spirit – is needed for genuine knowledge of God. Scripture teaches that God created the world out of nothing and sustains every part of it. Humanity, which was created good and with free will, has defaced itself and lost significant freedom due to its fall into sin. Calvin sees Christ the mediator as the fulfilment of the Old Testament offices of prophet, priest and king.

Calvin insists that God justifies sinners on the basis of grace and not works, forgiving their sins and imputing Christ's righteousness to them. Such justification, received by faith, glorifies God and relieves believers' anxiety about their status before God. On the basis of his will alone, God predestines some individuals to eternal life and others to eternal damnation.

Calvin dignifies even ordinary occupations by seeing them as service to God. He recognizes the distinction between civil government and the Church, although he says that government should protect true worship of God and Christians should obey and support their government. Calvin's thought was dominant in non-Lutheran Protestant churches until the eighteenth century and has enjoyed a resurgence since the mid nineteenth century.

1 Life

John Calvin was born in Noyon, France. He spent five years studying Latin grammar and the arts at the University of Paris, where he became acquainted with both scholastic and humanist thought. After his father withdrew him from preparation for an ecclesiastical career, Calvin studied civil law at the University of Orléans and the University of Bourges. He received the licentiate in law in 1532 and, in the same year, published a commentary on the Stoic philosopher Seneca's *De clementia*, thereby establishing his credentials as a humanist familiar with ancient thought.

By 1534 Calvin publicly advocated ecclesiastical reform in France, which meant that he had broken with the papacy; he spent the rest of his life as a refugee. The first edition of the *Institutes of the Christian Religion*, written while he was in exile in Basle, was published in 1536. Several major revisions and expansions of the work appeared in both Latin and French, including the definitive Latin edition of 1559. Addressed to King Francis I of France, the preface to the *Institutes* argues that, since the reform movement is the legitimate heir to the Christianity of the Scriptures and the early Church and is not seditious, it should be protected from persecution.

In 1536, during a stop in Geneva on his way to Strasbourg, Calvin was persuaded to stay and assist the ecclesiastical reformers. Tensions between the reformers and the city council led to Calvin's expulsion from Geneva in 1538. After ministering in Strasbourg, he returned to Geneva in 1541 and remained there until his death. His pastoral work in Geneva and Strasbourg focused on ministry to French Protestant refugees.

Calvin has been criticized for his involvement in the death of the notorious heretic Michael Servetus in 1555. Having already escaped execution elsewhere for his heterodox Trinitarian views, Servetus appeared in Geneva, was arrested at Calvin's insistence, and was condemned to death by the city council. He was burned at the stake despite Calvin's request that he be beheaded instead.

In addition to the *Institutes*, Calvin wrote many polemical works as well as commentaries on most of the books of the Bible, and engaged in preaching and pastoral work. He founded the Genevan Academy in 1559.

2 Religious epistemology

'Nearly the whole of sacred doctrine consists in these two parts: knowledge of God and of ourselves.' In this opening line of the 1536 edition of the *Institutes* (and every edition thereafter), Calvin announces his fundamental project of describing how we acquire this twofold knowledge and summarizing its content. Self-knowledge and knowledge of God are interrelated: self-knowledge leads us to be displeased with ourselves, thereby arousing us to seek God, the source of all good; and knowledge of God is required for a clear awareness of ourselves – especially of our folly and corruption.

Knowledge of God is not 'empty' or 'cold' speculation that 'merely flits in the brain', but rather knowledge that 'takes root in the heart' and includes the honouring of God (*Inst.*, 1.5.9; 1.12.1). Such reverence for and love of God, which Calvin calls 'piety', results from recognizing that we owe everything to God, are nourished by his fatherly care and should seek nothing beyond him.

Calvin insists that all humans have, by natural instinct, an awareness of divinity (*sensus divinitatis*). The universal need for religion – even idolatrous religion – shows that God has implanted in all people a seed of religion, a natural awareness 'that there is a God and that he is their Maker' (*Inst.*, 1.3.1). Religion was not 'invented by the subtlety and craft of a few to hold the simple folk in thrall' (*Inst.*, 1.3.2).

Lest anyone be excluded from access to happiness by lack of knowledge of God, says Calvin, God has also 'engraved unmistakable marks of his glory' upon the universe (*Inst.*, 1.5.1). The 'skillful ordering of the universe is for us a sort of mirror' reflecting the invisible God (*Inst.*, 1.5.1). And nursing infants 'have tongues so eloquent to preach [God's] glory that there is no need at all of other orators' (*Inst.*, 1.5.3). Although we have within ourselves 'a workshop graced with God's unnumbered works' that should lead us to break forth in praise of God, instead we are 'puffed up and swollen with all the more pride' because we see nature rather than God as the source of these good gifts (*Inst.*, 1.5.4).

God's glory is also displayed outside the ordinary course of nature, in his declaring clemency to the godly and showing severity to the wicked, protecting the innocent, and caring for the poor in their desperate straits. Yet most people, 'immersed in their own errors, are struck blind in such a dazzling theater', and do not recognize the glory of God (*Inst.*, 1.5.8).

Although God represents himself in the mirror of his works with great clarity, we grow dull towards such clear testimonies and presumptuously fashion a deity of our own imagining. Our minds are like springs pouring forth gods we have invented for ourselves. Even philosophers adore a shameful diversity of gods (*Inst.*, 1.5.11–12).

Since there is no pure religion founded upon common understanding alone, we need the witness of God himself, 'illumined by the inner revelation of God through faith' (*Inst.*, 1.5.13, 14). 'Just as old or bleary-eyed men and those with weak vision' can scarcely see until they put on spectacles, 'so Scripture, gathering up the otherwise confused knowledge of God in our minds, having dispersed our dullness, clearly shows us the true God' (*Inst.*, 1.6.1). Calvin recognizes, however, that Scripture must be confirmed as the living word of God. Neither the consent of the Church nor disputation in defence of Scripture will imprint on people's hearts the certainty and assurance that piety requires. The Spirit who spoke through the prophets must penetrate into our hearts to persuade us that they faithfully proclaimed what God spoke to them; the inner testimony of the Holy Spirit 'is more excellent than all reason' (*Inst.*, 1.7.4). In response to religious fanatics or enthusiasts who abandon Scripture and claim a new revelation from the Spirit, Calvin argues that God has forged a mutual bond between Word and Spirit, with the Spirit, as the author of Scripture, attesting the Word of God in Scripture and the Word leading us to recognize the true Spirit of God.

For Calvin, faith is 'a firm and certain knowledge of God's benevolence toward us, founded upon the truth of the freely given promise in Christ, both revealed to our minds and sealed upon our hearts through the Holy Spirit' (*Inst.*, 3.2.7). Knowledge of the unseen God does not involve comprehension, as with objects of sense perception, but rather consists in assurance of God's goodness towards us, which depends on our 'truly feeling its sweetness and experiencing it in ourselves' (*Inst.*, 3.2.15). Then, despite temptations and doubts, believers will 'either rise up out of the very gulf of temptations, or stand fast upon their watch', confident of God's mercy to them (*Inst.*, 3.2.21, 37).

3 God, creation and providence

Calvin emphasizes God's sovereignty and glory. He introduces the notion of accommodation in order to account for Scripture's speaking of God's mouth, ears, eyes, hands and feet (*Inst.*, 1.13.1); of God's repenting of having created the world or of having made Saul king of Israel (*Inst.*, 1.17.12); and even of God's wrath against sin (*Inst.*, 1.17.13; 2.16.2, 4). Such images 'do not so much express clearly what God is like as accommodate the knowledge of him to our slight capacity' (*Inst.*, 1.13.1).

Calvin affirms that God created the world by his own free will and follows Augustine in rejecting speculation about why God created the world when he did. He shows little interest in the duration or sequence of the events of creation, focusing instead on the spiritual value of observing that God created, out of nothing, an abundance and variety of creatures, each with its own nature and assigned functions, that God formed humanity as 'the most excellent example of his works', and that God has provided for the preservation of the entire creation (*Inst.*, 1.14.20). The goodness of creation should lead us to take 'pious delight in the works of God open and manifest in this most beautiful theater' (*Inst.*, 1.14.20).

Proper self-knowledge, says Calvin, is twofold: knowing what we were like when first created and knowing our condition after the Fall of Adam. As created, humans had rational minds to know their duty, and wills to direct the appetites under the guidance of reason. Only if humanity had not fallen would those philosophers be correct who hold that moral accountability depends on having free choice between good and evil. By sinning, Adam lost God's good gifts for himself and for his descendants, with the result that fallen human beings lack the ability to carry out their duty. Still, says Calvin, in being subject to the depravity and corruption of our nature, or original sin, we are not held liable for the transgression of another; the contagion imparted by Adam resides in us (see SIN §2).

Calvin insists that we see God's power as much in the continuing state of the universe as in its creation. God not only drives the 'celestial frame', but also 'sustains, nourishes, and cares for everything he has made, even to the least sparrow' (*Inst.*, 1.16.1). Since all events proceed from God's plan, 'nothing takes place by chance' – not even if a branch falls and kills a passing traveller (*Inst.*, 1.16.4, 6). Calvin argues that, unlike the Stoic dogma of fate, the doctrine of providence sees God as the ruler of all things who 'in accordance with his wisdom' has from eternity decreed what he was going to do and now carries it out (*Inst.*, 1.16.8).

If God wills all things, does he also will what is evil? Calvin argues that it is absurd to substitute 'bare permission' in the place of God's providence 'as if God sat in a watchtower awaiting chance events, and his judgments thus depended upon human will' (*Inst.*, 1.16.8; 1.18.1). Humans can accomplish nothing except by God's secret command. In response to the charge that God would then have two contrary wills – a revealed will that forbids sin and a secret will that decrees evil actions – Calvin says that God's will is one and simple in him but appears manifold to us because we cannot grasp how God both wills and does not will something to take place. Many Reformed theologians, while insisting with Calvin that all things are governed by God's providence, have departed from him by distinguishing between the active and the permissive will of God.

Calvin's affirmation of God's goodness in relation to evil events hinges on Augustine's insight that there is a great difference between what it is fitting for a human being to will and what is fitting for God. In opposition to those who 'wish nothing to be lawful for God beyond what their own reason prescribes for themselves', Calvin says that nothing but right flows from providence, although the reasons have been hidden from us (*Inst.*, 1.17.2). Conceding that his doctrine of providence might seem harsh, Calvin says we should not refuse to accept a teaching attested by clear Scriptural proofs just because it exceeds our understanding. In addition, believers can have gratitude for favourable outcomes, patience in adversity, and freedom from worry about the future because they know that all things are ruled by their heavenly father.

4   Christ and salvation

Even sinless humanity, says Calvin, would have needed a mediator in order to reach God. Yet the need for this mediator to be truly human as well as truly divine was due to our sin. The purpose of the incarnation was for Christ the mediator to become the redeemer, restoring the fallen world and assisting lost humanity in its distress.

Calvin's theology of the atonement emphasizes both Christ's victory over the powers of evil and his satisfaction of God's righteous judgment. Death held humanity captive, says Calvin, but Christ, in our stead, submitted to the power of death, grappled hand-to-hand with the armies of hell, and arose from the dead victorious over them. Alternatively, Calvin says that humanity's reconciliation with God requires the countering of disobedience with obedience, which Christ does in our place, paying what we could not pay and thereby acquiring righteousness for us (see ATONEMENT §4).

Like Martin LUTHER, Calvin says that the doctrine of justification is the main hinge on which true religion turns. To be *justified* in God's sight means that one is counted righteous by God; to be justified *by faith* means that one who is in fact a sinner 'grasps the righteousness of Christ through faith, and clothed

in it, appears in God's sight' not as sinful but as righteous (*Inst.*, 3.11.2). God justifies sinners by remitting their sins and imputing Christ's righteousness to them. God first freely embraces the sinner who is utterly void of good works and then conveys a sense of divine goodness that leads the sinner to despair of works and to rely wholly on God's mercy. So the faith through which sinners are justified is not itself a work that qualifies them for salvation, but rather God's gracious gift through which they receive God's mercy (see JUSTIFICATION, RELIGIOUS §4).

In his doctrine of predestination, Calvin attempts to avoid the twin dangers of either probing into matters that God wills to remain hidden or neglecting what Scripture says. Scripture presents two types of election: the general election of a nation or people, such as ancient Israel or the Church; and the election or predestination of individuals. Although God does not grant regeneration and perseverance to every member of an elect people, he works in the heart of each elect individual, granting perseverance so that this election is assured. Calvin observes that election involves the adoption 'in Christ into the eternal inheritance' of those who in themselves are unworthy of this adoption (*Inst.*, 3.22.1) (see PREDESTINATION; PROVIDENCE §§3–4; REPROBATION).

Predestination, then, is God's eternal decree regarding each individual, foreordaining eternal life for some and eternal damnation for others. This foreordination is not based on God's having foreseen the holiness of the elect or the sinfulness of the reprobate, but only in God's will, which to us is inscrutable. Mirroring election, reprobation is based in God's will, not in foreknowledge of the sinfulness of the reprobate. Calvin's doctrine of reprobation, which is rooted in his rejection of the idea of God's permissive will (see §3 above), differs from that of many Reformed theologians, who hold that God wills to elect some, thereby leaving the others in the ruin they incur by their sins.

5   Social and political thought

Calvin recognizes the dignity of each occupation – not just that of the clergy – as service to God. God has given each individual a calling or vocation 'as a sort of sentry post', to prevent heedless wandering about throughout life. Each person will fulfil his or her calling willingly, bearing its weariness and anxieties, if it is seen as a duty to God. 'No task', says Calvin, 'will be so sordid and base, provided you obey your calling in it, that it will not shine and be reckoned very precious in God's sight' (*Inst.*, 3.10.6).

Calvin argues that, since 'Christ's spiritual Kingdom and the civil jurisdiction are things completely distinct', legal or social distinctions of rank or privilege should not apply in Christ's realm (*Inst.*, 4.20.1). Nevertheless, civil government and the Church are to be mutually supportive. Accordingly, civil government should 'protect the outward worship of God' and even defend sound doctrine (*Inst.*, 4.20.2–3). Civil magistrates, who are given authority by God and serve as God's deputies, should embody divine providence, goodness, benevolence and justice. Governments may levy taxes, but should regard the revenues as treasuries of the people that must not be squandered.

Christians, for their part, must regard all magistrates as God's representatives, not as a necessary evil. Subjects should obey their government, pay taxes and accept service in public office or for military defence. Even wicked and unjust magistrates have been ordained by God and should be held by their subjects in the same esteem as they would hold the best of monarchs. Still, Calvin recognizes means for holding unjust rulers in check. Sometimes God raises up avengers to punish the wicked government, as when a just nation defeats a nation ruled by an evil leader; sometimes God appoints lesser magistrates to restrain unjust kings. Even common subjects must not allow their obedience to rulers to lead them to follow commands contrary to God's revealed will (*Inst.*, 4.20.32; *Comm.* on Daniel 6: 22) (see RELIGION AND POLITICAL PHILOSOPHY).

6 Influence

Calvin's thought has had a wide influence in the Church, society and the academic world. His theology sparked movements for ecclesiastical reform that led to Reformed churches in continental Europe, Presbyterian churches in the United Kingdom, and Puritan groups that sought refuge in the American colonies. Owing to the effects of the Enlightenment and liberal Protestant thought, Calvinist theology declined in influence during the eighteenth and nineteenth centuries. Since the middle of the nineteenth century, however, Calvin's thought has enjoyed a resurgence, having provided impetus to a Calvinist revival in the Netherlands led by Abraham Kuyper and to the neo-orthodoxy that flourished in the middle of the twentieth century under the leadership of Karl Barth and Emil Brunner. Calvin's religious epistemology has also influenced the development of 'Reformed epistemology' by Alvin Plantinga and Nicholas Wolterstorff (see RELIGION, HISTORY OF PHILOSOPHY OF §8; RELIGION AND EPISTEMOLOGY).

List of works

Calvin, J. (1528–64) *Ioannis Calvini opera quae supersunt omnia*, ed. J.W. Baum, A.E. Cunitz and E. Reuss, Brunswick and Berlin: C.A. Schwetschke, 1863–1900, 59 vols. (The standard scholarly edition of Calvin's works, published as part of the Corpus Reformatorum.)

—— (1528–64) *Selected Works of John Calvin: Tracts and Letters*, ed. H. Beveridge and J. Bonnet, 1844–58; repr. Grand Rapids, MI: Baker, 1983, 7 vols. (Reprint of a nineteenth-century translation of Calvin's tracts and letters.)

—— (1536) *Institutes of the Christian Religion*, trans. F.L. Battles, Grand Rapids, MI: Eerdmans, rev. edn, 1986. (A valuable translation of the first edition of the *Institutes*.)

—— (1540–64) *Calvin's Commentaries*, trans. Calvin Translation Society, 1843–55; reprint, Grand Rapids, MI: Baker, 1979, 22 vols. (Reprint of a good nineteenth-century translation of Calvin's commentaries, including the best English translation of his New Testament commentaries.)

—— (1551–64) *Calvin's Old Testament Commentaries*, Rutherford House translation, ed. D.F. Wright, Grand Rapids, MI: Eerdmans and Carlisle: Paternoster, 1993–. (The best English translation of Calvin's Old Testament commentaries.)

—— (1552) *Concerning the Eternal Predestination of God*, trans. J.K.S. Reid, Cambridge: James Clarke, 1961. (An important treatise by Calvin on predestination.)

—— (1559) *Institutes of the Christian Religion*, ed. J.T. McNeill, trans. F.L. Battles, The Library of Christian Classics, Philadelphia, PA: Westminster, 1960, 2 vols. (The standard translation of the definitive 1559 edition.)

References and further reading

Dowey, E.A., Jr (1952) *The Knowledge of God in Calvin's Theology*, New York: Columbia University Press; expanded edn, Grand Rapids, MI: Eerdmans, 1994. (A classic study of Calvin on the knowledge of God.)

Duke, A., Lewis, G. and Pettegree, A. (eds) (1992) *Calvinism in Europe, 1540–1610: A Collection of Documents*, Manchester and New York: Manchester University Press. (A selection and translation of important documents related to the development and spread of Calvinism.)

Ganoczy, A. (1987) *The Young Calvin*, trans. D. Foxgrover and W. Provo, Philadelphia, PA: Westminster. (An important study of Calvin's background and early theological development.)

Graham, W.F. (1971) *The Constructive Revolutionary: John Calvin and His Socio-Economic Impact*, Richmond, VA: John Knox. (A standard work on Calvin's social and political thought.)

Greef, W. de (1994) *The Writings of John Calvin: An Introductory Guide*, trans. L.D. Bierma, Grand Rapids, MI: Baker. (A solid introductory survey of Calvin's life and writings, with good primary and secondary bibliographies.)

McKim, D.K. (ed.) (1984) *Readings in Calvin's Theology*, Grand Rapids, MI: Baker. (Includes several important essays on Calvin's thought.)

McNeill, J.T. (1954) *The History and Character of Calvinism*, Oxford: Oxford University Press. (A classic study of Calvin, his background and his influence.)

Muller, R.A. (1986) *Christ and the Decree: Christology and Predestination in Reformed Theology from Calvin to Perkins*, Durham, NC: Labyrinth Press. (An important study of the doctrine of predestination in sixteenth-century Reformed theology.)

Niesel, W. (1956) *The Theology of Calvin*, trans. H. Knight, London: Lutterworth. (A classic study of Calvin's theological system.)

Parker, T.H.L. (1975) *John Calvin: A Biography*, Philadelphia, PA: Westminster. (A very good biography of Calvin.)

Pettegree, A, Duke, A. and Lewis, G. (eds) (1994) *Calvinism in Europe, 1540–1620*, Cambridge: Cambridge University Press. (A collection of original essays on the early development and spread of Calvinism.)

Plantinga, A. and Wolterstorff, N. (eds) (1983) *Faith and Rationality: Reason and Belief in God*, Notre Dame, IN and London: University of Notre Dame Press. (Includes seminal essays on Reformed epistemology.)

Prestwich, M. (ed.) (1985) *International Calvinism, 1541–1715*, Oxford: Clarendon Press. (Valuable essays on the development of Calvinism.)

Schreiner, S.E. (1991) *The Theater of His Glory: Nature and the Natural Order in the Thought of John Calvin*, Durham, NC: Labyrinth Press. (An important study of nature, providence and natural law in Calvin.)

Steinmetz, D. (1995) *Calvin in Context*, New York and Oxford: Oxford University Press. (A study of Calvin's thought in its historical context and in relation to his contemporaries.)

Wendel, F. (1963) *Calvin: Origins and Development of His Religious Thought*, trans. P. Mairet, New York: Harper & Row. (An excellent introduction to Calvin's life and to the *Institutes*.)

RONALD J. FEENSTRA

CALVINISM *see* CALVIN, JOHN

CAMBRIDGE PLATONISM

Cambridge Platonism was an intellectual movement broadly inspired by the Platonic tradition, centred in Cambridge from the 1630s to the 1680s. Its hallmark was a devotion to reason in metaphysics, religion and ethics. The Cambridge Platonists made reason rather than tradition and inspiration their ultimate criterion of knowledge. Their central aim was to reconcile the realms of reason and faith, the new natural philosophy and Christian revelation. Although loyal to the methods and naturalism of the new sciences, they opposed its mechanical model of explanation because it seemed to leave no room for spirit, God and life.

In epistemology the Cambridge Platonists were critics of empiricism and stressed the role of reason in knowledge; they also criticized conventionalism and held that there are essential or natural distinctions between things. In metaphysics they attempted to establish the existence of spirit, God and life in a manner consistent with the naturalism and method of the new sciences. And in ethics the Cambridge Platonists defended moral realism and freedom of the will against the voluntarism and determinism of Hobbes and Calvin. Cambridge Platonism was profoundly influential in the seventeenth and eighteenth centuries. It was the inspiration behind latitudinarianism and ethical rationalism, and many of its ideas were developed by Samuel Clarke, Isaac Newton and the Third Earl of Shaftesbury.

1 Origins and context
2 Epistemology
3 Metaphysics
4 Ethics

1 Origins and context

The term 'Cambridge Platonism' has been used to refer to a group of thinkers active in Cambridge from the late 1630s to the 1680s, who were in one form or another inspired by the Platonic tradition of philosophy. Most of them were either fellows or students of two colleges, Emmanuel and Christ's. Their inner circle consisted of Henry MORE (1614–87), Ralph CUDWORTH (1617–88), John Smith (1618–52) and Benjamin Whichcote (1609–83), who was its leading figure. Their outer circle of associates within Cambridge comprised John Sherman (d. 1666), John Worthington (1618–80), Peter Sterry (1613–72), George Rust (1626–70) and Nathaniel CULVERWELL

(1618–51). There were also thinkers outside Cambridge who were closely connected with, and often shared the views of, the Cambridge Platonists: John NORRIS (1657–1711), Joseph GLANVILL (1636–80) and Richard BURTHOGGE (c.1638–c.1704). Among the disciples of the Cambridge school were some important latitudinarian divines: Simon Patrick (1626–1707), Edward Fowler (1632–1714), John Tillotson (1630–94), John Moore (1646–1714), Gilbert Burnet (1643–1715), Edward Stillingfleet (1635–99) and Thomas Tenison (1636–1715).

Cambridge Platonism represents the most concerted and systematic attempt in seventeenth-century English thought to reconcile the claims of reason and faith, philosophy and religion. Cudworth and More were the first thinkers in the English Protestant tradition to develop a sophisticated natural theology. Some of their most substantive works – More's *Antidote to Atheism* (1653) and *Immortality of the Soul* (1659), Cudworth's *A Treatise concerning Eternal and Immutable Morality* (1731) and *True Intellectual System of the Universe* (1678) – were devoted to precise and detailed demonstrations of the existence of God, providence and immortality. True to the tradition of Florentine Platonism (see PLATONISM, RENAISSANCE §4), and contrary to BACON and orthodox Protestantism, the Cambridge men sometimes completely identified the realms of reason and faith, as if nature and revelation were only different hypostases or degrees of manifestation of the divine goodness. They held that the truths of revelation are only a more spiritual form of reason, and the truths of reason only a more natural form of revelation. But they did not always adhere to this equation and sometimes abandoned it in the face of the more recalcitrant Christian mysteries, such as the Trinity and Incarnation, which were conceded to be above, although never contrary to, reason.

Cambridge Platonism began as a reaction to the more severe tenets of Calvinist theology, especially its doctrine of predestination. In their early years Whichcote, Cudworth and More were repelled by Calvin's *deus absconditus*, which by some 'dark and inscrutable decrees' predestined people, regardless of their merits, to either salvation or damnation (see CALVIN, J. §4). This undermined not only certainty regarding salvation, but also moral responsibility. The great attraction of Platonism was that it made the ways of God accountable to man, so that he could be sure of his eternal election. Platonism meant that there are eternal forms of good and evil, which God never violates, and which are discernible by reason.

In the seventeenth-century dispute concerning 'the rule of faith' or the ultimate criterion of religious knowledge, the Cambridge Platonists stood firmly in the camp of reason. They opposed enthusiasm, which appealed to inspiration, no less than Roman Catholic 'dogmatism', which referred to apostolic tradition. It is important to recognize, however, that the Cambridge men defended reason only because they had a Platonic conception of it. They saw reason as a mystical faculty, a power of vision, which is guided by divine grace. They opposed the formal concept of reason prevalent in the nominalist tradition, according to which it is merely a power of inference. They also rejected Socinianism because of its critical attitude toward traditional Christian doctrine (see SOCINIANISM).

During the seventeenth-century controversy regarding ecclesiastical polity, the Cambridge Platonists attempted to walk a middle path between Laudianism and Puritanism, High-Church Anglicanism and Presbyterianism. They denied a common premise to these extreme positions: that church government and discipline is *jure divino*, prescribed by divine decree and determinable by Scripture. They argued that all such matters are indifferent, and should be determined by the civil sovereign alone. Anticipating the latitudinarians, they stressed the need for a comprehensive church whose creed was broad enough to accommodate all Christians (see LATITUDINARIANISM).

2 Epistemology

The epistemology of the Cambridge school was chiefly a defence of essentialism and rationalism against the conventionalism and empiricism of the nominalist tradition (see CONVENTIONALISM; EMPIRICISM; ESSENTIALISM; RATIONALISM). In his *A Treatise concerning Eternal and Immutable Morality*, the main epistemological work of the Cambridge school, Cudworth argued that things are what they are in virtue of the necessity of their nature or essence alone, and not in virtue of some divine command or power. God cannot make two plus two equal five, or the nature of a triangle such that its three angles are not equal to two right angles. It is an eternal and necessary truth that, given the concept of two and the concept of addition, two plus two equals four, and that, given the concept of a triangle, its three angles are equal to 180 degrees. Although the will of God is indeed the supreme efficient cause of all things, it is not their formal cause.

The Cambridge Platonists criticized empiricism as much as conventionalism. Anticipating Leibniz and Kant, Cudworth and More pointed out how the conditions of knowledge cannot be satisfied by the senses: knowledge requires judgment, but the senses do not judge. Knowledge also involves universality and necessity, whereas the senses show us only particularity and contingency. Furthermore, the senses are entirely passive, though knowledge demands activity, making sensations conform to innate laws. Finally, the object of the senses is given, distinct from the knower, but knowledge requires the identity of the knower and known, reason's contemplation of its own creations. Contrary to empiricism, Cudworth advocated a rationalist paradigm of knowledge, according to which true knowledge derives from deduction, consisting in 'a descending comprehension of a thing from the universal ideas of the mind, and not an ascending perception of them from individuals by sense'.

The Cambridge Platonists became notorious for their doctrine of innate ideas, which was the apparent target of Locke's famous polemic (see LOCKE, J. §2). But Cudworth, More and Culverwell explicitly rejected the view that the mind has pre-formed ideas prior to experience. They understood innateness in terms of the inherent *activities* and *faculties* of the mind, and stressed that these had to be stimulated by experience.

Cudworth and More had a clear response to Descartes' radical scepticism, which posed a serious challenge to the rationalism of the Cambridge school. They remarked that Descartes could not escape his radical doubt by his proof of the existence of God, since such a demonstration presupposes the truth of our faculties. They also maintained that there is a false premise behind Cartesian doubt: that knowledge requires the correspondence between concepts and an external reality. Since reason creates its object in the act of knowing it, we need not seek truth outside ourselves. Finally, they contended that we have no general reason to doubt our faculties if they normally supply clear and distinct ideas on specific occasions (see DESCARTES, R. §4).

3 Metaphysics

The Cambridge Platonists had an ambivalent attitude towards the new natural philosophy which blossomed during their era. They admired its methods of observation and experiment; they shared its distaste for the verbiage of the old scholasticism; and they accepted its naturalism, its belief that everything conforms to law. But they feared the consequences of the new mechanical model of explanation of Descartes and BOYLE. If this paradigm were generalized, then it would leave no room for spirit, life or God. The aim of the Cambridge Platonists was therefore to secure a place for spirit, life and God while upholding the naturalism and methods of the new philosophy.

Cudworth and More argued that mechanism alone cannot account for such phenomena as gravity and cohesion in the material world, or generation and growth in the organic world. To explain such phenomena, they postulated the existence of a 'plastic power' or 'spirit of nature', a concept deriving from the *logoi spermatikoi* or *rationes seminales* of the Stoic and Neoplatonic tradition (see STOICISM §5). This concept posits a living force within matter, a self-generating and self-organizing power. Although it is subconscious, this power is also purposive. It is the instrument of God himself, the means by which he achieves his ends in the material world. Cudworth and More denied that their spirit amounts to an occult force, and maintained that it alone avoids the extremes of supernaturalism and mechanism. If supernaturalism admits constant miracles in nature, mechanism derives design from chance. Only the plastic power explains design according to the requirements of naturalism.

To Henry More, the dangers of the new mechanism were most apparent in Descartes' distinction between the mind and body as thinking and extended substance. If *only* matter is extended, then spirit cannot exist, because what is unextended does not exist anywhere or in any place. If something exists, then it must be somewhere, and therefore extended. Boldly, More concluded that spirit too is extended. He maintained that its essential nature consists in a fourth dimension, 'spissitude', the power to expand or contract the space it occupies. Far from being the exclusive attribute of matter, infinite space has many attributes in common with God himself, and it amounts to the divine presence in nature itself. This conception of space later inspired Newton to call space 'the sensorium of God' (see DESCARTES, R. §8; NEWTON, I.).

Although the Cambridge Platonists criticized Cartesian dualism, they introduced one of their own. They attributed opposing characteristics to spirit and matter: spirit is indivisible, active and penetrable, while matter is divisible, passive and impenetrable. Although they postulated their plastic power partly to uphold the continuity of nature, they also understood it to be a spiritual substance distinct in kind from matter. Unlike the vital materialists of the eighteenth century, they did not employ this doctrine to show that mind and body differ only in degree, as if they were only more or less organized forms of living force (see DUALISM).

4 Ethics

The hallmarks of the ethics of Cambridge Platonism are realism and rationalism. Its realism grew from its reaction against Hobbes' and Calvin's voluntarism. What makes something good or evil, the Platonists contended, is not simply the will of some sovereign power, whether that is God or the civil ruler; rather, it is the thing's eternal essence or nature, which exists independent of contract, convention or will.

The rationalism of their ethics is apparent from the insistence that we know the nature of good and evil through reason alone. They stress that reason determines not only the means, but also the ends of action. Although they were rationalists, they did not advocate an ethics of duty in the modern Kantian sense. Unlike Kant, they did not distinguish between adherence to principle and conformity to nature, the promotion of human perfection.

The Cambridge men also opposed Hobbes' and Calvin's determinism no less than their voluntarism. They defended freedom of the will in the strong sense as a *liberum arbitrium*: the power to choose and act otherwise, and not simply to act on my desires without constraint. They contended that moral responsibility is incompatible with the necessity prevalent in nature. They were especially repelled by the bleak view of humanity in Hobbes and Calvin, and denied that human nature had been so ruined by the Fall that it could not do good by its own efforts. Although they did not dispute the reality of sin, they regarded it as a *perversion* or *disorder* of an inherently good human nature. They also insisted that people are not naturally selfish and competitive. They stressed the social nature of man, and maintained that a person is only happy and fulfilled through a moral life.

In general, ethics played a central role in Cambridge Platonism and its doctrines became especially influential. It maintains that action, not contemplation, is the end of life, and that the highest knowledge is only the result of good conduct. Its emphasis upon reason, the social nature of man and the goodness of human nature constantly reappear in the late seventeenth and early eighteenth centuries. The Cambridge school was particularly influential on Samuel BUTLER, SHAFTESBURY and Richard CUMBERLAND, and it was the inspiration behind the ethical rationalism of Samuel CLARKE, John Balguy and Richard PRICE.

See also: PLATO; NEOPLATONISM

References and further reading

Anderson, P. (1933) *Science in Defence of Liberal Religion: A Study of Henry More's Attempt to Link Seventeenth Century Religion with Science*, New York: Putnam. (Somewhat out of date, but clear and incisive.)

Cassirer, E. (1953) *The Platonic Renaissance in England*, London: Nelson. (Still the best study.)

Cragg, G. (ed.) (1968) *The Cambridge Platonists*, Oxford: Oxford University Press. (A useful anthology.)

* Cudworth, R. (1731) *A Treatise concerning Eternal and Immutable Morality*, ed. E. Chandler, London: Printed for James Knapton. (The fundamental ethical work of the Cambridge school.)

* —— (1678) *The True Intellectual System of the Universe*, London; repr. ed. J. Harrison, London, 1845; repr. Stuttgart-Bad Cannstatt, 1964. (The only major work of philosophy by Cudworth published in his lifetime.)

De Pauley, W.C. (1937) *The Candle of the Lord: Studies in the Cambridge Platonists*, London: Macmillan. (Sometimes helpful.)

Lichtenstein, A. (1962) *Henry More: The Rational Theology of a Cambridge Platonist*, Cambridge MA: Harvard University Press. (Incisive treatment of More.)

* More, H. (1662) *A Collection of Several Philosophical Writings*, London: William Morden. (An indispensible and important anthology.)

Passmore, J. (1951) *Ralph Cudworth: An Interpretation*, Cambridge: Cambridge University Press. (Helpful analysis).

Patrides, C.A. (ed.) (1968) *The Cambridge Platonists*, Cambridge: Cambridge University Press. (A good anthology.)

Smith, J. (1660) *Select Discourses*, London: Morden. (The only edition of Smith's writings.)

Stewart, J.A. (1910) 'The Cambridge Platonists', in J. Hastings (ed.) *Encyclopedia of Religion and Ethics*, Edinburgh: T&T Clark, vol. 3, 167–73. (A useful introduction to religious aspects).

Tulloch, J. (1874) *Rational Theology and Christian Philosophy in England in the Seventeenth Century*, vol. 2, Edinburgh: Blackwood. (A useful survey).

Whichcote, B. (1751) *The Works of the Learned Benjamin Whichcote*, Aberdeen: Chalmers, 4 vols. (Although indispensible, this is not a complete edition. It also lacks dating of texts.)

FREDERICK BEISER

CAMPANELLA, GIOVANNI DOMENICO *see* CAMPANELLA, TOMMASO

CAMPANELLA, TOMMASO (1568–1639)

Tommaso Campanella was a Counter-Reformation theologian, a Renaissance magus, a prophet, a poet and an astrologer, as well as a philosopher whose speculations assumed encyclopedic proportions. As a late Renaissance philosopher of nature, Campanella is notable for his early, and continuous, opposition to Aristotle. He rejected the fundamental Aristotelian principle of hylomorphism, namely the understanding of all physical substance in terms of form and matter. In its place he appropriated Telesio's understanding of reality in terms of the dialectical principles of heat and cold; and he adopted a form of empiricism found in Telesio's work that included pansensism, the doctrine that all things in nature are endowed with sense. Especially after 1602, Campanella's exposure to Renaissance Platonism also involved him in panpsychism, the view that all reality has a mental aspect. Thus his empiricism came to show a distinctly metaphysical and spiritualistic dimension that transformed his philosophy. At the same time his epistemology embraced a universal doubt and an emphasis on individual self-consciousness that are suggestive of Descartes' views.

Campanella's career as a religious dissident, radical reformer and leader of an apocalyptic movement presents a political radicalism that was oddly associated with more traditional notions of universal monarchy and the need for theocracy. The only one of his numerous writings that receives attention today, La Città del Sole *(The City of the Sun) (composed 1602, but not published until 1623), has come to occupy a prominent place in the literature of utopias though Campanella himself seems to have expected some form of astronomical/apocalyptic realization.*

Campanella's naturalism, especially its pansensism and panpsychism, enjoyed some currency in Germany and France during the 1620s, but in the last five years of his life it was emphatically rejected by the intellectual communities headed by Mersenne and Descartes, as well as by Galileo.

1 Life
2 Epistemology
3 Metaphysics
4 Moral and political philosophy

1 Life

Son of an illiterate Calabrian cobbler, Giovanni Domenico Campanella adopted the name 'Tommaso' when he joined the Dominican Order in 1582. He was attracted to Naples as an intellectual centre, where he encountered the primitive experimentalism and magic of Giambattista Della Porta and his circle. There too in 1591 he published his first work, *Philosophia sensibus demonstrata* (Philosophy Demonstrated by the Senses), which registered both his emphatic anti-Aristotelianism and his reception of Telesio's naturalism. As a result of his increasingly radical thought, he was hounded by the Inquisition. He suffered a series of trials, tortures and imprisonments, culminating with his twenty-seven year incarceration (1599–1626) by the Spanish viceregal regime for leading an abortive uprising. No matter how severe the conditions of his confinement, he managed to produce a vast number of works, some of which have never been recovered. It was through his writing that he managed to win his way out of prison to freedom in Rome (1626–34) where his astrological talents won him high favour from Pope Urban VIII. However, he was once more threatened by Spain, and fled to Paris where he was granted asylum by Louis XIII and Richelieu. During the last years of his life he prepared his works for publication while under royal protection.

2 Epistemology

It was in Campanella's *De sensu rerum et magia* (On the Sense and Feeling in All Things and On Magic), first composed in 1590 and published in 1620, that he initially presented his emerging empiricism and his view that the perceived world is alive and sentient in all its parts. This work became the most widely read and influential of all his philosophical works, and remains central to his combination of naturalism and a degree of magic that enables us to manipulate natural processes. However, the most comprehensive and formal presentation of his philosophy is found in his *Metafisica* (1602–24; first published in 1638), which is representative of his mature thought. He divides the work into three parts: *principia sciendi* (epistemology), *principia essendi* (metaphysics) and *principia operandi* (moral and political philosophy); and it is noteworthy that he begins with the theory of knowledge. Thus, before he constructs a metaphysics, Campanella finds it necessary to establish the reality of knowing and of individual self-consciousness. He seems to have been the first philosopher to feel the need of explicitly stating the problem of knowledge as an introduction to his philosophy.

Although he had previously been satisfied through his long exposure to Telesio that the nature of all things including human beings was basically sensory, by 1604 he had become convinced that the mind that God has infused into human beings not only has sensation and animal memory but something higher and more divine. This higher level of the intellect's functioning established individual self-consciousness. Here Campanella was more inspired by AUGUSTINE (§§5–6) than by AQUINAS (§10) (his ostensible guide in most matters), especially in his pursuit of a universal theoretical doubt. He entertained the possibility of his own self-deception, and he made explicit reference, paraphrasing it at length, to the famous passage in *De civitate Dei* (The City of God) where Augustine counters the Academic sceptics with his 'If I am mistaken, I am' (XI.26). It is this direct intuition of oneself, this direct knowledge of our being, our knowing and our willing that is now grafted onto the general sensory nature in which the self, like all other things, participates. Although between 1617 and 1623 DESCARTES (§§3, 7–8) read more of Campanella than he ever wished to admit, the striking similarities between Descartes' views and Campanella's universal doubt, his emphasis on self-consciousness, and his principle *cognoscere est esse* (knowing is being) are more apparent than real. While Descartes creates an emphatic distinction between soul and body, Campanella, instead of separating the two substances, makes a Neoplatonic identification of being with thought, in which all things now share. The difference between them is that between a philosophy of instinct, sensation and *élan vital*, and a philosophy of mathematical certitude, clear and distinct ideas, and a universal, impersonal reason.

By intellect, Campanella understands two distinct faculties. The first is sensation (the *intellectus sensualis*), which humans have in common with animals, and which is capable of grasping particulars but is unable to go beyond the senses. The second is mind (the *intellectus mentalis*) which aspires to invisible and eternal realities. This two-fold view of the intellect is quite similar to that offered by TELESIO (§5) in the later editions of his *De rerum natura iuxta propria principia* (On the Nature of Things According to Their Own Principles) (1586). Sense exhibits its own inherent certainty in its apprehension of singulars. Experience shows that to sense fire one need not apprehend the form of fire; rather it suffices simply to be slightly burned. On the basis of this initial passive perception, sense 'can infer the rest of the power of the object acting upon itself'. For Campanella, however, knowledge does not remain at this sensory, Telesian, level, but comes to involve a process of assimilation. Proceeding on the basis of his principle that knowing is being, he claims that things are known inasmuch as the knower becomes similar to them. However, he means by this something quite different from the assimilation of form to which Aristotle and Aquinas had referred. Each thing is sensed and known in so far as it is itself a sentient part

of nature, and the knowing essence of the thing becomes the object to be known.

In practical terms, Campanella's empiricism manifests a clear respect for *testimonia* (the evidence of direct witness or experience) in preference to *opinio* (traditional belief based upon some distant authority). The best and most repeated example of this distinction is the witness of Christopher Columbus against the authority of Augustine and Lactantius on the existence of antipodes. Sense, here reading from Nature, God's book, attests to things as they are; opinion to what we have read from others.

Especially in his *Apologia pro Galileo* (written in 1616, published in 1622), Campanella accepts and pays considerable attention to the popular notion of the two Books of Scripture and of Nature. In the *Apologia*, he presents an important statement about freedom of thought and the relationship between God's two Books, though without in any way committing himself to the Copernican system that Galileo had defended (see COPERNICUS, N.; GALILEI, GALILEO §§1, 4). In what seems to be a continuous adjustment of the evidence from the two Books in order to achieve their conformity or agreement, Campanella grants both precedence and pre-eminence to the first Book, that of Nature. Yet while the new discoveries provided by the first Book would seem to dictate a reinterpretation of the second that would bring Scripture into conformity with Nature, the entire intellectual enterprise is predicated on the underlying assumption and confidence that there can be no disagreement between what is offered in the Book of Scripture and the findings of the Book of Nature.

3 Metaphysics

Campanella's philosophy of nature is inspired by Telesio's effort to explain nature through its own principles (*iuxta propria principia*) (see TELESIO §2). From his first published work, he announced his opposition to Aristotle's hylomorphism. He rejects the idea of matter as pure potency actualized by form, and attributes to it a measure of reality all its own. Nor does he accept form in the scholastic sense, seeing it as the mode or quality of an object. Scorning the Aristotelian structure of matter as potency and form (whether substantial or accidental) as act, Campanella hoped to build a new edifice on the Telesian foundation of heat and cold as active principles contending for sole mastery of matter as passive substratum. Unfortunately, inconsistency in terminology obscures the clarity of his distinctions and he was by no means completely successful in disentangling himself from the conceptual world and terminology of the Aristotelian tradition.

Campanella confidently asserted that the senses perceived body directly: body is body in its own right without needing an abstract form to make it so. Having renounced substantial forms, he substituted the two active principles of heat and cold. Form is replaced by *temperamentum*, the arrangement and blending of internal parts, as the structure of matter. A more positive evaluation of Campanella's rejection of hylomorphism has detected in this departure from the traditional Aristotelian metaphysical supports a desire to reduce occult phenomena to mechanical contact, to some sort of material force, or to an inhering structural resonance in all things.

Also in reaction to Aristotle, Campanella presented a Neoplatonizing metaphysics that seeks to be in accord with Telesian physics. The subtitle to his *De sensu* (1620) reads: 'the world is shown to be a living and truly conscious image of God, and all its parts and details to be endowed with sense perception, some more clearly, some more obscurely to an extent sufficient for their preservation and that of the entirety in which they share sensation...'. Sense makes the entire world a gigantic, feeling creature.

Campanella goes on to explicate the nature and structure of Being by means of his original doctrine of the primalities (*primalitates*), Power, Wisdom and Love. His reading of the universe as consisting of power, sense or knowledge, and love seems to be a natural outgrowth both of his pansensism and his Augustinian base. The three primalities, his 'Monotriad', provided him with the philosophical counterpart to the central Christian theological doctrine of the Trinity. As metaphysical principles, the primalities are so inherent in the effects they produce that Campanella can speak of their 'essentiating' a being. Lesser beings do not merely participate in the primalities; they are totally pervaded or 'coessentiated' by them.

While the three principles of this 'coessentiation' are the same by virtue of their function, they differ in terms of their origin. Love derives from wisdom and power, and wisdom derives from power alone. Power is thus the source of the other two, though the operation and functioning of all three primalities presupposes their transcendent unity. These relationships are seen in all created beings, for being itself is a transcendental composite of power, knowledge and love. Wisdom, the second primality, is particularly important, for its effects help explain Campanella's doctrine of universal sensation. Primal wisdom endows all things, whether rational, animal, or material, with some measure of sense perception, and it is in this way that all created beings are

essentially related to one another and participate in the essence of the infinite being. Love as the third primality is the manifestation of wisdom, for love and knowledge, appetite and perception are conjoined. Love involves a process of becoming something else, the subject becoming imperfectly the object loved. Thus the doctrine that knowledge involves assimilation has a metaphysical basis. Here, as with Campanella's understanding of magic and of natural religion, a general indebtedness to FICINO (§§2, 4) is perceptible.

From this cosmology, the human being emerges as a microcosm or little universe, though Campanella preferred the term *epilogo* (epilogue) for this familiar Renaissance idea. The human microcosm conjoins five worlds or orders: (1) the archetypal world, which is infinite, eternal, and contains the archetypes of all possible worlds; (2) the mental or metaphysical world, that of angelic and human minds, composed of the primalities; (3) the mathematical world or universal space, which constitutes the basis or substratum of all bodies in an unchanging space; (4) the material world whose regular alterations place it above time, so that it participates in the perpetuity of the mathematical world; (5) the fifth, localized world, characterized by time, which is found within the fourth world and is the product of the two active principles. The five orders of being are so interrelated that whatever is in a superior world is by participation in the lower worlds, and whatever is in an inferior world is in an eminent way in those above. The human being as *epilogo* is understood as the ultimate epitome of all five worlds. This account of the microcosm is the corollary of the doctrine that the universe itself, the macrocosm, is a most perfect animal with its own body, spirit and soul (see COSMOLOGY §1).

4 Moral and political philosophy

Campanella distinguishes three aspects of moral or practical philosophy: ethics, economics and politics, the last of which far outweighed the other two in importance. In his ethics he rejects the idea of the supreme good as something extrinsic to humans, and he also rejects Aristotle's belief that the contemplation of truth is the supreme end for humans. Instead, he affirms the ideal of happiness as consisting in self-conservation, and the direction of all one's efforts towards God, who alone can guarantee this conservation. Beatitude then becomes a union effected with God through power, wisdom and love rather than through any intellectual contemplation. Campanella's understanding of virtue and the virtues follows from his understanding of the supreme good, for virtue has its ground in the three primalities. Virtue is seen as a power proceeding from the very nature of being, and manifesting itself in the operations of power, wisdom and love, which it helps perfect. In his deployment of a number of virtues, Campanella departed from the traditional framework of the four cardinal virtues, and made considerable use of St John Chrysostom, among the Church Fathers.

The focus and realization of the basically social nature of human beings occurs in the individual household, which includes the immediate family, its servants and even the domestic animals. In considering the economy of the family, which differs only in degree rather than in kind from the political state, Campanella asserts the centrality of marriage as a contract of natural law, sanctified by Christ as a sacrament. If some of his recipes for sexual relations, child-rearing and the education of the young suggest the calculations and concerns of the Solarians in his imaginary City of the Sun (see below), there is no hint of the Solarian community of women to be found in his treatment of marriage. Campanella is thus generally orthodox in his understanding of marriage within the present temporal dispensation, although the wife exercises a responsible role within the conservative structure headed by the *paterfamilias*.

Politics early became the pre-eminent consuming interest of the radical Dominican reformer – an interest, which when driven by the heady combination of astrology, magic and messianism led to a popular uprising, and to Campanella's long imprisonment. His famous work *La Città del Sole* (The City of the Sun) (first published in 1623), traditionally understood as being simply the account of an ideal society, and thus relegated to utopian literature (see UTOPIANISM §1), is more accurately understood as representing part of Campanella's millenarian expectation. It seems hardly accidental that he composed the work in 1602 only a year before the expected astronomical conjunction of planets figuring the sun's descent towards the earth, set for December 1603. Despite the apparent incommensurability of the then-current Christian economy with the rationally organized, communistic millenarian economy which Campanella saw as impending, there is a complementarity between the City of the Sun and the theocratic papal monarchy advanced by his other political writings: namely, the amalgamation of secular and spiritual into a comprehensive universal monarchy ruled by a priest-king.

From the very beginning two themes pervade Campanella's political philosophy: (1) the necessity of religion's informing politics; (2) the necessity for universal monarchy. These two threads, running through his entire thinking, intersect in his affirmation of the papal office as the effective expression and realization of power on earth. Monarchy is not simply the noblest form of government, but in Campanella's hands it came to be understood as something universal, all-inclusive and above the present clutter of kingdoms and empires. With Christ seen as the founder of universal monarchy, the designation of monarch properly pertains to the Pope, who when endowed with both temporal and spiritual arms, can serve as moderator among princes, and can prevent any Christian prince from arriving at the monarchy of Christendom. Campanella was scandalized by Dante's dualism of church and empire (see ALIGHIERI, DANTE §3), and wished to fuse secular and spiritual power in the monarchy of the priest-king. Thus one can only understand the monarchy of Spain (the ruler of Naples, and together with the Roman Inquisition, author of Campanella's misfortunes) as the Arm of God when it is in close association with, dependence on, and service to the papacy; the territorial aggrandizement of Spain can have the papal blessing only in so far as it serves the universal propagation of the true religion. After 1634, Campanella was to put France forward as the Pope's secular agent.

Campanella is a Machiavellian of sorts. Although apart from Aristotle himself no other so provoked the hostility of Campanella as did MACHIAVELLI and his reason of state, none the less Campanella could accept much of his predecessor's appreciation of power, its defence and increase through deception and harsh, sometimes immoral measures. On the other hand, he could not admit the divorce of politics from religion or the reduction of religion to some form of political manipulation and a mere means of ruling (see POLITICAL PHILOSOPHY, HISTORY OF §5). Affirming religion's political utility, Campanella seeks to incorporate the state into his church, empowering Christianity under the aegis of the armed priest-king. He wants to have his religion both ways: as justified on utilitarian grounds, and as the comprehensive, informing, living truth.

Campanella's entire thought reflects an emotional predisposition to innovation and a commitment to mint a new philosophy, eclectic and Platonizing, that is ostensibly more supportive of Christianity than the philosophy of Aristotle.

See also: ARISTOTELIANISM, RENAISSANCE; PLATONISM, RENAISSANCE; TELESIO, B.

List of works

Most of Campanella's works went through numerous stages of complex redaction before publication; for details see Firpo (1940) in references and further reading.

Campanella, T. (1591) *Philosophia sensibus demonstrata* (Philosophy Demonstrated by the Senses), Naples: Orazio Salviano; ed. L. de Franco, Naples: Vivarium, 1992. (Campanella's first publication and first formal venture into philosophy, composed 1589 but not published until 1591. Registers his emphatic anti-Aristotelianism, the reception of Telesio's philosophy and its transfer into a metaphysical key; precedes his magical, astrological and Gnostic speculations and his later interest in celestial, political and religious palingenesia.)

—— (1620) *De sensu rerum et magia* (Of the Sense and Feeling in All Things and on Magic), Frankfurt: Gottfried Tampach; repr. in L. Firpo (ed.) *Tommaso Campanella, Opera latina, Francofurti impressa annis 1617–1630*, Turin: Bottega d'Erasmo, 1975; English trans. of Book I and some chapters of Book IV (incorrectly designated Book V) in A.B. Fellico and H. Shapiro (eds) *Renaissance Philosophy; the Italian Philosophers*, New York: Modern Library, 1967, 338–79; partial English trans. of Book II by B. Dooley, *Baroque Italy: Selected Readings*, New York: Garland Press, 1995. (Composed first in Latin in 1590, then recomposed in Italian in 1604; a critical edition of the more definitive Italian version is available as *Del senso delle cose e della magia*, ed. Antonio Bruers, Bari: Gius. Laterza & Figli, 1925. After its publication in 1620, *De sensu* became the most widely read and influential of Campanella's philosophical works during the seventeenth century and remains central to his total naturalistic, magical position.)

—— (1622) *Apologia pro Galileo*, Frankfurt: Gottfried Tampach; repr. in L. Firpo (ed.) *Tommaso Campanella, Opera latina, Francofurti impressa annis 1617–1630*, Turin: Bottega d'Erasmo, 1975; trans. R.J. Blackwell, *A Defense of Galileo, the Mathematician from Florence*, Notre Dame, IN, and London: University of Notre Dame Press, 1994. (Composed in 1616, presents an important statement of *libertas philosophandi* and the relationship between God's two Books without in any way committing the author to the Copernican system; Blackwell's is the best English translation.)

—— (1623) *La Città del Sole: Dialogo Poetico; The City of the Sun: A Poetical Dialogue*, trans. and ed. D.J. Donno, Berkeley and Los Angeles, CA, and London: University of California Press, 1981. (Although composed in 1602, *La Città del Sole* was not published until 1623; most famous as a work of utopian literature.)

—— (1636) *De gentilismo non retinendo* (On that Paganism that must not be Maintained), Paris: Toussaint Dubray; Italian trans. R. Amerio, *Della necessità di una filosophia cristiana*, Turin: Società editrice internazionale, 1953. (Composed originally 1609–10; more than usually pungent effort on Campanella's part to mint a new Christian philosophy, eclectic but exclusive of Aristotle.)

—— (1638) *Metafisica: universalis philosophiae seu metaphysicarum rerum propria dogmata* (Metaphysics: The Essential Doctrines of Universal Philosophy or Metaphysical Things), ed. P. Ponzio, Bari: Levante, 1994; repr. L. Firpo, Turin: Bottega d'Erasmo, 1961; Latin-Italian abridged version, G. di Napoli (ed.) *Metafisica*, Bologna: Zanichelli, 1967, 3 vols. (First published in Paris in 1638, following four redactions 1602–24. Constitutes the most comprehensive, cumulative and formal presentation of Campanella's philosophy. One of the great dinosaurs of seventeenth-century philosophical production, di Napoli's Latin-Italian abridged version is more manageable.)

References and further reading

Amerio, R. (1972) *Il sistema teologico di Tommaso Campanella* (The Theological System of Tommaso Campanella), Milan and Naples: R. Riccardi. (The most formidable interpretation of Campanella as a Christian thinker, by the editor of Campanella's theological works.)

* Augustine (413–27) *De civitate Dei* (The City of God), trans. J. O'Meara, Harmondsworth: Penguin, 1972. (Quoted in §2. Several good English translations exist, of which this is the most notable.)

Badaloni, N. (1965) *Tommaso Campanella*, Milan: Feltrinelli. (A thematic, perceptive study, emphasizing the magical and the influence of Origen in Campanella's thought.)

Blanchet, L. (1920) *Campanella*, Paris; repr. New York: Burt Franklin, 1964. (Although somewhat dated, a brilliant, comprehensive treatment of Campanella as a radical philosopher of nature.)

Bock, G. (1974) *Thomas Campanella: Politisches Interesse und Philosophische Spekulation* (Thomas Campanella: Political Interest and Philosophical Speculation), Tübingen: Max Niemeyer. (A thorough, balanced Marxist interpretation of Campanella's political thought.)

Bolzoni, L. (1989) 'Tommaso Campanella e le donne: fascino e negazione della differenza' (Thomas Campanella and Women: Charm and the Denial of Difference), *Annali d'Italianistica* 7: 193–216. (Sensitive, perceptive analysis of Campanella's ambivalent view of women.)

Bonansea, B.M. (1969) *Tommaso Campanella: Renaissance Pioneer of Modern Thought*, Washington, DC: Catholic University of America Press. (Fundamental, though excessively scholastic and impervious to Renaissance intellectual currents.)

Copenhaver, B.P. and Schmitt, C.B. (1992) *A History of Western Philosophy: Vol. 3. Renaissance Philosophy*, Oxford and New York: Oxford University Press. (Contains an important, positive appreciation of Campanella as a critic of Aristotle who significantly undermined the current allegiance to occult qualities through his rejection of hylomorphism.)

Ernst, G. (1991) *Religone, ragione e natura: Ricerche su Tommaso Campanella e il tardo Rinascimento* (Religion, Reason and Nature: Research on Tommaso Campanella and the Late Renaissance), Milan: Franco Angeli. (An insightful thematic study of aspects of Campanella's thought.)

Firpo, L. (1940) *Bibliografia degli scritti di Tommaso Campanella* (Bibliography of Tommaso Campanella's Writings), Turin: Vincenzo Bona. (Fundamental for understanding the complicated history of Campanella's writings, though in need of revision.)

—— (1974) 'Campanella, Tommaso', in *Dizionario biografico degli Italiani* 17: 372–401, Rome: Società Grafica Romana. (Basic biographical and bibliographical information by the leading Campanella scholar.)

Headley, J.M. (1997) *Tommaso Campanella and the Transformation of the World*, Princeton, NJ: Princeton University Press, 1997. (Seeks to contextualize the thought of Campanella according to major issues in the Europe of the seventeenth century.)

Lerner, M.-P. (1987) 'Le "livre vivant" de Dieu: la cosmologie évolutive de Tommaso Campanella' (God's 'Living Book': the Developing Cosmology of Tommaso Campanella), in *Le discours scientifique du Baroque: Actes de la Xe session internationale d'étude du Baroque*, Montauban, 1983. (Thorough discussion of Campanella's interpretation of nature.)

Mönnich, M. (1990) *Tommaso Campanella: Sein Beitrag zur Medizin und Pharmazie der Renaissance* (Tommaso Campanella: His Contribution to the Medicine and Pharmacy of the Renaissance), Stuttgart: Wissenschaftliche Verlagsgesellschaft. (Excellent presentation of the scientific and medical features of Campanella's thought in their larger philosophical context; notable analyses of *sensus* and *spiritus*; good bibliography.)

JOHN M. HEADLEY

CAMPBELL, GEORGE (1719–96)

George Campbell, Scottish minister, professor and religious thinker, is now remembered primarily for The Philosophy of Rhetoric *(1776). Here he employed the Scottish Enlightenment's developing science of human nature to explain the effectiveness of the classical rules of rhetoric. He did this by relating the various ends of persuasive discourse to the natural faculties and propensities of the human mind. In his own time Campbell was better known as a religious apologist, using an enlightened theory of evidence in* A Dissertation on Miracles *(1762) to defend the believability of Christian miracles against the sceptical attack of David Hume.*

George Campbell was born in Aberdeen and educated at the town's Marischal College. He was ordained in the established Church of Scotland in 1748 and was minister of a country parish for nearly a decade. Upon returning to Aberdeen, he helped found the influential Aberdeen Philosophical Society, whose members included Thomas Reid, Alexander Gerard and James Beattie (see ABERDEEN PHILOSOPHICAL SOCIETY). He was appointed to the posts of Principal and Professor of Divinity in Marischal College in 1759 and 1771 respectively, which he held jointly until the year before his death.

Campbell's best known work today is *The Philosophy of Rhetoric* (1776), which earned its title by combining classical rhetorical theory with the Scottish Enlightenment's attempt to develop a comprehensive science of human nature (see ENLIGHTENMENT, SCOTTISH; HUMAN NATURE, 18TH-CENTURY SCIENCE OF). Campbell argued that the rhetorical standards established by the ancients were definitive, and could be used to explore the principles of human nature that made those standards universal. He linked the four ends of speaking, which were 'to enlighten the understanding, to please the imagination, to move the passions, or to influence the will', with the qualities of style, perspicuity and vivacity, that most effectively brought about persuasion (Campbell 1776: 1). He also employed the Scottish Enlightenment's principle of sympathy to explain how an orator communicated passions as well as believability to his audience.

Perhaps the most important philosophical aspect of *The Philosophy of Rhetoric* is its theory of evidence. Campbell divided evidence into two types, intuitive and deductive. Intuitive evidence is immediately convincing to the mind and provides a necessary foundation for rational and empirical argument. It includes evidence from pure intellection (self-evident mathematical axioms and definitions), consciousness (one's own being and sensations), and common sense (indemonstrable but indispensable premises of moral reasoning). Deductive evidence, by contrast, produces conviction mediately, by either logical or factual demonstration, denominated demonstrative and moral evidence. Demonstrative evidence concerns invariable mathematical and geometrical relations and is capable of absolute proof. Moral evidence concerns contingent matters of fact rather than necessary relations, and its proofs are only probable at best. It is, nevertheless, the most important kind of evidence, for it includes all human experience and testimony, and constitutes the proper province of rhetoric.

Campbell's philosophy was influenced by that of David HUME, though Campbell employed much effort in correcting Hume. Campbell followed Hume in equating experience with the habitual associations of ideas in the mind, but thought that Hume's extreme emphasis on personal experience seriously undervalued the importance of memory (the only voucher for the past evidence of the senses) and of testimony to human knowledge as a whole. He therefore employed Common Sense philosophy to defend the necessary reliance of human beings on their own memories and on the testimony of others (see COMMON SENSE SCHOOL). His theory of evidence was a significant and original contribution to Common Sense philosophy, particularly in its explication of intuitive knowledge and its emphasis on testimony, though his use of that philosophy was otherwise minimal and not nearly as extensive as the version employed by Thomas REID.

The methods and concerns of *The Philosophy of Rhetoric* were those of the Scottish Enlightenment, but its rhetorical strategy was aimed primarily at religious persuasion. Campbell's theory of evidence provided a philosophical foundation for his Christian apologetics, as exemplified by *A Dissertation on Miracles* (1762). This work was written against Hume's essay 'Of Miracles' (1748), which had claimed that a miracle could not be believed because the testimonial evidence in its favour necessarily contradicted our uniform experience of the laws of nature. Campbell argued that our knowledge of the laws of nature depended more upon the testimony of others than upon our personal experience. We could therefore no more reject the testimony of reliable witnesses concerning particular facts than we could the general testimony that had established the empirical laws of nature in the first place. He then attempted to demonstrate that only early Christian claims of miracles were

sufficiently reliable to overturn the general experience of human history.

Campbell was a relentless advocate for religious toleration and freedom of expression. His *Address to the People of Scotland* (1779; see Campbell 1762) defended the civil rights of Roman Catholics, though his outspokenness earned him the wrath of many of his Protestant countrymen. He argued that persecution was unchristian, counterproductive and philosophically indefensible. In a later manuscript (now in Aberdeen University Library) he contended that belief in abstract doctrines is the involuntary consequence of the passive mind's perception of evidence. Only argument and persuasion are compatible with the realities of the human mind and with the spirit of the gospel of Christ.

Campbell's reputation in his own lifetime rivalled that of almost any participant in the Scottish Enlightenment, and rested primarily on his religious writings, which included his posthumously-published divinity lectures. His contemporaries believed his masterpiece to be *The Four Gospels* (1789), which contained dissertations on the proper method of translating ancient documents, and which advocated enlightened principles of biblical criticism. Since his death, *The Philosophy of Rhetoric* has become a standard text on the subject as well as the object of considerable scholarly interest. It has eclipsed all his other writings.

See also: BLAIR, H.; MIRACLES; RHETORIC

List of works

Campbell, G. (1762) *A Dissertation on Miracles*, Edinburgh: Kincaid & Bell; 3rd edn, Edinburgh: Bell & Bradfute, 1797, 2 vols; repr. New York: Garland, 1983. (The third edition contains most of Campbell's sermons, including *An Address to the People of Scotland*.)
—— (1776) *The Philosophy of Rhetoric*, ed. L. Bitzer, Carbondale, IL and Edwardsville, IL: Southern Illinois University Press, 1988. (The now standard edition of the *Rhetoric*; Bitzer's introduction is the best short scholarly introduction to Campbell's life and thought.)

References and further reading

Bevilacqua, V. (1965) 'Philosophical Origins of George Campbell's *Philosophy of Rhetoric*', *Speech Monographs* 32: 1–12. (A reasonably accessible introduction to Campbell's rhetorical thought.)
Bitzer, L. (1969) 'Hume's Philosophy in George Campbell's *Philosophy of Rhetoric*', *Philosophy and*

Rhetoric 3: 139–66. (A compelling case for Campbell's debt to Hume.)

Burns, R. (1981) *The Great Debate on Miracles*, Lewisburg, PA: Bucknell University Press. (A treatment of the whole eighteenth-century miracles debate that puts Campbell's arguments in context.)

Howell, W. (1971) *Eighteenth-century British Logic and Rhetoric*, Princeton, NJ: Princeton University Press. (The standard account of the subject, which gives considerable space to Campbell.)

* Hume, D. (1748) 'Of Miracles', in *Enquiries Concerning the Human Understanding and Concerning the Principles of Morals*, ed. L.A. Selby-Bigge, Oxford: Clarendon Press, 2nd edn, 1972. (The most famous eighteenth-century attack on miracles, although coming rather late in the debate, and against which Campbell and many others wrote.)

JEFFEREY M. SUDERMAN

CAMPBELL, NORMAN ROBERT (1880–1949)

Campbell made important contributions to philosophy of science in the 1920s, influenced by Poincaré, Russell and his own work in physics. He produced pioneering analyses of the nature of physical theories and of measurement, but is mainly remembered for requiring a theory, for example, the kinetic theory of gases, to have an 'analogy', that is, an independent interpretation, for example, as laws of motion of a swarm of microscopic particles.

The British philosopher of science Norman Robert Campbell, who became a Fellow of Trinity College Cambridge in 1904, was also an experimental physicist, and worked on the research staff of the British General Electric Company from 1919 to 1944. His main contribution to philosophy, published in 1920, is his account of how physical theories explain laws. It maintains an absolute distinction between laws relating observable properties of objects, on which agreement can be achieved, and theories used to explain them. It could allow a weaker distinction, letting accepted theories come to state laws needing further explanation. But only an implausible view of the significance of the distinction can save its claim that theories need analogies.

Campbell's account of theories credits them with three components, illustrated by a simplified version of the kinetic theory of gases. First there is a theory's 'hypothesis', its mathematical propositions, empirically uninterpreted. Then there is a 'dictionary', linking terms of the hypothesis to observable terms used to state the laws the theory explains. Thus in his example the dictionary identifies the volume V, mass M, pressure P and absolute temperature T of a gas with combinations of constants and variables postulated by the hypothesis: for example, $V = l^3$, where l is a constant, $M = nm$, where m is a constant and $3n$ the number of variables dependent on the independent variable t (time). This hypothesis and dictionary entail the perfect gas law, $PV \propto T$.

But arbitrarily many formal systems, suitably interpreted, would also entail this law. To *explain* it, 'the propositions of the hypothesis must be analogous to some known laws': here 'the laws which would describe the motion of...[n] infinitely small and highly elastic particles [of mass m]...in a cubical box [of size l]' (1920: 128–9). Thus for Campbell an analogy is an essential part of a theory, not a dispensable aid to its formation: 'to regard analogy as an aid to the invention of theories is as absurd as to regard melody as an aid to the composition of sonatas' (1920: 130).

The importance of Campbell's main distinction, between propositions linking a theory's terms to each other and those linking them to others in the laws it explains, is now widely accepted if differently expressed. (For example, Nagel (1961) uses 'calculus' for Campbell's 'hypothesis' and 'correspondence rules' for his 'dictionary'.) But few now accept that a theory needs an analogy (which Nagel called a 'model'), a thesis that falls between two stools. First, a theory needs no analogy on an instrumentalist reading of it as a formal device linking laws statable in other terms: for then, since its hypothesis states nothing either true or false, its terms need no interpretation. But nor does it need an analogy on a realist reading of its hypothesis as consisting of true or false propositions. For then what these propositions state if true are not merely *analogous* to laws governing (for example) the motion of particles: they *are* laws governing the motion of the particles which the kinetic theory says compose a gas. Only if a hypothesis comprises propositions that are true or false but different in kind from those that state laws is Campbell's case for analogy tenable; but his – basically epistemological – argument for this was always weak and has been weakened further by later work on the meaning of theoretical terms in science (see THEORIES, SCIENTIFIC §§2, 7).

Although most physical laws relate measurable quantities, measurement remains an underrated topic in the philosophy of science. Campbell was one of the first philosophers to recognise its importance, observing that physics 'might almost be described as the science of measurement'. He saw that measurement itself depends on laws, like those giving physical sense to functions (addition, subtraction, multiplication) of the numbers used to measure quantities like length. His systematic account of this dependence, of the difference between fundamental and derived magnitudes, of the significance of units and dimensions, and of errors of measurement, set the agenda for later theories, which remain indebted to it.

See also: DUHEM, P.M.M.; MEASUREMENT, THEORY OF; MODELS; SCIENTIFIC REALISM AND ANTIREALISM

List of works

Campbell, N.R. (1920) *Physics: the Elements*, Cambridge: Cambridge University Press. (Republished in 1957 as *Foundations of Science*, New York: Dover Publications. Part I contains Campbell's account of theories, Part II his account of measurement.)

—— (1921) *What is Science?*, Cambridge: Cambridge University Press. (Republished in 1952, New York: Dover Publications. An introductory book on the scope of science, laws, measurement, mathematics in science, and its applications.)

—— (1928) *An Account of the Principles of Measurement and Calculation*, London: Longmans. (The final version of Campbell's account of measurement.)

References and further reading

Kyburg, H.E., Jr (1984) *Theory and Measurement*, Cambridge: Cambridge University Press. (A recent account of measurement, drawing on Campbell's work.)

* Nagel, E. (1961) *The Structure of Science*, New York: Harcourt Brace. (Chapters 5 (II–III) and 6 (I) of this classic work discuss Campbell's account of theories.)

D.H. MELLOR

CAMUS, ALBERT (1913–60)

Albert Camus was awarded the Nobel Prize in 1957 for having 'illuminated the problems of the human conscience in our times'. By mythologizing the experiences of a secular age struggling with an increasingly contested religious tradition, he dramatized the human effort to 'live and create without the aid of eternal values which, temporarily perhaps, are absent or distorted in contemporary Europe' (1943). Thus the challenge posed by 'the absurd' with which he is so universally identified.

Camus's most celebrated work is *L'Étranger* (1942) (*The Stranger*, 1988). Depicting the 'metaphysical' awakening of an ordinary Algerian worker, Camus concretizes the Pindarian injunction, provided as life's answer to 'the absurd' in an epigram to *Le Mythe de Sisyphe* (1943) (*The Myth of Sisyphus*, 1955): 'Oh my soul do not aspire to immortal heights but exhaust the field of the possible.'

But if the 'absurd' defines our world, it was never treated by Camus as a conclusion, only 'a point of departure'.

What else have I done except reason about an idea I discovered in the streets of my time? That I have nourished this idea (and a part of me nourishes it still) along with my whole generation goes without saying. I simply set it far enough away so that I could deal with it and decide on its logic.

(1954)

How and what morality is still possible, then, in view of the experience of 'the death of God' which has given birth to the experience of absurdity? While the absurd leaves humans without justification and direction, rebellion bears witness to the refusal of human beings to accept this incipient despair.

By demanding an end to oppression, rebellion seeks to transform – by revolution if necessary – the conditions that gave rise to it. Rebellion thus testifies to the human being's incessant demand for dignity. But it is often a vain yearning without a revolutionary transformation of the institutional structures of exploitation and oppression. Yet that transformation only promises further and even greater humiliation if it is not continually guided by the spirit and concerns of rebellion. Appalled by the totalitarian direction of many modern revolutionary movements, Camus thought he detected a messianic nostalgia lurking at the core of Western rebellions. He saw them driven by an often unexpressed need to replace the failed vertical transcendence of Judaeo-Christianity with a new horizontal transcendence.

L'Homme revolté (1951) (*The Rebel*, 1954) his major work in political theory, thus seeks to diagnose a way of thinking that has led rebellious thought from its initial generous impulses down the path of destruction, thus undermining one of the few sources of hope in our post-Christian world.

Rebellion and revolution have often, however, been falsely seen as polarized for Camus. Their opposition, rather than being necessary and celebrated, as has been claimed by both right- and left-wing detractors, is the death of both of them. The ground of any meaningful development of rebellion must be the implicit community of humans for whom value is demanded. Here is the crux of Camus's critique of 'legitimate murder', including capital punishment, which has led him, mistakenly, to be defined as a pacifist. Self-defence is justified, both individually and collectively, but pre-meditated or logical murder in the service of any cause whatsoever is not. It undermines the one undeniable community of humans confronting the universe, destroying the grounds of the possibility of coherent social values.

Thus Camus rejected any theory that argued that the ends justify the means. There are no transcendent ends. All ends are visions of transformed futures which themselves will simply be means for further action. If the ends justify the means, what then can justify the ends? His answer is the means – because they are simply more proximate ends in the service of a transformed quality of life that must always be lived concretely in the temporally unfolding present, ever confronted with injustice and exploitation, envisaging a transformed future that action may aspire to bring into being.

Throughout his life his thought was deeply marked by his experience. A French-Algerian from a poor working-class district of Algiers, Camus confronted Western civilization from the margins. Separated by ethnicity and culture from the Muslim majority, and by class from the ruling French *colons*, his attitude toward Europe remained ambivalent: drawn by the brilliance of its cultural expressions yet repelled by the scope of its brutalizing inhumanity.

To an emerging class sensitivity was added an anguished awareness of human finitude, poignantly brought home by contracting tuberculosis and facing death at the age of 17. A very personal urgency thus vitalized his metaphysical reflections. His mature work is marked by the conflicted awareness of the sensuality of the body in direct contact with a vibrant nature confronting the inevitability of ageing and death in a stark landscape without illusions.

Almost alone among traditional intellectuals, Camus remained tied by sensitivity and vision to his working-class origins. His values drew more from the communal experiences of college soccer than from the theoretical speculations of our greatest writers. The egalitarian collective effort of the Workers' Theatre that he led in the mid-1930s, where stars did not take bows and everyone pitched in with the staging, suggested to him the outlines of a truly just society.

An advocate of 'relative utopias', the renaissance, to the creation of which Camus always remained passionately committed, meant the qualitative transformation of daily life, the creation of dialogic communities at work and at home that gave voice and sustenance to the struggles for dignity of ordinary people. He continued to believe that only when the dignity of the worker and respect for intelligence are accorded their rightful place can human existence hope to realize its highest ideals, and our life find the collective meaning and purpose that alone can truly sustain us in the face of an infinite and indifferent universe.

See also: EXISTENTIALISM; EXISTENTIALIST ETHICS

List of works

Camus, A. (1938) *Noces*, Algiers: Charlot; trans. E. Conroy Kennedy, 'Nuptials', in *Lyrical and Critical Essays*, New York: Alfred A. Knopf, 1968.

—— (1942) *L'Étranger*, Paris: Gallimard; trans. M. Ward, *The Stranger*, New York: Alfred A. Knopf, 1988.

—— (1943) *Le Mythe de Sisyphe*, Paris: Gallimard; trans. J. O'Brien, *The Myth of Sisyphus and Other Essays*, New York: Alfred A. Knopf, 1955.

—— (1944) *Caligula*, Paris: Gallimard; trans. J. O'Brien, *Caligula and Three Other Plays*, New York: Alfred A. Knopf, 1958.

—— (1947) *La Peste*, Paris: Gallimard; trans S. Gilbert, *The Plague*, New York: Alfred A. Knopf, 1948.

—— (1950a) *Les Justes*, Paris: Gallimard; trans. J. O'Brien, The Just Assassins, in *Caligula and Three Other Plays*, New York: Alfred A. Knopf, 1958.

—— (1950b, 1956, 1958) *Actuelles*, vol. 1, *Chroniques 1944-1948*, vol. 2, *Chroniques 1948-53*, vol. 3, *Chroniques algériennes 1939-58*, Paris: Gallimard; trans. J. O'Brien, *Actualities*, and partially reprinted in *Resistance, Rebellion, and Death*, New York: Alfred A. Knopf, 1960.

—— (1951) *L'Homme revolté*, Paris: Gallimard; trans. A . Bower, *The Rebel*, New York: Alfred A. Knopf, 1954.

—— (1954) *L'Été*, Paris: Gallimard; trans. E. Conroy Kennedy, *Summer*, in *Lyrical and Critical Essays*, New York: Alfred A. Knopf, 1968.

—— (1956) *La Chute*, Paris: Gallimard; trans. J. O'Brien, *The Fall*, New York: Alfred A. Knopf, 1957.

—— (1957) *L'Éxile et le royaume*, Paris: Gallimard; trans. J. O'Brien, *Exile and the Kingdom*, New York: Alfred A. Knopf, 1957.

Camus, A. and Koestler, A. (1957) *Réflections sur le peine capitale: introduction et étude de Jean Bloch-Michel*, Paris: Calmann-Levy; trans. J. O'Brien, *Reflections on the Guillotine*, and partially reprinted in *Resistance, Rebellion, and Death*, New York: Alfred A. Knopf, 1960.

Camus, A. (1958) *'Discours de Suède' et 'L'Artiste et son temps'*, Paris: Gallimard; trans. J. O'Brien, 'Camus in Stockholm', *Atlantic Monthly* May 1958;

'The Artist and His Time', in *Resistance, Rebellion, and Death*, New York: Alfred A. Knopf, 1960.

—— (1994) *Le Premier Homme*, Paris: Gallimard; trans. D. Habgood, *The First Man*, New York: Alfred A. Knopf, 1995.

References and further reading

Bree, G. (1964) *Camus*, New York: Harcourt Brace & World. (Popular and sympathetic presentation from a literary perspective.)

Hanna, T. (1958) *The Thought and Art of Albert Camus*, Chicago, IL: Regnery. (A popular philosophical overview from a liberal perspective.)

Isaac, J.C. (1992) *Arendt, Camus, and Modern Rebellion*, New Haven, CT: Yale University Press. (A thoughtful, detailed and sympathetic critical comparison of the two thinkers.)

Lazere, D. (1973) *The Unique Creation of Albert Camus*, New Haven, CT: Yale University Press. (A serious study with a psychoanalytic bent.)

Lottman, H. (1979) *Albert Camus: A Biography*, Garden City, NJ: Doubleday & Co. (A very detailed factual account of Camus's life.)

Luppé, R. (1966) *Albert Camus*, trans. J. Cumming and J. Hargreaves. London: Merlin. (A succinct and original French interpretation.)

McCarthy, P. (1982) *Camus*, New York: Random House. (An intelligent critical review of Camus's philosophy that downplays the importance of *The Rebel*.)

O'Brien, C.C. (1970) *Albert Camus of Europe and North Africa*, New York: Viking Press. (An original analysis that critically evaluates the Cold War dimensions of Camus's life and writings.)

Parker, E. (1965) *Albert Camus: The Artist in the Arena*, Madison, WI: University of Wisconsin Press. (A presentation of Camus's journalistic writings in the immediate post-war period.)

Sprintzen, D.A. (1988) *Camus: A Critical Examination*, Philadelphia, PA: Temple University Press. (A comprehensive critical analysis of the philosophical structure and development of Camus's thought.)

Thody, P. (1961) *Albert Camus: 1913–1960*, London: Hamish Hamilton. (A popular literary overview of Camus's writings.)

DAVID A. SPRINTZEN

CANGUILHEM, GEORGES

see FRENCH PHILOSOPHY OF SCIENCE (§§3, 4)

CANTOR, GEORG (1845–1918)

Georg Cantor and set theory belong forever together. Although Dedekind had already introduced the concept of a set and naïve set theory in 1872, it was Cantor who single-handedly created transfinite set theory as a new branch of mathematics. In a series of papers written between 1874 and 1885, he developed the fundamental concepts of abstract set theory and proved the most important of its theorems. Although today set theory is accepted by the majority of scientists as an autonomous branch of mathematics, and perhaps the most fundamental, this was not always the case. Indeed, when Cantor set out to develop his conception of sets and to argue for its acceptance, he initiated an inquiry into the infinite which raised questions that have still not been completely resolved today.

1 Cantor's development of set theory
2 The philosophical implications

1 Cantor's development of set theory

Cantor was born to a wealthy merchant family in St Petersburg and first went to Germany (Frankfurt) at the age of eleven. He studied in Zurich, Göttingen and (mainly) in Berlin, under Kummer, who directed his dissertation (completed in 1867), Weierstrass and Kronecker. In 1869, after a brief intermezzo as a teacher, Cantor went to Halle as a *Privatdozent*. Despite persistent attempts to secure a better position at a more prestigious university, he spent his entire career there, dying in 1918 after several bouts of manic depression. Thanks to the efforts of Hilbert, Zermelo, Fraenkel and many others he did see his ideas accepted by the majority of mathematicians.

The beginnings of Cantor's work on set theory emerged towards the end of 1873 in an exchange of letters with his colleague Richard Dedekind (see Cantor and Dedekind 1937). In a letter dated 29 November Cantor asks whether there is a one-one correspondence between the real numbers and the natural numbers. He already knew, from Dedekind, that it was possible to put the algebraic numbers into one-one correspondence with the natural numbers. He doubted that the same was true of the real numbers because the reals form a continuum while the natural numbers are discrete. As far as we know,

Dedekind did not answer the question, believing it to be of no practical importance (although he saw its theoretical relevance).

In his next letter (7 December) Cantor answered his own question: he informed Dedekind that he had a proof of the impossibility of a one-one correspondence between the real numbers in the open unit interval (that is, those between, but not including, 0 and 1) and the natural numbers. This was the first proof that the real numbers are 'uncountable'. A few months later (1874), Cantor published his proof under the rather misleading title 'Über eine Eigenschaft des Inbegriffes aller reellen algebraischen Zahlen' (On a Property of the Set of all Real Algebraic Numbers). The main result, not mentioned in the title, had as a consequence the proof of the existence of 'transcendental' – that is, non-algebraic real – numbers.

This little-noticed paper showed for the first time that different 'levels' of infinity must be distinguished and this result, perhaps more than any other, triggered the further development of set theory. Dedekind was probably the only mathematician at the time who understood the real significance of this work, correcting his previous opinion of the practical unimportance of Cantor's question as 'conclusively rejected by Cantor's proof'. But what is its significance? First, the proof shows that the distinction between different levels of infinity is not empty – by no means a trivial result because until Cantor almost all mathematicians believed there to be essentially only one 'size' of infinity. Second, it challenges the Aristotelian dogma that the infinite exists merely potentially, but not actually.

In his next paper, 'Ein Beitrag zur Mannigfaltigkeitslehre' (1878), Cantor considered the 'power' of sets: two sets are of equal power (cardinality) if there is a one-one correspondence between their elements. He tried to show that there exist sets of higher cardinality than the continuum by showing that a continuum of two dimensions cannot be mapped one-one onto a continuum of one dimension. To his own surprise, however, the result was exactly the opposite: all continua of any countable dimension have the same cardinality as the linear continuum (the real numbers).

$$|\mathbb{R} \times \mathbb{R} \times \mathbb{R} \times \ldots| = \ldots = |\mathbb{R} \times \mathbb{R}| = |\mathbb{R}|$$

This unexpected result led Cantor to state for the first time his famous 'continuum hypothesis': that in the linear continuum of real numbers exactly two classes of infinities are represented – countable (the cardinality of the natural numbers) and uncountable (the cardinality of the reals) – with none in between (see CONTINUUM HYPOTHESIS; SET THEORY §3).

The following six years were the most fruitful of Cantor's life. Not only did he publish (in six parts) the paper 'Über unendliche lineare Punktmannigfaltigkeiten' (On Infinite Linear Manifolds of Points), but he also developed his 'arithmetical' theory of the infinite. The first step in the development was the introduction of 'derived sets' represented by the symbols '∞', '∞ + 1', and so on. Later he took these symbols as representing transfinite ordinal numbers. He defined a generalized 'successor' operation, and a 'supremum' operation which gives the limit of an infinite sequence of ordinal numbers. Starting from 0, the ordinal of the empty set, the 'successor' operation generates the sequence of natural numbers and the 'supremum' operation secures the existence of the first transfinite number – the ordinal of the set of natural numbers – called ω_0 or ω. The 'successor' operation in turn generates the numbers $\omega + 1, \omega + 2, \ldots$ and the 'supremum' operation then guarantees the existence of $\omega + \omega$, and so on. (See SET THEORY §2.)

Cantor divided the ordinals into number classes. The first number class is the class of natural numbers, which has cardinality $\aleph_0$ ('aleph-nought' or 'aleph-null'). It has to be exhausted before ω, the first number of the second number class, is created. The second number class is the set $\{\omega, \omega + 1, \omega + 2, \ldots, \}$, each element of which has cardinality $\aleph_0$. The cardinality of the second number class itself is $\aleph_1$. Cantor proved that $\aleph_1$ is the next largest cardinal after $\aleph_0$. In this terminology the continuum hypothesis becomes the conjecture that the cardinality of the continuum is $\aleph_1$ (see CONTINUUM HYPOTHESIS §2).

2 The philosophical implications

Cantor's work on the infinite did not end with his arithmetical analysis of it. In his 1883 essay 'Grundlagen einer allgemeinen Mannigfaltigkeitslehre', he also tried to answer philosophical objections to the idea of actually existing, completed infinite classes.

One objection rested on the supposition that infinite numbers must obey exactly the same laws as finite numbers. But, as Cantor had shown, transfinite numbers have their own peculiar arithmetical laws – for example, the commutative law of addition $(a + b = b + a)$ does not hold for ordinals. This means that transfinite numbers are not finite numbers but not that they are not numbers.

Another objection related to the impossibility of completing a limiting process such as that of approaching the transcendental number π. This was more difficult to deal with. Cantor developed his counter-argument in two steps: first, he argued that the infinite as it occurs in a limit-process is, properly speaking, only a variable approaching a certain limit but still itself always remaining finite. In the second step, he pointed to the logical aspect of quantification; in particular, to the fact that the use of a variable presupposes the specification of a closed domain over which it varies. Hence, a limit-process – like a general statement concerning all numbers – presupposes logically that the infinite domain of numbers is actually and not only potentially given.

Neither argument is, however, completely convincing. With respect to the first, it turned out that the question of consistency is more difficult to resolve than Cantor had imagined. Indeed, set theory, as it was conceived by Cantor, entailed also 'inconsistent sets' and, hence, inconsistencies as Cantor himself noted in a letter to Hilbert in 1897 (see PARADOXES OF SET AND PROPERTY §1). But even when the inconsistency had been removed by Zermelo, the problem of proving the consistency of the improved set theory remained.

The second argument blurs the distinction between mathematics and logic. This results from the fact that mathematical induction – as it is used in the limit-processes in analysis – is logically analysed as a universal claim about an infinite domain, which is supposed to be completely finished. 'In the system of set theory mathematics has no specific content, it is nothing but logic, which has come to maturity' as Weyl said (1925). Indeed Cantor's argument for the existence of transfinite numbers, or, as he says, for their 'immanent reality', rests on the assumption that we can 'run through' an infinite sequence of numbers and exhaust it. But this is – epistemically speaking – impossible. It presupposes, as Hilbert has shown (1926: 174–8), certain ideal assumptions regarding the logical notions of 'all' and 'existence'.

See also: CANTOR'S THEOREM; INFINITY §§6–7; LOGIC AND MATHEMATICAL TERMS, GLOSSARY OF; PARADOXES OF SET AND PROPERTY; SET THEORY

List of works

Cantor, G. (1932) *Gesammelte Abhandlungen mathematischen und philosophischen Inhalts* (Collected Papers), ed. E. Zermelo, Berlin: Springer, 1980. (With a biography by A. Fraenkel.)
—— (1874) 'Über eine Eigenschaft des Inbegriffs aller reellen algebraischen Zahlen' (On a Property of the Set of all Real Algebraic Numbers), *Crelle Journal* 77: 258–62. (The title of this paper is misleading because it describes only the first half of the content – the countability of the algebraic numbers. It refers neither to the main result – the uncountability of the open unit interval – nor to its main consequence – a new proof of the existence of 'transcendental' (that is, non-algebraic real) numbers.)

—— (1895, 1897) 'Beiträge zur Begründung der transfiniten Mengenlehre', parts 1 and 2, *Mathematische Annalen* 46: 481–512, 49: 207–48; trans. P.E.B. Jourdain (1915), *Contributions to the Founding of the Theory of Transfinite Numbers*, New York: Dover, 1955. (Two of Cantor's most important memoirs on transfinite numbers.)
—— (1991) *Briefe* (Letters), ed. H. Meschkowski and W. Nilson, Berlin: Springer. (Includes Cantor's 1899 letters to Dedekind and 1897–1900 letters to Hilbert relating to the paradoxes.)
Cantor, G. and Dedekind, R. (1937) *Briefwechsel Cantor–Dedekind* (Cantor–Dedekind Correspondence), ed. E. Noether and J. Cavaillès, Paris: Hermann; French trans. in J. Cavaillès, *Philosophie mathématique*, Paris: Hermann, 1962. (Includes most of the correspondence between Dedekind and Cantor.)

References and further reading

Dauben, J.W. (1979) *Georg Cantor: His Mathematics and Philosophy of the Infinite*, Cambridge, MA: Harvard University Press; repr. Princeton, NJ: Princeton University Press. (An excellent intellectual biography which traces the development of Cantor's mathematical ideas, putting them in the context of his philosophy and professional life.)
Ferreiros, J. (1993) 'On the Relation between Georg Cantor and Richard Dedekind', *Historia Mathematica* 20: 343–63. (An interesting re-examination of the mutual relation between Cantor and Dedekind.)
Hallett, M. (1984) *Cantorian Set Theory and Limitation of Size*, Oxford: Clarendon Press. (A detailed study of the historical development of set theory.)
Hilbert, D. (1926) 'Über das Unendliche', *Mathematische Annalen* 95: 161–90; trans. 'On the Infinite', in P. Benacerraf and H. Putnam (eds) *Philosophy of Mathematics: Selected Readings*, Cambridge: Cambridge University Press, 2nd edn, 1983. (An abridged version of an entire lecture held in the winter term 1924/1925.)
Majer, U. (1993) 'Das Unendliche – eine bloße Idee?', *Revue internationale de Philosophie* 47: 319–41. (A logico-philosophical investigation of the infinite.)
Purkert, W. and Ilgauds, H.J. (1987) *Georg Cantor 1845–1918*, Basle: Birkhäuser. (An extensive biography of Cantor's life and work.)
* Weyl, H. (1925) *Die heutige Erkenntnislage in der Mathematik* (The Present State of Knowledge in Mathematics), Erlangen: Weltkreis; repr. in *Gesammelte Abhandlungen*, vol. 2, ed. K. Chandrasekharan, Berlin: Springer, 1968. (A very condensed exposition of Weyl's point of view

regarding the relation between, on the one hand, logic and set theory and, on the other, arithmetic including analysis and the continuum.)

ULRICH MAJER

CANTOR'S THEOREM

Cantor's theorem states that the cardinal number ('size') of the set of subsets of any set is greater than the cardinal number of the set itself. So once the existence of one infinite set has been proved, sets of ever increasing infinite cardinality can be generated. The philosophical interest of this result lies (1) in the foundational role it played in Cantor's work, prior to the axiomatization of set theory, (2) in the similarity between its proof and arguments which lead to the set-theoretic paradoxes, and (3) in controversy between intuitionist and classical mathematicians concerning what exactly its proof proves.

Cantor's theorem states that the cardinal number ('size'; see SET THEORY §3) of the power set $\wp(A)$ of any set A (that is, the set of all subsets of A) is greater than the cardinal number of A itself.

One of the seemingly paradoxical properties of infinite sets is that they can be put into one-one correspondence with proper parts of themselves. For example, the function $f(n) = 2n$ maps each natural number to exactly one even number. If one-one correspondence is taken to indicate sameness of size for infinite sets, as it does for finite ones, then this means that the set of natural numbers must be said to be the same size as the set of even numbers, even though intuitively one would think that there should be twice as many natural numbers as there are even numbers. If any infinite set could be put into one-one correspondence with any other, there would be little point in trying to use 'numbers' as means of 'size' comparison for infinite sets. This is why Cantor's proof that there are infinite sets which cannot be put into one-one correspondence with each other was crucial to the development of his theory of transfinite ordinal and cardinal numbers.

Cantor was seeking a characterization of the structure of point continua and his original result (1874) was that no denumerable sequence of elements in an interval $[a, b]$ of the real line can contain all the elements of $[a, b]$. From this he concluded that a continuum of real numbers cannot be uniquely correlated with the natural numbers. To transform this result into what has become known as Cantor's theorem required making sense of the idea that every set, finite or infinite, has a cardinal number (sets between which there exists a one-one correspondence being deemed to have the same cardinal number); developing an arithmetic of infinite cardinal numbers; and establishing the existence of a one-one correspondence between the real numbers in any continuous interval and the set $\wp(\mathbb{N})$ of all subsets of the set $\mathbb{N}$ of natural numbers. The non-denumerability of the real numbers then becomes a special case of the more general set-theoretic result.

Russell was able to produce a contradiction in Frege's system of logic by considering the class of all classes that do not belong to themselves (see PARADOXES OF SET AND PROPERTY §4). A similar strategy is used to prove that there would be a contradiction if there were a one-one function f mapping a set A onto its power set $\wp(A)$. Consider $d = \{x \in A: x \notin f(x)\}$. This is a subset of A and hence $d \in \wp(A)$. Since f correlates every member of $\wp(A)$ with a unique member of A, there is a unique element $a_d \in A$ such that $d = f(a_d)$. But both $a_d \in d$ and $a_d \notin d$ entail contradictions. Since the existence of A and of $\wp(A)$ are not in question, there can be no such f which is both one-one and onto.

In the case where A is finite or denumerable, d coincides with the diagonal set, which is defined by interchanging 0's and 1's down the diagonal of a square array such as the following (in which 0 indicates that a_i belongs to $f(a_i)$ and 1 that it does not).

	$f(a_1)$	$f(a_2)$	$f(a_3)$	$f(a_4)$	$\cdots$
a_1	0	1	1	0	$\cdots$
a_2	0	0	1	1	$\cdots$
a_3	1	1	1	0	$\cdots$
a_4	1	0	0	1	$\cdots$
$\vdots$	$\vdots$	$\vdots$	$\vdots$	$\vdots$	$\vdots$

While there is general agreement that such an argument can be used to establish, for example, that for any given enumeration of the real numbers it is possible to specify a real number which is not included in that enumeration, the step to concluding from this that there exists a set whose cardinal number is greater than that of the natural numbers is disputed by those who, like the intuitionists, do not accept the existence of actually infinite totalities (see CONSTRUCTIVISM IN MATHEMATICS; INTUITIONISM). Instead they may interpret the result as reflecting the difference between natural numbers and real numbers. The latter must be defined via potentially infinite sequences of rational numbers or potentially infinite decimal expansions, and so are never fully determinate objects. A function from a domain of such entities to a collection of determinate objects can never be guaranteed to be one-one. It is thus concluded that the real numbers form a potentially infinite domain of a different kind from that of the natural numbers, but not one which could be said to have a higher cardinality.

See also: CONTINUUM HYPOTHESIS; LOGICAL AND MATHEMATICAL TERMS, GLOSSARY OF

References and further reading

Cantor, G. (1895, 1897) 'Beiträge zur Begründung der transfiniten Mengenlehre', parts 1 and 2, *Mathematische Annalen* 46: 481–512, 49: 207–46; trans. P.E.B. Jourdain (1915), *Contributions to the Founding of the Theory of Transfinite Numbers*, New York: Dover, 1955. (Two of Cantor's most important memoirs on transfinite numbers.)

Dauben, J.W. (1979) *Georg Cantor: His Mathematics and Philosophy of the Infinite*, Cambridge, MA: Harvard University Press. (An excellent intellectual biography which traces the development of Cantor's mathematical ideas, while putting them in the context of his philosophy of the infinite and his professional life.)

Dummett, M.A.E. (1978) *Truth and Other Enigmas*, London: Duckworth. (See the essays 'The Philosophical Significance of Gödel's Theorem', 'Platonism' and 'The Philosophical Basis of Intuitionistic Logic'.)

Wilder, R.L. (1952) *Introduction to the Foundations of Mathematics*, Krieger; 2nd edn, New York, London and Sydney: Wiley & Sons, 1965, 91–101. (Discussion of diagonal arguments.)

Wittgenstein, L.J.J. (1956) *Remarks on the Foundations of Mathematics*, ed. G.H. von Wright, R. Rhees and G.E.M. Anscombe, trans. G.E.M. Anscombe, Oxford: Blackwell, 2nd edn, 1967, part 1, appendix 2, 54–63; 3rd edn, 1978. (Includes a discussion of what exactly the proof of Cantor's theorem proves.)

MARY TILES

CAPREOLUS, JOHANNES (*c.*1380–1444)

Thomist philosopher and theologian, Capreolus composed a lengthy commentary on Aquinas' work on Peter Lombard's Sentences, *known as* Defensiones theologiae divi Thomae Aquinatis *(Defences of the Theology of Thomas Aquinas) (first printed in 1483–4). He sought to refute the criticisms of Thomism by competing scholastic traditions during the fourteenth century. The Thomistic school was so impressed with Capreolus' achievement that it came to refer to him as* Princeps Thomistarum *(leader of the Thomists). Twentieth-century Thomists have, generally, considered him more faithful to the teachings of Aquinas than later commentators such as Cajetan. His philosophical opinions which have received most attention concern analogy, the formal ontological constituent of the person and the individuation of material substances.*

Capreolus was born in Rodez, France, around 1380 and entered the Dominican Order there. In 1407 he was assigned to the University of Paris as bachelor of the *Sentences*. He was licensed to graduate as master of theology in 1411. He subsequently taught in Dominican convents in Toulouse and Rodez. He died in Rodez on 6 April 1444.

Capreolus' reflections on analogy appear in his attack on Duns Scotus' affirmation that the concept of being is predicated univocally of God and creatures (see DUNS SCOTUS, J. §5). He does not present a systematic theory of analogy but solely a tentative clarification of the analogy of being (see LANGUAGE, RENAISSANCE PHILOSOPHY OF §4).

He accepts as paradigmatic Aquinas' threefold division of analogy (see AQUINAS §9). It is the third part of the division that deals with the analogy between God and creatures: the analogical concept is predicated of things which have neither a proper notion nor their manner of being in common. To explain it, he uses the distinction between the formal and the objective concept thereafter adopted almost unanimously by the Thomistic school. The formal concept is the subjective, mental representation of a common nature produced by the possible intellect after it has been actualized by an impressed intelligible species abstracted by the agent intellect from a phantasm. The objective concept is the extramental common nature considered precisely in so far as it is the object of an act of understanding.

Duns Scotus would be correct, Capreolus claims, if he held that it is the formal concept of being that is predicated univocally of God and creatures. But Duns Scotus errs by asserting this of the objective concept of being which, in fact, is predicated analogically. An objective concept is analogical when it is predicated of several things 'by attribution'. Predication by attribution is the essential characteristic of analogical predication. By this Capreolus means a predication which reflects an order of priority and posteriority founded on real relations of causality, dependence or correlativity.

Capreolus proposes a theory of the formal,

ontological constituent of the person. The person is a complete being in the intellectual order. Being is predicated primarily of first or individual substances. The person is, then, an individual substance in the intellectual order. An individual substance does not derive the characteristics of its completeness (autonomy and incommunicability) so much from its essence as from its act of existence. The act of existence, which is the formal constituent not only of the essence but of the substance as such, must also be the formal constituent of the person. Accordingly, ontological personhood is to be distinguished from the instantiated intellectual nature in the same manner as the act of existence is distinguished from essence. Capreolus' theory has no place for the explanation of ontological personhood in terms of an added modality, as would be proposed by later commentators such as Cajetan, and is founded directly on Aquinas' real distinction between essence and the act of existence.

The problem of the individuation of material substances concerns the possibility of their solely numerical distinction and multiplication within a single species. The classic Thomistic answer is that such distinction and multiplication presupposes division, which in turn presupposes divisibility. Divisibility itself presupposes quantification, which in turn presupposes materiality. Individuation is to be explained, therefore, in terms of matter as marked (*signata*) by quantity. Divergences arise over the precise meaning of this marking (*signatio*). Capreolus' opinion is that it means the actual quantification of corporeal matter and not merely a capacity for, or some other kind of relation to, quantification on the part of prime matter. Later commentators, such as Cajetan, preferred one of these alternative interpretations and accused Capreolus of absurdly reducing the principle of individuation to an accident of material substances. But, for Capreolus, the principle of individuation is not this actual quantification but corporeal matter in so far as it is actually quantified.

Capreolus' work was very popular during the century which followed its first printing in 1483–4. This was due to the wide range of authors against whom he argued: Duns Scotus, WILLIAM OF OCKHAM, Peter AUREOL, GREGORY OF RIMINI, DURANDUS OF ST POURÇAIN, HERVAEUS NATALIS and many others. He seems to have relied, though, on the expositions of their views which he found in Aureol's commentary on the *Sentences*. Particularly important for the diffusion of his doctrines were the many digests, concordances and indices made at this time by such authors as Paul Soncinas, Sylvester Prierias and Matthias Aquarius. Since then his thought has been generally neglected with the exception of the few, especially controversial, issues mentioned above.

See also: AQUINAS, T.; CAJETAN; THOMISM

List of works

Capreolus, J. (1483–4) *Super libros IV Sententiarum (Defensiones theologiae divi Thomae Aquinatis)* (Defences of the Theology of Thomas Aquinas), Venice; ed. C. Paban and T. Pègues, Tours: Cattier, 1900–8, 7 vols; repr. Frankfurt am Main: Minerva, 1967. (The only modern edition of Capreolus' work.)

References and further reading

Bedouelle, G., Cessario, R. and White, K. (eds) (1997) *Jean Capreolus et son temps 1380–1444* (Capreolus and His Times), special issue of *Mémoire Dominicaine* 1. (Includes articles on Capreolus' background, doctrine and influence.)

Bellerate, B.M. (1960) 'L'analogia tomista nei grandi commentatori di S. Tommaso' (Thomistic Analogy in the Great Commentators on Aquinas), Rome: Salesian University, 28–44. (Abstract of a Ph.D. thesis that gives the most detailed account of Capreolus' theory of analogy.)

Degl'Innocenti, U. (1940) 'Il Capreolo e la questione sulla personalità' (Capreolus and the Question on Personality), *Divus Thomas* 43: 27–40. (Account of Capreolus' theory of ontological personhood.)

—— (1971) *Il principio di individuazione nella Scuola Tomistica* (The Principle of Individuation in the Thomistic School), Rome: Lateran University, 72–93. (Account of Capreolus' theory of individuation.)

Grabmann, M. (1956) 'Johannes Capreolus O.P., der *Princeps Thomistarum* (†1444), und seine Stellung in der Geschichte der Thomistenschule' (Capreolus, the *Prince of the Thomists*, and his place in the history of the Thomistic school), in *Mittelalterliches Geistesleben: Abhandlungen zur Geschichte der Scholastik und Mystik*, Munich: Hueber, vol. 3, 370–410. (Capreolus' influence on the Thomistic School.)

Hegyi, J. (1959) *Die Bedeutung des Seins bei den klassischen Kommentatoren des heiligen Thomas von Aquin: Capreolus, Silvester von Ferrara, Cajetan* (The Meaning of Being in the Classic Commentators on Aquinas: Capreolus, Silvestri and Cajetan), Pullacher Philosophische Forschungen 4, Pullach bei München: Berchmanskolleg, 9–51. (Account of Capreolus' metaphysics.)

Kaeppeli, T. (1975) *Scriptores Ordinis Praedicatorum*

Medii Aevi (Medieval Dominican Writers), Rome: Sabina, vol. 2, 395–6. (Essential biographical and bibliographical data.)

MICHAEL TAVUZZI

CARDANO, GIROLAMO (1501–76)

The Renaissance Italian Girolamo Cardano is famous for his colourful personality, as well as for his work in medicine and mathematics, and indeed in almost all the arts and sciences. He was an eclectic philosopher, and one of the founders of the so-called new philosophy of nature developed in the sixteenth century. He used both the Aristotelian and the Neoplatonic traditions as starting points, and following the medical paradigm of organic being, he transformed the traditional Aristotelian universe into an animated universe in which, thanks to their organic functional order, all individual parts strive towards the conservation both of themselves and of the whole universe. As a result, they can be subjected to a functional analysis. In his more casual writings on moral philosophy, Cardano showed his orientation to be basically Stoic.

1 Life
2 Non-philosophical achievements
3 Metaphysics
4 Physics
5 Epistemology
6 Main works in natural philosophy

1 Life

Girolamo Cardano (also known as Gerolamo Cardano or Hieronymus Cardanus) was the illegitimate son of a Milanese lawyer, and grew up in very difficult conditions. He studied medicine and mathematics at Pavia (1518–23) and Padua (1524–6). He received his MA and his MD from Padua, and practised as a physician, first at Saccolongo near Padua (1526–32) and then, after some controversy with his local colleagues, in Milan (1539–43). In 1552 he successfully cured John Hamilton, Bishop of Edinburgh, of asthma, and for the rest of his life enjoyed his reputation as a famous physician. Cardano started teaching mathematics at Milan in 1534, and medicine in Pavia from 1543. After the execution of his son for murder Cardano left Pavia, and he taught at Bologna from 1562. He was arrested by the Inquisition in 1570 for reasons which remain unknown, and was released on condition that he abandon teaching and publish-

ing. Cardano then went to Rome where he received an annuity from the Pope, and continued to practise as a physician. He also worked on his frank and self-revelatory autobiography up to the time of his death on 21 September 1576, a date that he had himself foretold from his horoscope.

Cardano was a prolific writer. In his will of 1571 he mentions 103 printed works and forty-three in manuscript form. In his autobiography *De vita propria liber* (*The Book of My Life*) he counts fifty-five works in print and forty-five in manuscript. His *Opera omnia* contains seventy-one works published during his lifetime and forty other works. His style is inelegant, his Latin faulty, his argumentation often incomplete and disorganized, and as a result his writings are often unclear and difficult to understand. This does not, however, mean that he had nothing of value to say.

2 Non-philosophical achievements

Cardano was extremely creative, and a torchbearer for scientific progress. He took pride in being called *vir inventionum* (the man of inventions) and opened up new perspectives on every field he entered. In medicine, Cardano claimed to have made 40,000 important and 200,000 less important inventions. In mathematics, he taught a method for solving cubic equations, though the mathematician Tartaglia accused him of plagiarism, and he made the first moves towards the theory of probability. In mechanics 'Cardano's suspension' is still regarded as a success. He wrote on music and on dreams, believed in demons, and was regarded as a reliable astrologer, who even cast the horoscope of Jesus Christ.

3 Metaphysics

Cardano claimed that PLOTINUS and ARISTOTLE were his main inspiration in philosophy, and though he argued explicitly against Aristotle, his theory is implicitly based on the Aristotelian tradition. While he was not a systematic thinker, his work rests on some basic assumptions which allow for a systematic understanding of his main philosophical teaching, and which are themselves of major philosophic interest.

His notion of unity is fundamental. It was developed in a little treatise *De uno* (On the One), written around 1560 and published in Basle in 1562. Cardano himself recommended it as an introduction to his natural philosophy. In it he argued that everything that exists is one, so that the structure of unity is identical to the structure of reality. Analysis of a given real being, a human being for example, shows that its unity consists both in the single principle behind its various operations and in the organic structure of its corporeal basis, which guarantees that its various parts cooperate in the effort to achieve self-conservation. Thus every real being can properly be regarded as a system constituted by a certain number of organic parts that cooperate in function. Every organ, in so far as it is a real being and therefore one, has necessarily to be such a system; and every real being, as part of a greater, more comprehensive, whole, has to function as an organ of this larger unit. As a result, reality is reduced to a system of functions, in which every individual being is at the same time an organ or subsystem of its supersystem, and the superior unit of its subsystems. This kind of ordering is also to be found in the sphere of history, which is governed by fate.

4 Physics

In Cardano's treatise *De natura* (On Nature), written at the same time as *De uno* (though not published in his lifetime) and like *De uno* recommended as introductory reading, Cardano developed his concept of nature in accordance with his basic ontological principle of unity. The single principle which coordinates the various operations of natural beings and causes the organic order of their unity is called the soul. As a result the whole of the material world is animated, and Aristotle's distinction between organic and non-organic nature is abandoned. Different souls are systematically ordered in the same way as the different natural beings which they animate. Their principal task is to care for the self-preservation of the bodies which correspond to them, so they are endowed with whatever means of cognition are necessary for that task. They act in accordance with the principles of sympathy and antipathy. The intellectual soul, being supernatural, is one and the same for all human beings, as Averroes had held (see IBN RUSHD §3).

Bodies themselves are constituted by the heat of the heavens. This heat is the active principle that serves the soul, and operates on the passive principle's density or extension. In *De subtilitate* (On Subtlety) Cardano identifies this passive principle with prime matter (*prima materia*) which, according to Averroes, is endowed with indefinite quantity; in *De natura* the passive principle is understood as moisture. Thus Cardano reduces and transforms Aristotle's doctrine of the four primary qualities (hot, cold, wet and dry) that constitute the four elements.

5 Epistemology

Natural beings are perceived as organic units through the senses, and it is the task of science, through a functional analysis, to transform this confused knowledge of the whole into a distinct knowledge of its parts and their ordering in a system. Thanks to the infinity of the universe's various parts, human beings will never be able to analyse and thereby know the whole of the universe. Moreover, thanks to the infinite subtlety of the smallest parts, which escape the senses, these too will necessarily remain unknown. As a result, as Cardano points out in *De arcanis aeternitatis* (On the Secrets of Eternity), it is the greatest and indeed most disastrous error to claim that humans can achieve absolute knowledge. Nonetheless, there are organic units which are not disproportionate to the human intellect in terms of the variety of their parts and the subtlety of their structure, and these can be the subject of scientific analysis. Moreover, they enjoy ontological autonomy as far as their place in the system's order is concerned, and hence can be known, if not according to their essence, at least according to their functional structure. It is this knowledge of the functional structure of natural beings that, if soundly based, can be used in technical or mechanical inventions.

6 Main works in natural philosophy

It is in the context of the principles discussed in §§3–5 that Cardano's main works in natural philosophy, the twenty-one books of *De subtilitate* from 1550, and their supplement, the seventeen books of *De rerum varietate* (On the Variety of Beings) written in 1557, should be read. While their titles refer to the aspects of reality that constitute the limits of human knowledge, the books themselves offer a comprehensive description of the whole universe. Following the order of the traditional Aristotelian doctrine of nature, they start with the principles of physics and descend to the elements, the mixed bodies, metals and stones, plants, animals, and human beings; then they ascend again from the psychological faculties of the senses, the will and the intellect, through their effects, the arts and sciences, to the demons, first substances, and God himself. This apparently Aristotelian order led Julius Caesar Scaliger to criticize Cardano from the perspective of orthodox Aristotelianism; the fact that, for no apparent reason, Cardano mixed the theoretical with the practical and the general with the particular does make it difficult to follow his arguments. However, contrary to Scaliger's belief, Cardano did not intend to teach Aristotelian natural philosophy. Nor did he, contrary to modern expectations, intend to display a comprehensive and consistent theory of nature. His way of writing and arguing must be understood in the light of his denial of the possibility of absolute truth and his doubts about the fruitfulness of merely theoretical argumentation. He was content to offer a functional analysis of individual natural beings through sense perception, and to validate his analysis through technical application.

See also: ARISTOTELIANISM, RENAISSANCE

List of works

Cardano, G. (*c.*1540–76) *Opera omnia*, ed. C. Spohn, Lyons, 1663, 10 vols; repr. New York and London: Johnson, 1967. (Only comprehensive edition of Cardano's works.)

—— (*c.*1540) *De arcanis aeternitatis* (On the Secrets of Eternity), in C. Spohn (ed.) *Opera omnia*, New York and London: Johnson, 1967, vol. 10, 1–49. (Incomplete; demonstrates the limits of human knowledge.)

—— (*c.*1541) *Liber de ludo aleae*, in C. Spohn (ed.) *Opera omnia*, New York and London: Johnson, 1967, vol. 1, 262–82; trans. S.H. Gould, 'The Book on Games of Chance', in O. Ore, *Cardano the Gambling Scholar*, Princeton, NJ: Princeton University Press, 1953; repr. New York: Dover, 1965. (Cardano's theory of probability.)

—— (1545) *Artis magnae sive de regulis algebraicis liber unus*, Nuremberg: Ioannes Petreius; ed. and trans. T.R. Witner, *The Great Art, or the Rules of Algebra*, Cambridge, MA: MIT Press, 1968. (Cardano's most important and influential algebra manual.)

—— (1550) *De subtilitate* (On Subtlety), Nuremberg: Ioannes Petreius; in C. Spohn (ed.) *Opera omnia*, New York and London: Johnson, 1967, vol. 3, 357–672; M.M. Cass (ed. and trans.) *The first book of Jerome Cardan's De subtilitate, Translated from the Original Latin with Text, Introduction and Commentary*, Williamsport, PA: Bayard Press, 1934. (Cardano's major work in natural philosophy.)

—— (1557) *De rerum varietate* (On the Variety of Beings), Basle: Henricus Petri; in C. Spohn (ed.) *Opera omnia*, New York and London: Johnson, 1967, vol. 2, 1–356. (Supplement to Cardano's *De subtilitate*; written in 1557.)

—— (*c.*1560) *De natura* (On Nature), in C. Spohn (ed.) *Opera omnia*, New York and London: Johnson, 1967, vol. 2, 283–98. (Written around 1560, *De natura* was only published posthumously.)

—— (1562) *De uno* (On the One), Basle; in C. Spohn (ed.) *Opera omnia*, New York and London: Johnson, 1967, vol. 1, 277–83. (Written around 1560, but not published until 1562; develops

Cardano's concept of what constitutes the 'oneness' of natural beings.)

—— (before 1576) *De vita propria liber*, in C. Spohn (ed.) *Opera omnia*, New York and London: Johnson, 1967, vol. 1, 1–54; trans. J. Stoner, *The Book of My Life*, New York: Dover, 1962. (Cardano's autobiography; he was working on this work up to his death in 1576.)

References and further reading

Eckman, J. (1946) 'Jerome Cardano', *Bulletin of the History of Medicine*, supplementary vol. 7, Baltimore, MD: Johns Hopkins University Press. (Discussion of Cardano's life and fortunes, with extensive bibliography in the notes.)

Fierz, M. (1977) *Girolamo Cardano (1501–1576)*, Basle and Stuttgart: Birkhäuser. (Discussion of Cardano's achievements as philosopher and scientist.)

Ingegno, A. (1980) *Saggio sulla filosofia di Cardano* (Essay on the Philosophy of Cardano), Florence: La Nuova Italia. (Describes the different aspects of Cardano's philosophy; bibliography on pages 21–31.)

Kessler, E. (ed.) (1994) *Girolamo Cardano. Philosoph, Arzt, Mathematiker* (Philosopher, Physician, Mathematician), Wiesbaden: Harrassowitz. (Contributions to the international Cardano Colloquium, held in Wolfenbüttel in 1989; covers the different aspects of Cardano's thought.)

Margolin, J.-C. (1976) 'Cardan, interprète d'Aristote' (Cardano as Interpreter of Aristotle), in *Platon et Aristote à la Renaissance. XVIe Colloque international de Tours*, Paris: Vrin, 307–33. (Places special emphasis on moral philosophy and the immortality of the soul.)

ECKHARD KESSLER

CARDANUS, HIERONYMUS
see CARDANO, GIROLAMO

CARE, ETHICS OF *see* FEMINIST ETHICS

CARLYLE, THOMAS (1795–1881)

Although widely influential as a historian, moralist and social critic, Carlyle has no real claim to be considered a philosopher. He does have some importance as one of the transmitters of the ideas of the German Idealists, such as Kant and Fichte, to Britain, and as one of the chief British spokesmen for the Romantic exaltation of the imagination above the understanding; but his grasp of philosophical issues is vague. His later writings are dominated by the idea, derived from his childhood Calvinism, of a divine justice working in history through the medium of great men ('heroes') who are its conscious or unconscious instruments.

Carlyle was born in Ecclefechan, Scotland, the eldest son of James Carlyle, a farmer and stonemason, and his wife Margaret. Educated at Annan Academy and Edinburgh University, he eked out a meagre living by private tutoring and journalism until leaving Scotland and moving to London in 1834. His first major work, *Sartor Resartus*, was published in 1833: the most significant of his later writings were *The French Revolution* (1837), *Past and Present* (1843), *Letters and Speeches of Oliver Cromwell* (1845) and *The History of Frederick the Great* (1858–65).

Carlyle is important as a literary figure, a moralist, a historian and a social critic, but has little serious claim to be considered a philosopher, though he was sometimes regarded as such by his contemporaries. His chief interest in this regard is as one of the transmitters of German Idealism to Britain in the 1820s. The tradition of Scottish Calvinism in which he had been brought up had been shaken by his encounter with the ideas of the Enlightenment at Edinburgh University, and he found in the German Idealist tradition a resolution of the problems this caused him. His enthusiasm for this tradition was expressed in a series of review articles from the 1820s which first brought his name before the public – notably on the 'State of German Literature' (1827) and 'Novalis' (1829) (see also 'Voltaire' (1829) and 'Diderot' (1833) for his repudiation of the rationalism of the Enlightenment).

In these articles he refers enthusiastically to the work of FICHTE and KANT, insisting particularly on the characteristic German Idealist distinction between *Vernunft* ('Reason') and *Verstand* ('Understanding'), and exalting 'Reason', understood as comprehending feeling and imagination, at the expense of the empirical and logical 'Understanding'. However, Carlyle was much more interested in the literature of the German renaissance than in its philosophy (it is

significant that he never wrote specifically on Kant or Fichte) – in particular, he idolized GOETHE – and his understanding of the strictly philosophical issues at stake was limited. He is accordingly less important as a transmitter of German Idealist philosophy than COLERIDGE – whom, in his later years, Carlyle knew, but whom he revealingly rejected, lacking patience for the fineness of Coleridge's distinctions and what he saw as his intellectual indecisiveness.

The fullest expression of Carlyle's philosophical position at this stage of his life is found in *Sartor Resartus*, the only one of his books which makes any claim to philosophical status. Its form – an examination of the life and writings of an imaginary 'Professor Teufelsdrockh' – is maverick, but the influence of German Idealism is manifest. The title ('The Tailor Re-Tailored') refers to Teufelsdrockh's supposed 'Philosophy of Clothes', in which clothes become the metaphor for the material world which simultaneously expresses and conceals the transcendental world within. This material world is conditioned by the categories of time and space, but these are themselves illusions, concealing the realities of eternity and infinity. These realities cannot be apprehended rationally, but only intuitively by the 'deep infinite faculties' of 'Fantasy and Heart'. In this plea for the imaginative faculties (anticipated in two important earlier essays, 'Signs of the Times' (1829) and 'Characteristics' (1831)) can be discerned one of the major manifestos of Romanticism, then at its height as a literary movement. The inspired artist – the ideal is Goethe – is seen by Carlyle as the hero who alone can discern and make clear to his readers the spiritual realities which underlie their material garments (the origin of the idea of 'hero worship', which becomes increasingly dominant in Carlyle's later work).

However, after *Sartor* Carlyle's concerns turned increasingly away from philosophy towards history and social criticism (the categories to which all his later writings listed above belong). His friends included both John Stuart MILL and Ralph Waldo EMERSON; but he passionately rejected both Mill's utilitarianism (which he characterized as 'Pig Philosophy') and his political liberalism, and showed little more enthusiasm for Emerson's transcendentalism. In his later writings, of which *The French Revolution* is the most remarkable, the influence of his earlier Calvinist heritage becomes increasingly apparent, in his insistence that the events of history can be properly understood only when they are seen as the workings of a vaguely-conceived divine providence which ensures the final triumph of justice in all the processes of history. This providence is purely moral – Carlyle does not see history as progressive (and seems not to have read Hegel). This sense of a providence working through history forms an approximate parallel to his earlier insistence on a transcendental order which can only be discerned through the material, but it is certainly not identical with it: it is moreover weakened by Carlyle's inability to provide any firm independent criterion of justice other than success, so that the argument becomes circular, and his biographies of Cromwell and Frederick the Great, especially the latter, are hard to distinguish from encomiums of *Realpolitik*.

A lack of close argument and clear definition pervades all Carlyle's work, and must undermine any serious claim for him as a philosopher. This very incoherence, however, enabled him to give forceful and sometimes memorable expression to a wide range of antirationalist and anti-empiricist attitudes characteristic of the Romantic reaction against the Enlightenment – a range that also includes a recurrent insistence on moral authenticity that sometimes anticipates some existentialist positions. His real significance, however, lies in other fields.

See also: GERMAN IDEALISM

List of Works

Carlyle, T. (1833–4) *Sartor Resartus*, ed. C.F. Harrold, New York: Doubleday, 1937. (Carlyle's only major work of philosophical interest.)

—— (1896) *The French Revolution*, London: Chapman and Hall, Centenary edition. (Generally recognized as the greatest of Carlyle's writings, this is interesting for its underlying philosophy of history, strongly influenced by German Idealism.)

—— (1896–9) *Critical and Miscellaneous Essays*, London: Chapman and Hall. (This Centenary edition contains 'Voltaire' and 'Diderot', marking Carlyle's repudiation of the Enlightenment; 'State of German Literature' and 'Novalis', summarizing his understanding of the German Idealist tradition; and 'Signs of the Times' and 'Characteristics', rejecting mechanical and utilitarian modes of thought in favour of imagination and faith.)

—— (1898) *Latter-Day Pamphlets*, London: Chapman and Hall, Centenary edition. (Interesting for the satirical attack on utilitarianism in the last chapter.)

References and further reading

Harris, K.M. (1986) 'Reason and Understanding Reconsidered: Coleridge, Carlyle, and Emerson', in *Essays in Literature* 13: 263–81, Macomb, IL: Western Illinois University. (Discusses Carlyle's understanding of Kant's distinction.)

Harrold, C.F. (1934) *Carlyle and German Thought*, Yale, NH: Yale University Press. (The only substantial treatment of the topic.)

Kaplan, F. (1983) *Thomas Carlyle*, Cambridge: Cambridge University Press. (The most recent authoritative biography.)

Tennyson, G.B. (1965) *Sartor Called Resartus*, Princeton, NJ: Princeton University Press. (The fullest study of *Sartor Resartus*.)

A.L. LE QUESNE

CARMICHAEL, GERSHOM (1672–1729)

Gershom Carmichael was a teacher and writer of pivotal importance for the Scottish Enlightenment of the eighteenth century. He was the first Professor of Moral Philosophy at the University of Glasgow, predecessor of Francis Hutcheson, Adam Smith and Thomas Reid. Carmichael introduced the natural law tradition of Grotius, Pufendorf and Locke to the moral philosophy courses he taught at the University of Glasgow (1694–1729). His commentaries on Samuel Pufendorf's work on the duty of man and citizen (1718 and 1724) made his teaching available to a wider readership in Great Britain and in Europe. He also composed an introduction to logic, Breviuscula Introductio ad Logicam, (1720 and 1722) and a brief system of natural theology, Synopsis Theologiae Naturalis (1729).

Gershom Carmichael began his teaching career at St Andrews University in 1693; he was appointed to the University of Glasgow in 1694, and became the first Professor of Moral Philosophy at that university in 1727. His moral philosophy is remarkable particularly for the manner in which he justified the natural rights of individuals. Those rights included self-defence, property and the natural right to services contracted for with others. He also argued that slavery is incompatible with the rights of men and citizens, and that subjects have a right to resist rulers who exceed the limits of their powers. His arguments for natural rights derived from his understanding of the divine or natural law that lasting happiness or beatitude may be found only in reverence for God. One may signify reverence or veneration directly; but reverence for God may also be signified indirectly, by reverence or respect for his creatures, and specifically by respect for mankind. The most evident manner in which the latter may be signified is by acknowledging the natural rights of all human beings. By such acknowledgement one signifies observance of the divine or natural law, and one finds, in such observance, beatitude or lasting happiness.

Carmichael's theory that rights derive from a universal longing for beatitude was consistent with the Reformed scholastic theology that was taught in Scottish universities in the late seventeenth and early eighteenth centuries. His theory of moral motivation presented a problem, however, for his successors. Was it possible for an action or a character to be moral or right or good if it was inspired by some motive other than veneration of God? HUTCHESON, SMITH and REID found in benevolence, in sympathy with others and in conscience, moral inspiration which they judged to be more consistent with experience than Carmichael's moral psychology. But, in their disagreements with Carmichael and with one another, they generated those fruitful speculations concerning the moral life of mankind that we have come to call the Scottish Enlightenment (see ENLIGHTENMENT, SCOTTISH). Carmichael's importance as a moral philosopher turns, then, not only upon his distinctive contribution to the natural rights tradition of GROTIUS, PUFENDORF and LOCKE; nor upon his redirection of Reformed or Presbyterian scholastic ethics to speculation on the divine inspiration for human rights and obligations; it was, above all, perhaps the manner in which he helped to shape the agenda of moral philosophy in eighteenth-century Scotland that makes him a figure worthy of attention in the history of philosophy.

See also: NATURAL LAW; RIGHTS

List of works

Carmichael, G. (1699) *Theses Philosophicae ... Sub Praesidio Gerschomi Carmichael, P.P., Glasguae MDCXIX* (Philosophical Theses [defended] under the presidency of Gershom Carmichael, Professor of Philosophy), Glasgow. (An early statement of Carmichael's ideas of thinking and acting which reflects the influence of the Port-Royal logic, Malebranche and Locke.)

—— (1707) *Theses Philosophicae ... Sub Praesidio Gerschomi Carmichael, P.P., Glasguae MDCCVII* (Philosophical Theses [defended] under the presidency of Gershom Carmichael, Professor of Philosophy), Glasgow. (An early version of Carmichael's theory of natural law).

—— (1718) *Supplementa et Observationes ad C[larissimi] V[iri] Sam[uelis] Pufendorfii. Libros Duos De Officio Hominis et Civis, Glasguae MDCCXVIII* (Supplements and Observations upon the distin-

guished Samuel Pufendorf's two books *On the Duty of Man and Citizen*), Glasgow. (The first edition.)

—— (1720) *Breviuscula Introductio ad Logicam, Glasguae MDCCXX* (A Short Introduction to Logic), Glasgow; 2nd edn, (Edinburgi MDCCXXII) Edinburgh, 1722. (An adaptation of the Port-Royal logic for students in British universities.)

—— (1724) *S[amuelis] Pufendorfii De Officio Hominis et Civis, Juxta Legem Naturalem, Libri Duo. Supplementis et Observationibus in Academicae Juventutis auxit et illustravit Gerschomus Carmichael, Philosophiae in Academia Glasguensi Professor. Editio Secunda priore Auctior et Emendatior. Edinburgi MDCCXXIV* (Supplements and Observations upon Samuel Pufendorf's On the Duty of Man and Citizen according to the Law of Nature composed for the use of Students in the Universities by Gershom Carmichael, Professor of Philosophy in the University of Glasgow), Edinburgh. (This is a second edition of the 1718 work with additions and amendments: it includes the text of Pufendorf's work and provides many observations not included in the edition of 1718.)

—— (1729) *Synopsis Theologiae Naturalis, sive Notitiae, De Existentia, Attributis et Operationibus, Summi Numinis, ex ipsa rerum Natura, Studiosae Juventutis usibus accomodata. Edinburgi MDCCXXIX* (Synopsis of Natural Theology, or Considerations upon the Existence, Attributes and Operations of the Divine Will, based upon the nature of things themselves, adapted for the use of young men in their studies), Edinburgh (A brief system of natural theology in the Reformed scholastic tradition.)

References and further reading

Hutcheson, F. (1747) *A Short Introduction to Moral Philosophy in three books, containing the Elements of Ethicks and the Law of Nature*, Glasgow. (Acknowledges his indebtedness to Carmichael's work in the introduction and in notes to the text.)

Moore, J. and Silverthorne, M. (1983) 'Gershom Carmichael and the natural jurisprudence tradition in eighteenth-century Scotland', in I. Hont and M. Ignatieff (eds) *Wealth and Virtue: the Shaping of Political Economy in the Scottish Enlightenment*, Cambridge: Cambridge University Press, 73–87. (Describes how John Locke's ideas of property and the original contract were communicated to Scottish students of moral philosophy.)

—— (1984) 'Natural Sociability and Natural Rights in the Moral Philosophy of Gershom Carmichael', in V. Hope (ed.) *Philosophers of the Scottish*

Enlightenment, Edinburgh: Edinburgh University Press, 1–12. (Contrasts Carmichael's understanding of moral ideas with the ideas of Pufendorf.)

Reid, T. (1990) *Practical Ethics: Being Lectures and Papers on Natural Religion, Self-Government, Natural Jurisprudence and the Law of Nations*, ed. K. Haakonssen, Princeton, NJ: Princeton University Press, 1990. (Edited from the manuscripts with an introduction and commentary. The commentary explores the relevance of Carmichael's natural rights theories and other juridical theories for Thomas Reid's lectures on jurisprudence.)

Stein, P. (1982) 'From Pufendorf to Adam Smith: the natural law tradition in Scotland', in N. Horn (ed.) *Europäisches Rechtsdenken in Geschichte und Gegenwart* (European Legal Thought in History and at the Present Time), Munich: C.H. Beck'sche Verlagsbuchhandlung, 667–79. (Examines continuities and differences in Scottish moral and legal philosophy from Carmichael to Adam Smith.)

Veitch, J. (1837) 'Philosophy in Scottish Universities', *Mind* 2: 74–91 and 207–34. (Remains a valuable account of the teaching of philosophy in early modern Scottish universities.)

JAMES MOORE
MICHAEL SILVERTHORNE

CARNAP, RUDOLF (1891–1970)

Carnap was one of the most significant philosophers of the twentieth century, and made important contributions to logic, philosophy of science, semantics, modal theory and probability. Viewed as an enfant terrible when he achieved fame in the Vienna Circle in the 1930s, Carnap is more accurately seen as one who held together its widely varying viewpoints as a coherent movement. In the 1930s he developed a daring pragmatic conventionalism according to which many traditional philosophical disputes are viewed as the expression of different linguistic frameworks, not genuine disagreements. This distinction between a language (framework) and what can be said within it was central to Carnap's philosophy, reconciling the apparently a priori domains such as logic and mathematics with a thoroughgoing empiricism: basic logical and mathematical commitments partially constitute the choice of language. There is no uniquely correct choice among alternative logics or foundations for mathematics; it is a question of practical expedience, not truth. Thereafter, the logic and mathematics may be taken as true in virtue of that language. The remaining substantive questions, those not settled by the language alone, should be addressed only by empirical means. There is no other source of news. Beyond pure logic and mathematics, Carnap's approach recognized within the sciences commitments aptly called a priori – those not tested straightforwardly by observable evidence, but, rather, presupposed in the gathering and manipulation of evidence. This a priori, too, is relativized to a framework and thus comports well with empiricism. The appropriate attitude towards alternative frameworks would be tolerance, and the appropriate mode of philosophizing the patient task of explicating and working out in detail the consequences of adopting this or that framework. While Carnap worked at this tirelessly and remained tolerant of alternative frameworks, his tolerance was not much imitated nor were his principles well understood and adopted. By the time of his death, philosophers were widely rejecting what they saw as logical empiricism, though often both their arguments and the views offered as improvements had been pioneered by Carnap and his associates. By his centenary, however, there emerged a new and fuller understanding of his ideas and of their importance for twentieth-century philosophy.

1　*Aufbau*
2　**Vienna**
3　**Syntax**
4　**America**
5　**Probability**

1　*Aufbau*

The last of twelve children, Carnap was born in Ronsdorf, a small village now incorporated into Wuppertal, Germany. His father, who died when Carnap was seven, was born poor but became a prosperous factory owner. Carnap's mother (née Dörpfeld) was from a more academic family. Her father was a well-known educational reformer, and her oldest brother, Wilhelm, was a renowned archaeologist who, along with Heinrich Schliemann, discovered the remains of Troy. Carnap's undergraduate studies at Freiburg and Jena were in physics, mathematics and philosophy, and Gottlob FREGE was among his teachers at Jena. While serving in the First World War he became familiar with relativity theory, and in 1919 with Whitehead and Russell's *Principia Mathematica* (1910–13) (see RUSSELL, B.; WHITEHEAD, A.N.). His doctoral dissertation in Jena, *Der Raum: Ein Beitrag zur Wissenschaftslehre* (Space: A Contribution to the Theory of Science) (1922), combined his undergraduate interests (as his career was to do). Anticipating his later principle of tolerance, this work argues that apparent disagreements among physicists, geometers and philosophers arise from the fact that they articulate wholly different concepts: physical, mathematical and visual space. The section on the last has a character reminiscent of Kant which he later repudiated, though some Kantian features continued to shape his work (see KANT, I. §5). This was especially true in the 1920s, during which he published papers on space, time and concept formation, as well as *Der logische Aufbau der Welt* (*The Logical Structure of the World*) (1928) and a textbook in mathematical logic. In 1923 he became friends with Hans REICHENBACH, who was then also a Neo-Kantian. In 1926, at the invitation of Moritz SCHLICK, Carnap became a *Privatdozent* at the University of Vienna, where an early version of the *Aufbau* was his *Habilitationsschrift*.

The *Aufbau* established his international reputation. Taken at face value, it is a system of definitions. He presents the first stages, constituting the objects of one's own experience, with great formal rigour, and the later stages carefully but in outline form. Finally he discusses the philosophic consequences of such a system. The *Aufbau* assumes a single undefined concept, partial, remembered similarity, ranging over time-points in the stream of experience. On that basis Carnap sets out to define (or constitute) every other concept and object in the whole system of science. The resulting system is constitution theory. Similarity is used to define properties, for every object having a given property must be similar to every other object having the same property. The partialness of the basic relation is exploited to order properties into families, and the 'rememberedness' of the basic relation is used to achieve a temporal ordering of experiences. Later, physical objects were to be defined, then other minds, and finally cultural objects.

Though plainly inspired by MACH and Russell, just what Carnap hoped to achieve by the *Aufbau* is unclear. One interpretation holds that the enterprise is straightforward ontological reduction to sensory phenomena, but Carnap seems not to have meant 'reduction' as understood by English-speaking philosophers. He shows complete indifference to such ontological issues and draws from his constitution theory a moral of metaphysical neutrality. Moreover, he says that a different basic relation or even a physical basis would have served his purposes equally well, and he calls his definitions 'epistemic analyses', not ontological ones. Carnap intends not to reproduce the actual processes of concept formation, but rather to give a rational reconstruction of them. This, and the fact that he starts, like Descartes, with one's own experiences and tries to range the various concepts and claims in a (rational) epistemic order, has suggested to some that Carnap is trying to justify the claims of science by providing them with a philosophical foundation. Against this, Carnap seems to take the results of contemporary science completely for granted; he claims no synonymy between defined and defining concepts, but only extensional equivalence in ways that presuppose rather than defend the science in question. This, surely, would undermine such a foundational programme. He denies that philosophers can make the sciences more certain. One intriguing interpretation developed by Michael Friedman (1992) among others, is that Carnap was undertaking the task of showing that intersubjectively applicable concepts can be developed, even though we each begin with our own subjective experience (see FOUNDATIONALISM).

Whatever the interpretation, are even those portions of the system that are fully worked out satisfactory? Notably, Nelson GOODMAN (1951) has argued that though each member of a 'property class' is indeed similar to each other, the class may fail to pick out a property because its members are similar in different respects. The seriousness of this problem will depend on the remedy and on how it serves Carnap's purposes.

2 Vienna

Moritz Schlick, named professor of inductive sciences in 1922, drew Carnap, Otto NEURATH, Hans Hahn and others as members of a new Vienna Circle, active in discussing scientific methodology (see VIENNA CIRCLE). With such figures as Wittgenstein, Popper and Gödel in the neighbourhood, Vienna in the late 1920s and early 1930s was lively indeed. The Circle combined serious interests in empirical science, its methods, and their logical analysis. Schlick had a doctorate in physics (under Max Planck); Carnap's speciality was logic, foundations of mathematics, and physics; Neurath was a sociologist, Hahn a mathematician, and others included economists and psychologists. The interest in scientific methodology was inspired largely by the writings of scientists: Mach, Duhem, Poincaré, Hilbert and Einstein. Members were uninterested or openly hostile to Cartesian methodological discussions, and they knew little of the British empirical philosophers, such as Berkeley, Hume and Mill. Russell was no ordinary British empiricist, and Viennese interest in him was very selective.

The nineteenth and early twentieth centuries witnessed major scientific and mathematical developments with implications for Kantian philosophy. First came non-Euclidean geometries which encouraged a distinction between physical geometry, which was synthetic, and mathematical geometry, which was a priori (see GEOMETRY, PHILOSOPHICAL ISSUES IN).

Hilbert dealt with the latter by deploying highly formal analyses and a theory of implicit definition. With the advent of Einstein's relativity theory, non-Euclidean structures invaded even physical geometry (see RELATIVITY THEORY, PHILOSOPHICAL SIGNIFICANCE OF). And Schlick was among the first philosophers to discuss and embrace the new physics. These developments did not refute the Kantians, but threw them into disarray. Rather than giving no answer, they had too many. Other nineteenth-century mathematical developments diminished the role for Kantian intuition. Finally, Frege and Russell developed modern symbolic logic and succeeded in deriving all of mathematics from it (and set theory) (see LOGICISM). In this they were inspired by the fear of both psychologism and empiricism in mathematics. Technically, their achievement only transferred mathematics from one Kantian classification (synthetic) to another (analytic) without saying much about what the analytic is. Russell himself seemed to prefer some sort of Platonistic account, and Frege preferred silence. Nevertheless, these achievements revealed how meagre and inadequate were Kant's discussions of the analysis of concepts. Both the geometric and arithmetic developments undermined the foundations of Kant's account of the synthetic a priori and showed the need for much more careful and systematic formal analyses. On neither front did the nineteenth-century empiricist tradition seem to have much to say that was useful.

Members of the Circle were empiricists, but of what sort? Schlick and Carnap were initially Neo-Kantian empiricists, and Neurath seems to have come from an Aristotelian empiricist tradition (see ARISTOTLE §9). Clearly they were not trying to reprise phenomenalism nor to substitute philosophic arguments and speculation for scientific evidence and methods. Perhaps what held them together was their conviction that science is not subservient to philosophy. Philosophers have no special source of news, and when they try to go beyond science or neglect it altogether they simply talk rubbish. There was a long tradition of calling this habit metaphysics, and deploring it (even, and perhaps especially, within the Kantian tradition). The result was the famous verification principle: that meaning is the mode of verification (or better, of confirmation) and that no claim is meaningful unless it can be confirmed or disconfirmed, either by logical (analytic) or empirical means. The verification principle itself is not an empirical claim, sociological or otherwise, about what claims people find meaningful. It is rather a proposal about how we should structure our language. If such a proposal were adopted, the principle would be an analytic claim in the metalanguage. In neither case would the verification principle be self-defeating (see MEANING AND VERIFICATION).

The Vienna Circle embraced a variety of evolving views. Among the most important cleavages was that between the 'right wing', led by Schlick and Frederick Waissmann and influenced strongly by Wittgenstein, and the 'left wing', led by Carnap and Neurath. One plank in the platform of the left was to liberalize the criterion of meaningfulness; a second was antifoundationalism. They argued that a physicalist language was sufficient for and conducive to the purposes of science, including its most basic observational evidence. They also embraced a confirmation holism and a thoroughgoing fallibilism about both observation reports and theories, and insisted that logic and mathematics were revisable (see FALLIBILISM). The left wing also emphasized the practical, especially the use of science as part of a programme of social reform. This practical emphasis eventuated in Carnap's intriguing suggestion that empiricism itself was a proposal to be adopted on pragmatic grounds. Carnap's version of the unity of science was that the language of science should be unified in having all of its concepts appropriately tied to a common, publicly testable, observational basis. Regarding the unity of the laws of science, he urged that while philosophers might have something to say about what the reduction of some laws to others might mean, we should avoid speculation and wait on experience to see whether that sort of unity really obtained. Such unity is neither foundationalist nor phenomenalist (see LOGICAL POSITIVISM).

3 Syntax

Carnap's most impressive undertaking of the 1930s was the development of a metalanguage that was adequate for discussing logic and the foundations of mathematics. In the process he worked out a new pragmatic and conventionalist epistemology with consequences for the character of observation and the interpretation of scientific theories. In the background were disputes among logicists, formalists and intuitionists over the foundations of mathematics, and between classicists and intuitionists over the character of logic. While Wittgenstein seemed to be saying that one could not talk about logical form, only show it, Carnap tried to develop a way of talking about logic in which its structure or form could be expressed. If the original language were suitably restricted, its structure could be described, even within that language itself, thanks to Gödel's device of arithmetization. Other object languages could be described in this metalanguage, and still more powerful object languages could be described in distinct metalanguages. This required a choice which could be settled neither by empirical means, nor, on pain of circularity, by logical ones. The issue resembled that which had faced geometers at the end of the nineteenth century, and Carnap met the new problem as Hilbert had met the old, with a version of a theory of implicit definition. The alternative logical structures are conventions defining the terms they contain, and we should tolerate alternatives. Hence, Carnap's famous principle of tolerance: 'In logic there are no morals', meaning roughly that there is no uniquely correct logic. The alternatives can be described, though not always in the language itself, and their consequences investigated and compared. Some may be more useful (more convenient, simpler, more powerful), and so a choice might be made on these grounds, but not because one of them is the right one. This is the central doctrine of *Logische Syntax der Sprache* (The Logical Syntax of Language) (1934a). The English translation included several sections containing a virtual semantics originally omitted for lack of space.

The doctrine was illustrated by presenting two languages. Language I is a coordinate language (using symbols of position rather than names of objects) and is highly restrictive, allowing, either in its formulas or in the definitions of terms, only quantifiers that can be replaced with finite conjunctions or finite disjunctions. Carnap thought this the language preferred by intuitionists, though they never entirely agreed. Language II is classical in using unlimited quantifiers and is sufficient for expressing classical mathematics. Gödel had shown that no language this rich could be both consistent and complete in the sense that every sentence or its negation would be derivable from the axioms. Carnap's striking innovation in Language II is to develop a consequence relation much more powerful than the traditional idea of derivation, and to show that mathematics could be complete in this new sense.

Most logical discussions, including those of Languages I and II, begin with lists of grammatical categories and of terms therein, and go on to specify what shall count as sentences, derivations, proofs and so on. But this provides no general terms which are useful for the discussion of other languages. Part IV of *Logical Syntax* provides definitions of grammatical categories and everything else to discuss and compare alternative languages, including translation. This is done with just two primitive terms: 'is a sentence' and 'is a direct consequence of'. The definitions do not always work, but, even so, are an amazing achievement. He tried to distinguish the logical from the descriptive vocabulary and specifically allowed rules of inference which were not wholly logical in

character. He also developed a general notion of analyticity, which he later modified. This discussion was essentially of a sort later called semantical, and in limited ways surpassed even Tarski's concurrent discussions (see SEMANTICS; TARSKI, A.). Carnap denied only that a syntactical discussion of truth was possible and, hence, that a truth theory was part of logic. Unsurprisingly, therefore, he soon changed his mind and embraced semantics. He and Tarski then viewed the new truth theory as lying within what Carnap meant by 'syntax'.

Characteristically, the last part of the book is devoted to the philosophical significance of the rest. Having discussed standards of translation, Carnap notes that many claims which seem to be about extra-linguistic objects can be translated into sentences about only words, sentences or other linguistic items. Before such translation, these sentences are said to be in material mode; after, in formal mode. Speaking in the material mode is fine, but it can disguise the implicit relativization of such claims to specific languages. This fosters the illusion that there is a uniquely correct answer to the unrelativized questions, and hence that there are genuine disagreements about it. Where we might be misled, we would do better to speak in the formal mode.

Carnap generalizes this observation. *All* philosophic questions, properly understood, are really about language. The traditional practice of philosophy is a mixture of empirical (psychological and sociological) questions with ones about the logical structure of language. This is not bad, but the concoction allowed metaphysicians, who certainly did not think their enterprise an empirical one, to think they were talking about extra-linguistic objects to which they somehow had a transcendent non-empirical access. To this Carnap says: Humbug! When the empirical component is assigned to science, where it belongs, only the logic of the language of science remains. Properly speaking, this is what philosophy is and all that it is. Such logic of science Carnap calls 'syntax', but his sense is far broader than that of later generations. Specifically, Carnap supposed that the grammatical form of observation sentences could be determined or at least marked syntactically and also that the question of which sentences implied which others could likewise be answered syntactically. Such an account of the structure of observation and inference would be the non-psychological core of a proper philosophic epistemology; it would be the logical structure of science.

This syntax project had two noteworthy dividends for philosophy of science. The first was 'Über Protokollsätze'('On Protocol Sentences') (1932a), Carnap's first presentation of the new conventionalist/pragmatist view. The Circle was debating the character of observational evidence. Is it certain? In cases of conflict with theory might the observational claims give way? Can or must it be about physical objects as opposed to private sensory states? Carnap says that the alternatives are not claims in conflict but rather the expression of different languages among which we must pragmatically choose. His own recommendation was a physicalist observational language (one far less regimented than Neurath's) in which the individual protocols could be revised in the light of other evidence and theory.

The second major dividend was the paper 'Testability and Meaning' (1936–7). Having decided that observation and implication relations were at the heart of logical analysis, Carnap saw that such analysis need not require that all empirically significant terms be explicitly definable in the observation language. Partial definitions would do if they reveal the implication relations between a given term and other terms antecedently established as empirically meaningful. These partial definitions Carnap calls reduction sentences, and they provide more adequately for disposition terms even if observational conditions which are jointly necessary and sufficient cannot be given. The reduction does not allow the elimination of the partially defined term. That this fact does not bother Carnap shows that the point of reduction in his sense is not economy, either in ontology or in conceptual resources. More likely, the point is a logical one, or epistemic in the structural sense just noted. This analysis of scientific terms also resulted in Carnap's denial in 'Wahrheit und Bewährung' ('Truth and Confirmation') (1936) that strict translations of claims from one language to another were always possible. Elsewhere in 'Testability and Meaning' he denies a sharp observational-theoretical distinction and suggests that it matters little where or how it is made more exact. Finally, he says that the varieties of empiricism themselves are conventions, though ones he strongly endorses, and he prefers the most liberal of those considered (see OBSERVATION; REDUCTION, PROBLEMS OF).

4 America

While Carnap is strongly associated with Vienna, he resided there for just five years. In 1931 he accepted a professorship in natural philosophy at the German University in Prague, though he still frequently attended Circle meetings. With the rise of Nazism, he moved in 1935 to the University of Chicago. This move coincided with his turn to explicitly semantical concerns, and the significance of his syntax project was largely lost on his new American audience. In Chicago an encyclopedia for unified science finally found a home, with the help of Charles Morris.

A preliminary result of the semantical work was *Foundations of Logic and Mathematics* (1939) with fuller accounts in *Introduction to Semantics* (1942) and *Formalization of Logic* (1943). These works broaden the previous syntax programme, which now clarifies meaning, rather than forbidding talk of it. They deal only with extensional languages, but in *Meaning and Necessity* (1947) Carnap provided a new semantical method of intension and extension in place of the older method of the name relation. This allowed the treatment of intensional languages (such as for modality) involving even quantification. Modality was taken as an essentially linguistic affair, rather than in metaphysically more profligate ways. He added a distinction between two senses of synonymy: a weak sense amounting to mutual entailment, and a stronger sense, called intensional isomorphism, which holds whenever expressions are built up in the same way out of weakly synonymous parts. Hence, any pair of arithmetic truths will be (weakly) synonymous but will not in general be intensionally isomorphic (see INTENSIONAL LOGICS).

5 Probability

A project to develop a theory of logical probability or degree of confirmation dominated the last three decades of Carnap's life. This notion of probability is essentially a generalization of deductive or logical implication, and, as such, a relation between sentences or propositions. Elementary statements of such probabilities are analytic or contradictory (just as claims of logical entailment would be). There is another concept of probability, the statistical frequency notion developed by Carnap's friends Richard von Mises and Hans Reichenbach, according to which the probabilities are factual ratios of classes of events. For Carnap, these two probability notions are not rivals, not even rival explications of the same ordinary concept. They are explications of two entirely different notions, both useful and both exhibiting the mathematical structure required to merit the term 'probability' (see PROBABILITY, INTERPRETATION OF).

Carnap developed this notion most extensively in *Logical Foundations of Probability* (1950a), which discusses what it is to explicate an ordinary concept and proceeds to provide the required analysis. Some results were initially implausible, such as that the degree of confirmation for any scientific law on any evidence is zero. This is mitigated, however, by the result that the instances of such a law need not have zero confirmation values. Kemeny and Bar-Hillel showed independently that Carnap's formulations exclude primitive predicates (such as disposition terms) having meaning relations to other primitive terms. Kemeny proposed a solution which Carnap adopted in 'Meaning Postulates' (1952), but still the account applied to a restricted range of languages, and Carnap's later years were devoted to broadening the theory's range and adequacy. Much of this new work appeared posthumously (see CONFIRMATION THEORY).

Throughout the 1940s Carnap happily spoke of abstracta, such as properties and propositions. This sparked fears of incompatibility with empiricism, and so, in 'Empiricism, Semantics, and Ontology' (1950b), Carnap argued persuasively that this fear was unfounded. The paper reaffirmed his longstanding linguistic conventionalism, now formulated in terms of a distinction between external and internal questions of existence. In the former, what is at issue is the adoption of a conceptual framework or language. There is no question of truth or falsity here, only of the utility of a way of speech. Once a framework has been adopted, genuine questions can be asked, but the answers are either factual (settled by empirical means) or logical. In neither case is there any deep metaphysical realism or any threat to empiricism.

While the issue was raised privately much earlier, in 1951 W.V. QUINE (§8) launched a public attack on the intelligibility of Carnap's notion of analyticity (or truth in virtue of meaning). Quine's view came to be very influential, though not universal. Whatever the merits of the case, Quine came to accept a notion of analyticity that applied to what had been the central examples under debate, namely, elementary logic and the so-called truths of essential predication (for example, 'All bachelors are unmarried'). This did not entirely resolve all of the issues, but it was unclear just how much any unresolvable disagreements should affect the evaluation of Carnap's philosophy (see ANALYTICITY).

From the early 1950s until its appearance in 1964 Carnap worked on the massive *The Philosophy of Rudolf Carnap*. It included an intellectual autobiography, a then-complete bibliography, and twenty-six critical essays with Carnap's extensive replies covering every aspect of his work.

In 1956 Carnap moved to UCLA (after two years at the Institute for Advanced Study in Princeton) to fill the post left vacant by Reichenbach's death. He continued to work on probability and confirmation, and also resumed work on topics which were more explicitly part of general philosophy of science. In 'The Methodological Character of Theoretical Concepts' (1956) he ventured a sophisticated criterion of empirical significance, and in other papers he advanced an account of analyticity for theoretical

concepts. The last book published in his lifetime was *Philosophical Foundations of Physics: An Introduction to the Philosophy of Science* (1966), which was essentially a reworked transcript of a course, and reissued under its less formidable subtitle a few years later. It contains wonderfully accessible treatments of quantitative concepts and measurement, non-Euclidean geometry, relativity and a variety of other issues, such as determinism and scientific realism.

Carnap left a legacy of clarity of thought, philosophic achievement and personal kindness that has rarely been equalled. After a period of eclipse, his work has been partially 'rediscovered', and it seems likely to inform and inspire succeeding generations of philosophers much as it had done throughout the middle third of the twentieth century.

See also: ANALYTICAL PHILOSOPHY

List of works

Carnap, R. (1922) *Der Raum: Ein Beitrag zur Wissenschaftslehre* (Space: A Contribution to the Theory of Science), Berlin: Reuther & Reichard. (Dissertation and first use of distinctions among senses in order to reconcile conflicting philosophic views.)

—— (1926) *Physikalische Begriffsbildung* (Physical Concept Formation), Karlsruhe: G. Braun. (Early discussion of qualitative and quantitative concepts.)

—— (1928) *Der logische Aufbau der Welt*, Berlin-Schlachtensee: Weltkreis-Verlag; trans. R. George, *The Logical Structure of the World*, Berkeley, CA: University of California, 1967. (Dramatic demonstration of constructional techniques.)

—— (1929a) *Abriß der Logistik* (Survey of Symbolic Logic), Vienna: Springer. (One of the first textbooks on symbolic logic, with applications, based on *Principia Mathematica*.)

Carnap, R., Hahn, H. and Neurath, O. (1929b) *Wissenschaftliche Weltauffassung* (The Scientific Conception of the World), Vienna: Wolf. (The so-called manifesto of the Viennese logical empiricists.)

Carnap, R. (1932a) 'Über Protokollsätze', *Erkenntnis* 3: 215–28; trans. R. Creath and R. Nollan, 'On Protocol Sentences', *Nous* (1987) 87: 457–70. (Carnap presents a conventionalist account of the form of observation reports.)

—— (1932b) 'Überwindung der Metaphysik durch logische Analyse der Sprache', *Erkenntnis* 2: 219–41; trans. A. Pap, 'The Elimination of Metaphysics Through the Logical Analysis of Language', in *Logical Positivism*, ed. A.J. Ayer, Glencoe, IL: Free Press, 1959, 60–81. (Carnap's most famous rejection of metaphysics.)

—— (1932c) 'Die physikalische Sprache as Universalsprache der Wissenschaft' (Physical Language as the Universal Language of Science), *Erkenntnis* 2: 432–65; trans. M. Black as *The Unity of Science*, London: Kegan Paul, Trench, Trubner & Co., 1934. (Along with 1932d, Carnap's classic statement of his physicalism.)

—— (1932d) 'Psychologie in physikalischer Sprache', *Erkenntnis* 3: 107–42; trans. G. Schick, 'Psychology in Physical Language' *Erkenntnis*. 165–98. (With 1932c, Carnap's classic statement of his physicalism.)

—— (1934a) *Logische Syntax der Sprache*, Vienna: Springer; trans. A. Smeaton, *The Logical Syntax of Language*, London: Kegan Paul, Trench, Trubner & Co., 1937. (Carnap's most important presentation of his conventionalism.)

—— (1934b) 'On the Character of Philosophic Problems', trans. W.M. Malisoff, *Philosophy of Science* 1: 5–19. (Carnap distinguished between assertions and proposals and identifies philosophy as the logical syntax of the language of science.)

—— (1935) *Philosophy and Logical Syntax*, London: Kegan Paul, Trench, Trubner & Co. (A less formal presentation of the basic ideas of the preceding item.)

—— (1936) 'Wahrheit und Bewährung', *Actes du Congrs international de philosophie scientifique, Sorbonne, Paris* 1935 4: 18–23; trans. H. Feigl, 'Truth and Confirmation', in *Readings in Philosophical Analysis*, ed. H. Feigl and W. Sellars, New York: Appleton-Century-Crofts, 1949. (Embraces semantics, a distinction between truth and confirmation, and a claim that meanings can change as theories do, so as to make exact translation impossible.)

—— (1936–7) 'Testability and Meaning', *Philosophy of Science* 3: 419–71; 4: 1–40. (Embraces partial definitions to treat disposition terms, makes further remarks about the theory-observation distinction, and treats empiricism as a proposal.)

—— (1939) *Foundations of Logic and Mathematics*, Chicago, IL: University of Chicago Press. (Treats a variety of philosophic issues, including the structure of scientific theories, from his emerging semantical point of view.)

—— (1942) *Introduction to Semantics*, Cambridge, MA: Harvard University Press. (Textbook-like presentation of Carnap's semantical views.)

—— (1943) *Formalization of Logic*, Cambridge, MA: Harvard University Press. (Extensive treatment of non-normal interpretations in the formalization of logic.)

—— (1947) *Meaning and Necessity*, Chicago, IL: University of Chicago Press. (Presents Carnap's distinction between intension and extension, a sophisticated account of synonymy, a surprising ambiguity about names, and a treatment of modalities and quantification.)

—— (1950a) *Logical Foundations of Probability*, Chicago, IL: University of Chicago Press. (Presents Carnap's first systematic treatment of his distinctive views on probability; though the view is not widely accepted the book is a gold mine of epistemological insight and argument.)

—— (1950b) 'Empiricism, Semantics, and Ontology', *Revue internationale de philosophie* 4: 20–40. (Presents Carnap's important distinction between external and internal questions.)

—— (1952a) *The Continuum of Inductive Methods*, Chicago, IL: University of Chicago Press. (Broadens the range of available treatments of probability.)

—— (1952b) 'Meaning Postulates', *Philosophical Studies* 3: 65–73. (Repairs a defect in Carnap's account of meaning generated by his work on probability.)

—— (1955) 'Meaning and Synonymy in Natural Languages', *Philosophical Studies* 6: 33–47. (Carnap's attempt to provide a pragmatics for natural languages, that is, to satisfy Quine's demand for behavioural criteria for meaning.)

—— (1956) 'The Methodological Character of Theoretical Concepts', *The Foundations of Science and the Concepts of Psychology and Psychoanalysis*, ed. H. Feigl and M. Scriven, Minneapolis, MN: University of Minnesota Press. (Carnap's most sophisticated criterion of meaningfulness.)

—— (1963) 'Intellectual Autobiography' and 'Replies and Systematic Expositions', *The Philosophy of Rudolf Carnap*, ed. P.A. Schilpp, La Salle, IL: Open Court, 3–84, 859–1013. (The volume, which includes twenty-six critical essays, is an impressive exploration of many facets of Carnap's philosophy.)

—— (1966) *Philosophical Foundations of Physics: An Introduction to the Philosophy of Science*, ed. M. Gardner, New York: Basic Books. (A clear and accessible treatment of Carnap's views on science; excellent discussions of measurement, non-Euclidean space and relativity.)

—— (1971, 1980) 'A Basic System of Inductive Logic', *Studies in Inductive Logic and Probability*, vol. 1, ed. R. Carnap and R. Jeffrey, vol. 2, ed. R. Jeffrey, Berkeley, CA: University of California Press, 33–165, 7–155. (A substantial revision and enrichment of the account given in *Logical Foundations of Probability*.)

Carnap, R. and Quine, W.V. (1990) *Dear Carnap, Dear Van: The Quine-Carnap Correspondence and Related Work*, ed. R. Creath, Berkeley, CA: University of California Press. (Besides the correspondence, the volume contains a previously unpublished reply to Quine's 'Two Dogmas of Empiricism'.)

References and further reading

Coffa, J.A. (1991) *The Semantic Tradition from Kant to Carnap: To the Vienna Station*, ed. L. Wessels, Cambridge: Cambridge University Press. (Pioneering re-evaluation of Carnap and the tradition out of which he comes.)

Creath, R. (1991) 'Every Dogma Has Its Day' *Erkenntnis* 35: 347–89. (Detailed review of the arguments of Quine's 'Two Dogmas of Empiricism' and surrounding literature.)

—— (1994) 'Functionalist Theories of Meaning and the Defense of Analyticity', in Salmon and Wolters (eds) 1994, 287–304. (An attempt to meet Quine's demands for behavioural criteria for natural languages.)

Friedman, M. (1992) 'Epistemology in the Aufbau', *Synthèse* 93: 15–57. (A significant reinterpretation of the Aufbau.)

—— (1994) 'Geometry, Convention, and the Relativized A Priori', in Salmon and Wolters (eds) 1994, 21–34. (An examination of a view of the a priori according to which it is both relativized and revisable.)

Goldfarb, W. and Ricketts, T. (1992) 'Carnap and the Philosophy of Mathematics', in *Science and Subjectivity*, ed. D. Bell and W. Vossenkuhl, Berlin: Akademie Verlag, 61–78. (An important modern discussion of Carnap's philosophy of mathematics.)

Goodman, N. (1951) *The Structure of Appearance*, Cambridge, MA: Harvard University Press. (Detailed technical discussion of Carnap's Aufbau.)

—— (1963) 'The Significance of the Aufbau', in Schilpp , 1963, 545–58. (A spirited defence of the Aufbau project by one of its major critics.)

Hintikka, J. (ed.) (1975) *Rudolf Carnap, Logical Empiricist*, Dordrecht: Reidel. (An important collection of essays on Carnap's work.)

Martin, R.M. (1952) 'On "Analytic"', *Philosophical Studies* 3: 42–7 (An important reply to Quine's 'Two Dogmas of Empiricism'.)

Oberdan, T. (1992) *Protocols, Truth, and Convention*, Amsterdam: Rodopi. (Extensive discussion of Carnap's views in the 1930s.)

Quine, W.V. (1951) 'Two Dogmas of Empiricism', *Philosophical Review* 60: 20–43. (Quine's most famous attack on Carnap's notion of analyticity.)

—— (1963) 'Carnap and Logical Truth', in Schilpp, 1963, 385–406. (Quine's most extensive attack on analyticity.)

Richardson, A. (1997) *Carnap's Construction of the World: The Aufbau and the Emergence of Logical Empiricism*, Cambridge: Cambridge University Press. (Important re-examination of Carnap's *Aufbau* and the Neo-Kantian tradition.)

Russell, B. and Whitehead, A.N. (1910–13) *Principia Mathematica*, Cambridge: Cambridge University Press, 3 vols; 2nd edn, 1927. (Enormously influential, this book carries out the reduction of mathematics to logic, including set theory.)

Salmon, W. and G. Wolters (eds) (1994) *Logic, Language, and the Structure of Scientific Theories*, Pittsburgh, PA: University of Pittsburgh Press, and Konstanz: Universitätsverlag Konstanz. (Significant collection of essays on Carnap and Reichenbach.)

Sarkar, S. (ed.) (1992) 'Carnap: A Centenary Reappraisal', *Synthèse* 93. (A centennial collection of essays on Carnap.)

* Schilpp, P.A. (ed.) (1963) *The Philosophy of Rudolf Carnap*, La Salle, IL: Open Court. (Its 1,100 pages contain twenty-six critical essays on Carnap's work, Carnap's autobiography, replies, and a bibliography.)

Spohn, W. (ed.) (1991) *Hans Reichenbach, Rudolf Carnap: A Centenary*, Dordrecht: Kluwer. (A centennial collection of essays on Reichenbach and Carnap.)

Übel, T. (1992) *Overcoming Logical Positivism from Within*, Amsterdam: Rodopi. (Extensive examination of the protocol sentences debate from Neurath's point of view.)

RICHARD CREATH

CARNEADES (214–129 BC)

The Greek philosopher Carneades was head of the Academy from 167 to 137 BC. Born in North Africa he migrated to Athens, where he studied logic with the Stoic Diogenes of Babylon; but he was soon seduced by the Academy, to which his allegiance was thereafter lifelong. He was a celebrated figure; and in 155 BC he was sent by Athens to Rome as a political ambassador, where he astounded the youth by his rhetorical powers and outraged their elders by his arguments against justice.

Under Carneades' direction the Academy remained sceptical. But he enlarged the sceptical armoury – in particular, he deployed sorites arguments against various dogmatic positions. He also broadened the target of sceptical attack: thus he showed an especial interest in ethics, where his 'division' of possible ethical theories served later as a standard framework for *thought on the subject. But his major innovation concerned the notion of 'the plausible' (*to pithanon*). Even if we cannot determine which appearances are true and which false, we are able to distinguish the plausible from the implausible – and further to distinguish among several grades of plausibility. It is disputed – and it was disputed among his immediate followers – how, if at all, Carneades' remarks on the plausible are to be reconciled with his scepticism.*

1 Life
2 Ethics
3 Theology
4 Scepticism

1 Life

Carneades' life is ill documented. He was born in 214 BC at Cyrene in North Africa. He moved to Athens where he studied logic with the Stoic Diogenes of Babylon and no doubt also listened to the other leading philosophers of the day. He gravitated to the Academy (see ACADEMY), which was still following the sceptical path laid down by ARCESILAUS, and in 167 BC he was chosen as scholarch. The school flourished under his leadership: later authors deemed that he had opened a new phase in its history. Blindness and miserable health obliged him to resign his position in 137; but he continued to philosophize vigorously until his death in 129. And when he died there was an eclipse of the moon.

He was a loud man, and admired even by his opponents for his powerful and persuasive style of argument: he had the irresistible force of a mighty river, the subtlety and resilience of a hunted beast. He lost no argument and left no hearer unmoved. When in 155 BC the Athenians petitioned the Roman Senate for the remission of a fine, they sent three philosophers as ambassadors – Diogenes the Stoic, Critolaus the Peripatetic, and Carneades. At Rome the three men displayed their professional talents to an enthusiastic public. Carneades revealed a particular power to charm and excite – the more so when, on successive days and with equal power, he urged the claims first of justice and then of injustice. Stern Cato hurried business through the Senate and bundled the Greeks off home before they could corrupt the Roman youth.

Like Arcesilaus – and SOCRATES – before him, Carneades wrote nothing. Several of his pupils took notes on his lectures and wrote memorials of his arguments; and our meagre knowledge of Carneades depends ultimately on these works – all of which are lost. Carneades was persuasive, but he was also elusive; and his pupils disagreed on how to interpret

him: his successor Clitomachus, who wrote voluminously about his master, confessed that 'he could never understand what Carneades believed' (Cicero, *Academics* II 139); and Metrodorus claimed that 'everyone has misunderstood Carneades' (Philodemus, *History of the Academy* XXVI 8–10).

Also like Arcesilaus – and Socrates – before him, Carneades argued against all-comers, showing himself 'the most acute and fertile' proponent of the *elenchos* or method of refutation (Cicero, *Tusculan Disputations* V 11). He also argued 'on both sides' – notoriously during his ambassadorial visit to Rome. And he was familiar with at least the rudiments of Stoic logic, so that his arguments against the Stoics were often and deliberately expressed as instances of Stoic inference patterns (see STOICISM §11).

In addition, he had a weakness for 'soritical' arguments – arguments which proceed 'little by little' from apparently true premises to an apparently false conclusion (see VAGUENESS §2). Such arguments were not invented by Carneades. Moreover, they had already been used against the Stoics; for CHRYSIPPUS had tried to answer them: before he came to the difficult cases he would 'fall silent' (*hēsychazein*). Carneades thought little of this reply:

> As for falling silent, as far as I'm concerned you may snore. What good does it do you? Someone has only to wake you up and pose the same question again.
>
> (Cicero, *Academics* II 93)

The sorites cannot be slept away (see further STOICISM §11).

Like Arcesilaus, Carneades was especially energetic in his attacks on the Stoa: he read Stoic texts assiduously, and confessed that 'had Chrysippus not existed, I would not have done either' (Diogenes Laertius IV 62). But his aim extended more widely – we happen to know that he discussed some aspects of Epicureanism; and Sextus Empiricus affirms that 'with regard to the criterion of truth, Carneades attacked not only the Stoics but all his predecessors' (*Against the Mathematicians* VII 159). Moreover, he maintained that, on some issues at least, 'the dispute between Stoics and Peripatetics concerned not substance but terminology' (Cicero, *On Ends* III 41), so that an argument against the former was thereby an argument against the latter (see ANTIOCHUS §2). It should not be thought (as some have thought) that his philosophy was purely polemical and *ad hominem*.

Carneades had a particular interest in ethics, where he not only discussed philosophical matters but also composed an idiosyncratic work on consolation. He also reflected on philosophical theology, and on such related issues as divination and the doctrine of fate.

But it was primarily for his epistemological attitudes that he was notorious: he argued for some version of scepticism – and at the same time he advocated a 'criterion', namely *to pithanon* or 'the plausible'. This last item was – or at any rate seemed to some of his disciples to be – a profound innovation; and it was presumably 'the plausible' which encouraged the suggestion that Carneades had not merely continued the tradition of Arcesilaus but had instituted a New Academy.

2 Ethics

Dogmatic philosophers disagreed over the *telos* or (Latin) *summum bonum*, the goal of life or the highest good. Carneades catalogued the differing doctrines and incorporated them into a schedule – the 'division of Carneades' – which set out 'not only the opinions on the highest good which have been championed by philosophers up to now but all opinions which can possibly be maintained' (Cicero, *On Ends* V 16). The division was celebrated, but no coherent version has survived. Carneades himself urged that the *telos* is 'the enjoyment of the goods to which nature first inclines us' (Cicero, *Academics* II 131): it is not known how he advocated the view – which in any event he advanced only as part of an *ad hominem* argument against the Stoics.

On the two Roman speeches on justice we have a little more information. The first speech was an anthology: Carneades 'put together everything which had been said in favour of justice' (Lactantius, *Divine Institutions* V 14.5). On the following day he first distinguished between 'civil' justice and 'natural' justice. He then urged that civil justice makes good sense: that is to say, it is in the interest of the legislators to enforce the laws which constitute civil justice and which they have conventionally established. But civil 'justice' is not just at all. Natural justice, on the other hand, is just – but it is either a phantom or a folly. If the Romans, with their wealth and their conquests, 'wish to be just, that is, to give back what is not theirs, then they must return to their cottages and live in poverty and misery'. For the community as a whole, natural justice is absurd. And for the individual too. Suppose that you are selling a house which you alone know to be riddled with dry rot: do you show the rot to a prospective purchaser? If you do not, you are prudent – and unjust. If you do, you are just – and foolish. Suppose that you have been shipwrecked and find a fellow sailor clinging weakly to a floating plank: do you dislodge him and grab the plank yourself? If you do, you are prudent – and unjust. If you do not, you are just – and dead.

The second speech, no less than the first, was a cento of familiar arguments and examples. Carneades' originality lay not in invention but in presentation. What he himself thought of the matter, and what he intended in arguing 'on both sides', we cannot tell. But he produced, as Socrates had produced, perplexity and disquiet and hostility. Cato was enraged. (But the Christian Lactantius was pleased; for Carneades had unwittingly shown that pagan philosophy, ignorant of divine truth, had no understanding of the nature and the glory of justice.)

3 Theology

Carneades collected arguments against the existence of gods. Some of these mockingly followed Stoic patterns of reasoning. Thus: the gods, being living creatures, must be capable of sense perception; anything which perceives is thereby pleased or displeased; anything which may be displeased may change for the worse; anything which may change for the worse may be destroyed: therefore if there are any gods they can be destroyed. But gods cannot be destroyed. Hence there are no gods. There was also a batch of soritical arguments. Thus:

> If Zeus is a god, then Poseidon is a god; if Poseidon is a god, then Achelous is a god; if Achelous is a god, then the Nile is a god;...then streams are gods. But streams are not gods. Therefore Zeus is not a god. But if there were any gods, then Zeus would be one. Hence there are no gods.
>
> (Sextus Empiricus,
> *Against the Mathematicians* IX 183)

According to Cicero, 'Carneades said these things not in order to do away with the gods – what could be less appropriate in a philosopher? – but in order to show that the Stoics explain nothing about the gods' (*On the Nature of the Gods* III 44). Perhaps so – in any event, it would be wrong to conclude that Carneades was a convinced atheist; for if even the arguments are not *ad hominem* – *ad Stoicos* – they will surely have formed the one half of a set of arguments 'on both sides'.

Carneades also argued against divine providence, and in particular he disputed the Stoic view that beasts exist for the benefit of mankind – what about bats and scorpions and crocodiles? And he rejected the science of divination (which the Stoics had generally applauded), urging that when a seer gets things right, the success is mere luck. Now divination, according to Carneades, presupposes causal determinism; for 'even Apollo cannot foretell an event unless there are causes in nature which so constrain it that it is necessary for it to occur' (Cicero, *On Fate* 32).

The Stoics, who defended divination, held that everything does depend on such naturally necessitating causes – such was their doctrine of fate (see STOICISM §20). The doctrine had been variously attacked. Carneades allowed that some of the arguments used against it were fallacious: they falsely conflated the thought that an event is causally determined with the thought that someone may have truly said in advance that it will occur. (To say truly that something will happen is not the same as to divine or foretell it.) And he produced a better argument:

> If everything comes about by antecedent causes... then necessity determines everything; if so, then nothing is in our power. Now some things are in our power. But if everything comes about by fate, then everything comes about by antecedent causes. Therefore not everything which comes about comes about by fate.
>
> (Cicero, *On Fate* 31)

The Epicureans also rejected fatalism. In doing so they introduced their celebrated theory of 'atomic swerves' (see EPICUREANISM §12): atoms may suddenly, and for no cause, change trajectory; and these swerves ensure that there may be 'voluntary motions of the mind' which leave some actions in our power. But Carneades criticised the Epicureans no less than the Stoics, maintaining (truly enough) that voluntary motion can be better defended than by the introduction of uncaused swerves.

4 Scepticism

> Carneades and Clitomachus and all their friends trample on the doctrines of everyone else and themselves expressly affirm that everything is inapprehensible and that a false appearance always neighbours a true one.
>
> (Hermias, *Mockery of the Pagan Philosophers* 15)

According to Carneades, we can apprehend nothing – not even (as Cicero adds) that we can apprehend nothing; for next to and indistinguishable from any true appearance there will always be found a false appearance.

Carneades fired broadsides against every philosophical attempt to provide a criterion of truth. He peppered them with bent oars and round towers and moving coastlines – with all the 'illusions' which have diverted later sceptics. In particular, he reflected on the reigning Stoic account of knowledge, which turned on the notion of an 'apprehensive appearance' (*phantasia katalēptikē*) (see STOICISM §12).

An appearance (*phantasia*), being the origin of cognition in animals, ought, like light, both to reveal itself and to indicate the evident item which produces it.

But *phantasiai*, like unreliable messengers, do not always report correctly the information with which they are charged. What is more, even if a *phantasia* does manage to give a correct report,

> none is true in such a way that it could not be false; rather, for any *phantasia* which is thought to be true, a false *phantasia* indistinguishable from it (*aparallaktos*) can be found.
>
> (Sextus Empiricus, *Against the Mathematicians* VII 163–4)

He offered numerous proofs and illustrations of this indistinguishability. Consider the twins, Castor and Pollux: it looks to me for all the world as though Castor is sitting opposite me at the dining table – and indeed he is sitting there. But is this appearance apprehensive, does it give me *knowledge* that Castor is there? No – for an indistinguishable appearance would have been caused by his twin, Pollux.

In general, if you know something, you must have apprehended it; apprehension is assent to an apprehensive appearance; and an appearance of something is apprehensive if it is true of that thing, if it was caused by that thing, and if it could not have been produced by anything else (see STOICISM §12). Like Arcesilaus, Carneades fastened on to the third condition:

> They say that they reject this one element, that something true can appear in such a way that what is false could not appear in the same way.
>
> (Cicero, *Academics* II 33)

If an appearance is apprehensive, then were it not the case that so-and-so it could not seem to me that so-and-so. But this is never so: it *could* seem to me that Castor was sitting opposite me even if (say) not he but Pollux were there. No appearances are apprehensive. Nothing is known.

Thus far, destruction. But there is also an apparently positive side to Carneades' scepticism. Alongside the distinction between true and false appearances there is a second and independent distinction between 'plausible' (*pithanos*) and implausible opinions. (The word *pithanos* was often Latinized as *probabilis* and hence rendered in English as 'probable'; but 'probable', in its modern sense, is a false translation of *pithanos*.) Truth and falsity are determined by the relation of an appearance to the items *of which* it is an appearance. Plausibility and implausibility are determined by the relation of an appearance to the item *to whom* it appears. An appearance is plausible if it tends to persuade or to evoke assent: it looks to me as if there is a coil of rope in the potting-shed – and the appearance is plausible in so far as I find myself inclined to accept that there is a coil of rope there.

What is plausible for me may not be plausible for you. And there are degrees of plausibility, some appearances being more persuasive than others. Moreover, we may *scrutinize* our appearances. Perhaps it is really a snake, not a coil of rope? I prod about in the potting-shed with a stick: nothing budges – and I now have a 'scrutinized' plausible appearance of a coil of rope. Again, appearances do not come to us as isolated atoms: they arrive in molecules, so that a plausible appearance may be controverted or *uncontroverted* by its associates. There seem to be no sloughed skins in the shed, I see no notice urging me to Beware of Serpents in the Grass, and so on. None of the other appearances associated with the appearance of the coil of rope controverts that appearance: I have an 'uncontroverted and scrutinized' plausible appearance of a coil of rope.

Plausible appearances, however well scrutinized and however uncontroverted, may always be false. None the less, we shall prefer the plausible to the implausible, the more plausible to the less plausible, and the uncontroverted and scrutinized plausible to anything else.

Such is Carneades' account of plausibility: herein appeared to lie his chief innovation – on account of which his 'New' Academy was later distinguished from the Middle Academy of Arcesilaus. What was the philosophical role and function of the account? The problem is this: on the one hand, the plausible, of which Carneades seems to approve, is that which evokes *assent*; on the other hand, Carneades apparently argues for a scepticism which *repudiates* any act of assent. Carneades' own pupils were puzzled, and interpreters have found no solution which commands general agreement.

One of Carneades' pupils probably construed the theory of plausibility as a theory of knowledge. Carneades' destructive arguments proved that the standard account of knowledge was flawed. Hence he had to devise another account – and the theory of the plausible lay at its heart. Carneades was not a sceptic – on the contrary, the point of the *pithanon* pricks the bubble of scepticism (see PHILO OF LARISSA §2). Later, St Augustine (on what authority is uncertain) affirmed that Carneades had never intended to attack 'ordinary' knowledge: his sceptical assault was limited to philosophical knowledge; and the theory of plausibility offered an account of our ordinary knowledge of ordinary things.

Or perhaps plausibility offers not knowledge but a knowledge substitute. We cannot strictly *know* anything – but that is no reason to suspend judgement, nor does it imply that all appearances are on an equal footing. Plausibility provides a criterion for rational belief – and rational belief is all we have on earth and all we need to have.

Sextus Empiricus presents Carneades' 'plausible' as a criterion of action: it is concerned with 'the discrimination of what is good and what is bad' (*Outlines of Pyrrhonism* I 226). Carneades suggests not that it is rational to *believe* what is plausible but that it is rational to *act on* what is plausible. (And rationality will recommend satisfaction with different degrees and types of plausibility in different practical circumstances.)

Or does the plausible play a purely descriptive and explanatory role? The question to which the plausible offers an answer is perhaps not 'How *should* a sceptic act?' but rather 'How *can* a sceptic act?' Dogmatists argued that without beliefs a sceptic could never stay alive (see ARCESILAUS §2). But according to Carneades, a sceptic's actions may be determined by the appearances; for not all appearances are equally plausible – and a sceptic will be moved by the most plausible appearance. Not, of course, that a sceptic will *believe* the appearance to be true: the appearance evokes 'assent' merely insofar as it is acted upon.

These brief suggestions do not exhaust the gamut of interpretations; and the surviving texts scarcely allow a rational choice among them: only in the Elysian fields – if anywhere – shall we learn the truth about Carneades.

References and further reading

Bett, R. (1989) 'Carneades' *Pithanon*: A Reappraisal of its Role and Status', *Oxford Studies in Ancient Philosophy* 7: 59–94. (Discusses the nature and the consistency of Carneades' account of plausible appearances.)

* Cicero (45 BC) *Academics*, trans. H. Rackham, Loeb Classical Library, Cambridge, MA: Harvard University Press and London: Heinemann, 1933. (Our most important single source on the sceptical Academy.)

* —— (mid 44 BC) *On Fate* (*De fato*), trans. R. Sharples, Warminster: Aris & Phillips, 1991. (Dialogue on causation and determinism; incompletely preserved.)

* Diogenes Laertius (*c.* early 3rd century AD) *Lives of the Philosophers*, trans. R.D. Hicks, *Diogenes Laertius: Lives of Eminent Philosophers*, Loeb Classical Library, Cambridge, MA: Harvard University Press and London: Heinemann, 1925, 2

vols. (Book IV includes a brief biography of Carneades.)

Mette, H.-J. (1985) 'Weitere Akademiker heute: von Lakydes bis zu Kleitomachos' (More Academics: Lacydes to Clitomachus), *Lustrum* 27: 39–148. (Collects the ancient testimonies on Carneades.)

* Philodemus (*c*.80–40 BC) *History of the Academy*, trans. T. Dorandi, *Filodemo. Storia dei filosofi. Platone e l'Academia*, Naples: Bibliopolis, 1991. (Greek text, with Italian translation and commentary; a biographical history.)

* Sextus Empiricus (*c.* AD 200) *Against the Mathematicians*, trans. R.G. Bury, Loeb Classical Library, Cambridge, MA: Harvard University Press and London: Heinemann, 1935. (Book VII includes a long presentation of some of Carneades' arguments.)

Striker, G. (1980) 'Sceptical Strategies', in M. Schofield, M.F. Burnyeat and J. Barnes (eds) *Doubt and Dogmatism*, Oxford: Clarendon Press. (An account of the aims and methods of Academic scepticism.)

JONATHAN BARNES

CAROLINGIAN RENAISSANCE

The 'Carolingian renaissance' is the name given to the cultural revival in northern Europe during the late eighth and ninth centuries, instigated by Charlemagne and his court scholars. Carolingian intellectual life centred around the recovery of classical Latin texts and learning, though in a strictly Christian setting. The only celebrated philosopher of the time is John Scottus Eriugena, but the daring Neoplatonic speculations of his masterpiece, the Periphyseon (On the Division of Nature) are not at all characteristic of the time and are based on Greek sources (Pseudo-Dionysius, Gregory of Nyssa, Maximus the Confessor) generally unknown to his contemporaries. The mainstream of Carolingian thought is important for the history of philosophy in three particular ways. First, it was at this time that logic first started to take the fundamental role it would have throughout the Middle Ages. Second, scholars began to consider how ideas they found in late antique Latin Neoplatonic texts could be interpreted in a way compatible with Christianity. Third (as would so often again be the case in the Middle Ages), controversies over Christian doctrine led thinkers to analyse some of the concepts they involved: for instance, the dispute in the mid-ninth century over predestination led to discussion about free will and punishment.

1 **General characteristics**
2 **The revival of logic**
3 **Platonism and Christianity**
4 **Doctrinal dispute and philosophical analysis**

1 General characteristics

It was Charlemagne himself who was in large part responsible for instigating the northern European cultural and intellectual renaissance of the late eighth and ninth centuries. From the mid-770s onwards, leading scholars gathered at his court, first men from southern Europe (where the tradition of classical learning still flourished) such as the Lombards Peter of Pisa, Paul the Deacon and Paulinus of Aquileia and the Spanish Goth Theodulf, who became bishop of Orleans, and then later the Anglo-Saxon Alcuin and his circle. During the reign of Louis the Pious (814–40) the intellectual movement, no longer encouraged at Court, was continued in the great monasteries such as Tours (where Alcuin had ended his life as abbot) and Fulda. By contrast, Charlemagne's grandson Charles the Bald (d. 877) was an enthusiastic promoter of learning and acted as patron and protector to the outstanding thinker of the period, Johannes Scottus ERIUGENA.

The Carolingian renaissance was one aspect of a wider renewal instituted by Charlemagne, which included reform of corruption and laxness in the clergy, restoration of correct latinity and the regularization of biblical and liturgical texts. The small elite of intellectuals at court, as well as writing history and engaging in theological dispute, composed classicizing poetry (quite often in panegyric of Charlemagne) in a self-conscious return to ancient models, parallel to the political renewal of antiquity which culminated in Charlemagne's imperial coronation in 800. Alcuin adopted the nickname 'Flaccus' (Horace) and addressed poems in classical metres to his group of intimate pupils. A library was built up at the court which contained copies of classical authors such as Lucan, Terence, Horace, Juvenal, Martial and Cicero; and after Charlemagne's death, Einhard wrote his life in a form imitated from Suetonius. In the mid-ninth century Lupus, Abbot of Ferrières, wrote elegant Latin letters which, in their concern for discovering and collating ancient texts, anticipate the interests of early modern humanists. Even Greek was studied in this period, especially by scholars of Irish origin such as Martin of Laon, Eriugena and Sedulius Scottus (also a fine Latin poet).

Historians often present the role of the Carolingian renaissance in the history of philosophy in terms simply of this rediscovery of ancient texts. Apart from Eriugena (who is envisaged as an isolated figure, inhabiting the thought world of Greek Neoplatonism or even nineteenth-century German idealism), Carolingian thinkers are described as passive assimilators of the ancient writings they began to study. Certainly, the forms and techniques favoured by thinkers of the time – excerption, paraphrase, compilation and glossing – give an impression of servility. Yet, through their particular interests and emphases, Carolingian thinkers set the direction for the subsequent course of medieval philosophy, a direction quite different from what late antique precedent would have suggested. With the exception of Eriugena, Carolingian thinkers did not take up the Neoplatonic systematizing of the Greek tradition after PLOTINUS, nor did they reflect the strong emphasis on rhetoric characteristic of classical Latin culture. Their thought is typified rather by the important place of logic and grammar; by the attempt to reach a Christian interpretation of pagan motifs and philosophical ideas; and by the importance of controversies over Christian doctrine in stimulating argument and analysis.

2 The revival of logic

It is no surprise that grammar should have been important in Carolingian education, since Latin was now (even in romance areas) not a mother tongue but a language which needed to be learned. But it is striking how, even in this period, grammarians went beyond straightforward linguistic instruction to explore some of the semantic problems raised in Priscian's *Institutiones grammaticae* (Principles of Grammar). There was no such obvious didactic reason for the study of logic, yet this subject was central to Carolingian education. Already in the *Libri Carolini*, (written very probably by Theodulf of Orleans, *circa* 789–92), ostentatious use is made of formal logical methods of argument. In the 790s, Alcuin prefaced a late antique paraphrase of the *Categories*, which he attributed to AUGUSTINE, with a dedicatory verse epistle to Charlemagne: the *Categoriae decem* (Ten Categories), as it was called, would be the most widely studied logical text in the next century. Alcuin also composed a treatise on logic; this was a patchwork of borrowed passages, especially from two late antique Christian encyclopaedists, Cassiodorus and Isidore of Seville (see ENCYCLOPE-DISTS, MEDIEVAL §§6–7), and from the *Categoriae decem*. Whereas Isidore had treated logic as a verbal art, and both he and Cassiodorus had placed great emphasis on syllogistic argument, Alcuin saw the ten categories as central to the subject, and he used them in understanding the Trinity and in order to distinguish God from his creation. Alcuin's pupils (especially a fellow Anglo-Saxon, Candidus) contin-

ued and extended these interests. A set of passages (the 'Munich passages', *circa* 800) connected with Candidus contains logical extracts and exercises, discussions of the Trinity and also a short dialogue which makes an original adaptation of Augustine's arguments for the existence of God. At much the same time another of Alcuin's pupils, Fredegisus, composed a little treatise *De substantia nihili et de tenebris* (On the Substance of Nothing and on Darkness), which attempts, rather unsuccessfully, to elucidate the reference of 'nothing'.

From the 850s onwards, interest in logic intensified. For example, in his *Liber de anima* (Book on the Soul) in the early 860s, Ratramnus, a monk at Corbie, turned a question raised by Augustine about the relationship between individual souls and the hypostasis Soul into a logical discussion about the relations between individual souls and the universal soul. The earliest glossed manuscripts of the *Categoriae decem* date from about ten years later. Some use the logical doctrines here as opportunities to develop the characteristic ideas of Eriugena (often without much real connection with the text). Others concentrate on more down-to-earth explanation of fundamental logical terms and concepts. They indicate the beginning of a process of careful study of ancient logical texts, which would ensure that, by the eleventh century, a high level of logical proficiency was common among well-trained thinkers (see LANGUAGE, MEDIEVAL THEORIES OF; LOGIC, MEDIEVAL).

3 Platonism and Christianity

The sources for ancient philosophy which first began to be used in the Carolingian period would remain the principal ones until the late twelfth century. On the one hand, there were writings by Church Fathers which were strongly marked by Neoplatonism – for example, Augustine's *De trinitate* (On the Trinity), heavily influenced by Plotinus, which was available earlier but not exploited by medieval writers until the time of Charlemagne (in, for instance, Alcuin's *De fide sanctae trinitatis* (On Faith in the Holy Trinity) (see AUGUSTINE; PATRISTIC PHILOSOPHY). There were also the pseudo-Dionysian writings, redolent of PROCLUS, which reached the West in 827 and were translated into Latin first by Hilduin, Abbot of St Denis and then, more successfully, by ERIUGENA in the late 850s (see PSEUDO-DIONYSIUS). On the other hand, there was a handful of more direct witnesses to ancient philosophy. Plato's *Timaeus*, in the partial translation of CALCIDIUS, was in Charlemagne's library. Alcuin is the first medieval author to use Boethius' *De consolatione philosophiae* (On the Consolation of Philosophy). The allegorical prosimetrum by Martianus Capella, *De nuptiis Philologiae et Mercurii* (On the Marriage of Philology and Mercury) began to be read in the early ninth century (and was being glossed intensively a few decades later), and Macrobius' commentary on Cicero's *Somnium Scipionis* (Scipio's Dream) came into use at much the same time (see ENCYCLOPEDISTS, MEDIEVAL §§3–4).

These direct witnesses posed Carolingian scholars with the problem of how to treat explicitly pagan material. This arose most directly in connection with the *De consolatione philosophiae*. Boethius was a Christian, but he omits any openly Christian doctrine from the *De consolatione* and, in sections such as the metrum (III, m.9) *O qui perpetua*, his epitome of the *Timaeus*, he mentions pagan ideas (reincarnation, the World Soul) which are rejected by Christianity (see BOETHIUS, A.M.S. §5). Two commentaries from the end of the ninth century illustrate diametrically opposed ways of tackling the problem. Remigius of Auxerre, the most prolific of late Carolingian commentators on secular texts, chooses to interpret everything in an explicitly Christian sense and either treats references to pagan doctrines as mere analogies or ignores them entirely. By contrast, Bovo, a monk of Corvey, begins his commentary (solely on *O qui perpetua*) by expressing surprise that Boethius, though a Christian, 'did not discuss anything of Church doctrine, but wished to reveal the teachings of the philosophers, especially the Platonists, to his readers'; and he then goes on, with obvious relish, to give a surprisingly accurate exegesis of the pagan ideas in the poem. But Bovo's bold position would have few imitators, whereas Remigius' Christianizing interpretation of pagan texts set a model for the next three centuries (see PLATONISM, MEDIEVAL).

4 Doctrinal dispute and philosophical analysis

Early in the Carolingian renaissance, the need to answer and convincingly reject the Greek position on image-worship proposed at the second Council of Nicaea provoked the most ambitious theological treatise of the period, the *Libri Carolini*. Throughout the period, doctrinal controversies (on Christology, the Trinity and predestination) continued to provide an impetus towards systematic thought. Not only did they force scholars to collect and order dossiers of authoritative material from the Church Fathers to support their case (as with Alcuin's voluminous works against the Adoptionist heresy), they also encouraged them to analyse and explore difficult and important concepts.

The mid-ninth-century controversy over predestination was particularly important in stimulating philosophical analysis. The dispute was begun by Gottschalk of Orbais, who, so his opponents claimed, held that divine predestination was dual: of the blessed to salvation and of the wicked to damnation. Eriugena's contribution to the debate in his *De praedestinatione* (On Predestination) is well known for its use of logic and its adoption of a number of Neoplatonic themes in establishing its radical conclusions. However, the sophistication of other participants in the controversy is less often noted. For example, both Hraban Maur (Hrabanus Maurus), Abbot of Fulda, and Hincmar, Archbishop of Rheims, made the distinction in their attacks on Gottschalk between predestining and foreknowing, and both recognized (though they did not fully overcome) the danger that, even if God is said to predestine only to salvation, he will seem arbitrary in his choice of whom so to predestine. Those who attacked Eriugena's treatise also showed greater acumen than is commonly recognized. For instance, Prudentius of Troyes challenges Eriugena's conceptual analysis of free will – especially his distinction between the will itself and its strength and power, and Florus of Lyons enters into a discussion of how different types of words signify in order to show the weakness of Eriugena's theory of sin (see PREDESTINATION).

See also: BYZANTINE PHILOSOPHY; CHARTRES, SCHOOL OF; ENCYCLOPEDISTS, MEDIEVAL; ERIUGENA, J.S.; LOGIC, MEDIEVAL; PLATONISM, MEDIEVAL

References and further reading

* Alcuin (795–802) *De dialectica* (On Dialectic), in J.-P. Migne (ed.) *Patrologia Latina*, Paris, 1851, vol. 101, col. 951–76. (The earliest medieval Latin logic textbook.)
* —— (795–802) *De fide sanctae Trinitatis* (On Faith in the Holy Trinity), in J.-P. Migne (ed.) *Patrologia Latina*, Paris, 1851, vol. 101, col. 11–58. (A discussion of the Trinity, based on Augustine's *De trinitate*.)
* Anonymous (after *c.*870) Glosses to *Categoriae Decem*. (A selection of these can be found in J. Marenbon, *From the Circle of Alcuin to the School of Auxerre*, Cambridge: Cambridge University Press, 1981.)
Bischoff, B. (ed.) (1965) *Karl der Grosse: Lebenswerk und Nachleben* (Charlemagne: His Life's Work and its Influence), vol. II *Das geistige Leben* (Cultural Life), Düsseldorf: Schwann. (Authoritative essays on all aspects of the early Carolingian renaissance.)
* Bovo of Corvey (*c.*880–90) Commentary on *O qui perpetua*, in R.B.C. Huygens, 'Mittelalterliche

Kommentare zum *O qui perpetua'*, *Sacris Erudiri* 6, 1954: 373–427. (Comments on what Bovo perceives as pagan ideas in Boethius' poem.)

Bullough, D. (1991) *Carolingian Renewal: Sources and Heritage*, Manchester: Manchester University Press. (Wide-ranging studies in Carolingian intellectual history and its political background.)

Candidus Wizo (*c.*800) Philosophical and theological passages, in J. Marenbon, *From the Circle of Alcuin to the School of Auxerre*, Cambridge: Cambridge University Press, 1981. (Discusses logic, trinitarian theology and quotes from Timaeus.)

Florus of Lyons (early 850s) *Adversus Ioannis Scoti Erigenae erroneas definitiones*, in J.-P. Migne (ed.) *Patrologia Latina*, Paris, 1852, vol. 119, col. 101–250. (Criticism of Eriugena's *De praedestinatione*.)

* Fredegisus of Tours (*c.*800?) *De substantia nihili et de tenebris* (On the Substance of Nothing and on Darkness), in Monumenta Germaniae Historica, Epistolae IV, *Epistolae Karolini Aevi II*, ed. E. Euemmler, Berlin: Weidmann, 1895, 552–5. (Considers what the referent of 'nothing' is.)

Gottschalk of Orbais (late 830s–840s) Works on Predestination, in C. Lambot (ed.) *Oeuvres théologiques et grammaticales de Godescalc d'Orbais*, Louvain: Spicilegium Sacrum Lovaniense, 1945. (Gottschalk sets out his theory of dual predestination, basing himself on Augustine.)

Hincmar of Rheims (849) *Ad reclusos et simplices* (Hincmar's letter against Gottschalk's theory of predestination), ed. W. Gundlach, 'Zwei Schriften des Erzbischofs Hinkmar von Reims – 2', *Zeitschrift für Kirchengeschichte* 10, 1889: 258–309. (Hincmar's attack on Gottschalk.)

Hrabanus Maurus (*c.*840) Letter to Bishop Noting (against Gottschalk on predestination), in J.-P. Migne (ed.) *Patrologia Latina*, Paris, 1852, vol. 112, cols. 1530–53. (Hrabanus attacks the idea of dual predestination.)

McKitterick, R. (ed.) (1994) *Carolingian Culture: Emulation and Innovation*, Cambridge: Cambridge University Press. (Essays by various specialists on Carolingian thought, music, literature, art and so on.)

Marenbon, J. (1981) *From the Circle of Alcuin to the School of Auxerre*, Cambridge Studies in Medieval Life and Thought, 3rd series, vol. 15, Cambridge: Cambridge University Press. (Logic, philosophy and theology from *circa* 790–890.)

Prudentius of Troyes (early 850s) *De praedestinatione* (On Predestination), in J.-P. Migne (ed.) *Patrologia Latina*, Paris, 1852, vol. 119, col. 101–250. (Attack on Eriugena's *De praedestinatione*.)

* Theodulf of Orleans (*c.*788–92) *Libri Carolini* (Caroline Books), ed. H. Bastgen, Monumenta Germaniae Historica Legum: III Concilia II, suppl., Hannover/Leipzig: Hahn, 1924. (The Western response, issued in Charlemagne's name, to the Greek position on image worship.)

* Ratramnus of Corbie (*c.*860–3) *Liber de anima* (Book on the Soul), ed. D.C. Lambot, Namur: Godenne; Lille: Giard, 1952. (Most important for its rejection of realist views about universals.)

* Remigius of Auxerre (*c.*900) Commentary on Boethius's *De consolatione philosophiae*, extracts in E.T. Silk (ed.) *Saeculi noni auctoris in Boetii consolationem Philosophiae commentarius*, appendix, Rome: American Academy in Rome, 1935. (Discovers hidden Christian meanings in Boethius' text.)

JOHN MARENBON

CARROLL, LEWIS *see* DODGSON, CHARLES LUTWIDGE

CARTESIANISM *see* DESCARTES, RENÉ; GEULINCX, ARNOLD; MALEBRANCHE, NICOLAS

CĀRVĀKA *see* MATERIALISM, INDIAN SCHOOL OF

CASSIODORUS
see ENCYCLOPEDISTS, MEDIEVAL

CASSIRER, ERNST (1874–1945)

Cassirer is one of the major figures in the development of philosophical idealism in the first half of the twentieth century. He is known for his philosophy of culture based on his conception of 'symbolic form', for his historical studies of the problem of knowledge in the rise of modern philosophy and science and for his works on the Renaissance and the Enlightenment. Cassirer expanded Kant's critique of reason to a critique of culture by regarding the symbol as the common denominator of all forms of human thought, imagination and experience. He delineates symbolic forms of myth, religion, language, art, history and science and

defines the human being as the 'symbolizing animal'.
All human experience occurs through systems of
symbols. Language is only one such system; the images
of myth, religion and art and the mathematical
structures of science are others.

Being of Jewish faith, Cassirer left Germany in 1933
with the rise of Nazism, going first to Oxford, then to
university positions in Sweden and the USA. In the last
period of his career he applied his philosophy of culture
generally and his conception of myth specifically to a
critique of political myths and to the study of irrational
forces in the state.

1   **Life**
2   **Philosophy of symbolic forms**
3   **Historical studies**
4   **Myth and the state**

1   Life

Ernst Cassirer was born in the German city of Breslau
(now Wroclaw, Poland) on 28 July 1874; he died
suddenly, of a heart attack, on the Columbia
University campus in New York on 13 April 1945.
His life was a personal and intellectual 'odyssey' that
took him from Europe to the USA, and led him from
the Marburg Neo-Kantianism of his teacher, Hermann Cohen, to his own broad vision of human
culture and a critique of the modern state. Cassirer
lectured as *Privatdozent* at the University of Berlin
from 1906 until 1919, when he accepted a professorship at the newly founded University of Hamburg; he
served as its rector in 1929–30.

After Hitler's assumption of the chancellorship of
Germany in January 1933, Cassirer left Germany. He
taught from 1933 to 1935 at All Souls College, Oxford
and then accepted a professorship at the University of
Göteborg, Sweden. In 1941 he moved to Yale
University in the USA, and then went to Columbia
University for the academic year 1944–5. Cassirer
published nearly 125 books, essays and reviews and
left a number of unpublished papers.

2   Philosophy of symbolic forms

Cassirer published the major work of his philosophy,
Philosophie der symbolischen Formen (The Philosophy
of Symbolic Forms: vol. 1, Language; vol. 2, Mythical
Thought; vol. 3, The Phenomenology of Knowledge),
from 1923 to 1929, but his conception of 'symbolic
form' goes back to the philosophy of science he
formed a decade earlier. Modern scientific thought,
Cassirer holds, is based on the 'functional concept'.
As opposed to the Aristotelian theory of concept
formation, in which a common substantial element is

sought through a comparison of the similarities and
differences of a class of particulars, the functional
concept is formed by articulating a principle by which
a set of particulars can be ordered as a series. This
principle of serial arrangement of a group of
particulars, unlike a substance, has no reality or
meaning independent of the elements it orders, and
these elements have meaning only in terms of the
positions they each occupy in the series. Cassirer
formulated this indissoluble bond between universal
and particular of the functional concept as F (a, b,
c, . . .). It suggested to him a model for how the mind
forms experience in all spheres of human activity,
cognitive and noncognitive.

The historical source for this insight is Kant's idea
of the 'schema', a conception of sensuous-intellectual
form that is presupposed by all acts of human
knowledge. What Kant delineates abstractly as one
of the principles of his first *Critique*, Cassirer finds as
a phenomenon within human experience: the symbol.
The critique of reason becomes the critique of culture.
Each area of human culture has its own way of
bringing sensed particulars together in symbolic
orders. Each area of culture has its own 'inner form'
– its own formation of the object, its own causality, its
own apprehensions of space, time and number. These
various symbolic forms of culture differ from each
other in their individual 'tonality', and human culture
as a whole is ideally a harmony of these forms.

The symbolic forms are frequently thought of as a
list, following the chapter titles of Cassirer's *An Essay
on Man* (1944): myth and religion, language, art,
history and science. Cassirer also suggests the
possibility of additional symbolic forms, such as
economics, morality and technology. In *The Phenomenology of Knowledge*, the third volume of *The
Philosophy of Symbolic Forms* (1923–9), Cassirer
presents three symbolic forms as corresponding to
the fundamental functions of the development of
consciousness. He makes clear that he is using the
term 'phenomenology' not in Husserl's sense but in
Hegel's, that is, as developmental, not descriptive
phenomenology. All knowledge and culture originates
in the 'phenomenon of expression', the *Ausdrucks-
funktion* of consciousness. At the level of 'expression',
(*Ausdruck*) the object is 'felt' in its immediacy.
Consciousness at this level takes the form of myth.
Symbol and symbolized occupy the same level of
reality. The dancer who dons the mask of the god *is*
the god. The mythic image in its felt immediacy gives
way to the logical powers inherent in language; this
produces the 'representational function' (*Darstel-
lungsfunktion*). This function builds a world of
common-sense objects, of thing-attribute relationships and classes. Symbol and symbolized now are

different orders of reality. Symbols refer to things. Beyond this is the purely 'significative function' (*Bedeutungsfunktion*) of scientific and theoretical thought. At this level the power of the symbol to generate 'symbolic systems' occurs. Here symbols can refer in fully determinate ways to other orders of symbols. The purest examples of this are mathematics and mathematical logic.

In a fourth volume of *The Philosophy of Symbolic Forms*, left incomplete in manuscript at his death, Cassirer considered 'the metaphysics of symbolic forms'. He examined how the expressive function of consciousness is the most fundamental manifestation of spirit (*Geist*) and how spirit is a transformation of life (*Leben*). Cassirer discusses a number of conceptions of life in modern philosophy and is led to his own doctrine of 'Basis-phenomena' (*Basisphänomene*), the foremost of which, he claims, is life. Life is the ongoing flow of existence that is first formed by the human power of expression, out of which, as described above, arise all forms of human culture.

3 Historical studies

Cassirer did not approve of 'hurling one's ideas into empty space' without showing their relation to the historical development of philosophy. Not only does he ground his original ideas in their historical sources and in the fields he discusses, he is the author of a large corpus of work in intellectual history. He wrote books and essays on Leibniz, Descartes, Kant and Rousseau, and edited a three-volume edition of Leibniz's philosophical works as well as one of the standard editions of Kant's works. Cassirer published essays on figures in humanist thought such as Hölderlin, Kleist, Humboldt, Schiller, Shaftesbury, Pico della Mirandola, Thomas Mann and Schweitzer. In the philosophy and history of science he wrote on Galileo, Newton, Einstein's relativity and Bohr's indeterminacy principle. Cassirer's systematic interpretation of the history of philosophy is centred on two series of works: his four-volume history, *Das Erkenntnisproblem in der Philosophie und Wissenschaft der neueren Zeit* (The Problem of Knowledge in Philosophy and Science in the Modern Age) (1906, 1907, 1920) and his trilogy, *Individuum und Kosmos in der Philosophie der Renaissance* (The Individual and the Cosmos in Renaissance Philosophy) (1927), *Die Platonische Renaissance in England und die Schule von Cambridge* (The Platonic Renaissance in England) (1932a) and *Die Philosophie der Aufklärung* (The Philosophy of the Enlightenment) (1932b). Cassirer began his study of the problem of knowledge intending to show how this problem develops in the simultaneous rise of modern philosophy and modern science, beginning with Nicholas of Cusa and culminating in Kant. Later he continued the theme in the post-Kantian systems through in Hegel, and much later, when in Sweden, he considered the shape of the contemporary sciences.

His trilogy of studies goes over some of the same ground as his earlier work, but in a more agile way and to a different purpose. He begins with Nicholas of Cusa, but his aim is to show how the Renaissance can be understood as a whole in terms of the problem of the individual and the cosmos. He then shows how the ideas of the Renaissance were transmitted via the Cambridge Platonists to culminate in the Enlightenment. Cassirer wishes to present a 'phenomenology of philosophic spirit'. This is not a progression of problems of pure thought, but the generation of a philosophical point of view on the individual, the world and society, in which the problems of knowledge are tied to the whole of human activity (see Platonism; Renaissance philosophy).

It is not possible to understand the basis of Cassirer's philosophy without an awareness of his debt to Goethe (see Goethe, J.W. von §3). Goethe's understanding of organic form is important for Cassirer's conception of the symbol, and his cosmopolitanism influences Cassirer's conception of culture. Goethe is the source of Cassirer's grasp of human creation as a process of self-liberation, a sentiment Cassirer extends to the whole of culture. He wrote on various aspects of Goethe's thought, but he was influenced more by Goethe's spirit and sense of life than by his interest in particular questions of interpretation.

4 Myth and the state

Cassirer does not have a political philosophy in the traditional sense. He has a critique of the modern state and a definite view of the relation of philosophy to politics. In his inaugural lecture at Göteborg in 1935, Cassirer recalled Kant's distinction between a 'scholastic' conception of philosophy and a conception of 'philosophy as related to the world' (*conceptus cosmicus*). Cassirer said that he as well as others have been guilty of the former and he aligns himself with the latter. He quotes Schweitzer, his ethical hero, who calls philosophy a 'watchman' who slept in the hour of peril, and did not keep watch over us during the rise of totalitarianism. Cassirer holds that philosophy does not and cannot cause the events of political life, nor can it resolve them, but it has a duty to act as our conscience, to inform us of them by the use of its powers of reflection. In *The Myth of the State* (1946) and other writings of this period, Cassirer attacks Heidegger's conception of 'thrownness' (*Geworfen-*

heit) as a conception of the human condition that puts philosophy in a position where it can no longer 'do its duty'. This goes back to Cassirer's debate with Heidegger in 1929 at Davos, Switzerland. Quoting Goethe, Cassirer sees human freedom as tied to the human project of spirit (*Geist*), of the creation of culture. Heidegger sees freedom as requiring a 'breakthrough' (*Einbruch*); freedom is not part of the human condition itself, but is contingent (*zufällig*) (see HEIDEGGER, M. §5).

Cassirer's philosophy of mythology is the most original part of his epistemology and phenomenology of knowledge. He shows that myth is not a collection of errors or a world of unchecked emotions but a total way of thinking and symbolizing, which exists at the beginning of human culture and is present as a phase in the development of any subsequent symbolic form. Myth is always present as the expressive moment in any act of cognition. In *An Essay on Man*, Cassirer claims that his philosophy of culture is an extension of the ancient ideal of self-knowledge and that human culture as a whole is the process of humanity's 'self-liberation'. The key to self-knowledge and culture is freedom from the immediacy of the object.

In *The Myth of the State*, Cassirer is able to apply the force of his entire philosophy of culture towards understanding the logic of modern political myths. They are a revival of the logic of the primordial forms of expressive consciousness. Modern political myths are not natural; they are manufactured products joined to the technology of mass communication. Such myths shape the life of the state and become the substitute for its rational principles. Cassirer sees this not only as true of Nazism, but also as a danger in the modern state itself. He claims that myth is impervious to argument, but that philosophy can warn us of it and allow us to understand it.

See also: STATE, THE §1

List of works

Cassirer, E. (1906, 1907, 1920) *Das Erkenntnisproblem in der Philosophie und Wissenschaft der neueren Zeit* (The Problem of Knowledge in Philosophy and Science in the Modern Age), Berlin: Bruno Cassirer, 3 vols. (History of the problem of knowledge from Nicholas of Cusa through in Hegel and Neo-Kantian systems of philosophy.)
—— (1910) *Substanzbegriff und Funktionsbegriff. Untersuchungen über die Grundfragen der Erkenntniskritik*, Berlin: Bruno Cassirer; trans. W.M. Swabey and M.C. Swabey, in *Substance and Function and Einstein's Theory of Relativity*, Chicago, IL: Open Court, 1923. (Cassirer's philosophy

of science, showing how the functional concept reflects the thought-form of modern science.)
—— (1923–9) *Philosophie der symbolischen Formen*, Berlin: Bruno Cassirer, 3 vols; trans. R. Manheim, *The Philosophy of Symbolic Forms*, New Haven, CT: Yale University Press, 3 vols, 1955–7: vol. 1, *Language*; vol. 2, *Mythical Thought*; vol. 3, *The Phenomenology of Knowledge*. (The major statement of Cassirer's systematic philosophy.)
—— (1925) *Sprache und Mythos. Ein Beitrag zum Problem der Götternamen*, vol. 6 of *Studien der Bibliothek Warburg*, Leipzig: Teubner; trans. S.K. Langer, *Language and Myth*, New York: Harper & Bros, 1946. (Study of the interconnections of the symbolic forms.)
—— (1927) *Individuum und Kosmos in der Philosophie der Renaissance*, vol. 10 of *Studien der Bibliothek Warburg*, Leipzig: Teubner; trans. M. Domandi, *The Individual and the Cosmos in Renaissance Philosophy*, New York: Harper & Row, 1963. (The major themes that unify Renaissance philosophy, with an emphasis on Nicholas of Cusa.)
—— (1932a) *Die Platonische Renaissance in England und die Schule von Cambridge*, vol. 24 of *Studien der Bibliothek Warburg*, Leipzig: Teubner; trans. J.P. Pettegrove, *The Platonic Renaissance in England*, Austin, TX: University of Texas Press, and Edinburgh: Nelson, 1953. (Emphasis on the Cambridge Platonists and Shaftesbury.)
—— (1932b) *Die Philosophie der Aufklärung*, Tübingen: Mohr; trans. F.C.A. Koelln and J.P. Pettegrove, *The Philosophy of the Enlightenment*, Princeton, NJ: Princeton University Press, 1951. (The unity of the Enlightenment's views of nature, religion, aesthetics and the state.)
—— (1942) *Zur Logik der Kulturwissenschaften. Fünf Studien*, vol. 47 of *Götesborgs Högskolas Arsskrift*, Göteborg: Wettergren & Kerbers; trans. C.S. Howe, *The Logic of the Humanities*, New Haven, CT: Yale University Press, 1961. (Five essays on the nature of the humanities, especially the differences between concept-formation in the sciences and the humanities.)
—— (1944) *An Essay on Man: An Introduction to a Philosophy of Human Culture*, New Haven, CT: Yale University Press. (Cassirer's summary of his philosophy of symbolic forms and the conception of human nature presupposed by it.)
—— (1946) *The Myth of the State*, New Haven, CT: Yale University Press. (Historical and systematic analysis of the modern state employing Cassirer's conception of mythical thought.)
—— (1950) *The Problem of Knowledge: Philosophy, Science and History since Hegel*, trans. from the German manuscript of 1940 by W.H. Woglom and

C.W. Handel, New Haven, CT: Yale University Press; German edn, *Das Erkenntnisproblem in der Philosophie und Wissenschaft der neueren Zeit. Von Hegels Tod bis zur Gegenwart (1832–1932)*. Stuttgart: Kohlhammer, 1957. (The final volume of *Das Erkenntnisproblem*, see above.)

—— (1979) *Symbol, Myth, and Culture: Essays and Lecturers of Ernst Cassirer 1935–1945*, ed. D.P. Verene, New Haven, CT: Yale University Press. (Essays and lectures from the last decade of Cassirer's life left in manuscript at the time of his death.)

—— (1995) *Zur Metaphysik der symbolischen Formen*, ed. J.M. Krois, vol. 1 of *Nachgelassene Manuskripte und Texte*, ed. J.M. Krois and O. Schwemmer, Hamburg: Meiner; trans. and ed. J.M. Krois and D.P. Verene as *The Metaphysics of Symbolic Logic*, vol. 4. of *The Philosophy of Symbolic Forms*, New Haven, CT: Yale University Press, 1996. (The fourth volume of Cassirer's major work (written in 1928), with further text on the conception of 'basis-phenomena' (written c.1940) left in manuscript at his death.)

References and further reading

Braun, H.-J. et al. (eds) (1988) *Über Ernst Cassirer's Philosophie der Symbolischen Formen* (On Ernst Cassirer's Philosophy of Symbolic Forms), Frankfurt: Suhrkamp. (Essays by European scholars on major themes in Cassirer's philosophy. From an international conference held in 1986 in Zurich.)

Eggers, W. and S. Mayer (1988) *Ernst Cassirer: An Annotated Bibliography*, New York: Garland. (Comprehensive bibliography of writings by and about Cassirer; annotations are uneven.)

Hamburg, C.H. (1964) 'A Cassirer–Heidegger Seminar', *Philosophy and Phenomenological Research* 25: 208–22. (Account of the exchange between Cassirer and Heidegger in 1929 at Davos, Switzerland.)

Heidegger, M. (1928) Review of Das mythische Denken by E. Cassirer, *Deutsche Literaturzeitung* 21: 1000–12; trans. J.G. Hart and J.C. Maraldo, 'Book Review of Ernst Cassirer's Mythical Thought', in *The Piety of Thinking: Essays by Martin Heidegger*, Bloomington, IN: Indiana University Press, 1976. (Heidegger's review of volume 2 of The Philosophy of Symbolic Forms.)

Krois, J.M. (1987) *Cassirer: Symbolic Forms and History*, New Haven, CT: Yale University Press. (Definitive study of the various aspects of Cassirer's philosophy.)

Langer, S.K. (1974) 'De Profondis', *Revue Internationale de Philosophie* 28: 449–55. (Comparison of Cassirer's and Freud's views of the symbol, by a philosopher who was greatly influenced by Cassirer.)

Schilpp, P.A. (1949) *The Philosophy of Ernst Cassirer*, Evanston, IL: The Library of Living Philosophers, Inc. (Twenty-three essays on aspects of Cassirer's thought, a biographical essay and a bibliography of his writings to 1946.)

Verene, D.P. (1969) 'Kant, Hegel and Cassirer: The Origins of the Philosophy of Symbolic Forms', *Journal of the History of Ideas* 30: 33–46. (Assesses the extent to which both Kant and Hegel are sources for Cassirer's philosophy of symbolic forms.)

DONALD PHILLIP VERENE

CASUISTRY

Casuistry, from the Latin casus *(cases), has been understood in three separate yet related senses. In its first sense casuistry is defined as a style of ethical reasoning associated closely with the tradition of practical philosophy influenced by Aristotle and Aquinas. In its second sense it is reasoning about 'cases of conscience' (*casus conscientiae*). The third sense, moral laxism, arose out of Pascal's famous critique of casuistry, which did much to diminish its influence. In recent years, however, a renewed interest in the first and second senses of casuistry has been witnessed in the areas of practical reasoning and applied philosophy.*

In its widest sense, casuistry can be described as a method of ethical reasoning which, drawing on the tradition of practical philosophy of Aristotle and Aquinas, aims to construct a 'dialectic' between the facts of particular cases and the antecedent assumptions, evaluations and convictions which individual agents bring to bear in their consideration of such cases. The purpose of the dialectic is to enable agents to arrive at informed decisions as to what is morally possible and impossible for them to do in particular cases. In a narrower sense, the term casuistry has been employed to characterize different systems of moral theology within the Christian, Jewish and Islamic traditions, in which all-inclusive norms are derived from judgments in particular cases, instead of being laid down in advance by absolute moral codes. In its narrowest sense, casuistry refers to the use of subtle definitional distinctions in the handling of the problems of moral theology, with the aim of drawing fine dividing lines between what is and is not permissible at the level of action. The technique has at times been used to excuse crimes and sins, thereby exculpating the immoral, and such is the extent of the modern association of casuistry with all varieties of obfuscation, quibbling and laxism, that a pejorative connotation of the word itself is now established in most European languages.

The identification of casuistry with its narrowest definition is due to Blaise Pascal's *Lettres écrites à un provincial (The Provincial Letters)* (1656–7) (see PASCAL, B.). This famous satire delivered to casuistry a near fatal blow, from which, in the popular mind, it has never recovered. It was Pascal's urbane yet brutal vilification of the Jesuit confessors of the University of Paris, individuals who had attempted to base an account of practical conduct on the analysis of cases (*casus*) and circumstances (*circumstantiae*), that stereotyped casuistry as the doctrine that sought 'to excuse the inexcusable'.

Pascal's attack on casuistry can be considered unjust since it was based on a partial understanding of the theories he was aiming to expose, and of the individual casuists he was attempting to ridicule. His aim in writing this work was to enlist the reader's support for a version of moral absolutism that was peculiar to Jansenism, a rigoristic Roman Catholic sect to which Pascal was aligned. Pascal was forever trying to illustrate the laxism inherent within Jesuit casuistry in order to establish an unfavourable contrast with the moral rigorism of the Jansenists.

The method embodied in the second definition of casuistry as case-reasoning was developed in the penitential handbooks of the Middle Ages and reached its fullest expression in Roman Catholic textbooks of moral theology of the Counter-Reformation. The method was also embraced by a number of Anglican divines and members of the Reformed tradition. The impetus behind the case-method lay in the desire among theologians and philosophers to discover the moral norms embodied in divine law in the circumstances of human life, rather than finding them in antecedent absolute norms which one could then apply to a set of cases. Thus, the case-reasoning of the theologians was able to respond to new situations and novel problems with a commendable degree of good sense, originality and doctrinal flexibility.

In recent times the case-method of the theologians has been revived in the field of bioethics (see BIOETHICS). For bioethicists the value of casuistry resides in its emphasis of practical problem-solving by means of a nuanced interpretation of individual cases. This is thought to have greater consonance with the actual conditions of medical practice and decision-making. Problems arise, however, when one attempts to achieve the transposition of the case-method of the theologians to the modern secular context of bioethics. The confessors of Roman Catholic casuistry, in particular, possessed both juridical authority and the authority of being experts within an institutional setting. Yet the new casuists of bioethics must rely on professional knowledge alone to determine morally adequate judgments in particular cases. The problem here is one of analogy. The older casuistical method relied upon interpretative authorities such as confessors and canonists which helped to bolster the idea that the judgments made in particular cases would reflect the assumptions of a common morality. Given the context of moral pluralism in which bioethical judgments are made, it is difficult to see how bioethics can draw upon the same type of paradigmatic examples of 'right' and 'wrong' moral judgment on which the earlier model of casuistry was based (see MORAL PLURALISM; MORAL EXPERTISE).

It is in its widest sense, in the context of moral philosophy, that casuistry holds its greatest promise. As a dialectical method of moral reasoning inspired by Aristotle and Aquinas, casuistry may well prove relevant here in virtue of its opposition to inflexible and literal interpretations of moral principles, and its resistance to any ethical attitude which first absolutizes a universal moral norm and then insists on its all-round and unyielding application, while denying any abatement or adjustment to changing contingencies.

See also: LOGIC OF ETHICAL DISCOURSE; MORAL JUDGMENT; SITUATION ETHICS

References and further reading

Aquinas, T. (1266–73) *Summa theologiae* (Synopsis of Theology), ed. T. Gilby, London: Eyre & Spottiswoode, 1966, vol. 28, IaIIae.90–97. (Questions 94 and following cover Aquinas' remarks on natural law. Many casuists conjoined Aquinas' remarks on natural law to Aristotle's account of the nature of ethics.)

Aristotle (*c.* mid 4th century BC) *Nicomachean Ethics*, trans. with notes by T. Irwin, Indianapolis, IN: Hackett Publishing Company, 1985, books I 3, V. (Provides discussion of the nature of ethics, and considers the importance of equity in law, both of which exerted a significant influence on the development of casuistry.)

Jonsen, A.J. and Toulmin, S. (1988) *The Abuse of Casuistry*, Berkeley, CA: University of California Press. (An influential defence of the casuistical tradition, particularly influential in applied philosophy, especially recent bioethics.)

Keenan, J.F. and Shannon, T.A. (eds) (1995) *The Context of Casuistry*, Washington, DC: Georgetown University Press. (A rich collection of articles which discuss the roots, practice and legacy of casuistry in moral philosophy and theology.)

Leites, E. (ed.) (1988) *Conscience and Casuistry in Early Modern Europe*, Cambridge: Cambridge University Press. (A collection of articles that illuminate the historical context in which casuistry was practiced.)

* Pascal, B. (1656–7) *Lettres écrites à un provincial*, trans. A.J. Krailsheimer, *The Provincial Letters*, Harmondsworth: Penguin, 1967, letters VI, VII. (A strong attack on Jesuit doctrines.)

Stone, M.W.F. (1998) *The Subtle Art of Casuistry: An Essay in the History of Moral Philosophy*, Oxford: Oxford University Press. (A defence of casuistry from the standpoint of recent moral philosophy. Emphasizes the Aristotelian-Thomistic roots of the casuistical method in contrast to other authors, most notably Jonsen and Toulmin.)

MARTIN STONE

CAT, SCHRÖDINGER'S

see QUANTUM MEASUREMENT PROBLEM

CATEGORICAL IMPERATIVE

see KANTIAN ETHICS

CATEGORIES

Categories are hard to describe, and even harder to define. This is in part a consequence of their complicated history, and in part because category theory must grapple with vexed questions concerning the relation between linguistic or conceptual categories on the one hand, and objective reality on the other. In the mid-fourth century BC, Aristotle initiates discussion of categories as a central enterprise of philosophy. In the Categories *he presents an 'ontological' scheme which classifies all being into ten ultimate types, but in the* Topics *introduces the categories as different kinds of predication, that is, of items such as 'goodness' or 'length of a tennis court' or 'red', which can be 'predicated of' subjects. He nowhere attempts either to justify what he includes in his list of categories or to establish its completeness, and relies throughout on the* unargued conviction that language faithfully represents the most basic features of reality. In the twentieth century, a test for category membership was recommended by Ryle, that of absurdity: concepts or expressions differ in logical type when their combination produces sentences which are palpable nonsense. Kant, working in the eighteenth century, derives his categories from a consideration of aspects of judgments, hoping in this manner to ensure that his scheme will consist exclusively of a priori concepts which might constitute an objective world. The Sinologist Graham argues that the categories familiar in the West mirror Indo-European linguistic structure, and that an experimental Chinese scheme exhibits suggestively different properties, but his relativism is highly contentious.*

1 **Categories in Aristotle**
2 **Categories in Ryle**
3 **Categories in Kant**
4 **Are categories universal?**

1 Categories in Aristotle

Despite the historical importance of category theory in Western philosophy, it is remarkably difficult to grasp what a category is and how a category theory might achieve legitimacy. To a degree, such elusiveness is simply the product of the lengthy and elaborate historical development these theories have sustained, but the profundity of the issues they broach also contributes to the puzzle – and hence to the abiding interest – of categories.

Orthodoxy has it that Aristotle in the treatise appropriately entitled *Categories* introduces categories to the Western tradition: 'of things said without any combination, each signifies either substance or quantity or qualification or a relative or where or when or being-in-a-position or having or doing or being-affected' (1b 25–7). Despite what his phrasing might easily be (and often has been) taken to imply, Aristotle plainly intends to refer, not to linguistic items, but rather to their referents. Thus his sentence might be paraphrased 'of things to which we can refer in uncombined (namely syntactically simple) language, each is. . . . .', and it enumerates all the types of being there are: substances, such as human beings; quantities, such as three feet long; qualities, such as red; and so forth. But although his manner of expression is in one sense misleading, it should not be deplored or dismissed as merely something like a trivial confusion of material and formal modes of speech. Rather, here, as so often elsewhere, Aristotle is moving from what we would regard as features of language to features of the world without so much as signalling any recognition that there is a transition to be made. Nor does he explain how he arrived at his list, or why one should feel confident that it is comprehensive (see ARISTOTLE §7).

To complicate matters further, there are compelling grounds for the belief that, despite the tradition, the genera of being with which the *Categories* deals are not (Aristotelian) categories. The word which we transliterate 'category' is employed by Aristotle to mean 'predicate' or '(type of) predication', so that a 'category theory' ought to be a theory of predication, not of being. And in a relatively unfamiliar text, *Topics* (I 9), this is just what we do find. After saying that the types of predication must be distinguished, Aristotle provides a list identical to that in the *Categories* – except that the first item is not 'substance', but 'what it is' (103b 21–3). In the *Categories*, individuals such as Socrates are substances pre-eminently, and species such as human being are substances secondarily: in the *Topics*, in contrast, colour is the 'what it is' of red no less than human being is the 'what it is' of Socrates.

What the *Topics* delivers, then, is a theory of predication according to which the predicates which can characterize any subject whatsoever will fall into ten ultimate kinds. Again, defence of this list in particular (or of the possibility of constructing *any* non-arbitrary, correct list) is lacking; but reflection on why the *Topics* was written might make the absence of this defence considerably less shocking, though at the cost, ironically enough, of undermining the status which the categories of the *Categories* have historically enjoyed. The *Topics* as a whole comprises prescriptions for the classification and analysis of a vast array of the sorts of argument then current in Greek philosophy. The intention is combative as well as constructive: Aristotle also teaches how to detect and dismember what he considers sorts of fallacious reasoning, and prime among these is ignorant or malicious exploitation of confusion in manner of predication. For example, what is good about food? That it does something – it produces pleasure. What is good about human beings? That they are 'of a certain quality, such as temperate or courageous or just' (*Topics* I 15.107A). So, if viewed as a digest of types of predication already familiar from the practices of Greek dialectic, the categories of the *Topics* require no defence beyond reasonable fidelity to the range of predicates actually found in the typical dialectical repertoire. In particular, there need be no presumption that predicational categories rooted in philosophical practice will correspond to a significant, let alone universal, ontological classification.

This is not to say that predicational and ontological categories are unrelated. Because Aristotle moves with disconcerting freedom from language to the world, he takes it for granted that predicate expressions do usually, without the possibility of radical misrepresentation, refer to real entities. So a scheme of predicational categories might indeed suggest at least the outline of a corresponding ontological scheme, one justified in detail and scope precisely to the extent that the original classification of predicates, and its extension, are well-founded. If this is the correct account of how these theories developed in Aristotle, what prompted the substitution of ontological 'substance' for predicational 'what it is'? Perhaps the governing idea of the *Categories* is that substance alone can serve as the subject in which items from other categories inhere: for instance, Socrates, but not his height, is pale-skinned and can properly be said to be pale-skinned. Therefore the design of the treatise is to convince us that, at its deepest level, ontology is marked by a crucial asymmetry between substantial and non-substantial being, quite possibly in a spirit hostile to the elevation of Platonic Forms which, far from being most real, would figure as no more than non-substantial, parasitic things. If so, a further irony is that the *Categories* was intended to establish a metaphysical thesis essentially independent of the grand classificatory ambitions with which it came to be historically associated. In the event, the philosophical tradition which was dominated by the followers of Aristotle since late antiquity, elevated the ontological categories into a system uniquely capable of displaying the lineaments of what is (see BEING §2; SUBSTANCE).

2 Categories in Ryle

The most noteworthy modern contribution to the theory of categories is that of Gilbert Ryle, in that he tries to throw light on the difficulty which Aristotle left entirely obscure: how to identify and discriminate between categories (see RYLE, G. §2). Ryle contends that one determines the logical category or type of an expression by ascertaining the field of sentence-forms into which it can enter without resultant absurdity. For example, 'four' can complete the frame '.....is a prime number' to yield a meaningful (if false) sentence, while 'Socrates', or so Ryle would urge, cannot. Such nonsense exemplifies what Ryle famously dubbed the 'category-mistake', the production of absurdity as the upshot not of lexical or grammatical irregularity but of the vain effort to combine the logically uncombinable. He conceived of category theory as a diagnostic tool for the exposure and resolution of chronic philosophical disputes. Ryle proposed that disputants on either side of, say, the mind–body problem are really at cross-purposes: they have put forward propositions which only seem to conflict, since their difference in type removes the possibility of any logical relations, whether of implication or of incompatibility, holding between them. At one point Ryle was willing to go so far as to proclaim that 'philosophy is the replacement of category-habits by category-disciplines' (1949: 10).

Although Ryle regarded Aristotle's theory as the ancestor of his own, an obvious dissimilarity is that Rylean categories, defined as they are by multiple logical relations, are potentially unlimited in number: Ryle was keen to explore what he termed 'the logical geography of concepts', not to engage in pigeon-holing. The great awkwardness looming over Ryle's theory is that all ventures to make out a principled difference between mere falsehood and the nonsense allegedly distinctive of category-mistakes have come to grief. But if Ryle did not finally achieve a strict criterion for the identification of categories, he nevertheless did successfully sharpen the powerful and once widely-shared intuition that certain propositions – some of philosophical importance – must be rejected not as false, but as (veiled) nonsense.

3 Categories in Kant

The basic problem of specifying what a category theory is, is unavoidably aggravated by Kant, the second major historical influence to shape the tradition (see KANT, I. §4). Kant arrives at his alternative categories by considering the conditions which allow there to be a logic of judgments, a procedure which he explicitly attributes to Aristotle, while emphasizing the divergence of their conclusions (Kant 1781/7: A80, B105). He asks: Which judgement forms does logic treat of? His answer is that all judgements have a 'quantity' (universal, particular or singular) and a 'quality' (affirmative, negative or infinite). They must all instantiate one of the 'relations' (categorical, hypothetical or disjunctive), and one of the 'modalities' (problematic, assertoric or apodeictic) (Kant 1781/7: A70, B95). Kant proposes to derive his categories from these forms or aspects of judgment, obtaining the corresponding list of unity, plurality and totality under 'quantity'; reality, negation and limitation under 'quality'; inherence and subsistence, causality and dependence, and community under 'relation'; and possibility–impossibility, existence–non-existence and necessity–contingency under 'modality' (Kant 1781/7: A80, B106). He pretends that their derivation from the types of judgement makes his categories superior to Aristotle's, because this procedure supposedly guarantees that all the concepts of pure understanding, and no others, are systematically discovered.

Every element of empirical reality must fall into place within this scheme, since the categories exhaust the understanding's a priori concepts. Kant's eventual aim in the Transcendental Deduction is to prove that, since every experience involves judgement, every possible experience must involve use of the categories. Specifically, his claim is that one must conceive of experience as experience of a world organized by the categories.

The conviction that Aristotelian genera of being and Kantian concepts of understanding cannot, *pace* Kant, be in competition, is hard to avoid since the philosophical projects which gave a point to these various theories are so diverse. But we should not hastily conclude that these schemes have nothing of philosophical importance in common. Aristotle's transitions from what we are likely to classify as linguistic or conceptual data to robustly realist theses seem surprisingly bold, even unmotivated; but that is precisely because we are heirs to the Kantian legacy which insists on our right to empirical realism but concedes the obligation to earn it by espousing transcendental idealism.

Aristotle blithely assumes that the fabric of the world is accessible to us, disclosed by the range of predications people, at any rate those of a philo-sophical disposition, have been disposed to make; he mounts no argument for the reliable accuracy of predication. True, it is not as if later Aristotelians ignored the issue of what the categories are categories of. Because the *Categories* was incorporated into the *Organon* – which came to be the traditional logic course, culminating in the analysis of arguments – some interpreters were indeed inclined to the position that the *Categories*, which began the logic course, ought to deal with the simples from which propo-sitions making up arguments are constructed, and so favoured the identification of categories with words. Other strands in the tradition preferred a realistic interpretation, while nevertheless asserting a thor-ough-going isomorphism between the structures of the world, our concepts and the words in which we express ourselves (this 'isomorphic' interpretation is vividly and compendiously presented in, for example, the Renaissance *Conimbricenses* commentary on the *Organon*). Still, even Aristotelians sensitive to the question 'what are categories categories of?', ne-glected the gulf which might separate our conceptual and linguistic resources from what really is: such isomorphism is viable only if grounded in a pre-modern assurance that an impersonal teleology or a divine providence secures and protects the fit between us and the world.

Kant's transcendentalism attempts to redeem such hostages to scepticism. We might accordingly con-ceive of both theories of categories as intimately concerned with the relation of language or our conceptual equipment to the world. To the Kantian, Aristotle seems primitive because he naïvely fails to perceive the paramount challenge confronting philosophy; to the modern follower of Aristotle, the Kantian seems the decadent victim of unjustifiable doubts.

4 Are categories universal?

The impression that Aristotelian and Kantian theories have a vital disagreement in common is strengthened if we move beyond the Western tradition in which they are such towering presences. Angus Graham (1989) endorses the contention, most frequently linked with the name of the famous linguist Benveniste, that the Aristotelian categories represent nothing more than yet another bogus reification of Indo-European linguistic forms. For example, 'quantity' in Aristotle's list is the translation of a Greek word which functions as both an interrogative ('how much?') and an indefinite adjective ('so much'). Thus it is argued that peculiarities of Indo-European grammar have encouraged the construction and success of a categorical scheme which, viewed from a broader linguistic perspective, is nothing more than the deluded inflation of quite parochial traits of familiar languages into general features of reality itself.

Graham goes on to try to substantiate this charge of Indo-European parochialism and to show that moderate versions of 'linguistic relativism' are acceptable – that is, that the narrowly linguistic properties of a language (its syntax, its degree of inflection and so on) encourage or discourage certain thought-patterns in its users. He sketches a scheme of Chinese categories derived from Chinese interrogative patterns, on the assumption that Aristotle had unreflectingly extrapolated his from Greek ones. For example, if the Aristotelian category of substance is the natural linguistic correlate of the question 'what is it?', the analogous Chinese interrogative *ho* solicits an answer in terms of *lei*, kind or type of thing (for example, human) rather than essence or basic nature (for example, rational biped). His global hypothesis is that the Chinese preference for 'which?' over 'what?' questions betrays a holistic cast of mind, felt throughout Eastern philosophy, originating in the inevitable congruence of Chinese thought with Chinese language.

Graham's version of linguistic relativism is arresting but very hard to vindicate. Quite apart from the obstacle that in the *Topics* the category 'what it is' groups non-substantial subjects as well as substances, Graham's relativistic interpretation presupposes that Aristotle proceeded in blinkered ignorance of the (alleged) fact that his native language variously stimulated and inhibited his tendency to propound ontological doctrines. But inspection of his works amply demonstrates that Aristotle is acutely aware of the linguistic traps into which philosophers are prone to fall. After all, in large measure the goal of the *Topics* is to alert us to such dangerous possibilities, and Aristotle's exercises in linguistic analysis often reach a pitch of extreme sophistication. This is not to say that gauging the impact of language on category theories is fruitless: only that they must not be reduced to a paltry imposition of fortuitous linguistic structure onto a world actually untouched by such strictly local projections. Relativistic objections do not foreclose the debate between Aristotelian confidence and Kantian caution.

See also: ONTOLOGY IN INDIAN PHILOSOPHY; UNIVERSALS

References and further reading

* Aristotle (4th century BC) *Categories*, trans. and notes J. Ackrill, Oxford: Clarendon Press, 1979. (Discussed in §1 above.)
* —— (4th century BC) *Topics*, Oxford: Clarendon Press, 1958. (Discussed in §1 above.)
* da Fonseca, P. (1606) *In universam dialecticam*, Coimbra. (Renaissance commentary on the *Organon*, written by several authors of whom de Fonseca is the sole one known.)
  Frede, M. (1987) 'The Title, Unity, and Authenticity of the Aristotelian *Categories*', in *Essays in Ancient Philosophy*, Oxford: Clarendon Press. (Magisterial exposition of the account relating the *Categories* and *Topics*, adopted in §1 above.)
* Graham, A.C. (1989) *Disputers of the Tao*, La Salle, IL: Open Court. (Appendix 2 is the source for the relativistic arguments relayed in §4.)
* Kant, I. (1781/7) *Critique of Pure Reason*, trans. N.K. Smith, London: Macmillan, 1929. (Discussed in §3.)
  Ryle, G. (1937–8) 'Categories', *Proceedings of the Aristotelian Society*, reprinted in A.G.N. Flew (ed.) *Logic and Language*, 2nd series, Oxford: Blackwell, 1959. (Pithily brilliant classic introduction of the views outlined in §2.)
* —— (1949) *The Concept of Mind*, Harmondsworth: Penguin, 1978. (The most sustained and influential attempt to do philosophy by uncovering category-mistakes.)
  Reding, J.-P. (1986) 'Greek and Chinese Categories', *Philosophy East and West* 36: 349–74. (Contains a thoughtful critique of Graham's relativism.)
  Sommers, F. (1963) 'Types and Ontology', *Philo-*

sophical Review 72: 327–63. (One of a series of works in which Sommers attempts to formalize and improve on criteria for types put forward by Ryle and others.)

ROBERT WARDY

CATEGORIES IN INDIAN PHILOSOPHY *see* ONTOLOGY IN INDIAN PHILOSOPHY

CATEGORY THEORY, APPLICATIONS TO THE FOUNDATIONS OF MATHEMATICS

Since the 1960s Lawvere has distinguished two senses of the foundations of mathematics. Logical foundations use formal axioms to organize the subject. The other sense aims to survey 'what is universal in mathematics'. The ontology of mathematics is a third, related issue.

Moderately categorical foundations use sets as axiomatized by the elementary theory of the category of sets (ETCS) rather than Zermelo–Fraenkel set theory (ZF). This claims to make set theory conceptually more like the rest of mathematics than ZF is. And it suggests that sets are not 'made of' anything determinate; they only have determinate functional relations to one another. The ZF and ETCS axioms both support classical mathematics.

Other categories have also been offered as logical foundations. The 'category of categories' takes categories and functors as fundamental. The 'free topos' (see Lambek and Couture 1991) stresses provability. These and others are certainly formally adequate. The question is how far they illuminate the most universal aspects of current mathematics.

*Radically categorical foundations say mathematics has no one starting point; each mathematical structure exists in its own right and can be described intrinsically. The most flexible way to do this to date is categorically. From this point of view various structures have their own logic. Sets have classical logic, or rather the topos **Set** has classical logic. But differential manifolds, for instance, fit neatly into a topos **Spaces** with nonclassical logic. This view urges a broader practice of mathematics than classical.*

This article assumes knowledge of category theory on the level of CATEGORY THEORY, INTRODUCTION TO *§1.*

1 Categorical thinking

The notion of 'isomorphism' aptly illustrates categorical thinking. In algebra two groups with the same group structure are 'isomorphic'. Two spaces with the same topological structure are 'homeomorphic'.

Before category theory, group isomorphism was defined group-theoretically, homeomorphism topologically, and so on. The definitions are unified in the categorical one (see CATEGORY THEORY, INTRODUCTION TO for an introduction to the concepts and notation). In any category, arrows $f : A \to B$ and $g : B \to A$ are called 'inverse' to one another if $gf = 1_A$ and $fg = 1_B$. Objects A and B are isomorphic if there are inverse arrows between them.

Category theory generally defines objects only up to isomorphism. That is, a categorical property will not have a unique instance in a category **A** but all its instances in **A** will be isomorphic and any object isomorphic to an instance will be an instance. For example, a 'terminal object' in a category **A** is an object T such that each object of **A** has exactly one arrow to T. A category **A** may have any number of terminal objects or none. Suppose T and T' are two such. Then there are arrows $T \to T'$ and $T' \to T$, and they are inverse since 1_T is the only arrow from T to T and similarly for T'. Hence T and T' are isomorphic. Conversely if T is terminal and there is an isomorphism $T \to T'$ then every object B of **A** has a unique arrow $B \to T \to T'$ to T', so T' is terminal.

2 The elementary theory of the category of sets (ETCS)

The 'elementary theory of the category of sets' (ETCS) axiomatizes the category **Set** (see CATEGORY THEORY, INTRODUCTION TO §1). We give the axioms in the next section.

In ETCS a 'singleton' is any set terminal in **Set**. We pick one and call it 1. We define an 'element' x of a set A to be a function from 1 to A, $x : 1 \to A$. Composing with any $f : A \to B$ gives an element of B, $fx : 1 \to B$. Trivially, each singleton has exactly one element.

We define a 'product' of sets B and C to be a set $B \times C$ and functions $p_1 : B \times C \to B$ and $p_2 : B \times C \to C$ such that for any set A and functions $f : A \to B$ and $g : A \to C$ there is a unique $u : A \to B \times C$ with $p_1 u = f$ and $p_2 u = g$. We can use $\langle f, g \rangle$ to name u, so $p_1 \langle f, g \rangle = f$ and $p_2 \langle f, g \rangle = g$. Thus elements $\langle x, y \rangle$ of $B \times C$ correspond to elements x of A and y of B.

Now 1 is only defined only up to isomorphism, as is the product $B \times C$, p_1, p_2. This is no laxity on our part. If a set S has any property expressible in ETCS without using names then so does every set isomorphic to S. Thus 1 is distinguished from other singletons only by its name. We can pick a product of B and C to call $B \times C$, p_1, p_2 but it is distinguished from other products of B and C only by its name.

The elements of an ETCS set are definite in number but without distinguishing properties. Each is merely an element of S and is itself and no other. Like Cantor's cardinals ETCS sets are distinguished only by cardinality and their elements are 'mere units' (see Lawvere 1994).

This is a point of controversy. In practice even in Zermelo–Fraenkel set theory (ZF) where sets can be uniquely defined we rarely bother to do so. We say 'Let S be a singleton' without saying which one. We speak of 'the product $B \times C$' without specifying its elements (that is, without choosing among the many ways to code ordered pairs $\langle b, c \rangle$ as sets in ZF). But some people claim this will not do in foundations (see Mayberry 1988).

Others favour such indeterminacy. Since Dedekind raised the issue for modern mathematics, some people claim mathematical objects should have only relevant properties. Natural numbers, say, should have only arithmetic properties. Every ZF set has non-arithmetic properties given by its particular elements. So on this view numbers cannot be ZF sets. But ETCS models of arithmetic have no irrelevant properties. So this view could say the numbers form an ETCS set (see Benacerraf 1965).

Specifically, 'recursion data' on a set S means an element x of S and a function $f : S \to S$. We define a 'natural number object' to be a set N with recursion data 0 and $s : N \to N$, called zero and successor, such that: for any recursion data x, f on any S there is a unique function $u : N \to S$ with

$$u(0) = x$$
$$u(sn) = f(u(n)) \text{ for all } n \in N$$

Provably in ETCS there are infinitely many different natural number objects but all are isomorphic. None has any properties but the shared ones which follow from the definition (see McLarty 1994).

A 'subset' of an ETCS set A is any one-to-one function $i : S \to A$, that is, a function such that for all elements x and y of S, $ix = iy$ implies $x = y$. An element x of A is a 'member' of i if there is some element z of S with $iz = x$. We often write $S \rightarrowtail A$ for a subset, leaving the function i implicit. A 'relation'

between sets A and B is a subset $R \rightarrowtail A \times B$ of the product. If $\langle x, y \rangle : 1 \to A \times B$ is a member of the subset we say x and y stand in the relation R or we write xRy.

A 'power set' of a set B is a set PB and an internal membership relation $\in^B \rightarrowtail B \times PB$ which ties subsets of B to elements of PB as follows: for each set A and relation $H \rightarrowtail B \times A$ there is exactly one function $h : A \to PB$, and vice versa, such that for all x in A, an element y of B has yHx if and only if $y \in^B hx$. Through H, each x in A defines a subset of B containing all y with yHx. Then hx is the element of PB tied to that subset. Power sets are defined up to isomorphism.

Now take any natural number object N and choose a power set PN, $\in^N$ for it, and then a power set for PN, and so on for as many levels as we want to work with. From these we can construct sets of rational, real and complex numbers in the usual way of arithmetized analysis. From here on ETCS works very much like ZF.

Mathematical practice, or even the typical set theory chapter in a maths text, relies on too few details and too much abuse of notation to say whether it is using ETCS or ZF. It can be cleaned up in either system. Yet ETCS claims to begin closer to practice. The basic ZF devices of transfinite accumulation, and coding pairs and numbers as sets, serve foundations only and are forgotten in practice. The basic devices of ETCS (the category axioms, finite limits, universal constructions – see Mac Lane 1986) are used throughout mathematics.

3 ETCS axioms and toposes

The topos axioms are the category axioms (see CATEGORY THEORY, INTRODUCTION TO §I) plus these two:

(1) There is a terminal object 1, and any objects A and B have a product $A \times B$, p_1, p_2.

(2) Each object B has a power set PB, $\in^B$.

Products and power objects are defined as in §2, reading 'object/arrow' for 'set/function'. We do the same for natural number objects, and many toposes satisfy the further 'axiom of infinity':

(3) There is a natural number object N, 0, s.

The characteristic feature of **Set** is that each function is uniquely determined by its effect on elements:

(4) Given any f and g both $A \to B$, if for all $x : 1 \to A$ we have $fx = gx$, then $f = g$.

The ETCS axioms are the category axioms plus (1)–(4).

In general topos theory any arrow $f : B \to A$ may be called a 'generalized element' of A. We call an arrow $i : S \to A$ 'monic' if it is one-to-one for all generalized elements of S: for any object T and arrows $h : T \to S$ and $k : T \to S$, $ih = ik$ implies $h = k$. We call any monic $i : S \to A$ a 'sub-object' of A. The definition of subsets in §2 agrees with this in **Set** but not in general.

We say i is 'included in' another sub-object $j : P \to A$ if there is some $f : S \to P$ with $i = jf$. Trivially, $1_A : A \to A$ is monic and includes all sub-objects of A. Call it all of A. Every topos has an initial object ϕ, and for each A the unique $\phi \to A$ is monic and included in every sub-object of A. Call it empty. Any two sub-objects of A have an intersection, defined as the largest sub-object included in both. They have a union defined as the smallest including both. Each sub-object i has a negation (or pseudo-complement), defined as the largest sub-object whose intersection with i is empty.

The operations on sub-objects give each topos a natural logic. For details see Johnstone (1977: ch.5) or other introductions to topos theory. The law of noncontradiction holds in every topos since by definition the intersection of any sub-object with its negation is empty. In terms of logic, every formula $P \,\&\, {\sim}P$ is false. But in many toposes the union of a sub-object of A with its negation need not be all of A, and so a formula $P \vee {\sim}P$ need not be true. The law of the excluded middle (LEM) fails in some toposes.

For example, in the topos **Spaces** every object has a spatial structure and every arrow has a derivative. There is an object R which we think of as the line. The arrows $R \to R$ are the classical differentiable functions on the real numbers. The line has a point 0, that is, an element $0 : 1 \to R$. So there is a sub-object $\{0\} \rightarrowtail R$ and its negation $\{x \neq 0\} \rightarrowtail R$. But the union $\{x \mid x = 0 \vee x \neq 0\}$ is not all of R. It is 'all of R except the cohesion at 0'. An arrow from this union to R may lack a derivative at 0 and even be discontinuous at 0 simply because it can be defined separately on the pieces $\{0\}$ and $\{x \neq 0\}$. So LEM fails in **Spaces** for the formula $x = 0$, among many others.

Heyting's first-order intuitionist logic is sound in **Spaces** as it is in every topos (see INTUITIONISM §7). It is not complete since in **Spaces** LEM holds for closed formulas. Every disjunction $P \vee {\sim}P$ with no free variables is true in **Spaces**. In **Set** the union of any subset and its negation is the whole set so LEM holds. Of course classical first-order logic is sound and complete in **Set**. Heyting's logic is complete in some toposes, and so for logic in toposes collectively.

The axiom of choice is false in many toposes. It is easy to see it must fail in **Spaces**. Consider the function $f : R \to R$ defined by $fx = x^3 - x$. For each y in R there is an x with $fx = y$ so if the axiom of choice held there would be a choice function $g : R \to R$ such that for each y, $f(gy) = y$. But the graph of f shows no such function g can be continuous everywhere (let alone differentiable), so no such function can exist in **Spaces**. In fact the axiom of choice fails in any topos where LEM fails, since it implies LEM (see Johnstone 1977 or other topos texts).

In another respect topos logic is not even formally intuitionistic. In the logic of any topos, for every object A, every formula with just one free variable of sort A defines a sub-object of A. Brouwer's philosophical misgivings about set formation find no reflection here.

When Grothendieck created toposes for applications in topology, algebraic geometry and number theory (see CATEGORY THEORY, INTRODUCTION TO §3) he paid no attention to intuitionistic mathematics, let alone to Brouwer's epistemology. And the theory today does not say reasoning must all be intuitionistic or constructive. Reasoning should be just as classical or constructive as will suit its context.

4 Radically categorical foundations

Lawvere offered ETCS as a logical foundation and to support an ontological claim. Since ETCS sets have no determinate contents, 'we seem to have partially demonstrated that even in foundations, not Substance but invariant Form is the carrier of the relevant mathematical information'. But ETCS is not his only logical foundation. For other purposes 'a more satisfactory foundation will involve a theory of the category of categories' (1964: 1,506, 1,510).

Lawvere (1966) axiomatized a 'category of categories'. We call these axioms CCAF. They give general theorems of category theory without implying the existence of many specific categories. Lawvere gave various stronger axioms. Positing that **Set** exists is one. The axioms then give all the categories constructed from **Set**.

Another would be to posit a 'category of all categories' as one object in the CCAF universe which represents the whole universe. The set theory NF (see SET THEORY, DIFFERENT SYSTEMS OF §7) includes a set of all sets. It also has a category of all categories in the most naïve sense. But this set theory works so awkwardly with functions that the category of all categories lacks crucial properties (it is not Cartesian closed). Axiomatizing this does not seem promising. A more promising approach not yet much explored would use 'fibered' categories in the sense of Bénabou (1985).

The radically categorical position, though, does not lean on any one logical foundation. It says mathematical objects exist each in its own right. Given any type of structure one goal should be to describe it as intrinsically as possible, and the most intrinsic descriptions of structures to date are categorical. For example, axioms for the topos **Spaces** describe differential manifolds including the line R in their own terms. These axioms do not presume set theory or anything else. They are on a par with ETCS or ZF in giving a self-contained logical foundation for their subject. But axioms only organize our knowledge. Spaces, sets and more exist whether we axiomatize them or not.

If spaces are as real as sets in this sense, then the logic of **Spaces** is as genuine a logic as that of **Set**. This is the point of controversy over topos logic. The axioms for **Spaces** can be modelled in classical set theory. (Moerdijk and Reyes (1991) give many variants.) And **Set** can be modelled in **Spaces** (McLarty 1988). You cannot have one without the other. But you could claim the logic of sets is genuine logic while **Spaces** and other toposes give merely formal interpretations. The radically categorical position says otherwise: each topos (and other categories we do not go into here) has its own genuine logic.

Logical foundations can also describe relations between various branches of mathematics. It is useful in geometry to know how spaces relate to sets. Plus, modelling **Spaces** in **Set** and vice versa gives relative consistency results – the **Spaces** axioms are consistent if ETCS is and vice versa. Johnstone (1977: ch.9) gives relative consistency results for variants of ZF and ETCS. This can increase our confidence in all the axiom systems.

What no logical foundations can do, on this view, is give a starting point to justify the rest of mathematics. No such powerful axiom system is transparently consistent and there is no prospect of proving any one consistent (see GÖDEL'S THEOREMS). The justification of mathematics rests on its whole place in our knowledge. All consistency proofs are relative consistency proofs.

See also: LOGICAL AND MATHEMATICAL TERMS, GLOSSARY OF

References and further reading

* Bénabou, J. (1985) 'Fibered Categories and the Foundations of Naïve Category Theory', *Journal of Symbolic Logic* 50: 10–37. (Requires basic category theory. Cited in §4.)
* Benacerraf, P. (1965) 'What Numbers Could Not Be', *Philosophical Review* 74: 47–73. (Discusses the classical problem for set-theoretic foundations that arithmetic has no unique set-theoretic representation. Requires basic logic.)

Corry, L. (1992) 'Nicolas Bourbaki and the Concept of Mathematical Structure', *Synthese* 92: 315–48. (Includes Bourbaki's internal debates over category theory.)
* Johnstone, P. (1977) *Topos Theory*, London: Academic Press. (The standard reference. Chapters 1–4 are quite demanding. Others are readable with basic topos theory. Cited in §§3–4.)

Lambek, J. and Couture, J. (1991) 'Philosophical Reflections on the Foundations of Mathematics', *Erkenntnis* 34: 187–209. (Claims moderate logicism, formalism, Platonism and intuitionism are all realized in the 'free topos'. Requires basic formal logic.)
* Lawvere, F.W. (1964) 'An Elementary Theory of the Category of Sets', *Proceedings of the National Academy of Science* 52: 1,506–11. (Requires basic category theory.)
* —— (1966) 'The Category of Categories as a Foundation for Mathematics', in S. Eilenberg (ed.) *Proceedings of a Conference on Categorical Algebra in La Jolla*, Berlin: Springer, 1–21. (Cited in §4. Requires basic category theory.)

—— (1969) 'Adjointness in Foundations', *Dialectica* 23: 281–96. (Includes a rapid introduction to the terms.)
* —— (1994) 'Cohesive Toposes and Cantor's "*lauter Einsen*"', *Philosophia Mathematica* 2 (3): 5–15. (Describes aspects of Cantor's thought, such as his cardinals, lost in ZF set theory. Cited in §2.)
* Mac Lane, S. (1986) *Mathematics Form and Function*, New York: Springer, 386–402. (Easy account of the categorical terms in §2.)

Marquis, J.-P. (1995) 'Category Theory and the Foundations of Mathematics: Philosophical Excavations', *Synthese* 103: 421–47. (Refers to much mathematics but readable without relevant background.)
* Mayberry, J. (1988) 'What are Numbers?', *Philosophical Studies* 54: 317–54. (Argues that working methods in mathematics since Newton have disguised the role of concrete foundations, as in §2.)
* McLarty, C. (1988) 'Defining Sets as Sets of Points of Spaces', *Journal of Philosophical Logic* 17: 75–90. (Compares the nineteenth-century creation of set theory from analysis to the relation between **Set** and **Spaces**. Requires basic logic. Cited in §4.)
* —— (1994) 'Numbers Can Be Just What They Have To', *Noûs* 27: 487–98. (Shows the structuralism of ETCS as in §2. No technical knowledge is required.)
* Moerdijk, I. and Reyes, G. (1991) *Models for Smooth*

Infinitesimal Analysis, New York: Springer. (Many variants on the **Spaces** of §3–4. Requires some differential geometry plus basic topos theory or skill in algebra.)

COLIN McLARTY

CATEGORY THEORY, INTRODUCTION TO

A 'category', in the mathematical sense, is a universe of structures and transformations. Category theory treats such a universe simply in terms of the network of transformations. For example, categorical set theory deals with the universe of sets and functions without saying what is in any set, or what any function 'does to' anything in its domain; it only talks about the patterns of functions that occur between sets.

This stress on patterns of functions originally served to clarify certain working techniques in topology. Grothendieck extended those techniques to number theory, in part by defining a kind of category which could itself represent a space. He called such a category a 'topos'. It turned out that a topos could also be seen as a category rich enough to do all the usual constructions of set-theoretic mathematics, but that may get very different results from standard set theory.

1 **Examples and the category axioms**
2 **Working with categories**
3 **Toposes**

1 Examples and the category axioms

Consider sets and functions. Write $f : A \to B$ to say f is a function defined on the set A and all its values are in the set B. Each set A has an identity function $1_A : A \to A$ with $1_A(x) = x$ for every x in A. Given any $f : A \to B$ and $g : B \to C$ there is a composite $gf : A \to C$ with $gf(x) = g(f(x))$ for all x in A.

Now consider a formal language with deductive rules. Let $f : A \to B$ say f is a proof whose sole assumption is the formula A and conclusion is the formula B. Each formula A gives a one-line proof $1_A : A \to A$ with A as assumption and conclusion. Proofs $f : A \to B$ and $g : B \to C$ concatenate to give $gf : A \to C$. We view a proof as transforming its assumption into its conclusion.

The features which are common to these two examples are widespread in mathematics. Category theory gives an axiomatic treatment of them. The category axioms speak abstractly of 'objects' and 'arrows': each arrow has an object as domain and

another as codomain. We write $f : A \to B$ to say f is an arrow with domain A and codomain B. If the codomain of one arrow is the domain of another, as in the case of $f : A \to B$ and $g : B \to C$, then the arrows have a 'composite' $gf : A \to C$. Each object A has an 'identity arrow' $1_A : A \to A$. The axioms require that for any arrows $f : A \to B$, $g : B \to C$ and $h : C \to D$ we have $h(gf) = (hg)f$, $f1_A = f$ and $1_B f = f$.

Thus we have the 'category' **Set**, whose objects are sets and whose arrows are functions, and the category **Proof**, whose objects are formulas and whose arrows are proofs (see Lambek 1994). The axioms clearly hold for **Set** and for **Proof**. Other useful categories include: **Top**, with topological spaces for objects and continuous functions for arrows; and **Group**, with groups (as in abstract algebra) for objects and group homomorphisms for arrows.

Picture a category as a network of arrows between points. So **Set** is an infinite network with a point for each set and an arrow for each function. Each path of arrows connected head-to-tail has a composite going from the first point on the path to the last.

2 Working with categories

We can look at some simple categorical structures. An object T of a category **A** is a 'terminal object' in **A** if each object of **A** has exactly one arrow to T. An object W of **A** is a 'weak terminal object' in **A** if each object of **A** has at least one arrow to W.

Terminal objects of **Set** are singleton sets. Weak terminal objects of **Set** are non-empty sets. In **Proof** the weak terminal objects are the provable formulas. If W is provable with no assumptions then it is provable from any assumption. Nothing is provable in only one way, so **Proof** has no terminal object.

Reversing arrows in the definition of a terminal object defines an 'initial object': an object I of **A** such that each object of **A** has exactly one arrow from I. Similarly for a 'weak initial object'. A set is initial in **Set** if and only if it is empty, and is weakly initial on the same condition. No formula is initial in **Proof**. Inconsistent formulas are weakly initial.

These definitions deal only with patterns of arrows. Yet in **Set** and **Proof** they coincide with specific concepts such as non-emptiness or provability. Other definitions give richer structures such as Cartesian products or power sets in **Set**, the several connectives in **Proof**, and topological or group structures in **Top** or **Group**. So category theory has a unifying role where one argument proves different theorems in different contexts. More importantly, it focuses on the relevant structural relations between objects, be they sets or spaces or whatever. To see this at work we ascend to transformations of categories, called 'functors'.

We write $\mathbf{F} : \mathbf{A} \to \mathbf{B}$ to say $\mathbf{F}$ is a functor from the category $\mathbf{A}$ to the category $\mathbf{B}$. This means that for each object A of $\mathbf{A}$ there is an object $\mathbf{F}A$ of $\mathbf{B}$, and for each arrow $f : A \to A'$ of $\mathbf{A}$ there is an arrow $\mathbf{F}f : \mathbf{F}A \to \mathbf{F}A'$ of $\mathbf{B}$, and $\mathbf{F}$ preserves identity arrows and composites. That is, for each A of $\mathbf{A}$ we have $\mathbf{F}(1_A) = 1_{\mathbf{F}A}$, and for any composite gf we have $\mathbf{F}(gf) = (\mathbf{F}g)(\mathbf{F}f)$. So $\mathbf{F}$ draws a picture of the network $\mathbf{A}$ in the network $\mathbf{B}$.

Each category $\mathbf{A}$ has an identity functor $1_{\mathbf{A}} : \mathbf{A} \to \mathbf{A}$ with $1_{\mathbf{A}}(A) = A$ and $1_{\mathbf{A}}(f) = f$ for all objects A and arrows f of $\mathbf{A}$. Functors compose in the obvious way. So categories and functors themselves are the objects and arrows of a category of categories (see CATEGORY THEORY, APPLICATIONS TO THE FOUNDATIONS OF MATHEMATICS §4).

Functors were invented to focus on relevant structure. Since about 1900 homology theory has been central to topology. To simplify somewhat, by 1940 homology theory was a way of taking each topological space S and constructing from it a family of groups $H_n(S)$, one for each natural number n. By a further construction each continuous function $f : S \to S'$ between topological spaces gives homomorphisms $H_n(f) : H_n(S) \to H_n(S')$. So group theory could be used to prove theorems of topology. But there were many different ways to construct the groups. The subject was thriving and chaotic.

Eilenberg and Mac Lane looked away from constructing the groups $H_n(S)$ and saw homology instead as drawing the network of continuous functions in the network of homomorphisms. They saw each H_n as a functor $H_n : \mathbf{Top} \to \mathbf{Group}$. To do this they created category theory and wrote their classic paper, 'The General Theory of Natural Equivalences' (1945). Category theory is now the standard language for homology. It cleared away old complexities and made room for vast new ones.

The new homology (and related cohomology) spread to algebra and number theory taking category theory with it. Then category theory took other new directions. (Applications before 1970 are surveyed in passing in Mac Lane (1971).)

3 Toposes

Around 1960 Grothendieck attacked some famous problems in geometry and number theory. His project achieved its initial aims in 1973 with Deligne's proof of the Weil conjectures, certain theorems concerning integer roots of polynomials (see McLarty 1990). For this project Grothendieck created 'toposes' (or, 'topoi'). These were categories which he viewed as spaces. Every ordinary topological space can be represented by a topos but toposes are considerably more general than that. The topological method of cohomology can be applied to all toposes and thus Grothendieck defined the 'étale' cohomology that Deligne used. This cohomology is now central to number theory but not all its applications require toposes.

About 1970 Lawvere and Tierney gave first-order axioms which apply to all of Grothendieck's toposes plus some other categories. Today we use 'topos' or 'elementary topos' to mean any model of the axioms, and 'Grothendieck topos' to mean one got by Grothendieck's method. To a logician a topos is analogous to the universe of sets. In any topos the constructions of ordinary mathematics exist, but not always in classical form. Classical logic is not valid in all toposes.

The category $\mathbf{Set}$ is a topos. Classical logic is valid in it and it gives classical mathematics. But there is also a topos $\mathbf{Eff}$ in which all functions from the natural numbers to themselves are recursive. Classical logic would prove there are non-recursive functions; but classical logic is not valid in $\mathbf{Eff}$. There is a topos $\mathbf{Spaces}$ in which each object has a spatial structure and each function is differentiable. This topos includes all the usual differentiable functions of calculus. Classical logic proves there are non-differentiable functions but it is not valid in $\mathbf{Spaces}$. In any topos the valid logic is somewhere between classical and intuitionistic. This is uncontroversial as a fact in model theory. For controversy over its philosophical interpretation see CATEGORY THEORY, APPLICATIONS TO THE FOUNDATIONS OF MATHEMATICS §4.

See also: LOGICAL AND MATHEMATICAL TERMS, GLOSSARY OF

References and further reading

Bell, J.L. (1988) *Toposes and Local Set Theories*, Oxford: Oxford University Press. (A logician's account of toposes using their analogy with the classical universe of sets. Requires facility with sets and formal logic. Includes a bibliography.)

* Eilenberg, S. and Mac Lane, S. (1945) 'The General Theory of Natural Equivalences', *Transactions of the American Mathematical Society* 58: 231–94. (The original paper. Requires basic knowledge of vector spaces and topology.)

* Lambek, J. (1994) 'What is a Deductive System?', in D.M. Gabbay (ed.) *What is a Logical System?*, Oxford: Oxford University Press, 145–64. (Surveys styles of proof theory including the categorical one in §1.)

* Mac Lane, S. (1971) *Categories for the Working Mathematician*, Berlin: Springer. (The standard. The main text requires some sophistication; the examples call for much background. Includes a thorough bibliography.)

—— (1986) *Mathematics Form and Function*, New York: Springer, 386–402. (Basic category theory, including **Set**, is described with no substantial prerequisites.)

Mac Lane, S. and Moerdijk, I. (1992) *Sheaves in Geometry and Logic*, Berlin: Springer. (The general theory of Grothendieck toposes, with many examples, including Cohen's forcing as a topos construction. Requires some category theory.)

* McLarty, C. (1990) 'The Uses and Abuses of the History of Topos Theory', *British Journal for the Philosophy of Science* 41: 351–75. (Debates some views of the history of toposes.)

—— (1992) *Elementary Categories, Elementary Toposes*, Oxford: Oxford University Press. (A categorical account, with chapters on **Set**, **Spaces** and **Eff**. Requires facility with algebraic thinking and formal logic. Includes a bibliography.)

COLIN McLARTY

CATHARSIS *see* EMOTION IN RESPONSE TO ART; KATHARSIS; TRAGEDY (§2)

CATTANEO, CARLO (1801–69)

The figurehead of the Italian democratic movement prior to the unification of Italy, Carlo Cattaneo developed a theory of federalism as a practice of self-government, envisaging a United States of Italy. He identified the bourgeoisie as the most dynamic force in contemporary history and regarded scientific culture as the engine of progress. Often dubbed the first Italian positivist, he perceived empirical philosophy as a kind of synthesis of all the sciences, but also stressed its anthropological and psychological dimensions and above all its character as a methodology of knowledge; his objective was to study human thought. The great themes of Cattaneo's philosophy are nature, the individual and society; particularly the last.

Cattaneo represents the most progressive trends in Italian thought in the first half of the nineteenth century. He aimed to encourage the propagation of technical and scientific knowledge in his native Lombardy in order to equip the entrepreneurial class with the expertise necessary for economic development; and to this end he founded the journal, *Il Politecnico* (1839–44; 1851–63). Until 1848, Cattaneo had formed part of the legal opposition to the regime, but when Milan rose against the Austrians on 18 March of that year, Cattaneo took an active, leading role in the Five Days' Uprising. He was critical of the provisional government, however, and when the Austrians returned, left for Paris, where he published *L'Insurrection de Milan en 1848* (The Milan Uprising of 1848). Shortly afterwards, he left Paris for Switzerland, where he settled permanently in Castagnola, near Lugano. From his exile in Switzerland, Cattaneo voiced his often fierce opposition to the principal political currents in Italy, and forged a role for himself as the great 'prompter' and moving spirit of the Italian democrats, and the leading proponent of federalism against unitary solutions.

Partly as a result of the influence of the philosopher G.D.R. Romagnosi, from whom he inherited the notion of sociability as the foundation of civil society, Cattaneo insisted on the need to intervene practically to shape the reality of one's society. Associated with this basic principle were his profound mistrust of the notion of the solitary consciousness and stress on human action in all its aspects. Rejecting the 'four opposing exaggerations' of idealism, materialism, scepticism and mysticism, Cattaneo saw the human environment as containing a balance of material and ideal forces. He hoped that the kind of renewal that had taken place in the natural sciences could also be brought about in the human sciences.

Cattaneo regarded history as the history of peoples and civilizations. It might even be studied through the examination of languages: a method which Cattaneo employed in a new and often anti-Romantic manner. The perspective adopted in his great historical canvasses is that of liberal, bourgeois culture, in which social changes and transformations are possible and necessary, and social mobility contains subversive forces. At least until 1848, Cattaneo regarded England as the apogee of modern economic development and triumphant capitalism (*Della conquista d'Inghilterra pei Normanni* (On the Norman Conquest) (1839); *Alcuni Stati moderni* (Some Modern States) (1842)), even though he did not ignore the effects of colonialism and its abuses of power (*Dell'India antica e moderna* (India, Past and Present) (1846)). Progress, for Cattaneo, is made up of cultural graftings, of conflicts and exchanges of ideas and principles between different peoples and cultures. Social conditions are the source of good or evil. Not for nothing have some critics seen Cattaneo's famous

Interdizioni israelitiche (Israeli Interdicts) of 1835 as containing the germs of historical materialism, in view of the importance he attributes there to economics as a factor in cultural development; while in his *Notizie naturali e civili sulla Lombardia* (Notes on the Natural and Social History of Lombardy) (1844) – perhaps his masterpiece – the portrait of a region becomes a model of historical method in its presentation of the dynamic interaction of the forces of economic interest and human intelligence.

Cattaneo's idealization of the Lombard bourgeoisie is just one aspect of his celebration of the bourgeoisie in general as the driving force of capitalism, within the context of which science and technology constitute the instruments of development and progress. Addressing himself to the problem of the origins of the Italian bourgeoisie, Cattaneo located them in the rise of the city, which interested him as the historically decisive force in the struggle against feudalism and as the catalyst for the whole process of socioeconomic development in Italy (*Della formazione e del progresso del Terzo Stato* (On the Genesis and Development of the Third Estate) (1854); *La città come principio ideale della istoria italiana* (The City as the Ideal Origin of Italian History) (1854). For Cattaneo, urban life was the typical and distinctive embodiment of Italian culture; and the city was also the birthplace of scientific culture and of modern empirical thought. It was no coincidence, for him, that the Italian revolutionary movement of 1848 had its roots in the cities.

It has been remarked of Cattaneo that his thought oscillates between a conception of philosophy as a synthesis of the empirical sciences and, contrastingly, as an analysis of the human spirit. Philosophy needed to draw on science, but at the same time it needed to be a psychological and anthropological exploration of collective life. In his *Collective Psychology* (five lectures delivered at the Lombard Institute of Sciences between 1859 and 1865), he takes as his object of study that most social of human acts: thought. And social ideology, the subject of his Lugano lectures, implies a study of human society from a perspective which foreshadows that of modern anthropology. Cattaneo employs the notion of a 'system'. A system may be closed, which is to say reactionary, or open and progressive; and it is the succession of one system by another that constitutes progress. In this way, Cattaneo develops the thought of VICO (§6) and integrates it with the notion of progress, the great common theme of eighteenth- and nineteenth-century writers.

During his exile, as he watched Italian society embark on a process of development very different from that for which he had hoped, Cattaneo abandoned political activism for the sphere of 'opinion' and ideas. He attached great importance to opinion-forming, which he regarded as essential as a means of combating the ignorance of the masses and preparing them for struggle on a national scale. Cattaneo's thought can thus be distinguished from socialist positions in that he envisaged the problems of the rural and industrial proletariat being dealt with by the bourgeoisie itself.

When attempts have been made to trace the ideological antecedents of twentieth-century Italian culture, Cattaneo has often been identified as the 'founding father' of the anti-moderate tradition in recent Italian history, the great protagonist of Italian 'anti-history' and the most authentic example the nineteenth century provides of a dissenting intellectual.

See also: ITALY, PHILOSOPHY IN §2

List of works

Cattaneo's writings were first published in his journal *Il Politecnico*.

Cattaneo, C. (1845) *Alcuni scritti* (A Selection of Writings), Milan: Borroni & Scotti. (Contains *Della conquista d'Inghilterra pei Normanni* (On the Norman Conquest) (1839), *Alcuni Stati moderni* (Some Modern States) (1842) and *Dell'India antica e moderna* (India, Past and Present) (1846).)

—— (1848) *L'Insurrection de Milan en 1848* (The Milan Uprising of 1848), Paris: Amyot. (Cattaneo's personal account of the Milan Uprising, highly critical of the provisional government.)

—— (1860) *Memorie di Economica pubblica dal 1833 al 1860* (Records of Public Economy from 1833 to 1860), Milan: Libreria F. Sanvito. (Contains *Ricerche economiche sulle interdizioni imposte dalla legge civile agli Israeliti* (Economic research on the bans imposed by civil law on the Israelites).)

—— (1948) *Scritti letterari, artistici, linguistici e vari* (Writings on Literary, Artistic, Linguistic and Other Subjects), ed. A. Bertani, Florence: Le Monnier, 2 vols. (Essays and articles by Cattaneo on aesthetics, linguistics and other subjects.)

—— (1949–56) *Epistolario* (Collected Letters), ed. R. Caddeo, Florence: Barbera, 4 vols. (Cattaneo's correspondence on a range of subjects.)

—— (1950) *Scritti filosofici* (Philosophical Writings), ed. N. Bobbio, Florence: Le Monnier, 3 vols. (This volume contains his lectures *Collective Psychology* (1859–65).)

—— (1955) *Scritti economici* (Writings on Economics), ed. A. Bertolino, Florence: Le Monnier, 3 vols. (Cattaneo's writings on industry, capitalism and economic issues.)

—— (1957) *Scritti storici e geografici* (Historical and Geographical Writings), ed. G. Salvemini and E. Sestan, Florence: Le Monnier, 4 vols. (The second volume contains *Notizie naturali e civili sulla Lombardia* (Notes on the Natural and Social History of Lombardy) (1844) and *Della formazione e del progresso del Terzo Stato* (On the Genesis and Development of the Third Estate) (1854).)

—— (1964–5) *Scritti politici* (Political Writings), ed. M. Boneschi, Florence: Le Monnier. (Cattaneo's political writings.)

—— (1968) *Scritti scientifici e tecnici, 1823–1848* (Scientific and Technical Writings, 1823–1848), ed. C.S. Lacaita, Florence: Giunti and Barbera. (Cattaneo's technical and scientific writings.)

—— (1972) *Opere scelte* (Selected Works), ed. D. Castelnuovo Frigessi, Turin: Einaudi, 4 vols. (A selection of Cattaneo's major writings in a range of subjects.)

References and further reading

Ambrosoli, L. (ed.) (1989) *'Il Politecnico', 1839–1844*, Turin: Bolleti Boringhieri, 2 vols. (A very full selection of articles from the famous Lombard journal, edited by Cattaneo, including extracts documenting its role in the diffusion of cultural and scientific knowledge.)

Ambrosoli, L. *et al.* (1975) *L'opera e l'eredità di Carlo Cattaneo. vol. 1, L'opera; vol. 2, L'eredità* (The Works of Carlo Cattaneo, their Fortunes and Influence: vol. 1, Cattaneo's Works; vol. 2, Fortunes and Influence), Bologna: Il Mulino. (A collection of essays that gives a good overall picture of the different tendencies in Cattaneo studies and indicates the reasons for the continuing interest in his works.)

Bobbio, N. (1971) *Una filosofia militante. Studi su Carlo Cattaneo* (A Militant Philosophy. Studies on Carlo Cattaneo), Turin: Einaudi. (Cattaneo is presented as a paradigm of rationalist thought in these studies, which cover his federalism, his philosophy and philosophical teaching and the critical fortunes of his works.)

Castelnuovo Frigessi, D. 'Lo specchio di Cattaneo' (Cattaneo's Mirror), *Studi storici* 11 (2): 254–78. (Interpretations of Cattaneo and their connection with the development of his thought.)

Cattaneo, C. (1943) *Lombardia antica e moderna* (Lombardy, Ancient and Modern), ed. M. Fubini under the pseudonym M. Fusi, Florence: Sansoni. (An edition of Cattaneo's famous *Notizie naturali e civili sulla Lombardia* (Notes on the Natural and Social History of Lombardy) brought out during the Fascist period by a distinguished Italian literary

scholar, in which Cattaneo is presented first and foremost as a great historian.)

Puccio, U. (1977) *Introduzione a Cattaneo* (Introduction to Cattaneo), Turin: Einaudi. (Marxist study, stressing the unity of Cattaneo's work as a historian and ideologue of capitalism and underlining the ideological element in his thought.)

Translated from the Italian by Virginia Cox

DELIA FRIGESSI

CAUSAL THEORY OF KNOWLEDGE *see* KNOWLEDGE, CAUSAL THEORY OF

CAUSALITY AND NECESSITY IN ISLAMIC THOUGHT

Discussions of causality and necessity in Islamic thought were the result of attempts to incorporate the wisdom of the Greeks into the legacy of the Qur'an, and specifically to find a philosophical way of expressing faith in the free creation of the universe by one God. Moreover, that article of faith was itself a result of the revelation of God's ways in the free bestowal of the Qur'an on a humanity otherwise locked in ignorance, which a purportedly Aristotelian account of the necessary connection of cause and effect might be taken to rule out. Thus free creation of the universe and free gift of the Qur'an formed a logical unit. The challenge, therefore, was to compose an account of metaphysical and ethical matters which permits rational discourse about them, without obscuring their ultimate source or precluding divine action in the course of world events and human actions.

*The scheme of emanation elaborated by al-Farabi sought to give 'the First' the place of pre-eminence which the Qur'an demanded for the Creator, but did so by modelling creation on a logical system whereby all things emanated necessarily from this One. It was this necessity, further articulated by Ibn Sina, which al-Ghazali took to jeopardize the freedom of God as Creator and as giver of the Qur'an. al-Ghazali's objections were honed by a previous debate among Muslim theologians (*mutakallimun*), who had elaborated diverse views on human freedom in an effort to reconcile the obvious demand for free acceptance of the Qur'an with its claims regarding God's utter sovereignty as Creator over all that is. Natural philosophy was also* *affected by these debates, specifically with regard to the ultimate constitution of bodies as well as accounts that could be given of their interaction. However, the primary focus was on human actions in the face of a free Creator.*

1 Metaphysical issues
2 Human action and divine action
3 Natural philosophy

1 Metaphysical issues

The understanding of causality that prevailed among the classical Islamic philosophers was decidedly Neoplatonic in character (see NEOPLATONISM §3). Intellectual coherence was assured by a scheme of emanation itself modelled on the necessity inherent in a logical system. Thus the connections between events shared in the connections between propositions that followed logically from one another. In this fashion, al-Farabi's emanation scheme offered a cosmic pattern for all causality as well as a master metaphor for causal interaction (see AL-FARABI §2). All that is and all that happens was conceived as depending, for its being and its intelligibility, ultimately on the first cause (or 'the One') by way of intermediary influences which are cosmic in character yet linked together by an intellectual inherence assuring necessary linkage between cause and effect. Aristotle's ideal of 'scientific explanation' in the *Posterior Analytics* could only have been projected, after all, if the world itself was so constructed that things and events were properly connected with one another so as to form a coherent whole (see ARISTOTLE §3).

That is the sense to be made of Ibn Sina's division of 'being' into 'necessary being' and 'possible being', with 'necessary being' restricted to the One from which all the rest emanates while the remainder is characterized as 'possible in itself yet necessary by virtue of another' (see IBN SINA §5). In this way the order of the natural world is assured, since it derives from the one principle of being in a way that is modelled on logical derivation. In this way also, the necessity of causal interaction becomes virtually identical with that of logical entailment, thereby linking the entire universe in a necessary order with the first cause. Furthermore, the pattern of logical entailment extends to the action of that first cause as well: the universe comes forth from it necessarily, as premises from a principle.

Such a model for causal activity cannot be easily imported into a world believed to be freely created by one God. The order described by the emanation scheme threatened the hegemony of the God revealed in the Qur'an, by removing the freedom of that God

to reveal as well as to create. Accommodation with Neoplatonic thought required too much by way of concession from believers in the Qur'an, and it was only a matter of time before this effort to harmonize creation with emanation was challenged. That challenge came notably from AL-GHAZALI, whose frontal attack, entitled *Tahafut al-falasifa* (The Incoherence of the Philosophers) was in turn countered by IBN RUSHD in his *Tahafut al-tahafut* (Incoherence of the Incoherence). But while Ibn Rushd's defence of a repristinated Aristotle would continue to influence Western thought, al-Ghazali's spirited attack succeeded in virtually marginalizing such philosophical reflection on metaphysical matters in the Islamic world to the activities of an elite who would come to be known as 'the philosophers', and whose adherence to Qur'anic faith would often be suspect.

2 Human action and divine action

If such quasi-logical necessity attributed to causality in the universe ran counter to the freedom of the divine agent, it also threatened by implication the freedom of human beings to respond to divine revelation; and such freedom is clearly presupposed by the very structure of the Qur'an, which calls constantly for a response to its warnings and means to elicit wholehearted response to the guidance it offers (see ISLAMIC THEOLOGY §3). Yet the controversy here was not carried out on the terrain staked out by the philosophers but rather among expressly religious thinkers (called *mutakallimun* because of their desire to articulate the faith by way of argument). The earliest among these, the Mu'tazilites, could only see their way to securing human freedom by considering free human actions as utterly autonomous, and so as the creations of human agents, not of God. These early Islamic thinkers fashioned their position on such matters without benefit of the later philosophical reflections noted above, and appear to have conflated notions of origination, causation and creation in an effort to assure that humans bear complete responsibility for the actions for which they will be rewarded or punished. Their concern was for justice, as it can be applied to human beings and to the God of the Qur'an.

Again, however, to withdraw a sector of creation from the purview of the creator of heaven and earth, and to insist that human actions be our creation and not God's, could hardly be sustained in Islam. The challenge this time came from one of the theologians' own number, al-Ash'ari, who shared their conceptual conflations; he developed a purportedly intermediate position, whereby human actions are *created* by God yet *performed* by us. The key notion introduced was *kasb* (or *iktisab*), which attempts to distinguish responsibility for one's actions from their sheer origination. Originating in the marketplace to describe transactions, it alludes to the fact that actions which God creates are 'acquired', or perhaps better, 'performed' by human beings as created agents (see ASH'ARIYYA AND MU'TAZILA §§1, 5).

While this position obviates the removal of human actions from the domain of God's creation, it seems to complicate unduly the issue of human agency and responsibility. The conceptual question turns on the extent to which the notion of 'agent' can be used of both creator and creature. Can there be an authentic agent other than the creator?

This is a question, of course, which touches every religious tradition which avers the free creation of the universe by one God: how does the first cause relate to other causes? Indeed, can there even be other causes in the face of a sovereign 'First'? The response of *kalam* thinkers to this question was complicated by their commitment to an atomistic metaphysics, which seemed designed to remove all causality other than the divine from the realm of nature: this is the celebrated 'Islamic occasionalism'. Later, however, the question was debated by al-Ghazali without reference to any such metaphysical theses. Rather, the terms were those introduced by 'the philosophers', turning on the necessity of the connections between events in nature, specifically between those which we recognize as causes and their effects. Clearly these connections could not be akin to logical necessity, or there would be no room whatsoever for miracles like the 'descent' of the Qur'an; yet if the universe is the result of God's free action and not of necessity, the creator will continue to be free to act within creation. Thus the account given of causal agency in general, and of personal agency in particular, will have to allow for just that: a kind of agency proper to creatures, yet always subordinate to the influence of a free creator. al-Ghazali responds to this challenge by comprehending created causes under a patterned regularity of the *sunna Allah*, action willed by God: creatures do indeed contain such powers, yet always subject to the will of the One who so created them. In this way, a key Islamic religious thinker such as al-Ghazali can simultaneously insist that God alone is the only agent and yet, by God's power, others are agents as well. Thus causality can be attributed to creatures, but not causal connections of the quasi-logical sort demanded by the emanation scheme.

3 Natural philosophy

Early *kalam* thinkers, as noted above, presumed an atomistic conception of nature by which the universe was divinely sustained by being freely created at 'each moment' by God. This conception is clearly an attempt to affirm the omnipresence of divine causal action in the universe God creates, and just as clearly evacuates created causal efficacy. It also runs foul of Aristotle's refutations of atomism in terms of the irreducibility of the continuum of time, space and matter to discrete moments (see ATOMISM, ANCIENT). It is these arguments which persuaded al-Ghazali that the Ash'arite presumption of the atomistic constitution of nature was gratuitous and unnecessary as a ploy to assure the omnipresence of the creator's action in nature. Thus Islamic thought has not been caught between the two extremes of 'occasionalism' (whereby all action is effectively God's) (see OCCASIONALISM) and the pervasive necessity associated with the Neoplatonic emanation scheme of its notable philosophers; there is a middle course, intimated by al-Ghazali and explicitly developed in the early twentieth century in Egypt in the celebrated Qur'an commentary *al-Manar*, whereby the *sunna Allah* is evoked to explain the consistency of a created world of nature.

In summary, Islamic thought must always reconcile the assertion that the entire universe is the free creation of God, who neither requires anything in order to create it nor stands to gain anything by creating it, with the fact that this created world has a consistency associated with causes and effects as we observe them and as we use them to explain natural phenomena. If that causal consistency is articulated in terms which presume a necessity inimical to the free action of a creator, either in the beginning or at any moment of the universe's duration, then Islamic thinkers will feel constrained, as some indeed have, to deny created causality in favour of divine sovereignty. However, as might be expected, developments internal to Islamic thought on this matter have found a way of affirming the free creation of the universe together with its causal consistency, and in doing so have suggested a pattern for causal connections in nature which distances them from the quasi-logical while respecting their reality, specifically by invoking an analogy with the patterns which the God who reveals the Qur'an sets up between human actions and their recompense: the *sunna Allah*. In this way the world of nature can be seen to have a consistency proper to it, yet at the same time is affirmed to be the result of an intentional agent whose order it reflects in the operations proper to it (see INTENTION §4). The pattern to be found by scientific investigation will be a reflection of that with which the natural world has been endowed by its creator: the celebrated *ayat*, or 'signs' of divine wisdom and ordering available to human reason.

See also: ARISTOTELIANISM IN ISLAMIC PHILOSOPHY; CAUSATION; CAUSATION, INDIAN THEORIES OF; CREATION AND CONSERVATION, RELIGIOUS DOCTRINE OF; AL-GHAZALI; ISLAMIC FUNDAMENTALISM; ISLAMIC THEOLOGY; NATURAL PHILOSOPHY, MEDIEVAL; NEOPLATONISM IN ISLAMIC PHILOSOPHY; OCCASIONALISM; OMNIPOTENCE

References and further reading

Alon, I. (1980) 'Al-Ghazali on Causality', *Journal of the American Oriental Society* 100 (4): 397–405. (A clear expositions of al-Ghazali's options.)

al-Ash'ari (873–936) *Kitab al-luma'* (The Book of Radiance), ed. and trans. R. McCarthy, *The Theology of al-Ash'ari*, Beirut: Imprimérie Catholique, 1953. (Edition of al-Ash'ari's major work.)

Fakhry, M. (1958) *Islamic Occasionalism*, London: Allen & Unwin. (Origin of the cliché.)

al-Farabi (c.870–950) *al-Madina al-fadila* (The Virtuous City), trans. R. Walzer, *Al-Farabi on the Perfect State*, Oxford: Clarendon, 1985. (Clear presentation of the emanation scheme.)

Frank, R. (1983) 'Moral Obligation in Classical Muslim Theology', *Journal of Religious Ethics* 11: 210, 228 n.19. (Argues that *kasb* should be translated as 'performance'.)

—— (1992) *Creation and the Cosmic System: Al-Ghazali and Avicenna*, Heidelberg: Carl Winter. (A careful study of al-Ghazali's relation to Ibn Sina.)

—— (1994) *Al-Ghazali and the Ash'arite School*, Durham, NC: Duke University Press. (Very innovative argument that al-Ghazali is in many ways closer to Ibn Sina than to the Ash'arites on a number of topics, including causality.)

Gardet, L. (1950a) *''illa'* (Cause), in *Encyclopedia of Islam* 3: 1127–32. (A classic compilation of sources on this topic.)

—— (1950b) *'Kasb'* (Acquisition), in *Encyclopedia of Islam* 4: 690–4. (A classic compilation of sources on this topic.)

* al-Ghazali (1095) *Tahafut al-falasifa* (The Incoherence of the Philosophers), ed. M. Bouyges, Beirut: Imprimerie Catholique, 1927; trans. S.A. Kamali, *Al-Ghazali's Tahafut al-Falasifah*, Lahore: Pakistan Philosophical Congress Publications, 1963. (Al-Ghazali's refutation of Islamic philosophy.)

Gimaret, D. (1980) *Théories de l'acte humain en théologie musulmane* (Theories of Human Action in Islamic Theology), Paris: Vrin. (A comprehensive study of human actions, with attention to *kasb*.)

—— (1990) *La doctrine d'al-Ash'ari*, Paris: Éditions du Cerf. (Places the work of al-Ash'ari in the perspective of *mutakallimun*.)

* Ibn Rushd (1180) *Tahafut al-tahafut* (The Incoherence of Incoherence), ed. and trans. S. Van den Bergh, London: Luzac, 1978. (Also contains the complete text of al-Ghazali's *Tahafut al-falasifa*, which it criticizes.)

Goodman, L. (1978) 'Did al-Ghazali deny Causality?', *Studia Islamica* 47: 83–120. (Examines a number of texts to find a coherent thread in his assertions.)

Schwartz, M. (1972) '"Acquisition" (*kasb*) in Early Kalam', in S.M. Stern and A. Hourani (eds) *Islamic Philosophy and the Classical Tradition*, Columbia, SC: University of South Carolina Press. (A careful tracing of Qur'anic and other early sources of *kasb*.)

DAVID BURRELL

CAUSATION

Two opposed viewpoints raise complementary problems about causation. The first is from Hume: watch the child kick the ball. You see the foot touch the ball and the ball move off. But do you see the foot cause *the ball to move? And if you do not see it, how do you know that that is what happened? Indeed if all our experience is like this, and all of our ideas come from experience, where could we get the idea of causation in the first place?*

The second is from Kant. We can have no ideas at all with which to experience nature – we cannot experience the child as a child nor the motion as a motion – unless we have organized the experience into a causal order in which one thing necessarily gives rise to another. The problem for the Kantian viewpoint is to explain how, in advance of experiencing nature in various specific ways, we are able to provide such a complex organization for our experience.

For the Kantian the objectivity of causality is a presupposition of our experience of events external to ourselves. The Humean viewpoint must find something in our experience that provides sufficient ground for causal claims. Regular associations between putative causes and effects are the proposed solution. This attention to regular associations connects the Humean tradition with modern statistical techniques used in the social sciences to establish causal laws.

Modern discussions focus on three levels of causal discourse. The first is about singular causation: about individual 'causings' that occur at specific times and places, for example, 'the cat lapped up the milk'. The second is about causal laws: laws about what features reliably cause or prevent other features, as in, 'rising inflation prevents unemployment'. The third is about causal powers. These are supposed to determine what kinds of singular causings a feature can produce or what kinds of causal laws can be true of it – 'aspirins have the power to relieve headaches' for example.

Contemporary anglophone work on causality has centred on two questions. First, 'what are the relations among these levels?' The second is from reductive empiricisms of various kinds that try to bar causality from the world, or at least from any aspects of the world that we can find intelligible: 'what is the relation between causality (on any one of the levels) and those features of the world that are supposed to be less problematic?' These latter are taken by different authors to include different things. Sensible or measurable properties like 'redness' or 'electric voltage' have been attributed a legitimacy not available to causal relations like 'lapping-up' or 'pushing over': sometimes it is 'the basic properties studied by physics'. So-called 'occurrent' properties have also been privileged over dispositional properties (like water-solubility) and powers. At the middle level where laws of nature are concerned, laws about regular associations between admissible features – whether these associations are deterministic or probabilistic – have been taken as superior to laws about what kinds of effects given features produce.

1   **Hume's legacy**
2   **Kant's reply**
3   **Mill's empiricism**
4   **Logical positivism**
5   **Causal laws**
6   **Singular causal claims**
7   **Causal powers**

1   Hume's legacy

The chief historical locus for the attack on causation is the work of David Hume, which is based on the associationist theory of concept formation that he shared with Locke and Berkeley. Ideas for Hume are either copies of sensory impressions or built out of other ideas, themselves copies of sensory impressions, by simple association. Sensory impressions are of the way things look, taste, feel and sound (see HUME, D. §2). We can have sensory impressions of redness and of hardness, of sourness and shrillness, but not of necessity or causality. Whence come these ideas then? In our experience events of one kind regularly follow those of another. By association we are led to expect the second when we experience the first. It is our impression of our own state of expectation that provides the idea of necessity or of causation. So the idea of causation, according to Hume, is a copy of an impression not of a feature of events in the outside world but of events that take place within us.

Hume therefore steered agnostically away from the direct question 'what is causality?', holding that the right answer (if there is one) must be unintelligible to us. Instead he asked what makes us believe in causal connections and what state of mind is such a belief. Much twentieth-century 'Humeanism' about causation is not so Hume-like as is often implied.

Hume's positive account has been developed in two different directions. The first attempts to analyse causal claims as claims about regular associations between sensible qualities (or others deemed acceptable) in the external world. The second bases causality in our particular ways of representing the world. A popular version of this looks not to how we represent the world but to how we intervene in it (Von Wright 1993): roughly, we regard as causes those kinds of features that we can manipulate. This idea needs careful formulation if it is to account for our usual causal discourse; for example, it is standardly assumed that craters on the moon cause their shadows but not the converse, though we typically manipulate neither.

As we have seen, Hume's theory of the one-to-one association of impressions and ideas lies at the heart of his answer to the second central question about causality, the question about the relation between causings and other 'less problematic' features of the world. This theory is also central to his answer to the first question about singular causation. There is no impression of one feature causing another, hence no corresponding idea about the world. What then about the world makes a singular causal claim true? The most that can be said is that we believe causal claims at the first level – that of singular causation – when they are instances of second-level claims – about causal laws – which in turn we believe when we meet with regular associations between sensible properties. The only facts that matter about the individual case are that the cause precedes the effect and is spatiotemporally contiguous with it. If in addition there is something about the world that makes effect follow cause we can have no comprehension of it and *a fortiori* no knowledge. Sometimes later accounts try to avoid the assumption that causes precede their effects in order to leave open the question of backward causation; other even aim to reduce claims about temporal order to ones about causal order (Reichenbach 1956) (see TIME §4; RELATIVITY THEORY, PHILOSOPHICAL SIGNIFICANCE OF §3). But this has proven difficult to do.

The associationist theory of concept formation central to Hume's account has been entirely abandoned in twentieth-century philosophy. But his conclusions have not. Modern day defenders of Hume's theses face three challenges:

(1) Explain why singular causal facts are less legitimate than noncausal facts like 'the cat was on the mat'.
(2) Show that no causal facts are required to make sense of those features counted as unproblematic and explain what makes these features superior.
(3) Produce a regularity account of causal laws that either accords with or corrects our usual judgments and the uses to which we put them.

The answers to questions (1) and (2) tend to be based on epistemological or methodological considerations: causal facts are so much harder to find out about than the privileged alternative that they can have no place in the known or intelligible world. This answer had a special grip in the heyday of sense-data when facts about our 'internal' experiences – which purportedly do not include causal facts – were supposed to be incorrigible. The construction of a reasonable sorting criterion is a more delicate job nowadays when it is widely assumed that nothing is incorrigible and the defence of any single claim will generally require a wealth of knowledge including some laws of nature. Similarly judgments about intelligibility are more difficult at a time when no theory of meaning seems entirely acceptable.

2   Kant's reply

In *Critique of Pure Reason* (1781/1787), Kant argued that our minds impose the category of causality on the otherwise unorganized manifold of sensory experience, and by this imposition constitute the external world of objects causally interacting within a uniform space and time. Therefore we have a priori assurance that all changes in the phenomenal world proceed in accordance with causal laws which we can discover by observation and experiment (see KANT, I. §§4–7).

Kant rejected Hume's suggestion that the mind is always passive in forming its expectations and that all our empirical beliefs arise from the association of ideas. The principle of determinism – that every event in the natural order is the effect of some cause – is a necessary truth because it is the presupposition of any experience of an objective world of things. Without this constraining principle we could not distinguish, as we in fact do, between the subjective order of our perceptual experience and the objective order of events in nature. Hume insisted that the proposition that nature is throughout regulated by causal laws could not itself be derived from experience and he was right to do so, according to Kant. This proposition is

rather the necessary presupposition of all experience of objects existing in an objective temporal order. We cannot but think of nature as the domain of universal laws valid for all observers.

3   Mill's empiricism

John Stuart MILL was an empiricist. He believed that all knowledge – even knowledge of mathematics – derives from experience. But he did not share Hume's concern about the idea of causation; nor did he embrace a regularity account of causal law. What occurs in nature is the consequence of a vast number of jointly acting causes. Seldom does any particular arrangement of causes stay in place long enough for regular behaviour to appear. Even if it were to, the regularity would not match with the causal laws we most need to know – laws about what each cause contributes separately.

In many domains there will be laws of this kind. In mechanics, for example, we can find the law governing the force due to gravity and that governing the force due to electricity. Mill called these 'tendency laws' because they tell what the cause contributes, or 'tends to do', but do not describe the effect that actually occurs (here, the 'total' force). What the cause tends to do and what it actually does would coincide exactly were the cause in a position to operate alone. The idea of a tendency law makes sense in mechanics because there is a well-defined rule for the composition of causes: when causes act together, the actual force produced is the vector sum of the forces ascribed to each individually by the basic tendency laws. Chemistry is different: when a cause acts jointly with another it may have no systematic relationship to what it does when the other is absent. In Mill's opinion political economy is like mechanics, not like chemistry.

Mill was concerned not with what causes are but with the proper empiricist question of how we find out about them. He was keen on the experimental method but realized that in many domains experiment is impossible. For these he articulated 'Mill's methods' which involve looking for factors that are present and absent in tandem with the effect and that co-vary in magnitude with it. These methods are a qualitative precursor to modern statistical techniques for confirming causal hypotheses from naturally occurring data (see STATISTICS AND SOCIAL SCIENCE §3). In political economy, where he supposed the fundamental driving factor to be behaviour resulting from 'the economic motive', Mill argued that basic causal laws can be found by looking inside ourselves at our motives and actions (ECONOMICS, PHILOSOPHY OF §3).

4 Logical positivism

Like various reductive empiricisms inspired by Hume, the logical positivism of the Vienna Circle also eschewed causes (see LOGICAL POSITIVISM §4; VIENNA CIRCLE §3). Causal talk, according to Rudolf CARNAP, imperspicuously casts in the material mode claims that properly belong in the formal mode: it looks as if we are talking about things in the world when instead we are talking about our representations of it. Causality for logical positivism became derivability: 'C causes E' if E can be derived from C in our representation of the world; that is, if we accept that all cases of C are cases of E. The account, however, was beset by problems about accidental regularities. 'All coins in my pocket are silver' does not ground a causal connection. So some notion of necessity or lawlikeness has generally been admitted: 'all Cs are *by law* Es'. Still whatever is involved in separating lawlike from accidental regularities has been supposed to be far weaker than a full-fledged concept of causation (see LAWS, NATURAL §2).

This account has obvious counter-intuitive results, pinpointed in an example by Sylvan Bromberger (1966). Given the angle of the sun and the laws of geometrical optics, from the height of the flagpole the length of its shadow can be derived – and the converse. Yet surely the height of the pole causes the length of the shadow and not the reverse. For staunch positivists this argument illustrates what is wrong with causal talk – it postulates differences in the world where in fact there are none. For others it constitutes a *reductio ad absurdum* of the reductivist/positivist position.

If strict derivability under universal laws is too weak as a stand-in for causal laws, it is also too strong, as C.G. HEMPEL admitted in his *inductive-statistical* model of explanation: E can be explained by (or accepted on the basis of) C if we admit as law that the probability of E given C is high, even though the association is not 100 per cent (see EXPLANATION §2). (Many would find the expression 'as law' redundant here for they take probability, as opposed to finite frequency, to be already a modal notion.) The move to less-than-universal associations is motivated not only by the irreducibly probabilistic nature of quantum associations but also because we could admit few explanations indeed in either the natural or the social sciences if universal (deterministic) association is demanded.

But high probability does not work either, as Michael Scriven argued with the example of paresis, which arises only in the last stages of syphilis. The probability of paresis given syphilis is low. Nevertheless when paresis occurs, syphilis is clearly the cause. This suggests that increase in probability is a better requirement: C causes E just in case the probability of E is higher than C than without.

Over and above these problems it is well-known that 'correlation is not causation'. Two kinds of cases illustrate. First, joint effects of a common cause are generally correlated with one another. For example, there is an anti-correlation between eating candy and getting divorced. But low candy consumption in a given period does not cause divorce during that period; rather, ageing is responsible for both. Second is a case due to Wesley Salmon *et al.* (1971). A box contains either of two radioactive elements, L and H, but never both. Each element produces W particles, L at a lower rate than H. L causes the presence of Ws in the box: if this situation persists L will predictably (or necessarily) produce Ws. Yet L may reduce the probability of W since the presence of L is correlated with the absence of even more effective cause H. Indeed, with a little care in the choice of the levels of intensity of L and H, the presence of L will raise the probability of W being present (see DETERMINISM AND INDETERMINISM; EXPLANATION §4).

The example suggests that there may be no universal rule for connecting probabilistic associations with causal laws although there may well be correct case-by-case connections. In the radioactivity case, the fact that Ls predictably cause Ws, plus facts about the situation, explain why the probability of W given L is exactly as it is. If one adopts some form of inference to the best explanation, the probabilities – whatever they are – will be evidence for the causal law (see INFERENCE TO THE BEST EXPLANATION). Moreover, given sufficient collateral information it is possible to deduce from the probabilistic facts that Ls produce Ws in this set up. (Although uncommon in the social sciences, this kind of 'bootstrapping inference' that allows the deduction of the hypothesis from data, given general background assumptions and other information specific to the situation, is familiar in experiments in physics.) Causality may after all be an umbrella notion with different criteria in different contexts.

5 Causal laws

By this point, it seems, the logical positivist account that locates the truth of causal-law claims in our representations of the world has merged with the Hume-inspired account that locates their truth in laws about regular associations. The difference between them depends on whether one talks about the regular associations we accept in our scientific theories – laws of science – or about laws of nature. Nevertheless they share the insistence that there must be a universal rule that connects causal laws and the laws of association, since neither tradition is willing to admit any concept of causation that cannot be reduced to facts they find less problematic. It remains to produce such a rule. The most promising attempts, originally formulated by Patrick Suppes (1970, 1973), try to restore increase in probability as the true sign of causality.

In both the candy-eating and radioactivity examples, the putative cause and the putative effect are each correlated with a third factor that is itself a cause of the putative effect. Candy consumption and divorce are correlated with age, which causes increase in divorce levels; L is correlated with H, itself a cause of W. Stratification is often used to control for features like age or the presence of other materials that may confound the correlations we expect between a genuine cause and its effects. The proposal then is that 'candy consumption prevents divorce' is true just in case candy consumption lowers the probability of divorce in subgroups where everyone is the same age. But what features should be used for stratification? Mathematically, correlations between C and E may appear and disappear if we stratify along any third variable correlated with both. The most natural choice is to use all and only other factors – like age – that are themselves causes of E.

Besides the obvious question of how exactly this suggestion should be formulated, the proposal faces three problems. First, in cases where a cause may produce two effects in tandem – cases of the production of products and by-products for example – joint effects may still be correlated with each other even though we look only at stratified subpopulations in which the cause is present to the same degree.

Second, the proposal abandons the programme of replacing causal laws with law-like regularities. Probabilistic associations may still help with causal inference, but only in so far as one has a great deal of causal information to begin with: no causes in, no causes out.

Third is the problem of validating the proposal – this one or any other. All available validations (Simon 1971; Spirtes, Glymour and Scheines 1993) put strong constraints on what kinds of causal relationships are possible among a set of variables as well as on the general relationship between causal laws and probabilities. Thus the task for those who wish to maintain some single situation-independent connection between causal laws and laws of associations is either to generalize these kinds of validations to cover laws or to produce convincing reasons why other kinds of cases are impossible.

The task for those who wish to reduce causal laws to probabilistic associations (Papineau 1993) is even more difficult, as can be seen by considering results of

groups working with Clark Glymour and Peter Sprites and with Judea Pearl (1988). These provide the most systematic treatment available of causal inference from probabilistic information. In this work, for a given set of variables it is assumed that both a causal structure (a set of causal laws satisfying certain conditions like asymmetry) and a probability measure over the variables exist and some plausible constraints are assumed to hold between the probabilities and the causal structure. It is then possible to generate the set of all causal structures consistent with any particular set of observed probabilities given the constraints. For most cases, however, the causal structure is not unique. The probabilistic associations do not seem enough to fix the causal laws. This is the problem of the flagpole and the shadow reasserting itself again after a long detour.

Alternative conclusions can be defended. The results are sympathetic to the view that causal laws do not reduce to laws of association but are rather about what kinds of singular causal events happen predictably or by law. On the other hand the results fit with a programme of locating the choice among different causal structures consistent with the same probabilities in facts about our perspective or our interests, or even with the claim that causal talk is hopelessly underdetermined and nothing fixes what we should say. And of course there is the project of articulating further constraints so that the probabilistic associations fix the causal laws uniquely. What definitely can be concluded is that no reduction of causal-law claims to claims about law-like or necessary associations has yet been achieved, let alone the stronger Hume-inspired view that causal-law talk can be reduced to claims about associations that employ no concepts of law or necessity at all.

A final outstanding problem for any account is to link the analysis of what causal claims say with our usual methods for confirming them. The regularity accounts described previously relate readily to standard techniques based on Mill's methods for the use of population data. The connection to results of controlled experiments is less clear (Cartwright 1995). Yet these are supposed to be our surest methods for causal inference; indeed so much so that some have taken causal-law claims simply to be claims about the results that would be obtained from controlled experiments (Holland 1986) (see EXPERIMENT; SCIENTIFIC METHOD).

6 Singular causal claims

Singular causal claims may be true because of singular causal facts. Two much discussed problems seem to presuppose this. First is 'overdetermination': two factors, each by law sufficient for an effect, occur and the effect ensues. Which is actually responsible? The second is 'causal pre-emption': a cause occurs sufficient by law to bring about an effect but a second cause intervenes and produces the effect first (Menzies 1996). Both problems suggest that there is more to causation in the single case than reductive empiricists and logical positivists allow. Yet some resist, feeling that this claim is unintelligible. The challenge they pose is to ground this claim in some plausible theory of meaning that will support their intuition.

Others reject singular causal facts because they find no grounds for judgments about them. To this writers like G.E.M. Anscombe (1971) reply that we can see the cat lapping up the milk as well as we can see anything! This defence is supported by theories of perception in which the ability to judge correctly that something has any feature at all by seeing it depends on having a good deal of collateral knowledge, including knowledge of both singular causal facts and causal laws. There are in addition, especially for causal processes in physics, accounts of singular causation in terms of other features conventionally admissible, such as energy interchange (Salmon 1984; Dowe 1992). It is also argued that the operation of a cause often leaves traces that can be used to determine its occurrence.

The question of whether there is significantly more to singular causation than lawful association is different from the question: for every singular causal fact is there a law that it can be brought under? Donald Davidson (1980) replies 'yes' to this latter question, and the same answer is presupposed by J.L. Mackie (1980), who takes causes to be INUS conditions – insufficient but non-redundant parts of unnecessary but sufficient conditions. Mackie's account supposes that there are general laws of the form

$$E \equiv (C_1^1 C_1^2 \ldots C_1^n) \vee (C_2^1 C_2^2 \ldots C_2^m) \vee \ldots \vee (C_p^1 C_p^2 \ldots C_p^k).$$

This allows us to focus on one of the contributing components, C_i^j, as the cause of interest in a given context, even though this component alone is not sufficient. (However it does not capture Anscombe 's denial that causes must be sufficient for their effects since she has in mind purely probabilistic or chance causation: could we not have a cause that is enough for the effect and yet the effect fail?) Some considerations of how to characterize properties enter here: if this C that is supposed to have caused an E is not doing what it does regularly, what makes it a C? But the usual arguments are epistemological: how could we know that a C caused E if this fact neither falls under a causal law nor is the expression of a known causal power? For instance, how could we count a

factor as a trace if there were no law ensuring that the operation of the cause generally produces this factor as a side-effect?

Midway between the view that there are singular causal facts and reductivist/positivist doctrines is the counterfactual account (Lewis 1986): roughly, C caused E just in case if C had not occurred E would not have. One task is to formulate this correctly, especially to avoid problems of overdetermination and pre-emption and to ensure that one effect of a common cause does not count as cause of a joint effect. The second task to explain is counterfactuals (see COUNTERFACTUAL CONDITIONALS). One common attempt offers a possible-world analysis. The counterfactual is true if in the nearest possible world where E fails, C fails too. Possible worlds are generally taken to be worlds which have the same laws as our own, except for small miracles to allow C to fail. On one reading possible worlds are mere calculational devices: one function maps from laws and non-causal facts to a set of structured descriptions ('the set of possible worlds'), and a second takes the set of descriptions plus the counterfactual in question into either 'true' or 'false'. Singular causal claims would then turn out to be indirect ways of talking about laws and non-causal facts, and the logical positivist programme would be in part borne out. If, however, the ontology of possible worlds plays a genuine role, the challenge is to defend the advantage of possible worlds over singular causal facts. A similar challenge must be met by probabilistic accounts of singular causation that use special notions of probability like single-case propensities (Eells 1991): why are these better than the cat's lapping up the milk?

7 Causal powers

The idea of a causal power or a disposition (Harré and Madden 1975) is closely bound to notions of potentiality and possibility related to the notions of necessity that reductive empiricists and logical positivists find unintelligible. They understand only claims about what occurs, or perhaps what occurs by natural law, not about what can occur by natural law. Proponents of causal powers often counter that there is no distinction between powers or dispositions and occurrent properties (Mellor 1971, 1991, 1995). Objects have properties and by virtue of having these properties they have the power to do a variety of things; otherwise the notion of property makes no sense. Perhaps properties are just nexus of causal powers (Shoemaker 1984). This raises the question of whether an object could have a particular power all on its own without thereby having any other usually related features (see Primary–secondary distinction; Property theory).

For the most part, however, questions centre on the relation between causal powers on the one hand and causal laws and singular causation on the other. Some powers are, in Gilbert Ryle's terminology, highly specific or determinate (1949). They tend to be back-named from some episodic verb that is taken to describe their natural expression (as in 'soluble' and 'dissolve'). This suggests a one-to-one correspondence between powers and laws. Aspirins have the power to relieve headaches just in case, by law, aspirins properly administered relieve headaches. Talk of powers then seems otiose.

The matter appears differently when more generic powers are considered. 'Electrons repel other electrons' describes a power that can be harnessed to produce an indefinite variety of different law-like behaviours in different situations; situations can even be rigged in which electrons reliably, by repelling other electrons, cause them to move closer. One can restore the one-to-one correspondence by inventing or choosing an appropriate episodic verb, though the attempt can seem strained. (As Ryle urges, grocers sell tea, wrap butter and weigh bacon. But do we want to say that grocers groce?) Nor does this unproblematically serve the reductivist/positivist purpose of rendering talk about powers as talk about laws, for is not 'repelling electrons' in the situation where they move closer a specific case of 'exercising a power'? The relationship between powers and the indefinite and un-inventoriable class of laws that express them thus remains a central philosophical concern.

See also: Causality and necessity in Islamic thought; Causation, Indian theories of; Paranormal phenomena

References and further reading

* Anscombe, G.E.M. (1971) *Causality and Determination*, Cambridge: Cambridge University Press. (Sophisticated but accessible to beginners.)
* Bromberger, S. (1966) 'Why-Questions', in R.G. Colodny (ed.) *Mind and Cosmos: Essays in Contemporary Science and Philosophy*, Pittsburgh, PA: University of Pittsburgh Press. (Accessible to beginners.)
  Carnap, R. (1934) *Logische Syntax der Sprache*, Vienna: Springer; trans. A. Smeaton, *The Logical Syntax of Language*, London: Kegan Paul, Trench, Trubner & Co., 1937. (Advanced study in logical positivism.)
  Cartwright, N. (1989) *Nature's Capacities and Their Measurement*, Oxford: Oxford University Press. (See chapter 3. Advanced.)
* —— (1995) 'Probabilities and Experiments', *Journal of Econometrics* 67: 47–59. (Advanced.)
* Davidson, D. (1980) *Essays on Actions and Events*, Oxford: Clarendon Press. (Intermediate-level study of singular causation.)
* Dowe, P. (1992) 'Wesley Salmon's Process Theory of Causality and Conserved Quantity Theory', *Philosophy of Science* 59: 195–216. (Intermediate.)
* Eells, E. (1991) *Probabilistic Causality*, Cambridge: Cambridge University Press. (Advanced study of singular causation.)
* Harré, R. and Madden, T.E. (1975) *Causal Powers*, Oxford: Blackwell.
  Hempel, C. (1966) *Philosophy of Natural Science*, Englewood Cliffs, NJ: Prentice Hall. (Very good for beginners.)
* Holland, P. (1986) 'Statistics and Causal Inference', *Journal of the American Statistical Association* 81: 945–60. (Advanced.)
  Hume, D. (1739–40) *A Treatise of Human Nature*, Oxford: Clarendon Press, 1988. (Essential.)
  —— (1902) *An Inquiry Concerning Human Understanding*, Oxford: Clarendon Press. (Essential.)
* Kant, I. (1781/1787) *The Critique of Pure Reason*; trans. N.K. Smith, London: Macmillan, 1929. (Essential; difficult.)
* Lewis, D. (1986) *Philosophical Papers*, Oxford: Oxford University Press, vol. 2, 159–84. (Advanced.)
* Mackie, J.L. (1980) *The Cement of the Universe: A Study of Causation*, Oxford: Clarendon Press. (Intermediate–advanced; a good survey.)
* Mellor, D.H. (1971) *The Matter of Chance*, Cambridge: Cambridge University Press. (See chapters 4 and 8. Intermediate.)
* —— (1991) *Matters of Metaphysics*, Cambridge: Cambridge University Press. (Intermediate.)
* —— (1995) *The Facts of Causation*, London: Routledge. (Intermediate.)
* Menzies, P. (1996) 'Probabilistic Causation and the Pre-emption Problem', *Mind* 105: 85–117. (Intermediate.)
* Papineau, D. (1993) 'Can We Reduce Causal Directions to Probabilities?', in A. Fine and M. Forbes (eds) *PSA 1992*, East Lansing, MI: Philosophy of Science Association, vol. 2, 238–52. (Intermediate.)
* Pearl, J. (1988) *Probabilistic Reasoning in Intelligent Systems: Networks of Plausible Inference*, San Mateo, CA: Morgan Kaufmann Publishers. (Advanced.)
* Reichenbach, H. (1956) *The Direction of Time*, Berkeley, CA: University of California Press. (Intermediate, but parts are good for beginners.)

* Ryle, G. (1949) *The Concept of Mind*, London: Hutchinson. (Good for beginners.)
* Salmon, W., Jeffrey, R.C. and Greeno, J.G. (1971) *Statistical Explanation and Statistical Relevance*, Princeton, NJ: Princeton University Press. (Intermediate, but parts are good for beginners.)
* Salmon, W. (1984) *Scientific Explanation and the Causal Structure of the World*, Princeton, NJ: Princeton University Press. (Intermediate, but parts are good for beginners.)
* Shoemaker, S. (1984) *Identity, Cause and Mind: Philosophy Essays*, Cambridge: Cambridge University Press. (Advanced.)
* Simon, H. (1971) 'Spurious Correlation: A Causal Interpretation', in H.M. Blalock (ed.) *Causal Models in the Social Sciences*, Chicago, IL: Atherton. (Advanced.)
* Spirtes, P., Glymour, C. and Scheines, R. (1993) *Causation, Prediction and Search*, Lecture notes on statistics 81, New York: Springer. (Advanced.)
* Suppes, P. (1970) *A Probabilistic Theory of Causality*, Amsterdam: North Holland. (Advanced.)
* —— (1973) 'Logic, Methodology and the Philosophy of Science', in E. Sosa and M. Tooley (eds) *Causation*, Oxford: Oxford University Press, 1993. (Intermediate–advanced.)
* Wright, G.H. Von (1993) 'On the Logic and Epistemology of Causal Relations', in E. Sosa and M. Tooley (eds) *Causation*, Oxford: Oxford University Press, 1993. (Intermediate–advanced.)

NANCY CARTWRIGHT

CAUSATION, INDIAN THEORIES OF

Causation was acknowledged as one of the central problems in Indian philosophy. The classical Indian philosophers' concern with the problem basically arose from two sources: first, the cosmogonic speculations of the Vedas and the Upaniṣads, with their search for some simple unitary cause for the origin of this complex universe; and second, the Vedic concern with ritual action (karman) and the causal mechanisms by which such actions bring about their unseen, but purportedly cosmic, effects. Once the goal of liberation (mokṣa) came to be accepted as the highest value, these two strands of thought entwined to generate intense interest in the notion of causation. The systematic philosophers of the classical and medieval periods criticized and defended competing theories of causation. These theories were motivated partly by a desire to guarantee the efficacy of action and hence the possibility of

attaining liberation, partly by a desire to understand the nature of the world and hence how to negotiate our way in it so as to attain liberation.

Indian philosophers extensively discussed a number of issues relating to causation, including the nature of the causal relation, the definitions of cause and effect, and classifications of kinds of causes. Typically they stressed the importance of the material cause, rather than (as in Western philosophy) the efficient cause. In India only the Cārvāka materialists denied causation or took it to be subjective. This is unsurprising given that a concern with demonstrating the possibility of liberation motivated the theories of causation, for only the Cārvākas denied this possibility. The orthodox Hindu philosophers and the heterodox Buddhists and Jainas all accepted both the possibility of liberation and the reality of causation, though they differed sharply (and polemically) about the details.

The Indian theories of causation are traditionally classified by reference to the question of whether the effect is a mode of the cause. According to this taxonomy there are two principal theories of causation. One is the identity theory (satkāryavāda), which holds that the effect is identical with the cause, a manifestation of what is potential in the cause. This is the Sāṅkhya-Yoga view, though that school's particular version of it is sometimes called transformation theory (pariṇāmavāda). Advaita Vedānta holds an appearance theory (vivartavāda), which is often considered a variant of the identity theory. According to the appearance theory effects are mere appearances of the underlying reality, Brahman. Since only Brahman truly exists, this theory is also sometimes called satkāraṇavāda (the theory that the cause is real but the effect is not).

The other principal theory of causation is the nonidentity theory (asatkāryavāda), which denies that the effect pre-exists in its cause and claims instead that the effect is an altogether new entity. Both adherents of Nyāya-Vaiśeṣika and the Buddhists are usually classified as nonidentity theorists, but they differ on many important details. One of these is whether the cause continues to exist after the appearance of the effect: Nyāya-Vaiśeṣika claims it does, the Buddhists mostly claim it does not.

Finally, some philosophers try to take the middle ground and claim that an effect is both identical and nonidentical with its cause. This is the position of the Jainas and of some theistic schools of Vedānta.

1 **The context of the Indian theories**
2 **Cārvāka scepticism**
3 **Sāṅkhya-Yoga and the transformation theory**
4 **Advaita Vedānta and the appearance theory**
5 **Nyāya-Vaiśeṣika and the nonidentity theory**

6 Buddhist theories
7 Jaina nonabsolutism

1 The context of the Indian theories

The commitment to the ideal of liberation (*mokṣa*) provides the context for understanding the classical Indian philosophers' concern with causation. Typically the theoretical problem of Indian philosophy is to provide an account of the world which allows for the possibility of our successfully entering into it as agents set on liberation from suffering (*duḥkha*). In order to guarantee the feasibility of liberation we need to be assured that there are reliable causal connections between events and actions such that it is possible for a person to enter into the course of events as a conscious agent whose actions have predictable consequences. To do this the Indian philosophers sought to identify those causal chains relevant to liberation, and to analyse the nature of the causal relation as exhibited among the members of those chains.

There are a number of such causal chains proposed. One of the oldest and best known is the Buddhist chain of dependent origination (*pratītyasamutpāda*). This twelvefold chain runs: ignorance; dispositions; consciousness; body and mind; the six sense fields; sense contact; sensation; desire; clinging; becoming; birth; old age and death. Each of these factors is both conditioning and conditioned. This is expressed in a traditional Buddhist formula characterizing the relation between the links: 'When *A* is, *B* is; *A* arising, *B* arises; when *A* is not, *B* is not; *A* ceasing, *B* ceases.' The possibility of liberation (called *nirvāṇa* in Buddhism) requires that we be able to break the chain at certain points where the links are only necessary conditions for what follows. In Buddhism the favoured weak links are ignorance (*avidyā*) and desire (*tṛṣṇa*), which can be eliminated with (respectively) knowledge and nonattachment (see SUFFERING, BUDDHIST VIEWS OF ORIGINATION OF).

The alternative causal chains of the Jainas, of Nyāya-Vaiśeṣika and of Sāṅkhya-Yoga differ in their details. However, all include ignorance as a link and hence guarantee the possibility of liberation through the possibility of the elimination of ignorance by right knowledge. It is essential for the possibility of liberation that the causal chains which bind us to suffering are such that at least some of the members are necessary but not sufficient conditions for other members, otherwise we could not enter the chain and reverse our condition of bondage. On the other hand, the chain must not have gaps, for if there is no necessary connection between the links none of our actions can be relied upon to bring about the goal of liberation. Thus once we have identified the causal chain that leads to bondage, we also need to say something more about the nature of the causal relation itself.

Two basic models dominate Indian thinking about the nature of the causal relation. One is the model favoured by the identity theory of Sāṅkhya-Yoga. A standard illustration is the case of milk and curds: the milk is the cause and the curds are the effect. But the milk is the same stuff as the curds; one is merely transformed into the other. Generalizing from this kind of example leads to the view that the effect pre-exists in its cause. In fact a cause and its effect are not two separate, discrete entities but instead two states of the same enduring substance. The major difficulty with this model (in both its Sāṅkhya and Advaitin versions) is that the causal relation threatens to be too strong. If nothing can become other than what it is already, how can we unenlightened beings ever achieve our own liberation?

The competing model of the causal relation is the one favoured by the nonidentity theory of Nyāya-Vaiśeṣika and (some) Buddhists. A standard Naiyāyika illustration is the pot and its two halves: the two halves of the pot are its causes and the pot is the effect. (Indian potters make a pot by first making two halves and then joining them.) According to this model the effect is not pre-existent in the cause. Effects are instead conceived of as wholes inhering in pre-existing parts which are the causes.

The Buddhist versions of the nonidentity theory are rather different because Buddhism generally denies that there are any persisting substances at all; everything is momentary. A standard illustration is the way in which whirling a flaming torch creates in watchers the impression of a persistent object: a circle of fire. Similarly, the momentary occurrences of things in certain patterns create the impression of persisting objects existing in the world.

Both versions of the nonidentity theory claim to avoid the error of making the causal relation too strong, for effects are not identical with their pre-existing causes. They also both claim to avoid making the causal relation too weak, for both in their different fashions try to guarantee the regularity of causal relations. However, to vindicate the latter claim each school has to develop a rather elaborate ontology and epistemology, the details of which come in for criticism from other schools.

A third position tries to occupy the middle ground between the identity theory and the nonidentity theory. This is the stance taken by the Jaina theory of nonabsolutism. According to this theory there is a variety of aspects any entity can be viewed from. Thus from one viewpoint the effect is pre-existent in the cause and from another viewpoint it is not. The theory attempts to provide a compromise account of the causal relation that is neither too strong (as the identity theory threatens to be), nor too weak (as the nonidentity theory threatens to be).

Common to all of these causal theories, however, is the assumption that causation is real and not merely subjective. This is natural enough, since all these theories accept the original problematic: how to analyse the nature of the causal chain so as to guarantee the feasibility of attaining liberation. The one exception to this in Indian philosophy is to be found in the views of the Cārvāka materialists. These philosophers were sceptics about both causation and the possibility of attaining liberation. They espoused an antireligious materialism and a subjectivist account of causation as being merely observed conjunctions of events.

We can arrange, then, the Indian theories of causation in the following sequence. First, we have Cārvāka scepticism about causation, with its attendant scepticism about the possibility of liberation. All the other theories can be represented as various defensive responses to this scepticism. Thus the identity theory seeks to guarantee the possibility of liberation with an account of causation that makes it a very strong relation. Two distinct versions of the theory are developed: the transformation theory of Sānkhya-Yoga and the appearance theory of Advaita Vedānta. The nonidentity theory, on the other hand, tries to preserve the possibility of liberation while making causation a rather weaker relation. Again, two versions of the theory are developed: the Nyāya-Vaiśeṣika theory and the Buddhist theory of conditioned origination. The Jaina theory is an attempted synthesis of the identity and nonidentity theories.

2 Cārvāka scepticism

As antireligious materialists, the Cārvākas had no interest in vindicating the possibility of liberation (see MATERIALISM, INDIAN SCHOOL OF §4). And as strict empiricists in their epistemology, they refused to admit anything but perception as a valid means of knowledge. Accordingly they refused to admit causation as an invariable and unconditional relation. All we can know is what we perceive and all we perceive are conjunctions of events, not a dependence relation between events. These conjunctions may be regarded as purely accidental: hence their views are sometimes known as accidentalism (yadṛcchāvāda). Rather than supposing some things are effects dependent on other things which are causes, the Cārvākas held that it is more reasonable to suppose things occur because of

their own natures (svabhāva): hence their views are sometimes called naturalism (svabhāvavāda).

This sceptical position was criticized by all the other schools. The most common criticism was of the overly restrictive epistemology that led to this sceptical result. Indeed, the Cārvāka position was often viewed as a reductio ad absurdum of its strict empiricist premises. Accordingly the response of the other schools was usually to try to develop from a less restrictive epistemology a more generous ontology which included causal relations.

Another common complaint, however, was that Cārvāka scepticism was self-refuting. One Naiyāyika version of this charge claims that the scepticism about causation is refuted by the sceptics' own behaviour: they purport to doubt the causal relation between fire and smoke, but light a fire when they want to produce smoke. Of course, the Cārvāka might just reply here that we are so constituted psychologically that we expect a uniform regularity between instances of fire and smoke. Notwithstanding this, there is no real justification for the expectation; it is just a habit of expecting what has previously occurred in certain circumstances to reoccur in similar circumstances. But for the liberation-oriented philosophers, the Cārvāka's philosophical anthropology here is far too pessimistic. The agent trapped in the patterns of habit is paradigmatically the unliberated being; liberation is freedom from such bondage and understanding the causal chains which lead to bondage also allows us to discover the route to freedom.

3 Sānkhya-Yoga and the transformation theory

Sānkhya-Yoga espouses the identity theory (satkāryavāda), so called because it holds that an effect (kārya) is already existent (sat) in its cause in a potential form. The Sānkhya version of the theory is also called transformation theory (pariṇāmavāda) because it holds that the cause undergoes a real transformation into its effect through the causal process.

The standard Sānkhya arguments for the identity theory presented in Īśvarakṛṣṇa's Sānkhyakārikā (Verses on Distinctionism) (verse 9) are basically that something cannot emerge out of nothing, that the effect must be of the same material as the cause and that specific causes can only produce specific effects. In order to guarantee all of this the effect must preexist in the cause; it is a modification of what was already present. Thus according to the metaphysics of Sānkhya the manifest world must have an existing cause that the effect pre-exists in. This is nature (prakṛti), conceived of as a unitary principle underlying observable phenomena, which are transformations of this substance. The self (*puruṣa*) is merely the passive witness of all this.

The key Sāṅkhya examples of causation all involve material causation: as when a seed grows into a plant, or milk is transformed into curd, or oil seeds into oil. In these cases a cause and its effect are plausibly just two states of a single continuing substance. The Naiyāyikas objected that the Sāṅkhya theory abolishes the distinction between material and efficient causes. But this is not quite true, for Sāṅkhya-Yoga also admits another type of cause: the efficient or instrumental cause (*nimittakāraṇa*). However, this is not supposed to act upon the material cause and transform it into an effect. Rather it simply removes the barriers which check the material cause (*prakṛti*) from transforming from a relatively unmanifested state to a more manifested state. The *Yogabhāṣya* (4.3) compares it to how a farmer allows water to flow from a filled bed to another just by removing the obstacles.

The transformation theory insists that there is a necessary relation between cause and effect. To this extent it responds to the Cārvāka sceptical challenge to the possibility of liberation: there is indeed an invariable concomitance between cause and effect, since the latter is just a manifested state of the former. But the theory threatens to make the causal relation too strong. Transformation theory holds causation to involve a real transformation of a common stuff. But then nothing can become other than it is already and the presently unenlightened can never attain liberation. Sāṅkhya-Yoga responds to this objection by developing a radical dualism between nature (*prakṛti*) and self (*puruṣa*). The self is essentially unaffected by the causal transformations of *prakṛti*. As the *Sāṅkhyakārikā* (62) startlingly puts it: 'No one, therefore, is bound; no one released, likewise no one transmigrates. Only *prakṛti* in its various forms transmigrates, is bound and is released'. Because the *puruṣa* is just pure, contentless consciousness it cannot be bound or liberated. Realizing the absolute separation of *prakṛti* and *puruṣa*, ceasing to misidentify ourselves with our bodies, we come to appreciate our true natures as pure consciousnesses. This realization leads to liberation (called *kaivalya* in Sāṅkhya-Yoga), a condition apart from all suffering. The difference between bondage and liberation, then, is not an ontological one, but an epistemological one. The removal of the epistemological condition of ignorance is sufficient for liberation (see SĀṄKHYA).

4 Advaita Vedānta and the appearance theory

The Sāṅkhya epistemological model of the route to freedom has much in common with the Advaitin approach to the problem. However, the Advaitin view came to be called appearance theory (*vivartavāda*), for it differs importantly from the Sāṅkhya-Yoga version of the identity theory. In particular, the transformation theory views an effect such as a pot as a genuine transformation of the clay which constitutes it; both cause and effect are real. By contrast, the appearance theory views the effect (the pot) as not real, but only an appearance (*vivarta*). This is because Advaita espouses a radical monism: only the Absolute (Brahman) is real and the Self (*ātman*) is identical with Brahman (see BRAHMAN; MONISM, INDIAN). Accordingly the Advaita theory of causation is a version of the identity theory in that the effect (the illusory world around us) is in a sense not different from its cause (Brahman/*ātman*). However, the effect is ultimately unreal, though the cause is real (thus the theory is sometimes called *satkāraṇavāda*, 'existent-cause-theory').

It is only on the level of phenomenal reality, then, that the Advaitins are willing to defend the identity theory. The Advaitin philosopher ŚAṄKARA, for instance, endorses on this level the familiar Sāṅkhya arguments that otherwise anything might come of anything and that clearly nothing comes of nothing. He also adds others of his own, including the suggestion that since the perceptibility of cause and effect are not independent it is reasonable to suppose they are identical. But ultimately, when we consider the relation between the world and Brahman, the effect is merely an *apparent* effect. This is because the Advaitins accept both that Brahman is an eternal being and that an eternal cause must have eternal effects. But since worldly phenomena are clearly not eternal, they conclude that they cannot be genuine effects of Brahman, merely illusory or apparent effects. In so far as Brahman underlies these appearances, however, it can be viewed as the material cause of the world. This is in accord with the Advaitin theory of perceptual error, according to which there must be something real that underlies a false appearance.

On the appearance theory, then, causality is an apparent relation between a (comparatively) unreal effect and a (comparatively) real cause, between a thought construction and that which grounds such a construction. The focus of the theory of causation thus shifts away from a concern with external relations between objects to a concern with the epistemic or awareness relation involved in such constructions. Accordingly liberation is conceived of epistemically as the realization of what one already essentially is: Brahman.

Clearly this theory of causation is only as plausible

as the concept of Brahman as pure being upon which it rests. But this latter notion was vigorously rejected by many other Indian philosophers and the appearance theory thus requires a controversial monism to support it. Moreover, the identity theory's attempt to guarantee the causal relation, begun by Sāṅkhya and continued by Advaita, seems to end up with too strong an account of causation. The only way out of this difficulty is to insist that, in some sense, we are already liberated but do not know it. Then liberation becomes an epistemological matter, not an ontological one. But with bondage no longer conceived in material terms, we have a corresponding drift both away from epistemological realism and towards metaphysical dualism or monism.

5 Nyāya-Vaiśeṣika and the nonidentity theory

Nyāya-Vaiśeṣika represents a robust commitment to both epistemological realism and metaphysical pluralism (see NYĀYA-VAIŚEṢIKA). The Naiyāyikas define a cause as an invariable and independently necessary antecedent of an effect. That is, the causal relation is a uniform temporal relation that is necessary in the sense that there can be no counterinstances (though the relation is not a logical one in the Western sense). Moreover, the constant conjunction involved is a relation between properties, rather than between particular events.

Nyāya recognizes three kinds of causal factor: inherent cause (samavāyikāraṇa); noninherent cause (asamavāyikāraṇa); and instrumental cause (nimittakāraṇa). The inherent cause is that substance in which the effect abides by the relation of inherence. Thus the pot-halves or the threads are the inherent causes of the pot or the cloth because the latter effects inhere in the former causes. Note that for Nyāya the halves or the threads are not that out of which the pot or the cloth are composed. Rather the effects inhere in the cause so that, for instance, the cloth is not produced *out of* the threads, but subsists *in* the threads.

The noninherent cause is a cause which (directly or indirectly) inheres in an inherent cause. For example, in the production of a pot, the pot-halves are the inherent cause of the pot and the contact between the pot-halves, which inheres in the pot-halves, is the noninherent cause of the pot.

The first two kinds of causal factor are together necessary but not sufficient to produce an effect. The category of instrumental (or efficient) cause lumps together all the remaining causal factors. These include the agents of actions and other supporting factors.

The Nyāya theory takes the effect to be an absolutely new thing. The Sāṅkhya argument that a nonexistent effect cannot be brought into existence is dismissed by the Naiyāyikas as confusing an absolute nonentity (like the hare's horn, which is nonexistent for all time) with what is merely nonexistent before a particular time (like the pot before it is produced by the potter).

Nyāya also rejects the Sāṅkhya argument that since not just anything can produce anything, there must be a necessary relation between cause and effect requiring that they coexist contemporaneously. The Naiyāyikas claim the relevant necessity is supplied by the fact that the relation is between universals, not particulars.

Essential to the Nyāya theory is the notion of inherence (samavāya). Inherence is the relation that connects wholes and parts (like pots and pot-halves, threads and cloth); it also connects substances and their qualities. Inherence is defined as the relation between two inseparable things related as located to locus. Inherence explains the relation of the pot to the pot-halves which are its material cause without falling into the identity theory's mistake of identifying the effect with its cause (and hence being unable to explain why the effect does not come into existence as soon as the cause does). Moreover, inherence relates the self (ātman) to its qualities, including wrong notions. This allows for the wrong notions to be destroyed without thereby destroying the self, thus guaranteeing the possibility of liberation.

The most popular objection to the Nyāya theory is the infinite regress argument against inherence: if two entities A and B are to be related by the inherence relation R, which is itself a distinct entity, then it is also necessary that A and R be related by a different inherence relation R*, itself a distinct entity. But then, of course, A and R* have to be related by a yet different inherence relation R**, and so on *ad infinitum*.

The Naiyāyikas reply that there is no regress because there is no other relation to connect inherence to its relatum. Clearly they cannot mean that the relatum and its relation are identical, for then, by the transitivity of identity, A would not only be identical with R, but also with B! Instead Navya-Nyāya ('New Nyāya', the later school of Nyāya) appeals to the notion of a self-linking connector (svarūpasambandha). The idea here is that while A requires the inherence relation R to connect it to B, A can be its own connector to R.

6 Buddhist theories

The Buddhists reject the Nyāya version of nonidentity theory because it seems to them that inherence is too strong a relation for causation. This is because the

Buddhist theory of momentariness (*kṣaṇikavāda*) implies that there can be no persisting relation between any two entities, nor any persisting entities (see MOMENTARINESS, BUDDHIST DOCTRINE OF). Instead they espouse an ontology of momentary events, each of which is causally efficacious, grouped into various patterns. Moreover, the theory of dependent origination is understood to imply that an effect is not the result of a single cause, but of many causes working together. The Buddhist schools attempted various classifications of this totality of causes and conditions.

The Abhidharma analyses reality into elements (*dharmas*) (see BUDDHISM, ĀBHIDHARMIKA SCHOOLS OF). A distinction is also admitted between a *dharma* and its characteristics (*lakṣaṇas*). But this distinction quickly leads to a quasi-substantialism in the Sarvāstivāda school, as the concept of a *dharma*'s enduring essence or 'own-nature' (*svabhāva*) is introduced as the bearer of a *dharma*'s 'own-characteristics' (*svalakṣaṇa*). The concept of *svabhāva* is utilized by the Sarvāstivādins to explain the continuity of phenomena, which are analysed into momentary existences: one aspect of a *dharma* changes while another (the *svabhāva*) remains unchanged. This idea is used to explain the connection between cause and effect: a mango seed gives rise only to a mango tree because of the unchanging essence of 'mango-ness' that is in the seed and which connects the seed and the tree. Thus *svabhāva* is a kind of underlying substratum of change, a quasi-substance.

The Sautrāntikas rejected this theory as incompatible with the Buddha's doctrine of 'no-self', for to say a thing arises from its 'own-nature' is just to say it arises from the self. Instead the Sautrāntikas held existence to be but a series of successive moments. A seed is but a series of such point-instants and the seed-series gives rise to the tree-series in the sense that the latter succeeds the former. Causality, then, is just contiguity or immediate succession. But what of the origin of the series themselves? The Sautrāntikas maintain that the seed-series, at one time nonexistent, comes into existence: that is, the effect does not pre-exist.

Hence the Sarvāstivādins, with their appeal to a quasi-substantial essence, end up with a causal theory that threatens to become a Buddhist version of the Sāṅkhya identity theory. The Sautrāntikas, on the other hand, espouse a Buddhist version of the nonidentity theory which fails to provide for any kind of necessity in the causal relation. Either way the possibility of liberation is not guaranteed: the first account is too strong, the second too weak.

This situation provides the context for the Mahāyāna developments. The Yogācārin idealists give up

the reality of the external object and join the drift away from epistemological realism (see BUDDHISM, YOGĀCĀRA SCHOOL OF §§1–4). But the Mādhyamikas take a different line, exemplified in the celebrated critique of causation by the second-century Buddhist philosopher NĀGĀRJUNA in his *Mūlamadhyamaka-kārikā* (Fundamental Verses on the Middle Way) (see BUDDHISM, MĀDHYAMIKA: INDIA AND TIBET). Nāgārjuna refers to and rejects four types of causal theory: (i) self-causation; (ii) external causation; (iii) both (that is, self- and external causation); and (iv) noncausation. The first type of theory includes the Sāṅkhya identity theory; it also includes the Sarvāstivādin theory. The second type includes the Nyāya nonidentity theory; it also includes the Sautrāntika theory. The third is the Jaina theory. The fourth is the Cārvāka theory.

In a virtuoso dialectical display Nāgārjuna argues that the first option is absurd since it supposes the production of what already exists. The second option is absurd because the cause cannot be totally extraneous to its effect, or anything might cause anything. The third option is also untenable, since it just combines the first two options. The fourth option is unacceptable because it implies randomness and the inefficacy of action.

The last claim makes it clear that Nāgārjuna does not deny causation *per se*. Rather causality is interdependence: that is, all things are on a par, dependent on one another. Accordingly everything is empty (*śūnya*) of an independent essence. But all the causal theories criticized understand causation as an asymmetrical dependence relation with one relatum self-existent and hence more real. Instead, the Buddha's teaching of dependent origination is that everything is interdependent, and this is equivalent to the truth of emptiness (*śūnyatā*), that nothing has any self-existence or essence. Liberation is the realization of this emptiness (see BUDDHIST CONCEPT OF EMPTINESS).

7 Jaina nonabsolutism

The Jainas also agree that everything is interdependent. However, they insist too that it is still possible to distinguish the more real from the less real. Jaina nonabsolutism (*anekāntavāda*) is the theory that everything in the world has various aspects which permit everything to be seen from various viewpoints (see MANIFOLDNESS, JAINA THEORY OF). With respect to causation this means that cause and effect are partly identical and partly nonidentical. A cause has a power (*śakti*) to produce an effect and from this viewpoint the effect is pre-existent in the cause. But the effect is a new substance *qua* its form and from this viewpoint the effect is not pre-existent in its cause. This explains both why a particular effect can only be produced from a particular cause and why an extra effort is necessary to bring about that effect. Thus a pot is pre-existent in the clay in so far as its matter is concerned, but not in so far as its shape is concerned. The potter's effort is required to shape the clay into a pot.

The Jaina view seeks, then, to combine the merits of both the identity and nonidentity theories, while avoiding the difficulties of each. The theory is also very close to the identity-in-difference (*bhedābheda*) theories of certain theistic Vedāntins. The major difficulty with the theory from its opponents' point of view is that it just doubles the trouble by trying to have things both ways. To the extent that the Jaina theory of causation is a version of the identity theory, the causal relation is too strong to guarantee the possibility of liberation; to the extent that it is a version of the nonidentity theory, the causal relation is too weak.

See also: CAUSATION

References and further reading

Āraṇya, Svāmī Hariharānanda (1963) *Yoga Philosophy of Patañjali*, Albany, NY: State University of New York Press, 1983. (Sanskrit texts and translations of the Yogasūtra and the Yogabhāsya.)

Bhaduri, S. (1947) *Studies in Nyāya-Vaiśeṣika Metaphysics*, Poona: Bhandarkar Oriental Research Institute, 2nd edn, 1975. (Chapter 12 reviews the Naiyāyika theory of causality.)

Bhartiya, M.C. (1973) *Causation in Indian Philosophy*, Ghaziabad: Vimal Prakashan. (Good comparative review with special reference to Nyāya-Vaiśeṣika.)

Garfield, J.L. (1995) *The Fundamental Wisdom of the Middle Way*, New York; Oxford University Press. (Translation of the Tibetan version of Nāgārjuna's *Mūlamadhyamakakārikā*, plus an extensive and valuable philosophical commentary thereon.)

* Īśvarakṛṣṇa (*c.* AD 350–450) *Sāṅkhyakarika* (Verses on Distinctionism), in G.J. Larson, *Classical Sāṃkhya*, Delhi: Motilal Banarsidass, 1969; 2nd rev. edn, 1979. (Sanskrit text and a translation, in a good study of Sāṅkhya.)

Kalupahana, D.J. (1975) *Causality: The Central Philosophy of Buddhism*, Honolulu, HI: University Press of Hawaii. (Good study of dependent origination with special reference to early Buddhism.)

* Nāgārjuna (*c.* AD 150–200) *Mūlamadhyamakakārikā* (Fundamental Verses on the Middle Way), trans. K. Inada, *Nāgārjuna: A Translation of his Mūla-*

madhyamakakārikā with an Introductory Essay, Tokyo: Hokuseido Press, 1970. (Includes the Sanskrit text.)

Potter, K.H. (1963) *Presuppositions of India's Philosophies*, Englewood Cliffs, NJ: Prentice-Hall. (Chapters 6–9 present an excellent and original philosophical treatment of the Indian problem of freedom and causation.)

—— (ed.) (1970) *Encyclopedia of Indian Philosophies*, vol. 1, *Bibliography*, Delhi: Motilal Banarsidass, 2nd rev. edn, 1983. (Standard bibliographical source; includes details of Sanskrit texts, translations and secondary literature.)

Radhakrishnan, S. and Moore, C.A. (eds) (1957) *A Source Book in Indian Philosophy*, Princeton, NJ: Princeton University Press. (A very useful collection of translated primary sources; see the index under 'causality'.)

Smart, N. (1964) *Doctrine and Argument in Indian Philosophy*, London: Allen & Unwin. (Chapter 14 offers a useful synoptic review of some of the Indian argumentation about causation.)

ROY W. PERRETT

CAUSATION, MENTAL
see MENTAL CAUSATION

CAVELL, STANLEY (1926–)

Born in Atlanta, Georgia, Stanley Cavell has held the Walter M. Cabot Chair in Aesthetics and the General Theory of Value at Harvard University since 1963. The range, diversity and distinctiveness of his writings are unparalleled in twentieth-century Anglo-American philosophy. As well as publishing essays on modernist painting and music, he has created a substantial body of work in film studies, literary theory and literary criticism; he has introduced new and fruitful ways of thinking about psychoanalysis and its relationship with philosophy; and his work on Heidegger and Derrida, taken together with his attempts to revitalize the tradition of Emersonian Transcendentalism, have defined new possibilities for a distinctively American contribution to philosophical culture. This complex oeuvre is unified by a set of thematic concerns – relating to scepticism and moral perfectionism – which are rooted in Cavell's commitment to the tradition of ordinary language philosophy, as represented in the work of J.L. Austin and Wittgenstein.

1   **Criteria and scepticism**
2   **Literature, cinema and psychoanalysis**
3   **Perfectionism and modernism**

1   Criteria and scepticism

Cavell's Ph.D. dissertation (later published, much revised, as *The Claim of Reason* (1979)) elaborates an unorthodox interpretation of the notion of a criterion – pivotal for both J.L. AUSTIN and WITTGENSTEIN as that which is elicited by their method of responding to philosophical confusions with reminders of 'what we say when', of how we apply words in the circumstances of everyday life. Cavell's position resembles orthodoxy in conceiving of criteria as fixing a word's grammar by linking it to other words in a schematism that aligns language with the world and users of those words with one another. However, he takes the precise extent of this linguistic community as something philosophical exploration helps to determine, not something it can take for granted; and he takes the capacity exercised in such explorations to be a species of self-knowledge rather than knowledge of a predetermined body of rules, since a word's complex grammatical schematism sets real but inherently flexible limits to its projectibility into new contexts of use, and so requires an ineliminably personal evaluation of the mutuality of words and world in specific contexts.

Cavell further argues that Wittgensteinian criteria go deeper than Austinian ones, by showing that grammatical reminders cannot be used to refute scepticism in the manner favoured by Austin and many Wittgensteinians (see CRITERIA; SCEPTICISM). Wittgensteinian criteria are criteria of identity rather than of existence; they specify what it is for something to count as a certain kind of thing, thus determining the applicability of a concept and making possible the judgments which deploy it, but they do not and could not determine the correctness of any such judgments. In this sense, sceptical denials that we can be certain of the existence of the external world or of other minds embody a truth; but they misrepresent this truth, since if criteria are not a species of knowledge-claim, they can no more be doubtful than they can be indubitable. Nevertheless, criteria so understood cannot be grounded in evidence or argument, but solely in our agreeing in their continued use; so the possibility of a sceptical refusal of that agreement is ineliminable. Since, however, our capacity to use words presupposes some such agreement, its sceptical refusal must result in emptiness – in the sceptics' saying something other than they take themselves to mean, or in saying nothing whatever. Accordingly, scepticism must be combatted not by claiming that

the repudiation of criteria is impossible or irrational, but by demonstrating its true cost.

That cost turns out to be high. In so far as criteria distinguish phenomena from one another, their repudiation amounts to transforming the world into an undifferentiated plenum. And in so far as they give expression to human interests in phenomena, marking out the distinctions which matter to us and so our shared responses to the world, their refusal amounts to a denial that the world matters, that its phenomena are of interest. But why, then, might such costs seem worth bearing? How can otherwise competent speakers come to relinquish the mastery of grammar which governs their everyday intercourse when under the pressure to philosophize? Any answer partly depends on which criteria are subject to repudiation; the needs and interests served by affirming a fantasy of the essential privacy of language are not those served by an emotivist fantasy of morality. But at its most general, the sceptical impulse refuses criteria as such – the conditions of human knowledge and meaning; and Cavell's claim is that the sceptic in us all is motivated by the sense that such conditions are constraints, that the limits of sense (that which makes thought and knowledge possible) are in fact limitations (perspectival blinkers imposed on an otherwise unmediated knowledge of the world). In other words, criteria are rejected in the name of a fantasized perspective on reality which transcends all limits, a view from nowhere; scepticism is a refusal of the conditioned nature of human knowledge, a denial of human finitude in the name of the unconditioned, the inhuman. But of course, nothing is more human than the desire to deny one's own humanity.

2   Literature, cinema and psychoanalysis

For Cavell, then, Wittgenstein's later philosophy aims at overcoming a variety of manifestations of scepticism in philosophy – scepticism understood not simply as an intellectual doctrine, but as the modern inflection of a perennial human impulse that finds expression in domains regarded as distinct from that of philosophy. By interpreting the repudiation of criteria as bringing about the death of the world and our interest in it, Cavell links ORDINARY LANGUAGE PHILOSOPHY with the concerns of Romanticism, in both its English and German forms – particularly the writings of Coleridge, Wordsworth and the Schlegels. He also interprets Shakespeare's plays and certain genres of Hollywood movie as responding to sceptical struggles, by following out the fates of human beings caught up in relationships in which scepticism about other minds is lived out and presented as exemplary of scepticism in general (see OTHER MINDS). The human capacity to revive self and world by recovering an interest in the latter's autonomous yet environing life is there figured by the capacity of these couples to acknowledge one another as separate and yet related; the vicissitudes of their weddedness to one another symbolize the vicissitudes of human weddedness to the world.

For Cavell, these readings are not literary illustrations of independently derived philosophical theses. Their focus on sceptical themes is rather understood to unsettle any received wisdom about divisions between philosophy and what lies outside it; and they are often Cavell's primary motivation for revising his more obviously philosophical investigations of these issues. For example, he takes his reading of *The Winter's Tale* to demonstrate that scepticism is inflected by gender; and the same reciprocity can be seen in his conception of the relationship between philosophy and psychoanalysis. Interpreting scepticism as a tragic repudiation of the humanity in oneself and others leads him to see Freud's attempts to recover human meaning from aberrant behaviour as a mode of overcoming scepticism, and to view the general psychoanalytic commitment to the reality of the unconscious mind as itself responding to Descartes' failure to refute scepticism by staking the mind's reality upon its existence as consciousness (see FREUD; DESCARTES). At the same time, he utilizes Freudian theory to diagnose the motivational sources of confusions in philosophy; and he uses Freud's fundamental but politically fraught alignment of masculinity with activity and femininity with passivity (understood as two dimensions of, or orientations towards, human experience) to argue that the essential passivity invoked in the Wittgensteinian practice of recalling the true significance of one's words (as well as in Heidegger's emphasis upon *Gelassenheit*) embodies a specifically feminine mode of philosophical thought and expression.

3 Perfectionism and modernism

Cavell's vision of the human mind as torn between its active and passive sides, between scepticism and its overcoming, is further underpinned by reference to EMERSON and THOREAU – and specifically by their perfectionist conception of the self as ineluctably split or doubled, as always capable of moving beyond the state in which it finds itself. When that capacity is active, the self embarks on an endless process of self-development, with each attained state neighbouring an attainable state that forms its possible future; when it is in eclipse, perhaps because of the attractions of one's attained state or by personal and social distractions from the draw of one's unattained state,

the self's capacity to grow is also eclipsed – and losing one's capacity to change oneself in the name of a better state of self and society means losing an essential aspect of the self's autonomy: the capacity to revise one's conception of the good. As this formulation suggests, Cavell concludes that Emersonian perfectionism should form an essential dimension of Rawlsian (and more generally, of Kantian) liberal democracy, since a non-autonomous self cannot internalize the moral law which should govern relations with others in a liberal society (see LIBERALISM).

Cavell's work is a species of philosophical modernism. His writings relate themselves to a number of intellectual and cultural traditions by regarding their continuation as an undismissible problem. He can neither accept their prevailing paradigms as they stand, nor reject them as no longer philosophically and humanly meaningful; so he aims to inherit them by subjecting them to a radical but internal critique that can ultimately be grounded only upon his own (and his readers') willingness to acknowledge his words as worthy continuations of those traditions. This means that his writings are bound to appear idiosyncratic and self-regarding; but it also means that that appearance can no more justify their dismissal than it can guarantee their value.

List of works

Cavell, S. (1969) *Must We Mean What We Say? A Book of Essays*, New York: Charles Scribner's Sons. (A set of interrelated essays on philosophical method and the arts, including a long and hugely influential essay on *King Lear*.)

—— (1971) *The World Viewed: Reflections on the Ontology of Film*, New York: Viking Press. (This analysis draws on Cavell's earlier work on theatre and painting; an expanded edition, published in 1979, includes replies to critics.)

—— (1972) *The Senses of Walden*, New York: Viking Press. (A highly compressed, detailed reading of Thoreau's famous text.)

—— (1979) *The Claim of Reason: Wittgenstein, Skepticism, Morality and Tragedy*, Oxford: Clarendon Press. (Cavell's much-revised dissertation, this contains his most detailed elaboration of his interpretation of criteria, and sets the scene for all his future writing.)

—— (1981) *Pursuits of Happiness: The Hollywood Comedy of Remarriage*, Cambridge, MA: Harvard University Press. (These six essays identify a genre of screwball comedies from Hollywood's golden age, in which issues of interpersonal acknowledgement are worked out in relation to Romanticism and scepticism.)

—— (1984) *Themes Out of School: Effects and Causes*, San Francisco: North Point Press. (A disparate collection, including an important early essay on existentialism and analytical philosophy.)

—— (1987) *Disowning Knowledge: In Six Plays of Shakespeare*, Cambridge: Cambridge University Press. (This collects a number of already-published pieces, as well as two new ones.)

—— (1988) *In Quest of the Ordinary: Lines of Skepticism and Romanticism*, Chicago, IL: University of Chicago Press. (The core of this collection is a sequence of lectures on American and English Romanticism in literature and philosophy.)

—— (1989) *This New Yet Unapproachable America: Lectures after Emerson after Wittgenstein*, Albequerque, NM: Living Batch Press, and Chicago, IL: University of Chicago Press. (Contains two lectures, including a long piece on Wittgenstein as a philosopher of culture.)

—— (1990) *Conditions Handsome and Unhandsome: The Constitution of Emersonian Perfectionism*, Chicago, IL: University of Chicago Press. (Cavell here relates his perfectionist concerns to recent work by Rawls and Kripke.)

—— (1994) *A Pitch Of Philosophy: Autobiographical Exercises*, Cambridge, MA: Harvard University Press. (As well as explicitly autobiographical reflections, this collection contains important essays on Derrida and J.L. Austin, and on opera.)

—— (1995) *Philosophical Passages: Wittgenstein, Emerson, Austin, Derrida*, Oxford: Blackwell. (Includes a much-revised version of Cavell's lectures on the opening of the *Philosophical Investigations*.)

—— (1996) *Contesting Tears: The Hollywood Melodrama of the Unknown Woman*, Chicago, IL, and London: University of Chicago Press. (This collection identifies a genre of film adjacent to that of the remarriage comedies studied in *Pursuits of Happiness*, and systematically relates cinema to psychoanalysis.)

References and further reading

Cohen, T., Guyer, P. and Putnam, H. (eds) (1993) *Pursuits of Reason: Essays in Honor of Stanley Cavell*, Lubbock, TX: Texas Tech University Press. (Festschrift, with some useful critical essays.)

Fischer, M. (1989) *Stanley Cavell and Literary Skepticism*, Chicago, IL: University of Chicago Press. (Applies Cavell's interpretation of scepticism to post-structuralist literary theory.)

Fleming, R. and Payne, M. (eds) (1989) *The Senses of Stanley Cavell*, Lewisburg, PA: Bucknell University Press. (Useful collection of critical essays, with two interviews with Cavell.)

Mulhall, S. (1994) *Stanley Cavell: Philosophy's Recounting of the Ordinary*, Oxford: Oxford University Press. (The first full-length general philosophical study of Cavell's work.)

—— (ed.) (1996) *The Cavell Reader*, Oxford: Blackwell. (Contains selections from every phase of Cavell's career, with a detailed bibliography, and a general introductory survey by the editor.)

STEPHEN MULHALL

CAVENDISH, MARGARET LUCAS (1623–73)

The only seventeenth-century woman to publish numerous books on natural philosophy, Cavendish presented her materialism in a wide range of literary forms. She abandoned her early commitment to Epicurean atomism and, rejecting the mechanical model of natural change, embraced an organicist materialism. She also addressed the relations that hold among philosophy, gender and literary genre.

1 **Philosophical influences**
2 **Organicist materialism**
3 **Theory of sense perception**
4 **Philosophy and gender**

1 Philosophical influences

Margaret Cavendish, Duchess of Newcastle, made contact with HOBBES, tutor to the Cavendish family, during the English Civil War. She became a member of the 'Newcastle Circle', which included Hobbes, CHARLETON and DIGBY, and which was influenced by interaction with MERSENNE and GASSENDI. While exiled in Paris, Rotterdam and Antwerp, she met DESCARTES and Roberval. In 1667, she became the first woman to attend a session of the Royal Society of London. She corresponded with Christian Huygens about 'Rupert's exploding drops', and with GLANVILL about witchcraft and Neoplatonic notions such as 'plastic faculties' and the 'soul of the world'. She was one of the first Englishwomen to gain recognition for her publications. In additional to writing treatises such as *Philosophical Fancies* (1653) and *Philosophical and Physical Opinions* (1655, 1663) she experimented with a wide range of genres to express her views: poetry, orations, plays, autobiobraphy (*Nature's Pictures...*, 1656), biography (*The Life of... William Cavindishe...*, 1667), allegories (*The World's Olio*,

1655), epistolary narrative (*CCXI Sociable Letters*, 1664a) and fiction (*The Description of a New World, called the Blazing-World*, 1668). Introduced to twentieth-century readers by Henry Ten Eyck Perry (1918) and Virginia Woolf (1925), her philosophy only came in for serious, sustained evaluation beginning in the 1980s.

2 Organicist materialism

Cavendish's earliest works, such as *Poems, and Fancies* (1653), combine a version of Epicurean atomism with Lucretius' strategy of using poetry to achieve the highest form of the good: intellectual pleasure (see EPICUREANISM §§3–5). But it is her *Philosophical Letters* (1664b), *Observations upon Experimental Philosophy* (1666), and *Grounds of Natural Philosophy* (1668) that present her mature natural philosophy. She attacks the Platonists' and hermeticists' postulation of incorporeals in their theory of natural change. She agrees with Hobbes that an incorporeal substance is inconceivable for 'natural reason', but concedes that, on the basis of faith, one might accept 'supernatural spiritual beings'.

Like Hobbes, she holds that all natural change is change of motion. But instead of mechanism, the model for change in her mature philosophy is one of vital agreement or sympathetic influence of parts, as within a single organism. For, she rejects Hobbes' principle: every motion in a body is produced by a contiguous body through impact. Rather, motion and vitality cannot be transferred from an external source, but are inherent in corporeal body. Cavendish rejects the transfer model of causation, which she thinks must underlie mechanical philosophy, for two main reasons. First, if motion is a mode of body, then it cannot be transferred outside of the substance in which it inheres. This would give to motion the unacceptable status of a 'real quality': a mere modification of substance that is none the less treated as if a 'complete thing'. Second, since motion is naturally inseparable from material body, if motion could be transferred, then a portion of body would be transferred too. But, since all change reduces to changes in motion, it follows that corporeal body would quickly be diminished. Cavendish here adapts a standard argument against atomism, cited by LUCRETIUS.

Corporeal individuals, that is to say parts of body, can act on others at a distance because of their sympathy and vital agreement, just as a seriously wounded appendage can affect change in the organism as a whole. Cavendish is even committed to a version of panpsychism, whereby all corporeal individuals contain some degree of sense and reason (see PANPSYCHISM). (In *De Corpore*, Hobbes admitted that he could not refute those who would ascribe sense to inanimate bodies.) She holds that corporeal nature is endowed with something analogous to understanding: Bodies know how to 'pattern out' the figure of a distant object in perception; they know how to duplicate themselves in generation. Her views – (1) that nature is a single, unified corporeal body, intrinsically possessing self-motion or vital force, (2) that all parts of corporeal nature have some degree of sense and intellect, (3) that causation is understood through the vital affinity one part of nature has for another, rather than via the mechanical model – are all adaptations from Stoicism. Cavendish appears to have been familiar with some version of Chrysippus' views, for she makes reference to some of his analogies and arguments (see STOICISM §3; CHRYSIPPUS).

3 Theory of sense perception

Cavendish characterizes her anti-mechanist model of change in the following way:

> A Watch-maker doth not give the watch its motion, but he is onely the occasion, that the watch moves after that manner, for the motion of the watch is the watches own motion, inherent in those parts ever since that matter was.... Wherefore one body may occasion another body to move so and so, but not give it any motion, but everybody (though occasioned by another, to move in such a way) moves by its own natural motion.
>
> (Cavendish 1664: 100)

She uses this vital concomitance model in her theory of sense perception: the 'corporeal motions' of external objects are the 'occasion' for the 'sensitive and rational motions' in creatures to imitate or 'pattern out' the motions and figures of the external objects. An 'occasion' is any circumstance which has no intrinsic connection to or direct influence on the effect, is not necessary for the production of the effect, but has an indirect influence on the production of the effect by inducing the primary cause through command or example. For Cavendish, a 'primary cause' is that which is necessary and sufficient for the production of the effect. An external object cannot be *necessary* for perception since 'the sensitive organs can make such like figurative actions were there no object present' (1668: 56). But neither is it *sufficient*; when the sense organs operate 'irregularly', misperception of objects takes place. So, the sensitive body is the principal cause of perceptions, and external objects are the exemplar causes that induce the body to pattern out one sense perception rather than another.

Cavendish's main argument against Descartes and Hobbes on perception is that their talk of translation of motion, or of imprinting an image, can only be interpreted via a transfer model of causation. But, as has been shown, such a model is inconsistent with their substance/mode ontology. Cavendish also has specific criticisms of Hobbes' theory of memory that derive from Stoic arguments. If sense is produced by imprinting and if, as Hobbes suggests, the bodily organs retain these imprints, then mechanism entails an eventual jumble of corporeal images. This criticism, derived from Chrysippus, was also proffered by Digby and Glanvill. Hobbes would have charged his critics with interpreting his metaphors too simplistically, since the impressions he refers to are infinitesimal motions. But without the mathematical model later provided by the calculus, the only models in terms of which to depict the impact of infinitesimally small motions were crude mechanical ones. So, however quaint these criticisms may seem to us, they were contemporary demands for an intelligible mechanical model of perception.

4 Philosophy and gender

In 'Female Orations', a section of *Orations of Divers Sorts* (1662), Cavendish explores the following questions: Is woman's social subordination to man a fact or no? If the former, is it due to oppression by men, to a natural inferiority in women, or to unfair cultural practices such as inferior education and constricted possibilities for acquiring moral, physical and intellectual experience? Finally, is woman's subordination to man inevitable? Rather than arguing for a position, Cavendish is content to lay out the logical space of the gender politics of her day. The prefaces and introductions to her books also contain defences of her desire to publish and her ability, as a woman, to do philosophy. Her experimentation with varied philosophical genres is, in part, an attempt to find a form which her readers would find acceptable: one in which a seventeenth-century woman, explicitly seeking fame as a natural philosopher, might give voice to her views.

See also: Atomism, ancient; Materialism

List of works

Cavendish, M. (1653) *Poems, and Fancies*, London; facsimile repr. Menston: Scolar Press, 1972; *Poems, and Phancies*, The Second Impression, much Altered and Corrected, London, 1664; *Poems, or Several Fancies in Verse: with the Animal Parliament, in Prose*, The Third Edition, London, 1668. (Atomism expressed in verse form, together with poems on moral topics such as cruelty to animals, and whimsical verses about fairies and other incorporeals.)

—— (1653) *Philosophicall Fancies*, London. (A prose exposition of her materialist natural philosophy.)

—— (1655) *Philosophical and Physical Opinions*, London; 2nd edn, London, 1663. (This revised version of *Philosophicall Fancies* is a transitional work, in which Cavendish begins to reject mechanistic atomism in favour of an organicist materialism; the substantially revised second edition, reissued as *Grounds of Natural Philosophy* (1668), expounds her mature system of natural philosophy.)

—— (1655) *The World's Olio*, London; The Second Edition, London, 1671. (A collection of mostly prose works, it also contains some poems on atomism first published as Part I of *Poems, and Fancies*.)

—— (1655/6) *Nature's Pictures Drawn by Fancie's Pencil to the Life*, London; 2nd edn, *Natures Picture Drawn by Fancies Pencil to the Life*, London, 1671. (The first edition of this collection of largely fictional sketches includes her autobiography, 'A True Relation of my Birth, Breeding and Life', which is not found in the second edition.)

—— (1662) *Playes*, London. (Some plays include discussions about gender politics, such as *The Female Academy* and *Bell in Campo*; excerpts from the latter play appear in *Women Writers of the Seventeenth Century*, ed. K. Wilson and F. Warnke, Athens, GA: University of Georgia Press, 1989.)

—— (1662/3) *Orations of Divers Sorts, Accomodated to Divers Places*, London; 2nd edn, London, 1668. (Includes 'The Female Orations' reprinted in *The Norton Anthology of Literature by Women*, ed. S. Gilbert and S. Gubar, New York and London: W.W. Norton & Co., 1985.)

—— (1664a) *CCXI Sociable Letters*, London; facsimile repr. Menston: Scholar Press, 1969. (An epistolary narrative praised by Charles Lamb, which has been compared to Samuel Richardson's works, it provides details of the historical and intellectual setting in which Cavendish was writing.)

—— (1664b) *Philosophical Letters: or, Modest Reflections Upon some Opinions in Natural Philosophy, maintained By several Famous and Learned Authors of this Age, Expressed by way of Letters: By the thrice Noble, Illustrious, and Excellent Princess, the Lady Marchioness of Newcastle*, London. (Letters to a fictious noblewoman, in which she criticizes the views of Descartes, Hobbes, More and van Helmont in light of her own system of natural philosophy; letters concerning Descartes are reprinted in Women Philosophers of the Early Modern Period, ed. M. Atherton, Indianapolis, IN: Hackett Publishing Company, 1994.)

—— (1666) *Observations upon Experimental Philosophy, To which is added, The Description of a New Blazing World*, London; the additional text was reissued as *The Description of a New World, called the Blazing-World*, London, 1668; repr. in *The Blazing World and Other Writings*, ed. K. Lilley, London and New York: Penguin, 1992. (A treatise of her natural philosophy, published with a utopian fiction that intimates some of her philosophical positions and parodies views about incorporeal spirits.)

—— (1667) *The Life of the thrice Noble, High and Puissant Prince William Cavendishe, Duke, Marquess, and Earl of Newcastle...* , London; 2nd edn, 1675; Latin trans. W. Charleton as *De vita et Rebus Gestis... Guilielmi Ducis Novo-Castrensis...* , London, 1668; numerous reprints. (This early English biography has gained Cavendish a place in literary history; she has been known primarily for this work.)

—— (1668a) *Plays, never before Printed*, London. (Some plays include discussions about gender politics, such as *The Convent of Pleasure*, excerpts from which appear in *First Feminists: British Women Writers 1578–1799*, ed. M. Ferguson, Bloomington, IN: Indiana University Press, 1985.)

—— (1668b) *Grounds of Natural Philosophy... The Second Edition, much altered from the First which went under the Name of Philosophical and Physical Opinions*, London. (A reissue of the 1663 work; together with *Philosophical Letters* and *Observations upon Experimental Philosophy*, this work constitutes the expressions of her mature natural philosophy.)

References and further reading

A Collection of Letters and Poems: Written by several Persons of Honour and Learning, Upon divers Important Subjects, to the Late Duke and Duchess of Newcastle (1678), London. (Documents important for reconstructing her intellectual circle, including letters to her by Hobbes, Glanvill, Charleton and Digby.)

Bowerbank, S. (1984) 'The Spider's Delight: Margaret Cavendish and the "Female Imagination"', *English Literary Renaissance* 14; repr. in *Women in the Renaissance: Selections from English Literary Renaissance*, ed. K. Farrell, E.H. Hageman and A.F. Kinney, Amherst, MA: University of Massachu-

setts Press, 1991. (A feminist examination of Cavendish's natural philosophy.)

Clucas, S. (1994) 'The Atomism of the Cavendish Circle: A Reappraisal', *The Seventeenth Century* 9 (2): 247–73. (Chronicles Cavendish's changing views in natural philosophy, arguing that she never entirely rejected atomism, broadly construed.)

Grant, D. (1957) *Margaret the First: A Biography of Margaret Cavendish, Duchess of Newcastle, 1623–1673*, London: R. Hart-Davis. (A standard source for biographical information.)

Jones, K. (1988) *A Glorious Fame: The Life of Margaret Cavendish, Duchess of Newcastle, 1623–1673*, London: Bloomsbury. (A biography which places Cavendish within the context of other women intellectuals of the period.)

Kargon, R.H. (1966) *Atomism in England from Hariot to Newton*, Oxford: Clarendon Press. (One of the few histories to treat the 'Newcastle Circle'; only Cavendish's earliest publications are discussed.)

Merchant, C. (1980) *The Death of Nature*, San Francisco, CA: Harper & Row. (A feminist/environmentalist revisionist history of science, which treats her rejection of mechanism.)

Meyer, G.D. (1955) *The Scientific Lady in England 1650–1760*, Berkeley, CA: University of California Press. (Focuses on her *Observations upon Experimental Philosophy* and places it in the context of other early modern scientific works by Englishwomen.)

Rogers, J. (1996) *The Matter of Revolution: Science, Poetry, and Politics in the Age of Milton*, Ithaca, NY and London: Cornell University Press. (Comparable to earlier treatments of Hobbes, this work explores the connection between Cavendish's natural philosophy and political views.)

Sarasohn, L.T. (1984) 'A Science Turned Upside Down: Feminism and the Natural Philosophy of Margaret Cavendish', *Huntington Library Quarterly* 47 (4): 299–307. (A treatment of Cavendish's natural philosophy that draws conclusions about the feminist implications of her work.)

Schiebinger, L. (1991) 'Margaret Cavendish, Duchess of Newcastle', in *A History of Women Philosophers*, vol. 3, ed. M.E. Waithe, Dordrecht: Kluwer. (A survey of Cavendish's natural philosophy.)

Ten Eyck Perry, H. (1918) *The First Duchess of Newcastle and Her Husband As Figures in Literary History*, Boston, MA and London: Ginn & Company. (An examination of Cavendish's corpus and a historically useful account of its critical reception.)

* Woolf, V. (1925) 'The Duchess of Newcastle', *The Common Reader*, London: Published by Leonard &

Virginia Woolf at the Hogarth Press. (An introduction of Cavendish to twentieth-century readers.)

EILEEN O'NEILL

CELSUS (late 2nd century AD)

The Greek philosopher Celsus of Alexandria was a Middle Platonist, known only for his anti-Christian work The True Account. *The work is lost, but we have Origen's reply to it,* Against Celsus. *In it Celsus defends a version of Platonist theology.*

Celsus is known only as the author of a polemical work against the Christians entitled *Alēthēs logos*, which may be translated *The True Account*, although other connotations of *logos* are also present in the title (see Logos). We know of this work only through the reply (*Against Celsus*) composed to it in AD 248 by the Church Father Origen, who does not in fact know who Celsus is (see Origen §1). We too know nothing about Celsus, but can date his work fairly closely from references in it to a persecution of Christians under a joint rulership which must be that Marcus Aurelius and Commodus (AD 177–80).

The title of Celsus' book may also refer to a passage of Plato's *Meno* (81a), where Socrates speaks of the ancient doctrine he has heard concerning the immortality of the soul as a 'true account' (see Plato §11). One of Celsus' polemical points certainly is that Platonic philosophy is in accord with the wisdom of the most ancient authorities, such as Orpheus and Homer – a common enough view among the Neoplatonists. As regards his own philosophical position, it is hard to pin him to any particular tendency within contemporary Platonism. He shows the expected contempt for a notion like the resurrection of the body (Origen, *Against Celsus* V 14), or the idea that god made man in his own image (VI 63), there being nothing that could resemble god. At VII 42, he gives a basic account of the Platonist view of the supreme god, which is incompatible with the notion of his involving himself too closely with matter. He alludes, indeed, to the notion of the supreme god being 'beyond being' (Plato, *Republic* 509b), and the title of his work may indicate his adoption of the *logos* as a secondary god, but we cannot be sure. He mentions three ways of attaining a conception of god – synthesis, analysis and analogy, which correspond approximately to the three ways distinguished by Alcinous in his *Didaskalikos*, chapter 10, although there is no indication that Celsus knows that work. Contact between man and

god is effected, of course, through the agency of daemons, whom the Christians are criticized for disdaining (VIII 28, 33, 35).

All this is very non-specific. *The True Account* is an interesting document, none the less, as a sign that Christians are coming to be of some weight in society, to the extent of meriting the sort of polemical refutation which hitherto the philosophical schools had directed against each other. Celsus' work is of the same genre as his contemporary Atticus' attack on the Peripatetics, Plutarch's attacks on the Epicureans and Stoics (see Plutarch of Chaeronea §1) and, later, Plotinus' treatise *Against the Gnostics* (Enneads II 9).

See also: Neoplatonism; Platonism, Early and Middle

List of works

Celsus (*c.* 180 AD) *The True Account*, ed. O. Glöckner, *Celsus' Alēthēs logos*, Bonn: A. Marcus und E. Webers Verlag, 1924; trans. R.J. Hoffman, *Celsus, On the True Doctrine*, Oxford: Oxford University Press, 1995. (Celsus' lost text as reconstructed from extracts of Origen's work *Against Celsus*.)

References and further reading

Andresen, C. (1955) *Logos und Nomos: Die Polemik des Kelsos wider das Urchristentum* (*Logos* and *Nomos*: Celsus' Polemic against Early Christianity), Berlin: de Gruyter. (Authoritative study of Celsus from a religious perspective.)
* Origen (AD 248) *Against Celsus*, trans. H. Chadwick, *Contra Celsum*, Cambridge: Cambridge University Press, 1965. (Our sole source on Celsus.)

JOHN DILLON

CENSORSHIP *see* Freedom of speech; Journalism, ethics of; Pornography

CERTAINTY

'Certainty' is not a univocal term. It is predicated of people, and it is predicated of propositions. When certainty is predicated of a person, as in 'Sally is certain that she parked her car in lot 359', we are ascribing an attitude to Sally. We can say that a person, S, is psychologically certain of a proposition, p, just in case

S believes p without any doubts. In general, psychological certainty has not been a topic which philosophers have found problematic.

On the other hand, certainty as a property of propositions, as in 'The proposition that Sally parked her car in lot 359 is certain for Sally', has been discussed widely by philosophers. Roughly, we can say that a proposition, *p*, is propositionally certain *for a person, S, just in case S is fully warranted in believing that p and there are no legitimate grounds whatsoever to doubt that p*. The philosophical issue, of course, is whether there are any such propositions and, if so, what makes them certain.

1   **Types of certainty**
2   **Propositional certainty**

1   Types of certainty

Before directly considering certainty, it would be useful to distinguish it from another notion – that of infallibility. Although neither concept has been employed in a universally accepted way by philosophers, generally it has been held that a person, *S*, is infallible with regard to a proposition, *p*, just in case it is not possible for *S* falsely to believe that *p*. For example, it might not be possible for persons falsely to believe of themselves that they have beliefs. But the range of such contingent propositions, if any, is very small indeed; and philosophers have been interested in whether certainty extends to a much wider range of contingent propositions. In addition, a person could be infallible with regard to some propositions, even if those propositions are not at all warranted. For example, consider any necessary truth. It would not be possible for *S* mistakenly to believe it, since it is not possible for that proposition to be false. But it may have little or no warrant for *S*. Since propositional certainty is inextricably connected with warrant, infallibility and certainty should not be conflated (see FALLIBILISM).

So let us turn to a direct examination of certainty. Psychological certainty is an attitude that persons can have towards a proposition, and propositional certainty is a measure of the epistemic warrant for a proposition. Thus, it is clear that psychological certainty and propositional certainty are logically independent. For *S* could be certain that *p* on inadequate grounds or, in some extreme cases, on no grounds whatsoever. On the other hand, a person could have the best grounds for believing *p* and no basis for doubt, but none the less fail to believe *p* with a high degree of resolve because of timidity.

Although the two types of certainty are logically independent, there is a connection between them.

Presumably a person would want the degree of belief in a proposition to parallel the degree of epistemic warrant for it. Descartes' *Meditations* (1641), one of the starting points of contemporary epistemology, can be seen as his attempt to determine which, if any, propositions are certain, in order to adjust his degree of belief accordingly (see DESCARTES, R. §4). If he is correct, very few propositions are certain (for example, 'I exist' and others revealed by the 'light of nature'). In particular, he argued that those based upon experience (for example, 'there is a table before me') are never certain because there is always some legitimate basis for doubt. Other philosophers, for example, G.E. Moore, argued that many propositions based upon experience can be certain (see MOORE, G.E. §3; COMMONSENSISM). The remainder of this entry discusses some of the more influential accounts of propositional certainty.

A contextualist account has been developed by both Moore and Wittgenstein (see CONTEXTUALISM, EPISTEMOLOGICAL). Although the specifics of the views vary, a contextualist account of propositional certainty claims, roughly, that the range of propositions that are fully warranted and beyond doubt or challenge is determined by the presuppositions of the context of discussion. As Aristotle remarked:

> [Some] people demand that a reason shall be given for everything, for they seek a starting point, and they seek to get this by demonstration, while it is obvious from their actions that they have no conviction. But their mistake is what we have stated it to be; they seek a reason for things for which no reason can be given; for the starting point of demonstration is not demonstration.
>
> (Aristotle *Metaphysics*: 1010a 8–14)

Wittgenstein (1949–51) and Moore (1959) have argued that the proposition, 'here's one hand', for example, is certain in most contexts. It might not be certain if, for example, we knew that there are several fake hands resting on a table and we also know that there is a hole in the table through which people sometimes put their hands just to fool us. But in the normal circumstances, it is certain. (It should be noted that Wittgenstein and Moore differ about whether knowledge entails certainty. Wittgenstein held that 'knowledge' and 'certainty' belong to different categories because knowing requires justification whereas a proposition is certain only if it does not require a justification.)

Contextualism can be challenged because it blurs the distinction between psychological and propositional certainty, for the latter is characterized in a way that makes it roughly equivalent to group psychological certainty, thus eschewing the notion of epistemic warrant. For example, in Salem, Massachusetts in the 1600s, it would have been propositionally certain (given a contextualist account) that there were witches. But, it could be argued that although such a proposition was taken for granted, it was never fully warranted and was always subject to legitimate doubt. More generally, it could be claimed that propositions that are certain might not be, and typically are not, equivalent to the ones that are taken for granted.

A modification of the contextualist view, suggested by David Lewis (1979), can be employed to mitigate this objection. Let us grant the basic contextualist point that in order for genuine doubt to occur, there must be some propositions that 'stand fast' (to use Wittgenstein's expression) which can be employed to remove or substantiate the doubt. None the less, what stands fast at the beginning of a discussion (even if held with oneself) could become doubtful as the discussion progresses. Grounds for doubt can increase as knowledge expands or simply because new possibilities are envisaged. Suppose, for example, that one of the participants asks 'Are you really sure that is a hand? After all, does not the certainty of that proposition depend upon the belief that your senses are generally reliable? Can you be certain of that?' Now, of course, the other participants can refuse to rise to the philosophical bait. But, by introducing the general question of the reliability of the senses, one of the participants has exposed one of the contextual presuppositions, thus making it eligible for doubt. Lewis's modification of the contextualist view provides a partial response to the objection because the worthiness of belief in a proposition that once stood fast can be addressed by participants by altering the context.

Nevertheless, the fundamental challenge to contextualism remains unanswered: Why should the contextual presuppositions, even the shifting ones as described by Lewis, determine which propositions are actually worthy of belief? Indeed, are any propositions worthy of belief, even those which play the quasi-foundational role ascribed to contextual presuppositions? That is the Cartesian question.

2 Propositional certainty

Some philosophers (for example, Hegel and Dewey) reject the Cartesian question, holding that it incorrectly presupposes an 'independently existing' reality whose nature is the object of inquiry (see IDEALISM; PRAGMATISM). Dewey wrote:

> Knowing is, for philosophical theory, a case of specially directed activity instead of something isolated from practice. The quest for certainty by means of exact possession in mind of immutable reality is exchanged for the search for security by means of active control of the changing course of events. Intelligence in operation, another name for method, becomes the thing most worth winning.
>
> (Dewey [1929] 1960: 204)

Other philosophers would argue that although *some* properties of *some* objects are affected by our interactions with them during the process of inquiry, it does not follow that *all* the properties of the object are affected or even that *all* objects have some properties that are affected by inquiry. To use an example cited by Dewey, suppose that the location or velocity of an atomic particle is altered when it is observed. None the less, its property of being within 100 miles of the earth's surface would not be affected. In addition, presumably, some very large objects can be observed without affecting them at all (stars that are millions of light years away, for example). Indeed, many properties (for example, being a conifer) or objects (for example, trees) appear to be mind-independent. But more importantly, even if all objects and properties are somehow mind-dependent, the Cartesian question appears to remain: Is any claim about objects and properties, whatever they are, fully warranted and not subject to any legitimate doubt?

In order to answer this question, it is important to note as did Peter Unger (1975) that in the relevant sense, 'certainty' (like, for example, 'perfect') is an absolute term. It does not come in degrees. Although we do say that some propositions are more certain than others, it has been pointed out that such expressions are equivalent to the claim that some propositions are more nearly certain than others. Certainty, like perfection, does not come in degrees although we can approach it by degrees.

Roderick Chisholm's (1977) account of certainty captures this absolute sense. He suggests that a proposition is certain just in case it is warranted and there is no proposition more warranted than it. None the less, although that account incorporates an important necessary condition of propositional certainty, it ignores two crucial features – namely that a proposition is certain only if it is fully warranted and it is beyond legitimate doubt. A proposition could satisfy the proposed condition and still be only partially warranted and subject to doubt, as long as no propositions are more warranted or subject to less doubt.

So, let us focus on what makes a proposition fully warranted and not the least bit doubtful. The first condition is rather easily defined. Given any account of warrant (for example, either an internalist or reliabilist account), we can say that a proposition is fully warranted just in case it is warranted and there is no incompatible proposition that is at all warranted (see JUSTIFICATION, EPISTEMIC §3).

Immunity to legitimate doubt is more difficult to characterize. None the less, two senses of doubt seem relevant here. We can say that a proposition, *p*, is *subjectively doubtful* for *S* if and only if there is some proposition which *S* is not warranted in denying which is such that it lowers the warrant of *p* (even the slightest degree). This is roughly equivalent to Descartes' account of certainty employed in the *Meditations* and is subjective because whether a proposition is immune to this type of doubt depends upon *S*'s particular prior beliefs. They could be false. Indeed, a proposition which is subjectively certain could be false. So, subjective immunity from doubt cannot be the entire story.

A second sense of propositional certainty is relevant: objective certainty. We can say that a proposition is *objectively doubtful* for *S* if and only if there is some *true* proposition which if added to *S*'s beliefs lowers the warrant of *p* (even to the slightest degree). This is objective because *S*'s warrant for *p* will be diminished if some of that warrant depends upon a false belief of *S* or if there is some true proposition that counts against *p* for which *S* has no explanation (based only on true propositions within the corpus of warranted beliefs). Finally, if *p* were false, its negation added to *S*'s beliefs would undercut the warrant for *p*. Hence, propositions immune to objective doubt are true.

It is now possible to suggest an account of propositional certainty. We can say that a proposition, *p*, is certain for *S* if and only if it is fully warranted and is neither subjectively nor objectively doubtful. Philosophers do not agree about either the range of such propositions or about whether knowledge entails certainty. Rationalists, typically, hold that certainty is a necessary condition of knowledge and that (only) a priori propositions are certain. Some – but only some – empiricists will hold that certainty is not a necessary condition of knowledge. Finally, many sceptics have held that knowledge entails certainty, and since no proposition is beyond legitimate doubt, no proposition is known.

See also: A POSTERIORI; A PRIORI; DOUBT; EMPIRICISM; INTERNALISM AND EXTERNALISM IN EPISTEMOLOGY; KNOWLEDGE CONCEPT OF; RATIONAL BELIEFS; RATIONALISM; SCEPTICISM

References and further reading

* Aristotle (3rd century BC) *Metaphysics*, trans. W.D. Ross, in Richard McKeon (ed.) *The Basic Works of Aristotle*, New York: Random House, 1941. (The account of foundational propositions is also developed in *Posterior Analytics*, translated by G.R.G. Mure in the McKeon collection.)

* Chisholm, R. (1966) *Theory of Knowledge*, Englewood Cliffs, NJ: Prentice-Hall, 2nd edn, 1977. (General introduction to contemporary epistemology. Later editions are equally good introductions.)

* Descartes, R. (1641) *Meditations on First Philosophy*, in E.S. Haldane and G.R.T. Ross (eds) *The Philosophical Works of Descartes*, vol. 1, Mineola, NY: Dover Publications, 1955. (Standard English edition of one of the starting points of contemporary epistemology.)

* Dewey, J. (1929) *The Quest for Certainty*, New York: Putnam, 1960. (Contains a defence of a pragmatic epistemology.)

Firth, R. (1976) 'The anatomy of certainty', *Philosophical Review* 76: 3–27. (Treatment of various accounts of what is termed 'objective' certainty in this entry.)

Klein, P. (1981) *Certainty*, Minneapolis, MN: University of Minnesota Press. (Development of the nature of objective propositional certainty discussed in this entry.)

—— (1986) 'Immune belief systems', *Philosophical Topics* 14 (1): 259–80. (Development of the nature of subjective certainty discussed in this entry.)

* Lewis, D. (1979) 'Scorekeeping in a language game', *Journal of Philosophical Logic* 8: 339–59. (Development of the modified contextualist account discussed in this entry.)

Markie, P. (1992) 'The cogito and its importance', in J. Cottingham (ed.) *The Cambridge Companion to Descartes*, Cambridge: Cambridge University Press. (Account of Descartes' discussion of the conditions of what was termed 'subjective certainty' in this entry.)

* Moore, G.E. (1959) *Philosophical Papers*, New York: Macmillan. (Contains several papers developing Moore's account of certainty and his defence of common sense.)

* Unger, P. (1975) *Ignorance: A Case for Scepticism*, Oxford: Oxford University Press. (Defence of scepticism based upon an analysis of psychological certainty, not propositional certainty, as is the more typical basis for scepticism.)

* Wittgenstein, L. (1949–51) *On Certainty*, Oxford: Blackwell, 1969. (The development of the contextualist account of certainty discussed in this entry.)

PETER KLEIN

CERTEAU, MICHEL DE (1925–86)

Michel de Certeau, a French philosopher trained in history and ethnography, was a peripatetic teacher in Europe, South America and North America. His thought has inflected four areas of philosophy. He studied how mysticism informs late-medieval epistemology and social practice. With the advent of the Scientific Revolution, the affinities the mystic shares with nature and the cosmos become, like religion itself, repressed or concealed. An adjunct discipline, heterology, thus constitutes an anthropology of alterity, studying the 'other' and the destiny of religion since the sixteenth century. De Certeau opens the hidden agendas that make representations of the past a function of social pressures, so that sometime histories are rearticulated in mirrored or subversive forms. This subversion makes accessible a general philosophy of invention that works within and against the strategic policies of official institutions. De Certeau's writings also belong to activism, the history of ideological structures, psychoanalysis, and post-1968 theories of writing (écriture) as defined by Deleuze, Derrida, Foucault and Lyotard.

For de Certeau, mystics are those strange beings who claim to have left the material and sensory world and encountered an unnameable being, or an unearthly experience, but have returned with visible marks – scars or mutilations – that attest to the truth of what they say. They eagerly tell of their visions to others. They are creatures of passage who invent places in which they disappear, and whose words convey to their listeners the supraterrestrial qualities of the world and language. They liberate those whom they meet, inspiring them to cognizance of areas that cannot be controlled by rational or symbolic means. Mystics are frequently female, often rootless, sometimes grimy and occasionally without formal education. The mystic belongs to all religions but appears on the European horizon at the time major edifices of belief slowly crumble under the pressure of science, oceanic travel, schematic reason (Ramus, Descartes) and pre-capitalist economy.

When the substantive *mysticism* is coined in the early seventeenth century, the behaviour and philosophy become the subject of scientific inquiry, thus relegating a formerly accepted, but almost unnameable condition to the margins of civilization. Mystical activity returns, however, in subjective areas of everyday life, has roots in politics (for example, ecology and feminism), and is a principal concern in Freudian and Lacanian psychoanalysis. Included in

de Certeau's studies are close readings of Jean-Joseph Surin, Nicolas of Cusa, Hieronymus Bosch and the wily, nomadic Freud of *Moses and Monotheism*.

De Certeau's contributions to the philosophy of history importantly concern the silencing of mystical language since the French classical age. Since the advent of print culture official historians have laboured to produce monuments reflecting the structures of power that sustain them. For de Certeau, the 'historiographical operation' constitutes the laws governing the creation of these pantheons of 'truth'. But the conceptual/social order of this historiography is also contested – by those (for example, Machiavelli) who tamper with its codes or who make visible its ideology.

Heterology, the second of de Certeau's philosophical inflections, is his name for the 'science' of otherness or alterity. Its topic is whatever resists being named, classified, or organized in a body of knowledge, often what generates or inspires it. This resistant other takes the form of those nocturnal musings, beings, impressions, dreams or epiphanic flashes that fascinate but cause consternation to the diurnal being. Frequently, the *other* who irrupts into the familiar world of sameness is the Indian (such as the Tupinamba in Jean de Léry's *Voyage to Brazil* of 1578), the wanderer (the footprint of Friday on Crusoe's island, or Panurge who disrupts the princely realm of Rabelais's *Pantagruel*), or the savage, the peasant isolated from urban development (those whom the Abbé Grégoire encounters in rural France in his 1791 study of the provinces). They can wear the garb of a literary double (Jekyll's Hyde) but may also resemble the *intercessor* (as Gilles Deleuze and Félix Guattari define the term in *What is Philosophy?*). The welcome extended to and cultivation of the other are vital, argues de Certeau, for the grounding displacement and deracination that mobilize inquiry, belief, affect and knowledge.

Invention, from its Latin sense (*invenire*, to happen upon, to choose) describes a vital area of de Certeau's philosophy of everyday life. Since capitalism has mapped out the world and, through mass media, colonized the subjective imagination, every individual becomes responsible for creating practices that do not serve the economy, but that give definition to autonomous and unofficial ways of living. Invention entails conceiving of *other* spaces in which the individual subject cannot be plotted, located or, as have been most third world natives, bartered, bled or tortured. Based in part on Lévi-Strauss's concept of *bricolage*, which is the indigenous 'science of concrete activity' that fashions new meanings from fragments of myth and quotidian objects, the art of invention includes practices of walking (a performative 'space act' analogous to J.L. Austin's 'speech act'; see SPEECH ACTS), of making different things from a gamut of inherited forms (cooking, playing), and of opening different mental spaces (via thinking or reading) in areas that otherwise lie under strict ideological control. In this way the anonymous subject, no matter what their origins, can philosophize and act so as to live within but also to change the tenor of inherited, often limiting, social conditions.

De Certeau's non-philosophical writings are no less varied than his philosophy. They range from dense and erudite historical studies (including critical editions) to collective and polemical tracts aimed at changing educational philosophy and the tradition of subjectivity. He ranks among the most important figures who pragmatized critical theory and the human sciences in France after the intellectual revolution of May 1968.

See also: ALTERITY AND IDENTITY, POSTMODERN THEORIES OF; DELEUZE, G.; DERRIDA, J.; FOUCAULT, M.; LACAN, J.; LYOTARD, J.F.; MYSTICISM, HISTORY OF; MYSTICISM, NATURE OF

List of works

Certeau, M. de with Julia, D. and Revel, J. (1975) *Une politique de la langue: la révolution française et les patois*, Paris: Gallimard. (Groundbreaking study that blends history, linguistics and ethnography of the 1789 era.)

Certeau, M. de (1980) *La Possession de Loudun*, Paris: Gallimard; trans. M. Smith, *The Possession of Loudun*, Chicago, IL: University of Chicago Press, 1997. (Studies how possessed women in witchcraft trials invented discursive space through language-play.)

Certeau, M. de with Giard, L. and Mayol, P. (1980) *L'Invention du quotidien*, vol. 2, *Habiter, cuisiner*, Paris: Union Générale d'Éditions; trans. T. Tomasik *The Practice of Everyday Life*, vol. 2, *Living, Cooking*, Minneapolis, MN: University of Minnesota Press, 1998. (Mobilizes the concept of everyday practice by analyzing space as it is lived in urban Paris and elsewhere.)

Certeau, M. de (1982a) *L'Écriture de l'histoire*, Paris: Gallimard; trans. with introduction T. Conley, *The Writing of History*, New York: Columbia University Press, 1988 and 1992. (Most synthetic of de Certeau's work in general; includes chapter on possessed women of Loudun.)

—— (1982b) *La Fable mystique*, Paris: Gallimard; trans .M. Smith *The Mystic Fable*, Chicago, IL: University of Chicago Press, 1993. (Comprehensive study of mysticism and heterology.)

—— (1987a) *Histoire et psychanalyse entre science et fiction*, ed. L. Giard, Paris: Gallimard; trans B. Massumi, introduction W. Godzich, *Heterologies*, Minneapolis, MN: University of Minnesota Press, 1986. (English translation contains an essay on South American Indian political federations.)

—— (1987b) *La Faiblesse de croire*, ed. L. Giard, Paris: Éditions du Seuil. (Argues that unstressed belief has political and ecological potential in an age of multinational capitalism.)

—— (1990) *L'Invention du quotidien*, vol. 1, *Arts de faire*, ed. L. Giard, Paris: Gallimard; trans. S. Rendall, *The Practice of Everyday Life*, Berkeley, CA: University of California Press, 1984. (First introduction to the philosophy in English; the translation is of the first edition, published in 1980.)

—— (1993 and 1994) *La Culture au pluriel*, and *La Prise de parole*, ed. L. Giard, Paris: Éditions du Seuil; trans. with introduction T. Conley, *Political Writings*, Minneapolis, MN: University of Minnesota Press, 1996. (Mobilizes the philosophy in terms of issues surrounding politics and cultural reform after 1968.)

References and further reading

Ahearne, J. (1995) *Michel de Certeau*, London: Polity Press. (Terse and informative study for anglophone readers.)

Conley, T. and Terdiman, R. (eds) (1992) 'Michel de Certeau', *Diacritics* 22 (1). (Includes translation of 'Mysticism' by de Certeau and articles by French and American scholars.)

Giard, L. (ed.) (1987) *Michel de Certeau*, Paris: Centre Georges Pompidou. (Incisive essays by Derrida, Rabinow, Terdiman, *et al.*)

—— (ed.) (1988) *Le Voyage mystique: Michel de Certeau*, Paris: Éditions du Cerf. (Contains complete bibliography of writings compiled by L. Giard and essays by students and followers.)

—— (ed.) (1991) *Histoire, mystique, et politique: Michel de Certeau*, Grenoble: Jérôme Millon. (Offers perspective on work by French philosophers and historians.)

TOM CONLEY

CETERIS PARIBUS LAWS

see CAUSATION; IDEALIZATIONS; LAWS, NATURAL

CHAADAEV, PËTR IAKOVLEVICH (1794–1856)

Pëtr Chaadaev was the first Russian thinker for whom his own country became a philosophical problem. His works initiated the powerful Russian tradition of reflecting on Russia's whence and whither: that is to say, the meaning of Russian history, the character of Russian national identity, and the possible, or necessary, paths of Russian historical development in the future. However, Chaadaev's answer to these questions was mostly negative: he defined Russia not by what it was, but by what it was not.

A paradoxical feature of Chaadaev's position was that his general philosophical views did not apply to his native country. He was a convinced Westernizer, identifying Western development with universal human history, but Russia was in his view the opposite of the West, an exception to the general rules. His general social philosophy, deeply influenced by the French theocratic traditionalists, was inherently conservative, stressing the importance of supra-individual unity and of continuous historical traditions; in contrast with this, his philosophy of Russian history defined Russia as a country without unity and without history, thus lacking the basic conditions for a genuine conservatism. This view provoked a strong reaction among Russian Romantic conservatives: they accepted some aspects of Chaadaev's conservative critique of atomistic individualism but tried to refute his pessimistic view of Russia, by arguing that, in fact, not Russia but the West represented atomistic disintegration and incapacity for organic development.

1 Metaphysics and philosophy of man
2 Philosophy of Russian history
3 Ecumenical ideas

1 Metaphysics and philosophy of man

In his youth Chaadaev, a promising Russian officer and a friend of Pushkin, was a Freemason (from 1814) and a sympathizer of the Decembrist movement, named after the ill-fated military uprising which took place in December 1825. During his travels in the West in 1822–6 he intensely studied the counter-Enlightenment trends in European thought and, as a result, underwent a spiritual crisis which confirmed him in his leanings towards Roman Catholicism. The failure of the Decembrist uprising he saw as an additional proof of the bankruptcy of the rationalistic belief in progress through political change. On his return to Russia in 1826 he withdrew into almost complete seclusion and devoted himself

entirely to the task of formulating his philosophical view of the world. He fulfilled this task in the eight 'Lettres Philosophiques' (Philosophical Letters) (written in French between 1828 and 1831), of which only the first, devoted to Russia, was published during his lifetime, in the journal *Teleskop* (Telescope) in 1836.

Following the French traditionalists – de Maistre, de Bonald and the early Lamennais – Chaadaev attacked in his Letters the moral and intellectual autonomy of the individual. The natural order of things, he argued, is based upon dependence and submissiveness. Moral law, like truth, is not something autonomous, as Kant claimed, but a force outside us; individual reason separates man from the universe and makes true understanding impossible; hence it should be subordinated to the universal reason of humankind. Being is hierarchically stratified: at the summit is the transcendent God; his emanation is the 'world consciousness', that is, supra-individual social consciousness, living in tradition and developing with it; below is the empirical consciousness of isolated individuals; on the lowest rung is pre-human nature. In this way Chaadaev combined the traditional theistic conception of a transcendent God with pantheistic emphasis on God's immanent presence in the world. This was in tune with Christian Neoplatonism (which reached Chaadaev through the esoteric tradition in Freemasonry, as well as through Schelling, whom he personally met in 1825) and with the panentheistic religious ideas of the German Romantics.

Chaadaev's conception of the 'social sphere' and supra-individual social consciousness provides the key to his philosophy of history. Knowledge, he argued, is a form of collective consciousness. Without society, that is, the supra-individual sphere which allows traditions to be handed down, human beings would never have emerged from the animal state. Also in religious experience the social sphere is of decisive importance: through it alone can the individual come to know God and to become a vessel for the divine truth. Therefore the surest way to God leads not through individualistic self-perfection or solitary asceticism but through strict observance of traditional norms and active participation in social life. The highest aim of man is 'the annihilation of his personal being and the substitution for it of a perfectly social or impersonal being'. The foundation of the inner unity of society is religion, whose necessary guardian is the institutionalized Church. Ecclesiastical mediation between man and God is indispensable for salvation, since efforts to achieve unmediated, individualized contact with God weaken the discipline of the soul and bring about social disintegration.

In his philosophy of history Chaadaev attempted to

reconcile the notion of a transcendent Providence with an immanentist approach, looking for the inner patterns that govern events and transform history into a meaningful process. The instruments of history are great, chosen individuals and historical nations, that is to say, nations which constitute supra-individual 'moral personalities'. The mission of historical nations is to rise towards universality; hence they cannot lock themselves up in nationalistic particularisms and superstitions. Since the time of Christ the substance of history and the focal point of 'world consciousness' is Christianity, and the purest, most 'historical' and 'social', manifestation of Christianity is Catholicism. The Renaissance and Reformation had destroyed the splendid unity of medieval Christendom and pushed humanity towards increasing social atomization and neo-paganism. Now, however, this great spiritual crisis was drawing to a close. The process of corruption had reached its lowest point but Christianity had not collapsed; on the contrary, there were signs of its imminent regeneration and progressive transformation.

In defining this transformation Chaadaev followed the favourite idea of the post-Revolutionary French thinkers, both traditionalist (like de Maistre), and utopian socialist (like the Saint-Simonians): the idea of a renewed, socialized Christianity which was to bring about the 'socialization of societies', the extension of Christianity from private life to public sphere, that is the effective 'ethicization' of social and political relations. Christianity, he felt, was becoming social, and humankind was entering the last phase of the establishment of the Kingdom of God on earth.

2 Philosophy of Russian history

In his views on Russian history Chaadaev drew a sharp contrast between Russia and the West, as well as between Russia and 'historical nations' in general.

According to Chaadaev, Russia had no history. He meant by this that Russian history was merely a collection of meaningless events, lacking the continuity of tradition and the unity of purpose. This was so because of Russia's separation from the universal Church, the Church of Rome. True, the Russians were Christians, but so were the Ethiopians; in both cases religious affiliation did not ensure membership of the Christian civilization. The European nations were marching through the centuries hand-in-hand, had fought together to free the Holy Sepulchre and prayed to God in one and the same language. The history of the West was sacred history, the Kingdom of God had to some extent already materialized in Europe. Russia, however, was a country forgotten by Providence, having no supraindividual consciousness and

moral personality of its own, not covered by the 'universal education of humankind'. Therefore the Russians had no guidelines and support in their past, lived without fixed customs and rules for anything, knew nothing about the ideas of duty, justice, rights and order. The 'Western syllogism' – logic and methodical thinking – was completely alien to their undisciplined minds. Small wonder that they grew but did not mature, that 'not a single useful thought had sprouted in the sterile soil' of their country.

The impression evoked by the publication of the 'Philosophical Letter' was enormous and almost completely negative. The most important exception was Aleksandr HERZEN who appreciated the 'Letter' as a powerful protest against the hopelessness of Russian life under autocracy. The Tsar Nicholas I decided that Chaadaev should be treated as a madman and subjected to compulsory supervision by physicians and the police. This explains the title of Chaadaev's text 'Apologie d'un fou' (The Apology of a Madman) (1837), in which he tried to make his views more palatable for Russian patriots. He admitted that his interpretation of Russian history was too severe and drew from his main thesis a different conclusion. The 'lack of history', he now argued, might also be a kind of privilege: without the burden of the past Russia would meet no obstacles in learning from the experience of Europe and in grounding its future on purely rational foundations.

In this way the Russian admirer of tradition formulated the view that being a blank sheet of paper made Russia a country of the future, destined to solve the grave social problems which had arisen in the West. This view, thanks to Herzen, was later to serve the purposes of Russian revolutionaries.

It is hard to say to what extent Chaadaev identified with his new view on Russia. It is likely that he really did admit the possibility of a great future for Russia, but was far from holding this view unreservedly. He could hardly be enthusiastic about the image of a civilization deprived of a religious basis and founded on purely scientific and anti-historical principles. Hence he tried to combine his new ideas with his old dream about Russia's inclusion into the universal history. This implied the removal of the main cause of Russia's 'lack of history' – its separation from the Church of Rome.

3 Ecumenical ideas

Chaadaev's manuscripts, especially his 'Fragments et pensées diverses 1828–1830' (Fragments and Thoughts 1828–1830), show that his overall view on the Orthodox Church was in fact far from the one-sidedly negative picture presented in 'Philosophical Letters'.

The Western Church, Chaadaev argued, was called to make history. It was ambitious, intolerant and did not despise the goods of this world, but this was the reverse side of its sublime mission in universal history. The mission of the Eastern Church was quite different, unhistorical, as it were. It developed the contemplative and ascetic aspect of Christianity, and hence all forms of secular ambition were forbidden to it as incompatible with its inner essence. In this way Chaadaev arrived at the conception of the Roman Catholic and the Orthodox Church as the two poles of the absolute truth. On the one side there was 'activism' and 'sociality', on the other, monastic concentration of spirit, contemplation and the evangelical purity of Christ's teaching. But there can be no doubt that Chaadaev wanted the Kingdom of God to be realized in history and saw the Church as its historical incarnation. It followed from this that the Catholic Church was historically much more important, although the Orthodox Church (unlike the Protestant churches) was also a legitimate and valuable part of the Christian heritage. Hence the need of reconciliation and union between the two Churches: not a simple conversion of the Orthodox Christians to Catholicism but a union on equal rights, with the due recognition of the separate traditions of both Churches.

Very similar, if not identical, views were developed later (partially under Chaadaev's influence) by Vladimir SOLOV'ËV. It is justified to see Chaadaev as an important precursor of Solov'ëv's philosophical ecumenism.

In the history of Russian thought Chaadaev's name was firmly associated with pro-Catholic sympathies. Even Herzen saw him as representing 'neo-Catholicism', or 'revolutionary Catholicism'. The first edition of Chaadaev's works was published by the Russian Jesuit, Father Ivan Gagarin, whose conversion to Catholicism was caused by Chaadaev's 'Philosophical Letter' on Russia. Small wonder that Chaadaev's heritage could not be fully appropriated by Russian religious thinkers; nor, of course, by the programmatically secularist ideologies of the 'progressive intelligentsia'. In Soviet Russia attempts were made to present Chaadaev as a 'progressive' thinker, but publishing his collected works, let alone honestly discussing his ideas, was impossible. In post-communist Russia Chaadaev's works have been published in full and, for the first time, widely distributed. None the less, his place in the rich tradition of Russian religious philosophy and in the history of Russia's national self-identification has not become sufficiently clarified.

See also: SLAVOPHILISM

List of works

Chaadaev, P.Ia. (1914) *Sochineniia i pis'ma* (Works and Letters), ed. M. Gershenzon, 2 vols, Moscow: A.I. Mamontov.

—— (1969) *The Major Works of Peter Chaadaev*, ed. and trans. R. McNally, Notre Dame, IL: University of Notre Dame Press. (Includes commentary and bibliographical notes.)

—— (1991) *Polnoe sobranie sochinenii i izbrannye pis'ma* (Collected Works and Selected Letters), ed. Z.A. Kamenskii, 2 vols, Moscow: Nauka. (In Russian and French, with bibliographical references.)

—— (1828–30) 'Fragments et pensées diverses 1828–1830' (Fragments and Thoughts 1828–1830), in [P. Tchaadaev], *Oeuvres inédites ou rares* (Unpublished or Rare Works), ed. R. McNally, F. Rouleau and R. Tempest, Meudon: Bibliothéque Slave, 1990. (This collection includes bibliographical references and indexes.)

—— (1828–31) 'Lettres Philosophiques' (Philosophical Letters), trans. M.-B. Zeldin, in *Philosophical Letters and Apology of a Madman*, Knoxville, TN: University of Tennessee Press, 1969. (Only the first of these letters was published in Chaadaev's lifetime, in *Teleskop*.)

—— (1837) 'Apologie d'un fou' (Apology of a Madman), trans. M.-B. Zeldin in *Philosophical Letters and Apology of a Madman*, Knoxville, TN: University of Tennessee Press, 1969. (Chaadaev's presentation of his views in a form more palatable to his contemporaries.)

—— [P. Tschaadaïeff] (1862) *Oeuvres choisies* (Selected Works), Paris-Leipzig: A Franck. (The first edition of Chaadaev's works, published by Father I. Gagarin.)

References and further reading

Gershenzon, M. (1908) *P.Ia. Chaadaev. Zhizn' i myshlenie* (P.Ia. Chaadaev, Life and Thought), St Petersburg: M.M. Stasiulevich.

Kamenskii, Z.A. (1991) '*Paradoksy Chaadaeva*', introduction to Chaadaev, *Polnoe sobranie sochinenii* (1991) (see above).

Koyré, A. (1950) *Études sur l'histoire de la pensée philosophique en Russie* (Studies in the History of Russian Philosophical Thought), Paris: J. Vrin.

McNally, R.T. (1971) *Chaadaev and His Friends*, Tallahassee, FL: Diplomatic Press.

Quénet, Ch. (1931) *Tchaadaev et les Lettres philoso-*

phiques (Chaadaev and the Philosophical Letters), Paris: H. Champion.

Walicki, A. (1975) 'The Paradox of Chaadaev', in *The Slavophile Controversy*, Oxford: Clarendon Press; 2nd edn, Notre Dame, IL: University of Notre Dame Press, 1989.

ANDRZEJ WALICKI

CHALCIDIUS *see* Calcidius

CHALDAEAN ORACLES

The Chaldaean Oracles were a collection of revelatory verses purportedly compiled in the second century AD. Along with the Orphic texts, Neoplatonists regarded them as divine words. When the Oracles appear in philosophical works, they lend support to select cosmological, metaphysical or psychological propositions which have already been formulated.

According to Neoplatonists, the *Chaldaika logia*, or Chaldaean Oracles, originated with a certain Julianus, a late second-century AD ex-soldier in the eastern Roman army, and with his son, also named Julianus, who was their author. The father, surnamed 'Chaldaean' and a 'philosopher', may have collected handed-down material which he passed on to his son, a 'theurgist', who was 'divinely inspired' to write new oracles. This origin, some seventy years before Porphyry, by whom they are first mentioned, is by no means certain. However, it may be corroborated by similar material in NUMENIUS, an important Neo-Pythagorean. Numenius flourished at that time in Apamea (Syria), where later Plotinus' theurgic-minded follower Amelius went to teach, as did Iamblichus, who was a major proponent of theurgy and the Oracles. Both Porphyry and Iamblichus had Syrian parentage. Moreover, in a unique fragment preserved by Proclus (Commentary on Plato's Parmenides, 594–5), 'the true theologians' used Syriac terms. Yet the question remains, how much was handed down and how much made up in a culture where Greek and Oriental had mixed since the third century BC and religions had absorbed Platonic ideas.

'Chaldaean' was often an honorific title for long-established wisdom, owing to the ancient astronomy of the Babylonians. In classical, and especially biblical, Greek, *logia theou* are God's own sayings (for example, the 'Hebrew *logia*' given to Moses, and those revealed in the New Testament). Neoplatonists,

such as the emperor Julian, Proclus and Damascius, referred to the Chaldaean sayings as 'of the gods' or 'God-given' (*theoparadota logia*; an expression later used by John Damascene for revelation in the Christian Church). For comparison, Iamblichus also spoke of 'Pythagoras' *logia*. Thus the *logia* are statements directly attributed to a supreme authority.

Of the various fragments, some cite distinctive entities particularly, the 'wry necked' (*iynges*) birds, as divine powers. Others reflect general Babylonian and Mithraic themes (fire as creative and divine). Many rely on Platonism: 'cyclo-spiral' time (from Plato's *Timaeus*, where the planets have compound orbits and are cosmic clocks); divinity is 'once' (*hapax*) and 'twice transcendent' (*dis epekeina*) (based on the Good in Plato's *Republic*). However, two cosmological themes seem to be Chaldaean and important. First, there is a hierarchy of divinity, of which the highest, called 'Father', is an 'abyss'. Neoplatonists tried to associate this highest divinity with their transcendent One, or with Being or essence, which is opaque to ordinary conception but intuitively intelligible. Second, the universe is divided into 'material', 'aetherial' and 'empyrean' 'zones', of which the 'aetherial' indicated the semi-materiality of vital soul, and the 'empyrean' the transcendent world. However, the Neoplatonists associated the 'material' with earth and physical matter; the 'aetherial' with the heavens populated by stars and planets; and the 'empyrean' (fiery) with the incorporeal domain. Later, when amalgamated with Aristotelian and Christian themes, the whole scheme flourished in graphic representations of the universe through the Middle Ages to the seventeenth century.

The Chaldaean Oracles are referred to by all the later Neoplatonists down to Simplicius (sixth century), and by some Christians. The Oracles also emerge in Byzantine sources; for example, Psellus (eleventh century) and Plethon (fifteenth century), who collected them in a manuscript titled 'Sayings of the Zoroastrian Magi'. Finally, they were transmitted to Renaissance Italy, where they were used mainly by PATRIZI DA CHERSO, FICINO and PICO DELLA MIRANDOLA for lending support to their own anti-Aristotelain arguments.

See also: IAMBLICHUS; NEOPLATONISM §1; PORPHYRY §2; PROCLUS §5

References and further reading

* *Chaldean Oracles* (2nd century? AD) *Oracles Chaldaïques*, ed. E. des Places, Paris: Les Belles Lettres, 1971; trans. R. Majercik, Leiden: Brill, 1989. (The former is parallel Greek text and French

translation with notes, and includes the treatises by Proclus and Psellus; the latter is parallel Greek with English translation of fragments and commentary, but without the tracts from Proclus and Psellus.)

Lewy, H. (1978) *Chaldaean Oracles and Theurgy*, ed. M. Tardieu, Paris: Études Augustiniennes, 2nd edn. (The seminal work on the Oracles, with updated evaluations, notes and articles.)

* Proclus (5th century AD) *On the Chaldaean Philosophy*, ed. E. des Places, Paris: Les Belles Lettres, 1971; trans. T. M. Johnson 1907; repr. in S. Neuville (ed.) *Iamblichus: Exhortation to Philosophy*, Grand Rapids: Phanes Press, 1988.

* —— (5th century AD) *Commentary on Plato's Parmenides*, trans. J.M. Dillon and G.R. Morrow, Princeton, NJ: Princeton University Press, 1987; repr. 1992. (English translation, including some Oracles and Orphic associations; see especially 593–5 for the fragment at 60 Klibansky, which is not cited in the current edition of the Chaldean Oracles.)

Saffrey, H.D. (1981) 'Les néoplatoniciens et les Oracles Chaldaïques' (The Neoplatonists and the Chaldaean Oracles), *Revue des Études Augustiniennes* 26: 209– 25. (Important study on Neoplatonism, theurgy and the origin of the Oracles.)

Suda (10th century AD) *Suidae Lexicon*, ed. E. Adler, Leibzig: Teubner, 1931; repr. Stuttgart, 1967. (Greek text of the dictionary, where many ancient reports survive; the Chaldaean Julians can be found at Iota numbers 433 and 434.)

LUCAS SIORVANES

CHANG TSAI *see* ZHANG ZAI

CHANGE

Change in general may be defined as the variation of properties (whether of things or of regions of space) over time. But this definition is incomplete in a number of respects. The reference to properties and time raises two important questions. The first concerns whether we need to specify further the kinds of properties which are involved in change. If we define change in an object as temporal variation of its properties we are faced with the problem that some properties of an object may alter without there being a consequent change in the object itself. The second question concerns the passage of time: does temporal variation constitute change only in

virtue of some feature of time itself, namely the fact (or putative fact) that time passes? Some philosophers have wished to reject the notion of time's passage. Are they thereby committed to a picture of the world as unchanging?

1 Cambridge change
2 Change and the passage of time

1 Cambridge change

In *The Principles of Mathematics* (1903), Russell defines change as follows:

> Change is the difference, in respect of truth or falsehood, between a proposition concerning an entity and the time T, and a proposition concerning the same entity and the time T', provided that these propositions differ only by the fact that T occurs in the one where T' occurs in the other.
>
> (Russell 1903: §442)

Geach (1969) has dubbed this kind of change 'Cambridge change', a term now familiar in the metaphysical vocabulary. Note that Russell defines change *simpliciter*, not specifically change in an entity, even though the definition is restricted to propositions about entities. But if we took it as a criterion for change in an entity, then we would have to allow that, for example, a cup of tea changes, not only when it cools down but when someone forms the intention to drink it. This second change passes Russell's test, since 'At T someone intends to drink the tea' is false, and 'At T' someone intends to drink the tea' is true. Yet, intuitively, someone's merely forming the intention to drink the tea is not a genuine change in the tea itself. We need something stronger than Russell's 'Cambridge criterion', as we might call it, if we wish to analyse genuine change in objects. Two possibilities will be briefly sketched here.

An object 'Cambridge-changes' if merely its relations to other objects change, as when for example it becomes smaller than another object simply because the latter has grown in size. If we can distinguish an object's *intrinsic* properties from its *extrinsic* properties, then we can define genuine change in an object as the variation over time of its intrinsic properties. We might attempt to characterize 'intrinsicness' as follows: *F* is an intrinsic property of *x* if and only if *x*'s being *F* does not logically depend upon the existence or properties of any other object. On this account, being an aunt, being ten yards from the top of Mount Etna and being read about do not count as intrinsic properties, whereas being ten yards in diameter and made of lead do count as intrinsic. However, this characterization is not without its difficulties. Change of shape is, surely, a genuine change in an object, but the shape of a thing does not count as intrinsic on the above criterion since having shape is, arguably, not logically independent of the existence of the containing space.

An alternative means of strengthening the Cambridge criterion employs the notion of causality. A genuine change in an object must, on this account, involve causal consequences contiguous to the object. This is not true of, for example, becoming an aunt or becoming famous – the effects of such 'changes' need not be near the object in question. Instead of defining real change in terms of intrinsic properties, we could define the intrinsic properties of an object as those whose alteration *must* involve contiguous effects. On this account, shape turns out, as we would expect, to be an intrinsic property of an object. But we cannot simply define real change in x as alteration which *must* have effects contiguous to x. The 'must' in italics is surely weaker than a logical must: there is no contradiction in supposing a change in mass, for example, to have no contiguous effects. But then if 'must' means instead 'must according to physical laws' then some mere Cambridge changes would pass the causal criterion. If x undergoes the Cambridge change of becoming less massive than some y as a result of y's increase in mass, then this must (in the physical sense) have gravitational consequences, however small, in x's vicinity. However, the chain of events leading to these effects in x's vicinity must have started in y's vicinity, so we could modify the account as follows: a real change in an object is such that, if it has effects, these must (in the physical sense) be mediated by effects contiguous to that object.

2   Change and the passage of time

In developing his famous argument for the unreality of time, McTaggart (1927) quotes, and proceeds to criticize, Russell's definition of change (see MCTAG-GART, J. §2). McTaggart's first criticism is, in effect, that real change must involve, not difference in truth-value between *different* propositions, but alteration in truth-value of the *same* proposition. Suppose, to use McTaggart's example, a poker is hot on Monday and cold thereafter. Now it is true at all times that the poker is hot on that particular Monday and cold thereafter, so these facts about the poker do not change. The only real change consists of the fact that the poker's being hot is first a present state and then a past state. In other words, real change implies the passage of time.

Why should we accept this objection of McTaggart's? Let us describe the event of the poker's cooling down, that is its being hot at T and cold at T', as a first-order change. Then McTaggart seems to require a second-order change: the change in the event as it shifts from future to present to past. So it remains to be seen why someone who denies the existence of second-order change, but accepts first-order change, should be thought to be denying change altogether.

McTaggart, however, has another objection. We can construct a spatial analogue of Russell's Cambridge change: there are two spatial points, S and S', such that the proposition 'At S [for example, London] the Greenwich meridian is within the UK' is true, while the proposition 'At S' [for example, Paris] the Greenwich meridian is within the UK' is false. Now this purely spatial variation is clearly not change, but why not? It will not do to say that Russell's definition of change involves times and so excludes purely spatial variation, for this leaves unanswered the deeper question of why time, not space, is the dimension of change. A number of writers who deny that time passes have addressed themselves to this question. One account has it that time is the dimension of causality (since causes must precede their effects) and real change involves causally connected states.

A third argument, not considered by McTaggart, may be advanced for the view that real change in objects must involve the passage of time. It is a commonplace that, for an object to be said to undergo change, it must be the same object which first has one property and then loses that property (see CONTINUANTS §1). However, if we deny that time passes, then we must also deny that things can 'move through' time in order to have different properties at different times. Or, if this kind of talk is too metaphorical, we may put the point in the following terms. In order to have a property (or at least an intrinsic property) at a time, an object must exist at that time. Since change takes place over time, an object cannot change unless it exists at more than one time. But now suppose that there is no passage of time and that every proposition about an object is, if true, true for all times. Then, if x is F at T and Not-F at T', then it is true for all times both that x exists at T and that it exists at T'. Is this not a contradiction? An influential solution to this problem is to say that objects are extended in time in the same way as they are extended in space: that is, they have different (temporal) parts at different times, just as your feet are located in different regions of space. But this introduces another problem, for neither the temporal parts of a thing, nor the collection of temporal parts which constitutes the temporally extended object, can be said to change in the sense we have defined it. A temporal part is confined to an unextended instant and so cannot have different (intrinsic) properties at different times; and the properties that can be attributed to the collection as a whole, such as occupying threescore years and ten, do not vary over time (see CONTINUANTS §2).

An adequate account of change, therefore, needs to address these questions: is there such a thing as McTaggart's second-order change in the temporal properties of events? If there is not, must we think of things as having temporal parts? If we must, can we reconcile this with the apparently obvious fact that things change?

See also: EVENTS; PROCESSES

References and further reading

* Geach, P.(1969) *God and the Soul*, London: Routledge & Kegan Paul. (Referred to in §1 above.)

Helm, P. (1975) 'Are "Cambridge" changes non-events?', *Analysis* 35 (4): 140–4. (Argues that mere Cambridge changes are not genuine events, and that therefore they cannot be the causes of other events, and are not examples of uncaused events.)

Le Poidevin, R. (1991) *Change, Cause and Contradiction*, London: Macmillan. (Argues against the passage of time, defends temporal part theory and attempts to show how this can be reconciled with the existence of change. Quite difficult.)

* McTaggart, J.M.E. (1927) *The Nature of Existence*, vol. 2, ed. C.D. Broad, Cambridge: Cambridge University Press. (See pgs 9–22 both for the material discussed in §2 above and for the famous proof of the unreality of time. Not an easy read, but does not presuppose a great deal of philosophical knowledge.)

Mellor, D.H. (1981) *Real Time*, Cambridge: Cambridge University Press. (Provides a causal criterion of genuine change, and argues that the denial of time's flow need not commit one to temporal parts and so can avoid the difficulties such parts raise for change. Lucid but quite demanding.)

* Russell, B. (1903) *The Principles of Mathematics*, London: Allen & Unwin. (Quoted in §1 above.)

ROBIN LE POIDEVIN

CHAOS THEORY

Chaos theory is the name given to the scientific investigation of mathematically simple systems that exhibit complex and unpredictable behaviour. Since the 1970s these systems have been used to model experimental situations ranging from the early stages of fluid turbulence to the fluctuations of brain wave activity. This complex behaviour does not arise as a result of the interaction of numerous sub-systems or from intrinsically probabilistic equations. Instead, chaotic behaviour involves the rapid growth of any inaccuracy. The slightest vagueness in specifying the initial state of such a system makes long-term predictions impossible, yielding behaviour that is effectively random. The existence of such behaviour raises questions about the extent to which predictability and determinism apply in the physical world. Chaos theory addresses the questions of how such behaviour arises and how it changes as the system is modified. Its new analytical techniques invite a reconsideration of scientific methodology.

1 **Defining chaos theory**
2 **Predictability**
3 **Determinism**
4 **Chaos and scientific understanding**
5 **Applications outside the natural sciences**

1 Defining chaos theory

Although there is controversy over the proper scientific definition of chaotic behaviour, chaos theory may be defined as the qualitative study of unstable aperiodic behaviour in deterministic nonlinear dynamical systems.

A dynamical system is a mathematical entity that usually results from the attempt to model a situation in the natural world (see MODELS). It has two components: a procedure for producing a mathematical description of the instantaneous state of a physical system, and a rule (the evolution equations) for transforming the current state description into a description for some other time. For some dynamical systems, the evolution equations yield a simple formula that allows the direct calculation of future states of the system.

The dynamical systems of interest for chaos theory contain nonlinear terms in the equations. These terms, such as x^2 or $\sin(x)$ or $5xy$, usually render an exact solution impossible. Researchers into chaotic phenomena instead seek a qualitative account of the system's behaviour, investigating the general character of its long-term behaviour, rather than seeking to arrive at numerical predictions of its exact future state (this special sense in which chaos theory is 'qualitative' must not be understood as contrasting with 'mathematical'). For example, a qualitative study of a planetary system would seek to discover what circumstances will lead to elliptical orbits as opposed to hyperbolic ones. This approach is called 'dynamical systems theory' (or sometimes simply 'dynamics') and began with the work of Henri POINCARÉ. Chaos theory is a specialized application of dynamical systems theory that typically treats such questions as: what characteristics will all solutions of this system ultimately exhibit? and, how does this system change from exhibiting one kind of behaviour to another kind?

Dynamical systems are usually studied in terms of trajectories in state space (sometimes called 'phase space'), a mathematically constructed abstract space where each dimension corresponds to one variable of the system. Every point in state space represents a full description of the system, and the evolution of the system manifests itself as the tracing out of a path, or trajectory, in state space. It is often possible to study the geometric features of these trajectories, even in actual experimental systems, without explicit knowledge of the solutions they represent. This allows one to characterize trajectories according to their topological features, and the investigation of how those features change as the parameters of the dynamical system are altered.

While qualitative questions can be asked about almost any dynamical system, chaos theory focuses on certain forms of behaviour – behaviour which is unstable and aperiodic. The form of instability known as sensitive dependence on initial conditions is a distinguishing characteristic of chaotic behaviour. A dynamical system that exhibits sensitive dependence on initial conditions will produce markedly different trajectories for two initial states that are initially very close together. In fact, given any specification of initial conditions, there is another set of initial conditions arbitrarily close to it that will diverge from it by some finite distance, given enough time. In most chaotic behaviour, sensitive dependence on initial conditions results from the exponential growth of any small initial difference. It is this instability that makes chaotic behaviour unpredictable (see §2).

Aperiodic behaviour occurs when no variable describing a property of the system undergoes a regular repetition of values. Furthermore, chaos is an appropriate label only when such behaviour occurs in a bounded system. An explosion thus does not qualify as chaotic behaviour. And systems studied by chaos theory bear the label 'deterministic' because their equations make no explicit reference to chance mechanisms (see §3).

For a dissipative dynamical system, characterized by the gradual loss of energy, trajectories in state space will asymptotically approach a shape known as an 'attractor' when transient effects have died away. Until the advent of chaos theory, only three types of attractor were generally recognized: the fixed point (corresponding to eventual equilibrium), the limit cycle (corresponding to periodic behaviour), and the torus (corresponding to behaviour with multiple periods in rationally incommensurable ratios). Chaotic behaviour in dissipative systems requires the introduction of a fourth variety: the so-called 'strange attractor'.

A crucial geometric feature of strange attractors is their combination of stretching and folding. The action of such a system takes nearby points and 'stretches' them apart in a certain direction, thus creating the exponential divergence responsible for unpredictability. But the system also acts to 'fold together' points that are at some distance, bringing about convergence of trajectories in a different direction, and hence asymptotic attraction.

The stretching and folding of chaotic systems gives strange attractors the distinguishing characteristic of a nonintegral, or fractal, dimension. These attractors often appear as stacks of two-dimensional sheets packed in a self-similar structure that seems to intrude into three-dimensional space. The dimension of such an object – more than two but less than three – describes its scaling properties, giving a quantitative indication of the stretching and folding at work in the dynamical system. Another quantitative characterization of chaotic systems is given by the Lyapunov exponents, which measure the degree of sensitivity to initial conditions and thus the degree of unpredictability.

It should be noted that strange attractors appear only in dissipative systems. For systems where energy is conserved, there is no convergence onto an attractor. Instead, trajectories are confined to a surface of constant energy in state space. Chaotic behaviour can occur in such systems, but the trajectories will fill the allowed energy surface (which may itself display an extremely complicated structure).

The examination of the transition to chaotic behaviour has yielded important results for understanding the way complex behaviour arises. For example, period-doubling behaviour is found in a wide variety of nonlinear systems, and this type of transition has certain universal features. This universality allows us to make exact predictions about a system's period-doubling behaviour as soon as we have verified that certain qualitative conditions hold.

Sensitive dependence on initial conditions, strange attractors and other elements of chaos theory have been reported in experimental systems in the physical and biological sciences. Some of these examples of chaotic behaviour have been convincingly documented in laboratory settings, while some of the examples of chaos outside the laboratory are the subject of lively debate.

2 Predictability

Moderately accurate initial conditions will always allow us to predict the chaotic behaviour of a system for some short time into the future, but since the vagueness in our initial conditions grows exponentially with time, we can see that for some chaotic systems, a useful prediction would require initial conditions to be specified with more accuracy than is possible. Inaccuracy can be due to equipment error, ineliminable perturbations from outside influences, round-off error in the representation of real numbers, or even the inherent indeterminacy of the quantity being measured.

Some may contend that so long as the prediction task for a chaotic system requires only some finite degree of accuracy, it is incorrect to say that such accuracy is impossible to achieve.

Since chaos theory, unlike special relativity or quantum mechanics, introduces no new fundamental postulates about the physical world, it provides no new physical theory that rules out the possibility of such predictions. Yet these same systems may nevertheless be unpredictable *in principle* because our inability to make such calculations in the longer term is not due to some constraint we could overcome. The very finitude of human resources implies that it is impossible to obtain the accuracy necessary for predictions.

The limitation posed by chaotic systems presents a challenge to the methodological assumption that a small amount of vagueness in measurements will lead to only a small amount of vagueness in predictions. The standard technique of perturbation analysis treats a difficult case as a version of a predictable system plus some small 'perturbation' that complicates the situation but keeps it mathematically tractable. Sensitive dependence guarantees that such approximative techniques will be worthless, thus calling into question some of the metaphysical beliefs that underwrite their general applicability. One such belief is the conviction that systems governed by simple rules must behave simply.

3 Determinism

Scientists and philosophers use the term 'determinism' in several senses (see DETERMINISM AND INDETERMINISM §1). By one criterion, a system is deterministic if the way it changes in time can be specified by a set of equations that make no reference to chance. That is, there are no probabilities built into the state description due to an averaging over many indistinguishable substates, and the evolution equations do not involve probabilistic branching. Thus,

the systems treated by chaos theory are deterministic by definition.

Another criterion consists in the uniqueness of a system's evolution: if two systems are identical in physical properties at one time, they must remain identical at all other times. That is, the complete instantaneous description of a deterministic system 'fixes' the past and future with no alternatives.

A third notion of determinism is that a system is predictable in principle by an all-powerful intelligence or computational scheme, given complete information of instantaneous conditions and the complete set of physical laws. Since measurements and calculations cannot be made with unlimited accuracy, a chaotic system will be unpredictable even though it satisfies other requirements for determinism. In other words, we may not be able to tell *which* unique trajectory a system is following, but that does not mean such trajectories do not exist.

On one interpretation, the randomness and apparent indeterminism of chaotic behaviour are merely artifacts of our epistemic limitations. Another interpretation would treat unique trajectories as inadmissible idealizations, arguing against uniqueness of evolution in chaotic behaviour. This instrumentalist approach argues that there is no point in insisting that the future is fixed, given the present, if that future cannot be predicted.

A third approach would draw on the implications of quantum mechanics to show that unique evolution encounters difficulty due to the workings of chaotic dynamics on intrinsically indeterminate quantities. Such an approach would require an account of how to combine the Newtonian formulations of nonlinear dynamics with the mathematical formalism of quantum mechanics – the difficult task of making sense of 'quantum chaos'.

4 Chaos and scientific understanding

One of the apparent paradoxes of chaos theory is that it represents a scientific study of unpredictable systems that actually has significant predictive power. Chaos theory provides an understanding of how predictable large-scale or long-term patterns appear in behaviour which is nonetheless unpredictable in detail. It may seem odd to assert that chaos theory has 'great predictive power', but such claims refer not to an ability to predict the exact value of some property of a system, but to an ability to foresee and understand changes in the overall behaviour of that system. The crucial point here is the distinction between specific *quantitative* predictions, which are typically impossible for chaotic systems, and *qualita-*

tive predictions, which are at the heart of dynamical systems theory.

The fruitfulness of chaos theory militates against the methodological assumption that it is always appropriate to seek to understand the behaviour of a system by trying to determine the equations governing the interactions of its parts (see REDUCTION, PROBLEMS OF). For most nonlinear dynamical systems, such a reductionist strategy does not help us understand how the chaotic behaviour sets in, or what kind of attractor characterizes it, or how the system will respond to changes in parameters. Understanding this behaviour requires the use of the new mathematical techniques of nonlinear dynamics. While chaos theory argues against the universal applicability of the method of reductionism, it provides no examples of 'holistic' properties which could serve as counter examples to metaphysical doctrines of reductionism, such as physicalism.

Chaos theory shows us the mechanisms responsible for unpredictable behaviour, but these mechanisms are best characterized as geometrical rather than causal. Systems with very different underlying causal substrata are grouped together in order to study their qualitative behaviour. Chaos theory does not need to reveal the causal process at work, and it would be impossible in principle to trace out the workings of the actual causal mechanism in a chaotic system. To do this would require calculations using the evolution equations of the system.

According to some accounts, science furnishes understanding by widening the scope of events that happen out of necessity and not contingency – by revealing laws of nature and subsuming phenomena under them (see EXPLANATION §2). While chaos theory establishes powerful generalizations, its practitioners do not portray their work as discovering new laws of nature. For instance, there is no set of necessary and sufficient conditions that would allow us to foresee which type of transition to chaotic behaviour a system will follow. Chaos theory emphasizes finding patterns and connections, while jettisoning the requirement that the patterns must yield necessity in a detailed and deterministic sense. Some may contend that this search for patterns actually constitutes striving to discover new laws governing qualitative features of systems.

Perhaps chaos theory does not provide us with any genuine understanding at all. After all, it does not introduce any fundamental revisions in our laws of nature. Some might argue that it merely introduces stop-gap measures for data analysis in systems with intractable equations. Perhaps it is only a source of new observations or empirical generalizations. But nonlinear dynamics does require a wholesale revision

of notions about the applicability of classical models, and provides powerful new analytic techniques. It should not be disparaged on the grounds that fundamental theoretical structures are left unchanged.

5 Applications outside the natural sciences

Chaos theory has attracted attention from outside the natural sciences. In the social sciences, the techniques developed for analysis of nonlinear systems have been applied to economic data, for instance. Such techniques can determine the extent to which random fluctuations in a chosen variable can be modelled with simple deterministic mechanisms.

Sensitive dependence on initial conditions has also served as a metaphor for the precarious swings of human history. Metaphorical interpretations of chaos theory have also appeared in natural theology and literary theory. Other areas where chaos theory may have philosophical implications are: the foundations of statistical mechanics, the problem of freedom of the will, and the role of the cultural context of science.

See also: RANDOMNESS

References and further reading

Batterman, R.W. (1991) 'Chaos, Quantization, and the Correspondence Principle', *Synthèse* 89: 189–227. (A useful discussion of some of the issues surrounding 'quantum chaos'.)

Bergé, P., Pomeau, Y. and Vidal, C. (1984) *Order Within Chaos*, trans. L. Tuckerman, Paris: Wiley & Sons. (Useful guide to chaos in the physical sciences.)

Devaney, R. (1986) *An Introduction to Chaotic Dynamical Systems*, Menlo Park, CA: Benjamin-Cummins Publishing. (A standard presentation of the mathematics of chaos at the introductory level.)

Dyke, C. (1990) 'Strange Attraction, Curious Liason: Clio Meets Chaos', *Philosophical Forum* 21: 369–92. (Examines the implications of chaos theory for history and the social sciences.)

Earman, J. (1986) *A Primer on Determinism*, Dordrecht: Reidel. (A comprehensive examination of philosophical issues about scientific determinism. Includes a technical discussion of chaos.)

Ford, J. (1989) 'What is Chaos, That We Should be Mindful of It?', in P. Davies (ed.) *The New Physics*, Cambridge: Cambridge University Press, 348–72. (Presents a number of arguments and speculations regarding predictability and determinism as they relate to chaos theory.)

Hao, B.-L. (ed.) (1984) *Chaos*, Singapore: World

Publishing Company. (A useful collection of historically important scientific papers on chaos.)

Hobbs, J. (1991) 'Chaos and Indeterminism', *Canadian Journal of Philosophy* 21: 141–64. (Presents an argument on the relevance of chaos theory to issues of determinism.)

Kellert, S.H. (1993) *In the Wake of Chaos*, Chicago, IL: University of Chicago Press. (Discusses the philosophical implications of chaos theory, especially regarding predictability, determinism, scientific understanding and social context.)

Smith, P. (1991) 'The Butterfly Effect', *Proceedings of the Aristotelian Society* 91: 247–67. (Presents an argument on the implications of chaos theory for scientific prediction.)

STEPHEN H. KELLERT

CHARITY

Within at least some branches of Christianity, the term 'charity' has been used to mean the love mandated by Jesus. In recent theological writings, however, there has been a tendency to replace it with the Greek word agapē. *There has been some disagreement in the twentieth century concerning the precise nature and functioning of Christian love, a major catalyst for debate having been Anders Nygren's book* Agape and Eros *(1930–6). Numerous scholars have complained that charity does not have a high profile nowadays and have noted that, in common parlance, the word usually has the meaning of benevolence or beneficence. Some attempts have been made to place greater emphasis on Christian love and relationships within Christian ethics. Of some interest in this regard is the notion of an ethic of care, which is not confined to Christian circles but has been the subject of some debate in recent times.*

1   Christian love
2   An ethic of care

1   Christian love

In much Christian literature, perhaps most especially in Roman Catholic theological writings, the word 'charity' has been used to denote the love for God and neighbour commanded by Jesus (John 15: 12) and extolled by St Paul (1 Corinthians 13). In the writings of Aquinas and others, charity (in Latin *caritas*) is also described as the greatest of the theological virtues (see THEOLOGICAL VIRTUES). The more generic term 'love', which is commonly used in the context of erotic relationships and friendship, has been said by many

authors to be too imprecise to convey the distinctiveness of Christian love (see LOVE §2). 'Charity' too, however, is not devoid of ambiguity. In fact, it is most commonly used nowadays to indicate benevolence, beneficence, philanthropy or an organization dedicated to philanthropic pursuits (see HELP AND BENEFICENCE). Some writers have made use of the expression 'charity-love', but, as Leandro Rossi has pointed out (1976), this term, in addition to being too complex and divorced from what is normal, might serve only to combine the ambiguities. The most suitable word, he concludes, is *agape*. This Greek word is, of course, widely used in the New Testament. Moreover, it would seem to be the preferred term nowadays in theological circles – including Roman Catholic ones. Indeed, Gene Outka goes so far as to say that, in current usage, *agape* 'is almost uniformly the referent for any alleged distinctiveness in Christian love' (1978: 7).

A mere change of word, however, does not suffice to eliminate all disputes about Christian love. Writing in the 1930s, Anders Nygren claimed that the classical Catholic idea of *caritas*, which stemmed largely from the writings of Augustine, has little to do with specifically Christian love. This is so, he maintains, because, in the Catholic notion, the primitive Christian *agape* motif is combined with the *eros* motif. *Eros* here means the human desire for union with God. *Agape*, on the other hand, is the distinguishing mark of Christianity. Christian fellowship with God depends entirely upon God's love (*agape*). On the human side, there is no way that leads to God. There is only a way for God to come to humans, and that is *agape*. In other words, there is simply no connection between *agape* and *eros*. They are totally incompatible. He goes on to say that Christians have nothing of their own. The love they show to others is the love that God has infused into them (Romans 5: 5).

The renowned Protestant scholar Karl Barth (1967) also saw the need to distinguish *eros* and *agape*. He went on to say, however, that the kind of relationship in which only God was at work and humans were mere channels of divine action could not be described as a covenant relationship, and yet, according to Scripture, that is the true relationship between them (see BARTH, K.). The initiative in this relationship is wholly and exclusively on the part of God, but that initiative aims at a correspondingly free human act, not the reaction of a puppet. The Roman Catholic moral theologian Bernard Häring (1979), on the other hand, takes the view that all human love can be redeemed. When, in response to God's *agape*, believers commit themselves to God, he says, all their prior dispositions, including *eros* and friendship, are gradually transformed, purified and raised to a higher level.

There has been some complaint in recent times that Christian love – whatever we wish to call it and whatever its relationship to *eros* may be – does not figure highly enough in Christian ethics. Referring specifically to Roman Catholic works, and writing in the 1950s, Gérard Gilleman noted that manuals of moral theology had law rather than love as their dominant theme. He therefore sought to establish 'a method of exposition in which charity will play the role of a vital principle, just as it does in the message of Christ and in Christian life' (1959: xxxvi). More recently, some Roman Catholic moral theologians have laid more emphasis than had previously been apparent in their discipline upon the distinction between personal goodness and the rightness of acts. Personal goodness exists when someone is truly loving (charitable). Mere rightness of acts does not necessarily indicate personal goodness. One could perform an ethically right act for a variety of motives, not all of them loving.

Within Protestantism, attempts to place greater emphasis on Christian love in Christian ethics can be found among some situation ethicists (see SITUATION ETHICS). One of the best known is Joseph Fletcher, who holds that principles and rules can be enlightening, but never the deciding factor. That status can only be given to love. In a given situation, one has to decide what is the loving thing to do. Numerous writers have lamented the fact, already noted, that the word 'charity' is now used chiefly to denote benevolence rather than Christian love. It could therefore seem surprising that Fletcher should describe Christian love as precisely benevolence. Having noted, however, that such words as 'benevolence' and 'goodwill' have taken on a tepid meaning, Fletcher goes on to say that 'Agapē goes out to our neighbors, not for our own sakes nor for theirs, really, but for God's' (1966: 105).

Whatever one makes of this contention or of Fletcher's situation ethics in general, the fact remains that, in recent times, the word charity has been used most often to refer to benevolence in a sense that is not specifically theological, or to beneficence. One can hardly claim, moreover, that the reason is purely linguistic – other senses of 'charity' having been taken over, so to speak, by *agape*. Outside the confines of theological circles, the Greek word is seldom encountered.

2   An ethic of care

Moreover, it is claimed by many that, beyond the confines of theological circles, there has been very little emphasis in recent times upon the demands of charity in ethics. Even discussions of philanthropic endeavours such as those aimed at the relief of poverty, it is pointed out, are discussed habitually in terms of justice. Given this state of affairs, recent discussion about an ethic of care has been particularly interesting (see FEMINIST ETHICS §1). The debate began with Carol Gilligan's book *In a Different Voice* (1982). Gilligan had noted that developmental psychology had been based largely on a study of men's lives. Lawrence Kohlberg's theory of moral development, moreover, was built on research that involved no females at all. His six stages of development in moral judgment through which he says one should pass in order to achieve maturity in moral reasoning are founded empirically on a study of eighty-four boys whose development he followed for over twenty years. Gilligan noted that groups not included in the original sample rarely reached the higher stages. This was particularly true of women, whose judgments, on the whole, seemed to exemplify Kohlberg's third stage. At that stage goodness is seen in terms of helping and pleasing other people, and morality is conceived in interpersonal terms. At the 'higher' stage four, 'relationships are', in Gilligan's words, 'subordinated to rules', while rules are, in turn, subordinated to universal principles of justice at stages five and six (1982: 18). Kohlberg's notion of maturity derives from a study of men's lives and, says Gilligan, 'reflects the importance of individuation in their development'. If, however, developmental constructs are derived from a study of women's lives, a conception of morality as concerned with care emerges. Moral development is then seen as centred around responsibility and relationships, whereas, when morality is seen in terms of fairness, moral development is tied to the understanding of rights and rules. Gilligan has noted, however, that the care perspective is not confined to women (see MORAL DEVELOPMENT).

An ethic of care does not necessarily involve the specifically Christian concept of charity or *agape*, but, no doubt, many would be of the opinion that it could, if it were adopted in Christian circles. Whether such charity is involved or not, however, it would seem that both philosophical ethics and specifically Christian ethics might benefit from further debate about Gilligan's basic idea. Interestingly, as John R. Donahue noted (1977), the biblical notion of justice could be described in terms of faithfulness to the demands of relationships.

See also: FAITH; HOPE; THEOLOGICAL VIRTUES

References and further reading

* Barth, K. (1967) *Church Dogmatics*, vol. 4, *The Doctrine of Reconciliation*, Edinburgh: T. & T. Clark, part II, 727–840. (A detailed exposition of Barth's ideas on Christian Love.)
* Donahue, J.R. (1977) 'Biblical Perspectives on Justice', in J.C. Haughey (ed.) *The Faith that Does Justice: Examining the Christian Sources for Social Change*, New York: Paulist Press, 68–112. (An analysis of the concept of justice in the Bible.)
* Fletcher, J. (1966) *Situation Ethics: The New Morality*, London: SCM Press. (A basic work on situation ethics seeing only love as always good.)
* Gilleman, G. (1959) *The Primacy of Charity in Moral Theology*, Westminster, MD: The Newman Press. (An attempt to centre morality in charity.)
* Gilligan, C. (1982) *In a Different Voice: Psychological Theory and Women's Development*, Cambridge, MA: Harvard University Press. (The book which is at the heart of the debate regarding an ethic of care.)
* Häring, B. (1979) *Free and Faithful in Christ*, vol. 2, *The Truth Will Set You Free*, Slough: St Paul Publications, 419–91. (A Roman Catholic view of Christian love.)
  Keenan, J.F. (1992) *Goodness and Rightness in Thomas Aquinas's Summa theologiae*, Washington, DC: Georgetown University Press. (A scholarly investigation of the goodness/rightness distinction, including reference to the role of charity in the distinction.)
  Larrabee, M.J. (ed.) (1993) *An Ethic of Care: Feminist and Interdisciplinary Perspectives*, London: Routledge. (A collection of contributions to the debate on an ethic of care by various authors, with particular attention being given to matters concerning moral philosophy, psychological aspects and cultural aspects.)
* Nygren, A. (1930–6) *Agape and Eros*, London: Society for Promoting Christian Knowledge. (A long and very detailed study of the meaning of Christian love. The author also sets out to show the major changes in meaning that have taken place in the course of history.)
* Outka, G. (1978) *Agape: An Ethical Analysis*, New Haven, CT and London: Yale University Press. (An examination of modern writings on *agape*, including those by Anders Nygren, M.C. D'Arcy, Gérard Gilleman, Reinhold Niebuhr, Paul Ramsey and Karl Barth, special attention being given to the work of the last-mentioned.)
* Rossi, L. (1976) 'Carità', in L. Rossi and A. Valsechi (eds) *Dizionario enciclopedico di teologia morale*, Rome: Edizioni Paoline, 89. (An analysis of Christian love.)

BERNARD HOOSE

CHARITY, PRINCIPLE OF

The principle of charity governs the interpretation of the beliefs and utterances of others. It urges charitable interpretation, meaning interpretation that maximizes the truth or rationality of what others think and say. Some formulations of the principle concern primarily rationality, recommending attributions of rational belief or assertion. Others concern primarily truth, recommending attributions of true belief or assertion. Versions of the principle differ in strength. The weakest urge charity as one consideration among many. The strongest hold that interpretation is impossible without the assumption of rationality or truth.

The principle has been put to various philosophical uses. Students are typically instructed to follow the principle when interpreting passages and formulating the arguments they contain. The principle also plays a role in philosophy of mind and language and in epistemology. Philosophers have argued that the principle of charity plays an essential role in characterizing the nature of belief and intentionality, with some philosophers contending that beliefs must be mostly true. A version of the principle has even served as a key premise in a widely discussed argument against epistemological scepticism.

1   **Versions of the principle of charity**
2   **Charity and critical thinking**
3   **Charity and philosophy of mind**
4   **Charity, philosophy of language and epistemology**

1   Versions of the principle of charity

The principle of charity is typically taken to be a principle about how to interpret the words and thoughts of others, favouring interpretations that maximize the accuracy and rationality of their utterances and beliefs. There are a variety of more precise formulations of the principle, emphasizing different aspects. Principles of charity also differ with regard to the strength and source of the commitment to charitable interpretation.

Truth and rationality are two dimensions along which one can urge charity. It can be that a person's situation is such that the most reasonable thing for them to believe happens to be false. If there is a question about how to interpret the person, where the choice is between attributing a reasonable but false belief and a true but unreasonable belief, the various versions of the principle of charity will choose differently.

Principles of charity can also differ in strength. The weakest merely recommend consideration of charitable interpretations, leaving open the possibility that in some circumstances one can properly interpret others in ways that make them irrational or mistaken. Moderate positions demand interpreting others as rational or right except in those rare cases in which there are compelling reasons to do otherwise. Stronger versions hold that it is never appropriate to interpret others as irrational or systematically mistaken. It is possible to regard the commitment to charity as merely a contingent but universal truth about the interpretation of humans by imperfect human interpreters or as an a priori requirement about all interpretation. Some versions of the principle are not primarily directives about how to interpret others but are, instead, principles to the effect that intentional states are by their nature rational or accurate so that interpreting others as irrational or mistaken is necessarily incorrect.

2 Charity and critical thinking

In courses on critical thinking (or argument analysis or informal logic), students learn a method for interpreting and evaluating the arguments and assertions that they read and hear. The principle of charity often plays a central role in the methodology taught in such courses. The version of the principle advanced in this context is typically one of the weaker ones mentioned above, recommending that charitable interpretations be favoured, but acknowledging other considerations as well. Advocates of charity differ over the basis for the principle. Some see it as an ethical matter. On this view, being charitable is part of being fair to those with whom one interacts. An alternative view emphasizes a more epistemological and pragmatic basis for being charitable: being charitable best contributes to one's own pursuit of the truth. Interpreting others in ways that make their words less plausible may make it easy to refute them. But interpreting and reflecting on the most plausible interpretation of their words is apt to increase the interpreter's own understanding of the issues addressed. When there is a more plausible and more insightful interpretation available, there is little point in considering a less plausible interpretation of the assertions or arguments of others.

3 Charity and philosophy of mind

Something resembling the principle of charity plays a key role in Daniel Dennett's influential philosophy of mind. According to DENNETT, when we describe a thing as an intentional system (a thing with propositional attitudes), we must take it to be rational. Dennett's claim is not endorsing any of the weaker theses described above. Rather, his claim is about the possibility of explaining or characterizing irrationality in intentional terms. He says of a purported case of irrationality, 'we must descend from the level of beliefs and desires to some other level of theory to describe' the case, since such cases 'defy description in ordinary terms of belief and desire' (Dennett 1982: 66–7). The claim here is not that we are always rational, but just that we cannot give intentional explanations of seemingly irrational behaviour. On Dennett's view, charity is not just a pragmatic, moral or epistemic principle to help guide interpretation. It is an essential part of intentional interpretation. Dennett argues for this partly by appeal to general considerations about belief and other intentional states, partly by appeal to the difficulty he finds in filling out the details of intentional explanations in cases of alleged irrationality.

4 Charity, philosophy of language and epistemology

The most widely explored use of the principle of charity is in discussions of radical translation. W.V. Quine and Donald Davidson are the most influential defenders of the principle in this setting. Quine discusses cases of radical translation – translation in cases in which the words to be translated are those of people in a foreign and unfamiliar culture. He contends that if we come up with a translation scheme that renders their beliefs and utterances regularly silly or mistaken, we will eventually be driven to question our translation scheme and replace it by one that makes more sense of them. Thus, if a person utters a certain sentence when and only when a rabbit passes by, one is to interpret that sentence to mean something like the true 'That's a rabbit', rather than the false 'That's a duck'. Of course, other things the person says might make the latter interpretation best, but then these other things are interpreted as truths, thereby preserving the truth of most of what the person says (see QUINE, W.V. §9; RADICAL TRANSLATION AND RADICAL INTERPRETATION).

Donald Davidson defends an account similar to Quine's, but he puts it to a surprising use, developing an influential argument against epistemological scepticism (see DAVIDSON, D. §5). Sceptics deny that we have knowledge, either globally or in some particular domain. Davidson appeals to the principle of charity in an argument against global scepticism. According to Davidson, what the principle of charity really requires is that the interpreter construe the subject's words so that the subject's beliefs mostly match the interpreter's. There's no guarantee of truth here; at best there is a guarantee of agreement. This would hardly worry a sceptic, as Davidson is willing to concede. But his argument has a second stage designed to overcome scepticism. He asks that we imagine an omniscient interpreter who believes all and only truths about the world of some subject. The omniscient interpreter is also bound by the principle of charity, and thus must interpret the subject's beliefs so that they largely match the interpreter's own. Since the corresponding beliefs of the omniscient interpreter are all true, the beliefs of the subject must be largely true. Thus, the nature of interpretation rules out the possibility that any interpretable being has beliefs that fail to be largely true. Hence, any scepticism based on the possibility that one's beliefs are mostly false is ruled out.

Quite a few philosophers have found Davidson's argument questionable, though they have differed over its fundamental flaw. Among the criticisms are these:

(1) The appeal to the omniscient interpreter raises a cluster of complex questions about possibility. Davidson surely does not want to rest his argument upon the assumption that there actually is an omniscient interpreter. Rather, his claim is merely that there could be one. Suppose that assumption is granted. Suppose further that in some possible world the omniscient interpreter interprets someone's beliefs. It may follow that, in that world, anyone interpreted must have mostly true beliefs. But nothing follows about the accuracy of anyone's beliefs in the actual world. Hence, nothing contrary to scepticism about actual humans follows.

There are various ways for Davidson to formulate his argument to try to get around this objection, perhaps the most promising being the following. There may be an omniscient interpreter in some other world who has true beliefs about the actual world and who interprets the beliefs of any individual, S, in the actual world. That interpreter is bound by the same rules of interpretation, and thus S's beliefs must largely coincide with the true beliefs of the interpreter. Hence, S has beliefs that are mostly true. Critics of this response may doubt the justifiability of assuming that there is a possible interpreter who is (a) omniscient, (b) capable of interpreting S, and (c) required to make S's beliefs match the interpreter's own beliefs.

(2) Even if we grant Davidson's conclusion that it is

impossible that most of S's beliefs are false, it does not follow that S knows much. From the fact that most of S's beliefs are true, and even from the fact that S knows this, it does not follow that with respect to almost any individual belief that S considers that S knows that it is true. Consider the analogy of a lottery in which most of the tickets will win small prizes. One can know that most tickets are winners without knowing of any particular ticket that it is a winner. Similarly, even if S knows that most of S's beliefs are true, it may be that there are none (other than that one and its consequences) that S knows to be true. Thus, even if sound, Davidson's argument leaves unscathed an extreme sceptical view. Davidson might reply that S's knowledge that S is mostly right provides justifying evidence for each of S's beliefs, thereby making each true belief justified, and thus knowledge. This, however, seems to rely on a remarkably low standard for knowledge-level justification.

(3) Much of the interest in Davidson's argument stems from the fact he attempts to draw such an epistemologically significant conclusion from a fact about the nature of radical interpretation. Thus, much of the criticism has focused on the connection between the principle of charity and scepticism. However, the principle itself is not without critics. Indeed, one may well wonder why Davidson thinks charity is essential for interpretation. Surely, in general interpreters do not always have to make their subject's beliefs largely agree with their own: interpreters will have many beliefs about their own home environment, beliefs remote subjects need not share. What may be more plausibly required is that interpreters attribute to subjects beliefs that the interpreters would hold given the subject's evidence. In other words, perhaps in interpretation one must assume that one's subjects respond to evidence in much the way one does oneself. Even this will seem dubious to many. Why, it could be asked, can one not take a subject to be responding erroneously to evidence? But even if this sort of principle of charity is granted, it is doubtful that the desired anti-sceptical conclusion follows. This is because one can grant that another person is responding properly to evidence but is nevertheless massively deceived. Thus, a brain in a vat, or a victim of the Evil Demon, might respond properly to evidence, but still have consistently false beliefs because that evidence is systematically misleading. Hence, a revised, and perhaps more plausible, version of the principle of charity requires only that interpreted subjects respond properly to evidence. This leaves open the possibility of massive deception and thus does not yield the anti-sceptical result.

(4) Facts about how best to interpret others are in

general logically independent of how those others actually must be. It would therefore be surprising if a requirement that we interpret others so as to make them not globally mistaken could yield the conclusion that they cannot actually be globally mistaken. It is, therefore, noteworthy that in some descriptions of his argument against scepticism, Davidson presents it in a way in which the principle of charity is not fundamentally a principle about how to interpret others but rather a principle about what intentional states must be like. He writes, 'What stands in the way of global skepticism is, in my view, the fact that we must, in the plainest and methodologically most basic cases, take the objects of a belief to be the causes of that belief. And what we, as interpreters, must take them to be is what they in fact are' (Davidson 1983 (1986): 317–18). The idea here is that the content of a belief is determined by the external states that cause it. Thus, for example, the belief that a subject has when undergoing a certain sort of sensory stimulation has as its content the external state regularly causing that sort of stimulation. This is a causal theory of meaning or content. On this view, it is the nature of language and belief that requires that our beliefs and utterances be largely true. This makes charitable interpretation appropriate, but only because independent facts about belief and language imply that uncharitable interpretations are always inaccurate.

Whatever the nature and role of the principle of charity in the version of Davidson's argument just described, the argument is not without its critics. Some dispute the causal theory of meaning upon which it depends. Others contend that even if it is sound, Davidson's argument does not really refute scepticism. They argue that even if it shows that that we know that our beliefs are true, we can still fail to know the content of our beliefs. This is because we cannot tell which external states are systematically causally connected to our beliefs. For example, it is possible that a particular sort of belief is systematically connected either to the presence in one's visual field of a certain kind of object or to a certain sort of computer state in the computer to which one's brain is connected. Davidson's view apparently implies that the content of the belief depends upon which sort of cause it has, and, the critics contend, Davidson has not shown how one can know which sort of cause one's belief has. This seems to leave intact a radical form of scepticism. Whether this objection succeeds depends upon whether there is room within Davidson's view for some sort of privileged access to the contents of one's beliefs.

See also: RATIONAL BELIEFS; SCEPTICISM

References and further reading

Brueckner, A.L. (1986) 'Charity and Skepticism', *Pacific Philosophical Quarterly* 67 (4): 264–8. (Develops the last objection to Davidson's argument mentioned in §4 above.)

—— (1991) 'The Omniscient Interpreter Rides Again', *Analysis* 51 (4): 199–205. (Defends Davidson's argument from objection 1 in §4 above.)

Davidson, D. (1982) 'Empirical Content', *Grazer Philosophische Studien* 16/17: 471–89; repr. in E. LePore (ed.) *Truth and Interpretation: Perspectives on the Philosophy of Donald Davidson*, Oxford: Blackwell, 1986, 320–32. (Includes a version of the anti-sceptical argument discussed in §4 above.)

* —— (1983) 'Coherence Theory of Truth and Knowledge', in D. Henrich (ed.) *Kant oder Hegel?*, Stuttgart: Klett-Cotta; repr. in E. LePore (ed.) *Truth and Interpretation: Perspectives on the Philosophy of Donald Davidson*, Oxford: Blackwell, 1986, 308–19. (Develops the argument discussed above in §4.)

* Dennett, D. (1982) 'Making Sense of Ourselves', in J.I. Biro and R.W. Shahan (eds) *Mind, Brain, and Function: Essays in the Philosophy of Mind*, Norman, OK: University of Oklahoma Press, 63–81. (Discusses the difficulty of attributing irrational beliefs to people.)

Foley, R. and Fumerton, R. (1985) 'Davidson's Theism?', *Philosophical Studies* 48 (1): 83–90. (Develops objection 1 from §4 above.)

Govier, T. (1987) *Problems in Argument Analysis and Evaluation*, Dordrecht: Foris Publications. (Discusses the role of charitable interpretation in critical thinking and argument analysis.)

Klein, P. (1986) 'Radical Interpretation and Global Skepticism', in E. LePore (ed.) *Truth and Interpretation: Perspectives on the Philosophy of Donald Davidson*, Oxford: Blackwell, 1986, 369–86. (Clarifies Davidson's anti-sceptical argument and develops objection 2 in §4 above.)

McGinn, C. (1986) 'Radical Interpretation and Epistemology', in E. LePore (ed.) *Truth and Interpretation: Perspectives on the Philosophy of Donald Davidson*, Oxford: Blackwell, 1986, 356–68. (Develops a version of objection 3 in §4 above.)

Quine, W.V.O. (1960) *Word and Object*, Cambridge, MA: MIT Press. (Most widely discussed statement of Quine's views about radical translation.)

RICHARD FELDMAN

CHARLETON, WALTER
(1620–1707)

The physician Walter Charleton was the first to introduce Epicurean atomism into England in the form advocated in France by Gassendi. Charleton's version of atomism, although largely derivative, was nevertheless influential. Together with his advocacy of a Christian hedonism, it helped to make both atomism in natural philosophy (with its associated mechanistic account of nature) and utilitarian theories in ethics acceptable to such thinkers as Robert Boyle, Isaac Newton, John Locke and others associated with the foundation of the Royal Society, of which Charleton was himself an active early member.

Walter Charleton was a physician who served both Charles I and Charles II, but his interests were always broader than medicine. He entered practice after studying at Magdalen Hall, Oxford, under John Wilkins, also one of the founders of the Royal Society. Charleton's quick rise to fame made him enemies, which in part explains his sad decline to poverty in later years after serving as President of the College of Physicians from 1689–91.

Charleton's major philosophical writings were two books on the philosophy of EPICURUS and two on central religious themes (the absurdity of atheism and the immortality of the soul). But it is important to appreciate that although he clearly saw himself as an exponent of a modified Christian version of the philosophy of Epicurus, in which he substantially followed in the footsteps of GASSENDI, he was also almost equally influenced by the philosophy of DESCARTES. In each of them he found a commitment to mechanism as the basic explanatory concept for an understanding of nature, together with a theism which rejected a materialist account of the mind.

In his *Physiologia Epicuro-Gassendo-Charletoniana: or a Fabrick of Science Natural upon the Hypothesis of Atoms* (1654), Charleton openly follows the radical natural philosophy espoused by Gassendi in considerable detail, even though its full exposition was not available until 1658, after Gassendi's death. The *Physiologia* offers a detailed and comprehensive account of matter and its properties in terms of atoms and motion. Although close to Epicurus, it is much fuller than any of the extant writings. Contrary to the traditional teaching of the Schools, the motion of atoms in the void is argued to be the basic explanation for all the phenomena of nature and of our awareness of those phenomena through sensation. In so doing, Charleton argues for the distinction between primary and secondary qualities, made famous by BOYLE and

LOCKE later in the century, and presents accounts of light, colours, sounds and other phenomena within the atomic model. Charleton makes no claim to absolute certainty – it is the *hypothesis* of atoms that he expounds. But he makes a very good case for the mechanical account of nature from within the new learning associated with BACON, Descartes, Gassendi and even his friend Thomas HOBBES, although he never accepted Hobbes' materialism.

Charleton had made clear his hostility to a full blown-materialism in *The Darknes of Atheism dispelled by the Light of Nature* (1652). A similar position was also presented in the later *Immortality of the Human Soul demonstrated by the Light of Nature* (1657). In these works Charleton follows Descartes rather than Gassendi, not only in his proof of God where he gives (with full acknowledgement) the causal argument offered by Descartes in the third Meditation, but also in a sharp dualism between mind and matter. The soul is a substance perfectly distinct from that of body, he claims, and it is endowed with immortality by the character of its essence. He follows Descartes, too, in holding that the idea of God is innate.

In drawing on Descartes' philosophy Charleton makes it clear that he wishes to distance himself from all those aspects of Epicurus that might be supposed to support atheism. Like Gassendi and Descartes he was keen to make his account of the new philosophy not just compatible with, but actually supportive of a Christian theology. At the same time he was quite sure that standard criticism of Epicurus was far too severe, as he made clear in the Introduction to his edition of Epicurus' moral philosophy, *Epicurus's Morals* (1655). Rather than being, as he was so often depicted, an advocate of impiety, gluttony and drunkenness, Epicurus was, Charleton urged, a great master of temperance, sobriety, continence and fortitude. Charleton is quite prepared not only to admit but to argue that Epicurus was wrong on several fundamentals. His three cardinal errors were his rejection of both the immortality of the soul and the worship of God, and his acceptance of suicide. There were, nevertheless, extenuating circumstances which went some way towards excusing Epicurus these undoubted errors, principally his living in a pagan country before the advent of Christianity. Granted the errors, Charleton, makes clear that he believes Epicurus has much to teach us about happiness and how it may be best obtained.

In all his writings Charleton is careful not to appear dogmatic. Nor was he ever an uncritical supporter of those who influenced him. This is especially true of his later writings. In his *Natural History of the Passions* (1674), for example, Charleton takes Descartes to task both for his bad anatomy (Charleton was an undoubted expert on anatomy) and for his inadequate explanation of the connection between mind and body.

Charleton died in poverty in Nantwich. His major influence was through the *Physiologia*, which introduced many English speakers to atomism, including the young Isaac NEWTON. His other works contributed to that assault on traditional teaching and the adoption of the mechanistic and hedonistic philosophies that came to dominate the eighteenth century.

See also: ATOMISM; HEDONISM

List of works

Charleton, W. (1652) *The Darknes of Atheism dispelled by the Light of Nature*, London. (A defence of theism against Hobbism and other supposedly atheistic philosophies.)
—— (1654) *Physiologia Epicuro-Gassendo-Charletoniana: or a Fabrick of Science Natural upon the Hypothesis of Atoms. Founded by Epicurus, Repaired by Petrus Gassendus, Augmented by Walter Charleton*, London. (Charleton's most important and influential work which argues for an Epicurean atomism, as compatible with traditional Christian doctrine, following Gassendi's interpretation.)
—— (1656) *Epicurus's Morals collected partly out of his owne Greek text in Diogenes Laertius, and partly out of the Rhapsodies of Marcus Antoninus, Plutarch, Cicero, and Seneca*, London. (Argues for the rehabilitation of Epicurus as a moral thinker.)
—— (1657) *The Immortality of the Human Soul demonstrated by the Light of Nature in two dialogues* London. (Rejects Epicurus' materialism but not his atomism.)
—— (1659) *Natural History of Nutrition, Life and Voluntary Motion*, London. (An important attempt to give a mechanistic and mathematically based physiology.)

References and further reading

Kargon, R.H. (1964) 'Walter Charleton, Robert Boyle and the Acceptance of Epicurean Atomism in England', *Isis* 5: 184–92. (Examines Charleton's impact on English matter theory.)
Webster, C. (1967) 'The College of Physicians. "Solomon's House" in Commonwealth England', *Bulletin of the History of Medicine* 61: 393–412. (Highlights scientific innovation in the College of Physicians and Charleton's role in it.)
Rattner Gelbart, N. (1971) 'The Intellectual Devel-

opment of Walter Charleton', *Ambix* 18: 149–68. (Important biographical paper.)
Sharp, L. (1973) 'Walter Charleton's Early Life and Relationship to Natural Philosophy in mid-Seventeenth-Century England', *Annals of Science* 30: 311–43. (Another important paper on Charleton's intellectual biography.)
Osler, M.J. (1979) 'Descartes and Charleton on Nature and God', *Journal of the History of Ideas* 40: 445–56. (Contrasts Descartes' rationalism with Gassendi's and Charleton's empiricism and its implications for their differing understandings of knowledge and of God.)

G.A.J. ROGERS

CHARRON, PIERRE (1541–1603)

Pierre Charron was a French Catholic priest of the late sixteenth century who used Montaigne's sceptical thought, which he presented in didactic form, in order to refute Calvinists, non-Christians, and atheists. He advanced a fideistic defence of religious thought which was based on accepting complete scepticism while appealing to faith alone as the source of religious knowledge. His De la Sagesse *(On Wisdom) (1601) is one of the first significant philosophical works to be written in a modern language. It is also one of the first modern works to set forth a naturalistic moral theory independent of religious considerations, and based primarily on Stoic ideas. Charron's views were extremely popular in the seventeenth century, and they influenced many sceptically inclined thinkers in France and England. His sceptical 'defence' of religion was regarded as insincere by some of the orthodox theologians, but other important religious thinkers defended him.*

1 Life and works
2 Theological thought
3 Sceptical philosophy

1 Life and works

Pierre Charron, philosopher and theologian, was born in Paris, one of twenty-five children. He studied Greek, Latin and philosophy at the Sorbonne, and then, after possibly studying law at Orleans and Bourges, went to the University of Montpellier from which he received the degree of Doctor of Law in 1571. After practising law unsuccessfully for a few years in Paris, he turned to theology and soon became renowned as a preacher and theologian. He was chosen by Queen Marguerite to be her regular preacher, and Henri IV, even before his conversion to Catholicism, often attended his sermons. He then became lecturer in divinity in various cities in the south of France, and canon and official teacher of the church of Bordeaux. Despite his great success he desired to give up worldly activities and to join a cloister, but he was turned away by two orders because of his age (forty-eight at the time). The most important event in Charron's life was his friendship with Michel de MONTAIGNE (though doubt has been cast on its extent). After Montaigne's death in 1592, Charron demonstrated his immense debt to Montaigne by presenting the union of scepticism and Catholicism in his writings.

Charron's first work, *Les Trois Veritez* (The Three Truths) (1594), was an apologetical work of theology which attacked Calvinists in particular. His major philosophical work, *De la Sagesse* (On Wisdom), appeared in 1601, as did his *Discours chrestiens* (Christian Discourses). His final work, *Le Petit Traicté de la sagesse* (Little Treatise on Wisdom), was written in 1603 and published posthumously in 1606. All of his works were very popular, and were often republished during the seventeenth century. *De la Sagesse* was most influential in disseminating sceptical ideas and arguments in the philosophical and theological discussions of the time.

There were several serious efforts to refute, reject and even suppress Charron's sceptical views. He was attacked by the Jesuit, François Garasse, who accused him of providing a breviary for libertines, and by the Protestant medical doctor, Pierre Chanet, among others. He was defended by the *libertins érudits* Guy Patin, Gabriel Naudé, François de La Mothe Le Vayer, and Pierre GASSENDI, as well as by some French leaders of the Counter-Reformation (see LIBERTINS). Pierre Bayle considered Charron a fine exemplar of Christian fideistic thought.

2 Theological thought

In his first work, *Les Trois Veritez*, Charron sought to undermine Calvinism by sceptical means. The three truths which he considered, that God exists, that Christianity presents the correct view of God, and that Catholicism is the true presentation of Christianity, are each supported by attacking the opponents in a negative manner rather than by presenting positive reasons for accepting the truths. Although most of the enormous work is devoted to the third truth, it begins with a brief discourse about knowledge of God, in which a scepticism is developed about the possibility of human beings having knowledge in

this area. Human rational capacities are so restricted and unreliable that it is doubtful that humans can know anything in either the natural or supernatural realms. Charron then joined his sceptical claims about the inadequacy and unreliability of human knowledge to the contention of the negative theologians that God is unknowable because his nature is infinite, and thus surpasses all human attempts to define or delimit it. Hence we cannot rationally know what he is, and as a result, the greatest philosophers and theologians know just as much or just as little about God as do the humblest persons. What we know is only what God is not. So, Charron said, 'the true knowledge of God is perfect ignorance about him'.

Charron's combination of negative theology and scepticism was then used to attack the claim of the atheist who denies that God exists. Such a denial, Charron argued, is presumably the consequence of a definition of God from which absurd or contradictory conclusions are drawn, but any such definition can only be the result of a human attempt to measure divinity by human means, an attempt which has no value, since atheists do not and cannot know what they are talking about.

Finally Charron argued negatively that it is unreasonable not to believe that God exists, and not to believe that Christianity is the correct statement of God and his role, and not to believe that Catholicism is the right form of Christian belief. He claimed that his opponents, especially the Calvinists of the day, argue on the basis of views derived by means of weak and miserable human capacities, and then use these unreliable results to measure divine truths.

3 Sceptical philosophy

Charron's sceptical defence of faith was elaborated in *De la Sagesse* and *Le Petit Traicté de la sagesse*. He claimed that since human beings can only discover truths by means of revelation, morality should be based on following nature except when it is guided by Divine Light. This view was first developed by setting forth Montaigne's scepticism in an organized didactic form. We must begin by knowing ourselves, which involves knowing the limits of what we can in fact know. Charron presents the traditional sceptical doubts about sense knowledge. Do we have the requisite sensory capacities to gain genuine knowledge? Are we able to distinguish illusions and dreams from veridical experiences? And can we ascertain which of our many varied sense experiences actually correspond to some objective state of affairs?

Charron then turned to questions that can be raised about our rational capabilities. He contended that we possess no certain or adequate criterion for distinguishing truth and falsehood. We in fact believe what we do as the result of our passions and of social pressures on us, rather than on the basis of reasons and evidence. We actually function as beasts do, rather than as rational beings. Hence we should accept Montaigne's claim that we possess no genuine principles unless God has revealed them to us. Everything else is just dreams, smoke, or illusion.

In the second book of *De la Sagesse* Charron set forth a discourse on method as a way of avoiding error and discovering truth in the light of the human situation. The Charronian method anticipates that of DESCARTES. First, one should examine each question freely and dispassionately. Next, one should keep prejudice and emotion out of all decisions. After that, one should develop a universality of mind. Finally, one should reject any decisions which are doubtful in even the slightest degree. This sceptical method or method of doubt was, Charron declared, of greater service to religion than any other possible method. If we followed it, we would reject all doubtful opinions until our minds became 'blank, naked and ready' to receive divine revelation on the basis of faith alone. So, Charron insisted, the complete sceptic will never be a heretic, for the sceptic, having no opinions, cannot have the wrong ones. On the other hand, if it pleases God to give the sceptic any information, he will possess true knowledge.

Until the sceptic receives any revelation, he ought to live according to a provisional morality. This is described in the third and final book of *De la Sagesse*, which sets forth Charron's theory of natural morality based on ancient sceptical and Stoic views. Without divine guidance the best one can do is live naturally as a Stoic sage or a noble savage. Here Charron is one of the first modern philosophers to set forth a moral theory independent of religious considerations.

At the time, some readers saw Charron's work as a basic didactic presentation of Pyrrhonian scepticism that challenged traditional philosophical claims to knowledge as well as religious views. By so doing, these readers believed, Charron was preparing the basis for a completely naturalistic view of human nature and conduct. However, Charron averred that *De la Sagesse* contained only part of his theory, namely that which deals with the human situation seen completely apart from divine guidance. When one considers the views in his different works taken as a whole, together with his ecclesiastical career and the religious sentiments that appear in his *Discours chrestiens*, one can find evidence for the case that Charron was a sincere fideist who propounded scepticism as a way of destroying those whom he saw as the enemies of the true faith, while preparing others for salvation by God's actions. Whatever his

true views, Charron greatly influenced the so-called *libertins*, and his ideas, as interpreted by them, provided some of the basis for irreligious naturalism in the Enlightenment.

See also: SCEPTICISM, RENAISSANCE; STOICISM

List of works

Charron, P. (1594–1603) *Oeuvres* (Works), Paris, 1635; repr. Geneva: Slatkine, 1970. (The only edition of Charron's works.)

—— (1594) *Les Trois Veritez* (The Three Truths), in *Oeuvres*, Geneva: Slatkine, 1970. (Uses sceptical arguments to attack Calvinist beliefs.)

—— (1601) *De la Sagesse* (On Wisdom), ed. A. Duval, Paris: Chassériau, 1824, 3 vols; repr. Geneva: Slatkine, 1968. (An important source of sceptical ideas for Renaissance theologians and philosophers. For a list of other editions and translations, see Charron 1961.)

—— (1606) *Le Petit Traicté de la sagesse* (Little Treatise on Wisdom), in *Oeuvres*, Geneva: Slatkine, 1970. (Presents a sceptical defence of faith; written in 1603, the treatise was first published posthumously in 1606.)

References and further reading

Busson, H. (1933) *La pensée religieuse française de Charron à Pascal* (French Religious Thought from Charron to Pascal), Paris: Vrin. (Discusses the irreligious consequences of Charron's thought in seventeenth-century France.)

Charron, J.D. (1961) *The 'Wisdom' of Pierre Charron, an Original and Orthodox Code of Morality*, University of North Carolina Studies in the Romance Languages and Literatures 34, Chapel Hill, NC: University of North Carolina. (Includes a list of editions and translations of *De la Sagesse* on pages 147–51.)

Horowitz, M.C. (1971) 'Pierre Charron's View of the Source of Wisdom', *Journal of the History of Philosophy* 9: 443–57. (Emphasizes the Stoic side of Charron's thought.)

Popkin, R.H. (1954) 'Charron and Descartes: the Fruits of Systematic Doubt', *Journal of Philosophy* 51: 831–37. (Shows the similarities and differences between Charron's and Descartes' methods of doubt.)

—— (1979) *The History of Scepticism from Erasmus to Spinoza*, Berkeley, CA: University of California Press. (Places Charron in the development of Renaissance scepticism.)

Rice, E.F. (1958) *The Renaissance Idea of Wisdom*,

Cambridge, MA: Harvard University Press. (An examination of how the notion of wisdom changed during the Renaissance, culminating in Charron's naturalistic, Stoic view.)

Sabrié, J.B. (1913) *De l'humanisme au rationalisme: Pierre Charron (1541–1603), l'homme, l'oeuvre, l'influence* (From Humanism to Rationalism: Pierre Charron, the Man, his Work and its Influence), Paris: Alcan. (Emphasizes the irreligious results of Charron's scepticism.)

Soman, A. (1970) 'Pierre Charron: A Revaluation', *Bibliothèque d'Humanisme et Renaissance* 32: 57–79. (Presents evidence that Charron was not a genuine friend and disciple of Montaigne.)

RICHARD H. POPKIN

CHARTRES, SCHOOL OF

In the first half of the twelfth century, the most advanced work in teaching and discussion of logic, philosophy and theology took place in the schools attached to the great cathedrals. Chartres was undoubtedly one of the more important of these schools, and Gilbert of Poitiers and Thierry of Chartres were certainly connected with it. To some historians, Chartres was the great intellectual centre of the period, and the greatest achievement of early twelfth-century thought was a brand of Platonism distinctive of this school. However, this view has been challenged by scholars who stress the pre-eminence of Paris, where the schools emphasized logic.

1   Who taught at Chartres?
2   'Chartrian Platonism'

1   Who taught at Chartres?

When Clerval (1895) first claimed the particular importance of early twelfth-century Chartres as an intellectual centre, he believed that he could point to four outstanding figures who had been schoolmasters there. First, there was Bernard, described as teaching at Chartres in John of Salisbury's *Metalogicon* (see JOHN OF SALISBURY); Clerval identified him with Bernard Silvestris (BERNARD OF TOURS), author of the *Cosmographia*, a prosimetrum recounting the creation of the world and of man in terms closely reminiscent of Plato's *Timaeus*. Second was the polymath THIERRY OF CHARTRES and third was GILBERT OF POITIERS, one of the leading theologians of the mid-twelfth century. Finally, most scholars of Clerval's time believed that WILLIAM OF CONCHES,

the grammarian and commentator on Platonic texts, was also a teacher at Chartres, although more recent research has cast doubt on various aspects of this claim.

The Bernard described in the *Metalogicon* – who was probably born *circa* 1060, and is mentioned in charters as master of the school at Chartres between 1114 and 1119 and as Chancellor between 1119 and 1124 – is no longer identified with Bernard Silvestris, who taught at Tours in the mid-twelfth century and whose only link with Chartres was his friendship with Thierry. The Chartrian Bernard was a grammarian, interested in Priscian and the theory of grammar as well as in expounding classical Latin tests. Although a commentary on Plato's *Timaeus* has been attributed to him with some plausibility, he was not, like the author of the *Cosmographia*, one of the great writers of the time.

The distinction between Bernard of Chartres and Bernard Silvestris is now accepted by all historians. The relation of other leading teachers to Chartres remains controversial: Sir Richard Southern (1970) has been the leading sceptic, while Edouard Jeauneau (1973), Peter Dronke (1969) and Nikolaus Häring (1974) have argued for the importance of Chartres. No one queries that Thierry ('the Breton' or 'of Chartres') was linked with Chartres, where he became Chancellor in about 1142. However, it is questionable how much teaching he did there; he is also known to have taught John of Salisbury on the Mont Sainte Geneviève in Paris in 1136–8. Where was his teaching predominantly based? A similar question applies to Gilbert of Poitiers, who was a canon of Chartres in 1124 and chancellor there from 1126 to 1137. Gilbert certainly taught in Paris, and one student mentions attending his lectures both at Paris among an audience of three hundred, and at Chartres in an audience of only four. Does this mean that Chartres was a scholastic backwater, or rather (as Dronke has argued) that Gilbert reserved his most advanced teaching for Chartres?

The connection of William of Conches with Chartres is even more problematic. He very probably studied at Chartres under Bernard and is regarded by John of Salisbury as a continuer of Bernard's approach. Jeauneau has found a few remarks in his work which might hint that he was himself teaching at Chartres, and an unclear and much discussed passage in John of Salisbury's *Metalogicon* (II.10) can be argued to support this surmise. However, this hardly constitutes solid evidence for placing him at Chartres, and there is much to recommend Southern's final view, that William taught neither at Paris nor at Chartres. In sum, Chartres may well have been a more important scholastic centre in the first half of the twelfth century than Southern allows, but there is no denying the pre-eminence of Paris in almost all branches of learning from about 1110 onwards.

2 'Chartrian Platonism'

The dispute about the school of Chartres has gone beyond the merely factual questions of who taught where, to become a debate about the very nature of twelfth-century thought. Many modern supporters of the school of Chartres hold that, in Dronke's words, it stands for 'what is freshest in thought, richest and most adventurous in learning, in northern Europe, in the earlier twelfth century' (Dronke 1969: 117), and some have suggested that 'Chartres' should be understood less as the name of a place where certain masters taught and more as the label for a distinctive brand of Platonism which was followed by masters such as Thierry, William of Conches, Gilbert of Poitiers and Bernard Silvestris.

Southern disputes this. In his first attack on the idea of a school of Chartres, he wrote of Bernard (of Chartres), Thierry and William of Conches that 'all their thoughts were old thoughts' (Southern 1970: 83). More recently, he has refined his criticisms. The Platonism of the masters who are described as 'Chartrian' was, he suggests, a very scholastic Platonism. It did not involve adopting, knowingly or instinctively, Plato's underlying positions or attitudes, nor some special 'poetic Platonism', but centred rather on the close scrutiny of the one work of Plato's they know, the *Timaeus* in Calcidius' partial translation. The 'Chartrian' scholars, he says (Southern 1979: 10), regarded Plato as an authority on 'the primitive organization of the elements of the universe' and used him not to reach a 'philosophical Platonism' but as 'a contribution to the vast jig-saw puzzle of universal knowledge about the origin of the world'. Such an authority was important as a doorway, but was quickly left behind when more scientific knowledge became available, especially from Arab sources. The 'Chartrian' scholars are better understood, he urges, 'by being freed from the school of Chartres and placed in the wider setting of a common scholastic enterprise' (Southern 1979: 40).

Powerful though it is, Southern's argument has some serious weaknesses. It overlooks the close link, in the work of Bernard of Chartres, William of Conches and Bernard Silvestris, between the study of grammar (which included both the interpretation of classical texts and the theory of grammar, based on Priscian) and what we would now call science. The breaking of this link in the course of the twelfth century should not be seen straightforwardly as scientific progress, but as a fundamental shift in assumptions and methods. Moreover, Southern fails to bring out an important peculiarity shared by at least three of these masters. Unlike most of the leading teachers of their time, Bernard of Chartres, William of Conches and Bernard Silvestris apparently remained arts masters and did not venture into sacred doctrine at all. Further, none of them seems to have been very interested in logic, the area to which (apart from theology) most twelfth-century masters gave the greatest attention (see LOGIC, MEDIEVAL). Thierry fits this pattern only partly, since he did write about the Trinity and the creation and seems to have been interested in logic. Gilbert of Poitiers fits it not at all, conforming rather to the more usual twelfth-century mould of the logician who goes on to write theology. Perhaps what the enthusiasts for the school of Chartres have hit upon, half unconsciously, is a group of twelfth-century masters (working in various centres) who rejected the pattern and priorities of intellectual life which were becoming the norm and who, in their lifelong dedication to the arts as opposed to theology, might be seen as forerunners of late thirteenth-century arts masters such as SIGER OF BRABANT and BOETHIUS OF DACIA.

See also: BERNARD OF TOURS; CLAREMBALD OF ARRAS; GILBERT OF POITIERS; PLATONISM, MEDIEVAL; JOHN OF SALISBURY; THIERRY OF CHARTRES; WILLIAM OF CONCHES

References and further reading

* Bernard Silvestris (early 1150s) *Cosmographia* (Cosmography), ed. P. Dronke, Leiden: Brill, 1978; trans. W Wetherbee, Ithaca, NY: Cornell University Press, 1973. (Describes the origins of the universe and man, strongly influenced by Plato's *Timaeus*.)

* Clerval, A. (1895) *Les écoles de Chartres au moyen-âge* (The Schools of Chartres in the Middle Ages), Paris: Picard. (Fundamental, though in some respects dated, study of the historical evidence for teaching at Chartres.)

Dutton, P.E. (1984) 'The Uncovering of the *Glosae super Platonem* of Bernard of Chartres', *Mediaeval Studies* 46: 192–221. (Dutton argues that a set of glosses to the *Timaeus* – which he has now edited in full – are the work of Bernard of Chartres).

* Dronke, P. (1969) 'New Approaches to the School of Chartres', *Anuario de estudios medievales* 6: 117–40; repr. with new bibliographical postscript in P. Dronke, *Intellectuals and Poets in Medieval Europe*, Rome: edizioni di storia e letteratura (Raccolta di studi e testi 183), 15–40. (Spirited

defence of the School of Chartres against Southern.)

* Häring, N. (1974) 'Chartres and Paris Revisited', in J.R. O'Donnell (ed.) *Essays in Honour of Anton Charles Pegis*, Toronto, Ont.: Pontifical Institute of Mediaeval Studies, 268–329. (Arguments against Southern.)

* Jeauneau, E. (1973) *Lectio philosophorum*, Amsterdam: Hakkert. (Collects Jeauneau's detailed and important essays on masters connected with Chartres.)

* John of Salisbury (1159) *Metalogicon*, ed. J.B. Hall, Corpus Christianorum, Continuatio Mediaeualis 98, Turnhout: Brepols, 1991; trans. D.D. McGarry, Berkeley, CA: University of California Press, 1955. (Defence of the study of ancient classics; important source for evidence about twelfth-century education.)

* Southern, R.W. (1970) 'Humanism and the School of Chartres', in R.W. Southern, *Medieval Humanism and Other Studies*, Oxford: Blackwell, 61–85. (Southern's original attack on the notion of a School of Chartres.)

* —— (1979) *Platonism, Scholastic Method and the School of Chartres*, Reading: University of Reading. (Describes Chartrian Platonism as scholastic rather than distinctive.)

—— (1982) 'The Schools of Paris and the School of Chartres', in R.L. Benson and G. Constable (eds) *Renaissance and Renewal in the Twelfth Century*, Oxford: Oxford University Press, 113–37. (Historical study, stressing the greater importance of Paris over Chartres.)

Wetherbee, W. (1972) *Platonism and Poetry in the Twelfth Century: The Literary Influence of the School of Chartres*, Princeton, NJ: Princeton University Press. (Urges an understanding of 'school of Chartres' as the label for a type of thought.)

JOHN MARENBON

CHATTON, WALTER
(*c.*1290–1343)

Chatton was an English philosopher and theologian who developed a detailed critique of the work of William of Ockham, causing the latter to revise some of his earlier writings. Chatton was also at times an opponent of Peter Aureol and Richard of Campsall; he generally, though not always, followed John Duns Scotus and responded to his critics. He is known also for his writings on physics, where he held views in line with those of Pythagoras and Plato, and on the Trinity, where he was strongly attacked by Adam Wodeham.

The English Franciscan philosopher and theologian Walter Chatton was born in the village of Catton, near Durham, around 1290. He was a contemporary of WILLIAM OF OCKHAM and Adam WODEHAM at the Franciscan custodial school in London from 1321 to 1323. There he delivered his *Reportatio* lectures on all four Books of the *Sentences* of Peter LOMBARD, in preparation for his later *Lectura* on the *Sentences* at Oxford sometime between 1324 and 1330 (most likely in 1328–30). He was one of the examiners of the works of DURANDUS OF SAINT-POURÇAIN and Thomas Waleys at the papal court in Avignon, and is believed to have died there in 1343.

Chatton was such a detailed critic of Ockham that it is impossible to follow many of the arguments in the latter's *Quodlibets* without having Chatton's *Reportatio* at hand. Ockham's famous razor was sharpened partly in response to Chatton's critique. Its early formulation, 'Beings should not be multiplied without necessity', was challenged by Chatton, who counters with an anti-razor that he calls 'my proposition': 'When a proposition is made true by things, if two things are not sufficient for its truth, then it is necessary to posit a third, and so on.' In response, Ockham in his later works reformulates his razor to say: 'When a proposition is made true by things, if two things are sufficient for its truth, then it is superfluous to posit a third, and so on.'

Chatton also attacked Ockham's view of concepts, at least the view Ockham held in the first redaction of his *Sentence* commentary, where he defends the *fictum* theory, which holds that the concept does not exist in the mind as in a subject but only has the reality of an object created by an act of understanding. Chatton himself held the *intellectio* theory, which contends that the concept is nothing else but the very act of knowing. Such an act of knowing is a true quality existing in the soul as in a subject, and is also a natural sign of the object that is immediately understood by means of it. Ockham not only did not despise Chatton's critique of the *fictum* theory, he incorporated his opponent's *intellectio* theory into his later treatments of concepts, at first reducing the *fictum* theory to a 'less probable' opinion and finally abandoning it.

The Ockham–Chatton exchange, however, is not limited to the period when both were in London. In discussing the dependence of a second cause on the first cause in essentially ordered causes, Chatton in his *Lectura* defends Duns Scotus' position against Ockham's challenges, quoting verbatim from Ockham's last philosophical work, the *Quaestiones in libros Physicorum Aristotelis* (Questions on Aristotle's *Physics*), probably written at Oxford about 1324.

In dealing with his own questions concerning Aristotle's *Physics*, Chatton is known especially for joining the early fourteenth-century minority including HENRY OF HARCLAY, GERARD OF ODO and Nicholas Bonet, thinkers who opposed Aristotle's claim that continua cannot be composed of indivisibles. Although Chatton had contemporary allies among the atomists, he seems to be alone in holding that continua are composed of finite numbers of indivisibles. Thomas BRADWARDINE, in his *Tractatus de continuo* (Treatise on the Nature of a Continuum), makes Chatton a follower of Pythagoras and Plato, who held the same position (see ARISTOTELIANISM, MEDIEVAL; PLATONISM, MEDIEVAL).

Besides Ockham, Chatton had a number of other debating partners. When Peter AUREOL attacked Duns Scotus' theory of the univocity of being, Chatton came to its defence. Aureol attacked Duns Scotus for claiming that we can have a univocal concept of being, a concept that is predicable in the same sense both of God and of creatures. Scotus achieved this univocal concept at a price, since his concept of being leaves outside its ambit the modes 'infinite' and 'finite' which, if they were included, would impede 'being' from being predicable both of God and of creatures. Chatton grants this objection, but considers it irrelevant. If Aureol, he argues, wants to include modes and differences in his concept of being, then 'being' becomes a most general concept of all that is opposed to nothing, and this is merely a logical and not a metaphysical concept. It is the latter, according to Chatton, that Scotus had in mind (see DUNS SCOTUS, J.).

Richard Campsall became Chatton's opponent when he argued that intuitive and abstractive cognition are not really distinct, 'since numerically the same knowledge is intuitive when the object is present and abstractive when it is absent, because plurality should not be admitted without necessity.' Against this position, Chatton raised twelve difficulties and then refuted Campsall by appealing to his anti-razor, arguing that it is not impossible that God conserve in existence the intellect with its abstractive cognition and make the object present without the intellect grasping it as present. Thus for the proposition 'He sees that object' to be true, it is not enough to have the intellect, its abstractive cognition and the object present. A distinct thing has to be added: intuitive cognition.

Chatton clashed with Campsall also over the logic involved in statements of non-identity related to the Christian teaching on the Trinity. Chatton's own treatment of the Trinity had its logical and meta-physical problems, turning the divine essence into a collection of persons. He was severely ridiculed and criticized for such Trinitarian views by Adam WODEHAM, who quite likely was the student who wrote down Chatton's *Reportatio*. In the margin of Chatton's text, Wodeham wrote: 'In all this discussion the report is not in accord with the mind of the speaker. Nor is there any wonder, since when the author said these things he was not quite sane. Later on, he thought things out better and had another go at it. And then the reporter naturally expressed things in a better way' (*Lectura secunda* I, 13*, n.28). Wodeham was Chatton's chief critic, often accusing him of misunderstanding or misrepresenting Ockham, or of accepting Ockham's views but pretending, by petty quibbles, that he was differing. Despite Wodeham's frequent attacks on him, however, the influence Chatton had on both Ockham and Wodeham shows his philosophical importance.

See also: BRADWARDINE, T.; HENRY OF HARCLAY; WILLIAM OF OCKHAM; WODEHAM, A.

List of works

Chatton, Walter (c.1321–30) *Reportatio et Lectura super Sententias: Collatio ad librum primum et prologus* (Commentary on Peter Lombard's *Sentences*), ed. J.C. Wey, Toronto, Ont.: Pontifical Institute of Mediaeval Studies, 1989. (This volume contains the introductory sermon and the prologue, which in effect is the prologue for both the *Reportatio* (1321–1323) and the *Lectura* (1324–1330). This work replaces earlier editions of separate prologue questions, but some earlier editions also contained excellent analyses and valuable studies; these are noted in the list of further readings, below. Other parts of the *Reportatio* and *Lectura* that have been edited can be found listed in Wey's introduction, 3–4, n. 10. Not included in Wey's list is *Lectura in I Sent.*, d. 4, q.1, aa.1–2, ed. S.F. Brown, *Medieval Philosophy and Theology* 3, 1993, 135–57, which discusses supposition theory.)

—— (c.1321–30) *Quaestio utrum quantum et continuum componantur ex indivisibilibus sicut ex partibus integrantibus*, eds J.E. Murdoch and E.A. Synan, *Franciscan Studies* 26, 1966, 234–66. (Contains Chatton's writings on the continuum; attributed to Chatton with some reservations (see Murdoch and Synan 1966).)

References and further reading

Adams, M.M. (1982) 'Universals in the Early Fourteenth Century', in N. Kretzmann, A. Kenny and J. Pinborg (eds) *Cambridge History of Later Medieval Philosophy*, Cambridge: Cambridge University Press, 411–39. (Includes an outline of Chatton's criticisms of William of Ockham, and the latter's response.)

Brown, S.F. (1985) 'Walter Chatton's *Lectura* and William of Ockham's *Quaestiones in libros Physicorum Aristotelis*', in W.A. Frank and G.J. Etzkorn (eds) *Essays Honoring Allan B. Wolter*, St Bonaventure, NY: Franciscan Institute, 81–93. (Shows the interrelationship of Chatton's *Lectura* and Ockham's *Quaestiones*.)

Campsall, Richard (c.1350–60), cited in Chatton, *Reportatio et Lectura super Sententias: Collatio ad librum primum et prologus* (Commentary on Peter Lombard's *Sentences*), ed. J.C. Wey, Toronto, Ont.: Pontifical Institute of Mediaeval Studies, 1989, prol., q.2, a.1, 77, n.3. (Campsall's argument, refuted by Chatton.)

Courtenay, W.J. (1978) *Adam Wodeham: An Introduction to his Life and Writings*, Leiden: Brill. (Provides Chatton's *curriculum vitae*.)

Cova, L. (1973) *Walter Catton, Commento alle Sentenze: Prologo, Questione Terza*, Rome: Edizione dell'Ateneo. (Analysis of the question as to whether we can have many concepts proper to God).

Etzkorn, G.J. (1987) 'A Heretofore Unknown *Quodlibet* of Walter Chatton', *Bulletin de philosophie médiévale* 29: 230. (Cod. Paris. Nat. lat. 15, 805 contains a Chatton *Quodlibet* that ends in the middle of Question 29.)

Fitzpatrick, N.A. (1971) 'Walter Chatton on the Univocity of Being: A Reaction to Peter Aureoli and William of Ockham', *Franciscan Studies* 31: 88–177. (Defends Scotus' teaching on univocity against Aureol and Ockham.)

Knudsen, C. (1982) 'Intentions and Impositions', in N. Kretzmann, A. Kenny and J. Pinborg (eds) *Cambridge History of Later Medieval Philosophy*, Cambridge: Cambridge University Press, 479–95. (Includes Chatton's criticisms of Ockham's work on intentions and impositions.)

—— (1985) 'Chatton contra Ockham über Gegenstand und Einheit von Wissenschaft und Theologie' (Chatton's Attack on Ockham Concerning the Object and Unity of Science and Theology), *Cahiers de l'Institut du moyen-âge grec et latin* 50: 3–112. (On the unity of the science of theology).

Maurer, A. (1984) 'Ockham's Razor and Chatton's Anti-Razor', *Mediaeval Studies* 46: 463–75. (Presents Ockham's reformulation of his famous razor in response to the criticism of Chatton.)

Murdoch, J.E. (1982) 'Infinity and Continuity', in N. Kretzmann, A. Kenny and J. Pinborg (eds) *Cambridge History of Later Medieval Philosophy*, Cambridge: Cambridge University Press, 564–94. (Contains a brief account of Chatton's views on indivisibles.)

Murdoch, J.E. and Synan, E.A. (1966) 'Two Questions of the Continuum: Walter Chatton (?) and Adam Wodeham, OFM', *Franciscan Studies* 26: 212–88. (Edition of the text concerning the nature of the continuum attributed to Chatton.)

Wodeham, Adam (1990) *Lectura Secunda*, ed. R Wood and G Gál, St Bonaventure, NY: St Bonaventure University, vol. I, 12*–18*. (Contains Wodeham's evaluation of Chatton).

STEPHEN F. BROWN

CHEMISTRY, PHILOSOPHICAL ASPECTS OF

Chemistry, like all theoretical sciences, is deeply rooted in philosophical inquiry. Early Greek atomism was a response to Parmenides' argument that the very concept of change is unintelligible. Aristotle in turn argued that a vacuum is impossible and proposed that qualitative change could be better understood in terms of four elements and an underlying prime matter.

During the Arabic and Latin Middle Ages, philosophical commentaries on the nature of materials were brought into juxtaposition with the practical arts of the alchemist, miner and pharmacist. As chemical speculations became more closely connected to observations during the time of the Scientific Revolution, natural philosophers became more and more interested in the methodological aspects of chemistry. Galileo and Locke tried to clarify the relationship between primary and secondary qualities. Boyle struggled to understand how the selective affinities so characteristic of chemical reagents could be explained within the framework of Descartes' mechanical philosophy. Lavoisier's textbook was organized around principles drawn from philo-philosophes such as Condillac.

As chemistry became an autonomous science, chemists turned less often to philosophy as a source of theoretical inspiration. However, they frequently appealed to philosophies of science in order to defend their own theories or criticize those of their opponents. The so-called 'atomic debates' amongst chemists in the British Association during the 1860s were primarily disputes about the epistemological legitimacy of appeals to unobservable entities. Many of the same issues were taken up at the end of the century by Ostwald, Mach and Duhem.

Logical empiricists in the twentieth century have often turned to chemistry as an example of the successful reduction of a secondary science to physics. Thus, it is claimed that the laws of classical thermodynamics, expressed using concepts such as enthalpy and entropy, can be derived from the laws of statistical mechanics describing the motions of particles. The details of this purported derivation have been questioned. Even more controversial is the attempt to derive accounts of the chemical bond and the shape of molecules from the first principles provided by quantum mechanics.

1   **Early concepts of atoms and elements**
2   **Corpuscles, forces and conservation**
3   **Positivism and nineteenth-century atomism**
4   **Chemistry with electrons**
5   **Current philosophical issues**

1   Early concepts of atoms and elements

To a modern student of chemistry there seems to be no tension between the concepts of atom and element. The periodic table of the elements illustrates how the chemical properties of a simple substance such as sulphur can be related to the physical properties of the atoms of which it is composed, especially its atomic number. Historically, however, there has often been conflict between atomic approaches and research programmes that talk about elements. Examples of the opposition already appear in pre-Socratic cosmological theories about the origins and composition of the world. The typical features of classical atomic theories are present in the fragmentary accounts we have of LEUCIPPUS and DEMOCRITUS (fifth century BC): the world is composed of atoms moving in a void (see ATOMISM, ANCIENT). The atoms themselves are unchanging, indivisible bits of matter which differ from each other only in size or shape. The processes we observe around us are the result of changing groupings or arrangements of atoms; the qualitative aspects of experience are the results of their collisions with the atoms of our soul or mind. However, Democritus is very explicit that we cannot expect to have knowledge of qualities.

> By convention are sweet and bitter, hot and cold, by convention is colour; in truth are atoms and the void. ... There are two forms of knowledge, one genuine, one obscure. To the obscure belong all of the following: sight, hearing, smell, taste, touch.
> (Kirk and Raven 1962: 422)

The atomistic tradition was continued by Plato who, in the *Timaeus*, gave an elaborate geometrical account of atoms in terms of the five regular polyhedra (see PLATO §16). In *The Nature of Things*, LUCRETIUS provided speculative corpuscular explanations of everything from evaporation to sexual attraction, but in part because of its historical connections to Epicurean moral philosophy, atomistic theorizing became theologically suspect and was not further developed until the rise of modern science (see EPICUREANISM §§3, 12).

The dominant theory of matter was Aristotle's sophisticated account of the four elements – earth, air, fire and water (an account earlier developed by Empedocles). Aristotle posited an underlying substratum of prime matter that could neither be created nor destroyed. On it were impressed various combinations of the four fundamental qualities, the hot or the cold, the wet or the dry. The four elements could be transmuted into each other. For example, by adding more warmth to water (formed from the cold and the wet) one could change it into air (characterized as the hot and the wet) (see MATTER §1).

In trying to explain the multiplicity of properties which we actually observe, Aristotle associated additional qualities with each element. Thus softness and ductility and a bland taste are characteristic of water. Brittle materials are earthy, while sour or spicy foods contain fire. Not only do ordinary materials contain varying proportions of the elements, they also differ in how intimately the parts are combined.

Although there are places where Aristotle seems to presuppose a sort of conservation law for his qualities, there are also passages in which he says that the more potent properties can completely transform the weaker. Thus if a great quantity of water is added to wine, in the end the water will actually convert the wine into water. In a similar way, Aristotle says, living things can transform food into flesh and bone (*De generatione et corruptione* I 5). The Aristotelian system thus provided the philosophical foundation for alchemy (see ALCHEMY).

2   Corpuscles, forces and conservation

Greek atomism had postulated that all processes could be understood as the result of collisions between, and regroupings of, invisible particles, but it had very little to say about how or why the atoms moved or what caused them to cohere into relatively stable clusters. Both of these deficiencies were addressed by the theories of motion developed in the seventeenth century. Although Descartes rejected the possibility of a vacuum, his programme of explaining all natural phenomena in terms of corpuscles moving in accordance with laws of inertia and collision was otherwise a continuation of the classical approach. Like Epicurus and Lucretius, Descartes wrestled with phenomena – colour, patterns of iron filings round a bar magnet, and physiology – which seemed particularly recalcitrant to mechanical explanations (see DESCARTES, R. §11).

Isaac NEWTON not only corrected the Cartesian laws of motion, he also revolutionized its ontology. The universal law of gravitation plus his three laws of motion gave a complete account of the movements of both heavenly bodies and middle-sized terrestrial objects such as projectiles. Newton was convinced that additional forces, each with a corresponding force law, would be needed to explain behaviour at the atomic level. Thus, he postulated a repulsive force varying inversely with the distance between nearest neighbours to explain the 'spring' in air which makes it resist compression. And in the famous thirty-first query of the Opticks Newton suggests that a variety of cohesive forces acting at short range may be needed to account for the 'sociability' of chemicals for each other. John Locke tried to give a philosophical account of how the world of sense experience with its rich diversity could be reduced to the 'solid, massy, hard, impenetrable, moveable particles' proposed by Newton which varied only in size, figure and velocity (see LOCKE, J. §4; PRIMARY-SECONDARY DISTINCTION §1).

Even if the relationship between primary and secondary qualities could be clarified to the satisfaction of philosophers, there still remained the difficulty of how working chemists, who dealt with what British schoolchildren came to know as the science of 'bangs and stinks', could relate atomic models to the practical problems of describing the properties and reactions of materials in the laboratory. And as chemists made progress in classifying materials according to their reactivities into, for example, acids, bases and salts or metals, calces and reducing agents, they found it more useful to think in terms of underlying elements or principles characterized in terms of their qualitative chemical natures, instead of the geometrical properties of corpuscles. The chemists working in this tradition, while not denying the possibility of underlying atoms, nevertheless ignored them when theorizing about chemical reactions.

Aristotle had accepted the Parmenidean axiom that a persisting underlying reality was a prerequisite for understanding change, and in his system prime matter is conserved. However, most of the things chemists were interested in, such as the elements themselves, were not conserved on Aristotle's account. By the eighteenth century there was a concerted effort to find a small fundamental number of chemical elements or principles which were conserved.

For the atomists, of course, conservation was built into the system – atoms are by definition invariant – and they prided themselves on the clarity and parsimony of their list of primary properties, size, figure, and so on. But atomists also had no way to limit or predict how many different types of atom there should be.

Those who postulated elements defined in terms of qualities permitted themselves a richer set of basic properties, but placed much stricter limits on the number of different kinds of element. Stahl, for example, retained a version of the four traditional elements but added to them the three 'earths' proposed by Becher: the saline earth (the principle of acidity), the sulphurous earth or phlogiston (the principle of inflammability) and the mercurial earth. Although originally called 'earths', these chemical principles were characterized by their great activity and, as became evident in later variants of the phlogiston theory when phlogiston was assigned a zero or even negative weight, their material nature was sometimes in doubt. But Stahl was adamant that the principles were conserved.

In his treatises on both the sulphurous and saline principles, Stahl extolled what he calls the joint method of analysis and synthesis. The standard chemical practice of determining the composition of a complex material by analysing it into its simpler constituents is fallible because either some of the analysands may be lost or something may be inadvertently added. Stahl recommends that chemists should 'complete the proof' by resynthesizing the material in question. Thus he believed that he had proved that sulphur contained phlogiston because he could prepare it using charcoal (a major source of phlogiston). It is an irony that Stahl's system was eventually rejected on the basis of Lavoisier's famous experiments in which the red calx of mercury was first analysed, thereby forming oxygen gas, and then resynthesized from the gas and metallic mercury.

Lavoisier's textbook of 1789 presents a list of dozens of elements, most of which are familiar to us today, and emphasized that not only mass but also the quantity of each individual element is conserved in all reactions. Lavoisier also gives the concept of element an operational definition – we are to take as elements those simple substances which cannot be further broken down in the laboratory. And, unlike Stahl, Lavoisier stressed the importance of tracking what happens to elements in reactions by weighing products and reactants. However, Lavoisier was not entirely consistent in his approach: two imponderable fluids which cannot be isolated, light and caloric, are the first elements on his list.

3 Positivism and nineteenth-century atomism

In 1808 Dalton provided a link between the atomistic research programme and Lavoisier's descriptive chemistry. Each material element on Lavoisier's list consisted of atoms of a characteristic weight surrounded by caloric. The relative weights of atoms could be calculated from empirically determined combining weights. At last there was a direct way to specify one of the primary properties attributed to atoms. Over the next century a great deal of experimental work went into determinations of atomic weights and molecular formulae.

However, Dalton's atomic theory provided no conceptual resources for explaining what held atoms together when they formed compounds. Unlike earlier 'hooks and eyes' speculations, Dalton pictured all atoms as spherical. And their effective volumes seemed to reflect how much caloric surrounded them rather than their intrinsic sizes. Caloric itself caused atoms to move apart, thus only heightening the mystery of the nature of chemical bonding.

Boscovich (1763) had developed Newtonian matter theory by drawing speculative graphs which showed alternating attractive and repulsive forces as a function of distance from the nucleus (see MECHANICS, CLASSICAL), but no one had any idea of how to relate these diagrams to chemical reactivities. Most puzzling was the fact that the reactivity of a material depends on its 'sociability' or compatibility with other reactants. Thus, as the alchemists were very aware, although gold is in general less reactive than silver, aqua regia will dissolve gold much more readily than it will silver. Aqua fortis, on the other hand attacks silver but not gold. Furthermore, the extent to which chemicals 'elected' to combine was sometimes a function of temperature or concentrations. It was difficult to fathom how Boscovichean forces could depend on such variables. This was one major reason why Kant concluded that chemistry would never be a theoretical science founded on universal mathematical laws. But after the discovery of electrochemical phenomena, philosophically minded chemists hoped that chemical affinities could be explained in terms of electrical attractions. After all, in voltaic cells electricity was produced from chemical reactions while in electrolytic cells electricity could be used to decompose complex bodies back into their elements. Berzelius' 'dualistic theory' proposed that all bonds were formed between electropositive and electronegative units. But this theory could not cope at all with the fact that the common atmospheric gases such as nitrogen and oxygen were diatomic and it was of little help in understanding the ever-growing number of organic compounds.

It is tempting to view nineteenth-century chemistry as the progressive articulation of atomic theory. To the laws of definite and multiple proportions were added Avogadro's hypothesis that equal volumes of gases contain equal numbers of particles and Kekulé's discovery that organic compounds could be represented as chains or rings of tetravalent carbon atoms. It even became possible to assign definite geometric structures to molecules.

Yet there was on-going scientific and philosophical resistance to the atomistic research programme. Some of it was a result of general methodological caution. Chemists were still very aware of the phlogiston debacle which John Herschel described as 'a lamentable epoch in which . . . as if to prove the perversity of the human mind, of two possible roads, the wrong was chosen' (1830: 300). The so-called 'atomic debates' at the British Chemical Society in 1869 illustrate the concern of chemists to avoid a naïve belief in hypothetical entities that were admittedly useful but not directly tied to experiment.

Other objections stemmed from specific conceptual lacunae or flaws within the contemporary theory. For example, if one took seriously the rigid geometrical structure attributed to carbon, how could one account for the so-called 'Walden inversion' in which the molecule apparently turned wrong-side out? Why should atoms have discrete valences or combining powers in the first place, such that nitrogen hooked up with three hydrogens and oxygen combined with two, while chlorine was satisfied with only one? And how could the family relationships and trends among the elements, so nicely summarized in Mendeleev's periodic table, ever be explained in terms of periodicities or trends within the numerical values of atomic weights?

By the end of the century the most vigorous opponents of atomism, Ostwald, MACH and DUHEM, could offer an alternative research programme, that of classical thermodynamics. This approach appeared to be much more closely tied to measurable quantities such as temperature and heats of reaction and its treatment of chemical processes required no assumptions about either mechanisms or the microstructure of the reactants. Mach and Duhem both had strong philosophical reasons for favouring phenomenological theories and Ostwald developed an entire metaphysical system based on 'energetics'.

Thermodynamics did indeed give valuable insights into reaction equilibria and the stability of chemical compounds, but it did not displace atomism. Instead, Boltzmann, PLANCK and others argued that it could be reduced to statistical mechanics, a theory of moving atomic particles (see THERMODYNAMICS). And through experiments with X-ray diffraction and radioactivity it became possible to measure quite directly exactly how many such particles there were in a gas sample and the distances between them in a crystal lattice.

4 Chemistry with electrons

In the early twentieth century chemistry was revolutionized by the discovery that the atom has parts, and by 1932, when the neutron was discovered, the basic features of our present picture of the chemical atom were firmly in place. The defining characteristic of a chemical element now became the number of protons in the nucleus – atomic weights were no longer universal constants but mere averages of isotopic distribution in the earth's crust. Valence, a useful empirical concept that had previously been devoid of theoretical interpretation, could now be related to the configurations of the outer electrons surrounding the chemical nucleus.

Since there was little opposition to the new chemistry, explicit recognition of just how radically concepts had been changed was slow in coming. Not only were chemical atoms divisible (through ionization as well as through nuclear fission), but even more fundamentally there were now no units that remained invariant during chemical processes. The closest candidate perhaps would be the kernel of the chemical atom – the nucleus plus the filled inner electron shells – but then, paradoxically it is the electrons outside of the kernel that are essential to chemical bonds.

The new concept of chemical element also deviated considerably from the traditional one. Not only was the law of conservation of matter revised by relativity theory, nuclear reactions violated Lavoisier's law of the conservation of elements. In a sense Lavoisier's operational definition of element as the last product of analysis could still be relied on to reveal the simplest homogeneous 'stuffs' out of which everything was constructed, but the arché of the universe now turned out to have no resemblance to the elements of the chemist, but to be instead the fundamental particles of the physicist. Even if one could restrict the methods of analysis to so-called chemical ones in a non-question-begging way, it was now clearer than ever that the relationship between the properties of the simple substance (for example, elemental carbon) and the properties of the stuff which was conserved in chemical reactions (for example, the element carbon) were extremely complex.

Of particular interest to philosophical accounts of the development of science are the interactions between chemical theories of bonding and atomic physics during the first quarter of the century. To chemists the discovery of the electron immediately provided the key to an understanding of all sorts of electrochemical phenomena, and a theory of ionization could account for properties of solutions of weak and strong electrolytes. Bohr's theory of discrete electron orbits, each containing a maximum number of electrons, also seemed to account for some of the similarities and trends summarized by the periodic table. However, the Bohr model, which was designed to account for the spectra of isolated atoms, postulated moving electrons, and it was not at all clear how it could be extended to cover the distribution of electrons in compounds. Theoretical chemists struck out on their own and in 1916 G.N. Lewis attempted to give a unified account of ionic and covalent bonding, which was based on the idea of the special stability of electron pairs and octets. According to Lewis, bonding electrons were always arranged at the corners of a cube, atoms could complete their octets by sharing corners or faces of their cubes, and ionic bonds formed when the sharing was unequal.

Lewis' account made a certain amount of sense to chemists although it predicted an inaccurate geometry for carbon compounds. It also served to dramatize the inadequacies of what we now call the old quantum theory.

Although scientists can live for some time with inconsistencies within a theory, or contradictions between mutually relevant theories, the drive for consistency is an enduring one and it was a great triumph when in 1926 Schrödinger proposed a quantum mechanical account of the atom which appeared to be applicable to chemical bonds as well as atomic spectra. By conceptualizing electrons as three-dimensional charged clouds one might hope to show that they were denser in just those regions of space where chemists were accustomed to draw lines or pairs of dots to represent chemical bonds. However, actually carrying out the derivations was a formidable problem. When the physicists Heitler and London set out to calculate the bond energy of H_2, the simplest molecule of all, they were forced to adopt a simplified representation of the interactions between four charged bodies (two protons and two electrons) and as a result were able only to approximate the observed values.

If quantum mechanics was to be of any benefit at all to chemists, more rough and ready methods of modelling complex systems had to be found. And there sprang up two rival schools of quantum chemistry: Linus Pauling's valence bond approach seemed well-suited to describing the geometry of covalent molecules, while Robert Mulliken's molecular-orbital approach was particularly useful in describing the vibrational spectra of molecules. There is still debate about the relative merits of these two approaches and both continue to be presented in contemporary chemistry textbooks.

5 Current philosophical issues

What has most intrigued philosophers about twentieth-century chemical theory is the question of whether chemistry is reducible to physics. While it is obviously desirable that theoretical chemistry be *compatible* with quantum mechanics, the demand that it be *reducible* is a much more stringent and controversial goal, for reduction requires that the entire theoretical and empirical corpus of chemistry be derivable from, or reproducible within, the explanatory structure of physics.

The quest for reduction is a recurring scientific ideal, but it was particularly popular with the logical positivists who founded a unity of science movement (see VIENNA CIRCLE §4; UNITY OF SCIENCE). The paradigm candidate for a successful reduction pair was classical and statistical thermodynamics, but it is also frequently claimed by both scientists and philosophers that it is no longer possible to do foundational theoretical work in chemistry because, after all, chemistry is really nothing more than the application of quantum mechanics to complicated arrays of electrons and nuclei.

While few would dispute the claim of reducibility in principle, there are many who find the project of analysing the actual relationships between the two disciplines to be a challenging and instructive one. Consider, for example, the puzzles surrounding the *aufbau* principle. It is often claimed that the striking chemical similarities among elements summarized by Mendeleev's periodic table can be given a straightforward explanation in terms of quantum mechanics. One simply 'builds up' the table by placing electrons in the lower energy levels first and demonstrates that elements in the same chemical group turn out to have similar electronic configurations. Thus, the outer electrons of fluorine ($2s^2p^5$) and chlorine ($3s^2p^5$) differ only in their principal quantum number. However, this simple procedure fails when one tries to build up the transition elements because the ordering of orbits by energy levels is not invariant with nuclear charge. So, for example, in nickel (atomic number 28) the 4s level is filled before the 3d level while in copper (atomic number 29) the 3d level is filled at the expense of the 4s! This 'crossing over' of energy levels can in theory be derived from first principles, but in practice, quantum chemists resort to *ad hoc* rules of thumb, referring to the increased stability of filled and half-filled sub-levels in order to

summarize such deviations from the simple *aufbau* recipe.

Philosophers, theoretical chemists and chemistry educators continue to wrestle with the many puzzling conceptual features of contemporary chemistry. Given the holistic character of quantum mechanics, how can we justify chemical explanations which treat atoms and molecules as discrete entities? It has even been argued that quantum mechanics does not permit talk about the shape of a molecule! Can one defend or at least clarify the eclecticism of chemists who switch from valence-bond thinking to an molecular-orbital account according to convenience?

Current chemistry also serves as a strategic site for philosophers who wish to develop more detailed and realistic accounts of methodological issues which arise in many sciences: how to deal with mathematically intractable representations, the role and evaluation of approximate explanations, the analysis of experimentation and instrumentation. Because of its central role in military, industrial and environmental affairs, chemical research has also come under the scrutiny of philosophers interested in the ethical and social dimensions of science (see RESPONSIBILITIES OF SCIENTISTS AND INTELLECTUALS).

See also: CONSERVATION PRINCIPLES; QUANTUM MECHANICS, INTERPRETATION OF; REDUCTION, PROBLEMS OF

References and further reading

* Boscovich, R.J. (1763) *Theoria philosophiae naturalis*, Venice; trans. J.M. Child, *A Theory of Natural Philosophy*, Cambridge, MA: MIT Press, 1966. (Relates matter to the concept of field.)

  Brock, W.H. (1992) *The Norton History of Chemistry*, London: Norton. (Useful bibliographic guide.)

* Herschel, J.F.W. (1830) *A Preliminary Discourse on the Study of Natural Philosophy*, London: Longmans, Rees, Orme, Brown & Green. (Treats chemistry as a branch of physics.)

* Kirk, G.S. and Raven, J.E. (1962) *The Presocratic Philosophers: A Critical History with a Selection of Texts*, London: Cambridge University Press. (Contains quotations from early Greek texts.)

* Lavoisier, A.-L. (1789) *Traité élémentaire de chimie*; trans. R. Kerr, *The Elements of Chemistry*, London: Wm. Creech, 1790. (A *very* influential textbook.)

  Paneth, F. (1961) 'The Epistemological Status of the Concept of Element', *British Journal for the Philosophy of Science* 13: 1–14, 144–60. (Clarifies relationships between atoms and elements.)

  Post, H.R. (1968) 'Atomism 1900', *Physics Education* 3: 1–13. (Summarizes the opposition to atomism.)

Primas, H. (1983) *Chemistry, Quantum Mechanics, and Reductionism*, New York: Springer. (Account of technical difficulties in carrying out the reduction.)

Scerri, E. (1989) 'Transition Metal Configurations and Limitations of the Orbital Approximation', *Journal of Chemical Education* 66: 481–3. (Explains the difficulties in applying the *aufbau* principle.)

NORETTA KOERTGE

CH'ENG *see* CHENG

CHENG

In early Confucian writings, cheng *describes the quality of authentically realizing or 'completing' a given thing's true nature. It appears together with* xin *(trustworthiness), a character to which it is related in sense.* Cheng *refers primarily to the fulfilment of a thing's true nature, while* xin *refers to the quality resulting from this. With regard to human beings,* cheng *is the authentic realization of ones nature. In texts such as the* Xunzi *and* Zhongyong, *the idea is related to the role human beings are believed to play in realizing or 'completing' a greater universal pattern. This development becomes centrally important for later neo-Confucian thinkers, who see these as different aspects of a single project.*

Cheng ('integrity' or 'sincerity') is not a central term of art for Confucius, but it takes on greater significance in the thought of MENCIUS and XUNZI. According to the *Mengzi* (4A12), *cheng* requires an understanding of the good. One cannot be *cheng* unless one understands why one is acting as one does. To be *cheng* is to be true to one's self, that is, one's true nature (hence 'sincerity'). Thus *cheng* is necessary for the cultivation of genuine virtue. Since such self-cultivation results in the most satisfying of lives (see SELF-CULTIVATION, CHINESE THEORIES OF), there is no greater joy than to find that one is *cheng*.

For Xunzi, *cheng* assumes greater prominence: 'Nothing is more beneficial for nourishing one's heart-mind', and 'the extension' of this excellence is the beginning and end of the moral life (*Xunzi* 3). Xunzi introduces the idea that one who is *cheng* has the power to transform both people and things. One who is *cheng* and *xin* (trustworthy) is 'like a spirit'.

All the above ideas are further developed in the DAXUE (Great Learning) and ZHONGYONG (Doctrine of the Mean). The former emphasizes that *cheng* is

primarily concerned with one's internal mental states by calling for all to *cheng* (make sincere) their *yi* (thoughts). One is to fulfil but not overstep the proper measure in one's perception of and response to things and events. In the *Zhongyong* we find the most complete development of the notion of *cheng*. Echoing Xunzi, the text gives *cheng* a strongly metaphysical sense: it is each thing's realization of its proper nature as part of a grand cosmic pattern. Bringing this state of affairs about is the highest purpose of human life. Thus, '*cheng* is the way of heaven and to realize *cheng* is the way of human beings'. One is to realize *cheng* by fulfilling (that is, completing) one's own nature. This in turn allows one to complete the nature of others and go on to complete the nature of all things, thus 'forming a triad with heaven and earth'.

The notion of *cheng* was extremely important for neo-Confucian thinkers. CHENG YI offered what became the standard interpretation. Discussing 'nature' and *cheng*, he explained that the former was a substantial thing while the latter was the quality of that thing's being fully realized as it should be: 'If you compare the nature to this fan, integrity (*cheng*) may be compared to this fan being properly made' (Graham 1992: 67).

See also: NEO-CONFUCIAN PHILOSOPHY; DAXUE; SELF-CULTIVATION, CHINESE THEORIES OF; VIRTUE ETHICS; XIN (TRUSTWORTHINESS); XUNZI; ZHONGYONG

References and further reading

* Graham, A.C. (1992) *Two Chinese Philosophers*, La Salle, IL: Open Court. (An insightful study of two neo-Confucian thinkers, Cheng Hao and Cheng Yi; contains helpful discussions of *cheng*, particular on pages 67–73.)

PHILIP J. IVANHOE

CH'ENG HAO *see* CHENG HAO

CHENG HAO (1032–85)

*Cheng Hao was a pivotal figure in the creation of a Confucian tradition that was to become the basis for intellectual and state orthodoxy in China from the thirteenth century to the twentieth century. His decision to seek the Confucian Way (*dao*) through a* *direct and personalized reading of the classics was later projected as the beginning of this movement. From a new perspective, he redirected Confucian discourse on such cardinal concepts as humaneness and human nature.*

Born into a family which for three generations had distinguished itself in high offices, Cheng Hao accompanied his father to a succession of posts in central China. At the age of twenty he passed the national civil service examination and, for most of the years until 1180, had a notable official career which culminated in 1169–70 with service at the emperor's court. During audiences with the emperor and in written memorials, he followed the example of MENCIUS in admonishing his ruler to follow benevolence and refusing even to discuss what would bring profit and advantages. So critical was he of Wang Anshi's utilitarian obsession with maximizing advantages and the happiness of the greatest number of people that Cheng was demoted to a local post and eventually dismissed entirely. The last five years of his life he devoted to teaching an increasing number of disciples, drawn in part by his exceptionally gracious and warm disposition.

Retrospective biographical accounts focused on his youthful fascination with Daoism and Buddhism, until his resolve to discover the Way (*dao*) led him to the classics (see CHINESE CLASSICS). Reading the classics in the context of his commitment to the Way, he was credited with a breakthrough in understanding the mind and heart of Mencius and reviving the transmission of the Way that had been lost since this last sage of the classical era.

Cheng Hao was the first to expound the idea of 'principle' (*li*), the normative patterns providing coherence to all things, as a Confucian concept, but his younger brother CHENG YI was the one who developed it into a Confucian philosophy (see LI). By equating human nature (see XING) with principle and the Way, neither brother regarded human nature as merely the raw human state. Although the younger brother would refer to human nature, principle and the Way as good, Cheng Hao considered them beyond any opposite, so he did not describe them as good. The opposite of good arose, like dysfunctional behaviour, from imbalance and deviation from the Mean. Cheng Hao also first broadened the Confucian idea of humaneness (*ren*) to encompass not only a profound sympathy with all beings but also a mystical oneness with the universe. Drawing support from a medical text, he noted that paralysis of the human limbs was described as an absence of *ren*; thus, it was the life force running through things. Seeking to teach spiritual cultivation of the self in order to realize the unity with all things, he condemned ego-centredness as a barrier to achieving this sense of oneness (see CONFUCIAN PHILOSOPHY, CHINESE §5; NEO-CONFUCIAN PHILOSOPHY §5).

Cheng has been interpreted primarily in two ways. Beginning with Zhu Xi's synthesis of the Confucian Way tradition (see ZHU XI), Cheng and his younger brother have been presented as a unified voice and as students of ZHOU DUNYI. This formulation facilitated Zhu's synthesis of diverse ideas, but even some of his contemporaries questioned his historical and philosophical accuracy. Other scholars, most notably Fung Yu-lan (1953), put Cheng Hao at the head of a subjective wing of Confucianism and his younger brother at the beginning of a rationalistic wing that culminated in Zhu Xi. Both conventional views have, since the 1980s, come to be regarded as exaggerated.

See also: CHENG YI; CONFUCIAN PHILOSOPHY, CHINESE; DAO; NEO-CONFUCIAN PHILOSOPHY; ZHOU DUNYI

List of works

Cheng Hao (1032–85) *Er Cheng ji* (Collected Works of the Two Chengs), Beijing: Zhonghua, 1981, 4 vols. (Cheng Hao's writings are included in this collection, most of which comes from his brother Cheng Yi. Many of the sayings and conversations recorded by their disciples do not make it clear which Cheng brother was talking.)

References and further reading

Chan Wing-tsit (1963) *A Source Book in Chinese Philosophy*, Princeton, NJ: Princeton University Press. (Convenient source of translations, and from the Zhu Xi school of interpretation.)

Zhu Xi [Chu Hsi] and Lü Zuqian (1175) *Reflections on Things at Hand*, trans. Chan Wing-tsit, New York: Columbia University Press. (A good translation of the most influential anthology centring on the works of the Chengs.)

* Feng, Youlan [Fung Yu-lan]. (1953) *A History of Chinese Philosophy*, trans. D. Bodde, Princeton, NJ: Princeton University Press, 2 vols. (A dated and controversial, but still useful, interpretation of the Chengs from his synthesis of Chinese and Western philosophy.)

Graham, A.C. (1958) *Two Chinese Philosophers: Ch'eng Ming-tao and Ch'eng Yi-ch'uan*, London: Lund Humphries; repr. La Salle, IL: Open Court, 1992. (Classic study by a significant modern philosopher, with copious translated passages from both Cheng brothers.)

HOYT CLEVELAND TILLMAN

CHENG HSÜAN *see* ZHENG XUAN

CH'ENG I *see* CHENG YI

CH'ENG MING-TAO *see* CHENG HAO

CHENG YI (1033–1107)

One of the most creative Chinese intellectuals, Cheng Yi was the most systematic and influential of a group of thinkers which channelled Confucian thinking into a new philosophical direction that gradually became dominant in East Asia for several centuries. Buddhism was still the most pervasive and sophisticated religious philosophy of his day; yet he effectively borrowed some of its ideas and methods to formulate a philosophy that would enable Confucian teachers to draw intellectuals away from the Buddhist masters.

Born to a scholar-official family, Cheng Yi lived most of his life around Luoyang, traditionally the secondary capital of China. Although he passed the major part of the highest civil service examination in 1059, he failed the culminating palace examination. Thereafter he lost interest in an official career and devoted himself to learning and teaching the 'Way' (*dao*) of the sages. Though he attracted a few early students, his prominence as a Confucian master came in his mid-fifties when he was appointed a lecturer to the emperor and subsequently a professor in the national academy. Even though his official career was thus limited to educational posts held late in life, his outspoken ideas and uncompromising demeanour eventually provoked the government to confiscate his land and exile him for three years. When he died in 1107, only the most loyal of his students dared to attend his funeral.

His followers developed a fellowship of Confucian intellectuals through which his ideas were disseminated. When in the twelfth century ZHU XI systematized philosophical reorientations of Confucian traditions for what soon became mainstream thinking and subsequently state orthodoxy, he drew more heavily on the ideas of Cheng Yi than any other eleventh-century master.

The central concept in Cheng Yi's philosophy was 'principle' (*li*), the normative patterns inherent in and providing coherence to each and every individual thing (see LI). While his elder brother CHENG HAO used 'principle' to point to a moral force alive in all things, Cheng Yi postulated it as the metaphysical basis of the harmony of the one and the many. Seeking to refute the Buddhist doctrine of 'emptiness' (*śūnyatā*) (see BUDDHIST CONCEPT OF EMPTINESS). Cheng Yi pointed to the linkage between the philosophical, ethical ultimate and the myriad things in daily life in order to fortify Confucian belief in the significance of structures, words and deeds in the sociopolitical realm. For instance, identifying human nature with principle provided a more philosophical basis for Mencius' doctrine of the goodness of human nature (see MENCIUS; XING). Moreover, as a way of explaining the existence of dysfunctional behaviour, Cheng Hao pointed to the interaction between principal and the psychological energy (qi) that constitutes the 'stuff' of all people and things (see QI). Ironically, as Yü Ying-shih (1987) shows, Cheng Yi developed Confucian 'this worldly' ethics after gaining insights into Chan disciplinary methods of meditation and spiritual cultivation. Perhaps because of the nature of his borrowings from Buddhism, his most frequent criticism of Buddhists was not their metaphysics, but their alleged selfishness in devaluing relations in family and society.

The concept of principle also provided a more sophisticated paradigm than the correlative cosmology developed over a thousand years earlier for explaining what was known about the natural world. Like that earlier synthesis, however, Cheng Yi was using the science of his day to bolster traditional values and roles associated with Confucian ethics. For instance, he rejected earlier Confucians' equating the cardinal virtue of humaneness (*ren*) with altruistic love (see CONFUCIAN PHILOSOPHY, CHINESE §5). Love was just a secondary attribute, because humaneness as principle denoted the oneness of all beings.

In Peter Bol's analysis, Cheng Yi made a radical break with the approach that the literati elite took to learning (Bol 1992). Whereas several centuries of intellectuals had focused on literary culture as the medium for understanding culture and values, Cheng announced that the mind could directly grasp the moral patterns inherent in the natural world. Thus, instead of responding primarily to the Buddhist challenge, Cheng was essentially intent on winning the sociopolitical elite to his view of the grounds of ethical values.

See also: BUDDHIST PHILOSOPHY, CHINESE; CHENG HAO; CONFUCIAN PHILOSOPHY, CHINESE; LI; NEO-CONFUCIAN PHILOSOPHY §5

List of works

Cheng Yi (1033–1107) *Er Cheng ji* (Collected Works of the Two Chengs), Beijing: Zhonghua, 1981, 4 vols. (Although Cheng Hao's writings are included, most of the four volumes comes from the work of Cheng Yi. Many of the sayings and conversations recorded by their disciples do not record which Cheng brother was talking.)

References and further reading

* Bol, P.K. (1992) *'This Culture of Ours': Intellectual Transitions in T'ang to Sung China*, Stanford, CA: Stanford University Press. (Using the paradigm of tension between the Way (*dao*) and literary culture (*wen*), Bol explains Cheng Yi's metaphysical philosophy as a radical departure from the Tang and early Song mainstream of literati thought.)
Graham, A.C. (1958) *Two Chinese Philosophers: Ch'eng Ming-tao and Ch'eng Yi-ch'uan*, London: Lund Humphries, reprinted 1992, La Salle, IL: Open Court. (Classic study by a significant modern philosopher and with copious translated passages from both Cheng brothers.)
—— (1986) 'What Was New in the Ch'eng–Chu Theory of Human Nature?', in Chan Wing-tsit (ed.) *Chu Hsi and Neo-Confucianism*, Honolulu, HI: University of Hawaii Press. (Perhaps the best study in English of Cheng Yi's view of the central Confucian problem of human nature.)
Tillman, H.C. (1992) *Confucian Discourse and Chu Hsi's Ascendancy*, Honolulu, HI: University of Hawaii Press. (A study of the Confucian fellowship and its ideas beginning with Cheng Yi and continuing through its establishment as orthodoxy in 1241.)
* Yu Yingshi [Yü Ying-shih] (1987) *Zhongguo jinshi congjiao lunli yu shangren jingshen* (The Religious Ethic and Mercantile Spirit in Modern China), Taibei: Lianjing. (Refutes Max Weber's findings about Chinese religion, but uses the question poised by Weber about the impact of religious values on merchant class values to explore changes in Buddhism and Confucianism, beginning respectively in the Tang and Song periods. An expanded English version is forthcoming.)

HOYT CLEVELAND TILLMAN

CH'ENG YI-CH'UAN

see CHENG YI

CHERNYSHEVSKII, NIKOLAI GAVRILOVICH (1828–89)

Nikolai Chernyshevskii was the main theorist of the Russian democratic radicalism of 'the 1860s' or, more precisely, of the period of political 'thaw' and liberal reforms which followed Russian defeat in the Crimean War and the enthronement (in 1855) of Alexander II. He was also the best representative of the non-conformist elements among the raznochintsy, *that is, the educated commoners, who at that time began to figure prominently in Russian intellectual and social life. As such, he exerted a powerful formative influence on the Russian intelligentsia.*

In 1862 Chernyshevskii was arrested, brought to trial and, despite insufficient evidence, condemned to lifetime banishment in Siberia. In exile, preserving his integrity to the end, he stoutly refused to ask for clemency (as a result, he remained in a remote Siberian village until 1883). In prison, waiting for trial, he wrote the novel Chto Delat' *(What Is To Be Done?) in which he showed the 'new men' of Russia – 'rational egoists', devoted to the cause of progress, and even a type of ascetic, self-sacrificing revolutionist. Thanks to a strange oversight of the censor the novel was serialized in the journal* Sovremennik *(The Contemporary) and, despite lack of literary distinction, became a powerful source of inspiration for several generations of Russian progressive youth.*

Chernyshevskii's philosophical reputation was created by the Russian Marxists. The 'father of Russian Marxism', G.V. Plekhanov, greatly impressed by Chernyshevskii's combination of Feuerbachian materialism and respect for Hegelian dialectics, described him as an important precursor of dialectical materialism. This view was taken up by Lenin who in Materialism and Empiriocriticism *called Chernyshevskii 'the great Russian Hegelian and materialist', the only Russian philosopher before Marxism who was able to defend 'integral materialism' against the agnosticism and subjectivism of Neo-Kantians, positivists, Machists and 'other muddleheads'. Soviet philosophers went even further: Chernyshevskii was treated by them not only as the greatest Russian philosopher before Marxism, but also as the greatest pre-Marxian philosopher of the world, founder of the highest form of pre-Marxian materialism. For several decades this was the obligatory dogma of the Soviet official ideology.*

After the breakdown of the Soviet Union, interest in Chernyshevskii's philosophy almost completely disappeared in Russia. It is impossible, however, to deny Chernyshevskii's importance in Russian intellectual history. Hence the need of rethinking his philosophical legacy.

1 Aesthetics
2 The anthropological principle
3 Political philosophy

1 Aesthetics

Nikolai Gavrilovich Chernyshevskii, son of an Orthodox priest in the city of Saratov, intended initially to become a priest himself. However, he changed his mind and, after graduating from a theological seminary, entered the faculty of history and philology at St Petersburg University. During his studies in St Petersburg he became acquainted with the works of Hegel and FEUERBACH, as well as with the writings of the French utopian socialists. His favourite Russian thinker was the literary critic V.G. BELINSKII. Young Chernyshevskii fully shared Belinskii's view on the special mission of literature and literary criticism in autocratic Russia. He decided, therefore, to provide literary critics with a theoretical clarification of the essence of art (with particular emphasis on literature) and of the role of art in society. He fulfilled this task in his master's dissertation 'Ėsteticheskie otnosheniia iskusstva k deistvitelnosti' (The Aesthetic Relations Between Art and Reality) (published and publicly defended in the spring of 1855).

Chernyshevskii's dissertation (as he himself explained in the preface to its third edition, 1888) was in fact a critique of Hegelian aesthetics from the point of view of Feuerbachian materialism. However, the Draconian censorship regulations, introduced in 1848 and still holding at the time of its writing, made it impossible to refer openly to Hegel and Feuerbach. Hence, Chernyshevskii's thesis took the form of a sharp critique of the Hegelian aesthetics of F.T. Visher, seen as a representative specimen of the 'dominant aesthetic theory'.

Against Hegelian idealism, defining beauty as a manifestation of the Absolute Idea, Chernyshevskii set his own conception, which reads as follows: 'Beauty is life; beautiful is that being in which we see life as it should be according to our conceptions'. In accordance with Feuerbach's anthropological materialism, this was to be a materialist and an anthropocentric conception: materialist, because 'life' was seen in it as rooted in nature and the beauty of art was interpreted a mere reflection of natural beauty; anthropocentric because the human being in the full

flowering of his faculties was made the measure of all things and the supreme ideal of beauty. Chernyshevskii conceded that this anthropological ideal could be interpreted in different ways, depending on historical and social circumstances, but strongly insisted that the aesthetic ideas of the privileged classes reflected an artificial life and were, therefore, normatively illegitimate. Only the working people, living in touch with nature, were the true representatives of the human species and thus the living embodiments of the supreme aesthetic ideal. In this way the Feuerbachian 'rehabilitation of nature' was linked with a cult of the common people and with the demand for the widest possible democratization of art.

Chernyshevskii's programmatic naturalism led to the conclusion that art was merely a surrogate for reality. Against aesthetic idealism Chernyshevskii set the view that works of art could only copy real life and that artists, therefore, could not claim to possess genuinely creative power. Nevertheless, he also stressed, somewhat inconsistently, that the function of art is not only to reproduce reality, but also to explain and evaluate it – to 'pass judgment' on the real-life phenomena that have been recreated in it. He made it explicit that because of this art, especially literature, could and should perform a socially useful didactic role, and that artists, especially writers, could and should become spiritual leaders of society.

Chernyshevskii's aesthetic ideas aroused very different reactions. Critics who defended uncommitted 'pure art' were horrified by them; Ivan Turgenev, expressing the views of many liberal-minded writers, reduced them to 'blind malice and stupidity'; in contrast with this Dmitrii Pisarev praised Chernyshevskii's thesis as a total elimination of aesthetics in the name of utilitarian values. On the whole, the acceptance or non-acceptance of the 'Aesthetic Relations Between Art and Reality' marked the difference between Russian liberals and democratic radicals. The latter enthusiastically embraced Chernyshevskii's ideas, treating them as obligatory guidelines for progressive literary criticism.

Soviet literary scholars used to emphasize that in *What Is To Be Done?* Chernyshevskii did not limit himself to a critical explanation and evaluation of the existing reality but also expounded positive ideals – an image of a revolutionary hero and a vision of a socialist society of the future. This allowed them to treat Chernyshevskii as an important precursor of 'socialist realism'.

2 The anthropological principle

Chernyshevskii's philosophical position was best

defined in his 'Antropologicheskii printsip v filosofii' (Anthropological Principle in Philosophy) (1860), a work written in connection with Lavrov's *Sketches* (see LAVROV, P.L. §1). (Contrary to most commentaries, Chernyshevskii endorsed Lavrov's anthropologism and only wanted to remove from it what he saw as concessions to idealism and eclecticism).

For Chernyshevskii the 'anthropological principle' supplied the theoretical foundation for the integral wholeness of man, the abolition of the eternal dualism of body and soul. The human individual, he argued, has only one indivisible nature and only as such can he represent an absolute value to other human beings. In Chernyshevskii's interpretation this principle was a cornerstone of an entire philosophical worldview (see RUSSIAN MATERIALISM: 'THE 1860S').

First, it was conceived as the reinstatement of a distinctively Feuerbachian, anthropocentric materialism, that is to say, a form of materialism capable of resisting all forms of idealism without becoming fully dependent on the dehumanized, mechanistic world of the natural sciences. Chernyshevskii intended his materialism to provide a basis for value-judgments; hence he had to distance himself from the cold abstractions of value-neutral objectivist scientism.

Second, Chernyshevskii's materialism was a theory of the human organism as both knower and object of knowledge – thus positing the indivisibility of matter and consciousness. For man, Chernyshevskii reasoned, the primary datum is not thinking but existence, including bodily existence in the material environment. He saw this standpoint as undermining the foundation of idealistic epistemology and proving decisive arguments against subjectivism and agnosticism.

Finally, the anthropological principle was conceived as a philosophical underpinning of the ethical conception of 'rational egoism' – a conception based on the premise that, ultimately, the guiding principle of conduct is individual interest. In the normative sphere this theory gave preference to utilitarianism, rationalism and egalitarianism. It postulated that the standard by which human actions must be judged is the benefit they bring – that good is not an autonomous value but only a lasting benefit, 'a very beneficial benefit'. The rational egoist accepts other people's right to be egoists because he knows that all people are equal; in controversial issues he is guided by the principle of the greatest good of the greatest number. In interpreting this utilitarian principle Chernyshevskii differed from Bentham's belief in the self-regulating market; he followed instead Feuerbach's view that truly rational individuals were communal beings, capable of conscious cooperation in pursuing mutually agreed common ends. His social

ideal was therefore a cooperative socialism, presupposing the full liberation of the individual from all sorts of blind faith and authoritarian compulsion. He outlined this vision in *What Is To Be Done?*, emphasizing in particular the full emancipation of women.

3 Political philosophy

Chernyshevskii's political philosophy concentrated on problems relevant to Russia as an underdeveloped country, a 'latecomer to the arena of history'.

In many points – in his commitment to the idea of the liberation of the individual, in his conviction that Russia should still learn from the West and humbly recognize the superiority of Western achievements – Chernyshevskii continued the line of Russian Westernism. In the essay 'O prichinakh padeniia Rima' (What Caused the Downfall of Rome?) (1861) he criticized all Russian conceptions of the 'senility' of the West, including Herzen's 'Russian socialism' (see HERZEN, A.I.). And yet there was a time (1856–7) when he thought it appropriate to cut himself off from the epigones of Westernism and to declare that in many respects he stood closer to the Slavophiles. He even proposed to the Slavophiles a kind of alliance for the joint defence of the peasant commune against the liberal economists, who demanded that it be abolished together with feudal bondage. This alliance, however, could not be concluded because the differences between the two partners were too important: the Slavophiles wanted to preserve pre-capitalist social relations, while Chernyshevskii saw the commune as a suitable means for a direct transition to a rational socialist collectivism.

In his articles on political economy (which were criticized but highly appreciated by Marx) Chernyshevskii set against bourgeois liberalism a conception of 'the political economy of the working people'. He fully recognized the progressiveness of capitalist development in the West, but was aware of its contradictions and wanted for his country a more humane and, at the same time, a more rapid type of progress. In his 'Kritika filosofskikh predubezhdenii protiv obshchinnogo zemlevladeniia' (Criticism of Philosophical Prejudices Against the Peasant Commune) (1859) he argued that Russia, and backward countries in general, could benefit from the experience and scientific achievements of the West and 'skip the intermediate stages of development or at least enormously reduce their length'. His main argument for the commune was based on a dialectical conception of progress: the first stage of any development is, as a rule, similar in form to the third; thus primitive communal collectivism is similar in form to the developed collectivism of a socialist society and can make easier a direct transition to it.

Chernyshevskii's criticism of the liberals was also levelled against political liberalism. He published in his journal *Sovremennik* a series of articles on the revolutions in France in which he sharply distinguished between liberals, who aimed at 'merely political' freedom, and democrats, whose main concern was the social welfare of the people. He did not hesitate to say that from the democratic point of view Siberia was a better country than England because Siberian peasants were better off than English proletarians ('Iulskaiia monarkhiia' (The July Monarchy) 1858). This populist conception of democracy exerted a mighty influence on the Russian revolutionary movement. Members of the revolutionary organization Land and Freedom treated Chernyshevskii as their intellectual leader and often asked him for advice.

However, Chernyshevskii himself did not embrace revolutionary solutions. Undemocratic methods used to prepare the abolition of serfdom in Russia, as well as his own unlawful arrest and trial, convinced him that the main obstacle on the way to true progress in Russia was lack of the rule of law and political freedom. Therefore in his 'Pis'ma bez adresa' (Letters Without Addressee) (1862) – whose addressee was actually Alexander II – he sided with the gentry liberals of Tver', who demanded a liberal constitution for Russia. In the penal settlement in Siberia he surprised his fellow prisoners by a total reversal of his previous view of political freedom. It is true, he argued, that political freedom cannot feed a hungry man, but without food people can survive several days, while without air they cannot live more than a few minutes. As air is necessary for the life of the human organism, so political freedom is necessary for the normal functioning of society.

Nevertheless, Russian liberals did not claim Chernyshevskii's legacy, thus allowing the revolutionists to take a monopolistic hold on it and to interpret it accordingly. The reception of Chernyshevskii's political ideas was therefore extremely one-sided. He was seen as an intransigent enemy of liberalism, preaching class struggle, categorically rejecting all half-way reforms and pushing Russia onto the path of agrarian revolution. This interpretation was radicalized by Lenin, in whose eyes Chernyshevskii was the greatest, most consistent representative of pre-Marxian 'revolutionary democracy' in Russia. The Soviet Marxists accepted this view and tried to present 'revolutionary democratism' as the most advanced political position before the emergence of Marxism.

List of works

Chernyshevskii, N.G. (1939–53) *Polnoe sobranie sochinenii* (Complete Works), Moscow: Khudozhestvennaiia literatura, 16 vols.

—— (1863) *Chto delat'*, in *Sovremennik*, St Petersburg; trans. B.R. Tucker, *What Is To Be Done?*, New York: Vintage Books, 1961. (Chernyshevskii's famous novel, first published in serial form.)

—— (1953) *Selected Philosophical Essays*, Moscow: Foreign Language Publishing House. (A representative selection of Chernyshevskii's philosophical thought in English. Includes 'Aesthetic Relations Between Art and Reality', 'Anthropological Principle in Philosophy' and 'Criticism of Philosophical Prejudices Against the Peasant Commune'.)

References and further reading

Lavretskii, A. (1941) *Belinskii, Chernyshevskii i Dobroliubov v bor'be za realism* (Belinskii, Chernyshevskii and Dobroliubov in the Struggle for Realism), Moscow: Khudozhestvennaiia literatura. (A representative Soviet work on Chernyshevskii's aesthetics and literary criticism, trying to present him as a precursor of 'socialist realism'.)

Lukács, G. (1956) *Einführung in die Aesthetik Tschernyschevskijs* (Introduction to Chernyshevskii's Aesthetics), in G. Lukács, *Beiträge zur Geschichte der Aesthetik*, Berlin. (Takes the view that Chernyshevskii's theory of realism represented the highest point in the development of pre-Marxist aesthetics.)

Pereira, N.G.O. (1975) *The Thought and Teachings of N.G. Černyševskij*, The Hague: Mouton. (A good introduction to Chernyshevskii's thought in English.)

Plekhanov, G.V. (1894) *N.G. Tschernischevsky. Eine literar-historische Studie* (N.G. Chernyshevskii. A Historical and Literary Study), Stuttgart: Dietz; *N.G. Chernyshevskii*, St Petersburg: Shipovnik, 1910. (The first comprehensive monograph on Chernyshevskii's philosophical view, by the 'Father of Marxism'.)

Steklov, Y.M. (1928) *N.G. Chernyshevskii, ego zhizn' i deiatelnost'* (N.G. Chernyshevskii, His Life and Activities), Moscow-Leningrad: Gosudarstvennoe izdatelstvo, 2 vols. (The crowning achievement of the early Soviet scholarship on Chernyshevskii.)

ANDRZEJ WALICKI

CH'I *see* QI

CHI *see* QI

CHIA I *see* JIA YI

CHICHERIN, B. *see* HEGELIANISM, RUSSIAN; LIBERALISM, RUSSIAN

CHIH *see* ZHI

CHIH TUN *see* ZHI DUN

CHIH-I *see* ZHIYI

CHILD'S THEORY OF MIND
see MIND, CHILD'S THEORY OF

CHILE, PHILOSOPHY IN
see POSITIVIST THOUGHT IN LATIN AMERICA

CHILLINGWORTH, WILLIAM (1602–44)

Chillingworth was one of the most notable English-speaking contributors to debates between Protestants and Catholics in the seventeenth century. His use of a distinction between metaphysical and moral certainty proved extremely influential, as did his rationalist and fallibilist approach to issues of faith and authority.

William Chillingworth was born in England at Oxford, and was educated there at Trinity College, where he became a fellow in 1628. In the same year he renounced his allegiance to the Church of England, resigned his fellowship and became a Roman Catholic. He travelled abroad to a Catholic seminary in the Netherlands, probably at Douai, possibly at St Omer, but soon found the life uncongenial and returned to England. In the early 1630s he had no clear religious allegiance, but was reconciled to the Church of England by 1635. From 1634 he lived at Viscount Falkland's house at Great Tew in Oxfordshire; Falkland's posthumously published *Discourse of Infallibility* (1645) owes much to Chillingworth's arguments. In the autumn of 1637 Chillingworth published his chief work, *The Religion of Protestants a Safe Way to Salvation*, directed against the Jesuit Edward Knott. When the Civil War broke out he sided with the King, and died as a prisoner of war in January 1644, following his capture at Arundel.

As its title indicates, *The Religion of Protestants* is a work of religious controversy, not a philosophical treatise. In this respect it resembles Hooker's *Laws of Ecclesiastical Polity* (1593–1600), but whereas Hooker adopted a strategy of laying down general principles and thereby out-flanking his opponents, Chillingworth chose to fight on his opponent's ground (see HOOKER, R.). The structure of the work is therefore dictated entirely by its target, Knott's *Mercy and Truth. Or Charity Maintained by Catholickes* (1634). This choice of tactics reflected the fundamental characteristics of Chillingworth's mind, essentially critical and combative rather than speculative or constructive. At Oxford he had acquired a near-legendary reputation for agility in debate, and he was understandably confident of his capacity to subdue any opponent.

Knott and Chillingworth both unequivocally accepted the infallibility of the Bible, but differed as to whether this was enough. For Knott, infallible Scriptures need to be expounded by an infallible interpreter; otherwise nothing could ever be certain in religion, and faith would degenerate into mere opinion. Chillingworth adamantly denied this. The Scriptures provide an infallible rule by which controversies are to be judged, but no infallible judge of their meaning exists on earth, either in the person of the Pope or anywhere else. No church has therefore the right to claim infallibility for its articles of faith. The Church of England claims no more than 'an Authority of determining Controversies of Faith, according to plain and evident Scripture and Universal Tradition' (Chillingworth 1638: ii.162); neither its articles nor those of the Lutherans or the Calvinists possess the infallibility of the Scriptures from which they are derived. It is this that lies behind Chillingworth's most often quoted dictum – so misleading when taken out of context – that 'The BIBLE, I say, the BIBLE only, is the Religion of Protestants!' (Chillingworth 1638: vi.56).

Chillingworth saw Knott's position as resting on two fundamental confusions – that of infallibility with authority, and of infallibility with certainty. Not all certainties are the same – indeed two quite separate kinds need to be distinguished. Metaphysical certainty belongs to direct revelations from God, to self-evident propositions and their logical consequences, and to the direct testimony of the senses. Faith cannot have this kind of certainty – if it could it would no longer be faith, but knowledge; it can, however, be morally certain – that is, probable to the highest degree. This is the only certainty that historical propositions can ever possess. Chillingworth naturally rejected Knott's scriptural and patristic arguments for papal infallibility, but he also insisted repeatedly that, even if successful, they could give the doctrine moral certainty only, not the infallible, metaphysical certainty that Knott's position required.

Chillingworth's approach to theology was unswervingly rationalist: 'neither God doth nor man may, require of us as our dutie, to give a greater assent to the conclusion, than the premises deserve' (Chillingworth 1638: ii.154). Blind faith is in no way meritorious: 'God hath given us our Reason to discern between Truth and Falshood, and he that makes not this use of it, but beleeves things he knowes not why, I say it is by chance that he believes the Truth, and not by choice: and that I cannot but feare, that God will not accept of this *Sacrifice of fooles*' (ii.113). It is hardly surprising that this did not find favour with Chillingworth's opponents, either Catholic or Protestant. Their doubts about the reality of Chillingworth's own faith were quite unfounded, as his sermons made plain, but suspicions that he might not be the safest of allies were more understandable. As Hobbes, who had met him at Great Tew, sardonically observed, 'he was like a lusty fighting fellow that did drive his enemies before him, but would often give his owne party smart back-blowes' (Aubrey 1898 vol. 1: 173).

Locke greatly admired Chillingworth, and the two men had much in common (see LOCKE, J. §7). Both were accused by hostile critics of Socinianism, wrongly in Chillingworth's case (see SOCINIANISM), and both can more fairly be regarded as credal minimalists: 'wee suppose that all the necessary points of Religion are plaine and easie, & consequently every man in this cause to be a competent Iudge for himself' (Chillingworth 1638: ii.16). They shared a deep loathing of religious persecution, not merely for its cruelty, but for its presumption: 'God hath authoriz'd no man to force all men to *Unity of Opinion*' (Chillingworth 1638: ii.85).

A few months before *The Religion of Protestants* appeared, Descartes' *Discourse on Method* was published in Holland. Chillingworth had no knowledge of Descartes' work and their two projects were utterly dissimilar; the fundamental congruence of their epistemology is therefore all the more striking (see DESCARTES, R. §3). Both take as basic the cognitive sovereignty of the individual. Authority may be accepted, but has first to be judged by reason, and this is something that each one of us has to do alone.

See also: FAITH

List of works

Chillingworth, W. (1727) *The Works of William Chillingworth*, London: Benjamin Motte. (This ninth edition contains Nine Sermons preached to the King and others, and Nine Additional Discourses, all quite short, on matters related to the Religion of Protestants.)

—— (1638) *The Religion of Protestants a Safe Way to Salvation*, Oxford: Leonard Lichfield; Menston: Scolar Press, 1972. (Chillingworth's most important philosophical work. Although published in the autumn of 1637, it is dated 1638 on the title page.)

References and further reading

* Aubrey, J. (1898) 'Chillingworth', in *'Brief Lives', chiefly of contemporaries... set down between 1669 &1696*, ed. A. Clark, Oxford: Oxford University Press, 2 vols. (Edited from the author's original manuscripts, this is the source of the description of Chillingworth attributed to Hobbes.)

* Cary, Sir Lucius, Viscount Falkland (1645) *Discourse of Infallibility*; repr. as *Sir Lucius Cary, Late Viscount of Falkland. His Discourse of Infallibility with an answer to it: And his Lordships Reply*, London: Gertrude Dawson, 1651. (Posthumously published work which owes much to Chillingworth's arguments.)

* Hooker, R. (1593–1600) Of the Laws of Ecclesiastical Polity, in W.S. Hill (ed.) *The Folger Library Edition of the Works of Richard Hooker*; vols 1–3, Cambridge, MA: Harvard University Press, 1977–81; vol. 6, Binghamton, NY: Medieval and Renaissance Texts and Studies, 1993. (Books I–V of the *Laws* were published between 1593 and 1600, and Books VI–VIII published posthumously between 1648 and 1662. Volumes 1–3 of this edition provide the main text; volume 6 gives discursive introductions and detailed commentary.)

* Knott, E. (Matthew Wilson) (1634) *Mercy and Truth. Or Charity Maintained by Catholickes*, St Omer (?). (The target of Chillingworth's Religion of Protestants.)

Leeuwen, H.G. Van (1963) *The Problem of Certainty in English Thought, 1630–1690*, The Hague: Martinus Nijhoff. (Not always accurate on Chillingworth, but a useful account of his influence.)

Orr, R.R. (1967) *Reason and Authority: the Thought of*

William Chillingworth, Oxford: Clarendon Press. (The fullest account of Chillingworth's life and thought, including a list of unpublished manuscripts.)

Trevor-Roper, H. (1987) *Catholics, Anglicans and Puritans*, London: Secker & Warburg. (Chapter 4 gives an excellent account of the Great Tew circle.)

J. R. MILTON

CHINESE CLASSICS

The Chinese Classics are a group of texts of divination, history, philosophy, poetry, ritual and lexicography that have, to a significant extent, defined the orthodox Ruhist (Confucian) tradition of China. Since the Song dynasty (960–1279), they have consisted of the following thirteen texts:

(1) The Shujing, *or* Shangshu *(Book of Documents, or Documents), the 'classic' of Chinese political philosophy. Allegedly compiled by Confucius, it contains a variety of historical documents, mostly dating from the fourth century* BC.

(2) The Yijing *(Book of Changes), a divinatory work using sixty-four permutations of broken (yin) and straight (yang) lines in six positions. It has two parts: the 'Zhouyi' (Zhou Changes), an ancient divination manual, and the* Shiyi *(Ten Wings), a commentary dating from the Warring States period (403–222* BC*).*

(3) The Shijing *(Book of Songs, or Odes), a collection of 305 poems, ostensibly selected by Confucius, on a wide variety of subjects. It includes songs of farming, feasting and love that are clearly of popular origin. It also contains a variety of court poetry including dynastic hymns, hunting and banquet songs and political satires from the Zhou court (1121–222* BC*).*

(4) The Yili *(Ceremony and Rites), a Warring States ritual text.*

(5) The Zhouli *(Rites of Zhou), another Warring States ritual text.*

(6) the Liji *(Book of Rites), a Han work that provides information about early Confucian philosophy and ritual. Together, works (4), (5) and (6) make up the* Lijing *(Classic of Rites).*

(7) The Zuozhuan *(Zuo Annals).*

(8) The Guliangzhuan *(Guliang Annals).*

(9) The Gongyangzhuan *(Gongyang Annals). Works (7), (8) and (9) are commentaries to the* Chunqiu *(Spring and Autumn Annals, or simply Annals), a chronicle of the reigns of twelve rulers of the state of Lu; its presentation of diplomatic and political events from 722–481* BC *is terse and factual, but the three*

commentaries provide substantial elaboration and exegesis.

(10) The Analects *of Confucius (Lunyu), containing anecdotes and short dialogues between Confucius and his disciples. In this work, Confucius established a new emphasis on humanistic ethics and political and social order.*

(11) The Xiaojing *(Book of Filial Piety), a short dialogue between Confucius and one of his disciples, concerned with filiality in both private and public life; it discusses children's filiality to their parents and subjects' filiality toward their rulers.*

(12) The Erya, *a book of glosses of Zhou dynasty terms (the title means 'Graceful and Refined').*

(13) The Mengzi, *which records a series of dialogues and debates between the philosopher Mencius and his students, several rulers and a variety of rhetorical and philosophical opponents. Mencius elaborated upon the* Analects, *arguing that human nature was inherently good and claiming that four 'sprouts' of goodness could be educated to create intuitive ability as the correct basis for moral judgments.*

The practice of appealing to authoritative texts appeared as early as the Analects *of Confucius, around 500* BC. *An explicit classical canon first appeared some four hundred years later during the Han dynasty (206* BC–AD 220*), when Emperor Wu institutionalized a set of five classics associated with Confucius. At the same time he established new procedures for recruiting officials, created official chairs for the study of the Five Classics, restricted official academic appointments to those five areas and founded an imperial academy for the study and transmission of those works. In this way he effectively created a new 'Confucian' state religion. The term 'classic' (jing) also appears as the first of six categories of literature in the classification system of the bibliographical chapter of the* Hanshu *(History of the Former Han Dynasty). Classics (jing) are distinguished from masters (zi), the latter being grouped into nine schools starting with the Ru, or Confucians.*

Since the Han dynasty, the content of the classical canon has grown from the original five (or seven) texts, as established during the Han dynasty. The original group of classical texts that acquired official sanction during the early Han empire was supplemented by additional texts during the Tang (617–907) and Song (960–1279) periods. The Chunqiu *(Spring and Autumn Annals) became known under the titles of three commentary editions, the* Gongyangzhuan, Guliangzhuan *and* Zuozhuan, *as noted above. The* Lijing *became known as three separate works on ritual, the* Yili, *the* Zhouli *and the* Liji, *again as noted above. The* Erya *was added to the classical canon during the Tang dynasty and the* Mengzi *during the Song dynasty, bringing the total to what became the standard thirteen texts.*

These works functioned as classics in a number of ways. They formed the core education of the bureaucratic elite, they provided an important source for imperial authority and they set the philosophical agenda for the dominant Confucian tradition. The classics are also significant for what they do not contain. Many of what are now considered the greatest philosophical works of the Warring States period are classified as masters, not classics; examples include the Zhuangzi, *the* Xunzi *and (until the Song dynasty) even the* Mengzi.

1   **Early ideas of textual authority**
2   **Definition of the canon**
3   **The thirteen classics**
4   **Significance**

1   Early ideas of textual authority

The practice of citing textual authority can be traced to the Zhou dynasty (1121–222 BC). There is evidence that the practice of poetic quotation of selected portions from the *Shijing* (Book of Songs) was highly valued by the Zhou elite. Quotation from the *Shijing* (and, to a lesser extent, the *Shujing* (Book of Documents)) could be used to lend the authority of tradition to particular utterances. The ambiguity of quotation could also be used in a variety of diplomatic, domestic and political contexts to diffuse tension or criticize a hierarchical superior. In this sense, the origins of the classics involve the notion of criticizing authority. In the *Analects* of CONFUCIUS, three texts are commonly appealed to as sources of authoritative utterance: the *Shijing*, the *Shujing* and the *Yijing* (Book of Changes). While the *Analects* thus contains a distinct notion of authoritative texts, there is no reference to an explicit classical canon of any kind.

Four works mark the beginning of what was later to become the Chinese classical tradition: the *Shujing*, the *Yijing*, the *Chunqiu* (Spring and Autumn Annals) and the *Shijing*. While tradition ascribes the compilation of these works to Confucius, they in fact date from the Zhou court between the ninth and sixth centuries BC. These annals and collections of poetry and ritual reflect the values and concerns of the Zhou aristocracy: sacrifice and warfare. The *Shujing* contains terse accounts of investitures, royal decisions and pronouncements and ritual dances, one of which, for example, celebrates the accession of King Wen of Zhou over the preceding Shang dynasty. The *Shijing* also contains sacrificial and ritual hymns from the

Zhou court, as well as a variety of other popular songs. The *Chunqiu* is a series of ritual documents in careful chronological order. These may have originated as an historical archive of fire divinations, performed by heating pieces of tortoise shell or animal bone on which a divinatory inquiry had been inscribed. A second form of divination entailed the manipulation of yarrow stalks, where even and odd numbers corresponded to broken or unbroken lines that represented yin and yang respectively, in a complex scheme of sixty-four permutations. Of the various yarrow-stalk divination systems (*yi*) used in various contexts, only the Zhou system has been preserved; the *Zhouyi (Zhou Changes)* forms the core of the *Yijing* (see YIJING).

2   Definition of the canon

Mention of a canon of six classics first appears in the *Zhuangzi*, itself a particularly non-canonical text (see ZHUANGZI). Chapter 14 of this work refers to six classics: *Shijing*, *Shujing*, *Lijing* (Book of Rites), *Yuejing* (Book of Music), *Yijing* and the *Chunqiu*. (A separate reference in the previous chapter mentions, but does not name, twelve classics.) The late Warring States philosopher XUNZI also refers to the same six, which he helped establish as canonical works of early Ruhist (Confucian) schools. The First Emperor of the Qin proscribed five of the six in 213 BC; the exception was the *Yijing*, presumably for its divinatory content. This imperial proscription, combined with the destruction of the Imperial Library in 207 BC, caused a serious breach in the transmission of these works, and the *Yuejing* may have been lost during this period.

The category of classics (*jing*) first appeared during the Han dynasty as an effort to create or re-create a textual canon. In 136 BC, under the influence of the philosopher DONG ZHONGSHU, the Emperor Wu of the Han promulgated a set of five classics associated with Confucius. He established five academic chairs for the specific study of five works, the *Yijing*, *Shijing*, *Shujing*, *Lijing* and *Chunqiu*. He further restricted the appointment of academicians to the specific study of those five classics. In 124 BC, also under the influence of Dong Zhongshu, he founded the Taixue, an imperial academy for the training and examination of students in those works, as a way of recruiting able officials. Students completing work at the academy were examined on the Five Classics in a written examination marking the beginning of the state examination system. These measures also established an explicit concept of a canon of classical texts in China, the importance of which cannot be underestimated. They raised Han Confucianism to the status of a state religion, and established these works as the basis for the education of officials. Despite this official recognition of both texts and institutions, however, the Han dynasty saw considerable debate about the legitimacy of both texts and editions of texts. While the Five Classics was the most frequent articulation of the Han Confucian canon, a set of seven classics added the *Analects* of Confucius and the *Xiaojing* (Book of Filial Piety) to the original five.

Also during the Han period a classification system of six classes of literature emerged, of which the category of the classics was first and foremost. The bibliographical chapter of the *Hanshu* (History of the Former Han Dynasty), edited by Ban Gu (AD 32–92) and based on an earlier compilation by Liu Xin (d. AD 23) lists the following six classes of literature: (1) the Six Classics (*jing*), (2) the masters (*zi*), grouped into nine schools, of which the Ru were most prominent, (3) poetry, (4) strategy manuals, (5) the numerical arts and (6) 'prescriptive techniques'. Much of the philosophical tradition of China is to be found not among the classics but among the masters (*zi*). These works are attributed to individuals to whose surnames the suffix *zi* or 'Master' has been added. Recent scholarship has shown that many of these texts are probably of composite authorship and are less the works of individuals than the core texts of 'schools' or lineages based on textual transmissions of these works (see GUANZI; HAN FEIZI; HUAINANZI; MENCIUS; MOZI; SUNZI; XUNZI; ZHUANGZI).

By Tang times, the number of classics expanded through the treatment of commentaries and component sections as individual works. The *Yili* (Ceremony and Rites), *Zhouli* (Rites of Zhou) and the *Liji* (Book of Rites), works on ritual that had presumably comprised the original *Lijing*, were now treated as separate works. The *Gongyangzhuan* (Gongyang Annals), *Guliangzhuan* (Guliang Annals) and *Zuozhuan* (Zuo Annals), three commentary editions of the *Chunqiu*, replaced the original in the classical canon. In addition, the *Erya* was recognized as a classic, as were the *Analects* and *Xiaojing*. During the Song dynasty the *Mengzi* was added, bringing the total to thirteen classics.

3 The thirteen classics

The *Shujing* or *Shangshu* (Book of Documents, or Documents), is a heterogeneous compendium of historical documents. Tradition names Confucius as the editor of this 'classic' of Chinese political philosophy, much of which was forged during the fourth century BC. The *Shujing* contains terse accounts of investitures, royal decisions and pronouncements, and ritual dances. It also contains dialogues between kings and ministers, including the advice of ministers to kings, all of which provides some insight into Warring States and Han political philosophy. The *Shujing* contains sections of philosophical exposition on principles of government which could be taken either as a standard of conduct for a discerning and virtuous emperor, or as a guide to conduct for a loyal minister.

The *Yijing* (Book of Changes) consists of an ancient manual of divination of uncertain provenance (the *Zhouyi*, or Zhou Changes) and a group of Warring States period commentaries (the Ten Wings). The divination system employs sixty-four permutations of broken (*yin*) and straight (*yang*) lines combined in six positions. As early as the Han dynasty, the *Yijing* was recognized as foremost among the classics and has functioned as a symbolic language of change and transformation. The *Yijing* provides a theoretical conception of the world as both sui generis and in a constant process of change and transformation according to discernible patterns of two complementary forces. The *yin–yang* theory first articulated in the *Yijing* provided the basis for later cosmologies of change and formed part of the foundation of early Daoist thought, medicine and the development of scientific thought in China (see DAOIST PHILOSOPHY; YIJING; YIN–YANG).

The *Shijing* is the earliest anthology of poetry in China. According to one tradition, Confucius selected compendium of 305 poems from a larger collection of three thousand poems of popular origin gathered at the Zhou court and dating from the beginning of the Zhou dynasty (tenth century BC) to the middle of the Spring and Autumn period (seventh century BC). It contains four sections of differing geographic origin and contents. The airs (*feng*), a northern collection of songs of community life, farming, feasting and love, preserve a subversive quality of 'pre-Confucian' society that at times conflicts with later use by Confucian exegetes. The odes or elegantiae (*ya*) are hunting and banquet songs and political complaints and satires, probably from the Zhou court. The lauds (*song*) are dynastic hymns used in court ceremony and sacrifice. Whatever the authorship of these diverse materials, quotation from the *Shijing* was widely used to support Ruhist argumentation and imperial authority within Han and Warring States texts. The Great Preface to the *Shijing* also contains a remarkable concise formulation of a theory of poetics and aesthetics.

The *Lijing* (Classic of Rites, or Three Rites) is a compendium of Zhou dynasty court religious and social ritual. It consists of three works: the *Zhouli* (Rites of Zhou), the *Yili* (Ceremony and Rites) and the *Liji* (Book of Rites). The *Lijing* was the worst preserved of the Five Classics, and the three extant versions of these works on ritual all date from later periods. The *Yili* dates from some time after Confucius, the *Zhouli* dates from the late Warring States period and the extant form of the *Liji* dates from the Han dynasty. The *Yili* provides details of ceremonies from the Spring and Autumn period; it includes detailed descriptions of sacrificial rituals for auspicious occasions, rituals for mourning and funerals, rituals for the reception of guests (including state visits and royal audiences) and rituals for various festive occasions (such as marriage, the capping ceremony for young men, archery contests and the reception of ministers). The *Zhouli* is an idealized description of the Zhou bureaucracy. It describes the ministries that formed the Zhou government, including such topics as the supervision control and appointment of officials, agriculture and marriage, state and religious rites, defense and security, legal administration and public works and civil engineering. It contains many interpolations by Han scholars and is of dubious historical value, but its detailed descriptions provide important insights into early Confucian views of government, law and administration. The *Liji* contains material that ranges in date from the late Warring States to the early Han. It provides information about both ritual and Ruhist philosophy, and contains a variety of Ruhist teachings from the late Zhou through the Han. It also contains essays on general principles of ritual. This section includes two works that the neo-Confucian scholar ZHU XI established as two of the Confucian Four Books: the *Zhongyong* (Doctrine of the Mean) and the *Daxue* (Great Preface) (see ZHONGYONG; DAXUE). Other sections include descriptions on the regulation of the rites, *yin–yang* theory, mourning, worship and sacrifice, auspicious rites, auspicious occasions and the *Yuejing*.

The *Chunqiu* (Spring and Autumn Annals) is a historical chronicle of the reigns of twelve rulers of the state of Lu. It provides a terse and impersonal factual chronicle of diplomatic and political events from 722–481 BC. According to MENCIUS, Confucius composed the *Chunqiu* as a historical object lesson of the lawlessness of his own age and his own state of Lu. The Chunqiu was of particular importance because of its use by the Han philosopher DONG ZHONGSHU, a major formulator of official Han Confucian metaphysics (see CONFUCIAN PHILOSOPHY, CHINESE). Dong claimed to have derived his ideas from the *Chunqiu*, and followed Mencius in believing that Confucius, having understood the heavenly patterns that governed the cosmos, applied them to human history. Dong gave CONFUCIUS the status of a 'hidden king', the moral and metaphysical arbiter whose praise and blame passed correct judgments on the actions of the kings of the past.

The *Chunqiu* was one of the Han dynasty's Five Classics. From the Tang dynasty onwards it was transmitted through three major commentaries, the *Gongyangzhuan* (Gongyang Annals), the *Guliangzhuan* (Guliang Annals) and the *Zuozhuan* (Zuo Annals). The *Guliangzhuan* and *Gongyangzhuan* both use question-and-answer dialogue to provide a morally normative interpretation of the *Chunqiu*. Tradition attributes the origins of the *Gongyangzhuan* to the oral teachings of Zixia, a disciple of Confucius; the *Guliangzhuan* borrows from and elaborates on the *Gongyangzhuan*. Both cover the historical span of the *Chunqiu*, and both employ the 'praise and blame' historiography of the latter. The *Zuozhuan* covers a longer period than the other two commentaries (722–453 BC) and contains more historical information. Its date and authorship are the source of considerable controversy.

The *Analects* of Confucius (*Lunyu*) is a collection of anecdotes, sayings and short dialogues, mostly between Confucius and his disciples. While Confucius himself claimed to be a transmitter of Zhou values rather than an innovator, the central concerns of the *Analects* moved away from divination of the will of spirits toward the ethics of the human world and the establishment and maintenance of political and social order. Confucius formulated new notions of humane benevolence (*ren*) and the right conduct of superior individuals (*junzi*) that were to remain hallmarks of later Confucian thought (see CONFUCIAN PHILOSOPHY, CHINESE; CONFUCIUS).

The *Xiaojing* (Book of Filial Piety) is a short dialogue between Confucius and his disciple Zengzu on filiality towards parents (by their children) and, by analogy, rulers (by their subjects). It is didactic in tone, and describes the virtues of filial piety as ostensibly practiced during the golden age of the Zhou. It includes quotations from the *Shijing* (Book of Songs) and is written in question and answer form. The *Xiaojing* was included among the Han seven classics, possibly because its articulation of appropriate behaviour of subjects toward rulers made it an attractive text for imperial patronage. Imperial patronage, as much as philosophical esteem within the tradition, conferred and maintained its status as a classic.

The *Erya* is a dictionary of Zhou terms. Various traditional accounts ascribe it to the Duke of Zhou, Confucius and the latter's disciple Zixia; recent scholarship dates it to the Qin or early Han dynasty. Its most important influence is in the nineteen categories into which words are grouped. These categories became the basis for the categories of encyclopedias and similar works. While many of the glosses in the *Erya* are cryptic, as a text it contains a variety of 'abstract' terms as well as entries on kinship terms, musical terminology, astronomic and calendrical terms, geographical terms, names of grasses, herbs, trees, wild and domestic animals and legendary animals. It was treated as an authoritative guide to the language of the classics.

The *Mengzi* consists of a series of extended conversations and debates between MENCIUS and various rulers, opponents and disciples. Mencius developed concepts that had been mentioned or suggested but not developed in the *Analects*. He stressed the inherent goodness of human nature and elaborated a theory of four inherent 'sprouts' of goodness: humane benevolence (*ren*), knowledge or wisdom (*zhi*), ceremony or ritual (*li*) and rectitude (*yi*). Mencius held that these sprouts could, with correct nurture, mature in any individual and create the intuitive ability that is the basis for moral conduct and moral judgment. Mencius also attacked a variety of opponents of Confucius, including the Mohists (see MOHIST PHILOSOPHY), the followers of YANGZHU and military strategists. The first imperial recognition accorded to the works of Mencius was by the Emperor Wen of the Han dynasty, who established a chair for the study of the *Mengzi*. The *Mengzi* is listed in the Han bibliography among the masters rather than the classics, and only appears in the classical canon during the Song dynasty.

4 Significance

During the approximately fifteen hundred years between Confucius and the Song dynasty, several classical schemata gained and lost sway, including the Six Classics of the Warring States period, the Five Classics of the Han, the Nine Classics of the Tang, and the Thirteen Classics of the Song. Nevertheless, although the content and size of Confucian classical canons changed over time, the notion of classics has been relatively continuous since the beginnings of philosophical thought in China. The classics are of philosophical importance because they articulate central ideas, values and dispositions of Chinese culture. They are also important because the definition of the classical canon effectively excluded other works of considerable philosophical significance.

The Chinese classics functioned as a classical canon in several senses. First, they provided a textual authority that could serve as a source of intellectual or political authority and legitimation for philosophers and rulers alike. For example, Confucius, Mencius and Xunzi all quote extensively from the *Shijing* and *Shujing*. (XUNZI differs from the other two in that he both quoted poetry as authoritative discourse and composed original verse, and is even listed at the head of a school of poets.)

Second, the classics formed the core of the education system that defined the bureaucratic elite. Despite competing claims from other textual canons and variations in emphasis, these works held a central role in the education (and definition) of the bureaucratic elite. The classical compendia defined the knowledge and the political and moral orientation of a learned scholar or official. Because they formed the root of the state examination system, their mastery was an important prerequisite for political office. Memorizing the classics was a large part of the early intellectual and moral education of boys. Additional 'classics' were developed for the separate education of women. The *Nuxiaojing* (Book of Filial Piety for Women) and the *Nulunyu* (Analects for Women) are both Tang works written by women for the education of women, the latter by a consort of the Tang emperor Dezong in the eighth century. These works were taken as repositories of knowledge, guides to conduct and a repertoire for use in situations that required literary elegance.

Finally, the classics set the philosophical agenda for what came to be known as the early Confucian tradition. They were centrally concerned with two related problems: how to maintain political and social order, and how to persuade rulers to voluntarily limit their own power. As such, all the classics functioned in a strongly hierarchical system and their style of argument or exposition reflects the social context in which they operated, for example, by the prevalence of persuasion over debate.

The thirteen classics are also noteworthy for what they do not contain. Many of the recognized classical works of Chinese philosophy appear in traditional classifications not among the classics but among the masters. Ruhist works include the *Mengzi* (until the Song dynasty) and *Xunzi* (see MENCIUS; XUNZI). Daoist 'masters' include the *Daodejing* and the *Zhuangzi* (see DAODEJING; ZHUANGZI). The one surviving Mohist work is the Mohist Canon (see MOHIST PHILOSOPHY; MOZI); the masters conventionally associated with the so-called Legalist school include Han Fei, Lord Shang, and Shen Buhai (see LEGALIST PHILOSOPHY, CHINESE; HAN FEIZI). Less well-known but important masters include the *Huainanzi* (compiled at the court of Liu An *circa* 140 BC) and the *Lushi chunqiu* (Springs and Autumns of Master Lu), attributed to Lu Buwei (d. 235 BC) (see HUAINANZI).

These works in turn function as the 'classics' – in the sense of a master text that defines a school – of several traditions. For example, the *Daodejing*, attributed to the apocryphal sage Laozi but probably dating from about 250 BC, is one of the canonical works of several Daoist traditions and may be the most widely read Chinese text outside China. Still other works, not listed among the masters but titled as classics or masters became the foundational texts for specific schools of expertise, for example, the *Huangdi neijing* (Yellow Thearch's Classic of Internal Medicine), a medical compendium dating from approximately 100 BC that became the master text for the high textual tradition of Chinese medical practice.

See also: CONFUCIAN PHILOSOPHY, CHINESE; CONFUCIUS; DAOIST PHILOSOPHY; AESTHETICS, CHINESE; DAODEJING; DONG ZHONGSHU; MENCIUS; YIJING

References and further reading

The dating of all classic texts is problematic and controversial. The dates of compilation given before are approximations.

Analects (4th–2nd century BC), trans. J. Legge, *The Confucian Analects*, Oxford, Clarendon Press, 1893; *repr. in The Chinese Classics*, vol. 1, Hong Kong: Hong Kong University, 1960; trans. A. Waley, *The Analects of Confucius*, New York: Random House, 1966; trans. D.C. Lau, *Confucius: The Analects (Lun yu)*, London: Penguin, 1979. (Lau is the standard English translation of the *Analects (Lunyu)*. The Legge edition contains facing Chinese text and notes.)

Erya (3rd century BC), in *Erya yinde* (Index to the *Erya*), Harvard–Yenching Institute Sinological Index Series, supplement 18, Beijing, 1941; ed. D.C. Lau and Chen Fong-ching, *A Concordance to the Erya and Xiaojing*, ICS Series, Hong Kong: Commercial Press, 1994. (There are no translations of this work.)

Gongyangzhuan (Gongyang Annals) (2nd century BC), trans. G. Malmqvist, 'Studies on the Gongyang and Guliang Commentaries', *Bulletin of the Museum of Far Eastern Antiquities* 43, 1971: 67–222; 47, 1975: 19–69; and 49, 1977: 33–215. (Partial translation of the Gongyang and Guliang commentaries to the *Chunqiu* (Spring and Autumn Annals).)

Guliangzhuan (Guliang Annals) (2nd–1st century BC) trans. G. Malmqvist, 'Studies on the Gongyang and Guliang Commentaries', *Bulletin of the Museum of Far Eastern Antiquities* 43, 1971: 67–222; 47, 1975: 19–69 and 49, 1977: 33–215. (Partial translation of the Gongyang and Guliang commentaries to the *Chunqiu* (Spring and Autumn Annals).)

Liji (Book of Rites) (2nd century BC–2nd century AD),

trans. J. Legge, *Li chi*, in *Sacred Books of the East*, vols 26–8, New York: University Books, 1926; repr. 1967; trans. S. Couvreur, *Li Ki: ou mémoires sur les bienséances et les cérémonies*, Ho Kien Fou [Hejianfu]: Imprimerie de la Mission Catholique, 1913, 2 vols. (English and French translations respectively of the *Liji*.)

Mengzi (2nd century BC–2nd century AD), trans. J. Legge, *The Works of Mencius*, in *The Chinese Classics*, vol. 2, 1895; trans. D.C. Lau, *Mencius*, New York: Penguin, 1970. (Lau is the standard English translation of the *Mengzi*. Legge contains facing Chinese text and notes.)

Shijing (Book of Songs) (5th century BC), trans. J. Legge, *The She King, or The Book of Poetry*, in *The Chinese Classics*, vol. 4, 1872; trans. B. Karlgren, *The Book of Odes*, Stockholm: Museum of Far Eastern Antiquities, 1950; trans. A. Waley, *The Book of Songs*, New York: Grove Press, 1960. (Karlgren's translation of the *Shijing* is highly literal; that of Waley is a literary translation.)

Shujing (Book of Documents) (5th century BC–4th century AD), trans. J. Legge, *The Shoo King or The Book of Historical Documents*, in J. Legge (ed.) *The Chinese Classics*, vol. 3, 1865; repr. Hong Kong: Hong Kong University Press, 1960; trans. B. Karlgren, *The Book of Documents*, Stockholm: Museum of Far Eastern Antiquities, 1950. (Karlgren translates the verifiably pre-Han portions of the *Shujing*, also known as the *Shangshu*. Legge does not distinguish between pre-Han materials and later interpolations.)

Xiaojing (Book of Filial Piety) (2nd or 1st century BC), trans. J. Legge, *The Hsiao ching*, in F.M. Muller (ed.) *Sacred Books of the East*, vol. 3, Oxford: Oxford University Press, 1899; trans. I. Chen, *The Book of Filial Piety*, London: John Murray, 1908; New York: E.P. Dutton, 1908–9; ed. P.K.T. Sih, trans. M.L. Makra, *The Hsiao ching*, New York: St. John's University Press, 1961. (Translations of the *Xiaojing*.)

Yijing (Book of Changes) (3rd–2nd century BC), trans. J. Legge, *The I Ching*, in F.M. Muller (ed.) *Sacred Books of the East*, vol. 16, Oxford: Oxford University Press, 1899; trans. R. Wilhelm and C.F. Baynes, *The I Ching or Book of Changes*, Bollingen Series 19, Princeton, NJ: Princeton University Press, 1950. (Wilhelm and Baynes is the standard English translation of the *Yijing*.)

Yili (Ceremony and Rites) (2nd or 1st century BC), trans. J. Steele, *The I li or Book of Etiquette and Ceremonial*, London: Probsthain and Co., 1917; trans. S. Couvreur, *Cérémonial*, Hsien hsien [Xian Xian]: Imprimerie de la Mission Catholique, 1916;

repr. Paris: Cathasia, 1951. (English and French translations respectively of the *Yili*.)

Zhouli (Rites of Zhou) (2nd or 1st century BC), trans. E. Biot, *Le Tcheou-li ou Rites des Tcheou*, Paris: Imprimerie Nationale, 1851; repr. Taipei: Ch'eng-wen, 1975. (French translation of the *Zhouli*.)

Zuozhuan (Zuo Annals) (2nd–1st century BC), trans. J. Legge, *The Ch'un Ts'ew with the Tso Chuen*, in *The Chinese Classics*, vol. 5, 1872; repr. Hong Kong: Hong Kong University Press, 1960; trans. S. Couvreur, *Tch'ouen st'ieou et Tso tschouan*, Ho Kien Fou, 1914, 3 vols; repr. Paris: Cathasia, 1951; trans. B. Watson, *The Tso Chuan: Selections from China's Oldest Narrative History*, New York: Columbia University Press, 1989. (Legge and Couvreur are the English and French translations of the *Chunqiu* (Spring and Autumn Annals) and the *Zuozhuan* commentary. Watson is a new partial translation of the *Zuozhuan*.)

LISA RAPHALS

CHINESE PHILOSOPHY

Any attempt to survey an intellectual tradition which encompasses more than four thousand years would be a daunting task even if it could be presumed that the reader shares, at least tacitly, many of the assumptions underlying that tradition. However, no such commonalities can be assumed in attempting to introduce Asian thinking to Western readers. Until the first Jesuit incursions in the late sixteenth century, China had developed in virtual independence of the Indo-European cultural experience and China and the Western world remained in almost complete ignorance of one another.

The dramatic contrast between Chinese and Western modes of philosophic thinking may be illustrated by the fact that the tendency of European philosophers to seek out the being of things, the essential reality lying behind appearances, would meet with little sympathy among Chinese thinkers, whose principal interests lie in the establishment and cultivation of harmonious relationships within their social ambiance. Contrasted with Anglo-European philosophic traditions, the thinking of the Chinese is far more concrete, this-worldly and, above all, practical.

One reason for this difference is suggested by the fact that cosmogonic and cosmological myths played such a minor role in the development of Chinese intellectual culture and that, as a consequence, Chinese eyes were focused not upon issues of cosmic order but upon more mundane questions of how to achieve communal harmony within a relatively small social nexus. The

rather profound linguistic and ethnic localism of what Pliny the Elder described as a 'stay-at-home' China, reinforced by a relative freedom from intercultural contact, generated traditional radial communities in which moral, aesthetic and spiritual values could remain relatively implicit and unarticulated. By contrast, in the West these norms had to be abstracted and raised to the level of consciousness to adjudicate conflicts occasioned by the complex ethnic and linguistic interactions associated with the development of a civilization rooted almost from the beginning in the confluence of Greek, Hebrew, and Latin civilizations.

The distinctive origins and histories of Chinese and Western civilizations are manifested in a number of important ways. The priority of logical reasoning in the West is paralleled in China by the prominence of less formal uses of analogical, parabolic and literary discourse. The Chinese are largely indifferent to abstract analyses that seek to maintain an objective perspective, and are decidedly anthropocentric in their motivations for the acquisition, organization and transmission of knowledge. The disinterest in dispassionate speculations upon the nature of things, and a passionate commitment to the goal of social harmony was dominant throughout most of Chinese history. Indeed, the interest in logical speculations on the part of groups such as the sophists and the later Mohists was short-lived in classical China.

The concrete, practical orientation of the Chinese toward the aim of communal harmony conditioned their approach toward philosophical differences. Ideological conflicts were seen, not only by the politicians but by the intellectuals themselves, to threaten societal well-being. Harmonious interaction was finally more important to these thinkers than abstract issues of who had arrived at the 'truth'. Perhaps the most obvious illustration of the way the Chinese handled their theoretical conflicts is to be found in mutual accommodation of the three emergent traditions of Chinese culture, Confucianism, Daoism and Buddhism. Beginning in the Han dynasty (206 BC–AD 220), the diverse themes inherited from the competing 'hundred schools' of pre-imperial China were harmonized within Confucianism as it ascended to become the state ideology. From the Han synthesis until approximately the tenth century AD, strong Buddhist and religious Daoist influences continued to compete with persistent Confucian themes, while from the eleventh century to the modern period, Neoconfucianism – a Chinese neoclassicism – absorbed into itself these existing tensions and those that would emerge as China, like it or not, confronted Western civilization.

In the development of modern China, when Western influence at last seemed a permanent part of Chinese culture, the values of traditional China have remained dominant. For a brief period, intellectual activity surrounding the May Fourth movement in 1919 seemed to be leading the Chinese into directions of Western philosophic interest. Visits by Bertrand Russell and John Dewey, coupled with a large number of Chinese students seeking education in Europe, Great Britain and the USA, promised a new epoch in China's relations with the rest of the world. However, the Marxism that Mao Zedong sponsored in China was 'a Western heresy with which to confront the West'. Mao's Marxism quickly took on a typically 'Chinese' flavour, and China's isolation from Western intellectual currents continued essentially unabated.

1 **Chinese thinking as *ars contextualis***
2 **The dominance of correlative thinking**
3 **The organization and transmission of knowledge**
4 **Confucius and Confucianism**
5 **Philosophical Daoism**
6 **The 'Hundred Schools'**
7 **Xunxi and rationalized Confucianism**
8 **First millennium syncretism**
9 **Neo-Confucianism: Zhu Xi and Wang Yangming**
10 **The modern period**

1 Chinese thinking as *ars contextualis*

Our traditional Western senses of order are grounded upon cosmogonic myths that celebrate the victory of an ordered cosmos over chaos. Chaos is a 'yawning gap', a 'gaping void'; it is an emptiness or absence, a nothingness; it is a confused mass of unorganized surds. Hesiod's *Theogony* tells how the yawning gap of Chaos separating Heaven and Earth was overcome by Eros – love thereby creating harmony (see HESIOD). The Book of Genesis tells how, from a 'dark, formless void', order was created by divine command. In the *Timaeus*, Plato's Demiurge 'persuades' the disorganized, intransigent matter into reasonable order, providing 'a victory of persuasion over necessity'. Classical Chinese culture, on the other hand, was little influenced by myths which contrasted an irrational Chaos with an ordered Cosmos. The relative unimportance of cosmogonic myths in China helps to account for the dramatically different intellectual contexts from which the Chinese and Western cultural sensibilities emerged.

In the Western tradition, thinking about the order of things began with questions such as 'What kinds of things are there?' and 'What is the nature (*physis*) of things?' This inquiry, which later came to be called 'metaphysics', took on two principal forms. One, which the scholastics later termed *ontologia generalis* (general ontology), is the investigation of the most essential features of things – the *being* of beings. A slightly less abstract mode of metaphysical thinking, *scientia universalis* (universal science), involves the attempt to construct a science of the sciences, a way of knowing which organizes the various ways of knowing the world about us. Both general ontology and universal science interpret the order of the cosmos. Both suppose that there are general characteristics – the being of beings, or universal principles – which tell us how things are ordered.

Neither of these forms of metaphysical thinking were influential in classical China. One reason for their unimportance is reflected in the character of the Chinese language. Simply put, the classical Chinese language does not employ a copulative verb. The Chinese terms usually used to translate 'being' and 'not-being' are *you* and *wu* (see YOU–WU). The Chinese *you* means, not that something 'is' (*esse* in Latin) in the sense that it exists in some essential way; it means rather that 'something is present'. 'To be' is 'to be available', 'to be around'. Likewise, *wu* as 'to not be' means 'not to be around'. Thus the Chinese sense of 'being' overlaps 'having'. A familiar line from the Daoist classic the *Laozi* or *Daodejing*, which is often translated 'Not-being is superior to Being', should more responsibly be translated as 'Not-having is superior to having' (or as a Marxist-inspired translator has rendered it, 'Not owning private property is superior to owning private property'). The Chinese language disposes those who employ the notions of *you* and *wu* to concern themselves with the presence or absence of concrete particular things and the effect of having or not having them at hand. Even in recent centuries, when the influence of translating Indo-European culture required the Chinese language to designate a term to do the work of the copula, the choice was *shi*, meaning 'this', thus indicating proximity and availability rather than 'existence'. One must assume that the practical, concrete disposition of Chinese thinkers is both cause and consequence of this characteristic feature of linguistic usage.

Perhaps the best designation for the most general 'science' of order in the Chinese tradition would be *ars contextualis*. 'The art of contextualizing' contrasts with both *scientia universalis* and *ontologia generalis*. Chinese thinkers sought the understanding of order through the artful disposition of things, a participatory process which does not presume that there are essential features, or antecedent-determining principles, serving as transcendent sources of order. The art of contextualizing seeks to understand and appreciate the manner in which particular things present-to-hand are, or may be, most harmoniously correlated. Classical Chinese thinkers located the energy of transformation and change within a world that is *ziran*, autogenerative or literally 'so-of-itself', and found the more or less harmonious interrelations among the particular things around them to be the natural condition of things, requiring no appeal to an ordering principle or agency for explanation.

The dominant Chinese understanding of the order of things advertises an important ambiguity in the notion of 'order' itself. The most familiar understanding of order in the West is associated with uniformity and pattern regularity. This 'logical' or 'rational' ordering is an implication of the cosmological assumptions which characterize the *logos* of a cosmos in terms of causal laws and formal patterns. A second sense of order is characterized by concrete particularities whose uniqueness is essential to the order itself. No final unity is possible in this view since, were this so, the order of the whole would dominate the order of the parts, cancelling the uniqueness of its constituent particulars. Thus, 'aesthetic' order is ultimately acosmological in the sense that no single order dominates.

The crucial difference between these two senses of order is that in the one case there is the presumption of an objective standard which one perforce must instantiate; in the other, there is no source of order other than the agency of the elements comprising the order. In the West, mathematical order has been thought the purest. In China, by contrast, any notion of order which abstracts from the concrete details of this-worldly existence has been seen as moving in a direction of decreasing relevance. Rational order depends upon the belief in a single-ordered world, a cosmos; aesthetic order speaks of the world in much less unitary terms. In China, the 'cosmos' is simply 'the ten thousand things'. The belief that the things of nature may be ordered in any number of ways is the basis of philosophical thinking as *ars contextualis*.

Each of these understandings of order existed at the beginnings of both Western and Chinese cultures, and both have persisted as interpretative options within them. It so happens that in the course of their respective histories, the two cultures made distinctly different choices which led to the variant senses of order as grounds for the organizing of personal, social and cosmic environs. These differing senses of order are reflected in the fact that the nineteenth-century Japanese had to coin the term *tetsugaku* (philosophy) to translate the Western philosophic tradition and to recover its Japanese counterpart, and that this same expression was soon thereafter imported into China as *zhexue* for the same purpose. The need to invent a term to refer to 'philosophy' suggests at least that these cultures had to reorganize patterns of indigenous intellectual experience in ways previously unfamiliar to them.

2 The dominance of correlative thinking

Rational or logical thinking, grounded in analytic, dialectical and analogical argumentation, stresses the explanatory power of physical causation. In contrast, Chinese thinking depends upon a species of analogy which may be called 'correlative thinking'. Correlative thinking, as it is found both in classical Chinese 'cosmologies' (the *Yijing* (Book of Changes), Daoism, the Yin–Yang school) and, less importantly, among the classical Greeks involves the association of image or concept-clusters related by meaningful disposition rather than physical causation. Correlative thinking is a species of spontaneous thinking grounded in informal and *ad hoc* analogical procedures presupposing both association and differentiation. The regulative element in this modality of thinking is shared patterns of culture and tradition rather than common assumptions about causal necessity.

The relative indifference of correlative thinking to logical analysis means that the ambiguity, vagueness and incoherence associable with images and metaphors are carried over into the more formal elements of thought. In fact, the chaotic factor in the underdetermined correlative order has a positive value as an opportunity for personalization and self-construal. In contradistinction to the rational mode of thinking which privileges univocity, correlative thinking involves the association of significances into clustered images which are treated as meaning complexes ultimately unanalyzable into any more basic components. In the Western tradition we are familiar with correlations such as those present in the humour theory of medicine, Pythagorean numerical correlations, Kepler's correlation of the perfections of the trinitarian God, the world and the soul, and so forth (see HIPPOCRATIC MEDICINE; PYTHAGORAS; KEPLER, J.). Astrological charts provide the most familiar illustration of correlative thinking. But, as may be seen particularly (although not exclusively) in the discussion of Daoist philosophy, correlativity is not only an anthropocentric mode of signification. The Daoist notion of *de* – 'particular focus' or 'virtuality' – extends the context of signification to all phenomena (see DAOIST PHILOSOPHY; DE).

Correlative thinking is the primary instrument in the creation, organization and transmission of the classical curriculum in China, from the *Book of Songs* to the *Analects* to the *Yijing* (see CHINESE CLASSICS; CONFUCIUS; YIJING). Perhaps the most overt illustrations of the Chinese resort to correlative thinking in the classical period are to be found in the period of the Han dynasty (206 BC–AD 220). During the Han period, vast tables of correspondences were employed

317

to identify and organize the sorts of things in the natural and social world which were thought to provide a meaningful context for one's life. One such set of tables, called 'tables of five', compared 'the five phases' (wood, fire, earth, metal, water), 'the five directions' (north, east, south, west and centre), 'the five colours' (green, red, yellow, white, black), 'the five notes', and so forth. Other types of correlation employed the twelve months, the twelve pitches, the twenty-eight constellations, the heavenly roots and the earthly branches. Such classifications include body parts, psycho-physical and affective states, styles of government, weather, domestic animals, technological instruments, heavenly bodies and much more.

One of the important devices for making such correlations is the contrast of *yin* and *yang*, literally, 'the shady side' and 'the sunny side' of the mountain (see YIN–YANG). These notions were employed to identify alternative patterns of hierarchical relationship. The old teacher, Laozi, is wiser than his young student and hence 'overshadows' him in this respect. Laozi is *yang* and the student is *yin*. The student, however, is stronger physically than the old master, and hence in physical prowess the student is *yang* to Laozi's *yin*. When these various strengths and weaknesses defining the relationship can be balanced to maximum effect, the relationship is most productive and harmonious. It is clear from this illustration that *yang* and *yin* are by no means to be understood as 'cosmic principles' or ontological contrasts rooted in the very nature of things. Rather, they are heuristics helpful in reading and characterizing the world as concretely experienced in a variety of ways.

Though the contents of many correlative schemata are often *prima facie* the same as the subject matters of the Western natural sciences, there is a crucial difference in the manner they are treated. In China, correlations were not employed as a means of dispassionately investigating the nature of things. Correlative descriptions are, in fact, prescriptions. Correlative schemes oriented human beings in a very practical manner to their external surroundings. Thus, the Chinese were concerned less with astronomy than with astrology; they were far more enthusiastic in the development of geomancy than geology. Science was always understood as ultimately subject to prevailing human values.

3 The organization and transmission of knowledge

The importance of correlative modes of thinking in classical Chinese culture is to be found not only in the acquisition of knowledge but also in its organization and transmission. Plato's employment of the 'Divided Line' allowed for the organization of knowledge by appeal to principles of clarity and coherence which were realized with the achievement of systematic unity (see PLATO). ARISTOTLE organized the body of the known into theoretical, practical and productive enterprises by appeal to the nature of the *psyche* as a thinking, acting and feeling creature. In each case there is the appeal to objective principles which serve to articulate the realms of knowledge.

There is a stark contrast between these Western models of classification and the one characteristically found in the traditional *leishu* (encyclopedic or classificatory works) of China. Chinese 'categories' (*lei*) are defined not by the presumption of a shared essence defining natural 'kinds', but by an identified functional similarity or association that obtains among unique particulars. Definitions are not framed in the terms of essential features and formal class membership; instead, definitions tend to be metaphorical and allusive, and invariably entail the human subject and human values. It is the earliest reference in the canons of classical literature, rather than principled scientific explanation grounded in the canons of reason and logic, that holds the weight of authority. In these compendia, there is little interest in the objective description of natural phenomena. The concern instead is with the relationship that the various contents of the world have to the social and cultural values which shape the human experience of it. As an example, the contemporary scholar Liang Congjie points out that 'of the fifty-five sections (*bu*) that make up the *Taiping yulan*, six of them – emperors, imperial relatives, officials, human affairs, ancestors, and ceremony – occupy thirty-five per cent of the work' (Hall and Ames 1995).

These Chinese encyclopedic works are hierarchical, with the human being self-consciously at the centre. Further, this 'human being' is no abstraction but is the specific imperial Chinese person, the emperor, who commissioned the work for the benefit of those examination candidates destined to assist him in governing his empire. Again in each category, individual entries begin from the most noble and conclude with the most base: animals begin from 'lion' and 'elephant' and finish with 'rat' and 'fox'; trees begin with 'pine tree' and 'cypress' and end with 'thistles' and 'brambles'. The world is not described objectively through an articulation of exclusive categories and subcategories, but is divided up prescriptively into natural and cultural elements which have an increasing influence on the experience of the Chinese court as they stand in proximity to the centre. In 'naming' (*ming*) his world, the ruler is 'commanding' (*ming*) it to be a certain way.

As for the transmission of knowledge, we are accustomed to the notion that philosophical ideas are disseminated through debate and dialectical interchange in which one theory or vision confronts another and arguments ensue as to the adequacy of each. However, this manner of looking at the transmission and alteration of ideas does not well suit the Chinese context. This is true primarily because such debate is rooted in rationalistic assumptions of the sort that privilege theories as relatively coherent patterns of belief and practice, which can be articulated apart from the institutions to which they are relevant. Things were quite different in China. Ancient China overcame the threat of the tensions and conflicts attendant upon ethnic and cultural pluralism by employing the contextualizing force of the Chinese language itself as means of transmitting culture. A class of literati developed; a canon of classical works was compiled and instituted along with a continuing commentarial tradition which served to translate and perpetuate the doctrines of these classical works; an examination system based upon these texts was introduced in the early Han period and persisted with relatively little change for two thousand years, being abolished only as recently as 1905.

With the dominance of Confucian orthodoxy in China, methods of adjudicating doctrinal conflicts were refined in a manner which took as its highest value the maintenance of social stability. Beginning in the early Han period, commentaries upon Confucian texts were produced which vied with each other for proximity to the canonical center. The authors of these commentaries were almost never interested in overthrowing the authority of the canon in favour of their own ideas, but sought to enrich the authority of the classic by claiming to better understand its original meaning. Further, since tradition was the sole ready resource for norms and doctrines, critics of a particular doctrine depended as much as proponents upon a shared cultural repository. This is evidenced in the conventional use of canonical allusions to focus social and political critique. The appeal to canonical authority is again a way of reinforcing a sense of shared community, and stands in sharp contrast to dialectical arguments which reference canons of reason or logic (see CHINESE CLASSICS).

Characteristic of scholarly dispute after the emergence of Han orthodoxy is a fundamental commitment to mutual accommodation. There is a general distaste for contentiousness and an active cultivation of the art of accommodation. In the exercise of criticism, the ritual basis of order comes into play since rituals serve as patterns of deference which accommodate and harmonize differences in desires, beliefs and actions. Criticism assumes a context of common concern and becomes thereby a cooperative exercise among responsible participants that proceeds to search for alternatives on which all can agree. One important constraint on self-assertiveness, as well as an encouragement for a consensual resolution, is that critics themselves are always implicated in the existing context; hence, any criticism is ultimately self-referential. Contentiousness, by contrast, betrays a concern for personal advantage. Such self-assertion threatens to disrupt rather than reinforce or improve the harmony of the existing context. From the *Analects* on, an appropriateness (*yi*) which respects social context has been advocated as the positive alternative to self-interested benefit (*li*). The proper goal of critical or constructive expression in China, whether it be scholarly, social or political, is the strengthening of communal harmony.

4 Confucius and Confucianism

While there may be some truth to the claim that in the West, every person is born either a Platonist or an Aristotelian, it is A.N. Whitehead's apothegm, 'All of Western philosophy is a series of footnotes to Plato', that, *mutatis mutandis*, resonates best with the Chinese context. For indeed, all of Chinese thinking is a series of commentaries on CONFUCIUS. In fact, the importance of Confucius in China may be said to outshine that of Plato in the Western tradition on at least two grounds. First, there is effectively no sort of pre-Confucian philosophic tradition to match that of the Presocratics. Confucius is not a synthesizer of past *thinkers*, but an interpreter and transmitter of past *institutions*, namely, the idealized Zhou rituals and customs which Confucius thought to be the key to social stability. Second, Confucius' thinking came to ground the tradition of Chinese culture for practically its entire intellectual tradition, from the early phases of the Han dynasty in the second century BC to at least the beginnings of the Republican period in the early twentieth century, and arguably down to the present day in a decidedly Chinese form of Marxism (see MARXISM, CHINESE).

The philosophy of Confucius begins from some basic assumptions, several of which can be derived from the following passage from the *Analects*:

> The Master said: 'Lead the people with administrative injunctions and put them in their place with penal law, and they will avoid punishments but will be without a sense of shame. Lead them with excellence and put them in their place through roles and ritual practices, and in addition to developing a sense of shame, will order themselves harmoniously.'

> (*Analects* 2/3)

First, Confucius believed in the radical malleability of the nascent human being through education and cultivation (see SELF-CULTIVATION, CHINESE THEORIES OF). Humanity for Confucius is not defined by anything 'given'; there is no essential human nature. Becoming human is a cultural achievement. Second, the formal instrument for pursuing personal refinement and self-articulation is *li*, often translated as ritual practice or propriety (see LAW AND RITUAL IN CHINESE PHILOSOPHY). Propriety, which includes everything from etiquette to social roles and institutions to the rites of life and death, is the underlying syntax of community. These formal structures reside in the conduct of those members of the community who serve as models of propriety.

The ultimate value of human experience lies in 'becoming a quality person' (*ren*), where the character which represents this accomplishment is constituted by 'person' and the numeral, 'two', suggesting its fundamentally social nature. It is because a person is shaped and articulated as a specific complex of roles and relationships that the Confucian person is irreducibly social. This social definition of person makes the promise of communal approbation an important encouragement for proper conduct, and the threat of shame an equally effective deterrent against undesirable conduct. Further, communal living becomes increasingly meaningful through the deepening quality of those particular relationships which constitute it: *this* person's son, *that* person's husband, *this* person's neighbour.

The goal of overcoming selfishness, fundamental in classical Confucianism, is not designed to be altruistic. The premise here is that selfishness is the greatest obstacle to the realization of one's social self. Since personal, familial, communal, political and even cosmic order are all coterminous and mutually entailing, commitment to community, far from being self-abnegating, is the road to personal fulfillment.

Excellence or virtue (*de*) achieved by members of the community empowers them as likely models of propriety for succeeding generations. Because the authority of community so constructed is internal to it, the community is self-regulating, dependent for its effectiveness upon authoritative leaders rather than the application of some external apparatus such as law and punishment. It is well worth noting that the importance of exemplary models of propriety in a Confucian society contrasts readily with the stress upon the resort to ethical principles so typical of rationalized societies. In the West, exemplary persons – Socrates or St Francis – are not typically thought to be ends in themselves; their lives point beyond to transcendent realities which ground their virtues. In Confucian societies, however, the sage Kings Yao and

Shun, the Duke of Zhou – and Confucius himself – are self-realized individuals who serve as distinctly immanent and historical individuals whose lives constitute models for emulation.

The distinction between a society of principles and a society shaped by models of propriety helps us to understand the distinctly 'aesthetic' quality of Confucian morality. Propriety leads to 'proper' conduct in one's relationships by at once reinforcing traditionally appropriate norms while at the same time insisting that they be internalized and 'made one's own' (*yi*). The notion of propriety or 'rightness' (*yi*) in a Confucian society, since it applies always within a social context, must involve notions of 'harmony'. Proper actions are 'fitting' in the sense that they fit and harmonize with other such actions. The notion of the 'right' action, therefore, has much in common with the artist's choice of the 'right' brush or the 'right' colour in the execution of a painting.

The failure to understand the aesthetic character of Confucian ethics has reinforced the tendency for Western philosophers to understand Confucian ritualization (*li*) as the imposition of external guides to conduct, mere forms imposed upon one from outside. Hegel's depiction of China as a culture without *Geist* in his *Philosophy of History* is representative of interpretations by the best minds of Europe and America. This truncated reading has in turn perpetuated the stereotypical opinion of Confucius as a purveyor of trite moral truisms, rather than as a founder of a social order which, by its dependence upon the sort of balanced complexity associated with aesthetic creations, has lasted longer than any other on the face of the planet.

5 Philosophical Daoism

Daoism is a complex movement in early China (see DAOIST PHILOSOPHY). A proto-Daoist religious sensibility seems to have been a stratum of Chinese popular culture centuries before the emergence of 'religious Daoism' as a formal iconoclastic movement in the second century AD. During the late Warring States period, Daoism developed a sublimated and sophisticated intellectual dimension as a response to rival traditions of thought. Because this school of political and philosophical anarchism was articulated in two primary compilations, the *Daodejing* (or *Laozi*) and the *Zhuangzi*, it came to be known as 'Lao-Zhuang' Daoism (see DAODEJING and ZHUANGZI).

The central message of this school is captured by the title of the *Daodejing* – literally, 'the classic of *dao* and *de*'. In fact, the name '*dao*-ism' itself is an abbreviation of the earliest designation of this tradition as '*dao-de*-ism', reflecting the core question which pervades the Daoist texts: what is the relationship between *dao* and *de*? This can be interpreted and restated as: what constitutes excellence (*de*) and how does one achieve it within one's particular place (*de*) in the world (*dao*)? Since one's 'place' is both spatial and temporal, *de* is the excellence achieved as one treads one's 'pathway' (or *dao*) through life (see DAO; DE).

A central Lao–Zhuang complaint against rival Confucianism is ecological, denouncing the anthropocentric limits it imposes on personal realization. While early Confucianism argues that human beings are the product of harmoniously orchestrated interpersonal relationships, the Daoists insist that the relational definition of humanity be extended to encompass the world more broadly. Human beings inhere in social, cultural *and* natural environments, and these environments are continuous and mutually shaping. The rhythm and regularity of human community is embedded in, and hence must be responsive to, the cadence and flow of all of nature's complex orders. To ignore the responsibility of humanity to participate fully in the harmony of our non-human surroundings leads inevitably to the distortion of our natural impulses by the imposition of often ossified conventions and institutions on the intuitive ground of human experience. Impositional conduct leads to coercion which, in the human world as our most immediate example, reduces the creative possibilities of community by denying the full participation of some of its participants.

The *Daodejing* expresses this notion of teasing an integrated and dynamic harmony out of available differences: 'The myriad things shoulder *yin* and embrace *yang* and blend their energies (*qi*) together to constitute a harmony (*he*)' (see QI). The 'myriad things' denotes the natural world as a complex of unique and particular thing-events (*de*). This complex of things lacks the suggestion of a single-ordered unity or coherence carried by terms such as 'cosmos' or 'universe', where the inventory of things is thought to be organized according to unifying natural laws and causal relationships. To the extent that the myriad things achieve 'order', it is constituted by the sum of a contingent set of aesthetic harmonies construed from the perspective of each of the participants as they dispose and express themselves in the world.

The intelligible patterns created by the many different things which collaborate to constitute the world are all pathways or *dao*s which can, in varying degrees, be traced out to map one's own place and its context, and in this mapping, to find coherence and meaning. *Dao* is always reflexive in that there is no final distinction between an independent source of order and that which it orders. One's world and its

order are constituted by the collaboration of oneself with a myriad other self-causing and mutually shaping particulars. *Dao* is, at any given time and place, both *what* the world is and *how* it is, as entertained from that perspective. For this reason, from a human point of view, explanation does not lie in the discovery of some antecedent agency or the isolation and disclosure of relevant causes. Rather, any particular event or phenomenon can be understood by mapping out the conditions which collaborate to sponsor it. Once broadly understood, these same conditions can be manipulated therapeutically to anticipate the next moment, and to prescribe for it.

The *Daodejing* is primarily a political treatise. It is by bringing this anarchic and ecological sensibility to the operations of human governance that government in its relationship to community can become *wuwei*, free of any coercive activity and free to orchestrate the full talents of its constituent population (see DAODEJING).

The *Zhuangzi*, focusing more on personal than political realization, is without question one of the richest and most celebrated pieces of philosophical literature in the Chinese tradition. While expressing an unrelenting scepticism about those evidential claims for certainty and objectivity which empower competing philosophical voices, this text uses a collage of anecdotes, parables, provocative images and other such rhetorical tropes and strategies to defend creativity as a fundamental value. It is through an appreciation of the role of creativity in the world that one comes to an understanding of an inclusively 'proper' order, where the 'anarchic' harmony, eschewing as it does any sense of determinative principle or *archē*, is 'made mine' by the fullest expression of all participating elements. The functional value of such an anarchic understanding of order in the world lies in overcoming any fear of personal injury or death by recognizing and relying upon the discernible regularity and continuity in the world, and by respecting the contribution that transformative change makes to the quality of life (see ZHUANGZI).

Daoism, like Confucianism, becomes porous and eclectic as it enters the Han dynasty, and serves as a freewheeling counterpoint to the Confucian state ideology throughout the two millennia of Imperial China. In the *Huainanzi*, an early Han compendium of knowledge representative of this syncretic turn, Daoism serves as a primary ore, being alloyed with the concerns and perspectives of competing schools to produce a more malleable and practical amalgam. The coherence of the *Huainanzi*, however, is one true to the spirit of Lao–Zhuang in that conflicting and divided opinions are happily juxtaposed as necessary for providing the fullest summary of China's cultural achievements. It is richness and intensity rather than some rationalized order that is the signature of Huainanzi's version of syncretic Daoism (see HUAI-NANZI).

There were also 'Huang–Lao' Daoists in late Qin and Eastern Han dynasties who combined the seemingly incompatible bureaucratic and technocratic designs associated with the Yellow Emperor (Huangdi) with Daoistic sensibilities as a strategy for participating effectively in the political order. These thinkers coupled the institutional structures and institutions of centralized government with Daoist notions of sagely government to constitute a kind of instrumental Daoism. Recent archaeological discoveries are providing an increasing amount of evidence from which to bring this movement into clearer focus.

The qualitative, aesthetic concerns which pervade Daoism continued to have an important influence throughout the evolution of Chinese culture, most notably in the productive and literary arts: painting, calligraphy, poetry, ceramics and so on. The vocabulary of Daoism was also instrumental in transforming imported Mahāyāna Buddhism from an exotic religion into a source of spiritual growth with largely indigenous aspirations (see BUDDHIST PHILOSOPHY, CHINESE).

6 The 'Hundred Schools'

Granted the disposition on the part of the Chinese to promote a harmonious narrative of China's cultural development, a closer look at the actual events yields a slightly greater sense of conflict. In the approximately one hundred years intervening between the death of Confucius in 481 BC and the birth of his most influential disciple, MENCIUS, in *circa* 380 BC, a complex variety of philosophical schools developed. In the Daoist work the *Zhuangzi*, this growth in diversity is referred to as the period of the 'Hundred Schools'. Far from seeing in this a healthy pluralism of opinion, the *Mengzi* (3B/9), as a representative of the Confucian tradition, described this phenomenon in the most negative of terms: 'Sage-kings do not arise, the various nobles do as they please, scholars without position speak freely on any number of topics, and the words of Yang Zhu and Mo Di fill the empire.'

The period of the conflicting schools began when Mo Di, the founder of Mohism, called Confucian ideas into question. Mohist thinking, generally characterized as a kind of utilitarianism, constituted a significant challenge to the ritually grounded traditionalism of Confucius (see MOHIST PHILOSOPHY; MOZI; LOGIC IN CHINA). Legalism, associated

with Shang Yang (d. 338 BC) and HAN FEIZI, differed from both Confucianism and Mohism by beginning its social thinking not with the people but with positive laws and sanctions presumed to be external devices necessary to bring order to the turmoil of its day. With the Legalists came at least the adumbration of a theory of rational political order (see LEGALIST PHILOSOPHY, CHINESE; LAW AND RITUAL IN CHINESE PHILOSOPHY). During the succeeding centuries leading up to the founding of the Han dynasty, a plethora of alternative schools emerged and court-sponsored academies were established in different parts of the empire reminiscent of the great academies of classical Greece. The most famous representative of these academies during the fourth and early third centuries was Jixia at the Qi capital of Linzi, attracting over time a range of such notables as ZHUANGZI, Song Xing, Shen Dao, MENCIUS, Gaozi, XUNZI and Zou Yan.

In the beginning, the competing schools engaged primarily in debates over doctrine, although they were also quite ready to offer commentary on the ever changing political situation. Conservative Confucians who sought the meaning of life by appeal to family and social obligations were opposed by those Daoists who sought to attune the human world to the regular rhythms and patterns of nature. There were fierce debates among the Confucians, Daoists, Mohists, Sophists and Yangists (and many others) concerning the goodness or evil or neutrality of human nature. In due course, as the contest became increasingly complex, the debates took a procedural and logical turn. Thinkers such as Zhuangzi, Sophists such as Hui Shi and Gongsun Longzi and the later Mohist logicians began to argue about the meaning of argument itself, and to worry over standards of evidence. Mohism and the School of Names developed a complex and technical vocabulary for disputation, and puzzled over the linguistic paradoxes which advertise the limits of language (see LOGIC IN CHINA). Thus, as was the case in the history of early Greek thinking, a second-order rationalism developed in China primarily as a means of adjudicating doctrinal conflict.

One of the most puzzling questions in Chinese intellectual history is why the rational and proto-scientific activities illustrated by the disputations of the late fourth and third centuries BC had virtually vanished by the early years of the Han dynasty. Perhaps the most plausible explanation for this phenomenon is one best couched in terms of the sociology of knowledge. As noted above in our discussions on the transmission of knowledge in China, the civilizing process in China was not one of urbanization as in the West, where the very word 'civilization' means 'citification'. Politics was explicitly concerned with the *polis*, and thus had to confront the complex patterns of trade and commerce associated with interactions among diverse languages and ethnicities, along with the growth of a plurality of institutions – banks, universities, trading companies – each with its own ideological axe to grind. Politics then became the art of compromise applied essentially to pluralistic urban centers.

In China, civilization was effected by the contextualizing power of a common written language. Thus, the same logical tools which could effectively serve the cause of adjudicating disputes in a pluralistic urban society such as developed in Europe would be unacceptably disruptive in a society whose stability was dependent upon the existence of communal affect associated with a common literature which both shaped and was shaped by a common language. The art historian George Rowley once remarked that for the Chinese, truth is not truth unless it is subtle. This is but to say that the bare bones logical propositions, bereft of subjective forms of feeling, cannot be 'true'. The affective and connotative features of language must always be present if language is to serve its function of harmonizing and stabilizing social interactions.

Herein lies a productive illustration of the greatest of contrasts between the politics of China and of the West. For the Western cultures, which are characterized by a pluralism of beliefs and practices, logical tools are essential as instruments of conflict resolution. For the Chinese culture, characterized by a far greater homogeneity of language and ethnicity, those same tools threaten the community of affect which guarantees social harmony. Thus in China, the seeds of 'rationalism' and the contentiousness it entails could be expected to have fallen upon rocky soil, and indeed they did.

7 Xunxi and rationalized Confucianism

A decisive figure in both the emergence and ultimate decline of rationalism in early China was the Confucian philosopher XUNZI. Xunzi is often touted as the most 'rationalistic' of the classical Confucians, and in one sense he deserves to be so described. However, because his so-called rationalism is grounded in history and culture without appeal to metaphysical, grammatical or sociological determinants, he is rationalistic in a rather Pickwickian sense. Xunzi's project does not illustrate a development of the incipient rationalism of the later Mohists and the School of Names. His is a distinctly historicist programme – and a historicist rationalism is, strictly speaking, oxymoronic. Thus in an analysis of argumentation in Xunzi, one must distinguish Xunzi's concrete, historical rationality from notions of abstract and impersonal reason familiar in classical Western metaphysical thinking.

There is, in spite of many similarities, also a fundamental difference between Xunzi's rationality and the peculiar kind of reasoning which grounds the later Mohist *Canons*. The rationality shared by Xunzi and the later Mohists is based upon their nominalist stances. However, the almost total congruence between the later Mohists and Xunzi on the nature of language and logic, which among other things allows Xunzi to utilize most of the technical vocabulary of the Mohist disputers, must be qualified by the fact that Mohist nominalism shares with physicalist nominalism of the Western tradition the importance of logical (and causal) necessity (see NOMINALISM). For the Mohists, necessity (*bi*) is what is 'unending' (*bu yi ye*), a condition of logical and scientific disputation which is invulnerable to time. Thus, even though the later Mohist has no explicit metaphysical theory, there is a belief that the world is comprised by concrete particulars with necessary logical relations one to the other (see MOHIST PHILOSOPHY).

By contrast, there are no metaphysical, linguistic or behavioural determinants to be found in Xunzi. Rationality for Xunzi is formed dialectically amid cultural, social and natural forces, both shaping and being shaped by them. Valid reasoning is the discovery and articulation of appropriate and efficacious historical instances of reasonableness. 'Reasoning' (*li*) and historical analogy are inseparable (see LI). On the one hand, *li* – the mapping out of patterns – can only operate on the basis of assumed classifications (*lei*); at the same time, it is the 'mapping' operation of *li*, including and excluding on the basis of perceived similarities and differences, that establishes classifications (*lei*) in the first place.

Xunzi's nominalism must be understood, much as that of the Greek Sophists, as a tropic rather than a metaphysical device. Nominalism of the 'rhetorical' as opposed to the 'logical' or 'atomistic' variety does not arise from a conviction that universals do not exist, or that there are no abstract entities, or that there are no such things as non-individuals. Xunzi's rhetorical or linguistic nominalism is essentially an anti-metaphysical and an anti-logical methodology that is quite similar to the sophistic nominalisms of many of the early Greek rhetoricians.

Though Mencius was later to emerge in the Chinese tradition as the most prominent of Confucius's interpreters, it was Xunzi's ritual-centred Confucianism that held sway in the formative years of Confucianism as a state ideology. This was emphatically the case during the first century of the

Han dynasty and the founding of empire. The institutionalization of academic positions which the Han dynasty inherited from the Qin helped to perpetuate and galvanize the influence of Xunzi. Several of Xunzi's immediate students were responsible for the transmission of specific classics which comprised the Confucian curriculum, including the *Guliang Commentary* to the *Spring and Autumn Annals* and the *Zuozhuan* historical narrative. Even the 'Mao' orthodox version of the *Book of Songs* was named for a lineage of Xunzi disciples. The preface to Xunzi's collected works written two hundred years after his death by the court bibliographer Liu Xiang (79–8 BC), reported that Lanling, still under the influence of Xunzi, continued to produce fine scholars.

Perhaps Xunzi's greatest and most enduring influence came from the extent to which he continued Confucius' emphasis on ritual practice as an instrument for socializing, enculturating and humanizing the Chinese world. His description of the function of ritual in society is cited extensively in the histories and the many canons of ritual that were compiled during this period, and looms large in the syncretic philosophical literature that was to become the signature of the Han. The *Huainanzi*, for example, is by and large a text representing a variety of often conflicting philosophical positions, but the crown of this Han dynasty work is its final chapter, the 'Greatest Clan' (*taizu*), which develops a philosophical position in many aspects reminiscent of Xunzi, especially with respect to the importance of ritual and learning (see HUAINANZI).

It can be argued that Xunzi, by co-opting the philosophic concerns of the early rationalists for the emerging Confucian program, made the formal continuation of these competing schools redundant. Put another way, the nascent rationalism which was emerging in those thinkers interested in argument for its own sake was overwhelmed by the conventionalist rationalism of Xunzi and the large following he attracted in the early years of the Han dynasty. The signature of the Confucian sense of order that persists far beyond the temporal borders of the Han dynasty is typified by Xunzi's ritually constituted community, a movement from contesting diversity to an absorbent and inclusive harmony. The emergence of what we might call 'Han' thinking in this period had a determinative effect on the style which Chinese philosophy was to assume throughout its long history.

8 First millennium syncretism

With the emergence of a Confucian orthodoxy in the Han dynasty based on the Xunzi branch of Con-

fucianism, scholarly dispute was tempered by a fundamental commitment to mutual accommodation. In the exercise of criticism the ritual basis of order comes into play, since rituals serve as patterns of deference which accommodate and harmonize differences in desires, attitudes and actions. Ideally, 'dispute' is a cooperative exercise among responsible participants that proceeds beyond obstinacy to search for alternatives on which all can agree. There is a fundamental dis-esteem for coercion of any kind, because aggressiveness or violence threatens to disrupt rather than reinforce or improve upon the existing social order. The goal of protest is not victory in contest, which is necessarily divisive, but the strengthening of communal harmony.

The interest in logic and rationality as tools of disputation which had emerged briefly in the pre-Qin days of the Hundred Schools, along with the analytical and dialectical modes of discourse attendant upon these methodologies, soon faded into the counter-current of Chinese intellectual culture. With the ascent of a Confucian ideology, China emerged as a culture grounded in the immanent aesthetic order of a ritually-constituted society, in large measure precluding the kind of rational conflict familiar in the Western tradition. With the Han thinkers came the emergence of a fortified Confucian orthodoxy, complete with canon and commentary.

By the beginning of the first century BC, Confucianism had become the clear and enduring victor over all contending voices, a success due in important degree to its ability to accommodate within a ritually-grounded intellectual society the most profound elements of Daoism, Legalism and Mohism, a pattern that would be repeated in Confucianism's gradual appropriation of Buddhist elements by its medieval adherents. It is generally recognized that the intellectual orthodoxy which came to dominance in the Han dynasty was a river fed by three powerful streams: Confucianism, Daoism and Buddhism. The stress here is upon the harmony of the three traditions. Though Confucianism remains dominant, the three sensibilities provide distinct foci in accordance with which one can construe one's life.

Confucians are often distinguished from Daoists by the observation that though both seek aesthetic harmony, the Daoists seek harmony with nature while Confucians are concerned with harmony in the social sphere. 'Nature' ('the ten thousand things') and 'society', as contexts, are both aesthetic products whose order is a creation of the elements of the contexts (see AESTHETICS, CHINESE). In the Daoist text the *Zhuangzi*, there is the statement that each of the ten thousand things comes into being out of its own inner reflection and yet none can tell how it comes to be so. The Confucian version of this claim is that 'it is the person who extends order in the world (*dao*), not order that extends the person' (*Analects* 15/29).

In China, the phrase 'the continuity between man and Heaven' (*tianren heyi*) has been construed to mean that personal, societal, political and cosmic order are coterminous and mutually entailing, and that from the human perspective, this order is emergent in the process of one's own self-cultivation and articulation. If we think of the various contexts which are to be harmonized as concentric circles, we can see that there is an interdependence between one's self-realization at the center and world order at the outer extreme. Classically, this is expressed through the notion of the Sage as exemplar both of tradition in its broadest sense and 'the will of Heaven' – that is, the specific environing conditions that set up the viable possibilities in a particular social situation or historical epoch. This is the sense of Mencius' assertions that 'all of the myriad things are complete here in me' and 'one who applies exhaustively his heart-and-mind realizes his character, and in thus realizing his character, realizes Heaven (*tian*)' (*Mengzi* 7A/4 and 7A/1).

There are continuous and dynamic patterns discernable in the developmental flow of Chinese philosophy that provide us with a way of organizing the tradition beyond its consolidation in the Han dynasty. First, the membrane that divides Chinese intellectual culture into 'schools' and 'traditions' is highly porous. Intellectual diversity, like political diversity, follows a pattern of being absorbed and assimilated into a harmony dominated by some central doctrine, and then precipitating out of this same harmony in periods of disunity. When the centre is strong, the dominant school draws into itself and co-opts competing elements, thereby fortifying itself against opposition. When, over time, the centre weakens, disintegration sets in and those intellectual resources that have been marginalized by the dominant centre move in to reshape the core.

As noted above, Confucianism, fortified by precepts and concerns drawn from the 'Hundred Schools' of the pre-Qin period, emerges as the prevailing Han ideology. As the Han dynasty declines in the second century AD, religious Daoism and Buddhism move in from the periphery to recolour the intellectual ideology, transforming state-centred Confucianism into the more esoteric and reclusive 'pure conversation' (*qingtan*) and neo-Daoist (*xuanxue*) movements of the Northern and Southern dynasties. However, the influence is mutual. As Buddhism takes root and flourishes in Chinese soil, it is interpreted through indigenous categories which overwhelm many of its original concerns, gradually translating it into a religion and philosophy consonant with the assumptions of the Sinitic world view. By the time the Huayan and Chan sects of Buddhism appear in the Tang dynasty (see BUDDHIST PHILOSOPHY, CHINESE), doctrinal affinities with Daoism and Confucianism have transformed an erstwhile foreign doctrine into a Chinese institution.

9 Neo-Confucianism: Zhu Xi and Wang Yangming

As the Empire regrouped and neo-Confucianism (see NEO-CONFUCIAN PHILOSOPHY), referred to as '*dao* learning' in Chinese, began to take shape in the medieval period, the speculative and the practical extremes of Buddhism came to exert an influence on the revival of Confucianism and to set the agenda for rival claims to orthodoxy within the neo-Confucian ranks. On one extreme, the Cheng–Zhu school favoured broad text-based learning and 'the investigation of things' (*gewu*) while the competing Lu–Wang school rejected canonical studies for a more subjective, meditative approach to personal realization. What these contesting traditions shared in common was philosophical ambition encouraged by the presumption that there is a direct line between personal cultivation and an understanding of natural and moral order. This led to extended reflections on the nature and order of all things, and heated discussions about the relationships that obtained among the most abstract distinctions which could be marshalled in explanation of cosmic regularities. Where these two extremes of neo-Confucianism disagreed most fundamentally was on the most effective method of self-cultivation (see SELF-CULTIVATION, CHINESE THEORIES OF).

ZHU XI is representative of the systematic and theoretical wing of neo-Confucianism. His extensive commentaries established the Four Books (the *Analects*, the *Mengzi*, the *Daxue* (Great Learning) and the *Zhongyong* (Doctrine of the Mean)) as the core curriculum for official examinations, an orthodoxy that persisted into the twentieth century. The authority of Zhu Xi's project lay in his claim to retrieve and revive the import of classical Confucianism. In so doing, he made use of the traditional philosophical vocabulary, but augmented it with complex theoretical discussions of *li* (the patterned regularity of existence) and *qi* (the psychosomatic stuff of existence), giving precedence to the former as identical with the grounding principle of Zhou Dunyi's cosmology, the Great Ultimate (*taiji*) (see LI; QI; ZHOU DUNYI). Hence, Zhu Xi's wing of neo-Confucianism is often referred to as '*li* learning'. These abstract distinctions had moral significance.

They could be appealed to qualitatively in explanation of both the goodness of humanity and how to realize it. Although Zhu Xi did not rule out introspection as a means to illumination, the emphasis of his programme was clearly on scholarly learning.

The most eminent of the thinkers representing an emphasis upon internal cultivation was WANG YANGMING. He rejected the intellectualization of personal realization by identifying the heart-and-mind (see XIN (HEART AND MIND)) with *li*, or pattern. For Wang, the human mind is both the locus and the standard of sagehood. Perhaps the most celebrated theme in Wang is his belief in the continuity and inseparability of knowledge and practice.

There is some question among contemporary scholars as to whether neo-Confucian philosophy, launched with the eleventh century cosmological speculations of SHAO YONG and Zhou Dunyi, abandoned the tradition of *ars contextualis* and became metaphysical in a more recognizably Western sense. This involves the question as to whether notions of 'transcendence', 'objective essences' and 'natural kinds' were at least tacitly introduced. At the very least, one can say that Western philosophers would find the language of neo-Confucian philosophers more familiar than that of most other Chinese thinkers. Having allowed this surface familiarity, one must consider that the philosophical substance of tradition weighs heavily against any assumption that neo-Confucianism was dualistic, and was thus disposed to move in an essentialist direction.

Historically, the speculative, cosmological turn in Chinese philosophy came under formidable attack with the founding of the Qing dynasty in the seventeenth century. Evidential research (*kaozheng-xue*) brought with it an attempt to get behind the 'empty' commentaries of neo-Confucianism and a return to the philologically-centered historical scholarship of 'Han learning' (*Hanxue*). On the premise that new problems require new solutions, the abstract theorizing and universalistic tendencies of Song–Ming '*dao* learning' gave way to the analysis of particular historical events and cultural artifacts as a resource for finding answers to the specific issues of the day. Thinkers such as WANG FUZHI and DAI ZHEN recovered and reaffirmed the correlative and interdependent relationship between historical event and the principles of order. Once again, it can be seen how the pragmatic concerns of most Chinese intellectuals militate against the exercise of philosophical speculations that move too far afield from the concrete problems of human beings, or which could conceivably serve to introduce contentiousness among intellectuals.

10 The modern period

Beginning with the Buddhist incursion into China at the beginning of the Common Era, the question of the degree to which 'Western' influences have effected significant changes in China's cultural life has been vigorously debated. HAN YU, like MENCIUS a thousand years earlier, railed against the pernicious influence upon the Confucian community of competing ideologies. Yet, as we have argued above, the Chinese genius for realizing social stability through the harmonious integration of novel influences led to the effective transformation of Buddhist ideology and practice into a distinctly Chinese institution.

In modern times, events surrounding the May Fourth movement in 1919 seemed likely to lead to the Chinese acceptance of Western ideological influences. Hu Shi, a student of John DEWEY and later a distinguished Chinese philosopher, helped arrange Dewey's twenty-six month lecture tour of China in 1919–21), and later sought to disseminate his mentor's ideas. Bertrand RUSSELL, whose lectures in China overlapped Dewey's, was equally well-received by the intelligentsia. However, the final result of the May Fourth uprising, which occurred just three days after Dewey's arrival in China, was not the realization of democratic reform but the founding of the Chinese Communist Party in 1921. The widespread assumption that Marxism has effectively westernized Chinese philosophical culture is seriously challenged by Mao's own claim, upon adopting Marxist ideology, that he was using a Western heresy to confront the West (see MARXISM, CHINESE).

The Chinese transformation of Marxist into Maoist thinking in contemporary China reveals the inertia of Chinese tradition. The single most distinctive change that Mao made to Marxism was a commitment to particularity and site-specificity. Dialectical materialism is revised to reflect a *yin–yang ad hoc* relationship between economic principle and social superstructure. Although hierarchical, these forces are seen as interdependent and mutually determining. Human malleability and the fluidity of social nature goes far beyond the standard Marxian line. Where Marx places emphasis on the uniformity of class-originated nature, Mao emphasizes the importance of those differences derived from ways of living and thinking that must be factored into the evaluation of any particular 'concrete' personality. There is in Mao a basic suspicion of abstract, general claims, and a recurrent return to specific cases and historical examples. The contemporary Chinese view so historicizes the Marxist sensibility as to make room for an almost unlimited flexibility with regard to the shaping of individual personalities and the development of individual skills (see MARXISM, CHINESE).

There is little evidence to suggest that contemporary China has abandoned any significant elements of its syncretic Confucian orthodoxy. The dynastic leadership of contemporary China maintains many of the same characteristics that have dominated since the Han dynasty: a governing state ideology that gives all people their respective place in their community, an understanding of the nation as a 'family', a programmatic constitution which functions more like a Bill of 'Rites' than a Bill of Rights, a filial respect for the ruler as 'father and mother' of the people, and the consequent sense of rule as a personal exercise. With respect to the personal character of rule, it continues to be the case in China that to object to the policies that articulate the existing order is in fact to condemn the ruler's person.

As a ritually-constituted society, without grounding in the objective principles associated with reason or natural law, contemporary China is defined by the exemplars of its tradition. The members of the society are themselves possessed of their 'humanity' not as a gift from God or a common genetic inheritance, but as created by ritual enactment. The Chinese have no inalienable rights. Citizens have been deemed to possess only those rights granted by China's various constitutions. The Chinese would see the Enlightenment insistence upon the universality of certain values and principles as an instance of ethnocentric dogmatism. Chinese ethnocentrism is, perhaps, more consistent than its Western counterpart since it is grounded in the self-conscious insistence upon the centrality of its peculiar ethos, defined by racial and linguistic identity.

China remains a culture grounded in the model of the family which cultivates filial dependency. Thus, the Chinese have no means of cultivating that 'healthy suspicion' of governmental power which we take for granted without undermining the community of affect that binds ruler and people. As a rational means of organizing social and economic interactions, the technology so prized in the West cannot but erode the ritual grounding of interpersonal relationships. One of the catchwords of the Tiananmen protests in 1989 was 'democracy'. But, in a society where individualism remains a symptom of selfishness and license, and freedom of speech must be qualified by the Confucian understanding that not only saying but *thinking* involves a disposition to act, Chinese democracy must certainly take on an unfamiliar form. Indeed, the inhibition of individualism and freedom of speech is not a modern invention of Chinese communists but a persistent feature of a Confucian society in which ideas are always dispositions to act.

One can hardly look closely at the intellectual culture of contemporary China without coming to respect the power of China's traditions. The intransigent sense of 'Chineseness' which coalesced in the Han dynasty continues to determine the shape of Chinese intellectual culture. For good or ill, the Chinese remain the people of the Han.

See also: AESTHETICS, CHINESE; BUDDHIST PHILOSOPHY, CHINESE; CHINESE CLASSICS; CONFUCIAN PHILOSOPHY, CHINESE; CONFUCIUS; DAODEJING; DAOIST PHILOSOPHY; GUANZI; HISTORY, CHINESE THEORIES OF; HUAINANZI; LAW AND RITUAL IN CHINESE PHILOSOPHY; LEGALIST PHILOSOPHY, CHINESE; LOGIC IN CHINA; LUSHI CHUNQIU; MARXISM, CHINESE; MOHIST PHILOSOPHY; NEO-CONFUCIAN PHILOSOPHY; SELF-CULTIVATION, CHINESE THEORIES OF; WANG CHONG; YIJING

References and further reading

Bodde, D. (1991) *Chinese Thought, Society, and Science*, Honolulu, HI: University of Hawaii Press. (Examines the social and intellectual forces that influenced the development of science and technology.)

Chan Wing-tsit (1963) *A Source Book in Chinese Philosophy*, Princeton, NJ: Princeton University Press. (A basic resource of original sources in translation.)

de Bary, W.T. *et al.* (1960) *Sources of Chinese Tradition*, New York: Columbia University Press. (A representative selection of philosophical literature translated from original sources.)

Gernet, J. (1985) *China and the Christian Impact: A Conflict of Cultures*, trans. J. Lloyd, Cambridge: Cambridge University Press. (Uses journals, correspondence and other sources to place the Jesuits and Chinese intelligentsia in conversation and to reveal their different presuppositions.)

Graham, A.C. (1978) *Later Mohist Logic, Ethics and Science*, Hong Kong: The Chinese University Press. (A detailed look at the analytic side of classical Chinese philosophy.)

—— (1989) *Disputers of the Tao*, La Salle, IL: Open Court. (The most sophisticated overview of major philosophical developments in China's formative period.)

Granet, M. (1950) *La pensée chinoise* (Chinese Thought), Paris: Éditions Albin Michel. (A pioneering attempt to characterize Chinese philosophical thinking.)

Hall, D.L., and Ames, R.T. (1987) *Thinking Through Confucius*, Albany, NY: State University of New

York Press. (A comparative study which attempts to identify underlying assumptions in Confucian thinking.)

* —— (1995) *Anticipating China: Thinking Through the Narratives of Chinese and Western Culture*, Albany, NY: State University of New York Press. (A sequel to *Thinking Through Confucius* which further elaborates differences in thinking, arguing that these differences must be factored into discussions of contemporary issues such as gender, rights and so on.)

—— (1997) *Thinking from the Han: Self, Truth and Transcendence in Chinese and Western Culture*, Albany, NY: State University of New York Press. (A discussion of cultural differences that emerge in the contrasting narratives of the Chinese and Western traditions.)

Henderson, J.B. (1984) *The Development and Decline of Chinese Cosmology*, New York: Columbia University Press. (Traces correlative cosmology in China from its origins to late imperial times.)

Maspero, H. (1981) *Taoism and Chinese Religion*, trans. F. Kierman, Jr, Amherst, MA: University of Massachusetts Press. (Argues for the influence of Daoism, rejecting the assumption that Confucianism was the dominant philosophical orientation in Chinese history.)

Schwartz, B.I. (1985) *The World of Thought in Ancient China*, Cambridge, MA: Harvard University Press. (An accessible history of classical Chinese philosophy emphasizing continuities with Western culture.)

DAVID L. HALL
ROGER T. AMES

CHINESE ROOM ARGUMENT

John Searle's 'Chinese room' argument aims to refute 'strong AI' (artificial intelligence), the view that instantiating a computer program is sufficient for having contentful mental states. Imagine a program that produces conversationally appropriate Chinese responses to Chinese utterances. Suppose Searle, who understands no Chinese, sits in a room and is passed slips of paper bearing strings of shapes which, unbeknown to him, are Chinese sentences. Searle performs the formal manipulations of the program and passes back slips bearing conversationally appropriate Chinese responses. Searle seems to instantiate the program, but understands no Chinese. So, Searle concludes, strong AI is false.

SEARLE (1980) argues that, since in the imaginary case he does everything the computer would do and he still does not understand a word of Chinese, it follows that a computer successfully programmed to pass a Chinese Turing test (see TURING, A.M. §3) would not understand Chinese either. The problem, according to Searle, is that computer programs, whether executed by electronic devices or by Searle inside the room, concern only *syntax*, or strings of symbols characterized only by *spelling*, not *meaning*, while thought and understanding require meaning and semantics. And he claims you cannot get semantics from mere syntax, no matter how subtle or complicated it may be.

An underlying assumption of Searle's interpretation is that real mentality and genuine intentional content (what he calls 'intrinsic intentionality') require consciousness. In later publications Searle (1990a) has made this explicit in terms of his 'connection principle', which states that the notion of an unconscious or non-conscious thought can be coherently understood only as a disposition to have a corresponding conscious thought; an unconscious belief that *p* or desire for *x* is nothing more than the disposition to have a conscious belief that *p* or desire for *x* under apt circumstances. He argues that the notion of a thought that is in principle inaccessible to consciousness is incoherent (see UNCONSCIOUS MENTAL STATES §5).

Many objections have been raised against the Chinese room. Searle pre-emptively discussed and tried to refute several of them at the time of his original publication. Two have been especially important: those which Searle labels the 'systems reply' and the 'robot reply'.

The systems reply concedes that in the imagined case Searle does not understand Chinese, but insists that the whole organized system consisting of Searle, the rule books, paper, pencil and room *does*. According to the systems reply the example errs in comparing Searle with the whole computer when in fact his role is analogous only to that of the central processing unit (CPU) of the computer, a small part of it, to which there is no need to attribute the understanding that is displayed by the entire system (see SEMANTICS, CONCEPTUAL ROLE).

Searle offers a two-part response. First, he labels absurd the very suggestion that a system consisting of a person, some books, paper and a pencil could literally understand things or have a mind over and above that of the person alone. Such an ensemble he asserts is just the wrong sort of thing literally to understand or to have a mind. Second, he tries to avoid the objection by altering his example and removing himself from the room to a wide open field and committing all the rule books to memory. In such a case he would perform all the purely formal operations in his head, re-establishing his analogy with the whole computer. He asserts he would still not understand a word of Chinese (though some of his critics claim otherwise).

The robot reply concedes that the original Chinese room might not suffice for understanding Chinese. Since all its behaviour is strictly verbal, it is able to make connections between words and words, but not between words and the world: it might give coherent answers to questions about boiled eggs, but not have any ability to recognize an egg. The robot reply thus imagines a program installed within a robot that allows it to simulate the full range of human behaviour, verbal and non-verbal; and *that*, it is claimed, would count as understanding Chinese and having a mind.

Searle, however, disagrees. He notes that the robot's sensors would supply its internal processors only with more formal symbolic inputs. Were he and his Chinese room installed within the robot with additional rule books specifying how to respond to those additional symbols, and were these responses to drive the robot's apt behaviour, he, Searle, would still not understand a single word of Chinese. Nor, he argues, would the robot. Again, the assumption that mentality requires consciousness seems in part to drive Searle's intuition. Critics less sympathetic to that assumption and more inclined to analyse intentionality in terms of causal interactive relations have been predictably more persuaded by the robot reply, especially if it is combined with the systems reply (see SEMANTICS, INFORMATIONAL).

Other objections to the Chinese room have sought to discredit it as a source of unreliable and misleading intuitions. Some have focused on the enormous disparity between the complexity and speed that would be required in a computer able to pass a Turing test, which the man in the room could not match. Others have stressed that strong AI need not be committed to the Turing test, and that the specific program by which behaviour is produced is crucial to whether something has a mind. In reply, Searle denies that speed or style of program is of any importance; what matters, he argues, is that the operations he performs are merely formal.

See also: ARTIFICIAL INTELLIGENCE; CONSCIOUSNESS; INTENTIONALITY

References and further reading

Dennett, D.C. and Hofstadter, D. (eds) (1981) *The Mind's I*, New York: Basic Books. (A diverse and delightful collection with commentary by the editors including critical discussion of the Chinese room.)

* Searle, J. (1980) 'Minds, Brains, and Programs', *Behavioral and Brain Sciences* 3: 417–24. (Original publication of the Chinese room.)

* —— (1990a) 'Consciousness, Explanatory Inversion and Cognitive Science', *Behavioral and Brain Sciences* 13: 585–96. (Discussion of the connection principle.)

—— (1990b) 'Is the Brain's Mind a Computer Program?', *Scientific American* 262: 26–31. (A clear and simple introduction to the Chinese room debate.)

Van Gulick, R. (1988) 'Consciousness, Intrinsic Intentionality and Self-Understanding Machines', in A. Marcel and E. Bisiach (eds) *Consciousness in Contemporary Science*, Oxford: Oxford University Press. (Places the Chinese room in the context of general issues about mind, machines, meaning and consciousness.)

ROBERT VAN GULICK

CHINUL (1158–1210)

Chinul was the founder of the Korean Chogye school of Buddhism. He sought to reconcile the bifurcation between Kyo (doctrinal) thought and Sôn (Zen) practice that rent the Korean Buddhist tradition of his time, by showing the symbiotic connection between Buddhist philosophy and meditation. He also advocated a distinctive program of soteriology that became emblematic of Korean Buddhism from that time forward: an initial sudden awakening to the nature of the mind followed by gradual cultivation of that awakening until full enlightenment was achieved.

1 Life
2 Buddhist ecumenicalism
3 Introspection and the mind
4 Soteriology

1 Life

Chinul, the National Master Puril Pojo, ordained as a monk when he was seven years old and passed the ecclesiastical examinations in the Sôn (Zen) branch of the Korean Buddhist tradition in 1182. According to his biography, however, Chinul became disillusioned with his colleagues' pursuit of worldly fame and profit, and soon afterwards decided to abandon ecclesiastical advancement for a contemplative life in the south of the Korean peninsula. Unlike many of his peers, Chinul did not make the incumbent pilgrimage to the mecca of the Chinese mainland and, despite his Sôn ecclesiastical affiliation, seems also not to have had close personal contacts with any teacher of meditation in Korea. A virtual autodidact, Chinul made up for this lack of individual instruction by drawing on sources that were readily available to him: the scriptures and scholastic commentaries of Kyo and the discourse records of previous masters of Sôn. His reading of scriptures and of Sôn texts catalyzed three separate awakenings, which led to his realization of the fundamental identity between Kyo and Sôn.

Chinul eventually established a number of monasteries and hermitages in the south of the Korean peninsula, including what became one of the three most important monasteries in the Korean Buddhist tradition, the Songgwang-sa (Piny Expanse Monastery). Chinul's works all date from this period of contemplation, starting with his earliest work, *Kwôn su Chônghye kyôlsa mun* (Encouragement to Practice: The Compact of the Samādhi and Prajñā Community), written in 1190 upon the establishment of his first retreat society. *Susim kyôl* (Secrets on Cultivating the Mind), arguably his most popular treatise, was composed between 1203 and 1205, and his *magnum opus*, *Pôpchip pyôrhaengnok chôryo pyôngip sagi* (Excerpts from the Dharma Collection and Special Practice Record with Personal Notes), was completed in 1209, one year before his death. His remaining works were edited and published posthumously by his successor Chin'gak Hyesim (1178–1234).

The approach to Buddhism that Chinul outlined in his writings was marked by a strong reliance on correct doctrinal understanding at the inception of practice. Only after correct understanding had been forged regarding the justification and rationale of Buddhist practice would the student then go on to formal meditation training. That training could run the gamut from techniques heavily beholden to Kyo contemplative exercises, to the joint cultivation of concentration and wisdom (an approach deriving from one of the earliest stratum in Chinese Chan literature), to a new style of meditation just then developing on the Chinese mainland, the investigation of the 'critical phrase' (*kongan*; in Japanese, *kōan*). By synthesizing several antecedent strands of Buddhism, Chinul produced a uniquely Korean Buddhist school called Chogye (after the Korean pronunciation of Caogi Mountain, the monastic home of the sixth patriarch of the Chinese Chan school, Huineng (638–713)). Chinul's Chogye school became the dominant school of Korean Buddhism from the thirteenth century onward and Chinul's distinctive approach to Buddhist thought and practice became

the model followed by most subsequent teachers within the Korean tradition (see BUDDHIST PHILOSOPHY, KOREAN).

2 Buddhist ecumenicalism

Although Chinul was principally a Sôn meditator, he nevertheless retained a strong personal interest in the scriptural teachings of Kyo. Chinul's attempted reconciliation of the two branches of Buddhism sought to authenticate the Sôn approach in the scriptures of Kyo, thereby demonstrating the veracity of both. Chinul reviewed the entire Buddhist canon, seeking scriptural substantiation for the Sôn claim that enlightenment could be achieved solely through meditative introspection. While reading a text from the Flower Garland school, he finally found such substantiation and declared, 'What the Buddha said with his lips is Kyo; what the patriarchs of Sôn transmitted with their minds is Sôn. The mind and the words of the Buddha and patriarchs can certainly not be contradictory.' From that point on Chinul was convinced of the affinities between scriptural testimony and meditative experience, and his main ambition was to bring about a rapprochement between the Kyo and Sôn strands of the Korean Buddhist tradition.

3 Introspection and the mind

For Chinul, the essential unity of Sôn and Kyo would be recognized once Buddhist adepts perceived their original natures: the quality of sentience that was most fundamental to all 'sentient' beings. Such insight was achieved through introspection, looking into the mind itself in order to verify the truth of one's innate buddhahood. It was through introspection – what Chinul termed 'tracing back the light of the mind' (*panjo*) or 'tracing the radiance emanating from the mind back to its source' (*hoegwang panjo*) – that students would overcome all limited conceptions about their true natures and perceive the vast web of interrelationships connecting themselves to all other things in the universe. This state of enlightenment achieved through Sôn practice was, Chinul claimed, what the Flower Garland school of Kyo called the unimpeded interpenetration between all phenomena.

Introspection was a technique that took the usual propulsion of the mind out into the world of the senses and turned it back in upon itself, until the mind's radiant source was discovered. To trace this inherent radiance of the mind back to its source meant to realize instantaneously that oneself was inherently enlightened, that one's mind was congenitally luminous. This brightness of mind was the faculty that illuminated sense objects, allowing them to be cognized. Hence, by tracing the radiance emanating from the mind back to its source, meditators discovered that core of luminosity that was fundamental to all sentient beings (see ILLUMINATION; ILLUMINATIONIST PHILOSOPHY). This discovery of their true nature constituted the initial understanding of the experience of enlightenment.

4 Soteriology

Chinul derived from this vision of the inherence of enlightenment a soteriological stratagem that came to be the hallmark of Korean Sôn: sudden awakening followed by gradual cultivation. This soteriological programme advocated that the optimal approach to Buddhist practice involved an initial understanding-awakening (*haeo*) to the true nature of the mind, which generated correct comprehension of both the absolute reality of all things (their nature) and their phenomenal appearances (their characteristics). This awakening, which occurred instantaneously, caused students to know that they were in fact innately enlightened and identical in principle with all the buddhas.

However, in Chinul's schema, simply knowing that one was enlightened was not sufficient to be able to act in an enlightened way. It was through a gradual process of subsequent spiritual cultivation that the understanding achieved through the initial awakening permeated all of one's behaviour, leading ultimately to realization-awakening (*chûngo*), or full enlightenment. The habitual patterns of thought and action developed during innumerable previous lifetimes were so deeply engrained that there was little hope of bringing them to an abrupt end; to change the inertial force of these habits required a long process of gradual cultivation. But, because students understood through the awakening that occurred at the very inception of practice that their minds were inherently pure and free of defilements, they could eliminate mental defilements while knowing that there was really nothing that needed to be eliminated. Similarly, students could also develop wholesome qualities of mind while realizing that there was nothing that needed to be developed. Chinul compared this interpretation of cultivation to the gradual calming of waves (mental defilements) after the wind that has whipped them up (the ignorance of one's innate buddhahood) had stopped: one was simply allowing a natural process to complete itself. Hence at the consummation of training one simply 'realized' in all facets of one's life the same truths that one had

'understood' initially. Chinul's soteriological stratagem of sudden awakening followed by gradual cultivation therefore accommodated a developmental component, while remaining strongly beholden to the subitist orientation that dominated much of Zen thought and practice throughout East Asia.

See also: BUDDHIST PHILOSOPHY, KOREAN

List of works

Chinul (1190–1209) Collected works, in *Han'guk Pulgyo chônsô* (Collected Works of Korean Buddhism), ed. Han'guk Pulgyo chônsô p'yônch'an wiwônhoe, Seoul: Tongguk University Press, 1980, vol. 4, 698–869; ed. and trans. R. Buswell, *The Korean Approach to Zen: The Collected Works of Chinul*, Honolulu, HI: University of Hawaii Press, 1983. (The standard Korean edition of all of Chinul's works; Buswell's edition is the standard English edition and translation of Chinul's major works. A paperback abridged version of the latter is R. Buswell, *Tracing Back the Radiance: Chinul's Korean Way of Zen*, Classics in East Asian Buddhism 2, Honolulu, HI: University of Hawaii Press.)

—— (1190) *Kwôn su Chônghye kyôlsa mun* (Encouragement to Practice: The Compact of the Samādhi and Prajñā Community), ed. and trans. R. Buswell, *The Korean Approach to Zen: The Collected Works of Chinul*, Honolulu, HI: University of Hawaii Press, 1983. (Written on the establishment of his first retreat society.)

—— (1203–5) *Susim kyôl* (Secrets on Cultivating the Mind), ed. and trans. R. Buswell, *The Korean Approach to Zen: The Collected Works of Chinul*, Honolulu, HI: University of Hawaii Press, 1983. (Chinul's most popular treatise.)

—— (1209) *Pôpchip pyôrhaengnok chôryo pyôngip sagi* (Excerpts from the Dharma Collection and Special Practice Record with Personal Notes), ed. and trans. R. Buswell, *The Korean Approach to Zen: The Collected Works of Chinul*, Honolulu, HI: University of Hawaii Press, 1983. (Chinul's major work.)

References and further reading

Buswell, R. (1983) *The Korean Approach to Zen: The Collected Works of Chinul*, Honolulu, HI: University of Hawaii Press. (The standard English edition and translation of virtually all of Chinul's works. Includes complete annotation, an extensive introduction to Chinul's life and thought with a survey of the history of Korean Buddhism, and a thorough bibliography to Western and East Asian sources.

Abridged in paper back as *Tracing Back the Radiance: Chinul's Korean Way of Zen*, Classics in East Asian Buddhism 2, Honolulu, HI: University of Hawaii Press, 1991.)

—— (1986) 'Chinul's Systematization of Chinese Meditative Techniques in Korean Sŏn Buddhism', in P.N. Gregory (ed.) *Traditions of Meditation in Chinese Buddhism*, Honolulu, HI: University of Hawaii Press, 199–242. (The ecumenical approach to practice developed by Chinul.)

—— (1988) 'Ch'an Hermeneutics: A Korean View', in D.S. Lopez (ed.) *Buddhist Hermeneutics*, Studies in East Asian Buddhism 6, Honolulu, HI: University of Hawaii Press, 231–56. (Describes the hermeneutical stratagems Chinul uses to reconcile statements in Kyo and Sŏn materials.)

—— (1989) 'Chinul's Ambivalent Critique of Radical Subitism in Korean Sŏn Buddhism', *Journal of the International Association of Buddhist Studies* 12 (2): 20–44. (Chinul's treatment of the soteriological stratagem of sudden awakening/sudden cultivation.)

—— (1990) 'Chinul's Alternative Vision of Kanhwa Sŏn and Its Implications for Sudden Awakening/Sudden Cultivation', *Pojo sasang* 4: 423–63. (Technical discussion of how Chinul seeks to reconcile a radical-subitist form of meditation with his moderate subitism of sudden awakening/gradual cultivation.)

Keel, H. (1984) *Chinul: The Founder of the Korean Sŏn Tradition*, Berkeley Buddhist Studies Series vol. 6, Berkeley, CA: Center for South and Southeast Asian Studies. (A valuable expository study of Chinul's contributions to Korean Buddhist philosophy.)

Park Sung-Bae (1983) *Buddhist Faith and Sudden Enlightenment*, Albany, NY: State University of New York Press. (A provocative monograph on Korean Sŏn practice, which focuses especially on Chinul and the tension he posits between faith and doubt in Sŏn meditation.)

—— (1994) 'On the Subitist/Gradualist Debate in Korean Buddhism: Sŏngch'ŏl's Theory of Sudden Enlightenment and Sudden Practice', in D. Suh (ed.) *Korean Studies: New Pacific Currents*, Pacific Association for Korean Studies I, Honolulu, HI: Center for Korean Studies, 163–74. (Analysis of a contemporary Korean argument against Chinul's preferred soteriology.)

Shim Jae-Ryong (1979) 'The Philosophical Foundation of Korean Zen Buddhism: The Integration of Sŏn and Kyo by Chinul (1158–1210)', Ph.D. dissertation, University of Hawaii. (Extensive treatment of Chinul's ecumenical philosophy.)

ROBERT E. BUSWELL, JR

CHISHOLM, RODERICK MILTON (1916–)

Chisholm is an important analytic philosopher of the second half of the twentieth century. His work in epistemology, metaphysics and ethics is characterized by scrupulous attention to detail, the use of a few basic, undefined or primitive terms, and extraordinary clarity. One of the first Anglo-American philosophers to make fruitful use of Brentano and Meinong, Chisholm translated many of Brentano's philosophical writings. As one of the great teachers, Chisholm is widely known for the three editions of Theory of Knowledge, *a short book and the standard text in US graduate epistemology courses. An ontological Platonist, Chisholm defends human free will and a strict sense of personal identity.*

Roderick Milton Chisholm (born in North Attleboro, Massachusetts, USA) has come as close as any philosopher ever does to actually living the good life: marrying happily, teaching graduate philosophy at his Alma Mater and, in later years, living by the ocean. Upon completing an undergraduate philosophy major at Brown University, Chisholm entered the doctoral programme at Harvard, finishing in 1942. The subsequent three years of military experience, administering psychological tests to recruits, had little influence on his philosophy, nor did his brief stint at the Barnes Foundation lecturing on the philosophy of art. Chisholm returned to Brown in 1947 where he taught for the next forty years, heavily influencing Anglo-American epistemology and metaphysics.

Chisholm remained remarkably consistent throughout his career, opposing a variety of fashionable philosophical movements (phenomenalism, linguistic reductions of any sort and extensionalism) and simultaneously developing and elaborating original views on knowledge and justification, intentionality and ontology. In the early years he was most concerned to resist the dominant – and then popular – strains of positivism. For example, against phenomenalists who proposed to translate material-object statements into sensation statements, Chisholm convincingly argued that the requisite boundary or background conditions themselves could never be adequately stated using only sensation statements (see PHENOMENALISM §2).

It is easy to see in this pattern of reasoning the beginnings of his view, later known as 'the primacy of the intentional'. This doctrine would be elaborated in greater detail as Chisholm debated with Wilfrid SELLARS and others who sought to reduce various human referential or intentional capacities to dispositions to engage in certain linguistic behaviour (see INTENTIONALITY §§1, 3). The central tenet of the primacy of the intentional is that the ability of humans to use language to refer to things in the world is to be explicated in terms of their ability to think of these same things. Sellars and others held the reverse.

Chisholm was inspired by the work of Franz BRENTANO to spend years searching for a mark or criterion of the mental. During this period he translated Brentano's *Wahrheit und Evidenz* (The True and the Evident) and many other works by Brentano and MEINONG. He lectured frequently in Graz, Austria, winning in 1972 an honorary degree from the University, which was, according to him, the 'high spot' of his philosophical career.

Chisholm published three editions of his *Theory of Knowledge*. In all three, he was a pure foundationalist for a priori knowing, claiming that any a priori knowledge was either intuitively certain or known to be deducible from what was intuitively certain (see A PRIORI §3). However, his account of empirical knowledge was a much more complicated story, containing a strong coherentist component. While claiming that certain internal mental states were 'self-presenting' and thus not in need of any evidential support, Chisholm consistently required substantial coherence among one's internal beliefs before one was justified in believing any proposition which went beyond the internal.

The foundational or anchoring self-presenting states and their corresponding beliefs consist of a variety of 'seemings'. What one seems to believe, seems to intend, seems to hope for or fear and, most importantly, seems to perceive, are all self-presenting; that is, if one is in any of these states and believes that one is in the state, then that belief is certain. Chisholm, following up a suggestion of his colleague Curt Ducasse, developed an adverbial theory of sensory experiencing. Chisholm urged that when referring to internal experiencing, we replace talk of 'sense-data' with adverbial expressions such as 'being appeared to redly'. In Chisholm's view, having the property of being appeared to redly was self-presenting and, thus, certain. The main advantage of this artificial way of speaking was the avoidance of ontological and epistemic puzzles about sense data. While 'being appeared to redly' is somewhat comprehensible, the approach requires similar adverbs for all the other possible modes of sensing and suffers some implausibility because of their absence from ordinary language (see MENTAL STATES, ADVERBIAL THEORY OF).

A fundamental characteristic of Chisholm's approach was to employ a fertile primitive term together with simple logical relationships to define other more complex concepts. For example, in the 3rd edition of *Theory of Knowledge* (1989b) the central foundational category of the 'certain' was defined in terms of the primitive comparative term 'more justified than' as follows:

p is certain for *S* =Df For every *q*, believing *p* is more justified for *S* than withholding *q*, and believing *p* is at least as justified for *S* as is believing *q*.

Definitions such as these occur throughout his work and it would not be inappropriate to label his approach 'Definitionalism'. Because of their clarity and simplicity, Chisholm's definitions generated numerous responses, mostly proposed counter-instances. Chisholm welcomed every example and never tired of modifying or 'chisholming away at' his definitions.

Chisholm handled epistemological scepticism by assuming that we have particular justified beliefs and the ability to examine them critically and thereby to discover principles of justification. These principles enabled Chisholm to construct a fifteen-category epistemic hierarchy, ranging from the certainly false to the certainly true. Each of the categories is defined in terms of the primitive 'more justified than'. Chisholm glosses this primitive in terms of an epistemic requirement to prefer. That is, when *S* is more justified in believing *p* than in believing *q*, *S* is required to prefer *p* to *q*. This epistemic requirement would then compete with all one's other kinds of requirement (including ethical), and from the competitive fray one's overall or real obligation would then emerge.

Chisholm was throughout his career inclined towards Platonism, always regarding attributes as abstract and eternal. The details of his ontology evolved and led him to seek a comprehensive theory of ontological categories. In *The First Person* (1981) Chisholm developed a theory of objective reference based around the primitive notion of 'direct attribution'. Direct attribution usually involves the 'emphatic reflexive' typified by such sentences as 'he believes that he himself is wise'. Chisholm uses his account of attribution to explain all *de re* or objective attributions.

Chisholm approached ethics theoretically, developing a theory of intrinsic value, and practically defending a kind of 'indeterminism'. The theory of intrinsic value employed undefined primitive terms to develop hierarchically arranged categories of both value and obligation. Chisholm's indeterminism, or theory of agent causation, affirmed free choices for which there were no internal or external conditions causally sufficient for that choice. Responsible agents themselves contribute the final condition which then brings about the actual choice and leads to the action.

See also: A POSTERIORI §2; COMMONSENSISM; FOUNDATIONALISM; FREE WILL; INTERNALISM AND EXTERNALISM IN EPISTEMOLOGY; KNOWLEDGE AND JUSTIFICATION, COHERENCE THEORY OF; PERCEPTION; SCEPTICISM

List of works

A full bibliography can be found in Bogdan (1986).

Chisholm, R. (1957) *Perceiving: A Philosophical Study*, Ithaca, NY: Cornell University Press. (Exposition of the adverbial theory of perception, an account of adequate evidence based on an ethical primitive, and a Brentano-like view of intentionality. Carefully argued, yet accessible to the diligent beginning reader.)

—— (ed.) (1960) *Realism and the Background of Phenomenology*, Glencoe, IL: Free Press. (Collection of articles from 1870 to 1940 by German, British and American philosophers and psychologists concerned with the reality of objects of perception and thought. The editor's introduction is exceptionally useful and accessible, the articles themselves are of moderate complexity.)

—— (1966) *Theory of Knowledge*, Englewood Cliffs, NJ: Prentice Hall, 1st edn. (Closely argued exposition of entire epistemic system including a discussion of the metaphilosophical issues relevant to scepticism. Textbook for advanced students)

Chisholm, R. and Swartz, R. (eds) (1973) *Empirical Knowledge: Readings from Contemporary Sources*, Englewood Cliffs, NJ: Prentice Hall. (Collection of influential essays on scepticism, foundationalism, memory and belief. Most are accessible, but the essay by Sellars is difficult.)

Chisholm, R. (1976) *Person and Object: A Metaphysical Study*, La Salle, IL: Open Court. (Expanded version of the Carus Lectures on the self, agency, identity through time, and states of affairs; contains several appendices on justified belief and the part–whole relation. Readable but filled with definitions.)

—— (1977) *Theory of Knowledge*, Englewood Cliffs, NJ: Prentice Hall, 2nd edn. (Significantly revised and lengthened, with greater emphasis on the use of primitive terms to define complex concepts. Textbook for advanced students.)

Chisholm, R. and Haller, R. (eds) (1978) *Die Philosophie Franz Brentanos: Beiträge zur Brentano-Konferenz, Graz, 1977,* The philosophy of Franz Brentano: Papers from the Brentano conference, Graz, 1977, Amsterdam: Editions Rodopi N.V. (Contributions to the 1977 Conference on Brentano's philosophy in Graz, Austria.)

Chisholm, R. (1981) *The First Person: An Essay on Reference and Intentionality*, Minneapolis, MN: University of Minnesota Press. (Analysis of all reference, especially the referring capacity of linguistic expressions, in terms of first person reference. Concise and rather technical.)

—— (1982) *The Foundations of Knowing*, Minneapolis, MN: University of Minnesota Press. (Collection of previously published but slightly revised essays and an update of his epistemic system involving three new, short essays. Most parts are highly readable.)

—— (1986) *Brentano and Intrinsic Value*, New York: Cambridge University Press. (Exposition and interpretation of Brentano's theory of value, linking it to his general views on intentionality. Rather technical)

—— (1989a) *On Metaphysics*, Minneapolis, MN: University of Minnesota Press. (Collection of previously published, but revised, essays on action, identity, reference, and ontology; almost all views expressed here are worked out in greater detail elsewhere. Readable.)

—— (1989b) *Theory of Knowledge*, Englewood Cliffs, NJ: Prentice Hall, 3rd edn. (Substantially revised and shortened, with several chapters devoted to the metaphilosophical issues raised by the internalism–externalism and foundationalism–coherentism debates. Textbook for advanced students.)

—— (1996) *A Realistic Theory of Categories: An Essay on Ontology*, New York: Cambridge University Press. (An extremely concise reduction of all ontological entities using eight undefined categorial locutions. Includes all major metaphysical doctrines and central epistemological views, few real-world examples and many technical formulations. For advanced readers only.)

References and further reading

Bogdan, R.J. (ed.) (1986) *Roderick M. Chisholm*, Boston, MA: Reidel. (Contains a complete bibliography and a useful self-profile essay by Chisholm)

Brentano, F. (1889) *Vom Ursprung sittlicher Erkenntnis*, ed. and co-trans. R. Chisholm as *The Origin of Our Knowledge of Right and Wrong*, London: Routledge & Kegan Paul, 1969. (Translation of the third edition of 1934. A compact statement of Brentano's ethics which includes a theory of intrinsic value defined in terms of correct interests and preferences, supplemented by a utilitarian account of instrumental value.)

* —— (1930) *Wahrheit und Evidenz*, ed. and co-trans. R. Chisholm as *The True and the Evident*, London: Routledge & Kegan Paul, 1966. (Chronologically arranged lectures, letters, fragments and notes on the subject of truth, beginning with Brentano's version of the correspondence theory and ending with his view that true judgments are those which someone judging with evidence would accept.)

—— (1976) *Philosophische Untersuchungen zu Raum, Zeit, und Kontinuuum*, ed. R. Chisholm and S. Kourner, Hamburg: Felix Meiner Verlag; trans. B. Smith, *Philosophical Investigations on Space, Time, and the Continuum*, London: Croom Helm, 1988. (Brentano's account of time-consciousness, his anti-Cantorian theory of the continuum and his unorthodox views on boundaries.)

—— (1978) *Aristotle and his World-View*, ed. and co-trans. R. Chisholm, Los Angeles, CA: University of California Press. (Brentano's views as to what is essential in Aristotle. The sections on various aspects of Aristotle's Deity serve as an excellent introduction to Brentano's own views.)

—— (1981) *The Theory of the Categories*, ed. and co-trans. R. Chisholm, The Hague: Martinus Nijhoff. (Brentano's views on various ontological issues.)

Fichte, J. (1800) *The Vocation of Man*, ed. and co-trans. R. Chisholm, New York: Liberal Arts Press, 1955. (Edited and readable translation which contains a very useful, yet concise, introduction to Fichte's Idealism and general philosophical stance.)

Kim, J. (1986) 'Critical review of *The First Person*', *Philosophy and Phenomenological Research* 46 (3): 483–507. (Sympathetic examination of the central doctrine that all reference is ultimately *de se* reference.)

Meinong, A. (1968–78) *Alexius Meinong Gesamtausgabe* Complete works of Alexius Meinong, Graz: Akademische Druck- und Verlagsanstalt, 8 vols. (All the books and essays that Meinong published, together with his intellectual self-portrait and major reviews. Volumes 4 and 5 are edited by Chisholm. Volume 7 contains a comprehensive index. The supplementary volume contains a selection of posthumous material including lecture notes, notes on other philosophers' writings, and a lexicon of logic and epistemology.)

DAVID BENFIELD

CH'OE CHE-U *see* Tonghak

CHOICE, AXIOM OF *see* Axiom of choice

CHOMSKY, NOAM (1928–)

Fish swim, birds fly, people talk. The talents displayed by fish and birds rest on specific biological structures whose intricate detail is attributable to genetic endowment. Human linguistic capacity similarly rests on dedicated mental structures many of whose specific details are an innate biological endowment of the species. One of Chomsky's central concerns has been to press this analogy and uncover its implications for theories of mind, meaning and knowledge.

This work has proceeded along two broad fronts.

First, Chomsky has fundamentally restructured grammatical research. Due to his work, the central object of study in linguistics is 'the language faculty', a postulated mental organ which is dedicated to acquiring linguistic knowledge and is involved in various aspects of language-use, including the production and understanding of utterances. The aim of linguistic theory is to describe the initial state of this faculty and how it changes with exposure to linguistic data. Chomsky (1981) characterizes the initial state of the language faculty as a set of principles and parameters. Language acquisition consists in setting these open parameter values on the basis of linguistic data available to a child. The initial state of the system is a Universal Grammar (UG): a super-recipe for concocting language-specific grammars. Grammars constitute the knowledge of particular languages that result when parametric values are fixed.

Linguistic theory, given these views, has a double mission. First, it aims to 'adequately' characterize the grammars (and hence the mental states) attained by native speakers. Theories are 'descriptively adequate' if they attain this goal. In addition, linguistic theory aims to explain how grammatical competence is attained. Theories are 'explanatorily adequate' if they show how descriptively adequate grammars can arise on the basis of exposure to 'primary linguistic data' (PLD): the data children are exposed to and use in attaining their native grammars. Explanatory adequacy rests on an articulated theory of UG, and in particular a detailed theory of the general principles and open parameters that characterize the initial state of the language faculty (that is, the biologically endowed mental structures).

Chomsky has also pursued a second set of concerns. He has vigorously criticized many philosophical nostrums from the perspective of this revitalized approach to linguistics. Three topics he has consistently returned to are:

- *Knowledge of language and its general epistemological implications*
- *Indeterminacy and underdetermination in linguistic theory*
- *Person-specific 'I-languages' versus socially constituted 'E-languages' as the proper objects of scientific study.*

1 **The aims and principles of linguistic theory**
2 **Knowledge of language**
3 **Indeterminacy and underdetermination**
4 **I-language versus E-language**

1   The aims and principles of linguistic theory

There is an intimate relation between how a problem is conceived and the kinds of explanations one should offer. Chomsky proposes that we identify explanation in linguistics with a solution to the problem of how children can attain mastery of their native languages on the basis of a rather slender database. This is often referred to as 'the logical problem of language acquisition'.

A natural language assigns meanings to an unbounded number of sentences. Humans typically come to master at least one such language in a surprisingly short time, without conscious effort, explicit instruction or apparent difficulty. How is this possible? There are significant constraints on any acceptable answer.

First, a human can acquire any language if placed in the appropriate speech community. Grow up in Boston and one grows up speaking English the way Bostonians do. However, the 'primary linguistic data' (PLD) available to the child are unable to guide the task unaided. There are four kinds of problems with the data that prevent it from shaping the outcome:

(a) The set of sentences the child is exposed to is finite. However, the knowledge attained extends over an unbounded domain of sentences.

(b) The child is exposed not to sentences but to utterances of sentences. These are imperfect vehicles for the transmission of sentential information as they can be defective in various ways. Slurred speech, half sentences, slips of the tongue and mispronunciations are only a few of the ways that utterances can obscure sentence structure.

(c) Acquisition takes place without explicit guidance by the speech community. This is so for a variety of reasons. Children do not make many errors to begin with when one considers the range of logically possible mistakes. Moreover, adults do

not engage in systematic corrections of errors that do occur and even when correction is offered children seem neither to notice nor to care. At any rate, children seem surprisingly immune to any form of adult linguistic intrusion (see Lightfoot 1982).

(d) Last of all, and most importantly, of the linguistic evidence theoretically available to the child, it is likely that only simple sentences are absorbed. The gap between input and intake is attributable to various cognitive limitations such as short attention span and limited memory. This implies that the acquisition process is primarily guided by the information available in well-formed simple sentences. Negative data (the information available in unacceptable ill-formed sentences) and complex data (the information yielded by complex constructions) are not among the PLD that guide the process of grammar acquisition. The child constructing its native grammar is limited to an informationally restricted subset of the relevant data. In contrast to the evidence that the linguist exploits in theory construction, the information the child uses in building its grammar is severely restricted. This suggests that whenever the linguistic properties of complex clauses diverge from simple ones, the acquisition of this knowledge cannot be driven by data. Induction is insufficient as the relevant information is simply unavailable in the PLD.

The general picture that emerges from these considerations is that attaining linguistic competence involves the acquisition of a grammar, and that humans come equipped with a rich innate system that guides the process of grammar construction. This system is supple enough to allow for the acquisition of any natural language grammar, yet rigid enough to guide the process despite the degeneracy and deficiency of the PLD. Linguistic theorizing takes the above facts as boundary conditions and aims both at descriptive adequacy (that is, to characterize the knowledge that speakers have of their native grammars) and explanatory adequacy (that is, to adumbrate the fine structure of the innate capacity) (see LANGUAGE, INNATENESS OF).

Issues of descriptive and explanatory adequacy have loomed large in Chomsky's work since the beginning. Chomsky's objection, for example, to 'Markov models' of human linguistic competence was that they were incapable of dealing with long distance dependencies exemplified by conditional constructions in English and hence could not be descriptively adequate. His argument in favour of a transformational approach to grammar rested on the claim that it allowed for the statement of crucial generalizations evident in the judgments of native speakers and so advanced the goal of descriptive adequacy (Chomsky 1957). Similarly, his influential critique (1959) of Skinner's *Verbal Behavior* consisted in showing that the learning theory presented therein was explanatorily inadequate. It was either too vague to be of scientific value or clearly incorrect given even moderately precise notions of stimulus or reinforcement.

The shift from the early *Syntactic Structures* (1957) theory to the one in *Aspects of a Theory of Syntax* (1965) was also motivated by concerns of explanatory adequacy. In the earlier model the recursive application of transformations allows for the generation of more and more complex sentences from the sentences produced by the 'phrase structure' component of the grammar. In the *Aspects* theory, recursion is incorporated into the phrase structure component itself, and removed from the transformational part of the theory (see SYNTAX §3). The impetus for this was the observation that greater explanatory adequacy could be attained by grammars that had a level of 'Deep Structure' incorporating a recursive base component. In particular, Fillmore (1963) observed that the various optional transformations in a *Syntactic Structures* theory always applied in a particular order in any given derivation. This order is unexplained in a *Syntactic Structures* theory; in *Aspects* it is deduced. Thus, the move to an Aspects-style grammar is motivated on grounds of greater explanatory adequacy: introducing Deep Structure and moving recursion to the base allows for a more restricted theory of Universal Grammar. All things being equal, restricting UG is always desirable as it advances a central goal of grammatical theory; the more restricted the options innately available for grammar construction, the easier it is to explain how language acquisition is possible, despite the difficulties in the PLD noted above.

The same logic motivates various later additions to and shifts in grammatical theory. For example, a major move in the 1970s was radically to simplify transformational operations so as to make their acquisition easier. This involves eliminating any mention of construction-specific properties from transformational rules. For example, an *Aspects* rule for passive constructions looks like (1), the left-hand side being the Structural Description (SD) and the right hand side being the Structural Change (SC):

(1) $X - NP1 - V - NP2 - Y \rightarrow$

        $X - NP2 - be + en \ V - by + NP1 - Y$

This rule would explain, for instance the grammaticality of 'the ball is kicked by John' given that of 'John kicks the ball'. Observe that the SC involves the constants 'be + en' and 'by'. The SD mentions three general expressions, 'NP1', 'V' and 'NP2' and treats these as part of the context for the application of the rule. In place of this, Chomsky proposed eliminating the passive rule and replacing it with a more general rule that moves NPs (Chomsky 1977, 1986). The passive rule in (1) involves two applications of the 'Move NP' rule, one moving the subject 'NP1' to the 'by' phrase, and another moving the object 'NP2' to the subject position. In effect, all the elements that make the passive rule in (1) specific to transitive constructions are deleted and a simpler rule ('Move NP') replaces it.

There is a potential empirical cost to simple rules, however. The simpler a transformation the more it generates unacceptable outputs. Thus, while a grammar with (1) would not derive 'was jumped by John' from 'John jumped', a grammar eschewing (1) and opting for the simpler 'Move NP' rule is not similarly restricted. To prevent overgeneration, therefore, the structure of UG must be enriched with general grammatical conditions that function to reign in the undesired overgeneration (Chomsky 1973, 1977, 1986). Chomsky has repeatedly emphasized the tension inherent in developing theories with both wide empirical coverage and reasonable levels of explanatory adequacy.

A high point of this research agenda is Chomsky's *Lectures on Government and Binding* (1981). Here the transformational component is reduced to the extremely simple rule 'Move a' – that is, move anything anywhere. To ensure that this transformational liberty does not result in generative chaos, various additions to the grammar are incorporated, many conditions on grammatical operations and outputs are proposed, and many earlier proposals (by both Chomsky and others) are refined. Among these are trace theory, the binding theory, bounding theory, case theory, theta theory and the Empty Category Principle. The picture of the grammar that Chomsky's *Lectures* presents is that of a highly modular series of interacting subsystems which in concert restrict the operation of very general and very simple grammatical rules. In contrast to earlier traditional approaches to grammar, *Lectures* witnesses the virtual elimination of grammatical constructions as theoretical constructs. Thus, in Government Binding (GB)-style theories there are no rules of Passive, Raising, Relativization or Question Formation as there were in earlier theories. Within GB, language variation is not a matter of different grammars having different rules. Rather, the phenomena attested in different languages are deduced by variously setting the parameters of Universal Grammar. Given the interaction of the grammatical modules, a few parametric changes can result in what appear on the surface to be very different linguistic configurations. In contrast to earlier approaches to language, variation consists not in employing different kinds of rules, but in having set the parameters of an otherwise fixed system in somewhat different ways (see Chomsky 1983).

The GB research programme has proven to be quite successful in both its descriptive range and its explanatory appeal. Despite this, Chomsky has urged a yet more ambitious avenue of research. He has embarked on the development of a rationalist approach to grammar that goes under the name of 'Minimalism' (Chomsky 1995). The theory is 'rationalist' both in that it is grounded on very simple and perspicuous first principles, and in that it makes use only of notions required by 'virtual conceptual necessity'. Chomsky hopes to make do with concepts that no approach to grammar can conceivably do without and remain true to the most obvious features of linguistic competence. For example, every theory of grammar treats sentences as pairings of sounds and meanings. Thus, any theory will require that every sentence have a phonological and an interpretative structure. In GB theories, these sorts of information are encoded in the PF (Phonetic Form) and LF (Logical Form) phrase markers respectively. In addition, GB theories recognize two other distinctive grammatical levels: S-structure and D-structure. A minimal theory, Chomsky argues, should dispense with everything but LF and PF. It will be based on natural 'economy' principles and indispensable primitives. Chomsky has suggested reanalysing many of the restrictions that GB theories impose in terms of 'least effort' notions such as 'shortest move' and 'last resort movement'. For example, he proposes that the unacceptability of sentences such as 'John is expected will win', are ultimately due to the fact that the moved NP 'John' need not have moved from the embedded subject position (between 'expected' and 'will') as it fulfils no grammatical requirement by so moving. This work is still in its infancy, but it has already prompted significant revisions of earlier conclusions. For example, with the elimination of D-structure, the recursive engine of the grammar has once again become the province of generalized transformations. Whatever its ultimate success, however, Minimalism continues the pursuit of the broad goals of descriptive and explanatory adequacy enunciated in Chomsky's earliest work.

2 Knowledge of language

According to Chomsky, the three fundamental epistemological questions in the domain of language are 'What constitutes knowledge of language?', 'How is knowledge of language acquired?' and 'How is this knowledge put to use?'. The answer to the first question is given by a particular generative grammar. Harold's knowledge of English is identified with Harold's being in a particular mental/brain state. A descriptively adequate grammar characterizes this part of Harold's mental/brain make-up. An answer to the second question is provided by a specification of UG and the principles that take the initial state of the language faculty to the knowledgeable state on exposure to PLD. Harold knows English in virtue of being genetically endowed with a language faculty and having been normally brought up in an English-speaking community. Beyond this, further issues of grounding are unnecessary. Issues of epistemological justification and grounding in the data are replaced by questions concerning the fine structure of the initial state of the language faculty and how its open parameters are set on the basis of PLD. The third question is answered by outlining how linguistic knowledge interacts with other cognitive capacities and abilities to issue in various linguistic acts such as expressing one's thoughts, parsing incoming speech and so on (see Chomsky 1986).

How much does the language case tell us about epistemological issues in other domains? In other words, should knowledge of quantum mechanics be analysed in a similar vein, that is, being in a particular mental state, grounded in specific innate capacities and so on. Chomsky only makes sparse comments on this general issue, but those he advances suggest that he believes that knowledge in these domains should be approached in much the same way they are approached in the domain of language. This suggests that humans have an innate science-forming capacity that underlies our success in the few domains of inquiry in which there has indeed been scientific success. As in the domain of language, this capacity is focused and modular rather than being a general all-purpose tool and this, Chomsky speculates, might well underlie the patchiness of our successes. Where we have the right biological propensities, we develop rich insightful theories that far outpace the data from which they are projected. Where this mind/brain structure is lacking, mysteries abound that seem recalcitrant to systematic inquiry. Stressing our cognitive limits is a staple of Chomsky's general epistemological reflections. If humans are part of the natural world we should expect there to be problems that fall within our cognitive grasp and mysteries that lie outside it. The rich theoretical insights allowed in the natural sciences are the result of a chance convergence between properties of the natural world and properties of the human mind/brain (see Chomsky 1975).

3 Indeterminacy and underdetermination

Knowledge of language, Chomsky has argued, presents a strong argument in favour of traditional rationalist approaches to mind and against traditional empiricist approaches (see LEARNING §1; RATIONAL-ISM). In particular, 'learning' is treated as more akin to growth and the course of acquisition is seen more as the unfolding of innate propensities under the trigger of experiential input than as the result of the shaping effects of the environment. This rationalist perspective is now quite common and this is largely due to Chomsky's efforts. Chomsky has consistently warned against empiricist prejudices in philosophy, and in no instance more strongly than in his critique of Quine's methodological remarks on linguistics (for example, see Quine 1960).

Chomsky takes Quine to be arguing that linguistic investigations are beset with problems greater than those endemic to inquiry in general. Whereas empirical investigation in general suffers from underdetermination of theory by evidence, linguistic study is beset with the added problem of indeterminacy (see RADICAL TRANSLATION AND RADICAL INTERPRETATION §§2–3). Indeterminacy differs from standard inductive underdetermination (see UNDERDETERMINATION) in that where there is indeterminacy 'there is no real question of right choice' among competing proposals. Chomsky interprets Quine as arguing that 'determining truth in the study of language differs from the problem of determining truth in the study of physics' (Chomsky 1975: 182–3).

In reply, Chomsky (1969) argues that Quine's thesis rests on classical empiricist assumptions about how languages are acquired. Quine, he argues, supposes that humans have 'an innate quality space with a built-in distance measure'... to certain 'simple physical correlates'. In addition, certain kinds of induction in this space are permitted. Beyond this, however, 'language-learning is a matter of association of sentences to one another and to certain stimuli through conditioning'. Further, one cannot 'make significant generalizations about language or common-sense theories, and the child has no concept of language or of "common-sense" prior to this training' (Chomsky 1969: 54–5, 63).

Chomsky notes that Quine provides no evidence to support these assumptions. Nor can there be any good evidence to support them if the nature of the learning problem in the domain of language is characterized as Chomsky has argued it must be. Chomsky concludes that 'Quine's thesis of the indeterminacy of transla-tion amounts to an implausible and quite unsubstantiated empirical claim about what the mind brings to the problem of acquisition of language (or of knowledge in general) as an innate property' (Chomsky 1969: 66). Stripped of these tendentious empirical assumptions, Quine fails to show that indeterminacy is anything other than the familiar problem of underdetermination of theory by evidence as applied to linguistics. Chomsky (1996) has since argued that the ultimate source of many critiques of the mental sciences in general and linguistics in particular (including Quine's indeterminacy thesis) is a kind of methodological dualism that takes humans to be separate from the natural world. This dualism is manifest in the a priori constraints that philosophers place on explanations in the mental sciences, which would be regarded as inappropriate if applied to the physical sciences.

In this vein Chomsky asks, for example, why access to consciousness is so often taken to be crucial in substantiating the claim that humans have I-language or follow rules. Suppose, he asks, we had a theory that perfectly described what happens when sound waves hit the ear, stimulating the performance system to access the cognitive system and construct a logical form that interacts with other cognitive systems to yield comprehension, in so far as the language faculty enters into this process. What more could be desired? The insistence that this entire process be accessible to consciousness in order for the account to be credible, he argues, is a demand beyond naturalism, a form of methodological dualism of dubious standing that would be summarily rejected if raised elsewhere.

Or consider the oft-voiced suspicions concerning mentalist approaches in psychology. Many philosophers are ready to accept these as perhaps temporarily necessary but ultimately, the view seems to be, mentalist theories must reduce to physical ones to be truly legitimate. Chomsky argues that this sentiment is another manifestation of methodological dualism and should be rejected. First, it presupposes that there is a tenable distinction between the mental and the physical. However, Chomsky argues that since Newton undermined the Cartesian theory of body by showing that more 'occult' forces were required in an adequate physics, mind–body dualism has lost all grounding. Second, even if reduction were possible, reduction comes in many varieties and there is little reason to believe that the contours of the reducing physical theory would be left unaffected by the process. Since Newton, Chomsky notes, 'physical' has been an honorific term that signifies those areas in which we have some nontrivial degree of theoretical understanding. The relevant scientific question is whether some theory or other offers interesting descriptions and explanations. The further insistence that its primitives be couched in physical vocabulary is either vacuous (because 'physical' has no general connotation) or illegitimate (another instance of methodological dualism).

The general conclusion Chomsky draws is that whatever problems linguistic theory encounters, it is no more methodologically problematic than theories in other domains. He attributes the qualms of philosophers to lingering empiricist dogma or an indefensible epistemological dualism.

4 I-language versus E-language

Given the aims of Chomskian linguistic theory, the proper objects of study are the I-languages internalized by native speakers, rather than public E(xternal)-languages used by populations. Chomsky denies that public E-languages are interesting objects of scientific study. Indeed he denies that E-languages can be coherently specified as they simply do not exist. The proper objects of inquiry are I-languages; 'I' standing for intensional, internal and individual. An I-language is individual in that each speaker has one. This focus turns the common wisdom on its head. E-languages like English, Swahili and so forth are (at best) radical idealizations for Chomsky, or (at worst) incoherent pseudo-objects. At best, E-languages are the intersection of the common properties of various I-languages. Thus, for example, it is not that speakers communicate because they have a language in common; rather wherever I-languages *overlap* communication is possible.

An I-language is internal in the sense of being part of a speaker's individual mental make-up. It is neither a Platonic object nor a social construct. Also, an I-language is intensional, not extensional. Comprised as it is of an unbounded number of sentences, a language cannot be 'given' except via a specification of the function that generates them, that is a grammar for that language. Thus, it is languages in intension, languages dressed in all of their grammatical robes, not simple concatenations of words, that are the proper objects of scientific interest. One consequence of this is that weak generative capacity (that is, the extensional equivalence of languages generated by different grammars) is of dubious interest. In short, the shift from E-language to I-language turns many long-standing questions around, raising some to prominence that were considered secondary and relegating many that previously were considered crucial to the status of pseudo-questions.

Many philosophers have found Chomsky's focus on I-language problematic. To illustrate, we will consider an important philosophical critique and Chomsky's reply.

Dummett (1986) argues against internalist approaches to language that they fail to provide an account of notions like 'language of a community' or 'community norms' in the sense presupposed by virtually all work in the philosophy of language and philosophical semantics. These notions, Dummett claims, are required to provide a notion of a common public language which 'exists independently of any particular speakers' and of which native speakers have a 'partial, and partially erroneous, grasp' (see LANGUAGE, SOCIAL NATURE OF §2).

The naturalistic study of language, Chomsky counters, has no place for a Platonistic notion of language, a notion of language outside the mind/brain that is common to various speakers and to which each speaker stands in some cognitive relation. The reason is that this Platonistic reification rests on notions like 'language' and 'community' that are hopelessly underspecified. Asking if two people speak the same language is, in Chomsky's opinion, to ask a highly context-dependent question – much like asking whether Boston is near New York. What counts as a community depends on shifting expectations of individuals and groups. Human society is not neatly divided into communities with languages and their norms. Thus, what counts as a community is too under-specified to be useful for theoretical purposes. Therefore, it is not a defect of linguistic theory that these notions play no role within it.

From Chomsky's perspective E-languages are epiphenomenal objects, if coherent at all. I-language in its universal aspects is part of the human genotype and specifies one aspect of the human mind/brain. Under the triggering effects of experience a particular grammar arises in the mind/brain of an individual. From this perspective, universal grammar and the steady-state grammars that arise from them are real objects. They will be physically realized in the genetic code and the adult brain. E-language, in contrast, has a murky ontological status. Chomsky (1980) argues that the priority of I-language cannot be reasonably doubted once we observe that languages involve an infinite pairing of sounds and meanings. Given that language is infinite, it cannot be specified except in so far as some finite characterization – a function in intension – is provided. It might be possible to give some characterization to the notion 'a language used by a population' but only indirectly via a grammatical specification of the language. But this concedes the priority of I-language as the claim unpacks into something like: each person in the relevant population has a grammar in their mind/brain that determines the E-language. Thus, at best, an E-language is that object which the I-language specifies. However, even this might be giving too much reality to E-languages, for there is nothing in the notion I-language that requires that what they specify corresponds to languages as commonly construed, that is, things like French, English and so on. It is consistent with Chomsky's viewpoint that I-language never specifies any object that we might pre-theoretically call a language. Whether this is indeed the case, the key point is to realize that the move from grammar to language is a step away from real mechanisms to objects of a higher degree of abstraction. I-language is epistemologically and ontologically hardier than E-language, much philosophical opinion to the contrary.

See also: LANGUAGE, INNATENESS OF; LANGUAGE, PHILOSOPHY OF; LANGUAGE, SOCIAL NATURE OF §3; NATIVISM; UNCONSCIOUS MENTAL STATES §4

List of works

Chomsky, N. (1957) *Syntactic Structures*, The Hague: Mouton. (First work on Transformational Grammar.)

—— (1959) 'Review of *Verbal Behavior* by B.F. Skinner', *Language* 35: 26–58. (A critique of behaviourist approaches to learning.)

—— (1965) *Aspects of a Theory of Syntax*, Cambridge, MA: MIT Press. (Outlines the Standard Model.)

—— (1969) 'Quine's Empirical Assumptions', in D. Davidson and J. Hintikka (eds) *Words and Objections*, Dordrecht: Reidel.

—— (1973) 'Conditions on Transformations', in S.R. Anderson and P. Kiparsky (eds) *A Festschrift for Morris Halle*, New York: Holt, Rinehart & Winston. (Begins the move away from rule-based approaches to grammar.)

—— (1975) *Reflections on Language*, New York: Pantheon. (A good non-technical review of the extended standard theory and various philosophical issues related to generative grammar.)

—— (1977) *Essays on Form and Interpretation*, Amsterdam: North Holland. (Essays in the extended standard theory.)

—— (1980) *Rules and Representations*, New York: Columbia University Press. (Essays on linguistics and philosophy.)

—— (1981) *Lectures on Government and Binding*, Dordrecht: Foris.

—— (1983) 'Some Conceptual Shifts in the Study of Language', in L. Cauman, I. Levi, C. Parsons and R. Schwartz (eds) *How Many Questions?: essays in honor of Sidney Morgenbesser*, Indianapolis, IN: Hackett. (A description of how linguistic theory has

changed from Syntactic Structures to Local Government Binding.)

—— (1986) *Knowledge of Language*, New York: Praeger. (Chapter 3 provides an informal yet challenging overview of Government Binding Theory.)

—— (1995) *The Minimalist Program*, Cambridge, MA: MIT Press. (Chomsky's best current text on Minimalism.)

—— (1996) *Powers and Prospects*, Boston, MA: South End Press. (More recent philosophical esays on E-language and dualism.)

References and further reading

* Dummett, M.A.E. (1986) 'Comments on Davidson and Hacking', in E. Lepore (ed.) *Truth and Interpretation*, Oxford: Blackwell. (Argues in favour of the importance of E-languages.)

* Fillmore, C.J. (1963) 'The Position of Embedding Transformations in a Grammar', *Word* 19: 208–31. (A technical critique of Generalized Transformations.)

Haegeman, L. (1994) *Introduction to Government and Binding Theory*, Oxford: Blackwell. (A good textbook on Government Binding Theory.)

Lightfoot, D.W. (1982) *The Language Lottery*, Cambridge, MA: MIT Press. (A good introduction to the logic of linguistic research.)

Pinker, S. (1994) *The Language Instinct*, New York: Morrow. (Combines Darwin and Chomsky to argue that linguistic competence is a human instinct rather than cultural phenomenon. Good introduction to linguistic research.)

* Quine, W.V. (1960) *Word and Object*, Cambridge, MA: MIT Press. (Argues for the radical indeterminacy of certain aspects of linguistic theory.)

* Skinner, B.F. (1957) *Verbal Behavior*, New York: Appleton-Century-Crofts. (Presents the behaviourist account of language that Chomsky influentially criticized.)

Webelhuth, G. (ed.) (1995) *Government and Binding Theory and the Minimalist Program*, Oxford: Blackwell. (A very good advanced text on Government Binding Theory.)

NORBERT HORNSTEIN

CHÔNG YAGYONG (TASAN) (1762–1836)

Chông Yagyong was a government official and a scholar of the Sirhak (Practical Learning) school in the late Chosôn dynasty of Korea. He is also known by his literary name Tasan. A man of independent mind, Chông was not satisfied with the conventional interpretation of the Confucian classics. He immersed himself in research on the Six Classics and the Four Books, investigating a whole range of writings by scholars from the Han through the Qing dynasties and searching for the true and original intents of the ancient sages uncorrupted by later interpretations. In the course of clarifying ancient terms and concepts, he frequently challenged the orthodox views of the Song neo-Confucianism that had largely dominated the intellectual climate of Chosôn Korea. Although he frequently praised Zhu Xi, he did not hesitate to point out the shortcomings of the neo-Confucian masters.

In his youth, Chông Yagyong came under the influence of the scholarship of Yi Ik (1681–1763). In 1784 he was first introduced to the teachings of Catholicism by his friend Yi Pyôk (1754–86), who provided him with a copy of Matteo Ricci's *The True Meaning of Our Lord in Heaven*, and thereafter he was exposed to Catholicism and Western learning. Having passed the higher civil examination in 1789, he held various government posts, such as local magistrate, Secret Inspector, Third Minister and Royal Secretary. Because of his association with Catholicism his official career was not smooth, but he nevertheless became one of the favorites of King Chôngjo who, recognizing his brilliance, protected him as much as possible. In 1801, during the persecution of Catholics, Chông was forced out of office and had to spend the next eighteen years in exile. His earlier renunciation of Catholicism may have saved him from certain death, and there are conflicting accounts as to whether his public disclaimer was genuine. While in exile, Chông devoted his energy to scholarship, mostly writing commentaries on the classics. In 1818 he was released from exile and allowed to return to his home at Mahyôn, an eastern suburb of present-day Seoul, where he lived until his death. He wrote extensively on a wide range of subjects, but he is better known for his scholarly commentaries on the Six Classics and the Four Books, and his three studies on government and economy.

Not satisfied with the neo-Confucian cosmology based on principle (*i*; in Chinese, *li*) and material force (*ki*; in Chinese, *qi*), Chông developed his own concept of heaven (see QI; TIAN). He sees heaven or the heavenly ruler as a monotheistic spirit who created the universe and presides over all beings. Unlike plants or animals, every person is endowed by heaven with its spiritual quality, enabling them to transcend all things. At the same time, people are equipped with dual qualities: the autonomy to choose good or evil and the natural inclination 'to take pleasure in the

good and to be ashamed of evil'. Chông then explains that the reason why 'the superior man does not wait till he sees things, to be cautious' is because he is aware of the presence of the heavenly ruler even in a dark room. Thus men have the obligation to obey and respect heaven, from whence emanates all ethical and moral value. One can see the influence of Catholicism in Chông's concept of heaven, and similarly in his studies of the Six Classics and the Four Books, he built up his own system of philosophy through an eclectic approach.

Chông also valued practical applications of knowledge, and thus declared that 'the teaching of the School of the Principle is to know the Way through self-awareness so that one can exert his utmost toward realizing the right principle'. Of the many works on government and economy that he wrote, three are best known: *Kyôngse yup'yo* (Designs for Good Government), *Mongmin simsô* (Admonitions on Governing the People) and *Hûmhûm sinsô* (Towards a New Jurisprudence). Not unlike John LOCKE, Chông believed that the first governments were formed when people in a community agreed to let a judicious man settle a dispute that arose. Accordingly, he maintained that government exists on behalf of the people. In place of the chaotic land system that prevailed in Korea at the time, he proposed a 'village land' (*yôjôn*) system whereby land would be owned and cultivated jointly by village members and the harvest distributed according to the amount of work contributed by each individual. His overriding goal for the government was to promote and protect the well-being of the people as a whole. A man of practical mind, he also devised cranes that were used in the construction of the fortifications at Suwôn, set up a pontoon bridge over the Han River and experimented with smallpox and measles inoculations. A versatile scholar, he wrote on a wide range of subjects including history, geography, philology and military science. He is regarded as the greatest of all the Sirhak scholars who stood between the traditional and the modern periods in Korea.

See also: CONFUCIAN PHILOSOPHY, KOREAN; NEO-CONFUCIAN PHILOSOPHY; QI; SIRHAK

List of works

Chông Yagyong [Tasan] (1762–1836) *Chông Tasan chônjip* (Complete Works of Chông Tasan), Seoul: Munhôn p'yônch'an wiwônhoe, 1960–1, 4 vols. (This is a facsimile reproduction in reduced size of the original, published in 1936.)

—— (1817) *Kyôngse yup'yo* (Designs for Good Government), in *Chông Tasan chônjip*, Seoul:

Munhôn p'yônch'an wiwônhoe, 1960–1. (Embodies Chông Yagyong's proposals for reform in governmental structure and administration as well as the land and tax system.)

—— (1818) *Mongmin simsô* (Admonitions on Governing the People), in *Chông Tasan chônjip*, Seoul: Munhôn p'yônch'an wiwônhoe, 1960–1. (A handbook for local magistrates on how to manage local administration, along with views on the problems of the common people.)

—— (1819) *Hûmhûm sinsô* (Towards a New Jurisprudence), in *Chông Tasan chônjip*, Seoul: Munhôn p'yônch'an wiwônhoe, 1960–1. (Study and proposal for the reform of the handling of penal cases for murder.)

References and further reading

Henderson, G. (1957) 'Chông Tasan: A Study in Korea's Intellectual History', Journal of Asian Studies 16 (3): 377–86. (A general survey of his career and association with his Catholic friends.)

Kang Man'gil *et al.* (1999) *Tasanhak ûi t'amgu* (In Search of the Tasan School), Seoul: Minûmsa. (Seven South Korean scholars examine various aspects of Chông's views on subjects including criminal law, social structure, the tax system, finance, the classics and Catholicism.)

Kûm Changt'ae (1987) *Han'guk sirhak sasang yôngu* (Study of the Thought of the Practical Learning in Korea), Seoul: Chimmundang. (Part 2 of this book is devoted to the study of Chông's philosophy such as view on Heaven and the *Yijing*.)

Kwahagwôn Ch'ôrhak Yônguso (1962) *Chông Tasan yôngu* (Studies of Chông Tasan), Pyôngyang: Kwahagwôn. (North Korean scholars examine Chông's views on philosophy, society and economy, language, literature, history, education and natural science.)

Setton, M. (1996) *Chông Yagyong: Korea's Challenge to Orthodox Neo-Confucianism*, Albany, NY: State University of New York Press. (A penetrating study of the worldview behind Chông Yagyong's reform ideas, with comparative perspectives of China and Japan.)

Yi Urho (1966) *Tasan kyônghak sasang yôngu* (Study of Chông Yagyong's Thought on the Classics), Seoul: Uryu munhwasa. (A pioneering study of Chông focusing on his views on the Confucian classics.)

—— (1975) *Tasanhak ûi ihae* (Understanding Chông Yagyong), Seoul: Hyônamsa. (Collection of articles from other sources, dealing mostly with Chông's study of the Confucian classics.)

Yi Urho *et al.* (1989) *Chông Tasan ûi kyônghak* (Classical Studies of Chông Tasan), Seoul: Minûmsa. (Four Korean scholars examine Chông's study of the *Daxue*, *Zhongyong*, *Mengzi* and *Analects*.)

YÔNG-HO CH'OE

CHOU TUN-I *see* ZHOU DUNYI

CHRISTIAN PHILOSOPHY, EARLY *see* PATRISTIC PHILOSOPHY

CHRISTIANITY AND SCIENCE *see* RELIGION AND SCIENCE

CHRISTINE DE PIZAN (1365–*c*.1430)

Christine de Pizan, France's 'first woman of letters', is primarily remembered as a courtly poet and a propagandist for women. Her extensive writings were influenced by the early humanists, reflecting an interest in education (particularly for women and young people) and in government. Following Aquinas, Christine defined wisdom as the highest intellectual virtue and tried to apply the concept of the just war to contemporary problems. Her works are also noteworthy for their contribution to the transmission of Italian literature to Parisian intellectual circles.

Christine de Pizan was born in Venice. Her father and grandfather, city officials in Venice and graduates of the University of Bologna, would undoubtedly have known Petrarch (see PETRARCA, F.), and possibly Boccaccio. Christine's father, an astrologer and medical man of some reputation, was invited to the French court of the cultivated King Charles V, and Christine grew up as part of Charles' entourage. Her father encouraged Christine's early taste for study, and she probably received a basic education alongside her two brothers until her marriage, at the age of fifteen, to Etienne Castel, a young notary who was soon appointed a royal secretary. Widowed at twenty-five, with her father already dead, Christine found herself in desperate financial straits with three children to support. However, she managed to obtain patronage through her taste for study and subsequently for writing. Her attachment to early humanistic interests can be attributed to her programme of self-education during these early years of widowhood, as well as to her father's early influence and possibly to his library.

A debate with young Parisian intellectuals, in which Christine insisted on the superiority of Dante's work over Jean de Meun's *Roman de la Rose* (Romance of the Rose), strengthened her reputation. Becoming successful as a court poet, Christine was one of the first scholars to introduce Dante to France, using him in her first long work, *L'Epître d'Othéa à Hector* (*The Letter of Othea to Hector*) (c.1400) and her semi-autobiographical poem *Le Chemin de Long Estude* (The Long Road of Study) (c.1403). Her *Livre de la Cité des Dames* (*Book of the City of Ladies*) (1405) was inspired in large measure by Boccaccio's *De Claris Mulieribus* (Concerning Outstanding Women), and to a lesser degree by his *Decameron*, retelling selected tales from a woman's point of view. In addition, the influence of Boccaccio's concept of poetry (as expressed in his *De Genealogia Deorum Gentilium* (A Genealogy of Gentile Gods)) can be discerned in her *Letter of Othea*. Her debt to Petrarch is more elusive, although she mentions him in *The City of Ladies* and reworks his version of the Griselda story there.

Her long allegorical poem *La Mutacion de Fortune* (The Mutation of Fortune) (1403) led to a commission from the duke of Burgundy to write a biography of his late brother, *Les Fais et Bonnes Meurs du Sage Roy Charles V* (The Deeds and Good Customs of the Wise King Charles V). In this work she did not just give a historical account of Charles' life, but portrayed him as an exemplary ruler and a philosopher, a model of the philosopher-king. Drawing inspiration from Aquinas' commentary on Aristotle's *Metaphysics* she proposed a definition of wisdom as the highest intellectual virtue and the philosophical life as the prerogative of the free individual.

In common with other early humanists, Christine shows particular interest in the education of the young, notably the French dauphin, Louis de Guyenne. She wrote *Le Livre du Corps de Policie* (*The Book of the Body Politic*) (c.1406) and *Le Livre de la Paix* (The Book of Peace) (1413) for Louis, and her *Les Fais d'Armes et de Chevalerie* (Deeds of Arms and of Chivalry) (1410) was probably intended to form part of his military education. Inspired by the Roman author Vegetius as well as by contemporary needs, *Les Fais d'Armes* was the first professional military treatise to have appeared in some time. The first chapters comprise a significant discussion of the concept of the just war, with Christine attempting to apply traditional ideas to the problems of her own time. The book subsequently played a role in the reform of the French army in the second half of the fifteenth century. Her *Livre des Trois Vertus* (Book of Three Virtues) (1405), devoted to the education of women and dedicated to the dauphin's wife, Marguerite of Burgundy, was also significant: it was reprinted as late as 1536, and influenced European leaders including Margaret of Austria, Anne of France and Louise of Savoy.

See also: HUMANISM, RENAISSANCE

List of works

Christine de Pizan (c.1400) *L'Epître d'Othéa à Hector*, trans. J. Chance, *The Letter of Othea to Hector, with Introduction, Notes, and Interpretive Essay*, Newport, RI: Focus Library of Medieval Women, 1990.

—— (c.1403) *Le Livre du Chemin de Long Estude* (The Long Road of Study), ed. R. Püschel, Berlin: Damköhler and Paris: Le Soudier, 1881; new edn, Berlin: Hettler, 1887; repr. of 1887 edn, Geneva: Slatkine, 1974. (A good text, but limited critical apparatus.)

—— (1403) *Le Livre de la Mutacion de Fortune* (The Mutation of Fortune), ed. S. Solente, Paris: Picard, 1959–1966, 4 vols. (An excellent first edition.)

—— (1404) *Le Livre des Fais et Bonnes Meurs du Sage Roy Charles V* (The Deeds and Good Customs of the Wise King Charles V), ed. S. Solente, Paris: Champion, 1936–40. (An excellent edition; fully documented.)

—— (1405) *Le Livre de la Cité des Dames*, trans. E.J. Richards, *The Book of the City of Ladies*, New York: Persea, 1982. (Argues for the equality of women.)

—— (1405) *Le Livre des Trois Vertus* (Book of Three Virtues), trans. C.C. Willard, in M. Pelner Cosman (ed.) *A Medieval Women's Mirror of Honor, the Treasury of the City of Ladies*, New York: Bard Hall Press/Persea, 1989.

—— (c.1406) *Le Livre du Corps de Policie*, trans. and ed. K. Langdon Forhan, *The Book of the Body Politic*, Cambridge: Cambridge University Press, 1994. (Major political work; argues for the interdependence of rulers and subjects.)

—— (1410) *Le Livre des Fais d'Armes et de Chevalerie*, trans. W. Caxton, *The Book of Faytes of Armes and Chyvalrye*, ed. A.T.P. Byles, London: Early English Text Society, 1932; revised edn, 1937.

—— (1413) *Le Livre de la Paix* (The Book of Peace), ed. C.C. Willard, The Hague: Mouton, 1958. (An excellent edition with introduction and notes.)

—— (1993) *The Writings of Christine de Pizan*, ed.

C.C. Willard, New York: Persea. (A wide selection of Christine's writings in English translation with notes and bibliography.)

—— (1997) *The Selected Writings of Christine de Pizan*, trans. R. Blumenfield-Kosinski and K. Brownlee, ed. R. Blumenfield-Kosinski, New York and London: W.W. Norton.

References and further reading

Batard, Y. (1973) 'Dante et Christine de Pisan', in *Missions et Démarches de la Critique: Mélanges offerts au Professeur J.A. Vier*, Paris: Klincksieck, 345–55. (Basic study of Christine's influence.)

Bozzolo, C. (1967) 'Il *Decameron* come fonte del *Livre de la Cité des Dames* de Christine de Pisan' (The *Decameron* as the Source of Christine de Pizan's *The Book of the City of the Ladies*), in F. Simone (ed.) *Miscellanea di Studi e Richerche sul Quattrocento Francese*, Torino: Giappichelli, 3–24. (Good analysis of Christine's literary borrowings.)

Davis, N.Z. (1980) 'Gender and Genre: Woman as Historical Writers, 1400–1820', in P.H. Labalme (ed.) *Beyond Their Sex: Learned Women in the European Past*, New York: New York University Press, 153–60. (Brief view of Christine as a writer of history, notably in her biography of Charles V.)

Hicks, E. (ed.) (1977) *Le Débat sur le Roman de la Rose*, Paris: Champion. (Good discussion of the debate over the relative merit of Dante and Jean de Meun; includes work by the participants.)

Ornato, E. (1961) 'La prima fortuna del Petrarca in Francia' (The Early Fortunes of Petrarch in France), *Studi Francesi* 5: 201–17, 401–14. (Basic study of Christine de Pizan's influence in the popularization of Petrarch's work.)

Willard, C.C. (1984) *Christine de Pizan. Her Life and Works*, New York: Persea. (General discussion with modern bibliography.)

CHARITY CANNON WILLARD

CHRISTOLOGY *see* INCARNATION AND CHRISTOLOGY

CHRYSIPPUS (*c.*280–*c.*206 BC)

The Greek philosopher Chrysippus of Soli was the third and greatest head of the Stoic school in Athens. He wrote voluminously, and in particular developed Stoic logic into a truly formidable system. His philosophy is effectively identical with 'early Stoicism'.

Chrysippus was born at Soli in Cilicia (southern Turkey). He came to Athens to study philosophy, initially with the Academic sceptic Arcesilaus. By the time he transferred his allegiance to the Stoic school, its founder ZENO OF CITIUM was dead and had been succeeded by Cleanthes, who became Chrysippus' teacher. For a while he taught philosophy outside the Stoa, but in 232 BC CLEANTHES died and Chrysippus succeeded him, holding the office till his own death.

Chrysippus may well have been relatively poor. In his work *On Livelihoods* he tackled the question of how a philosopher might appropriately earn a living. The only three acceptable means, he concluded, were serving a king (if one could not oneself be a king), reliance on friends, and teaching. There is no evidence that Chrysippus, like some other Stoics, adopted the first of these practices.

From the long excerpts of his writings which have survived in other authors, it seems that his Greek was clumsy and often obscure. (The people of his native Soli were so notorious for their poor Greek as to have given the 'solecism' its name.) Nevertheless, he wrote prolifically, his works totalling at least 705 rolls of papyrus, and what he wrote was widely read. Often he returned to the same topic several times in different treatises. His writings were also accused of beng padded out with endless quotations. Not all were doctrinal expositions – some were investigative and open-ended.

'If there had been no Chryippus', it was said, 'there would have been no Stoa'. Chrysippus is generally regarded as the person who built the full Stoic system. (The entry STOICISM is therefore in effect an account of his philosophy.) Whether Chrysippean Stoicism should be, as it often is, called 'orthodox' Stoicism is less clear. Later Stoics did not treat him as altogether authoritative: some, including his successor Antipater as well as POSIDONIUS, were openly critical of him. On the other hand, his writings became and remained the classic Stoic texts to cite and analyse. Exegesis of passages from Chrysippus was a later Stoic teaching method, for example in the school of Epictetus, and conversely his writings were the primary target of anti-Stoic polemicists such as Plutarch and Galen. But Chrysippus presented Zeno rather than himself as the voice of authority, and many of his ideas were developed as defences and interpretations of Zeno's pronouncements, often against the rival interpretations of Cleanthes and others.

Chrysippus contributed extensively to every area of Stoic thought, with the possible exception of epistemology. Above all, he was the school's master logician, and the list of his writings partially preserved by Diogenes Laertius includes an astonishing 118 titles of logical treatises. They include at least seven works, filling fifteen rolls, on the Liar Paradox alone.

See also: LOGIC, ANCIENT

References and further reading

Arnim, H. von (1903–5) *Stoicorum Veterum Fragmenta* (Fragments of the Early Stoics), Leipzig: Teubner, with vol. 4, indexes, by M. Adler, 1924. (The standard collection of early Stoic fragments, in Greek and Latin, commonly abbreviated as *SVF.* Chrysippus fills almost the whole of volumes 2–3, although only a minority of the fragments include an explicit attribution to him.)

Brehier, E. (1910) *Chrysippe et l'ancien stoïcisme*, Paris: Presses Universitaires de France; 2nd edn, Paris: Alcan, 1951. (A still valuable assessment of Chrysippus' contribution to Stoicism.)

* Diogenes Laertius (*c.* early 3rd century AD) *Lives of the Philosophers*, trans. R.D. Hicks, *Diogenes Laertius Lives of Eminent Philosophers*, Loeb Classical Library, Cambridge, MA: Harvard University Press and London: Heinemann, 1925, 2 vols. (Book VII 179–202 is a life of Chrysippus, including an incompletely preserved catalogue of his works.)

Galen (*c.* AD 175) *On the Doctrines of Hippocrates and Plato*, ed. and trans. P.H. de Lacy, *Galeni de Placitis Hippocratis et Platonis (Corpus Medicorum Graecorum* V 4 2 1), Berlin: Akademie-Verlag, 3 vols, 1978–83. (Includes long excerpts from Chrysippus' writings on psychology.)

Gould, J.B. (1970) *The Philosophy of Chrysippus*, Albany, NY: State University of New York Press. (Lucid survey.)

DAVID SEDLEY

CHU HSI *see* ZHU XI

CHUANG TZU *see* ZHUANGZI

CHUNG YUNG *see* ZHONGYONG

CHURCH, ALONZO (1903–95)

Alonzo Church was one of the twentieth century's leading logicians. His work covers an extensive range of topics in logic and in other areas of mathematics. His most influential work relates to three areas: the general properties of functions, as presented in his 'calculus of lambda conversion'; the theory of computability and the decision problem, to which he made fundamental contributions, known as Church's thesis and Church's theorem; and intensional logic, developing Frege's theory of sense and denotation. In the last four decades of his life Church continued working mostly in this last area.

1 Life
2 A theory of functions
3 The logic of sense and denotation

1 Life

Alonzo Church was born in Washington, DC. After receiving his Ph.D. from Princeton in 1927 he spent two years as a National Research Fellow at Harvard, Göttingen and Amsterdam. He then held positions in mathematics and philosophy at Princeton (1929–67) and UCLA (1967–90).

Church's work covers an extensive range of topics in mathematics and logic, including the Lorentz transformation, differentials, recursive arithmetic, postulate theory, the law of the excluded middle, non-standard interpretations of propositional logic, higher-order logic, a theory of weak implication and notes on the history of logic. His most influential work, however, relates to three areas: (1) the general properties of functions, in his 'calculus of lambda conversion' (see LAMBDA CALCULUS), first presented in 1932 and developed in 1941; (2) effective calculability – his influential proposal that the effectively calculable functions can be identified with the recursive functions (see CHURCH'S THESIS) and his negative solution to the decision problem ('*Entscheidungsproblem*') for predicate logic (see CHURCH'S THEOREM AND THE DECISION PROBLEM) were first published in 1936; and (3) intensional logic and a development of Frege's theory of sense and denotation (see Church 1951; FREGE, G. §3). In the last four decades of his life Church continued working mostly in this last area. Particularly important is his series of papers on its 'revised' formulations (1973, 1974, 1993).

While at Princeton Church became one of the principal founders of the *Journal of Symbolic Logic*, the first volume of which appeared in 1936. He was an editor of the journal for its first forty-four volumes.

2 A theory of functions

The notion of mathematical function dominated Church's early work. He concentrated only on the general properties of functions 'independently of their appearance in any particular mathematical (or other) domain'. In his explanation of the notion of function, Church diverged from the standard view in mathematics and logic. Of importance is his emphasis on the intensional aspect of functions according to which they are not identified with a set of ordered tuples as is usual in mathematics, but are regarded as *operations* – items which are applied to tuples of objects (their arguments) to yield other single objects as values. The general properties of functions were studied in his λ-calculus, which presented a language permitting unambiguous denotation of functions. The principal expression of this language is an abstraction operator which is used to construct an expression for a function from an expression for an arbitrary value. For example, '$\lambda x.x^2$' denotes the function which takes any number to its square. The rules of transformation (conversion) of the calculus provide a guide for derivations among expressions of the above type.

The λ-calculus has had a significant effect on the development of logic. It was shown that the original formulation of the calculus is equivalent to the combinatory logic of Schönfinkel and, for this reason, Church is considered to be one of the founders of combinatory logic. The λ-calculus also played an important role in the development of intensional logic, particularly in that part of it which takes intensions as functions of a certain type.

A study of general properties of functions led Church to two seminal discoveries concerning the problem of whether it is possible to make all of mathematics algorithmic. The first of these was his conjecture concerning a precise demarcation of the class of functions characterized intuitively as algorithmically or effectively computable. This conjecture, which has come to be known as 'Church's thesis', is that this intuitively characterized class of functions is identical with the precisely characterized class of functions known as general recursive (see COMPUTABILITY THEORY §2). The second is Church's proof that the so-called 'decision problem' is unsolvable. The general decision problem for mathematics asks whether for every class of mathematical problems there is an algorithm which decides the answer. More particularly, the decision problem for predicate logic asks whether there is an algorithm for deciding logical truth. Church established a negative answer to both questions (see CHURCH'S THEOREM AND THE DECISION PROBLEM).

3 The logic of sense and denotation

Church's work on functions is partly responsible for his interest in developing a theory of intensions. His λ-calculus utilizes a notion of 'function-in-intension' (as opposed to 'function-in-extension') and he notes that two functions-in-intension f and g might be different – might, that is, differ in intension or 'meaning' – even if they share the same domain of arguments and for each n-tuple of objects $a_1,\ldots,a_n$ of that domain, $f(a_1,\ldots,a_n) = g(a_1,\ldots,a_n)$. In his earlier work, the notion of difference in meaning was left unexplained. The last four decades, however, he devoted to developing a theory of this difference in meaning. The result was his 'logic of sense and denotation', based on Frege's theory of proper names (see PROPER NAMES §1; FREGE, G. §§2–3). Church follows Frege in assigning two sorts of semantic values to proper names. A proper name is said to *express* its 'sense' and to *name* its 'denotation' (or 'reference'). Frege and Church are of the view that two names having the same denotation might none the less differ in sense.

Another characteristic feature of the Frege–Church theory is that declarative sentences are treated as names. They express their senses (propositions), and denote (or name) their truth-values.

Like Frege, Church also distinguished between two uses of proper names: the ordinary and the oblique. The principal criterion for obliqueness is the failure of substitutivity for equality (=), and for material equivalence ($\equiv$). Examples include contexts with modalities (possibility or necessity) and sentences expressing belief or knowledge ('propositional attitudes'). Church states that in oblique contexts a proper name does not have its 'usual' denotation but rather denotes what in ordinary contexts is its sense.

Church also accepted the following Fregean views concerning the role played by names in determining the sense and denotation of their larger contexts: if a name is replaced by another having the same sense, the sense of the whole context remains unchanged; and if a name is replaced by another having the same denotation, the denotation of the whole context remains unchanged.

In spite of these similarities between Church and Frege, there are also significant differences. For example, to avoid antinomies found in Frege's theory by Russell, Church built his logic of sense and denotation on a theory of types (see THEORY OF TYPES). Also, unlike Frege's informal treatment, Church's was formal. Using this method, he formulated exact criteria of identity for 'concepts' or senses and identified three alternative forms for the theory, depending upon the particular criterion of identity adopted.

One of these (known as 'Alternative (2)') is designed to treat oblique contexts with modalities but is ill-suited for contexts expressing knowledge and belief, for which purpose the so-called 'Alternative (0)' was developed.

Powerful arguments against any Fregean theory of proper names were presented by Kripke and others. Nevertheless, many aspects of his theory can still be salvaged and it retains a strong appeal as a theory of propositional attitudes. Church offered compelling arguments that attitudes such as belief are relations between agents and propositions rather than between agents and sentences. Further, Alternative (0) offers a sufficiently fine-grained notion of proposition, by use of which Church was able to resolve a number of philosophical and logical puzzles relating to propositional attitudes, for example, those relating to the failure of substitutivity of coreferential expressions in propositional attitudes (see SENSE AND REFERENCE §§4–5), the paradox of analysis and Mates' puzzle concerning iterated epistemic operators. Church's analysis of intensions for expressions other than proper names is also suggestive – particularly those parts of it that pertain to his Fregean theory of definite descriptions (including his criticisms of Russell's theory of such descriptions).

See also: COMBINATORY LOGIC; DESCRIPTIONS; INTENSIONAL LOGICS; LOGICAL AND MATHEMATICAL TERMS, GLOSSARY OF

List of works

Church, A. (1999) *Collected Papers*, ed. T. Burge, H.B. Enderton and M. Zeleny, Cambridge, MA: MIT Press. (A new two-volume collection of Church's work.)

Church, A. (1932, 1933) 'A Set of Postulates for the Foundation of Logic', papers 1 and 2, *Annals of Mathematics* 33: 346–66, 34: 839–64. (Church's first published formulation of the calculus of lambda-conversion.)

—— (1936a) 'An Unsolvable Problem of Elementary Number Theory', *American Journal of Mathematics* 58: 345–63. (A seminal paper of mathematical logic; the first publication of Church's thesis and Church's theorem.)

—— (1936b) 'A Note on the *Entscheidungsproblem*', and correction, *Journal of Symbolic Logic* 1: 40–1, 101–2. (Church's theorem applied to the classical predicate calculus to show that it is undecidable.)

—— (1940) 'A Formulation of the Simple Theory of Types', *Journal of Symbolic Logic* 5: 56–68. (Includes a version of the calculus of lambda-conversion based on the simple theory of types (which played a major role in his logic of sense and denotation).)

—— (1941) *The Calculi of Lambda-Conversion*, Princeton, NJ: Princeton University Press. (Classic source for the calculus of lambda-conversion.)

—— (1943) 'Carnap's *Introduction to Semantics*', *The Philosophical Review* 52: 298–304. (A review in which Church suggests and 'proves' the thesis that the denotation of a declarative sentence is a truth-value.)

—— (1950) 'On Carnap's Analysis of Statements of Assertion and Belief', *Analysis* 10: 97–9. (A classic paper in logical semantics and the philosophy of language; develops Langford's test of translation and shows that verbs such as 'believes', 'knows', 'says' cannot be treated as expressing relations between agents and sentences but rather as expressing relations between agents and propositions.)

—— (1951) 'A Formulation of the Logic of Sense and Denotation', in *Structure, Method and Meaning: Essays in Honor of Henry M. Sheffer*, New York: Liberal Arts Press, 3–24. (Classic source but requires considerable training in formal logic.)

—— (1954) 'Intensional Isomorphism and Identity of Belief', *Philosophical Studies* 5: 65–73. (Informal presentation of Church's notion of synonymous isomorphism; forms a foundation for his Alternative (0).)

—— (1956) *Introduction to Mathematical Logic*, vol. 1, Princeton, NJ: Princeton University Press. (An excellent introduction to mathematical logic. The introduction provides a clear, extensive and informal exposition of Church's views on the theory of sense and denotation; helpful for those interested in Church's logistic treatment of intensions.)

—— (1960) 'Logic and Analysis', in *Atti del XII Congresso Internazionale di Filosofia*, Florence, 77–81. (A relatively 'unknown' paper that presents Church's views on the relation of logic to philosophy and of the place of logic in analysis of epistemic matters.)

—— (1973, 1974) 'Outline of a Revised Formulation of the Logic of Sense and Denotation', parts 1 and 2, *Noûs* 7: 24–33, 8: 135–56. (Incorporates the notion of possible world.)

—— (1974) 'Russellian Simple Type Theory', *Proceedings and Addresses of the American Philosophical Association* 47: 21–33. (A re-formulation of Russell's mathematical logic in terms of a simple theory of types. Church argues that if the re-formulation is to be presented as intensional logic then Frege's distinction between sense and denotation will have to be introduced.)

—— (1976) 'Comparison of Russell's Resolution of the Semantical Antinomies with that of Tarski',

Journal of Symbolic Logic 41: 747–60. (Two resolutions of the semantic antinomies are compared: Russell's based on a ramified theory of types and Tarski's based on the object-language/metalanguage distinction. Church shows that the former resolution is a special case of the latter.)

—— (1993) 'A Revised Formulation of the Logic of Sense and Denotation. Alternative (1)', *Noûs* 27: 141–57. (Presents a system of logical axioms characterizing propositions that might be taken as objects of assertion and belief. The system is based on a simple theory of types and it is shown that it is set-theoretically consistent. Requires a considerable training in formal logic.)

References and further reading

Anderson, C.A. (1980) 'Some New Axioms for the Logic of Sense and Denotation. Alternative (0)', *Noûs* 14: 217–34. (A modification of Church's Alternative (0); informal explanation of some of Church's important ideas and axioms.)

—— (1984) 'General Intensional Logic', in D. Gabbay and F. Guenthner (eds) *Handbook of Philosophical Logic*, Dordrecht: Reidel, vol. 2, 355–85. (Development of intuitive motivations for Church's logic of sense and denotation as well as an introduction to its formalization. Also provides a useful comparison with Montague's intensional logic.)

Bealer, G. (1994) 'Property Theory: The Type-Free Approach v. The Church Approach', *Journal of Philosophical Logic* 23: 139–71. (A comparison of Church's view of properties with that of Bealer.)

PETER DOLNÍK

CHURCH'S THEOREM AND THE DECISION PROBLEM

Church's theorem, published in 1936, states that the set of valid formulas of first-order logic is not effectively decidable: there is no method or algorithm for deciding which formulas of first-order logic are valid. Church's paper exhibited an undecidable combinatorial problem $\mathcal{P}$ and showed that $\mathcal{P}$ was representable in first-order logic. If first-order logic were decidable, $\mathcal{P}$ would also be decidable. Since $\mathcal{P}$ is undecidable, first-order logic must also be undecidable.

Church's theorem is a negative solution to the decision problem (Entscheidungsproblem), the problem of finding a method for deciding whether a given formula of first-order logic is valid, or satisfiable, or neither. The great contribution of Church (and, independently, Turing) was not merely to prove that there is no method but also to propose a mathematical definition of the notion of 'effectively solvable problem', that is, a problem solvable by means of a method or algorithm.

The period 1929–37 was very eventful for logic. It began with Gödel's proof that first-order logic is semantically complete, that is, that the set of provable formulas coincides with the set of logically valid formulas. It included the incompleteness theorems of Gödel (see GÖDEL'S THEOREMS §§3–4), Church's theorem showing the undecidability of first-order logic, and the statement by Church and Alan Turing of Church's thesis equating the intuitive notion of effectiveness and the mathematical notion of recursiveness. The paper by Turing, which exhibited a universal Turing machine and introduced the notion of a computer program, was the culmination of the period.

Church's theorem, published in 1936 (see Davis 1965), states that the set of valid formulas of first-order logic is not effectively decidable: there is no method or algorithm for deciding which formulas of first-order logic are valid. Turing's slightly later paper proved the same result in a slightly different way. Both papers followed the same pattern. They exhibited an undecidable combinatorial problem $\mathcal{P}$ and showed that $\mathcal{P}$ was representable in first-order logic. If first-order logic were decidable, $\mathcal{P}$ would also be decidable. Since $\mathcal{P}$ is undecidable, first-order logic must also be undecidable.

Hilbert and Ackermann had formulated the *Entscheidungsproblem* (the decision problem) as the problem of finding a method for deciding whether a given formula of first-order logic is valid, or satisfiable, or neither; that is, whether all, some, or none of its possible interpretations are true. Church's theorem is a negative solution to the *Entscheidungsproblem*.

Hilbert and Ackermann had not proposed a mathematical definition of what constitutes a method, and the great contribution of Church and Turing was not merely to prove that there is no method but also to propose a mathematical definition of the notion of 'effectively solvable problem', that is, a problem solvable by means of a method or algorithm.

The technical result proved by Church only showed that the set of *provable* formulas of first-order logic is not λ-definable, that is, not definable in the λ-calculus, a logical calculus invented by Church (see LAMBDA CALCULUS). To conclude that the set of *valid* formulas in first-order logic is not 'effectively' decidable, we need two additional facts. We need to equate validity in first-order logic with provability in a particular formal system, a result proved already by Gödel, but about which Church had some qualms due to the non-constructive nature of the proof. We also need to equate the mathematical notion of λ-definability (or the provably equivalent notions of recursiveness and Turing computability) with the *intuitive* notion of effective computability. This second equality is Church's thesis (see CHURCH'S THESIS). Assuming Church's thesis, Church's theorem constitutes a negative solution to the problem of giving a uniform procedure for deciding which formulas of first-order logic are valid.

The particular version of first-order logic which Church used to prove his theorem included, as part of the language, the equality symbol, a constant and several function symbols. However, such a rich vocabulary is not actually necessary. Even first-order logic with a single dyadic predicate symbol is undecidable. (This is in sharp contrast to the decidability of the special case where the language consists solely of monadic predicates, a result first proved by Löwenheim (1915).)

Also, despite Church's qualms about the non-constructiveness of Gödel's completeness proof, Church's theorem is rather sturdy. It is known that, for Gödel's completeness result to hold, one must allow formulas with non-recursive models to be considered to be satisfiable. However, even if one restricts the possible models – for example, if one confines oneself to finite models or to constructive (recursive) models – the set of valid formulas remains non-recursive, and Church's theorem remains true, although first-order logic is no longer complete relative to these restricted classes of models.

Hilbert's *Entscheidungsproblem* as formulated by Hilbert and Ackermann inquired about the decision problem for logic as such. This would also include second-order logic, whose undecidability follows of course from that of the (weaker) first-order logic. But here a slightly more complex situation prevails. First-order logic, while not decidable, is none the less semi-decidable in that we do have a procedure to enumerate the set of all valid formulas. What prevents first-order logic from being decidable is that we do not have a procedure to enumerate the complementary set of all formulas which are *not* valid, that is, of all formulas whose negations are satisfiable (have at least one true interpretation). However, second-order logic is not even semi-decidable, a fact which is already implicit in Gödel's incompleteness result for arithmetic, and which pre-dated Church's theorem by about five years (see GÖDEL'S THEOREMS §1). Thus, at the time that Church proved his theorem, only the question for first-order logic was really open.

Note that a positive solution to the *Entscheidungsproblem* would not have required a mathematical definition of effectiveness. It would have sufficed to present a method for deciding which formulas of first-order logic were valid and to rely on our mathematical intuition to see that the method qualified as a genuine algorithm. However, a negative solution requires us to delimit the notion of effective computability to show that validity in first-order logic lies outside it, and such a delimitation necessarily requires that the notion of effectiveness be given a mathematical definition, or at least be mathematically circumscribed.

Church himself did not provide in his paper an independent definition of the intuitive notion of effectiveness. Rather he proposed that his technical notion, λ-definability, be taken to be a definition of the intuitive notion of effectiveness. A more substantial analysis was provided by Alan Turing in his paper (see Davis 1965). Turing analysed the possible mental algorithms that a human being could carry out and claimed that his machines, Turing machines, could also carry them out. A crucial element in Turing's argument was the claim that a human computer (sic) would only be able to carry out algorithms which utilized a finite number of distinct symbols, and that while he was carrying out an algorithm, his mind could only occupy a finite number of distinct states. Turing's argument for the first claim is that if the process of calculation used infinitely many basic symbols, then some of these symbols would be very close to others and confusion could not be avoided. He remarks that the same also holds of states of mind, but offers no argument. (See TURING MACHINES.) Gödel, in fact, describes Turing's remarks in this context as a 'philosophical error'. If we do accept Turing's justification that effectiveness equals Turing computability, then since λ-definability and Turing computability are provably equivalent, Turing's analysis also provides substantial ammunition for Church's own claim.

See also: CHURCH'S THESIS; LOGICAL AND MATHEMATICAL TERMS, GLOSSARY OF

References and further reading

* Davis, M. (ed.) (1965) *The Undecidable: Basic Papers on Undecidable Propositions, Unsolvable Problems and Computable Functions*, Hewlett, NY: Raven Press. (Includes a corrected version of Church's original paper, and Turing's article.)

Gödel, K. (1990) 'Some Remarks on the Undecidability Results', in *Collected Works*, ed. S. Feferman *et al.*, New York and Oxford: Oxford University Press, vol. 2, 305–6. (An excellent account of Gödel's own views.)

Herken, R. (ed.) (1988) *The Universal Turing Machine: A Half-Century Survey*, Oxford: Oxford University Press. (An excellent collection of papers by contemporary researchers; see especially R. Gandy, 'The Confluence of Ideas in 1936', 55–111.)

* Löwenheim, L. (1915) 'Über Möglichkeiten im Relativkalkül', *Mathematische Annalen* 76: 447–70; trans. S. Bauer-Mengelberg, 'On Possibilities in the Calculus of Relatives', in J. van Heijenoort (ed.) *From Frege to Gödel: A Source Book in Mathematical Logic, 1879–1931*, Cambridge, MA: Harvard University Press, 1967, 232–51. (Decidability of the special case of first-order logic with a language consisting solely of monadic predicates.)

ROHIT PARIKH

CHURCH'S THESIS

An algorithm or mechanical procedure A is said to 'compute' a function f if, for any n in the domain of f, when given n as input, A eventually produces fn as output. A function is 'computable' if there is an algorithm that computes it. A set S is 'decidable' if there is an algorithm that decides membership in S: if, given any appropriate n as input, the algorithm would output 'yes' if n ∈ S, and 'no' if n ∉ S. The notions of 'algorithm', 'computable' and 'decidable' are informal (or pre-formal) in that they have meaning independently of, and prior to, attempts at rigorous formulation.

Church's thesis, first proposed by Alonzo Church in a paper published in 1936, is the assertion that a function is computable if and only if it is recursive: 'We now define the notion... of an effectively calculable function... by identifying it with the notion of a recursive function....' Independently, Alan Turing argued that a function is computable if and only if there is a Turing machine that computes it; and he showed that a function is Turing-computable if and only if it is recursive.

Church's thesis is widely accepted today. Since an algorithm can be 'read off' a recursive derivation, every recursive function is computable. Three types of 'evidence' have been cited for the converse. First, every algorithm that has been examined has been shown to compute a recursive function. Second, Turing, Church and others provided analyses of the moves available to a person following a mechanical procedure, arguing that everything can be simulated by a Turing machine, a recursive derivation, and so on. The third consideration is 'confluence'. Several different characterizations, developed more or less independently, have been shown to be coextensive, suggesting that all of them are on target. The list includes recursiveness, Turing computability, Herbrand–Gödel derivability, λ-definability and Markov algorithm computability.

1 **Computability and decidability**
2 **What is Church's thesis?**
3 **Epistemic status**
4 **Other theses**

1 Computability and decidability

The algorithms or mechanical procedures envisaged here must determine what is to be done at each step, involving no creativity or intuition on the part of the agent (other than an ability to recognize symbols). The paradigm is a recipe for routine calculation, or a computer program.

An algorithm (or mechanical procedure) A 'computes' a function f if, for any n in the domain of f, when given n as input, A produces fn as output. A function is 'computable' if there is an algorithm that computes it. (See COMPUTABILITY THEORY §2.) There is no fixed limit on the amount of materials or memory required for a computation, nor on the number of steps an algorithm might take. If a function were computed only by an algorithm whose execution required more memory than there are particles in the solar system, it would not be capable of computation in any realistic sense, yet it would still be computable. What is required is that the algorithm have only finitely many steps. A set S is 'decidable' if there is an algorithm that 'decides' membership in S: if, given any appropriate n as input, the algorithm outputs 'yes' if $n \in S$, and 'no' if $n \notin S$.

Strictly speaking, computability should apply only to functions on things like marks on paper and magnetic media, since these are the items that can be manipulated by computers and algorithms. It is common to take computability to apply to functions on 'strings', which are the abstract forms of sequences of characters. For example, the string '$abc23$' is the form of all actual and possible concrete inscriptions of these three letters and two numerals. It is also common to think of computability as applying to functions on natural numbers, via canonical notation.

The root meaning of 'computability' would be something like 'capable of computation', and the root meaning of 'decidability', something like 'capable of decision'. Thus, these are modal notions. Computability is also an 'extensional' notion: it applies to functions themselves, not to descriptions or presentations of functions. Moreover, the quantifier 'there is an algorithm' does not involve (*de re*) knowledge of an algorithm (see DE RE/DE DICTO §1). For example, let

$fn = 1$ if there is a string of at least n consecutive 5's in the decimal expansion of π, and $fn = 0$ otherwise. No one knows of any algorithm A such that A computes f. Nevertheless, the function f is computable. If there are indefinitely long strings of consecutive 5's in the expansion of π, then f is computed by an algorithm that produces '1' no matter the input. Otherwise, let N be the longest string of consecutive 5's in the expansion. Then f is computed by an algorithm that outputs '1' for all inputs less than or equal to N, and outputs '0' for all other inputs. In all cases, then, f is computable.

The notions of recursiveness (see COMPUTABILITY THEORY §1) and λ-definability (see LAMBDA CALCULUS §4) arose as part of various foundational programmes earlier in the twentieth century. Church and his students became interested in the extension of the λ-definable functions. They set themselves the task of investigating various (computable) functions, to see if they could be shown to be λ-definable. Shortly after Kleene proved that the predecessor function is λ-definable, Church proposed his thesis: that a function is computable if and only if it is recursive. He published it after Kleene established the connection with recursiveness.

Although algorithms have been constructed since antiquity, it is curious that no one attempted a precise characterization of computability *per se* before the mid-1930s, at which time a number of more or less independent characterizations appeared almost simultaneously. One motivation was the desire, or need, to establish *negative* results about computability and decidability. Notice that the straightforward way to show that a given function is computable is to give an algorithm. This does not require a rigorous definition of computability, since most theorists can recognize an algorithm when they see one. To establish that a given function is *not* computable, on the other hand, one needs to show that *no* algorithm computes the function. This requires the formulation of a property shared by all algorithms or all computable functions. The straightforward route to such a property is a careful characterization of computability. At the time, the construction of algorithms for various purposes was a central item on the agenda of mathematical logic (see HILBERT'S PROGRAMME AND FORMALISM). Virtually all of the original characterizations of computability include theorems that certain functions are not computable or that certain sets are not decidable.

A related motivation was the desire to understand the extent of Gödel's incompleteness theorem. The original proof only applied to a particular system, but it is clear that the proof could be generalized to any common axiomatization of arithmetic. This, and the work on Hilbert's programme, led to the problem of characterizing just what a formal deductive system is. One requirement is that the syntax should be 'effective', in the sense that the collections of well-formed formulas, axioms and rules of inference should all be decidable. The natural generalization of the incompleteness theorem is that there is no sufficiently rich, effective and complete deductive system for arithmetic. As above, to establish this generalization, one needs a grasp of the limits of algorithms, and this came with the characterization of computability (see GÖDEL'S THEOREMS; FORMAL LANGUAGES AND SYSTEMS).

The modern notion of a function as an arbitrary correspondence between sets has emerged only towards the end of the twentieth century. In the past, the very idea of a 'non-computable' function might have been questioned, as it is today by constructivists and intuitionists. It might be added that from the constructivist perspective, Church's thesis has a sharp formulation. For a constructivist, a formula of the form $\forall x \exists! y \Phi(x, y)$ states that, given any x, *one can find* a unique y such that $\Phi(x, y)$ holds. This amounts to an assertion that a certain function is computable. Thus, Church's thesis is the scheme that if $\forall x \exists! y \Phi(x, y)$ then there is a *recursive* function f such that $\forall x \Phi(x, fx)$. In other words, for a constructivist, Church's thesis is a claim that *all* number-theoretic functions are recursive. Among intuitionists and constructivists, Church's thesis is controversial (see INTUITIONISM; CONSTRUCTIVISM IN MATHEMATICS; Beeson 1985; McCarty 1987).

As noted, however, there is a consensus among (non-constructivist) mathematicians and logicians that Church's thesis is correct. Within recursive function theory, a technique has been developed, sometimes called 'argument by Church's thesis', wherein one concludes that a function is recursive, or that a set is decidable, just because there is an algorithm for it. For example, for each natural number n, let $g(n)$ be the sum of the divisors of n. Since it is routine to give an algorithm to factor a number and add its divisors, one can conclude, by Church's thesis, that g is recursive. One does not have to deal with the details of recursive derivations, Turing machines and so on. By avoiding tedious detail, the perspective is broadened, leading to greater insight (see Rogers 1967).

2 What is Church's thesis?

Despite the consensus on the correctness of Church's thesis, there is not much agreement over what the correctness amounts to. What does Church's thesis mean? Does it have a determinate truth-value? Can it be known and, if so, how?

Computability is a pragmatic, pre-theoretic property of functions. It relates somehow to human abilities, suitably idealized. As such, Church's thesis is an important case study for the philosophical problem of accounting for the relationship between mathematics and material or human reality. Some authors have gone so far as to call computability a 'psychological' concept, since it relates to competence in grasping and executing procedures. One of the founders of computability, Emil Post, wrote that

for full generality a complete analysis would have to be made of all the possible ways in which the human mind could set up finite processes... we have to do with a certain activity of the human mind as situated in the universe. As activity, this logico-mathematical process has certain temporal properties; as situated in the universe it has certain spatial properties.

(Davis 1965: 408–19)

This passage also notes the aforementioned modal nature of computability. Notice, however, that recursiveness, Turing computability, λ-definability and so on are at least *prima facie* non-modal. They are defined in terms of quantifiers ranging over abstract entities, such as natural numbers, strings on a finite alphabet and so on. Thus, Church's thesis identifies the extension of an idealized, pragmatic, modal property of functions with the extension of a formal, rigorously defined, *prima facie* non-modal arithmetic property. On the surface, then, Church's thesis proposes an exchange of modality for ontology. How are such proposals to be evaluated?

A closely related matter concerns vagueness. Typically, pragmatic, modal notions do not have sharp boundaries. There are, for example, borderline cases of 'climbable mountains', 'liftable weights' and 'teachable students'. Clearly, there are also borderline cases of functions 'capable of computation', if we do not idealize. Slogans such as 'ignoring limits on memory and materials' sharpen the notion, but it is still not clear that idealized computability, as defined above, is an unequivocal property with *completely* precise boundaries. Recursiveness and Turing computability, on the other hand, do appear to have precise boundaries. *Prima facie*, then, Church's thesis identifies a vague notion with a precise one.

Clearly, a vague property cannot *exactly* coincide with a precise one. So, if computability is in fact vague, Church's thesis does not literally have a determinate truth-value or else it is false. Church's thesis might then be thought of as a proposal that recursiveness be *substituted* for computability, for certain purposes. It would be similar to a pronounce-ment such as 'For the purposes of this form, a resident is defined to be...'.

The value of 'definitions' or 'precisifications' of vague terms depends on the purposes at hand. Given the extensive idealizations, Church's thesis seems best suited for establishing *negative* results about computability. If one shows, for example, that a function is not recursive, that is conclusive reason to hold that it is not 'capable of computation': one should give up trying to compute it. Suppose, on the other hand, that a function has been shown to be recursive. By itself, this gives no information on the feasibility of an algorithm, and thus it does not establish that the function can be calculated, in any realistic sense. Moreover, it is of little value to anyone interested in actually computing the function. For this purpose, there are other, less idealized models, such as 'finite state' computability, 'push down' computability, primitive recursiveness and computability in polynomial time or space (see COMPLEXITY, COMPUTATIONAL).

A different interpretation of Church's thesis is that even though computability is a pre-theoretic notion, it is nevertheless a precise, mathematical property of functions. One might hold, for example, that there are determinate mathematical structures underlying idealized human abilities to calculate, write programs, or even think. Understood this way, Church's thesis states that this property is coextensive with another precise mathematical notion, recursiveness. Thus, Church's thesis has a truth-value. The 'arguments from confluence' support this interpretation. The fact that a number of *prima facie* different attempts to characterize computability lead to the same extension suggests that recursiveness, Turing computability and so on delimit the boundaries of a 'natural kind' underlying computation.

3 Epistemic status

The Goldbach conjecture (that every even number greater than 4 is the sum of two primes) and the 'twin prime' conjecture (that there are infinitely many numbers n such that n and $n+2$ are both prime) are long-standing open problems in number theory. They can be settled, if at all, by mathematical proof. It is widely held that Church's thesis is not like this. Its evidence is not mathematical. Because of the connection with human abilities, and perhaps because of the supposed vagueness, Church's thesis has been called an 'empirical' or 'quasi-empirical' matter.

As noted above, one type of evidence cited for Church's thesis is that every algorithm that has been investigated has been shown to compute a recursive function. This is consonant with the quasi-empirical nature of Church's thesis (on a certain view of scientific hypotheses). The intuitive ability to recognize algorithms is analogous to 'observation', and showing that an algorithm computes a recursive function amounts to 'confirmation' of Church's thesis (see CONFIRMATION THEORY). This type of evidence was prominent in the thought of Church and Kleene.

Some theorists, on the other hand, do regard Church's thesis as a mathematical matter, capable of whatever epistemic standards are applicable there, and some regard the thesis as proved. Robin Gandy (1988), for example, suggests that Turing's direct argument that every algorithm can be simulated on a Turing machine does not merely provide evidence for an inductive, scientific hypothesis; rather, it 'proves a theorem'. Turing provides a careful analysis of a human executing an algorithm, showing how each 'step' can be simulated on a Turing machine. There are lemmas that the number of symbols and the number of 'states of mind' must be finite. Gandy regards the analysis to be as convincing as typical mathematical work. Apparently, Gödel was also convinced by Turing's arguments, and not by the 'quasi-empirical' evidence (see Davis 1982).

On these views, the pragmatic nature of computability, and its potential vagueness, do not automatically disqualify Church's thesis from mathematics. This is consistent with a widely held position that there is no sharp boundary between mathematics and empirical science (see DUHEM, P.M.M.; QUINE, W.V.O.). Mathematics has its roots in everyday life, and cannot be severed from it. Even a cursory look at the history of the notions underlying recursiveness reveals ambivalence, ambiguity and vagueness, especially in the notion of 'set' (see Mendelson 1990). Yet no one doubts that sets and recursive functions belong to mathematics. According to the view at hand, computability is no different.

4 Other theses

There are similar 'theses' in the history of mathematics and science. Consideration of these may shed some light on the philosophical issues here.

The notion of a grammatical sentence of a natural language is clearly pragmatic, modal and at least *prima facie* vague. This is contrasted with formal, mathematical characterizations of grammaticality, as proposed by linguists. Unlike Church's thesis, however, there is no consensus on one of these grammars.

Closer to home, the notion of 'validity', or 'logical consequence', is *prima facie* pragmatic and modal, if not vague. In typical logic textbooks, validity is related to inference abilities, and an argument is said to be valid if it is not possible for the premises to be true and the conclusion false. Yet, when one reads on,

validity is formally defined in terms of models, which are mathematical constructions on sets. Thus, we have another exchange of modality and ontology. The identification of the pre-formal validity with model-theoretic consequence may be called 'Tarski's thesis'. Notice that there is a consideration of confluence here. Gödel's completeness theorem shows that for first-order languages, the model-theoretic notion of consequence coincides in extension with a deductive one (see CONSEQUENCE, CONCEPTIONS OF; MODEL THEORY; PROOF THEORY).

Within more traditional mathematics, consider notions such as 'area', 'volume' and 'continuity'. While these do not appear pragmatic and modal, they did have clear meanings before their rigorous formulations in analysis and measure theory. Moreover, the notions do have uses in everyday and scientific life and there seem to be borderline cases of the pre-theoretic notions. In modern mathematics, however, these notions all have rigorous, precise definitions. The various identifications with the pre-theoretic notions may be called Euclid's thesis, Lebesgue's thesis, Weierstrass' thesis, Cauchy's thesis, and so on. The reader may decide the extent to which these theses have determinate truth-values, whether they are mathematical or 'quasi-empirical', and whether they have been (or can be) established with characteristic mathematical rigour.

See also: COMPUTABILITY THEORY; COMPLEXITY, COMPUTATIONAL; COMPUTABILITY AND INFORMATION; LOGIC MACHINES AND DIAGRAMS; LOGICAL AND MATHEMATICAL TERMS, GLOSSARY OF

References and further reading

* Beeson, M.J. (1985) *Foundations of Constructive Mathematics*, New York: Springer. (Includes an account of Church's thesis from a constructivist perspective.)
* Davis, M. (ed.) (1965) *The Undecidable: Basic Papers on Undecidable Propositions, Unsolvable Problems and Computable Functions*, Hewlett, NY: Raven Press. (Original papers, or English translations, by Gödel, Church, Turing, Rosser, Kleene and Post; includes some items not published elsewhere.)
* —— (1982) 'Why Gödel Didn't Have Church's Thesis', *Information and Control* 54: 3–24. (Careful historical discussion of what convinced some of the major players of Church's thesis.)
* Gandy, R. (1988) 'The Confluence of Ideas in 1936', in R. Herken (ed.) *The Universal Turing Machine: A Half-Century Survey*, New York: Oxford University Press, 55–111. (Extensive historical study of the development of computability.)

Kleene, S. (1979) 'Origins of Recursive Function Theory', in *Twentieth Annual Symposium on Foundations of Computer Science*, New York: IEEE, 371–82. (Reminiscent account, by one of the founders of recursive function theory; good source on the development of the λ-calculus and on Church's thought on logic and computability.)

—— (1987) 'Reflections on Church's Thesis', *Notre Dame Journal of Formal Logic* 28: 490–8. (Philosophical discussion of Church's thesis.)

* McCarty, C. (1987) 'Variations on a Thesis: Intuitionism and Computability', *Notre Dame Journal of Formal Logic* 28: 536–80. (An intuitionistic view of Church's thesis.)

* Mendelson, E. (1990) 'Second Thoughts about Church's Thesis and Mathematical Proofs', *Journal of Philosophy* 87: 225–33. (Argument that Church's thesis is provable.)

Myhill, J. (1952) 'Some Philosophical Implications of Mathematical Logic', *Review of Metaphysics* 6: 165–98. (Philosophical account of the argument that computability is partly psychological.)

* Rogers, H. (1967) *Theory of Recursive Functions and Effective Computability*, New York: McGraw-Hill. (Comprehensive mathematical development, based on 'argument by Church's thesis'.)

Shapiro, S. (1981) 'Understanding Church's Thesis', *Journal of Philosophical Logic* 10: 353–65. (Discussion of the philosophical status of Church's thesis.)

—— (1983) 'Remarks on the Development of Computability', *History and Philosophy of Logic* 4: 203–20. (Historical account.)

—— (1993) 'Understanding Church's Thesis, Again', *Acta Analytica* 11: 59–77. (A further discussion of the philosophical status of Church's thesis, including its modal status, its vagueness and the view that Church's thesis is a mathematical matter.)

Sieg, W. (1994) 'Mechanical Procedures and Mathematical Experience', in A. George (ed.) *Mathematics and Mind*, Oxford: Oxford University Press, 71–117. (Philosophical account of Church's thesis and its relationships with mechanism.)

STEWART SHAPIRO

CICERO, MARCUS TULLIUS (106–43 BC)

Cicero, pre-eminent Roman statesman and orator of the first century BC and a prolific writer, composed the first substantial body of philosophical work in Latin. Rising from small-town obscurity to the pinnacle of Rome's staunchly conservative aristocracy, he devoted most of his life to public affairs. But he was deeply interested in philosophy throughout his life, and during two intervals of forced withdrawal from politics wrote two series of dialogues, first elaborating his political ideals and later examining central issues in epistemology, ethics and theology. Designed to establish philosophical study as an integral part of Roman culture, these works are heavily indebted to Greek philosophy, and some of the later dialogues are largely summaries of Hellenistic debates. But Cicero reworked his sources substantially, and his methodical expositions are thoughtful, judicious and, on questions of politics and morals, often creative. An adherent of the sceptical New Academy, he was opposed to dogmatism but ready to accept the most cogent arguments on topics important to him. His vigorously argued and eloquent critical discussions of perennial problems greatly enriched the intellectual and moral heritage of Rome and shaped Western traditions of liberal education, republican government and rationalism in religion and ethics. These works also afford invaluable insight into the course of philosophy during the three centuries after Aristotle.

1 **Life and writings**
2 **Classical republicanism**
3 **Scepticism and natural theology**
4 **Humanist ethics**
5 **Influence**

1 Life and writings

Marcus Tullius Cicero, elder son of a locally influential family in the town of Arpinum, moved to Rome in his youth to pursue a career in law and government. There he studied with several Greek philosophers, including the Academic PHILO OF LARISSA, and after a brilliant legal debut he spent two years in Greece studying philosophy and rhetoric with ANTIOCHUS and the Stoic POSIDONIUS. Upon his return he won election to a major office that brought lifelong membership of the Senate (Rome's supreme governing body) and soon established himself as the foremost advocate of the age. Elected consul (Rome's chief executive office) in 63 BC, he suppressed an insurrection and was hailed his country's saviour. But opponents contrived his exile in 58 BC, and when he returned the following year, he found his influence severely diminished. Turning to writing, he formulated and defended his political ideals in three pioneering dialogues (see §2). When Julius Caesar precipitated civil war in 49 BC, Cicero sided reluctantly with the opposition as the lesser threat to Roman institutions. Caesar's swift victory brought dictatorship, and Cicero, although granted clemency, was excluded from politics. Returning to writing, he championed free political discussion in a series of rhetorical works, then composed in twenty months a dozen works (nine survive whole or in large part) discussing central problems in Hellenistic philosophy (see §§3–4) (see HELLENISTIC PHILO-SOPHY). The political turmoil that followed Caesar's assassination in March 44 BC slowed, then halted this astonishing pace as he rallied resistance to Mark Antony's despotic designs. His campaign might well have succeeded had Antony not colluded with Caesar's adoptive heir, the future Augustus: Cicero was assassinated and his head impaled in the Forum where he had spoken so often and so eloquently.

Cicero's extant works, although only part of his enormous output, comprise over fifty speeches, nearly a thousand letters to friends and associates, several works on rhetorical theory and practice, and twelve on philosophical topics. This vast corpus, besides displaying great intellectual range and stylistic virtuosity, embodies Cicero's conviction that philosophy and rhetoric are interdependent and both essential for the improvement of human life and society. His oratory bears the stamp of his theoretical studies, and his treatises and dialogues are richly oratorical. The philosophical works in particular unite the rhetorical techniques and ample style of Roman oratory with the analytical methods and conceptual apparatus of Greek philosophy in a unique fusion of eloquence and insight. All but one of these works are fictional dialogues. Some portray Cicero or eminent Romans of the previous century discoursing at length among friends; others, employing a format that reflects Roman political and legal practice but also the critical spirit Cicero admired in Plato and his sceptical heirs in the New Academy (see §3), present paired speeches for and against Epicurean and Stoic theories. Composed for audiences unused to abstract theory and systematic analysis, the discussions lapse at times into earnest declamation, and the close questioning found in Plato's dialogues is rare. However, they are methodically organized and often incisive, and by presenting opposing views and arguments in clear and engaging terms, they dramatize the significance of fundamental problems and encourage critical reflection.

2 Classical republicanism

Cicero's first philosophical works are three long dialogues that analyse and evaluate the political institutions and practices of contemporary Rome in the light of Greek theory. Although largely conservative, they provided the first political theory in Latin and remain the most systematic ancient account of

Roman government; while others described events, only Cicero advanced a structural analysis. Written when Rome's republican traditions were collapsing under unprecedented concentrations of economic and military power, these dialogues champion political liberty, rational debate and rule by law. Articulating the principles behind his lifelong goal of harmonizing Rome's competing interests in a just and stable 'concord of the orders', they propound a comprehensive vision of civil society directed by an elected elite schooled in rhetoric and philosophy, devoted to constitutional government and able to shape public opinion through effective oratory.

The first of these works, *On the Orator*, explores the role of rhetoric and philosophy in public life. Oratory had long been a potent tool in Roman politics, and Cicero aims to reinforce its prestige and legitimize its influence by showing that its success requires wide learning and sound reasoning. Much of the discussion focuses on education, as he weighs the merits of the traditional Roman emphasis on history, poetry and practical experience against the Greek disciplines of formal rhetoric and philosophy. His model orator, who clearly reflects Cicero's own proficiencies, unites thorough knowledge of history and law with complete command of logical method, philosophical theory and rhetorical techniques in a Romanized version of Plato's philosopher-rulers. Both expect philosophical education to produce the best statesmen; but whereas Plato's ideal hinges on mathematical training and transcendental metaphysics, Cicero proposes a thoroughly pragmatic programme of instruction designed to foster eloquence and informed civic debate.

Cicero delineates the institutional framework behind his conception of leadership in *On the Republic*, which was almost entirely lost until most of the first third was recovered in 1820. Challenging the utopian bent of Greek political theory exemplified by Plato's *Republic*, Cicero argues that the best constitution, far from being unattainable, was largely realized in Rome, where a unique blend of monarchy, aristocracy and democracy formed a 'mixed constitution' that provided a system of government ostensibly stable and just. This account, which recasts Rome's narrow oligarchy as a paradigm of aristocratic paternalism, rests on an incisive and apparently original analysis of political legitimacy. Defining a republic (*res publica*) as 'a people's affair' (*res populi*) and a people as a community 'united by consensus about right and by mutual interest', Cicero criticizes all other constitutions for contravening the people's rights and interests, then argues that no political system is legitimate unless it distributes legal rights equally to all, but electoral, legislative and judicial authority proportionally according to merit and wealth. Other extant sections of the dialogue classify types of constitution in classical Greek fashion and survey the development of Roman institutions; lost or poorly preserved sections summarized Hellenistic debates about the nature and rewards of justice, discussed Roman education and measured past Roman statesman against Cicero's ideal. Ending the work is the famous 'dream of Scipio', which interweaves astronomy and eschatology to sketch a theodicy that rewrites Plato's myth of Er in the light of Stoic cosmology and exalts public service by reserving the finest posthumous rewards for outstanding statesmen.

On Laws, a sequel probably left incomplete and published only after Cicero's death, fills in his constitutional model by outlining a comprehensive legal system. Vying with Plato's *Laws* this time, he continues his argument that Rome already embodied much of the ideal. His treatment of religion and political administration, which is all that survives, is deeply conservative, largely an explanation and defence of existing statutes and institutions by appeal to Greek theory and Roman history, with proposals for change limited to streamlining and archaizing reforms rather than extensive revision or thorough codification. The work was extremely influential, especially on Christian and early modern thought, because it contains the fullest surviving ancient account of natural law (see NATURAL LAW). Drawing heavily on Stoic ideas, Cicero argues that the natural world exhibits a divinely ordained and rationally intelligible order that can be codified in legislation and provides the ultimate tribunal for all positive law.

Civil war interrupted Cicero's writing and he never returned to constitutional or legal theory. But his very last book rounds out his political thinking by examining the role of personal morality in public life. In the guise of an extended epistle to his son, *On Duties* maps out a code of conduct for the Roman nobility that emphasizes justice, benefaction and public service. The focus throughout is on men of high station and the problems of integrating personal ambitions and social obligations. Borrowing heavily from the Stoic PANAETIUS (§2), Cicero argues that virtuous conduct is always expedient as well as morally required, and that apparent conflicts between morality and personal advantage are illusory because virtuous action is always the best option.

3 Scepticism and natural theology

Cicero embraced the sceptical stance of the New Academy in his youth when he studied under Philo of Larissa. Modern scholars debate whether he shifted soon afterward to positions he learned from Antiochus, or remained an Academic sceptic throughout life. But a likely explanation for this debate is the moderate tenor of Cicero's scepticism, which eschews dogmatic certainty but accepts 'convincing' (*probabile*) arguments. Inclined by profession to adversarial argument, Cicero employed the Academic strategy of arguing on both sides of questions in his earlier as well as his later dialogues. But his aim was never suspension of judgment, as in the early New Academy under ARCESILAUS (§2). Rather, adopting a pragmatic fallibilism that derives from CARNEADES (§4) but probably owes most to Philo, he considered the careful weighing of opposing arguments the most reliable route to truth. On this basis, he endorsed an eclectic synthesis of ideas derived mainly from Antiochus and Stoics but also from Aristotle and Plato (whom he styles the prince of philosophers and quotes often in original translations); and while reserving judgment on many theoretical issues, he held firm views about many practical matters of politics and morality.

Cicero discusses his sceptical stance most fully in *Academics*, which inaugurates his second series of dialogues by recounting a pivotal debate within the later New Academy about the nature and possibility of knowledge. Only parts of the work survive. But one fully preserved book (entitled *Lucullus*) summarizes Antiochus' heavily Stoicizing brand of empiricism, then rehearses a battery of sceptical objections drawn mainly from Carneades and Philo. Debate centres on Antiochus' defence of the Stoic 'criterion of truth' (see STOICISM §§12–13), a class of allegedly self-certifying perceptions that would be the source and foundation of any knowledge. Cicero himself delivers the sceptical rebuttal, arguing forcefully that knowledge requires certainty, but that certainty is neither attainable nor necessary for the rational conduct of life. Both sides are powerfully argued, and in line with Philo's fallibilism, readers are obliged to assess which seems more 'convincing'. Though frequently elliptical, the discussion maintains a level of argument rarely matched in Latin before Augustine.

Cicero continued to use this Academic method of presenting opposing arguments in most of his subsequent dialogues. *On the Nature of the Gods* presents two pairs of speeches expounding, then criticizing, Epicurean and Stoic theology. The central issue is not whether gods exist, but rather their role in nature and human affairs. Epicureanism envisages immortals residing far beyond this world and oblivious to human affairs; Stoicism maintains that the world itself is rational and divine, operating in accord with providence to the benefit of humanity; and the Academic critiques, without denying the existence of gods, argue that both schools rely on highly dubious assumptions and wholly fail to prove their cases. The debate covers questions of cosmology at length, including both an impassioned defence and sustained criticism of Stoic arguments from design; and the beliefs and rituals of Greek and Roman polytheism are criticized and reinterpreted throughout. The whole discussion, in its reliance on canons of rational inquiry and analysis, is a model of natural theology. Refusing to rely on revelation or authority, all sides agree that religious issues must be decided by evidence and argument; Stoic appeals to divination and widespread belief in gods, for example, are advanced as inferences to the best explanation. In the end, Cicero endorses the Stoic conception of the world as governed benevolently by divine reason, which he clearly found more compelling both intellectually and morally than either the stark amorality of Epicurean atomism or the official religion of Rome which his public station obliged him to uphold.

Two subsequent works examine related problems of knowledge and causation. *On Divination* presents a richly illustrated defence followed by a scathing critique of various religious claims to foreknowledge. Highlighting epistemological issues, Cicero constructs remarkably balanced cases. The defence, appealing to Stoic arguments that divination is a natural consequence of divine providence and often based on systematic observation, assembles a vast gallery of empirical evidence; his reply, in keeping with the rigorous rationalism of Academic scepticism, challenges the validity of this evidence and argues that divination is inexplicable and inconsistent with the evident regularity of nature. But Cicero, despite ridiculing the defence and pronouncing much of Roman religion sheer superstition, offers no final verdict and endorses traditional rites on grounds of social utility. *On Fate* analyses the closely connected topic of determinism. Cicero defends a theory of free will which he attributes to Carneades, while criticizing the Epicureans for postulating uncaused atomic 'swerves' (see EPICUREANISM §12), and arguing that the Stoic conception of fate as a universal and eternal causal web precludes voluntary action and moral responsibility. Detailed analysis of Stoic theories of causation and logical consequence makes this perhaps Cicero's most exacting work.

4 Humanist ethics

Informing all of Cicero's work is a profound faith in the natural goodness of humanity and the power of reason to direct and improve human life. The assumptions behind this humanist outlook, which is probably Cicero's most constructive synthesis of Greek ideas, are systematically examined in *On the Ends of Good and Evil* (usually known as the *De finibus*). Tackling the central question of ancient ethical theory, the dialogue inquires into the ultimate end of human action and how happiness is attained (see EUDAIMONIA). Paired speeches expound and criticize Epicurean and Stoic accounts of human nature and the status of moral virtue; ending the work and receiving only brief criticism is a neo-Aristotelian account derived from Antiochus. Cicero speaks throughout as an Academic sceptic, arguing that Epicurean hedonism is incoherent and morally subversive, and challenging the Stoic doctrine that moral virtue is the sole good and hence sufficient for happiness. But he commends the moral austerity and theoretical rigour of Stoic ethics, and while he finds the Aristotelian position intuitively attractive and most conducive to public service, he questions whether Antiochus' view that non-moral interests are also intrinsically good undermines the supremacy of moral virtue.

Setting aside sceptical worries to address practical questions, Cicero explores some applications of his ethical rationalism in two substantial works and a pair of earnest but elegant moralizing essays. *On Duties* employs a Stoic framework to spell out systematic rules of conduct (see §2). *Tusculan Disputations* similarly uses Stoic theory to analyse problems in moral psychology. Adopting a format used by Carneades, Cicero presents five lengthy disquisitions refuting common beliefs about the emotions; but since each speech upholds a Stoic paradox, the result is a sustained defence of Stoic doctrines. Invoking a legion of philosophical and literary authorities, Cicero argues vigorously that philosophy is the medicine of the soul, and that it alone enables us to scorn death, endure pain, overcome grief and other passions, and lead good lives. Much of the argument rests on an acute Stoic analysis of emotions as governed by beliefs. But Cicero's ideal of rational restraint and self-control as the source of mental tranquillity and happiness distills ideas central to Greek and Roman culture alike. Two shorter dialogues portray eminent Romans from the previous century as sage advisors on more personal topics. *On Old Age* enumerates the lasting rewards of honourable character and education, including a glorious afterlife. *On Friendship* extols a paradigm of aristocratic male companionship based on mutual benefit but also integrity and loyalty. Both works, while distinctly less systematic than Cicero's other dialogues, exemplify his ability to illuminate vital human concerns with philosophical insight and graceful eloquence.

5 Influence

Cicero was the most influential writer and intellect of his time, and his impact on Western culture has been lasting and profound. His philosophical writings, by forging expressions essential for theoretical discussion, inaugurated over sixteen centuries of philosophy in Latin. They also fuelled the rise of Christianity in the West, as the Latin Fathers mined his dialogues in their campaigns against pagan religion and philosophy (see PATRISTIC PHILOSOPHY). AUGUSTINE, whose life was transformed by the exhortation to philosophy in Cicero's lost *Hortensius*, drew on his writings extensively, especially in *Against the Academics* and *City of God*. Through these and other writers, most notably Ambrose, Jerome and the pagan Macrobius (whose Neoplatonic commentary on 'Scipio's dream' was widely studied), Cicero's ideas shaped medieval thought, especially ethics and theories of natural law. His influence reached its zenith in the Renaissance, when Erasmus and other humanists emulated his critical spirit and reaffirmed his secular outlook and ecumenical ideals (see RENAISSANCE PHILOSOPHY). By making his writings the foundation of a liberal education, they also increased his moral authority; and in the following centuries his ethical and political works (above all *On Duties*, dubbed 'Tully's Offices' in English) fostered the revival of republicanism and the development of liberalism, while his dialogues on religion were inspirational to deism. VOLTAIRE proclaimed him the model of enlightened reason; and HUME was deeply indebted to Cicero, especially in his critique of religious dogmatism and his conception of 'mitigated' scepticism. The rise of idealism in the nineteenth century lowered Cicero's philosophical reputation considerably. But renewed interest in scepticism and virtue ethics, along with improved understanding of Hellenistic philosophy, has in recent decades stimulated intense discussion of his work yet again.

List of works

Cicero, M.T. (80s BC) *On Invention* (*De inventione*), in two books, trans. H. Hubbell, Loeb Classical Library, Cambridge, MA: Harvard University Press and London: Heinemann, 1949. (Handbook on rhetoric and informal argument; includes Latin text with translation.)

—— (55 BC) *On the Orator* (*De oratore*), in three books, trans. E. Sutton and H. Rackham, Loeb Classical Library, Cambridge, MA: Harvard University Press and London: Heinemann, 1942. (Dialogue debating the place of rhetoric and philosophy in politics and education.)

—— (54–51 BC) *On the Republic* (*De republica*), in six books, trans. G. Sabine and S. Smith, *On the Commonwealth*, Columbus, OH: Ohio State University Press, 1929. (Dialogue analyzing the structure and legitimacy of the Roman state; less than a third preserved.)

—— (late 50s BC) *On Laws* (*De legibus*), in three books, trans. C. Keyes, Loeb Classical Library, Cambridge, MA: Harvard University Press and London: Heinemann, 1928. (Dialogue on the Roman legal system; incomplete.)

—— (46 BC) *Stoic Paradoxes* (*Paradoxa Stoicorum*), trans. M.R. Wright, in *On Stoic Good and Evil*, Warminster: Aris & Phillips, 1991. (Short declamations defending six claims of Stoic ethics.)

—— (late 46 BC) *Hortensius*; ed. A. Grilli, Milan: Istituto Editoriale Cisalpino, 1962. (Lost dialogue proclaiming the value of philosophy; only fragments and reports survive.)

—— (early 45 BC) *Academics*, trans. H. Rackham, Loeb Classical Library, Cambridge, MA: Harvard University Press and London: Heinemann, 1933. (Dialogue on the nature and possibility of knowledge. Substantial parts of two versions survive: the second of two books from the first version, entitled *Lucullus* but often called *Prior Academics* or *Academics* II; and the first of four books from a thorough revision, entitled *Varro* but often called *Posterior Academics* or *Academics* I.)

—— (mid 45 BC) *On the Ends of Good and Evil* (*De finibus bonorum et malorum*), in five books, trans. H. Rackham, Loeb Classical Library, Cambridge, MA: Harvard University Press and London: Heinemann, 1914; book III trans. M.R. Wright, in *On Stoic Good and Evil*, Warminster: Aris & Phillips, 1991; book V trans. S. White, Oxford: Oxford University Press, forthcoming. (Three dialogues summarizing and criticizing Epicurean, Stoic, and Aristotelian ethical theories.)

—— (late 45 BC) *Tusculan Disputations* (*Tusculanae disputationes*), in five books, trans. J.E. King, Loeb Classical Library, Cambridge, MA: Harvard University Press and London: Heinemann, 2nd edn, 1945; books I, II and V trans. A.E. Douglas, Warminster: Aris & Phillips, 1985 and 1990. (Five disquisitions on topics in moral psychology.)

—— (late 45 BC) *On the Nature of the Gods* (*De natura deorum*), in three books but incomplete, trans. P.G. Walsh, Oxford: Oxford University Press, 1997. (Dialogue summarizing and criticizing Epicurean and Stoic views about divinity.)

—— (45 or 44 BC) *Timaeus*, ed. R. Giomini, Leipzig: Teubner, 1975. (Latin translation of part of Plato's Timaeus: 27d-47b, with gaps.)

—— (early 44 BC) *Cato the Elder: On Old Age* (*Cato

maior, De senectute), trans. F. Copley, Ann Arbor, MI: University of Michigan Press, 1967. (Dialogue on how to live after retiring from public life.)

—— (early 44 BC) *On Divination* (*De divinatione*), in two books, trans. H.M. Poteat, Chicago, IL: University of Chicago Press, 1950. (Dialogue arguing first for, then against a religious basis for knowledge about the future.)

—— (mid 44 BC) *On Fate* (*De fato*), trans. R. Sharples, Warminster: Aris & Phillips, 1991. (Dialogue on causation and determinism; incompletely preserved.)

—— (mid 44 BC) *Topics*, trans. H. Hubbell, Loeb Classical Library, Cambridge, MA: Harvard University Press and London: Heinemann, 1949. (Synopsis of informal reasoning.)

—— (mid 44 BC) *Laelius: On Friendship* (*Laelius, De amicitia*), trans. J.G.F. Powell, Warminster: Aris & Phillips, 1990. (Dialogue on the nature and value of friendship.)

—— (late 44 BC) *On Duties* (*De officiis*), in three books, trans. M. Griffin and E.M. Atkins, Cambridge: Cambridge University Press, 1991. (Treatise examining virtuous conduct and its relation to personal advantage.)

References and further reading

Gawlick, G. and Görler, W. (1994) 'Cicero', in H. Flashar (ed.) *Die Philosophie der Antike* 4, Basle: Schwabe, 991–1168. (Comprehensive survey in German of Cicero's philosophical *oeuvre*, with full bibliography.)

Glucker, J. (1988) 'Cicero's Philosophical Affiliations', in J. Dillon and A.A. Long (eds) *The Question of 'Eclecticism'*, Berkeley, CA: University of California Press. (Influential paper arguing that Cicero initially embraced Philo's scepticism but adopted views of Antiochus for most of his career and reverted to scepticism only in his sixties.)

Griffin, M. and Barnes, J. (eds) (1991) *Philosophia togata: Essays on Philosophy and Roman Society*, Oxford: Oxford University Press. (Several papers discuss Cicero at length; useful analytical bibliography.)

Laks, A. and Schofield, M. (eds) (1995) *Justice and Generosity: Studies in Hellenistic Social and Political Philosophy*, Cambridge: Cambridge University Press. (Includes studies of Cicero's thought by J.-L. Ferrary, A. A. Long and M. Schofield.)

Powell, J.G.F. (ed.) (1995) *Cicero the Philosopher*, Oxford: Oxford University Press. (A dozen studies on diverse topics, including a rejoinder to Glucker by W. Görler.)

Rawson, E. (1983) *Cicero: A Portrait*, Ithaca, NY:

Cornell University Press, 2nd edn. (Thoughtful and engaging biography emphasizing intellectual and ethical aspects.)

STEPHEN A. WHITE

CIESZKOWSKI, AUGUST VON (1814–94)

Cieszkowski is perhaps best known for being the first to revise Hegel's philosophy of history into a basis for future social reform. His introduction of the idea of 'praxis' as a synthesis between abstract theory and undirected practice was fundamental in the development of the Young Hegelian school, which formed shortly after Hegel's death and sought the radical transformation of all then-existing political, religious and economic orders.

August was born of a wealthy, aristocratic Polish family. He received an excellent education, particularly in languages. His concern with democratic reform was first shown by his participation in the Polish anti-Russian revolutions of 1830–1. In 1832, he transferred from the Jagiellonian University of Cracow to the University of Berlin. There he joined the circle of Hegel's more liberal interpreters and soon developed an appreciation of the practical possibilities of Hegelian theory.

At the time, most of Hegel's students, inspired by the French Revolution of 1830, were impatient to begin the project which they took to be implied in Hegelian theory: the practical reformation of their age. To this end, both orthodox religion and politics had to be completely revised. Cieszkowski became particularly close to two young professors at the University: Eduard Gans and Carl-Ludwig Michelet. Unlike some of their colleagues, they understood Hegel as supporting liberal doctrines, and they led Cieszkowski towards developing a Hegelian basis for political action. In 1838, Cieszkowski proceeded to revise theoretical Hegelianism in order to reveal its revolutionary content. The result was *Die Prolegomena zur Historiosophie* (Prolegomena to the Wisdom of History). This work was immediately and enthusiastically approved by the progressive Hegelians, in particular by the extreme 'Young Hegelians' – a group which included such radicals as Moses Hess, Ludwig Feuerbach, Max Stirner, Arnold Ruge, Karl Marx and Bruno Bauer.

Although David F. Strauss' *Das Leben Jesu* (Life of Jesus) (1835–6) is rightly credited with being the first Young Hegelian work, it was nevertheless

Cieszkowski's work which set the general pattern for the Young Hegelian school. Prior to it, a major difficulty confronting liberal activists was Hegel's own evident lack of concern with the future course of world history (see HEGEL, G.W.F. §8). Hegel's view, expressed throughout his works, held that philosophy played no role in '*teaching* what the world ought to be'. This attitude did not sit well with the Young Hegelians. Cieszkowski proposed a radical restructuring of Hegel's own fourfold division of historical ages (Oriental, Greek, Roman and Christian-Germanic) into a triadic and so more 'dialectical' structure: past, present and future. The past, which linked Adam to Christ, was characterized by a focus on practice; the present, from Christ to Hegel, by a focus on theory. The past, with its direct engagement with the practical and concrete issues of reality, had been followed by an age of equal and opposite focus, one in which theoretical speculation drew mankind away from everyday concerns into an abstract mental realm. The theoretical age, which began with Christ's proclamation of the 'Kingdom of God', asserted the ascendancy of the soul over the body. This age ended in the perfected theory of Hegel. After his final and conclusive theory, the post-Hegelian future would be characterized by a synthesis of past practice and present theory – a new era of 'praxis'. This new division of history obviously justified the study of Hegelian theory by giving theorists a major role in setting a future agenda. Praxis, as expressed in the 'deed' linking the abstract theory of Hegelianism with practical action, would engage future thinkers in an ongoing process of rationalizing the real. In sum, the final result of Hegelian theory was, in a proper dialectical manner, the return of that theory into the practical world from which it had emerged. Cieszkowski's work not only redirected Hegelian interest from religion to politics, but also established a programme for Hegelians. Henceforth, given that Hegelianism was the perfected philosophical theory, there only remained the practical task of conforming the world to it (see HEGELIANISM §2).

In 1842 Cieszkowski published another philosophical work, *Gott und Palingenesie* (God and Regeneration), directed against Michelet's reduction of God to an impersonal ideal. For Cieszkowski this implied a failure to grasp the concreteness of the divine personality, and was a step back from the threshold of future praxis into the earlier age of abstract theorizing. However, due to its opaque style and the obscurity of its subject, the work was unsatisfying even to its author.

In the year following the publication of the *Prolegomena*, Cieszkowski visited France, where he become deeply interested in an alternative to German philosophic theory: that is, French economic practice. Moving in the social circles of such eminent liberal French economists as Auguste Blanqui, Hippolyte de Passy, and P.L.E. Rossi, as well as with such thinkers as Pierre-Joseph Proudhon, Royer-Collard and Louis Blanc, it was not long before Cieszkowski's first economic work appeared: *Du crédit et de la circulation* (Concerning Credit and Circulation) (1838b). It advocated the reform of the monetary system by introducing a new type of interest-bearing note. The work, based upon several years of research into economic issues, proposed to balance both private and public economic interests. In 1844 he wrote a short work proposing a reform of the decadent French Upper House, *De la pairie et de l'aristocratie moderne* (On the Peerage and Modern Aristocracy). An indirect critique of the French bourgeoisie, it reasserted the need for a strong legislative body representing universal interests, a 'popular patriciate' defending the public order threatened by the anarchic individualism of the Lower House.

After the abortive revolutions of 1848, Cieszkowski became a member of the Prussian Lower House, and supported the cause of Polish nationalism. In 1866 he retired from politics to his estate in Poland, where, until his death, he pursued varied public-interest projects and worked on a lengthy treatise entitled *Ojcze Nasz* (Our Father). He considered this his major work. But although begun in the 1830s, it remained unfinished at his death in 1894. It is a grand and cloudy romantic vision of a political order inspired by theological principles – principles which Cieszkowski thought were embedded in the Lord's Prayer. The Prayer was the revelation of God's plan, the divine praxis required for the establishment of a new and harmonious social order – an earthly 'Kingdom of God'.

See also: HISTORY, PHILOSOPHY OF

List of works

Cieszkowski, A. von (1838a) *Die Prolegomena zur Historiosophie* (Prolegomena to the Wisdom of History), Berlin: Viet. (The author's major study revising Hegel's philosophy of history.)

—— (1838b) *Du crédit et de la circulation* (Concerning Credit and Circulation), Paris: Treuttel et Wurtz. (An economic proposal to reform French government monetary policy.)

—— (1842) *Gott und Palingenesie* (God and Regeneration), Berlin: E.H. Schröder. (A speculative exercise attempting to personalize the Hegelian absolute spirit.)

—— (1844a) *De la pairie et de l'aristocratie moderne*

(On the Peerage and Modern Aristocracy), Paris: Amyot. (A proposal to liberalize and reform the French Upper House towards making it an effective instrument of government.)

—— (1844b) *Ojcze Nasz* (Our Father), Paris: Maulde et Renou. (A reading of the Lord's Prayer as a key to social reform.)

—— (1979) *Selected Writings of August Cieszkowski*, ed., trans. and intro. A. Liebich, Cambridge: Cambridge University Press. (Contains a comprehensive bibliographic essay.)

References and further reading

Liebich, A. (1979) *Between Ideology and Utopia: The Politics and Philosophy of August Cieszkowski*, Dordrecht: Reidel. (A comprehensive study of the whole of Cieszkowski's life and works.)

Lobkowicz, N. (1967) *Theory and Practice: History of a Concept from Aristotle to Marx*, Notre Dame, IN: Notre Dame University Press, 193–204. (A study placing Cieszkowski in the context of philosophic history.)

Stepelevich, L.S. (1974) 'August von Cieszkowski: From Theory to Practice', *History and Theory* 13 (1): 39–53. (Relates Cieszkowski to the Young Hegelian school.)

—— (1987) 'Making Hegel Into a Better Hegelian: August von Cieszkowski', *Journal of the History of Philosophy* 25 (4): 263–73. (A critique of Cieszkowski's revision of Hegel's philosophy of history.)

* Strauss, D.F. (1835–6) *Das Leben Jesu*, Tübingen: Osiander; trans. M.A. Evans (George Eliot), *Life of Jesus*, Philadelphia, PA, Fortress, 1972. (Argues that the messianic Christ was merely a mythic figure.)

LAWRENCE S. STEPELEVICH

CITIZENSHIP

Within political philosophy, citizenship refers not only to a legal status, but also to a normative ideal – the governed should be full and equal participants in the political process. As such, it is a distinctively democratic ideal. People who are governed by monarchs or military dictators are subjects, not citizens. Most philosophers therefore view citizenship theory as an extension of democratic theory. Democratic theory focuses on political institutions and procedures; citizenship theory focuses on the attributes of individual participants.

One important topic in citizenship theory concerns the need for citizens to actively participate in political life. In most countries participation in politics is not obligatory, and people are free to place private commitments ahead of political involvement. Yet if too many citizens are apathetic, democratic institutions will collapse. Another topic concerns the identity of citizens. Citizenship is intended to provide a common status and identity which helps integrate members of society. However, some theorists question whether common citizenship can accommodate the increasing social and cultural pluralism of modern societies.

1 Citizenship and democratic theory
2 The responsibilities of citizenship
3 Citizenship, identity and difference

1 Citizenship and democratic theory

'Citizenship' is a term the philosophical meaning of which differs from its everyday usage. In everyday speech, citizenship is often used as a synonym for 'nationality', to refer to one's legal status as a member of a particular country. To be a citizen entails having certain rights and responsibilities, but these vary greatly from country to country. For example, citizens in a liberal democracy have political rights and religious liberties, whereas citizens in a monarchy, military dictatorship or religious theocracy may have neither.

In philosophical contexts, citizenship refers to a substantive normative ideal of membership and participation in a political community. To be a citizen, in this sense, is to be recognized as a full and equal member of society, with the right to participate in the political process. As such, it is a distinctively democratic ideal. People who are governed by monarchs or military dictators are subjects, not citizens.

This link between citizenship and democracy is evident in the history of Western thought. Citizenship was a prominent theme among philosophers of the ancient Greek and Roman republics, but disappeared from feudal thought, only to be revived with the rebirth of republicanism during the Renaissance (see POLITICAL PHILOSOPHY, HISTORY OF §§2, 4). Indeed, it is sometimes difficult to distinguish citizenship, as a philosophical topic, from democracy. However, theories of democracy primarily focus on institutions and procedures – political parties, elections, legislatures and constitutions – while theories of citizenship focus on the attributes of individual citizens.

Theories of citizenship are important because democratic institutions will collapse if citizens lack certain virtues, such as civic-mindedness and mutual goodwill. Indeed, many democracies suffer from voter apathy, racial and religious intolerance, and significant non-compliance with taxation or environmental policies that rely on voluntary cooperation. The health of a democracy depends not only on the structure of its institutions, but also on the qualities of its citizens: for example, their loyalties and how they view potentially competing forms of national, ethnic or religious identities; their ability to work with others who are different from themselves; their desire to participate in public life; their willingness to exercise self-restraint in their economic demands and in personal choices affecting their health and the environment.

2 The responsibilities of citizenship

In ancient Athens, citizenship was viewed primarily in terms of duties. Citizens were legally obliged to take their turn in public office and sacrificed part of their private life to do so. In the modern world, however, citizenship is viewed more as a matter of rights than duties. Citizens have the right to participate in politics, but also the right to place private commitments ahead of political involvement.

An influential exposition of this conception of 'citizenship-as-rights' is T.H. Marshall's *Citizenship and Social Class* (1950). Marshall divides citizenship rights into three categories: civil rights, which arose in England in the eighteenth century; political rights, which arose in the nineteenth century; and social rights – for example, to education, health care, unemployment insurance and old-age pension – which have become established in the twentieth century (see RIGHTS §§4–5). For Marshall, the culmination of the citizenship ideal is the social-democratic welfare state. By guaranteeing civil, political and social rights to all, the welfare state ensures that every member of society is able to participate fully in the common life of society (see SOCIAL DEMOCRACY).

This is often called 'passive' citizenship, because of its emphasis on passive entitlements and the absence of any civic duties. While it has helped secure a reasonable degree of security, prosperity and freedom for most members of Western societies, most theorists believe that the passive acceptance of rights must be supplemented with the active exercise of responsibilities and virtues. Theorists disagree, however, about which virtues are most important and how best to promote them.

Conservatives emphasize the virtue of self-reliance. Whereas Marshall argued that social rights enable the disadvantaged to participate in the mainstream of society, conservatives argue that the welfare state has promoted passivity and dependence among the poor. To promote active citizenship, we should reduce welfare entitlements and emphasize the responsibility to earn a living, which is the key to self-respect and social acceptance (see CONSERVATISM). Critics respond that cutting welfare benefits further marginalizes the underclass. Also, as feminists note, gender-neutral talk about 'self-reliance' is often a code for the view that men should financially support the family while women look after the household and care for the elderly, sick, and young. This reinforces the barriers to women's full participation in society (see FEMINIST POLITICAL PHILOSOPHY).

Civil society theorists focus on how we learn to be responsible citizens. They argue that it is in the voluntary organizations of civil society – churches, families, unions, ethnic associations, environmental groups, neighbourhood associations, support groups – that we learn civic virtues. Because these groups are voluntary, failure to live up to the responsibilities they entail is met with disapproval rather than legal punishment. Yet because the disapproval comes from family, friends and colleagues, it is often a more powerful incentive to act responsibly than punishment by an impersonal state (see CIVIL SOCIETY).

The claim that civil society is the seedbed of civic virtue is debatable. The family teaches civility and self-restraint, but it can also be 'a school of despotism' that teaches male dominance over women. Similarly, churches often teach deference to authority and intolerance of other faiths; ethnic groups often teach prejudice against other races, and so on.

Liberal virtue theorists emphasize the importance of citizens' ability to engage in public discourse. This does not mean simply making one's views known. It also involves the virtue of 'public reasonableness'. Citizens must give reasons for their political demands, not just state preferences or make threats. Moreover, these reasons must be 'public' reasons, in the sense that they are capable of persuading people of different faiths and nationalities. It is not enough to invoke scripture or tradition; a conscientious effort is required to distinguish those beliefs which are matters of private faith from those which are capable of public defence.

Where do we learn this virtue? Liberal virtue theorists often suggest that schools should teach children to distance themselves from their own cultural traditions when engaging in public discourse and to consider other points of view. However, traditionalists object that this encourages children to question parental or religious authority in private life. Those groups which rely on an uncritical acceptance of tradition and authority are threatened by the open-minded and pluralistic attitudes which liberal education encourages. Hence some religious groups see compulsory liberal education as an act of intolerance towards them, even if it is carried out in the name of teaching the virtue of tolerance (see TOLERATION).

Civic republicans offer another approach to responsible citizenship. In its most general sense, 'civic republican' refers to anyone who believes in the need for active and responsible citizens. But there is a narrower conception of civic republicanism, distinguished by its belief (following Aristotle) in the intrinsic value of political participation. Such participation is, in Adrian Oldfield's words, 'the highest form of human living-together that most individuals can aspire to' (1990: 6). On this view, political life is superior to the merely private pleasures of family, neighbourhood and profession, and so should occupy the centre of people's lives.

This view conflicts with modern understandings of the good life in the Western world. Most people today find the greatest happiness in their family life, work, religion or leisure, not in politics. Political participation is seen as an occasional, often burdensome, activity necessary to ensure that government respects and supports people's freedom to pursue their personal projects and attachments. The assumption that politics is primarily a means to protect and promote private life underlies most modern views of citizenship. This attitude may reflect the impoverishment of public life today, compared to the active citizenship of ancient Greece. Political debate seems less meaningful, and people feel less able to participate effectively. But it also reflects the enrichment of private life, given the increased prominence of romantic love and the nuclear family (with its emphasis on intimacy and privacy); increased prosperity (and so richer forms of leisure and consumption); and modern beliefs in the dignity of labour (which the Greeks despised). The call for active citizenship today must compete with the powerful attractions of private life (see LIBERALISM §§3–4).

3 Citizenship, identity and difference

Citizenship is not just a status, defined by a set of rights and responsibilities. It is also an identity, an expression of one's membership in a political community. Moreover, it is a shared identity, common to the diverse groups in society. Citizenship therefore serves an integrative function. Extending citizenship rights has helped integrate previously excluded groups, like the working class, into society.

Some groups, however – for example, African-Americans, indigenous peoples, ethnic and religious minorities, gays and lesbians – still feel excluded from the mainstream of society, despite possessing the common rights of citizenship. According to cultural pluralists, citizenship must reflect the distinct socio-cultural identity of these groups – their 'difference'. The common rights of citizenship, originally defined by and for white men, cannot accommodate the needs of marginalized groups. These groups can only be fully integrated through what Iris Marion Young calls 'differentiated citizenship' (1989). That is, the members of certain groups should be incorporated into the political community, not only as individuals, but also through the group, and their rights should depend in part on their group membership.

This view challenges traditional conceptions of citizenship, which define citizenship in terms of treating people as individuals with equal rights under the law. This is how democratic citizenship is standardly distinguished from feudal and other pre-modern views that determined people's political status by their religion, ethnicity, class or gender. The idea of differentiated citizenship, therefore, is seen by many as a contradiction in terms. Moreover, if groups are encouraged by the very terms of citizenship to turn inward and focus on their 'difference', how can citizenship provide a source of commonality and solidarity for the various groups in society?

It is important to distinguish here two broad categories of differentiated citizenship. For some groups – such as the poor, women, racial minorities and immigrants – the demand for group rights is usually a demand for greater inclusion and participation in the mainstream society. For example, these groups may feel underrepresented in the political process due to historic barriers, and so seek special group-based representation (see REPRESENTATION, POLITICAL §2). Or they may want the school curriculum to recognize their contributions to society's culture and history. Or they may seek exemptions from laws that disadvantage them economically, given their beliefs and practices. These groups share the goal of national integration – that is, that historically disadvantaged groups should become full and equal participants in the mainstream society. They simply claim that recognition and accommodation of their 'difference' is needed to ensure integration.

Other groups demanding differentiated citizenship reject the goal of national integration. They wish to govern themselves, apart from the larger society. This is particularly true of national minorities – that is, distinct historical communities, occupying their own homeland or territory and sharing a distinct language and history. These groups find themselves within the boundaries of a larger political community, but claim the right to govern themselves in certain matters in order to ensure the free development of their culture.

What these national minorities want is not primarily better representation in the central government, but rather the transfer of power from the central government to their own communities, often through some system of federalism or local autonomy (see FEDERALISM AND CONFEDERALISM). Rather than seeking greater inclusion into the larger society, they seek greater autonomy from it.

This sort of demand challenges traditional accounts of citizenship identity, which presuppose that people view themselves as members of the same society. If democracy is the rule of the people, demands for self-government raise the question of who 'the people' really are. National minorities claim that they are distinct 'nations' or 'peoples', with inherent rights of self-determination which were not relinquished by their (often involuntary) federation with other nations within a larger country. Self-government rights divide the people into separate peoples, each with its own rights, territories and powers of self-government; and each, therefore, with its own political community. If citizenship is membership of a political community, then self-government rights give rise to a sort of dual citizenship, and to conflicts about which community – the national group or the state – citizens identify with most deeply. Moreover, if limited autonomy is desirable for a national minority, why not secede completely and have a fully autonomous nation-state?

In effect, countries with national minorities face the problem of conflicting nationalisms (see NATION AND NATIONALISM). The state seeks to promote a single national identity through common citizenship; the minority seeks to promote its distinct national identity through differentiated citizenship. Finding a source of social unity in such multination countries is a fundamental question facing theorists of citizenship.

See also: DEMOCRACY; REPUBLICANISM

References and further reading

All of these works are written in nontechnical language, accessible to those with little or no background in political philosophy.

Beiner, R. (1994) *Theorizing Citizenship*, Albany, NY: State University of New York Press. (A collection of prominent contemporary essays on citizenship, covering most of the theories and issues discussed in this article.)

Clarke, P.B. (1994) *Citizenship*, London: Pluto Press. (A collection of historical writings on citizenship, from Aristotle to the present day.)

Galston, W. (1991) *Liberal Purposes: Goods, Virtues, and Duties in the Liberal State*, Cambridge: Cambridge University Press. (A prominent statement of the liberal virtue theory discussed in §2.)

Kymlicka, W. (1995) *Multicultural Citizenship*, Oxford: Oxford University Press. (An evaluation of the cultural pluralist critique of universal citizenship, discussed in §3.)

Kymlicka, W. and Norman, W. (1994) 'Return of the Citizen: A Survey of Recent Work on Citizenship Theory', *Ethics* 104 (2): 352–81. (A summary of the recent literature on citizenship, with an extensive bibliography.)

Macedo, S. (1990) *Liberal Virtues: Citizenship, Virtue and Community*, Oxford: Oxford University Press. (A statement of the liberal virtue theory, discussed in §2.)

* Marshall, T.H. (1965) *Citizenship and Social Class*, Cambridge: Cambridge University Press. (The classic exposition of the modern theory of citizenship-as-rights, discussed in §2.)

Mouffe, C. (1992) *Dimensions of Radical Democracy: Pluralism, Citizenship and Community*, London: Routledge. (A collection of essays on citizenship theory, covering issues of both civic virtue and cultural pluralism.)

* Oldfield, A. (1990) *Citizenship and Community: Civic Republicanism and the Modern World*, London: Routledge. (An exposition of the civic republican view, discussed in §2.)

Spinner, J. (1994) *The Boundaries of Citizenship: Race, Ethnicity and Nationality in the Liberal State*, Baltimore, MD: Johns Hopkins University Press. (A liberal response to the cultural pluralist critique of universal citizenship, discussed in §3.)

Walzer, M. (1989) 'Citizenship', in T. Ball and J. Farr (eds) *Political Innovation and Conceptual Change*, Cambridge: Cambridge University Press. (A concise history of the concept of citizenship.)

—— (1992) 'The Civil Society Argument', in C. Mouffe *Dimensions of Radical Democracy: Pluralism, Citizenship and Community*, London: Routledge; also in R. Beiner *Theorizing Citizenship*, Albany, NY: State University of New York Press, 1994. (A clear statement of the civil society theory, discussed in §2.)

* Young, I.M. (1989) 'Polity and Group Difference: A Critique of the Ideal of Universal Citizenship', *Ethics* 99 (2): 250–74; repr. in R. Beiner *Theorizing Citizenship*, Albany, NY: State University of New York Press, 1994. (A prominent statement of the cultural pluralist critique of universal citizenship, discussed in §3.)

WILL KYMLICKA

CIVIL DISOBEDIENCE

According to common definitions, civil disobedience involves a public and nonviolent breach of law that is committed in order to change a law or policy, and in order to better society. More, those classed as civilly disobedient must be willing to accept punishment. Why is the categorization of what counts as civil disobedience of practical importance? The usual assumption is that acts of civil disobedience are easier to justify morally than other illegal acts. Acts of civil disobedience, such as those committed by abolitionists, by followers of Mahatma Gandhi and Martin Luther King, Jr and by opponents of the Vietnam War, have been an important form of social protest.

The decision as to what exactly should count as civil disobedience should be guided both by an ordinary understanding of what the term conveys and by what factors are relevant for moral justification. For justification, nonviolence and publicness matter because they reduce the damage of violating the law. Tactics should be proportionate to the evil against which civil disobedience is aimed; someone who assesses the morality of a particular act of civil disobedience should distinguish an evaluation of tactics from an evaluation of objectives.

1 **What constitutes civil disobedience?**
2 **Justifying civil disobedience**

1 What constitutes civil disobedience?

People care about definitions of civil disobedience because they believe that acts of civil disobedience are easier to defend than ordinary illegal acts. To understand that assumption, it helps to see how any approach to civil disobedience fits within a larger sense of the moral wrongness of most law breaking. Reasons against violating the law are founded on moral rights or justice (deontological reasons) or on harmful consequences (consequential reasons) (see DEONTOLOGICAL ETHICS; CONSEQUENTIALISM). Many acts that breach standards of criminal and civil law are independently immoral. Thus, murders breach the moral rights of victims and are undesirable measured by consequences. Whether or not people have some general responsibility to obey the law, simply because it is the law, the existence of duties to other members of the community and reasons of consequence support keeping the law on many other occasions. For instance, at least within a fair and reasonably effective legal system, taxpayers should pay their taxes (see OBLIGATION, POLITICAL).

For acts of civil disobedience to be morally justified, reasons in their favour must outrank or outweigh whatever moral reasons lie behind obeying the law. The significance of an act's constituting civil disobedience is that reasons in favour of obedience are reduced or reasons for disobeying are strengthened, or both. An approach to what counts as civil disobedience should be responsive to widespread understanding of the term's meaning and to factors that matter morally.

Any effort to isolate the phenomenon of civil disobedience must distinguish between what we may call full disobedience of law and violating some 'lower'-level rule whilst hoping or expecting that one will be regarded as justified by some higher *legal* rule. In regimes with written constitutions, for example, someone may claim a constitutional privilege to disobey a statute. Such an action, based on an accepted constitutional right, is not true civil disobedience. However, classification becomes more troublesome when someone breaks a law believing that the law should be declared unconstitutional, but strongly expecting that courts will disagree. This essay disregards this subtlety and concentrates on persons who lack any serious claim that their behaviour is protected by another, higher legal rule.

People usually disobey laws from self-interest or strong emotion, without any belief that they are justified morally. But not infrequently people think they have good moral reason to disobey. They may believe that because the precise terms of a law are not regarded seriously or are widely disobeyed, they have little moral reason to obey. (Many Americans feel this way about speed limits on highways.) Even when they perceive substantial reasons to obey, people may think disobedience is justified because they cannot conscientiously perform the required acts, because they face conflicting moral claims in the circumstances or because they seek to achieve broader social goals. The first sort of reason is exemplified by the refusal on a religious basis to submit to conscription. Those engaging in these conscientious refusals would welcome legal change, but their disobedience has a more personal point. Someone who lies under oath to protect a friend lacks such a conscientious objection, but may believe duties of friendship are stronger than the responsibility to testify truthfully. Other illegal acts have some broader social objective. Acts of civil disobedience have such broader social objectives.

An extremely expansive definition of civil disobedience is any 'deliberate violation of law for a vital social purpose' (Zinn 1968: 39). According to this definition, the poisoning of Rasputin, and even the rape of Muslim women in Bosnia – if done to help impose Serbian rule – would qualify as civil disobedience. Such an understanding strays too far from the basic conception that 'civil' in 'civil disobedience' relates not only to the civil order but also to the kinds of tactics that are used. On this view, 'civil' is opposed to 'violent', although the line between the two is hardly transparent (see VIOLENCE).

At the other end of the spectrum of definitions is John Rawls' account (see RAWLS, J. §4). Rawls states that someone who engages in civil disobedience 'invokes the commonly shared conception of justice that underlies the political order', declaring that principles of justice are not being respected and aiming to make the majority reconsider the justice of its actions (1971: 364–5). This approach is part of Rawls' comprehensive theory of justice for liberal democracies (and does not indicate what counts as civil disobedience for tyrannies). Although not ruling out all other forms of resistance for democracies, Rawls thinks acts of civil disobedience are easier to justify.

Rawls' account disqualifies many acts commonly regarded as involving civil disobedience. Vegetarians publicize their moral abhorrence of killing animals for food by blocking entrances to stockyards; pacifists trespass peacefully on an army base to object to a popular war. In countries where dominant views are neither vegetarian nor pacifist, such demonstrations do not qualify as civil disobedience for Rawls. Analysis is more complicated if objectors trespass on nuclear power facilities. A demonstrator convinced that shared principles of justice have not been respected will be engaging in civil disobedience, but one who sees the problem as one of government stupidity will be doing something else. Such shades of evaluation probably should not determine whether someone's participation constitutes civil disobedience.

Rawls' idea that civil disobedience makes the majority reconsider the justice of its actions oversimplifies the objectives underlying most such activities. Suppose people block construction work where officials have approved destruction of a forest in order that expensive housing may be build. The demonstrators have a triple message: that the government acted unjustly on the facts available; that the government should now change course in light of the demonstrated intensity of opposition; and that inconvenience and embarrassment will attend continuation of the present policy. Demonstrators often seek to manipulate costs and benefits to persuade officials that the present course is too expensive. *Pure* appeals to justice are rare; civil disobedience usually involves calculated elements of pressure. Some of Rawls' definitional criteria may be better understood as factors relevant to deciding whether acts of civil disobedience are justified. For deciding that acts count as civil disobedience, an account drawn from common definitions is preferable.

2 Justifying civil disobedience

The main argument in favour of engaging in civil disobedience is that an overt violation of law may be effective in a way that neither ordinary speech nor lawful demonstrations can achieve. If one's objectives are important enough, reasons in favour of obeying the law may be overridden. Acts of civil disobedience do less damage to the values of law observance than do most other violations of law that are intended to achieve similar objectives.

The requirement of nonviolence is directly relevant to the issue of damage. Acts of civil disobedience typically cause inconvenience, to a greater or lesser degree. Some also involve breaches of property rights, such as trespasses. However, they do not threaten the safety of persons, the most important interest that the law protects.

The publicness of civil disobedience is mainly significant because it ensures that violators can be identified and arrested, and can be punished if authorities proceed against them. Voluntary submission to punishment goes some way towards satisfying one's duty to be fair to others in respect to law. Ordinary violations of law take advantage of those who 'play by the rules'. But when people act openly in a way that makes punishment simple, they implicitly declare that they seek no personal advantage from their action and are willing to pay the appropriate penalty. They also openly commit their fate to legal processes. Even if submission to punishment does not *fully* satisfy a duty of fairness in respect to law, it reduces greatly the degree of unfairness (see CRIME AND PUNISHMENT §1). The consequences of illegal action are also different when violators act openly and submit to punishment. The frustration, resentment and insecurity people feel when their interests are jeopardized are reduced if they realize that those who threaten them are willing to pay an even more costly price. By acting openly, the violators demonstrate the depth of their convictions, showing that they take their claims very seriously. They also signify their respect for their fellow citizens and for the law, especially if they not only submit to punishment willingly but also acknowledge its appropriateness. Openness also reduces the destructive potentiality of illegal actions as examples to others with various social grievances.

Since the main significance of publicness or openness is in its connection to identification and punishment, openness should be understood in a way that corresponds with this significance. Suppose war protesters surreptitiously enter a government office at night, pour blood on some military files and openly declare the following morning exactly what they have done and why. This behaviour may count as 'open' for the purpose of classification as civil disobedience, even though the violation itself was covert. Some open actions do not involve the element of submission to punishment. If police who know they are easily identifiable block traffic but are counting on their bargaining power as indispensable peace keepers to ensure that no punishment is imposed, their unwillingness to submit to the law is little affected by the openness of their actions. For this reason, their behaviour probably should not count as civil disobedience.

What constitutes the conditions for civil disobedience to be morally justified? Perhaps the most common suggestion is that lawful means of protest have been pursued unsuccessfully. This condition makes obvious sense. If a law or policy may be altered by legal means, resort to more drastic illegal means is not yet appropriate. Thus, speeches, letters to politicians and lawful demonstrations should precede unlawful demonstrations. The principle is sound, although people often disagree over when lawful means have proved unsuccessful. The principle does not apply in its usual form in emergency situations, say when the government undertakes an unexpected invasion of another country, and, perhaps, it does not apply when the unproductiveness of legal means of protest is patently clear in advance.

Former US Supreme Court Justice Abe Fortas once suggested that disobedience is never justified unless the law being violated is the target of the protest (Fortas 1968). Although disobedience is usually easier to justify when a close connection exists between the injustice people protest against and the law they disobey, no absolute principle of the kind Fortas proposed is defensible. Among other objections, the principle might leave some laws and policies – for example, a highly unjust definition of treason or an egregious use of military force abroad – entirely immune from law-violating protest; and it would also preclude such protests for the government's failure to enact laws to prevent injustice.

Rawls has proposed that ordinarily, justified civil disobedience will be limited 'to instances of substantial and clear injustice, and preferably to those which obstruct the path of removing other injustices' (1971: 372). The clearer an injustice, the stronger the justification for illegal protest. But what of parents blocking a street in order to get a traffic light installed? Contained instances of civil disobedience may be warranted to combat less than grave injustices, so long as the tactics used are not disproportionate to the evil that they protest against. Rawls' insistence that protesters appeal to a shared sense of justice might be taken as a condition for justified civil disobedience in a liberal democracy (even if it is rejected as a criterion of what constitutes civil disobedience). When protesters do appeal to a shared sense of justice, they importantly indicate their fidelity to the existing political system. But one should not rule out the possibility that civil disobedience may sometimes be justified to shift the moral sense of the community, as in the examples of protests by vegetarians and pacifists, or to respond to stupidity and ineptitude, which parents may see as the dominant obstacle to having the traffic light installed.

Those considering whether civil disobedience is justified will need to consider the likely effects of their actions in accomplishing their objectives. They must also ask whether their actions will have a serious negative effect on political stability or will lead to reprisals against persons whose interests they represent but who do not endorse the tactics they employ.

No easy formula presents itself for determining whether any particular exercise of civil disobedience is justified. Moreover, since civil disobedience typically accompanies highly controversial social issues, even clarity of evaluation is difficult. Suppose 'pro-life' demonstrators illegally block access to an abortion facility, believing that actions of this kind can help alert people to the horrors of abortion, save unborn children and increase the likelihood that the law will become more restrictive. Is this civil disobedience justified? A person might think it is not: (1) because all opposition to women's choice is not justified; or (2) because the protesters' actions will disserve their own objectives; or (3) because civil disobedience is not warranted, even if one assumes the pro-life view is sound and the protest will have the hoped-for effect. Only the third view directly confronts the demonstrators' judgment about the appropriateness of civil disobedience as a tactic. Too often, ostensible objections to tactics end up being reducible to disagreement with objectives. Careful, dispassionate analysis is required to focus upon genuine differences of views about the technique of civil disobedience itself.

See also: GANDHI, M.K.

References and further reading

Adams, J.L. (1970) 'Civil Disobedience: Its Occasions and Limits', in J.R. Pennock and J.W. Chapman (eds) *Nomos X: Political and Legal Obligations*, New York: Atherton, 293–331. (A useful overall view.)

Bedau, H. (ed.) (1969) *Civil Disobedience: Theory and Practice*, Indianapolis, IN: Pegasus. (Contains important writings by theorists and by leaders of acts of civil disobedience, with an illuminating introductory essay.)

* Fortas, A. (1968) *Concerning Dissent and Civil Disobedience*, New York: Signet Books. (Asserts strong limits on justifiable civil disobedience; popular nonphilosophical treatment.)

Greenawalt, K. (1987) *Conflicts of Law and Morality*, New York: Oxford University Press, 226–43; repr. Oxford: Clarendon Press, 1989. (Relates civil disobedience to more general themes about obligation to obey the law and expands on analysis in this essay.)

* Rawls, J. (1971) *A Theory of Justice*, Cambridge, MA: Harvard University Press. (In chapter 6, pages 363–91, Rawls develops a powerful theory of how civil disobedience can be justified in a liberal democracy; asserts a restrictive view of what counts as civil disobedience and of when civil disobedience is justified.)

Singer, P. (1973) *Democracy and Disobedience*, Oxford: Clarendon Press. (Considers whether and when it is permissible to disobey decisions arrived at by democratic means.)

* Zinn H. (1968) *Disobedience and Democracy: Nine Fallacies on Law and Order*, New York: Vint. (Expansive account of civil disobedience and when it is justified; nonphilosophical treatment.)

KENT GREENAWALT

CIVIL SOCIETY

In modern social and political philosophy civil society has come to refer to a sphere of human activity and a set of institutions outside state or government. It embraces families, churches, voluntary associations and social movements. The contrast between civil society and state was first drawn by eighteenth-century liberals for the purpose of attacking absolutism. Originally the term civil society (in Aristotelian Greek, politike koinonia) referred to a political community of equal citizens who participate in ruling and being ruled

In the twentieth century the separation of philosophy from social sciences, and the greatly expanded role of the state in economic and social life, have seemed to deprive the concept of both its intellectual home and its critical force. Yet, approaching the end of the century, the discourse of civil society is now enormously influential. What explains the concept's revival? Does it have any application in societies that are not constitutional democracies? From a normative point of view, what distinguishes civil society from both the state and the formal economy?

1 **Conceptual history**
2 **Revival of the discourse of civil society**
3 **Critiques and responses**

1 Conceptual history

The concept of *civil society* was introduced into modern European political philosophy through Latin translations of the Aristotelian Greek term, *politike koinonia*. In Aristotle's work, *politike koinonia* was defined as an ethical-political community of free and equal citizens who participate in ruling and being ruled under a legally defined system of public procedures and shared values. The term has since come to refer to very different organizations of the sphere regulated by public law – city republics, estate polities, dualistic structures of prince and country, the society of orders within the absolutist state (Riedel 1975). However, the Aristotelian identification of the political and the civil was maintained until the eighteenth century.

The early liberal polemical juxtaposition of society and state, originating in pre-revolutionary intellectual discourses critical of absolutism, decisively affected the meaning of civil society. Ever since, civil society has referred to a sphere of activity and set of institutions outside the state or government, representing an order of legitimacy that properly constructed political organizations ought to serve. The normative ideal of free and equal citizens comprising the body politic (civil society) was retained, but the body politic itself became differentiated in various ways from the state.

Nineteenth-century liberalism in all its versions maintained the society/state dualism. Yet the category of civil society developed primarily at the conservative, revolutionary and republican margins of liberal thought. Although he insisted upon the ethical dignity of the modern state, HEGEL (§8) nevertheless conceived civil society as a complex framework of economic activities, legal institutions, intermediary associations and publics upon which modern political culture and identity were to rest (Hegel 1821). Drawing on Hegel's concept of the 'system of needs', MARX (§4) identified the civil with the bourgeois, and reconceptualized civil society from two points of view: as class society and as economic society. Marx also worked with a differentiated model of state and civil society but, unlike Hegel, he sought a revolutionary reunification of the civil and the political (Marx 1843). Finally, TOCQUEVILLE worked with a three-part model that differentiated, albeit unsystematically, between a civil society of economic and cultural associations and publics, a political society of local, provincial and national assemblies, and the administrative apparatus of the state (Tocqueville 1835–40).

The professionalization of philosophy and the emergence of differentiated social sciences in the twentieth century seemed to leave the concept of civil society without an intellectual home. Nevertheless it continued to play a role outside, and even within, the disciplines. In Marxian social philosophy, GRAMSCI (§3) and his followers made the concept of civil society central to their strategy of maintaining a Hegelianized Western Marxism distinct from Soviet Marxism (see MARXISM, WESTERN §2). Albeit without using the term, the Durkheimian–Parsonian tradition in sociology continued to develop the idea of intermediary associations and a community of free and equal citizens in order to promote normative integration and combat the atomizing tendencies of the modern state and the capitalist economy. In political theory, the idea of pluralistic limits on the centralizing impulse of the modern state continued to play a role, from Gierke to the British philosophical and the US empirical pluralists. Yet, with the emergence of the structuralist school in Marxism, and the decline of functionalism in sociology and of pluralism in political science, these efforts to translate the originally philosophical concept of civil society into the language of social science and theory apparently came to an end.

2 Revival of the discourse of civil society

Nevertheless, the concept of civil society began to reappear about fifteen years ago in the milieu of neo-Marxist critics of socialist authoritarianism. The pioneering theorists of this revival were Kolakowski, Mlynar, Vajda and Michnik in the East, Habermas, Lefort, Touraine and Bobbio in the West, Weffort, Cardoso and O'Donnell in the South. All knew the works of Hegel, the young Marx or Gramsci and thus had access to the concept of civil society and the idea of a state/society dichotomy. At an earlier stage, neo-Marxists had sought to deepen Marxian social philosophy by drawing upon non-Marxist theorists such as Weber, Simmel, Croce and Freud. They used concepts like alienation, fetishism, hegemony, reification and rationalization to explain and target the endurance of capitalism in the West, as well as new forms of domination and injustice in the East. The recent revival of the concept of civil society seemed to be an analogous move, since its presence in the young Marx justified a critical appropriation of the ideas of another series of non-Marxist thinkers, from Tocqueville to Carl SCHMITT and Hannah ARENDT (§1). This time, however, instead of invoking Marx to criticize orthodox Marxism, the theorists of civil society

located the conceptual origins of communist totalitarianism in the young Marx's demand that the differentiation of state and civil society be overcome (see TOTALITARIANISM). With this self-critique, neo-Marxists became 'post-Marxist'.

The historical success of the revival of the concept of civil society was due to its anticipation of and convergence with a new radical reformist strategy for the transformation of dictatorships, first in the East and subsequently in Latin America. The underlying project of 'societal self-organization' was geared towards rebuilding solidarities outside the authoritarian state. It appealed to a civil public sphere independent of all official, state or party-controlled communication. As a result, there is now vastly expanded discussion, not only in the East (most recently in China) and in the Middle East, but also in many Western countries with established civil societies, where the focus is on the strategic and normative possibilities of further democratizing existing democracies. Yet here too, the discussion has involved an analysis of the specific types of civic solidarities and civil institutions that secure social integration, provide public spaces for participation and reinforce the vibrant civic cultures which, in Robert Putnam's words, 'make democracy work' (1993).

Success in political discourse has led to revival in political science, and to a lesser extent in philosophy and sociology. It has also led to a more explicit critique of the concept.

3 Critiques and responses

On the methodological and analytical levels the concept of civil society is plagued by ambiguities. Even once it is differentiated from political and economic society, it remains unclear what civil society actually comprises. If it entails civil publics, voluntary associations and families, stabilized by basic rights (to association, assembly, expression, press, privacy), we come up against the heterogeneity of these institutions. There are publics in the differentiated domains of society – in science, art, law, religion – admission to which cannot be open to all. Voluntary associations vary in size, purpose, and political function. These in turn differ from social movements, which are also extremely diverse in form and orientation. Family types vary greatly. The question inevitably arises: what is the point of referring to this whole complex as civil society?

One could, of course, ask the same question about the institutions comprising the 'economy' or the 'state'. But in those cases the concepts of money and (political) power do seem to indicate the outlines of differentiation. The concept of communicative action coordination reconstructed by Habermas (1981) may solve the problem in principle for civil society. Yet on the institutional level, ambiguities remain. Surely political parliaments and corporate boards do not exclude deliberation any more than civil associations and publics exclude money or power. Do state, economic and civil institutions have organizing principles that differ in kind or only in degree?

One solution is to argue the distinctiveness of civil society from the normative point of view. The actors and institutions of the polity and the economy are directly oriented to the exercise of state power, to issues of collective goal setting, efficient administration and/or profit. They cannot afford to subordinate strategic or instrumental criteria to those patterns of normative integration that generate solidarities or collective identities and build civic culture and which are characteristic of civil society. Moreover, the publics in state and economic institutions are constrained by pressures of decision-making that preclude in principle the ideal of *open-ended* communication and contestation, an ideal that serves as a standard, however counterfactual, for interaction in civil and associational publics.

However, even on the level of normative political theory the coherence of the concept of civil society remains in question. Indeed, each of the core elements of civil society has been articulated by *competing* and apparently incompatible traditions of political philosophy. Concerned with the danger of state absolutism, the liberal tradition has focused on individual rights (see LIBERALISM §3). The threat of anomie and social disintegration in modern society motivates the communitarian's stress on social solidarity, social integration and 'intermediary institutions' (see COMMUNITY AND COMMUNITARIANISM). Fearing corruption paternalism and/or political apathy, republican and democratic theorists focus on civic virtue, participation and public space (see REPUBLICANISM). The question remains: can the gaps between these distinct positions be papered over by a conception of civil society that tries to bring together the categories of rights, social solidarity, participation and public space?

The concept of civil society cannot serve as the centrepiece of a political philosophy that is construed either as an alternative to, or a synthesis of, these normative perspectives. Nor can it serve to harmonize competing political projects. However, it can help us to articulate the contested terrain that is at stake in the competing political theoretical traditions. From this perspective, the question is not whether the concept of civil society is still relevant to contemporary political theory, but rather, which version of civil society a particular theoretical approach presupposes. Once this is made clear, the concept can be useful to efforts to develop specific interpretations of rights, solidarities, participatory forms and public spaces that make liberal, communitarian, democratic and republican insights at least compatible. Nevertheless, it is bound to remain what Gallie (1955–6) once called an essentially contested concept.

References and further reading

* Aristotle (*c.* mid 4th century BC) *Politics*, trans. and with notes by E. Barker, London: Oxford University Press, 1968. (Earliest normative development of the concept of civil society.)

Cohen, J. (1982) *Class and Civil Society: The Limits of Marxian Critical Theory*, Amherst, MA: University of Massachusetts Press. (Thorough analysis of Marx's treatment of the concept of civil society.)

Cohen, J.L. and Arato, A. (1992) *Civil Society and Political Theory*, Cambridge, MA: MIT Press. (The most comprehensive theoretical statement to date.)

* Gallie, W.B. (1955–6) 'Essentially Contested Concepts', *Proceedings of the Aristotelian Society* 56: 167–98. (Discusses what is meant by essentially contested concepts.)

Gramsci, A. (1929–35) *Prison Notebooks*, New York: International Publishers, 1971. (Best twentieth-century Marxist elaboration of the concept of civil society.)

* Habermas, J. (1981) *The Theory of Communicative Action*, Boston, MA: Beacon Press, 2 vols. (Theoretical framework for the discursive concept of civil society.)

* Hegel, G.W.F. (1821) *Grundlinien der Philosophie des Rechts*, trans. and with notes by T.M. Knox, *Hegel's Philosophy of Right*, New York: Oxford University Press, 1967. (Best nineteenth-century synthetic articulation of the concept.)

Keane, J. (ed.) (1988) *Civil Society and the State*, London: Verso. (Collection of seminal essays on the civil society.)

* Marx, K. (1843) 'Contribution to the Critique of Hegel's *Philosophy of Right*', and 'On the Jewish Question', in *The Marx–Engels Reader*, ed. and with notes by R.C. Tucker, New York: W.W. Norton, 1978, 16–52. (Most important nineteenth-century critique of the bourgeois character of civil society.)

Parsons, T. (1971) *The System of Modern Societies*, Englewood Cliffs, NJ: Prentice Hall. (Best twentieth-century analysis of the integrating role of civil institutions.)

* Putnam, R. (1993) *Making Democracy Work: Civic Traditions in Modern Italy*, Princeton, NJ:

Princeton University Press. (Best recent analysis of the importance of civil society to successful democratic polities.)

* Riedel, M. (1975) 'Gesellschaft, bürgerliche' (Civil Society), in O. Brunner, W. Conze and R. Koselleck (eds) *Geschichtliche Grundbegriffe* (Fundamental Philosophical Concepts) , Stuttgart: Klett, vol. 2. (Best work on conceptual history of civil society.)

* Tocqueville, A. de (1835–40) *Democracy in America*, Garden City, NY: Doubleday, 1969. (Important analytical distinction between civil and political society.)

Touraine, A. (1981) *The Voice and the Eye*, New York: Cambridge University Press. (Best work on the dynamic social movement aspect of civil society.)

JEAN L. COHEN

CIVILIAN TRADITION

see ROMAN LAW

CIXOUS, HÉLÈNE (1937–)

Hélène Cixous, a prolific French author born in Algeria, works between poetry and philosophy. She is part of a larger intellectual community in France that, since the 1960s, has sought a critique of the Western (male) subject, claiming that the 'metaphysical' notion of the subject has for three centuries contributed to the repression of nature, women and other cultures by construing human existence in terms of the separation of mind from body, and more generally of concept from metaphor.

Influenced by Nietzsche and Freud, Cixous privileges the artistic and poetic but all her work has philosophical underpinnings, especially those proposed by Derrida. Like his, her thought champions notions of difference, multiplicity and life over identity, univocity and death. She seeks to displace the unified, narcissistic (male) subject, which in her view is on the side of death. Cixous is also importantly influenced by her critical reception of Hegel and Heidegger.

Though she declares herself primarily a poet and a thinker, Cixous has kept close ties with the academy and has undertaken a variety of political activities. After helping to found, in 1968, the experimental University of Paris VIII at Vincennes – an institution both politically controversial and intellectually scintillating – she established there, in 1974, one of France's few Centres for Women's Studies. Her

seminars have attracted students from around the world and have become, not merely intellectual experiences, but spiritual training grounds. Her struggle for a different approach to the other and for giving a voice to others has led her to espouse many political causes. But politics for Cixous are, like philosophy, never separated from poetry: from the invention of new languages without which, in her words, no social change can come about.

The critique of a subject identified as 'male' leads, from Cixous's earliest work on, to broadly psychoanalytical concerns. Her acute perceptions of others' psychic 'vibrations' has made her an excellent reader and critic, as evidenced in the early essays on Freud, Joyce, Kleist, and Poe collected in *Prénoms de personne* (1974). But she has also subjected psychoanalysis to intense, deconstructive scrutiny, in which supposed psychoanalytic 'truths' are rejected in favour of open-ended, personal narratives. Her avant-garde writings of the late 1960s and early 1970s conceived of a subject that is no longer masterful and autonomous but always in dialogue – or transference – with other textual or living subjects or voices. In this conception, the subject constructs itself, or is actively 'born' and 'reborn', at the interstices of various texts and history. The philosophical underpinning for this is a critique of Hegel and his brand of dialectical reasoning, as exemplified in the account of the master–slave relation in the *Phenomenology of Spirit* (see HEGEL, G.W.F §5) – a relation which Cixous sees as the basis of much of Western dualistic thinking, including the existential humanism of SARTRE and de BEAUVOIR.

In one of her most widely read books, *La Jeune Née* (1975) (*The Newly Born Woman*, 1986) co-authored with Catherine Clément, Cixous began a lengthy detour through the cause of women. In this phase of her work, she 'deconstructively' criticized symbolic practices that organize culture through hierarchically ordered oppositions such as nature/culture, speech/writing and man/woman (see DECONSTRUCTION). These oppositions, themselves produced historically, were to be displaced into mere differences. The simultaneous exclusion in metaphysics of the terms 'writing' and 'woman', argued for by DERRIDA, enabled her to coin the productive but controversial expression, 'feminine writing' (*écriture feminine*). This phrase, read in the derivative sense of a woman writing, was used to raise consciousness. But in a Derridean sense, writing is always related to and occurs within an (unconscious) scene. Thus, Cixous argued that the body is never a brute given but is always already encoded, and disarms accusations of essentialism. 'I' is more than one, for it is in constant dialogue with others, and any identity is imposed from the outside. Cixous destabilized the fixed sexual identities imposed by a reigning cultural order through her concern with bisexuality.

In Cixous's enterprise of feminine writing, philosophy intersects with anthropology as well as with psychoanalysis. Bataille's reading of Mauss's classic essay, *Essai sur le don* (1925) (*The Gift*, 1967) prompted her to look at cultures that practise modes of exchange different from those of Western retention and accumulation (such as Kwakiutl tribes, known for their ritual of *potlatch*). This led her poetically to invent ways of giving and receiving unconditioned by a restricted (male) economy infused with feelings of guilt and debt. She argued that women, because of their marginal status in society, practise the art of the gift more often than men, who are caught in scenarios of castration. 'Feminine writing' itself therefore exemplified an art of giving at the level of content and form. Her texts, speaking of generosity, exemplify it through an excess of meaning. In this, 'feminine' serves to designate, not an enduring attribute, but a transitional step toward other modes of exchanging where it will be replaced with other adjectives.

In the early 1980s, Cixous's critique of the Hegelian dialectic of recognition and sublation gave way to other approaches. Her reading of the Brazilian novelist, Clarice Lispector, first published in the review *Poétique* in 1979, inaugurated a shift toward Heidegger's philosophy of language. With it came a change in style. Emphasis on surface gave way to depth; earlier 'explosions of the subject' were discarded in favour of a return to 'man' (*l'homme*). Heidegger's notion of poetry, a *technē* that he favours over instrumental technology of repression, was welcomed. In this stage of her work, Cixous combined her devotion to writing more explicitly with philosophy, as a new brand of 'writing-thinking' enabled her to work through personal, cultural and historical issues. Her texts of this period are concerned with philosophical questions such as, who leaves and who arrives where? How does one give and receive? How does one have what one has? Her continued dialogue with Derrida also led her to deal with questions similar to his, such as the promise and the secret.

In her recent work, the emphasis on individual pleasure (*jouissance*) fades. Her concern with the cause of women, though not abandoned, opens out to others. This is evident in her writings for the theatre. Her plays on Cambodia (1985) and India (1987), on apartheid and the gulag (*Manne*, 1988) broach issues of history and collective voice in terms of neo-colonialism. All these plays and texts oppose a lofty sphere of combat for truth to a low sphere of political battles and sheer power. In this period Cixous has continued her personal meditations, now focusing on her childhood and her Jewish origins. She is also returning more to the classroom, navigating deftly between national literatures and philosophies, between genres and media.

How such a hybrid writing-thinking fares either as poetry or as philosophy remains to be seen. To date, all of Cixous's production, whatever its genre, has been critical of metaphysical closure and its repressive conceptual and syntactic structures. Her reading and writing of differences performed through a variety of topics undo totalizing systems based on inclusion, exclusion and negation – or, in psychoanalytic terms, on castration. Yet birth – no longer just anatomical and natural – and *sorties*, ways out, do not simply lead to an outside. They must, for Cixous, be continually re-enacted in an ongoing writing-thinking at the interstices of personal, cultural and social history.

See also: DERRIDA, J.; FEMINISM AND PSYCHOANALYSIS

List of works

Cixous, H. (1974) *Prénoms de personne*, Paris: Éditions du Seuil. (Collection of early essays on Freud, Joyce, Kleist and Poe.)

—— (1975) *La Jeune Née*, with Catherine Clément, Paris: Christian Bourgois; trans. B. Wing, *The Newly Born Woman*, Minneapolis, MN: University of Minnesota Press, 1986. (A militant essay that focuses on the previous exclusion of women from cultural discourses and invents new cultural practices through writing.)

—— (1979) 'L'Approche de Clarice Lispector', *Poétique* 40; trans. D. Jensen, in *Coming to Writing and Other Essays*, Cambridge, MA: Harvard University Press. (A reading of Lispector's 'feminine writing'. A marked shift toward Heidegger in its general use of language and the use of a notion of approach.)

—— (1985) *L'Histoire terrible mais inachevée de Norodom Sihanouk, roi du Cambodge*, Paris: Théâtre du Soleil; trans. J. MacCannell, J. Pike and L. Groth, *The Terrible but Unfinished Story of Norodom Sihanouk, King of Cambodia*, Lincoln, NE: University of Nebraska Press, 1994. (King Sihanouk's generous attempt to save his country from political fanatics and technocrats out to destroy it.)

—— (1987) *L'Indiade ou l'Inde de leurs rêves*, Paris: Théâtre du Soleil. (Gandhi's politics of renunciation, non-violence and 'maternal' love triumph over the adversaries' cravings for personal power that lead to death and destruction.)

—— (1988) *Manne*, Paris: Éditions des Femmes;

trans. C. MacGillivray, *Manna*, Minneapolis, MN: University of Minnesota Press. (A denunciation of apartheid and the gulag as tribute to the courage of Nelson and Winnie Mandela, Osip and Nadezhda Mandelstam, and the Russian poetess Anna Akhmatova. A study of the relation between poetry and history.)

References and further reading

All these works are expository, non-technical and accessible.

Conley, V.A. (1984) *Hélène Cixous: Writing the Feminine*, Lincoln, NE and London: University of Nebraska Press, expanded edn, 1991. (A critical, introductory study especially of Cixous's early writings. Contains interview.)

MacGillivray, C. (1994) 'Introduction' to *Manna*, Minneapolis, MN: University of Minnesota Press. (A helpful, close reading of Cixous's textual strategies.)

* Mauss, M. (1925) *Essai sur le don*, Paris: Alcan, L'année sociologique; trans. Ian Cunnison, *The Gift*, New York: W.W. Norton, 1967. (The first systematic study of the custom of exchanging gifts as part of all human, personal relationships between individuals and groups.)

Moi, T. (1985) 'Hélène Cixous: An Imaginary Utopia', in *Sexual/Textual Politics*. London: Methuen. (A critical reading of Cixous's 'essentialism'.)

Sellers, S. (1988) *Writing Differences*, Milton Keynes: Open University Press. (A collection of textual readings by Cixous and her seminar participants. Includes interview.)

Shiach, M. (1992) *Hélène Cixous: The Politics of Writing*, London and New York: Routledge. (Focuses on the relations between feminism and writing. Deals with the theatre.)

VERENA ANDERMATT CONLEY

CLANDESTINE LITERATURE

Clandestine philosophical (anti-Christian) literature of the seventeenth century circulated in manuscript form until its publication by the philosophes in the later eighteenth century. Since research began, the list of texts has grown and now includes some 260 titles which cover the classical heritage of the Renaissance, the works of La Peyrère and Cyrano, the influence of Spinoza, the growth of rationalism which accompanied the splintering of Protestant churches and sects, and the development of the deist debate in Britain.

Clandestine philosophical literature has been considered a serious object of study since 1912 when G. Lanson discovered a number of manuscript copies of 'philosophical' (that is, anti-Christian) texts in French public libraries. The search for such texts was pursued by I.O. Wade (1938), stimulated by N.L. Torrey's work on Voltaire's library in St Petersburg. Wade thus put forward a list of 102 philosophical texts distributed between 1700 and 1750. These results have been extended by recent research, in particular by M. Benítez, and some 260 titles distributed in Europe from the sixteenth to the eighteenth century are now known. New discoveries will certainly be made and new texts revealed, as suggested by the catalogues of private libraries of that period. This literature raises questions for philosophy, intellectual history, apologetics, printing and the book-trade; it constitutes the roots of anti-Christian thought in the eighteenth century, and the texts of the prestigious *philosophes* of the Enlightenment must now be related to this intellectual context.

The development of this field of study has raised new problems. Research now covers the sixteenth, seventeenth and eighteenth centuries, and there is great risk of anachronism in the interpretation of early texts in relation to later events. Nevertheless, currents of thought can be defined which act as signposts from one century to the next: the clandestine philosophers of the eighteenth century regarded themselves as inheritors of a long anti-Christian and anti-ecclesiastical tradition.

In France, this anti-Catholic literature is not to be confused with Protestant, Socinian, Anabaptist or even Jansenist polemics, but the multiplication of sects and churches had an obvious effect on clandestine authors, who represent all possible positions in relation to Catholic orthodoxy (see SOCINIANISM). In this sense, the barrier between orthodoxy and heterodoxy becomes vague and confusing. Recent research on SPINOZA and the Dutch 'collegiants' (such as Bredenburg) has illustrated how philosophical rationalism was enriched by religious thought. A symmetrical development of philosophical ideas within Christian apologetics is evidence of prevalent uncertainty towards traditional barriers between deism and Christianity, belief and unbelief. The 'inner light' and the philosophical 'Enlightenment' enriched each other.

Similar relations can be discerned in the distribution of clandestine literature. The archives of the Bastille yield few names of clandestine philosophers, but reveal the full breadth of unorthodoxy and the full weight of the censorship prevalent in the seventeenth century. The successive waves of Huguenots and Jansenists are easy to discern: throughout the classical age book-pedlars and printers of political, religious or obscene pamphlets are imprisoned; the diffusion of philosophical ideas thus follows in the footsteps of other unorthodox currents of thought. Philosophical writings are distributed by specialists in political satire, in Marrano, Protestant and Jansenist propaganda. The history of clandestine ideas in Europe is thus closely linked to the history of the book-trade and censorship.

An important aspect of 'scribal publication' in the seventeenth century has been underlined by H. Love (1993). The manuscripts, of course, preceded the printed work, but they survived beyond the printing of the text (or rather, one version of the text) and continued to be amended and altered by subsequent scribes: in this sense, they are evidence of the evolution of philosophical ideas. Clandestine literature can thus be studied from the point of view of textual genetics: variants are to be interpreted not as mistakes, not as lessons unfaithful to the original, but as indications of a living and changing philosophy.

Clandestine philosophical literature reflects the main currents of intellectual history and reveals their significance for anti-Christian thought. Thus, in 1659 an enormous compendium of classical thought was constituted under the title *Theophrastus redivivus*, presenting the classical heritage in the form of extracts from ancient authors on a variety of crucial themes: the existence of the gods, the nature of the material world, the status of religion, the existence of the soul, the existence of hell, the consequences of physical death, the precepts of life according to Nature and so on. It is an anthology of free thought concocted from Ancient texts. At the same period, various versions of Cyrano de Bergerac's *L'Autre monde* were distributed, and Isaac La Peyrère composed his vast trilogy which leads us from the 'pre-Adamites' to the conversion of the Jews. A number of manuscripts reflect debates around the 'new philosophy' of Descartes and a dozen texts deal with aspects of Spinoza's philosophy. Clandestine philosophical literature of the end of the seventeenth century thus developed in the intellectual context of the rivalry between the 'systems' of DESCARTES, GASSENDI, HOBBES, MALEBRANCHE, Spinoza and LOCKE – and soon of LEIBNIZ. Machiavelli, Naudé, La Mothe Le Vayer, Hobbes, Vanini were systematically exploited, while MONTAIGNE and BAYLE were inexhaustible sources of plagiarism and imitation. The English context of debates around Deism weighed heavily on the evolution of French thought: Toland, COLLINS, Tindal, MANDEVILLE, Blount,

Middleton, Bolingbroke and Woolston were soon to be translated, as also were the Marranos Isaak de Troki and Orobio de Castro (see DEISM).

Clandestine philosophical literature can thus be interpreted within the context of the history of philosophical scepticism recently traced by R.H. Popkin and others. Central to this history in the seventeenth century was the rivalry between the Pyrrhonism inherited from Montaigne by La Mothe Le Vayer, Gassendi and Pascal and the rationalism developed by Descartes, Malebranche and Leibniz (see PYRRHONISM; RATIONALISM). The philosophy of the Enlightenment can thus be shown to derive from a crisis in Christian philosophy of the seventeenth century.

See also: LIBERTINS; PASCAL, B.

List of works

Bergerac, C. de (1657) *L'Autre monde ou les estats et empires de la lune* (The other world or the estates and empires of the moon), ed. M. Alcover, Paris: Champion, 1977; repr. Paris: Klincksiek, 1996. (Well-known imaginary voyage by a disciple of Gassendi.)

La Peyrère, I. (1643) *Du Rappel des Juifs* (Of the recalling of the Jews); *Systema theologicum ex Præadamitarum hypothesi* (Theological system drawn from the hypothesis of the pre-Adamites), 1655. (Original theological system built on the reinterpretation of the Old Testament as being the history of the Jewish nation only, and not of the whole of humanity.)

Theophrastus redivivus (1659), ed. G. Canziani and G. Paganini, Florence: Franco Angeli editore, 1981–2. (A compendium of classical thought in the form of extracts from ancient authors on a variety of crucial themes.)

References and further reading

Aylmer, G.E. (1982) 'Unbelief in 17th-century England', in D. Pennington and K. Thomas (eds), *Puritans and Revolutionaries: Essays in 17th-century History presented to Christopher Hill*, Oxford: O.U.P., 22–46. (Historical evidence to be read in the context of L. Febvre's well-known 1942 work *The Problem of Unbelief in the Sixteenth Century: The Religion of Rabelais*, trans. B. Gottlieb, Cambridge, MA: Harvard University Press, 1982.)

Benítez, M. (1988) 'Matériaux pour un inventaire des manuscrits philosophiques clandestins des XVIIe et XVIIIe siècles', *Rivista di storia della filosofia* 3:

501–31. (An inventory of 148 clandestine manuscripts and bibliography of recent work.)

—— (1995) *La Face cachée des Lumières. Recherches sur les manuscrits philosophiques clandestins de l'Age classique*, Oxford: The Voltaire Foundation; Paris: Universitas. (A new inventory of some 260 titles of clandestine works, an introduction dealing with the definition of clandestine philosophy and a collection of articles on materialism and pantheism in clandestine works.)

Berman, D. (1988) *The History of Atheism in England: from Hobbes to Russell*, London: Croom Helm. (Good general account covering Hobbes and the early English Deists.)

Bloch, O. (1982) *Le Matérialisme du XVIIIe siècle et la littérature clandestine*, Paris: Vrin. (Collection of articles dealing with a variety of clandestine manuscripts.)

Canziani, G. (ed.) (1994) *Filosofia e religione nella litteratura clandestina (secoli XVII e XVIII)*, Milan: Franco Angeli. (Collection of articles on clandestine literature, with two editions of clandestine texts.)

Gregory, T., Paganini, G., Canziani, G., Pompeo Faracovi, O. and Pastine, D. (eds) (1981) *Ricerche su letteratura libertina e letteratura clandestina nel Seicento*, Florence: La Nuova Italia. (Collection of articles dealing with seventeenth-century free thought.)

Kors, A.C. (1990) *Atheism in France, 1650–1729, vol. 1: The Orthodox sources of disbelief*, Princeton, NJ: Princeton University Press, 1990; vol. 2: *Naturalism and Disbelief*, Princeton, NJ: Princeton University Press, 1997. (An ambitious analysis of causes of unbelief, traced back to contradictions and uncertainties in Christian thought and followed through to the effects in clandestine literature.)

La Lettre clandestine: Bulletin d'information sur la littérature philosophique clandestine à l'âge classique (1992–), Paris: Saint-Etienne. (This journal, directed by O. Bloch and A. McKenna, appears annually and provides a current bibliography.)

* Lanson, G. (1912) 'Questions diverses sur l'histoire de l'esprit philosophique en France avant 1750', *Révue d'histoire littéraire de la France* 19: 1–29, 293–317. (Pioneer work in the discovery of clandestine manuscripts.)

* Love, H. (1993) *Scribal Publication in Seventeenth-Century England*, Oxford: Clarendon Press. (Details the prevalence of scribal publications in the seventeenth century in all fields of thought and the conclusions to be drawn by the modern editor from this method of diffusion.)

McKenna, A. and Mothu, A. (eds) (1997) *La Littérature clandestine: Actes du colloque de Saint-Etienne, octobre 1993*, Oxford: The Voltaire Foundation; Paris, Universitas. (Papers from a conference on clandestine literature: a variety of manuscripts are analysed.)

Popkin R. (1979) *The History of Scepticism from Erasmus to Spinoza*, Berkeley and Los Angeles, CA, and London: University of California Press. (The first general account of the influence of Pyrrhonism in the seventeenth century: Pyrrho, Sextus Empiricus, Montaigne and the early editions and translations; reaction of the 'libertins érudits' and Counter-Reformation, leading first to Descartes', then to Spinoza's anti-Pyrrhonist rationalism.)

—— (1990) *The Third Force in 17th century Philosophy*, Leiden: Brill. (A collection of essays dealing with Millenarianism in the seventeenth century and its influence on contemporary philosophical thought.)

Popkin, R. and Vanderjagt, A. (1993) *Scepticism and Irreligion in the Seventeenth and Eighteenth centuries*, Leiden: Brill. (A collection of essays detailing recent research on the history of free thought.)

* Torrey, N.L. (1930) *Voltaire and the English Deists*, Yale University Press; repr. Oxford: Marston Press, 1963. (First systematic study of this important question, through Voltaire's library in Leningrad.)

* Wade, I.O. (1938) *The Clandestine Organisation and Diffusion of Philosophic ideas in France from 1700 to 1750*, Princeton, NJ: Princeton University Press; New York: Octagon, 1967. (A first inventory of 102 clandestine manuscript titles in France.)

ANTONY McKENNA

CLAREMBALD OF ARRAS (1110/20–*c*.1187)

A teacher of philosophy at Laon and commentator on Boethius, Clarembald was a product of the School of Chartres. His principal philosophical work, the Tractatulus *(Short Treatise on Genesis), is an attempt to link Platonic theories of creation with the account given in Scripture, and includes a discussion of the nature of form and matter.*

Clarembald most likely was born between 1110 and 1120. He studied at Paris under THIERRY OF CHARTRES and HUGH OF ST VICTOR in the late 1130s, and directed the schools of Laon for a short while around 1160. Most of his life, however, was an active one: he was provost and archdeacon of the diocese of Arras, and was chaplain in Laon during the last years of his life.

Clarembald's principal philosophic work links him to the school of Chartres. He wrote an introductory letter to Thierry of Chartres' *De sex dierum operibus* (On the Works of the Six Days of Creation) and a *Tractatulus* (Short Treatise on Genesis). In the introductory letter, Clarembald claims credit only for the special effort he has made in his *Tractatulus* 'to reconcile many views of the philosophers with the Christian truth so that the word of Scripture might receive strength and protection even from its adversaries.'

The *Tractatulus* thus attempts to reconcile the portion of Plato's *Timaeus* that was translated and commented on by Calcidius with the message of Genesis as interpreted by Ambrose, Augustine, Isidore of Seville and Bede. The scriptural account, according to Clarembald, does not conflict with philosophical explanations of order in the world. The opening words of Genesis, 'In the beginning God created heaven and earth', bring out the deeper meaning of philosophical arguments. They provide an introduction, even for pagans and non-believers, to a knowledge of the Creator. The world (heaven and earth) is made up of contrary elements: hot ones and cold ones, moist ones and dry ones. It is either nature, chance or a maker that has joined together these opposed elements. Nature cannot produce such an order, since it unites only things that are alike; neither can chance produce such a universe, since chance presupposes already existing causes that come together to produce an unexpected happening. These causes thus would be prior to chance, the agent that allegedly joins them together. The only cause capable of uniting these contrary elements into an ordered whole is their maker, the Creator who brought these elements into existence.

The Genesis account adds that 'the earth was void and empty'. AUGUSTINE (§8) speaks of the primordial matter as 'formlessness', or the capacity to receive a form. PLATO (§16) describes the same formless matter as that which exists between nothingness and substance. His pupil ARISTOTLE (§12) at times calls this *aptitudo* (ability), and at times *carentia* (lack of form). We grasp it, according to Clarembald, by removing forms. When we remove from a formed object its forms, then nothing remains but the potential to receive these forms. If we take away the form of a brass statue, for example, then only the brass is left; if we strip the brass of its properties, then only the element of earth remains. If we remove the characteristics of earth (dryness and frigidity), then that which remains is not nothing, but formless matter. Such formless primordial matter is called by

the philosophers *possibilitas* (potency), since it is capable of receiving all forms. When it receives such forms, then it becomes *possibilitas definita* (specified possibility) (see MATTER).

Formless matter does not receive its forms from itself, but from what the philosophers call *necessitas absoluta* (absolute necessity). 'Absolute necessity', according to Clarembald, is what BOETHIUS calls 'Divine Providence', what Augustine names 'Word' or 'Divine Wisdom' and what PYTHAGORAS describes as 'One'. 'Divine Wisdom' implants *rationes seminales* (seminal reasons) in the formless matter and it is by means of them that things reproduce other things of the same kind. These seminal reasons, or what the philosophers call *similitudines nascendi* (reproductive likenesses), account for the normal course of nature (see AUGUSTINE).

Clarembald's earlier commentaries on Boethius' *De trinitate* (On the Trinity) and *De hebdomadibus* (On the Groups of Seven) already make many of the philosophic points he develops in the *Tractatulus*, but they also reveal his view of the nature of a properly conceived and formulated *quaestio* (question) (Commentary on *De trinitate* Prol. 5–14), his theory of the categories (Commentary on *De trinitate* 4, 1–46), the distinction between dialectical, demonstrative and sophistical syllogisms (Commentary on *De hebdomadibus* i, 1–2), and his interpretation of Boethius' different levels of abstraction (Commentary on *De trinitate* 2, 17–9). Although strongly influenced by THIERRY OF CHARTRES and HUGH OF ST VICTOR, Clarembald was on theological issues also a strong critic of Peter ABELARD and a more cautious opponent of GILBERT OF POITIERS.

See also: CHARTRES, SCHOOL OF; THIERRY OF CHARTRES

List of works

Clarembald of Arras (*c.*1157) *Tractatus super librum Boetii De trinitate* (Exposition of Boethius' *De trinitate*), in N.M. Häring in *Life and Works of Clarembald of Arras*, Toronto, Ont.: Pontifical Institute of Mediaeval Studies, 1965. (Contains his description of a correctly formulated *quaestio* or question, and his interpretation of Aristotle's ten categories.)

—— (*c.*1158) *Expositio super librum Boetii De hebdomadibus* (Commentary on Boethius' *De hebdomadibus*), in N.M. Häring, *Life and Works of Clarembald of Arras*, Toronto, Ont.: Pontifical Institute of Mediaeval Studies, 1965. (Contains his understanding of dialectical, demonstrative and sophistical syllogisms.)

—— (c.1160s) *Tractatulus* (Short Treatise on Genesis), in N.M. Häring, *Life and Works of Clarembald of Arras*, Toronto, Ont.: Pontifical Institute of Mediaeval Studies, 1965. (Clarembald's short commentary on Genesis.)

References and further reading

Häring, N.M. (1955) 'The Creation and Creator of the World according to Thierry of Chartres and Clarenbaldus of Arras', *Archives d'histoire doctrinale et litteraire du moyen-âge* 22: 137–216. (Clarembald's account of creation.)

STEPHEN F. BROWN

CLARKE, SAMUEL (1675–1729)

Regarded in his lifetime along with Locke as the leading English philosopher, Clarke was best known in his role as an advocate of a thoroughgoing natural theology and as a defender of Newtonianism, most notably in his famous correspondence with Leibniz. His natural theology was set out in his Boyle lectures of 1704 and 1705, but it left little room for revelation, and endeared him to neither side in the quarrel between deists and orthodox Anglicans. A staunch proponent of Newtonian natural philosophy, he defended it against criticisms of its notions of gravity and absolute space.

1   Natural theology
2   Doctrine of the soul
3   Defence of Newton

1   Natural theology

Samuel Clarke was born at Norwich, England, and studied at Gonville and Caius College, Cambridge, where he remained until 1700. He was a fine classicist and while still a student he published a Latin translation of the standard Cartesian natural philosophy textbook of the time, Rohault's *Traité de Physique*, which replaced the inferior translation of Théophile Bonnet (see ROHAULT, J.). In 1697 he was converted to the cause of Arianism, and from this time until his death in 1729 – after many years as rector of St James's, Westminster and chaplain to Queen Anne – he devoted his main energies to the development of a natural theology.

Among the key theological issues within the Anglican Church at this time were an internal dispute between defenders of the Athanasian Creed (which established the notion of the Trinity) and Arians, and an external dispute between Anglicans and deists. Arianism or unitarianism had significant support within rationalist theology in England in the late seventeenth and early eighteenth centuries. Deism – the notion that there is a natural religion with precedence over any revealed religion – had become a significant force with the posthumous publication of the works of Charles Blount (1654–93) in 1695, and reached its apogee in the 1730s. English deists, unlike French Enlightenment writers, generally considered themselves Christians, with the result that the distance between deists and writers like Clarke, who defended natural theology at the expense of revelation, was sometimes very small.

Clarke's aim was to reconstruct religion and ethics on the basis of natural philosophy and natural theology. His proof of the existence of God is a version of the cosmological argument. Its core is that if something exists now, something always must have existed because things cannot come into existence from nothing; but what it is that always has existed must be 'self-existent', that is, it must depend on nothing else for its existence; and what is self-existent is necessarily existent. All these steps are questionable but, even if supposed valid, the argument establishes a very abstract God rather than a personal God who is moral, just and truthful. Consequently Clarke needed to bridge the gap between this God and the God of Christianity (even in its unitarian version).

His account of God harbours a deep and familiar problem. On the one hand, God is completely free, and orders the world in a way that is constrained by nothing, for nothing could constrain such a perfect being. On the other hand, goodness and truth are not arbitrary, and in particular God's action must reflect natural standards of truth and goodness rather than instantiate such standards arbitrarily. Clarke attempts to reconcile these principles by means of a doctrine of the 'fitness of things', whereby nature has a moral aspect which mirrors its physical aspect, moral and physical aspects both being knowable by reason. The idea is that any rational being will guide its conduct in terms of these moral principles. Since God is completely rational, he follows them of necessity, but we are also influenced by passions which act against reason and cause us to behave immorally on occasion, and it is from this that the need for established religions arises.

2   Doctrine of the soul

The Boyle Lectures were set up – on a bequest of £50 per annum from Boyle – to counter deism, Hobbesianism, atheism and other unorthodox views, and in his Boyle Lectures for 1705 Clarke attacked what he perceived to be the reductionism of Hobbesian and Spinozistic accounts of mind (see DEISM §2; HOBBES, T. §3; SPINOZA, B. §§5–6). The problem had come to the fore because of Locke's passing statement that it is not inconceivable that God could 'superadd to matter the faculty of thinking' (see LOCKE, J. §5). Like other critics of Locke, Clarke believed that this was tantamount to materialism. His response was to deny that perception and intelligence can derive from matter – either reductively or in virtue of a combination of matter and motion – on the grounds that only what possesses a perfection can cause or communicate it: something that lacks the perfection of thought cannot produce this perfection in something else.

Two critics took Clarke to task – Henry Dodwell and Anthony Collins. Collins, in particular, accuses Clarke of failing to distinguish between the powers of the parts of matter and the powers of organized combinations of parts: the latter powers are different from the former and serve to explain thought and action. Clarke denies that there can be powers in the whole that are not powers of the parts, distinguishing various kinds of genuine from non-genuine properties of things: colours, for example, seem to be properties of the whole but not the part, yet they are in fact not genuine properties of the object at all. Collins accuses Clarke of asserting that the whole cannot have powers lacking in its parts, whereas he should be demonstrating it. The question is not simply one of onus of proof, however, for Clarke himself subsequently admits that something can have qualities or powers, such as roundness, which are not present in its parts. But consciousness, he maintains, is not like this: it is a power which must inhere in the parts if it is to be present at all (see COLLINS, A. §§3–4).

The dispute is inconclusive, but it hard to avoid the conclusion that Clarke set off on the wrong foot in denying that whole and parts can have different properties, and the claim that consciousness must be in all of the parts is not supported by any compelling argument.

3 Defence of Newton

Clarke is often praised for the way in which his notes to his translation of Rohault undermine Rohault's Cartesianism in favour of a Newtonian account. But in fact the notes to the first edition are very uncritical, accepting the vortex theory and making no mention of gravitation. It was only in later editions that the notes took on a Newtonian edge, and by that time Newton's *Principia* had a wide circulation. Clarke was, however, an able defender of Newtonianism in the 1700s, being the first to distinguish clearly between momentum and kinetic energy, and he was chosen to respond to Leibniz's accusation that the ideas of Newton and Locke were responsible for the decline of religion in England (see LEIBNIZ, G.W. §11).

Some of the questions at issue between Clarke and Leibniz are on points of interpretation, as in Leibniz's rejection of Newton's claim that space is simply God's *sensorium*. Leibniz points out that if God needed an organ to perceive things, those things could not depend on him, and Clarke replies by construing Newton's doctrine as meaning that God is omnipresent and so, far from requiring sense organs, has unmediated perceptual grasp. Other disputes involve substantive questions in natural philosophy, and the fundamentals of Leibniz's philosophy – notably his principles of sufficient reason and the identity of indiscernibles – are called into question. Many of the issues in the dispute are essentially continuations of the clash between Cartesian and Newtonian natural philosophy. Descartes had provided a model in which planets were carried around a centrally rotating sun by the swirling motion of the ether around this sun, an account which dispensed with any need for action at a distance. This is essentially the account that Leibniz defends, and Clarke defends both the existence of a void (which undermines the idea of a swirling ether) and action at a distance, which he points out has been shown to exist, even if its causes have not been discovered.

Other questions in dispute raise new problems, and a key issue is the nature of space and time. Leibniz considered these to be relations, and hence to be relative, whereas Clarke considered them to be real and absolute. Newton had considered that, although we cannot tell of any inertial state whether it is a state of rest or a state of uniform rectilinear motion, there is a way in which we can detect the existence of absolute space, and he believed that the concave deformation of the surface of water in a rotating bucket can only be explained by a rotation relative to absolute space (see NEWTON, I. §3). Leibniz did not accept that the idea of absolute space made sense, for in such a space no part is different from any other, and there would be no reason for God to create things in one place rather than another. Clarke's response is effectively that God does not need sufficient reason: God creates through an act of will. Moreover, points in space are not merely relational: they have real properties that distinguish them from one another, as the bucket experiment indicates. Clarke is in a strong position here, and the challenge to Leibniz is to indicate how differences in inert forces can be explained except by reference to space and time.

List of Works

Clarke, S. (1738) *The Works of Samuel Clarke*, London: John & Paul Knapton, 4 vols; repr. New York: Garland, 1978. (This edition contains everything of any philosophical or theological significance by Clarke – except his notes on Rohault – and provides useful biographical material.)

—— (ed.) (1697) *Jacobi Rohaulti Physica, Latine reddit et annotatiunculis quibusdam illustravit S. Clarke...*, London: Jacob Knapton. (Latin translation of Rohault's *Physics* with notes by Clarke; subsequent editions appeared in 1708 and 1718).

References and further reading

Alexander, H.G. (1956) *The Leibniz–Clarke Correspondence*, Manchester: Manchester University Press. (Contains a useful introduction and notes to the translation of this exchange.)

* Blount, C. (1695) *The Miscellaneous Works of Charles Blount*, London, 1697; repr. New York: Garland, 1979. (Blount's attacks, in the 1680s on the necessity for miracles, and his call for a natural religion devised by lay people, are generally seen as marking the beginnings of deism in England.)

Priestly, F.E.L. (1970) 'The Clarke–Leibniz Controversy', in R.W. Butts and J.W. Davis (eds.), *The Methodological Heritage of Newton*, Oxford: Blackwell. (Clear account of the controversy.)

Ray, C. (1991) *Time, Space and Philosophy*, London: Routledge. (Chapter 5 looks at the Leibniz–Clarke controversy with an eye to its implications for later developments in physical theory.)

Reventlow, H.G. (1985) *The Authority of the Bible and the Rise of the Modern World*, Philadelphia, PA: Fortress Press, II, ch. 3. (A good account of the context of Clarke's natural theology.)

Yolton, J. (1984) *Thinking Matter*, Oxford: Blackwell. (Chapter 2 deals with the Clarke–Collins dispute.)

STEPHEN GAUKROGER

CLASSICAL FIELD THEORY
see FIELD THEORY, CLASSICAL

CLASSICAL MECHANICS
see MECHANICS, CLASSICAL

CLASSIFICATION *see* TAXONOMY

CLAUBERG, JOHANNES (1622–65)

Johannes Clauberg was a member of the Cartesian school in the years immediately following Descartes' death, and is extremely important as an early expositor of Descartes and a spirited defender of the Cartesian philosophy. His writings include a number of direct commentaries on Descartes' published works, as well as extensions and elaborations of the master's views.

Clauberg was born to Protestant parents in Solingen, Westphalia. He studied at Bremen, then at Groningen, where the Cartesian Tobias Andraea and the anti-Cartesian Martinus Schoock both taught. In 1646 he visited France and England, and in the late 1640s he studied at the University of Leiden, where he attended the lectures of the Cartesian Johannes de Raey. Clauberg's *Elementa philosophiae sive ontosophia*, published in 1647 although probably written in 1645, was a defence of Aristotelian metaphysics against Ramist attacks, and contains nothing recognizably Cartesian (see RAMUS, P). While it is not impossible that he met Descartes himself, he was probably converted to Cartesianism by either Andraea or de Raey before April 1648, when he transcribed the notes of a conversation between Descartes and the young theologian Frans Burman. In 1649, at the request of Count Louis Henry of Nassau, he was appointed professor of philosophy and theology at the University of Herborn in Germany, where he taught Cartesianism for two years in the face of considerable opposition. The count tried to stabilize Clauberg's position by writing to some Dutch universities for their opinions on the new Cartesian philosophy, and while there were some positive responses, they were too few and too late to make a difference. In 1651, along with the Cartesian Christopher Wittich who was his school friend from Groningen days, Clauberg left Herborn for the University of Duisburg, where he taught until his death.

Clauberg's *Logica vetus et nova* (1654) was an attempt to combine the principles of traditional logic with those of a 'Cartesian' logic, something not unlike what Arnauld was to do in the Port-Royal logic a few years later, despite the fact that Descartes himself rejected the enterprise of formal logic (see ARNAULD, A. §2; PORT-ROYAL). His *Metaphysica de ente* (1664), sometimes mistaken for a second edition of his earlier *Elementa philosophiae sive ontosophia*, was in reality a completely separate work, presenting a metaphysics in scholastic style but with Cartesian content. Its subject matter was the science of being as such. Clauberg treated the notions of being, essence, existence, the One, the True, the Good and so on – all found in traditional Aristotelian treatises on metaphysics. However, Clauberg's metaphysics was grounded in the Cartesian distinction between mind and body, which he takes to replace the ten Aristotelian categories as the highest division of things into classes. Again, this is somewhat paradoxical, since Descartes himself seemed to reject the idea of a metaphysics in the sense of a science of being as such. His logic and metaphysics in particular earned Clauberg the reputation of the learned Cartesian, and his presentation of Cartesian ideas in scholastic form, complete with scholarly references, probably eased the way for Descartes' philosophy in the German universities.

Of particular philosophical interest is his *Physica* (1664), a collection of treatises including one on living things and another on the union between mind and body. Like other Cartesians writing in this decade, including the French circle of Cartesians (CORDEMOY, LA FORGE, Clerselier and so on), with whom he was probably in contact, Clauberg put forward a kind of occasionalism (see OCCASIONALISM). First, matter as such is inert, and God is the only genuine efficient cause of motion in the physical world; like Descartes, Clauberg held that the soul or mind, a substance whose essence is thought, is really distinct from body, a substance whose essence is extension. But unlike Descartes, he held that the two are not genuine ('physical') causes of changes in one another, and that mind and body are united simply by virtue of the quasi-causal relations between them. The mind is what he called a 'moral cause' of changes in the body; mind does not create new motion, but only changes the direction of the motion already there, otherwise the Cartesian law of the conservation of quantity of motion would be violated. Conversely, body, being less noble than mind, is only the 'procatarctic cause' of ideas in the mind, giving mind the 'occasion to have these or those ideas, which it always has the power to have within it'.

See also: DESCARTES, R.

List of works

Clauberg, J. (1691) *Opera Omnia Philosophica* (Collected philosophical works), Amsterdam, 2 vols; repr. Hildesheim: Olms Verlag, 1968. (A collection of virtually all Clauberg's philosophical writings, as well as a biographical sketch of the author, all in Latin. Since this edition includes many notes and comments not in the originals, it must be used with care.)

—— (1647) *Elementa philosophiae sive ontosophia* (The elements of philosophy, that is, the ontosophia), Gronigen. (An early Aristotelian treatise on metaphysics, not reprinted in the *Opera Omnia*.)

—— (1652) *Defensio Cartesiana adversus Jacobum Revium* (A defence of Descartes against Jacob Revius), Amsterdam; repr. in *Opera Omnia Philosophica*, Hildesheim: Olms Verlag, 1968, vol. 2. (A contribution to a controversy at the University of Leiden over Descartes' philosophy, this also is a close discussion and defence of Descartes' *Discourse on the Method*.)

—— (1654) *Logica vetus et nova (Logic, old and new)*, Amsterdam; repr. in *Opera Omnia Philosophica*, Hildesheim: Olms Verlag, 1968, vol. 2. (An attempt to combine the principles of traditional logic with those of a 'Cartesian' logic. A second edition was published in 1658.)

—— (1655) *Initiatio Philosophi sive dubitatio cartesiana* (An initiation into philosophy, or, Cartesian doubt), Duisburg; repr. in *Opera Omnia Philosophica*, Hildesheim: Olms Verlag, 1968, vol. 2. (A commentary on and defence of Cartesian doubt as a starting-place for philosophy.)

—— (1656) *De Cognitione Dei et nostri… Exercitationes centum* (One-hundred exercises concerning the knowledge of God and of ourselves), Duisburg; repr. in *Opera Omnia Philosophica*, Hildesheim: Olms Verlag, 1968, vol. 2. (Largely a commentary on Descartes' views concerning God and the mind, it also contains assorted lectures and disputations on related subjects.)

—— (1657) *Unterschejd zwischen den Cartesianischen, und der sonst in Schulen gebräuchlichen Philosophie Beschriebene* (The difference between the Cartesian philosophy and that normally used in the schools), Duisburg; repr. in *Opera Omnia Philosophica*, Hildesheim: Olms Verlag, 1968, vol. 2. (This may have been written originally for the examination of Cartesianism at Herborn in 1651. It appeared in Latin translation in 1680.)

—— (1658) *Paraphrasis in Renati Descartes meditationes de prima Philosophia* (Paraphrase of René Descartes' *Meditations on First Philosophy*), Duisburg; repr. in *Opera Omnia Philosophica*, Hildesheim: Olms Verlag, 1968, vol. 1. (A virtual reprint of Descartes' Meditations, with extensive commentary.)

—— (1664) *Physica quibus rerum corporearum vis et natura, Mentis ad Corpus relatae proprietates, denique Corporis ac Mentis arcta et admirabilis in Homine conjunctio explicantur* (The Physics, in which is explained the force and nature of corporeal things, the properties of the mind as it relates to the body, and finally the close and wondrous connection between the mind and the body in man), Amsterdam; repr. in *Opera Omnia Philosophica*, Hildesheim: Olms Verlag, 1968, vol. 1. (A collection of shorter treatises, including the *Physica contracta* (The short physics), the *Disputationes quibus principia Physica latius explicantur* (Physical disputations in which the principles of physics are explained more fully), the *Theoria corporum viventium* (The theory of living bodies), and the *Corporis et animae in homine conjunctio* (The connection between body and soul in man).)

—— (1664) *Metaphysica de ente quae rectius Ontosophia (Metaphysics concerning being, more properly called ontosophia)*, Amsterdam; repr. in *Opera Omnia Philosophica*, Hildesheim: Olms Verlag, 1968, vol. 1. (There may have been an earlier edition of this published in 1660. Despite the similarity of the titles, this is *not* a second edition of the 1647 work.)

References and further reading

Balz, A.G.A. (1951) 'Clauberg and the Development of Occasionalism', in *Cartesian Studies*, New York: Columbia University Press. (A study of Clauberg with special attention to his occasionalism.)

Bohatec, J. (1912) *Die Cartesianische Scholastik in der Philosophie und Theologie der reformierten Dogmatik des 17. Jahrhunderts*, Leipzig: Deichert. (Classic work on Cartesianism in Protestant thought, in which Clauberg plays an important role.)

Menk, G. (1985) "Omnis novitas est periculosa': Der frühe Cartesianismus an der Hohen Schole Herborn (1649-1651) und die reformierte Geisteswelt nach dem dreißigjährigen Krieg', in K. Schaller (ed.) *Comenius: Erkennen, Glauben, Handeln*, St. Augustin: Richarz, 1985. (A very good account in German of Clauberg's early years, as well as a discussion of the crisis over Cartesianism at Herborn in 1651.)

Trevisani, F. (1992) *Descartes in Germania*, Milan: FrancoAngeli. (A careful study of Cartesianism in the seventeenth century at the University of Duisburg, where Clauberg taught.)

Verbeek, T. (1992) *Descartes and the Dutch: Early Reactions to Cartesian Philosophy, 1637–1650*, Carbondale, IL: Southern Illinois University Press. (A general study of Dutch Cartesianism, in which Clauberg plays a significant role.)

Weier, W. (1970) 'Cartesianischer Aristotelismus im siebzehnten Jahrhundert', *Salzburger Jahrbuch für Philosophie* 14: 35–65. (A study of Clauberg as an example of the attempt to combine elements of Aristotelian and Cartesian thought.)

—— (1982) 'Der Okkasionalismus des J. Clauberg

und sein Verhältnis zu Descartes, Geulincx, Malebranche', *Studia Cartesiana* 2: 43–62. (A study of Clauberg's occasionalism.)

DANIEL GARBER

CLEANTHES (331–232 BC)

The Greek philosopher Cleanthes of Assos played a leading role in the formation of Stoicism. He was at once the most physicalist and the most religious of the Stoics. Pupil, and eventual successor (in 262), of the school's founder Zeno, he wrote numerous philosophical works, including some poetry. In particular, he developed the notion of fire as the world's governing principle.

Born at Assos in Asia Minor (modern Turkey), Cleanthes is said to have had his first career as a boxer. Moving to Athens, he joined the newly emerging Stoic school, led by ZENO OF CITIUM. Poverty forced him to work at night, drawing water, and to attend Zeno's classes during the day. He became Zeno's closest ally in the school, and in 262 BC succeeded him as its head. He died at a very advanced age, to be succeeded by CHRYSIPPUS.

Cleanthes was a prolific writer: we know the titles of some 57 works. Either in addition to these works, or more probably within them, he composed passages of philosophical poetry, of which his short but very powerful *Hymn to Zeus* survives intact. His philosophical outlook was distinctive in three strikingly different ways. (1) He was the most physicalist of the Stoics, with a special interest in the role of fire. (2) He was perhaps the main logician in the school's first generation, and was probably responsible for developing the key notion of the incorporeal *lekton* (see STOICISM §8). (3) He was the most deeply religious of Stoic thinkers.

Cleanthes, even more than other Stoics, revered HERACLITUS as an authority on cosmological matters. From Heraclitus he acquired and developed the doctrine of the primacy of fire, which he viewed as the vehicle of divine 'reason' (*logos*), varying according to its degree of 'tension'. Not only does the world begin and end in fire, as nearly all Stoics agreed (see STOICISM §5), but fire – which includes warmth – is the main creative force throughout nature. Here he was not in actual disagreement with other Stoics, but he was the school's leading fire theorist, while after him the emphasis shifted from fire to *pneuma*, which includes air as well as fire (see STOICISM §3).

Zeno had identified the virtues as various kinds or

aspects of wisdom – using a description which left the nature of their unity (see STOICISM §16) unclear. Cleanthes interpreted this as referring to a suitably tensioned 'stroke of fire' in the soul, constituting a kind of mental strength which, in different circumstances, comes to be called 'justice', 'courage' and so on. While not incompatible with the usual Stoic intellectualist view of virtue, this analysis has a strikingly physicalist emphasis. Similarly, where Zeno had called a mental impression (*phantasia*) a 'printing' in the soul, Cleanthes was criticized by his successor Chrysippus for treating this as a literal imprint, as if in wax.

Cleanthes' deeply religious temperament is evident from his *Hymn to Zeus*. There, uniquely among Stoics as far as we know, he enhances god's majesty by absolving him of willing the actions of the bad. Another symptom is his outrage at the contemporary astronomer Aristarchus, who alone in antiquity suggested that the earth might orbit the sun rather than vice versa, while revolving on its own axis. Cleanthes proposed that he be prosecuted for impiety, because his theory 'moved the world's hearth'. Yet he is also the author of some surprisingly rationalistic explanations of the origin of religion (Cicero, *On the Nature of the Gods* II 13–15).

Cleanthes' interest in logic is attested by the solution he provided to the Master Argument (see DIODORUS CRONUS §5), which was being used to argue for the necessity of the future. He responded by rejecting its premise 'Every past truth is necessary', perhaps on the ground that present and future events determine the truth-value of past predictions.

References and further reading

Arnim, H. von (1903–5) *Stoicorum Veterum Fragmenta* (Fragments of the Early Stoics), Leipzig: Teubner, with vol. 4, indexes, by M. Adler, 1924. (The standard collection of early Stoic fragments, in Greek and Latin, commonly abbreviated as *SVF*; Cleanthes is in volume 1, 103–39.)

* Cicero (45 BC) *On the Nature of the Gods*, trans. H. Rackham, Loeb Classical Library, Cambridge, MA: Harvard University Press and London: Heinemann, 1933. (Latin text with English translation. Book II is an eloquent presentation of Stoic theology; see 13–15, 24, 40–1 for Cleanthes' contributions.)

* Cleanthes (331–232 BC) Fragments, in A.C. Pearson, *The Fragments of Zeno and Cleanthes*, Cambridge: Cambridge University Press, 1891. (Still useful, but mainly for specialists.)

Long, A.A. (1975–6) 'Heraclitus and Stoicism', *Philosophia* 5–6: 133–56; repr. in A.A. Long, *Stoic Studies*, Cambridge: Cambridge University Press, 1996, 35–57. (Includes much on Cleanthes' debt to his favourite Presocratic.)

Solmsen, F. (1968) 'Cleanthes or Posidonius? The Basis of Stoic Physics', in F. Solmsen, *Kleine Schriften*, Hildesheim: Olms, vol. 1, 436–60. (On Cleanthes' theory of vital heat.)

DAVID SEDLEY

CLEMENT OF ALEXANDRIA (AD 150–215)

Clement of Alexandria, a Christian Platonist, came to conversion through philosophy. In a series of allusive writings he presented a Hellenized Christianity along with the philosophical syncretism of his age: Stoic ethics, Aristotelian logic and especially Platonic metaphysics. Just as Paul saw the Hebrew prophets and law as a preparation for the Gospel, Clement saw Christianity as making possible a confluence of Plato and the Old Testament, both offering anticipations of Jesus' teaching. Clement's fusion of Platonism and Christianity vehemently opposed the dualism and determinism of gnostic theosophy, and stressed free choice and responsibility as fundamental to moral values. Central to his writing is the vindication of faith as the foundation for growth in religious knowledge by philosophical contemplation and biblical study.

Clement's principal works are *Protreptikos* (Exhortation to Conversion) attacking polytheism, *Paidagogos* (Moral Tutor) on etiquette and Christian ethics, and above all the *Stromateis* (Miscellany), left incomplete. The eighth and last book of *Stromateis*, Clement's commonplace work on logic and epistemology, was not part of the original plan. He intended to make the third work in his trilogy a systematic statement of religious philosophy entitled *Didaskalos* (Teacher), but wisely, since it would have been controversial, he never wrote it.

The *Stromateis* touches elusively on profound issues but then changes the subject. The reader is invited to participate in the quest for religious truth, granted to those who strenuously search but also receive divine help. If one had to make a choice between eternal salvation and continuing growth in the knowledge of God, one would certainly choose the latter (a saying plagiarized without acknowledgement by G.E. Lessing in *Duplik*).

Platonic language appears in Clement's theme of the mysteriousness of faith in God. Echoes of Plato's seventh letter are heard in his diffidence about putting advanced theology into writing, and the third book of the *Republic* provides his model for attacks on the clever and conceited who scorn such topics.

Clement's objective is to defend educated Christians who see no reason to jettison good philosophy merely because they have renounced the world, the flesh and the devil. Many in the Church were suspicious of philosophers because of the appeal made to them by gnostic sects claiming to offer a higher understanding (*gnosis*). The 'orthodox' (Clement uses the word with an ironical touch) were confident that faith alone sufficed for salvation. Some asserted (following Enoch 16:3) that philosophy was the invention of the devil, transmitted to humanity through the fallen angels' mating with women. Clement noticed that even this negative notion implicitly conceded that in philosophy, perhaps in confused form, there was heavenly truth. He was sure that Plato on God's transcendence, on the aspiration that the soul be 'as like God as possible' and on the goal of the vision of God (as in *Phaedrus*) was so close to Christian faith as to be virtually indistinguishable. The Stoics, on the therapy of the emotions and on the absolutes of the moral life, were similarly stating what he knew to be true. Here Clement owed much to PHILO OF ALEXANDRIA, especially for the thesis that philosophy prepares the mind for theology just as the liberal arts prepare it for philosophy.

How the philosophers succeeded in getting so much right was a question with more than one possible answer. Clement's main answer is that all human beings, being made in God's image, possess a 'shared mind', a 'natural conception' as the Stoics had put it, and so have a universal intuition for God and for virtue and righteousness. The philosophers' ability to 'reflect the truth' may therefore be ascribed to the exercise of natural endowment. Moreover, there can be special inspiration imparted to selected individuals; that this inspiration is Christian in nature is evident from Jesus' parable of the sower.

Philo and NUMENIUS of Apamea had earlier supposed that Plato had been able to get so much right because of his studies in the writings of Moses, who could be shown by chronographers to have lived centuries earlier. Clement develops at length the theme of Greek plagiarism from barbarian traditions, inverting an argument deployed against Christianity by the pagan Platonist CELSUS, whose work *Alethes Logos* (The True Account) Clement probably knew. Celsus also thought the oldest and most venerable religious tradition was to be found among primeval barbarian peoples uncorrupted by civilization. Clement was not therefore implausible to his contemporaries in suggesting that classical philosophy was dependent on older, non-Greek tradition for religious

truth; and such a lack of religious originality in Plato or PYTHAGORAS was, for him, no demerit.

The nature of faith was a problem never far from the centre of Clement's stage. It was under attack on one side from gnostics who scorned simple catechetical teaching (see GNOSTICISM); on the other side, educated pagans thought the Christian exhortation to 'believe' denied rational investigation and asked for mere submission to authority. Clement drily remarked that the latter method was a famous principle of no less a figure than Pythagoras. Religious faith he saw as related to natural assent. We assent, without a full prior inquiry, to the presuppositions of rational demonstration. We use the term 'faith' (*pistis*) for the state of satisfied conviction at the conclusion of a sound argument, or for the immediacy of assent to what our senses perceive. The word also contains some element of the commitment of loyalty to a cause or a person. In Christianity, faith is the necessary precondition of advance in the knowledge and love of God through meditation on the inner, symbolic, meaning of Scripture, linked to contemplation of higher things. Thereby the soul may be gradually freed from the distractions of passion and enabled to rise to the mystical vision of God.

Much technical Stoic and some Aristotelian language enters Clement's description of the conflict between reason and emotion. To live according to nature is to obey the Creator–Logos, Reason for all things, who for Clement is known in Christ and who is able to bring power to moderate the passions and, at the highest level of ascetic contemplation, suppress them. Passionlessness (*apatheia*) is synonymous with Plato's 'likeness to God', and with the perfection of which Jesus spoke in the sermon on the mount.

See also: FAITH; GNOSTICISM; ORIGEN; PLATONISM, EARLY AND MIDDLE; PLATONISM, MEDIEVAL

List of works

Clement of Alexandria (150–215) *Clemens Alexandrinus*, Leipzig: J.C. Hinrichs. (Standard Greek edition of Clement's works by O. Stählin, 4 vols with index, later reprints with revised text; includes the *Protreptikos*, *Paidogogos* and *Stromateis*.)

—— (150–215) *Protreptikos* (Exhortation to Conversion), trans. G.W. Butterworth in *Clement of Alexandria*, Cambridge, MA: Harvard University Press, 1919.

—— (150–215) *Stromateis* (Miscellany), vols 1–3 trans. J. Ferguson, Washington, DC: Catholic University Press, 1991. (There is also a translation by W. Wilson, consisting of all but *Stromateis* 3 on sex, in *The Writings of Clement of Alexandria*, Edinburgh: T. & T. Clark, vol. 4; repr. Grand Rapids, MI: Eerdmans, 1979, but this should be regarded as a brave failure; nevertheless, it is the only English translation of much of Clement.)

References and further reading

Bigg, C. (1913) *The Christian Platonists of Alexandria*, 2nd edn, Oxford: Clarendon Press. (A classic portrait of Clement and Origen.)

Chadwick, H. (1966) *Early Christian Thought and the Classical Tradition*, Oxford: Clarendon Press. (Covers the work of Justin, Clement and Origen.)

de Faye, E. (1906) *Clément d'Alexandrie* (Clement of Alexandria), 2nd edn, Paris: E. Leroux. (Standard liberal portrait.)

Lilla, S. (1971) *Clement of Alexandria: A Study in Christian Platonism and Gnosticism*, London: Oxford University Press. (The best study of Clement's middle Platonism.)

Osborn. E.F. (1957) *The Philosophy of Clement of Alexandria*, Cambridge: Cambridge University Press. (Systematic treatment.)

Spanneut, M. (1957) *Le Stoicisme des Pères de l'Église* (The Stoicism of the Church Fathers), Paris: Éditions du Seuil. (Clement's transformation of Stoic ethics.)

Wyrwa, D. (1983) *Die christliche Platonaneignung in den Stromateis des Clemens von Alexandrien* (Christian Platonism in the *Stromateis* of Clement of Alexandria), Berlin: de Gruyter. (Detailed examination of the appropriation of Platonic themes in the *Stromateis*.)

HENRY CHADWICK

CLEOMEDES (*c.* 2nd century AD)

Cleomedes was the author of On the Heavens, *a Greek treatise on elementary astronomy surviving from a larger exposition of Stoic philosophy. Its account of measurements of the earth, and its applications of Stoic epistemology and philosophy of science, make it important evidence on poorly documented subjects.*

Since Cleomedes refers to POSIDONIUS (*c.*135–*c.*50 BC), and conducts polemics against Peripatetics and Epicureans, he could not have been active much later than AD 200. *On the Heavens*, his presentation of elementary astronomy, is part of a larger exposition to which he himself alludes (see I 1.7, and I 1.94–5). Book I deals with celestial and terrestrial zones,

seasonal and climatic differences (I 1–4), the sphericity and centrality of the earth (I 5 and 6) and the earth's transparency in celestial observations (I 8). The account in I 7 of Posidonius' and Eratosthenes' measurements of the size of the earth is indispensable evidence for historians of science. The subjects of book II 1–3 are the size of the heavenly bodies, and in particular the Epicurean view that they are no larger than they appear, and lunar theory (II 4–6). A brief appendix (II 7) deals with planetary latitudes, elongations and periods. The work is non-technical, eschews discussion of the complexities of planetary motion and presents material in the stylized fashion typical of ancient elementary pedagogy.

In Byzantium and Renaissance Europe *On the Heavens* was exclusively used as a textbook of elementary astronomy. In the late nineteenth and early twentieth centuries scholars mined it for specific doctrines of Posidonius. But it is Posidonius' philosophy of science that is of the greatest significance for Cleomedes (see POSIDONIUS §6). Posidonius (fr. 18) had defined astronomy as a science subordinate to physical theory, and as employing the ancillary sciences of mathematics and geometry. Cleomedes' work may not precisely embody this programme, but it does fall within its general orbit. Thus it specifies the role of assumptions from physics and geometry in calculations of the size of the earth, sun and moon (I 7; II 1.282, 304–5). Also, the treatise opens by defining, with detailed supporting arguments, the physical context for spherical astronomy as the standard Stoic cosmology of a finite world in infinite void. Elsewhere the theories of the Stoic continuum play a much larger role than physical theory normally would in astronomical handbooks (see for example I 5.6–9, 126–38; I 6.40–3; I 8.79–99; II 4–). The epistemological problems raised by astronomical observations, to which Posidonius (fr. 18) also alludes, are reflected in references to the Stoic theory of the criterion of truth (I 5.1–6; II 1.1–4), and in the lengthy polemic in book II 1 against the Epicurean claim that the sun is no larger than it appears.

It may be unfortunate that Cleomedes' Stoicism is embedded in a survey of elementary astronomy, but in the absence of his other works, *On the Heavens* at least shows that the Stoicism of late antiquity was not, as has been traditionally thought, exclusively preoccupied with prescriptive ethics.

List of works

Cleomedes (*c.* 2nd century AD) *On the Heavens*, ed. R.B. Todd, *Cleomedis Caelestia*, Leipzig: Teubner; 1990; trans. R. Goulet, *Cléomède: Théorie*

Élémentaire, Paris: Vrin, 1980. (Respectively, Greek text and French translation with commentary.)

References and further reading

Barnes, J. (1989) 'The Size of the Sun in Antiquity', *Acta Classica* (Debrecen) XXV: 29–41. (A survey of the arguments in *On the Heavens*, II 1 in their wider context.)

Kidd, I.G. (1988) *Posidonius: II. The Commentary*, Cambridge: Cambridge University Press. (Includes important commentary on several Cleomedean texts.)

* Posidonius (*c.*135–*c.*50 BC) Fragments, in *Posidonius: I. The Fragments*, ed. L. Edelstein and I.G. Kidd, Cambridge: Cambridge University Press, 1989, 2nd edn. (This contains all the Cleomedean passages in which Posidonius is named, and is the edition from which the fragments (fr.) and testimonia (T) of Posidonius are cited.)

Todd, R.B. (1989) 'The Stoics and their Cosmology in the First and Second Centuries A.D.', in W. Haase (ed.) *Aufstieg und Niedergang der römischen Welt*, Berlin and New York: de Gruyter, II.36: 3, 1365–78. (On the wider historical context of *On the Heavens*.)

—— (1992) 'Cleomedes', *Catalogus Translationum et Commentariorum*, VII: 1–11. (A survey of Cleomedes' reception, with particular reference to the Renaissance.)

—— (forthcoming) 'Physics and Astronomy in Post-Posidonian Stoicism: The Case of Cleomedes', in W. Haase (ed.) *Aufstieg und Niedergang der römischen Welt*, Berlin and New York: de Gruyter, II.37: 5. (An analysis of the secondary literature on Cleomedes and an assessment of his relation to Posidonius.)

ROBERT B. TODD

COCKBURN, CATHARINE (1679–1749)

Catharine Cockburn (Catharine Trotter) was a British moral philosopher who turned to philosophy after a successful career as one of the first woman playwrights. She wrote no substantial systematic treatise of her own, but intervened ably and anonymously in philosophical and theological debates of her day, in particular the debate on ethical rationalism triggered by Samuel Clarke's 1704–5 Boyle lectures. Her adversaries included Thomas Rutherforth, William Warburton, Isaac Watts, Francis Hutcheson and Lord Shaftesbury. Her most famous contribution to the philosophy of her time was her able 1702 defence of Locke's Essay Concerning Human Understanding. *Her letters, published posthumously, discuss a range of philosophical topics.*

Born Catharine Trotter, in London of Scottish parentage, Cockburn appears to have been largely self-taught in philosophy. She was linked to circles around, first, the playwright William Congreve, and later Gilbert Burnet, Bishop of Salisbury. The latter may have been instrumental in persuading her to give up writing plays in favour of philosophy. After her marriage in 1708 to the Scottish clergyman Patrick Cockburn, the adverse pressures of rearing a family in reduced financial circumstances combined with deteriorating eyesight to hamper her pursuit of philosophy.

Throughout her writings Cockburn is consistent and nondogmatic in her philosophical position. Among the topics she discusses are necessary existence, infinite space, the idea of substance and the nature of spirit, but her main focus is on ethical questions, in particular the nature of virtue and of moral obligation. Opposing the ethical relativism of Hobbes, she argues that morality is neither arbitrary nor conventional in foundation (see HOBBES, T. §5). Against latter-day would-be defenders of morality, she denies that moral virtues exist in the abstract and that the obligation to virtue is founded in innate moral sense. Nor does moral obligation depend on externally imposed sanctions. Rather, moral obligation and the principles of moral conduct can be understood from the 'reason, nature and fitness of things' (1751a, vol. 2: 44). Human beings are rational and social beings, so for human beings to act in accordance with their own nature is to act rationally and for the good of all. By the exercise of reason we arrive at a knowledge of the principles of right and wrong from ideas of sensation and reflection. Having thus acquired a concept of goodness, we deduce that God is good and deserves our obedience, and that it is most fit for a reasonable being to act in conformity with God's moral perfections.

The outlines of the philosophical position from which Cockburn defended CLARKE are already evident in her defence of LOCKE in which she wrote 'I know no philosopher before him that has fixed morality upon so solid a foundation' (1702: 48). It is to her credit that, although she did not agree with Locke in all particulars, she defended him against misunderstandings and misreadings that imputed to him scepticism or deism, exposing the inconsistencies and fallacious arguments of his opponents: as she reminded his critics, 'the question is not what Mr. Locke thinks, but what may be proved upon his principles' (1702: 60). She rallied twice more to Locke's defence in *A Letter* (1826) and *Vindication* (1751b), defending his philosophy from charges that it undermined Christian orthodoxy.

Catherine Cockburn was recognized as an astute mind by her contemporaries, among them Locke, who gratefully acknowledged her defence of his philosophy. Leibniz, too, praised her writings, and she was dubbed 'Sappho Ecossoise' by Leibniz's patron, Sophie Charlotte of Hanover.

See also: HUTCHESON, F.; SHAFTESBURY

List of Works

Cockburn, C. (1751a) *The Works of Mrs Catharine Cockburn*, ed. T. Birch, London: J. and P. Knapton. (Collected philosophical writings, with extracts from letters and a biographical introduction.)

—— (1702) *A Defence of Mr Locke's Essay of Human Understanding*, London: W. Turner and J. Nutt. (Defence of Locke's *Essay*, published anonymously.)

—— (1726) *A Letter to Dr Holdworth . . . concerning the Resurrection of the same Body. In which the passages that concern Mr Locke are chiefly considered*, London: S. Motte. (Further defence of Locke.)

—— (1743) *Remarks upon Some Writers in the Controversy Concerning the Foundation of Moral Virtue and Moral Obligation*, London. (Defence of Samuel Clarke.)

—— (1747) *Remarks upon the Principles and Reasonings of Dr Rutherforth's Essay on the Nature and Obligations of Virtue, in Vindication of . . . the late Dr Samuel Clarke*, London: J. and P. Knapton. (Defends Samuel Clarke.)

—— (1751b) *Vindication of Mr Locke's Christian Principles*, in *The Works of Mrs Catharine Cockburn*, vol.1, ed. T. Birch, London. (Defends Locke on resurrection.)

References and further reading

Bolton, M. (1994) 'Aspects of the Philosophical Work of Catharine Trotter', *Journal of the History of Philosophy* 31: 565–88. (The only serious study of Cockburn's philosophy to date.)

Gosse, E. (1916) 'Catharine Trotter, Precursor to the Blue Stockings', *Transactions of the Royal Society of Literature* 34: 87–118; repr. in *Some Diversions of a Man of Letters*, London: William Heinemann, 1919. (Largely of literary interest.)

SARAH HUTTON

COERCION

Coercion (also called 'duress') is one of the basic exculpating excuses both in morality and in some systems of criminal law. Unlike various kinds of direct compulsion that give a victim no choice, a coercee is left with a choice, albeit a very unappealing one. They can do what is demanded, or can refuse, opting instead for the consequences, with which they are threatened. Sometimes courts find that the coercive threat that led the defendant to act as they did was objectively resistible by any person of reasonable fortitude, especially when the defendant's conduct was gravely harmful to others or to the state.

A proposal is an offer when it projects for the recipient's consideration a prospect that is welcome in itself, and not harmful or unwelcome beyond what would happen in the normal course of events. Coercive offers, according to some writers, are those that force a specific choice from the victim while actually enhancing their freedom. Some argue, however, that genuine coercion requires the active and deliberate creation of a vulnerability, and not mere opportunistic exploitation of a vulnerability discovered fortuitously.

1   Coercion and compulsion
2   Threats and offers
3   Coercive and noncoercive proposals
4   Coercion and exploitation

1   Coercion and compulsion

Coercion is a technique for forcing people to act as the coercer wants them to act, and presumably contrary to their own preferences. It usually employs a threat of some dire consequence if the actor does not do what the coercer demands, although it is controversial whether a non-threatening offer might in some contexts be coercive (see §2). There is a contrast between coercion, in which the victim can choose one or the other of the two alternatives allowed by the coercer (for example, 'your money or your life'), and what we might call compulsion, in which the victim has no choice at all, as for example when the victim is knocked unconscious and dragged away. In compulsion, options are closed by physical force, making alternatives to what the coercer demands physically impossible. In contrast, coercion does not destroy the preferred alternative as much as destroy its appeal by increasing its cost. The cost is the alternative specified in the coercer's threat.

2   Threats and offers

If such things as 'coercive offers' exist they must not,

by definition, be a species of threat, but rather be in essential contrast to the more typical instances of coercion which involve a demand enforced by a threat. Coercive offers would also be in contrast to the more familiar noncoercive inducement; attractive prospects which function as enticements that one 'cannot resist'. With few exceptions, philosophers have held that allegedly 'irresistible' attractiveness does not negate voluntariness or excuse the attracted party from responsibility.

The common genus of which threats and offers are species is that of preference-affecting proposals – those proposals not likely to be received with perfect indifference. To begin with, an offer is a proposal to contribute to a person something that they want or find welcome, something they would prefer having to not having. A threat, on the other hand, is a proposal to inflict something they would not welcome. But, threats and offers are more than 'proposals.' They also contain a reciprocation condition; a 'demand' in the case of threats, and a 'request' in the case of offers. These elements amount to the coercer's *quid pro quo*: 'what is in it for them'. In the case of coercive threats, at least, far more is in it for them than for the other party. This way of speaking makes it clear that credible threats in support of demands are a kind of contractual transaction, but a transaction so lopsided as to be unconscionable, involuntary on one side, and legally invalid.

One kind of preference-affecting proposal is a demand backed by a threat; another is a request backed by an inducement. Both of these can be construed as typically biconditional in form: the action that A requests or demands from B is taken to be both a necessary and a sufficient condition of A's reciprocation: 'I will do x to (or for) you *if and only if* you will do y for me'. A's offer of $11,000 for B's car thus translates:

(1) If you give me your car, I will give you $11,000.
(2) If you do not give me your car, I will not give you $11,000.

The first preference-affecting proposal (1) – 'I will give you $11,000' – is obviously an offer. The second – 'I will not give you $11,000' – is not an offer, but neither is it a threat. 'I will not give you $11,000' would count as a threat only if the speaker paid that amount regularly and was now proposing to withhold it, thus disappointing the other party's natural expectation. Since the proposal is part offer and part neither offer nor threat, it is an offer overall.

Such an example is an easy case. It would be more difficult if it were unclear what the 'normal course of events' was, or what is in the circumstances a 'reasonable expectation'. An important element of

the analysis then would be some proposed 'norms of expectability'. Some writers employ for this purpose a kind of statistical test while others employ a test of moral requiredness (Nozick 1969). Suppose the consequent clause in the second biconditional (2) is something like: 'I will not pull you out of the lake in which you are about to drown' (unless you promise to sign over all your worldly goods to me). Such a proposal violates a moral norm. We not only expect most people in such circumstances to attempt easy rescue (statistical norm); our morality *requires* it (moral norm). Thus the proposal not to rescue would be a threatened deviation both from statistical and from moral norms. And when the projected behaviour deviates from one of these norms but not the other, it can be sufficient to classify it as a threat. In summary, if A's projected consequences of B's failure to do y are worse (or less welcome) than they would be in the normal and expected course of events (where 'expected' straddles 'predicted' and 'morally required'), then A's proposal is a threat. If it correctly portrays those consequences as improvements, it is an offer.

3 Coercive and noncoercive proposals

Various examples, actual and hypothetical, have convinced some writers that there are such things as coercive offers. One rather standard example is that of the 'lecherous millionaire': B's child will die unless the child receives expensive surgery. A, a millionaire, proposes to pay for the surgery if, but only if, B will agree to become his mistress (Wertheimer 1987: 229). The millionaire's proposal, which does not project any harm beyond what would happen without his gratuitous intervention, is clearly an offer; an 'illicit offer', but an offer none the less. The controversy over this example has been mainly over whether the offer is coercive or not. On the one side, it has been argued that the example, at least from B's point of view, is coercive in just the sense in which the standard gunman's threat is coercive (Feinberg 1986). In both examples, the powerful wrongdoer (A) uses superior advantages (weapons or money) to manipulate B's options so that B has 'no choice' but to do what A wants. In either case, the option seen from the victim's point of view is: 'Sleep with me or your baby dies'.

On the other side, it is frequently argued that it is misleading to label as 'coercion' a proposal the effect of which is to create a net *increase* in a person's options, giving them a valued choice not previously possible (Zimmerman 1981). Thus B has been given an option she did not have before, without losing any options that she did have before, so that in a sense her freedom has been increased. Yet to some the suggestion that a coercive proposal could be freedom-enhancing is intolerably paradoxical.

4 Coercion and exploitation

A different solution is proposed by David Zimmerman (1981), who employs a critical distinction between coercion, understood as necessarily restrictive of freedom, and exploitation, understood as not necessarily coercive. In the lecherous millionaire example, *A* is an opportunist who happens to chance upon a vulnerable party, but who played no role himself in creating her vulnerability. In Zimmerman's terms, that makes *A* an exploiter. For him to be a genuine coercer, it must be the case that he deliberately created the situation in which *B* is helpless. Zimmerman illustrates the distinction between exploitative offers that are, and those that are not coercive, with the following example:

A kidnaps *B*, brings him to the island where *A*'s factory is located, and abandons him on the beach. All the jobs in *A*'s factory are considerably worse than those available on the mainland. The next day *A* approaches *B* with the proposal 'Take a job in my factory and I won't let you starve'.

This example is a genuine coercive offer, according to Zimmerman, but if there were two factories on the island, and the owner of the second learns of *B*'s plight and rushes to the beach before *A* can get there in order to make the same kind of offer to the kidnapped worker, then *A*'s offer is merely opportunistic exploitation: 'Coercing goes beyond exploiting, however objectionable the latter may be' (Zimmerman 1981: 122). The effect on the victim appears to be coercive whether the exploiter deliberately created the vulnerability or only took advantage of it opportunistically. 'Work or starve' is as coercive in effect as 'Sleep with me or your baby dies'. However, in the example that Zimmerman uses, *A* inflicts a kind of double blow on *B*, first by undermining *B*'s freedom (the act of kidnapping) and then by taking advantage of his undermined state with a 'coercive offer'. The lecherous millionaire, in contrast, was a mere opportunist. Whilst his behaviour may be viewed as morally reprehensible, it can be argued that his unsavoury conduct did not violate the vulnerable party's right; nor did it threaten any harm to *B* beyond what she could expect to occur anyway in the normal course of events.

See also: Freedom and liberty; Responsiblity

References and further reading

* Feinberg, J. (1986) *Harm to Self*, Oxford: Oxford University Press, 189–268. (Argues against paternalistic justifications for coercive interference with a person's voluntary conduct. Considers the ways in which one person's consent to another's action can fall short of voluntariness, including the case in which 'consent' is acquired through the use of coercive action. Includes a discussion of the 'lecherous millionaire', §3.)

Fletcher, G. (1978) *Rethinking Criminal Law*, Boston, MA: Little, Brown, 759–876. (Discusses the theory of criminal defences, both justifications and excuses, in particular, those of duress and necessity and the relations between the two.)

Frankfurt, H. (1973) 'Coercion and Moral Responsibility', in T. Honderich (ed.) *Essays on Freedom of Action*, London: Routledge & Kegan Paul. (Discusses coercion as an exercise in moral discourse. An influential article.)

Gross, H. (1979) *A Theory of Criminal Justice*, Oxford: Oxford University Press, 276–91. (A systematic theory of criminal law which includes a discussion of coercion as an excuse in criminal law.)

* Nozick, R. (1969) 'Coercion', in S. Morgenbesser, P. Suppes and M. White (eds) *Philosophy, Science and Method*, New York: St Martin's Press. (A classic source for discussion of 'norms of expectability' and their use in distinguishing threats from offers.)

Taylor, M. (1982) *Community, Anarchy and Liberty*, Cambridge: Cambridge University Press. (Asks whether a society without state coercion could ever achieve durable stability, and if so, under what conditions. Examines the relations – conceptual and empirical – between coercion and community.)

* Wertheimer, A. (1987) *Coercion*, Princeton, NJ: Princeton University Press. (One of the few book-length analyses of the concept of coercion, both in law and everyday life. Contains detailed discussion of the relation between coercive threats and offers, coercion and exploitation, and coercion and voluntariness.)

Williams, G. (1961) *Criminal Law: The General Part*, London: Stevens & Sons Limited, 751–69. (A thorough and authoritative examination of the treatment of coercion in English law. Attempts to resolve various controversies about coercion among criminal law theorists.)

* Zimmerman, D. (1981) 'Coercive Wage Offers', *Philosophy and Public Affairs* 10 (12): 121–45. (An influential article defending an analysis of

economic exploitation and coercion, and the differences between the two.)

JOEL FEINBERG

COGNITION, INFANT

In the past thirty years developmental psychologists have developed techniques for investigating the cognitive resources of infants. These techniques show that an infant's initial representation of the world is richer and more abstract than traditional empiricists supposed. For instance, infants seem to have at least some understanding of distance, of the continued existence of objects which are out of sight, and of the mental states of others. Such results have led philosophers to reconsider the idea – to be found in Plato – that there may be innate constraints on the way we view the world, and to examine the extent to which innate 'knowledge' may be revised as a result of learning.

How do we ask prelinguistic infants what they know? Infants' behaviour may initially look random and confused, but with closer observation, and particularly with the aid of videotape, we have discovered that it is quite systematic and structured. Very young infants show distinct emotional expressions. They act on objects in distinct and appropriate ways. Infants imitate the actions of others. We can use these patterns of action and emotion to test experimentally how infants behave when we present them with new events.

But we can also use other techniques that do not depend on spontaneous behaviour. Infants show characteristic shifts of visual attention and these shifts have been widely used to assess infant knowledge. An infant is first shown some event over a period of time. Infants typically look attentively at the event at first and then their attention declines, a process called habituation. We can then show the infant a new event. If the infants think the new event is different from the earlier event their attention will return; they will, once again, look attentively, a process called *dis*habituation. But if they think the new event is only a minor variant of the original event it will not capture their attention.

Philosophers have puzzled over the gap between our ordinary conception of the physical world as three-dimensional enduring objects moving in space and the information that arrives at our senses. For example, one classic question is how we infer a three-dimensional world from a two-dimensional retinal image (see EMPIRICISM; PHENOMENALISM; VISION).

Newborn infants seem to have at least some understanding of distance. Even very young infants will extend their arms towards objects within reach, but not out of reach. Similarly, newborn infants show size constancy. They recognize that an object that has moved away from them is still the same object, in spite of the fact that the retinal image is smaller.

A similar puzzle about object knowledge is the Molyneux problem (see MOLYNEUX PROBLEM). How do we link information about the same object that comes from different sensory modalities? Intermodal mapping is found in very young infants. Newborn infants imitate visually perceived facial gestures, although they cannot see their own faces, suggesting a mapping between tactile and visual experience. Similarly, in one experiment, infants sucked on either a bumpy or smooth object without ever being allowed to see it. Then they saw a visual image of either a bumpy or smooth object without touching it. Infants consistently looked more at the visual image that matched their previous tactile experience. Infants show a similar appreciation of the congruence between the temporal pattern of a sequence of noises and a sequence of flashes.

Yet another question is how we understand that objects endure even when they move out of sight. Infants appear to make some predictions about the possible movements of visible objects. Even very young infants reach for objects in the dark, suggesting that they can also represent objects that are out of sight for at least a brief time. However, infants will not search for objects that are hidden behind screens or under cloths until they are about 9 months old. This is in spite of the fact that they have the motor capacity to search under screens, and can remember seeing the objects being hidden. Their actions suggest that they believe the object no longer exists.

In contrast, some visual attention experiments suggest that young infants can draw inferences about objects behind screens. For example, we can show 5-month-old infants a screen that folds backwards to a flat position until they habituate to that event. Then we can show them an object in the path of the folding screen. The screen either folds flat (apparently going through the space that should have been occupied by the object), or the screen stops when it reaches the appropriate angle, as if blocked by the hidden object. Infants look more at the first event than the second, in spite of the fact that the first event is actually more superficially similar to the habituating event. In the case of distance and intermodal matching, the action and attention experiments give similar results. However, in this case there appears to be a discrepancy between the findings from studies of action and of attention. Children apparently demonstrate one set of beliefs when they act on objects and another contradictory set of beliefs when they look at objects. There is an ongoing debate about whether the attention-effects imply that infants understand enduring objects.

Another classic problem is how we infer that others have mental states like our own, given only the evidence of their behaviour (see OTHER MINDS). Very young infants act in ways that seem coordinated with the actions and emotions of others, and at around 9 months show signs of understanding that mental states are directed at objects. At this point infants begin to point at objects and to follow the gaze and pointings of others (see MIND, CHILD'S THEORY OF).

What philosophical conclusions can we draw from these empirical results? One theoretical possibility might be the sort of strong nativism advocated in Plato's *Meno*, in which Socrates wonders how it is that we have abstract and complex representations of the world, when the evidence of our senses is so limited and concrete? He answers the question by conducting a psychological experiment on a child, Meno's slave boy, testing whether he has the abstract representations in question (*Meno* 82b–86b). When it turns out that he does, Socrates concludes that the representations are innate, a view later echoed by Descartes and Kant. In its modern version, the nativist view suggests that there are strong and unchanging innate constraints on the way we view the world, a kind of 'core knowledge' (see INNATE KNOWLEDGE; NATIVISM). On an alternative view, the ability of infants to learn and change their beliefs is as impressive as their innate endowment. On this view infants begin with rich innate representations of the world, but those representations are subject to often quite radical revision as the infant learns more about the world. On this view, the infant is like a scientist who constructs and revises theories, and the innate representations are initial theories (see LEARNING). On either view, infants are an important and often neglected source of information about basic epistemological questions.

See also: INNATE KNOWLEDGE; LANGUAGE, INNATENESS OF; COGNITIVE DEVELOPMENT; PIAGET, J.

References and further reading

Baillargeon, R. (1993) 'The Object Concept Revisited: New Directions in the Investigation of Infants' Physical Knowledge', in C. Granrud (ed.) *Visual Perception and Cognition in Infancy*, Hillsdale, NJ: Erlbaum. (A review of work investigating very early object knowledge using the habituation technique.)

Bower, T.G.R. (1982) *Development in Infancy*, San Francisco, CA: W.H. Freeman. (A seminal and philosophically sophisticated (if sometimes controversial) look at infant perception and cognition.)

Butterworth, G. (1991) 'The Ontogeny and Phylogeny of Joint Visual Attention', in A. Whiten (ed.) *Natural Theories of Mind: Evolution, Development and Simulation of Everyday Mindreading*, Oxford: Blackwell, 223–32. (Work on early understanding of other minds.)

Cohen, L.B. (1979) 'Our Developing Knowledge of Infant Perception and Cognition', *American Psychologist* 34: 894–9. (A classic review of the habituation technique and work using it to investigate infant categorization.)

Gopnik, A. (1988) 'Conceptual and Semantic Development as Theory Change', *Mind and Language* 3: 197–217. (A theoretical statement of the 'theory theory' of infant cognition.)

Gopnik, A. and Meltzoff, A.N. (1997) *Words, Thoughts and Theories*, Cambridge, MA: MIT Press. (Considers several domains of infant knowledge and their philosophical implications. Chapters review infant object knowledge, infant theory of mind and infant categorization, as well as presenting alternative theoretical accounts of knowledge in infancy.)

Meltzoff, A.N. (1993) 'Molyneux's Babies: Cross-Modal Perception, Imitation, and the Mind of the Preverbal Infant', in N. Eilan, R. McCarthy and B. Brewer (eds) *Spatial Representation: Problems in Philosophy and Psychology*, Cambridge, MA: Blackwell. (Implications of imitation and cross-modal matching research for philosophical problems about objects and minds.)

Piaget, J. (1952) *The Origins of Intelligence in Childhood*, New York: Basic Books. (Classic discussion of infant action and cognition.)

—— (1954) *The Construction of Reality in the Child*, New York: Basic Books. (Another classic discussion of infant action and cognition.)

Rovee-Collier, C. (1990) 'The "Memory System" of Prelinguistic Infants', in A. Diamond (ed.) *The Development and Neural Bases of Higher Cognitive Functions*, Annals of the New York Academy of Sciences, vol. 608, 517–42. (A review of work using the 'conjugate reinforcement' technique, in which infants learn to act in order to produce particular types of interesting events, with special reference to memory and categorization.)

Spelke, E. (1990) 'Origins of Visual Knowledge', in D. Osherson and L. Smith (eds) *Visual Cognition and Action: An Invitation to Cognitive Science*, vol. 3, Cambridge, MA: MIT Press. (A review of new data on early perception and object knowledge.)

Spelke, E., Breinlinger, K., Macomber, J. and

Jacobson, K. (1992) 'Origins of Knowledge', *Psychological Review* 4: 605–12. (A theoretical statement of the 'core knowledge' view of infant cognition.)

Trevarthen, C. (1979) 'Communication and Cooperation in Early Infancy: A Description of Primary Intersubjectivity', in M. Bulllowa (ed.) *Before Speech*, New York: Cambridge University Press, 231–347. (Descriptions of very early social behaviour in infants.)

Wellman, H.W. (1993) 'Early Understanding of Mind: The Normal Case', in S. Baron-Cohen, H. Tager-Flusberg and D. Cohen (eds) *Understanding Other Minds: Perspectives from Autism*, Oxford: Oxford University Press. (A review of work on infant 'theory of mind'.)

ALISON GOPNIK
ANDREW N. MELTZOFF

COGNITIVE ARCHITECTURE

Cognitive architecture involves the properties of mental structures and mental mechanisms that do not vary when people have different goals, beliefs, precepts or other cognitive states. A serious computational theory of mind (CTM) requires that the architecture be constrained independently of such states. One consequence of taking the distinction between architecture and representation-governed process seriously is that it provides a reply to those who are sceptical about the role of rules in cognition, on the grounds that following rules leads to an infinite regress: in CTM, rules are executed by the causal structure of the architecture, and hence do not require further rules for following rules.

The notion of cognitive architecture in the context of the computational theory of mind (CTM) comes directly from the notion of computer architecture, which refers to the relatively fixed set of computational resources available to a programmer in designing a program for a given computer system. Among other properties, this includes the type of memory that the computer has, the way it encodes information (the system of symbolic codes or language it uses), the basic operations that are available, and the constraints on the application of these operations (as in serial v. parallel sequencing). The architecture is a functional characterization of the computer system on which the program runs (see MIND, COMPUTATIONAL THEORIES OF).

It is important to bear in mind that computer architecture reflects the physical properties or 'hardware' only indirectly, since the architecture visible to the programmer might itself be simulated in software or firmware. For this reason it is sometimes referred to as the 'functional architecture' or even as the 'architecture of the virtual machine'. Someone writing a program in, say, LISP or C, has available the resources (operations, datastructures and programming constraints) of those languages and is not concerned with their physical instantiations: LISP or C in that case *is* the architecture of the relevant virtual machine.

In theories of cognition, the notion of architecture is particularly important because it represents the dividing line between cognitive and non-cognitive aspects of a model. In CTM, mental processes are modelled as computer programs, but the process of executing these programs itself lies outside the domain of CTM. What makes the computer model run, or generate token instances of behaviour, is the causal structure of the underlying computational mechanism, the computational architecture.

The architecture of computational models was often taken for granted in modelling cognitive processes. In the 1950s, information-processing models were typically expressed in terms of whatever architecture was available or seemed intuitively reasonable – usually a so-called 'von Neumann' architecture which uses a serial fetch–execute computational regime and location-addressable register memory. But in more recent years, under the influence of Simon and Newell's literal interpretation of programs-as-theories (see Simon and Newell 1964; developed more fully in Newell 1990), it became clear that the assumptions one made about the underlying architecture strongly influenced which programs it could implement (not which functions it could compute, since with suitable external memory it could compute any computable function) and hence constituted a strong claim about the nature of mind.

Mapping out the cognitive architecture in detail is important if the CTM is to provide a literal scientific hypothesis about the causes of cognitive behaviour. Programs can only be individuated relative to an architecture. According to the way in which computer scientists and cognitive scientists individuate programs, two different architectures cannot execute the same program, although the universality of such machines guarantees that (subject to memory requirements) they can compute the same function. The kind of 'strong equivalence' of computational models with mental processes that many cognitive scientists demand is not achieved just by providing a detailed characterization of the process in the form of a program. Because the form of such a program depends on the architecture on which it runs, the theory must specify an independently motivated architecture, including a specification of the representational system it uses. In such a fully articulated model the individual operations – as well as the symbolic expressions they operate over – the sequencing discipline that is imposed on the program execution, the memory constraints that it must adhere to, and so on, all constitute empirical claims. Only when one has independently specified both the architecture and the representations can one's computational model lay claims to being 'strongly equivalent' to the cognitive process being modelled (see Pylyshyn 1984).

In recent years there has been a great deal of debate about which class of architecture is the right one for modelling cognition. In particular there have been proposals that the class of computational architectures that operate over syntactic strings, as in the Turing machine or in proof theory, are inappropriate for modelling psychological processes (see TURING MACHINES; PROOF THEORY). Instead, some people have proposed so-called 'connectionist' or 'neural net' architectures, consisting of a network of simple threshold elements that compute certain functions (the precise class being unknown) by passing activation among the elements over weighted links (see CONNECTIONISM). Such networks, it is claimed, compute without reading or writing symbolic expressions. The debate raises the philosophic issue of whether mind can or should be modelled as a syntactic engine, computing in a 'language of thought', as is generally assumed in the CTM (see Fodor and Pylyshin 1988; LANGUAGE OF THOUGHT).

Distinguishing architecture and representations (including representations of processes in terms of programs which run on that architecture) is important to the philosopher for a number of reasons (see Pylyshyn 1996). For one, it represents an attempt to understand the nature of the relatively fixed mental structures that instantiate psychological processes: the basic cognitive *capacities* of the mind within which representation-governed processes are instantiated. Some of these structures are likely to be universal and perhaps even innate (we put aside for now the issue of how architecture changes, except to note that it does not change in response to new knowledge – by definition it is not 'cognitively penetrable').

Recognizing the role of architecture also helps to resolve a problem about rule following raised by Wittgenstein (1953): how is a system to know how to follow a rule? If by using another rule, this invites an infinite regress (see WITTGENSTEIN, L. §10). In CTM the regress does not arise because the architecture executes the rules and it does not do this by using rule-following rules, but, instead, by virtue of its causal structure. In a computer we do not have to

have algorithms for executing algorithms; instead the physical instantiation of the algorithm in the machine, together with the structure of the machine, simply causes the behaviour to unfold. The relevant abstract description of these causal-structural properties constitutes a description of the architecture of the system.

See also: COMPUTABILITY THEORY; LANGUAGE OF THOUGHT; MODULARITY OF MIND

References and further reading

* Fodor, J.A. and Pylyshyn, Z. (1988) 'Connectionism and Cognitive Architecture', *Cognition* 28: 3–71. (Provides a detailed analysis of the requirements on cognitive architecture and why these are not met by 'neural net' or 'connectionist' proposals.)
* Newell, A. (1990) *Unified Theories of Cognition*, Cambridge, MA: Harvard University Press. (The definitive last work by Newell on a proposed cognitive architecture.)
* Pylyshyn, Z. (1984) *Computation and Cognition: Towards a Foundation for Cognitive Science*, Cambridge, MA: MIT Press. (Much of this book is concerned with explicating the notion of cognitive architecture and the criterion of 'cognitive impenetrability' by which it is identified. Discusses 'strong equivalence'.)
* —— (1996) 'The Study of Cognitive Architecture', in D. Steier and T. Mitchell (eds) *Mind Matters: Contributions to Cognitive Science in Honor of Allen Newell*, Hilldale, NJ: Erlbaum. (A general, as well as historical, discussion of the issue of cognitive architecture, with emphasis on Allen Newell's important contribution – and some criticism of his assumption of architectural homogeneity as well.)
* Simon, H.A. and Newell, A. (1964) 'Information Processing in Computers and Man', *American Scientist* 52 (3). (An early, readable statement of the project of taking programs seriously as models of mental processes.)
* Wittgenstein, L. (1953) *Philosophical Investigations*, New York: Macmillan, esp. §§198–292. (An influential discussion of rule-following, and the fact that at some point a rule must be followed 'blindly', without recourse to any further rule.)

ZENON W. PYLYSHYN

COGNITIVE DEVELOPMENT

Psychological research of the last two decades has produced a surge of surprising results regarding cognitive development in children that has challenged a number of traditional philosophical assumptions about the nature of knowledge. The developing cognitive system seems organized in terms of specific domains, rather than as a general, all-purpose processor to which traditional empiricism was committed. Children's conceptual development is often guided by highly abstract principles and parameters that are present in a child's mind long before concrete details of a domain are encountered. Moreover, the data seem to indicate that development consists predominantly of gradual conceptual enrichment over time, rather than radical change.

Research in cognitive development addresses the nature of thought and perception, focusing specifically on the origins of cognition, and its changes over time. Thus, it addresses such questions as what sorts of innate expectations infants possess about the kinds of things to be learned; whether development is continuous or stage-like in nature; whether it proceeds from more concrete to more abstract forms of thought; and finally, the nature of cognition itself as either a global and general learning system, or a set of more specialized and separable domain-specific systems (see MODULARITY OF MIND).

The emergence of the experimental study of cognitive development in the twentieth century is largely attributed to a few key figures, most notably Jean PIAGET, Lev VYGOTSKII and Heinz Werner. All three favoured stage-like transitions in cognitive development that had sweeping influences across all domains of thought. Although significant portions of their theories are no longer widely believed, the phenomena they uncovered still remain the focus of most contemporary experimental work: knowledge of, for example, arithmetic, spatial layout, physical object mechanics and social interaction.

The last two decades of empirical research on these phenomena have produced a surge of new results that support increasingly strong claims about the nature of cognitive development. Contrary to the associationist assumptions of traditional empiricism, it seems to be guided by highly abstract principles and parameters about specific domains of inquiry – for example, language, causal relations among material objects, biology, intentional psychology – long before the domain is actually encountered. Indeed, along the lines of traditional Rationalism, many of them are arguably innate (see EMPIRICISM; NATIVISM; RATIONALISM).

Much of this recent work has been influenced by the revolution in linguistics brought about by Noam CHOMSKY. Chomsky provided convincing evidence that, in the normal human environment, language is unlearnable unless the learner has specific sets of innate expectations about the nature of grammar. For example, children make systematic errors they have never heard spoken, and use syntactic rules that they have never been taught. Although the nature of this language-specific endowment is still actively debated, the vast majority of language acquisition researchers now acknowledge the need for an a innate set of predetermined expectations about linguistic structure (see LANGUAGE, INNATENESS OF).

Following this proposal in linguistics, many psychologists now argue that children possess innate or early-developing predispositions that guide the development of their understanding of other types of knowledge domains, such as the mechanics of physical objects (see COGNITION, INFANT) and human social behaviour (see MIND, CHILD'S THEORY OF). As with language, this domain-specific approach has been proposed to explain both children's impressive cognitive abilities, and their puzzling defects. For example, young infants clearly see objects as solid three-dimensional things (solidity) that move in predictable ways (continuity), but fail to understand gravity, even though evidence for all three is roughly equally present (and important) in the environment (Spelke *et al.* 1992). Infants seem to have a 'theory' of physical objects that ignores gravity until much later in development. This theory may not be as elaborate or extensive as that used by adults, but clearly it guides children's developing understanding of the world in ways similar to adults'.

At least by the age of 3 or 4, children also seem to have a special 'teleological' framework for interpreting some phenomena. Preschool children are more prone to ask such questions as 'What's this for?' when asking about a property of a living kind than of a non-living natural kind, such as a rock, about which they are more likely to ask merely 'What is that?', or 'What is that *P* [property]?', without any presumption that it serves any purpose. They seem to recognize that the features of living kinds are interconnected and designed in some manner to be causally linked in a way not true of non-living natural kinds. This bias towards teleological explanation may be a fundamental component of conceptual development (Keil 1995). Moreover, when told that human beings possess specific biological properties such as eating, sleeping and having hearts, preschool children will show highly structured patterns of generalization of these properties to living as opposed to non-living kinds (Carey 1985).

It is important to note that these explanatory frameworks go beyond mere associative principles. For example, although being curved is a property equally associated with both bananas and boomerangs, it is causal and central only in the latter case. A straight banana is clearly still a banana, but a straight boomerang is a stick (see Medin and Shobin 1988; BEHAVIOURISM, METHODOLOGICAL AND SCIENTIFIC; LEARNING §2).

Contrary to earlier claims, recent research also suggests that development consists predominantly of gradual conceptual enrichment over time, rather than radical change. Rather than undergoing a series of cognitive metamorphoses as Piaget supposed, the infant's world contains many parameters of understanding that continue to play a role across development, and into the conceptual systems of adults. For example, 6-month-olds understand that objects continue to exist even when they cannot see them (Diamond 1991), and infants have a surprising understanding of numerosity and some aspects of counting (Gallistel and Gelman 1992).

Research on cognitive development is currently being conducted in a manner that crosses traditional research boundaries and more closely follows the spirit of cognitive science. Carey (1991) has found striking parallels between conceptual development in children and conceptual developments in the history of science. Anthropologists find exciting commonalities in what people in all cultures regard as fundamental categories such as living kinds (Atran 1995). The relevance of linguistics to conceptual development is clearly apparent. Philosophical contributions to such efforts come from many directions, including logic and the nature of inductive learning devices (see INDUCTIVE INFERENCE), conceptual change in science (see CONCEPTS), the formal nature of reasoning (see COMMON-SENSE REASONING, THEORIES OF), clarifying relations between metaphysics and epistemology, and how the nature of thought might be revealed through language (see LANGUAGE, PHILOSOPHY OF).

See also: LEARNING; MORAL DEVELOPMENT

References and further reading

* Atran, S. (1995) 'Causal Constraints on Categories and Categorical Constraints on Biological Reasoning Across Cultures', in E. Sperber, D. Premack and A.J. Premak (eds) Causal Cognition: A Multidisciplinary Debate, Oxford: Clarendon Press, 205–33. (Explores universals in biological thought across different cultures and relations to causal thinking.)
* Carey, S. (1985) Conceptual Change in Childhood, Cambridge, MA: MIT Press. (Proposes a model of conceptual change for biology in which biological thought emerges largely out of a native psychology.)
* —— (1991) 'Knowledge Acquisition: Enrichment or Conceptual Change?', in S. Carey and R. Gelman (eds) The Epigenesis of Mind: Essays on Biology and Cognition, Hillsdale, NJ: Erlbaum, 257–91. (An examination of the difficulties of certain conceptual changes – for example, distinguishing heat from temperature – in both childhood development and the history of science.)
* Diamond, A. (1991) 'Neuropsychological Insights into the Meaning of Object Concept Development', in S. Carey and R. Gelman (eds) The Epigenesis of the Mind: Essays on Biology and Cognition, Hillsdale, NJ: Erlbaum, 67–110. (Discusses how developmental changes of the infant's object concept might be related to underlying maturational changes in brain function.)
* Gallistel, C.R. and Gelman, R. (1992) 'Preverbal and Verbal Counting and Numerical Cognition', Cognition 44: 43–74. (Discusses how aspects of counting might be present in infancy and come to guide the emergence of verbal counting.)
* Keil, F. (1995) 'The Growth of Causal Understanding in Natural Kinds', in E. Sperber, D. Premack and A.J. Premak (eds) Causal Cognition: A Multidisciplinary Debate, Oxford: Clarendon Press, 234–62. (Discusses how the emergence of causal understandings of natural kinds can be dramatically different from other sorts of entities such as artefacts.)
* Medin, D. and Shobin, E.J. (1988) 'Context and Structure in Conceptual Combination', Cognitive Psychology 20: 158–90. (Shows how conceptual combination can reveal the importance of theoretical relations in concepts in ways that override mere frequency-based information.)
* Spelke, E.S., Breinlinger, K., Macomber, J. and Jacobson, K. (1992) 'Origins of Knowledge', Psychological Review 95: 605–32. (Presents a systematic survey of how the infant's knowledge of the physical world might develop and how it reflects a rich array of cognitive principles from very early on.)

F.C. KEIL
G. GUTHEIL

COGNITIVE PLURALISM

Descriptive cognitive pluralism claims that different people, or people in different cultures, go about the business of reasoning (that is, forming and revising beliefs) in significantly different ways. If descriptive cognitive pluralism is true, it lends considerable urgency to the venerable philosophical problem of deciding which strategies of belief formation and revision we ourselves should use. Normative cognitive pluralism claims that various quite different systems of reasoning may all be equally good. Epistemic relativism, which claims that different strategies of reasoning are best for different people, is a species of normative cognitive pluralism. Evaluative-concept pluralism claims that different people in different cultures use very different concepts of cognitive evaluation. Their notions of rationality and justification (or the closest equivalents in their culture) are quite different from ours. If this is right, it poses a prima facie challenge to a central strategy in analytic epistemology which tries to arbitrate between different systems of reasoning by determining which system best comports with our own concepts of epistemic evaluation.

1   Descriptive pluralism
2   Normative pluralism
3   Evaluative-concept pluralism

1   Descriptive pluralism

'Cognitive pluralism' might be used to label at least three distinct though related claims. One of these, which I call 'descriptive cognitive pluralism', has been much debated in anthropology, comparative psychology and the history of science. Descriptive pluralism maintains that different people go about the business of cognition – the forming and revising of beliefs and other cognitive states – in significantly different ways. For example, it has been urged that people in certain pre-literate societies think or reason very differently from the way modern, Western, scientifically educated people do. Closer to home, it has been suggested that different individuals or groups in our own society (men versus women, artists versus scientists, well-educated versus poorly educated) form beliefs and solve cognitive problems in markedly different ways – ways that indicate differences in underlying cognitive processes (see FEMINIST EPISTEMOLOGY §4).

The denial of descriptive cognitive pluralism is descriptive monism, the thesis that all people exploit more or less the same cognitive processes. The distinction between descriptive monism and descriptive pluralism is best viewed not as a hard and fast one, but as a matter of degree. No one would deny that people differ from one another to some extent in the speed and cleverness of their inferences; nor would it be denied that in attempting to solve cognitive problems, different people try different strategies first. But if these are the only sorts of cognitive differences to be found among people, descriptive monism will be vindicated. If, on the other hand, it should turn out that different people, different groups or different cultures use radically different 'psycho-logics' – that the revising and updating of their cognitive states is governed by substantially different principles – pluralism will have a firm foot in the door. The more radical the differences, the further we will be towards the pluralistic end of the spectrum.

If descriptive cognitive pluralism turns out to be true, it is possible that some of the diversity in reasoning strategies may be due to genetic differences among individuals or groups. But it might also be the case that some of the diversity, or all of it, is attributable to environmental variables that differ in important ways from one culture to another. Some of the rules of reasoning that people internalize and use, or all of them, may be analogous to the grammatical rules that subserve the production and comprehension of sentences in natural languages. The possibility that there is a fair amount of acquired diversity in human cognitive processes, and that patterns of reasoning or cognitive processing are to a substantial degree moulded by cultural influences, adds a certain urgency to one of the more venerable problems of epistemology. For if there are lots of different ways in which the human mind/brain can go about ordering and re-ordering its beliefs and other cognitive states, if different cultures could or do go about the business of reasoning in very different ways, it becomes quite pressing to ask which of these ways should we use and which cognitive processes are the good ones? Here the analogy with grammatical rules breaks down in an illuminating way. Most of us are inclined to think that one language is as good as another. The one you should use is the one spoken and understood by the people around you. By contrast, most of us are not inclined to accept this sort of thorough-going relativism about cognitive processes. If pre-literate tribes or pre-modern scientists or members of a contemporary sub-culture or our own distant descendants think in ways that are quite different from the ways we think, few of us would be inclined to suggest that all of these ways are equally good. Some ways of going about the business of belief revision are better than others. But just what is it that makes one system of cognitive processes better than another, and how are we to tell which system of reasoning is best? These are among the most basic and the most disquieting questions that epistemology tries to answer.

2   Normative pluralism

Normative cognitive pluralism is not a claim about the cognitive processes people do use; rather it is a claim about good cognitive processes – those that people ought to use. It asserts that there is no unique system of cognitive processes that people should use, because various systems that are very different from each other may all be equally good. The distinction between normative pluralism and normative monism, like the parallel distinction between descriptive notions, is best viewed as a matter of degree, with the monist end of the spectrum urging that all normatively sanctioned systems of cognitive processing are minor variations of one another. The more substantial the differences among normatively sanctioned systems, the further we move in the direction of pluralism. Epistemic relativism is a species of normative cognitive pluralism. An account of what makes a system of reasoning a good one is relativistic if it entails that different systems are good for different people or different groups of people (see EPISTEMIC RELATIVISM). Not all pluralistic accounts of good reasoning are relativistic, since some accounts entail that different systems of reasoning are equally good for everyone.

Historically, it is probably true that much of the support for normative pluralism among social scientists derived from the discovery (or putative discovery) of descriptive pluralism, along with a certain ideologically inspired reluctance to pass negative judgments on the traditions or practices of other cultures. But normative pluralism was certainly not the only response to descriptive pluralism among social scientists. Many reacted to the alleged discovery of odd reasoning patterns among pre-modern peoples by insisting on monism at the normative level, and concluding that the reasoning of pre-modern folk was 'primitive,' 'pre-logical' or otherwise normatively substandard. Among philosophers, both historical and contemporary, normative cognitive pluralism is a minority view. The dominant philosophical view is that there is only one good way to go about the business of reasoning, or at most a small cluster of similar ways.

3 Evaluative-concept pluralism

Evaluative-concept pluralism is a descriptive thesis, not a normative one. It maintains that people's intuitive concepts of cognitive evaluation, concepts like those that we express with terms like 'justified' or 'rational', vary significantly from culture to culture. If evaluative-concept pluralism is correct, the terms of cognitive evaluation exploited in other cultures or intellectual traditions may differ in both meaning and extension from the terms of cognitive evaluation that are embedded in our own everyday thought and language.

Though the issue is controversial, some philosophers think that evaluative-concept pluralism poses a serious challenge to the tradition of analytic epistemology. That tradition tries to resolve normative questions in epistemology by analysing or explicating our ordinary concepts of epistemic evaluation. If we want to know whether our own system of cognitive processes is better or worse than some alternative system, the analytic epistemologist proposes that we settle the question by determining which system does a better job of producing beliefs that comport with our concept of justification (or rationality) (see NORMATIVE EPISTEMOLOGY §1). But the analytic epistemologist typically offers us no reason to think that the notions of evaluation prevailing in our own language and culture are any better than the alternative evaluative notions that might or do prevail in other cultures. In the absence of any reason to think that the locally prevailing notions of epistemic evaluation are superior to the alternatives, it is hard to see why we should care whether the cognitive processes we use are sanctioned by those local evaluative concepts.

Imagine that we have located some exotic culture that does in fact exploit cognitive processes very different from our own, and that the notions of epistemic evaluation embedded in their language also differ from ours. Suppose further that the cognitive processes prevailing in that culture accord quite well with their evaluative notions, while the cognitive processes prevailing in our own culture accord quite well with ours. Would any of this be of any help in deciding which cognitive processes we should use? Without some reason to think that one set of evaluative notions was preferable to the other, it seems clear that for most of us it would be of no help at all.

See also: FEMINIST EPISTEMOLOGY; GENDER AND SCIENCE; POSTCOLONIAL PHILOSOPHY OF SCIENCE; RATIONAL BELIEFS

References and further reading

Hollis, M. and Lukes, S. (eds) (1982) *Rationality and Relativism*, Cambridge, MA: MIT Press. (A collection of essays by philosophers, anthropologists and historians of science debating the evidence for descriptive pluralism and the merits of relativism.)

Hutchins, E. (1980) *Culture and Inference: A Trobriand Case Study*, Cambridge, MA: Harvard University Press. (A sophisticated study in cognitive anthropology that supports descriptive cognitive monism.)

Levy-Bruhl, L. (1966) *Primitive Mentality*, Boston, MA: Beacon Press. (Classical anthropological defence of descriptive pluralism and normative monism.)

Quine, W.V. (1960) *Word and Object*, Cambridge, MA: MIT Press. (Chapters 1 and 2 offer an important argument against the possibility of descriptive pluralism.)

Stich, S. (1990) *The Fragmentation of Reason*, Cambridge, MA: MIT Press. (Chapters 1, 4 and 6 are especially relevant and expand on the material in this entry.)

Wilson, B. (ed.) (1979) *Rationality*, Oxford; Blackwell. (Collection of essays by philosophers, anthropologists and others exploring various aspects of cognitive pluralism.)

STEPHEN P. STICH

COHEN DE HERRERA, ABRAHAM *see* HERRERA, ABRAHAM COHEN DE

COHEN, HERMANN (1842–1918)

Hermann Cohen was the founder of the Marburg School of Neo-Kantianism and a major influence on twentieth-century Jewish thought. Die Religion der Vernunft aus den Quellen des Judentums *(Religion of Reason out of the Sources of Judaism) (1919) is widely credited with the renewal of Jewish religious philosophy. Cohen's philosophy of Judaism is inextricably linked with his general philosophical position. But his system of critical idealism in logic, ethics, aesthetics and psychology did not originally include a philosophy of religion. The mainly Protestant Marburg School in fact regarded Cohen's Jewish philosophy as an insufficient solution to the philosophical problem of human existence and to that of determining the role of religion in human culture. Thinkers who favoured a new, more existentialist approach in Jewish thought, however, saw Cohen's introduction of religion into the system as a daring departure from the confines of philosophical idealism.*

Cohen identified the central Jewish contribution to human culture as the development of a religion that unites historical particularity with ethical universality. At the core of this religion of reason is the interdependence of the idea of God and that of the human being. Cohen derives this theme from the Jewish canon

through a philosophical analysis based on his transcendental idealism.

1 Life and work
2 'Critical idealism' as the basis of the sciences and the humanities
3 Ethics and the philosophy of religion

1 Life and work

Hermann Cohen was the son of a cantor in the provincial town of Coswig in the state of Anhalt. He abandoned his rabbinical studies at the Jewish Theological Seminary (Breslau) after witnessing the rift between reform and orthodox Jews over the divine revelation of the Mishnah (the ancient code of rabbinic law). Seeking orientation in the conflict between religion and modern consciousness, Cohen turned to philosophy and the sciences. After receiving his doctorate at Halle in 1865, he published studies on mythological, philosophical and aesthetic topics (God and the soul, Plato's theory of Forms), influenced by the then compelling idea of a 'mechanism of consciousness'; but he gradually abandoned the methodologies of Helmholtz and Steinthal and immersed himself in the philosophy of KANT. His 1871 exposition of Kant's first critique, *Kants Theorie der Erfahrung* (Kant's Theory of Experience), brought him to the centre of the Neo-Kantian movement and led to his appointment as a Privatdozent at Marburg. Subsequent publications, especially *Kants Begründung der Ethik nebst ihren Anwendungen auf Recht, Religion und Geschichte* (Kant's Justification of Ethics and its Application to Law, Religion and History) (1877) and *Das Prinzip der Infinitesimalmethode* (The Principle of the Method of Infinitesimals) (1883) made original contributions to Kantian thought. Cohen's mature philosophical system follows the classic structure of Kant's three critiques but projects a fourth part, on psychology, and seeks to establish a 'critical idealism' faithful in broad outline to the tradition of PLATO, DESCARTES, LEIBNIZ and KANT. Cohen ascribed the continuity of this tradition to a perennial philosophical problematic that arises from the idealism inherent in scientific thought.

The Marburg School, represented by Cohen and his colleague Paul Natorp, attracted students from as far away as St Petersburg (Boris Pasternak) and Madrid (Ortega y Gasset). Those who became philosophers – Ernst Cassirer, Nicolai Hartmann, Heinz Heimsoeth and Hans-Georg Gadamer – gradually emancipated themselves from Marburg Neo-Kantianism. But the tendency of some philosophers to ignore Cohen's contributions expressed ideological biases – thus Heidegger's 1929 verdict of having 'overcome' Neo-Kantianism.

In 1876 Cohen succeeded his mentor Friedrich Albert Lange, author of the *Geschichte des Materialismus und Kritik seiner Bedeutung in der Gegenwart* (History of Materialism), to a highly visible position as practically the only non-baptized Jew to hold a chair in philosophy at a Prussian university. Three years later he found himself compelled to defend Judaism against the charges of Heinrich von Treitschke that it was alien to the values of German culture. From then on, Cohen's public engagement on behalf of Judaism and Judaic studies increased steadily, extending in time to the renewal of Jewish religious philosophy, a field often neglected among the more historically oriented disciplines of *Wissenschaft des Judentums* (the 'Science of Judaism').

From 1903 Cohen was active in the *Hochschule für die Wissenschaft des Judentums* in Berlin, where, after retiring from Marburg, he lectured on the biblical prophets, the Psalms, the Greek philosophical roots of medieval Jewish thought, Maimonides, Descartes, and philosophical psychology (see MAIMONIDES, M.). Shortly before his death, Cohen also helped found an academy dedicated to the science of Judaism, at the suggestion of his former student Franz ROSENZWEIG.

2 'Critical idealism' as the basis of the sciences and the humanities

Unprecedented scientific progress in the later nineteenth century speeded the collapse of German Idealism. Empirical studies of brain function eclipsed intellectual inquiries into the nature of thought, and in many philosophy departments experimental psychology displaced traditional philosophy. Opposing the tide of positivism and materialism, Cohen championed idealism both for what he saw as its ethical implications and because he conceived of idealism as the true groundwork of scientific thought. Like his mentor Lange, Cohen did not malign materialism but saw it as a heuristic principle, itself a product of critical thought, a hypothesis meant to make scientific cognition possible. Materialism itself, then, showed the fertility of critical idealism (see Köhnke 1991).

Cohen's logic, set out in *System der Philosophie, Erster Teil: Logik der reinen Erkenntnis* (System of Philosophy Part One: The Logic of Pure Cognition) (1902), constructs transcendental philosophy rather differently from Kant. Beginning not from the senses and the a priori forms of sensibility and thought but from the science found in 'printed books', Cohen finds knowledge grounded in mathematical principles. These are products not of experience but of pure

thought. Only such knowledge is relevant for the logic of cognition. The 'being' it discovers is 'given' only in the mathematical abstractions that we metaphorically call laws of nature. Sense perception, then, including the refined perception of the laboratory, must be relegated to the role of a methodological principle. The limited rules of syllogistic logic (based as they are on grammar rather than mathematical ideas) are similarly relegated to the methodology of research. While sense perception and syllogistic logic are tools in the verification of hypotheses, the hypotheses themselves are the 'origin' (*Ursprung*) of the objects of cognition. Hence, the 'logic of the origin' determines the foundation of being in thought: thought as the origin of being. Reflecting the constantly progressing sciences with their shifting paradigms, the system of categories and judgments represented in Cohen's logic is open-ended – quite a contrast to Kant's efforts to find fixed normative patterns in our thinking as earnest of its objectivity.

There are other deviations: most strikingly, Kant's 'thing-in-itself' (noumena) (see KANT, I. §3) is eliminated as a superfluous dogmatic prejudice. In another notable reform, to avoid psychologistic readings of the Kantian a priori that would confuse the a priori forms of consciousness with innate functions of the brain, Cohen identifies the knowing subject as the 'unity of cultural consciousness' (*Einheit des Kulturbewußtseins*). The quest for a unity underlying the distinct 'directions of culture' (science, law, art) was the ultimate goal of Cohen's system. The transcendental conditions of that unity were to be addressed in the final part (on psychology) of Cohen's philosophical edifice, which he did not live to complete.

Cohen's revision of transcendental logic pivots on the 'principle of the infinitesimal method' whose paradigm is the physicist's reliance not on the senses but on mathematical models (1902: 126). Cognition, we find, begins, counterintuitively, in a 'no-thing' and an 'adventurous detour' (1902: 84) in which reason itself constitutes the object: the non-sensory infinitesimal becomes the origin of all finite reality.

The anti-materialist, anti-determinist implications of Cohen's conception of reality come to the fore in the humanities and ethics. Once it is understood that reality is discovered in judgments, not sense experiences, morality seems far less ephemeral than materialism might seem to make it – provided it can be shown that the ethical concept of a human being is the actual operative principle in some valid mode of discourse. Cohen finds such a 'direction of culture' in law, which must presuppose a concept of the human being transcending the biological. Ethics, then, is constructed analogously to logic, with the human being as the analogue of nature and the laws that regulate humanity's historical and political existence as analogues of the laws of nature. Since ethics seeks the principles of a reality that presupposes the idea of a human being, Cohen's *Ethik des reinen Willen* (Ethics of Pure Will) (1904) becomes a philosophy of law.

Ethics, as 'the teaching about the human being', becomes the 'centre of philosophy' and lays the groundwork for all disciplines dealing with the products of human action (law, economics, the humanities). Overawed by the sciences, the humanities have sometimes mistakenly adopted the biological notion of the human being, but what they require is the ethical notion of a human being: ethics is 'the positive logic of the humanities' (1904: 1).

3 Ethics and the philosophy of religion

Will, action and consciousness are the 'constitutive concepts' (1904: 389) of an ethics that rests on the 'methodology of the exact concepts of the science of law', to which ethics 'listens attentively for the sake of its problems of person and action' (1904: vii). Will, action and consciousness are defined in the end so as to unite all ethical concepts. All the actions of a moral subject become transformations of the 'pure will'. Beyond the bare idea of will, however, the concepts of freedom and autonomy are presuppositions of the realization of any good. For this reason, Cohen introduces into his ethics traditional Jewish concepts of sin and repentance. Religious rather than philosophical, in his view, these concepts introduce a crucial element of morality that ethics alone cannot provide: the concrete individual. The state, the community, and other such social agencies operate in the ideal time of legal progress. But only the individual can originate moral decisions in actual time.

Ethics, strictly conceived, can address the problem of guilt (*dolus*, *culpa*) but not that of sin (*peccatum*). It cannot deal with concrete human failure. For the law has no power over sin in the sense of guilt but only over culpability (1904: 366–). Ethics similarly lacks a principle of self-transformation. But this principle is found in the biblical and rabbinic idea of 'repentance' (*teshuvah*). Religion can address the concrete individual; but for ethics, by its very structure, the concrete individual is a mere fiction.

Ethics and religion share the goal of advancing a humane civilization. But ethics deals with individuals only as members of collectivities. Religion is charged with the reconstitution of particular individuals in psychological or liturgical time, redirecting each toward the future, through a regeneration of the individual moral consciousness, whose existence is endangered by transgression of the law.

Ethics orients the philosophy of religion toward interpreting particular truths of faith in so far as they contribute to the ethical goal. Religion must demonstrate that its principles not only do not contradict the progress of the state towards the ethical ideal but contribute to its realization. Such a formal directive cannot by itself generate particular truths of faith. These arise in the self-transformation of mythology into a religion which each faith must achieve, in so far as it has a 'share in reason'. Religion continuously transforms myths into ethically justifiable truths of faith. Thus a religion of reason can direct the individual and the community toward moral progress by contributing to the generation of moral consciousness. The task of a philosophy of religion is exposition of the truths of faith of a particular tradition, in so far as they can be conceived as transcending its myths (1904: 337, 388, 586).

The correlation of God and man, fully developed only in *Die Religion der Vernunft aus den Quellen des Judentums (Religion of Reason out of the Sources of Judaism)* (1919), serves to clarify both the historical development and the systematic structure of the truths of the Jewish faith: God and man are correlated as coordinates that progressively determine each other. Reason here aims continually to reconstitute the moral direction of the individual and the community by generating the whole set of moral conditions in the language of the Jewish faith. Accordingly, the religious correlation of God and man must construct the whole apparatus of moral responsibility and law within itself as a condition for the regeneration of individual moral consciousness.

Cohen's thought revolves around this correlational idea of God, which is, for him, the decisive contribution of Judaism to civilization. Even in *Ethik des reinen Willen*, God is the systematic capstone uniting ethics with logic. Addressing the 'being of the ought', ethics has no grounding in reality unless the human spirit has recourse to a principle that unites the present reality (nature) with the ideal of its future. The realization of the ethical ideal in the actual world rests on the assumption of a common origin of both nature and man. Cohen (1919) supports the same idea from within the sources of Judaism that are concretized in the speech-acts of the liturgy.

See also: LOGIC OF ETHICAL DISCOURSE; NEO-KANTIANISM

List of works

Cohen, H. (1977–) *Werke*, ed. Hermann-Cohen-

Archiv am Philosophischen Seminar der Universität Zürich unter der Leitung von Helmut Holzhey, Hildesheim, Zurich and New York: Georg Olms, 18 vols. (Including one published and six forthcoming volumes of minor writings and a forthcoming new edition of *Religion der Vernunft*, the *Werke* constitute the first comprehensive edition of Cohen's works, with mostly excellent introductions, comparison of editions, notes, and so on.)

—— (1871) *Kants Theorie der Erfahrung* (Kant's Theory of Experience), ed. G. Edel, Berlin: Dümmler; 3rd edn, 1918; 1st and 3rd edns repr. in *Werke*, vol. 1.1—1.3, Hildesheim: Georg Olms, 1987. (Volume 1.1 of the *Werke* edition consists of a reprint of the 3rd edition, Berlin, 1918; vol. 1.2 lists the variations between the earlier editions and offers an index; vol. 1.3 is a reprint of the 1st edition. The variations between the volumes indicate the progress from Cohen's first exposition of Kantian thought to his own mature system of philosophy, masterfully analysed by the editor.)

—— (1877) *Kants Begründung der Ethik nebst ihren Anwendungen auf Recht, Religion und Geschichte* (Kant's Justification of Ethics and its Application to Law, Religion and History), Berlin: Dümmler; 2nd edn, 1910. (The 1st edition of this work presented a considerable step beyond a mere exposition of Kantian thought. It is here that Cohen first 'eliminates' the Kantian 'thing-in-itself' and presents the foundation of his own philosophical approach. The 2nd edition is much revised, especially in its programmatic approach to the relation of ethics to the humanities. This edition is to be reprinted in volume 2 of *Werke*.)

—— (1883) *Das Prinzip der Infinitesimalmethode und seine Geschichte: Ein Kapitel zur Grundlegung der Erkenntniskritik* (The Principle of the Method of Infinitesimals and its History: A Chapter in the Foundation of the Critique of Cognition), Berlin: Dümmler; 4th edn repr. in *Werke*, vol. 5.1, Hildesheim: Georg Olms, with an introduction by P. Schultheß, 1984. (This study first established the link between the method of scientific validity and the principle of the origin of cognition in thought that became the cornerstone of Cohen (1902).)

—— (1889) *Kants Begründung der Ästhetik* (Kant's Justification of Aesthetics), Berlin: Dümmler. (Rounding out the tripartite structure of studies based on Kant's three critiques, this is Cohen's foray into the field of aesthetics. The work found little resonance at the time. It is to be reprinted in volume 11 of *Werke*.)

—— (1896) 'Biographisches Vorwort und Einleitung mit kritischem Nachtrag' (Biographical Preface and Introduction with a Critical Postscript), in F.A.

Lange (ed.) *Geschichte des Materialismus* (History of Materialism), Leipzig: Baedecker, 5th edn; repr. in *Werke*, vol. 5.2, with an introduction by H. Holzhey, Hildesheim: Georg Olms, 1984. (F.A. Lange had been Cohen's benefactor in that he was responsible for Cohen's call to the University of Marburg, where Cohen became Lange's successor. Cohen was responsible for several subsequent editions of Lange's best-selling philosophical study of the history of materialism. Yet in his 'Introduction with a Critical Postscript', revised in 1914, Cohen also criticized Lange and gave a précis of his own philosophical programme. The edition of 1896 was hailed by Vaihinger as 'no less than a new foundation of critical idealism'.)

—— (1902) *System der Philosophie, Erster Teil: Logik der reinen Erkenntnis* (System of Philosophy Part One: The Logic of Pure Cognition), Berlin: Bruno Cassirer; repr. in *Werke*, vol. 6, Hildesheim: Georg Olms, 1977. (The first part of the mature philosophical system which is clearly no longer Kantian but original.)

—— (1904) *System der Philosophie, Zweiter Teil: Ethik des reinen Willen* (System of Philosophy Part Two: Ethics of Pure Will), Berlin: Bruno Cassirer, 1904; repr. in *Werke*, vol. 7, with an English introduction by S.S. Schwarzschild, Hildesheim: Georg Olms, 1981. (A philosophy of the relation between state, community and individuals based on the conceptual tools of jurisprudence. Lays the foundations of a moral philosophy of law and of religion.)

—— (1912) *System der Philosophie, Dritter Teil: Ästhetik des reinen Gefühls* (System of Philosophy Part Three: Aesthetics of Pure Feeling), Berlin: Bruno Cassirer; repr. in *Werke*, vols 8 and 9, with an introduction by G. Wolandt, Hildesheim: Georg Olms, 1982. (Cohen's aesthetics aims to unite natural and moral aspects in the sentiments of *Erhabenheit* (sublimeness) and *Humor* (humour). Walter Benjamin was one of the few appreciative readers of this work. Other contemporaries considered it an unreadable book and a collection of professorial ramblings.)

—— (1915) *Der Begriff der Religion im System der Philosophie* (The Concept of Religion in the System of Philosophy), Gießen: Töpelmann; repr. in *Werke*, vol. 10, ed. H. Holzhey, with an introduction by A. Poma, Hildesheim: Georg Olms, 1996. (In this work, dedicated to the Marburg School's discussions on religion, Cohen first argued for an integration of religion into the system of philosophy without 'sublating' it into ethics.)

—— (1919) *Die Religion der Vernunft aus den Quellen des Judentums*, Leipzig: Fock; trans. S. Kaplan with an introduction by L. Strauss, *Religion of Reason out of the Sources of Judaism*, New York: Frederick Ungar, 1972. (The title of the first edition included a definite article before the word 'religion' as if to say Judaism was the only religion of reason. Since this seemed contrary to Cohen's opinion, subsequent editions dropped the definitie article, reading *Religion der Vernunft*. Hailed by Julius Guttmann as having renewed the discipline of Jewish philosophy, this work nevertheless failed to have a serious impact until its current rediscovery as a serious interpretation of a classical religion in the spirit of humanistic philosophy.)

—— (1924) *Hermann Cohens Jüdische Schriften* (Hermann Cohen's Jewish Writings), ed. B. Straub, with an introduction by F. Rosenzweig, Berlin: Schwetschke; partial English translation by E. Jospe, *Reason and Hope: Selections from the Jewish Writings of Hermann Cohen*, New York: W.W. Norton, 1971. (The forthcoming six volumes of *Kleinere Schriften*, published as volumes 13 through 17 of *Werke*, will do away with the unhelpful division between this collection and the one published in 1928. Contains a wealth of material of interest to students of the history of philosophy and religion in Wilhelminian Germany.)

—— (1928) *Schriften zur Philosophie und Zeitgeschichte* (Philosophical and Political Writings), eds A. Görland and E. Cassirer, Berlin: Akademieverlag, 2 vols. (Contains political and philosophical writings that will be reissued in chronological order and integrated with Cohen (1924) in the *Werke* edition.)

References and further reading

* Adelmann, D. (1968) *Einheit des Bewußtseins als Grundproblem der Philosophie Hermann Cohens*, Inaugural-Dissertation, Heidelberg: Ruprecht-Karl-Universität, 1968. (The first attempt to understand Cohen's philosophy under the aspect of the 'unity of the cultural consciousness'.)

Altmann, A. (1962) 'Hermann Cohens Begriff der Korrelation', in H. Tramer (ed.) *Zwei Welten: Siegfried Moses zum Fünfundsiebzigsten Geburtstag*, Tel Aviv, 366–99. (The first challenge to the, until then pervasive, interpretation of Cohen's Jewish thought associated with Franz Rosenzweig's 'Einleitung' (1924) in Hermann Cohen's *Jüdische Schriften*.)

Brandt, R. and Orlik, F. (1993) *Philosophisches Denken – Politisches Wirken. Hermann-Cohen-Kolloquium Marburg 1992*, Hildesheim, Zurich and New York: Georg Olms. (A collection of essays representing contemporary European scholarship on various aspects of Cohen's philosophy.)

* Brelage, M. (1965) *Studien zur Transzendentalphilosophie*, Berlin: de Gruyter. (Evaluates Cohen's theoretical philosophy in the context of the approaches of Husserl, Hartmann, Hönigswald and Heidegger.)

Edel, G. (1988) *Von der Vernunftkritik zur Erkenntnislogik: Die Entwicklung der theoretischen Philosophie Hermann Cohens*, Freiburg i.Br.: Alber. (The most lucid exposition of the development of Cohen's theoretical philosophy to date. With a bibliography of literature on Cohen.)

Holzhey, H. (1986) *Cohen und Natorp*, vol. 1, *Ursprung und Einheit: Die Geschichte der 'Marburger Schule' als Auseinandersetzung um die Logik des Denkens*, and vol. 2, *Der Marburger Neukantianismus in Quellen: Zeugnisse kritischer Lektüre: Briefe der Marburger: Dokumente zur Philosophiepolitik der Schule*, Basle and Stuttgart: Schwabe. (Written by the founder of the Hermann-Cohen-Archiv at Philosophisches Seminar der Universität Zürich, vol. 1 clarifies the basic differences between the theoretical philosophies of the two 'heads' of the Marburg School; vol. 2 contains documents and comprehensive bibliographies.)

* Köhnke, K.C. (1991) *The Rise of Neokantianism: German Academic Philosophy between Idealism and Positivism*, trans. R.J. Hollingdale, Cambridge and New York: Cambridge University Press. (Excellent background for the rise of Neo-Kantianism. Weak in its chapter on Cohen.)

Orlik, F. (1992) *Hermann Cohen (1842–1918): Kantinterpret – Begründer der 'Marburger Schule' – Jüdischer Religionsphilosoph*, Schriften der Universitätsbibliothek Marburg 63, Marburg: Universitätsbibliothek. (Excellent biographical resource.)

Poma, A. (1988) *Filosofia critica di Hermann Cohen*, Milan: Ugo Mursia Editore, 1988; trans. J. Denton, *The Critical Philosophy of Hermann Cohen*, Albany, NY: State University of New York Press, 1997. (A well-researched and elegantly written comprehensive introduction to the philosophy of Hermann Cohen.)

Schwarzschild, S.S. (1975) 'The Tenability of Hermann Cohen's Construction of the Self', *Journal of the History of Philosophy* 13: 361–84. (The pioneer of US scholarship on Cohen addressing the key problem of Cohen's philosophy of religion.)

Wiedebach, H. (1997) *Die Bedeutung der Nationalität für Hermann Cohen*, Hildesheim, Zurich and New York: Georg Olms. (A masterful pioneering study on the political dimension in Cohen's thought.)

Winter, E. (1980) *Ethik und Rechtswissenschaft. Eine*

historisch-sytematische Untersuchung zur Ethik-Konzeption des Marburger Neukantianismus im Werke Hermann Cohens, Berlin: Duncker & Humblot. (On Cohen's ethics, compared to contemporary philosophies of law.)

Zank, M. (1994) 'Reconciling Judaism and "Cultural Consciousness": The Idea of Versöhnung in Hermann Cohen's Philosophy of Religion', Ph.D. dissertation, Waltham, MA: Brandeis University. (Analyses the development of Cohen's religious philosophy; with documents and bibliographies.)

—— (1996) '"The Individual as I" in Hermann Cohen's Jewish Thought', *The Journal of Jewish Thought and Philosophy* 5: 281–96. (A study of the ambiguity of Cohen's late philosophy of religion, between idealism and existentialism.)

MICHAEL ZANK

COHERENCE THEORY OF JUSTIFICATION AND KNOWLEDGE *see* KNOWLEDGE AND JUSTIFICATION, COHERENCE THEORY OF

COHERENCE THEORY OF TRUTH *see* TRUTH, COHERENCE THEORY OF

COIMBRA GROUP
see COLLEGIUM CONIMBRICENSE

COLERIDGE, SAMUEL TAYLOR (1772–1834)

Although much of Coleridge's life and his best critical and creative powers were devoted to the attempt to develop a philosophical system, he is less well known as a philosopher than as a romantic poet. This is partly because many of his writings remained unpublished until recent years; they now shed new light on the extent of his knowledge of intellectual history, and on the significance of his philosophical synthesis.

As a young man, Coleridge was attracted by the materialist philosophies and theories of human nature which had become part of the Enlightenment's 'Science of Man'. These coincided with his support for the drive towards progress and human brotherhood which he thought inspired the French Revolution. At Cambridge (1791–4) religious doubt accompanied his radical politics and he turned from orthodox Christianity to Unitarianism.

Gradually, however, he became dissatisfied with the 'mechanistic' reductive principles of British eighteenth-century thought. His visit to Germany (1798–9) and his subsequent study of German ideas convinced him that here was a spectrum of philosophical insights which was more adequate to the whole *of human nature; one through which 'head and heart' might be reconciled.*

Coleridge's work reflects his experience of a world subject to violent revolutionary upheavals and his sense of widespread intellectual and moral confusion. Becoming convinced in the early years of the nineteenth century of both the intellectual and spiritual value of Christianity, he sought to re-establish a unity between religious faith and experience and critical philosophy. His 'ideal Realism' reconciled elements of Greek and German philosophy with reinterpretations of Judaeo-Christian themes and doctrines, and with the moral lessons he believed history provided. Any sound philosophy must, he insisted, do justice to every aspect of human nature. He declared that he was not concerned to be 'original' but to provide a new synthesis, and boldly claimed to have been the first to have 'attempted to reduce all knowledges into harmony'; although his copious notes intended for an Opus Maximum, *the 'Logosophia', were never organized into publishable form.*

1 Metaphysics
2 Political philosophy

1 Metaphysics

German philosophy showed Coleridge that he was not alone in seeking a new philosophical ground beyond either dogmatic empiricism or ungrounded metaphysical speculation. He was deeply influenced by, for example, KANT, F.H. JACOBI, FICHTE and SCHELLING, but also examined them critically. In general, he believed idealist philosophy had failed to discern the true nature of a 'self' and its inherent relationality. Other central focuses in his work include the dynamic and constitutive nature of Ideas, the primacy of absolute Will over Being or Mind, and the relation of words as 'living powers' to thought and being.

Coleridge's epistemology is inseparable from his moral philosophy. His insistence in the 'Essay on Faith' that conscience is a precondition of true self-consciousness, for example, is related to his theory of Ideas. He is often categorized as belonging to the

Platonist and idealist traditions of thought; certainly he rejects the view that Ideas are merely abstract concepts opposed to reality or (as they were for Kant) merely regulative; they are constitutive of the world, and so must never be confused with mere images or objects of thought. He agrees with Plato that ideal and real are not opposed, and with Descartes that all ideas (as opposed to beliefs or opinions) are their own evidence; but his own theory of ideas is coloured by his agreement with Fichte, that if knowledge is possible at all, it begins with an 'act of will'. There has to be an affirmation given to the inner witness of experience and feeling, even in the first step of perception; though at this stage the 'yes' is pure act, not a cognitive response. Like Fichte, he recognized that, without this, philosophy was powerless to refute scepticism; if, on the other hand, ideas have a dynamic of will, then conscience and consciousness must be intimately connected.

Coleridge's theory of ideas is linked to his development of the German distinction between *Vernunft* (Reason) and *Verstand* (Understanding) (see KANT, I. §8; HEGEL, G.W.F. §4). Reason is the faculty of Ideas, a unifying, uniquely human faculty which, in its unity with the will, is inaccessible to causal explanation. The Understanding, by contrast, is the faculty of 'speculative intellect'; the power of analysis, of logical deduction, of calculation, quantification and explanation. Reason includes the faculty of imagination, the image of divine creativity. Imagination creates and interprets the symbols through which universal principles or Ideas are revealed in particular form. It recognizes that what appear to the Understanding to be contradictions (for example, a reality which is both universal and particular) are in fact the necessary polarities by which reality is constituted.

An important theme in Coleridge's writings is that of 'distinction-in-unity'. Drawn from a synthesis of the philosophies of Pythagoras, Plato and the Alexandrian Jew, Philo, with the Christian model of Trinity, this principle provides the basis of his contribution to the debate on the nature of the self and self-consciousness. Distinction-in-unity was not merely a logical, regulative concept but represented dynamic relationship; that through which, for example, the self is constituted. It is also the means of moral development by which individuals become persons. Coleridge argued that the necessary conditions of personhood (relationship, free will, reason and love) require a transcendent source of 'personeity'. His Absolute is a primacy of Will, self-realized in Mind (Idea) and Being. Throughout his mature writings the nature and function of will and 'act' in relation to reason is constantly reassessed.

Coleridge found in Christianity a language through which the principle of self-consciousness was perfectly expressed. The Trinity was representable as 'ipseity' ('this-ness' or 'self-ness'), 'alterity' ('other-ness') and 'community' (the former two realized in relationship). 'Alterity' is symbolized by *Logos* as the 'Word' or Idea of God; God-other-and-the-same, the first principle of relationship. The 'Community' (Spirit) of the Godhead is a self-realizing, self-limiting love of the 'Other' as another Self. These relations, Coleridge argued, constituted the principle of Humanity. The human self is only fully realized in relation to a Thou ('Essay on Faith').

Distinction-in-unity also provided the basis of his philosophy of nature. He agreed with the German *Naturphilosophen* that life must be understood not in terms of organization, mechanisms or configurations of atoms, but as polarities of forces and powers, and their products (see NATURPHILOSOPHIE). Throughout his life he followed the latest scientific theories and developments in academic journals, and his *Note-books* reveal strenuous efforts to show how moral and natural philosophy might be reconciled.

Coleridge saw philosophical integrity and linguistic veracity as interdependent. The abuse of language, with its lack of attention to etymology and to the relation of grammar and language to the processes of thought, resulted in intellectual and moral corruption (*Aids To Reflection*, 1825). It was necessary to 'desynonymize'; to understand the unique, living quality of each word, and therefore its true relation to others. Words should reflect their true source – the *Logos*, the incarnate Word of God.

The *Logos*, as the unifying principle of the 'Logosophia', is first an epistemological principle representing the birth of language, of self-consciousness and therefore of philosophy. *Logos* is also an aesthetic medium; as 'Word' it is the archetypal symbol of the revelatory power of words and imagination. As the principle of polarity ('alterity') it is also the 'life and light' of nature's powers, forces and products. Finally, *Logos* may be defined as ideal Humanity (universal and individual).

2 Political philosophy

As a young man, Coleridge was influenced by the political radicalism of friends such as John Thelwall and William GODWIN, and by the reforming zeal of Joseph Priestley's Unitarianism (see PRIESTLEY, J.). He agreed with the latter's view that Jesus was himself a true radical and a free-thinking teacher whose humanity was devalued by the attribution of divinity. By the mid-1790s he had distanced himself from Godwin's radical atheism and from Thelwall's view of the irrelevance of Christianity to reform. Soon after, he was to become dissatisfied with Priestley's materialism. However, his Bristol Lectures (1795) and his journal *The Watchman* (1796) reflect his continuing admiration for the principles (if not the practical reality) of the French Revolution, his criticism of the established Church, and his critique of property.

Coleridge contributed essays and leaders to newspapers on all aspects of social and political thought: on economics, government, foreign affairs, relations of church and state, on monarchy, and on representation. He consistently supported the antislavery movement and opposed the bills, acts and political movements that he thought endangered 'nationality' and the principles of true humanity. As his theory of nationhood developed, based on the relation between 'national church', monarch and state (*On the Constitution of Church and State*, 1830) the tone of Coleridge's political and social criticism changed. His later views are all related to his concept of the state in the widest sense of nation or 'body politic'. This, in its ideal form, contained the unity of state and national church. In any particular historical representation of the idea, national church and state are *opposing* poles. Together with the sovereign, they maintain the harmony and balance of the whole.

Coleridge contrasted 'party-spirit' and 'clanship' to true 'national spirit'. On this basis, he denounced the 'false patriotism' of the Irish movements for independence and Catholic emancipation. While Roman Catholics were not to be excluded from the Christian church, their fealty to Rome amounted to self-exclusion from the *national* church, and therefore from full citizenship. For this reason, he found that he could not support the 1829 bill for emancipation. Catholics could not, for example, belong to the 'clerisy'; the leaders who would foster the ideal characteristics of humanity. These would ensure the development of Reason, the religious sense, a philosophical and moral understanding of history, attention to the true meaning of words and a recognition of the state as (potentially) a living unity of Will and Reason rather than a Hobbesian 'Leviathan'.

'Nation', Coleridge agreed with Kant, was not to be identified with 'people'; he was not a democrat, and did not equate the desires of the aggregate of the people with the interests of the nation. He distrusted the foreshadowings of mass labour movements, as his later notebooks show, declaring them to be the result of bad government which had ignored the moral lessons of history and abandoned the fundamental question of what it is to be human. He vehemently criticized leading politicians and statesmen, such as William Pitt and Charles Grey, for failing to preserve the 'nationalty'; that is, a reserve for the nation in the form of 'a *wealth* not consisting of lands, but yet derivative from the land, and rightfully inseparable from the same'. This was the opposite pole to the division of land into 'propriety', or 'hereditable estates' among individuals; these were 'the two constituent factors, the opposite, but correspondent and reciprocally supporting, counter-weights, of the *commonwealth*'. He rejected the 'political economy' of such thinkers as Adam SMITH and Thomas Malthus as 'a science which begins with *abstractions*, in order to exclude whatever is not subject to a technical calculation'. These 'abstractions' it assumes 'as the whole of human nature'.

Coleridge described the nation as 'a moral unity, an organic whole'. Its archetype was that of the Jewish people in the time of Moses. Despite his criticism of 'party-spirit', he often openly declared the superiority of the English nation; of its constitution, and its development through the creative tension of the opposing principles of 'progression' and 'conservation'. He became increasingly fearful that the nation was under threat of a moral vacuum, but abandoned his earlier political radicalism in favour of philosophical combat against an encroaching 'mechanism' that ignored not only the human ideal, but also human nature, need and experience.

See also: GERMAN IDEALISM

List of works

Coleridge, S.T. (1969–) *The Collected Works*, ed. various, Princeton, NJ, and London: Princeton University Press and Routledge. (The grand project of this critical edition, together with the *Letters* and the *Notebooks* will, when complete, represent the whole of Coleridge's vast achievement, much of it for the first time in published form. Begun at the end of the 1960s, its aim has been to give his writings the widest possible circulation by providing accurate readable transcriptions, and by attempting to make sense of fragments, trace references and allusions by detailed cross-referencing and editorial commentary. The *Collected Works* includes *The Watchman* (vol. 2) and the 'Essay on Faith', in the volume *Shorter Works and Fragments*, ed. H. and J.R. de J. Jackson, 1995.)

—— (1966–71) *Collected Letters of Samuel Taylor Coleridge*, ed. E.L. Griggs, Oxford: Clarendon Press, 6 vols. (E.L. Grigg's edition of the *Collected Letters* gives access to Coleridge's correspondence with family, friends, publishers, fellow scholars, poets and other eminent men and women of his time. They reveal the chronology of his preoccupations, his hopes and fears, the details of his daily life and the development of his thought.)

—— (1957–) *The Coleridge Notebooks*, ed. K. Coburn and M. Christensen, Princeton, NJ: Princeton University Press, 5 vols. (*The Coleridge Notebooks* reveal not only the vast range of Coleridge's reading and his intellectual brilliance and profundity, but show his repeated return to struggle with certain topics and the sources of influence on which he drew. Here are fragments of his thought on the physical sciences, on history, religion, psychology, politics, grammar – all witnessing to his continual attempt to show the ultimate unity of nature and mind, philosophy and religion, thought, feeling and experience.)

References and further reading

Colmer, J. (1959) *Coleridge, Critic of Society*, Oxford: Oxford University Press. (Still one of the best studies of the whole range of Coleridge's political thought.)

Jasper, D. (ed.) (1986) *The Interpretation of Belief: Coleridge, Schleiermacher and Romanticism*, London: Macmillan. (An interesting compendium of short critical studies of religious, literary and philosophical themes in Coleridge.)

McKusick, J.C. (1986) *Coleridge's Philosophy of Language*, New Haven, CT: Yale University Press. (A lively and stimulating account of this aspect of Coleridge's thought; of moderate difficulty in its specialism.)

Modiano, R. (1985) *Coleridge and the Concept of Nature*, London: Macmillan. (A very good and readable account of the relation of Coleridge's thought to German philosophies of nature.)

Morrow, J. (1990) *Coleridge's Political Thought: Property, Morality and the Limits of Traditional Discourse*, London: Macmillan. (Clear and useful in the relationship which it draws between Coleridge's moral philosophy and his political criticism. A good bibliography.)

Muirhead, J.H. (1930) *Coleridge as Philosopher*, London: Allen & Unwin. (One of the best and most enduring attempts to take Coleridge's philosophical claims seriously; of moderate difficulty.)

Newsome, D. (1974) *Two Classes of Men*, London: John Murray. (Clear and stimulating, based on Coleridge's division of thinkers into Platonists or Aristotelians; accessible.)

Perkins, M.A. (1994) *Coleridge's Philosophy: the Logos as Unifying Principle*, Oxford: Oxford University Press. (A thorough, sometimes demanding overview of Coleridge's thought in the light of his search for unity.)

Skorupski, J. (1993) *English Language Philosophy 1750–1945*, Oxford: Oxford University Press. (The first chapter here is useful).

Uehlein, F.A. (1982) *Die Manifestation des Selbstbewusstseins im konkreten 'Ich bin'* (The Manifestation of Self-Consciousness in the Concrete 'I am'), Hamburg: Felix Meiner Verlag. (One of the best analyses of the role of self-consciousness. Again, intellectually demanding in places and unfortunately not yet in translation.)

MARY ANNE PERKINS

COLLEGIUM CONIMBRICENSE

The Collegium Conimbricense ('Coimbra group') or the Conimbricenses were late sixteenth- and early seventeenth-century Jesuit philosophy professors at the University of Coimbra, specifically in the College of Arts, which in 1555 had been placed under the direction of the Society of Jesus. Encouraged by their religious superiors and especially by Pedro da Fonseca, between 1592 and 1606 the Conimbricenses published five volumes containing eight treatises of commentary on Aristotle. Distributed particularly through the Jesuits, these volumes were widely influential in Europe, America, and the Far East, including Japan and China. On this last, Sommervogel (1891) has cited the seventeenth-century Jesuit, Athanasius Kircher, to the effect that by his time all the Coimbra commentaries had been translated into Chinese.

Chief members of the Collegium Conimbricense were Emmanuel de Goes (1542–97), Cosmas de Magelhães (1551–1624), Balthasar Alvarez (1561–1630), and Sebastian de Couto (1567–1639). In order of appearance, their treatises were: (1) *Commentarii Collegii Conimbricensis Societatis Jesu in octo libros Physicorum Aristotelis Stagyritae* (Commentaries... on the Eight Books of Aristotle's *Physics*) (1592); (2) *Commentarii Collegii Conimbricensis Societatis Jesu in quatuor libros de Coelo* (Commentaries... on the Four Books of *On the Heavens*) (1592); (3) *Commentarii Collegii Conimbricensis Societatis Jesu in libros meteorum* (Commentaries... on the Books of the *Meteorology*) (1592); (4) *Commentarii Collegii Conimbricensis Societatis Jesu in parva naturalia* (Commentaries... on the *Parva Naturalia*) (1592); (5) *Commentarii Collegii Conimbricensis Societatis Jesu in libros Ethicorum ad Nichomachum* (Commentaries ... on the Books of the *Nicomachean Ethics*) (1595);

(6) *Commentarii Collegii Conimbricensis Societatis Jesu in libros de generatione et corruptione Aristotelis Stagiritae* (Commentaries...on Aristotle's *On Generation and Corruption*) (1595); (7) *Commentarii Collegii Conimbricensis Societatis Jesu in libros de anima Aristotelis Stagiritae* (Commentaries...on Aristotle's *On the Soul*) (1595) (this work was edited by Magelhães, who added his 'Tractatio aliquot problematum ad quinque sensus spectantium' (A Treatment of Some Problems regarding the Five Senses) and attached a treatise by Alvarez called 'De Anima Separata' (On the Separated Soul), because Aristotle had not discussed the separated soul in the previous books); and (8) *Commentarii Collegii Conimbricensis et Societatis Jesu in Universam Dialecticam Aristotelis* (Commentaries...on the Whole Logic of Aristotle) (1606).

This last volume, which was edited and published by de Couto, shows the Conimbricenses at their best. Through its two main parts, following the style of Fonseca's commentaries on the *Metaphysics* of Aristotle (see FONSECA, P. DA §3), they have reviewed individual treatises of the Organon. For each of these, they give the Greek of Aristotle, translate it into Latin, summarize and explain its philosophical doctrine, and then comment on it by raising *questions* which it had occasioned among the scholastics of the sixteenth and earlier centuries. Their scholarship, with regard to Greek, Latin, philosophy and the scholastic tradition before themselves, is quite evident. Evident also is the sincerity and depth of their own philosophical interest.

A good example is the first chapter of their commentary on Aristotle's *De interpretatione*. Entitled *De signo* (On the Sign), it is more than sixty pages long. While some treatment of signs in Aristotelian commentary was common among the scholastics, these pages of the Conimbricenses represent the first really major seventeenth-century treatise on signs. Five principal issues are raised: (1) the nature and conditions common to signs; (2) the divisions of signs; (3) the signification of spoken words and of writing; (4) whether concepts are the same among all, and (going into the question of a natural primitive language) whether spoken words are different; and (5) whether some concepts in our minds are true or false, and others devoid of truth and falsity. Along the way there are sub-questions about the essence of a sign, the possibility of something being a sign of itself, signs as natural or conventional, signs as formal or instrumental, signs as actual or aptitudinal, the relations involved in signs, and so forth. Although their commentary is a work of logic, the Conimbricenses show awareness of many epistemological, psychological, metaphysical and theological questions which can be raised with regard to signs and signification. They also display a remarkable understanding of the breadth and scope of semiotics itself.

Some of the items which they have touched on in different ways are the following: language, syntactical speech, laughing, nodding, coughing, people talking in their sleep, people lying, people emitting words without thought. They consider the signification of negative words, of syncategorematic words such as 'if', nonsense words like 'Blictri', and words like 'chimera' and 'goat-stag' to which no real things correspond. They are interested in the signs involved in writing and reading, especially voiceless reading. Coupled with a short discussion of the physiological bases of speech and hearing, they treat the relation between deafness and an inability to speak or communicate. Relying on Herodotus' account of King Psamittachus, who deliberately reared children with animals to see what language they would naturally speak, as well as on an account, from Jesuit missionaries at the court of Akbar the Great, Mogul of India, of a similar experiment conducted by that prince in 1596, the Conimbricenses discuss the language of what amount to feral children. Probably also relying on accounts of Portuguese Jesuit missionaries, they briefly speak of the difference between written languages which use pictograms (they mention hieroglyphics, as well as Chinese and Japanese characters) and those which use an alphabet. Connected with this they touch upon the signification of arithmetical numbers as well as astronomical signs. Topics occasioned by the Bible are the language of Adam and Eve, the language of Adam when giving 'proper' names to the animals, the sign of Cain (which following St Jerome they regard as a tremor), the rainbow given to Noah, and the phenomenon of different languages at the Tower of Babel (see LANGUAGE, RENAISSANCE PHILOSOPHY OF §2). In the area of zoosemiosis, they mention Aristotle's study of the song of birds, and they discuss the formation of words by parrots and magpies, as well as different kinds of communication among brute animals. Against a general background of optics, they discuss images as signs, especially images in mirrors. While it does not fully express their semiotic theory, one very revealing sentence is the following: 'There is nothing which leads to the cognition of anything else which cannot be reduced to some sort of sign' (*In universam dialecticam* II q.2 a.3).

See also: ARISTOTELIANISM IN THE 17TH CENTURY §2; ARISTOTELIANISM, RENAISSANCE; FONSECA, P. DA; LANGUAGE OF THOUGHT; LANGUAGE, RENAISSANCE PHILOSOPHY OF

List of works

Commentarii Collegii Conimbricensis Societatis Jesu in octo libros Physicorum Aristotelis Stagyritae (Commentaries... on the Eight Books of Aristotle's *Physics*), 1592; Lyons, 1594; repr. Hildesheim: Olms, 1984. (Contains commentary questions on change, substance, accidents and other topics treated in Aristotle's *Physics*.)

Commentarii Collegii Conimbricensis Societatis Jesu in libros de generatione et corruptione Aristotelis Stagiritae (Commentaries... on Aristotle's *On Generation and Corruption*), 1595; Mainz, 1606; repr. Hildesheim: Olms, forthcoming. (Contains commentary questions on coming to be and passing away and other topics treated in Aristotle's *On Generation and Corruption*.)

Commentarii Collegii Conimbricensis Societatis Jesu in libros de anima Aristotelis Stagiritae (Commentaries... on Aristotle's *On the Soul*), 1595; repr. Lyons: Horatio Cardon, 1627. (Contains Greek text, Latin translation, explanation of chapters of Aristotle's *On the Soul*, with commentary questions on Books 2 and 3 of this work.)

Commentarii Collegii Conimbricensis Societatis Jesu in libros Ethicorum ad Nichomachum (Commentaries... on the Books of the *Nicomachean Ethics*), 1595; repr. Lyons: Horatio Cardon, 1616. (This work, which is without text or translation of Aristotle, is ninety-five columns long and made up of nine disputations each divided into questions on the *Nicomachean Ethics*.)

Commentarii Collegii Conimbricensis Societatis Jesu in quatuor libros de caelo, meteorologicos, et parva naturalia, Aristotelis Stagiritae (Commentaries... on Aristotle's *On the Heavens, Meterology* and *Parva Naturalia*), Cologne: Impensis Lazari Zetzneri, 1603. (Contains commentary questions on three works of Aristotle).

Commentarii Collegii Conimbricensis et Societatis Jesu. In Universam Dialecticam Aristotelis Stagiritae (Commentaries... on the Whole Logic of Aristotle), Cologne, 1607; repr. Hildesheim: Olms, 1976. (The treatise *De signo* (On the Sign) is in the second part. The reprinted 1607 edition, unlike the 1606 edition cited in the main text, does not contain the Greek text.)

References and further reading

Doyle, J.P. (1985) 'The *Conimbricenses* on the Relations Involved in Signs', in *Semiotics 1984*, New York: Plenum Press, 567–76. (Introduction to the sign theory of the Conimbricenses.)

Lohr, C.H. (1987) *Latin Aristotle Commentaries. II Renaissance Authors*, Florence: Olschki, 98–9. (Contains bibliographical information on the commentaries of the Collegium Conimbricense.)

Risse, W. (1964) *Die Logik der Neuzeit* (The Logic of the Modern Period), Stuttgart and Bad Cannstatt: Frommann, 373–8. (Conimbricenses' logic treated within its historical context.)

Solana, M. (1940) *Historia de la filosof–a española. Época del renacimiento (siglo XVI)* (History of Spanish Philosophy. The Time of the Renaissance (16th Century)), Madrid: Asociación Española para el Progreso de las Ciencias, vol. 3, 366–71. (Contains some treatment of the Conimbricenses' doctrine on sensation.)

* Sommervogel, C. (1891) *Bibliothèque de la Compagnie de Jésus* (Booklist of the Society of Jesus), Bruxelles: Oscar Schepens, vol. 2, cols 1273–8. (Referred to in the introduction; contains information about the editions of the Conimbricenses' commentaries.)

Stegmüller, F. (1959) *Filosofia e teologia nas universidades de Coimbra e Evora no seculo XVI* (Philosophy and Theology in the Universities of Coimbra and Evora in the 16th Century), Coimbra: Universidade de Coimbra, 95–9. (The Conimbricenses treated within a wider context.)

Tavares, S. and Bacalar Oliveira, J. (1967) 'Conimbricensi', in *Enciclopedia Filosofica*, Florence: Sansoni, vol. 1, cols. 1590–1. (Contains information about the diffusion and the methods of the volumes of the Collegium Conimbricense.)

JOHN P. DOYLE

COLLIER, ARTHUR (1680–1732)

Arthur Collier was an English parish priest who arrived, independently, at a version of immaterialism strikingly similar to that of Berkeley. In his 1713 work Clavis Universalis *('universal key'), Collier contends that matter exists 'in, or in dependence on' the mind. Like Berkeley, he defends immaterialism as the only alternative to scepticism. He admits that bodies appear to be external, but their apparent or 'quasi' externeity is, he argues, merely the effect of God's will, and not a sign of 'real' externeity or mind-independence. In Part I of the* Clavis, *Collier argues (as Berkeley had in his* New Theory of Vision*) that the visible world is not external. In Part II he argues (as Berkeley had in both the* Principles *and the* Three Dialogues*) that the external world 'is a being utterly impossible'.*

1 Life

Collier was born at Langford Magna, near Salisbury in Wiltshire, England. He entered Pembroke College, Oxford in 1697 and transferred to Balliol in 1698. In 1704 he became rector of Langford Magna, a position he held until his death. While at Langford, Collier may have met John NORRIS whose *Essay towards a Theory of the Ideal or Intelligible World* (1701/4) he admired. Norris argued that the existence of the external world could not be demonstrated, but he did not deny that it exists. In the *Clavis Universalis* (1713) Collier set out to demonstrate this more radical conclusion.

By 'external', Collier writes, 'I understand the same as is usually understood by the words, absolute, self-existent, independent, etc.' ([1713a] 1909: 6). 'All matter, body, extension, etc. exists in, or in dependence on mind, thought, or perception, and ... is not capable of an existence, which is not thus dependent' – dependent, that is, not on any mind in particular, but on 'some mind or other' ([1713a] 1909: 6). There is, in fact, a material world in the mind of God that is numerically distinct from the world perceived by any of God's creatures. Collier insists that he makes 'no doubt or question' of the existence of bodies. But their existence, he contends, is an 'in-existence'. He compares it to the existence of objects seen in a mirror, and to the images that float before a fevered imagination.

2 The visible world

The *Clavis* is divided into two main parts: in the first, Collier, 'content for a while to grant that there is an external world' ([1713a] 1909: 33), argues that the visible world is not external; in the second, he argues that an external world is utterly impossible. The first part begins with the argument that we cannot justly infer real externeity from visible or apparent externeity. Sounds, smells, tastes and heat, which seem to exist 'altogether without' the mind, have been proven by DESCARTES, MALEBRANCHE and NORRIS to exist entirely within it. Light and colours, objects of sight which seem to be distant from or external to the mind, are not really external at all, any more than the visions seen by prophets, or the delusions of drunkards and madmen. If Apelles imagines a centaur, Collier says, the centaur seems to be external, even though it is, as an object of imagination, wholly within the mind.

God can turn the imaginary object into an object of sight, he proposes, without creating an external centaur, simply by *intensifying* Apelles' perception. The faint and languid image of a centaur will then become a vivid perception or object of sense. All the difference between imagining and seeing, Collier contends, is a difference of degree.

Collier offers several reasons why visible objects are not and cannot be external. If we press our eye as we look at the moon, we see two moons, not one. Both moons are equally vivid and they seem to be equally external. It follows, he claims, that either both are external or neither is. But 'we are agreed ... that they are not both so' ([1713a] 1909: 30). He therefore concludes that neither moon is external, observing that this pattern of reasoning can be extended to any visible object whatsoever. A second argument purports to show that the moon in the heavens is not the moon that humans see. The moon in the heavens is dark, opaque, spherical and large; the moon that humans see is luminous, flat and 'so little, as to be entirely covered by a shilling' ([1713a] 1909: 33). According to a third argument, a thing can be seen only if it is present to our mind. But an object cannot be present to the mind if it is external to it. Hence a visible object cannot possibly be external.

Part 1 of the *Clavis* concludes with a series of objections and replies. According to one objection, Descartes has shown that the existence of an external world can be derived from the goodness of God. Collier replies that although we are inclined to believe in an external world, the judgment that there is such a world is not involuntary. If it is mistaken, the blame falls not on God but on ourselves.

3 The external world

Part 2 of the *Clavis* is as relentlessly argumentative as Part 1: Collier presents nine separate arguments against an external world and concludes by replying to three objections. He begins by arguing that because an external world must be invisible (as established in Part 1), it must be unknowable. This is, he admits, no 'demonstration' that there is no external world, but it is 'near of kin to demonstration' and serves the same purpose, because it is an acknowledged rule of reasoning that an unknown thing should never be supposed to exist. Later he considers the objection (attributed to Malebranche) that Scripture assures us of an external world. Collier replies that it does not. He expands on his reply in *A Specimen of True Philosophy* (1730), where he develops an immaterialist interpretation of the opening verse of Genesis.

Collier's second argument is that God would have no reason to create an external world. It is therefore 'extrinsically impossible', or impossible in view of its cause. He goes on to claim, in arguments that resemble Kant's first and second antinomies, that it is also 'intrinsically impossible', or impossible in its own nature (see KANT, I. §8). He argues, for example, that the external world is both finite and infinite. The contradiction can be avoided, he claims, only by denying that the world is external to the mind. Arthur O. Lovejoy and Ethel Bowman are among the commentators who have noticed the resemblance to Kant. As Lovejoy (1908) points out, a German translation of the *Clavis* (bound with a translation of Berkeley's *Dialogues*) was published in 1756, but as Lovejoy admits (and as H.J. de Vleeschauwer (1938) argues in more detail) there is no persuasive evidence that Kant was actually influenced by Collier.

Collier also argues that because the external world is a created thing, it must 'subsist on the mind, or will, or power, of God' ([1713a] 1909: 87). He also argues, much as Berkeley had, that philosophical definitions of matter come to nothing, and that if the world is external, there is no theory of vision compatible with our seeing it. In a brief conclusion, Collier surveys the consequences of his doctrine. The survey is meant to fulfil his promise of a 'universal key' – a way of unlocking 'almost all the general questions that [the reader] has been used to account very difficult, or perhaps indissoluble' ([1713a] 1909: 131) – but apart from observing that his doctrine undermines the Catholic doctrine of transubstantiation, Collier discusses no particular question in detail. He admits that ordinary language is almost wholly built on the supposition of an external world. But he is no more disturbed by this than he was by the objection that the external existence of the visible world enjoys universal consent. Indeed the motto on the title page of the *Clavis*, borrowed from the Latin translation of Malebranche's *Search after Truth*, boldly proclaims that 'the popular approval of an opinion on a difficult matter is a certain sign of falsehood'.

4 Collier and Berkeley

Some scholars suspect that Collier deliberately concealed his debt to BERKELEY; most accept his report (in the first paragraph of the *Clavis*) that he arrived at his views ten years before he published them. Collier first refers to Berkeley in letters written in 1714–15. In *A Specimen of True Philosophy* (1730), he writes that 'except a single passage or two' in Berkeley's *Dialogues*, there is no other book 'which I ever heard of in the World' on the same subject as the *Clavis* (1730: 21). This is a puzzling remark on several counts, one being that in the Preface to the *Dialogues*, Berkeley describes both of his earlier books. Robert

Benson, Collier's biographer, reports seeing among his papers an outline, dated 1708, on the question of the visible world being without us or not, but says no more about it. Benson concludes that Collier's independence cannot reasonably be doubted; perhaps the outline would, if unearthed, establish this. There is, however, internal evidence for Collier's independence. As Charles J. McCracken (1983) shows, Collier's most important arguments have parallels in Malebranche and John Norris (who are among Collier's acknowledged sources) and in BAYLE (who is not). If we are determined to find Collier unoriginal, then we can do so without supposing that he borrowed from Berkeley.

See also: IDEALISM

List of Works

Collier, A. (1713a) *Clavis universalis: or, a new inquiry after truth. Being a demonstration of the non-existence, or impossibility, of an external world*, London: Printed for R. Gosling; ed. E. Bowman, Chicago, IL: Open Court, 1909; repr. New York: Garland, 1978. (Collier's defence of immaterialism. The Bowman edition has an introduction and notes.).

—— (1713b) *Christian principles of obedience to the higher powers. In a sermon preach'd . . . at the cathedral church of Sarum* [Salisbury], London: Printed for R. Gosling. (On the subjection of Christians to civil authority.)

—— (1716) *Of justification by faith, as in opposition to justification by works: in a sermon . . . preached at the cathedral church of Sarum* [Salisbury], London: Printed and sold by J. Downing. (Concludes with some remarks on systems of ethics.)

—— (1730) *A specimen of true philosophy in a discourse on Genesis: the first chapter and the first verse*, Sarum [Salisbury]: Printed by Charles Hooton. (An immaterialist interpretation of the opening verse of *Genesis*.)

Parr, S. (ed.) (1837) *Metaphysical tracts by English philosophers of the eighteenth century*, London: E. Lumley; repr. Hildersheim: Georg Olms, 1974; repr. Bristol: Thoemmes Press, 1992. (Includes both the *Clavis* and *A Specimen of True Philosophy*.)

References and further reading

* Benson, R. (1837) *Memoirs of the life and writings of the Rev. Arthur Collier*, London: E. Lumley; repr. Bristol: Thoemmes Press, 1990. (A biography, with long selections from Collier's correspondence. Chapter 2 contains several letters of philosophical

interest. Collier's theological views, examined in Chapter 3, are summarized in an unpublished manuscript that appears as Appendix A.)

* Eschenbach, J.C. (1756) *Sammlung der vornehmsten Schriftsteller die die Würklichkeit ihres Eignen Körpers und der ganzen Körperwelt Läugnen* (A collection of the leading authors who deny the reality of their own bodies and of the whole corporeal world), Rostock: A.F. Röse. (Contains German translations of both the Clavis and Berkeley's *Dialogues*, with extensive critical notes.)

Johnston, G.A. (1923) *The Development of Berkeley's Philosophy*, London: Macmillan. (For Berkeley's relation to Collier see Appendix I, pages 360–82. Refers to earlier discussions of Collier by Thomas Reid and Dugald Stewart.)

* Lovejoy, A.O. (1908) 'Kant and the English Platonists', in *Essays Philosophical and Psychological in Honor of William James*, New York: Longman, Green, 1908, 265–302. (Kant and Collier are discussed on pages 284–90.)

* McCracken, C. (1983) *Malebranche and British Philosophy*, Oxford: Clarendon. (Chapter 5 includes an accessible survey of Collier's main arguments, emphasizing his debt to Malebranche and Norris.)

* Vleeschauwer, H.J. de (1938) 'Les antinomies Kantiennes et la Clavis Universalis d'Arthur Collier' ('The Kantian antinomies and the Clavis Universalis of Arthur Collier'), *Mind* 47: 303–20. (Argues against the suggestion that Collier influenced Kant.)

KENNETH P. WINKLER

COLLINGWOOD, ROBIN GEORGE (1889–1943)

Collingwood was the greatest British philosopher of history of the twentieth century. His experience as a practising historian of Roman Britain led him to believe that the besetting vice of philosophy is to abstract propositions away from the context of the practical problems and questions that gave rise to them. Until we know the practical context of problems and questions to which a proposition is supposed to be an answer, we do not know what it means. In this respect his concern with the living activities of language users parallels that of the later Wittgenstein. Collingwood also believed that the interpretation of others was not a scientific exercise of fitting their behaviour into a network of generalizations, but a matter of rethinking their thoughts for oneself. His conviction that this ability, which he identified with historical thinking, was the neglected and crucial component of all human thought stamped him as original, or even a maverick, during his own lifetime. He also shared with Wittgenstein the belief that quite apart from containing propositions that can be evaluated as true or false, systems of thought depend upon 'absolute presuppositions', or a framework or scaffolding of ideas that may change with time. The business of metaphysics is to reconstruct the framework that operated at particular periods of history. Collingwood had extensive moral and political interests, and his writings on art, religion and science confirm his stature as one of the greatest polymaths of twentieth-century British philosophy.

1 Overview
2 Major themes
3 Other works and topics

1 Overview

Collingwood was born in the Lake District of England, and educated until the age of 13 by his father, a painter and friend of Ruskin. It was during his childhood that he absorbed his admiration for practical problem-solving, whether the problems were those of a painter, an archaeologist or a sailor: 'I learned to think of a picture not as a finished product exposed for the admiration of virtuosi, but as the visible record...of an attempt to solve a definite problem in painting, so far as the attempt has gone' (1939: 2). He subsequently attended Rugby School and University College, Oxford, where he had a brilliant career as a classicist. He was the only pupil of F.J. Haverfield, the Romano-British historian, to survive the First World War, and conceived it his duty to carry on Haverfield's work. So he effectively combined two careers, as a teacher of philosophy at Pembroke College, Oxford, from 1912, and as a practising archaeologist and classicist. In the second capacity he made extensive contributions to the corpus of Roman inscriptions recorded in Britain, and wrote the sections on Roman Britain in the *Oxford History of England*. Although in his *Autobiography* (completed in 1938) he liked to portray himself as a philosophical outsider, his distinction was acknowledged by the Waynflete Chair of metaphysical philosophy, to which he was elected in 1936, and which he held until a series of strokes forced him to retire in 1941.

Collingwood characterized the philosophical situation at the Oxford of his time as one of opposition between the lingering 'school of Green' and the 'realists', whose members included John Cook-Wilson, H.W.B. Joseph and H.A. Prichard. Similar tendencies to realism in Cambridge were represented by G.E. Moore and Bertrand Russell. By the 'school of Green' Collingwood referred to what is often called 'absolute idealism', although he is careful to note that the leading representative of that school in his time, F.H. Bradley, repudiated the label of idealist, as Collingwood himself did. Although educated as a realist, Collingwood locates his progressive disenchantment, in the years before the First World War, in his realization that the historical understanding that the realists brought to philosophy was totally inadequate. Moore criticized Berkeley for views which Berkeley never held; Cook-Wilson criticized Bradley for views that Bradley never held. As a historian Collingwood found himself offended by the lack of historical scholarship demonstrated by such performances. He differs from the analytic tradition most fundamentally over history. If one reads Moore, or Wittgenstein, it might seem that philosophy and history have nothing to do with one another, and if Moore made a historical mistake about Berkeley, that need not diminish the importance of his philosophical thought. But Collingwood sees thought as something that is essentially historically embodied: the idea of a worthwhile philosophy with no reflection on its own historical situation would be a contradiction. We can understand where we are only by understanding our own historical embedding: how we got there and the thoughts of those who would wish us to have got somewhere else. For Collingwood, therefore, there is no split, of the kind that has been made much of in recent philosophy, between treating historical philosophers as great, but unlearned, contemporaries and treating them as historical material: in all the important respects, the past lives in the present and the present cannot be understood without it (see HISTORY, PHILOSOPHY OF §4).

2 Major themes

According to Collingwood, the realists of his time thought of knowledge as the static, direct apprehension of the truth of a proposition: a mysterious unity that arises when mind confronts fact. Collingwood, making use of his experience as a working historian, insisted that knowledge is never that, but must be the outcome of a moving, active, dynamic process of hypothesis formation and testing. Questioning is one half of the act of which the other half is forming an answer, and it takes both halves to make up a situation of knowing anything. It should be noticed that this is not an opposition to realism on behalf of any kind of idealism, and the label is of little diagnostic value in attempting to understand Collingwood.

Applying this doctrine to the interpretation of historical texts, Collingwood insists that you cannot know what a philosopher meant by a doctrine until you know the question to which the doctrine was intended as an answer and how that question arose. Immediately it follows that you cannot tell whether propositions contradict each other unless you know that they are answers to the same question. This is partly a plea for intelligent appreciation of the space of problems within which different writers work, and in effect Collingwood is highlighting a version of what later became called the principle of charity (see CHARITY, PRINCIPLE OF §1). Indeed, he sometimes embraces one extreme consequence of a method based on the principle of charity, namely that since we have to read the questions to which philosophers address themselves back from their answers, there is no possibility of saying that their answers are inadequate or muddled or mistaken. Using his favourite analogy of naval history he asks: 'How can we discover what the tactical problem was that Nelson set himself at Trafalgar? Only by studying the tactics he pursued in the battle. We argue back from the solution to the problem' (1939: 70). He himself notes that this works at least mainly because Nelson won the battle, and we may legitimately wonder whether it is right to assume that the great dead philosophers won all their battles. But for Collingwood the integrity of the historical quest requires interpreting them substantially as if they did.

The upshot is that the scope for fundamental criticism of a philosopher diminishes markedly, and this leads to the second theme of constant importance to Collingwood: the identification of metaphysics with history. At first blush it may seem that he must believe that metaphysics, at least as it is done in critical discussion of the views of great past thinkers, has been entirely superseded by the historical problem of discovering the questions and answers they are proposing. However, the twist is that solving this historical problem, for Collingwood, requires reliving the problem and rethinking the issue for oneself. It requires making the words of the text into one's own, re-centring one's concerns and seeing how these things are to be said or these actions performed in answer to them. So if the metaphysical problem gives way to a historical one, it is equally true that a historical problem gives way to a metaphysical one: for example, to understand Plato historically requires fully grasping the problem to which the theory of Forms provides an answer.

Collingwood's *rapprochement* between history and metaphysics here depends upon his insistence that historical thinking is in this way a matter of living through the thinking of the person confronted with a problem. This is perhaps the best-known of his doctrines, and he has several interlocking reasons for it. He holds that to study a person in respect of their mental features is to study their own self-understanding, and that means the concepts that determine their plans and activities. Understanding these concepts is not an atomistic project, a matter of finding individual elements, perhaps written in the brain, connected by scientific law with other elements. It is an essentially holistic enterprise that needs to draw on the wider knowledge of the person's human context. When I come to understand why you acted as you did I am not concerned to place you in a law-like causal network, but to see the point of your doings. In the modern jargon, rationalizing you is a distinct normative activity, not reducible to seeing your behaviour just as part of what generally happens, part of a scientifically repeatable pattern. By the normativity of thought Collingwood means not just that as bystanders we can assess the thoughts of others for truth or falsity, rationality or the reverse. He means that thinking itself is essentially a process of which such assessments are a part. The thinker is actively engaged in solving a problem, and is constantly evaluating proposals, withdrawing some and improving others. What is being done cannot be clocked or recorded or understood in terms of a succession of passive occurrences.

In all his works, from the early *Religion and Philosophy* (1916), he opposes this theory of interpretation to 'scientific' psychology. He sees the scientific psychologist as one who treats the phenomena of mental life as natural events, surveyable from the outside, and who seeks to generate laws of association and development. But, he says, the mind regarded in this way ceases to be a mind at all. He has no objection to this treatment of essentially passive mental phenomena, such as he takes feelings to be. It is when the approach is tried upon thinking that he objects. He is at his most scathing when describing the grotesque failure of psychologists of his day to engage with thought, even when they purport to be giving its scientific nature. His critique goes to the heart of the question of method in gaining human understanding. For although he calls his epistemology a theory of history, it is what is with less dignity called a theory of folk psychology (see FOLK PSYCHOLOGY). He is quite clear that he is not only concerned with the remote past: 'If it is by historical thinking that we re-think and so rediscover the thought of Hammurabi or Solon, it is in the same way that we discover the thought of a friend who writes us a letter, or a stranger who crosses the street' (1946: 219) – and, he adds, our own thoughts of ten years or five minutes ago. The inclusion of self-knowledge is deliberate and

impressive, for Collingwood held that there was no division between knowing one's own mind and knowing that of others. In this respect his approach is more sophisticated than the *verstehen* method of Wilhelm Dilthey. Its closest successor in current philosophy is the view that ascription of belief and desire to others is best seen as an 'off-line simulation' of their active processes of thought. Collingwood's view that the self-controlling normativity of thought unfits it for being the subject of a self-standing science strikingly anticipates the later discussions of interpretation of others given by writers such as Davidson and Dennett. His hostility to the external, objectifying, professedly 'scientific' approach to the human world is as radical as anything to be found in more recent debates.

A final theme that can be isolated as a constant in his work is the dependence of all thought upon absolute presuppositions. Collingwood is not here thinking of the a priori, for, this time anticipating Quine, he has no use for the category. Rather, at a particular time the identification of questions and the production of answers in response to them must go on against a largely unnoticed background of presuppositions. These themselves are not posed in answer to any questions, and therefore cannot be assessed as true or false. To use the analogy with which Wittgenstein in *On Certainty* characterized the same doctrine (which he held for the same reason – the absence of a method for raising and answering the question of truth) they are the hinges on which the door swings. Collingwood has in mind something like the paradigms of Thomas Kuhn: the resources for thought and the devices for structuring it that, in a particular period of time, form the framework within which ordinary investigation proceeds. Again, his prescience in isolating such a category and insisting that historical research be directed at uncovering its operations in the history of science and philosophy has been amply confirmed by later writing.

3 Other works and topics

If one thinks of British philosophy of the 1920s and 1930s as mainly concerned with Russellian and Moorean approaches to mind and matter, or as easing itself into some kind of relationship to logical positivism, then Collingwood's interests will seem unusual. His first attempt at a system of his own is *Speculum Mentis* (1924), which reviews five forms of experience as modes of discovering the truth. These are art, religion, science, history and philosophy. Art and religion stand at the bottom, since neither aims at expressed knowledge, although religion aims at symbolizing our relationship with the world. Science aims at truth, but its categories are inadequate to capture human experience. History suffers because historians can be seen as spectators of the events that they write down, and their own perspectives are distorting influences. Only in philosophy does the possibility of transcending these partial perspectives arise, and with it an understanding of the relative place of the four inferior modes of experience. The hierarchy of different modes of knowledge is an example of what he later explored as a 'scale of forms' or dialectically related set of categories whereby the essence of a phenomenon becomes more perfectly instanced. There are echoes here of the idealism to which Collingwood was not formally committed. His later reaction to this work was that it misunderstood the nature of history: historians are not spectators, but by reliving past thought become one with the histories they are writing (see OAKESHOTT, M. §2).

The theme of artistic experience is the topic of his justly famous *The Principles of Art* (1938). Collingwood considers, and rejects, several views about the nature of art: that it is craft, representation or imitation, magic or amusement. He finds its essence in expression and imagination, which gives definite form to what is hitherto unconscious. Arguably the least successful part of the work is the attempt to examine what is involved in expression, which leads to the paradoxical doctrine that successful artists achieve their success in their own imagination, while externalizing or expressing what has been imagined is mere craft. This separation of thought and expression seems to witness a surprising and naive separation of mind and body, and his full view may be more complex. He certainly held, for instance, that there is no such thing as an unexpressed emotion (1938: 238), which is hardly consistent with a simple-minded dualism.

Throughout his life Collingwood wanted to put his theoretical concerns into close relationship with practical, moral and political activity. His deep hostility to utilitarianism, especially visible in his *Essays in Political Philosophy* (1989) and *The New Leviathan* (1942), probably originated in the work of the 'school of Green' although it is also fertilized by continental moral philosophy. Proper living, for Collingwood, is not the repeated satisfaction of a stream of arbitrary desires or caprices, but an exercise of rational, free agency, in conformity with duty. Rationality and freedom are equated with knowledge. Collingwood here sympathized not only with Kant, but with the tradition of European liberalism of such writers as Giovanni Gentile and Guido de Ruggiero. For such thinkers the conditions for freedom include an especial sort of community, whose members acknowledge the same freedom in each other, and in which the institutions are organized so as to promote this mutual recognition (see FREEDOM AND LIBERTY §2). Like Benedetto Croce, Collingwood believed that, properly understood, liberalism tempers democracy with aristocracy. In any body politic there will be rulers and ruled; the rulers will be objects of emulation, and therefore under an obligation to comport themselves aristocratically, in the sense of possessing full awareness of the dignity due to their station. In a liberal society the ranks of the rulers would be replenished from those of the ruled, and systems of education and freedom of ideas would be the devices for ensuring the ongoing quality of the intake.

Collingwood's writing is undoubtedly infuriating. Along with passages and doctrines of great depth and interest there are casual formulations of argument and a rather donnish delight in pugnacious overstatement and paradox that have left him easy prey to unsympathetic critics. Nevertheless the depth and range of his thought have seldom been equalled, and the years since his death have only slowly revealed the central importance of his problems, and the interest of his discussions of them.

List of works

Collingwood, R.G. (1916) *Religion and Philosophy*, London: Macmillan. (A juvenile work notable for its containing the equation of history and philosophy.)

—— (1924) *Speculum Mentis*, Oxford: Oxford University Press. (The first attempt at a systematic metaphysics, relating different areas of knowledge: art, religion, science, history and philosophy.)

—— (1933) *An Essay on Philosophical Method*, Oxford: Oxford University Press. (An attempt to interpret philosophy through the different 'forms' of the categories that it treats; the work is vaguely reminiscent of Kant.)

—— (1938) *The Principles of Art*, Oxford: Oxford University Press. (The most influential and readable work on aesthetics in English.)

—— (1939) *An Autobiography*, Oxford: Oxford University Press. (A slightly paranoid but amusing exercise in self-interpretation.)

—— (1940) *An Essay on Metaphysics*, Oxford: Oxford University Press. (A rejection of positivism in favour of metaphysics as the science of the presuppositions of thought at a time.)

—— (1942) *The New Leviathan*, Oxford: Oxford University Press. (Collingwood's only treatise on political philosophy, celebrated for its equation of freedom and knowledge.)

—— (1945) *The Idea of Nature*, Oxford: Oxford

University Press. (A superb and under-appreciated exercise in the history and philosophy of science.)

—— (1946) *The Idea of History*, Oxford: Oxford University Press. (Collingwood's most widely read and influential work, covering history and historiography from Herodotus to Toynbee and Spengler.)

—— (1989) *Essays in Political Philosophy*, ed. D. Boucher, Oxford: Clarendon Press. (Diverse essays from 1924 onwards, concerned both with the structure of political association and the underpinnings of civilization.)

References and further reading

Boucher, D. (1989) *The Social and Political Thought of R.G. Collingwood*, New York: Cambridge University Press. (A clear and useful guide to Collingwood's political thought.)

Donagan, A. (1962) *The Later Philosophy of R.G. Collingwood*, Oxford: Clarendon Press. (A predominantly hostile presentation of Collingwood from the standpoint of the following generation of Oxford philosophy.)

Dussen, W.J. van der (1981) *History as a Science: The Philosophy of R.G. Collingwood*, The Hague: Nijhoff. (A scholarly and close reading of the major writings on history, including commentary on his work as a historian.)

Mink, L.O. (1969) *Mind, History, and Dialectic*, Bloomington, IN: Indiana University Press. (Probably the best overall introduction to Collingwood. It includes revealing discussions of the 'scale of forms' and Collingwood's more general metaphysical standpoint.)

SIMON BLACKBURN

COLLINS, ANTHONY (1676–1729)

Anthony Collins was an English freethinker, best-known to philosophers for his reconciliation of liberty and necessity, and his criticisms of Samuel Clarke's arguments for the immateriality and immortality of the soul. 'I was early convinced', Collins wrote, 'that it was my duty to enquire into, and judge for my self about matters of Religion' (1727: 4). This is a fair summary of Collins' lifelong project: to judge the claims of religion as an impartial scientist would judge the claims of a theory, not by 'the Way of Authority', but by reason or 'the Way of private Judgment' (1727: 107). Collins took on almost the whole of religion as affirmed and practised in the eighteenth-century Church of England: its philosophical foundations, its theological doctrines, its methods of scriptural interpretation and its views on the politics of church and state. He found most of it wanting. His conclusions were at least deistic and perhaps atheistic (though he remained a practising member of the established church): the irony of his writing and the reactive character of virtually everything he published make it difficult to know for sure.

1 Life
2 The defence of freethinking
3 Liberty and necessity
4 The immateriality and immortality of the soul
5 Analogical predication
6 Biblical interpretation
7 Toleration

1 Life

Collins was born in Middlesex, England. He studied at Eton and at King's College, Cambridge (though he did not stand for a degree), and later studied law at London's Middle Temple. When he married his first wife in 1698, his father gave him an estate in Essex. There Collins met John LOCKE, who was living in retirement nearby, and in the last two years of Locke's life they became devoted friends. Locke's rationalism was an important early influence on Collins. A second important personal influence was the French refugee intellectual Pierre Desmaizeaux. Collins also knew John TOLAND, who visited Collins several times at his country home. Collins travelled to Holland in 1711 and 1713, where he met Jean LE CLERC. Between 1717 and 1724 he played an active role in Essex government, serving, for example as county treasurer.

2 The defence of freethinking

In his first book, *An Essay concerning the Use of Reason, in Propositions whereof the Evidence is Human Testimony* which appeared anonymously in 1707, Collins had worked to establish the authority of reason over matters of religion. He had, for example, rejected the prevailing distinction between what is *agreeable* to reason, what is *contrary to* reason and what is *above* reason, insisting that every belief belongs in one of the first two categories. If a report of a miracle is consistent in itself and is compatible with what we know intuitively or demonstratively, then it is, so far, not contrary to reason. It is agreeable to reason if the witness reporting it is credible, and contrary to reason if not.

Collins' full-scale defence of the authority of reason came in his anonymously published *A*

Discourse of Free-thinking (1713). He defines free-thinking as 'the Use of the Understanding, in endeavouring to find out the Meaning of any Proposition whatsoever, in considering the nature of the Evidence for or against it, and in judging of it according to the seeming Force or Weakness of the Evidence' (1713: 45). Everything Collins published in his lifetime performs one or more of the three tasks identified in this definition: determining meaning, assessing evidence and judging in accordance with the evidence. According to Collins' theory of judgment (as presented in his 1717 work *A Philosophical Inquiry concerning Human Liberty*), we cannot help but judge according to the 'apparent degrees of light' – the apparent evidence – that propositions possess. His plea for freedom in judgment, then, is really a plea that our pronouncements not be forced to diverge from what the evidence indicates.

Collins' main argument for freethinking is that truth is good (required by God, useful to society, neither forbidden by God nor hurtful to anyone), and that there is no way to discover it except by applying reason. Against this there was one particularly pressing objection: true opinion (not *reasoned* true opinion) is what salvation depends on, and true opinion can be arrived at by revelation. Reasoning would either reinforce revealed truth (in which case it would be superfluous) or subvert it (in which case it would deprive us of the most vitally important thing). It seems that reasoning is hardly worth the risk. Collins' response to this objection is largely implicit. He distinguishes between 'what God speaks plainly to the whole World' – what God says to the reasoning power with which everyone is endowed – and 'what [some] suppose he has communicated to a few' (1713: 72). He then argues that claims to revelation can be evaluated only by reason. (He takes evident pleasure in documenting priestly disagreements about the interpretation of Scripture – disagreements that reason alone can adjudicate.) What God speaks plainly to everyone, he insists, is that 'he can require nothing of Men in any Country or Condition of Life, but that whereof he has given them an opportunity of being convinc'd by Evidence and Reason in the Place where they are, and in that Condition of Life to which Birth or any other Chance has directed them' (1713: 30). The good of society is, he argues, 'the Rule of whatever is to be allow'd or restrain'd' (1713: 90), and it is a mistake to think that removing restraints on reason would breed disorder.

Richard Bentley's *Remarks upon a Late Discourse of Free-Thinking* (1713) is best-known for its criticisms of Collins' classical and Biblical scholarship, but Bentley also objects to Collins' conception and defence of freethinking. Bentley thinks his definition

is trivial, 'for it comprehends the whole herd of Human Race, even Fools, Madmen, and Children; for they use what *Understanding* they have; and judge as things *seem*' (Bentley 1713: 10). Collins' definition is really a definition of the understanding; it contains 'not a Syllable about *Freedom*' (Bentley 1713: 10), and in practice, Collins' so-called freedom is nothing but 'an inward Promptness and Forwardness to decide about Matters beyond the reach of [the freethinkers'] Studies, in *opposition* to the rest of Mankind' (Bentley 1713: 11). Collins' oppositional creed, in Bentley's opinion, amounts to atheism:

> that the Soul is material and mortal, Christianity an imposture, the Scriptures a forgery, the Worship of God superstition, Hell a fable, and Heaven a dream, our life without providence, and our Death without hope like that of Asses and Dogs.
> (Bentley 1713: 14)

There is, according to Bentley, an 'occult meaning' in Collins' discussions of disputes about Scripture: 'from the variety of Scripture to insinuate none is true' (Bentley 1713: 45), (see BENTLEY, R.).

3 Liberty and necessity

In his first book Collins briefly defended a version of compatibilism. He rejected the view that liberty is self-determination, 'without regard to any extrinsecal Causes' (1707a: 34). It is, instead, merely 'a Power to do or forbear several Actions, according to the Determination of [the] Mind' (1707a: 35). It follows that liberty is consistent with Necessity, and 'ought not to be oppos'd to it, but only to Compulsion' (1707a: 38).

Collins embraced the doctrine of necessity in his first book ('no one action', he wrote, 'could possibly not happen' [1707a: 36]), but a full defence was presented only in *A Philosophical Inquiry Concerning Human Liberty*. There Collins argues as follows (1717:57): (1) 'All...actions have a beginning' and (2) 'Whatever has a beginning must have a cause'. It follows that every action has a cause. Collins then claims that (3) 'Every cause is a necessary cause'. It follows that every action has a necessary cause. Collins supports (3) by arguing against 'the Epicurean System of chance' (see EPICUREANISM §§4, 12).

Collins argues in the *Inquiry* that experience is no proof of a liberty incompatible with necessity. We deceive ourselves by considering actions of which we now repent. Because we are now in a repentant humour, we find no present cause of the action. But the circumstances we were in and the causes we were under made the action 'unavoidably determin'd'. It is this determination, in fact, that is a matter of experience: 'for are we not manifestly determin'd by pleasure or pain, and by what seems reasonable or unreasonable to us, to judge or will or act?' (1717: 24). Collins also argues that necessity is 'the sole foundation of morality and laws' (1717: iv). It is, for one thing, a presupposition of effective punishment, for if human beings were not necessary agents determined by pleasure and pain, the threat of pain could not motivate them. He even argues that a grasp of the very distinction between virtue and vice depends on being a necessary agent.

Collins often speaks against liberty, but his real target, as he sometimes makes clear, is liberty inconsistent with necessity. We have, as he emphasizes at the close of the *Inquiry*, 'a truly valuable liberty of another kind' (1717: 116) – the power to do as we will, or as we please. Had we this power or liberty in all things, he concludes, we would be omnipotent. Collins also admits there is a difference between the 'moral necessity' (determination by reason and the senses) to which human beings are subject – and the 'absolute, physical, *or* mechanical necessity' to which stones and clocks are subject. Throughout the *Inquiry*, Collins portrays the hypothesis of necessity as an opinion friendly to religion, and the belief in liberty inconsistent with necessity as atheistic. He claims that even 'most of those who assert *liberty* in words' – liberty inconsistent with necessity, that is – 'deny the thing, when the question is rightly stated' (1717: 111), an observation that anticipates Hume.

In his *Remarks upon a Book Entitled, A Philosophical Enquiry concerning Human Liberty* (1717), Samuel Clarke agreed that every action has a cause, but denied that every cause is a necessary cause. The cause of an action is the 'self-moving power' of the person. Motives and reasons *influence* action, but they do not cause it. Collins' final work on the topic, *A Dissertation on Liberty and Necessity* was published in 1729, after Clarke's death. He claimed that Clarke, in his criticisms of the *Inquiry*, simply assumed that the soul is a self-moving power (see CLARKE, S. §2).

4 The immateriality and immortality of the soul

In *A Letter to the Learned Mr. Henry Dodwell* (1707), Collins took aim at Clarke's arguments for the immateriality and immortality of the soul. In *A Letter to Mr. Dodwell*, Clarke had argued that because a material thing is divisible, it cannot be an individual consciousness. A mind or individual consciousness must therefore be immaterial, and if it is immaterial, it is naturally immortal: it cannot be destroyed (or robbed of its essential powers) by any natural process. Collins made several objections. First, he claimed, Clarke simply assumes that think-

ing is an 'individual power' – a power that can belong only to an indivisible thing. But there are, Collins maintained, powers (such as the sweet smell of a rose) that belong to divisible things, and cannot be reduced to the sum or aggregate of the powers of their parts. Thinking may be such a power, and for all we know, a human being may be a system of matter 'fitly disposed' (as John Locke had put it) to think (see LOCKE, J. §5). Second, Collins asked, even if Clarke managed to show that an immaterial substance must continue to exist, what proof is there that it must continue to think?

Clarke replied to Collins' *Letter*, and Collins to Clarke's reply. (When the controversy ended, each author had contributed four pieces, in addition to the original statement of Clarke's case in his *Letter to Dodwell*.) The central point at issue was the interpretation and application of Clarke's thesis (offered in reply to the first objection above) that 'every Power or Quality, that is or can be *inherent* in any System of Matter, is nothing else than the Sum or Aggregate of so many Powers or Qualities *of the same kind*, inherent in all its Parts' (Clarke [1707] 1738 vol. 3: 759) (see CLARKE, S. §2).

5 Analogical predication

In *A Vindication of the Divine Attributes* (1710), Collins argues against the proposal (made by William King in *Divine predestination and fore-knowledge* [1709]) that wisdom, goodness, justice and mercy are 'attributed to God in the same improper analogous Sense' (1710: 14) as parts or passions. Collins objects that if *all* of God's attributes are analogical, we cannot differentiate between theism and atheism. Nor can we make it our duty to imitate the divine perfections.

6 Biblical interpretation

William Warburton regarded Collins' *A Discourse of the Grounds and Reasons of the Christian Religion* (1724) as one of the most plausible arguments ever made against Christianity (Warburton [1738] 1765 vol. 5: 281). In *The Reasonableness of Christianity* (1695), Locke had put forward as the one essential doctrine of Christianity the belief that Jesus is the Messiah. In Part 1 of the *Grounds and Reasons*, Collins argues that it can be established that Jesus is the Messiah only if it can be shown that Jesus, as described in the Gospels, fulfils the Old Testament prophecies. But the Old and New Testaments, Collins argues, do not agree 'according to the literal and obvious sense' (1724: 39). The Old Testament must therefore be interpreted allegorically – 'in a secondary or typical, or mystical, or allegorical sense' (1724: 53). Collins insinuates that no reasonably controlled method of interpretation could arrive at the desired results. He mockingly presents a long list of rules meant to transform 'the mean literal sense of... words into a noble and spiritual sense' (1724: 59); the climactic rule permits a simultaneous change in the order of words, the addition of new words and the deletion of others.

In Part 2 Collins takes up William Whiston's proposal, in his *Essay towards Restoring the True text of the Old Testament* (1722), that the Old and New Testaments once agreed, and that the apostles argued literally. Since that time, however, the text of the Old Testament has been corrupted. Whiston proposes to establish the text as it stood in the days of Jesus and the apostles; Collins argues that this simply cannot be done (see HERMENEUTICS, BIBLICAL).

7 Toleration

In *A Letter to the Reverend Dr. Rogers* (1727) Collins presents the following argument, among many others, for toleration:

(1) I judged the Christian religion true and joined the Church of England.

(2) I also judged that if I resided in Spain or Scotland, it would be my duty to worship God publicly, according to the way of the Church of England, and that the magistrate ought to protect me in this.

Collins does not infer the judgment in (2) from the judgment in (1). But (2) is, he suggests, a natural accompaniment of (1). And this suggests that magistrates in England should extend the same toleration to Spanish Catholics or Scottish Presbyterians that those who embrace the Anglican Church would expect from magistrates in Spain or Scotland (see TOLERATION; LATITUDINARIANISM).

List of works

Collins, A. (1707a) *An essay concerning the use of reason in propositions, the evidence whereof depends upon human testimony*, London. (Argues for the authority of reason in matters of religion.)

—— (1707b) A letter to the learned Mr. Henry Dodwell; containing some remarks on a (pretended) demonstration of the immateriality and natural immortality of the soul, in Mr. Clarke's answer, London; A reply to Mr. Clarke's defence of his letter to Mr. Dodwell, London, 1707; Reflections on Mr. Clarke's second defence of his letter to Mr.

Dodwell, London, 1707; and An answer to Mr. Clarke's third defence of his letter to Mr. Dodwell, London, 1708, in *The Works of Samuel Clarke*, vol. 4, London, 1738, 719–909; repr. New York and London: Garland, 1978. (On Samuel Clarke's proofs of the soul's immateriality and immortality. Clarke's Works includes both sides of the controversy.)

—— (1710) *A vindication of the divine attributes*, London: H. Hills. (A criticism of William King's analogical theology.)

—— (1713) *A discourse of free-thinking, occasion'd by the rise and growth of a sect call'd free-thinkers*, London; repr. New York: Garland, 1976. (Collins' defence of freethinking.)

—— (1717) *A philosophical inquiry concerning human liberty*, London: R. Robinson; repr. as *Determinism and Free Will*, ed. J. O'Higgins, The Hague: Martinus Nijhoff, 1976. (Argues that liberty is compatible with necessity. The modern edition contains a detailed introduction and notes.)

—— (1724) *A discourse of the grounds and reasons of the christian religion*, London; repr. New York: Garland, 1976. (Contends that Jesus cannot be shown to fulfil Old Testament prophecies.)

—— (1727) *A letter to the reverend Dr. Rogers on occasion of his eight sermons concerning the necessity of divine revelation*, London. (Argues in defence of toleration.)

—— (1729a) *A dissertation on liberty and necessity*, London: J. Shuckburgh. (A reply to Samuel Clarke's criticisms of 1717.)

—— (1729b) *A discourse concerning ridicule and irony in writing*, London: J. Brotherton; repr. Los Angeles, CA: William Andrews Clark Memorial Library, University of California, Los Angeles, 1970. (Defends the use of ridicule, irony, mockery, and raillery in writing on religion; observes that defenders of the established church often resort to it.)

References and further reading

Attfield, R. (1977) 'Clarke, Collins and Compounds', *Journal of the History of Philosophy* 15: 45–54. (An account of the Clarke–Collins debate on the immateriality of the soul. Assesses Clarke's 'reductionist premiss' – his claim that the powers or qualities of a system of matter must be the sum or aggregate of qualities of the same sort in the parts.)

* Bentley, R. (1713) *Remarks upon a late discourse of free-thinking*, London: J. Morphew & E. Curll. (An attack on the *Discourse of free-thinking*.)

Berkeley, G. (1732) *Alciphron*, in A.A. Luce and T.E. Jessop (eds) *The Works of George Berkeley, Bishop of Cloyne*, vol. 3, London: Thomas Nelson, 1950. (An attack on freethinking; Collins is discussed – but not named – in the Sixth and Seventh Dialogues.)

Berman, D. (1975) 'Anthony Collins: aspects of his thought and writings', *Hermathena* 119: 49–70. (Supplements the 1970 work by O'Higgins; describes Collins' place in eighteenth-century British philosophy, particularly in relation to Locke and Berkeley.)

—— (1988) *A History of Atheism in Britain: from Hobbes to Russell*, London: Croom Helm. (Chapter 3 argues, against O'Higgins, that Collins was not a deist but an atheist. On pages 78 to 82 Berman attempts to reconstruct a pantheistic argument for atheism attributed to Collins by Berkeley, who claimed, in the 'Advertisement' to Alciphron, that Collins boasted of such an argument in conversation.)

Clarke, S. (1707) A letter to Mr. Dodwell; wherein all the arguments in his epistolary discourse against the immortality of the soul are particularly answered, London, followed by four later pamphlets defending the argument, in *The works of Samuel Clarke*, vol. 3, London, 1738, 719–909; repr. New York and London: Garland, 1978. (Clarke's argument for the immateriality and immortality of the soul, which replies to Collins' criticisms. The *Works* includes both sides of the controversy.)

—— (1717) 'Remarks on a book, entitled, a philosophical enquiry concerning human liberty', in *The Works of Samuel Clarke*, vol. 4, London, 1738, 719–35; repr. New York and London: Garland, 1978. (Criticism of Collins' 1717 work.)

* King, W. (1709) *Divine predestination and fore-knowledge, consistent with the freedom of man's will*, Dublin: J. Baker. (King's analogical theology is criticized by Collins in his 1710 work.)

O'Higgins, J. (1970) *Anthony Collins: The Man and His Works*, The Hague: Martinus Nijhoff. (A richly documented study of Collins' life, work and influence on, for example, Voltaire and d'Holbach.)

Rowe, W. (1987) 'Causality and Free Will in the Controversy Between Collins and Clarke', *Journal of the History of Philosophy* 25: 1–67. (A very helpful account of the main points at issue. Defends Clarke against some of Collins' criticisms.)

Stephen, L. (1876) *History of English Thought in the Eighteenth Century*, London: Smith, Elder. (Collins is discussed in chapter 4, pages 201–28.)

* Warburton, W. (1738) *The divine legation of Moses demonstrated*, London: A. Millar and J. and R. Tonson, 4th edn, 5 vols, 1765. (Book VI §6 is a criticism of Collins' 1724 work.)

* Whiston, W. (1722) *An essay towards restoring the true text of the Old Testament; and for vindicating the citations made thence in the New Testament*, London. (Collins' target in the second part of his 1724 work.)

KENNETH P. WINKLER

COLOUR AND QUALIA

There are two basic philosophical problems about colour. The first concerns the nature of colour itself. That is, what sort of property is it? When I say of the shirt that I am wearing that it is red, what sort of fact about the shirt am I describing? The second problem concerns the nature of colour experience. When I look at the red shirt I have a visual experience with a certain qualitative character – a 'reddish' one. Thus colour seems in some sense to be a property of my sensory experience, as well as a property of my shirt. What sort of mental property is it?

Obviously, the two problems are intimately related. In particular, there is a great deal of controversy over the following question: if we call the first sort of property 'objective colour' and the second 'subjective colour', which of the two, objective or subjective colour, is basic? Or do they both have an independent ontological status?

Most philosophers adhere to the doctrine of physicalism, the view that all objects and events are ultimately constituted by the fundamental physical particles, properties and relations described in physical theory. The phenomena of both objective and subjective colour present problems for physicalism. With respect to objective colour, it is difficult to find any natural physical candidate with which to identify it. Our visual system responds in a similar manner to surfaces that vary along a wide range of physical parameters, even with respect to the reflection of light waves. Yet what could be more obvious than the fact that objects are coloured?

In the case of subjective colour, the principal topic of this entry, there is an even deeper puzzle. It is natural to think of the reddishness of a visual experience – its qualitative character – as an intrinsic property of the experience. Intrinsic properties are distinguished from relational properties in that an object's possession of the former does not depend on its relation to other objects, whereas its possession of the latter does. If subjective colour is intrinsic, then it would seem to be a neural property of a brain state. But what sort of neural property could explain the reddishness of an experience? Furthermore, reduction of subjective colour to a neural property would rule out even the possibility that forms of life with different physiological structures, or intelligent robots, could have experiences of the same qualitative type as our experiences of red. While some philosophers endorse this consequence, many find it quite implausible.

Neural properties seem best suited to explain how certain functions are carried out, and therefore it might seem better to identify subjective colour with the property of playing a certain functional role within the entire cognitive system realized by the brain. This allows the possibility that structures physically different from human brains could support colour experiences of the same type as our own. However, various puzzles undermine the plausibility of this claim. For instance, it seems possible that two people could agree in all their judgments of relative similarity and yet one sees green where the other sees red. If this 'inverted spectrum' case is a genuine logical possibility, as many philosophers advocate, then it appears that subjective colour must not be a matter of functional role, but rather an intrinsic property of experience.

Faced with the dilemmas posed by subjective colour for physicalist doctrine, some philosophers opt for eliminativism, the doctrine that subjective colour is not a genuine, or real, phenomenon after all. On this view the source of the puzzle is a conceptual confusion; a tendency to extend our judgments concerning objective colour, what appear to be intrinsic properties of the surfaces of physical objects, onto the properties of our mental states. Once we see that all that is happening 'inside' is a perceptual judgment concerning the properties of external objects, we will understand why we cannot locate any state or property of the brain with which to identify subjective colour.

The controversy over the nature of subjective colour is part of a wider debate about the subjective aspect of conscious experience more generally. How does the qualitative character of experience – what it is like to see, hear and smell – fit into a physicalist scientific framework? At present all of the options just presented have their adherents, and no general consensus exists.

1 **Physicalism and objective colour**
2 **Subjective, 'qualitative' colour**
3 **The identity theory and its problems**
4 **Functionalism**
5 **Objections to functionalism**
6 **Replies**
7 **Eliminativism**

1 Physicalism and objective colour

The question 'What sort of property is the redness of the shirt?' is sensible only against a background of assumptions regarding what counts as an informative answer. Otherwise, the following naïve response seems appropriate. Colour is one of the features physical objects have, and red is a type of colour. What else is there to say? What makes the question substantive, however, is the background assumption of the doctrine of physicalism.

Physicalism is a doctrine accepted by a wide variety of philosophers, despite wide disagreement about its detailed characterization. There are two basic tenets: (1) that there is a privileged level of basic physical properties, its precise inventory being the business of physical science to determine; and (2) that all causal transactions in nature occur by virtue of mechanisms that are ultimately realized by the properties of this basic class. This doctrine is sometimes expressed by the slogan, 'no change without a (basic) physical change' (see MATERIALISM IN THE PHILOSOPHY OF MIND; SUPERVENIENCE OF THE MENTAL).

Acceptance of physicalism generates a problem about colour in the following way. The colour of my shirt – its being red – has causal influence; most notably, on the visual experiences of sentient beings. By the second principle of physicalism there must be physical mechanisms that mediate this influence. So how do these mechanisms relate to the colour?

There seem to be four possible answers. First, colour is itself a basic physical property, akin to mass, charge, charm and the like. Second, colour is reducible to other physical properties, in something like the way that heat is reducible to mean kinetic energy or water is reducible to H_2O (see REDUCTIONISM IN THE PHILOSOPHY OF MIND). Third, there is no natural physical property with which to identify colour: colours are mind-dependent properties in the sense that they can only be characterized by reference to their effects on human visual systems. Finally, colours are not real properties of objects at all: in a sense they are an illusion (see COLOUR, THEORIES OF; PROPERTY THEORY).

The first alternative is clearly a non-starter, since colour is not a basic physical property. There is controversy about the second. To explain the controversy, we must review some basic facts about colour vision. What we normally think of as perceived colour is a combination of three properties: hue, brightness and saturation. Hue (essentially the shade of colour itself) is determined by the wavelength composition of the light hitting the eye; brightness is determined by the relative intensity of the light; and saturation is a matter of how much hue relative to white light there is in the stimulus.

Now, it might be thought that a specific colour could be identified with light of a specific wavelength, intensity and saturation. Then the colour of a physical object could be identified with a tendency to reflect just that composition of light. However, it turns out that bundles of light with quite different distributions of wavelengths can produce the same effect on the visual system and therefore are perceived as the same colour. (Such distributions are called 'metamers'.) Also, there is the phenomenon of colour constancy. As illumination changes, say from bright outdoors to indoors, or noon to late afternoon, the composition of the light reflected from my red shirt changes. Yet it continues to look red throughout. One standard explanation of colour constancy is that the visual system takes changes of illumination into account by comparing the light reflected from many objects at once, thus using the contrast as a major determinant of perceived colour. But this makes the identification of colour with any property of the light reflected from an object quite complicated, if not hopeless.

In response to this problem, David Hilbert (1987) proposes that we identify colour with the complex, but quite objective, property of 'spectral reflectance'. An object's spectral reflectance is a function that takes specific distributions of light contained in illuminants as input and specific distributions of light reflected as output. He argues that it is precisely this property that is preserved in cases of colour constancy. What we perceive when we perceive the shirt as red throughout changes of lighting conditions is its surface spectral reflectance. There are various problems with this view, the most notable being the problem of metamers. As mentioned above, two very different light distributions, even against the same background illumination, can yield the same perceived colour. Yet, in Hilbert's view, since the two objects reflecting these two different distributions have different spectral reflectances, they must count as differently coloured. This seems quite counterintuitive, especially if the background illumination in question is broad daylight. (Hardin (1988) dismisses the spectral reflectance view largely for this reason. Hilbert (1987) responds at length to the objection, and the interested reader should consult his discussion.)

In view of the difficulties with the second alternative, it might be thought that colour is best thought of as a disposition on the part of objects to cause certain experiences in us. So what makes the shirt red is its disposition, however grounded in its physical properties, to cause a normal human observer, under normal conditions, to have a reddish visual experience. (The historical roots of this position can be found in Locke's discussion of primary and secondary qualities; see PRIMARY–SECONDARY DISTINCTION; LOCKE, J. §4.) Note that on the dispositional view, colour is a real, but mind-dependent property of objects. That is, objects are really coloured, though their being so is dependent on properties of us.

Hardin (1988) disputes the dispositional view on the grounds that there is no principled analysis of the phrases 'normal conditions' and 'normal human observer'. Thus there is no unequivocal way to attribute colours to objects, since as we change observer and conditions we change the object's colour. On his view the appropriate locus of colour attribution is experience: there are chromatic experiences, but no coloured objects. In our terms, there is only subjective colour, no objective colour.

2 Subjective, 'qualitative' colour

The puzzle concerning subjective colour is an instance – perhaps the most discussed instance – of the general puzzle concerning the qualitative, or phenomenal, character of conscious mental states: the puzzle of 'qualia'. We will continue to restrict our attention to colour experience, but most of the positions and arguments we review can be applied to the more general issue of phenomenal experience as a whole. Moreover, when it comes to visual experience, colour provides the most compelling challenge to an account consistent with physicalism. Indeed, we now need to ask the same question about subjective that we asked about objective colour: what sort of physical property could it be?

One obvious way of sorting properties is to distinguish intrinsic from relational properties. To a first approximation, intrinsic properties are those that an object possesses in virtue of conditions wholly within the object. Relational properties are those that an object possesses in virtue of its standing in some relation to other objects. So, for instance, my body's mass is an intrinsic property, whereas its weight is relational, since it depends on my body's location relative to the gravitational field generated by another object. (I weigh less on the moon than on the earth, though my mass is the same.)

Let us call the reddish qualitative character of my visual experience of the shirt 'subjective red'. Is subjective red an intrinsic property of my experience? At first blush, it certainly seems to be. But, given the constraints of physicalism, if subjective red is an intrinsic property of my experience, and if my experience enters causal transactions with other states (or events) in virtue of its qualitative character, then subjective red must be somehow reducible to, or composed of, a physical property of my nervous system.

3 The identity theory and its problems

This latter line of reasoning has led many to what has been called the 'central state identity theory'. On this view, an experience is identifiable with a neural state, and its (intrinsic) properties are ultimately neural in character (see MIND, IDENTITY THEORY OF). Three sorts of challenges have been mounted against this identification: (1) the conceivability argument, (2) the multiple-realizability argument, and (3) the knowledge argument.

According to the first, since it seems conceivable that one could be having an experience of a reddish sort but not be in the neural state in question, the experience cannot be the same as the neural state. However, put so baldly, this argument is clearly fallacious. It is conceivable that water might not have been H_2O, but that is no reason to deny that it is in fact identical to it (see INTENTIONALITY; PROPOSITIONAL ATTITUDE STATEMENTS). However, the conceivability argument seems to many to be getting at something not so easily dismissed, and this is brought out by considering the second argument, about multirealizability: subjective red cannot be identical to a neural state because it seems possible that there could be creatures with a different sort of physical constitution (say, Martians, or robots) that could nevertheless experience reddish visual sensations like ours. This seems more interesting than mere conceivability, since the possibility seems to survive the discovery that, among all the instances we have observed, subjective red always happens to be realized by a certain neural state. This does not seem to be the case with, for example, water and H_2O: if all the water we have observed is H_2O, that seems to be a good reason to think that all water is (see Kripke 1980; ESSENTIALISM).

The last argument, the knowledge argument, is due to Frank Jackson (1982). If subjective red is a physical property, then if one knows all the relevant physical facts pertaining to colour vision one will know all there is to know about subjective red. Imagine Mary, a vision scientist who possesses the complete physical theory of colour vision, but who has lived in a totally achromatic environment her entire life; she has only seen the world in black and white. Upon release from this restricted environment, she encounters a ripe tomato, and exclaims, 'So that's what red looks like!' It seems she has learned something new, and yet, Jackson argues, if physicalism is true she should already have known all there was to know about colour experience. Hence, subjective red is not a physical property.

Now, one reply to this argument is the same as to the conceivability argument. 'Knowledge', another intentional term, is referentially opaque: the fact that Mary knows all the physical facts and yet cannot recognize subjective red from its physical description does not show that subjective red is not identical to a

physical property; after all, the fact that she might know all the physical facts about H_2O without recognizing that it is water does not show that water is not H_2O. Mary may, in one sense, know everything there is to know when she learns all the physical facts, just not under every possible description. But that constitutes no problem for physicalism.

Still, however, many philosophers feel that these replies are missing the point. What provides plausibility to the three arguments is that appeal to the neural properties of one's visual state does not seem to *explain* its qualitative properties. The fact that these neurons are firing in this way does not really explain the shirt's looking 'reddish'. This is known as the 'explanatory gap' argument (see Levine 1983, 1993; EXPLANATION).

It could be put this way: once we discover the chemical composition of water, and know various chemical laws governing the states and interactions of physical substances, we can explain the features of water that we initially used in picking it out. For instance, we can explain why it freezes and boils at the temperatures it does, why it is necessary for life, and a host of its other properties. In fact, it is not really conceivable that something could be H_2O and yet fail to manifest these various properties, at least so long as we fix basic chemical laws. This seems to be what at least the conceivability and knowledge arguments are getting at: that the physical facts do not 'upwardly necessitate' facts about qualitative experience in the way that chemical facts necessitate facts about water. No matter how detailed our knowledge of the physical mechanisms by which neurons transmit their impulses from one to the other, we are still left with the question of why all this electrochemical activity should constitute an experience with a reddish (as opposed to a greenish, say) qualitative character. It still seems quite conceivable that such electrochemical activity should occur and yet not the experience of subjective red, and this residual conceivability is a manifestation of the explanatory gap. To put the matter in terms of the knowledge argument, the fact that Mary would learn something new upon emerging from her achromatic world is evidence that the physical theory of colour vision does not really explain the qualitative character. Even if she knew the meaning of ordinary 'red' she could not deduce from the rest of her knowledge that tomatoes look red (in the way that she could deduce that water freezes at $32°F$).

One might object that appeals to neurophysiology can indeed provide an explanation of subjective red. For one thing, if we were to find a stable correlation between subjects' reports of reddish sensations and their occupying certain neurophysiological states, then we could predict the occurrence of these sensations from knowledge of their brain states. For another, knowledge of the neurophysiological properties explains the mechanisms by which subjective red performs its cognitive functions. Colour perception involves selective sensitivity to fairly complicated properties of the light reflected from physical surfaces, and we now know a lot about how that sensitivity is implemented in neural hardware.

The problem with the first consideration is that in place of a genuine explanation all we are given is a brute correlation. I may be able to predict with perfect confidence that when someone occupies this particular neurophysiological state they are having a reddish sensation, but my ability to make this prediction does not manifest an understanding of why this brain state should go with reddish, and not bluish or greenish sensations. Brute facts are just that; they are not explicable. Moreover, they do not support counterfactuals: how are we to judge whether something lacking a specific physical property we possess really would not be having a reddish experience? What could satisfy us about the modal claim that not only are reddish experiences correlated with a certain neural state *in fact*, but *must* be so correlated?

Of course sometimes we admit that certain facts are brute facts; for instance, the value of the gravitational constant, the basic laws of physics, and the like. But notice it is a methodological assumption of current scientific practice, a corollary of physicalism, that only at the basic physical level are brute facts to be found. The idea that something as complicated as the brain should just give rise to reddish experience, and there be no explanation of this fact, is inconsistent with fundamental Physicalist assumptions.

If there is any hope for explaining subjective colour within a Physicalist framework, it would seem to depend on the second consideration: showing how the neurophysiological states of the brain provide the mechanisms by which colour sensations perform their cognitive functions. But to make this work it is necessary to analyse subjective colour in terms of its function, for otherwise explaining that function would not count as a full explanation of subjective colour itself. In other words, we need to abandon the treatment of subjective colour as an intrinsic property of sensation, and treat it instead as a relational, or functional, property.

4 Functionalism

Functionalism is the view that mental states are definable in terms of their causal roles, their causal relations with stimuli, behaviour and other mental states (see FUNCTIONALISM). Thus, arguably, something is a belief if and only if it is the result of perception or reasoning and the cause, with desires, of action. So a state would be an experience of subjective red just in case it was normally caused by viewing red things, it tended to cause judgments to the effect that something was red, and it generally related to other mental states – in particular through similarity judgments – in the way that is typical of experiences of red. Let us call the functional role in question 'functional red'.

A more specific form of the functional/relational approach is to treat qualitative states as essentially representational, and qualitative content as representational content. The idea is this. When I have a reddish experience I am in the state of representing the object I perceive as having a certain property, in this case the property of being red. Immediately, of course, the question arises how to distinguish colour experience from mere colour belief. The standard reply is to appeal to the special functional role of the visual system, for example, by attributing to it some distinctive representational system all its own. The point is that to have a reddish experience is to represent an external object as red in this special visual way. This is a relational theory since subjective red's identity is determined by its representational content, which is a matter of its relation to external objects, and it is a functional theory, since the particular functional organization of the visual system provides the basis for distinguishing experience from mere judgment.

One thorny problem for the representational approach involves the alleged representational content of the sensation. Above we said that subjective red is a representation that some object is red. But what is 'being red'? As our earlier discussion showed, it is not easy to specify what property objective redness is, so it is correspondingly difficult to specify what the representational content of subjective red is supposed to be. There are various ways a representationalist can respond. If one believes that colour is identifiable with a spectral reflectance function, then that could be the content of the sensory representation. If, however, one denies the existence of objective colour, one could say that our sensory systems represent objects as having a property that they in fact do not have. This is the so-called 'error theory'. Finally, one might be subjectivist about the content of subjective red itself. That is, one could say that a reddish experience is a report from the visual system concerning its own state – a way of saying, 'I'm experiencing redly now' (see MENTAL STATES, ADVERBIAL THEORY OF).

Note that it is no objection to the first proposal

that the alleged content has a complex theoretical structure and therefore could not plausibly be attributed to our sensory system. There are many representations we employ which in their internal structure are relatively simple and yet they refer to properties or objects which have a complex structure, and about which experts possess sophisticated theories. Take the well-worn example of water. According to most philosophers of language and mind, when I think about water I am thinking about a substance with the structure H_2O. But of course I do not have to know this, and it certainly is not plausible to claim that my mental representation of water contains representations of hydrogen and oxygen. Similarly, subjective red could function to detect, or register, a certain complicated property of an object's surface without itself possessing complex structure.

5   Objections to functionalism

The basic objection to a functionalist account of subjective colour, or of any qualitative experience, is that it just seems intuitively plausible that functional red and subjective red could come apart. The mismatch goes in both directions. That is, according to the famous absent and inverted qualia hypotheses, it seems quite possible that a creature could satisfy the conditions for functional red even though not experiencing subjective red, or, for that matter, having any qualitative experience at all. On the other hand, it also seems quite possible that a creature could experience subjective red even though most of the causal relations it normally maintains were absent (this is less emphasized in the literature).

An example of the first sort of problem is the famous 'inverted spectrum' thought experiment. As we noted above, colour experience is a function of three basic features: hue, brightness and saturation. Colour quality space can be modelled then as a three-dimensional solid; in fact, a cone. The vertical dimension represents brightness, the horizontal represents saturation, and the circular dimension represents hue. Given this model, there seems to be a mapping of points in the space onto their complements around an axis that bisects the cone through the middle. Reds would be mapped onto greens, blues onto yellows, and so on. The resulting cone would be isomorphic to the original in the sense that all the distance/similarity relations among points would be maintained.

Given this characterization of an inversion, take two creatures, one of whom has a colour quality space described by the original cone and the other of whom has one described by the inverted cone. If we are just looking at the relational properties – those involving causal relations to external stimuli, internal mental states, and behaviour – it seems that the two creatures would be functionally isomorphic. Yet, when looking at a red fire engine one would be having a reddish experience and the other would be having a greenish one. In other words, while they would both satisfy the criteria for functional red, one would be having an experience of subjective red and the other of subjective green. So, subjective red cannot be identical to functional red.

The 'absent qualia' hypothesis represents an even more extreme possibility. Ned Block (1980) asks us to imagine the entire nation of China (or any similarly large group of individuals) organized, say, by telephone, so as to realize the functional organization of a human brain. Let us also imagine that this vast network is connected to a robot which has a video camera for an 'eye'. When the robot is stimulated by light from a fire engine the network will go into a state of functional red, by hypothesis. Yet, it seems quite bizarre to claim that the robot, the network, or the system comprising both, is having a qualitative experience. Thus we have a case of functional red without subjective red (or any qualitative character at all).

An example of subjective red without the normal causal connections could occur if someone's normal functioning were disturbed, so that various relations between their colour experience and memory, belief and the like no longer held. It seems possible that this could happen while the qualitative character of their experience remained unchanged. One concrete case of this is colour blindness. The fact that someone cannot distinguish red from green obviously affects the structure of their colour space, yet it is not obvious that this makes their experiences of blue any different from mine.

6   Replies

There have been three basic responses to these anti-functionalist arguments. The first is to grant their cogency and claim that for experiences such as subjective red, as opposed to cognitive states such as belief, functionalism is wrong and the traditional identity theory is right. But then one must confront the objections to that theory discussed above: the multiple-realizability argument and the explanatory gap.

The second sort of response is to attempt to undermine the intuitive resistance to a relational account represented by the absent and inverted qualia hypotheses. Numerous such attempts have been made, but we will focus on two related strategies in particular: what might be called the 'asymmetries' strategy and the 'subtle role' strategy. In the end they are both problematic, but they represent serious attempts to meet the challenge and their problems are instructive.

The basic idea behind the asymmetries strategy is to argue that an appropriately chosen and sufficiently rich relational description can uniquely identify a type of qualitative character, and thereby get around the sorts of counterexamples just discussed. Consider the inverted spectrum argument. As presented above, it seems to make the assumption that there exists a natural axis of symmetry dividing the colour cone. However, there is empirical evidence to the effect that this is not so (see COLOUR, THEORIES OF).

First, there is the question of the location of the primaries. It seems evident that some hues are experienced as combinations of others, while some seem not to be. Contrast a pure red or green with orange or purple. One might have thought that pure examples of each of these primaries would occupy points in the three-dimensional colour solid equidistant from the origin, representing equal amounts of brightness and saturation, and equidistant from complex hues. But not so. Yellow, for instance, occupies a point of higher perceived brightness than do the other primaries. Also, some primaries occupy a larger region than do others; that is, there are more steps to be taken before we describe what we see as a combined hue. Furthermore, there is the anomaly of brown, which results from darkening yellow, yet is not thought of as merely dark yellow but another hue altogether. The point is that if you were to invert along the red–green and blue–yellow axis, it does not look as if all the relational judgments would be the same. Normals would consider dark and light blues to have the same hue, but inverts would not. Normals and inverts would differ in when they considered hues to be combinations, as opposed to primaries. Functional identity between normals and inverts could not be maintained. Hence, they would not be functionally identical to us, and spectrum inversion would not constitute a counterexample to functionalism. (See Harrison 1973; Clark 1993; Hardin 1988 for arguments along these lines.)

The second, 'subtle role' strategy is aimed more at the absent qualia hypothesis. The idea here is to attack the notion that a creature could be functionally identical to us and yet lack qualia by demonstrating that qualitative character is itself essential to normal functioning. Van Gulick (1993) notes that there is some evidence, for example, from blindsight cases – in which a patient claims not to see anything within a certain region of their visual field and yet can correctly 'guess', upon prompting, whether or not something is there – that consciousness is necessary for carrying out certain functions (see CONSCIOUSNESS §7; UNCONSCIOUS MENTAL STATES). For instance, blindsight patients tend not to initiate action with respect to the objects that they can passively detect in their blind field. If, as such cases suggest, consciousness is essential to the performance of certain functional roles, then it is not possible for a non-conscious state to play the same functional role. Hence, absent qualia are not possible.

We said above that there are problems with both strategies. With respect to the asymmetries strategy, there are two basic objections. First, even if the geometric space that characterizes our colour experience is in fact asymmetrical in the way described above, this seems to be a contingent feature of it. Why should this matter? So long as it is not demonstrated that it is essential to qualitative experience that it be immune to inversion, we have no reason to believe that all forms of qualia will have this feature. But if any form of qualitative experience is susceptible to inversion, functionalism is in trouble.

Moreover, as suggested earlier by the case of red–green colour blindness, there could easily be cases of individuals whose colour experience is somewhat, but not completely, different from our own. Suppose that theirs is symmetrical, and therefore subject to inversion. Would it not make sense to say that when such a person looked at a red fire engine they were having an experience that was more like our subjective red than, say, our subjective green? But, if inversion were possible for them, we could not say this solely on the basis of their functional organization.

The second problem with the asymmetrical approach is that it does nothing to address the absent qualia hypothesis. Suppose that any inversion of primaries would be detectable. Still, given cases like Block's China-head, it seems possible that a creature could realize a structure onto which the complete set of similarity relations definitive of the colour solid could be mapped, and yet there be *nothing* it is like to be that creature. Addressing the inverted qualia argument alone does not save functionalism.

The 'subtle role' strategy is, of course, specifically addressed to absent qualia. But here too there is a problem. Suppose we have to grant that there may be jobs, or roles, that only qualitative states can fill. That still does not mean that filling that role is what it is to be a qualitative experience. In fact, that very way of putting it – that being qualitative is essential, or necessary to playing the role – seems to imply just the reverse; that being qualitative is one thing, playing the role quite another. Suppose it turned out that being red was essential to some plant's playing the ecological role it played; nothing that was not red could do it. We would not say that being red is to play that role, but rather that being red is what makes the plant in question especially suited to play that role. It seems that the same goes for subjective red – the qualitative experience of seeing red – in the scenario Van Gulick envisaged.

Nor is it clear how the 'subtle role' strategy addresses Block's counterexample concerning the nation of China. Either one would have to admit that the entire nation experienced subjective red, or one would have to argue that the lack of qualitative character in this case posed an insuperable obstacle to realizing the relevant functional description. Both positions are difficult to defend. However, some (see Lycan 1987) have argued that there are other constraints – for instance, extremely fine-grained functional descriptions couched in teleological terms – that would rule out the nation of China as a legitimate realization (see FUNCTIONAL EXPLANATION).

In discussing the problems for functional accounts of colour qualia, we have not distinguished among various forms of functionalism. In particular, we have not addressed the representational version of functionalism, according to which colour qualia are functionally specific forms of representations of colour properties. It is sufficient to note here that the absent and inverted qualia hypotheses cause problems for this version of functionalism as much as any other. For suppose that an inverted spectrum is possible. Then two states could differ in their qualitative character and yet carry the same information concerning the reflectance properties of distal stimuli. Or, if absent qualia are possible, then a state could carry information concerning the reflectance properties of a distal stimulus and yet there be nothing at all it is like to occupy the state. If either case is possible, one cannot identify qualitative character with the representation of such properties (see SEMANTICS, INFORMATIONAL).

7 Eliminativism

We have seen that functional/relational analyses of colour qualia face serious difficulties. We have also seen that treating colour qualia as intrinsic properties also encounters a serious obstacle, in the form of the explanatory gap. Of course there are possible replies to these difficulties, and many contemporary philosophers hold one or the other of these views. Yet, the persistence of objections to the various accounts of qualia has led some philosophers to embrace eliminativism about subjective colour (whether or not they, like Hardin, are eliminativists about the objective sort). That is, they see the philosophical

problem of qualia as our attempting to identify a real phenomenon in the world which corresponds to a conception to which no real phenomenon does, nor even could, correspond. Belief in qualia is something like belief in ghosts. Just as we do not bother to find some real phenomenon to serve as the referent of our idea of a ghost, so too we should abandon the idea that a real phenomenon could serve as the referent of our idea of subjective red (see ELIMINATIVISM).

Eliminativism is quite naturally joined to the representational position just described. No one literally denies that we experience sensations of colour. That the fire engine looks red to me is a genuine fact. However, the eliminativist teases apart what is genuine about this fact from what is illusory in the following manner. That I see, and therefore judge, the fire engine to be a certain way, is undeniable. But it is wrong to infer from my perceptual judgment concerning the surface of the fire engine to the existence of a colour-like property of my experience itself – a colour *quale*. It is the existence of this inner property – around which inversion and absence puzzles take hold – that the eliminativist denies.

A major source for eliminativist sentiment is Wittgenstein's famous attack on the coherence of any notion of inner experience that did not manifest itself in outwardly observable behaviour (see CRITERIA; PRIVATE LANGUAGE ARGUMENT). While Wittgenstein had many targets in mind with his 'private language argument' – his argument against the possibility of a language that only one person could possibly understand – certainly the idea that I could introspect and discover qualia as properties of my inner experiences was one of them. A number of philosophers have extended this Wittgensteinian critique, most notably Daniel Dennett (1991). As Dennett characterizes them, believers in qualia are tied to a picture of the mind as a theatre (the 'Cartesian theatre'), in which mental entities are on display before the mind's eye. He has coined the term 'figment' to capture the unjustified inference from the reality of colours as properties of physical objects to the reality of colour qualia as properties of internal states.

Suggestive as this diagnosis of the problem of colour qualia is, it alone does not really constitute an argument in favour of eliminativism. However, various further arguments have been presented in the recent literature. First, the believer in qualia is accused of allegiance to a dualist metaphysics. Second, qualia are disparaged as posits of common-sense psychology, a theory that, like many common-sense theories of the world, must give way before its more rigorous and detailed scientific competitors.

Third, thought experiments like the inverted and absent qualia hypotheses are attacked as internally incoherent. Finally, belief in qualia is alleged to lead to unsavoury sceptical consequences. For instance, if someone could be functionally identical to me without having qualia, how do I know I really have them? (Of course some of these same arguments could serve to support a reduction of qualia to functional states, rather than their elimination. The line between eliminativism and reductionism, either of the functional or neurophysiological variety, is not always easy to draw.)

Advocates of colour qualia have responded to these arguments. Those who do not straightforwardly embrace dualism deny that their position entails it. Qualia, on their view, are not posits of an outmoded theory, but among the primary data that any adequate psychological theory must explain. The discussion above demonstrates how hard it is really to undermine the inverted qualia hypothesis. As for the charge of scepticism, many dismiss it as just that. Sceptical worries attach to most phenomena, they argue. But whether or not these replies succeed, eliminativist challenges of the sort just described will find adherents so long as a truly explanatory connection between qualitative character and neurophysiological or functional organization is still lacking.

See also: COLOUR, THEORIES OF; CONSCIOUSNESS; QUALIA; SECONDARY QUALITIES; VISION

References and further reading

* Block, N. (1980) 'Troubles with Functionalism', in N. Block (ed.) *Readings in Philosophy of Psychology*, Cambridge, MA: Harvard University Press, vol. 1, 268–305. (Good presentation of the varieties of functionalism, and source for the 'China-head' example. The first part employs some technical notation.)
* Clark, A. (1993) *Sensory Qualities*, Oxford: Oxford University Press. (Presents a theory of sensory qualities as points in a multidimensional quality space defined in terms of similarity judgments. Very detailed and somewhat technical.)
* Dennett, D.C. (1991) *Consciousness Explained*, Boston: Little, Brown. (Makes the case for eliminativism about qualia.)
* Hardin, C.L. (1988) *Colour for Philosophers: Unweaving the Rainbow*, Indianapolis, IN: Hackett Publishing Company. (Excellent review of the empirical literature regarding colour. Argues both for irrealism about objective colour and against the inverted

spectrum argument in support of a functional analysis.)
* Harrison, B. (1973) *Form and Content*, Oxford: Blackwell. (One of the earliest attempts to combat the inverted spectrum argument through a close consideration of the actual structure of colour experience.)
* Hilbert, D.R. (1987) *Colour and Colour Perception: A Study in Anthropocentric Realism*, Stanford, CA: Center for the Study of Language and Information, Stanford University. (Argues for a realist account of objective colour. Extensive use of empirical findings.)
* Jackson, F. (1982) 'Epiphenomenal Qualia', *Philosophical Quarterly* 32: 127–36. (Source for the example about Mary the vision scientist. Argues that sensory qualia are non-physical and do not causally interact with physical states.)
* Kripke, S. (1980) *Naming and Necessity*, Cambridge, MA: Harvard University Press. (Classic presentation of the position that the reference of 'natural kind' terms, such as 'water' and 'gold', is determined by scientifically discovered essences.)
* Levine, J. (1983) 'Materialism and Qualia: The Explanatory Gap', *Pacific Philosophical Quarterly* 64: 354–61. (Raises the problem of the 'explanatory gap').
* —— (1993) 'On Leaving Out What It's Like', in M. Davies and G. Humphreys (eds) *Consciousness: Psychological and Philosophical Essays*, Oxford: Blackwell, 121–36. (Argues for the claim, presented in §3, that the explanatory gap underlies standard objections to identity theory, as well as the claim that the reduction of water to H_2O is different from the reduction of subjective red to a neural state.)
* Lycan, W.G. (1987) *Consciousness*, Cambridge, MA: Bradford Books/MIT Press. (Defends a thoroughgoing functionalist theory of conscious states.)
  Rey, G. (1992) 'Sensational Sentences Switched', *Philosophical Studies* 67: 77–103. (Combines a version of the representational theory of sensory qualities with eliminativist arguments, as described in §7, and applies it to the inverted spectrum problem.)
  Shoemaker, S. (1981) 'The Inverted Spectrum', *Journal of Philosophy* 74: 357–81. (Ingenious defence of functionalism in the face of the inverted spectrum argument, which Shoemaker, unlike other functionalists, endorses.)
  Smart, J.J.C. (1959) 'Sensations and Brain Processes', *Philosophical Review* 68: 141–56. (Classic presentation of the identity theory. The discussion of colour experience foreshadows functionalist theories.)
* Van Gulick, R. (1993) 'Understanding the Phenomenal Mind: Are We All Just Armadillos?', in M.

Davies and G. Humphreys (eds) *Consciousness: Psychological and Philosophical Essays*, Oxford: Blackwell, 137–54. (Good survey of the various anti-functionalist arguments, with lines of reply to each.)

JOSEPH LEVINE

COLOUR, THEORIES OF

The world as perceived by human beings is full of colour. The world as described by physical scientists is composed of colourless particles and fields. Philosophical theories of colour since the Scientific Revolution have been driven primarily by a desire to harmonize these two apparently conflicting pictures of the world. Any adequate theory of colour has to be consistent with the characteristics of colour as perceived without contradicting the deliverances of the physical sciences.

Given this conception of the aim of a theory of colour, there are three possibilities for resolving the apparent conflict between the scientific and perceptual facts. The first is to deny that physical objects have colours. Theories of this kind admit that objects appear coloured but maintain that these appearances are misleading. The conflict is resolved by removing colour from the external world. Second, it might be that colour is a relational property. For an object to possess a particular colour it must be related in the right way to a perceiver. One common version of this view analyses colour as a disposition to cause particular kinds of perceptual experience in a human being. Since the physical sciences deal only with the intrinsic properties of physical objects and their relations to other physical objects and not their relations to perceiving subjects, the possibility of conflict is removed. A third possible response is to maintain that colour really is a property of external objects and that the conflict is merely apparent. Some theories of this form maintain that colour is identical to a physical property of objects. Others maintain that colour is a property that physical objects possess over and above all their physical properties. Philosophical discussions of colour typically take the form of either elaborating on one of these three possibilities or attempting to show more generally that one of these three types of response is to be preferred to the others.

1 **Eliminativist theories of colour**
2 **Relational theories of colour**
3 **Realist theories of colour**

1 Eliminativist theories of colour

The association between atomistic metaphysics and the denial that colour has any place in the external world is both ancient and common. It can be found in authors as widely separated in time and other views as Democritus and Galileo. Although metaphysics is no longer atomistic in a strict sense, many contemporary scientists hold similar views about the absence of colour from the external world. Colours as perceived are commonly seen by those acquainted with scientific metaphysics to have features that preclude all attempts at the identification of colour with a physical property of external objects.

Once colour has been excluded from the external world there still remains the question of which objects, if any, possess colour. One possible answer to this question is to maintain that colours are genuine properties of some perceptual experiences. This view is a kind of phenomenalism with regard to colour (see PHENOMENALISM). Although colour phenomenalists maintain that no tomato is red, strictly speaking, it may be that the visual experience obtained by looking at a ripe tomato in good light genuinely does possess the property of being red (Jackson 1977). Something like this answer combined with a reductive account of mental properties may explain the repeated claims by visual scientists of the last two centuries that colours are properties of the brain. This form of subjectivism requires a commitment to the existence of *qualia* or sense-data: in other words, intrinsic properties of visual experience to which we have unmediated conscious access (see QUALIA).

Alternatively, it may be argued that nothing, including visual experience, has colour. C.L. Hardin (1988) has argued, first, that there are essential properties of colour as perceived that no physical property possesses, then further that there are no mental items which could be the bearers of colour. The upshot is that although there are objects which *appear* coloured, there is nothing that *is* coloured.

The main difficulties faced by the various forms of colour eliminativism all derive from its failure to produce an adequate resolution of the apparent conflict between the scientific world and the perceptual world. Our visual experience is an experience of coloured objects. The external focus of our visual experience is also reflected in much of our thought and talk about colour. All forms of colour subjectivism are forced to maintain that our visual experience is profoundly misleading and most of our talk and thought about colour, if taken literally, profoundly confused. Colour subjectivism removes any possibility of conflict between perception and science by either moving the location or denying the reality of the world as we perceive it. Colours are properties of visual experience mistakenly projected in perception and thought onto external objects. The main motivation for attributing such widespread confusion to our ordinary thought and language is the failure of any less radical account successfully to accommodate all the relevant facts.

2 Relational theories of colour

One motivation for adopting eliminativism about colour is the obvious dependence of perceived colour on the characteristics of our visual system. Organisms whose visual systems differ from ours will divide the spectrum in different ways. Objects that look the same in colour to us may look very different in colour to organisms whose sensory apparatus differs in certain ways from ours. In general, neither the categories nor the similarity relations that arise from human colour vision map in a straightforward way onto any physical property. Two coloured surfaces that are an exact perceptual match can be physically very different and, in general, similarity in perceived colour (of whatever degree) is no reliable guide to similarity in any interesting physical property. Eliminativism is not, however, the only possible theory of colour capable of accommodating these facts. Rather than eliminating colour from the world, relational theories of colour take colour to consist in a relation between the external perceived object and the perceiving subject.

The most common form of relational theory has taken colours to be dispositions or powers to cause characteristic kinds of perceptual experience. Dispositional theories of colour date back at least to the seventeenth century and continue to have widespread currency among philosophers. The most famous early exponent of this view of colour is John Locke (see LOCKE, J. §§3–4; PRIMARY-SECONDARY DISTINCTION §1). According to a theory of this kind, an object is red, for example, if and only if it has the power or disposition to cause a characteristic kind of experience in an appropriately situated human being.

Colours are to be thought of, according to relational theories, as analogous in important respects to physical properties like solubility and more precisely to qualities like nutritiousness or poisonousness. A substance is poisonous, for example, if it causes degradation in bodily function if taken into the body. Whether or not a substance is poisonous depends on what kind of organism is under consideration. Some substances cause bodily harm to some organisms while being harmless or even beneficial to other organisms. Thus the very same

substance can be poisonous to one kind of organism and nutritious to another. Whether or not a substance brings about degradation in bodily function can also depend on the circumstances in which it is ingested. Substances that are harmless if taken by themselves can be poisonous if taken in conjunction with other substances. According to relational views of colour, an object can be red to one kind of perceiver and green to another in virtue of possessing exactly the same intrinsic physical characteristics. What matters is the kind of causal effect the object has on the perceiver, which depends in turn on the characteristics of the perceiver's visual system. The kind of effect an object has on a perceiver can also vary with changes in the viewing conditions, notoriously the character of the illumination, and consequently the colour of an object can change with viewing conditions. According to relational views of colour, no object has any particular colour if considered independently of how it is related to perceiving organisms.

One difficulty with relational views of colour is that they seem on the surface to be incompatible with the way we ordinarily talk about colours. We often make claims like 'that tomato is red' without offering any further explanation of who it is red for and in which circumstances. In addition, if someone were to claim of a beautiful ripe tomato that it is black, the ordinary response would be denial or puzzlement in spite of the fact that there are clearly viewing conditions under which the tomato would produce the characteristic effect that is associated with black things. The typical response of adherents of relational views of colour to this kind of difficulty is to claim that ordinary colour claims contain an implicit reference to a particular class of perceivers and a particular kind of viewing condition. To say that a tomato is red without qualification is to say that it produces the effect characteristic of red things on *normal* (human) perceivers in *normal* (for humans) viewing conditions. If we fix one term of the relation, then we can talk about colour as if it were an intrinsic property of the object being described.

The main problems that relational views of colour face fall into two categories. As we have seen, the theory attempts to account for ordinary colour talk by making use of the notions of a normal perceiver and normal conditions. There are serious questions, however, about whether a suitable conception of normality actually exists. It is possible to specify precisely the characteristics of a normal perceiver, but then it follows from the substantial variation in human colour vision that there will be extremely few normal perceivers. Thus most people will not be in a position to determine visually the colours of objects. If we offer a more relaxed standard for who counts as a normal perceiver, then there will be variation in the effects of objects within the class of normal perceivers, and the determinacy in colour attribution that the appeal to normal perceivers was supposed to provide will be lost. Similar problems arise in trying to specify which viewing conditions count as normal. The other main difficulty facing relational theories of colour arises from the necessity of describing the characteristics, the production of which gives an object its colour. In ordinary talk we use words like 'red' indiscriminately to describe both the external property and the perceptual experience with which it is associated. Relational theories of colour must find some way of independently characterizing perceptual experiences while avoiding circularity and vacuity.

3 Realist theories of colour

Realist theories of colour hold that colour is a genuine property of physical objects and that objects possess this property independently of their relation to perceiving subjects (see REALISM AND ANTIREALISM §2). Realist theories can be divided into two categories depending on whether or not they take colour to be reducible to physical properties. Physicalist theories of colour hold that colour is a physical property, possibly a complicated one, and that to see the colour of an object is to see that it has a physical property. Physicalist theories of colour bear some analogy to materialist theories of mind and share some of the same advantages and problems (see MATERIALISM IN THE PHILOSOPHY OF MIND). In spite of the resemblance in logical structure between the two types of theory, there is no logical connection between materialist theories of mind and physicalist theories of colour, and it is possible consistently to maintain every combination of affirming and denying the two theories.

The early defenders of physicalist theories of colour were somewhat vague about exactly which physical property they took colour to be identical with and largely confined their attention to defending the possibility that there could be some physical property identical with colour. It is obvious, however, that the relevant physical property must be one that has to do with light, or the reflection of light, since these are the prominent elements in the causal chain leading to the perception of colour. The most suitable candidate, as has been argued by D.R. Hilbert (1987), is the way in which objects reflect light. This property, surface spectral reflectance, is a relatively stable property of the surfaces of objects, which does not vary with changes in the illumination. Unlike its reflectance, the light reaching the eye from an object varies with changes in the illumination in ways that match neither

our perceptual judgments of object colour nor our inclination to attribute stable colour properties to objects.

The main problems facing physicalist theories revolve around two connected questions: how is the content of colour experience determined and what is the structure of our colour concepts? Armstrong (1968) clearly saw that any very rich concept of colour is incompatible with physicalism. Most people who use and apply colour concepts are ignorant of the relevant physical and physiological facts. If we build a large amount of colour lore and phenomenology into the concept of colour, then there will be no physical property which will fit the bill. Many of the objections to physicalist theories of colour consist in arguing that some part of our concept of colour is incompatible with the empirical facts. The physicalist's only response to these arguments is to show that either the empirical facts are misrepresented or the claimed necessary truth about colour is not really necessary at all. Physicalist theories of colour require that colour perception not be transparent, in the sense that any colour perceiver necessarily knows all there is to know about colour. The easiest way to avoid this kind of difficulty is to adopt an externalist theory of content. Externalist theories of content have the effect of breaking any necessary connection between internal perceptual states and what they represent and thereby provide the resources for a defence of physicalism against a class of objections drawn from the assumption of transparency (see CONTENT: WIDE VERSUS NARROW).

Not all colour realists are physicalists, and there have been some philosophers who have claimed that colours are intrinsic properties of physical objects that cannot be identified with any physical property. There are two possibilities available to the defender of such a theory. Either colours are properties over and above all the physical properties and bearing no necessary connection to them, or colours are properties that supervene on physical properties but cannot be reduced to them. These two views bear obvious analogies to dualism and non-reductive materialism in the philosophy of mind. The main difficulty the dualist theory faces is that colours, as perceived, will have no place in the causal chain leading to the perception of colour, which raises serious epistemological problems as to how we could ever know the colour of an object. Taking colour to supervene on the physical properties of objects avoids this difficulty and has the virtue of avoiding many of the other difficulties faced by the theories of colour discussed above. The main difficulties facing the theory of colours as supervenient properties are the general difficulties of understanding the relation of supervenience and what kind of evidence could ever support a conclusion of this kind.

See also: Colour; Secondary qualities

References and further reading

* Armstrong, D.M. (1968) *A Materialist Theory of the Mind*, New York: Humanities Press. (Referred to in §3. Chapter 12 defends a physicalist theory of colour in the context of a materialist theory of mind.)

Byrne, A. and Hilbert, D.R. (1997) 'Readings on Color', in *The Philosophy of Color*, vol. 1, Cambridge, MA: MIT Press. (A collection of recent philosophical work on colour. The referenced works by Campbell, Johnston and Peacocke are reprinted here.)

Campbell, J. (1993) 'A Simple View of Colour', in J. Haldane and C. Wright (eds) *Reality, Representation, and Projection*, Oxford: Oxford University Press. (Defends a version of non-physicalist realism about colour.)

Galileo, G. (1623) *The Assayer*; trans. and ed. S. Drake in *Discoveries and Opinions of Galileo*, Garden City, NY: Doubleday, 1957. (Referred to in §1. A presentation of Galileo's metaphysical views.)

* Hardin, C.L. (1988) *Color for Philosophers*, Indianapolis, IN: Hackett; repr. expanded edn, 1993. (Referred to in §1. Argues for an eliminativist theory of colour. Also presents a useful introduction to colour science.)

* Hilbert, D.R. (1987) *Color and Color Perception*, Stanford, CA: Centre for the Study of Language and Information. (Referred to in §3. Defends a physicalist theory of colour.)

* Jackson, F. (1977) *Perception*, Cambridge: Cambridge University Press. (Referred to in §1. Defends a phenomenalist theory of colour in the context of a general theory of perception.)

Johnston, M. (1992) 'How to Speak of the Colors', *Philosophical Studies* 68: 221–63. (Defends a version of dispositionalism and contains a discussion of the features common-sense attributes to colour.)

Kirk, G.S., Raven, J.E. and Schofield, M. (1983) *The Presocratic Philosophers*, Cambridge, Cambridge University Press. (A standard collection of writings by Presocratic philosophers, Democritus included.)

Locke, J. (1689) *Essay Concerning Human Understanding*; Oxford: Oxford University Press, 1975. (Referred to in §2. The origin of modern philosophical debates about the nature of colour.)

Peacocke, C. (1984) 'Colour Concepts and Colour Experience', *Synthèse* 58: 365–81. (Defends a version of dispositionalism and worries about the problem of circularity that faces dispositional theories.)

DAVID R. HILBERT

COMBINATORY LOGIC

Combinatory logic comprises a battery of formalisms for expressing and studying properties of operations constitutive to contemporary logic and its applications. The sole syntactic category in combinatory logic is that of the applicative term. Closed terms are called 'combinators'; there is no binding of variables. Systems containing the basic combinators S and K exhibit the crucial property of combinatorial completeness: every routine expressible in the system can be captured by a term composed of these two combinators alone. Combinatory logic is a close relative of Church's lambda calculus. M. Schönfinkel first introduced and defined basic combinators in 1920 in assaying foundations for mathematics that avoid bound variables and take operations, rather than sets, as fundamental. H. Curry later rediscovered the combinators (and coined the term 'combinatory logic') independently of Schönfinkel. Curry constructed various formal systems for combinatory logic and, throughout most of the subject's history, was the central figure in the research. In 1969, D. Scott succeeded in constructing set-theoretic, functional models for the lambda calculus and combinatory logic. Since then semantic studies of combinatory systems, together with research on their applications to computer science and further development as foundational systems, have dominated the field.

1 Combinators and the elimination of variables
2 Combinatory logic
3 Combinatory logic as a foundation for mathematics

1 Combinators and the elimination of variables

In his *On the Building Blocks of Mathematical Logic* (1924), M. Schönfinkel sought to surpass Whitehead and Russell's *Principia Mathematica* and Frege's *Grundgesetze* in isolating notions absolutely fundamental to mathematical logic. In addition to employing a Sheffer stroke-like operator for predicate calculus (Sheffer (1913) showed that all truth-functional connectives could be expressed in terms of 'not...and'), Schönfinkel proposed abandoning the type-stratified logical universe of *Principia Mathematica* in favour of one consisting entirely of type-free functions, mathematical operations presupposed by all others, unlimited in their allowed inputs and, hence, self-applicable. Moreover, he looked to reduce the number of all logical symbols (of both first- and higher-order logic) to three: the stroke-like function, a constant function and a 'fusion' function. These were the building blocks from which Schönfinkel intended to analyse logical expressions as compounds of basic operations. In this way, the ultimate operations on which mathematical logic depends – operations usually left implicit and unformalized – were to be revealed to the foundational gaze. As a bonus, this universal analysis was to require a wholesale elimination from logic of the variable.

For a simple example of variable elimination, consider a binary operation ○ which is 'idempotent'; that is, for all x, $x \circ x = x$. To render this relation without bound variable x, one introduces operation symbols or, to use terminology due to H. Curry, 'combinators'. In this case, let O and I be such that $Ox = x \circ x$ and $Ix = x$. Then, to claim idempotency for ○, one writes merely $O = I$. The variable x becomes redundant, for, if we apply both sides of the combinator equation to x, we return the original: $x \circ x = Ox = Ix = x$. Combinators then serve to express general laws, such as those of function application, without bound variables, and knotty issues of substitutability and illicit variable capture are avoided.

In general, a combinator is a variable-free name for an operation (on operations) defined using an equation. A number of combinators are standard and bear conventional names. Some of the most common are S, K, I, B and W, defined as follows: $Sxyz = xz(yz)$, $Kxy = x$, $Ix = x$, $Bxyz = x(yz)$ and $Wxy = xyy$. Schönfinkel, in effect, introduced combinators S and K for the operations he called 'fusion' (*Verschmelzung*) and 'constant' (*Konstanz*). S performs a generalized composition operation and K, when applied to x, yields Kx, the constantly x-valued function of y. I is a universal identity function. B denotes conventional composition of functions, since Bfg, applied to x, gives $f(gx)$. Finally, W realizes diagonalization: Wf, applied to x, yields fxx. If we think of f as a binary function, Wf is the unary function which is f with arguments identified. (Incidentally, here we are exploiting a device known to Schönfinkel, as well as to Frege, but now called 'currying', after Curry. By that device, combinators denote unary operations but achieve the effect of n-ary operations ($n > 1$) when iterated.)

2 Combinatory logic

Curry (1900–82), a student of Hilbert who redis-covered the combinators independently of

Schönfinkel, devised the first formal systems for (what he termed) 'combinatory logic'. In Curry's systems, the fundamental syntactic category is that of (combinatory) term, where basic terms are either variables or constants. Compound terms denote applications: if t and u are terms, then so is tu, expressing the application of t to u. Among the constants are the basic combinators K and S. Any term built up entirely from K and S is also called a combinator.

As with the lambda calculus, we can define appropriate notions of reduction, normal form and equality for combinatory terms (see LAMBDA CALCULUS). The 'reduction' of one combinatory term to another is conceived by analogy with simplifying computation, for example, the reduction of $(3 + 6) \times (10 - 2)$ to 72 by calculation. A 'normal form' is a term which can be simplified no further. Terms t and u are equal whenever they can be linked by a finite sequence of terms $t_0, t_1, \ldots, t_n$ such that, for every k and l, either t_k reduces to t_l or conversely.

Since operations may be viewed both extensionally and non-extensionally, there are extensional ('strong') and non-extensional ('weak') conceptions of reduction and normality, on either of which Kxy reduces to x and $Sxyz$ to $xz(yz)$. Both kinds of reduction are univocal in that, if t reduces to a normal form, it does so uniquely. This is guaranteed by the 'Church–Rosser theorem', which states that, if t reduces to u and to v, then there is a term w to which u and v both reduce. As in the lambda calculus, select combinators can serve as numerals and an arithmetic can be so developed that every partial recursive function is representable within combinatory logic.

It is readily seen that some combinators are definable from others. For example, I is recovered as SKK, since, for any x, $SKKx = Kx(Kx) = x = Ix$. The principle here is general: S and K comprise a 'complete' set of combinators in that every other combinator is derivable from these alone. Indeed, let t be any term, simple or complex, containing only variables from a finite set, say, x, y, z. Then there is a combinator, denoted $[x, y, z]t$, called 'the abstraction of t with respect to x, y and z', containing no free variables and constructed entirely from S and K such that $((([x, y, z]tx)y)z$ reduces (weakly) to t. In effect, Schönfinkel was the first to recognize the completeness of combinatory logic.

The notation '$[x, y, z]t$' is entirely metatheoretic; it denotes a term containing neither free nor bound variables and connotes that the abstraction $[x, y, z]$-operation plays a role in combinatory logic analogous to that played in the lambda calculus by the $\lambda x \lambda y \lambda z$ abstractor (see LAMBDA CALCULUS). This loose analogy is made precise by defining functions which inject the set of combinatory terms into those of the lambda calculus so that relevant equality relations coincide. There are metatheoretic functions Λ and C, where Λ maps combinatory terms into lambda terms and C the reverse, so that, for combinatory terms t and u, $C\Lambda(t)$ is the same term as t and, as far as extensional equality is concerned, $t = u$ in combinatory logic if and only if, in the lambda calculus, $\Lambda(t)$ equals $\Lambda(u)$. (The non-extensional versions of the respective calculi are also comparable but the matter is more complex.) The function C employs abstraction in dealing with lambda terms: $C(\lambda x \lambda y.t)$, for example, is $[x,y]C(t)$.

Intuitively, a model for (non-extensional) combinatory logic would be a universe D with a binary operation $\bullet$ – representing application – and containing elements k and s which behave, with respect to $\bullet$, as K and S do. It is easy to verify that such a model satisfies all the equalities of the weak or non-extensional combinatory logic. However, combinatory logic was originally conceived as a doctrine of operations or functions and real difficulties arise in rendering these functions in set-theoretic terms. For one thing, combinatory logic allows self-application: the combinator SS is perfectly well-formed. But no standard set-theoretic function can be a member of its own domain. Moreover, every combinator, unlike every set-theoretic function, admits fixed points. Curry discovered a 'paradoxical' combinator Y, which may be defined $WS(BWB)$, that computes a fixed point for any term: if t is a term, Yt is equal to $t(Yt)$.

In 1969, D. Scott (1976) was the first to overcome these obstacles and give set-theoretic constructions of models (in the above sense) for combinatory logic in which the terms name functions. A key idea was to let combinatory terms name functions which are not arbitrary but continuous. Here, a continuous function on a partial order with limits preserves the order and the limits which exist. Scott's original construction was quite complex; models less complicated to build were soon forthcoming. These semantic breakthroughs inaugurated a period of intense research on combinatory logic and the lambda calculus, stimulating numerous applications of both to computer science.

3 Combinatory logic as a foundation for mathematics

Schönfinkel's original goal, which Curry nurtured and pursued under the rubric 'illative combinatory logic', was the construction of a comprehensive system for the foundation of mathematics free of types and bound variables, and highlighting those operations essential to logical thought. To be comprehensive, no significant notion was to be banished to the metatheory. Other than the assertion sign, every concept which bears on the system was to be amenable to combination with combinators inside the system.

The strongest of Curry's early illative systems, which appeared in print in 1934, proved excessively comprehensive: Church's students S. Kleene and J. Rosser demonstrated its inconsistency in 1935. Curry himself refined the core of their argument, obtaining the elegant 'Curry's paradox', which shows plainly that even a simple logic of implication cannot be developed in the presence of combinatorial completeness. Curry and his co-workers then sought to avoid paradox by inventing systems to circumscribe, within the class of legal terms, canonical terms standing for propositions. Unfortunately, consistent versions of these systems were too weak to support a comprehensive mathematics. Throughout the middle and late twentieth century, a number of logicians contributed significantly to achieving the goal of Curry and Schönfinkel (a task known as 'Curry's programme' – see Seldin 1980) for illative systems, among them P. Aczel, M. Bunder, S. Feferman, F. Fitch, J. Hindley, D. Scott and J. Seldin. In 1983, M. Bunder published his system HOPC ('Higher-Order Predicate Calculus'), which is an illative system with internal typing and in which a significant portion of Zermelo–Fraenkel set theory can be interpreted.

See also: LOGICAL AND MATHEMATICAL TERMS, GLOSSARY OF

References and further reading

Barendregt, H. (1981) *The Lambda Calculus: Its Syntax and Semantics*, Amsterdam: North Holland, 2nd edn, 1984. (A bible of lambda calculus research. Authoritative and detailed.)

* Curry, H. (1934) 'Functionality in Combinatory Logic', *Proceedings of the National Academy of Sciences of the USA* 20: 584–90. (An article crucial to later research in illative combinatory logic.)

Curry, H. and Feys, R. (1958) *Combinatory Logic*, vol. 1, Amsterdam: North Holland. (Once the premier work on the subject; it remains an excellent reference.)

Hindley, J. and Seldin, J. (1986) *Introduction to Combinators and λ-Calculus*, London Mathematical Society Student Texts no. 1, Cambridge: Cambridge University Press. (An excellent introduction, highly recommended for beginners.)

* Kleene, S. and Rosser, J. (1935) 'The Inconsistency of Certain Formal Logics', *Annals of Mathematics* 36: 630–6. (A technical application of gödelization to proving the inconsistency of early systems of Church and Curry.)

* Schönfinkel, M. (1924) 'Über die Bausteine der mathematischen Logik', *Mathematische Annalen* 92: 305–16; trans. *On the Building Blocks of Mathematical Logic*, ed. H. Behmann; repr. in J. van Heijenoort (ed.) *From Frege to Gödel: A Source Book in Mathematical Logic, 1879–1931*, Cambridge, MA: Harvard University Press, 1967, 355–66. (From a 1920 presentation to the Mathematical Society at Göttingen. Introduction in the 1967 version by W.V. Quine.)

* Scott, D. (1976) 'Data Types as Lattices', *SIAM Journal of Computing* 5: 522–87. (A characteristically charming exposition of results by Scott, Plotkin and others on the graph model.)

* Seldin, J. (1980) 'Curry's Program', in J. Hindley and J. Seldin (eds) *To H.B. Curry: Essays on Combinatory Logic, Lambda Calculus and Formalism*, New York: Academic Press, 3–34. (An authoritative presentation of Curry's vision for combinatory logic.)

* Sheffer, H.M. (1913) 'A Set of Five Independent Postulates for Boolean Algebras, With Application To Logical Constants', *Transactions of the American Mathematical Society* 14: 481–8. (The first publication of the fact that there is a single connective that is expressively complete for sentential logic.)

Stenlund, S. (1972) *Combinators, λ-Terms and Proof Theory*, Dordrecht: Reidel. (A laudably concise introduction to combinatory logic and its role in proof theory.)

DAVID CHARLES McCARTY

COMEDY

In the narrowest sense, comedy is drama that makes us laugh and has a happy ending. In a wider sense it is also humorous narrative literature with a happy ending. In the widest sense, comedy includes any literary or graphic work, performance or other art intended to amuse us. This article will leave aside theories of humour and concentrate on comedy as a dramatic and literary form.

Comedy began at about the same time as tragedy, and because they represent alternative attitudes toward basic issues in life, it is useful to consider them together. Unfortunately, several traditional prejudices discriminate against comedy and in favour of tragedy. There are four standard charges against comedy: it emphasizes the animal aspects of human life, encourages disrespect for leaders and institutions, is based on malice, and endangers our morality. These charges are easily answered, for none picks out something that is both essential to comedy and inherently vicious. In fact, once we get past traditional prejudices, several of the differences between comedy and tragedy can be seen as advantages. While tragedy tends to be idealistic and elitist, for example, comedy tends to be pragmatic and egalitarian. While tragedy values honour, even above life itself, comedy puts little stock in honour and instead emphasizes survival. Tragic heroes preserve their dignity but die in the process; comic characters lose their dignity but live to tell the tale. Most generally, comedy celebrates mental flexibility and a realistic acceptance of the limitations of human life. The comic vision of life, in short, embodies a good deal of wisdom.

1　**The demeaning of comedy**
2　**Answering the charges**
3　**Comedy and tragedy**
4　**Comic wisdom**

1　The demeaning of comedy

Although comedy and tragedy grew up together, and many dramatists from Sophocles to Shakespeare wrote both, tragedy is usually thought superior to comedy, and is often judged the only important dramatic form. Tragedy is called 'serious' drama, comedy 'light' drama. The low status traditionally held by comedy is revealed by two meanings that arose for the word 'comical': 'befitting comedy; trivial, mean, low; the opposite of tragical, elevated, dignified' and 'of persons: low, mean, base, ignoble or clownish'.

The demeaning of comedy, and of humour generally, began with PLATO. Four main charges are traditionally offered. One is that comedy, which had its origins in animal masquerades, phallic processions and similar revelry, emphasizes the animal side of human nature. Plato found the Old Comedy of his time still wild and vulgar. In his mind the licence of comedy encouraged the undermining of our rationality by our lower physical nature. When laying down rules for the education of the young guardians in his ideal state, Plato insisted that they must not be prone to laughter and that the literature they read should not show the heroes and gods laughing too heartily.

Comedy is also charged with encouraging irreverence toward leaders and institutions. A society, like an individual, needs rational control, and that requires respect for leaders and traditions. But comedy can make fun of anything; Greek comedy even lampooned the gods. Plato was probably especially resentful of the ridicule his teacher Socrates suffered in the comedy of Aristophanes.

Throughout history, opposition to comedy and

laughter has been strongest in societies which emphasize physical restraint, decorum and conformity. Many medieval monastic orders had statutes forbidding laughter. The Puritan and Victorian eras saw many condemnations of comedy and laughter. The more authoritarian the regime, the greater its suppression of comedy. Hitler even set up 'joke courts' to punish those who made fun of his regime – one Berlin cabaret comic was executed for naming his horse Adolf.

The third charge against comedy, and humour generally, is that laughter is inherently mean-spirited. According to Plato, the object of laughter is vice, and specifically people's ignorance about themselves. Dramatic characters and real people are comic to the extent that they think of themselves as wealthier, better-looking, more virtuous or wiser than they really are. Our laughter at their self-ignorance involves a kind of malice toward them – a 'pain in the soul', as Plato called it – that is not only antisocial but harmful to our own character.

ARISTOTLE agreed with Plato that the essence of laughter is ridicule. Most people carry humour too far, he claimed, not worrying about hurting the feelings of those at whom they laugh. This view of laughter was later called the superiority theory. Its most famous proponent was the seventeenth-century philosopher Thomas HOBBES, who said that the cause of laughter is the sudden glory we feel when we judge ourselves to be doing better than someone else. Those who laugh the most, according to Hobbes, are those who are conscious of the fewest abilities in themselves. They have to search out the imperfections of others in order to feel good about themselves.

The last charge against comedy is that it is full of gluttons, drunkards, liars, adulterers and other base characters, who are bound to have a bad influence on our own morality. Aristotle said that comic characters are worse than real people and warned that children should not be allowed to attend comedies because they would be led to imitate the vices they saw on the stage. The purported danger of comedy to morality has been cited many times. It was part of the English Puritans' rationale for outlawing drama. Rousseau used it against the comedies of Molière. The weight attached to it can be judged from the number of writers and critics who felt obliged to argue that in laughing at immoral behaviour, we reject it, so that comedy discourages rather than encourages vice. Ben Jonson, Sir Philip Sidney, John Dryden, Henry Fielding, George Meredith, Henri Bergson and dozens of others defended comedy by citing its moral utility in this way.

2   Answering the charges

While the four charges against comedy apply to some plays and comic works, none applies to all of them, and none makes a convincing case that some characteristic is both essentially vicious and essential to comedy.

Comedy's emphasis on the animal side of human nature may be a fault if we share Plato's low opinion of the body and of the physical side of life. Similarly, the irreverence of comedy may be objectionable if we agree that our leaders and institutions deserve reverence and not critical questioning. But we need not share Plato's views on these issues. Indeed, a good case can be made for saying that comedy is valuable precisely because it reminds us of our physicality and because it keeps us thinking critically about our leaders and institutions.

The other two charges against comedy – that laughter is an expression of feelings of superiority and malice, and that the base behaviour of comic characters might rub off on us – do focus on two things that are reasonably considered objectionable. But they fail to show a necessary connection between either of these and comedy.

Although the first of these charges has a long history, it has seldom been carefully examined. If the superiority theory is right, then our laughter is always directed at a person, and in laughing we must be comparing ourselves favourably with that person. But, as Francis Hutcheson showed a century after Hobbes, neither of these consequences is true. We sometimes laugh when no one else is involved, and we sometimes laugh when someone seems superior to us. If I open my front door on a November morning to find a foot of snow where there was grass the night before, I may laugh – not at anyone, not even at the snow (in the sense of ridicule), but simply out of surprise. Similarly, I may laugh at clever rhymes or other wordplay in a comedy without comparing myself to the character speaking the lines or to anyone else. Some action which is better than we expected may also make us laugh in surprise. A stock character in early film comedy, for example, is the plucky hero, such as Charlie Chaplin or Buster Keaton, who gets out of trouble with an ingenious acrobatic stunt that we would never have thought of, much less been able to execute. The stunt makes us laugh, though the character looks superior to us.

The last charge against comedy – that we are likely to imitate its base characters – has probably been made more often than any other. But seldom has any evidence been given for it. Do people who see a lot of comedies have a higher rate of drunkenness or adultery? Are people who laugh at hypocrisy more likely to become hypocrites themselves? These are empirical questions calling for empirical research. Several characters, such as the boor, the windbag and the pompous ass, seem to be comic only if we think that their traits are undesirable – someone who emulated them would not find them funny. It may be that other comic characters, such as the smooth-talking liar, do elicit emulation from some people. But that has never been established, nor has it been shown that these characters outnumber the ones who discourage emulation. In short, like the other charges against it, the claim that comedy threatens our morality is largely an ancient prejudice.

3   Comedy and tragedy

Once we set aside traditional prejudices against comedy, we can compare it more equitably with tragedy. The most general similarity between the two is their focus on the incongruities in human life – the ways in which our experiences do not match our expectations. As William Hazlitt said, humans are the only animals who laugh and weep because they are the only ones who are struck by the difference between what things are and what they ought to be.

It is in their responses to life's incongruities that comedy and tragedy differ. Both see misfortune, vice, folly, and, in general, the gap between the real and the ideal as part of the human condition. But tragedy sees these leading to downfall and death, while comedy sees them as something we can live with and even enjoy.

Comedy and tragedy also have different attitudes towards the physical side of human nature. Comedy accepts the limitations of our bodily existence and celebrates acts like eating and sex. Tragedy bemoans our physical limitations and often identifies the human being with the mind, spirit or soul. In general, comedy is more physical and active, and tragedy more intellectual and contemplative. Falstaff might deliver a monologue while gnawing on a leg of mutton: it is inconceivable that Hamlet would do so.

The idealism and dualism of tragedy carry over to its vision of society. In tragedy only a few people are important and only their lives are of interest. The main characters in tragedy, as in the epic, are heroes, typically male rulers or warriors. In comedy, by contrast, there is a greater variety of characters, women are more prominent, and central characters may come from any social class. While the language of tragedy is elevated, the language of comedy is common speech.

Tragedy usually focuses on the suffering of one elite character in an extraordinary situation; comedy involves several characters from different social classes in ordinary situations. When comedy has a central character, that person, unlike the tragic hero, is not exalted above other human beings. Tragedy emphasizes the dignity and pride of the hero, which are often based on the code of honour of a male-dominated, power-based, militarist ideology. Indeed, it is often just this ideology which gets the hero into the tragic situation. Comic characters, not bound by codes of honour, may lack dignity, but at the end of the comedy they are still alive. Indeed, they are often found attending a wedding or another life-affirming celebration.

Furthermore, because comedy values life – especially the life of the community – over honour, it emphasizes the social support we all need. In tragedy, by contrast, the hero is more of a 'loner'. Many comic plots are based on reconciliation and peacemaking, while no tragic plots are. As Aristotle noted, in comedy enemies sometimes become friends, but in tragedy they never do.

4   Comic wisdom

The popularity and value of comedy lie largely in its vision of human life, which contrasts sharply with the dominant ideologies of Western culture. Those ideologies treat as virtues such traits as respect for authority, duty, honour, single-mindedness, courage and a capacity for hard work. These have been promoted by armies and other patriarchal institutions since ancient times. An important way of inculcating them in society at large has been to celebrate them in epic and tragic art, which are full of military imagery. Indeed, patriarchies try to get us to think of everything in military terms. In the USA, social programmes are called 'the war on poverty'; medical research is called 'the war on breast cancer'; even programmes to stop violence are 'the war on violence'! When military metaphors sink deep enough into our culture, life itself becomes a series of battles.

While blind obedience, single-mindedness, the ability to work constantly, and the willingness to die or kill on command are important for the conduct of war, it is not at all clear that they are virtues in all areas of life. Thus alongside the official ideology promulgated by epics and tragedy there has always existed an alternative ideology of comedy. Instead of promoting military virtues, comedy promotes the questioning of authority, mental flexibility, playfulness and the value of life. All of these threaten institutions of power in various ways, and as a result comedy has been suppressed in most cultures. However, because it addresses deep human needs, it has survived.

Comedies have different kinds of characters. Many

serve as negative role models, examples of how not to act. In laughing at the miser, the prude and the pedant, as Henri Bergson pointed out, we are recognizing their mechanicalness, their ineptness at living a human life. But most comedies also have at least one character that we identify with and may even admire. Many of the roles played by Charlie Chaplin, Mae West and Groucho Marx are of this type. These characters are so different from epic and tragic heroes that their usual name, 'comic heroes', is misleading. We can call them comic protagonists.

The attitudes of these characters embody what is most valuable in comedy. Unlike tragic heroes, they play as well as work. They are not unwaveringly committed to any cause; nor are they prepared to die, or kill, to achieve their goals. Like tragic heroes, they face problems and enemies, but instead of confronting them head on with violence, they use trickery, perhaps by turning the power of the threat against itself, or with reverse psychology. When all else fails, they are not ashamed to run away. As the old saying goes, you're a coward for only a moment, but you're dead for the rest of your life.

Comic protagonists differ most notably from tragic heroes in their mental flexibility, a trait which comedy celebrates. The characters who lose in comedy are rigid creatures of habit; those who succeed are adaptable and think on their feet. Unlike tragic heroes, comic protagonists do not have fixed categories for thinking or acting. They can view situations from several perspectives and see many possibilities. Much of their thinking is lateral rather than vertical, to use Edward de Bono's terms.

When confronted by problems, tragic heroes are given to emotions that make them mentally rigid and even obsessive. Comic protagonists keep an unemotional clearheadedness in the face of misfortune that allows them to think rather than feel their way through challenges. They do not engage in self-pity or curse their fate, but are more likely to laugh at their problems, as tragic heroes never do. As a result, they are more likely to bounce back from their mistakes and learn from them. The contrast here is fittingly generalized by Walpole's maxim, 'This world is a comedy to those that think, a tragedy to those that feel'.

Since emotional disengagement and the ability to imagine alternatives are a big part of human freedom, comic protagonists are considerably freer than tragic heroes. They are often in charge of their lives as tragic heroes are not, and they end up victors, while tragic heroes end up victims.

It is often said that the tragic vision of life embodies wisdom. Solemnity and pessimism are considered hallmarks of wisdom. Western thinkers, with a few exceptions such as Democritus and Nietzsche, have usually thought wisdom to be a kind of seriousness about life. But that is all part of the traditional prejudice against comedy. Judged fairly, the comic vision reveals at least as much wisdom as the tragic.

Indeed, if wisdom includes emotional disengagement, seeing life from a higher perspective than usual and seeing it objectively rather than from a self-privileging position, then comedy seems wiser than tragedy. If wisdom includes a realistic attitude towards life, comedy's tolerance for human limitations and its emphasis on adapting ourselves to an imperfect world seem to make it more realistic than tragedy. More fully than tragedy, too, comedy represents the richness of life – especially social life – in the many ways it may be lived and appreciated.

Comic characters make mistakes and suffer misfortunes, but through it all they are at home in their world, and they get by with a little help from their friends. Tragic characters, with their elitism and idealism, are not satisfied with living a merely human life. The central lesson of comedy is that we are finite and prone to error, but with a sense of humour we can still be happy.

The capacity for happiness seems to need some psychological technique for coping with finitude and fallibility, and humour is easily the most effective. Psychological studies have shown that humour is correlated not only with self-esteem but with creativity and a tolerance for ambiguity, diversity and change. Furthermore, humour has medical benefits – it blocks negative emotions, counteracts stress, boosts the activity of the immune system, reduces pain, and even has a laxative effect!

Both comedy and tragedy are reactions to the human condition, but as a dramatic form, an artistic sensibility, and an attitude toward life itself, comedy seems truer to human nature. The displacement of tragedy by comedy and tragicomedy in the twentieth century seems a step towards the acknowledgement of this fact.

See also: BERGSON, H.-L. §6; HUMOUR; TRAGEDY

References and further reading

* Bergson, H. (1956) 'Laughter', in Wylie Sypher (ed.) *Comedy*, Garden City, NY: Doubleday. (An explanation of laughter as the corrective response of a group to an individual's 'mechanical inelasticity'. Difficult style.)

Gutwirth, M. (1993) *Laughing Matter: An Essay on the Comic*, Ithaca, NY, and London: Cornell University Press. (A synthesis of previous theories of laughter and an exploration of the values of comedy. Moderately difficult.)

* Morreall, J. (ed.) (1987) *The Philosophy of Laughter and Humor*, Albany, NY: State University of New York Press. (An anthology of philosophical writings on laughter and humour from Plato to Roger Scruton, including all philosophers cited in this article.)

—— (1989) 'The Rejection of Humour in Western Thought', *Philosophy East and West*, 39 (3): 244–65. (Traces the development of philosophical theories of humour, and philosophical opposition to humour; suggests overlooked philosophical values of humour, discussing humour in Zen. Easy to read.)

* Plato (*c*.380–367 BC) *Republic*, trans. P. Shorey, Cambridge, MA: Loeb Classical Library, Harvard University Press, 1930, esp. 388e–389a. (Parallel Greek text and English translation.)

JOHN MORREALL

COMENIUS, JOHN AMOS (1592–1670)

Comenius (Jan Amos Komensky), a Czech philosopher and theologian, was one of the founders of modern educational theory. As a Protestant minister he had to leave Bohemia during the Counter-Reformation, spending most of his life in various European countries. His greatest work (not published during his lifetime) is De rerum humanarum emendatione consultatio catholica (A General Consultation on the Reform of Human Affairs), whose leading idea is the demand for a harmonious arrangement of human relations on the basis of rational enlightenment, the development of education, and the instruction of all humankind. Comenius builds his philosophy on an idea of human nature understood as grounded in an active creative force perpetually leading to improvement: instruction and education are the tools to fulfil this humanitarian ideal. To lend force to this, Comenius constructs a whole ontological system, in which a harmonious development of the whole of existence leads to human reality as its highest tier.

Comenius was born in southern Moravia; his family belonged to the Czech reformist church known as the Unity of Brethren. After studies at the Union's schools in his own country and at the Universities of Herborn and Heidelberg, Comenius became a preacher of the reformed church, and later its bishop. His activities in his homeland – where he had started

working on a great encyclopedia of universal knowledge in the Czech language and on his first educational works – were interrupted by the anti-Habsburg uprising of the Bohemian Estates (1618–20) which ended in the loss of the kingdom's independence. Enforced re-Catholicization and persecution of other religions followed. For a few years Comenius went into hiding while writing his best-known Czech book, the symbolic prose *Labyrint světa a ráj srdce (The Labyrinth of the World and the Paradise of the Heart)*, but in 1628 he left his country for good and settled in Leszno (Lissa) in Poland. Here he created his important educational works, *Didactica* and *Janua linguarum reserata*, where he demands equal rights to education for all people, and also his first pansophic works, *Pansophiae prodromus* and *Conatuum pansophicarum dilucidatio*, where he makes proposals for reforming political relations in the world ravaged by the Thirty Years' War.

Comenius' educational and pansophic work found much support in Europe, and the English Parliament invited him to come to London to reform the education system and pursue his general efforts at universal improvement there. He recruited influential patrons such as James Ussher, John SELDEN, John Pym, Samuel Hartlib and others. Impulses from Comenius' stay in England contributed to the appearance of his *Via lucis* which contains – in addition to a proposal for an international organization of scientific work – Comenius' historical philosophy: Darkness (feudalism, the rule of the papacy and the Habsburgs, and general backwardness) will be driven away by Light because history is a tiered process where the amount of Light grows continuously out of the struggle with Darkness, in the form of rays of general education and rational enlightenment. Comenius expected that the period of the voyages of discovery, expansion of trade, book printing, science and technology will soon usher in an era of enlightenment, peace, international co-operation and prosperity. This should be helped by the spread of education into all layers of society, and to each individual.

The outbreak of the Civil War curtailed Comenius' activities in England. He left for Sweden to reform its educational system, hoping at the same time that Sweden's policy and participation in the Thirty Years' War might result in the liberation of the Kingdom of Bohemia from the rule of the Habsburgs and facilitate the repatriation of its political emigrants, a hope soon to be proved forlorn. During his stay he continued to expand his pansophic plans but found the Swedes uninterested. The years 1651–4 were spent in Hungary reforming its educational system, and Comenius then returned to Leszno where a fire in the town destroyed his library and all his manuscripts. Due to the change of political climate in Poland he could not stay there much longer, and in 1656 he left for Amsterdam where he spent the remainder of his life.

In the Netherlands Comenius published (with the help of the City of Amsterdam) his educational work *Opera didactica omnia* (1657–8). At the same time he pressed on with *De rerum humanarum emendatione consultatio catholica* (A General Consultation on the Reform of Human Affairs), a six-volume work which represents a synthesis of his life efforts. He almost succeeded in finishing it: some parts were published, but he found no support for a complete edition. Nor could his heirs arrange publication, for the same reason. For a long time the manuscript was believed lost. Only in 1935 was it discovered in the library of the Pietistic Orphanage in Halle, and the first complete version was published in Prague in 1966.

The *Consultation*, in addition to its prologue 'To the Lights of Europe' which addresses Europe's educated elite, consists of seven parts: 'Panegersia' (Universal Awakening) defines human matters, analyses their disconsolate state and calls for a quest for improvement; 'Panaugia' (Universal Enlightenment) explores possible ways to reform, and selects the most effective of them, 'the bright light of Minds spreading everywhere and to everything'; 'Pantaxia' (Universal Order) or 'Pansophia' (Universal Science), the fundamental section of this work, outlines Comenius' ontology by describing different tiers of world affairs right to the top one – an ideal human society; 'Pampaedia' (Universal Education) proclaims education for all, including adults, throughout their lives, including even 'entirely barbaric nations' which should be freed from 'the darkness of their ignorance'; 'Panglottia' (Universal Eloquence), a general study of languages as a means for spreading the light, including an artificial philosophical language; 'Panorthosia' (Universal Improvement) shows how – thanks to all so far discussed – the state of education, religion and public administration can be improved 'so that by God's command an Enlightened Pious and Peaceful Age can be brought to Earth'; 'Pannuthesia' (Universal Call), a challenge to all educated people, lords spiritual and temporal, 'as well as all Christians without difference, consciously to press for the bringing about of these desired and desirable things'.

Comenius' thought is characterized by his effort to achieve synthesis. He accepts all sorts of intellectual ideas from the present and past, transforms them and incorporates them into his conceptual structures. First and foremost he brings to fruition the Czech Reformation tradition, the roots of which go back to Jan Hus. From this tradition stems his emphasis on the activity of humans – free beings who, in striving for perfection, come close to God, and transform the world through their action. In this he does not consider humans to be just a 'res cogitans' (a thinking substance), and does not reduce them to mere intellectual subjectivity. He sees humans in their complexity, with a developed emotional component and above all with a will which dominates other forces and attributes of human existence. Such a being has all the prerequisites for working upwards again to human perfection, once lost by succumbing to evil and vice.

Comenius built his early philosophy on the empiricism of BACON. But this did not entirely satisfy him, and he searched for a universal knowledge which would be not just an agglomeration of empirical data but a logically structured whole where empirical findings would exactly fit into a solid framework of fundamental principles, to be found with the help of metaphysics. Comenius' image of the world was initiated by Neoplatonism and by NICHOLAS OF CUSA but these impulses are again re-shaped. He combines the dynamic descendancy of Neoplatonic Nature with the non-dynamic ascendancy of Aristotelian-Scholastic Nature, creating the picture of a dynamic ascendant world where practical human activity plays an active part. It is not a purely linear process as it has its regresses, but as a basic direction it points to the highest step – an ideal, harmonious human society. Comenius' lifelong efforts for a universal reform aim at this ideal, as illustrated by his final project outlined in *Consultation*.

See also: CZECH REPUBLIC, PHILOSOPHY IN; MEDIEVAL PHILOSOPHY; NEOPLATONISM

List of works

Comenius, J.A. (1969–) *Johannis Amos Comenii Opera omnia*, ed. M. Steiner, Prague: Academia. (A critical edition of all his works in the original languages. Twenty-seven volumes are planned in total, of which thirteen have been published to date.)

—— (1957) *John Amos Comenius 1592–1670. Selections*, intro. J. Piaget, trans. I. Urwin, Paris: UNESCO. (Produced in commemoration of the third centenary of the publication of *Opera didactica omnia*. Popular anthology of known Comenius' philosophical and pedagogic texts.)

—— (1623) *Labyrint světa a ráj srdce* (The Labyrinth of the World and the Paradise of the Heart), trans. Count Lützow, London: The Golden Cockerel Press, 1950. (The greatest Czech work of Comenius – a symbolic and critical picture of the society of that time.)

—— (1633) *Janua linguarum reserata*, Lipsiae: Gohofredi Grosii (Gottfried Gross), trans. as *The Gate of Tongues Unlocked and Opened*, London: T. Cotes, 1633. (The English translation of textbook of new methods of foreign language education.)

—— (1639) *Panosophiae Prodromus*, London: L. Fawne and S. Gellibrand. (The first sketch of Comenius' pansophism.)

—— (1644) *Conatuum pansophicarum dilucidatio*, Lugduni Batavorum (Leyden): David Lopez de Haro. (New version of pansophic theory.)

—— (1657–8) *Magna Didactica J.A. Comenii*, ed. F.C. Hultgren, Farnborough: Gregg, 1968; trans. and ed. M.W. Keatinge as *The Great Didactic of John Amos Comenius*, New York: Russel & Russel, 1967. (The Hultgreen edition is a facsimile of the original Amsterdam collected edition. Keatinge's translation contains bibliographical, historical and critical introductions.)

—— (1659) *Orbis Pictus*, ed. J.E. Sadler, London: Oxford University Press, 1968. (The reprint is a facsimile of the first English edition of 1659.)

—— (c.1660s) *De rerum humanarum emendatione consultatio catholica* (A General Consultation on the Reform of Human Affairs), ed. J. Červenka and V.T. Miškovská-Kozáková with J. Brambora, D. Čapková-Votrubová, J. Hora, J. Kopecký, J. Kyrášek and J. Moravec, 1st edn preface by J. Váňa with an epilogue by J. Patočka, Prague: Academia, 1966. (The synthesis of Comenius' life work not published in its entirety until 1966 – a critical edition. English translation by A.M.O. Dobbie of individual parts of the Consultation: Pampaedia, London: Buckland Ltd, 1986; Panaugia or Universal Light (1987), Panegersia or Universal Awakening (1990), Panglottia or Universal Language (1989), Pannuthesia or Universal Warning (1991), all Shipston-on-Stour, Warwickshire: Peter I. Drinkwater; *Panorthosia or Universal Reform* chapters 19–26 (1993), chapters 1–18 (1996), Sheffield: Sheffield Academic Press.)

—— (1668) *Via Lucis*, Amsterdam: Ch. Cunrad; trans. as *The Way of Light*, Liverpool–London: The University Press, 1938. (A proposal for an international organization of scientific work.)

References and further reading

Acta Comeniana. International Review of Comenius Studies and Early Modern Intellectual History, (1969–), Prague. (Periodical containing papers by Czech and other researchers in the principal European languages.)

Studia Comenia et historica, ed. Musaeum Comenii Hunno-Brodense, Uherský Brod (1971–). (Periodical which brings articles from a wide field of history and philosophy, mostly in Czech or German.)

Pešková, J., Cach, J. and Svatoš, M. (eds) (1991) *Homage to J.A. Comenius*, Prague: Karolinum. (A collection of papers in English, exploring a wide range of Comenius' ideas.)

Sadler, J.E. (1966) *J.A. Comenius and the Concept of Universal Education*, London: Allen & Unwin. (An attempt at systematic interpretation of Comenius' philosophical and pedagogic views.)

Turnbull, G.H. (1947) *Hartlib, Dury and Comenius. Gleanings from Hartlib's Papers*, London: Hodder & Stoughton/University Press of Liverpool. (Profiles of Hartlib, Dury and Comenius, based on materials stored in Hartlib Papers in Sheffield.)

JOSEF ZUMR

COMMON LAW

Common law and custom are features of most enduring legal orders. In English law the concepts have taken on special and interrelated significance, since English law is said to be grounded in common law and that in turn is said to derive from custom. According to classical common law theory, which crystallized in the seventeenth century, common law grew from the customs of the English people. It was not made by legal officials, as statutes are. Change was accommodated in this theory, on the basis not of identity of elements of law over time but of continuity, a continuity of authority and reception of legal customs, and of the traditional legal order which declared them to be law. The role of legal officials – particularly judges – was to interpret and declare legal custom; their judgments provided evidence of it. They did not make it or invent it. This mode of development through continual interpretation and reinterpretation of the significance and bearing of the legal inheritance was, according to common lawyers, better adapted to social complexity, change and variety, and also to human epistemological and practical limitations, than attempts to cover any field with legislation.

This theory was largely eclipsed in nineteenth-century England by the theory of legal positivism, and with it were eclipsed for a time some useful insights into social complexity and institutional limitations. Also lost was a sense of the complex dialectic between continuity and change in legal and institutionalized traditions. In its best moments, common law theory had such a sense.

1   **Common law as custom**
2   **Change and continuity in the common law**

1 Common law as custom

Common law is a term employed in many legal systems to mark a contrast between law which is in some way general or 'common' in scope – though the ways considered relevant differ markedly between different legal orders – and more particular types or branches of law once or concurrently applied in the same legal order. Custom, too, has figured widely as a significant term of art within complex legal orders (Kelley 1990). It typically refers to an element or source of law – unwritten, traditional, old, local – to be distinguished from other, usually newer, more deliberate, more explicit, written sources, which apply on a territorial rather than a communal or 'personal' basis, and which are administered by officials (Constable 1994). Both common law and custom are then, in part, contrast terms by reference to other aspects of legal systems; and frequently the contrast in mind is between the two of them.

Today when the common law is mentioned, however, it is usually in connection with the English legal tradition, and that tradition is distinctive in the way in which it has purported to connect, rather than contrast, common law and custom. For while it is acknowledged in this tradition that the institutions that administered common law supplanted those of customary law to form a national law, common lawyers have long insisted that the substance of English common law is drawn, and derives its legitimacy from, custom.

After the eleventh-century Norman conquest of England, the King's Courts gradually extended their sway throughout the kingdom. Institutionally this was at the expense of a variety of local assemblies, tribunals, customary bodies and practices. Substantively, too, the centralized application of written laws had profound transformative effects on oral customs and traditions, even when the courts claimed to be applying customary law (Constable 1994). The law dispensed by the King's Courts came to be known as the common law. This has led to one broad and two somewhat narrower uses of the term.

In its now most familiar usage, 'common law' is a global term for the legal tradition that was developed in Britain by these courts over centuries, and spread to its legal offshoots, such as the USA, Canada, Australia and New Zealand. The common law, in this sense, is most often contrasted with the civilian tradition (see ROMAN LAW §3) of continental Europe (and erstwhile colonies of European countries).

In a second and narrower usage, internal to the common law tradition, the law dispensed by the common law courts was distinguished from the specific 'equitable' interventions by the Lord Chancellor and the Court of Chancery to supplement traditional common law remedies (see JUSTICE, EQUITY AND LAW §4).

Third, when statutes enacted by Parliament became prominent sources of English law, they were also distinguished from the common law developed by the courts. This third distinction persists, though statutes are more and more general in scope and effect and in many areas have come to override the common law.

English common law practice had many features that distinguished it from other legal traditions. The common law also spawned a distinctive theory of law. Classical common law theory crystallized most clearly in the seventeenth century and maintained its influence through the eighteenth. It insisted – to the dismay of Hobbes, Bentham and other legal positivists – that the common law, far from being made by any identifiable institutions or persons – kings or parliaments or even judges – grew from the customs of the English people. As Sir William BLACKSTONE put it in the eighteenth century, the common law was an 'antient collection of unwritten maxims and customs' (Blackstone [1765–9] 1979, vol. 1: 17), and '[t]he only method of proving, that this or that maxim is a rule of the common law, is by shewing that it hath been always the custom to observe it' (Blackstone [1765–9] 1979, vol. 1: 68). Although the decisions of judges were acknowledged to be crucial elements in the development of the tradition in this perception, they did not make the common law, but were merely evidence of it.

The claim that the common law is grounded in custom addresses, often without much differentiation, descriptive, explanatory and normative issues, as well as social theory and legal and political philosophy. Several matters need to be unravelled, central among them the following three. First, whether, and if so how, an account of law as custom can make sense of legal change. Second, if law is popular custom, what is the role of legal officials? Third, what are the normative implications of the customary character attributed to the common law; what, if any, are its particular virtues?

2 Change and continuity in the common law

One of the most important interpreters of the language of the common law, Pocock (1987), has argued that the common lawyers' identification of common law and custom involved them in a paradox, stemming from an ambiguity inherent in the concept of custom itself. On the one hand, '[i]f the idea that law is custom implies anything, it is that law is in constant change and adaptation, altered to meet each new experience in the life of the people' (Pocock 1987: 36). On the other hand, 'it is equally possible to regard [custom] as that which has been retained throughout the centuries and derives its authority from its having survived unchanged all changes of circumstances' (Pocock 1987: 37). Pocock took the views of Sir Edward Coke, the seventeenth-century common lawyer and (from 1606–16) Chief Justice, as emblematic of the tradition, and emphasized that Coke and his contemporaries seemed largely in thrall to the second, unhistorical, interpretation. Later scholarship (Burgess 1992), and some clarifications by Pocock himself, suggest than even Coke might have been less single-mindedly ahistorical than Pocock was taken originally to suggest and, more important, that Coke's was never the interpretation widespread among the most distinguished and sophisticated common lawyers.

Such lawyers, among them in the seventeenth century Spelman, Vaughan, SELDEN and Hale, in the eighteenth Blackstone and Lord Mansfield, had no time for immemorial origins. Since evidence was poor and incomplete, there was no way of knowing such origins with any exactness. In any event it is not in the nature of law to remain unchanged:

> From the Nature of Laws themselves in general, which being to be accommodated to the Conditions, Exigencies and Conveniencies of the People, for or by whom they are appointed, as those Exigencies and Conveniencies do insensibly grow upon the People, so many times there grows insensibly a Variation of Laws, especially in a long tract of Time.
>
> (Hale [1713] 1971: 39)

Indeed, while Hale believed that deliberate legal change should be approached with caution and humility, he also thought it absurd to imagine that the law should remain unchanged: 'The matter changeth the custom; the contracts the commerce; the dispositions, educations and tempers of men and societies change in a long tract of time; and so must their lawes in some measure be changed, or they will not be usefull for their state and condition' (Hale [1665] 1787: 269–70).

If there was all the adding, subtracting, altering and creating that Hale describes, what held things together, in the absence of the glue of identity; what made all these different laws part of the same 'common law'? For Hale, and the common law tradition more broadly, change was an intrinsic characteristic of a law in constant organic evolution.

Like a person, the law maintained its continuity through a process of continual change and growth. Or, to change the metaphor as several of them did, the common law survived change just as 'the Argonauts Ship was the same when it returned home, as it was when it went out, tho' in the long Voyage it had successive Amendments, and scarce came back with any of its former Materials' (Hale [1713] 1971: 40). What made all its elements part of the same law was not their changelessness but their continuity. And this continuity had more to do with the continuing authority and reception of the law than it did with any demonstrable objective longevity of all its elements.

The source and ground of this continuity was twofold. First, it stemmed from the anchoring of the common law, developed by the courts, in popular customs which had been 'handed down by tradition, use and experience' (Blackstone [1765–9] 1979, vol. 1: 17) and had survived by constant transmission, reception, interpretation, refinement, transformation and application, from 'time whereof the memory of man runneth not to the contrary' (Blackstone [1765–9] 1979, vol. 1: 67). These customs had developed over the life of the country, and had indeed become constitutive of 'the people, into whom their ancient laws and customes are twisted and woven as a part of their nature...' (Hale [1665] 1787: 255). As these customs displayed continuity through change, so too did the common law, whose officials continuously drew upon them, interpreted them, rendered them explicit and made them binding.

Second, continuity was embedded in the characteristic practices of the legal institutions themselves, for these practices – and particularly those of the common law courts – were best understood as customary ones. As A.W.B. Simpson has revived and endorsed this aspect of the common law account:

> the common law system is properly located as a customary system of law in this sense, that it consists of a body of practices observed and ideas received by a caste of lawyers.... The ideas and practices which comprise the common law are customary in that their status is thought to be dependent upon conformity with the past, and they are traditional in the sense that they are transmitted through time as a received body of knowledge and learning.
>
> (Simpson 1987: 376)

Given such continuity, it was possible to accept, even to advocate, reform of the law, so long as it was done by common law methods, materials and institutions. And much of the most distinguished common law thought of the eighteenth century was devoted to advocating legal reform of precisely that sort (Lieberman 1989).

3 Judges and the common law

Notwithstanding their insistence that the common law reflects and rests upon the customs of the English people, not every custom was law. Customs became recognizably legal in the common law when legal officials recognized them (though this was not, for common lawyers, the source of their authority). Coke, Hale and Blackstone all paid great attention to the activities of such officials. However, whereas legal positivists insisted upon the primacy of legislators, the common law tradition did not. Instead its focus was on the common law judge. The declaration, determination, refinement, alteration and transformation characteristic of common law development were primarily the work of the judges of the common law courts: 'the depositary of the laws; the living oracles, who must decide in all cases of doubt, and who are bound by an oath to decide according to the law of the land' (Blackstone [1765–9] 1979, vol. 1: 69).

Given the acknowledged centrality of judicial pronouncements in its development, it is not surprising that, increasingly from the eighteenth century, the common law has been referred to as 'judge-made' law, distinguished in this character from statutes, which are made by parliaments. To put things this way, however, is implicitly (and today typically unconsciously) to reject the common law understanding of law altogether, in favour of understandings from within the tradition of legal positivism, which – in legal philosophy – has largely overwhelmed that of the common law. For the common lawyers did not view the judge as lawmaker, but as interpreter and declarer of custom, directly or as filtered through earlier judicial decisions; in Coke's words, 'the mouth of the law (for *judex est lex loquens* [the judge is the law speaking])'. This is not a passive role, but nor is it a legislative one. And while common law theory may not furnish an adequate account as it stands, it is neither unperceptive nor absurd.

The positivist critics of common law theory conceived of law as a system of substantive rules, made deliberately by particular persons or institutions (see LEGAL POSITIVISM). Existing rules would either cover a particular case, or not. If the former, the judge's obligation was to apply the rule to the case. If the latter, the judge would have to supplement the rule in a legislative or quasi-legislative manner. To common lawyers, this set of alternatives would seem unrealistic and impoverished.

On the one hand, well into the nineteenth century common law *practitioners* tended not to think of the law as a collection of substantive rules at all. Rather it was a system of reasoning, and a collection of procedures and remedies, to be adapted to cases as they came before the court. Substance, on this view, came 'from below, in a constant feeding from society' (Lobban 1991: 79).

On the other hand, common law *theorists* did believe that there were substantive rules of the common law, but did not regard them as simply to be applied or made. In any event, unlike statutes, they did not come in a fixed and delimited textual form, ready to be applied. The meaning and bearing of customs and precedents was rather of continual argument, interpretation and reinterpretation. More generally, common law theorists regarded the law, not as a systematic collection of discrete rules, but as a traditional or customary order, of language, thought, maxims, principles, understandings, values and rules – with its own ways of knowing, thinking and arguing, handed down over generations. Lawyers and judges are trained and participate in this order, and interpret it. The judges are the authoritative guardians of this tradition. They conserve it, bring it to bear on particular cases, adapt, apply and transmit it. New things are said and done, of course, on this 'Argonauts Ship' – but by experts working from inside, not out, with materials already on board, and with a keen and experienced sense of the risks involved in straying too far.

The notion here is one of skilled and experienced participants in a familiar and intricate customary order, who deal with both repeated and new problems and changing circumstances by working with old materials. Moreover they do not merely work with those materials, but think in terms that they provide, making distinctions and analogies that make sense in their terms, terms endogenous to the legal materials rather than imposed on them from without. Here, to vary the metaphor yet again, not merely is the statue within the block of stone, but so too are the tools and even the sculptor as well.

Morever, the common law judges are not merely participants in the legal tradition; they are *experts* in the law. This is an expertise not available to everyone without long experience and training. Rather, as Hale observed, 'men are not borne Comon Lawyers' (Hale 1966: 505). Without training and long experience they lack what Coke called 'the artificial reason and judgment of law, which law is an act which requires long study and experience, before that a man can attain to the cognizance of it' (Coke [1608] 1907: 1342–3).

4 The virtues of the common law

An intensely live question, perhaps even now, was

what, if anything, England gained from law which was predominantly of this sort: grounded in custom, and determined by judges. More generally, what might any legal order have to gain from law which, unlike legislation 'is not laid down; customs, we know, grow up' (Simpson 1987: 363)? Simply put, the answer of Jeremy BENTHAM and his followers to these questions was: nothing much and nothing good. For the early positivists' model for law was overwhelmingly legislative. Legislation was the model both for what law is and for what good it can do. Laws are the general commands of legally unlimited sovereigns to habitually obedient subjects. They can do good if clear-headed, deliberate, purposeful legislators issue explicit and unambiguous general commands to deal with social problems and to reform the law – particularly the common law. On this view, either the 'common law' really is inchoate custom or judicial resolution of particular disputes – and then it is no law at all, for no general commands have been issued – or it is purported general commands wrested from individual cases, but in that case power has been arrogated by the 'sinister interests' of 'judge and co.', as Bentham described the masters of the common law.

The common lawyers, by contrast, believed that the common law owed its moral authority (which they did not always sharply distinguish from its legal validity) to its immemorial reception, rather than to its legally irresistible imposition. And they praised it above all for those features which most distinguished it from legislation. Many of the themes of common law theory were elaborated more famously by Edmund BURKE (§3) and more recently by F.A. HAYEK. They are elements of what might be called the methodological conservatism of common law theory.

First, there is a stress on the irreducible complexity and interconnectedness of social life. The problems and circumstances of life are extraordinarily various, complex, interdependent and changing. Many of the most successful institutions have been the products of no one's design, and the reasons for their success might be unknown to anyone in particular. There is too much to know for any individual adequately to understand what makes for success in legal arrangements or social arrangements generally – even those that already exist – let alone confidently to predict the results of legal interventions (see SOCIAL THEORY AND LAW §5).

Given the inherent complexity of the world, then, and the inescapable limitations on what we can know and what we can hope to do, thoughtful, cautious, corrigible elaboration and refinement of solutions is preferable to imperious imposition of them. The incremental methods of the common law are suited to the first; legislation to the second. For unlike

legislators, as the eighteenth-century Scottish jurist Lord Kames (see HOME, H. (LORD KAMES)) insisted, '[a] court of justice determines nothing in general; their decisions are adapted to particular circumstances.... They creep along with wary steps, until at last, by induction of many cases...a general rule is with safety formed' (quoted in Lieberman 1989: 162).

Moreover, common law judges do not creep unguided, with just their puny individual 'natural' reason to light their way. For the common law in which they are immersed provides them with a great deal on which to draw. Given the difficulties in doing so, customs that have survived some long time must, at the very least, be presumed to have weathered and adapted to many trials, both literal and metaphorical. Common law judges have the vast storehouse of cases and decisions to draw upon. This law, in its organic and recorded development, encompasses multitudes of cumulative decisions, and these draw upon social customs since time immemorial. These customs – and the judicial reflection upon and refinement of them – embody, or at the very least should be presumed to embody, wisdom far deeper than could be available to any unaided individual, for 'time is the wisest thing under heaven' (Hale [1665] 1787: 270) and the common law is 'fraught with the accumulated wisdom of ages' (Blackstone [1765–9] 1979, vol. 4: 435).

Some interpreters have suggested that the common lawyers favoured custom over reason, but that is not the way they saw it or put it. On the contrary, they insisted that the common law combined both; indeed that its attention to the former uniquely revealed the dictates of the latter. At its most philosophical, this is a variation on Aquinas' distinction (see AQUINAS, T. §13) between *deduction* as one way in which particular conclusions can be derived from the natural law, and *determination*, 'of certain general features...like that of the arts in which some common form is determined to a particular instance.... So the natural law establishes that whoever transgresses shall be punished. But that a man should be punished by a specific penalty is a particular determination of the natural law' (*Summa theologiae*, IaIIae.95.2). Determinations will vary according to the ways in which circumstances, customs, other particular conditions and human ingenuity themselves vary. Determinations cannot conflict with the natural law from which they are derived, but nor are they uniquely correct implications of them. For there are no such uniquely correct implications. The common law, dealing with the complex particularities of social life, had general elements of the first sort, but in its detail was mainly of the second. Indeed it is a remarkable store of such determinations, as adapted to and coloured by the particular, complex and variable conditions in which the law must operate, and refined by the sustained application of the 'artificial reason and judgment of law'.

In this way one could insist on the existence of a law of nature, accessible to reason, which the common law could not violate, and at the same time insist that laws apt for some people at some times could not simply be transplanted to other people and other times. In this way, too, one could, by praising the reason immanent in the common law, deny that the common law was simply whatever judges had decided. One could insist, on the contrary – and the eighteenth-century common lawyers increasingly did – that deeper principles underlay the common law, could be discerned through expert interpretation of it, and furnished grounds for decisions which appeared to depart from particular precedents. Such decisions furthered or were said to further values immanent in the common law – general principles 'which run through the cases', in Mansfield's phrase.

To modern positivists this appears to be a sophistical mask for judicial legislation, but this is not how it appeared then, nor is it necessarily so. Rather, underlying it are conceptions which emphasize the particularity and practicality of the judges' task, the collective nature of the publicly justified reasoning processes in which they indulge, and the wisdom of reflecting in a sustained manner on what the tradition in which one works has done in similar circumstances. It is not necessarily the mere reactionary resistance to change, and obscurantist deference to authority, that Jeremy Bentham took it to be.

5 Conclusions

The common lawyers had many commitments on which most contemporary observers would be at best agnostic. They shared, for example, a hagiographic commitment to the common law as the accumulation of the wisdom of ages. And while they did not claim that all of the common law merely stems from the customs of the people – for one of its sources is old statutes – the common lawyers saw no difficulty in claiming that it was grounded directly in the customs of the people rather than merely in the activities of the lawyers and the decisions of the judges.

Many critics have found extremely questionable this premonition of historical jurisprudence, with its homogenization of official law with social life, and of social life itself (see JURISPRUDENCE, HISTORICAL). Of course the common law has a continuing link with the common life, if only because some cases are brought by ordinary folk, and lawyers and judges are required to meditate on whatever problems are brought before them. It is one thing, however, to say that as a reactive

social institution which is driven by the cases brought before it, the common law is likely to adapt over time to the 'Conditions, Exigencies and Conveniencies of the People'; although even this is not a simple matter, for the cases that come before the courts – particularly the higher courts – are not random samples, and there are open and difficult questions about how and how much that adaptation occurs, about what law responds to in society and about what in law responds. It is another thing entirely to say that judicial law meshes directly, smoothly and constantly with popular custom. Questions abound not only about the degree of autonomy of official law from other social practices and traditions, but also about the complex and variable relationships between official and lay customs and traditions, and about the significance of social and political power in maintaining elite practices. There are also a host of other questions, for example, about what elements in plural, stratified, heterogeneous societies – including England, notwithstanding its insularity – judges' law might be related to. While it is obvious and important, then, that law and life are intimately related, the relationships are not simple, unidirectional, unmediated or uniform. To say that the products of specialized and differentiated institutions represent a distillation of national mores and customs is to raise and to beg a host of questions of fact, morals and social theory upon which it is difficult to pronounce in general or even with regard to the long history of the common law.

Nevertheless, the common lawyers had a better appreciation than many of their successors of the complexity of social affairs, of the significance of continuity in legal life, of the need for social grounding of legal institutions, of some of the resources available to schooled participants in a traditional order, and of the inextricable relationships between continuity and continuous change that are characteristic of enduring and complex normative traditions, such as the common law. Not all of these insights were retained when the cloying hagiography of common law partisans was thrown out of philosophical discussions of law.

See also: LAW, PHILOSOPHY OF; SAVIGNY, F.K. VON; SELDEN, J.; STAIR, J.D.

References and further reading

* Blackstone, Sir W. (1765–9) *Commentaries on the Laws of England*, 4 vols, Oxford: Clarendon Press, 1787; Chicago, IL: Chicago University Press, 1979. (The 1979 edition contains valuable editorial introductions to each volume.)

* Burgess, G. (1992) *The Politics of the Ancient Constitution*, London: Macmillan. (Excellent account of English political and legal thought in the seventeenth century, with thorough and thoughtful revisions to Pocock's theses about the 'common law mind'.)

* Coke, Sir E. (1608) 'Prohibitions del Roy', in *77 English Reports*, London: Stevens and Sons, 1907, 1342–3. (The case was 1608, but is incorporated in the 1907 *English Reports*.)

* Constable, M. (1994) *The Law of the Other*, Chicago, IL: University of Chicago Press. (Study of transformation of the customary institution of the 'mixed jury' with interesting reflections on the replacement of customary law by 'official' law.)

* Hale, Sir M. (1665) 'Considerations Touching the Amendment or Alteration of Lawes', in F. Hargrave (ed.), *A Collection of Tracts Relating to the Law of England*, vol. 1, 1787, 249–89; repr. Oxford: Professional Books, 1982. (See §2 above for discussion.)

* —— (1713) *The History of the Common Law of England*, ed. C.M. Gray, Chicago, IL: University of Chicago Press, 1971. (Published posthumously; printed three times, 1713, 1716, 1739, virtually as it stood in manuscript and numerous times thereafter with editorial additions.)

* —— (1966) 'Sir Matthew Hale's Criticisms on Hobbes's Dialogue of the Common Laws', repr. in Sir W. Holdsworth, *A History of English Law*, vol. 5, 2nd edn, London: Methuen, 419–513. (Unpublished in Hale's lifetime.)

* Kelley, D.R. (1990) *The Human Measure*, Cambridge, MA: Harvard University Press. (Masterly historical discussion of the role of custom in European legal and social theory.)

* Lieberman, D. (1989) *The Province of Legislation Determined*, Cambridge: Cambridge University Press. (Excellent discussion of eighteenth-century English and Scottish, common law and positivist, views on the rival claims of common law and legislation – especially as sources of law reform.)

* Lobban, M. (1991) *The Common Law and English Jurisprudence, 1760–1850*, Oxford: Clarendon Press. (Study of the tensions between common law practitioners' remedies-focused assumptions about the nature of the common law and the more rule-based focus of eighteenth-century common law system builders, such as Blackstone, and critics of the common law tradition, such as Bentham.)

* Pocock, J.G.A. (1987) *The Ancient Constitution and the Feudal Law: A Reissue with a Retrospect*, Cambridge: Cambridge University Press. (Classic study of the 'common law mind' with extensive reply to critics of the first edition.)

Postema, G.J. (1986) *Bentham and the Common Law Tradition*, Oxford: Clarendon Press. (One of the best available accounts of the legal theory of the common law tradition, and of Jermey Bentham's criticisms of, and alternative to, that theory.)

* Simpson, A.W.B. (1987) 'The Common Law and Legal Theory', in A.W.B. Simpson, *Legal Theory and Legal History*, London: Hambledon Press, 359–82. (Excellent critique of positivist accounts of the common law, in favour of a slightly modified common law theory.)

MARTIN KRYGIER

COMMON SENSE SCHOOL

The term 'Common Sense School' refers to the works of Thomas Reid and to the tradition of Scottish realist philosophy for which Reid's works were the main source. The ideas of the school were carried abroad – to France; and to the USA, where they were highly influential, particularly among leading academics critical of Calvinism. Interest in Reid and the tradition to which he gave rise was revived almost a century later by leading American philosophers and their students.

P. Royer Collard introduced Thomas Reid's work to France, and Victor COUSIN and Théodore Jouffroy became disciples of the Scot, though they were sometimes loathe to give full credit to their mentor. Through Cousin's influence Reid's expressionist theory of art had a continuous influence throughout the nineteenth century on French aesthetics, culminating in a modern version of expressionism developed by René Sully-Prudhomme, the first recipient of the Nobel prize in literature in 1901.

John WITHERSPOON emigrated early in life to the United States and introduced Reid and Stewart to the young republic, where they, along with Cousin, exerted a major philosophical influence for fifty years. Their free-will agency theories were used effectively in undermining the Old School Calvinism of the Congregational and Presbyterian Churches. Among the most effective followers of Reid, STEWART and Cousin – all critics of Calvinism – were Francis Wayland (Brown University, RI), Asa Mahan (Oberlin College, OH), Henry P. Tappan (University of Michigan, MI), and Alexander Campbell (Bethany College, WV). Like Witherspoon and George CAMPBELL before him, James McCosh emigrated from Scotland to be the president of Princeton and the last great light of the Scottish tradition in America, providing what the tradition had hitherto lacked – a realistic analysis of causality. The interest in Reid and the Scottish tradition as a whole was revived in the United States in the twentieth century by the writings of C.J. DUCASSE, Roderick CHISHOLM, Wilfred SELLARS and their students.

While it must not be thought that all the members of the tradition held identical views, there was a common core to the Scottish realistic tradition to which most of these people adhered.

According to Reid, a number of concepts and principles in daily use could not in principle be learned from experience. The concept of space, for example, could not be learned from experience since every perception presupposes it. Hence concepts and judgments which cannot be learned must be the result of nativistic epistemic input, since that is the only other alternative. The judgments supplied nativistically are numerous and constitute what Reid called the principles of common sense. The following is a small sampling of these principles: every event must have a cause; people have some degree of power over their own actions and decisions; qualities perceived by the senses must have a subject called body or substance. These principles and numerous others proclaim what is either evident or self-evident and hence require no justification other than rebuttal of criticism. Any judgment may be accepted at face value unless there is a reason to doubt it. But the only acceptable reason for doubting such a judgment would be that it conflicts with other evident judgments. Hence no discursive philosophy can throw doubt on them singly or as a class. Such judgments carry more authority than any discursive arguments that are designed to show them to be false. Moreover, common-sensical principles are inviolable because they are universally held, and they are unavoidable in the sense that denying them is pointless (in that further sense that doing so never gets rid of them). The philosopher who momentarily denies them reaffirms them in the market place or, even while denying them, acts upon them unwittingly. That Hume pointed out this state of affairs (see HUME, D. §2) was, for Reid, a very honest if self-defeating thing for a sceptic to do.

Philosophies which deny the truths of common sense principles must contain a fallacy, and the job of the philosopher is to detect that fallacy. That such philosophies must contain a fallacy follows from the fact that denying them leads to absurd consequences and from the fact that evident and self-evident judgments always constitute a better reason for keeping such principles than discursive reasons can provide for disallowing them. Since philosophers on the whole are clever reasoners we must not usually look for the fallacies in their arguments but for some faulty premise with which they begin.

An example of a faulty premise which leads to absurd consequences by rejecting an evident universal and unavoidable judgment is the premise shared by LOCKE, BERKELEY, and Hume. Locke's premise is that the only things of which we are directly aware are our own ideas, impressions, sensations, phenomena, or whatever else the alleged non-physical entity of direct awareness insisted upon might be called. Once granted this premise, the slippery slope from Locke to Berkeley to Hume's scepticism is inevitable. Since no sensation can in principle in any way resemble an object, Locke's representative realism is untenable and we are left with the equally untenable alternatives: Berkeley's subjective idealism, which avoids scepticism only by inconsistently allowing direct knowledge of the self, or Hume's scepticism, the claim that we can never know or have any good reason to believe that our senses ever give us reliable information. Reid found no good argument to support Locke's premise – indeed, Locke and most philosophers generally take it for granted – and he argued convincingly that Hume's 'diminishing table' argument to bolster this premise was not only not successful but proved the opposite viewpoint. Having dismissed Locke's premise, Reid offered instead his adverbial-like analysis of sensation, which construed sensation as an act of the mind and dispensed with non-physical entities altogether (Reid 1872: 245–306; 'diminishing table' argument, 303– 5). It was this aspect of the common sense tradition which re-emerged in the work of contemporary adverbial theorists like Ducasse, Chisholm, and Sellars.

See also: ABERDEEN PHILOSOPHICAL SOCIETY; BEATTIE; BUFFIER; COMMONSENSISM; MOORE, G.E. §3

List of works

Cousin, V. (1828) *Cours de l'histoire de la philosophie moderne*, Paris: Pichon & Didier, 3 vols; trans. O.W. Wight *Course of the History of Modern Philosophy*, New York: Appleton 1852. (Cousin's use of the word 'absolute' has misled numerous commentators into characterizing him as an absolute idealist.)

—— (1853) *Du vrai, du beau, du bien*, Paris: Didier; trans. O.W. Wight *The True, the Beautiful and the Good*, New York: Appleton, 1854. (Shortened version of Cousin's lectures and a nineteenth-century translation of the 3rd edition.)

Jouffroy, T. (1838) *Philosophical Miscellanies*, Boston: Hilliard, Gray. (Collection of philosophical and literary essays which, despite the title, is crucial for understanding Jouffroy's thought.)

—— (1840) *Introduction to Ethics, Including a Critical Survey of Moral Systems*, trans. W.H. Channing, Boston: Hilliard, Gray. (This book was a standard text for ethics courses in American universities during the long dominance of Reid's philosophy in America.)

Mahan, A. (1881) *A Critical History of Philosophy*, London: Elliot Stock. (Probably Mahan's most important work. He developed his own version of Reid's doctrine in volume 2; note particularly his discussion of Kant.)

McCosh, J. (1867) *Intuitions of the Mind*, revised edn, New York: Carter. (McCosh's most important book, containing a more sophisticated analysis of the concept of cause than had heretofore appeared in the common sense tradition.)

Reid, T. (1785) *Essays on the Intellectual Powers of Man*, ed. B. Brody, Cambridge, MA: M.I.T. Press, 1969. (The best edition since it avoids all of Hamilton's footnotes which are systematically misleading.)

—— (1788) *Essays on the Active Powers of the Human Mind*, ed. B. Brody, Cambridge, MA: M.I.T. Press, 1969. (The best edition since it avoids all of Hamilton's footnotes which are systematically misleading.)

—— (1872) *Collected Works*, ed. W. Hamilton, Edinburgh: Maclachlan & Stewart, 7th edn. (Hamilton's footnotes are systematically misleading.)

Stewart, D. (1826) *Esquisses de philosophie morale* (Outline of moral philosophy), trans. T. Jouffroy, Paris: Johanneau. (This book was influential in the formulation of Jouffroy's own moral philosophy.)

—— (1854–60) *Collected Works*, ed. W. Hamilton, Edinburgh: Constable. (Text is good, but the footnotes should be avoided. Strangely, Hamilton never had a clear understanding of the common sense tradition.)

Wayland, F. (1835) *The Elements of Moral Science*, ed. J.L. Blau, Cambridge, MA: Harvard University Press, 1963. (Blau's text is by far the best available; his Introduction throws much light on the Reidian tradition in America.)

References and further reading

Barker, S.F. and Beauchamp, T.C. (eds.) (1976) *Thomas Reid: Critical Interpretations*, Philadelphia, PA: Monograph Series. (Analyses and clarifies numerous aspects of Reid's philosophy.)

Grave, S.A. (1960) *The Scottish Philosophy of Common Sense*, Oxford: Clarendon Press. (Presents a flawed interpretation of Reid's views on sensation and perception, but helpfully promoted the resurgence of the new interest in the Common Sense School.)

Lehrer, Keith (1989) *Thomas Reid*, London: Routledge. (Claims Reid's major contribution is his combining nativism, psychology and epistemology.)

Madden, E.H. (1968) *Civil Disobedience and Moral Law*, Seattle: University of Washington Press. (Deals with the deontological ethics and moral reforms of American common sense advocates.)

—— (1986) 'Stewart's Enrichment of the Common Sense Tradition', *History of Philosophy Quarterly* 3 (1): 45–63. (Portrays Stewart as a significant philosopher, by no means a shadow of Reid.)

Manns, J.W. (1993) *Reid and his French Disciples*, Leyden: Brill. (Exhibits the best understanding of the common sense tradition yet written.)

Rowe, W.L. (1991) *Thomas Reid on Freedom and Morality*, Ithaca, NY: Cornell University Press. (Constitutes the most thorough examination of Reid's agency theory.)

Stewart, D. (1803) *Account of the Life and Writings of Thomas Reid*, Edinburgh, William Creech. (Portrays Reid as a gentle, modest and amiable man and casts significant light on the nature and scope of Reid's philosophy.)

EDWARD H. MADDEN

COMMON-SENSE ETHICS

'Common-sense ethics' refers to the pre-theoretical moral judgments of ordinary people. Moral philosophers have taken different attitudes towards the pre-theoretical judgments of ordinary people. For some they are the 'facts' which any successful moral theory must explain and justify, while for others the point of moral theory is to refine and improve them. 'Common Sense ethics' as a specific kind of moral theory was developed in Scotland during the latter part of the eighteenth century to counter what its proponents saw as the moral scepticism of David Hume. Thomas Reid, the main figure in this school, and his followers argued that moral knowledge and the motives to abide by it are within the reach of everyone. They believed that a plurality of basic self-evident moral principles is revealed by conscience to all mature moral agents. Conscience is an original and natural power of the human mind and this shows that God meant it to guide our will. A deeply Christian outlook underwrites their theory.

'Common-sense ethics' refers to the pre-theoretical moral judgments of ordinary people (see MORAL JUDGMENT). Moral philosophers have taken different positions on the significance of such pre-theoretical judgments with respect to moral theory. Some see our pre-theoretical judgments as the 'facts' which any successful moral theory must systematize, explain and/or justify. Others claim that moral theory should improve our common-sense moral judgments which without theory may be distorted by local prejudices and biases. 'Common Sense ethics', however, is a specific type of moral theory, which originated in Scotland during the latter part of the eighteenth century and the early nineteenth century. Thomas Reid (1785; 1788) originally developed the Common Sense moral theory in response to what he perceived as David Hume's sceptical attacks on morality. There are two central features of Hume's moral theory which Reid took to be sceptical. The first is Hume's claim that moral approval is a matter of sentiment. According to Hume (1739/40), moral approval is a sentiment, a calm form of love: when we consider persons' characters impartially, sympathy with the persons themselves and those with whom they usually associate causes us to feel love for their good qualities, and this love is moral approval. Reid interpreted Hume's claim that approval is a matter of sentiment in a way which anticipated the emotivist analysis of moral 'judgments' (see EMOTIVISM; HUME, D. §4.6). According to Reid, for Hume moral approval and disapproval are merely expressions of agreeable or disagreeable feelings which are neither true nor false. When I condemn a person, I am not making a judgment about the person, but am only expressing some uneasy feeling I have (see MORAL SCEPTICISM §3).

The second point which Reid found to be sceptical concerns Hume's notorious claim that 'reason is and ought only to be the slave of the passions' (1739/40: 415) (see REASONING/RATIONALITY: PRACTICAL §1; PRACTICAL REASON AND ETHICS §2). Hume argued that, strictly speaking, the idea of rational action makes no sense. Reason helps us to discern the means to our ends, but it neither selects nor ranks ends. It does not provide us with motives of either prudence or duty. Reid interpreted this as implying that reason has no say in determining our ends. Reason does not even help us to form a conception of our ends. Our ends are supplied by brute feelings.

Reid addressed both of these points in his theory of conscience: conscience is an original and natural power of the mind, common to all human beings. Reid thought this showed that God meant it to guide our wills. It is both an intellectual and active power. As an intellectual power, it enables us to intuit directly the first principles of morality. Reid thought that

moral reasoning, and indeed all reasoning, must start from self-evident first principles which we perceive immediately. If we had to figure out the basic principles of morality by a process of ratiocination, as Locke maintained, morality would not be within the reach of everyone. Since morality is required of everyone, 'the knowledge that is necessary for all, must be attainable by all' (1785: 481). But only mature moral agents, those of 'ripe understanding', and free of interest, passion and prejudice, are in a position to see the self-evident moral principles. Moral education is therefore necessary.

Reid did not object to calling conscience a moral sense since he believed that a correct analysis of sensing shows that it involves judgment and so reason. Hume's mistake, according to Reid, was that he failed to see that approval is a complex act of the mind with feeling as only one component. Reid insisted that we all know the difference between feeling and judging. He granted that when I approve of someone, I experience an agreeable feeling, but claimed that this feeling is different from and dependent upon the prior judgment that the person's conduct merits esteem. Persuade me that the agent was bribed and both my esteem and agreeable feeling vanish (see MORAL SENSE THEORIES).

Conscience is also an active power. Reid followed Joseph BUTLER in arguing that there are several distinct sources of motivation. Reid called the motives which do not presuppose judgment or reason 'animal' principles of action; these include our appetites, desires and affections. Those which require the use of reason are, in contrast, rational principles of action. One rational principle is our overall good. Reid argued that without reasoning we could not even form a conception of our overall good and, once we arrive at a conception of it, we necessarily seek it. It is a governing principle, to which our animal principles ought to be subordinated. The other rational principle is duty, which conscience reveals to us and which motivates us to do our duty for duty's sake. Reid thought that the concept of duty is simple and refers to a relation between an agent and an action. Conscience's authority, its right to govern us, is self-evident and superior to that of interest. God's wisdom and benevolence guarantees that no agent will be a 'loser' by doing his duty.

Reid believed that there is a plurality of equally fundamental moral truths. Some of these concern the preconditions and range of moral judgments, for example, that only voluntary acts deserve praise. Others are substantive self-evident principles and concern our basic duties to ourselves, others and God. Reid's list of self-evident axioms includes such principles as that we ought to act benevolently towards others, that we should treat others as we would judge it right for them to treat us, and that we owe God veneration and submission. Reid addressed an important problem which the earlier rationalists failed to see and his own followers ignored: if there is a plurality of substantive self-evident moral principles, they may come into conflict. According to Reid, the virtues, as dispositions to act according to moral principles, support and strengthen one another. But in concrete instances one principle may direct us to perform an action, while another principle forbids its performance. To use Reid's example, 'what generosity solicits, justice may forbid' (1788: 639). Reid thought that in such cases we rely on self-evident priority rules, for instance, that 'unmerited generosity should yield to generosity and both to justice' (see MORAL PLURALISM).

Reid's followers, such as James BEATTIE and Dugald Stewart (1793; 1828) accepted the main elements of his moral theory. They agreed that the first principles of morality are self-evident and that there is a plurality of them (see STEWART, D.). They distinguished among animal and rational principles of action. They shared Reid's belief that God meant conscience to be our guide and that it is an intellectual and active power of the human mind. On the whole they were noncritical proponents of the Common Sense moral theory, adding little to it.

Kant's famous reaction to the philosophers of the Common Sense school was a characteristic one. Instead of answering Hume's sceptical challenge, according to Kant (1783), they merely appealed to the common sense of humankind, without any proper insight into the question. While this may be true of Reid in his more unguarded moments and of his disciples more generally, the Common Sense moral theory was influential not only in France and England but also in the US. By the mid-nineteenth century, William Whewell's version of rational intuitionism became dominant (1845), overshadowing the Common Sense moral theory.

There is a relation between common-sense ethics and the Common Sense moral philosophers: the Common Sense moral philosophers trusted the conscience of ordinary people. Philosophical ethics, although useful in bringing self-evident moral truths to light and systematizing them, has a limited role to play in revising them. If there is a conflict between 'the practical rules of morality, which have been received in all ages' and those advanced by theorists, as Reid says, 'the practical rules ought to be the standard by which the theory is corrected' (1788: 646). But the Common Sense moral philosophers' confidence in the judgments of ordinary people sprang from their conviction that conscience is 'the

candle of the Lord set up within us' (Reid 1788: 597). It is grounded in the belief that God gave us the capacity not only to know what we ought to do but also to do it.

See also: INTUITIONISM IN ETHICS; MORAL JUSTIFICATION; MORAL KNOWLEDGE

References and further reading

Beattie, J. (1790–3) *Elements of Moral Science*, New York: Garland Publishing Company, 2 vols, 1977. (A collection of lectures delivered at Marischal College on psychology, natural theology, moral philosophy, politics and economics.)

Grave, S.A. (1960) *The Scottish Philosophy of Common Sense*, Oxford: Clarendon Press. (The most comprehensive critical discussion of Common Sense moral philosophy, including coverage of Reid, Stewart and Beattie.)

* Hume, D. (1739/40) *A Treatise of Human Nature*, ed. L.A. Selby-Bigge, revised by P.H. Nidditch, Oxford: Clarendon Press, 2nd edn, 1978, books II, III. (Contains Hume's discussion of reason's role in action and his theory of moral approval.)

* Kant, I. (1783) *Prologomena zur einer jeden künftigen Metaphysik die als Wissenchaft wird auftreten können*, trans. J. Ellington, *Prolegomena to Any Future Metaphysics*, Indianapolis, IN: Hackett Publishing Company, 1971. (Kant disparages the appeal of the Common Sense moral philosophers to common sense in their attempt to settle metaphysical questions; in the introduction, Kant argues that the Comon Sense philosophers failed to understand Hume's sceptical challenge to our concept of causality and the implications of this challenge for metaphysics as a whole.)

Mill, J.S. (1861) *Utilitarianism*, Indianapolis, IN: Hackett Publishing Company, 1979, esp. ch. 2. (Seeks to make utilitarianism acceptable by working hard at minimizing the conflicts between the deliverances of utilitarian theory and those of common-sense ethics.)

Rawls, J. (1971) *A Theory of Justice*, Cambridge, MA: Harvard University Press. (Rawls' idea of 'reflective equilibrium' incorporates the idea of testing principles of justice with what he calls our 'considered judgments'. These are the moral judgments we are most confident in since self-interest or other biases have been filtered out.)

* Reid, T. (1785) 'Of Reasoning', in *Essays on the Intellectual Powers of Man*; in W. Hamilton (ed.) *Works*, Edinburgh, 1846–63, 2 vols; repr. Hildesheim: Georg Olms Verlagsbuchhandlung, 1967. (The page number given for the quotation cited in

the above entry comes from Hamilton's edition. In ch. 2 of the essay, 'Whether Morality be capable of demonstration', Reid argues against the Lockean view that we arrive at the first principles of morality by means of demonstrative reasoning.)

* —— (1788) 'Of the Rational Principles of Action' and 'Of Morals', in *Essays on the Active Powers of Man*; in W. Hamilton (ed.) *Works*, Edinburgh, 1846–63, 2 vols; repr. Hildesheim: Georg Olms Verlagsbuchhandlung, 1967. (The page numbers given for the quotations cited in the above entry come from Hamilton's edition. This work contains Reid's moral theory. It also includes Reid's libertarian account of freedom. Although Reid often misinterprets Hume, some of his criticisms of Hume are insightful. Reid thought that Hume uncritically accepted the theory of ideas and that his mistakes may be traced to this. Includes an appendix in which Hamilton explains the idea of common sense.)

Schneewind, J.B. (1977) *Sidgwick's Ethics and Victorian Moral Philosophy*, Oxford: Clarendon Press, ch. 2. (Contains a clear, concise and informative discussion of the main elements of Reid's moral psychology, his account of the liberty of the will, and justice. Also included is a short but helpful discussion of Reid's followers who wrote about morality.)

* Stewart, D. (1793) 'Of the Active and Moral Powers of Man', in *Outlines of Moral Philosophy*; in W. Hamilton (ed.) *Collected Works*, Edinburgh: T. & T. Clark, Constable 1854–77; repr. Westmead: Gregg International, 1971. (Based on his lectures, Stewart wrote this for the use of students at Edinburgh. This work includes a discussion of the various springs to action, the origin of our moral ideas, and our duties to God, others and ourselves. An appendix contains an outline of his political theory.)

* —— (1828) *Philosophy of the Active and Moral Powers of Man*, ed. and abridged by J. Walker, Boston, MA: Phillips, Samson and Co., 1868. (An expanded version of the *Outlines*, this work contains a critical survey of British modern moral philosophy. Stewart argues against Hobbes and others that the sense of duty cannot be reduced to self-love. He opposes Paley's associationism and Bentham's utilitarianism. The influence of Reid is especially evident, as well as that of Cudworth, Shaftesbury, Butler and Price. Stewart tends to avoid appeals to a common sense.)

* Whewell, W. (1845) *The Elements of Morality, Including Polity*, London: J.W. Parker, and New York: Harper & Bros, 2 vols. (Whewell's account of rational intuition is sometimes closer to that of

Kant's than Reid's. He emphasizes that intuition is an activity of reason and not just a passive perception of first principles.)

CHARLOTTE R. BROWN

COMMON-SENSE REASONING, THEORIES OF

The task of formalizing common-sense reasoning within a logical framework can be viewed as an extension of the programme of formalizing mathematical and scientific reasoning that has occupied philosophers throughout much of the twentieth century. The most significant progress in applying logical techniques to the study of common-sense reasoning has been made, however, not by philosophers, but by researchers in artificial intelligence, and the logical study of common-sense reasoning is now a recognized sub-field of that discipline.

The work involved in this area is similar to what one finds in philosophical logic, but it tends to be more detailed, since the ultimate goal is to encode the information that would actually be needed to drive a reasoning agent. Still, the formal study of common-sense reasoning is not just a matter of applied logic, but has led to theoretical advances within logic itself. The most important of these is the development of a new field of 'non-monotonic' logic, in which the conclusions supported by a set of premises might have to be withdrawn as the premise set is supplemented with new information.

The formal study of common-sense reasoning is a field in which the concerns of philosophy and artificial intelligence converge. From a philosophical point of view, it is motivated by a popular approach to the philosophy of mind – known as the 'language of thought' hypothesis – that postulates a domain of mental representations as the primary bearers of meaning, and then analyses cognition as the rule-governed manipulation of these representations. In order for an approach along these lines to be useful, some account must be provided of the structure of the internal representations, and of the rules governing their manipulation (see LANGUAGE OF THOUGHT).

These issues have been studied extensively within cognitive psychology, of course. Here, the idea is to focus on an existing system capable of intelligent behaviour in a wide range of circumstances – a human being – and to attempt to infer the symbolic processes underlying this intelligence. But the issues are studied also within the area of artificial intelligence, and from a perspective that offers a different kind of illumination: the goal here is to build an intelligent system, rather than attempting to discover the structure of a system that already exists. Although the performance exhibited by the artificial systems designed to date is significantly less impressive than that of humans when evaluated across a broad range of circumstances, the symbolic processes underlying the behaviour of these systems are at least well understood.

Among the various research methodologies that have emerged within artificial intelligence, one of the most powerful is the logic-based approach first advanced by John McCarthy; and it is primarily this approach that has motivated the formal study of common-sense reasoning. In fact, the logic-based approach in artificial intelligence has much in common with the project of formalizing mathematical and scientific reasoning that has been carried on throughout the twentieth century. Within artificial intelligence, the idea is that much of the knowledge necessary for achieving intelligent action even in everyday situations can be represented in a machine through the formulas of some logical language, and that the reasoning tasks underlying this intelligence can then be accomplished by means of logical deduction.

Both the idea of using logic as an underlying representation language for artificial intelligence and the emphasis on formalizing common-sense knowledge are present even in McCarthy's very early work (for example, McCarthy 1959), but the project receives its clearest articulation in a paper jointly authored by McCarthy and Patrick Hayes (1969), which isolates the task of defining 'a naïve, common-sense view of the world precisely enough to programme a computer to act accordingly'.

Much of the work now produced within artificial intelligence on the topic of formalizing common-sense reasoning is similar to what one finds in philosophical logic – attempts to adapt or generalize logical techniques to apply to some new area – and there is now a good deal of interaction between these two fields. Still, the research that takes place within artificial intelligence has a somewhat different character from standard philosophical logic. For one thing, the matter of implementation is always in the background, and sometimes in the foreground; but even apart from that, the studies generated within artificial intelligence are often focused on very detailed representational problems that would seem peculiar to a philosopher. It would not be unusual, for example, to find a research project in artificial intelligence with the goal of representing what an agent would have to know about the objects in their kitchen in order to prepare a meal.

This kind of detailed work is necessary, of course, since the ultimate goal is to encode information in such a way that it could actually be used to drive a reasoning agent. Still, it is not as if the project of providing a logical representation of common-sense knowledge were simply a matter of applied logic. In fact, the problems presented by the task of representing this kind of information explicitly have led to a number of theoretical advances within logic itself: the most important of these is the development of the new field of 'non-monotonic' logic.

In most standard logics, the addition of new information to a given set of premises might lead us to draw new conclusions, but never to withdraw conclusions already reached. The set of consequences of a given set of premises is thus said to grow monotonically as the premise set grows: the consequence set can only increase, never decrease, as the premise set is supplemented with new information. A non-monotonic logic is simply a logic in which this property fails – a logic in which the addition of new information to a given premise set might force us to retract some conclusion drawn from the original set of premises (see NON-MONOTONIC LOGIC).

The study of non-monotonic logics within artificial intelligence was motivated by the realization that much of our common-sense knowledge concerns defeasible information – generalizations subject to exceptions, such as 'Birds fly' or 'Things remain where you put them'. Of course, philosophers had always known that these defeasible generalizations could not be represented naturally in ordinary logic: the statement 'Birds fly', for example, cannot be represented by a formula of the form $\forall x(Bx \supset Fx)$. But it was not until the practical need arose for reasoning with defeasible statements such as these that serious attention was focused on the problem; and it then became apparent that the appropriate notion of defeasible consequence would have to be non-monotonic.

To take a standard example, given only the information that Tweety is a bird and that birds tend to fly, it is natural to conclude defeasibly that Tweety flies. But if this premise set were supplemented, consistently, with the additional information that Tweety does not fly (perhaps Tweety is a penguin), it would then seem reasonable to withdraw our initial conclusion.

The monotonicity property flows from assumptions that are deeply rooted in both the proof theory and the semantics of most ordinary logics. From a proof-theoretic point of view, this property follows from the fact that a proof based on a set of premises also counts as a proof based an expansion of the same set of premises; from a semantic point of view, the property results from the assumption that the models of a set of premises are models also of any of its subsets. Because the features underlying the monotonicity property are so basic to the conception of most standard logical systems, researchers concerned with non- monotonic reasoning have been led to explore fundamentally new ideas in both proof theory and semantics.

The first proof-theoretic treatment of non-monotonic reasoning is found in Raymond Reiter's default logic (1980), which supplements ordinary logic with new rules of inference, known as 'default rules'. The semantic approach to non-monotonic reasoning was first explored in McCarthy's own theory of circumscription (1980).

Because of its intrinsic interest and practical importance, the study of non-monotonic logic has grown into a significant area of research. The fixed-point and minimal model approaches pioneered by Reiter and McCarthy are still the best-known and most widely applied techniques in non-monotonic reasoning, but a number of other approaches have been explored as well; a series of articles surveying these different approaches can be found in Gabbay *et al.* (1994). In recent years, the techniques developed within the field of non-monotonic logic have begun to find applications also to a number of philosophical issues, such as the understanding of *ceteris paribus* clauses in scientific generalizations and the formalization of *prima facie* obligations.

See also: ARTIFICIAL INTELLIGENCE

References and further reading

Davis, E. (1990) *Representations of Commonsense Knowledge*, San Mateo, CA: Morgan-Kaufmann. (A textbook in the field of formalizing commonsense reasoning.)

* Gabbay, D., Hogger, C.J. and Robinson, J.A. (eds) (1994) *Handbook of Logic in Artificial Intelligence and Logic Programming*, vol. 3, *Nonmonotonic Reasoning and Uncertain Reasoning*, Oxford: Oxford University Press. (Definitive and detailed survey articles on a variety of non-monotonic logics.)

Horty, J. (1994) 'Moral Dilemmas and Non-Monotonic Logic', *Journal of Philosophical Logic* 23: 35–65. (An application of non-monotonic logic to problems in moral reasoning.)

* McCarthy, J. (1959) 'Programs with Common Sense', in D.V. Blake and A.M. Uttley (eds) *Proceedings of the Symposium on Mechanization of Thought Processes*, London: H.M. Stationery Office; expanded version repr. in R. Brachman and H.

Levesque (eds) *Readings in Knowledge Representation*, San Mateo, CA: Morgan-Kaufmann, 1985. (An early statement of McCarthy's views.)

* —— (1980) 'Circumscription – A Form of Non-Monotonic Reasoning', *Artificial Intelligence* 13: 27–39.

* McCarthy, J. and Hayes, P. (1969) 'Some Philosophical Problems from the Standpoint of Artificial Intelligence', in B. Meltzer and D. Michie (eds) *Machine Intelligence*, vol. 4, Edinburgh: Edinburgh University Press.

* Reiter, R. (1980) 'A Logic for Default Reasoning', *Artificial Intelligence* 13: 81–132.

Thomason, R. (1988) *Philosophical Logic and Artificial Intelligence*, Dordrecht: Kluwer. (Some essays at the intersection of philosophical logic and artificial intelligence.)

—— (1991) 'Logicism, Artificial Intelligence, and Common Sense: John McCarthy's Program in Philosophical Perspective', in V. Lifschitz (ed.) *Artificial Intelligence and Mathematical Theory of Computation*, San Diego, CA: Academic Press. (An article relating the project of formalizing common-sense knowledge to the logicist programme in philosophy.)

JOHN HORTY

COMMONSENSISM

'Commonsensism' refers to one of the principal approaches to traditional theory of knowledge where one asks oneself the following Socratic questions: (1) What can I know?; (2) How can I distinguish beliefs that are reasonable for me to have from beliefs that are not reasonable for me to have? and (3) What can I do to replace unreasonable beliefs by reasonable beliefs about the same subject-matter, and to replace beliefs that are less reasonable by beliefs that are more reasonable? The mark of commonsensism is essentially a faith in oneself – a conviction that a human being, by proceeding cautiously, is capable of knowing the world in which it finds itself.

Any inquiry must set out with some *beliefs. If you had no beliefs at all, you could not even begin to inquire. Hence any set of beliefs is better than none. Moreover, the beliefs that we do find ourselves with at any given time have so far survived previous inquiry and experience. And it is psychologically impossible to reject everything that you believe. 'Doubting', Peirce says, 'is not as easy as lying'. Inquiry, guided by common sense, leads us to a set of beliefs which indicates that common sense is on the whole a reliable guide to knowledge. And if inquiry were not thus guided by common sense, how would it be able to answer the three Socratic questions with which it begins?*

1 **Background: Reid and Peirce**
2 **Commonsensism and metaphysics**
3 **Critical commonsensism: a systematic treatment**

1 Background: Reid and Peirce

The term 'commonsensism' was introduced by Charles Sanders PEIRCE who was concerned to contrast his own 'critical commonsensism' with the views of Thomas REID and with those of the other members of the Scottish Common Sense school of philosophy. According to Reid, the 'principles of common sense' are intuitive truths that all sane people accept when they are not doing philosophy. They are no less reasonable than the truths of logic and mathematics.

Reid is most persuasive in criticizing those philosophers who reject the principles of common sense. He calls our attention to the extremes of British empiricism, culminating in the absurdities of Hume's empirical system. These alleged absurdities include the following: we cannot know anything about the past; we cannot know whether there are any material things; and we cannot even know that we ourselves exist. Reid observes: 'A traveller of good judgment may mistake his way, but when it ends in a coal-pit, it requires no great judgment to know that he hath gone wrong, nor perhaps to find out what misled him'. The committed empiricist who is not yet prepared to abandon his extreme epistemological views may point out that Reid cannot demonstrate, to the empiricist's satisfaction, that the empiricist is not in a delirium. 'But how does he know that he is not in a delirium? I cannot tell; neither can I tell how a man knows that he exists. But, if any man seriously doubts whether he is in a delirium, I think it is highly probable that he is, and that it is time to seek for a cure' (Reid 1764 (1854): 107).

A somewhat more patient and difficult response may be found in the critical commonsensism of Peirce, which may be thought of as a refinement upon the views of Reid. Peirce says that his own view 'arises out of a contrite fallibilism, combined with a high faith in the reality of knowledge, and an intense desire to find things out' (Peirce 1931–5: 1.14) (see FALLIBILISM).

2 Critical commonsensism: a systematic treatment

'The slogans are impressive enough,' one may say, 'but how are they to be applied?' In setting out, one presupposes that, by contemplating various possible beliefs, we can find out that some of them logically imply others, that some contradict others, that some are such that they serve to confirm others (they make the others probable) and that some are such as to disconfirm others (they make the others improbable). Probability, as Peirce conceives it, is 'a thing to be inferred upon evidence'.

Two quite different procedures are involved. The first is that of ridding ourselves of beliefs that we should not have. The second is that of reconstruction – that of 'building anew'. We may call the second procedure 'the road back'. Descartes distinguishes the two steps in the first of his *Meditations*: 'I was convinced that I must once for all seriously undertake to rid myself of all the opinions which I had formerly accepted, and commence to build anew from the foundation'. Critical commonsensism, therefore, is a version of foundationalism (see FOUNDATIONALISM).

To see how commonsensism is applied in the theory of knowledge, we should consider the 'building anew' that is involved in the road back. Having some faith in ourselves, we start out with our native common sense – with what we find ourselves inclined to believe. Where else, after all, could we start out? If, like Peirce, we accept critical commonsensism, we will make this assumption: the mere fact that we find ourselves believing one thing rather than another is itself a *prima facie* reason for believing that thing. One way to improve upon this mass of uncritical beliefs is to sift it down and try to cast away the things that should not be there. If we find a set of beliefs that contradict each other, we will try to sift it down in such a way that the remaining set is not contradictory. If we then find that the remaining set disconfirms some of its members, then we will proceed in analogous fashion, in the hope that the surviving set will not thus disconfirm any of its members.

We also appeal to the experiences of perceiving and remembering. Suppose you think that you are perceiving a sheep. That you think you are perceiving a sheep gives some *prima facie* justification for that belief. And at this stage of the road back, there may be still more to be said for the belief. If the belief is confirmed by the set of other beliefs that has so far survived your critical scrutiny, then it is more reasonable than any belief not so confirmed.

What has been said about perceiving may also be said, *mutatis mutandis*, about remembering. Traditional empiricism, Peirce points out, is not adequate to the epistemic status of memory (see EMPIRICISM).

Still another source of epistemic respectability is the possibility of concurrence (also called 'coherence' and 'mutual support'). A set of beliefs may be said to concur, or to be related by mutual support, provided that any of its members is confirmed by the conjunction of all the others. If we find such a set among the beliefs that we still have, then we may say that the whole now has a still greater degree of epistemic respectability (see KNOWLEDGE AND JUSTIFICATION, COHERENCE THEORY OF).

In summarizing his approach to the theory of knowledge, Peirce calls attention to 'one of the most wonderful features of reasoning and one of the most important philosophemes in the doctrine of science, of which, however, you will search in vain in any book I can think of: namely, that reasoning tends to correct itself, and the more so, the more wisely its plan is laid. Nay, it not only corrects its conclusions, it even corrects its premises' (Peirce 1931–5: 5.575).

3 Commonsensism and metaphysics

The 'defence of common sense' associated with G.E. Moore should not be considered as being primarily an attempt to deal with the problems of the traditional theory of knowledge. It is intended, rather, as a corrective to what Moore felt were some of the excesses of the metaphysicians of his day, particularly those in the tradition of absolute idealism (see MOORE, G.E. §§2–3). Some of these philosophers, for example, tried to prove that there is no valid distinction between appearance and reality. In lectures on this topic, Moore would refute such views in the following way. He would hold up his hand, saying 'Here is a hand', and he would then point out that this obvious fact was inconsistent with the proposed theory about appearance and reality. If their reasoning were sound, then they would not be justified 'in believing that this is a hand'. Some of these philosophers had also felt that they could prove that 'time is unreal'. Moore calls to their attention what, apparently, many of them had not noticed – that their thesis has the absurd consequence that no one ever knows whether or not they had their breakfast before having their lunch. Such refutations met with considerable indignation but not with any very convincing rejoinders.

See also: CONTEXTUALISM, EPISTEMOLOGICAL; RATIONAL BELIEFS §2

References and further reading

Chisholm, R.M. (1966) *Theory of Knowledge*, Englewood Cliffs, NJ: Prentice Hall, 3rd edn, 1991. (A contemporary statement and defence of critical commonsensism.)

—— (1996) *A Realistic Theory of Categories: An Essay on Ontology*, Cambridge: Cambridge University Press. (A summation of Chisholm's views on an enormous range of topics.)

* Descartes, R. (1641) *Meditations on First Philosophy*, in *The Philosophical Writings of Descartes*, vol. 2, ed. and trans. J. Cottingham, R. Stoothoff, D. Murdoch and A. Kenny, Cambridge: Cambridge University Press, 1984–91. (Descartes' main metaphysical work, mentioned in §2 above.)

Moore, G.E. (1922) *Philosophical Studies*, London: Routledge & Kegan Paul. (See especially chapter 6 entitled 'The Conception of Reality'.)

—— (1959) *Philosophical Papers*, London: George Allen & Unwin. (Chapter 2 'A Defence of Common Sense', and chapter 7 'Proof of an External World', are perhaps the clearest writings that exist on the relation of common sense to philosophy.)

* Peirce, C.S. (1931–58) *The Collected Papers of Charles Sanders Peirce*, vols 1–6 ed. C. Hartshorne and P. Weiss, vols 7–8 ed. A. Burks, Cambridge, MA: Harvard University Press. (The indexes should be consulted, as references to commonsensism abound throughout the volumes.)

* Reid, T. (1764) *An Inquiry into the Human Mind on the Principles of Common Sense*, in *The Collected Works of Thomas Reid*, ed. Sir William Hamilton, Edinburgh: Maclachlan & Stewart, 1854. (Reid's clearest statement of his views about common sense can be found in this early work.)

RODERICK M. CHISHOLM

COMMUNICATION AND INTENTION

The classic attempt to understand communication in terms of the intentions of a person making an utterance was put forward by Paul Grice in 1957. Grice was concerned with actions in which a speaker means something by what they do and what is meant might just as much be false as true. He looked for the essence of such cases in actions intended to effect a change in the recipient. Grice saw successful communication as depending on the recognition by the audience of the speaker's intention. Since then there have been many attempts to refine Grice's work, and to protect it against various problems. There has also been worry that Grice's approach depends on a false priority of psychology over semantics, seeing complex psychologi-

cal states as existing independently of whether the agent has linguistic means of expressing them.

1 Grice's theory
2 Reactions
3 Prospects and alliances

1 Grice's theory

The classic attempt to understand communication in terms of the intentions of a person making an utterance was put forward by Paul GRICE in his 1957 article. Grice takes as his subject what he calls 'non-natural meaning' (meaning$_{NN}$), which he contrasts with the wider class of cases of natural meaning in which we say, for instance, that 'those spots mean measles' or 'those clouds mean rain'. It cannot be true that those spots mean measles but the patient has not got measles; meaning is simply a correlation or signalling. Whereas Grice is concerned with actions in which a speaker (or, in general, an agent) means something by what they do and what is meant might just as well be false as true. Here too he makes a distinction: between a wider class of actions that predictably cause a recipient to believe something, and a narrower class of actions that not only may cause the belief that p, but also themselves mean that p. The wider class would include such actions as leaving photographs around, expecting the recipient to believe that the events shown had happened. The narrower class should take us somewhere near the domain of linguistic communication.

Grice looks for the essence of such cases in actions intended to effect a change in the recipient. He eventually located the difference in the manner in which the change in belief is expected to come about. In the wider class, the action may simply be a natural sign of the state of affairs, but in the narrower class of non-natural meaning there is an element of reflexivity involved, since the intended mechanism, through which the recipient is expected to come to the belief, is that the agent is recognized as acting with the intention that the recipient come to believe it: it is only if the agent's intention is recognized that the change in belief will ensue. So, for example, deliberately ignoring someone in the street might be said to mean$_{NN}$ that the agent is angry with the recipient, because getting the recipient to believe this depends upon their recognizing the intention with which the action was performed. Grice proposes that 'A meant$_{NN}$ something by x' is roughly equivalent to 'A uttered x with the intention of inducing a belief by means of the recognition of this intention'. He sees successful communication as requiring recognition of the speaker's intention in communicating. Of course,

the account could be extended to speech acts other than assertion: for example, intentions to get people to perform actions or supply information can be used to fix what is meant by imperatives and questions.

Armed with an account of the speaker's meaning on an occasion, Grice goes on to propose that 'the utterance x meant something' is roughly equivalent to 'someone meant something by x'. For a sentence to mean something 'timelessly' is for people in general to use it to mean that thing. We can thus progress from an account of communication in a 'one-off' case to a more general account of the kind of meaning possessed by the sentences of a public language.

2 Reactions

Grice's short article spawned a huge literature, and various modifications were suggested. One is that it may not be quite right to identify the speaker's intention as one of changing the hearer's belief. I may say that p without caring whether my hearer accepts or indeed already believes that p. A change in belief might be one effect of my utterance, but it is not always one I intend (in the terms introduced by Austin, it is a 'perlocutionary' effect), whereas we are looking for a characterization of what a speaker is doing in uttering anything (the 'illocutionary' act; see SPEECH ACTS §1). It seems rather that the only reliable intention behind an utterance is that the speaker intends the hearer to understand something by it, not necessarily to believe it or react to it in any other way. But already it is a matter of fine judgment whether this is important, and, after all, one can say things with the intention that the hearer not even understand them, for example when showing off one's grasp of some technical term. Certainly, a defence of Grice would go, once the whole social practice of communication with language is in place, we can say things with the most devious of intentions. Nevertheless, it may be true that the central or paradigm case is that of imparting information, and indeed any account that fails to put this function of language at the centre risks distortions of its own. So Grice may simply be following the proper path by concentrating upon the central or basic case and hoping that deviations will become explicable in the light of what is said about it.

A more elaborate debate queried whether Grice's conditions are sufficient for meaning. It concentrates on cases where there is an element of deceit. As Bennett puts it, 'in real communication everything is open and above board' (1976: 126), but a range of cases suggest that Grice's conditions could be met while there are hidden and devious intentions around. Grice's conditions could be satisfied while, further up the hierarchy of intentions, I have the intention that you misunderstand something about the situation. Complex counterexamples of this structure were rapidly concocted. However, what Grice called 'sneaky intentions' can be blocked by a number of strategies. One such is to require that all the speaker's intentions be known to the hearer, and another is that the intentions in question should be 'mutually known', where this means that the hearer knows the speaker's intentions, the speaker knows that the hearer knows, the hearer knows that the speaker knows...and so on.

There is a cost to piling up the reflexive intentions with which speakers are credited, for it is easy to wonder whether there is a psychological reality to these complex layers of intention, or whether they are simply an artefact of the theory. In fact, some unease arises when we realise that Grice's approach requires that the reflexive intention – the intention that the hearer's belief be modified by means of their recognition of my intention in speaking – be typically present throughout the field of linguistic communication. It would seem to be to overload the psychology of the young child or not-very-aware adult to credit them with intentions of such complexity: typical speakers, we might say, just do not know or care *how* their messages get across, so long as they do. Certainly a strategist faced with a hitherto unknown type of problem of communication may do something with the hope that the intention with which they do it is recognized, but this seems to be a sophisticated plan for coping with precisely the kind of situation where normal communication has broken down.

This kind of thought suggests that Grice is too much concerned with one-off cases. At least in typical cases of communication we are not involved in one-off strategies, but can rely upon the conventional meanings of our terms. (For Grice himself, as we have seen, the existence of these conventions would simply be the existence of enough people inclined to use a term to effect communication in enough cases.) While reflexive intentions may be necessary to solve new problems of communication, as when we confront someone with whom we share no language, it may be that they drop out of the picture when a rule-governed or conventional medium of communication is available: it may be that reliance on conventions and rules supplants the mechanism of recognizing the speaker's intention, rather than supplementing it. Once we have language I do not have to know even whether you intended me to understand you in order to know what you said. Similarly, there may be sentences whose typical use is not to convey the messages that their strict and literal meanings suggest, but nevertheless, when uttering one of them, one can be held to have said whatever it is that its strict and literal meaning

identifies. In short, a conventional and deeply normative system (that is, one in which the speaker is *liable* to be held to have said things, regardless of what was intended) takes on a life of its own, independent of the detailed case-by-case intentions of participants.

Behind this objection there lies the deeper unease that Grice's approach sets things up so that the speaker has intentions of considerable complexity, and we then try to understand meaning and linguistic communication given so much rich psychology. Whereas a permanent strand in modern philosophy of language has been to try to identify the mastery of language with the ability to have thoughts (or, at least, thoughts of this kind of complexity) at all. From this standpoint it may seem perverse arbitrarily to enrich the psychology of the actors, and on that basis to explain their use of sentences as vehicles of their given, antecedent intentions. You cannot intend, the thought goes, without representing to yourself what you intend, and typically this will be by using the best representative medium known to us, which is our natural language. In forming an intention we typically speak to ourselves, saying that we will do this or that, and if this process is itself seen as a kind of internal communication then intentions are not suitable for giving an analysis of communication in general. So we should be thinking of social communication as one of the activities that makes possible the enriched psychology that we find in participants in conversational exchanges. The problems in this area are, however, deeply intractable. Some philosophers, notably John Searle (1983), insist that the 'intentionality' of language (that is, its directedness or power to represent absent or merely possible states of affairs) must be understood as being derived from a more fundamental power of the 'mind/brain'; in such a scheme there is no problem with Grice's direction of attack. To others it merely mystifies things to postulate intentional powers in the mind/brain, and our capacity to represent absent states of affairs to ourselves must be seen as essentially linguistic, since language is the only representational system that we actually know anything about.

A final radical criticism is that Gricean proposals try to secure openness in communication by adding to the speaker's intentions. But, it has been argued (Meijers 1994), openness cannot be secured that way. It is a matter of a relationship between the speaker and hearer, not a one-way matter of the speaker having sufficiently open intentions. A speaker must not only have the intention to be open, but there must also be a commitment to being open (and liability to penalty if they are not). Arguably this takes us into the domain of collective intentions; ones based on an understanding between the different parties about what they, collectively, are trying to do. The relation between speaker and hearer, by such an account, is more like that between us when we together plan that *we* sing a duet, than when I unilaterally intend that *I* do something with some effect on you. Again, there are various proposals about the nature of such common intentions, and whether they reduce to a kind of aggregate of individual intentions.

3 Prospects and alliances

Sir Peter Strawson (1971) detected a 'Homeric opposition' between followers of Grice and philosophers of language, such as Davidson, who put the notion of a truth-condition at the centre of their picture. It is fair to say that this opposition has softened in the intervening years. Clearly there is no formal contradiction between supposing that a remark in the mouths of members of some community means that *p* if and only if there exists a practice of using it with the intention of communicating that *p*, and saying that the same remark means that *p* if and only if it represents the state of affairs that *p*, or has the truth-condition that *p*, or would be interpreted by an ideal interpreter as saying that *p*. The opposition is a question of whether we give priority to representation over communication, or vice versa. If we think of sentences possessing meaning by way of some kind of accord with things and facts, then their role in communication will seem a kind of bonus; if we think of the seamless way in which linguistic behaviour is woven into communication (and other activities involving the world) then we will reject any appeal to basic representative powers of elements of the 'mind/brain', in favour of a clearer understanding of the representative powers of the whole person, here meaning the linguistically active, socially embodied person communicating with others of the same nature.

The perennial importance of Grice's work is that intention and communication cannot be separated for long. If I intend to tell you that the cat is sick, we have not communicated unless this is how you take my utterance. If I intend a remark ironically or condescendingly, then we have not communicated unless you understand the irony or the condescension. And there is a limit to the possibility of unintended meaning: although on an occasion someone may mean something by an utterance that they did not intend, or fail to mean something that they did intend, such occasions are essentially parasitic. If they occur too often, then the conventions shift, and the meaning of the remark in the language realigns itself with the way the speakers intend it. There is no

separating semantics and psychology, but there is the perennial question of priority. The strange and intriguing interdependency of intention and language seems to be two-way: our words can convey no more than we intend by them, but we ourselves can intend only what our words will carry.

Further work on these topics clearly requires a better understanding of whether meaning is essentially social. Work on rule-following has sometimes issued in the view that it must be so, and that determinate meaning only emerges in a fully social, normative practice in which the applications of words are routinely subject to criticism and correction. If this kind of thought can finally be defended, then Grice's programme will have been thoroughly vindicated, in its direction if not in every detail.

See also: MEANING AND COMMUNICATION; MEANING AND RULE-FOLLOWING

References and further reading

Avramides, A. (1989) *Meaning and Mind*, Cambridge, MA: MIT Press. (A thorough investigation particularly of the issue of reduction of semantics to psychology, and whether Grice's approach requires belief in it.)

* Bennett, J. (1976) *Linguistic Behaviour*, Cambridge: Cambridge University Press. (A lively development of Grice's work, especially valuable for its discussion of the relation between full intentionality and more primitive signalling systems.)

* Grice, P. (1957) 'Meaning', *Philosophical Review* 66: 377–88; repr. in *Studies in the Way of Words*, Cambridge, MA, and London: Harvard University Press, 1989. (The seminal article in the field.)

Lewis, D.K. (1969) *Convention: A Philosophical Study*, Cambridge, MA: Harvard University Press. (The classic modern analysis of the concept.)

* Meijers, A. (1994) *Speech Acts, Communication and Collective Intentionality*, Utrecht: Leiden University. (An impressive defence of the ineliminable presence of collective intentions in communication.)

Searle, J.R. (1969) *Speech Acts*, Cambridge: Cambridge University Press. (A lucid development of J.L. Austin's work on the actions we perform in conversation.)

* —— (1983) *Intentionality: An Essay in the Philosophy of Mind*, Cambridge: Cambridge University Press. (Searle's work is perhaps the most impressive development of the notion of acts performed in speech, but also controversial through his firm belief that the intentional powers of language are

derived from a prior biologically engendered capacity.)

* Strawson, P.F. (1971) 'Meaning and Truth', in *Logico-Linguistic Papers*, London: Methuen. (An early reflection upon the relations between communication and representation.)

SIMON BLACKBURN

COMMUNICATION AND MEANING *see* MEANING AND COMMUNICATION

COMMUNICATIVE RATIONALITY

The concept of 'communicative rationality' is primarily associated with the work of the philosopher and social theorist Jürgen Habermas. According to Habermas, communication through language necessarily involves the raising of 'validity-claims' (distinguished as 'truth', 'rightness' and 'sincerity'), the status of which, when contested, can ultimately only be resolved through discussion. Habermas further contends that speakers of a language possess an implicit knowledge of the conditions under which such discussion would produce an objectively correct result, and these he has spelled out in terms of the features of an egalitarian 'ideal speech situation'. Communicative rationality refers to the capacity to engage in argumentation under conditions approximating to this ideal situation ('discourse', in Habermas' terminology), with the aim of achieving consensus.

Habermas relies on the concept of communicative rationality to argue that democratic forms of social organization express more than simply the preferences of a particular cultural and political tradition. In his view, we cannot even understand a speech-act without taking a stance towards the validity-claim it raises, and this stance in turn anticipates the unconstrained discussion which would resolve the status of the claim. Social and political arrangements which inhibit such discussion can therefore be criticized from a standpoint which does not depend on any specific value-commitments, since for Habermas achieving agreement (Verständigung) is a 'telos' or goal which is internal to human language as such. A similar philosophical programme has also been developed by Karl-Otto Apel, who lays more stress on the 'transcendental' features of the argumentation involved.

1 **Instrumental and communicative rationality: Habermas and the Frankfurt School**
2 **Objections to Habermas' approach**
3 **Apel's approach and his critique of Habermas**

1 Instrumental and communicative rationality: Habermas and the Frankfurt School

Jürgen Habermas, the leading thinker of the second generation of the Frankfurt School, introduced the concept of communicative rationality in order to correct what he perceives to be the 'normative deficit' in the work of earlier thinkers in this tradition. This deficit consists in the lack of any philosophically perspicuous grounding for their critique of modern society. The thought of the Frankfurt School before Habermas, classically summarized in Theodor Adorno and Max Horkheimer's *Dialectic of Enlightenment* (1944), viewed social relations within the most advanced capitalist societies as being almost entirely shaped by the demands of 'instrumental reason'. Strongly reminiscent of Max Weber's 'purposive rationality' (*Zweckrationalität*), the concept of instrumental reason refers to the capacity to maximize efficiency in the control of objective processes through a knowledge of the determinants of such processes. For Adorno and Horkheimer the predominant institutionalization of this *aspect* of reason, reflected in its pervasive philosophical equation with reason as such, has socially disastrous consequences. It leaves the ends to be collectively pursued beyond the scope of rational determination, and gives rise to a 'totally administered society'. At the same time however, as Habermas repeatedly complains, the earlier Critical Theorists propose no alternative broader conception of reason, from the standpoint of which the restriction of reason to its instrumental aspect could be coherently criticized (see FRANKFURT SCHOOL; CRITICAL THEORY).

The contrast between instrumental and communicative rationality, which represents Habermas' attempt to remedy this situation, is anchored in the philosophical anthropology systematically presented in *Knowledge and Human Interests* (1971). Here Habermas argues that any society, in order to reproduce itself, must be capable both of productive exchange with nature (in the form of labour), and of the communicative coordination of collective activities. Labour gives rise to concepts which articulate a 'technical interest' in instrumental control, whereas the need for agreement generates the distinct categorial framework of a 'practical interest' in hermeneutic understanding. In later writings Habermas specifies that participants in 'communicative action' must be capable of regarding the statements raised in the

459

course of discussion from the standpoint of their *validity*, and must possess an implicit knowledge both of the appropriate procedures for settling disputed validity-claims and of the (invariably counterfactual) conditions under which following such procedures would produce an objectively correct result. Such knowledge is mobilized, for example, when discovery of covert coercion renders a previously achieved consensus invalid.

In the Western philosophical tradition, the concept of rationality has long been connected with the ability to reflect on and give grounds for one's beliefs and the actions they inform. However, in modern philosophy, it is often only beliefs capable of guiding goal-oriented action which are considered as candidates for rationality. Against this, Habermas argues that the type of action oriented towards reaching agreement in language is irreducible to that which is oriented towards successful intervention in the objective world. The illocutionary aims of speech acts can only be achieved through cooperation, based on a free acceptance by others of the validity-claims raised by the speaker, which cannot be reduced to a causally producible effect. Hence the ability to achieve consensus by offering grounds reflects a distinct form of rationality which 'inhabits everyday communicative practice', and which Habermas therefore describes as 'communicative rationality'.

With regard to the problem of grounding a critical social theory, two aspects of Habermas' proposal are significant. First, Habermas extends the scope of validity beyond 'truth' (*Wahrheit*). He argues that claims to normative rightness (*Richtigkeit*), typically moral or legal claims, are in principle susceptible of the same form of resolution through discussion as cognitive claims. There can thus be an equivalent of truth in practical matters, although Habermas admits that the status of a claim to 'sincerity' (*Wahrhaftigkeit*) cannot be resolved through discussion. (An additional claim, concerning the 'intelligibility' (*Verständlichkeit*) of one's utterance, is only discussed sporadically by Habermas, and is perhaps best considered as a *precondition* of these principal validity-claims.) Second, canons of argument are themselves not merely relative to specific cultural and institutional contexts. Whenever we engage in argumentation, Habermas proposes, we must implicitly assume (however counterfactually) that the conditions of an 'ideal speech situation', in which the 'unforced force of the better argument' would indeed ultimately triumph, have been fulfilled, otherwise discussion would lose its point. Such a speech situation would be characterized by the equal right of all participants to raise issues, ask questions, pose objections and so on, and therefore provides a

normative yardstick against which current decision-making procedures can be critically assessed. In particular, the widespread dominance of the functional requirements of 'social systems' such as the market economy and modern bureaucracy can be seen as embodying a one-sided 'rationalization' which suppresses the rational potential of those democratic principles which are equally fundamental to modernity.

2 Objections to Habermas' approach

The concept of communicative rationality faces objections from a variety of quarters. If such rationality is to represent more than the ability to adhere to culturally specific canons of argumentation, then Habermas must show the universal necessity of those pragmatic presuppositions of communication which form the ideal speech situation. The first step towards this is to argue for an internal relation between meaning and validity. Habermas contends that 'we understand a speech-act when we know what makes it acceptable' ([1981] 1984:400), where acceptability refers to intersubjective recognition of validity and not to correspondence with a reality whose structure would supposedly be given prior to language. He then draws the conclusion that 'an orientation towards the possible validity of utterances belongs not just to the pragmatic conditions of reaching understanding, but to the understanding of language as such' (1988: 76).

However, Habermas' account of the preconditions for grasping linguistic meaning may be implausibly strong. Herbert Schnädelbach (1991), for example, has objected that to understand what makes an utterance acceptable does not require one to take a stand on whether it is, in the present instance, valid. We can observe communicative action – the exchanging of reasons – from a third-person perspective without being drawn into the process of judging validity-claims, so that a normative standpoint is not internal to the very application of the concept of communicative rationality. In reply, Habermas has argued that even in apparently unfavourable cases, such as a sudden burst of laughter during a speech, we cannot understand the laughter without knowing if it is genuine or not (and thus a valid 'utterance'), and this involves *assessing* the grounds for it. The methodological suspension of our spontaneous yes/no attitude towards validity-claims merely indicates that the task of interpretation is being postponed.

A further major objection to Habermas' views has been raised by Albrecht Wellmer, among others. It is that there may indeed be certain idealizations which function as necessary pragmatic presuppositions of linguistic communication, but that the notion of an ideal speech situation represents an 'objectivistic misinterpretation' of these. This is because an ideal speech situation, exempt from the fallibility, opacity and temporality of human language, would be beyond the conditions which make communication itself necessary and possible. To regard the striving for such a situation as morally incumbent upon us would be to regard us as obliged to attain the impossible, which is absurd. According to Wellmer (1986), communication indeed relies upon 'performative idealizations' (for example, the conviction that the reasons we have for a claim are sound and will stand the test of time), but to transform these idealizations into an ideal to be practically pursued is to fall prey to a 'dialectical semblance' (*Schein*). Habermas, however, continues to maintain that it is meaningful to idealize forms of communication, just as we idealize physical measurements; in other words, to anticipate the full realization of conditions we must already presume to hold to some degree when engaged in serious argumentation.

Other critics have focused on Habermas' claim that reaching an understanding can be seen as the primary function of language, to which we are implicitly committed as soon as we speak. Thinkers influenced by post-structuralism, in particular, have objected that the commitment to achieving consensual truth cannot, except by begging the question, be considered more fundamental than playful, ironic or fictional uses of language. More generally, it is contended that an essential semantic instability of language, or the relativity of meaning to context, undermines even the assumption that identical meanings are exchanged in communication.

In reply to this, Habermas suggests that joking, playful, ironic and fictional uses of language depend on an intentional confusion of contrasting modes correlated to validity-claims (being/illusion, is/ought, essence/appearance), which is simultaneously seen through as such. These uses therefore depend on a prior recognition of the distinctions between validity dimensions. Habermas also emphasizes that belief in the identity of communicated meanings has no *metaphysical* status, but is merely a pragmatic presupposition which can (indeed must) be unproblematically relied on, up to the point where communication actually breaks down.

3 Apel's approach and his critique of Habermas

Habermas' account of communicative rationality has developed over the years in tandem with that of his Frankfurt colleague Karl-Otto Apel. However, Apel's programme is more strongly connected to the tradi-

tion of transcendental philosophy (Apel prefers the term 'transcendental pragmatics' to Habermas' 'universal pragmatics' for the general theory of communicative competence). The key conflict between Apel and Habermas concerns their attitude to the possibility of an 'ultimate grounding' (*Letztbegründung*) for a universalistic moral standpoint. In a critical essay (1992), Apel contends that Habermas is mistaken to play down the 'transcendental difference' between empirically testable reconstructions of communicative competence and philosophical reflection which reveals the unconditional validity of certain basic presuppositions of argumentation. Apel sees here a confusion which leads to paradoxical consequences – for example, that the 'principle of fallibilism' (the principle that no empirical consensus can be immune to revision) must itself be regarded as fallible. Habermas, however, replies that the normative preconditions of communication should be considered only as 'factually indispensable': they cannot be imagined as inoperative given our human sociocultural form of life. To show this, however, we do not need to set philosophical truths in a position of qualitative precedence over knowledge obtained by scientific methods.

The concept of communicative rationality has thus been, and continues to be, the subject of intense debate. These reflect that fact that the project of defining a concept of rationality more encompassing that instrumental rationality, one internally connected to the idea of *reciprocal* and *egalitarian* relations between human beings, has deep roots in the German philosophical tradition since Kant. Because of this, whatever future transformations this project may undergo, it is unlikely to be entirely abandoned.

See also: HABERMAS, J.; RATIONALITY: BELIEF; REASONING/RATIONALITY: PRACTICAL

References and further reading

* Adorno, T.W. and Horkheimer, M. (1944) *Dialectic of Enlightenment*, London: Verso, 1979. (Referred to in §1. Presents the classic Frankfurt School critique of instrumental reason.)

Apel, K.-O. (1973) *Transformation der Philosophie*, Frankfurt am Main: Suhrkamp Verlag, 2 vols; partial trans. G. Adey and D. Frisby, *Towards a Transformation of Philosophy*, London: Routledge & Kegan Paul, 1980. (Sets out Apel's theory of communicative rationality, based on the regulative idea of an unlimited communication community.)

* —— (1992) 'Normative Begründung der "Kritischen Theorie" durch Rekurs auf Lebensweltliche Sittlichkeit? Ein Transzendental-pragmatisch orien-

tierter Versuch mit Habermas gegen Habermas zu denken' ('Normatively Grounding "Critical Theory" through Recourse to the Lifeworld? A Transcendental-Pragmatic Attempt to Think with Habermas against Habermas'), in A. Honneth, T. McCarthy, C. Offe and A. Wellmar (eds) *Zwischenbetrachtungen. Im Prozess der Aufklärung (Philosophical Interventions in the Unfinished Project of Enlightenment)*, Frankfurt am Main: Suhrkamp Verlag; trans. B. Rehg, Cambridge MA: MIT Press, 125–72. (Referred to in §3. The fullest statement of Apel's critique of Habermas.)

Cooke, M. (1994) *Language and Reason: A Study of Habermas' Pragmatics*, Cambridge MA: MIT Press. (A detailed, sympathetic but critical analysis of Habermas' concept of communicative rationality.)

* Habermas, J. (1968) *Erkenntnis und Interesse*, Frankfurt am Main: Suhrkamp Verlag; trans. J.J. Shapiro as *Knowledge and Human Interests*, London: Heinemann, 1971. (Referred to in §1. Develops the distinction between instrumental action and communicative action as two distinct forms of action.)

—— (1976) 'Was heißt Universalpragmatik', in K.-O. Apel (ed.) *Sprachpragmatik und Philosophie*, Frankfurt am Main: Suhrkamp Verlag; trans. T. McCarthy as 'What is Universal Pragmatics?', in *Communication and the Evolution of Society*, London: Heinemann, 1979, 1– 68. (Habermas' most detailed statement of his programme for a universal pragmatics)

* —— (1981) *Theorie des Kommunikative Handelns. Band 1: Handlungsrationalität und gesellschaftliche Rationalisierung*, Frankfurt am Main: Suhrkamp Verlag; trans. T. McCarthy as *Reason and the Rationalization of Society*, vol. 1 of *The Theory of Communicative Action*, Boston MA: Beacon Press, 1984. (Contains important discussions of the concept of communicative rationality.)

* —— (1988) 'Handlungen, Sprechakte, sprachlich vermittelte Interaktionen und Lebenswelt', in *Nachmetaphysiches Denken* (Postmetaphysical thinking), Frankfurt am Main: Suhrkamp Verlag. (Source of the second quotation in §2 above.)

* Schnädelbach, H. (1991) 'Transformation der Kritischen Theorie' ('The Transformation of Critical Theory'), in A. Honneth and H. Joas (eds) *Kommunikatives Handeln (Communicative Action)*, trans. J. Gaines and D.L. Jones, Cambridge: Polity Press, 7–22. (Referred to in §2. Criticizes Habermas for suggesting that identifying grounds involves evaluating them, thereby making any description of communicative rationality normative.)

* Wellmer, A. (1986) *Ethik und Dialog. Elemente des moralischen Urteils bei Kant und in der Diskursethik*, Frankfurt am Main: Suhrkamp Verlag; trans. D. Midgeley as 'Ethics and Dialogue: Elements of Moral Judgement in Kant and Discourse Ethics', ch. 4 of *The Persistence of Modernity*, Cambridge: Polity Press, 1991, 113–231. (Referred to in §2. An important critique of the idealizations built into Habermas' theory of communicative rationality.)

PETER DEWS

COMMUNISM

Communism is the belief that society should be organized without private property, all productive property being held communally, publicly or in common. A communist system is one based on a community of goods. It is generally presented as a positive alternative to competition, a system that is thought to divide people; communism is expected to draw people together and to create a community. In most cases the arguments for communism advocate replacing competition with cooperation either for its own sake or to promote a goal such as equality, or to free specific groups of people to serve a higher ideal such as the state or God.

The word *communism* appears to have first been used in the above sense in France in the 1840s to refer to the ideas of thinkers such as Françoise Émile Babeuf (1760–97) and Étienne Cabet (1788–1856), both of whom advocated the collectivization of all productive property. The concept is ancient, however. Early versions of a community of goods exist in myths that describe the earliest stages of human culture; it was a major issue in ancient Athens, a key component of monasticism and became the basis for much criticism of industrial capitalism.

The word communism later became associated with the teachings of Karl MARX (§12) and his followers and came to refer to an authoritarian political system combined with a centralized economic system run by the state. This form of communism has roots in the earlier idea because the ultimate goal of communism, as seen by Marx, was a society in which goods are distributed to people on the basis of need. The older usage continues to exist in a worldwide communal movement and as a standard by which to criticize both capitalism and Marxian communism.

The idea of communism as collectively owned property first appears in the Western tradition in classical Greece. Plato's *Republic* contains a notable early defence (see PLATO §14). Prior to the invention of the word, major communist theories can be found in some parts of the Christian Bible, in medieval monasticism and in Thomas More's *Utopia* (1516). In all these cases the basis for collectively owned property is that members of society are freed from the need to devote their time to earning a living or caring for private property so that they can devote themselves to something more important such as the pursuit of knowledge, God or personal fulfilment. The assumption is that the need to provide for oneself or one's family gets in the way of matters considered more important. For example, Plato advocates abolishing the family in his *Republic* because he fears that family ties will both distract the individual from higher things and tempt people to favour one group (family members) over others (non-family members). In monastic communism, which also abolishes the family, all property is owned by the community and each individual member of the community owns nothing, not even their clothes. Everything is provided by the community for each monk or nun; they are, thereby, freed from the burden of property to devote themselves to God. In More's *Utopia* all houses and their furnishings are as near identical as possible and, since location cannot be identical, people move from house to house in regular rotation.

Later, secularized versions of communism stressed the equitable (not necessarily equal) distribution of, or at least access to, resources, but the underlying principle is quite similar. Rather than freeing some or even all people in a society to devote themselves to a higher cause, secular communism is designed to allow everyone to pursue personal fulfilment. It may best be characterized by a slogan adopted by Marx that appears to have been first published on the title page of Cabet's *Voyage en Icarie* (1840): 'From each according to his ability, to each according to his need'. In other words, each person contributes to society to the best of their ability in the areas of work for which they are suited; in return, society provides their basic needs. The underlying assumption is that all human beings deserve to have their needs met simply because they are human beings; differential ability and talent does not make one person more deserving than another. A specific case is the assumption by most communist theorists that there should be no difference in treatment of those who contribute to society through physical labour and those who contribute through mental labour. For example, in 1888 Edward Bellamy published *Looking Backward*, a utopian novel that became an instant bestseller and produced a worldwide movement. In it, Bellamy advocated an absolutely equal income for all members of society that could then be used by each individual to meet their own felt needs. An approach

adopted by many intentional communities is for the group to make collective or social decisions (either by consensus or by majority rule) about economic matters that affect the community as a whole but to provide each individual member of the community with a discretionary income to use as they wish.

Marx maintained major aspects of this approach in the stage of human development that he called 'full' or 'pure' communism or just communism. The non-alienated people of this future communism will create a world in which income will be distributed on the basis of need (see ALIENATION §§3–4; MARX, K. §4); since everyone will be a productive labourer, there will no longer be any classes; and, because there will no longer be a need for political power to enforce class dominance, the state will gradually disappear to be replaced with decentralized, non-political administrative agencies. Since everyone will work, there will be high productivity and, therefore, plenty for all. Given the changed social situation, people will begin to think differently and social distinctions between occupations and between city and country will disappear. Thus, this form of communism is, in its essentials, identical to the earliest communist tradition. At least one major twentieth-century Marxist theorist, Ernst Bloch (1885–1977) in *Das Prinzip Hoffnung* (The Principle of Hope) (1959) argued that this utopian goal should be at the centre of Marxist theory (see UTOPIANISM §4).

While Marxism and its version of communism predominantly took a different road, the more fundamental and historically earlier theory did not disappear. Non-Marxist forms of collective property have existed and been defended as part of the communal movement best represented by the Israeli kibbutzim and the US communal movement of the early nineteenth and mid-twentieth centuries, and by some forms of anarchism (see ANARCHISM §3). Communism as common property and as a vision of a better life for all is still a living tradition.

The arguments against communism take a number of different forms. The simplest rely on assumptions about human nature radically at variance with those of communism's proponents. The assumption is made, with little real evidence, that human beings are 'naturally' competitive and that therefore communism cannot work (see HUMAN NATURE §1). A more developed analysis argues that communism is necessarily economically inefficient and will, therefore, be unable to provide as high a standard of living as a non-communist system. Some go so far as to argue that communism is impossible to sustain over long periods of time because its inefficiency is so great that the economic system must sooner or later collapse. Of course, economic efficiency is very low in the scale of values held by most supporters of traditional communism. Proponents of communism generally take the position that economic efficiency symbolizes the competitive system that they oppose and stands in the way of the cooperative community they hope to achieve.

Today, many believe that the time of communism has passed, largely because Marxist communism has been discredited in much of the world. But communism is not, and never has been, reducible to the Marxist version. Most fundamentally, it is the economic basis for dreams of complete human fulfilment, whether it is sought in monastic orders, intentional communities or whole societies. That dream persists, and with it the ideals of communism.

See also: EQUALITY; SOCIALISM

References and further reading

* Bellamy, E. (1888) *Looking Backward: 2000–1887*, ed. C. Tichi, Harmondsworth: Penguin, 1982. (A popular novel depicting an egalitarian society.)

Bernstein, E. (1930) *Cromwell and Communism*, London: Allen & Unwin. (A study by a prominent Marxist of communism in seventeenth-century Britain.)

* Cabet, É. (1840) *Voyage et adventures de Lord Villiam Carisdell en Icarie*, Paris: Bureau au Populaire. (A utopian novel in which Cabet popularized communism.)

Cole, G.D.H. (1953–6) *A History of Socialist Thought*, London: MacMillan, 5 vols in 7. (General history of most variants of collective ownership.)

Dawson, D. (1992) *Cities of the Gods: Communist Utopias in Greek Thought*, New York: Oxford University Press. (Early developments of communism.)

Hillery, G.A., Jr. and Morrow, P.C. (1976) 'The Monastery as a Commune', *International Review of Modern Sociology* 6 (1): 139–54; reprinted as Hillery, G.A. in *Communes: Historical and Contemporary*, ed. R. Shonle Cavan and M. Singh Das, New Delhi: Vikas Publishing House, 1979, 152–69. (The best introduction to monastic communism.)

Kenyon, T. (1989) *Utopian Communism and Political Thought in Early Modern England*, London: Pinter. (A recent study of communism in the UK.)

Lugon, C. (1949) *La République communiste chrétienne des Guaranis (1610–1766)*, Paris: Les Éditions Ouvrières. (A study of Christian communism under the Jesuits in Paraguay.)

* More, T. (1516) *Utopia*, ed. G.M. Logan and R.M. Adams, Cambridge: Cambridge University Press, 1989. (The origin of the word utopia and an early statement of communism and religious toleration.)

* Plato (c.380–367 BC) *Republic*, trans. D. Lee, Harmondsworth: Penguin, 2nd edn, 1974. (One of the earliest works usually called an utopia.)

Prudhommeaux, J. (1907) *Étienne Cabet et les Origines du Communisme Icarien*, Nimes: Imprimerie 'La Laborieuse'. (A study of one of the earliest people to call hiimself a communist.)

Surtz, E.L., S.–J. (Society of Jesus) (1957) *The Praise of Pleasure: Philosophy, Education and Communism in More's 'Utopia'*, Cambridge, MA: Harvard University Press. (The best discussion of communism in the thought of Thomas More.)

Wiles, P.J.D. (1962) *The Political Economy of Communism*, Cambridge, MA: Harvard University Press. (Includes a good discussion of 'full' or 'pure' communism.)

LYMAN TOWER SARGENT

COMMUNITARIANISM

see COMMUNITY AND COMMUNITARIANISM

COMMUNITY AND COMMUNITARIANISM

Reflections on the nature and significance of community have figured prominently in the history of Western ethics and political philosophy, both secular and religious. In ethics and political philosophy the term 'community' refers to a form of connection among individuals that is qualitatively stronger and deeper than a mere association. The concept of a community includes at least two elements: (1) individuals belonging to a community have ends that are in a robust sense common, not merely congruent private ends, and that are conceived of and valued as common ends by the members of the group; and (2) for the individuals involved, their awareness of themselves as belonging to the group is a significant constituent of their identity, their sense of who they are.

In the past two decades, an important and influential strand of secular ethical and political thought in the English-speaking countries has emerged under the banner of communitarianism. The term 'communitarianism' is applied to the views of a broad range of contemporary thinkers, including Alasdair MacIntyre, Charles Taylor, Michael Sandel, and sometimes

Michael Walzer (MacIntyre 1981; Sandel 1982; Taylor 1979, 1989; Walzer 1983). It is important to note, however, that there is no common creed to which these thinkers all subscribe and that for the most part they avoid the term.

There are two closely related ways to characterize what communitarians have in common; one positive, the other negative. As a positive view, communitarianism is a perspective on ethics and political philosophy that emphasizes the psycho-social and ethical importance of belonging to communities, and which holds that the possibilities for justifying ethical judgments are determined by the fact that ethical reasoning must proceed within the context of a community's traditions and cultural understandings (Bell 1993: 24–45). As a negative view, communitarianism is a variety of anti-liberalism, one that criticizes liberal thought for failing to appreciate the importance of community.

At present the communitarian critique of liberalism is more developed than is communitarianism as a systematic ethical or political philosophy. Existing communitarian literature lacks anything comparable to Rawls' theory of justice or Feinberg's theory of the moral limits of criminal law, both of which are paradigmatic examples of systematic liberal ethical and political theory. For the most part, the positive content of the communitarians' views must be inferred from their criticisms of liberalism. Thus, to a large extent communitarianism so far is chiefly a way of thinking about ethics and political life that stands in fundamental opposition to liberalism. To some, communitarian thinking seems a healthy antidote to what they take to be excessive individualism and obsessive preoccupation with personal autonomy. To others, communitarianism represents a failure to appreciate the value – and the fragility – of liberal social institutions. The success of communitarianism as an ethical theory depends upon whether an account of ethical reasoning can be developed that emphasizes the importance of social roles and cultural values in the justification of moral judgments without lapsing into an extreme ethical relativism that makes fundamental ethical criticism's of one's own community impossible. The success of communitarianism as a political theory depends upon whether it can be demonstrated that liberal political institutions cannot provide adequate conditions for the flourishing of community or secure appropriate support for persons' identities so far as their identities are determined by their membership in communities.

1   Community

If I am a member of a community, I conceive of the goals and values I share with my fellows as essentially *our* goals and values, not just as goals and values that happen to be the same for all of us because of a contingent convergence of our individual interests. Each member thinks of furthering the community's ends primarily as gains for *us*, not as a gain for themselves that happens to be accompanied by similar gains for other individuals in the group. In the activities that are the life of the community, individuals think of themselves first and foremost as members of the group. Thus, at least in the course of these activities, the distinction between what is in your interest, as opposed to mine or ours, breaks down or recedes into the background.

In contrast, in an association individuals typically conceive of their interests as distinct, even if their goals are collective; that is, as states of affairs that necessarily involve the group. For example, if they are an association rather than a community, when the employees in a firm work together to secure an important contract for the company (the collective goal), each will cooperate with others only to further their own interest, conceiving of it as distinct from, although congruent with, that of the others.

A contrast can also be drawn between how the members of a community regard the process of pursuing the common goal and how that process is regarded in an association. In a community, the process itself (or rather the relationships among members of the group that constitute the process) is seen by members of the group to be valuable in itself, independently of whether it is effective in achieving the goal of the process. In an association, the relationships that exist in the process of pursuing the collective goal are viewed as being of only instrumental value for attaining private goods for each of the individuals involved.

Since a community is defined at least in large part by a set of shared values and goals, the second element in our analysis of community, shared identity, is at least partly normative. In other words, if in saying who I am I feel it important to identify myself as, for example, a Catholic, then this characterization of who I am is not a description of myself as being a member of a certain religious group; it also includes the awareness that I have certain commitments, an allegiance to certain values and the perception that I have certain obligations by virtue of being a member of this group.

These familiar ways of contrasting communities with mere associations have the virtue of throwing the distinction between the two into bold relief, but they oversimplify. Being a community is a matter of degree: groups fall along a continuum, from communities in the strict sense, in which the sense of a shared identity is fundamental to a person's most basic conception of themselves and in which allegiance to the common interest eclipses any distinct conception of private interest, to mere associations, whose members are connected by the most tenuous and transitory ties of private interests or tastes and whose identity derives chiefly from sources other than membership of the group (Feinberg 1988: 81–122). For example, in many groups, individuals will be motivated to cooperate with others both by a sense of community, according to which what counts is whether 'we' succeed, and by their own private interests in the outcome of the common endeavour, which they will be able to distinguish quite clearly from the interest of the group. Similarly, the extent to which the members will conceive of their membership as being an important component of who they are (what their values and commitments are, and so on) will vary across different groups. Thus the extent to which a group is a community will depend upon how dominant the sense of common, not merely congruent, goals is, and how large a role the sense of allegiance to the values and ends of the group plays in each individual's sense of who they are.

2 Communitarianism

To determine what, according to communitarians, the true significance of participation in community is, we must see the ways in which communitarians believe liberalism has failed to acknowledge that significance.

The first obstacle to reconstructing a positive communitarian view from the communitarian critiques of liberalism is the fact that communitarians have sometimes been unclear about what liberalism is, and in some cases apparently have made uncharitable assumptions about what liberalism is committed to (Feinberg 1988: 86–8; Buchanan 1988: 853–7). One useful place to begin is with a rather narrow but clear articulation of liberalism as a minimal political philosophy – a thesis about the proper role of the state. What I shall call the *liberal normative political thesis* is simply that the state is to place a priority on the enforcement of the basic individual and civil rights, those rights which, roughly speaking, are found in the US Constitution's Bill of Rights and in Rawls' First Principle of Justice, the Greatest Equal Liberty Principle (Rawls 1971: 61) (see RAWLS, J. §1). These include the rights to freedom of religion, expression, thought and association, the right of political participation (including the right to vote and

to run for office), and the rights of legal due process and equality before the law.

This fundamental thesis of liberal political philosophy implies another: namely, that the proper role of the state is to protect these basic rights, not to make its citizens virtuous or to impose upon them any particular or substantive conception of the good life or of the common good. By honouring this commitment to protect individual and civil political rights and forgoing any other projects that would violate them, the state recognizes a distinction between the private and the public spheres, and hence a limit on its own authority as well as a domain of autonomy for individuals (see LAW, LIMITS OF §4).

In marking off a private sphere through the protection of individual rights liberalism not only demarcates a domain of autonomy for individuals, it also makes room for a variety of associations – and communities. For this reason it is misleading to say that liberalism protects individual freedom rather than community.

3 Communitarian criticisms of liberalism

The following four criticisms form the core of the communitarian attack on liberalism. Not all are advanced by every thinker usually labelled communitarian.

(1) Liberalism rests on an individualism that is both ontologically and motivationally false. Liberal ontology asserts that only individuals exist and that all putative properties of groups can be reduced to properties of individuals; liberal motivational theory assumes that individuals are motivated solely by preferences for private goods, and that they desire participation in groups only as a means to achieving such goods.

(2) Liberalism undervalues political life, viewing participation in the political community as a mere instrumental good, valuable only as a means toward the attainment of the various private ends that individuals have, rather than as something valuable in itself.

(3) Liberalism presupposes a defective conception of the self, not recognizing that the self is 'embedded' in and partly constituted by communal commitments that are not objects of choice. Thus liberalism fails to understand that what one's obligations are is determined, to a large extent, by one's identity as a member of the community and the roles one occupies within the community (see OBLIGATION, POLITICAL §2).

(4) The liberal emphasis on individual rights devalues, neglects, and ultimately undermines commu-

nity; yet participation in community is a fundamental and irreplaceable ingredient in the good life for human beings.

Only the fourth communitarian criticism is a direct attack on the liberal normative political thesis. The other three are instances of a characteristic communitarian move, one which is most explicit perhaps in Sandel and TAYLOR: namely, that of attempting to undermine the liberal normative political thesis by exposing flaws in the system of beliefs upon which it supposedly rests. As we shall see, one problem with this strategy is the tendency on the part of those who employ it to fail to appreciate the range of different considerations that the liberal can invoke to support the liberal normative political thesis. At most, only some of these justifications may include beliefs which communitarianism shows to be false. Other justifications for liberalism – including what appear to be the most plausible – may remain intact.

The first criticism is easily rebutted. The liberal normative political thesis does rest on an individualistic premise, but the premise is neither the ontological individualism nor the motivational individualism which communitarians rightly have attacked. Liberalism is individualistic only in a *moral* sense. Liberals hold that what matters ultimately, morally speaking, is individuals – their autonomy and wellbeing.

Moral individualism does not commit the liberal to ontological individualism: holding that individuals are morally primary does not commit one to denying that groups exist or that they are reducible without remainder to the properties of individuals. Similarly, liberalism can readily admit that in order to describe the interest that individuals have in participating in groups it is necessary to make reference to institutions and practices. Liberals can also agree that the institutional or social concepts used to describe the interests that individuals have in belonging to groups and pursuing shared ends are not reducible to pre-institutional or pre-social concepts (such as that of the 'atomistic' individual existing in a state of nature). Liberalism, as a normative political thesis about the priority of the basic civil and political rights (and the proper role of the state and the limits of its authority), does not entail any such individualistic views; nor do the more plausible lines of justification invoked to support the liberal normative political thesis include such views among their premises. The latter justifications are simply attempts to show how a political order that protects the basic civil and political rights, and hence has a rather limited role for the state and a large private sphere in which diverse individuals (and groups) can flourish, will, in the long run, and in the

majority of cases, best serve the autonomy and welfare of individuals.

The second communitarian criticism, that liberalism undervalues participation in the political community, is harder to assess. Those who voice it sometimes neglect to distinguish clearly between two quite different theses. The first is that participation in the political community is valuable in itself, as a significant ingredient in the good life for all or most human beings. Liberalism need not, and does not, deny this. The second is that the good life requires that one participate in what may be called an all-inclusive political community or in some rather direct and substantial way in the highest-level political organization in one's society.

The first thesis is more controversial than the bare claim that participation in some form of community or other is an essential ingredient in the good life. It is the claim that participation in *political* community is essential. Although clearly in need of systematic defence, the latter claim is not implausible. It can be supported by arguing, as Aristotle seems to have done, that the good life for human beings, or at least the best life, requires the exercise and development of certain powers of will and intellect that can only be achieved through participation in activities in which one rules and is ruled in turn (see ARISTOTLE).

Notice, however, that even if this first thesis is granted, we are still a great distance from the second. For one may be able to achieve the good of participation in political community without participating in any significant way in an overarching political community, or the highest level of political organization. All that is necessary is that one participate in one or more political subcommunities, which might include not only local governments but also many other types of communities, religious and secular, in so far as they include a substantial political dimension in their internal activities.

Given the apparent diversity of the conditions of human flourishing, the sweeping pronouncement that the good life or even the best life for all (or even most) human beings requires significant participation in the most inclusive form or highest level of political organization appears rather dogmatic. To my knowledge no communitarian has shouldered the burden of supporting this second thesis.

The third communitarian criticism is sometimes formulated as the slogan that liberalism – at least the liberalism of theorists such as John Rawls and Ronald Dworkin – conceives of 'the self as being given prior to its ends' (Sandel 1984a: 115). Put more positively, this is the thesis that an individual's identity is to a significant degree constituted by an allegiance to the ends to which they are committed by virtue of their membership of the community, and more specifically by the roles they occupy in it.

Liberals need not and should not deny that when human beings become aware of themselves as moral agents and when they confront questions about what they ought to do, they already recognize themselves as having an identity. Nor should they fail to acknowledge that this identity is constituted to a large extent by the various roles in which they find themselves in the practices of their community (or communities), and that these roles carry with them certain obligations and commitments. Liberalism need not deny this commonsensical truth, which we may call 'the fact of embeddedness'. There is, however, a more radical interpretation of the thesis that which liberal thinkers do not espouse – but one which appears to be quite implausible. This is the view that the ends that are 'given' as part of a person's socially generated identity are *incorrigible* for that individual, that they cannot meaningfully be objects of criticism by the individual, and hence that they can neither be chosen or rejected by them.

It would be uncharitable to say that communitarians unequivocally hold this more radical interpretation of the embeddedness thesis, but there are passages in their writings that suggest that they do:

> I can only answer the question 'What am I to do?' if I can answer the prior question 'Of what story or stories do I find myself a part'? We enter human society, that is, with one or more imputed characters – roles into which we have been drafted. . . . I am someone's son or daughter, someone else's cousin or uncle; I am a citizen of this or that city, a member of this or that guild or profession; I belong to this or that clan, that tribe, this nation. Hence what is good for me has to be the good for one who inhabits these roles. As such I inherit from the past of my family, my city, my tribe, my nation, a variety of debts, inheritances, rightful expectations, and obligations.
>
> (MacIntyre 1981: 203–5)

If the point is that the self is embedded in the sense that the obligations a person has are given, *irrevocably* so, by their membership of and particular role within a community, that the obligations that are imputed along with membership and roles are not subject to criticism, and that a person cannot rationally choose to reject such roles, then liberalism does deny the embeddedness of the self. For liberalism, to the extent that it emphasizes individual autonomy, stresses the ability of individuals, at least under favourable conditions in which social practices and institutions allow the free flow of information and untrammelled discussion, to exercise critical judgment about the

suitability of their roles and the validity of the values of their communities, and hence to question the obligations that are imputed to them.

To put the same point in terms of what may be called the normative significance of identity, communitarians sometimes appear to hold that an individual cannot critically assess those putative obligations that are constitutive of their identity. On the face of it, however, this seems quite wrong. The fact that I am a racist – that racism is partly constitutive of my identity – does not show that I am obliged to treat white people as if they were superior to black people, nor that it is impossible for me to criticize my racist beliefs and reconstitute my identity as that of one who is dedicated to racial equality. It makes perfectly good sense to say that I ought to disavow my racist identity and strive to construct a new, nonracist identity.

The communitarian might reply that even when criticism of culturally-imputed obligations and values does occur, it must always proceed by drawing on conceptual, factual and moral resources that are themselves available only through the culture in question. This may in fact be what MacIntyre has in mind when, immediately following the passage cited above, he states that the obligations one inherits from one's social roles are one's moral starting point. The implication is that one may not remain at this starting point. One may come to revise one's conception of what is valuable, what one's obligations are, and so on – but only by utilizing tools of criticism that are also given by one's community.

On this interpretation, the embeddedness thesis is the claim that if an individual is able to exercise critical judgment about whether to act on the values and perceived obligations that are imputed to them by their community, this is only possible by drawing on perspectives that are available within the very communal normative structure that imputes the values in the first place.

If this means that all factual assumptions, concepts and moral principles that an individual relies on to criticize the values of his own community must be wholly endogenous to that community, must originate there or must be widely accepted there, then it not only appears to be false, but would seem to rest upon a view of communities which, ironically, is 'atomistic individualism' writ large. On this view, communities and the systems of values they embody are like the self-contained, *sui generis* and impermeable 'bare individuals' which communitarians believe to people the illusory world of liberal theory. But surely it cannot be denied that communities interact and that they borrow from one another's cultures, any more than it can be denied that the values of individuals are shaped by the social forces within which they develop.

In fact, modern societies are characterized by not only a plurality of interpenetrating communal cultures within the boundaries of a given society, but also by increasing interaction among different societies as the global economy and the global culture it brings with it expand. For example, Western principles concerning human rights in general and the equality of women in particular have been used, with some success, to criticize the assigned roles and perceived values and obligations of non-Western societies. Once it is recognized that criticism of acculturated values sometimes relies at least in part on beliefs, concepts or principles that originate outside the culture, then even the more moderate version of the embeddedness thesis is seen to be implausible.

Nevertheless an important truth remains: even if one is able to criticize obligations that are constitutive of one's culturally-assigned identity, all reasoning about what one ought to do must begin with a recognition of who one is and what one's obligations are as determined by one's identity. If this is what is meant by embeddedness, then communitarians have articulated an important truth about the nature of ethical reasoning and critical ethical reflection – one which liberal thinkers have perhaps generally neglected. What is not clear, however, is how taking this fact of embeddedness seriously affects the conclusions about the state and individual rights which liberalism seeks to defend.

The fourth and final communitarian criticism of liberalism is potentially more telling. The claim is that liberalism exalts individual autonomy to the neglect and detriment of community. The communitarians' point, presumably, is both that: (1) the justifications liberals offer to support the normative political thesis concerning the priority of basic individual, civil and political rights rest on an excessively positive valuation of individual choice or autonomy; and that (2) implementing the liberal priority on these individual rights is damaging to communities.

Contemporary liberals have offered strong arguments against both elements of the communitarian attack. First, liberal theorists can and do explicitly recognize the importance of community, and to that extent do not assume that individual autonomy is the sole value to be protected. Some of the most prominent contemporary liberal theorists, including Rawls, Dworkin and Feinberg, are most naturally read as ascribing to a moral individualism that bases the case for individual rights ultimately on both the autonomy and the wellbeing of individuals (Buchanan 1988: 878–81). If this is the case, then all that is needed to incorporate a fundamental appreciation for community into the heart of the liberal justification for individual rights is the commonsensical thesis: for

all or most human beings, participation in communities is an important ingredient in their wellbeing, as something that is intrinsically valuable. Once again, there is nothing in liberal theory, or at least in its more plausible variants, that precludes a recognition of the truth of this thesis.

Some contemporary liberal thinkers have argued that participation in community is also valuable because the community's shared values provide a context for meaningful choice (Kymlicka 1989: 205–19). To the extent that this is so, the opportunity to participate in flourishing communities is valuable not only from the perspective of individual wellbeing but also from that of individual autonomy, since autonomy can flourish only where meaningful choices are possible.

Liberalism, therefore, can include a proper recognition of the importance of participation in communities for individuals and can avoid an exclusive emphasis on individual autonomy that would neglect the importance of community for individual wellbeing. In addition, a number of liberal thinkers have pointed out that liberalism's priority on individual civil and political rights not only provides scope for individual autonomy but also serves to protect communities and to allow them to flourish (Feinberg 1988: 108–12; Buchanan 1994: 11–15).

To understand how individual rights protect communities, consider the rights to freedom of association, expression and religion. Historically these rights, as well as political participation rights and legal due process rights, have provided a strong bulwark against attempts by the state or rival communities to destroy or dominate minority communities. They allow individuals to partake of the essential good of community, and to enjoy the context for meaningful choice that community values provide, both by protecting existing communities from interference and by giving individuals the freedom to unite with like-minded others to form new communities. It is wrong to assume, then, that because the rights which liberals champion are individual rights, the purposes those rights serve and the values upon which they rest are purely individualistic.

This is not to say, of course, that any existing liberal theory provides a fully satisfactory way of accommodating both the importance of individual autonomy and the importance of participation in community. Nor is it to suggest that the particular understandings of the scope and limits of individual rights that liberals typically advocate successfully resolve all conflicts between the interests of individuals *qua* individuals and the interests of communities. Perhaps the most obvious instances of such unresolved conflicts – and of the challenge to liberalism that they represent – lie in the area of tensions between the interest in preserving a community's longstanding culture (or certain central features of it) and the liberal commitment to ensuring that children are educated so as to be able to make their own choices as to how to live. For example, some religious communities in the USA and elsewhere have sought an exemption from public schooling requirements on the grounds that exposure to ideas and values dominant in the majority culture would weaken their own community's traditions. Here there seems to be a direct conflict between liberalism's emphasis on individual autonomy and freedom of expression, and the value of preserving a community. And to say, as I have done, that liberalism ought to and can recognize the importance of participation in community for the wellbeing and autonomy of individuals does not in itself shed any light on how the balance should be struck between the individual rights liberalism has traditionally championed and the need to protect cultures when the former and the latter are in conflict.

If striking an adequate balance requires rejecting what I have taken to be the core of liberalism – the normative political thesis of the priority of individual rights – then the fourth major communitarian criticism of liberalism will be telling: the liberal priority on individual rights will be seen to rest on an inadequate appreciation of the value of community. If this is the case, then perhaps the most fruitful line of development for communitarian thought would be a concerted effort to show how political systems that only recognize individual rights as basic fail to respond satisfactorily to the need to preserve communities.

One important element of this line of inquiry is the question of whether states should recognize *group* rights that are justified according to the protection they provide for communities or their cultural values and that are basic rights in the sense of not being generated through the exercise of the individual rights which liberalism recognizes, such as the right to freedom of association and the legal right to make contracts. (Examples of basic group rights – those not generated through the exercise of individual rights – might include language rights for national minorities and collective land rights for indigenous peoples). If the liberal thesis of the primacy of individual rights rules out recognition of any basic group rights, then a successful case for basic group rights (as needed to provide sufficient protection for communities) would be a conclusive communitarian objection to liberalism thus interpreted. As a way of developing system-atically communitarianism both as a positive view and

as a critique of liberalism, this line of research may prove crucial (see MULTICULTURALISM).

4 Conclusions

If communitarianism is understood as being, or as centrally including, a radical critique of liberalism, where the latter is construed narrowly as the normative political thesis that the proper role of the state is to uphold the basic individual civil and political rights, then the communitarian project has thus far proven inconclusive. For liberalism can, and a growing number of contemporary liberal thinkers do, take the value of participation in community seriously – thus acknowledging the central tenets of communitarianism while denying that liberalism cannot incorporate them. However, if liberalism is understood to exclude entirely any role for basic group rights in the protection of cultural communities, then the communitarian critique of liberalism may well turn out to be telling.

Alternately, communitarianism might be viewed more positively, not primarily as a criticism of the liberal normative political thesis but as a rationale for an expanded and enriched research agenda in ethics and political philosophy. Taking the importance of community seriously in political philosophy would mean acknowledging and attempting to resolve systematically the conflicts that can arise in any theory that recognizes the importance of both individual autonomy and participation in communities. And doing so may require rethinking the scope and limits of theories of individual rights and a willingness to entertain the possibility that these rights must be supplemented with special group rights designed to provide added protection to especially vulnerable communities (Buchanan 1994: 11–15).

In ethical theory the communitarian message is to take seriously the fact that to a large extent moral obligations are the product of explicit choices or voluntary agreements made not by autonomous individuals operating in a social and institutional vacuum, but by individuals who regard themselves and are regarded by others as members of communities, as occupants of particular social roles. In addition, communitarianism stresses a fundamental truth about how ethical reflection and argumentation must begin; namely, in the concrete context of social practices in which individuals find themselves and in an awareness that the sense of self and the recognition of moral values are inextricably bound together. Thus, another important item on the agenda for a communitarian ethical theory is a careful articulation of the extent to which the social starting place that supplies one's identity places unsurpassable limitations on the sorts of moral conclusions one can draw and the kinds of moral commitments one can come to make through a process of rational reflection.

See also: CONFUCIAN PHILOSOPHY, CHINESE §5; INTERNATIONAL RELATIONS, PHILOSOPHY OF §3; NATION AND NATIONALISM; RAWLS, J.

References and further reading

Avineri, S. and de-Shalit, A. (1992) (eds) *Communitarianism and Individualism*, Oxford: Oxford University Press. (A useful collection of articles from both sides of the debate between communitarians and liberals.)

* Bell, D. (1993) *Communitarianism and Its Critics*, Oxford: Clarendon Press. (An imaginative defence, in dialogue form, of communitarian approaches to social and political philosophy.)

* Buchanan, A. (1988) 'Assessing the Communitarian Critique of Liberalism', *Ethics* 99 (4): 852–82. (A critical reconstruction and evaluation of communitarian criticisms of liberalism.)

* —— (1994) 'Liberalism and Group Rights', in J. Coleman and A. Buchanan (eds) *In Harm's Way*, Cambridge: Cambridge University Press. (A defence of the view that liberalism can recognize group rights.)

* Feinberg, J. (1988) *Harmless Wrongdoing*, vol. 4, *The Moral Limits of the Criminal Law*, New York: Oxford University Press. (A theory of the moral principles legislators ought to take into account in formulating criminal law concerning harmless wrongdoings.)

* Kymlicka, W. (1989) *Liberalism, Community, and Culture*, Oxford: Oxford University Press. (An account of how liberalism can and ought to take into account the value of culture to individuals.)

* MacIntyre, A. (1981) *After Virtue: A Study in Moral Theory*, London: Duckworth. (A critique of post-Enlightenment Western religious thought, from a communitarian perspective.)

Mulhall, S. and Swift, A. (1992) *Liberals and Communitarians*, Oxford: Oxford University Press. (An introduction to the thought of Sandel, MacIntyre, Taylor and Walzer, and the liberal responders, Rawls, Rorty and Raz.)

Plant, R. (1974) *Community and Ideology*, London: Routledge & Kegan Paul. (Examines the concept of community and different conceptions of community in political philosophy.)

* Rawls, J. (1971) *A Theory of Justice*, Cambridge, MA: Harvard University Press. (The most systematic account available of justice at the level of the basic structure of social institutions.)

* Sandel, M. (1982) *Liberalism and the Limits of Justice*, Cambridge: Cambridge University Press. (A critique of liberal theories of justice, focusing on Rawls; taken from the standpoint of a communitarian view of obligation and ethical reasoning.)

* —— (1984a) 'Justice and the Good', in *Liberalism and Its Critics*, New York: New York University Press. (Argues that the attempt of liberal theorists to develop an account of justice that is prior to and independent of the good must fail.)

—— (1984b) 'The Political Theory of the Procedural Republic' in *Liberalism and Its Critics*, New York: New York University Press. (Argues that political decision making requires agreement on a substantive conception of the good.)

* Taylor, C. (1979) *Hegel and Modern Society*, Cambridge: Cambridge University Press. (Reflections on Hegelian themes.)

—— (1985) 'Atomism', in C. Taylor (ed.) *Philosophy and the Human Sciences*, Cambridge: Cambridge University Press. (Critique of atomistic conceptions of society and of rights-based political philosophy.)

* —— (1989) 'Cross-purposes: The Liberal–Communitarian Debate', in N. Rosenblum (ed.) *Liberalism and the Moral Life*, Cambridge, MA: Harvard University Press. (Argues that the usual division between liberals and communitarians is confused, and that the real dividing line runs between procedural liberals and their republican critics.)

* Walzer, M. (1983) *Spheres of Justice*, New York: Basic Books. (Claims that ideas of justice depend on the meanings attached to social goods by the members of a particular community.)

ALLEN BUCHANAN

COMPLEXITY, COMPUTATIONAL

The theory of computational complexity is concerned with estimating the resources a computer needs to solve a given problem. The basic resources are time (number of steps executed) and space (amount of memory used). There are problems in logic, algebra and combinatorial games that are solvable in principle by a computer, but computationally intractable because the resources required by relatively small instances are practically infeasible.

The theory of $\mathcal{N}P$-completeness concerns a common type of problem in which a solution is easy to check but may be hard to find. Such problems belong to the class $\mathcal{N}P$; the hardest ones of this type are the $\mathcal{N}P$-complete *problems. The problem of determining whether a formula of propositional logic is satisfiable or not is $\mathcal{NP}$-complete. The class of problems with feasible solutions is commonly identified with the class $\mathcal{P}$ of problems solvable in polynomial time. Assuming this identification, the conjecture that some $\mathcal{NP}$ problems require infeasibly long times for their solution is equivalent to the conjecture that $\mathcal{P} \neq \mathcal{NP}$. Although the conjecture remains open, it is widely believed that $\mathcal{NP}$-complete problems are computationally intractable.*

1   **Time and space in computation**
2   **Hierarchies and reductions**
3   **Provably intractable problems**
4   **$\mathcal{NP}$ and the polynomial-time hierarchy**

1   Time and space in computation

The theory of complexity analyses the computational resources necessary to solve a problem. The most important of these resources are *time* (number of steps in a computation) and *space* (memory capacity of the computer). This entry is mainly concerned with the complexity of decision problems having infinitely many instances. There is another approach to complexity applicable to individual finite objects, in which the complexity of an object is measured by the size of the shortest programme that produces a description of it (see COMPUTABILITY AND INFORMATION).

The model for computation chosen here is the Turing machine (see TURING MACHINES). The *time* for a computation is the number of steps taken before the machine halts; the *space* is the number of cells of the tape visited by the reading head during the computation. Several other models of sequential computation have been proposed. The time and space complexity of a problem clearly depend on the machine model adopted. However, the basic concepts of complexity theory defined in this entry are robust in the sense that they coincide for any reasonable model of sequential computation.

Let Σ be a finite alphabet, and Σ^* the set of all finite strings in this alphabet. A subset of Σ^* is said to be a 'problem'. The size $|s|$ of a string s is its length, that is, the number of occurrences of symbols in it. A function f defined on Σ^* and having strings as its values is computed by a Turing machine M if for any string s in Σ^*, if M is started with s on its tape, then it halts with $f(s)$ on its tape. A problem L is solvable if there is a Turing machine that computes the characteristic function of L (the function f such that $f(s) = 1$ if s is in L and $f(s) = 0$ otherwise). For example, the problem Satisfiability of determining

whether a formula of propositional logic is satisfiable or not is solvable by the familiar method of truth tables.

Solvable problems can be classified according to the time and space required for their solution. If f is a computable function, then we say that f is computable in time $T(n)$ if there is a Turing machine M computing f and a constant c such that for any input s, M halts with output $f(s)$ in at most $c \cdot T(|s|)$ steps. A function f is computable in space $S(n)$ if there is a machine M computing f and a constant c such that for any input s, M halts after visiting at most $c \cdot S(|s|)$ squares on its tape. A problem L is solvable in time $T(n)$ if the characteristic function of L is computable in time $T(n)$; L is solvable in space $S(n)$ if the characteristic function of L is computable in space $S(n)$. For example, the truth table method shows that Satisfiability can be solved in time 2^n and space n (we need only enough tape space to evaluate the truth table one row at a time).

One of the most significant complexity classes is the class $\mathcal{P}$ of problems solvable in polynomial time. A function is polynomial-time computable if there exists a k for which f is computable in time n^k. A problem is solvable in polynomial time if its characteristic function is polynomial-time computable. The importance of this class rests on the widely accepted working hypothesis that the class of practically feasible algorithms can be identified with those algorithms that operate in polynomial time. Similarly, the class $\mathcal{PSPACE}$ contains those problems solvable in polynomial space. The class $\mathcal{EXPTIME}$ consists of the problems solvable in exponential time; a problem is solvable in exponential time if there is a k for which it is solvable in time 2^{n^k}. The class $\mathcal{EXPSPACE}$ contains those problems solvable in exponential space. The problem Satisfiability is in $\mathcal{EXPTIME}$; whether it is in $\mathcal{P}$ is a major open problem.

2   Hierarchies and reductions

The complexity classes defined above represent only a few levels within detailed hierarchies defined by space and time bounds. To state results on the hierarchies, we define a class of functions that includes all the complexity bounds considered here. A function $S(n)$ is said to be fully space constructible if there is a Turing machine that uses exactly $S(n)$ tape cells for any input of length n. With this definition we can state the space hierarchy theorem (Hartmanis, Lewis and Stearns 1965):

> If $S_1(n)$ and $S_2(n)$ are fully space constructible functions and if

$$\liminf_{n \to \infty} \frac{S_1(n)}{S_2(n)} = 0,$$

then there exists a problem solvable in space $S_2(n)$ but not in space $S_1(n)$.

In informal terms, the theorem says that if $S_1(n)$ and $S_2(n)$ are 'reasonable' mathematical functions and asymptotically $S_2(n)$ grows faster than $S_1(n)$, then there is a problem solvable in space $S_2(n)$ but not in $S_1(n)$. For example, there is a problem solvable in space n^3, but not in space n^2. A similar but slightly weaker time hierarchy theorem can be proved for complexity classes defined by time bounds.

The problems in these theorems that separate the complexity classes are defined by diagonalization. Applications of the theorems to naturally occurring problems in logic and mathematics are obtained by using the tool of efficient reductions. These are the complexity-theoretic analogue of the notion of Turing reducibility in recursion theory.

Let L_1 and L_2 be problems expressed in alphabets Σ_1 and Σ_2, respectively. L_1 is said to be polynomial-time reducible to L_2 (briefly, reducible to L_2) if there is a polynomial-time computable function f from Σ_1^* to Σ_2^* such that for any s in Σ_1^*, $s \in L_1$ if and only if $f(s) \in L_2$. Many other notions of reducibility have been considered. The important property of polynomial-time reducibility is that it is compatible with the main complexity classes $\mathcal{C}$ considered in this entry; this means that if L_2 is in a complexity class $\mathcal{C}$ and L_1 is reducible to L_2, then L_1 is also in $\mathcal{C}$.

3 Provably intractable problems

If $\mathcal{C}$ is a complexity class and L is a problem in $\mathcal{C}$ such that any problem in $\mathcal{C}$ is reducible to L, then L is said to be $\mathcal{C}$-complete. Such problems are the hardest problems in $\mathcal{C}$; if any problem in $\mathcal{C}$ is computationally intractable, then a $\mathcal{C}$-complete problem is intractable.

The time hierarchy theorem implies that there are problems in $\mathcal{EXPTIME}$ requiring exponential time for their solution, no matter what algorithm is employed. It follows that the same is true for any problem that is $\mathcal{EXPTIME}$-complete. Such problems can be shown to exist in the area of combinatorial games. For example, we can define generalized chess to be a game similar to standard chess, but played on an $n \times n$ board. The problem of determining of an arbitrary position in generalized chess whether or not the first player has a winning move is $\mathcal{EXPTIME}$-complete (Fraenkel and Lichtenstein 1981). If M is a Turing machine that solves this problem, there is a constant $c > 1$ such that infinitely many $n \times n$ chess positions exist for which M requires time greater than c^n to determine whether the first player has a win or not. In this sense, chess can be said to be a provably difficult game.

Problems that are $\mathcal{EXPSPACE}$-complete are also inherently intractable. In algebra, the word problem for commutative semigroups has been proved $\mathcal{EXPSPACE}$-complete (Mayr and Meyer 1982). An instance of this problem is a finite sequence of equations of the form $s = t$ where the terms s and t are constructed from a set of constants using a single binary operation; the problem to be solved is whether or not the last equation in the sequence can be inferred from the earlier equations by the usual rules for equations, assuming the commutative and associative laws for the operation. It follows that any Turing machine solving this problem requires an exponential amount of space for infinitely many inputs.

Logical theories are a source of solvable decision problems for which no feasible algorithm exists. An example is first-order arithmetic, restricted to addition. The language of this theory is a first-order language based on identity, the addition symbol and the constants 0 and 1. The decision problem consists in determining whether or not a sentence in this language is true in the natural numbers. Presburger in 1930 showed that this problem is decidable by the method of eliminating quantifiers. In 1973 Rabin and Fischer showed that the complexity of the problem is doubly exponential. This means that for any machine solving this problem, there is a constant $c > 0$ such that for infinitely many sentences of length n the machine takes at least $2^{2^{cn}}$ steps to determine whether it is true or not.

Still more powerful lower bounds can be proved by allowing second-order quantifiers. The weakest such extension allows quantifiers ranging over finite sets. Let WS1S be the weak monadic second-order theory of one successor. This theory is formulated in a second-order language with equality, based on the constant 0 and the successor function. The decision problem consists of deciding whether a sentence of WS1S is true in the natural numbers when the second-order quantifiers range over finite sets of natural numbers. It was shown decidable by Büchi in 1960. Define a function $F(n,m)$ by the recursion

$$F(n,1) = 2^n$$
$$F(n,m+1) = 2^{F(n,m)}.$$

If d is a real number greater than 0, then $f(d,n) = F(n,[dn])$ represents exponentiation by a stack of $[dn]$ 2's, where $[x]$ is the integer part of x. Albert Meyer in 1972 showed that an algorithm deciding WS1S must use space $f(d,n)$ infinitely often for some $d > 0$. This result shows that the decidability of WS1S is of a purely theoretical nature, so that the theory may be considered undecidable from a practical point of view.

The conclusion of the previous paragraph could be challenged by pointing out that Meyer's lower bound is an asymptotic result that does not rule out a practical decision procedure for sentences of practically feasible size. However, a further result shows that astronomical lower bounds can be proved for WS1S even if we restrict the length of sentences. A Boolean network or circuit is an acyclic directed graph in which each node is labelled with a variable of one of the logical operators 'and', 'not'. The nodes labelled with a variable have no incoming edges, while those labelled 'and' have two, and those labelled 'not' have one. There is exactly one node (the output node) with no outgoing edge. A circuit computes a Boolean function (truth-function) of the variables labelling its input nodes in an obvious way. Meyer and Stockmeyer showed that any such network that decides the truth of all sentences of WS1S of length 616 or less (encoded as binary strings) must contain at least 10^{123} nodes. Even if the nodes were the size of a proton and connected by infinitely thin wires, the network would densely fill the known universe.

4 $\mathcal{NP}$ and the polynomial-time hierarchy

A very common type of practical computational problem takes the form of searching for a solution to a set of conditions, where a proposed solution can be checked easily for correctness. Problems of this kind appear naturally in fields such as operations research, automated theorem proving, computer algebra, linear programming, graph theory and many other areas of discrete mathematics. The features common to such problems have been formalized in the theory of $\mathcal{NP}$-completeness.

A k-place relation holding between finite strings of symbols in a finite alphabet Σ is said to be polynomial-time computable (see §1 above) if its characteristic function is polynomial-time computable. (The characteristic function of a relation R is the function f such that $f(\langle s_1, \ldots, s_k \rangle) = 1$ if $R(s_1, \ldots, s_k)$, and $f(\langle s_1, \ldots, s_k \rangle) = 0$ otherwise.) Let L be a problem expressed in an alphabet Σ. L belongs to the class $\mathcal{NP}$ if there is a polynomial-time computable relation R and a polynomial $p(x)$ such that for any s in Σ^*, s is in L if and only if there exists a y such that $|y| \leqslant p(|s|)$ and $R(s, y)$.

The abbreviation '$\mathcal{NP}$' stands for 'non-deterministic polynomial-time', and is derived from an alternative definition of the class using non-deterministic Turing machines. The instructions for such a machine give for each pair consisting of a scanned symbol and the current state a finite set of permissible actions. A language is in $\mathcal{NP}$ if and only if it is accepted by a non-deterministic Turing machine the length of whose computations is bounded by a polynomial in the size of the input. (A string is accepted by such a machine if there is a computation consisting of permissible actions at each step that ends in an accepting configuration.)

Informally, we could describe the relation between $\mathcal{P}$ and $\mathcal{NP}$ as follows. The class $\mathcal{P}$ consists of problems with a feasible decision method; the class $\mathcal{NP}$ consists of problems where we can guess a solution, and check in a feasible amount of time if our guess was correct.

The problem Satisfiability belongs to $\mathcal{NP}$ since we can take the relation $R(s, y)$ to be the relation 'y is a truth-value assignment that satisfies the formula s'. Satisfiability occupies a central position in the theory of $\mathcal{NP}$-completeness as perhaps the simplest and most natural example of an $\mathcal{NP}$-complete problem. Cook's theorem of 1971 showing that Satisfiability is $\mathcal{NP}$-complete led to the identification of hundreds of $\mathcal{NP}$-complete problems in computer science and discrete mathematics. The book by Garey and Johnson (1979) includes a partial list of such problems.

If a problem is $\mathcal{NP}$-complete, then a polynomial-time algorithm for the problem would lead to a polynomial-time algorithm for any problem in $\mathcal{NP}$ so that the equation $\mathcal{P} = \mathcal{NP}$ would be true. A polynomial-time algorithm for the satisfiability problem for propositional logic would lead to polynomial-time algorithms for hundreds of important problems in discrete mathematics; this follows immediately from the definition of $\mathcal{NP}$-completeness. Because such algorithms have been sought in vain for several decades, it is commonly conjectured that none exists, although no proof of this conjecture has been found. The problem '$\mathcal{P} = \mathcal{NP}$?' is widely considered the most important open problem in theoretical computer science.

The recursive sets can be identified with the computable sets; if we accept the identification of 'feasibly computable' with 'polynomial-time computable' then $\mathcal{P}$ is the class of problems with feasible solutions. The recursively enumerable sets are obtained from recursive relations by unbounded quantification; similarly, the problems in $\mathcal{NP}$ are obtained from relations in $\mathcal{P}$ by polynomially bounded quantification. Thus the class $\mathcal{NP}$ is the complexity-theoretic analogue of the class of recursively enumerable sets, and the $\mathcal{NP}$-complete problems correspond to problems of the highest degree of unsolvability among recursively enumerable sets, such as the halting problem (see COMPUTABILITY THEORY §5; TURING MACHINES §3).

The analogy with recursion theory has been extended by defining a complexity-theoretic analogue of the Kleene arithmetical hierarchy of recursion theory. The class Σ_k^p is defined as the class of problems expressible in the form

$$\{s: (\exists y_1, |y_1| \leqslant p(|s|))(\forall y_2, |y_2| \leqslant p(|s|))$$
$$\ldots R(s, y_1, \ldots, y_k)\},$$

where there are k alternating bounded quantifiers in the prefix of the defining formula, $p(x)$ is a polynomial and R is a polynomial-time computable relation. In particular, $\mathcal{NP} = \Sigma_1^p$. The class Π_k^p is given by a definition dual to that for Σ_k^p, where bounded existential quantifiers are replaced by bounded universal quantifiers, and universal by existential.

It is conjectured that all the classes in the polynomial hierarchy are distinct, but no proof is known. If $\mathcal{P} = \mathcal{NP}$, then all the classes in the hierarchy collapse to $\mathcal{P}$. All of the classes in the polynomial hierarchy are contained in $\mathcal{PSPACE}$. The equality $\mathcal{P} = \mathcal{PSPACE}$ is consistent with current knowledge, even though $\mathcal{PSPACE}$ appears to be a much more extensive class than $\mathcal{P}$.

The space and hierarchy theorems above were proved by diagonal arguments similar to those used to prove Church's theorem (see CHURCH'S THEOREM AND THE DECISION PROBLEM). There are reasons to think that diagonalization cannot be used to separate $\mathcal{P}$ and $\mathcal{NP}$ or other low-level complexity classes (the analogy with recursion theory breaks down at this point). These reasons are based on results about oracle machines. If A is a set of strings then a Turing machine with oracle A is defined to be a Turing machine that in addition to the normal type of instruction also has instructions of the form (q_i, σ, q_j, q_k), where q_i, q_j, q_k are machine states and σ is a symbol from the tape alphabet (see TURING MACHINES §3). The instruction is interpreted by the machine as follows: when the current state is q_i and the string of symbols to the right of the reading head (starting with the current symbol σ) is in A, then the machine's next state is q_j, otherwise its next state is q_k. Thus a Turing machine with oracle A has the ability to answer in a single step questions of the type 'Is this string in the set A?'. Time and space of a computation by an oracle machine is computed just as for an ordinary Turing machine, counting the time taken for the answer to the oracle query as one step (the oracle answers any query instantaneously).

If A is any set of strings, then by imitating the definitions of the complexity classes above, but substituting 'Turing machine with oracle A' every-

where for 'Turing machine' we can define relativized complexity classes $\mathcal{P}^A$, $\mathcal{NP}^A$ and so on. Then we have the following theorem (Baker, Gill and Solovay 1975):

There is a recursive oracle A for which $\mathcal{P}^A = \mathcal{NP}^A$ and a recursive oracle B for which $\mathcal{P}^B \neq \mathcal{NP}^B$.

The significance of this theorem lies in the fact that known techniques of diagonalization, such as are used in recursion theory, relativize in the presence of oracles. Thus it provides evidence that standard diagonal techniques are inadequate to settle such questions as '$\mathcal{P} = \mathcal{NP}$?'.

See also: COMPUTABILITY THEORY; LOGICAL AND MATHEMATICAL TERMS, GLOSSARY OF

References and further reading

* Baker, T., Gill, J. and Solovay, R. (1975) 'Relativizations of the $\mathcal{P} = ?\mathcal{NP}$ Question', *SIAM Journal of Computation* 4: 431–42. (This paper shows that diagonalization techniques very likely do not suffice to answer the $\mathcal{P} = ?\mathcal{NP}$ question.)
* Cook, S.A. (1971) 'The Complexity of Theorem-Proving Procedures', in *Proceedings of the 3rd Annual ACM Symposium on Theory of Computing*, New York: Association for Computing Machinery, 151–8. (The fundamental paper introducing the theory of $\mathcal{NP}$-completeness.)
* Fraenkel, A.S. and Lichtenstein, D. (1981) 'Computing a Perfect Strategy for $n \times n$ Chess Requires Time Exponential in n', *Journal of Combinatorial Theory*, series A, 31: 199–213. (This paper shows generalized chess to be a hard game in the computational sense.)
* Garey, M.R. and Johnson, D.S. (1979) *Computers and Intractability: A Guide to the Theory of $\mathcal{NP}$-Completeness*, San Francisco, CA: Freeman. (Includes an extensive list of $\mathcal{NP}$-complete problems from many areas.)
* Hartmanis, J., Lewis, P.M., II and Stearns, R.E. (1965) 'Classification of Computations by Time and Memory Requirements', in *Proceedings of the IFIP Congress 1965*, New York: Spartan Books, 31–5. (The first appearance of the space and time hierarchy theorems.)
Hopcroft, J.E. and Ullman, J.D. (1979) *Introduction to Automata Theory, Languages and Computation*, Reading, MA: Addison-Wesley. (A clearly written textbook giving the basic definitions and results of complexity theory.)
Leeuwen, J. van (ed.) (1990) *Handbook of Theoretical Computer Science*, vol. A, *Algorithms and Complexity*, Amsterdam: Elsevier. (A collection of

detailed survey articles covering many topics not included in this entry, such as parallel complexity and cryptography.)

* Mayr, E.W. and Meyer, A.R. (1982) 'The Complexity of the Word Problem for Commutative Semigroups and Polynomial Ideals', *Advances in Mathematics* 46: 305–29. (One of the earliest papers showing the existence of computationally intractable problems in classical algebra.)

Sipser, M. (1997) *Introduction to the Theory of Computation*, Boston, MA: PWS. (An elegant introduction to the basics of computational complexity theory, written by a major figure in the area.)

Stockmeyer, L. (1987) 'Classifying the Computational Complexity of Problems', *Journal of Symbolic Logic* 52: 1–43. (A very informative survey article.)

ALASDAIR URQUHART

COMPOSITIONALITY

A language is compositional if the meaning of each of its complex expressions (for example, 'black dog') is determined entirely by the meanings its parts ('black', 'dog') and its syntax. Principles of compositionality provide precise statements of this idea. A compositional semantics for a language is a (finite) theory which explains how semantically important properties such as truth-conditions are determined by the meanings of parts and syntax. Supposing English to have a compositional semantics helps explain how finite creatures like ourselves have the ability to understand English's infinitely many sentences. Whether human languages are in fact compositional, however, is quite controversial.

It is often supposed that meaning, within a context of use, determines truth-value. Meaning and context are also generally thought to determine what terms refer to, and what predicates are true of – that is, to determine extensions. Because of this, compositionality is generally taken to license a principle of substitutivity: if expressions have the same meaning, and substituting one for another in a sentence does not change the sentence's syntax, the substitution can have no effect on truth. Given this, the idea that meaning is compositionally determined constrains what can be identified with meaning. For example, expressions with the same extension cannot always be substituted for one another without change of truth-value (see PROPOSITIONAL ATTITUDE STATEMENTS §2; MODAL LOGIC, PHILOSOPHICAL ISSUES IN §3).

Natural languages obey a principle of composi-

tionality (PC) only if something more 'fine-grained' than extensions plays the role of meanings, so that expressions with the same extension can still have different meanings. Some say that no matter how fine-grained we make meaning, there will be counter-examples to the claim that meaning is compositionally determined. For example, 'woodchuck' and 'groundhog' are synonymous. But the sentences 'Mae thinks Woody is a woodchuck' and 'Mae thinks Woody is a groundhog' apparently may diverge in truth-value. (Certainly Mae may assert, with understanding, that Woody is a woodchuck, while denying, with understanding, that Woody is a groundhog. For she can understand 'woodchuck' and 'groundhog' but not realize that they are synonymous.) Such arguments lead to the conclusion that meaning is not compositionally determined (or that different forms cannot share meanings).

There is no consensus about such arguments. All agree PCs need *some* restrictions – they do not, for instance, apply to words in quotational constructions. So if 'thinks' is implicitly quotational, the argument loses its force (see USE/MENTION DISTINCTION AND QUOTATION). If 'thinks', as Frege held, produces a (more or less) systematic shift in the semantic properties of the expressions in its scope, this perhaps reduces the threat to compositionality (see SENSE AND REFERENCE §§4, 5). Some find such accounts of 'thinks' incredible (Davidson 1984).

Linguists often understand the claim that a language is compositional as asserting an extremely tight correspondence between its syntax and semantics (see SYNTAX). A (simplified) version of such a claim is that (after disambiguating simple word forms), there is, for each (simple) word, a meaning and, for each syntactic rule used in sentence construction, an operation on meanings, such that the meaning of any sentence is mechanically determined by applying the operations on meanings (given by the rules used in constructing the sentence) to the meanings of the simple parts. (Often a host of extra restrictions are incorporated. For example: the operations may be limited to applying function to argument; the order in which operations are applied may be settled by the structure of the sentence.) Some see such principles as providing significant constraints on semantical theories, constraints which may help us decide between theories which are in other respects equivalent (for example, Montague 1974).

Such strong PCs imply that every ambiguous sentence is either syntactically ambiguous or contains simple expressions which are themselves ambiguous (see AMBIGUITY). There are putative counterexamples to this. For instance, it has been alleged that 'The women lifted the piano' has two meanings, a 'collective' one (the group lifted it) and a 'distributive' one (each individual lifted it) (see Pelletier 1994).

Context sensitivity makes the formulation of PCs a delicate matter. In some important sense, differing uses of 'that is dead' have like meanings and syntax. But obviously they may differ in truth; presumably such differences may arise even within one context. How can this be reconciled with compositionality?

We might (implausibly) say that demonstrative word forms, strictly speaking, lack meanings (only tokens have such). An alternative (see Kaplan 1989) sees the meaning of the word type 'that' as 'incomplete', needing contextual supplementation to determine a meaning of the sort other terms have. A third strategy insists that if 'that is dead but that is not' is true, its 'that's are different demonstrative word types. (Advocates of this view are good at seeing very small subscripts.) This view makes it generally opaque to speakers whether tokens are tokens of the same word type, and thus opaque whether their arguments are logically valid. A fourth strategy sees context as providing an assignment of referents to *uses* of a type in a context. On most ways of working this out, it seems there is no true fleshing out of the principle: the meaning of a sentence type (a) is determined by the meanings of parts and syntax, and (b) determines, in context, the sentence's truth-value. This approach also seems to undermine the idea that an argument like *that is dead; so that is dead* is formally valid (see DEMONSTRATIVES AND INDEXICALS).

Even if relatively tight PCs should prove untenable (as claims about natural languages), it would not follow that natural languages did not have compositional semantics – finite theories which assign truth-conditions and other semantically relevant properties to sentence types or their uses. It has been argued that only if they do would it be possible for finite creatures like ourselves to learn them (since the languages involve infinite pairings of sounds and meanings); analogous arguments hold that our ability to understand (in principle) natural languages requires the existence of such semantics. Such arguments apparently presuppose that learning and understanding a language requires knowing a theory from which semantic facts (such as the fact that, for any speaker x and time t, a use of 'J'existe encore' by x at t says that, at t, x still exists) are deducible. While such a view is not implausible, alternative plausible views of competence do not support this sort of argument. For example, one might identify linguistic competence with the possession of *syntactic* knowledge (or even just with the possession of syntactic abilities) by someone with appropriate social and environmental relations and behavioural dispositions. Whether natural languages have compositional semantics,

and whether the meanings of their sentences are determined simply by the meanings of their parts and syntax, is still not settled.

See also: MEANING AND TRUTH; SEMANTICS

References and further reading

* Davidson, D. (1984) *Inquiries into Truth and Understanding*, Oxford: Oxford University Press. (Essay 1 argues that learnable languages have compositional semantics; essay 7 argues against Fregean accounts of 'thinks'.)
Grandy, R. (1990) 'Understanding and the Principle of Compositionality', in J.E. Tomberlin (ed.) *Philosophical Perspectives*, Atascadero, CA: Ridgeview Publishing Company, vol. 4, 557–72. (Defends compositional semantics against the attacks of Schiffer and others.)
* Kaplan, D. (1989) 'Demonstratives', in J. Almog, J. Perry and H. Wettstein (eds) *Themes From Kaplan*, Oxford: Oxford University Press. (Gives Kaplan's views of demonstrative meaning.)
* Montague, R.M. (1974) *Formal Philosophy*, New Haven, CT: Yale University Press. (Essays 6–8 give formulations of compositionality principles. Very difficult.)
Partee, B. (1984) 'Compositionality', in F. Landman and F. Veltman (eds) *Varieties of Formal Semantics*, Dordrecht: Foris, 281–311. (Evaluates Montague-style principles of compositionality. Difficult but illuminating.)
* Pelletier, F.J. (1994) 'The Principle of Semantic Compositionality', *Topoi* 13: 11–24. (A good introduction to arguments for and against principles of compositionality.)
Schiffer, S. (1987) *Remnants of Meaning*, Cambridge, MA: MIT Press. (Contains arguments against the existence of compositional semantics for natural languages.)

MARK RICHARD

COMPUTABILITY AND INFORMATION

The standard definition of randomness as considered in probability theory and used, for example, in quantum mechanics, allows one to speak of a process (such as tossing a coin, or measuring the diagonal polarization of a horizontally polarized photon) as being random. It does not allow one to call a particular outcome (or string of outcomes, or sequence of outcomes) 'random', except in an intuitive, heuristic sense. Information-theoretic complexity makes this possible. An algorithmically random string is one which cannot be produced by a description significantly shorter than itself; an algorithmically random sequence is one whose initial finite segments are almost random strings.

Gödel's incompleteness theorem states that every axiomatizable theory which is sufficiently rich and sound is incomplete. Chaitin's information-theoretic version of Gödel's theorem goes a step further, revealing the reason for incompleteness: a set of axioms of complexity N cannot yield a theorem that asserts that a specific object is of complexity substantially greater than N. This suggests that incompleteness is not only natural, but pervasive; it can no longer be ignored by everyday mathematics. It also provides a theoretical support for a quasi-empirical and pragmatic attitude to the foundations of mathematics.

Information-theoretic complexity is also relevant to physics and biology. For physics it is convenient to reformulate it as the size of the shortest message specifying a microstate, uniquely up to the assumed resolution. In this way we get a rigorous, entropy-like measure of disorder of an individual, microscopic, definite state of a physical system. The regulatory genes of a developing embryo can be ultimately conceived as a program for constructing an organism. The information contained by this biochemical computer program can be measured by information-theoretic complexity.

1   The paradox of randomness
2   Random strings
3   Random sequences
4   Chaitin's Omega number
5   Randomness in physics
6   Logical depth

1   The paradox of randomness

Suppose that persons A and B each give us a string of 32 bits, saying that they were obtained from independent coin flips. If A gives the string

$$x = 01101000100110101101100110100101$$

and B gives the string

$$y = 00000000000000000000000000000000,$$

then we will believe A and will not believe B: the string x *seems* random, but the string y does not. Why? The strings are extremely different from the point of view of regularity. The string y has a maximum regularity which allows us to express it in a very compact way – 'only zeros' – while x appears to have no shortened definition at all. The distinction between regular and

irregular strings becomes sharper as the strings get longer: it is clearly easier to specify the number

$$10^{10^{10^{10}}}$$

than the first 1,000 digits of π. Classical probability theory is not sensitive to the above distinction, as strings are all equally probable. However, even Laplace (1749–1827) was, in a sense, aware of this paradox; he suggested that non-random strings are strings possessing some kind of regularity, and since the number of all those strings (of a given length) is small, the occurrence of such a string is extraordinary.

Borel (1909), von Mises ([1928] 1919), Ville (1939) and Church (1940) all elaborated on this idea, but a formal model of irregularity was not found until the mid-1960s. Information-theoretic complexity was introduced independently by Solomonoff (1964), Kolmogorov (1965) and Chaitin (1966). The basic idea is to measure the informational complexity of an object by the size of the smallest program computing it. There are two principal applications: (1) to provide a new conceptual foundation for probability theory and statistics by making it possible to define rigorously the notions of random string and random sequence; and (2) to describe the major limitative theorems in mathematical logic in an information-theoretic form.

Let $A = \{a_1, a_2, \ldots, a_Q\}$, $Q \geqslant 2$, be a finite alphabet, and consider the set of all strings $x_1 x_2 \ldots x_n$ of elements in A. We denote by $|x|$ the length of the string x.

It is convenient to think of a computer as a decoding device at the receiving end of a communication channel. Its programs can be viewed as code words, or strings over the alphabet A, and the result of the computation as the decoded message. It is natural to require that successive programs (for example, subroutines) sent across the channel can be separated. This can be achieved by stipulating that programs are 'self-delimiting', that is, no meaningful program is a prefix of another. Self-delimiting programs carry within them information about their size, in the sense that they allow the computer to decide when to stop reading the input; they act as 'atomic' programs having no significant sub-programmatic structure. Formally, a 'computer' is a self-delimiting partial recursive function C which carries strings (programs) into strings (see COMPUTABILITY THEORY §§2–3). The (Chaitin) complexity $H_C(x)$ of a string x induced by the computer C is the length of the shortest program for C that outputs x, and halts:

$$H_C(x) = \min\{|y| \mid C(y) = x\}.$$

This notion of complexity is machine-dependent. It is possible to make it 'asymptotically' independent of the choice of the computer. The price paid amounts to at most an O(1) uncertainty in the numerical values, and is expressed by the following 'invariance theorem': there exists a computer U such that for all computers C one has

$$H_U(x) \leqslant H_C(x) + O(1).$$

($O(f)$ denotes a function $g(n)$ whose absolute value is bounded by a constant times $f(n)$, for sufficiently large n.)

A universal self-delimiting Turing machine (see COMPUTABILITY THEORY §4; TURING MACHINES §2) is a possible candidate for U. Indeed, U simulates the computation of every computer C in the most efficient way: there exists a prefix δ such that the program δx makes U simulate the computation of C on x. The prefix δ depends upon U and C; it is independent of x. From now on we fix a computer U (called universal) and put $H_U = H$.

The set of meaningful programs for U is an instantaneous code, in the sense that each program can be decoded as soon as we come to the end of the string corresponding to it. In view of the invariance theorem it follows that the set of meaningful programs for U is an asymptotically optimal code for the set of all strings: every string can be coded by such a program, with minimum expected length.

In this context the joint complexity $H(x,y)$ of two strings x, y, defined to be the size of the smallest program that makes U output both of them, satisfies the classical inequality:

$$H(x,y) \leqslant H(x) + H(y) + O(1),$$

that is, the complexity is asymptotically sub-additive. In the original formulation of these definitions the sub-additivity failed to be true. Chaitin (1974) and Levin (1974) independently found the solution: computers have to be self-delimiting.

2 Random strings

Randomness is not absolute, but relative. It makes more sense to ask 'To what extent is x random?' than 'What is a random string?'.

To define random strings we try to capture the idea that a string is random if it cannot be algorithmically compressed. Formally, a string is 'random' if it has 'almost' maximal complexity within the set of all strings of the same length. The maximal value of the complexity of strings of length n is given by the formula

$$\max_{|x|=n} H(x) = n + H(\text{string}(n)) + O(1),$$

where $\text{string}(n)$ is the nth string according to the

lexicographic order. (Strings are enumerated in order of increasing length: all strings of length one, followed by all strings of length two, and so on.)

We are naturally motivated to adopt the following definition. A string x is (Chaitin) 'm-random' (m a natural number) if

$$H(x) \geqslant |x| + H(\text{string}(|x|)) - m.$$

x is random if it is 0-random.

To validate the above model of randomness one has to show that random strings defined in this way possess (almost) all properties intuitively associated with randomness. We discuss here only two such properties: (1) the absence of any algorithmic rule for defining random strings; and (2) the equi-distribution of letters and blocks of letters. Property (1) holds true in a strong sense: the set of random strings is 'immune', that is, it is infinite and contains no infinite recursively enumerable subset (see COMPUTABILITY THEORY §5). The intuition motivating (2) is that in a 'truly random' string each letter has to appear with approximately the same frequency, namely Q^{-1}. Moreover, the same property should extend to substrings. Indeed, one proves that all 'reasonably long' substrings of a random string have approximately the same frequency, which depends only on the length of substrings.

3 Random sequences

An infinite sequence $\mathbf{x} = x_1 x_2 \ldots x_n \ldots$ is uniquely determined by its prefixes

$$\mathbf{x}(n) = x_1 x_2 \ldots x_n, \quad n = 1, 2 \ldots.$$

Is it possible to define the randomness of a sequence by means of the degree of randomness of its prefixes? The answer is affirmative. A sequence $\mathbf{x}$ is random if and only if there exists a natural number c such that $H(\mathbf{x}(n)) \geqslant n - c$ for all natural $n \geqslant 1$. This condition is equivalent to the following, apparently stronger, requirement (Chaitin 1974): a sequence $\mathbf{x}$ is random if and only if

$$\lim_{n \to \infty} H(\mathbf{x}(n)) - n = \infty.$$

Martin-Löf (1966) made use of constructive probability theory in order to define random sequences. The set of all sequences can be equipped with the product probability (induced by the uniform distribution of letters in the alphabet). A constructive null set (of sequences) is a set which can be recursively covered by recursively enumerable sets having arbitrarily small probabilities. The union of all constructive null sets is still a null set, in fact, a maximal one. It can be shown that the set of random sequences coincides exactly with the complement of the maximal null set. It follows that with probability one every sequence is random. However, from a topological point of view, the set of random sequences is of first Baire category, which is a rather small set.

Random sequences share many properties associated with randomness; for instance, they are Borel normal (every string x appears in a random sequence with the probability $Q^{-|x|}$, which depends only on the length of the string), they pass almost all stochasticity tests, they are incompatible with the slightest form of computability (the possibility to compute an infinite part of a sequence makes that sequence non-random). Random sequences generate, in a sense, all sequences; that is, every sequence is effectively reducible, via a fixed process, to a random one. Randomness is an invariant of number representations: the usual representations of a real number are either random for all bases, or not so for any base.

4 Chaitin's Omega number

Consider a universal self-delimiting program which, instead of being given a specific program at the beginning of the computation, is fed with a 'random string' of bits. Whenever the universal program requests another input bit we just toss a fair coin and input 1 or 0, according to whether the coin comes up heads or tails. Finally we ask the question 'When the above procedure is begun, what is the probability that the universal program will eventually halt?'. The answer is Chaitin's Omega number, Ω.

The sequence of digits of Ω is random. This means that we will never know more than a handful of digits of Ω. This number appears to be cabalistic: it can be known of, but not itself known.

The fascination of Ω comes from the fact that it is computationally equivalent to the halting problem (see COMPUTABILITY THEORY §5), but contains the same information in a fantastically compressed form. An oracle supplying a few digits of Ω would be of invaluable help in answering many mathematical questions, such as Goldbach's conjecture (we may construct a computer which halts if and only if it finds an even number greater than 2 which is not the sum of two primes), or Riemann's hypothesis.

From a practical point of view, even having access to all digits of Ω would not make the task of solving problems very easy, as the time (see COMPLEXITY, COMPUTATIONAL) to decompress Ω grows extremely rapidly, that is, non-recursively.

The classical opinion that an axiom should be self-evident appears to be too restrictive. Neither Riemann's hypothesis, nor Schrödinger's equation are self-evident, but both are very useful. The possibility of finding new axioms for the positive integers should

perhaps get more attention. This quasi-empirical attitude seems to be consistent with Gödel's own views:

> axioms need not be evident in themselves, but rather their justification lies (exactly as in physics) in the fact that they make it possible for these 'sense perceptions' to be deduced... I think that... this view has been largely justified by subsequent developments, and it is to be expected that it will be still more so in the future.
>
> ([1944] 1990: 121)

5 Randomness in physics

All science is founded on the assumption that the physical universe is ordered and rational. The most powerful expression of this state of affairs is found in the successful application of mathematics to make predictions expressed by means of the laws of physics. Where do these laws come from? Why do they operate universally and unfailingly? Nobody seems to have reasonable answers to these questions. The most we can do is to explain that the hypothesis of order is supported by our daily observations: the rhythm of day and night; the regular ticking of clocks. However, there is a limit to this perceived order. How are we to reconcile these seemingly random processes with the supposed order? How can the same physical process (for example, the spin of a roulette wheel) obey two contradictory laws, the laws of chance and the laws of physics?

As our direct information refers to finite experiments, it is not out of the question to discover local rules, functioning on large, but finite scales, even if the global behaviour of the process is truly random. But, to perceive this global randomness we have to have access to infinity, which is not physically possible. It is important to notice that, consistently with our common experience, facing global randomness does not imply the impossibility of making predictions. Space scientists can pinpoint and predict planetary locations and velocities 'well enough' to plan missions years in advance. Astronomers can predict solar or lunar eclipses centuries before their occurrence. However, we have to be aware that all these results – superb as they may be – are only true within a certain degree of precision, which can hardly be evaluated.

This suggests the idea that the universe might be random (see Calude and Salomaa 1994). Here is an example illustrating this idea. Consider reversible transformations of a string x, $x_{t+1} = T(x_t)$. This equation can be regarded as a deterministic law of motion generating the phase-space trajectory of a simple, idealized system. The complexity $H(x_t)$ tends to increase in the course of evolution, provided the initial state is not too complex. It approaches the equilibrium value consistently with the Boltzmann estimate of the entropy, and fluctuates around the equilibrium. This shows how a reversible, deterministic, dynamic evolution can lead to a significant increase of complexity (see Zurek 1989).

Any physical system may be perceived as a computational process. One could even go further and speculate (with Wheeler, Fredkin, Toffoli) that the universe is a gigantic information-processing system, in which the output is as yet undetermined. In Wheeler's compact form: 'It from bit!', that is, 'it' – every force, particle, and so on – is ultimately present through 'bits' of information. Under this interpretation Ω – which represents the halting probability of the system – acquires physical significance. This constant is not only non-computable, but reflects, in a sense, the indeterministic, chaotic nature of the universe, consistently with Svozil's thesis (1993) according to which chaos in physics corresponds to randomness in mathematics.

6 Logical depth

Charles Bennett's thesis (1988) is that a structure is 'deep' if it is superficially random but subtly redundant; in other words, if almost all its algorithmic probability is contributed by slow-running programs. The value of a message is only slightly related to its information content. For example, a typical sequence of coin tosses has high information content, but little message value. According to Bennett, the 'logical depth' of a message can be measured by the amount of computational work required by its originator, which its receiver is saved from having to repeat. Here we include things which are computable in principle, but only at a considerable cost in resources. Tolstoy's *War and Peace*, Leonardo da Vinci's portrait of *Mona Lisa*, or phase-space sheets that evolve from simple coarse-grained cells via the chaotic dynamics of a simple Hamiltonian are objects with large logical depth.

See also: LOGICAL AND MATHEMATICAL TERMS, GLOSSARY OF

References and further reading

Atiyah, M. *et al.* (1994) 'Responses to "Theoretical Mathematics: Toward a Cultural Synthesis of Mathematics and Theoretical Physics", by A. Jaffe and F. Quinn', *Bulletin of the American Mathematical Society* 30: 178–207. (Enlightening and provocative essays by, among others, M. Atiyah, A. Borel, G. Chaitin, S. Mac Lane, B. Mandelbroit and R. Thom, on the nature of mathematics.)

* Bennett, C.H. (1988) 'Logical Depth and Physical Complexity', in R. Herken (ed.) *The Universal Turing Machine: A Half-Century Survey*, Oxford: Oxford University Press, 227–58. (Expansion of the material of §6.)
* Borel, É. (1909) 'Les probabilités dénombrables et leurs applications arithmétiques' (Enumerable Probabilities and their Arithmetical Applications), *Rendiconti del Circolo Matematico di Palermo* 27: 247–71. (An important paper inaugurating the modern analysis of randomness.)
  Brisson, L. and Meyerstein, F.W. (1994) *Inventing the Universe*, New York: State University of New York Press. (Some philosophical consequences of Chaitin's work.)
  Calude, C. (1994) *Information and Randomness: An Algorithmic Perspective*, Berlin: Springer. (An informative introduction to basic results in algorithmic information theory in a general setting.)
  Calude, C. and Jürgensen, H. (1994) 'Randomness as an Invariant for Number Representations', in H. Maurer, J. Karhumäki and G. Rozenberg (eds) *Results and Trends in Theoretical Computer Science*, Berlin: Springer, 44–66. (A proof of the invariance of randomness with respect to number representations and a discussion of random real numbers.)
  Calude, C., Jürgensen, H. and Zimand, M. (1994) 'Is Independence an Exception?', *Applied Mathematics and Computation* 66: 63–76. (A topological proof showing that the set of all true but unprovable statements is large.)
* Calude, C. and Salomaa, A. (1994) 'Algorithmically Coding the Universe', in G. Rozenberg and A. Salomaa (eds) *Developments in Language Theory*, Singapore: World Scientific, 472–92. (An informal discussion of the randomness hypothesis discussed in §5.)
* Chaitin, G.J. (1966) 'On the Length of Programs for Computing Finite Binary Sequences', *Journal of the Association for Computing Machinery* 13: 547–69. (Chaitin's first contribution to the subject.)
* —— (1974) 'A Theory of Program Size Formally Identical to Information Theory', in *Abstracts of Papers, 1974 IEEE International Symposium on Information Theory*, Indiana, IN: University of Notre Dame Press; repr. in *Journal of the Association for Computing Machinery* 22: 329–40, 1975. (The first systematic presentation of self-delimiting computers and their complexities; discusses complexity-theoretic characterization of random sequences.)
—— (1987a) *Algorithmic Information Theory*, Cambridge: Cambridge University Press. (The classic introduction to the subject.)
—— (1987b) *Information, Randomness and Incomple-*

teness: Papers on Algorithmic Information Theory, Singapore: World Scientific; 2nd edn, 1990. (An anthology of Chaitin's seminal papers.)

—— (1992) *Information-Theoretic Incompleteness*, Singapore: World Scientific. (An original and systematic examination of the incompleteness phenomenon from an information-theoretic point of view.)

* Church, A. (1940) 'On the Concept of a Random Sequence', *Bulletin of the American Mathematical Society* 46: 130–5. (Develops von Mises' ideas in the framework of computability theory.)

Gács, P. (1992) 'Every Sequence is Reducible to a Random One', *Information and Control* 70: 186–92. (A proof of the reducibility of any sequence to a random one.)

* Gödel, K. (1944) 'Russell's Mathematical Logic', in P.A. Schlipp (ed.) *The Philosophy of Bertrand Russell*, Evanston, IL: Northwestern University Press, 123–53; repr. in *Collected Works*, ed. S. Feferman *et al.*, Oxford: Oxford University Press, 1990, vol. 2, 119–41. (Source of the quote in §4.)

* Kolmogorov, A.N. (1965) 'Three Approaches for Defining the Concept of "Information Quantity"', *Problems in Information Transmission* 1: 3–11. (Expounds the considerations leading to the algorithmic definition of random strings.)

* Levin, L.A. (1974) 'Randomness Conservation Inequalities: Information and Independence in Mathematical Theories', *Problems in Information Transmission* 10: 206–10. (Discussion of self-delimiting computers and their complexities.)

Li, M. and Vitányi, P.M. (1993) *An Introduction to Kolmogorov Complexity and Its Applications*, Berlin: Springer. (A comprehensive treatise on descriptional complexities.)

* Martin-Löf, P. (1966) 'The Definition of Random Sequences', *Information and Control* 9: 602–19. (An important piece of work describing random sequences in the framework of constructive probability theory.)

* Mises, R. von (1928) *Wahrscheinlichkeit Statistik und Wahrheit*, Vienna: Springer; trans. *Probability, Statistics and Truth*, London: Allen & Unwin; 2nd revised edn prepared by H. Geiringer, New York: Macmillan, 1961. (Expounds the frequential analysis of randomness, as started by the author in his 1919 paper 'Grundlagen der Wahrscheinlichkeitsrechnung', *Mathematische Zeitschrift* 5: 52–99.)

Rozenberg, G. and Salomaa, A. (1994) *Cornerstones of Undecidability*, Englewood Cliffs, NJ: Prentice-Hall. (An enlightening presentation of undecidability and randomness.)

Schnorr, C.P. (1981) *Zufälligkeit und Wahrscheinlichkeit. Eine algorithmische Behandlung der Wahrscheinlichkeitstheorie* (Randomness and Probability: An Algorithmic Foundation of Probability Theory), Berlin: Springer. (The first monograph on algorithmic information theory.)

Shannon, C.E. and Weaver, C.E. (1949) *The Mathematical Theory of Communication*, Urbana, IL: University of Illinois Press. (The first and still one of the best books on classical information theory.)

* Solomonoff, R.J. (1964) 'A Formal Theory of Inductive Inference, Part 1 and Part 2', *Information and Control* 7: 1–22, 224–54. (The first paper dealing with descriptional complexity.)

Solovay, R.M. (1975) 'Draft of a paper (or series of papers) on Chaitin's work . . . done for the most part during the period of Sept.–Dec. 1974', unpublished manuscript, Yorktown Heights, NY: IBM Thomas J. Watson Research Center. (A highly technical and original presentation of Chaitin's results.)

* Svozil, K. (1993) *Randomness & Undecidability in Physics*, Singapore: World Scientific. (The first systematic presentation of algorithmic randomness in physics.)

* Ville, J. (1939) *Étude critique de la notion de collectif* (A Critical Study of the Notion of Collective), Paris: Gauthier-Villars. (Critical examination of von Mises' model of randomness.)

* Zurek, W.H. (1989) 'Algorithmic Randomness and Physical Entropy', *Physical Review A* 40: 4,731–51. (A detailed discussion of the relevance of information-theoretic complexity for physics.)

CRISTIAN S. CALUDE

COMPUTABILITY THEORY

The effective calculability of number-theoretic functions such as addition and multiplication has always been recognized, and for that judgment a rigorous notion of 'computable function' is not required. A sharp mathematical concept was defined only in the twentieth century, when issues including the decision problem for predicate logic required a precise delimitation of functions that can be viewed as effectively calculable. Predicate logic emerged from Frege's fundamental 'Begriffsschrift' (1879) as an expressive formal language and was described with mathematical precision by Hilbert in lectures given during the winter of 1917–18. The logical calculus Frege had also developed allowed proofs to proceed as computations in accordance with a fixed set of rules; in principle, according to Gödel, the rules could be applied 'by someone who knew nothing about mathematics, or by a machine'.

Hilbert grasped the potential of this mechanical aspect and formulated the decision problem for predicate logic as follows: 'The Entscheidungsproblem *[decision problem] is solved if one knows a procedure that permits the decision concerning the validity, respectively, satisfiability of a given logical expression by a finite number of operations.' Some, for example, von Neumann (1927), believed that the inherent freedom of mathematical thought provided a sufficient reason to expect a negative solution to the problem. But how could a proof of undecidability be given? The unsolvability results of other mathematical problems had always been established relative to a determinate class of admissible operations, for example, the impossibility of doubling the cube relative to ruler and compass constructions. A negative solution to the decision problem obviously required the characterization of 'effectively calculable functions'.*

For two other important issues a characterization of that informal notion was also needed, namely, the general formulation of the incompleteness theorems and the effective unsolvability of mathematical problems (for example, of Hilbert's tenth problem). The first task of computability theory was thus to answer the question 'What is a precise notion of "effectively calculable function"?'. Many different answers invariably characterized the same class of number-theoretic functions: the partial recursive ones. Today recursiveness or, equivalently, Turing computability is considered to be the precise mathematical counterpart to 'effective calculability'. Relative to these notions undecidability results have been established, in particular, the undecidability of the decision problem for predicate logic. The notions are idealized in the sense that no time or space limitations are imposed on the calculations; the concept of 'feasibility' is crucial in computer science when trying to capture the subclass of recursive functions whose values can actually be determined.

1 **Primitive recursive functions**
2 **Finite computations**
3 **Effective descriptions**
4 **Basic results**
5 **Undecidable problems**
6 **Physical steps**

1 Primitive recursive functions

Let us start with the class of 'primitive recursive' functions (from n-tuples of natural numbers to the natural numbers). A precise definition of this class was given by Gödel in 1931 (see van Heijenoort 1967), although he then called it simply the class of recursive functions. The main definitional schema of primitive recursion used in the generation of the elements of

this class was well-known in mathematics, having been presented most clearly by Dedekind (1888), who had given a set-theoretic reconstruction that turned out to be of importance also in computability theory. Skolem established in 1923 that most functions in elementary number theory are primitive recursive. The foundational significance of this function class was emphasized by Hilbert and Bernays (1934, 1939): the values of the functions (for any argument) can be determined in finitely many steps, proceeding purely 'mechanically'. This point is also expressed by saying that the functions are 'effectively calculable'.

The class $\mathcal{PR}$ of primitive recursive functions is specified inductively and contains as its initial functions the zero-function Z, the successor function S, and the projection functions P_i^n for each n and each i with $1 \leqslant i \leqslant n$. These functions satisfy the equations $Z(x) = 0$, $S(x) = x'$ and $P_i^n(x_1, \ldots, x_n) = x_i$, for all $x, x_1, \ldots, x_n$; x' is the 'successor' of x. The class is, first of all, closed under the 'schema of composition': given an m-place function ψ and n-place functions $\varphi_1, \ldots, \varphi_m$ all in $\mathcal{PR}$, the function ϕ defined by

$$\phi(x_1, \ldots, x_n) = \psi(\varphi_1(x_1, \ldots, x_n), \ldots, \varphi_m(x_1, \ldots, x_n))$$

is also in $\mathcal{PR}$; ϕ is then said to be obtained 'by composition' from ψ and $\varphi_1, \ldots, \varphi_m$. $\mathcal{PR}$ is also closed under the 'schema of primitive recursion': given an n-place function ψ and an $(n+2)$-place function φ both in $\mathcal{PR}$, the function ϕ defined by

$$\phi(x_1, \ldots, x_n, 0) = \psi(x_1, \ldots, x_n)$$
$$\phi(x_1, \ldots, x_n, y') = \varphi(x_1, \ldots, x_n, y, \phi(x_1, \ldots, x_n, y))$$

is also a function in $\mathcal{PR}$; ϕ is said to be obtained 'by primitive recursion' from ψ and φ. A function is 'primitive recursive' if and only if it can be obtained from the initial functions by finitely many applications of the composition and primitive recursion schemas.

The primitive recursive functions do not exhaust the class of effectively calculable functions; that was shown by Ackermann and independently by Gabriel Sudan, who constructed functions that are obviously effectively calculable, but not primitive recursive (see van Heijenoort 1967 for detailed references). The 'Ackermann function' can be defined by the following recursion equations.

$$\phi_0(x, y) = S(y)$$
$$\phi_{n'}(x, 0) = \begin{cases} x & \text{if } n = 0 \\ 0 & \text{if } n = 1 \\ 1 & \text{otherwise} \end{cases}$$
$$\phi_{n'}(x, y') = \phi_n(x, \phi_{n'}(x, y))$$

Notice that ϕ_1 is addition, ϕ_2 is multiplication, ϕ_3 is exponentiation, and so on; that is, the next function is always obtained by iterating the previous one. For each n, the function $\phi_n(x,x)$ is primitive recursive, but $\phi_x(x,x)$ is not!

We can construct another example of an effectively calculable, but not primitive recursive function ψ by effectively listing all primitive recursive unary functions $\varphi_0, \varphi_1, \varphi_2, \varphi_3, \ldots$ and then setting $\psi(x) = 1 + \varphi_x(x)$. Since ψ differs from every φ_i, ψ cannot be primitive recursive; but the effectiveness of our listing of the functions φ_i ensures that ψ can be effectively calculated.

For working with this class of functions it is indispensable to establish further closure properties. To allow, for example, directly general explicit definitions (without the cumbersome detour of projections) of functions such as

$$f(x,y,z) = (xy+z)^2 + 789,$$

one establishes that variables can be permuted, substitutions can be carried out, and that the constant functions $\mathrm{con}_m^n(x_1, \ldots, x_n) = m$ are primitive recursive. Beyond addition, multiplication and exponentiation it is useful to know that the following functions are also in $\mathcal{PR}$.

$x!$	(factorial)
$\mathrm{pred}(x)$	(predecessor)
$x \dot{-} y$	(arithmetic subtraction, $\max(0, x-y)$)
$\overline{\mathrm{sg}}(x)$	$(= 1 \dot{-} x)$
$\mathrm{sg}(x)$	$(= 1 \dot{-} \overline{\mathrm{sg}}(x))$

Then it is very easy to define the bounded sum of an $(n+1)$-place function ϕ in $\mathcal{PR}$ as follows.

$$\phi(x_1, \ldots, x_n, 0) = 0$$
$$\sum_{x < y'} \phi(x_1, \ldots, x_n, x) = \sum_{x < y} \phi(x_1, \ldots, x_n, x)$$
$$+ \phi(x_1, \ldots, x_n, y).$$

The bounded product is defined similarly.

The functions we listed are useful for the investigation of primitive recursive relations; an n-place relation R between natural numbers is called primitive recursive if and only if its characteristic function χ_R is in $\mathcal{PR}$. (For recursion-theoretic purposes it is convenient to consider 0 to be the truth-value T and 1 the truth-value F.) It is now possible to show directly that the primitive recursive relations are closed under Boolean operations – particularly, '$\neg$' (not), '$\&$' (and), '$\vee$' (or), '$\rightarrow$' (if...then) – and bounded quantification, that is, '$(\forall x < y)$' (for all x less than y) and '$(\exists x < y)$' (for some x less than y).

Finally, we discuss bounded minimization: if for some x less than y $R(x_1, \ldots, x_n, x)$, then the function $\mu x < y.R(x_1, \ldots, x_n, x)$ yields the smallest such x, otherwise the function yields y. Define first

$$\phi_1(x_1, \ldots, x_n, x) = \begin{cases} 0 & \text{if } (\exists z \leqslant x) R(x_1, \ldots, x_n, z) \\ 1 & \text{otherwise} \end{cases}$$

and notice that

$$\mu x < y.R(x_1, \ldots, x_n, x) = \sum_{x < y} \phi_1(x_1, \ldots, x_n, x).$$

Thus, if the relation R is primitive recursive, bounded minimization leads to a function in $\mathcal{PR}$.

Given this list of functions in $\mathcal{PR}$ and the closure conditions for primitive recursive relations, we have a convenient framework in which we can show the primitive recursiveness of number-theoretic relations; for example, the characteristic function $\chi_<$ of the 'less than' relation ' $<$ ' is given by

$$\chi_<(x,y) = \overline{\mathrm{sg}}(y \dot{-} x);$$

equality, being a divisor of, and being prime are all defined easily. This indicates that the class is mathematically rather rich.

2 Finite computations

In 1931 and in his Princeton lectures of 1934, Gödel used primitive recursive functions and relations to describe the syntax of particular 'formal' theories – after Gödel-numbering the syntactic configurations that make up the theory. Since he strove to arrive at a general concept of formality through the underlying concept of calculability for functions, there was no reason to focus attention on theories whose syntax could be presented primitive recursively. He viewed primitive recursive definability of formulas and proofs as a precise condition which *in practice* sufficed to describe formal systems, but he was searching for a condition that would suffice *in principle*.

In his Princeton lectures, Gödel considered it a very important property that the values of primitive recursive functions can be calculated by a finite computation for arbitrary arguments. He added in a footnote:

The converse seems to be true if, besides recursions according to the scheme (2) [of primitive recursion], recursions of other forms...are admitted. This cannot be proved, since the notion of finite computation is not defined, but it can serve as a heuristic principle.

(1934)

Parenthetically, we note that this remark does not contain a formulation of Church's thesis (see

CHURCH'S THESIS); that (prima facie plausible) reading was explicitly ruled out by Gödel in a letter to Martin Davis (1982). It does, however, indicate the motivation for the considerations in the last part of Gödel's lectures: there he used quite general forms of recursion to introduce 'general recursive functions'. (The relation of Gödel's proposal to suggestions of Herbrand is discussed in Sieg (1994).) These functions are obtained as unique solutions of a system E of equations, and their values must be computable in an equational calculus with just two obviously mechanical rules: the first rule allows the substitution of numerals for variables in any equation derived from E; the second rule allows the replacement of terms $t(v_1, \ldots, v_n)$ in a derived equation by μ, in case $t(v_1, \ldots, v_n) = \mu$ is a derived equation. (Lower-case Greek letters stand here for numerals.)

This class of general recursive functions very quickly turned out to be characterizable in a variety of ways: Church and Kleene showed the equivalence to λ-definability, Kleene to μ-recursiveness (discussed below), and Turing to computability by his machines (see LAMBDA CALCULUS; COMBINATORY LOGIC; TURING MACHINES). The class introduced by Gödel was used by Church in his first formulation of 'Church's thesis' (see Sieg 1997). The early, pre-Turing attempts to argue for the thesis are captured in a mathematically concise way through the concept of a function 'reckonable according to rules' (*regelrecht auswertbare Funktion*). These functions were introduced by Hilbert and Bernays in the second volume of their *Grundlagen der Mathematik* (1934, 1939); they were characterized as being calculable in deductive formalisms satisfying general recursiveness conditions; the critical condition required the proof predicate of the formalisms to be primitive recursive. It was shown that the calculations could be carried out in a particular subsystem of arithmetic; Gödel took this fact in 1946 as the basis for his claim that computability is an 'absolute' concept (see Sieg 1994). The analysis of Hilbert and Bernays also clearly revealed the 'stumbling block' all these analyses encountered: they tried to characterize the elementary nature of steps in calculations, but could not do so without referring to recursiveness (Church), primitive recursiveness (Hilbert and Bernays), or to very specific rules (Gödel).

Only Turing was able, in his ground-breaking 1936 paper 'On Computable Numbers' (see Davis 1965), to circumvent the stumbling block by focusing on the calculations of a human 'computor' proceeding mechanically (see TURING MACHINES §1). He formulated general boundedness and locality conditions for such a computor and showed that any number-theoretic function whose values can be calculated by a computor satisfying these conditions can actually be computed by a Turing machine (see Mundici and Sieg 1995). The latter fact is sometimes called 'Turing's theorem'. The restricted formulation of Turing machines allows a uniform and simple description of computations; its adequacy for linear computations is guaranteed by Turing's theorem. The starting point of Turing's analysis was, however, the mechanical behaviour of a human computor operating on finite configurations in the plane. This behaviour can be described generally and mathematically precisely. To arrive at such a more general description, we take a preliminary step and replace the states of mind by what Turing described as 'physical and definite counterparts'. This is done by considering 'state of mind' not as a property of the working computor, but rather as part of the configuration which is operated on. Turing discussed this replacement very vividly in his 1936 paper:

> It is always possible for the computer [in our terminology, the computor] to break off from his work, to go away and forget all about it, and later to come back and go on with it. If he does this he must leave a note of instructions (written in some standard form) explaining how the work is to be continued. This note is the counterpart of the 'state of mind'. We will suppose that the computer works in such a desultory manner that he never does more than one step at a sitting. The note of instructions must enable him to carry out one step and write the next note.

> ('On Computable Numbers', in Davis 1965)

This was achieved quite beautifully by Post in 1947, and Post's approach of describing Turing machine computations is used by Davis (1958). The configurations on which the machine works are instantaneous descriptions (IDs). These are finite sequences in the alphabet of a Turing machine containing exactly one state symbol; the position of the state symbol indicates which symbol is being scanned. A program of a Turing machine can now be viewed as a set of Post production rules operating on (a single symbol of) such IDs. If in this way of describing Turing machines one replaces finite sequences by finite graphs (with a few well-motivated properties) and the simple Post–Turing operations on one symbol at a time by operations on a fixed finite number of distinguished graphs, then one arrives at the notion of a 'Kolmogorov machine'. This latter notion, or rather a general concept of algorithm, was introduced by Kolmogorov and Uspensky (1958): Kolmogorov machines compute exactly the Turing computable number-theoretic functions.

Which number-theoretic functions can be computed by Turing machines or other computing devices? Kleene's analysis of the equational calculus led to the introduction of the 'regular minimization' operator and to an inductive characterization of Gödel's class of general recursive functions. Suppose the $(n+1)$-place function ϕ has the property that for every $x_1, \ldots, x_n$ there is a y such that $\phi(x_1, \ldots, x_n, y) = 0$. Denote by $\mu y . \phi(x_1, \ldots, x_n, y) = 0$ the least such y. Under these conditions, the function ψ given by

$$\psi(x_1, \ldots, x_n) = \mu y . \phi(x_1, \ldots, x_n, y) = 0$$

is said to be obtained from ϕ 'by regular minimization'. A function is '(μ-)recursive' if and only if it can be obtained from the initial functions by a finite number of applications of composition, primitive recursion and regular minimization. That is, the class $\mathcal{R}$ of recursive functions is obtained from $\mathcal{PR}$ by closure under regular minimization.

Up to now we have considered total (that is, everywhere defined) functions and operations that do not lead outside the class of total functions. Gödel (after Kleene) emphasized the importance of partial functions defined only for a subset of $\mathbb{N}$ or $\mathbb{N} \times \ldots \times \mathbb{N}$. For example, while $\mu y . xy = 0$ is an equivalent definition of the zero function, an expression such as $\mu y . x + y = 0$ is undefined for each $x > 0$. For partial functions ϕ we liberalize the regularity condition for minimization:

$$u = \mu y . \phi(x_1, \ldots, x_n, y) = 0$$

holds if and only if the following two conditions are satisfied:

(1) For any $i = 0, 1, \ldots, u-1$, $\phi(x_1, \ldots, x_n, i)$ is defined and different from 0;

(2) $\qquad \phi(x_1, \ldots, x_n, u) = 0$.

Given $x_1, \ldots, x_n$, at most one number u can satisfy both (1) and (2). If no such u exists then the n-tuple $(x_1, \ldots, x_n)$ is outside the domain of the function

$$\mu y . \phi(x_1, \ldots, x_n, y) = 0$$

or, stated differently, this function is undefined at $(x_1, \ldots, x_n)$. A function is 'partial recursive' if and only if it can be obtained from the initial functions by a finite number of applications of composition, primitive recursion and (unrestricted) minimization. Note that the partial recursive functions can be enumerated by a partial recursive function; that is obviously not possible in the case of total functions: a standard diagonal construction leads immediately to a contradiction. This fact (for partial recursive functions) and its significance are described in §3 and the beginning of §4.

One can explicitly construct Turing machines for the initial functions and for those operations on programs that correspond to composition, primitive recursion and regular, as well as unrestricted, minimization. Thus, these operations do not lead outside the class of Turing computable functions. This immediately yields the following theorem, showing the power of Turing machines: all partial recursive functions are Turing computable.

3 Effective descriptions

To prove the converse of the theorem just stated, we follow Pythagoras' ontological prescription and use Gödel's device to assign numbers e and y as 'codes' to Turing machines M and finite sequences of IDs. The coding introduced by Gödel for formal theories in 1931 (and adapted for Turing machines in Davis' book) will do. Once a machine is coded as a number, the code can be supplied as an input to any machine; this adumbrates the metamorphosis of hardware into software, culminating in the stored-program computer. Programming the first computers virtually amounted to inserting wires into plugboards, but von Neumann – influenced by Turing's treatment of his paper machines – realized that programs can be coded and stored as strings of symbols in the same way as data.

For any effective Gödel-numbering it is easy, though somewhat tedious, to establish that simple syntactic notions and operations concerning machines and their IDs can be represented by number-theoretic, indeed primitive recursive, predicates and functions. For instance, the ternary predicate $T(e, x, y)$ expressing that y is (the code of) a computation of Turing machine (M with code) e for input x is primitive recursive; also, the unary 'result-extracting' function U is primitive recursive, where $U(y)$ is either the number on the tape of the last ID of the computation y or, in case y is not the code of a computation, $U(y) = 0$. (Our choice of the default value 0 is only to guarantee that U is a total function.)

Given a Turing computable function ϕ and a machine M with code e computing ϕ, there are two possibilities for any input x:

Case 1. M terminates. Then there is a (first) computation y^* of M for input x, that is, y^* is the smallest number y such that $T(e, x, y)$; the number $U(y^*)$ read on the tape in the final configuration of y^* coincides with the value $\phi(x)$; writing $\mu y . T(e, x, y)$ as an abbreviation for $\mu y . \chi_T(e, x, y) = 0$, we have

(3) $\qquad \phi(x) = U(\mu y . T(e, x, y))$.

Case 2. M does not terminate. Then for any y, the predicate $T(e, x, y)$ will be false, that is, $\chi_T(e, x, y) = 1$ for all y, and condition (2) in the definition of the unrestricted μ-operator will never hold. Thus, both $\mu y . T(e, x, y)$ and $U(\mu y . T(e, x, y))$ are undefined.

This establishes (3) for both cases, and we have proved 'Kleene's normal form theorem' for unary Turing computable functions:

Let φ be an n-place number-theoretic function that can be computed by a Turing machine with code e; then for each $x_1, \ldots, x_n$ in the domain of φ we have

$$\varphi(x_1, \ldots, x_n) = U(\mu y . T(e, x_1, \ldots, x_n, y)).$$

Kleene's theorem holds also, with the same proof, for functions having any finite number of arguments. Kleene established this normal form theorem not for Turing computable functions, but for total functions that can be calculated in Gödel's equational calculus. He concluded that Gödel's general recursive functions are recursive, a conclusion we can draw now for Turing computable partial functions: every Turing computable function is partial recursive.

Using the theorem formulated at the very end of §2, it follows that Turing computability for number-theoretic functions is equivalent to partial recursiveness and, indeed, to all the other characterizations discussed in that section. Kleene's theorem has most interesting additional consequences, to be discussed in the next section. This is done not just to present elegant mathematical results, but to reinforce the conceptual analysis, as these results (are taken by some to) lend additional support to Church's thesis (see CHURCH'S THESIS).

4 Basic results

Kleene's normal form theorem has important consequences for the theory of computability. Consider, first of all, the two-place function

$$\psi(e, x) = U(\mu y . T(e, x, y));$$

ψ is partial recursive and provides an enumeration of all unary partial recursive functions. This is 'Kleene's enumeration theorem'. This theorem – together with the equivalence of partial recursiveness and Turing computability – guarantees the existence of a 'universal' Turing machine. Indeed, consider a Turing machine $M[\psi]$ computing ψ. For any pair of arguments e and x, $M[\psi]$ interprets its first argument as the code of a Turing machine $M[\varphi]$ (computing a unary partial recursive function φ) and its second argument as the input for $M[\varphi]$. Then $M[\psi]$ proceeds to compute $\varphi(x)$ following the program of $M[\varphi]$. Since $M[\varphi]$ was arbitrary, $M[\psi]$ is able to simulate any Turing machine. Similarly, for each $n = 2, 3, 4, \ldots$, there is a partial recursive $(n+1)$-place function $\psi^{(n)}$

such that every n-place partial recursive function φ can be written as

$$\varphi(x_1, \ldots, x_n) = \psi^{(n)}(e, x_1, \ldots, x_n)$$

for a suitable index e for φ.

Given a function $\varphi(p_1, \ldots, p_m, x_1, \ldots, x_n)$ of $m+n$ variables, let us 'parametrize' φ, that is, assign values $p_1^*, \ldots, p_m^*$ to the first m variables. We then obtain a new n-place function ϕ as follows:

$$\phi(x_1, \ldots, x_n) = \varphi(p_1^*, \ldots, p_m^*, x_1, \ldots, x_n).$$

Intuitively, ϕ is the 'slice' of φ with coordinates $(p_1^*, \ldots, p_m^*)$. By Kleene's enumeration theorem we can write, for suitable indices e and e^*:

$$\varphi(p_1, \ldots, p_m, x_1, \ldots, x_n) = \\ \psi^{(m+n)}(e, p_1, \ldots, p_m, x_1, \ldots, x_n)$$

and

$$\phi(x_1, \ldots, x_n) = \psi^{(n)}(e^*, x_1, \ldots, x_n).$$

The following 'parameter (or S_n^m-) theorem' tells us that the slicing operation leading from e to e^* can be performed uniformly and effectively:

For each $m, n > 0$ there is a primitive recursive $(n+1)$-place function S_n^m such that

$$\psi^{(m+n)}(e, p_1, \ldots, p_m, x_1, \ldots, x_n) \\ = \psi^{(m)}(S_n^m(e, p_1, \ldots, p_m), x_1, \ldots, x_n).$$

This theorem was established by Kleene at first for Gödel's general recursive functions; it amounts in that context to replacing effectively the first m variables of the function φ computed from equations with code e by numerals for $p_1, \ldots, p_m$. This theorem is used to prove the following central result, also due to Kleene, the 'recursion theorem':

Let ϕ be a partial recursive function with $(n+1)$ places. Then there is a number e such that for all $x_1, \ldots, x_n$

$$\psi^{(n)}(e, x_1, \ldots, x_n) = \phi(e, x_1, \ldots, x_n).$$

The theorem finds many uses in establishing that implicitly defined functions are actually partial recursive. For example, letting $n = 1$ and writing ψ instead of $\psi^{(1)}$, an application of the recursion theorem to the function $g(y, x) = y$ immediately yields the 'fixed point theorem':

There is a constant e^* such that for all x

$$\psi(e^*, x) = e^*.$$

Intuitively, for every possible input x, the program with number e^* uses x to output a copy of itself – just like a self-replicating organism. More generally, for every recursive function $r(z)$, we obtain by applying the recursion theorem to the function $\psi(r(z), x)$ a number e such that for all x, $\psi(e, x) = \psi(r(e), x)$.

Kleene's enumeration theorem allows us to reformulate properties of partial recursive functions as number-theoretic properties of their codes. A set P of natural numbers is called an 'input-output property' (of unary partial recursive functions) if and only if, whenever e' is in P and e'' codes the same function as e' (in the sense that $\psi(e', x) = \psi(e'', x)$ for all x in their common domain), then e'' is also in P. The following theorem, 'Rice's theorem', states that non-trivial input-output properties are not recursive: if P is an input-output property such that neither it nor its complement is empty, then P is not recursive.

There are important non-trivial input-output properties of programs. For instance, the set of codes of Turing machines computing total functions is one such property; as a consequence of Rice's theorem we know that there is no Turing machine that decides whether or not a given Turing computable function is total. We will discuss additional undecidable problems in the next section; however, undecidability will be established there in quite different ways.

5 Undecidable problems

'Problems' are identified with (characteristic functions of) one-place predicates or, equivalently, with subsets of $\mathbb{N}$. Let K be the problem corresponding to the question 'Does the computation of machine M with code e terminate, if the input is the natural number e?'. This problem was formulated by Turing and is known as the 'halting problem' (see TURING MACHINES §3). A diagonal argument (using the existence of a universal machine) settles the undecidability of K without resorting to Rice's theorem.

The halting problem is the progenitor of a multitude of undecidable problems, arising in virtually all fields of mathematics. Consider, for instance, the following problem. Let there be a presentation P of a group G via generators and relations (P looks like a multiplication table for G) and two expressions v and w built up from these generators, using the multiplication operation and its inverse. Do v and w represent the same element of G? This is known as the 'word problem for groups'. Novikov and, independently, Boone proved that the problem is undecidable.

Markov proved the undecidability of the following problem for four-dimensional manifolds. Consider a suitable combinatorial description of two manifolds. Are they homeomorphic? In the two-dimensional case the problem becomes decidable; it is not known whether the three-dimensional problem is decidable or not.

Yet another logic-free undecidable problem is given by elementary functions, that is, those functions f of a real variable x which can be built up using exponentials, logarithms, nth roots, trigonometric functions and their inverses by addition, multiplication, and composition. While the derivative operation does not lead outside the realm of elementary functions, the integral of, say, $(\sin x)/x$ is not elementary. Indeed, Richardson proved that the following problem is undecidable: is the integral of an elementary function elementary?

Finally, the tenth problem in Hilbert's list presented at the International Congress of Mathematicians in 1900 asks for an algorithm to decide of a Diophantine equation – that is, a polynomial equation $p(x_1, \ldots, x_n) = 0$, with integer coefficients – whether or not it has integer solutions (see Hilbert 1900). Following important work by J. Robinson, Davis and Putnam, Matijasevic proved in 1970 that this problem is undecidable (see Matijasevic 1993).

Let us go back to the halting problem, K. Recalling the discussion in §3, it is clear that the predicate $K(e)$ can be defined by the statement 'There exists a y, such that $T(e, e, y)$'. K is thus an example of a 'recursively enumerable' (RE) set of natural numbers: it can be defined by prefixing one existential quantifier to a decidable binary predicate. Trying for each n in $\mathbb{N}$ all possible pairs (e, y) such that $e + y = n$ and singling out e whenever $T(e, e, y)$ is true, we can effectively list all members of K. Recursively enumerable sets were named because of the following equivalent characterization: a subset of $\mathbb{N}$ is RE if and only if it is either empty or the range of a (primitive) recursive function. Furthermore, a set R is recursive if and only if both R and its complement are RE. This latter fact allows a different route into computability theory: recursive enumerability is taken as the basic concept, and recursive sets are defined as those RE sets whose complements are also RE; this is done in Post's approach.

The importance of K among RE sets stems from its being 'complete', that is, maximally difficult among all RE sets; by this we mean that every RE set can be effectively reduced to K. A problem P is effectively reducible to Q if and only if there is a recursive function f such that for all natural numbers x, $x \in P$ if and only if $f(x) \in Q$. Thus, if we want to see that x is a solution of problem P we compute $f(x)$ and test whether $f(x)$ solves Q! Clearly, Q is at least as difficult as P, in the sense that effective solutions for Q yield effective solutions for P. By effectively reducing the halting problem K to the *Entscheidungsproblem* (decision problem) E, Turing concluded from the undecidability of K that also E cannot be decidable. Turing's reduction is nothing but a transcription of the ternary predicate $T(e,e,y)$ into a first-order arithmetical theory with sufficient demonstrative power.

The halting problem K, the most complex among RE problems, is the simplest in an infinite sequence of manifestly undecidable problems, the so-called 'jumps'. In order to obtain the jump hierarchy, the concept of computation is relativized to sets of natural numbers whose membership relations are revealed by 'oracles'. The jump K' of K, for example, is defined as the halting problem, when an oracle for K is available. This hierarchy can be associated in a most informative way with definability questions in the language of arithmetic: all jumps can be defined by increasingly complex arithmetical formulas, and all arithmetically definable sets are reducible to some jump. The above construction underlies the arithmetic hierarchy introduced by Kleene and Mostowski in the fifties.

Certain interesting sets of natural numbers are not definable by arithmetic formulas; one example is the set of all Gödel numbers of true arithmetic statements. If this set were arithmetically definable, one could formulate arithmetically the liar sentence that expresses its own falsity. This observation of Gödel and Tarski (see GÖDEL'S THEOREMS) is the cornerstone for proving the incompleteness of every formal theory of arithmetic that contains symbols for addition and multiplication and has semantically sound axioms and rules of inference: no matter which (true) statements we choose as axioms, and no matter which inference rules we adopt (provided they are truth-preserving) there are statements which, albeit true for the natural numbers, are not provable in the theory. Arithmetic truth can be defined, however, in second-order languages that allow quantification over functions.

6 Physical steps

Turing appealed in his analysis of mechanical calculability to the limitations of the human sensory apparatus; he claimed that the justification for his thesis lies ultimately 'in the fact that the human memory is necessarily limited'. This remark is not expanded on at all, and we can only speculate as to Turing's understanding of this 'fact': did he have in mind more than the spatial limitations for 'encoding' finite configurations? If not, the restrictions can be motivated by physical considerations. The question of whether there are ways of getting around the effect of such physical limitations is discussed with references to the literature by Mundici and Sieg (1995); and Mundici (1981).

Assume that a Kolmogorov machine operates on configurations containing z different symbols, each symbol being physically 'coded' by at least one atom – an altogether reasonable assumption. Then there must be at least z pairwise disjoint regions containing the codes (of the symbols). Otherwise, the electron clouds of two different codes might overlap, making the codes indistinguishable. Let c and a denote the speed of light and Bohr's radius of the hydrogen atom, respectively, so that $a/c = 0.176 \times 10^{-18}$ seconds. It follows that the codes will be contained in a volume of at least $z(4/3)\pi a^3$ cubic metres; that forces the diameter of the machine to be larger than $2az^{\frac{1}{3}}$ metres – the diameter being the largest possible distance between two codes in this volume. Let f be the frequency of our machine; thus, $1/f$ is the time available for each computation step. Since signals cannot travel faster than light and since a computation step involves the whole configuration, it follows that f cannot exceed $c/(2az^{\frac{1}{3}})$ steps per second. Thus, we obtain the inequality

$$fz^{\frac{1}{3}} < 2.828 \times 10^{18} \text{ steps per second,}$$

which points out a fundamental incompatibility between high number of codes (that is, size of configurations) and high computational speed. The operations of Kolmogorov machines are thus restricted in complexity, as they have to lead from distinguished graphs to distinguished graphs; and within the given physical boundaries only finitely many different graphs are realizable.

If we focus on physical devices and analyse machine, not human mechanical, computability we have to take into account the possibility of parallel procedures as incorporated, for example, in cellular automata. Gandy (1980) provided the first conceptual analysis and a general description of parallel algorithms. These algorithms are thought to be carried out by 'discrete deterministic mechanical devices', that is, machines satisfying the physical assumptions explicit in our discussion above; in Gandy's words,

> The only physical assumptions made about mechanical devices... are that there is a lower bound on the linear dimensions of every atomic part of the device and that there is an upper bound (the velocity of light) on the speed of propagation of changes.
>
> (1980: 126)

He formulated axiomatic principles for these devices and proved that whatever can be calculated by devices satisfying the principles ('Gandy machines') is also computable by a Turing machine.

See also: LOGICAL AND MATHEMATICAL TERMS, GLOSSARY OF

References and further reading

All the classic papers referred to in this entry have been reprinted in either van Heijenoort (1967) or Davis (1965); careful discussions of the history of the subject are given by Gandy in Herken (1988) and by Sieg (1994).

Cutland, N. (1980) *Computability – An Introduction to Recursive Function Theory*, Cambridge: Cambridge University Press. (An informative introduction to basic results.)

* Davis, M. (1958) *Computability and Unsolvability*, New York: McGraw-Hill; repr. New York: Dover, 1982. (A classic, detailed presentation of the basic parts of computability theory.)

* —— (ed.) (1965) *The Undecidable: Basic Papers on Undecidable Propositions, Unsolvable Problems and Computable Functions*, Hewlett, NY: Raven Press. (Anthology of the fundamental papers on the subject by Gödel, Church, Turing, Kleene, Rosser and Post.)

* —— (1982) 'Why Gödel Didn't Have Church's Thesis', *Information and Control* 54: 3–24. (Provides fascinating historical information on the developments in Princeton in 1933 to 1936.)

* Dedekind, R. (1888) *Was sind und was sollen die Zahlen?*, Braunschweig: Vieweg; repr. in *Gesammelte mathematische Werke* (Collected Mathematical Works), ed. R. Fricke, E. Noether and Ö. Ore, Braunschweig: Vieweg, 1932, vol. 3, 335–90; trans. W.W. Beman (1901), 'The Nature and Meaning of Numbers', in *Essays on the Theory of Numbers*, New York: Dover, 1963; trans. *What are Numbers and What Should They Be?*, Orono, ME: Research Institute for Mathematics, 1995. (*The* 'modern' set-theoretic foundation of number theory.)

* Frege, G. (1879) *Begriffsschrift, eine der arithmetischen nachgebildete Formelsprache des reinen Denkens*, Halle: Nebert; trans. '*Begriffsschrift*, a Formula Language, Modelled Upon That of Arithmetic, for Pure Thought', in J. van Heijenoort (ed.) *From Frege to Gödel: A Source Book in Mathematical Logic, 1879–1931*, Cambridge, MA: Harvard University Press, 1967, 1–82. (This small booklet includes the most significant step from Aristotelian to modern logic.)

* Gandy, R. (1980) 'Church's Thesis and Principles for Mechanisms', in J. Barwise, H.J. Keisler and K. Kunen (eds) *The Kleene Symposium*, Amsterdam: North Holland, 123–45. (Axiomatic characterization of machine, not human mechanical, computability including parallel computations.)

* Gödel, K. (1934) Notes of Princeton Lectures, in *Collected Works*, ed. S. Feferman *et al.*, vol. 1, *Publications 1929–1936*, New York and Oxford: Oxford University Press, 1986. (Quoted in §2. German originals and English translations.)

* Heijenoort, J. van (ed.) (1967) *From Frege to Gödel: A Source Book in Mathematical Logic, 1879–1931*, Cambridge, MA: Harvard University Press. (Anthology of fundamental papers in logic starting with Frege's *Begriffsschrift* (1879) and ending with Gödel and Herbrand.)

* Herken, R. (ed.) (1988) *The Universal Turing Machine: A Half-Century Survey*, Oxford: Oxford University Press. (This book includes informed, systematic, enlightening, historical and provocative essays by, among others, Kleene, Gandy, Davis, Feferman and Penrose.)

* Hilbert, D. (1900) 'Mathematische Probleme. Vortrag, gehalten auf dem internationalen Mathematiker-Kongress zu Paris 1900', *Nachrichten von der königlichen Gesellschaft der Wissenschaften zu Göttingen. Geschäftliche Mitteilungen* 253–97; repr. in *Archiv der Mathematik und Physik* 1: 44–63, 213–37, 1901; trans. 'Mathematical Problems', *Bulletin of the American Mathematical Society* 8: 437– 79, 1902. (The most influential list of open mathematical problems in the twentieth century.)

* Hilbert, D. and Bernays, P. (1934, 1939) *Grundlagen der Mathematik* (Foundations of Mathematics), Berlin: Springer, 2 vols; 2nd edn, 1968, 1970. (A most comprehensive presentation of the work in proof theory done in the Hilbert school and of related developments; for example, volume 2 includes the first detailed proof of Gödel's second incompleteness theorem.)

* Kolmogorov, A.N. and Uspensky, V.A. (1958) 'On the Definition of an Algorithm', trans. in *American Mathematical Society Translations* 2 (21): 217–45, 1963. (This paper gives a very interesting analysis of 'algorithms'.)

* Matijasevic, Y.V. (1993) *Hilbert's Tenth Problem*, Cambridge, MA: MIT Press. (A beautiful and thorough presentation of the solution to Hilbert's tenth problem, originally solved by Matijasevic in a paper of 1970, 'Enumerable Sets are Diophantine'.)

* Mundici, D. (1981) 'Irreversibility, Uncertainty, Relativity and Computer Limitations', *Il Nuovo Cimento, Europhysics Journal* 61 B (2): 297–305. (Discusses physical limitations of computer steps, arising from relativity and quantum mechanical principles, such as Pauli indistinguishability.)

* Mundici, D. and Sieg, W. (1995) 'Paper Machines', *Philosophia Mathematica* 3: 5–30. (A nontechnical essay on the development of the main ideas of computability, also covering physical computation.)

* Neumann, J. von (1927) 'Zur Hilbertschen Beweistheorie' (On Hilbert's Proof Theory), *Mathematische*

Zeitschrift 26. (This paper includes the central contribution of von Neumann to the development of proof theory: he proves the consistency of a fragment of number theory.)

Odifreddi, P. (1992) *Classical Recursion Theory*, Amsterdam: North Holland, 2 vols. (A comprehensive modern treatise on computability theory.)

Rogers, H. (1967) *Theory of Recursive Functions and Effective Computability*, New York: McGraw-Hill. (The standard reference on recursion theory before Odifreddi (1992) and Soare (1987).)

* Sieg, W. (1994) 'Mechanical Procedures and Mathematical Experience', in A. George (ed.) *Mathematics and Mind*, Oxford: Oxford University Press, 71–117. (Examination of the conceptual analyses underlying computability theory, in particular in Turing's fundamental paper; presents the historical development in detail and emphasizes connections to investigations in the foundations of mathematics.)

* —— (1997) 'Step by Recursive Step: Church's Analysis of Effective Calculability', *Bulletin of Symbolic Logic*. (Describes in detail the approach Church took to the conceptual issues underlying his work on computability and undecidability. New historical material is taken into account to complement (and correct) the discussion in Davis (1982).)

Soare, R.I. (1987) *Recursively Enumerable Sets and Degrees*, Berlin and New York: Springer. (Brings the reader to the frontiers of research on computable functions, featuring Post's problem, oracles, priority methods and lattices of RE sets.)

DANIELE MUNDICI
WILFRIED SIEG

COMPUTATIONAL COMPLEXITY *see* COMPLEXITY, COMPUTATIONAL

COMPUTATIONAL THEORIES OF MIND *see* MIND, COMPUTATIONAL THEORIES OF

COMPUTER SCIENCE

At first sight, computers would seem to be of minimal philosophical importance; mere symbol manipulators that do the sort of things that we can do anyway, only faster and more conveniently. Nevertheless, computers are being used to illuminate the cognitive abilities of the human and animal mind, explore the organizational principles of life, and open up new approaches to modelling nature. Furthermore, the study of computation has changed our conception of the limits and methodology of scientific knowledge.

Computers have been able to do all this for two reasons. The first is that material computing power (accuracy, storage and speed) permits the development and exploration of models of physical (and mental) systems that combine structural complexity with mathematical intransigence. Through simulation, computational power allows exploration where mathematical analysis falters. The second reason is that a computer is not merely a concrete device, but also can be studied as an abstract object whose rules of operation can be specified with mathematical precision; consequently, its strengths and limitations can be systematically investigated, exploited and appreciated. Herein lies that area of computer science of most interest to philosophers: the theory of computation and algorithms. It is here where we have learned what computers can and cannot do in principle.

1 Turing machines and computability
2 The Church–Turing thesis
3 The Halting problem
4 Problems that are computationally intractable

1 Turing machines and computability

In his classic paper 'On Computable Numbers, with an Application to the *Entscheidungsproblem*' (1936) Alan TURING investigated the problem of characterizing the computable real numbers. The real numbers are those numbers that correspond to the points on a straight line: the positive and negative integers, the fractions or rational numbers, and finally, the irrational numbers, such as π and the square root of 2. Whereas the values of the integers and fractions can be specified using a finite set of symbols and computed exactly, the same is not true for the irrationals. Some of the irrationals like π or the square root of 2 can be computed to as many decimal places as we like; other irrationals, however, cannot be computed at all. Intuitively, the difference between the two kinds of numbers lies in the fact that the former can be determined to arbitrarily high degrees of precision, in Turing's words, 'using finite means', whereas to obtain an arbitrarily precise value of the latter sort of number would require infinite means.

Turing proceeds to give a precise account of what it means to compute 'using finite means'. Imagine a machine that at any given time is in one of a finite number of states $Q = \{q_0, q_1, \ldots, q_i\}$. At the same time, the machine is scanning a square of a finite but extendible tape on which is printed one of a finite number of symbols $S = \{s_0, s_1, \ldots, s_k\}$. The machine is capable of doing just three things. First, it writes a symbol on the square (possibly the same symbol that it is scanning). Next, it moves one square to the left or one square to the right. And finally, it enters a (possibly) new state. The key idea is that what the machine does is determined only by its current state and the symbol currently being scanned. Exactly what the machine is to do in a given situation is specified by a rule which is stated in the form of a 'quintuple' such as the following:

$$q_2 * \# R q_3,$$

which may be read, 'if in state q_2 and scanning the symbol *, then write the symbol #, go to the right and enter state q_3'. A Turing machine is formally defined as a set of such instructions, subject to the proviso that no two quintuples begin with the same two items. (This ensures that there is no ambiguity as to what the machine is to do when in a certain internal state and scanning a given symbol.) Often, the state q_0 is designated as the starting state of the machine, and the symbol s_0 is considered to be the 'blank' symbol B. A Turing machine halts when it is in a certain internal state q_i, scanning a symbol s_i, and there is no quintuple beginning with $q_i s_i$. (What to do, what to do...?) Using these conventions, and assuming that the machine is started on the right-most symbol of a finite string of 1s, then the machine described by the quintuples:

$$q_0 \, 1 \, 1 \, L \, q_0$$

$$q_0 \, B \, 1 \, L \, q_1$$

will (as the reader can verify easily) move to the left leaving all of the 1s intact until it finds the first blank ('B') which it will then replace by a 1, move one more square to the left, and then halt (see TURING MACHINES).

Let us call the symbols $S^* = \{s_1, s_2, \ldots, s_k\}$ the (proper) *alphabet* of the Turing machine. (Notice that the 'blank' symbol q_0 is hereby excluded.) The *words* of this alphabet are now defined as the set of all the finite strings of the members of the alphabet. A function on this alphabet is simply a map that takes any word to a unique word; that is, a map from the set *words* to itself. (For simplicity's sake, only functions taking a single argument will be considered here.) Such a function is said to be *Turing computable* just in case there is a Turing machine M which, when started on the right-most letter of a word, eventually halts leaving on its tape the string that is the function's value on the original word. Roughly, a Turing computable function is a function that can be computed by some Turing machine.

Of all the functions on an alphabet, how many are Turing computable? With the aid of Cantor's theory of infinite sets (see CANTOR'S THEOREM), we can answer this question fairly easily. Basically, since a Turing machine is determined by (and can thus be regarded as defined by) a finite set of quintuples, Turing machines can (in principle) be ordered 'alphabetically'. So there are only a countable infinity of Turing machines and hence at most a countable infinity of Turing computable functions (since each Turing computable function requires at least one Turing machine to compute it). But there are an uncountable infinite number of functions from (any) set of words to itself. Hence, although there are an infinite number of Turing computable functions, there are an uncountable number of functions that are not Turing computable. So to the question, 'of all the functions from words to words, how many are computable?', the answer is 'a countable infinity, that is, almost none of them'. Later, we shall examine an interesting function – the Halting function – that is not computable.

Although we have considered functions from and to the words of any finite alphabet of symbols, the same results may be obtained by confining our attention to functions from the set N of natural numbers $0, 1, 2, \ldots$, to itself. To see this, think of the symbols $S^* = \{s_1, s_2, \ldots, s_i\}$ as the digits $\{0, 1, \ldots, i-1\}$. Then, corresponding to a finite string of letters in S^*, we have a string of digits, which can then be regarded as representing a natural number using base i. In this way, the words of S^* become mapped to numbers in N, and functions from *words* to *words* become functions from N to N. This allows us to restrict our attention to the Turing computable functions from N to N without any important loss of generality.

2 The Church–Turing thesis

In work carried out prior to Turing's 1936 paper (presented to the American Mathematical Society in 1935), Alonzo CHURCH (1936) had defined a class of computable functions from the set $N = \{0, 1, 2, \ldots\}$ of natural numbers to itself which he called the 'recursive' functions. The recursive functions are defined, roughly, as those that can be obtained from a few basic computable functions (in the sense that we have algorithms for them) by applying 'computable' operations such as functional composition or recursion. For example, one of the basic functions is the *successor* function which takes a number n to $n+1$. Another is multiplication. Composing these two functions we obtain $(n+1)m$. Church's basic functions, Turing showed, were Turing computable, and the operations for their combination could also be mimicked by Turing machines. For example, the function $mn+1$ can be computed by a Turing machine that chains together the Turing machines that compute mn and $n+1$. In this way, Turing showed that the recursive functions are all Turing computable. In addition, he also proved the converse: any Turing computable function from N to N is recursive. As a result, the Turing computable functions and the recursive functions are identical (Boolos and Jeffrey 1982, chs 7 and 8).

In his 1936 paper, Church had conjectured that the recursive functions were just the computable functions from and to the natural numbers N. In his paper of the same year, Turing also conjectured that the functions computable by his machines were also just the computable functions. Since the two sets of functions are identical, these conjectures have since been joined and are known as the *Church–Turing thesis*, namely,

> Any computable function from N to N is recursive, that is, Turing computable

(see also CHURCH'S THESIS). Let us see what reasons there are for holding this thesis to be correct.

First of all, notice that in the above statement of the thesis, the first occurrence of the term 'computable' has not been given a precise definition. The intuitive idea is that a function is computable if we can calculate its output using means that are of the same sort that we use to do calculations in arithmetic. But what, exactly, are these 'means'? We have examples galore, but no precise general account of what sort of procedures these examples embody. We could, of course, simply take Church's recursive functions or Turing's machine to *define* just those procedures. But in that case, the Church–Turing thesis becomes a tautology.

So let us stick with 'computable' as a pre-analytic term and see where that gets us. Consider the following example. Suppose that we consider a new kind of machine model, very much like a Turing machine, except that instead of a one-dimensional tape, the new machine operates on a 'board' of two dimensions, a potentially infinite checkerboard. Such a *2D Turing machine*, as I shall call it, will have quintuples just like a Turing machine, except that the move instructions R, L are expanded to eight possibilities: N, S, E, W, NE, NW, SE, and SW. Imagine that we now write out a set of quintuples and proceed to use them in the same way that we previously used a Turing machine – say, to determine what results from putting the string !#* down on the board and starting at the eastmost symbol (*). Clearly, if we could show that such a machine would stop when provided with any such input, then we would agree that a function was thereby *computed* by this 2D Turing machine. In short, the same intuitions which assure us that any function which is Turing computable is *computable* in the ordinary sense – the uncontested converse of the Church–Turing thesis – also work here to yield the conviction that any function that is 2D Turing machine computable is *computable*. But if this be granted, it can now be seen that there is – at least in principle – a way to show the *falsity* of the Church–Turing thesis: produce a machine model, such as a 2D Turing machine, that clearly *computes*, and then prove that there are some functions that *it* can compute that a standard Turing machine cannot.

In this spirit (and perhaps just for the fun of it), there has been a great deal of work on developing alternative models of computation. The 2D Turing machine model given above, along with its n-dimensional counterparts, can be shown to be no more powerful than a standard linear tape machine. Adding finitely many tapes with their own read/write heads does not help either: any function computable by these enhanced machines can be proven to be computable (perhaps more slowly) by a lowly standard Turing machine. Other models that are not simple variations of Turing machines have also been explored, such as abacus or register machines, post systems and generalized digital computers. While these alternative models might usefully focus on one or more features of computation systems, they all are incapable of computing a function that cannot likewise be computed by a 'plain vanilla' Turing machine. As a result, although there is no way of proving the Church–Turing thesis to be correct, it is widely held to be so.

The Turing machines that we have considered so far have all been dedicated to some particular computational task. A *universal Turing machine* (UTM) would be capable of computing anything that a Turing machine can. In his 1936 paper, Turing showed how to construct machines of this type, and, roughly, here is how they work. A section of the tape of a UTM is set aside (perhaps surrounded by *s or some other symbol in its alphabet reserved for this purpose) for the program that the machine is to execute. This program will be another Turing

493

machine's quintuples (probably suitably encoded). A suitable input is now provided in some input area of the tape, and the UTM passes back and forth from the program and input areas to the work area, performing the computation in accord with the program on its tape. When one considers that much the same sort of activity is precisely what undergraduates do when, in a purely mechanical way, they work out on paper the behaviour of a Turing machine provided by the instructor, then the existence of a universal Turing machine should not come as much of a surprise. What is more remarkable is that such a machine is described in some detail in Turing's 1936 paper. Later work has produced some very concise UTMs, such as Marvin Minsky's, which uses only four symbols and seven states (Minsky 1967: §14.8.). Turing's basic idea – put the program on the tape (in the temporary memory, RAM) of a universal computer – was later taken up by von Neumann, and became one of the pillars of current digital computer architecture.

3 The Halting problem

As we have already seen, 'most' functions from N to N are not computable. Let us now look at a particular function that bears this affliction, the Halting function. Given a particular Turing machine or more generally, a particular program, it would be useful to be able to know whether that program will halt when provided with a given input. Of course, in some cases, the answer is obvious. The problem here is to find a general method, another program, that can compute the answer to the halting problem for *any* given input program and its input. Putting the matter in terms of Turing machines: is there a Turing machine that, when provided with a (suitably encoded version of a) program on its tape, together with an input to that program, will output, say, a '1' if the program will halt on that input and a '0' otherwise. (It is assumed here that, after delivering its verdict, the Halter machine itself then halts.)

It turns out that no such Turing machine exists. This result is sometimes referred to as the undecidability of the Halting problem. One reason this is so important is that it is the basis of showing that a number of other such problems are undecidable (by reducing them to the Halting problem); another reason is that it shows that there is a strong connection between the failure of computability and a wide class of unsolved problems in number theory. For example, in 1742 Goldbach conjectured that every even number (greater than 2) can be expressed as the sum of two prime numbers; to this day, his conjecture has been neither proven nor disproven.

Now it is a simple matter to write a program that will check an even number to see if it is expressible as the sum of two primes, and do this for successively greater even numbers. If such a program were to find an even number not equal to the sum of two primes, then it could be designed to halt and print out some message like 'Goldbach has been refuted!'. On the other hand, if Goldbach was right, then the program will go on checking even numbers indefinitely, and thus never halt. If the Halting problem were decidable, then such problems – and there are a great many such problems – could (in principle, at least) be settled according to the Leibnizian saying: 'Let us compute!' (For a survey of results on uncomputable functions, see Harel 1992, ch. 8.)

4 Problems that are computationally intractable

Even when we consider only computable functions, there are some problems whose solutions will probably forever remain beyond our reach. A classic example is the travelling salesperson problem. Imagine a set of N towns laid out on a map, together with the various roads connecting these towns. The length of each road is given. The problem now is to find the shortest itinerary for the salesperson to take which starts at a given town, returns to that town at the finish, and visits every other town exactly once. Clearly, the solution is computable: enumerate each of the possible paths, computing and recording its length along the way, and return as the answer the path requiring the minimum total distance. The problem is that the number of steps required to execute this algorithm goes up drastically as the number of towns involved gets larger. Thus, for 100 towns, the number of steps required by the best current programs is greater than 2^{100}, a very large number. (Assuming our algorithm executes one million steps per second, such an algorithm would require over 10^{16} years to complete its task; the accepted upper limit on the age of the universe is, however, only around 15 billion, that is, 15×10^9 years.)

The travelling salesperson problem is only one of a wide class of problems, called *NP complete* problems, that require, as far as we know, solutions on the order of 2^N steps. (The reason that *NP* complete problems are so-called may be found in Harel 1992, ch. 7.) If any one of the problems in this class could be shown to be solvable by an algorithm that was, say, linear in N or polynomial in N, then the same would be true for all the problems in this class. While it is widely believed that the *NP* complete problems require algorithms that work in exponential time, this has not yet been proven, and remains one of the most difficult unsolved problems in the theory of computation.

Problems having an input of size N that *require* 2^N or more steps for their solution are said to be *intractable*. While there remains some (dim) hope for the tractability of the NP complete problems, there are many other problems that are provably intractable, and thus require algorithms operating in exponential time or worse. For example, a complete examination of the game tree of checkers could determine whether or not the side that moves first has a guaranteed winning strategy. Consider now generalized checkers, played not on an 8×8 board, but on an $N \times N$ board. It has been shown that the problem of determining the existence of a guaranteed first-mover winning strategy is intractable in N; that is, there is no algorithm for solving this problem which does so in fewer than K^N steps ($K > 1$). This is not the end of it, however. Some problems can be shown to be solvable in at best doubly exponential time 2^{2^N}, or even worse. Similar results have been established for problems that involve unreasonably large amounts of memory space (Harel 1992, ch. 7).

The situation is not altogether bleak. There are tractable algorithms for solving NP complete problems that give correct or nearly correct answers most of the time. For example, there are tractable algorithms designed to tackle the travelling salesperson problem that routinely come up with paths that are surely far shorter than most routes. Another possible way around intractability is an algorithm that generates the correct answer (say, to a decision problem) with a certain high probability, regardless of the size N of the input. More precisely, suppose that we can show that if the answer to our question is truly 'yes', then there is an algorithm that will output 'yes' with a probability $P > K$, regardless of the size N of the input; on the other hand, if the correct answer is 'no', then our algorithm will quickly yield that result. Clearly, such an algorithm is almost as good as one that provides answers whose correctness can be guaranteed.

One such probabilistic algorithm was presented by Solovay and Strassen (1977). It is designed to test an arbitrary natural number for compositeness. (Does the number have nontrivial factors?) Number theorists have been able to show that if a number is composite (that is, not prime), then over half of the numbers less than that number will have a quickly computable property W that will be a conclusive witness to that fact. Thus if a number is not composite, no such witness will exist. A candidate N for compositeness is now input into the algorithm and a number less than N is chosen at random. If the randomly chosen number has the 'witness' property W, then the original number N must be composite, so the program outputs 'Composite!' and halts. On the other hand, if the randomly chosen number does not have the witness property W, then the algorithm chooses another number less than N at random. If 100 or so random choices fail to turn up a witness to Ns compositeness, then the program outputs 'Not composite!'. A little thought shows that since over $1:2$ of the numbers less than N will have W if N is composite, then if we fail to find such a witness after 100 random trials, the chances of Ns being composite are less than $1:2^{100}$, a very small chance indeed. Provided we are willing to take a small risk of error, this method results in a very fast probabilistic algorithm for testing compositeness.

Whether the existence of such an algorithm shows that probabilistic algorithms can tame intractable problems is, however, still unclear. The hitch is that the compositeness problem is not *known* to be intractable. Furthermore, there are no cases of problems *known* to be intractable that have succumbed to a probabilistic algorithm (although some NP complete problems have been tamed). The issue of whether or not there are probabilistic algorithms that can solve (provably) intractable problems remains open. It *has* been shown, however, that probabilistic algorithms cannot tame problems that are not computable, a result that follows from the fact that any probabilistic algorithm can be simulated deterministically.

The theory of deterministic algorithms has also contributed to our understanding of what apparently stands in direct opposition to determinism: randomness (see RANDOMNESS §4).

See also: COMPLEXITY, COMPUTATIONAL; COMPUTABILITY AND INFORMATION; COMPUTABILITY THEORY; TURING REDUCIBILITY AND TURING DEGREES

References and further reading

* Boolos, G.S. and Jeffrey, R. (1974) *Computability and Logic*, Cambridge: Cambridge University Press; 2nd edn, 1982. (A classic, easy to read text on computation theory and its relation to logic.)

Chaitin, G. (1969) 'On the Length of Programs for Computing Finite Binary Sequences: Statistical Considerations', *Journal of the Association for Computing Machinery* 16: 145–59. (Chaitin's improvement on the Kolmogorov definition of algorithmic complexity.)

* Church, A. (1936) 'An Unsolvable Problem of Elementary Number Theory', *American Journal of Mathematics* 58: 345–63; repr. in M. Davis (ed.)

The Undecidable, New York: Raven Press, 1965, 89–107. (Church's original paper on the lambda calculus approach to the theory of computation.)

Davis, M. (ed.) (1965) *The Undecidable*, New York: Raven Press. (A sourcebook of classic papers on computation theory.)

Davis, M., Sigal, R. and Weyuker, E. (1983) *Computability, Complexity, and Languages: Fundamentals of Theoretical Computer Science*, Boston, MA: Academic Press; 2nd edn, 1994. (A handbook, perhaps *the* handbook, of the current state of computation theory. A work of moderate technical difficulty.)

Garey, M. and Johnson, D. (1979) *Computers and Intractability*, New York: W.H. Freeman. (A detailed but only moderately technical account of the theory of computational intractability.)

* Harel, D. (1992) *Algorithmics*, Reading, MA: Addison-Wesley. (An excellent, easy to read survey of the current state of computation theory.)

Kolmogorov, A.N. (1965) 'Three Approaches to the Quantitative Theory of Information', *Problems in Information Transmission* 1: 1–7. (The paper in which Kolmogorov introduces algorithmic measures of complexity.)

Li, M. and Vitanyi, P. (1993) *An Introduction to Kolmogorov Complexity and its Applications*, New York: Springer. (A thorough, fairly technical, account of Kolmogorov and Chaitin's ideas on complexity.)

* Minsky, M. (1967) *Computation: Finite and Infinite Machines*, Englewood Cliffs, NJ: Prentice Hall. (A lively, easy to read survey of computation theory as things stood in the early 1960s.)

Solomonoff, R.J. (1964) 'A Formal Theory of Inductive Inference, Part 1 and Part 2', *Information and Control* 7: 1–22, 224–54. (The first of the classic trio of papers (Solomonoff, Kolmogorov, Chaitin) on the foundations of algorithmic information theory.)

* Solovay, R. and Strassen, V. (1977) 'A Fast Monte-Carlo Test for Primality', *Society for Industrial and Applied Mathematics Journal of Computing* 6: 84–5. (An early probabilistic algorithm for testing a number for primality, discussed in the text.)

* Turing, A. (1936, 1937) 'On Computable Numbers, with an Application to the *Entscheidungsproblem*', *Proceedings of the London Mathematical Society*, series 2, 42: 230–65; corrections, 43: 544–6; repr. in M. David (ed.) *The Undecidable*, New York: Raven Press, 1966, 116–54. (The classic paper on Turing machines: difficult, brilliant, containing many errors.)

JOHN WINNIE

COMTE, ISIDORE-AUGUSTE-MARIE-FRANÇOIS-XAVIER (1798–1857)

The French philosopher and social theorist Auguste Comte is known as the originator of sociology and 'positivism', a philosophical system by which he aimed to discover and perfect the proper political arrangements of modern industrial society. He was the first thinker to advocate the use of scientific procedures in the study of economics, politics and social behaviour, and, motivated by the social and moral problems caused by the French Revolution, he held that the practice of such a science would lead inevitably to social regeneration and progress.

Comte's positivism can be characterized as an approach which rejects as illegitimate all that cannot be directly observed in the investigation and study of any subject. His system of 'positive philosophy' had two laws at its foundation: a historical or logical law, 'the law of three stages', and an epistemological law, the classification or hierarchy of the sciences. The law of three stages governs the development of human intelligence and society: in the first stage, early societies base their knowledge on theological grounds, giving ultimately divine explanations for all phenomena; later, in the metaphysical stage, forces and essences are sought as explanations, but these are equally chimerical and untestable; finally, in the positive or scientific stage, knowledge is secured solely on observations, by their correlation and sequence. Comte saw this process occurring not only in European society, but also in the lives of every individual. We seek theological solutions in childhood, metaphysical solutions in youth, and scientific explanations in adulthood.

His second, epistemological law fixed a classification or hierarchy of sciences according to their arrival at the positive stage of knowledge. In order of historical development and thus of increasing complexity, these are mathematics, astronomy, physics, chemistry, biology and sociology. (Comte rejected psychology as a science, on the grounds that its data were unobservable and therefore untestable.) Knowledge of one science rested partly on the findings of the preceding science; for Comte, students must progress through the sciences in the correct order, using the simpler and more precise methods of the preceding science to tackle the more complex issues of later ones. In his six-volume Cours de philosophie positive *(The Positive Philosophy) (1830–42), Comte gave an encyclopedic account of these sciences, ending with an exposition of what he regarded as the most advanced: social physics or 'sociology' (a term he invented). The sociologist's job would be to discover the laws that govern human behaviour on a large scale, and the ways in which social institutions and norms operate together in a complex yet ultimately predictable system.*

In his later work, Comte fleshed out his vision of the positive society, describing among other things a Religion of Humanity in which historical figures would be worshipped according to their contribution to society. Despite such extravagances, however, the broader themes of his positivism – especially the idea that long-standing social problems should be approached scientifically – proved influential both in France and, through J.S. Mill's early support, in England.

1   Life

Auguste Comte was born in Montpellier, France. He attended the École Polytechnique, from which he was expelled in 1816, for political reasons. Comte's main concern throughout his life was resolving the political, social and moral problems caused by the French Revolution. To that end, he embarked upon an encyclopedic work, which he first conceived under the inspiration of Henri de SAINT-SIMON, for whom he worked as secretary from 1817 to 1824. At that time, he proposed several plans for a competition to create an encyclopedia modelled on that of Denis DIDEROT, but designed to bring together the 'positive ideas' of the period, that is, ideas conceived in their relation to modern science and free from the bonds of traditional theology and metaphysics. Comte's encyclopedic project developed into the famous *Cours de philosophie positive* (Course in Positive Philosophy) (1830–42), a complete system of philosophy in six volumes which aimed to provide the foundations for political and social organization in modern industrial society. Meanwhile, he wrote a series of minor works in social philosophy, which became known as the 'opuscules'. The third, *Plan des travaux scientifiques nécessaires pour réorganiser la société* (Plan of the Scientific Operations Necessary for Reorganizing Society) (1822), which is often called 'the fundamental opuscule', presented the first outline of the concepts which would become central to Comte's positivism – the 'law of three stages' and the classification of the sciences (see §3 below).

While pursuing his intellectual career, Comte earned his living first as a mathematics tutor at the École Polytechnique, then as admissions examiner at the same school. When he lost the latter job , he was forced in 1848 to seek financial support from his disciples in order to survive. All his life Comte regretted his failure to be appointed a tenured professor; he accused François Arago, among others, of deliberately blocking his academic career. He was also unsuccessful when he requested the creation of chairs at the Collège de France: in 1832 the chair of the General History of the Physical and Mathematical Sciences, and in 1846 the chair of the General History of the Positive Sciences.

Comte always linked his theoretical research to the practical aim of moral, social and political reorganization. He considered this reorganization from the theoretical aspect of political science – 'sociology' or 'positive politics' – and from the practical aspect of the union of the social classes. Moreover, it was for the benefit of the proletarians that he gave public courses in popular astronomy between 1831 and 1848. He considered these lectures the prelude to the reorganization of the intellectual system, which, thanks to the scientific knowledge of society, would finally result in 'a politics finally freed from the arbitrary and the utopian' (Larizza-Lolli 1993: 76). Comte wrote the *Discours sur l'esprit positif* (A Discourse on the Positive Spirit) (1844) as a basic introduction to this reorganization. The *Discours sur l'ensemble du positivisme* (A General View of Positivism), which appeared in 1848, derived from a similar intention, that of presenting to the workers a synthesized vision of positivist philosophy. From 1847, Comte devoted his lectures to the refutation of communism.

The epistemological foundation of Comte's political project tends to be problematic. For Comte, 'epistemology' involved the history, philosophy and methodologies of the sciences, as well as their basic concepts and theories. His positivist politics is based, on the one hand, on historical and logical law, the law of the three stages (theological, metaphysical and positive stages) and, on the other hand, on an epistemological law: the classification or hierarchy of the sciences, fixed according to the order of their arrival at the positive stage of knowledge (mathematics, astronomy, physics, chemistry, biology, sociology). Thus, as a fundamental epistemological concept, 'positivism' designates an intellectual attitude founded on the practice of rational and experimental scientific methods. At the same time, Comte's scientific positivism is a philosophy of the positive sciences, though initially it is also a philosophy of scientific creativity. Comte allowed certain new sciences that had not yet been fully regularized to be classed as positive: for instance, he confirmed the advance of biology to the level of a positive science. The most advanced of all positive sciences – social physics or sociology – allowed for the transformation of society based on the progress of the sciences.

Under the aegis of his Religion of Humanity, first described in the sixth volume of the *Cours de philosophie positive* (The Positive Philosophy) (1842), Comte articulates his vast political project in the *Système de politique positive* (System of Positive Polity) (1851–4). In this work, he gives his project a social and moral goal, founding it on altruism – a term he originated, according to Emile Littré. Comte's last book was *La Synthèse subjective* (Subjective Synthesis) (1856). Never completed, it re-evaluates the role of the sciences from the perspective of a positivist education. Comte died, probably of stomach cancer, on 5 September 1857.

2 Speculation and action

Following the example of Francis BACON, who stressed the efficacy of combining knowing (*scire*) and doing (*posse*), Comte held that power is proportionate to knowledge: 'From science, comes foresight; from foresight, comes action' ([1830–42] 1975 I: 45). Even though he clearly separates theory and practice in the scientific study of phenomena, Comte orients his positive philosophy towards a constant interrelationship between speculation and action, while keeping it equidistant between rationalism and empiricism.

The pragmatic aspect of Comte's thought goes back to ideas he first expressed in 1816, while still a student at the École Polytechnique. He affirmed the necessity of pragmatism in a letter of 28 September 1819 to his best friend, Pierre Valat, declaring that he could not conceive of a scientific work that would have no useful goal for humanity. Conversely, he added that political research would have to be intellectually challenging in order to interest him; otherwise, it would have no validity in his eyes. This also explains why he underlined the necessity of basing political studies on a scientific foundation.

On the one hand, Comte was interested in a discipline that would soon be known as 'epistemology'. For him, it encompassed the history and philosophy of the sciences, the various methodologies which they used, fundamental scientific concepts and theories, and what he as well as Bacon called 'primary philosophy', which constituted the synthesis of the regular means of scientific knowledge and their principal, universally valid results. His epistemological concerns later led Comte to establish a 'Table of

the Fifteen Universal Laws' in the fourth volume of the *Système de politique positive* (see §§2, 3 below), settling three groups of universal laws about (1) laws formation, (2) static and dynamic theories of understanding, and (3) movement/existence, action/reaction classification and relation. Yet he never worried about defining 'facts', 'scientific verification' or 'observation'. Nor did the problem of the origin of knowledge concern him. Robert C. Scharff rightly emphasizes Comte's insistence 'that such issues [could] not even be understood as issues without recourse to philosophy's history' (1991: 193).

On the other hand, Comte was very conscious of the political, social and cultural problems posed by the French Revolution. As the third opuscule clearly states, he placed himself politically between 'the people' and 'the kings' (1970a: 57), between the 'retrograde' ideas of the latter and the 'critical' ones of the former; in effect, he had rebelled against the royalism and Catholicism of his parents, but at the same time opposed the destructive spirit of the revolutionaries. Similarly, he did not favour the mixture of the retrograde and critical currents advocated by the 'doctrinaires' such as Pierre Royer-Collard, François Guizot, Charles de Rémusat, and Prosper Duvergier de Hauranne, whom Comte grouped in the 'stationary school' (1970a: 69; 1975 II: 43), characterized by 'organic emptiness'. From 1822, after the fading of the spiritual power of the Church, Comte reproached the French body politic for neglecting to create an organization with analogous power. In spite of French politicians' efforts to recast a temporal power, they had, according to Comte, also failed here. He pointed to the absence of any explicit positive theory as proof of the double failure of French politics.

Before his encyclopedic enterprise was sufficiently developed to become the *Cours de philosophie positive*, Comte, in his role of secretary to Saint-Simon and with his approval, edited some research projects which he called 'Programmes'. One example is the *Programme d'un travail sur les rapports des sciences théoriques avec les sciences d'application* (Programme of work on the relations between the pure and applied sciences), which he published in 1817. From 1817 to 1820, he began a certain number of preparatory works, which were at least initially encouraged, if not conceived, by Saint-Simon. They would continue after 1820, but in a totally different form.

Just as in the fundamental opuscule of May 1822, Comte resolutely insisted on linking his theoretical work to the practical goal of social reorganization in the *Cours de philosophie positive*, the two *Discours* of 1844 and 1848, the *Système de politique positive* and his last writings. Very early, in fact, he had made a definitive and fundamental observation that the development of human intelligence was closely tied to the history of societies, which he formulated as follows: 'intelligence arrives at a higher stage of development when altruism itself is more developed' (1851: 693). It closely connected the development of intelligence with that of the individual's interest in his or her peers, intelligence and altruism both being clear signs of the progress of humanity.

Comte considered the theoretical discipline of sociology to be concerned with the real nature of humanity, and so he gave a higher status to its method, which was originally objective, defining it instead as 'subjective', that is, as situated beyond objective cosmological observation. The objective method employed in the *Cours de philosophie positive* had permitted the passage from the world to humankind. Now it was necessary to go from humankind to the world; hence the designation of this method as 'subjective', that is, as dependent on the real nature of humankind.

3 Comtean epistemology

Comte's epistemology focused on considering and evaluating the social phenomena that the fundamental sciences recognized as subject matter for a 'positive science' – a science based on observation with a legitimate place in the system of recognized sciences. His epistemology reverses the accepted hierarchy of the sciences – astronomy, physics, chemistry and biology, all of which were traditionally subordinated under mathematics – and places them under the domination of sociology. Comte thought that once the principle of sociality was accepted by scientists, the new science should be called 'anthropology'; he presents this in the *Discours sur l'esprit positif* (1844), where he defines the underlying nature of the scientific approach as necessarily social. First, a 'semiotic principle' justifies it as social, because it originates in the constitution of the different systems of signs produced by society, especially the society of scientists. Second, it is social because it obeys a 'principle of homology' (Kremer-Marietti 1980: 53–69), which applies to all relations and then expresses the possibility of applying the scientific norm of theoretical unification – a norm that Comte shared with Henri POINCARÉ. The principle of 'classification', which would also be recognized by Pierre DUHEM, is justified by the principle of homology; the latter belongs logically to a more general thesis (which Poincaé would later formulate) according to which 'it is illegitimate to take into consideration a single isolated hypothesis in order to verify it' (Duhem 1914: 393; Kremer-Marietti 1992:

372). In Comte's case, it gives rise to the conception of the 'Table of the Fifteen Universal Laws'; the theoretical unity achieved by Comtean epistemology thanks to this table is due to the organization of all laws through a classification of scientific facts. Comte distrusted a logic isolated from science, a fact isolated from theory, a doctrine isolated from method, and a method isolated from its object. It was necessary to have a theory in order to locate the observations which, if isolated, would have no scientific value. Comte never stopped saying that the 'crudest' phenomena explain the 'noblest' ones.

Oddly enough, without this holistic type of explanation ordering the homology of the concepts of the world and man, abstract morality could not gain access to the positive system. For Comte, the reference to a system obeying the principle of homology was a universally practicable theoretical necessity – a criterion of verification which he could use to assess the value of experiments and conclusions.

In his 'Oral Course in Positive Philosophy', given from 1826, Comte developed his general review of the positive sciences, which he subjected to the historical and logical law of three stages. His teaching plan followed the classification or hierarchy of the sciences, which he saw as a fertile classificatory model. Henceforth he would elevate this model to the status of a key or grid of concepts. Not only did he depend on it to determine, according to the law of three stages, the historical and logical necessity of sociology, a new discipline dealing with social, historical and political points of view, but even more important, this classification permitted him to proceed in certain areas where observation was not yet possible. It is on this principle of classification that Comte established his 'cerebral theory' (see §4 below). He also drew the necessity of 'abstract morality' (the seventh fundamental science) from his view that the order of the individual, concerned with abstract morality, is at the very heart of sociology, where it is subordinate to the social order, exactly as the social order is subordinate to the vital order and as the latter in its turn is subordinate to the material order. In Comte's eyes, these successive subordinations do not exclude either the specificity or the originality peculiar to the different orders of phenomena and their respective sciences. The seventh degree of the series of sciences 'arrives', according to Comte, 'at man envisaged in the most precise fashion'. Because the double weight of the material and vital orders is in reality borne by the social order, which helps to modify them, the 'order of the individual', the most dependent of all, becomes the 'immediate regulator of our destinies' at the same time that it experiences the pressure of all the orders through the social order, to which it is subordinate.

4 The logic of systems and the semiotic principle

Comte highlighted a history of human logics by emphasizing the necessary and reciprocal connection between the systems and institutions of signs, which are languages, and social systems. He saw social history as being affected by the systems of logic which he recognized as existing at three levels: the 'logic of sentiments', the 'logic of images' and the 'logic of signs'. This tripartition into sentiments, images and signs contains the semiotic elements that we can recognize in Charles Peirce's semiotic as Firstness, Secondness and Thirdness (Peirce 1966: 241) (see PEIRCE, C. §7).

Language appeared as a dynamic system relating political life to domestic life. It allowed for the creation of a positive science whose basis was observation but whose ideal reference was mathematical language, which arose from the logic of signs. Comte's semiotic position explains his mathematical views. He called attention to the fact that physical science depended as much on observation guided by theory as on the proper use of a model of language, which, to him, was the language of mathematics.

As early as 1819, Comte maintained a general theory of language and signs in his *Essais sur la philosophie des mathématiques* (Essays on the Philosophy of Mathematics). This logic of the systems of signs in both science and aesthetics was clearly confirmed in 1852 in the second volume of *Système de philosophie positive*. Written long after the first and long before the second of these works, the *Cours de philosophie positive* contains an epistemology concerned with revealing the scientific means of demonstrating the final necessity of the human and social sciences. These sciences are ruled by a logic of systems, of which the law of three stages is the determining operational element.

The 'positive logic' of the *Système de philosophie positive* is nothing other than a combination of systems of signs (affective, imaginary and intellectual), subjected to the unification of the three systems governing sentiments, images and linguistic or mathematical symbols. Comte wanted every 'logic of signs' to be expressly connected with the 'logic of images' and the 'logic of sentiments'. He reaffirmed the semiotic principle in 1856, in *Synthèse subjective*, and this led to a complete formulation showing how 'the regular conjuncture of sentiments, images and signs' was able 'to inspire in us conceptions that meet our moral, intellectual and physical needs' (1856: 27).

The logic of the systems of signs arises from 'the interior function of language' because, according to Hobbes, people communicate by signs, with one phenomenon becoming the sign of another phenomenon. The Table of the Fifteen Universal Laws may be considered the outcome of this logic. The reason is that this table achieves an intellectual unity through its reduction to a precise and definite number of signs, which are specific laws, valid for all phenomena.

Evidently, there is a link between the three Comtean logics and the three-stage law and an even closer link between these logics and the three sub-states of the theological stage. In fact, Comte thought that fetishism, polytheism and monotheism were at the origin of these three logics, whose development was closely connected with the system of society. The logic of sentiments originated in fetishism, the logic of images was created under polytheism, and the logic of signs (linguistic and mathematic) arose from monotheism. It is clear that this semiotic principle has important implications for Comte's epistemology as well as for his theory of language and art.

5 The moral and political plan

The opuscules of his youth, appended to the fourth volume of the *Système de philosophie positive*, demonstrate Comte's constant interest in moral and political reconstruction, in which semiotics played a role. As mentioned above, semiotics was connected with the law of three stages and the three theological sub-states. In Comte's eyes, fetishism was superior to the other two sub-states because it founded human language. For Comte, the 'fetishist thinker' was closer to phenomenal reality than the 'theologicist dreamer'. Yet the theologians taught us to consider purely ideal existences, without which we would not have been able to create the scientific realm. In addition, without monotheism, abstraction would have been impossible.

It is important to remember that mental states have their ontological foundation in the corresponding social state. It is impossible, for example, to speak abstractly of a society that embraces a specific intellectual and mental state. Thus man and society advance in correlation with the development of intelligence. As a result, the positivist project for society studies the different forms of learning, from the most ancient to the most advanced, by means of knowledge of the various forms of civilization.

The study of 'social statics' brings out the principle of solidarity that is crucial for the coexistence and cohesion underlying all social systems. The study of 'social dynamics' highlights the principle of the continuity and tradition of societies. In brief, scientific positivism demands that we act so that theory and practice are in harmony. This harmony in turn generates the harmony between the knowledge of the environment that surrounds us and our reaction to this environment.

If knowledge leads to power over the outside world, our industrial society should be able to realize an equitable political project only by developing an all-embracing moral project. If Comte had limited himself to considering the use of abstract science in the 'sciences of application', or the results of the latter on industry, the industrial activity arising from positive science would not suffice to constitute a project for society. Because of his familiarity with all scientific areas, Comte turned to a complete knowledge of man; he contended that abstract morality, the 'final science', could 'systematize the special knowledge of our individual nature by combining the biological point of view with the sociological' (1851–4: 2, 438). To this end, Comte provided the essential epistemological basis with the 'cerebral chart', established in 1851 from his method of classification. 'Abstract morality' usually precedes 'concrete morality'; from the 'cerebral chart' emerges the principle of man's action in society: 'Act out of affection, and think in order to act' (1851–4: 1, 680–733). The phrenology of Franz Josef Gall, which he criticized for separating the brain from the whole nervous system and detaching the individual from his social milieu, permitted Comte to maintain the innateness of human qualities and the importance of the emotions, as well as the distinction between the mind and the heart: their harmony constitutes the soul. For Comte, the rule of positive society will be love, a basic feature of humanity and thus something which it is possible to expect human beings to develop.

6   The human sciences and the standard conduct of nations

A fundamental question remains: How does Comte's epistemological system make it possible for him to create a political project?

The analysis of the human psyche (§5 above) showed that the need for love transcends natural egoism by means of altruism. The cerebral chart claimed that both speculation and action are dominated by affection and that social consensus depends on the affective life. Comte, who recognized the permanence of affectivity, expressed it by the phrase, 'One tires of thinking and even acting; one never tires of loving', a progressive division in intermediate items between extreme terms. Using a process of binary decomposition, Comte was able to derive the scale of all the intermediary affections between complete egoism and pure altruism. His analytical method

was inherent in the taxonomic method that he usually used. It permitted him to maintain that altruism 'when it is energetic, is always better able than egoism to direct and stimulate the intelligence, even among the animals' (1851–4: 1, 693). The cerebral theory thus represents the fundamental order of our natural make-up and can be applied to social existence.

Social statics deals with the play of the permanent social forces revealed by Comte. What is the material power of Western society? Comte answered that it is 'number' (the proletariat) and 'wealth' (the administrators of capital). What is its intellectual power? It is the aesthetic and scientific spirit (its representatives in society). What about sentiment? Sentiment is concerned with the heart, which is both masculine and feminine, for man and woman share masculine and feminine traits. Even if Comte considers women intellectually inferior to men, he recognizes in them a superiority in terms of sensibility and makes them the guardians of universal morality; yet women remain auxiliary to men. No doubt it was from his romantic love for Clotilde de Vaux, which lasted a year (1845–6), that Comte obtained his experience of the feminine condition. Theoretically, Comte applies an Aristotelian principle governing the different forces of society: the double principle of the separation of functions and the combination of efforts.

Property, family and language are the necessary elements of social statics, which owes its unity to 'religion'. To Comte, religion is a synthesis of 'dogma', which represents the philosophical unity of scientific theories; 'worship', which directs sentiments; and 'regulations', which govern behaviour. Worship and regulations form the subjective domain of love, which is subordinated to the objective realm of philosophical dogma. Social dynamics can be summarized in the law of three stages; it is the permanent substratum of human action. The harmony between the social static and the social dynamic expresses itself in the principle of progress, which is conceived as the development of order. The postulate of harmony is evoked in the perspective of that which governs and rallies, that is, religion, which is destined to 'bind the interior and to link it to the outside'.

The *Cours* deals with the creation of the system of scientific systems as does the *Système de philosophie positive*, which also proposes the new construction of a political synthesis inspired by religion. This completes the human unity to which the synthesis tends through loving, thinking and acting. Religion thus becomes a super-theory of the immediately applicable unity; it permits human intervention in the historical and social dynamic, for it puts morality and politics in the service of social progress. The Religion of Humanity is 'proven' because it is founded on cosmological and human knowledge, and is thus the only answer to moral and political questions. Civil society cannot answer these questions even if its mechanisms permitted it, and it would in any case be unable to set its solutions in motion, since it is nothing but a battleground for divergent opinions. The same criticism is found in the works of HEGEL, who limits the civil objective to the satisfaction of needs. While the Hegelian state is called upon to transcend the egoistic civil society by an objective moral idea, Comte wants to orient the will towards the superior reality of humanity, a subjective moral idea. For 'Humanity breaks up first into Cities, then into Families, but never into individuals' (1851–4: 4, 31). Morality takes the individual into consideration; families and homelands are, nevertheless, still important to it as the necessary introduction to Humanity. In terms of its composition, the Great Being is defined as 'the continuous totality of converging beings'.

Comte envisages a future where positive morality determines the discipline of existence. His concept of altruism recalls the principle of friendship or philia, which Aristotle made the cement of the ancient cities. While earlier Comte assigned temporal power to the proletarians, he later entrusts it to those who favoured the 'universal union'. From 1842, he foresees that the spiritual power has to be 'the true philosophical class'; he therefore gives it the title of 'Western Positive Committee' and already imagines it to be a 'Positive Church'. Comte intends it to direct the intellectual and moral regeneration of modern societies, with the assistance of the proletariat, at least after the latter has ended the transitional dictatorship towards positivism. Just as with all women (who do not form a class), the proletariat is the servant of the spiritual power; it watches over the temporal power to see that it respects the general principles of the social regime.

As for the positive economy, Comte hoped that it would be nothing other than the 'universal and continuous systematization of human toil'. He wanted work to be systematized for the sake of future generations. Capitalization supported the sociocracy, which, according to the evidence of those who recognized its inner workings, involved the collaboration of the social classes based on the functions and organs of the body. (Sociocracy was related to regulation, while sociolatry dealt with worship. Both were founded on sociology, which served as their dogma.) Comte's positivist economic theory was summed up in two laws: first, that each man can produce more than what he consumes, and second, that the products obtained can be preserved beyond the time required for their reproduction. The

institution of capital is justified by the preponderance of human work over consumption. Comte's detractors, such as Herbert MARCUSE, did not understand his view of the origin and social destination of capital funds. Yet Comte maintained that these capital funds made each active citizen the agent of all the others: each one had to function above all for others by applying the positivist motto 'Live for others'. Others' obligations emanated naturally from the social consensus.

Once the altruistic sentiments were recognized and generalized, Comte thought it possible to treat the three principal obligations – moral, judicial and civic – as one. But there was also an economic obligation to work, and to sustain the products of that work as long as possible; for the importance of solidarity among people would only become clear from the perspective of future generations.

7 The complete positivism

Comte had persuaded his disciples that the active class should nourish the contemplative class. After 1852, thanks to an increase in the Positivist Subsidy, he was able to devote himself entirely to his writings and to represent the priesthood of the Religion of Humanity. He concentrated on asserting the ultimate importance of morality and politics, in this way inaugurating the 'second part of the great revolution'. He affirmed the autonomy of the philosopher as well as that of the positivist movement. Since the appearance in July 1851 of the first volume of the *Système de philosophie positive*, Comte felt that he had completed the philosophical part of his work; he was now free to work on the religious part, which was basically a combination of morality and politics. The *Système de philosophie positive* was to conclude the French Revolution. Comte summed up his solution in the ideas 'Order' and 'Progress', which he combined in a unified and radical way. The positivist mission was to attain not a mixture but a 'necessary harmony' between the retrogression of Comte's time and anarchy. Comte loudly claimed to have answered the needs of the people and satisfied the poor, at the same reassuring the rich. He recommended not intervening in the contemporary political scene, but contented himself with constructing a provisional programme which consisted mainly in the spiritual reorganization of the West, while denouncing the powerlessness and instability of the 'incomplete positivists'.

It was impossible to conceive of an isolated people, far from the great human fraternity. Spiritual unity had to make the totality of human affairs prevail over parties and frontiers. Social positivism (the new religion) had to realize and complete intellectual positivism (the new epistemology). The prestige of progress explained the success that intellectual positivism had obtained. Social positivism would be able to achieve its goals only by reconstructing the spiritual order. As an opponent of theoretical materialism, which privileged the cosmological sciences, Comte believed that it was necessary to ensure the preeminence of the human and social sciences – for him, sociology and abstract morality. In 1856, he called attention to the great trilogy that consisted of his three most important works: *Cours de philosophie positive*, *Système de philosophie positive* and *Synthèse subjective*. According to Comte, the reign of solidarity had arrived – that of individuals and of peoples.

8 Influence

Comte's ideas were initially well received in England after the excellent review of the first two volumes of *Cours de philosophie positive* in the *Edinburgh Review* (1838). Later, John Stuart MILL confirmed his support in *System of Logic* (1843), in which he presents social statics as the science of the 'coexistences of social phenomena' and social dynamics as that of their progressions. Mill saw in social statics a theory of the consensus between the different parts of the social organization, whereas social dynamics was a theory of society in its progressive movement; their combination led to a law of correspondence between the spontaneous stages and their simultaneous transformations, from which one could then discover the scientific law governing the development of humanity. Like Comte, Mill regarded the speculative faculties of human nature as the agents of social progress, and he also advocated the historical method (his 'Inverse Deductive Method') in the social sciences. In politics, he favoured the separation of powers and the establishment of a consensus based on a common public doctrine. In 1841 he began a six-year correspondence with Comte with an enthusiastic letter, but continued it in opposition to him in three areas: psychology, political economy and feminine intelligence. In *Auguste Comte and Positivism* (1865), Mill categorically rejected the Religion of Humanity, though he still accepted Comte's method.

Alexander Bain, the founder of the journal *Mind*, rallied, if not directly to Comtism, at least to the English positivist school. Like Comte, Bain (1855) connected his psychology to the spontaneous activity of the brain. Similarly, though he explicitly differentiated his own philosophy from that of Comte, Herbert SPENCER, who wrote *Social Statics* (1851) on the basis of extreme individualism, then applied the doctrine of evolution to sociology, while at the same time rejecting Comte's conclusions. The English positivist Frederick Harrison, founder of *The Positivist Review*, was also the author of a *Social Statics* (1875). He engaged in a polemic with Spencer to force him to recognize the links between his philosophy and that of Comte. Spencer did at least admit that he owed the concept of social consensus to Comte. Other notable supporters are Richard Congreve (1818–99), who devoted himself to the propagation of English positivism, and Harriet MARTINEAU, who edited a summary of Comte's philosophy, *The Positive Philosophy* (Comte 1830–42).

In France, Comte drew support from certain workers, such as Fabien Magnin, the author of *Études Sociales* (Social Studies) (1913), but his main devotee was the academic Pierre Laffitte, who published numerous positivist texts. Many people who did not strictly adhere to positivism nevertheless came under Comte's influence: Claude Bernard advanced the discipline of experimental medicine and studied the internal environment of advanced living organisms; and Pierre Duhem became well-known for his work on the elements of a natural classification, the epistemological independence of the fundamental sciences, and the holistic thesis. On the other hand, many French thinkers were critical of Comte, notably Émile MEYERSON.

In general, Comte's positivism was received in two ways: some absorbed his central themes of the importance of scientific method in resolving social issues but rejected his religious movement; others were deeply impressed by his diagnosis of the crises afflicting modern society and were inspired by his vision for its redemption. In France, the former were led by Émile Littré, who was critical but friendly towards Comte's thought; the latter by Pierre Laffitte, a supporter of the positivist religion and from 1892 Professor of History of Science at the Collège de France. Two positivist reviews were published, *La philosophie positive* (1867–82) under the direction of Littré and G. Wyrouboff, and the *Revue occidentale* (1878–1914) created by Laffitte. The *Revue positiviste internationale* (1906–30) was founded later under the direction of Emile Corra. The religious aspect of Comte's positivism was developed by an English-born American, Henry Edger, who published *The Positivist Calendar* in 1856.

See also: NISHI AMANE

List of works

Comte, A. (1830–42) *Cours de philosophie positive* (Course in Positive Philosophy), Paris: Société Positiviste, 5th edn (identical to the first), 1892, 6 vols; ed. M. Serres *et al.*, Paris: Hermann, 1975, 2 vols; trans. and condensed H. Martineau, *The Positive Philosophy*, London: G. Bell, 1896, 3 vols. (Comte's major work.)

—— (1844) *Discours sur l'esprit positif* (A Discourse on the Positive Spirit), Paris: Vrin, 1990. (An attempt to introduce and popularize positivism.)

—— (1848) *Discours sur l'ensemble du positivisme* (A General View of Positivism), Paris: Société Positiviste, 1907. (A further introduction to positivism.)

—— (1851–4) *Système de politique positive ou Traité de sociologie instituant la religion de l'Humanité*, Paris: L. Mathias, 1928, 4 vols; Osnabrück: Zeller, 1967; trans. J.H. Bridges, F. Harrison *et al.*, *System of Positive Polity*, London, 1875, 4 vols; repr. New York: Burt & Franklin, 1966. (Presents Comte's scheme for a new society.)

—— (1856) *Synthèse subjective ou Système universel des conceptions propres à l'état normal de l'Humanité* (Subjective Synthesis), vol. 1: *Traité de philosophie mathématique*, Paris: Société Positiviste. (Comte's last, uncompleted, work.)

—— (1970a) *Plan des travaux scientifique nécessaires pour réorganiser la société* (Plan of the scientific operations necessary for reorganizing society), Paris: Subier Montaigne. (The fundamental opuscule, dating from 1822.)

—— (1970b) *Écrits de jeunesse, 1816–28* (Early Writings, 1816–28), ed. P.E. de Berrêdo Carneiro and P. Arnaud, Paris: Mouton. (Includes *Opuscules de philosophie sociale* and *Mémoire sur la Cosmogonie de Laplace* and *Essais sur la philosophie des mathématiques*.)

—— (1973–90) *Correspondance générale et confessions* (General correspondence and Confessions), ed. P.E. de Berredo Carneiro, P. Arnaud, P. Arbousse-Bastide and A. Kremer-Marietti, Paris: École des Hautes Etudes en Sciences Sociales, 8 vols. (A scholarly edition of Comte's correspondence.)

—— (1995) *The Correspondence of John Stuart Mill and Auguste Comte*, trans. with foreword A. Haac, intro. A. Kremer-Marietti, New Brunswick, NJ: Transaction Publishers. (A translation of the correspondence between Comte and Mill.)

References and further reading

* Bain, A. (1855) *The Senses and The Intellect*, London. (Applies the findings of physiology to psychology.)

* Brewster, D. (ed.) (1838) Review of *Cours de philosophie positive*, *Edinburgh Review* 67. (An unsigned and sympathetic review of the first two volumes of Comte's *Cours de philosophie positive*.)

* Duhem, P. (1914) *La théorie physique – son objet – sa structure* (Physical theory: its object and structure), Paris: M. Rivière. (Famous study by the French physicist.)

* Edger, H. (1856) *The Positivist Calendar*, New York. (A guidebook for the practice of Positivism.)

Gouhier, H. (1933–41) *La Jeunesse d'Auguste Comte et la formation du positivisme* (The young Comte and the formation of Positivism), Paris: Vrin, 3 vols. (A good basis for understanding the evolution of Comte's thought.)

* Harrison, F. (1875) *Social Statics*, London. (An essay from one of the leaders of the Positivist movement in England.)

* Kremer-Marietti, A. (1980) *Le Projet anthropologique d'Auguste Comte* (Auguste Comte's anthropological project), Paris: SEDES. (Examines the principle of homology and epistemology.)

—— (1982) *Entre le Signe et l'Histoire: l'Anthropologie positiviste d'Auguste Comte* (Between the sign and history: The positivist anthropology of Auguste Comte), Paris: Méridiens Klincksieck. (Expansion of the material in §§2–5 of this entry. Historical and semiotic approach to the theoretical structures of positivist epistemology.)

—— (1983) *Le Concept de Science positive. Ses tenants et ses aboutissants dans les structures anthropologiques du positivisme* (The concept of positive science), Paris: Méridiens Klincksieck. (How the concept of positive science is taken as a model: complements §2 of this entry.)

—— (1987) 'Positivist Anthropology', *Encylopedia of Library and Information Science*, New York: Marcel Dekker INC. (Compares the theories of language and classification of Alexander Bryan Johnson and Comte.)

—— (1988) 'Auguste Comte et la sémiotique' (Auguste Comte and Semiotics), *RSSI* 8 (1–2): 131–44. (Seeks out the semiotic principle; see §4 above.)

* —— (1992) 'Measurement and Principles. The Structure of Physical Theories', *Revue Internationale de Philosophie* 3 (182): 361–75. (Includes a view on holism.)

Larizza-Lolli, M. (1993) 'Le premier rayonnement en France des idées d'Auguste Comte (1824–48): les milieux, les institutions, les hommes' (The initial reception in France of Auguste Comte's ideas (1824–48): the environment, the institutions, the people), *Bulletin de la Société d'Histoire de la Révolution de 1848 et des Révolutions du XIXème siècle*, Paris, 69–101. (A historical essay on Comte's scientific environment.)

Laudan, L. (1971) 'Towards a Reassessment of Comte's "Méthode Positive"', *Philosophy of Science* 37: 35–53; also in *Science and Hypothesis: Historical Essays on Scientific Methodology*, ed. L.

Laudan, Dordrecht: Reidel, 1981, 141–62. (An essay on Comte's scientific method.)

* Magnin, F. (1913) *Etudes Sociales* (Social Studies), Paris. (The essays of a manual worker inspired by positivism.)

* Mill, J.S. (1843) *System of Logic: Ratiocinative and Inductive*, in *Collected Works of John Stuart Mill*, vols 7 and 8, London: Routledge, 1991. (Emphasizes the study of human nature (psychology) and the study of human character (ethology).)

* —— (1865) *Auguste Comte and Positivism*, in *Collected Works of John Stuart Mill*, vol. 10, 261–368, London: Routledge, 1991. (Mill criticizes Comte.)

* Peirce, C.S. (1966) *Collected Papers*, vols 1–8, ed. C. Hartshorne, P. Weiss and A. Burks, Cambridge, MA: Harvard University Press. (Contributes to the logic of scientific methodology.)

Petit, A. (1991) 'La Révolution occidentale selon Auguste Comte: entre l'Histoire et l'Utopie' (The western revolution according to Auguste Comte: between History and Utopia), *Revue de Synthèse* CXIII (1): 21–40. (Presents utopia as the servant of history.)

* Pickering, M. (1993) *Auguste Comte: An Intellectual Biography*, vol. 1, Cambridge: Cambridge University Press. (The newest and very important history of Comte's thought and life.)

Plé, B. (1996) *Die Welte 'aus' den Wissenschaften* (The world 'out of' the sciences), Stuttgart: Klein-Cotta. (Study of sociology of science: positivism in France, England and Italy from 1848 to 1910.)

* Scharff, R. (1991) 'Comte, Philosophy, and the Question of History', *Philosophical Topics* 19: 177–204. (Observations pertinent to Comte's epistemology. Referred to in §1.)

—— (1995) *Comte after Positivism*, Cambridge, Cambridge University Press. (A recent study of Comte's thought.)

Schmaus, W. (1982) 'A Reappraisal of Comte's Three-State Law', *History and Theory* 21 (2): 248–66. (An interesting essay on Comte's famous law of three stages.)

* Spencer, H. (1851) *Social Statics: or the Conditions Essential to Human Happiness and the First of them Developed*, London: Chapman. (Spencer's first important work, advocating extreme individualism.)

Translated from the French by Mary Pickering

ANGÈLE KREMER-MARIETTI

CONCEPTS

The topic of concepts lies at the intersection of semantics and philosophy of mind. A concept is supposed to be a constituent of a thought (or 'proposition') rather in the way that a word is a constituent of a sentence that typically expresses a thought. Indeed, concepts are often thought to be the meanings *of words (and will be designated by enclosing the words for them in brackets: [city] is expressed by 'city' and by 'metropolis'). However, the two topics can diverge: non-linguistic animals may possess concepts, and standard linguistic meanings involve conventions in ways that concepts do not.*

Concepts seem essential to ordinary and scientific psychological explanation, which would be undermined were it not possible for the same concept *to occur in different thought episodes: someone could not even recall something unless the concepts they have now overlap the concepts they had earlier. If a disagreement between people is to be more than 'merely verbal', their words must express the same concepts. And if psychologists are to describe shared patterns of thought across people, they need to advert to shared concepts.*

Concepts also seem essential to categorizing the world, for example, recognizing a cow *and classifying it as a* mammal. *Concepts are also* compositional: *concepts can be combined to form a virtual infinitude of complex categories, in such a way that someone can understand a novel combination, for example, [smallest sub-atomic particle], by understanding its constituents.*

Concepts, however, are not always studied as part of psychology. Some logicians and formal semanticists study the deductive relations among concepts and propositions in abstraction from any mind. Philosophers doing 'philosophical analysis' try to specify the conditions that make something the kind *of thing it is – for example, what it is that makes an act good – an enterprise they take to consist in the analysis of concepts.*

Given these diverse interests, there is considerable disagreement about what exactly a concept is. Psychologists tend to use 'concept' for internal representations, for example, images, stereotypes, words that may be the vehicles for thought in the mind or brain. Logicians and formal semanticists tend to use it for sets *of real and possible objects, and* functions *defined over them; and philosophers of mind have variously proposed proper-properties, 'senses', inferential rules or discrimination abilities.*

A related issue is what it is for someone to possess *a concept. The 'classical view' presumed concepts had 'definitions' known by competent users. For example, grasping [bachelor] seemed to consist in grasping the definition, [adult, unmarried male]. However, if definitions are not to go on forever, there must be primitive concepts that are not defined but are grasped in some other way. Empiricism claimed that these definitions were provided by sensory conditions for a concept's application. Thus, [material object] was defined in terms of certain possibilities of sensation.*

The classical view suffers from the fact that few successful definitions have ever been provided. Wittgenstein suggested that concept possession need not consist in knowing a definition, but in appreciating the role of a concept in thought and practice. Moreover, he claimed, a concept need not apply to things by virtue of some closed set of features captured by a definition, but rather by virtue of 'family resemblances' among the things, a suggestion that has given rise in psychology to 'prototype' theories of concepts.

Most traditional approaches to possession conditions have been concerned with the internal *states, especially the beliefs, of the conceptualizer. Quine raised a challenge for such an approach in his doctrine of 'confirmation holism', which stressed that a person's beliefs are fixed by what they find plausible overall. Separating out any particular beliefs as defining a concept seemed to him arbitrary and in conflict with actual practice, where concepts seem shared by people with different beliefs. This led Quine himself to be sceptical about talk of concepts generally, denying that there was* any *principled way to distinguish 'analytic' claims that express definitional claims about a concept from 'synthetic' ones that express merely common beliefs about the things to which a concept applies.*

However, recent philosophers suggest that people share concepts not by virtue of any internal facts, but by virtue of facts about their external (social) environment. For example, people arguably have the concept [water] by virtue of interacting in certain ways with H_2O and deferring to experts in defining it. This work has given rise to a variety of externalist *theories of concepts and semantics generally.*

Many also think, however, that psychology could generalize about people's minds independently of the external contexts they happen to inhabit, and so have proposed 'two-factor theories', according to which there is an internal *component to a concept that may play a role in psychological explanation, as opposed to an* external *component that determines the application of the concept to the world.*

1 Concepts as shareable constituents of thought

Constituents of thought. It is widely thought that 'intentional' explanation in terms of such states as belief, thought and desire affords the best explanation of the behaviour and states of people, many animals and perhaps some machines: someone drinks water because they have a thirst which they think water will quench. By and large, philosophers and psychologists such as Fodor (1975, 1991) or Peacocke (1992) who are interested in intentional explanation take themselves to be committed to the existence of concepts, whereas those sceptical of this form of explanation, for example, Quine (1960), tend to avoid them (see ANIMAL LANGUAGE AND THOUGHT; COGNITIVE DEVELOPMENT; INTENTIONALITY).

Suppose one person thinks that water dissolves salt, and another that it does not. Call the thing that they disagree about a 'proposition' – for example, [Water dissolves salt]. It is in some sense shared by them as the object of their disagreement, and it is expressed by the sentence that follows the verb 'thinks that'. Concepts are the constituents of such propositions (in at least one understanding of them; see PROPOSITIONS, SENTENCES AND STATEMENTS), just as the words 'water', 'dissolves' and 'salt' are constituents of the sentence. Thus, these people could have these beliefs only if they had, *inter alia*, the concepts [water], [dissolves], [salt].

Just which sentential constituents express concepts is a matter of some debate. The central cases that are discussed tend to be the concepts expressed by predicates or general terms, such as 'is water' or 'x dissolves y', terms potentially true of many different individual things. But there are presumably concepts associated with logical words (for example, [not], [some]), as well as with individual things (for example, [Rome], [2]).

Shareability. If we are to make sense of processes of reasoning and communication, and have a basis for generalization in a cognitive psychology, then concepts must be shareable. Consequently, concepts need to be distinguished from the particular ideas, images, sensations that, consciously or unconsciously, pass through people's minds at a particular time. The concept [cat] could not be some individual experience someone has, since in that case no two people could share it and a single person probably could not have the same one twice. Just what kind of shareable object a concept might be is a matter of considerable disagreement among theorists. In much of the psychological literature, where the concern is often with features of actual mental processing, concepts are regarded as mental representations, on such as words or images.

It will be important with respect to this and later proposals to invoke a distinction from the study of language between types and tokens (see TYPE/TOKEN DISTINCTION). A linguistic *token*, such as an inscription of 'café' on a door, has a specific spacetime location: one can ask when and where it occurs; whereas a linguistic *type* – the word 'café' – like any 'universal', is an abstract object outside space and time. One can erase a token of the word 'café', but the type word would still exist. Similarly, concepts could be regarded as internal representation types that have individual ideas as their specific tokens. On this view, you and I could share the concept [water] if you and I have tokens of the same representation type in our minds or brains. There is a good deal of discussion in psychology as to whether concepts in this sense are (type) words, phrases, pictures, maps, diagrams or other kinds of representations, for example, 'prototypes' or 'exemplars' (see §7 below; and Smith and Medin (1981); Rips (1995) for reviews of the psychological literature).

But many philosophers take the view that these mental representation types would no more be identical to concepts than are the type words in a natural language. Words in a language are usually individuated syntactically, allowing both spoken and written tokens of a word to be of the same type, and syntactically identical tokens (for example, of 'bank') to be ambiguous, or of different semantic types. Moreover, different syntactic types – for example, 'city', 'metropolis' – can be synonymous, that is, be of the same semantic type. Similarly, one person might express the concept [city] by a mental representation 'city', another by 'metropolis'; still another perhaps by a mental image of bustling boulevards. But, for all that, they might have the same concept [city]: one could believe and another doubt that cities are healthy places to live. Moreover, different people could employ the same representation to express different concepts: one person might use an image of bustling boulevards to express [city], another to express [pollution]. So, on the standard philosophical reading (which we shall follow here), concepts are to be individuated differently from the representations that express them.

However, although concepts understood in this latter way are arguably also indispensable to psychology, they raise different issues from those concerning representations that standardly interest psychologists. Questions about representations typically involve just the issues that psychologists have tended to investi-gate: processing time, ease of judgment, susceptibility to errors. If one person represents cities and their relations 'spatially', where another represents them by names and descriptions, this may explain differences in how rapidly the two of them can answer questions about cities; but, again, presumably they both still have the concept [city]. Just why they would, what the possession conditions for [city] or any concept might be, is not easy to say (see §5 below): the point here is that they seem to involve issues different from the issue of identifying a syntactically defined representation.

This difference between the psychologist's and philosopher's typical interest is sometimes obscured by ambiguous phrasing. When KANT identifies 'analytic' claims (or claims that express the 'analysis' of a concept) as those in which one concept is 'contained in' another, he glosses this by saying: 'I have merely to analyse the concept, that is, to become conscious to myself of the manifold which I always think in that concept' (1781/1787: A7). In our terms, this could be read as a claim about representations, or (presumably what he intended) about the concepts they express. My mental representation of freedom might invariably involve an image of dancing people, but surely neither Kant nor I would want to say that the analysis of my concept of freedom involved dancing. Conversely, there is no reason that a good analysis should serve as a representation in ordinary, rapid reasonings (for example, identifying something as a bird): indeed, vivid images might serve better.

2 Meanings of words

As most of our examples suggest, concepts are presumed to serve as the meanings of linguistic items, underwriting relations of translation, definition, synonymy, antinomy and semantic implication (Katz 1972). Indeed, much work in the semantics of natural languages (see Jackendoff 1987) takes itself to be addressing 'conceptual structure'. This is partly motivated by Grice's proposal to understand linguistic meaning ultimately in terms of the intentions with which speakers produce linguistic tokens (1957): 'good' means what it does at least partly because of what users of the word have intended to mean by it; that is, because of the concept they have intended to express (see MEANING AND COMMUNICATION; GRICE, H.P. §2).

One problem with this role for concepts is that it is by no means clear just what a theory of meaning is supposed to involve. Some of the issues are exactly the issues we are considering here. However, some issues seem peculiar to language: for example, how much of what is understood in the uttering of a sentence is part of its meaning, or semantics, and how much is part of its use, and so an issue of pragmatics? (See PRAGMATICS.) If I say of someone 'He is not very good at chess', is the meaning simply that 'It is not the case that he is very good', or 'He is bad at chess'?

3 Concepts and analysis

Objects of analysis. At least since Plato's *Euthyphro*, philosophers have been fascinated by a certain sort of question about constitutiveness: in virtue of *what* is something the kind of thing it is – for example, what is 'essential' to something's being good, a piece of knowledge, a free act? Obviously, not just any truth about the target phenomenon will suffice as an answer: to take Plato's *Euthyphro* example, merely the fact that the gods love the good is no reason to think that that is what makes something good, any more than that all bachelors eat is what makes them bachelors (see CONCEPTUAL ANALYSIS).

Some philosophers think such questions are answered by natural science. This certainly seems to be true in the case of 'natural kinds' such as water or polio, which arguably have 'real essences' largely independently of us (see Kripke [1972] 1980; Putnam 1975; ESSENTIALISM). But many concepts, such as [magic], [freedom], [soul] may not pick out any real kind of thing at all (much less one studiable by science): in these cases, all that seems shareable by different possessors of the concept is some belief or other. But even in the natural science cases, some conceptual analysis seems to many unavoidable, if only to determine exactly what the science is about (what makes an investigation one about water, or polio, or consciousness; Bealer 1987).

There is a related question that concepts are also sometimes recruited to answer; not a metaphysical question about 'the nature of things', but an epistemological one about how people seem to know a priori (or 'independently of experience') various necessary truths, for example, that there is an infinity of prime numbers or that equiangular triangles are equilateral ones. However, it should be seen as a substantive and controversial hypothesis, to which we will return, whether this epistemological interest should coincide with the above metaphysical one (see A PRIORI; §5 below).

Philosophers have also sometimes hoped that conceptual analysis would help (dis)solve certain philosophical questions about, for example, truth, free will, personal identity, either by clarifying the commitments of the relevant concepts, or by showing that they were somehow defective. A once popular strategy was to show that the application of a concept was not 'verifiable' (§5 below). A more recent strategy

is to show that the application of a purported concept would be unintelligible, as in the case of [absolute space] (Peacocke 1992: ch. 8).

Whatever its ultimate philosophical benefits, conceptual analysis does seem to involve the sort of facts that are relevant to the question of concept possession. Returning to our pair of people who represent cites differently: what seems relevant to the question of whether, despite their different representations, they still have the same concept [city] is what sorts of things they believe are essential to being a city; what things they would and would not count as cities (which is not to say that this would be decisive; see §5). This difference can lend an air of unreality to philosophical as opposed to psychological discussions of concepts, depending, as it does, upon difficult questions about what (one would think) is possible in various often very outlandish situations.

Vagueness. One supposed defect of many concepts should be set aside from the start. The belief in constitutive analyses of a concept is often thought to be undermined by the existence of difficult, borderline cases for its application (Wittgenstein 1953: §§66–7; Smith and Medin 1981: 31). Now, it certainly cannot be denied that the world is full of genuine borderline cases: 'Is drizzle rain?', 'Are viruses alive?'. Arguably, the world does not supply determinate answers: all kinds in the world may have vague boundaries, any precise delimitation of which may depend upon human decision. But this does not imply that all applications of concepts are up to human decision, much less that there are no defining essences of the phenomena they pick out. [Unmarried adult male] may be a perfectly good analysis of [bachelor] not only despite hard cases, but because the hard cases for the one correspond exactly to the hard cases for the other. (See VAGUENESS.)

4 Referential views

One candidate for the common object of people's thoughts has been simply the referents of their representations, that is, the objects in the world picked out by them. Someone might say that two representations express the same concept if and only if they refer to the same thing(s) in the world. Putting aside the difficult problem of explaining 'reference', this seems an appealing suggestion, clearest in the case of (token) proper names such as 'Aristotle' where the name refers to a specific person (see PROPER NAMES). When we turn to predicates, however, things are not so clear. There are a number of different candidates for what counts as the 'referent' of a predicate and so of the concept it would express: (1) its extension, (2) its intension (as function), and (3) the property that all the (possible) objects satisfying it have in common.

Extensions. The 'extension' is the set of actual objects that satisfy the concept. For example, the extension of [city] might be the set of cities: {Paris, London, Madrid,...}. Russell (1956) proposed an account of 'propositions' according to which they were composed of real objects in the world combined with properties (see also Kaplan 1979). Extensional logicians such as Goodman (1951) and Quine (1960) think that sets of actual objects are all that are needed for serious science: all that needs to be mentioned are actual lions, tigers and quarks. They realize that this suggestion clashes with our ordinary understanding. [Cordate] is not the same as [renate], despite the fact that (let us suppose) all and only actual creatures with kidneys are creatures with hearts ([renate] and [cordate] are 'coextensive'). It seems reasonable to require concepts to cover *possible* cases, for example, possible creatures that are renates but do not have hearts. Goodman would not agree, since, as he famously argues (1951: 5), 'the notion of "possible" cases, of cases that do not exist but might have existed, is far from clear' (see COUNTERFACTUAL CONDITIONALS; GOODMAN, N. §3). But he and Quine would also be wary of talk of concepts generally; and semanticists such as Kaplan (1979) and Salmon (1986) are anxious to avoid introducing talk of them into talk of the semantics of language.

Intensions as functions. Although one might agree that modal notions such as possibility and necessity are not as clear as one would like, it is by no means agreed that science can actually dispense with them. Many philosophers think that the laws essential to causal explanation in any science require modal and counterfactual talk. But, especially in psychology, it seems doubtful that extensions would perform all the explanatory work concepts are needed to perform. Whether or not biology need worry about the possibility of renates lacking hearts, someone could *think* something is a renate without thinking it has a heart. Consequently, many philosophers have claimed that, in addition to extensions, there must be 'intensions', or entities distinguished more finely than mere extensions permit (see INTENSIONAL ENTITIES; INTENSIONAL LOGICS).

Intensions have been defined in a number of ways. One approach is in terms of 'senses' or 'modes of presentation', to which we shall turn shortly (§5). Another approach simply amplifies the extensional characterization to include sets of possible as well as actual objects. Modal logicians and formal semanticists such as Montague (1974), D. Lewis (1972) and Stalnaker (1984), interested in presenting a formal account of the semantics of natural languages, have regarded intensions as functions that map a possible world to the extension of the concept in that world (see SEMANTICS, POSSIBLE WORLDS).

However, mere appeals to possibilia may still not cut things finely enough: for there are concepts that are different even though they apply to all the same things in all possible worlds, for example, [equiangular triangle] and [equilateral triangle], or, following Kripke ([1972] 1980), [water] and [H_2O]; or, to take cases of necessarily *empty* extensions, [square circle] and [married bachelor], which both refer to nothing in all possible worlds. Particularly interesting examples of this latter category have been suggested by Kripke ([1972] 1980) and Slote (1975), who argue in different ways that nothing could possibly satisfy the specific demands of [unicorn] or [monster]. How are we to distinguish these concepts by reference to possible objects?

Properties. Some philosophers think the appropriate reference for predicate concepts is not provided by the objects that the concepts pick out (whether in the actual or merely possible worlds), but rather by the properties those objects share. Thus, [city] is not individuated by the set of all actual or possible cities, but rather by the property, 'being a city'.

Historically, concepts have not always been clearly distinguished from properties, both being regarded as 'universals' (see UNIVERSALS). Thus, the *mortality* one found widespread among men was often assumed to be the same as the concept [mortality] that was a constituent of one's fears. Sometimes this identification seems terminological, as in Frege (1892a) (who uses 'concept' in a quite special way and discusses 'senses' independently), but at other times it is substantive, as in Carnap (1952). Most writers these days would distinguish the two (Putnam 1970; Bealer 1982), even if they also think that there is a property for every concept.

An interesting issue raised by FREGE (1892a) that does seem common to both general concepts and properties is the difficulty of specifying exactly what sort of entities they are. As Frege noted, they seem to be incomplete, or 'unsaturated', having places in them awaiting completion by objects, in the way that predicates in language, such as 'x loves y', have variables awaiting substitution with names (such as 'Romeo' and 'Juliet'). This issue becomes important when we try to specify how general and singular concepts combine to form a thought, or how properties and objects combine to constitute facts (Russell 1903: ch. 4; Wittgenstein 1921).

Many worry that appealing to properties to individuate concepts is gratuitous metaphysics, a free invention of a property for every concept, encouraged by the loose presumption that properties, such as 'immortality', can exist even without being instantiated. To answer this charge, philosophers often claim that properties are provided by the actual causal structure of the world: having kidneys and having a heart enter differently into causal relations, as perhaps do equiangularity and equilaterality (Sober 1982). Particularly philosophers of mind such as Dretske (1981, 1988), Millikan (1984) and Fodor (1991), interested in causal interactions between an organism and the world, find this way of thinking about concepts attractive (see SEMANTICS, INFORMATIONAL; SEMANTICS, TELEOLOGICAL).

However, it is not clear that causal properties will suffice. Are all our concepts really of causally efficacious properties? What about the concept [an inefficacious property]? Or concepts of secondary properties ([red], [sweet]), or ethics and aesthetics ([good], [comical]), which, many have argued, do not pick out genuine causal properties? Or consider, again, necessarily coextensive concepts such as [water] and [H₂O] – which arguably correspond to the same property – or [round square] and [married bachelor], which arguably correspond to none. How could they differentially enter into the causal structure of the world? Or should we suppose that properties can be distinguished even though they are indistinguishable not only in the actual, but in all possible worlds? Are there any constraints?

Moreover, even if we could distinguish concepts by properties, that would not suffice for conceptual analysis. Plato's *Euthyphro* question – is something good because the gods love it, or do they love it because it is good? – brings this out nicely, since the question remains even if we assume that that gods love the good in all possible worlds (so that [good] and [god-beloved] are necessarily coextensive): the *direction* of analysis still needs to be specified.

5 Possession conditions: external v. internal

Many philosophers might not think that Plato's *Euthyphro* question needs an answer: for purposes of logic, and perhaps even formal semantics, appeal to any of these external phenomena (extensions, intensions or properties) may suffice, 'analysis' be hanged. However, if concepts are to play a role in psychology, then one at least wants to know what sort of relation someone must bear to these external phenomena in order to qualify as a competent user of the concept. This is a question about the possession conditions for a concept to which many have thought analyses are crucial.

In considering possession conditions, special care is needed with the peculiar idiom 'concept of *x*' and the

ontology it involves. Psychologists often speak of such things as the child's 'concept of causality'. This could mean the representation the child employs of the concept [causality] that the child shares with adults; or it could mean any of the extension, intension or rule that children associate with the English word 'cause'; or it could mean (as in fact it very often does mean) merely the standard beliefs – what some call the 'conception' – that children associate with the extension, intension: [causality]. Which of these is intended all depends upon what entity one thinks of as the concept and what a mere accompaniment of it. What cannot be seriously intended is the suggestion that a child has a concept [causality] that is both identical to but different from the adults'. (What invites confusion here is the 'of' that implies no relation: just as 'the nation of China' means 'the nation, China', so 'the concept of *x*' often means 'the concept, [*x*]'.)

It might be thought that none of the external identifications of concepts could ever be viable for psychology, since psychology is about what is 'in the mind' (or 'in the head'), not what is in the world external to it (see Jackendoff 1987: 126). This would be an error. We have already seen one way in which it cannot be true: in so far as concepts are shareable, they must be distinguished from individual mental episodes. But still it might be thought that a concept must be a *type* of internally specified mental state, since, after all, surely psychology aims to talk about individual minds, even if it categorizes them in various ways. However, an interest in characterizing what is going on in the mind need not exclude alluding to external objects: the fact that extensions or properties may be external to the head is no reason to think them unsuitable candidates for classifying things that are in the head, just as classifying various words in a book as 'about Vienna' does not prevent those words from existing entirely inside the book.

There have been a variety of external relations that philosophers have proposed that would link internal representations to external phenomena in a way that might constitute concept possession. Influential articles by Kripke ([1972] 1980, 1982), Putnam (1975) and Burge (1979) have given rise to a variety of externalist theories of concepts, which look to such facts as actual causal history (Devitt 1981), various co-variation conditions (Dretske 1981, 1988; Fodor 1991) and evolutionary selection (Millikan 1984; Papineau 1987). However, in so far as they rely on real phenomena in the external world, they are subject to certain limitations that many feel can only be surmounted by appealing to some kind of conditions that are 'in the head'.

Intensions: 'senses'. What argues for the need for

some internal condition on concept is the difficulty for any purely external account of capturing psychologically real distinctions. The examples of necessarily unextended concepts, such as [round square], suggest that the mind can somehow make distinctions for which there is no possible external reality. Consequently, many philosophers have argued that, in addition to the referent of a general term, there must also be (following Frege 1892b) its 'sense', or 'mode of presentation' (occasionally 'intension' is used here as well; see SENSE AND REFERENCE). Thus, what really seems to distinguish [equiangular triangles] and [equilateral triangles] is not the actual or possible things to which they refer, but rather the way the mind conceives them: it is one thing to think of something as (or *qua*) an equilateral triangle, another to think of it *qua* an equiangular triangle (which is why the proof that they are necessarily coextensive is informative). And this obviously helps with the problem of the necessarily coextensive: what distinguishes, for example, [water] and [H_2O] are the different 'ways of thinking', not reflected in any even possible difference in the world. For some (for example, Peacocke 1992) concepts are senses so understood. But, of course, we then need a theory of senses.

6 The classical view and empiricism

One conception of senses is provided by the classical view of concepts. This view has two independent parts that are not always clearly distinguished, one making a claim about the nature of concepts, the other about what is to possess them: (a) concepts have an 'analysis' consisting of conditions that are necessary and sufficient for their satisfaction; and (b) these 'defining' conditions are known to any competent user. An interesting, but problematic, example has been [knowledge], whose analysis was traditionally thought to be [justified true belief], but which has turned out to be far subtler, due to counterexamples raised by philosophers such as Gettier (1963) (see KNOWLEDGE, CONCEPT OF).

The example of [knowledge] brings out an important caveat for the classical view: the proper analysis of a concept need not be readily available to a competent user of it. It was not easy for Athenians to reply to Plato's inquiries about [good], nor for recent philosophers to reply to Gettier. According to a reasonable version of the classical view, a competent user's knowledge of an analysis may be 'tacit' or 'unconscious', rather like the 'knowledge' people have of the grammatical rules of their language, which they seem dependably to obey despite being unable to articulate them (see Evans 1981; Katz 1971; KNOWLEDGE, TACIT; UNCONSCIOUS MENTAL STATES). For

Plato, the analyses could only be extracted from someone by a process of 'dialectic', involving consideration of various examples and arguments to a point of 'reflective equilibrium' (Bealer 1987: 322; Jackson and Pettit 1995).

The classical view, however, has always had to face the difficulty of primitive concepts: how are they to be defined? An influential (but not the only possible) answer was provided by seventeenth-century British empiricists, who claimed that all the primitives were sensory. Indeed, the classical view has often been uncritically burdened with this further claim, or, anyway, the claim that all concepts are 'derived from experience'. Locke (1689), Berkeley (1710) and Hume (1739–40) seemed to take this to mean that concepts were somehow composed of introspectible mental items – 'images', 'impressions' – that were ultimately decomposable into basic sensory parts (see EMPIRICISM; SENSE-DATA).

Berkeley ([1710] 1982: 13) noticed a problem with this approach that every generation has had to rediscover: if a concept is a sensory impression, like an image, then how does one distinguish a general concept [triangle] from a more particular one – say, [isosceles triangle] – that would serve in imagining the general one? In any case, images seem quite hopeless for capturing the concepts associated with logical terms (what is the image for negation or for possibility?). Whatever the role of images, concepts and our competence with them involve something more (see IMAGERY).

Indeed, in addition to images and impressions and other sensory items, a full account of concepts needs to consider issues of logical structure. This is precisely what the logical positivists did, focusing on logically structured propositions and transforming the empiricist claim into their famous 'verifiability theory of meaning': the meaning of a proposition is the means by which it is confirmed or refuted, ultimately by sensory experience; the concept expressed by a predicate is the statement of the (perhaps logically complex) sensory conditions under which people confirm or refute whether something satisfies it (see MEANING AND VERIFICATION). Thus, [acid] might be analysed by reference to tendencies to cause litmus paper to turn red; [belief] by observable behavioural dispositions (see BEHAVIOURISM, ANALYTIC); [material object] by enduring possibilities of sensation (see PHENOMENALISM).

This once popular position has come under much attack in the last fifty years. Few, if any, successful 'reductions' of ordinary concepts (such as [material object], [cause]) to purely sensory concepts have ever been achieved, and there seems to be a pattern to the failures (Chisholm 1957). There have been four main diagnoses: (1) the classical search for 'necessary and sufficient' conditions is misguided and ought to be replaced by an appreciation of the role of a concept in our reasonings and theories of the world; (2) concepts should be regarded as 'family resemblance' structures, or 'prototypes', (3) because of the 'holism of confirmation', attempts to analyse concepts in terms of any verification conditions cannot succeed; and (4) we should stop looking for characterizations of concepts in terms of epistemic conditions, but rather, more metaphysically, in terms of the actual phenomena in the world to which people are referring, but about which they might be ignorant (thus, we would abandon clause (b) of the classical view, which requires analyses to be known by competent users). We will discuss each in turn.

7 Inferential roles and prototypes

Inferential roles. The first alternative, inspired by Wittgenstein's famous dictum, 'the meaning of a word is its use' (1953: §43), treats concepts as involving some or other role of a representation, either in a theory or in thought. Thus, many (for example, Kuhn 1962) have argued that someone possesses a concepts such as [witch] or [phlogiston] only if they understand the theories in which they play a role, or can reason with it in certain appropriate ways (see SEMANTICS, CONCEPTUAL ROLE).

A vexing problem with this approach has been the fact that it is hard to identify just which roles are essential to a concept. It would appear that people can be wrong and/or disagree about almost anything: Berkeley claimed that material objects were ideas, some creationists that people are not animals, some nominalists that numbers are concrete objects. If people are genuinely to disagree with these views, they must share the relevant concepts; otherwise their use of the same words would be equivocal, their disagreement 'merely verbal'. But then it seems very hard to insist upon any specific inferential role being essential to possessing a concept.

Prototypes. Another proposal also inspired by Wittgenstein (1953: §66) is to appeal to 'family resemblances' among the things to which a concept applies: he claimed that games, for example, share no single property, but are similar to each other in various ways that cluster together (some involve winning/losing, others mere entertainment; some are played in groups, others alone). This speculation was taken by psychologists (for example, Rosch 1973; Smith and Medin 1981) to be a testable psychological hypothesis. They showed that people respond differently (in terms of response time and other measures) to questions about whether, for example, penguins rather than robins are birds, in a fashion that suggested that concept membership was a matter not of possessing a classical analysis, but of 'distance' from a 'prototype' or typical 'exemplar'. Thus, a robin satisfies many more of the features of a typical bird than does a penguin and so is a 'better' member of the category; and a malicious lie is a better case of a lie than a well-intentioned one.

It has not always been clear precisely what sort of thing a prototype or exemplar might be. One must take care not to import into the mind procedures, such as comparing one actual bird with another, that make sense only outside of it. Presumably either a prototype or an exemplar is some sort of representation (a list, or an 'image') indicating selected properties, and a metric for determining the distance of a candidate from those properties. Some writers have exploited the resources of 'fuzzy set theory' to capture the intended structure, whereby membership of a category is understood not as an 'all or none' affair, but as a matter of degree: everything satisfies every concept to some degree, however small (see Zadeh 1982; FUZZY LOGIC).

Quite apart from specifying just what the view involves, there are, however, a number of problems with appeals to prototypicality as a theory of concepts. In the first place, loosening the conditions on a concept's application from 'defining' conditions to mere 'family resemblances' risks leaving that application far too unconstrained. Everything after all bears some resemblance to everything else (Goodman 1970): returning to Wittgenstein's example, anything, *x*, resembles standard games in some way or other (if only in belonging to some arbitrary set that contains all games and that thing *x*!). The question is which resemblances are *essential* to the concept, and which merely *accidental* – a question that returns us to the question the classical view tries to answer (see ESSENTIALISM).

Second, prototypes seem poor candidates for handling the crucial phenomenon of conceptual combination: the prototype for [tropical fish] does not seem constructible from the prototypes for [tropical] and [fish], yet someone could grasp [tropical fish] none the less (Osherson and Smith 1982).

Third, prototypicality, which presumably involves distances among a complex cluster of diverse properties, must be distinguished from both vagueness and estimation. As we have already observed (§1), nearly every concept admits of vague cases, in which it is not clear whether the concept applies. But this does not imply that the concept does not have a (correspondingly vague) definition. Similarly, estimation of whether or not something satisfies a concept is a question that arises with regard to *any* concept. But it is clearly not a *metaphysical* issue of the actual conditions something must satisfy in order to satisfy a concept, but rather an *epistemological* one concerning the belief or epistemic probability that something satisfies the conditions, given certain evidence (see REALISM AND ANTIREALISM). The sight of someone with a toupee may mean that there is a 90 per cent probability that he is actually 50 per cent bald, or a 40 per cent probability that he is actually 95 per cent bald. The question of whether [bald] has a classical analysis is untouched by this issue as well (Rey 1983).

8 Metaphysics v. epistemology

These latter distinctions may turn on the different interests we have already noted (§1) in psychologists' and philosophers' use of 'concept', applying respectively to representations or to their shareable meanings. The fact that people are quicker to say that robins rather than penguins are birds may tell us something about people's representations of [bird], but nothing about the definition of the concept [bird] itself, that is, what is in fact required to satisfy that concept (on reflection, after all, most of us agree that penguins are bona fide birds, despite our initial hesitation). This is not to say that the definitional issue is not relevant to psychology: what people take to be required to be a bird is as much a psychological issue as how they figure out whether those requirements have been met. It is just that prototype theory seems to be addressed largely to the latter issue, the classical view to the former.

However, the differences may be deeper than merely terminological. As the example of estimation shows, it is extremely easy to conflate metaphysical issues about the conditions for something's satisfying a concept with the epistemic ones of estimating whether something actually satisfies those conditions. One reason is that English can encourage running the two together, phrasing the metaphysical question as 'What determines what is what?' and the epistemic one as 'How does someone determine what is what?'. A second reason is that epistemic conditions are as likely to 'come to mind' in thinking with a concept as are its defining conditions (see §1 above).

But a more important reason is that empiricism made a policy of connecting the two: the defining conditions for a concept were to be stated in terms of experiential evidence. As anti-empiricists from Plato on have argued, however, many of our concepts seem to 'transcend experience', in that they seem to be graspable and sometimes applicable in the absence of it. For lack of any genuine Euclidean triangles in the world, it is unclear how our concept of them could be derived from experience. And even instantiated concepts such as [material object], [causation] and [prehistoric] seem to go far beyond mere sensory experience: we seem to be able to think coherently about material objects causally interacting in prehistoric times, even in the absence of any sensory evidence of that interaction. In any case, many of our concepts transcend their stereotypes: most of us understand the concept [female doctor], and recognize that [even number] has a perfectly good definition, despite our demonstrable reliance on stereotypes in both cases (Armstrong, Gleitman and Gleitman 1983).

Moreover, it can often seem arbitrary and unduly restrictive to tie a concept to any particular method of verification (or confirmation). Taking a page from Pierre Duhem (1914), Quine (1953) argued that 'our beliefs confront the tribunal of experience only as a corporate body': litmus paper turning red confirms that a solution is acidic only in conjunction with a great deal of background chemical and physical theory; indeed, Quine claims, only in conjunction with the whole of a person's system of beliefs (a view called 'confirmation holism'; see ANALYTICITY; CONFIRMATION THEORY; QUINE, W.V.). Hence, if a concept is to be analysed as its verification conditions, its meaning would be similarly holistic ('meaning holism'). Given that no two persons' beliefs are likely to be precisely the same, this has the consequence that no two people ever share precisely the same concepts – and no one could, strictly speaking, remember the same thing over any amount of time that included a change of any belief! Fodor and LePore (1992) have recently argued that this sort of conceptual (or semantic) holism would undermine serious psychology, but, fortunately, that the arguments for it are less than compelling (see HOLISM: MENTAL AND SEMANTIC; ATOMISM, ANCIENT).

9 Difficulties for an internalist approach

Even if one distinguishes epistemological from metaphysical issues in determining concept identity, there remain a number of problems for any purely internalist theory of concepts. Whether classical or prototypical, any internalist theory of concepts requires distinguishing internal features – beliefs, inferential roles, prototypes – that are essential to (or defining of) a concept from those that are accidental, and many feel that it really is this distinction that is undermined by Quine's observations about holism. Indeed, 'sameness of concept' for Quine becomes by and large an 'indeterminate' issue (see RADICAL TRANSLATION AND RADICAL INTERPRETATION). The most one might expect is a similarity of inferential role between symbols in different theories or symbol systems (Harman 1972; Block 1986): which similarities are selected may vary for different explanatory tasks, and may be a pragmatic affair (Bilgrami 1992; Lormand 1996).

A second problem emerged from the externalist approaches of Kripke ([1972] 1980), Putnam (1975) and Burge (1979), and has come to be represented by Putnam's example of 'twin earth' (1975): suppose there were a planet exactly like the earth in every way except that, wherever the earth has H_2O, twin earth has a different, but superficially similar chemical XYZ. Putnam argues that twin-earthlings would not mean by the word 'water' what we mean (for example, their tokens of the sentence 'Water is wet' would not have the same truth-conditions as ours), despite the fact that, *ex hypothesi*, twin-earthlings would have our same internal structure. (Burge (1979) and Stich (1983) present less outlandish examples.) As Putnam famously put it, 'meanings just ain't in the head'; rather, he argues, they depend at least in part upon the relations between internal states and external phenomena (see CONTENT: WIDE AND NARROW).

In view of both these examples, and the Quinian worries, FODOR (1991, 1998) opts for an entirely 'atomistic' account of concepts, arguing that concepts have no 'analyses' whatsoever: they are simply ways in which people are directly related to individual properties in their environments, any one of which they might enjoy without the others. In principle, someone might have the concept [bachelor] and no other concepts at all, much less any 'analysis' of it, simply by virtue of having some internal state that is causally connected with bachelorhood in the local environment. Such a view goes hand in hand with Fodor's rejection of not only verificationist, but any empiricist, account of concept learning and construction. Indeed, given the failure of empiricist constructions, Fodor (1975, 1979) argues that concepts are not constructed or 'derived from experience' at all, but are (nearly enough) all innate (see NATIVISM). Devitt (1995) defends a more moderate, 'molecularist' position, allowing that many innate primitives are non-sensory (for example, [cause], [object]) but that others are susceptible to definition, especially in view of the thereby enlarged primitive base.

10 Two-factor theories and a modified classical view

Although externalism does seem to account both for the stability of concepts through variation in belief and for variations in concept due to variations in environment, it still must confront the issues we mentioned earlier (§5) that invite internalism, namely, that there seem to be more distinctions in the mind than are available in the external world. An increasingly popular approach is to separate the internal and external work concepts are asked to perform. According to 'two-factor' theories, 'concepts' should be regarded as having two components: one 'in the head', consisting of an internal representation playing a certain psychological role; and the other, some sort of co-variational law or evolutionary fact that, in a historical context, determines the reference and truth-conditions of the concept. (Sometimes 'concept' is restricted to the internal factor, 'content' to the external; and 'two-factor theory' is sometimes applied only to those views in which the two factors are relatively independent of one another.)

A two-factor theory leaves a place for a modified classical view, as well as for something like philosophical analysis. The internal factor would determine a full semantic content to a conceptual representation only in a particular context, so that the full analysis of (the content of) a concept might await empirical investigation of that context and not be available to its user. But this is perhaps as it should be: philosophical analysis of 'the nature of' a phenomenon may depend both upon the internal rule one is deploying and the actual phenomenon that, in a context, the rule picks out (Bealer 1987; Jackson and Pettit 1995).

See also: CONTENT, NON-CONCEPTUAL; SEMANTICS

References and further reading

* Armstrong, S., Gleitman, L. and Gleitman, H. (1983) 'What Some Concepts Might Not Be', *Cognition* 13 (3): 263–308. (Discussion of experiments demonstrating prototypicality effects even with concepts, such as [even number], that have obvious classical definitions.)

Ayer, A.J. (1936) *Language, Truth and Logic*, London: Gollancz. (The classic defence of the logical positivist programme, including efforts to analyse all empirically meaningful statements into statements about possible sense experience.)

* Bealer, G. (1982) *Quality and Concept*, Oxford: Oxford University Press. (A recent effort to distinguish concepts from properties, and to provide a logical framework for discussing them both.)

* —— (1987) 'The Limits of Scientific Essentialism', in J. Tomberlin (ed.) *Philosophical Perspectives*, vol. 1, *Metaphysics*, Atascadero, CA: Ridgeview Press. (An argument that externalist theories of meaning and concepts must rely on certain internal conditions, knowable a priori.)

* Berkeley, G. (1710) *A Treatise concerning the Principles of Knowledge*, Indianapolis, IN: Hackett Publishing Company, 1982. (Thirteen raises an important problem for an empiricism that derives 'ideas' too directly from sense 'impressions'.)

* Bilgrami, A. (1992) *Belief and Meaning: The Unity and Locality of Mental Content*, Oxford: Blackwell. (A strategy for how meaning holism can be made compatible with interpersonal comparisons of meaning and concepts.)

* Block, N. (1986) 'Advertisement for a Semantics for Psychology', in P.A. French, T.E. Uehling, Jr and H.K. Wettstein (eds) *Midwest Studies in Philosophy*, vol. 10, *Studies in the Philosophy of Mind*, Minneapolis, MN: University of Minnesota Press. (A defence of an inferential role theory of meaning and concepts as involving merely similarity, not identity among those roles.)

* Burge, T. (1979) 'Individualism and the Mental', in P.A. French, T.E. Uehling, Jr and H.K. Wettstein (eds) *Midwest Studies in Philosophy*, vol. 4, Minneapolis, MN: University of Minnesota Press. (Subtle defence of an externalist account of concept possession.)

* Carnap, R. (1952) *Fundamentals of Concept Formation in Empirical Science*, Chicago, IL: University of Chicago Press. (Good example of a work in which concepts and properties are identified.)

* Chisholm, R. (1957) *Perceiving: A Philosophical Study*, Ithaca, NY: Cornell University Press. (Classic critique of 'phenomenalist' and 'behaviourist' efforts to 'reduce' talk about material objects to talk about sensations, and talk about mental states to talk about external behaviour.)

* Devitt, M. (1981) *Designation*, New York: Columbia University Press. (A defence of a causal theory of the reference of names – plausible as part of an externalist account of concepts of individuals.)

* —— (1995) *Coming to Our Senses*, Cambridge: Cambridge University Press. (A defence of a moderate conceptual molecularism, combining an externalist account of some non-sensory concepts, but also an inferential role account of others.)

* Dretske, F. (1981) *Knowledge and the Flow of Information*, Cambridge, MA: MIT Press. (An effort to base an externalist theory of concepts on the notion of 'information'.)

* —— (1988) *Explaining Behavior: Reasons in a World of Causes*, Cambridge, MA: MIT Press. (Further development of an informational semantics, linking informational roles to behavioural consequences.)

* Duhem, P. (1914) *The Aim and Structure of Physical Theory*, trans. P. Wiener, New York: Atheneum, 1954. (Early statement of confirmation holism and, thereby, for an empiricist like Quine, for meaning, or conceptual, holism.).

* Evans, G. (1981) 'Semantic Theory and Tacit Knowledge', in S. Holtzman and C. Leich (eds) *Wittgenstein: To Follow a Rule*, London: Routledge & Kegan Paul, 118–37. (Discussion of the view that knowledge of the semantics of one's language might be tacit.)

* Fodor, J.A. (1975) *The Language of Thought*, New York: Crowell. (Now classic statement of the claim that thought consists in computations on representations encoded in the brain, presumed throughout much cognitive psychology and in this entry; also, independently, initiates the argument that almost all concepts are innate.)

* —— (1979) 'The Present Status of the Innateness Controversy', in *RePresentations: Essays on the Foundations of Cognitive Science*, Cambridge, MA: MIT Press. (Rich discussion of the issues underlying the claim that almost concepts are innate.)

* —— (1991) *A Theory of Content*, Cambridge, MA: MIT Press. (Vigorous defence of a radically externalist theory of meaning and concepts – although he tends to use the latter term for the internal representation of an externally determined 'content'.)

* —— (1998) *Concepts: Where Cognitive Science Went Wrong*, Oxford: Oxford University Press. (Extended critique of conceptual role and other analyses of concepts in current linguistics, philosophy and psychology.)

* Fodor, J.A. and LePore, E. (1992) *Holism: A Shoppers' Guide*, Oxford: Blackwell. (A critique of arguments for semantic and conceptual holism.)

* Frege, G. (1892a) 'Über Begriff und Gegenstand', *Vierteljahrsschrift für wissenschaftliche Philosophie* 16: 192–205; trans. P.T. Geach, 'On Concept and Object', in *Translations from the Philosophical Writings of Gottlob Frege*, ed. P.T. Geach and M. Black, Oxford: Blackwell, 3rd edn, 1980. (Frege himself used 'concept' for something like what is more commonly called a 'property'; but the subtle issues he raises here apply to both.)

* —— (1892b) 'Über Sinn und Bedeutung', *Zeitschrift für Philosophie und philosophische Kritik* 100: 25–50; trans. M. Black, 'On Sense and Reference', in *Translations from the Philosophical Writings of Gottlob Frege*, ed. P.T. Geach and M. Black, Oxford: Blackwell, 3rd edn, 1980. (*Locus classicus* of a 'sense' theory of meaning and what many regard as concepts.)

* Gettier, E. (1963) 'Is Justified True Belief Knowledge?', *Analysis* 23: 121–3. (Short and highly influential article presenting counterexamples to the traditional 'analysis' of [knowledge]; excellent as a paradigm of the philosopher's interest in concepts.)

* Goodman, N. (1951) *Structure of Appearance*, Indianapolis, IN: Bobbs-Merrill, 1966. (A classic

effort at empiricist analysis of objective into sensory concepts, wholly within an extensional conception.)

* —— (1970) 'Seven Strictures on Similarity', in L. Foster and J. Swanson (eds) *Experience and Theory*, Amherst, MA: University of Massachusetts Press. (Excellent discussion of the perils of appealing to 'similarity' in theories of concepts.)

* Grice, H.P. (1957) 'Meaning', *Philosophical Review* 66: 377–88. (Classic sketch of a programme for deriving the meaning of sentences from the intentions of speakers.)

* Harman, G. (1972) *Thought*, Princeton, NJ: Princeton University Press. (Defence of an inferential role theory of meaning and concepts as involving merely similarity, not identity among those roles.)

* Hume, D. (1739–40) *A Treatise of Human Nature*, ed. L.A. Selby-Bigge, revised P.H. Nidditch, Oxford: Clarendon Press, 1975. (Classic development of an early empiricist theory of concepts.)

* Jackendoff, R. (1987) *Consciousness and Computation*, Cambridge, MA: MIT Press. (Lively and imaginative internalist account of conceptual structure as it appears to be revealed by the semantics of natural language.)

* Jackson, F. and Pettit, P. (1995) 'Moral Foundationalism and Moral Motivation', *Philosophical Quarterly* 45 (178): 20–40. (Recent 'two-factor' proposal to provide definitions by the role of terms in ordinary thought, which, given a context of utterance, determines a propositional content.)

* Kant, I. (1781/1787) *Critique of Pure Reason*, trans. N. Kemp Smith, New York: St. Martin's Press, 1968. (Classic study of the basic concepts arguably required for any understanding of an objective world.)

* Kaplan, D. (1979) 'Dthat', in P. French, T. Uehling and H. Wettstein (eds) *Contemporary Studies in the Philosophy of Language*, Minneapolis, MN: University of Minnesota Press, 383–400. (Highly influential development of a 'direct reference' theory of demonstratives (for example, 'that', 'this'), indexicals ('I', 'her') and other expressions, according to which 'concepts' play much less of a role than traditionally supposed.)

* Katz, J. (1971) *The Underlying Reality of Language and its Philosophical Import*, New York: Harper & Row. (Early proposal modelling knowledge of semantics and concepts on the kind of tacit knowledge of syntax postulated by Chomsky.)

* —— (1972) *Semantic Theory*, New York: Harper & Row. (Defence of the classical view on behalf of a semantics of natural language.)

* Kripke, S.A. (1972) 'Naming and Necessity', in D. Davidson and G. Harman (eds) *Semantics of*

Natural Language, Dordrecht: Reidel, 252–355; expanded version published as *Naming and Necessity*, Oxford and New York: Blackwell, 1980. (One of the original defences of an externalist account of proper names and natural kind terms; suggestive of a similar account of the corresponding concepts.)

* —— (1982) *Wittgenstein on Rules and Private Language*, Cambridge, MA: Harvard University Press. (An attack on an internalist account of concept possession, and a suggestion of an externalist 'social' theory instead.)

* Kuhn, T. (1962) *The Structure of Scientific Revolutions*, Chicago, IL: University of Chicago Press. (Influential defence of a holistic, inferential role theory of concept possession.)

Laurence, S. and Margolis, E. (eds) (1998) *Concepts*, Cambridge, MA: MIT Press. (An excellent collection of leading articles on the topic by philosophers, psychologists and logicians.)

* Lewis, D.K. (1972) 'General Semantics', in D. Davidson and G. Harman (eds) *Semantics of Natural Language*, Dordrecht: Reidel. (Systematic presentation of a theory of meaning and concepts as intension-functions on possible worlds.)

* Locke, J. (1689) *An Essay concerning Human Understanding*, New York: Dutton (Everyman), 1961. (The original proposal of an empiricist theory of concepts.)

* Lormand, E. (1996) 'How to Be a Meaning Holist', *Journal of Philosophy* 93: 51–73. (Defence of the view that a token representation may have many different meanings, for different explanatory purposes.)

* Millikan, R. (1984) *Language, Thought and Other Biological Categories*, Cambridge, MA: MIT Press. (The original statement of an evolutionary/teleological theory of meaning and concepts.)

* Montague, R. (1974) *Formal Philosophy*, ed. R. Thomason, New Haven, CT: Yale University Press. (A systematic development of a theory of meaning and concepts as intension-functions on possible worlds.)

* Osherson, D. and Smith, E. (1982) 'Gradedness and Conceptual Combination', *Cognition* 12: 299–318. (Examination of the difficulties of conceptual combination for prototype theories.)

* Papineau, D. (1987) *Reality and Representation*, Oxford: Blackwell. (Defence of an evolutionary approach to concept ascription.)

* Peacocke, C. (1992) *A Study of Concepts*, Cambridge, MA: MIT Press. (Sophisticated and influential defence of a 'sense' theory of concepts.)

* Plato (395–347 BC) *Euthyphro*, in *The Collected Dialogues of Plato including the Letters*, ed. E.

Hamilton and H. Cairns, Princeton, NJ: Princeton University Press, 1961. (Raises an important kind of question for conceptual analysis: is something good because the gods love it, or do they love it because it is good?)

* Putnam, H. (1970) 'On Properties', in *Philosophical Papers*, vol. 1, Cambridge: Cambridge University Press, 1975, 305–22. (Excellent discussion distinguishing properties from concepts.)

* —— (1975) 'The Meaning of "Meaning"', in *Philosophical Papers*, vol. 2, *Mind, Language, and Reality*, Cambridge: Cambridge University Press. (Highly influential, lively and readable defence of an 'externalist' theory of meaning and concepts.)

* Quine, W.V. (1953) 'Two Dogmas of Empiricism', in *From a Logical Point of View and Other Essays*, Cambridge, MA: Harvard University Press. (Important source of attacks on the scientific significance of conceptual analysis and on the classical view.)

—— (1954) 'Carnap and Logical Truth', in *Ways of Paradox and Other Essays*, Cambridge, MA: Harvard University Press, 2nd edn, 1976. (Superb essay on the history of 'conceptual analysis', as well as important arguments on behalf of his meaning holism and against the scientific significance of analyses.)

* —— (1960) *Word and Object*, Cambridge, MA: MIT Press. (Classic exposition of an account of mind and language without appeals to concepts or meanings.)

* Rey, G. (1983) 'Concepts and Stereotypes', *Cognition* 15: 237–62; repr. in S. Laurence and E. Margolis (eds) *Concepts*, Cambridge, MA: MIT Press, 1998. (Criticism of prototype theories for conflating epistemological with metaphysical issues.)

—— (forthcoming) 'A Naturalistic A Priori', *Philosophical Studies*. (Argues that the classical view can be defended against Quinian attacks by supposing analyses are sub-doxastic, like the rules of grammar.)

* Rips, L. (1995) 'The Current Status of Research on Concept Combination', *Mind and Language* 10 (1/2): 72–104. (Excellent review of psychological research on concepts to that date.)

* Rosch, E. (1973) 'On the Internal Structure of Perceptual and Semantic Categories', in T.E. Moore (ed.) *Cognitive Development and Acquisition of Language*, New York: Academic Press. (Influential discussion of the role of 'prototypes' in categorization tasks.)

* Russell, B. (1903) *Principles of Mathematics*, New York: Norton, 2nd edn, 1938. (Chapter 4 wrestles with the problem of distinguishing a sentence from mere lists of words, which involves thinking about

how a general concept is related to the individual (concept?) that satisfies it; connected to discussions in Frege (1892a) and Wittgenstein (1921).)

* —— (1956) *Logic and Knowledge, Essays 1901–1950*, ed. R.C. Marsh, London: Allen & Unwin; repr. London: Routledge, 1992. (Influential essays presenting a highly 'referential' conception of the constituents of thoughts and propositions.)

* Salmon, N. (1986) *Frege's Puzzle*, Cambridge, MA: MIT Press/Bradford Books. (Argues against 'sense' theories of linguistic meaning.)

* Slote, M. (1975) 'Necessarily Inapplicable Concepts', *Philosophical Studies* 28: 265–71. (Argues that certain familiar concepts, such as [miracle] and [evil], could not possibly be instantiated.)

* Smith, E. and Medin, D. (1981) *Concepts and Categories*, Cambridge, MA: Harvard University Press. (Useful discussion of psychological research supporting prototype theories.)

* Sober, E. (1982) 'Why Logically Equivalent Predicates May Pick Out Different Properties', *American Philosophical Quarterly* 19: 183–9. (Argues that predicates such as 'equiangular' and 'equilateral' may pick out not only different concepts, but also different properties.)

* Stalnaker, R. (1984) *Inquiry*, Cambridge, MA: MIT Press/Bradford Books. (Clear and readable defence of a theory of meaning and concepts as intension-functions on possible worlds.)

* Stich, S. (1983) *From Folk Psychology to Cognitive Science: The Case Against Belief*, Cambridge, MA: MIT Press. (Proposes an essentially pragmatic approach to concept ascription across people; good discussion of intuitions leading us to different descriptions.)

* Wittgenstein, L. (1921) *Tractatus Logico-Philosophicus*, trans. D.F. Pears and B.F. McGuinness, London: Routledge & Kegan Paul, 1961. (Proposes an interesting 'picture' theory of meaning to solve the problem of how predicates combine with names to form sentential representations; suggestive of a similar treatment of mental representations and/or concepts.)

* —— (1953) *Philosophical Investigations*, New York: Macmillan. (The source of 'use' and 'inferential role' theories of concept possession, as well as of the suggestion that concepts might have a prototype or 'family resemblance' structure.)

* Zadeh, L. (1982) 'A Note on Prototype Theory and Fuzzy Sets', *Cognition* 12: 291–7. (Application of the formalism of 'fuzzy set theory' to a prototype theory of concepts.)

GEORGES REY

CONCEPTUAL ANALYSIS

A distinction must be made between the philosophical theory of conceptual analysis and the historical philosophical movement of Conceptual Analysis.

The theory of conceptual analysis holds that concepts – general meanings of linguistic predicates – are the fundamental objects of philosophical inquiry, and that insights into conceptual contents are expressed in necessary 'conceptual truths' (analytic propositions). There are two methods for obtaining these truths:

(1) direct a priori definition of concepts;
(2) indirect 'transcendental' argumentation.

The movement of Conceptual Analysis arose at Cambridge during the first half of the twentieth century, and flourished at Oxford and many American departments of philosophy in the 1950s and early 1960s. In the USA its doctrines came under heavy criticism, and its proponents were not able to respond effectively; by the end of the 1970s the movement was widely regarded as defunct. This reversal of fortunes can be traced primarily to the conjunction of several powerful objections: the attack on intensions and on the analytic/synthetic distinction; the paradox of analysis; the 'scientific essentialist' theory of propositions; and the critique of transcendental arguments. Nevertheless a closer examination indicates that each of these objections presupposes a covert appeal to concepts and conceptual truths. In the light of this dissonance between the conventional wisdom of the critics on the one hand, and the implicit commitments of their arguments on the other, there is a manifest need for a careful re-examination of conceptual analysis.

1 **Origins and career of Conceptual Analysis**
2 **The theory and methods of conceptual analysis**
3 **Five fundamental objections**
4 **The inescapability of conceptual analysis**

1   Origins and career of Conceptual Analysis

Many of the elements of Conceptual Analysis are present already in John Locke's *Essay Concerning Human Understanding* (1689) – in his doctrines of general ideas and definitions (decompositions of complex general ideas into sets of simple ideas); in his distinction between 'trifling' and 'instructive' universally certain propositions; and in his closely related distinction between 'intuitive' and 'demonstrative' knowledge (see LOCKE, J. §§3–4). An even more important source of influence is Immanuel Kant's *Critique of Pure Reason* (1781/1787). There Kant makes three crucial sets of distinctions. The first

is between 'analytic' and 'synthetic' propositions, that is, between propositions true by virtue of conceptual content alone, and propositions true by virtue of conceptual content together with a non-conceptual semantic element ('intuition'). The second is between a priori (necessary, experience-independent) and a posteriori (contingent, experience-dependent) truths. The third is a threefold division between proofs by empirical methods, 'constructive' proofs in mathematics, and 'transcendental' proofs. Transcendental proofs establish the truth of non-mathematical synthetic a priori propositions by showing how the natural sciences – and human experience itself – presuppose a set of primitive pure concepts or 'categories' (see KANT, I. §4).

Kant's important idea that conceptual truths can be either analytic a priori or synthetic a priori is effectively erased by Gottlob Frege in his *Foundations of Arithmetic* (1884). Frege's overriding philosophical aim is to put mathematical proof on a firm footing by reducing the truths of arithmetic to analytic truths of logic. In view of this, the proper goal of an analysis is the production of non-circular, explanatory, yet meaning-preserving general definitions of fundamental concepts – as exemplified in Frege's famous definition of a number as a class of equinumerous classes (see LOGICISM; FREGE, G. §§7–8). Analytic a priori truths for Frege are propositions that follow deductively either from the self-evident, unprovable laws of pure logic alone, or else from the laws of logic together with logical definitions.

Frege's method was enthusiastically developed and subtly transformed by G.E. Moore in what may be regarded as the first phase of Conceptual Analysis. Moore supplemented Frege's austere logicism with a Kant-inspired attentiveness to the multiplicity of different sorts of concepts, propositions and logico-semantic relations, and with a predilection for arguments resting on appeals to common sense (see MOORE, G.E. §§3–4). Moorean analysis then travelled from Cambridge to Oxford, where J.L. AUSTIN and Gilbert RYLE added to it a special focus on the uses and abuses of ordinary language. This led directly to the vigorous growth in the 1950s of the second phase of Conceptual Analysis, sometimes also called 'Oxford Philosophy'. Conceptual analysis was exported to the USA in the 1950s and early 1960s, primarily through the writings of H.P. GRICE and P.F. STRAWSON. While it found a niche for a time in many American philosophy departments, it did not ultimately survive. It was attacked on several fronts by leading American philosophers (most damagingly, perhaps, by W.V. QUINE – see §3 of this entry for details), and by the end of the 1970s had largely succumbed.

2 The theory and methods of conceptual analysis

The career of Conceptual Analysis was rather brief and embattled, but its underlying philosophical theory, conceptual analysis, should be analysed and judged on its own merits. For simplicity's sake, we can think of conceptual analysis as defined by the conjunction of the following five theses:

(1) *The content thesis.* A concept is a general content possessing intrinsic, individuating structures and relations (an intension), and having a corresponding application either to sets of actual or possible objects (an extension), or to other concepts.

(2) *The linguistic thesis.* A concept is the meaning of a predicate-expression; and all such words have meanings only in the context of whole sentences used (first and foremost) in making statements in ordinary discourse.

(3) *The modal thesis.* Every true proposition expressing conceptual interconnections is necessary and analytic.

(4) *The knowledge thesis.* Purely conceptual inquiry produces important a priori knowledge. This knowledge is expressed in analytic propositions known to be true either by (a) direct definitional analysis of conceptual contents, or by (b) indirect 'transcendental' arguments.

(5) *The metaphilosophical thesis.* All fundamental philosophical errors arise from misunderstandings of concepts, and can be corrected only by proper conceptual analyses.

The first two theses convey a theory of concepts. Being general, concepts play the role traditionally assigned to universals (see UNIVERSALS). Yet because they are ontologically dependent upon ordinary language, concepts are not otherworldly, Platonic entities. And because concept-possession depends upon linguistic use and mastery, concepts are immediately accessible to all competent speakers.

Concepts bear necessary relations to one another and also have fixed internal structures; these relations and structures are open to the process of analysis; and a capacity for analytical insight is guaranteed by linguistic mastery. Concepts, however, are of two quite different sorts: 'categorematic' and 'syncategorematic'. Categorematic concepts (for example, 'bachelor' or 'being taller than') are 'material' intensional contents that uniquely and independently determine concept-extensions. Syncategorematic concepts, by contrast, are 'formal' intensions that apply in a rule-like way to other concepts or conceptual complexes. These in turn are of two sorts:

(1) 'logical concepts' (such as 'conjunction') expressing logical operations; and

(2) 'categorical concepts' (such as 'objecthood') expressing higher-order conditions of the applicability of lower-order concepts.

Analytical insight into categorematic and syncategorematic concepts permits the capture of both non-logical and logical truths (for example, 'bachelors are unmarried males' and '$\sim (P \& \sim P)$') within the general class of conceptual truths.

The modal thesis tells us that all conceptual truths are analytic and necessary; such truths reflect conceptual contents alone and bear no connections to the disposition of things in the actual world or any possible world. They are therefore 'topic-neutral'. This makes is relatively easy to see why, as the knowledge thesis asserts, the cognition of analytic propositions is a priori: the insight into conceptual content requires no appeal to empirical facts or individuals. And certainly in the case of such simple definitional propositions as 'bachelors are unmarried males', it appears to be the case that a direct awareness of conceptual identity – guaranteed by linguistic competence and the grasp of word-synonymy – requires no appeal to experience in order to be known. But the very idea of a conceptual identity is not so simple as one might think; nor does insight into conceptual truth always result from definitional inquiries alone. This is manifest in three ways.

In the first place, definitional truths do express conceptual identities or synonymies of words, but the criterion of identity cannot be merely that concepts are identical, or words synonymous, when they share the same extensions necessarily. The concepts 'creature with a heart' and 'creature with a kidney', for example, share actual extensions, but are clearly not identical. And as C.I. Lewis first pointed out in 'Modes of Meaning' (1943–4) there are also concepts – such as 'equilateral triangle' and 'equiangular triangle' – that are necessarily co-extensional, but not precisely identical. Hence a stricter criterion of conceptual identity, involving an isomorphism of the concepts' internal structures, must be invoked.

In the second place, there are analytic propositions expressing conceptual relations that reflect only partial identities of concepts, for example: (A) 'bachelors are males'. And most logical truths appear not to reflect *either* complete *or* partial conceptual identities. Here, however, it is possible to appeal to a criterion of analyticity used by Kant, namely that the denial of an analytic proposition leads to a contradiction. This is closely connected with the idea that when terms in partially definitional propositions *are* replaced by their full definitions, or perfect synonyms, logical truths will result. Thus substituting 'unmarried males' into (A) for 'bachelors' produces the logical truth, (A*) 'unmarried males are males'. The denial of (A*) is obviously logically contradictory. So an a priori grasp of conceptual identities and logical concepts appears to be sufficient for knowledge of definitional propositions and logical truths alike.

Third, however, there are conceptually true propositions, such as (B) 'nothing can be simultaneously coloured in two different ways all over' and (C) 'the world as we experience it contains reidentifiable objective particulars in a single spatiotemporal scheme', that do not seem to reflect logical truths, or even complete or partial identities of concepts, but rather conceptual connections of a somewhat different sort. Here we are strongly reminded of Kant's view that some conceptual truths are not analytic, but instead synthetic. And indeed, although conceptual analysts generally eschew the existence of the synthetic a priori, this is precisely where the appeal to transcendental arguments comes in. A transcendental argument aims to show that a proposition *P* (say, (B) or (C)) is conceptually true because it is presupposed by another proposition *Q* (say, '*a* is red; so it is not green' or '*a* is not being perceived by me now; but it is still over there just the same'), which is taken by hypothesis to be perfectly acceptable and a 'paradigm case' of some class of statements. Not only is *P* a necessary condition of the truth of *Q*, but more profoundly *P* is a necessary condition of the *real possibility* or *meaningfulness* of *Q* – of its being true or false in the first place. This is because the concepts expressed in *P* are categorial concepts having a 'conceptual priority' over the concepts expressed in *Q*, which is to say that the concepts in *P* have a central place in the overall 'conceptual scheme' by which language-using human beings organize their common sense experience in the ways exemplified by *Q*. Thus the conceptual truth (B) expresses an insight about the very nature of human experience of colour; and the conceptual truth (C) expresses an insight about the very nature of human perception of objects. Transcendental arguments thus extend the scope of conceptual analysis from the mere definitional or logical exploration of conceptual contents (sometimes also called 'philosophical grammar'), towards insights into first principles expressing the 'conceptual geography' of the common sense world (see TRANSCENDENTAL ARGUMENTS).

The metaphilosophical thesis follows directly from the other four. Concepts govern the ways we think about all things and other concepts; thus not only all philosophical truths, but also all philosophical errors, are conceptual. The two methods of conceptual analysis – definitional and transcendental – must be employed not merely as means of philosophical insight but also for the unmasking and diagnosis of conceptual confusions.

3 Five fundamental objections

The many different lines and styles of criticism directed against conceptual analysis tend to converge on five basic objections:

(1) *The flight from intensions.* If concepts are linguistic intensions, then obviously any sceptical argument showing that intensions do not exist will undermine the linguistic thesis. Just such an argument has been influentially promoted by Quine, in two parts. First, intensions are said to be either ontologically 'mysterious' or purely psychological entities that intervene between language (or linguistic behaviour) and reference, and should be ruled out of any properly logical and scientific approach to semantic issues. Second, all the explanatory roles traditionally played by intensions – as what words signify, as truth-vehicles, as grounds of synonymy, as grounds of modality, as objects of the propositional attitudes, and as objects of philosophical analysis – can be functionally mimicked by logical or linguistic devices that make no appeals whatsoever to intensional entities (see INTENSIONAL ENTITIES).

(2) *The death of analyticity.* Perhaps even more famous than Quine's attack on intensions is his attack, in 'Two Dogmas of Empiricism' (1951), on the very idea of analyticity (see QUINE, W.V. §8). Setting aside logical truth, Quine argues that non-logical analyticity is based on the concept of synonymy. But every plausible attempt to give an explanation of synonymy (by appeal to the notions of definition, linguistic interchangeability, or semantical rules) ends either in circularity or vacuity. In the absence of a clear account of synonymy, no clear boundary between analytic and synthetic (factual, contingent) propositions can be established. If sound, this argument forces the rejection of the modal thesis (see ANALYTICITY).

(3) *The paradox of analysis.* In 'Moore's Notion of Analysis' (1942), C.H. Langford points up a deep difficulty in the conception of a definitional analysis. In order for a proposition expressing the results of such an analysis to be correct or true, it must establish a complete or partial identity between concepts. But if an identity is so established, then the very same concept, wholly or in part, redundantly shows up twice in the same conceptual truth, as expressed by two different words or phrases. Thus every correct

definitional analysis of a concept is non-informative and trivial; and the very project of definitionally analysing a concept is epistemically pointless. If true, it follows directly from the paradox that the first part of the Knowledge Thesis, which states that all conceptual truths express important a priori knowledge, is false.

(4) *Scientific essentialism and the contingency of conceptual truths.* Enshrined in the linguistic thesis, the modal thesis and the knowledge thesis, are claims to the effect that the meanings of words are conceptual intensions, and that conceptual truths are analytic, a priori and necessary. But it has been influentially argued by Hilary Putnam (1975) that the extensions of some general words – 'natural-kind' terms such as 'water' or 'cats' – are not in fact determined by their corresponding concepts. The extension of a natural-kind word, says Putnam, is instead determined by a strict relation of identity between the natural kind and the microphysical stuff that locally predominates in the samples used by scientists in their empirical investigations (see REFERENCE §3). The stuff's physical microstructure – say, water's being H_2O – is its scientific *essence*; and propositions expressing this essence – say, 'Water is H_2O' – are necessary and a posteriori. But this immediately implies that the conceptual propositions expressed by the use of sentences including natural-kind terms will not be necessary truths. For example, consider the apparently necessary (because analytic by partial definition) proposition 'Water is a liquid'. The natural-kind word 'water' will pick out only whatever stuff in a given world has the microstructure H_2O. But it is possible that on a different world, under different physical conditions, the stuff that is H_2O and a liquid here on Earth might look very different and have very different surface properties: it might be solid, for example. So the conceptual proposition 'Water is a liquid' is false in that possible world; and thus it is only contingently true in the actual world, even if grasped a priori.

(5) *Transcendental arguments presuppose verificationism.* Even supposing that definitional conceptual truths are empty tautologies, and not always necessary, still conceptual truths gained by transcendental arguments would remain cognitively significant and modally secure. But as Barry Stroud (1968) has pointed out, the theory of transcendental arguments assumes a strongly verificationistic theory of meaningfulness for concepts and propositions. Verificationism, however, is afflicted with insurmountable problems. So transcendental arguments are semantically suspect, and the second part of the Knowledge Thesis would thereby seem to be undermined too.

4 The inescapability of conceptual analysis

On the assumption that these criticisms are sound, things look very bleak for conceptual analysis. And it is true that the movement of Conceptual Analysis did eventually break up under the weight of the criticisms just described. But a closer inspection reveals a striking feature of the philosophical dialectic: In order to gain the acceptance of any argument aimed *against* conceptual analysis, it appears that the critic must finally appeal to the truth of some premises that implicitly invoke concepts and conceptual truths.

To take only one central example. Quine's famous arguments against intensions and analyticity all assume the notion of a logical truth. According to Quine in 'Truth by Convention' (1936), a logical truth is a sentence that contains certain words (logical constants) 'essentially': these words preserve their interpretations across every uniform assignment of values to the non-logical constants in the sentence, ensuring that it 'comes out true' no matter what. Now logical constants, with their 'essential occurrence', are semantically equivalent to the conceptual analyst's *logical concepts*; and in this way Quinean logical truths are (covertly) conceptual truths. Moreover, although Quine suggests in 'Two Dogmas of Empiricism' (1951) that even logical truths are revisable, he states in his later *Philosophy of Logic* that 'every logical truth is obvious, actually or potentially' ([1970] 1986: 82), and that the very attempt to deny a logical truth would involve a change of meaning of the logical constants. In other words, logical constants and logical truths are ineliminable parts of any rational conceptual scheme recognizable as our own. This recognition is epistemically equivalent to what conceptual analysts mean by the a priori grasp of a conceptual truth; the only difference is that whereas most analysts hold that logical truths are known and justified by direct conceptual insight, Quine persuasively appeals instead to a transcendental proof.

If sound, this argument smoothly generalizes. No philosopher can do without logic; and if logic is itself necessarily such as to contain concepts and conceptual truths that are grasped a priori, and whose existence and validity can be established only via transcendental argument, then no philosopher can ultimately avoid the analysis of concepts. Supposing that conceptual analysis is – even in this minimalistic way – philosophically inescapable, the demand for a re-examination and re-working of its basic theses seems self-evident.

See also: ANALYTICAL PHILOSOPHY; CONCEPTS; MEANING AND VERIFICATION

References and further reading

Austin, J.L. (1961) *Philosophical Papers*, ed. J.O. Urmson and G.J. Warnock, Oxford: Oxford University Press, 3rd edn, 1979. (Conceptual analyses with a bias towards ordinary language; see especially essays 2, 4–5, 8 and 11–2.)

Flew, A. (ed.) (1956) *Essays in Conceptual Analysis*, London: Macmillan. (Essay 6, by Urmson, discusses the 'paradigm case argument'.)

* Frege, G. (1884) *The Foundations of Arithmetic*, trans. J.L. Austin, Evanston, IL: Northwestern University Press, 2nd edn, 1953. (See especially §§1–4, 12–7 and 55–91.)

Grice, H.P. (1989) *Studies in the Way of Words*, Cambridge, MA: Harvard University Press. (A thematically organized collection of Grice's writings; see especially chapters 1, 10–1, 13, 15, and the 'Retrospective Epilogue'.)

Hempel, C. (1950) 'Problems and Changes in the Empiricist Criterion of Meaning', *Revue Internationale de Philosophie* 11: 41–63. (A summary of objections to verificationism.)

* Kant, I. (1781/1787) *Critique of Pure Reason*, trans. N.K. Smith, London: Macmillan, 1929. (See especially the introduction.)

* Langford, C.H. (1942) 'Moore's Notion of Analysis', in P.A. Schilpp (ed.) *The Philosophy of G.E. Moore*, New York: Tudor, 2nd edn, 1952. (For Moore's reply to Langford, see part III.iii.)

* Lewis, C.I. (1943–4) 'Modes of Meaning', *Philosophy and Phenomenological Research* 4: 236–49. (A sketch of basic principles of conceptual-intensional semantics.)

* Locke, J. (1689) *Essay Concerning Human Understanding*, ed. P.H. Nidditch, Oxford: Clarendon Press, 1975. (See especially books III and IV.)

Moore, G.E. (1922) *Philosophical Studies*, London: Kegan Paul, Trubner, Trench & Co. (A collection of Moore's early essays.)

—— (1959) *Philosophical Papers*, London: George Allen & Unwin. (A collection of Moore's later essays, with special applications of conceptual analyses to anti-sceptical arguments.)

* Putnam, H. (1975) 'The Meaning of "Meaning"', in K. Gunderson (ed.) *Midwest Studies in Philosophy: Language, Mind, and Knowledge*, Minneapolis, MN: University of Minnesota Press, 131–93. (Defends scientific essentialism.)

* Quine, W.V. (1936) 'Truth by Convention', repr. in H. Geigl and W. Sellars (eds) *Readings in Philosophical Analysis*, New York: Appleton-Century-Crofts, 1949, 250–73. (An anticipation of many of the main themes in 'Two Dogmas'.)

* —— (1951) 'Two Dogmas of Empiricism', repr. in *From a Logical Point of View*, New York: Harper & Row, 1961, 20–47. (Rejects the very idea of analytic truths.)

* —— (1970) *Philosophy of Logic*, Cambridge, MA: Harvard University Press, 2nd edn, 1986. (Discusses the nature of logical truth.)

—— (1960) *Word and Object*, Cambridge, MA: MIT Press. (See especially chapters 2 and 6.)

Ryle, G. (1971) *Collected Papers*, vol. 2, London: Hutchinson. (Exercises in conceptual analysis, mostly deflationary in tone and import; see especially essay 12 for a treatment of syncategorematic concepts.)

Strawson, P.F. (1959) *Individuals: An Essay in Descriptive Metaphysics*, London: Methuen. (Conceptual Analysis takes a 'transcendental turn'.)

—— (1992) *Analysis and Metaphysics*, Oxford: Oxford University Press. (An introduction to Strawsonian conceptual analysis.)

* Stroud, B. (1968) 'Transcendental Arguments', *Journal of Philosophy* 65: 241–56. (An influential discussion.)

ROBERT HANNA

CONCEPTUAL ROLE SEMANTICS *see* SEMANTICS, CONCEPTUAL ROLE

CONDILLAC, ETIENNE BONNOT DE (1715–80)

One of the leading figures of the French Enlightenment period, Condillac is the author of three highly influential books, published between 1746 and 1754, in which he attempted to refine and expand the empirical method of inquiry so as to make it applicable to a broader range of studies than hitherto. In the half-century following the publication of Newton's Principia Mathematica *in 1687, intellectual life in Europe had been engaged upon a fierce debate between the partisans of Cartesian physics, who accepted Descartes' principles of metaphysical dualism and God's veracity as the hallmark of scientific truth, and those who accepted Newton's demonstration that the natural order constituted a single system under laws which could be known through painstaking observation and experi-*

ment. By the mid-eighteenth century Newton had gained the ascendancy, and it was the guiding inspiration of the French thinkers, known collectively as the philosophes, *to appropriate the methods by which Newton had achieved his awesome results and apply them across a broader range of inquiries in the hope of attaining a similar expansion of human knowledge. Condillac was at the centre of this campaign.*

Condillac's first book, An Essay on the Origin of Human Knowledge *(1746), bears the subtitle* A Supplement to Mr. Locke's Essay on the Human Understanding. *While Condillac is usually seen as merely a disciple and popularizer of Locke offering little of any genuine originality, and while he did indeed agree with Locke that experience is the sole source of human knowledge, he attempted to improve on Locke by arguing that sensation alone – and not sensation together with reflection – provided the foundation for knowledge. His most famous book, the* Treatise on the Sensations *(1754) is based upon the thought-experiment of a statue whose senses are activated one by one, beginning with the sense of smell, with the intention of showing how all the higher cognitive faculties of the mind can be shown to derive from the notice the mind takes of the primitive inputs of the sense organs. Condillac also went beyond Locke in his carefully argued claims regarding the extent to which language affects the growth and reliability of knowledge. His* Treatise on Systems *(1749) offers a detailed critique of how language had beguiled the great seventeenth-century systems-builders like Descartes, Leibniz and Spinoza and led them into erroneous conceptions of the mind and human knowledge, the influence of which conceptions was as insidious as it was difficult to eradicate.*

1 **Life and historical context**
2 **Epistemology**
3 **Knowledge and nature as systems**
4 **Reputation and influence**

1 Life and historical context

Etienne Bonnot, Abbé de Condillac, was born in Grenoble. His father was a successful lawyer and the family was prosperous. He was educated for the priesthood and took holy orders in 1740. While he remained a priest and was accustomed to wearing the cassock throughout his life, it appears that he celebrated Mass only once and neglected for the most part the other duties which attended his office. Dissatisfied with the education provided for him, he devoted himself to the study of philosophy, immersing himself in the works of Descartes, Malebranche, Leibniz and Spinoza. He read no English, but

acquired his knowledge of Locke through the French translation of the *Essay concerning Human Understanding* (1689) by Pierre Coste and read Voltaire's books on Newton. He was the contemporary of such Enlightenment luminaries as Helvetius, Diderot, Buffon, La Mettrie and Holbach. Voltaire and Diderot both expressed the very highest regard for his writings. Condillac was on friendly terms with Rousseau, and was frequently to be seen at the salons in and around Paris where so much of the intellectual activity of the Enlightenment took place. He spent nine years (1758–67) in Italy as tutor to the prince of Parma, and wrote a thirteen-volume course of studies which encompassed history, grammar, poetics and scientific methodology.

The Enlightenment was a period of intense intellectual ferment whose major currents are both multifarious and complex (see ENLIGHTENMENT, CONTINENTAL). It is possible nonetheless to isolate several trends and commitments which define more or less the general tendency of thought and the aspirations of those who worked to articulate them. The *philosophes* thought of themselves, perhaps first and foremost, as the champions of the new methods in the natural sciences. They could see important progress being made in so many areas, not only in physics under the aegis of Newton but in chemistry, in navigational technique, in medicine and so on. Their first commitment was to bring the method of the new sciences to bear on as many different lines of inquiry as possible, their guiding assumption being that there was no field of research that could be placed beyond the purview of scientific investigation. But this commitment to the ways of natural science inevitably brought them into conflict with the authority and power of the religious establishment. Though the prestige and political strength of the Catholic Church had been eroding in France over the first decades of the eighteenth century, it was still a force to be reckoned with, especially where its authority to pronounce on matters of fundamental truth about the world and about the human place within it were challenged. In their attempts to advance the cause of science, the *philosophes* had to contend at every turn with what they called the powers of 'superstition' and 'enthusiasm', slightly veiled code words for the doctrinal chauvinism of the Church and what to their minds was its reactionary and stultifying influence upon the political institutions and social conditions of the day. These three currents, the defence and advancement of the cause of natural science, the challenge to the traditional authority and power of the Church and a political agenda directed towards the progress of humanity, define what may be taken as the essential thrust of the Enlightenment as an intellectual movement. Condillac's own contribution to this movement must be set in this context. His philosophy as a whole may be understood as the attempt to hold science and theology together in a single systematic vision of nature, together with a more benign and accommodating perception of man's place within the natural order.

2 Epistemology

All Condillac's philosophy begins in the empiricism of John LOCKE, but he introduces a further methodological component which, he believes, takes him beyond Locke in his treatment of the nature of human knowledge. Disappointed with what appeared to him the idle speculation and dogmatism of the philosophers of the seventeenth century, he writes,

> It seemed to me that we might reason in metaphysics and in morals with as great exactness as in geometry; that we might frame as accurate ideas as the geometricians; that we might determine, as well as they, the meaning of words in a precise and invariable manner; in short that we might prescribe, perhaps better than they have done, a plain and easy order for the attainment of demonstration.
>
> (1746: 2)

Condillac's epistemology represents the attempt to bring together Locke's insistence that all knowledge begins with experience with the rigour of a quasi-geometrical method of inference. With Locke, Condillac rejects Descartes' doctrine of innate ideas, but he wishes to preserve something of the latter's deductive logic as we move from the simple ideas received through sensation to the more abstract and complex ideas of scientific theory (see DESCARTES, R.). This attempt to combine elements of Lockean empiricism with Cartesian rationalism is representative of one of the most important aspirations of the Enlightenment thinkers generally. Condillac's historical importance lies in the fact that he, more than anyone else, tried to work out the details of such a combination with care and precision, and to formulate once and for all the method by which a sure and steady progress could be attained in virtually all areas of human inquiry. It was his hope, and that of all the French thinkers of the time, that the broader application of such a method would yield the same remarkable results in any number of different domains that Newton had achieved in physics through his combination of painstaking observation and mathematical rigour.

Condillac believed that he had made two important advances on Locke by showing, first, how sensation

alone, and not sensation and reflection as Locke held, provided all the ideational resources necessary for knowledge and, second, how 'signs' or language provided the essential means for moving beyond our personal awareness of our sensations in the direction of objective knowledge. It is for the sake of demonstrating the first of these claims that Condillac constructed the elaborate thought-experiment of the living statue he discusses in his most famous book, the *Treatise on the Sensations* (1754). He asks the reader to imagine a statue whose senses are to be activated one at a time beginning with the sense of smell. His purpose is to show how all the higher cognitive faculties of the mind are generated out of the sequential occurrence of the most primitive of sensory experiences. The statue is presented with the smell of a rose. It immediately discerns the alteration of its 'mode' from the utter lack of sensation to the manifestation of the rose's scent. This awareness of alteration within itself constitutes what Condillac calls 'attention', the first and most basic operation of the mind upon the input provided by sensation. The statue is then presented with the scent of jasmine. It attends to the alteration of its own mode and immediately perceives the difference between the rose and the jasmine. This immediate recognition of the difference between the two, and then again the recognition of identity when presented subsequently with the rose, is a manifestation of the mind's power of judgment. 'A judgment', Condillac writes, 'is only the perception of a relation between two ideas which are compared', arising from the mind's implicit capacity to attend to the ideas separately (1754). The larger significance here is that identity and difference, two notions of fundamental importance for logic itself, are shown to derive from sensation and not to repose in the mind as innate principles or 'clear and distinct ideas' available a priori and suited to provide an initiation point for the construction of knowledge.

The statue is able not only to attend to the single presented sensation but to retain an 'impression' of the rose while attending to the jasmine. This is memory, which too, according to Condillac, is only a function of sensation. The mind, then, is both passive, in receiving sensations, and active, in making comparisons between sensations present and remembered. With this much of the mind's capacities described, Condillac asks what might have occurred if the statue had first been presented with an unpleasant smell. If it lacked all experience of pleasant scents, the statue would not, in the presence of the unpleasant one, immediately have experience of anything we could call discomfort or pain, nor would it desire the removal of the unpleasant smell and a return to its former state of utter privation: 'Suffering can no more make it desire a good it does not know than enjoyment can make it fear an ill it does not know' (1754: 5). Pleasure and pain, desire and aversion are thus also shown to arise from primitive sensations, but only through the operation of the mind's capacity for retention, comparison and judgment. Simply put, pleasure and pain are not themselves primitive sensations but learned responses to the mind's reflection upon the various sensations which come through to conscious experience by way of the organs of sense.

Nonetheless, Condillac claims, no sensations are completely indifferent, as any two of them will inspire within the statue not only a recognition of their difference but also a preference for one over the other. This immediately discernible preference of one sensation over another engenders, over time, the whole vast range of our desires and aversions; with the experience of desire and aversion the primitive capacities of the mind are magnified. On Condillac's view, our preference for one sensation over another provides a stimulus to the power of attention, enhancing the mind's ability to focus more keenly and resolutely on ideas stored in memory and leading in turn to a greater discernment and affinity for those sensations which are preferred. 'If we bear in mind that there are absolutely no indifferent sensations', Condillac writes, 'we shall conclude that the different degrees of pleasure and pain are the law by which the germ of all we are is developed, and that they have produced all our faculties' (1754: 46). Towards the end of the Treatise Condillac reaffirms this claim: 'As without experience there is no knowledge, so without needs there is no experience, and there are no needs without the alternatives of pleasures and pains. Everything then results from the principle which we laid down at the beginning of this work' (1754: 209).

In the ensuing pages of the Treatise Condillac's statue is endowed, one by one, with the remaining four senses. Condillac attaches special importance to the sense of touch, arguing that it is only with the addition of this inlet of sensory experience that the statue comes to have ideas of space, extension and external objects, and to acquire awareness of itself as something distinct from its own representations of objects.

3 Knowledge and nature as systems

While the Treatise on the Sensations is Condillac's most famous and influential text, it is only in the Treatise on Systems (1749) and several less well known works, especially The Logic (1780), that Condillac offers his most thoroughgoing exposition of what he conceived of as a system of human knowledge. Having demonstrated the merits of Lockean empiricism in the Essay on the Origin of Human Knowledge, he proceeds, in the Treatise on Systems, to offer a critical analysis of the rationalistic systems of thought contrived by the great seventeenth-century philosophers, Descartes, Malebranche, Leibniz and Spinoza. Condillac argues that it was their failure to understand the nature and function of language, and the need to derive even the most general and abstract terms from materials provided through sensation, which led these thinkers astray from the very outset of their labours. Much of their deductive method could be preserved, but each link in the chain of inferences must be subjected to linguistic scrutiny to assure that the developing system of concepts allowed in nothing that could not ultimately be shown to derive from sensory experience. 'The language of philosophy has been nothing else but a gibberish for many centuries past. At length that gibberish has been banished from the sciences' (The Logic: 64).

Condillac believed that the language of science might be brought to a clarity and precision analogous to mathematical symbols and equations through what he called the method of analysis. This method requires that we examine each term in our language and try to trace it back to the point at which it connects up with immediate experience. At a simpler, more primitive point in their history, Condillac conjectures, humans were able to make an apt assignment of 'signs' to those things in our experience which stood out as particularly relevant to our needs and wants. The human capacity for speech is itself a natural endowment neatly insinuated amidst the various other faculties of the mind where it augments and facilitates their operation. 'There is an innate language, though there are no innate ideas' (1780: 56). Nature itself teaches us the method of analysis. So long as we had hitherto comported ourselves in the construction of our language in accordance with its natural tendency, and to the extent today that we come to understand better the ways in which it was originally adapted to our needs and wants, the knowledge we construct on the basis of our growing stock of abstract terms and concepts can be certified as valid and reliable. 'Error begins when nature ceases to inform us of our mistakes; that is, where judging of things which have little relation to the wants of first necessity, we do not know how to try our judgments in order to discover whether they are true or false' (1780: 6).

Condillac's method of analysis can and must be applied in other directions also. Once the basic terms of our scientific vocabulary are correlated accurately and unambiguously with experientially derived ideas, we are able to exercise the power of judgment over the propositions in which they occur in such a way as to extract and formulate with precision the relations and interconnections our linguistic signs implicitly bear to one another. In this way a systematic structure of concepts begins to emerge which in turn enables us to attend more carefully, especially through the use of controlled experiments, to the continued stream of input from sensation. Our knowledge of the world grows through a sequence of inferential steps, and the emergent system of knowledge could be imbued with the same precision and rigour as is to be found in mathematics itself if we would but attend to the clarity and accuracy of our basic terms.

There is much in Condillac which might plausibly be construed as anticipating certain basic themes in the mid-twentieth century movement of LOGICAL POSITIVISM. It would be a mistake, however, to impute too great a prescience to Condillac as a precursor of later philosophical movements because there are other, deeply ingrained aspects of his thought which are wholly characteristic of his historical moment and utterly foreign to the later developments. According to Condillac, all human knowledge will ultimately fall together into one vast system of concepts which reflects with perfect accuracy the systematic structure of nature itself. In using the analytic method to trace the meanings of our words back to their origins in sensory experience we are only following out the order in which our ideas themselves were generated in our encounter with nature. The perfect congruence between human knowledge as a system of concepts and nature itself as a systematic whole is ultimately a reflection of the divine intelligence which designed and brought nature into existence. Human nature, and human intelligence as the highest expression of our nature, have been 'conformed' by the creator as an integral part of the natural order and all our needs, desires and cognitive faculties can be brought to reside in perfect harmony with that order. By coming to understand nature as a system we grow in our knowledge of God.

Condillac, in short, was a deist and his philosophy as a whole gives magnificent expression to the eighteenth-century conception of God as cosmic law-giver (see DEISM). The laws of nature which Newton had articulated, and all the other laws of nature which science was in process of discovering, were written into the natural order at its inception. But just as nature had its laws, so too there was a set of laws governing human nature, every bit as objective and every bit as amenable to the method of analysis as any other domain of science.

The faculties and wants of man being given, the

laws are given themselves; and though we make them, yet God who created us with such wants and such faculties, is, in truth, our sole legislator. When, therefore we follow these laws which are conformable to our nature, it is Him we obey, and this accomplishes the morality of actions.

(1780: 27)

It was not only human knowledge which could be brought into perfect systematic harmony between all the parts; human conduct too, all of our various personal and social interrelations could be harmonized in accordance with the law of human nature. It was one of the highest aspirations of the Enlightenment period, and of Condillac as one of its philosophically most astute representatives, to raise humankind to the more civilized and prosperous state that would emerge as we gained better knowledge of God's laws, both natural and human. The 'moral sciences' themselves – including the nascent sciences of economics, psychology and politics – could be fully integrated into the whole vast system of natural laws, and to the extent that they were thus integrated and conceived in such a way as to permit a thoroughgoing application of the method of analysis, it was only to be expected that our knowledge of the human order and hence our ability to secure for ourselves a greater happiness in this world would be enhanced.

4 Reputation and influence

In his own day, Condillac enjoyed a very high reputation in French intellectual circles as the one writer who had devoted his energies to the elaboration of the theory of knowledge required to support the ideals and political agenda of the Enlightenment movement. His works continued to be published in new editions well into the nineteenth century. His philosophy provided the stimulus and inspiration for the early nineteenth-century thinkers known as the *idéologues*, such as Destutt de Tracy and CABANIS. Condillac is often cited in textbooks on the history of psychology as one of the first to bring methodical scrutiny to bear on the subtle dynamics of such cognitive functions as attention, memory and habit formation.

It remains a matter of scholarly controversy whether Condillac really made any important advances over Locke in his treatment of the empirical basis of knowledge. With regard to the two specific points on which Condillac himself believed he had gone beyond Locke, in reducing the source of ideas to sensation alone instead of sensation and reflection and in his theory of language, there is much that could be argued in Locke's defence. Nonetheless, it can hardly be denied that Condillac brought a much greater coherence and clarity to Locke's often tentative and disorganized discussions in the *Essay concerning Human Understanding*. By doing so he is responsible for bringing the empirical spirit of inquiry into a much broader currency on the Continent that it might otherwise have enjoyed. Condillac has not yet been given the careful attention that he deserves, and the full story of how his philosophy has influenced and shaped the later course of the history of ideas has yet to be written.

See also: EMPIRICISM; NEWTON, I.; RATIONALISM

List of works

Condillac, E.B. de (1947–51) *Œuvres philosophiques*, ed. G. Le Roy, Paris: Presses Universitaires de France, 3 vols.

—— (1746) *Essai sur l'origine des connaissances humaines: ouvrage où l'on réduit à un seul principe tout ce qui concerne l'entendement humain*, trans. T. Nugent, in J.H. Stam (ed.) *An Essay on the Origin of Human Knowledge*, New York: AMS Press, 1974. (A facsimile reproduction of the original 1756 translation by Thomas Nugent; introduction by J.H. Stam.)

—— (1749) *Traité des sistèmes, où l'on en démêle les inconvéniens et les avantages* (Treatise on Systems), La Haye. (Regrettably, there is as yet no English translation of this work.)

—— (1754) *Traité des sensations*, trans. G. Carr, in H.W. Carr (ed.) *Treatise on the Sensations*, Los Angeles: University of Southern California, 1930. (This is Condillac's best-known and most frequently cited book, containing his famous example of the statue which is endowed one by one with the five senses. The book is frequently acknowledged as a seminal text in the history of psychology.)

—— (1780) *La logique; ou, Les prémiers dévélopemens de l'art de penser*, Paris: Chez Petit Libraire; repr. in G. Le Roy (ed.) *Œuvres philosophiques*, vol. 2, Paris: Presses Universitaires de France, 1947–51; trans. J. Neef, in D.N. Robinson (ed.), *The Logic*, Washington, DC: University Publications of America, 1977. (The 1997 edition is a reprint of the original 1809 translation by J. Neef. This text offers the most succinct and accessible statement of Condillac's philosophy as a whole, including his conception of scientific method, his religious views and moral theory. Highly recommended.)

References and further reading

Cassirer, E. (1951) *The Philosophy of the Enlightenment*, Princeton, NJ: Princeton University Press. (A classic text in Enlightenment studies. Cassirer acknowledges Condillac's importance and gives him a prominent role as he traces the intellectual developments of the age.)

Frankel, C. (1969) *The Faith of Reason: The Idea of Progress in the French Enlightenment*, New York: Octagon Books. (Though more generally concerned with the French Enlightenment as a whole, Frankel also recognizes Condillac's central importance for the philosophy of the period and keeps him well within view throughout his study. An excellent general introduction to the Enlightenment.)

Hine, E.M. (1979) *A Critical Study of Condillac's Traité des Systèmes*, The Hague: Nijhoff. (An excellent in-depth study of one of Condillac's most important texts. Provides a thorough analysis of Condillac's thought within the context of eighteenth-century intellectual controversies. Includes a comprehensive bibliography for further research.)

Knight, I.F. (1968) *The Geometric Spirit: The Abbé de Condillac and the French Enlightenment*, New Haven, CT: Yale University Press. (The only book in English devoted to a comprehensive survey of Condillac's life and work. Written in a readily accessible style, it provides an excellent introduction to the philosophy of the Enlightenment in general, and also offers researchers and specialists important insights into the philosophies which influenced Condillac, as well as his influence upon later developments in the history of thought.)

Schaupp, Z. (1925) *The Naturalism of Condillac*. (The first full-length treatment of Condillac in English, this obscure little book is still worth reading. Includes a careful discussion of Condillac's relation to Locke.)

PAUL F. JOHNSON

CONDITIONALS

see COUNTERFACTUAL CONDITIONALS; INDICATIVE CONDITIONALS

CONDORCET, MARIE-JEAN-ANTOINE-NICOLAS CARITAT DE (1743–94)

The Marquis de Condorcet belongs to the second generation of eighteenth-century French philosophes.

He was by training and inclination a mathematician, and his work marks a major stage in the development of what is known today as the social sciences. He was held in high regard by contemporaries for his contributions to probability theory, and he published a number of seminal treatises on the theory and application of probabilism. He is best known today for the Esquisse d'un tableau historique des progrès de l'esprit humain *(1795), his monumental, secularized historical analysis of the dynamics of man's progress from the primitive state of nature to modernity.*

Condorcet's principal aim was to establish a science of man that would be as concise and certain in its methods and results as the natural and physical sciences. For Condorcet there could be no true basis to science without the model of mathematics, and there was no branch of human knowledge to which the mathematical approach was not relevant. He called the application of mathematics to human behaviour and organization 'social arithmetic'.

The central epistemological assumption, upon which his philosophy was based, was that the truths of observation, whether in the context of the physical or the moral and social sciences, were nothing more than probabilities, but that their varying degrees of certainty could be measured by means of the calculus of probabilities. Condorcet was thus able, through mathematical logic, to counteract the negative implications of Pyrrhonic scepticism for the notions of truth and progress, the calculus providing not only the link between the different orders of knowledge but also the way out of the Pyrrhonic trap by demonstrating man's capacity and freedom to understand and direct the march of progress in a rationally-ordered way.

In his Esquisse *Condorcet set out to record not only the history of man's progress through nine 'epochs', from the presocial state of nature to the societies of modern Europe, but in the tenth 'epoch' of this work he also held out the promise of continuing progress in the future. He saw the gradual emancipation of human society and the achievement of human happiness as the consequence of man having been endowed by nature with the capacity to learn from experience and of the cumulative, beneficial effects of the growth of knowledge and enlightenment. Condorcet's* Esquisse *laid the basis for the positivism of the nineteenth century, and had a particularly significant impact on the work of Saint-Simon and Auguste Comte.*

1 Life
2 The science of the probable
3 Progress and the science of man

1 Life

Condorcet was one of the outstanding French mathematicians of his time. He was the only eighteenth-century French *philosophe* of stature to have participated in the Revolution and, as a legislator, to have had an impact on events after 1789. Born in Ribemont, his early education took place at Reims, and by 1758 he had entered the University of Paris where he studied ethics, metaphysics, logic and mathematics at the prestigious Collège de Navarre. There he was taught by the Abbé Nollet, a proponent of Newtonian physics, and he worked closely with Georges Girault de Kéroudon on philosophical matters and on the crucial problems of the integral calculus. In later years he also came under the influence of Euler, Fontaine, the Bernouillis and, above all, of the distinguished mathematician and academician, Jean Le Rond D'ALEMBERT, who became his patron. He was elected Perpetual Secretary of the Academy of Sciences in 1773, and in 1782 became a member of the French Academy. An enthusiastic supporter and theorist of the Revolution, he played an important role in the drafting of the *Déclaration des droits* in 1789. Suspected later of being a Girondin, he was denounced, and died, possibly a suicide, in Bourg-la-Reine while awaiting the guillotine.

His first major work, *Du calcul intégral*, was published in 1765 as part of the Academy of Science's proceedings, and was widely acclaimed. This was followed by a series of essays and mathematical papers, published between 1766 and 1769, including important work on the applications of the integral calculus to the still unresolved mathematical obscurities of Newton's *Principia*. The extensions of the methodology of differential calculus, probability (the 'mathematics of hope') and their application to nonscientific areas, particularly the moral, political and social sciences, were to remain at the core of his thinking, especially during and after Turgot's ministry (1774–6). His exploration of the potential of the calculus of probabilities was developed further in the *Essai sur l'application de l'analyse à la probabilité des décisions rendues à la pluralité des voix* in 1785. The *Essai* is complemented by the *Eléments du calcul des probabilités et son application aux jeux de hasard*, not published in its own right until 1805.

Condorcet was part of that new-wave reformist movement in late eighteenth-century France that included Turgot, the *idéologues*, and the physiocrats, all united in their understanding of how the world of ideas could and must interact with the world of political and social reality. Other major publications include the *Essai sur la constitution et les fonctions des assemblées provinciales* (1788), *Sur l'Instruction publique* (1791–2), *Réflexions sur la jurisprudence criminelle* (1775), *De l'Influence de la Révolution de l'Amérique sur l'Europe* (1786), *Quatres lettres d'un bourgeois de Newh(e)aven á un citoyen de Virginie* (1788), *Lettres sur le commerce des grains* (1775), and the *Réflexions sur l'esclavage des nègres* (1781). In addition, he wrote innumerable pamphlets, drafts of bills and other legislative material for the National Convention. He was also interested in the development of a symbolic logic to give precise expression to intellectual operations and which would be appropriate to the formulation of a universal language of the sciences, although his treatise on this subject, the *Essai d'une langue universelle*, was to remain unfinished. In the non-mathematical area his greatest and most influential work is the *Esquisse d'un tableau historique des progrès de l'esprit humain*, published posthumously in 1795.

2   The science of the probable

Condorcet used mathematics as a model upon which to build a philosophy of social science, and to establish a methodology as applicable to the science of man as it was to the physical sciences. In Condorcet's hands mathematics became an instrument of social and philosophical analysis and, following the lead given by D'Alembert, he set out to integrate the Newtonian view of a rationally determined order of nature into an analagous framework of moral, social and political order. He postulated the view that all human sciences were underpinned by positive fact in the same way as the physical sciences, and open to a rigorous system of analysis made meaningful through the use of a precise, well-determined 'universal' language, capable of unambiguous use across the whole spectrum of scientific enquiry.

Greatly influenced by LOCKE and HUME, as well as by the French sensationalist philosopher CONDILLAC, Condorcet devoted much of his intellectual life to the development of a concept of 'social arithmetic' based on the calculus of probabilities. He saw probabilism as constituting the essential epistemological link between the social and the physcial sciences. By utilising the calculus of probabilities, the uncertainties and ambivalences inherent in previous attempts to study and evaluate man's behaviour, which had resulted in the case of many philosophers in a profound scepticism, could be dissipated. He was convinced that this 'true philosophy' would provide the foundation for a systematic 'science of man'. The clearest elaboration of this philosophy of probable belief and the methodological principles for its application are to

be found in general, tentative outline in the notes to Condorcet's reception speech to the French Academy in 1782, and in more sophisticated mathematical detail in the *Mémoire sur le calcul des probabilités* (1784), in the *Essai sur l'application de l'analyse à la probabilité des décisions rendues à la pluralité des voix* and in the *Eléments du calcul des probabilités et son application aux jeux de hasard*.

In the preliminary discourse to the *Essai sur l'application de l'analyse*, he postulated two key principles governing the processes of human reasoning: (1) that 'nature follows invariable laws' and (2) that these laws 'are made known to us by observable phenomena'. What leads us to believe in the truth of such a postulation is our phenomenological experience of the facts and of the ways in which that experience accords with these two principles. A perfect and definitive calculation of the probability of their truth can never be fully realized, as it is impossible to take cognizance of the totality of the factors that shape our experience. Condorcet insisted, on the other hand, that such a calculation, were it possible, would indicate a very high degree of probability of the truth of these principles. In the light of this probable truth, Condorcet then added a third working proposition, namely that all human reasoning that informs judgment, decision making, choice and conduct is based ultimately on probability.

'The truths proved by experience are simply probabilities.' For Condorcet this insistence on uncertainty did not, however, lead to the *impasse* of Pyrrhonism. On the contrary, although all knowledge was founded only on probabilities, the value, or degree of probability could be determined with relative precision.

Condorcet fully accepted the Lockean view on epistemological modesty. Uncertainty characterized all human understanding (exception being made for the mathematical model itself), but for Condorcet, as for Locke, uncertainty was not an invincible, action-denying absolute. In the *Essai sur l'application de l'analyse* he sought to demonstrate, by means of the calculus of probabilities, how the defeatist scepticism of the past could be made to give way before the new positivism.

The calculus of probabilities was applicable in theory to all aspects of human life and behaviour, and in demonstrating the logical foundation for this principle Condorcet developed a view of rational belief that owed as much to Hume as to Locke. Belief in both the moral and physical sciences was in his system simply the representation of things as having to exist in a certain way, based on our experience that what has occurred will tend to recur within a frame of constant laws. Belief was not, however, the result of a raw process of reaction to sense impressions. Man obeys an automatic sentiment that leads him to belief, but in order to avoid

judgment and opinion degenerating into prejudice and irrationality, Condorcet took care to distinguish between the *sentiment* of belief and the actual *grounds* for belief. Reason and experience must play their part if man was to be rescued from the illusions of the senses and the fleeting impressions made upon the senses. To this end, he advanced the view that reason had found a powerful weapon in the form of the calculus of probabilities, which offered a dependable methodology for the estimation of the *grounds* for belief. The calculus would provide the necessary mechanism for the correction of any error arising from the passive, automatic and uncritical *sentiment* of belief, particularly important in the case of the moral and social sciences.

The principles of probabilistic philosophy enabled Condorcet to elaborate a model of calculation that permitted the objective evaluation of man in society, and with it he sought to transform the calculus of probabilities into a mathematically-based language of rational decision-making and action. The *Essai sur l'application de l'analyse* was an attempt to illuminate the ways in which the calculus could work in a practical context, in this case the constitutional process itself, so that the unpredictable and the contingent could be measured and minimized. This particular treatise represents Condorcet's most detailed and sustained attempt to 'discover the probability that assures the validity of a law passed by the smallest possible majority, such that one can believe that it is not unjust to subject others to this law and that it is useful for oneself to submit to it'. The mathematics that he then deployed exemplify the pioneering methodology that he would adopt in other contexts, such as crime, jurisprudence and taxation theory, to locate the human sciences within the realm of the probable, and to attempt to address the otherwise intractable problem of accounting for chance in human behaviour.

3 Progress and the science of man

Condorcet's name has been associated most commonly with the 'idea of progress', and the work in which he developed this idea in depth is the *Esquisse d'un tableau historique des progrès de l'esprit humain*. Based on the empirical observation of data and the statistical analysis of that data, the *Esquisse* traces the trajectory of human achievement using a de-christianized chronology of historical periods or 'epochs'. The tableau starts with primitive man in the state of presocial nature and culminates in the ninth 'epoch',

covering the years from Descartes and the late seventeenth century to the birth of the first French republic. A tenth 'epoch' offers a vision of the postmillenium future and holds out the promise of unlimited human perfectibility. Condorcet paid particular attention to two factors in man's advancement: (1) the growth of language as the principal vehicle of social progress and intellectual advancement, and (2) the development of technology and the physical sciences as instruments facilitating the progressive liberation of man from the darkness of past error and servitude.

Lockean sensationalist psychology deeply influenced Condorcet, particularly with regard to his doctrine of moral sentiment. At the start of the *Esquisse* primitive man emerges as the one creature with the faculty of receiving sensations, of reflecting upon them, of analysing them and recombining them. In Condorcet's view, the pleasure-pain principle engendered in early man moral feelings, and eventually relationships, based on controlled self-interest. The sensations facilitated man's difficult, but irreversible, climb out the of the darkness of primitive presocial life into the light of civilisation. Condorcet understood the implications for the moral sciences of Lockean reversion to the origins of knowledge in sense experience, together with its consequential destruction of the myth of innate ideas, and he saw Lockean sensationalism as an intellectual event whose importance was matched only by that of the Newtonian revolution in physics.

Condorcet wanted to show in the *Esquisse* that history was not the creation of random forces, with man cast in the role of passive spectator/victim. The gradual emancipation of man from the limitations imposed upon him by nature, and the consequential liberation of the individual, was itself a natural process, and the reflection of an order inherent in man's condition that could be made intelligible. Man's progress was enacted within the framework of an exclusively human condition, free from the intervention of transcendental forces. Progress was for Condorcet an entirely secular concept, the fruit of human dynamics interacting with the natural currents of history alone. Evil was not a consequence of man's nature but of the absence of enlightenment, and would recede inevitably as knowledge in the moral sciences caught up with the advances being made in the physical sciences, and extended its beneficial effects.

In linking the pursuit of knowledge, and the inexorable logic of scientific advances, to the mission of progress, Condorcet had to demonstrate necessarily that there was a relationship between advances made in the physical and natural sciences and those made in the moral and social sciences, and that as man learned to order his natural environment by means of the physical sciences he would also learn to order his social environment through the advancement of the moral sciences and their political and sociological extensions. The historical portrait of man in the *Esquisse* is drawn with that demonstration in mind in the context of each successive 'epoch'.

Progress for Condorcet was always a cumulative, collective phenomenon, dependent upon the free pursuit of knowledge and upon the rational application of that knowledge. His view of progress assumed that the laws of nature were constant, and that there was an analogous constancy at work in historical processes to which the calculus of probabilities in relation to the future was relevant. A scientific, mathematically-informed study of history would reveal constant principles, many of which would confirm the truth of human progress, as far as this truth could be defined in probabilistic terms.

The power of mathematics allowed man to rise above the facts of random phenomena and to take advantage of the 'law of calculated observations'. This was the law that permitted a scientific understanding of causes, effects and relationships, that allowed for the determination of those recurring patterns of phenomena in human history that made a given truth probable, and that facilitated the measurement of degrees of certainty, and therefore control, in human affairs. It was the key that would open the way to a rationally-planned application of the 'science of man'. The 'science of man', anchored firmly to what were essentially Baconian traditions of thought – observation, experiment, calculation – and Lockean–Humean epistemology, would establish the basis for a radical reordering of the processes of human understanding to create 'a new understanding admitting only precise ideas, exact notions and truths whose degree of certainty or probability has been rigorously weighed'.

Condorcet argued throughout the *Esquisse* the case for the indefinite perfectibility of human society. His vision entailed the construction of a future in which man's potential for social and political choice of action was theoretically infinite. Condorcet's positivism was not facile, however, nor was his optimism Panglossian. The tenth 'epoch' of the *Esquisse*, in some ways naïvely utopian, is a projection of probabilities set out within a cautiously defined context of preconditions, reservations and contingencies. Condorcet never lost sight of the essential fragility of human civilization; progress remained dependent ultimately on the rational exercise of the human will alone, and without that vital driving-force progress would not take place.

See also: COMTE, A.; HUMAN NATURE, SCIENCE OF, IN THE 18TH CENTURY; POSITIVISM IN THE SOCIAL SCIENCES; PYRRHONISM; SAINT-SIMON, C.-H. DE R.

List of works

Condorcet, M.J.A.N. (1968) *Œuvres de Condorcet*, ed. A. Condorcet-O'Connor and F. Arago, Stuttgart-Bad Canstatt: Friederich Fromann Verlag, 12 vols. (This is a reprint of the 1847–9 edition of Condorcet's collective works; still the standard edition.)

—— (1785) *Essai sur l'application de l'analyse à la probabilité des décisions rendues à la pluralité des voix* (Essay on the Application of Analysis to the Probability of Majority Decisions), Paris: Imprimerie royale; repr. New York: Chelsea, 1972.

—— (1795) *Esquisse d'un tableau historique des progrès de l'esprit humain*, Paris: Agasse; repr. A. Pons (ed.), Paris: Flammarion, 1988; trans. J. Barraclough, in S. Hampshire (ed.), *Sketch for a Historical Tableau of the Progress of the Human Mind*, London: Weidenfeld and Nicolson.

—— (1805) *Éléments du calcul des probabilités et son application aux jeux de hasard, à la loterie et aux jugements des hommes* (Elements of the Calculus of Probabilities and its Application to Games of Chance, to the Lottery and to Men's Judgements), Paris: Fayolle. (This treatise first appeared as an appendix to Euler's correspondence with a German princess (1787–9). There is no modern edition, and it was not included in the O'Connor-Arago edition of Condorcet's works.)

References and further reading

Badinter, E. and R. (1968) *Condorcet 1743–94. Un Intellectuel en politique* (Condorcet 1743–94. An Intellectual in Politics), Paris: Fayard. (A biographical study with some account of intellectual development. Aimed at the general reader.)

Baker, K. (1975) *Condorcet. From Natural Philosophy to Social Mathematics*, Chicago, IL and London: University of Chicago Press. (The most comprehensive and authoritative analysis of Condorcet's ideas so far published. Particularly useful for the *Essai sur l'application de l'analyse* and the *Éléments du calcul*, as well as for an understanding of the philosophical and historical implications of the *Esquisse*. Excellent bibliography. Suitable for specialists and general readers.)

Granger, G.-G. (1956) *La Mathématique sociale du marquis de Condorcet* (The Social Mathematics of the Marquis de Condorcet), Paris: Presses Universitaires de France. (Still a very useful study of the originality of Condorcet's contribution to the concept of social science for the general reader.)

Popkin, R. (1987) 'Condorcet and Hume and Turgot', *Condorcet Studies* 2: 47–62. (A closely argued account of the philosophical divisions between Condorcet and Hume, with particular reference to the impact of Hume's break with Turgot. A clear account of the ideas of two of the greatest social scientists of the Enlightenment. Aimed at the specialist.)

Shapiro, J. (1978) *Condorcet and the Rise of Liberalism*, New York: Octagon Books. (A general account of Condorcet's philosophy of progress, with particular reference to the *Esquisse*. A good and lively introduction to Condorcet for the general reader.)

DAVID WILLIAMS

CONFEDERALISM

see FEDERALISM AND CONFEDERALISM

CONFIRMATION THEORY

The result of a test of a general hypothesis can be positive, negative or neutral. The first, qualitative, task of confirmation theory is to explicate these types of test result. However, as soon as one also takes individual hypotheses into consideration, the interest shifts to the second, quantitative, task of confirmation theory: probabilistically evaluating individual and general hypotheses in the light of an increasing number of test results. This immediately suggests conceiving of the confirmation of an hypothesis as increasing its probability due to new evidence.

Rudolf Carnap initiated a research programme in quantitative confirmation theory by designing a continuum of probability systems with plausible probabilistic properties for the hypothesis that the next test result will be of a certain kind. This continuum of inductive systems has guided the search for optimum systems and for systems that take analogy into account.

Carnapian systems, however, assign zero probability to universal hypotheses. Jaakko Hintikka was the first to reconsider the confirmation of such hypotheses and using Carnap's continuum for this purpose has set the stage for a whole spectrum of inductive systems of this type.

1 **Qualitative and quantitative confirmation theory**
2 **The continuum of inductive systems**
3 **Optimum inductive systems**
4 **Inductive analogy by similarity**
5 **Universal generalizations**
6 **Applications**

1 Qualitative and quantitative confirmation theory

According to the hypothetico-deductive method a theory is tested by examining its implications. The result of an individual test of a general hypothesis stated in observation terms can be positive, negative or neutral. If it is neutral the test was not well devised; if it is negative, the hypothesis, and hence the theory, has been falsified. *Qualitative* confirmation theory primarily aims at further explicating the intuitive notions of neutral and positive test results. Some paradoxical features discovered by Hempel and some queer predicates defined by Goodman show that this is not an easy task.

Assuming that a black raven confirms the hypothesis 'All ravens are black' and that confirmation is not affected by logically equivalent reformulations, Hempel argued (1965) that not only a non-black non-raven but, even more counterintuitively, also a black non-raven confirms it (see HEMPEL, C.G. §2). Goodman (1955) argued that not all predicates guarantee the 'projectibility' of a universal hypothesis from observed to non-observed cases. For example, if 'grue' means 'green, if examined before *t*' and 'blue, if not examined before *t*', a green emerald discovered before *t* would not only confirm 'All emeralds are green' but also 'All emeralds are grue', and hence, assuming that consequences are also confirmed, even 'All emeralds not examined before *t* are blue' (see GOODMAN, N. §3). Whereas Goodman succeeded in formulating criteria for acceptable predicates, in terms of their relative 'entrenchment' in previously successfully projected generalizations, up to now nobody has given a generally accepted qualitative solution to Hempel's riddles (see UNDERDETERMINATION §2).

Below we treat *quantitative*, more specifically, probabilistic confirmation theory, which aims at explicating the idea of confirmation as increasing probability due to new evidence. Carnap introduced this perspective and pointed confirmation theory towards the search for a suitable notion of logical or inductive probability (see PROBABILITY, INTERPRETATIONS OF §5). Generally speaking, such probabilities combine indifference properties with inductive properties.

2 The continuum of inductive systems

Mainly in his *The Continuum of Inductive Methods* (1952), Rudolf CARNAP started a fruitful research programme centering around the famous λ-continuum. The probability systems in this programme can be described in terms of individuals and observation predicates or in terms of trials and observable outcomes. The latter way of presentation will be used here. Moreover, we will presuppose an objective probability process, although the systems to be presented can be applied in other situations as well.

Consider a hidden wheel of fortune. You are told, truthfully, only that it has precisely four coloured segments, BLUE, GREEN, RED, and YELLOW, without further information about the relative size of the segments. So you do not know the objective probabilities. What you subsequently learn are only the outcomes of successive trials. Given the sequence of outcomes e_n of the first n trials, your task is to assign reasonable probabilities, $p(R/e_n)$, to the hypothesis that the next trial will result in, for example, RED.

There are several ways of introducing the λ-continuum, but the basic idea behind it is that it reflects gradually learning from experience. In fact, as Zabell (1982) rediscovered, C-systems were anticipated by Johnson. According to Carnap's favourite approach $p(R/e_n)$ should depend only on n and the number of occurrences of RED thus far, n_R. More specifically, it should be a special weighted mean of the observed relative frequency n_R/n and the (reasonable) initial probability 1/4. This turns out to leave room for a continuum of (C-)systems, the (λ-continuum, $0 < \lambda < \infty$:

$$p(R/e_n) = (n_R + \lambda/4)/(n+\lambda) =$$
$$n/(n+\lambda) \cdot (n_R/n) + \lambda/(n+\lambda) \cdot (1/4)$$

Note that the weights $n/(n+\lambda)$ and $\lambda/(n+\lambda)$ add up to 1 and that the larger the value of λ the slower the first increases at the expense of the second; that is, the slower one is willing to learn from experience.

C-systems have several attractive indifference, confirmation and convergence properties. The most important are these:

(a) order indifference or exchangeability: the resulting prior probability, $p(e_n)$, for e_n, does not depend on the order of the results of the trials, that is, $p(R/e_n) = p(e_n^*)$ for any permutation e_n^* of e_n;

(b) instantial confirmation: if e_n is followed by RED this is favourable for RED, that is, $p(R/e_nR) > p(R/e_n)$;

(c) instantial convergence: $p(R/e_n)$ approaches n_R/n for increasing n.

However, confirmation and convergence of universal hypotheses are excluded in C-systems. The reason is

that C-systems in fact assign zero prior probability to all universal generalizations, for instance to the hypothesis that all results will be RED. Of course, this is desirable in the described situation, but if you were told only that there are *at most* four coloured segments, you would like to leave room for this possibility.

3 Optimum inductive systems

Carnap proved that for certain kinds of objective probability process, such as a wheel of fortune, there is an optimal value of λ, depending on the objective probabilities, in the sense that the average mistake may be expected to be lowest for this value. Surprisingly, this optimal value is independent of n. Of course, in actual research, where we do not know the objective probabilities, this optimal value cannot be calculated. Carnap did not raise the question of a reasonable estimate of the optimal value for a specific objective process, for he saw the problem of selecting a value of λ primarily as a choice that each scientist had to make in general. However, the question of a reasonable estimate has attracted the attention of other researchers.

Festa (1993) proposed basing the estimate on 'contextual' knowledge of similar processes in nature. For example, in ecology one may know the relative frequencies of certain species in different habitats before one starts the investigation of a new habitat. For a quite general class of systems, Festa formulates a solution to the estimation problem that relates the research area of confirmation theory to that of truth approximation: the optimum solution may be expected to be the most efficient way of approaching the objective or true probabilities.

Unfortunately, wheels of fortune do not constitute a technological (let alone a biological) kind for which you can use information about previously investigated instances. But if you had knowledge of a random sample of all existing wheels of fortune, Festa's approach would work on the average for a new, randomly drawn, one.

4 Inductive analogy by similarity

Carnap struggled with the question of how to include analogy considerations into inductive probabilities. His important distinction between two kinds of analogy – by similarity and by proximity – was posthumously published (Carnap 1980). Here we will consider only the first kind.

Suppose you find GREEN more similar to BLUE than to RED. Carnap's intuition of analogy by similarity is that, for instance, the posterior probability of GREEN should be higher if, other things being equal, some occurrences of RED are replaced by occurrences of BLUE. The background intuition, not valid for artificial wheels of fortune, is that similarity in one respect (for example, colour) will go together with similarities in other respects (for example, objective probabilities). However, explicating which precise principle of analogy one wants to fulfil has turned out to be very difficult.

One interesting approach is in terms of *virtual trials*, which is a way of determining how analogy influence is to be distributed after n trials. In the case above, BLUE would get more analogy credits than RED from an occurrence of GREEN. The resulting systems of virtual analogy have the same confirmation and convergence properties as C-systems. Moreover, they satisfy a principle of analogy that is in general more plausible than Carnap's. Roughly, the new principle says that replacement of a previous occurrence of BLUE by GREEN makes less difference for the probability that the next trial will be BLUE than does replacement of a previous occurrence of RED by GREEN for the probability that the next trial will be RED.

Unfortunately, systems of virtual analogy are not exchangeable: the order of results makes a difference. There are, however, exchangeable systems with some kind of analogy by similarity. For example, Skyrms (1993) has sketched a Bayesian approach that uses information about possible gravitational bias of a symmetric wheel of fortune to determine the influence of analogy, and di Maio (1995) follows a suggestion of Carnap.

5   Universal generalizations

Carnap was well aware that C-systems do not leave room for non-analytic universal generalizations. In fact, all systems presented thus far have this problem. Although tolerant of other views, Carnap himself was inclined to downplay the theoretical importance of universal statements.

Hintikka (1966) took up the problem of universal statements. His basic idea was to apply Bayesian conditionalization to Carnap's C-systems with uniform λ, using a specific prior distribution on universal statements containing a parameter α. The systems belonging to the resulting α–λ-continuum have the instantial confirmation and convergence properties and also the desired property of universal confirmation; that is, that the probability of a not yet falsified universal statement increases with another instance of it. Moreover, they satisfy universal convergence: $p(H_R/e_n)$ approaches 1 for increasing n as long as only RED continues to occur (where H_R indicates the

universal statement that only RED will occur in the long run). For increasing parameter α, universal confirmation is smaller and universal convergence slower.

In fact, systems based on an arbitrary prior distribution and C-systems with arbitrary λ, here called H-systems, already have the general properties of instantial and universal confirmation and convergence. The subclass of H-systems based on an arbitrary prior distribution and C-systems with λ proportional to the corresponding number of possible outcomes is particularly interesting. For this subclass appears to be co-extensive with a class of systems introduced by Hintikka and by Niiniluoto (1988), very differently from H-systems, using principles and parameters related only to finite sequences of outcomes.

There is also a plausible 'delabelled' reformulation of H-systems that can be extended to the very interesting case of an unknown denumerable number of possible outcomes. Presenting the delabelling in terms of exchangeable partitions, Zabell (1996) has studied this case by principles leading to a class of systems with three parameters.

6   Applications

The Carnap–Hintikka programme in confirmation theory, also called inductive probability theory, has applications in several directions. Systems of inductive probability were intended primarily for explicating confirmation as increasing probability. One may even define a quantitative degree of confirmation: namely, as the difference or ratio of the posterior and the initial or prior probability. There are other interesting types of application as well. Carnap (1971) and Stegmüller (1973) stressed that they can be used in decision making, and Skyrms (1991) applies them in game theory (see DECISION AND GAME THEORY). Costantini *et al.* (1982) use them in a rational reconstruction of elementary particle statistics. Festa suggests several areas of empirical science where optimum inductive systems can be used. Finally, for universal hypotheses, Hintikka, Hilpinen (1968) and Pietarinen (1972) use systems of inductive probability to formulate rules of acceptance and Niiniluoto uses these systems to estimate degrees of verisimilitude.

See also: INDUCTION, EPISTEMIC ISSUES IN; INDUCTIVE INFERENCE; LEARNING; PROBABILITY, INTERPRETATIONS OF; PROBABILITY THEORY AND EPISTEMOLOGY; RATIONALITY OF BELIEF; STATISTICS

References and further reading

Almost all items presuppose some elementary mathematical training.

* Carnap, R. (1952) *The Continuum of Inductive Methods*, Chicago, IL: University of Chicago Press. (Introduces the λ-continuum as a way of gradually learning from experience and proves that there is an optimal value of λ, depending on the underlying objective probabilities. See §§2, 3.)

* —— (1971) 'Inductive Logic and Rational Decisions', in R. Carnap and R. Jeffrey (eds) *Studies in Inductive Logic and Probability*, Berkeley, CA: University of California Press, vol. I, 5–31. (Presents the general aims of inductive logic and in particular its role in rational decision making. §6.)

* —— (1980) 'A Basic System of Inductive Logic, Part 2', in R. Jeffrey (ed.) *Studies in Inductive Logic and Probability*, Berkeley, CA: University of California Press, vol. II, 7–155. (Continues the foundational analysis of systems of inductive probability, started in Part 1 of Volume I of 1971, with special emphasis on analogy, introducing the important distinction between analogy by similarity and analogy by proximity. §4.)

* Costantini, D., Galavotti, M.C. and Rosa, R. (1982) 'A Rational Reconstruction of Elementary Particle Statistics', *Scientia* 76 (117): 151–9. (Presents a rational reconstruction of elementary particle statistics in terms of principles underlying Carnap's λ-continuum. §6.)

* Festa, R. (1993) *Optimum Inductive Methods*, Dordrecht: Kluwer. (Gives a detailed analysis of the relation between the generalization of Carnap's λ-continuum, Bayesian statistics, notably Dirichlet distributions, and verisimilitude. Proposes an estimate of the optimal value of λ on the basis of 'contextual' knowledge of similar processes and suggests several areas of empirical science where optimum inductive systems can be used. §§3, 6.)

* Goodman, N. (1955) *Fact, Fiction, and Forecast*, Cambridge, MA: Harvard University Press. (Contains discussion of intuitive ideas about qualitative confirmation and argues that they should be restricted to well-entrenched predicates in order to exclude the confirmation of generalizations in terms of queer predicates, like 'grue'. §1.)

* Hempel, C.G. (1965) *Aspects of Scientific Explanation*, New York: Free Press. (Contains, among other things, Hempel's most important writings on qualitative confirmation, including the raven paradoxes, induction and rational belief. §1.)

* Hilpinen, R. (1968) *Rules of Acceptance and Inductive Logic*, Amsterdam: North Holland. (Gives a detailed analysis of Hintikka's two-dimensional continuum and corresponding rules of acceptance. §6.)

* Hintikka, J. (1966) 'A Two-dimensional Continuum of Inductive Methods', in J. Hintikka and P. Suppes (eds) *Aspects of Inductive Logic*, Amsterdam: North Holland, 1966, 113–32. (Presents the two-dimensional α–λ-continuum, leaving room for universal hypotheses, based on Carnap's λ-continuum and a specific prior distribution related to a virtual universe of α individuals. §5.)

Kuipers, T. (1978) *Studies in Inductive Probability and Rational Expectation*, Dordrecht: Reidel. (Studies the systems of Carnap, Hintikka and Niiniluoto, and their generalization, in great detail. Refers also to the related work of Carnap and Hintikka, and to the work of Hilpinen, Pietarinen and Stegmüller. §§2, 5, 6.)

—— (1988) 'Inductive Analogy by Similarity and Proximity', in D.H. Hellman (ed.) *Analogical Reasoning*, Dordrecht: Kluwer, 299–313. (Presents systems with virtual inductive analogy by similarity, and also studies analogy by proximity. §4.)

* Maio, M.C. di (1995) 'Predictive Probability and Analogy by Similarity in Inductive Logic', *Erkenntnis* 43: 369–94. (Weakens restricted relevance such that it leads to exchangeable systems which are sensitive to analogy by similarity. §4.)

* Niiniluoto, I. (1988) 'Analogy and Similarity in Scientific Reasoning', in D.H. Hellman (ed.) *Analogical Reasoning*, Dordrecht: Kluwer. (Discusses, among others, proposals for inductive analogy by similarity by Costantini, Kuipers, Niiniluoto and Spohn. §4.)

* Pietarinen, J. (1972) *Lawlikeness, Analogy and Inductive Logic*, Amsterdam: North Holland. (Gives an overview of the main ideas and problems in the Carnap–Hintikka programme around 1970. §6.)

* Skyrms, B. (1991) 'Inductive Deliberation, Admissable Acts and Perfect Equilibrium', in M. Bacharach and S. Hurley (eds) *Foundations of Decision Theory*, Oxford: Blackwell, 220–41. (Applies Carnap's λ-continuum in game theory by letting players update their beliefs according to it. §6.)

* —— (1993) 'Analogy by Similarity in HyperCarnapian Inductive Logic', in J. Earman (ed.) *Philosophical Problems of the Internal and External Worlds. Essays concerning the Philosophy of Adolf Grünbaum*, Pittsburgh, PA: University of Pittsburgh Press, 973–82. (Presents a Bayesian approach to analogy that uses information about possible gravitational bias of a symmetric wheel of fortune to determine the influence of analogy. §4.)

* Stegmüller, W. (1973) *Carnap II: Normative Theorie des Induktiven Räsonierens*, Berlin: Springer. (Em-

phasizing the role in rational decision it presents Carnap's λ-continuum and generalizes it to arbitrary initial probabilities. §§2, 6.)

* Zabell, S.L. (1982) 'W.E. Johnson's "Sufficientness" Postulate', *Annals of Statistics* 10 (4): 1,091–9. (Points out that Johnson anticipated C-systems in 1932, including its axiomatic foundation. §2.)

* —— (1996) 'The Continuum of Inductive Methods Revisited', in J. Earman and J. Norton (eds) *The Cosmos of Science*, Pittsburgh, PA: University of Pittsburgh Press, and Konstanz: Universitätsverlag Konstanz, 349–83. (Studies 'delabelled' probability systems in terms of exchangeable partitions, by imposing additional principles, leading to a class of systems with three parameters. §5.)

THEO A.F. KUIPERS

CONFUCIAN ANALECTS

see CONFUCIUS

CONFUCIAN PHILOSOPHY, CHINESE

Chinese Confucian philosophy is primarily a set of ethical ideas oriented toward practice. Characteristically, it stresses the traditional boundaries of ethical responsibility and dao, *or the ideal of the good human life as a whole. It may be characterized as an ethics of virtue in the light of its conception of* dao *and* de *(virtue). Comprising the conceptual framework of Confucian ethics are notions of basic virtues such as* ren *(benevolence),* yi *(rightness, righteousness), and* li *(rites, propriety). There are also notions of dependent virtues such as filiality, loyalty, respectfulness and integrity. Basic virtues are considered fundamental, leading or action-guiding, cardinal and the most comprehensive. In the classic Confucian sense,* ren *pertains to affectionate concern for the well-being of fellows in one's community. Notably,* ren *is often used in an extended sense by major Song and Ming Confucians as interchangeable with* dao *for the ideal of the universe as a moral community.* Yi *pertains to the sense of rightness, especially exercised in coping with changing circumstances of human life, those situations that fall outside the scope of* li. Li *focuses on rules of proper conduct, which have three functions: delimiting, supportive and ennobling. That is, the* li *define the boundaries of proper behaviour, provide opportunities for satisfying desires of moral agents within these boundaries, and encourage the development of noble characters which markedly embody cultural refinement and communal concerns. The* li *are the depository of insights of the Confucian tradition as a living ethical tradition. This tradition is subject to changing interpretation governed by the exercise of* quan *or the weighing of circumstances informed by the sense of rightness* (yi).

However, the common Confucian appeal to historical events and paradigmatic individuals is criticized because of lack of understanding of the ethical uses of such a historical appeal. The pedagogical use stresses the study of the classics in terms of the standards of ren, yi *and* li. *Learning, however, is not a mere acquisition of knowledge, but requires understanding and insight. Also, the companion study of paradigmatic individuals is important, not only because they point to models of emulation but also because they are, so to speak, exemplary personifications of the spirits of* ren, yi *and* li. *Moreover, they also function as reminders of moral learning and conduct that appeal especially to what is deemed in the real interest of the learner. The rhetorical use of the historical appeal is basically an appeal to plausible presumptions, or shared beliefs and trustworthiness. These presumptions are subject to further challenge, but they can be accepted as starting points in discourse. The elucidative use of historical appeal purports to clarify the relevance of the past for the present. Perhaps most important for argumentative discourse is the evaluative function of historical appeal. It focuses our knowledge and understanding of our present problematic situations as a basis for exerting the unexamined claims based on the past as a guidance for the present. Thus, both the elucidative and evaluative uses of historical appeal are critical and attentive to evidential grounding of ethical claims.*

Because of its primary ethical orientation and its influence on traditional Chinese life and thought, Confucianism occupies a pre-eminent place in the history of Chinese philosophy. The core of Confucian thought lies in the teachings of Confucius (551–479 BC) contained in the Analects *(Lunyu), along with the brilliant and divergent contributions of Mencius (372?–289 BC) and Xunzi (fl. 298–238 BC), as well as the* Daxue *(Great Learning) and the* Zhongyong *(Doctrine of the Mean), originally chapters in the* Liji *(Book of Rites). Significant and original developments, particularly along a quasi-metaphysical route, are to be found in the works of Zhou Dunyi (1017–73), Zhang Zai (1020–77), Cheng Hao (1032–85), Cheng Yi (1033–1107), Zhu Xi (1130–1200), Lu Xiangshan (1139–93), and Wang Yangming (1472–1529). Li Gou (1009–59), Wang Fuzhi (1619–92), and Dai Zhen (1723–77) have also made noteworthy contributions to the critical development of Confucian philosophy. In the twentieth century, the revitalization and transformation of Confucian philosophy has taken a new turn in response to Western philosophical traditions. Important advances have been made by Feng Youlan, Tang Junyi, Thomé H. Fang, and Mou Zongsan. Most of the recent works in critical reconstruction are marked by a self-conscious concern with analytic methodology and the relevance of existentialism, phenomenology, and hermeneutics. Still lacking is a comprehensive and systematic Confucian theory informed by both the history and the problems of Western philosophy.*

1 **The conceptual framework**
2 **An ethics of virtue:** *dao* **and** *de*
3 **Basic notions and the problem of conceptual unity**
4 **The ethical framework of Confucianism**
5 *Ren*
6 *Yi* **and** *li*
7 **The scope and function of** *li*
8 **The Confucian tradition**
9 **Xunzi and Zhu Xi**
10 **Transformation of the Confucian tradition**
11 **Historical appeal**

1 The conceptual framework

A student or scholar of moral philosophy, approaching the classical core of Confucian ethics for the first time, is likely to be faced with a major difficulty in the lack of systematic exposition of basic Confucian notions such as *ren* (benevolence), *li* (rites), and *yi* (rightness), and their interconnection. Unlike major Western philosophers, Confucian thinkers are not concerned with definitions. As William Theodore de Bary (1970: v) has pointed out, most Chinese thinkers are not interested in the definition and analysis of concepts: 'generally, the more crucial or central the idea, the greater the ambiguity'. Instead, they are concerned with the expansive uses of ideas that suggest the widest possible range of meaning.

From the point of view of contemporary moral philosophy, this pervasive feature of Confucian discourses may appear to be an anomaly, given the classical emphasis on the right use of terms (*zhengming*). A serious student of the works of XUNZI, the one classical Confucian generally considered to be the most rationalistic and systematic philosopher, will be frustrated in the attempt to find definitions, in the sense of necessary and sufficient conditions, for the application of basic Confucian terms. This fact is all the more surprising in view of Xunzi's recurrent employment of certain definitional locutions or quasi-definitional formulas for explaining his theses on human nature and the mind. Like most major Confucians, Xunzi has a pragmatic attitude toward

the use of language, that is, the uses of terms that require explanation are those that are liable to misunderstanding in the context of particular discourse. The Confucian explanations of the use of ethical terms are context-dependent and are addressed to a particular rather than universal audience.

Two different assumptions underlying this attitude toward language may account for the absence of Chinese interest in context-independent explanation of the use of ethical terms. First, there is an assumption of the primacy of practice implicit in the Confucian doctrine of the unity of knowledge and action (*zhixing heyi*). Definition, in the sense of meaning explanation, is a matter of practical rather than theoretical necessity. This assumption does not depreciate the importance of theoretical inquiry, but rather focuses on its relevance to the requirements of practice, particularly those that promote unity and harmony among people in the community. Such requirements vary in time and place. A viable ethical theory is thus subject to pragmatic assessment in the light of changing circumstances. In general, ethical requirements cannot be stated in terms of absolute or fixed principles or rules. It is this assumption of the primacy of practice that renders plausible Donald Munro's claim that the consideration important to the Chinese is the behavioural implications of the belief or proposition in question (Munro 1969). What effect does adherence to the belief have on people? What implications for social action can be drawn from the statement? In Confucianism, there was no thought of 'knowing' that did not entail some consequence for action.

Related to the primacy of practice is the assumption that reasoned discourse may legitimately appeal to what Nicholas Rescher calls 'plausible presumptions,' that is, an appeal to shared knowledge, belief or experience, as well as to established or operative standards of discourse (Rescher 1977: 38). For Confucian thinkers, most of these presumptions, at least among the well-educated, represent the shared understanding of a common tradition and a living cultural heritage. These presumptions are often suppressed and mainly form the background of discourse. Thus Confucian reasoning and argumentation appears to be highly vague and inexplicit. From the Aristotelian point of view, Confucian reasoning is 'rhetorical', as it frequently involves enthymemes and arguments from examples.

Given the assumptions of the primacy of practice and appeal to plausible presumptions, any attempt at introducing Confucian ethics to students of Western philosophy involves a basic task in philosophical reconstruction. This is a task in constructive interpretation, not only in providing a general characterization but also in reshaping the basic notions and concerns of Confucian ethics in response to some problems of moral philosophy. Such an exploration serves two important and connected aims: first, a plausible explication of the Confucian outlook in philosophically relevant idioms, and second, a critical development of Confucian ethical thought.

2 An ethics of virtue: *dao* and *de*

While major Confucianists (for example, Mencius and Xunzi) differ in their conceptions of human nature in relation to conduct, most of them accept Confucius' ideal of a well-ordered society based on good government (see XING; MENCIUS; XUNZI). Good government is responsive to the basic needs of the people, to issues of wise management of natural resources and to just distribution of burdens and benefits. In this vision of socio-political order, special emphasis is put on harmonious human relationships (*lun*) in accord with *de*, virtues or standards of excellence. This vision is often called *dao*, a term that has been appropriated by different classical schools of Chinese thought, including Daoism and Legalism (see LEGALIST PHILOSOPHY, CHINESE; DAOIST PHILO-SOPHY). In the Analects, *dao* is sometimes used as a verb, meaning 'to guide'; sometimes it is used as a concrete noun, meaning literally 'road'. In the latter sense, it can be rendered as 'way'. But in distinct Confucian ethical usage, as commonly acknowledged by commentators, it is *dao* as an abstract noun that is meant, and more especially in the evaluative rather than descriptive sense, that is, as referring to the ethical ideal of a good human life as a whole (see DAO).

Throughout its long history, Confucianism has stressed character formation or personal cultivation of virtues (*de*) (see DE). Thus it seems appropriate to characterize Confucian ethics as an ethics of virtue, not an ethics of rules or principles. To avoid misunderstanding, two explanations are in order. In the first place, the Confucian focus on the centrality of virtues assumes that the notion of *de* can be rendered as 'virtue'. In the second place, this focus does not depreciate the importance of rule-governed conduct (see MORAL DEVELOPMENT).

Sinologists differ in their interpretation of the Confucian use of *de*. Some insist that *de* should be construed as 'power', 'force' or 'potency', and in Confucian usage it should be qualified as moral in contrast to physical force. Others argue for 'virtue' in the distinctively ethical sense, as pertaining to the excellence of a character trait or disposition. Inter-estingly, these two construals of *de* are not incompa-tible in the light of some English uses of 'virtue' (see VIRTUE ETHICS). In *Webster's Third New Interna-*

tional Dictionary, for example, the sixth definition of 'virtue' is: 'an active quality or power whether of physical or of moral nature; the capacity or power adequate to the production of a given effect', and the fifth definition is: 'a characteristic, quality, or trait known or felt to be excellent'. The *Oxford English Dictionary* likewise offers as definitions 'a good quality' and 'efficacy; inherent power'. Both these senses of 'virtue' are found in the classical Chinese uses of *de*.

There is, of course, the value-neutral sense of *de* that leaves open the question whether personal traits or qualities merit ethical approval, and this question is reflected in the distinction, still current in Modern Chinese, between *meide* and *ede*. The former pertains to 'beautiful' or 'commendable' *de*, and the latter to its contrary. *Meide* are those traits that are acquired through personal cultivation. The *Encyclopedia Dic-tionary of the Chinese Language* offers the following two entries for *de* in the ethical sense, one suggested by an interpretation of its homophone, meaning 'to get' or 'to obtain', found in the *Liji* (Book of Rites): 'that which is obtained in the heart-and-mind as a result of personal cultivation', and 'the nature that is formed after successful personal cultivation'. Both these definitions involve *meide*, commendable, ac-quired qualities or traits of character, much in the sense of David Hume's 'personal merits' (see HUME, D.) *Ede*, on the other hand, are personal demerits or 'detestable' qualities of character.

Also important is the sense of *de* as power or force, in view of the Confucian notion of *junzi* (ethically superior or paradigmatic individuals). By virtue of ethical achievement, a *junzi* possesses the power of attraction or influence indicative of effective agency (see MORAL AGENTS). As Confucius remarks, the *junzi*, equipped with the virtues (*de*), never stands alone: 'He is bound to have neighbours.' 'The virtue (*de*) of the gentleman (*junzi*) is like the wind; the virtue (*de*) of the small man is like grass. Let the wind blow over the grass and it is sure to bend' (*Analects* 12.19, in Lau 1979: 115–16). In sum, the Confucian notion of *de* can be properly construed as ethical virtues that possess a dual aspect: an achieved condition of a person through self-cultivation of commendable character traits in accordance with the ideal *dao*, and a condition that is deemed to have the peculiar potency or power of efficacy in influencing the course of human life. The difficult problem is to present the Confucian *dao* and *de* as an ethics of virtue with a coherent conceptual scheme.

3 Basic notions and the problem of conceptual unity

The *Analects*, a composite work, is commonly

considered the main and most reliable source of Confucius' teachings (see CONFUCIUS). It bequeaths to the Chinese tradition a large and complex ethical vocabulary, which contains a significant number of virtue (*de*) terms with implicit reference to the Confucian ideal of *dao*. Terms such as *ren* (benevolence), *yi* (rightness) and *li* (rites) seem to occupy a central position both in the *Analects* and throughout the history of Confucian discourse. Until recent times, however, few philosophical scholars of Confucianism attended to the problem of conceptual explication and the unity of these basic notions, that is, their presumed interconnection or interdependence in the light of *dao* as an ideal, unifying perspective. While most Confucian terms for particular virtues can be rendered into English without the need of elaborate explanation – for example, *xiao* (filiality), *yong* (courage), *wei* (dignity), *zhong* (fidelity), *ci* (kindness), *jing* (respectfulness) – the apparently basic notions (*ren*, *li* and *yi*) are not amenable to the simple expedience of translation and thus pose a problem for conceptual analysis and interpretation. Moreover, existing translations of these terms ineluctably embody the writer's interpretation, a sort of implicit commentary, representing the writer's prior understanding of the translated texts.

Similarly, an explication of basic Confucian notions involves philosophical commentary, a familiar feature in the development of the history of Chinese thought. However, attempts at explication have been beset by a formidable difficulty, especially in defining the basic concepts of the Confucian framework. The pioneering study of the conceptual aspect of Confucian ethics is Chen Daqi's *Kongzi xueshuo* (Teachings of Confucius) (Chen 1976). Chen reminds us that prior to interpreting the ideas of Confucius, it is essential to inquire into the conceptual status of some recurrent terms in the text. For determining the centrality or basic status of notions or concepts, Chen proposes four criteria, according to which basic concepts are (1) fundamental, (2) leading or guiding, (3) the most important (cardinal) or (4) the most comprehensive.

Fundamental concepts suggest the distinction between basic and derivative concepts. However, it is more plausible and accords better with Chen's discussion to construe his distinction as one between basic and dependent concepts. Given our characterization of Confucian ethics as an ethics of virtues, this is a conceptual distinction between basic and dependent virtues. A concept may depend on another for its ethical significance without being a logical derivation. For instance, one cannot derive the concept of love from *ren*, yet its ethical significance depends on its connection with *ren*. This is perhaps the principal ground for Zhu Xi's famous contention that *ren* cannot be equated with love, for it is the rationale of love (*ai zhi li*) (see ZHU XI).

Leading or guiding concepts recall the purport of ethical terms as guides for action, informing the Confucian agent that the enduring significance of ethical endeavours lies in the pursuit of *dao* or the ideal of the good human life as a whole. *Cardinal concepts* and *comprehensive concepts* are the chief mark of basic ethical concepts. Comprehensive concepts also raise an issue in Confucian scholarship. Perhaps the issue can be settled if comprehensiveness is ascribed to *dao* or *ren* in the broad sense as signifying the holistic, ideal unifying perspective of Confucian discourse. Again, consider Zhu Xi's thesis that *ren* (in the broad sense) embraces the four: *ren* (in the narrow sense), *yi* (rightness), *li* (rites) and *zhi* (wisdom). In terms of an ethics of virtue, the fundamental distinction is the distinction between cardinal and dependent virtues. Accordingly, Chen proposes that in addition to *dao* and *de*, the Confucian scheme consists of *ren*, *li* and *yi* as the basic, cardinal concepts. This thesis is well-supported by the recurrence of such concepts and their fundamental importance throughout the history of Confucianism.

4 The ethical framework of Confucianism

The foregoing pertains to the question of identifying basic, cardinal concepts as contrasted with dependent concepts. A more formidable problem remains as to how these basic concepts are related to one another. The following discussion presents a sketch of a philosophical reconstruction, which is essentially a conceptual experiment. The sketch offers a general characterization of Confucian ethics as a form of virtue ethics, and provides a sample of how such basic notions as *li* and *yi* can be shaped in response to questions deemed important for the development of a Confucian moral philosophy.

The Confucian ethical framework comprises the five basic concepts: *dao*, *de*, *ren*, *yi* and *li*. The best initial approach is to regard these, with a minimum of interpretation, as 'focal notions', that is, terms that function like focal lenses for conveying distinct though not unrelated centres of ethical concern. As generic terms, focal notions are amenable to specification in particular contexts, thus acquiring specific or narrower senses. This distinction is an adaptation of Xunzi's distinction between generic terms (*gongming*) and specific terms (*bieming*). However, a term used as a specific term in one context may in another context be used as a generic term subject to further specification. In other words, the use of a term in either the generic or specific sense is entirely relative to the speaker's purpose on a particular occasion, rather than to any theory concerning the intrinsic characters of terms or the essential attributes of things.

As noted earlier, *dao* is an evaluative term. Its focal point of interest lies in the Confucian vision of the good human life as a whole or the ideal of human excellence. Commonly rendered as 'the way', *dao* is functionally equivalent to the ideal 'way of life'. Unlike other basic terms, *dao* is most distinctive as an abstract, formal term in the highest generic sense, that is, subject to general specification by way of such virtue (*de*) words as *ren*, *li* and *yi*. As *de* is an individual achievement through personal cultivation, when a person succeeds in realizing *dao*, they have attained such basic *de* as *ren*, *li* and *yi*. The specification of *de*, apart from *ren*, *li* and *yi*, can take a variety of forms or dependent virtues such as filiality, respectfulness or trustworthiness. In this sense, *de* is an abstract noun like *dao*, but it depends on *dao* for its distinctive character. *De* is thus functionally equivalent to ethical virtue. Thus, the opening remark of the *Daxue* (Great Learning) points out that the way of great learning or adult, ethical education lies in the clear exemplification of the virtues (*ming mingde*) (see DAXUE; MORAL EDUCATION; MORAL DEVELOPMENT). With its emphasis on *dao* and *de*, Confucian ethics is properly characterized as an ethics of virtue, but more informatively as an ethics of *ren*, *li* and *yi*, relative to their concrete specification or particularization by terms of dependent virtues (for example, filiality, respectfulness, integrity). As generic, focal terms, *ren*, *li* and *yi* are specific terms relative to *dao* as a generic term. Differently put, implicit in Chen's account is a distinction between basic, interdependent virtues (*ren*, *li* and *yi*) and dependent virtues (filiality, respectfulness and so on) (Chen 1976). As indicated earlier, the latter are dependent in the sense that their ethical import depends on direct or indirect reference to one or more of the basic, interdependent virtues of *ren*, *li* and *yi* (see VIRTUE ETHICS).

5 *Ren*

While *ren*, commonly translated as 'benevolence', has a long history of conceptual evolution and interpretation, as a focal notion it centres its ethical interest on love and care for one's fellows, that is, an affectionate concern for the well-being of others – the one persistent idea in the Confucian tradition. For this reason, English translators often render *ren* as 'benevolence', suggestive of the use of 'benevolence' in Francis HUTCHESON and David HUME. Perhaps a

more literal translation of *ren*, however, is 'human-heartedness' or 'humanity', since *ren* is basically an idea of love or concern for the well-being of human community, a specification of the concrete significance of the Confucian *dao* (see COMMUNITY AND COMMUNITARIANISM §1). This core meaning of *ren* as fellow-feeling is found in the *Analects*; it is reported that Confucius once said to his disciple Zengzi, 'My *dao* has one thread that runs through it.' Zengzi construed this *dao* to consist of *zhong* and *shu*, an interpretation widely acknowledged as a method for pursuing *ren* (*Analects* 4.15, in Lau 1979: 74) While the relation between *zhong* and *shu* has divergent interpretations, *zhong* may be rendered as 'doing one's best', and *shu* as 'consideration' (of other people's feelings and desires). In this light, Confucian ethics displays a concern for both self-regarding and other-regarding virtues.

However, the acquisition of these virtues presupposes a locus in which these particular, dependent virtues are exercised. Thus among the dependent virtues, filiality, brotherhood or sisterhood are primary, for the family is the natural home and the foundation for the extension of *ren*-affection. Thus friendship is viewed as a fundamental human relationship along with those of husband–wife and parent–child. In Song and Ming Confucianism (for example, in CHENG HAO and WANG YANGMING), *dao* is sometimes used interchangeably with *ren*. In this manner, *ren* attained the status of a supreme, all-embracing ethical ideal of the well-being of every existent thing, human or non-human, animate or inanimate. Confucius' vision of a well-ordered human society is transformed into the vision of the universe as a moral community. In this conception, anything that is an actual or potential object of human attention is considered an object of human concern. Exploitation of human and natural resources must be subject to evaluation in terms of *dao* as an all embracing ethical ideal of existence. This ideal of *dao* makes no specific demands on ordinary humans. For the most part, conflict of values is left to individual determination, though the welfare of the parents is always the first consideration. Thus, the concrete significance of *dao* is open to the exercise of *yi*, the agent's sense of rightness.

6 *Yi* and *li*

The exercise of *yi*, usually rendered as righteousness or rightness, depends on ethical education based on *daotong* or the tradition of the community of interpretation; that is, the reasoned interpretation of the educated members of the community informed by *sensus communis*, a sense of common interest, a regard for *dao* as the ideal unifying perspective. Disagreement or dispute on the pragmatic import of *dao* is expected, as members of the community of interpretation have their own conceptions of human excellence (*shan*) and possibilities of fulfilment. The ethical solution of conflict of interpretation lies in transforming the disagreement into agreement in the light of *sensus communis*, not in a solution defined by agonistic debate which presumes that there are impartial judges who can render their corporate decision in terms of majority vote. Unlike contemporary democratic polity, the majority rule cannot be reasonably accepted as a standard for setting ethical disagreement. The ethical tradition provides the background and guidelines to ethical conduct. Normative ethical theories have value because they provide different ways of assessing the significance of tradition. Like the basic concepts of Confucian ethics, they are focal notions for important centres of ethical concern, for example, duty and interest (private or public), or in recent terminology, agent-relative and agent-neutral reasons for action (see MORAL AGENTS).

The notion of *li* focuses on the ritual code (see LAW AND RITUAL IN CHINESE PHILOSOPHY). For this reason, it is commonly rendered as 'rites', 'ritual', 'propriety', or 'ceremonials'. The ritual code is essentially a set of rules of proper conduct pertaining to the manner or style of performance. As *yi* is incompatible with exclusive regard for personal gain, the *li* set forth the rules of ethical responsibility. For Confucius and his followers, the *li* represent an enlightened tradition. As D.C. Lau has put it:

> The rites (*li*) were a body of rules governing action in every aspect of life and they were the repository of past insights into morality. It is, therefore, important that one should, unless there are strong reasons to the contrary, observe them. Though there is no guarantee that observance of the rites necessarily leads, in every case, to behaviour that is right, the chances are it will, in fact, do so.
> (Lau 1979: 20)

Yet, the ethical significance of *li* is determined by the presence of the spirit of *ren*. As Confucius once said, 'If a man has no *ren*, what has he to do with *li*?' (*Analects* 3.3, in Lau 1979: 67). Since the ritual code represents a customary practice, the early Confucians, particularly Xunzi and the writers of some chapters in the *Liji*, were concerned with providing a reasoned justification for compliance with *li* or traditional rules of proper conduct. As Arthur Waley aptly remarks: 'it was with the relation of ritual [*li*] as a whole to morality and not with the details of etiquette and precedence that the early Confucianists were chiefly

concerned' (Waley 1938: 67) The same concern with reasoned justification is evident in Song and Ming Confucianists (for example, Zhu Xi and Wang Yangming) who maintain that the significance of *li* (ritual) lies in its rationale (*li zhi li*).

The ethical significance of *yi*, in part, is an attempt to provide a rationale for the acceptance of *li*. *Yi* focuses principally on what is right or fitting. The equation of *yi* with its homophone meaning 'appropriateness' is explicit in the *Zhongyong*, 20 (see ZHONGYONG), and is generally accepted by Confucianists (for example, Xunzi, Li Gou and Zhu Xi). However, what is right or fitting depends on reasoned judgement. As XUNZI observes: 'The person concerned with *yi* follows reason' (*Xunzi* XV, in Li 1979: 328) Thus, *yi* may be construed as reasoned judgement concerning the right thing to do in particular exigencies. Li Gou, a Song Confucian, justly reminds his readers that *yi* is 'decisive judgement' that is appropriate to the situation at hand.

In light of the foregoing, the interdependence of basic notions may be stated as follows. Given *dao* as the ideal of the good human life as a whole, *ren*, *li* and *yi*, the basic Confucian virtues (*de*), are constitutive rather than mere instrumental means to its actualization. In other words, the actualization of *dao* requires the co-satisfaction of the standards expressed in *ren*, *li* and *yi*. Since these focal notions pertain to different foci of ethical interest, we may also say that the actualization of *dao* requires a coordination of three equally important centres of ethical interest and endeavour. The connection between these foci is one of interdependence rather than subordination. Thus in the ideal case, *ren*, *li* and *yi* are mutually supportive and adherent to the same ideal of *dao*. When *dao* is in fact realized, *ren*, *li* and yi would be deemed constituents of this condition of achievement. When, on the other hand, one attends to the prospect of *dao*-realization, *ren*, *li* and *yi* would be regarded as complementary foci and means to *dao* as an end. In sum, *ren*, *li* and *yi* are complementary foci of human interest.

7 The scope and functions of *li*

Because of its distinctive character and role in Confucian ethics and its pervasive influence in traditional China and contemporary critique, the notion of *li* requires special attention (see LAW AND RITUAL IN CHINESE PHILOSOPHY). Implicit in the notion of *li* is an idea of rule-governed conduct. In the *Liji* (Book of Rites), the subject matter ranges from ritual rules (or formal prescriptions) concerning mourning, sacrifices, marriage and communal festivities to the more ordinary occasions relating to conduct towards ruler, superior, parent, elder, teacher and guest. Because of its emphasis on the form or manner of behaviour, *li* is often translated as 'religious rites', 'ceremony', 'deportment', 'decorum', 'propriety', 'formality', 'politeness', 'courtesy', 'etiquette', 'good form' or 'good behaviour'. These renderings are misleading without understanding the different functions of *li*. At the outset, it is important to note that for Confucians the *li* are an embodiment of a living cultural tradition; that is, they are subject to modification in response to changing circumstances of society. Thus some writers of the *Liji* point out that the *li* are the prescriptions of reason, and that any ritual rule that is deemed right and reasonable (*yi*) can be considered a part of *li*. On one plausible interpretation, the traditional ritual code represents no more than a codification of ethical experiences based on the concern with *ren* and *yi*. In this light, the *li* are in principle subject to revision or replacement. In the spirit of ZHU XI, we may say that a Confucian must reject ritual rules that are burdensome and superfluous and accept those that are practicable and essential to the maintenance of a harmonious social order. However, any reasoned attempt to revise or replace *li* presupposes an understanding of their functions. It is this understanding that distinguishes the Confucian scholar from a pedant, who may have a mastery of rules without understanding their underlying rationales. For elucidation, we rely mainly on a reconstruction of Xunzi's view, since we find in some of his essays the most articulate concern for and defence of *li* as an embodiment of a living, cultural tradition (see XUNZI).

With regard to any system of rules governing human conduct, one can always raise questions concerning its purpose. In Confucian ethics, the *li*, as a set of formal prescriptions for proper behaviour, have a threefold function: delimiting, supportive and ennobling. The *delimiting* function is primary, in that the *li* are fundamentally directed to the prevention of human conflict. They comprise a set of constraints that delineate the boundaries of pursuit of individual needs, desires and interests. The *li* purport to set forth rules of proceeding in an orderly fashion, ultimately to promote the unity and harmony of human association in a state ruled by a sage king imbued with the spirit of *ren* and *yi*. This orderliness consists of social distinctions or divisions in various kinds of human relationships (*lun*), namely, the distinctions between ruler and minister, father and son, the eminent and the humble, the elder and the younger, the rich and the poor, and the important and unimportant members of society. In abstraction from the connection with *ren* and *yi*, the delimiting function of *li* may be compared to that of negative

moral rules or criminal laws. Like rules against killing, stealing or lying, the *li* impose constraints on conduct. They create paths of obstruction, thus blocking certain moves of agents in the pursuit of their desires or interests. The *li*, in effect, stipulate the conditions of eligibility or permissibility of actions. They do not prejudge the substantive character or value of individual pursuit. They provide information on the limiting conditions of action, but no positive guidance as to how one's desires may be properly satisfied. Put differently, the *li* tell agents what goals *not* to pursue, but they do not tell them how to go about pursuing goals within the prescribed limits of action.

Apart from the delimiting function, the *li* have also a *supportive* function; that is, they provide conditions or opportunities for satisfaction of desires within the prescribed limits of action. Instead of suppressing desires, the *li* provide acceptable channels or outlets for their fulfilment. In an important sense, the supportive function of *li* acknowledges the integrity of our natural desires. So long as they are satisfied within the bounds of propriety, we accept them for what they are whether reasonable or unreasonable, wise or foolish, good or bad. The main supportive function of *li* is the redirection of the course of individual self-seeking activities, not the suppression of motivating desires. Just as the delimiting function of *li* may be compared with that of criminal law, their supportive function may be compared with that of procedural law, which contains rules that enable us to carry out our wishes and desires (for example, the law of wills and contracts). The *li*, like these procedural rules, aid the realization of desires without pronouncing value judgments.

The focus on the *ennobling* function of *li* is a distinctive feature of Confucian ethics and traditional Chinese culture (see SELF-CULTIVATION, CHINESE THEORIES OF). The keynote of the ennobling function is 'cultural refinement', the education and nourishment (*yang*) of emotions or their transformation in accord with the spirit of *ren* and *yi*. The characteristic concern with the form of proper behaviour is still present. However, the form stressed is not just a matter of fitting into an established social structure or set of distinctions, nor is it a matter of methodical procedure that facilitates the satisfaction of the agent's desires and wishes; rather, it involves the elegant form (*wen*) for the expression of ethical character. In other words, the ennobling function of *li* is directed primarily to the development of commendable or beautiful virtues (*meide*). The 'beauty' (*mei*) of the expression of an ethical character lies in the balance between emotions and form. What is deemed admirable in the virtuous conduct of an ethically superior person (*junzi*) is the harmonious fusion of elegant form and feelings. In the ideal case, a *li*-performance may be said to have an aesthetic dimension. In two different and related ways, a *li*-performance may be said to be an object of delight. In the first place, the elegant form is something that delights our senses. It can be contemplated with delight quite apart from the expressed emotional quality. In the second place, when we attend to the emotion or emotional quality expressed by the action, which we perceive as a sign of an ethical virtue or character, our mind is delighted and exalted, presuming of course that we are also agents interested in the promotion of ethical virtues in general. Respect for traditional rites of mourning and sacrifices is an expression for the concern with *ren* and *li*, because such practices exemplify the Confucian ideal of humanity; it is a sort of religious concern without endorsing any religious beliefs and practices.

8 The Confucian tradition

If the set of *li*, or rules of proper conduct, is viewed as a repository of traditional insights, a question then arises concerning the Confucians' conception of their own tradition. Like other enduring ethical or religious traditions which extend across history (such as Buddhism or Christianity), the Confucian or Ru tradition, as embodied in the notion of *daotong*, has often been the target of the contemporary critique. According to one familiar appraisal, the Ru tradition is out of tune with our times. Like any cherished cultural artefact, it is best revered as a relic of the past. Moreover, many adherents of the Confucian tradition are dogmatic; they are unwilling to accept reasonable proposal for change or modification of some components of the tradition.

Replying to this charge, a Confucian thinker or scholar might point out that, to a certain extent, the critique is reasonable. Throughout its long history, there is a recurrent tendency of many adherents of the Confucian tradition to institute orthodoxy and uphold their perceived values of the tradition as the true values of the tradition, indifferent to the distinction between perceived and real values. A personal ascription of value to an object cannot be logically equated with the value inherent in the object. Understanding a living tradition requires an appreciation of the distinction between the actual past and the perceived past, and the distinction between a living, robust tradition and a dying, decaying tradition. In the words of Jaroslav Pelikan, 'Tradition is the living faith of the dead, traditionalism is the dead faith of the living' (Pelikan 1984: 65).

Confucianism, in the words of Thomé Fang, is 'a constructive philosophy of comprehensive harmony invested with creative energies of life' (Fang 1981: 33). Although this is a summary statement of the outcome of Fang's metaphysical inquiry, it is an apt characterization of the vitality of the Confucian *dao* or way as an ethical vision of the good human life, an ideal amenable to varying interpretations of its concrete significance in different times and places. *Dao* is an ideal theme rather than an ideal norm or supreme principle of conduct (Cua 1978, ch. 8). It is fundamentally a unifying perspective for harmonizing the diverse elements of moral experience. To adopt the *dao* is to see human life, in its morally excellent form, as possessing a coherence in which apparently conflicting elements are viewed as eligible components of an achievable harmonious order (Cua 1982, ch. 3). It is this vision of *dao* that renders intelligible the idea of a Confucian ethical tradition as a living tradition enriched by its historic past, interpreted by adherents as having a present and prospective significance (see DAO).

9 Xunzi and Zhu Xi

XUNZI and ZHU XI are perhaps the most articulate proponents of the importance of learning the classics as an indispensable means to inculcating a respect for the historical aspect of tradition. Xunzi points out that learning is an unceasing process of accumulation of goodness, knowledge, and practical understanding: 'If an ethically superior person (*junzi*) studies widely and daily engages in self-examination, his intellect will become enlightened and his conduct be without fault.' In general, the programme of learning 'commences with the recitation of the classics and ends with the study of *li* (rituals)'. Its purpose, however, is 'first to learn to become a scholar and ultimately to become a sage'. The classics are presumed to embody the concrete significance of *dao*. For example, 'the *Odes* give expression to the will (*zhi*) or determination [to realize *dao*]; the *History* or *Book of Documents* to its significance in human affairs; the *Li* or *Rites* to its significance in conduct; the *Music* to its significance in promoting harmony; and the *Spring and Autumn Annals* to its subtleties.' Notably, these classics are not self-explanatory, thus guidance from perceptive teachers is required. For example, 'the *Li* and *Music* present us with models, but no explanations; the *Odes* and the *History* deal with ancient matters and are not always pertinent; the *Spring and Autumn Annals* are terse and cannot be quickly understood' (*Xunzi* I, in Li 1979: 2–14; trans. in Watson 1963: 15–20).

Indeed, for Confucius as for MENCIUS and Xunzi, the *li* represent an ethical and cultural tradition (see CONFUCIUS). Learning to be a moral agent consists in part in appreciating 'the accumulated wisdom of the past'. Compliance with *li* as a set of formal prescriptions of proper behaviour without regard to *ren* and particular circumstances would be deemed unreasonable. It is perhaps for this reason that Confucius stresses *yi* (a sense of rightness) rather than preconceived opinions in coping with novel and exigent situations. Mencius is emphatic that the relevance of a *li*-requirement must be considered in the light of weighing (*quan*) particular circumstances. In a similar spirit, Xunzi emphasizes the exercise of *yi* in responding to changing circumstances of human life. In general, the enforcement of laws and other rules of conduct depends on superior or exemplary persons (*junzi*) who have not only a knowledge of the subject matter but also an understanding of their underlying purposes, in addition to having a sense of priority and an ability to respond appropriately to changing affairs. Learning to become a sage (*shengren*) must begin with the study of the classics with a view to discerning their actuating significance in living contexts (see CHINESE CLASSICS).

The Confucian respect for the authority of the past in relation to the present requires not only a critical understanding of the practical significance of the classics but, more importantly, a critical assessment of the ethical character and achievement of contemporary adherents of the tradition. Thus Xunzi urges his readers to distinguish common people from three sorts of Confucians (Ru): the vulgar or conventional (*suru*), the refined or cultured (*yaru*) and the great or sagely Confucians (*daru*). This distinction between three types of Confucians may be seen to be motivated by Xunzi's desire to respond to the internal challenges within the Confucian tradition – a reminder and a warning to his fellow Confucians against uncritical intellectual and practical affiliation (*Xunzi* VIII, in Li 1979). His critique of Mencius on the relation between morality and human nature is a well-known illustration of an internal conflict between different interpretations of a key aspect of Confucian ethical tradition. Like Mencius, Xunzi is also quite aware of the need to engage in argumentation to answer external challenges to the Confucian tradition (*Xunzi* XXIII, in Li 1979). For Mencius, there was no alternative but to engage in disputation since the *dao* of the sages, embodied in Yao and Shun, had in his own time been obscured by the prevailing teachings of YANG ZHU and MOZI.

In a similar spirit, Xunzi attacks the views of a number of philosophers, for example, Mozi, Hui Shi, Songzi and Shen Dao, as well as Laozi and Zhuangzi. Xunzi considers most of their doctrines pernicious because, though often presented in elegant language and composition, they also present erroneous conceptions of the distinction between right and wrong and between order and disorder. However, it is noteworthy that Xunzi's critique explicitly acknowledges that 'some of what they advocate has a reasoned basis, and thus their statements appear plausible' (*Xunzi* VI, in Li 1979: 94). In the light of his holistic conception of *dao*, many philosophical views are unacceptable not because they are totally erroneous, but because they grasp only partial aspects of *dao* and exaggerate these at the expense of other aspects. In sum, in Xunzi we find a Confucian philosopher who exemplifies a concern with defending the Confucian tradition against both internal and external challenges, and who is at the same time quite capable of critical adoption of non-Confucian views which he deems reasonably acceptable.

Zhu Xi's conception of the Confucian tradition, *daotong*, commonly rendered as 'transmission of *dao*', is a conception central to the orthodox tradition of neo-Confucianism (see NEO-CONFUCIAN PHILOSOPHY). Because of its religious connotation, the notion of orthodoxy quite naturally suggests an uncritical adherence to conventional or currently accepted beliefs as possessing an unquestioned authoritative status. As de Bary has instructively shown, however, *daotong* is better construed as 'repossession of *dao*' or 'reconstitution of *dao*', recalling Pelikan's distinction between a living tradition and traditionalism (de Bary 1981: 2).

As Tu Wei-ming remarks, Zhu Xi's study of the classics represents 'serious efforts to revitalize the tradition [which] involved creative adaptation as well as faithful interpretations' (Tu 1979: 134). For example, in his detailed recommendations of classics for examinations, apart from some commentaries, Zhu Xi stresses the self-critical study of original texts: 'In studying the classics one must have regard for the considered views of former scholars and extrapolate from them, aware that they are not necessarily conclusive but must be weighed as to what they understood and what they missed; then finally all this must be reflected upon in one's own mind to verify it' (*Zhuzi yulei* 3:37, in Li 1962, 1638–42). Zhu Xi also recommends non-orthodox philosophers of early China such as Xunzi, HAN FEIZI, Laozi (see DAODEJING) and ZHUANGZI. De Bary rightly reminds us that Zhu Xi's notion of *daotong* should not be construed in a manner that suggests a passive reception and transmission of the Confucian Way, for it involves an activity of revitalization and rediscovery as well as recovery of the meaning of the tradition or, in contemporary language, an activity of constructive or reconstructive interpretation of the tradition: 'In fact, Chu Hsi [Zhu Xi] emphasized the discontinuities in the tradition almost more than the continuities, and underscored the contributions of inspired individuals who rediscovered or "clarified" the Way in new forms' (de Bary 1981: 99).

Both Xunzi and Zhu Xi emphasize the role of inspired and insightful persons regarding classical learning. This emphasis somewhat echoes Confucius' notion of *junzi* or paradigmatic individuals, that is, persons, who through their life and conduct embody *ren*, *li*, *yi* and other ethical excellences (see §2). The *junzi* are the exemplars of the actuating significance of the Confucian tradition, serving as standards of inspiration for committed agents. These paradigmatic individuals are generally ascribed an authority by their contemporary adherents. The authority, however, is based on the acknowledgement of their superior knowledge and achievement, and especially their exercise of yi in interpretive judgements concerning the relevance of rules in exigent situations, or in Xunzi's words, on *dao* and *de* (virtue). However, while possessed of an authoritative ethical status, as standard bearers and interpreters of culture the *junzi* are not arbiters of moral disputes, for their interpretations of the Confucian tradition represent individual efforts toward the repossession or reconstitution of *dao*, thus essentially contestable and subject to reasoned assessment of their contemporaries and posterity.

Implicit in the foregoing characterization of the Confucian tradition as a living tradition is the notion of tradition as an interpretive concept. For the most part, major Confucian philosophers stress the importance of classical education and the role of teachers as *junzi* or paradigmatic individuals, because they are thought to exemplify the best spirit of Confucius. Notably, Confucius' conception of *junzi* focuses on some salient characteristics. In addition to their pursuit of *dao*, the concern with *ren*, *li* and *yi*, they are also persons of integrity, catholicity and neutrality. The integrity is exemplified in their unwavering concern with the harmony of words and deeds (Cua 1978, ch. 5). This stress on the role of *junzi* as a guiding standard of education and moral conduct naturally gives rise to the question on the possibility of modification and transformation of the Confucian tradition. Indeed, if tradition is an interpretive concept, some account must be given on how changes may be viewed as consistent with the conservation of tradition.

10 Transformation of the Confucian tradition

In the Confucian context, this problem of transformation of the tradition is best considered in terms of the distinction and connection between *jing* (the standard) and *quan* (the weighing of circumstances). The former pertains to the operative, established standards of conduct, the latter to the specific circumstances. *Quan* may be regarded as *jing* prior to the determination of its significance in actual, particular situations. In other words, *jing*, the established standards of conduct, depend on *quan* in the sense that their application is undetermined prior to actual circumstances. When such a determination is made, *quan* would become part of *jing*, given the assumption that the judgments are accepted by the Confucian community of interpretation. Concisely put, *jing* is the determinate *quan*, and *quan* is the indeterminate *jing*. Of course, both represent the constant (*chang*) and the changing (*bian*) aspects of *dao*.

More importantly, the exercise of *quan* entails a concern with *yi* or rightness of judgement. Right judgement is necessary not only in dealing with the hard cases of the moral life, but also with normal situations (*jing*) where the intelligent adherent of the tradition confronts the problem of interpretation and application. In both sorts of situation the agent has the same moral objective, that is, to do the right thing. This is perhaps the point of Zhu Xi's saying that *quan* is unavoidably exercised in changing situations that fall outside the scope of the regular practice of *daoli* (moral norm):

'When *quan* attains equilibrium (*zhong*), it does not differ from *jing*', that is, they have achieved the same moral objective. In both cases they are governed by the exercise of *yi* or one's sense of rightness. For ZHU XI, *yi* constitutes the *guan*, the thread that runs though *jing* and *quan*
(*Zhuzi yulei* 3:37, in Li 1962, 1638–42).

The foregoing reflections on the distinction and connection between *jing* and *quan* afford us an answer to the question of the possibility of change or modification of the Confucian tradition of *dao*. Intelligent adherents of the Confucian tradition can deploy the sceptical challenge without fear of the corruption of the tradition (see MORAL SCEPTICISM). The dynamic interplay of *jing* and *quan* in relation to constancy (chang) and change (bian) shows that the distinction is not a fixed or absolute distinction. As DAI ZHEN points out, what is deemed important or unimportant in our assessment will vary in different times and places (Dai 1777 [1975]: 125). Put differently, the substantive content of the tradition of *dao* cannot be considered settled without prejudging the merits of particular circumstances. The exercise of *quan* in any situation requires a careful examination and analysis of all the relevant factors involved.

Quite naturally, one may raise the question of justification for such judgements in exigent circumstances. In normal situations, the *li* are quite sufficient for action guidance insofar as they are informed by a concern for *ren*. The problem of reasoned justification for such judgments has not received attention from most Confucian thinkers, except Xunzi. However, even in the works of Xunzi we do not find any articulate answer to this problem, though his works do provide materials for constructing a response. In the first place, Xunzi is explicit that any discussion is valuable because there exist certain standards for assessment, and these standards pertain principally to conceptual clarity, respect for linguistic practices and evidence, and the requirement of consistency and coherence in discourse. A philosophical reconstruction along the lines of the theory of argumentation presents an interesting Confucian view of justification in terms of rational and empirical standards of competence, along with certain desirable qualities of participants in ethical discourse. In this reconstruction of Xunzi's works, ethical justification is a phase of discourse, preceded by explanatory efforts in the clarification of normative claims responsive to a problem of common concern among participants. This in turn presupposes that queries concerning the proper uses of terms are understood by participants in ethical argumentation (Cua 1985a).

11 Historical appeal

As widely noted by contemporary writers on Confucian ethics, in argumentative discourse the Confucians are fond of appeal to historical events and paradigmatic individuals. This ethical use of historical knowledge and beliefs is a pervasive feature of Confucianism. A serious student of Chinese philosophy cannot accept the common view that Chinese thinkers are inclined to be uncritical towards their history, or that they believe that history provides the exclusive guidance for present problems and perplexities. A careful examination of the works of Xunzi refutes this thesis. The Confucian respect for tradition and its history, and for exemplary historical persons and events, is best appreciated in terms of four ethical, argumentative uses of the past or historical appeal. These are the pedagogical, rhetorical, elucidative and evaluative uses (see History, Chinese theories of).

For Xunzi, the primary aim of moral education is the transformation of man's native but problematic motivational structure (for example, feelings and desires) by way of knowledge of standards of *ren*, *yi* and *li*. One learns for the sake of doing; knowing the right and the good is for the sake of acting in accord with such knowledge. Learning, however, is not equivalent to the mere acquisition of knowledge but more essentially requires understanding and insight.

For Xunzi, the basic philosophical issue in moral education pertains to the rational coordination of the intellectual and volitional activities of the mind (xin) by means of the *dao*. Given the autonomy of mind, one can choose to accept or reject its guidance. If the mind is directed by reason and nourished with clarity and is not perturbed by extraneous matters, 'it will be capable of determining right and wrong and of resolving doubts' (*Xunzi* XXI, in Li 1979: 490; trans. in Watson 1963: 131). In sum, the pedagogical use of the historical appeal points not only to models who are worthy or unworthy of emulation, but more significantly to models functioning as reminders in moral learning and conduct that appeal especially to what is deemed in the real interests of the learner. Notably, gentle suasion rather than coercion is involved, as the individual still retains the freedom to accept or reject it. This constitutes the argumentative value of the pedagogical function of the historical appeal rather than the mere exhibition of moral exemplars. The latter's effectiveness lies primarily in the appeal to paradigmatic individuals (*junzi*) (see Moral education; Moral development).

The rhetorical function of the historical appeal is essentially a problem of assurance, of appeal to plausible presumptions or shared beliefs and trustworthiness (*xin*) (see Xin). When I present reasons supporting my interpretation of the Confucian tradition, I will deploy those unquestioned assumptions in discourse. Also, I expect my fellow Confucians to believe me when I cite information that is presumably known to members of my community. Obviously, the historical appeal functions as a technique for assuring the audience that the thesis maintained is consonant with shared historical beliefs, and obviates having to state reasons for their support. It also constitutes a technique of discounting alternative views, shifting the burden of proof to a possible adversary. These uses, of course, are subject to further challenge, for the rational acceptability of the thesis and an assurance that the thesis is not a mere imaginative contrivance to avoid questioning.

The elucidative function of the use of history attempts to clarify the relevance of the past for the present. This is basically an expression of the respect for tradition, clarifying, in interpretation, one's intelligent, critical understanding of the tradition. Of course, the question of evaluation arises in serious Confucian discourse. Inherent in the use of historical characters for elucidating and demonstrating the applicability of an ethical thesis is the implicit claim that human history is the proper subject of ethical appraisal. However, this claim is explicit in the evaluative use of the historical appeal.

Notably, the elucidative use of the historical appeal

is retrospective; that is, it is the use of the appeal to the past for judging the present (*yigu chijin*); while the evaluative use is prospective, that is, for the sake of determining the relevance of the past to the present (*yijin chigu*). In the retrospective use, Xunzi is clearly recommending the adoption of a standpoint based on historical knowledge or beliefs for the purpose of maintaining or assessing the adequacy of current beliefs. The prospective use, however, stresses our knowledge and understanding of our present problematic situations as a basis for assessing the unexamined claims based on the past as a guidance to the present. Both the retrospective and prospective uses of the historical appeal are essentially critical, and can be used either in the positive defence of one's thesis or in the negative evaluation of another's thesis or both. In J.O. Urmson's words, we have here a distinction between *standard-invoking* and *standard-setting* aspects of normative discourse (Urmson 1968: 68). In effect, the retrospective use of the historical appeal invokes an established framework with its operative criteria or standards for justification of ethical judgments. Of course, one can always raise external questions about an established practice.

The prospective use of the historical appeal reverses the standpoint of the retrospective one. Human history is seen as a subject matter rather than as a basis for ethical judgment. In adopting this standpoint, one can no longer avail oneself of the presumption of the truth of historical beliefs without critical examination, nor can one presume the existence of shared historical knowledge. The key issue here lies in the present evidential grounding of ethical claims (for further discussion see Cua 1985b).

In closing, it may be noted that Confucian ethics, like any normative system, presents conceptual problems of interpretation and reconstruction. Attention here has been focused on the Confucian scheme of basic notions and the idea of Confucian tradition (*daotong*). Doing full justice to the range of Confucian concerns also involves a critical consideration of divergent views on such topics as the relation of the basic notions to human nature, the role of emotions in ethical deliberation and justification, the place of law in an ideal social, political union, and the metaphysical grounding of *dao*, particularly in the connection of the human and the natural orders. A serious student of Confucian philosophy must consider these problems with reference both to the divisive efforts and tension within the history of Chinese philosophy, and to the significance of these efforts to of Western philosophical inquiries.

See also: CHENG HAO; CHENG YI; CHINESE PHILOSOPHY; BUDDHIST PHILOSOPHY, CHINESE; CHINESE CLASSICS; LEGALIST PHILOSOPHY, CHINESE; NEO-CONFUCIAN PHILOSOPHY; HISTORY, CHINESE THEORIES OF; CONFUCIUS; DAI ZHEN; DAO; DAOIST PHILOSOPHY; DAXUE; DE; DONG ZHONGSHU; ETHICAL SYSTEMS, AFRICAN; ETHICS IN ISLAMIC PHILOSOPHY; FAMILY, ETHICS AND THE; HAN YU; CONFUCIAN PHILOSOPHY, JAPANESE; JIA YI; CONFUCIAN PHILOSOPHY, KOREAN; LAW AND RITUAL IN CHINESE PHILOSOPHY; LI; LU XIANGSHAN; MORAL EDUCATION; MORAL DEVELOPMENT; MORALITY AND ETHICS; SELF-CULTIVATION, CHINESE THEORIES OF; SHAO YONG; VIRTUE ETHICS; WANG FUZHI; WANG YANGMING; XUNZI; ZHANG ZAI; ZHONGYONG; ZHOU DUNYI; ZHU XI

References and further readings

Chan Wing-tsit (1955) 'The Evolution of the Confucian Concept *Jen* [*ren*]', *Philosophy East and West* 4: 295–319. (A classic study of the concept of *ren* in the history of Confucianism.)

—— (1963) *A Source Book in Chinese Philosophy*, Princeton, NJ: Princeton University Press. (A translation of and commentary on selections from the Chinese philosophical tradition.)

—— (1975) 'Chinese and Western Interpretation of *Jen* [*ren*] (Humanity)', *Journal of Chinese Philosophy* 2: 107–29. (An informative survey of contemporary interpretations of *ren*.)

Chan Wing-tsit and Fu, C. (1978) *Guide to Chinese Philosophy*, Boston: C.K. Hall. (A contemporary bibliography of scholarly work on Chinese philosophy.)

Chang, C. (1962) *The Development of Neo-Confucian Thought*, New York: Bookman, 2 vols. (A standard interpretation of medieval Chinese philosophy.)

* Chen Daqi (1976) *Kongzi xueshuo* (Teachings of Confucius), Taibei: Zhengchong. (A reconstruction of Confucian philosophical terms.)

—— (1977) *Pingfan de daode guan* (Ordinary View of Morality), Taibei: Chonghuan.

* Cua, A.S. (1978) *Dimensions of Moral Creativity: Paradigms, Principles, and Ideals*, University Park, PA: Pennsylvania State University Press. (Chapters 4 and 5 deal with Confucian ethics focusing on paradigmatic individuals as embodiments of *ren*, *yi* and *li*.)

* —— (1982) *The Unity of Knowledge and Action: A Study in Wang Yang-ming's Moral Psychology*, Honolulu, HI: Unversity of Hawaii Press. (Emphasis on the practical import of moral learning against the background of a Confucian vision of the universe as a moral community.)

* —— (1985a) *Ethical Argumentation: A Study in Hsün Tzu's [Xunzi's] Moral Epistemology*, Honolulu,

HI: University of Hawaii Press. (A Xunzi-based philosophical study of Confucian ethical argumentation with emphasis on the character of the participants, standards of competence, uses of definition and diagnosis of erroneous ethical beliefs.)

* —— (1985b) 'Ethical Uses of the Past in Early Confucianism: The Case of Hsün Tzu [Xunzi]', *Philosophy East and West* 35 (2): 133–56. (Examination of Xunzi's Confucianism.)

—— (1989) 'The Concept of *Li* in Confucian Moral Theory', in R.E. Allison (ed.) *Understanding the Chinese Mind: Philosophical Roots*, Hong Kong: Oxford University Press. (Discussion of the delimiting, supportive and ennobling functions of *li* and their justification.)

—— (1992) 'The Idea of Confucian Tradition', *Review of Metaphysics* 45: 803–40. (Discussion of the concept of living ethical tradition and its application to Confucian ethics.)

—— (1997) *Moral Vision and Tradition: Essays on Chinese Ethics*, Washington, DC: Catholic University of America Press. (Fourteen essays on Chinese ethics dealing with such topics as opposites as complements and 'forgetting morality' in Laozi and Zhuangzi, the Daoist vision and Confucian vision of *ren*, self-deception, tradition and conceptual framework, and ground rules for settling intercultural conflicts.)

* Dai Zhen (1777) *Mengzi ziyi shucheng* (Commentary on the Meanings of Terms in the Book of Mencius), Taibei: Holu, 1975; trans. A. Chen and M. Freeman, New Haven, CT: Yale University Press, 1990. (A commentary on some of the key notions in the works of Mencius and other Confucian classics.)

* de Bary, W.T. (ed.) (1970) *Self and Society in Ming Thought*, New York: Columbia University Press. (An anthology of studies of different schools of thought on these subjects.)

* —— (1981) *Neo-Confucian Orthodoxy and the Learning of the Mind-and-Heart*, New York: Columbia University Press. (A study of the neo-Confucian conception of orthodoxy tracing the idea of orthodoxy from Zhu Xi through the early Ming times, and *xinxue*, the development of Zhu Xi's ideas of learning of mind and heart, and their influence in Tokugawa Japan.)

—— (1983) *The Liberal Tradition in China*, Hong Kong and New York: Chinese University of Hong Kong Press. (A discussion of this topic in terms of the history and contemporary significance of neo-Confucianism, emphasizing such problems as education, individualism, moral cultivation and critiques of political despotism.)

* Fang, T.H. (1981) *The Chinese View of Life: The Philosophy of Comprehensive Harmony*, Taipei: Linking. (An important contribution to the unity of Chinese thought by an influential Chinese philosopher in the Chinese-speaking world. More extensive work is found in T.H. Fang, *Chinese Philosophy: Its Spirit and Development*, Taipei: Linking, 1981.)

Fingarette, H. (1972) *Confucius: The Secular as Sacred*, New York: Harper & Row. (A revision of the classical evaluation of Confucius.)

Fung Yu-lan (1952) *A History of Chinese Philosophy*, trans. D. Bodde, Princeton, NJ: Princeton University Press. (The standard history of Chinese philosophy.)

Graham, A.C. (1989) *Disputers of the Tao: Philosophical Argument in Ancient China*, La Salle, IL: Open Court. (A detailed philosophical engagement with the classical period.)

Hall, D.L. and Ames, R.T. (1987) *Thinking Through Confucius*, Albany, NY: State University of New York Press. (A conceptual reconstruction of Confucian terms based primarily on the *Analects*.)

Kao Ming (1986) 'Chu Hsi [Zhu Xi] and the Discipline of Propriety', in W. Chan (ed.) *Chu Hsi and Neo-Confucianism*, Honolulu, HI: University of Hawaii Press. (A discussion of the role of propriety (*li*) in the philosophy of Zhu Xi.)

Knoblock, J. (ed. and trans.) (1988–94) *Xunzi: A Translation and Study of the Complete Works*, Stanford, CA: Stanford University Press. (The new standard translation.)

* Lau, D.C. (ed. and trans.) (1979) *Confucius: The Analects*, New York: Penguin. (A standard translation of the *Analects* with a good introduction.)

* Li Disheng (ed.) (1979) *Xunzi jishi*, Taibei: Xuesheng. (A good modern Chinese annotated edition of *Xunzi*.)

Moore, C. (ed.) (1967) *The Chinese Mind: Essentials of Chinese Philosophy and Culture*, Honolulu, HI: East–West Center Press. (A selection of papers from the proceedings of four East–West Philosopher's Conferences (1939, 1949, 1959, 1964). This volume presents informative papers on some general aspects of Chinese ethics, epistemological methods, scientific spirit, metaphysics and so on.)

Munro, D.J. (1969) *The Concept of Man in Early China*, Stanford, CA: Stanford University Press. (A discussion of what it means to be a person in the classical schools of Chinese philosophy.)

Naess, A. and Hannay, A. (eds) (1972) *Invitation to Chinese Philosophy*, Oslo: Universitetsforlaget. (An important anthology of recent comparative Chinese and Western introductions to Chinese philosophy, dealing with such topics as Chinese wisdom, paradigmatic individuals, neo-Confucianism, Daoism, Chan (Zen) Buddhism and so on. Seven of the eight essays by different authors were reprinted from *Inquiry* (1971).)

* Pelikan, J. (1984) *Vindication of Tradition*, New Haven, CT: Yale University Press. (A notable, brief defence of tradition as a basis of thought and action by an eminent historian of Christianity.)

* Rescher, N. (1977) *Dialectics*, Albany, NY: State University of New York Press. (An excellent introduction to the disputational approach to inquiry from a socially oriented perspective.)

Schwartz, B. (1985) *The World of Thought in Ancient China*, Cambridge, MA: Harvard University Press. (A broad-ranging and critical interpretation of the classical tradition.)

* Tu Wei-ming (1979) *Humanity and Self-Cultivation*, Berkeley, CA: Asian Humanities Press. (A collection of interpretive essays on the Confucian tradition.)

* Urmson, J.O. (1968) *The Emotive Theory of Ethics*, London: Hutchinson University Library. (A critical discussion of the development of emotive theory from C.K. Ogden and I.A. Richards to C. Stevenson's *Ethics and Language.*)

* Waley, A. (ed. and trans.) (1938) *The Analects of Confucius*, New York: Random House. (A readable translation of the *Analects* of Confucius with a good introduction to some of its principal concepts.)

* Watson, B. (trans.) (1963) *Hsün Tzu [Xunzi]: Basic Writings*, New York: Columbia University Press. (An accessible and readable translation of ten of Xunzi's major essays.)

* Zhu Xi (1130–1200) *Zhuzi yulei* (Classified Conversations of Zhu Xi), ed. Li Chengde, Taipei: Zhengzhong, 1962, 3 vols. (An important collection of Zhu Xi's discourses on various aspects of his thought; an indispensable source.)

A.S. CUA

CONFUCIAN PHILOSOPHY, JAPANESE

Confucian philosophy is said to have arrived in Japan as early as the third century AD, but it did not become a subject of meaningful scholarly inquiry until the seventh century. The 'Confucianism' to which Japanese elites and scholars were first attracted represented fields of knowledge concerned more with ontology and divination than with social ethics and politics. Because of the priority given to birth over talent in official appointments, Confucianism in Japan remained more a gentlemanly accomplishment and never approached the status it had in China, where mastery of its teachings represented a gateway to officialdom. Intellectually, Confucian philosophy was overshadowed both in Japan and on the continent at this time by the teachings of Buddhism, which provided answers both to spiritual and metaphysical concerns.

Confucianism in China was refashioned in the eleventh and twelfth centuries by a number of scholars, of whom Zhu Xi was the most prominent. He revised the curriculum, restored social and ethical concerns to positions of centrality within the tradition and formulated a new rationalistic ontology. His teachings won a broad following among intellectuals in China and eventually earned the government's endorsement as the official interpretation for China's examination system.

From the seventeenth century onwards, Zhu Xi's teachings reached a comparably distinguished position within scholarly circles in Japan, though the government's endorsement of the Hayashi family as official interpreters of Zhu Xi's teachings was the limit of the official authorization of that philosophy in Japan. Though the idealistic Wang Yangming school challenged Zhu Xi's teachings in Japan as it had in China, the more effective challenge was mounted by the classicist teachings known as Ancient Studies. These scholars, of whom the best known was Ogyū Sorai, sought the 'true message of the sages' by emphasizing direct study of the ancient core texts of Confucianism rather than the exegesis on those classics by Zhu Xi and others.

Confucian philosophy contributed to the rationalism, humanism, ethnocentrism and 'historical mindedness' of Tokugawa Japan. The teachings were also responsible for changing fundamental ontological and epistemological assumptions, while also opening intellectual circles to unprecedented pluralism and diversity. Towards the end of the Tokugawa period in the mid-nineteenth century, Confucian philosophy (particularly in the variety fashioned by Wang Yangming) also provided inspiration and justification for those activist reformers who succeeded in overthrowing the old order.

During the modern period, Confucian philosophy has been identified with the Tokugawa tradition which has been at times idealized and and at other times vilified. Nonetheless, a number of the assumptions central to Confucian philosophy continue to characterize much popular and intellectual thought in contemporary Japan, as well as those ethics that tend to be most admired, even though actual knowledge of Confucian philosophy does not appear to be widespread any longer in Japan.

1 Confucian philosophy in early Japan

549

1 Confucian philosophy in early Japan

The earliest extant Japanese histories record that in AD 285 – the actual date was probably a century or so later – Wani, of the Korean kingdom of Paekche, brought copies of the *Analects* (*Lunyu*; in Japanese, *Rongo*) of Confucius and the *Qianziwen* (Thousand Character Classic; *Senjimon* in Japanese) from Korea to Japan (see CONFUCIAN PHILOSOPHY, KOREAN). Even though most scholarship on Japan tends to identify this introduction of Confucian texts with the introduction of Confucian philosophy, it is nonetheless clear that immigrants from China and Korea who were familiar with the Confucian classics surely preceded the gift of these texts and probably themselves represent the actual introduction of Confucianism to Japan.

Confucianism does not appear to have provoked the same measure of suspicion or antagonism as other forms of continental East Asian civilization being introduced to Japan at this time, and the fact that Japanese interest in Confucianism continued to grow is suggested by the arrival in the sixth century of authorities from Paekche on the Confucian classics. Thereafter, with the coincident introduction of Buddhism (also from Korea), Confucian philosophy came to be regarded in Japan as one component of the richly variegated culture and civilization of continental East Asia, both of which were increasingly welcomed and responsible for major changes in Japan.

The 'Confucianism' to which Japanese elites were first exposed, however, was not the ethical sociopolitical teaching represented by texts like the *Analects* or the *Mengzi* (see CONFUCIUS; MENCIUS) which were not at that time regarded as the core of the tradition. Instead, this early continental Confucianism represented the elaboration of metaphysical and cosmological constructions dating from Han dynasty China (206 BC–AD 220) (see CHINESE PHILOSOPHY). According to these teachings, an emperor was the supreme Son of Heaven whose correct performance of his role as an intermediary between Heaven above and Earth below was essential to the harmonious processes of the cosmos (see TIAN). According to this doctrine human responsibilities lay principally in the area of governmental administration, which if properly executed would then ensure that everything from seasonal change to plentiful harvest would contribute to terrestrial well-being, and of course the greatest responsibility thus rested with those in the highest positions. Accordingly, those in Japan who aspired to a more powerful Chinese-style imperial institution often invoked these claims to further their own interests. Further, by positing the interrelatedness of all phenomena in the human realm with those of the celestial and terrestrial realms, this early form of Confucianism also taught that an understanding of the whole might be inferred from an understanding of individual particulars, and so it came to include such divinatory exercises as geomancy, astrology and numerology. These too enjoyed considerable appeal in Japan.

However, because long-standing aristocratic principles in Japan gave priority to pedigree over either virtue or administrative performance, Japanese Confucianism differed from that on the continent by marginalizing both discussion of imperial virtue as it was believed to promote effective government, and assessment of administrative performance as it was likewise believed to entitle one to career advancement. Thus, it was characteristic in Japan before the seventeenth century to consult 'Confucian' philosophy on such matters as determining auspicious dates or sites for important events or constructions, but only rarely does one find meaningful engagement of Confucian wisdom on how best to order the affairs of human beings or the state.

One example of this peripheral role for Confucian philosophy may be discerned in Japan's first important statement of goals for the polity in terms of the new political thought from the continent, the so-called 'Seventeen Article Constitution' of 604. In this document, its author Prince Shōtoku exhorts Japanese leaders to accept the continental imperial principle using references to Confucianism as only one possible source of justification, with other often more persuasive arguments drawn from such alternative forms of thought as Buddhism and Legalism (see SHŌTOKU CONSTITUTION). Buddhism in Japan, as in China, succeeded in preempting Confucian claims to authority in the realm of governance by itself asserting its role in 'protecting' the government from both natural and supernatural threats (see BUDDHIST PHILOSOPHY, CHINESE).

This, however, did not prevent Confucianism from making contributions in other areas. For example, one may discern the influence of Confucian philosophy in the seventh- and eighth-century impulse to record Japanese history for posterity, and it is clear that the early refashioning of the previously oral historical tradition sought to depict at least some emperors in the classic guise of benevolent Confucian-style monarchs. These earliest histories in Japan, however, did not reflect certain other perhaps more fundamental Confucian historiographical principles, such as the notion of dynastic change, the Mandate of Heaven as conferred upon those whose virtue entitles them to rule, and historical evidence of Heaven's rewarding the rectification of names whereby responsibilities were expected to conform to title and position.

Further, from time to time as during the reigns of Emperors Daigo (897–930) and Murakami (946–67), Confucianism did receive attention at the imperial court, but such occasions were the exception rather than the rule. Despite the fact that Confucian texts remained part of the curriculum of those aristocrats who trained for positions in service to the imperial court – positions to which their aristocratic birth gave them first claim – Confucian philosophy *per se* was quickly subordinated to Buddhism and came to be regarded for the most part as a teaching of only secular value whose larger truths might all be found in more developed fashion within Buddhism. Indeed, when the Buddhist pioneer KŪKAI sought to represent all religious consciousness in terms of ten stages, he ranked Confucianism near the very bottom and second only to the debased consciousness of animal passions, a perspective that was shared widely during succeeding centuries in Japan.

2 Zhu Xi and the Confucian revival

During the eleventh and twelfth centuries in China, where Confucian philosophy had similarly been subordinated to Buddhism, Confucian teachings were revitalized. The curriculum was refashioned to restore the ethical writings of figures like CONFUCIUS and his interpreters to a central position, and metaphysical and cosmological teachings were restructured in a manner that undermined Buddhism's heretofore hegemonic claims to authority in those areas. The central figure in this development was ZHU XI (1130–1200) who, without diminishing his achievement, is often described as having synthesized the teachings of a number of earlier figures including ZHOU DUNYI, ZHANG ZAI, SHAO YONG and the brothers CHENG HAO and CHENG YI.

Zhu Xi understood the world to be constructed of a combination of principle (*li*; in Japanese, *ri*) and material force (*qi*; in Japanese, *ki*). Principle, a singular term which included both natural and moral principles, has ontological priority over material force and is complete, unchanging, eternal and good. Material force, by contrast, represents the physical stuff of the universe, is changeable, and contains both good and bad elements (see QI). Together, principle and material force were thus seen by Zhu Xi as comprising the entire physical universe and as

operating according to the same rhythms of change and stasis that govern the cosmos.

Within human beings, according to Zhu Xi, principle corresponds to one's original nature (*benran zhi xing*; in Japanese, *honzen no sei*), or in other words, that disposition which humans share at the moment of birth and which is likewise naturally and equally good among all people (see XING). Similarly, in humans material force is represented by one's specific nature (*qizhi zhi xing*; in Japanese, *kishitsu no sei*), that disposition which is specific to oneself and which varies in its turbidity from one person to the next. Under ideal circumstances when one's emotions are not aroused to excess, one can respond naturally to one's original nature and one's behaviour accordingly will seemingly spontaneously conform to correct norms. At other times, however, one's emotions and desires are agitated to the extent that they interfere with the ability to respond to others with goodness or in a humane manner. Thus the key to goodness, Zhu Xi taught, was learning how to still one's specific nature so that one's original nature might be manifested in all its excellence. This exercise in turn can be facilitated by either of two ways: first, one can study the external world in order to discern the role of principle within it, recognizing that by apprehending truths concerning principle in the world, one has likewise learned something about one's original nature; alternatively, one may cultivate the quality of seriousness (*qing*; in Japanese, *kei*) through such practices as quiet sitting or study of the canonical literature, thereby learning how to still one's potentially disruptive emotional excesses. This twofold praxis gave Zhu Xi's philosophy both intellectually and spiritually compelling properties.

These teachings, often styled 'neo-Confucianism' in European and North American scholarship, reached Japan in the thirteenth century, but aside from a brief period of vogue at the imperial court of Emperors Hanazono (1308–18) and Godaigo (1318–39), they were taught almost exclusively in Zen monasteries and hence were not regarded as a subject for serious study independent from Buddhism. Such practises as Confucian quiet sitting were thus represented in the monasteries as simply less well-developed versions of such Zen teachings as 'sitting in meditation' (*zazen*). Thus, even though Confucian texts were also included in the curriculum of the Ashikaga *gakkō* (academy) at which scions of this distinguished family trained for service in the *bakufu* (central government), the teachings had the status more of one of the polite gentlemanly accomplishments than that of political philosophy with its own intellectual integrity. The contrast with the continent could not in this respect have been much greater, for there Zhu Xi's teachings were at the root of a radical change in both ontology and epistemology from a fundamentally Buddhist orientation to one which was grounded in Confucianism (see NEO-CONFUCIAN PHILOSOPHY).

3 Tokugawa Confucianism

The relatively low regard in which Confucian philosophy was held in Japan prior to the seventeenth century changed during the Tokugawa period (1600–1868). Spurred on the one hand by the arrival of new Confucian texts from Korea as part of the booty from Japan's unsuccessful invasion of that country, and on the other hand by the Tokugawa government's eventual understanding of the utility of secular ideology in bolstering its claims to legitimate rule, Confucian teachings for the first time in Japan enjoyed the status of an independent subject of scholarly inquiry. Recent scholarship has demonstrated, however, that Confucianism's displacement of Buddhism's hegemony in these areas was a somewhat slower process than had previously been understood, and required the better part of a century to accomplish.

A pioneering figure in this development was FUJIWARA SEIKA (1561–1617), a former Zen priest who became fascinated with the rich diversity of continental Confucian philosophy reflected in the newly imported texts. Seika was attracted to and taught doctrines from a broad range of Chinese and Korean Confucian scholars, including those who challenged the authority of Zhu Xi's teachings. It was Seika's disciple Hayashi Razan (1583–1657) who, by contrast, became an early champion of the version represented by the teachings of Zhu Xi. Since these teachings had been sanctioned in China since the early fourteenth century as the correct interpretation for the official state-sponsored exams, they were essential to the curriculum of all who aspired to government service in China, and if anything they enjoyed even greater favour among aristocratic and official elites in Korea (see CONFUCIAN PHILOSOPHY, KOREAN). Hayashi Razan initiated efforts, later continued by his son Hayashi Gahō (1618–80), to win official endorsement of these teachings by Japan's central military government with the Hayashi themselves as the authorized interpreters of this tradition. These efforts bore fruit later when, in 1691, the Shogun Tokugawa Tsunayoshi donated land for the relocation of the Hayashi family's school in Edo (modern Tokyo) and appointed Razan's grandson Hayashi Hōkō (1644–1732) as its head, a position that the Hayashi maintained within their family through the remainder of the Tokugawa period.

Outside the Hayashi family, Yamazaki Ansai (1618–82) was probably the best known Japanese spokesman for Zhu Xi's teachings. Yamazaki Ansai founded his own school, the Kimon, in which he stressed an uncompromising moral rigour in one's pursuit of sagehood, with particular emphasis on the cultivation of seriousness. Ansai also formulated his own version of Shintō called Suika in which somewhat arbitrary correspondences were drawn between elements in the Confucian metaphysic and Shintō noumena. The Kimon was by far the most successful private academy in Japan devoted to the teachings of Zhu Xi, though Ansai's attempt to reconcile Confucianism with Shintō and his tradition of moralism meant that the academy was never without its share of controversies.

Zhu Xi's teachings were responsible in Japan for a complex intellectual legacy which included humanism, rationalism, ethnocentrism and 'historical mindedness'. The humanism was related to Zhu Xi's conviction that the responsibility for maintaining the delicate balance that lay at the heart of both the individual and the cosmos lay squarely on the shoulders of human beings. The rationalism emerged in response to the Confucian belief that the world and all its phenomena were ultimately understandable, and even though the understandings might vary among Confucian teachers, the mere assumption of intelligibility encouraged a broad range of scholarly enquiries. The ethnocentrism was related to the fact that Confucians in China had traditionally regarded their own heritage and tradition as paramount, and so despite the fact that Confucians in Japan were at times regarded as excessively Sinophilic, Japanese Confucians often manifested patriotic qualities that were in no way secondary to those of their Chinese counterparts. Finally, the historical mindedness derived from the fact that Confucianism taught that all examples or virtue and vice necessary to demonstrate the essentially self-correcting property of historical principles might be found within the copious records of the past.

Furthermore, with the ontological and epistemological shift that Confucian philosophy provoked, one observes the transformation of a host of related fields of study of which Shintō provides perhaps the best example (see SHINTŌ). Shintō had heretofore existed in comfortable equilibrium with Buddhism and had reconciled its teachings to Buddhism, but from the very start of the Tokugawa period, and with increasing frequency through the seventeenth century, one observes Shintō scholars seeking to refashion their theologies, dropping Buddhist epistemes and replacing them with Confucian vocabulary and assumptions. Many Confucian scholars in Japan, in particular those identified with the Zhu Xi tradition, were for their part similarly impelled to reconcile the 'truths' of Confucian philosophy with the traditional spirituality of Shintō.

In China the principal challenge within the Confucian tradition to the teachings of Zhu Xi was identified with the teachings of the scholar and celebrated general WANG YANGMING (1472–1528) who identified the mind as the seat of original goodness within human beings. His philosophy emphasized what he styled the 'unity of thought and action' whereby, for example, the concept of filial piety was regarded as the genesis of filial action, and filial action was regarded as the completion of the filial impulse. Further, by emphasizing the mind's intuitive understanding of goodness, Wang Yangming and his followers de-emphasized the study either of texts to glean their truths or the physical world to plumb its principles. This philosophy, known as Yōmeigaku (literally 'Yangming studies') in Japan, had proponents there during the seventeenth century, of whom the two best known were Nakae Tōju (1608–48) and KUMAZAWA BANZAN (1619–91), who was also celebrated as a reformer of the *samurai* class. Nonetheless, Yōmeigaku did not command a large audience in Japan until the closing years of the Tokugawa period when its idealistic orientation proved attractive to a wide range of politically activist reformers.

In Japan, however, a more significant Confucian challenge to Zhu Xi's teachings was mounted by those scholars whose teachings are collectively referred to as Ancient Studies (*kogaku*). Though the various scholars identified with Ancient Studies differed significantly, they shared the premise that if truths representing a Way lay within the core texts of ancient Confucianism, then those truths might be better apprehended through the study of the ancient texts themselves, than by reading the exegesis on those texts written centuries later by scholars like Zhu Xi. Ancient Studies is said to have begun with the writings of Yamaga Sokō (1622–85), who described how he came to understand that his 'misunderstandings' derived from his reliance on Chinese commentaries, but that once he turned directly to the writings of Confucius and the other ancient sages, he finally understood their message. A similar approach was used by ITŌ JINSAI (1627–1705) and his son Itō Tōgai (1670–1736) whose school, the Kogidō (Hall of Ancient Meaning), represents the first financially successful private Confucian academy in Japan.

The most prominent of the Ancient Studies scholars, however, was OGYŪ SORAI (1666–1728). Where other Confucian scholars in Japan had accepted naturalist ontologies and without exception regarded the sage as a figure of great wisdom who discovered the Way and its truths, Ogyū Sorai applied a historicist perspective to this question. Sorai regarded the Way as a 'comprehensive term' which included those laws, rituals and other practices that ancient rulers invented and applied successfully to rectify the ills of their own ages. If, Sorai argued, the ills of the present are to be similarly rectified, then one must account for the altered circumstances that prevail in another time and place for the application of this redefined 'Way' to be successful. Further, the manner in which one learns of the ancient Way is through the study of ancient texts in which the Way is encoded, but since the words that comprise those texts have themselves changed over time, Sorai insisted that his students become proficient in historical linguistics. Known as the Ken'en, the Sorai school is believed to have been the most popular of all Confucian schools in Japan through the mid-eighteenth century.

Confucian philosophy influenced the Tokugawa polity in a variety of ways. Perhaps the most conspicuous was the tendency within the society to see itself as comprised of four classes with *samurai* (*shi*) at the top, followed by agriculturalists, artisans and merchants in that order. Notwithstanding the fact that this ideal came to deviate significantly from the mercantilist realities of urban Japan, this paradigm was of Confucian origin in China and represented the attempt to identify the Japanese samurai class with the scholar-bureaucrat (*shi*) class of China. Similarly, the study of Confucian philosophy came to be of vocational advantage to *samurai* who found their martial skills no longer as useful to a society that remained essentially at peace for over two centuries. In this way, many *samurai* became sufficiently expert in Confucian philosophy to themselves become instructors of the subject within their own private academies. One benefit that Japanese society later derived from this development in the study of Confucian philosophy was a well-developed literate and patriotic managerial class available to serve the nation in its later modernization efforts.

Throughout the seventeenth and early eighteenth centuries, there was no academic tension between the study of Confucian philosophy and the study of subject material from the native tradition, but during the eighteenth century, scholars devoted to the study of things Japanese criticized Confucians in Japan for not only neglecting but even harming their own tradition by engaging in the study of a 'foreign' humanly constructed Way. Notwithstanding that this argument both applied and owed more to the followers of Ogyū Sorai than other Confucian schools, one does observe a new tension between Confucian and nativist pursuits during much of the eighteenth century, a tension which is essentially overcome through the reconvergence of these academic fields during the nineteenth century.

The scholars who most successfully represented this synthesis of Confucian and native ideals were largely identified with the Mito domain. The *daimyō* (or lords) of Mito had aggressively sponsored scholarship on Japanese history and ancient classics since the seventeenth century, devoting as much as one-third of the domain's revenue to sponsored research. As the shortcomings of the Tokugawa state became steadily more apparent, it was Confucian scholars from Mito who sought to identify within the Japanese traditions paradigms of such Confucian virtues as loyalty and filial piety, arguing that the study of Japanese history revealed those virtues to have existed in more persuasive forms in Japan than in China.

In the same manner, one can observe within Japanese Confucian philosophy itself the fracturing of Confucianism into competing schools in the eighteenth century, followed by the nineteenth-century resurgence of certain syncretic tendencies within the Confucian tradition. For example, even though the popularity of the various Ancient Studies schools of Confucianism contributed unprecedented pluralism and intellectual vitality to Confucian philosophic circles, the often contentious relations between schools represented a scholarly atmosphere that some regarded as indecorous. Alarmed over what it regarded as an unhealthy degree of intellectual heterodoxy within Confucian circles generally, and the Hayashi school in particular, the Tokugawa government issued a directive in 1790 ordering the head of the Hayashi school to maintain greater fidelity to the teachings of Zhu Xi. This concern with philosophical orthodoxy was, in fact, just one way in which the government at this time was attempting to return to those 'fundamentals' which it believed to have been responsible for the success of the Tokugawa state in the seventeenth century.

Numerous Confucian philosophers of the late Tokugawa regarded what they perceived to be the ills of their age as related on the one hand to this contentious intellectual atmosphere and on the other to an excessive tendency toward activism on the part of other Confucians. These scholars sought solace in and believed that they might affect reform through eclectic approaches to the exegesis of traditional Confucian texts. Their scholarship lacks the vitality of that evidenced within Confucian circles of the first half of the Tokugawa period, and in most studies they have been overshadowed by their more activist contemporaries; yet their scholarship provides compelling evidence of the degree to which Confucian

philosophy represented an intellectual sanctuary for many late-Tokugawa intellectuals.

4 Confucianism in modern Japan

Confucian philosophy contributed to the rationales used by ideologues who led the Meiji Restoration of 1868. For example, the slogan 'Loyalty to sovereign (*chū*) and filial piety (*kō*) are one' argued that Confucian loyalty to one's lord, here understood to mean the emperor, was no less fundamental than those Confucian virtues that bound family relationships, of which filial piety was always regarded as the foundational virtue. Similarly, the slogan *taigi meibun* used Confucian vocabulary to argue that there was a correct fixed position for each person within an essentially immutable social order, and when each person performed their duty the social order was harmonious. Both of these slogans reflect the fact that Confucianism generally appears both during the Meiji Restoration and thereafter primarily in terms of its social and political ethics, with the emphasis on individual duty and responsibility.

During the Meiji period, when much that was traditional in nature was overwhelmed by the rapid reforms, Confucian philosophy demonstrated remarkable resiliency as its vocabulary and reasoning were used in various ways to reinforce an understanding of the Japanese polity as a quasi-family state. This is particularly evident in the Imperial Rescript on Education promulgated in 1890 under what is believed to be the influence of the Meiji emperor's Confucian tutor, Motoda Nagazane (1818–91). The Rescript speaks of the Japanese people as subjects who are 'united in loyalty and filial piety', representing the 'fundamental character' of the Japanese empire and the foundation of its education. Other Meiji scholars such as Nishimura Shigeki (1828–1902) sought to reconcile the 'truths' of Confucianism with the 'truths' of Western culture and civilization, often under one or another variation of the binary theme 'Eastern ethics and Western science'.

Despite the fact that Confucian philosophy has been alternatively vilified in Japan as synonymous with all that is old-fashioned and hence bad, and lionized as embodying all that is noble and of enduring value within the traditional culture, it is evident that a number of assumptions that are characteristic of Confucian ontology and ethics remain widely accepted within present-day Japan. Conspicuous among these are the assumptions that there are enduring metaphysical principles that undergird the physical world, and that these principles have a self-correcting quality. For this reason, a fundamental moral optimism is justified. These principles have an analogue within human beings in the form of an originally good disposition which is instinctively capable of moral and ethical behavior. Human relations are similarly governed by enduring principles, where these relations tend overwhelmingly to be vertical in character with clear superiors and subordinates. One's most important relationships are those within the family, and it is these domestic relationships that provide the training ground for the more complex relationships one enters into outside the home. Since both the material world and the realm of human society are governed by identical principles, all phenomena and things, all persons and other creatures are interrelated, making it possible to gain insight into the whole from mastery of any of its parts.

There are other ways in which Confucian philosophy is said to have contributed its legacy to the intellectual and social fabric of contemporary Japan. Most prominent among these are the assertions that the high value attached to education, the high levels of respect accorded to those in authority, the reverence shown toward one's ancestors and forebears, and the willingness to subordinate one's own interests to the interests of larger collectivities in modern Japan are all attributable to the influence of Confucian philosophy. More recent scholarship, however, has tended to see these tendencies as features that either have antecedents in pre-Confucian times or that can be traced to other influences, though there is broad agreement that Confucian philosophy at the very minimum contributed to the reinforcement of these values, each of which remains prominent in modern Japan.

See also: CONFUCIAN PHILOSOPHY, CHINESE; FUJIWARA SEIKA; JAPANESE PHILOSOPHY; ITŌ JINSAI; KUMAZAWA BANZAN; NEO-CONFUCIAN PHILOSOPHY; OGYŪ SORAI; SHINTŌ; SHŌTOKU CONSTITUTION; WANG YANGMING; ZHU XI

References and further reading

de Bary, W.T. (1959) 'Some Common Tendencies in Neo-Confucianism', in D.S. Nivison and A. Wright (eds) *Confucianism in Action*, Stanford, CA: Stanford University Press, 25–49. (A valuable essay for understanding Confucianism's contributions to intellectual circles in Japan and throughout East Asia.)

Hall, J.W. (1959) 'The Confucian Teacher in Tokugawa Japan', in D.S. Nivison and A. Wright (eds) *Confucianism in Action*, Stanford, CA: Stanford University Press, 268–301. (Helpful for understand-ing the institutional context of instruction in Confucianism.)

Inoue, Y. (1992) *Confucius*, trans. R.K. Thomas, London: Peter Owen. (A best-selling historical novel in Japan, that suggests some ways in which Confucius is preceived in popular culture.)

Maruyama, M. (1974) *Studies in the Intellectual History of Tokugawa Japan*, trans. M. Hane, Princeton, NJ: Princeton University Press. (Pioneer-ing study of Ogyū Sorai and his contributions to modern thought in Japan.)

Mercer, R. (1991) *Deep Words: Miura Baien's System of Natural Philosophy*, Leiden: Brill. (Contains translations of three eighteenth-century works help-ful to understanding Confucianism's impact on one philosopher.)

Nosco, P. (ed.) (1986) *Confucianism and Tokugawa Culture*, Princeton, NJ: Princeton University Press. (Contains nine essays and an introduction on the general theme of responses to Confucianism.)

Spae, J.J. (1967) *Itō Jinsai: A Philosopher, Educator and Sinologist of the Tokugawa Period*, New York: Paragon Reprints. (Initially published in 1948, this remains the standard introduction to a key figure in Ancient Studies.)

Tsunoda, R. *et al.* (eds) (1964) *Sources of Japanese Tradition*, New York: Columbia University Press, 2 vols. (A valuable collection of translated exerpts from the writings of a number of major Japanese Confucian philosophers.)

Tucker, M.E. (1989) *Moral and Spritual Cultivation in Japanese Neo-Confucianism: The Life and Thought of Kaibara Ekken, 1630-1714*, Albany, NY: State University of New York Press. (A thoughtful analysis of a Japanese Confucian philosopher and the intellectual context of his times.)

PETER NOSCO

CONFUCIAN PHILOSOPHY, KOREAN

Confucianism came to Korea in the late fourth century AD. While Buddhism, which had arrived at the same time, was for centuries the central spiritual and intellectual tradition of Korea, Confucianism was viewed as largely limited to the world of government functionaries. In China during the Song dynasty (979–1279) a creative Confucian movement revitalized and reshaped the tradition, giving rise to what Western Scholars call 'neo-Confucianism'. By the end of the fourteenth century neo-Confucian learning had pene-trated deeply among young scholar-officials in Korea, who used it as a lever against the deeply entrenched Buddhist establishment. In 1392, in history's only neo-Confucian revolution, a new dynasty was founded in Korea. The Chosôn dynasty (1392–1910), ruling a country smaller in scale and more centrally unified than China, was to make Korea the most (neo)Confucian of all East Asian societies.

The scale, control, and temper of Korean society had important consequences for the development of the neo-Confucian tradition. In China the Cheng–Zhu school of neo-Confucian thought held privileged status as the orthodox standard for the all-important civil service examinations. Zhu Xi (1130–1200) was the great creative synthesizer of this school and its foremost authority, but his synthesis drew especially upon the work of the Cheng brothers. The Cheng–Zhu school was rivalled and even eclipsed in popularity later by the school of Wang Yangming (1472–1529), whose more Zen-like approach also found great favour in Japan. Korea, in contrast to both China and Japan, remained almost exclusively devoted to the Cheng–Zhu school.

This exclusive and intensive development of the Cheng–Zhu school of neo-Confucian thought is the most generally distinctive characteristic of Korean neo-Confucianism. When the thinkers of a culture devote themselves for centuries to a single complex body of learning, as was the case for example with Aristotle and medieval Europe, the result is a mode of philosophical discourse described as 'scholasticism'. Scholastic philosophy is renowned for the intricacy and closeness of its argumentation, though this may be an obstacle for the outsider for whom it is often difficult to recapture the intense and absorbing vision which inspired major controversy about seemingly minor differences. Korea, with its exclusive cultivation of Zhu Xi's complex synthesis, produced the most scholastic version of neo-Confucian thought. The writings of scholars or scholar-officials of note were commonly collected and published after their death, so the centuries of 'collected works', written in literary Chinese, are a vast resource in which the twists and turns, the problems and potentials for development in the Cheng–Zhu school are examined with unequalled thoroughness.

To understand the particular contribution this Korean scholasticism made to neo-Confucian thought one must be aware of the scope and complexity of Zhu Xi's synthesis. The intellectual culture within which the Confucian revivalists of the Song dynasty worked had for seven or eight centuries been predominantly shaped by Daoist and Buddhist influences, so the questions in their minds as they returned to the Confucian classics included dimensions neglected by more traditional Confucianism. Read with new eyes, an entirely new level of meaning was uncovered in the ancient texts: they discovered a Confucian foundation for the meditative cultivation of consciousness that had been a particular strength of the Buddhists, and to frame it and provide an account of sagehood equal to Buddhist talk of enlightenment, they found a complete metaphysical system, a Confucian version of the kind of thinking that had been elaborated mainly under Daoist auspices. Thus Zhu Xi's synthesis knit together not just disparate thinkers of the Song dynasty, but contemporary questions with texts well over a thousand years old. It incorporated Daoist metaphysics with Buddhist meditative cultivation in a new structure with Confucian moral values and social concerns at that structure's core. Implicit in this was the conflation of the distinctive world views of India, the origin of Buddhism, and China. This has important metaphysical consequences, for the central paradigm for Indian reflection on the nature of existence was consciousness, while for the Chinese it was the image of a single living physical body.

A synthesis of this scope cannot be a seamless whole, though the conceptual system with which Zhu Xi knit it together achieved a remarkable degree of verbal consistency. This, in fact, is where Korean neo-Confucian thought makes a special contribution. For it is at the seams, where differences and tensions inherent in a synthesis are conceptually masked, that the kind of problems occur that become the source of endless scholastic controversy. Korean neo-Confucianism contains two such controversies; each has occupied minds for centuries. Though the points being debated resist any ultimate solution, the disputes themselves disclose the creative tensions at the heart of Zhu Xi's synthesis.

The first of these controversies arose in the middle of the sixteenth century and decisively shaped the intellectual agenda for the remainder of the Chosôn dynasty. The protagonists in the controversy, Yi Hwang and Yi I, are the two most famous names in Korean thought, and allegiance to each became the central dividing line of Korean neo-Confucianism. Known as the 'Four–Seven Debate,' this controversy is the most famous philosophical dispute in Korean history. On the surface it involves the question of feelings and how they arise. Some feelings, such as commiseration or shame at doing evil, seem spontaneously human and correct, while others, such as fear, anger, or pleasure, seem more questionable. Are there then two kinds of feelings that arise from different sources? The question is of great philosophical importance, because ultimately it discloses tensions at the heart of the dualistic monism/monistic dualism which is the fundamental structure of Zhu Xi's metaphysical system.

The second great controversy arose among followers of Yi I in the early eighteenth century. Neo-Confucian metaphysics views the entire universe as possessing a *single nature, which is manifested differently at different levels of existence due to the differing capacities of the concrete, psychophysical component of various sorts of creatures. The Horak controversy swirled about the question of whether the fundamental or 'original' nature of things is the same or different. The fundamental nature is normative, and it would be absurd to say the norm for a cow is the same as for a human; but the fundamental nature is fundamental and normative precisely because it is considered as anterior to the limitation/distortion of the imperfect psychophysical component. How then can it be considered as differentiated into cow and human? Pulling at these seemingly verbal loose ends leads again deep into Zhu Xi's metaphysics, revealing between its Indian and Chinese (Buddhist and Daoist) motifs tensions which come to a focus more clearly here perhaps than anywhere else in neo-Confucian thought.*

1   **Historical development**
2   **The centre of philosophical reflection**
3–4 **The Four–Seven Debate**
5–6 **The Horak Debate**

1   Historical development

Neo-Confucianism has dimensions similar to Marxism in Western thought: that is, although it can be considered as a philosophical system its scope includes the practice of government, social structure and relationships, and the individual's way of life. The object of the life of the mind is not abstracted as 'truth,' but is integrated with the whole of life: Confucian thought aims beyond intellectual apprehension at the actual practice of a full and integral human life in a harmonious, well-ordered society. (see CONFUCIAN PHILOSOPHY, CHINESE; NEO-CONFUCIAN PHILOSOPHY).

Thus the neo-Confucian revolution that inaugurated the Chosôn dynasty in 1392 was also a social revolution. Energies for the first century were largely absorbed in institution building and reform of unacceptable but deeply rooted custom such as matrilocal marriages. Contrary to Confucian theory, Korean society maintained its aristocratic structure, but the Korean aristocracy (*yangban*) in other respects became highly orthodox, correct adherence to neo-Confucian norms becoming a mark of their social distinction. The aristocratic social structure also had the effect of making the Korean ruler much more a first-among-equals, much more subject, as orthodox Confucian theory prescribed, to the remonstrance and persuasion of his ministers than was the case in Ming or Qing-dynasty China.

Towards the end of the first century, remonstrance,

the right of government officials to object, criticize, and offer contrary advice to superiors and particularly to the ruler, became a central and bloody issue. Zealous Korean neo-Confucians had enshrined the right to remonstrance in three government ministries, and when these acted in concert they were able to bring the government to a standstill: they could effectively thwart the king and his highest ministers, always on grounds framed in the language of lofty Confucian moral principles. The result of this systemic tension was a series of purges from the end of the fifteenth to the middle of the sixteenth centuries; the purged were the remonstrating officials, who paid with their lives or with exile when the throne and high ministers were pushed beyond the limit. These 'literati purges' left a deep imprint on the Korean neo-Confucian tradition. All Confucian learning was supposed to be for the sake of character formation, but as the established core of civil service examinations it was also the way to get ahead, and the way to secure a high reputation. In the Cheng–Zhu school a movement by earnest scholars who focused on self-cultivation and despised the ambitious motives of 'worldly Confucians' appropriated for itself the label '*daoxue*', (in Korean *tohak*), 'the learning of the true Way'. The effect of the early history of purge and martyrdom was to give special luster to the *tohak* dimension of the tradition, making it a predominant feature in the lives and thought of virtually all major Korean neo-Confucians.

he record of the development of neo-Confucian thought during this early period is somewhat sparse. The major focus initially was on institution building, while the philosophically interesting aspects of neo-Confucian thought are most closely linked with spiritual self-cultivation and its metaphysical framework. Those most likely to produce writings of interest were thus also the most likely purge victims, and what they may have written is lost. What we possess reflects the diversity and unevenness one might expect: during this period Cheng–Zhu orthodoxy had not fully settled in, nor was there a complete and systematic grasp of the integrated whole of this school's complex synthesis. The most famous name of the period, Sô Kyôngdôk (1489–1546), espoused a monism of material force (*ki*; in Chinese *qi*) similar to that of the early Chinese neo-Confucian, ZHANG ZAI (see QI). Sô has a great reputation for independence and originality, but unfortunately what remains of his writings is not enough to give a very adequate picture of his ideas. Others, such as the famous martyr of the 1519 purge, Cho Kwangjo (1482–1519), reflect a situation in which those most involved with the self-cultivation side of the tradition had a very inadequate grasp of the delicate balance between theory and

557

practice, study and meditation, that characterizes the Cheng–Zhu school. Cho's writings perished with him, but his students, we are told, often spent the day sitting in meditation rather than studying.

It is generally agreed that a full, balanced, and mature grasp of Zhu Xi's complex synthesis first came with the work of YI HWANG (1501–70). He and a thinker of the next generation, YI YULGOK (1536– 84), are considered the foremost neo-Confucian philosophers of Korea. Particularly important was the Four–Seven Debate, initiated between Yi Hwang and Ki Taesûng (1527–72) and continued by Yi Yulgok and Sông Hon (1535–98), with Yi I taking up the position advocated by Ki Taesûng (see §§3–4). The debate had the effect of permanently dividing the neo-Confucian intellectual world of Korea into two major schools professing allegiance to Yi Hwang and Yi Yulgok, a division further complicated by complex regional and factional ties as time progressed.

Invasions first by the Japanese under Hideoshi and then by the Manchus devastated the country. The seventeenth century is remembered principally for extreme factional division and conflict by neo-Confucians in government and for the development of a rigid, orthodox tone that caused the persecution of several scholars labelled as 'heterodox' because they questioned elements of Cheng–Zhu learning.

Zhu Xi's synthesis was sufficiently vast, however, to permit major divisions and significantly different interpretations within it. The Yi Hwang–Yi Yulgok split was already evidence of this, and in the early eighteenth century the Horak controversy confirmed it. Named for the regions associated with the principle figures in the debate, the Horak controversy caught the attention and drew in major thinkers of the eighteenth century and beyond. Its participants were all followers of Yi Yulgok, and in some ways, as will be discussed below, the controversy could be considered a final working through of problems deeply embedded in Yi Yulgok's insistence on philosophical consistency in handling the Four–Seven question.

The eighteenth and nineteenth centuries are also celebrated by Korean intellectual historians for the rise of sirhak or 'practical learning', a broad and disparate movement among some neo-Confucian scholars towards focusing their scholarly efforts on more concrete issues of political, social and economic concern, bringing the borderless discourse of neo-Confucian thought more within the confines of actual life on the Korean peninsula. The movement historically did not develop a cohesive self-consciousness, and the label 'sirhak' was applied to it by twentieth century historians, who saw in it the indigenous development of values and types of learning that have become the essence of modernity.

Their attention has brought to light a sirhak dimension in a number of significant thinkers of the period, among whom the figure of CHÔNG YAGYONG (1762–1836) overshadows all. A true polymath, in addition to extensive writing on practical affairs his works include a voluminous review of the changing interpretation of the Confucian classics over the centuries and a critique of Cheng–Zhu metaphysics from a theistic perspective grounded in the most ancient classics. His restoration of a theistic Confucianism occurred under the influence of the writings of the Roman Catholic missionary to China, Matteo Ricci. The work itself is thoroughly Confucian, however, and since it was worked out by a thinker who also had mastery of the Cheng–Zhu synthesis it is possibly the most thoroughgoing and systematic theistic philosophy produced by a Confucian thinker. In his day Chông had no significant intellectual heirs, but he may well be the most studied thinker of the Chosôn dynasty.

2 The centre of philosophical reflection

Among the East Asian neo-Confucian traditions what is most distinctive about Korea is the depth and continuity of its commitment to the orthodox Cheng–Zhu school. Thus even those like Chông Yagyong who struck out in new directions did so with a deep grounding in Cheng–Zhu thought. For the vast majority of thinkers the fundamental truth of Zhu Xi's vision was a given, and the essential task of every generation was to understand how their particular problems and insights fit into, or 'already were', the original meaning intended by ZHU XI or the ancient authorities such as CONFUCIUS and MENCIUS as interpreted by Zhu Xi. Over four centuries of Korean reflection in this mode served to develop both the potentialities and the problems inherent in Zhu Xi's synthesis to an unprecedented degree. Korean insight in this respect is captured particularly in the two great controversies mentioned in §1, the Four–Seven and Horak debates.

Both debates focus on the same general area of neo-Confucian thought, sôngnihak (in Chinese, xinglixue), the study of the nature (sông) and principle (i) (see XING; LI). It is no accident that the most complex and philosophically interesting controversies occur in sôngnihak, for it is the systematic nexus of every area of neo-Confucian thought: here converge what the West would call metaphysics, philosophy of man, psychology, ethics and ascetical theory or spiritual practice. The motive of Confucian, Daoist and Buddhist thought alike is the full realization of human potential, which demands self-cultivation. But self-cultivation involves an implicit or explicit metaphysical framework, which is necessary to understand in what the full realization of human potential may consist (see SELF-CULTIVATION, CHINESE THEORIES OF). Buddhist meditative cultivation techniques assumed a monistic background. Huayan Buddhism used the indigenous Chinese term *li* (in Korean, *i*, meaning 'truth', 'rationale', 'principle' or 'pattern') to convey this monistic 'Buddha nature', the ultimate single reality of all phenomenal existence. Chan (Zen) Buddhism focused less on such intellectual formulation and stressed instead the direct and immediate realization of this as the reality of one's own and all being (see BUDDHIST PHILOSOPHY, CHINESE; BUDDHIST PHILOSOPHY, KOREAN). Neo-Confucians, in close touch with this background, were aware of the importance of techniques of cultivating consciousness, but wanted nothing of Buddhist monism; thus they sought a more concrete metaphysics with a more secure grounding in phenomenal reality. Their remedy was to pair *i* with another traditional term, *qi* (in Korean, *ki*), the animating 'life force' of body and psyche and, philosophically, the very 'stuff' of the universe (see QI). In its most coarse, turbid and condensed form, *ki* thus accounted for the concreteness of the divisible world the West knows as 'matter'; but in its original, pure and rarified condition it is also the stuff of psyche and mind, embracing the characteristics the West incorporates in terms such as 'spirit' and 'soul'.

In neo-Confucian metaphysics, *i* is made concrete and existential through its embodiment in *ki*. The focal point in its spectrum of meanings also shifts somewhat: as a stand-in for Buddha-nature, *i* was more on the side of 'ultimate truth', while in the neo-Confucian context its ancient connections with pattern or order are exploited in a way that makes it virtually interchangeable in many contexts with the much used *dao*, the Way, the inner pattern, the nature that structures all existence and activity. Instead of Buddhist monism, this dualism of *i* and *ki* gives us a modified, organismic monism: *i* is one, but embodied and manifested diversely through the many diverse conditions of *ki*. The many beings of the universe may thus be likened to the members of a single living body, truly different from one another and yet ultimately manifestations of a single unity beyond all name or distinctness: *i* is the single pattern or principle running throughout, while *ki* accounts for the real but not ultimate diversity.

This neo-Confucian metaphysics thus yields a very traditional East Asian organismic vision of the universe, in which every element at every level is interdependently woven together with every other in a patterned, normative whole (see NEO-CONFUCIAN PHILOSOPHY). The cosmic dimensions of this tradition had found clearest manifestation in Daoism, while Confucianism had explored mainly the social ramifications; as united in neo-Confucian thought, these become respectively the framework for and the outcome of self-cultivation. The theory of self-cultivation is related to metaphysics much as epistemology is in western thought. The organismic unity of *i* solves the western problem of how distinct individuals can know 'the other', for in spite of the manifold diversity of their ways of manifesting it, all share in the same *i*. In particular, because of the high purity of the *ki* which constitutes the human psyche, *i*, the pattern of all things, is possessed in its integral fullness by the human heart-and-mind (see XIN). This means we have within ourselves the guiding pattern for appropriate responsiveness to any thing or any situation. If we are out of touch and inappropriately responsive, that is because of some adventitious factor such as an element of turbidity or coarseness in the *ki* of our psychophysical constitution which blocks or distorts our true connectedness. Neo-Confucians compared this to the way a paralyzed limb, even though connected, no longer responds appropriately to the needs and messages of the body. The ideal sage, endowed with perfect *ki*, responds to all things with spontaneous perfection; being perfectly in touch, he need not be concerned about prolonged thought or self-discipline. Less perfectly endowed individuals, however, need both. They must follow the more laborious path, regaining their apprehension of *i* by the discipline of focused attention externally and clear calmness internally. Meditative practice, 'quiet sitting', could nurture the quiet and calm that self-possession promotes and is a means to our harmonious integration in the *i* that is our nature within and also the structure of the world without.

Sôngnihak, 'the study of the nature and *i*', thus addresses itself to the anthropocosmic core of neo-Confucian learning, where the metaphysics of the universe transmutes into a description of the working of our inner life in relation to every life situation. *I* is not only the pattern of the universe, but the ground of our psyche which prepares us to participate properly in the universe; *ki* is not only the stuff through which all things have their concrete actuality and diversity, but also the factor that distorts the potentially perfect continuity of *i* without and within. Unlike dualisms of spirit and matter which carve out a unique and special place for human beings, the challenge here is to describe all the complexity and conflict of the human heart-and-mind in continuity with the conceptual system used for all other natural phenomena. Korean neo-Confucianism pushes the limits and reveals hidden tensions in the Cheng–Zhu version of this endeavour.

3 The Four–Seven Debate

In the history of philosophy, the Cheng–Zhu metaphysics and anthropology of *i* and *ki* occupy a very special and interesting place. The patterning *i* and the concertizing, activating *ki* bring to mind the Aristotelian dualism of form and matter (see ARISTOTLE §§11–14); but in this case, although *i* is manifested as many forms it is ultimately one form which runs through all things. Thus the universe is truly a single organic unity, rather than a plurality of formally and materially discrete beings as in the Aristotelian case. This is a monistic dualism. Recalling the Buddhist usage of *i* and the vitalistic background of the concept of *ki*, one also sees in the dualism traces of the mind/body split and the spirit/matter dualism of western thought. But here too the parallel is instructive because it breaks down: mind and body alike are comprised of *i* and *ki*, so they too are an organic continuum. As we shall see, each of the great Korean controversies pushes and tests the meaning and resources of the *i–ki* dualism along these lines.

The Four–Seven debate arose in 1549, and was carried out in lengthy correspondence first between YI HWANG and Ki Taesûng, then between YI YULGOK and Sông Hon. The central question of the debate focused on the metaphysical explanation of good and evil. In a pluralistic western context this is commonly a question of will and choice, premised on the human individual's distinctive characteristic of rationality and self-determination (see FREE WILL; EVIL, PROBLEM OF). But in a culture and philosophy of organicism the question is posed in terms of response rather than choice: as seen in §2, the question of evil is more like why a limb does not respond appropriately than why individuals choose what is wrong. Hence questions of will and choice are secondary in Confucian moral discourse. Of primary concern rather are the feelings and the nature which is manifested in the way the feelings respond. In a famous classical passage, MENCIUS had argued that human nature is fundamentally or originally good, citing as evidence the spontaneous feelings of alarm and commiseration that arise at the sight of a dire event such as a toddler about to fall into a well (see XING). He expanded this argument by describing four such spontaneously good feelings or tendencies: in addition to commiseration, there are the feelings of shame and dislike for evil, the tendency to yield and defer to others, and the sense of right and wrong. These innate tendencies, he said, if nurtured properly become respectively the mature characteristics of humanity, righteousness, propriety and wisdom.

The innate tendencies described by Mencius were referred to by later Confucians as the 'four beginnings', and they constitute the 'four' of the Four–Seven debate. Neo-Confucians took the four mature characteristics as descriptions of the composition of human nature, which metaphysically is equated with *i*, the normative inner pattern of all things. Concrete, actual feelings such as the Four Beginnings, are the manifestation of *i* on the level of the active, phenomenal world, the level of *i* combined with *ki*. Because *i*, the norm, is inherently good, so the feelings which manifest it are also naturally good unless imperfections in *ki*, the stuff of our psychophysical constitution, somehow interrupt and distort the way in which it is manifested.

The 'seven' of the Four–Seven debate comes from a different source, the classic *Lijing* (Book of Rites), which describes a list of seven feelings: desire, hate, love, fear, grief, anger, and joy. These conventional human feelings are obviously the sort of tendencies that can be either right or wrong, appropriate or inappropriate. They are the object of endless Confucian exhortations to cultivate careful attention and discernment of the movement of the feelings. The initial movement in particular is critical, for a tiny discrepancy at the beginning can become a gap of a thousand miles as things unfold.

On the level of traditional moral discourse none of this poses any special problem. The disruption of feelings and responses from their appropriate course could be accounted for by individualistic self-centredness, long identified as the root of all evil. But the special advance of neo-Confucian thought was that its new dualistic metaphysics could support a metaphysical explanation of the source of evil/disruption as well. This was of critical importance, for the description of the distorting role of *ki* with regard to the inherently perfect *i* provided a precise description of sagehood and the hinderance to sagehood, and hence an understanding of the rationale and effectiveness of approaches to self-cultivation.

In Western thought, spirit/matter dualisms, or rationality versus animal nature, set up clear value hierarchies which become the basis for explaining why it is wrong to subordinate higher values to lower. *I* and *ki*, being associated respectively with the normative and distorting roles, appear to invite a similar value discrimination. There is then an initial plausibility in suggesting that inherently good feelings such as the Four Beginnings are on the side of *i*, while more doubtful ones such as the Seven Feelings must be on the side of *ki*. This is what Yi Hwang did, almost incidentally, in the course of going over a diagrammatic treatise by another scholar. However, Ki Taesûng, a younger contemporary, reproached him. *I* and *ki* are absolutely interdependent, have no separate existence, and cannot separately be the source of different kinds of feeling; rather, he argued, there is really only one kind of feelings, for all feelings arise in precisely the same way, *i* being the formative source and *ki* the element of concrete actualization. There is, he said, actually no real (metaphysical) distinction between the Four Beginnings and Seven Feelings: the Seven Feelings are a general term for all human feelings, and the Four Beginnings are just a subset, singling out feelings when they are appropriate. Yi Hwang fought for a real distinction, even finding a passage in which Zhu Xi himself paired the Four Beginnings with *i* and the Seven Feelings with *ki*. Finally he came up with a formula that attempted to take full account of the inseparability and interdependence of *i* and *ki* and at the same time could support some feelings which are inherently more whole and human than others: in the case of the Four Beginnings, he said, *i* gives issuance and *ki* follows; in the case of the Seven Feelings, *ki* issues and *i* mounts it.

Ki Taesŭng eventually yielded to Yi Hwang's formula, but after Yi Hwang's death the debate was resurrected when Yi Yulgok's friend Sông Hon read Yi Hwang's treatise in conjunction with some similarly dualistic remarks by Zhu Xi and was persuaded. YI YULGOK, perhaps the most brilliant and systematic philosophical mind produced by the Korean neo-Confucian tradition, countered forcefully that such extreme dualism was absolutely wrong. *I* and *ki* could not vary their role and relationship as if they were two independent entities; in the metaphysics of the cosmos, he argued, it was always *ki* that was in the concrete issuing role and *i* 'mounting it' as the formative pattern that made things be and act as they did. If this was the cosmic case, it could be no different when it came to the human psyche. The dualistic expressions frequent in Zhu Xi and other authoritative sources should be understood appropriately in their moralizing context, but not transformed into a metaphysical dualism that would disrupt the delicate one-but-two, two-but-one perfect interdependence and complimentarity of *i* and *ki*.

The Korean neo-Confucian intellectual world subsequently split between followers of Yi Hwang and Yi Yulgok; infrequent thinkers attempted various sorts of syntheses, but the problem has never been resolved. On Yi Hwang's side are the dualistic phenomena common to the moral life; self-cultivation above all was the controlling factor in Yi Hwang's thought. However, Yi Yulgok has the appearance of greater philosophical consistency and rigor; he truly removed insupportable ambiguities in Zhu Xi's system and brought it to a new level of coherence.

4 The Four–Seven Debate (cont.)

What do we learn from this controversy? The two positions and the unresolvable dispute offer a unique window on the Cheng–Zhu philosophical enterprise. Yi Hwang is a faithful reflection of the motivation behind the neo-Confucian project, which is ultimately to bring about good character formation and proper order in society and the world. Yi Yulgok shows us the most careful philosophical crystalization of the deep East Asian assumption that there is no final distinction between humanity and the rest of existence: we are an integral and organic part of the universe. In the West morality has often been treated as a uniquely human phenomenon, something that marks us off from the rest of the world. As seen through the frame of the Four–Seven debate, the challenge taken up by neo-Confucian metaphysics is whether a philosophy of organic unity can adequately account for the phenomena of human moral experience, particularly the conflicting tendencies to which we are subject and which seem less evident in the life of the rest of nature.

In its historical context the Four–Seven debate concerns the adequacy of the neo-Confucian incorporation of Mencius' explanation that human nature is good. The deep issue is, how can the normative human nature (*i*) be considered a dynamic element assisting in this process? Health and life are normative but not abstract: the body fights for health, injured trees and plants heal themselves if given time. Mencius used such examples in a more than metaphorical sense: he saw human psychic or moral life as part of the same natural system with a similar dynamism, and the neo-Confucians certainly meant to carry forward this vision. Equating the nature with *i*, the normative of each and all things, seemed to be a metaphysical version of Mencius' view. But *ki*, its counterpart, raises questions: it was introduced not only to insure an objectively real world versus the Buddhist monism of consciousness, but also to objectify the moral problem. The latter was perhaps the more important issue in Confucian eyes: Buddhism claimed ultimately to transcend the dualism of good and evil, and neo-Confucians were bitterly critical of the anti-nomian potential in such views. With its degrees of coarseness or turbidity, *ki*, by contrast, objectifies the problem of moral distortion. The neo-Confucian elaboration of a systematic philosophical explanation for a source of evil within the human constitution that does not negate the inherent goodness of human nature was a great triumph. But the solution may have succeeded too well, for the turbidity of *ki* in the psychophysical constitution seemed to put a formidable barrier between the person and the kind of spontaneously good tendencies of which Mencius spoke. In China this resulted in the radical split in which WANG YANGMING simply equated the human heart-and-mind with *i* and thus opened the way to immediate intuition and spontaneous perfection in stark contrast to the kind of prolonged book learning and rigorous ascetical practice demanded in the Cheng–Zhu approach. The orthodox followers of Zhu Xi claimed this amounted to another form of Chan (Zen) Buddhism, but Wang's school was nonetheless immensely successful in China and Japan, although not in Korea.

The position worked out by Yi Hwang is an answer to this problem that remains totally within the Cheng–Zhu tradition; in comparison, the Wang Yangming solution appears an extreme and perhaps unnecessary alternative. By granting *i* the possibility of some kind of initiative to set the current in the proper direction before the disrupting influence of *ki* could take over, he was providing grounds for the spontaneous and appropriately human responsiveness Mencius had spoken of: '*I* gives issue and *ki* follows.' But the price is emphasizing the dualistic potential in Cheng–Zhu thought, for perfect complimentarity demands *ki* alone have such a concrete actualizing function. This was Yi Yulgok's objection; but in demanding that Yi Hwang's formula for the more dubious Seven Feelings, '*ki* gives issue and *i* mounts it', be the only one, he is hard pressed to really save Mencius. It would seem that if imperfect *ki* is in at the origin of all feelings in exactly the same sort of way, then the normative goodness of *i* is a mere abstraction, not something that is manifest in the actual tendencies of our inner life. The only way the perfection of *i* can spontaneously manifest in the phenomenal world would seem to be through the agency of perfectly pure *ki*.

The tightness of Yi Yulgok's consistent insistence on the absolute complementarity and interdependence took Cheng–Zhu thought to a new level of systematization. At the same time, the question remains as to whether this systematization could settle the kind of issues solved by Yi Hwang's more dualistic approach. The real test of his system came more than a century later with the Horak debate.

5 The Horak Debate

The Horak debate arose in the early decades of the eighteenth century among scholars belonging to Yi Yulgok's school of thought. Once launched, it was the source of philosophical debate down to the twentieth century, second only to the Four–Seven debate in length, notoriety and intellectual importance among Chosôn dynasty neo-Confucian controversies. Its

chief protagonists were HAN WÔNJIN (1682–1751) and YI KAN (1677–1727). Both were students of the same prominent master, Kwôn Sangha, and both at different times held the prestigious position of Royal Lecturer, reflecting their recognition as leading scholars of their time. The debate takes its name from the geographical regions with which the major participants were associated: the 'ho' group was centered in Ch'ungch'ôngdo and supported the position of Han Wônjin, while the 'Nak' scholars who supported Yi Kan hailed mainly from Kyônggido.

The Horak controversy began on grounds that can be considered in some ways a continuation of the Four–Seven debate, driving Yi Yulgok's position to its final ramifications. However, in addition to pushing to the ultimate the question of a non-dualistic metaphysics of *i* and *ki* and its meaning for self-cultivation, the controversy took a new turn that brought out hidden tensions and ambiguities in the concept of *i* itself.

The Four–Seven debate pushed the issue of the ramifications of the metaphysics of *i* and *ki* for the responsive life of the heart-and-mind; the Horak debate revisited the question, but this time with a focus on how to understand the meditative practice that was an important feature of self-cultivation. After centuries of Buddhist predominance, it was natural for early neo-Confucian thinkers to assume that consciousness itself, not just moral habits and self-discipline, is a key object of cultivation. Likewise, long familiarity with meditative discipline affected the way they understood the paradigmatic yin–yang pattern of alternating activity and quiet as it applied to consciousness: quiet was taken to mean not just relative inactivity, but absolute inactivity, that is, the condition of objectless consciousness familiar to trance meditation. Thus classical references to a condition before the feelings were aroused became a warrant for a meditative discipline known as 'quiet sitting': the mind resting in objectless consciousness, in this view, is but the natural compliment to the mind actively engaged with some sort of object. Both of these conditions should have their appropriate role in self-cultivation.

Just as they framed the understanding of the feelings, *i* and *ki* served to interpret the place and meaning of meditation practice. Turbid *ki* translated easily into literal psychic turbidity and tumult; clarifying and calming one's consciousness was also a matter of clarifying and calming one's *ki*. In this conceptualization there is an easy movement from the philosophical usage of the term *ki* in metaphysics to the more popular use of the term in which *ki* is the life force and the force of the feelings. What then would be the meaning of a perfectly clear, calm, objectless state of consciousness? Obviously this would be a condition of pure, undistorted unity with *i*, one's perfect nature which is, as we have seen, the formative grounds for all activity of the heart-and-mind. From this integral contact with the inner pattern for relating to all things, one might expect to gradually develop an ease and spontaneous appropriateness of one's responses in the active life; and this would also be facilitated as the practice fostered increased calm and mental focus in all areas of life. *I* as our own nature and the nature of all things lays the grounds for our appropriate interaction in all circumstances, and this practice seems highly effective as a means of removing the distortions introduced by our turbid *ki*.

One can see here the life context of the *i–ki* metaphysics of the neo-Confucians. Clearly, philosophical reflection here grows out of and returns to the task of spiritual cultivation. The importance in practice of *i* as not only an abstract norm but as a formative, dynamic factor in spiritual cultivation is evident. Conceptually this was captured in the idea of the 'original nature', that is, *i* as it is in itself, undistorted by the imperfection that may be present in *ki*. This again, like the Four Beginnings, is a reference to Mencius, for neo-Confucians explain that his argument that human nature is good was in fact pointing to the 'original nature' before there ever was such terminology. Of course the negative side is equally important in understanding self-cultivation. The potentially 'bent out of shape' natures of actual human beings with all the concrete reality of imperfect *ki* was conceptualized, in contrast with the 'original nature', as the 'physical (*kijil*; in Chinese, *qizhi*) nature'.

Neo-Confucians stressed that the double terminology did not mean we have two natures: the 'original nature' terminology was necessary because if one only observed the actual humans with their imperfect 'physical nature', the original perfection of *i* would not be evident. In actuality, of course, there is only one nature: the only nature (*i*) is *i* embodied in *ki*. The point of the dual terminology is that even as embodied and hence manifested in a distorted and imperfect way, the original perfection of the nature is never lost.

But what then is the point? Since all actuality occurs only in the context of *i*-with-*ki*, is the original nature anything but a way of paying lip-service to Mencius' teaching about a good human nature? The same problem we saw in the Four–Seven debate regarding the issuance of the feelings recurs here on the level of the nature, the source of the feelings. The issue is more explosive, however, for the original nature is a central aspect of self-cultivation theory: it is the dynamic base of tendencies to be cultivated and

enlarged upon in activity, and meditative quiescence, the 'condition before the mind is aroused', was commonly understood as putting one in touch with the original nature.

6 The Horak Debate (cont.)

Han Wŏnjin ignited the controversy by remarks he made in 1707 in a short treatise on the original nature and the physical nature. As a typical follower of Yi Yulgok, his main concern was to attack dualistic misunderstandings that sometimes stemmed from this terminology. Almost incidentally, he remarked that, regarding the original nature in the condition before the mind is aroused, since it must still inhere in *ki*, one could also take that fact into account and refer to it as the physical nature. The pure perfection of the original nature could be reached only by an 'exclusive reference' that simply did not take *ki* into account; in reality, of course, *ki* had to be there. In quiescence, Han observed, the imperfection that might be present in *ki* could not be observed, but that does not mean it is not there.

To speak of the condition before the mind is aroused and the physical nature in the same breath was novel and provoked a storm of protest, for it deeply challenged the conventional conceptual framework of self-cultivation theory. Han's chief opponent was Yi Kan, a man deeply steeped in self-cultivation practice who himself had experienced the problems of a turbulent consciousness and the benefits of quiet sitting. The original nature was a reality that functioned in his spiritual practice and explained his positive experience. It could not, he argued, be reduced to a mere matter of 'exclusive reference'.

In the course of the controversy, Han's position proved intellectually unassailable and he never modified it, even though more scholars sided with Yi Kan than with him. The logic of a consistent, non-dualistic interpretation of Cheng–Zhu metaphysics supported him: no *i* without *ki*, and hence no *i*-originated actuality without the mediation of *ki*. It was rather Yi Kan who was forced, step-by-step, to modify his position. Finally, in order to support a living contact with the original nature, he introduced the notion of an 'original mind', arguing that the turbidity of *ki* applied to the body but that the heart-and-mind remained essentially pure. This is the closest neo-Confucian thought approaches the mind/body dualism common in western thought; but it is a dualism of *ki*, reflecting that the stuff of both, unlike spirit/matter, is ultimately the same.

In the Four–Seven debate, Yi Hwang gave a dualistic twist to *i–ki* metaphysics in order to maintain the the status of Mencius' Four Beginnings.

Here Yi Kan, in a similar defense of a Mencius-inspired vision of self-cultivation, when Yi Hwang's kind of *i–ki* dualism is unthinkable, must resort to a division of *ki* itself in terms of mind and body. In the overall structure and intent of Cheng–Zhu thought, the role of *i* goes beyond merely explaining formal intelligibility or grounding an intellectual norm: it is a dynamic, active force in the process of becoming a full human being, but this dynamic side threatens to cast *i* and *ki* as competitive forces in a form of dualism out of tune with the deep structure of neo-Confucian metaphysics. The language of Zhu Xi's synthesis is continuously ambiguous, sounding in some passages quite dualistic and then, especially in more systematic metaphysical discussion, sounding non-dualistic and emphasizing perfect complementary and interdependence between *i* and *ki*. The history of these two controversies in Korea shows clearly that the ambiguities cannot be removed without a significant and creative recasting of the basic conceptual framework.

The question of the original nature in the condition before the mind is aroused led Han Wônjin into reflection on the whole question of the nature. Cheng Yi's famous dictum, '*I* is one but manifested diversely', is one of the cornerstones of the Cheng–Zhu understanding of the nature. The comprehensive one *i* of all things is the 'Supreme Ultimate', as ZHOU DUNYI put it in his famous *Diagram of the Supreme Ultimate*. Zhu Xi's comment reflects Cheng's dictum: 'Each thing has its own nature and all things are the one Supreme Ultimate.' This metaphysics accounts for the diverse manifestation of *i* whereby each thing has its own nature in terms of the varying degrees of the coarseness or turbidity of *ki*. Just as this accounts for the different degrees of intellectual and moral qualities of humans, so on a broader scale it accounts for entirely different species.

In self-cultivation discourse, it is of course the perfectly good original nature which is normative, and this led to a stress on *i*'s transcendence of the concrete limitation of *ki*: the pure and vital original nature remains unsullied, however bent out of shape it may be as manifested in a given individual. A criminal with a turbid psyche thus strives to become a better human, not a better criminal. But how does this apply to other species, similarly differentiated by the imperfection of *ki*? Is the normative, original nature of a cow the same as the original nature of a human? Han observed that according to the classics each creature should follow its nature, which implies that it is the nature *as differentiated* by *ki* that is normative: a good cow acts like a cow, not like a human.

Such reflections led Han Wônjin in 1708 to propose a novel, tripartite way of viewing the nature: (1) the nature as pure *i*, with no reference to *ki*, and hence no differentiation (the nature in this sense is unitary and ineffable); (2) the nature as 'based on *ki*', that is, as differentiated into species but undistorted and hence normative; and (3) the concrete physical nature according to which every individual, even of the same species, is different from every other. The 'original nature', he suggested, is a differentiated norm, and this demands the distinctive second category, the nature as based on *ki*.

Han's opponents, led by Yi Kan, mocked the novel language of a nature 'based on ki' which somehow was not yet the real, concrete physical nature of an individual being. Yi held firmly to the common understanding of a unitary *i* as the 'single origin', common to and within all things, and *i* as concretely manifested in diverse individuals. With *ki* comes limitation and distortion, and hence separation from the norm; hence the original nature must be identified with the 'single origin,' and its diversity as norm must somehow be likewise contained in that.

This dispute involved the most fundamental elements of Cheng–Zhu thought, the equation of *i* with the nature of things and the use of *ki* to account for both individual (especially moral) differences and the differentiation of various kinds of creatures. It thus was pursued with intensity, but over the years no consensus could be reached. Part of the reason for this lies in a deep ambiguity in Cheng Yi's foundational proposition, '*I* is one and manifested diversely.' Is the diverse manifestation totally the consequence of *ki*? Such was the understanding of Han Wônjin, who demanded the explicit reference to *ki* to account for any kind of diversified norm. Or is *ki* the means of implementing a diversity that has its more profound source in *i* itself? Such was the understanding of Yi Kan, who treated the 'Single Origin' as a self-diversifying, normative *i*. One can find support for both of these interpretations of Cheng's dictum in the writings of Zhu Xi, but the ambiguity runs through most discourse treating of the diversification of *i* through *ki*.

The fundamental ambiguity explored in the Horak debate points ultimately to the seam by which the organismic metaphysics typified by Chinese Daoism is stitched together with the consciousness-oriented participation metaphysics (all creatures are the manifestation of One Mind) which is part of Buddhism's Indian heritage (see DAOIST PHILOSOPHY). *I* as self-diversifying follows the organismic paradigm of the single pattern which accounts for both the unity and the diversity of a living body; *i* as unitary but manifested in varying degrees of fullness through the varying perfection of *ki* represents a kind of monism quite different from this one-body image, bringing to mind more the One Mind which never becomes plural in spite of its manifold manifestation. Mind and body have been subtly united here in a way unparalleled by any other of the world's great traditions. Bodies are differentiated by kinds and consciousness permits of degrees. neo-Confucians utilize *i* in both these ways, explicating through it the distinctness and commonality of all things, the transcendence of a normative nature, and the universal responsiveness of human consciousness which is the highest degree of participation in *i*. As the Horak debate makes clear, this feat involves a varied conceptualization of *i*'s relationship with *ki* as the price of such an accomplishment.

See also: HAN WÔNJIN; LI; NEO-CONFUCIAN PHILOSOPHY; QI; SELF-CULTIVATION, CHINESE THEORIES OF; YI HWANG; YI KAN; YI YULGOK

References and further reading

de Bary, W.T. and Haboush, J.K. (eds) (1985) *The Rise of Neo-Confucianism in Korea*, New York: Columbia University Press. (Useful collection of articles on major figures and features of the Korean neo-Confucian tradition.)

Deuchler, M. (1992) *The Confucian Transformation of Korea*, Cambridge, MA: Harvard University Press. (Excellent analysis of process by which Korea became East Asia's 'most Confucian' society.)

Haboush, J.K. (1988) *A Heritage of Kings*, New York: Columbia University Press. (A study of the functioning of neo-Confucian ideology and symbols in the reign of one of Korea's most outstanding kings.)

Kalton, M.C. (ed. and trans.) (1988) *To Become a Sage*, New York: Columbia University Press. (An annotated translation and commentary of the most famous work of Yi Hwang (T'oegye), one of the two leading neo-Confucian thinkers of Korea.)

Kalton, M.C., Kim Oaksook, C., Park Sung-Bae, Ro Youngchan, Tu Weiming and Yamashita, S. (trans) (1993) *The Four–Seven Debate*, Albany, NY: State University of New Work Press. (An annotated translation of the most famous controversy in Korean neo-Confucian thought.)

Lee, P.H., Baker, D., Ch'oe Yongho, Kang, H.H. and Kim Han-kyo (eds) (1993) *Sources of Korean Tradition*, New York: Columbia University Press. (An extensive collection of translations from original sources, including neo-Confucian works.)

Ro Youngchan (1988) *The Korean Neo-Confucianism of Yi Yulgok*, Albany, NY: Sate University of New York Press. (A study of the thought of one of the two leading neo-Confucian thinkers of Korea.)

MICHAEL C. KALTON

CONFUCIUS (551–479 BC)

Confucius is arguably the most influential philosopher in human history – 'is' because, taking Chinese philosophy on its own terms, he is still very much alive. Recognized as China's first teacher both chronologically and in importance, his ideas have been the rich soil in which the Chinese cultural tradition has grown and flourished. In fact, whatever we might mean by 'Chineseness' today, some two and a half millennia after his death, is inseparable from the example of personal character that Confucius provided for posterity. Nor was his influence restricted to China; all of the Sinitic cultures – especially Korea, Japan and Vietnam – have evolved around ways of living and thinking derived from the wisdom of the Sage.

A couple of centuries before Plato founded his Academy to train statesmen for the political life of Athens, Confucius had established a school with the explicit purpose of educating the next generation for political leadership. As his curriculum, Confucius is credited with having over his lifetime edited what were to become the Chinese classics, a collection of poetry, music, historical documents and annals that chronicled the events at the Lu court, along with an extensive commentary on the Yijing (Book of Changes). These classics provided a shared cultural vocabulary for his students, and became the standard curriculum for the Chinese literati in subsequent centuries.

Confucius began the practice of independent philosophers travelling from state to state in an effort to persuade political leaders that their particular teachings were a practicable formula for social and political success. In the decades that followed the death of Confucius, intellectuals of every stripe – Confucians, Legalists, Mohists, Yin–yang theorists, Militarists – would take to the road, attracted by court academies which sprung up to host them. Within these seats of learning, the viability of their various strategies for political and social unity would be hotly debated.

1 Life, works and influence
2 Teachings
3 Disciples
4 The *Analects*: texts and commentaries

1 Life, works and influence

Although Confucius enjoyed great popularity as a teacher and many of his students found their way into political office, his enduring frustration was that personally he achieved only marginal influence in the practical politics of the day. He was a *philosophe* rather than a theoretical philosopher; he wanted desperately to hold sway over intellectual and social trends, and to improve the quality of life that was dependent upon them. Although there were occasions on which important political figures sought his advice and services, over his years in the state of Lu, he held only minor offices at court.

Early on, however, and certainly by the time of his death, Confucius had risen in reputation to become a model of erudition, attracting attention from all segments of society. As time passed and the stock in Confucius rose, the historical records began to 'recall' details about his official career that had been supposedly lost. Over time, his later disciples altered the wording of his biographical record in his favour, effectively promoting him from minor official to several of the highest positions in the land.

Nor does the story end there. By the time of the Han dynasty (206 BC–AD 220), Confucius was celebrated as the 'uncrowned king' of the state of Lu, and by the fourth century AD, any prefecture wanting to define itself as a political entity was required by imperial decree to erect a temple to Confucius. Gods in China are local cultural heroes who are remembered by history as having contributed meaning and value to the tradition, and of these revered ancestors, that god called Confucius has been remembered best.

Confucius was certainly a flesh and blood historical figure, as real as Jesus or George Washington. But the received Confucius was and still is a 'living corporate person', in the sense that generation after generation of descendants have written commentaries on the legacy of Confucius in an effort to make his teachings appropriate for their own times and places. 'Confucianism' is a lineage of scholars who have continued to elaborate upon the canonical texts passed on after the life of Confucius came to an end, extending the way of living that Confucius had begun.

Although the ascent of Confucius to exalted status began early in the tradition with the continuation of his work by his many disciples, it was not until Confucianism was established as the state ideology during the Han dynasty (206 BC–AD 220) that his school of thought became an unchallenged orthodoxy. By developing his insights around the most basic and enduring aspects of the human experience – family, friendship, education, community and so on – Confucius had guaranteed their continuing relevance. One characteristic of Confucianism that began with Confucius himself, and made it so resilient in the Chinese tradition, is its porousness and adaptability. Confucius said of himself that he only transmitted traditional culture, he did not create it; his contribution was simply to take ownership of the tradition, and adapt the wisdom of the past to his own present historical moment.

Just as Confucius reinvented the culture of the Zhou and earlier dynasties for his own era, Han dynasty Confucianism drew into itself many of the ideas owned by competing schools in the earlier centuries, and in so doing, fortified itself against their challenge. This pattern – absorbing competing ideas and adapting them to the specific conditions of the time – sustained Confucianism across the centuries as the official doctrine of the Chinese empire until the fall of the Qing dynasty in 1911. In fact, an argument can be made that just as the composite of Buddhism and Confucianism produced neo-Confucianism, the combination of Marxism and Confucianism in this century has created a kind of neo-neo-Confucianism.

As recently as the Cultural Revolution (1966–76), Jiang Qing, Mao Zedong's wife, and her cohorts mounted an Anti-Confucius campaign that swept the country. The great irony of this Anti-Confucius campaign was that during this period one could not acquire a copy of the *Analects*, not because they had been banned or suppressed but because they were sold out; the entire country was put to work reading the teachings of Confucius in order to criticize them.

2 Teachings

There are many sources for the teachings of Confucius that have been passed down to us today. The most authoritative among them are the *Lunyu* Analects. (*Lunyu* literally means 'discourses'; a better translation is 'analects', coming from the Greek *analekta*, which has the root meaning of 'leftovers after a feast'.) It is probably the case that the first fifteen books of these literary 'leftovers' were assembled and edited by a congress of Confucius' disciples shortly after his death. It would seem the disciples concluded that a very special person had walked among them, and that his way – what he said and did – should be preserved for future generations. Much of this portion of the text is devoted to remembering Confucius, a personal narrative of what he had to say, to whom he said it and how he said it. The middle three chapters are like snapshots of his life-habits – Confucius never sat down without first straightening his mat; he never slept in the posture of a corpse; he never sang on a day that he attended a funeral; he drank freely, but never to the point of being confused of mind.

The last five books of the *Analects* appear to have been compiled some time later, after the most prominent disciples of Confucius had launched their own teaching careers and had taken it upon themselves to elaborate on the philosophy of their late Master. Confucius is less prominent in these chapters, yet he is referenced with more honorific terms, while the now mature disciples are themselves often quoted.

In addition to the *Analects*, the other two most important resources for the life and teachings of Confucius are the *Zuozhuan* (the Zuo commentary on the *Spring and Autumn Annals*), and the *Mencius*. The Zuo commentary is a narrative history which purports to interpret the chronicle of the court history of the state of Lu up until the death of Confucius. The *Mencius* is a text named after a disciple who elaborated the doctrines of Confucius some century and a half after his death (see MENCIUS), and became one of the Four Books in the Song dynasty, which were from then onwards the core of the Confucian classics (see CHINESE CLASSICS).

One thing is clear about the *Analects* and these supplementary texts: they do not purport to lay out a formula by which everyone should live. Rather, they provide an account of one man: how he cultivated his humanity, and how he lived a satisfying life, much to the admiration of those around him. The way (*dao*) of Confucius is nothing more or less than the way in which he as a particular person chose to live his life. The power and lasting value of his ideas lie in the fact that they are intuitively persuasive, and readily adaptable.

Confucius begins from the insight that the life of every human being is played out within the context of their particular family, for better or for worse. For Confucius and generations of Chinese to come, it is one's family and the complex of relationships that constitute it, rather than the solitary individual, that is the basic unit of humanity. In fact, for Confucius, there is no individual – no 'self' or 'soul' – that remains once the layers of social relations are peeled away. One is one's roles and relationships. The goal of living, then, is to achieve harmony and enjoyment for oneself and others through acting appropriately in those roles and relationships that constitute one.

Given that we all live within the web of family relationships, it is entirely natural that we should project this institution out onto the community, the polity and the cosmos as an organizing metaphor. The Confucian community is an extension of aunts and uncles, sisters and cousins; the teacher is 'teacher–father' and one's senior classmates are 'elder–brother students'; 'the ruler is father and mother to the people, and is the son of "Heaven"'. 'Heaven' itself is a faceless amalgam of ancestors rather than some transcendent Creator deity (see TIAN). As Confucius says, 'The exemplary person works hard at the root, for where the root has taken firm hold, the way will grow.' What then is the root? He continues: 'Treating your family members properly – this is the root of becoming a person.'

For Confucius, the way to live is not dictated for us by some power beyond; it is something we all must participate in constructing. On one occasion, Confucius said 'It is not the way that broadens people, but people who broaden the way.' The way is our passage through life, the road we take. Our forbearers mapped out their way and built their roads, and in so doing, have provided a bearing for succeeding generations. They have given us the culture and institutions that structure our lives and give them value and meaning. But each new generation must be roadbuilders too, and continue the efforts that have gone before.

Confucius saw living as an art rather than a science. There are no blueprints, no formulae, no replications. He once said, 'The exemplary person seeks harmony, not sameness.' In a family, each member has his or her unique and particular role. Harmony is simply getting the most out of these differences. Similarly, Confucius saw harmony in community emerging out of the uninhibited contributions of its diverse people. Communal enjoyment is like Chinese cooking – getting the most out of your ingredients.

Confucius was extraordinarily fond of good music, because making music is conducent to harmony, bringing different voices into productive relationships. Music is tolerant in allowing each voice and instrument to have its own place, its own integrity, while at the same time, requiring that each ingredient find a complementary role in which it can add the most to the ensemble. Music is always unique in that each performance has a life of its own.

What Confucius calls *ren* – literally, 'becoming a person' – is the recognition that personal character is the consequence of cultivating one's relationships with others (see CONFUCIAN PHILOSOPHY, CHINESE §5). There is nothing more defining of humanity for Confucius than the practical consideration of one human being for another. Importantly, *ren* does not precede practical employment; it is not a principle or standard that has some existence beyond the day to day lives of the people who realize it in their relationships. Rather, *ren* is fostered in the deepening of relationships that occur as one takes on the responsibility and obligations of communal living, and comes fully to life. *Ren* is shared human flourishing. It is the achievement of the quality of relationships which, like the lines in calligraphy or landscape painting, collaborate to maximum aesthetic effect.

Wisdom for Confucius is relevant knowledge: not knowing 'what' in some abstract and theoretical sense, but knowing 'how' to map one's way through life and get the most happiness out of it. Happiness for oneself and for others is isomorphic; it is mutually entailing. In discussing knowledge, Confucius says that being fond of something is better than just knowing it, and finding enjoyment in it is better than just being fond of it. Confucius associates *ren* with mountains; it is spiritual and enduring, a constant geographical marker from which we can all take our bearings. Wisdom is like water, pure, flowing and nurturing. The exemplary person is both *ren* and wise, both mountain and water.

A good way to think about 'the way' is the notion of passage. On one occasion, Confucius observed while standing on the bank of a river, 'Isn't its passing just like this, never ceasing day or night!' Life is at its very best a pleasant journey, where the inherited body of cultural institutions and the pattern of roles and relationships that locate us within community – what Confucius calls 'propriety' (*li*) – are a code of formal behaviours for stabilizing and disciplining our ever-changing circumstances. 'Propriety' covers everything from table manners to the three years of mourning on the loss of one's parent, from the institution of parenthood to the appropriate posture for expressing commiseration. It is a social syntax that brings the particular members of community into meaningful relationships. Propriety is a discourse, which like language, enables people to communicate, and to locate themselves appropriately, one with the other.

What distinguishes 'propriety' from rules and regulations is that these cultural norms must be personalized, and are open to refinement. Only I can be father to my sons; only I can be this son to my mother; only I can sacrifice to my ancestors. And if I act properly, performing my roles and cultivating my relationships so that they are rich and fruitful, other people in community will see me as a model of appropriate conduct, and will defer. It is precisely this power of example that Confucius called 'excellence' (*de*). Excellence is the propensity of people to behave a certain way when provided with an inspiring model.

The other side to what Confucius calls 'propriety' is the cultivation of a sense of shame. Shame is community-based. It is an awareness of and a concern for how others perceive one's conduct. Persons with a sense of shame genuinely care about what other people think of them. Self-sufficient individuals, on the other hand, need not be concerned about the judgments of others. Such individuals can thus be capable of acting shamelessly, using any means at all to take what they want when they want it.

3 Disciples

Confucius was tolerant of difference. In fact, on six separate occasions in the *Analects*, he is asked what he means by *ren*, an idea that is at the heart of his teachings, and six times he gives different answers. For Confucius, instructing disciples in *ren* requires that the message be tailored to the conditions of the person asking the question. We have said that, for Confucius, persons are no more than the sum of their specific familial and communal roles and relationships, and that *ren* emerges out of the quality that they are able to achieve in cultivating them. It stands to reason, then, that to know Confucius, we do best to familiarize ourselves with his community of disciples. The Teacher can best be known by his students.

Some of these disciples come to life in a careful reading of the *Analects*. For example, although Confucius was reluctant to use the term *ren* to describe anyone, he did use it of his favourite disciple, Yan Hui, also called Yan Yuan. Living on a bowl of rice and a ladle of water, Yan Hui's eagerness to learn and his sincerity endeared him to the Master; but he was also possessed of an incomparable character, and was so intelligent that Confucius said of him, 'When he is told one thing he understands ten'. Although Yan Hui was some thirty years younger than Confucius, it was only him among his many disciples that Confucius saw as his equal. It is no surprise, then, that Confucius was totally devastated by the death of Yan Hui at the young age of thirty-one.

Zilu was another of Confucius' best-known and favourite disciples. He was a person of courage and action who was sometimes upbraided by Confucius for being too bold and impetuous. When he asked Confucius if courage was indeed the highest virtue, Confucius tried to rein him in by replying that a person who has courage without a sense of appropriateness will be a trouble-maker, and a lesser person will be a thief. Confucius' feelings for Zilu were mixed. On the one hand, he was constantly critical of Zilu's rashness and immodesty; and impatient with his seeming indifference to book learning. On the other hand, Confucius appreciated Zilu's unswerving loyalty and directness; he never delayed on fulfilling his commitments. Being nearer Confucius in age, Zilu with his military temper was not one to take criticism without giving it back; on several occasions, especially in the apocryphal literature, Zilu challenges Confucius' judgment in associating with political figures of questionable character and immodest reputation. However, Confucius' enormous affection for the irrepressible Zilu comes through the text.

Confucius was also critical of his disciples. Zai Yu, also called Ziwo, was devoted to Confucius, yet on numerous occasions Confucius criticised him roundly for a lack of character. It was as a metaphorical reference to attempting to educate Ziwo that Confucius said, 'You cannot carve rotten wood, nor can you whitewash a wall made from dry manure.'

Zigong excelled as a statesman and as a merchant, and was perhaps second only to Yan Hui in Confucius' affections. Confucius was respectful of Zigong's abilities, and in particular his intellect, but less impressed with Zigong's use of this intellect to amass personal wealth. Coming from a wealthy, educated home, Zigong was well-spoken, and as such, Confucius' most persistent criticism of him is that his deeds could not keep pace with his words. Even so, much of the flattering profile of Confucius collected in the *Analects* is cast in the words of the eloquent Zigong.

Zengzi is best remembered as a proponent of filial piety – devotion and service to one's parents. A natural extension of this affection for one's family is friendship. Zengzi rose to prominence after the death of Confucius as one of his leading advocates.

These and many other disciples came from around the central states of China, gravitating to the state of Lu to study with Confucius. In spite of the sometimes severe opinions which Confucius expressed freely about them – and he admonishes almost every one of them – they were devoted to the Master, and responded to him with reverence. There is no greater proof of this enduring respect for Confucius than the fact that they had a hand in recording Confucius' criticisms of themselves, and then went on to found branch schools based on these same criticisms to perpetuate his teachings.

4 The *Analects*: texts and commentaries

The work known as the *Analects* is mainly a collection of sayings and conversations of Confucius. In the time of Emperor Wu (140–87 BC) of the Han there were three versions of the work, the *Lulun*, the *Qilun* and the *Gulun*. In the first century BC, Zhang Yu taught a version known as *Lunyu according to Marquis Zhang*, which incorporated readings from both the *Lulun* and the *Qilun*. Zheng Xuan (AD 127–200) further adopted readings from the *Gulun*. The text that has come down to us is that of He Yan (AD 190–249) in his *Lunyu jijie* (Collected Commentaries on the *Lunyu*).

The extant *Analects* is in twenty books. Of the three early versions, only the *Lulun* had twenty books; the

Qilun and the *Gulun* both had twenty-two books, though the extra books were not identical. According to the *Xinlun* of Huan Tan (24 BC–AD 56) the order of the chapters in the *Gulun* was different and there were more than four hundred variant readings. Lu Deming (AD 556–637) of the Tang dynasty also remarked that in the *Qilun*, besides the two extra books, 'the chapters and verses were considerably more numerous than in the *Lulun*'. Some of the variant readings were recorded by scholars before the three versions were lost and these have been collected by textual critics over the centuries, but these consist mainly of variant forms of graphs. Only a handful affect the interpretation of the text. For instance, the text of VII.17 in the traditional text reads, 'Grant me a few more years so that I may continue to study the *Yijing* at the age of fifty, and I shall be free from major errors.' According to Lu Deming, the *Lulun* reads *yi* (grammatical particle) in place of *yi* (meaning the *Yijing* (Book of Changes)). This can only be rendered 'Grant me a few more years so that I may continue to learn at the age of fifty, and I shall, perhaps, be free from major errors.' Thus the variant reading has a bearing on the substantive point whether Confucius was a keen student of the *Yijing*. Of the two eclectic versions, the *Lunyu according to Marquis Zhang* was based on the *Lulun* while incorporating readings from the *Qilun*. As for Zheng Xuan's version, it has been the common view that this was likewise based on the *Lulun* but incorporating readings from the *Gulun*. However, this may not be the case, as there is some evidence that Zheng also adopted some readings of the *Qilun*. On their versions of the *Lunyu*, both Zhang and Zheng wrote commentaries. Zhang's commentary was in an independent work known as *Lu Anchang hou shuo* (Marquis Anchang's Exegesis of the Lu [lun]). Unfortunately this was lost at a very early age and we do not possess even a single quotation from it.

Zheng's commentary was attached to his text of the *Analects*, and although the work is lost, numerous quotations, particularly through He Yan's *Collected Commentaries*, have come down to us. In the present century a number of fragments came to light in Dunhuang and Turfan, the most notable of which is a partial manuscript copy done by a twelve-year-old schoolboy in 710 and discovered in 1969. In all, we now possess over half of Zheng's total commentary, and this has spurred on the study of this commentary. In Bajiaolang in Ding Xian, Hebei province, a copy of the *Analects* on bamboo slips was unearthed in 1971 in a tomb of the late Western Han, consisting of over half of the whole text. The exciting part of the discovery is that the text antedates the version of Marquis Zhang, and may represent the school of the

Qilun. Unfortunately, the publication of this text so far has not revealed any major differences.

Of the numerous commentaries on the *Analects*, only a few landmarks can be mentioned. The *Lunyu zhushu* (Subcommentary on the *Lunyu*) by Xing Bing (932–1010) and *Lunyu jizhu* (Collected Commentaries on the *Lunyu*) by the great neo-Confucian thinker ZHU XI (1130–1200) were authoritative works for the educated reader. In the Qing dynasty, as a reaction against the neo-Confucian approach, there were new commentaries on the classics with greater philological emphasis. On the *Analects* in particular, we have Liu Baonan's *Lunyu zhengyi* (The True Interpretation of the *Lunyu*).

There is finally the question of the composition of the *Analects*. First (as noted in §2), the work as we have it was not put into the present form once and for all. The later books were likely to have been added on at a later editing. Second, within a single book, some material must have been taken from existing collections of sayings of Confucius *en bloc* and some chapters added subsequently. Finally, sayings of disciples must have been incorporated by their own disciples to enhance their standing in the Confucian tradition. This is particularly true of Book I, in which are found sayings by younger disciples such as Youzi and Zengzi who played an important role in the formation of the Confucian tradition.

List of works

Confucius (551–479 BC) *Lunyu* (Analects), trans. D.C. Lau, *Confucius: The Analects (Lun-yu)*, Hong Kong: Chinese University Press, 1992. (Although the dates given are for Confucius' own life, the *Analects* were in fact compiled over a long period after his death, as noted in the text of the entry. Lau provides a revised bilingual translation of the *Analects*, complete with a philosophical introduction, appendices on the history of the text, events in the life of Confucius and a characterization of his various disciples. The standard English translation.)

References and further reading

Fingarette, H.A. (1972) *Confucius: The Secular as Sacred*, New York: Harper & Row. (A pioneering re-evaluation of the philosophy of Confucius, and its relevance to contemporary philosophy.)

Hall, D.L. and Ames, R.T. (1987) *Thinking Through Confucius*, Albany, NY: State University of New York Press. (A reconstruction of the philosophical insights of Confucius, comparing the presuppositions of his way of thinking with presuppositions that underlie the Western traditions of philosophy.)

D.C. LAU
ROGER T. AMES

CONIMBRICENSES
see COLLEGIUM CONIMBRICENSE

CONNECTIONISM

Connectionism is an approach to computation that uses connectionist networks. A connectionist network is composed of information-processing units (or nodes); typically, many units process information simultaneously, giving rise to massively 'parallel distributed processing'. Units process information only locally: they respond only to their specific input lines by changing or retaining their activation values; and they causally influence the activation values of their output units by transmitting amounts of activation along connections of various weights or strengths. As a result of such local unit processing, networks themselves can behave in rule-like ways to compute functions.

The study of connectionist computation has grown rapidly since the early 1980s and now extends to every area of cognitive science. For the philosophy of psychology, the primary interest of connectionist computation is its potential role in the computational theory of cognition – the theory that cognitive processes are computational. Networks are employed in the study of perception, memory, learning and categorization; and it has been claimed that connectionism has the potential to yield an alternative to the classical view of cognition as rule-governed symbol manipulation.

Since cognitive capacities are realized in the central nervous system, perhaps the most attractive feature of the connectionist approach to cognitive modelling is the neural-like aspects of network architectures. The members of a certain family of connectionist networks, artificial neural networks, have proved to be a valuable tool for investigating information processing within the nervous system. In artificial neural networks, units are neuron-like; connections, axon-like; and the weights of connections function in ways analogous to synapses.

Another attraction is that connectionist networks, with their units sensitive to varying strengths of multiple inputs, carry out in natural ways 'multiple soft constraint satisfaction' tasks – assessing the extent to which a number of non-mandatory, weighted constraints are satisfied. Tasks of this sort occur in motor-control, early vision, memory, and in categorization and pattern recognition. Moreover, typical networks can re-programme themselves by adjusting the weights of the connections among their units, thereby engaging in a kind of 'learning'; and they can do so even on the basis of the sorts of noisy and/or incomplete data people typically encounter.

The potential role of connectionist architectures in the computational theory of cognition is, however, an open question. One possibility is that cognitive architecture is a 'mixed architecture', with classical and connectionist modules. But the most widely discussed view is that cognitive architecture is thoroughly connectionist. The leading challenge to this view is that an adequate cognitive theory must explain high-level cognitive phenomena such as the systematicity of thought (someone who can think 'The dog chases the cat' can also think 'The cat chases the dog'), its productivity (our ability to think a potential infinity of thoughts) and its inferential coherence (people can infer 'p' from 'p and q'). It has been argued that a connectionist architecture could explain such phenomena only if it implements a classical, language-like symbolic architecture. Whether this is so, however, and, indeed, even whether there are such phenomena to be explained, are currently subjects of intense debate.

1   **What is a connectionist network?**
2   **Computation, representation and learning**
3   **Networks and multiple soft constraint satisfaction**
4   **Connectionism and artificial intelligence**
5   **Connectionism and neuroscience**
6   **Connectionism and the philosophy of psychology**
7   **Crux of the classical/connectionist debate**

1   What is a connectionist network?

Units and their activation. A unit in a connectionist network can be an input unit, an output unit or a 'hidden' unit. Input units can directly receive signals from sources external to the network; output units can directly send signals outside the network. Input and output units are sometimes called 'visible' units because of their direct interaction with external factors. The 'hidden' units of a network are those units (if any) that send or receive signals from outside the network only by means of sending or receiving signals from other units, as in the following 'Hamming net':

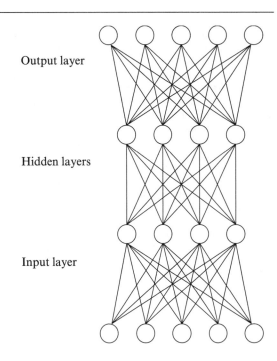

Output layer

Hidden layers

Input layer

Simple connectionist network (from Dinsmore 1992: 9)

A network can have one or more layers of hidden units, or no hidden units at all.

At any time, a unit is in an activation state. The kinds of activation states units occupy can vary from one network architecture to another, from being merely active or inactive, to being in discrete states of three or more levels of activation, or to having continuous degrees of activation, either bounded or unbounded. The activation state of a unit is indexed by a real number, typically on the interval [0,1], called the 'activation value' of the state.

Each unit computes an output function that maps its current state of activation to an output signal. The signal is not an encoded message such as a data structure, but a degree of activation indexed by a real number. While an output function can be linear, typically it is some threshold function. If a unit has a negative bias, it may send 0 (or the null signal) unless its activation value exceeds a certain threshold; if it has a positive bias, the unit may send a certain output value unless its activation value falls below a specific threshold. Networks in which units compute non-linear output functions exceed in computational power networks in which units compute only linear ones.

Patterns of connectivity. The activation state of a

unit U_i causally influences the degree of activation of a unit U_j by means of the activation output U_i sends to U_j. The direction of such causal influence is the direction of activation spread or flow. There is a connection from a unit U_i to a unit U_j when, but only when, the output of U_i can exert an influence on the activation state of U_j via a direct path within the network – one along which there is no intermediate unit. Connections are thus the direct causal routes along which units send signals to their output units. In some networks, two units can mutually influence each other, and thus a unit can be related to another both as input and output. In 'auto-associative' networks, each unit is connected to every other unit, including itself; in other networks, there are various restrictions on which units are connected.

When units can mutually influence each other, information processing is interactive. In 'recurrent' networks, there are connection patterns that contain loops. That is, a unit is either related to itself as an input unit or there is a series of unit connections from the unit back to itself; thus, the output of a unit at one time can causally influence its activation state at another via activation flow. In 'feed-forward' networks, information processing is non-interactive: activation flows in a single direction from input units to output units via whatever layers, if any, of hidden units the network contains. The Hamming net, for instance, is a feed-forward network with three layers of units, one of which is a layer of hidden units (see diagram above).

The causal influence a sending unit exerts on a receiving unit depends on two intrinsic properties of their connection: its weight (or strength); and whether it acts to increase (excite) or decrease (inhibit) the level of activation of the receiving unit. The notation 'w_{ij}' is used to stand for a real number which indexes the connection from unit U_i to unit U_j by its weight and kind; the number is positive/negative when the connection is excitatory/inhibitory, respectively. The weight of the connection is the absolute value of w_{ij}.

In many networks, the extent and kind of causal influence a unit U_i exerts on a unit U_j is indexed by the product of w_{ij} and the activation value of U_i. The total network activity input to U_j is the sum of all such causal influences: it is the sum of the product of each input activation value and the real number indexing the weight and kind of connection it bears to U_j. (If there are inputs from sources external to the network, they must likewise be indexed by real numbers and included in the summing.) But in some networks, the net input function to a unit – called the 'propagation rule' – is more complex. In 'competitive' networks, units form pools: the units in a pool are all mutually inhibitory – that is, they bear inhibitory connections to each other – while units outside the pool are excitatory to one or more units in the pool. And still more complex patterns of connectivity are possible.

Units respond to the signals they receive either by changing their level of activation or by remaining at the same level. Which response occurs is a function of three factors: the total activity input to the unit, the unit's current activation state, and the unit's bias (if any). The activation function for a unit maps the unit's net input (a sum or weighted sum) and current activation state to an activation state of the unit. In Hopfield networks, units have a sigmoidal (S-shaped) response to net input: their activation levels only increase by a given amount given an increase in net input; after that, they level off and increase no further. But units can also have Gaussian (bell-shaped) activation functions and other sorts of non-linear ones as well.

Local and global effects. Units process information by computing an activation function and an output function. By means of such local interactions among units, global consequences ensue. The behaviour of a network as a whole is a consequence of the pattern of connectivity exhibited by its units at a time and the global activation state of the network at that time. The latter is indexed by a vector (ordered list) of real numbers, the activation value of each unit in the network at that time being indexed by one and only one element of the vector.

Network information processing is characterized as the evolution through time of global patterns of activation. The set of all possible global activation states of a network is its activation space, whose dimensionality is exactly equal to the number of units in the network. The vectors that index possible global states of the network pick out points in the activation space, and the temporal evolution of the network is characterized as a trajectory through that space.

2 Computation, representation and learning

A network itself can behave in a rule-like way to compute functions from one vector to another. The argument of the function is a vector indexing a pattern of activation over input units, and the value of the function for that argument is a vector indexing a pattern of activation over output units. In response to any input activation pattern representing an argument of a particular function, a network with a specific pattern of connectivity can be disposed to produce the output activation pattern representing the value of the function for that argument. The network computes the function when this disposition is activated.

Representations within a network can be of one of

two kinds: local or distributed. A representation is *local* if it is (or is realized by) an *individual* unit in a certain activation state. A representation is *distributed* if it is (or is realized by) a pattern of activation over a *group* of two or more units. A network computes functions from one sort of representation to another by computing the corresponding vector-to-vector function in the manner described in the preceding paragraph.

The pattern of connectivity exhibited by the units in a network functions like an 'implicit' look-up table program. A look-up table program looks up (unique) answers to questions posed to it. Patterns of activation over input units function like questions posed to the network (for example, 'To what category does this belong?'), and patterns of activation over output units function like answers to the questions ('To category C.'). Unlike typical classical look-up mechanisms, networks do not *explicitly* store the answers as data structures; rather, the answers are, so to speak, *implicitly* contained in the pattern of connectivity. The patterns of activation over output units can be construed as data structures. But such patterns are produced in response to the network's inputs as a result of the network's pattern of connectivity, rather than retrieved from some storage location in the network. A network's memory, it is said, is in its pattern of connectivity.

A network's pattern of connectivity is not architecturally fixed, for the weights of connections are not. Connectionist networks can programme themselves, via weight change, to execute a given look-up table program. Thus, the look-up table need not be pre-programmed into the network; the network can develop it in response to training. It is taught to recognize a pattern, for instance, by being trained on examples of the pattern: presented with examples of the target pattern as inputs, its outputs are assessed by some evaluation procedure and the weights of connections are then adjusted (see the discussion of learning rules below); the network passes through a number of cycles of this procedure until it acquires the disposition to respond to each input in the right way (or to some desired degree of accuracy). Networks can be trained to associate patterns and to extract features from data sets in response to statistical regularities in them.

During training, weight change occurs in accordance with learning rules. One of the earliest is *Hebb's rule*: when two units are activated at the same time, the strength of the connection between them will be increased (see Hebb 1949). By conforming to this rule a network can learn associations that depend on correlations between activations of units in the network. The generalized *delta rule*, typically called 'back-propagation', is currently the most widely used learning rule in connectionist research. For a given input activation pattern, the actual output pattern is compared with a target output pattern. The difference between the two is then propagated back into whatever connections were used to get the actual output. If the match is good, then the connections among units which contributed to the output are strengthened; if the match is poor, then the relevant connections are reduced in strength. Back-propagation is worthy of special note because it dispelled concerns about the possible computational limitations of network architectures raised by Minsky and Papert's critique of perceptrons – simple two-layered networks (Minsky and Papert 1969).

Back-propagation is a kind of supervised learning rule since it results in weight changes based on an externally generated report on the network's performance – an error signal. Networks can engage in unsupervised learning by monitoring their performance by means of internal feedback via direct or indirect loops.

3 Networks and multiple soft constraint satisfaction

Many kinds of networks are capable of finding optimal (or near-optimal) solutions to problems whose solution involves assessing multiple soft constraint satisfaction – problems Minsky and Papert (1969) called 'best-match' problems. There has been considerable success in analysing a wide range of cognitive problems as such problems. Content-addressable memory – recalling something or someone on the basis of a partial characterization (for example, 'a game played on a court with a ball that players try to drop through a hoop') – is analysed as a pattern-completion task involving multiple soft constraint satisfaction. And categorization using conceptual schemata has been analysed similarly. This seems to many to capture Wittgenstein's 'family resemblance' account of concepts, whereby objects satisfy a concept by virtue of sharing any of a variety of resemblances, as well as Rosch's related account of concepts in terms of the resemblance of an object to a 'prototype' (see CONCEPTS §7). And recently Prince and Smolensky's optimality theory (1993) outlines how parsers using multiple soft constraint satisfaction might serve for the parsing of natural language.

The basic network approach to such problems is due to Hinton (1977). Each unit represents a hypothesis (note that such representations are local and unstructured), and each connection puts constraints among hypotheses. If, for example, hypothesis H is evidence for hypothesis H', there is a positive connection from the unit representing H to the unit representing H'; and the connection is negative if H is evidence against H'. The tighter the confirming or disconfirming evidential relation, the greater the strength of the connection. If one hypothesis implies another, the connection from the first to the second will be such that the output unit must be on if the input unit is on; if two hypotheses are incompatible, they may be mutually connected in such a way that they cannot both be on. Since input units can also receive external input, the corresponding hypotheses can receive direct confirming or disconfirming evidence from the environment. The fact that different hypotheses may have different a priori probabilities is handled by biasing the relevant units. The overall goodness of fit of a particular hypothesis to the evidence is measured by the sum of the individual constraints on the activation value of the unit representing the hypothesis. The activation values of units range between a minimum and a maximum. The maximum value means that the hypothesis should be accepted, the minimum that it should be rejected, and intermediate values correspond to intermediate states of certainty. The constraint satisfaction problem is thus reduced to one of maximizing this overall goodness of constraint fit.

Implementing such a procedure by a network has proved fruitful in many areas of cognitive science. For example, one of the basic problems in computational vision is to characterize the computational procedure by which the visual system arrives at representations of the scene before the subject's eyes from the subject's retinal images (see VISION). A leading research programme characterizes the computational procedure as a Bayesian decision procedure implemented by a network (see PROBABILITY, INTERPRETATIONS OF).

One problem that arises for procedures for solving best-match problems is avoiding local maxima of goodness of fit. The Boltzmann machine, developed by J. Hinton and Terence Sejnowski, employs the standard method for avoiding them. Exploiting a computational analogue of the metallurgical process of annealing – whereby metals are heated to a little below their melting point and then cooled very slowly so that all their atoms have time to settle into a single orientation – random noise (heat) is introduced into network activity. The noise functions to jar the network out of local landscape valleys (which correspond to low goodness peaks) so it can explore other parts of the energy landscape to find the global energy minimum (the highest goodness peak). When the network reaches a stable state, it has settled or relaxed into a solution. Given sufficient time, the Boltzmann machine can solve any computational problem for which weights exist.

4 Connectionism and artificial intelligence

Work in connectionist computation has had perhaps its greatest impact in the field of artificial intelligence (AI), which attempts to develop intelligent machines (see ARTIFICIAL INTELLIGENCE). AI research into connectionist networks has yielded fruit in many areas of business and industry. (The connectionist machines are, however, virtually always simulated on standard commercial computers, rather than actually manufactured.)

Networks are especially proficient at solving so-called connected problems – ones that do not divide into independently solvable subproblems. Consider, for example, 'the travelling salesman' problem: a salesman must visit each of a number of cities, beginning and ending his journey at the same city, and visiting all the others only once. The problem is to find the shortest route he can take. (If there are, for instance, twenty cities, then there are over 6.5 billion combinations of routes.) Since which city the salesman visits depends on which cities he has already visited, the problem does not divide into independently solvable subproblems. Such problems are decidable, and can thus be solved by classical methods. However, as the connected parameters of the problem increase, there is an exponential increase in the computational resources required to solve them by classical means. Connectionist networks are able to solve such problems much more efficiently. Hopfield's network is able to find a nearly optimal solution to the travelling salesman problem in a small number of training cycles.

Networks are also proficient at pattern-recognition tasks and at learning to perform such tasks. One network that has received a great deal of attention in the popular press is Sejnowski and Rosenberg's NETtalk (1987), which learns to associate letters with phonemes. The network drives a synthesizer that produces pronunciations of the phonemes. After sufficient network training, the synthesizer sounds like a robotic voice literally reading English texts presented to it.

There have been some comparative studies between networks employing back-propagation and classical learning systems employing various members of the family of 'top-down inductive decision trees' (TDIDT), which are kinds of 'production systems' (Quinlan 1987). The studies compared decision trees and networks with respect to speed and predictive accuracy of learning categorization tasks, both from accurate data and from noisy and/or incomplete data (for example, Fisher and McKusick 1989; Mooney *et al.* 1989; Shavlik *et al.* 1991). One data set used in a comparative study is Sejnowski's and Rosenberg's

'NETtalk Full' (Shavlik *et al.* 1991). The TDIDT member that figured in the study was ID3. There was no statistically significant difference in the predictive accuracy of the network using back-propagation and ID3. ID3 was 64.8% accurate; the network was 63.0% accurate. Moreover, both ID3 and back-propagation degraded at roughly the same rate as features were removed from the data set, but ID3 was five times faster than back-propagation. On the NETtalk-A data set, ID3 was 63.1% accurate and the network was 66.4% accurate; and ID3 was 100 times faster. (In studies for some data sets, TDIDTs are as much as 1,000 times faster than networks using back-propagation; but that is unsurprising since back-propagation is notoriously slow.) Speed aside, other such comparative studies indicate that networks using back-propagation are roughly equivalent to various TDIDT members in terms of predictive accuracy and graceful degradation in the face of noisy and/or incomplete data.

New learning algorithms for networks are being explored, as are new TDIDT algorithms. Moreover, in the field of machine learning, there is currently much research into machines that integrate networks and TDIDTs into a single machine architecture. This research proceeds without regard to either neural or psychological plausibility; its aim is not to model how cognizers actually learn, but rather to build better learning machines.

5 Connectionism and neuroscience

The nervous system appears to be a system of neural networks. We are, however, largely ignorant of its workings. By and large, it is unknown what functions any type of neuron computes, and how information generally is encoded in the brain. But enough is known to know that, while connectionist networks were inspired by neural networks, extant connectionist networks are not neurally realistic: no type of connectionist network yet proposed is instantiated by any actual neural network. On the basis of anatomical and immunocytochemical criteria of type individuation, it is estimated that the number of types of cortical neurons is somewhere between fifty and 500 (Sereno 1988). Different types of neurons appear to perform specialized functions. These functions are not well understood, but there is no evidence that any type computes activation functions or output functions computed by units in any extant network model. Further, there is no neural analogue of back-propagation. And while parts of dendrites appear to be able to act as independent information-processing units, this has no analogue in extant connectionist networks (Churchland and Sejnowski 1992).

None the less, work in computational neuroscience with the members of a certain family of connectionist networks, namely artificial neural networks, is playing an important role in increasing our knowledge of the nervous system. Computational neuroscience strives for more and more realistic networks with the aim of someday modelling actual neural-network information-processing (Churchland and Sejnowski 1992). Important pioneer work has already been done. For example, there has been considerable development of artificial neural network models of low-level vision phenomena such as stereopsis (binocular vision) and colour constancy, and of motor-control phenomena such as the vestibular-ocular reflex (that enables eyes to focus on a fixed point as the head moves). Indeed, artificial neural network theory is presently the only approach to understanding information processing in neural networks.

6 Connectionism and the philosophy of psychology

The bulk of the philosophical literature on connectionism has focused on one of two issues: first, the prospects of cognitive architecture proving to be thoroughly connectionist; and, second, the consequences for folk psychology should it prove to be so.

There is nothing approaching a consensus regarding the second issue. Some philosophers argue that connectionism could vindicate folk psychology (for example, Horgan and Tienson 1995); others, that it would entail the elimination of many folk-psychological notions, for example, belief (Ramsey *et al.* 1990). One obstacle to adjudicating such disputes is that it is unclear how wrong folk psychology must be for eliminativism to follow; another is that it is controversial exactly what folk psychology entails (Stich and Warfield 1995). For example, it has been claimed that folk psychology is committed to the view that having beliefs requires having sentence-like mental representations. It is true that according to the *classical computational* theory of belief, a belief that *P* consists in a disposition to compute in certain ways with a mental sentence that means that *P*. However, this account of belief is a scientific hypothesis, not something implied by folk psychology. Similarly, it has been claimed that folk psychology is committed to the view that when an agent acts, some, but not all, of the agent's beliefs and desires play a causal role in producing the action. However, this too is an open question: some philosophers view folk psychology as an interpretive device, rather than as a system of causal hypotheses (see FOLK PSYCHOLOGY; ELIMINATIVISM).

Perhaps the most serious obstacle to adjudicating these disputes is that there is nothing approaching a consensus about what connectionist *cognitive* architecture would be like. For example, some connectionists maintain that a connectionist cognitive architecture would contain sentence-like representations as a phenomenon emerging from the network (Smolensky *et al.* 1992). Indeed, there is no consensus about what kinds of network activity would count as realizing mental activity or what sorts of network states would count as realizing beliefs, desires, intentions or the like. While there has been much interesting connectionist work in cognitive modelling, a connectionist alternative to the classical conception of cognition as rule-governed symbol manipulation has yet to be articulated. The value of discussions of whether folk psychology would be vindicated is that they bring this issue of an alternative conception into bold relief (see COGNITIVE ARCHITECTURE; LANGUAGE OF THOUGHT).

7 Crux of the classical/connectionist debate

Discussions of the prospects of cognitive architecture proving to be thoroughly connectionist have taken place in the context of discussions of whether a connectionist theory of cognition could replace the classical theory.

It is universally acknowledged that cognitive architecture is not a Turing machine architecture (in which a scanner reads and prints symbols on an infinitely long tape – see TURING MACHINES), nor a von Neumann architecture (in which a central processor controls what occurs in different addresses – see NEUMANN, J. VON). The classical theory of cognition is not committed to either of these classical architectures. Neither is it committed to any extant classical programming languages such as LISP (or 'list processor'), nor to rules being explicitly represented, to processing being sequential ('serial' as opposed to 'parallel'), to data structures being explicitly stored in memory locations, nor to there being an executive overseer. Classicism is committed only to our cognitive architecture including (1) a symbol system with a compositional syntax (a 'language of thought') and (2) types of algorithmic and heuristic causal processes in which complex symbols participate in virtue of their logico-syntactic structure (see LANGUAGE OF THOUGHT; MIND, COMPUTATIONAL THEORIES OF). The crux of the classicism/connectionist architecture debate is whether an adequate cognitive architecture could fail to include both (1) and (2).

According to proponents of replacement connectionism, connectionism can yield an adequate, alternative theory of cognitive architecture to the classical theory. Jerry Fodor and Zenon Pylyshyn (1988) have raised the most widely discussed challenge to this position. They point out that classicism can explain systematic relationships among capacities to have thoughts involving the exercise of the same concepts in the same intentional mode (for example, belief, desire, intention and so on): for example, that someone able to think that the dog is chasing the cat would normally be able to think that the cat is chasing the dog, and that someone able to want the cat to be on the mat would normally be able to want the mat to be on the cat. They point out, further, that classicism can explain the 'productivity' of thought – that is, the fact that people can have a potential infinitude of thoughts; and that it can explain the inferential coherence of thought processes, for example, the truth-preserving relations between premises and conclusions in a valid argument. They challenge replacement connectionists to show how a connectionist architecture could explain such phenomena without implementing a classical one.

One response to the challenge is to concede that it cannot be met, and to embrace the implementational option, or propose some mixed architecture. Another is to reject the challenge on the grounds that there are no such cognitive phenomena to be explained. A third is to attempt to meet the challenge: to show how connectionism could explain such phenomena without implementing a classical architecture. While each response has defenders, discussion has focused mainly on the third. It is generally acknowledged that networks with only local representations are inadequate to explain the cognitive phenomena in question. However, some connectionists (most notably Smolensky 1991, 1995) argue that it is possible for a network architecture with distributed representations to yield explanations of systematicity, productivity and inferential coherence without implementing a classical architecture. Whether this is so is a subject of intense debate (see, for example, Fodor and McLaughlin 1990; McLaughlin 1993a, 1993b, 1997). The potential role of connectionism in the computational theory of cognition remains unresolved.

See also: COGNITIVE ARCHITECTURE; MODULARITY OF MIND

References and further reading

Aizawa, K. (1992) 'Connectionism and Artificial Intelligence: History and Philosophical Interpretation', *Journal of Experimental Artificial Intelligence* 4: 295–313. (Excellent historical discussion of connectionism.)

Bechtel, W. and Abrahamsen, A. (1991) *Connectionism and the Mind*, Oxford: Blackwell. (Presently the most comprehensive philosophical discussion of the connectionist approach to cognition.)

Broadbent, D. (1985) 'A Question of Levels: Comments on McClelland and Rumelhart', *Journal of Experimental Psychology* 114: 89–192. (Raises the issue of whether connectionism and classicism may be concerned with phenomena at different levels of organization or description.)

Churchland, P.M. (1995) *The Engine of Reason, the Seat of the Soul: A Philosophical Journey into the Brain*, Cambridge, MA: MIT Press/Bradford Books. (Includes an examination of the role of connectionism in understanding the mind/brain.)

* Churchland, P.S. and Sejnowski, T.J. (1992) *The Computational Brain*, Cambridge, MA: MIT Press/Bradford Books. (An excellent primer on the study of neural computation using artificial neural networks; and a key source for §5.)

Clark, A. (1989) *Microcognition*, Cambridge, MA: MIT Press/Bradford Books. (Examines the potential role of connectionism in the understanding of cognition.)

—— (1993) *Associative Engines: Connectionism, Concepts, and Representational Change*, Cambridge, MA: MIT Press/Bradford Books. (Addresses various problems faced by connectionist models of cognitive phenomena.)

Davies, M. (1991) 'Concepts, Connectionism, and the Language of Thought', in W. Ramsey, S. Stich and D. Rumelhart (eds) *Philosophy and Connectionist Theory*, Hillsdale, NJ: Erlbaum. (Argues that it may be a priori true that thought capacities are systematic; and discusses the prospects for eliminativism concerning beliefs and desires should cognitive architecture prove to be thoroughly connectionist.)

Dietterich, T.G., Hild, H. and Bakirir, G. (1990) 'A Comparative Study of ID3 and Backpropagation for English Text-to-Speech Mapping', *Proceedings of the Seventh International Conference on Machine Learning* 24–31. (Comparative study of a classical learning system and a network using back-propagation on NETtalk data sets.)

* Dinsmore, J. (1992) 'Thunder in the Gap', in J. Dinsmore (ed.) *The Symbolic and Connectionist Paradigms: Closing the Gap*, Hillsdale, NJ: Lawrence Erlbaum, 1–23. (Source of §1 diagram.)

Feldman, J.A. and Ballard, D.H. (1982) 'Connectionist Models and Their Properties', *Cognitive Science* 6: 205–54. (In addition to popularizing the term 'connectionism', this essay proposed the controversial 'one hundred step constraint' on algorithms based on the fact that a neuron can fire only about 100 times in the time it takes a human cognizer to perform various recognition tasks, such as recognizing a familiar word.)

* Fisher, D. and McKusick, K.B. (1989) 'An Empirical Comparison of ID3 and Backpropagation', *Proceedings of the Sixth Workshop on Machine Learning* 169–73. (Comparative study of classical learning systems and a network using backpropagation.)

* Fodor, J. and McLaughlin, B.P. (1990) 'Connectionism and the Problem of Systematicity: Why Smolensky's Solution Doesn't Work', *Cognition* 35: 183–204. (Responds to an attempt by Smolensky (1991) to show how a connectionist architecture could explain systematicity without implementing a classical architecture.)

* Fodor, J. and Pylyshyn, Z. (1988) 'Connectionism and Cognitive Architecture: A Critical Analysis', *Cognition* 28: 3–71. (Argues that if connectionism is to provide an adequate, alternative theory of cognition to classicism, a connectionist architecture must be able to explain systematicity, productivity and inferential coherence without implementing a classical (language of thought) architecture.)

Gelder, T. van (1991a) 'Classical Questions, Radical Answers: Connectionism and the Structure of Mental Representations', in T. Horgan and J. Tienson (eds) *Connectionism and the Philosophy of Mind*, Dordrecht: Kluwer, 355–1. (Argues that cognitive psychology is undergoing a Kuhnian paradigm shift from the classical to a connectionist paradigm, and that the new connectionist paradigm need not answer questions framed in terms of the old classical paradigm.)

—— (1991b) 'What is the "D" in "PDP"? A Survey of the Concept of Distribution', in W. Ramsey, S. Stich and D. Rumelhart (eds) *Philosophy and Connectionist Theory*, Hillsdale, NJ: Erlbaum, 33–60. (Attempts to explicate the notion of a distributed representation.)

* Hebb, D. (1949) *The Organization of Behavior*, New York: Wiley & Sons. (An important early work on neural networks.)

* Hinton, G.E. (1977) 'Relaxation and its Role in Vision', unpublished doctoral dissertation, University of Edinburgh. (Presents the network approach to best-match problems described in §3.)

Horgan, T. and Tienson, J. (eds) (1991) *Connectionism and the Philosophy of Mind*, Dordrecht: Kluwer. (Anthology of papers examining the potential role of connectionism in understanding cognition.)

* —— (1995) 'Connectionism and the Commitments of Folk Psychology', *Philosophical Perspectives* 9: 127–52. (Argues that connectionism may well be able to vindicate folk psychology.)

—— (1996) *Connectionism and the Philosophy of*

Psychology, Cambridge, MA: MIT Press/Bradford Books. (Defends the view that the mind is a dynamic system realized in a system of neural networks.)

Marinov, M.S. (1993) 'On the Spuriousness of the Symbolic/Subsymbolic Distinction', *Minds and Machines* 3: 253–70. (Examines comparative studies of networks using back-propagation and classical top-down inductive decision trees; and argues that classicism, like connectionism, can avail itself of 'subsymbols', that is, symbols for microfeatures.)

McClelland, J.L. and Rumelhart, D.E. (1988) *Explorations in Parallel Distributed Processing: A Handbook of Models, Programs, and Exercises*, Cambridge, MA: MIT Press/Bradford Books. (An excellent beginning work book in connectionist modelling, which contains a discussion of best-match problems and Hinton's method for solving them that served as a source for §3. Readers who seek a working knowledge of such modelling should begin here.)

McClelland, J.L., Rumelhart, D.E. and the PDP Research Group (1986) *Parallel Distributed Processing: Explorations in the Microstructure of Cognition,* vol. 2, *Psychological and Biological Models*, Cambridge, MA: MIT Press/Bradford Books. (Volume 2 of the two 'bibles' of connectionism. Obligatory reading for students of connectionism.)

* McLaughlin, B.P. (1993a) 'The Connectionism/Classicism Battle to Win Souls', *Philosophical Studies* 70: 45–72. (Examines various aspects of the connectionism/classicism debate about the nature of cognitive architecture.)

* —— (1993b) 'Systematicity, Conceptual Truth, and Evolution', in C. Hookway and D. Peterson (eds) *Royal Institute of Philosophy*, supplement 34: 217–34. (Argues that the Fodor–Pylyshyn challenge to connectionism would remain even if it is a conceptual truth that thought capacities are systematic; argues that capacities for perceptual representations may be systematic; and argues that the systematicity of thought cannot be explained solely by appeal to natural selection.)

* —— (1997) 'Classical Constituents in Smolensky's ICS Architecture', in M.L. dalla Chiara, K. Doets, D. Mundici and J. van Benthem (eds) *The Tenth International Congress of Logic, Methodology and Philosophy of Science, Florence, August 1995*, vol. 2, *Structures and Norms in Science*, Dordrecht: Kluwer, 331–43. (A response to Smolensky (1995).)

McLaughlin, B.P. and Warfield, T.A. (1994) 'The Allure of Connectionism Reexamined', *Synthese* 101: 365–400. (Argues against the widespread misconception that connectionist architectures are better suited to modelling the learning of pattern recognition abilities than are classical architectures.)

* Minsky, M.A. and Papert, S. (1969) *Perceptrons*, Cambridge, MA: MIT Press. (A famous critique of perceptrons – simple two-layered networks – which, they argue, cannot compute exclusive 'or'.)

* Mooney, R., Shavlik, J., Towell, G. and Gove, A. (1989) 'An Experimental Comparison of Symbol and Connectionist Learning Algorithms', *Proceedings of the Eleventh International Joint Conference on Artificial Intelligence* 775–70. (Comparative study of classical learning systems and a network using back-propagation.)

Pinker, S. and Prince, A. (1988) 'On Language and Connectionism: Analysis of a Parallel Distributed Processing Model of Language Acquisition', *Cognition* 28: 73–193. (A critique of Rumelhart and McClelland's connectionist model of verbs in the past tense; also contains a discussion of general issues concerning the potential role of connectionism in cognitive science.)

* Prince, S. and Smolensky P. (1993) *Optimality Theory: Constraint and Interaction in Generative Grammar*, technical report TR-2, New Brunswick, NJ: Rutgers Center for Cognitive Science, Rutgers University. (Development of an account of grammar along connectionist lines.)

* Quinlan, J.R. (1987) 'Generating Production Rules from Decision Trees', *Proceedings of the Eleventh International Conference on Artificial Intelligence* 304–7. (Argues that top-down inductive decision trees are production systems.)

Raggett, J. and Bains, W. (1992) *Artificial Intelligence from A to Z*, London: Chapman and Hall. (A valuable source of simple explanations for many of the technical terms used in this entry.)

* Ramsey, W., Stich, S. and Garon, J. (1990) 'Connectionism, Eliminativism and the Future of Folk Psychology', *Philosophical Perspectives* 4: 499–533. (Argues that connectionist architectures cannot capture the propositional modularity of beliefs and desires: the fact that some but not all beliefs and desires will play a causal role in producing intentional actions; and they argue further that given this, if cognitive architecture is thoroughly connectionist, eliminativism concerning belief and desire will be warranted.)

Ramsey, W., Stich, S. and Rumelhart, D. (eds) (1991) *Philosophy and Connectionist Theory*, Hillsdale, NJ: Erlbaum. (Anthology containing original essays on philosophical issues concerning connectionism.)

Rey, G. (1991) 'An Explanatory Budget for Connectionism and Eliminativism', in T. Horgan and J. Tienson (eds) *Connectionism and the Philosophy of Mind*, Dordrecht: Kluwer, 219–40. (Spells out a variety features of propositional attitudes that are explained by classicism and challenges connectionists to say how they can capture them.)

Rumelhart, D.E., McClelland, J.L. and the PDP Research Group (1986) *Parallel Distributed Processing: Explorations in the Microstructure of Cognition*, vol. 1, *Foundations*, Cambridge, MA: MIT Press/Bradford Books. (Volume 1 of the two 'bibles' of connectionism; a key source for §1. Begin your reading here.)

* Sejnowski, J. and Rosenberg, C. (1987) 'Parallel Networks That Learn to Pronounce English Text', *Complex Systems* 1: 145–68. (Presents NETtalk.)

* Sereno, M. (1988) 'The Visual System', in I.W. Seelen, U.M. Leinhos and G. Shaw (eds) *Organization of Neural Networks*, Wienheim: VCH, 167–84. (Examination of aspects of the visual system in terms of neural networks.)

Sethi, I.K., and Jain, A.K. (eds) (1991) *Artificial Neural Networks and Statistical Pattern Recognition*, Amsterdam: Elsevier/North Holland. (Essays on neural networks, top-down inductive decision trees and pattern recognition.)

* Shavlik, J., Mooney, R. and Towell, G. (1991) 'Symbolic and Neural Learning Algorithms: An Experimental Comparison', *Machine Learning* 6: 111–43. (Includes some of the comparative studies between TDIDTs and networks using back-propagation, described in §4.)

Smolensky, P. (1988) 'On the Proper Treatment of Connectionism', *Behavioral and Brain Sciences* 11: 1–74. (Explicates a connectionist view of cognition.)

* —— (1991) 'Connectionism, Constituency and the Language of Thought', in B. Loewer and G. Rey (eds) *Meaning in Mind: Fodor and His Critics*, Oxford: Blackwell, 223–90. (A response to the Fodor–Pylyshyn challenge to explain how a connectionist architecture can explain systematicity without implementing a classical architecture.)

* —— (1995) 'Reply: Constituent Structure and Explanation in an Integrated Connectionist/Symbolic Architecture', in C. Macdonald and G. Macdonald (eds) *Connectionism: Debates on Psychological Explanation*, Oxford: Blackwell, 223–90. (Further develops the response in Smolensky (1991) to the Fodor–Pylyshyn challenge; and responds to Fodor and McLaughlin (1990).)

* Smolensky, P., Legendre, G. and Miyata, Y. (1992) 'Principles for an Integrated Connectionist/Symbolic Theory of Higher Cognition', technical report CU-CS-600–92, Boulder, CO: Department of Computer Science, University of Colorado. (Develops an architecture that integrates features of connectionist and symbolic architectures; an architecture Smolensky (1995) claims can be used to explain systematicity and productivity without implementing a classical architecture.)

* Stich, S. and Warfield, T. (1995) 'Reply to Clark and Smolensky: Do Connectionist Minds Have Beliefs?', in C. Macdonald and G. Macdonald (eds) *Connectionism: Debates on Psychological Explanation*, Oxford: Blackwell. (A reply to papers by Clark and Smolensky arguing that, contra Ramsey, Stich and Garon (1990), connectionist architectures can accommodate beliefs.)

BRIAN P. McLAUGHLIN

CONSCIENCE

To have a conscience involves being conscious of the moral quality of what one has done, or intends to do. There are several elements under the idea of conscience. First, conscience can signify those very moral convictions persons cleave to most firmly and judge themselves by. Second, the notion may cover the faculty by which we come to know moral truths (assuming there to be such) and apply them to ourselves. Third, conscience can be said to concern the examination by a person of the morality of their desires, actions and so on. Finally, conscience can involve guilt: one can suffer from a 'bad conscience'. In the Christian tradition, conscience can be viewed as 'the voice of God within' each of us. Several of these aspects of conscience are expressed in Milton's lines from Paradise Lost, *when God says: 'And I will place within them as a guide/My umpire Conscience' (III: 194–5).*

There are many elements comprehended under the idea of conscience, and it is sensible to consider these separately since they do not always occur together. First, someone's conscience may be considered to comprise those fundamental moral convictions by keeping to which they retain a sense of their moral integrity and decency as people. In this sense something is 'a matter of conscience', or raises 'questions of conscience', if it touches on such central personal principles. According to this signification, different people can have markedly different consciences, but, it would be argued, we should still respect each person's conscience since to force them to violate the demands of their conscience is to force them to give up their sense of their own integrity. This line of argument may be resisted, however. We are told that some Nazis saw carrying out the extermination programme as a matter of conscience. To force them not to do this does not seem to involve a moral problem. In reply, it can be said that only consciences which are 'enlightened' require respect. The question whether conscience can be enlightened, or fallible and perverted, leads on to a second strand in thinking about conscience.

According to this strand, a person's conscience comprises their capacity to come to acquire moral standards for their own conduct; or, more specifically, their capacity to come to know moral truths (see MORAL KNOWLEDGE §1). This sense, strictly more basic than *conscientia* itself, is referred to as *synderesis* or *synteresis* by Aquinas (*Summa theologiae*), by which he means the power to grasp fundamental moral principles, a power supposedly common to all persons and one which, if functioning appropriately, results in our all knowing the same basic principles. However these very basic principles (such as 'Do good' and 'Eschew evil') are too general to help us know how to act in particular circumstances. We require also a capacity to derive more concrete principles which will give us moral guidance, and a capacity to apply these appropriately to our own circumstances. These two secondary functions are the province of conscience strictly understood, according to Aquinas. Errors in conscience can arise in deriving these more specific rules of conduct or in their application even if *synderesis* is held to be infallible. Questions can arise, analogous to those referred to earlier, about whether it is better to follow one's conscience even though it may prove to be fallible or to violate one's conscience which, if it is erroneous, may then mean one ends up doing the right thing. Talk of a 'perverted' conscience may mean that a person's ultimate convictions are judged to be perverse, as in the first strand identified; or that their capacity to know good from evil, in general or in the particular case, has been distorted or corrupted.

Building on the above, we may note a third emphasis in the idea of conscience, to do with the care, intensity and frequency with which someone examines the moral credentials of their desires, feelings, actions and omissions. Someone may have an 'overworked' or 'oversensitive' conscience, by making too much a matter of moral self-scrutiny or by being too scrupulous about any and every moral doubt which may arise (if one can be overscrupulous about such things). On the other hand, a person's conscience may be 'fast asleep' and need 'awakening' or 'quickening', as in the famous painting by Holman Hunt, 'The Awakening Conscience' (1852). They do not lack a conscience, but rather the will or disposition to use it. Joseph Butler (1726), in a sensitive and important discussion of the moral significance of conscience, emphasized that conscience sometimes 'without being consulted, without being advised with, magisterially exerts itself' (Sermon II) (see BUTLER, J. §§2–4). I take this to mean that sometimes without, or against, our will or deliberate intention we find ourselves judging our own intentions and deeds critically and in condemnation. This thought leads on to the last aspect of conscience to be considered.

A person may first become aware that they have done something they feel to be wrong or wicked through experiencing feelings of uneasiness, guilt, or a vague sense of oppression. It may take some thought to discover what deed these feelings attach to, but they can be regarded as central manifestations of having a 'bad conscience' about it. Feelings of remorse, shame, dismay, torment and guilt, all forms of self-punishment following from self-condemnation, are major elements in the functioning of conscience. A clear, easy or happy conscience does not usually bring self-congratulatory feelings with it (that would be more like self-righteousness), merely the absence of the pains of a troubled conscience. Popular morality likes to believe that no-one can escape from the toils of a guilty conscience in the end if they commit some terrible deed, however hard they try.

The self-punitive strand in conscience has particularly attracted the attention of psychoanalysts including Freud (1930). Some people can be crippled in their capacity for active life by the savagery and relentlessness of self-punitive guilt incident to, say, feeling aggressive or sexual impulses. Freud held that children 'internalize' powerful parental figures as part of their development and, in doing so, can subject themselves to very severe judgments felt to be emanating from these figures. The 'super-ego' thus conceived can confront and harangue the child's ego, and inhibit its expression (see FREUD, S. §8; PSYCHOANALYSIS, POST-FREUDIAN §2). To gain relief from such savage self-censure is not, of course, to become amoral or conscienceless; it is simply to adopt a less punitive attitude to moral endeavour.

It has been argued that moral regulation via the medium of an inner witness, self-judgment and self-punishment, is not so central to all cultures as it has been to our own. Some anthropologists contrast 'guilt' cultures with 'shame' cultures; in the latter it is fear of public exposure and loss of 'face' which is the principal vehicle of moral regulation (see MORAL SENTIMENTS §3).

It is inappropriate to ask which of the above four aspects of conscience comprises its essence or makes up what it 'really' is. In different contexts one or more of these aspects may be in view and it is more important to appreciate the variety of elements here than it is to determine which of them is definitive of conscience.

See also: COMMON-SENSE ETHICS; INTUITIONISM IN ETHICS; MORAL AGENTS

References and further reading

* Aquinas, T. (1266–73) *Summa theologiae* (Synopsis of Theology), ed. T. Gilby, London: Eyre & Spottiswoode, 1970, vol. 11, Ia.79.11–13; 1966, vol. 18, IaIIae.19.5–8. (Foundational discussion of profound significance.)

Benedict, R. (1946) *The Chrysanthemum and the Sword*, Rutland, VT: Charles E. Tuttle, ch. 10. (Important discussion of guilt and shame cultures.)

Bennett, J. (1974) 'The Conscience of Huckleberry Finn', *Philosophy* 49: 123–34. (A very witty and incisive discussion of erroneous conscience.)

* Butler, J. (1726) *Fifteen Sermons Preached at the Rolls Chapel*, Sermons I, II, III, XI, XII; repr. in *Five Sermons Preached at the Rolls Chapel and A Dissertation Upon the Nature of Virtue*, ed. S. Darwall, Indianapolis, IN: Hackett Publishing Company, 1983. (Another foundational discussion of great importance, in which conscience is presented as part of a hierarchical account of the elements of human motivation.)

D'Arcy, E. (1961) *Conscience and Its Right to Freedom*, London: Sheed and Ward. (Through an examination of the historical sources and of contemporary debate, argues for a moral obligation to follow judgments of conscience made in good faith and for a right to religious freedom.)

Freud, S. (1912) 'Totem Und Tabu', *IMAGO* 1: 213–27, 301–333; trans. and ed. J. Strachey, 'Totem and Taboo', in *The Standard Edition of the Complete Psychological Works of Sigmund Freud*, vol. 13, London: Hogarth Press, 1955, part II, 'Totem and Emotional Ambivalence'. (Considers problems of social psychology from the point of view of psychoanalysis, and compares taboo prohibitions with obsessional neuroses.)

—— (1927) *Die Zukunft Einer Illusion*, Leipzig, Vienna and Zurich: Internationaler Psychoanalytischer Verlag; trans. and ed. J. Strachey, *The Future of an Illusion*, in *The Standard Edition of the Complete Psychological Works of Sigmund Freud*, vol. 21, London: Hogarth Press, 1955. (Presents an account of conscience in terms of the work of a punitive super-ego.)

* —— (1930) *Das Unbehagen In Der Kultur*, Leipzig, Vienna and Zurich: Internationaler Psychoanalytischer Verlag; trans. and ed. J. Strachey, *Civilisation and its Discontents*, in *The Standard Edition of the Complete Psychological Works of Sigmund Freud*, vol. 21, London: Hogarth Press, 1955. (A more extensive account of the development of conscience in terms of the renunciation of instinctive gratification and the formation of the super-ego.)

Jones, D.H. (1966) 'Freud's Theory of the Moral Conscience', *Philosophy* 41: 34–57. (Critical assessment of Freud's theories.)

Lewis, C.S. (1967) *Studies in Words*, Cambridge: Cambridge University Press, ch. 8. (An exceptionally illuminating etymological essay, in which the evolution of the terms related to the nature and exercise of conscience is related to deepening understanding of its significance.)

Potts, T.C. (1982) 'Conscience', in N. Kretzmann, A. Kenny, J. Pinborg (eds) *The Cambridge History of Later Medieval Philosophy*, Cambridge: Cambridge University Press. (A survey of medieval theories of conscience.)

Wallace, J.D. (1978) *Virtues and Vices*, Ithaca, NY: Cornell University Press, ch. 4. (A careful discussion of many aspects of conscience.)

NICHOLAS DENT

CONSCIOUSNESS

Philosophers have used the term 'consciousness' for four main topics: knowledge in general, intentionality, introspection (and the knowledge it specifically generates) and phenomenal experience. This entry discusses the last two uses. Something within one's mind is 'introspectively conscious' just in case one introspects it (or is poised to do so). Introspection is often thought to deliver one's primary knowledge of one's mental life. An experience or other mental entity is 'phenomenally conscious' just in case there is 'something it is like' for one to have it. The clearest examples are: perceptual experiences, such as tastings and seeings; bodily-sensational experiences, such as those of pains, tickles and itches; imaginative experiences, such as those of one's own actions or perceptions; and streams of thought, as in the experience of thinking 'in words' or 'in images'. Introspection and phenomenality seem independent, or dissociable, although this is controversial.

Phenomenally conscious experiences have been argued to be nonphysical, or at least inexplicable in the manner of other physical entities. Several such arguments allege that phenomenal experience is 'subjective'; that understanding some experiences requires undergoing them (or their components). The claim is that any objective physical science would leave an 'explanatory gap', failing to describe what it is like to have a particular experience and failing to explain why

581

there are phenomenal experiences at all. From this, some philosophers infer 'dualism' rather than 'physicalism' about consciousness, concluding that some facts about consciousness are not wholly constituted by physical facts. This dualist conclusion threatens claims that phenomenal consciousness has causal power, and that it is knowable in others and in oneself.

In reaction, surprisingly much can be said in favour of 'eliminativism' about phenomenal consciousness; the denial of any realm of phenomenal objects and properties of experience. Most (but not all) philosophers deny that there are phenomenal objects – mental images with colour and shape, pain-objects that throb or burn, inner speech with pitch and rhythm, and so on. Instead, experiences may simply seem to involve such objects. The central disagreement concerns whether these experiences have phenomenal properties – 'qualia'; particular aspects of what experiences are like for their bearers. Some philosophers deny that there are phenomenal properties – especially if these are thought to be intrinsic, completely and immediately introspectible, ineffable, subjective or otherwise potentially difficult to explain on physicalist theories. More commonly, philosophers acknowledge qualia of experiences, either articulating less bold conceptions of qualia, or defending dualism about boldly conceived qualia.

Introspective consciousness has seemed less puzzling than phenomenal consciousness. Most thinkers agree that introspection is far from complete about the mind and far from infallible. Perhaps the most familiar account of introspection is that, in addition to 'outwardly perceiving' non-mental entities in one's environment and body, one 'inwardly perceives' one's mental entities, as when one seems to see visual images with one's 'mind's eye'. This view faces several serious objections. Rival views of introspective consciousness fall into three categories, according to whether they treat introspective access (1) as epistemically looser or less direct than inner perception, (2) as tighter or more direct, or (3) as fundamentally non-epistemic or nonrepresentational. Theories in category (1) explain introspection as always retrospective, or as typically based on self-directed theoretical inferences. Rivals from category (2) maintain that an introspectively conscious mental state reflexively represents itself, or treat introspection as involving no mechanism of access at all. Category (3) theories treat a mental state as introspectively conscious if it is distinctively available for linguistic or rational processing, even if it is not itself perceived or otherwise thought about.

1 **Pre-Cartesian uses of 'consciousness'**
2 **Post-Cartesian uses of 'consciousness'**
3 **Subjectivity and the phenomenal**
4 **Dualism and the phenomenal**
5 **Eliminativism and the phenomenal**
6 **Introspection and the phenomenal**
7 **Completeness of introspection**
8 **Reliability of introspection**
9 **Introspection as inner perception**
10 **Alternatives to inner perception**

1 Pre-Cartesian uses of 'consciousness'

As elsewhere in philosophy, Descartes' writings mark a major shift in philosophical preoccupation with consciousness (see DESCARTES, R.). Pre-Cartesian philosophers of mind rarely emphasize the terms 'conscious' or 'consciousness' (or clear equivalents). Post-Cartesian philosophers of mind rarely avoid such emphasis. This section compares Descartes' usage with earlier usage.

Descartes typically speaks of being 'conscious' to refer to an allegedly *intimate* source of knowledge about *one's own* mental occurrences. In the 'Conversation with Burman' he says that 'to be conscious is both to think and to reflect on one's thought' (1648: 335), where the term 'thought' extends widely, as in the 'Second Replies', to 'everything that is within us in such a way that we are immediately conscious of it' including 'all the operations of the will, the intellect, the imagination and the senses' (1641: 113). Descartes seems to treat everything mental as introspectively conscious, in these passages and elsewhere (see the 'Fourth Replies', 1641: 171). Elsewhere, however, Descartes seems to deny that introspection is complete, as in the *Discourse on Method*: 'many people do not know what they believe, since believing something and knowing that one believes it are different acts of thinking, and the one often occurs without the other' (1637: 122).

The resulting focus on the scope and limits of introspective knowledge (see §§6–7) is apparently responsible for the modern uses of 'conscious' and 'non-conscious' to mark a potential distinction between two kinds of mental states. Introspected states are (introspectively) conscious, while others, if any, are (introspectively) unconscious. Pre-Cartesian authors do not use the word 'conscious' to mark such a distinction, although some may be committed to the distinction, either implicitly or in other terms (Whyte 1962). To take a rather spectacular example, SOCRATES claims in Plato's *Meno* that since one's soul 'has been born many times' and 'has learned everything that there is', 'seeking and learning are in fact nothing but recollection' (81c–d). This seems to require that one has latent knowledge of which one can at best become aware with great difficulty (see PLATO §11).

Many pre-Cartesian writers share commitment to a special fountain of reflective knowledge, often called 'inner sense'. In *Summa theologiae* Aquinas posits a 'common sense' which enables one, for example, to 'tell white from sweet', and adds that this common sense 'is also able to sense sensation itself, as when somebody sees that he is seeing' (I.78.4). This responds to Aristotle's apparent claim, in *On the Soul*, that it is 'by sight that one perceives that one sees' rather than by another sense (III 2, 425b12). On these views, the subject matter of such inner awareness is more restricted than for Descartes, including sensation but perhaps not other mental processes. It may even be that, for Aristotle, the relevant 'inner' perception – by which one sees that one sees – is directed at one's external sense organs *themselves* and not at anything Descartes would consider strictly 'mental'.

A nearer equivalent to 'introspective consciousness' is the Sanskrit term '*manas*', used widely in Hindu texts for a 'mind-organ' that functions like the external sense organs. For instance, the *Vaiśeṣika Sūtra* (*c*. 3rd century BC) claims that 'Intellect, pleasure, pain, desire, aversion, effort are perceptible by the internal organ' (Radhakrishnan and Moore 1957: 411). This inner perception is carefully distinguished from 'inferential knowledge', and is framed so as not to involve introspection of a 'self'. Indeed, while Descartes holds that he can introspect himself as a 'thinking thing', Hinduism characteristically claims that introspection reveals no 'true self' distinct from one's mental states, and Buddhism characteristically denies that there are 'thinking things' at all (see MOMENTARINESS, BUDDHIST DOCTRINE OF; SELF, INDIAN THEORIES OF).

The word 'conscious' derives from the Latin words '*cum*' ('together with') and '*scire*' ('knowing'). In the original sense, two people who know something together are said to be conscious of it 'to one another', with the irresistible connotation that they are privy to a scandalous secret. By extension, one can be conscious 'to oneself' of secret shames – whence the original use of 'consciousness' for conscience, the inner accuser silently sharing knowledge of one's transgressions. This archaic moral sense of 'consciousness' is not a concern in this entry (see CONSCIENCE).

The Latin conjunction of '*cum*' and '*scire*' also has a use in which the prefix is merely emphatic, so that being 'conscious of' something simply means knowing it, or knowing it well. In this sense the word 'conscious' can also be used as an adjective: a 'knowing' being such as a normal person is a conscious being, while an 'unknowing' being such as a plant or sleeping person is an unconscious being.

'Conscious', like 'knowing', can be used in this way for things *with* minds but not for things with*in* minds, such as mental states. People and animals know things – are conscious of things – but mental states do not themselves know things. Thus, for example, Aquinas uses 'conscious' to describe *bearers* of mental states – such as human beings, animals and God – but not to describe mental states – not even 'seen' seeings. Since the main philosophical problems about consciousness concern the more modern distinction between conscious and unconscious *states*, this entry focuses neither on the distinction between conscious and unconscious *subjects*, nor on the broad 'knowing' sense of 'conscious' (see KNOWLEDGE, CONCEPT OF). In effect, Descartes refashions the 'knowing well' sense of 'conscious', regimenting it for a *particular* source of knowing, introspection. Issues about the specific epistemological status of introspection are a central concern of this entry.

2 Post-Cartesian uses of 'consciousness'

Descartes' use of 'consciousness' for reflective knowledge spread rapidly through the next generation of European philosophers. In *An Essay concerning Human Understanding* Locke writes, as he does of 'reflection', that 'Consciousness is the perception of what passes in a Man's own mind' (1689: II.i.19); Leibniz's term for this is 'apperception'. In his *Critique of Pure Reason* Kant goes on to distinguish between 'empirical apperception' of a 'flux of inner appearances' – mentioning that 'Such consciousness is usually named *inner sense*' – and 'transcendental apperception' which is alleged to be a 'pure original unchangeable consciousness' that reveals a 'fixed and abiding self' (A107; see KANT, I. §6). This entry discusses one's introspective access to the 'flux' of particular events within one's mind, rather than substantive introspective knowledge about one's self – about whether one is made of physical or spiritual components, and whether one persists through time (see MIND, BUNDLE THEORY OF; INTROSPECTION, EPISTEMOLOGY OF §4; PERSONAL IDENTITY).

In the broader 'knowing' sense (see §1), a creature is conscious of something just in case it knows something, independently of whether this knowing is itself introspectible. This ancient sense of 'conscious' lingers on, and broadens to cover any kind of belief or cognition (whether or not it is 'knowledge'), and any kind of attitude about something (whether or not it is 'cognitive'). In this sense, a creature has consciousness if it has any kind of 'intentional' mental state. By extension, the state itself can be said to be a state of consciousness, even if it is not introspectible. (This is distinct from the widespread claim that all conscious states are intentional – that 'all consciousness...is consciousness of something' (Sartre 1943: 11). On this broad sense of 'conscious', by definition, all 'ofness' is conscious ofness.) As twentieth-century philosophers of mind and language most often pursue concerns about intentionality using terms other than 'consciousness', intentionality will not be explored in this entry (see INTENTIONALITY).

In a still broader sense, 'mind' and 'consciousness' are synonyms, as are 'being mindful of' something and 'being conscious of' it, so that any kind of mental state (whether or not it is an 'attitude') is a state of consciousness. When HEGEL (§5), MARX or LUKÁCS speak of 'unhappy', 'false' or 'class' consciousness, or when political activists attempt to 'raise' conscious-ness, their concerns are usually equally well rendered using a general term such as 'knowledge', 'thinking', 'attitudes' or 'mentality' in place of 'consciousness'. It is not clear that their concern is with introspection, since they refer mainly to thoughts about (or seemingly about) non-mental things, independently of whether these thoughts are themselves introspec-tively conscious. (When Hegel refers to thoughts explicitly about the mind, he uses 'self-consciousness' rather than 'consciousness'.) Likewise, many scientific writings officially on 'consciousness' are about mentation and mentation-like activity in general, avoiding any question of whether the activity is introspectively conscious. Since these broad uses of 'consciousness' seem to introduce no distinctive philosophical perplexities, this entry puts them aside.

With the dawn of scientific psychology in the late nineteenth century, the central philosophical contro-versies about consciousness centre around whether consciousness can ever be explained by an objective science of the mind. The biologist Thomas Huxley provides an early attempt to express the sense of mystery: 'How it is that anything so remarkable as a state of consciousness comes about as a result of irritating nervous tissue, is just as unaccountable as the appearance of Djin when Aladdin rubbed his lamp' (1866: 210). Since that time there have been many scientific advances in understanding the me-chanisms of perception, thought and communication, and many philosophical advances in understanding the nature of intentionality and meaning. According to Thomas Nagel and many other philosophers, such advances must leave an unexplained residue, concern-ing *what it is like* to have phenomenally conscious experiences (as illustrated in the introduction; see NAGEL, T. §4). Nagel writes that 'Consciousness is what makes the mind–body problem really intract-able', identifying 'subjectivity' as its most troublesome feature:

Fundamentally an organism has conscious mental states if and only if there is something it is like to *be* that organism – something it is like *for* the organism. We may call this the subjective character of experience...every subjective phenomenon is essentially connected with a single point of view, and it seems inevitable that an objective, physical theory will abandon that point of view.

(1974: 166–7)

Until quite recently, the agenda for the philosophy of mind has been set more by epistemology than by the sciences of mind. Consequently, introspective consciousness has been the most central and im-portant philosophical notion of consciousness. The remainder of the entry is divided between the explanation of phenomenal consciousness and the epistemology of introspective consciousness.

3 Subjectivity and the phenomenal

Nagel argues that physical theories cannot explain one's phenomenal consciousness, because they aban-don one's point of view (see §2). Science does indeed abandon one's point of view, in so far as one need not be able to understand or defend the theory (if one lacks relevant concepts or evidence), and in so far as subjects with other points of view should be able to understand and defend the theory. But does abandon-ing a point of view prevent *describing* the point of view, or the features viewed from that point? Even if Nagel is correct that one's point of view and one's phenomenal experience are 'essentially' connected, they may not be *exclusively* connected. An objective physical theory of phenomenal consciousness would presumably allow that phenomenal features are accessible from multiple points of view – for instance, both by some form of introspection and by some form of neurophysiological or psychological observation and theory. Furthermore, if experiences are *necessa-rily* introspectible or introspected (see §6) this might explain Nagel's claim that phenomenal features are 'essentially connected with a single point of view'.

Frank Jackson (1982) amplifies Nagel's challenge in his 'knowledge argument' against 'physicalism', the thesis that the world is wholly physical. He imagines a super-scientist, Mary, who has never seen anything coloured because she lives her life in a black-and-white room. From a black-and-white television in this room, she learns *all* the objectively specifiable physical (and causal or 'functional') facts in the world. When she finally leaves the room and first sees colour, Jackson argues, she learns a *new* fact about the nature of phenomenal experience; she might exclaim, 'Oh! It is like *this* to see red!' The new fact Mary learns cannot be identical to a physical or functional fact, or else it would be among the facts Mary already knows before leaving the room. So no wholly physicalist account of phenomenal facts can be true (see COLOUR AND QUALIA; QUALIA).

Most responses to Jackson's argument involve denying that Mary learns a new fact upon experiencing red. On some views, she learns *how* to do new things – to imagine experiencing redness or to recognize redness visually – without coming to know *that* any new fact obtains. On others, she learns that an *old* physical fact about experience obtains, but comes to know it *in a new way* – via introspective access or via new concepts. For example, one proposal (Lycan 1990) compares the relevant introspective ways of representing one's experiences with *simple inner-perceptual demonstratives*, ways of knowing colour experience that would be unavailable to Mary from within the black-and-white room. Consider an analogy: when one perceives a banana and thinks of it demonstratively – as 'this' – those who do not perceive the banana cannot think of it in the same way – simply as 'this' (while staring at something else). Likewise, if one's introspections of one's experiences involve some demonstratives of them, this would explain why these representations cannot strictly be shared by someone who does not 'perceive' the same experiences but merely thinks *about* them. (For marks against this strategy, see Raffman 1995; for further elaboration, see Tye 1995: 173–8.)

Even among philosophers who accept that phenomenal consciousness is *some* physical or functional process, there are doubts about the possibility of explaining it. Colin McGinn (1991) suggests that human beings are forever blocked from knowing the 'link' between the brain and consciousness, roughly because introspective consciousness gives no knowledge of brains, while neuroscientific access to brains gives no access to consciousness. Critics respond that one might learn the explanatory link by theoretical inference from *joint* introspective and scientific data, such as correlations between phenomenal features and brain states (see Flanagan 1992: ch. 6).

In slightly different ways, Jackson, Joseph Levine (1993) and David Chalmers (1996) argue that even if one can know what this 'link' *in fact* is, explanations based upon it cannot be as satisfying as other scientific explanations. In essence, the argument is that for any objective, scientific account of phenomenal consciousness, one can *conceive* of a creature that meets the conditions in the account but *lacks* phenomenal consciousness. In the extreme case, it is said, one can conceive of a world that is an exact *physical* duplicate of the actual world – complete with duplicate stars, planets, rocks, plants, animals and

philosophers – but which lacks any phenomenal consciousness. All the human-like beings in that world would be non-phenomenal 'zombies'. So the prescientific concept of phenomenal consciousness is not such that scientific premises could necessitate, a priori, conclusions about the phenomenal. In Levine's terms, there is an 'explanatory gap' between physical reality and phenomenal consciousness. By contrast, for example, it is claimed that the prescientific concept of 'water' is such that scientific premises about H_2O, can necessitate, a priori, conclusions about water. In particular, it is held to be part of our *concept* of water that *if* there is anything roughly unique in the lakes and rivers around us that has a preponderance of features such as boiling, eroding rocks, quenching thirst and so on, then it is water. If science establishes that H_2O meets this condition, then there is no further conceptual possibility that H_2O is not water.

At least three lines of response may be advanced against the explanatory gap argument. One concedes that no scientific premises a priori necessitate conclusions about the phenomenal, but insists that the same is true for scientific explanations of water, and so on. Perhaps someone who believes in water but denies that it boils, is in lakes and so on is making a *false* and *bizarre* claim but are not strictly *contradicting* themselves. The fate of this response presumably depends on the fate of general reservations about a priori or conceptual necessity (see ESSENTIALISM; A PRIORI).

The second strategy also concedes the lack of a priori necessity, but attributes it to the idiosyncratic ways in which phenomenal facts are represented – for example, by introspection-based demonstratives (see Tye 1995: 178–81; DEMONSTRATIVES AND INDEXICALS). By comparison, suppose that agent *A* holds banana *B* in front of his face, and comes to accept the demonstrative '*This* is a banana'. This conclusion cannot strictly be deduced from any demonstrative-free *descriptions* of the banana – that *B* is a banana in *A*'s hand, that *A* sees *B*, and so on. The subject could believe all of these premises, and still *conceive* that this is not a banana – perhaps by conceiving that he is not in fact agent *A*. This response to the explanatory gap seems at best to apply only to particular phenomenal conclusions, of the form: it is like *this* to have a given experience. It is an *incomplete* response, since there are phenomenal conclusions without demonstratives, namely, those of the form: there is *something* it is like to have a given experience.

The third strategy is to deny that there is an unbridgeable conceptual gap; in effect, to deny that zombies (non-phenomenal physical duplicates of phenomenal creatures) are even *conceptually* possible. In Nagel-like fashion, Robert Kirk analyses the concept of phenomenality as follows: a creature's phenomenal states are those with different 'characters' that are 'for the creature as a whole' (1994: ch. 5). He explains this in terms of neural states with different 'patterns of activation' that are 'directly available' to 'have different effects on processes of assessment, decision-making, and action initiation'. It follows that if a creature has states with characters for the creature, any physical duplicate of the creature does also. The problem is that Kirk's 'having character' does not express the same concept as Nagel's 'being like something'. Perhaps Kirk demonstrates how states can be 'for a creature', but he does not demonstrate that they are 'like something' for the creature, that is, phenomenal, in Nagel's full-blown sense. For example, *beliefs* may also be realized in different patterns of activation with the relevant direct availability, and so in that sense beliefs may be 'for' a creature, but beliefs are not clearly *themselves* 'like something' for a creature (see §6). Further analysis of the 'like something' idiom would be needed to complete this line of response to the explanatory gap (see BELIEF).

4 Dualism and the phenomenal

The attraction of subjectivity-based arguments against physicalism makes it important to understand the potential ramifications of various non-physicalist alternatives. The central metaphysical issues concern 'mental causation' and 'emergence' (see MENTAL CAUSATION). The two central epistemological ramifications concern knowledge of other minds and knowledge of one's own mind (see OTHER MINDS).

Physical science promises an explanation of physical events wholly in terms of other physical events. For example, unsupported objects fall, not because they *want* to fall, but because of gravitational forces. Similarly, a large group of neurons cause another neuron to fire, not because of its embarrassment due to peer pressure or its fear of a mob, but because of electrochemical forces. In this way, there should be a purely physical explanation of the activities of brains in producing (reflex or non-reflex) behaviour. Yet *phenomenal consciousness* also seems to have physical consequences on behaviour. When one feels an itch, one scratches; this seems to be in large part *because* of what it is like to itch. But how can an itchy *feel* make a difference, if there is a purely physical explanation of one's hand motions? The physicalist may make room for phenomenal causation by maintaining that the feel of an itch is *wholly constituted by* (or, perhaps, identical with) features of the brain and body (see MIND, IDENTITY THEORY OF). The *feel* causes the hand motion, because it is *made of* things that do so,

just as the *brain* causes the hand motion by being composed of things that do so (that is, neurons). But this strategy is unavailable to the non-physicalist who thinks there are mental objects, properties or states that are not wholly composed of physical entities (see DUALISM). One possibility for the dualist is to maintain that some physical events are *inexplicable* purely in physical terms – this is Descartes' own position about non-reflex behaviour. Another prominent strategy is to defend 'epiphenomenalism' about the phenomenal, or the idea that, contrary to appearances, phenomenal features are irrelevant to the generation of physical events (see Jackson 1982; Chalmers 1996: ch. 4; EPIPHENOMINALISM).

If phenomenal states and features are not wholly constituted by physical states and features, how *are* they constituted? One idea, prevalent among neuroscientists, is that the phenomenal 'emerges' from physical *interactions*. By analogy, water has properties that are not explicable by the properties of hydrogen and oxygen separately. Water dissolves salt, but neither hydrogen nor oxygen does so separately (nor does hydrogen dissolve *part* of salt and oxygen the rest). Analogously, the whole of a phenomenal experience is taken to be more than the sum of its physical parts (that is, the physical entities that help realize it). The initial plausibility of such analogies seems to depend on a too-narrow conception of the 'parts' of a complex entity. A water molecule does have hydrogen and oxygen atoms as parts, but it also has various *relations* among these atoms as other 'parts'. The physical relation of *bonding*, for instance, is as necessary for water as the atoms are. If *all* of the parts of water are counted, it is not clear that water has properties inexplicable by the properties of these parts. This kind of 'emergence' conclusion – one that forgets to 'sum' some of the parts of a whole – is compatible with a wholly physicalist account of water, and of consciousness. In the absence of better analogies, non-physicalist philosophers have more commonly denied that there is *genuine* emergence, emergence of new features that are *inexplicable* in terms of combinations of other features. This leads some non-physicalists to the startling 'panpsychist' claim that mental 'ingredients' of phenomenal consciousness must be present in the tiniest bits of matter capable of comprising brains, and to the claim that phenomenal consciousness is a *fundamental* part of nature – perhaps along with subatomic mass and charge (see Chalmers 1996: 8; PANPSYCHISM).

Epiphenomenalism and panpsychism exacerbate the epistemological problem of other minds, but in opposite directions. It seems that we have excellent, even if not quite *perfect*, justification for believing that other people have experiences. Plausibly, talk of experiences is not simply disguised talk of others' observable behaviour, but is instead to be *inferred* from behaviour with some degree of theoretical risk. Perhaps the inference is in part grounded on drawing an analogy between oneself and others, but inference from a *single* case gives one at best meagre justification for conclusions about others. The residual problem of other minds, then, is to explain how one attains an appropriate level of justification. The physicalist can maintain that one is justified in part because the phenomenal features of experience help explain behaviour – in fact, help cause it. But the epiphenomenalist seems forced to deny this, potentially rendering it *too hard* to attain knowledge of other minds. The panpsychist, on the other hand, renders it *too easy* to attain such knowledge; not only other people but other animals, plants, rocks and protons have mental features.

A final danger with the idea that phenomenal consciousness depends on nonphysical features is that it threatens self-knowledge about one's phenomenal states. The nonphysicalist who believes that zombies are possible believes that two people could be alike in all non-phenomenal respects, while one has phenomenal experience and the other does not. Each could be fully convinced of their own rich, detailed phenomenal experience, but one would be wrong. It is difficult to see how either could justify their belief that they are *not* a zombie, if zombies are possible. Chalmers tries to address this problem by stipulating that non-zombies are *necessarily* distinctively justified:

> To have an experience is automatically to stand in some sort of intimate epistemic relation to the experience – a relation that we might call 'acquaintance.' There is not even a conceptual possibility that a subject could have a red experience like this one without having *any* epistemic contact with it: to have the experience is to be related to it in this way.... [This] is to stand in a relationship to it more primitive than belief: it provides *evidence* for our beliefs, but it does not in itself constitute belief.
> (1996: 196–7)

This conclusion anticipates the idea that inner perceptions of one's experiences – taken to be more 'primitive' than reflective beliefs about one's experiences – are necessary for phenomenal consciousness (see §6). But where the non-zombie has inner perceptual states, by hypothesis the zombie has them also. Perhaps what zombies have are *misperceptions*, but this need not lessen their *justification* in accepting these misperceptions at face value, and in believing they have experiences.

Also, the heavy reliance on introspections of experience opens up two alternatives for physicalism.

The first is to deny that there is experience at all, but only the favoured kind of introspections *as of* experience. The second – perhaps the more attractive – is to maintain that the favoured kind of introspections are *sufficient* for experience. This is to invert Chalmers' claim that 'to have the experience is to be related to it in this [inner perceptual] way'; if so, this is precisely because to be related to a state in this inner perceptual way is to have an experience. Neither strategy carries obvious commitment to anything nonphysical. (For related objections to 'absent qualia', see Shoemaker (1984: chaps 9, 14); and for a response, see Block (1980). Rey (1986) extends the point, arguing that *non*-psychological requirements on phenomenal consciousness – perhaps biological or neurophysiological ones – would also jeopardize introspective knowledge of experience; see also Chalmers (1996: 7).)

5   Eliminativism and the phenomenal

In addition to subjectivity-based arguments, phenomenally conscious experiences provide other interesting arguments against physicalism. In certain experiences one seems to be aware of phenomenal denizens of an inner mental world: coloured and shaped mental 'images', bodily 'sensations' such as 'pains' that may be throbbing or in one's limb, and inner 'speech' with 'private' volume and pitch. Such alleged mental objects as afterimages, pains and inner speeches, that are naturally reported as having properties of non-mental objects (for example, roundness, throbbingness or loudness), may be called 'phenomenal objects'. The argument against physicalism based on reports of phenomenal objects is simple. In such experiences nothing in one's brain or body or (causally relevant) environment is literally purple and round, literally throbbing in a limb, or literally soft and medium-pitched. So if phenomenal objects do exist with these properties, they are not among the things in one's brain or body or environment. One must be either a dualist (see §4) or an 'eliminativist' about mental entities with these properties; that is, the physicalist must deny that objects with such properties exist (see ELIMINATIVISM).

The challenge for the eliminativist about phenomenal objects is to explain why people are often *tempted* to claims of phenomenal objects, with ordinary perceptible properties. Broadly, the temptation may be attributed to an *ambiguity* or *looseness* in ordinary reports of experiences, or to an *illusion* built into the experiences themselves, which may then be reported strictly and faithfully. Following a suggestion due to Ned Block, Michael Tye (1995) pursues the former strategy by pointing out that people often describe representations as *having* properties that they merely *represent*: the phrase 'a warm thermostat setting' may be used for a thermostat setting *of* warmth, and 'a nude painting' may be used for a painting *of* nudity. It should be no surprise then that people describe experiences *of* colour and shape as themselves *being* coloured and shaped, and so no surprise that, speaking freely, they treat them as images. The other strategy is latent in J.J.C. Smart's suggestion that 'There is, in a sense, no such thing as an after-image... though there is such a thing as the experience of having an image' (1959: 151). On one straightforward construal of 'the experience of having an image', an experience itself *represents* that there is an image with certain features, although there is no such thing (compare with Sartre's 'illusion of immanence', 1940: 5). The illusory-experience view has an advantage over the reporting-based view to the extent that afterimages *look* purple and round, pains *feel* dull or in motion, and inner speech seems to *sound* faint or high-pitched. By contrast, a warm thermostat setting need not itself feel warm, and a nude painting need not itself look nude (any more than other paintings look *clothed*). However, without an account of why experiences misrepresent phenomenal objects, the illusory-experience view does not adequately discharge the eliminativist's explanatory burden (for one account, see Rey 1997).

In addition to phenomenal objects, eliminativists have targeted alleged 'phenomenal properties' of experiences, or 'qualia'. There is not merely 'something' it is like to have a phenomenally conscious experience, but some *particular* 'thing' or things it is like. People sometimes *try* to describe these particular properties, for example, by saying that a given pain is 'sharp' or 'throbbing' to some degree, or that a given visual image is 'blurry' or 'moving'. Even if the eliminativist about phenomenal objects is correct that there are only experiences *as of* sharp throbbing pains and *as of* blurry moving images, descriptions such as 'sharp' and 'blurry' seem in some indirect or nonliteral way to convey particular aspects of what it is like to have these experiences. In a relatively cautious use of the word 'qualia', particular what-it-is-like properties, whatever their nature turns out to be, are qualia.

There are bolder uses of 'qualia' on which the word can apply only to properties of experience that pose challenges to scientific explanation. Some require qualia to be infallibly and completely accessible to introspection, which is puzzling on any plausible scientific explanation of introspection (see §§7–8). Some require qualia to be inaccessible without introspection – for instance by purely behavioural or neurophysiological tests that one may perform on other people, without relying on an introspective understanding of one's own experience; this seems to preclude explanation of qualia as physical properties discoverable in multiple objective ways (see §3). Perhaps the most controversial philosophical idea about qualia, however, is that they are 'intrinsic' properties of experience. Metaphysicians dispute the correct account of intrinsicality, but the following may serve to convey the intuitive idea, as it applies to experience: for an experience to have a property intrinsically, the experience must have the property solely in virtue of the *spatiotemporal parts* of what realizes the experience. (This is meant to exclude everything that even in part exists when or where the experience does not, for example, stimuli that cause the experience, and behaviour and other mental states that the experience causes.) This seems to preclude explaining qualia in 'functionalist' terms by appeal to the causal role of experiences, or in 'intentionalist' terms by appeal to the representational content of experiences (see FUNCTIONALISM). Defenders of the intrinsicality of qualia often argue for the possibility of 'inverted qualia', cases in which two experiences differ in qualia even though they have identical causal or representational relations to their mental and non-mental surroundings (see Block 1990).

Qualia in such bold senses have been rejected most forcefully by Dennett (§3). He describes several examples in which changes in whether we like or dislike certain tastes seem to change the tastes themselves, concluding that when someone 'thinks of "that taste" he thinks equivocally or vaguely' and 'need not try – or be able – to settle whether he is including any or all of his reactions' (1988: 61–3). Nevertheless he accepts that, through the changes in likes and dislikes, 'the taste is (sort of) the same', and defenders of intrinsicality may hope to explain such taste similarities by appeal to reaction-independent components of experiences (see Lormand 1994 for further defence of bold qualia).

An argument against the existence of intrinsic qualia can be built upon what G.E. Moore calls the 'diaphanousness' of perceptual experience:

The moment we try to fix our attention upon consciousness and to see *what*, distinctively, it is, it seems to vanish: it seems as if we had before us a mere emptiness. When we try to introspect the sensation of blue, all we can see is the blue: the other element is as if it were diaphanous.

(1903: 450)

Gilbert Harman argues as follows:

When you see a tree, you do not experience any features as intrinsic features of your experience.

Look at a tree and try to turn your attention to intrinsic features of your visual experience. I predict that you will find that the only features there to turn your attention to will be features of the presented tree, including relational features of the tree 'from here'.

(1990: 39)

Defenders of intrinsicality may claim not to satisfy Harman's prediction. This response gains plausibility in cases of degraded perception (for example, blurred or double vision), and it is not clear how Harman's argument is supposed to generalize from perceptual experiences to bodily-sensational, imaginative or thought experiences (see BODILY SENSATIONS; IMAGERY). (For discussion of imagery by a philosopher in sympathy with Harman, see Tye (1995).) The prediction may hold for non-degraded perceptual experiences and perhaps 'upgraded' imaginings such as dreams, and in these cases perhaps it shows that no experienced features *seem* intrinsic to experience. One may hold that some experienced features *are* intrinsic to experience, but only by incurring a burden of explaining why these features seem to belong to trees and other non-mental objects. In fact, this burden remains even if qualia are taken to be *relational* features of perceptual experience, since the relevant experienced features are experienced as if they belong *objectively* to trees, and do not seem in experience to depend on the participation of the perceiver. Just as the eliminativist about phenomenal *objects* of experiences would do well to explain the illusory experience of their *presence*, so the *non*-eliminativist about phenomenal *properties* of experience – whether intrinsic or relational – would do well to explain the illusory experience of their *absence* (see QUALIA).

6 Introspection and the phenomenal

Here the discussion begins to shift from phenomenality to introspection. To clarify the apparent difference between phenomenal and introspective consciousness, consider whether a state can be conscious in one but not the other sense. Can there be *nothing* it is like to have a state, even when one is introspectively aware of it? Can there be *something* it is like to have a state, even when one is wholly unaware of it? The *facts* are murky and controversial, but it is important to be clear about the *possibilities*.

The introduction lists four kinds of states that are most clearly phenomenal: perceptual experiences, bodily-sensational experiences, imaginative experiences and streams of thought. There are mental states not explicitly on this list, notably 'propositional attitudes' such as the belief that snow is white (see

PROPOSITIONAL ATTITUDES). Usually one's belief that snow is white is latent and unintrospected, though one can raise it to introspective consciousness easily. Normally there seems to be something it is like to have such an introspectively conscious belief (see BELIEF). However, there is another possibility to explore. What having the belief 'is like' may be completely accounted for by what it is like to have experiences *accompanying* the belief, such as auditory imaginings of asserting the words 'Snow is white' (or 'I believe snow is white', or 'Mon Dieu! La neige! Blanche!'), or visual imaginings of some fictitious white expanse of snow, together with what William James (1890: 287–8) describes as feelings or imaginings of moving eyeballs, eyelids, brow, breath, jaw-muscles and so on as one thinks. Pending evidence of further aspects of what it is like to have the belief, this illustrates how there can be something it is like *when* one has an introspectively conscious state, although the state itself has no phenomenal character (Lormand 1996). Introspective consciousness – at least of the sorts available to beliefs – is unlikely simply to *be* phenomenal consciousness, and is unlikely to be *sufficient* for it.

Might introspection nevertheless be *necessary* for phenomenality? There is a tension between a 'yes' answer and the view that many species of animals can have experiences – that there is something it is like for cats and dogs to feel pain or to see bright lights, for instance. It is implausible that these beings have Cartesian reflective knowledge *that* they feel pain and see. This would require having *concepts* of feeling pain and of seeing, and perhaps a *self*-concept, and all this would seem to involve capacities beyond the reach of most nonhuman animals – for example, the ability to conceive of *others* as feeling pain and seeing, and the ability to *remember* or *envisage* oneself feeling pain and seeing (see ANIMAL LANGUAGE AND THOUGHT). Notoriously, Descartes himself accepts that nonhuman animals are 'automata' without mental states of any sort. Defenders of a reflective-knowledge requirement may either mimic this strategy, denying that animals have conscious experiences (Carruthers 1992), or else attempt to minimize the conceptual sophistication needed for the reflective knowledge (Rosenthal 1990).

This tension is more commonly taken to be a serious strike against a reflective-knowledge requirement on phenomenality (see, for example, McGinn 1982: 52; Dretske 1995: 18), especially given that a similar tension arises in the case of human infants. Thomas Reid objects against Locke that 'reflection ought to be distinguished from consciousness', since:

From infancy, till we come to the years of understanding, we are employed solely about external objects. And, although the mind is conscious of its operations, it does not attend to them; its attention is turned solely to the external objects, about which those operations are employed.

([1785] 1969: 57)

Even for beings with the requisite conceptual capacities, it seems implausible that reflective knowledge must accompany *each* of their experiences. At any given moment one can attend only to a small proportion of the sensory stimuli one encounters. It is also difficult to attend simultaneously to the outside world and to one's experience of it, as Auguste Comte argues (1842: 21): 'The thinking individual cannot cut himself in two – one of the parts reasoning, while the other is looking on' (see INTROSPECTION, PSYCHOLOGY OF). Nevertheless, plausibly, there is something many inattentive perceptions of unattended stimuli are like; experience would be quite impoverished were it not for the contributions of background noises and odours, pressures on one's feet or seat, moisture under one's tongue, peripheral vision and so on. It is possible to maintain that one continually forms reflective *beliefs* about these experiences, but this fits poorly with the difficulty of *remembering* these experiences (after they change, for example).

An introspective requirement on phenomenality can blunt much of the force of these objections by distinguishing inner *perception* from the formation of reflective *beliefs*, and by distinguishing *inattentive* introspection from *attentive* introspection. Just as one might sense a daffodil without having a concept of daffodils, or a tendency to remember the daffodil, so perhaps one can inwardly sense an experience without having a concept of experiences, or a tendency to remember the experience. Animals and babies might sense even if they cannot form beliefs; likewise, perhaps they can inwardly sense even if they cannot form reflective beliefs (see BELIEF). Also, according to Locke, just as there can be passive sensation, so reflection need not be done intentionally or with attention (1689: II.i.7). Along these lines, Brentano distinguishes between inner *perception*, which may be automatic and inattentive, and inner *observation*, which is actively guided by purposeful attention (1874: 29). It is true that a creature's most pressing cognitive needs require mental resources to be directed at the *external* world, but if inner perception is normally inattentive, it need not draw resources away from attentive outer perception (see BODILY SENSATIONS). It is an open question whether there can be phenomenal experiences without any kind of introspective awareness of them, even of a primitive sort (but see §7 below).

7 Completeness of introspection

Perhaps more thoroughly than Descartes (see §1), Locke identifies the mental with the introspectively conscious, claiming that it is unintelligible 'that any thing *thinks without being conscious of it*, or perceiving, that it does so' because 'thinking consists in being conscious that one thinks' (1689: II.i.19). This completeness claim has been rejected by most subsequent philosophers, with the prominent exception of some in the broadly phenomenological tradition, following Franz Brentano and Edmund Husserl (see §10).

The main evidence for introspectively unconscious mental processes is that they would fill certain theoretical gaps in the scientific explanation of behaviour and introspectible mental activity. This inferential strategy is most prominent in psychoanalytic attempts to explain otherwise bizarre dreams, associations among concepts, apparent slips of the tongue, emotional disorders, neurotic physiological reactions and so on (see FREUD, S.; PSYCHOANALYSIS, POST-FREUDIAN; UNCONSCIOUS MENTAL STATES). Although the scientific status of such clinically-based explanations is controversial (see PSYCHOANALYSIS, METHODOLOGICAL ISSUES IN), alternative explanations are elusive; witness Sartre's difficulties in trying to explain self-deception and 'bad faith' without appeal to unconscious mentation (1943).

Furthermore, many replicable psychological experiments lead to parallel conclusions about introspectively unconscious mentation in more mundane settings. In one family of experiments (Lackner and Garrett 1972), subjects are presented with an ambiguous sentence in one ear, and disambiguating words in the other ear, but so quietly as not to be noticed consciously by the subjects – typically the stimulus is reported as a meaningless noise. Nevertheless, the subjects' interpretations of the ambiguous sentence are predictable from the meanings of the disambiguating words. This is evidence that subjects not only identify but *understand* the words, without introspective consciousness of doing so.

Similarly, there is evidence of vision without introspective consciousness of vision in cases of subliminal visual perception (Dixon 1987) and 'blindsight' (Weiskrantz 1988). In these cases subjects act on the basis of information about the visual features of objects, despite denying – sincerely – that they have relevant visual experiences. Blindsight subjects have damage to certain neural pathways connecting portions of the retina to the visual cortex, yet in some sense they have perceptual states sensitive to these stimuli. For example, some ability to discriminate an 'X' from an 'O' is intact. This is evidenced by the preponderance of correct answers they can give to questions about the stimuli. When asked to reach for objects in blindsight regions, also, some subjects reflexively pre-orient their hand and fingers in ways suited to the specific shapes of the objects. What blindsight patients lack most clearly is any ability to *introspect* their perceptual states and abilities: they deny that they are perceiving; they respond to the stimuli only when coaxed to do so; and even then they take themselves merely to be guessing. Nevertheless, their guesses tend to be correct and their behaviour appropriate to the stimuli.

It is not only in unusual cases that there seem to be introspectively unconscious perceptual states. On virtually all detailed theories of normal vision, for example, cells in each retina register the amount of incoming light at various points, and cause further states representing sudden discontinuities of incoming brightness, which cause further representational states and, eventually, introspectively conscious visual experiences (see VISION). These early layers of visual processing seem well beyond the reach of introspection. Although these processes (unlike, say, blood flow in the brain) have many mentation-like features – they are assessable as correct or incorrect in relation to external stimuli; they may increase gradually in stability as evidence for them mounts; they may play a direct role in modulating intentional visuomotor action, and so on – they are at best somewhere in the vague boundary between the mental and the non-mental.

To the extent that introspectively unconscious perceptual states are phenomenal, they present a new threat to the claim that introspection is necessary for phenomenality (see §6). Disagreement arises about whether cases of subliminal perception or blindsight involve phenomenal consciousness – perhaps blind-seeing is like something, despite the subject's sincere denials; at any rate the cases are not clear enough to weigh decisively against the necessity claim.

There is more dispute about whether non-intro-spectible information-bearing states in early visual processing are phenomenally conscious. On the view that they are, it would be difficult to explain why phenomenal visual experiences are not continually like double images, given that one has *separate* left-eye-caused and right-eye-caused early visual states. On behalf of the view, one possibility is that there is something it is like *for one's early visual systems* to have certain states, although there is nothing it is like *for one* to have them. Although this is a possibility, it seems no more likely than the possibility that there is something it is like *for one's neurons* when they fire.

8 Reliability of introspection

Even if introspective consciousness is limited, it may be epistemologically interesting as an especially reliable means of access within its domain (see INTROSPECTION, EPISTEMOLOGY OF). Many philosophers have thought that introspective access to mental facts is more reliable than access to other empirical facts. Augustine writes in *On the Trinity* that 'nothing can be more present to the mind than the mind itself' (X.3.5), and asks rhetorically, 'what is so intimately known as the mind, which perceives that it itself exists and is that by which all other things are perceived?' (VIII.6.9). Descartes devotes his *Second Meditation* to an argument that the mind is 'better known' than the body, and Locke also claims that our knowledge of 'Things without us' is 'not altogether so certain, as our intuitive Knowledge' (1689: IV.xi.3). As with completeness, most subsequent philosophers reject the *infallibility* of introspection, although many would agree that it is *relatively* reliable.

The claim of introspective infallibility is extremely bold. In other empirical domains, at best certain mechanisms keep one's beliefs in rough accord with the facts (for example, mechanisms of perception, reason and memory, and the persistence of facts when one is not continually checking them). But mechanisms fail; a mechanism of this complexity that could never possibly fail would be a miracle 'at least as mysterious as papal infallibility', according to Dennett (1988: 55). The same reason to expect fallibility holds for introspection: if there is the slightest mechanism correlating one's thoughts with one's thoughts about them, it should be breakable, and if there is no mechanism, a perfect correlation between the two would seem to be sheer luck.

Furthermore, scientific investigations of introspection have revealed widespread 'confabulation' in self-access. In identifying one's beliefs and motivations, one systematically but sincerely reports attitudes one thinks rational or statistically normal in the circumstances, even if one does not have them (see Nisbett and Wilson 1977; INTROSPECTION, PSYCHOLOGY OF). For instance, in the 'bystander effect', increasing the number of joint witnesses to a person's need decreases the likelihood that any of them will assist. But bystanders rarely report this as a factor in their decision whether to help, often claiming instead to have reached a decision based solely on their own likelihood of success. According to Nisbett and Wilson, much allegedly 'introspective' access to attitudes consists of self-directed, fallible guesses, based at best on common-sense abilities to rationalize behaviour. Also, since these abilities are at work in one's access to others' mental states, this self-directed guesswork provides some reason to suppose, with Ryle (1949), that introspective consciousness is not interestingly more reliable than access to other minds.

In the face of this evidence, the Cartesian may attempt to identify a restricted domain in which a kind of introspection is comparatively reliable (Ericsson and Simon 1993) or even infallible (Lormand 1994). The model of rationalizing or statistical guesswork does not extend easily to introspection of phenomenally conscious experiences. For example, untutored subjects offer consistent and apparently reliable reports of 'feelings' of stinging (rather than throbbing) pain when a limb has restricted blood flow. They seem not to infer these feelings in the way one might form beliefs about another's pain feelings, since no common-sense principles of rationality dictate that one should feel stinging rather than throbbing, and since the subject need know no relevant statistical information about how people feel in these circumstances.

Against any attempt to find a restricted domain safe for infallibility, Dennett argues that one can easily be wrong about the 'changes and constancies' in one's experience over even brief intervals of time (1988: 59). This weighs against infallible *memory* access to what it was like to have *past* experiences, though not against infallible or especially reliable access to *current* experiences.

9 Introspection as inner perception

How should introspective consciousness be explained? While Lockean inner perception (see §2) has some contemporary defenders, most notably David Armstrong (1980), this view has fallen on hard times in philosophy of mind.

How is inner perception supposed to be distinctively analogous to outer perception? Of course, inner perceptions are not generated by literal inner eyes, ears and their attendant experience-forming processes. Armstrong explains inner perception as being, like outer perception, 'selective' (incomplete), 'fallible' and 'causal'. This illuminates little, since probably all cognitive processes have these features, even one's most theoretical (versus perceptual) scientific beliefs, for example, those about quantum mechanics or cosmology. Another initially tempting idea is the Hindu one (see §1) that inner perception is a causal but *non-inferential* source of evidence about mental states (or, more cautiously, that it is as low as outer perception on flexible, all-things-considered inference). Might a mental state be introspectively conscious only if its bearer inwardly perceives the state, in this sense? One strong objection is that introspective access often involves self-directed theo-

retical inferences, often confabulatory ones (see §8). It is therefore best to restrict inner-perception views to current phenomenal experience (in accordance with the suggestions at the end of §8).

An influential objection is that inner perception requires phenomenal 'sense data' interposed between physical objects and one's perceptions of them (see SENSE-DATA; PERCEPTION). Accepting inner perception may seem to involve accepting that one at best perceives outer objects *indirectly* through perceptions of phenomenal mental entities. But such a mediation theory would have difficulty explaining why inwardly perceiving sense-data did not in turn require perceiving further entities ('sense-data data') and so on, infinitely. Such arguments against sense-data have been mounted against inner perception (as in Shoemaker 1994), but with unclear effect. Inner perceptions need not be *interposed* between objects and one's perceptions of them – the causal chain in perceiving a table need not proceed from the table to an inner perception and then to a perception of the table. Rather, on a more natural view, the causal chain goes directly from the table to a perception of the table, and then (in cases in which the table perception is introspectively conscious) to an inner perception of the perception of the table.

Dennett argues that inner perception of a 'Cartesian theatre' of consciousness would be too sharp to explain the vague conscious/unconscious distinction, and that inner perception is wasteful – 'once a discrimination has been made once [in outer perception], it does not have to be made again' (1991: 127). Yet it can be vague whether something is inwardly (or outwardly) perceived, and inner perception of an outer perception need not re-represent features the outer perception is *of*, but instead may newly represent features *of* the outer perception (see Lormand 1994, for further defence of inner theatres).

Perhaps the most influential objection to inner-perceptual introspection is based on Moore's 'diaphanousness' claim (see §5). The objection is that, since each outer-perceptual modality (seeing, hearing and so on) makes its own distinctive contribution to what experience is like, an additional modality of inner perception should be expected to make *its* own contribution, to change what it is like. But what it is like to introspect a perceptual experience seems simply borrowed from what it is like to have the experience itself (McGinn 1982: 50–1). When one tries to attend to features of normal experiences, one normally 'sees through' the experiences to outer objects. So a fundamental disanalogy between outer perception and alleged inner 'perception' is that the former, but not the latter, has its own phenomenology or perceptual quality. This is evidence against inner perception of current phenomenal experiences.

On the other hand, if inner perception is necessary for phenomenality (see §6), then instead of *borrowing* phenomenal qualities from an outer perception, as the diaphanousness objection alleges, inner perception helps *generate* these qualities together with the (otherwise phenomenally unconscious) outer perception. This may explain why inner perception does not add further qualia to an outer-perceptual experience; inner perception may *already* make its phenomenal contribution in the generation of an outer experience with qualia (see QUALIA).

10 Alternatives to inner perception

Two rivals to inner-perception accounts treat introspective access as epistemically *less* intimate than inner perception. First, James maintains that introspection is always retrospective (1890: 187–), largely in reaction to Comte's denial that the mind can simultaneously split between ordinary thinking and awareness of that thinking (see §6). James is unhappy with Brentano's response to Comte – that *inattentive perception* can be split between outer and inner domains – because James seeks to defend the reliance on careful, attentive introspective reports in experimental psychology (see JAMES, W. §2). Second, some maintain that introspection is always laden with theoretical (versus perceptual) inferences. The experimental evidence for confabulation and expectation-driven inference (see §8; compare with Lyons 1986) suggests that introspection is *often* theory-laden and retrospective, but does not suggest that *all* cases of introspective consciousness are, including the *seemingly* non-inferential consciousness of phenomenal experiences that *seem* to persist while being accessed.

One theory of consciousness that combines naturally with theory-ladenness is Rosenthal's 'higher-order thought' theory (1990). (A thought or belief is 'higher-order' in virtue of being about mental entities rather than non-mental entities.) According to Rosenthal's view, a mental state is conscious just in case one forms, in a suitably direct way, a thought that one has the state. The state may generate its higher-order thought through inference so long as these inferences are not themselves conscious. This condition is intended to rule out cases in which one comes to think about a state through very indirect inference – say, solely through believing the testimony of a psychologist. On this view, even if introspective access to phenomenally conscious experiences is somehow inferential, it would *seem* non-inferential simply because one lacks higher-order thoughts about the inferences.

At the other extreme from defenders of theory-ladenness and retrospection, many phenomenologists reject inner perception as not being intimate *enough* to explain introspective access. On one suggestion, some introspectively conscious mental states 'reflexively' represent *themselves* (in addition to representing other things). This conclusion is often embraced to avoid an infinite regress threatening the assumption that introspection is complete (see §6): an experience represents itself rather than being represented by a separate introspective state which (assuming completeness) must in turn be represented by a separate introspection of the introspection, and so on. BRENTANO argues that 'The presentation which accompanies a mental act and refers to it is part of the object on which it is directed' (1874: 128). HUSSERL also suggests that 'In the case of a perception directed to something immanent [that is, roughly, mental], . . . perception and perceived form essentially an unmediated unity, that of a single concrete cogitatio' (1913: 112). And SARTRE insists that 'the first consciousness of consciousness' – what he calls 'pre-reflective consciousness' – 'is one with the consciousness of which it is [a] consciousness' (1943: 13–14). Given the prevalence of inferential, confabulatory access to one's mental states, reflexivity theories, like inner-perceptual ones, are best restricted to current phenomenally conscious experiences rather than to other mental states. Again, there is a possibility that one's only access even to these experiences is somehow much more confabulatory or inferentially sensitive to expectations than ordinary perception is, but pending evidence for this possibility the restriction to phenomenal experiences is reflexivity's best hope.

Since one often suffers ordinary perceptual illusions, the more analogous introspection is to perception, the more likely it would be that one would suffer naïve introspective illusions about what one's conscious experiences are like. But it rarely if ever happens that one mistakes, say, a dull pain for a sharp pain, in the way that one mistakes a roadside cow for a horse. This may be evidence that introspection is sometimes neither inner perception nor self-directed theoretical inference, but a process with fewer breakable causal links. Some introspective access may be like one's psychologically *primitive* abilities to shift among mental states. Just as the transition from believing *that p and q* to believing *that p* presumably takes place without intermediate inference or inner perception, so might the transition from (say) believing *that p* to believing *that I believe that p*, or the transition from *having a dull pain* to believing *that I have a dull pain*. As Shoemaker proposes:

Our minds are so constituted, or our brains are so wired, that, for a wide range of mental states, one's being in a certain mental state produces in one, under certain conditions, the belief that one is in that mental state. This is what our introspective access to our own mental states consists in. The 'certain conditions' may include one's considering whether one is in that mental state.... The beliefs thus produced will count as knowledge, not because of the quantity or quality of the evidence on which they are based (for they are based on no evidence), but because of the reliability of the mechanism by which they are produced.

(1994: 268)

A challenge for this view is to explain lawful and systematic *patterns* among introspectible and non-introspectible states, without an *ad hoc* assumption, for each pattern, that it happens to be 'wired' to higher-order beliefs in the right way. For example, why are brain states governing autonomic bodily functions not introspectible? Why are perceptual experiences introspectible but not subliminal perceptions and early perceptual states? Why does it seem easier to introspect one's fleeting thoughts than one's deeply held beliefs?

All of the theories described thus far in this section reject the etymological suggestion that 'introspection' is a kind of inner perception, while retaining the assumption that a subject's introspective 'access' to a mental state is always a matter of somehow *representing* the state. Further alternatives emphasize other forms of access to a state, or the state's functional relations to processes other than a subject's awareness of them. Verbal reportability is the process most frequently appealed to as an alternative requirement for introspective consciousness (Dennett 1978), in keeping with ordinary and scientific reliance on reportability as a symptom of consciousness. One threat is that reportability may only seem relevant to consciousness because it correlates somewhat with inner-directed representation. Normally, in reporting, one *perceives* one's reporting – hears one's speech, feels one's facial motions, and so on – and is thereby in a position to *understand* one's reports – to recognize one's own voice and realize which mental states one's words express. By contrast, if there is speech without any kind of self-perception, perhaps as in some forms of hypnosis or sleeptalking, this may not seem sufficient for, or even relevant to, introspective consciousness.

Dennett's construct is nearer to Block's notion (1995) of 'access consciousness', as distinguished from introspection and from phenomenality. In Block's terms, a mental state is access conscious if it is poised for free rational control of inference and action. The relevant actions may, but need not, include verbal actions, and the relevant inferences may, but need not, include Cartesian reflective knowledge. Although access consciousness has played little role in the history of philosophical discussions of consciousness, many contemporary writers employ comparable notions in attempts to explain consciousness generally (Dennett 1991; Tye 1995; Chalmers 1996).

See also: AWARENESS IN INDIAN THOUGHT; COLOUR AND QUALIA; DUALISM; MATERIALISM IN THE PHILOSOPHY OF MIND; MIND, INDIAN PHILOSOPHY OF; NIRVĀṆA; PHENOMENOLOGICAL MOVEMENT; QUALIA; REDUCTIONISM IN THE PHILOSOPHY OF MIND; SPLIT BRAINS; SUPERVENIENCE OF THE MENTAL

References and further reading

* Armstrong, D. (1980) 'What is Consciousness?', in *The Nature of Mind*, Ithaca, NY: Cornell University Press, 55–67. (A sketch of an inner-perception view.)
* Block, N. (1980) 'Are Absent Qualia Impossible?', *Philosophical Review* 89: 257–74. (Answers 'no', in response to Shoemaker (1984: ch. 9). Clear but increasingly intricate as possible replies mount.)
* —— (1990) 'Inverted Earth', in J. Tomberlin (ed.) *Philosophical Perspectives*, vol. 4, Atascadero, CA: Ridgeview. (The inverted qualia argument mentioned in §5 is a sidelight to a novel argument against functionalism.)
* —— (1995) 'On a Confusion about a Function of Consciousness', *Behavioral and Brain Sciences* 18: 227–87. (Distinguishes access consciousness from phenomenal consciousness – see §10.)
* Brentano, F. (1874) *Psychology from an Empirical Standpoint*, trans. A. Rancurello *et al.*, London: Routledge & Kegan Paul, 1973. (Study of intentionality and reflexive consciousness.)
* Carruthers, P. (1992) *The Animals Issue*, Cambridge: Cambridge University Press. (Uses a higher-order-thought theory of consciousness to argue that nonhuman animals lack phenomenal experience.)
* Chalmers, D. (1996) *The Conscious Mind*, Oxford: Oxford University Press. (Appeals to subjectivity in a defence of dualism, epiphenomenalism and panpsychism about phenomenal consciousness.)
* Comte, A. (1842) *Introduction to Positive Philosophy*, trans. F. Ferré, Indianapolis, IN: Bobbs-Merrill, 1970. (Rejects introspection as a reliable means of knowledge.)
* Dennett, D. (1978) 'Toward a Cognitive Theory of Consciousness', in *Brainstorms*, Cambridge, MA:

MIT Press. (Characterizes conscious states as those available for linguistic report.)

* —— (1988) 'Quining Qualia', in A. Marcel and E. Bisiatch (eds) *Consciousness in Contemporary Science*, Oxford: Oxford University Press. (Challenges qualia claims, including intrinsicality and reliable access.)

* —— (1991) *Consciousness Explained*, Boston, MA: Little, Brown. (An attack on introspective theories of phenomenal consciousness, with some leanings towards eliminativism.)

* Dretske, F. (1995) *Naturalizing the Mind*, Cambridge, MA: MIT Press. (An attempt to explain consciousness in terms of 'information functions'; criticizes introspective theories of phenomenality.)

* Descartes, R. (1637, 1641, 1648) *The Philosophical Writings of Descartes*, trans. J. Cottingham, R. Stoothoff, D. Murdoch and A. Kenny, Cambridge: Cambridge University Press, 3 vols, 1984–91. (The boldest epistemological claims for introspection are in the *Fourth Replies*. I have used 'conscious' in place of the translator's 'aware' to render Descartes' Latin 'conscius' and French 'connaissant' and 'conscient'.)

* Dixon, N. (1987) 'Subliminal Perception', in R. Gregory (ed.) *The Oxford Companion to the Mind*, Oxford: Oxford University Press. (Brief overview of the research and controversies.)

* Ericsson, K. and Simon, H. (1993) *Protocol Analysis*, Cambridge, MA: MIT Press. (A scientific defence of introspective reliability against Nisbett and Wilson (1977) and others.)

* Flanagan, O. (1992) *Consciousness Reconsidered*, Cambridge, MA: MIT Press. (A good extended introduction to the central philosophical issues. Responds to McGinn (1991).)

* Harman, G. (1990) 'The Intrinsic Quality of Experience', in J. Tomberlin (ed.) *Philosophical Perspectives*, vol. 4, Atascadero, CA: Ridgeview. (Argues against intrinsic qualia using diaphanousness and the rejection of sense-data.)

* Husserl, E. (1913) *Ideas*, trans. W. Gibson, New York: Macmillan, 1962. (The classic work of phenomenology as a reflexive study of consciousness.)

* Huxley, T. (1866) *Lessons in Experimental Physiology* 8. (Early example of a long line of biologists who accept epiphenomenalism.)

* Jackson, F. (1982) 'Epiphenomenal Qualia', *Philosophical Quarterly* 32: 127–36. (Includes the 'knowledge argument' against physicalism and a defence of epiphenomenalism.)

* James, W. (1890) *The Principles of Psychology*, repr. Cambridge, MA: Harvard University Press, 1993. (Packed with sensitive but reasonably cautious

reports from the heyday of introspective psychology. Defends introspection as retrospection.)

* Kirk, R. (1994) *Raw Feeling*, Oxford: Clarendon Press. (Argues that phenomenal 'zombies' are conceptually impossible – see §4.)

* Lackner, J. and Garrett, M. (1972) 'Resolving Ambiguity: Effects of Biasing Context in the Unattended Ear', *Cognition* 1: 359–72. (Psycholinguistic experimental paradigm with implications for subliminal perception.)

* Levine, J. (1993) 'On Leaving out What it's Like', in M. Davies and G. Humphreys (eds) *Consciousness*, Oxford: Blackwell. (Careful statement of the 'explanatory gap' argument; emphasizes epistemological rather than metaphysical conclusions.)

* Locke, J. (1689) *An Essay concerning Human Understanding*, ed. P.H. Nidditch, Oxford: Oxford University Press, 1975. (Classic work of empiricism; treats consciousness as complete and infallible 'reflection'.)

* Lormand, E. (1994) 'Qualia! (Now Showing at a Theater near You)', *Philosophical Topics* 22: 127–56. (A defence of qualia and introspective theories of phenomenal consciousness against Dennett (1988, 1991).)

* —— (1996) 'Nonphenomenal Consciousness', *Noûs* 30: 242–61. (Argues that conscious moods and attitudes are non-phenomenal and uses this to criticize theories of phenomenal consciousness.)

* Lycan, W. (1990) 'What is the Subjectivity of the Mental?', in J. Tomberlin (ed.) *Philosophical Perspectives*, vol. 4, Atascadero, CA: Ridgeview. (A friend of inner perception treats subjectivity.)

* Lyons, W. (1986) *The Disappearance of Introspection*, Cambridge, MA: MIT Press. (A valuable historical survey of theories of introspection, and a defence of theory-ladenness.)

* McGinn, C. (1982) *The Character of Mind*, Oxford: Oxford University Press. (A brief but rich introduction to philosophy of mind; criticizes inner sense.)

* —— (1991) *The Problem of Consciousness*, Oxford: Blackwell. (Denies that human beings can ever grasp *how* consciousness is physical, even if it is.)

* Moore, G.E. (1903) 'The Refutation of Idealism', *Mind* 12: 433–53. (Introduces diaphanousness by way of arguing against the claim that *esse* is *percipi*.)

* Nagel, T. (1974) 'What is it Like to be a Bat?', repr. in *Mortal Questions*, Cambridge: Cambridge University Press, 1979. (Made the 'what it is like' idiom and subjectivity arguments popular in philosophical discussions of qualia.)

* Nisbett, R. and T. Wilson (1977) 'Telling More Than We Can Know: Verbal Reports on Mental

Processes', *Psychological Review* 84 (3): 231–59. (Influential psychological case for confabulatory and expectation-driven access to attitudes.)

* Radhakrishnan, S. and Moore, C. (1957) *A Source Book in Indian Philosophy*, Princeton, NJ: Princeton University Press. (Includes ancient references to inner perception among both defenders of Hindu tradition and sceptics.)

* Raffman, D. (1995) 'On the Persistence of Phenomenology', in T. Metzinger (ed.) *Conscious Experience*, Thorverton: Imprint Academic. (Argues that the physicalist cannot use demonstrative or descriptive introspection to explain subjectivity.)

* Reid, T. (1785) *Essays on the Intellectual Powers of Man*, repr. Cambridge, MA: MIT Press, 1969. (An attempt to inject 'common sense' into empiricism; emphasizes existence of pre-attentive consciousness.)

* Rey, G. (1986) 'A Question about Consciousness', in H. Otto and J. Tuedio (eds) *Perspectives on Mind*, Dordrecht: Reidel. (Argues that our concept of consciousness is over-simple and incoherent; uses first-person knowledge against spiritual and biological accounts.)

* —— (1997) *Contemporary Philosophy of Mind: A Contentiously Classical Approach*, Oxford: Blackwell. (Chapter 11 provides a relatively detailed functionalist theory of some phenomenal states, and attempts to explain mistaken 'reification' of phenomenal properties.)

* Rosenthal, D. (1990) 'A Theory of Consciousness', ZIF Report 40, Bielefeld: Center for Interdisciplinary Research. (A higher-order-thought theory.)

* Ryle, G. (1949) *The Concept of Mind*, London: Hutchinson. (Attack on Descartes' dualism and epistemological claims, and defence of philosophical behaviourism.)

* Sartre, J.-P. (1940) *The Psychology of Imagination*, trans. New York: Philosophical Library, 1948. (Sustained attack on the illusion of immanence.)

* —— (1943) *Being and Nothingness*, trans. H. Barnes, New York: Philosophical Library, 1956. (Classic work of existential phenomenology; defends 'pre-reflexive consciousness'.)

* Shoemaker, S. (1984) *Identity, Cause, and Mind*, Cambridge: Cambridge University Press. (Chapter 9 is an intricate defence of functionalism against zombies; chapter 14 is an intricate reply to Block (1980).)

* —— (1994) 'Self-Knowledge and "Inner Sense"', *Philosophy and Phenomenological Research* 54: 249–314. (An extended attack on inner perception.)

* Smart, J. (1959) 'Sensations and Brain Processes', *Philosophical Review* 68: 141–56. (Defence of materialism against phenomenal-object and other objections.)

* Tye, M. (1995) *Ten Problems of Consciousness*, Cambridge, MA: MIT Press. (An attempt to explain phenomenality in terms of intentional content that is 'poised' for cognitive influence; appeals to demonstrative introspection against subjectivity arguments; also appeals to diaphanousness against intrinsic qualia.)

* Weiskrantz, L. (1988) 'Some Contributions of Neuropsychology of Vision and Memory to the Problem of Consciousness', in A. Marcel and E. Bisiatch (eds) *Consciousness in Contemporary Science*, Oxford: Oxford University Press. (Brief, directed discussion from the leading authority on blindsight.)

* Whyte, L. (1962) *The Unconscious Before Freud*, London: Tavistock. (A compendium of pre-modern and early modern views of 'hidden' behavioural influences. Citations are lax.)

ERIC LORMAND

CONSENT

A concept of central importance in moral, political and legal philosophy, consent is widely recognized as justifying or legitimating acts, arrangements or expectations. In standard cases, a person's consent to another person's acts removes moral or legal objections to or liability for the performance of those acts. Thus, in medical practice the informed consent of a patient to a procedure can justify the physician's actions. In law, the maxim 'volenti non fit injuria' (the willing person is not wronged) governs a wide range of acts and transactions, from the economic to the sexual. And in politics, it is often supposed that it is 'the consent of the governed' that justifies or makes permissible both governmental policies and the use of official coercion to compel obedience to law. Consent may be given in a variety of more and less direct forms, but its binding force always rests on the satisfaction of conditions of knowledge, intention, competence, voluntariness and acceptability of content.

1   **Meaning and importance**
2   **Forms and conditions**
3   **Philosophical applications**

1   Meaning and importance

Consent is an act by which one freely changes the existing structure of rights and obligations, typically by undertaking new obligations and authorizing others to act in ways which would otherwise have been impermissible for them. In standard cases, one consents to an act or arrangement in response to a request by others; but consenting is so strongly linked with such acts as promising, contracting, taking oaths and entrusting, that it is best to regard all of these sources of self-assumed obligations as kinds of consent (as in Locke's political philosophy; see LOCKE, J. §10). In the most general terms, then, consent is any act by which an agent deliberately and suitably communicates to another the intention to undertake by that act new obligations and to convey by that act new rights to others. Given the satisfaction of various conditions, consent then authorizes, permits, justifies or legitimates actions by others or arrangements on which they may rely.

It is important to distinguish consent thus understood as a positive act from the weaker notions of consent – an attitude of approval, acceptance or agreement or as mere passivity, acquiescence or submission. These weaker forms of consent are far less important than and quite different from consent properly so-called. A 'pro-attitude' is neither necessary nor sufficient for true (morally binding) consent. Cases of grudging, off-hand or insincere consent show that a positive attitude is not necessary, while commonplace cases in which we approve of an arrangement without having in any way altered (or attempted to alter) the existing structure of rights and duties show that such an attitude is not sufficient. Similarly, one may passively submit to or even acquiesce in the control of a bully without thereby incurring new obligations of future compliance. Binding consent must be a positive act with the explicit, conventional, or otherwise clear meaning of a voluntary undertaking.

Justification by appeal to consent is especially important within the philosophical structure of liberal thought. Liberalism conceives of persons as self-conscious sources of value, whose choices of plans and actions are morally important and who have rights to govern themselves (within the bounds set by the rights of others) (see LIBERALISM). Consent is seen as the means by which this individual moral liberty may be limited in a fashion consistent with respect for liberty. For the consensual undertaking of obligation is one kind of use of personal liberty, a use which makes morally possible new and beneficial forms of social interaction. Justification by consent also has the advantage of being a relatively uncontroversial style of justification, since nearly everyone allows that what one has freely agreed to do ought to be done.

2 Forms and conditions

Attempted justifications by consent have appealed to a wide variety of forms of consent. The most fundamental divisions are those between personal and impersonal consent and between actual and hypothetical consent. Consensual justification of an act or policy with respect to some individual usually involves showing that the individual (expressly or tacitly) personally consented to it; but theorists have also appealed to the consent of the majority of an individual's colleagues (for example, fellow citizens) or to the consent of an individual's ancestors (for example, the founders of the society). Justification by appeal to personal consent is by far the most convincing of these options, since the authority of majorities over us seems to depend on our prior personal consent to be governed by them, and our forebears could not possibly have been authorized to consent for us.

Justification by consent also standardly appeals to the actual consent of the affected persons. This actual consent may be given either by some discrete act or by some ongoing series of acts (such as active participation in the practices of some group). And actual consent may be either express or tacit (implicit, indirect). Express consent is consent given by an explicit verbal or written undertaking or by other direct but nonverbal consensual acts (such as raising one's hand). Tacit consent is given by actions or omissions (such as inactivity or silence) that do not involve an explicit undertaking, but that none the less constitute the making of a morally significant choice in the context of a clear, noncoercive choice situation. Some attempted justifications, however, appeal not to actual but to hypothetical consent. Hypothetical consent can be ideal (what fully rational persons would consent to), counterfactual (what real persons could or would have consented to, had they been pressed to give their consent) or dispositional (what real persons would have consented to, had they been able). Only appeals to the last of these (by which we justify, for example, imposing medical treatment on an unconscious injured person) seem to be genuine justifications by consent. Appeals to the others are really attempts to justify by showing that an arrangement is best or acceptable, independent of people's consent.

Consent of whatever form can only justify acts or arrangements given the satisfaction of a complex set of conditions for binding consent. These conditions can be divided into five categories. First, there are knowledge conditions. Where one is deceived or misled about an arrangement, or where one is otherwise non-negligently ignorant of crucial facts, apparent consensual acts may not bind (because consent is not 'informed'). Second, binding consent must be intentional, not only in the sense that the acts themselves must be intentionally performed, but also that they must involve the intention to give consent and thereby alter existing moral relations. Third, consent can only be given by the competent, which may exclude in various contexts apparent consent given by the insane, severely retarded, emotionally disturbed, immature, intoxicated and so on. Fourth, binding consent must be voluntary, limiting it to cases not involving the extraction of consent by coercion, undue influence, exploitation, unfair bargaining advantage and so on. Finally, consent only binds given acceptability of content. In most legal systems, for instance, agreements you make to commit crimes, become a slave or allow yourself to be killed are not enforceable. The moral basis for such rules could be either the alleged inalienability of the rights at issue or the contradiction supposedly involved in the creation of moral obligations to do the immoral.

3 Philosophical applications

Discussions of consent are most common in three areas of philosophical debate. In medical ethics the idea of informed consent is basic (see MEDICAL ETHICS). Agreements to undergo some surgical procedure, for instance, are binding (and limit the physician's liability) only if patients understand (as far as they are able) basic facts about the nature of the procedure, its risks, costs and alternatives. In legal philosophy, much discussion of the proper structure of contract law turns on analyses of consent. And what constitutes consent is central to the definition of crimes like rape and sexual assault, where a showing of free consent to an act by a competent adult generally defeats criminal charges.

But by far the most numerous philosophical treatments of consent occur in political philosophy, where theorists argue the merits of consent theories of political obligation and authority (see OBLIGATION, POLITICAL; AUTHORITY). According to consent theory, the obligations of citizens to obey the law and support their governments and the authority or rights their governments have over them derive only from consent. The sort of consent relevant to this political justification is variously claimed to be actual and personal (Locke 1690; Beran 1987; Simmons 1993), impersonal or hypothetical (Rawls 1971; Pitkin 1965–6), discrete or ongoing (Walzer 1970; Pateman 1979). Since express consent is relatively rare in political life, it is commonly argued that consent can be given tacitly by continued residence in a state one is free to leave (Locke 1690), by voting (or possessing the right to vote) in democratic elections (Plamenatz 1968; Weale 1978) or by full and direct participation in political life (Pateman 1979). Many also argue, however, both that the conditions of knowledge, intention and voluntariness rule out many of those alleged sources of political consent and that taking seriously the ideal of government by consent forces the acknowledgement that no existing governments are in fact legitimate under these terms (Simmons; Green 1988; Pateman).

See also: FREEDOM AND LIBERTY; RIGHTS; LIBERALISM §5

References and further reading

All of the following involve detailed and sometimes subtle argument, but all are also accessible to readers without formal training in philosophy.

* Beran, H. (1987) *The Consent Theory of Political Obligation*, London: Croom Helm. (The most complete presentation of consent theory in political philosophy.)

Feinberg, J. (1986) *Harm to Self*, New York: Oxford University Press. (The best discussion of the conditions on consent is given in chapters 22–6.)

* Green, L. (1988) *The Authority of the State*, Oxford: Oxford University Press. (Careful discussion in chapter 6 of the relation between consent and political authority.)

Kleinig, J. (1982) 'The Ethics of Consent', *Canadian Journal of Philosophy* supplementary vol. 8: 91–118. (Thorough treatment of the nature of and conditions on consent.)

* Locke, J. (1690) *The Second Treatise of Government*, in *Two Treatises of Government*, ed. P. Laslett, Cambridge: Cambridge University Press, 1960. (The classic statement of the consent theory of political obligation and authority, centred in chapters 7 and 8.)

* Pateman, C. (1979) *The Problem of Political Obligation*, Berkeley, CA: University of California Press. (Discusses the history and many varieties of consent theory in chapters 4–7, favouring a Rousseauian version.)

* Pitkin, H. (1965–6) 'Obligation and Consent, I and II', *American Political Science Review* 59 (4): 990–9, 60 (1): 39–52. (Develops a hypothetical consent theory of political obligation.)

* Plamenatz, J.P. (1968) *Consent, Freedom and Political Obligation*, Oxford: Oxford University Press, 2nd edn. (Discussion of consent theory, with a defence of voting as an expression of consent in the 'Postscript'.)

* Rawls, J. (1971) *A Theory of Justice*, Cambridge, MA: Harvard University Press. (Powerful defence of political justification by appeal to hypothetical consent, with the implications for political obligation in chapter 6.)
* Simmons, A.J. (1993) *On the Edge of Anarchy: Locke, Consent, and the Limits of Society*, Princeton, NJ: Princeton University Press. (Discussion of Locke and the implications of consent theory in chapters 3, 4, 7 and 8; extensive bibliography.)
* Walzer, M. (1970) *Obligations: Essays on Disobedience, War, and Citizenship*, New York: Simon & Schuster. (Applies a distinctive conception of consent theory to various practical political problems.)
* Weale, A. (1978) 'Consent', *Political Studies* 26 (1): 65–77. (Analysis of consent in terms of inducing reliance.)

A. JOHN SIMMONS

CONSEQUENCE, CONCEPTIONS OF

The idea of one proposition's following from others – of their implying it – is central to argument. It is, however, an idea that comes with a history attached to it, and those who blithely appeal to an 'intuitive' or 'pretheoretic' idea of consequence are likely to have got hold of just one strand in a string of diverse theories. This entry introduces the main alternatives – to call them rivals would be too strong, since it suggests that they are necessarily in competition with one another. Simply put, consequence may be conceived as a relation that is or is not modal in character, and is or is not formal. Thus for Aristotle, consequence is both necessary and formal; for Chrysippus it is necessary but not formal; for Bolzano and Tarski it is formal but not necessary; and for Philo and Russell it is neither necessary nor formal. Conceptions of consequence that are neither necessary nor formal are also needed if justice is to be done to deduction in science, the law and daily life. Cutting across all these other differences there is a perennial controversy about relevance. Does implication always require a full-blooded connection between premises and conclusion, or may it hold simply because of some property of either separately, for example, because the premises are impossible?

1 **Aristotle**
2 **Chrysippus, Philo and Diodorus**
3 **Medieval logic**
4 **Bolzano**
5 **Tarski**
6 **Enthymemes**

1 Aristotle

Alone among the persons discussed here, Aristotle never defined his conception of consequence. A definition can be supplied, however, that brings out its distinctive features: necessity, formality and relevance. Namely, a number of premises imply a conclusion if, for all premises $P, \ldots$ and conclusions Q of the same logical form as the given ones, if $P, \ldots$ are (or were) true, then necessarily Q is (would be) true.

The ingredient of necessity here (unlike formality) features in Aristotle's definition of a syllogism. It is required by his demand that proofs should produce 'understanding' (*epistēmē*), coupled with his claim that understanding something involves seeing that it cannot be otherwise. Hence, a proof needs to establish the necessity as well as the truth of its conclusion, which means not only starting from necessarily true axioms but proceeding by steps that preserve necessity as well as truth.

A part of Aristotle's project of axiomatizing science was to separate out those lines of argument that are applicable to all the sciences because they depend purely on topic-neutral terms such as 'every', 'some' and 'not'. These arguments are 'logical' in the special sense in which Aristotle sometimes – not always approvingly – uses the word to signify 'abstract'. The distinction between logical – that is, topic-neutral – and extralogical terms is not clear cut, but he sidesteps the difficulties by selecting a fixed handful of logical terms for study at any one time. Logicians have done the same ever since, splitting consequence in predicate logic, modal logic and so on, rather than lumping them into one broad relation of logical consequence.

Since an extralogical term does no work in making a logical argument valid, the argument remains valid if the term is replaced by any other. In other words, as the definition emphasizes, logical consequence is 'formal'. This feature is exploited by Aristotle's innovation of inference schemes, in which letters take the place of the non-working terms. The combination of formality and an artful selection of working terms creates opportunities for systematization and a mathematical treatment of the subject.

The definition uses counterfactuals because that seems to give the best fit with Aristotle's position on relevance. Where P is impossible and Q unconnected with it, 'If P were true Q would be true' is quite impossible to assess, and such cases are duly excluded by his dictum that premises only imply conclusions involving the same terms. But if a scheme is valid whenever its instances can be assessed (as with the syllogistic moods), he assumes that it holds universally; that is, even when the premises are impossible.

2 Chrysippus, Philo and Diodorus

Our knowledge of the fourth century BC dialecticians Chrysippus, Philo and Diodorus is fragmentary and second-hand, but they appear to have made two lasting contributions to the subject of consequence, one distinctly unhelpful, the other of enormous importance (see PHILO THE DIALECTICIAN §2; DIODORUS CRONUS §3).

Expressions of the form '___ follows from ___' or '___ implies ___' need to be completed by sentences embedded in quotation marks or 'that' clauses. As any logic teacher knows, this is not something that comes naturally, and the simpler 'If *P*, *Q*' form is a convenient shorthand. The Greek dialecticians seem to have turned it into a regular convention, making the conditional *the* vehicle for discussing consequence. Apart from the other drawbacks of the convention, its blurring of an object language–metalanguage distinction is liable to make a study of consequence look like a contribution to propositional logic. This is especially unfortunate, since their great contribution was to propose the first definitions of consequence and inaugurate a debate about it.

For Chrysippus (the attribution is not certain but strongly probable), premises imply a conclusion if their truth is incompatible with its falsity. 'A man is running' thus implies 'An animal is moving'. As a class, such analytic implications are logical in a broad sense but not in Aristotle's special one; they are necessary without being formal.

For Philo of Megara, an implication holds if – for whatever reason – it is not the case that the premises are true and the conclusion false.

Diodorus Cronus' definition is that 'it neither was nor is possible' that the premises be true and the conclusion false. But since he equates the possible with what is or will be true, this amounts to saying that an implication holds if and only if Philo's condition is satisfied at every time.

Little has survived of the debate itself, alas, but relevance was certainly one issue, for we know that where *P* is impossible, 'If *P*, not-*P*' was acceptable to Diodorus but not Chrysippus. Another issue is likely to have been the extreme weakness of Philo's definition, to which Diodorus' looks like a critical rejoinder. To defend (and perhaps motivate) Philo's definition, one need only ask why there should be a higher standard for the steps of an argument than for its starting point. Premises do not have to be necessarily true, so why should conclusions have to

follow *necessarily*? Weak as it is, Philo's definition captures what *Principia Mathematica* (1910–13) calls the 'essential property' of implication; that what is implied by a true proposition is true. It still seems far-fetched to suggest that, for example, all true propositions imply one another, but Philo has been defended even on this point. Russell (1919) distinguishes the presence of an implication from its practical utility for inference. To infer any truths from any others would indeed be *valid* (his word, his italics), but if they are already known to be true there will be no need to infer them, so that inference will in fact only take place if Philo's condition is known to obtain independently, a much stricter requirement.

3 Medieval logic

Medieval logicians tended to follow the ancient dialecticians' expository convention. Thus their 'sequences' (*consequentiae*) tend to be conditional propositions, though their discussion is appropriate to consequence: a sequence is typically said to be 'sound' (*bona*; *valet*) rather than true. The conditional convention lingered into modern times, as witnessed in the ambiguous status of Gentzen's '*Sequenzen*' and Russell's 'material implication'.

As this suggests, medieval logicians were familiar with all the ancient conceptions of consequence. They classified them into 'formal', that is, Aristotelian, and 'material'. Material consequence was subdivided into '*simpliciter*' (absolute), that is, Chrysippian; and '*ut nunc*' (as things are), that is, Philonian, the maxim '*ex falso sequitur quodlibet*' (from a falsehood anything follows) being a reminder of the latter. A few writers created a further subdivision, '*per accidens*' (incidental), to cover a Diodorean conception.

One medieval contribution has left a lasting mark on the subject. We have seen that different ancient conceptions produced different answers about relevance. The medieval development of propositional logic appeared to settle the question by producing a proof that *any* conclusion *Q* really does follow from an impossible premise *P*. The proof runs from *P* to *P* or *Q*, and thence, together with the necessary truth not-*P*, to *Q*. Ironically, the credit for this is generally given not to, say, William of Soissons, but to C.I. Lewis, a logician and historian of logic who had no time for the Middle Ages. The topic is still controversial: Bolzano argued that nothing at all follows from an impossibility, and not all modern logicians accept the Lewis proof (see RELEVANCE LOGIC AND ENTAILMENT §1). However, most follow the medieval line, which, when used to reform Chrysippian consequence, produces the familiar textbook formula for validity: 'It is impossible for the premises to be true and the conclusion false'.

4 Bolzano

We saw that Aristotelian consequence is formal, but this does not depend on its being specifically logical: a comparable relation based on *any* division between working and non-working terms will automatically be formal with respect to the latter. Bolzano exploits this insight in the context of a theory of propositions that are – unlike the propositions mentioned elsewhere in this entry – non-linguistic items, composed of 'ideas' (1837). A conclusion is said to follow from a number of premises with respect to an arbitrary choice of ideas if every substitution for those ideas that turns the premises into true propositions also turns the conclusion into a true one. The other logical notions are relativized in a similar way. Bolzano is happy to include 'logical consequence' as a special case, that is, consequence when every extralogical idea is treated as substitutable. But his heart is in proving theorems about relative consequence in general. (Since he also broke with the old conditional expository convention, his results are unambiguously intelligible to the modern reader.)

Bolzano's definition is non-modal. Indeed, a modal relation seems to be ruled out by his theory of ideas. His emphasis on the immutability of ideas and propositions and their reference to the actual, suggests that he cannot allow, as Frege can, that a false proposition P could be true in different circumstances. In different circumstances P itself would stay false; what would be true would, by hypothesis, be a different proposition. (Moreover, his resolutely non-linguistic stance prevents him from identifying it.) It follows that a modal definition of consequence on the lines of 'Whatever the circumstances might be, if P were true Q would be true' will not work (and cannot be rescued by appealing to 'the proposition corresponding to P').

5 Tarski

A century after Bolzano, Tarski took a similar approach to logical consequence, but where Bolzano had worked with non-linguistic propositions, he dealt in sentences. Given this choice, the obvious first step would be to replace Bolzano's substitutions of ideas by substitutions of words. This would produce the following definition (labelled (F) by Tarski, 1936):

(F) A conclusion follows logically from a number of premises if every substitution for the extralogical vocabulary that makes the premises true, makes the conclusion true.

Indeed, Quine takes just this line when he defines a logical truth as a sentence that remains true under every substitution for its extralogical vocabulary. But the problem with such definitions is that in a particular language there may not be enough words of the right kind, so that an inference may come out as logically valid, or a sentence as logically true, simply because the counter-instances happen to be inexpressible. Quine plays down the difficulty by claiming that it will not arise if the language is 'reasonably rich', that is, capable of expressing arithmetic. His claim may be correct for logical truth but, as Boolos (1975) has shown, it does not extend to consequence.

Tarski had already come across this problem in his work on the concept of truth in formalized languages (1933). A first shot at the truth-conditions of a universally quantified sentence would be to say that it is true if and only if every particular instance of it is true; but this will not work if there are insufficient constants available, for example, if not every individual has a name. Tarski's solution was to get round any shortage of genuine constants by treating free variables as roving constants, capable of taking each object of the appropriate type (individuals, relations, and so on) in turn as their 'value'. Using the idea of a sentential function, in which free variables replace constants, he defined the 'satisfaction' (making true) of a sentential function by an assignment of values to its variables. The truth of $(x)Fx$ can then be equated with the universal satisfaction of the sentential function Fx.

It was a natural step to apply the same ideas to the definition (F). For brevity, let a 'model' of a sentence be an assignment of values that satisfies the sentential function obtained by replacing all the extralogical constants in the sentence by variables. Then, Tarski says, a conclusion follows logically from a number of premises if every model of the premises is a model of the conclusion.

This definition leaves open where to draw the line between logical and extralogical. In particular, it leaves one free to treat 'thing' (as in 'everything Fs', 'something Fs') as a logical constant or not. On the second option each assignment of values involves choosing a 'domain of individuals' as value for the variable that replaces 'thing'. The notion of an assignment of values then becomes that of a structure, in the familiar sense of a collection of objects structured by various relations. If too the logical constants are restricted to a mathematically amenable few (for example, $\supset$ instead of 'if'), the notions of satisfaction and model may be defined in purely set-theoretic terms (see MODEL THEORY). Because of this, the resulting *model-theoretic* conception of consequence has been enthusiastically adopted by many mathematical logicians. Its intimate identification with set theory does, however, expose it to the troubles of that discipline. For, on the prevailing conception, the universe of sets is too large to be a set, and is therefore ineligible to be the domain of any model. For special reasons, first-order logic is unaffected, but the model-theoretic approach to second-order consequence has a question mark over it.

In keeping with the positivism of his day, Tarski wanted nothing to do with modality. (Granted, he uses 'must' when formulating (F) as a scheme, but only to indicate that the scheme holds universally; indeed, he stresses that (F) involves no notion more problematic than that of truth.) The non-modal aspect of his definition has been attacked, by Kneale (1961) and subsequently by Etchemendy (1990). A debate is called for, but it will be more fruitful if it asks for what purposes necessity is an essential ingredient of consequence. For example, someone who does not endorse Aristotle's doctrine of proof and *epistēmē* may well be content with proofs that establish the bare truth of theorems, and it is not obvious that this requires a modal relation of consequence. Again, one motive for developing (say) group theory in the abstract is to derive laws that can be applied to all possible groups. But here a 'possible group' does not mean a non-existent structure composed of possibilia, but an actual structure waiting to be recognized as a group (compare with 'a possible hiding-place'). Once more, a modal conception of consequence is not obviously required.

6 Enthymemes

For a genuinely pre-theoretic notion of consequence one needs to look outside the logic books, and to remember too that a philosopher's conception of modality is not the only legitimate one: lawyers, scientists and others deal in *real* possibilities, not mere notional logical possibilities. In such circles, arguments take place on the basis of some propositions and some inferences which are common ground and taken for granted; call these an argument's 'basis'. But this is not peculiar to everyday argument. A striking example is the predicate calculus, with its built-in presumption that domains of individuals are non-empty (and the corollary that what it holds out as logical consequence fails the test of formality with respect to the extralogical term 'thing'). Indeed *all* deduction has to proceed on some basis or other, for if every step were challengeable, argument could never get moving.

Historically, adherents of one conception of consequence have tried to exclude any other by the doctrine of the 'enthymeme', or incomplete argument. If an argument '*P*, so *Q*' looks sound but does not measure up to the favoured standard, some part of its basis (call it *B*) is declared to be a missing, 'suppressed' premise. The original arguer was either incompetent or deluded: their argument should have been, or really was, '*P*, *B*, so *Q*'. This expanded version will satisfy the favoured standard, which is thereby vindicated. As well as using this weapon against everyday consequence, logicians have turned it on each other. Traditional logicians use it to claim that all consequence is really syllogistic. Formal logicians of every stripe use it to claim that all necessary consequence is really formal (that is, someone who takes for granted the transitivity of 'before' is guilty of suppressing a premise, though someone who takes for granted the transitivity of 'implies' is not).

The self-serving character of the enthymeme doctrine is plain. Perhaps what is needed is, rather, an inclusive theory of consequence that will accommodate all kinds of basis for arguments. Let *B* be any basis; then a number of premises imply a conclusion on the basis of *B* if the conclusion belongs to the closure of the premises with respect to *B*. In the spirit of Bolzano, one can go on to develop the general theory of consequence relative to a basis. It needs to be complemented, however, by a quite different kind of discussion, about what bases are appropriate to what purposes and circumstances. In this connection (setting aside any differences over relevance), the broad conceptions of consequence descried in the previous sections can be seen as lumping together a class of eligible bases. Thus Chrysippian consequence covers – more exactly, it is the union of – consequence taken over all bases composed exclusively of analytic propositions and steps. Similarly, Philonian consequence is the union of consequence taken over all bases composed of true propositions and truth-preserving steps, though its paradoxical characteristics suggest that this is not the best way of dealing with so diverse a class.

See also: LOGICAL AND MATHEMATICAL TERMS, GLOSSARY OF

References and further reading

* Bolzano, B. (1837) *Wissenschaftslehre*, trans. R. George, *Theory of Science*, Oxford: Blackwell, 1972. (Discussed in §4. The relevant sections of this readable but wide-ranging book are §§12, 19, 48, 66, 125, 147, 154–5, 182.)

* Boolos, G. (1975) 'On Second-Order Logic', *Journal of Philosophy* 72: 509–27. (The appendix includes the technical result cited in §5. Despite the title, Boolos' result, like Quine's, relates to first-order logic.)

Carnap, R. (1934) *Logische Syntax der Sprache*, Vienna: Springer; trans. A. Smeaton, *The Logical Syntax of Language*, London: Kegan Paul, 1937. (Carnap briefly introduces consequence as closure with respect to arbitrary 'P-rules'. Tarski had anticipated the idea of closure under rules but, as his 'On the Concept of Logical Consequence' reveals, he was unwilling to take it beyond effective, finitary rules, that is, unwilling to use it to define consequence rather than deducibility.)

* Etchemendy, J. (1990) *The Concept of Logical Consequence*, Cambridge, MA: Harvard University Press. (Uses a distinction between 'representational' and 'interpretational' semantics to develop Kneale's criticism of Tarski, from a standpoint of uncritical adherence to Chrysippian consequence, relevance and all.)

* Kneale, W.C. (1961) 'Universality and Necessity', *British Journal for the Philosophy of Science* 12: 89–102. (Criticizes Bolzano and Tarski.)

Kneale, W. and Kneale, M. (1962) *The Development of Logic*, Oxford: Oxford University Press. (Chapters 2–4 include an invaluable introduction to the early history of consequence.)

* Russell, B.A.W. (1919) *Introduction to Mathematical Philosophy*, London: Allen & Unwin. (Cited in §2. Philonian consequence is defended in chapter 14.)

Smiley, T. (1995) 'A Tale of Two Tortoises', *Mind* 104: 725–36. (Expands the theme of §6 of this entry.)

* Tarski, A. (1933) *Pojęcie prawdy w językach nauk dedukcyjnych*, Warsaw; trans. J.H. Woodger, 'The Concept of Truth in Formalized Languages', in *Logic, Semantics, Metamathematics: Papers from 1923 to 1938*, Oxford: Oxford University Press, 1956, 152–278. (Cited in §5.)

* —— (1936) 'O pojęciu wynikania logicznego', *Przegląd filozoficzny* 39: 58–68; trans. J.H. Woodger, 'On the Concept of Logical Consequence', in *Logic, Semantics, Metamathematics: Papers from 1923 to 1938*, Oxford: Oxford University Press, 1956, 409–20. (This non-technical article is where Tarski expounds the idea of formal, non-necessary consequence discussed in §5. Although the option of varying the domain of individuals is not mentioned, it is given a thorough airing in his more technical 1933 piece.)

* Whitehead, A.N. and Russell, B.A.W. (1910) *Principia Mathematica*, Cambridge: Cambridge University Press, vol. 1, §1; 2nd edn, 1925. (Cited in §2.)

TIMOTHY SMILEY

CONSEQUENTIALISM

Consequentialism assesses the rightness or wrongness of actions in terms of the value of their consequences. The most popular version is act-consequentialism, which states that, of all the actions open to the agent, the right one is that which produces the most good.

Act-consequentialism is at odds with ordinary moral thinking in three respects. First, it seems excessively onerous, because the requirement to make the world a better place would demand all our time and effort; second, it leaves no room for the special duties which we take ourselves to have to those close to us: family, friends and fellow citizens; and third, it might require us, on occasion, to do dreadful things in order to bring about a good result.

Consequentialists standardly try to bring their theory more into line with common thinking by amending the theory in one of two ways. Indirect act-consequentialism holds that we should not necessarily aim to do what is right. We may get closer to making the world the best possible place by behaviour which accords more with ordinary moral thought. Rule-consequentialism holds that an action is right if it is in accordance with a set of rules whose general acceptance would best promote the good. Such rules will bear a fairly close resemblance to the moral rules with which we now operate.

1　Act-consequentialism
2　Criticisms of act-consequentialism
3　Indirect act-consequentialism
4　Rule-consequentialism

1　Act-consequentialism

Although the term 'consequentialism' is a recent coinage – it appears to have first been used in its present sense by Anscombe (1958) – it refers to a type of theory which has a long history. Consequentialism builds on what may seem to be the merest truism, namely that morality is concerned with making the world a better place for all. Consequentialist considerations certainly figure importantly in issues of public policy. Penal, economic or educational programmes are standardly judged by the goodness or badness of their results.

All moral theories offer an account both of the right and of the good. They all tell us, that is, both what makes an action right or wrong, and what kinds of thing are good or valuable. It is characteristic of consequentialist theories to assess whether an action is right in terms of the amount of good it produces (see §4). Deontological ethical theories, by contrast, hold that the right is independent of the good: certain kinds of action are wrong, and others right, independently of the goodness or badness of their consequences (see DEONTOLOGICAL ETHICS; RIGHT AND GOOD).

Act-consequentialism, the simplest form of the theory, holds that the right action – the one you should do – is the one which would produce the greatest balance of good over bad consequences; that is, the one which would maximize the good. (Where two or more actions come out equal best, then it is right to do any one of them.) Which action is in fact the right one will depend on what account of the good any particular act-consequentialist theory offers.

A theory of the good is an account of those things which are intrinsically good, good in themselves, and not merely good as a means to something else which is good (see GOOD, THEORIES OF THE §2). A visit to the dentist is only extrinsically good, because it leads to healthy teeth and the avoidance of toothache, but it is not in itself a good thing; it is a necessary evil. By far the most popular and influential account of the good within the consequentialist camp is that offered by utilitarianism (see UTILITARIANISM). On this view, usually known as hedonism or welfarism, the good is pleasure, happiness or wellbeing (see HEDONISM; HAPPINESS). The act-utilitarian holds, therefore, that the right action is the one which maximizes happiness.

Many consequentialists reject hedonism. A pioneer in this respect was G.E. Moore (1903), whose theory, somewhat confusingly, used to be referred to as ideal utilitarianism, in contrast to the hedonistic variety (see MOORE, G.E. §1). Among the things which have been held to be intrinsically good are knowledge, virtue, beauty, justice, and the flourishing of the environment as a whole. Many of these alternative accounts of the good are pluralist: that is, they claim that there are several different kinds of good thing which cannot all be brought under one head (see MORAL PLURALISM). Pluralist act-consequentialism faces a difficulty. In order to determine which of the possible actions is the right one, agents must be able to rank the outcomes of each action, from the worst to the best. But if there are several distinct values which cannot be reduced to a common measure, how can one kind of value be compared with another in order to produce a definitive ranking? This is the problem of incommensurability of value.

The term 'consequentialism', though hallowed by frequent philosophical use, may be misleading since it might naturally be taken to imply that an action itself can have no intrinsic value; its value is all to be found in its consequences. Utilitarianism is indeed committed to this view – for what matters on the utilitarian account is not the nature of the act itself but the pleasure which it produces in anyone affected by it – but it is not an essential feature of consequentialism as such. Some consequentialists wish to leave room for the thought that certain kinds of action, such as lying, cheating, and killing the innocent, are intrinsically bad, while other kinds of act, such as generous, loyal, or just ones, are intrinsically good. Consequentialism can take such values into account in calculating which course of action produces the best results. In deciding whether one course of action is preferable to another, a consequentialist needs to know the total value that would be produced by taking each course of action, and that will include not only the value of the consequences but the value, if any, which attaches to the action itself.

Consequentialism is sometimes described as a teleological theory, because it conceives of a moral theory as setting a goal which we should strive to achieve (see TELEOLOGICAL ETHICS). The goal which consequentialism sets is to bring about a world containing the greatest balance of good over bad. Such a classification risks confusion, however, since a virtue ethics, such as Aristotle's, is also usually classified as teleological, yet Aristotle's theory differs from consequentialism in at least two crucial respects. First, the good at which agents aim, on Aristotle's view (outlined in *Nicomachean Ethics*), is not the best state of the world, but the good life for humans; agents are to seek to realize distinctively human goods in their own lives. Second, Aristotle's theory, unlike consequentialism, does not define the right in terms of the good. On the contrary, a full understanding of the good life rests on a prior conception of the right, for an important part of the good life consists in acting rightly (see ARISTOTLE §§21–6; RIGHT AND GOOD §2; VIRTUE ETHICS).

We also need to distinguish the kind of consequentialism with which we are here concerned from ethical egoism, which is sometimes classified as a consequentialist theory (see EGOISM AND ALTRUISM). Ethical egoism, which holds that the right action is the one which would best promote the agent's own interests, is structurally similar to consequentialism in that the right action is the one which maximizes a good, in this case, the agent's own good. What distinguishes egoism from the sort of consequentialism discussed here is that the latter is an *impartial* theory, giving equal weight to each person's good (see IMPARTIALITY).

2 Criticisms of act-consequentialism

How should consequentialists set about deciding what to do? A natural answer is: by calculating, as best they may, what would produce the most good on any particular occasion when they are called upon to act.

Of course, lack of time and knowledge limit what they can do by way of calculation, but they must do the best they can. So interpreted, however, act-consequentialism can be criticized for running counter to our intuitive moral convictions in a number of ways.

First, it seems excessively demanding; I shall only be acting rightly in so far as I maximize the good. Given all the bad things in the world, and the fact that few of us do much to improve them, it is clear that, in order to do what act-consequentialism requires, I would have to devote virtually all my energy and resources to making the world a better place (see HELP AND BENEFICENCE §2). This would give me no time or money to pursue my own interests, or even to relax, except to refresh me ready to redouble my moral efforts on the morrow. The degree of self-sacrifice required would make the lives of the saints look self-indulgent. Ordinary morality is surely not as demanding as this; it gives us permission to pursue our own goals, provided that we are not in breach of any of our fundamental duties. Some have proposed, in order to meet this point, that the theory be modified so that an act is right if its consequences are good, or good enough, even if they are not the best. This suggestion has not been widely adopted, for it is usually held that a rational agent will always prefer the greater good to the less.

Second, act-consequentialism appears to leave no place for the duties we take ourselves to have to our family and friends (see FAMILY, ETHICS AND THE; FRIENDSHIP). Such duties are often classified as agent-relative: each of us should help *their own* family and friends, so that the persons to whom the duties are owed vary from agent to agent. Act-consequentialism, however, is an agent-neutral moral theory; the goal at which we should aim does not depend on who the agent is. I should direct my efforts towards those for whom I can do the most good; their relationship to me is irrelevant. Even if act-consequentialism places special value on the cultivation of certain relationships, such as friendship, this will still not yield a duty of friendship, as traditionally understood. If friendship is a great good, then my duty as a consequentialist is to promote friendship in general between all persons; that will not necessarily require me to give special attention to *my* friends, as distinct from helping others to give special attention to their friends.

Third, if act-consequentialism is too demanding in one respect it seems too permissive in another. For it leaves no room for the thought, central to much ordinary moral thinking, that there are certain constraints on our action, certain kinds of act, such as cheating, torturing and killing, which we ought not to contemplate, even if acting in one of these forbidden ways would maximize the good. The end, as we often say, does not justify the means. Once again, constraints seem to be agent-relative. Each of us is required not to kill or torture the innocent *ourselves* even if, by doing so, we could prevent two such tortures or killings.

3 Indirect act-consequentialism

Because it generates these counter-intuitive results, few consequentialists hold that agents should decide what to do by asking what will produce the best results. There are two theories which offer a less direct link between the overall goal of making things go as well as possible and how one should decide to act on any particular occasion. The first of these is known as indirect act-consequentialism. It retains the claim that the right action is the one with the best consequences, but denies that the virtuous agent need be guided directly by consequentialist thoughts when deciding how to act.

Indirect act-consequentialism builds on the thought that we do not necessarily hit the target if we aim directly at it. The gunner must make allowances for wind, gravity and poorly aligned sights; the moralist may have to direct our thoughts away from the goal if we are to achieve it. Act-consequentialism, on this view, tells us what the target is, but not how to hit it. It is not itself a good guide to action for a number of reasons: the calculations are tricky and time-consuming; we may be tempted to skew the results in our favour; doing the right action may require us to go against dispositions which are both deeply rooted and generally useful. So we may actually do better, in terms of achieving the goals which consequentialism sets us, if we do not aim to do what is right, but follow a few fairly simple moral rules of the traditional type, or encourage within ourselves the development of dispositions, such as kindness and loyalty, which will normally lead us to act in beneficial ways. In adopting such rules, or developing such dispositions, we know that we will sometimes act wrongly when we could, perhaps, have acted rightly. Yet we may still get closer, in the long run, to achieving the consequentialist goal than we would have if we had attempted to aim at it directly.

Some indirect act-consequentialists go further. Since we make better decisions if we eschew consequentialist calculations, it might be best if we rejected consequentialism. It seems possible that agents might behave worse, in consequentialist terms, if they were taught the truth of consequentialism than if they were brought up to believe some other moral theory. In which case consequentialists would do well to prevent its truth being generally known. Opponents see this position as incoherent. If the adoption of consequentialism demands its suppression then in what sense can we adopt it? How could a society be said to be governed by a moral code if no-one in that society believed it?

4 Rule-consequentialism

The second alternative to direct act-consequentialism is rule-consequentialism, which offers a more substantive role for moral rules or principles. Individual acts are judged right or wrong by reference to the rules; the rules, but not the individual acts, are judged by the results of accepting them. The right action is, roughly, the one that is in conformity with a set of moral rules which, if generally accepted, would tend to produce better results than any other set of viable rules we might accept. Rule-consequentialism differs from indirect act-consequentialism in two ways. It maintains that each decision should be guided by thoughts about which action is the right one, and denies that the right action is necessarily the one with the best results. In deciding which rules to accept we should bear in mind that the rules need to be clear, reasonably simple and not too difficult to comply with, given human nature. If they meet these requirements, it is likely that such rules will not be too dissimilar to our present ones.

Rule-consequentialism might be a plausible moral theory, but should it properly be seen as a form of consequentialism? It apparently abandons a central tenet of consequentialism: the claim that our goal should be to maximize the good. The rule I should follow, on this view, is the one that *would* have better consequences, if generally accepted, than any other rule. If it is not, in fact, generally accepted, then in following it I may not get as close to maximizing the good as I would if I followed some other policy. For that reason, perhaps, act-consequentialism has remained most popular among defenders of the theory, despite its difficulties.

See also: PERFECTIONISM

References and further reading

* Anscombe, G.E.M. (1958) 'Modern Moral Philosophy', *Philosophy* 33: 1–19. (A vigorous rebuttal, among other things, of what she saw as the pervasive strand of consequentialism in English moral philosophy.)
* Aristotle (*c.* mid 4th century BC) *Nicomachean Ethics*, trans. W.D. Ross, Oxford: Oxford University Press, 1972. (Arguably the greatest work on ethics in Western thought; considers what is required to live a full and satisfying life, in which the finest human capacities are exercised properly.)
* Moore, G.E. (1903) *Principia Ethica*, Cambridge: Cambridge University Press, 1966, esp. ch. 5. (Argues that to say that an act is right is equivalent to saying that its total results will be the best possible, and claims that by far the most valuable things are personal relationships and the appreciation of beauty.)
Pettit, P. (1993) 'Consequentialism', in P. Singer (ed.) *A Companion to Ethics*, Oxford: Blackwell, 230–40. (A clear introduction to the topic.)
Parfit, D. (1984) *Reasons and Persons*, Oxford: Clarendon Press, esp. sections 10–14, 37, 41–4. (Contains one of the most sophisticated recent discussions and defences of consequentialism.)
Scheffler, S. (1982) *The Rejection of Consequentialism*, Oxford: Clarendon Press. (Argues for a 'hybrid' theory in which agents are permitted, but cannot be required, not to maximize the good.)
—— (1988) *Consequentialism and Its Critics*, Oxford: Oxford University Press. (A very useful collection of seminal articles.)
Sidgwick, H. (1874) *The Methods of Ethics*, London: Macmillan; 7th edn, 1907, esp. I (ch. 9), II (ch. 1), III (chaps 11, 13), IV (chaps 2–5). (The classic source of many of the strategies now discussed by consequentialists and their opponents.)
Smart, J. and Williams, B. (1973) *Utilitarianism For and Against*, Cambridge: Cambridge University Press. (Two fine essays. Williams' piece introduces many of the objections to consequentialism that have figured in subsequent debate, including the notorious example of Jim and the Indians.)

DAVID McNAUGHTON

CONSERVATION PRINCIPLES

In antiquity 'self-evident' principles were used to argue for the conservation of certain quantities. The concept of quantitative conservation laws, such as those of mass and energy, is of much later origin. Even prior to the development of modern mechanics, symmetries were employed to solve some dynamical problems. The relation between conserved quantities and symmetries has come to play a central role in the physical sciences. Conservation laws may reflect as much about the way the human mind organizes the phenomena of the world as they do about physical reality itself.

One can distinguish between broad metaphysical principles of conservation and empirical conservation laws. Here we shall be concerned mainly with the latter. Historically, the development of each concept influenced that of the other. In the sixth and fifth centuries BC, several Greek thinkers (Thales, Anaximander, Anaximenes, Empedocles, Leucippus and Democritus) promulgated a range of materialistic philosophies, which included a belief that all substances in the cosmos are derived from some single substrate (or, at most, from a few of them) or that matter has an atomistic structure (see MATTER §1). Like these ancient materialists, Antoine Lavoisier (1743–94) in his *Elements of Chemistry* (1789) took it as axiomatic that in natural processes no matter is ever created or destroyed. John Dalton's (1766–1844) atomic hypothesis, based on 'ultimate particles' of matter, also assumed conservation of matter or, in modern terminology, of mass. René DESCARTES (1596–1650), on basically theological grounds, adumbrated a law of conservation of momentum, while he and Christiaan Huygens (1629–95) had a proper conception of the law of inertia which is closely related to momentum conservation. However, it was only with Isaac Newton's (1642–1727) *Principia* (1687) that mechanics was provided with a sufficiently complete and consistent dynamical scheme from which conservation laws could be derived. In modern terminology, by a conserved quantity we mean one that is a constant in time by virtue of the dynamical equations of motion. The elegant formulations of classical mechanics by Leonhard Euler (1707–83), Joseph-Louis Lagrange (1736–1813) and Pierre-Simon Laplace (1749–1827) allowed one to find the conserved quantity corresponding to an invariance property of a mechanical system (see MECHANICS, CLASSICAL §5). As an example, the invariance of a physical system under rotation about some axis fixed in space implies the conservation of angular momentum about that axis. Given the dynamics, one then derives certain invariances and conservation laws.

The law of conservation of energy is one of the most important in physics. This law is very broad and extends far beyond mechanics. The physicists Benjamin Thompson (1753–1814) and James Joule (1818–89), and the chemist Humphrey Davy (1778–1829), were instrumental in demonstrating the interconvertibility of mechanical energy and heat. The first formulation of the concept of energy conservation was given by the physician and physicist Julius von Mayer (1814–78), although he received proper recognition only after Hermann von HELMHOLTZ (1821–94) rediscovered his work. Albert Einstein (1879–1955) unified the conservation of mass and of energy into a single law by arguing for the equivalence, or interchangeability, of mass and energy (see EINSTEIN, A. §2). As ever more forms of energy are included in a generalization of the law of conservation of energy, the status of that law becomes almost definitional (but still extremely useful). In fact, Émile MEYERSON held that there are principles of lawfulness and of causality which reflect basic and universal characteristics of human thought and understanding. This suggests that our various conservation laws may be rooted as much in the human mind as they are in any external reality.

Much of the fundamental work in twentieth-century theoretical physics is based on an intimate connection between conserved quantities and the symmetries of physical systems. In common usage the term 'symmetry' often refers to a certain pleasing proportion or balance. However, here we are concerned with a technical sense of this term, as in geometrical symmetries or in the crystalline symmetry of a snowflake. As an illustration, a plane equilateral triangle is left invariant under successive rotations of 120 degrees about an axis perpendicular to the plane of the triangle and through its centre. The figure looks the same after the rotation as before. Similarly, we can consider those transformations that leave unchanged the *form* of the mathematical equations describing a physical system. This connection between symmetries and conserved quantities had long been familiar in classical Lagrangian mechanics, but the mathematician Emmy Noether (1882–1935) proved a general result that continues to hold in relativity and in quantum theory. Just as invariance under displacements in space and time yields energy and momentum conservation, so, for example, what is termed the 'internal' symmetry of gauge invariance (a mathematical operation that leaves Maxwell's equations for electrodynamics unchanged) leads to the conservation of electrical charge. Another type of gauge invariance (a change of the arbitrary phase of the wave function in the Schrödinger equation) implies conservation of probability in quantum mechanics. What are termed higher symmetries can account for other conservation laws, such as that of baryon (or nucleon) number in elementary-particle physics. In a sense, physics has come full circle, building into theories those symmetries that will ensure certain conservation laws. When we have a complete dynamics, we use it to derive conservation laws. When searching for new theories, symmetries are a guide to discovery (see ELECTRODYNAMICS; FIELD THEORY, QUANTUM).

References and further reading

Elkana, Y. (1974) *The Discovery of the Conservation of Energy*, Cambridge, MA: Harvard University Press. (An examination of the origins of this concept in modern science.)

Gillispie, C.C. (1960) *The Edge of Objectivity*, Princeton, NJ: Princeton University Press. (A history of scientific ideas.)

Goldstein, H. (1950) *Classical Mechanics*, Reading, MA: Addison-Wesley. (A lucid and thorough exposition of the principles of mechanics, including the relation between symmetries and conservation laws.)

Hill, E.L. (1951) 'Hamilton's Principle and the Conservation Theorems of Mathematical Physics', *Reviews of Modern Physics* 23: 253–60. (Noether's theorem applied to continuous groups as used in physics.)

Sambursky, S. (1975) *Physical Thought From the PreSocratics to the Quantum Physicists*, New York: Pica Press. (An intellectual history of Western physical science.)

Weyl, H. (1952) *Symmetry*, Princeton, NJ: Princeton University Press. (A very readable discussion of the role that symmetry has played throughout the ages in various cultures generally and in mathematics.)

Wigner, E.P. (1967) *Symmetries and Reflections*, Bloomington, IN: Indiana University Press. (A collection of essays, both technical and philosophical, on symmetries applied to modern physics.)

Wilson, L.S. (1970) *The Conflict Between Atomism and Conservation Theory 1644–1860*, London: MacDonald & Co. (An internalist history of the evolution of these two traditions.)

JAMES T. CUSHING

CONSERVATISM

Conservatism is an approach to human affairs which mistrusts both a priori reasoning and revolution, preferring to put its trust in experience and in the gradual improvement of tried and tested arrangements. As a conscious statement of position, it dates from the reaction of Burke and de Maistre to the Enlightenment and Revolutionary thought and practices in the eighteenth century. Its roots, however, go far deeper. From Plato, conservatives derive a sense of the complexity and danger of human nature, although they reject emphatically his belief in the desirability of philosophical governance. From Aristotle, conservatives derive their sense of the need for practical experience in judging both moral and political matters, and their understanding of the role of tradition in inculcating habits of virtue and wisdom in the young.

Against Plato, conservatives prefer the limited government advocated by Hobbes, because of their belief in the ignorance and corruptibility of rulers, and because of their wish to encourage the self-reliance of subjects. They do, however, reject any conception of a social contract. In this, they follow de Maistre, who argued that creatures with the institutions and reactions necessary to form a social contract will already be in a society and hence have no need of such a thing.

While de Maistre emphasized the terror underlying political power, more characteristic of modern Anglo-Saxon conservatism is the position of Burke. For Burke, a good constitution is one adorned with 'pleasing illusions' to make 'power gentle and obedience liberal'. It is also one which dissipates power in a society through autonomous institutions independent of the state. For both these reasons the communist regimes of eastern Europe could not be defended by conservatives, even though for a time they represented a form of social order.

While conservatism is not antithetical to the free market, and while the market embodies virtues the conservative will approve of, for the conservative the market needs to be supplemented by the morality, the institutions and the authority necessary to sustain it. Human beings are by nature political, and also inevitably derive their identity from the society to which they belong. Our sense of self is established through our family relationships and also through the wider recognition and apportionment of roles we achieve in the public world beyond the family. According to Hegel, who since Aristotle has written most profoundly on the interplay of the private and the public in human life, both family and the public world of civil society need to be sustained through the authority of the state. On the other hand, the distinctions between family, civil society and the state need to be maintained against the characteristically modern tendency to treat them collectively. In his insistence both on authority and on the checks and balances needed in a good society, Hegel may be said to be the most articulate and systematic of conservative thinkers.

Conservatism has been much criticized for its tendency towards complacency and to accept the status quo even when it is unacceptable. However, in its stress on the imperfectibility of human nature and on the dangers of wholesale revolution, it may be said to be more realistic than its opponents. Conservatives can also be quite content with the claim that societies animated by conservative political structures have been more successful morally and materially than socialist or liberal societies. This claim they believe to be true, and it is a fundamental aspect of their position that the dispute between them and their opponents is, at bottom, an empirical one.

1   The conservative temper
2   Plato and Aristotle

1 The conservative temper

Many strands of thought make up conservatism, and thinkers who are regarded as conservative have held a wide variety of opinions on many crucial issues, both philosophical and political. The protean and, to the intellectual mind, untidy character of conservatism is, however, part of its essence. Indeed, it is an important aspect of what distinguishes conservatism from other ideologies, or, as conservatives would say, from ideologies. For conservatism is an approach to human and, more specifically, to political affairs which mistrusts the power of human reason. Its temper is sceptical and empirical. It places more faith in tried and tested arrangements than in ideas, however brilliant. It recognizes the extent to which individuals are situated within their societies, and the extent to which societies are fashioned by their histories. Conservatism is also acutely conscious of the flaws in human nature, as well as its potential for good, and of the way in which civilized life depends on a context of order and tradition.

It has rightly been said that prior to the Reformation, it was impossible to distinguish conservatism in politics, not because none existed but because there was nothing else. However, even between the time of Luther and that of the French Revolution, while we can certainly discern conservative themes in writers such as Hobbes, Swift, Pascal and Hume, it is not until Edmund Burke's *Reflections on the Revolution in France* (1790) and Joseph de Maistre's *Considérations sur la France* (*Considerations on France*) (1797) that we find comprehensive and self-conscious statements of a conservative position. It is no coincidence that both these impassioned diatribes were conceived as reactions to what their authors perceived as a deadly threat to the established order of society, and in de Maistre's case, to the divine order as well.

The conservative position is one that is better unarticulated not, as its opponents might insist, because it is intellectually threadbare, but because its preference is for the harmony which arises from an unquestioning and untroubled acceptance of settled ways of doing things. In making articulate what is better left unsaid, conservatism is, from its own point of view, in danger of lapsing into ideology, into the erection of principle and dogma over practice and habit. As we will see, neither de Maistre nor certain modern conservatives have proved immune to this temptation.

2 Plato and Aristotle

While explicit conservatism may be a characteristically modern phenomenon, the intellectual roots of much conservatism can be found in the thoughts of Plato and, more particularly, Aristotle. From Plato conservatives derive a keen sense of the dividedness of human nature. For most conservatives would assuredly recognize the image in *Phaedrus* of the soul consisting of a charioteer struggling to harness together a good horse and a bad horse (*c.*366–360 BC; 253c–). For conservatives one incontrovertible lesson of history is the danger of licence and anarchy, and the human and political folly of the romanticism which would do away with political order in the name of freedom or even reason. Individuals do not have reason enough to order their own affairs, nor even do whole societies starting from scratch; and freedom, in practice, is too often freedom for one person's bad horse to do violence both to his or her own better nature and to those around. Thus conservatives would sympathize with the Platonic insistence on the need for order provided by a strong state, as featured in both *Republic* (*c.*380–367 BC) and *Laws* (*c.*360–347 BC) (see PLATO §§14,17).

Conservatives would, however, have rather less sympathy with other aspects of Platonic thought. Conservatism is not committed to the view that decline is inevitable, nor indeed to the myth of a past golden age. Being more aware than non-conservatives of the problems involved in change is not synonymous with an obdurate refusal of all reform. Indeed, wholeheartedly rejecting the central Platonic doctrine of the possibility of infinitely enlightened rulers, conservatism must embrace mechanisms for gradual reforms necessitated by errors of policy, errors often visible only after experience of the effects of policy, and particularly to the ruled who suffer most from the effects.

Central to conservatism is the belief that even the best-intentioned action can have unexpected and undesired consequences. The ramifications of the unintended consequences are the greater when the actions in question are policies whose effects will bear upon a whole society. Even the cleverest and most beneficent agencies will inevitably be unable to predict all the effects of their policies in advance. Because of their inevitable ignorance and because, in any case, they are unlikely to remain completely uncorrupted by power, in contrast to Plato conservatives favour a system in which the scope of the actions of rulers is limited, and in which revision and reform is a real possibility.

Overall, in fact, the empiricism of Aristotle is far more congenial to conservatives than the rationalism of Plato. For Aristotle, both ethical enquiry and politics are areas in which there is no substitute for the wisdom which derives jointly from experience and the patient cultivation of good habits. If politics were simply a matter of cleverness, then we would expect to be able to learn about it from sophists, who profess to be able to teach it, but who are far from being able to practise it to good effect. We cannot learn about medicine or painting from people who are not doctors or artists. In like manner, the would-be legislator needs experience of life and politics, over and above intelligence; guidance is needed also from those versed in the intricacies of human affairs, rather than from the merely clever. Moreover:

> The soul of the student must first have been cultivated by means of habits for noble joy and noble hatred, like earth which is to nourish the seed. For he who lives as passion directs will not hear argument that dissuades him nor understand it if he does.
>
> (*Nichomachean Ethics* 1179,b,25–6)

Aristotle's assumption (see ARISTOTLE §§27, 28), in contrast to that of moral educators in the romantic and rationalist traditions, who would have even young children submit all their moral beliefs to critical scrutiny, is that moral reasoning can proceed properly only on the basis of good habits, already ingested and ingrained. Aristotle's clear assumption, like that of the conservative, is that moral and political virtues emerge as the fruits of experience, and are passed on to the newcomer brought up within the tradition which recognizes experience as the wisdom of the past. To the newcomer this process of transmission is initially an unthinking one, purely a matter of habit.

As well as his moral conservatism, Aristotle insisted on hierarchies of talent and ability, albeit in a less rigid and doctrinaire manner that Plato. He also argued strongly that justice is not equality, but the giving to each of what each are owed. It is hard to think of any conservative dissenting from Aristotle's inegalitarianism, firmly based as it is in facts about human nature and in the actual development of history and culture. Nor would a conservative be likely to favour Plato's holist state over Aristotle's more limited type of rule in which, although the state is logically prior to the individual, private property, the family and other activities independent of the state are clearly envisaged.

3 Hobbes

Conservatives are dispositionally inclined towards a Hobbesian polity for at least two reasons. First, a strong government is needed in order to protect individuals and communities against injustice and the depredations of the strong, and to turn what would otherwise be a war of all against all into a settled, peaceful existence (see HOBBES, T. §6). Second, limited government is favoured both because of the ignorance and corruptibility of rulers and also to encourage the self-reliance of subjects.

Where, however, conservatives depart from Hobbes and all liberals of a contractarian sort is on the notion of a social contract (see LIBERALISM §5). A contract, as even Hobbes admits, is, *in extremis*, defeasible (Hobbes 1651). Whereas if, following Burke, conservatives see life as a partnership between the living, the dead and the unborn, it is not a partnership in which we, the living, can be absolved from our duties to our partners, if only because they are not here to release us. In any case, for conservatives the very idea of non-social animals – or as they view them, savages fleeing from the war of all against all – coming together to contract is a nonsense; such beings could never construct a system depending on the mutual recognition of obligations and enforcement of promises. Meanwhile, those creatures who could enact a social contract, with the rewarding, punishing and respecting of each other's rights and freedoms which such a notion requires, are already in a society, and so have no need of a primeval contract (de Maistre 1797) (see CONTRACTARIANISM §§2–6).

4 De Maistre and Burke

De Maistre, whose criticism of the social contract is given above, held that society is not made by man, weak as he is and his 'reason' a feeble pretence, but by God. Thus, any attack on the social order amounts to a blasphemy. Furthermore, society is held together only by the executioner, 'the terror of human society and the tie that holds it together'. This is conservatism as reactionary ideology. De Maistre takes every cherished doctrine of the Enlightenment and turns it on its head. In so doing, he shows the same cavalier disregard for human life as those he attacks, to such a degree that he is led to compliment the Jacobins on the grounds that they, unlike their liberal-minded predecessors, at least killed people and restored order of a sort.

In so arguing, de Maistre falsifies what, since Burke, has become a central tenet of Anglo-Saxon conservatism; that the main defence against anarchy and against the war of all against all is not the brute power of the state. Burke had no more illusions about human motivation or ability than de Maistre, but he saw that sentiment had to be added to power in order for a state to become a community, tolerable for all to live in. Burke, like de Maistre, believed that 'no great human institution results from deliberation' but is the result of evaluation over time in ways often undreamt of by its founders, and also that 'human works are fragile in proportion to.... the degree to which science and reasoning' have been involved in their construction (1797: 57). Both men pour scorn on the attempt to formulate a constitution or a bill of rights which is not simply an articulation of existing practice, and even more upon the characteristically modern delusion that liberty, rather than its opposite, can be secured by such a procedure. Furthermore, de Maistre's adage that 'threads which can be broken by a child at play can nevertheless be joined to form a cable capable of supporting the anchor of a great vessel' (1797: 75) is entirely in the spirit of Burkean conservatism, in both its positive and negative aspects; negatively, that seemingly trivial criticism can undermine the spirit of a great enterprise; positively, that what binds a great society need not, indeed must not, seem onerous, or the cause is dead.

And it is here that Burke and de Maistre part company. For Burke, and those of his followers supporting the tradition of Anglo-Saxon conservatism, what is crucial in a successful constitution are 'the pleasing illusions' which make 'power gentle and obedience liberal', which harmonize 'the different shades of life and which, by a bland assimilation' incorporate 'into politics the sentiments which beautify and soften private society'. Revolutions tear off all this 'decent drapery of life' and expose our 'naked shivering nature'.

> On this scheme of things, a king is but a man; a queen is but a woman; a woman is but an animal; and an animal not of the highest order. All homage paid to the sex in general as such, and without distinct views, is to be regarded as romance and folly. Regicide, and parricide, and sacrilege, are but fictions of superstition, corrupting jurisprudence by destroying its simplicity. The murder of a king, or a queen, or a bishop, or a father are only common homicide; and if the people are by any chance, or in any way, gainers by it, a sort of homicide much the most pardonable, and into which we ought not to make too severe a scrutiny.
>
> (Burke 1790: 171)

Burke goes on to contrast this conservatism with the barbarous philosophy, the offspring of cold hearts and muddy understanding, in which 'laws are to be supported only by their own terrors' (see BURKE, E.).

De Maistre was certainly as guilty as some of his opponents of subscribing to a barbarous philosophy, and to that extent should be regarded as outside the conservative mainstream. Moreover, the spirit of what Burke says need not require sentiment invested in any particular form of government; only that it is genuinely invested somewhere, or else government – and human life as a whole – will reveal itself in its most repulsive and reductive form. It is thus clear that conservatism does not sanction any form of established power. In particular, it would not sanction a form of established power incapable of sustaining public affection, as was the case in eastern Europe during the Cold War. There the Communist party was the only authority and only power, running every aspect of society through a series of front institutions in whose legitimacy and independence few believed.

Even if the eastern European dictatorships had commanded more public affection than they did, and however long lasting and successful they had been, they would not in any case have been acceptable to conservatives. Following Burke, conservatives put considerable stress on the necessity for autonomous institutions and sources of power, so as to balance state power and to mitigate the consequences of centralized ignorance. It is here that there is an overlap between conservatism and the classical liberalism of Adam Smith and his followers (see LIBERALISM §2; SMITH, A. §4).

5 Conservatism and the market

Adam Smith's model of the free market is based on the assumption that the most efficient way of organizing an economy is one that has evolved without planning, and which runs best without interference from the centre. It is impossible to know how agents in a large society will act economically before they actually engage in market transactions. If there are many entrepreneurs and producers there is a greater likelihood of real needs and desires being met than if there is only one agency of production. Those producers who, by a combination of luck and design, manage to tap into actual demand will benefit; and so will consumers, who, from the range of goods and services offered, will pick those which satisfy their wants at the cheapest price. In Smith's view, those of us in capitalist societies have stumbled on a system in which producers and consumers are enabled to benefit each other, and which will produce both a measure of economic stability and productive drive, even though each individual in the system acts only on his or her private desires (to maximize profit, to purchase the best at the cheapest price). The system will, however, break down if central agencies attempt to restrict what is, in effect, the flow of information to and from producers and consumers, and so disturb its natural albeit unplanned tendency towards equilibrium.

Both the evolutionary aspect and the anti-statism of Smithian economic theory is likely to appeal to conservatives, who are also aware of the limitations of planning. But a true conservative would never, as Hayek did, utter any general edict against planning, even planning of a centralized sort (see HAYEK, F.A. VON §3). Making anti-planning into a principle or economic liberalism into an ideology offends the pragmatic and sceptical temper of the true conservative, who could cheerfully admit a role for state planning and even for economic interference were such things necessary, as in the modern world they no doubt are in order to make one's country, as Burke would have it, 'lovely' to one's compatriots. As Michael Oakeshott put it:

A plan to resist all planning may be better than its opposite, but it belongs to the same style of politics. And only in a society already deeply infected with Rationalism will the conversion of the traditional resources of resistance to the tyranny of Rationalism into a self-conscious ideology be considered a strengthening of those resources. It seems that now, in order to participate in politics and expect a hearing, it is necessary to have, in the strict sense, a doctrine; not to have a doctrine appears frivolous, even disreputable. And the sanctity, which in some societies was the property of a politics piously attached to traditional ways, has now come to belong exclusively to Rationalist politics.

(Oakeshott 1962: 21–2)

For Oakeshott, conservatism is to be contrasted principally with Rationalism, which is the belief that politics is to be understood in terms of getting things done, of achieving ends laid down by predetermined blueprints. For Oakeshott, this approach embodies the dual fallacy of thinking first that ends can be laid down independently of the means one consider appropriate in the light of one's way of life, and second, of failing to appreciate that the most important things in life are ends in themselves, worth having and cherishing for what they are, not for what they enable one to achieve. One of the deformations of the modern world is the introduction of methods and ideas appropriate to instrumental rationality into areas where they are inappropriate, such as the law, education and the arts. Above all, the introduction of means–end thinking is undesirable in connection with

the state itself, not least because we have no choice in regard to membership of it (see OAKESHOTT, M.J. §3).

For Oakeshottian conservatism, politics should be seen in terms of a people elaborating ways of living together in the light of its particular history and traditions, and because of the compulsion involved, governmental and political intervention should be as light as possible. Political activity should not be seen as an enterprise driven by the pursuit of universally determinable extrinsic goals, such as equality or the elimination of poverty. To those who think otherwise, it might be pointed out that even if what is said is couched in the abstract language of universal rights, what will at any given point count as equality or the elimination of poverty will depend very much on the thought and practice of the time (see TRADITION AND TRADITIONALISM).

Much of the transformation of politics into enterprise and instrument has occurred because of collectivist approaches to institutions; much has happened because of market-led thinking. It is a moot point as to whether classical liberals would have favoured the prevalent instrumentalist view of politics and institutions, which Oakeshott criticizes. Adam Smith himself believed the weakening of traditional allegiances to be one of the 'inconveniences' of market societies. He, along with more recent neo-liberals such as Hayek, also recognized the need for a strong, if minimal, state to enforce contracts and to provide the social stability within which the market can operate. Thus, the supposed conflict between economic liberalism and conservatism often cited as a criticism of Mrs Thatcher's project of a strong national state combined with a free market does not appear as such in the works of her mentors. Nevertheless, from the conservative point of view economic liberalism certainly needs supplementation if it is to provide an adequate account either of man or of society.

6 Hegel

At this point, conservatives will point to a need to generalize de Maistre's criticism of social contract theories of the state. The social contract is a nonsense because it has to assume that what it purports to set up already exists. But equally nonsensical is the idea of the abstract ahistorical individual rational agents envisaged in so much Kantian and post-Kantian moral philosophy, the self who (in Rawls' terms) is prior to the ends affirmed by it. As F.H. Bradley put it: 'the man into whose essence his community with others does not enter, does not include relations to others in his very being, is a fiction' (1876 (1927): 168). Here Bradley is echoing Hegel, who in turn is drawing on de Maistre and Burke and, more remotely, Aristotle (see BRADLEY, F.H.).

For Aristotle, man is, by nature, a political animal, bound by his very identity to family and city. In Hegel's hands this involves recognition that we are born into a network of relationships and obligations, which we did not choose, and to which we owe indissoluble debts of piety. Our sense of self arises first in the reciprocity involved in our natural family, and it is then extended into the public world of mutual but impersonal recognition through which we escape the war of all against all. (For Hegel this is civil society, in which is resolved the life and death struggle of master and slave.) As our identity as self-conscious agents is only made possible by this social network, in being disloyal to it, we are disloyal to the very self whose emancipation we vainly seek in our disloyalty. But while it is through the family and the institutions of civil society that we all derive our initial identity and the possibility of developing a life and career in the public world, they in turn owe their existence and wellbeing to an all-protecting state (Hegel 1833) (see HEGEL, G.W.F. §8).

Against the liberals, then, Hegel will insist on the priority of the state and its independence from individual, family and the institutions of civil society. Like Burke and de Maistre, he believes that order, family and civil society will collapse without the state, and without cultivation of habits of obedience to the state (and, particularly, of loyalty to the sovereign). On the other hand, collectivists, who include individual, family and civil society within the state, forget the state's *raison d'être* and the way its role and the respect it warrants demand that it should be above particularity, faction and caprice. While Hegel was not a democrat, neither was he a totalitarian. He argued for the personal, and no doubt in practice unequal, accumulation of capital as a means to protect individual and family and to assure generational continuity; for the welfare state as a means of ensuring cooperation from subjects; and for autonomous institutions against the might of the executive. In this intimate and delicate balancing of individual freedom and state power, the insistence on both authority and on checks and balances, Hegel escapes the one-sidedness of liberals and collectivists alike, and at the same time lays claim to be regarded as the most subtle and far-reaching of conservative thinkers.

7 An assessment of conservatism

While a fully expounded Hegelian conservatism contains within itself the resources to answer many of the objections which can be raised to a theoretical conservatism, in practice those who see their actual

society riddled with defects and inadequacies are likely to be impatient with the temperamental resistance to change which they find in Burke and his followers in real politics. Furthermore, the stress on human ignorance and on the wisdom of generations – which would not get a hearing in other fields of endeavour – are too often simply an evasion of the hard task of shaking ourselves out of our complacency and working hard to do things better. To its critics, when faced with what they see as its blindness to pressing human problems, conservatism looks like little more than lazy self-interest bolstered by rhetoric and obscurantism.

It is certainly true that conservatism, in certain circumstances, will tend to uphold hierarchies and social distinctions. Conservatism is certainly not committed to egalitarianism, believing as it does in the right of individuals to make their own way through life and to benefit or not accordingly. Freedom of this sort is an important concomitant of the belief common to conservatives and classical liberals alike that individuals rather than the state are the best judges of their own interests. It is also an aspect of the traditional virtues of self-reliance and responsibility to family, qualities which conservatives also stress. But while not committed to equality, as we saw with Hegel, and in contrast to *laissez-faire* liberalism there is nothing in conservatism *per se* to rule out welfarism up to a point. It may indeed be a required part of life in a society that has any claim to be a community deserving of the allegiance of its members, something which is of great importance to conservatives.

None the less, there is no denying that in so far as it does not aim at egalitarianism and regards the means necessary to produce such an aim as likely to cause far more harm than good (and less equality, if the experiences of the French and Russian revolutions are any guide), conservatism does sometimes uphold hierarchies or inequalities. But it must be emphasized that it does not, and will not, uphold *all* or *any* hierarchies. In particular, precisely because of its belief in political ignorance and the imperfectibility of men, especially rulers, conservatism will not uphold totalitarian hierarchies (see TOTALITARIANISM). It will also, in Aristotelian mode, assert that in matters of morality and politics, in contrast to natural science, there are no special experts. Rather, in these areas the experience of the whole of mankind over generations is the main source of moral knowledge, against which should be balanced the pretensions of particular groups of people to moral expertise, however clever they are in their own fields.

As already stated, conservatism should not be identified with blind or dogmatic reaction. Far from being opposed to reform, the principle of reform is central to conservatism, and follows from its scepticism and empiricism regarding human affairs. If obvious abuses exist, then principles and policies must be modified to accommodate improvement. But the modifications must be suitably cautious and their effects monitored. Ancient institutions should be treated with respect, because they embody a kind of tacit wisdom. Because of their ignorance about the way things work and the effects of change, conservatives, although open to reform, are wary of large-scale upsets of what is working reasonably well. And they tend to prefer the tolerable, and even the tolerably bad, to the promise of an unknown and untried good.

Conservatives have no principled objection to a welfare state, providing it allows plenty of room for autonomous institutions and initiatives. But they are more aware than their socialist opponents of the tendency for welfare systems to stifle initiative and self-reliance, and are also more sensitive to bureaucratic bossiness and the inborn tendency of bureaucracies to serve themselves first and their clients second.

Perhaps in the end the issue between conservatives and their political opponents, whether liberal or socialist, is an empirical one. Against socialists, conservatives argue, plausibly enough, that societies with autonomous institutions and unplanned economies have done rather better for all than those with centralized planning and large bureaucracies. Against classical liberals, conservatives will point to the constant splintering of a society which encourages too much choice and diversity, and to the need in a coherent society for a sense of tradition and a deference to generally recognized authority. If these points can be adequately argued, conservatives can rebut the argument commonly made against them that in their resistance to change they are motivated primarily by self-interest. And if this form of argument seems to make the choice for conservatism rest in part on empirical considerations, this will not unsettle conservatives, for their claim is that their position is rooted in a better understanding of human nature and human history than those of their opponents.

See also: HUMAN NATURE

References and further reading

* Aristotle (*c.*mid 4th century BC) *Nicomachean Ethics* and *Politics*, in *The Works of Aristotle Translated into English*, ed. W.D. Ross, Oxford: Oxford University Press, 12 vols, 1908–52. (Important here because of the stress on the importance of experience in practical wisdom. Referred to in §2.)

Berlin, I. (1990) 'Joseph de Maistre and the Origins of Fascism' in *The Crooked Timber of Humanity*, ed. H. Hardy, London: John Murray. (A fascinating study of de Maistre.)

* Bradley, F.H. (1876) *Ethical Studies*, Oxford: Oxford University Press, 1927. (Stresses 'my station and its duties', and the plain man's view of right and wrong, against theory-based moral systems; but does not believe morality is completely defined by its conservative underpinnings. Referred to in §6.)

* Burke, E. (1790) *Reflections on the Revolution in France*, Harmondsworth: Penguin, 1986. (Classic statement of a conservative position. Referred to in §4.)

Grant, R.A.D. (1992) 'The Politics of Equilibrium', *Inquiry* 35: 423–46. (Contains an excellent rebuttal of the view that conservatism would conserve *anything*.)

Hayek, F.A. (1988) *The Fatal Conceit*, London: Routledge. (Defends the market in economics and conservatism in morals.)

* Hegel, G.W.F. (1833) *The Philosophy of Right*, ed. A.W. Word, Cambridge: Cambridge University Press, 1991. (The most succinct exposition of Hegel's political philosophy and that most relevant to conservatism. Referred to in §6.)

* Hobbes, T. (1651) *Leviathan*, ed. R. Tuck, Cambridge: Cambridge University Press, 1991. (In its stress on the limited role of the state and on the need for a state, the text is a source of much conservative thinking. Referred to in §3.)

Honderich, T. (1990) *Conservatism*, London: Penguin. (A blistering attack on conservatism, containing all stock objections, and more.)

* Maistre, J. de (1797) *Considerations on France*, trans. R.A. Lebrun, Cambridge: Cambridge University Press. (Shares many conservative themes with Burke. Referred to in §4.)

* Oakeshott, M. (1962) *Rationalism in Politics*, London: Methuen. (The best modern version of a Burkean position. Referred to in §5.)

* Plato (*c.*380–347 BC) *Republic*, *Phaedrus* and *Laws*, in *The Dialogues of Plato*, trans. B. Jowett, Oxford: Oxford University Press, 4th edn revised, 1953. (In his assessment of the complexity of human nature, Plato anticipates conservative thinking. Referred to in §2.)

Quinton, A. (1978) *The Politics of Imperfection*, London: Faber. (An elegant defence of conservatism.)

Scruton, R. (1980) *The Meaning of Conservatism*, London: Penguin. (A strong exposition of conservatism.)

Tannsjo, T. (1990) *Conservatism for our Time*, London: Routledge. (Argues that in certain circumstances conservatives should defend a communist regime. Attacked by Grant (1992).)

ANTHONY O'HEAR

CONSILIENCE OF INDUCTION *see* CONFIRMATION THEORY; SCIENCE, 19TH-CENTURY PHILOSOPHY OF; WHEWELL, WILLIAM

CONSTANT, BENJAMIN

see CONSTANT DE REBECQUE, HENRI-BENJAMIN

CONSTANT DE REBECQUE, HENRI-BENJAMIN (1767–1830)

Benjamin Constant combined the activities of a religious historian, autobiographer and novelist with a career as a political theorist and politician. Constant's intellectual outlook was shaped by French Enlightenment thought and two years spent at Edinburgh University in 1783–5 added experience of observing the British government and constitution at work. Through all of Constant's writings runs a consistent theme: the necessity of safeguarding the freedom of the individual in modern society. At the end of his life he summed up his liberalism thus: 'Freedom in all things, in religion, philosophy, literature, industry and politics. And by freedom I mean the triumph of the individual both over an authority that would wish to govern by despotic means and over the masses who would claim the right to make a minority subservient to a majority' (1957: 835). Constant's political activity and his writings, which some consider prophetic of the growth of modern totalitarian regimes, have been influential in the development of liberal thought in Europe and the USA.

1 **Political activity and thought**
2 **Religious thought**

1 Political activity and thought

The thought of Henri-Benjamin Constant de Rebec-que, known as Benjamin Constant (born Lausanne, Switzerland, died Paris) needs to be seen against the background both of his complex and subtle mind – ever sceptical and alive to paradox and ambiguity in all human transactions – and his long observation of the abuse of political power during one of the most turbulent periods of French history. Even during his childhood, Constant had experienced political oppression in Lausanne under the rule of the Bernese, and this instilled in him a lifelong libertarianism. This was reinforced by six years as chamberlain at the court of the Duke of Brunswick, during which time his sympathies veered towards Jacobinism. In Paris after *Thermidor* – and under the influence of Germaine de STAËL, with whom he had a long and stormy liaison – Constant tried to bring about the establishment of a moderate republican government in France, using pamphlets and, subsequently, his role as a member of Bonaparte's Tribunate. This remained his ideal during his long period of opposition to the despotism of Napoleon. After twelve years of enforced political inactivity and self-imposed exile in Germany, he sought a political career during the first Restoration and then, notoriously, collaborated with Napoleon during the Hundred Days of 1815. Despite criticism of his action, Constant maintained that the personality of a head of state was of little importance; the ex-dictator's declared intention to act henceforth as a constitutional monarch made him preferable to a restored, autocratic and repressive Bourbon. During his last years, Constant became unofficial leader of left-wing liberals in the French Assembly and one of its greatest orators, campaigning for such causes as press freedom and the abolition of slavery. The July Revolution of 1830, in which he was an important figure, saw the (short-lived) triumph of many of Constant's ideals.

Constant's political thought therefore was not shaped by abstract speculation alone. It developed out of opposition to the cult of antiquity prevalent in eighteenth-century France, and in particular to Jean-Jacques Rousseau's idealization of the small Greek city state. For Constant, Rousseau's notion of the supremacy of the general will over the will of the individual as set out in his *Du Contrat social* (The Social Contract) (1762) and his notorious ban on atheism led inexorably to a tyranny such as had been seen during Robespierre's Terror (see GENERAL WILL §2; ROUSSEAU, J.-J. §3). France had experienced a police state that felt justified in interfering in the lives of individual citizens and even in attempting to invade the inner sanctum of private thoughts and beliefs. Such a view of the individual's relationship with society was regressive and anachronistic, ignoring more than 2,000 years of human development. What may have been appropriate for the Greek *polis* in antiquity was certainly no longer so in the modern world, where personal independence and privacy had become essential in large commerce-based societies. These views, set out in *De la Liberté des anciens comparée à celle des modernes* (Freedom in Antiquity Compared With Freedom in the Modern Age) (1820), drew a clear distinction between freedom in the ancient world and modern freedom. In Constant's memory were Robespierre's communitarian rhetoric and exaltation of Spartan virtues, which demonstrated the dangers of re-establishing a form of society and social relationships where there were no clear boundaries between the public and private spheres. Where the supposed demands of the community were allowed precedence over individual rights, anything might be permissible in the name of the general good. He felt the same concern when it came to scientifically organized utopias of the future, such as that of the Saint-Simonians, which promised greater productivity and human happiness (see SAINT-SIMON, C. DE; UTOPIANISM).

Freedom in modern times demanded clearly defined areas where government interference was not allowed. Not only did the essential right to privacy of the individual need to be protected, due legal processes had to be scrupulously respected and preserved at all times as a bulwark for the individual against arbitrary persecution by an authoritarian government. Yet the Constant who steadfastly defended individual liberty and privacy, so abused by the Jacobins during the Revolution, nevertheless held throughout his career to the ideals of 1789: egalitarianism (as far as the rights of individuals, nations and races were concerned), religious toleration (despite the bitter anticlericalism of his own youth), absolute freedom of speech and of the press, and representative institutions which would be a vehicle for the exercise of popular sovereignty.

Constant's opposition to the usurper and dictator Napoleon, so powerfully expressed in *De l'Esprit de conquête et de l'usurpation* (On the Spirit of Conquest and Usurpation) (1814), was based on the same philosophical grounds. Caesarism, that is, rule by a military dictatorship that consciously echoed the republics of Graeco-Roman antiquity, was as much a brutalizing anachronism as Robespierre's Terror. Wars of conquest by a tyrannical demagogue were the norm in antiquity, but were out of tune with a modern world based on industry, banking and commerce, where peace, tolerance and justice were the order of the day. The *res publica* of antiquity had been replaced as the focus of importance by private pursuits and needs. 'The least government [is] the best government', Constant had written under the Directory,

anticipating the thinking of modern liberals for whom the legitimate spheres of government activity should be limited to national defence and the maintenance of law and order (see LIBERALISM §2).

Individual citizens with their private concerns and activities and their inalienable right to own property, to enjoy personal security, and to have freedom of self-expression, of belief and of movement should be expected to play no greater role in the running of the state than that of casting their vote and choosing their representative in a governing assembly. Gone was the claustrophobic world of the small city state so beloved of Rousseau, where every citizen played a direct role in popular democracy and people could legitimately involve themselves in everyone else's views and business. In its place Constant proposed a constitutional monarchy on the British model, with an essentially figurehead monarch and a bicameral assembly comprising an upper hereditary body, limited in its powers and ensuring stability, continuity and moderation, and an elected lower chamber reflecting the views and life of a society in constant evolution.

2 Religious thought

In a well-known fragment of an unpublished Preface to his novel *Adolphe* (1816), Constant wrote that 'all things are connected in nature' and suggested a link between 'religious belief' and 'enthusiasm for liberty'. Behind his lifelong work on the history of world religions, represented by *De la Religion considérée dans sa source, ses formes et ses développements* (Religion Considered in its Source, its Forms and its Development) (1824–31) and *Du Polythéisme romain* (Roman Polytheism) (1833), lay Constant's conviction that two related needs were fundamental to human beings: the need for freedom and the need to believe. For Constant 'le sentiment religieux' was not the illusion excoriated by D'Holbach, Helvétius and other Enlightenment philosophers (see ENLIGHTENMENT, CONTINENTAL). It was a real and permanent facet of human nature. Societies had evolved through the stages of theocracy, slavery, feudalism, absolute monarchy to rule by a privileged aristocracy; and at each stage the permanent human longing for freedom had brought resistance to oppression and the casting aside of outworn forms of government. Similarly, men and women of all historical periods had in them a religious sense or feeling, an inner need to rise above mere egoism that expressed itself in self-sacrifice and self-denial. All cultures had seen a constant struggle between the religious feeling of individuals, which was a living thing and needed to evolve and change, and the static outward shape imposed on it by a priestly caste in terms of forms of worship and dogma.

The parallel is clear: as an optimist and believer in human perfectibility, Constant believes that there is a law of movement in history in both in politics and religion that cannot be resisted. The need for liberty inherent in human nature will always ensure that those forms of government or of religious belief which are fixed, stagnant and unchanging are replaced by forms better adapted to the needs of the historical moment. In 'De la Perfectibilité de l'espèce humaine' (On the Perfectibility of the Human Race) (1829), it is unlimited human perfectibility that gives meaning to life – and indeed a form of survival beyond death in the progressive development of intellectual and spiritual qualities from generation to generation. Religious feeling had developed through history from primitive polytheism through theism to Christianity and had reached its highest form in modern Protestantism – open-minded, tolerant and pluralistic. Yet every form of belief, like every form of government, was a provisional one and would ultimately be outgrown. Political wisdom required an eventual change in institutions to reflect the evolution of society (the ultimate goal being a society that allowed the greatest personal freedom), and likewise a tolerant state would enable religious feeling to be expressed in a form appropriate to a new age.

List of works

Constant, B. (1957) *Œuvres*, ed. A. Roulin and C. Roth, Paris: Gallimard (Bibliothèque de la Pléiade). (Offers the most comprehensive modern selection of Constant's political and religious writings; another edition of *Œuvres complètes* is in progress (Tübingen: Max Niemeyer, 1993–) but will take many years to complete.)

—— (1806) *Principes de politique applicables à tous les gouvernements* (Political Principles Applicable to All Governments), ed. E. Hofmann, Geneva: Droz, 1980. (A summary of Constant's political beliefs.)

—— (1814) *De l'Esprit de conquête et de l'usurpation* (On the Spirit of Conquest and Usurpation), Hahn: Hanover; repr. in E. Harpaz (ed.), Paris: Flammarion, 1986; trans. and ed. H. Byrne Lippmann, *Prophecy from the Past: Benjamin Constant on Conquest and Usurpation*, New York: Reynal & Hitchcock, 1941. (An analysis and indictment of military dictatorships inspired by Napoleon's example.)

—— (1816) *Adolphe: anecdote trouvée dans les papiers d'un inconnu* (Adolphe: An Anecdote Found Among the Papers of an Unknown Person), London: Colburn and Paris: Tröttel et Wurtz; ed.

F. Tilkin, in *Benjamin Constant: Écrits littéraires (1800–1813)* (Benjamin Constant: Literary Works (1800–1813)), Tübingen: Max Niemeyer, 1995, 81–203; trans. with introduction by L.W. Tancock, London: Penguin, 1964. (A first-person novel of close self-analysis centring on the protagonists's inability to free himself from a love relationship.)

—— (1820) *De la Liberté des anciens comparée à celle des modernes*, vol. IV, in *Cours de politique constitutionnelle* (Freedom in Antiquity Compared With Freedom in the Modern Age), Paris: Béchet aîné and Rouen: Béchet fils; repr. in the collection, *Benjamin Constant: De la Liberté chez les modernes*, ed. M. Gauchet, Paris: Le Livre de poche, 1980. (Contrasts the notion of freedom in the ancient *polis* with the modern need for individual freedom and privacy.)

—— (1820–22) *Mémoires sur les Cent-Jours* (Memoirs concerning the Hundred Days), ed. K. Kloocke and A. Cabanis, Tübingen: Max Niemeyer, 1993. (An explanation of Constant's conduct in rallying to Napoleon during the Hundred Days in 1815.)

—— (1824–31) *De la Religion considérée dans sa source, ses formes et ses développements* (Religion Considered in its Source, its Forms and its Development), Paris: Bossange père *et al.*; repr. in P. Deguise (ed.), Lausanne: Bibliothèque romande, 1971 (extracts). (A study of the development of religious feeling through human history.)

—— (1829a) *Mélanges de littérature et de politique*, Paris: Pichon and Didier.; trans., with introductory and critical notices, by G. Ripley, *Philosophical Miscellanies translated from the French of Cousin, Jouffroy, and B. Constant*, Boston, MA: Hilliard, Gray, and Co., 1838, 2 vols. (A collection of essays on literary and political themes published shortly before Constant's death.)

—— (1829b) 'De la Perfectibilité de l'espèce humaine' (On the Perfectibility of the Human Race), in *Mélanges de littérature et de politique*, Paris: Pichon et Didier; repr. in P. Deguise (ed.), Lausanne: L'Age d'Homme, 1967. (Good all-round text.)

—— (1833) *Du Polythéisme romain, considéré dans ses rapports avec la philosophie grecque et la religion chrétienne* (Roman Polytheism Considered in Relation to Greek Philosophy and the Christian Religion), ed. M.-J. Matter, Paris: Béchet aîné, 2 vols. (A study of Roman belief in many gods that has links with Constant's *De la Religion*.)

—— (1988) *Political Writings*, ed. B. Fontana, Cambridge: Cambridge University Press. (The only available modern selection in translation.)

References and further reading

Bastid, P. (1966) *Benjamin Constant et sa doctrine* (The Political Thought of Benjamin Constant), Paris: Armand Colin, 2 vols. (A highly detailed account of Constant's political thought.)

Berlin, I. (1969) *Four Essays on Liberty*, Oxford: Oxford University Press. (Constant as 'the most eloquent of all defenders of freedom and privacy'.)

Deguise, P. (1966) *Benjamin Constant méconnu: Le livre 'De la Religion'* (A Neglected Work by Benjamin Constant: On Religion), Geneva: Droz. (The standard text covering Constant's work on religion.)

Dodge, G.H. (1980) *Benjamin Constant's Philosophy of Liberalism. A Study in Politics and Religion*, Chapel Hill, NC: University of North Carolina Press. (A clear and accessible account of Constant's work in these related areas.)

Fontana, B. (1991) *Benjamin Constant and the Post-Revolutionary Mind*, New Haven, CT, and London: Yale University Press. (An account of Constant's relation to predecessors such as Montesquieu, Rousseau and Sieyès, and an assessment of his originality.)

Holmes, S. (1984) *Benjamin Constant and the Making of Modern Liberalism*, New Haven, CT, and London: Yale University Press. (The standard exegesis of Constant's contribution to modern liberal thought.)

DENNIS WOOD

CONSTANTS, LOGICAL

see LOGICAL CONSTANTS

CONSTATIVES

see PERFORMATIVES; SPEECH ACTS (§4)

CONSTITUTIONALISM

Constitutionalism comprises a set of ideas, principles and rules, all of which deal with the question of how to develop a political system which excludes as far as possible the chance of arbitrary rule. While according to one of the classic sources of constitutionalism, article sixteen of the 1789 French Declaration of the Rights of Man and of the Citizen, 'any society in which rights are not guaranteed, or in which the separation of powers is not defined, has no constitution', the scope of constitu-tional principles is in fact broader. In addition to these two defining principles, the following are essential: popular sovereignty; the rule of law; rules about the selection of powerholders and about their accountability to the ruled; and principles about the making, unmaking, revision, interpretation and enforcement of a constitution. Despite close affiliations, constitution-alism and democracy are not the same. Whereas democracy is an institutional device which realizes the right of the people to govern themselves, constitution-alism aims to establish institutional restraints on the power of the rulers, even if they are popularly elected and legitimized. Constitutionalism embodies the self-rationalizing and self-restraining principles of popular government.

1 **The concept, its historical roots and main variants**
2 **Problems, tensions and difficulties**
3 **Future developments**

1 **The concept, its historical roots and main variants**

Constitutionalism in the modern sense of the term embodies the philosophical and juridical response to man's quest for political freedom. It encompasses the values, principles, reasoning, institutional devices and procedures which shape the idea of an institutional framework by which political freedom is secured. This framework is called constitutional government, and the instrument by which it is established is the constitution. The components which make up con-stitutional government vary considerably in different countries, to the point that what is regarded as a core element of constitutionalism in one country is considered incompatible with constitutionalism in another. However, there are a small number of properties that over a long period have been taken to define the very essence of constitutionalism, and about which there is a broad consensus.

The following precepts are basic to modern constitutionalism. First, the claim that the arbitrary will of the political ruler(s) must be submitted to rules. A government under law, a rule that governs the governors or, in the most pointed version, the rule of law and not of men, are but different ways of expressing the essence of modern constitutionalism. The term 'rule' means 'legal rule'; however, in particular cases extra-legal (political, moral) rules may also acquire constitutional quality if they are accepted as binding by both the ruled and the rulers (see RULE OF LAW (RECHTSSTAAT) §1). Second, constitutionalism implies the principle of popular sovereignty. Although in nineteenth-century Germany the 'graciously granted' rules whereby sovereign princes affirmed certain limitations on their sovereign power were called constitutions, the concept of constitutionalism requires the constituent, or constitution-making power of the people. This follows from the premise that in modern societies the 'people' is the ultimate source of sovereign power; since constitutions shape the sovereign power, they can only be ordained by the sovereign (see SOVEREIGNTY). The third essential element of constitutionalism is the idea of limited government. This means that both the purposes of government, and the instruments available to power-holders to realize those purposes, are delineated – something implicit in the term 'constituted power'. This entails, as the most important institutional consequence for the form constitutional government is to take, some kind of separation of powers. Furthermore, constitutional government calls for rules which define the accountability of the rulers to the citizenry. Finally, constitutionalism requires that changes to the constitutional rules must be effected according to the rules of the constitution itself. Based on these minimum requirements, constitutional documents normally extend over three main issues: individual rights; the structure of government; and rules about the revision of the constitution.

These characteristics distinguish modern from ancient and medieval constitutionalism, neither of which knew the concept of sovereign power or that of the natural freedom of the individual. The demise of ecclesiastical power, and the resulting disruption of the balance between secular and ecclesiastical authority characteristic of medieval society, gave birth to the idea of supreme power originating from a single sovereign source, paralleled by the idea of natural, equally unlimited, individual freedom. As a new political structure based on the monistic character of power was created, the word 'constitution' was progressively used to counteract the unlimited power of the sovereign prince. Gradually it became associated with the concept of political freedom. Originally appearing in English political discourse at the beginning of the seventeenth century, and signifying the empirical state of the body politic by analogy with the human body, 'constitution' had acquired its modern and narrower meaning by the end of that century. The term no longer referred to the social structure of a particular country, but to its government as formed by the law of the land. The locus of power and the domestication of power through law became the main point of interest. Moreover, during the seventeenth century, the age when the modern absolutist territorial state was consolidated, it became common to use the word 'constitution' in the sense of an eternal and supreme law.

Constitutional government has turned out to be the only viable alternative to either despotism or anarchy, the two main threats to political freedom. This was essentially Montesquieu's perception that among all states England was the only nation 'whose constitution has political liberty for its direct purpose'. This statement referred to the final triumph of constitutionalism in England's Glorious Revolution of 1688 which imported the three elements characteristic of what has become known as the Westminster model of constitutionalism; namely, parliamentary sovereignty; the rule of law; and the operation of so-called constitutional conventions. The latter element refers to legally non-binding political and moral conventions which ensure that the conduct of parliament (which by virtue of its very supremacy cannot be subject to laws) conforms to the sovereignty of the people, namely, to the will of the majority of the electors (see MONTESQUIEU, C. §3).

Although England is undoubtedly the homeland of modern constitutionalism, since the last quarter of the eighteenth century its notion of constitutionalism and particular form of constitutional government no longer embody the definitive model. In its US colonies the English model became itself the object of a constitutional revolution: the Constitution of the United States was drawn up in 1787, and became effective in 1789, the first year of the French Revolution. Quite different understandings of constitutional government came to prevail in the USA and France, greatly expanding the idea of constitutionalism. While the essentials – the submission of political rule to rules, popular sovereignty, limited government and the accountability of the rulers to the ruled – remained untouched, the ensuing institutions stood in clear, even hostile, opposition to those of the Westminster model. The Americans, who felt that the English version of constitutionalism did not protect them against the arbitrariness of parliament, reinvented, although with a quite different meaning, the medieval distinction between constitution and ordinary laws, a move inconsistent with the notion of parliamentary sovereignty. From this they drew three ideas. First, the constitution is superior to government and ordinary law, hence it creates, defines and limits government, including the legislature itself. Placing the constitution at the top of a legal hierarchy entails, second, that the constitution as the ultimate source of authority of political power be fixed, ordained in an act of extraordinary legislation and written in a document. This in turn generated a third element, namely the precept that the superiority of the constitution over ordinary laws includes the authority of the courts to invalidate laws incompatible with the constitution ('judicial review'). One of the most significant implications of this is the protection of constitutional rights not just against the executive, but against the legislature as well.

In its turn, the French Revolution, in which the US notion of the constitution as a written document enacted by a constituent power and superior to ordinary laws was adopted, gave birth to a notion of rights which stood in stark contrast to the English notion. The latter is based on the inseparable connection between a right and the institutional remedies against its violation so that, in the words of Dicey, 'in England the law of the constitution is little else than a generalisation of rights which the Courts secure to individuals' ([1915] 1982: 119). The French model, in contrast, proclaimed the rights of the individuals as being assured by, and hence dependent upon, the constitution, so that the whole burden of guaranteeing rights was placed on the constitution.

This notion of rights is part of a more comprehensive set of ideas which the French Revolution has contributed to the conceptual development of constitutionalism. Its main characteristic is the understanding of the constitution as the written embodiment of universally valid principles and doctrinal truths which render it a kind of rational plan for an utterly rational and smoothly functioning polity. This constitutional standard of complete rationality entails an incessant quest for the perfection of the polity and has inserted a spirit of political dynamism into the concept of constitutionalism which is lacking in both the English and the US versions. Consequently, in the French variant legal mechanisms to enforce the constitution are less important than political means. Thus what seems paradoxical at first glance, namely that the truly revolutionary and philosophically extremely influential Declaration of the Rights of Man and of the Citizen of 1789 has played only a minor role in the constitutional life of France, is quite understandable. Constitutional rights embody political claims and are primarily satisfied in the sphere of politics. Likewise, French constitutions have never allowed judicial review. They have mostly relied instead on the operation of the political process in general and parliament in particular to enforce the constitution. On the other hand, the French constitutional model's responsiveness to the political process has facilitated the incorporation of substantive policy goals (like social rights or state goals) in the constitution. Such a purposive constitutionalism is alien to US constitutional reasoning, which views it as a potential risk to the legal normativity of the constitution. Moreover, given the origin of US constitutionalism, Americans trust the courts more than parliaments.

2 Problems, tensions and difficulties

Since the basic idea of constitutionalism is essentially the substitution of reason and rule for the arbitrary will of man, a pivotal element of constitutionalism is the conceptual clarification of the binding force of constitutional rules. If the concept of popular sovereignty includes the supreme power of the people to establish whatever political order it pleases, and if at the same time constitutionalism embodies the idea of forming, and hence restraining, sovereign power, do these not represent inconsistent principles? Moreover, is not the term 'constitutional democracy' an oxymoron? Traditional answers to these questions affirm that indeed there is a tension between constitutionalism and democracy, but they regard constitutional government as a justifiable restraint on democratic rule in order to protect minorities against the will of the majority (see DEMOCRACY §3). More recent analyses of constitutionalism emphasize the dialectics of self-binding and point to the fact that constitutions are not only devices against majorities, but serve equally to protect majorities themselves from myopia, moral weakness and a lack of self-restraint. In this understanding both democracy and constitutionalism share the goal of limiting the risks of political liberty and of politics generally, but employ different means: the former protects the individual right to an equal share in the political process, the latter 'lowers the stakes of politics' by enabling the sovereign to exercise governmental self-restraint through institutional devices (Murphy 1993). On this view constitutions are not primarily disabling devices; rather, they serve as a support for democratic self-government in that they enable the people to preserve the conditions of political freedom and democracy, better to recognize the options open to democratic choice, to reduce the risk of irreversible mistakes, to develop the capacity for self-correction and to enhance their democratic capabilities through learning.

There is abundant evidence that the strategy of self-binding need not weaken an agent's capacity but frequently increases their options. The prime example is Ulysses, who had himself bound to the mast in order to be able to listen to the sirens without losing his life. Another instance is the prohibition of contracts to sell oneself into slavery: this does not restrict, but promotes, freedom. Having the collapse of the Weimar constitution in mind, the drafters of the German Basic Law wanted to shield the German people from the temptation of once again embracing totalitarian rule, and thus definitively excluded the option of abolishing basic constitutional institutions through any kind of constitutional amendment.

Likewise, the prohibition to print money imposed on the states in article 1, section 10, paragraph 1 of the US constitution can be understood as a mechanism of self-binding against the temptation to pursue policies which induce inflation (Holmes 1988).

3 Future developments

The main political impulse which has given constitutionalism worldwide recognition as the concept of a well-ordered polity has been the desire to 'tame the Leviathan' which was born in the religious struggles of the sixteenth and seventeenth centuries. Despite the manifold refinements which it has undergone, and notwithstanding a growing awareness of the aforementioned enabling functions of constitutions, constitutionalism is still widely associated with the purely negative functions of limited government. It is therefore often wrongly conflated with liberalism. This view does not take sufficiently into account that constitutions, although rarely containing solutions to particular substantive policy problems, can be credited with having resolved difficulties besides those that result from arbitrary state power. Thus, for example, the modern welfare state is the result of amalgamating the working-class demand for social justice with the idea of citizenship, which is a pivotal element of constitutionalism (see CITIZENSHIP §§1–2). Likewise, the inherent learning potential of constitutional devices has allowed constitutional states to cope more successfully with the challenges posed by the destabilizing technological, economic, social and cultural changes since the middle of the twentieth century than political systems which for one reason or another lacked constitutional arrangements.

However, approaching the end of the twentieth century, modern societies suffer from difficulties for which the traditional concept of constitutionalism has no answer. Economic inefficiency, civic apathy, a lack of concern for future generations, the seemingly irresistible decay of educational institutions and the continual worldwide impoverishment of urban life are just a few examples of phenomena which until now have hardly been touched upon by constitutional reasoning, even though they are of utmost importance for the quality of a polity. These problems facing a modern polity, which go beyond the traditional goal of preventing the arbitrary exercise of political power increasingly have been addressed by a school of thought which invokes the idea of a 'new constitutionalism'. This is characterized by concern for a good polity and hence completely revokes the basic assumption of traditional constitutionalism; namely, that for the sake of civil peace any striving after the common good and common values had to be excluded altogether from the realm of politics. Paradoxically, with this the 'new constitutionalism' returns to the Aristotelian point of departure in reasoning about constitutionalism; namely, to the idea of the *politeia* (see ARISTOTLE §§27–28).

See also: SHŌTOKU CONSTITUTION

References and further reading

* Dicey, A.V. (1915) *Introduction to the Study of the Law of the Constitution*, reprint of the 8th edn, Indianapolis, IN: Liberty Fund, 1982. (Classic treatise of English constitutional law with broad comparative views on French and US constitutionalism; expounds on the material in §1 of this entry.)

Elkin, S.L. and Soltan, K.E. (eds) (1993) *A New Constitutionalism. Designing Political Institutions for a Good Society*, Chicago, IL, and London: University of Chicago Press. (Thorough and multi-faceted reflections about the possible meaning of a new constitutionalism and how it differs from traditional constitutionalism.)

Friedrich, C.J. (1974) *Limited Government. A Comparison*, Englewood Cliffs, NJ: Prentice Hall. (A lucid and comprehensive account of the history and theory of modern constitutionalism from a traditional perspective.)

Greenberg, D., Katz, S.N., Olivero, M.B. and Wheatley, S.C. (eds) (1993) *Constitutionalism and Democracy. Transitions in the Contemporary World*, New York and Oxford: Oxford University Press. (Good account of the role of constitutionalism not only in Europe, but also in other parts of the world such as Latin America and southern Asia.)

Grey, T.C. (1979) 'Constitutionalism: An Analytic Framework', in J.R. Pennock and J.W. Chapman (eds) *Constitutionalism*, New York: New York University Press. (Contains a conceptual framework for the analysis of constitutions along particular properties like textuality, quality as supreme law and amendment procedures.)

Grimm, D. (1991) *Die Zukunft der Verfassung* (The Future of the Constitution), Frankfurt: Suhrkamp. (Contains a historical and analytic perspective on constitutionalism in the framework of social change and development.)

* Holmes, S. (1988) 'Precommitment and the Paradox of Democracy', in J. Elster and R. Slagstad (eds) *Constitutionalism and Democracy*, Cambridge: Cambridge University Press. (Expansion of the topic of self-binding referred to in §2 of this entry.)

Kasper, G. (1986) 'Constitutionalism', in L.W. Levy, K.L. Karst and D.J. Mahoney (eds) *Encyclopedia of the American Constitution*, New York and London: Macmillan. (Contains an elaborate account of the institutions and functions of modern constitutions, largely referring to the US constitution.)

McIlwain, C.H. (1966) *Constitutionalism: Ancient and Modern*, Ithaca, NY: Cornell University Press. (Indispensable for the understanding of the historical emergence of modern constitutionalism; particular emphasis on England.)

* Murphy, W.F. (1993) 'Constitutions, Constitutionalism, and Democracy', in D. Greenberg, S.N. Katz, M.B.Olivero and S.C. Wheatley (eds) *Constitutionalism and Democracy. Transitions in the Contemporary World*, New York and Oxford: Oxford University Press. (Illuminating conceptual distinctions with respect to the problems raised in §2 of this entry.)

Wood, G.S. (1969) *The Creation of the American Republic, 1776–1787*, New York: W.W. Norton. (Comprehensive and thoughtful narrative of the debates about the US constitution.)

ULRICH K. PREUß

THE CONSTRUCTIBLE UNIVERSE

The 'universe' of constructible sets was introduced by Kurt Gödel in order to prove the consistency of the axiom of choice (AC) and the continuum hypothesis (CH) with the basic (ZF) axioms of set theory. The hypothesis that all sets are constructible is the axiom of constructibility *(V = L). Gödel showed that if ZF is consistent, then ZF + V = L is consistent, and that AC and CH are provable in ZF + V = L.*

1   **The universe of constructible sets**
2   **The axiom of constructibility**

1   The universe of constructible sets

The 'universe' of constructible sets was the first example of an inner model (see SET THEORY, especially §7, the notation and terminology from which will be used throughout). The 'universe' of all sets consists of a hierarchy of (transitive) levels $V(\alpha)$, where:

$$V(0) = \emptyset \quad V(\rho + 1) = V(\rho) \cup \wp(V(\rho))$$
$$\text{at limits } V(\tau) = \cup\{V(\sigma) \mid \sigma < \tau\}$$

The universe of constructible sets has two equivalent definitions. According to the first definition, the constructible universe consists of a hierarchy of (transitive) levels $L(\rho) \subseteq V(\rho)$ where:

$$L(0) = \emptyset \quad L(\rho + 1) = L(\rho) \cup \lambda(L(\rho))$$
$$\text{at limits } L(\tau) = \cup\{L(\sigma) \mid \sigma < \tau\}$$

where the elements of $\lambda(X)$ are those subsets of X that are obtainable from elements of $X \cup \{X\}$ by a few simple set-theoretic operations:

$$G_1(u,v) = \{u,v\}$$
$$G_2(u,v) = u - v$$
$$G_3(u,v) = u \otimes v$$
$$G_4(u) = \text{dom}(u)$$
$$G_5(u) = \in_u = \{(w,v) \mid w \in v \in u\}$$
$$G_6(u) = \{((a,b),c) \mid ((b,c),a) \in u\}$$
$$G_7(u) = \{((a,b),c) \mid ((c,b),a) \in u\}$$
$$G_8(u) = \{((a,b),c) \mid ((a,c),b) \in u\}$$

According to the second definition, the constructible universe consists of a hierarchy of (transitive) levels $M(\rho) \subseteq V(\rho)$ where:

$$M(0) = \emptyset \quad M(\rho + 1) = M(\rho) \cup \mu(M(\rho))$$
$$\text{at limits } M(\tau) = \cup\{M(\sigma) \mid \sigma < \tau\}$$

where the elements of $\mu(X)$ are those subsets Y of X that are *definable* over X, in the sense that for some formula $\Phi(u,v,w,\ldots)$ and some $y,z,\ldots \in X$, $Y = \{x \in X \mid \Phi^X(x,y,z,\ldots)\}$. The highly technical proof of the equivalence of the two definitions involves correlating the set operations $G_1,\ldots,G_8$ with certain syntactic operations by which a complicated formula Φ can be built up from simpler formulas. A set x is *constructible* if $x \in L(\rho)$ for some ordinal ρ, or equivalently if $x \in M(\rho)$ for some ρ.

The condition 'x is constructible' is expressible by a formula $\Xi(x)$ of the symbolic language of set theory. Gödel showed that if Ψ is an axiom of ZF+V=L, then Ψ^Ξ is provable in ZF, where Ψ^Ξ is obtained from Ψ by restricting all quantifiers 'for all x' and 'for some x' to read 'for all x such that $\Xi(x)$' and 'for some x such that $\Xi(x)$', in other words, by restricting them to read 'for all constructible x' and 'for some constructible x'. The highly technical proof involves heavy use of 'absoluteness' considerations and of various necessary and sufficient conditions for being a model of this or that axiom of set theory (see SET THEORY §6).

In handling the axioms of ZF, it is generally most convenient to use the second definition of constructibility. For instance, to handle the axiom of union, one must show that if x is constructible, then $\cup x$ is constructible: If $x \in M(\rho)$ for some ρ, then $\cup x \in M(\sigma)$ for some σ. To do this, one observes that the formula $\Phi(x,z)$ or '$z \in y$ for some '$y \in x$', which expresses the condition '$z \in \cup x$', is limited and therefore absolute for transitive sets such as the levels $M(\rho)$, so that

$$\cup x = \{z \mid \Phi(z,x)\}$$
$$= \{z \in M(\rho) \mid \Phi^{M(\rho)}(z,x)\} \in \mu(M(\rho)) \subseteq M(\rho+1).$$

The separation axiom of ZF requires special handling. To handle it, one must show that for any formula Φ, if x is constructible, then $\{y \in x \mid \Phi^\Xi(y)\}$ is constructible. Now if $x \in M(\rho)$ one has $\{y \in x \mid \Phi^{M(\rho)}(y)\} \in M(\rho+1)$, so it would suffice to show that for any formula Φ there are arbitrarily large ordinals ρ such that for any $y \in M(\rho)$, $\Phi^\Xi(y)$ holds if and only if $\Phi^{M(\rho)}(y)$ holds. This result can be established, and indeed it is a fairly straightforward variant of the reflection principle (see SET THEORY §7).

In addition to handling the axioms of ZF, the axiom of constructibility must also be handled, for which purpose it is most convenient to use the first definition of constructibility. The axiom of constructibility asserts that $\Xi(x)$ holds for all x. What one must prove is the assertion that results when all quantifiers in this axiom are restricted to sets x such that $\Xi(x)$: What one must prove is the assertion that $\Xi^\Xi(x)$ holds for all x such that $\Xi(x)$, where Ξ^Ξ is the result of taking the rather complicated formula Ξ expressing constructibility and restricting all its quantifiers to constructible sets. Considerations of absoluteness are crucial. One successively establishes the absoluteness of the formulas expressing the conditions '$w = G_i(u,v)$', '$Y = \lambda(X)$', '$X = L(\rho)$'.

2   The axiom of constructibility

By basic ordinal arithmetic (see SET THEORY §4), if there is a well-order of a set X of order type σ, then there is a well-order of $X \otimes X = \{(u,v) \mid u,v \in X\}$ of order type σ^2. This basic fact, together with the fact that each element of $\lambda(X)$ is of the form $G_i(u,v)$ for some i and some $(u,v) \in X$, can be used to show that if there is a well-order of a transitive set X, then there is a well-order of the transitive set $X \cup \lambda(X)$ in which the elements of X come before those of $\lambda(X) - X$. In particular, if there is a well-order of $L(\rho)$, then there is a well-order of $L(\rho+1)$ in which the elements of $L(\rho)$ come before the elements of $L(\rho+1) - L(\rho)$. This fact can be used to prove by transfinite induction that there is a well-order of $L(\rho)$ for every ρ. It follows that for any set x that belongs to some $L(\rho)$ there is a well-order of x, namely the well-order of $L(\rho)$ restricted to x. It follows that if the axiom of constructibility V = L holds, so that every set belongs to some $L(\rho)$, then for every set x there is a well-order of x, so that the well-

ordering principle WO holds. But WO is a well-known equivalent of the axiom of choice AC. Thus V = L implies AC.

By basic cardinal arithmetic (see SET THEORY §3, notation and terminology from which is used throughout), if X is countable, then so is $X \otimes X$. This basic fact, together with the fact that each element of $\lambda(X)$ is of the form $G_i(u,v)$ for some i and some $(u,v) \in X$, can be used to show that if a transitive set X is countable, then so is $X \cup \lambda(X)$. In particular, if $L(\rho)$ is countable, then so is $L(\rho+1)$. This fact can be used to prove by transfinite induction that $L(\rho)$ is countable for every countable ρ. It follows that the set of those sets A of natural numbers such that $A \in L(\rho)$ for some countable ρ cannot have cardinal greater than $\aleph_1$. Gödel proved that if A is a set of natural numbers is constructible, so that $A \in L(\sigma)$ for some σ, then in fact $A \in L(\rho)$ for some *countable* ρ. His proof combined heavy use of absoluteness considerations with a celebrated result of mathematical logic (see LÖWENHEIM–SKOLEM THEOREMS AND NONSTANDARD MODELS). It follows that the set of constructible sets of natural numbers cannot have cardinal greater than $\aleph_1$. It follows that if the axiom of constructibility V = L holds, so that every set (of natural numbers or of anything else) is constructible, then the set $\wp(\omega)$ of *all* sets of natural numbers must have cardinal exactly $\aleph_1$ so that the continuum hypothesis CH holds. A generalization establishes that V = L in fact implies the generalized continuum hypothesis GCH.

V = L also has implications for descriptive set theory (see SET THEORY §5): in descriptive set theory, well-orders and AC are used both to produce sets with desirable properties (uniformizability) and to produce sets with undesirable properties (non-measurability). Assuming V = L, the well-order of the real numbers **R** obtained as above, when considered as a subset of the plane $\mathbf{R} \otimes \mathbf{R}$, turns out to be not too complicated (a Σ_2^1 set). It follows that Σ_p^1-uniformization for all p, and hence projective uniformization PU, can be proved assuming V = L; but Σ_2^1-measurability, and hence projective measurability PM, can be refuted.

V = L also has implications for combinatorial set theory (for which see SET THEORY §4, notation and terminology from which will be used). One such consequence of V = L is the principle $\diamond$, asserting that there is a function S from Ω to $\wp(\Omega)$ with $S(\rho) \subseteq \rho$ for all $\rho < \Omega$ such that for any $X \subseteq \Omega$, $\{\rho < \Omega \mid S(\rho) = X \cap \rho\}$ is stationary. While the significance of this principle is hardly obvious on first reading, it has an important consequence, namely ~SH, the negation of Suslin's hypothesis SH about the order type θ of the usual order on the real numbers. Much more complicated combinatorial principles, implying or implying the negation of various historic conjectures have been derived from V = L through a minute analysis of the fine structure of the constructible universe by Ronald Jensen.

While the addition of certain hypotheses to ZFC as new axioms has sometimes been advocated (see SET THEORY §6), the addition of V = L to ZF as a new axiom has seldom been so proposed (and was not so proposed by Gödel). This is because V = L seems contrary to the intuition that the universe of all sets is as 'wide' as possible, containing wholly arbitrary collections, and because its consequences in descriptive set theory are not all desirable or attractive. Indeed, strong large cardinal and determinacy axioms, which imply both PU and PM, and which *have* often been often advocated, are incompatible with V = L. But even in investigating these other axioms, the method of 'inner models', of which the constructible model is the prototype, has been widely useful, as have variants of the constructible universe itself. (For instance, the variant $L[\mathbf{R}]$, which starts with $L(0) = \mathbf{R}$ rather than $L(0) = \emptyset$, plays a role in such investigations: The proof that SC implies PD proceeds by proving that SC implies that AD holds in $L[\mathbf{R}]$, and that AD holding in $L[\mathbf{R}]$ implies PD.)

See also: AXIOM OF CHOICE; CONTINUUM HYPOTHESIS

References and further reading

Devlin, K.J. (1977) 'Constructibility', in J. Barwise (ed.) *Handbook of Mathematical Logic*, Amsterdam: North Holland, 453–89. (An authoritative survey covering both Gödel's and Jensen's work.)

Gödel, K. (1940) *The Consistency of the Continuum Hypothesis*, Princeton, NJ: Princeton University Press, 1994. (The original source.)

JOHN P. BURGESS

CONSTRUCTIVISM

Originally proposed by sociologists of science, constructivism or social constructivism is a view about the nature of scientific knowledge held by many philosophers of science. Constructivists maintain that scientific knowledge is made by scientists and not determined by the world. This makes constructivists antirealists. Constructivism here should not be confused with constructivism in mathematics or logic, although there are some similarities. Constructivism is more aptly compared with Berkeley's idealism.

Most constructivist research involves empirical study of a historical or a contemporary episode in science, with the aim of learning how scientists experiment and theorize. Constructivists try not to bias their case studies with presuppositions about how scientific research is directed. Thus their approach contrasts with approaches in philosophy of science that assume scientists are guided by a particular method. From their case studies, constructivists have concluded that scientific practice is not guided by any one set of methods. Thus constructivism is relativist or antirationalist.

There are two familiar (and related) criticisms of constructivism. First, since constructivists are self-avowed relativists, some philosophers argue that constructivism fails for the same reasons that relativism fails. But many philosophers of science note that relativism can be characterized in various ways and that versions of relativism can be useful in the interpretation of science. Therefore, constructivism's relativism does not by itself render it unacceptable. Second, constructivists are accused of believing that scientists literally 'make the world', in the way some make houses or cars. This is probably not the best way to understand constructivism. Rather, constructivism requires only the weaker thesis that scientific knowledge is 'produced' primarily by scientists and only to a lesser extent determined by fixed structures in the world. This interprets constructivism as a thesis about our access to the world via scientific representations. For example, constructivists claim that the way we represent the structure of DNA is a result of many interrelated scientific practices and is not dictated by some ultimate underlying structure of reality. Constructivist research provides important tools for epistemologists specializing in the study of scientific knowledge.

1   Constructivism and social constructivism
2   The development of constructivism
3   Criticisms and replies
4   Constructivism as an epistemological thesis

1   Constructivism and social constructivism

The term 'constructivism' refers to a cluster of related approaches to the study of science. All these approaches involve empirical studies of science emphasizing the social nature of scientific practice. Some constructivists draw the following theoretical conclusion from their empirical studies of science: namely, the truth or falsehood of scientific beliefs derives not from their relation to the world but from the social arrangements of scientists. Social constructivists maintain that social interests or factors in the micro-structure of scientific practice determine which beliefs are held to be true or false. Social constructivist case studies often focus on scientific controversies where resolution does not appear to depend on hard evidence or data, but on 'other factors'. Thus the claim that scientific knowledge is socially constituted results from the generalization of these other factors. This view is similar to a social-determinist view about belief formation. It is best exemplified by the Edinburgh School sociologists of science (see Bloor 1992) and Harry Collins' empirical programme of relativism (Collins and Pinch 1993). Another constructivist view is that scientific facts are constituted by arrangements of scientists, and animate and inanimate objects. This view challenges social determinism on the grounds that society is no better understood than nature, and so claiming that to understand the study of nature one needs to understand society is premature. This view is shared by actor-network theorists such as Bruno Latour (1987), and reflexivists such as Steve Woolgar (1988) (see also Latour and Woolgar 1986). They develop the view in different ways, though we will refer to them both as constructivist.

Actor-network theorists, such as Latour, maintain that scientific knowledge results from the establishment of connections between objects, animals and humans. For example, our knowledge of the structure of DNA connects together several different scientific practices, instruments and techniques. Challenging the structure of DNA involves challenging an established set of connections between these domains. Since constructivist case studies aim to show how scientific activity leads to this connectivity, often the case studies have a historical dimension, starting at the time before a particular scientific fact was established.

The terms 'fact' and 'belief' are often conflated in constructivist literature, leading to some confusion. To avoid further confusion we will define these terms as they are used here. Beliefs are propositions or sentences that are candidates for truth or falsehood. Individual scientists have various beliefs about their world. Facts are established pieces of scientific knowledge, as found in scientific textbooks. Though not the standard philosophical definition of 'fact', this definition will help in understanding constructivism.

Constructivism as discussed here is distinct from constructivism in mathematics or logic (see CONSTRUCTIVISM IN MATHEMATICS), and distinct from constructive empiricism in the philosophy of science. Constructivism shares antirealism with both these views and a kind of empiricism with the latter view. The antirealism in constructivism is expressed in the claim that the truth and falsity of scientific beliefs can

be established independently of any evidence from the real world (Collins and Pinch 1993) (see SCIENTIFIC REALISM AND ANTIREALISM §4). The empiricism in constructivism is a methodological tenet: all studies of science should be empirical studies of scientific practice. Versions of constructivism, for example the reflexivist view, are more readily compared to some kinds of scepticism or idealism. These forms of constructivism, claiming that scientists have access to nothing other than representations, are reminiscent of BERKELEY's idealism (Woolgar 1988).

Constructivism is antirealist and relativist: constructivists reject the view that science discovers a determinate structure to reality and they reject the view that scientific knowledge is achieved by following one particular rational method. According to critics, the rejection of these views constitutes a fatal flaw in constructivism. Nonetheless most constructivists enthusiastically embrace the antirealist and relativist consequences of their position.

2 The development of constructivism

Constructivism has a long heritage in philosophy. However, its modern history consists of refinements to the view developed by the Edinburgh School in the sociology of knowledge.

The roots of constructivism are in the sociology of knowledge which can be traced as far back as Plato, who proposed a relationship between a citizen's knowledge and their place in society. Marx provided the starting point for modern sociology of knowledge when he claimed that 'it is not men's consciousness which determines their existence, but on the contrary their social existence which determines their consciousness' (Marx and Engels 1970: 51). Hence, to explain the genesis of human ideas Marx looked to social structures (see MARXIST PHILOSOPHY OF SCIENCE). The discipline addresses issues such as: what is the relationship between a society or social structure and what is known? Does society affect science or the knowledge of nature more or less than it does the knowledge of culture? What kinds of social force produce knowledge and what kind of analysis of society reveals these social forces?

The Edinburgh School of sociologists of scientific knowledge (Bloor 1992) are direct descendants of Marx. Bloor starts out from a critique of the Marxist sociologist of knowledge, Mannheim, who maintained that all knowledge, except for that generated by the physical sciences and mathematics, is socially determined. Bloor expands the sociology of knowledge to include the study of mathematics and scientific knowledge.

As well as responding to Mannheim, Edinburgh

School constructivists are reacting to two other strands of thought. The first is American sociology of science, represented by Robert Merton (Merton 1973). Although Merton argues that the rise of science and its success results from social forces, he stops short of claiming any relation between the content of scientific knowledge and society at large. Merton studies science as an institution within society, divided up in particular ways. There are reward systems and hierarchies designed to maintain its social order in accordance with certain norms. Merton is sympathetic towards a logical empiricist account of the status of scientific knowledge. He agrees that philosophical analysis can uncover the method by which scientists achieve knowledge. The Edinburgh School maintains, contra Merton, that scientific knowledge can be examined sociologically.

Edinburgh School sociologists react to a second strand of thought that they call 'traditional philosophy of science'. They reject any philosophical approach that explains the attainment of scientific knowledge in terms of a method or set of methods. They also reject any approach that proposes only one standard of rationality. In Edinburgh School literature 'traditional philosophy of science' includes logical positivism, logical empiricism, POPPER, LAKATOS and Laudan (see LOGICAL POSITIVISM; SCIENTIFIC METHOD). Further, Edinburgh School sociologists claim that traditional philosophers of science ignore empirical information about scientific practice in their studies.

The Edinburgh School defends a view known as 'interest theory' in the sociology of scientific knowledge. This view can be understood as a set of methodological directives for the study of science. Since they argue that the truth or falsehood of scientists' beliefs are determined by social interests, they explain the validation of all scientific beliefs using the same causal model. Empirical studies of science are therefore undertaken to establish the derivation of particular scientific beliefs. The results of these studies lead them to conclude that scientific beliefs are not made true by any rational method that aided in their acquisition. Philosophers of science are often confused by the presentation of this position as the Edinburgh School deliberately conflates a method for explaining how they arise and a method for explaining how these beliefs are validated. This is a troublesome conflation, if one takes seriously the distinction between justification and discovery. But in fact, the Edinburgh School attacks this distinction explicitly; the conflation is an important tactical move. It is difficult to decide, however, what a causal explanation of belief validation amounts to (Roth 1994).

Finally, the Edinburgh School argues reflexively that the methodological directives should be applicable to the studies of science that result. In other words, any knowledge obtained about science can be explained by the interest model. In their view such reflexivity ensures that the social study of science is as scientific as the natural science under scrutiny (Bloor 1992).

What all constructivists accept from the Edinburgh School's account is a method, or loose set of directives, for how to study science. Minimally they accept the injunction to study science empirically as it is practised on a day to day basis. The historical version of this method – which is to move away from a study of scientific texts to the social context the texts arose from – also reveals that science is a messy business, a far cry from the linear and tidy affair implied by rationalist reconstruction.

Despite accepting the methodological directives, other constructivists try to avoid some of the more obviously problematic claims of the Edinburgh School. The Edinburgh School focused on beliefs as the unit of analysis, arguing that scientists' beliefs are determined by their social interests. Constructivists such as Latour and Woolgar (1986) concentrate more on 'scientific facts'. This changes the focus of study from knowledge as the possession of individuals to knowledge as a commodity or shared object. This approach introduces a more materialist view of knowledge. An example may help illustrate this point.

A scientific fact is represented in any key content statement from a scientific textbook. For example, a popular neuroscience textbook points out that dopamine-beta-hydroxilase is only present in terminal buttons of nerve cells producing nor-epinepherin. This statement is established in neurobiology and has a key place in research. Latour (1987) refers to such facts as 'black boxes': once in place they are never challenged or re-investigated. Fifty years ago the textbook statement would have made no sense, because there was no application for its use. The statement was a conjecture even half-way through the testing of the difference between nor-epinepherin terminal buttons and dopamine terminal buttons. Later it becomes a strong hypothesis, and, finally, is accepted by all researchers in the field.

What constructivists investigate is the 'hardening' of such facts, the transformation of conjecture into established background knowledge in a field. Constructivism is the view that such facts are not revealed to scientists, but are constructed by them. But this construction of scientific facts is not merely a social process. Constructivists, such as Latour (1987), challenge the Edinburgh School social-determinist assumption that scientific knowledge is determined solely by social factors, arguing that: the social determinist thesis fails because we do not understand society any better than we do the natural world. For social factors to be a suitable candidate for the sole explananda of scientific knowledge we require a well-developed understanding of society. These constructivists claim, however, that by studying science as the connecting point between society and nature, we improve both our understanding of society and scientific knowledge.

From their empirical discoveries about that nature of scientific practice, constructivists go on to make general claims about science. Importantly, they claim that scientific knowledge is constructed by scientists, not discovered (Woolgar 1988). Constructivists get into difficulty cashing out this claim. Several philosophers criticize careless presentations of constructivism, which imply that scientists literally make the world by negotiating among themselves. What is important about constructivism is the emphasis on the construction of scientific knowledge: constructivists do not emphasise the construction of the world, but the construction and acceptance of representations of the world.

3 Criticisms and replies

Critics of constructivism charge that the view is necessarily relativist. Next they conclude that since relativism is *prima facie* unsatisfactory, so is constructivism. Can this charge of relativism be answered? Though constructivists have not answered all charges of relativism, they have suggested ways around some of its forms. In what follows we will first survey the many kinds of relativism and then discuss constructivists'responses to this kind of criticism (see RELATIVISM; EPISTEMIC RELATIVISM).

Philosophers of science have presented relativism as a menace to science, knowledge, rationality and just about everything else. For example, Larry Laudan says:

> The displacement of the idea that facts and evidence matter by the idea that everything boils down to subjective interests and perspectives is – second only to American political campaigns – the most prominent and pernicious manifestation of anti-intellectualism in our time.
>
> (Laudan 1990: x)

In contrast, many sociologists of science cheerfully embrace relativism. Let us look at some of the forms of relativism that constructivists embrace, before critically assessing them.

Relativists are reacting to two main types of opponent: the realist and the rationalist. We can thus distinguish two broad categories of relativism: anti-realism and antirationalism. Laudan characterizes relativism with respect to scientific knowledge as 'the thesis that the natural world and such evidence as we have about that world do little or nothing to constrain our beliefs' (1990: viii). He adds that the relativist slogan is 'the way we take things to be is quite independent of the way things are' (1990: viii). This is antirealist relativism. The negative thesis of antirealism can be formulated as several different positive theses, versions of which are common in the literature. For example:

(a) Scientific knowledge is produced by the whim and fancy of indiviual scientists.
(b) Scientific knowledge is determined by social arrangements of the community of scientists.
(c) Scientific knowledge is determined by the wider political and social interests of individual scientists.

The realist here would argue that scientific knowledge is in some way determined by the real nature of the world. A weaker version of this claim is that knowledge is constrained by the nature of the world.

Another criticism of relativism is that scientific knowledge is further determined by scientists following particular rational methods. This is a thesis about the rationality of scientists and is independent of the realist criticism. The rationalist thesis is opposed by antirationalist relativists who insist that there is no one set of methods guiding scientists to the truth. Critics claim that antirationalism entails that no one set of knowledge claims has any special claim to validity over any others. But this latter position involves an extra step of reasoning and should be distinguished from antirationalist relativism: it can be called judgmental relativism (Knorr-Cetina and Mulkay 1982).

One final distinction is worth making: relativism is not equivalent to subjectivism, although subjectivism is a kind of relativism. A subjectivist believes that the truth of a scientific statement is decided by an individual scientist. Those who hold thesis (a) above are subjectivist and relativist. But there are those who believe that establishing the truth or falsehood of a claim has little to do with individual whim, and yet still has nothing to do with the real world or the scientific method. Those who hold thesis (b) above are in this position. Only thesis (a) above is subjectivist.

Constructivism is not wedded to either subjectivism or judgmental relativism. The assumption that all forms of relativism collapse into one or other of these positions is mistaken. An example of judgmental relativism about scientific knowledge is the claim that it is no more valid than a collection of beliefs about witches. Constructivists will join anyone else in acknowledging that, as a result of advances in scientific knowledge, diseases can be held at bay, we speak to each other across continents and fly around the world. Meanwhile belief in witches' remedies and broomstick travel simply have not caught on throughout society. Constructivists want to answer questions about why science is more successful than 'witchcraft', and so judgmental relativism is not a fruitful theoretical tenet for them. Subjectivism is no more promising as a theoretical basis for addressing such questions.

Critics could still maintain that even if constructivism is not wedded to judgmental relativism or subjectivism, it is still relativist. Why would anyone attempting to give a coherent account of scientific knowledge production be relativist? Constructivists' defences of relativism derive in part from methodological considerations about the study of scientific practice. Bloor's symmetry principle (1992) is motivated by these kinds of consideration. The principle states that the causes of a scientific belief can be of the same kind irrespective of that belief's later acknowledged truth or falsehood. False beliefs, according to Bloor, are not caused by special irrational means. The results of studies guided by this methodological assumption lead Bloor and others to conclude that impartial empirical studies of scientific practice do not lead to rationalism or realism about science. (Paul FEYERABEND endorsed similar kinds of conclusion in his historical studies.) This kind of argument amounts to an issue of the burden of proof. Some constructivists, however, reject this argument, resorting to the higher level claim that distinctions between relativism and rationalism or relativism and realism are simply the products of a form of analysis. They suggest that, with a shift of emphasis in the study of science, such distinctions will be rendered obsolete. Latour (1987) adopts this approach.

Latour argues that scientists make claims credible by placing them in a network of objects, other scientists, instruments and other knowledge claims. The following illustrative contrast illuminates this point. There are no widely available textbooks on broom travel, few flying brooms have been seen supporting human weight, and no brooms have challenged aeroplanes as vehicles of commercial air travel. By way of contrast aeroplane travel enjoys much support. In challenging the viability of airplane travel, however, we realize how physically and socially entrenched it is: there are textbooks on fluid dynamics and jet propulsion, and flight schedules are kept daily. Though few scientific facts are as indubitable or widely believed as the fact that 747s fly, all scientific facts are connected to a set of instruments, practices,

prominent scientists, observable effects and objects. Latour's suggestion is that it is possible to tell a constructivist story about how some beliefs have more perseverance than others, without invoking philosopher's traditional standards of rationality, by accounting for all the connections between the various objects, instruments and social intitutions that constitute the facts that the beliefs pertain to. Notice that on this account, contra antirealist relativism, objects do play a part in determining the validity of scientific beliefs. On this view scientific beliefs acquire authority from the role scientific facts play in connecting social and natural systems. Purported facts supporting other belief systems lack this authority.

This proposed way around relativism rids constructivism of an obviously self-destructive judgmental relativist or subjectivist component; but constructivism is still relativist. Certainly, scientific knowledge is validated by different methods in different fields, and was validated by different methods in earlier epochs; but uncovering these methods is part of the study of science. If this is relativism, then constructivism is relativist. But acquiescence to this kind of relativism is not a disaster.

Though constructivism may not suffer from a disastrous relativism, some argue the view is simply absurd (Devitt 1991). Constructivist sociologists often make an ontological claim that scientists construct objects, and this, according to many critics, is absurd. Of course, scientists do construct objects, thousands of them: telescopes, microscopes, oscilloscopes, micropipettes; and, on the smaller side, synthesized enzymes, proteins and chemicals of all kinds. Claiming this is surely not absurd; it is simply stating what goes on in scientific practice. Devitt and others worry that Latour and Woolgar's (1986) claim that Guillemin and his team *made* Thyrotropin Releasing Factor (Hormone) implies they did not discover it. And Devitt quotes Latour and Woolgar generalizing this point, saying:

> Despite the fact that our scientists held the belief that the inscriptions could be representations or indicators of some entity with an independent existence 'out there', we have argued that such entities were construed solely through the use of these inscriptions... objects... are constituted through the artful creativity of scientists.
>
> (Devitt 1991: 256)

A defence against Devitt's accusation can be made from Latour and Woolgar's comments about their methodological strategy. They emphasize that their claims about making the world are part of a rhetorical strategy whose methodological point is to detach us from the simple, and predominantly accepted, picture that scientists simply divulge facts about the world that are out there pre-packaged and ready for the taking. But, Latour and Woolgar's defence aside, many constructivists appear to make the ontological, and not methodological, claim that scientists make up the world (Woolgar 1988). This kind of idealism is not a productive approach to the study of science. Fortunately constructivism does not require this view and nor do constructivists' methodological and epistemological claims require a grounding in any form of idealism (Fine 1996).

Some constructivists tackle ontological questions head on and, rather than endorsing an idealist position, they view nature as a source of resistance to human action (Pickering 1994). The natural world, they argue, is ill-defined and scientific research is a kind of social action that characterizes the world's resistance with various kinds of representation. This view of the world as an as yet undifferentiated source of resistance is the closest constructivists come to a version of realism. It should be noted that critics such as Devitt would not regard this constructivist version of realism as realist.

4 Constructivism as an epistemological thesis

Constructivists claim that a detailed description of what goes into the consolidation of a scientific fact is epistemologically relevant. Scientists consolidate facts with a great deal of effort, moving from a hypothesis about a particular experimental effect to a fact that connects with accepted knowledge in the field. Their effort to consolidate the fact contributes to its authority. Describing how facts accumulate authority helps constructivists understand the distinctive nature of scientific knowledge. This is one version of a story familiar to naturalistic epistemologists (see NATURALIZED EPISTEMOLOGY; SOCIAL EPISTEMOLOGY). Understood in this way, constructivism is part epistemological and part methodological, and need make no ontological claims.

On the constructivist view, scientific facts acquire authority by passing through several kinds of legitimation strategy. One of the most important of these strategies is for a fact to guide all future practice in a particular area of research. One cannot investigate energy transfer in the mitochondrion without accepting the fact that there are mitochondria, and that they are the loci of energy transfer. Facts accumulate authority by attaching to experimental practice, constraining future experimental practice, being embodied in pieces of equipment, and being unquestioned by members of the scientific community. Constructivists claim to have established empiri-

cally that scientific facts do not gain their authority by satisfying standards of certainty or rationality for individual scientists.

Philosophers of science who share the view that empirical studies of scientific practice make an important contribution to understanding science may think that constructivists will contribute to epistemology (Nelson 1994). An epistemology suited to the practicalities of scientific practice has to account for all of science's particularity. Constructivism is most fruitfully interpreted as a contribution to naturalized philosophy of science and as joining in the attempt to give a naturalistic account of the attainment of scientific knowledge.

See also: FRENCH PHILOSOPHY OF SCIENCE; GENDER AND SCIENCE; NATURALIZED PHILOSOPHY OF SCIENCE; POSTCOLONIAL PHILOSOPHY OF SCIENCE

References and further reading

* Bloor, D. (1992) *Knowledge and Social Imagery*, Chicago, IL: University of Chicago Press, 2nd edn. (A coherent statement of the Edinburgh School's view. Includes a postscript responding to critics.)
* Collins, H. and Pinch, T. (1993) *The Golem*, Cambridge: Cambridge University Press. (A useful introduction to constructivist methodology, which is accessible to all readers. Empirical programme of relativism.)
* Devitt, M. (1991) *Realism and Truth*, Oxford: Blackwell, 2nd edn. (This edition includes a chapter criticizing constructivism and which presents a realist alternative.)
* Fine, A. (1996) 'Science Made Up: Constructivist Sociology of Scientific Knowledge', in P. Galison and D. Stump (eds) *The Disunity of Science*, Stanford, CA: Stanford University Press, 231–54. (Develops the view that the methodological insights of constructivists are important for philosophy of science. Connects constructivism to a consensus theory of truth.)
  Hacking, I. (1989) 'The Participant Irrealist at Large in the Laboratory', *British Journal for the Philosophy of Science* 39: 277–94. (A sympathetic critical appraisal of Latour and Woolgar's work.)
  Kitcher, P. (1993) *The Advancement of Science*, Oxford: Oxford University Press. (Contains detailed criticisms of Latour and others' views on realism and rationality.)
  Knorr-Cetina, K. (1981) *The Manufacture of Knowledge: An Essay on the Constructivist and Contextual Nature of Science*, Oxford: Pergamon Press. (One of the first constructivist laboratory studies.)

* Knorr-Cetina, K. and Mulkay, M. (1982) *Science in Context*, London: Sage. (A useful collection of case studies and theoretical debates about constructivism.)
* Latour, B. (1987) *Science in Action*, Cambridge, MA: Harvard University Press. (Develops the constructivist view via case studies and criticisms of traditional approaches in philosophy of science. Actor-network theory.)
* Latour, B. and Woolgar, S. (1986) *Laboratory Life*, Princeton, NJ: Princeton University Press, 2nd edn. (The first constructivist laboratory study published.)
* Laudan, L. (1990) *Science and Relativism*, Chicago, IL: University of Chicago Press. (A discussion of the place of relativism in philosophy of science. Introductory level.)
* Marx, K. and Engels, F. (1970) *The German Ideology*, ed. C.J. Arthur New York: International Publishers. (Modern sociology of knowledge, background reading.)
  Megill, A. (ed.) (1994) *Rethinking Objectivity*, Durham: Duke University Press. (A collection of constructivist, historicist and feminist approaches to defining objectivity.)
* Merton, R. (1973) *Sociology of Science*, Chicago, IL: University of Chicago Press. (An influential collection of theoretical papers on sociology of science.)
* Nelson, A. (1994) 'How Could Scientific Facts Be Socially Constructed?', *Studies in the History and Philosophy of Science* 25: 535–47. (Argues that there is an important philosophical challenge embodied in constructivist studies of science.)
  Pickering, A. (1984) *Constructing Quarks*, Chicago, IL: University of Chicago Press. (A case study from the interest theory perspective. Edinburgh School.)
  —— (1992) *Science as Cultural Practice*, Chicago, IL: University of Chicago Press. (A collection of theoretical debates about the status of constructivism.)
* —— (1994) 'Objectivity and the Mangle of Practice', in A. Megill (ed.) *Rethinking Objectivity*, Durham: Duke University Press, 1994. (See Megill 1994.)
* Roth, P.A. (1994) 'What Does the Sociology of Scientific Knowledge Explain?: Or, When Epistemological Chickens Come Home to Roost', *History of the Human Sciences* 7: 95–108. (A detailed criticism of the Edinburgh School account of belief causation.)
  Shapin, S. and Shaffer, S. (1985) *Leviathan and the Airpump*, Princeton, NJ: Princeton University Press. (Much-cited groundbreaking case study from the interest theory perspective. Edinburgh School.)
* Woolgar, S. (1988) *Science: The Very Idea*, London: Tavistock. (Sustained argument for a radical constructivism disguised as an introductory text. Reflexivist approach.)

STEPHEN M. DOWNES

CONSTRUCTIVISM IN ETHICS

There have been many forms of the idea that there are no distinctively ethical properties, and that ethical claims are composed or constructed out of other considerations. In some sociological writing the term is used for the view that ethics is artificial or socially constructed, for example out of social norms or attitudes. However, constructivism in ethics is now identified mainly with certain views not of the source but of the justification of ethics, which have their origin in Kant's work and have been revived and developed by John Rawls. Constructivism in ethics seeks to show how substantive principles, and in particular principles of justice, can be built out of minimal, uncontroversial elements, such as a slender account of action and reason.

1　Social constructivism and constructivism in ethics
2　Kantian constructivism: Rawls
3　Kantian constructivism: other possibilities

1　Social constructivism and constructivism in ethics

The idea that ethical ideas and institutions, like other ideas and institutions, are not basic features of the world but are *made* or *constructed* by human beings has a long history. Protagoras claimed that man is the measure of all things; Hobbes depicted the state and justice as a mortal God made by men; Hume argued that justice is an artificial virtue (see PROTAGORAS §3; HOBBES, T. §§6–7; HUME, D. §4). The twentieth century has seen a wide range of claims that standards of right and wrong, good and bad are constructed. Most of these claims assert that actual ethical norms are the *social constructs* of particular human societies, without relevance or validity beyond the societies in which they arose. Their proponents speak of the social construction of reality (of meaning, of science), the construction of social identity, the construction of political attitudes – and the construction of ethics (see CONSTRUCTIVISM). When ethical norms are viewed as social constructions the aim is to explain rather than to justify them; in general social constructivism has interested sociologists more than it has interested philosophers.

A more specific and philosophically significant

view of the construction of ethics identifies it with the claim that ethical principles can be justified by appeal to elementary and uncontroversial features of action and reason. Constructivism in ethics can be contrasted both with forms of ethical realism and with many conventionalist or relativist views of ethics (see MORAL REALISM; MORAL RELATIVISM). Unlike realists, constructivists deny that there are any distinctively moral facts or properties, whether natural or non-natural, which can be *discovered* or *intuited* and which provide the foundations of ethics (see FACT/VALUE DISTINCTION; NATURALISM IN ETHICS). Unlike conventionalists or relativists, constructivists think that it is possible to justify universal ethical principles (see UNIVERSALISM IN ETHICS). The distinctive feature of constructivism in ethics is the claim that universal ethical principles can be built out of quite minimal accounts of action and reason.

2 Kantian constructivism: Rawls

At first glance it might seem that most utilitarian and kindred ethical theories are constructivist, because they do not assume that there are objective moral facts and properties, and they aim to justify universally valid ethical claims (see UTILITARIANISM). However, the term 'constructivist' is not generally applied to utilitarian ethical theories, because their arguments appeal not only to conceptions of action and reason but to individual desires and preferences. It is usually reserved for positions which do not draw on assumptions about the content of desires and preferences in justifying ethical conclusions. For this reason constructivism in ethics is often spoken of as 'Kantian constructivism' (see KANTIAN ETHICS).

The leading exponent of Kantian forms of constructivism is John RAWLS, who has developed a range of arguments for constructivist approaches to the justification of principles of justice. In *A Theory of Justice* (1971), he uses the term 'constructive' very broadly to refer to ethical positions, including utilitarianism and his own contractualism, which seek to provide procedures for resolving moral problems (see CONTRACTARIANISM §§7–9). He contrasts constructive positions with theories, such as intuitionism, which provide only a plurality of unranked principles, hence no adequate procedures for resolving ethical problems (see INTUITIONISM IN ETHICS).

In his later work, beginning with 'Kantian Constructivism in Moral Theory' (1980) and continuing through *Political Liberalism* (1993), Rawls uses the term 'constructivist' more narrowly to refer to methods of reasoning in ethics which not merely offer ways of justifying substantive principles, but do so on the basis of minimal and supposedly uncon-

troversial claims about reason and action, and without referring to agents' desires or preferences. In these later writings Rawls no longer views utilitarianism as a constructive position and argues only for a constructive theory of the right, and so of justice. He also concludes that no constructive account of the good or of virtue can be given, and that we must accept that there is no rational way of choosing among conceptions of the good.

The most controversial features of Rawls' subtly differing versions of ethical constructivism are his considerations about the resources out of which an account of substantive ethical principles is to be constructed. His justificatory arguments assume that we can appeal not merely to instrumental but to other conceptions of reason or reasonableness. In *A Theory of Justice*, he had argued that principles of justice were justified if they were in *reflective equilibrium* with our considered moral judgments. In 'Kantian Constructivism in Moral Theory' (1980) he viewed persons as 'agents of construction' who appealed to certain ideals, such as a Kantian ideal of the person, in justifying principles of justice. In 'Justice as Fairness: Political not Metaphysical' (1985), he went on to argue that justifications could appeal to ideals which are constitutive of the identities of citizens of liberal societies. In *Political Liberalism* (1993) he argued that 'persons are reasonable... when... they are ready to propose principles and standards as fair terms of cooperation and to abide by them willingly, given the assurance that others will likewise do so' (49) and that this conception of 'public reason is characteristic of a democratic people: it is the reason of its citizens, of those sharing the status of equal citizenship' (213). Discussions of Rawls' versions of constructivism have questioned whether appeals to the ideals or identities of citizens, or to their conception of fair terms of cooperation, can count as forms of reasonableness.

3 Kantian constructivism: other possibilities

Several other recent writers have proposed alternative versions of ethical constructivism, and have argued that these can be used to justify universally valid ethical principles. Thomas Scanlon (1982) has proposed that moral principles are those which parties similarly motivated could have no reason to reject. Thomas Hill (1989) has suggested that Kant's 'Kingdom of Ends' can be seen as a constructive model for deliberating about moral principles. Onora O'Neill (1989, 1996) has proposed ways of reading Kant and of developing Kantian ethics that not only construct substantive ethical principles out of elementary conceptions of agency and reason, but construct an account of practical reason itself out of the necessary conditions for principles to be adoptable by all relevant parties, so explicating the Kantian identification of practical reason with universalizability.

See also: PRACTICAL REASON AND ETHICS

References and further reading

* Hill, T.E, Jr (1989) 'Kantian Constructivism in Ethics', *Ethics* 99: 752–70; repr. in *Dignity and Practical Reason*, Ithaca, NY: Cornell University Press, 1992, 226–50. (Interprets Kant's 'Kingdom of Ends' as model for constructing ethical principles.)
  McCarthy T. (1994) 'Kantian Constructivism and Reconstructivism: Rawls and Habermas in Dialogue', *Ethics* 105: 44–63. (Compares the conceptions of practical reason used in the later works of Rawls and Habermas.)
* O'Neill, O. (1989) *Constructions of Reason: Explorations of Kant's Practical Philosophy*, Cambridge: Cambridge University Press. (Papers on Kant's vindication of reason and on his ethics; emphasis on their constructive character.)
* —— (1996) *Towards Justice and Virtue: A Constructive Account of Practical Reasoning*, Cambridge: Cambridge University Press. (A constructive account of practical reason, justice and virtue.)
* Rawls, J. (1971) *A Theory of Justice*, Cambridge, MA: Harvard University Press. (His magnum opus: the most influential work in political philosophy of the late twentieth century.)
* —— (1980) 'Kantian Constructivism in Moral Theory' (The Dewey Lectures), *Journal of Philosophy* 77: 515–72. (Substantial revision of *Theory of Justice*; emphasis on procedures by which agents can reach agreement about justice.)
* —— (1985) 'Justice as Fairness: Political not Metaphysical', *Philosophy and Public Affairs* 14: 223–51. (Further revision; emphasis on the political rather than metaphysical basis of justification in ethics.)
* —— (1993) *Political Liberalism*, New York: Columbia University Press. (Substantial reworking of earlier papers; argues for the political justification of a liberal conception of justice, and the impossibility of justifying any 'conception of the good' in pluralistic societies.)
* Scanlon, T.M. (1982) 'Contractualism and Utilitarianism', in A. Sen and B. Williams (eds) *Utilitarianism and Beyond*, Cambridge: Cambridge University Press, 103–28. (Defends a contractualist account of practical reason: rules are to be accepted if nobody motivated to find agreement could reject them.)

ONORA O'NEILL

CONSTRUCTIVISM IN MATHEMATICS

Constructivism is not a matter of principles: there are no specifically constructive mathematical axioms which all constructivists accept. Even so, it is traditional to view constructivists as insisting, in one way or another, that proofs of crucial existential theorems in mathematics respect constructive existence: that a crucial existential claim which is constructively admissible must afford means for constructing an instance of it which is also admissible. Allegiance to this idea often demands changes in conventional views about mathematical objects, operations and logic, and, hence, demands reworkings of ordinary mathematics along nonclassical lines. Constructive existence may be so interpreted as to require the abrogation of the law of the excluded middle and the adoption of nonstandard laws of constructive logic and mathematics in its place.

There has been great variation in the forms of constructivism, each form distinguished in its interpretation of constructive existence, in its approaches to mathematical ontology and constructive logic, and in the methods chosen to prove theorems, particularly, theorems of real analysis. In the twentieth century, Russian constructivism, new constructivism, Brouwerian intuitionism, finitism and predicativism have been the most influential forms of constructivism.

1 Orientation
2 Russian constructivism
3 New constructivism
4 Brouwerian intuitionism
5 Finitism
6 Predicativism

1 Orientation

A call for 'constructive existence', standardly thought a hallmark of constructivism in mathematics, represents a general, revisionary attitude towards certain crucial statements of existence. That attitude is expressible as E:

(E) A mathematical statement $\exists x M(x)$, if crucial, is admissible only if a well-defined a can be constructed such that $M(\mathbf{a})$ is admissible, where $\mathbf{a}$ denotes a.

For E to be revisionary, the constructivist must indicate which claims are to be crucial, provide accounts of well-definedness and constructibility, and respond to any disruptions in traditional logic incited by E. It is in terms of these requirements that the outlines of influential forms of constructivism are demarcated.

Well-definedness. E need not govern all existential statements. Forms of constructivism are earmarked by choices of crucial statements, statements to which E is to be applied. Predicativists impose a version of E on claims about classes, but sometimes ignore E in elementary number theory. Russian constructivists put all their mathematics under the aegis of a strict reading of E.

As a call for revision, E is nugatory without strictures on well-definedness and constructibility. Conventionally, whenever $\exists n A(n)$ holds of natural numbers, there is a determinate m which is the least number for which $A(x)$ holds. However $\exists n A(n)$ is proved, one might then think to 'construct' an n such that $A(\mathbf{n})$ by using the computable function which outputs the number m on any input. So, unless the constructivist supplies further explanation, any proof of $\exists n A(n)$ might seem to satisfy E.

In general, well-definedness is explained in terms of canonical notations. Some constructivists count a natural number canonically denoted once a tally-mark numeral is available for it. Constructivist E. Bishop identified well-defined integers with number descriptions which are convertible into base-ten numerals. A real number may be deemed well-defined once a finitary recipe for approximating it is at hand. A predicativist about classes refuses classes not admitting definition in suitably predicative terms.

If well-definedness depends upon supplies of notations, it is natural to imagine constructive mathematical realms as nominalistic in that everything in them be nameable. It is also common to picture constructive realms as expanding over time as more notations are created. Some see in this image a contemporary rendering of Aristotle's notion of potential infinities, of domains which are inexhaustible not because there now exist infinitely many elements in them but because, over time, more elements always appear. Explicit treatment of time enters infrequently into constructive mathematics itself, Brouwer's use of the creative subject affording a celebrated exception (see INTUITIONISM §3).

Constructions. Constructibility is explicated in functional or operational terms. In general, a value is constructible just in case there is a recipe for computing that value in principle. Again, definite restrictions are needed if E is to fulfil a desire which often motivates constructivism: that acceptable definitions in mathematics lead to algorithmic computation. This desire is explicit in E*, a generalization of E many constructivists endorse.

(E*) The statement $\forall x \exists y A(x, y)$ is, if crucial, admissible only when there is a construction o which computes, given any well-defined value a for x, a well-defined $o(a)$ such that $A(\mathbf{a}, \mathbf{o(a)})$ is admissible.

Conventionally, axioms of choice ensure that, when $\forall x \exists y A(x, y)$ holds, there is a function f such that $\forall x A(x, \mathbf{f}(x))$ holds too. Hence, talk of 'constructions' must amount to more than talk of conventional functions. Once again, forms of constructivism are differentiated in the kinds of construction allowed. Traditional intuitionists demand that the class of constructions include only those operations given by computing recipes which humans can, in principle, follow. Finitists seem to want more: that recipes be guaranteed to output on any admissible input. Given their nominalistic leanings, certain constructivists identify operations with explicit rules or linguistic expressions of rules.

Constructive logics. Constructivism almost always calls for radical revisions in conventional mathematics. E may require, of any statement, that its admissibility entail the availability of constructions. To see why, take a statement S and define a predicate $A(x)$ so that $A(x)$ is true of 0 alone, if S holds, and of 1 alone otherwise. Trivially, when S holds, there is an m such that $A(\mathbf{m})$ and, given E, there must be a construction of such an m. But there is more to see from this example. If the law of the excluded middle (LEM) is valid, there is a simple proof of $\exists n A(n)$. But, if the truth or falsity of S is unknown, this simple proof appears to violate E. Short of settling S, one cannot construct a well-defined m such that $A(\mathbf{m})$, if 'construction' and 'well-definedness' are interpreted restrictively, since such an m equals 0 just in case S is true. Therefore, E is so interpretable as to conflict with the validity of LEM.

It has also been said that constructivism requires changes in logic for the reason that mathematical claims, constructively treated, hold extra information in the form of recipes for construction. Supplying this information is a requirement on any constructively correct proof. Presumably, the proof of $\exists n A(n)$ just described does not bear appropriate information when S is unknown. In this regard, it is important to note that the impact of E upon logic should not be thought wholly restrictive. Constructive claims can feature in proofs not only as conclusions but also as premises and, hence, as yielding up extra information. Some constructivists, for example, read E* as underwriting logical principles for deducing, directly from $\forall x \exists y$ premises, axioms of choice.

One way constructivists delimit needed alterations to logic is by establishing canons for correct constructive proof. Given such canons, a principle of inference is to be allowed when it licenses inferences that preserve correct provability. Intuitionists and Russian constructivists, for example, require of disjunctive and universal claims that

(E∨) a constructive proof of $(A \vee B)$ include an effective marker and a further constructive proof. If the marker has value 0, the further proof is one of A and, if the marker is 1, the proof is of B and

(E∀) a constructive proof of $\forall n A(n)$ involve an operation f such that, for any number m, $f(m)$ yields a constructive proof of $A(\mathbf{m})$.

The basic idea of using canons of abstract proof to assess logical principles is apparent in the writings of Brouwer. A. Heyting and A.N. Kolmogorov were the first to devise both proof specifications for each form of mathematical statement and formal logics arguably correct with respect to them. (Kolmogorov's logic was not complete, however.) Allegiance to the logic of Heyting, if not to any particular formalization of it, is shared by many constructivists.

Logics obeying E∨ and E∀ may fail to certify LEM. To see this, let $A(n)$ be an undecidable predicate of natural numbers. Then, $\forall n(A(n) \vee \sim A(n))$ plausibly lacks a constructive proof. For, were there such a proof, it would yield a recipe f giving, computably in n, a marker $f(n)$ signalling, in each case, the truth or the falsity of $A(\mathbf{n})$ and contradicting the supposition that $A(\mathbf{n})$ be undecidable.

2 Russian constructivism

Prominent among Russian (or Markovian) constructivists have been A.A. Markov, who initiated the approach around 1950, N.A. Shanin and G.S. Ceitin. As constructivists, the Russians might be thought most exacting, since E is imposed on existential quantifications over any domain. Entities are well-defined only if they admit encoding as natural numbers or as words on a finite alphabet. Encodings must be, as Markov wrote, 'potentially realizable' as concrete notation (1962: 2). Accordingly, Russian constructivists require operations to be given as Turing machines or Markov algorithms and, hence, as finite words. Sets are identified with arithmetic formulas with one free variable.

In virtue of their views on operations, a belief in (a version of) Church's thesis (CT) is ascribed to Russian constructivists. CT's most straightforward version is 'Every total numerical function is Turing computable'. This CT is not, as in recursion theory, a hypothesis about the meaning of 'informally computable', but a powerful mathematical axiom. For example, CT entails, in Russian constructivism, the falsity of the general LEM. The Markovian implementation of E, then, enjoins upon Russian constructivists markedly anti-classical principles of logic and mathematics.

Unlike new constructivists and Brouwerian intuitionists, Russian constructivists adopt (a form of) Heyting's logic as an official formal system. They employ an understanding of the system's signs devised by Shanin on which the truth of an existential claim S records the existence of an algorithm on whose operation S is a specification. In the name of this understanding, mathematical principles including CT get adopted which are permitted by neither intuitionists nor new constructivists. Among these is Markov's principle:

(MP) Whenever a natural number predicate $A(x)$ is decidable, $\exists n A(n)$ is provable constructively from $\sim\forall n \sim A(n)$.

When MP is rendered in algorithmic terms, a motive for adopting it is plainest. The decidability of $A(x)$ then requires a recipe R for determining membership in $\{n: A(n)\}$. If one runs R successively on inputs $0, 1, 2, \ldots$ searching for members of $\{n: A(n)\}$, a proof of $\sim\forall n\sim A(n)$ guarantees that this search cannot fail. MP says that, in these circumstances, there is an m such that $A(\mathbf{m})$ to which the search procedure will lead.

Adherence to CT lends Russian constructive analysis a computable cast throughout. As O. Aberth wrote, the mathematics 'may be informally described as an analysis wherein a computation algorithm is required for every entity employed. The functions, the sequences, even the numbers of computable analysis are defined by means of algorithms. In this way definition and evaluation are made inseparable' (1980: 2). There is no single conception of real number within Russian constructivism. A real is an 'FR-number', for example, when it is given in terms of a pair of algorithms, the first yielding a Cauchy sequence of rational approximants and the second a modulus of convergence. ('FR' stands for 'fundamental sequence with regulator of convergence'.) The most famous mathematical theorem of Russian constructivism is that proved by Ceitin (and, independently, by Kreisel, Lacombe and Schoenfield), which implies that every function from the reals to the reals is continuous. In Russian constructivism, this does not entail, as it would conventionally, that every real-valued function on a closed interval is uniformly continuous. Using a result of E. Specker, Russian constructivists prove that there are continuous functions which are unbounded on closed intervals.

3 New constructivism

New constructivists (or Bishop constructivists) comprise a relatively small group of mathematicians inspired by E. Bishop. Bishop's influential *Foundations of Constructive Analysis* banished lingering doubts that a significant mathematics could survive constructivization. It was consequent to the book's 1967 publication that new constructivism had its greatest impact upon mathematics.

As for well-defined entities, new constructivists do not require that everything be coded as integers. In addition to numbers, they embrace abstract operations, functions (akin to extensional operations), proofs and sets. There is canonical number notation but no special notations for sets or operations. A set S is said to be 'constructed' once recipes are given for constructing S-elements and conditions are specified under which equalities between those elements can be proved. For example, a new constructivist real number is a triple $\langle r,p,s \rangle$ of operations r and s and a proof p wherein r is a sequence of rationals, s a sequence of natural numbers and p a proof that s is a modulus of convergence for r.

As far as constructions are concerned, only mathematical operations representable by demonstrably computable recipes are allowed. Even so, new constructivists refuse CT and set no a priori limit on the way recipes must be expressed. Nor do new constructivists endorse a particular formalism for constructive logic. Certain working limitations are, however, discernible from a metamathematical viewpoint: CT has been proven consistent with systems reflecting Bishop's ideas. Metamathematical experience also suggests that all new constructive theorems are formally provable from suitable axioms via Heyting's logic.

Bishop insisted that new constructive mathematics capture the 'numerical meaning' of mathematical claims. Numerical meaning, he averred, is the sole clear and legitimate meaning for any mathematics. This meaning was to be cashed out in predicting the outcomes of performable computations on the integers, computations that come from realizing constructive theorems as computer programs. Bishop encouraged a comparison between formalizations of new constructivism and high-level specification and programming languages, ones whose proofs could be compiled into implementable code. This general idea

of 'programming constructive mathematics' has since been taken up by a number of computer scientists.

The principal effort in new constructivism, which Bishop called 'the most urgent task of the constructivist' (1970: 54), is not a wholly autonomous construction of mathematics under the guidance of E but a painstaking *re*construction of classical mathematics intended to reveal its numerical meaning. The goal is to set as many traditional theorems as possible onto a constructive basis without offending conventional sensibilities. Conflict never erupts between theorems of new constructivism and those of conventional mathematics since new constructivists shun any anti-classical consequences of E.

Without benefit of nonclassical assumptions, new constructivists cannot prove, as their Russian colleagues do, that every real-valued function of a real variable is continuous. Moreover, Specker's theorem shows that they cannot expect to prove that continuous functions are bounded in range, even on closed unit intervals. In order to retain the boundedness theorem for continuous functions on such intervals, new constructivists supplement the traditional statement of the theorem with the extra hypothesis that the function is uniformly continuous. This kind of hypothesis supplementation has become a feature of all branches of new constructive mathematics.

4 Brouwerian intuitionism

The most celebrated of contemporary mathematical constructivisms, at least before 1967, was Brouwerian (Dutch or neo-) intuitionism. To an extent, the celebrity of intuitionism was allied to that of its leading exponent, L.E.J. Brouwer, who first presented the approach in articles appearing between 1907 and 1930 (see INTUITIONISM §§2–3). Brouwer and his followers maintained a relative liberality in the matter of well-definedness. Besides natural numbers, intuitionists granted full status to non-algorithmic or 'free choice' sequences, kinds of sets, abstract proofs (including infinitary ones) and moments of time. Brouwer refused nominalistic constraints: mathematical existence for him did not await the fashioning of notations. Mathematics was to be constructed as a free creation, unaided by realist metaphysics, linguistic representation or empirical data. Brouwer deemed an entity legitimate if it was apparent to a Neo-Kantian inner intuition. A well-defined entity could be displayed in intuition either as a mental construction from the perception of a passage in time or as a choice sequence or set of items so constructed.

From among a panoply of legitimate operations on numbers, intuitionists denominate as 'law-like' those functions which are computable by recipe. In keeping with his anti-linguistic bent, Brouwer did not establish strict limits on the means by which recipes are to be communicated and CT for law-like sequences is not intuitionistically acceptable. Brouwer expressed a concern (one which both Bishop and Markov later proved unfounded) that the law-like continuum – in which reals are identified with law-like sequences – would not support a satisfactory real analysis. This concern seems to have led him to import into intuitionistic mathematics an analogue of the probabilistic 'choice sequences' of Borel. For Brouwer, choice sequences need not be law-like or even fully determinate. There may be some restrictions set upon sequence terms to appear in future but, beyond that, nothing about the course of a sequence may be presumed known.

Traditionally, there are two intuitionistic analogues to the conventional notion of set: 'species' and 'spread'. Species are properties determined by extensional mathematical predicates and individuated extensionally: pairs of species are identical when they have the same members. Spreads, on which Brouwer laid great emphasis, are either species of choice sequences constrained to obey a 'spread law' or species of sequences obtained from those via continuous mappings. The generators of real numbers comprise a spread in the latter sense.

The quintessential intuitionistic result is 'Brouwer's theorem': every real-valued function of a real variable on a closed, bounded interval is uniformly continuous. Brouwer concluded from this that every real-valued function on the reals is continuous. Brouwer's proof of the latter is markedly different from that which leads to Ceitin's theorem in Russian constructivism; it relies upon mathematical principles inconsistent with CT (see INTUITIONISM §3).

5 Finitism

As the name suggests, finitism requires that one eschew reference to infinite collections. In the case of Hilbert's finitism, this requirement was coupled with a desire, epistemically motivated, to replace abstract concepts with concrete, visualizable notation. Hilbert's idea was that a metamathematics confined to the realm of the visualizable would secure conventional mathematics against the paradoxes. Besides Hilbert's finitistic metamathematics, notable forms of twentieth-century finitism are represented by Skolem's primitive recursive arithmetic and Yessenin-Volpin's ultra-intuitionism.

For most finitists, only natural numbers or items encodable as natural numbers count as fully well-defined. Numbers are not conceived as constituting an infinite totality but as individually realizable in

concrete notation. Hilbert would have had it that talk of natural number, finitistically construed, comes down to talk of (the intuitable forms of) strings of tally marks. He wrote, 'The subject matter of mathematics is, in accordance with this theory, the concrete symbols themselves whose structure is immediately clear and recognizable' ([1926] 1983: 142) (see HILBERT'S PROGRAMME AND FORMALISM).

If the use of unbounded existential quantification is believed to require infinite totalities, as it was by Hilbert, restriction E will be implemented finitistically using constructions carrying explicit bounds. Bounded existential quantifications over the natural numbers are usually finitistically admissible and other existentially quantified claims, when allowed, get treated as 'incomplete statements', abbreviations for bounded quantifications. Universal quantifications are, if admissible, finitistically reconstrued as free variable expressions each instance of which is verifiable or falsifiable by direct calculation.

Constructions do enter into finitistic mathematics, but not as members of an infinite domain of number operations, as in intuitionism. Nor are they identified with members of a category of abstract rules or infinite graphs. An operation on natural numbers is a finitistic construction if realizable as a combinatorial transformation of concrete signs for which explicit bounds on the number of steps required to complete the transformation have been given. Primitive recursive functions are natural candidates for finitistic constructions on the natural numbers since these functions are Turing computable functions definable without unbounded search routines. Whether the class of finitistically admissible functions includes more than the primitive recursive functions is a topic of disagreement.

In Hilbertian finitism, admissible statements are said to capture mathematical claims which are '*inhaltlich*' or contentual. Statements refusing finitistic reconstrual were considered not contentual but ideal, expressions lacking full content. For Skolem, only those statements whose truth-values are fully determinable via primitive recursive calculations are admitted. Arithmetical predicates which are composed of simple equations between primitive recursive terms combined by connectives and bounded quantifiers Skolem treated as primitive recursive functions. Therefore, systems representing this approach are called 'logic-free', since quantifiers and connective signs are not required. Because of the limitations on the kinds of claim permitted, the proofs in Skolem's and Hilbert's finitistic arithmetics obeyed conventional logic.

Finitistic number theory and analysis, in the style of Skolem, has undergone some development, notably by R. Goodstein. Various constructions of real number are examined, among them that of primitive recursive real number: a primitive recursive sequence armed with a primitive recursive modulus. Anticlassical mathematical axioms are refused; hence, there are no finitistic continuity theorems like Ceitin's. However, since finitistic mathematics is intuitionistically acceptable, neither will it be possible to contradict Brouwer's theorems. According to Goodstein, a finitist in the style of Skolem cannot prove that a bounded, monotone sequence of rational numbers is convergent.

The so-called 'ultra-intuitionism' of A.S. Yessenin-Volpin differs radically from the views just described. Standard concepts of natural number and Skolem's 'recursive mode of thought' are not accepted as unequivocally correct. Yessenin-Volpin limits well-definedness to numbers which are feasible rather than potentially realizable: to be well-defined, an ultra-intuitionistic number must be literally displayed as a notation. One might say that the well-defined numbers of ultra-intuitionism do not constitute a single potentially infinite series but form a tree, each branch of which represents a temporally expanding series of tokens from some numeral system. From P. Bernays and G. Kreisel, commentators have adopted the term 'strict finitism' for application to such positions as Yessenin-Volpin's in distinguishing them from more liberal finitistic conceptions. Among philosophers of language, the viability of strict finitism has proved a subject of controversy. M. Dummett (1975) has maintained that sorites-like paradoxes would so haunt strict finitism that it is revealed as incoherent; C. Wright (1982) has since raised serious questions about the correctness of Dummett's conclusions.

6 Predicativism

Predicativism took impetus from the writings of Poincaré and Russell on the paradoxes and received influential, but troubled, expression in Whitehead and Russell's *Principia Mathematica* (1910–13) (see THEORY OF TYPES). Predicativistic approaches to the foundations of mathematics were later instigated or investigated by C. Chihara, S. Feferman, G. Kreisel, P. Lorenzen, H. Wang and H. Weyl, among others.

Predicativists would have it that all mathematical entities – or all higher-order entities – are logical classes and that their existence is governed by a version of E. A logical class $\{x: A(x)\}$ is predicatively well-defined on condition that all quantifiers in $A(x)$ are restricted to a range of classes or entities already known to be well-defined and including neither $\{x: A(x)\}$ nor any class presupposing it for its

definition. Definitions $\{x: A(x)\}$ satisfying this condition are termed 'predicative' and others 'impredicative'. Russell put forward the requirement that all classes be predicative in the form of what came to be known as the 'vicious-circle principle'. According to Russell, predicative classes must be organized into types so that 'any expression containing an apparent [bound] variable is of higher type than that variable' ([1908] 1967: 182). Consequently, the favoured way to implement bans against impredicativity has been to devise hierarchical formal systems (predicative type theories) for class definition and manipulation.

An intended model of predicative formalism, greatly simplified, is segmented into an ascending sequence of orders or levels indexed by natural or ordinal numbers. At the lowest or 0 level is a collection of given elements such as the natural numbers. Level 1 contains those classes whose definitions involve quantifiers ranging only over the given elements, level 2 contains classes specifiable using quantifiers ranging either over the given elements or over classes of level 1, and so on. Each class has a level, so impredicative classes are ruled out. Formalisms embodying an idea of levels include the 'ramified type theory' of *Principia Mathematica* and Wang's systems Σ.

A class is predicative thanks to a suitable definition or notation for it; that notation cannot be grasped before notations for classes of lower level are grasped. As Wang put it, 'new objects are only to be introduced stage by stage without disturbing the arrangement of things already introduced or depending for determinedness on objects yet to be introduced at a later stage' (1970: 640). Following Poincaré, one often imagines predicative universes as expanding over time.

As for constructions, we can think of each predicative class as the result of a well-founded construction process involving conventional logical or class operations such as complementation, intersection and union, and quantification which is predicatively restricted. Hence, the imposition of E upon predicative mathematics seems to call for no great alteration in the fundamental inferences of conventional higher-order logic, apart perhaps from variable indexing. Each variable may wear an ordinal index and quantifier rules be so restricted that bound variables share indices with substituted parameters.

Predicativism has not spawned a programme for reworking mathematics as influential as Brouwerian intuitionism or new constructivism. Even so, a wide variety of mathematical results are known. Weyl saw that the theorem that every non-empty bounded class of reals has a least upper bound is unobtainable in complete generality within (a restricted) predicative mathematics if reals get defined in terms of classes. He showed that, by treating reals as sequences, the theorem that every bounded, monotonically increasing sequence approaches a limit is predicatively provable, as are other theorems of analysis. Wang has argued that predicativists cannot retain Cantor's theorem on the existence of uncountable sets.

See also: LOGICAL AND MATHEMATICAL TERMS, GLOSSARY OF

References and further reading

* Aberth, O. (1980) *Computable Analysis*, New York: McGraw-Hill. (An attractive technical introduction to analysis in the style of Russian constructivism.)

Beeson, M.J. (1985) *Foundations of Constructive Mathematics*, Berlin: Springer. (An overview of the metamathematics of constructive formal systems. Requires considerable formal experience.)

Benacerraf, P. and Putnam, H. (eds) (1964) *Philosophy of Mathematics: Selected Readings*, Englewood Cliffs, NJ: Prentice Hall, 2nd edn, 1983. (An invaluable collection of classic essays on the foundations of mathematics; most are nontechnical.)

* Bishop, E. (1967) *Foundations of Constructive Analysis*, New York: McGraw-Hill. (The bible of new constructivism. A technical work with a lucid nontechnical introduction.)

* —— (1970) 'Mathematics as a Numerical Language', in J. Myhill, R.E. Vesley and A. Kino (eds) *Intuitionism and Proof Theory*, Amsterdam: North Holland, 53–71. (A clear statement of Bishop's central philosophical ideas.)

Bridges, D. and Richman, F. (1987) *Varieties of Constructive Mathematics*, Cambridge: Cambridge University Press. (A mathematical introduction to constructivism, contrasting theorems of new constructivism with those of intuitionism and Markovian constructivism. A background in conventional analysis is required.)

Brouwer, L.E.J. (1981) *Brouwer's Cambridge Lectures on Intuitionism*, ed. D. van Dalen, Cambridge: Cambridge University Press. (A compact sample of Brouwer's thinking; well edited but quite technical.)

Chihara, C. (1973) *Ontology and the Vicious-Circle Principle*, Ithaca, NY: Cornell University Press. (Includes an exposition, for philosophers, of traditional issues surrounding predicativity.)

* Dummett, M.A.E. (1975) 'Wang's Paradox', *Synthese* 30: 301–24; repr. in *Truth and Other Enigmas*, Cambridge, MA: Harvard University Press, 1978, 248–68. (A thought-provoking exploration of issues from philosophy of language which may affect the legitimacy of finitism.)

—— (1977) *Elements of Intuitionism*, Oxford: Clarendon Press, 1990. (An influential text in which great emphasis is placed upon the metalogic of intuitionism.)

Feferman, S. (1964) 'Systems of Predicative Analysis', *Journal of Symbolic Logic* 29: 1–30. (A brilliant introduction to predicativism and its systematic formulation. The second section requires technical knowledge.)

Hazen, A. (1983) 'Predicative Logics', in D. Gabbay and F. Guenthner (eds) *Handbook of Philosophical Logic*, vol. 1, *Elements of Classical Logic*, Dordrecht: Reidel. (A helpful overview of and introduction to predicativism and predicative logics.)

Heijenoort, J. van (ed.) (1967) *From Frege to Gödel: A Source Book in Mathematical Logic, 1879–1931*, Cambridge, MA: Harvard University Press. (An invaluable collection of significant articles by Gödel, Hilbert, Brouwer, Skolem and others. Technical knowledge often required.)

Heyting, A. (1956) *Intuitionism: An Introduction*, Amsterdam: North Holland; 3rd revised edn, 1971. (The first – and still the most charming – popular technical account of Brouwer's intuitionism.)

* Hilbert, D. (1926) 'Über das Unendliche', *Mathematische Annalen* 95: 161–90; trans. 'On the Infinite', in P. Benacerraf and H. Putnam (eds) *Philosophy of Mathematics: Selected Readings*, Cambridge: Cambridge University Press, 2nd edn, 1983; and in J. van Heijenoort (ed.) *From Frege to Gödel: A Source Book in Mathematical Logic 1879–1931*, Cambridge, MA: Harvard University Press, 1967. (A classic statement of Hilbert's views on metamathematics; largely nontechnical.)

* Markov, A.A. (1962) 'O Konstruktivnoii Matematike', *Trudy Matematicheskogo Instituta imeni V.A. Steklova* 67: 8–14; trans. 'On Constructive Mathematics', *American Mathematical Society Translations*, series 2, 98: 1–9, 1971. (A brief introduction to Russian constructivism; relatively nontechnical.)

* Russell, B.A.W. (1908) 'Mathematical Logic as Based on the Theory of Types', *American Journal of Mathematics* 30: 222–62; repr. in J. van Heijenoort (ed.) *From Frege to Gödel: A Source Book in Mathematical Logic 1879–1931*, Cambridge, MA: Harvard University Press, 1967, 150–82. (Includes Russell's diagnosis of the paradoxes and an explanation of his ramified type theory.)

Skolem, T. (1923) 'Begründung der elementaren Arithmetik durch die rekurrierende Denkweise ohne Anwendung scheinbarer Veränderlichen mit unendlichem Ausdehnungsbereich', *Skrifter utgit av Videnskapsselskapet I Kristiania, I. Matematisk-naturvidenskabelig Klasse* 6: 1–38; trans. 'The Foundations of Elementary Arithmetic Established by Means of the Recursive Mode of Thought, Without the Use of Apparent Variables Ranging Over Infinite Domains', in J. van Heijenoort (ed.) *From Frege to Gödel: A Source Book in Mathematical Logic 1879–1931*, Cambridge, MA: Harvard University Press, 1967, 302–33. (A brilliant and careful formal development of a finitistic arithmetic.)

Tait, W.W. (1981) 'Finitism', *Journal of Symbolic Logic* 78 (9): 524–46. (A lucid exposition of one approach to the foundational issues surrounding finitism.)

* Troelstra, A.S. and Dalen, D. van (1988) *Constructivism in Mathematics: An Introduction*, Amsterdam: North Holland, 2 vols. (A comprehensive technical overview of the current state of constructive mathematics, with emphasis on intuitionism and mathematical logic.)

* Wang, H. (1970) *Logic, Computers and Sets*, New York: Chelsea. (Includes several articles by Wang on the historical and technical background to predicativism.)

Weyl, H. (1918) *Das Kontinuum: Kritische Untersuchungen über die Grundlagen der Analysis*, Leipzig: Veit; trans. T. Bole, *The Continuum: A Critical Examination of the Foundations of Analysis*, New York: Dover, 1994. (Historically influential but, at times, idiosyncratic treatment of mathematical and logical foundations for predicative analysis.)

* Whitehead, A.N. and Russell, B.A.W. (1910) *Principia Mathematica*, vol. 1, Cambridge: Cambridge University Press; 2nd edn, 1925. (The classic effort to demonstrate the logicistic thesis; highly technical.)

* Wright, C. (1982) 'Strict Finitism', *Synthese* 51; repr. in *Realism, Meaning and Truth*, Oxford: Blackwell, 1986, 107–75. (A detailed reconsideration of issues raised in Dummett (1975).)

DAVID CHARLES McCARTY

CONTENT, INDEXICAL

Many of our thoughts are about particular individuals (persons, things, places, . . .). For example, one can spot a certain Ferrari and think that it is red. What enables this thought to latch onto that particular object? It cannot be how the Ferrari looks, for this could not distinguish one Ferrari from another just like it. In general, how a thought represents something cannot determine which thing it represents. What a singular thought latches onto seems to depend also on features of the context in which the thought occurs. This suggests that its content is essentially indexical, contextually variable much as the content of an utterance such as 'I am hungry' depends on who utters it and when. The indexical model of singular thought is not limited to thoughts about individuals one perceives, but applies also to thoughts about individuals one remembers or has been informed of, such as an old bicycle or Christopher Columbus. In each case, a certain contextual relation, based on perception, memory or communication, connects thought to object.

Our thoughts do not merely represent what the world is like. Many of our thoughts manage to latch onto particular individuals (persons, things, places, . . .), and how this is accomplished needs to be explained. If, for example, one thinks of the bird on the window sill that it is a sparrow (the thought is expressible by 'That bird is a sparrow'), there must be something about the thought which makes it about *that* bird (see DEMONSTRATIVES AND INDEXICALS). It might seem that the object of a thought must be uniquely determined by some component of the thought. This view is analogous to Frege's view that the 'sense' of a linguistic expression determines its reference (see FREGE, G. §3; SENSE AND REFERENCE). The idea is that *how* something is represented determines which thing is represented. That is, the subject component of the thought, expressible in this example by the demonstrative description 'that bird', imposes a certain condition whose satisfaction by a certain individual makes it the object of the thought. This condition is the same no matter who entertains the thought, no matter where or when. The trouble with this view is that one might not represent the thing in question with enough specificity to single it out from all other birds. Indeed, one might even misrepresent it – perhaps what one takes to be a sparrow is actually a porcelain figure.

Here is an alternative view. An individual is singled out as the object of the thought not because it satisfies a condition represented in the thought but because the thought is causally connected to it. That is, as Tyler Burge (1977) has suggested, a thought latches onto something by way of bearing a certain contextual relation to that particular individual. If this is correct, then facts about the circumstances in which the thought occurs, and not just atemporal facts about its character, are relevant to the determination of its object. Two widely separated people with similar perceptual experiences (or the same person at different times) could have thoughts of exactly the same character, expressible by 'That bird is a sparrow', and yet be having these thoughts about different birds. One might be correct, the other mistaken. This suggests that singular thoughts are true or false only relative to a context. As John Perry (1993) describes them, they are 'essentially indexical'.

To explain how this can be, we need to distinguish the type of thought that both people have from the particular occurrence (or token) of that type which each has (see TYPE/TOKEN DISTINCTION). Tokens of the same thought type can be about distinct objects because singular thoughts are 'token-reflexive', much like indexical expressions. For example, the reference of the indexical 'I' depends on who utters it; of 'here' on where it is uttered; and of 'tomorrow' on when it is uttered. As a result, the sentence 'I will be here tomorrow' is neither true nor false in itself but only relative to a particular tokening of it. That is, a given utterance of it is true if the maker of that utterance will be at the place of the utterance on the day after the utterance. Different people, or the same person at a different place or time, would say different things with these words. Notice that there is also a sense in which everyone who utters 'I will be here tomorrow' says the same thing – utterances of the sentence are type-identical, but their truth-conditional contents differ in the way just described. Singular thoughts are similarly token-reflexive and indexical in content, because their objects are determined only relative to their context of occurrence. The object is not thought of as the unique object of a certain sort, that is, under a definite description (see DESCRIPTIONS), but in some contextually sensitive way. On this indexical view of singular thought, a thought represents a certain object in a context but without representing the context itself. The truth-condition of a particular token of the thought type, such as the one expressible as 'That bird is a sparrow', is not absolute but is contextually variable, in this case varying with the context of perception.

Not only can singular thoughts be about objects of perception, they can also be about individuals one remembers or has been informed of. François Recanati (1993) and Kent Bach (1987) both suggest that these cases involve uses of 'mental indexicals'. One suggestive idea, developed most fully by Graeme Forbes (1989), is that, when we are introduced to (or otherwise learn of) an individual by name, we form a 'mental file' labelled with the name. We can later call up the individual by name. These mental files on persons and things are relatively permanent, but, as Recanati suggests, we seem to operate also with temporary files, labelled with mental counterparts of pronouns, on individuals currently singled out in perception or in conversation.

See also: CONTENT: WIDE AND NARROW; REFERENCE

References and further reading

* Bach, K. (1987) *Thought and Reference*, Oxford: Oxford University Press, chaps 1, 2. (Develops a relational account of perception-, memory- and communication-based singular thought, according to which percepts, memories and names [as labels on mental files] function as mental indexicals.)
* Burge, T. (1977) 'Belief *de re*', *Journal of Philosophy* 74: 338–62. (Contends that singular thoughts are not reducible to descriptional thoughts and are true or false only relative to contexts.)
—— (1979) 'Sinning against Frege', *Philosophical Review* 88: 398–432. (Argues that Frege's theory of context-insensitive senses, if properly understood and suitably refined, is not vulnerable to certain objections based on indexical thoughts.)
Evans, G. (1982) *The Varieties of Reference*, Oxford: Oxford University Press, chaps 5, 6. (Proposes an information-based account of singular thought.)
* Forbes, G. (1989) 'Cognitive Architecture and the Semantics of Belief', in P. French *et al.* (eds) *Midwest Studies in Philosophy*, vol. 14, Minneapolis, MN: University of Minnesota Press. (Proposes an account of singular thought, as well as thoughts about natural kinds, according to which the subject term takes the explicitly indexical form, 'the subject of this dossier'.)
* Perry, J. (1993) *The Problem of the Essential Indexical and Other Essays*, Oxford: Oxford University Press. (Collects the author's influential papers on irreducibly indexical aspects of content.)
* Recanati, F. (1993) *Direct Reference: From Language to Thought*, Oxford: Blackwell, chaps 5, 6. (Develops an account of non-descriptive modes of presentation, on which names function as labels on permanent mental files and indexicals as labels on temporary files.)

KENT BACH

CONTENT, NON-CONCEPTUAL

To say that a mental state has intentional content is to say that it represents features of the world. The intentional content of a belief can be characterized in terms of concepts: the content of the belief that fish swim is characterized by the concepts 'fish' and 'swimming'. The contents of beliefs are, for this reason, often described as conceptual. One way to explain this idea is to say that to have a belief, one has to possess the concepts which characterize the belief's content. However, some philosophers believe that certain mental states have non-conceptual contents: these states represent the world without the subject having to possess the concepts which characterize their contents. The main examples of these putative states are conscious perceptual experiences and the non-conscious states of cognitive information-processing systems (such as the visual system).

1 Conceptual and non-conceptual content
2 Varieties of non-conceptual content
3 Problems with non-conceptual content

1 Conceptual and non-conceptual content

Beliefs and other propositional attitudes are individuated in terms of their contents. It is natural to think that having these propositional attitudes involves having concepts, construed here as items in the mind. If someone believes that *a is F*, then they must have the concept *F*, and the concept *a* – whatever concepts may be. This can be summed up by saying that beliefs have conceptual contents (see PROPOSITIONAL ATTITUDES). Some philosophers, for example Evans (1982) and Peacocke (1993), think that not all intentional mental states have conceptual contents. They hold that some intentional states have 'non-conceptual' contents: the contents of these states do not, in some sense, involve concepts.

How can a thinker's state have the content that *a is F* without the state 'involving' the concepts *a* and *F*? The best way to answer this question is to focus on the idea of 'possessing' concepts. In the case of states with conceptual contents – like beliefs – we can say that in order for a subject to be in these states, the subject has to possess certain concepts. Likewise, we can say that in order to be in a state with *non-*conceptual content, a subject does not have to possess certain concepts. But which concepts? It would be too strong to say that being in non-conceptual states does not require having any concepts at all – this issue should not be settled by the very definition of non-conceptual content. Rather, we should say that for a subject *S* to be in a non-conceptual state with content *P*, *S* does not have to possess the concepts which *S would* have to possess if *S were* in a conceptual state with content *P*.

If we call these concepts the concepts which are 'canonical' for *P*, then we can say that a state with non-conceptual content is one of which the following is true:

> in order for a subject, *S*, to be in a state with a content *P*, *S* does not have to possess the concepts canonical for *P*.

The idea of concepts canonical for a certain content is just the idea that there are concepts which *essentially* characterize a given content (Cussins 1990: 382–3).

The content expressed by the sentence 'snow is white', for example, is essentially characterized in terms of the concepts expressed by the words 'snow' and 'white'.

Why should anyone be interested in the category of non-conceptual content? Why should it be of any more philosophical interest than the category of non-red things? The reason is that intentionality seems closely bound up with having concepts. So it is a substantial thesis that there can be intentionality without possession of (the relevant) concepts (see INTENTIONALITY; CONCEPTS). However, simply defining 'non-conceptual content' leaves open the question of whether there actually is any. So are there any states with non-conceptual content?

2 Varieties of non-conceptual content

The definition of non-conceptual content just given applies straightforwardly to some notions of content. States which carry 'information' (in Dretske's (1981) sense) have non-conceptual contents, since a state's carrying information is a matter of its co-varying in a nomic or reliable way with a certain phenomenon. For example: on this view we can say that a weather vane represents or indicates the direction of the wind. But it is obvious that the weather vane does not possess the concept of the direction of the wind.

However, it is debatable whether a state's carrying information is sufficient for the state to have representational content in any interesting sense. For one thing, since nomic co-variation is present wherever there is causation, this theory stretches the notion of representation to the point where it can apply to almost everything in the universe. Another problem is that informational states seem incapable of representing incorrectly; but the possibility of incorrect representation seems essential to genuine representation. Something more must be added to turn mere informational states into states with genuine representational content (see SEMANTICS, INFORMATIONAL).

Two other kinds of state are claimed to have non-conceptual contents: states of the information-processing cognitive systems (for example the visual system) postulated by many psychological theories; and conscious perceptual experiences. Computational psychological theories claim that systems within the brain perform computations: that is, these cognitive systems compute functions by processing representations algorithmically. So the thinker (or the cognitive system) is in certain representational states, or states with content. These representational states are essentially specified in terms of certain concepts, but there is no need for the thinker to possess these concepts in order to be in these states. For example, Marr's (1982) theory of vision analyses visual information processing in terms of complex mathematical concepts; one need not master these concepts in order to process visual information. So these computational states, if they exist, are non-conceptual (see MIND, COMPUTATIONAL THEORIES OF; VISION).

The other kind of states which have been attributed non-conceptual contents are conscious perceptual experiences. The general idea here is that in perception many aspects of the world are presented to the perceiver; yet there is no need to suppose that the perceiver has a distinct concept for each aspect of the world which is so presented. Consider colour experience: is it plausible that each of us has a distinct concept for each precise shade of colour we are able to perceive? If it is not, this can be a reason for holding that perceptual experiences have non-conceptual contents: perception has a 'phenomenological richness' which is not constrained by the concepts the perceiver has (Evans 1982: 229–; other motivations for attributing non-conceptual contents to experiences are offered in Crane 1992 and Martin 1992).

Given that experiences have non-conceptual contents, how should this be explained? One of the most detailed accounts has been given by Peacocke (1993: ch. 3). At one level, the content of a perceptual experience is what he calls a 'scenario': a set of ways of filling out the space around a perceiver with properties and relations – for instance, with colour and shape properties. The experience's representational content is given by the scenario, because the experience is correct just in case the actual distribution of properties and relations around the perceiver belongs in the scenario. However, there is no requirement that the perceiver has all the concepts which essentially characterize the properties and relations in the scenario.

Opinions differ on whether the content of experience is wholly conceptual, wholly non-conceptual, or some mixture. Evans (1982) holds that it is wholly non-conceptual, while Peacocke (1993) holds that experiences can have many layers of content, some of which are conceptual and some non-conceptual (see PERCEPTION).

3 Problems with non-conceptual content

The notion of non-conceptual content could be criticized on two fronts. First, the application of the notion to a particular kind of mental state (perception, for example) could be criticized. Second, the very notion of non-conceptual content itself could be criticized.

John McDowell (1994: ch. 3) argues that to treat the content of experience as non-conceptual is to commit oneself to the idea which Wilfrid Sellars criticized as 'the myth of the given': the idea that experience involves being presented with an unconceptualized 'given' which the mind then goes on to conceptualize (Sellars 1956). McDowell argues that accepting this picture renders the relation between mind and world deeply problematic. By contrast, he argues that the content of experience is wholly conceptual. McDowell therefore accounts for the phenomenological richness of experience in a different way: he claims that where we have (for example) discrimination between colours, we may not have a distinct word for each colour, but we do have 'a recognitional capacity, possibly quite short-lived, that sets in with the experience' (1994: 57). And such a recognitional capacity is, he argues, fully conceptual.

Scepticism about the very idea of non-conceptual content can arise out of scepticism about the claim that there are concepts one must have if one is to be capable of having certain intentional states. Accepting this claim amounts to accepting a mentalistic version of a sharp distinction between analytic and synthetic statements – a distinction which has proved highly controversial (see ANALYTICITY).

References and further reading

* Crane, T. (1992) 'The Nonconceptual Content of Experience', in T. Crane (ed.) *The Contents of Experience*, Cambridge: Cambridge University Press. (Defines non-conceptual content and argues that perceptual experience has non-conceptual content, on the basis of a contrast between the different inferential roles of perception and belief. Sections 1–3 provide a straightforward introduction to the topic of non-conceptual content as understood in §1 above.)

* Cussins, A. (1990) 'The Connectionist Construction of Concepts', in M. Boden (ed.) *The Philosophy of Artificial Intelligence*, Oxford: Oxford University Press. (An attempt to show how states with conceptual content emerge out of states with non-conceptual content.)

* Dretske, F.I. (1981) *Knowledge and the Flow of Information*, Oxford: Blackwell. (A physicalist theory of intentional content, based on the mathematical concept of information. Though it presents an original theory, this is a very clearly written book.)

* Evans, G. (1982) *The Varieties of Reference*, Oxford: Clarendon Press. (Influential and wide-ranging account of reference and thought. At various points in the book the claim that experiences have

non-conceptual content is defended. Difficult in parts.)

* Marr, D. (1982) *Vision*, San Francisco, CA: Freeman. (Pioneering and influential computational theory of vision. After the introduction, some knowledge of mathematics is needed.)
* Martin, M.G.F. (1992) 'Perception, Concepts and Memory', *Philosophical Review* 101: 745–63. (Argues that perceptual experiences have non-conceptual contents, based on an examination of the relation between memory and perception.)
* McDowell, J. (1994) *Mind and World*, Cambridge, MA: Harvard University Press. (Chapter 3 argues that experience is fully conceptual. A difficult work, though not technical.)
* Peacocke, C. (1993) *A Study of Concepts*, Cambridge, MA: MIT Press. (Lucid though difficult, chapter 3 defends an account of the non-conceptual content of perceptual experience.)
* Sellars, W. (1956) 'Empiricism and the Philosophy of Mind', in H. Feigl and M. Scriven (eds) *Minnesota Studies in the Philosophy of Science*, vol. 1, Minneapolis, MN: University of Minnesota Press. (Classic statement of Sellars' argument against the 'myth of the given'. Difficult.)

TIM CRANE

CONTENT: WIDE AND NARROW

A central problem in philosophy is to explain, in a way consistent with their causal efficacy, how mental states can represent states of affairs in the world. Consider, for example, that wanting water and thinking there is some in the tap can lead one to turn on the tap. The contents of these mental states pertain to things in the world (water and the tap), and yet it would seem that their causal efficacy should depend solely on their internal characteristics, not on their external relations. That is, a person could be in just those states and those states could play just the same psychological roles, even if there were no water or tap for them to refer to. However, certain arguments, based on some imaginative thought experiments, have persuaded many philosophers that thought contents do depend on external factors, both physical and social. A tempting solution to this dilemma has been to suppose that there are two kinds of content, wide and narrow. Wide content comprises the referential relations that mental states bear to things and their properties. Narrow content comprises the determinants of psychological role. Philosophers have debated whether both notions of content are viable and, if so, how they are connected.

1   **Motivating the distinction**
2   **Twin earth thought experiments**
3   **Two kinds of content?**

1   Motivating the distinction

Many of our mental states, including our perceptions, memories and beliefs, represent things in the world and properties of those things (see PROPOSITIONAL ATTITUDES). But this fact seems to produce a dilemma. On the one hand, representational states are what they are in virtue of how they represent things to be. That is, they are most appropriately individuated (distinguished from one another) by their different contents, which are comprised of things in the world (objects and their properties and relations; see INTENTIONALITY). On the other hand, in so far as these states play causal roles in our psychologies, they do so because of how the world seems to us, and presumably that is solely a matter of what is 'in the head'. Their psychological roles would be just the same even if one were a brain in a vat or a victim of Descartes' evil demon. The dilemma, then, is to reconcile the apparent facts that the representational character of mental states depends on their external relations and that their causal efficacy depends on their internal properties (see METHODOLOGICAL INDIVIDUALISM). The distinction between wide and narrow content has been thought to resolve this dilemma.

Is this a genuine dilemma? Leaving aside such sceptical suggestions as that the contents of psychological states have no causal efficacy (see MENTAL CAUSATION), one might argue that the dilemma is illusory because, strictly speaking, contents *are* internal properties. Contrary to what many philosophers have supposed, the mere fact that the notion of content is connected with notions such as reference and truth-conditions does not mean that content is external. For this is compatible with a Fregean conception of content. FREGE held that linguistic expressions have sense as well as reference, and the same might be suggested about concepts. Each concept expresses a condition of reference (a sense) and what it refers to is whatever satisfies that condition; and this condition is not dependent on external features of the thinker's situation and is not otherwise sensitive to contextual factors (see SENSE AND REFERENCE). If concepts are Fregean in this way, then any two thinkers entertaining thoughts with the same conceptual composition are, regardless of their external circumstances, thinking thoughts with the same truth-conditions. This rules out the possibility that, because of sensitivity to circumstances, one could be thinking something true and the other, something false.

One difficulty with this Fregean view is its inability to handle thoughts that are about particular individuals. Thoughts such as 'That's a canary' seem to be essentially indexical, in that their truth-conditions are relative to their contexts of occurrence (see CONTENT, INDEXICAL): different people, having qualitatively identical experiences, could think thoughts of that form but be thinking of different birds.

A similar problem for the Fregean picture is posed by recognitional concepts: one might see a certain exotic insect and think, referring to its type, for which one might have no name, 'That must be indigenous to the Amazon'. One might later observe a similar specimen and think, 'It must be another one of those', referring to the same type. One would be mistaken if, no matter how much the second looks like the first, it is actually an insect of a different type. Thus the property of being of the type initially picked out is not a matter of fitting a certain image or conception. Whether or not one's concept of that type applies to the next specimen depends not on whether it fits one's conception but on whether it is in fact a thing of the same sort as the one originally picked out. So it seems that the Fregean picture does not apply to recognitional concepts.

2 Twin earth thought experiments

A similar difficulty was revealed by Putnam's celebrated 'twin earth' thought experiments (1975), which introduced the distinction between wide and narrow content (see PUTNAM, H.). Twin earth is a place where everything is just like it is on earth, except as otherwise specified. In one scenario, two men, Art and Bart (Art's counterpart on twin earth), each have thoughts that they express with the words 'Water quenches thirst'. However, on twin earth the clear liquid that fills the seas and falls from the skies is composed not of H_2O but of some other stuff, XYZ. It is 1750 and Art and Bart, like everyone else, are ignorant of chemistry and could not, even if they had the opportunity, tell the difference between H_2O and XYZ. Nevertheless, Putnam contends, Art and Bart use the word 'water' to express different concepts. If Art were to classify a sample of XYZ as water, he would be wrong, for it would not be a substance of the same kind as water. As for Bart, he does not take XYZ to be water, for he does not have the concept 'water'. So Art and Bart, even though they are not different neurally, have different concepts, with different conditions of correct application. Their

concepts are not determined solely by what is in their heads (see CONCEPTS §5; METHODOLOGICAL INDIVIDUALISM).

Burge (1979) conducts another thought experiment designed to show that differences in people's social environments can make for differences in mental content. An arthritic patient called Al complains, 'My arthritis has spread to my thigh'. Nothing in his acquisition of the term 'arthritis' has kept him from supposing that this inflammatory disease can occur in the bones as well as the joints. Meanwhile, Cal, his twin earth counterpart, registers a similar complaint. There, however, the term 'arthritis' is used to refer to an inflammatory disease of either the joints or the bones. Cal's exposure to the term 'arthritis' is the same as Al's, but, given how it is used on twin earth, he understands it correctly. Now, according to Burge, both patients are correctly said, on their respective planets, to believe that arthritis can occur in the bones, but, since Cal's belief is true and Al's is false, what they believe is different. However, there is no internal difference between them. Therefore, what they believe is partly an external matter. Contents are not, and do not supervene upon, what is in the head.

These thought experiments have met with considerable enthusiasm but also with neglected criticism (see Unger 1984; Bach 1987; Crane 1991). For one thing, they are conducted selectively: varying their details can yield contrary intuitions, for example, that XYZ is a kind of water. Also, even granting the correctness of the intuition, for example, that XYZ is not a kind of water, they leave it a mystery why the references of different concepts should be determined in different ways. The reference of the concept we express with 'water' depends on the nature (H_2O) of the clear, plentiful liquid around us, but this is not the situation with the concepts we express with the terms 'earth', 'air' and 'fire', whose references are chemically heterogeneous and are determined by the satisfaction of certain phenomenological conditions. Putnam and his followers do not explain why the fact that water is a chemical natural kind, and earth, air and fire are not, should make the concept water a different kind of concept from the concepts earth, air and fire, with its reference determined in a fundamentally different way, even back in 1750.

The arthritis argument depends essentially on the supposition that one can have beliefs with contents one 'incompletely understands'. It assumes, for example, that Al not only misunderstands the word 'arthritis' but operates with the concept arthritis rather than with some broader concept (call it 'tharthritis') that he mistakenly associates with the word. So, it might be objected, Al understands the term 'arthritis' in precisely the same way as Cal does, and has the very same belief, namely that his tharthritis has spread to his thigh. Whatever evidence there is that he also believes that his arthritis has spread to his thigh is overridden by his idiosyncratic understanding of the term 'arthritis' (we are not tempted to say that he believes that he has inflammation of the joints in his thigh).

In any case, we cannot assume that what 'that'-clauses capture is the sort of content relevant to psychology, that is, to characterizing people's perspectives and explaining their actions and inferences. As Loar (1988) and Patterson (1990) have both argued, one can grant that the thought experiments succeed in showing that the truth-conditions of attitude ascriptions are sensitive to aspects of the physical and social environment without granting that 'that'-clauses capture psychological content (see PROPOSITIONAL ATTITUDE STATEMENTS). After all, semantics (of natural language) is not psychology.

3 Two kinds of content?

Burge is satisfied that there is only one kind of content, the externalist kind revealed by the thought experiments and specified by 'that'-clauses in attitude ascriptions, and that no other kind is needed for psychology. Other philosophers, such as Loar (1988) and Block (1986), accept the thought experiments but propose another kind of content – narrow as opposed to wide – which captures the person's subjective point of view and serves the purposes of psychological explanation. Narrow contents capture what earthlings and their twin earth counterparts have in common, and explanations that ignore narrow contents miss crucial generalizations. If so, what is narrow content and how is it connected to wide content?

Loar and Block take narrow content to be 'conceptual role', which is defined in terms of a concept's inferential connections to other concepts. The main challenge for this view is to find a non-arbitrary way of constraining the relevant connections, so that each psychological state can turn out to possess a determinate narrow content, and to explain how this constrains its truth-condition (see SEMANTICS, CONCEPTUAL ROLE). Another conception of narrow content, originated by White (1982) and championed by Fodor (1987), is that narrow content is a function from context to wide content. One challenge for this approach is to define the operative notion of context and to specify narrow contents informatively, rather than by abstraction from wide contents. Also, although the distinction between wide and narrow content acknowledges a systematic discrepancy between ordinary attitude attributions and scientific psychological explanation, and is

motivated by a respect for both, one might wonder whether there really are two kinds of content or merely one kind described in two different ways.

It is difficult to assess the competing views because none of them has yet been developed in any great detail. A plausible if tentative assessment is that the distinction between wide and narrow content is well-motivated but not well-formulated. It is well-motivated since, in many cases, a thought's truth-condition is not wholly determined by what is in the head, and yet what is in the head does determine, independently of environmental factors, the thinker's perspective. Also, as Frege first recognized, wide content is too coarse to distinguish distinct perspectives on the same state of affairs or otherwise mark relevant differences in cognitive role. Realizing this, opponents of narrow content have suggested syntactic form or computational role as a surrogate for narrow content. However, this suggestion cuts things too finely: it fails to reckon with the possibility that mental representations of different forms or different computational roles might nevertheless embody the same cognitive perspective.

See also: CONTENT, INDEXICAL; HOLISM: MENTAL AND SEMANTIC; METHODOLOGICAL INDIVIDUALISM; SEMANTICS

References and further reading

* Bach, K. (1987) *Thought and Reference*, Oxford: Oxford University Press. (Chapter 13 challenges Putnam's and Burge's twin earth thought experiments.)
* Block, N. (1986) 'Advertisement for a Semantics for Psychology', in P. French *et al.* (eds) *Midwest Studies in Philosophy*, vol. 10, Minneapolis, MN: University of Minnesota Press. (Surveys a wide variety of theories and defends a conceptual role theory of narrow content.)
* Burge, T. (1979) 'Individualism and the Mental', in P. French *et al.* (eds) *Midwest Studies in Philosophy*, vol. 4, Minneapolis, MN: University of Minnesota Press. (Employs a variety of twin earth thought experiments to argue that mental contents are to a degree socially constituted.)
* Crane, T. (1991) 'All the Difference in the World', *Philosophical Quarterly* 41: 1–25. (Challenges Putnam's and Burge's twin earth thought experiments.)
* Fodor, J. (1987) *Psychosemantics: The Problem of Meaning in the Philosophy of Mind*, Cambridge, MA: MIT Press. (Explores White's idea that narrow content is a function from context to wide content.)

—— (1994) *The Elm and the Expert*, Cambridge, MA: MIT Press. (Argues that wide content is the only notion of content needed for the purposes of psychological explanation.)

* Loar, B. (1988) 'Social Content and Psychological Content' and 'Reply to Bilgrami', in R. Grimm and P. Merrill (eds) *Contents of Thoughts*, Tucson, AZ: University of Arizona Press. (Argues, contrary to Burge, that psychological content is not in general what is captured by oblique 'that'-clauses.)

Loewer, B. and Rey, G. (eds) (1991) *Meaning in Mind: Fodor and His Critics*, Oxford: Blackwell. (Articles, with replies by Fodor, addressing main issues in the theory of content.)

* Patterson, S. (1990) 'The Explanatory Role of Belief Ascriptions', *Philosophical Studies* 59: 313–32. (Argues that the orthodox interpretation of Burge's twin earth thought experiments does not do justice to the ways in which intentional states are individuated in common-sense psychology.)

* Putnam, H. (1975) 'The Meaning of "Meaning"', in K. Gunderson (ed.) *Language, Mind, and Knowledge*, Minneapolis, MN: University of Minnesota Press. (Devises twin earth thought experiments to argue that meanings cannot both determine reference and be 'in the head'.)

Stich, S. and Warfield, T. (eds) (1994) *Mental Representation: A Reader*, Oxford: Blackwell. (Includes important articles on major theories of content.)

* Unger, P. (1984) *Philosophical Relativity*, Minneapolis, MN: University of Minnesota Press. (Chapter 5 challenges the twin earth thought experiments by showing how varying their details yields conflicting intuitions.)

Wallace, J. and Mason, H.E. (1990) 'Some Thought Experiments about Mind and Meaning', in C.A. Anderson and J. Owens (eds) *Propositional Attitudes: The Role of Content in Logic, Language, and Mind*, Stanford, CA: Center for the Study of Language and Information, Stanford University. (Argues that ordinary language provides much richer and subtler ways of attributing mental contents than is allowed by the orthodox interpretation of Burge's twin earth thought experiments.)

* White, S. (1982) 'Partial Character and the Language of Thought', *Pacific Philosophical Quarterly* 63: 347–65. (Proposes a conception of narrow content as a function from context to wide content.)

KENT BACH

CONTEXTUALISM, EPISTEMOLOGICAL

The idea that norms vary with social setting has long been recognized, but it is only in the late twentieth century that philosophers have developed precise versions of epistemological contextualism, the theory that standards of knowledge and justification vary with context. Ordinary practice seems to support this rather than the 'invariantist' view that epistemological standards are uniform.

Suppose, for example, that having seen my children a minute ago, I assert 'I know my children are in the garden'. My neighbour Harold then says, 'Good, because an escaped prisoner is seeking hostages nearby'. I may then appropriately claim, 'On second thoughts, I do not know, I should check carefully'. Standards for knowledge appear to have shifted, since they now require further investigation.

Contextualism's greatest advantage is its response to scepticism. Sceptics raise radical possibilities, such as that we might be dreaming. The contextualist grants that such doubts are legitimate in the sceptical context, but holds they are illegitimate in everyday situations. Yet contextualism can appear to be an objectionable form of relativism, and may be accused of confusing standards that we apply in practical conversational contexts with the true standards that determine whether someone has knowledge.

1   Elements of the theory
2   Advantages of contextualism
3   Contextualism as relativism
4   Further objections

1   Elements of the theory

Epistemological contextualism holds that standards of knowledge and justification vary with context. One form of the theory, call it 'subject-based contextualism', holds that epistemic standards depend on the knower's context. A more radical form, 'attributor-based contextualism', treats standards as varying with contexts of attribution. On this latter view, one attributor may legitimately claim that a person knows something while another may legitimately deny that the same person has the knowledge in question. Suppose Susan asserts, 'I know your children are in your garden; I saw them there a minute ago'. When my concern is to call the children to dinner, I attribute knowledge to Susan. But Harold, aware of an escaped prisoner seeking hostages nearby, would not attribute knowledge to her. What Susan knows depends on attributors' contexts, not only on her situation.

Contextualists also vary regarding contextual elements that determine standards. In the examples above, the relative importance of having correct information determines the strength of justification required. Other factors affecting epistemic standards might include: (1) doubts entertained; (2) doubts mentioned; (3) the topic under consideration; and (4) elements of the situation that affect the knower's reliability. David Lewis (1996) suggests that we follow a 'rule of accommodation', such that we tend to adjust our standards so as to count knowledge claims as true. Michael Williams (1991) argues for 'methodological necessities' which exempt propositions from doubt if considering them demands a shift in disciplinary focus. For instance, a molecular biologist may ignore concerns that shift the topic to particle physics.

Some contextualists believe that knowledge has a foundational structure (see FOUNDATIONALISM). Foundationalists typically claim that knowledge is grounded in basic beliefs which have intrinsic epistemic credibility, and have that credibility as a result of belonging to some type of beliefs, such as beliefs about sensory experience. Contextualists deny both claims. Basic non-inferential beliefs have their status because they are permissible in context, and the belief type that is basic varies with context. We might expect that when discussing where to eat lunch, for example, basic beliefs include beliefs about ordinary material objects, whereas in conversation between physicists, basic beliefs include those about widely accepted theoretical views.

2 Advantages of contextualism

Beyond its compatibility with everyday practice, contextualism provides attractive responses to major philosophical problems. Here, let us consider the regress argument and scepticism. Suppose we hold that knowledge requires justification. The regress argument for foundationalism examines the nature of such justification. Either a belief has intrinsic credibility, and so is 'self-justifying', or it is justified by inference. If the latter, then the belief is ultimately inferred from (1) intrinsically credible beliefs, (2) unjustified beliefs, (3) an infinite regress of justification, or (4) a circular justification in which some beliefs appear in their own support. Foundationalists claim (1) is the only acceptable alternative, but they have had problems explaining and defending the notion of intrinsic credibility.

Those contextualists who allow a foundational structure propose an alternative resolution: justification ends in beliefs that are unjustified in their context. This is made plausible in two ways. First,

the contextualist cites contextual factors that make it reasonable for agents to limit justification. For example, where all parties to an investigation agree on certain beliefs, there is no need to provide further justification. The contextualist may also appeal to Williams' concept of methodological necessity, according to which asking for justification can force inquirers to ignore disciplinary constraints. Second, contextualists claim that while justification ends with unjustified belief, demand for further justification can always be legitimated by special doubts about the unjustified belief.

The contextualist response to scepticism is even more attractive. Contextualists claim that sceptical doubts are legitimate, but only in the sceptical context (see SCEPTICISM). Williams (1991) gives an illuminating response along these lines. He contends that scepticism presupposes 'epistemological realism', the view that there is only one correct order of appropriate epistemic inference. Sceptics believe that knowledge of 'the external world' must be justified on the basis of immediate experience. If so, we must argue from beliefs about sense impressions, or how things appear, to beliefs about the material world. Williams claims this order of inference is necessary only within the sceptical context. In other contexts, it is permissible to begin our justifications with beliefs about the material world; and in some situations, such as psychological investigations of perception, we may begin with beliefs about external objects and draw inferences about appearances. Epistemological realism is false, since context determines the proper order of inference.

Keith DeRose (1995) proposes, in contrast, a contextualist 'conditional theory' of knowledge. Suppose S has a true belief p. Where S would not believe p if p were false, the belief is 'sensitive'; where S would believe p even if p were false, the belief is 'insensitive'. DeRose endorses a 'rule of sensitivity': whenever someone asserts that S knows p, standards of knowledge are raised to require S's belief p to be sensitive and the resulting standard applies for all beliefs in that context.

Suppose the belief p is that 'S's house is red'. If someone claims S knows p, the rule of sensitivity requires that if S's house were another colour, S would not believe p. Philosophers typically evaluate subjunctive conditionals by considering whether, in possible worlds 'close' to the actual world but in which the antecedent of the subjunctive is true, the consequent is also true. 'If not p, S would still believe p', is true if, in worlds similar to our own but in which S's house is not red, S can tell the colour of the house. Intuitively, at close worlds, S can determine the colour if S employs normal perceptual abilities. In contrast, let the belief q be 'I am a brain in a vat', where we have in mind the sceptical possibility that a brain is connected to a complex computer which simulates everyday experience. If someone claims S knows not-q, the rule of sensitivity demands that if q were true, S would not believe not-q (that is, S would believe q). This requires great epistemic ability, for we evaluate it by considering whether S believes q in worlds where S is a brain in a vat. The closest such world is far from the actual world, since in the actual world we cannot find out whether we are brains in vats. Once the rule of sensitivity raises standards so that we must consider such worlds, it does so for other beliefs in the context, including p. But in a world where S is a brain in vat, S will believe p even though p is false – in that world, S cannot determine the colour of anything! Thus, in contexts where p alone is considered, S knows p. But when S entertains p and a sceptical hypothesis, the rule of sensitivity raises standards to a level at which ordinary beliefs such as p are no longer known.

These responses to scepticism have the consequence, which Williams calls 'instability' and Lewis labels 'elusiveness', that when we raise sceptical doubts about ordinary knowledge, we change context and thereby 'destroy' that knowledge. In the sceptical context, the sceptic wins the debate. But this may be advantageous for contextualism, since it can explain both our judgment that we have knowledge in everyday situations and our feeling that sceptical doubts should be taken seriously.

3   Contextualism as relativism

In the case of contextualism, two objections underlie the charge of relativism. First, contextualism seems to accept statements of this form: 'S knew p, but now, S's evidence and reliability staying the same, S does not know p'. How can people know something at one time but not know it at a later time if they have the same justification they always had?

The second objection is more pressing. Straightforward relativists about truth – those who claim a proposition may be true for one group yet false for another group – appear to hold that a single proposition can be both true and false. This seems incoherent; the notion of truth is no longer in play but has been replaced by 'truth for' or 'truth from a point of view'. Subject-based contextualism escapes this worry, for while 'S knows p' is true or false depending on S's context, 'S knows p in context C' is true from all points of view. The attributor-based contextualist, however, holds that truth of statements having the form 'S knows p', or 'S knows p in context C' (where 'C' refers to the subject S's context) are relative to

attributors' context. It seems that there is no truth about whether S knows p, but only 'truth for' or 'truth from a point of view'.

To answer these objections we must treat 'knows' as an indexical term, analogous to 'I' or the demonstrative 'that' (see DEMONSTRATIVES AND INDEXICALS). Following David Kaplan (1989), we may distinguish the 'character' of an indexical, the part of meaning that is constant, from the 'content', which changes. Roughly, the character of 'I' is a function from context to speaker, and the content of 'I' is the speaker on a given occasion of use. According to DeRose (1992), the character of 'S knows p' requires that S should believe p, that p should be true, and that S should be in good enough epistemic position with respect to p. But what is 'good enough' varies with context, hence the content of a knowledge attribution is the level of epistemic position that counts as good enough in that context.

For example, the character of 'knows' in (w) 'Clara knows there is water in the glass' will require that Clara should believe there is water in the glass, that this belief should be true and that Clara should be in a good enough position to determine that there is water in the glass. But whether Clara is in a good enough position will vary with the attributor's context. Where the attributor's interest is in watering plants, the content of 'know' in (w) requires that Clara's position is good enough if she has the typical person's ability to identify water, in which case (w) is true. If, however, the attributor is engaged in important experiments, the content of 'know' in (w) requires that Clara's position is good enough only if she performed a chemical analysis, in which case (w) is false (assuming she has not done the analysis). There is no more mystery about the way truth conditions of (w) vary with context than there is about the way truth conditions of 'I lost my keys' and 'That is a rose' vary with context.

The second objection to relativism is easily handled, then: truth is relative to the attributor's context, but the notion of truth is preserved by treating knowledge claims as having an indexical component. What about the first objection? In any context, epistemic standards are set at one level, so we cannot employ two different sets of standards in evaluating a single sentence within that context. Therefore, we will reject statements of the form 'S knew p, but, S's evidence and reliability remaining the same, S no longer knows p'. Nevertheless, a corresponding 'metalinguistic' statement may be correct: '"S knows p" was true, but now, S's evidence and reliability remaining the same, "S knows p" is false'. The contextualist argues that this is unobjectionable, given the indexicality of knowledge attributions.

4 Further objections

Let us consider four other objections:

(1) Knowledge may require greater uniformity than contextualism allows. Edward Craig (1993) has argued that the function of knowledge claims is to tag reliable information. But if epistemic standards regularly shift, we cannot rely on information gained in another context without continually re-evaluating our knowledge in each new situation. At the least, we need uniform standards of evaluation across broad areas of inquiry. The contextualist reply must grant that a core set of standards applies when special contextual factors are absent.

(2) In one context, Harold may say, 'Your children are in the garden', but once he learns about an escaped prisoner seeking hostages nearby, he would not make the same assertion. Assertibility conditions for the claim have changed, yet surely truth conditions have not. Does not the same thing hold for knowledge ascriptions? Assertibility conditions for knowledge claims vary with context, but why does this show that truth conditions for knowledge claims change also? The contextualist answer depends on arguing that speakers legitimately assert *p* only when they have adequate justification for claiming to know *p*. Thus, knowledge claims may not admit of a divide between assertibility conditions and truth conditions.

(3) Contextualism that allows unjustified beliefs is problematic. If there is no ground for non-inferential beliefs, surely we have not really provided justification. Foundationalists and coherentists will claim they can account for our permitting the absence of explicit justification. First, they would endorse the above view that contextualism conflates assertibility conditions in a practical context with truth conditions that are not contextually determined. Foundationalists might argue that basic beliefs have minimal intrinsic credibility, but must be further justifiable given a legitimate challenge. Some coherentists claim that the most coherent theory provides grounds for accepting initial cognitive output from our sensory mechanisms. This output provides basic beliefs in a context, but is always justifiable in terms of broader theory. Contextualist response to such views requires detailed arguments about the plausibility of foundationalism and coherentism.

(4) Many sceptics believe they point to facts about the human condition that are so important they throw ordinary knowledge claims into doubt. As Barry Stroud (1996) argues, we have an 'objective conception of the world' which entails that almost all our beliefs about it can be mistaken. If this is a fundamental truth, then we cannot avoid scepticism merely by noting that in certain contexts we habitually ignore sceptical worries. The reply to this objection stresses first, that contextualism grants some truth to scepticism and, second, that unlike scepticism, contextualism emphasizes the practical origins of discourse about knowledge.

See also: JUSTIFICATION, EPISTEMIC; KNOWLEDGE, CONCEPT OF

References and further reading

Annis, D. (1978) 'A Contextual Theory of Epistemic Justification', *American Philosophical Quarterly* 15: 213–19. (One of the first clear statements of contextualism.)

Aristotle (mid 3rd century BC) *Metaphysics*, ed. W.D. Ross, Oxford: Oxford University Press, 1924, 2 vols. (Although Aristotle does not endorse all aspects of contextualism, a basis for foundational contextualism can be located in his writings: 1011a–14 are especially relevant.)

Cohen, S. (1987) 'Knowledge, Context, and Social Standards', *Synthese* 73: 3–26. (Crucial discussion of how ability as a contextual factor affects the legitimacy of doubts and defeating considerations.)

* Craig, E. (1993) 'Understanding Scepticism', in J. Haldane and C. Wright (eds) *Reality, Representation and Projection*, Oxford: Oxford University Press. (Response to contextualism that develops an important alternative way of understanding the social role of knowledge claims.)

* DeRose, K. (1992) 'Contextualism and Knowledge Attributions', *Philosophy and Phenomenological Research* 52: 913–29. (Contextualist account of truth conditions for knowledge claims and a good introduction to attributor-based contextualism.)

* —— (1995) 'Solving the Sceptical Problem', *The Philosophical Review* 104: 1–53. (Sophisticated contextualist response to scepticism.)

Hambourger, R. (1981) 'Justified Assertion and the Relativity of Knowledge', *Philosophical Studies* 40: 241–69. (Contains a careful examination of the relation between assertion and knowledge.

* Kaplan, D. (1989) 'Demonstratives', in J. Almog, J. Perry and H. Wettstein (eds) *Themes From Kaplan*, Oxford: Oxford University Press, 481–563. (Important work on the logic of demonstratives and indexicals. The theory developed here may be extended to versions of contextualism that treat 'know' as an indexical.)

* Lewis, D. (1996) 'Elusive Knowledge', *Australasian Journal of Philosophy* 74: 549–67. (Investigation of how knowledge loses its status once we reflect on it; contains an important list of contextual factors.)

* Stroud, B. (1996) 'Epistemological Reflection on

Knowledge of the External World', *Philosophy and Phenomenological Research* 56: 345–58 (Response to Williams by a leading sceptic.)

Unger, P. (1984) *Philosophical Relativity*, Minneapolis, MN: University of Minnesota Press. (Contains an original and carefully developed account of contextualism and invariantism.)

* Williams, M. (1991) *Unnatural Doubts: Epistemological Realism and the Basis of Scepticism*, Oxford: Blackwell. (Thorough study of scepticism that develops the contextualist alternative.)

Wittgenstein, L.J.J. (1969) *On Certainty*, Oxford: Blackwell. (Contains a foundationalist-contextualist account of justification and certainty. See especially paragraphs 82–110, 151–66 and 224–5.)

BRUCE W. BROWER

CONTINGENCY

People are often puzzled about the apparent contingency of the world. To say that something happens contingently is to say that it might not have happened, and to think of the world as contingent is to think that it might not have existed. Is it contingent? Those who ask this are asking whether there might not have been a world at all, or none that was at all like ours. Usually they are not asking whether there could have been a world which differed from ours only in its details: for example, one in which free agents made slightly different choices. That is an important question too, but a separate one. Some people reject the question of the contingency of the world as meaningless because they do not see how any answer to it could be verified. But such verificationism is controversial, and even if there is something wrong with the question it is still worth asking why people find it compelling.

On the classical medieval view, the existence of the world is contingent: it depends on God's choice. God's existence, however, is not contingent but necessary. It belongs to God's essence that he should exist. But there has long been the alternative idea, that the existence of the world is itself necessary. Many Neo-Platonists held (some still do) that the world exists because it is best that it should. If it is best that something should come about, then it must come about, and there is no room for God's choice in the matter. Other philosophers think that the world exists necessarily because it exists in virtue of scientific laws, which are themselves necessary. The idea that it is contingent, they suggest, is due to the confusion of scientific necessity with logical necessity. Logical

necessity attaches only to statements – those that are instances of logical laws, often called analytic. The existence of the world itself is (scientifically) necessary; but the statement 'There exists a world like ours' is logically contingent – alternatives can be imagined without contradiction.

Spinoza also held that the world exists necessarily, but for neither of these reasons (see SPINOZA, B. §4). For him it is necessary in its own right; existence belongs to the world's essence, as for the medievals it belongs to the essence of God. The necessity here is neither scientific nor logical, but metaphysical. Spinoza (1677) called the world 'God', but it lacks the personality of the orthodox God and is identified with Nature. He infers that because the world itself exists necessarily, there is no room for contingent events within it, but this is a mistake: one could hold, as Hegel did, that the nature of the world requires that there be certain contingencies within it.

It 'exists by the necessity of its nature alone': it is hard to see what this means, either for Spinoza or for his medieval predecessors who had said the same of God. It is not that it exists by definition – that we have formulated a concept of God or Nature in which existence is taken to be a defining characteristic. Spinoza was well aware (as were ANSELM and DESCARTES) that our conceptions are likely to be defective and our definitions consequently irrelevant. It is that existence belongs to its essence as solubility in water belongs to the essence of sugar. So just as sugar is soluble necessarily, so God or Nature exists necessarily. Like Anselm and Descartes, Spinoza inferred that it exists. Aquinas and other medievals were more cautious, and held that this does not follow: what follows is that if there is a God its existence is necessary (see GOD, ARGUMENTS FOR THE EXISTENCE OF §§1, 2).

Spinoza also said that God is *causa sui*, here again following many predecessors, including Descartes (1641). This is often translated as 'cause of itself', but 'self-explanatory' might be better. Spinoza equated something's existing necessarily with its being self-explanatory, or requiring no explanation. Unfortunately this is a mistake. If to exist is part of something's essence we can still ask why it exists, just as we can ask why sugar is soluble. No doubt if it is sugar it is necessarily soluble, but we may derive that necessity from more general laws, and we may ask why there should be sugar at all. In general the fact that something is necessary does not remove the need to explain it. Complex mathematical truths can be explained in terms of simpler ones; perhaps elementary logical laws do not need explanation. But Descartes thought they did – they were fixed by God. Among those who hold that the basic laws of physics are necessary, some deny that they need explanation and others insist that they do. Some of these would feel that it strengthens, or at least fills out, their case to say that although these laws are scientifically necessary they are metaphysically contingent; in other words, that this world is itself metaphysically contingent – other worlds with alternative laws could have existed instead. But this is to repeat the mistake of equating what is necessary with what does not need explanation, and what is contingent with what does.

This mistake explains why people puzzle over the contingency of the world. What they really want to know is whether the world's existence requires explanation. It is a difficult question; but if we could solve it, any explanation we provided would automatically tell us whether the world is contingent or not. Thus if the world is the free creation of God, it would not have existed if God had chosen differently, and it is metaphysically contingent. If, alternatively, as thought, it was created by a God who is bound to create the best of all possible worlds, there is no real possibility of God's choosing differently, and the world is metaphysically necessary (see LEIBNIZ, G.W. §3). Leibniz (1697) refused to put the matter like this, and insisted on calling it contingent, just because it is created by God. There may be various reasons for this refusal, including a wish to continue to call God's choice 'free' even though God's own perfection left no alternative. But one of them is the thought that the world requires explanation, and that to call it necessary would be to imply otherwise.

We always seek explanations wherever possible. Leibniz (and many others) believed in a principle of sufficient reason, which says there is an adequate explanation for everything that exists or occurs. It is natural to hope that there is such an explanation; but then either there must be chains of explanations stretching back infinitely, or else there is some thing or event the nature of which removes the need for further explanation. Some have seen the Big Bang in this way, but it is evidently possible to speculate about why it occurred. There is no incoherence in the idea of something which had no cause and which did not depend on anything, but it would remain natural for us to seek an explanation for it even though there was none to be found. There is room for dispute as to what an explanation is, but if to explain the fact that Φ is to render it intelligible by reference to the fact that Ψ, it would seem that there might be some facts which were, in their own right, as intelligible as possible, like (perhaps) the fact that if p then p. The demand for further explanations could be terminated if we came to a fact of this kind. Some have thought the existence of God to be maximally intelligible, and

the existence of the world not to be; but if 'intelligible' means 'intelligible to us', it seems plain that neither is maximally intelligible, and if that is not what it means, it is unclear what else it means.

A more defensible view would be that God's existence is 'self-explanatory' in that what makes his existence intelligible is his existence itself. It is arguable that we cannot explain anything except by tacitly presupposing the existence of God, because every explanation rests on certain principles of reasoning, and to suppose that these principles yield truth about the world is to suppose the sort of systematic match between the way we think and the way things are that could only be due to a purposive agent. If that were so, God's existence would be required to render anything intelligible, and if anything were proposed as an explanation of God, its explanatory power would derive from God's existence itself. This is as close as we could come, I think, to capturing the idea that God is *causa sui*. But it would not terminate the demand for explanations: we could still ask *why* God exists, and hope to find an answer which makes it more intelligible why there should be a God. And it does not entail the thesis that God's existence is necessary; nor does it follow from it.

References and further reading

Barrow, J.D. and Tipler, F.H. (1986) *The Anthropic Cosmological Principle*, Oxford: Clarendon Press. (A careful discussion of whether the fact that the universe is such as to allow intelligent life makes it necessary to seek an explanation for it. Combines sophisticated material from physics and biology with intriguing speculation. Not for beginners.)

* Descartes, R. (1641) *Meditations on First Philosophy* with *Objections and Replies*, in *The Philosophical Writings of Descartes*, vol. 2, trans. J. Cottingham, R. Stoothoff and D. Murdoch, Cambridge: Cambridge University Press, 1984. (The third Meditation and the first and fourth Replies give Descartes's account of God as *causa sui*. The sixth Reply commits him to holding that logical laws depend on God's choice, though some commentators question whether he really meant this.)

* Leibniz, G.W. von (1697) 'On the Ultimate Origination of Things' in *Leibniz: Philosophical Writings*, trans. M. Morris and G.H.R. Parkinson, London: Everyman's Library, Dent, 1973; also in *G.W. Leibniz: Philosophical Essays*, trans. R. Ariew and D. Garber, Indianapolis, IN and Cambridge: Hackett, 1989. (A neat statement of Leibniz's position on the contingency of the world – or one of his positions, since he had several, to the annoyance of Leibniz scholars.)

Leslie, J. (1989) *Universes*, London: Routledge. (Argues that the universe requires an explanation. Favours an account described as theistic, but the theism is Neoplatonic: God is said to be 'the world's creative ethical requiredness', and the universe came about because it was good that it should – on this see especially ch. 8.)

Mackie, J.L. (1981) *The Miracle of Theism*, Oxford, Clarendon Press. (Chs 5, 8 and 13 are particularly relevant. Criticizes the idea that the universe, as a whole, requires explanation, as well as the Neoplatonic account and Leslie's version of it in particular. Clear and trenchant.)

Prevost, R. (1990) *Probability and Theistic Explanation*, Oxford: Clarendon Press. (See especially ch. 7. Capable defence of the traditional view that a necessarily existent God is needed to explain a contingent world.)

* Spinoza, B. (1677) *Ethics*, trans. with notes E. Curley in *The Collected Works of Spinoza*, vol. 1, Princeton, NJ: Princeton University Press, 1985. (Sets out Spinoza's views about God and necessity. The first part is particularly relevant.)

RALPH C.S. WALKER

CONTINUANTS

There is a common-sense distinction between terms such as 'statue' or 'chair' on the one hand, and 'concert' or 'war' on the other. A long-standing tradition in metaphysics has attached some significance to this distinction, holding that the first kind of term is used to name continuants, whereas the second kind is used to name events or processes. The difference is that continuants can be said to change, and therefore persist through change, whereas events do not. However, the distinction between continuants and events has been challenged on the grounds that no concrete object does, in fact, retain its identity through time. It has been suggested, for example, that unless we give up the notion of identity through time, we are faced with questions that we cannot answer. In addition, the notion that things persist through change is, apparently, threatened by a certain view of time. On this view there is in reality no past, present and future, but rather unchanging temporal relations between events. It has been suggested that such a view is committed to the idea that objects have temporal parts, and these by definition cannot persist through time.

1   Do objects persist?
2   Continuants and tenseless time

1   Do objects persist?

Intuitively, you are the same individual as someone who existed yesterday, even though you have fewer brain-cells, your body temperature will have fluctuated and some of your desires may have changed. In contrast, a performance of a piece of music does not itself change: rather, it *consists* of a series of changes. An important part of the motivation for a distinction between continuants and events concerns our notion of responsibility. You can only be held responsible for the actions you performed yesterday if they really were your actions: you now and the person who performed those acts must be one and the same. This connection with responsibility might incline us to widen the class of continuants to include football clubs, religious orders and companies. Someone taking a company to court presumes that the company being taken to court today is the same as the one that violated the law last year.

For material objects, identity through time might plausibly be thought to be no more than spatio-temporal continuity. Put briefly, the continuity criterion states that an object, *a*, existing at one time *t* at place *s*, is identical with *b*, existing at a later time *t'* at place *s'*, if and only if there is a continuous series of spatio-temporal points between *s* at *t* and *s'* at *t'* such that no point in that series is unoccupied by an object. This rules out the possibility of an object going out of existence for a period and then coming back into existence again. It also rules out discontinuous spatial motion. Two kinds of problem case arise for this account, however. Consider first a lump of bronze which is moulded into a statue of an old man by Rodin. This later falls into the hands of Henry Moore, who remoulds the statue to represent a pregnant woman. Finally, it comes into the possession of Elizabeth Frink, who turns it into an enormous head. What this obviously fictional example of aesthetic vandalism illustrates is that, although Frink's statue is spatio-temporally continuous with Rodin's statue, they are nevertheless not the same statue. Consider next an amoeba, A, which divides to form two amoebae, B and C. Both B and C are spatio-temporally continuous with A, but they cannot both be identical with A, for then (since 'identical with' is a transitive relation) they would be identical with each other. Clearly, spatio-temporal continuity is not the same relation as identity (see IDENTITY §1).

In the face of this, we could look for a way of strengthening the spatio-temporal continuity criterion, or we could simply regard identity through time as a primitive relation, irreducible to any other. But both these options leave us with the apparently unanswerable question of whether it is B, or C, or neither, that is identical with amoeba A. A third, radical, approach is to reject altogether the notion of identity through time and with it the notion of a continuant. On this view, associated with Quine (1960), things, strictly speaking, do not persist through time. Rather, they are temporally extended in a sense closely analogous to the sense in which they are spatially extended (see QUINE, W.V.O. §5). Just as a thing has different spatial parts at different places, so it has different *temporal* parts at different times. There is no question of a temporal part being identical to a later or earlier temporal part, any more than there is a question concerning whether your left foot is identical to your right foot. In the language of temporal parts, we can redescribe the cases above as follows: the collection of temporal parts that is Rodin's statue shares no temporal parts with either the Moore collection or with the Frink collection, though it does share a temporal part with the collection that is the lump of bronze. As for the amoeba, since no temporal part existing before the division can be identical with any part existing afterwards, there can be no question of B or C being the same as A. What we have is simply a branching collection of temporal parts.

However, the notion of temporal parts is a controversial one. Effectively, it dissolves the distinction between objects and events in treating the former, more or less, as extended processes. So the temporal-parts view needs to explain why it is objects, not events, that are thought to change (see EVENTS). In addition, the view must explain why we are apparently entitled to hold people responsible for past acts if the temporal part held responsible is not the temporal part that performed the act. Indeed, since temporal parts do not have duration, but exist only for an instant, how can the temporal parts of people be said to perform acts at all? The temporal-parts view can preserve the common-sense distinction between such things as chairs and concerts by pointing out that every temporal part of a chair is itself a chair, whereas it is *not* true that every temporal part of a concert is itself a concert. But is this enough to explain the facts about change and responsibility mentioned above?

2 Continuants and tenseless time

The appeal to temporal parts in dealing with the problem cases above is not simply a desperate manoeuvre: further motivation for the temporal-parts view comes from a certain view of time, namely one which denies the passage of time (see CHANGE §2). Just what is involved in this denial should, however, be made more precise.

According to the *tensed theory of time*, tensed expressions such as 'now', 'last year', 'in a few days'

time', reveal a significant feature of time itself. For example, the presentness of a certain event is, on this view, a non-relational property of the time of that event; and also a transient property, in that the event will soon be past. The tensed theory is therefore associated with the view that time passes. According to the *tenseless theory of time*, in contrast, the presentness of an event is a relational feature of it: it is present only with respect to a particular time. Similarly, an event is only past with respect to a time, or group of times. On this view 'present with respect to' simply means 'simultaneous with', and 'past with respect to' simply means 'earlier than'. So the only facts about presentness are trivial ones: a time is present with respect to (that is, simultaneous with) itself, past with respect to later times, and future with respect to earlier times. Times, therefore, do not on this view change in respect of their presentness. The tenseless theory is thus associated with the *denial* of time's passage. We can present the contrast between the tensed and tenseless theories in terms of the account they give of what makes tensed assertions true:

Tensed theory

A particular utterance of 'It is *now* very windy' is true if and only if it is now very windy (or, equivalently, extreme windiness is present).

A particular utterance of 'It *was* very windy' is true if and only if it was very windy (or, equivalently, extreme windiness is past).

Tenseless theory

A particular utterance of 'It is now very windy', uttered at time t, is true if and only if it is very windy at t;

A particular utterance of 'It was very windy', uttered at time t, is true if and only if it is very windy at some time earlier than t;

where t is specified in tenseless terms (for example, '4 pm on 31 December 1999').

It has often been assumed that the tenseless theory is committed to temporal parts, and the assumption is a natural one, for tenseless theory does away with what might have seemed a crucial disanalogy between time and space. As a place is 'here' to us just because we happen to be at that place, so, on tenseless theory, an event is 'present' to us just because we are at a point simultaneous with that event. Since objects have spatial parts, it is natural to assume that the tenseless theorist will suppose them to have temporal parts. There have, however, been attempts to reconcile the tenseless theory with the notion of continuants.

In temporal-part theory, the fact that x is F at time t is represented by the formulation 'x-at-t is F', where 'x-at-t' names a temporal part of x. There are, however, different ways of reporting the fact in question. For example, instead of qualifying the subject, x, with the term denoting a time, we could qualify the predicate: 'x is F-at-t'. Alternatively, we could treat properties as *relations*, linking an object and a time: 'x bears relation F to t'. Why are these ways of representing the facts thought to be alternatives to temporal parts? Because it is the whole, temporally extended, object which is F-at-t (on the first account) or which stands in certain relation to a time (on the second account).

An objection to these supposed alternatives says that the intuition underlying the notion of continuants is that an object (in contrast to an event) is *wholly present* at each of the instants which compose its temporal extension. There can be no spatial analogue of this: an object is not thought to be wholly located at each of the points which constitute its spatial extension. The idea that something can be wholly present at different times avoids contradiction if we think of time as passing – that is the time at which an object is present as itself changing. Once we give up the idea that times can change in this way, and adopt the tenseless theory of time, we surely also give up the idea that an object can be wholly located at a time. Treating properties as relations between times and a temporally extended object merely disguises this fact (see TIME §2).

See also: PROCESSES

References and further reading

Geach, P. (1965) 'Some problems about time', *Proceedings of the British Academy* 51: 321–36. (Accessible, wide-ranging paper. Argues against the notion of temporal parts.)

Johnston, M. (1987) 'Is there a problem about persistence?', *Aristotelian Society* supplementary vol. 62: 107–35. (Discusses alternative formulations of the proposition that a thing has a property at a certain time, and defends an 'adverbial' treatment of the temporal qualifier. Quite technical.)

Le Poidevin, R. (1991) *Change, Cause and Contradiction*, London: Macmillan. (Develops and defends the tenseless theory of time. Ch. 4 expands on the material of §2 above. Mostly quite difficult.)

Mellor, D.H. (1981) *Real Time*, Cambridge: Cambridge University Press. (Defends the tenseless theory of time and attempts to reconcile the theory with the existence of continuants, by treating properties as relations between objects and times.
A good but relatively demanding introduction to the tenseless theory of time.)

Noonan, H.W. (1980) *Objects and Identity*, The Hague: Martinus Nijhoff. (A detailed and often quite difficult discussion of synchronic and diachronic identity and the debate over continuants, coming down in favour of Quine's ontology of temporal parts.)

* Quine, W.V. (1960) *Word and Object*, Cambridge, MA: M.I.T. Press. (Referred to in §1 above. See especially page 171 for his view that objects are not to be distinguished from events.)

Simmons, P.M. (1987) *Parts: A Study in Ontology*, Oxford: Clarendon Press. (A detailed and technically demanding application of mereology – the formal study of part-whole relationships – to metaphysical issues such as the nature of continuants. Chapter 5 is especially relevant.)

ROBIN LE POIDEVIN

CONTINUUM HYPOTHESIS

The 'continuum hypothesis' (CH) asserts that there is no set intermediate in cardinality ('size') between the set of real numbers (the 'continuum') and the set of natural numbers. Since the continuum can be shown to have the same cardinality as the power set (that is, the set of subsets) of the natural numbers, CH is a special case of the 'generalized continuum hypothesis' (GCH), which says that for any infinite set, there is no set intermediate in cardinality between it and its power set.

Cantor first proposed CH believing it to be true, but, despite persistent efforts, failed to prove it. König proved that the cardinality of the continuum cannot be the sum of denumerably many smaller cardinals, and it has been shown that this is the only restriction the accepted axioms of set theory place on its cardinality. Gödel showed that CH was consistent with these axioms and Cohen that its negation was. Together these results prove the independence of CH from the accepted axioms.

Cantor proposed CH in the context of seeking to answer the question 'What is the identifying nature of continuity?'. These independence results show that, whatever else has been gained from the introduction of transfinite set theory – including greater insight into the import of CH – it has not provided a basis for finally answering this question. This remains the case even when the axioms are supplemented in various plausible ways.

1 **The continuous, the discrete and the infinite**
2 **Numbering the continuum**
3 **Reactions to independence**

1 The continuous, the discrete and the infinite

Greek mathematics was divided into arithmetic – the science of discrete magnitudes – and geometry – the science of continuous magnitudes. The basis for this division can be found in Aristotle's sophisticated discussions of space and time. The existence of incommensurable magnitudes, such as the side of a square and its diagonal (the ratio of which is $\sqrt{2}$), was already well known, as was the distinction between points and extended parts, however small, of a continuous whole. Aristotle argued that since two points can never be contiguous (either there is a separation between them or they coincide), a continuum can never be built up out of points. He defined a continuously extended whole as one which may be divided at any point into continuously extended wholes and concluded that it is necessary to draw a fundamental distinction between those wholes which are collections of parts and those which are 'given before their parts', that is, between discrete and continuous magnitudes.

So long as this division was in place (that is, until the seventeenth century) a question such as 'What is the (cardinal) number of points in a continuous line?' could not arise because it could not sensibly be asked. 'Continuity' was a primitive geometric concept. The situation changed, however, with the acceptance of Descartes' introduction of algebraic methods into the heart of geometry, allowing geometric curves to be defined by equations of 'motions' of points 'generating' them. This effectively swept aside the division between arithmetic and geometry, but without in any way confronting or resolving the problem of how to model the continuous by the discrete.

Newton and Leibniz explored and exploited the infinite divisibility of continua in their attempts to study continuous motions algebraically. Initially this exploration (infinitesimal calculus, analysis; see ANA-LYSIS, PHILOSOPHICAL ISSUES IN §1) moved freely between algebraic expression and geometric intuition, mediated by the concept of continuous motion. However, this led to the discovery of a number of 'pathological' functions, whose graphs cannot be pictured. For example, in a continuous plane, unlimited in extent, there is no limit to the number of wavelike, and hence continuous, oscillations that a point might execute within a given finite interval. So one might ask whether there might be a function which corresponds to a point oscillating with infinite frequency (that is, which is such that no matter how small an interval we take there will be an oscillation contained within it). Weierstrass' everywhere continuous but nowhere differentiable function seemed to 'describe' such a 'motion'. This kind of function contradicts the assumption, based on cases which can be pictured, that continuity and differentiability go together. So an account of continuity was required in terms not based on geometric intuition.

2 Numbering the continuum

Cantor's early attempts to characterize the structure of continua were natural extensions of the kind of work in analysis which led to discovery of these pathological functions. He established that the cardinality of the set $\mathbb{R}$ of real numbers is greater than that of the set $\mathbb{N}$ of natural numbers (see CANTOR'S THEOREM). He further proved that there is a one-one correspondence between the points in a plane (the two-dimensional continuum) and the points in a line. So he already knew (writing $|A|$ for the cardinality of A) that

$$|\mathbb{R} \times \mathbb{R}| = |\mathbb{R}| > |\mathbb{N}|.$$

Cantor thus interpreted the problem of how to identify the nature of continuity as that of how to say when a given set of points in an n-dimensional space is to be considered a continuum. Having already defined the real numbers in terms of limits of convergent sequences of rational numbers, he made use of the more general notion of a 'limit point'. A point p is defined to be a limit point of a set P of points if in any neighbourhood of p there are infinitely many points of P. It can be proved that if P is infinite then it has at least one limit point. The set of limit points of P is denoted by $P^{(1)}$. The set $\mathbb{R}$ of real numbers (the 'continuum') is such that $\mathbb{R}^{(1)} = \mathbb{R}$. Sets with this property were called 'perfect'. But perfection does not serve to characterize continuity, as Cantor demonstrated with his 'ternary set', also called 'Cantor's discontinuum' (see SET THEORY §5). This is the set of points of the closed interval (a 'closed' interval includes the points at either end) $[0, 1]$ which remain after infinitely many repetitions of the following procedure: divide each interval of the set into thirds, and in each case discard ('blank out') the middle third, leaving behind two closed intervals.

This set is dense in no interval of the continuum ($B \subseteq A$ is 'dense' in A if it is disjoint from no open interval of A), closed, perfect and contains no interior points: it is completely discontinuous.

Nevertheless, Cantor felt that perfect sets held the key since he was able to prove that no *denumerable* point set (that is, a set with the cardinality of the natural numbers) could be perfect. If a set P is finite, its first derived set $P^{(1)}$ is empty. For any P, either there is some finite n such that $P^{(n)}$ is finite and hence $P^{(n+1)}$ is empty, or there is not. For perfect sets there is no such finite n. So if this idea is to differentiate between continuous and discontinuous perfect sets it seems that *transfinite* indices of iteration need to be used. This was the context in which Cantor originally introduced transfinite ordinal numbers (see SET THEORY §2). He divided the ordinals into first and second number classes:

(1) $0, 1, 2, 3, \ldots$

(2) $\omega, \omega + 1, \omega + 2, \ldots \omega.2, \omega.2 + 1, \ldots \omega.3, \ldots \omega.\omega \ldots$

(1) is the set of natural numbers, $\mathbb{N}$, which has cardinality $\aleph_0$ ('aleph-nought' or 'aleph-null'). Every ordinal α in (2) is such that the cardinality of $\{x : x < \alpha\}$ is $\aleph_0$. That is, these numbers represent all the possible orderings of a denumerably infinite set. Cantor proved ([1895, 1897] 1955: 169–73) that these two number classes cannot be put into one-one correspondence and that there can be no set with a cardinality in between the two. This justified calling the cardinality of (2) '$\aleph_1$'.

In this way the extension of the ordinal number sequence into the transfinite generates not only infinite ordinal numbers α but also infinite cardinal numbers $\aleph_\alpha$. It thus provides a scale of cardinal numbers on which one might hope to locate $2^{\aleph_0}$. The 'continuum hypothesis' (CH) expresses the claim that there is a one-one correspondence between the real numbers and the numbers in the second number class (in symbols, $2^{\aleph_0} = \aleph_1$), and another way of interpreting the claim made by the generalized continuum hypothesis (GCH) would be as saying that the two routes to generating higher infinite cardinalities (via power sets and via the number classes) coincide (in symbols, $2^{\aleph_\alpha} = \aleph_{\alpha+1}$ for every ordinal α). Although Cantor believed CH to be true (and Gödel (1939) proved it to be consistent with the axioms of set theory), he realized that there is no immediate guarantee that every cardinality will have a representative among the cardinalities of the number classes unless it can also be assumed that every set can be well-ordered, and hence has an ordinal number. If it were not the case that every set could be well-ordered, the cardinalities of those sets which cannot be so ordered would not be represented by cardinal numbers arising from the construction of the ordinal number sequence. Indeed it can be shown that in Zermelo–Fraenkel set theory (ZF), GCH entails the

axiom of choice and hence that every set can be well-ordered, whereas Cohen's independence result proves that the converse does not hold (see Cohen 1963–4).

3 Reactions to independence

Proof of the independence of CH (GCH) from ZFC (ZF plus the axiom of choice – see SET THEORY, DIFFERENT SYSTEMS OF §3) stimulated renewed interest in philosophical questions about the status of set theory and the epistemology of mathematics. Is there a universe of sets in virtue of which CH is either true or false, although at present we do not know which? If this is the case, how would we come to know more about it and hence hope to determine the truth-value of CH? The most radical reaction would undercut even these questions by interpreting the independence results as showing that the whole set-theoretic approach to problems of continuity was misguided: CH is undecidable because it does not make any real mathematical sense; it presupposes that we can sensibly talk about actually infinite sets, whereas we cannot. Less radical reactions assume that CH does make mathematical sense. The problem then is not merely how to determine whether or not it should be accepted, but to decide whether there is a basis for acceptance or rejection and, if so, what this might be. It might be argued that the situation of CH is analogous to that of the parallel postulate after it was proved to be independent of the remaining axioms of Euclidean geometry. The result in that case was a widening of the field of mathematical investigation to consider a whole variety of geometries in which the parallel axiom fails. Analogously, in set theory, explorations of systems in which CH holds and in which it fails have been carried out. Gödel (1947), however, contrasts the epistemological situations in geometry and set theory. In geometry the question of the truth or falsity of the parallel postulate retains its sense if the geometric axioms are interpreted as referring to the behaviour of rigid bodies, light rays and so on, but not otherwise – that is, the question of its truth or falsity has become an empirical question to be answered by reference to the contexts in which geometry is used; it is no longer a mathematical question. The question of the truth or falsity of CH, however, retains its sense only if the axioms of set theory are interpreted as referring to mathematical objects (sets), since these axioms have no direct empirical interpretation. Gödel himself believed that sets are mathematical objects which have an independent existence. He would thus interpret the proof of the independence of CH from ZFC as a demonstration that the axioms of ZFC do not contain a complete description of the set-theoretic universe. In this case there is a need to look for new axioms to complete the description. Several such axioms have been suggested and their consequences studied (see SET THEORY §1), but none has yielded anything approaching consensus on either their acceptability or that of CH.

Gödel's mathematical realism is not the only philosophical position which would underwrite attempts to resolve questions about the status of CH (and other proposed axioms of set theory) by studying the consequences for other areas of mathematics of accepting or denying it. It might be argued that what mathematical sense CH has is derived from its preformal connections with the problem of characterizing the continuous in terms of the discrete. If so, any determination should be based on its impact on the ever-widening area of mathematics connected with this problem. This approach relates philosophical issues about the status of set theory with other areas of mathematics, it does not resolve them.

See also: LOGICAL AND MATHEMATICAL TERMS, GLOSSARY OF

References and further reading

* Cantor, G. (1895, 1897) 'Beiträge zur Begründung der transfiniten Mengenlehre', parts 1 and 2, *Mathematische Annalen* 46: 481–512, 49: 207–46; trans. P.E.B. Jourdain (1915), *Contributions to the Founding of the Theory of Transfinite Numbers*, New York: Dover, 1955. (Two of Cantor's most important memoirs on transfinite numbers.)

* Cohen, P.J. (1963–4) 'The Independence of the Continuum Hypothesis', *Proceedings of the National Academy of Science, USA* 50: 1,143–8, 51: 105–10; repr. in *Set Theory and the Continuum Hypothesis*, New York: Benjamin, 1966. (The original version of his proof.)

Dauben, J.W. (1979) *Georg Cantor: His Mathematics and Philosophy of the Infinite*, Cambridge, MA: Harvard University Press. (An excellent intellectual biography which traces the development of Cantor's mathematical ideas, while putting them in the context of his philosophy of the infinite and his professional life.)

* Gödel, K. (1939) 'Consistency Proof for the Generalized Continuum Hypothesis', *Proceedings of the National Academy of Science, USA* 25: 220–4. (Original publication of the proof.)

—— (1940) *The Consistency of the Continuum Hypothesis*, Princeton, NJ: Princeton University Press, 1994. (Revised and more complete version of the original proof.)

* —— (1947) 'What is Cantor's Continuum Problem?', *American Mathematical Monthly* 54: 515–25; repr. in P. Benacerraf and H. Putnam (eds) *Philosophy of Mathematics: Selected Readings*, Cambridge: Cambridge University Press, 2nd edn, 1983. (A very valuable discussion which gives some of the context of debate about CH.)

Hallett, M. (1984) *Cantorian Set Theory and Limitation of Size*, Oxford: Clarendon Press. (Includes an integrated account of Cantor's metaphysical and mathematical theories of infinity together with discussion of the relation between Cantorian and modern set theory.)

Tiles, M.E. (1989) *The Philosophy of Set Theory: An Introduction to Cantor's Paradise*, Oxford: Blackwell. (Traces the philosophical and mathematical background to the formulation of CH and considers whether it can be decided.)

MARY TILES

CONTRACEPTION

see LIFE AND DEATH (§5); SEXUALITY, PHILOSOPHY OF

CONTRACTARIANISM

The idea that political relations originate in contract or agreement has been applied in several ways. In Plato's Republic *Glaucon suggests that justice is but a pact among rational egoists. Thomas Hobbes developed this idea to analyse the nature of political power. Given the predominantly self-centred nature of humankind, government is necessary for society. Government's role is to stabilize social cooperation. By exercising enforcement powers, government provides each with the assurance that everyone else will abide by cooperative rules, thereby making it rational for all to cooperate. To fulfil this stabilizing role, Hobbes argued that it is rational for each individual to agree to authorize one person to exercise absolute political power. Neo-Hobbesians eschew absolutism and apply the theory of rational choice to argue that rules of justice, perhaps even all morality, can be construed in terms of a rational bargain among self-interested individuals.*

John Locke, working from different premises than Hobbes, appealed to a social compact to argue for a constitutional government with limited powers. All men are born with a natural right to equal freedom, and a natural duty to God to preserve themselves and the rest of mankind. No government is just unless it could be commonly agreed to form a position of equal freedom, where agreement is subject to the moral constraints of natural law. Absolutism is unjust according to this criterion.

Rousseau developed egalitarian features of Locke's view to contend for a democratic constitution. The Social Contract embodies the General Will of society, not the unconstrained private wills of its members. The General Will wills the common good, the good of society and all of its members. Only by bringing our individual wills into accord with the General Will can we achieve civic and moral freedom.

In this century, John Rawls has recast natural rights theories of the social contract to argue for a liberal egalitarian conception of justice. From a position of equality, where each person abstracts from knowledge of their historical situations, it is rational for all to agree on principles of justice that guarantee equal basic freedoms and resources adequate for each person's independence.

T.M. Scanlon, meanwhile, has outlined a right-based contractualist account of morality. An act is right if it accords with principles that could not be reasonably rejected by persons who are motivated by a desire to justify their actions according to principles that no one else can reasonably reject.

1   **The role of agreement**
2   **Interest-based contracts and Hobbes**
3   **Contemporary Hobbesian views**
4   **Conventionalism**
5   **Democratic contract views and Locke**
6   **Rousseau's democratic contract view**
7   **Rawls' democratic contract**
8   **Right-based versus interest-based views**
9   **Moral contractualism**

1   The role of agreement

Contract accounts of justice are intuitively appealing. One explanation of their appeal is promissory obligation; if we agree to something we accept it, and when we agree on condition that others do, there is mutual reliance and grounds for holding all to their commitments. But the obligation of fidelity to promises does not adequately account for the intuitive force of agreement. Not all agreements involve promises. Also, it still must be explained why we should keep our promises, and a contractual promise cannot explain this duty. Hume (1748) explained promissory and contractual obligations by their public utility, and dismissed contractarian accounts of political relations as superficial.

But suppose we see the intuitive force of agreement as deriving not from promising, but from the liberal idea that rules of social cooperation should be based in individuals' consent and for their reciprocal benefit. Hume's argument cannot easily account for these ideas, for there is no clear connection between general utility and free consent; moreover, utilitarian principles do not guarantee institutions that benefit each individually. Here the idea of agreement calls upon deeper associations with democratic ideals of freedom and equality. Assuming that individuals are free and equal by nature or by right, it is natural to think that the political and social requirements they are subject to are contingent on their free agreement. Approached in this way, the ideas of contract and agreement can be applied to elucidate the requirements of freedom and equality.

Contract views differ depending on how the idea of agreement is specified. Who are the parties to the agreement? How are they situated (status quo, state of nature or strict equality)? What are their intentions, capacities and interests? What rights and powers do they have? What is the purpose of the agreement (political obligations, a constitution or social duties and institutions too)? Is the agreement actual or hypothetical, historical or non-historical? There is not one, but several contract views.

Two distinctions help to organize different views. First, *political contractarianism* concerns political and social relations associated with the idea of justice, including the legitimate role and powers of governments, basic rights and duties of citizens, property and its distribution, and the structure of economic relations. Issues of political justice underlie the work of the major representatives of social contract doctrine: Hobbes, Locke, Rousseau, Kant and Rawls. *Moral contractarianism* extends the idea of agreement to other moral relations. The most ambitious view would hold that all our duties and obligations, political and non-political, have their bases in agreement. None of the figures above profess this view.

Next, a *social contract view* maintains that certain basic duties and institutions are grounded in a unanimous agreement among all society's (competent) members. Unanimity illuminates the idea that justice, or morality generally, involves uniform public rules impartially applied to all individuals, which benefit each equally in some way. An *individual contract view* holds that certain basic duties or institutions originate in private or non-social agreement. Robert Nozick's libertarianism is an example (Nozick 1974); he depicts legitimate political power as originating not in social agreement, but in a series of discrete private contracts among isolated individuals (see LIBERTARIANISM).

Attention here is devoted to political and moral

versions of the social contract tradition. There are two major traditions of social contract thought that deal with issues of political justice: *interest-based contract views* stem from Hobbes; *democratic contract views* derive from the natural rights theories of Locke, Rousseau and Kant.

2 Interest-based contracts and Hobbes

The common aim of interest-based views is to account for justice (or morality generally) in terms of what best promotes each person's enlightened interests. Norms of justice are depicted as the outcome of a mutually advantageous agreement. To carry this idea through, interest-based views contend that the basic desires and interests of individuals are fixed by their nature or circumstances, and are definable without any moral notions. Normally interests are explained as self-regarding or focused on oneself, although they need not be purely so (for example, Hobbes recognized 'conjugal affection' as widespread). What is important is that our final ends conflict. Agreement is then depicted as a rational compromise or bargain among essentially conflicting interests, where each party is willing to qualify the direct pursuit of their interests on condition that others do too. Essential to interest-based views is that all parties to the agreement must be made better off (or at least not worse off) than they would be without it.

Interest-based agreements are *historical* in that the parties have knowledge of their particular desires and circumstances. In Hobbesian interest-based views, historical circumstances are defined by a hypothetical, presocial and non-cooperative state of nature. The purpose of agreement from this baseline is to arrive at conditions of peaceable and efficient social cooperation, on the assumption that humans are mainly concerned with advancing their particular interests, are indifferent to the welfare of strangers and have no concern for morality and justice for their own sake. In interest views based on *convention*, the parties are similarly motivated, but their historical circumstances are defined by the current status quo. Because these views take the status quo as given, they do not so much seek to justify or critically assess prevailing cooperative norms as to explain them. Primary attention in this entry is devoted to Hobbesian views.

Hobbes' social contract has two roles (see HOBBES, T. §§6,7). Its first purpose is as an analytical device designed to clarify the nature and necessities of political society. Its second purpose is normative: to justify absolute political power (see ABSOLUTISM §1). To discover the nature of political power, Hobbes imaginatively dissolves political society into its constituent parts, individuals, and then asks how it could come about from this initial situation. In the absence of effective political power individuals (or families) would inhabit a non-cooperative state of nature. Human nature is such that the primary ends of individuals are self-focused (or family-focused at best) and conflicting. Hobbes contends that the three motivations dearest to us are self-preservation, 'conjugal affection' and the means for commodious living. Given these and other motives, and uncertainty about the future, our desires are insatiable. But resources are scarce, so humankind is naturally competitive. Moreover, we are equal enough in strength of body and mind for the weakest to pose a threat to the strongest. Assuming these conditions, Hobbes' thesis is that a state of nature tends towards a state of war. In the absence of effective political power, it is irrational to be cooperative by keeping one's promises and commitments or trusting in the goodwill of others. To protect one's person and possessions, each person's most rational strategy is one of 'anticipation', being prepared to attack others whenever circumstances seem favourable. The outcome is a collectively irrational situation where each person does what is best for themselves but all end up worse off than if they (jointly) had acted differently.

Hobbes' state of nature is the first recognition of 'prisoner's dilemma' situations central to modern game theory (see DECISION AND GAME THEORY §3). Hobbes resolves the state of nature dilemma with the social contract. What is needed to deliver those captured in a state of nature, or to avoid falling into one, is: (1) a system of norms which make social cooperation possible ('the laws of nature'); and (2) an effective sovereign to publicize and uniformly enforce positive laws that specify these 'articles of peace'. Hobbes' contract commissions one person to exercise political power sufficient to specify and enforce such laws. The contract is everyone's *mutual authorization* of a sovereign, not an agreement with him (a contract of government), for the sovereign cannot be contractually bound and remain sovereign (see SOVEREIGNTY). For Hobbes, to be adequate to its role, political power must be effectively absolute. The sovereign's role is to *stabilize* social cooperation by providing all with the assurance that cooperative norms are being enforced and that others will abide by them.

Locke argued that agreement to absolute political power is irrational. Constitutional regimes that limit power and secure individual rights provide better alternatives. Hobbes contests the stability of constitutionalism: effective sovereign power cannot be limited, divided or subject to the rule of law. History has decided matters differently. What endures in Hobbes is not his argument for absolutism, but the structure of his social contract (see CONSTITUTION-ALISM).

3 Contemporary Hobbesian views

This enduring legacy of Hobbes' social contract becomes apparent in the work of two contemporary Hobbesians, David Gauthier and James Buchanan. Both defend the classical liberalism of the *laissez-faire* economists. Gauthier does not try to justify executive political authority – it is unnecessary among fully rational beings. Instead he aims to (1) give a 'rational reconstruction' or morality, and (2) show how Western market society is grounded in reason (Gauthier 1986). Regarding (1), Gauthier contends that rationality is individual utility maximization. Morality, while it constrains the direct pursuit of utility, can be construed as an extension of principles of rational choice: rules which are rational to follow on condition that others do. Morality is then reduced to enlightened self-interest. It constitutes the restrictions on action that rational persons would mutually agree on to maximize individual utility.

Gauthier exhibits this neo-Hobbesian theme in (2), his defence of the 'system of natural liberty'. For Gauthier (and Buchanan) 'Economic Man' best characterizes human behaviour outside families: 'Economic Man is a radical contractarian in that *all* his free or non-coercive interpersonal relationships are contractual' (Gauthier 1986: 319). Contractual bargains typify market behaviour. Markets are 'an ideal of human interaction' because there we act free of moral constraints and perfect markets are efficient. But due to externalities markets often fail; each acts to maximize individual utility, and the outcome is non-efficient (see MARKET, ETHICS OF §1). It seeks to approximate the efficient equilibrium of perfect competition. But this requires cooperation, a joint strategy of mutual adherence to constraints on utility maximization. Gauthier's social contract supplies the cooperative norms needed to approximate perfect market interaction.

Hobbes contends that markets and property are not possible without political power; a sovereign must define property claims and enforce contracts. But Gauthier argues that rational agents in a state of nature would realize that the benefits of market relations outweigh the costs of predation and strife, so natural property and exchange would evolve among physical equals prior to any social contract. Market behaviour and private property are then presocial, part of our natural condition. Gauthier's social contract is not an agreement on political power, on the design of property or on markets as the mechanism for distribution. It is a bargain yielding a principle ('minimax relative concession') for correcting the externalities behind market failures and for distributing the fruits of cooperation (the 'cooperative surplus') arising outside private propertied market relations. This principle mimics the perfect market in that it distributes the benefits and burdens of cooperation according to each person's marginal contribution. Gauthier's social contract has a limited function, but a necessary one he believes, if peaceable and efficient social cooperation are to be possible.

Hobbesian views depict justice and morality as mutually advantageous norms that are rational to observe so long as others do too. Providing everyone with assurance that cooperative terms will be uniformly complied with is essential for stability. However, even assuming that each benefits from the compliance of others, moral constraints often seem to conflict with our rational interests, and for many this is sufficient reason to disregard them. How can such 'free-riders' be persuaded that it is irrational to disregard moral constraints when circumstances appear favourable? To argue that virtue and justice are their own reward makes no sense on Hobbesians' instrumental view of morals. This problem explains why Hobbes gave the sovereign absolute power: no other way insures against free-riding, which undermines everyone's belief in the rationality of compliance. Gauthier's solution is non-political: free-riders acquire a reputation for unreliability and others refuse to cooperate with them; rationality therefore requires developing a disposition always to comply. This may convince people who continually interact, but what about strangers? The larger a society, the less effective reputation is as a deterrent, so under modern conditions it appears inadequate for stability. (For this reason Buchanan (1975) advocates a 'protective state' as one end of the social contract, to stabilize pre-political market relations.)

Hobbesian views collapse questions of justification into questions of (rational) motivation: to justify norms is to show they promote each person's existing interests. But many who currently benefit from the status quo would be greatly disadvantaged if Gauthier's or Buchanan's *laissez-faire* schemes were enacted (for example, monopolists, oligopolists, beneficiaries of government regulation and subsidies, and recipients of public assistance). What reason do they have for accepting contract arguments for reform? Can it seriously be argued that in mixed Western economies everyone would benefit by reverting to *laissez-faire*? History tells us this shift promises only further adverse consequences for those already naturally and socially disadvantaged, and even greater benefits for most who are already better off. Without resolving this motivational problem, the justificatory task of modern Hobbesian theories cannot be carried through on its own terms.

4 Conventionalism

HUME (§5) attacks Locke's contractarian account of political legitimacy and obligation. But he argues that rules of property and economic exchange, of promising, and of allegiance to governments might be explained as 'a kind of contract' (Hume 1748). A *convention* is a mutually beneficial social rule which people publicly accept and comply with because they believe others will too, and where the rule's benefits can be gained only if there is general compliance. The idea is often used for analytic or explanatory purposes, to clarify institutions or practices commonly accepted as part of the status quo. Conventional explanations of law and morality have been attempted (Harman 1977). The term 'social contract' is often applied, particularly by social scientists, to practices that exhibit the features of Humean conventions. Conventions are, like social contracts, mutually beneficial, but only in the weak sense that each person who participates is better off than they would be in the absence of any such rules. For example, virtually any property scheme can be explained as a convention, or 'social contract' in this weak sense. To call conventional accounts 'contractarian' is acceptable if it is recognized that, standing alone, they are explanatory and not normative. Each person's benefiting from a practice does not justify it, although it may explain why people continue to comply.

5 Democratic contract views and Locke

Freedom and equality are primary democratic ideals. The role of a social contract in LOCKE (§10), Rousseau, Kant and Rawls is to elucidate the requirements of these ideals in matters of political justice. If free persons all could, or would, agree to something from a suitable position of equality, the standards they would endorse embody requirements of democratic justice applicable to us so far as we aim to cooperate on terms of equal freedom and mutual respect.

Unanimous agreement among free persons equally situated serves different purposes for these thinkers. For Locke the social contract is a test of the legitimacy of existing constitutions; for Rousseau and Kant, it is also a standard for just legislation; and for Rawls it provides criteria for designing the basic institutions of society. Each defines the conditions of equality and the freedom of the parties to the agreement differently. But the general idea shared in common is that the justice of political institutions depends on whether they could, or would, be agreed to from a position of equal political jurisdiction (see JUSTICE §5).

Democratic contract views maintain that, whatever the differences among individuals *de facto*, all persons are free and equal *de jure*, when each has the requisite capacities of reason, intellect and self-control to decide on their good and comply with social requirements. Democratic contract views are therefore right-based, since they define agreement as subject to antecedent principles of right and justice, which are depicted as not reducible to non-moral interests (or any prior agreement based therein). Among these principles of right may be certain moral rights and duties which cannot be infringed upon or bargained away (as in Locke, Rousseau and Kant). Alternatively, principles of right may be implicit in an ideal of the person as free, equal and endowed with certain moral powers (as in Rawls), that is purportedly implicit in the public culture of a democratic society.

The democratic contract tradition originates with Locke's argument against royal absolutism. Locke contends that all are born with a natural right of equal freedom, by virtue of which no one may legitimately exercise political jurisdiction over another without their consent. Moreover, all have a natural duty to God to preserve themselves and the rest of humankind. Given these rights and duties (the 'fundamental law of nature'), Locke asks, how could legitimate political authority come about from a state of equal right as defined by a non-political but socialized state of nature? Locke contends that no constitution is just unless it could have been contracted into from this initial situation by a series of agreements wherein no one agrees to anything that makes them worse off than in a state of nature, and no one agrees to anything that causes them to violate the rights of others or their own duties. Royal absolutism could not be contracted into compatibly with these conditions, so it is unjust. A constitutional monarchy with a limited franchise could be contracted into, as could other constitutional schemes; each is then, according to Locke's criterion, a legitimate constitution (see LIBERALISM §5; LEGITIMACY §2).

Locke's social contract, like those of Hobbes, Rousseau, Kant and Rawls, is hypothetical. Locke's claim is not (as Hume thought) that a constitution is legitimate only if it actually originated in agreement in the past among our forebears: one '*cannot* by any *Compact* whatsoever, bind *his Children* or Posterity' (Locke 1690: §116; original emphasis). Rather, it is legitimate only if it could have originated in agreement from a state of equal political right. Actual agreement is irrelevant for purposes of applying this criterion.

Locke's social contract is also historical, for it envisages agreement from a (hypothetical) state of nature where everyone has full knowledge of their situation and interests there. Unlike Hobbes' state of nature, this situation is moralized – a 'natural community' – for each therein recognizes natural rights and duties as constraints upon everyone's pursuit of their interests, and upon what can legitimately be agreed to.

It is objected that hypothetical contracts have no binding force (see, for example, Dworkin 1977). This assumes that hypothetical agreements provide an account of the political obligations of individuals. But this is not the primary purpose of Locke's social contract (or Rawls', Kant's or Rousseau's either). The main purpose of Locke's agreement is not to explain the duties of individuals, but the justice of political institutions. Promising plays no role in explaining the effectiveness of Locke's criterion when construed as a test of political legitimacy. Locke does give an individual contract account of political obligation. Persons are obligated as citizens and subjects to bear allegiance to a legitimate government in perpetuity, not by birth, but only once they actually give their express consent to join a regime. Those who withhold such express consent to join still consent tacitly to obey the laws upon benefiting from them. Express and tacit consent are actual, not hypothetical; moreover they are individual commitments, not social agreements requiring participation by all society's members. Locke's account of political obligation is subject to many objections (see CONSENT; OBLIGATION, POLITICAL §3), but it is not essential to his social contract view.

6 Rousseau's democratic contract view

In ROUSSEAU (see §3) and KANT the social contract provides a point of view from which to decide on just legislation and articulates the ideas of moral freedom (autonomy) and the common good (Rousseau 1762; Kant 1797).

All social contract views assume that everyone benefits by social cooperation. Rousseau makes a stronger claim: certain essential human capacities and interests can only be realized in society, and only then where society has been structured democratically. While natural freedom typifies a state of nature, there we are not (in contrast to Hobbes) rationally prudent, but 'stupid, short-sighted animals', moved by instinct and appetite tempered by natural compassion. Our capacities for reason (prudential and moral) are socially interdependent. But human reason, moral

sensibilities and deeper human affections have always been distorted by gross inequalities in power and property. Consequently, humankind has been prevented from realizing these great goods and moral and civic freedom. How is it possible to achieve a society where people realize these benefits, without arousing the will to domination, subservience and other vices of history? Rousseau addresses this problem with his *contrat social*.

The general will expresses the idea that moral and civic freedom are attainable only when institutions satisfy principles free and equal citizens can give to themselves. One's particular will is the interests constituting one's individual good. Hobbes' social contract underscores the inevitable conflict among particular wills, and arbitrates by requiring all to compromise for mutual benefit. Rousseau calls this 'sum of particular wills', the 'will of all'. The general will, by contrast, is what we would jointly will if we subordinated our particular wills and adopted the perspective of free and equal citizens, each motivated by the good of the public and all its members (see GENERAL WILL).

The general will is initially expressed through the social contract. Its object is the common good. For Rousseau (Kant and Rawls too) divergences among individual wills does not mean there cannot be a supreme end all might share which regulates individuals' free pursuit of their particular ends. Such a common good is possible, and is necessary if all are to realize moral and civic freedom. The common good is, first, the institutions and laws that protect the fundamental ('natural') rights of individuals and define a just constitution. Among these are democratic institutions which provide for the civic freedom of citizens and their equal (and for Rousseau direct) participation in legislative deliberation and decision. Beyond this, the common good is whatever laws are willed in legitimate democratic procedures that advance the interests of each member of society in their freedom and security.

For Rousseau (and Kant), the social contract and the general will also express the elusive idea of moral autonomy (see AUTONOMY, ETHICAL). Natural liberty, or acting as one pleases on the basis of inclination, is a kind of slavery, 'while obedience to a law we prescribe to ourselves is liberty' (Rousseau 1762: I, 8). We have a fundamental interest in realizing such freedom, since then (according to Kant) we fully realize the powers of practical reason constituting our humanity. Moral freedom, or autonomy, is attainable only in society, and (for Rousseau) only then where regulative institutions conform to principles free and equal citizens could give to themselves reciprocally. To act autonomously is to act compatibly with the general will for its own sake: to willingly subordinate the free pursuit of one's particular good to the common good, as articulated by the social contract.

7 Rawls' democratic contract

RAWLS (see §1) transforms and develops the contract views of Kant, Rousseau and Locke. The object of agreement is principles of justice that apply not just to laws and the constitution, but to other basic social institutions that regulate the distribution of wealth and opportunities to occupy favourable social positions. Rawls aims to provide 'the most appropriate moral basis for a democratic society' (1971: viii).

Consider a problem in Locke's social contract: since the parties have historical knowledge of their differences in a state of nature, it is not irrational for some to agree to alienate their rights of equal political jurisdiction to gain the benefits of political society. Nor is it wrong; for Locke political rights, unlike liberty of conscience and basic freedoms of the person, are not inalienable. If so, it is not unjust to restrict voting rights constitutionally to propertied males, making the rest 'passive citizens'. However democratic Locke's starting position, he does not require a democratic constitution with equal political rights.

Rawls' contract is designed to prevent arbitrary contingencies (for example, prevailing property distributions) from affecting the justice of political and social institutions. A contract is non-historical the more those party to it abstract from knowledge of circumstances (actual or hypothetical) that would advantage or disadvantage people who occupy certain positions. (The idea is already implicit in Rousseau and Kant, for neither envisage social agreement as transpiring in a state of nature.) Rawls' original position is wholly non-historical since contractors are placed behind a complete 'veil of ignorance' regarding their particular situations, so none can take advantage of their social circumstances, their natural talents, their particular conceptions of the good or prevailing historical conditions. By situating his parties symmetrically, Rawls makes them strictly equals, and carries to the limit the ideal of equality behind democratic contractualism.

Rawls argues that the conception of justice that would be agreed to in the original position is neither utilitarian nor perfectionist, but a Kantian account: justice as fairness. Its main principles afford equal rights to certain basic liberties and opportunities and regulate distributions of wealth and access to social positions so that they benefit everyone, with primary attention given to those least advantaged. These principles for institutions, along with individual duties of justice, mutual aid and mutual respect, comprise the general will of free and equal moral persons. Just laws and institutions constitute their common good. In complying with and acting for the sake of these principles and institutions, citizens are morally autonomous, for they act on and from a law they give to themselves, out of their rational and moral powers.

HEGEL (1821) argued that contract doctrines are individualistic and incompatible with community. This criticism may apply to Hobbesian accounts of our relations with strangers but, as for Rousseau and Kant, arguably Hegel misunderstood the role of the general will. Contemporary communitarians (for example, Sandel 1982) restate Hegel's criticism, contending that Rawls' original position presupposes abstract individualism (see COMMUNITY AND COMMUNITARIANISM). Rawls (1993) contends this interpretation is mistaken.

8 Right-based versus interest-based views

Hobbesians and others object that right-based views (especially non-historical ones) are not genuinely contractual, since they involve little or no bargaining. Given their moral assumptions and shared interests in a common good, agreement is superfluous; the same standards can be derived by impartial decision by one individual. Now, one can simply stipulate that contracts and agreements involve bargains among essentially conflicting interests. This has the peculiar consequence that most major proponents of social contract theory (Locke, Kant, Rousseau, Rawls) are not contractarians at all. (Even Hobbes' contract is not a negotiated bargain but a mutual authorization of an effective sovereign.) But not all agreements involve bargains or negotiated compromises among conflicting interests. People with diverse ends often commit themselves to norms on condition that others do, to achieve a shared end of great importance (for example, in religious associations or marital vows). The point of agreement is not to resolve conflict (there may be none), but to tie down the future to keep the parties from deviating from the shared purposes and norms of association. Democratic views involve agreement in this sense of a *shared precommitment* among citizens to relations that maintain their freedom and equal status. This agreement is not effective because of mutual promises. Rather, it establishes principles and institutions which bind citizens perpetually into political relations as equals, and so prevent them from later changing their minds or surrendering to temptations that undermine the good of others or everyone's shared interest in justice.

Being rational bargains, interest-based contracts involve mutual advantage: each person gains, given their historical starting position (status quo or state of nature). Being shared precommitments, right-based agreements involve reciprocity: everyone benefits as measured from a fair baseline of equality. Interest-based agreements between serfs and landlords to increase productivity on condition that serfs get 10 per cent of the surplus are mutually advantageous but not reciprocal, for the terms are unfair and the starting position is unjust. In the reciprocal agreements of democratic views, there is no guarantee that each person will benefit compared to the status quo. The purpose of reciprocal agreements is not to improve on the status quo by preserving its injustices, but to provide a criterion for assessing current injustice and the measures required for reform.

But if there is no guarantee that one will benefit, how can everyone be expected to accept the terms of reciprocal agreements? Many favoured by an unjust status quo will not; if their sense of justice is weak or vacillating, it may be irrational for them to. For democratic theorists this does not count against the validity or reasonableness of right-based contracts. It is a motivation problem belonging to the process of transition from an unjust to a just society. Unlike Hobbesians, for democratic views justice is not defined as a compromise among given and essentially conflicting interests. So justifying a moral conception does not involve showing each person, whatever their desires, that justice benefits them. Rather, a conception is justified when it conforms to reasonable persons' considered judgments of justice and reasonableness.

To Hobbesians this appears circular and unenlightening. They construe moral justifications reductively, as questions of rational motivation given non-moral interests. Hobbesians encounter a different problem; namely persuading those now advantaged by the status quo that it is rational to accept norms that would be agreed to by self-interested members of a hypothetical state of nature. Some sort of motivation problem is then confronted by any contract view that does not take the current status quo as the basis for agreement. And in the history of social contract thought, there are no significant normative doctrines of status quo agreement.

9 Moral contractualism

The idea that not only justice, but morality generally, is based in general agreement has not been worked out in detail. Rawls and Gauthier suggest it, but their arguments are limited to justice. The primary difficulty with this thesis is that many duties do not

seem to involve reciprocity or mutual advantage. The duties of parents to their young children are not contingent upon children observing their duties to honour and obey their parents. And duties forbidding cruelty to animals or the destruction of nature and valuable species are not easily explained in contractual terms.

One significant effort to account contractually for, not all, but many moral duties is T.M. Scanlon's right-based view. Scanlon (1982,1988) is influenced by the idea of universal acceptability implicit in Kant's claims that as moral beings we should regard ourselves as legislative members of a kingdom of ends. Scanlon depicts morality as the result of 'hypothetical co-deliberation'. It is 'a theory according to which an act is right if it would be required or allowed by principles which no one, suitably motivated, could reasonably reject as a basis for informed, unforced general agreement' (1988: 15). Interpreting this, imagine a community of free and informed agents, each of whom is conscientious, sincere and motivated by a desire to justify their actions, ends and expectations to everyone else similarly motivated. Morality is the set of public norms which such idealized persons would jointly affirm and commit to, aware that these norms are to regulate their activities and serve as the final standards for justification, criticism and settling conflict.

Reasonableness is a central idea in Scanlon, Rawls and right-based views. It is conceived of as a fundamental moral category, not reducible to rationality. One can be fully rational, by acting best to promote one's interests, and still be unreasonable. A reasonable person respects the needs and interests of others and is not prone to overreaching. To be reasonable is to be responsive to the individual reasons of others. It involves a willingness to limit one's expectations and constrain one's actions and ends by rules that respect the legitimate pursuits of others. Reasonableness also includes a willingness to justify one's actions by reasons others could publicly endorse in uncoerced general agreement. Reasonableness is not altruism. One can be unreasonably altruistic, by promoting a majority's interests while undermining the needs of the few. Reasonable persons are equitably fair-minded; they regulate their acts in ways that respect everyone's basic interests.

Scanlon's contractualism yields an account of morality's subject matter, and so of moral objectivity and validity. Many moral theories assume there is a perspective from which to achieve unanimity, at least among rational persons similarly informed. For example, in Locke's intuitionist moral epistemology, the fundamental law of nature is self-evident to the right reason of every informed and unbiased rational being. Contractualism reverses the order of dependence between unanimity of judgment and moral principles. Rather than moral judgments being true when they match a prior moral order, the moral order is specified in terms of ideal judgment and agreement. Moral truth is then defined by referring to the principles to which free persons would agree under ideal conditions. There is no order of moral facts antecedent to hypothetical co-deliberation and agreement. Moral truth is then discoverable by us, not by rational intuition or moral sense, but by deliberating on what free, informed moral agents equally situated would reasonably agree to.

See also: INTERNATIONAL RELATIONS, PHILOSOPHY OF; LIBERALISM

References and further reading

Binmore, K. (1994) *Game Theory and the Social Contract*, Cambridge, MA: MIT Press. (An economist's application of game theory to social contract doctrine.)

* Buchanan, J. (1975) *The Limits of Liberty*, Chicago, IL: University of Chicago Press. (Hobbesian argument for classical liberalism.)

Cohen, J. (1986) 'Reflections on Rousseau', *Philosophy and Public Affairs* 15 (3): 275–97. (Critical review of recent books on Rousseau.)

* Dworkin, R. (1977) 'Justice and Rights', in *Taking Rights Seriously*, London: Duckworth. (Notable assessment of Rawls' earlier work.)

Freeman, S. (1990) 'Reason and Agreement in Social Contract Views', in *Philosophy and Public Affairs* 19 (2): 122–157 (Contrasts Hobbesian and democratic contract views.)

* Gauthier, D. (1986) *Morals by Agreement*, Oxford: Clarendon Press. (Central work by major modern representative of Hobbesian contract doctrine.)

—— (1990) *Moral Dealing*, Ithaca, NY: Cornell University Press. (Collected papers.)

Gough, J. (1957) *The Social Contract*, Oxford: Clarendon Press, 2nd edn. (Pre-Rawlsian account of the tradition.)

Hampton, J. (1986) *Hobbes and the Social Contract Tradition*, Cambridge: Cambridge University Press. (Prominent interpretation of Hobbesian tradition.)

* Harman, G. (1977) *The Nature of Morality*, New York: Oxford University Press, ch. 9. (Covers moral conventionalism.)

* Hegel, G. (1821) *The Philosophy of Right*, trans. H.B. Nisbet, ed. A. Wood, Cambridge: Cambridge University Press, 1991. (Criticism of social contract and general will as individualistic.)

* Hobbes, T. (1649) *Leviathan*, ed. R. Tuck, Cambridge: Cambridge University Press, 1991. (Hobbes' primary statement of his doctrine.)

* Hume, D. (1748) 'Of the Original Contract' in *Essays Moral, Political, and Literary*, ed. E. Miller, Indianapolis, IN: Liberty Classics, 1985. (Historically effective criticism of Locke's contract doctrine.)

* Kant, I. (1797) *Metaphysical Elements of Justice*, trans. J. Ladd, Indianapolis, IN: Bobbs-Merrill, 1965. (Contains Kant's account of the Original Contract.)

* Locke, J. (1690) *Two Treatises of Government*, ed. P. Laslett, Cambridge: Cambridge University Press, 1963. (The second treatise contains the doctrine that government must be based in consent.)

* Nagel, T. (1991) *Equality and Partiality*, New York: Oxford University Press, chaps 4–5. (On political contractualism.)

* Nozick, R. (1974) *Anarchy, State and Utopia*, New York: Basic Books. (Individualist contract account of political authority, and libertarian criticism of Rawls.)

* Rawls, J. (1971) *A Theory of Justice*, Cambridge, MA: Harvard University Press. (The major contemporary statement of democratic contractarianism.)

* —— (1993) *Political Liberalism*, New York: Columbia University Press. (Develops the Kantian conception of the person informing Rawls' contract view.)

* Rousseau, J. (1762) *Du contrat social* (Of the Social Contract), in *Rousseau's Political Writings*, ed. A. Ritter and J.C. Bondanella, New York: W.W. Norton, 1988. (Account of the General Will and the Social Contract.)

* Sandel, M. (1982) *Liberalism and the Limits of Justice*, Cambridge: Cambridge University Press. (Communitarian criticism of Rawlsian liberalism.)

* Scanlon, T. (1982) 'Contractualism and Utilitarianism', in A. Sen and B. Williams (eds) *Utilitarianism and Beyond*, Cambridge: Cambridge University Press. (Initial presentation of moral contractualism.)

* —— (1988) 'The Significance of Choice', in *The Tanner Lectures on Human Values*, vol. 8, ed. S.M. McMurrin, Salt Lake City, UT: University of Utah Press, 149–216. (Develops contractualism and discusses freedom of the will.)

Simmons, A.J. (1993) *On the Edge of Anarchy: Locke, Consent, and the Limits of Society*, Princeton, NJ: Princeton University Press. (On the role of consent in Locke's political doctrine.)

SAMUEL FREEMAN

CONVENTION AND NATURE

see NATURE AND CONVENTION

CONVENTION AND NECESSARY TRUTH

see NECESSARY TRUTH AND CONVENTION

CONVENTIONALISM

How is it known that every number has a successor, that straight lines can intersect each other no more than once, that causes precede their events, and that the electron either went through the slit or it did not? In cases like these it is not easy to find observable evidence, and it is implausible to postulate special modes of intuitive access to the phenomena in question. Yet such theses are relied on in scientific discourse and can hardly be dismissed as meaningless metaphysical excess. In response to this problem the positivists and empiricists (notably Poincaré, Hilbert, Carnap, Reichenbach and Ayer) developed a strategy known as conventionalism. The idea was that certain statements, including fundamental principles of logic, arithmetic and geometry, are asserted as a matter of conventional stipulation, being no more than definitions of some of their constituent terms; consequently they must be true, our commitment to them cannot but be justified, and the facts in virtue of which they are true are simply the facts of our having made those particular decisions about the use of words. This doctrine was a compelling and powerful weapon in the positivist–empiricist arsenal, evolving throughout the 1920s, 1930s and 1940s. But it fell into disfavour under a barrage of serious challenges due mainly to Quine. How are 'conventions' to be identified as such? How could they possibly provide words with meanings, or have the epistemological import that is claimed for them? How could arbitrary, contingent decisions about the use of words result in the existence of necessary facts? In the absence of satisfactory replies to these objections few philosophers these days believe that conventionalism can settle the semantic, epistemological and metaphysical questions that it was intended to answer. However, certain aspects of the view remain defensible and interesting.

1 The scope and nature of conventionalism
2 The definition of 'convention'
3 The semantic component of conventionalism
4 The epistemological component of conventionalism
5 The metaphysical component of conventionalism
6 Prospects for the defence of conventionalism

1 The scope and nature of conventionalism

Conventionalism is the strategy of supposing that certain theses are implicit definitions – hence mere choices of language – and hoping thereby to explain how their adoption can be justified and to specify that in which their truth consists. It has been applied to the principles of deductive inference, to the claims of mathematics, and to 'bridge laws' specifying the observational consequences of theoretical hypotheses – all domains in which methods of *empirical* verification might seem to be inappropriate. For example, it was said that the axioms and rules of classical deductive logic are nothing more than implicit definitions of the logical constants, 'and', 'not', 'every', and so on; and this was supposed to show both how our reasoning could be justified and to articulate what it is to be a logical truth. Another famous application was to questions about the structure of space. It was maintained by H. POINCARÉ (1905) that geometrical facts are matters of convention: thus if we decide to use Euclidean geometry, we thereby implicitly define the terms 'point' and 'line' in such a way that the theorems of Euclidean geometry are true. We are therefore justified in employing any geometry we please; for there are no facts about the structure of space that could make some choices correct and others incorrect. A variant form of conventionalism about space and time was urged by Reichenbach (1968). In his view what stand in need of stipulation are certain correlations between spatio-temporal and physical properties (for example, that light travels in straight lines, and that pendulum swings consume equal periods of time). The idea here was that only once such 'coordinative definitions' had been decided upon would it become possible to investigate empirically the structure of space and time; alternate conventions will yield alternate answers, and so there are no facts of the matter as to which answers are correct (see REICHENBACH, H. §4; RELATIVITY THEORY, PHILOSOPHICAL SIGNIFICANCE OF §3).

Thus, to whatever domain it was applied, conventionalism in its standard form consisted in the following four elements: one, that some specified, determinate body of sentences (or rules) is accepted as a matter of conventional stipulation; two, that these commitments implicitly define certain constituent terms; three, that the propositions which the sentences express are known a priori; and four that those propositions are true – and the corresponding facts exist – in virtue of our conventional stipulations. In the following sections we shall consider objections to each of these components of the doctrine.

2   The definition of 'convention'

In the ordinary sense of the word a *convention* is an explicit agreement to act in some specified way. But, in that sense, no convention has ever been adopted to go around saying '$1+1=2$'; and similarly for the other cases in which conventionalism was deployed. Thus emerges one of the fundamental difficulties faced by this philosophy: that of explaining how to demarcate 'conventions' or 'stipulations' (in the intended technical sense) from other utterances we are inclined to make. R. CARNAP (1950), perhaps the most sophisticated practitioner of the strategy, equated 'linguistic conventions' with the analytic (framework) sentences that determine what our words mean and which language we are using. These were in turn identified as the sentences which we decide to accept on the basis of pragmatic rather than epistemological considerations, and it was concluded that the propositions expressed by those sentences are known a priori. However, Quine's (1935, 1951, 1954) influential critique of conventionalism made a strong case that although these conceptions of 'convention', 'meaning', 'language', 'pragmatic reason', 'analytic' and 'a priori' may well be linked in the way that Carnap supposed, they are all equally obscure and equally in need of clarification, and that it remains to find a way of breaking out of the circle of inter-definable ideas in order to characterize any one of them objectively (see QUINE, W.V. §8).

3   The semantic component of conventionalism

The legitimacy of *deciding* that a certain set of sentences (or rules of inference) is to qualify as correct rested on two assumptions: first, that we are at liberty to decide which language to speak, for example, what our words are to mean; and, second, that in stipulating that a sentence be true we are merely fixing the meaning of one or more of its constituent terms. But the second of these assumptions has received considerable criticism, notably in the writings of Frege (1903, 1906), Prior (1960), Belnap (1962) and Dummett (1977). The thesis in question tends to be construed as follows: that in deciding to regard '#F' as true, one is implicitly deciding to give 'F' whatever meaning it would need to have in order that '#F' be true, given the already established meaning of the rest of the sentence, '#_'. But this thesis is far from obviously correct. In the first place, how can we be sure that there exists *any*

meaning which could be assigned to 'F' and which would render '#F' true? Second, how can we be sure that there is only *one* such meaning? Third, even if there is such a meaning, what reason is there to suppose that this is the meaning that 'F' acquires? And fourth, even if it is, how does our treating '#F' as true *bring it about* that 'F' acquires that meaning: what account of the nature of meaning could explain how this happens? The difficulty of answering these questions casts doubt on the possibility of implicit definition.

4   The epistemological component of conventionalism

The main point of the doctrine was to show how our views about logic, arithmetic, spatiotemporal structure, and theory–observation relations could be rational, despite the absence of intuitive or empirical access to those domains. The idea was that our claims are justified a priori – independently of intuition or experience – because they merely fix the meanings of terms, which are commitments that are not subject to a posteriori constraint. Now we have just seen how the feasibility of implicit definition may well be questioned. But there is an additional problem concerning the alleged non-empirical character of such conventions. For even if it is conceded that by regarding a sentence as true one can fix the meaning of one of its constituents, there can remain a doubt as to whether the truth of that sentence is known a priori. The grounds for this doubt derive from Quine's web-of-belief model of theoretical development, according to which our total theory formulation evolves under the constraints of empirical adequacy, global simplicity and conservativism (see QUINE, W.V. §3). For if this model is correct then every element in the web earns its keep empirically by contributing towards the overall system that 'best' satisfies these three desiderata, and so everything we believe is a posteriori. This is not to deny that our commitment to '#F' might implicitly define a constituent term 'F'. The point rather is that given Quine's model not even such meaning-constituting principles would be known a priori (see A PRIORI).

5   The metaphysical component of conventionalism

On the metaphysical front, the standard conventionalist stance is blatantly antirealist; for insofar as a certain fact is merely a matter of convention, it evidently does not exist independently of us and our practices (see SCIENTIFIC REALISM AND ANTIREALISM). And this metaphysical thesis has provided a glaring target for criticism. For although it is no doubt a fact about us that we decide to commit ourselves to the truth of, for example, '$1 + 1 = 2$', this fact regarding our commitment is not plausibly identifiable with the arithmetical fact that $1 + 1 = 2$. The former fact concerns words, the latter numbers. Moreover, the former is contingent – there are possible worlds in which we decide to adopt different conventions – whereas the latter is necessarily the case – there is no possibility that $1 + 1 = 3$. Thus the conventionalist's metaphysical thesis, implying as it does that if we had spoken a different language then perhaps $1 + 1$ would have been equal to 3, is extremely unattractive and has helped bring the entire doctrine into disrepute.

6   Prospects for the defence of conventionalism

The above criticisms need not be considered decisive. In each case replies might be devised, involving modifications of the standard four-pronged doctrine. Thus, in response to the challenge to demarcate the class of conventional stipulations, one might abandon the intuitive concept of 'convention', with the presumption that it is evident when such things occur, and look to empirical linguistics for a characterization of which regularities in the use of a term (including assertions containing it) are explanatorily basic and hence implicitly define it. As for the difficulties with implicit definition, one might hope to pre-empt them by altering the assumption that, in regarding '#F' as true, one is giving 'F' the meaning it would need to have for '#F' to be true. Instead, again invoking a use-conception of meaning, one might suppose that, in regarding '#F' as true, one is giving 'F' the meaning that is constituted by that rule of use (Horwich 1997). In that case the four above-mentioned difficulties could not arise. For the existence and uniqueness of a meaning is ensured by the existence of the regularity, and the explanation of how the convention provides meaning would be trivial.

Turning to the epistemological objection, one might resist the thesis that *everything* is a priori, which seemed to follow from the web-of-belief model. For there can surely be different formulations of the same theory – notational variants of each other. Therefore the decision to adopt one rather than another way of expressing one's beliefs is a convention that is not subject to a posteriori revision. Thus the acceptance of a theory, Tabc, formulated using new terms 'a', 'b' and 'c', may be regarded as the product of two commitments: one being the substantive existential belief that there are unique theoretical properties, x, y and z, satisfying Txyz; and the other being the linguistic decision to call those properties 'a', 'b' and 'c'. This conditional thesis,

$(\exists!xyz)(Txyz) \rightarrow$ Tabc, would not be held a priori (Lewis 1970; Horwich 1986).

Finally, the metaphysical critique of conventionalism could be accepted and accommodated by jettisoning the antirealist component of the standard doctrine. It would still be supposed that certain sentences ('conventions') implicitly define certain of their constituents; but it would no longer be maintained that the facts expressed by those sentences are reducible to facts about our practices, hence matters of convention.

Thus one might respond to the variety of objections to conventionalism. But this can hardly qualify as a vindication of the doctrine. For the revised defensible position which the objections have compelled solves none of the epistemological or metaphysical problems for which conventionalism was invented. Moreover, there is now reason to suspect that there were no real problems here in the first place. For Quine's model suggests that logic, geometry, arithmetic and our theory–observation bridge principles have an epistemological and metaphysical status that is no different from the rest of what we believe. This still leaves open the possibility of implicit definition: the conventional a priori decision to use these words rather than those in the articulation of our beliefs, including those of logic, mathematics and science. But this is such a pale shadow of the original positivistic idea, it might be as well to reserve the term 'conventionalism' for that doctrine and consider it refuted.

See also: LANGUAGE, CONVENTIONALITY OF; LOGICAL POSITIVISM; NECESSARY TRUTH AND CONVENTION

References and further reading

Ayer, A.J. (1936) *Language, Truth and Logic*, New York: Dover. (Forcefully advocates conventionalism and elaborates its extensive philosophical ramifications.)

* Belnap, N.D. (1962) 'Tonk, Plonk and Plink', *Analysis* 22, 130–3. (Discusses implicit definition and the question of whether a *unique* meaning is determined. See §3.)

* Carnap, R. (1950) 'Empiricism, Semantics and Ontology', in *Meaning and Necessity*, Chicago, IL: University of Chicago Press; 2nd edn, 1956. (The most detailed and plausible articulation of pre-Quinean logical empiricism. See introduction and §2.)

* Dummett, M. (1977) *Elements of Intuitionism*, Oxford: Clarendon Press. (Argues that the logical constants are not implicitly defined by the laws in

which they appear, and hence that classical logic cannot be justified by regarding its fundamental principles as implicit definitions. See §3.)

Frege, G. (1895–1903) 'Correspondence between Frege and Hilbert', in *Philosophical and Mathematical Correspondence*, Chicago, IL: University of Chicago Press, 1986, 31–52. (Contains Hilbert's idea – and Frege's criticism of it – that the axioms of a theory can fix the meanings of its terms.)

* —— (1903, 1906) 'On the Foundations of Geometry', in B. McGuiness (ed.) *Collected Papers on Mathematical Logic and Philosophy*, Oxford: Blackwell, 1983. (1903, series 1, 1906, series 2. Further articulates Frege's critique of implicit definition. See §3.)

* Horwich, P. (1986) 'A Defence of Conventionalism', in G. MacDonald and C. Wright (eds) *Fact, Science and Morality*, Oxford: Blackwell. (Argues that Quine's critique leaves open a form of 'global conventionalism' concerning the language with which to express our total theory formulation. See §6.)

* —— (1997) 'Implicit Definition, Analytic Truth, and A Priori Knowledge', *Nous*. (Argues that objections to the standard conception of implicit definition may be dissolved in the context of a use-theory of meaning. See §§3, 4, 6.)

* Lewis, D. (1970) 'How to Define Theoretical Terms', *Journal of Philosophy* LVII (July): 427–66. (Articulates the strategy, suggested by Carnap, Russell and Ramsey in the 1920s, that any theory can be factored into two independent components: a substantive existential claim and an a priori conditional which defines the theoretical terms. See §6.)

* Poincaré, H. (1905) *Science and Hypothesis*, London: Walter Scott Publishing. (Maintains that the facts of geometry are mere matters of convention. See introduction and §1.)

* Prior, A.N. (1960) 'The Runabout Inference-Ticket', *Analysis* 21, 38–9. (Shows that an alleged implicit definition presupposes what may well be false: that there exists a meaning that, if possessed by the term in question, would render true the sentences defining the term. See §3.)

* Quine, W.V. (1935) 'Truth by Convention', in *The Ways of Paradox*, Cambridge, MA: Harvard University Press, 1976. (Argues that logic cannot derive from explicit conventions. See introduction and §2.)

* —— (1951) 'Two Dogmas of Empiricism', in *From a Logical Point of View*, Cambridge, MA: Harvard University Press, 1953. (Suggests that the alleged distinction between analytic and synthetic statements (and related notions such as synonymy and

rule of language) resist clarification and are of dubious coherence. See introduction and §§2, 4.)

* —— (1954) 'Carnap and Logical Truth', in *The Ways of Paradox*, Cambridge, MA: Harvard University Press, 1976. (Argues against the view that the fundamental principles of logic are conventions of language. See introduction and §§2, 4.)

* Reichenbach, H. (1968) *The Philosophy of Space and Time*, New York: Dover. (Maintains that assumptions about the physical manifestation of straight lines and other geometrical objects are matters of convention, hence that geometry, which results from such assumptions, is also conventional. See introduction and §1.)

PAUL HORWICH

CONVERSATION *see* DISCOURSE SEMANTICS; PRAGMATICS

CONWAY, ANNE (*c*.1630–79)

Anne Conway (née Finch) was the most important of the few English women who engaged in philosophy in the seventeenth century. Her reputation derives from one work published after her death, Principia philosophiae antiquissimae et · recentissimae *(1690), which proposes a Neoplatonic system of metaphysics featuring a monistic concept of created substance. The work entails a critique of the dualism of both Descartes and Henry More, as well as of the materialism (as she saw it) of Hobbes and Spinoza. In her concept of the monad and her emphasis on the benevolence of God, Conway's system has some interesting affinities with that of Leibniz.*

Anne Conway (née Finch) studied philosophy with the Cambridge Platonist, Henry MORE, who instructed her by letter since, as a woman, she was debarred from attending university (see CAMBRIDGE PLATONISM). She was introduced to philosophy through the study of Cartesianism in the modified – and therefore critical – version accepted by More. Later in life she encountered the physician and thinker, Francis Mercurius van HELMONT, who brought her into contact with alchemical thought and the Jewish Kabbalah, and appears to have provided the catalyst for her turning away from the dualism of her Cartesian and Cambridge-Platonist background. Conway's *Principia philosophiae antiquissimae et recentissimae* (1690) is a Latin translation of a manuscript found among her effects after her death and published under the auspices of van Helmont in a collection entitled *Opuscula philosophica*. It was translated back into English and published as *The Principles of the Most Ancient and Modern Philosophy* in 1692. The original manuscript is lost and the printed version is probably incomplete.

Conway posits three orders of being: God, Christ or *Logos*, and 'Creature' or created substance. Where God is essentially unchanging ('a Spirit, Light, and Life, infinitely Wise, Good, Just, Mighty, Omniscient, Omnipresent, Omnipotent, Creator and Maker of all things visible and invisible', [1690] 1982: 149), creatures are characterized by mutability, with Christ as 'Middle Nature' linking God with creation. Created beings or species are modes of one single spiritual substance which comprises an infinite number of hierarchically arranged spiritual particles or monads. What is commonly taken to be matter is in fact less refined spirit – congealed spirit, as it were. All creatures are made up of a combination of both refined and congealed spirit. Created substance may increase in perfection, becoming more spiritual, or fall away from perfection, becoming more like matter. So also creatures themselves can move up or down the ontological scale, transmuting into higher or lower orders of creature: a grain of dust or sand 'through various and succedaneous Transmutations' may come to acquire the noblest attributes of substance, namely 'a capacity of all kind of Feeling, Sense, and Knowledge, Love, Joy, and Fruition, and all kind of Power and Virtue' ([1690] 1982: 225).

Conway developed her scheme in part as an answer to what she saw as the shortcomings of contemporary philosophy, the key error of which was, in her view, the mechanical concept of matter as inert, devoid of life and sense. As a result, mechanism was unable to account for action and life. Although she commends DESCARTES for his 'Mechanical Skill and Wisdom' she denies that understanding the laws of local motion can explain the vital operations of nature. HOBBES and SPINOZA compound the problem by conceiving God in material terms and thereby confounding God with created things. While she accepts an instrumental role for local motion in the operations of nature, Conway conceives motion to entail change in general, defining it more broadly as a vital operation of the 'Strength, Power and Virtue', intrinsically present in substance as modes of substance and capable of extending their influence beyond that substance. Interaction between creatures is by a process analogous to emanation or radiation. Conway calls this 'virtual extension', that is 'a Motion or Action which a Creature hath . . . proceeding from the innermost parts' ([1690] 1982: 229) and reaching to other creatures through a proper spiritual medium. This spiritual principle of causality may be likened to a field of force, and provides the dynamics of perfectionism in Conway's ontology.

These modal transmutations of substance are also spiritual in the religious sense of that term, since the degeneration away from perfect spiritual substance which is entailed in the monads' becoming more like matter is also a falling away from the goodness of God. By the same token the purification of substance to become more spirit-like involves a return towards goodness and hence towards God. Conway's concept of substance thus underpins her soteriology: she denies the eternity of Hell, regarding the punishment of sin as corrective and ultimately salvific. Thus her overall ontological and spiritual scheme is in the end ameliorative, suffering being explained as part of the process of moral and substantial purification by which 'creature' is restored to a more spiritual and therefore more divine state. Both in her concept of the monad and in her emphasis on God's benevolence, her system has obvious affinities with that of LEIBNIZ. Yet, although he expressed admiration for her, it is unlikely that she influenced him directly.

See also: SALVATION

List of works

Conway, A. (1690) *Principia philosophiae antiquissimae et recentissimae de Deo, Christo et Creatura id est de materia et spiritu in genere*, in *Opuscula Philosophica*, Amsterdam; trans. as *The Principles of the Most Ancient and Modern Philosophy*, London, 1692; repr. ed. P. Loptson, Dordrecht: Kluwer Academic Publishers, 1982. New trans. by A. Condert and T. Corse, Cambridge: Cambridge University Press, 1996. (Latin translation of a now-lost English original, and an English translation of this. The introduction to the modern reprint is not wholly reliable.)

—— (1992) *The Conway Letters: the Correspondence of Anne, Viscountess Conway, Henry More and their Friends, 1642–1684*, ed. M. Nicolson and S. Hutton, Oxford: Clarendon Press. (Letters with introduction to the intellectual context, bibliography and biographical commentary.)

References and further reading

Brown, S. (1990) 'Leibniz and Henry More's Cabbalistic Circle', in S. Hutton (ed.) *Henry More (1614–1687): Tercentenary Studies*, Dordrecht: Kluwer Academic Publishers. (Challenges the view that Conway influenced Leibniz.)

Coudert, A. (1975) 'A Cambridge Platonist's Kabbalist Nightmare', *Journal of the History of Ideas* 36: 633–52. (On Henry More, F.M. van Helmont, Anne Conway and the *Kabbala denudata*.)

Gabbey, A. (1977) 'Anne Conway et Henry More: lettres sur Descartes' (Anne Conway and Henry More: Letters on Descartes), *Archives de Philosophie* 40: 379–404. (On the discussion of Cartesianism in the early correspondence of More and Conway.)

Hutton, S. (1995) 'Anne Conway critique de Henry More: l'esprit et la matière' (Anne Conway, critic of Henry More: spirit and matter), *Archives de Philosophie* 58: 371–84. (On the relationship of Conway's thought to that of Henry More.)

Merchant, C. (1979) 'The Vitalism of Anne Conway: its Impact on Leibniz's Concept of the Monad', *Journal of the History of Philosophy* 17: 255–69. (Argues that Conway influenced Leibniz by showing parallels between Leibniz and Conway.)

Popkin, R.H. (1990) 'The Spiritualistic Cosmologies of Henry More and Anne Conway', in S. Hutton (ed.) *Henry More (1614–1687): Tercentenary Studies*, Dordrecht: Kluwer Academic Publishers. (On Conway's and More's alternative to the mechanical philosophy.)

SARAH HUTTON

COOPER, ANTHONY ASHLEY

see SHAFTESBURY, THIRD EARL OF

COPERNICUS, NICOLAUS (1473–1543)

Copernicus argued that the earth is a planet revolving around the sun, as well as rotating on its own axis. His work marked the culmination of a tradition of mathematical astronomy stretching back beyond Ptolemy, to the Greeks and Babylonians. Though it was associated with methods and assumptions that had been familiar for centuries, it was also revolutionary because of its implications for the relations between humankind and the universe at large.

Around 1513 Copernicus composed the *Commentariolus*, a brief draft describing a new sun-centred system of astronomy. A few copies were circulated among astronomers, but it was not published until rediscovered in 1878. In the years that followed, he worked on a systematic programme of observation to allow accurate recomputation of the parameters needed for his heliocentric model. Despite his own conviction, however, Copernicus could not find a cogent argument for the counterintuitive claim that the earth *really* moves. It was only in 1540, when his disciple Georg Rheticus gave the first published account of the new system in his *Narratio prima*, that Copernicus was encouraged to complete and publish his long-planned work, the *De revolutionibus orbium coelestium* (1543). His friend, the Lutheran theologian Andreas Osiander, prefaced the work with an anonymous foreword asserting the hypotheses of the work were to be regarded as 'useful mathematical fictions only', thus misleading the first generation of readers into an underestimation of the revolutionary character of Copernicus' proposal. Only later did readers like BRUNO and KEPLER draw attention to the discrepancy between the message of the foreword and that of the main text.

In the opening lines of the *Commentariolus*, Copernicus describes what prompted him to undertake the immense labour of reconstructing and recomputing the entire system of astronomy. Ptolemy's equants, mathematical devices that allowed planets to move nonuniformly on the circumference of their circles, 'seemed neither sufficiently absolute nor sufficiently pleasing to the mind' (see PTOLEMY). Copernicus discovered that placing the sun at the centre not only allowed him to save the phenomena, but also explained a variety of puzzling features of the planetary motions that Ptolemy had to leave as brute fact. In the heliocentric system, these turn out to be 'natural', necessitated by the fact that we are observing the sky, not from the centre, but from a moving vantage-point. Thus he could claim to have brought closer the 'mathematical' and the 'physical' approaches to astronomy that had so long been separated.

Copernicus attributed three motions to the earth. The first was a daily rotation on its own axis, the second a yearly revolution around the sun, the third, an annual motion in declination of the earth's axis (which later turned out to be unneeded). Attributing an annual motion to the earth allowed him to dispense with the larger planetary epicycles of Ptolemy, but the planets still required smaller epicycles in order to eliminate the equants. The first major achievement of Copernicus' system was that the relative distances of the planets could be determined, which the Ptolemaic model could not do. But other advantages were also plain. Making the earth the third planet explained the retrograde motions of the planets: the earth was lapping the outer planets and being lapped by the inner ones. The dimensions and periods of these apparent loops in the planetary paths could now be derived from the relative distances of the planets from the sun and their periods of revolution; in the Ptolemaic model, by contrast, the retrograde motions were an 'add-on', requiring arbitrary stipulation of epicycle parameters. Copernicus also noted why the outer planets are nearest and therefore brightest when in opposition (at the opposite side of the sky from the sun); in Ptolemy's scheme there is no particular reason why this should be the case. Finally, he could explain why Venus and Mercury are 'tied', as it were, to the sun, never appearing more than a certain maximum angular distance from it in the sky. Inner planets in a heliocentric system will *necessarily* appear 'tied' in this way; a puzzle for Ptolemy, because it linked the motions of these planets to the motion of the sun in a way that could be arbitrarily postulated but that defied explanation in his model.

Copernicus was a scientific realist (see SCIENTIFIC REALISM AND ANTIREALISM §1). He knew that the constructions of mathematical astronomers were traditionally regarded as no more than helpful fictions. He knew too that objections to the earth's motion would be urged by those who took a literalist approach to the wording of the Bible. Yet he was confident that he had shown that the earth *really* is in motion. Some recent historians have suggested that he was motivated by a Neoplatonic metaphysical belief in the cosmic primacy of the sun but there is little real evidence for this. In book one of *De revolutionibus*, he makes the reasons for his realistic stand clear enough. He does not appeal to a superior accuracy of prediction nor to a reduction in the number of circles deployed. Rather, his system displays, he says, a 'harmony' that its rivals lack. And this is not an expression merely of an aesthetic preference. Superior explanatory power was for Copernicus something more than saving the phenomena: it convinced him that he had hit on the truth with regard to the earth's motions.

See also: COSMOLOGY; EXPLANATION; KUHN, T.S.

List of works

Copernicus, N. (1543) *De revolutionibus orbium coelestium* (On the Revolutions of the Heavenly Spheres), in J. Dobrzycki (ed.) and E. Rosen (trans. and commentary) London: Macmillan, 1978. (Copernicus' major work, with a detailed commentary.)
—— (1939) E. Rosen (ed.) *Three Copernican Treatises*, New York: Dover. (Translations of the *Commentariolus*, Copernicus' *Letter against Werner*, and

Rheticus' *Narratio prima*. Also a useful annotated bibliography.)

References and further reading

Armitage, A. (1947) *The World of Copernicus*, New York: Mentor. (Popular biography.)
Kuhn, T. (1957) *The Copernican Revolution*, New York: Random House. (A classic work, containing a particularly useful chapter on Copernican astronomy.)
* Rosen, E. (1970) 'Was Copernicus a Hermetist?', in R.G. Stuewer (ed.) *Historical and Philosophical Perspectives of Science*, Minnesota Studies in the Philosophy of Science, Minneapolis, MN: University of Minnesota Press, vol. 5, 163–71. (A decided 'no' to the question posed.)
* Swerdlow, N.M. and Neugebauer, O. (1984) *Mathematical Astronomy in Copernicus's De Revolutionibus*, New York: Springer, 2 vols. (A detailed technical analysis of every aspect of Copernicus' work, with a useful short biography.)
Westman, R. (ed.) (1975) *The Copernican Achievement*, Berkeley, CA: University of California Press. (A set of essays marking the fifth centenary of Copernicus' birth. Lively scholarship on a wide array of Copernican topics.)
—— (1994) 'Two Cultures or One? A Second Look at Kuhn's *The Copernican Revolution*', *Isis* 85: 79–115. (Review of recent scholarship on the Copernican revolution generally.)

ERNAN McMULLIN

CORDEMOY, GÉRAUD DE (1626–84)

Géraud de Cordemoy was, by profession, first a lawyer, then a tutor to the Dauphin (the future Louis XV). But he was also one of the more important Cartesian philosophers in seventeenth-century France. In Le discernement du corps et de l'ame, Cordemoy defended a strict dualist and mechanist philosophy. But his Cartesianism was unorthodox, since he introduced indivisible atoms into his natural philosophy and was one of the first to argue for occasionalism, the doctrine that God alone is a true causal agent. He also wrote an important work on the nature and origins of speech and language, Le discours physique de la parole.

Géraud de Cordemoy was born in Paris on 6 October 1626. A lawyer by profession, from 1657 onwards he regularly attended occasions at which Cartesian philosophical ideas were discussed, and his *Discours de l'action des corps* was incorporated into the 1664 edition of Descartes' *Le Monde*. His major philosophical work, *Le discernement du corps et de l'ame* (1666), was thoroughly Cartesian in inspiration, and was followed two years later by *Le Discours physique de la parole*. By this time his broad interests included politics, pedagogy and history. In 1673, through the influence of Bossuet, he was appointed *lecteur ordinaire* to the Dauphin and joined the vibrant intellectual circles at the court of Louis XIV. He also began research into the history of France, published posthumously as *Histoire de France*. In 1675 he was elected to the Académie Française, of which he later became director. He died on 15 October 1684.

Most of Cordemoy's philosophical work involved an unorthodox defence and development of Descartes' system. He worked hard, for example, at reconciling Descartes' cosmogony with the biblical account of creation. More important, however, are the modifications he introduced into Cartesian metaphysics and natural philosophy with respect to the nature of matter and causation.

Descartes' matter, or body, understood as pure extension, is by nature divisible *ad indefinitum*. (Descartes preferred to say that the extension of the world is indefinite but not infinite – only God is 'infinite.') Hence, there are no in-principle indivisible atoms. Moreover, whatever is extended is body, so that the universe is a plenum. Cordemoy accepted the Cartesian project of mechanistic physics according to which all natural phenomena are to be explained solely by means of the motion and rest of insensible particles of matter, each of which is characterized by geometrical features alone. But he held that the only consistent form of mechanism is atomism. In the *Discernement*, he distinguished matter from extended substance, or body. Substance is essentially indivisible. Bodily substances, then, are indivisible, impenetrable, extended atoms, each with an invariable figure. Matter, on the other hand, is constituted by collections of atomic bodies, between which there are empty spaces. Cordemoy argued that only an atomism can consistently account in a non-relative way for the individuality and integrity of bodies. Moreover, a material plenum would render motion problematic and rectilinear motion unnatural, contrary to Descartes' own physical laws.

The *Discernement* next turns to the nature of causal relations, both between bodies and between bodies and minds. Cordemoy is generally regarded (along with LA FORGE) as one of the originators of the modern doctrine of occasionalism (see OCCASIONALISM; MALEBRANCHE §3). According to Cordemoy, bodies and minds are devoid of any real causal efficacy. One body cannot cause motion in itself or in another body, nor can it cause an event in the mind. And finite minds cannot cause mental events or move bodies. Only God, an infinite spirit, is a true causal agent. Cordemoy's argumentation proceeds in an a priori manner, starting from definitions and self-evident axioms. In the body-body case, one body cannot be the cause of motion in another body because motion is a state of a body, and states cannot be communicated from one substance to another. Moreover, no body causes motion in itself, since nothing has 'from itself' that which it can lose without ceasing to be what it is (one of Cordemoy's axioms), and a body can lose its motion without ceasing to be a body. It follows that the first mover of bodies is not a body, since such a first mover must have motion from itself. But there are only two sorts of substances: mind and body. Hence, the first mover of bodies must be a mind. Another axiom then states that an action can be continued only by the agent that initiated it. Thus, the mind that first moved bodies continues to move them. It is not *our* minds that move bodies. This is especially clear from the fact that bodies are usually moved independently of the volitions of any finite mind. This is true not just of inanimate bodies, but also of a great deal of the motion that takes place in the human body. What misleads us into attributing causal efficacy to minds and bodies is just the constant regularity in the succession of states of things. But, Cordemoy says (as Hume would repeat), this regular succession is *all* that experience reveals to us (see HUME, D. §2). The true cause can only be an infinite, all-powerful mind – God – who, acting on the occasion of the antecedent event, brings about the appropriate effect. Taken in a broader context, Cordemoy's occasionalist project is to demonstrate the ultimate metaphysical foundations of the physics of Cartesian (but atomistic) bodies.

Cordemoy's other important philosophical contribution, while not present in the *Discernement* itself, is none the less intimately related to that work's mechanistic science of body and dualist anthropology. In *Le Discours physique de la parole*, Cordemoy's stated aim is an examination of the nature of speech and language. He studies both that part played in linguistic communication by the purely physical mechanisms of the body, and the semantic aspect contributed by the mind. He considers, as well, the process of learning language and certain questions (some ethical) related to eloquence.

Cordemoy's atomist and occasionalist modifications of Descartes' philosophy drew strong critical responses from other Cartesians (such as Dom Robert DESGABETS). But he also impressed later thinkers, and Malebranche and Leibniz acknowledged his influence. More recently, the linguist Noam CHOMSKY identifies Cordemoy as an important contributor to the development of rationalist linguistics.

See also: ATOMISM, ANCIENT; DESCARTES, R.; GASSENDI, P.

List of works

Cordemoy, G. (1968) *Oeuvres philosophiques* (Philosophical works), ed. P. Clair and F. Girbal, Paris: Presses Universitaires de France. (Contains most of the works listed below, along with a 'Bio-Bibliography'.)

—— (1664) *Discours de l'action des corps* (Discourse on the action on bodies), incorporated into Descartes' *Le Monde*, Paris: Jacques Le Gras. (A treatise on mechanist physics.)

—— (1666) *Le Discernement du Corps et de l'Ame en six discours pour servir à l'éclaircissement de la physique* (The distinction of the body and the soul in six discourses to serve as the elucidation of physics), Paris. (Cordemoy's analysis of body and of its distinction from and relationship to the mind.)

—— (1668a) *Discours physique de la parole* (Physical discourse on language), Paris. (An influential study of the nature, origin, and uses of speech and language.)

—— (1668b) *Lettre écrite au R.P. Cossart de la Compagnie de Jésus* (Letter written to Father Cossart of the Jesuits), in *Les Oeuvres de feu M. de Cordemoy* (The works of the late M. de Cordemoy), Paris: Remy, 1704. (Cordemoy's attempt to reconcile Descartes' cosmogony with the biblical account of creation.)

—— (1691) *Traité de Metaphysique* (Treatise on metaphysics), Paris. (A brief discussion of human happiness and freedom.)

—— (1704) *Histoire de France* (History of France), in *Les Oeuvres de feu M. de Cordemoy* (The works of the late M. de Cordemoy), Paris: Remy. (Cordemoy's research into the history of France.)

References and further reading

Balz, A.G.A. (1951) *Cartesian Studies*, New York: Columbia University Press. (Contains a useful chapter on Cordemoy's philosophy in general.)

Battail, J.-F. (1973) *L'avocat philosophe Géraud de Cordemoy* (The lawyer-philosopher Géraud de Cordemoy), The Hague: Martinus Nijhoff. (A first-rate study of Cordemoy's life and thought.)

Chomsky, N. (1966) *Cartesian Linguistics*, Lanham, MD: University Press of America, 1983. (Places Cordemoy's work on language in the history of what the author calls 'rationalist linguistics'.)

Mouy, P. (1934) *Le développement de la physique cartésienne 1646–1712* (The development of Cartesian physics), Paris: J.Vrin. (Still the best account of the history of Cartesian physics in the seventeenth century, with some material on Cordemoy's atomism.)

Prost, J. (1907) *Essai sur l'atomisme et l'occasionalisme dans la philosophie cartésienne* (Essay on atomism and occasionalism in Cartesian philosophy), Paris: Henry Paulin. (Contains several chapters on Cordemoy, focusing on both his atomism and his role in the genesis of occasionalism.)

STEVEN NADLER

CORRESPONDENCE THEORY OF TRUTH *see* TRUTH, CORRESPONDENCE THEORY OF

CORRUPTION

Corruption denotes decay or perversion. The term implies that there is a natural or normal standard of functioning or conduct from which the corrupt state of affairs or action deviates. When we talk of a person becoming corrupt, we mean not just that they have broken a rule, but that the basic norms of ethical conduct no longer have any force for them. Corruption strikes at the root of a thing.

Political corruption involves the decay or perversion of political rule. Broadly, this occurs when a group or individual subverts a society's publicly endorsed practices for conciliating conflicts and pursuing the common good so as to gain illegitimate advantage for their interests in the political process. The precise specification of the nature and dynamics of corruption is inherently controversial. Classical accounts associate it with a collapse of civic virtue and the eventual destruction of the state. Modern theories focus more narrowly on the misuse of public office for private gain.

1 **The historical tradition**
2 **Corruption in political science**
3 **The core of political corruption**

1 The historical tradition

The corruption of politics, as the decay of the capacity to pursue justice or the common good, was a central concern for political philosophers in antiquity, and it remained so for their republican successors until the end of the eighteenth century. Two paradigmatic accounts of this process are in books 8 and 9 of Plato's *Republic* (*c.*380–367 BC), which sketch a political sociology and social psychology of the decay of the ideal state into ever more debased and less fully human forms (see PLATO); and book 3 of Thucydides' *History of the Peloponnesian War* (*c.*424–399 BC), in which the fall of Corcyrus is depicted in terms of the complete subversion of the political, social and moral order of the state (see THUCYDIDES). For classical authors, corruption was only incidentally a case of bribery, malfeasance or profiteering; its core sense concerned the systematic subversion of those practices, institutions and beliefs that provided a society with a shared understanding and a shared set of purposes. Within this tradition we find accounts, of varying degrees of sociological subtlety, of the causal and material preconditions for political rule and for its decay. These centre around the destabilizing effects of economic inequality among citizens, the enervating effects of luxury, concern with the size of states and their populations, the role of military training and combat, the appropriate education for citizens, the threat of foreign contamination and the best constitutional structure for the state. Without attention to these factors, the capacity of citizens to live virtuously and to recognize the demands of the common good becomes corrupted and the state falls.

This part-normative, part-sociological project of theorizing about the material and cultural preconditions for the stability of states exerted a powerful influence on Western traditions of political thought from Polybius to Rousseau, with MACHIAVELLI playing a central role. Through Aristotle, it had still wider influence on thinkers such as the fourteenth-century North African philosopher of history, IBN KHALDUN. In the UK it played a major part in the language of political opposition in the eighteenth century; thence it came to influence both American and French revolutionaries.

From the early modern period, however, there have been two counter-tendencies to this classical tradition. One denies that there is a common good for politics to pursue; instead, politics involves the pursuit of interests within institutional constraints, and claims about corruption are dismissed as emotive and as wholly motivated by factional or individual interests (as in Hobbes). The other narrows the focus, understanding corruption not as a systemic phenomenon but as a form of rule infraction or deviance by holders of public office. A precondition for this view is the separation of state and society, and the belief that civil society functions relatively autonomously from the state – corruption in government becomes seen as unrelated to the activities of social and economic life, and its solution is believed to lie with the construction of systems of scrutiny and mechanisms of accountability, rather than with the creation and sustaining of widespread citizen virtue.

2 Corruption in political science

Modern conceptions of corruption have tended to follow the more restricted ambitions of this view of corruption as individual rule infraction. Political scientists operate with two main, rival definitions: one centred around public office and one centred around public interest. The public office conception of corruption is exemplified by Nye: 'Corruption is behaviour which deviates from the formal duties of a public role because of private regarding (personal, close family, private clique) pecuniary or status gains; or violates rules against the exercise of certain types of private regarding influence' (1967: 966).

For Nye, questions of the public interest are questions about the effects of corruption and should not be taken as definitional of the phenomenon. Others, however, have sought to define political corruption precisely in terms of a conception of the public interest. Carl Friedrich argues that we have corruption wherever an office-holder or functionary is induced by non-legitimated rewards to act in ways favouring the rewarder and thereby doing damage to the public and its interests (Heidenheimer *et al.* 1989: 10) (see PUBLIC INTEREST §3).

Both public office and public interest definitions of corruption, however, must identify the norms by which we are to define the character and scope of public office or the public interest. Both definitions rely on such norms, but it is not obvious which norms we should accept. There may be little consensus within a society; official and popular mores may not coincide; and what people say about these norms may not coincide with how they behave. The law is equally deficient as a definitive source for norms, not least because laws can be the product of corrupt practices. Moreover, laws regulating political conduct rest on prior assumptions about the character of political office and the appropriate rules for its conduct – as such, legal norms are better understood as drawing on, rather than underpinning our understanding of public office.

These difficulties in identifying the norms of public office or the standard for the public interest ensure that the study of political corruption remains an unavoidably normative exercise. They also show that any theory of political corruption will require an understanding of the distinctive character of political activity and an account of the conditions in which this activity can resist subversion by competing values and activities in society.

A similar conclusion can be drawn by pressing the distinction between definitions of public-office and of public-interest. The conduct of public office, for the most part, is not (and cannot be) exhaustively prescribed by systems of rules. Most offices carry considerable discretion and flexibility, so as to allow occupants to respond to the contingencies of political life. But although the rules of office are open in this sense, the end or basic purpose of the office is unquestionably that it be guided by considerations of the public interest. Moreover, in identifying a rule violation as corrupt we are inevitably led to ask in whose interests the rule was broken. Depending on the answer to that question, we may judge an action as foolish, high-handed or misconceived, rather than corrupt.

3 The core of political corruption

These definitional problems, it should be emphasized, do not arise because the term corruption is unclear. On the contrary, its meaning is relatively uncontentious: it is rooted in the sense of a thing being changed from its naturally sound condition. The problem arises in applying this to politics since there is no general consensus on the 'naturally sound condition of politics'. Public office and public interest definitions focus on different aspects of the political; their disagreement is not over corruption, but over which criteria are appropriate to identify the naturally sound condition from which corrupt behaviour deviates.

It is at this point that the classical republican tradition, conceiving corruption in terms of the decay of the distinctive realm of human action which is politics, has renewed appeal (see REPUBLICANISM). Classical views identified a natural condition to politics, conceived in teleological terms, which provided the normative basis or standard which corrupt acts were seen as subverting or otherwise destroying. Modern political science is deeply uncomfortable with such normative commitments and yet, if we are to use the term coherently, such normative commitments are essential. They are essential because we cannot identify political corruption – and if we cannot identify it we cannot understand or explain it – without a commitment to some conception of the nature of politics which these acts subvert. Corruption is, then, the 'other' of politics; it is what must be

overcome for properly political rule to be possible. The classical republican tradition had the conceptual and normative framework to recognize this relationship, but the scientism and historicism of the nineteenth and twentieth centuries, and the shift in concern from the conditions for attaining a commonality of purpose and interest within the polity to the problem of integrating the potentially insurgent masses into the bureaucratic politics of the modern nation state, served to displace the insights of this older paradigm. Indeed, political scientists have tended to concentrate their efforts on the understanding of corruption in deviant cases, such as in authoritarian states and command economies or as a transitional phenomenon in newly democratized regimes undergoing rapid economic development and social change, and have generally assumed that the modernization and liberalization of the state solves such problems. Above all, in sharp contrast to the classical model, there has been very little attention paid to the correlation between the maintenance of an active civic culture and the incidence of corruption within the political domain. The result has been the development of models of politics which have, by eschewing questions of the distinctive nature or character of politics and underplaying the relevance of the mores and beliefs of civil society in the incidence of corruption, largely failed to provide an adequate understanding of what remains a widespread phenomenon in many modern states.

References and further reading

Dobel, J.P. (1978) 'Corruption of a State', *American Political Science Review*, 72 (3): 958–73. (An account of the classical tradition of conceptualizing corruption.)
Euben, J.P. (1989) 'Corruption', in T. Ball, J. Farr and R.L. Hanson (eds) *Political Innovation and Conceptual Change*, Cambridge: Cambridge University Press, 220–46. (Contrasts the classical tradition with more modern traditions in political theory.)
Friedrich, C.J. (1966) 'Political Pathology', *Political Quarterly* 37 (1): 74; and Heidenheimer *et al.* (1989) *Political Corruption: A Handbook*, New Brunswick, NJ: Transaction Press, 10.
Heidenheimer, A.J. (1970) *Political Corruption: Readings in Comparative Analysis*, New York: Holt, Reinhart & Winston. (An early collection of articles, many of which also appear in Heidenheimer *et al.* (1989).)
* Heidenheimer, A.J., Johnston, M. and Levine, V.T. (eds) (1989) *Political Corruption: A Handbook*, New Brunswick, NJ: Transaction Press. (The standard work on the subject in politics.)

Ibn Khaldun (1377) *The Muqaddimah: An Introduction to History*, trans. F. Rosenthal, London: Routledge & Kegan Paul, 3 vols, 1958. (See volume 1, chapters 2 and 3, for a succinct statement of Khaldun's understanding of the corruption of the state.)

* Nye, J.S. (1967) 'Corruption and Political Development: A Cost–Benefit Analysis', *American Political Science Review* 61 (2): 417–27; reprinted in and cited from Heidenheimer *et al.* (1989) *Political Corruption: A Handbook*, New Brunswick, NJ: Transaction Press, 963–83. (A major exponent of the view that corruption may be beneficial to the economic development of a society.)

Philp, M. (1996) 'Defining Political Corruption', *Political Studies* 45 (3). (An examination of the problems of defining political corruption which links the definition to competing conceptions of the nature of politics.)

* Plato (c. 380–367 BC) *Republic*, trans. P. Shorey, Loeb Classical Library, Cambridge, MA: Harvard University Press, 1930. (See especially books 8 and 9.)

Putnam, R.D. (1993) *Making Democracy Work: Civic Traditions in Modern Italy*, Princeton, NJ: Princeton University Press. (An attempt to show empirically the connection between civic virtue and low levels of corruption.)

Scott, J.C. (1972) *Comparative Political Corruption*, Englewood Cliffs, NJ: Prentice Hall. (A classic study of corruption, focusing primarily on machine politics.)

* Thucydides (c. 424–399 BC) *History of the Peloponnesian War*, trans. C.F. Smith, Loeb Classical Library, Cambridge, MA: Harvard University Press, 1921. (See especially book 3, §§69–85.)

MARK PHILP

COSMOLOGICAL ARGUMENT *see* GOD, ARGUMENTS FOR THE EXISTENCE OF

COSMOLOGY

The term 'cosmology' has three main uses. At its most general, it designates a worldview, for example, the Mayan cosmology. In the early eighteenth century, shortly after the term made its first appearance, Christian Wolff used it to draw a distinction between physics, the empirical study of the material world, and cosmology, the branch of metaphysics dealing with material nature in its most general aspects. This usage remained popular into the twentieth century, especially among Kantian and neo-scholastic philosophers. But recent developments in science that allow the construction of plausible universe models have, effectively, pre-empted the use of the term in order to designate the science that deals with the origins and structure of the physical universe as a whole.

Cosmology may be said to have gone through three major phases, each associated with a single major figure – Aristotle, Newton and Einstein. The ancient Greeks were the first to attempt to give a reasoned account of the cosmos. Aristotle constructed a complex interlocking set of spheres centred on an immovable central earth to account for the motions of the heavenly bodies. Newton formulated a theory of gravitational force that required space and time to be both absolute and infinite. Though the laws of nature could, in principle, be specified, nothing could be said about the origins or overall structure of the cosmos. In 1915, Einstein proposed a general theory of relativity whose field-equations could be satisfied by numerous universe-models. Hubble's discovery of the galactic red shift in 1929 led Lemaître in 1931 to choose from among these alternatives an expanding-universe model, which, though challenged in the 1950s by a rival steady-state theory, became the 'standard' view after the cosmic microwave background radiation it had predicted was observed in 1964. The 'Big Bang' theory has since been modified in one important respect by the addition of an inflationary episode in the first fraction of a second of cosmic expansion. As a 'cosmic' theory, it continues to raise issues of special interest to philosophers.

1 Aristotle's cosmos
2 Newton's infinites
3 The expanding universe

1 Aristotle's cosmos

Cosmology and philosophy came into existence together in the Greek-speaking world of the sixth century BC when some daring minds sought a 'reasoned account' of the origins and nature of the universe. They assumed that the complex must originally have come from the simple, and thus sought clues in the world around them for the elements and processes responsible, resting their claims on argument rather than on the authority of a tradition. Plato was sharply critical of his predecessors' lack of attention to the traces of mind he saw everywhere in the world around; his *Timaeus* took the universe to be the work of a demiurge (artificer) who imposed partial order on a pre-existent and recalcitrant receptacle (see

PLATO §16). He acknowledged that his account fell short of knowledge proper. But it could still claim the status of a likely story.

Aristotle went much further, and the cosmology he constructed would substantially endure for two millennia. Beginning from the sophisticated geometrical combinations of circles whereby his contemporaries EUDOXUS and Callippus had sought to 'save' the motions of the seven 'wandering stars', he proposed a set of fifty-five rotating concentric spheres, the poles of each carried by the sphere next outside it, and each given its own motion of rotation by an immanent mover, akin to a soul. The complex motion of each planet is the resultant of the motions of its own cluster of spheres, the innermost of which carries the planet. The physics of earth does not apply to these spheres, whose eternal circular motions are quite unlike the rectilinear natural motions found on earth. Nothing much further can be said about the nature of the spheres and the celestial bodies they carry except that they are incorruptible (see ARISTOTLE §16).

The aim of Aristotle's cosmology was to give a plausible causal explanation of the planetary motions, and in this it succeeded. It was not of much practical use for the needs of working astronomers, and its concentric spheres could not explain the known regular variations in planetary brightness. The epicycles and eccentrics first introduced by Apollonius and Hipparchus and later welded by Ptolemy into an accurately predictive geometrical scheme were of much more use for practical ends, but could not compete with Aristotle's ingenious model in explanatory appeal. The fact that the two approaches could not be reconciled was troublesome, but medieval philosophers grew accustomed to arguing that the truth of things would be found in 'physics', that is, in causal explanation, even though 'mathematics' would perhaps be more effective for saving the phenomena.

2 Newton's infinites

Aristotle's cosmology fell as the Copernican heliocentric model (see COPERNICUS) gradually proved itself in the hands of Kepler and Galileo. In his *Astronomia nova* (1609), Kepler argued that a proper cosmology, one that could claim to give a true account of the motions and distances of the planets, would have to elucidate the causes of those motions and not merely save the phenomena. His own attempts to explain the motions in terms of forces acting at a distance were not successful. It was left to Newton to carry this programme through, utilizing a gravitational attraction that varied inversely as the square of the distance. Leibniz and the Cartesian physicists of the day were willing to concede that the

new mechanics of Newton's *Principia* (1687) could save the phenomena, but they insisted that action at a distance could not be accounted an explanation, and hence that the *Principia* did not support a genuine cosmology (see MECHANICS, CLASSICAL §3; NEWTON, I.).

In order to support the reality of the forces he postulated, Newton introduced the idea of 'absolute' motion (changes in which would be the indication of forces acting) and its corollaries, absolute space and absolute time. Absolute space is Euclidean and thus boundless; it exists independently of any material contents, unlike an Aristotelian place. Absolute time 'flows equably without relation to anything external'; it is thus independent of actual physical change (unlike Aristotelian time) and it is without beginning or end. Not much purchase here for questions about the origin and extent of the material universe! A century later, indeed, Kant would argue that the proclivity of human reason to pose cosmological questions such as these, which necessarily (in his view) lead to antinomy, forces a radical critique of pure reason itself (see KANT, I. §8).

Newton made one significant cosmological claim. In Aristotle's universe, terrestrial and celestial bodies were altogether different in nature, so that a simple science of the two was impossible. Newton showed, however, that a single mechanics governed earth and planets, and in the boldly inductivist third rule of reasoning of the *Principia* postulated that qualities characterizing bodies at the local level should be deemed to characterize the universe generally. The inverse square law of gravitation could, on this basis, be portrayed as a cosmological law governing the attraction between any two particles in the universe. Kant was the first to see just how this might explain the origin of such stable cosmic structures as planetary systems or even the Milky Way. Questions about origin or structure at the level of the universe, however, still seemed fruitless.

3 The expanding universe

In 1915, EINSTEIN formulated a general theory of relativity, employing non-Euclidean geometry to describe a unified spacetime in which the curvature of spacetime replaces gravitational force as a cause of motion (see SPACETIME §3; RELATIVITY THEORY, PHILOSOPHICAL SIGNIFICANCE OF §§4–7). Universe models could now be constructed as solutions to the field equations of the new theory, though constraints were needed on the large number of possible solutions. A variety of 'natural assumptions' were introduced regarding large-scale cosmic structure, some of them given the status of 'cosmological principles'. Notable amongst these was Einstein's daring conjecture that matter should be distributed uniformly over space on the largest scale. When Einstein discovered that his equations tended to yield unstable models, he added a cosmological constant representing a repulsion that increased with distance, since he assumed that a plausible universe model ought to be static. Alexander Friedmann (1924) and Georges Lemaître (1927) proposed, instead, nonstatic solutions in which space itself could be expanding.

Hubble's discovery of the galactic red shift in 1929 was the next significant development. It indicated that the galaxies are moving away from us, and from one another, at speeds proportional to their distances. Lemaître (1931) realized how neatly this fitted the nonstatic models of general relativity and formulated the theory of the expanding universe, later called the 'Big Bang' theory. From the rate of expansion, one could calculate an upper limit on the length of time since the expansion began from a single enormously condensed volume. An answer to the ancient cosmological query about origins suddenly seemed to be within reach. But a disappointment was in store. Using Hubble's figure for the expansion constant, the limit-age came out as roughly two billion years, much shorter than the estimated age of the solar system or of the oldest stars.

This was one, though not the principal, motivation for the construction of an alternative 'steady-state' model by Bondi and Gold (1947). It rested on what they described as the 'perfect' cosmological principle, requiring a homogeneous distribution of matter in an infinite space and throughout an infinite time. To account for the Hubble expansion, they postulated the continuous creation of hydrogen throughout space at a rate too low to be detectable, sufficient to allow new galaxies to replace the old as the old move out of view. Baade (1952) showed that Hubble's estimate for galactic distances was too low and that the 'Big Bang' age in consequence was a much safer ten to twenty billion years. And in the late 1950s, evidence began to mount that the relative abundance of galaxies of different types varied with distance, contrary to the 'perfect' principle.

But it was the discovery by Penzias and Wilson of the uniform cosmic microwave background radiation, reflecting a 3K black-body temperature distribution, that proved decisive (1965). Alpher and Herman had predicted long before (1948) that just such a relic of radiation should be expected from the original Big Bang. The effect of the discovery was not only to bring over most cosmologists to the Big Bang theory but also, to a significant extent, it validated cosmology itself as a respectable branch of science. Fresh data concerning the observed cosmic helium abundance (25 per cent by mass) also fitted the Big Bang account of helium formation in the first minutes of the cosmic expansion.

Still, some serious challenges remained. In the Big Bang model, the universe might be (geometrically) 'open', in which case it would be infinite and galaxies would continue to expand indefinitely, or it could be 'closed', finite, with the galaxies ultimately collapsing again inwards, or 'flat', poised between. The decisive factor is the average cosmic mass-density. Collins and Hawking (1973) showed that for a long-lived universe like ours to develop, one in which the background radiation is isotropic, the early universe would have had to be 'flat' to an almost unbelievably exact degree. Cosmologists had always assumed that no particular initial cosmic parameter setting would be needed, so this discovery was both unexpected and unwelcome. Collins and Hawking responded with what Carter (1974) dubbed the 'anthropic principle': the fact that we have observed the universe to be long-lived and isotropic is merely a consequence of our own existence. Were it not to be of that sort, we would not be here! To convert this 'principle' into an explanation, a further premise was necessary. Their choice was a many-universe hypothesis: if our universe is one among a large number of actual universes, we would naturally find ourselves in one that is suited for human existence. Other writers, most of them philosophers of religion, pointed out on the other hand that such 'fine tuning' would be what one would expect were the universe to be the work of a provident Creator (see GOD, ARGUMENTS FOR THE EXISTENCE OF §5). Here, then, were two unconventional sorts of anthropic *explanation*, each requiring a much broader context than usual to make it acceptable. (It seems doubtful that there is a nontrivial anthropic *principle*, strictly speaking.) The same two alternatives were also proposed in response to a rather different sort of fine tuning. Were the physical constants, notably the relative strengths of the four fundamental forces, to be even very slightly different, a long-lived galactic universe containing the heavy elements needed for complex life would not have developed.

Alan Guth (1981) took a more conventional approach to the 'flatness' problem. He proposed a modification of the Big Bang model that would automatically bring about the critical mass-density needed: a gigantic inflation within the first fraction of a second of the cosmic expansion. This would also eliminate several other troublesome anomalies in the original Big Bang theory; it would, for example, achieve the needed causal coordination across different spatial regions of the early universe. The inflationary hypothesis illustrates the extent to which quantum theory has entered into the cosmological debate. On the one hand, standard quantum ideas have permitted physicists to reconstruct the probable sequence of the early expansion, allowing the derivation of testable predictions concerning, for example, the relative cosmic abundance of the lighter elements. On the other, the enormous energies and densities of the very first moments of the (hypothetical) expansion have become a conceptual testing-ground for quantum field theory of a sort that the particle accelerators of earth could never provide.

Cosmology is, as it has always been, a testing-ground for philosophical ideas, lying at the limits of our notions of space, time and causality. Inductivist doubts as to whether a unique object such as the universe could ever become a legitimate object of knowledge have been to some extent quieted. A theory of the universe can be tested as theory normally is, by such criteria as coherence, predictive novelty and consilience. The vast expansion in our conceptual horizons that Big Bang theory and its inflationary addendum have brought about have led philosophers to be more wary than they were of the sort of appeal to intuition on which philosophies of nature in the past were often based. For the same reason, reliance on 'cosmological principles' as anything more than idealizations of a regulative sort has become increasingly suspect. Discussions of anthropic forms of explanation have forced scientists and philosophers alike to clarify what counts as 'explaining' and what resources can legitimately be drawn on in the process. The many-universe models, particularly those prompted by the inflationary hypothesis, have raised new questions about what should count as a distinct universe. It is less than a century since Einstein opened the new era in cosmology. No doubt surprises as great as those already encountered still lie ahead.

See also: ANAXIMANDER; COSMOLOGY AND COSMOGONY, INDIAN THEORIES OF; DAO; LI; PYTHAGOREANISM; SPACE; XING

References and further reading

Ellis, G.F.R. (1989) 'The Expanding Universe: A History of Cosmology from 1917 to 1960', in D. Howard and J. Stachel (eds) *Einstein and the History of General Relativity*, Boston, MA: Birkhäusen, 367–431. (Good summary history. Detailed bibliography; includes publications mentioned by date in the text.)

Harrison, E.R. (1981) *Cosmology: The Science of the Universe*, Cambridge: Cambridge University Press. (A widely praised textbook.)

Hetherington, N.S. (ed.) (1993) *Encyclopedia of Cosmology*, New York: Garland. (An excellent reference work. Special attention is paid to historical and philosophical aspects on cosmology. Several of the scientific essays were written by those who contributed to the fundamental advances described.)

Isham, C.J. (1993) 'Quantum Theories of the Creation of the Universe', in R.J. Russell, N. Murphy and C.J. Isham (eds) *Quantum Cosmology and the Laws of Nature*, Notre Dame, IN: University of Notre Dame Press, 49–89. (Technical but readable account of various attempts to use quantum theory to illuminate the mode of origination of the universe.)

Kragh, H. (1996) *Cosmology and Controversy*, Princeton, NJ: Princeton University Press. (A careful account of the debate between defenders of the steady-state and Big Bang cosmological models. Includes a helpful chapter on the philosophical issues involved.)

Leslie, J. (1989) *Universes*, London: Routledge. (An extensive review of the evidence for 'fine tuning' in recent cosmology and of the various responses to it. Concludes that either God (in the form of an ethical requirement) is real or that there exist many varied universes.)

—— (ed.) (1990) *Physical Cosmology and Philosophy*, New York: Macmillan. (A useful anthology containing some classic papers by major cosmologists, where the authors reflect on such philosophical issues as the propriety of anthropic forms of cosmological explanation.)

McMullin, E. (1994) 'Long Ago and Faraway: Cosmology as Extrapolation', in R. Fuller (ed.) *Bang: The Evolving Cosmos*, Lanham, MD: University Press of America, 105–45. (Can there be a proper science of structures and events as remote from us in space and in time as those that recent cosmology purports to establish? What is to count here as 'proper science'? A review of the credentials of the Big Bang theory, concluding positively.)

* Munitz, M.K. (ed.) (1957) *Theories of the Universe from Babylonian Myth to Modern Science*, Glencoe, IL: Free Press. (Selection of readings from those who shaped the science of cosmology, ranging from Aristotle and Lucretius, through Newton and Kant, to Lemaître and Gamow.)

—— (1986) *Cosmic Understanding: Philosophy and Science of the Universe*, Princeton, NJ: Princeton University Press. (Munitz has done more than any other philosopher writing in English to turn the attention of philosophers to the intriguing issues raised by cosmology, both ancient and modern. A readable account of those issues.)

Rhook, G. and Zangari, M. (1994) 'Should We

Believe in the Big Bang? A Critique of the Integrity of Modern Cosmology', in D. Hull, M. Forbes and R.M. Burian (eds) *PSA 1994*, East Lansing, MI: Philosophy of Science Association, vol. 1, 228–37. (The authors argue that the weight of anomalies currently facing the Big Bang theory indicates that the confidence it presently enjoys may be misplaced.)

ERNAN McMULLIN

COSMOLOGY AND COSMOGONY, INDIAN THEORIES OF

Theories of the origin of the universe have been told as stories, riddles and instruction in India since early times. The three prominent religious movements, Hinduism, Buddhism and Jainism each had their own myths and speculations.

In the Hindu tradition there was never one single theory. Among the divergent ideas we can distinguish: an early stage, which included themes such as there being nothing at the beginning, or the universe being created by mutual birth, or creation as the dismemberment of a sacrificial victim, or the gods arriving after the first moment of creation; and a later stage, in which Viṣṇu or Brahmā was regarded as the creator of the universe. Simultaneously, the old Sāṅkhya idea of the self-creating universe, in which the original material stuff transforms itself into the different parts of the universe, coexisted with the idea of a god creating the universe.

The early Buddhist tradition neglected questions such as 'Does the universe exist?' The first mention of such topics occurred in the Pāli Canon, where they were condemned. A few centuries later, these cosmological ideas were taken up by Vasubandhu, who collected them and formulated them in a comprehensive way. Without a creator god, the universe is primarily a reflection of meditational experiences of the world, a Single Circular System. There are several other systems, such as the Thousand Universe System, the Immeasurable Universe System and the Pure Land.

The Jaina tradition had a very detailed theory of the spatial arrangement of the universe. This was essential for understanding where all the individual selves travel to after death, given their spiritual accomplishments (or lack of them). From earth they go to heavens or hells, the aim being eventually to reach the place of bliss and thus to gain final freedom.

1 **Vedic period**
2 **Upaniṣads and classical Hinduism**
3 **Later Hinduism**
4 **Buddhism**
5 **Jainism**

1 Vedic period

Just as the earliest speculations in many cultures revolved around questions and theories of the origin of the universe and related topics, so in India the earliest available document of the culture, the *Ṛg Veda* (*c.*1200 BC), preserves such ideas. It predates any divergence of the ideological movements. The references are scattered. In the oldest parts, cycles 2–9, the topics centre around separating heaven from earth. The creation of the universe is likened to the building of a house, and measuring is one of the main activities. The doors of the house face east and let in the morning light. Other artistic activities, such as weaving or forging, are used to describe the creation of the universe. But interpretations of the myths and speculations on the origin of the universe can be found only later, in the youngest parts of the *Ṛg Veda*, specifically the tenth cycle.

The tenth cycle contains a number of cosmological hymns. Several themes are discernible: in one hymn there is nothing at the beginning, in another there is mutual birth, another describes the dismemberment of a sacrificial victim, yet another the arrival of gods after the first moments of creation. Early cosmological questions such as 'Where did anything come from?' receive some intriguing treatment; hymn 10.129 says that 'At the beginning there was neither existence nor nonexistence.' The questions were often answered in the form of riddles.

Similarly, the Aditi hymn (*Ṛg Veda* 10.72) is ambiguous. First, Reality or Being arises from Nothing. After this, the skies come into being, born from vast spaces. The earth is born of the vast spaces. Often in the *Ṛg Veda* the sky and the earth are considered to be the parents of the various gods. Then Dakṣa is born of Aditi, the mother goddess. In the same hymn, Aditi is the daughter of Dakṣa. It is something like a mutual birth or an incestuous birth. The very same process of birth is found in the well-known 'Puruṣasūkta' (*Ṛg Veda* 10.90.), where Virāj (who is female) is born of Puruṣa, but in turn Puruṣa is born of Virāj. After the mutual birth in the Aditi hymn the gods come into existence and Aditi gives birth to seven sons, whom she takes to the gods. She also gives birth to an eighth son, whom she sets aside to be the human who procreates and dies.

The hymn of dismemberment of the sacrificial victim is called the 'Puruṣasūkta'. It describes the

681

sacrifice of the Primeval Man, through which the world becomes filled with animals as well as all things and populated with people, who are grouped into four categories. Different parts of the Primeval Man are the sources of the social hierarchy and division of labour in Hindu society. Thus from the head of the Man come the priests, from his arms spring the warriors, from his thighs come the farmers and merchants, and from his feet emerge those who provide services for the other groups. The dismemberment depicts the different strata of society while justifying class divisions that survive to the present day.

2   Upaniṣads and classical Hinduism

The main background for the variety of often unrelated and even contradictory speculations in Indian cosmology was provided at the time of the late Veda, especially during the time of the *Atharvaveda*, the Brāhmaṇas and the Upaniṣads (1000–600 BC).

The Upaniṣads do not form a uniform ideology, but rather represent a collection of speculations on the nature of things. Here we find, for example, a refutation of the early statement about the universe as born from nothing. In Chāndogya Upaniṣad 6, a father instructs his son, telling him that at the beginning there was only one being and from it all was born (see MONISM, INDIAN §4).

In Chāndogya Upaniṣad 6 and other parts of the early Upaniṣads there is a convention of listing. Frequently we find lists of three items: fire, water, solid matter (called food), each of which in turn becomes threefold. The first sets of ontological categories were presented as lists, and this constituted the scientific method of the early period. The number four often plays an important role in lists of the basic elements: heat, water, the solid matter (called 'food') and the wind. Some thinkers added a fifth, space (*ākāśa*). Before the differentiation of separate religious and cultural movements, there was something of an obsession with these lists. This habit continued in the philosophical schools, such as the School of Logic (Nyāya), the School of Categorization (Sāṅkhya) and the School of Particulars (Vaiśeṣika).

After the early suppositions of a god creating the universe in separating the earth from heaven, or something nonexistent willing itself into existence, we find that the large segments of population in India becoming Vaiṣṇavite adopted an evolutionary scheme that most identify with Sāṅkhya teachings (see SĀṄKHYA). The Sāṅkhya school vacillated between the numbers two and three: there exists only the material stuff and consciousness, yet the material stuff is of two kinds – undifferentiated, when unmanifest,

and manifest when created into separate entities – so together with consciousness we get a list of three. The primeval material stuff is undifferentiated until it is disturbed. Once disturbed, it evolves into twenty-three primal entities, from which the world is formed. According to Sāṅkhya, in containing these primal entities within itself in the pre-existent form, the cause contains the effect (see CAUSATION, INDIAN THEORIES OF §3). A distinct entity, consciousness (*puruṣa*), brings about the initial disturbance in the primeval material stuff (*prakṛti*). The exact manner in which this disturbance is effected, or what is the relation of consciousness to this material stuff, has never been satisfactorily explained.

Twenty-three primal entities evolve from the primeval material stuff. These are all material, even though the initial ones comprise what we ordinarily consider to be our mental faculties: reason, ego and mind. Consciousness makes these otherwise material entities conscious through its 'proximity'. These first three entities are followed by five sense faculties, five action faculties, five subtle elements and five gross elements. These evolved parts, the material stuff, together with consciousness comprise everything there is.

But what accounts for the differences among entities within the world, some of them light and active and others heavy and dull? The answer is that the primeval material stuff is composed of three elemental forces: 'intelligence', energy and inertia. Different combinations of these forces account for the differences among worldly things. None of the forces is ever found by itself. Each exists only in different combinations with the others, separating and recombining in differing degrees.

3   Later Hinduism

In the later Hindu tradition, the gods become responsible for the process of the creation of the universe, and its destruction in order to create it again. This is one of the major themes of the Purāṇas. The Purāṇas ('Old Stories'), composed from about the fourth century AD onwards, centre around the creation and dissolution of the universe, time periods and genealogies. They are actually the second round of so-called 'old stories', the first one being collected in the epic of the *Mahābhārata*.

In contrast to the diverse early ideas of the universe, its arrangement and timescale, the Purāṇic ideas reflect a synthesizing effort to organize the material into some kind of coherence. There is still no single creation myth, but instead we can recognize several major themes, such as the creation scheme involving *puruṣa* and *prakṛti*. This pair is responsible for the creation of whatever exists. Another theme is that of the universe as an egg. A third theme is that of a god, whether Viṣṇu, Puruṣa or Brahmā, often depicted with very human features, who creates this universe.

The interaction between *puruṣa* and *prakṛti* is often interpreted in terms of an interaction between a male and a female. This produces an egg, but it does not break open to give life; rather the universe comes alive within the unbroken egg. It has seven heavens, where the gods and some higher beings spend their allotted time. The egg also contains seven nether worlds, the dwelling place of the ogres (*asuras*) and other fantastic beings. These nether worlds are lavish places with graceful gardens and comfortable houses. Between the heavens and the nether worlds is the earth. India, the ancient name for which was 'Jambudvīpa', is in the centre, surrounded by six other lands, with Mount Meru as the *axis mundi*. It seems that this is all the spatial arrangement there is of the physical world. Hells are described vividly in terms of various punishments, but they do not have a physical existence and appear to be moral spaces. Neither the heavens nor the hells are permanent dwelling places. After one's merit or demerit is exhausted, the next stop may be in the opposite quarter.

The moral aspect of this cosmology is also reflected in the four ages: *kṛta*, *treta*, *dvāpara* and *kali*. These were the terms used for the throws of a popular dice game much enjoyed at the time. The four ages, which constitute one of several theories of time, are described as involving a gradual loss of grace for humankind. The earliest period, *kṛta*, is posited as the ideal state, the past golden age. Things deteriorate in each successive age, until the fourth age, our present, in which we are more or less miserable. A favourite illustration is the cow or the bull of *dharma*, which stands on all four legs in the golden age of *kṛta*. In each successive age, the cow stands on one leg less, becoming less secure as time goes on. In our time, she stands on a single leg and thus has a hard time standing up at all.

There are other theories of time. One is a calendar, based on observations of the moon and sun, that divides time into days, months and years. This calendar has a magnified counterpart in the lifetime of Brahmā. He is the ultimate creator of the universe and his lifetime, a complicated maze of calendars, spans 12,000,000 divine years. Each divine year is 360 human years. So Brahmā's lifetime is 4,320,000,000 earthly years. At its end, the universe dies too. This is the dissolution of the universe before its new creation, a cycle that repeats itself endlessly and is referred to as the pulsating universe.

4   Buddhism

Originally, questions about the beginning and the functioning of the world were not considered relevant in Buddhism. Whenever he was asked about such topics, Lord Buddha refused to discuss them, referring to them as vain and useless intellectual endeavour. They did not contribute to liberation.

During the next few centuries, these questions gave rise to speculations and theories which form the basis for the Ābhidharmika schools of Buddhism. VASU-BANDHU (fourth century AD) examines them in his monumental *Abhidharmakośa* (Compendium of Abhidharma, that is, of theories beyond the teaching of the Buddha). In the third chapter, he describes the world, the universe and the levels through which an accomplished spiritual being will pass on the way to *nirvāṇa*.

Vasubandhu believed in a Single Circular System. At the centre of the universe is Mount Meru. Past this are another seven mountain ranges, all of gold and all circular. Beyond these there are four islands. Yet another mountain range encircles all of this. There are bodies of water between each of the mountain ranges. All but the last consist of fresh water; the last one is salt water. Below Jambudvīpa (India) are the sixteen hells. At the summit of Mount Meru are the thirty-three gods.

If we shift to a nonlocational arrangement, there is a threefold division: the sphere of desire, the sphere of form, and the formless sphere. The sphere of form is further subdivided into four meditational levels. In the formless sphere the beings themselves have no form. Liberation takes place beyond the formless sphere. These three spheres are the different levels in meditation that gradually cultivate the aspirant for the final goal of *nirvāṇa*. This is a vision of a physical universe mixed with a universe known through meditation.

There are other systems in addition to the Single Circular System. We can speak basically of two major types of cosmology: single-world cosmology, and systems based on the coexistence of multiple worlds. These cosmologies are best viewed as conceptualizations of liberation, as reflected in the different schools. In the single-world cosmology, the mechanism for rebirth involves effort, but can be manipulated: it is possible to avoid hell and go instead to heaven by doing meritorious actions. *Nirvāṇa* is liberation from a single-world cosmology, and is often described as being above the formless heavens (of the nonlocational arrangement). In multiple-world cosmologies, liberation is interpreted differently. It is rebirth in a celestial Buddha's Pure Land. This rebirth is the last rebirth, during which it is possible to attain enlightenment just by listening to Buddha's teaching.

5 Jainism

The Jainas took a keen interest in cosmography, the depiction of the organization of the universe, in order that the destinations of individuals according to their behaviour could be explained. The universe depicted was a representation of mental states experienced in meditational practices, rather than of actual or imaginary physical locations. An important source for the study of Jaina cosmography is Umāsvāti's *Tattvārthasūtra*, of around the fourth to fifth centuries AD. Chapters three and four describe the Jaina universe in painstaking detail.

The Jaina cosmology excludes cosmogony because there is no beginning of time, no beginning or creation of the universe. Time is eternal. Frequently the universe is pictured as a woman, with arms bent outward, although sometimes it is depicted as a male figure. Just as in the Hindu cosmography, the earth is in the middle of the universe. The island of the earth is divided into two parts by two mountain ranges extending north to south. There are two Mount Merus, one in the east and one in the west. Below the earth are the hells, which get progressively wider towards the bottom. The heavens, which are above the earth, first become wider (the arms bent outward), then further on they become narrower. Space, as opposed to time, is finite. The inhabited universe (*loka*) is delimited first by thick air, then by thin air, and finally is surrounded by the uninhabited universe (*aloka*), which is empty of anything. Above the heavens, in a circular region, the liberated selves bask in bliss.

This entry has given representative samples of the major trends in Indian cosmological and cosmogonic thought. There is a large body of literature that deals with a number of other things, but contains many ideas that can be considered cosmology. The *Mahābhārata*, the Purāṇas, and the Mānava Dharmaśāstra are almost inexhaustible sources for the Hindu cosmologies and cosmogonies. As compared to the random, organic growth of cosmological ideas in Hinduism, both the Buddhists and the Jainas formulated their cosmological theories after their traditions were well established, and so they reflect a more deliberate ideology.

See also: BUDDHIST PHILOSOPHY, INDIAN; GOD, INDIAN CONCEPTIONS OF; HEAVEN, INDIAN CONCEPTIONS OF; HINDU PHILOSOPHY; JAINA PHILOSOPHY

References and further reading

Gombrich, R. (1975) 'Ancient Indian Cosmology', in C. Blacker and M. Loewe (eds) *Ancient Cosmologies*, London: Allen & Unwin. (Single, short survey covering all the major facets of cosmologies.)

Kloetzli, R. (1983) *Buddhist Cosmology. From Single World System to Pure Land: Science and Theology in the Images of Motion and Light*, Delhi: Motilal Banarsidass. (A good, comprehensive introduction.)

* *Ṛg Veda* (c.2000 BC), trans. W.H. Maurer, *Pinnacles of India's Past: Selections from the Ṛg Veda*, University of Pennsylvania Studies in South Asia 2, Amsterdam and Philadelphia, PA: John Benjamin, 1986. (A literary and precise translation.)

Schubring, W. (1962) *The Doctrine of the Jainas Described after the Old Sources*, trans. W. Beurlen, Delhi: Motilal Banarsidass. (Contains a thorough discussion of Jaina cosmology and cosmography.)

* Umāsvāti (4th–5th century) *Tattvārthasūtra*, ed. and trans. N. Tatia, *Tattvārtha Sūtra: That Which Is*, San Francisco, CA: HarperCollins, 1994. (An authoritative edition, containing text in transcription and translation, of a classic Jaina manual.)

* Upaniṣads (1000–600 BC), trans. P. Olivelle, *Upaniṣads*, World's Classics Series, Oxford: Oxford University Press, 1996. (The latest, most up-to-date translation of twelve Upaniṣads, with excellent annotations which resolve many hitherto unintelligible passages.)

EDELTRAUD HARZER CLEAR

COUNT TERMS *see* MASS TERMS

COUNTERFACTUAL CONDITIONALS

'If bats were deaf, they would hunt during the day.' What you have just read is called a 'counterfactual' conditional; it is an 'If... then...' statement the components of which are 'counter to fact', in this case counter to the fact that bats hear well and sleep during the day. Among the analyses proposed for such statements, two have been especially prominent. According to the first, a counterfactual asserts that there is a sound argument from the antecedent ('bats are deaf') to the consequent ('bats hunt during the day'). The argument uses certain implicit background conditions and laws of nature as

additional premises. A variant of this analysis says that a counterfactual is itself a condensed version of such an argument. The analysis is called 'metalinguistic' because of its reference to linguistic items such as premises and arguments. The second analysis refers instead to possible worlds. (One may think of possible worlds as ways things might have gone.) This analysis says that the example is true just in case bats hunt during the day in the closest possible world(s) where they are deaf.

1 **Classification issues and familiar logical connectives**
2 **The metalinguistic view**
3 **Possible worlds semantics**
4 **Similarity**
5 **Comparisons**

1 **Classification issues and familiar logical connectives**

'Counterfactual' conditionals serve to summarize hypothetical reasoning and to justify or explain action and inaction ('I didn't tell you because, had I told you, everyone in the office would have known'). They serve to state particular causal contingencies ('If the battery were flat, the starter would not turn') and various kinds of necessity ('If he were dead, she would be a widow'). Counterfactuals have also been enlisted for philosophical analyses of dispositions ('X is soluble just in case it would dissolve if it were immersed in water'), causality ('Had A not occurred, B would not have occurred'), freedom of action ('I would have acted otherwise if I had so chosen'), knowledge ('If p were false, Mary would not believe that p') and laws of nature, which have been characterized as generalizations that are not merely true but support counterfactuals.

Counterfactuals are commonly contrasted with indicative conditionals (see INDICATIVE CONDITIONALS). The following pair conveys a feeling for the difference:

(1) If Shakespeare hadn't written *Hamlet*, then someone else would have (counterfactual).

(2) If Shakespeare didn't write *Hamlet*, then someone else did (indicative).

Instead of 'counterfactual conditional', sometimes the term 'subjunctive conditional' is used. The former refers to a property of the statement made by uttering a conditional sentence in an appropriate context, the latter refers to the grammatical form of the sentence uttered. Neither label is satisfactory. A problem with 'counterfactual' is that not all assertions of counterfactuals are, or are meant to be, counter to fact, as, for

example, 'If you did the cooking, I would clean up afterwards' (put forward as a suggestion before the cooking has started). 'Subjunctive' is problematic because the grammatical form in question is not the subjunctive in English (where this form is all but extinct) nor in other European languages (where it is widely used). Moreover, 'subjunctive' contrasts with 'indicative', yet indicatives such as (3) below go much more naturally with 'subjunctives' such as (1) than with indicatives such as (2):

(3) If Shakespeare does not write *Hamlet*, then someone else will.

It is surprisingly difficult to characterize the difference between the two kinds of conditional. It is not even agreed at which linguistic level – morphosyntactic, semantic or pragmatic – the distinction is to be drawn. We will content ourselves here with defining counterfactual *sentences* as the likes of (1) above. Our question is then which *statements* these sentences normally serve to express.

In the view of most authors, an analysis must state non-circular and informative truth-conditions. It should also be 'compositional': the truth-conditions of '$A \rightarrow B$' should be a function of the truth-conditions of A and B (see COMPOSITIONALITY). (Read '$A \rightarrow B$' as 'If it were the case that A, then it would be the case that B'.) The material conditional of classical logic and the strict conditional of modal logic both meet these demands, but their truth-conditions are unsuitable. A material conditional is true just in case either its antecedent is false or its consequent true. Since most counterfactuals have false antecedents, they would come out true irrespective of their consequents if they were treated as material conditionals. But many are not true (for example, (1) above); hence the material conditional cannot be the right analysis. A strict conditional is true just in case the corresponding material conditional is necessarily true, or, in possible worlds parlance, just in case in all worlds in which the antecedent is true the consequent is also true. If the material conditional is too easy to satisfy, the strict conditional is too hard. Consider

(4) If fewer people smoked, fewer would contract lung cancer,

which is true if any counterfactual is. Yet there are possible worlds where the antecedent is true and the consequent false, for example, worlds in which lung cancer is caused by eating chocolate. So the strict conditional is too strict. We might confine our attention to less exotic worlds; ones governed by the same natural laws as the actual world. But that still would not do because among the lawful worlds where fewer people smoke there are worlds where more people work in coal mines and the overall incidence of lung cancer is the same. The worlds in which we are interested must resemble the actual world more closely. We imagine that fewer people smoke in these worlds, but that otherwise things are very much as in the actual world. It is this idea of a minimal departure from actuality (or purported actuality) that underlies, in one form or another, all theories of counterfactuals.

2   The metalinguistic view

Nelson Goodman (1954) put forward an influential view in which '$A \rightarrow B$' is true if and only if (1) there is an appropriate subset of all the true initial conditions that, in conjunction with A and the laws of nature, entails B; and (2) there is no other subset of the initial conditions that in the same manner entails not-B. The minimal departure from actuality lies in the appropriate choice of initial conditions. Two problems beset Goodman's proposal: the characterization of the relevant initial conditions and the definition of laws. The second problem is serious, but not as serious as the first.

Apart from being true, the relevant initial conditions must be jointly compatible with A (as long as A is consistent), for otherwise any consequent whatever could be inferred and the corresponding counterfactual would be true. The conditions must also be compatible with not-B, for otherwise A and the laws would play no role in the inference to $B - B$ would follow from the initial conditions by themselves. ('Compatible' statements are ones which do not jointly entail a contradiction.) But compatibility alone is not a strong enough condition. Consider

(5)   If match m had been struck, it would have lighted.

Let O = 'oxygen is present', D = 'm is dry', S = 'm is struck', L = 'm lights' and N = 'If O, D and S, then L' (our natural law). Suppose that we start with the situation of O, D and N being true and that the match has not been struck and has not lighted. O, D and N are jointly compatible with S and jointly compatible with not-L, and together with S they imply L. Therefore (5) should be true.

However, not-L is also true, not-L, O and N are jointly compatible with S and jointly compatible with D; and O, N and not-L together with S imply not-D. Thus

(6)   If match m had been struck, it would not have been dry

should be true as well. This is unacceptable. Hence logical compatibility is not enough. The relevant conditions must be jointly tenable or 'cotenable' with the antecedent. (B is said to be cotenable with A if it is not the case that B would be false if A were true.) In this case, not lighting is compatible with, but not cotenable with, striking, because, had m been struck, it would have lighted; so (5) is true and (6) is not. But now we are caught in a circle or regress because cotenability is defined in terms of counterfactuals, while counterfactuals are defined in terms of cotenability. Goodman saw no way out of this quandary.

3   Possible worlds semantics

In the 1960s, modal logicians turned talk of possible worlds into a powerful analytic tool. Robert Stalnaker and David LEWIS applied it to the analysis of counterfactuals. Both saw counterfactuals as devices to locate the actual world within a certain similarity structure in logical space. The intuition they built on is that '$A \rightarrow B$' is true in the actual world just in case B is true in the most similar A-world(s) (an A-world being a world where A is true). Stalnaker (1968) represents the minimal departure from actuality by a selection function on possible worlds, Lewis (1973) by ordering worlds so that given any two worlds u and v, either u is more similar to the actual world than v, or vice versa, or else u and v are equally similar to the actual world. For Stalnaker, '$A \rightarrow B$' is true if and only if B is true at $f(A, w^*)$, the world picked out by applying the selection function f to antecedent A and the actual world w^*. f selects a world in which A is true and which, intuitively, resembles w^* as closely as the truth of A permits. For Lewis, '$A \rightarrow B$' is true if and only if either there is no A-world, or some A & B-world is more similar to the actual world than any A & not-B-world. Lewis' analysis makes '$A \rightarrow B$' trivially true when A is impossible, which is when there is no A-world. So does Stalnaker's analysis because, for impossible A, f selects 'the impossible world' in which every statement is true.

An argument form is valid if and only if it has no instance with true premise(s) and a false conclusion. The following is an example of an invalid argument:

> If Ronald Reagan had been born a Russian, he would have been a communist.
>
> If he had been a communist, he would have been a traitor.
>
> Therefore, if he had been born a Russian, he would have been a traitor.

The premises seem true, but not the conclusion. The argument is an instance of 'hypothetical syllogism':

$$A \rightarrow B, \quad B \rightarrow C \quad \therefore A \rightarrow C$$

The possible worlds theory explains how hypothetical syllogism can fail to be valid. World c, the closest world where Reagan was a communist, is closer to the actual world than world r, the closest world where he was born a Russian. In c, his career is as we know it, except for that traitorous affiliation. In r, he grows up in Russia, becomes a loyal party member there and never dreams of being president of the USA. So c makes the second premise of the argument true, while r makes the first premise true and the conclusion false.

On the Lewis–Stalnaker analyses, a number of argument forms that are valid for the material and various strict conditionals are invalid. Hypothetical syllogism is only one of them. Others are:

$A \rightarrow B$ $\therefore$ not-$B \rightarrow$ not-A ('contraposition')

$A \rightarrow B$ $\therefore$ $C \rightarrow B$, where C entails A ('strengthening the antecedent')

$A \rightarrow (B \rightarrow C)$ $\therefore$ $(A \& B) \rightarrow C$ and $(A \& B) \rightarrow C$ $\therefore$ $A \rightarrow (B \rightarrow C)$ ('import-export')

For practical purposes, the invalid argument forms can often be replaced by similar valid ones, for example, hypothetical syllogism by

$A \rightarrow B$, $(A \& B) \rightarrow C$ $\therefore$ $A \rightarrow C$.

The distinction between valid and invalid argument forms ought to match natural language usage. Examples like the one about Reagan therefore carry heavy weight. If they were rejected and any of the argument forms in question added to the logics that emerge from the Lewis–Stalnaker analyses, '$\rightarrow$' would collapse into the material conditional. Attacks on the counterexamples are therefore indirect attacks on the core of the analyses. (For more discussion, see Stalnaker 1984.)

4 Similarity

Lewis allows ties in the relative similarity between worlds, as well as no limit to how closely worlds can resemble each other. Stalnaker's theory can be seen as a special case of Lewis' that does not make these allowances. For Stalnaker, there is to be always exactly one most similar antecedent-world. The difference is reflected in a disagreement about the principle of 'conditional excluded middle' which says that '$A \rightarrow B$' and '$A \rightarrow$ not-B' cannot both be false. The principle holds in Stalnaker's view but not in Lewis'. In Lewis' view, there may be, for any $A \& B$-world, an equidistant or closer $A \&$ not-B-world and vice versa, so that both counterfactuals can be false. For Stalnaker, there is exactly one closest A-world in which either B or not-B is true. Consider the pair

If Bizet and Verdi had been compatriots, Bizet would have been Italian.

If Bizet and Verdi had been compatriots, Verdi would have been French.

We hesitate to affirm either. Doesn't this show that Lewis is right? Not necessarily. We also hesitate to deny either of the two, and the best explanation may be that the relevant standard of similarity between worlds has not been made clear, so that we do not know exactly what claims are at issue. Conditional excluded middle holds relative to a given selection function f, but it does not apply to cases where f has not been determined. Any theory of counterfactuals must allow for a good measure of indeterminacy if it is to account for actual usage.

Goodman's theory can be transposed into the possible worlds framework. With the right definition of cotenability, it becomes equivalent to Lewis'. Does Lewis therefore solve Goodman's problem about cotenability? In some sense, yes, because there is no longer a circle in the truth-conditional schema. In another sense, no, because Goodman's worry was less about the abstract form of the analysis than about how particular cotenability judgments can be grounded. For an answer to this question, the notion of relative similarity between worlds is probably too vague.

The relevant notion of similarity cannot be the one we use when we compare ordinary objects. For otherwise we should reject

If Nixon had pushed the button, there would have been a nuclear holocaust,

because among the worlds where Nixon pushes the ominous button those where nothing happens are more similar to ours, in the everyday sense of similarity, than those where the doomsday machinery goes off. But given that there is (or was) such a button, the counterfactual looks true. Lewis suggests that the similarity relation relevant for counterfactuals has the most similar worlds agree with the actual world throughout the past until shortly before the time of the antecedent. Then a small miracle (a deviation from the laws of the actual world, not from those of the world in question) brings about the antecedent, and from then on history evolves in accordance with the laws of the actual world. The proposal has limited scope. It does not apply to 'counterlegals' about what would be the case if this or that law of nature were different. It also does not deal with disjunctive antecedents pertaining to different times. Maximizing agreement throughout the past would naturally lead here to a selection of worlds in which only the disjunct pertaining to the latest time holds. Other authors favour total agreement in laws over miracles of any size. Miracles prevent a counterfactual extrapolation of what the past would have had to have been in order to bring about the antecedent. Yet such 'backtracking' is perfectly intelligible. Jim and Jack quarrelled yesterday and Jack is still furious. If Jim asked a favour of Jack today, Jack would oblige him none the less. For in order that Jim ask, there would have had to have been no quarrel before. The significance of backtracking and Lewis' proposal about similarity remain contested.

5 Comparisons

Metaphysical and other qualms about the possible worlds analyses rekindled an interest in metalinguistic theories in the 1980s. There have also been proposals for an epistemic analysis based on the idea that '$A \to B$' is 'acceptable' with respect to a body of beliefs K just in case K, minimally changed so as to accommodate A, entails B. Formally, most of these theories are equivalent to Lewis' or slight variants thereof, but they avoid the ontological cost of possible worlds. In so far as they do not provide truth-conditions, the epistemic theories have difficulty explaining the role of counterfactuals embedded in truth-conditional constructions such as conjunctions or disjunctions. Moreover, the idea of revising a body of beliefs seems better suited for evaluating indicative conditionals than counterfactuals. For example, if you add to your present beliefs the assumption that Shakespeare did not write *Hamlet* and make the minimal changes necessary to restore consistency, you will infer that someone else must have written the piece because you have no reason to give up your belief in its existence. This yields the correct judgment for the indicative (2) but not for the counterfactual (1). It is not obvious how to adapt procedures of belief change to counterfactuals.

Goodman and many others believed that an analysis of counterfactuals was indispensable for the philosophy of science. Few still share this opinion. The cotenability problem, the indeterminacy of many counterfactuals, and doubts about possible worlds and their similarities have convinced many that counterfactuals do not belong in the ultimate scientific description of the world. In decision and game theory, by contrast, the peculiarity and importance of counterfactual reasoning has only just begun to be appreciated. The solution of decision problems requires answers to questions about situations that, as a result of the very decision at issue, will be counterfactual. Counterfactuals also continue to play an important role in philosophical analyses, and

their use and misuse in daily commerce is largely unhampered by difficulties of interpretation.

See also: LOGICAL AND MATHEMATICAL TERMS, GLOSSARY OF; RELEVANCE LOGIC AND ENTAILMENT; POSSIBLE WORLDS

References and further reading

Edgington, D. (1995) 'On Conditionals', *Mind* 104.414: 235–329. (Gives an excellent overview and synthesis of the various issues surrounding conditionals.)

* Goodman, N. (1954) *Fact, Fiction, and Forecast*, Atlantic Highlands, NJ: Athlone Press. (See §3. A non-technical classic.)

Harper, W.L., Stalnaker, R. and Pearce, G. (eds) (1981) *IFS: Conditionals, Belief, Decision, Chance, and Time*, Dordrecht and Boston, MA: Reidel. (A collection of important papers of varying degrees of technicality.)

Jackson, F. (ed.) (1991) *Conditionals: Oxford Readings in Philosophy*, Oxford: Oxford University Press. (A collection of important papers, including Lewis' on the similarity between worlds.)

* Lewis, D.K. (1973) *Counterfactuals*, Cambridge, MA: Harvard University Press. (See §4. The philosophical discussion demands no technical expertise, but the details of the semantics and the logic get very technical.)

Sanford, D.H. (1989) *If P then Q: Conditionals and the Foundations of Reasoning*, London and New York: Routledge. (An informative historical overview.)

* Stalnaker, R. (1968) 'A Theory of Conditionals', *Studies in Logical Theory: American Philosophical Quarterly Monograph Series* 2: 98–112; repr. in W.L. Harper, R. Stalnaker and G. Pearce (eds) *IFS: Conditionals, Belief, Decision, Chance, and Time*, Dordrecht and Boston, MA: Reidel, 1981, 41–56. (See §4. The first statement of Stalnaker's position; no technical expertise required.)

* —— (1984) *Inquiry*, Cambridge, MA: Bradford Books. (An excellent non-technical discussion of counterfactual and indicative conditionals and their role in reasoning.)

FRANK DÖRING

COURNOT, ANTOINE AUGUSTIN (1801–77)

Cournot is best known for his work in applying mathematical techniques to economic and social affairs and is generally acknowledged to be the founder of econometrics. His work in philosophy, however, is at least as distinguished. His philosophy may be seen as a meditation on continuity and discontinuity, on law and brute empirical fact, which is unassimilable to law. Empiricism is exclusively preoccupied with the latter phenomenon, rationalism with the former. Cournot affirmed the reality of both. His philosophy thus mediates between empiricism (which, when it is consistent, leads on his view to scepticism) and rationalism (which, when it is consistent, loses contact with reality).

Continuity is real because the world is not a chaos; it is a network of events, forming various series, which reveal necessary and determinable relations. But discontinuity is also real, for the order we discern in the various events is not a single order. The series are independent and the points where they intersect cannot be predicted from within the series themselves. Brute contingency is therefore as real as law. Consequently, though the world may be known, it can never be reduced to a single scheme.

Antoine Augustin Cournot was born in the town of Gray, near Dijon. He was raised in his grandmother's house, being especially influenced by an uncle, who was a Jesuit, and by a maiden aunt, whose views were directly opposed to those of the uncle. At an early age, he learned to balance different views, to form his own conclusions, and to keep his peace. He was educated at Gray and at the École Normale in Paris, specializing in mathematics and science. He spent his working life in the university, holding chairs at Lyons and Grenoble. In 1838, he was named Inspector General and in 1854 was appointed as Rector of the Academie at Dijon. Involved in teaching and administration, he continued to work on fundamental problems in many fields. In 1851, he published his most important philosophical work, *Essai sur les fondements de nos connaissances* (*An Essay on the Foundations of Our Knowledge*). Failing eyesight led to his retirement in 1862. But he continued to work at philosophy and in his last years published another important work, *Matérialisme, Vitalisme, Rationalisme* (Materialism, Vitalism and Rationalism).

Like KANT, Cournot held that knowledge is relative. We know the world not in its ultimate nature but in its relations to ourselves. Cournot, however, rejected what he took to be Kant's subjective idealism, denying that the order we discern in nature is the product of our own minds. The central problem in philosophy is precisely to clarify how the mind makes contact with reality through its grasp of order. Empiricism is inadequate for this purpose, for the senses serve neither as the basis nor as the criterion

for knowledge. A simple example will illustrate the point. Consider a law, such as Boyle's law, which is consistent with numerous observations. The observations, however numerous, are a random selection from those that might be made. They represent an element of chance. We accept Boyle's law because we cannot believe that under those chance conditions the law would always be confirmed, unless it represented an order in the gases which is independent of the conditions themselves. It is not the observations which explain the law; it is the law which provides the best explanation for the observations. The point is evident on other grounds. First, observations, being discontinuous, cannot correspond to law, which is continuous; a law holds, whatever the observations. Second, with sufficient ingenuity one can think of many different laws which are consistent with those same observations. Science, according to Cournot, depends on a feeling for order which cannot be quantified and which is akin to the feeling for beauty.

Law in itself, however, is not sufficient for knowledge. The laws of planetary motion will enable us to fix the positions of the planets at any time in the future or the past. But suppose, in the remote past, a comet entered the planetary system, disturbed its arrangement and then disappeared. No trace of this event would appear in our knowledge of astronomy. Consequently, in fixing the positions of the planets, prior to its occurrence, we should be led into systematic error. It is impossible to believe that such events have never occurred. Much in history, therefore, is likely to be not simply unknown but unknowable. In short, scientific rationalism is as inadequate as empiricism.

Cournot anticipated Darwin's theory of evolution (see DARWIN, C. §§2–3). He discussed what is virtually the same theory, in his *Essay*, some eight years before Darwin's work appeared, arguing that it could not provide a comprehensive explanation of the evolutionary process. He agreed that the environment has an important role in selecting organic forms for survival. What the theory cannot explain, however, are the organic forms themselves, which cannot evolve through an accumulation of chance variations. Each organic form is an order, involving an interrelation of its parts. The forms therefore are discontinuous; to get from one to another through continuous variation one would have to pass through stages which do not constitute possible organic forms. Thus a wing which is slightly too weak for flight is entirely useless as a wing. The evolutionary process can be understood only as a phenomenon involving both continuity and discontinuity, order and chance. The pattern of a leaf is definite, so far as its principle veins are concerned, but, in its ultimate ramifications, is so modified by contingent forces that no individual leaf is exactly the same as another. Similarly, the world itself is governed by general laws the detailed fulfilment of which is left to contingent circumstances. Consequently there is no conflict between contingency and finality or purpose. It is through contingency that finality or purpose works. Thus it is not in order to serve the needs of the bee that the flower exists. The flower exists for its own sake, exhibits finality in itself, and simultaneously serves the needs of the bee. For Cournot, the world is a composition, overwhelming in its beauty and complexity, which is executed simultaneously on different planes.

See also: EMPIRICISM; EVOLUTION, THEORY OF; RATIONALISM

List of works

Cournot, A.A. (1838) *Recherches sur les principes mathématique de la théorie des richesses*, Paris; trans. N.I. Bacon, *Researches into the Mathematical Principles of the Theory of Wealth*, London: Economic Classics series, 1938. (His most influential work.)

—— (1861) *Essai sur les fondements de nos connaissances et sur les caracteres de la critique philosophique*, Paris, 2 vols; trans. M.H. Moore, *An Essay on the Foundations of Our Knowledge*, New York: The Liberal Arts Press, 1956. (His main work in philosophy.)

—— (1922) *Traité de l'enchaînement des idées fondamental dans les sciences et dans l'histoire* (Treatise on the Structure of the Fundamental Ideas of Science and History), Paris, 2 vols. (This edition contains a foreword by Lévy-Bruhl.)

—— (1934) *Matérialisme, vitalisme, rationalisme: Études sur l'emploi des données de la science en philosophie* (Materialism, Vitalism, Rationalism: Studies in the Use of Scientific Assumptions in Philosophy), Paris. (A work of comparable importance to the *Essai*.)

References and further reading

Moore, M.H. (1934) 'The Place of A.A. Cournot in the History of Philosophy', *Philosophical Review* 43: 380–401. (The best introduction to Cournot in English.)

Poincaré, H. *et al.* (1905) *Revue de metaphysique et de morale* 13: 3. (An edition devoted entirely to Cournot's work. Contains contributions by leading French thinkers.)

Ruddick, C.T. (1940) 'Cournot's Doctrine of Philo-sophical Probability', *Philosophical Review* 49: 415–23. (Another competent survey.)

H.O. MOUNCE

COUSIN, VICTOR (1792–1867)

French philosopher, educationalist and historian, Victor Cousin is primarily associated with 'Eclecticism' and the history of philosophy, but his work also includes contributions to aesthetics, philosophy of history and political theory. He was a prolific writer and editor, and a significant figure in the development of philosophy as a professional discipline in France.

Victor Cousin was born in Paris, the son of an artisan. His education was funded by a wealthy sponsor, and culminated in the prix d'honneur and study at the École normale, where his formative influences included Laromiguière, Royer-Collard and Maine de Biran. His subsequent academic career at the École normale and the Sorbonne progressed rapidly, his lectures attracting large audiences and much publicity. In the early 1820s Cousin became a victim of the reaction against liberalism; his university lecturers were suspended and the École normale closed. Employed as a private tutor, Cousin worked on the history of philosophy and studied contemporary German idealism. On a visit to Prussia in 1824, French police reports and his association with members of the Carbonari led to his imprisonment. Hegel, with whom Cousin had established a relatively warm association, intervened on his behalf with the authorities, and he was subsequently released. Restored to his University post in 1828, Cousin's lectures received great acclaim and, especially under the July Monarchy, public recognition followed on a grand scale. He became a member of the Académie Française and of the Académie des Sciences Morales et Politiques, a peer of France, Commander of the Légion d'Honneur, member of the Conseil Supérieur de l'Instruction Publique and, briefly, in Theirs' second cabinet, minister for public instruction. From 1830, Cousin increasingly devoted his energies to administrative and educational affairs. Using his position as director of the École normale, he presided over the development of philosophy as a professional (and non-theological) discipline in France. Cousin also influenced the reform of French primary education, publishing reports on the school systems of Prussia, Saxony and Holland. Following the 'tragic experience' of 1848, he fell out of favour, and with the coup d'état of 2 December 1851, was increasingly removed from public life. His last years were spent quietly, surrounded by his books in rooms in the Sorbonne, writing a series of historical studies, mainly portraits of women notables of the seventeenth century. He died in Cannes.

Cousin was probably the best known exponent of Eclecticism, maintaining that schools of philosophical thought (which, for him, fell into four categories) all contained elements of the truth that, once recovered, could be reconciled. Sensationalism, idealism, scepticism and mysticism, he averred, were 'not false but incomplete'. Cousin denied the charge of facile syncretism, insisting that Eclecticism was grounded in a tripartite model of human psychology revealed by observation and experiment, human nature being composed of the three distinct but complementary faculties of sensibility, will and reason. Various philosophical schools were chided for their neglect of one or more of these capacities; thus Cousin charged the epistemology of CONDILLAC (and of his materialist successors) with mistakenly reducing human experience to the passive faculty of sensation.

For Cousin, the reason revealed by psychological introspection was universal and necessary, and by virtue of this impersonal character – and in a manner not always clear to his critics – it provided the conditions for both the existence of, and our knowledge of, humanity and nature. His apparent assertion of the immanentism of reason led to charges of pantheism or even Neoplatonism (see PANTHEISM; NEOPLATONISM). Clerical critics were scarcely reassured when Cousin insisted that, since the masses could not attain philosophical understanding, his system preserved a place for religion as a socially necessary and seemingly inferior (because symbolic) parallel of Eclectic metaphysics.

Art (like religion and philosophy) was a mode in which the infinite, or God, became apparent. It formed an independent sphere in which human nature provided the criteria by which to judge an ideal beauty. For Cousin, the aesthetic hierarchy that resulted was headed by imaginative poetry.

Cousin also discerned a 'manifestation of God' in the historical development of epochs and cultures. History followed a tripartite spiritual progression, as philosophical concerns turned from the infinite, to the finite, to the relation between the two. The resulting Oriental, Greek and Modern worlds were characterized successively by pantheism (and monarchy), polytheism (and democracy), and theism (and constitutionalism). Cousin described this philosophy of history as both speculative and empirical, although critics found it easier to discern evidence of the former than the latter quality. Furthermore, here as elsewhere in Cousin's work, the distinction between his own

opinions and his reproduction of certain themes in contemporary German philosophy is not always apparent.

In rejecting all exclusive doctrines, Eclecticism claimed to have a political parallel in the repudiation of political doctrines and practice based on faction. Cousin was a moderate liberal, committed to constitutional monarchy, the Charter and the interests of the 'juste milieu'. He distinguished a sphere of enforceable individual rights to equal respect and private property, and a subordinate sphere of voluntary duties to protect and promote the wellbeing of others. Cousin attributed a positive role to the state, not least in the provision of moral and educational instruction.

Claiming to recover and reconcile the truth embedded in previous schools of thought, Eclecticism encouraged work in the history of philosophy. Cousin's own efforts in this area were prodigious. His editorial labours included a six-volume edition of Proclus (1820–7); an eleven-volume edition of Descartes (1826); and single-volume editions of Abélard and Maine de Biran. Cousin was also responsible for a thirteen-volume translation of Plato (1822–40). His interpretative studies included works on Aristotle, Locke, the Scottish Enlightenment and Kant, together with an inflammatory contribution to l'affaire Pascal (an acrimonious dispute about editorial and interpretative standards in contemporary Pascal scholarship).

The contrast between Cousin's intellectual hegemony in nineteenth-century France and the subsequent neglect of his work is striking. Although Cousin's historical significance is undeniable, claims for the intrinsic philosophical interest of his work remain muted. Eclecticism strikes many as empty or flawed, while Cousin's role as an interpreter and popularizer of post-Kantian German philosophy largely rests on the unsystematic, and often unacknowledged, incorporation of elements of Schelling and Hegel into his own work. Even Cousin's endeavours in the history of philosophy, although not without interest, and unquestionably important in opening up French philosophy to new influences, frequently fall short of modern scholarly standards.

See also: HEGELIANISM §3; GERMAN IDEALISM

List of works

Cousin, V. (1828) *Cours de l'histoire de la philosophie moderne*, Paris: Pichon & Didier, 3 vols; trans. O.W. Wright as *Course of the History of Modern Philosophy*, New York: D. Appleton, 1852, 2 vols. (Published version of Cousin's lectures, and a nineteenth-century translation of a variant of the text.)

—— (1833) *De l'instruction publique dans quelques pays de l'Allemagne et particulièrement en Prusse*, Paris: Pitois-Levrault, 3rd edn, 1840; trans S. Austin as *Report on the State of Public Instruction in Prussia*, London: E. Wilson, 1834. (Cousin's influential account of German schooling, and an English translation of the first edition.)

—— (1838) *Fragmens philosophiques* (Philosophical Fragments), Paris: Ladrange, 3rd edn, 2 vols. (A collection of Cousin's early writings.)

—— (1848) *Justice et charité*, Paris: Pagnerre; trans. W. Hazlitt as *Justice and Charity*, London: Samson Low, 1858. (A short pamphlet outlining the different demands of justice and charity, and a nineteenth-century translation.)

—— (1851) *Discours politiques avec une introduction sur les principes de la Révolution française et du gouvernment representatif* (Political speeches with an introduction to the principles of the French Revolution and of representative government), Paris: Didier. (Cousin's interpretation of recent French history and his defence of constitutional monarchy.)

—— (1853) *Du vrai, du beau, du bien*, Paris: Didier; trans. O.W. Wright as *The True, the Beautiful and the Good*, Edinburgh: T. & T. Clark, 1854. (Shortened version of Cousin's lectures and a nineteenth-century translation of the third edition.)

—— (1866) *Fragments philosophiques pour servir à l'histoire de la philosophy* (Philosophical fragments to serve as a history of philosophy), Paris: Slatkine, 1970. (Reprint of a five-volume edition of Cousin's lectures.)

References and further reading

Boas, G. (1925) *French Philosophies of the Romantic Period*, Baltimore, MD: Johns Hopkins University Press. (Includes a chapter on Eclecticism.)

Kelly, G.A. (1992) *The Humane Comedy*, Cambridge: Cambridge University Press. (A thoughtful study of French liberalism which includes material on Cousin.)

Ody, H.J. (1953) *Victor Cousin. Ein Legensbild im deutsch-französischen Kulturraum* (Victor Cousin. A study in Franco-German culture), Saarbrucken: West-Ost-Verlag. (A modern German study of Cousin.)

Simon J. (1887) *Victor Cousin*, trans. G. Masson, London: George Routledge & Sons, 1888. (A general work by a student and contemporary of Cousin.)

Spitzer, A.B. (1987) *The French Generation of 1820*, Princeton, NJ: Princeton University Press. (An interesting historical account of Cousin's age cohort.)

Will, F. (1965) *Flumen Historicum: Victor Cousin's Aesthetic and its Sources*, Chapel Hill, NC: University of North Carolina Press. (A study of the Platonic, neoclassical and German Idealist sources of Cousin's aesthetic.)

DAVID LEOPOLD

CRAIG'S INTERPOLATION THEOREM *see* BETH'S THEOREM AND CRAIG'S THEOREM

CRATHORN, WILLIAM (*fl. c.*1330)

An English scholastic a generation younger than William of Ockham, Crathorn's theological writings confront the central metaphysical and epistemological problems of his day. He is of interest largely because of his willingness to pursue the logical implications of his views to the most extreme conclusions. This characteristic makes Crathorn a provocative and idiosyncratic thinker, although not always a coherent one.

Crathorn was a Dominican friar from northern England who lectured at Oxford on Peter Lombard's *Sentences* during the academic years 1330–2 (see LOMBARD, P.). These lectures, his *Quaestiones in primum librum Sententiarum* (Questions on the First Book of the *Sentences*), are our best guide to Crathorn's philosophy. In them he discusses the most controversial philosophical problems of his day, such as divine foreknowledge and human freedom, the ontological status of the Aristotelian categories and the distinction between intuitive and abstractive cognition. His philosophical agenda owes much to WILLIAM OF OCKHAM, but he is not in any sense Ockham's disciple; at almost every juncture Crathorn explicitly rejects Ockham's views.

Crathorn's theory of universals, developed in his *Quaestiones*, is central to his thought. He begins by rejecting competing views, including those of Thomas AQUINAS and John DUNS SCOTUS as well as Ockham's early *fictum* account. Crathorn's treatment of Aquinas, a fellow Dominican, is particularly interesting. After faithfully describing what Aquinas said about universals, Crathorn denies that this was what Aquinas actually meant. Perhaps, Crathorn suggests, Aquinas advanced such a view 'by way of conforming himself to the way men of his time spoke'. Evidently, any pressure that Crathorn may have felt to adhere to the views of his great *confrère* was not enough to force a substantive change in Crathorn's own thought.

At first glance, Crathorn's own theory of universals appears to be a rather ordinary nominalism. A universal, he says, is anything that either causes, resembles or is conventionally predicated of more than one thing. Only words and concepts can be universals in the ordinary sense of the term. Words can be universal in the third way: by convention, they are predicated of more than one thing. Concepts can be universals in either the second or the third way.

It is here that the peculiarity of Crathorn's position emerges. How can concepts either resemble or be conventionally predicated of external things? The first of these may seem less peculiar, since most scholastics spoke of mental representation in terms of similarity. However, Crathorn is unique in holding this doctrine in a completely literal way. For him, the concept of whiteness really is white. He in effect asks how anything could resemble what is white otherwise than by being white (*Quaestiones* q.1, concl.7). But Crathorn does not hold that all concepts are likenesses of this sort; he notices, for instance, that there is nothing in the external world for the general concept of colour to resemble (*Quaestiones* q.11, concl.4). Here Crathorn faces a problem. Whiteness, like colour, is a determinable property, so there is no one shade of white in the external world for the concept 'whiteness' to resemble. In fact, however, Crathorn does find something in the external world for non-determinate concepts like 'colour' to resemble: they resemble (again, literally) the written or spoken words used to express that concept. Thus our concept of colour is literally a likeness of the word 'colour'. Crathorn says that this concept is conventionally predicated of colours inasmuch as it resembles the word 'colour', which is itself conventionally predicated.

Crathorn explicitly holds that these concepts are the immediate objects of intellective cognition. Likewise, sensory impressions are what we immediately perceive, and they, too, literally resemble features of the external world. This leads him to confront the notorious sceptical problem of how we know anything about the external world if all we directly perceive is internal impressions (see SCEPTICISM). At the outset of his commentary, Crathorn develops on this basis a series of ever more serious sceptical conclusions, culminating in the claim that on the basis of our sensory impressions alone we can have no knowledge of the external world. However, Crathorn averts an epistemological crisis by appealing to the knowledge, available to us a priori, that God would not let us be deceived in this way – at least not regularly.

According to his contemporary and rival Robert HOLCOT, Crathorn later publicly lectured on the Bible, but no record of these lectures has been found. Richter (1972) describes a manuscript containing what purports to be quodlibetal questions by Crathorn; some of these questions are from the *Quaestiones*, others not. This additional material, largely philosophical rather than specifically theological, has been neither edited nor studied.

See also: ARISTOTELIANISM, MEDIEVAL; NOMINALISM; UNIVERSALS

List of works

Crathorn, W. (*c*.1330) *Quaestiones in primum librum Sententiarum* (Questions on the First Book of the *Sentences*); ed. F. Hoffmann, *Quästionen zum ersten Sentenzenbuch*, Beiträge zur Geschichte der Philosophie und Theologie des Mittelalters NF29, Münster: Aschendorff, 1988 (Although unevenly edited, this is the only edition of the entire Latin text of the *Quaestiones*. No translations of Crathorn's work have been published.)

References and further reading

Gelber, H. (1984) 'I Cannot Tell a Lie: Hugh Lawton's Critique of Ockham on Mental Language', *Franciscan Studies* 44: 141–79. (Summarizes Crathorn's account of mental language.)

Nuchelmans, G. (1973) *Theories of the Proposition: Ancient and Medieval Conceptions of the Bearers of Truth and Falsity*, North Holland Linguistic Series 8, Amsterdam: North Holland. (A sophisticated discussion of Crathorn's use of the things signified by a proposition as the objects of knowledge.)

Pasnau, R. (1997) *Theories of Cognition in the Later Middle Ages*, New York: Cambridge University Press. (Gives an extended discussion of Crathorn's likeness theory of mental representation (Chapter 3) and his treatment of scepticism (Chapter 7).)

* Richter, V. (1972) 'Handschriftliches zu Crathorn' (Manuscripts Associated with Crathorn), *Zeitschrift für katholische Theologie* 94: 445–9. (A groundbreaking investigation into Crathorn's life and work.)

Schepers, H. (1970) 'Holcot contra dicta Crathorn' (Holcot Against the Claims of Crathorn), *Philosophisches Jahrbuch* 77: 320–54. (Assesses the philosophical dispute between Crathorn and Holcot, with particular reference to their dispute over the objects of knowledge.)

—— (1972) 'Holkot contra dicta Crathorn II' (Holkot Against the Claims of Crathorn II), *Philosophisches Jahrbuch* 79: 106–36. (Assesses the philosophical dispute between Crathorn and Holcot, with particular reference to their dispute over the objects of knowledge.)

Tachau, K. (1988) *Vision and Certitude in the Age of Ockham: Optics, Epistemology and the Foundations of Semantics, 1250–1345*, Leiden: Brill. (Contains a good discussion of Crathorn's epistemology.)

—— (1995) 'Introduction', in R. Holcot, *Seeing the Future Clearly: Questions on Future Contingents*, Toronto, Ont.: Pontifical Institute of Medieval Studies. (Offers the latest and most persuasive reconstruction of Crathorn's career and works.)

Wood, R. (1988) 'Introduction', in Adam de Wodeham, *Tractatus de Indivisibilibus*, Dordrecht: Reidel. (Outlines Crathorn's view that the continuum is composed of a finite number of indivisibles.)

ROBERT PASNAU

CRATYLUS (late 5th/early 4th century BC)

Probably an Athenain, Cratylus was a radical Heraclitean, holding that the world is in constant and total flux. Through this doctrine he had a seminal influence on Plato. Cratylus also, for some time at least, defended the natural correctness of names.

Taking 'Everything is in flux' to be the core of Heraclitus' philosophy (see HERACLITUS §3), Cratylus concluded (Aristotle, Metaphysics 1010a9) that Heraclitus was wrong to deny the possibility of stepping twice into the same river: total flux excludes stepping into the same river even once, and it also implies that one should say nothing. Accordingly, Cratylus 'finally' disavowed speech and merely waggled his finger. In the words of Aristotle (Aristotle, Metaphysics 987a32), the young Plato 'became familiar with Cratylus and with the Heraclitean doctrines that all phenomena are always in a state of flux, and that there is no knowledge about them'. These doctrines, Plato himself later espoused.

Both Plato and Aristotle regularly associate Heraclitus with the constant flux of everything. Some scholars take this to be a misinterpretation of Heraclitus, mediated by Cratylus, with little support in Heraclitus' transmitted words. Yet Aristotle's remarks about Cratylus only make sense on the assumption that Cratylus took himself to be improving the consistency and implications of Heraclitus' own flux doctrine. Total flux excludes everything, including a river, from ever being 'the same'. The inference that nothing has an intrinsic identity if everything is in total flux is drawn by Socrates in Plato's *Theaetetus* (156a–157c) (see PLATO §15). There is also a probable echo of Cratylus' recommendations about refraining from speech when Socrates argues that no names are legitimate that 'make anything stand still'. Plato's dialogue *Cratylus* ends with Socrates arguing that knowledge is impossible 'if everything is changing and nothing persists'. Plato responded to Cratylus by arguing that even if total flux holds true for the phenomenal world, it does not pertain to the stable and everlasting Forms, which are the only genuine objects of knowledge.

As a linguistic naturalist, Cratylus denied that usage has any bearing on the correctness of names. All names that are really names are correct, and their correctness is due to their capacity, irrespective of particular languages, to signify the nature of things. A phonetic item that is inappropriate to the nature of the thing cannot be that thing's name. He rejected therefore the possibility of speaking falsely. In Plato's portrayal Cratylus, as a Heraclitean, approves Socrates' efforts to explain the phonetics of Greek words as natural signifiers of flux even after Socrates has shown that the hypothesis cannot be valid for all names. By the time Cratylus decided to waggle his finger instead of speaking, had he abandoned this linguistic naturalism? Many have thought so, but the supposition is not necessary. Cratylus may have still believed that the only correct names must be names that reveal the nature of things. His final position was probably not the abandonment of this thesis but the inference that things in total flux have no nature that names could reveal.

References and further reading

Allan, D.J. (1954) 'The Problem of Cratylus', *American Journal of Philology* 75: 271–87. (Develops the theory that Cratylus abandoned his linguistic naturalism in later life.)

* Aristotle (*c.* mid fourth century BC) *Metaphysics*, trans in J. Barnes (ed.) *The Complete Works of Aristotle*, Princeton, NJ: Princeton University Press, 1984. (Includes an important survey of earlier thought.)

* Cratylus (late 5th/early 4th century BC) Fragments, in H. Diels and W. Kranz (eds) *Die Fragmente der Vorsokratiker* (Fragments of the Presocratics),

Berlin: Weidemann, 6th edn, 1952, vol. 2: 69–70. (The standard edition of the writings of the Presocratic philosophers; includes Greek texts, with translations in German, of the testimonia from Aristotle and a selection from Plato's *Cratylus*.)

Mouraviev, S.N. (1994) 'Cratylos (d' Athènes?)', in *Dictionnaire des Philosophes Antiques*, ed. R. Goulet, Paris: CRNS Éditions, 1994, vol. 2, 503–10. (Lucid guide to the evidence and modern scholarship.)

* Plato (*c.*380–367 BC) *Theaetetus*, trans. M.J. Levett, revised M. Burnyeat, *The Theaetetus of Plato*, Indianapolis, IN: Hackett Publishing Company, 1990.

—— (*c.*380–367 BC) *Cratylus*, trans. in J. M. Cooper (ed.) *Plato: Complete Works*, Indianapolis: Hachett, 1997. (Our main source on Cratylus, especially his linguistc naturalism.)

A.A. LONG

CREATION AND CONSERVATION, RELIGIOUS DOCTRINE OF

The doctrine of the creation of the universe by God is common to the monotheistic religions of Judaism, Christianity and Islam; reflection on creation has been most extensively developed within the Christian tradition. Creation is by a single supreme God, not a group of deities, and is an 'absolute' creation (creation ex nihilo, 'out of nothing') rather than being either a 'making' out of previously existing material or an 'emanation' (outflow) from God's own nature. Creation, furthermore, is a free act on God's part; he has no 'need' to create but has done so out of love and generosity. He not only created the universe 'in the beginning', but he sustains ('conserves') it by his power at each moment of its existence; without God's support it would instantly collapse into nothingness. It is controversial whether the belief in divine creation receives support from contemporary cosmology, as seen in the 'Big Bang' theory.

1   Creation and polytheism
2   Creator or Demiurge?
3   Creation and emanation
4   Creation as temporal or eternal?
5   Conservation, continuous creation and deism
6   Contemporary issues

1   Creation and polytheism

That the universe has been created by God is one of the most fundamental tenets of Judaism, Christianity and Islam. Creation plays a key role in the theistic worldview and is rich with implications. Every major alternative confronting the theistic worldview has presented a different kind of challenge to the belief in creation. Here we consider several such challenges, taken roughly in historical order.

The biblical belief in divine creation took form in the midst of the conflict between the monotheistic faith of Israel and ancient polytheism. Particularly significant was Mesopotamia, which was both the region from which Abraham came ('Ur of the Chaldees') and the scene of the formative experience of the Babylonian exile. The creation narrative in Genesis 1 has marked parallels with the Babylonian *Enuma Elish* but the theological context and emphasis are vastly different (see Heidel 1951). Here we do not have the numerous gods in their rivalry and occasional strife, but rather the single creator God ordering all things in accordance with his Word. That God simply speaks, with effortless mastery – 'and it was so' – contrasts with the various means of creation in contemporary mythology. There is no trace in Genesis of a struggle in which the earth is fashioned out of the corpse of a slain monster, or of a divine 'begetting' in which some part of the cosmos comes from the deity by sexual generation (or vice versa). Particularly noteworthy is the treatment of the heavenly bodies, which in Babylon as in most ancient cultures were worshipped as divine. Rather than being given divine honours, they are assigned an important but strictly functional role in the creation ('to give light upon the earth, to rule over the day and over the night, and to separate the light from the darkness'); the stars are added almost as an afterthought.

2   Creator or Demiurge?

When the Christians of the second and third centuries began to reflect upon their faith in the light of Greek philosophy, one of the readily available conceptual models for creation was the one presented by PLATO (§16) in the *Timaeus*, where the Demiurge in his beneficence 'desired that all things should come as near as possible to being like himself' (*Timaeus* 29e). But certain deficiencies were evident, as compared with what Christians wished to say about their God. The Demiurge is not ontologically supreme, but clearly is subordinate to the Forms. The good intentions of the Demiurge are limited and often frustrated by the recalcitrant matter with which he must work, but which he had no part in creating. In

695

later Gnostic worldviews, the status of matter becomes even more problematic: it is evil in itself, and the fundamental source of evil in human life. The Demiurge, who has imprisoned humans in mortal bodies, is contrasted with and inferior to the High God, who seeks to liberate them from material contamination (see GNOSTICISM).

In opposition to this, the Church Fathers insisted that God is the supreme source of all concrete existence other than himself: he has created all things *ex nihilo*, 'out of nothing'. The idea is not, of course, that 'nothing' is the name of some negative, peculiarly elusive 'stuff' out of which creation came. On the contrary, creation *ex nihilo* means precisely that there is no pre-existing 'stuff' whatsoever – that things have come to exist solely because of the Word and creative power of God. To be sure, creation *ex nihilo* is not to be found in Genesis; the chaos of Genesis 1: 2 is not said to be created, but is presupposed in the later acts of creation. But creation out of nothing is at least strongly suggested in the New Testament (for example, Romans 4: 17, Hebrews 11: 3), was clearly affirmed by the early Church Fathers (for example, Irenaeus), and has been the consistent teaching of Christian theologians, apart from occasional lapses in the direction of emanationism (see §3). And matter, the physical realm, is not some negative, inhibiting factor which impedes God in the achievement of his purpose; rather, it is itself created by God and is an integral part of the creation which he pronounced 'very good'.

3 Creation and emanation

Among the philosophical options offered by the ancient world, one of the most attractive to Christian thought was the Neoplatonism of Plotinus (see NEOPLATONISM; PLOTINUS §§3–5). This theory emphasized the vast difference between the transcendent God (or 'One') and the mundane realm, and urged human beings, in pursuit of their true good, to seek reunion with the divine source from which they had come. Neoplatonism furnished a rational, philosophical account of the derivation of the world from that source, one that had to be taken seriously by theologians who needed to free themselves from crude, anthropomorphic images of divine 'making'. The idea of evil as 'privation', taken from Neoplatonism, went far towards an understanding of how evil can exist in a world wholly created by God without God's having created evil. Evil, on this account, is not a positive existence in itself, but simply a deficiency in a created being which is, as created, good. And since to be created is as such to be less than God and thus subject to imperfection, there is no occasion for

surprise (or for any reproach to God) in the existence of such imperfections in the creation. Finally, some of the 'emanations' from the One were fairly readily assimilated to the emerging doctrine of the Trinity, thus enhancing both the rational appeal of that doctrine and the attractiveness for Christians of the Neoplatonic philosophy.

For Neoplatonism, the fundamental concept for relating the One (that is, God) to the world is that of emanation. In general, emanationist schemes have the following characteristics:

1 God, or the One, is conceived in terms of extreme transcendence, so remote from everyday reality that he (or it) can be described only in negations.

2 God is linked to the world of everyday experience through a graded series of levels. For Plotinus, these are Mind, then Soul (itself divided into an upper and a lower aspect), and then the individual souls of humans and animals, until finally the lowest level, that of material bodies, is reached.

3 Each lower level in the series is derived from the next higher level through the process of emanation. The lower level 'flows out' from the upper level without diminishing it; illustrative analogies include the outflow of a stream from a spring, and light radiating from a lamp. Thus the lower level is inferior in ontological status, yet shares in the nature of the higher level which produces it.

4 The emanation of a lower level from a higher is eternal and necessary; it follows from the nature of the higher level, and does not involve or depend on a decision of will.

This general scheme was adopted with only minor modifications by some Christians, such as PSEUDO-DIONYSIUS and Johannes Scottus ERIUGENA. It was also taken over by the Muslim philosophers AL-FARABI (§2) and IBN SINA (§5). But it was rejected or severely modified by the major theologians of Judaism (see MAIMONIDES §3), Christianity (for example, Augustine and Aquinas) and Islam (see AL-GHAZALI §3; NEOPLATONISM IN ISLAMIC PHILOSOPHY). In general, the following aspects of emanationism are objectionable from the standpoint of biblical or Qur'anic thought:

1 The extreme separation of the Source from the everyday world, and the refusal to apply ordinary predicates to it, make it problematic to equate it with the personal God of theism. In particular, the need for a series of intermediaries linking God and the world is in conflict with the biblical and Qur'anic witness to the immediate presence and activity of God in all aspects of existence.

2 On the other hand, the nature of the process of

emanation threatens the fundamental distinction between God and creatures that is essential to theism. 'Creation' in this scheme is really not *ex nihilo* but rather *ex deo* – a conclusion which is hardly welcome to any of the monotheistic religions.

3 Finally, the necessary, nonvolitional character of the process of emanation undermines the freedom of God in creation, and thus also the sense of gratitude to God for the generous gift of existence he has bestowed on us and on the world.

The concept of creation, as developed by theistic philosophers and theologians, agrees with emanationism in strongly emphasizing the dependence of creatures on God. But it insists on a fundamental ontological distinction between the creator and the creatures: creation is *by* God, but not *out of* God. God bestows on creatures a being that is their own and not his, though it is always dependent upon him. Furthermore, it is insisted that creation is a free and gratuitous act on God's part: there was and is no necessity for God to create a world. To this it might be objected that, since it is obviously better for there to be a universe than for there not to be one, a wise and good God must of necessity have created a world. The answer to this objection is rather startling: God is infinitely greater than creatures, so the value of God plus the entire creation is no greater than the value of God by himself. (Adding a finite quantity, no matter how large, to infinity still leaves you with just infinity, not 'infinity plus'.)

4 Creation as temporal or eternal?

One further question raised by emanationism is not answered by the considerations discussed above. Is creation temporal or eternal? Does the universe have a temporal beginning or is it beginningless? This question was especially acute for medieval thinkers because it was claimed that Aristotle had demonstrated the eternity of the world; on the other hand, the Scriptures seemed to point definitely towards a temporal beginning (see ETERNITY OF THE WORLD, MEDIEVAL VIEWS OF). In response to this, Maimonides pointed out that even if the eternity of the world had been demonstrated, it would be perfectly possible to give a figurative interpretation of those biblical texts that seem to imply a temporal beginning. Aquinas and other Christian writers had less freedom, because the Fourth Lateran Council (1215) had defined it as a doctrine of faith that the universe had a beginning in time.

The predominant view at the time among both Christians (such as BONAVENTURE (§5)) and ortho-

dox Muslims was that, contrary to the claims of the Aristotelians, the temporal finitude of the universe could be conclusively demonstrated. This was argued on the basis of certain problems with the idea of an 'actual' (already realized) infinity, such as seems to be involved in the concept of an infinite past. For example: if the past is infinite, then there has occurred a time which was an infinite number of years prior to the present. But if this were so, it would be impossible that, through the passing of years one by one, an infinite number would be traversed and we would find ourselves in the present. So if the past were infinite, the present would never have been reached, which is absurd. (This problem does not arise for an infinite future, because future eternity, unlike past eternity, is only a 'potential' infinity; there will never come a future time separated from the present by an infinite number of years.)

The response of both Maimonides and Aquinas at this point is that neither the finitude nor the infinity of the past has been demonstrated; philosophically, the question remains open. (The answer given to the argument described above was that, even if the past is infinite, it still is not the case that there exists some time which occurred an infinite number of years before the present. Any given time in the past preceded the present by only a finite number of years – and was itself preceded by an already infinite past.) Both Maimonides and Aquinas, then, were free to affirm on the basis of Scripture that the past is finite and that the world has a temporal beginning.

It is important to see, however, that the question of the world's eternity is not settled by the considerations discussed in §3 above. For suppose that, contrary to the conclusion of Maimonides and Aquinas, the world does indeed have an infinite, beginningless past. It could still be said that the universe is created *ex nihilo*, in the sense that it has no existence except that which is wholly dependent on the will and power of God. Its relation to God would then be just what theists suppose the relation to God of the actual universe to be, at every moment subsequent to the first. It could, furthermore, still be the case that God is entirely free in creating the universe – that it is simply by God's free decision that there is eternally a universe distinct from God, rather than God existing alone in self-sufficient perfection.

That is not to say that the issue of a temporal creation is religiously indifferent; there are, after all, the biblical and Qur'anic texts that seem to imply such a beginning. It is clear, furthermore, that the notion of an eternal creation strongly suggests, even if it does not logically imply, some sort of necessity for the creation process – either because God has some kind of need for a creation, or because the universe is produced from the divine nature by some sort of necessity. A belief in the eternity of creation tends towards a denial of the freedom of God in creation, even if it does not force us to that conclusion.

5   Conservation, continuous creation and deism

Belief in God as creator has almost always involved the affirmation that God not only produced the universe in the beginning, but sustains it in being from moment to moment. The New Testament says of Christ that 'in him all things hold together' (Colossians 1: 17), and describes him as 'sustaining all things by his powerful word' (Hebrews 1: 3). And the Psalms are pervaded by the sense of the immediate dependence of the creatures on their creator: 'When thou sendest forth thy Spirit, they are created; and thou renewest the face of the ground' (Psalms 104: 30). So theistic philosophers and theologians have affirmed the divine conservation of creatures, claiming that no creature exists at any moment unless God actively sustains its existence at that moment; without this support it would instantly vanish into nothingness.

There has been debate, however, about the use of the phrase 'continuous creation' to describe this process. Descartes wrote that 'the same power and action are needed to preserve anything at each individual moment of its duration as would be required to create that thing anew if it were not yet in existence' ([1641] 1984: 33). But this does not seem quite correct. No doubt it is true that a being already in existence is as unable to exist without divine power as one which newly comes into existence this very moment. But it is not strictly true that God does exactly the same thing in the two cases. When he newly creates something *ex nihilo*, he brings into existence something that previously did not exist, either as a whole or in its several parts. When he conserves some being, then he sustains the continued existence of a being that is already in existence. And this point is crucial for countering the argument for occasionalism (see OCCASIONALISM). When God newly creates a being *ex nihilo*, then God alone must determine all that being's characteristics; there is nothing else that might perform this task. But when God conserves a being that is already in existence, then the previous state and causal powers of that being can play a part – often a large part – in determining the being's state and characteristics at the time in question.

So it does not seem to be the case that God does exactly the same thing when he creates something anew as when he conserves it in existence. The expression 'continuous creation' might still be used as a dramatic way of calling attention to the fact that

an already existing being has no more power to maintain itself in existence than a nonexistent and merely possible being has to bring itself into existence. But a straightforward equating of creation with conservation seems to be ruled out.

It should be noted here that most medieval theologians held that, in addition to conserving the world in existence, God 'concurs' in each and every instance of creaturely action. This concurrence is not mere permission, but is rather an active causal contribution by God in cooperation with the creaturely action, which apart from this cannot bring about its result. This doctrine of divine *concursus* has not played a major role in recent discussions of creation; it remains to be seen whether a convincing case can be made for it.

The deists rejected the doctrine of conservation, asking in effect why God could not create beings which, once created, could go on about their business without further direct help from him (see DEISM). But the religious case for divine conservation is compelling, even aside from scriptural texts. If God did not act to conserve creatures in existence, then his present action in the world would be limited to special miraculous acts of divine intervention – a highly undesirable result, even if one has no objection to the idea of miracle as such. The religious sense of dependence upon God and of being sustained by God, an important part of the religious life for a great many believers, would have to be either rejected as illusory or radically reinterpreted. (It could hardly be maintained that we are able to have, now, an experience of 'dependence' on a long-ago act of initial creation.) It could still be said that we are 'dependent' on God in the sense that he could annihilate us at any moment – but that is precisely the sense in which hostages become dependent upon terrorists to spare their lives; it is hardly of much use to religion. To be sure, it may be that none of these arguments would have persuaded the deists, who seem to have felt that although religion is somehow necessary, the course of prudence is to get along with as little of it as one can manage.

6   Contemporary issues

For most of the nineteenth and twentieth centuries, such metaphysical reflections as these were out of fashion, and various other issues came to the fore. A problem of some importance in the mid twentieth century was the question of the meaningfulness and intelligibility of the doctrine of creation. It was noted quite correctly that, once we get beyond crude anthropomorphic ideas of 'making', the terms used in speaking of creation are employed in ways far removed from their familiar uses. The question, then, is whether the ordinary meaning of the terms has not been eroded away without remainder, and without anything else having been put in its place. There are indeed analogies that can be adduced here: our experience of the instability of many things (for example, of a home constructed in an earthquake zone) may illuminate the 'ontological instability' of things and thus their dependence upon God. And we speak of God as 'planning' for the world by analogy with our own planning for future contingencies. But the instabilities we are aware of are instabilities *within the world*, remediable by ordinary, intra-worldly means; our experience of planning presupposes all sorts of limitations on our part which are explicitly excluded in the case of God. So the meaning which our analogies seem to provide may well prove to be illusory.

It is fair to say that this sort of objection became progressively less compelling during the second half of the twentieth century. To speak about the doctrine of creation with some accuracy it is indeed necessary to speak in explicitly metaphysical terms – something which philosophers have increasingly found themselves willing and able to do (for example, Richard Swinburne and Alvin Plantinga). The analogies with ordinary experience are undoubtedly important in enabling us to grasp the significance of the doctrine. But the analogies are abused if we demand that the very same relation which obtains between God and creatures should be exemplified in the relations between creatures.

Most contemporary discussion of creation concerns its relation to natural science. Much of this discussion is over points in contention between the worldviews of theism and scientific naturalism, and cannot be considered here. But there are two points at which science impinges directly on traditional thinking about creation: evolutionary biology, and cosmology.

There is a broad consensus among theologians, including most conservative theologians, that biological evolution as such poses no threat to the doctrine of creation. There is, however, a need to contest philosophical interpretations of evolution in terms of scientific naturalism, interpretations which are sometimes propounded by leading scientists. There is also a need to rethink certain areas of theology (especially theological anthropology) in the light of the acceptance of human evolution. There are differences among theologians over the extent to which evolution should be incorporated into positive theological teaching. Neo-orthodox theologians such as Karl Barth and Emil Brunner accepted evolution, but it was peripheral to their major theological concerns.

Teilhard de Chardin, on the other hand, sought to establish a strong positive relationship between Christian hope and evolutionary optimism.

An area of particular interest is the relationship between the doctrine of creation and scientific cosmology (see GOD, ARGUMENTS FOR THE EXISTENCE OF §5; RELIGION AND SCIENCE §6). Here theology seems to be in the unusual position that it cannot be harmed by science but might be in a position to benefit from it. The key theological point at issue is the age of the universe as finite or infinite. It seems theology has nothing to fear from cosmology on this point. There is for one thing the possibility (though not a favoured possibility) for theology to accept an eternal universe (see §4 above). On the other hand, it seems that it would not be possible for science to establish that the universe is infinitely old: what might a scientific proof of that look like? If science were to find no evidence for a 'beginning', then at worst theology would be back in the same position as that accepted by Aquinas – able to say that reason cannot settle the issue, but that revelation informs us of a temporal creation. In fact, however, the triumph of 'Big Bang' cosmology over the 'steady state' theory (with additional help from the second law of thermodynamics) seems to provide substantial support for the idea of a temporal origin of the universe. It would be unwise for theists to cite these scientific developments as 'proof' of an absolute beginning, and thus of the need for a First Cause. Such a claim would underestimate the ingenuity of scientists, who continue to produce scenarios which permit an eternal universe. (To be sure, the scenarios available at present are highly speculative, and some of them may be motivated as much by aversion to the idea of an absolute beginning, and therefore a possible creation, as by empirical data.) But one may at least conclude, with Ernan McMullin, that 'if the universe began in time through the act of a Creator, from our vantage point it would look something like the Big Bang that cosmologists are now talking about' (1981: 39).

See also: ETERNITY; FREEDOM, DIVINE; GOD, CONCEPTS OF; MOTOORI NORINAGA; MIRACLES; PANTHEISM; TIAN

References and further reading

Burrell, D.B. (1993) *Freedom and Creation in Three Traditions*, Notre Dame, IN: University of Notre Dame Press. (Comparative analysis of medieval thought on freedom and creation in Judaism, Christianity and Islam.)

Clifford, R.J. (1988) 'Creation in the Hebrew Bible', in *Physics, Philosophy, and Theology: A Common*

Quest for Understanding, Vatican City State: Vatican Observatory, 151–70. (Concise analysis of the teaching of the Hebrew Bible on creation.)

Craig, W.L. and Smith, Q. (1993) *Theism, Atheism, and Big Bang Cosmology*, Oxford: Clarendon Press. (Debate on the implications of Big Bang cosmology with a finite past for the universe.)

* Descartes, R. (1641) *Meditations on First Philosophy*, trans. J. Cottingham, R. Stoothoff and D. Murdoch, *The Philosophical Writings of Descartes*, vol. 2, Cambridge: Cambridge University Press, 1984. (The passage cited in §5 is found in Meditation III.)

Drees, W.B. (1990) *Beyond the Big Bang: Quantum Cosmologies and God*, La Salle, IL: Open Court. (Excellent, accessible summary of the state of cosmology as of the publication date; somewhat limited in philosophical analysis.)

Flew, A. and MacKinnon, D.M. (1955) 'Creation', in A. Flew and A. MacIntyre (eds) *New Essays in Philosophical Theology*, London: Macmillan, 170–86. (Contains a good presentation by Flew of the doubts about the intelligibility of creation language.)

Freddoso, A.J. (1988) 'Medieval Aristotelianism and the Case against Secondary Causation in Nature', in T.V. Morris (ed.) *Divine and Human Action: Essays in the Metaphysics of Theism*, Ithaca, NY, and London: Cornell University Press, 74–118. (Metaphysical analysis of occasionalism, the 'third alternative' to concurrentism and mere conservationism.)

—— (1991) 'God's General Concurrence with Secondary Causes: Why Conservation is not Enough', *Philosophical Perspectives* 5: 553–85. (Analysis of the positions of concurrentism and mere conservationism, with Suarez's arguments for concurrentism.)

—— (1994) 'God's General Concurrence with Secondary Causes: Pitfalls and Prospects', *American Catholic Philosophical Quarterly* 68 (2): 131–56. (Analyses concurrentism and defends it against the arguments of Durandus.)

* Heidel, A. (trans. and ed.) (1951) *The Babylonian Genesis: The Story of Creation*, Chicago, IL: University of Chicago Press, 2nd edn. (Contains *Enuma Elish* and other Babylonian creation narratives, with a discussion of Old Testament parallels.)

Kretzmann, N. (1985) 'Ockham and the Creation of the Beginningless World', *Franciscan Studies*, vol. 45, annual XXIII: 1–31. (Analyses Ockham's responses to the arguments claiming to prove a temporal creation.)

Kvanvig, J.L. and McCann, H.J. (1988) 'Divine Conservation and the Persistence of the World', in T.V. Morris (ed.) *Divine and Human Action: Essays in the Metaphysics of Theism*, Ithaca, NY, and London: Cornell University Press, 13–49. (Argues that the persistence of the world in being requires a divine cause.)

* McMullin, E. (1981) 'How Should Cosmology Relate to Theology?' in A.J. Peacocke (ed.) *The Sciences and Theology in the Twentieth Century*, Notre Dame, IN: University of Notre Dame Press, 17–57. (An accurate and very cautious assessment of the relationship between cosmology and theology.)

—— (ed.) (1985) *Evolution and Creation*, Notre Dame, IN: University of Notre Dame Press. (Several essays deal with the relationship of evolution to theology; the editor's introduction provides a valuable historical summary.)

* Plato (*c.*366–360 BC) *Timaeus*, trans. F.M. Cornford, Indianapolis, IN: Library of Liberal Arts, 1959. (Plato's 'likely story' concerning the origin and structure of the cosmos.)

Quinn, P.L. (1988) 'Divine Conservation, Secondary Causes, and Occasionalism', in T.V. Morris (ed.) *Divine and Human Action: Essays in the Metaphysics of Theism*, Ithaca, NY, and London: Cornell University Press, 50–73. (Argues for mere conservationism, and refutes the charge that the doctrine of divine conservation leads to occasionalism.)

Westermann, C. (1971) *Schöpfung*, Stuttgart: Kreuz-Verlag; trans. J.J. Scullion, *Creation*, Philadelphia, PA: Fortress Press, 1974. (Interesting discussion of the biblical narratives of creation and Fall in the light of ancient Near-Eastern parallels.)

WILLIAM HASKER

CRESCAS, HASDAI
(*c.*1340–1410)

During the most tragic period of Spanish-Jewish history (1391–1492), Hasdai Crescas wrote a philosophical-theological treatise, Or Adonai (Light of the Lord), *seeking to define and fortify the Jewish faith in the face of constant Christian attack. It is a polemical book, aiming to defend a traditional version of Judaism by criticizing the Aristotelian formulations proposed by such Jewish philosophers as Moses Maimonides and Levi ben Gershom (Gersonides). Since they relied on Aristotelian physics, Crescas began his reconstruction of Jewish theology with a demolition of Aristotle's natural philosophy. He then turned to metaphysics in general and Jewish theology in particular. His constructive work was especially novel in its treatment of human choice, divine omniscience and creation. Aiming to defend traditional Jewish ideas, Crescas in the end broached some of the most radical challenges to be found within the medieval philosophical tradition, including the proposal that there might be numerous worlds other than our own, infinite magnitudes, and a void, or vacuum.*

1 Crescas' motives
2 Critique of Aristotle
3 Divine omniscience and human choice
4 Creation
5 Plurality of worlds

1 Crescas' motives

Perhaps the most original and acute of all medieval Jewish philosophers, Hasdai Crescas lived through one of the most difficult periods of Jewish history. From 1391 to 1492, Spanish Jewry, the traditional repository of Jewish philosophy, suffered one defeat after another, culminating in the expulsion of the Jews who remained loyal to their faith in 1492. As chief rabbi of Aragonese Jewry, Crescas was continually called upon to defend both Jews and Judaism against the onslaughts of the Spanish clergy and populace. It is in this context that one must understand the purpose, tone and content of his major work, *Or Adonai* (1410), and his polemical tract, *Bittul 'Iqqarei ha-Notzrim* (Refutation of Christian Principles) (1398). The former work is the focus of our attention here, but it is noteworthy that the latter employs philosophical arguments throughout. One of its main theses is that core Christian dogmas are incompatible with reason.

One of the main threats to Judaism, Crescas believed, was internal: an 'alien woman', namely Aristotelian philosophy, had seduced Jewish thinkers and their followers into a misguided conception of Judaism, which made it easy for the Christians to convert Jews. To defend the Judaism he deemed authentic, Crescas proposed to banish the foreign influence by exposing its pretensions and demolishing its foundations. To this end, he was bold enough to focus his attack on the chief conveyer of the Aristotelian philosophy that had been imported into the sacred domain of the Torah, Moses MAIMONIDES, whose Jewish creed was rooted in the conceptual framework of Aristotelian natural philosophy and metaphysics. *Or Adonai* constructs a new creed on very different conceptual foundations. In elaborating his views, Crescas is concerned to show that the authentic Jewish position is not to be formulated in or defended by Aristotelian language or arguments. Nevertheless, his method is philosophical throughout: to refute the Aristotelians he employs rigorous argumentation and fine analysis worthy of the best of his adversaries.

The credal structure of Judaism, Crescas claimed, is a fourfold system whose foundational axioms are the 'root beliefs' in the existence, unity and incorporeality of God. These three doctrines define religion generically, but only minimally. A higher tier is constituted by the ideas that make up a revealed religion, such as divine omniscience and prophecy. On the 'third floor' are the beliefs taught by the religion Crescas takes to be the true revealed religion – Judaism. These include the creation of the world, the primacy of Mosaic prophecy, and the coming of the messiah. Acceptance of these doctrines is obligatory for all Jews, but their truth is not entailed in the general concept of a revealed religion. Finally, in the 'attic' are views upheld by various Jewish sages which have no binding force, although one may believe in them. Examples include the plurality of universes, the existence of demons, and theories about the nature of the First Mover.

2 Critique of Aristotle

For the Aristotelian philosopher or theologian, metaphysics in general and theology in particular rest on natural philosophy. Thus Crescas' reconstruction of Jewish theology begins with a radical critique of Aristotelian physics. Maimonides had prefaced his exposition of the arguments of the Aristotelian school for the existence, unity and incorporeality of God by laying down twenty-six principles of Aristotelian natural philosophy. Although Maimonides himself had parted company with the Aristotelian tradition, he had explicitly criticized in detail only one of the Aristotelian philosophers' first premises that he listed, the eternity of the cosmos, treating the rest, by and large, as useful cosmological axioms. Crescas targets the premises of the Aristotelian philosophers at large, aiming, through them, at what he conceives as unreasonable and damaging admissions of Aristotelian views by Maimonides.

The theological thrust of Crescas' 'scientific innovations' can be seen in his critique of several of the standard medieval proofs for the existence of God. Many of these arguments presuppose the impossibility of an actual infinity, an impossibility that Aristotle believed he had proved. There were arguments, for example, which assumed that there cannot be an infinite series of moving causes, so that there must be an Unmoved Mover as the ultimate cause of motion. Or, it was assumed, there cannot be an infinite series of causes and effects existing simultaneously, so there must be a First Cause to produce and sustain the whole series.

But why, Crescas asks, can there not be an actual infinity? After exposing flaws in Aristotle's arguments, Crescas affirms not only the possibility of an actual infinity but its existence. Space, he argues, the vacuum, is actually infinite. Here Crescas compounds his critique by identifying the void as infinite. For Aristotle had denied not only the possibility of an actual infinite, but also the possibility of a vacuum or void, which had seemed to him to involve a variety of absurd implications.

Aristotle and his followers had faced a vexing problem when asked what lies beyond their finite world. Aristotle's answer was that there is nothing – no vacuum, no space, no other world. In effect, he rejected even the question. To Crescas this seemed arbitrary at best. His own answer seemed more sensible: that there is infinite space beyond our world, extension, in which there is a real possibility of other worlds.

Having opened the door to the actual infinite, Crescas begins to open other doors as well: perhaps there is an infinite number of actual individuals or an infinitely large body. None of these hypotheses is absurd or improbable. Crescas' hospitality to an actual infinite was appreciated by Spinoza, who became a powerful advocate in behalf of an idea once widely taken by philosophers to be absurd on the face of it (see SPINOZA, B. DE §3).

3 Divine omniscience and human choice

The second part of Crescas' treatise discusses the theological dogmas presupposed by any revealed religion. His most penetrating discussions are found in his treatment of divine omniscience and human choice. He analyses these separately, but they can be discussed together since they are closely related in most medieval treatments. Like most medievals, Crescas defends a strong version of divine omniscience: God knows all truths. Many ancient and medieval thinkers had thought God's knowledge of future contingent facts problematic if not impossible. Gersonides (1288–1344), Crescas' 'philosophical litigant', had concluded that God does not know the future doings of human beings as individual events, but only the general laws pertaining to them. Crescas deems this not just false but heretical. After all, if God did not know Moses as an individual, how could God speak to him and give him the Torah? For Crescas, Gersonides' doctrine makes nonsense of the very idea of prophecy and revelation.

Crescas does not rest his case on revelation. He analyses each of Gersonides' arguments and finds them all invalid. He argues, for example, that even if it were true that temporal facts are known by temporal beings through sense-perception, it does not follow that this is the only way they are knowable. Why could a nontemporal being not know them in some nontemporal way? Since everyone agrees that God is eternal, it should also be admitted that God knows everything, including facts about the future, eternally, that is, timelessly. Strictly, there is no future or past to God. Crescas' solution is similar to that reached by many late ancient and medieval thinkers, such as Proclus, Boethius and Aquinas, but he was the first to propose it in the Jewish philosophical literature.

Now if God knows future contingents timelessly, can we still say that our choices are themselves contingent, or free? If not, all legal and moral obligations would be pointless. Crescas' response to this ancient dilemma, as he himself realized, is more novel and daring than his answer to the question about divine knowledge. He declares boldly that in one sense, in so far as they have causes, our choices and the actions based upon them are determined and necessary.

Crescas is an explicit and unabashed defender of causal determinism, not only in nature at large but in human behaviour specifically. If our choice to give charity were uncaused, it would be inexplicable and groundless. But should such an event be the subject of praise and reward? Crescas' answer is that, even though the event is necessary in so far as it is caused, it is contingent as such, that is, considered in itself, for it is a logically possible state of affairs, not a necessary truth like the theorems of logic or mathematics. My act of charity has a cause, and in this sense is determined and necessary, but it is still free, since it is, in itself, merely a logically contingent state of affairs. As long as I am not subject to external compulsion, such that I feel forced, an action can be deemed voluntary. So what I do tomorrow remains contingent, despite God's eternal knowledge. Indeed, in different circumstances I could have acted otherwise. And God, in that case, would eternally have known otherwise.

4 Creation

In Part Three of *Or Adonai*, Crescas discusses those beliefs that are not essential to all revealed religions but are taught by the one revealed religion that Crescas takes to be true, that of the Torah. He begins by discussing creation, which is the first belief explained in the Torah. By Crescas' time, creation had become one of the most controversial issues in philosophy. Three theories were widely debated: (1) the eternalism of Aristotle and his followers; (2) the theory of *formatio mundi* attributed to Plato, creation understood as the formation of an orderly cosmos out of formless matter; and (3) the doctrine by now most generally regarded as orthodox among Jews, Christians and Muslims, *creatio ex nihilo* (see CREATION AND CONSERVATION, RELIGIOUS DOCTRINE OF; ETERNITY OF THE WORLD, MEDIEVAL VIEWS OF).

Crescas focuses chiefly on Gersonides' modified version of the second theory and Maimonides' support of the third. He rejects his two predecessors' rebuttals of Aristotle's arguments in favour of eternity and against creation, finding them either invalid or dependent on theorems of Aristotelian physics which were shown in Part One of *Or Adonai* to be false or unproved. As in his treatment of divine omniscience, Crescas is especially incensed by Gersonides, whose defence of *formatio mundi* he believes to be a misreading of the Torah and demonstrably false. Gersonides had relied heavily on the claim that *ex nihilo* creation implies the existence of a vacuum before creation and its persistence outside the world even afterwards. But, as we have seen, Crescas is prepared to defend the possibility of a vacuum. Besides, Gersonides' argument is unsound: in creating the universe God created its spatial dimensions along with it; no empty space was needed before creation.

After disposing of the arguments of Gersonides and Maimonides, Crescas presents his own solution, redefining *ex nihilo* creation to refer to the world's causal dependence on God. No 'prior' matter is needed. Indeed, the whole formulation is temporally neutral: the universe could be eternal albeit created, that is, eternally dependent upon God. A similar view had been defended by the Muslim Neoplatonists AL-FARABI and Avicenna (see IBN SINA). Crescas understands that dependence on their approach might offend some of his readers, so he offers a weaker, more traditional version of the idea: instead of one eternally existing world, an infinite series of worlds might be created by God. Our world, in that case, did have a definite temporal beginning, as tradition teaches, but God's creativity continues at all times. Both doctrines preserve the important dogma of divine omnipotence.

5 Plurality of worlds

The final part of Crescas' treatise contains thirteen short disquisitions on various topics about which there is no unanimity among the sages, but where plausible arguments have been adduced in favour of diverse positions. Since these doctrines have no dogmatic status, a Jew is free to affirm or deny them, or to withhold judgment.

The first of these questions is whether this world could be destroyed and replaced. Is ours only one of a series of successive created universes? This was a question of considerable interest to Christian theologians in the fourteenth century. Few Jewish philosophers had devoted much discussion to the question, although there are hints of the idea in the Rabbinic literature, and Maimonides and Gersonides had defended the indestructibility of our universe. Crescas finds none of the arguments for or against a succession of worlds compelling. But his previous suggestion that God can create an infinite series of worlds shows his attraction to this view. It is quite possible, he says, that God could destroy this world and create a more perfect one. But if so, Crescas insists, God would destroy the earth only; the heavenly bodies are everlasting. It remains in doubt whether this last is consistent with Crescas' views on eternal creation.

In the second question Crescas wonders whether there could be a plurality of coexisting worlds. Gersonides, following Aristotle, had defended the uniqueness of the cosmos: one God, one world. Crescas is not so sure. He seems to lean towards the view that other worlds might coexist with ours. Aristotle had urged (among other arguments) that since each of the physical elements has a natural place towards which it moves if nothing impedes it (such as fire, which naturally moves upwards towards the outermost region of the earth) then if there were another world, fire *there* would move towards the outermost region in *our* world. Since this seems untenable, our world must contain all the matter there is, and no other universe is possible. Crescas rejects this argument. Even if the theory of natural places is true – and Crescas denies it – the fire in another world would move towards the outermost region of *that* world, not ours. The doctrine of natural places, if true, must be relativized.

There is a certain unintended irony in Crescas' enterprise. He set out to defend a traditional Jewish theology, purified of Aristotelian intrusions. Yet the conclusions he reaches are novel, sometimes radical. He rejects the Aristotelian cosmology that had served for centuries as the backdrop for medieval philosophical speculations. He redefines key theological ideas. Even his pupil, Joseph Albo, criticized and rejected Crescas' deterministic account of choice. And his ill-concealed sympathy for 'eternal creation' is hardly unanimously hailed among later thinkers. The (somewhat Epicurean sounding) proposals about an infinite void and multiple worlds fell largely upon deaf ears, until, in the aftermath of the modern discrediting of the medieval worldview, Crescas' ideas found a sympathetic reader in Spinoza.

See also: ARISTOTLE §§10, 16; ARISTOTELIANISM, MEDIEVAL; GERSONIDES; SPINOZA, B. DE

List of works

Crescas, H. (1398) *Bittul 'Iqqarei ha-Notzrim* (Refutation of Christian Principles), trans. D.J. Lasker, *The Refutation of Christian Principles by Hasdai Crescas*, Albany, NY: State University of New York Press, 1992. (Crescas' philosophical critique of the basic dogmas of Christianity.)

—— (1410) *Or Adonai* (Light of the Lord), ed. S. Fischer, Jerusalem: Sifrei Ramot, 1990; 'Choice' (Book 2: 5), trans. S. Feldman, in J.D. Bleich (ed.) *With Perfect Faith*, New York: Ktav, 1983, 472–91; 'Resurrection and Immortality' (Book 3: 1, part 2), trans. W. Harvey, in Bleich (ed.), 663–80; 'Divine Knowledge' (Book 2:1), trans. W. Harvey, in Bleich (ed.), 466–71. (Crescas' systematic philosophical reconstruction of Jewish theology, based upon a radical critique of Aristotelian philosophy and physics.)

References and further reading

Feldman, S. (1980) 'The Theory of Eternal Creation in Hasdai Crescas and Some of his Predecessors', *Viator* 11: 289–320. (Exposition of Crescas' cosmology in its historical-philosophical context.)

—— (1982) 'Crescas' Theological Determinism', *Da'at* 9: 3–28. (Philosophical critique of Crescas' doctrine of divine omniscience.)

—— (1984) 'A Debate Concerning Determinism in Late Medieval Jewish Philosophy', *Proceedings of the American Academy for Jewish Research* 51: 15–54. (A philosophical analysis and critique of Crescas' determinism using material from Crescas' successors.)

Harvey, W. (1973) 'Hasdai Crescas' Critique of the Theory of the Acquired Intellect', unpublished Ph.D. dissertation, Columbia University, New York. (Contains several translations from Crescas, and an excellent analysis of some major themes in his philosophy.)

Kellner, M. (1986) *Dogma in Medieval Jewish Thought*, Oxford: Oxford University Press. (Includes a useful study of Crescas' creed.)

Pines, S. (1967) *Scholasticism After Thomas Aquinas and the Teachings of Hasdai Crescas and His Predecessors*, Jerusalem: Israel Academy of Sciences and Humanities. (Seeks to show the influence of Christian thought on Crescas and some of his predecessors.)

Ravitzky, A. (1988) *Crescas' Sermon on the Passover and Studies in his Philosophy*, Jerusalem: Israel Academy of Sciences and Humanities. (Detailed historical-literary analysis of the development of Crescas' views on determinism and miracles.)

Rudavsky, T. (1990) 'The Theory of Time in Maimonides and Crescas', *Maimonidean Studies* 1: 143–62. (Challenging, but perceptive and stimulating.)

Schweid, E. (1970) 'The Religious Philosophy of Hasdai Crescas', in *Or Adonai*, Jerusalem: Makor Publishing. (Included as an introduction to the reprinting of the 1555 edition of *Or Adonai*. Excellent and comprehensive study of the major themes.)

Touati, C. (1974) 'Hasdai Crescas et ses paradoxes sur la liberté', *Mélanges d'histoire des religions offerts à Charles H. Puech*, Paris, 573–8. (Good exposure of some of the difficulties in Crescas' doctrine of divine omniscience.)

—— (1983) 'La Providence divine chez Hasdai Crescas', *Da'at* 10: 15–31. (A fine exposition of Crescas' complex theory of providence.)

Wolfson, H. (1916–17) 'Crescas on the Problem of Divine Atributes', *Jewish Quarterly Review*, n.s. 7: 1–44, 175–221; repr. in *Studies in the History and Philosophy of Religion*, Cambridge, MA: Harvard University Press, 1977, vol. 2, 247–337. (Detailed terminological study of the problem of divine attributes in Crescas and other late medieval Jewish philosophers.)

—— (1929) *Crescas' Critique of Aristotle*, Cambridge, MA: Harvard University Press. (The major study of Crescas' critique of Aristotelian natural philosophy; contains a critical edition, translation and commentary on Book 1 of *Or Adonai*.)

SEYMOUR FELDMAN

CRIME AND PUNISHMENT

An account of how state punishment can be justified requires an account of the state, as having the authority to punish, and of crime, as that which is punished. Crime, as socially proscribed wrongdoing, may be formally censured, and may lead to the payment of compensation to those injured by it – but why should it also attract the kind of 'hard-treatment' punishment which characterizes a system of criminal law? How should we decide which kinds of wrongdoing should count as crimes?

Consequentialists justify punishment by its beneficial effects, notably in preventing crime by deterring, reforming or incapacitating potential criminals. They face the objection that the wholehearted pursuit of such goals would lead to injustice – punishment of those who do not deserve it. Even if that objection is met by imposing non-consequentialist constraints on the sys-

tem, they also face the objection that a consequentialist system fails to respect criminals as responsible moral agents.

Retributivists hold that punishment must be deserved if it is to be justified, and that the guilty (and only the guilty) deserve punishment. Positive retributivists hold that the guilty should be punished as they deserve, even if this will achieve no consequential good. Negative retributivists hold that only the guilty may be punished, but that they should be punished only if their punishment will be beneficial. The main objection to retributivism is that it fails to explain why the guilty deserve punishment.

Some retributivists have argued that the guilty deserve censure, and that punishment serves to communicate that censure. But why should we use 'hard treatment' such as imprisonment or fines to communicate censure? Does the hard treatment function as a consequentialist deterrent? Or could such punishments serve to reform or educate criminals, thus bringing them to repent their crimes and restoring their relationships with those they have wronged?

A theory of justified punishment must be related to our existing penal institutions. It must, in particular, have something to say about sentencing: about what kinds of punishment should be imposed, and about how sentencers should decide on the appropriate severity of punishment. A central issue concerns the role of the principle of proportionality: the demand that the severity of punishment should be proportionate to the seriousness of the crime.

But we must also ask whether our existing penal practices can be justified at all. We must face the abolitionists' argument that punishment should be abolished in favour of social practices which treat 'crimes' not as wrongdoings that must be punished, but as 'conflicts' which must be resolved by a reconciliatory rather than a punitive process.

1 **Punishment, the state and the criminal law**
2 **Consequentialism and retributivism**
3 **Punishment and communication**
4 **Penal theory and sentencing**
5 **Can punishment be justified?**

1 Punishment, the state and the criminal law

Our focus is on punishment imposed by the state for breaches of the criminal law. Punishment can be initially defined as the deliberate infliction of something meant to be burdensome, by an authority, on an alleged offender, for an alleged offence. It needs justification because it involves doing things (depriving people of life, liberty or money) which are normally wrong. Different moral perspectives, how-

ever, generate different accounts of why punishment is morally problematic and thus of what could justify it. Is what matters the infliction of pain, for instance; or the apparent coercive infringement of rights which punishment involves?

A justification of state punishment presupposes a normative theory of the state, as having the authority to punish. Different theories of the state generate different conceptions of punishment: a liberal theory, for example, might set more modest aims for state punishment, and subject it to stricter constraints, than would a communitarian theory (see LIBERALISM §5; COMMUNITY AND COMMUNITARIANISM §§2, 3).

A justification of punishment also requires an account of crime, since it is crimes that are punished. Crime can be minimally defined as socially proscribed wrongdoing, breaching an authoritative social norm (see SOCIAL NORMS). We require an account of the proper character and scope of such norms (and of what it is to be responsible for breaching them, since crime involves a criminal who can be held responsible for it) (see RESPONSIBILITY §1). But not all breaches of socially (or legally) authoritative norms count as crimes which merit punishment: we must ask what kinds of response are appropriate to different kinds of wrongdoing.

Censure is one proper response to breaches of authoritative norms, and the expression of censure may be a further defining feature of punishment; this distinguishes fines, for instance, from taxes (see §3). But censure can be expressed by formal declarations, or by symbolic punishments which are painful only in virtue of their expressive meaning, whereas criminal punishments typically inflict 'hard treatment' (the loss of liberty, money or life) which is painful independently of its expressive meaning. Why should such hard treatment be an appropriate response to socially proscribed wrongdoing?

Another response to such wrongdoing is the enforced payment of compensation to those harmed by it; this is a central feature of the civil as distinct from the criminal law. But though punishment may involve the payment of compensation, it also inflicts hard treatment that is not directly compensatory (nor do crimes always harm identifiable victims). Why should such punitive hard treatment ever be appropriate, and for what kinds of conduct? Which should count as crimes, rather than merely as civil wrongs?

Some theorists appeal to the 'harm principle' (see LAW AND MORALITY §2): only conduct which harms or endangers others should be criminal. But this provides at most a necessary, not a sufficient, condition for criminalization: not every kind of (even seriously) harmful conduct is a plausible candidate for criminalization. And, apart from the question of whether paternalistic laws, prohibiting conduct that harms only the agent, can ever be justified, we must ask what counts as 'harm'. Can we distinguish harmful from merely offensive conduct? Might we count some conduct as 'harmful' purely because of its moral character (as, for example, a breach of trust or a denial of rights) rather than because of its material effects?

Whether we talk of conduct that harms interests, or that infringes rights, or that flouts community values, we must ask which interests, rights or values should be protected by the criminal rather than the civil law. Crimes are often said to be public, rather than private or individual, wrongs: wrongs not just against some individual who may then claim damages, but against the community or state. That is why while civil cases are brought (and may be dropped) by individual plaintiffs, criminal cases are brought by the state or community, even when they involve an attack on an individual victim. But can we explain crimes as public wrongs, without distorting the way in which many crimes attack individual victims? To say, for instance, that murder and rape should be crimes not because of what they do to their particular victims, but because they threaten public order, seems to deny the significance of the victim's suffering. We might suggest that even crimes against individual victims should count as 'public' wrongs in that the community should identify itself with the victim, counting the victim's wrong as 'ours'. Or we might abandon the idea of crimes as public wrongs (except for those which directly injure the collective rather than any individual, like tax evasion), and portray crimes as attacks on those central rights or interests which the state should protect. Either approach, however, leaves us with the question of which rights or interests should be thus protected, or which wrongs should thus be seen as public wrongs. Or if we say that the criminal law should protect the values which are essential to the identity or existence of the community, we must ask which those values are. (Any account of crime must also explain the distinction between *mala in se*, acts which are wrong independently of any legal rule, and *mala prohibita*, acts which are wrong only because prohibited. *Mala prohibita*, however, include many offences (notably 'regulatory' offences, such as minor traffic violations) which some think should not count as true 'crimes': they should be dealt with, not by a criminal process which censures and punishes, but by some distinct regulatory procedure.)

Instead of asking directly which kinds of conduct should be criminalized, we might ask what justifies criminal punishment, and found our principles of criminalization on our answer to that question. If the central justifying aim of punishment is deterrence, we

can ask which kinds of conduct should be thus deterred; if its proper aim is 'retribution', we can ask which kinds of conduct merit such a retributive response.

2 Consequentialism and retributivism

Penal theory has long been a battleground between consequentialists and retributivists. After a period of consequentialist domination, the 1970s saw a revival in retributivist thought, as part of a wider rights-based reaction against consequentialism in social policy.

Consequentialists justify punishment by its instrumental contribution to certain goods: most obviously, the good of crime-prevention. A penal system is justified if its crime-preventive and other benefits outweigh its costs, and no alternative practice could achieve such goods more cost-effectively. Punishment prevents crime by deterring, incapacitating or reforming potential offenders: by giving them prudential disincentives to crime, by subjecting them to restraints which make it harder for them to break the law, or by so modifying their attitudes that they will obey the law willingly (see BENTHAM, J. §3; CONSEQUENTIALISM).

It is at most a contingent truth that such effects on potential offenders are efficiently achieved by punishing actual offenders. This generates the familiar objection to any purely consequentialist theory, that it sanctions injustice. A system of deterrent punishment must appear to punish actual offenders: but that leaves open the possibility of framing innocent scapegoats to deter others or to reassure the public. And unless actual offending is the only reliable predictor of the future crimes which reformative or incapacitative measures aim to prevent, such measures might be efficiently (but surely unjustly) inflicted on those who have not yet broken the law but are thought likely to do so. Indeed, since a person's subjection to coercive treatment by the state must depend on the predicted effects of such treatment, rather than on their past conduct, we might wonder whether consequentialists can justify a system of punishment, of measures imposed for a crime, at all.

Some consequentialists do argue that we should replace punishment by other, more efficient methods of dealing with socially dangerous people. Others argue that we should accept the 'injustices' that a strictly consequentialist penal system might perpetrate (noting that we already accept, for instance, the pre-emptive detention of the mentally disordered). Most accept, however, that a justified system of punishment cannot perpetrate the kinds of gross injustice noted above.

Consequentialists might meet this objection by providing a fuller account of the goods to be achieved or protected, and of the methods by which they might practically be achieved. Thus some argue that individual freedom is an essential good, whose protection precludes the deliberate punishment of those who have not voluntarily broken the law. Others argue that, given the fallibility of human agents, the only safe way to pursue the appropriate goods is to set strict constraints on the penal system: for instance, strictly to forbid the deliberate punishment of an innocent. Such consequentialist defences, however, depend on large empirical claims about the likely effects of penal strategies, which cannot easily be verified. Can the demands of justice to which this objection appeals really be adequately grounded in the contingencies on which this consequentialist argument depends?

Another strategy is to abandon pure consequentialism, and impose non-consequentialist side-constraints of justice on our pursuit of the consequentialist's goals: to insist, for instance, that only those who have voluntarily broken the law may be punished, since responsible agents have a right not to be subjected to such coercive measures unless they voluntarily make themselves liable to them.

One objection to even a side-constrained consequentialist theory concerns the moral standing of those who are punished or threatened with punishment: that a consequentialist system fails to respect its citizens (criminals and non-criminals) as responsible agents. A system of deterrent punishments, Hegel argued, treats all those whom it threatens with punishment like 'dogs': rather than seeking their allegiance to the law by appeal to the moral reasons which justify its demands, it coerces their obedience by threats (see HEGEL, G.W.F. §8). A consequentialist system of reform similarly treats those subjected to it as objects to be remoulded, rather than as responsible agents who must determine their own conduct.

Against such objections, some argue that a side-constrained system of deterrent punishments can respect the moral standing of those it threatens and punishes; or that 'rehabilitation' and 'reform' need not be improperly manipulative or coercive. But one stimulus to the retributivist revival in the 1970s was the claim that only retributivism respects the moral standing of criminals: their right to receive 'fair and certain punishment', rather than being 'used merely as means' to the deterrence of others, or being subjected to indefinite terms of reformative 'treatment'.

The central retributivist slogan is that (only) the guilty deserve punishment, and deserve punishments proportionate to the seriousness of their crimes. This demand for 'just deserts' may be interpreted nega-

tively, as forbidding the punishment of the innocent (or the excessive punishment of the guilty); or positively, as requiring that the guilty be punished as they deserve. The negative reading makes guilt a necessary, but not sufficient, condition of justified punishment: it suggests a 'mixed' account, which gives punishment a consequentialist aim but subjects our pursuit of that aim to retributivist side-constraints, requiring that punishment be both deserved and consequentially beneficial. The positive reading makes guilt a necessary and sufficient condition of justified punishment: the guilty should be punished because they deserve it, whether or not their punishment achieves any consequential good (see KANT, I. §10).

The central task for any retributivist is to explain this supposed justificatory relation between guilt and punishment: what is it about crime that makes punishment an appropriate response to it? The central objection to all retributivist theories is that they fail to discharge this task: they either fail to explain this notion of penal desert, falling back on unexplained intuition or metaphysical mystery-mongering, or offer covertly consequentialist explanations.

The 'new retributivism' of the 1970s offered various accounts of the idea of penal desert. One was that criminals gained by their crimes an unfair advantage over the law-abiding, since they accepted the benefits of the law-abiding self-restraint of others, but evaded that burden of self-restraint themselves: their punishment removed that unfair advantage, thus restoring the fair balance of benefits and burdens which the law should preserve. One objection to this account is that it distorts the nature of crime: what makes rape punishable as a crime is surely the wrong done to its victim, not the unfair advantage the rapist supposedly takes over all those who obey the law.

Another trend in recent retributivist thought has rather built on the idea of punishment as an expressive or communicative practice.

3 Punishment and communication

Expressive accounts of punishment need not be retributivist: since by expressing censure we can modify wrongdoers' conduct, consequentialists can advocate expressive punishments. But the expressive or communicative aspect of punishment can explain the retributivist's slogan that the guilty deserve punishment: if they have broken a law which justifiably claimed their obedience, they deserve censure; and it is a proper task for the state, speaking on behalf of the community, to communicate that censure to them.

We should talk of communication rather than of expression here. For communication is a process

707

which addresses (as expression need not) another as a rational agent; it captures the idea (central to recent versions of retributivism), that we must address criminals as rational and responsible agents.

But even if criminal wrongdoers should be censured, and hard-treatment punishments of the sort imposed by our penal systems can communicate that censure, we must ask why it should be communicated in this way, rather than by formal declarations or purely symbolic punishments (see §1).

Some suggest that hard treatment is necessary if the censure which wrongdoing merits is to be communicated effectively to the criminal, who might not attend to merely symbolic punishments; or that it may be necessary to 'defeat' the claim to superiority which was implicit in the wrongdoer's crime (but do all crimes make such a claim?). But why, if not for the consequentialist reason that this will make the punishment a more effective deterrent, is effective communication so crucial that we must inflict hard-treatment punishments to achieve it?

Others accept that a communicative retributivism cannot by itself justify the use of hard treatment as the communicative vehicle: it must be justified by a consequentialist concern for deterrence. This need not be the kind of 'mixed' account which portrays retributivist values merely as side-constraints on the consequentialist ends which give the penal system its positive aim. The communication of censure can itself be the central justifying aim of punishment, so that the law addresses the citizen as a responsible moral agent, appealing to the moral reasons which justify its demands and the censure that it imposes on those who flout those demands. But recognizing that, as fallible human beings, we will not always be adequately motivated by such moral reasons for obeying the law, we communicate that censure through hard treatment in order to provide an additional prudential incentive for obedience. On one version of this account, the hard treatment should provide only a modest prudential supplement which does not replace or drown the law's moral voice: the question then is whether such modest supplements will be effective. On another version, the hard treatment may be harsh enough to provide by itself an effective deterrent; but this will revive the objections noted earlier to a deterrent conception of punishment.

More ambitiously communicative accounts of punishment portray the hard treatment as a mode of moral communication which aims to reform or educate. Punishment aims to bring wrongdoers to understand and to repent their crimes, and thus to reform their future conduct. Hard treatment assists this purpose by helping to bring home to them the meaning and implications of what they have done; it can also, if it is willingly undergone, enable them to express their repentance and thus reconcile themselves with their victims and the community. Such accounts are retributivist, since punishment must be focused on the past crime as an appropriate censuring response to it, but they also give punishment a forward-looking purpose: the offender's reform or rehabilitation, the restoration of the relationships which the crime damaged, the making of symbolic (and perhaps material) reparation to the victim and the community. Such purposes, however, are not to be understood in strictly consequentialist terms, as independent ends to which punishment is a contingent means: they can be achieved only through a punitive process which aims to persuade wrongdoers that they must suffer punishment for what they have done.

We must ask, however, whether hard-treatment punishment could ever be an appropriate vehicle for such a communicative, reformative and penitential endeavour; and whether, even if it could (as it might be in, for instance, a religious community that practises penance), the state should take such a coercive interest in the moral condition of its citizens. This conception of punishment might be at home within a communitarian perspective according to which individuals can find their identity and their good only as members of a community united by shared values and mutual concerns; but it seems incompatible with a liberal insistence on the need to protect individual rights and privacy against intrusive state or community power. Liberals can argue that punishment's primary purpose should be the communication of appropriate censure, but may deny that the state should try, by such coercive means, to secure repentance and reform; in which case hard-treatment punishments could be justified only as prudential deterrents which do not seek to invade the criminal's soul.

4 Penal theory and sentencing

Philosophical discussions of punishment are typically conducted at a level of high abstraction, remote both from the actualities of penal practices and from the pressing concerns of penal practitioners. But we must try to relate them to the real penal world.

One central issue is that of sentencing. What kinds of punishment should be available to the courts (capital punishment; imprisonment; fines; community service; probation)? What makes a particular kind of punishment appropriate, either generally or for a particular crime? How should sentencers determine the severity of punishment to be imposed on particular crimes or criminals?

Discussion of the last question often focuses on the principle of proportionality: the severity of punishment should be proportionate to the seriousness of the crime. Some such principle is integral to any retributivist theory, including communicative theories: for if punishment is to communicate an appropriate degree of censure, its severity must be proportionate to the seriousness of the crime. The application of such a principle requires some way of assessing and comparing the seriousness of different crimes, and the severity of different punishments; and it is not clear either just how, or how precisely, this can be done. Furthermore, while such a principle can help to determine the relative severity of sentences, requiring that more serious crimes be punished more severely, and so on, it is not clear whether it can help to fix absolute levels of punishment.

How important is the principle of proportionality? On some views, it is paramount: the primary aim of sentencing is to do justice by assigning proportionate sentences. This means, in practice, that the available range of punishments must be limited, and that the courts should have only very limited discretion in sentencing. Others argue that the demand for proportionality must be weighed against other relevant principles, such as a principle of penal parsimony which requires courts to impose the lightest acceptable sentence, even if that is lighter than is required for strict proportionality; on this view proportionality might be seen as a limiting principle requiring that criminals be punished no more severely than is proportionate to their crimes.

There is also a tension between the demand for proportionality and any ambitious account of punishment as communication. If punishment is given an educative, reformative or penitential aim, courts should seek punishments which are materially appropriate, rather than just formally proportionate, to the crime and the criminal: punishments which will appropriately address the particular criminal. But this would require the courts to be given a more flexible and creative discretion in sentencing, to find or construct sentences appropriate to the particular case: a discretion which might undermine demands for strict and formal proportionality.

Here again we face a conflict between a liberal perspective which emphasizes the demands of formal justice, and seeks to protect the citizen against the coercive and discretionary power of the state; and a more ambitious conception of the proper role of the state and the criminal law in seeking the moral good of the citizens.

5 Can punishment be justified?

Any plausible normative theory of punishment will show our existing penal institutions to be radically imperfect. The kind and degree of suffering that they inflict cannot be plausibly portrayed as either consequentially cost-effective or retributively just, or well-suited to the aims of a communicative theory of punishment. Nor is it clear that the preconditions of justified punishment are satisfied in our own societies, especially if punishment is portrayed in retributive or communicative terms: can we truly say that most of those who are convicted by our courts have culpably flouted laws which justifiably claimed their allegiance, or that we (in whose name the law speaks) have the moral standing to censure them?

The radical imperfection of our existing penal institutions raises a serious question for any citizen. Should we accept those existing institutions (while also striving for their reform) as necessary to the prevention of yet greater disorder or injustice; or may we have to recognize that they perpetrate such serious injustice, or cause so much harm, that they cannot be justified at all?

The suggestion that, even if a practice of state punishment could in principle be justified, our existing penal institutions may lack any adequate justification, might seem frivolous: can we honestly argue that they should be abolished? But this is just what is argued by 'abolitionists', many of whom indeed argue that punishment cannot even in principle be justified: we should work not for the reform of our penal institutions, but for their abolition. Such arguments are not often considered in the philosophical literature, which tends to assume that the key issue is not whether, but how, state punishment can be justified; but they present a challenge that must be taken seriously.

Various themes run through abolitionist writings. One concerns the very concept of 'crime' as that which merits a punitive response: we should reconceptualize crimes as 'conflicts' that require resolution rather than punishment. Relatedly, we should 'civilize' our response to crime, favouring a civil law rather than a criminal model: rather than seeking 'retributive' justice by condemning and punishing those judged to have done wrong, we should seek 'restorative' justice by striving to reconcile the conflicting parties and (where necessary) negotiating reparation for whatever harm has been done. These themes are often accompanied by an advocacy of 'informal justice': rather than allowing the state to 'steal' conflicts from the individuals and local communities to whom they properly belong, we should look for informal, participatory modes of conflict-resolution.

But punishment (the deliberate infliction of suffering) is never justified: neither as retribution (which is not a proper aim), nor as deterrence (which denies the moral standing of those who are threatened and punished). And while rehabilitative facilities may be offered to those who need and seek them, they can never properly be imposed on citizens.

Against such views it may be argued that some 'conflicts' involve the commission of genuine wrongs which should be condemned; that any morally acceptable 'reconciliation' must involve the recognition and acceptance of guilt by the wrongdoer (these considerations argue in favour of a communicative conception of punishment as censure); and that a society which truly forswore the whole coercive apparatus of criminal justice would be unable to protect itself or its members against seriously destructive wrongs and social disorder. We might imagine a more perfect society in which the kinds of hard-treatment punishment currently imposed would be unjustified, because unnecessary. We may agree that we now punish too much, too harshly, that our penal institutions do not serve the ends that punishment should serve, and that too often they inflict further suffering on those who are already seriously disadvantaged by the political and economic structures from which many of us benefit. Abolitionists forcibly remind us of these points; but this is not to agree that punishment can never be justified.

See also: JUSTICE; LAW, PHILOSOPHY OF

References and further reading

Bianchi, H. and Swaaningen, R. van (eds) (1986) *Abolitionism: Towards a Non-repressive Approach to Crime*, Amsterdam: Free University Press. (A useful collection of abolitionist papers.)

Braithwaite, J. and Pettit, P. (1990) *Not Just Deserts*, Oxford: Oxford University Press. (A consequentialist account of punishment and criminal justice, setting individual freedom under the law as the aim to be pursued, and focusing on punishment as 'reintegrative shaming'.)

Christie, N. (1981) *Limits to Pain*, London: Martin Robertson. (An abolitionist critique of punishment.)

Duff, R.A. (1986) *Trials and Punishments*, Cambridge: Cambridge University Press. (A communicative account of punishment as penance.)

—— (1996) 'Penal Communications: Recent Work in the Philosophy of Punishment', *Crime and Justice* 20: 1–97. (A critical survey of penal philosophy from 1970–93; includes a full bibliography.)

Farrell, D. (1985) 'The Justification of General Deterrence', *Philosophical Review* 94: 367–94. (Argues that deterrence is consistent with proper respect for rights.)

Feinberg, J. (1970) 'The Expressive Function of Punishment', in J. Feinberg *Doing and Deserving*, Princeton, NJ: Princeton University Press, 95–118. (A seminal discussion of punishment as expressive.)

—— (1984–7) *The Moral Limits of the Criminal Law*, Oxford: Oxford University Press, 4 vols. (An exhaustive discussion of the proper scope of the criminal law, focusing especially on the 'harm principle'.)

Hampton, J. (1984) 'The Moral Education Theory of Punishment', *Philosophy and Public Affairs* 13: 208–38. (Punishment as moral education which respects the criminal's autonomy.)

—— (1992) 'Correcting Harms versus Righting Wrongs: The Goal of Retribution', *UCLA Law Review* 39: 201–44. (Punishment as communicative retribution which 'defeats' the wrongdoer.)

Hart, H.L.A. (1968) *Punishment and Responsibility*, Oxford: Oxford University Press. (A collection of influential papers, developing a side-constrained consequentialist account of punishment.)

Hirsch, A. von (1976) *Doing Justice: The Choice of Punishments*, New York: Hill and Wang. (An important early contribution to the revival of retributivism.)

—— (1993) *Censure and Sanctions*, Oxford: Oxford University Press. (Punishment as censure, with hard treatment providing a prudential supplement; the role of the principle of proportionality.)

Hirsch, A. von and Ashworth, A .J. (eds) (1992) *Principled Sentencing*, Boston, MA: Northeastern University Press; Edinburgh: Edinburgh University Press. (A useful collection of materials on the principles of sentencing.)

Honderich, T. (1984) *Punishment: The Supposed Justifications*, Harmondsworth: Penguin, revised edn. (A critical discussion of the standard theories of punishment.)

Lacey, N. (1988) *State Punishment*, London: Routledge. (A communitarian, 'mixed' account of punishment as aiming to secure both individual autonomy and social goods.)

Morris, H. (1968) 'Persons and Punishment', *The Monist* 52: 475–501. (Criticizes 'treatment' conceptions of punishment, offers a 'benefits and burdens' account.)

—— (1981) 'A Paternalistic Theory of Punishment', *American Philosophical Quarterly* 18: 263–71. (Punishment as moral education and reform.)

Morris, N. and Tonry, M. (1990) *Between Prison and Probation*, New York: Oxford University Press.

(Theoretical and practical issues of sentencing, especially in relation to non-custodial penalties.)

Murphy, J.G. (1973) 'Marxism and Retribution', *Philosophy and Public Affairs* 2: 217–43; repr. in *Retribution, Justice, and Therapy*, Dordrecht: Reidel, 1979, pp. 93–115. (The 'benefits and burdens' theory of punishment; also discusses the problem of the gap between ideal theory and actual practice.)

—— (1984) 'Crime and Punishment', in J.G. Murphy and J. Coleman, *The Philosophy of Law*, Totowa, NJ: Rowman and Allanheld, 113–65. (An introductory discussion of many of the issues covered in this entry, including the distinction between crimes and civil wrongs.)

Primoratz, I. (1989) *Justifying Legal Punishment*, Atlantic Highlands, NJ: Humanities Press. (A useful introductory text, criticizing utilitarian and 'mixed' accounts, arguing for retributivism.)

Walker, N. (1991) *Why Punish?*, Oxford: Oxford University Press. (Defends a firmly consequentialist theory of punishment.)

R.A. DUFF

CRITERIA

The concept of criteria has been interpreted as the central notion in the later Wittgenstein's account of how language functions, in contrast to the realist semantics of the Tractatus. *According to this later account, a concept possesses a sense in so far as there are conditions that constitute non-inductive evidence for its application in a particular case. This condition on a concept's possessing a sense has been thought to enable Wittgenstein to refute both solipsism and scepticism about other minds. There are powerful objections to this conception of criteria, which have led some philosophers to look for an alternative account of the role of criteria in Wittgenstein's later philosophy.*

1   **Criteria and scepticism**
2   **Criteria and grammar**

1   Criteria and scepticism

Norman Malcolm (1963) sets out the central argument by means of which Wittgenstein allegedly refutes solipsism and scepticism about other minds. Wittgenstein is held to expose the incoherence of the argument from analogy, and thereby to show that if we make the assumption that we know, for example, what pain is only from our own case, then we could

never transfer the idea to others. This allegedly forces the defender of the view that 'pain' refers to a private object within a psychological realm into endorsing solipsism. Wittgenstein is then held to use the private language argument to show that solipsism is incoherent (see WITTGENSTEIN, L. §13; PRIVATE LANGUAGE ARGUMENT).

The solipsist has a concept of pain only if it makes sense to talk of identifying a sensation as a sensation of pain correctly or incorrectly. But what does it mean to say that the solipsist has correctly identified a given sensation as one of pain? The solipsist has neither a standard, a sample nor a customary practice of using the word 'pain' against which the inclination to apply the concept can be judged. There is nothing independent of this inclination that enables the solipsist to determine whether the application is correct or incorrect. But in so far as there is nothing to determine whether the application is correct or incorrect, the idea of using the word correctly or incorrectly makes no sense. And in so far as the solipsist lacks a criterion of correct application, the solipsist lacks a concept of pain.

Thus, the assumption that one knows what pain is only from one's own case is shown to lead to a contradiction: if we know about sensations only from our own case, then we cannot know about them even in our own case. It follows, Malcolm argues, that it is a condition of our being able to attribute sensations to ourselves that there should exist *criteria* on the basis of which we are necessarily justified in ascribing them to others. When these criteria are fulfilled, speakers do not merely have good inductive evidence that another is in pain (as the argument from analogy holds); they possess evidence that *establishes beyond question* that another is in pain.

This initially powerful rebuttal of scepticism is weakened, however, when Malcolm is forced to concede that there is a wide range of circumstances (being in a play, being hypnotized, pretending and so on) in which behaviour that would, in other circumstances, constitute criterial evidence for another's being in pain, does not count as fulfilling the criteria. Thus, what looks initially like an argument that establishes that there must be logically necessary and sufficient conditions for another's being in pain – that is, that there must be circumstances in which the behavioural evidence would make it a contradiction for the sceptic to deny that another is in pain – receives a fatal qualification. For given that a doubt may arise over whether the circumstances are ones in which criteria are satisfied (or really satisfied), it seems that the sceptic could always raise a question about any particular case. What looked like an argument to establish that our belief in another's pain is, on particular occasions, logically justified, is now reduced to the much weaker claim that there must be circumstances in which a speaker *accepts* that the criteria for another's being in pain are fulfilled.

There are a number of familiar objections to the argument that Malcolm attributes to Wittgenstein. First of all, it has been seen as amounting to little more than a version of verificationism, and as such it is thought not to warrant the status or the degree of significance that Malcolm ascribes to it. Secondly, it has been objected that the promise to provide a refutation of scepticism is undermined by the qualifications set out in the previous paragraph. It looked as if criteria were to enable us to show that our belief in another's pain is logically justified, but it turns out that the satisfaction of criteria on particular occasions is something that we must ultimately just accept, even though a doubt is, in some sense, still possible. The sceptic could be forgiven for regarding this as vindication, rather than refutation, for there remains a gap between evidence and truth that must be filled by brute faith that our criteria are satisfied. At this point we seem justified in returning to Wittgenstein's texts to see if there is an alternative interpretation of his use of the concept of criteria.

2 Criteria and grammar

The principal concerns of Wittgenstein's later philosophy are the false pictures of language and of psychological phenomena that plague us in philosophy. These myths and false pictures arise, Wittgenstein believes, when we treat the phenomena that characterize our human form of life – language, consciousness, thought, action and so on – as things whose essence lies hidden from us. We both discover the emptiness of the pictures we construct, and achieve the understanding that we seek, through what Wittgenstein calls a 'grammatical investigation'. His idea of a grammatical investigation is characteristically rich. He describes such an investigation as one in which 'we remind ourselves of the kind of statement that we make about phenomena'. Because the essence of language and psychological phenomena lies open to view in the forms of our ordinary practice, it is through a careful description of our actual employment of expressions that we come to understand the nature of these phenomena. The understanding which a grammatical investigation achieves simply sets before us 'what already lies open to view', but in such a way that it no longer puzzles us or cries out for further explanation. Part of the difficulty in understanding Wittgenstein's later philosophy is that he does not believe that the understanding which a grammatical investigation achieves can be expressed

in the form of a clear, unambiguous description of the structure and function of language in general, or of our psychological language game in particular.

It is possible to see Wittgenstein's concept of criteria not as a theoretical term of art but as linked in important ways with this idea of a grammatical investigation. Thus, asking for the criteria that ordinarily establish, in the sense of *identify*, something as an instance of a specific kind of thing (as a mistake, as expecting someone between 4.00 and 4.30, as understanding the order 'Add two' in the way that it was meant and so on) is one particular form of grammatical investigation. Other forms include asking how we teach someone a concept, asking how we would explain it, asking whether we would apply it in certain non-standard cases, asking whether certain facts being different would make it unusable, comparing it with a concept that Wittgenstein invents, and so on. Wittgenstein uses these forms of investigation to induce the clarified vision of the workings of our ordinary language games that he believes is essential to our coming to recognize that everything we need to understand language and psychological phenomena is already there before our eyes.

One of the principal lessons of the grammatical investigation of our ordinary criteria is that the criteria governing our concepts are much more complicated, our language games much more subtle and involved, than at first appears. In the case of psychological concepts this complexity is expressed, not only by the first-person–third-person asymmetry which characterizes these concepts (for example in the case of pain, I do not attribute pain to myself on the basis of observation, the concept of a mistake does not apply in the first-person case, and it makes no sense for me to doubt whether I am in pain), but also by an indeterminacy and uncertainty which Wittgenstein again takes to be a defining feature of our psychological language game. Wittgenstein believes that it is in part these grammatical features of our psychological concepts that prompts the philosopher to form a picture of the mental as an inner realm. For not only is the first-person–third-person asymmetry captured in the distinction between inner and outer, but the idea of the inner allows us to interpret the indeterminacy and uncertainty that is inherent in the language game as merely epistemic: the facts are there alright, but hidden beneath the surface that the other presents to the world.

Wittgenstein's grammatical investigation is directed at a complete overcoming of the philosophical myth of the inner. On the one hand, he tries to show that the picture of a determinate inner realm not only plays no role in our ordinary language game, but that it has no real application. His tactic here is not to try to refute the philosopher's claims, but to develop and explore them in such a way that we come to see, not only that no such thing is ever ordinarily in question, but that the picture of a private inner realm, which initially seems so clear to us, has no real content. He does not argue that no precise system of concepts linked, for example, with exact physiological readings of what is occurring in our brain and nervous system could never be constructed, but he tries to show us that such a system of concepts would not tell us what pain, or thought, or understanding really are; it would in no sense be a refinement of our system of psychological concepts, or constitute an explication of the phenomena that make up our form of life.

On the other hand, Wittgenstein's detailed exploration of the complex, infinitely nuanced language game that the process of acculturation initiates us into, gradually enables us to see how our language game actually functions, and to resist the temptation to misrepresent it in the myth of the inner. He works to overcome our sense that to abandon the idea of a private inner realm is to deny something vital, something without which we are mere machines. He uses the techniques of grammatical investigation to show that our philosophical picture of the inner is grounded in a fundamentally mistaken idea of the relation between our ordinary psychological concepts and the characteristic forms of movement, gesture and expression of the living bodies of humans and other animals. The division which we are mistakenly inclined to draw between an inner and outer realm is shown to be one that is actually grounded in the grammatical distinctions between psychological and non-psychological concepts.

Thus, we gradually come to see that our ordinary psychological language game is distinctive, not in that it describes a hidden realm of facts, but in its grammar. The grammar of our psychological language game reveals the nature of the facts it describes, and in recognizing the distinctiveness of this grammar, we recognize the distinctive form of the phenomena with which we are concerned. Thus, the first-person–third-person asymmetry which characterizes psychological concepts is not something that needs to be explained by (the empty) appeal to a special sort of fact (private facts); rather, this asymmetry itself reveals the distinctive form of mental phenomena.

Likewise, pretence, deceit, betrayal, as well as the ordinary dissemblings that constitute polite behaviour, are part of the form of our psychological language game, and not an unfortunate or incidental addition to it. These phenomena should not lead us to downgrade the 'outer evidence', but to recognize the subtlety and the complexity of the criteria we operate with. Sometimes we are sure of our judgment that another's feeling is genuine, sometimes anyone who is not a lunatic will share our certainty, but at other times we are uncertain and the judgment of different speakers may vary. What Wittgenstein tries to show is that this reflects the essential complexity and ambiguity of our criteria, and not the hiddenness of the facts; our uncertainty arises from the complexity and the subtlety of our relations with others and of the patterns that our psychological concepts require us to discern, and not from the indirectness of our evidence.

Wittgenstein's later philosophy of psychology clearly does constitute a concerted attack on the myth of the inner. This attack does not, however, take the form of a theory of how language functions that imposes on psychological concepts the requirement that what is inner is criterially linked with what is outer. The understanding of psychological phenomena that Wittgenstein's grammatical investigation offers is, in a sense, much more radical than this suggests. What we are gradually brought to see is that the nature of psychological phenomena is not hidden; that the evidence for their existence is not indirect, but involved and complex; that everything that we need to understand the essence of these phenomena is already there in the distinctive grammar of our language game, as this is revealed, for example, by the nature of the criteria with which we operate.

See also: CONTEXTUALISM, EPISTEMOLOGICAL; OTHER MINDS

References and further reading

Albritton, R. (1959) 'On Wittgenstein's Use of the Term "Criterion"', *The Journal of Philosophy* 56: 845–57. (Explores the view that criteria are logically necessary and sufficient conditions.)

Cavell, S. (1979) *The Claim of Reason*, Oxford: Clarendon Press. (This provides the excellent criticisms of Malcolm and the best introduction to the anti-Malcolm view of criteria. See especially part 1, chapters 1 and 2.)

* Malcolm, N. (1963) 'Wittgenstein's *Philosophical Investigations*', and 'Knowledge of Other Minds', in *Knowledge and Certainty*, Englewood Cliffs, NJ: Prentice Hall. (Sets out Wittgenstein's alleged refutation of solipsism and scepticism about other minds.)

McDowell, J. (1982) 'Criteria, Defeasibility, and Knowledge', *Proceedings of the British Academy*, 68: 455–79. (Provides good criticism of Malcolm's view.)

Wittgenstein, L. (1978) *Blue and Brown Books*,

Oxford: Blackwell. (Pages 23–5 are especially important.)

—— (1992) *Last Writings on the Philosophy of Psychology: The Inner and the Outer*, Oxford: Blackwell. (Provides the most sustained treatment of the topic of criteria. But note that it is in the nature of Wittgenstein's philosophical method that remarks on criteria are spread throughout his works and that these remarks bear complex relations both with each other and with other topics discussed.)

Wright, C. (1982) 'Anti-Realist Semantics: The Role of *Criteria*', in G. Vesey (ed.) *Idealism Past and Present*, Cambridge: Cambridge University Press. (Provides an alternative to Malcolm's view.)

MARIE McGINN

CRITICAL LEGAL STUDIES

Critical Legal Studies first developed in the USA in the latter half of the 1970s. Drawing on the political inspiration of the contemporary New Left, it was an intellectual movement committed to radicalizing legal theory by bringing together US legal realism and modern European social theory. In so doing, it sought to provide a fundamental critique of the nature and place of law in modern capitalist society.

In its first phase, its main target was the liberal positivist theories of law that dominate Anglo-American jurisprudence. Such theories inform both the organization of the traditional legal curriculum and the nature of legal practice. By contrast, Critical Legal Studies saw law as based upon deeply contradictory premises, so that the orthodox positivist claim that law could be in principle rational and coherent was rejected in favour of the 'indeterminacy thesis'. Legal decisions were in truth a matter not of logical deduction but of choice. They could always go one way or the other. Ultimately, therefore, it was an open political decision made by a judge which determined a legal conclusion. The idea of the 'rule of law' operating above politics was rejected, but regarded as important in terms of the political legitimation function it served in Western societies.

While the name 'Critical Legal Studies' has a US provenance, a number of different critical legal projects can be identified. These projects reflect the broader character of the national traditions of which they are a part. European approaches, particularly the German and the British, reveal a more sustained engagement with modern and postmodern social theory. However, as a result of problems in the original project, Critical Legal Studies has entered into a second phase in the

USA in which there is an increasing interest in social theory. The result has been a convergence of European and US concerns, but around a highly fragmented group of modern and postmodern social theories. Nietzsche, Foucault, Derrida and Habermas have been introduced into legal theory while Marx and Weber, the original theoretical mainstays of a critical approach to law, have been sidelined. There is a danger in this that Critical Legal Studies will become little more than a group of theorists talking among themselves. While the original US critique of legal doctrine may have run out of steam for want of sufficient theoretical sophistication, it is important not to lose sight of its direct focus on law and legal forms. It is arguable that the recent 'turn to theory' must validate itself in terms of the contribution it is able to make to a critical understanding of law and its practices; also that an important, as yet unaddressed, question concerns the relationship between postmodern forms of criticism and sociological analyses of the development of law.

1   **Introduction**
2   **Critical Legal Studies in the USA**
3   **Critical Legal Studies in Germany and Britain**
4   **Theoretical overview**
5   **The future**

1   Introduction

Critical Legal Studies as an approach to legal theory is a relatively recent phenomenon beginning in the second half of the 1970s and continuing to the present. It therefore comprises a body of thought that is hard to summarize or judge conclusively. Contributing to the problem is the variety of approaches within it, such that one can talk more easily of a 'movement' than a 'school' or a 'canon'. Notwithstanding the common New Left political heritage, the problem is further compounded by the existence of distinct Critical Legal Studies approaches in the USA and in a variety of west European countries, and by the dynamic, unstable and increasingly fragmentary character of their development. Critical Legal Studies in the early 1990s has a substantially different agenda and set of interests from that of a decade ago. In the light of these problems, it is proposed to begin with a picture of the trends of development in three different countries, the USA, Germany and Britain, before proceeding to offer a general assessment. With regard to this second objective, it is important to consider the relationship between Critical Legal Studies, legal studies in general, and broader movements in social theory. It is only in that context that a deeper perspective on the character, potential and limits of Critical Legal

Studies can be achieved. A caveat must however be entered that in relation to so broad, disparate and currently evolving a movement, all generalizations and judgments are more than usually tentative.

2 Critical Legal Studies in the USA

A Critical Legal Studies movement first began in the late 1970s in the USA. The approach was characterized by the marriage of an existing legal realist tradition (see LEGAL REALISM §3) with a radical leftist antipathy to law which, while nominally committed to theoretical critique, was in general only weakly informed by an understanding of radical theoretical traditions. A recent survey of Critical Legal Studies (Boyle 1991) refers to the relevance of socialist, structuralist, deconstructionist, feminist, phenomenological and Hegelian theory. Critical Legal Studies in the USA was always catholic in its sources, but never particularly deeply engaged with theory. It was more comfortable with a relatively narrow critique of the dominant legal tradition and its closer theoretical supports – economic analysis of law or a narrowly philosophical liberalism for example – than with a synthesis of the legal realist tradition and broader social theory (see SOCIAL THEORY AND LAW §4). In recent times, the balance has been redressed through a deep interest in theory, but this has been accompanied by a move away from the earlier critiques of doctrinal analysis, in their time so powerful.

Critical Legal Studies in the USA directed itself against the dominant rationalist and formalist approach to legal studies. Legal realism had already introduced a sceptical critique of the possibility of coherence or consistency within a system of legal rules. Principles could always be opposed by counter-principles or by policies; rules were always subject to exceptions which threatened to swallow them up; the demand for fixed rules always existed in tension with broader standards which could be invoked against them; supposedly clear distinctions such as that between the private and the public were ultimately untenable. Realism's critique flowed from a dissatisfaction with formalistic and positivistic accounts of law (see LEGAL POSITIVISM §3), but its aim was pragmatic: to find a better way of comprehending law in order to put it to better use. Critical Legal Studies by contrast was informed by a more radical political standpoint that saw law not as an instrument to be used in the service of reform but as itself, in its very form, a barrier to social change. In its abstraction and pretence of rationality, law was essentially alienating and disempowering. The critique of law was therefore aimed at breaking the grip of traditional legal

thinking upon the consciousness of lawyers and, in an unclearly defined way, 'the people' as a whole. In place of pragmatism, Critical Legal Studies substituted another peculiarly US intellectual current, populism.

A key concept (that was later to be repudiated) was that of a fundamental contradiction in a capitalist society – or, perhaps, all social life – between the individual and the social (Kennedy 1979). The conflict between self and others manifested itself in a variety of forms within law: in the clash of individualist and altruist principles, in the distinction between the private and the public (see PRIVACY), or between the subjective and the objective. Because this contradiction was fundamental, any attempt to reconcile its two sides was impossible, and legal rationalism was no more than a means of suppressing or hiding it. The existence of contradiction within law also explained the practical adversarial method of the lawyer, and illustrated the central contention of Critical Legal Studies that legal decision-making was essentially a matter of choice that could only be made according to political, as opposed to compelling internal, legal, criteria. The trick of the law was to make this political choice appear to be based upon apolitical rational grounds. The resulting 'legal consciousness' constituted the basis for legitimating forms of ideology in the broader society.

From this brief description, it will be seen that Critical Legal Studies contained a number of strands that did not necessarily add up to a coherent alternative perspective. That law and politics are intertwined is a claim that is not incompatible with more flexible varieties of legal positivism; nor is the argument about the fundamental contradiction within Western thought and law necessarily linked to it. With regard to the latter, it is important to know whether the contradiction is historical or existential. If it is a condition of all sociality or of an evolutionary modernity, then law will be regarded in a different light than if it is seen as a product of capitalist society with its own particular alienating forms. If the resulting legal consciousness is a significant mode of legitimation in the broader society, what are the mechanisms through which this occurs? The problem for Critical Legal Studies was that it remained unclear about the bigger questions that were necessarily inherent in its project. It could lead both to a call to the barricades and to a reconstructive legal project, both to a rejection of law in favour of a radical remaking of the world through informal communitarian modes of regulation and to a commitment to a revised liberal legalism (a 'super-liberalism' in R.M. Unger's 1986 account). It could also lead to individual nihilism, personal angst and intellectual incoherence as two hundred years of liberal legal thought was 'trashed' without much to put in its place.

In its earlier, stronger phase, Critical Legal Studies never moved from what Alan Hunt (1986) has called 'theory adoption' to 'theory construction'. It therefore found itself resting on insufficiently theorized premises that were hard to defend, and which left it vulnerable to counterattack. The 'fundamental contradiction' was eventually, somewhat cavalierly, renounced (Gabel and Kennedy 1984) while the precise scope of the 'indeterminacy thesis' has remained indeterminate. James Boyle (1991) has recently reflected upon the problems of transition from critical legal thought to social theory and of the eclectic quality of the former. Yet it is to be doubted whether his suggestion that Critical Legal Studies should be content with what he calls 'local theory' will assist it in reaching beyond some of its impasses. This is not to deny the value of much recent work on law and culture, as well as critical race theory and feminist legal analysis (see FEMINIST JURISPRUDENCE), but the more specific direction of this often sophisticated critical work leaves broader issues necessarily unaddressed. The consequence has turned out to be a theoretical turn which frequently leads away from law and into an engagement with modern and postmodern trends in social theory. Compare in the area of feminist critique of law, for example, MacKinnon's (over-)direct analysis of the gendered character of law (1987) with the later, more sophisticated but abstract deconstructionist approach of Cornell (1991). As Goodrich (1993) comments, this route will ultimately be validated only if it leads to new and deeper understanding of law, as opposed to further, more *recherché*, repetitions and (mis)translations of Continental theory.

3 Critical Legal Studies in Germany and Britain

If US Critical Legal Studies in its first phase was reluctant to link theoretical analysis to the critique of legal formalism, the same cannot be said of the parallel German tradition. In Germany, *Politische Rechtstheorie*, the counterpart to Critical Legal Studies in the USA, coupled an interest in the critique of legal formalism with analysis based upon historical materialism, Enlightenment philosophy and post-Weberian sociology of law. Just as Critical Legal Studies drew upon the native critical tradition provided by US pragmatism, populism and legal realism, so German critical legal theory has drawn on the wider traditions of modern classical and post-classical European thought.

The major axes of German thought are provided by the Enlightenment commitment to a philosophical rationalization and legitimation of law, and by the Marxist materialist tradition. Modern debates within these two approaches are also substantially mediated by what might be called the 'Weberian problematic' which involves the post-classical conflict within specifically legal thought between formal and substantive justice. German critical legal thought in this regard has been much concerned with the problem of the 'materialization' of law in the twentieth century, and how legal theory between Hegel and Marx should orient itself to it.

Three primary routes can be identified. The first, fundamentally Marxist, route sought to derive forms of law and the state directly from the logic of capitalist economic development (Holloway and Picciotto 1978). Such an approach came to be regarded as ahistorical and aprioristic and fell into disfavour in the late 1970s, yet it retains a broad residual presence within critical legal thought. It is an approach that compares and contrasts with a second route developed in particular by Jürgen HABERMAS (§4), which seeks to understand law both as a 'control medium' for capitalism linked with strategic political and economic action, and as a universalistic form linked to the life world and rational communication (see COMMUNICATIVE RATIONALITY). In his earlier work on legitimation crises, Habermas (1976) used this emerging dualist perspective in order to analyse critically the social contradictions of law in the welfare state, but his more recent work reveals an endorsement of legal formalism, at the same time as it finds it difficult to recognize the concrete legal forms within which formalism could be instantiated (Habermas 1988). Habermas' work can be seen as an Enlightenment-inspired attempt to establish the possible legitimacy of legal institutions in a post-classical world that has rejected in theory and practice the possibility of a formal justice rooted in positive law.

A third route extends the biological conception of the 'autopoietic' (self-referential and self-sustaining) system to legal and other social systems. This theory responds to the multiple conflicts between formal and substantive law by embracing them and at the same time rejecting the role of law as legitimative. In this account of law, emphasis is placed upon the autonomous and self-reflexive character of law within a social system that is differentiated into heteronomous, self-operating sub-systems. These sub-systems are largely closed to each other, and operate according to their own languages and imperatives. They receive inputs from other sub-systems and provide outputs to them, but all such inputs and outputs must be translated into the language of the sub-system itself. Autopoiesis proposed a radical form of system closure, which has been used to explain the propensity to regulative failure built into legal systems, and to provide a critique of 'juridification' as a system-imperative of the legal sub-system. The problem for autopoietic theory is that, despite its critical rhetoric, it presents a view of law that is little different from that of the self-understanding of the lawyer. Its roots in biological metaphor and its aprioristic method lead it to a sociological view of law's functionality unrelated to social or historical development, teetering on the brink of solipsism. Autopoiesis has rejected the linkage between law and an immanent morality explored by Habermas and his associates, but it has not established a sufficiently critical purchase point from which to understand law. Its view of law can in some respects be compared with that of Weber, for whom modern legal rationality was part of the 'iron cage' of bureaucracy which entrapped humankind, and from which there was little chance of escape (see WEBER, M. §2). It might be said to reflect the proclaimed problems of modernity without possessing the critical resources to deal with them.

British Critical Legal Studies can be seen as characteristically resting somewhere between the USA and the German traditions. Compared to the latter, the British have largely been entrapped within an empirical and utilitarian intellectual tradition that has hardly encouraged a deep interest in or respect for the value of theoretical approaches to law. British Critical Legal Studies lack, the German adherence to a sense of 'schools of thought' or of the necessity of locating oneself within a particular theoretical tradition (other than the positivist, of course). While one should stress a common background in the Marxism of the 1970s, the British approach is now more eclectic, more inclined to draw according to interest or fashion from a variety of Continental theories. Compared to the USA, however, the British critical theorists reject the value of populist or pragmatic modes of thought, and are more deeply committed to theoretical engagement with law. By comparison, they benefit from a deeper engagement with theoretical traditions in the sociology of law which goes back to structuralist, form-derivational and feminist debates of the 1970s. The result has been that, in a comparatively small intellectual community with a common background, there has emerged a relative diversity of approaches of some depth to critical legal analysis.

While it is therefore difficult to speak of a British approach to Critical Legal Studies, a range of individual British critical approaches can be identified. To name three of the more recent authors, Peter Goodrich (1990) has drawn upon Nietzsche and Heidegger to establish a critical counter-aesthetics of law and judgment to weigh against English legal traditions; Peter Fitzpatrick (1992) has brought together a Derridean sense of myth and a critique of colonialism to establish what he describes as the mythical foundations of modern law; and Alan Norrie (1993) has combined form analysis, social history and critical realism to establish a praxiological account of criminal law and punishment. These works share themes, but their intellectual allegiances and methodologies – within the current critical canon – vary.

4 Theoretical overview

Critical Legal Studies in the USA, Germany and Britain are characterized by a wide range of intellectual sources which include elements of Marxism, deconstruction, legal realism and Neo-Kantianism (as in autopoietic theory), as well as attempts to recreate the Enlightenment project (such as that of Habermas). They have in common a political and intellectual desire to transcend the positivist and formalist tradition; but with their diverse starting points, is there any way to analyse Critical Legal Studies approaches save in terms of what they are against?

One possibility is to locate Critical Legal Studies within the 'dialectic of the Enlightenment' and in particular the fragmentation of the Enlightenment project after Hegel and Marx. The breakdown of the Hegelian synthesis between legal and rational thought, together with the impact of Marxism, led in the nineteenth century to a threefold division in thinking about law and philosophy. What followed was a complex development with many overlapping strands, but one can identify schematically three theoretical approaches in order to locate Critical Legal Studies. The first is the development of positivist modes of thought which discarded the need for an external, overall system of philosophical reason with which to legitimate law's operation (the positivist approach) (see POSITIVISM IN THE SOCIAL SCIENCES). Second, within ethical philosophy and critical theory, rationalist thought was subjected to increasing scrutiny and subversion (the approach of philosophical critique) (see CRITICAL THEORY). Third, with Marxism, a historical and materialist method was developed that sought to understand both law and reason as expressions of historically developed social relations (the approach of sociological critique) (see SOCIALISM). These three different approaches to social theory and law constitute the parameters within which Critical Legal Studies operate.

Drawing on the second and third approaches, Critical Legal Studies provides a critique of the idea that law and legal reasoning can be understood independently of broader social, moral and political questions, so that the positivist developments of the nineteenth century (the first approach), together with their modern derivatives, are a primary target. It is this target that gives Critical Legal Studies what unity it has; thereafter, the adoption of any critical perspective is a rather 'free' matter of picking from the range of critical resources available within Marxist and post-Enlightenment political philosophy (the second and third approaches). Because of its leftist political interests and its roots in 1970s social movements, Critical Legal Studies has always drawn significantly upon Marxism, but more recently there has been a greater emphasis on the method of deconstruction and the work of French post-structuralists such as Foucault, Levinas, Derrida and Lyotard. While the relationship between post-structuralism and Marxism is controversial, these critical approaches have in common a desire to relate law to an 'outside' or a 'beyond' and to deny its autonomy. In Derrida (1990), the assertion of 'the other' as the beyond of law is explicit, while in Marxism, the external is to be found in the social relations of which law is a specific part, but which it also helps to constitute. In contrast to these trends, however, it should be noted that the German approaches as represented by Habermas (at least in his more recent (1988) work; see also Murphy 1989) and autopoietic theory seek to establish a critical basis 'inside' the law. Indeed in the latter case it is questionable how much more autopoiesis offers than a sociological variant of the Neo-Kantian positivist tradition in European legal philosophy.

The dialectic of the Enlightenment is both theoretical and historical. The radical rationalism of the Enlightenment became conservative in the work of Hegel, and then collapsed in the context of the 'well ordered bourgeois state'. Legal positivism derived its strength from precisely this order, which was in important respects juridical. The role of theory came to be the 'rational reconstruction' (MacCormick 1993) of actual legal relations and practices, and legal positivism found its place within society and the academy as a result (Cotterrell 1983). Yet positivism was always vulnerable. Its linkage to the rationalization of a particular social practice (the law) created a tension with a range of social theories for which such a link was politically and intellectually problematic (see LEGAL REASONING AND INTERPRETATION §3). Critical legal theory brings to bear a critical perspective on legal thought by exploiting this tension between positivistic legal-academic practice and broader social, moral and political concerns. It operates in the conflictual space between the three approaches established by the fragmentation of the Enlightenment project. So doing, it is able to expose legal thought to broader traditions in philosophy and sociology in ways that are at their best creative and critical. It remains on an 'edge' of legal-academic theory and practice and is vulnerable to changes in political and intellectual fashion. None the less it provides those who are justifiably dissatisfied with the narrow orthodoxy of traditional legal thought with some critical tools to go beyond the taken-for-granted reality of the mainstream.

5 The future

It is fitting to conclude an account of a new theoretical approach to law with consideration of its possible future directions. I discuss this in the Anglo-American context with reference to two reviews of Critical Legal Studies, one by an original US participant, the other by a recent British commentator.

Mark Tushnet (1991) offers a bleak picture of the current state of Critical Legal Studies in the USA. While he recognizes the need for a credible theoretical programme, he argues that Critical Legal Studies does not in fact have any essential intellectual components. Indeed he recommends that it be treated as a political rather than theoretical location for a left-leaning diaspora of feminists, critical race theorists, postmodernists, cultural radicals and political economists (see FEMINIST JURISPRUDENCE). What is more, the indeterminacy thesis at the heart of the original movement has now been to an extent both abandoned by its proponents and accepted by the mainstream. The gap between the two sides is now mainly one of degree. The only route forward that Tushnet suggests is a return to the classical social theory of Marx and Weber, but the recommendation is lukewarm. Yet if the indeterminacy thesis is partly abandoned by the critics and partly accepted by the mainstream, it is surely the question of how legal systems achieve determinacy under particular social and political conditions that becomes relevant. It is the historical analyses of classical social theory which consider such conditions and recognize the social and political significance of formalist and positivist concepts of law. These approaches therefore hold out the possibility of protecting Critical Legal Studies against absorption into a revised but still orthodox positivism. Tushnet outlines the theoretical process of engagement and disenchantment with Marx and Weber undergone by US critical theorists, but his account only confirms the pragmatic and populist nature and limits of that engagement. It therefore urges by implication a less half-hearted reappraisal of what such theories have to offer a critical legal project.

An alternative orientation to critical legal theory is provided by Peter Goodrich (1993) from within the present current of post-structuralist theory. He argues that critical thought 'should investigate the conditions of possibility of the text and its interpretation' (1993: 232). This involves, first, the use of history to reconstruct the intellectual development of the doctrinal tradition, leading to a recognition of the cultural specificity of forms of law, and a critique of their modes of tradition, representation, repetition and reproduction. Second, such a historical perspective focuses on systems of classification, on conceptual grids and schemata, and on the forms of knowledge which pass as law. This represents a genuine programme for critical legal theory, but Goodrich's account raises questions about how it can be achieved. In particular, the relationship between the social history of legal forms and their critical interpretation remains problematic. In the concrete case of contract law, for example, Goodrich separates the 'historical' from the 'interpretive' stage of his critique. At the historical stage, he cites the existing institutional legal histories of contract, while the interpretive stage draws on literary theory or discourse analysis.

The result is an antinomian form of critique in which the first stage is undertheorized from a critical standpoint, and the second stage is abstractly theorized in a way that is unintegrated with the first. The critical punch of the second stage is provided by Goodrich's discussion of Carole Pateman's feminist criticism (1986) that the political social contract is also a sexual contract that marginalizes women, but nothing is said about the specifically legal institution discussed by the historians of contract. No doubt something could be said to link the two, but what is missing from, or marginalized within, Goodrich's account is any consideration of contract as a social phenomenon along the lines outlined by Marxism and Weber. Such accounts, which are nowadays sometimes treated as *passé*, none the less provide a substantial social and historical context within which the discourses of lawyers and legal historians can be read, and an important starting point for their critique. The point is not negatively to oppose classical social theory to postmodernism, but rather to ask how they can be fruitfully articulated, as surely they ought to be, in any analysis that seeks genuinely to be historically critical.

Treating these two reviews as representative of its current state of development, two dangers confront critical legal theory. The first is that, undertheorized, it will lose its distinctiveness and disappear into the mainstream. The second is that, abstractly theorized, it will lose the grip on law as a specific social and political phenomenon that Critical Legal Studies originally promised, but ultimately failed to deliver. A way beyond both these dangers is provided by a retrieval and integration of, but not an uncritical return to, the traditions of classical social theory represented by Weber and Marx (see MARXISM, WESTERN). If Critical Legal Studies does not address these in a more constructive way than it has done over the last decade it risks one of two fates. Either it will dissolve into the orthodox positivist tradition it sought to criticize, or it will lose itself in the abstract ethical theorizing that constitutes a large part of postmodernism.

See also: CRITICAL THEORY; LAW, PHILOSOPHY OF; POSTMODERNISM; SOCIAL THEORY AND LAW

References and further reading

* Boyle, J. (1991) 'Editor's Introduction', *Critical Legal Studies*, Aldershot: Dartmouth. (Useful collection of previously published US Critical Legal Studies essays.)
* Cornell, D. (1991) *Beyond Accommodation: Ethical Feminism, Deconstruction and the Law*, London: Routledge. (Important but difficult attempt to provide an ethical basis for feminist legal theory.)
* Cotterrell, R. (1983) 'English Conceptions of the Role of Theory in Legal Analysis', *Modern Law Review* 46: 481. (Analyses the role of positivist legal theory in rationalizing and legitimating the work of the legal profession.)
* Derrida, J. (1990) 'Force of Law: The "Mystical Foundation of Authority"', *Cardozo Law Review*, 11: 919–1045. (Derrida's accessible discussion of law and justice from a deconstructionist standpoint.)
  Douzinas, C. and Warrington, R. (1995) *Justice Miscarried*, Brighton: Harvester Wheatsheaf. (Application of Levinas to legal studies.)
* Fitzpatrick, P. (1992) *The Mythology of Modern Law*, London: Routledge. (Critical analysis of Western law as 'white myth' (Derrida): as founded on racist and nationalist mythologies.)
* Gabel, P. and Kennedy, D. (1984) 'Roll Over Beethoven', *Stanford Law Review* 36: 1–55. (Zany dialogue illuminating the intellectual and existential concerns of two leading critical legal scholars in the USA. The entire volume is devoted to Critical Legal Studies.)
* Goodrich, P. (1990) *Languages of Law: From Logics of Memory to Nomadic Masks*, London: Weidenfeld and Nicolson. (A complex and sophisticated

postmodern critique of the history, symbols and language of the English common law.)

* —— (1993) 'Sleeping with the Enemy', *New York University Law Review* 68: 389–425. (British commentary on the current state of US Critical Legal Studies.)

* Habermas, J. (1976) *Legitimation Crisis*, London: Heinemann. (Sophisticated development of the concept of legitimation in modern capitalist society beyond Weber's conception of legal-rational legitimacy.)

* —— (1988) 'Law and Morality', ed. S.M. McMurrin, *Tanner Lectures on Human Values*, vol. 8, Cambridge: Cambridge University Press, 219–79. (Argues for 'a rationality of legislative and judicial procedures guaranteeing impartiality': a position which appears to place Habermas within mainstream liberal thought.)

* Holloway, J. and Picciotto, S. (1978) *State and Capital: A Marxist Debate*, London: Edward Arnold. (English translation of the German debate which had a considerable contemporary impact.)

* Hunt, A. (1986) 'The Theory of Critical Legal Studies', *Oxford Journal of Legal Studies* 6: 1–45. (An early attempt to survey Critical Legal Studies in the USA by a British Marxist.)

Joerges, C. (1989) '*Politische Rechtstheorie* and Critical Legal Studies: Points of Contact and Divergencies', in C. Joerges and D. Trubek (eds), *Critical Legal Thought: An American-German Debate*, Baden-Baden: Nomos. (Useful comparison of US and German critical legal approaches.)

Kelman, M. (1987) *A Guide to Critical Legal Studies*, Cambridge, MA: Harvard University Press. (An insider's analysis and reconstruction of the Critical Legal Studies movement in the USA.)

* Kennedy, D. (1979) 'The Structure of Blackstone's Commentaries', *Buffalo Law Review* 28: 205. (A seminal Critical Legal Studies essay in the USA.)

* MacCormick, D.N. (1993) 'Reconstruction after Deconstruction: Closing in on Critique', in A. Norrie (ed.), *Closure or Critique: New Directions in Legal Theory*, Edinburgh: Edinburgh University Press. (Attempts to defend legal positivism against the Critical Legal Studies attack.)

* MacKinnon, C. (1987) *Feminism Unmodified*, Cambridge, MA: Harvard University Press. (Argues that men exploit women through their sexuality, and that law operates to support this.)

* Murphy, W.T. (1989) 'The Habermas Effect: Critical Theory and Academic Law', *Current Legal Problems* 42: 135–65. (Salutary reminder of the critical distance – that is not always recognized by 'critical' lawyers – between 'system' and 'life world' in Habermas' project.)

* Norrie, A. (1993) *Crime, Reason and History*, London: Weidenfeld and Nicolson. (A critical analysis of English criminal law, focusing on the tensions and contradictions in its general principles.)

* Pateman, C. (1986) *The Sexual Contract*, London: Routledge. (A feminist critique of the exclusion of women from the social contract in Western liberal political philosophy.)

Teubner, G. (1992) *Law as Autopoietic System*, Oxford: Blackwell. (Teubner's statement of the autopoietic theory of law.)

* Tushnet, M. (1991) 'Critical Legal Studies: A Political History', *Yale Law Journal* 100: 1515–44. (Retrospective account of the history and politics of the Critical Legal Studies movement in the USA by an original member.)

* Unger, R.M. (1986) *The Critical Legal Studies Movement*, Cambridge, MA: Harvard University Press. (A virtuoso 'manifesto' for the Critical Legal Studies movement in the USA by one of its leading figures.)

ALAN NORRIE

CRITICAL REALISM

Critical realism is a movement in philosophy and the human sciences starting from Roy Bhaskar's writings. It claims that causal laws state the tendencies of things grounded in their structures, not invariable conjunctions, which are rare outside experiments. Therefore, positivist accounts of science are wrong, but so is the refusal to explain the human world causally. Critical realism holds that there is more to 'what is' than 'what is known', more to powers than their use, and more to society than the individuals composing it. It rejects the widespread view that explanation is always neutral – to explain can be to criticize.

Bhaskar originally called his general philosophy of science 'transcendental realism' (see Bhaskar 1978) and his philosophy of the human sciences 'critical naturalism' (see Bhaskar 1979). The term 'critical realism' arose by elision of these two phrases, but Bhaskar and others in this movement have accepted it since 'critical', like 'transcendental', suggests parallels with Kant's philosophy, while 'realism' indicates the differences from it (see KANT, I. §5).

Critical realism starts from the transcendental question 'how are informative experiments possible?', which includes the question 'why are they necessary?'; that is, why can we not rely on spontaneous observations, but have to set up test-situations artificially, and how can these artificial tests disclose what happens spontaneously outside the laboratory? Bhaskar's answer is that experiments set up, as near as possible, 'closed systems', defined as systems in which something like Humean causation works: whenever A happens B happens.

In closed systems, particular mechanisms of nature can be isolated and studied accurately, but elsewhere in the open systems of which the world is made up, a multiplicity of these mechanisms co-determine events. Experimentally closed systems are of special value to science because they uncover mechanisms of nature, but these mechanisms are only of interest because they also operate in those open systems of which almost all the world consists, outside artificially contrived experimental conditions. Astronomy alone finds approximations to closed systems in nature, due to the lack of forces capable of deflecting heavenly bodies from their courses.

On this basis, critical realism postulates three kinds of 'depth' in nature, and identifies three common fallacies which arise from ignoring them.

(1) Not only may one distinguish, as common-sense realism does, between the contents of experience ('the empirical') and the actual course of events ('the actual'); one may also distinguish 'generative mechanisms' in nature, which are real even if not actualized. Gravity is real, even when the roof is not falling in. Failure to recognize this leads to 'actualism', the attempt to locate laws at the level of the actual (spontaneously occurring constant conjunctions). As against this, laws should be analysed as tendencies: bodies tend to persist in a state of rest or uniform motion in a straight line; hoppy beer tends to make you sleepy; capitalist enterprises tend to get bigger and fewer.

(2) The real multiplicity of natural mechanisms grounds a real plurality of sciences which study them. Even though one kind of mechanism may be explained by another (for instance, biological mechanisms by chemical ones), it may not be reduced to the other. Nature is stratified, with some strata rooted in but emergent from others; the course of events is different from what it would be if the more 'basic' strata alone existed. So the attempt to reduce human to natural or biological to physico-chemical science is ruled out by the nature of the subject-matter.

(3) Science is a social product, the result of experimental work; but the mechanisms it discovers operate in nature prior to and independently of their discovery. So we must distinguish the 'transitive object' of science – the knowledge it has produced – and its 'intransitive object' – the reality it is about, which exists independently of our knowledge, and always has unexplored depths to it. When this is not recognized, we fall into the 'epistemic fallacy', reducing questions about what is to questions about what we can know. Concepts like 'the empirical world' encapsulate this fallacy.

Several conclusions may be drawn for the human sciences.

(1) Most controversies between positivistic and hermeneutic views assume, on both sides, a positivist account of natural science (see POSITIVISM IN THE SOCIAL SCIENCES §1). Therefore, positivists expect the human sciences to find constant conjunctions in the human world, though they are scarce enough in the natural; and hermeneuticists conclude from the absence of such conjunctions that the human sciences are radically unlike the natural ones (see SOCIAL SCIENCE, CONTEMPORARY PHILOSOPHY OF §§1–3). A critical realist account of science makes possible a non-reductive naturalism in human science.

(2) Closed systems cannot even be established artificially in the human sciences. So experimental method is irrelevant here. More to the point are the detective-like skills of those natural scientists who study open systems: geologists, natural historians, meteorologists.

(3) Since we are humans, we have in our conceptualized social practices a ready-made starting point for the human sciences. This is the truth in hermeneutics. But there are no grounds either for regarding these data as infallible or for treating their operation as non-causal. Once we reject Humean causality and recognize emergence, we can accept that reasons for actions can be their causes – but also that they may be rationalizations of actions whose causes are elsewhere. Human sciences may be interpretive and non-reductive, but at the same time causally explanatory and corrective of agents' conceptions (psychoanalysis, Chomskyan linguistics and certain versions of Marxism seem to fit this model best) (see CHOMSKY, N.; SOCIAL SCIENCE, HISTORY OF PHILOSOPHY OF §12). This makes them potentially emancipatory, in that they can correct enslaving illusions (as psychoanalysis claims to), or illusions that subserve social oppression (compare Marx on ideology). In this connection, Bhaskar introduces the notion of an explanatory critique: some beliefs are incompatible with their own true explanation, and since this can apply to moral beliefs, the fact/value gap is bridged.

Critical realist interventions in debates about particular disciplines in the human sciences include Pateman (1987) on linguistics, Will (1980, 1984) on psychoanalysis, Collier (1989) on Marxism, and Soper (1995) on ecology.

See also: EXPERIMENT; EXPERIMENTS IN SOCIAL SCIENCE; EXPLANATION IN HISTORY AND SOCIAL SCIENCE; NATURALISM IN SOCIAL SCIENCE §1

References and further reading

Archer, M. (1995) *Realist Social Theory: the Morphogenetic Approach*, Cambridge: Cambridge University Press. (An elaborated defence of the mutual irreducibility of social structure and intentional agency, as propounded by critical realism.)

* Bhaskar, R. (1978) *A Realist Theory of Science*, Hemel Hempstead: The Harvester Press. (Basic text on transcendental realist philosophy of science.)

* —— (1979) *The Possibility of Naturalism*, Hemel Hempstead: The Harvester Press. (Basic text on critical naturalist philosophy of the human sciences.)

—— (1986) *Scientific Realism and Human Emancipation*, London: Verso. (Ramifies the above theories, introduces the concept of explanatory critique, and concludes with a critique of positivism. Very difficult reading.)

—— (1989) *Reclaiming Reality*, London: Verso. (Essays on various matters and at various levels. The best Bhaskar text to read as an introduction or a sampler.)

—— (1991) *Philosophy and the Idea of Freedom*, Oxford: Blackwell. (Mainly a critique of Rorty, with some comments on critical realism and Marxism.)

—— (1993) *Dialectic*, London: Verso. (Further developments of critical realism, focusing on the concepts of negativity and totality. Very difficult reading.)

—— (1994) *Plato Etc.*, London: Verso. (An essay in the critical realist resolution of the traditional problems of philosophy. Difficult reading.)

* Collier, A. (1989) *Scientific Realism and Socialist Thought*, Hemel Hempstead: The Harvester Press. (Suggests critical realist solutions to some problems of Althusserian Marxism.)

—— (1993) *Critical Realism*, London: Verso. (General introductory exposition of critical realism.)

Lawson, T. (1997) *Economics and Reality*, London: Routledge. (A critique of contemporary economic theory from a critical realist standpoint.)

Manicas, P. (1987) *A History and Philosophy of the Social Sciences*, Oxford and New York: Blackwell.

(An account of the development of social scientific theories from a critical realist point of view, concluding with a realist critique of empiricism.)

New, C. (1996) *Agency, Health and Social Survival*, London and Bristol, PA: Taylor and Francis. (A readable critical realist comparison and critique of various theories in psychology and psychoanalysis.)

* Pateman, T. (1987) *Language in Mind and Language in Society*, Oxford: Clarendon Press. (Critical realist interventions in philosophical disputes about linguistics. Some prior knowledge of Chomsky's theories helps.)

* Soper, K. (1995) *What is Nature?*, Oxford: Blackwell. (Untangles various concepts of nature, from a standpoint which is at once critical realist, feminist and ecological.)

* Will, D. (1980) 'Psychoanalysis as a Human Science', *British Journal of Medical Psychology*, 53: 201–11. (Argues that psychoanalysis conforms to the best current model of science, that is, critical realism.)

* —— (1984) 'The Progeny of Positivism: The Maudsley School and Anti-Psychiatry', *British Journal of Psychotherapy*, 1 (1): 50–67. (Uses critical realism to defend psychoanalysis from positivist and anti-scientific criticism.)

ANDREW COLLIER

CRITICAL THEORY

The term 'critical theory' designates the approach to the study of society developed between 1930 and 1970 by the so-called 'Frankfurt School'. A group of theorists associated with the Institute for Social Research, the School was founded in Frankfurt, Germany in 1923. The three most important philosophers belonging to it were Max Horkheimer, Theodor Wiesengrund Adorno and Herbert Marcuse.

Horkheimer, Adorno and Marcuse feared that modern Western societies were turning into closed, totalitarian systems in which all individual autonomy was eliminated. In their earliest writings from the 1930s they presented this tendency towards totalitarianism as one result of the capitalist mode of production. In later accounts they give more prominence to the role of science and technology in modern society, and to the concomitant, purely 'instrumental', conception of reason. This conception of reason denies that there can be any such thing as inherently rational ends or goals for human action and asserts that reason is concerned exclusively with the choice of effective instruments or means for attaining arbitrary ends.

'Critical theory' was to be a form of resistance to contemporary society; its basic method was to be that of 'internal' or 'immanent' criticism. Every society, it was claimed, must be seen as making a tacit claim to substantive (and not merely instrumental) rationality; that is, making the claim that it allows its members to lead a good life. This claim gives critical theory a standard for criticism which is internal to the society being criticized. Critical theory demonstrates in what ways contemporary society fails to live up to its own claims. The conception of the good life to which each society makes tacit appeal in legitimizing itself will usually not be fully propositionally explicit, so any critical theory will have to begin by extracting a tacit conception of the good life from the beliefs, cultural artefacts and forms of experience present in the society in question. One of the particular difficulties confronting a critical theory of contemporary society is the disappearance of traditional substantive conceptions of the good life that could serve as a basis for internal criticism, and their replacement with the view that modern society needs no legitimation beyond simple reference to its actual efficient functioning, to its 'instrumental' rationality. The ideology of 'instrumental rationality' thus itself becomes a major target for critical theory.

1 Historical background

In 1923 a group of intellectuals in Frankfurt, Germany, founded an 'Institute for Social Research' as a centre for the interdisciplinary study of social and economic issues in contemporary society from a broadly socialist perspective. The term 'critical theory' is used to designate the approach to social theory developed by the members of the Institute (who came to be known collectively as 'The Frankfurt School') between 1930 and 1970. The philosophers most closely associated with the genesis of critical theory were Max HORKHEIMER, Theodor Wiesengrund ADORNO and Herbert MARCUSE. When the National Socialists seized power in Germany in 1933 the Institute moved to New York, where it remained until 1949. Much of the most original work of the Frankfurt School was produced during this period of exile in the USA.

In their early papers, Horkheimer and Marcuse outline the conception of an interdisciplinary social theory that would be guided by an interest in the normative goal of human emancipation. Translations of the most important papers from this period are collected in *Critical Theory* (Horkheimer 1968) and *Negations* (Marcuse 1968).

Although Horkheimer, Adorno and Marcuse took themselves to be rationalists (of a sort), in the 1940s they found themselves becoming increasingly sceptical of the Enlightenment assumption that scientific and technological progress is an unproblematic human good. Empirical science, they thought, was based on a form of rationality – 'instrumental rationality' – which was inherently manipulative and which would have disastrous social and moral consequences if not strictly subordinated to a more encompassing notion of rationality. The 'critique of instrumental reason' is elaborated most fully in *The Dialectic of Enlightenment*, written jointly by Adorno and Horkheimer and published in 1947. The 1940s also saw the completion of Adorno's *The Philosophy of Modern Music* (1949) and, in *Minima Moralia* (1951), his reflections on the impossibility of leading a good life in the contemporary world.

In 1949 Horkheimer negotiated a return of the Institute to Frankfurt. Marcuse, however, elected to remain in the USA. During the 1950s and 1960s he held positions at various US universities and wrote the two books on which his reputation as a theorist of the New Left mainly rests: *Eros and Civilization* (1955) and *One-Dimensional Man* (1964).

Upon their return to Frankfurt Adorno and Horkheimer became prominent public figures, while continuing to practise their form of cultural criticism. In 1958 Horkheimer retired to Switzerland where he died in 1973. In 1966 Adorno published a lengthy philosophical account of his version of the critical theory, *Negative Dialectics*. He seems to have been surprised by the student movement of the 1960s. Many participants were inspired by his writings and thought of themselves as putting critical theory into practice, however Adorno repudiated their activism. In contrast, Marcuse attempted to the very end of his life to maintain a theoretical commitment to action for radical social change.

2 Conception of 'theory'

Members of the Frankfurt School agreed in rejecting a widely held view about what a 'theory' is. In normal parlance a 'theory' is a set of formally specified and interconnected general propositions that can be used for the successful explanation and prediction of the phenomena in some object domain. This conception of theory, the members of the Frankfurt School argued, is extremely misleading because it directs attention away from the social context within which theories necessarily arise, are tested and are applied, and within which alone they are fully comprehensible. The term 'theory' should be used in the first instance to designate a form of (ideally social) activity with an especially salient cognitive component, and only derivatively for the propositions that might be formulated in the course of such activity. Human societies are engaged in a constant process of assimilating nature through labour in order to reproduce themselves; they develop forms of cognitive activity in order to make this self-reproduction more secure and more efficient. Horkheimer, Adorno and Marcuse call such cognitive activity 'traditional theory'. Virtually everything we would in normal parlance call a theory (including all scientific theories) is what the members of the Frankfurt School would call a derivative form of traditional theory. However, they would claim there is another possible kind of cognitive activity, one which is not directed at reproducing society in its present form or making its assimilation of nature more efficient, but rather is directed at changing the existing society radically so as to make it more substantively rational. Essentially it is an attempt to do away with those fundamental features of the society that prevent agents from being able to lead a good life. 'Critical theory' is the name given to such inherently oppositional forms of thinking. In a derivative sense the propositions or specific theses brought forward by agents engaged in such oppositional thinking at some particular time may also be called critical theory. A critical theory thus is historically specific, being directed at a particular society that stunts the possible realization of the good life. It is inherently negative, and it depends on a conception of substantive reason.

3 Critique of instrumental reason

Critical theorists argue that in the ancient world the concept of 'reason' was an objective and normative one. Reason was thought to refer to a structure or order of what ought to be which was inherent in reality itself and which prescribed a certain way of life as objectively rational. Human beings were thought to have a (subjective) faculty which allowed them to perceive and respond to this objective structure of the world; this faculty could then also be called reason in a derivative sense. Even when ancient philosophers spoke of reason as a human faculty (rather than as a structure of the world), their conception of it was 'substantive'; humans were thought to be able to use reason to determine which goals or ends of human action were worthy of pursuit.

In the post-Enlightenment world the 'objective' conception of reason becomes increasingly implausible. Reason comes to be conceived as essentially a subjective ability to find efficient means to arbitrarily given ends; that is, to whatever ends the agent in question happens to have. The very idea that there could be inherently rational ends is abandoned. Reason becomes subjective, formal and instrumental.

The historical process by which reason is instrumentalized is in some sense inevitable and irreversible. The philosophical position called 'positivism' draws from this the conclusion that reason itself should simply be identified with the kind of reason used in natural science. Scientific reason, the critical theorists claim, is a particularly highly developed form of instrumental reason. The point of getting an exact depiction of reality as it is and of the causal laws that govern events is to allow humans to manipulate the world successfully so as to attain their ends. For this to be possible, the positivists believe, the terms that figure in significant scientific discourse must be clearly defined and their relation to possible confirming or disconfirming perceptual experience must be clearly specified. Reason, the positivists think, can be a guide to life only in a very limited sense. Its role is restricted to discharging three tasks: (1) it can criticize a set of beliefs and ends for failing to satisfy certain minimal principles of logical consistency; (2) it can criticize a given choice of means towards a given end on a variety of possible empirical grounds, such as that the means in question will not actually lead to the envisaged end or will have undesirable side effects, and it can propose more appropriate means; (3) it can unmask inherently non-cognitive beliefs, for instance value judgments, that are presenting themselves as if they had cognitive content. The role of reason in discharging the third of these tasks is especially important in the view of the positivists because any statements that do not belong to the descriptive and explanatory apparatus of science, and in particular any statement about what ought to be the case, stand wholly outside the domain of rational argumentation and can be nothing but the expression of arbitrary choice or personal preference (see POSITIVISM IN THE SOCIAL SCIENCES).

Critical theorists think that this line of argument is seductive, but dangerous and false. Although it is true that reason cannot directly prescribe some set of ends as inherently rational and worthy of pursuit for their own sake, it retains an essential function that goes beyond those the positivists would allow it. This further function is that of 'internal' or 'immanent' criticism.

4   Internal or immanent criticism

To understand the Frankfurt School's doctrine of internal criticism it is necessary to see it in the context of their general conception of society. Horkheimer, Adorno and Marcuse reject all four components of the positivist approach to the study of human society:

1   the view that human societies are just bundles of separate facts, events and institutions ('atomism');
2   the view that social facts and institutions are what they are regardless of what people think of them ('objectivism');
3   the view that the concepts we use to give an account of a society are just tools which we are free to define in whatever way seems convenient ('nominalism');
4   the view that the concepts we form should be purely descriptive, that is, defined exclusively in terms of purely observable properties with no evaluative component ('the fact/value distinction').

Contrary to this, members of the Frankfurt School hold that every society is a 'totality' in which each feature is essentially connected with all others and that social reality is partly constituted by the forms of belief, understanding and evaluation that exist in the society in question. Thus atomism and objectivism are false. Furthermore, the actual practices and institutions in a society would make no sense unless they were seen as inherently oriented towards the realization of some socially specified conception of the good life. Thus the more naïve versions of the fact/value distinction are problematic for the study of societies. To use the favoured Hegelian terminology: each institution in a society must be seen in relation to its (objective) 'concept', an ideal form of itself which it aspires to approximate, thereby playing its assigned role in the realization of the good life. The concept of an institution is objective in that the agents who participate in the institution need not be fully and explicitly aware of it – it cannot be determined by simply reading off the contents of their beliefs. It is also objective in that if we as researchers fail to formulate the concept correctly, we will have misunderstood the institution in question fundamentally. Thus 'nominalism' in the study of society is wrong, too. Although the concept of a social institution is objective in this sense, it is not, of course, objective in the sense in which a natural phenomenon is; it is *finally* constituted by human subjects and their activities, although this process of 'constitution' may be a very highly mediated one, lasting through a long historical time. To discover the concept is a very complex, constructive, theoretical activity requiring the social philosopher to enter into the history of the institution and study the ways in which people in the past understood it, the hopes, aspirations and values that were associated with it and their consequences.

A critical theory elicits the concept of a given institution in a given society, formulates it and confronts the actual reality of the institution with this ideal concept. There will be a discrepancy which the critical theory will point out and analyse. This analysis can be called internal or immanent criticism because the standards used in it are derived from the concept of the institution itself. Use of this internal method allows criticism to proceed without it being necessary for the critic to have an unconditional commitment to or to give an independent justification of the standards of criticism used. The common view held by all the critical theorists until 1969 (the year of Adorno's death) was that substantive reason in the modern world must remain relentlessly negative: one cannot extract from reason the image of a good society or indeed any unconditional set of positive ideals. Reason cannot describe utopia, but can at best specify a 'determinate negation' of some particular feature of contemporary society that has been subject to internal criticism. Just as Marx does not describe the socio-economic formation he believes will succeed capitalism in positive and detailed terms, but only in negative terms as a 'class-*less* society', so similarly the most Adorno is ever willing to assert is that it would be desirable to be able 'to be different without *angst*' (1951: 656). In 1969 Marcuse announced (in the 'Introduction' to *An Essay on Liberation*) that he was breaking with the prohibition on utopian speculation that had been an integral part of the original critical theory; his post-1969 views will be discussed below (see §7) (see Utopianism).

5   The dialectic of enlightenment

Horkheimer and Adorno held that the final framework for social criticism had to be a speculative philosophy of history. In *The Dialectic of Enlightenment* (1947) they set out to provide the global interpretation of human history they believe is necessary.

Human history is a dialectic of 'enlightenment' on the one hand and 'myth/barbarism' on the other. 'Enlightenment' as used by Adorno and Horkheimer means both: (1) a certain theory – that is a specification of goals for society, a set of views about individual morality, the nature of knowledge, rationality and so on; and (2) the actual state of society which results from the massive application of this theory. 'Myth' is the opposite of enlightenment in sense (1); 'barbarism' the opposite of enlightenment in sense (2).

Enlightenment as a theory comprises five central tenets.

1 Commitment to certain ideals; autonomy, individuality, non-coercion, human happiness and so on.
2 Commitment to the view that 'genuine' knowledge is knowledge that is (a) 'objectifying', based on a clear and strict separation between the human subject and nature (as object of knowledge); (b) 'identifying', subsuming individual instances (of whatever it is that is to be known) under unitary general concepts and thus presenting them as in some sense 'the same'; (c) inherently technologically or instrumentally efficacious.
3 Commitment to the view that an increase in genuine knowledge in a society would lead to a greater realization of the ideals of the Enlightenment (as formulated in 1 above).
4 Commitment to a principle of universal criticism; that is nothing is to be taken on faith or authority or because of ' tradition' but every belief must show a warrant that will be recognized by the Tribunal of Reason.
5 Commitment to seeing itself (that is, to seeing enlightenment) as absolutely different from and opposed to barbarism and myth.

Horkheimer and Adorno have a number of criticisms of this theoretical position. First of all they claim that item 5 is false. The enlightenment is wrong to see itself as utterly and radically different from myth. Rather the relation between myth and enlightenment is a 'dialectical' one. Both have a common origin as reactions to the same phenomenon: primeval terror. Human history in fact is nothing but a series of attempts to deal with our overwhelming fear of what is other or unknown. Myth arises from a mimetic reaction to this terror: by making ourselves like that which we fear, by identifying with it, we attempt to do away with its otherness, as primitive hunters might try to deal with their fear of a predator by mimicking its movements in a dance. Another way to react to fear of the unknown is by separating it strictly from the self and subjecting it to a system of identifying categories the better to keep track of it and perhaps eventually control it. This second reaction is that of enlightenment: a rigid fixation on self-preservation as the absolute overriding goal and an incipiently paranoid concern to classify everything so as to be able to subordinate it to the attainment of that goal. Looked at, then, from sufficient distance enlightenment and myth seem similar. Both are attempts to use a form of identity to deal with the *angst* induced by difference. The direction (as it were) of 'identification' runs, however, in the opposite direction in the two cases. In myth we make ourselves like the other; in enlightenment we try to make the other like our category (by subsuming it). Close inspection of myths moreover reveals them to be historically superseded forms of enlightenment. The pantheon of Olympian gods – archetype of mythic thinking in the West – is not just a creation of the mimetic impulse, but must also be seen as a form of enlightenment relative to the religious beliefs and practices associated with the nameless, chthonic deities of pre-Homeric Greece. What counts as myth and what ·as enlightenment is not given absolutely once and for all, but is historically relative.

Adorno and Horkheimer's second criticism is that the enlightenment tends to overlook or downplay the price humanity has had to pay for enlightenment. The instrumentally manipulative attitude the enlightenment bids us adopt towards nature will necessarily tend to extend itself to our relations with our fellow humans. Furthermore, effective instrumental control of nature requires that I control and finally repress my own spontaneity. Spontaneity is, however, an essential part of a human's capacity for happiness. Modern subjectivity itself is a result of this process of enlightenment, in which self-preservation is ensured at the cost of impairing our capacity for happiness.

The third line of criticism is that enlightenment has an inherent tendency to destroy itself. The original substantive ideals of the enlightenment (autonomy, individuality and so on) are not themselves exempt from the demands of the principle of universal criticism; that is, from the requirement of giving an account of themselves before the Tribunal of Reason. It becomes increasingly clear, however, that it is not possible to argue from the results of empirical science or from some more general principles of instrumental reason (that is, from some bit of what the enlightenment itself would consider 'genuine knowledge') to the validity of those ideals. In the end the ideals themselves come to look like myths or prejudices which ought to be discarded. The Marquis de Sade, a legitimate child of the enlightenment, finds no 'rational' arguments against cruelty (and much to be said in its favour).

Fourth, the history of the twentieth century has shown that the increase in technological control over the world and the spread of scientific knowledge does not in fact necessarily make people more autonomous, more highly individuated or more happy.

Their final criticism starts from the rigidity and paranoia of the enlightenment project, from its need to encompass *everything* in a single, definitive, closed system of concepts. This means that enlightenment is potentially totalitarian and has an inherent tendency to absolutize itself; that is, (falsely) to declare itself to be not just a given historically relative stage in the global process of enlightenment, but rather the final and definitive form of enlightenment. In thus absolutizing itself and resisting change, the given stage of enlightenment turns itself into a form of myth. This transformation is the final stage of the 'dialectic of enlightenment'.

Despite this battery of criticisms Horkheimer and Adorno do not reject the enlightenment outright. Rather they see their task as one of furthering the underlying enlightenment project by enlightening the enlightenment about itself. By analysing its inherent tendency towards totalitarianism, they hope to save its ideals (even if only in negative form) and prevent it from turning itself into a form of myth and barbarism (see TOTALITARIANISM §4).

6 Negative dialectics

In his *Negative Dialectics* (1966), Adorno tries to give a philosophical account of the kind of thinking that is constitutive of critical theory: a form of substantive reason which is however purely negative.

Both everyday thinking and science, he claims, proceed by subsuming particulars under general concepts. By doing this, however – by claiming that *this* (tree) is a tree and that *that* (tree) is (also) a tree – we are tacitly asserting an identity between the two individuals and between each individual and the concept. To engage in such 'identity thinking' is to be tacitly trying to make identical what is in fact in some sense different – no two trees are exactly alike. Using an identifying concept is a way of trying to crush or suppress difference. The appropriate form of resistance to this reprehensible project is to remain aware of 'non-identity'; that is, of the ways in which instances are not identical with the concepts under which they are subsumed (and with each other). 'Negative dialectics' tacks back and forth between concept and instances, continually pointing out in what concrete ways they are not identical. Such a negative dialectics is a kind of cognition of the non-identical, although the process of moving back and forth negatively between concept and instance has no natural stopping point and will not ever result in some positive, detachable conclusion or new, more adequate concept.

Adorno rejected the usual standards of clarity and communicability for philosophical writing, seeing in them forms of repression', ways of preventing novel thoughts from being thought. He thus consciously wrote in an elusive, convoluted style, and claimed that (his) philosophy could not be summarized. This view makes good sense if one thinks of philosophy as essentially a concrete attempt to specify a 'determi-

nate negation' that cannot in principle be turned into anything positive.

7 Conclusion

The philosophy of art had always played an important part in Adorno's thinking. Art and philosophical reflection on it form one of the few remaining oases for the play of free, spontaneous, human subjectivity in an increasingly regimented world. By the end of the 1960s, however, it had become hard to see how such reflection on high art, negative dialectics or the meditative essays on religion, pessimism and the philosophy of Schopenhauer Horkheimer had begun writing could be seen as part of the 'self consciousness of a revolutionary process of social change', or indeed how the late form of critical theory could be connected with any kind of action at all.

Toward the end of the 1960s Marcuse tried to break out of this impasse by giving up the traditional self-imposed ban among the members of the Frankfurt School on giving a 'positive' theory of any kind or engaging in utopian speculation (see §4). In *An Essay on Liberation* (1969) and *Counter-Revolution and Revolt* (1972) Marcuse claimed that the modern world had brought into existence a 'new sensibility' which he saw expressed most clearly in the emerging student counter-culture. This 'new sensibility', with its demand for aesthetically satisfying forms of immediate experience and its refusal to participate in consumer society, represented a significant new political force in the world. The social change necessary to accommodate the 'new sensibility' had become a vital individual need, and so one could even speak of a 'biological foundation for socialism'.

Since the mid-1960s a group of younger philosophers, most notably Jürgen HABERMAS, have tried to develop further some of the central components of critical theory. Although there are many similarities between the work of this second-generation of Frankfurt philosophers and the programme of critical theory, there are also some striking and important differences. In a sense the second generation marks a return to the kind of Neo-Kantian philosophy the critical theorists of the 1930s were reacting against. Adorno in particular was uncompromising in his opposition to the idea that philosophy should consist of a closed system of interconnected propositions that rested on a purportedly firm foundation and claimed universal validity. In the work of Habermas and his associates, however, the Kantian themes of finding a fixed universal framework for theorizing, giving firm foundations for knowledge claims of various sorts, and investigating the conditions of the possibility of various human activities, structure much of the discussion.

In retrospect the most important contribution of critical theory to philosophy in the late twentieth century would seem to be their criticism of positivism and their demand that social theory be reflective; that is, that theorists try to be as aware as possible of their own position, the origin of their beliefs and attitudes, and the possible consequences their theorizing might have on what they are studying.

See also: FRANKFURT SCHOOL

References and further reading

* *Zeitschrift für Sozialforschung* (Journal of Social Research) (1932–42). (The house organ of the Institute for Social Research in which the members of the Frankfurt School published their most important theoretical work during the 1930s and the very early 1940s. Most of the essays translated in Horkheimer's *Critical Theory* (1972) and in Marcuse's *Negations* (1968) originally appeared here. The journal has a complicated publishing history. In 1932 it began being published by Hirschfeld Verlag, Leipzig. Between 1933 and 1940 it was published (in German) by Librairie Alcan, Paris. In 1939 it changed its name to *Studies in Philosophy and Social Science* and was published (in English) by The Institute for Social Research, Morningside Heights, New York City. The last issue appeared in 1942. In 1980 the Deutscher Taschenbuchverlag, Munich photomechanically reproduced all of the issues of the *Zeitschrift für Sozialforschung/Studies in Philosophy and Social Science* in a set of nine paperback volumes.)
Adorno, T. (1949) *The Philosophy of Modern Music*, trans. A.G. Mitchell and W.V. Blomster, London: Sheed & Ward, 1973.
* —— (1951) *Minima Moralia*, trans. E.F.N. Jephcott, London: New Left Books, 1974.
* —— (1966) *Negative Dialectics*, trans. E.B. Ashton, New York: Seabury Press, 1973.
* Adorno, T.W. and Horkheimer, M. (1944) *Dialectic of Enlightenment*, trans. J. Cumming, New York: Herder & Herder, 1972.
Benhabib, S. (1986) *Critique, Norm and Utopia*, New York: Columbia University Press. (An especially full discussion of the Hegelian and Marxist background.)
Geuss, R. (1981) *The Idea of A Critical Theory*, Cambridge: Cambridge University Press. (Discusses concepts of 'ideology' and 'real interests' and the epistemology of a critical theory.)
Held, D. (1980) *Introduction to Critical Theory*, Berkeley and Los Angeles, CA: University of California Press. (Best general introduction.)
Horkheimer, M. (1947) *The Eclipse of Reason*, New York: Oxford University Press.
* —— (1968) *Critical Theory*, trans. M.J. O'Connell, *et al.*, New York: Herder & Herder, 1972. (Translation of the more important of Horkheimer's essays from the 1930s, all originally published in *Zeitschrift für Sozialforschung*.)
Jay, M. (1973) *The Dialectical Imagination*, Boston, MA: Little, Brown. (Historical account of the Institute for Social Research.)
* Marcuse, H. (1955) *Eros and Civilization*, Boston, MA: Beacon Press.
* —— (1964) *One-Dimensional Man*, Boston, MA: Beacon Press.
* —— (1968) *Negations*, trans. J.J. Shapiro, Boston, MA: Beacon Press. (Contains translations of the most important essays from the 1930s originally published in *Zeitschrift für Sozialforschung*.)
* —— (1969) *An Essay on Liberation*, Boston, MA: Beacon Press.
* —— (1972) *Counter-Revolution & Revolt*, Boston, MA: Beacon Press.
Theunissen, M. (1969) *Gesellschaft und Geschichte* (History and Society), Berlin: Walter de Gruyter. (Best philosophical analysis.)

RAYMOND GEUSS

CROCE, BENEDETTO (1866–1952)

The leading Italian philosopher of his day, Croce presented his philosophy as a humanist alternative to the consolations of religion. A Hegelian idealist, he argued that all human activity was orientated towards either the Beautiful, the True, the Useful or the Good. These ideals were the four aspects of what, following Hegel, he termed spirit or human consciousness. The first two corresponded to the theoretical dimensions of spirit, namely intuition and logic respectively, the last two to spirit's practical aspects of economic and ethical willing. He contended that the four eternal ideals were 'pure concepts' whose content derived from human thought and action. Spirit or consciousness progressively unfolded through human history as our ideas of beauty, truth, usefulness and morality were steadily reworked and developed.

Croce insisted that his idealism was a form of 'absolute historicism', since it involved the claim that all meaning and value evolved immanently through the historical process. He strenuously denied that spirit could be regarded as some form of transcendent puppet-master that existed apart from the human beings through which it expressed itself. He accused Hegel of making this mistake. He also maintained that Hegel's conception of the dialectic as a synthesis of opposites had paid insufficient attention to the need to retain the distinct moments of spirit. He argued that the Beautiful, the True, the Useful and the Good, though linked, ought never to be confused, and he criticized aestheticism and utilitarianism accordingly.

Croce developed his thesis both in philosophical works devoted to aesthetics, ethics, politics and the philosophy of history, and in detailed historical studies of Italian and European literature, culture, politics and society. Opposition to the Fascist regime led him to identify his philosophy with liberalism on the grounds that it emphasized the creativity and autonomy of the individual. In practical politics, however, he was a conservative.

1   **Life and works**
2   **Aesthetics**
3   **Logic and history**
4   **Ethics and politics**

1   Life and works

Born in 1866 at Pescasseroli, in the Abruzzi in Southern Italy, Croce's family were wealthy land-owners; Croce himself never had to pursue a career. In 1883 his parents and sister were killed in an earth-quake in which he too was buried. For the next three years he lived in Rome with his uncle, Silvio Spaventa, a prominent liberal statesman of the Cavourian party known as the Historical Right and brother of the prominent Hegelian philosopher Bertrando Spaventa, whose own political thinking also drew on Hegelian themes. Although Croce never took a degree, he attended lectures at Rome university, where he came under the influence of Antonio LABRIOLA who introduced him to the writings of Johann Friedrich Herbart and later Karl Marx. Croce's political views reflected the conservative liberalism of his uncle, but he claimed never to have been attracted by Bertrando Spaventa's brand of HEGELIANISM or his doctrine of the ethical State. Herbart's Neo-Kantian position, in contrast, inspired his later theory of concept-formation, while his early studies of Marx led him to his view of the Useful as a category distinct from the Good, towards which most practical activity was aimed (see HERBART, J.F.; MARX, K. §11).

Resisting family pressure to enter the law, Croce left Rome in 1886 and settled in Naples, where he determined to become a private scholar. Initially he devoted his energies to numerous antiquarian studies centred on various aspects of southern Italian history in the sixteenth, seventeenth and eighteenth centuries. This research formed the basis of his later books on the Kingdom of Naples and the Baroque era in Italy. This period culminated in his study of Neapolitan theatre from the Renaissance to the Enlightenment, published in 1891. The fusion of cultural and social history in these early writings was highly innovative and contained the germs of many of his later philosophical preoccupations – particularly with respect to the nature of human creativity and action.

These theoretical concerns began to come to the fore when in 1893 he published his first essay in philosophy, 'La storia ridotto sotto il concetto generale dell'arte' (History Subsumed under the General Concept of Art). Croce used an article by the Italian positivist Pasquale Villari entitled 'Is History a Science?' as an excuse both to attack the positivism then dominant in Italy and to enter the contemporary German debate between Windelband and Dilthey over the identity of the human sciences (see DILTHEY, W. §3; HISTORY, PHILOSOPHY OF §4). Croce argued that while history was like art in representing particular events rather than elaborating general laws, as in the natural sciences, it differed in dealing with what actually occurred, rather than with what might have happened. Prompted by Labriola, he followed up this essay with a number of articles attacking crude quasi-Darwinian materialist interpre-tations of Marxism, although he went beyond his brief to criticize Marx's economic doctrines as well. These writings, collected together in book form in 1900 as *Materialismo storico ed economia marxista* (Historical Materialism and the Economics of Karl Marx), brought him to the attention of an interna-tional public including Georges Sorel and Vilfredo Pareto, whose interpretation of Marxism as a secular religion he came to share. His friendship with Giovanni Gentile, then working on a doctoral dissertation on Marx's philosophy, also began at this time (see GENTILE, G. §1). Their collaboration over the next twenty years was to transform Italian philosophy, producing a revival of Hegelian Idealism.

In 1903 Croce began to publish his bimonthly journal *La critica*, devoted to reviews of the latest Italian and European books in the humanities and including general surveys of Italian literature and philosophy since unification written by Croce and Gentile respectively. Croce's *Estetica come scienza dell'espressione e linguistica generale* (Aesthetic) had appeared in 1902. This book became the first volume of his *Philosophy of Spirit*, and was followed by his *Logica come scienza del concetto puro* (Logic) (1905, completely reworked in 1909), the *Filosofia della pratica. Economia ed etica* (Philosophy of the

Practical) (1909), and the *Teoria e storia della storiografia* (Theory and History of Historiography) (1917). Prompted by Gentile, Croce's philosophy took an increasingly historicist direction from 1905 onwards, a shift that led to the rewriting of the *Logica)*. This development also prompted him to write detailed studies of Hegel, *Cio che è vivo e cio che è morto nella filosofia di Hegel* (What is Living and What is Dead in the Philosophy of Hegel) (1907), and of Vico, *La filosofia di Giambattista Vico* (The Philosophy of Giambattista Vico) (1911).

Croce became a life senator in 1910 but only began to write on and participate in politics with the advent of First World War, when he campaigned for Italy to remain neutral. He acted as Minister of Education in the last cabinet of the liberal politician Giovanni Giolitti from 1920 to 1921, putting forward reforms in schools and higher education that he and Gentile in particular had long advocated and which were finally implemented in the Fascist *Riforma Gentile*. Sympathetic to Fascism as long as he felt it was controlled by the old liberal elite as a bulwark against socialism, he never subscribed to its ideology and broke with it after 1924. Relations with Gentile, already strained due to his aversion to his friend's extreme subjectivist 'actual' idealism, finally collapsed with the latter's entry into the Fascist Party, of which he became the self-styled philosopher. Croce became a leading opponent of the regime, penning a famous protest against Gentile's *'Manifesto of Fascist Intellectuals'* in 1925. Opposition gave him a new lease of life and led him to characterize his philosophy as a form of liberalism – most particularly in two series of essays: *Etica e politica* (Politics and Morals) written largely in 1924–8 and collected in 1931, in which he put forward his ethico-political theory of history, and *La storia come pensiero e come azione* (History as the Story of Liberty) (1938), where he defined history as the 'story of liberty'. He also illustrated these theses in four historical studies: *La storia del regno di Napoli* (A History of the Kingdom of Naples) (1925), *Storia d'Italia dal 1871–1915* (History of Italy 1871–1915) (1928a), *Storia dell'eta barocca in Italia* (A History of the Baroque Era in Italy) (1929) and *Storia d'Europa nel secolo XIX* (History of Europe in the Nineteenth Century) (1932). He made corresponding changes to his aesthetic doctrine, culminating in *La poesia* (Poetry) in 1936. Only the allied invasion caused him to stop publishing *La critica*, and he continued to produce books and essays and occasional *Quaderni della critica* right up to his death in 1952.

2 Aesthetics

Croce's aesthetics were tied both to his activity as a literary critic, which was copious, and developments in his general philosophy. He confessed to having no appreciation of music and wrote comparatively little on architecture or the figurative arts, leading some commentators to suggest that his theory is biased towards poetry. As the major influences on his own thinking, he claimed Francesco De Sanctis, whose *La storia della letteratura italiana* (History of Italian Literature) (1870–1) he continued through to the late nineteenth and early twentieth centuries, and Giambattista Vico, whose aesthetic thought he first brought to prominence.

Commentators commonly identify four phases within Croce's aesthetic doctrine, roughly corresponding to changes in his philosophy, although opinions differ over their compatibility with each other. The first phase, associated with the *Aesthetic* of 1902, consists of Croce's identification of art with intuition. His main targets were positivist or empiricist theories, on the one hand, and intellectualist or rationalist views on the other. Against the first, he claimed that feeling and emotion have to be expressed to have any existence, and that this is a cognitive process. Against the second, he distinguished logical from intuitive knowledge. Whereas the former works through concepts and deals with universal relations between things, the latter is obtained through images of particular things. Adopting a Herbartian reading of Kant, he argued that we organize the world of experience and sensation through the intuitive faculty of the imagination that gave expression to them. Form and content, intuition and expression were identical. That which was not expressed had not been intuited and remained 'a mere natural fact'. The logical categorization of this intuitive knowledge was a subsequent stage. He also contended that the theoretical activity of the imagination was distinct from any practical or ethical purpose. True art, therefore, was concerned neither with the True, the Useful or the Good – an argument he deployed against the Italian *verismo* school of naturalist writers influenced by Emile Zola.

The second phase of Croce's aesthetics came with his theory of the lyrical nature of art. First enunciated in an article of 1908, and subsequently elaborated in the *Breviario di estetica* (The Essence of Aesthetic) (1913), this doctrine attempted to specify further just what artistic expression consisted of: namely the lyrical intuition of 'intense feelings' or emotions. Such feelings, he still insisted, could not be described in sensationist terms, but could only be expressed through images. For analogous reasons, he also rejected romantic theories that treated art as no more than a spontaneous outpouring of emotion. Art is a spiritual activity that transforms our bare animal existence. However, he continued to distinguish the images of intuition from the categories of logical thought, and he criticized the artificial canons and rules of classical theorists for ignoring this fact.

While distinct from either philosophy or practice, art was related to them. Drawing on his contemporaneous revision of Hegel and the resulting thesis that spirit evolved via a dialectic of distincts rather than of opposites, Croce argued that intuition tends to give way to perception and so to conceptual thought or judgment. Furthermore, such knowledge leads us to take up a new attitude to life and so affects our practice. This new will in its turn solicits new passions and feelings that find expression in a new lyric and fresh art, constituting a process which Croce termed the 'circle of spirit', in which each moment is both independent and dependent, condition and conditioned.

The third phase of Croce's aesthetics builds on this thesis by insisting on the 'cosmic' or 'universal' character of art. Put forward in his article 'Il carattere di totalità dell'espressione artistica' (The Totality of Artistic Expression) (1918a), this doctrine served to underline the cognitive aspect of his theory by stressing that as an aspect of spirit 'every genuine artistic representation is itself and is the universe, the universe in that individual form' (1926: 122). However, intuition formed only a part of the 'circle of spirit', and he rebutted criticisms of mysticism or aestheticism which accused him of reducing all knowledge to artistic intuition. Nevertheless, at this time Croce tended to reify spirit and treat human activity as a mere manifestation of its unfolding, a position he later rectified. Croce illustrated his argument in studies of *Goethe* (1919a), *Ariosto, Shakespeare, Corneille* (1920) and *La poesia di Dante* (The Poetry of Dante) (1921).

The final phase was signalled by *La poesia* (1936). Croce regarded this book as incorporating all the subsequent revisions of his aesthetic theory and replacing the *Aesthetic* of 1902. He argued that there were four types of 'expression': the 'sentimental or immediate', the 'poetic', the 'prosaic' and the 'rhetorical'. True poetry, he argued, only arose when these types originated from a 'lyrical expression' and had no ulterior utilitarian, moral or philosophical purpose. When lyricism was absent, one had literature, which he further subdivided into the sentimental, moralistic, entertaining or instructive.

3 Logic and history

Croce's *Logic* centred on his notion of the 'pure concept' as a universal idea that could not be confused with the particular representations it encompassed. As such, it was to be distinguished from 'pseudo-concepts', which were mere classes of objects. These latter were empirical rather than theoretical categories.

The content of 'pure concepts' came through history. The identification of history and philosophy in the second edition of the *Logic* (1909) was the most important revision Croce was to make to his theory. Judgment, he argued, is essentially historical in nature, involving the union of a pure universal concept with a historically given particular object. When we say 'Peter is a man' we not only define a characteristic of Peter with a preformed concept of what a man is, we reaffirm and change the concept of man in relation to Peter. Our notions of maleness are historical products of past meetings with other Peters and Pauls, and modifiable by other future encounters. Similarly, Peter's conception of himself was equally defined by a given notion of man. In this way, Croce argued, philosophy proved both conditioned by history and a means, through conceptual innovation, for the making of new history. Likewise, theory and practice are mutually related, the one influencing the other.

Croce carried this thesis further in the final volume of the *Philosophy of Spirit*, the *Theory and History of Historiography*. Here he famously claimed that 'All history is contemporary history' because 'it meets a present need' (1917: 5–17). The collection of facts about the past, while a necessary preliminary for historical writing, was not yet history but 'chronicle'. It was a 'dead' past because it had yet to be interpreted and given a meaning. Interpretation involved entering the minds of the historical actors and understanding the inner significance of their actions by reliving these events in the historian's own consciousness. Croce believed that this was possible because we are what our past has made us, so that our knowledge of ourselves is historically conditioned. The past literally lives within us.

Croce was careful to avoid any suggestion of relativism or subjectivism. He denied that history was whatever we took it to be. Indeed, at times he appeared to argue that it was not so much individuals, as spirit 'eternally individualizing itself' that was the true subject of history. This thesis, together with his contention that we are all products of the past, risked denying individuals the possibility for any creative action at all. During the 1920s and 1930s he modified his position on both these fronts. In a series of essays written in 1922–4, he proposed the view that history was 'ethico-political' in nature. In other words, the conflict of different individual ideals was the true dynamic of history, a view he deployed against both Marxism and Fascism. Historicism, therefore, buttressed liberalism. He was not thereby advocating voluntarism, however. As he made clear in his final major work, *History as the Story of Liberty*, successful action depends on a correct appraisal of one's current situation – itself a matter of historical judgment. Knowing the world in thought gives an impetus to the ethical desire to transform it through action.

4 Ethics and politics

Croce's initial concern in the field of practical philosophy was to distinguish the concepts of the Useful and the Good and to combat both utilitarian moralities and moralistic politics as category mistakes. Although this distinction figured in his writings on Marx and formed the basis of an influential debate with Vilfredo Pareto on the relation of economics to ethics, he did not expound it fully until the *Filosofia della pratica: economia ed etica*, where he integrated it into his general theory of the circle of spirit within history.

He did not draw any practical inferences from this doctrine until the First World War. In a series of articles later collected as *Pagine sulla guerra* (Writings on the War) (1919b), he attacked those who maintained that the war was between two rival moralities – the democratic and the autocratic. Croce contended that war, like politics in general, was pre-moral in being orientated towards the Useful. The state had no purpose but that of power and no means other than force, so that the military struggle should be seen as a matter of pure *realpolitik*. He strenuously denied that this view entailed identifying might with right. However, in essays published as *Frammenti di etica* (The Conduct of Life) (1922), he did insist that morality was not something that could be pursued directly, but was a matter of the judgment of history. Accordingly, he argued that each person should simply fulfil the duties of their appointed station and trust in Providence.

The dangers of this deeply conservative position became evident with the rise of Fascism (see FASCISM). Croce initially supported it, albeit lukewarmly, as leading to a strengthening of the state. However, Gentile, now a keen supporter of Fascism, made precisely the jump that Croce feared of identifying the force of the state with its moral strength. This move, and his resulting doctrine of the ethical state, led Croce to clarify his position. He accused Gentile and the Fascists of putting forward a 'governmental morality'. While he continued to regard the state in the narrow sense as belonging to the realm of the Useful, he now maintained that politics in general had an ethical dimension in the struggle to realize certain ideals and he endorsed

liberal democracy for allowing the widest possible competition between different points of view. However, he claimed his liberalism to be 'metapolitical' rather than narrowly party political. While he believed that liberalism entailed a free market in ideas, he argued that different economic and political policies might be appropriate in different historical circumstances – even communism. This argument provoked a debate with the economist Luigi Einaudi over whether moral and political liberalism entailed libertarianism. Against Einaudi, Croce maintained that economic liberals erred in attempting to categorize everything in terms of the Useful and so failed to see that liberalism was the dialectic of spirit in all of its moments throughout the whole of history. Croce made the same criticism of left-of-centre liberals such as Guido Calogero and Guido de Ruggiero, who campaigned for a social welfare view of liberalism similar to that of the English New Liberals, such as L.T. Hobhouse. While Croce's 'metapolitical' position proved useful in uniting the various opponents of Fascism, it yielded little except a certain pragmatism when it came to practical politics. After the war, Croce acted as President of a new formed Liberal Party. However, he was unable to forge a broad non-Catholic non-Socialist bloc, as he had hoped. Instead, he found himself presiding over an increasingly right-wing party and ultimately resigned.

The shifts in Croce's politics highlight a constant tension in his philosophy as a whole between historicism and idealism, realism and rationalism, politics and ethics, the Hegelian and the Kantian aspects of his thought. In some respects, his chief claim was to have made a virtue out of this tension, rather than attempting to synthesize these two elements. The constant revisions that his thought underwent, however, suggests that he found himself constantly pulled in different directions, emphasizing one then the other.

See also: ECONOMICS AND ETHICS §5; ARTISTIC EXPRESSION §4; HEGELIANISM §6; HISTORICISM §1; POETRY §4; SOCIAL DEMOCRACY §1

List of works

Croce, B. (1906–52) *Opere complete*, Bari: Laterza, 74 vols. (This excludes his correspondence and is not exhaustive. A National Edition is planned, and Adelphi Edizioni of Milan have recently published semi-critical editions of some of his more important works. Croce also made a selection of his works published in 1951 as *Filosofia-Poesia-Storia*, Milan and Naples: Riccardo Ricciardi; trans. C. Sprigge, *Philosophy, Poetry,*

History: An Anthology of Essays, London: Oxford University Press, 1966.)

—— (1891) *I teatri di Napoli del Secolo XV–XVIII* (The Theatres of Naples from the Fifteenth to the Eighteenth Centuries), Naples: Pierro. (The culmination of Croce's only archival research into Neapolitan history of this period.)

—— (1893) 'La storia ridotto sotto il concetto generale dell'arte' (History Subsumed under the General Concept of Art), *Atti dell'Accademia Pontaniana* 24: 1–32. (Croce's first foray into philosophy.)

—— (1900) *Materialismo storico ed economia marxista*, Palermo: Sandron; trans. C.M. Meredith, *Historical Materialism and the Economics of Karl Marx*, London: Latimer, 1914. (Contains his critique of vulgar Marxism and Marxist economics, and his debate with Pareto.)

—— (1902) *Estetica come scienza dell'espressione e linguistica generale*, Milan, Palermo, Naples: Sandron; trans. D. Ainslie, *Aesthetic*, London: Macmillan, 1909; 2nd complete edn, 1922. (The first volume of his *Philosophy of Spirit*, which provides both the first version of his aesthetic doctrine and of his philosophy as a whole – each of which were subsequently much modified.)

—— (1905) *Logica come scienza del concetto puro*, Bari: Laterza; 2nd edn, 1909; trans. D. Ainslie, *Logic*, London: Macmillan, 1917. (The second volume of the *Philosophy of Spirit*. The changes to the second edition were occasioned by criticisms of the first by Gentile, whose influence is duly acknowledged, which led Croce in a more pronounced historicist direction.)

—— (1907) *Cio che è vivo e cio che è morto nella filosofia de Hegel*, Bari: Laterza; trans. D. Ainslie, *What Is Living and What Is Dead in the Philosophy of Hegel*, London: Macmillan, 1915. (A classic study of the German philosopher, which marked Croce's passage from a Neo-Kantian to a more Hegelian position, albeit with important reservations.)

—— (1909) *Filosofia della pratica, economia ed etica*, Bari: Laterza; trans. D. Ainslie, *Philosophy of the Practical*, London: Macmillan, 1913. (The third volume of the *Philosophy of Spirit*.)

—— (1911) *La filosofia de Giambattista Vico*, Bari: Laterza; trans. R.G. Collingwood, *The Philosophy of Giambattista Vico*, London: Latimer, 1913. (One of the earliest studies of the eighteenth-century Neapolitan philosopher, whose thought Croce did much to promote. As with his study of Hegel, his technique is to separate the living from the dead on the basis of those elements which are absorbed or rejected by his own philosophy.)

—— (1913) *Breviario de estetica*, Bari: Laterza; trans. D. Ainslie, *The Essence of Aesthetic*, London: Heinemann, 1921; first published in *The Book of the Opening of the Rice Institute*, Houston, TX, 1912. (Marks the second phase of his aesthetic doctrine.)

—— (1917) *Teoria e storia della storiografia*, Bari: Laterza; trans. D. Ainslie, *Theory and History of Historiography*, London: Harrop, 1921. (The fourth and final volume of his *Philosophy of Spirit*, in which he gives his first full exposition of his historicist views.)

—— (1918) *Contributo alla critica de me stesso*, privately printed in Naples for distribution to friends; trans. R.G. Collingwood, *Autobiography*, Oxford: Clarendon Press, 1927. (Subsequently extended, and republished as an appendix to *Etica e politica*, it focuses on the evolution of his thought and takes Vico's *Autobiography* as its model. He periodically brought it up to date in later editions of *Etica e politica*.)

—— (1919a) *Goethe*, Bari: Laterza; trans. E. Anderson, London: Methuen, 1923. (A study of the German poet Goethe in which Croce seeks to illustrate his 'lyrical' account of poetic expression. The Italian edition included translations of his poetry by Croce.)

—— (1919b) *Pagine sulla guerra (Writings on the War)*, ed. G. Castellano, Naples: Ricciardi; 2nd expanded edn, Bari: Laterza, 1928. (A collection of journalistic pieces in which Croce advocated Italian neutrality and, once Italy had entered the war, argued for a realist view of politics, which he associated with Germany, against the idealist view he linked with the allies.)

—— (1920) *Ariosto, Shakespeare, Corneille*, Bari: Laterza; trans. D. Ainslie, New York: Holt, 1920. (Originally published separately, Croce employed these studies of three great dramatists to further develop his theory of poetry.)

—— (1921) *La poesia di Dante*, Bari: Laterza; trans. D. Ainslie, *The Poetry of Dante*, London: Macmillan, 1922. (A study of Dante's poetry.)

—— (1922) *Frammenti di etica*, Bari: Laterza; trans. A. Livingston, *The Conduct of Life*, New York, 1924. (Collects articles mainly written in 1915–18 which attempt to elaborate a historicist ethics against the background of the First World War.)

—— (1925) *La storia del regno de Napoli*, Bari: Laterza; trans. F. Frenaye, *History of the Kingdom of Naples*, Chicago, IL: Chicago University Press, 1970. (An attempt at 'ethico-political' history that focuses on the role played by intellectuals.)

—— (1926) *Nuovi saggi di estetica* (New Essays on Aesthetics), 2nd edn, Bari: Laterza. (Collects together the various essays in which Croce progressively revised his philosophy of aesthetics. Includes 'Il carattere di totalità della espressione artistica' (1918).)

—— (1928a) *Storia d'Italia dal 1871 al 1915*, Bari: Laterza; trans. C.M. Ady, *History of Italy 1871–1915*, Oxford: Clarendon Press, 1929. (A defence of the liberal regime of Giolitti, with important chapters on the cultural life of the period.)

—— (1928b) *Aesthetica in nuce*, Bari: Laterza; trans. R.G. Collingwood, 'Aesthetics', in *Encyclopaedia Britannica*, New York and London, 14th edn, 1929, vol. 7. (The most accessible account of the third phase of Croce's aesthetic doctrine.)

—— (1929) *Storia dell'eta barocca in Italia* (A History of the Baroque Era in Italy), Bari: Laterza. (Written in 1924–5 and published in instalments in *La critica* between 1924 and 1928, this was a path-breaking work that prompted study of a relatively neglected period of Italian history.)

—— (1931) *Etica e Politica*, Bari: Laterza; trans. S. Castiglione, *Politics and Morals*, London: Allen & Unwin, 1946. (Collects essays written in 1924–8, and represents Croce's attempt to defend a specifically liberal political order against Fascism and to revise his historicism in an 'ethico-political' direction that gave greater play to the creative action of individuals.)

—— (1932) *Storia d'Europa nel secolo XIX* , Bari: Laterza; trans. H. Furst, *History of Europe in the Nineteenth Century*, New York: Harcourt Brace, 1933. (The most 'philosophical' of Croce's histories, which is presented in terms of an apologia for the nineteenth-century liberal culture with which he strongly identified.)

—— (1936) *La poesia*, Bari: Laterza. (The final version of his aesthetic.)

—— (1938) *La storia come pensiero e come azione*, Bari: Laterza, trans S. Sprigge, *History as the Story of Liberty*, New York: W.W. Norton, 1941. (A major revision of his earlier historicism that links it firmly with a 'metapolitical' liberalism through its emphasis on the creative role of human thought and action.)

—— (1949) *My Philosophy, and Other Essays on the Moral and Political Problems of Our Time*, London: Allen & Unwin, selected by R. Klibansky, trans. E.F. Carritt. (A selection from Croce's later works.)

—— (1981) *Lettere a Giovanni Gentile* (1896–1924), ed. A. Croce, Milan: Arnaldo Mondadori. (Contains invaluable accounts of his disagreements with Gentile that allows one to trace the development of his thought and the influence of his one-time

colleague upon it. Gentile's letters are republished in his Collected Works.)

References and further reading

Bellamy, R.P. (1986) 'Liberalism and Historicism: Benedetto Croce and the Political Role of Idealism in Modern Italy 1890–1952', in A. Moulakis (ed.) *The Promise of History: Essays in Political Philosophy*, Berlin and New York: de Gruyter. (Locates Croce's thought in the cultural and political context of the times.)

—— (1987) *Modern Italian Social Theory: Ideology and Politics from Pareto to the Present* , Cambridge: Polity Press, ch. 5. (Focuses on the development of Croce's historicism.)

—— (1991) 'Between Economic and Ethical Liberalism: Benedetto Croce and the Dilemmas of Liberal Politics', *History of the Human Sciences* 4: 175–95. (An account of Croce's political ideas.)

Borsari, S. (1964), *L'opera di Benedetto Croce* (The Works of Benedetto Croce), Naples: Istituto italiano per gli studi storici. (The definitive bibliography of the various editions of Croce's works, although now a little dated.)

Corsi, M. (1974) *Le origini del pensiero di Benedetto Croce* (The Origins of Benedetto Croce's Thought), Naples: Giannini, 2nd edn. (An excellent study of Croce's writings pre-1903, which traces the origins of his later thought in his earlier work.)

De Sanctis, F. (1870–1) La storia de letteratura italiana (History of Italian Literature), in *Opere di De Sanctis*, Turin: Einaudi, 1958, vols 8 and 9. (Croce produced the first critical edition of this work in 1912. In the volumes of *La critica* preceeding the First World War he sought to continue it with studies of authors and literary schools that had developed in Italy since unification.)

Galasso, G. (1990) *Croce e lo spirito del suo tempo* (Croce and the Spirit of His Times), Milan: Mondadori. (A historical study of Croce's philosophy.)

Jacobitti, E.E. (1981) *Revolutionary Humanism and Historicism in Modern Italy*, New Haven, CT: Yale University Press. (Looks at Croce's writings pre-1914 and relates them to the Italian idealist tradition of the nineteenth century.)

Orsini, G.N.G. (1961) *Benedetto Croce, Philosopher of Art and Literary Critic*, Carbondale, IL: Southern Illinois University Press. (The best account in English of Croce's aesthetics.)

Roberts, D.D. (1987) *Benedetto Croce and the Uses of Historicism*, Berkeley and Los Angeles, CA, and

London: University of California Press. (A defence Croce's historicism.)

Rossi, P. (1957) 'Benedetto Croce e lo storicismo assoluto' (Benedetto Croce and Absolute Historicism), *Il Mulino* 6: 322–4. (An excellent critical study of the evolution of Croce's historicism.)

Sainati, V. (1953) *L'estetica di Croce* (Croce's Aesthetics), Florence: Felice Le Monnier. (A fine account of the different phases of Croce's aesthetic.)

Sasso, G. (1975) *Benedetto Croce: la ricerca della dialettica*, Naples: Morano. (A critical defence of the Crocean project, that attempts to trace an internal logic to the progressive evolution of Croce's thought.)

RICHARD BELLAMY

CRUCIAL EXPERIMENTS

A 'crucial experiment' allegedly establishes the truth of one of a set of competing theories. Francis Bacon (1620) held that such experiments are frequent in the empirical sciences and are particularly important for terminating an investigation. These claims were denied by Pierre Duhem (1905), who maintained that crucial experiments are impossible in the physical sciences because they require a complete enumeration of all possible theories to explain a phenomenon – something that cannot be achieved. Despite Duhem, scientists frequently regard certain experiments as crucial in the sense that the experimental result helps make one theory among a set of competitors very probable and the others very improbable, given what is currently known.

Francis BACON was the first to discuss the idea of a 'crucial experiment' at length. He called results of such experiments 'instances of the cross' (hence *experimentum crucis*), borrowing our metaphor from the crosses erected where two roads meet to point out the different directions. Bacon claimed that such decisive instances are to be found both among ones already obtained and, more frequently, among new ones produced expressly for that purpose. He offered several scientific examples, including experiments to decide between competing theories of the tides, of the apparent diurnal rotation of the heavens, of the weight of bodies, of magnetism, and of exploding gunpowder. According to Bacon (1620), such experiments 'afford great light, and are of great weight, so that the course of interpretation sometimes terminates, and is completed in them'.

The most famous attack on the idea of crucial experiments was offered by DUHEM, who boldly asserted (1905) that 'a "Crucial Experiment" is impossible in physics'. He gave two arguments. The first, an expression of Duhem's 'holistic' view of science, is that what is tested is not a single hypothesis or theory by itself, but a 'whole theoretical group', including assumptions regarding the laboratory instruments to be used in testing it. Secondly, and more importantly, even if only a 'theoretical group' rather than an individual hypothesis is tested, for a crucial experiment to be decisive:

> it would be necessary to enumerate completely the various [competing] hypotheses which may cover a determinate group of phenomena; but the physicist is never sure he has exhausted all the imaginable assumptions. The truth of a physical theory is not decided by heads or tails.
>
> (Duhem 1905: 190)

What lies behind the idea of a crucial experiment, according to Duhem, is an 'argument by elimination' with a form such as E_1:

(a) Some phenomenon O is observed.

(b) O can be explained by, and only by, exactly one of the theories $T_1, \ldots, T_n$.

(c) But $T_2, \ldots, T_n$ are false, because each entails some observable consequence which the crucial experiment shows to be false.

(d) So T_1 must be true.

In order to use such an argument, one must consider among $T_1, \ldots, T_n$ not just known theories, but all possible ones that could explain the phenomenon; and this, as Duhem points out, is impossible. If crucial experiments depend on such eliminative arguments, they must be impossible.

Yet scientists frequently do offer eliminative arguments, and of a form not subject to Duhem's major objection. In the early nineteenth century, proponents of the wave theory of light, such as Thomas Young and Augustin Fresnel, sought to establish their theory over the then entrenched particle theory by using an eliminative argument consisting of these steps: (1) Because light travels in space with a finite velocity, and the only known methods of communication of motion from one point in space to another are via the transference of bodies or the propagation of a wave disturbance through a medium, it is highly probable that light consists either of waves or of particles. (2) Some optical phenomena, for example, rectilinear propagation of light, reflection and refraction, can be shown to follow from both the wave and particle theories without difficulty. But in explaining certain other optical phenomena, most notably diffraction, the particle theory, but not the wave theory, introduces auxiliary assumptions that are very probable assuming the particle theory is true but very improbable given everything else that is known. (3) Wave theorists conclude that, given what is known (including all the observed optical phenomena), the wave theory is highly probable (see Achinstein 1991) (see OPTICS §1).

This argument is not refuted by Duhem's logical claims. Wave theorists do not assert, nor do they need to, that the particle and wave theories are the only *possible* ones (which is false, as was shown by twentieth-century quantum theory). They assert only that, relative to what is known at the time, it is highly probable that one theory or the other is true. And they offer reasons for this claim from known causes of motion. Their eliminative argument has a form expressed not by E_1 but by E_2:

(a) Some phenomenon O is observed.

(b) In the case of phenomena of the same type as O, the only known causes are C_1 and C_2; so probably either T_1 (which postulates cause C_1) or T_2 (which postulates C_2) is true.

(c) But T_2 is probably false because, in order to explain related phenomena, T_2, but not T_1, introduces auxiliary assumptions that although probable given T_2 are very improbable otherwise.

(d) So, given what is known, probably T_1 is true.

How do 'crucial experiments' enter the picture? Experiments that reveal phenomena which one theory but not the other explains without introducing highly improbable assumptions may be considered 'crucial' ones in establishing the high probability of the former theory. Fresnel's 1819 experiments on the diffraction of light showed the positions and intensities of the observed diffraction bands. These results were derivable from the wave theory without difficulty. To obtain them from the particle theory one had to introduce special forces acting at a distance that produce effects completely different from any ever observed in nature. Fresnel considered his experiments crucial in so far as they helped make the wave theory highly probable and the particle theory highly improbable.

References and further reading

* Achinstein, P. (1991) *Particles and Waves*, New York: Oxford University Press. (Co-winner of the Lakatos Award in 1993, this work discusses methodological issues in nineteenth-century physics, and includes an analysis of arguments given by wave theorists of light.)

* Bacon, F. (1620) *Novum Organum*; Chicago, IL: University of Chicago Press, 1952. (Book II, section 36, of this classic contains Bacon's discussion of crucial experiments.)

* Duhem, P. (1905) *The Aim and Structure of Physical Theory*, Princeton, NJ: Princeton University Press, 1991. (One of the greatest and most readable twentieth-century works in the philosophy of science.)

Glymour, C. (1980) *Theory and Evidence*, Princeton, NJ: Princeton University Press. (Argues, contra Duhem, that individual hypotheses in a theory can be confirmed.)

PETER ACHINSTEIN

CRUSIUS, CHRISTIAN AUGUST (1715–75)

Crusius was a pivotal figure in the middle period of the German Enlightenment, linking Pufendorf and Thomasius with Kant. Though sometimes wrongly characterized (for example, by Hegel) as a Wolffian, he was instead an important critic of that position. His system reflected a new alliance between Pietism and Lutheran orthodoxy, offering a comprehensive antirationalist, realist, and voluntarist alternative to the neoscholastic tradition as renovated by Leibniz. Crusius was important in Kant's development and helps us understand the latter's philosophical Protestantism.

Born a pastor's son in Leuna bei Merseburg, in Saxony, Crusius was educated at Leipzig and much influenced there by the Thomasian professor A.F. Hoffmann (1703–41). Interested in both philosophy and theology throughout his career, he accepted a chair as extraordinary professor of philosophy at Leipzig in 1744. In 1750, however, he became ordinary professor of theology, also retaining his teaching post in philosophy until his death. His reputation as a philosopher peaked in Germany during the 1750s and 1760s, mainly on the basis of four scholastic manuals published in German during 1744–9. His greater theological reputation as founder of a 'biblico-prophetic' school emphasizing the inspirational unity of Scripture lasted well into the mid-nineteenth century.

1 Philosophical intentions

Crusius' works divide not only into philosophical and theological, but also into Latin and German. In the latter case, which includes his four scholastic manuals *Anweisung* (1744), *Entwurf* (1745), *Weg* (1747) and *Anleitung* (1749), there is disagreement over which are more important, and one gets differing accounts depending on their respective bases. The Latin essays, including *De usu et limitibus principii rationis determinantis* (On the Use and Limits of the Principle of Determining Reason) (1743), cover much the same ground as the manuals, but they are more focused, less didactic and together yield better insight into Crusius' philosophical concerns. Collected in revised form in the *Opuscula philosophico-theologica* (Small Philosophical and Theological Works) of 1750, most of them received approved German translations within a decade or two. Several works from Crusius' 'theological' period also help to clarify his notion of philosophy and its tasks. They include the *Epistola...de summis rationis principiis* (Letter...on the Highest Principles of Reason) (1752), *Dissertationes II–IV de superstitione* (Discourses II–IV on Superstition) (1766), *Kurzer Lehrbegriff der Moraltheologie* (A Short Outline of Moral Theology) (1772: vol. 1), and the prefaces to later editions of the manuals.

These sources reveal Crusius' opposition to 'the newer philosophy', which is inaccurately characterized as 'the Leibnizian–Wolffian system'. For Wolff himself rejected the term, claiming that he knew little of Leibniz when he wrote his so-called 'German Metaphysics' (1719), and Crusius did not use it until 1753 in the preface to the second edition of his *Entwurf*, having previously described the *praeceptor Germaniae* as a 'propagator of Leibnizian philosophy'. Leibniz and Wolff are often mentioned in the Latin writings (the manuals intentionally omit authorial references) and the similarities between them noted, but they are not regarded as having a joint system. Instead, the 'newer philosophy' consisted for Crusius of Leibnizian doctrines about sufficient reason, pre-established harmony, monadic substances, and the best of all possible worlds, with Wolff playing the role of systematizer and elaborator (see LEIBNIZ, G.W.; WOLFF, C.).

Carboncini (1986) suggests that Crusius saw the 'newer philosophy' as a general type. This emerges especially from the theological works, which link it with ancient superstition opposed to sound human understanding, particularly with Stoic fatalism. Beside this objection to its content, Crusius also criticized its syncretistic form and its methodological reliance on sectarian prejudices. His own philosophy, by contrast, emphasized freedom, clarity of concepts (rather than the formal necessity and certainty of arguments) and critical thinking for oneself. These notions link him with the Pietist, 'eclectic' tradition with which he has other, more specific affinities. They also suggest a connection between his philosophical and theological interests and provide a wider context for the needed developmental account of his thought.

2 Basic elements of Crusius' system

Since they were meant to counter Wolff's influence, Crusius' four scholastic manuals are themselves quite Wolffian: thorough, explicit, systematic and full of definitions, multiple arguments and cross-references. They also address many topics treated by Wolff and clearly complement one another.

Least original among them is the *Anleitung*, which was the first Pietist tract to interpret nonliving nature in mechanistic terms, though Crusius still rejected Newtonian gravity. It also emphasized humans' merely hypothetical knowledge of basic natures and powers, and developed a position about the probable status of empirical generalizations or 'presumptions' (for example, nature makes no leaps) similar to Hume's (see HUME, D.).

A 'logic' in the broad sense of a methodology of knowledge, Crusius' *Weg* covers many topics treated by Wolff under empirical psychology. This is because philosophy was for him not merely a science of the possible but one dealing with really existing things. The general 'thinkability' (*cogitabilitas*) criterion that regulates it was therefore elaborated into three principles instead of one. To the formal principle of (A) non-contradiction from which Wolff had sought to derive all other truths (see WOLFF, C. §6), Crusius thought it necessary to add two other, material principles: those of (B) inseparability (*das Nichtzutrennenden*) and (C) unconjoinability (*das Nichtzuverbindenden*). What can or cannot be conceptually separated or joined is not a question of logical possibility only but depends on the nature of the human understanding and the general content of experience. Accordingly Crusius also rejected Wolff's attempt to employ the mathematical method in philosophy, citing no less than nine differences between them, including the fact that mathematics begins with simple ideas whereas philosophy must discover them through an analysis of experience.

Like its counterpart, the will, the human understanding is composed of several basic powers, including sensation, reason, memory, and judgment. We have no clear grasp of these, nor of most other basic concepts, but know them only indirectly or relatively, through comparisons or their effects, in what Crusius calls symbolic as opposed to intuitive knowledge. Symbolic knowledge is regulated by principles (B) and (C) and can be (morally) certain even though it is incomplete. Its conclusions may not be ontologically valid and may, indeed, involve antinomic 'conflicting proofs', but this only reflects the fact that for Crusius some truths are not only beyond but even opposed to our limited human understanding.

Crusius' epistemology combines a Lockean doctrine of simple ideas, discovered through an analysis of experience, with a Leibnizian innatism prefiguring Kant (see LOCKE, J.; KANT, I.). This becomes clearer in the *Entwurf*, which is sectioned into a reordered Wolffian scheme of ontology, theology, cosmology and pneumatology (rational psychology). Here Crusius discusses the (renamed) principle of determining reason, the distinction between the ideal (*ratio cognoscendi*) and the real (*ratio essendi vel fiendi*) ground of things, his doctrine of basic concepts (which he once called 'categories'), particularly space, time and causality, the failure of the ontological argument for God's existence, the nature and interaction of material and spiritual substances, and the two fundamental powers of the human soul, understanding and will.

The fact that the *Anweisung* was the first of Crusius' manuals to appear indicates the primacy of the practical in his thought. Its opening 'thelematology' discussing the human will and its component basic desires and essential freedom is followed by sections on ethics, natural moral theology, natural law, and prudence. These reflect both the standard natural law schema of duties to self, God and others, and the eudaimonist-perfectionist orientation of Leibniz and Wolff (see NATURAL LAW). What distinguishes Crusius is his integration of the intellectualist and voluntarist strains in ethics that had uneasily coexisted since PUFENDORF into a form for which Kant has received most credit. Yet much of Kant's moral apparatus is Crusian, including the central notions of duty, obligation, law, right, virtue, happiness, the highest good, and the moral postulates (see KANT, I.§§9–11). Indeed, since Crusius clearly distinguished prudential and moral necessity, as well as action in accordance with and for the sake of duty, Kant's classification of him as a 'theological moralist' in the analytic of the *Critique of Practical Reason* (1788) is, while technically correct, also misleading. By not doing justice to Crusius it hides Kant's philosophical debts and thereby distorts the history of ethics.

3 Influence

Kant scholars rediscovered Crusius in the late nine-teenth century. Yet even this relationship (most evident in Kant's *Reflexionen* of 1774–5 and lectures) is insufficiently understood, despite the seminal work of Heimsoeth (1956), Wundt (1964b), Schmucker (1961) and Tonelli (1967, 1969). Crusius' influence on the *Nova Dilucidatio* (1755) and the 'Prize Essay' (1764), where Kant distanced himself from Wolffianism, is clear, but his role in Kant's later theoretical and practical philosophy awaits more comprehensive assessment.

Little is known about Crusius' influence beyond Kant. He had numerous disciples into the 1770s, including A.F. Reinhard (1726–83), who received the 1755 Berlin Academy prize on the question of optimism. The Academy itself, led since 1745 by Maupertuis, had broad affinities with Crusianism because of its opposition to Leibniz and Wolff, but these too remain unelaborated. Other links requiring study are those with J.H. Lambert, M. Mendelssohn, J.B. Basedow (who shaped Kant's views on education), and Fichte, who knew Crusius through C.F. Pezold's important 1766 German edition of the *De usu* (see FICHTE, J.G.).

See also: ENLIGHTENMENT, CONTINENTAL; PIETISM; THOMASIUS, C.

List of works

Crusius, C.A. (1964–) *Die philosophischen Hauptwerke* (The Main Philosophical Works), ed. Tonelli, G., Hildesheim: Olms, 4 vols. (Volume 4.2, *Namenregister und wissenschaftlicher Apparat zu den Bänden I–IV,1* (Register of names and critical apparatus for vols I–IV.1) is to appear in 1996.)

—— (1744) *Anweisung vernünftig zu leben* (Guide to Rational Living), Leipzig; in Crusius (1964–), vol 1. (Crusius' 'ethics'.)

—— (1745) *Entwurf der nothwendigen Vernunft-Wahrheiten, wiefern sie den zufälligen entgegen gesetzt werden* (Sketch of the Necessary Truths of Reason, insofar as they are Opposed to Contingent Truths), Leipzig; in Crusius (1964–), vol 2. (Crusius' 'metaphysics'.)

—— (1747) *Weg zur Gewissheit und Zuverlässigkeit der menschlichen Erkenntnis* (The Way to the Certainty and Dependability of Human Knowledge), Leipzig; in Crusius (1964–), vol 3. (Crusius' 'logic'.)

—— (1749) *Kleinere philosophische Schriften* (Minor Philosophical Writings), Leipzig; in Crusius (1964–), vol 4.1. (Crusius' most important Latin essays and the philosophically relevant portions of his 'physics', that is, chaps 1–2 of the *Anleitung, über natürliche Begebenheiten ordentlich und vorsich-*

tlich nachzudenken (Guide to Thinking about Natural Events in an Orderly and Careful Manner). (See Carboncini and Finster (1987), vol. 4.1)

Schneewind, J.B. (trans.) (1990) 'Christian August Crusius', in J.B. Schneewind (ed.) *Moral Philosophy from Montaigne to Kant*, vol. 2: 568–85, New York: Cambridge University Press. (These excerpts from the *Anweisung* are the only translation of Crusius into English.)

References and further reading

Beck, L.W. (1969) *Early German Philosophy*, Cambridge, MA: Belknap Press, 394–402. (Reliable but limited mainly to Crusius' *Entwurf*.)

Benden, M. (1972) *Christian August Crusius. Wille und Verstand als Prinzipien des Handelns*, Bonn: Bouvier. (Thorough, but repetitive and tedious.)

* Carboncini, S. (1986) 'Christian August Crusius und die Leibniz–Wolffsche Philosophie', in A. Heinekamp (ed.), *Beiträge zur Wirkungs- und Rezeptionsgeschichte von Gottfried Wilhelm Leibniz*, Stuttgart: Franz Steiner, 110–25; repr. *Studia Leibnitiana Supplementa* 26. (Referred to in §1. Important for its reconsideration of Crusius' relation to Leibniz and Wolff.)

—— (1989) 'Die thomasianisch-pietistische Tradition und ihre Fortsetzung durch Christian August Crusius', in W. Schneiders (ed.) *Christian Thomasius 1655–1728. Interpretationen zu Werk und Wirkung*, Hamburg: Felix Meiner, 287–304. (Refreshingly different in linking Crusius, and so indirectly Kant, to 'eclecticism'.)

Carboncini, S. and Finster, R. (1987) 'Einleitung', in G. Tonelli (ed.) *Die philosophischen Hauptwerke*, vol. 4.1, Hildesheim and New York: Olms, i–xxxvi. (Essential supplement to Tonelli's 'Introduction' in *Hauptwerke*, vol. 1.)

* Heimsoeth, H. (1956) 'Metaphysik und Kritik bei Chr. A. Crusius. Ein Beitrag zur ontologischen Vorgeschichte der *Kritik der reinen Vernunft* im 18. Jahrhundert' (A contribution to the history of the *Kritik der reinen Vernunft* in the eighteenth century), *Studien zur Philosophie Immanuel Kants. Metaphysische Ursprünge und Ontologische Grundlagen*, Cologne: Kölner Universitätsverlag, ch. 3, 125–88. (An acute treatment of Crusius' many anticipations of Kant's metaphysics of experience.)

Krieger, M. (1993) *Geist, Welt und Gott bei Christian August Crusius*, Würzburg: Königshausen & Neumann. (The latest study of Crusius, focusing on his 'special metaphysics'; chapter 1 contains a full discussion of the previous Crusius literature.)

* Schmucker, J. (1961) *Die Ursprünge der Ethik Kants in*

seinen vorkritischen Schriften und Reflektionen (The Sources of Kant's Ethics in his Precritical Writings and Reflections), Meisenheim am Glan: Anton Hain, 81–98. (Still the most explicit source for Crusius' influence on Kant's mature moral philosophy.)

* Tonelli, G. (1967) 'Crusius, Christian August', in P. Edwards (ed.) *The Encyclopedia of Philosophy*, vol. 2: 268–71, New York: Macmillan. (Good general introduction, particularly for English readers.)

* —— (ed.) (1969) 'Einleitung' (Introduction), *Die philosophischen Hauptwerke*, vol. 1, Hildesheim: Olms, vii–lxv. (The standard overview article on Crusius and his works.)

Wundt, M. (1945) *Die deutsche Schulphilosophie im Zeitalter der Aufklärung*, Tübingen: Mohr; repr. Hildesheim: Olms, 1964, 254–64. (Brief treatment based on Crusius' scholastic manuals.)

* —— (1964) *Kant als Metaphysiker*, Stuttgart: Enke, 52–81. (A good account based primarily on Crusius' Latin works.)

MICHAEL J. SEIDLER

CUDWORTH, DAMARIS
see MASHAM, DAMARIS

CUDWORTH, RALPH (1617–88)

Ralph Cudworth was the leading philosopher of the group known as the Cambridge Platonists. In his lifetime he published only one work of philosophy, his True Intellectual System of the Universe *(1678). This was intended as the first of a series of three volumes dealing with the general topic of liberty and necessity. Two further parts of this project were published posthumously, from the papers he left when he died:* A Treatise Concerning Eternal and Immutable Morality *(1731) and* A Treatise of Freewill *(1838).*

Cudworth's so-called Cambridge Platonism is broadly Neoplatonic, but he was receptive to other currents of thought, both ancient and modern. In philosophy he was an antideterminist who strove to defend theism in rational terms, and to establish the certainty of knowledge and the existence of unchangeable moral principles in the face of the challenge of Hobbes and Spinoza. He admired and borrowed from Descartes, but also criticized aspects of Cartesianism.

Cudworth's starting point is his fundamental belief in the existence of God, conceived as a fully perfect being, infinitely powerful, wise and good. A major part of his True Intellectual System *is taken up with the demonstration of the existence of God, largely through* consensus gentium *(universal consent) arguments and the argument from design. The intellect behind his 'intellectual system' is the divine understanding. Mind is antecedent to the world, which is intelligible by virtue of the fact that it bears the stamp of its wise creator. The human mind is capable of knowing the world since it participates in the wisdom of God, whence epistemological certainty derives. The created world is also the best possible world, although not bound by necessity. A central element of Cudworth's philosophy is his defence of the freedom of will – a meaningful system of morals would be impossible without this freedom. Natural justice and morality are founded in the goodness and justice of God rather than in an arbitrary divine will. The principles of virtue and goodness, like the elements of truth, exist independently of human beings. A* Treatise Concerning Eternal and Immutable Morality *contains the most fully worked-out epistemology of any of the Cambridge Platonists and constitutes the most important statement of innate-idea epistemology by any British philosopher of the seventeenth century.*

1 **Life**
2 *The True Intellectual System of the Universe*
3 **Plastic Nature**
4 **Epistemology**
5 **Free will**
6 **Relation to Descartes**
7 **Influence**

1 Life

Cudworth was born in England at Aller, Somerset. Educated at Emmanuel College, Cambridge, he was elected to a fellowship in 1639. During the Civil War, in the wake of the Parliamentary purge of Cambridge dons, he was appointed Master of Clare Hall and Regius Professor of Hebrew. In 1654 he became master of Christ's College, a position which, along with the Regius Professorship, he retained at the restoration of the monarchy and occupied until his death. Cudworth was also one of the most learned classicists of his day. Although his religious background was in predestinarian Calvinism, he rejected his theological roots in favour of a more Arminian theology which stressed the role of reason in religion. This antivoluntarist stance went hand in hand with a tolerant outlook and an interest in millenarianism. He was consulted by Cromwell on the re-admission of the Jews to England.

Cudworth's philosophical antideterminism is the counterpart of his theological antivoluntarism. Common to both is his conception of the deity, which emphasizes divine goodness, wisdom and justice rather than the divine will. His antivoluntarism has fundamental philosophical implications. First, voluntarism leads to scepticism: if truth depends on God's arbitrary will, there can be no certainty. Second, if the will of God determined all human actions, then human beings would not be responsible for their actions and could not act morally. Furthermore, if the arbitrary will of God decided what was right and wrong, there could be no principles of morality. Voluntarism is the theological counterpart of the false intellectual systems of the philosophical determinists (see VOLUNTARISM).

Cudworth was one of the first philosophers to write consistently in the English language. His philosophical reputation rests on a group of incomplete or posthumously-published treatises. The only philosophical work published in his lifetime was his *True Intellectual System of the Universe* (1678). This was originally conceived as part of a larger work on liberty and necessity, which he never completed. His posthumously published *Treatise Concerning Eternal and Immutable Morality* (1731) was originally intended as the epistemological prolegomenon to a projected treatise on ethics (never completed) of which *A Treatise of Free Will* (1838) was intended to form part. The latter prints one of three discussions of the subject which exist in manuscript. Both posthumously published works of Cudworth as well as the unpublished writings develop philosophical themes sounded in his *True Intellectual System*.

2 *The True Intellectual System of the Universe*

The larger part of Cudworth's *True Intellectual System* is taken up with *consensus gentium* arguments for belief in a supreme deity. Cudworth marshals his immense classical erudition to demonstrate that belief in a deity is natural to humans, by showing that all humans at all times have had some kind of belief in a deity. Cudworth's survey of classical writings was also intended to vindicate corpuscularian natural philosophy from the charge of that it is intrinsically atheistic. Although Cudworth's *System* appears antiquarian, the arguments are relevant to the philosophy of his time and the whole work is underpinned by a concept of philosophy as a unified, timeless whole which has been the same since the beginning of time and which is concerned to discover the same single truth. This *philosophia perennis*, or perennial philosophy, derives from Renaissance models of the history of philosophy propounded by figures such as Agostino Steucho. It is dependent on syncretic and selective readings of philosophical texts, concentrating on noting parallels in doctrines rather than on analysing individual systems. On such a model, contemporary philosophy is not a new development but a recent manifestation of doctrines and arguments for which there are many analogues in antiquity.

For Cudworth, true philosophy is a combination of atomistic, mechanistic natural philosophy and a metaphysics concerned with the immortality of the soul and the existence of God. But this philosophy, originally propounded by Moses, has been corrupted over time. Cudworth distinguishes four distortions of the original atomism in four varieties of atheism: atomical atheism (according to which all things come about by chance), Hylozoic atheism (which imputes life to matter, associated with STRATO of Lampsacus), Hylopathian atheism (which is merely materialistic, associated with ANAXIMANDER) and Cosmo-plastic atheism (which makes the world soul the highest *numen*). These schools of atheistic philosophy have their contemporary proponents: because he imputes the properties of spirit to matter, SPINOZA is a Hylozoist, whereas HOBBES, by denying the existence of spirit, is a Hylopathian atheist.

Cudworth's taxonomy of atomistic philosophies is designed to distinguish between theistic and non-theistic forms of atomism. In this way he attempts to supply contemporary atomism with an impeccably theistic pedigree, clearing it of the imputation that all atomism is materialistic and therefore atheistic. True natural philosophy, he argues, leads inevitably to belief in God. Corpuscularian mechanism supports theism because it is impossible to explain movement, life or thought in terms of the properties attributed to material substance according to the mechanical philosophy, that is in terms of size, shape, position, motion and rest. Since these properties cannot by themselves account for 'Life and Cogitation, Sense and Consciousness, Reason and Understanding, Appetite and Will' (1678: 36), there must be some other cause, necessarily immaterial, namely a spirit or soul. Furthermore, the properties of matter may be deduced from the very idea of it. Matter is therefore intelligible without the useless and unintelligible scholastic apparatus of intentional species and substantial forms. In so far as Cudworth adopted the mechanical theory of matter, he was a modern in his natural philosophy.

3 Plastic Nature

In response to the shortcomings of the mechanical account of motion, Cudworth formulated his distinctive doctrine of Plastic Nature, a formative agency which acts as an intermediary between God and nature, maintaining the orderly day-to-day operations of the physical universe. The concept is indebted to the Platonic doctrine of *anima mundi*, and its functions are associated by Cudworth with the vegetable soul of Aristotelianism. Although he conceives of it as a spiritual agent, he insists that it operates unconsciously, performing the directives of God without question or foresight. Cudworth put forward his theory of Plastic Nature as an alternative to 'Fortuitous Mechanism' on the one hand, which explains all physical phenomena as the result of chance, and occasionalism, on the other, which requires God to intervene in even the most minute details of day-to-day natural occurrences (see OCCASIONALISM). Occasionalist intervention is, in Cudworth's view, unbecoming to God, and it tends to atheism by undermining divine providence, rendering it 'operose, Sollicitous and Distractious'. Even when the mechanistic alternative to occasionalism admits the existence of a deity, it too tends towards atheism by reducing God to an 'idle Spectator'. The doctrine of Plastic Nature is thus designed to rescue divine providence. Its existence shows that nature is not the supreme *numen* but is subordinate to a Perfect Mind. Plastic Nature is the means whereby God imprints his presence on his creation, displaying his wisdom and goodness therein and rendering it intelligible.

4 Epistemology

Contrary to what its title might suggest, *A Treatise Concerning Eternal and Immutable Morality* is largely a work of epistemology. Cudworth originally intended it to serve as prolegomenon to a work on ethics which he never completed, and of which *A Treatise of Freewill* constitutes a section on moral psychology. The fundamental ethical question posed in the overall work is that of Plato's *Euthyphro*: whether things are good because the gods will them, or whether the gods will them because they are good. The treatise is directed against the epistemology and moral relativism of Hobbes, though some of the discussion takes the form of a commentary on the views of Protagoras from Plato's *Theaetetus*. It is a fundamental tenet for Cudworth that moral values are really existing absolutes founded in the goodness and wisdom of God and that knowledge of moral principles is innate to the mind. He sets out the epistemological basis of this view by arguing that all intelligible things exist independently of human minds and even the world. Truth and the principles of knowledge are contained in the mind of God. Certain knowledge is possible because individual minds participate in the divine mind.

Cudworth's epistemology is constructed round the basic Platonic principles of archetype and ectype (form and copy): divine wisdom and knowledge is imprinted in individual minds as well as being reflected in the make-up of the physical world. Since knowledge is in this way innate to the mind, the process of cognition is an act of recollection. Here Cudworth employs the Platonic theory of *anamnesis*, as well as the Stoic concepts of *koinai ennoiai* (common notions) and *prolepsis* (anticipation) to develop the idea that the mind operates by a kind of foreknowledge or anticipation (see PLATO §11; STOICISM §9). This a priori account of cognition accords with his fundamentally Platonic tenet that intellect precedes the world, ideas pre-exist things. But his theory of knowledge is not based on simple correspondence of ideas and things. Mind is not a passive receptor, but an active participant in cognition. Since truth is known from within the mind, not from without, sensory input is insufficient for understanding the external world. Sense data are received passively and piecemeal. Knowledge cannot be derived from them without a comprehending mind able apply 'conceptions or intelligible ideas' to sensory input. The mind focuses on the intelligible aspects of an object, the *scheses* or relationships between its parts, and so penetrates to its essence, understands its function. In the same way, the atomical philosophy can give a meaningful account of the nature of matter, undistracted by sense appearances. It is thus 'the triumph of reason over sense' because it 'solves all the phenomena of the corporeal world by those intelligible principles of magnitude, figure, site and motion, and thereby makes sensible things intelligible' (1731: 544).

5 Free will

In all probability Cudworth's unpublished writings on the subject of free will were a continuation of *Eternal and Immutable Morality*. The three surviving manuscripts on that subject overlap with one another in content, but none is complete (the first was printed in 1831, but the others contain important additions to the discussion). In these papers Cudworth argues that freedom of the will is an essential attribute of rational beings. Without free will moral responsibility would be impossible, and rational beings would be reduced to the level of mere machines. Cudworth conceives of free will as a 'ruling principle' or 'hegemonicon' of the soul which directs the actions of the individual being. More particularly, free will is a power of the soul which directs its actions towards the good. This conception of the beneficent partiality of the will leads Cudworth to repudiate any view that the will is

indifferent. In so far as free will entails the power of furthering the perfection of a creature, it properly belongs only to beings capable of improvement. Consequently it is not an attribute of perfect beings and does not pertain to God. Furthermore, in so far as it may misdirect the soul towards spurious goods, it can lead to wrong doing. It is therefore, in Cudworth's phrase, 'a mungrell thing', since it combines the imperfection of the being to which it belongs and the perfection towards which that being aspires (see FREE WILL; WILL, THE).

The soul is not constrained to act morally by external incentives or disincentives (such as rewards and punishments in the afterlife) but it contains within it the principles of virtue and vice, 'all moral habits' and conscience. This internal moral sense of the soul is superior to intellection and a token of the presence of the divine. Error is a consequence of the imperfection of created beings, who cannot always see the truth clearly and consequently often make judgments about action without clearly and distinctly perceiving the truth.

Cudworth's concept of free will is sustained by a unitary concept of the soul and its powers. The soul is a single, uncompartmentalized unity, compounded of powers or principles, two higher and one lower. It is the function of the middle principle, or free will, to control the lower appetites and to direct the soul towards the highest principle, the *summum bonum*, just as the charioteer in Plato's *Phaedrus* controls the contrary impulses of his two horses to make them pull in the same direction. The term Cudworth uses to describe the exercise of the power of the controlling principle is 'conatus' (striving).

Cudworth's emphasis on the unitary function of the will, and its integration with the soul as a whole, enables him to side-step what he sees as the irresolvable dilemma of philosophers about the priority of reason over will, or will over reason. Furthermore, the integrative function of his 'middle' principle makes it possible to explain close interaction of mind and body, since the domain of the middle principle extends both to the lower, animal appetites and to the higher principles of the soul. In this respect his conception of free will enables him to avoid the problems associated with Cartesian dualism of mind and body (see DUALISM).

6 Relation to Descartes

Cudworth kept abreast of contemporary developments in philosophy and in what we now call science. Indeed, he regarded his 'intellectual system' as the counterpart in philosophy of the physical world system of Copernicus and Galileo. Cudworth was a perceptive critic of contemporary philosophy. His negative assessment of Hobbes and Spinoza was related to his critique of determinism and materialism. His relationship to Descartes was more complex: his philosophy is indebted to Cartesianism in many fundamentals, but he was also critical of Descartes in important particulars. He took over Cartesian dualism of mind and body, and drew on Descartes' theory of the passions. He incorporated the Cartesian account of body into his own philosophy (regarding Descartes as a reviver of Democritean atomism). In epistemology he adopted the Cartesian principle of 'Clear Perceptibility or Intelligibility' as the criterion of truth and used it to underwrite his Platonist identification of being with truth: 'whatsoever is clearly and distinctly perceived to *Be, Is*'. None the less Cudworth put forward a number of criticisms of Descartes, all with sceptical implications. In his *System* (I.iv) he argues that Descartes' proof of the existence of God in the *Meditations* is circular – Descartes first employs the faculties of reason and understanding to prove that God exists, and then proves the truth of those faculties from the existence of God. The argument for the existence of God from the idea of necessary existence, is fallacious because it draws an absolute conclusion from a mere hypothesis. Cudworth offers a number of amendments to Descartes' arguments in an attempt to strengthen them (for example, replacing the argument from necessary existence by one based on possible existence). His other criticisms of Cartesianism are theological, though with important philosophical implications. He argues that Descartes' voluntarism leads to scepticism and his denial of final causes undermines providence. On both these counts Cartesianism is potentially atheistic and Descartes has not been true to his own principles (see DESCARTES, R. §6).

7   Influence

The weighty humanist erudition which encumbers *The True Intellectual System* is largely responsible for the fact that Cudworth is less well known than he deserves to be. But his philosophy continued to arouse interest in both Britain and the rest of Europe during the last part of the seventeenth and throughout the eighteenth centuries. Cudworth's British legacy remains to be charted in detail, but mention should be made of John Ray, Locke (his critique of innate ideas notwithstanding), Shaftesbury, Ramsay, Price and Reid. Thomas Wise produced a severely pruned edition of *The True Intellectual System* in 1703, designed to focus on theological issues of the early eighteenth century. *A Treatise Concerning Eternal and Immutable Morality* was published by Edward

Chandler during the course of the eighteenth-century debate on ethical rationalism sparked by criticisms of Samuel Clarke. Thanks to J.L. Mosheim's Latin translation (1733), Cudworth's writings were known in Germany in the time of Kant. Through extracts published by Jean Le Clerc in the *Bibliothèque choisie* (1703–6), and the controversy between Le Clerc and Bayle which ensued, aspects of Cudworth's philosophy (especially his theory of Plastic Nature) entered enlightenment debates. The doctrine of Plastic Nature was defended by Paul Janet in France as late as the nineteenth-century (Simonutti 1993); and in 1823, Cudworth's philosophy was translated into Italian by Luigi Benedetti.

See also: CAMBRIDGE PLATONISM; LOCKE, J.; NEOPLATONISM

List of works

Cudworth, R. (1678) *The True Intellectual System of the Universe*, London; repr. ed. J. Harrison, London, 1845; repr. Stuttgart-Bad Cannstatt, 1964. (The only major work of philosophy by Cudworth to be published in his lifetime.)

—— (c. 1678–88) 'On Liberty and Necessity', British Library Additional MSS 4978–82. (Three separate treatises on free will, only one of which has been published. See *A Treatise of Freewill* (1838) below.)

—— (1731) *A Treatise Concerning Eternal and Immutable Morality*, London; repr. in *True Intellectual System*, 1845, vol. 2; ed. S. Hutton, Cambridge: Cambridge University Press, 1996. (First published posthumously by Edward Chandler, this contains Cudworth's epistemology.)

—— (1838) *A Treatise of Freewill*, ed. J. Allen, London; ed. S. Hutton, Cambridge: Cambridge University Press, 1996. (British Library Additional MS 4978, one of the three manuscript versions on the subject of free will by Cudworth.)

References and further reading

Aspelin, G. (1943) 'Ralph Cudworth's Interpretation of Greek Philosophy. A Study in the History of English Philosophical Ideas', *Göteborgs Högskolas Arsskrift* 49: 1–47. (Cudworth's interpretation of Greek philosophy.)

Cassirer, E. (1932) *Die Platonische Renaissance in England und die Schule von Cambridge*, Leipzig and Berlin: Studiender Bibliothek Warburg; trans. J.P. Pettigrove, *The Platonic Renaissance in England*, Edinburgh: Nelson, 1953. (Discusses Cambridge Platonism in relation to European philosophy.)

Colie, R. (1957) *Light and Enlightenment*, Cambridge:

Cambridge University Press. (On the Cambridge Platonists and the Republic of Letters, including Cudworth, Bayle and vitalism.)

Cragg, G.R. (ed.) (1968) *The Cambridge Platonists*, New York: Oxford University Press. (Selections from *Eternal and Immutable Morality*.)

Darwall, S. (1995) *The British Moralists and the Internal Ought*, Cambridge: Cambridge University Press. (Chapter 5 discusses Cudworth's moral philosophy, especially his writings on free will.)

Gregory, T. (1967) 'Studi sull'atomismo del seicento: III Cudworth e l'atomismo' (Studies on seventeenth century atomism: Cudworth and atomism), *Giornale critico della filosofia italiana* 46: 528–41. (Cudworth and Atomism.)

Hunter, W.B. (1950) 'The Seventeenth-century Doctrine of Plastic Nature', *Harvard Theological Review* 4: 197–213. (Includes discussion of Cudworth's theory of plastic nature.)

Hutton, S. (1995) 'Lord Herbert and the Cambridge Platonists', in S. Brown (ed.) *British Philosophy and the Age of Enlightenment, Routledge History of Philosophy*, vol. 5: 20–42. London: Routledge. (Includes a section on Cudworth's philosophy.)

Passmore, J.A. (1951) *Ralph Cudworth, an Interpretation*, Cambridge: Cambridge University Press. (The only monograph on Cudworth, this deals mainly with posthumous publications and manuscripts. Useful – if dated – bibliography, with incorrect attribution of some manuscripts to Cudworth.)

Popkin, R.H.(1992) 'Cudworth', in *The Third Force in Seventeenth-century Philosophy*, Leiden: Brill, 333–50. (Cudworth and Scepticism.)

Rogers, G.A.J. (1988) 'Die Cambridge Platoniker' and 'Ralph Cudworth', *Ueberwegs Grundriss der Geschichte der Philosophie: die Philosophie des 17. Jahrhunderts* 3 (1): 245–6, 267–72, 285–90. (Includes a comprehensive and recent bibliography.)

Sailor, D.B. (1962) 'Cudworth and Descartes', *Journal of the History of Ideas* 23: 133–40. (Cudworth and Descartes.)

Scott, D. (1990) 'Platonic Recollection and Cambridge Platonism', *Hermathena* 149: 73–97. (On the theory of knowledge of Cudworth, More and Whichcote.)

Simonutti, L. (1993) 'Bayle and Le Clerc as readers of Cudworth. Elements of the debate on Plastic Nature,' in the Dutch Learned Journals *Geschiedenis van de Wijsbegeerte in Nederland* 4: 147–165. (Cudworth's fortuna in Enlightenment Europe.)

SARAH HUTTON

CULTURAL IDENTITY

If cultural identity means that a person achieves the fullest humanity within an accepted context of traditional symbols, judgments, values, behaviour and relationships with specific others who self-consciously think of themselves as a community, then it must be seen as a great contemporary challenge to many Western philosophical assertions about the person, society, meaning and truth.

This sense of cultural identity, as well as more extreme forms, can amount to classic determinism: individuals are subsumed under the relations with meaning and people surrounding them. Advocates of the centrality of cultural identity often make an argument rooted in an 'authenticity' which purports that, to fully encounter oneself, each of us must grasp and fully accept one's psychological and social location within a specific group of people who interpret life in terms of the particular civilization that contains them.

1   **Philosophy and cultural identity**
2   **Community and belonging**
3   **Alternative perspectives**

1   Philosophy and cultural identity

In the twentieth century Western philosophy has endured many assaults on the claims of some of its practitioners that it somehow constitutes a foundational discipline whose concerns are basic to any comprehensive analysis of what it means to be human. In some intellectual quarters the most formidable challenges arise from both scientific practice and the dominant models and images therein. This view is often found among analytic philosophers trained in the Anglo-American traditions. These traditions have emphasized the close study of 'linguistic claims' and sentences whose truth these philosophers seek to ascertain by appealing to logic and 'common language usage'.

Usually quite separate from that tradition have been other continental ones whose fundamental texts were first written in German, French, or more rarely for English-speaking students of philosophy, Russian, Italian, or Spanish. At least some of these European advocates have been influenced by Friedrich NIETZSCHE and other thinkers (including those commonly called philosophers but also literary figures, artists and social theorists) of an intellectual tradition descended from Nietzsche.

From such a Nietzschean perspective, concepts like cultural identity pose problems of the range and possibility of philosophy quite different from those of science. The Spanish thinker José ORTEGA Y GASSET has described himself as a human creature who is both 'myself and my circumstance'. In that duality Ortega Y Gasset demonstrates what it means to have become aware of context, or what some existentialists have called 'situationality'. Even when people think it is better to seek truth, they still exist within a situation of having been influenced both consciously and unconsciously by their circumstances in the world.

Thus issues of cultural identity can cause a crisis of legitimacy for any human activity which stresses the search for basic truths, fundamental realities and those thoughts or ideas which serve to ground our lives. If we are creatures with identities rooted in specific cultures, then the ancient Western idealist sense of the humanly universal is either suspect or defunct. This might be because we become products of cultural contexts so that we and the people we encounter across the world may be more fundamentally different than similar.

2 Community and belonging

The decline of empires in the twentieth century has contributed to new senses of this issue of the problematic commonality of individuals and societies. In recent centuries imperial Europeans, the people of the USA, as well as the Japanese, Chinese, Russian, Turkish, Incan, Aztec and various dominant tribes in other continents could confidently view other peoples as still being in need of protection, advancement, development and civilizing enlightenment. Late in this century in numerous areas of the world, the question of what it is to be fully human has arisen, with the conclusion that individuals must define themselves in terms native to the people or community to which they belong. Put radically, 'belonging' within such theories of cultural identity becomes the first condition for achieving full adulthood for members of our species. It is only when we acknowledge to which group we belong that we can discover who we are and what being human truly means.

This perspective has the effect of making most intellectual activity regional. Our symbols and their meaning essentially become products of those others who collectively give us our neighbouring human groups. This is a process connected to psychology in personal and social senses: adult consciousness is a result of belonging to a group, or community. Self-image necessarily evolved from and continues to comprise elements derived from our personal situations in tandem with others.

Politically this appeal to the region of nearby others and their established meanings for our selfhood has the effect of determining to what group we belong within other neighbourhoods of the world and thus where else we can expect both to be welcome and express the best of ourselves. Such perspectives permit cultural identity to provide people both like and unlike ourselves with the certainty of boundaries. From a psychosocial position, these perspectives of cultural identity can be seen as safe and 'authentic', however, they can also be anti-cosmopolitan, anti-individualistic and relativistic. Their appeal may be seen on two levels: for the relatively powerless there is the possibility of successful initiation and nurture within a tradition of relations and symbolic expression; for the powerful within such a self-defining community there is a means to unify the group and establish both its continuity of power and ready-made 'outsiders' to serve whatever purposes might sustain that power as well as the group's position among other groups.

In the West, within the great democracies and among the ruins of the old empires, appeals to cultural identity have tended to be voiced in three ways. Some groups have insisted on the inevitable alienation their members experience when left as unintegrated, unhappy, unfulfilled, though nominal citizens of such states as the former Soviet Union, Eastern Europe and China. In countries like the USA, Canada, many European countries and other technologically advanced nations like Australia, New Zealand and Japan, some have demanded that the dominant culture admit the presence of and provide significant resources for (sometimes as restitution for past suppressions) groups either fully in possession of their cultural inheritances or struggling before the indifference or hostility of some members of dominant groups. Finally, in some developing nations a combination of two other tendencies has arisen: some communities or peoples wish to escape traditional control by the central metropolitan powers, while others want a better deal from those powers as they continue to be valued components of the nation. This mix can be found in countries such as India, Brazil, Mexico, Malaysia, Indonesia, the Philippines, Nigeria and Zaïre.

In terms of such topics, discussions of cultural identity are difficult to find outside issues arising from the remnants of empire and the countervailing gestures of liberation. In the context of theories of liberation from the old empires, some religious movements seem deeply committed to advancing accompanying cultural identities. Variants of Islam fit this model, as do evangelical Protestants in Catholic countries in Latin America.

More controversially, in the most developed areas of the world cultural identity has sometimes been transformed into a self-defining paradigm for the liberation of women, gays and lesbians. In these cases some have argued that a mix of roles, attitudes, values, personalities, interpersonal styles, language patterns, behaviour, ethics and other expressions constitute a separate origin for identity that is parallel in form to and more powerful than more traditional concepts such as ethnicity or race. From such perspectives being feminist or gay conveys a centrality or origin of personhood that is foundational to personal identity, which manifests itself coincidentally in what these theorists call a separate culture.

However, determinisms tend to crowd and frustrate people when the search for a fundamental essence becomes serious. Most advocates of personhood which focuses on cultural identity do not want to accept gender or sexual preference as competing forms of personal identity. Their usual position is to stress how these aspects of humanity bear out the evidence of the effects of particular cultures, or subcultures within larger social units like nation states and thus provide arenas within behaviour for seeing the power and separateness of cultural identity. Instead of stressing common forms of the feminine, such advocates choose to emphasize the differences of women's roles from one community to another.

Cultural identity, in its purer forms, should be seen as an assertion of an essentialist argument: we are what those among whom we have been raised have made us. We cannot find ourselves fully without embracing these community-based relations: from them we get a sense of what is important and definitional about our lives.

3 Alternative perspectives

There are at least three alternatives which oppose such notions: first, advocates of human generality, often expressed as 'universal humanity', stress intuitions and evidence that common structures arise routinely within the lives of people supposedly living within other, sometimes 'opposed' cultures. From such a perspective, placing a stress on polarized cultural identities is tangential, narrow and by definition dehumanizing and thus dangerous. Second, cultural identity is a stance rooted more in the politics of the decline of empires than in anything foundational. The reservations inscribed in this stance might be that advocates of cultural identity practise a form of 'local politics' whereby they seek to take advantage of guilt arising from the legacy of empires and stigmatized hegemonic attitudes. This criticism emphasizes the political and social advantages accrued by the leaders of movements who wish to be compensated for past gestures directed at the affected group by dominant cultures and societies. The third opposition to previously discussed notions of community and

belonging is that we are individuals whose lives are particularized by the accidents of space, time, biology and history in ways which are unique. Within the terms of this model, cultural origins are extremely important, but they themselves can become critical topics: their elements can become other for us and can be altered or disowned. Options from other human cultures can be substituted or adopted by us.

See also: COMMUNITY AND COMMUNITARIANISM; PERSONS

References and further reading

Schutte, O. (1993) *Cultural Identity and Social Liberation in Latin American Thought*, Albany, NY: State University of New York Press. (A thorough analysis of the positive features of cultural identity in Latin America.)

Unamuno, M. de (1954) *The Tragic Sense of Life*, New York: Dover. (Argues that the person creates persona, only some of which stress relations to ancestors or neighbours as foundational to personhood.)

Weinstein, M.A. (1976) *The Tragic Sense of Political Life*, Columbia, SC: University of South Carolina Press. (Contains the argument that the individual is badly served by identification with, or belonging to a 'people', or nation-state.)

—— (1978) *Meaning and Appreciation*, West Lafayette, IN: Purdue University Press. (Describes human consciousness as existing prior to membership in a people or community.)

JOHN A. LOUGHNEY

CULTURAL RELATIVISM
see RATIONALITY AND CULTURAL RELATIVISM

CULTURE

Culture comprises those aspects of human activity which are socially rather than genetically transmitted. Each social group is characterized by its own culture, which informs the thought and activity of its members in myriad ways, perceptible and imperceptible. The notion of culture, as an explanatory concept, gained prominence at the end of the eighteenth century, as a reaction against the Enlightenment's belief in the unity of mankind and universal progress. According to J.G.

Herder, each culture is different and has its own systems of meaning and value, and cannot be ranked on any universal scale. Followers of Herder, such as Nietzsche and Spengler, stressed the organic nature of culture and praised cultural particularity against what Spengler called civilization, the world city in which cultural distinctions are eroded. It is difficult, however, to see how Herder and his followers avoid an ultimately self-defeating cultural relativism; the task of those who understand the significance of human culture is to make sense of it without sealing cultures off from one another and making interplay between them impossible.

Over and above the anthropological sense of culture, there is also the sense of culture as that through which a people's highest spiritual and artistic aspirations are articulated. Culture in this sense has been seen by Matthew Arnold and others as a substitute for religion, or as a kind of secular religion. While culture in this sense can certainly inveigh against materialism, it is less clear that it can do this effectively without a basis in religion. Nor is it clear that a rigid distinction between high and low culture is desirable. It is, in fact, only the artistic modernists of the twentieth century who have articulated such a distinction in their work, to the detriment of the high and the low culture of our time.

1 Definition of culture

In human history, culture in its broadest sense is that which is socially rather than genetically transmitted. It is that which children learn by virtue of their being brought up in one group rather than another, and, in its totality, it is that which distinguishes one human group from another. To human culture belong language, customs, morality, types of economy and technology, art and architecture, modes of entertainment, legal systems, religion, systems of education and upbringing, and much else besides; everything, in other words, by virtue of which members of a group endow their activities with meaning and significance. Even from the brief list of elements comprising a culture, it will be evident that there is no clear criterion for identity in the case of human culture. Cultures are characteristically permeable, evolving, open to influence from outside and inside in unpredictable ways, liable to be divided into subcultures, and to generate offspring with their own lives and development. And while individuals from a given culture are formed by it in all sorts of ways, conscious and unconscious,

theoretical and practical, individuals are not prisoners within their cultures, but can affect them, react against them and contribute to their development.

2 Herder and the centrality of culture

In view of the all-encompassing nature of culture and of the multiple vaguenesses connected with the notion, one might be tempted to wonder whether it is a useful concept at all. That it is not just useful, but central to the analysis of history, was strongly urged by HERDER (§4) in a sustained onslaught on Enlightenment thinking. Against the Enlightenment's conception of the unity of mankind and its belief in progress, Herder stressed the plurality of human societies and the incommensurability of their values (and hence the impossibility of talking of historical progress in any uncontested way). According to Herder, each of us is what we are because of the group to which we belong. Activity and self-expression are valuable in the degree to which they express the personality of the individual agent and that of the group to which they belong. Stressing the organic nature of human societies and the interplay between societies and cultures, Herder rejects centralization, bureaucracy, the elimination of cultural diversity and, above all, imperialism. In his *Briefe zur Beförderung der Humanität* (Letters for the Advancement of Mankind), he asks:

> Can you name a land where Europeans have entered without defiling themselves forever before defenceless, trusting mankind?... Our part of the earth should not be called the wisest, but the most arrogant, aggressive, money-minded: what it has given these peoples (the colonies) is not civilization but the destruction of the rudiments of their own cultures wherever they could achieve this.
>
> (Herder, in Berlin 1976: 160–1)

The world in which each of us lives is a particular cultural inheritance, binding us to our forefathers and to our descendants, and distinguishing us from members of other cultures. Herder is clearly right to make what is, in effect, the distinction between causal explanations and explanations in terms of meaning. Human beings are not machines, and our activities cannot be accounted for in terms of scientific psychology; while we doubtless have animal needs and urges, our lives are lived for the most part in realms of meaning, even in pursuit of such elementary needs as food, shelter and sex. The human *Lebenswelt* is a world of *intelligibilia*, of norms and normativity, of activities regulated by standards and fashions and criteria demanding our allegiance, on pain of lapse into brutishness, outlawry and, ultimately, incoherence.

If Herder had done no more than draw attention to the importance of culture and meaning in human affairs, and to the equivocal nature of the concept of progress, there would be few who would dissent. His position, however, becomes more problematic when wrestling with the consequences he derives from it. Thus, Herder's dislike of nationalism and repudiation of the idea of a *Favoritvolk* leads him into a cultural relativism which has at least as many difficulties as the nationalist supremacism of successors such as Fichte (see NATION AND NATIONALISM). At the same time, his insistence on the organic nature of culture and his rejection of cosmopolitanism (even if in the form of imperialism) may well have provided encouragement to the very nationalism he deplored. Certainly, it is hard not to see Spengler's celebrated distinction between civilization and culture as owing as much to Herder as to Nietzsche (who was himself no mean exponent of cultural essences). For Spengler, the very idea of a cosmopolis, a world city, is a symptom of decline from the higher state of culture.

3 Culture and civilization

For Spengler (who is in his own way elaborating themes from Nietzsche's *The Birth of Tragedy*), civilization is the movement away from the strong local and unquestioned bonds which constitute organic culture:

> In place of a type-true people, born of and grown on the soil, there is a new type of nomad, cohering unstably in fluid masses, the parasitical city-dweller, traditionless, utterly matter-of-fact, religionless, clever, unfaithful, deeply contemptuous of the countryman, and especially that highest form of countryman, the country gentleman.
> (Spengler [1917–22] 1926–8: 32)

Along with the decline of organic culture comes science, rationalism, socialism, internationalism, a preoccupation with trade and luxury, wage disputes and football grounds; all, in other words, which is characteristic of modernity. Like Herder, Spengler does not see any of this as progress, although one wonders whether the deep-seated relativism to which both are committed entitles them to see it as decline either.

4 Cultural relativism

Cultural relativism, indeed, is the pathos of strong theories of culture. What in the hands of Herder and Spengler began as a reasonable reaction against the facile optimism and scientism of the Enlightenment and its offshoots, such as socialism and utilitarianism, can turn all too quickly into an enervating and disabling relativism. This relativism deprives itself of the resources to criticize barbaric societies, old and new. It is noteworthy that for all his invective against both Rome and what he calls its lack of soul, and against the twentieth-century world, Spengler is carefully even-handed in praising the Colosseum and 'the brown massiveness' of Roman brickwork, as well as the aero-engines, the precision lathes and the steel structures of his own day (Spengler 1917–22: introduction). Moreover, there is a worrying determinism in making culture too definitive of the group to which it belongs, in that any reception of outside influence is going to seem either impossible in appealing to values not recognized by insiders or undesirable in diluting the purity and distinctiveness of a culture; or, at different times, both before and after it has happened.

While with regard to culture neither Herder nor Spengler avoid the traps laid by relativism, determinism and prescriptivism, no important thinker who has seen the significance of culture has shown clearly how attendant dangers are to be avoided without lapsing into a kind of universalism which cannot accommodate any significant understanding of culture (see RELATIVISM; SOCIAL RELATIVISM).

5 Common culture and high culture

So far, this entry has focused on what might be called the anthropological sense of culture: that memorably described by T.S. Eliot as involving all the characteristic activities and interests of a people (Eliot 1948). Speaking of English culture, Eliot lists Derby Day, Henley Regatta, Cowes, the Twelfth of August, a cup final, the dog races, the pin-table, the dartboard, Wensleydale cheese, boiled cabbage cut into sections, beetroot in vinegar, nineteenth-century Gothic churches and the music of Elgar. Eliot, being an American, was rather better positioned to describe *English* culture than most Englishmen. So much of a culture is traditional, unspoken, taken for granted, even unrealized by its adherents. It nevertheless gives form and meaning and moral direction to the experience of those who belong to it. It is partly because of its tacit dimension that theorists of culture fear that too much explicitness, too much reasoning and too much change will unbalance the common culture of a people, and so change or even subvert its identity. Why is the cabbage cut into sections? Isn't Wensleydale cheese hard to make conform to Euro-standards? Shouldn't the cup final be played so as to fit the demands of television? After not very much of this, the whole world, or so it seems, starts to dance to the tune of McDonald's and satellite TV.

After giving his list, Eliot goes on to enunciate what he calls 'the strange idea that what is part of our culture is also part of our *lived* religion' (Eliot [1948] 1962: 31; original emphasis). Eliot's own idea was that a people's culture is the incarnation of its religion, although as he concedes that materialism could be a religion in the required sense, it is hard to assess the force of this claim.

More characteristic of thinking about culture over the last 200 years is the claim associated first with SCHILLER and, in the English-speaking world, with CARLYLE, Ruskin, Matthew Arnold and F.R. Leavis; namely, that culture or, more precisely, high culture can somehow substitute for religions. The thought is that in the absence of an acceptable dogmatic religion, people's highest aspirations and spiritual life are best expressed in works of art.

Leavis' continual complaint was that in so much of contemporary life we find 'no goals having any real authority except those capable of measurement' (Leavis 1972). In such circumstances, we lose our sense of the value and meaning and potential of life; there is 'no wealth, but life', as Ruskin put it, but we no longer have any sure sense of what wealth in life is, or how life should be lived to mine its wealth. The thought is that in some works of art, (in Leavis' view, such as in Eliot's poetry, in D.H. Lawrence and in Blake), we are brought up short against a harder reality than we normally encounter in the utilitarian, hedonistic, calculating world in which we spend most of our lives, and we glimpse possibilities of something higher or deeper.

Certainly Beethoven's symphonies and quartets, the painting of Turner and Van Gogh, the poetry of Rilke and the writing of Proust, are for many today epiphanic or revelatory in the way religion once was. Artists of this calibre seem to Leavis to form a league against the philistine, Benthamite world (which includes among its characteristic products most contemporary analytical philosophy). And art, in this highest sense, spreads messages more terrifying than the insipid 'sweetness and light' which Arnold thought could form a bulwark against anarchy.

It must, however, be a moot point as to whether any of the exponents of the arts mentioned above would have seen themselves as unreligious or in competition with religion as such, rather than as hostile to some very specific forms of religion. It is, in other words, a moot point as to whether art can uplift in the way Leavis and the other critics hope if all doors are closed against religious hope, or whether an explicitly humanistic, atheistical art would not be likely simply to reinforce the very materialism Leavis hopes literature will rebut.

Whether high culture can perform the role foisted on it or not, the very notion of a high culture is increasingly questioned, not least by contemporary artists and critics themselves. Eliot argued that hereditary class divisions were essential for a healthy culture and a healthy art, and however romantically we may look at the groundlings in Shakespeare's theatre or the whole city enraptured by Aeschylus, it is undeniable that there are elements in Shakespeare and Aeschylus which repay and demand the highest levels of attention, ability and concentration, levels clearly beyond the majority of any population known in history.

What, however, is not in doubt is that there have been times and places in which the majority of a culture have been capable of responding in some way to Aeschylus and Shakespeare; as also to Raphael or Rembrandt or Mozart or to the Authorized Version of the Bible. In the same way, 'high' artists, such as Bach, Schubert, Scott, Dickens, Hogarth and David, have drawn on popular forms and created popular forms themselves. The truth is that at least until this century, culture and art have operated at different levels, but in a way in which there were continuities and overlaps. It is only with the giants of twentieth-century modernism – Schoenberg, Le Corbusier and, to a lesser degree, Picasso and Braque – that exponents of high culture have deliberately cut themselves off from their roots in the surrounding popular culture. The result has been a hermetic and self-referential high culture lacking popular appeal, and a popular culture with few values other than those of advertising and the mass media. The conclusion prompted by this observation is that in cultural matters, the important distinction is not so much that between high culture and popular culture as that between good cultural times and bad cultural times; and that just as good works can be found at both the high and the popular ends of the spectrum, so in bad times works low in ambition and achievement can be found in prestigious galleries and concert halls just as much as in the mass media.

See also: IBN KHALDUN

References and further reading

Arnold, M. (1869) *Culture and Anarchy*, Cambridge: Cambridge University Press. (Puts the argument for culture's civilizing force.)

* Berlin, I. (1976) *Vico and Herder*, London: Chatto & Windus. (An excellent and readable account of Herder.)

Barnard, F.M. (ed.) (1969) *J.G.Herder on Social and Political Culture*, Cambridge: Cambridge University Press. (Classic source on the importance of culture for the history of a people.)

* Eliot, T.S. (1948) *Notes Towards the Definition of Culture*, London: Faber & Faber; repr. 1962. (Explores the complexity and necessity of the idea of culture. Referred to in §5.)

* Herder, J.G. (1784–91) *Briefe zur Beförderung der Humanität* (Letters for the advancement of Mankind), trans. T.O. Churchill in *Outlines of a Philosophy of the History of Man*, London, 1800. (Stresses the particularity of different cultures and the absurdity of looking for invariant laws of human behaviour.)

* Leavis, F.R. (1972) *Nor Shall My Sword*, London: Chatto & Windus. (Defends a sense of culture against utilitarian consensus. Referred to in §5.)

Scruton, R. (1990) *The Philosopher on Dover Beach*, Manchester: Carcanet. (Much intelligent reflection on the subject matter in §5.)

* Spengler, O. (1917–22) *Der Untergang des Abendlanders* (The Decline of the West), trans. C.F. Atkinson, New York: Alfred A. Knopf, 2 vols, 1926–8. (Significant for its distinction between culture and civilization. Referred to in §3.)

Taylor, C. (1989) *Sources of the Self*, Cambridge: Cambridge University Press. (An excellent, although difficult, discussion of the whole area..)

ANTHONY O'HEAR

CULVERWELL, NATHANIEL (*c*.1618–*c*.51)

Nathaniel Culverwell (or Culverwel) was one of the first natural law theorists in seventeenth-century England, and one of the first moral philosophers to stress the primacy of reason. His aim was to revive the natural law tradition of Aquinas and Suarez, which had fallen into disrepute in English Calvinism. Culverwell's theory is a synthesis of rationalism and voluntarism. It attempts to do justice to both the normative and coercive, to the moral and punitive aspects of law. The emphasis of his theory is, however, strongly rationalist, a reaction against the voluntarist legacy of Calvinism. Culverwell had close connections with some of the leading figures of Cambridge Platonism. He is not, however, a typical member of this school, because of the strong Calvinist strands of his early sermons.

1 Life
2 Natural law
3 Cambridge Platonism

1 Life and work

Not much is known about Nathaniel Culverwell's life. Born into a prominent family of Puritan clergymen, he was christened on 13 January 1619. In 1633 he was admitted to Emmanuel College, Cambridge, where he took his B.A. in 1636 and his M.A. in 1640. Emmanuel College was then notorious as a 'Puritan nursery', but it was also the cradle of Cambridge Platonism (see CAMBRIDGE PLATONISM). Among Culverwell's fellow undergraduates were Ralph CUDWORTH, John Smith and John Worthington, and it is probable that Culverwell's tutor was Benjamin Whichcote. Culverwell was made a Fellow of Emmanuel in 1642. He died young, probably in 1651.

Culverwell published nothing in his lifetime. His most important work is *An Elegant and Learned Discourse of the Light of Nature* (1652), edited by his colleague William Dillingham. This work was probably written during the university year 1645–6, when it was delivered as a series of sermons in Emmanuel College chapel. Culverwell also wrote eight sermons, which were published with the *Discourse*. The most important of these are 'The White Stone', whose theme is the need to make our election sure, and 'Spiritual Opticks', whose subject is the imperfection of our knowledge of God in this life.

2 Natural law

Culverwell's *Discourse* occupies an important place in the history of English moral philosophy. Appearing before the ethical works of Richard CUMBERLAND, John Locke, Jeremy Taylor, Ralph Cudworth and Henry MORE, it is one of the first attempts in English Protestantism to stress the role of reason in ethics and to develop a doctrine of natural law. Like Richard HOOKER, Culverwell wanted to revive the natural law tradition of Aquinas and Suarez, and to combat the nominalist legacy of Protestantism, which had reduced natural law to divine commands (see AQUINAS, T. §13; CUDWORTH, R. §§4–5; LOCKE, J. §9; SUAREZ, F. §4).

The general purpose of the *Discourse* was to determine the proper relationship between reason and faith. Culverwell attempted to strike a middle path between the Socinians, who praised reason at the expense of faith (see SOCINIANISM), and the radical sects, who demoted reason for the sake of the gospel. He maintained that although reason cannot discover or demonstrate the essential mysteries of the gospel – the Trinity, Incarnation and salvation – it can determine the law of nature, which is a reflection of the eternal law of God. Although Culverwell aimed at a *via media*, his chief goal was to defend the powers of reason. He wrote mainly to combat the rise of antinomian sects which taught that all moral laws had been abrogated by the gospel. Their teaching not only posed the dangers of immoralism and anarchism, but it also impugned Calvinism itself, which always stressed the role of grace over reason. In introducing natural law into Calvinism, then, Culverwell's intention was to clear it of the charge of antinomianism (see CALVIN, J.).

The basics of Culverwell's doctrine of natural law closely follow Aquinas and Suarez. Like Aquinas, Culverwell holds that the law of nature is the participation of our reason in the eternal law of God. And, true to Suarez, Culverwell argues that the law of nature is essential to a rational being, and cannot apply to animals or nature in general, for 'where there is no Liberty, there's no Law, a Law being nothing else, but a Rational restraint, and limitation of absolute Liberty'. Although he admired the modern natural law theorists John SELDEN, Hugo GROTIUS and Claudius Salmasius, Culverwell criticized them because they presupposed but did not examine the general concept of nature. In explaining this concept, Culverwell again returned to the scholastic tradition, defining the nature of a thing as its essence, its characteristic manner of acting.

Although he has been described as a 'voluntarist', Culverwell attempts to avoid the extremes of both voluntarism and rationalism (see VOLUNTARISM; RATIONALISM). The foundation of his position is the scholastic distinction between the normative and coercive, or demonstrative and preceptive aspects of law. The normative or demonstrative aspect is its moral justification, the reasons for acting according to it; the coercive or preceptive aspect is the will that decrees it and the power that enforces it. Again following Aquinas and Suarez, Culverwell maintains that both these elements are necessary to an adequate concept of the law of nature. On the one hand, like all laws, the law of nature involves an act of will, a power of enforcement; hence, contrary to rationalism, there could not be a law of nature if God did not exist. On the other hand, the law of nature has a moral validity, a ground of obligation, independent of the will; contrary to voluntarism, then, nothing is right or wrong simply because God commands it. Although Culverwell stresses the importance of the divine will as the source of law, the emphasis of his theory is on reason, which had been underrated in the voluntarist tradition of Calvinism.

For Culverwell, the foundation of the law of nature rests upon the innate faculties of man, which express themselves in self-evident principles such as 'do unto others as you would have them do unto you'.

Culverwell denies, however, that we have pre-existing ideas and argues that only our faculties are innate. Unlike the Cambridge Platonists, he stresses that knowledge requires experience as much as the activity of reason.

3 Cambridge Platonism

Culverwell's position within Cambridge Platonism has been the subject of dispute. Some regard him as a paradigmatic Platonist, while others place him outside this movement because of his Calvinism. Undoubtedly, there are deeper strains of Calvinism in Culverwell than in most of the Cambridge Platonists, so that it is misleading to regard him as typical of the movement. Some of the early sermons, especially 'The Act of Oblivion', 'The White Stone' and 'Spiritual Opticks', stress some standard Calvinist doctrines: predestination, the necessity of grace, the distinction between the elect and reprobate, and the inadequacy of human reason to understand salvation. These were doctrines that were decisively rejected by Whichcote, Cudworth and More in the 1640s. On the other hand, it is important to recognize that, in the 1640s, many of the rationalist strands of Cambridge Platonism were still only nascent. There are indeed strong Calvinist remnants in Whichcote, Cudworth and More, who stress the necessity of grace no less than Culverwell. Any sharp distinction between Culverwell and Cambridge Platonism therefore runs the risk of anachronism, reading the early years of Cambridge Platonism in the light of its later doctrines. The distinction becomes sharp only by overrating the rationalist strands, and underrating the Calvinist ones, in Cambridge Platonism.

It is more accurate to regard Culverwell as a transitional figure between Calvinism and Cambridge Platonism. It is also likely that Culverwell's doctrines were in evolution, moving away from Calvinism and towards a greater rationalism, since there is a greater emphasis upon the value of reason in the *Discourse* than in the earlier sermons. It is a sad fact that, given his early death, we can only speculate about the final result of Culverwell's intellectual development.

See also: MEDIEVAL PHILOSOPHY; NATURAL LAW

List of works

Culverwell, N. (1652) *An Elegant and Learned Discourse of the Light of Nature, with several other Treatises*, London: Rothwell. (The classic first edition, reissued in 1654, 1661 and 1669. The other treatises included, among others, 'The White

Stone', 'Spiritual Opticks' and 'The Act of Oblivion'.)

References and further reading

Brown, J. and Caird E. (1857) *The 'preface' and 'critical essay' to Of the Light of Nature: A Discourse by Nathanael Culverwel*, Edinburgh: Constable. (Still useful.)

De Pauley, W.C. (1937) *The Candle of the Lord: Studies in the Cambridge Platonists*, New York: Macmillan, ch. 7, 163–74. (A helpful analysis.)

Greene, R. (1971) 'Introduction' to the critical edition of An Elegant and Learned Discourse of the Light of Nature, *University of Toronto Department of English Studies and Texts* No. 17, ix-lv, Toronto, Ont.: University of Toronto Press. (Invaluable study of Culverwell's context.)

Passmore, J. (1967) 'Culverwel, Nathaniel', *Encyclopedia of Philosophy*, ed. P. Edwards, New York: Macmillan, vol. 2, 276–7. (Useful, but exaggerates Culverwell's distance from Cambridge Platonism.)

Tulloch, J. (1874) *Rational Theology and Christian Philosophy in England in the Seventeenth Century*, Edinburgh: Blackwood, vol. 2, 410–26. (Old but good.)

FREDERICK BEISER

CUMBERLAND, RICHARD (1632–1718)

Richard Cumberland developed his ideas in response to Hobbes' Leviathan. He introduced concepts of aggregate goodness (later used in utilitarianism), of benevolence (used in moral-sense theory), of moral self-obligation, of empirical proofs of providence and of the moral importance of tradition à lá Burke. The philosophical basis for Cumberland's views was a theory of natural law which was strongly anti-voluntarist and committed to objective moral values, but recognizing institutions such as governments of state and church as conventional or traditional. Cumberland was often seen as the third co-founder, with Pufendorf and Grotius, of modern natural law.

The English philosopher Richard Cumberland was educated at Magdalene College, Cambridge, and in several respects was close to the Cambridge Platonists as well as to Nathaniel CULVERWELL (see CAMBRIDGE PLATONISM). He subscribed to an extreme Erastianism that saw him through both the Restoration of 1660 and the Revolution of 1688–9. He was in fact on the far latitudinarian wing of the Anglican Church, and it is fitting that he was made Bishop of Peterborough as part of the Revolution settlement in 1691. His only philosophical work, *De legibus naturae*, appeared in 1672, the same year as Pufendorf's *De iure naturae et gentium* (see PUFENDORF, S.). His other works were in such areas as patriarchal law, Jewish weights and measures, and Phoenician history.

The primary objective of Cumberland's philosophical work was to refute Hobbes by showing that morals has an objective basis and that it cannot simply be the imposition of a sovereign power (see HOBBES, T. §5). This objective basis is to be found in the common good, by which he means the good of the universal moral community of God and humanity through all times. By promoting this common good, we will inevitably promote our own good, but we in fact have a natural inclination (an active power) to pursue the common good, namely benevolence. This natural inclination can be regulated by reason through precepts.

Once we learn through experience, systematized in the science of morals, that benevolence is universal and thus part of God's will, we will realize that the rational precepts which we have developed are, in fact, natural laws prescribed by God; we will see that the natural inclinations to benevolence are also moral virtues; and we will understand that the common good is not just a natural good but a moral good .

Behind all this lies the common idea that morality is a matter of obligation to the law of a superior. Yet, Cumberland avoids a voluntarist view of law and obligation (see VOLUNTARISM). God himself wills as law what is for the common good, but he obliges humanity to obey the law, not by his mere willing it nor by an appeal to the human rational calculation of pleasures and pains, but by an invitation to unify each person's particular will with the general will of God. God is the perfect intuitionist utilitarian who alone is capable of self-obligation, and humans can imperfectly take part in his unity of intuition and will. God's invitation to humanity – revelation apart – is expressed in the rewards and punishments that are naturally connected with compliance with, and transgression of, the law of nature. These are not, as a common utilitarian reading will have it, sanctions for or grounds of obligation to the law of nature; they are grounds of discovery of the law of nature (see UTILITARIANISM).

While his language is often vague, Cumberland clearly eschews hedonism as an account of the good, including the common good (see HEDONISM). He seems to be aiming at a notion of self-perfection as the ideal good, but the perfection in question is, in turn, formalistically understood. It consists in an approximation to the general will of God which, if achieved, would establish a harmonious system of all the individuals making up the moral universe. Like his contemporary, Malebranche, but independently of him, Cumberland is thus coming close to a notion of universalizability (see MALEBRANCHE, N. §§5–6).

Cumberland's idea of the harmonious moral system of mutually interdependent individuals was a conscious attempt to transfer Descartes' theory of the full physical world, or *plenum*, to morals. It contributed to the subsequent age's development of an empirical science of morals and thus to the breach with Locke's idea of morals as a demonstrative science (see DESCARTES, R. §11; LOCKE, J. §9). The science of morals he regarded as a system of cohering individuals, but the mechanisms that made them cohere were a matter of empirical investigation. Cumberland thus joined Locke in rejecting innate ideas. But one of the empirical factors in accounting for the mind was teleological, namely the mind's possible understanding of, and associated striving for, the common good. By accounting for the universal moral system as a possibility, moral science acquired a normative function. This role of moral science as self-fulfilling prediction, while rudimentary in Cumberland, became a lasting feature of British moral thought for more than a century.

As with so many natural lawyers, Cumberland has no strong theory of contract. The duties undertaken in contractual relations are, in so far as they are just, nothing but duties imposed by natural law, and rights are simply derivative from the duties. Contracts thus function only to make explicit what is implied by natural law. What is more, Cumberland is keen to acknowledge historically-given moral institutions. In language that often is strikingly Burkean, he maintains that such given institutions provide the best contribution to the common good simply because of the losses to be expected from major reform. Hand in hand with this, he points out that natural benevolence tends to establish social relations, including economic ones, that are independent of political society. When Dugald STEWART, early in the nineteenth century, maintained that Cumberland was an inspiration for the Scottish school of moral thought in the intervening century, he thus had a strong point.

See also: NATURAL LAW

List of works

Cumberland, R. (1672) *De legibus naturae*, London; trans. J. Maxwell as *A Treatise of the Law of Nature*, London, 1727, repr. New York, 1978; French trans.

J. Barbeyrac as *Traité philosophique des loix naturelles*, Amsterdam, 1744. (Barbeyrac's translation has important editorial notes. Another English version is John Tower's 1750 translation, *A Philosophical Enquiry into the Laws of Nature*. James Tyrrell based his *A Brief Disquisition of the Law of Nature*, (London, 1692; rev. 1701; repr. Littleton, CO: Rothman, 1987) on Cumberland, but it does not give a clear idea of the latter's work.)

References and further reading

Haakonssen, K. (1997) 'The Character and Obligation of Natural Law According to Richard Cumberland', in M.A. Stewart (ed.) *Studies in Seventeenth-Century Philosophy*, Oxford: Clarendon Press. (Full interpretation, along the lines indicated above, of the coherence of Cumberland's thought.)

Kirk, L. (1987) *Richard Cumberland and Natural Law: Secularisation of Thought in Seventeenth-Century England*, Cambridge: James Clarke & Co. (The only modern monograph; strong on biography and textual problems.)

Schneewind, J.B. (1995) 'Voluntarism and the Origins of Utilitarianism', *Utilitas* 7: 87–96. (Sets Cumberland in the wider context indicated by the title.)

Sharpe, F.C. (1912) 'The Ethical System of Richard Cumberland and Its Place in the History of British Ethics', *Mind* 21: 371–98. (Classic study of Cumberland as proto-utilitarian.)

KNUD HAAKONSSEN

CUSANUS *see* NICHOLAS OF CUSA

CUSTOM *see* COMMON LAW

CYNICS

Cynicism (originating in the mid-fourth century BC) was arguably the most original and influential branch of the Socratic tradition in antiquity, whether we consider its impact on the formation of Stoicism or its role in the Roman Empire as a popular philosophy and literary tradition. The self-imposed nickname 'Cynic', literally 'doglike', was originally applied to Antisthenes and to Diogenes of Sinope, considered the founders of Cynicism, and later to their followers, including Crates of Thebes and Menippus. It emphasizes one of the most fundamental and controversial features of Cynic thought and practice – its radical re-examination of the animal nature of the human being. Their decision to 'play the dog' revolutionized moral discourse, since humans had traditionally been defined by their place in both a natural (animal → human → god) and a civic hierarchy. By calling such hierarchies into question, Cynicism re-evaluated the place of humankind in nature and the role of civilization in human life.

*Cynicism includes an innovative and influential literary tradition of satire, parody and aphorism devoted to 'defacing the currency' (that is, the dominant ideologies of the time). It proposes a new morality based on minimizing creaturely needs in pursuit of self-sufficiency (*autarkeia*), achieved in part by physical training (*askēsis*), and on maximizing both freedom of speech (*parrhēsia*) and freedom of action (*eleutheria*) in open defiance of the most entrenched social taboos; and an anti-politics which sees existing governments as a betrayal of human nature, and traditional culture as an obstacle to happiness. In their place, Cynics advocated an immediate relationship to nature and coined the oxymoron* kosmopolitēs *or 'citizen of the cosmos'. However the literary, ethical and political elements of Cynicism are interrelated, all are most easily defined by what they oppose – the inherited beliefs and practices of classical Greek civilization.*

The virtual loss of all early Cynic writings means that the history of Cynicism must be reconstructed from much later sources dating from the Roman Empire, the most important of which is Diogenes Laertius (third century AD*).*

1 The early Cynics
2 Diogenes' conception of the human being
3 Diogenes' successors
4 Cynics in the Roman Empire

1 The early Cynics

While ancient tradition consistently viewed ANTI-STHENES (*c.*445–365 BC) as the first Cynic and DIOGENES OF SINOPE as his pupil, modern scholarship has systematically questioned this view on chronological, numismatic and other grounds. What is at stake is nothing less than the relationship of Cynicism to SOCRATES, since Antisthenes was a prominent pupil of Socrates (present at his death) as well as of Gorgias the rhetorician.

Antisthenes wrote a great deal and, unlike later Cynics, his interests included theoretical as well as literary and ethical topics. It is probably more accurate to see him as an important forerunner (rather than as a founder) whose teachings provided Diogenes' practice with some basis in theory. Particularly relevant would be his beliefs that virtue (see

ARETĒ) 'is a matter of deeds and does not needs lots of discourses and learning' and that it is sufficient for happiness 'since happiness requires nothing else except the strength of a Socrates'. If Xenophon follows Antisthenes in his representation of Socrates, then Antisthenes must have laid particular stress on Socrates' 'self-mastery' (*enkrateia*). In his *Symposium* Xenophon represents Antisthenes as actually praising poverty, which certainly resonates with Cynicism. The biographer Diogenes Laertius says that Antisthenes provided the model for Crates' 'self-mastery' and Diogenes' 'imperturbability' (*apatheia*), which he learned by imitating Socrates, thereby inaugurating the Cynic way of life.

Whatever his relationship to Antisthenes, Diogenes of Sinope (412/403–324/321 BC) was the paradigmatic Cynic of antiquity. While Diogenes probably produced written works that do not survive, including a *Republic*, for us his life and thought are inseparable, since the latter is conveyed almost entirely by a tradition of biographical anecdotes that was over 500 years old by the time of our primary source, Diogenes Laertius. Diogenes Laertius preserves over 150 sayings or anecdotes that purport to quote Diogenes verbatim, as well as some brief paraphrases of his philosophy (VI 70– 3), which may be even less reliable in so far as they reflect Stoic and other influences. Their historicity is always problematic, but their representation of Diogenes is the most valuable evidence we possess. Almost one in six of the anecdotes involves some form of word play or allusion to poetry. The form in which Diogenes is transmitted has two crucial features that a summary of his teachings might fail to convey. First, most of the anecdotes involve Diogenes responding wittily to some challenging question or circumstance: he is shown as a satiric provocateur as well as a heterodox moralist, and both sides of his nature need to be kept in view; if what Diogenes represents is reduced to a simple, practical morality much that made him influential is lost. Second, the biographical form necessarily makes the philosopher the embodiment of his thought; this unity of theory and practice was to become an explicit principle of Cynicism and an important source of Diogenes' authority as a philosopher. It made him (like Socrates) emblematic of the philosophic life in antiquity.

If the anecdotes, and the metaphors and slogans they inspired, are the core of ancient Cynicism, Diogenes' philosophy begins with the fact of his exile from Sinope for (literally) defacing the local currency. When reproached for his exile, he replied: 'But that was how I became a philosopher, you miserable fool!' Asked what good he had got from philosophy, he replied: 'If nothing else, then to be prepared for every kind of luck.' Diogenes describes himself by quoting a fragment from an unidentified tragedy:

Without a city, without a house

without a fatherland

A beggar with a single day's bread.

This is the starting point of Cynicism: it is, among other things, an attempt to show that we are so constituted by nature that, given proper training (*askēsis*), happiness is possible under the most adverse conditions.

It is tempting to see Diogenes as transforming into an act of conscious defiance the exclusion he suffered involuntarily when forced into exile. This defiant stance became his 'philosophy' in a concerted attempt to demonstrate by his own example that happiness does not depend on society or on any contingent circumstance, the domain of Fortune, but wholly on the autonomous self – a self brought into existence, not by years of laborious text-based studies such as those advocated by other philosophers, but by Cynic discipline based on exemplary acts and corporeal training. This is why Cynicism came to be called a 'shortcut to virtue'.

The Cynic shortcut 'defaced' the value philosophers attached to theoretical disciplines as well as the conventional value society attached to such externals as money, status, family and political power. (Yet the most influential Hellenistic schools – STOICISM and EPICUREANISM – would follow the Cynics in arguing that the happiness of the sage *should be* independent of context.) Thus Diogenes' life becomes an extended counter-example meant to refute his critics, both popular and philosophical, as he turns the cause of his exile into a metaphor for his activity as a philosopher – 'defacing the currency' of conventional wisdom. 'Defacing' took the form of literary parody and satire, provocative acts of free speech (*parrhēsia*) and public exhibitions of the Cynic way of life. The laughter they were meant to provoke is an indispensable element of Diogenes' practice and served to reinforce his independence by distancing him from the rules that everyone else obeyed.

2   Diogenes' conception of the human being

If Diogenes differed from his contemporaries on the sufficient conditions for happiness, it is because they differed in their conception of the human being. Some of the most famous anecdotes dramatize Diogenes' rejection of the prevailing conceptions of the human, such as when he lit a lamp in broad daylight and walked around saying 'I'm looking for a human being', or when Plato defined a human being as a 'featherless biped' and Diogenes produced a plucked chicken, saying, 'Here is Plato's human being'.

Diogenes' positive conception of human nature is given, as always, by his own example, not by definitions. From it we can infer that for the Cynic human beings are animals who have much to learn about freedom and self-sufficiency from their fellow creatures. As well as offering ethical instruction, the use of animals as examples served to illustrate the intrinsic superiority of nature to culture. Theophrastus reports that Diogenes discovered how to adapt to circumstances by carefully observing a mouse. Such adaptability enabled him to test the limits of his species by living like a dog in an abandoned wine-jar (*pithos*). A string of anecdotes develop different aspects of the canine metaphor: among Diogenes' canine characteristics was a shameless indifference to social norms, which enabled him to discard traditional morality based on shame in favour of living naturally and freely – that is, fulfilling his essential creaturely needs for food, sex and shelter without regard for the restraints and prohibitions of culture. Yet unlike sophists such as CALLICLES, the Cynics never used nature to sanction dominating others (although theft was another matter). Clearly, the Cynic rejection of shame cannot be reduced to a matter of manners as opposed to morals: Diogenes' pursuit of life according to nature led him to question the rational basis of such fundamental dietary and sexual taboos as those against cannibalism and incest, citing examples from nature and non-Hellenic cultures.

While advocating a rigorous physical training intended to inure one to inevitable hardship, Diogenes showed no aversion to pleasures compatible with his way of life. Indeed, he used 'any place for any purpose', exemplifying the Cynic conception of freedom, which applied to sexual activity – from free love to public masturbation – as well as to eating, sleeping and talking. But the ultimate aim of imitating the freedom and self-sufficiency of animals is neither instinctual satisfaction nor mere 'imperturbability' (*apatheia*), but the Olympian independence of the gods, who, 'needing nothing', live easily free of mortal cares. Hence, Heracles, the one mortal to reach Olympus by triumphing over his famous labours, was adopted and re-interpreted by the Cynics as their mythical prototype. Diogenes explicitly claimed that their life had 'the same character' because both 'deemed nothing more important than freedom'.

Of course Diogenes' Cynicism is full of paradoxes. While teaching life according to nature and denouncing existing social arrangements, Diogenes went on living in cities, which he made no attempt to reform. While advocating freedom and self-sufficiency as paramount values, he both practised and advocated begging for a living. We must resist the temptation to turn a remarkable experiment, which challenged the most fundamental ideas of Greek civilization, into a mere system.

While Diogenes probably had no pupils as such, his example (whether conveyed orally or by written works) effectively established a philosophical model that invited imitation and interpretation. In the absence of a systematic body of doctrine, the nature of Cynicism was always up for debate; all the Cynics of antiquity as well as those who represent them (for example, LUCIAN, Dio Chrysostom) were of necessity actively engaged in interpreting the tradition, whether by word or deed.

3 Diogenes' successors

The most influential Cynic in antiquity after Diogenes was Crates of Thebes (c.368–c.283 BC), a wealthy landowner and therefore at the opposite end of the social spectrum from a poor exile like Diogenes. He was a hunchback and several anecdotes refer to his comic appearance. He married Hipparchia of Maronea, who, along with her brother Metrocles, became a practising Cynic and, as such, the most famous female philosopher of antiquity. Their Cynic marriage (*kynogamia*), based only on mutual consent, was consistent with Diogenes' views but radically at odds with Greek custom. The tradition holds that Hipparchia adopted the simple Cynic garb of Diogenes – a rough cloak, knapsack and staff – and lived on equal terms with her husband, attending events usually reserved for men and successfully defending her decision to pursue philosophy instead of weaving. Crates and Hipparchia were also notorious for living and sleeping together in public places, Cynically indifferent to shame and public opinion. It was Crates who described the fruits of philosophy as 'a quart of beans and to care for naught'.

However Crates came to know Diogenes, his life was a remarkable application of the Cynic's principles. He clearly regarded himself as a follower, calling himself a 'fellow citizen of Diogenes'. There are several (probably fictitious) accounts of how Crates became a Cynic, which revolve around the fact that he evidently sold all his possessions and gave the proceeds to his fellow citizens, thereby embracing poverty, as had Diogenes. In contrast to Diogenes with his combative style and acerbic tongue, Crates was remembered as a benevolent figure and, thanks to his role as arbiter of family quarrels, actually revered as a household deity in Athens. But his fragments are clearly informed by a satiric (or seriocomic) perspective, the hallmark of Cynic discourse: 'He used to say

that we should study philosophy until we see in generals nothing but donkey-drivers.'

Crates was one of the most influential literary figures of the fourth century and his writings did much to disseminate Cynic ideology and establish parody as a distinctly Cynic mode of 'defacing' tradition. His *oeuvre* is notable both for its originality and its variety. He composed 'tragedies', elegies and epistles, and parodies such as his poem in hexameters entitled *Pēra* (Knapsack), a hymn to frugality, a *Praise of the Lentil*, and an *Ephēmerides* (Diary).

After Crates came Menippus (first half of the third century BC). The unreliable biographical tradition depicts him as a Phoenician slave who acquired his freedom by begging or usury and hanged himself when his business failed. Be that as it may, Menippus is among the most influential of Hellenistic authors. He is the only Cynic expressly called *spoudogeloios* ('seriocomic') in antiquity, and is credited with the invention of Menippean satire, a form of narrative satire that parodies both myth and philosophy. The imitations and adaptations of his work by Varro (116–26 BC) and Lucian gave Menippean forms a long and influential afterlife in antiquity and the Renaissance, making Cynicism one of the primary sources of satiric literature in Europe.

Bion of Borysthenes (c.335–c.245 BC) also played an important role in early Cynicism, especially in the domain of literature. Tradition holds that he was sold into slavery as a boy but was bought by a rhetorician and received a rhetorical education. Later, he evidently received an eclectic education in philosophy at Athens: he studied with the Academics (under Xenocrates and Crates), with the Cynics, Cyrenaics and, finally, the Peripatetics. Bion probably originated the literary form of the diatribe – an argumentative monologue with imagined interlocutors, which was an important model for satirists and essayists of the Empire. Because Bion's Cynicism seems less radical and more opportunistic than that of Diogenes, it has sometimes been characterized as a 'hedonizing Cynicism'. References in Horace and other writers suggest an eclectic thinker with remarkable literary talents, as do his witty fragments.

Teles (*fl. c.*235) was a teacher and moralist who quoted extensively from such philosophers as Diogenes, Crates, Metrocles, Stilpo and Bion, his favourite authority and model. The surviving seven excerpts of his *Diatribes* are the earliest examples we possess of this influential Cynic tradition.

The works of Cercidas (c.290–220 BC), the last important early Cynic, take a surprising political turn. Cercidas was unusual for a Cynic in being a soldier, politician and lawmaker as well as a poet. He is best-known for his *Meliambi* (written in the Doric dialect), in which he uses a lyric form to mount a serious Cynic critique of contemporary politics.

4 Cynics in the Roman Empire

Whatever the causes of its apparent decline after Cercidas, when Cynicism re-emerges in the Roman Empire, it has changed, as has the world. In a series of confrontations under the emperors Nero, Vespasian and Domitian, Roman aristocrats with republican sympathies were put to death and the philosophers associated with them – both Stoics and Cynics – were banished from Rome. The best known Cynic of the period, Demetrius, a friend and hero of Seneca, is the most conspicuous example of the Cynic involvement in the 'philosophical opposition' to the emperor.

The emergence of Cynicism as a potent political ideology – opposed to hereditary monarchy – in the first century AD is highly significant but potentially misleading: most Cynics did not live in Rome nor in the West but in the Greek-speaking cities of the East from Athens to Alexandria. Most were not politically active but busily engaged in living the Cynic way of life – begging their daily bread and bearing witness to the example of Diogenes. Socially their status had been extremely mixed from the beginning, but as a rule they were not the associates of men of wealth and power such as Seneca. The sight of vagrant Cynics living in groups, travelling from city to city dressed in the Cynic garb, was not uncommon in the Empire. In the centuries since its inception Cynicism (alone among the philosophical sects) had become a popular movement attracting adherents from those strata of society outside the traditional audience for philosophy. It is impossible to quantify the movement, but more than eighty known Cynics have now been identified.

The most prominent Cynics of the Empire – Demetrius, Demonax of Cyprus (second century AD) and Peregrinus Proteus of Parium (c. AD 100–65) – were, unlike the early Cynics, teachers, not writers, and what we know of them is filtered through writers with their own philosophic interests, such as the Stoic Seneca and the satirist and sophist Lucian. Indeed, one of the central paradoxes of Cynicism's reception in the Empire is that the influence of Cynic ideology reached its apogee (in the second century AD) when very little in the way of original Cynic literature was being produced by practising Cynics. Oenomaus of Gadara (second century AD) is the only Cynic of the Empire known to us by his written work, *Charlatans Unmasked*, a lively, if not particularly original, attack on the veracity of oracles that survives because it is quoted by Eusebius, but does not seem to have made a great impression on Oenomaus' contemporaries.

His other works, including 'tragedies' that scandalized the pious emperor Julian, are lost.

The only literature produced by Cynics in the Empire that we can set beside that of Oenomaus are the *Cynic Epistles*, a collection of fictitious letters attributed to the early Cynics and other sages. The authors of the letters are unknown and their dates of composition may vary considerably (from the third century BC to the second century AD). The epistles offer an informative survey of the topics, slogans and anecdotes that must have fuelled many a 'diatribe', the term conventionally used to describe the oral performances of the Cynic street preachers so often remarked on by our sources. These oral performances were probably the primary means by which Cynic teachings were disseminated among the general populace. The *Cynic Epistles* confirm the impression that Cynic literary production in the Empire was no longer marked by the innovative parodies and polemics of the classical period and now served primarily to propagate Cynicism as a popular ideology and collective moral praxis.

We must remember, however, that our most important sources (other than Diogenes Laertius and the *Cynic Epistles*), the sophists Lucian (c. AD 120–80) and Dio (c. AD 40–111), the Stoic Epictetus (c. AD 55–120) and the emperor Julian (c. AD 332–61) probably had access to classic works by the early Cynics as well as a secondary literature that grew up around them. Both Dio and Lucian draw on these lost traditions to create a contemporary Cynic literature in which Diogenes and other legendary Cynics (Antisthenes, Crates, Menippus) appear as characters. Their works give us the liveliest images we have of what the lost Cynic classics might have been like and (along with Diogenes Laertius) are among the primary means whereby Cynicism became part of the philosophical and literary culture of Europe.

Lucian's use of Cynic traditions is too complex to characterize briefly, but Cynic ideology and the example of the Cynic classics were indispensable to him: they gave him a licence to satirize all things Greek, which now of course included Cynics and Cynicism itself. It is Cynicism as a radical form of cultural criticism – of 'defacing' the idols of the tribe through parody, satire and free speech – that led Lucian to adopt Cynic forms (for example, Menippean satire) and voices in so many works. But his *Life of Demonax* also shows a serious interest in using Cynic (and Socratic) traditions eclectically to construct a contemporary ethical model.

Similarly, Dio – who claims to have lived as a Cynic when in exile – uses the authority of Diogenes' persona in an important series of speeches to advocate Cynic values of particular importance to him as a courtier, particularly autonomy and freedom of speech. While lacking some of the Cynic seriocomic qualities that Diogenes has in Diogenes Laertius or Lucian, Dio's Diogenes is, on the whole, surprisingly true to his persona in the anecdotal tradition. Epictetus, by contrast, offers a distinctly idealized, quasi-religious account of Cynicism as a philosophical vocation and practical philosophy. His emphasis on praxis invites comparison with that of the *Cynic Epistles*. Julian echoes some of Epictetus' religious tendencies while arguing that Cynicism is a universal philosophy founded not by Diogenes nor Antisthenes, but by Apollo and based on the dictum 'Know thyself'.

Yet despite the obvious affinities all these authorities have for Cynic traditions, all denounce contemporary Cynics in the harshest terms as ignorant impostors. It is clear that the Cynic movement had split along the lines of class, wealth and education – the very distinctions Cynicism sought to annul. What we hear in the denunciations of our sources are the traces of a heated argument over the Cynic legacy. What is the ultimate value of Cynicism? As a practical ascetic morality for the have-nots, as a universal ethical model of freedom and autonomy, or as a cultural practice devoted to 'defacing' the false values of the dominant culture? Who has the right to speak out in the name of Diogenes? It is an argument that would resound from the humanists of the Renaissance to the *philosophes* of the eighteenth century, when DIDEROT wrote his Encyclopedia article on the Cynics and his Cynic masterpiece, *Rameau's Nephew*, exploring the relation between Cynicism, cynicism and the nature of enlightenment.

See also: ARISTON OF CHIOS; SOCRATIC SCHOOLS; ZENO OF CITIUM

References and further reading

Billerbeck, M. (ed.) (1991) *Die Kyniker in der modernen Forschung* (The Cynics in Modern Research), Amsterdam: Grüner. (Includes a selection of modern studies, 1851–1980, and a complete bibliography.)

Branham, R.B. and Goulet-Cazé, M.-O. (eds) (1996) *The Cynics: The Cynic Movement in Antiquity and its Legacy* . Berkeley, CA: University of California Press. (Surveys the history of the movement and its reception; includes a comprehensive catalogue of the ancient Cynics and an annotated bibliography.)

Dio Chrysostom (*c.* AD 100) *Discourses*, vol. 1, trans. J.C. Cahoon and H. Crosby, Loeb Classical Library, Cambridge, MA: Harvard University Press and London: Heinemann, 1932. (Parallel Greek text and English translation; Diogenes is represented in Orations 4, 6, 8–10, but Cynic (and Stoic) thinking pervades his works.)

* Diogenes Laertius (*c.* early 3rd century AD) *Lives of the Philosophers*, trans. R.D. Hicks, *Diogenes Laertius Lives of Eminent Philosophers*, Loeb Classical Library, Cambridge, MA: Harvard University Press and London: Heinemann, 1925, 2 vols. (Parallel Greek text and English translation; Book VI is our most important source for the Cynics.)

Downing, F.G. (1992) *Cynics and Christian Origins*, Edinburgh: T. & T. Clark. (Studies the Cynic influence on Christianity.)

Dudley, D.R. (1937) *A History of Cynicism: From Diogenes to the Sixth Century* AD, London: Methuen; repr. Chicago, IL: Ares,1990. (The best general introduction to the ancient Cynics.)

* Epictetus (*c.* AD 50–*c.*120) *Discourses and Enchiridion*, trans. W.A. Oldfather, Loeb Classical Library, Cambridge, MA: Harvard University Press and London: Heinemann, 1925–8, 2 vols. (Parallel Greek text and English translation; Cynicism is discussed at III 22, IV 8.30–43.)

Giannantoni, G. (1990) *Socratis et Socraticorum Reliquiae* (The Fragments of Socrates and the Socratics), Naples: Bibliopolis, 4 vols. (Ancient sources in Greek and Latin, with discussion in Italian; includes all the documentation relevant to the Cynics.)

Goulet-Cazé, M.-O. (1986) *L'Ascèse Cynique: Un commentaire de Diogene Laërce VI 70–71* (Cynic Asceticism: A Commentary on Diogenes Laertius VI 70–71), Paris: Vrin. (Analyses the central ideas of Diogenes' ethics in the context of the Socratic tradition.)

—— (1990) 'Le cynisme à l'époque impériale' (Cynicism in the Imperial Era), in W. Haase (ed.) *Aufstieg und Niedergang der römischen Welt*, Berlin and New York: De Gruyter, II 36 4: 2,720–833. (A lucid survey of Cynicism in the Roman Empire.)

Goulet-Cazé, M.-O. and Goulet, R. (1993) *Le cynisme ancien et ses prolongements* (Ancient Cynicism and its Influence), Paris: Presses Universitaires de France. (A valuable survey of current work on the Cynics based on an international colloquium (Paris 1991).)

Höistad, R. (1948) *Cynic Hero and Cynic King: Studies in the Cynic Conception of Man*, Lund: Carl Bloms. (A useful introduction vitiated by its rejection of the anecdotal tradition.)

* Julian (*c.* AD 140–80) *Discourses*, trans. W.C. Wright, Loeb Classical Library, Cambridge, MA: Harvard University Press and London: Heinemann, 1913, 2 vols. (Parallel Greek text and English translation;

Orations 6, 7 and the *Letter to Themistius* treat the Cynics.)

Kindstrand, J.F. (1976) *Bion of Borysthenes: A Collection of the Fragments with Introduction and Commentary*, Uppsala: Acta Universitatis Uppsaliensis, Studia Graeca Uppsaliensa. (Greek text, with commentary in English.)

—— (1980) 'Demetrius the Cynic', *Philologus* 124: 83–98. (Short study of Demetrius.)

* Lucian (c. AD 140–80) *Works*, trans. A.M. Harmon, K. Kilburn and M.D. Macleod, Loeb Classical Library, Cambridge, MA: Harvard University Press and London: Heinemann, 1913–17, 8 vols. (Parallel Greek text and English translation; important works for the Cynics include *Demonax, The Cynic, Peregrinus, The Runaways, The Fisherman, Zeus Refuted, Philosophers for Sale! The Double Indictment* and *The Dialogues of the Dead*. Also relevant are *Nigrinus, Hermotimus, Symposium, On Sacrifices, On Mourning* and *Zeus the Tragic Actor*.)

Malherbe, A.J. (1977) *The Cynic Epistles: A Study Edition*, Atlanta, GA: Scholars Press. (Parallel Greek text and English translation of most of the Cynic letters.)

Marshall, P. (1922) *Demanding the Impossible: A History of Anarchism*, London: Harper Collins. (Places Cynicism in the history of anarchism.)

Niehues-Pröbsting, H. (1979) *Der Kynismus des Diogenes und der Begriff des Zynismus* (The Cynicism of Diogenes and the Modern Concept of Cynicism), Munich: Wilhelm Fink. (The best account of the whole tradition (ancient and modern) in one volume.)

O'Neil, E.N. (1977) *Teles: The Cynic Teacher*, Missoula, MT: Scholars Press. (English translation of Teles' fragments.)

Paquet, L. (1988) *Les Cyniques grecs: Fragments et témoinages*, Ottawa, Ont.: Les Presses de l'Université d'Ottawa. (An annotated French translation of the main Cynic fragments and testimonia.)

Relihan, J.C. (1992) *Ancient Menippean Satire*, Baltimore, MD: Johns Hopkins University Press. (The best history of the genre.)

Sayre, F. (1948) *The Greek Cynics*, Baltimore, MD: Furst. (Often eccentric, but surveys much of the ancient evidence in English translation.)

Seneca (c. AD 52–62) *On Benefits*, in *Moral Essays*, vol. 3, trans. J.W. Basore, Loeb Classical Library, Cambridge, MA: Harvard University Press and London: Heinemann, 1920. (Parallel Latin text and English translation; VII 1.4–7 summarizes Demetrius' teaching.)

—— (c. AD early 60s) *Letters*, trans. R.M. Gummere, Loeb Classical Library, Cambridge, MA: Harvard University Press and London: Heinemann, 1917–25, 3 vols. (Parallel Latin text and English translation; Cynic (and Stoic) themes abound; see letters 20, 24, 47, 62, 67, 90, 91.)

Sloterdijk, P. (1988) *Critique of Cynical Reason*, trans. M. Eldred, London: Verso. (An influential interpretation of Cynicism focusing on its reception in Germany and its significance for critical theory.)

* Xenophon (c.370s BC) *Symposium*, trans. O.J. Todd, Loeb Classical Library, Cambridge, MA: Harvard University Press and London: Heinemann, 1923. (Parallel Greek text and English translation.)

BRACHT BRANHAM

CYRENAICS

The Cyrenaic school was a Greek philosophical school which flourished in the fourth and early third centuries BC. It took its name from the native city of its founder, Aristippus of Cyrene, a member of Socrates' entourage. His most important successors were his grandson, Aristippus the Younger, and Theodorus, Anniceris and Hegesias, the heads of three separate Cyrenaic sects.

The basis of Cyrenaic philosophy is physiological and psychological. It focuses on the individual feelings of pleasure and pain which are classed as pathē, *experiences produced in a subject by its contact with an object. They are described, respectively, in terms of smooth and rough movements, of the flesh or of the soul. A third category of* pathē, *described as intermediate between pleasure and pain, is also defined as movements and related to one's perception of individual properties or qualities. All* pathē *are short-lived and have no value beyond the actual time of their occurrence.*

These physiological characteristics are encountered both in the ethics and in the epistemology of the school. Although the Cyrenaics differed in their ethical doctrines, all of them attributed a central role in their systems to the individual bodily pleasure experienced in the present moment, and some of them considered it the moral end: it is pursued for its own sake, whereas happiness, conceived as the particular collection of pleasures that one experiences during a lifetime, is sought for the sake of its component pleasures. The goodness of individual pathē *of pleasure is supported by an elaborate epistemological doctrine whose central claims are that we are infallibly and incorrigibly aware of the occurrence and content of our own* pathē, *but that we cannot apprehend the properties of external objects. A striking feature of this doctrine is the neologisms designating the perception of qualities, such* as 'I am whitened' and 'I am affected whitely'. This, and other features of Cyrenaic subjectivism, anticipate some modern philosophical analyses of subjective experience.

1   History of the school

The Cyrenaic school was founded by a close associate of SOCRATES, Aristippus of Cyrene (see ARISTIPPUS THE ELDER), after Socrates' death (399 BC) and probably after Aristippus' numerous travels. For three successive generations its scholarchs (school heads) were members of the same family: Aristippus was succeeded by his daughter Arete (born c.400 BC) and then by his grandson, Aristippus the Younger (born c.380 BC). Our sources mention also Antipater of Cyrene, Aethiops and, later, Epitimides and Paraebates, but almost nothing is known about their careers as scholarch. Aristoteles of Cyrene apparently belonged to the same generation as Aristippus the Younger. At the beginning of the Hellenistic period (323–31 BC), the Cyrenaics Theodorus, Anniceris and Hegesias each founded a separate sect. Each sect was identified by the name of its leader ('Theodorians', 'Annicerians', 'Hegesians') but also preserved its Cyrenaic affiliation. It seems likely that, during the same period, there was yet another sect bearing the original name of the school and claiming to represent Cyrenaic orthodoxy. The Cyrenaic sects disappeared in the second half of the third century BC, some time between Arcesilaus' death and Chrysippus' appointment as head of the Stoa.

Of the Cyrenaics' writings, only some titles survive. Aristippus the Elder is credited with several Socratic dialogues on various ethical themes and with a three-volume history of Libya. Theodorus was the author of an influential treatise entitled *On the Gods* which attempted to refute traditional Greek theological beliefs. Hegesias composed a book entitled *The Self-Starver* enumerating the calamities of life, which may have aimed to procure an empirical basis for his moral pessimism.

Some sources maintain that the Cyrenaics devoted themselves exclusively to ethics, disallowing physics and logic as branches of philosophy. However, there is good evidence that they accepted logic as a tool of philosophical argumentation, and that they developed epistemology as a separate subject of inquiry, not as part of ethics or logic.

2   Epistemology

The origins of Cyrenaic philosophy were ethical, the epistemology probably being developed in the third generation of the school by Aristippus the Younger. However, the founder of the school laid the physiological and psychological foundations of the Cyrenaic theory of knowledge, mainly by his analysis of the notions of pleasure and pain, which was endorsed by his successors.

Pleasure and pain are *pathē*. The term belongs to a group of words related to the Greek verb *paschein* (to undergo) and refers to effects upon a subject, usually caused by an external object. The word can be used both regarding an inanimate substance and regarding a perceiving subject: a stone exposed to the sun may turn hot, or a person in a warm room may feel hot. Although the Cyrenaics focused on the *pathē* in connection with perceivers, their analysis preserves physicalist overtones. These are particularly obvious in the definitions of pleasure and pain as smooth and rough movements, of the flesh or of the soul, related to pleasurable and painful feelings. Some sources define that relation as an identity, but there is good evidence that the Cyrenaics drew a distinction between the physical motion associated with pleasure or pain and the subjective experience of *feeling* pleasure or pain. Since the motions associated with the *pathē* disappear with time, the *pathē* are short-lived. The memory of past pleasures and the anticipation of future ones is not really a pleasure, and presumably the same holds for pain as well. There are conditions in which a perceiver experiences neither pleasure nor pain: according to the Annicerians, the states of the absence of pleasure (*aēdonia*) and of the absence of pain (*aponia*) are not *pathē*, for they are not related to motions but are comparable to the state of someone asleep. On the other hand, Aristippus the Younger introduced a third category of *pathē*, which are associated with motions and defined as intermediate between pleasure and pain. They represent the manner in which one is affected by one's perception of the empirical qualities of an object and are reported by verbal or adverbial neologisms, such as 'being whitened' or 'being affected whitely', and 'being sweetened' or 'being disposed sweetly'. Pleasure and pain, as well as the intermediates, are sensed by 'inmost' or 'internal' touch. Although the sources say nothing further about this, it seems likely that the function of internal touch is to register the qualitative alterations of the flesh, and thus to provide a necessary and sufficient condition for one's awareness of one's own *pathē*.

These characteristics of the *pathē* constitute the basis for the Cyrenaic theory of knowledge, whose full formulation probably coincided with the introduction of the intermediates into the doctrine. It is centred on the subjectivist claim that the only knowledge accessible to one is the awareness of one's own *pathē*, and on the dogmatic assertion that the nature of external objects cannot be known.

Although the Cyrenaics draw no sharp distinctions between the physical and mental aspects of the *pathē*, in the context of their epistemology they clearly concentrate on the latter: one's apprehension of the *pathē* concerns primarily the subjective experience that one has. For, first, the Cyrenaics distinguish between the smooth movement associated with pleasure and the sensation or consciousness (*aisthēsis*) of it. Second, their use of adverbial expressions, such as 'being disposed whitely', is applicable to perceivers only, and inapplicable to inanimate objects undergoing purely physical change. And third, the *pathē* are, according to the Cyrenaics, self-presenting states which cannot yield false information about themselves to the person who experiences them. This only makes sense if the *pathē* are taken to be the immediate contents of experience rather than objective physical states.

This is confirmed by their insistence on the privacy of experience: each *pathos* is private (*idion*) to the individual perceiver experiencing it. Autobiographical reports regarding one's own *pathē* are infallible (*adiapseusta*), incorrigible (*anexelenkta*), always firm (*bebaia*) and true (*alēthē*). Thus, one has privileged access to one's own *pathē*, which may be related to the way in which they are detected by 'internal touch'. By contrast, the Cyrenaics stressed the structural and definitional inaccessibility of other people's *pathē* by arguing that people cannot have a common, that is, publicly shared, *pathos* which might be used as a common criterion of truth. The private character of the *pathē* is also said to make them incommunicable to others.

The incorrigible awareness of the *pathē* is contrasted with one's ignorance of external objects. The scope of Cyrenaic scepticism is limited in that it does not question in a radical and systematic way the actual existence of objects and, consequently, does not raise the so-called problem of the external world. It concerns mainly our knowledge of empirical properties or qualities and is supported by the argument that our beliefs about them are in reality beliefs about the content of our *pathē*, and that no one can transcend the barrier between objective properties and our perception of them. Since the causal history of a *pathos* cannot be traced back to the objective property which it is ordinarily supposed to represent, our beliefs regarding the properties of objects can be neither confirmed nor refuted by further evidence of any kind.

The Cyrenaics appear to have focused on specific problems, mostly related to the perception of secondary qualities, and did not try to provide a general epistemological theory. Important criticisms that can be brought against their position include the following: (1) the claim that only the *pathē* are apprehensible is too narrow to justify our ordinary assumptions about what we know; (2) the theory is either inexpressible or self-refuting; (3) it entails a radical subjectivization of all experience, which raises doubts, unwelcome to the Cyrenaics themselves, about the very existence of the external world and of other people.

3 Early Cyrenaic ethics

It has been commonly held that the Cyrenaics were the only philosophers in antiquity to abandon the traditional position of Greek ethics; that the moral end is happiness (see EUDAIMONIA), and to identify it instead with individual bodily pleasure experienced in the present moment. However, this position overlooks the value that the Cyrenaics attributed to happiness as well as to individual pleasures, and fails to account for the significant differences between the ethical doctrines of various members of the school.

There are two groups of testimony about the ethical views of Aristippus the Elder. According to one, he was a hedonist (see HEDONISM) who defined the moral end as a smooth movement resulting in a short-lived pleasure of the body. He distinguished it from happiness, the particular collection of individual pleasures experienced over a lifetime. But according to the second body of testimony, Aristippus did not define pleasure as the only thing which is intrinsically good, nor did he maintain that it is only pleasure and not happiness that is pursued for its own sake. Although he appears to have conceived of happiness in compositional terms and to have considered pleasure its major constituent, he believed that the enjoyment of pleasure should be conditional upon the capacity to master oneself. This is acquired by means of philosophical education, which also secures spiritual freedom, self-awareness and, more generally, the well-being of one's soul. Provided that these goods are obtained, one may indulge in many and intense pleasures without the fear of enslaving one's soul.

Regardless of the origins of the two traditions, there are good reasons for accepting the latter. First, there is evidence that Aristippus never lectured in defence of a particular moral end and that he detested adopting a didactic tone. This tells against his having argued on behalf of a well-defined hedonistic position and, perhaps, in favour of his having shared the common assumption that the supreme good is happiness, however defined. Second, one source, the Peripatetic Aristocles, flatly denies that Aristippus was a hedonist, and adds that he was only thought to be so on the grounds of his intemperate habits. Third, the importance which he attributed to long-term activities such as philosophy, and his statements that he aims at the easiest and pleasantest life and that he wishes to live a life of freedom leading to happiness (Xenophon, Memoirs of Socrates II 1) indicate that he perceived his life as a continuous whole, not as a series of disconnected pleasurable episodes. On that account, too, he seems closer to eudaimonism than to hedonism. Finally, the relationship of Aristippus to Socrates and the claim of his school to a Socratic pedigree make it difficult to believe that he would have held a view which entailed that any means to the pleasure of the present is acceptable and which, therefore, would have verged on the immoral.

The value that Aristippus attributed to a life of freedom and happiness recurs in his political stance. According to Xenophon, he declined to assume the civic roles of ruling or of being ruled which were necessarily attached to the political condition of citizenship and, instead, chose for himself the apolitical stance of 'living as a foreigner in every land'. Thus, he defined freedom not only as internal freedom, but also as freedom from duties and obligations with regard to any particular city. His motivation for assuming this position was eudaimonistic: only the life of a foreigner affords the type of freedom that leads to happiness.

Aristippus the Younger was probably the first Cyrenaic philosopher to single out momentary bodily pleasure as the moral end. He appears to have conceived of the moral end as complete and perfect, for he maintained that bodily pleasures do not differ in intensity or degree: none is more pleasurable than another, presumably because no particular instance of the moral end can be more perfect, and therefore more worthy of choice, than another. He distinguished between happiness and the moral end by defining happiness as a particular collection of individual pleasures experienced over one's lifetime, and by claiming that happiness is not desirable for its own sake but for the sake of the pleasures composing it. However, his hedonistic ethics is not altogether devoid of eudaimonistic considerations. For he believed that the overall moral goal is to live a pleasurable life, thus emphasizing the importance of accumulating the particular pleasures which jointly compose a happy life. Such considerations arguably precluded him from holding the view that all means are permissible for obtaining pleasures. For some means to a particular pleasure may obstruct the achievement of subsequent pleasures or may have painful after-effects, and thus may affect one's enjoyment of a happy life.

4 Later Cyrenaic ethics

The ethics of Anniceris and of Hegesias also rest on a delicate balance between hedonism and eudaimonistic elements. Anniceris and his disciples further clarified the notion of the moral end by emphasizing that pleasure and pain are necessarily related to motion and by arguing that, since the condition of mere absence of pain is not characterized by motion, it cannot be part of the moral end. Their thesis should be contrasted with the position of the rival school of EPICURUS, according to which the supreme moral good is static pleasure, characterized by the complete absence of pain (see EPICUREANISM §10). They broadened Aristippus the Younger's definition of the moral good by attributing intrinsic moral value to mental as well as bodily pleasure, and allowed for circumstances in which sages will act altruistically and deprive themselves of pleasures, but will none the less be happy. Anniceris' concern with the repetition of individual pleasures and the enjoyment of new pleasures over an extended period of time is also indicated by his recommendation of forming good habits in order to correct a naturally bad disposition, and friendships on account of the repeated good feelings that they cause us.

Hegesias was a hedonist in principle, since he too defined the momentary present pleasure as the moral end. However, he added that one scarcely enjoys such pleasures, whereas one suffers numerous pains during one's lifetime. On these grounds, he concluded that the collection of individual pleasures constituting happiness cannot be achieved. The unattainability of happiness led him to maintain that life is a matter of indifference, and that life and death are each desirable in turn. His pessimism is moderated by the intellectualist position that no one errs voluntarily, and by the philanthropic concern that one should not despise other people but teach them.

Theodorus radically modified the hedonism of the other Cyrenaic sects. He introduced the concepts of joy and grief, defining joy as the supreme moral good, and claimed that pleasure and pain are intermediate between good and evil. Although he did not speak openly of happiness, his position has clearly eudaimonistic dimensions. For he viewed particular pleasures instrumentally, as means to joy, and he believed that joy results from the exercise of wisdom and justice. For these reasons, it seems likely that he conceived of joy as a long-term pleasurable state akin to happiness. His doctrine is comparable to the views of Aristippus the Elder: he considered wisdom and justice to be goods and emphasized their importance for achieving the moral end; he maintained that the sage need not be temperate in the enjoyment of pleasure, but unlike Aristippus the Elder did not make it conditional upon the capacity for mastering oneself; and he stressed the self-sufficiency of the sage, advocated cosmopolitanism and considered irrational the performance of military duty for any particular city. On the other hand, Theodorus introduced into Cyrenaic ethics an atheism and an amoralism which are not encountered in the doctrines of his predecessors.

The ethical doctrines of the Cyrenaics, regarding both the central role of pleasure and the importance of happiness, appear to find support in their epistemology. Since any momentary pleasure is a *pathos*, the manner in which it affects one is infallibly apprehended. It could be argued that we infallibly apprehend not only the pleasurable nature of the experience but also its self-evident goodness. Regarding the desirability of a happy life, the Cyrenaics could maintain either that it is itself a *pathos*, so that its content is indubitable, or that the goodness of a pleasurable life is self-evident in so far as the goodness of its component pleasures is self-evident. This connection between their ethics and their epistemology is admittedly no more than a conjecture and invites the objection that moral properties such as goodness are not part of the self-evident content of a *pathos*. Further, even if the goodness of every individual *pathos* of pleasure were self-evident, it would not straightforwardly follow that a collection of such *pathē* must preserve the goodness of the pleasures constituting it.

5 The Socratic connection

Historically, the Cyrenaic school owes its Socratic pedigree to the inclusion of its founder, Aristippus of Cyrene, in Socrates' entourage (see SOCRATIC SCHOOLS). Philosophically, there are several elements both in its epistemology and in its ethical doctrines that would justify the claim that it remained close to the spirit of Socrates' teachings.

Concerning their theory of knowledge, the Cyrenaics might argue that, like Socrates, they obeyed the Delphic maxim 'Know yourself!' and came to the conclusion that one cannot know anything but oneself. Thus, both the description of the physical states related to the *pathē* and the epistemic analysis of our apprehension of them could be inscribed in the context of an effort to pursue further the Socratic example of self-knowledge. Further, they could appeal to Socrates' disavowal of knowledge in support of their position that one is necessarily bound to be ignorant about external objects, thus endorsing, or perhaps even inaugurating, the tradition which made Socrates the founder of scepticism.

As regards their ethical doctrines, the Cyrenaics could make the general remark that even the Platonic Socrates, whether or not a hedonist, considered the enjoyment of mental pleasures compatible with the existence of a virtuous state of soul, and did not disallow all bodily pleasures, but only those which endanger self-mastery and moderation. Finally, most Cyrenaic philosophers appear to have endorsed some version of Socratic intellectualism – perhaps the most important motivation for calling them a Socratic school.

References and further reading

Doering, K. (1988) *Der Sokratesschüler Aristipp und die Kyrenaiker* (Aristippus the Pupil of Socrates and the Cyrenaics), Wiesbaden and Stuttgart. (The most recent book-length study of Cyrenaic philosophy.)

Giannantoni, G. (1990) *Socratis et Socraticorum Reliquiae* (The Fragments of Socrates and the Socratics), Naples: Bibliopolis. (Volume 2 contains the Greek and Latin testimonies for the Cyrenaics.)

Irwin, T. (1991) 'Aristippus Against Happiness', *The Monist* 74: 55–82. (Explores the nature of Cyrenaic hedonism and its epistemological support.)

Tsouna, V. (1998) *The Epistemology of the Cyrenaic School*, Cambridge: Cambridge University Press. (The only full-scale study of this topic, with translations of the relevant texts.)

* Xenophon (c. 360s BC) *Memoirs of Socrates*, trans. H. Tredennick, revised R. Waterfield, Harmondsworth: Penguin, 1990. (Aristippus appears as one of Socrates' interlocutors in II 1 and III 8.)

VOULA TSOUNA

CZECH REPUBLIC, PHILOSOPHY IN

The foundation of the University of Prague in 1348 contributed significantly to establishing Bohemia as a centre of philosophical thought. The main philosophers and theologians from the University favoured the Platonic tradition, and from this position they criticised corruption in the Church. The most important representative of this trend was Jan Hus who followed the teaching of John Wyclif in the spirit of rationalism and humanism. His ideas became an ideological base for the anti-feudal Hussite Revolution in the fifteenth century and the later Czech Reformation. Theoreticians on the extreme wing of the Revolution held a natural world-view, opposing the notion of transcendence. Social thinking in this era found expression in Petr Chelčický, who preached a strict pacifism and a classless society. The Revolution broke the power of the Church's ideological monopoly, and had a positive impact on the development of Czech society for the following two centuries. The atmosphere of relative tolerance allowed Renaissance thinking and Czech Reformation rationalism and humanism to enrich each other. This tradition culminated in the work of Jan Amos Comenius, who aimed to improve social relations through rational enlightenment and education, promoting harmony and justice for the development of all humankind.

After 1620, Czech spiritual life was paralysed for many centuries by a forced anti-Reformation and the emigration of many of the country's leading intellectuals. A revival started only at the end of the eighteenth century. František Palacký, inspired by the neohumanism of his era and by the Czech Reformation, formed a new philosophy of Czech history. B. Bolzano achieved impressive results in philosophy of science and logic, while A. Smetana created an independent variant of the philosophy of identity. In the second half of the nineteenth century Herbartism became very influential, contributing to social psychology and aesthetics.

The most important representative of modern Czech thinking is T.G. Masaryk, creator of a philosophical concept of democracy understood in the context of a humanistic world view. Masaryk's philosophy has been followed by many philosophers and theologians in the twentieth century. In the period between the wars, important concepts based on structuralism were created by J.L. Fischer (philosophy, sociology), J. Mukařovský (aesthetics), V. Příhoda (psychology, pedagogy), and many linguists. J. Patočka contributed to the development of phenomenology with his concept of the natural world. In opposition to 'school' philosophy L.Klíma preached extreme subjectivism and individualism. Non-dogmatic Marxists wrote internationally regarded works. Well known in analytical philosophy and modern logic are the achievements of L. Tondl, O. Weinberger, K. Teige, R.Kalivoda and K. Kosík and P. Tichý.

1 **Early period**
2 **From the National Revival to 1918**
3 **From the foundation of an independent state**

1 Early period

Philosophy in the Czech Republic is connected to national history in a manner unlike any other European 'philosophical' country. It has sometimes had to disregard academic problems and interests to

join the social battles of the era, and so it has played a major ideological role. Often it has had to reach beyond itself to develop ideas in other spheres of spiritual life, from the literary and historical to the natural sciences. The beginnings of philosophy in Bohemia go back as far as the thirteenth century to the Prague Cathedral School, which had contact with other European centres of philosophy. The founding of Prague University in 1348 was a positive stage in the development of philosophical scholarship, and important philosophical trends were evident at the University from the beginning. With time, however, realism in opposition to nominalism prevailed, based on the Platonic traditions of European thinking (see NOMINALISM). The chief representative was Vojtěch Raňkuv of Ježov (Adalbert Rankonis) (d. 1388), a Rector of the Sorbonne who introduced the writings of John WYCLIF to Prague University. Others include Jan Milíč of Kroměříž (d. 1374), a severe critic of both secular and Church power who influenced later Hussite thinkers with his chiliastic image of the coming doomsday and the 'era of justice'; Matěj (Mathias) of Janova (d. *circa* 1394), who denounced the institution of the church and demanded the creation of a *communio sanctorum* (community of saints) modelled on the first Christians; and Tomáš of Štítný (d. *circa* 1405), the first scholar to write his critical essays in Czech and the founder of Czech philosophical terminology.

This movement culminated in the early fifteenth century with Jan HUS, whose philosophy built on the achievements of Wyclif to reach humanistic and rationally critical conclusions. Hus believed that every Christian has the right to use their reason to judge the laws of the secular world as well as Church powers, as well as the right to refuse to obey if they find any discrepancies between these and God's law (understood as a Platonic Idea). The truth wins only when a man is willing to sacrifice his own life for it. Hus attempted to defend his ideas before the Church Council in Konstanz, but failed and was burnt at the stake. After his death, his ideas became an ideological starting point for the Hussite Revolution (1419–34) and the Reformation that followed. His influence was widespread: Jakoubek of Stříbro' (Jacobellus of Mies) (d. 1429), an ideologist of the mild wing of the Hussite Revolution, introduced Holy Communion from the chalice as a symbol of Christian equality for all believers; Mikuláš Biskupec (d. *circa* 1460) represented the radical wing and preached the 'liberal law of the Lord' which was based on the spiritual and social emancipation of human beings; Martin Húska (d. 1421), an extreme left-wing Hussite ideologist, refused to accept any notion of transcendence and denied theist dogmas – for him, God lives in human beings and the Eucharist is a real material feast, all people are equal and sexual life should be free; Petr Chelčický (d. 1460), a social reformer, believed the feudal division of society to be unjust and claimed equal rights for everyone, calling for universal love and condemning all violence (his ideas later influenced L.N. TOLSTOI).

The Hussite Revolution inspired the Czech Reformation, the first victorious reformation in Europe, and in 1457 a new Church was founded in Bohemia. Known as *Jednota bratrská* (Unity of Brethren), this new Church, was based on the teachings of Chelčický. Later it became an important centre of spiritual and cultural life in Czech society. (Many of its members emigrated in the seventeenth century before the violent anti-reformation broke out, and one of its branches still exists in the USA as the Moravian Brethren.) The 'Unity' proclaimed the idea of religious tolerance and, combined with other Reformation ideas, contributed to the forming of the 'Czech confession' (1575) which demanded freedom of belief for all – including serfs, thereby going against the feudal principle that they follow the beliefs of their ruler ('*cuius regio, eius religio*'). Among the representatives of the Unity was Jan Blahoslav (d. 1571), an outstanding bishop who wrote many theological and pedagogical essays, as well as the first Czech book on aesthetics and musical theory.

In Bohemia as elsewhere, the Reformation was followed by a surge in Renaissance humanism, both existing simultaneously and having mutual influence. In fact, representatives of both sides aimed to bring the two movements together. Viktorin Kornel of Všehrdy (d. *circa* 1520), a founder of the first Czech law school, worked on the philosophy of natural law, which reflected the self-awareness of the new class of citizens. He was also the creator of a philosophy of Czech history that overemphasized the importance of the Hussite period. Řehoř Hrubý of Jelení (Gelenius) (d.1514), a translator of Cicero, Petrarch and Erasmus of Rotterdam, was influenced by Stoicism and united his patriotism with the idea of Universal Goodness into a universally understood world view. Jan Jessenius (d.1621), a rector of Prague University who was executed for his part in the anti-Habsburg uprising, was a physician and a follower of Renaissance natural philosophy (inspired by Franciscus Patritius). He also supported Heliocentrists, as did the outstanding mathematician and astronomer Tadeáš Hájek (d.1600), whose work was used by Tycho de Brahe, Kepler and Galileo.

Prague at this time was also an important centre of Jewish culture. Its most important representative was Jehuda ben Becalel Liva (d.1609), the legendary Rabbi Löw who, in his chief philosophical and theological document *Be'er ha-gola* (1600) expresses his understanding of a free man opening himself to the outside world through his activity. Rabbi Löw also wanted the Jewish community to engage other nations in dialogue on equal terms.

Czech Reformation thinking, which was enriched by many elements from the Renaissance, culminates in the synthetic work of Jan Amos COMENIUS, the last bishop of the Unity. In his major work, *De rerum humanarum emendatione consultatio catholica*, he created a philosophical system dominated by the idea of amelioration and the harmonious arrangement of human relations, based on rational enlightenment and general education. He believed in human nature as an active force capable of constant improvement. Didacticism and pedagogy were to serve as an instrument to reach this aim. At he deepest layer of this conception there is an ontology based on a modified Neo-Platonist scheme, whose highest degree is the harmonious development of all beings into a new human reality.

The movement in Czech philosophical thinking which culminated in the work of Comenius was interrupted after the Battle of White Mountain in 1620. The Czech State ceased to exist and a forced re-Catholicization of the country followed. The elite of Protestant intellectuals, including Comenius, had to leave the country and their place was taken by Catholic priests, mostly of foreign origin, who brought with them other intellectual traditions. Some of them contributed to the history of seventeenth-century philosophical thinking, including Roderigo Arriaga, a follower of the neoscholastics, who tried to find a compromise between the teaching of Thomas AQUINAS and William of OCKHAM in a spirit of mild realism; Jan Caramuel of Lobkowicz, considered a father of modern logic of relations; and Valerianus Magni, a Franciscan who developed the Scotistic tradition, opposed neoscholasticism and was close to Descartes' rationalism (see DESCARTES, R.; DUNS SCOTUS, J.; RATIONALISM). Jan Marcus Marci of Kronland was a different type of thinker, a natural scientist rooted in Platonism and Neoplatonism who preached the analogical construction of microcosm and macrocosm – through studying the activity of nerves he arrived at ideas anticipating later associative psychology (see NEOPLATONISM; PLATONISM, RENAISSANCE). Hieronymus Hirnheim belonged to the anti-Jesuit opposition. He stressed the ethical ideas of original Christianity, the primacy of life-praxis over speculative scholasticism and the importance of subjective belief oriented to a philosophy close to Jansenism.

2 From the National Revival to 1918

After the long period of oppression, Czech intellectual life was slowly revived in the last third of the eighteenth century. It was inspired first by the Enlightenment, later by neohumanism and romanticism, and at the same time by the older national tradition of the Reformation. It paid great attention to the development of the most important branches of scientific research. Consequently Slavic philology, history and natural sciences were studied, and these soon reached European academic levels.

The founder of Czech and Slavic philology, Josef Dobrovský (d.1829), was also a founder of modern critical rationalistic methods of research rooted in the Enlightenment. Bernard BOLZANO, the greatest philosopher of this era, developed on the traditions of the Enlightenment and criticized Kantian and post-Kantian philosophy. An inventive mathematician and one of the founders of the philosophy of science and modern logic, he investigated the semantic basis of logical systems. His pursuit of the relationship between idea (*Vorstellung*) and notion, of the notion of consciousness, and of the function of *Vorstellungen* in a sentence, was later expanded by Husserl (see HUSSERL, E. §6). Jiří Procházka (d.1820), a physiologist, initiated the reflexive theory of spiritual activity. (His 1784 essay *De functionibus systematis nervosi commentatio* was translated into English in 1851, and influenced the theory of Marshall Hall.) Later on, in the spirit of German *Naturphilosophie*, he created a dynamic picture of nature according to the law of polarity derived from the science of electricity. Jan Evangelista Purkyně (d.1869) was also influenced by the German tradition. A founder of the theory of cellular construction of living organisms, he added a historical dimension to his dynamic concept of nature, and held a pantheist ontology (see PANTHEISM). František Palacký (d. 1876), author of the monumental 'History of the Czech nation', had pursued philosophy in his youth. He was influenced by neo-humanism, and especially by Schiller on whose ideas he formed a model of perfect humanity and thus his humanistic philosophy of Czech history, which for a long time was a basis for Czech policy (see SCHILLER, F.C.S.).

The revolution of 1848 was philosophically reflected in the work of Augustin Smetana (d. 1851), whose roots were in left-wing Hegelianism. In his philosophy of human spirituality he created an independent variant on the philosophy of identity, based on the relative identity of knowledge (*Wissen*) and existence (*Sein*). He interpreted the Hegelian historical scheme of the development of *Weltgeist* so that it envisaged that the era to come would bring a dominant role and social justice for the Slavs. However, the impact of Hegel's philosophy was not very strong in Bohemia.

The dominant trend in philosophical thinking in the second half of the nineteenth century in Bohemia was Herbartism, introduced to Bohemia by Franz Exner (d. 1853) who opposed Hegel's idealism and criticized his psychology (see HERBART, J.F.). Robert Zimmermann (d. 1898), a student of Bolzano, managed to influence this trend through his historic and synthetic works in aesthetics while working at Prague University. Some followers of Herbartism developed single philosophical disciplines, others originated completely new ideas in the philosophy of religion, the history of philosophy, sociology, social psychology, and logic. Otakar Hostinský (d. 1910) created an aesthetic concept of 'concrete formalism' and the philosophy of art, and some of his ideas were employed by the Prague structuralist school (see STRUCTURALISM IN LINGUISTICS). Herbartism was very influential throughout central Europe, and to some extent it fulfilled the role of positivism in Czech intellectual life (that is why classical positivism appeared relatively late; but it lasted well into the twentieth century). Herbartism tried to react positively to impulses from contemporary sciences (empirical psychology and Darwinism for example) and provided the first steps to a variety of new concepts and inventions such as *Gestaltqualitäten*, the neopositivism of the Vienna circle, and the relationship of consciousness and subconsciousness in FREUD (see VIENNA CIRCLE).

Miroslav Tyrš (d. 1884) stood outside this trend. He transformed Schopenhauer's pessimistic concept of the will into a philosophy of human activity of a subject who is both a counterplayer and a co-player in the struggle of life (Darwin's influence) and formulated a new plan for the development of a small nation, working it out in practical terms by founding a mass physical training organisation 'Sokol' which is still in existence (see SCHOPENHAUER, A.). Tomáš Garrigue MASARYK began his philosophical career by opposing Herbartism and German post-Kantian philosophy, and he gradually succeeded in weakening their positions. His philosophical roots were in French and English positivism, but he used these solely as a research methodology to investigate the general crisis of values. He sought to resolve this crisis by using the concept of a human being as a harmonious unity of reason, will and emotion. His thought was based on religious values of the Czech Reformation and on the idea of democracy, understood as a humanistic world outlook. After 1918, this concept became the central idea of the newly formed Czechoslovak state, of which Masaryk was the first president.

3 From the foundation of an independent state

The culture and political climate of the new democratic state was conducive to philosophical investigation, and philosophy was an integral part of the curriculum in the newly formed universities and colleges. Among the many trends, positivism was still in fashion and even became a sort of national philosophy. It was mostly true to J.S. Mill's principles of positive methodology and to Comte's schemes of development, although attempts were made to modernize these (see COMTE, A.; MILL, J.S.). Josef Tvrdý (d. 1942) introduced the emergentism of Samuel ALEXANDER to the qualitative understanding of evolutionary processes. However, Josef Král (d.1978) worked out his concept of the history of Czech thought in a traditional spirit. Emanuel Chalupný (d.1958) also pursued the philosophy of Czech history and created his own sociological system. Spiritual fathers of neo-positivism like Ernst MACH (a longserving professor at Prague University), Rudolf CARNAP and Philip Frank, who both worked in Prague for some time, had less direct impact on Czech philosophy.

Masaryk's humanistic philosophy based on religion was adopted mainly by Protestant thinkers, including Emanuel Rádl (a proponent of 'intuitive realism' and critic of positivist scientism), Josef L. Hromádka (an independent follower of so called dialectic theology), and Jan B. Kozák (who was influenced by phenomenology and attempted to solve the problems inherent in the relationship between science and belief, and the question of objective ethical values). Masaryk's influence extended into many different fields and he found followers in a wide range of disciplines.

In the period between the First and Second World Wars, the three basic streams of structuralism, phenomenology and non-orthodox Marxism constituted mainstream philosophy, and their impact was to prove of major importance. About 1930, structuralism became a methodological basis for some of the humanities and social sciences and took a specific dynamic form with an expressive historical aspect. Its noetical, ontological and sociological principles were worked out by Josef Ludvík Fischer who also created a model of structural democracy, freeing all social forces for the benefit of the individual and society as a whole. Theoretical bases for sociology were formed in an analogical way by In. Arnošt Bláha. The *Cercle linguistique de Prague* became an internationally acclaimed propagator of the structural and functional understanding of language, literature and the arts, enriching the philosophy of all three in the works of Jan Mukařovský and Roman Jakobson. Additionally, structural philosophy of education and structuralist methods in psychology were advocated by Václav Příhoda (see STRUCTURALISM).

The Czech-German *Cercle philosophique de Prague*, founded on the initiative of the aesthetician Emil Utitz, with J.B. Kozák, became an ideological centre of the phenomenological movement. In 1935 HUSSERL was invited to Prague and the lectures he delivered were the basis for his final book *The Crisis of the European Sciences*. Jan PATOČKA, Husserl's pupil, became the most important representative of phenomenology in Bohemia. In the 1930s he worked on the problem of the original, predetermined natural world (*Lebenswelt*), its structure, and the activity of human beings in it. This was a very progressive project and it was some time before it gained a following in the phenomenological literature. Also some structuralists of the era had an interest in phenomenology and duly modified their concept of the function and tasks of art in the context of human existence (see PHENOMENOLOGICAL MOVEMENT).

Marxist philosophy in the first half of the twentieth century had a social basis in a strong left-wing political movement. Apart from the ideologists who took their starting point from the Communist Party, there were those who took Marxism as a starting point for independent thinking. One such thinker was Karel Teige, an important theoretician of avant-garde art. He regarded artistic activities a means to realize an ideal of a free human being and to apply his creative force in the contemporary social conditions. Jaroslav Kabeš, who was influenced by the young Marx and later on by great representatives of Czech culture, persisted in questioning the purpose of human existence. The problems of a materialistic concept of history, and particularly its relation to Czech history and the history of European revolutions, attracted the attention of Kurt Konrad and Záviš Kalandra. The latter was also one of the first Czech Marxists to consider the importance of Freud's work in understanding the role of the psychological factor in history and the structure of personality.

Other philosophers of the first half of the twentieth century also had significant influence and impact. They include Ladislav Klíma, a radical subjectivist and philosopher of free existence in an absurd world, anticipating later existentialism (see EXISTENTIALISM); natural scientists František Mareš and Karel Vorovka who argued against positivistic scientism from an idealistic starting point; Vladimír Hoppe who emphasized intuitivism and mysticism; and Karel Engliš who created a philosophical system based on the teleological understanding of social relations (see FUNCTIONALISM IN SOCIAL SCIENCE). Among Catholic researchers, neo-scholastic Josef Kratochvil attracted most attention. He called his standpoint 'neo-idealism' and aimed to overcome the positivist view of unknowable transcendence. The group of philosophers and theologians gathered around the journal *Filosofická Revue* was also neo-thomistically oriented, while those German philosophers in Prague who gathered round the Brentano-Gesellschaft, formed from the second generation of Brentano's pupils, were also very active.

During the Nazi occupation and the following six years of the Second World War, the continuity of philosophical investigation in Bohemia was interrupted. Universities and colleges were closed down and severe censorship was introduced. Some important philosophical figures were executed, some imprisoned in concentration camps and others forced into exile. The end of the war did not mean a return to pre-war conditions, the shift towards socialism creating a new situation. In the relatively free political situation of the years 1945–8 the ideological influence of Marxism was increasing. This process was supported by Arnošt Kolman who came back from the Soviet Union, as well as by many philosophers of socialist orientation who accepted Marxism and those who had previously been closer to it. Some non-Marxists continued to hold on to their former views.

This situation changed in February 1948 when the Communist Party came to power. Stalinism became the official ideology and all other philosophical and ideological schools of thought were prohibited. Many philosophers, especially Catholics, were imprisoned, and some of the younger ones left the country. Marxists were also persecuted. It took almost ten years for the ideological opposition to get more space for freer philosophical investigations. Meanwhile, Masaryk continued to have followers at home and abroad, Fischer continued his ontological work based on structuralism, and Patočka proceeded in his phenomenological investigations, trying to synthesize his ideas with those of HEIDEGGER, while also maintaining an interest in the history of philosophy.

In the 1960s, young non-Marxist intellectuals gathered round the cultural journal *Tvář* (Face) – its spiritual agent was a playwright, Václav Havel, and philosophical essayists Ladislav Hejdánek and Jiří Němec were among the contributors. The freer atmosphere was also favourable to the development of non-orthodox Marxism, and the tendency to integrate elements of contemporary European thinking with Marxism became stronger, manifesting itself in many ways. An important experiment aimed at solving phenomenological-existential problems on the basis of Marxism was carried out by Karel Kosík, and similar efforts were made by other philosophers of the same generation. Questions of philosophical anthropology and ethical study also attracted attention. The

problems of structuralism and the philosophical message of the artistic avant-garde were considered using Marxist categories by Robert Kalivoda (d. 1989) and simultaneously by other theoreticians in different variants. Other philosophers researched analytical philosophy, cybernetics, semantics and modern logic. In this connection are works written by Ladislav Tondl, Otto Weinberger and Pavel Tichý. At this time, much light was shed on the many periods of the history of philosophy, including that of Bohemia, while at the same time systematic questions raised by the material were widely discussed.

The third catastrophe of Czech philosophy in this century was the defeat of the 'Prague Spring', and the subsequent inauguration of another totalitarian regime. The majority of philosophers in the movements discussed above were dismissed from their posts at universities and research institutions, were prohibited from publishing and their books were removed from public libraries. Those who did not leave the country were compelled to work as unskilled manual workers. This gave rise to vigorous unofficial intellectual activity. In spite of police repression, lectures and seminars were organized in private houses, sometimes with the participation of philosophers from France, England, Germany and The Netherlands. Dozens of books and some magazines were issued independently (*samizdat*), and many works were published abroad. This situation was not without precedent – the philosopher and poet known as Egon Bondy (real name Z. Fišer), a legendary personality of the Czech underground, had been involved in such activity since 1948. Students of Patočka took part in the preparation of a twenty-seven volume edition of Patočka's Collected Works, and the youngest generation of his pupils continued in his tradition after their teacher's death. This time also saw the formation of an active group of Catholic-orientated philosophers who concentrated their efforts on publishing the illegal magazine *Paraf* (whose name derived from *Paralelní filosofie*, parallel philosophy, in opposition to the official philosophy). In the 1980s, as the pressure of the regime gradually decreased, many (mostly younger) philosophers were given the opportunity to work in the official institutions.

The fall of the totalitarian regime at the end of 1989 allowed the necessary conditions for the resumption of Czech philosophy to be re-established. Such freedom had existed in modern times only in the period between the two world wars. Many philosophers of the older generation returned to their original profession, as did some younger philosophers who had been forbidden to work in their field of study after graduating. E. Kohák, I. Sviták, J.M. Lochman and K. Chvatík were some of the philosophers living in exile who now renewed contacts with home. Besides these there was the Catholic thinker M. Loblowicz, analytic philosophers and logicians O. WEINBERGER, P. Tichý and J. Šebestík, phenomenologist I. Šrubař, postmodernist V. Bélohradský and others. Active philosophical life could now resume.

See also: MARXIST PHILOSOPHY, RUSSIAN AND SOVIET; SLOVAKIA, PHILOSOPHY IN

References and further reading

* Comenius, J.A. (*c.*1660s) *De rerum humanarum emendatione consultatio catholica* (General consultation on the reform of human affairs), Prague: Academia, 1966. (The synthesis of Comenius's life work not published in its entirety until 1966. Mentioned in §1 above.)

Gabriel, Jiří-Nový, Lubomír (eds) (1993) 'Czech Philosophy in the 20th Century', *Czech Philosophical Studies II*, Cultural Heritage and Contemporary Change IV, Washington, DC: The Council for Research in Values and Philosophy. (Summary of separate trends of Czech thinking written by a team of authors.)

Jakovenko, B. (1935) 'La philosophie tchécoslovaque contemporaine' (Contemporary Czech Philosophy), in *Der russische Gedanke* IVe Prague: Supplément de la revue. (Chapter about leading thinkers of the twenties and thirties with bibliographies: texts are in French, German, English and Italian.)

* Jehuda ben Becalel Liva (1600) *Be'er ha-gola*, Prague. (Rabbi Löw's chief philosophical and theological document, mentioned in §1 above.)

Král, J. (1934) *La philosophie en Tchécoslovaquie* (Philosophy in Czecheslovakia), Prague: Bibliothèque des problèmes sociaux. (Digest of history of philosophy in Bohemia and Slovakia with a separate chapter about German philosophy in Bohemia.)

Lobkowicz, Nikolaus (1961) *Marxismus-Leninismus in der ESR, Die tschechoslowakische Philosophie seit 1945*, Dortrecht: Reidel (Detailed analysis of Czech and Slovak Marxism with consideration of other trends.)

Mácha, Karel (1985–9) *Glaube und Vernunft: Die Böhmische Philosophie in geschichtlicher Übersicht*, I–III. Munich, New York, London, Paris: KG Saur. (Broad history. The author's judgment is at times somewhat subjective.)

* Procházka, Jiří (1784) *De functionibus systematis nervosi commentatio*, Prague: Academia, 1954. (Treatise on the functions of the nervous system, mentioned in §2 above.)

Zumr, Josef (1971) 'Philosophie der Gegenwart in der Tschechoslowakei', in R. Klibansky (ed.) *Contemporary Philosophy*, Florence: La nuova italia editrice, 455–73. (Digest of Czech and Slovak thinking between 1930 and 1969.)

Translated from the Czech by G.R.F. Burša

JOSEF ZUMR

D

DAI ZHEN (1724–77)

Dai Zhen, a neo-Confucian philosopher, argues against the received neo-Confucian view of dao *as a metaphysical entity. On the contrary,* dao *is immanent in the world and, in the case of the human world specifically, in the everyday lives of ordinary people irrespective of social status. His philosophical views had important political and social implications.*

Dai Zhen came from Huizhou in Anhui Province. During his early years, Dai often accompanied his father, a cloth merchant, on business trips which brought him in touch with the political and social realities in many parts of China. In 1754 he became entangled in a lawsuit with a powerful clansman who was a friend of the local magistrate and, on being informed that he was about to be arrested, left home in great haste and went to Beijing. This background exerted no small influence on the formulation of his philosophical critique of the dominant Confucian ideology in decades to come.

Dai wrote three important philosophical treatises: *Yuanshan* (Inquiry into Goodness), *Xuyan* (Surviving Words) and *Mengzi ziyi shuzeng* (Commentary on the Meanings of Terms in the Book of Mencius). A central concern of all his writings is the immanental status of *dao*. He contends by way of etymology that this is the original meaning of *dao* in early Confucian texts. Understood analytically, *dao* consists of all the principles or patterns (*li*) discoverable in the world. Song dynasty neo-Confucians are wrong, due to the influence of Buddhism, in assuming that *li* is a gift from Heaven and resides in the human mind/heart as if it were a thing. Viewed objectively, *li* is none other than the internal texture and structure in things (see DAO; LI).

True to Confucian humanism, Dai makes an important distinction between what is natural (*ziran*) and what is necessary (*biran*). The former refers to principles or patterns governing all the activities in the world whereas the latter refers to those in the human world exclusively. In this view, not only is the human world continuous with the natural world but the two worlds are also marked by a clear break, thereby distinguishing human beings from all other kinds of beings. He understands the idea of goodness (*shan*) in this light. In his own words: 'Goodness is what is

necessary whereas nature (*xing*) is what is natural (see XING). What is natural will be fully completed only when it is developed into what is necessary. This is known as developing the natural to the utmost' (*Mengzi ziyi shuzeng*: 195). This suggests that the world will not be complete without human beings.

Following the same logic, Dai rejects the neo-Confucian bifurcation between moral principles (*li*) on the one hand, and human desires (*yu*) and feelings (*qing*) on the other. Moral norms are capable of regulating human desires and feeling precisely because they are the internal texture and structure in the everyday life of human beings rather than something imposed on it from outside. His objectification of *dao* and *li* naturally leads him to emphasize the central importance of intellectual inquiry known as 'investigation of things' (*gewu*) in the Confucian tradition (see NEO-CONFUCIAN PHILOSOPHY §9). Intellect or intelligence (*zhi*) is what distinguishes human beings from other phenomena (see ZHI).

Dai draws important political and social implications from his philosophical views. He believes that the neo-Confucian concept of *li* as Heavenly Principle always serves to justify the oppression of the helpless common people by those in power. The struggle of the common people to satisfy their basic needs in life are denounced as 'selfish desires' and anyone who has the audacity to defy the norm imposed on the common people by the ruling elite often ends up being condemned to a moral death. Clearly, he is deeply dissatisfied with the Song dynasty neo-Confucian definition of *li* as 'heavenly principles', which has been used by those in power to justify the oppression of the helpless common people. Thus in Dai's philosophical system, we see an unmistakeable beginning of a modern spirituality uniquely China's own.

See also: DAO; NEO-CONFUCIAN PHILOSOPHY; LI; ZHI

List of works

Dai Zhen (1766) *Yuanshan* (Inquiry into Goodness), in *Dai Zhen guanji* (Complete Works of Dai Zhen), Beijing: Qinghua University Press, 1991, vol. 1, 9–27; trans. Cheng Chung-Ying, *Tai Chen's Inquiry into Goodness*, Honolulu, HI: East–West Center Press, 1971. (Edition and translation.)

—— (1769) *Xuyan* (Surviving Words), in *Dai Zhen guanji* (Complete Works of Dai Zhen), Beijing: Qinghua University Press, 1991, vol. 1, 64–116. (No modern translation of this work exists at present.)

—— (1777) *Mengzi ziyi shuzheng* (Commentary on the Meanings of Terms in the Book of Mencius), in *Dai Zhen guanji* (Complete Works of Dai Zhen), Beijing: Qinghua University Press, 1991, vol. 1, 149–210; trans. T. Loden, 'Dai Zhen's Evidential Commentary on the Meaning of the Words of Mencius', *Bulletin of the Museum of Far Eastern Antiquities* 60, Stockholm, 1988: 165–313. (Edition and translation.)

References and further readings

Chin Ann-ping and Freeman, M. (1996) *Tai Chen on Mencius*, New Haven, CN: Yale University Press. (An analysis of Dai Zhen's writings on Mencius.)

Yü Ying-shih (1989) 'Tai Chen's Choice Between Philosophy and Philology', *Asia Major*, third series, 11 (1): 79–108. (Article on Dai Zhen's philosophical outlook.)

YÜ YING-SHIH

DAMASCIUS (*c.*462–540)

The late Neoplatonist philosopher Damascius was the last head of the Platonist school in Athens. He largely accepted the metaphysical system of the Athenian School of Syrianus and Proclus, but subjected it to acute dialectical scrutiny in a series of commentaries, and especially in his treatise On First Principles. *His philosophical position is not comprehensible without bearing in mind that of Proclus, although on certain issues, such as the nature of the first principle and of the soul, he prefers the solutions of the earlier Iamblichus.*

Damascius was probably born *c.*462 in Damascus. He studied rhetoric first in Alexandria and then moved to Athens shortly before the death of Proclus in 485. He practised in Athens as a professor of rhetoric and, although he attended lectures in philosophy, he experienced a real 'conversion' to philosophy only in around 491, under the influence of the Platonist Isidorus, whose life he later wrote. At about this time, following Isidorus, he returned to Alexandria for a spell, where he attended also the lectures of the Platonist AMMONIUS, SON OF HERMEAS .

Around 510–15, Damascius himself succeeded as head of the Platonist school, and from then until 529 he presided over an intellectual and financial revival of that institution, which had fallen into some obscurity. His students included SIMPLICIUS (§§1,3), who testifies to the acuteness of his intellect and the excellence of his instruction (*On Aristotle's Physics* 624.38).

In 529, the emperor Justinian issued his famous decree against non-Christian teachers. This effectively closed the Platonic school. In its wake (*c.* autumn of 531), following on the accession to the throne of Persia of the young Chosroes, who had a lively interest in philosophy, Damascius and a group of other philosophers decided to emigrate to Persia. They returned after a year, however, under a safe conduct arranged by Chosroes, which enabled them to philosophize in private. Damascius' last years were probably spent at Emesa in Syria, where he died.

Damascius' works are only partly preserved, and often in an unsatisfactory state. We have no surviving commentaries by him on Aristotle, but Simplicius, in his commentary *On Aristotle's Physics*, quotes extensively from a special treatise of his *On Number, Space and Time*. His commentaries on Plato have survived somewhat better, but even the surviving ones on the *Phaedo and Philebus* are in the form of students' notes. His only properly surviving works are the treatise *Problems and Solutions on First Principles*, and his *Commentary on Plato's Parmenides*.

It is chiefly from these two latter works that we can appreciate the particular quality of Damascius' philosophizing. Situated at what was effectively the end of a long philosophical tradition, he exhibits a remarkable blend of scholastic elaboration and critical acumen. He accepts all the metaphysical convolutions of Syrianus and PROCLUS, and those of IAMBLICHUS before them. Indeed, one of his distinctive features is a tendency to revive positions of Iamblichus in opposition to those of the later Athenian School, as well as their penchant for syncretistic theology, and such documents as the Chaldaean Oracles and the Orphic Theogonies (see CHALDAEAN ORACLES). In contrast, however, he rigorously puts all the basic principles of Neoplatonism to the test of dialectic, with most stimulating results.

There are four main topics examined in *On First Principles*. First, the nature of the first principle, in which Damascius examines the case for an absolutely ineffable principle prior to the One proper, while analysing the contradictions involved in postulating a first principle which is both entirely simple and transcendent, and the source of all creation and diversity. Second, an analysis of the components of the henadic realm, the triad of One–many (Monad), many–One (Indefinite Dyad) and 'the unified', which is the union of the two. Third, arising out of this, a penetrating discussion of the central dynamic of Neoplatonic metaphysics, the triple process of remaining, procession and return (*monē-proodos-epistrophē*). And finally, the relationship of the intelligible realm as a whole to its parts, the Forms. In his *Commentary on Plato's Parmenides* we find his views on the nature of the soul, which he sees as a radically median entity, subject to change even in its essence.

To ask what is distinctive in Damascius' philosophy, however, results in a complex answer. His philosophy is unashamedly that of his predecessors. Where he differs from Syrianus and Proclus, as he does on such questions as the nature of the first principle and the economy of the henadic realm, or on the nature and status of the soul, he is often only reverting to the doctrines of Iamblichus. Even his views on space and time, and his postulation of archetypal forms of both these entities, largely develop positions of Iamblichus. Damascius' particular genius lies rather in the dialectical analysis to which he subjects all these questions, and it is for this that he is valuable.

See also: NEOPLATONISM §§1, 4

List of works

Damascius' texts cannot be dated relative to each other.

Damascius (c.462–540) *Problems and Solutions on First Principles*, ed. L.G. Westerink and J. Combès, *Damascius, Traité des premier principes*, Paris: Les Belles Lettres, 1986– 9, 3 vols. (Contains French translation and notes.)

—— (c.462–540) *Commentary on Plato's Parmenides*, ed. C.A. Ruelle, *Damascii Successoris Dubitationes et solutiones in Platonis Parmenidem*, Paris: Klincksieck, 1899, 2 vols; repr. Amsterdam, 1966. (Also contains Problems and Solutions on First Principles.)

—— (c.462–540) *Commentary on Plato's Philebus*, ed. L.G. Westerink, *Damascius, Lectures on the Philebus*, Amsterdam: North Holland, 1959. (Contains text, translation and notes.)

—— (c.462–540) *Commentary on Plato's Phaedo*, ed. L.G. Westerink, *The Greek Commentaries on Plato's Phaedo* , vol. 2, Amsterdam: North Holland, 1973. (Text and translation.)

—— (c.462–540) *Life of Isidorus*, ed. C. Zintzen, *Damascii vitae Isidori reliquiae*, Hildesheim: Olms, 1976. (Greek text.)

References and further reading

Combès, J. (1989) *Études néoplatoniciennes* (Neoplatonist Studies), Grenoble: Millon. (Collection of articles in French, mainly on Damascius.)

Gersh, S. (1978) *From Iamblichus to Eriugena*, Leiden: Brill. (Contains much discussion of Damascius' philosophy.)

Sambursky, S. (1982) *The Concept of Place in Late Neoplatonism*, Jerusalem: Israel Academy. (Contains texts and translations relative to Damascius' doctrine on subject of place.)

Sambursky, S. and Pines, S. (1971) *The Concept of Time in Late Neoplatonism*, Jerusalem: Israel Academy. (Contains texts and translations relative to Damascius' doctrine on time.)

* Simplicius (after 538) *On Aristotle's Physics*, ed. H. Diels, *Commentaria in Aristotelem Graeca IX–X*, Berlin: Reimer, 1882–5; trans. C. Hagen, *On Aristotle's Physics 7: Simplicius*, London: Duckworth, 1994.

Steel, C. (1978) *The Changing Self, A Study on the Soul in Later Neoplatonism: Iamblichus, Damascius and Priscianus*, Brussels: Paleis der Academien. (An excellent discussion of Damascius' theory of the soul.)

JOHN DILLON

DAMIAN, PETER (1007–72)

Peter Damian is noted for his asceticism, contributions to church reform and literary style, the latter in writings that are primarily religious in character. Because of his hostility to the unbridled use of the disciplines of grammar and dialectic in religious matters, Damian is sometimes depicted as an opponent of philosophy. A more accurate assessment of his attitude is that the liberal arts, including philosophy, must remain subservient to religion. Damian's major work De divina omnipotentia *(On Divine Omnipotence) shows that he was willing and able to use philosophical argument in theology.*

Peter Damian was born in Ravenna in 1007, entered monastic life with the Benedictine Order at Fonte Avellana around 1036, became prior in 1043, was made cardinal around 1057 and died in 1072. He was actively involved in monastic reform, writing opinions on such topics as simony, married clergy and sexual abuses committed by clergy. Damian's usual mode of writing was the epistle, of which some 180 survive, displaying considerable rhetorical skill on the part of their author.

Damian entered an ongoing controversy over the relation between secular learning – exemplified in the study of grammar, dialectic and philosophy – and divine revelation as contained in the Bible. Although he has sometimes been interpreted as a champion of anti-intellectual fideism, the attitude discernible in Damian's writings is more inchoate than the interpretation suggests. He believes that the Bible contains all the knowledge necessary for personal salvation, and that monks spend their time most profitably in its study. At the same time, however, in insisting that secular learning should be chastened and made subordinate to the study of the word of God, he seems willing to grant secular studies some legitimacy. He offers no delineation of what form that legitimacy might take. The debate about the relation between secular learning and revelation was soon to be subsumed under a larger debate about the respective roles of reason and faith in human understanding. Less than a generation after Damian's flourishing, for example, one can find more sophisticated observations in the writings of ANSELM.

In a lengthy letter, now known as *De divina omnipotentia* (On Divine Omnipotence), to Desiderius, Abbot of Monte Cassino, Damian displays his skills both as philosophical critic and theologian. The question to be determined is whether God's omnipotence includes the ability so to act that what has happened never happened. Damian criticizes Desiderius' claim that God is unable so to act because he does not will so to act. He thinks that Desiderius' claim amounts to (1) God does not will to do *A* if and only if God cannot do *A*, and argues that claim (1), along with the principle (2) God does *A* if and only if God wills to do *A*, entails (3) if God does not do *A*, then God cannot do *A*.

Claim (1) entails that if God does not will to do *A*, then God cannot do *A*. Principle (2) entails that if God wills to do *A*, then God does *A*. Since either God wills to do *A* or God does not will do to *A*, it follows that either God does *A* or God cannot do *A*, which is equivalent to (3). Because (3) means that God is able to do only what God in fact does, Damian thinks that Desiderius' claim (1) must be rejected.

Damian proceeds to offer two separate solutions to the original question. According to the first solution, it is true that everything that has happened necessarily has happened, but that fact is irrelevant to the issue of God's omnipotence. The sentence, 'everything that has happened, necessarily has happened', is trivially true, 'according to the order of speaking'. Although Damian lacked the terminological distinctions that later medieval philosophers had at their disposal, his point can be expressed in their terminology by saying that 'everything that has happened, has happened' is necessarily true *de dicto*, and is not to be confused with the *de re* interpretation, 'everything that has happened has happened necessarily'. Only the latter would impinge on God's omnipotence.

Damian's second resolution maintains that there is a way in which God can still bring it about that Rome, which was founded, never was founded. God lives not in time but in eternity, in which the temporal past, present and future are all equally present to God. Thus, according to Damian, the founding of Rome, although past from our temporal perspective, is eternally present to God's power. As such, God can still cause Rome not to be founded, a situation that we, living after the time of the founding of Rome, describe as God's power to cause Rome never to have been founded.

See also: ETERNITY; OMNIPOTENCE

List of works

Damian, P. (1007–72) *De divina omnipotentia* (On Divine Omnipotence); in A. Cantin (ed.) *Lettre sur la toute-puissance divine*, Sources Chrétiennes 191, Paris: Éditions du Cerf, 1972. (Contains the complete Latin text with a French translation. The translation by O.J. Blum in *Medieval Philosophy: From St Augustine to Nicholas of Cusa*, eds J.F. Wippel and A.B. Wolter, New York: Free Press, 1969, presents a translation of only a part, with the sections not in sequence.)

—— (1007–72) Letters, ed. O.J. Blum, Washington, DC: Catholic University of America Press, 1989–. (A part of The Fathers of the Church: Medieval Continuation series. The following volumes have appeared: 1, Letters 1–30, 1989; 2, Letters 31–60, 1990; 3, Letters 61–90, 1992.)

—— (1007–72) Sermons, ed. G. Lucchesi, *Sancti Petri Damiani Sermones*, Corpus Christianorum, Continuatio Mediaevalis 57, Turnhout: Brepols, 1983. (Contains seventy-five sermons or fragments, twenty-four of which are deemed not to be by Damian.)

References and further reading

Kenny, A. (1979) *The God of the Philosophers*, Oxford: Clarendon Press. (Emphasizes, on pages 100–3, that Damian points out that in the sense in which God cannot alter the past, it would also follow that God cannot alter the future, which is absurd. Also argues that Damian's conception of omnipotence does not commit him to maintaining that God can violate the principles of logic.)

Weinberg. J. (1964) *A Short History of Medieval Philosophy*, Princeton, NJ: Princeton University

Press, 60–1. (Claims that Damian maintains that God's omnipotence extends over even the principles of logic.)

WILLIAM E. MANN

DANCE, AESTHETICS OF

The aesthetics of dance is the philosophical investigation of the nature of dance, of our interest in it, especially as an art form, and of the variety of aesthetic judgments we make about it – judgments of beauty, grace, line and other aesthetic qualities. Most philosophical issues concerning dance result from considering philosophical questions that arise in other areas: another art form, art in general, or human action. Sometimes the issue for dance can usefully be seen as a combination of issues from other areas. Often, one's response to such issues gives a possible direction for one's thoughts about dance.

A selection of such questions can be taken from the characteristics of dance. Since some dances are works of art, is there a kind of judgment characteristic of an interest in art, and, if so, what are its features? In particular, and in parallel with questions for other arts, does knowledge of the choreographer's intention have any role in understanding the dance? What follows for the understanding of dance from the fact that dance is a multiple art: that a particular dance (like a particular piece of music) can be performed in London at the same time as it is performed in New York? What follows from dance's status as a performing art (like music)? Is any special role for the understanding of dance to be assigned to a notated score in a dance notation? (If so, does this differ from music?) How is the special place of the dancer to fit into accounts of understanding dance? As some dances are regularly thought to be communicative, how does dance differ (if at all) from so-called 'nonverbal communication'? More generally, dance study must address far-reaching philosophical issues: the place of dance as human action; the 'role' of dance, for example, in ritual; the relevance of the history and traditions of dance-forms to the understanding of those forms.

1   Introduction

Dance has not been a major topic for philosophical enquiry for the contemporary aesthetician, because aestheticians have focused on problems in literature, music or painting, and because dance is viewed correctly as having few problems of its own: for example, discussion of the place of the choreographer's intention for criticism or understanding of his work will largely reproduce similar discussions for other artists (see ARTIST'S INTENTION) and theorists might be expected to take similar positions in both cases. Again, any discussion of dance must acknowledge that only some dances can be considered to be works of art, just as only some paintings are considered works of art. For dance, just as for other 'objects of aesthetic appreciation', aestheticians must ask whether the appreciation of art works is importantly different from the rest of 'aesthetic appreciation' or whether, instead, these cases should be understood in terms of one, underlying experience.

More specifically, the status of dance as a multiple art form, which allows the same dance to be performed in two or more places at the same time, and as a performing art are both shared by music. Thus, questioning the appropriateness of, for example, a type/token analysis for the relationship between the work itself and performances of it will be shared with the aesthetics of music, and it will be reasonable to expect analogous answers. Equally, issues resulting from the recording of dance using notation will be shared with those in music. This entry considers a selection from the many issues potentially lying within the ambit of the aesthetics of dance and provides remarks on each.

2   Dance, art and aesthetic appreciation

Does the philosophical aesthetics of dance concern only those dances or dance-forms that are, or could be, art forms, or should its net be cast more widely? In so far as its central interest lies in art-type dance, the aesthetics of dance will reflect concerns beyond the mere appreciation of grace, line, beauty and other aesthetic qualities in human movement. Then any value attributed to dance can begin from ascriptions of whatever value is proper to art, and issues in the aesthetics of dance will align with those in the aesthetics of other arts, especially other performing arts.

3   The distinctiveness of dance?

Dance is characterized by its *physicality*: it is an essentially physical art form and in this it differs from music, literature and visual art. Music and visual art require human action for their creation and existence, but the art objects are not physical (that is, not human action) in quite the same sense. Moreover, most dance – in contrast to music – has a 'mixed' character: a typical dance performance involves not merely movement but costume, music, staging and the like. (In this respect, the typical dance resembles the typical opera.) What exactly are the roles of these other elements, some already having status as art? For example, attending the ballet *The Rite of Spring* involves hearing Stravinsky's music. How is this to be integrated into our analysis of the art form? Of particular interest here are the ways in which elements of costume – often thought variable across different performances – can sometimes be entirely fixed by the choreographer, for example, in certain works by Alwin Nikolais. Equally, elements normally taken as fixed – for example, the music – may, in certain works, turn out not to be completely determined. For instance, Twyla Tharp's *The Bix Pieces* (1971) has a variable musical element.

4 Dance as a multiple art and as a performing art

Dance and music share their performing character: one encounters the work of art itself only in some performance of it. So performing arts generate, as it were, two objects for discussion: the work itself and particular performances of it – *Swan Lake* itself and, say, Tuesday night's performance of it. This fact has interesting implications. First, the dance itself is an abstract object – one never meets it, although, in another way, seeing the performances constitutes seeing it. Second, the dance can be seen in two places at the same time – by groups seeing different performances. So *Swan Lake* could be performed simultaneously in London and New York. Third, London's *Swan Lake* and New York's *Swan Lake* will differ, since they use different casts and are performed on stages of different sizes. In London, the producer may emphasize certain characteristics of *Swan Lake*, perhaps to suit the dancers in the cast. For similar reasons, different aspects may be stressed when the dance is staged in New York.

A type/token contrast (see TYPE/TOKEN DISTINCTION) that takes the work itself as the type and the particular performance as the token might be introduced here. Such an analysis would generate the three points noted above. Since *Swan Lake* is a type, it follows that it is an abstract object (the first point). As an abstract object, it is encountered only through encountering tokens: hence there can be more than one token at any particular time (the second point). But all the various performances are equally *Swan Lake*, despite their differences (the third point).

However, the type/token distinction cannot itself determine what is to count as a token of a particular type. There is a fine borderline between restaging a dance and re-choreographing to produce a different dance: for example, are some of Nureyev's productions re-choreographed or merely restaged? This consideration recognizes a difficulty in deciding whether a particular performance is or is not a token of a particular type. For recognizing re-choreography as the production of a different work of art is a way of saying that its performances are tokens of a different type.

Three possible objections to a type/token analysis of dance illustrate the complexity of this issue. First, has the analysis identified the crucial elements? One might think that, as with music, the interpretation of the performer or of the stager was also of crucial importance: yet the proposed analysis leaves no room for it. Second, does the type/token contrast focus on the right characteristics of multiple art form or is Nelson Goodman's autographic/allographic contrast more appropriate (see ART WORKS, ONTOLOGY OF §4)? Third, does the analysis tell us enough? Are we not still struggling to decide both when we have a token of a particular type and how the type 'constrains' its tokens?

5 Dance notation and understanding

One characteristic feature of dance as art is the possibility of its notation. There are three well-developed notation systems for dance: Labanotation, Benesh and Eshkol Wachman. Goodman has sketched the criteria of adequacy for any notation system for any art form: for example, the symbols must be clearly differentiated in order to pick out different states of affairs. One practical question is, 'To what degree do the notation systems mentioned above fulfil such criteria?' Alternatively, a philosophical issue arises concerning the uses to which notated scores might be put. Might they, for instance, play a role in the solution of (numerical) identity questions, such that any performance satisfying a notated score for *Swan Lake* was thereby bound to be an instance of that art work?

Two aspects of such notation systems have direct implications for the aesthetics of dance. First, dance notations radically under-determine the dance, by not guaranteeing that the movements they describe are dance rather than something else; by telling us nothing about costume, staging, music and the like; and by not fully determining the movements to be performed. Notated scores embody perceptions of the movements in question. The movements are objects that have been analysed, in the choice of what are to count as the key characteristics of a particular pattern of movement, and are not potential objects for analysis. So notation systems offer *interpretative* descriptions rather than neutral documentations of movements. Second, recording a particular dance in different notation systems imposes different sets of constraints on the dancer. The two recordings might be satisfied by slightly different sequences of movements. For instance, a performance which satisfied a notated score for *Swan Lake* in Labanotation might fail to do so for a score in Benesh, and vice versa. All that can be urged is that only reputable notation systems count here: those knowledgable about an art form decide what is reputable.

Further, positive use of the phrase 'those knowledgable about a particular art form' is an admission that, in the end, it is a matter for judgment by dance critics whether or not something is an instance of a particular work of art. If Nureyev's changes mean that his production no longer satisfies a particular notated score for *Swan Lake*, one alternative would be to doubt the appropriateness of that notation. It may, then, be a matter for art criticism, or more precisely for the critics of dance, whether a particular performance genuinely counts as a performance of *Swan Lake*.

6 The role of the dancer

The aesthetics of any performing art must address the role of the performer. The choreographer is the central artist, yet dancers should not be considered mere puppets of the choreographer, even when they have not been specifically involved in the initial creation of the particular dance. (As dances can typically be performed at a later date, there is an inherent possibility of dancers performing previously choreographed pieces.)

Revealingly, the term 'interpretation' is used in two distinct ways in performing arts, which I shall call 'critic's interpretation' and 'performer's interpretation'. The first characteristically consists of strings of sentences that discuss the structure and value of the work in question. But a pianist's rendering of a particular piano piece is also an interpretation. Here interpretation typically consists of some set of actions that are performed in producing the witnessable work. For dance, it consists in performing (at least) movements of the body. This second sort – performer's interpretation – is unique to the performing arts, while critic's interpretations are possible for all works of art. So any problems we have in understanding the idea of critic's interpretation, or in seeing the basis of

such interpretation are problems for all the arts equally. But concerns about making the interpretation an interpretation of a particular work of art, and of no other, and about ruling out inappropriate interpretations, have two dimensions for the performing arts. They apply not only to critic's interpretation – a difficulty shared with other art forms – but also to performer's interpretation.

When one witnesses a work in the performing arts, it has already become a performer's interpretation. Works in any performing art are under-determined at their creation just as they are under-determined by their notations: they are only brought to determinacy by performance. In this sense, works in the performing arts typically come as recipes, with an instruction to perform them – an instruction to produce a performer's interpretation. But once that interpretation is complete, the dance in that performance is determinate, and hence in the same position as works of the particular object sort, or non-performing works of the multiple sort, such as works of literature. Each has a physical instantiation which is available for critic's interpretation and such critic's interpretation will draw on the traditions and conventions of that art form. One important function of the dancer is thus as the creator of the performer's interpretation. We can therefore understand the virtues of one dancer over another in terms of their respective abilities to produce interesting and sustainable performer's interpretations.

7 Verbal and nonverbal communication

The distinctiveness of dance's expressive character seems to have no parallel in music, and so requires different treatment. How, if at all, does the expressiveness of dance relate to the more general expressiveness of bodily movement: to so-called 'nonverbal communication'? For the 'instrument' of dance is that very same human body in which we recognize, for instance, the sadness of another person through their posture, their words, and so on.

Activities that embody the intention to communicate can be distinguished from those that do not, even though actions of the latter type can teach us something about those who perform them – for example, their state of mind. Such a contrast, if sustainable, clearly places much dance, with verbal language and sign language, in one category, and much else that is nonverbal in the other. If we distinguish art-type dance from dance that is not art, then any expressive or communicative power of the latter would be that of 'other movement'. But should the expressive and communicative power of art-type dance be treated in the same way? If we conclude that it should, we have scarcely any reason for drawing the distinction between our interest in art and that in non-art. This in turn has implications for the value of dance, and in particular its educational value.

8 General philosophical issues

Finally, a significant number of general philosophical questions raise important issues for the aesthetics of dance. For instance, dance is a kind of human action: but how should we recognize or value, if at all, the dances of chimps or, in the future, of robots? Tentative solutions to various problems in the philosophy of action may be needed before events can be adequately characterized as dance at all, especially given the diversity of dances. Again, considering 'dance in other societies' raises a number of familiar questions concerning the beliefs of other cultures or societies. For instance, having recognized that the North American Indian ghost dances have a specific purpose (namely, to rid the continent of the white man), we will have difficulty concluding that they are art; can we even conclude that they are dance? For philosophical purposes the issue differs little from questions arising from, say, the Lascaux cave paintings.

As with other art forms, a developed aesthetics of dance would explore both the history of dance, at least as an art form, and the history of dance criticism. Thus, the question will arise of when it is appropriate to date the beginnings of dance. Should we, in parallel with Kristeller's work on the concept 'art', think of art-type dance coming into being with the baroque ballet in, say, the court of Louis XIV? Or should we conclude that, since the Greeks had a muse for dance (Terpsichore), there must have been art-type dance in classical Greece? Resolving such questions is partly a matter for history, but also calls for philosophical reflection on the implications of calling the activity *dance* rather than something else.

See also: ACTION; ARTISTIC INTERPRETATION; MUSIC, AESTHETICS OF; ART, PERFORMING

References and further reading

Copeland, R. and Cohen, M. (eds) (1983) *What is Dance?*, Oxford: Oxford University Press. (A useful anthology, including both the work of philosophers and of dance critics and dance theorists. Especially useful for some classic sources.)

Fancher, G. and Myers, G. (eds) (1981) *Philosophical Essays on Dance*, Brooklyn, NY: American Dance Festival Inc. (An anthology bringing together artists, critics and philosophers, with responses to some of the papers by choreographers and other dance practitioners. Some pieces difficult.)

* Goodman, N. (1968) *Languages of Art*, Indianapolis, IN: Bobbs–Merrill. (A classic text on notation, with a distinctive view of the nature of symbolism and of representation in art. Complex and technical.)

* Kristeller, P.O. (1951) 'The Modern System of the Arts: A Study in the History of Aesthetics I', *Journal of the History of Ideas* 12: 495–527; and (1952) 'The Modern System of the Arts: A Study in the History of Aesthetics II', *Journal of the History of Ideas* 13: 17–46; both repr. as 'The Modern System of the Arts', in *Renaissance Thought and the Arts*, Princeton, NJ: Princeton University Press, 1990. (Two important papers arguing for an eighteenth-century beginning to a roughly contemporary conception of the nature of art.)

McFee, G. (1992) *Understanding Dance*, London: Routledge. (An introductory text raising all of the issues discussed here and focusing on the art form of dance.)

—— (1994) *The Concept of Dance Education*, London: Routledge. (Application to education of ideas from the aesthetics of dance, taking the provisions of the National Curriculum for England and Wales as an example. Introductory.)

Sheets-Johnstone, M. (ed.) (1984) *Illuminating Dance: Philosophical Explorations*, Cranbury, NJ: Associated University Presses. (A collection including work by many of the leading figures in the aesthetics of dance. Some articles technical.)

Sparshott, F. (1988) *Off the Ground: First Steps to a Philosophical Consideration of Dance*, Princeton, NJ: Princeton University Press. (A systematic attempt to address the whole of the aesthetics of dance. Especially good on questions other than those relating to dance as an art form. Some technicality.)

—— (1995) *A Measured Pace: Towards a Philosophical Understanding of the Arts of Dance*, Toronto: University of Toronto Press. (Companion to the above, approaching the art forms of dance with due emphasis on the perspective of the dancer. Grounded in detailed account of the arts in general. Some passages technical.)

GRAHAM McFEE

DANTE ALIGHIERI

see ALIGHIERI, DANTE

DAO

Dao*, conventionally translated 'the Way', is probably the most pervasive and widely recognized idea in Chinese philosophy. The specific character of Chinese philosophy arises because a dominant cultural factor in the tradition, now and then, has been the priority of process and change over form and stasis, a privileging of cosmology over metaphysics. That the* Yijing *(Book of Changes) is first among the Chinese classics in every sense bears witness to the priority of cosmological questions – how, or in what way (*dao*) should the world hang together? – over metaphysical and ontological questions – what is the reality behind appearance, the Being behind the beings, the One behind the many, the true behind the false? The contrast lies in finding a way rather than seeking the truth.*

To contrast the difference between the search for metaphysical 'truth' – the way things really are – and the mapping of an appropriate and productive 'way' (*dao*) in the human world, we might consider the philosophical questions being asked by representative texts. The project in the Confucian *Analects*, for example, is not to speculate on *what* the ultimate source of value in the world might be, but to recount biographically *how* one sensitive person, Confucius, made his way in the world as a possible model for others (see CONFUCIUS). The *Daodejing* does not purport to provide an adequate and compelling description of what *dao* and *de* might mean as an ontological explanation for the world around us; rather, it seeks to engage us and to provide guidance in how we ought to interact with the phenomena, human and otherwise, that give us context in the world (see DAODEJING). Likewise the *Yijing* is not a systematic cosmology that seeks to explain the sum of all possible situations we might encounter in order to provide algorithmic insight into what to do, but is a resource providing a vocabulary of images that enable us to think through and articulate an appropriate response to the unique and always changing conditions of our lives (see YIJING).

Although the way of living to be discovered in the canonical texts, the *dao*, has historical antecedents, it is not simply to be discovered and walked. As the *Zhuangzi* 2 says, 'The path is made in the walking of it' (see ZHUANGZI). *Dao* means both to lead along a path, and to be led along it. In the Confucian *Analects*

15.29 we read, 'It is the human being that can broaden the way (*dao*), not the way that broadens the human being.' The human being must be a road-builder because human culture – the human *dao* – is always under construction.

The parts of speech which order Western languages – nouns, verbs, adjectives and adverbs – encourage us to divide up the world in a culturally specific manner. Under the influence of these grammatical determinants, we are inclined to separate things from actions, attributes from modalities, where from when and when from what (see SYNTAX). However, given the fluidity between time, space and matter assumed in classical Chinese cosmology, these categories do not govern the way in which the world is divided. The categories used to define a Chinese world must be seen as crossing the borders of time, space, and matter. *Dao* is both 'what is' (things and their attributes) and 'how things are' (actions and their modalities). *Dao* has as much to do with the subjects of knowing and their quality of understanding as it does with the object of knowledge and its attributes. There are no clear lines between things and events, and hence we cannot separate 'the Way' as *what* from a way as *how*.

In classical Western metaphysics, the equivocation between one as 'unity' and one as 'uniqueness' tends to be resolved in favour of 'unity.' Thus, in any of the various conceptions of a single-ordered universe assumed by the early systematic philosophers, the many phenomena comprising the world are defined in accordance with unifying first principles which determine the essential reality of the things of the world (see COSMOLOGY). *Dao* is often taken to be this familiar search for the One behind the many.

In classical Chinese reflections on world order, however, the equivocation between one as 'unity' and as 'uniqueness' is usually resolved in favour of the unique. The natural cosmology of classical China does not require a single-ordered cosmos, but invokes an understanding of a 'world' constituted by 'the ten thousand things' (see CHINESE PHILOSOPHY §1). There is no Being behind the beings – only beings are. And *in toto*, these beings are *dao*. Continuity makes *dao* one; difference makes *dao* myriad; change makes *dao* processional and provisional. *Dao* is thus both the One and the many, or better, the field and foci through which it is entertained.

The Chinese 'world as such' is constituted by 'worlding' (*ziran*), a process of spontaneous arising, or literally, uncaused 'self-so-ing', which references no external principle or agency to account for it. The one and the many stand in a holographic relationship: there is the indiscriminate field (*dao*) and its particular focus (*de*). *Dao* as field is always entertained and focused from some perspective or another, from some particular *de* (see DE). Just as in a holographic display where each detail contains the whole in an adumbrated form, so each item of the totality focuses the totality as its particular field.

See also: CHINESE PHILOSOPHY; CONFUCIUS; DAODEJING; DAOIST PHILOSOPHY; DE; QI; YIJING

References and further reading

Graham, A.C. (1989) *Disputers of the Tao: Philosophical Argument in Ancient China*, La Salle, IL: Open Court. (A survey of ancient Chinese thought.)

Hall, D.L. and Ames, R.T. (1995) *Anticipating China: Thinking Through the Narratives of Chinese and Western Culture*, Albany, NY: State University of New York Press. (A comparative study of the uncommon assumptions that ground the Chinese and Western philosophical traditions.)

Hansen, C. (1992) *A Daoist Theory of Chinese Thought*, New York: Oxford University Press. (An account of ancient Chinese philosophy that emphasizes language and *dao* as a guiding discourse.)

DAVID L. HALL
ROGER T. AMES

DAODEJING

The Daodejing *(or* Tao Te Ching*) is a brief work probably composed during the period 350–250 BC. It later became the most authoritative 'scripture' in the Daoist religious and philosophical tradition, and in modern times has become among the most often-translated and popular works in world religious literature. It recommends cultivating mental calm, an intuitive, non-conceptual understanding of the world, an integrated and balanced personality, a self-effacing manner and a low-key and non-intrusive leadership style. One who has this spirit has* dao *(tao), which is also conceived of as a cosmic reality, the origin of the world.*

1 Origin and composition
2 Concrete advice
3 Deeper dimensions

1 Origin and composition

We have no reliable direct information about the origins of the *Daodejing* (the title means 'Classic of *Dao* and *De*'). Its traditional attribution to the legendary and later deified sage Laozi (Lao Tzu) is now widely questioned (see Chan (1963); Graham (1990)). It is traditionally divided into eighty-one very brief numbered 'chapters', each probably consisting of several oral sayings originally coined in a close-knit community, with unifying editorial additions. The term 'Laoist' is used here to refer to the thought of this book so as to differentiate it from other contemporary and later forms of Daoism (see DAOIST PHILOSOPHY).

2 Concrete advice

The *Daodejing* repeatedly criticizes egotistic self-assertion and boastful self-promotion, and competing with others for social status. It also criticizes 'working' at impressing others by external refinements such as polished speech and cultivated manners; this is the basis for its criticism of contemporary Confucian self-cultivation. Many paradoxical sayings praise ways of being at the opposite extreme: self-effacing public service, appearing 'empty', 'compromised' or 'dull and stupid', and cultivating softness, 'weakness' and femininity (in contrast to the masculine strength much admired by contemporaries).

The *Daodejing* warns against the mental disturbance caused by external stimulation and the attraction of 'desirable' things. It advocates finding contentment in oneself (*Daodejing* 44, 46) and cultivating mental stillness (16, 52). This will give one an inexhaustible source of energy, ensuring good health and enabling one to 'last long', possibly gaining immortality (33).

The *Daodejing* criticizes confidence in the ability of conceptual ('naming') knowledge to grasp reality, probably a criticism of Mohist logicians and the Confucian programme of 'rectifying names' (see LOGIC IN CHINA). It emphasizes the unpredictability of the world as well as the impossibility of capturing true norms in exact verbal formulas. One must rely instead on the intuitive understandings of a properly cultivated mind. The ultimate basis for norms (*dao*) is 'nameless' and can only be conveyed by 'wordless teaching' (*Daodejing* 2, 43).

Much of the *Daodejing* consists of advice about how to rule, probably reflecting its origins in a group of shi, men aspiring to administrative or advisory positions in government (Hsu 1965). It criticizes contemporary rulers who exploit peasant society for their own advantage (53, 72, 75), or who rely on physical violence (war-making and capital punishment) to achieve their ends (30, 31, 69, 74). It also strongly criticizes ruling styles that are in any way overbearing or intrusive. A ruler should not strive to be 'awesome' (72), even by trying to set a high moral example for the people (this is probably an anti-

Confucian polemic). Again many paradoxical sayings advocate the extreme opposite of these normal tendencies of rulers. Rather than lording it over his subjects, he should attract their allegiance and cooperation by his deferential attitude, treating them as though he is someone 'lower' than they (61, 66, 68). Rather than searching for ego-gratification by high-profile achievements, the best kind of ruler strives to go unnoticed, giving the people the impression that social order is happening 'naturally' (17). A ruler should not try to mould the society according to his own values and ideas; this is 'working on' society, in contrast to which Laoists advise 'not working' (*wuwei*), 'taking the mind of the people as his mind' (49), and fostering and maintaining the organic social harmony already present in the communities he governs ('helping along [their] naturalness' (64)). Rather than being strict, the ruler should have the 'dull and incompetent' appearance (58) of one with a 'muddled mind' (49). When he has to intrude, he should be as non-confrontational as possible, defeating opposition by 'soft' indirect means, or by nipping bad tendencies in the bud (36, 64).

The *Daodejing* expresses opposition to several contemporary 'progressive' movements, such as the encouragement of personal ambition or rational-utilitarian thought among the peasantry, as a means of increasing material production and political strength. This causes discontent and contention and upsets social harmony, making it difficult for rulers to maintain a healthy (that is, simple traditional agrarian) social order.

3 Deeper dimensions

Many passages in the *Daodejing* speak about a deeper dimension of reality, most notably those that picture *dao* as the origin of the world; the *Daodejing* and the *Zhuangzi* are largely responsible for giving dao the pregnant meaning it came to have in later Chinese tradition (see DAO; ZHUANGZI). However, these passages present a set of overlapping images rather than a system of doctrines, and there is no very explicit indication as to how they relate to each other or to the concrete advice outlined above. Consequently, interpretations of this facet of the *Daodejing*'s thought vary widely, and at present nothing can be regarded as settled.

Philosophically inclined modern interpreters have tended to construe this area of Laoist thought on the model of Western 'metaphysics'. On this view, teachings about *dao* constitute an objective transcendent foundation of the worldview taught by the *Daodejing* as a whole. The implicit model here is very often (Fung 1937; Kaltenmark 1969; Schwartz 1985)

speculative mysticism, as found in Neoplatonism or Vedānta (see NEOPLATONISM; VEDĀNTA), or German Idealism (see GERMAN IDEALISM) as found in Hegel and Heidegger: *dao* is an unmanifest Absolute Being underlying but pervading the phenomenal world of beings. Its 'namelessness' refers to the fact that it is beyond all finite determinations that characterize the world of appearances. One then has to posit also a 'manifest' aspect of *dao* which has some positive and definite content, in order to ground the obvious bias of the *Daodejing* towards one side of the various polarities it poses (softness versus hardness, femininity versus masculinity and so on). There are also, however, several anti-mystical philosophical interpreters who construe *dao* in a more naturalist way as something immanent in the world, or as something like 'natural law' (Needham 1962). Finally, Hansen (1992) thinks the *Daodejing* argues a primarily negative and sceptical thesis, that no socially conditioned value judgments have any objective grounding.

However, it can also be argued that self-cultivation rather than speculative philosophy or mysticism is the background for the thought of the *Daodejing* (Roth 1991), and that its teachings about *dao* are to be construed imaginally rather than as philosophical metaphysics (Girardot 1974). On this view (argued in LaFargue 1994), the *Daodejing* imagines a primordial level of human conscious being that is inactive, unaroused, undifferentiated (*pu* (uncarved), *Daodejing* 15, 28, 32, 19), and not involved in conceptual thought ('nameless' and *tong* (merged), 1, 56). Society in general does not value this, but gravitates instead towards more active, 'excited' states, towards the specialized development of prized and admired 'virtues', towards grasping reality by means of refined conceptual (learned) thought, and towards striving to make one's mark on the world. Each of these disturbs the state of organic harmony, both internal and social, that Laoists regard as 'natural'. Laoists want to reverse this conventional value-orientation, insisting that the inactive, undifferentiated, organically harmonious state is the more valuable, and indeed the source of all that is most valuable in life. Expressed in chronological imagery, this is the 'prior' or 'root' state; people ought to reverse their normal tendencies and 'turn back' to cultivating this level of their being (Chapter 10 contains meditation instruction connected with this self-cultivation practice). The idea is not to remain literally inactive, but to 'dwell in' this layer of one's being and let it express itself in the manner of one's active involvement in the world. This will be a manner different from those whose value-orientation is more conventional: it will make one appear feminine rather than masculine, soft and weak rather than hard and strong, and 'empty' (that is, without a strongly felt, sharply defined presence) rather than solid.

One who cultivates this level of being experiences more mental clarity and also has a different perspective, dominated by a distinctive value-orientation. The world appears different to such a person than it does to conventional society. (This is the view of the world expressed in the more practical aphorisms of the *Daodejing*.) Laoists are aware that the character of this changed world has its origin in the state of mind they cultivate. They imagine this state to be a deeper layer of the world itself, expressed by saying it is 'the world's origin'.

On this view, *dao* was for Laoists primarily an internal spirit to be cultivated, imagined as an independent cosmic force or entity informing an ideal state of mind and expressing itself in certain ideal patterns of conduct. This 'subjective' reality of *dao*-as-experienced served as a basis for the vision of a world with *dao* as its source. The *Daodejing* had not yet transformed this into an objectified doctrine about the world that (as in the metaphysical interpretation) a person could adopt intellectually and 'believe in', even in the absence of self-cultivation and the concrete experience of *dao* (although such an objectifying transformation did happen rather soon after, and can be seen already in the earliest commentaries of HAN FEIZI and Wang Bi.)

Laoist 'mysticism' was not speculative – mystical insights did not serve as the basis for a set of doctrines about reality – nor was it unitive – Laoists did not strive for union with *dao* for its own sake. Rather, it was developed in practical directions. Dao was valued as a constantly dependable and nourishing internal 'mother' (*Daodejing* 20), sustaining those whose values deprived them of external social support. It also had a strongly political dimension: *dao* as the highest reality gave whoever possessed it the spiritual status of 'pattern/norm for the world', taking over this religious role which previous tradition had assigned to the Zhou Emperor. When such a person attained an administrative or advisory position in government, the *dao* he possessed would ideally inform the policies he promoted, and above all his leadership style (32, 37). Thus, as *dao* radiated from his person as *de*, subtle 'charisma', it would set the tone for the entire society and become the foundation for an ideal social order. This union of 'spiritual' and political interests is a distinctive feature of the *Daodejing*, at least in its final recension; some scholars argue that early Laoist thought was apolitical, and that applying Laoist ideas to problems of governing represents a later stage of development.

See also: DAO; DAOIST PHILOSOPHY; DE; SELF-CULTIVATION, CHINESE THEORIES OF

References and further reading

Daodejing: recommended translations

Addis, S. and Lombardo, S. (trans.) (1993) *Lao Tzu Tao Te Ching*, Indianapolis, IN: Hackett. (A succinct, fairly literal translation.)

Carus, P. (trans.) (1913) *The Canon of Reason and Virtue–being Lao-Tze's Tao te king. Chinese and English*, Chicago, IL: Open Court. (Gives English equivalent of each Chinese character in the text; however, works with an unreliable Chinese text.)

Chan Wing-tsit (trans.) (1963) *The Way of Lao Tzu (Tao te ching)*, Chicago, IL: University of Chicago Press. (Translation with useful commentary and introduction, recommended for novice reader; includes a critical review of traditional evidence concerning 'Laozi' on pages 35–59.)

Duyvendak, J.J.L. (trans.) (1954) *The Book of the Way and its Virtue*, London: John Murray; repr. Boston: Charles E. Tuttle, 1992. (Translation with useful textual analysis and contemporary parallel passages.)

Henricks, R.G. (trans.) (1989) *Lao-Tzu Te-Tao Ching*, New York: Ballantine. (A translation of the newly discovered Mawangdui manuscripts of the *Daodejing* dating from *circa* 200 BC, with useful notes on differences between this and traditional manuscripts.)

Karlgren, B. (trans.) (1975) 'Notes on Lao Tze', *Museum of Far Eastern Antiquities Bulletin* 47: 1–13. (An exceedingly literal translation by a noted authority on ancient Chinese language.)

LaFargue, M. (trans.) (1992) *The Tao of the Tao Te Ching*, Albany, NY: State University of New York Press. (Translation, detailed commentary and essays on main themes; analyzes text into oral sayings and editorial additions; translation recommended for novice reader.)

Lau, D.C. (trans.) (1963) *Lao Tzu Tao Te Ching*, Baltimore, MD: Penguin. (A widely used translation with long introduction.)

—— (1982) *Tao Te Ching*, Hong Kong: Chinese University Press. (Translates both the traditional and the Mawangdui texts, with long introductions to each; Chinese and English on facing pages.)

Waley, A. (trans.) (1958) *The Way and its Power*, New York: Grove Press. (Translation with good historical introduction and some commentary.)

Secondary works

Chan, A.K.L. (1991) *Two Visions of the Way: A Study of the Wang Pi and Ho-shang Kung Commentaries on the Lao-Tzu*, Albany, NY: State University of New York Press. (Detailed comparison of the two earliest Chinese commentaries on the *Daodejing*.)

Creel, H.G. (1970) *What is Taoism?*, Chicago, IL: University of Chicago Press, 1–47. (First proposed the now widely accepted distinction between the 'purposive' Daoism of the *Daodejing* and the 'contemplative' Daoism of *Zhuangzi*.)

Erkes, E. (trans.) (1950) *Ho-Shang-Kung's commentary on Lao-Tse*, Ascona: Artibus Asiae Publishers. (A translation of an early Chinese commentary (*circa* AD 180), which reads into the *Daodejing* the more complex self-cultivation theories of later Daoism, while still retaining the idea that self-cultivation is preparation for ruling well.)

* Fung Yu-lan (1937) *A History of Chinese Philosophy*, Vol. 1, *The Period of the Philosophers*, Peiping: Henri Vetch, 170–91. (A metaphysical interpretation of *dao*, with descriptions also of the *Daodejing*'s practical advice, by a Chinese scholar who trained also in Western philosophy.)

* Girardot, N. (1974) *Myth and Meaning in Early Taoism*, Berkeley, CA: University of California Press, 47–76. (Emphasizes the theme of primordial undifferentiated 'chaos' in the *Daodejing*.)

* Graham, A.C. (1990) 'The Origins of the Legend of Lao Tan', in *Studies in Chinese Philosophy and Philosophical Literature*, Albany, NY: State University of New York Press, 111–24. (A detailed analysis of the historical development of the legends surrounding 'Laozi', and how the *Daodejing* came to be attributed to him; intricate historical argumentation will be difficult for the general reader.)

* *Han Feizi* (c.280–233 BC), bk. 6, chaps 20–1, trans. W.K. Lao, *The Complete Works of Han Fei Tzu*, London: Arthur Probsthain, 1938. (The earliest commentator on selected chapters from the *Daodejing*, showing how the *Daodejing*'s teaching can be integrated into a Legalist framework.)

* Hansen, C. (1992) *A Daoist Theory of Chinese Thought: a Philosophical Interpretation*, New York: Oxford University Press, 210–30. (Argues that the purpose of the *Daodejing* is to undermine socially induced value judgments by showing that no way of evaluatively 'naming' things has any objective and unchanging basis; for philosophically advanced readers.)

* Hsu Cho-yun (1965) *Ancient China in Transition: An Analysis of Social Mobility, 722–222*, Stanford, CA:

Stanford University Press. (The best sociological analysis of China at the time of the *Daodejing*'s composition; see especially the discussion of shi (pages 86–106), the class to which the *Daodejing*'s authors probably belonged.)

Julien, S. (1842) *La Livre de la Voie et de la Vertu* (The Book of the Way and Virtue), Paris: L'Imprimerie Royale. (One of the earliest Western translations of the *Daodejing*; includes interesting excerpts from many traditional Chinese commentators.)

* Kaltenmark, M. (1969) *Lao Tzu and Taoism*, Stanford, CA: Stanford University Press, 19–69. (A detailed metaphysical interpretation of *dao*.)

* LaFargue, M. (1994) *Tao and Method: a Reasoned Interpretation of the Tao Te Ching*, Albany, NY: State University of New York Press. (Argues the interpretation of the *Daodejing* presented in this article. Detailed discussion of the social background of *Daodejing* and of major methodological problems in its interpretation; detailed philosophical and methodological discussions will be difficult for general reader.)

* Lau, D.C. (1958) 'The Treatment of Opposites in Lao-tzu', *Bulletin of the School of Oriental and African Studies* 21 (2): 344–60. (Surveys Chinese interpreters that assimilate *Daodejing* to the 'balancing of opposites' theme of the *Yijing*; argues that the *Daodejing* consistently favors the soft/weak over the hard/strong.)

* Needham, J. (1962) *Science and Civilisation in China*, Vol. 2, *History of Scientific Thought*, Cambridge: Cambridge University Press, 33–164. (Argues that the *Daodejing* reflects proto-scientific attempts to discover natural laws, arriving however at a more 'organicist' view that contrasts with the atomism of modern Western science; it also rejects Zhou feudalism in favor of more 'primitive' organic communities. Difficult for the general reader.)

* Roth, H. (1991) 'Psychology and Self-Cultivation in Early Taoistic Thought', *Harvard Journal of Asian Studies* 51 (2): 599–650. (Discusses self-cultivation practices reflected in other early 'Daoistic' writings, important for understanding the *Daodejing*'s background in self-cultivation. Difficult for the general reader.)

* Schwartz, B. (1985) *The World of Thought in Ancient China*, Cambridge, MA: Harvard University Press, 192–215. (The most persuasive and nuanced version of the mystical/metaphysical interpretation of *dao* in the *Daodejing*; includes also a detailed discussion of its relation to the concrete advice given; for the general reader.)

* Wang Bi (AD 226–49) *Commentary on the Lao Tzu by Wang Pi*, trans. A. Rump, Honolulu, HI: University

of Hawaii Press, 1979. (Translation of an insightful early Chinese philosophical commentary.)

MICHAEL LAFARGUE

DAOIST PHILOSOPHY

Early Daoist philosophy has had an incalculable influence on the development of Chinese philosophy and culture. Philosophical Daoism is often called 'Lao–Zhuang' philosophy, referring directly to the two central and most influential texts, the Daodejing *(or* Laozi*) and the* Zhuangzi, *both of which were composite, probably compiled in the fourth and third centuries BC. Beyond these two texts we might include the syncretic* Huainanzi *(circa 140 BC) and the* Liezi, *reconstituted around the fourth century AD, as part of the traditional Daoist corpus.*

Second in influence only to the Confucian school, the classical Daoist philosophers in many ways have been construed as both a critique on and a complement to the more conservative, regulatory precepts of their Confucian rivals. Daoism has frequently and unfortunately been characterized in terms of passivity, femininity, quietism and spirituality, a doctrine embraced by artists, recluses and religious mystics. Confucianism, by contrast, has been cast in the language of moral precepts, virtues, imperial edicts and regulative methods, a doctrine embodied in and administered by the state official. The injudicious application of this yin–yang-like concept to Daoism and Confucianism tends to impoverish our appreciation of the richness and complexity of these two traditions. Used in a heavy-handed way, it obfuscates the fundamental wholeness of both the Confucian and Daoist visions of meaningful human existence by imposing an unwarranted conservatism on classical Confucianism, and an unjustified radicalism on Daoism.

There is a common ground shared by the teachings of classical Confucianism and Daoism in the advocacy of self-cultivation. In general terms, both traditions treat life as an art rather than a science. Both express a 'this-wordly' concern for the concrete details of immediate existence rather than exercising their minds in the service of grand abstractions and ideals. Both acknowledge the uniqueness, importance and primacy of the particular person and the person's contribution to the world, while at the same time stressing the ecological interrelatedness and interdependence of this person with their context.

However, there are also important differences. For the Daoists, the Confucian penchant for reading the 'constant dao' myopically as the 'human dao' is to experience the world at a level that generates a dichotomy between the human and natural worlds. The argument against the Confucian seems to be that the Confucians do not take the ecological sensitivity far enough, defining self-cultivation in purely human terms. It is the focused concern for the overcoming of discreteness by a spiritual extension and integration in the human world that gives classical Confucianism its sociopolitical and practical orientation. But from the Daoist perspective, 'overcoming discreteness' is not simply the redefinition of the limits of one's concerns and responsibilities within the confines of the human sphere. The Daoists reject the notion that human experience occurs in a vacuum, and that the whole process of existence can be reduced to human values and purposes.

*To the extent that Daoism is prescriptive, it is so not by articulating rules to follow or asserting the existence of some underlying moral principle, but by describing the conduct of an achieved human being – the sage (*shengren*) or the Authentic Person (*zhenren*) – as a recommended object of emulation. The model for this human ideal, in turn, is the orderly, elegant and harmonious processes of nature. Throughout the philosophical Daoist corpus, there is a 'grand' analogy established in the shared vocabulary used to describe the conduct of the achieved human being on the one hand, and the harmony achieved in the mutual accomodations of natural phenomena on the other.*

The perceived order is an achievement, not a given. Because dao *is an emergent, 'bottom-up' order rather than something imposed, the question is: what is the optimal relationship between de and dao, between a particular and its environing conditions? The Daoist response is the self-dispositioning of particulars into relationships which allow the fullest degree of self-disclosure and development. In the Daoist literature, this kind of optimally appropriate action is often described as* wuwei, *'not acting wilfully', 'acting naturally' or 'non-assertive activity'. Wuwei, then, is the negation of that kind of 'making' or 'doing' which requires that a particular sacrifice its own integrity in acting on behalf of something 'other', a negation of that kind of engagement that makes something false to itself. Wuwei activity 'characterizes' – that is, produces the character or ethos of – an aesthetically contrived composition. There is no ideal, no closed perfectedness. Ongoing creative achievement itself provides novel possibilities for a richer creativity. Wuwei activity is thus fundamentally qualitative: an aesthetic category and, only derivatively, an ethical one. Wuwei can be evaluated on aesthetic grounds, allowing that some relationships are more productively* wuwei *than others. Some relationships are more successful than others in maximizing the creative possibilities of oneself in one's environments.*

This classical Daoist aesthetic, while articulated in these early texts with inimitable flavour and imagination, was, like most philosophical anarchisms, too intangible and impractical to ever be a serious contender as a formal structure for social and political order. In the early years of the Han dynasty (206 BC–AD 220), there was an attempt in the Huainanzi *to encourage the Daoist sense of ethos by tempering the lofty ideals with a functional practicality. It appropriates a syncretic political framework as a compromise for promoting a kind of practicable Daoism – an anarchism within expedient bounds. While historically the* Huainanzi *fell on deaf ears, it helped to set a pattern for the Daoist contribution to Chinese culture across the sweep of history. Over and over again, in the currency of anecdote and metaphor, identifiably Daoist sensibilities would be expressed through a range of theoretical structures and social grammars, from military strategies, to the dialectical progress of distinctively Chinese schools of Buddhism, to the constantly changing face of poetics and art. It can certainly be argued that the richest models of Confucianism, represented as the convergence of Daoism, Buddhism and Confucianism itself, were an attempt to integrate Confucian concerns with human community with the broader Daoist commitment to an ecologically sensitive humanity.*

1   **Classical Daoism**
2–3   **Fundamental notions: *dao* and *de***
4–7   **Person and world: the *wu*-forms**
8–9   **The transformation of things: *wuhua***

1   Classical Daoism

Before attempting to characterize the lineaments of Daoist philosophy, a brief discussion of the meaning of the term 'classical Daoism' is necessary. Unlike Confucianism, the 'school' of Daoism, *daojia*, does not name a tradition constituted by a founding thinker. Indeed, the term 'Daoism' is itself an *ex post facto* creation of subsequent editors and historians.

Daoism is first named as a school by Sima Tan in the *Shiji* (Records of the Historian) in the second century BC; and because Sima Tan's concern was classifying schools in terms of their contributions to 'the art of rulership', there was no expressed connection at this time between Zhuangzi and Laozi, later recognized as the two principal Daoist thinkers. In Sima Tan's classification, the Daoists are listed as one of six schools of thought, the others being the Yin–Yang school (see YIN–YANG), the Confucians (see CONFUCIAN PHILOSOPHY, CHINESE), the Mohists

(see MOHIST PHILOSOPHY), the Legalists (see LEGALIST PHILOSOPHY, CHINESE) and the School of Names (see LOGIC IN CHINA).

In the first century AD, Ban Gu in the *Hanshu* (History of the Former Han Dynasty) included the writings of Zhuangzi and Laozi together under the heading of 'Daoism' as one of nine philosophical schools. By the first quarter of the fourth century, the principal texts of Daoism were recognized as the *Daodejing* (also called the *Laozi*) and the *Zhuangzi* (see DAODEJING; ZHUANGZI), along with the respective commentaries by Wang Bi (AD 226–49) and Guo Xiang (d. early fourth century), texts such as the *Guanzi* and *Heguanzi* and writings attributed to the Yellow Emperor (Huangdi). In 1973, an early Han tomb was excavated at Mawangdui and two silk copies of the *Daodejing* were discovered, along with four texts originally attributed to the Yellow Emperor that have a distinctly Legalist flavor. The bundling of these texts together suggests an attempt to borrow the authority of Emperor Huangdi, the legendary founder of the Chinese state, for a Legalist interpretation of Laozi's doctrines. There is some scholarly opinion that it was this Legalistic Daoism, called Huang–Lao, rather than Lao–Zhuang Daoism which actually defined the school during the Han dynasty.

A further complication in explaining the sense of 'Daoism' results from the fact that 'the School of the Way', *daojia*, is to be distinguished from *daojiao*, what may be termed the 'the Doctrine of the Way', with the latter traditionally dating from the middle of the second century. *Daojiao* is the foundation of the organized Daoist religion which has persisted down to the present day. On the surface at least, many of the rituals and doctrines of this religious Daoism do not seem to cohere with the spirit of the more philosophical form of Daoism. Until recently scholars of Daoism, particularly those in the West, have typically drawn a rather sharp distinction between the *daojia* and *daojiao*. More recently, with the translations of Daoist 'religious' texts of the medieval period, there have been attempts to identify a 'mystical philosophy' in the *daojiao* which has its roots in the thought of Laozi and Zhuangzi. It should also be said that many of the contemporary practitioners of so-called religious Daoism distinguish themselves from the philosophical Daoists in terms of the esoteric or 'inner' teachings and practices constituting the central identity of their community versus the exoteric or 'outer' teachings of the *daojia*. Having acknowledged this distinction, there is some contemporary scholarly concern regarding the tendency to over-intellectualize the philosophical tradition at the expense of a meditative and hygenic regimen that seems implicit in these texts.

Perhaps it is fitting that the historical roots of what has come to be identified as Daoist thinking should be obscure. In fact, relatively fluid identity of the Daoist tradition has in part been responsible for its widespread influence beyond the borders of China. Both the *Daodejing* and the writings of Zhuangzi have become classics of world philosophical and spiritual literature, taking their place as expressions of that *philosophia perennis* which touches the deepest layers of human sensibility. Certainly the hundreds of translations of the *Daodejing* attest to this status.

The usual distinction made between the classical forms of Confucianism and Daoism is in terms of the most general context with which each is concerned. Confucians focus upon issues relevant to a ritualized human society (see CONFUCIAN PHILOSOPHY, CHINESE; CONFUCIUS), while Daoists concern themselves with the natural ambiance. Such a distinction has but qualified merit, however, since it really characterizes only the overall emphasis of the contrasting models of thinking. The familial or bureaucratic metaphor employed by the broad Confucian tradition is most relevant to the concerns of social structure and harmony, though Han speculations led to the extension of this metaphor to the broadest of cosmological issues. In a similar manner, the more naturalistically inclined Daoists begin with the 'Six Realms' – heaven, earth and the four directions – but are quite capable of bringing the model of accommodation, developed with reference to the ten thousand things, to bear upon concrete social and political concerns in a variety of both constructive and critical manners. Indeed, the *Daodejing* is generally considered to be a political manual dealing with the proper guidance of society.

Thus the distinction between Daoism and Confucianism, at what we in the West would term the 'philosophical' level, is perhaps not as great as the majority of commentators have claimed. In fact, were we to search for something like a central insight or commitment giving rise to the most general speculations associated with the two visions, we might find that there is a 'single thread' running through both Confucianism and Daoism. The central focus of both Confucian and Daoist forms of thinking is the form of engagement which might be termed 'deference'. In Confucianism one may discuss this deferential activity in terms of the notion of *shu*, a sort of analogical activity which encourages one to put oneself in another's place as a strategy for determining appropriate conduct. This activity is broadly shaped by a system of rituals (*li*) which characterize the structures of society and the roles through which various human activities are expressed (see LAW AND RITUAL IN CHINESE PHILOSOPHY).

In Daoism, deference involves a yielding (and being yielded to) grounded in a recognition of the uniqueness of that to which deference is paid. One may best express the meanings of deferential activity in Daoism through the notions of *dao*, *de* and the so-called *wu*-forms: *wuwei*, *wuzhi* and *wuyu*.

2 Fundamental notions: *dao*

Dao engenders one,
One engenders two,
Two engenders three,
And three engenders the myriad things.
The myriad things shoulder *yin* and embrace *yang*,
And mix the *qi* to achieve harmony.

(*Daodejing* 42)

Dao is the process of the world itself, the 'way' of things. In Daoism, the relevant contrast is not between the cosmological 'whatness' of things and the ontological 'thatness' of things, but rather between the world as 'chaos' (*hundun*) – the sum of all orders – and any given world as construed from some particular perspective (*de*), that is, in terms of any particular one of the orders (see DAO).

Dao is not organic in the sense that a single pattern or *telos* could be said to characterize its processes. It is not *a* whole, but many such wholes. It is not a One to which the Many reduce. Its order is not rational or logical, but aesthetic; there is no transcendent pattern determining the existence or efficacy of the order. The order is a consequence of the particulars comprising the totality of existing things. This interpretation of *dao* makes of it a totality not in the sense of a single-ordered cosmos, but rather as the sum of all potential orders. Any given order is an existing world that is construed from the perspective of a particular element within the totality; but, as a single world, it is a selective abstraction from the totality of possible orders. Such a limited order cannot serve as fundament or ground. In the Daoist sensibility, all differences are cosmological differences, that is, differences among particular components which, at some moment, comprise the order.

The Daoists understanding of the world is not as an ordered whole but as 'the ten thousand things' (*wanwu*). As this term indicates, there is in effect no concept of 'cosmos' at all, insofar as that notion could be said to entail a coherent, single-ordered world which is any sense enclosed or defined. The Daoists are therefore primarily 'acosmological' thinkers. In the absence of some overarching *archē* or 'beginning' as an explanation of the creative process, and under conditions which are thus 'anarchic' in the philosophic sense of this term, although nature might indeed be conventionally classified in terms of 'kinds', such categories would by no means be natural kinds. Difference is always prior to similarities.

The Chinese binomial most frequently translated as 'cosmos' is *yuzhou*, a term that overtly expresses the interdependence between time and space. For the Daoists – indeed for the classical Chinese generally – time pervades everything and is not to be denied; it is not derivative of matter, but a fundamental aspect of it. Unlike traditions which devalue time and change in pursuit of the timeless and eternal, in classical China things are always processional and transforming (*wuhua*) and hence are always provisional. In fact, in the absence of some claim to objectivity that 'objectifies' and thus makes 'objects' of phenomena, the Chinese tradition does not have the separation between time and entities that would allow for either time without entities or entities without time: there is no possibility of either an empty temporal corridor or an eternal anything (in the sense of being timeless).

What encourages us within a Western metaphysical tradition to separate time and space is our inclination inherited from the Greeks to see things in the world as fixed in their formal aspect, and thus as bounded and limited (see TIME §1). But if, instead of giving ontological privilege to the formal aspect of phenomena, we observe them in light of their ceaseless transformation, we are able to temporalize them and perceive them as 'events' rather than 'things', where each phenomenon is some current or impulse within a temporal flow. In fact, the pervasive capacity of the world to transform continuously is the meaning of time itself. It is because things in the world are reproductive that time is reproductive. Since the world is always entertained from one perspective or another, and since the temporal aspect is never abstract, fictive or replicated, any perspective is an advancing path that is neither linear nor cyclical, but both. Time–space–matter is an advancing spiral. The expression 'advancing path' is particularly appropriate, because it is this image of our passage in the world that is captured in *dao* as a grounding metaphor pervasive in the tradition (see PROCESSES).

The most provocative characterization of *dao* in the *Daodejing* is as both 'nameless' and 'nameable':

Dao can be spoken of, but that is not constant dao;

The name can be named, but that is not the constant name;

The nameless is the beginning of the heavens and the earth;

The named is the mother of the myriad things.

Dwell constantly in nothing in order to observe its mysteries;

Dwell constantly in something in order to observe its boundaries.

(*Daodejing* 1)

If *dao per se* is the 'way' of things, construed as all of the processes of becoming, then nameless and nameable *dao* characterize the functions of 'not-being present' and 'being present' respectively, as abstracted from the process of becoming-itself. *Dao* is the *that which*: that which *is* and that which *is not* are the polar elements of 'becoming-itself'.

3 Fundamental notions: *de*

It would be easy to misunderstand this interpretation as claiming a far greater coherence for the Daoist vision than is likely. One must look carefully at the meanings of the explanatory categories *you* and *wu*, conventionally translated as 'being' and 'not-being', in the Chinese tradition (see YOU–WU). For example, *wu* means 'have not' or 'there is not', which readily contrasts with the sense of not-being as 'nothing' or 'no entity'. The sense of *wu* is of the absence of specific concrete things. The correlative sense of you in this context is the presence of these same concrete things.

If one looks at Daoism with the appropriately adjusted senses of 'being' and 'not-being', the notion of *dao* as the 'that which' loses its ontological tone. There is only 'this' and 'that'. To translate this idea as 'only beings are' is quite appropriate provided one does not look for any Being standing behind or beneath or beyond these beings, and provided one does not interpret 'are' in an existential sense. The best manner of avoiding such a confusion is simply to say, since there are only 'thises' and 'thats', the locution 'only beings are' is more aptly expressed as 'beings only' or 'these beings'.

Beings are 'thises' and 'thats'. *Dao*, construed as 'that which is' and 'that which is not' – nameable and nameless *dao* – characterizes the process of existence and experience as 'becoming-itself'. This reflexive notion, however, does not name an 'itself' which becomes; rather, the locution 'becoming-itself' refers simply to the unsummed processes of becoming *per se*. It is these processes that are entailed by the notion of *dao*.

What this means, of course, is that Daoism expresses a radical acosmology. If we wish to understand the sense in which 'difference' is to be understood relative to the parity of things, we must restrict ourselves solely to the question of the differences among particular things. Each particular element in the totality has its own *de*. *De* is best understood as a particular focus that orients an item in a field of significances such that it achieves its own intrinsic excellence (see DE). The *de* of an element provides the perspective from which it construes all other items in its environs. In this manner each item with respect to its *de* 'names' and creates a world. *Dao* and *de* are related as field and focus respectively. The relations of *dao* and *de* are 'holographic': that is, each element in the totality of things contains the totality in an adumbrated form. The particular focus of an item establishes its world, its environment; the totality as a noncoherent sum of all possible orders is adumbrated by each item.

The *Zhuangzi* contains a passage in which this notion of 'locus' or 'place' is presented as being integral to what it means to know:

Zhuangzi and Huizi were strolling across the bridge over the Hao river. Zhuangzi observed, 'The minnows swim out and about as they please – this is the way they enjoy themselves.'

Huizi replied, 'You are not a fish – how do you know what they enjoy?'

Zhuangzi returned, 'You are not me – how do you know that I don't know what is enjoyable for the fish?'

Huizi said, 'I am not you, so I certainly don't know what you know; but it follows that, since you are certainly not the fish, you don't know what is enjoyment for the fish either.'

Zhuangzi said, 'Let's get back to your basic question. When you asked *From where* do you know what the fish enjoy?' you already knew that I know what the fish enjoy, or you wouldn't have asked me. I know it from here above the Hao river.'

(*Zhuangzi* 17)

Zhuangzi is not just depending upon linguistic ambiguity in order to win an argument. He has a more philosophic point to make: he wants to deny the objectivity of knowledge in the sense of the independence of the world as known, from the knower. For Zhuangzi, knowledge is performative and a function of fruitful correlations. It is a 'realizing' of a world in the sense of 'making it real', and the knower and the known are inseparable aspects of this same event. Agency cannot be isolated from action. One and one's posture or perspective is thus integral to what is known; where you are and how you know are mutually entailing. Knowledge is proximity. Zhuangzi's experience with the fish makes his world continuous with the world of the fish, and as such, his claim to knowledge is a claim to having been there. Being continuous with the fish and collaborating with them in the experience does not deny the fish their difference. In fact, it is only through Zhuangzi's deference to their difference – allowing them to be what they are – that the experience can be optimally fruitful and he can really come to know these particular fish (see KNOWLEDGE, CONCEPT OF).

The Daoist belief in the 'the parity of things' celebrates the *differences* that exist among the items of the totality. The manner in which all things are *similar* is easily stated: although the *de* of things, being ever unique, are hierarchical in their relations one to the other, at the same time they have parity in the sense that each *de* is necessary for every other *de* to be what it is. With no Being behind the beings of the world, the way of things is both continuous and radically perspectival. There can be no standards such as the 'great chain of being' or the 'ladder of perfection' establishing ontological hierarchies (see BEING §§1–2). What we have instead is both the uniqueness of each perspective, and parity among them.

4   Person and world: the *wu*-forms

Having indicated the sense of parity affirmed by the Daoists, and the deferential activity such an understanding entails, we may now attempt to grasp in greater detail how the Daoists seek to respond to their natural and social environs. As noted earlier, in Confucianism, deference (*shu*) operates within ritual patterns (*li*) shaped in accordance with the familial relationships extending outward into society and culture (see CONFUCIAN PHILOSOPHY, CHINESE). By contrast, Daoism expresses its deferential activity through what we shall call the *wu*-forms, *wuzhi*, *wuwei* and *wuyu*: that is, 'no-knowledge', a sort of knowing without resort to rules or principles; 'no-action', or actions in accordance with the *de* (particular perspective) of things, and 'no-desire', or desiring which does not seek to own or control its 'object' (which in effect makes it an 'objectless desire'). In each of these cases, it is necessary to remain sensitive and responsive to the particular perspective (*de*) of what is to be known, what is to be acted in accordance with, or what is to be desired.

Since the *wu*-forms bear some skewed resemblance to the faculties of the tripartite *psychē* which has played such an important role in Western speculations since Plato, we shall begin by noting the contrasting problematics underlying the distinctive interpretations of knowledge, action and desire in classical Daoism and dominant strains of the Western tradition. The Platonic *psychē*, and its permutations throughout the subsequent history of Western thought, has provided us with a wealth of interpretations of the modalities of knowing, acting and desiring which comprise the structure of the self (see PSYCHĒ). The heritage of the self construed as a tripartite structure is one of conflict, the soul at war with itself. In PLATO, the primary conflict of course is between knowledge and ignorance, reflected in such mottos as 'To know the Truth is to do the truth' and 'You shall know the Truth and the Truth shall make you free'. Allied with this conflict, internal to reason itself, is that tension between the appetitive and the spirited elements on the one hand, and the rational elements on the other. This is essentially a conflict between mind and body, ramified with the confluence of Hebraic and Hellenic sensibilities. It is well expressed in the words of St Paul: 'The good that I would do, I do not do; the evil that I would not do, that I do', and receives perhaps its profoundest expression in Augustine's *Confessiones* in the form of a war between passions and the will, one demanding the satisfactions of desire, the other seeking obedience to the will of God (see AUGUSTINE). The conflict is again succinctly stated in a familiar doctrine of David HUME: 'Reason is and always shall be, a slave to the passions' (see DUALISM; EMOTIONS, PHILOSOPHY OF; HUMAN NATURE).

These permutations of the soul at war are so deeply embedded in our own intellectual culture as to shape unconsciously much of our analysis of alternative psychological and cultural sensibilities. It is essential, therefore, to recognize that the model of the tripartite self has little relevance to the dynamics of Chinese models of the person, and the relation of those models to their larger social and cultural context. A signal of this fact is that there is no fundamental mind–body dualism with which to contend; and since this dualism sets up the principal conflict within the self between reason on the one hand and the affective and volitional components on the other, any conflict in the Daoist understanding of person obviously cannot be between heart and mind, or mind and will. In fact, the goal of cultivation of the self for the Daoist is predicated upon a different dynamic altogether: the attempt to move from activities of knowing, feeling and action shaped by construal to those shaped by deference (see SELF-CULTIVATION, CHINESE THEORIES OF).

Having said all this, there are terms such as *zhi*, *wei* and *yu* which initially seem to correlate rather closely with what we in the Western tradition call knowing, acting and desiring. If the Daoist self is not divided in the manner of the Western model of the tripartite soul, how are we to account for these three modalities? The *wu*-forms must be thought of as activities that establish the deferential relations which constitute the self at any given moment.

5 Person and world: the *wu*-forms (cont.)

Wuzhi, as 'no-knowledge', means the absence of a certain kind of knowledge, specifically the sort dependent upon ontological presence (see ZHI). Knowledge grounded in a denial of ontological presence does not presuppose a single-ordered world and its intellectual accoutrements. It is therefore 'unprincipled knowing', the sort of knowing that does not appeal to rules or principles determining the existence, meaning or activity of a phenomenon. *Wuzhi* provides one with a sense of the *de* of a thing, its particular focus, rather than yielding some understanding of that thing in relation to some concept or natural kind or universal. Ultimately, *wuzhi* is expressed as a grasp of the *daode* relationship of each encountered item, which permits an understanding of the totality construed from the particular focus (*de*) of that item.

Wuzhi, or 'knowing without principles', is tacit and, though inexpressible in literal terms, may be communicated though parabolic and imagistic language. A Confucian critic challenged the Daoist claim which begins the *Daodejing* – 'Dao can be spoken of, but it is not constant *dao*' – by asking: 'If constant *dao* cannot be spoken of, how is it that the author of the *Daodejing* used several thousand characters in speaking of it?' The Daoist replied: 'I make for you a beautiful embroidery of drakes and pass it along to you for your admiration. I cannot, however, show you the golden needle by which it was made.' Such parabolic language does not presuppose a literal ground. Parabolic language, therefore, is constitutive of discourse itself. Language is, from the beginning, a language of difference and particularity. It is this language that permits the communication of the results of *wuzhi*.

Knowledge, as unprincipled knowing, is the entertainment of the world on its own terms without recourse to rules of discrimination which separate one sort of thing from another sort. The *Huainanzi*, a Han dynasty eclectic text with a strong Daoist colouration (see HUAINANZI), reports on this kind of mirror-like 'knowing':

Therefore, the sage is like a mirror –

He neither sees things off nor goes out to meet them,

He responds to everything without storing anything up.

Thus, he is never injured through the myriad transformations he undergoes...

It is because the mirror and water do not install cleverness beforehand that when they come into contact with shapes that are square, round, bent and straight, they are unable to escape being shown for what they are.

(Huainanzi 6 and 1)

Rules of thumb, habits of action, customs, fixed standards, methods, stipulated concepts, categories, commandments, principles, laws of nature: all these require us to 'welcome things as they come and escort them as they go'. Having stored past experience and organized it in terms of fixed standards or principles, we anticipate, celebrate and recall a world patterned by these discriminations. The sage, however, mirrors the world and 'neither sees things off nor goes out to meet them'. As such, he 'responds to everything without storing anything up'. This means that he mirrors the world *at the moment* in a way that is undetermined by the shape of a world passed away, or by anticipations of a world yet to come.

6   Person and world: the *wu*-forms (cont.)

Wuwei, often misleadingly translated as 'no action' or 'non-action', involves the absence of a specific sort of action, namely, coercive action which interferes with the particular focus *(de)* of those things within one's field of influence. Actions untainted by stored knowledge or ingrained habits are unmediated, unstructured, unprincipled and spontaneous. As such, they are consequences of deferential responses to the item or event in accordance with which, or in relation to which, one is acting. These actions are *ziran*: 'spontaneous' and 'self-so-ing'. They are *nonassertive* actions.

The 'grand analogy' in the *Daodejing* is that dao is to world as ruler is to people. *Dao*, as the discernible rhythm and regularity in the world around us, is non-impositional: '*Dao* is constantly non-assertive *(wuwei)* yet there is nothing which is not done' *(Daodejing 37)*.

In the Chinese exercise form known as *taijiquan*, there is a practice known as 'push-hands' *(duishou)* which well-illustrates *wuwei*. Two individuals facing one another perform various circular movements of the arms while maintaining minimal hand contact. The movement of each individual mirrors that of the other. *Wuwei* is realized when the movements of each are sensed, by both parties, to be uninitiated and effortless – that is, *spontaneous*. Presumably, one can employ such mirroring responses in 'the art of rulership', providing a sort of nonconstruing model for the guidance of the state. Such is the testimony of the *Daodejing*:

Thus, the sage says:

I am nonassertive *(wuwei)*

And the people transform themselves;

I cherish stillness,

And the people attune themselves;

I do not intervene,

And the people are prosperous of their own accord;

I am objectless in my desires,

And the people retain their natural genuineness of their own accord.

(Daodejing 57)

And again:

[The sage] constantly causes the people to seek 'unprincipled understanding' and to be objectless in their desires,

And as for the erudite – they wouldn't dare to do anything.

In simply acting non-assertively,

Everything is properly ordered.

(Daodejing 3 (following the Mawangdui text for the last line))

This attitude is carried over into the human world: in government, impositional power is a major concern so the consummate political model in Daoism, corresponding to *dao*, is described as *wuwei* and *ziran*:

The most excellent ruler: the people do not even know that there is a ruler.

The second best: they love and praise him.

The next: they stand in awe of him.

And the worst: they look on him with contempt.

Inadequate integrity in government

Will result in people not trusting those who govern.

So hesitant, the ruler does not speak thoughtlessly.

His job done and the affairs of state in order,

The people all say: 'We are naturally like this [*ziran*].'

(Daodejing 17)

Spontaneous action is a mirroring response. As such, it is action which accommodates the other to whom one is responding on their own terms. Such spontaneity involves recognizing the continuity between oneself and the other, and responding in such a way that one's own actions, while serving one's own ends, at the same time promote the interests and well-being of the other. This does not lead to imitation but to complementarity. Handshakes and embraces are actions which both presuppose a recognition of the stance of the other, and complete that stance. When the music starts to play and your partner opens his arms, the dance proceeds as a dyadic harmony of nonassertive actions: provided, of course, you and your partner defer to one another.

7 Person and world: the *wu*-forms (cont.)

Perhaps the best characterization of the term *wuyu* is 'objectless desire'. Since neither unprincipled knowing nor nonassertive action can in the strict sense objectify a world or any element in it – that is, make discrete and independent objects out of one's environment – the kind of desiring associated with the Daoist sensibility is in the strictest sense 'objectless'. The 'enjoyments' associated with *wuyu* are possible without the need to define, possess or control the occasion of one's enjoyment.

Thus, *wuyu*, rather than involving the cessation of desire, represents the achievement of *deferential desire*. Desire, based upon a mirroring understanding (*wuzhi*) and a nonassertive relationship (*wuwei*), thus allowing for the integrity of whatever is entertained, is shaped not by the desire to own, control or consume but simply to celebrate and to enjoy. Desire is for those things desirable in part because they *stand to be desired*. But those things which stand to be desired must themselves be deferential, which means that they cannot *demand* to be desired; for to demand to be desired is to seek a kind of seductive control over the desirer. In a world of events and processes in which discriminations are recognized as conventional and transient, desire is predicated upon the ability at any given moment to 'let go'. It is in this sense that wuyu is a nonconstruing, objectless, desire.

The problematic of desire familiar to the Western tradition is expressed by Plato's definition of Eros as 'the son of Resource and Need'. Erotic desire is predicated upon a motivation to attain an absent object. Once attained, desire ceases. The resolution of the problem of desire in Plato comes from learning what is truly desirable – namely, knowledge. Complete attainment of knowledge is not possible in this life, so desire continues as an unabated, ultimately harmonizing, motivation to increase one's understanding, rather than as a movement from one desired object to the next in a frustrated attempt to achieve final satisfaction (see DESIRE).

The Daoist problematic with respect to desire does not concern what is desired, but rather the manner of the desiring. Objectless desire always allows for letting go. Enjoyment for the Daoist is realized not in spite of the fact that one might lose what is desired, but because of this fact. The world is a complex set of processes of transformation, never at rest. In Plato, the desire for knowledge is the only thing that can define both embodied and disembodied existence; it is the only desire that can be permanent and eternal. In Daoism, transient desire is the only desire that lets things be, that does not construe the world in a certain manner, and that does not seek to apply the brakes on a world of changing things.

The key to understanding *wuyu* – indeed of all these wu-forms that are constitutive of the Daoist self – lies in the contrast between 'objects' and 'objectivity'. From a Western perspective, it appears that the thoughts expressed in both the *Zhuangzi* and the *Daodejing* represent something like what would in the West be termed a realism (see REALISM AND ANTI-REALISM). Beyond the confusions introduced by language, and by our own distorted perceptions and tendentious categorizations, there is, with properly Daoist qualifications, an 'objectively' real world. Our task is to entertain that world as 'objectively' as possible. The problem begins when we believe that the objective world is a world of objects: concrete, unchangeable things which we encounter as over against us, things which announce themselves to us by saying 'I object!' For the Daoist, the objective world cannot be objective in this sense. It is a constantly transforming set of events or processes which belie the sorts of discriminations that would permit a final inventory of the furniture of the world:

> Maojiang and Lady Li were beauties for human beings, but fish upon seeing them would seek the deeps, birds on seeing them would fly high, and deer upon seeing them would dash off. Which of these four understands what is really handsome in this world?
>
> (*Zhuangzi* 2)

The moment we begin to discount these other views of Lady Li, we have drained a great deal of significance from the notion of 'beauty' by setting up exclusive standards which determine not only the truly beautiful but the unacceptably ugly. Further, these fixed standards – whether of beauty or goodness or justice – are the means of creating a world of fixed objects. Those things or situations which meet the standards are themselves defined and delimited, closed to any other changes than those involved in degradation and decay, that is, failure to realize the demands set by the standard.

Paradoxically, therefore, for the Daoist the objective world is objectless. The sage envisions a world of transforming events which may, for whatever reason, be frozen momentarily into a pattern of discrimination, but which can be recognized, when seen clearly, as beyond such distinctions:

> There is nothing which is not a 'that', and nothing which is not a 'this'. Because we cannot see from a 'that' perspective but can only know from our own

perspective, it is said that 'that' arises out of 'this' and 'this' further accommodates 'that'. This is the notion that 'this' and 'that' are born simultaneously. And even though this is so, being born is simultaneously dying and vice versa; being acceptable is simultaneously being unacceptable and vice versa; accommodating right is accommodating wrong and vice versa. It is for this reason that the sage, illuminating this situation with the way things really are rather than going along with discriminations, is also a case of accommodating what is right and what is 'this'. But 'this' is also 'that' and vice versa. And a 'this's' 'that' further has one set of right and wrong while 'this' has another. In truth, is there really such a thing as 'this' and 'that' or not?

> Where neither 'this' nor 'that' has an opposite
>
> Is called the hinge of *dao*,
>
> And as soon as the hinge is fitted to its bracket
>
> It can respond endlessly
>
> (*Zhuangzi* 2)

The *wu*-forms – *wuzhi*, *wuwei*, *wuyu* – all provide a way of entertaining and deferring to an object-less world. Thus the sage is concerned with that sort of knowing, acting and desiring which does not depend upon objects. This point is crucial to the Daoist understanding of both self and world. The discriminated, and discriminating, self of the sort recognized in the contemporary West comes into being through encountering a world of things which effectively stand over against and object to him (see PERCEPTION). In Daoism, however, personality is forgotten to the extent that discriminated objects no longer constitute the environs of the self.

The consequence of this transformed vision is that knowing, acting and desiring are no longer based upon *construal*. The affirmation of principles as fixed guides for thought and conduct leads us to construe the object of our knowledge by recourse to those principles. An item becomes one of a *kind*, or an instrument for the achievement of an end. Feeling ourselves in tension with objectified others leads us to act in an aggressive or defensive manner to effect our will. Desire motivated by an object leads us to seek possession of that which is desired, allowing it significance only insofar as it meets our need. An individual intoxicated by objects narrows, truncates, and obfuscates the world as it is. Such a person fails to recognize the bottomlessness of each particular phenomenon, leaving off an appreciation of it at the point that the phenomenon ceases to resonate with one's own expectations of it. On the other hand, unprincipled knowing, nonassertive action and

objectless desire have this in common: to the extent they are successful, *they leave the world as it is*.

8 The transformation of things: *wuhua*

As we have said, the Daoist self is above all deferential. Deferring to the ways of things as they truly present themselves involves the expression of mirroring responses to environing circumstances. Mirroring such a world in fact involves the mirroring of an indefinite number of worlds since each item is the particular focus of a world. In his commentary on the *Daodejing* 5, Wang Bi notes that 'the myriad things acquire proper order and patterning among themselves'. In ordering themselves, they thereby order a world. Mirroring the individual things in their distinctive particularities therefore involves mirroring a complex set of overlapping orders, each with its own distinctive centre.

Obviously, the construing individual could not but treat such a world as chaotic in the extreme. The deferential self, on the other hand, sees these overlapping orders as a richly spontaneous array of patternings. The famous account of Lord Hundun – Lord Chaos – which closes the Inner Chapters of the *Zhuangzi* is appropriate here:

> The ruler of the North Sea was 'Swift', the ruler of the South Sea was 'Sudden', and the ruler of the Central Sea was 'Chaos'. Swift and Sudden had on several occasions encountered each other in the territory of Chaos, and Chaos had treated them with great hospitality. Swift and Sudden, devising a way to repay Chaos' generosity, said: 'Human beings all have seven orifices through which they see, hear, eat, and breathe. Chaos alone is without them.' They then attempted to bore holes in Chaos, each day boring one hole. On the seventh day, Chaos died.
>
> (*Zhuangzi* 7)

The construing self, relying upon its own seven orifices alone as its strategy for shaping the world, closes down the spontaneity of the unordered totality. But why shouldn't one wish to bring order out of Chaos? A reasonable question indeed, if chaos is the confusion and disarray which Western mythology describes. But if 'chaos' is a noncoherent sum of all orders – perhaps better rendered positively as 'spontaneity' – then imposing order on it means simply selecting one of a myriad candidates for order and privileging that one over the rest.

Obviously something more needs to be said concerning how one might go about actually mirroring the parity of all things. After all, the practical effect of giving each thing its due, when that means allowing it to focus a world from its own peculiar perspective, would seem to be disastrous. We can, however, follow the 'logic' of the Daoist sage at least this far: The most profound experience of the sage is not that of the Oneness of all things, or of Oneness *with* all things; it is closer to the experience of the particularity of all things. The experience of unity relevant to the Daoist is of 'this one' and 'that one'. Daoists do not 'become one with all things'; rather, as deferential, they approach becoming one with this or that thing. In effect, the sage becomes one with *all* other things only through celebrating continuity with other things based upon an intuition of parity.

When the *Zhuangzi* recommends that we become 'one with all things', this is not a Vedānta-like call to surrender one's particularity and dissolve into a unitary and perfect whole. Rather, it is a recognition that each and every unique phenomenon is continuous with every other phenomenon within one's field of experience. Is this an exhaustive claim: are we talking about *all* phenomena? Because the world is processional and because its creativity is *ab initio* rather than *ex nihilo* – a creativity expressed across the careers of its constitutive phenomena – any answer to this question would have to be provisional. Phenomena are never either atomistically discrete nor complete. The *Zhuangzi* recounts:

> With the ancients, understanding had gotten somewhere. Where was that? Its height, its extreme, that to which no more could be added was this: some of them thought that there had never begun to be things. The next lot thought that there are things, but that there had never begun to have boundaries among them. The next lot thought that there are boundaries among things, but that there had never begun to be the acceptable and unacceptable among them...
>
> (*Zhuangzi* 2)

But if the world is not a single, unitary cosmos, with rules and standards and laws finally determining its order – if the world, on the contrary, is the noncoherent totality of all possible orders – how does the deferential sage survive deferring to chaos? Ostensibly, the sage must discriminate as much as we ordinary folk. The difference that makes all the difference is that the sage recognizes the arbitrariness, transitoriness and merely conventional status of such discriminations.

Only 'thises' and 'thats' exist, by virtue of their distinctive *de*. When discriminations are made, as perforce they must be, one treats or 'deems' things in the mode of a transitory discrimination. This involves the utterance of a 'that's it!' which deems something to be the case. The sage discriminates as is deemed necessary, always acting in a deferential mode. However, such discriminations are qualified in two important ways. First, the sage recognizes that such discriminations are conventional and transitory. Secondly, to the extent possible, even these discriminated items are engaged in the modes of unprincipled knowing, nonassertive action and objectless desire.

The Daoist posture of mirroring the world cannot be either dialectical or analytic, since both analysis and dialectic require a putative whole: the former in order to divide into parts, the latter in order to form the opposing parts into some synthetic whole. Neither the 'ten thousand things' nor the self which plies its way among them may be summed to a coherent whole. The Daoist way is *analogical*; that is to say, it involves the correlation of elements with presumed similarities of structure, character or function without the necessity of assuming a holistic context. Such a method emphasizes the *ad hoc* nature of any sorts of discrimination or organization.

The employment of correlativity without the necessity of positing a cosmic whole as background of one's ruminations is a defining characteristic of philosophical Daoism. From that insight follows the irrelevance of dialectical and analytic modes of discourse; and from the irrelevance of the dialectical and analytic modes of discourse follows the implausibility of precise concepts, or of univocal language. From the irrelevance of conceptual language derives the impossibility of having objects or explanations of those objects with any final integrity or comprehensiveness. This means that neither the world nor the self can constitute a coherent unity.

9 The transformation of things: *wuhua* (cont.)

We have seen thus far that the Daoist engages the world in a mirroring manner which accepts order to be a function of the focal activity of each item in the totality of things. In such a world, 'order' is the same as 'chaos'; that is, it is an indefinite set of overlapping orders. While the sage recognizes the hierarchical relationships which obtain among things, the *de* of the individual things must be deferred to because each thing also has parity with the others as an inimical and unsubstitutable defining condition.

We have tried to understand the notions of person and world in classical Daoism by articulating some of the consequences of the sage's act of mirroring which allows things to be seen in their original order(s). One way of doing this is to ask, as we have just done, 'what sort of being is it who engages a world constituted by a complex set of overlapping orders shaped by the individual perspectives or particular foci (*de*), of each of 'the ten thousand things'?' Responding to this question has led us to the notion of the deferential self characterized by the modes of engagement identified as *wuzhi*, *wuwei* and *wuyu*. Another fruitful route toward understanding the Daoist version of the deferential self is by noting that the employment of the wu-forms as a means of mirroring the world as it is, has direct consequences for establishing the 'mood', 'temperament', or 'humour' with which the Daoist engages the ten thousand things.

The Daoist, by virtue of deferential activity, is characterized by a 'light-minded' or 'light-hearted' mood. As a popular translation of one of the chapter titles of the *Zhuangzi* has it, this mood is one of 'free and easy rambling'. Such a mood is often contrasted with the more serious-minded Confucian, and is even more dramatically contrasted with the 'high serious-ness' of the Anglo-European culture. The dominant sensibility of Western philosophy is imbued with a commitment to a single-ordered world, hierarchically arranged with human beings near the top of the ladder ('a little less than the Angels'). The high-seriousness of the Western individual is an appropriate response to the fixed and permanent status of his world. Daoists, by contrast, respond to a more horizontal world of things possessed of an indefinite number of orders. Their's is thus a more flexible and light-hearted response. We propose to pursue this contrast between the 'serious' and the 'light-hearted' as means of highlighting the distinctive character of the Daoist world.

The first thing to be said has to do with the rather standard perception of Daoism as a relativistic mode of understanding. In the West, relativism is usually an epistemological doctrine: that is to say, 'relativity' is a theoretical notion. The relativities recognized are not thought to be ontologically constitutive of the way of things, and are seldom thought to involve practical consequences. Relativists do not normally wish to claim that the world itself actually exists in a number of different ways, but only that we have a number of different theories of the way of things, and that there is no satisfactory means of deciding which gets at the way things really are. Secondly, a consistent relativist must claim that nothing practically follows from relativism but inaction. If one tacitly or explicitly commits to one of a number of ways of acting, relativism has been practically abandoned. Thus, the issue of relativism in Western philosophy is, mainly, a red herring (see RELATIVISM).

Philosophical Daoism avoids this sort of relativism by asserting a ground for parity by virtue of the continuity among things, associated with Zhuangzi's 'transformation of things' (*wuhua*). *Dao* is the total process of becoming which constitutes the ways of things. These things form 'worlds' characterizable

from the perspective of each and every item in the total process. Given the uniqueness of each thing as a starting point, particulars must with reference to any given issue stand in hierarchical relationship. This is the ground of deference. All things defer, in this way or that, to everything else. This is why a correlative and hierarchical *yin–yang* vocabulary usually works to articulate relationships. We say usually because, given the porous nature and attendant vagueness of particular things and events, there are occasions on which the yin–yang language is not functional. As is stated in the *Yijing* (Book of Changes), 'What yin–yang does not fathom is called inscrutability'.

The transformation of all things entails two important consequences. First, there are always myriad alternative postures which challenge the ultimacy of one's present configuration. Second, the processional nature of experience guarantees that one will in fact actually proceed through an indefinite number of such configurations. The sagely recognition of this fact is the source of Daoist light-heartedness.

With Daoism, and specifically the Zhuangzian variety, the issue of relativism is usually seen to be irrelevant. Though the assumption that ZHUANGZI is a realist would doubtless be challenged by many scholars who would insist that he is an extremely subtle proponent of a kind of sceptical relativism, Zhuangzi's transformation of things seems to commit him to the belief that the world actually exists as a shifting set of ways of being, a myriad set of overlapping worlds, a chaos of 'thises' and 'thats', a multifarious congeries of orders. 'Chaos' (*hundun*), understood as the totality of all orders, names the way of things. Further, Zhuangzi seems to believe that there are crucial and direct practical consequences of such ontological pluralism. The deferential self, expressed through the modalities of the *wu*-forms, spontaneously engages in mirroring responses which take into account the *de* of the items or events he or she encounters. Thus, Zhuangzi's 'relativism' is seriously moderated at the level of practice since deference entails commitment. There are, therefore, direct practical consequences of mirroring the vast indifferent complex of the ways of things in a manner that allows one to see all things as viable candidates for deferential response.

The paradigm for Daoist light-heartedness turns out to be something like this:

If people sleep in damp places, they ache at the waist and end up half-paralyzed, but is this the case with the loach? If they live in the trees, they tremble with fear, but is this the case with the ape?

(*Zhuangzi* 2)

The paradigm of high seriousness on the other hand is something like:

What is sauce for the goose is sauce for the gander.

Daoist light-heartedness depends upon the coexistence of a plurality of viable world orders. On this view, the world – if by this we mean that *the* World is one, single-ordered, rational, coherent, internally consistent cosmos – is singularly humourless. Even if the totality is acknowledged to possess many orders, as long as there is any hint of a logical or axiological priority given to one or some orders *vis-à-vis* an other or other orders, the ground of any real light-mindedness or light-heartedness is undermined. This is the case because the notion of a privileged order implies a non-deferential, determinative stance. It is such a notion of superiority which cancels true light-heartedness. However, it is not simply a matter of taking up a variety of sympathetic stances. For Zhuangzi, one actually becomes all of the potential objects and beings with respect to which such stances may be taken:

Before long, Master Lai fell ill. Wheezing and panting, he was on the brink of death. His wife and children gathered about him and wept. Master Li, having gone to enquire after him, scolded them, saying: 'Get away! Don't impede his transformations!'

Leaning against the door, Master Li talked with him, saying: 'Extraordinary, these transformations! What are you going to be made into next? Where are you going to be sent? Will you be made into a rat's liver? Or will you be made into an insect's arm?...

Now if a great ironsmith were in the process of casting metal, and the metal leapt about saying: 'I must be forged into a Mo Ye sword!' the great ironsmith would certainly consider it to be an inauspicious bit of metal. Now, if once having been cast in the human form, I were to whine: 'Make me into a human being! Make me into a human being!' the transformer of things would certainly take me to be an inauspicious person. Now once we take the heavens and earth to be a giant forge and transformation to be the great ironsmith, where ever I go is just fine. Relaxed I nod off and happily I awake.

(*Zhuangzi* 6)

The transformative processes (*wuhua*) are not to be interfered with, but are to be met with deference. To this extent, the sage is in agreement with Faust who proclaims to Mephistopheles:

If I ever say to the moment, 'Hold! Thou art so fair!'

then thou canst require my soul of me.

What distinguishes the life of the Daoist sage from that of the pleasure-seeking Faust lies in the difference between aggressive desiring and *wuyu*. For Faust each moment brings a new object of desire to be seduced, consumed or otherwise enjoyed, and then abandoned.

The Daoist neither demands constant transformation for the sake of the ever-new, nor objects to transformation, attempting to apply the brakes and hold onto the moment. The deferential self yields to the moment, without constraint.

Daoists such as Zhuangzi are light-hearted by virtue of being freed from the serious responsibilities entailed by 'being right', or 'having the truth'. Were one to seek a coherent theory to house Zhuangzi's teachings, he would risk constructing a platform from which he may proclaim (implicitly) the superiority of those teachings. And if we presume that Daoist light-heartedness is used in the defence of a vision of things which necessarily denies the validity of other visions, we have simply made any attempts at light-heartedness secondary to the 'true philosophical enterprise', namely, the defence of a particular way of envisaging things.

The character of light-heartedness lies in a felt incongruity or contradiction. The Daoist treats these incongruities as existing among things and events which are on a par with the others. The pluralist vision of Daoism plays upon the sense of the contradiction between one perspective and a myriad others: between Zhuangzi and a butterfly, among fishes, birds, cicadas and turtle doves, between men and monkeys. Light-heartedness is an essential means of teasing one into the recognition of the variety of perspectives permitted by the totality of existing things. The need for allusiveness lies in the fact that one cannot fully appreciate the differences without some sense of the reality of those differences. However, one cannot confront these differences in too direct a manner; they may at best be hinted at.

We should note here that though the term 'irony' has often been used to name the Daoist form of light-heartedness, it is hardly an altogether appropriate one. There can be no real philosophic irony without something like the dialectic of tragedy and comedy as it developed in ancient Greece, and Zhuangzi's doctrine of the transformation of things precludes the development of a tragic sense. The tragic sense is predicated upon loss. But the transformation of things guarantees that there is no final loss: there are only processes of transformation which realizes the becoming of what has not yet become.

See also: AESTHETICS, CHINESE; CONFUCIAN PHILOSOPHY, CHINESE; LEGALIST PHILOSOPHY, CHINESE; NEO-CONFUCIAN PHILOSOPHY; CHINESE PHILOSOPHY; DAO; DAODEJING; DE; GUANZI; HUAINANZI; QI; YIJING; YIN–YANG; YOU–WU; ZHI; ZHUANGZI

References and further readings

Ames, R.T. (1989) 'Putting the *te* Back in Taoism', in J.B. Callicott and R.T. Ames (eds) *Nature in Asian Traditions of Thought*, Albany, NY: State University of New York Press. (An argument for an 'aesthetic' interpretation of Daoism.)

Chang Chung-yuan (1963) *Creativity and Taoism*, New York: Harper & Row. (A discussion of the influence of Daoism on Chinese culture and aesthetics.)

* *Daodejing*, (c. 350–250 BC), trans. D.C. Lau, *Tao Te Ching*, Chinese Classics: Chinese–English Series, Hong Kong: The Chinese University Press, 1982. (A reliable translation of the text revised on the basis of the Mawangdui archaeological discoveries.)

Graham, A.C. (1989) *Disputers of the Tao*, La Salle, IL: Open Court. (A contextualization of Daoist thinking within classical Chinese philosophy.)

Hall, D.L. (1978) 'Process and Anarchy – A Taoist Vision of Creativity', *Philosophy East and West* 28 (3): 271–85. (A new vocabulary for interpreting Daoism.)

—— (1982) *The Uncertain Phoenix*, New York: Fordham University Press. (Daoism as a philosophical resource for contemporary philosophical issues, especially technology.)

Hall, D.L. and Ames, R.T. (1995) *Anticipating China: Thinking Through the Narratives of Chinese and Western Culture*, Albany, NY: State University of New York Press. (A narrative understanding of the difference between Chinese and Western philosophical sensibilities.)

—— (1997) *Thinking from the Han: Self, Truth, and Transcendence in China and the West*, Albany, NY: State University of New York Press. (An exploration of several central philosophical issues that illustrate the distance between Chinese and Western assumptions.)

LaFargue, M. (1992) *The Tao of the Tao Te Ching*, Albany, NY: State University of New York Press. (A translation and commentary on how to read the Daodejing.)

Needham, J. (1956) *Science and Civilisation in China*, vol. 2, Cambridge: Cambridge University Press. (A well-known statement of the role of Daoism in classical Chinese thought.)

Waley, A. (1934) *The Way and Its Power: A Study of the Tao Te Ching and its Place in Chinese Thought*, London: George Allen & Unwin. (A pioneering translation of the Daodejing with a discussion of many of the central concepts.)

Wu Kuang-ming (1990) *The Butterfly as Companion: Meditations on the First Three Chapters of the Chuang Tzu*, Albany, NY: State University of New York Press. (A Zhuangzian commentary on several core chapters of *Zhuangzi*.)

* *Zhuangzi* (c. 4th century BC), trans. B. Watson, *The Complete Works of Chuang Tzu*, New York: Columbia University Press, 1968; trans. A.C. Graham, *Chuang-tzu: The Inner Chapters*, London: George Allen & Unwin, 1981. (Watson is an elegant, literary translation of the *Zhuangzi* influenced by Japanese commentators; Graham is a philosophically sensitive translation of about 85 per cent of the *Zhuangzi*.)

DAVID L. HALL
ROGER T. AMES

DARWIN, CHARLES ROBERT (1809–82)

Darwin's On the Origin of Species *(1859) popularized the theory that all living things have evolved by natural processes from pre-existing forms. This displaced the traditional belief that species were designed by a wise and benevolent God. Darwin showed how many biological phenomena could be explained on the assumption that related species are descended from a common ancestor. Furthermore, he proposed a radical mechanism to explain how the transformations came about, namely, natural selection. This harsh and apparently purposeless mechanism was seen as a major threat to the claim that the universe has a transcendent goal.*

Because Darwin openly extended his evolutionism to include the human race, it was necessary to re-examine the foundations of psychology, ethics and social theory. Moral values might be merely the rationalization of instinctive behaviour patterns. Since the process which produced these patterns was driven by struggle, it could be argued that society must inevitably reflect the harshness of nature ('social Darwinism'). Darwin's book has been seen as the trigger for a 'scientific revolution'. It took many decades for both science and Western culture to assimilate the more radical aspects of Darwin's theory. But since the mid-twentieth century Darwin's selection mechanism has become the basis for a highly successful theory of evolution, the human consequences of which are still being debated.

1 Scientific work

Darwin was born in 1809 in Shrewsbury, England. After a brief spell as a medical student he moved to Cambridge, where he received extra-curricular training in natural history and geology. Travelling on the survey ship HMS *Beagle* (1831–6), he studied the geology of South America and accepted what he took to be Charles Lyell's uniformitarian theory of geological change (see GEOLOGY, PHILOSOPHY OF §1). He proposed a new theory to explain the formation of coral reefs, and collected fossils and studied the geographical distribution of South American animals. In particular he was struck by the existence of distinct but related species of birds on the individual islands of the Galapagos group, off the west coast of South America.

Soon after his return to England, he became convinced that the Galapagos species could only be explained as the modified descendants of migrants from the mainland. Evolution theories were highly controversial at the time, but Darwin was soon a complete convert. He studied animal breeding and was led to the theory of natural selection. Having been active in the scientific life of London, in 1842 he moved to Down House in Kent, where he spent the rest of his life suffering from a debilitating illness. He kept up his studies of biogeography and produced a major taxonomic survey of barnacles. This work was intended to throw light on his theory, which remained unpublished until a similar idea was proposed by A.R. WALLACE in 1858. *On the Origin of Species* was published at the end of 1859; following an intense controversy, the basic idea of evolution was accepted by the majority of scientists.

In *The Descent of Man* (1871) Darwin extended his theory to the human race. Much of his later scientific work centred on the application of his theory in botany, to explain the activity of climbing and insectivorous plants, and the relationship between flower structure and insect pollination. He also wrote a study of earthworms.

2 The evolutionary worldview

Conventional histories of the Darwinian revolution have assumed that, prior to the publication of the *Origin of Species*, everyone accepted that each species was designed by a wise and benevolent God. Darwin's materialistic theory thus upset a vision of a perfectly ordered universe. In fact, the idea of evolution had been widely discussed in the previous decades. Robert Chambers' *Vestiges of the Natural History of Creation* (1844), promoted the image of life progressing towards higher levels of physical and mental organization under the control of divinely implanted laws. Historians still debate the extent to which Darwin himself saw evolution as necessarily progressive. There was certainly an element of progressionism in his thinking, but his theory was built on different foundations and in later life he was unable to accept that the whole process was designed by the Creator. Darwin may have begun his work believing that the laws governing natural development were instituted by God, but he ended up seeing the universe as a scene of perpetual struggle and suffering.

Darwin argued that each population changes by adapting to its local environment. When members of a population migrate to new areas, they will adapt to the new conditions and thus come to differ from the parent group. If the degree of difference becomes sufficient, the two populations would find it difficult to interbreed even if they came into contact, and would thus count as distinct species. Local varieties or subspecies are the first steps on the way to full speciation. The overall pattern of evolution must thus be visualized as an irregularly branching tree, not as the ascent of a ladder towards a fixed goal.

Darwin believed that evolution was an immensely slow process, and thus that it was unrealistic to expect ever to observe one species being transmuted into another. Opponents of the theory argued that we only observe minor changes within species, from which it is illegitimate to infer that change spead over a longer timespan will generate a new species distinct from the parent form. Darwin realized that the case for evolution would have to be argued by showing that the theory accounted for a range of otherwise inexplicable phenomena. He showed that the classification of species could be understood as a reflection of the tree-like model of genealogical relationships (see TAXONOMY §§3–4). Each major taxon was founded by a single ancestral form which had developed some important evolutionary innovation; the descendants of this ancestor radiated out through the local adaptation of sub-populations, thus creating the genera and species we recognize today. Homologies such as the similar bone structures of the forelimb in humans, horses and bats were explained as adaptive modifications of similar structures inherited from a common ancestor. Relationships between dissimilar adult forms could often be traced in their early embryos, which were not subject to the same degree of modification. Darwin knew that evolutionary change could not be demonstrated from the fossil record, which often gave the appearance of sudden 'leaps'. He argued that the record is very imperfect, the 'leaps' are in fact gaps concealing gradual evolutionary transformations. Once this factor was taken into account, the fossil record could be reconciled with the tree model. The geographical distribution of organisms could also be explained in terms of species migrating outward from their point of origin, adapting themselves to the new territories they entered (see EVOLUTION, THEORY OF).

3 Natural selection

The basic idea of evolution was accepted quite rapidly in the 1860s, although many people, scientists included, were unwilling to admit that the development of life on earth had no preordained goal. This meant that they were particularly worried about Darwin's proposed mechanism of natural selection. In this theory, the species could not be regarded as having an underlying 'type' on which all the individual organisms were modelled. The species was just the breeding population, and if the average structure of the individuals making up the population changed, then so did the species. The natural world could not be composed of a range of fixed, specific types or forms (see SPECIES §2).

There was much debate over whether natural selection could be considered a *vera causa* or true cause capable of producing significant changes in species. Darwin knew that each component of the effect could be demonstrated individually, but doubted that selection could produce a new population incapable of interbreeding with the parental type within an observable timescale. For him, selection was a plausible mechanism of change, and probably the most important one – but he never ruled out the possibility of other mechanisms. Much of the initial opposition to the selection theory was based on an unwillingness to believe that the species does not have some sort of essence which prevents individuals becoming modified beyond a fixed range.

Darwin's studies of domesticated animals convinced him that the individuals making up any population differ significantly among themselves. This is sometimes called 'random' variation, because there seems to be no apparent purpose to the differences. Darwin knew that there was an underlying mechanism to explain the production of individual differences and their transmission through heredity, although his own explanation did not stand the test of time. Many of Darwin's contemporaries found it difficult to accept that the variations which accumulate to give evolution could be produced by a process that imposed no fixed direction. They preferred to believe that the variations were directed along a predetermined channel by forces arising from within the organism, or were produced in response to the organism's own purposeful activities. If characteristics acquired in response to new behaviour-patterns were inherited, this would give the rival evolutionary mechanism known as 'Lamarckism'. Darwin himself accepted a subsidiary Lamarckian effect, but stressed the natural selection of random variation. Modern genetics has shown that acquired characteristics cannot be inherited and that mutations produce many different characteristics within a population. In the modern Darwinian theory, selection works by changing the frequencies of genes within the population (see GENETICS).

Natural selection depends upon the elimination of those variant characteristics which are maladaptive, and the superior reproductive fitness of those which confer some adaptive benefit. Following Malthus, Darwin believed that the tendency for a population to breed beyond the capacity of its food supply would lead to a 'struggle for existence' in which the least fit would be eliminated. This was what H. SPENCER called the 'survival of the fittest'. Contrary to a popular anti-Darwinian argument, natural selection is not based on a tautology (the survival of those who survive), because fitness is defined in terms of the adaptation which enables an organism to live and breed more effectively. Darwin did, however, argue that there is a different mechanism, sexual selection, capable of enhancing those characteristics which, even if maladaptive, improve the organism's chances of reproducing. Thus the peacock has developed its large tail because this characteristic has become involved with the birds' mating behaviour – a bigger tail attracts peahens more effectively, and the reproductive advantage this confers outweighs the disadvantages of a large tail when escaping from predators.

4 Human origins

From the start, Darwin accepted that the human species would have to be included within the evolutionary worldview. If humans were to be treated as merely advanced animals, the mental and moral faculties traditionally seen as products of the soul would have to be explained as extensions of those faculties already possessed by animals. In his *Descent of Man* (1871) and *Expression of the Emotions in Man and the Animals* (1872), Darwin tried to justify this proposition and to explain how the human mind had developed so much further than those of our closest animal relatives. He did not believe that the mind was a *tabula rasa* or blank slate capable of indefinite modification by experience. Many mental activities are governed by instincts imprinted by evolution. He showed that many aspects of human behaviour, especially the way we express emotions, are relics of our animal ancestry. He also took seriously many stories that interpreted animal behaviour in anthropomorphic terms, thus providing apparent evidence that animals possess rudiments of even the highest mental and moral faculties.

Darwin accepted that the mental faculties were produced by the brain, and that the increased brain size of the 'higher' animals is reponsible for their increased intelligence and more complex behaviour. Many of his contemporaries assumed that evolution would inevitably produce a steady increase in the level of animal intelligence. In *The Descent of Man*, however, Darwin anticipated the modern position in which (since evolution is not inherently progressive) it is necessary to explain why the branch leading to humans has experienced a much greater expansion in intelligence than that leading to our closest cousins, the great apes. He argued that the distant ancestors of humans had stood upright as a means of walking on the open plains, while the apes had stayed in the trees. Human intellengence was a by-product of this change of habitat, produced as a means of exploiting the hand's ability to manipulate the environment.

Darwin argued that the higher animals exhibit social behaviour which provides the foundation for human moral values. Social behaviour is governed by instincts, and natural selection can act upon the variations in such instincts to promote useful behaviour patterns. Since our distant ancestors lived in social groups, we have inherited their social instincts, and our moral values are rationalizations of behavioural tendencies which we feel automatically. Modern efforts to explain some aspects of human behaviour in terms of biologically implanted instincts make use of the same argument (see SOCIOBIOLOGY).

Although Darwin anticipated some modern ideas on human evolution, he shared the prejudices of his own time and was convinced that Europeans were superior to other races and that modern industrial civilization is the highest expression of social evolution. His ideas were taken up by some social evolutionists who argued that here, as in the biological realm, progress would only result if individuals or races were left to struggle among themselves to determine which was fit enough to survive. This social philosophy came to be known as 'social Darwinism' – although one of its leading proponents, Herbert Spencer, was more a Lamarckian than a Darwinian. The claim that struggle was a spur to progress was developed in many other forms besides Darwin's theory of natural selection.

See also: AL-AFGHANI §2; EVOLUTION AND ETHICS; EVOLUTIONARY THEORY IN SOCIAL SCIENCES; HUXLEY, T.H.

List of works

Darwin, C. (1845) *Journal of Researches into the Geology and Natural History of the Countries Visited during the Voyage of H.M.S. Beagle*, London: John Murray. (A semi-popular account of the voyage, frequently reprinted.)

—— (1859) *On the Origin of Species by means of Natural Selection, or the Preservation of Favoured Races in the Struggle for Life*, London: John Murray. (Darwin's main work on evolution; the much-revised sixth edition of 1872 is the one most frequently reprinted.)

—— (1871) *The Descent of Man and Selection in Relation to Sex*, London: John Murray, 2 vols; repr. Princeton, NJ: Princeton University Press, 1981. (Darwin's main work on human origins, with a long account of sexual selection and an attempt to apply that theory to explain human characteristics.)

References and further reading

Bowler, P. (1984) *Evolution: The History of an Idea*, Berkeley, CA: University of California Press; revised edn 1989. (General survey of the history of evolutionism, with extensive bibliography.)

—— (1988) *The Non-Darwinian Revolution: Reinterpreting a Historical Myth*, Baltimore, MD: Johns Hopkins University Press. (A reassessment of Darwin's impact on nineteenth-century thought.)

—— (1990) *Charles Darwin: The Man and his Influence*, Oxford: Blackwell. (Biography and assessment of Darwin's influence.)

Desmond, A. and Moore, J. (1991) *Darwin*, London: Micheal Joseph. (Massive biography stressing the social context of Darwin's thought.)

Ghiselin, M. (1969) *The Triumph of the Darwinian Method*, Berkeley, CA: University of California Press. (Detailed account of Darwin's scientific work.)

Kohn, D. (ed.) (1985) *The Darwinian Heritage*, Princeton, NJ: Princeton University Press. (Major compilation of Darwin scholarship.)

Richards, R. (1987) *Darwin and the Emergence of Evolutionary Theories of Mind and Behavior*, Chicago, IL: University of Chicago Press. (The evolution of mental powers according to Darwin and later writers.)

Young, R. (1985) *Darwin's Metaphor: Nature's Place in Victorian Culture*, Cambridge: Cambridge

University Press. (Essays on the social context of Darwinism.)

PETER J. BOWLER

DASHENG QIXIN LUN

see AWAKENING OF FAITH IN MAHĀYĀNA

DAVID OF DINANT (*fl. c.*1210)

A twelfth- and early thirteenth-century philosopher who may have taught at Paris, David of Dinant was noted for a heretical, pantheistic view that identified God, mind and matter. None of his works survive intact, and we know of them primarily through the works of other authors. His major work, the Quaternuli, *was condemned at Paris in 1210. His heretical views were influential enough to receive critical attention in the works of Albert the Great and Thomas Aquinas.*

Very little is known for certain about David of Dinant's life. He was born, probably at Dinant, Belgium, but possibly in Dinan in Brittany, in the middle of the twelfth century. He may have taught at the University of Paris. A work of his identified as *Quaternuli*, perhaps the first word of the work's text, was condemned in 1210: all copies of it were to be brought to the Bishop of Paris and burned, and anyone discovered possessing the work after Christmas of that year was to be regarded as a heretic. This work may be identical to one attributed to David with the title *De Tomis hoc est de Divisionibus* (On the Volume Known as 'On Divisions'). David died most likely in the second decade of the thirteenth century, perhaps while a fugitive from France.

Some fragments of his writings appear to have survived, but his most distinctive views are to be gleaned from the accounts of his philosophical opponents. Chief among these are ALBERT THE GREAT and Thomas AQUINAS. Although NICHOLAS OF CUSA also refers to David, he may have acquired his knowledge from reading Albert or Aquinas.

According to Aquinas, David divided reality into three parts, bodies, souls and eternal, separated substances. Bodies are composed of *hyle* or prime matter, souls are constituted from *nous* or mind, and eternal, separated substances are constituted from God. Albert and Aquinas both attribute to David the additional thesis that prime matter, mind and God are

one and the same. It follows that God, mind and prime matter constitute all things, or, as Aquinas puts it, that everything is one essence. David's views thus contradict several doctrines of philosophical theology, defended particularly by scholastic philosophers; these include the doctrines that God is an immaterial being, that God is perfectly simple, having no parts or plurality of any kind, that the created world is separate from God, that God created the world out of nothing, and that human souls are not divine (see GOD, CONCEPTS OF).

Aquinas claims that David's identification of God and prime matter was based on the argument that, if they were not identical, God would have to differ from prime matter by means of some differentiae. But if they possessed differentiae, God and prime matter would not be metaphysically simple, contrary to the assertion that they are simple. Aquinas, and apparently David, presuppose a theory of predication deriving from Aristotle by way of Porphyry's *Isagōgē* (see PORPHYRY). On that theory, questions concerning what natural kinds have in common and questions concerning how natural kinds differ from one another are to be answered by specifying the genera and differentiae of the respective natural kinds. Horses and humans, for example, are the same in genus insofar as they are both sensitive, animate corporeal substances, but different in species because horses possess the differentiae of being ungulate while lacking the differentiae of being bipedal and rational, and humans possess the differentiae of being bipedal and rational while not being ungulate. As reported by Aquinas, David's argument begins with the premise that God and prime matter are metaphysically simple, proceeds by inferring that they can thus have no differentiae (for the possession of any differentiae entails that its possessor is metaphysically complex), and concludes that because there is no specific difference between them, God and prime matter are identical.

Aquinas claims that David's argument is fallacious; it confuses *difference* with *diversity*. It is true that two distinct kinds of thing in the same genus must differ by means of some differentiae, but the same does not hold for kinds that share no genus in common. Although horses share something in common with humans, horses and humans share nothing in common with, for example, cerulean blue. There are no differentiae that distinguish colours from animate substances, but it does not follow that colours and animals are identical; they are simply diverse. Similarly, Aquinas argues, God and prime matter are diverse in themselves. In Aristotelian terms, prime matter is pure potentiality, having no actuality of its own, and God is pure actuality, a being having no unactualized potentiality.

See also: ARISTOTELIANISM, MEDIEVAL; MATTER; SIMPLICITY, DIVINE

List of works

David of Dinant (before 1210) *Quaternuli*. (This work may also be identical with work attributed to David known as *De Tomis hoc est de Divisionibus*. There are no printed versions of David's work, and only fragments of his writings survive. Knowledge of his work is to be obtained primarily from the work of Albert the Great and Thomas Aquinas.)

References and further reading

Denifle, H. and Chatelaine, E. (eds) (1889) *Chartularium Universitatis Parisiensis* (Charters of the University of Paris), Paris: Delalain, vol. 1. (Contains the text of the decree of 1210, condemning the *Quaternuli*.)

Albert the Great (1270–80) *Summa theologiae sive de mirabili scientia Dei*, book 1, part 1, questions 1–50A; published in *Opera Omnia*, vol. 34, part 1, Aschendorff: Westphalia Monastery, 1978. (David of Dinant is discussed briefly in treatise 6, question 29, chapter 1, article 2, 'Whether the divine unity admits any plurality'.)

Aquinas, Thomas (1252–73) *Opera omnia* (Collected Works), ed. R. Busa, Stuttgart–Bad Canstatt: Friedrich Fromman Verlag Günther Holzboog, 1980, 7 vols. (Volume 1 contains the Latin text of Aquinas' commentary on the *Sentences* of Peter Lombard. Aquinas mentions David's threefold division and the thesis that everything is one in essence in book 2, distinction 17, question 1, article 1, 'Whether the human soul is of the divine essence'. Volume 2 contains the Latin texts of *Summa contra gentiles* and *Summa theologiae*.)

—— (1259–65) *Summa contra gentiles* (Synopsis [of Christina Doctrine] Directed Against Unbelievers); trans. A.C. Pegis, *On the Truth of the Catholic Faith*, Garden City, NY: Image Books, 1955–7, 5 vols. (Aquinas offers the argument presented above against David's identification of God and prime matter in book 1, chapter 17, 'That there is no matter in God'.)

—— (1266–73) *Summa theologiae*, published as *Summa Theologica*, Westminster, MD: Christian Classics, 1981, 5 vols. (A reprint of the translation of the Fathers of the English Dominican Province. Volume 1 contains the first part of the *Summa theologiae*. Aquinas says that David 'most stupidly'

identified God and prime matter (part 1, question 3, article 8, 'Whether God enters into the composition of other things').)

WILLIAM E. MANN

DAVIDSON, DONALD (1917–)

Donald Davidson's views about the relationship between our conceptions of ourselves as people and as complex physical objects have had significant impact on contemporary discussions of such topics as intention, action, causal explanation and weakness of the will. His collection of essays, Actions and Events *(1980), contains many seminal contributions in these areas. But perhaps even greater has been the influence of Davidson's philosophy of language, as reflected especially in* Inquires into Truth and Interpretation *(1984). Among the philosophical issues connected to language on which Davidson has been influential are the nature of truth, the semantic paradoxes, first person authority, indexicals, modality, reference, quotation, metaphor, indeterminacy, convention, realism and the publicity of language.*

1 **Reasons and causes**
2 **Events**
3 **The mind–body problem**
4 **Theory of meaning**
5 **Radical interpretation**
6 **Indirect quotation**
7 **Adverbial modification**
8 **Animal thought**
9 **Conceptual schemes**
10 **Against facts**

1 Reasons and causes

Since 1963, with the publication of 'Actions, Reasons, and Causes', Donald Davidson's philosophical work has taken centre stage in analytic philosophy. He begins this essay with the question: what is the relation between a reason and an action when that reason explains the action by giving the agent's reasons for performing it? Prior to this essay, something like a consensus had formed in philosophy that this relationship was not causal. Discussion tended to centre around why it could not be causal and the consequences of its not being so.

Davidson's central purpose was 'to defend the ancient – and commonsense – position that rationalization is a species of causal explanation' (Davidson 1980: 3). A large portion of the essay is devoted to refuting various arguments, quite popular then, that purported to show that reasons could not be causes of the actions they rationalize. The arguments are too many and varied to be properly treated here, but in passing I note that they were largely inspired by remarks made by Wittgenstein and/or certain interpretations of Humean strictures on causation. Each argument proposes that a necessary condition for two items to interact causally is not satisfied by reasons and actions. Davidson replies to the leading arguments by showing in each case either that reasons and actions indeed satisfy the necessary condition in question or that the allegedly necessary condition for causal interaction is not necessary at all (see ACTION).

2   Events

Davidson's chief claim about events is that they are concrete particulars – that is, unrepeatable entities with location in space and time. He regards the mind–body problem as the problem of the relation between mental and physical events. He treats causation as a relation between events and he takes action to be a species of event, so that events comprise the very subject matter of action theory. He argues for the existence of events and for specific claims as to their nature.

In 'Causal Relations' (1980) Davidson argues that the most plausible interpretation of singular causal statements like 'The short circuit caused the fire' treats them as two-place predicate statements with their singular terms (in this case, 'the short circuit' and 'the fire') designating events. In 'The Individuation of Events' (1980), Davidson argues that an adequate theory of action must recognize that we can describe the same action differently. This seems crucial in making sense of perfectly natural claims like 'Jones managed to apologize in saying "I apologize"', wherein apparently one event is described both as an apology and as an utterance (see EVENTS).

3   The mind–body problem

Consider claims (1)–(3):

(1) No mental event is a physical event.
(2) Some mental events cause physical events.
(3) The only causes of physical events are physical events.

Although much can be said in favour of each, together they clearly are inconsistent. The dilemma posed by the plausibility of each of (1)–(3) and by their apparent incompatibility is the traditional mind–body problem. Davidson's resolution of the

dilemma is to abandon (1). Davidson's account accepts the following principles about the gap between the mental (M) and the physical (P) and about causation:

(4) There are no exceptionless psychological or psychophysical laws and in fact all exceptionless causal laws can be expressed in a purely physical vocabulary.
(5) Event c causes event e only if there is an exceptionless causal law which subsumes c and e.

It is commonly held that a property expressed by M is reducible to a property expressed by P only if there is an exceptionless law that links them. So, it follows from (4) that mental and physical properties are distinct. Thesis (5) says that c causes e only if there are descriptions D of c and D' of e and an exceptionless causal law L such that L and 'D occurred' entail 'D caused D''. Theses (4) and (5) entail that physical events have only physical causes and that all event causation is physically grounded.

Davidson shows that theses (2)–(5) can all be true if (and only if) mental events are identical to physical events. Say that an event e is a physical event just in case e satisfies a predicate of our basic physical sciences. These are the predicates appearing in exceptionless laws. Since only physical predicates (or predicates expressing properties reducible to basic physical properties) appear in such laws, it follows that every event that enters into causal relations satisfies a basic physical predicate. So, mental events which enter into causal relations are also physical events. The mental and physical are still distinct in so far as mental and physical events *so-described* are not linked by exceptionless law; but still mental events are physical events (see ANOMALOUS MONISM).

4   Theory of meaning

Davidson's work in the philosophy of language began later than his seminal work in the philosophy of action. I will discuss primarily the first two essays in his 1984 collection, where he identifies an adequacy criterion for theories of meaning for natural languages, and then applies it critically to a number of then-prominent views about natural language. He also sketches a programme in which a Tarski-style truth theory plays the role of a theory of meaning which meets the criterion he initially articulated.

Like the nineteenth-century mathematician/philosopher Gottlob FREGE, Davidson requires that we specify what every sentence means by exhibiting its meaning as a function of the meanings of its significant parts (and their arrangement in the sentence). Call any such theory for a language 'a compositional meaning theory' for that language (see COMPOSITIONALITY). That there must be a compositional meaning theory for natural languages, such as English, seems mandatory because natural languages are spoken by finite speakers without magical abilities, but natural languages themselves have an infinity of meaningful (and nonsynonymous) sentences, each one of which, at least potentially, a speaker understands (at a given time). This seems to require that our knowledge of meanings be based on (a finite number of) rules which determine from a finite set of semantic primitives what count as meaningful compositions, where an expression is semantically primitive if the 'rules which give the meaning for the sentences in which it does not appear do not suffice to determine the meaning of the sentences in which it does appear' (Davidson 1984: 9).

According to Davidson, a compositional theory of meaning for a language L is such that anyone who knows it is in a position to understand every sentence of L. By specifying the meaning of a sentence S in L, it is clear that what Davidson has in mind requires that the specification enable anyone who understands the language in which the specification is given, to understand S. Davidson's idea is that to provide a compositional meaning theory, we can produce a Tarski-like *truth theory* for L (see TARSKI, A.). A theory is a truth theory for language L if and only if for each sentence S of L, the theory entails a 'T-sentence' of the form:

(T) S is true-in-L iff p,

where the sentence (T) is in a metalanguage M used to talk about L. An adequate theory of meaning for German, for example, should issue in theorems like (S):

(S) 'Schnee ist weiss' is true in German iff snow is white.

Davidson's twist on Tarski is that, instead of requiring (for a compositional meaning theory) that for each T-sentence the condition that 'p' translates S is satisfied, Davidson merely requires that each T-sentence be true. While we thus can avoid the danger of circularity attendant on using the notion of 'correct translation' in characterizing what it takes to explain meaning, it may seem that the requirement of merely issuing in *true* T-sentences is too weak. All the 'iff' in a T-sentence requires is that the sentences surrounding it are either both true or both false, so that the following is true, though not at all helpful about meaning:

(S*) 'Schnee ist weiss' is true in German iff grass is green.

Davidson points out, however, that the need for a *finitely stated* adequate theory of meaning to contain recursive apparatus plausibly would lead the theory to issue in (S) rather than (S*). Still, he imposes further constraints on an adequate meaning theory, as we will see in the next section (see MEANING AND TRUTH).

5 Radical interpretation

Davidson requires of the meaning-giving T-theory that it be empirically warranted under the practice of radical interpretation. This means that empirical considerations must be respected in choosing between different but true truth theories for, say, German, between a theory that issues in (S) and one that issues in the true but non-interpretive (S*). The favoured T-theory is to be selected on the basis of evidence plausibly available to a radical interpreter (RI), 'someone who does not already know how to interpret utterances the theory is designed to cover' (1984: 128). More particularly, an RI does not know the language they are trying to interpret and has no access to bilingual informants, prior dictionaries and the like. An RI can generally tell when an informant 'holds-true' a sentence even though they do not know the interpretation of the sentence (1984: 135). So, among the primary data for an RI are, for example:

(E) Kurt belongs to the German speech community, Kurt holds-true 'Es regnet' on Saturday at noon, and it is raining near Kurt on Saturday at noon.

Data like (E) are collected from a variety of speakers across a variety of times to confirm or support a generalization like:

(GE) For all speakers x in the German speech community, for any time t, x holds-true 'Es regnet' at t iff it is raining near x at t.

Sentences like (GE) provide evidence that the speakers of the community take some form of words to express a certain truth. Davidson, remarkably, does not consider anything else as potential evidence for interpreting another (1984: 135).

What licenses an inference from data like (GE) to the corresponding T-sentences? Davidson's answer is that a principle of charity is presupposed. According to this principle, the favoured truth theory for a language L must entail T-sentences according to which most of the sentences that speakers of L hold true are true. Under radical interpretation, sentences held true must usually be true because interpretation is partly constituted by this principle of charity. So, once sentences like (GE) are collected, we can infer corresponding T-sentences via a principle of charity (see CHARITY, PRINCIPLE OF §4; MEANING AND

UNDERSTANDING §2; RADICAL TRANSLATION AND RADICAL INTERPRETATION §§7–10).

6 Indirect quotation

Indirect quotation attributions have long been known to possess features which frustrate the construction of satisfactory theories of meaning. For example, the inference (1)–(3) is an apparent instance of substitutivity of identity but it is invalid:

(1) Galileo said that the earth moves.
(2) The earth = the third planet from the sun.
(3) So, Galileo said that the third planet from the sun moves.

Davidson's analysis of indirect discourse is driven by the desire to find a way of incorporating contexts like (1) into a truth theory for a language containing them (1984: 176). His proposal is that we analyse utterances of (1) as consisting of two distinct utterances:

(4) Galileo said that. [The earth moves.]

The first part of (4) is just a relational statement; the second part does not function semantically as part of what is said, but rather is there to serve as the referent of the demonstrative 'that' in an utterance of the first part. How does this get the truth-conditions right? According to Davidson, (4) is true just in case what the speaker has referred to as 'that' is an utterance which *samesays* some assertive utterance by Galileo. 'Samesays' is treated somewhat casually: it is whatever relation between the utterances is required for things to come out intuitively right; two utterances samesay each other just in case they agree in content, import or purport.

Since paraphrase (4) of (1) contains a demonstrative, it is true or false only relative to a context of utterance. A typical utterance of (1) creates a context relative to which 'that' refers to an utterance of the bracketed sentence in (4). And since in most contexts the occurrences of 'that' in (1) and (3) refer to different utterances, (1)–(3) is invalid. It is also clear that (1)–(3) is not an instance of substitutivity of identity, since, on Davidson's analysis, the singular terms 'the earth' and 'the third planet from the sun' do not even occur in (1) and (3).

Despite important virtues, Davidson's account has not won anything like general acceptance. The literature is replete with objections: for example, Lepore and Loewer (1989). Some authors complain the account is too strong; others that it is too weak, and others that it fails to generalize, for example, to other propositional attitudinal ascriptions or to *de re* constructions (see PROPOSITIONAL ATTITUDE STATEMENTS §3).

7 Adverbial modification

We began with Davidson on events. The strongest argument he advances for the existence of events and for his conception of their nature derives, surprisingly, from his views in the philosophy of language. Any theory of meaning for a language must embody a view of the relationship between language and reality. Davidson's conviction is that a theory of meaning, by providing a view about this relationship, offers substantive answers to the various metaphysical questions about reality. In particular, it will require events in order to explain the semantic (logical) form of action, event and causal statements.

Consider the English sentence (1). One obvious candidate for its truth-condition is (2):

(1) John hit Bill.
(2) 'John hit Bill' is true if and only if John hit Bill.

In (2) language is both mentioned and used, and in this sense (2) 'hooks up' language to reality. This hook-up remains silent on the nature of reality. It simply tells us that the English sentence (2) requires for its truth that John hit Bill. Since an adequate theory of meaning must be finite (1984: 4–15), if we try to construct a theory for, say, English, we are forced to read structure into English sentences (see §4). There does not seem to be another way to generate infinitely many sentences from a finite vocabulary. But now consider sentences like (3)–(5):

(3) John hit Bill at six.
(4) John hit Bill at six in the bedroom.
(5) John hit Bill at six in the bedroom with the stick.

There are no specifiable limits upon the number of kinds of adverbial modifiers which can sensibly attach to these sorts of sentences. Therefore, treating each distinctively modified sentence as attributing between John and Bill a distinct *primitive* relation (such as hitting-at-six-in-the-bedroom) threatens to offend against the condition that the theory be finite. On the basis of considerations of this sort, Davidson proffers a proposal which reveals the common elements in these sentences, issues in the correct semantic truth-conditions, and validates the requisite implications – for instance, that (4) implies (3), and so forth. He takes sentences like (1) and (3)–(5) to harbour existential quantifiers ranging over events. The thesis that there are events is true because the best semantics for English requires quantification over them, as witnessed by their counterparts in first order logic (1′), and (3′)–(4′) respectively:

(1′) There is an event e and e is a hitting of Bill by John.
(3′) There is an event e and e is a hitting of Bill by

John and *e* occurs at six.

(4′) There is an event *e* and *e* is a hitting of Bill by John and *e* occurs at six and *e* occurs in the bedroom.

This technique for discerning ontological commitments extends to all cases where quantification and predication are required in order to construct a satisfactory semantics for natural language. The method is a general method for doing ontology (see ADVERBS; ONTOLOGICAL COMMITMENT).

8 Animal thought

According to Davidson, the capacity to think requires facility with language, so that only creatures with a language can think. He defends this controversial thesis in 'Thought and Talk' (1984) and 'Rational Animals' (1985). His argument begins by noting that ascriptions of propositional attitudes – belief, desire, intentions and the like – exhibit semantic opacity. In attributing, for example, to a dog the belief that the cat went up the tree we might wonder whether the propriety of this ascription would be affected were we to substitute for 'the tree' another expression that refers to the tree. If not, this would disclose that our attribution of belief to the dog falls short of literalness. If a dog holds a belief about a tree, it must do so under some description or other (1985: 475).

Davidson's main contention is that semantic opacity could be had only by connecting thought to language. He advances two different lines of argument to this conclusion. The first appeals to holism and it is of the form that since we could never have grounds for ascribing the required background beliefs to creatures without a language, we could never be warranted in ascribing to such creatures any thoughts at all. The argument is that since ascriptions of belief exhibit semantic opacity and since semantic opacity requires that we regard beliefs as possessing some definite intentional content and since the possession of a belief with a definite content presupposes 'endless' further beliefs, it follows that a creature to whom we are warranted in ascribing a belief is one possessing a sophisticated behavioural repertoire; and only linguistic behaviour exhibits the sort of complex pattern that might warrant such ascriptions.

Even if sound, this argument at most establishes that we are unlikely ever to have decisive evidence that a speechless creature has beliefs. Davidson, however, draws the stronger conclusion that 'unless there is actually such a complex pattern of behavior, there is no thought' (1985: 476). He is aware of this shortcoming in his argument and offers another. He argues

that propositional attitudes require a dense network of beliefs, that 'in order to have a belief, it is necessary to have the concept of belief', and that 'in order to have the concept of belief one must have language', that is, one must be a member of a 'speech community' (1985: 478). How, it will be asked, does Davidson get from the ubiquity of belief and the claim that beliefs in turn require second-order beliefs to the conclusion that 'a creature must be a member of a speech community if it is to have the concept of belief' (1984: 170)?

Davidson argues as follows: the possibility of belief or thought generally depends on the concept of a representation that might be true or false; and a concept of truth and falsity includes some notion of an objective, public domain. And this, in turn, is possible only for an interpreter (1984: 170; 1985: 480). Davidson seems to hold that only utterances can afford the fine-grained structure required for attributing thought; for only a creature whose behaviour exhibits the kind of structure implied by a theory of meaning is a creature in which semantically opaque representations can make an appearance (see ANIMAL LANGUAGE AND THOUGHT).

9 Conceptual schemes

In 'On the Very Idea Of a Conceptual Scheme' (1984), Davidson argues that no good sense can be made of the idea that different people, communities, cultures or periods view, conceptualize, or make the world (or their worlds) in different ways; or of the distinction between conceptual scheme and empirical content. He associates conceptual schemes with sets of intertranslatable languages (1984: 191). Different conceptual schemes then correspond to non-intertranslatable languages. He then argues that it is hard to make sense of a total failure of translatability between languages (1984: 185). No one could be in a position to judge that others had concepts or beliefs radically different from their own (1984: 197).

In part, Davidson holds this view both because strong pressures arise from the very nature of radical interpretation (RI) and because 'all understanding of the speech of another involves radical interpretation' (1984: 125). Since RI, and therefore, all interpretation, has a holistic character, it makes no sense to ascribe a single belief to a person except against the background of a very large number of other beliefs. Furthermore, 'belief is in its nature veridical'. That it is so, can be seen 'by considering what determines the existence and contents of a belief' (1986: 432). It all comes back to Davidson's views about the conditions of correct attribution of beliefs and other propositional attitudes, that is, the possibility of RI. In interpreting another, an interpreter ventures hypotheses as to what in the circumstances in question causes the speaker to hold-true the sentence in question and this is supposed to provide them (normally) with the meaning of that sentence. In every case there will be many different causal chains leading to the same utterance. An interpreter must choose one cause and does so by responding to something in the environment ('triangulating') and so converging on something that is a common cause both of their own response and of the utterance of the speaker, thereby correlating the two and thus giving content of the speaker's utterances (Davidson 1991: 159–60).

One immediate consequence is that an RI cannot find speakers to have beliefs if they themselves have no opinion as to their general truth and falsity. Given what beliefs are and how their contents are determined on this story, Davidson is committed to its being impossible that all a person's beliefs about the world might be false. An RI must therefore have beliefs about the world in order to succeed in ascribing beliefs about the world to others. But they also must find that others – if they have beliefs at all – largely agree with them in those beliefs. If Davidson is right, then the crucial aspect of his theory of RI is the importance of causality in determining what someone means or believes. We cannot 'in general fix what someone means independently of what he believes and independently of what caused the belief... The causality plays an indispensable role in determining the content of what we say and believe' (Davidson 1986: 435). So, it is the central role of causation in the fixing of the contents of beliefs that ensures the truth of everything we believe is not in general 'logically independent' of having those very beliefs; and that others cannot differ too much from us about what it is they believe. The way in which the contents of beliefs are determined puts limits on the extent of falsity and diversity discriminable in a coherent set of beliefs. The method of RI 'enforces' on any successful interpreter the conclusion that a speaker's beliefs are largely true and largely like their own. Thus, the possibility of global scepticism is ruled out.

10 Against facts

In recent writings, for example, 'The Myth of the Subjective' (1989) and 'The Structure and Content of Truth' (1990), Davidson attempts to refute the claim that there are representations of reality. In the latter he argues against 'the popular assumption that sentences, or their spoken tokens, or sentence-like entities or configurations in our brains can properly be called "representations", since there is nothing for them to represent' (Davidson 1990). If facts do not make sentences true, then in what sense are they representations? On Davidson's approach to meaning no entities (facts, objects or events) correspond to sentences.

Davidson's main argument against facts and correspondence theories of truth appears in his 'True to the Facts' (1984). There we find the Great Fact argument that given certain plausible assumptions there is at most one fact. The assumptions are 'that a true sentence cannot be made to correspond to something quite different by the substitution of coreferring singular terms, or by the substitution of logically equivalent sentences' and from these assumptions one can prove that 'if true sentences correspond to anything, they all correspond to the same thing' (Davidson 1990: 303). Rightly or wrongly, Davidson takes these assumptions to embody traditional wisdom about facts (see Neale 1995). The main point is that if a context satisfies these two assumptions, then that context is truth functional. So, if a sentence is made true by some fact f, then every materially equivalent sentence is made true by f as well, and thus, f is the Great Fact (see FACTS §2).

See also: AKRASIA §2; ANOMALOUS MONISM; INDIRECT DISCOURSE §2; INTENTION §3; MEANING AND UNDERSTANDING §2; LANGUAGE, SOCIAL NATURE OF §4; RADICAL TRANSLATION AND RADICAL INTERPRETATION §§6–8

List of works

Davidson, D. (1980) *Actions and Events*, Oxford: Oxford University Press. (Contains all of Davidson's essays on action and events mentioned in §§1–2: 'Actions, Reasons, and Causes', 'Causal Relations' and 'The Individuation of Events'.)

—— (1984) *Inquiries into Truth and Interpretation*, Oxford: Oxford University Press. (Includes essays on the philosophy of language ('Thought and Talk' and 'On the Very Idea of a Conceptual Scheme') and 'True to the Facts'. Others mentioned in the article are listed under separate titles.)

—— (1985) 'Rational Animals', in E. Lepore and B. McLaughlin (eds) *Actions and Events: Perspectives on the Philosophy of Donald Davidson*, Oxford: Blackwell, 1985. (Argues against the idea of nonlinguistic thinkers.)

—— (1986) 'A Coherence Theory of Truth and Knowledge', in E. Lepore (ed.) *Truth and Interpretation: Perspectives on the Philosophy of Donald Davidson*, Oxford: Blackwell. (Elaborates a theory of the nature and content of beliefs.)

—— (1989) 'The Myth of the Subjective', in M. Karusz (ed.) *Relativism: Interpretation and Confrontation*,

Paris: University of Notre Dame Press, 1989. (One strand of Davidson's argument that there are no representations of reality.)

—— (1990) 'The Structure and Content of Truth', *The Journal of Philosophy* 87: 279–328. (Argues that there is nothing in reality for sentences to represent.)

—— (1991) 'Epistemology Externalized', *Dialectica* 45: 191–202. (Includes discussion of 'triangulation', contributing to Davidson's argument against the coherence of non-intertranslatable languages.)

References and further reading

Fodor, J. and Lepore, E. (1992) *Holism: A Shopper's Guide*, Oxford: Blackwell. (An extended consideration of arguments, including Davidson's, that the contents of thoughts, concepts and words are fixed only 'holistically' – in concert – rather than each in isolation.)

Lepore, E. (ed.) (1986) *Truth and Interpretation: Perspectives on the Philosophy of Donald Davidson*, Oxford: Blackwell. (Useful essays on this aspect of Davidson's work.)

* Lepore, E. and Loewer, B. (1989) 'You Can Say That Again', *Midwest Studies in Philosophy* 14: 338–56. (Explores criticisms and defences of Davidson's account of propositional attitude ascriptions.)

Lepore, E. and McLaughlin, B. (eds) (1985) *Actions and Events: Perspectives on the Philosophy of Donald Davidson*, Oxford: Blackwell. (Useful essays on this aspect of Davidson's work.)

* Neale, S. (1995) 'Gödel and the Best of All Possible Slingshots', *Mind* 104: 761–825. (A detailed look at arguments by Davidson and others for denying that sentences stand for entities more specific than truth-values.)

ERNIE LEPORE

AL-DAWANI, JALAL AL-DIN (1426–1502)

Jalal al-Din al-Dawani was a prominent philosopher and theologian from Shiraz, who came to the note of Western scholars through an English translation of his ethical treatise the Akhlaq-e Jalali *(Jalalean Ethics), published in 1839. Although the larger part of his work written in Arabic has been little studied, he did write extensively and engaged in a famous and lengthy philosophical dispute with another leading philosopher, Sadr al-Din al-Dashtaki. His metaphysical views were quoted, and refuted, by Mulla Sadra. He emerges as a thinker who combined elements of illuminationist and Peripatetic philosophy (and possibly also interests in Ibn al-'Arabi) to confront theological, ethical, political and mystical concerns.*

Jalal al-Din Muhammad ibn As'ad al-Dawani (or Dawwani) was born near Kazarun, southern Iran, in the village of Davan in AH 830 (AD 1426). He first studied there with his father, who had been taught by the Sayyid al-Sharif al-Jurjani (d. AH 816/AD 1413), before going on to further and complete his education in philosophy, theology and law in Shiraz. In common with the other leading religious scholars of his time and place, he was directly caught up in the turbulent politics of Iran in the second half of the ninth century AH (fifteenth century AD). He was inducted into various religious offices, and many of his works were dedicated to Aq Qoyunlu and other Timurid rulers and princes. He also achieved fame as a teacher in the Begum *madrasa* (Dar al-Aytam) in Shiraz. The question of his religious allegiance, whether Sunni or Shi'i (he wrote theological works of both persuasions), has always been the subject of debate and of many fanciful stories, but it may be of comparatively slight significance given the situation in the Iran of his time, which was marked by a Sunnism with a strong Shi'i colouring. He died in AH 908/AD 1502 near Kazarun, a year or so before the Safavid capture of Shiraz, and is buried in his home town.

Al-Dawani first came to the attention of Western scholarship through the 1839 English translation of his Persian ethical work, the *Akhlaq-e Jalali* (Jalalean Ethics), more correctly known under its original title of *Lawami' al-ishraq fi makarim al-akhlaq* (Lustres of Illumination on the Noble Virtues). Al-Dawani's text marks a third stage in the development of the ethical strand of writing begun by IBN MISKAWAYH with the *Tahdhib al-akhlaq* (Cultivation of Morals) and continued by Nasir al-Din AL-TUSI with his *Akhlaq-e Nasiri* (Nasirean Ethics), on which al-Dawani's work is closely modelled. Al-Dawani retains al-Tusi's division of the text into three sections – ethics, economics and politics – and subdivides his work similarly, although significantly he entirely omits al-Tusi's theoretical first section of the ethics. The title, *Lawami' al-ishraq* (Lustres of Illumination), may indicate the author's *ishraqi* (illuminationist) and mystical concerns. The political content of the work has been of some interest to historians, as regards both its descriptions of the ideal ruler and the titles used for its dedicatee, the Aq Qoyunlu Uzun Hasan, which betray a possible *ishraqi* influence and seem to foreshadow the extravagant claims of Isma'il, the first Safavid monarch of Iran.

The *Akhlaq-e Jalali* is generally acknowledged to

be a less satisfactory work than al-Tusi's, being weaker in argument and encumbered with anecdotal material (following the literary taste of the period) from both Greek (indirectly) and Islamic sources, being more 'Ciceronian', as its 1839 translator, W.F. Thompson, apologetically expressed it. It is therefore easier to admire the work for its style than for its intellectual rigour. Thompson's translation does not improve matters, thanks to its baroque literary style and ponderous sentiments.

Apart from the *Akhlaq-e Jalali*, over seventy-five works by al-Dawani are recorded, covering the fields of philosophy, mysticism, theology and exegesis. Of particular interest to subsequent philosophers were his commentary on al-Suhrawardi's *Hayakil al-nur* (The Temples of Light), *Shawakil al-hur fi sharh Hayakil al-nur* (The Houri's Haunches in Commentary of the Temple of Light) and his series of glosses on the commentary by 'Ala' al-Din al-Qushji (d. AH 879/AD 1474) on al-Tusi's *Tajrid al-kalam* (Abstract of Theology). In both works he engaged with his contemporary Sadr al-Din al-Dashtaki (and subsequently the latter's son Ghiyath al-Din). All three were greatly influenced by AL-SUHRAWARDI, although the Dashtakis perhaps more than al-Dawani. Sadr al-Din denied any reality to existence, either mental or extramental, and could thus be described as an extreme essentialist. Al-Dawani, on the other hand, held a view which harks back to Fakhr al-Din AL-RAZI. Existence in the outside world, for al-Dawani, is a single necessary reality, absolutely devoid of multiplicity, and is thus equal to God. Everything else is contingent: 'entities' whose existence is not real but only various 'portions of existence' (*hisas*) conceived by the mind. The reality of the external world is established solely through quiddities. Al-Dawani's illuminationism is thus a modified one, but it proved more influential than al-Dashtaki's extreme form, for it was adopted by MIR DAMAD and initially by the latter's pupil MULLA SADRA before he turned to his radical existentialism.

See also: IBN AL-'ARABI; ILLUMINATIONIST PHILOSOPHY; MYSTICAL PHILOSOPHY IN ISLAM

List of works

al-Dawani (1467–77?) *Akhlaq-e Jalali* (Jalalean Ethics), ed. M.K. Shirazi, Calcutta: printed at Habl-ul-Matin Press, 1911; trans. W.F. Thompson, *Practical philosophy of the Mohammadan people...*, *being a translation of the Akhlaq-i-Jalaly...from the Persian of Fakir Jany Muhammad Asaad...*, London: Oriental Translation Fund of Great Britain and Ireland, 1839; repr. Karachi, 1977.

(No critical edition has yet been done of this work and the Shirazi edition is only one of several lithographs and printings. Thompson's translation, which is only partial, suffers from an overweight style, and the translator's attempts to stress in his notes the common Greek ancestry of Islamic and European philosophical ethics at the expense of the Islamic content of the work is now probably of little interest except to students of early nineteenth-century British thought.)

—— (1426–1502) *Shawakil-al-hur fi sharh-i-Hayakil-al-nur* (The Houri's Haunches in Commentary on the Temple of Light), ed. M. Abdul Haq and M.Y. Kokan, Madras: Government Oriental Manuscripts Library, 1953. (Arabic text only, though there is a brief English introduction.)

References and further reading

Newman, A.J. (1994) 'Davani, Jalal al-Din Mohammad', *Encyclopaedia Iranica*, vol. VII, fasc. 2, Costa Meza, CA: Mazda Publishers, 132–3. (A mainly biographical article giving most of the relevant sources.)

Rosenthal, E.I.J. (1962) *Political Thought in Medieval Islam*, Cambridge: Cambridge University Press, 210–23. (A chapter in this work examines the political section of the *Akhlaq-e Jalali*.)

Wickens, G.M. (1984) 'Aklaq-e Jalali', *Encyclopaedia Iranica*, vol. I, fasc. 7, London: Routledge & Kegan Paul, 724. (A brief article on al-Dawani's best known work.)

JOHN COOPER

DAXUE

Originally a chapter in the Liji *(Book of Rites), one of the Five Classics in the Confucian tradition, the Daxue (Great Learning) has for centuries attained the status of a canon, arguably the most influential foundational text in East Asian Confucian humanism. When the great neo-Confucian thinker Zhu Xi grouped the* Daxue *with the Zhongyong (Doctrine of the Mean), another chapter in the* Liji, *the Confucian* Analects *and the* Mengzi *as the Four Books, its prominence in the Confucian scriptural tradition was assured. Since the Four Books with Master Zhu's commentaries became the required readings for the civil service examinations in 1313, and since Master Zhu insisted that the* Daxue *must be studied first among the Four, it has been widely acknowledged as the quintessential Confucian text.*

Intent on presenting the case of Confucian moral and political agenda, the *Daxue* (Great Learning) establishes the three basic principles: enlightening the enlightened virtue, loving the people and abiding in the highest good. These neatly outline the basic concerns of the Confucian project: self-cultivation, social responsibility and ultimate human flourishing (see CONFUCIAN PHILOSOPHY, CHINESE). Enlightening the enlightened virtue is based on the premise that although human nature is naturally endowed with 'enlightened virtue' (*mingde*), a life-long moral self-cultivation is necessary so that our innate virtue will continue to be enlightened (see SELF-CULTIVATION, CHINESE THEORIES OF). This paradox is central to Confucian teaching: while ontologically we are already sages, existentially we must always try to become sages. The second principle, 'loving the people', specifies that self-cultivation, far from being the quest for inner spirituality as a lonely struggle, necessarily involves communication with others. The self as a centre of relationships entails an ever-expanding network of human-relatedness. Loving the people, comparable to the Christian dictum of 'loving thy neighbour', is, according to WANG YANGMING (1472–1529), a constitutive aspect of self-cultivation. However, ZHU XI interpreted this particular principle significantly differently, as 'renew the people'. He was able to do so by changing one single word *qinmin* (to be close in the sense of loving and caring) to *xinmin* (to renew the people). This conflict of interpretation has profound implications for the style of governance implicit in the *Daxue*. The third principle, 'abiding in the highest good', does not raise philological issues, but the semantic significance is difficult to determine. Does it mean that the loftiest moral aspiration must serve as guidance for ordinary human existence, or that we must strive to approximate that which is always beyond our reach?

However, it is the eight steps in the *Daxue* that offer a holistic vision and a practical programme of self-cultivation, a way of learning to be human. These eight steps are: (1) investigation of things, (2) extension of knowledge, (3) authentication of the will, (4) rectification of the heart-and-mind, (5) cultivation of the person, (6) regulation of the family, (7) governance of the state and (8) universal peace. All are centred around self-cultivation (step 5). Thus, steps 1–4 constitute the inner dimension and 6–8 symbolize the outer manifestation of self-cultivation. The centrality of self-cultivation is unequivocal:

> From the Son of Heaven down to the common people, all must regard cultivation of the person as the root. There is never a case where the root is in disorder and yet the branches are in order. There

has never been a case when what is treated with great importance becomes a matter of slight importance and what is treated with slight importance becomes a matter of great importance.

> (*Daxue*)

The sense of priority and sequence is crucial in the *Daxue*. The life orientation implicit in the text demands that a sense of direction (toward the highest good) can provide an anchorage for our moral self-realization. With this anchorage, we can have a fixed purpose which leads to tranquility of the mind. With tranquility of the mind, we can attain serene repose and only in serene repose can we cogitate. Only through cogitation can we fully embody the virtue that is originally ours. The Confucian project so conceived esteems learning, both as an acquisition of knowledge and as a process of self-transformation. However, it seems obvious that the acquisition of knowledge through the investigation of things is not empirical work for the sake of enhancing our cognitive intelligence; rather, it is the cultivation of moral knowledge as an integral part of our self-understanding.

The relationship between knowledge and morality raises challenging questions in Chinese philosophy. Is it possible that the investigation of things and the extension of knowledge naturally lead to the authentication of the will? Must we begin the process of self-cultivation by making up our mind that the knowledge of the good is not empirically acquired but experientially confirmed? Should the investigation of things be understood as learning about the external world or should it be conceived as a form of self-reflection in the lifeworld? Understandably, the *Daxue* has become a basic reference and a primary source for numerous fruitful scholarly and philosophical debates in Chinese intellectual history.

However, it is beyond dispute that this approach to learning presupposes that the primary purpose of education is character building. The *Daxue*, as a form of adult education, offers a comprehensive programme for human flourishing. The programme, built upon the 'Elementary Learning', a highly ritualized guide to self-improvement, focuses on political leadership. In the modern context, the argument makes sense only if we think of it as addressed to rulers and their ministers, rather than to any ordinary person in search of moral guidance. Nevertheless, the strength of the argument lies in its assumptive reason that rulership, or leadership in general, proves to be identical with the moral self-cultivation of all people in ordinary human existence in the lifeworld. Indeed, how we exercise power and influence in the presumed privacy of our homes is politically meaningful and, thus, ought to be made publicly accountable. The *Daxue*, a brief essay of some 1,750 words, carries a profound message for cultivating politically significant ethical intelligence for the global community.

See also: CHINESE CLASSICS; CHINESE PHILOSOPHY; CONFUCIAN PHILOSOPHY, CHINESE; SELF-CULTIVATION, CHINESE THEORIES OF; ZHONGYONG

References and further reading

* Chan Wing-tsit (1963) *A Source Book in Chinese Philosophy*, Princeton, NJ: Princeton University Press. (A standard translation of the *Daxue*, with commentary.)

Schwartz, B.I. (1985) *The World of Thought in Ancient China*, Cambridge, MA: Harvard University Press. (A discussion of the philosophical content of this short yet influential document.)

Tu Wei-ming (1989) *Centrality and Commonality: An Essay on Confucian Religiousness*, Albany, NY: State University of New York Press. (Although focused primarily on the *Zhongyong*, this monograph provides a philosophical context for the *Daxue*.)

TU WEIMING

DE

Across the corpus of pre-Qin philosophical literature, de, conventionally translated as 'potency' or 'virtue', seems to have a fundamental cosmological significance from which its other connotations are derived. We begin from the pervasive assumption that existence is an uncaused, spontaneous process. It is ziran: *so-of-itself. As a total field, this dynamic process is called* dao; *the individuated existents in this field – its various foci – are called* de.

In the Daoist literature, *de* denotes the particular as a focus of potency in this process conception of existence. *De* is any particular disposition of the totality. The *Daodejing* – literally, the classic of *dao* and *de* – states: 'The great *dao* is so expansive. It reaches in all directions. All of individuated existence arises because of it' (*Daodejing* 34) (see DAODEJING).

When *de* is cultivated and accumulated, so that the particular is integrated utterly with its environments, the distinction between *dao* and *de* – between field and focus – collapses. *De* as an individuating notion is transformed into *de* as an integrating notion. The *Daodejing* 28 observes: 'One who possesses *de* in

abundance is comparable to a new-born babe.' In this literature, both Daoist and Confucian, the infant, the uncarved block and the exemplary person are all metaphors for a condition in which one does not distinguish oneself from one's environments. These metaphors illustrate the assumption that any particular, when viewed in terms of its intrinsic relatedness, entails the full process of existence. Such being the case, because the babe is a matrix through which the full consequence of undiscriminated existence can be brought to focus and experienced, it can be used as a metaphor for the *de* which is *dao*.

The early Confucian tradition limited its concerns to the social and political problems of the human community. At this level, the cultivation of *de* is to overcome the discreteness and discontinuity of the inchoate self in the direction of continuity and social harmony. Through achieved excellence, one becomes a model for others and an object of deference. *De* is both 'potency' and 'virtue' in the sense that each person is a meaning-creating and meaning-disclosing focus. As one becomes extended in community through patterns of deference, one's capacity for valuation is proportionately increased. The human being is a world maker, and the greater one's proportions, the great one's efficacy as a maker of values.

The extension of *de* entails both an act of intending and the attraction of the support necessary to effect what is intended. The particular initiating the direction focuses this support as coextensive with its own particularity. At the same time, the particular becomes coextensive with 'other' by overcoming its particularity and accommodating the natural direction and volition of the 'other' to integrate them into its own field of interpretation. As artist, as communal leader, as teacher, one is able to organize one's natural, social and cultural environments and disclose their possibilities for productive harmony. One is able to manifest, interpret and display the local culture.

On the political level, the relationship between ruler and people is described in terms of *de*. To the extent that the ruler reaches out to become coextensive with the prevailing cultural propensities of the people, he expresses the values of the community. To the extent that he becomes culturally coextensive with them through deference, they come to share his values and moral insights, and he wins them over. If we consider agency, *de* means literally 'bounty' or 'beneficence' as it extends down from the ruler, and 'gratitude' as it is disclosed in the deference of the people. If, more appropriate to the Chinese tradition, we think situationally, *de* is the disposition of being both benefactor and beneficiary through productive, non-coercive communal relations. As the *de* of the people is manifest within the ruler's *de*, his potency is enhanced and he becomes the wind that bends the grass, the north star around which the other stars revolve, the maker and transmitter of culture to which other persons subscribe. It is in this sense that the emperor is the empire, and the patriarch is the family.

There is a coextensiveness of ruler and people in the sense that the ruler expresses the people through his government by accommodating their cultural proclivities and thus orchestrating an interpretation of culture that is both his and theirs. There is always, in this conception of *de*, a tension between attempting to maximize the possibilities for harmony provided by attending conditions, and the expression of an interpretation that does justice to one's own uniqueness and sense of appropriateness. It is the sensitive balancing of these forces that produces harmony within all human environments (see CULTURE; SOVEREIGNTY).

See also: CHINESE PHILOSOPHY; CONFUCIUS; DAO; DAOIST PHILOSOPHY

References and further reading

Ames, R.T. (1991) 'Nietzsche's "Will to Power" and Chinese "Virtuality" (*De*): A Comparative Study' in G. Parkes (ed.) *Nietzsche and Asian Thought*, Chicago, IL: University of Chicago Press. (A discussion of *de* that seeks to shed light on Nietzschean creativity.)

Hall, D.L. and Ames, R.T. (1987) *Thinking Through Confucius*, Albany, NY: State University of New York Press. (A study of the central vocabulary of classical Confucianism.)

DAVID L. HALL
ROGER T. AMES

DE BEAUVOIR, SIMONE

see BEAUVOIR, SIMONE DE

DE BIRAN, PIERRE FRANÇOIS MAINE *see* MAINE DE BIRAN, PIERRE-FRANÇOIS

DE BUFFON, COMTE GEORGES LOUIS LECLERC

see BUFFON, GEORGES LOUIS LECLERC, COMTE DE

DE CORDEMOY, GÉRAUD

see CORDEMOY, GÉRAUD DE

DE DICTO *see* DE RE/DE DICTO

DE FONTENELLE, BERNARD

see FONTENELLE, BERNARD DE

DE LA FORGE, LOUIS

see LA FORGE, LOUIS DE

DE LA METTRIE, JULIEN OFFROY *see* LA METTRIE, JULIEN OFFROY DE

DE MAN, PAUL (1919–83)

De Man's work is among the most renowned and influential in American literary theory of the latter twentieth century, especially regarding literary theory's emergence as an interdisciplinary and philosophically ambitious discourse. Always emphasizing the linguistic aspects of a literary work over thematic, semantic or evaluative ones, de Man specifically focuses on the figurative features of literary language and their consequences for the undecidability of meaning. His extension of his mode of 'rhetorical reading' to philosophic texts also participates in the blurring of generic and institutional distinctions between literature and philosophy, a tendency pronounced in French philosophy of the latter twentieth century.

1 **Deconstruction and Derrida**
2 **Literary theory**
3 **Philosophical critique**

1 **Deconstruction and Derrida**

Paul de Man, born in Belgium and educated in

comparative literature at Harvard, taught comparative literature at Cornell, Johns Hopkins and Yale universities. Associated with Jacques DERRIDA and deconstruction, and more generally with post-structuralism, de Man already exerted considerable influence through his teaching before the advent of deconstruction and his publication of an essay on Derrida. His association with Derrida and deconstruction is in part due to their subsequent friendship and colleagueship, but it is in part the artefact of the observer. De Man shares with Derrida the unrelenting attention to questions of language, and the rigorous practice of close reading of texts; with regard to deconstruction, he shares that practice's 'reversal' and 'reinscription' of assumed priorities – in de Man's case, the priority of meaning over the linguistic and tropological devices that ostensibly convey meaning, reversed and reinscribed by him as the irreducible textual productivity of tropes (metaphor, chiasmus, prosopopeia) and other linguistic 'materiality' that leaves meaning suspended in undecidability and reading suspended in rhetorical repetitions and 'disfigurations' of the text before it. But he differs from Derrida in that he believes (as he argued in 'The Rhetoric of Blindness', in de Man 1971) that deconstruction is not something that one does to texts – as a philosopher, say, operating against the dominant grain of institutional philosophy – but rather something that texts do by themselves and to their readers. Thus de Man also de-emphasizes the 'institutional' aspect of Derridean deconstruction's 'reinscription' of problematic priorities back upon the institutional loci of their teaching and application, although in his later work issues of authority, ideology and critiques of falsehood are increasingly pronounced.

2 Literary theory

De Man's literary theory developed by way of studies of novels and poetry as well as philosophic texts, but it always displays several dominant features: drawing primarily upon romantic and modern authors, he foregrounds the rhetorical language of texts and explores its consequences for what texts actually, rather than apparently, mean; how they actually, if contradictorily, function; and how, ultimately, they may resist meaning and any satisfied aesthetic sense of their formal and structural workings. In essays from the 1950s and 1960s, borrowing from European phenomenology and its terminologies of consciousness, intentionality, temporality and being, de Man accents the difference and tension between poetic language's power to posit and imagine linguistically determined conditions on the one hand, and literature's false attractions – representational and nostalgic – toward natural objects and ontological being on the other. His highly influential essay 'The Rhetoric of Temporality' (1969), which also signals his turn toward a focus upon rhetorical language, analyses as allegory the perpetual reinstating of a temporal distance between a subject and its origin, and as irony the unbridgeable discrepancy between a linguistic and an empirical self. In his equally influential collection *Blindness and Insight* (1971), de Man studies European writers and critics (Husserl, Heidegger, Binswanger, Lukács, Blanchot, Poulet, Nietzsche, Derrida, Baudelaire, Mallarmé) to demonstrate the priority of a text's 'insight' or self-knowing 'rhetoricity' over the 'blindness' of its readers who unwittingly ('blindly') repeat the text's structure and statement when they believe they are critically most distant from them. De Man here extends the category of the 'literary' to include philosophic texts as well as literature conventionally construed: 'any text that implicity or explicitly signifies its own rhetorical mode and prefigures its own misunderstanding as the correlative of its rhetorical nature' (1971: 136). *Allegories of Reading* (1979) expands the sense of rhetoricity as the undecidability between literal and figurative meanings of a text, in a series of analyses of the 'allegories' or figurative narratives of mis- and non-understanding that generate themselves in response to the textual figures and rhetoric of such authors as Yeats, Rilke and Proust but also Nietzsche and above all, Rousseau. In this book as well as in subsequent essays on Wordsworth, Shelley, Baudelaire and others (collected in *The Rhetoric of Romanticism*, 1984), de Man increasingly emphasizes what he calls the 'materiality' of language, its 'inscription', meaning the nonsemantic, noncognitive dimensions of language that subtend all linguistic acts not only as grammar, for example, subtends semantics, but also as the sheer positing of linguistic signifiers and their frequent interference with or 'disfiguring' of signification subtend all possible logical, grammatical or semiotic codifications and decodings of language. This latter aspect of his work marks de Man as post-structuralist, in resolutely refusing any reduction of language and signification to code.

3 Philosophical critique

Throughout his work de Man draws with seeming indifference from philosophy as well as literature and criticism to develop his literary theory. This leads to a deliberate blurring of distinctions between the two kinds of discourse, which is perhaps an easy and uncontroversial manoeuvre when he treats authors who themselves challenged or ignored the difference (Pascal, Rousseau, Nietzsche, Benjamin, Heidegger, Blanchot), as, for example, in his reconfounding of Rousseau's confusing differentiations between natural, fictional and historical conditions. But in a number of essays, some left unfinished by him and just recently (1996) published, de Man attempts a more frontal critique of certain assumptions and goals of mainline Western philosophy. Writing on Locke, Kant and Hegel, de Man not only signals the tropological substratum that enables but also destabilizes the establishment of certain philosophic concepts (for example, a 'ground'), he also calls into question the claims that there is thought that is distinguishable from – nobler, more ideal than – language in its materiality (Hegel), and that language ought to or can be modelled on phenomenal and cognitive presentation of meaning from the world (Kant). He subsumes the 'matching' of language, and with it of grammar and logic, to a phenomenal-cognitive model of nature and its human experience, under the names of an 'aesthetic formalization' or 'aesthetic ideology'; and he criticizes it in the name of language's tropological, material and ultimately non-signifying otherness from all aesthetics and other rational-logical extensions that would establish a truthful continuity between the world and language or vice versa. De Man's work, then, a collection of radical, unique and often incisive readings of literary and philosophic texts that remains (1997) unconsidered by most professional philosophers, offers a view of language and textuality that is an anti-theory of philosophy as well as a controversial theory of literature.

See also: DECONSTRUCTION; POST-STRUCTURALISM

List of works

Man, P. de (1969) 'The Rhetoric of Temporality ', in C.S. Singleton (ed.) *Interpretation: Theory and Practice*, Baltimore, MD: Johns Hopkins University Press; repr. in *Blindness and Insight*, 2nd edn, Minneapolis, MN: University of Minnesota Press. (De Man's single most influential piece of writing.)

—— (1971) *Blindness and Insight: Essays in the Rhetoric of Contemporary Criticism*, New York: Oxford University Press. (Includes the important critique of Derrida, 'The Rhetoric of Blindness'.)

—— (1979) *Allegories of Reading: Figural Language in Rousseau, Nietzsche, Rilke and Proust*, New Haven, CT: Yale University Press. (The second part is a sustained deconstructive reading of Rousseau.)

—— (1984) *The Rhetoric of Romanticism*, New York:

Columbia University Press. (Collection of essays, principally on poets, from 1960 to his death.)

—— (1986) *The Resistance to Theory*, Minneapolis, MN: University of Minnesota Press. (The title essay is especially important for his critique of philosophy.)

—— (1996) *Aesthetic Ideology*, Minneapolis, MN: University of Minnesota Press. (Collects his most important papers on philosophy.)

References and further reading

Chase, C. (1994) 'De Man, Paul', in M. Groden and M. Kresiwirth (eds) *The Johns Hopkins Guide to Literary Theory and Criticism*, Baltimore, MD: Johns Hopkins University Press. (An authoritative and comprehensive introduction to de Man's literary theory.)

Derrida, J. (1986) *Mémoires for Paul de Man*, trans. C. Linsay, J. Culler and E. Cadava, New York: Columbia University Press. (A profound meditation, at once analytic, speculative and memoiristic, about de Man's work and the place of deconstruction in the USA.)

Gasché, R. (1989) 'In-Difference to Philosophy: De Man on Kant, Hegel and Nietzsche', in L. Waters and W. Godzich (eds) *Reading de Man Reading*, Minneapolis, MN: University of Minnesota Press. (A rigorously critical analysis of de Man's 'in-difference' to some of philosophy's assumptions and procedures.)

Godzich, W. (1983) 'Caution! Reader at Work!', introduction to 2nd edn of P. de Man, *Blindness and Insight*, Minneapolis, MN: University of Minnesota Press. (A useful introduction, distinguishing de Man's 'reading' from other critical and interpretive practices.)

—— (1986) 'The Tiger of the Paper Mat', Foreword to P. de Man, *The Resistance to Theory*, Minneapolis, MN: University of Minnesota Press. (Especially helpful in sketching the philosophical background and importance of de Man's use of resistance.)

Hamacher, W. (1989) 'LECTIO: De Man's Imperative', in L. Waters and W. Godzich (eds) *Reading de Man Reading*, Minneapolis, MN: University of Minnesota Press. (The most incisive analysis thus far of the active or performative aspects of 'reading' in de Man's writings.)

Jacobs, C. (1989) 'Allegories of Reading Paul de Man', in L. Waters and W. Godzich (eds) *Reading de Man Reading*, Minneapolis, MN: University of Minnesota Press. (The best example of deploying de

Man's reading of allegory to read de Man on allegory.)

TIMOTHY BAHTI

DE MONTESQUIEU, CHARLES BARON

see MONTESQUIEU, CHARLES BARON DE

DE MORGAN, AUGUSTUS (1806–71)

Augustus De Morgan was an important British mathematician and logician. Much of his logical work was directed to expanding the traditional syllogistic theory, and to meeting the objections of Sir William Hamilton and his allies to the techniques he used. More important for the future of logic, though, was De Morgan's work in two areas: the logic of complex (compound) terms, in which he essentially developed the theory of Boolean algebra, and his introduction of the logic of relations as a serious topic for formal logic. His work on probability logic, while flawed, was also significant.

Augustus De Morgan was born in Madura, India. He grew up in England and graduated from Trinity College, Cambridge in 1827. His mathematical abilities were such that he was appointed Professor of Mathematics at the newly founded University of London (now University College) the following year. He resigned on grounds of principle in 1831, but returned in 1836. He then held his professorship for thirty years, resigning, once again for reasons of principle, in 1866.

De Morgan was an amazingly prolific writer for both specialist and general audiences. As a mathematician, he clarified the concepts of mathematical induction and of limits, and he proved an important result about infinite series. He made significant contributions to the foundations and philosophy of algebra, and was deeply interested in the history and bibliography of mathematics. He is best known for the logical works which he published from 1847 to 1862. Their interpretation is difficult, however, for De Morgan's unusually fertile imagination was often constrained by being placed at the service of an essentially conservative attempt to extend the theory of the syllogism.

Much of De Morgan's published work arose from his highly publicized controversy with Sir William HAMILTON over the quantification of the predicate. At first this dispute concerned Hamilton's charge that De Morgan had plagiarized from Hamilton's work, but it was soon resolved in De Morgan's favour. It then became a lively controversy over the comparative merits of Hamilton's and De Morgan's modifications of traditional logic. To the modern reader, much of this dispute seems very dated. However, De Morgan's analyses of categorical propositions remain interesting. He introduced into logic the concept of the universe of discourse, and he allowed that for each term, 'X', there would also be its contrary, 'x'. With this notation, there are eight possible categorical propositions:

(1) All Xs are Ys
(2) All xs are ys
(3) All Xs are ys
(4) All xs are Ys
(5) Some Xs are Ys
(6) Some xs are ys
(7) Some Xs are ys
(8) Some xs are Ys

All except (4) and (6) can be expressed as traditional categorical propositions using only 'X' and 'Y'; (4), however, must be stated as 'Everything is X or Y', and (6), its negation, as 'Some things are neither Xs or Ys'. De Morgan devised an ingenious 'spicular' notation for expressing these forms, which allowed him to state concisely the rules of inference for this enlarged system.

If De Morgan's syllogistic modifications look backwards, two facets of his work look forwards. The first is the often neglected logic of complex (or compound) terms in his *Formal Logic* (1847: ch. 6). In this treatment, 'XY' stands for the 'conjunction' of the classes X and Y, and 'X, Y' stands for their 'disjunction'. The most familiar feature of this section is 'De Morgan's laws':

$$\text{non-}(XY) = x,y \text{ and non-}(X, Y) = xy$$

However, there is much more to this section than these laws; it contains, in essence, the full theory of Boolean algebra. In fact, De Morgan's system is probably closer to modern Boolean algebra than Boole's (see BOOLE, G.; BOOLEAN ALGEBRA).

One interesting feature of De Morgan's account is his characterization of conjunction and disjunction. Where '$X)P$' stands for 'Every X is P', the Conjunctive Principle is

If $X)P$ and $X)Q$ then $X)PQ$,

and the Disjunctive Principle is

If $P)X$ and $Q)X$ then $P,Q)X$.

These laws for conjunction and disjunction (intersection and union) today provide the basis for one of the two common formulations of Boolean algebra.

De Morgan's other main contribution to logic was his powerful logic of relations. Philosophical considerations led him to give a relational analysis of all propositions; and this resulted, in turn, in his formal logic of relations ('On the Syllogism IV', 1860).

Where 'X' and 'Y' are singular terms, and 'L' and 'M' are relational expressions, De Morgan used the following notation:

$X..LY$	X is an L of Y
$X.LY$	X is not an L of Y
$X..lY$	X is a non-L of Y
$X..LMY$	X is an L of an M of Y
$X..LM'Y$	X is an L of every M of Y
$X..L,MY$	X is an L of none but Ms of Y
$L))M$	L is included in M

De Morgan stated a great many relational identities, such as

$$not(L^{-1}) = l^{-1}$$

and

$$(LM)^{-1} = M^{-1}L^{-1}$$

One of De Morgan's most interesting propositions is 'Theorem K':

$$\text{If } LM))N, \text{ then } nM^{-1}))1,$$

for which he provided an elegant demonstration.

De Morgan seemed most interested in applying his logic of relations to the analysis of the syllogism. Thus, while he hinted at some of the elaborations of this logic which would come later, he did not carry them out, nor did he work further on the logic of relations.

Some of De Morgan's other ideas, such as that of the numerically definite syllogism, have had only a minor impact on the history of logic. However, his attempt to include within logic the theory of probability, conceived of as the theory of rational degrees of belief, was of considerable importance. His concern was in calculating the probability of the conclusion of a logically valid argument whose premises are merely probable. Within this domain, he emphasized traditional problems about the uses of authority and testimony in argument. While his analyses of such cases were insightful, they were often flawed by a failure to require the stochastic independence of the elements of a conjunction when replacing the probability of a conjunction by the product of the probabilities of its conjuncts (see PROBABILITY THEORY AND EPISTEMOLOGY).

See also: LOGIC IN THE 19TH CENTURY §§3–4

List of works

De Morgan, A. (1838) *An Essay on Probabilities*, London: Longman's; repr. New York: Arno Press, 1981. (Contains a useful introduction to De Morgan's philosophy of probability.)

—— (1847) *Formal Logic*, London: Taylor & Walton; repr. London: Open Court, 1926. (De Morgan's major early work.)

—— (1966) *On the Syllogism and Other Logical Writings*, ed. P. Heath, New Haven, CT: Yale University Press. (A carefully prepared comprehensive edition of De Morgan's other logical writings. His essay 'On the Syllogism IV' (1860) appears on pages 208–46.)

References and further reading

Hailperin, T. (1988) 'The Development of Probability Logic from Leibniz to MacColl', *History and Philosophy of Logic* 9: 131–91. (A critical study of several attempts at devising a probability logic, including De Morgan's.)

Heath, P. (1966) 'Introduction' to *On the Syllogism and Other Logical Writings*, vii–xxxi. (An account of De Morgan's life and works, especially strong on the controversy with Hamilton.)

Mansel, H.L. (1851) 'Recent Extensions of Formal Logic', *North British Review* 15: 90–121. (An extended criticism of the new logical work of De Morgan and others from a more traditional point of view.)

Martin, R.M. (1979) 'De Morgan and the Logic of Relations', in R.M. Martin, *Peirce's Logic of Relations and Other Studies*, Lisse: Peter de Ridder Press, 46–53. (An interpretation of De Morgan's logic of relations using the language of contemporary symbolic logic.)

Merrill, D.D. (1990) *Augustus De Morgan and the Logic of Relations*, Dordrecht: Kluwer. (A study of the philosophical and technical aspects of De Morgan's logic of relations.)

DANIEL D. MERRILL

DE PIZAN, CHRISTINE

see CHRISTINE DE PIZAN

DE RE/DE DICTO

'*De re*' *and* '*de dicto*' *have been used to label a host of different, albeit interrelated, distinctions.* '*De dicto*' *means* '*of, or concerning, a dictum*', *that is, something having representative content, such as a sentence, statement or proposition.* '*De re*' *means* '*of, or concerning, a thing*'. *For example, a* de dicto *belief is a belief that a bearer of representative content is true, while a* de re *belief is a belief concerning some thing, that it has a particular characteristic.*

Consider the following example:

> *John believes his next-door neighbour is a Buddhist.*

This statement is ambiguous. Construed de dicto, *it is true in the following circumstance. John has never had any contact with his next-door neighbour. Nevertheless, John believes that his next-door neighbour is bound to be a Buddhist. Construed in this* de dicto *fashion, the statement does not attribute to John a belief that is distinctively about a particular individual. In contrast, construed* de re, *it does attribute to John a belief that is about a particular individual. For example, construed* de re, *the statement is true in the following circumstance. John encounters his next-door neighbour, Fred, at a party without realizing that Fred is his next-door neighbour. On the basis of his conversation with Fred, John forms a belief about the individual who is in fact his next-door neighbour to the effect that he is a Buddhist.*

1 **The different distinctions**
2 **Relationships between the different distinctions**

1 The different distinctions

'*De dicto*' means 'of, or concerning, a dictum'. '*De re*' means 'of, or concerning, a thing'. Roughly, a *de dicto* belief is a belief that a bearer of representative content (that is, a statement, sentence, proposition or such like) is true, while a *de re* belief is a belief concerning some thing, that it has a particular characteristic. (I)–(IX) below are a number of different distinctions that have been described as *de re/de dicto* distinctions in the literature.

(I) In the case of modality and belief we can draw scope distinctions. Consider the following sentences:

(1)　Every effect necessarily has a cause.

(2)　Joan believes her husband is an axe murderer.

(1) and (2) manifest a scope ambiguity. (1) is ambiguous between:

(1′)　□ (if *e* is an effect then *e* has a cause),

in which the entire sentence 'If *e* is an effect then *e* has a cause' falls within the scope of '□'; and:

(1*)　If *e* is an effect, □ (*e* has a cause),

in which only the part '*e* has a cause' falls within the scope of '□'. (2) may, likewise, be disambiguated as:

(2′)　Joan believes that her husband is an axe murderer

or:

(2*)　Joan's husband is believed by Joan to be an axe murderer.

(1′) and (2′) give the *de dicto* readings of (1) and (2). (1*) and (2*) give their *de re* readings. According to (1′), it is impossible for something to be an effect without having a cause – something few would dispute. According to (1*), it is impossible for anything which is an effect not to have been caused – a much more controversial claim. (2′) implies that Joan has the disconcerting belief she could express by uttering, 'My husband is an axe murderer'. (2*) implies that Joan has a less disconcerting belief. According to (2*), she believes that someone, whom, perhaps unbeknownst to her, she is married to, is an axe murderer (see PROPOSITIONAL ATTITUDES §2).

(II) A sentence expresses a *de re* modality provided that some object essentially features in its truth-condition in the following sense: its truth-value depends on the characteristics that the object might have. For example, the sentence 'Possibly Fred is a Buddhist' expresses a *de re* modality because its truth-value depends on whether a certain individual, Fred, could have the characteristic of being a Buddhist.

(III) Some hold that predicates such as 'is necessarily human' or 'is possibly six feet tall' attribute a special kind of property known as a modal property. A *de re* modal attribution attributes a modal property. For example, 'John is necessarily human' expresses a *de re* modal attribution if it attributes to John the modal property of being necessarily human.

(IV) Another *de re/de dicto* distinction depends on the distinction between rigid and non-rigid designators. Proper names such as 'Napoleon' are said to be rigid designators because they designate the same thing in any possible situation in which they designate at all (see PROPER NAMES §2). According to this way of drawing the distinction, a modal sentence expresses a *de re* modality if it contains a rigid designator falling within the scope of a modal operator. For example, 'It might have been the case that Napoleon spoke Chinese' expresses a *de re* modality, in contrast to 'It might have been the case that the most famous French general spoke Chinese'.

(V) Quine (1953) insists that modalities are invariably relativized to a description in the following sense. We cannot say that something necessarily or possibly has a characteristic absolutely: we can only say that something necessarily or possibly has a characteristic relative to a description. Bill Clinton is necessarily a president relative to the description '42nd President'. He is contingently a president relative to the description 'husband of Hillary'. In Quine's view all modalities are *de dicto*. *De re* modalities, if, contra Quine, they existed, would be those not relativized to a description.

Some further distinctions taken to be distinctions between the *de re* and the *de dicto* are illustrated in application to belief.

(VI) It has been argued that we should distinguish between two kinds of belief. Having a *de dicto* belief amounts to standing in a two place relation to a dictum. Having a *de re* belief amounts to standing in an at least three place relation to an object and a property. Suppose John believes that all prominent politicians are wealthy. In consequence, without knowing who is president, he believes that the president is wealthy. In that case, John will have a *de dicto* belief in virtue of standing in the two place belief relation to the sentence 'The president is wealthy'.

Now suppose that Sally meets Bill Clinton, and judges from the cut of his clothes that he is wealthy. Whether or not she believes he is president, Sally believes of the president that he is wealthy. According to this way of distinguishing *de re* from *de dicto* beliefs, Sally stands in the three place belief relation to the president and the characteristic of being wealthy.

(VII) In another way of distinguishing between *de re* and *de dicto* beliefs, a *de re* belief is about a particular individual or individuals, whereas a *de dicto* belief is general. Sally's belief about the president that he is wealthy is a belief about a particular individual to the effect that he is wealthy. On the other hand, John's belief that the president is wealthy is the general belief that whoever occupies the presidency is wealthy.

(VIII) A different epistemic distinction between *de re* and *de dicto* beliefs is as follows. In contrast with a *de dicto* belief, in order to have a *de re* belief one must be epistemically acquainted with the subject of one's belief: one must know who, which or what it is.

(IX) A final distinction is that between object-dependent and object-independent beliefs. Sally sees a cat and forms the belief that she expresses by uttering,

'That cat has mange'. Some say that she cannot hold this belief about the cat unless it exists. If so, her belief is object-dependent. It is sometimes held that *de re*, as opposed to *de dicto*, beliefs are object-dependent in this sense.

2 Relationships between the different distinctions

Consider the following examples:

(3) □ (the subject of Gance's best-known film was human).

(3') The subject of Gance's best-known film is such that □ it was human.

Abel Gance's best-known film was about Napoleon. According to distinction (I) above, sentence (3) expresses a *de dicto* modality and (3') a *de re* modality. 'The subject of Gance's best-known film' falls within the scope of '□' in (3), and outside the scope of that modal operator in (3'). So Napoleon does not essentially feature in the truth-condition of (3). Hence, distinctions (I) and (II) above would agree in counting (3) as a *de dicto* modality. Since 'the subject of Gance's best-known film' falls outside the scope of '□' in (3'), (3') is true if and only if it is impossible for Napoleon to have been nonhuman. So (I) and (II) likewise agree in counting (3') as a *de re* modality.

Distinction (III) has it that sentences expressing *de re* modalities attribute modal properties. The truth-value of (3) does not depend on Napoleon having the modal property of being necessarily human. Arguably, the truth-value of (3') does depend on his having that modal property. So (III), like (I) and (II), decrees that (3) is a *de dicto* modality and (3') is *de re*.

'The subject of Gance's best-known film' is a non-rigid designator because it designates different things in different possible situations. Since 'the subject of Gance's best-known film' falls within the scope of the modal operator in (3), (IV) deems (3) to be a *de dicto* modality. In (3'), 'the subject of Gance's best-known film' falling outside the scope of '□' has the same effect as replacing 'the subject of Gance's best-known film' with a rigid designator such as 'Napoleon' in (3).

(3*) □ (Napoleon was human).

The truth-value of (3*) depends on whether the actual referent of 'Napoleon' might have been nonhuman. According to (IV), (3*) expresses a *de re* modality for basically the same reason that (3') does according to (II) and (III).

Distinction (V) implies that a modality is *de dicto* if it is relativized to a description. Otherwise, it is *de re*. (3) is true if and only if nothing could be nonhuman which satisfies the description 'the subject of Gance's best-known film'. In Quine's sense the modality in (3) is relativized to a description, and is an example of a *de dicto* modality. In contrast, since the definite description in (3′) falls outside the scope of the modal operator, the truth of (3′) requires that the individual who actually satisfies that definite description must be human. (3′) is true if and only if Napoleon, the individual actually referred to by 'the subject of Gance's best-known film', must be human. (V) implies that (3′) is a *de re* modality.

Now consider:

(4)   John believes that the president is wealthy.

(4′)   The president is such that Sally believes he is wealthy.

According to (VI) above, a *de dicto* belief relates a believer to a proposition, sentence or statement, whereas a *de re* belief relates a believer to something that may be extralinguistic. John's *de dicto* belief that the president is wealthy relates John to the sentence 'The president is wealthy'. The *de re* belief attributed to Sally by (4′) relates her to Bill Clinton.

Since Sally's *de re* belief about the president relates her to Clinton, she could not have that belief unless Clinton exists. Hence, the belief attributed to Sally by (4′) turns out to be object-dependent in conformity with distinction (IX). Moreover, if Sally's *de re* belief about the president relates her to Clinton, it is about a specific individual. Hence, it is *de re* in conformity with (VII). Since Sally knows who it is she believes to be wealthy, her belief is also *de re* in the terms of distinction (VIII).

See also: ESSENTIALISM; LOGICAL AND MATHEMATICAL TERMS, GLOSSARY OF; USE/MENTION DISTINCTION AND QUOTATION

References and further reading

Burge, T. (1977) 'Belief *De Re*', *Journal of Philosophy* 74: 317–38. (A classic attempt to articulate the notion of a *de re* belief, and argue that it is more fundamental than the notion of a *de dicto* belief.)

Dennett, D. (1982) 'Beyond Belief', in A. Woodfield (ed.) *Thought and Object*, Oxford and New York: Oxford University Press. (A sustained attempt to call into question the distinction between *de re* and *de dicto* beliefs.)

Fine, K. (1989) 'The Problem of *De Re* Modality', in J. Almog, J. Perry and H.K. Wettstein (eds) *Themes From Kaplan*, Oxford and New York: Oxford University Press, 197–272. (A somewhat difficult, but rewarding, discussion of key distinctions related to *de re* modalities.)

Kneale, W. (1960) 'Modality *De Dicto* and *De Re*', in E. Nagel, P. Suppes and A. Tarski (eds) *Logic, Methodology and the Philosophy of Science: Proceedings of the 1960 International Conference*, Stanford, CA: Stanford University Press, 1962, 622–33. (Particularly useful in providing a historical background to the distinction between *de re* and *de dicto* modalities.)

Kraut, R. (1983) 'There are No *De Dicto* Attitudes', *Synthese* 54: 275–94. (A defence of scepticism about the distinction between *de re* and *de dicto* attitudes.)

McDowell, J. (1984) '*De Re* Senses', *Philosophical Quarterly* 34: 283–94. (Includes a discussion of the alleged object dependence of *de re* thoughts.)

Plantinga, A. (1969) '*De dicto* et *de re*', *Noûs* (3): 235–58. (An attempt to reduce *de re* to *de dicto* modalities.)

* Quine, W.V. (1953) 'Reference and Modality', in *From a Logical Point of View*, New York: Harper, 139–59. (Includes Quine's argument against the meaningfulness of *de re* modal attributions.)

—— (1976) 'Quantifiers and Propositional Attitudes', in *Ways of Paradox and Other Essays*, Cambridge: Cambridge University Press, 185–96. (A classic statement of one way of distinguishing between *de re* and *de dicto* beliefs.)

—— (1979) 'Intensions Revisited', in P.A. French, T.E. Uehling, Jr and H.K. Wettstein (eds) *Contemporary Perspectives in the Philosophy of Language*, Minneapolis, MN: University of Minnesota Press, 268–74. (Quine's second thoughts about the *de re/de dicto* distinction.)

ANDRÉ GALLOIS

DE VIO, THOMAS *see* CAJETAN

DEATH

Reflection on death gives rise to a variety of philosophical questions. One of the deepest of these is a question about the nature of death. Typically, philosophers interpret this question as a call for an analysis or definition of the concept of death. Plato, for example, proposed to define death as the separation of soul from body. However, this definition is not acceptable to those who think that there are no souls. It is also unacceptable to anyone who thinks that plants and lower animals have no souls, but can nonetheless die. Others have defined death simply as the cessation of life. This too is problematic, since an organism that goes into suspended animation ceases to live, but may not actually die.

Death is described as 'mysterious', but neither is it clear what this means. Suppose we cannot formulate a satisfactory analysis of the concept of death: in this respect death would be mysterious, but no more so than any other concept that defies analysis. Some have said that what makes death especially mysterious and frightening is the fact that we cannot know what it will be like. Death is typically regarded as a great evil, especially if it strikes someone too soon. However, Epicurus and others argued that death cannot harm those who die, since people go out of existence when they die, and people cannot be harmed at times when they do not exist. Others have countered that the evil of death may lie in the fact that death deprives us of the goods we would have enjoyed if we had lived. On this view, death may be a great evil for a person, even if they cease to exist at the moment of death.

Philosophers have also been concerned with the question of whether people can survive death. This is open to several interpretations, depending on what we understand to be people and what we mean by 'survive'. Traditional materialists take each person to be a purely physical object – a human body. Since human bodies generally continue to exist after death, such materialists presumably must say that we generally survive death. However, such survival would be of little value to the deceased, since the surviving entity is just a lifeless corpse. Dualists take each person to have both a body and a soul. A dualist may maintain that at death the soul separates from the body, thereby continuing to enjoy (or suffer) various experiences after the body has died.

Some who believe in survival think that the eternal life of the soul after bodily death can be a good beyond comparison. But Bernard Williams has argued that eternal life would be profoundly unattractive. If we imagine ourselves perpetually stuck at a given age, we may reasonably fear that eternal life will eventually become rather boring. On the other hand, if we imagine ourselves experiencing an endless sequence of varied 'lives', each disconnected from the others, then it is questionable whether it will in fact be 'one person' who lives eternally.

Finally, there are questions about death and the meaning of life. Suppose death marks the end of all conscious experience – would our lives be then rendered meaningless? Or would the fact of impending death help us to recognize the value of our lives, and thereby give deeper meaning to life?

1 Analysis of death versus criterion of death

The most fundamental philosophical question about death is the question concerning its nature or essence – 'What is death?'. When philosophers offer answers to this question, they may be said to be defining death. It is important to recognize that two distinct projects may be confused under the single name 'defining death'. The first is a project in conceptual analysis which tries to give an account of the nature of death. Since death is the event that takes place when an organism dies, one way to explain the nature of death would be to formulate a definition of '*x* dies at *t*'. If successful, such a definition would tell us what we mean when we say that something dies, and thus reveal the nature of death. Among the most popular proposals is:

(D1) x dies at $t =_{df.} x$ ceases to be alive at t

A definition of this sort is successful if it is true. A fully adequate definition of death would display the structure of the concept of death.

The second (or 'criterial') project is one of public policy. For many practical purposes, it is important to have agreement on the question of whether a person is dead or alive. Furthermore, for practical purposes, it is important that there should be agreement about the time of death. Even if we agreed that (D1) is true, we might still be in grave doubt about whether certain people are dead. For example, consider a person whose brain has been irreparably destroyed in an accident, but whose blood is being oxygenated and circulated by life-support mechanisms. Since it is unclear whether people such as this have ceased to be alive, it is unclear whether they are dead. Those who engage in the criterial project try to formulate a criterion of human death that is relatively easy to apply. Such a criterion would pick out an observable change that occurs around the time on which most would agree that humans die. The proposal would then be that this change (for example, cessation of electrical activity in the brain, cessation of respiration, cessation of heartbeat, and so on) should be taken to be the legal mark of death. If the proposal were accepted, then medical personnel and undertakers, among others, could appeal to this criterion as a legal defence.

Conceptual analysis would yield a necessary truth about the structure of the concept of death. The search for such analyses fits into a philosophical tradition going back to Plato and Aristotle. It resembles attempts to analyse such concepts as knowledge, causation, goodness and truth, so the analytical project is classically philosophical. The criterial project, if successful, would lead to a contingently useful criterion of human death. If it were accepted by the courts, it might remain in use for decades (until medical technology made it obsolete). But at best it would be a contingent principle with just temporary and practical value. The project itself requires knowledge of medical details and legal precedents, but does not seem to be a project for which philosophers are especially well qualified.

2 Death as separation of body from soul

In the *Phaedo*, Plato has Socrates say:

> Is it [death] not the separation of soul and body? And to be dead is the completion of this; when the soul exists in herself, and is released from the body and the body is released from the soul, what is this but death?
>
> (*Phaedo* [Jowett, 1937 vol. 1]: 447)

These remarks suggest a view about the nature of death:

(D2) *x* dies at $t =_{df.}$ *x*'s soul separates from *x*'s body at *t*

This is problematic, one problem being that (D2) entails that if a thing is to die, it must have a soul. Yet many find it hard to believe that plants (which clearly can die) have souls. Similarly, many find it hard to believe that every living cell has a soul, and yet cells can die.

Many philosophers accept a materialist conception of people. They think that people are material objects – their bodies. Materialists of this sort think that people have no souls. Unless they want to say that people never die, (D2) is clearly unacceptable to such materialists (see MATERIALISM).

3 Death as the cessation of life

The most popular analysis of the concept of death is expressed by (D1). One problem with (D1), however, is its obscurity. There is great controversy about the concept of life. Some claim that to be alive is to be able to engage in life processes, such as nutrition, respiration, and reproduction. Others say that life requires the presence of a soul or some other animating substance. Still others define life by appeal to the notion that living things are able to resist the force of entropy. A number of incompatible accounts of the nature of life have been proposed, but none enjoys universal acceptance. Hence, it is not entirely clear that we know precisely what we mean when we say that something is alive. Since in (D1) death is defined by appeal to the concept of life, (D1) inherits the obscurity of the concept of life.

Furthermore, (D1) seems to be inconsistent with certain empirical facts. One fact concerns suspended animation. Freezing, drying and certain other procedures may be used to arrest the life functions of formerly living entities. Viruses, bacteria and other micro-organisms are placed in suspended animation in laboratories as a matter of course. Sperm, eggs and blastulas of horses, cows and even human beings may be held in this state for months or years. Since all the life functions of such entities have been suspended, it seems that they have ceased to live. But since they can return to life again later, it seems that they have not died. (D1) therefore fails, since it implies that when such organisms go into suspended animation, they die.

In light of this difficulty with suspended animation, it might appear that it would be better to define death not as the mere cessation of life, but as the *permanent* cessation of life:

(D3) *x* dies at $t =_{df.}$ *x* ceases permanently to be alive at *t*.

If an organism goes into suspended animation but will later return to life, (D3) implies that it has not died as its loss of life was not permanent. Thus, (D3) seems to be an improvement over (D1).

Nevertheless, (D3) is still problematic. Suppose two similar organisms go into suspended animation at some time. Suppose one is later brought back to life, whereas the other is not. Then during the period when both were in suspended animation, the first was not dead (since it had not *permanently* ceased to live) but the second was already dead (since it had *permanently* ceased to be alive). This may seem odd, since the two organisms might have been cell-for-cell duplicates during the period of suspended animation, yet according to (D3) one was already dead and the other was not. This shows that (D3) conflicts with the intuitively plausible notion that the life and death of an organism depends upon the intrinsic character of that organism. Thus none of the traditional analyses of the concept of death is definitively correct. The fundamental question about death remains unanswered: we do not know precisely what death is.

4 The mystery of death

A recurrent theme about death in popular thought (as well as in some philosophical circles) is the idea that death is mysterious. As we have seen, it is difficult to formulate a satisfactory philosophical analysis of the concept of death. If it is impossible to analyse the concept of death, then it is impossible to explain precisely what we mean when we say that something dies. It might be said therefore that, in virtue of this fact, death is mysterious. Of course, death is not *distinctively* mysterious – all other unanalysable concepts are equally mysterious in this way.

Yet it is widely thought that there is a special mystery about death. Some seem to take the mystery to be that we cannot know or even conceive of what being dead will be like. This might be thought to follow from the fact that most of us who are living have no recollection of ever having been dead, and thus we lack first-hand experience of what death is like. Furthermore, since there is considerable doubt about the veracity of the testimony of those few who claim to recall having been dead, none of us has a reliable second-hand report of what death is like.

A deeper reason for thinking death difficult to imagine becomes evident if we suppose that death is an 'experiential blank' – that is, if we suppose that the dead have absolutely no experiences. It has been claimed that being dead is impossible to conceptualize precisely because being dead is like this. However, while it must be admitted that it is quite difficult to form any clear conception of what an experiential blank would feel like, this may be a bogus problem. Perhaps it is difficult to imagine this feeling not because it is mysterious or hidden, but rather because there is no such feeling. If the dead have no experiences, then it is no wonder and no mystery that we cannot imagine what the experiences of the dead feel like.

5 The evil of death

If we cease to have experiences at death then we cannot experience pain or any other sort of misfortune while dead. How then can death harm us? And if death cannot harm us, how can it be reasonable for us to fear death? Lucretius claimed that it would be more reasonable for us to view death with the same calm indifference with which we view the infinite stretch of time prior to our creation. These are ancient questions: they were discussed by Plato and by Epicurus and his followers, just as they are still discussed today (see PLATO §§7, 13; EPICURUS §2).

Dualists who believe that our souls continue to live after our bodies die have an easy reply to these questions. They can say that we do not cease to have experiences at death. If we go to hell, we will suffer eternal torment. Thus, death can harm us and (if we have been bad) it is quite reasonable for us to fear death. Our deaths will mark the beginning of the

worst and longest period of misery we will ever experience.

The questions about the evil of death are more puzzling for materialists and others who accept the notion that the dead cannot experience pains or other misfortunes. How can such a person explain the evil of death? Some, such as Thomas Nagel, reject the principle that we cannot be harmed by something that we do not experience. They cite the harms of deprivation: suppose a person suffers a brain injury and is reduced to the mental state of a contented infant – they may experience no pain, and may not be aware of any misfortune, yet they have been seriously harmed simply by the deprivation of their mental capacities. According to a more extreme view, a person may be harmed by falling into nonexistence. Consider a girl who dies painlessly in her youth. Suppose that if she had lived, she would have been quite happy. Her death therefore seems to deprive her of a lifetime of happiness. Some (for example, McMahan or Feldman) see this as a grave harm – though of course a harm of which the victim has no conscious experience. These philosophers claim that it may be reasonable for us to view death as a great evil – even if we will have no experiences while dead. Perhaps the fear of death is not entirely irrational.

6 The survival of death

For a variety of reasons, many are deeply troubled by the question of whether we will survive death. The question is open to several interpretations. Different interpretations arise from different conceptions of the metaphysics of persons, and from different conceptions of death and survival.

Materialists of one traditional sort maintain that people are just physical objects – their own bodies. On this view, there are no souls. People have psychological properties simply because their brains are functioning properly. A materialist of this sort might take the question about survival to be 'will I (= my body) continue to exist after I die?'. On this interpretation, the person is taken to be the human body, the survival of which is taken to be continued existence. If we interpret the question in this way, the answer is fairly obvious. In the vast majority of cases the human body does continue to exist for at least a few months after it dies. However, since the brain is no longer functioning, it presumably has no experiences. It is difficult to understand how anyone could take this sort of survival to be of any value to the deceased.

Such a materialist might reinterpret the question to mean 'will I continue to *live* after I die?'. Almost certainly, the answer to this question must be no. If you are just your body, and your body becomes dead and ceases forever to live when it dies, then you become dead and cease forever to live when you die.

Dualists maintain that each person has both a body and a soul. In classical forms of dualism, the soul is taken to be a non-physical object – not made of atoms or molecules. During life, the soul and body are intimately associated. Some would say that during life the soul 'animates' the body. Dualists of one tradition take each person to be a unified complex of body and soul. Descartes sometimes seems to endorse this view of persons ('I am not lodged in my body merely as a pilot in a ship, but so intimately conjoined, and as it were intermingled with it, that with it I form a unitary whole' – *Meditations* VI (1958): 239). It would be natural for such a dualist to adopt the Platonic conception and take death to be the dissolution of the soul-body compound. For such a philosopher, the question about survival may be put thus: 'Will I (= this complex of body and soul) continue to exist after I am dissolved by death and my parts have gone their separate ways?'. Once we have accepted the metaphysical assumptions of this sort of dualism, the answer to this question seems to be no. If the person is the complex of body and soul, and the complex is destroyed by death, then the person is destroyed by death. Though the parts may continue to exist, the compound itself must cease to exist and to live at death (see DESCARTES, R. §8) .

Dualists of another tradition take persons to be embodied souls. On this view, each living person is a soul that happens to be attached to a body. Descartes seems in other passages to endorse this view of persons ('I have a body with which I am very closely conjoined, yet . . . I am truly distinct from my body, and can exist without it' – *Meditations* VI (1958): 239). A philosopher who accepts this metaphysical conception of persons might understand the question about survival in this way: 'Will I (= my soul) continue to have experiences after my body has died?'. Although some have denied it, the correct answer to this question is conceivably yes, and it is somewhat easier to understand why someone who accepts this metaphysical conception of persons might be interested in this sort of survival.

It is interesting to note that on this second dualistic conception, it is not quite clear that *people* actually die. Of course, *human bodies* die. However, on the view in question, no person is a human body. Each living person is just a soul – albeit a soul that happens to be ensconced in a mortal body. That which continues to live after the death of the body is a thing that does not die – the soul. That which dies – the body – typically deteriorates and eventually goes out of existence after death (see DUALISM §1).

7 Immortality

We might think that the concept of immortality is the concept of never dying. However, this would be slightly misleading since it would imply that non-biological objects such as rocks and bricks, atoms and planets, numbers and properties, are all immortal: since they never live, they never die. It would also be misleading to suppose that the concept of immortality is the concept of living at some time but never dying, since this would also have odd implications. Consider a living thing that goes into eternal suspended animation. It never dies, but this sort of immortality is hardly better than death. It is better, therefore, to take the concept of immortality to be the concept of living forever. This seems more interesting, and is probably closer to the concept that has been discussed.

Some say that eternal life would be a great blessing – something of unsurpassable value. Perhaps they reason as follows: life is good; more of a good thing is always better than less; therefore eternal life is exceedingly good. But others (most notably Bernard Williams) have argued that eternal life could not possibly be desirable. Williams considers several possible 'models' of eternal life. On one, a person (identified as 'E.M.') remains eternally at the same biological age (in his example, the age is forty-two). Williams claims that after a few hundred years, this person would inevitably become bored with life. The boredom is inevitable, he insists, in virtue of the fact that 'everything that could happen and make sense to one particular human being of 42 had already happened to her' (1973: 90).

On another model we imagine that E.M. does not remain at a constant biological age of forty-two, and does not retain a certain character. Rather, we imagine that E.M. lives out an endless succession of different lives, each with a new character and personality. In this way, E.M. avoids the tedium of the first model. Williams suggests that this is not a model on which a single person lives forever. Rather, it is a model on which a series of distinct persons live. Thus, it has no bearing on the question of the desirability of eternal life.

It could be argued, however, that Williams has neglected certain important possibilities. One is the possibility that there are activities whose pleasure does not decrease with repetition. Another is that people may grow and change gradually over time, and thereby come to have new interests without losing their identities as individuals. Such growth might make it possible for a single individual to live forever without falling into the tedium that might result from steadfast pursuit of just one interest over an endless stretch of time.

8 Death and the meaning of life

A number of thinkers have suggested that there is some important connection between death and 'the meaning of life'. A person who thinks that death is not followed by any sort of afterlife may think that death makes life meaningless. Schopenhauer sometimes seems to have expressed this view (see SCHOPENHAUER, A. §6). Others who believe in God and immortality may see it this way: God placed us here on earth in order that we may either sin or achieve our salvation. If we sin, we are punished with eternal damnation. If we achieve salvation, we are rewarded with eternal bliss. A person who accepts this picture might say that if there were no God and no afterlife in which to receive reward or punishment, then life would be (to quote Shakespeare) 'a tale told by an idiot, full of sound and fury, signifying nothing'. In other words, if there were no God and no afterlife, our lives would not be components of a larger and purposeful scheme – we would live for a while and then simply die. For many, if it were like this, life would be meaningless. Those who believe in an afterlife may take comfort in thoughts of this afterlife, and think that its existence serves to make ordinary life here on earth meaningful.

Yet it appears that sense can be made of the idea that life is meaningful even if it ends in death. If people have worthwhile goals and exert themselves to achieve these goals, taking some pleasure in both the exertion and the achievement, then their lives may be said to be meaningful – at least in what Paul Edwards calls 'the terrestrial sense'. Death, of course, may bring an end to such meaningfulness, but the fact that they will someday die seems not to be able to rob people's lives of this sort of meaningfulness while they are alive.

According to an even more extreme view, life is made *more* meaningful by the recognition that it will end with death. According to this view, we gain a deeper appreciation for the common satisfactions of our everyday experience when we fully realize that someday we will die, and will then have nothing at all.

See also: LIFE AND DEATH; LIFE, MEANING OF; SOUL, NATURE AND IMMORTALITY OF

References and further reading

* Descartes, R. (1641) *Meditations on First Philosophy*, in N. Kemp Smith (ed. and trans.) *Descartes: Philosophical Writings*, New York: Random House, 1958. (Descartes' presentation of his dualistic conception of persons.)

Donnelly, J. (ed.) (1994) *Language, Metaphysics, and Death*, 2nd edn, New York: Fordham University Press. (Useful and well-organized collection of essays on the nature and meaning of death, the nature of the soul, and immortality. Includes papers by Nagel, Williams, Rosenbaum, Edwards, Feldman and others.)

* Edwards, P. (1967) 'Life, Meaning and Value of', in P. Edwards (ed.) *The Encyclopedia of Philosophy*, New York and London: Macmillan Publishing Company & The Free Press. (Clear exposition of main views on meaning of life. Explains and criticizes Schopenhauer's arguments for pessimism.)

Edwards, P. (ed.) (1992) *Immortality*, New York: Macmillan Publishing Company. (Anthology of thirty-four readings on immortality, including selections from Plato, Lucretius, Aquinas, Descartes, Hume, Reid, Mill, Broad and others. Extensive, detailed annotated bibliography.)

* Epicurus (c.300 BC) 'Letter to Menoecceus', trans. C. Bailey in W. J. Oates (ed.) *The Stoic and Epicurean Philosophers*, New York: The Modern Library, 1940, 30–4. (Classic statement of the view that since we will not exist once we are dead, death cannot harm us. Claims that the fear of death is wholly irrational.)

* Feldman, F. (1992) *Confrontations with the Reaper: A Philosophical Study of the Nature and Value of Death*, New York: Oxford University Press. (Defends a materialist conceptual scheme for death and associated concepts; argues for a version of the deprivation approach to the evil of death; presents a modified utilitarian theory about the wrongness of killing.)

Fischer, J.M. (1993) *The Metaphysics of Death*, Stanford, CA: Stanford University Press. (Clear and well-organized introduction by Fischer, followed by sixteen papers on death. Includes papers by Nagel, Williams, Parfit, McMahan, Feldman and others. Excellent bibliography.)

Kamm, F.M. (1993) *Morality, Mortality, Volume 1: Death and Whom to Save From It*, Oxford: Oxford University Press. (Extensive discussion of the evil of death, focusing on the question why non-existence after death seems so much worse than non-existence before birth. Also discusses moral questions concerning the allocation of transplantable bodily organs.)

* Nagel, T. (1973) 'Death' in *Mortal Questions*, Cambridge: Cambridge University Press, 1–10. (Discusses whether it is a bad thing to die. See §5 above.)

* Plato (c.330 BC) *Phaedo*, trans. B. Jowett in *The Dialogues of Plato*, New York: Random House, 1937. (Introduction by R. Demos. Represents a dialogue about death, the nature of the person, and

the role of the philosopher. Socrates is the leading character in the discussion, which takes place in his cell in jail, on the day of his death.)

President's Commission for the Study of Ethical Problems in Medicine and Biomedical and Behavioral Research (1981) *Defining Death: Medical, Legal and Ethical Issues in the Determination of Death*, Washington, DC: President's Commission. (Report of U.S. Presidential Commission directed to investigate ethical and legal implications of proposed and enacted legal criteria of death. Contains a review of actual statutes as well as thoughtful discussion of a proposed new uniform statute.)

* Williams, B. (1973) *Problems of the Self*, New York: Cambridge University Press. (Contains 'The Makropoulos Case: Reflections on the Tedium of Immortality', and other essays by Williams.)

FRED FELDMAN

DEBORIN, A. *see* MARXIST PHILOSOPHY, RUSSIAN AND SOVIET

DECISION AND GAME THEORY

Decision theory studies individual decision-making in situations in which an individual's choice neither affects nor is affected by other individuals' choices; while game theory studies decision-making in situations where individuals' choices do affect each other. Decision theory asks questions like: what does it mean to choose rationally? How should we make choices when the consequences of our actions are uncertain? Buying insurance and deciding which job to take are examples of the kind of decisions studied by this discipline. Game theory instead applies to all decisions that have a strategic component. The choices of an oligopolist, voting strategies, military tactical problems, deterrence, but also common phenomena such as threatening, promising, conflict and cooperation are its subject matter. In a strategic situation, the goal is not just to choose rationally, but to choose in such a way that a mutual solution is achieved, so that choices 'coordinate' in the right way. The formal methods developed by game theory do not require that the subject making a choice be an intentional agent: coordinated interaction between animals or computers can be successfully modelled as well.

1 **Probability as a guide to life**
2 **Expected utility**
3 **Games in normal form**
4 **Games in extensive form**
5 **Selection by evolution**
6 **Repeated games**
7 **Bargaining games**
8 **Cooperative games**

1 Probability as a guide to life

The thesis that reasonable decisions must be based on probability was already regarded as common-sensical in the eighteenth century. It is presented most clearly in Joseph BUTLER (1736), who claimed that 'probability is the very guide to life'. The thesis was first explicitly formulated by Antoine ARNAULD (1662), who aimed to dispel the common illusion 'of considering only the magnitude and importance of the expected gain or the feared loss rather than considering the probability of the gain or loss'. A decision made under conditions of uncertainty thus had to depend upon *two* factors: an evaluation of the probability of the possible events and an evaluation of the gains or losses following such events. Take, for example, a gamble in which one of n outcomes will occur. Let the outcomes be worth $x_1, x_2, \ldots, x_n$ dollars, respectively. The probability of each outcome is known, therefore we have $p_1, p_2, \ldots, p_n$, where $0 \leq p \leq 1$ and $\Sigma_{i=1}^{n} p_i = 1$. How much is it worth to participate in this gamble? The answer was that the expected monetary value $\Sigma_{i=1}^{n} x_i p_i$ is the fair 'price' of the gamble.

For centuries, then, it was taken for granted that proper choice meant maximizing expected monetary value. Suppose, however, that you face the following gamble. A fair coin is to be tossed until a head appears. You receive 2^n dollars if the first head occurs on the nth trial. The expected monetary value of this gamble is $\Sigma_{n=1}^{\infty} 2^n (1/2)^n = 1 + 1 + 1 + \ldots$, an infinite value. Thus, on the account we are considering, you should be willing to pay any finite stake to play it. Introspection tells us that no one will act like that: how then do we explain the discrepancy between theory and experience?

In 1738 Daniel Bernoulli, provoked by the above paradox (the so-called St Petersburg paradox), suggested that to determine the value of a gamble one should not consider its monetary value but instead the *utility* that such money has for the gambler. Bernoulli recognized that the utility of a given sum of money may not be the same for different people, and may even differ for the same person at different times. In general, any increase in wealth will produce a utility increase that is inversely proportional to the quantity of goods already possessed.

According to Bernoulli, one should maximize some concave function of money (he suggested the logarithmic function), to reflect its diminishing marginal utility. In the example above, if we take the utility of a sum of money to be proportional to its logarithm, and we take the mathematical expectation of utility (rather than money), we have a finite value, so that the gambler is willing to pay only a finite stake. The fair price of the gamble is now the monetary equivalent of its expected utility value, for example, $\Sigma_{n=1}^{\infty} \log_{10} 2^n (1/2)^n = \log_{10} 2 \times \Sigma_{n=1}^{\infty} n(1/2^n)$. In the limit, this sum approaches a finite value. Expected utility was born.

2 Expected utility

Almost 200 years later, von Neumann and Morgenstern (1944) proved that if individual preferences satisfy a given set of axioms, they can be represented by the expectation of some utility function. Their theory applies to agents who must choose one among a set of feasible actions without being able to predict with certainty what the outcome of a given choice will be. Each action may result in one of several possible outcomes, depending on which state of the world occurs, and there exists a known probability distribution over the states. In this case, we say that the choice is one under *risk*, to distinguish it from a choice situation in which there are no known probabilities. Their results initiated a vast research field known as *decision theory*. We shall highlight here only a few of the main concepts of decision theory that are particularly relevant to game theory.

Suppose action A has two possible outcomes, a and a', and that these outcomes occur with probabilities p and $(1-p)$, respectively. Choosing A is thus like choosing a lottery that gives you prize a with probability p and prize a' with probability $(1-p)$. Denote this lottery by $(ap, a'(1-p))$. Agents are completely defined by their preferences over such lotteries. Let us denote lotteries by X, Y, Z, and probabilistic mixtures of lotteries (compound lotteries) by $pX + (1-p)Y$. Specific outcomes are just degenerate lotteries with an outcome probability of one, and are denoted by x, y, z. Denote 'X preferred to Y' by $X \succ Y$, 'X indifferent to Y' by $X \sim Y$. The von Neumann–Morgenstern axioms concerning individuals' preferences over lotteries are:

(1) *Ordering.* Preferences are complete: either $X \succ Y$, $Y \succ X$, or $X \sim Y$, and transitive: $X \succ Y$ and $Y \succ Z$ implies $X \succ Z$.

(2) *Preference increasing with probability.* If $x \succ x'$ and $X = (px, (1-p)x')$, $Y = (qx, (1-q)x')$, then $X \succ Y$ if and only if $p > q$.

(3) *Continuity.* For all lotteries $X \succ Y \succ Z$, there exists a unique p such that $(pX, (1-p)Z) \sim Y$. (A consequence of this axiom is the following: given that there is a best lottery outcome b and a worst lottery outcome w, for any lottery outcome x there will always be some probability combination of b and w such that the agent is indifferent between that combination and x. For given x, define u_x such that $x \sim (u_x b, (1-u_x)w)$. u_x is called the von Neumann–Morgenstern *utility index* of x.)

(4) *Independence.* If $X \succ Y$, then $(pX, (1-p)Z) \succ (pY, (1-p)Z)$, for all $p \in (0,1)$ and Z.

(5) *Rules for combining probabilities.* Consider the lottery $(px, (1-p)x')$. By continuity, we have that $X \sim [p(u_x b, (1-u_x)w), (1-p)(u_{x'}b, (1-u_{x'})w)]$. Denote the compound lottery by X^*. The probability of obtaining b in the lottery X^* is $pu_x + (1-p)u_{x'}$. Similarly, the probability of obtaining w is $p(1-u_x) + (1-p)(1-u_{x'})$. So X is indifferent to $[pu_x(b) + (1-p)u_{x'}(b), p(1-u_x)(w) + (1-p)(1-u_{x'})(w)]$. Now consider a lottery $Z = (zq, z'(1-q))$. It must be the case that $Z \sim [(qu_z(b) + (1-q)u_{z'}(b), q(1-u_z)(w) + (1-q)(1-u_{z'}(w)]$. Using (2) we have that $X \succ Z$ when $pu_x + (1-p)u_{x'} > qu_z + (1-q)u_{z'}$. Since u_x is the utility index of x, we can say that X is preferred to Z when the expected utility of X is greater than the expected utility of Z.

A *rational* agent is understood to be one who chooses an action that best fulfils their goals. This is a minimal definition of rationality, since it does not encompass beliefs (beyond consistency of probability assessments) or goals. Given a goal, an agent will usually have several alternative actions that satisfy it, and a preference ranking over them. A rational agent will act according to that ranking and choose one among the maximally preferred alternatives (there may be more than one). If their preference ordering satifies conditions (1)–(5), the agent is choosing the action with the highest expected utility.

The major result of von Neumann and Morgenstern is the proof that – when conditions (1)–(5) hold – there exists a real-valued utility function U over consequences (which is unique up to a positive linear transformation) such that for any two lotteries X and Y, $X \succ Y$ if and only if $\Sigma_{x \in X} p(x)U(x) > \Sigma_{y \in Y} p(y)U(y)$. A rational decision maker is thus represented as acting so as to maximize his expected utility.

Most choices, however, involve uncertain consequences whose probability cannot be objectively quantified. Savage (1954) proved a representation theorem showing that if preferences for actions are transitive and satisfy certain other mathematical conditions, then there is a utility function on consequences (unique up to a linear transformation) and a unique subjective probability distribution on states of the world such that action A is preferred to action B if and only if A has greater expected utility than B (see RATIONALITY, PRACTICAL).

Expected utility theory was never meant to be descriptive of how agents behave under risk or uncertainty. Rationality should be viewed as an idealization, a useful benchmark for measuring how much actual choices deviate from the ideal. Some of the most interesting recent research on decision theory has been motivated by empirical results which reveal systematic violations of the expected utility axioms, as well as by the so-called paradoxes of Allais (1953) and Ellsberg (1961). Alternative utility models have been proposed by Kahneman and Tversky (1979), Machina (1982) and Fishburn (1982) (see RATIONAL BELIEFS).

Strategic interactions. Many of the consequences of our decisions depend not just on our choice and the occurrence of some state of the world, but also on how *other* agents choose. In a *strategic* context, people interact and make decisions on the basis of expectations about other people's behaviour. These are the kind of situations to which *game theory* applies. Von Neumann and Morgenstern introduced their decision theory as a tool for playing a special type of game in which whatever one player gains the other loses. An example of such a *zero-sum game* is matching pennies, where each player privately turns a penny either heads up or tails up. If the choices match, player 1 gives the penny to player 2; if they do not, player 2 gives player 1 the penny. In this game, rational player 1 should maximize his *security level*, where the security level of a strategy (see §3) is defined as the worst that strategy can bring the player; player 2 instead should minimize her *hazard level*, the best that a strategy can bring the opponent. Using pure strategies, neither player can guarantee himself more than -1. But if each player randomizes between heads up and tails up with probability $1/2$, each can guarantee himself an expected payoff of 0. The expected payoff combination $(0,0)$ is the only one that yields each player his security level, hence it is – in von Neumann's words – *individually rational*. In 1928 von Neumann proved the so-called *Minimax theorem*: every two-person zero-sum game with finitely many pure strategies (see §3) has precisely one individually rational payoff vector. In von Neumann's early work, outcomes were always expressed in money, and it was implicitly assumed that the marginal utility of money was the same for all players. To fend off objections to this assumption,

a monetary outcome was replaced by its utility, and it is precisely the formulation of expected utility theory that allowed for a rigorous treatment of the expected payoffs that result from players' randomization over pure strategies (see §3).

Strictly competitive games like the zero-sum example above are rarely encountered in economic and political applications. Much more common are *mixed-motive games*, in which players' interests are only in partial conflict, or *coordination games*, in which players' interests often coincide. Research in game theory in the last half of the twentieth century has been almost exclusively focused upon the latter kind of games.

3 Games in normal form

A *normal form* game is completely defined by three elements: a list of players $i = 1, \ldots, n$; for each player i, a finite set of pure strategies S_i; a payoff function u_i that gives player i's payoff $u_i(s)$ for each n-tuple of strategies $(s_1, \ldots, s_n)$, where $u_i : X_{j=1}^n S_i \to R$. All players other than some given player i are customarily denoted as '$-i$'. A player may want to randomize over his pure strategies; a probability distribution over pure strategies is called a *mixed-strategy* and is denoted by σ_i. Each player's randomization is assumed to be statistically independent of that of the opponents, and the payoffs to a mixed-strategies' profile are the expected values of the corresponding pure strategies payoffs. If the players were jointly to choose a random device and condition their strategy choices on the outcome of this joint randomization, then they would play a *correlated strategy*.

The matrix in Figure 1 depicts a normal form game: each player picks a strategy independently and without communicating with the other, and the outcome is the joint result of these two strategies. The game is one of *complete information*, in that the players know the rules of the game and other players' payoffs. It is usually assumed that players have *common knowledge* that both possess this information (Aumann 1976). If the players are allowed to enter into binding agreements before the game is played, we say that the game is *cooperative*. *Noncooperative games* instead make no allowance for the existence of an enforcement mechanism that would make the terms of the agreement binding on the players. If preplay negotiation leads to an agreement, and there is no enforcement mechanism available, we should ask whether the agreement is self-enforcing, by virtue of its being in the best interest of each player to adhere to.

2

	C	D
C	2, 2	0, 3
D	3, 0	1, 1

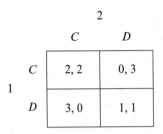

Figure 1

Nash equilibrium. The standard solution concept for noncooperative games is that of Nash equilibrium (Nash 1951). Informally, a Nash equilibrium specifies players' actions and beliefs such that (i) each player's action is optimal given that players' beliefs about other players' choices; (ii) players' beliefs are correct. Thus an outcome that is not a Nash equilibrium requires either that a player chooses a suboptimal strategy, or that some players 'misperceive' the situation.

More formally, a *Nash equilibrium* is a vector of strategies $(\sigma_1^*, \ldots, \sigma_n^*)$, one for each of the n players in the game, such that each σ_i^* is optimal given (or is a best reply to) σ_{-i}^*. Note that optimality is only conditional on a fixed σ_{-i}, not on all possible σ_{-i}.

A common interpretation of Nash equilibrium is that of a self-enforcing agreement. That is, were players to agree in preplay negotiation to play a particular strategy combination, they would have an incentive to stick to the agreement only in case the agreed upon combination is a Nash equilibrium. While this is generally true of pure strategy Nash equilibria, it is not true of equilibria in mixed strategies. Consider the game in Figure 2.

2

	t_1	t_2
s_1	8, 3	3, 8
s_2	5, 6	7, 2

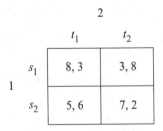

Figure 2

This game has no Nash equilibrium in pure strategies, but Nash proved that – provided certain restrictions are imposed on strategy sets and payoff functions – a game will have at least an equilibrium in mixed strategies. Nash's result generalizes von Neumann's theorem (1928) that every game with finitely many strategies has an equilibrium in mixed strategies.

Suppose A plays $((4/9)s_1, (5/9)s_2)$. Then if B chooses t_1, her expected utility is $3(4/9) + 6(5/9) = 42/9$. If B chooses t_2, she nets $8(4/9) + 2(5/9) = 42/9$. So if A randomizes with probabilities $(4/9, 5/9)$, B is indifferent between t_1 and t_2 and can thus randomize between them. Suppose B chooses $((4/7)t_1, (3/7)t_2)$; then A nets $41/7$ if he plays s_1, and $41/7$ if he plays s_2. Thus A is indifferent between s_1 and s_2, and can randomize between them. The combination $((4/9)s_1, (5/9)s_2)$, $((4/7)t_1, (3/7)t_2)$ is a mixed-strategy Nash equilibrium. In a mixed-strategy equilibrium, the equilibrium strategy of each player makes the other indifferent between the strategies on which he is randomizing; thus if A were to know that B randomizes with probabilities $(4/7, 3/7)$, any of his strategies (pure or mixed) would be a best reply to B's choice and conversely, were B to know that A randomizes with probabilities $4/9, 5/9$, any of her strategies would be a best reply. Paradoxically, if players were to agree to play a mixed-strategy equilibrium, they would have no particular incentive to play their equilibrium mixed strategies. A mixed-strategy equilibrium is thus a self-enforcing agreement only in the weak sense that, given the other players' equilibrium behaviour, each player is indifferent between all the strategies taken from the support of his equilibrium strategy.

A better justification of mixed-strategy equilibria comes from a different understanding of mixed strategies. This is the *purification* idea, according to which a player's mixed-strategy consists in uncertainties in the minds of other players as to the real values of his payoffs (Harsanyi 1973). That is, player A does not randomize between his strategies with probabilities 5/9 and 4/9; it is just that player B attaches probability 5/9 to the event that A has payoffs such that he will pick the first strategy and probability 4/9 to the event that A has different payoffs, in which case he would choose the second strategy. When players are uncertain about the payoffs of other players, the game is one of *incomplete information*. In this case, players cannot predict what would be a best response for the other players, and consequently cannot determine their own optimal behaviour.

Harsanyi (1967) provided a method for transforming games of incomplete information into games of imperfect information, for which optimal choices and equilibrium behaviour are well defined. The basic idea is simple. A player who is uncertain about another player's payoff will be treated as if he were uncertain about the *type* of player he faces. A player's type embodies the player's private information. In our example, it is information about one's payoff function, but it may include beliefs about other players' payoff functions or even about other players' beliefs. Players' types are randomly drawn by nature according to an initial probability distribution. Each player knows his type but cannot observe nature's choice; players know, however, the prior type distribution as well as all the possible types. Furthermore, the types and the prior distribution are assumed to be common knowledge among the players. A player's strategy choice depends on his type. If a player knows the strategies of the opponents (as functions of their types), and once he is informed about his own type, he will calculate the conditional probability of the opponents' types (given his own type), compute his expected utility using this probability and choose a strategy that maximizes his payoff function. A *Bayesian equilibrium* in a game of incomplete information with a finite number of types for each player, a prior type distribution and a set of pure strategies for each type of player, is a Nash equilibrium of the 'expanded game' where each player can be one of several types, each playing a different strategy. Harsanyi (1973) showed that a mixed-strategy equilibrium of a game of complete information can be justified as the limit of pure strategy equilibria of slightly perturbed games of incomplete information. In a Bayesian game, once players' type-contingent strategies have been computed, each player behaves as if he was facing opponents who play mixed strategies. Uncertainty thus arises from the distribution of types rather than from use of randomizing devices on the part of the players.

Correlated equilibrium. In a game of incomplete information, a player receives a 'signal' from nature about his type. Such signals are assumed to be private and independent. When signals are public and are not independent, we have correlation. Correlation may be perfect, as when the players observe the same random variable (for example, a coin toss), or imperfect, as when there is a random variable that can take three values, x, y, z, and player 1 knows that the realization is either x or a member of $\{y, z\}$, whereas player 2 knows that it is either z or a member of $\{x, y\}$. Even with imperfect correlation, players can do much better than playing a Nash equilibrium. Consider the game in Figure 3.

There are three Nash equilibria in this game: (H, D), (D, H) and $((1/2)D, (1/2)H; (1/2)D, (1/2)H)$. When multiple equilibria are present, and there is some conflict of interest among the players, it becomes difficult to see how a preplay negotiation process may end in an agreement to play one of the equilibria. Schelling (1960) proposed the notion of *focal point* to explain how, in such games, an equilibrium could be reached. For example, if player 1 is much more senior than player 2, (H, D) may seem the natural solution to both. However, notions like

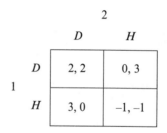

Figure 3

focal point or salience (Lewis 1969) refer to information external to the game, are difficult to formalize, and presuppose that players share the same information. Even in games of *pure coordination* like, for example, the game in Figure 5, where players' interests perfectly coincide, we may expect (a, c) to be played because it is the only Pareto optimal outcome, but such confidence can only be grounded in the assumption that players have common knowledge that Pareto optimality makes it a focal point for both. In games of pure coordination, however, preplay negotiation will easily identify an equilibrium, therefore the possibility of preplay communication among the players would easily solve the multiplicity problem. The game of Figure 3 is a more difficult case. Obviously player 1 prefers (H, D) and 2 prefers (D, H). (D, D) is not self-enforcing, and the mixed-strategy equilibrium only offers a meagre expected payoff of 1 to each player. Suppose now that the players can jointly watch the toss of a fair coin, and agree to play (D, H) if heads, and (H, D) if tails. This lottery is worth 1.5 to each player, and $(1.5, 1.5)$ is a better outcome than the mixed-strategy equilibrium. The agreement is self-fulfilling: observing heads establishes (D, H) as a focal point. The case of imperfect correlation is similar. Suppose that the two players engage a referee at no cost. The referee will use a random device to select one of the cells according to the following probabilities: $p(D, D) = p(H, D) = p(D, H) = 1/3, p(H, H) = 0$. The referee will not inform the players about the chosen cell, but will secretly tell 1 to use the row in which the cell occurs, and 2 to use the column in which the cell occurs. The players agree to do whatever the referee suggests. If they honour the agreement, (D, D), (D, H) and (H, D) will be played with probability 1/3 each. This agreement is self-fulfilling and corresponds to the outcome $(1.66, 1.66)$. It is, in Aumann's words, a *correlated equilibrium*, and it can be proved that the set of correlated equilibria always contains the Nash equilibria of the game (Aumann 1974).

827

Rationalizability. Notice that, in order to justify equilibrium play, we introduce self-enforcing agreements, and the possibility of preplay negotiation that would allow such agreements to take shape. In most games, common knowledge of the structure of the game and of players' rationality are not sufficient to predict that an equilibrium will be played, even if it is the unique equilibrium for the game. The concept of Nash equilibrium embodies a notion of individual rationality, since each player's equilibrium strategy is a best reply to the opponents' strategies, but unfortunately it does not specify how players can arrive to form the beliefs about each other's strategies that support equilibrium play. Beliefs, that is, can be internally consistent but fail to achieve the interpersonal consistency that guarantees that an equilibrium will be reached. Bernheim (1984) and Pearce (1984) have argued that assuming players' rationality (and common knowledge thereof) can only guarantee that a strategy will be *rationalizable*, in the sense of being supported by coherent beliefs about other players' choices and beliefs. But a combination of rationalizable choices need not constitute a Nash equilibrium. Take the game of Figure 2. Player 1 thinks player 2 will choose t_2 because he might think 1 will play s_1, on the assumption that 2 will play t_1 because 1 plays s_2. If 1 is expected to play s_2, it is rationalizable that 2 plays t_1. t_1 is a rationalizable strategy because player 2 can tell a coherent story about why 1 might choose s_2. Note that in this game all four combinations of strategies are rationalizable, yet none of them is an equilibrium.

Dominance. In a Nash equilibrium, the optimality of a strategy is only conditional on a fixed σ_{-i}, not on all possible σ_{-i}. In the game of Figure 1, however, the two Nash equilibrium strategies (D,D) are also optimal with respect to any strategy choice of the opponent. Whatever player 1 does, player 2 is better off by choosing D, and the same is true for player 1. We say that D is a *strictly dominant* strategy, in that it guarantees a player a better payoff than any other strategy, irrespective of the opponent's choice. If instead a strategy guarantees a player payoffs that are greater than or equal to the payoffs of any other strategy, that strategy is only *weakly dominant* for the player. Note that a *strictly dominant equilibrium* does not guarantee an optimal outcome; Figure 1 is the well-known prisoner's dilemma, where (D,D) is the unique, strictly dominant equilibrium, but playing (C,C) would have been better for both players. In this case, rationality dictates choosing (D,D), and indeed this is the unique prediction for the game. Notice that a strictly dominated strategy is never rationalizable, hence in this game the unique rationalizable combination of strategies is the Nash equilibrium.

Sometimes games can be solved by *iterated dominance*. Consider the game of Figure 4.

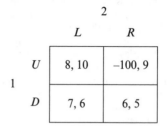

Figure 4

L is a strictly dominant strategy for player 2, and since rationality is common knowledge, 2 is expected to eliminate R. Now U dominates D for player 1, who eliminates it. In this case iterated dominance succeeds in reducing each player's set of available strategies to a singleton, so we can predict that the unique resulting profile of undominated strategies is the solution to the game. It is also easy to prove that such strategy profile is a Nash equilibrium (Bicchieri 1993). Note that assuming common knowledge of rationality (or at least some level of mutual knowledge of rationality) is crucial to obtaining the (U,L) solution. If there is some doubt that a player may not be fully rational – for example, if 1 thinks there is a 0.01 chance that R is chosen – then he does better by choosing D.

In Figure 5 there are two Nash equilibria in pure strategies: (a,c) and (b,d), and in the (a,c) equilibrium each player plays a weakly dominant strategy. Should we confidently predict that (a,c) will be the solution of the game? When a player has a strictly dominant strategy, rationality dictates choosing it, hence predicting behaviour is a simple matter. The case of weakly dominant strategies is not so straightforward. For one thing, it is not true that a weakly dominated strategy cannot be a best reply to any beliefs. In fact, for any weakly dominated strategy there is always some belief for which the strategy is a best reply. Putting the point differently, weak dominance means that there is at least one choice on the part of an opponent that makes one indifferent between the weakly dominated strategy and other strategies. In our example, were player 2 to believe that 1 plays b, her best reply would be d, and conversely, were player 1 to expect 2 to play d, his optimal strategy would be b.

Principles such as iterated strict dominance, rationalizability and Skyrms' (1990) deliberation dynamics are examples of how it is possible to restrict the set of predictions using rationality arguments alone. A very different approach is to start from the

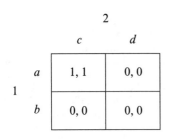

2

		c	*d*
	a	1, 1	0, 0
1			
	b	0, 0	0, 0

Figure 5

set of Nash equilibria, and ask whether some of them should be eliminated because they are in some sense 'unreasonable'. This is the approach taken by the *refinement* programme.

Normal form refinements. Consider again the game in Figure 5. How reasonable is the equilibrium (b, d)? Under what circumstances would players agree to play it, and then stick to the agreement? If the problem is that players should not be too sure of the opponents' choices, one should try to model this uncertainty in the game. Selten's insight was to treat perfect rationality as a limit case (Selten 1965). His 'trembling hand' metaphor suggests that deciding and acting might be two separate processes, in that even if one decides to take a particular action, one may end up doing something else by mistake. More precisely, it is required that an equilibrium strategy is not only optimal against the opponents' strategies, but also some very small probability $\varepsilon > 0$ that the opponents make 'mistakes'. Such an equilibrium is *trembling-hand perfect*. Is the equilibrium (b, d) perfect? If so, b must be optimal against c being played with probability ε and d being played with probability $1 - \varepsilon$ for some small $\varepsilon > 0$. But the payoff to a is ε, while the payoff to b is 0. Hence for all $\varepsilon > 0$, a is a better strategy choice. The equilibrium (b, d) is not perfect, but (a, c) is. A prudent player will thus rule out (b, d). In this simple game, checking the perfection of some action is easy, since only one 'mistake' is possible. With many actions, there are many more possible mistakes to take into account. Similarly, with many players we may need to worry about who is most likely to make a mistake. Note that the starting point of this approach is the set of Nash equilibria of the game. It is assumed that players will coordinate upon one of them, and thus the problem becomes that of ruling out all those equilibria that, for one reason or another, are not reasonable agreement points. Specifying why an equilibrium might be unacceptable is easier if one can consider what *would* happen were some of the players to 'deviate' from the agreed upon equilibrium. This is why much of the refinement

literature refers to games in extensive form, where the dynamic structure of games, the order in which players move and the kind of information they have when making a choice are made explicit.

4 Games in extensive form

The *extensive form* of a game specifies the following information: a finite set of players $i = 1, \ldots, n$, one of which might be nature (N); the order of moves; the players' choices at each move and what each player knows when he has to choose; the players' payoffs as a function of their moves; finally, moves by nature correspond to probability distributions over exogenous events. The order of play is represented by a game tree T, which is a finite set of partially ordered nodes $t \in T$ that satisfy a precedence relation denoted by ' $<$ '. The information a player has when he is choosing an action is represented using *information sets*, which partition the nodes of the tree. Since an information set can contain more than one node, the player who has to make a choice at an information set that contains, say, nodes t and t' will be uncertain as to which node he is at. If a game contains information sets that are not singletons, the game is one of *imperfect information*, in that one or more players will not know, at the moment of making a choice, what the preceding player did. A *subgame* is a collection of branches of a game which start from the same node and which, together with the node, form a game tree by itself. In Figure 6, player 2's decision node as well as her moves form a subgame of the game. Finally, the games I shall consider here are all games of *perfect recall*, in that a player always remembers what she did and knew previously. A *strategy* for player i is a complete plan of action that specifies an action at every node at which it is i's turn to move. Note that a strategy specifies actions even at nodes that will never be reached if that strategy is played. The game in Figure 6 is a finite game of perfect information where player 1 moves first. If he chooses D at the first node, the game ends and he nets a payoff of 1, whereas player 2 only gets 0. But choosing D at the first node is only *part* of a strategy of player 1; for example, it can be part of a strategy that says 'play D at the first node, and x at the last node'. It is important that a strategy specifies actions even at nodes that will not be reached: this allows players to say what *would* happen were those nodes to be reached by mistake or for some other reason. The game of Figure 6 has two Nash equilibria in pure strategies: (Dx, d) and (Dy, d). This is easy to verify by looking at Figure 6', the normal form representation of the game. Is there a way to eliminate one of the two equilibria?

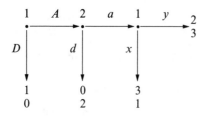

Figure 6

	d	a
Dx	1, 0	1, 0
Ax	0, 2	3, 1
Dy	1, 0	1, 0
Ay	0, 2	2, 3

2 (top of table); 1 (left of table)

Figure 6'

Suppose player 1 were to play at his last node. Since he is rational, he would choose x, which guarantees him a payoff of 3. Knowing by assumption that 1 is rational, player 2 – if she were to reach her decision node – would play d, since by playing a she would net a lower payoff. Finally, since by assumption player 1 knows that 2 is rational and that she knows that 1 is rational, he will choose D at his first decision node. (Dy, d) should thus be ruled out, since it recommends an irrational move at the last node. In the normal form, iterated elimination of weakly dominated strategies allows both equilibria to survive. The reason is simple: if 1 plans to choose D and 2 plans to choose d, it does not matter what player 1 would do at the last node, since that node will never be reached. The procedure used in the extensive form to conclude that only (Dx, d) is a reasonable solution is referred to as *backwards induction* (Zermelo 1913). In finite games of perfect information in which there are no ties in payoffs, backwards induction always identifies a unique equilibrium. The use of backwards induction to solve our game presupposes that players analyse the game from the end up and that, once a subgame has been reached, the conclusion about what is rational to do in that subgame is independent of any consideration of how that subgame was reached.

The strategic irrelevance of past moves – which is crucial to backwards induction – has been questioned by many philosophers and game theorists. If player 2 were to reach her decision node, would she keep thinking that player 1 is rational? Clearly her choice will depend on how she answers this question. Binmore (1987), Bicchieri (1989, 1993) and Reny (1992) were the first to point out that backwards induction may be inconsistent with common knowledge of rationality. The jury is still out and in recent years much foundational work has been devoted to model more precisely players' knowledge and reasoning in games.

Extensive form refinements. The goal of the refinement programme is that of eliminating implausible equilibria. In the normal form, Selten's trembling-hand perfection requires that players ask how a strategy will perform were another player to take an action that has zero probability in equilibrium. In the extensive form representation, we ask what would happen off-equilibrium, at points in the game tree that will never be reached if a given equilibrium is played. In both cases, the starting point is an equilibrium, which is checked for *stability* against possible deviations. By its nature, the Nash equilibrium concept does not restrict action choices off the equilibrium path, since those choices do not affect the payoff of the player who moves there. For example, the equilibrium (Dy, d) in Figure 6 lets player 1 make an irrational choice at the last node, since that choice is not going to affect his payoff (which is determined by his choosing D at the beginning of the game). However, the strategy of a player at an off-equilibrium information set can affect what other players choose at their equilibrium information sets: in Figure 6, in order to choose D, player 1 will have to decide what would happen were he to play A instead. He thus has to think about player 2's choice at an off-equilibrium node. His conclusion about 2's choice will obviously affect his own move. *Subgame perfection* is a criterion proposed by Selten (1965) to rule out implausible equilibria in extensive games of perfect information. A subgame perfect equilibrium is a Nash equilibrium such that the strategies, when restricted to any subgame, remain a Nash equilibrium of the subgame. The equilibrium (Dy, d) is not subgame perfect. Note that in these games, the equilibrium obtained by backwards induction is also the unique subgame perfect equilibrium.

However, as Figure 7 suggests, not all subgame perfect equilibria are sensible. In this game both (c, L) and (a, R) are trivially subgame perfect, since this game has no proper subgames. To obviate this problem, further refinements have been proposed. I will mention here only some of the most important.

Kreps and Wilson (1982) introduced the concept of *sequential equilibrium*. Briefly, a sequential equilibrium is a strategy combination and a system of beliefs with the following properties: each player has a belief over the nodes at each of his information sets. Beginning at any information set, given a player's belief there and given the strategies of the other players, his own strategy for the rest of the game still maximizes his expected payoff. Beliefs must be obtained from the beliefs at earlier information sets and the equilibrium strategies by Bayes' rule. A *perfect equilibrium* (Selten 1975) is an equilibrium that is robust to small perturbations of players' equilibrium strategies. A *proper equilibrium* (Myerson 1978) is an equilibrium that is robust with respect to 'plausible' deviations, interpreted as deviations that do not involve costly mistakes. An alternative refinement that does not involve consideration of mistakes is the idea of *forward induction* (Kohlberg and Mertens 1986). The main idea is that off-equilibrium beliefs should be consistent with interpretations of deviations as rational moves, or *signals* that the deviating player intends to play something different.

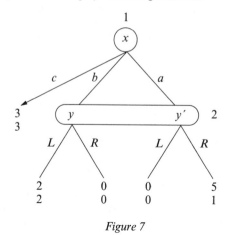

Figure 7

5   Selection by evolution

An alternative way of dealing with multiple equilibria is to suppose that the selection process is made by nature. In an *evolutionary game* players are endowed with rules (strategies) and are randomly matched with other players in repeated encounters. A well known evolutionary model is Axelrod's (1984) prisoner's dilemma tournament in which strategies were matched against each other in turn. Survival of the fittest favours rules that are not exploitable by other rules and do well when played against themselves,

because otherwise as the rule invaded the population and thus became more frequent, it would become weakened by lack of success. Maynard Smith (1982) has defined an *evolutionarily stable strategy* (ESS) as a strategy p^* which (i) is a best reply to itself and (ii) if there is any other strategy p that is a best reply to p^*, then p^* must be a better reply to p than p is to itself. As an example, consider a modified version of the game in Figure 3, one in which the payoffs for HD are (4,0), and those for DH are (0,4), and suppose that the two strategies are 'hawk' and 'dove'. A hawk always fights and escalates contests until it wins or is badly hurt. A dove never escalates; if it fights with another dove, they will settle the contest by sharing the resource. Suppose injury has a payoff in terms of loss of fitness equal to -6. A victory nets 4. If hawk meets hawk or dove meets dove, each has a 50 per cent chance of victory. So a hawk meeting another hawk has an expected payoff of $1/2 \times 4 + 1/2 \times (-6) = -1$. If hawk meets dove, hawk gets 4 and dove gets 0; finally, two doves can expect a payoff of $1/2 \times 4 = 2$. The unique ESS turns out to be the mixed-strategy Nash equilibrium of the game: play hawk with probability 2/3 and dove with probability 1/3. If it were the case that 'hawkishness' and 'doveness' are genetic traits, we would expect the population to evolve so that two thirds of it is made up of hawks and one third of doves. Note that the evolutionary model gives a natural interpretation to mixed strategies as the proportions of certain strategies (or traits) in a population. This is an example of how evolution can select one equilibrium among many. In this particular game there are three equilibria – HD, DH, and (1/3 D, 2/3 H) – but only one of them is evolutionarily stable.

6   Repeated games

Repeated games model ongoing interactions and are thus suitable models for phenomena like cooperation, trust, revenge, punishment and reputation formation. Take the prisoner's dilemma depicted in Figure 1, where C stands for 'cooperate' and D for 'defect'. Suppose this game is repeated N times. At each stage, players know the actions taken by all players at the previous stage, and the payoffs to each player are simply the sum of the payoffs he receives at each stage. Since the game is noncooperative, players cannot make enforceable agreements to cooperate. Moreover, a promise to cooperate or a threat to retaliate if the other does not cooperate, in order to be effective, must be credible. Both players know that in the last Nth repetition both will defect, no matter what they did before. So they might as well defect in the $N-1$th repetition, too. Proceeding inductively, both players defect in each period, and indeed this is the unique subgame perfect equilibrium (see §4) of the repeated game. Consequently a promise to cooperate is not credible, nor is a threat to retaliate. They are not credible because they involve irrational behaviour, and rationality is common knowledge among the players.

When the game is infinitely repeated, the inductive argument that leads players to defect at each stage fails. In such games mutual cooperation is possible, indeed is one of many possible equilibria. This result is knows as the *Folk theorem* – so called because it is part of the folk literature of game theory but its authorship is obscure (Aumann 1981). It states that any feasible expected payoff combination can be sustained in an equilibrium provided that each player has an expected payoff at least as large as she can guarantee for herself even if all other players pick strategies solely to punish her. In our example, any pair of feasible payoffs that gives each player more than 1 can be sustained in equilibrium. This result also holds for games in which players discount future payoffs, provided the discount rate is small. And it holds for games with an expected finite number of repetitions but a small probability that the game ends at each period.

As an example, consider indefinitely repeating the game in Figure 1, where players roll a fair dice after each stage and continue playing if and only if neither 5 nor 6 appears. There is a probability of 1/3 that each stage is the last, and the probability that the game will continue until at least the Nth stage is $(2/3)^{N-1}$. Since $(2/3)^N$ goes to zero as N goes to infinity, the probability that the game will go on forever is zero. Suppose player 1 announces that they will cooperate as long as player 2 is cooperative, but as soon as 2 defects, 1 will defect forever. The expected payoff of mutual cooperation (C) is $2 + 2(2/3) + \ldots + 2(2/3)^N + \ldots + 2(2/3)^{N+2} + \ldots$. Can player 2 gain by deviating and, say, play D (defect) at the $N+1$th stage? In this case 2 will at most get $2 + 2(2/3) + \ldots + 2(2/3)^{N-1} + 3(2/3)^N + 1(2/3)^{N+1}1(2/3)^{N+2} + \ldots$. Since the expected payoff of C is better than the expected payoff of D, it is better for player 2 to cooperate. Mutual cooperation is a Nash equilibrium (see §3).

Cooperation can be achieved also in a finitely repeated game, provided the players involved are not too sure about each other's rationality. Suppose that one player assigns a small probability that the other is a *tit-for-tat* player, that is, that he cooperates in the first period, and then mimics what the other player did in the preceding period. Kreps *et al.* (1982) showed that if the game is one of incomplete information (see §3), a small probability that one of the players is using the tit-for-tat strategy is enough to guarantee that both will cooperate until near the last period. Cooperation for several periods of the game is a rational strategy for both players, provided that the prior probability of one of them playing tit-for-tat is common knowledge. This is an important result, as it explains at least some of the experimental evidence about cooperative behaviour in situations that have a known finite time-horizon. Furthermore, it shows that cooperative behaviour is possible, and compatible with individual rationality, even in the absence of external enforcing mechanisms.

7 Bargaining games

Consider a game in which two players must split three (indivisible) dollars between them. They must choose shares x_1, x_2 simultaneously. Their payoffs are defined as follows: if $x_1 + x_2 \leq 3$, each player gets the share he proposed; if $x_1 + x_2 > 3$, each gets nothing. There are four Nash equilibria in pure strategies: $(0,3)$, $(3,0)$ $(1,2)$ and $(2,1)$. One way to solve this indeterminacy is to allow the players to make a sequence of offers and counter-offers. For example, player 1 may be allowed to make the first offer; if it is accepted, player 2 gets the remainder and the game ends. If it is rejected, it is now player 2's turn to make an offer, and player 1 can accept or reject it. If he rejects, each player gets a payoff of zero. It is now possible to apply backwards induction, and predict that player 2 will offer one dollar to player 1 at the second stage, knowing that he will accept. Thus player 1 knows that at the first stage the only acceptable offer is two dollars to player 2. Further specification of the bargaining process thus determines the outcome of the bargaining problem as a subgame perfect equilibrium, in which player 1 gets one dollar and player 2 gets two dollars. The outcome, however, is very sensitive to the details of the process, in this case who moves first.

An alternative way to get a prediction for the outcome of a bargaining problem is to list a set of properties that an outcome is expected to have. Consider again our bargaining problem, but assume now the three dollars are divisible, and that players' marginal utility of money is positive and constant. As before, if the players do not reach an agreement, they get nothing, $(x_0, y_0) = (0,0)$. Acceptable shares need not sum to $3.

In the case of two-person bargaining, we can draw the set of possible money combinations (the outcome set) on a graph with x representing the share as well as the utility of player 1 on one axis, and y representing the share as well as the utility of player 2 on the other.

In Figure 8, the origin has been placed at that utility combination that corresponds to total disagreement (x_0, y_0).

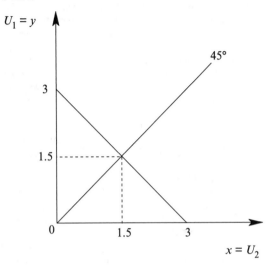

Figure 8

Nash (1950, 1953) suggested that it is reasonable to expect the outcome of a bargaining process to satisfy the following conditions:

(1) *Pareto optimality*: whatever agreement is reached, it will not be possible to improve it without damaging one of the players.
(2) *Independence of irrelevant alternatives*: if we drop some possible utility combinations from the outcome set, and if the actual outcome of the original game is also a possible outcome in the restricted game, then it will be the final outcome for the restricted game as well.
(3) *Symmetry*: if the set of possible outcomes is symmetric (that is, if for every point $x = a$, $y = b$ in the outcome set, the point $x = b$, $y = a$ is also in the set), then the outcome of bargaining will give $x = y$.
(4) *Invariance*: the solution is independent of the units in which we measure utility.

Nash proved that there is a unique point that satisfies the four conditions, namely the utility combination (x^*, y^*) such that $(x^* - x_0)(y^* - y_0) \geq (x - x_0)(y - y_0)$ for all (x, y) in the outcome set.

The bargaining set of our example is symmetric, hence the outcome must lie on the 45°-line, and Pareto optimality requires it to be on the Pareto frontier. This identifies $(x^*, y^*) = (1.5, 1.5)$ as the unique outcome. Clearly our prediction of the outcome of a bargaining problem will depend upon our degree of confidence in the conditions that a solution should satisfy. There is, however, a link between the latter approach and the strategic one: Nash himself suggested that any set of conditions that identifies a particular outcome should be supplemented by a bargaining process that results in that outcome.

8 Cooperative games

In a noncooperative game, there is no way for the players to enter into binding agreements, or to commit themselves to playing a particular strategy. Agreements are of course possible in such games, but to be honoured they have to be self-enforcing, that is, they must be Nash equilibria. In a cooperative game on the other hand, agreements between the players are enforceable. The Nash bargaining solution introduced an approach to games that overlooks moves and strategies in favour of considering the set of all possible outcomes of an interaction and selecting a particular outcome based on some prior conditions. This approach makes sense if we allow for the possibility of enforcing contracts, since in this case every outcome that can be jointly achieved by the players is a feasible agreement.

While the Nash solution can be generalized to n players (Harsanyi 1977), the possibility of coalition formations among the players raises new problems. Games in which coalitions can arise are described in *characteristic function* form. Such games are completely described by the players, the coalition structure, and the specification of what each coalition can guarantee itself. An example of a game in characteristic function form is the following: there are three players who must divide a dollar between themselves with the convention that a majority of two rules. Since a majority can decide on how to split the dollar, a single player cannot guarantee any amount. Two players can together guarantee a total of one dollar, and the coalition consisting of all the players (the grand coalition) can guarantee itself one dollar. We define an *imputation* as a vector $x = \{x_1, \ldots, x_n\}$ such that $\Sigma_{i \in N} x_i = V(N)$, the total amount the grand coalition can guarantee itself if there is a total of N players; in the game above this sum is one dollar. We also require that each x_i must be at least as great as what player i can guarantee himself. The imputation thus refers to the amount each player receives in a given outcome. It does not yet indicate the solution of the game. A solution for such games is a proposed distribution of the joint payoff to the players that is accepted. There are many ways to characterize payoff vectors as acceptable. One approach is to provide criteria that an acceptable allocation should satisfy.

Two such criteria are Pareto optimality and symmetry. The *Shapley value* (Shapley 1953) is the unique payoff allocation that satisfies the above criteria. It is such that the value of each player i in a game turns out to be the average of all marginal contributions that player i can make to all coalitions.

A natural requirement for any payoff vector to be mutually agreeable seems to be that no subgroup could do better by breaking the agreement. The core concept captures this idea formally. The *core* consists of all imputations satisfying $\Sigma_{i \in S} x_i = V(S)$, the amount coalition S can guarantee, for all possible S. In the dollar division game the core is empty, indicating that there is no allocation that is stable against deviations by subgroups.

See also: BEHAVIOURISM IN THE SOCIAL SCIENCES; ECONOMICS, PHILOSOPHY OF; PROBABILITY, INTERPRETATIONS OF; RATIONAL BELIEFS; RATIONAL CHOICE THEORY; SEMANTICS, GAME-THEORETIC; SOCIAL ACTION

References and further reading

* Allais, M. (1953) 'Le comportement de l'homme rationnel devant le risque: critique des postulats et axiomes de l'école américaine', *Econometrica* 21: 503–46. (Shows how the von Neumann–Morgenstern Independence axiom is sometimes violated.)
* Arnauld, A. (1662) *La Logique, ou l'art de penser*, Paris; 2nd edn, Amsterdam: Wolfgang, 1685. (A very early theory of decision-making under uncertainty. See specifically chapter XVI, part III.)
* Aumann, R. (1974) 'Subjectivity and Correlation in Randomized Strategies', *Journal of Mathematical Economics* 1: 67–96. (Introduces the concept of *correlated equilibrium*.)
* —— (1976) 'Agreeing to Disagree', *Annals of Statistics* 4: 1,236–9. (Defines *common knowledge* in games.)
* —— (1981) 'Survey of repeated games', in R. Aumann (ed.) *Essays in Game Theory and Mathematical Economics in Honor of Oscar Morgenstern*, Mannheim: Bibliographisches Institut. (A good introduction to repeated games.)
* Axelrod, R. (1984) *The Evolution of Cooperation*, New York: Basic Books. (Shows how a cooperative strategy can do well in computer tournaments, and how cooperation can evolve in a mixed population.)
* Bernheim, B.D. (1984) 'Rationalizable Strategic Behavior', *Econometrica* 52: 1,007–28. (With Pearce's (1984) article, the classic definition of *rationalizability*.)
* Bernoulli, D. (1738) 'Specimen theoriae novae de

mensura sortis', *Commentarii Academiae Scientiarum Imperialis Petropolitanae* V: 75–92; trans. L. Sommer, 'Exposition of a New Theory on the Measurement of Wealth', *Econometrica* 22: 23–36. (Provides the oldest definition of expected utility and applies it to solving the St Petersburg paradox.)
* Bicchieri, C. (1989) 'Self-Refuting Theories of Strategic Interaction: A Paradox of Common Knowledge', *Erkenntnis* 30: 69–85. (Shows how common knowledge of rationality is inconsistent with backwards induction.)
* —— (1993) *Rationality and Coordination*, Cambridge: Cambridge University Press. (A comprehensive introduction to the philosophical foundations of game theory.)
* Binmore, K. (1987) 'Modeling Rational Players: I', *Economics and Philosophy* 3: 179–214. (A criticism of traditional justifications of backwards induction and a reflection on the meaning of rationality in strategic contexts.)
* Butler, J. (1736) *The Analogy of Religion, Natural and Revealed, to the Constitution and Course of Nature*, London. (Classic text refered to in §1.)
* Ellsberg, D. (1961) 'Risk, Ambiguity, and the Savage Axioms', *Quarterly Journal of Economics* 75: 643–69. (Documents a famous violation of the von Neumann and Morgenstern Independence axiom.)
* Fishburn, P.C. (1982) *The Foundations of Expected Utility*, Dordrecht: Reidel. (Comprehensive introduction to decision theory.)
* Harsanyi, J. (1967) 'Games with Incomplete Information Played by Bayesian Players', *Management Science* 14: 159–82, 320–34, 486–502. (Reduces games of incomplete information to games of complete information.)
* —— (1973) 'Games with Randomly Disturbed Payoffs: A New Rationale for Mixed Strategy Equilibrium Points', *International Journal of Game Theory* 2: 1–23. (Introduces the idea of *purification* of mixed strategies.)
* —— (1977) *Rational Behaviour and Bargaining Equilibrium*, Cambridge: Cambridge University Press. (A comprehensive treatise on bargaining games.)
* Kahneman, D. and Tversky, A. (1979) 'Prospect Theory: An Analysis of Decision Under Risk', *Econometrica* 47: 263–91. (A classical criticism of decision theory based on experimental evidence.)
* Kohlberg, E. and Mertens, J.-F. (1986) 'On the strategic stability of equilibria', *Econometrica* 54: 1,003–37. (Introduces the idea of *forward induction* as a refinement of Nash equilibrium.)
* Kreps, D. and Wilson, R. (1982) 'Sequential

Equilibria', *Econometrica* 50: 863–94. (Defines the concept of *sequential equilibrium* as a refinement of Nash equilibrium.)

* Kreps, D., Milgrom, P., Roberts, J. and Wilson, R. (1982) 'Rational Cooperation in the Finitely Repeated Prisoner's Dilemma', *Journal of Economic Theory* 27: 245–52. (Shows how incomplete information allows players to cooperate in a finitely repeated prisoner's dilemma.)
* Lewis, D. (1969) *Convention: A Philosophical Study*, Cambridge, MA: Harvard University Press. (A study of conventions as coordination equilibria.)
* Machina, M. (1982) 'Expected Utility Analysis Without the Independence Axiom', *Econometrica* 50: 277–323. (An alternative axiomatization of expected utility.)
* Maynard Smith, J. (1982) *Evolution and the Theory of Games*, Cambridge: Cambridge University Press. (A classic application of game theory to biology.)
* Myerson, R. (1978) 'Refinements of the Nash Equilibrium Concept', *International Journal of Game Theory* 7: 73–80. (Introduces the concept of *proper equilibrium*.)
* Nash, J. (1950) 'The Bargaining Problem', *Econometrica* 18: 155–62. (Introduces the *Nash bargaining solution*.)
* —— (1951) 'Noncooperative Games', *Annals of Mathematics* 54: 289–95. (Defines and proves the existence of *Nash equilibrium*.)
* —— (1953) 'Two-person Cooperative Games', *Econometrica* 21: 128–40. (Proves there exists a solution for such games that satisfies certain desirable properties.)
* Neumann, J. von (1928) 'Zur theorie der gesellschaftsspiele', *Mathematische Annalen* 100: 295–320. (Contains the proof of the *minimax theorem*.)
* Neumann, J. von and Morgenstern, O. (1944) *Theory of Games and Economic Behavior*, Princeton, NJ: Princeton University Press. (The classic, if outdated, introduction to games theory.)
  Osborne, M. and Rubinstein, A. (1994) *A Course in Games Theory*, Cambridge, MA: MIT Press. (An excellent, comprehensive textbook.)
* Pearce, D.G. (1984) 'Rationalizable Strategic Behavior and the Problem of Perfection', *Econometrica* 52: 1,029–50. (Introduces the concept of *rationalizability* independently of Bernheim.)
* Reny, P. (1992) 'Rationality in Extensive Form Games', *Journal of Economic Perspectives* 6: 92–100. (Shows how common knowledge assumptions may be inconsistent with backwards induction.)
* Savage, L. (1954) *The Foundations of Statistics*, New York: Dover. (Seminal work on decisions under uncertainty.)
* Schelling, T. (1960) *The Strategy of Conflict*, Cambridge, MA: Harvard University Press. (Contains a simple but comprehensive analysis of coordination games.)
* Selten, R. (1965) 'Spieltheorethische Behandlung eines Oligopolmodels mit Nachfragetragheit', *Zeitschrift für die gesamte Staatswissenschaft* 121: 301–24. (Introduces the idea of *trembling hand perfection* for games in normal form.)
* —— (1975) 'Re-examination of the Perfectness Concept for Equilibrium Points in Extensive Games', *International Journal of Game Theory* 4: 22–55. (Introduces the concept of *perfect equilibrium*.)
* Shapley, L.S. (1953) 'A Value for n-person Games', in H.W. Kuhn and A.W. Tucker (eds) *Contributions to the Theory of Games*, Princeton, NJ: Princeton University Press, vol. II, 307–17. (Introduces the now classical solution concept for cooperative games.)
* Skyrms, B. (1990) *The Dynamics of Rational Deliberation*, Cambridge, MA: Harvard University Press. (See §3. Deliberation dynamics, an example of how it is possible to restrict the set of predictions using rationality arguments alone.)
* Zermelo, E. (1913) 'Über eine Anwendung der Mengenlehre auf die Theorie des Schachspiels', in *Proceedings of the Fifth International Congress of Mathematicians*, vol. II, Cambridge: Cambridge University Press. (The original statement of the *backwards induction* algorithm.)

CRISTINA BICCHIERI

DECISION PROBLEM *see*
CHURCH'S THEOREM AND THE DECISION PROBLEM

DECONSTRUCTION

Although the term is often used interchangeably (and loosely) alongside others like 'post-structuralism' and 'postmodernism', deconstruction differs from these other movements. Unlike post-structuralism, its sources lie squarely within the tradition of Western philosophical debate about truth, knowledge, logic, language and representation. Where post-structuralism follows the linguist Saussure – or its own version of Saussure – in espousing a radically conventionalist (hence sceptical

*and relativist) approach to these issues, deconstruction
pursues a more complex and critical path, examining
the texts of philosophy with an eye to their various
blindspots and contradictions. Where postmodernism
blithely declares an end to the typecast 'Enlightenment'
or 'modernist' project of truth-seeking rational enquiry,
deconstruction preserves the critical spirit of Enlightenment thought while questioning its more dogmatic or
complacent habits of belief. It does so primarily
through the close reading of philosophical and other
texts and by drawing attention to the moments of
'aporia' (unresolved tension or conflict) that tend to be
ignored by mainstream exegetes. Yet this is not to say
(as its detractors often do) that deconstruction is a
kind of all-licensing textualist 'freeplay' which abandons every last standard of interpretive fidelity, rigour
or truth. At any rate it is a charge that finds no warrant
in the writings of those – Jacques Derrida and Paul de
Man chief among them – whose work is discussed
below.*

1   **Is there a logic of deconstruction?**
2   **Paul de Man and 'aesthetic ideology'**
3   **Some analytical bearings**

1   Is there a logic of deconstruction?

What is 'deconstruction' and what does it do? There is
a problem here in that DERRIDA often goes out of his
way to disown any summary treatment of the topic or
any attempt to define (and so delimit) deconstruction
in 'adequate' conceptual terms. Nevertheless one can
offer at least some attempt at a working definition.
What typically occurs in a deconstructive reading is
that the text in question is shown to harbour
contradictory logics which are standardly ignored –
or concealed from view – on other, more orthodox
accounts. Very often it is a matter of locating certain
clearly-marked binary oppositions (as for instance
between nature and culture, speech and writing,
concept and metaphor, or philosophy and literature)
and showing that their order of priority is by no
means as stable or secure as the text seeks to
maintain. That is to say, there is a counter-logic at
work whereby those distinctions can be shown to
break down, or to generate a reading markedly at
odds with the author's overt intent. Not that intention
is simply ruled out as irrelevant for the purposes of a
deconstructive reading. On the contrary, it offers an
'indispensable guardrail' (Derrida [1967b] 1975: 158)
which saves interpretation from running wild in
endless subtleties of its own ingenious devising.
However, this leaves open the possibility that texts
may mean something other – and more – than is

allowed for by any straightforward appeal to the
warrant of authorial intention.

Thus in each of the above-mentioned cases one
term (the first) is conventionally assigned a positive or
superior value while the other is construed – by author
and mainstream interpreters alike – as self-evidently
standing in a dependent, derivative or supplementary
relation to it. For Rousseau, nature both precedes
culture and represents a better, more authentic way of
life, while writing is regarded as a bad 'supplement' to
speech, one that involves all manner of corrupting
artifice and which infects the very sources of
spontaneous 'natural' expression. Yet he cannot
describe that idealized 'state of nature' except in
terms that perforce acknowledge the *impossibility* of
any such state having ever existed. For there is clearly
a logical or conceptual problem about an argument
that sets up this rigid opposition between nature and
culture, but which then proceeds to identify the best
(that is, the most primitive, least 'civilized') cultures
with an early stage of social evolution that would
somehow *not yet* have embarked upon the path to
civilization and ruin. The case with speech and writing
is somewhat more complex but can be stated along
much the same lines (see ROUSSEAU, J. §2).

For Rousseau, speech – in its 'natural' condition –
is a mode of utterance that expresses sentiments so
directly (with so little room for civilized pretence) that
it allows human beings to communicate face-to-face
without any need for the kinds of elaborate convention that characterize other, more articulate forms of
linguistic exchange. What is bad about writing is
precisely its dependence on a graphic notation which
involves such artifice as the very condition of its
possibility, and which thus stands at the furthest
remove from the passional origins of speech. However
this argument fails to take account of the conventional character of *all* language, spoken and written
alike; that is to say, the extent to which speech
partakes of various signifying systems (phonetic,
semantic, syntactic and so on) in the absence of
which it would simply not qualify as language.
Furthermore it is just this reliance on conventions –
a matter of structural necessity – that Rousseau has to
recognize (against his own wishes) as an intrinsic
condition of language-in-general. For it would then
be the case that writing (not speech) might offer the
best model for explaining those constitutive features
of language – its structural properties, conventional
character, capacity to signify in various contexts
irrespective of self-present utterer's intentions, and
so forth – which necessarily pertain to *all* language,
whether written or spoken (Derrida 1989).

There is a parallel here with Wittgenstein's argument against the possibility of a private language, that

is to say, his contention that any such 'language' would not in fact constitute a language since it would lack the criteria for shared understanding and hence be wholly unintelligible even to its solitary user (see PRIVATE LANGUAGE ARGUMENT; WITTGENSTEIN, L.). What is distinctive about Derrida's approach to such issues is also what sets deconstruction apart from most work in the 'other' (analytic or Anglo-American) tradition. That is, he treats them as issues specific to the reading of certain problematical passages in certain texts, passages whose overt or manifest sense is shown to be at odds with the structural logic that governs the argument as a whole. Hence Derrida's claim with regard to Rousseau that 'his declared intention is not annulled by this but rather *inscribed* within a system which it no longer dominates' (Derrida [1967b] 1975: 243). However this emphasis on textual close-reading goes along with a keen analytical grasp of the philosophic issues involved and should not, therefore, be taken as evidence that Derrida is practising literary criticism (or a mode of 'merely' rhetorical exegesis) under the guise of linguistic philosophy. Rather he argues from the *conditions of possibility* for raising such questions about meaning, context, authorial intention and so forth, questions that clearly point beyond the sphere of localized interpretative insight or thematic commentary. Thus he is not so much concerned with particular instances of paradox, aporia or self-contradiction in Rousseau's texts. What chiefly engages Derrida's interest is that pervasive 'logic of supplementarity' whereby the second (supposedly inferior or derivative) term in each pair turns out to be always already presupposed in any definition of the first (supposedly original and self-sufficient) term. This logic may resist formalized statement through its complexities of modal structure – which Derrida brings out to striking effect in his reading of Rousseau – and its apparent suspension of classical axioms like bivalence or non-contradiction. But this should hardly place his work beyond the pale for philosophers with a knowledge of developments in recent post-classical (for example, intuitionist or many-valued) logic.

2   Paul de Man and 'aesthetic ideology'

Paul DE MAN is another thinker whose writing occupies the currently contested zone between philosophy and literary theory. In de Man's case also, the suspicion is often voiced that his practice of minute close-reading – especially when applied to philosophic texts – must go along with a lack of genuine analytic rigour or merely a desire to make trouble by inventing all manner of pseudo-problems. I should not wish to

claim that this characterization is entirely wide of the mark, at least as regards de Man's more tortuous attempts to outdo Nietzsche in deconstructing all the concepts and categories of logic, epistemology, causal explanation and other 'metaphysical' notions (de Man 1979). All too often these claims have been taken on trust or treated as a deconstructive *fait accompli* by literary theorists keen to upstage their colleagues in philosophy or the natural sciences. At its best, however, de Man's work cannot be dismissed as simply a product of the turf-battle between rival academic disciplines. In late essays like 'The Epistemology of Metaphor' (1978) on Locke, Condillac and Kant, and 'Pascal's Allegory of Persuasion' (1981) on the relation between suasive or performative language and the language of logical proof-procedures, his thought exhibits an exceptional degree of analytic acuity and rigour. Certainly he is far from advancing the sorts of blanket 'textualist' claim – such as 'all concepts are metaphors', 'all philosophy is a kind of literature', 'all talk of "truth" is just a species of rhetorical imposture', and so forth – that are often attributed to him (and to Derrida) by disciples and opponents alike.

Above all, de Man insists that textual exegesis in the deconstructive mode can at times produce readings sharply at odds with established or mainstream critical opinion. This produces an extreme – some would say perverse – attentiveness to just those kinds of aberrant textual detail (tropological swerves, displacements, substitutions or elisions) which complicate the reading-process beyond any notion of straightforward fidelity to the author's presumed intent. Of course this description might also apply to that mode of 'rational reconstruction' by which some philosophers have lately seen fit to treat the texts of past thinkers with a view to their own, mainly analytic concerns. However it is the aim of this approach to discover some viable (constructive) solution to problems whose importance is taken to justify the strong-revisionist line. For de Man, conversely, it is the purpose of a deconstructive reading to respect the very letter of the text even where this leads to a stage of aporetic deadlock where the text turns out to contest or subvert its own statements of intent.

Hence his insistence on the stubborn *literality* of deconstruction, that is to say, its power to hold out against the seductive ('eudaimonic') appeal of other, more compliant and therefore – he would argue – less rigorous modes of understanding. For de Man much depends on the way that we read certain passages in the work of philosophers and literary theorists who have reflected – in a more or less self-conscious or critical mode – on these issues of language, knowledge and representation. What he often discovers is an alternating rhythm of co-implicated 'blindness' and 'insight', a rhythm characterized by moments of apparent naïvety (for example, with regard to the supposed organic or consubstantial relation between language and nature) which none the less exist in close proximity to moments of un-self-deceiving rigour (de Man 1983). His aim is to expose the workings of a deep-laid 'aesthetic ideology' whose effect – so he argues – is chiefly manifest in the discourse of post-Kantian philosophy and literary theory. Most often it results from a confusion between linguistic (especially metaphorical) structures and those forms of phenom-enal or sensory perception that characterize our knowledge of natural-world objects and processes. Thus: 'literature is fiction not because it somehow refuses to acknowledge "reality", but because it is not *a priori* certain that language functions according to principles which are those, or which are *like* those, of the phenomenal world' (de Man 1986: 11). To suppose otherwise is to fall into a way of thinking that can all too easily be co-opted for the purposes of ideological mystification.

Such is, for instance, the Cratylist delusion – revived by Romantic poet-philosophers like Schiller and Coleridge – according to which it is possible for language (especially the language of symbol and metaphor) to achieve a condition of organic form beyond all the Kantian antinomies of subject and object, mind and nature, or intuitive and conceptual knowledge. Aesthetic ideology can thus be seen as the source of some far-reaching errors, among them – most crucially for de Man – the idea that particular (national) languages and cultures can likewise mani-fest the kind of predestined, organic development and growth that grants them an inherent superiority over other, more fractured or dissociated forms of cultural-linguistic expression. De Man's notorious wartime journalism, published in Nazi-occupied Belgium, often attributed just such a natural, predestined eminence to German thought and culture. It seems plausible to claim that his later writings were concerned in various ways to challenge or resist what he subsequently saw as the seductive power of an aesthetic creed with large implications for our thinking about issues of culture, politics and moral responsibility. Thus: 'what we call ideology is precisely the confusion of linguistic with natural reality, of reference with phenomenalism'. And again, more pointedly, those who charge deconstruction with a culpable indifference to issues of history and politics 'are merely stating their fear at having their own ideological mystifications exposed by the tool they are trying to discredit. They are, in short, very

poor readers of Marx's German Ideology' (de Man 1986: 11).

3 Some analytic bearings

Gilbert RYLE lost patience with the so-called 'psychologism' of Husserl, despite having previously published some detailed and constructive (albeit critical) studies of his work (Ryle 1971 – see RYLE, G. §1). So it was – or so the story is often told – that a rift emerged between phenomenology (along with various derivative 'continental' schools of thought) and later developments in the Anglo-American analytic tradition. This view fitted in with the received idea – initiated by Russell and Frege, and erected into a full-scale programme by logical empiricists like Rudolf Carnap – that philosophy should work to clear away those errors and confu-sions of natural language that could best be revealed by analysis in the formal or logico-semantic mode (see ANALYTICAL PHILOSOPHY §2). It would also help to resist the kinds of metaphysical bewitchment by language to be seen at their worst (so Carnap thought) in Heidegger's obscurantist appeal to the primordial wisdom supposedly enshrined in Greek and German etymology. Derrida's work has indeed been much influenced by Heidegger, especially as regards its questioning of those various deep-laid 'logocentric' priorities and values whose presence in the Western philosophical tradition is a constant theme of his writing, early and late. However he has also criticicized some aspects of Heidegger's thought, among them precisely the harking-back to a lost originary plenitude of Being (Derrida 1967b). For it is here that Heidegger himself falls prey to a potent irrationalist mystique, an appeal to language – or to certain privileged *national* languages and cultures – as the source of a wisdom supposedly concealed throughout the history of so-called 'Western meta-physics' (see HEIDEGGER, M. §6).

In de Man's work also, Heidegger figures as a prime example of that alternating pattern of 'blind-ness' and 'insight' which in turn can enable the reader to attain a less prejudiced (if never fully adequate, transparent or demystified) level of understanding (de Man 1983). Such arguments will scarcely be convincing to those for whom 'deconstruction' is pretty much synonymous with the obscurantist 'jargon of authenticity' that Heidegger promoted and that Derrida has supplied with its latest fashion-able twist. However this notion cannot stand up to the sort of close reading which Derrida brings to his commentary on Heidegger and others, and which his own texts properly require on the part of responsible critics. Here again what has most often got in its way is the fixed preconception – handed down from the logical empiricists – that analytic (that is, genuine or serious) thought should have no truck with such extravagant forms of 'continental' pseudo-philosophy.

If the prospects look fair for a mending of this rift, then one clear sign is the current reappraisal (by Michael Dummett (1993) among others) of the strong continuities that exist within and between these two lines of descent. Another is the willingness of some commentators to look again, for example, at Derrida's reading of J.L. Austin – the target of a well-known hostile response by John Searle (1977) – and to discover not only points of genuine philosophical interest but also a certain affinity between the thought of Austin and Derrida (Austin 1961, Derrida 1989). This emerges, for instance, in their shared alertness to the ways that language (so-called 'ordinary' language) can prove more complex and resistant to codification than anything allowed for by speech-act theory in its systematized form. If 'undecidability' is in question here – as so often in Derrida's work – then it is the upshot of a reading closely attentive to the detail and the logic of Austin's arguments.

See also: POST-STRUCTURALISM

References and further reading

* Austin, J.L. (1961) *How to Do Things With Words*, London: Oxford University Press. (A classic exposition of speech-act theory, 'deconstructed' with relish – though by no means attacked or dismissed – by Derrida in *Limited Inc.*)

* de Man, P. (1978) 'The Epistemology of Metaphor', *Critical Inquiry* 5 (1): 13–30. (On metaphor in the texts of Locke, Condillac and Kant.)

* —— (1979) *Allegories of Reading: figural language in Rousseau, Nietzsche, Rilke, and Proust*, New Haven, CT: Yale University Press. (Essays in his typical late mode of deconstructive textual exegesis.)

* —— (1981) 'Pascal's Allegory of Persuasion', in S.J. Greenblatt (ed.) *Allegory and Representation*, Baltimore, MD: Johns Hopkins University Press, 1–25. (Analyses the relationship between constative and performative language in Pascal's writings on geometry, mathematics and religious faith.)

* —— (1983) *Blindness and Insight: essays in the rhetoric of contemporary criticism*, London: Methuen, 2nd edn. (Examines the blind-spots of presupposition and ideological prejudice in various twentieth-century critics and philosophers.)

* —— (1986) *The Resistance to Theory*, Minneapolis, MN: University of Minnesota Press. (On 'aesthetic ideology' and the resistance to it through a deconstructive reading of various – mainly literary-critical – texts.)

Derrida, J. (1967a) *La Voix et le Phénomène*; trans. D. Allison as *Speech and Phenomena and Other Essays on Husserl's Theory of Signs*, Evanston, IL: Northwestern University Press, 1973. (Represents Derrida's early, intensive, and critical engagement with Husserl.)

* —— (1967b) *De la Grammatologie*; trans. G. Spivak as *Of Grammatology*, Baltimore, MD: Johns Hopkins University Press, 1975. (On Rousseau, speech/writing, nature/culture, and other key themes of Derrida's early work.)

—— (1967c) *L'Écriture et la Différence*; trans. A. Bass as *Writing and Difference*, Chicago, IL: The University of Chicago Press, 1978. (Essays on Husserl, Levinas, Foucault, structuralism and the human sciences.)

—— (1972a) *Marges de la Philosophie*; trans. A. Bass as *Margins of Philosophy*, Chicago, IL: University of Chicago Press, 1982. (Contains some of Derrida's most important and powerfully-argued essays, among them 'White Mythology: metaphor in the text of philosophy'.)

—— (1972b) *La Dissémination*; trans. B. Johnson as *Dissemination*, London: Athlone Press, 1981. ('Plato's Pharmacy' and other essays in the border-zone between philosophy and literature.)

* —— (1989) *Limited Inc*, ed. G. Graff, Evanston, IL: Northwestern University Press. (Includes Derrida's essay on Austin; also his response to Searle (1977) and further reflections on speech-act philosophy.)

* Dummett, M. (1993) *On the Origins of Analytic Philosophy*, Cambridge, MA: Harvard University Press. (Comparative/contrastive account of work in the two traditions, with reference mainly to Frege and Husserl.)

Norris, C. (1987) *Derrida*, London: Fontana. (Introductory work for students of philosophy and literary theory.)

—— (1988) *Paul de Man and the Critique of Aesthetic Ideology*, London: Routledge. (Critical survey of de Man's writings; develops some of the arguments outlined above.)

* Ryle, G. (1971) *Collected Papers*, vol. 1, London: Hutchinson. (Includes Ryle's early review-articles on Husserl and Heidegger.)

* Searle, J.R. (1977) 'Reiterating the Differences', *Glyph*, vol. 1, Baltimore, MD: Johns Hopkins University Press. (Highly critical response to Derrida on the topic of Austinian speech-act philosophy.)

CHRISTOPHER NORRIS

DEDEKIND, JULIUS WILHELM RICHARD (1831–1916)

Dedekind is known chiefly, among philosophers, for contributions to the foundations of the arithmetic of the real and the natural numbers. These made available for the first time a systematic and explicit way, starting from very general notions (which Dedekind himself regarded as belonging to logic), to ground the differential and integral calculus without appeal to geometric 'intuition'. This work also forms a pioneering contribution to set theory (further advanced in Dedekind's correspondence with Georg Cantor) and to the general notion of a 'mathematical structure'.

Dedekind's foundational work had a close connection with his advancement of substantive mathematical knowledge, particularly in the theories of algebraic numbers and algebraic functions. His achievements in these fields make him one of the greatest mathematicians of the nineteenth century.

1 Career
2 Algebraic numbers and algebraic functions; new conception of mathematical 'objects'
3 Real and natural numbers; their basis in logic

1 Career

Richard Dedekind was born in Braunschweig, Germany. In 1848 he entered the Collegium Carolinum in that city to study 'mathematics and science', but it was for mathematics that he had already decided. In 1850 he matriculated at the University of Göttingen, and two years later received his doctorate, under the sponsorship of the great C.F. Gauss. In 1854 he 'habilitated' (qualified as a private lecturer) at Göttingen, a few weeks after Bernhard Riemann, who had been a fellow student and who was one of the two greatest influences upon Dedekind's mathematical – and philosophical – career. The second was J.P.G. Lejeune Dirichlet, who succeeded Gauss on his death in 1855. On Dedekind's later testimony, Dirichlet had 'inaugurated a new era for the study of mathematics at Göttingen', and had 'made a new man' of him.

In external details, the story of Dedekind's career is brief: he became a professor at the Polytechnic Institute of Zurich in 1858, then, in 1862, accepted a professorship at the Collegium Carolinum (itself by then a Technical Institute). This position he held until his retirement in 1894, having several times declined offers of university appointments (preferring to remain in his home town and near his ancestral

family). After formally retiring he continued to offer occasional courses of lectures until shortly before his death.

Dedekind's style of thought in general was to ponder slowly over the subjects that engaged him; he tended not to publish until he had brought a piece of work to a degree of classic perfection and could display for his readers the heart of the matter with a maximum of clarity. (A word Dedekind uses to characterize this quality he valued in mathematical exposition is 'quietness'. The motto of his work might well have been that explicitly invoked by Gauss: *pauca sed matura* (few, but ripe).)

2 Algebraic numbers and algebraic functions; new conception of mathematical 'objects'

A considerable part of Dedekind's energy during the early years of his career was devoted to the posthumous publication of works by his friends: Dirichlet's lectures on number theory; then Riemann's papers, both published and unpublished.

It was in the elaboration of themes arising from Dirichlet's number-theoretic lectures that Dedekind found the central theme of his own great contributions to mathematics – in the first place, a very far-reaching generalization (and clearer grounding) of the then new theory of algebraic numbers. Dedekind's major publication on this subject took the modest form of a supplement, among a whole series of supplements designed to clarify points arising from the main text, in his edition of the Dirichlet lectures. This work first appeared in the second edition (1871) as 'Über die Komposition der binären quadratischen Formen' ('On the Composition of Binary Quadratic Forms'). It was revised in subsequent editions (1879, 1894), appearing as 'Über die Theorie der ganzen algebraischen Zahlen' ('On the Theory of Integral Algebraic Numbers').

Characteristic of this work from the first was the introduction of a series of notions that have come to form the basis of modern algebra – among them, those of 'field', 'module', 'ideal' (and 'algebraic integer' itself) – on the basis of what we would now describe as structural axiomatic characterizations: thus, for instance, Dedekind defines not only a particular field, but the conditions to be satisfied for any system to be a field. Thus Dedekind effected a move towards regarding mathematics itself as concerned with species of structure explicitly characterized, rather than with particular kinds of 'objects', grasped by 'intuition'. (In this one may see the influence of Riemann, whose characterization of geometry was quite the same.) It was also characteristic that Dedekind made extensive use of sets ('systems' in his terminology) as 'mathematical objects' on which operations might be performed; and that he introduced as fundamental the consideration of mappings, both within and between particular structures.

The generality of Dedekind's formulations in this work opened the way for another significant development: his establishment (in collaboration with Heinrich Weber) of a rigorous foundation for the theory, initiated by Riemann, of algebraic functions of one variable ('compact Riemann surfaces'), bringing to light a deep algebraic analogy between this theory and that of algebraic integers. The resulting paper (1882) has become a cornerstone of twentieth-century algebraic geometry.

3   Real and natural numbers; their basis in logic

Dedekind's theory of real numbers and continuity, published in 1872, was motivated, he tells us, by his first obligation to teach the differential calculus (in 1858), and his dissatisfaction with the 'geometrical' reasoning upon which one traditionally relied. Beginning from the system of rational numbers, Dedekind remarks that this ordered system contains what we may call 'gaps', in the following sense: there exist certain splittings of the system into two non-empty, exhaustive parts, with each element of the one less than each element of the other, such that the 'lower' part contains no greatest element and the 'upper' part no least (for example, negative numbers and those positive numbers with squares less than 2, on the one hand; and positive numbers with squares greater than 2, on the other). He calls a system *continuous* if such gaps never occur; remarks that, whereas ordinary geometry tacitly assumes continuity for the system of points on a line, this is by no means a conceptually necessary property of space – it should rather be postulated explicitly when desired; and shows how, for a non-continuous system such as that of the rational numbers, one can construct a continuous extension by introducing a new element for each 'gap', so placed in the ordering as to 'fill' the gap. Most crucially, Dedekind (1) proves that the new system so constructed automatically fulfils the requirement of continuity, and (2) defines, in the numerical case, arithmetic operations for the new ('irrational') numbers (and between them and the rationals), and demonstrates that all the properties needed for traditional mathematics hold.

Dedekind's work on the natural numbers was done between 1872 and 1878, but published only in 1888. It is based on the definition of a 'simply infinite system': a set N, with a one-to-one mapping ϕ of N into itself, and an element (called '1') in N that is not taken on as

a value by ϕ, such that every element in N belongs to what Dedekind calls the 'chain' of 1, that is, the intersection of all sets that contain 1 and are 'closed under ϕ' – that is, contain, together with any element x, its image $\phi(x)$. Dedekind shows how this definition justifies the principle of mathematical induction for any simply infinite system (see LOGICISM §3), and how it also justifies the powerful technique of recursive definition. According to Dedekind, 'the system of the natural numbers' is just any simply infinite system, whose elements are regarded without respect to anything but their position in that system. This characterization (from which Giuseppe Peano directly borrowed his axioms for arithmetic) has been crucial for subsequent foundational work in mathematics (see ARITHMETIC, PHILOSOPHICAL ISSUES IN §4).

Besides his published work, Dedekind made significant contributions, in his correspondence with Georg Cantor (1937), to set theory and to point–set topology, which the latter was then developing.

See also: CANTOR, G.; KRONECKER, L.; LOGICAL AND MATHEMATICAL TERMS, GLOSSARY OF; LOGICISM

List of Works

Dedekind, R. (1930–32) *Gesammelte mathematische Werke* (Collected Mathematical Works), ed. R. Fricke, E. Noether and Ö. Ore, Braunschweig: Vieweg, 3 vols. (Dedekind's collected works. Volume 3 reproduces several of the works given here.)

—— (1871) 'Über die Komposition der binären quadratischen Formen' ('On the Composition of Binary Quadratic Forms'), in P.G. Lejeune Dirichlet, *Vorlesungen über Zahlentheorie* (Lectures on Number Theory), ed. R. Dedekind, Braunschweig: Vieweg, 2nd edn, supplement 10; passages significantly altered in subsequent edns are repr. in Dedekind (1932), vol. 3, 223–61. (The first version of Dedekind's fundamental work on the theory of algebraic integers. Later versions were published in 1879 and 1894 (see below).)

—— (1872) *Stetigkeit und Irrationalzahlen*, repr. in Dedekind (1932), vol. 3, 315–34; trans. W.W. Beman, 'Continuity and Irrational Numbers', in *Essays on the Theory of Numbers*, New York: Dover, 1963. (His classic work on the construction of the real numbers and the notion of 'continuity' or 'Dedekind completeness'.)

—— (1879, 1894) 'Über die Theorie der ganzen algebraischen Zahlen' ('On the Theory of Integral Algebraic Numbers'), in P.G. Lejeune Dirichlet, *Vorlesungen über Zahlentheorie* (Lectures on Number Theory), ed. R. Dedekind, Braunschweig: Vieweg, 3rd and 4th edns, supplement 11; repr. in

Dedekind (1932), vol. 3, 1–222, 297–313; 4th edn repr. New York: Chelsea, 1968. (The later versions – each very significantly reworked – of the theory first published in 1871.)

Dedekind, R. and Weber, H. (1882) 'Theorie der algebraischen Funktionen einer Veränderlichen' ('Theory of the Algebraic Functions of One Variable'), *Journal für reine und angewandte Mathematik* 92: 181–290; repr. in Dedekind (1930), vol. 1, 238–349. (A fundamental contribution to algebraic geometry.)

Dedekind, R. (1888) *Was sind und was sollen die Zahlen?*, Braunschweig: Vieweg; repr. in Dedekind (1932), vol. 3, 335–90; trans. W.W. Beman, 'The Nature and Meaning of Numbers', in *Essays on the Theory of Numbers*, New York: Dover, 1963; trans. *What are Numbers and What Should They Be?*, Orono, ME: Research Institute for Mathematics, 1995. (His classic work on the foundations of the theory of the natural numbers. Characterized by Dedekind's usual clarity, but a little laborious in its working-out of basic set-theoretic relations. The title is somewhat misconstrued in translation as it should more properly be rendered as 'What are Numbers and What are They For?' or 'The Nature and Function of Numbers' – see Stein (1988: 246–7).)

—— (1890) *Letter to H. Keferstein*, trans. H. Wang and S. Bauer-Mengelberg, in J. van Heijenoort (ed.) *From Frege to Gödel: A Source Book in Mathematical Logic, 1879–1931*, Cambridge, MA: Harvard University Press, 1967, 99–103. (A masterly presentation, in a short space, of the basic ideas of Dedekind (1888). A very useful guide for the beginner.)

Dedekind, R. and Cantor, G. (1937) *Briefwechsel Cantor–Dedekind* (Cantor–Dedekind Correspondence), ed. E. Noether and J. Cavaillès, Paris: Hermann; French trans. in J. Cavaillès, *Philosophie mathématique*, Paris: Hermann, 1962. (Includes most of the correspondence of Dedekind and Georg Cantor. The surviving portion of the correspondence not included in this collection is published in Dugac (1976).)

References and further reading

Dugac, P. (1976) *Richard Dedekind et les fondements des mathématiques* (Richard Dedekind and the Foundations of Mathematics), Paris: Vrin. (Includes biographical material, commentary, otherwise unpublished correspondence, preliminary notes for the works of 1872 and 1888, and manuscript material.)

* Landau, E. (1917) 'Richard Dedekind', *Nachrichten*

von der königlichen Gesellschaft der Wissenschaften zu Göttingen. Geschäftliche Mitteilungen 50–70; repr. in *Collected Works*, ed. P.T. Bateman *et al.*, Essen: Thales, 449–65. (A biographical eulogy.)

Stein, H. (1988) 'Logos, Logic, and Logistiké: Some Philosophical Remarks on the Nineteenth-Century Transformation of Mathematics', in W. Aspray and P. Kitcher (eds) *History and Philosophy of Modern Mathematics*, Minneapolis, MN: University of Minnesota Press, 238–59. (Discusses the work of Dedekind in relation to the general development of mathematics in his century, and especially his relation to Dirichlet, Riemann, Kronecker and Hilbert.)

HOWARD STEIN

DEDUCTIVE CLOSURE PRINCIPLE

It seems that one can expand one's body of knowledge by making deductive inferences from propositions one knows. The 'deductive closure principle' captures this idea: if S knows that P, and S correctly deduces Q from P, then S knows that Q. A closely related principle is that knowledge is closed under known logical implication: if S knows that P and S knows that P logically implies Q, then S knows that Q. These principles, if they hold, are guaranteed by general features of the concept of knowledge. They would form part of a logic of knowledge.

An influential argument for scepticism about knowledge of the external world employs the deductive closure principle. The sceptic begins by sketching a logically possible hypothesis, or counter-possibility (for example, that one is a brain in a vat, with computer-induced sense experience) which is logically incompatible with various things one claims to know (such as that one has hands). The proposition that one has hands logically implies the falsity of the sceptical hypothesis. Supposing that one is aware of this implication, the deductive closure principle yields the consequence that if one knows that one has hands, then one knows that one is not a brain in a vat. The sceptic argues that one does not know this: if one were in a vat, then one would have just the sensory evidence one actually has. It follows that one does not know that one has hands. Some philosophers have sought to block this argument by denying the deductive closure principle.

1   **Closure principles**
2   **Justification and relevant alternatives**
3   **Closure and reliabilist theories of knowledge**

1 Closure principles

According to the 'deductive closure principle', if S knows that *P*, and S correctly deduces *Q* from *P*, then S knows that *Q* (call this principle 'Closure'). The set *X* of propositions which one knows is not closed (in the mathematical sense) under logical implication *simpliciter*. This is because there are countless propositions which are logical consequences of what one knows which one does not recognize as such. Since one does not believe these logically implied propositions, one does not know them, and so they are not members of *X*. A similar point holds for the closure principle for known logical implication: it seems possible for one to know that *P*, know that *P* implies *Q*, and yet fail to deduce *Q*. According to Closure, those logical consequences which one deduces from what one knows are members of *X*. Such deduced consequences meet two of the conditions for knowledge: they are true (since they follow from known, and therefore true, propositions), and they are believed. If these deduced consequences are to be known, as Closure says, then they must satisfy whatever further necessary conditions for knowledge there might be.

Suppose that *having justification for believing that P* is a necessary condition for knowing that *P* (see KNOWLEDGE, CONCEPT OF §2; JUSTIFICATION, EPISTEMIC). Then it is plausible to suppose that Closure will hold only if *closure for justification* holds: if S has justification for believing that *P*, and S correctly deduces *Q* from *P*, then S has justification for believing that *Q*. This principle is used in constructing Gettier examples in which one starts with a justified belief of a false proposition (such as that Jones has ten coins in his pocket and will win the race) and deduces a proposition (say, that someone who has ten coins in his pocket will win the race) which just happens to be true. If closure for justification holds, then one will have a justified, true belief that does not amount to knowledge (see GETTIER PROBLEMS).

S may have justification for believing that *P* without actually believing that *P* (for example, S may fail to realize that S's evidence justifies a belief about the identity of the killer). Thus it is plausible to hold that justification is closed under logical implication *simpliciter*: if S has justification for believing propositions which logically imply *Q*, then S has justification for believing that *Q*. This principle is employed in generating the lottery paradox. One holds a ticket in a very large, fair lottery which one justifiably believes will have just one winner. Assume that the very high probability that one's ticket will not win justifies one in believing that one's ticket will not win. Since similar reasoning will apply to every other ticket, one has justification for believing that the first will not win,

one has justification for believing that the second will not win, and so on. Given that these propositions logically imply that no ticket will win, the closure principle now under consideration implies that, paradoxically, one has justification for believing that no ticket will win (see PARADOXES, EPISTEMIC §1).

2 Justification and relevant alternatives

Fred Dretske (1970) describes a case which appears to be a counterexample to both closure for justification and Closure itself (assuming that justification is a necessary condition for knowledge). Here we see again that the assessment of Closure depends on one's views about the analysis of the concept of knowledge. At the local zoo, one sees some striped animals in an enclosure marked 'Zebras'. One's evidence justifies a belief that these animals are zebras. However, one's evidence does not count towards their *not* being cleverly disguised mules (since one would have exactly similar evidence were it a hoax). Therefore, one's evidence does not justify one in believing the proposition that these animals are not cleverly disguised mules, even though one recognizes (we will suppose) that that proposition is logically implied by the zebra proposition for which one has justification.

A sceptically minded philosopher might well object that it is far from clear that one's evidence does justify a belief that the animals are zebras. To the extent that one's evidence does not count against the cleverly disguised mule hypothesis, the sceptic would say, it does not count in favour of the zebra hypothesis.

Dretske sketches a general theory of knowledge which bolsters his appeal to brute intuition about the proper analysis of the zebra case (intuition which might beg the question against scepticism). He holds that when S knows that *P* in some particular context, there is a range of *relevant alternatives* (counterpossibilities) to *P* which is a subset of the set of *all* alternatives to *P*. To know that *P*, it is only required that S be able to rule out the relevant alternatives to *P*. On this theory, Closure fails, because there will be situations in which S knows that *P*, knows that *R* is an alternative to *P* (knows that not-*R* is logically implied by *P*), and yet is unable to rule out *R* (fails to know that not-*R*). These are situations in which *R* is an *irrelevant* alternative to *P*.

The main motivation behind the relevant-alternatives theory is to provide a way of blocking the Cartesian sceptical argument. Therefore, we need an account of *relevance* according to which the sceptic's bizarre alternatives to ordinary propositions about the external world turn out to be irrelevant. This will make it possible for one to know that one has hands while lacking knowledge that one is not a disembodied brain in a vat. There is little agreement among relevant-alternative theorists on the analysis of the concept of relevance. One view is that an alternative R is relevant with respect to a particular claim to know that P if and only if the objective probability of R meets some specified level. If there are hoaxing zoos in one's vicinity, then this could render the cleverly disguised mule possibility a relevant alternative in the zebra case. Another view is that alternative relevance is determined by various features of the conversational context in which a knowledge attribution is made (a context which might not include the putative knower). The mentioning of alternatives might be such a contextual feature, so that the brain in a vat alternative can become relevant in a philosophical discussion of knowledge.

It has been argued (Klein 1981) that closure for justification holds even though (as Dretske claims) one's evidence E may justify a belief that P without justifying a belief of a deduced proposition, such as that one is not in a vat. On this view, even though E does not justify one's belief that one is not in a vat, one still has an adequate reason for believing that proposition. This is because P itself becomes available as evidence for the deduced proposition, given that E justifies one's belief that P.

3   Closure and reliabilist theories of knowledge

Let us consider the *reliabilist* approach to the analysis of the concept of knowledge, according to which knowing that P is a matter of having a reliably produced true belief that P. On many such accounts, the justification condition for knowledge is either analysed as, or replaced by, a reliability condition (see RELIABILISM). Whether Closure fails on such an analysis depends on how reliability is conceived. On one conception (Goldman 1976), in order for S's belief that P to count as reliably produced, S must be able to discriminate the actual situation in which P is true from those *relevant possible situations* in which P is false. This is close to the relevant alternatives theory, and Closure will accordingly fail. If a possible situation in which P is false and S is envatted is not a relevant one, then S can know that P without being able to discriminate the actual situation from the one in which S is envatted. Now consider S's claim to know the logically implied proposition that S is not envatted. A possible situation in which S *is* envatted is plausibly regarded in this case as a relevant alternative possibility. Since, as we assumed, S is unable to discriminate the actual situation from a vat situation, it follows that S does not know that S is not in a vat. Thus Closure fails, since S can know that P without knowing that S is not envatted.

Reliability is sometimes conceived as having an explicitly counterfactual dimension. For example, Robert Nozick's (1981) 'tracking' analysis of knowledge contains this counterfactual condition: if P were false, then S would not mistakenly believe that P. Suppose that S claims to know that S is sitting, on an occasion when S is sitting in a perfectly normal environment. If S were not sitting, then, presumably, S would be standing, or lying down, or the like. In such a counterfactual circumstance, S would *not* mistakenly believe that S is sitting. So S's claim to know that S is sitting satisfies Nozick's counterfactual condition (as well as the other conditions for knowing, we may suppose). Now consider S's claim to know the logically implied proposition that S is not in a vat. If S *were* in a vat, then, presumably, S *would* mistakenly believe that S is *not* in a vat. So S does not satisfy the counterfactual condition for knowing that S is not in a vat. Thus on the present analysis, S knows that S is sitting but fails to know that S is not a brain in a vat.

According to an alternative counterfactual conception of reliability, whether a belief that P is reliably produced does not necessarily depend on what one would believe in counterfactual circumstances in which P is false. Instead, we focus on the process which issues in the belief. A belief-forming process will count as reliable just in case the process actually yields a sufficiently high ratio of true beliefs and also would yield the required ratio in counterfactual circumstances similar to one's actual circumstances (which might not include circumstances in which P is false). Closure will hold on this version of reliabilism. Suppose that one forms the correct belief that one has hands via an ordinary perceptual process. Then one forms the further belief that one is not disembodied in a vat, via the belief-forming process of deductive inference. This inferential belief issues from a process that is obviously reliable in the sense under consideration. Thus if the original belief issues from a process which is reliable in that sense and therefore amounts to knowledge, then so will the inferential belief.

In the end, we see that even though the denial of the closure principles we have discussed would aid in the refutation of scepticism, whether these principles hold is a controversial matter which depends on the nature of knowledge and justification.

See also: EPISTEMIC LOGIC; KNOWLEDGE, CONCEPT OF §§7–10; SCEPTICISM

References and further reading

Brueckner, A. (1985) 'Skepticism and Epistemic Closure', *Philosophical Topics* 13 (3): 89–117.

(Critical overview of the issues discussed in this entry.)

* Dretske, F.I. (1970) 'Epistemic Operators', *Journal of Philosophy* 67 (24): 1007–23. (*Locus classicus* of the relevant alternatives theory discussed in §2 above, and includes the zebra case discussed in that section; contains a sketch of a view like Nozick's, considered above in §3.)

—— (1981) 'The Pragmatic Dimension of Knowledge', *Philosophical Studies* 40 (3): 363–78. (Useful discussion of the concept of a relevant alternative.)

Gettier, E. (1963) 'Is Justified True Belief Knowledge?', *Analysis* 23 (6): 121–3. (The origin of the Gettier problem discussed above in §1.)

* Goldman, A.I. (1976) 'Discrimination and Perceptual Knowledge', *Journal of Philosophy* 73 (20): 771–91. (Reliability as discrimination, as discussed in §3 above; contains a useful discussion of the concept of a relevant alternative.)

* Klein, P. (1981) *Certainty: A Refutation of Scepticism*, Minneapolis, MN: University of Minnesota Press. (Discussion of the argument for the closure of justification discussed in §2 above; discussion of the relation between closure principles and the problem of scepticism.)

—— (1987) 'On Behalf of the Skeptic', in S. Luper-Foy (ed.) *The Possibility of Knowledge: Nozick and his Critics*, Totowa, NJ: Rowman & Littlefield. (Contains an argument that reliabilism can provide support for Closure, as discussed above in §3; the book contains many trenchant critical articles about the anti-sceptical strategy of Nozick, as well as a helpful bibliography.)

Kyburg, H.E. (1970) *Probability and Inductive Logic*, Toronto, Ont.: Macmillan. (Chapter 13 gives a presentation of the lottery paradox discussed in §1 above.)

* Nozick, R. (1981) *Philosophical Explanations*, Cambridge, MA: Harvard University Press. (Chapter 3 contains a discussion of the anti-sceptical strategy discussed in §3 above.)

Williams, M. (1991) *Unnatural Doubts: Epistemological Realism and the Basis of Scepticism*, Oxford: Blackwell. (Chapter 8 contains arguments that reliabilism does not induce the failure of Closure, as discussed above in §3.)

ANTHONY BRUECKNER

DEEP ECOLOGY *see* ECOLOGICAL PHILOSOPHY; NÆSS, ARNE

DEFEASIBILITY THEORY OF KNOWLEDGE *see* KNOWLEDGE, DEFEASIBILITY THEORY OF

DEFINITE DESCRIPTIONS *see* DESCRIPTIONS

DEFINITION

A definition is a statement, declaration or proposal establishing the meaning of an expression. In virtue of the definition, the expression being defined (the 'definiendum') is to acquire the same meaning as the expression in terms of which it is defined (the 'definiens'). For example, 'Man is a rational animal' determines the meaning of the term 'man' by making it synonymous with 'rational animal'. Classical theory maintains that a good definition captures the 'real nature' of what is defined: 'A "definition" is a phrase signifying a thing's essence' (Aristotle). Historically, philosophers have come to distinguish these 'real' definitions from 'nominal' definitions that specify the meaning of a linguistic expression rather than signify the essential nature of an object, 'making another understand by Words, what Idea, the term defined stands for' (Locke).

A further distinction can be drawn between contextual or implicit definitions, on the one hand, and explicit definitions, on the other. Often a definition fixes meaning directly and explicitly: for example, the definition of a proper name might well take the form of an explicit identity statement ('Pegasus = the winged horse') and a definition of a predicate is usually given (or can be re-cast) in the form of an equivalence ('For every x: x is a man if and only if x is a rational animal'). But sometimes the meaning of a term is specified in context, by way of the meaning of larger expressions in which the term occurs. A paradigmatic example of this is Bertrand Russell's analysis of the meaning of the definite article.

1 The role of definitions
2 Formal conditions on definability
3 Contextual definitions
4 'Circular' definitions

1 The role of definitions

A definition is a statement, declaration or proposal (the 'definiens') establishing the meaning of an expression (the 'definiendum'). Explicit definitions can be viewed as providing useful abbreviations for complex expressions. It follows that, strictly speaking, they are theoretically dispensable, in so far as we can always replace the definiendum by the definiens in any context. This was already noted by Whitehead and Russell in *Principia Mathematica*, according to whom definitions are 'mere typographical conveniences' ([1910] 1925: 11). However, they also point out that from a more pragmatic point of view, the use of a definition (whether explicit or not) conveys additional information besides the literal meaning of the sentence in which the definiendum occurs.

This can happen in two ways. First, a definition calls attention to the fact that the (complex) concept expressed by the definiens plays an important role in the discourse in which the definiendum is used: for instance, agreeing to mean by 'prime' a number that can be divided without remainder only by 1 and itself calls attention to the importance of this notion for number theory. 'Hence the collection of definitions embodies our choice of subjects and our judgment as to what is most important' ([1910] 1925: 11–12). Second, a definition may sometimes supply an analysis of an already existing concept that had not previously been made precise. In this case the newly introduced concept shares most or all of the traits of its informal counterpart, although realizing those traits in a more specific and precise manner. It should be observed that in general many competing, equally precise and sometimes formally equivalent analyses of the same informal idea are possible, and the choice among them is then inspired by considerations such as simplicity, elegance and adaptability to the particular context of application.

A related view of definitions was put forward by Carnap (1947), who characterizes certain definitions as 'rational reconstructions' of less precise concepts derived from everyday life or earlier stages of scientific development. Such a definition is called an 'explication', and the newly defined term the 'explicatum'; the earlier, less precise concept is referred to as the 'explicandum'. In giving an explication, one 'sharpens' a vague, pre-existing concept, making it precise; or even replaces it with a new, more exact one. In general it is not required that the explicandum have the same meaning as the explicatum. All that is required is some sort of correspondence between the two concepts, in such a way that the latter can be used instead of the former. This task of rational reconstruction is 'one of the most important ... of logical analysis and logical construction' ([1947] 1956: 7–8).

2 Formal conditions on definability

From a purely formal point of view, a definition given in the context of some theory behaves just like any other axiom of the theory, in that it can be used to infer propositions (theorems). However, as already noted by Whitehead and Russell, a definition should not convey any new information: the theory T' obtained by supplementing some theory T by a definition should, in some sense, be equivalent to T.

It is possible to make this requirement precise by laying down two criteria that a definition should satisfy: eliminability and non-creativity. It appears that these criteria were first formulated by the Polish logician S. Leśniewski (1931), but the presentation given here follows P. Suppes (1957).

In order to explain the two criteria, we will suppose that we are working within a formalized background theory T, that is, a set of axioms expressed in some formal language. In such a language, as is customary, free variables are to be construed as implicitly universally quantified; moreover, T is assumed to be consistent. A definition then is just a sentence ϕ that involves some new symbol not already in T. In particular, ϕ is allowed to occur in inferences from the axioms of T. The two criteria can be formulated as follows. A sentence ϕ introducing a new symbol satisfies the criterion of eliminability if and only if whenever η is a formula in which the new symbol occurs, then there is a formula θ in which the new symbol does not occur and such that $(\eta \leftrightarrow \theta)$ can be inferred from T augmented with ϕ. Similarly, we say that ϕ satisfies the criterion of non-creativity if and only if whenever θ is a sentence not involving the new symbol and such that $\phi \rightarrow \theta$ can be inferred from T, then θ can already be inferred from T; in other words, the introduction of the definition does not make possible the derivation of any new theorems that do not involve the new symbol. (One then says that $T + \phi$ is a 'conservative extension' of T.) Notice that the second criterion implies, in particular, that the theory supplemented by the definition be free of contradictions: inconsistency is a strong form of creativity.

Although the two criteria apply to explicit and implicit definitions alike, in the case of explicit definitions it is possible to lay down certain constraints on the syntactic form of the sentence ϕ ensuring that the two criteria are automatically satisfied. For simplicity, we will review these constraints only for the case in which the definiendum is a relation symbol or an individual constant (name), but a similar constraint can be formulated for the definition of function symbols.

A formula ϕ is an acceptable definition of an *n*-

place relation symbol R if and only if ϕ has the form $R(x_1, \ldots, x_n) \leftrightarrow \theta$, where $x_1, \ldots, x_n$ are all distinct variables and θ is a formula all of whose free variables are among $x_1, \ldots, x_n$ and in which R does not occur. The requirement that the variables $x_1, \ldots, x_n$ all be distinct is necessary to ensure that the eliminability criterion is satisfied, as is the further requirement that the definiendum R not be allowed to occur in the definiens; jointly, the two requirements are also sufficient for the satisfaction of the eliminability criterion.

The requirement that the definiens not contain any variables that do not already occur in the definiendum is meant to ensure non-creativity. To see that the constraint expresses a necessary condition, consider, for instance, the definition '$G(x) \leftrightarrow x > y$'. Since free variables are implicitly universally quantified, the definition is equivalent to the conjunction of '$G(x) \rightarrow \forall y (x > y)$' and '$\exists y (x > y) \rightarrow G(x)$'; by transitivity of implication we obtain that if $\exists y (x > y)$ then $\forall y (x > y)$, which, when interpreted as a statement of arithmetic, is false. The definition is therefore creative. (The constraint on variables is also sufficient for non-creativity if and only if the definiendum is not allowed to occur in the definiens.)

The constraint on the explicit definition of individual constants is slightly more complex, due to the existential import of such constants in ordinary logic. Rather than considering definitions in the form of an explicit identity '$c =$ the so-and-so', we will give a constraint using the more general form of an equivalence. A sentence ϕ is an acceptable definition of an individual constant c if and only if ϕ has the form $c = x \leftrightarrow \theta$, where θ is a formula not containing c with x as its only free variable, and such that $\exists! x \theta$ (that is, there is one and only one x such that θ) is derivable from the theory.

3 Contextual definitions

Sometimes it is neither possible nor convenient to give a definition in the explicit form of an equivalence or identity. Indeed, given that formally definitions are just further axioms, any sentence containing a new symbol could be taken to be a candidate for a definition of that symbol. Such definitions are called 'contextual', in that the meaning of the new symbol is specified (at least partially) by giving the meaning of some larger expression in which it occurs; the symbol itself, when occurring in isolation, need not be endowed with any meaning at all. Perhaps the first and most conspicuous example of contextual definition is given by Russell (see, for example, Whitehead and Russell [1910] 1925: 66; but see also Frege 1884, 1903), when specifying the meaning of the definite

article by giving explicit truth-conditions for sentences in which it occurs. As is well known, Russell proposes to analyse sentences of the form 'The ϕ is ψ' as the conjunction of the three following sentences in which the definite article no longer occurs: (1) There is at least one ϕ; (2) There is at most one ϕ; and (3) Whatever is a ϕ is a ψ. Other examples are the contextual definition of the membership symbol '$\in$' given by the axioms of set theory, and the usual recursive definition of '$+$' in the context of arithmetic (the latter is given by the conjunction of the two equations $x + 0 = x$ and $x + y' = (x + y)'$, where x' denotes the successor of x).

Of course, in general, one would not expect the criterion of eliminability to be satisfied, for a contextual definition need only tell us how to find an equivalent not involving the new symbol for a restricted class of sentences, namely those in which the definiendum occurs in the context given by the definition. For instance, the usual recursive definition of '$+$' does not tell us how to eliminate this symbol in the context $\forall x \forall y (x + y = y + x)$. But the criterion of non-creativity still applies, along with the weaker requirement that the theory augmented by the definition still be consistent.

As a related question one might consider whether, within the framework of a particular theory, a contextual definition can be replaced by an explicit one. A useful tool in answering this question is a method invented by A. Padoa (1902) and further developed by Tarski (1956: 296–320). The method relies on the fact that if a symbol α is explicitly definable within a given theory T, then any two interpretations on which all sentences of T are true must agree on the interpretation of α. Therefore, in order to show that α is not explicitly definable in T it suffices to exhibit two interpretations of T that assign different values to α.

Padoa's method also has a converse of sorts, which is a deep result about the expressive power of first-order logic. Let us say that a symbol α is 'implicitly definable' in T if any two interpretations of T agree on the value they assign to α. (So implicit definitions are a particular case of contextual definitions.) The proposition that any symbol implicitly definable in T is also explicitly definable is known as Beth's definability theorem (see BETH'S THEOREM AND CRAIG'S THEOREM). This is a powerful theorem, and one of the results of model theory with the most far-reaching philosophical implications.

4 'Circular' definitions

We have seen that one of the constraints on the syntactic form of definitions meant to ensure the satisfaction of the criterion of eliminability is that the definiendum itself not occur in the definiens. That is, the requirement rules out 'circular' definitions. This is in keeping with the idea that a definition, among other things, should also provide a way to determine the extension of the defined term, that is, the set of entities that fall under it. Indeed, a way of determining whether an object x falls in the extension of, say, a predicate P is to ascertain whether x satisfies the definiens of P: if the definiens itself is allowed to have occurrences of P, then it might be impossible to determine whether anything satisfies it without knowing the extension of P. So circularly defined terms would lack a definite criterion of applicability.

However, there are circumstances in which it appears that no non-circular definition is available for a given concept. Consider, for instance, the concept of truth, construed as a predicate of sentences of a given language. If the language in question itself contains the truth-predicate then we can have circularity as follows. Tarski (1944) suggested that for any sentence ϕ, the following equivalence (known as a 'T-biconditional') might be regarded as a *partial* definition of truth: t is true if and only if ϕ, where t is a term denoting ϕ (for instance, t could be obtained by enclosing ϕ in quotes). If ϕ itself contains occurrences of 'is true', the T-biconditional for ϕ exhibits a form of circularity. As is well known, this circularity can lead to paradoxes, as in the case of the so-called liar paradox arising from the consideration of the T-biconditional for the sentence λ: λ is not true. As another example, consider the kind of (harmless) circularity that arises when we are trying to specify a function f by means of the two equations $f(x,0) = x$ and $f(x,y') = (f(x,y))'$, where as before x' is the successor of x (this is harmless because, as is well known, the two equations above identify a unique function over the natural numbers, namely addition).

A general theory of possibly circular definitions was put forward by A. Gupta and N. Belnap (1993). They regard a definition not as supplying a way to fix the extension of a term, but as providing a 'rule of revision', that is, a way of improving upon hypothetical extensions. Suppose we have a possibly circular definition of a 1-place predicate P, which has the form $P(x) \leftrightarrow \phi(P)$, where the definiendum P occurs in the definiens. This can be viewed as an operation defined over the space of the possible extensions of P (that is, over the set of all subsets of the domain): given a possible extension E as input the rule of revision returns the value of $\phi(P)$ when P is interpreted as E. In turn, a revision rule can be used to give rise to a revision process, that is, an infinite sequence of possible extensions, defined as follows. We begin with an arbitrary extension E as a 'bootstrapper' or initial

guess; we then let E_1 be the result of applying the revision rule to E, E_2 the result of applying the revision rule to E_1, and so on. In this way we obtain an infinite sequence. Say that an extension E' 'coheres' with such a sequence if it contains all items that are eventually in every member of the sequence, that is, all items x such that for some E_n, x is in E_i for every $i \geqslant n$. We can then extend the sequence into the transfinite by letting E^∞ come after each member of the sequence, where E^∞ is an arbitrary extension that coheres with the sequence, and start applying the revision rule again.

So each revision rule specifies a class of revision processes, each one of which is characterized by a different 'bootstrapper' and different 'guesses' at limit stages. Should a revision process culminate in a fixed point, that is, an extension that is returned unchanged by the revision rule, we have found a 'good' candidate for the extension of P. But it should be noted that this is a by-product of the definition: the meaning of the definition is not given by the extension (which might not exist), but by the pattern of variation exhibited by the various revision processes to which it gives rise.

See also: FREGE, G. §§6, 8, 9; LOGICAL AND MATHEMATICAL TERMS, GLOSSARY OF; PARADOXES OF SET AND PROPERTY §3

References and further reading

Belnap, N.D. (1993) 'On Rigorous Definitions', *Philosophical Studies* 72: 115–46. (Expanded treatment of the issues covered here; rigorous yet accessible both from a philosophical and technical point of view; emphasizes definition as an act of conceptual clarification.)

* Carnap, R. (1947) *Meaning and Necessity: A Study in Semantics and Modal Logic*, Chicago, IL: University of Chicago Press; 2nd, enlarged edn, 1956. (Presents Carnap's notion of explication.)

* Frege, G. (1884) *Die Grundlagen der Arithmetik: eine logisch-mathematische Untersuchung über den Begriff der Zahl*, Breslau: Koebner; trans. J.L. Austin, *The Foundations of Arithmetic: A Logico-Mathematical Enquiry into the Concept of Number*, Oxford: Blackwell, 2nd edn, 1980. (Numbers are defined contextually – as extensions of particular concepts – by giving their identity conditions.)

* —— (1903) *Grundgesetze der Arithmetik: begriffsschriftlich abgeleitet*, Jena: Pohle, vol. 2; fragments, including 'Frege on Definitions', in *Translations from the Philosophical Writings of Gottlob Frege*, trans. and ed. P.T. Geach and M. Black, Oxford: Blackwell, 3rd edn, 1980. (Gives the 'sharp

boundary' condition, emphasizing that definitions should be complete and not leave any cases undecided. Also, the inconsistent axiom (V) can be viewed as a (creative!) contextual definition of the extension of a concept.)

* Gupta, A. and Belnap, N.D. (1993) *The Revision Theory of Truth*, Cambridge, MA: MIT Press. (Includes the first full presentation of revision theory as a general theory of definition.)

* Leśniewski, S. (1931) 'Über Definitionen in der sogenannten Theorie der Deduktion', *Comptes Rendus des Séances de la Société des Sciences et des Lettres de Varsovie* (Classe 3) 24; trans. in *Collected Works*, ed. S.J. Surma, J.T. Srzednicki and D.I. Barnett, with an annotated bibliography by V.F. Rickey, Boston, MA: Reidel, 2 vols, 1981, 629–48. (The original source for the theory of definition in first-order logic.)

* Padoa, A. (1902) 'Un nouveau système irréductible de postulats pour l'algebre', in *Deuxième Congrès International des Mathematiciens*, Paris, 249–56. (First appearance of a necessary condition for implicit definability, later developed by Tarski.)

Robinson, R. (1950) *Definition*, Oxford: Oxford University Press. (A good source for the nontechnical issues in the theory of definition. Includes some history.)

* Suppes, P. (1957) *Introduction to Logic*, Princeton, NJ: Van Nostrand. (Possibly the best treatment of definitions in first-order logic from an elementary point of view.)

* Tarski, A. (1944) 'The Semantic Conception of Truth', *Journal of Philosophy and Phenomenological Research* 4: 341–76; repr. in L. Linsky (ed.) *Semantics and the Philosophy of Language: A Collection of Readings*, Champaign, IL: University of Illinois Press, 1969. (Tarski's more philosophical treatment of the concept of truth, including the partial definition of truth as given by the T-biconditionals.)

* —— (1956) *Logic, Semantics, Metamathematics: Papers from 1923 to 1938*, trans. and ed. J.H. Woodger, Oxford: Clarendon Press; repr. and ed. J. Corcoran, Indianapolis, IN: Hackett Publishing Company, 2nd edn, 1983. (Tarski's development of Padoa's method. See also his remarks on formal and material correctness in 'The Concept of Truth in Formalized Languages'.)

* Whitehead, A.N. and Russell, B.A.W. (1910) *Principia Mathematica*, vol. 1, Cambridge: Cambridge University Press, 2nd edn, 1925. (The source for contextual definitions – sums up Russell's work published elsewhere.)

G. ALDO ANTONELLI

DEFINITION, INDIAN CONCEPTS OF

Definitions in Indian philosophy are conceived very differently from definitions in Western philosophy. In Western philosophy and logic, it is usual to define a term or a linguistic expression. A definition here consists of a 'definiens', typically a longer expression, statement or proposal, and a 'definiendum', a shorter expression or term whose meaning is established by the definiens. Definitions permit the definiendum to be put in place of the definiens and are thus 'abbreviations' (for example, 'father' is an abbrevation of 'male parent'). In India, definitions in the sense of abbreviations were regularly used in grammar from the earliest times, as in the work of Pāṇini (c.800 BC).

In Indian philosophy, however, definitions are not conceived of as abbreviations. We may have direct acquaintance with an object; this is one way of knowing it. We may also know an object or many objects through their properties or features; this is another way of knowing them. These properties or features are the modes under which objects are cognized. If we know objects through the properties that belong to all of them and only to them, then the objects are collected together through their properties to form a group. A group is nothing real; it is a way of collecting objects by knowing them under one mode. When we know a group of objects through properties common to all of them and only to them, we may also want to know another set of properties or features which also belongs to all the objects and only to them. The second set of properties is the defining mark (lakṣaṇa), or, simply, the definition, of the objects collected together into a group by being known under one mode. The objects themselves are the definienda of the definition. The first set of properties through which the definienda are collected together to form a group is called 'the limiting properties of being the definienda of the definition'. The defining mark, that is, the definition, is not an essential property of the definienda, but is only a property (or set of properties) common to all of them and only them.

1 General features of definition
2 Navya-Nyāya theory of definition
3 Navya-Nyāya theory of relations
4 First type of definition
5 Second type of definition
6 Relation between the two types

1 General features of definition

There are two stages in the Indian theory of definition: (1) the objects to be defined must all be known under one mode ('the limiting property of being the definienda'); and (2) the definition of those objects must be a property coextensive with the limiting property. The limiting property and the definition cannot be identical, although they must be coextensive. A single object, too, can be defined. Its defining mark, that is, its definition, depends upon the prior act of identifying it. The object's criterion of identity is the limiting property of being the definiendum, which has to be different from the defining mark.

A sentence stating the defining mark of a group of objects is called 'the sentence of definition'. It has some special features which should be noted. A sentence of definition has to be a general sentence applicable to all the definienda. In Indian philosophy, variables are not used; pronouns are used to attain generality. For example a true cognition (not 'a true cognition') is defined as a cognition having *that* as a predicate in a *that*-possessor. For example, if a thing has potness (that is, is a pot), then the cognition that the thing has potness (that it is a pot) is a true cognition. Using the pronoun 'that' twice in the sentence makes it a general sentence. For we may write any property term for 'that'.

As objects belonging to very different ontological categories can be the definienda of a definition, the defining mark may belong to the different kinds of definienda by very different ontological relations. This is a peculiarity of the Indian theory which distinguishes it from the theories of traditional Western logic.

2 Navya-Nyāya theory of definition

Only Navya-Nyāya ('New Logic'), created by GAṄGEŚA (*c.*1325) and developed by Raghunātha (*c.*1530), Jagadīśa (*c.*1620), GADĀDHARA (1604–1709) and later philosophers, has a fully developed theory of definition.

There are two fundamental ways in which the Navya-Nyāya theory of definition differs logically from Western theories, apart from the ontological point of view. First, it differs from Plato's theory in that whereas Plato tries to find out the essence or the universal of, say, justice, in Navya-Nyāya, definitions are properties, not necessarily universals or essences, and may even be individual properties belonging to single individuals.

In Plato, Aristotle and Porphyry, there is a hierarchy of genus and species, and definition is *per genus et differentiam*. Thus every definition must have at least two components – the generic property and the differentia; the defining property of 'human', for example, is animality-and-rationality. The Navya-

Nyāya theory of definition is fundamentally different because the structure of the defining property is not always composite, especially when it is a proper universal in the sense of Nyāya. A universal is an unanalysable property, even though it may be subsumed under a wider universal. No universal is a composite of a generic property and differentia. Thus the defining property of humans is just humanity, even though it is subsumed under the generic property of animality. According to Navya-Nyāya, humanity as a property is as simple as animality and cannot be obtained by adding differentia to the generic property. Analysis of a concept is possible only in the case of composite properties, which are not proper universals. Universals, when not referred to by an expression, are known in and through themselves and not under the mode of some other property, and therefore do not stand in need of analysis; indeed, they cannot be analysed at all. It has been objected that although it is correct to say that what games have in common is their being games, it is not at all enlightening. But enlightenment, if sought by further analysis, is not possible in this case.

3 Navya-Nyāya theory of relations

The second fundamental point of difference between the Navya-Nyāya theory and traditional Western theories of definition stems from the Navya-Nyāya doctrine that a defining property need not be a universal. A proper universal is related to all its instances by one relation, inherence, according to Navya-Nyāya. The defining property is very often a property different from a proper universal and is often related to different types of objects by different types of relations. Navya-Nyāya therefore developed a very elaborate technique of showing how the defining property can be said to be 'common' to objects which very often belong to ontologically different categories. This is done by determining the specific nature of the relation by which the defining property can be said to be 'common to' the different types of objects. This specific relation between the defining property and the different types of objects is very often the sum of the different relations by which the defining property is related to different types of objects. This sum of relations is necessary, for it is by this relation that the defining property can be said to be 'common to' all the different types of objects. As an example of this technique of showing how a defining property is 'common to' all the objects to be defined, we may explain the definition of *being a positive object* (*bhāvatva*). According to Navya-Nyāya, there are six ontological categories of positive reals. There is one proper universal common to the first three categories of positive reals, namely existence (*sattā*), which is the highest universal (*parā jāti*). This universal is related to six categories: (1) substance, (2) quality, (3) motion, (4) universal, 5) ultimate differentia, and (6) inherence (see NYĀYA-VAIŚEṢIKA §§4–5; ONTOLOGY IN INDIAN PHILOSOPHY).

Existence is a property common to the first three categories in the sense of being related to them by inherence. Now, according to Navya-Nyāya, the remaining three categories of objects do not have existence inhering in them. Thus, if existence is to be the defining property of being a positive object it must be related to the last three categories of objects by other relations. Navya-Nyāya shows how existence can be indirectly related to the fourth and fifth categories of objects. Universals and ultimate differentia inhere in, say, substances, in which existence also inheres. In Navya-Nyāya terminology, existence is related to universals (and ultimate differentia) as both inhere in the same object.

Still there is the problem of showing how existence can be related to inherence itself, for inherence is the sixth category of positive reals. Existence cannot inhere in inherence, for according to Navya-Nyāya, existence inheres in only the first three categories of positive reals. According to Navya-Nyāya, existence is related to, is located in, inherence by a self-linking relation which is ontologically inherence itself. There is no need to postulate an ontologically different relation between existence and inherence. Inherence, which is the second term of the relation, also functions as the relation. Thus, although the relation between existence and inherence is not *inherence as inherence*, but only *inherence as a self-linking relation*, still it is inherence which is ontologically the same as this relation.

In Western logic, universal laws are formulated by means of variables. These variables are signs bound by some operators, and also act as place-holders for names of their values. Because of the convention that the same name in to be written at all places where a variable occurs (within the scope of one quantifier, or in the same formula if it occurs freely), the variables perform the function of relative pronouns.

Although variables have been used in Indian algebra for a long time, they were not used in Nyāya. In algebra before the introduction of variables, the pronouns *yāvat* and *tāvat* were used. In Nyāya, there is a very popular method similar to this practice which uses the relative pronouns *yat* and *tat* ('that' and 'which') and *sva* ('its', or 'one's own'). Consider the following definition: 'Pervasion is the co-presence of that with that which is not limited by the limiter of the counterpositiveness to the constant absence that has a common locus with it and has no common locus with

its counterpositive.' In this definition the first 'that' stands for the probans, the second 'that' for the probandum, and the 'its' for the constant absence. (The 'its' occurs only in the translation; in Sanskrit it is eliminated by a compound.)

4 First type of definition

Two different types of definition are admitted in Navya-Nyāya, corresponding to two different purposes for which defining marks of objects are determined. The first purpose for finding a defining mark of objects collected under a mode is to find out a mark by which all the objects can be distinguished from everything else. Thus the defining mark in this case becomes the probans (corresponding to the middle term of a syllogism) for inferring that every one of the objects to be defined is different from everything else. This inference has to be for the sake of others; for according to Navya-Nyāya, the defining mark is used to prove to others that it excludes the objects to be defined, *P*s, from every non-*P*. This proof, which takes the form of an inference for the sake of others, has to be put in the negative form (see INFERENCE, INDIAN THEORIES OF §5).

This point may be explained with an example. The defining mark of earth is smell. By smell all earthen things are differentiated from non-earth. The inference is of the form: 'Earth is different from non-earth, the reason being smell.' This can be put in the form of a syllogism thus: 'Whatever is not different from non-earth has no smell. Earth has smell; therefore earth is different from non-earth.' Here earth is *P* (the minor term), difference from non-earth is the probandum (the major term) and smell is the probans (the middle term).

This example shows a fundamental difference between Western theories and Indian theories in general, and Navya-Nyāya in particular. In Western philosophy, 'earth is different from non-earth' ('earth is not non-earth') is regarded as an analytical sentence. In traditional Western logic, 'earth is not non-earth' is the obverse of 'earth is earth', which is an identity sentence. But in Navya-Nyāya, no analytic sentence is significant. Although one can know (always truly) that earth is earth, there is no point in saying it, for a sentence expressing it will not communicate any information. So, according to Navya-Nyāya, there is analytical judgment, but there is no analytical sentence. But the sentence 'earth is different from non-earth' ('earth is not non-earth') is not an analytical sentence; it can be used as the conclusion of an inference. This is not true a priori; it needs to be proved. Every definition in this sense is the probans of a conclusion of the form: *P* is different from non-*P*.

5 Second type of definition

The second type of definition is used to explain why a word applies to whatever it applies to. According to Nyāya, a word becomes applicable to its referents if and only if there is a sufficient reason for its application to them. This reason must be a property of the referents, and this property is the defining property of the referents being the referents of that word. The defining mark is the nature of the referents of the word, and is denoted by the abstract noun formed from the word. For example, jarness is the nature of jars and is denoted by the abstract noun 'jarness' formed from the word 'jar' by the abstraction suffix '-ness'.

There may be different properties which belong to all and only those objects which are denoted by a word, and the problem is to decide which of them is to be regarded as the defining mark of the objects considered as the referents of the word. Not all coextensive properties are necessarily identical, even though two coextensive universals are. For example, all jars and only jars have the two properties of (1) having a neck like a conch shell and (2) jarness. Now these two properties, although coextensive, are still different, for (1) is an analysable property while (2) is not. It is to be noted that jarness cannot be used as a probans to infer that jars are different from non-jars, for here the limiting property of being objects to be defined, jarness, becomes the same as the defining mark. Thus jarness cannot be regarded as the defining mark of jars, in the first sense of the term. Jarness can, however, be the defining mark of jars in the sense of being the sufficient reason for the application of the word 'jar' to jars. In this case, the limiting property of being objects to be defined does not become identical with the defining mark, jarness, for the limiting property is not, in this case, jarness, but the property 'being the referent of the word "jar"'. In this type of definition we are considering jars only as referents of the word 'jar', and are trying to discover the sufficient reason for its application to them.

6 Relation between the two types

There are two different motives for finding defining marks. First, when one hears the word 'earth', one may want to know the distinguishing mark of earth. Here the limiter of being objects to be defined is a property of the objects denoted by the word. Second, one may want to know why the word 'earth' is applicable to whatever it is applicable. Here the limiter of being objects to be defined is being a referent of the word 'earth'.

There are three different theories of the relation between the two kinds of defining marks. First, the most commonly accepted theory is that these are of two different kinds. The second theory is that a defining mark in the proper sense is only a distinguishing mark; the so-called usage-explaining marks, too, can be used as probantia for inferring difference from all others by only reinterpreting the limiter of being objects to be defined as the property of being referents of the words. If this property is regarded as the limiter, then all usage-explaining marks can be used as distinguishing marks. The third theory is that a distinguishing mark can also be used as a usage-explaining mark by conceiving a usage-explaining mark as a mark whose cognition enables one to infer the correct applicability of the word. Thus there are only distinguishing defining marks, and no special type of usage-explaining defining marks.

See also: DEFINITION

References and further reading

Bhattacharyya, S. (1987) *Doubt, Belief and Knowledge*, New Delhi: Allied Publishers, esp. chaps 17–18. (General introduction to the Navya-Nyāya theory of inference.)

—— (1990) *Gadādhara's Theory of Objectivity*, New Delhi: Motilal Banarsidass, esp. part 1, ch. 5. (For detailed discussion of the Navya-Nyāya theory of definition.)

Bhattacharyya, S. and Potter, K.H. (eds) (1993) *Encyclopedia of Indian Philosophies*, vol. 6, *Indian Philosophical Analysis: Nyāya-Vaiśeṣika from Gaṅgeśa to Raghunātha Śiromaṇi*, Princeton, NJ: Princeton University Press, and New Delhi: Motilal Banarsidass. (For a general introduction to Navya-Nyāya theory; see especially the introduction.)

Potter, K.H. (ed.) (1974) *Encyclopedia of Indian Philosophies*, vol. 1, *Bibliography*, Princeton, NJ: Princeton University Press, and New Delhi: Motilal Banarsidass. (For the dates and works of Navya-Nyāya authors mentioned in the present entry.)

—— (ed.) (1977) *Encyclopedia of Indian Philosophies*, vol. 2, *Indian Metaphysics and Epistemology: The Tradition of Nyāya-Vaiśeṣika up to Gaṅgeśa*, Princeton, NJ: Princeton University Press, and New Delhi: Motilal Banarsidass. (For a general introduction to Nyāya theory.)

SIBAJIBAN BHATTACHARYYA

DEISM

In the popular sense, a deist is someone who believes that God created the world but thereafter has exercised no providential control over what goes on in it. In the proper sense, a deist is someone who affirms a divine creator but denies any divine revelation, holding that human reason alone can give us everything we need to know to live a correct moral and religious life. In this sense of 'deism' some deists held that God exercises providential control over the world and provides for a future state of rewards and punishments, while other deists denied this. However, they all agreed that human reason alone was the basis on which religious questions had to be settled, rejecting the orthodox claim to a special divine revelation of truths that go beyond human reason. Deism flourished in the seventeenth and eighteenth centuries, principally in England, France and America.

1   The meaning of 'deism'
2   Four kinds of deist
3   Deism's period of influence
4   Significance of deism

1   The meaning of 'deism'

Deism in the popular sense asserts that a supreme being created the world but then, like an absentee landlord, left it to run on its own. Deism in the proper sense affirms a divine creator of the world but denies any divine revelation, holding that human reason alone is sufficient to provide us with whatever knowledge is necessary for a correct moral and religious life. (The *Oxford English Dictionary* defines 'deist' as 'one who acknowledges the existence of a God upon the testimony of reason, but rejects revealed religion'.) What is the connection between the popular and proper senses of deism? Someone who believed that God created the world but left it and its inhabitants to shift for themselves would surely deny that God acted in the world to provide us with a special revelation. So a deist in the popular sense will be a deist in the proper sense. But one may be a deist in the proper sense without being a deist in the popular sense. A person who believes in God but denies divine revelation may hold, nevertheless, that human reason is sufficient to establish that God exercises providential control over his creation. Indeed, a deist in the proper sense may even insist that reason shows us that the supreme being who created the world not only exercises providential control over his creation but is also perfectly good and just and has provided for rewards and punishments for human beings in a life to come. Thus, the basic, common point that separates deists from traditional theists is the issue of divine revelation. The deist denies that God reveals to us truths that are important for us to believe but which human reason cannot discover on its own. (Some deists were prepared to allow the existence of a revelation provided that its contents were not utterly mysterious to reason, claiming that God would have no interest in revealing things to us that we could not comprehend.) This is basic deism. On top of this one may add additional items that distinguish more radical deists from the traditional theist who believes that God has provided by special revelation truths that are important for us to believe but which our reason is insufficient to comprehend or establish on its own. The deist who sees God as creator of the world but uninterested in its future and the welfare of its human inhabitants is a basic deist who has added denials of other important ideas in traditional theism.

2   Four kinds of deist

In the second series of his Boyle Lectures, delivered in 1705, the philosopher and theologian Samuel CLARKE (§§1–2) distinguished four kinds of deist. The most important kind of deist, according to Clarke, believes in the existence of God in the sense of a supreme being who is infinitely powerful, all-knowing, perfectly good and the creator of the world. Furthermore, this deist believes that God exercises providential control over the world, has created human beings who have moral and religious duties, and has provided them with a future life in which the good will be rewarded and the wicked punished. But this deist rejects the idea of divine revelation, accepting only what is discoverable by natural reason. The next kind of deist holds the same view of God's attributes and providential control over the world, but in addition to denying divine revelation also denies human immortality and any future state of rewards and punishments. A further kind of deist believes that the supreme author of the world exercises control over the natural operations of the world but, lacking the moral attributes of goodness and justice, is indifferent to human welfare. It is understood that this deist also rejects divine revelation and a future state of rewards and punishments. The most radical kind of deist not only denies the moral attributes of the supreme being and any providential concern for human welfare, but also denies that the supreme being exercises control over the natural operations of the world. According to this deist, the supreme being, although infinitely powerful and intelligent, just created matter in motion without causing any particular natural happenings in the world or even establishing the natural laws according to which these happenings take place.

It is apparent from Clarke's discussion that the denial of divine revelation is common to all four kinds of deist. In his view, the most plausible kind of deism affirms that God is morally perfect and has provided for a future state of rewards and punishments. Against this kind of deist Clarke argues that it is eminently reasonable to believe that God would provide a revelation detailing our duties towards him and towards one another, particularly our need to repent of sin and establish a right relationship with him. Clarke also contends that fulfilled prophesies and the evidence for miracles rationally justify us in taking the Bible to contain this divine revelation. The next kind of deist also ascribes moral perfection to God but is encumbered with the difficulty of explaining why such a being would not provide for a future state of rewards and punishments. The last two kinds of deist deny that the creator has any moral attributes. Against both kinds Clarke argues that there are objective moral truths independent of any divine will and that, consequently, an infinitely intelligent, all-powerful being could not fail to have the moral attributes of goodness, justice and truth. For, he argues, knowing what is best to be done is itself a motive for doing it. And since God knows perfectly the principles of duty and has no needs that might conflict with his acting in accordance with duty, he always does what is best and, therefore, is perfectly good.

3 Deism's period of influence

Deism could emerge as an important movement only in a period when belief in a divine creator is not only virtually unquestioned but taken to be provable by human reason. Deism also requires a climate of enormous confidence in the power of human reason to disclose the basic truths about God, the world, morality and human destiny. And finally, deism can flourish best, if at all, only when there is general agreement that the traditions and authority of the established religion should be subject to the test of reason, and when there is some degree of toleration for different views on religious questions. In the latter half of the seventeenth century these conditions came to prevail in England, with the result that deism took root there, spreading then to Europe and America. But by the late eighteenth century its influence in England and elsewhere had declined.

The father of deism in England, Lord HERBERT OF CHERBURY (§§3–4) (1583–1648), argued that from the very beginning of the human race God implanted in our minds a disposition to believe in the existence of a supreme being, in the obligation to worship this being by pursuing a life of piety and virtue, and in the existence of a future life in which the good will be rewarded and the wicked punished. These basic ideas he held to be at the heart of all religious traditions, constituting a universal, natural religion apprehended solely by human reason. Later deistic writers followed Herbert's lead in taking human reason as the sole source of a basic religion of nature, viewing with scepticism, if not disbelief, appeals to the authority of the Bible, the authority of the Church and its traditions, and the testimony of the inner light. Among these deistic writers in England were John Toland (1670–1722), Anthony COLLINS (1676–1729), Thomas Woolston (1660–1724) and Matthew TINDAL (1657–1730). Toland, an Irishman, published *Christianity not Mysterious* (1696), in which he argued that nothing in Christianity that is true is either contrary to reason or above reason, attributing the mysteries in Christianity to paganism and the interests of priests. He also expressed doubts about the authenticity of parts of the Bible. His book raised such a storm that it was condemned by the Irish parliament, and he fled to England to avoid imprisonment. He professed to be a disciple of Locke, and it is instructive to compare their views. In his opposition to enthusiasm, Locke had advocated the use of reason in religion and was prepared to reject anything in Scripture that was contrary to reason. But he allowed for divine revelation of truths that were beyond reason as well as truths that were supported by reason. Thus he accepted the mysteries of the virgin birth, the resurrection and the divinity of Christ. Toland, and deists generally, departed from Locke in rejecting anything in Scripture that was mysterious or above reason (see LOCKE, J. §7).

The case for Christianity rested in large part on two claims: that the Old Testament prophecies regarding the messiah were fulfilled in Christ and that the miracles reported in the New Testament, particularly the resurrection of Christ, are well confirmed. If neither claim could be sustained in the court of reason, deism would appear to be intellectually superior to traditional Christianity. At least this is how the deists saw it. Consequently, they directed their attacks at the Old Testament prophecies and the New Testament miracles. In *A Discourse of the Grounds and Reason of the Christian Religion* (1724), which received thirty-five critical replies, Collins argued in some detail that on any literal interpretation of the prophecies it is simply unreasonable to see their fulfilment in the New Testament. In *Discourses on the Miracles of Our Saviour* (1727–29), Woolston attacked the argument based on the New Testament miracles. Arguing that taken literally the miracle stories were full of absurdities, Woolston claimed that even the Church Fathers recognized that they could only be taken figuratively. His work sold widely, receiving numerous critical replies. He was fined and imprisoned for his efforts.

Tindal's influential work *Christianity as Old as the Creation* (1730) reaffirmed and developed the deists' favourite claim that God had instilled in all human beings sufficient reason to discover the simple truths expressing our duties both towards himself and our fellow human beings. Tindal argued that the fundamental teachings of Christianity express these duties and, by doing so, make Christianity as old as the creation. He proceeded to argue that this religion of nature which God wrote in our hearts from the dawn of creation is the criterion against which the teachings of all religions must be measured. Any purported new revelation must be judged by reason in light of the original religion of nature.

Voltaire, the most prominent of the French deists, came into contact with English deism during his extended stay in London (1726–9). Returning to France, he attacked both the superstition and deceit he felt to be rampant in the Catholic Church and the materialism and atheism of younger philosophers. His own deism involved a belief in God, in absolute moral values and in personal immortality. Rousseau moved from Calvinism to Catholicism and finally to deism. His deism was similar to Voltaire's in stressing belief in God and a future life, but he particularly emphasized the role of conscience in establishing a personal relationship with God.

In eighteenth-century America, the works of English religious thinkers, including deists, were well known. In the latter half of the century Voltaire and Rousseau were read. Franklin, Jefferson, Washington and Thomas Paine were deists, although Paine was far and away the most outspoken. Paine believed deeply in the existence of God and the practice of virtue. Although less concerned with human immortality, he accepted the idea of a future life. He regarded deism as the rational replacement for revealed religion and viewed the rise of atheism as a reaction to the irrationality, fanaticism and political conservatism of revealed religion. To promote deism he undertook to destroy the authority of traditional Christianity by attacking its foundation in the Bible as the revealed word of God. In *The Age of Reason* (1794) he mounted the traditional arguments against the general idea of a supernatural revelation and then focused on the claims for the Bible, arguing that Moses was not the author of the first five books of the Old Testament and that the Gospels were not written by the apostles. He denied that Jesus was divine, claiming that the life of Christ depicted in the Gospels is a fable. The great importance of Paine's book is that it brought the ideas of deism to the general public.

4 The significance of deism

In an age of reason, deism had some advantages over orthodoxy. That there is a God, that we have duties to him and our fellow humans, and that there is a future state of rewards and punishments appeared to many to be truths firmly supported by reason. Indeed, many followers of orthodoxy also held that these three points are well supported by reason. But in the fight over the need for and the existence of special revelation, orthodoxy was put on the defensive. For it was not overly difficult for the deists to point out serious weaknesses in the case for special revelation built on Old Testament prophecies and New Testament miracles. Thus, so long as reason was the only testing ground, deism appeared to have the advantage. But deism was not without problems and excesses of its own. First, deists never could agree on which beliefs were essential. Some rejected immortality, whereas others took it to be central to the religion of nature. Second, the idea that there is a fundamental, universal religion of nature common to all human beings from the dawn of creation turned out to be a myth, wholly unsupported by historical studies. And, finally, as reason's ability to settle such ultimate questions came under serious attack, deism itself was called into question. For, unlike orthodoxy, deism rejected any religious claim that could not be established by reason. Thus, although deistic beliefs (such as belief in a divine reality, belief in moral duties towards others, and so on) survive, deism's belief in the power of reason to disclose to us a universal religion of nature is largely a thing of the past.

See also: MIRACLES; NATURAL THEOLOGY; PROVIDENCE; RELIGION AND SCIENCE; RELIGION, HISTORY OF PHILOSOPHY OF

References and further reading

Byrne, P. (1989) *Natural Religion and the Nature of Religion: The Legacy of Deism*, London and New York: Routledge. (Contains a valuable discussion of deism.)

* Clarke, S. (1706; 9th edn 1738) *A Discourse Concerning the Being and Attributes of God, the Obligations of Natural Religion, and the Truth and Certainty of the Christian Revelation*, British Philosophers and Theologians of the 17th and 18th Centuries, New York: Garland, 1978. (Clarke's introduction contains his careful classification of four kinds of deist; the Garland reprint is of the ninth (1738) edition.)

* Collins, A. (1724) *A Discourse of the Grounds and Reason of the Christian Religion*, British Philosophers and Theologians of the 17th and 18th

Centuries, New York: Garland, 1976. (Important historical attack against revelation and prophecies as adequate rational support for Christianity.)

Herbert of Cherbury, E. (1624) *De Veritate*, trans. and ed. M.H. Carre, Bristol: J.W. Arrowsmith, 1937. (Argues for an original, natural religion common to the human race.)

Morais, H.M. (1960) *Deism in Eighteenth Century America*, New York: Russell & Russell. (Useful summary of the views of a number of eighteenth-century American deists.)

* Paine, T. (1794) *The Age of Reason*, Indianapolis, IN: Bobbs-Merrill, 1957. (Popular deistic work attacking what Paine took to be the foundations of Christianity in superstitions and myths.)

Stromberg, R.N. (1954) *Religious Liberalism in Eighteenth-Century England*, Oxford: Oxford University Press. (Contains an illuminating discussion of the rise of deism in England.)

* Tindal, M. (1730) *Christianity as Old as the Creation*, British Philosophers and Theologians of the 17th and 18th Centuries, New York: Garland, 1978. (Argues that whatever is true in Christianity is apparent to natural reason. A major work in English deism that occasioned considerable controversy.)

* Toland, J. (1696) *Christianity not Mysterious*, British Philosophers and Theologians of the 17th and 18th Centuries, New York: Garland, 1978. (Widely read work insisting that the true gospel can contain nothing contrary to reason, nor above it.)

* Woolston, T. (1727–9) *Discourses on the Miracles of Our Saviour*, British Philosophers and Theologians of the 17th and 18th Centuries, New York: Garland, 1979. (Popular work arguing that a literal interpretation of the miracles attributed to Jesus leads to absurdities and inconsistencies.)

WILLIAM L. ROWE

DELEUZE, GILLES (1925–95)

Although grounded in the history of philosophy, Gilles Deleuze's work does not begin with first principles but grasps the philosophical terrain 'in the middle'. This method overthrows subject–object relations in order to initiate a philosophy of difference and chance that is not derived from static being; a philosophy of the event, not of the signifier–signified; a form of content that consists of a complex of forces that are not separable from their form of expression; the assemblage or body without organs, not the organized ego; time, intensity and duration instead of space; in short, a world in constant

motion consisting of becomings and encounters with the 'outside' that such concepts do not grasp.

This radical philosophical project is rendered most clearly in Deleuze (and his collaborator Guattari's concept of the 'rhizome'). The rhizome is a multiplicity without any unity that could fix a subject or object. Any point of the rhizome can and must be connected to any other, though in no fixed order and with no homogeneity. It can break or rupture at any point, yet old connections will start up again or new connections will be made; the rhizome's connections thus have the character of a map, not a structural or generative formation. The rhizome, then, is no model, but a 'line of flight' that opens up the route for encounters and makes philosophy into cartography.

1   **Histories of philosophy and philosophical works**
2   **Collaborations with Félix Guattari**
3   **Minor literature and nomad arts**

1   Histories of philosophy and philosophical works

Born in Paris, Gilles Deleuze spent the period of the Second World War studying philosophy at the Sorbonne. His teachers included Ferdinand Alquié, Georges Canguilhem, Maurice de Gandillac and Jean Hyppolite. Deleuze particularly admired Alquié and Hyppolite, but found them both to be stuck in the history of philosophy. For him, only Sartre escaped that history, and introduced a breath of fresh air into the post-Liberation situation of the intellectual in France. Deleuze's academic career proceeded in the usual manner: Professeur de Lycée, Professeur de l'Université de Provence, researcher at the Centre National des Recherches Scientifiques, Professeur de l'Université de Paris VIII. His public life is perhaps defined more by what did not happen than what did. He seldom travelled outside France, never joined the Communist Party, never embraced existentialism, phenomenology, or Heidegger; but he never renounced Marx, nor was Deleuze himself denounced during the upheavals of May 1968 in France. He died in 1995, by suicide, under conditions of deteriorating health.

By his own account, all the authors in the history of philosophy who interested Deleuze had something in common: they all escaped from the history of philosophy in some respect. Beyond this they had few relationships with one another: the Stoics, Hume, Bergson, Nietzsche, Leibniz, and especially Spinoza. Their likeness had to be produced by a technique that explored what happens between them, in an encounter for which no single philosopher served as a model. In Deleuze's rewritings of the history of philosophy, as well as in his two early philosophical works,

Différence et répétition (1968a) (*Difference and Repetition*, 1994) and *Logique du sens* (1969) (*The Logic of Sense*, 1990), what results is the production, not of history at all, but of 'philosophical geography', the line between two ideas forming an ideal space that is neither the one nor the other, but is in flux. Deleuze carries this out by grasping each philosophy 'in the middle' rather than by seeking its first principle.

An example of Deleuze's monstrous production can be found in his engagement with KANT in *La Philosophie critique de Kant* (1963) (*Kant's Critical Philosophy*, 1984) which he called 'a book on the enemy'. If Kant harmonizes the faculties in order to ground the architectonic of rationality, Deleuze focuses on how Kant makes possible the *disjunction* of the faculties. This incites the terrible struggle between imagination and reason and understanding and inner sense, a struggle whose importance lies in the notion that this discord produces an accord, even though the faculties are no longer determined by their succession in time or their contiguity in space, and are unregulated, as well, by any law.

Such a reading is no doubt indebted to Deleuze's admiration for HUME: not the Hume whose empiricism is claimed by the binary first principle: sensible ideas-intelligible ideas, but the Hume who substitutes the external and changing relation A *and* B, for the internal and essential relation A *is* B. Such a move realizes philosophical geography by undermining the verb 'to be' and establishing the moving series: *and, and, and*. Of equal importance, the substitution of 'and' for 'is' makes way for the concept of systems, unities or wholes that are open, as opposed to unities that transcend their parts. Finally, since philosophers have by and large begun with the concept of unity and then derived multiplicity from it as its contrary, to think multiplicity as what is, without a closed unity, Deleuze insists that we have to learn to think in terms of time instead of space. This is Deleuze's view of Bergson's contribution to philosophy, that in the world (and equally in cinema) matter, the movement-image, is produced by the expansion or relaxation of memory-duration, the time-image. Bergson – upon whom, Deleuze remarks, so much hatred was focused within the French university – argued, against Riemann and Einstein, that duration is what differs with itself originally. It is internal difference, a world of intensive magnitudes preserved, virtually coexistent in memory as the repetition of multiple planes, and so not as a numerically multiple exteriority.

Even before Bergson, Deleuze found in NIETZSCHE the guarantee that memory is the return, not of 'to be', of what is the same, but of becoming and difference. Following Hume, Deleuze argues that, for Nietzsche, all bodies consist of multiple relations between forces; will to power wills becoming and difference when it experiments with forces. When a force extends its power as far as it is able, its will is the expression of the power that it is and, in willing, it affirms difference and chance.

Connecting Hume, Nietzsche, the Stoics, and especially, SPINOZA, Deleuze discovered what he called 'a secret link which resides in the critique of negation, the cultivation of joy, the hatred of interiority, the exteriority of forces and relations, the denunciation of power'. What guides this is, in part, a profound and consistent anti-Hegelianism. In *Le Bergsonisme* (1966) (*Bergsonism*, 1988) this anti-Hegelianism is oriented by Bergson's objection to the imprecision and generality of Hegel's notions of unity and multiplicity. In *Nietzsche et la philosophie* (1962) (*Nietzsche and Philosophy*, 1983) it is guided by Nietzsche's critique of negative slave morality, values based upon a logic that states, 'You are evil; therefore, I am good', and upon the false conception of action as external rather than internal to power. This critique is clarified in Deleuze's work on the Stoics and Spinoza, where it is played out in terms of a conception of the body as multiple and active.

For the Stoics, there are two planes of being: bodies and events. Bodies are beings in depth; they are real, existing in space and temporally, in the present. On the other plane, we find 'incorporeal acts' – sense, the formalization of expression, ideational events at the surface of bodies. Mixtures deep inside bodies are the *causes* of incorporeal events, that is, of sense: becoming green, becoming poisoned. These becomings are the effects of bodily mixtures and are not reducible to bodies. Deleuze's logic of becoming undermines propositional logic, for the attribute is not a quality related to a subject by the indicative 'is'; any verb in the infinitive operates as limitless becoming. This has the additional effect of referring to no subject, no I claims the event which is always referred to simply as 'it'.

Deleuze wrote two books on Spinoza: *Spinoza et le problème de l'expression* (1968b) (*Expressionism in Philosophy: Spinoza*, 1990) which served as part of his doctoral thesis, and *Spinoza: philosophie pratique* (1970) (*Spinoza: Practical Philosophy*, 1988). For Deleuze's project of geographical philosophy, Spinoza's importance lies in the fact that, practically alone among philosophers, Spinoza asks what a body, understood as an assemblage of affects or becomings, can do, and how this leads to the practical or ethical question of how to increase our power to think, exist and act. The answer is, on Deleuze's account, a matter of a body's capacity to be affected in encounters among bodies, each of which is a dynamic and open multiplicity, an assemblage. Bodies that are

857

compatible increase one another's power to act; incompatible bodies decrease power for one or both of them. As a decrease in power is the normal situation for human beings, so the 'sadness' that characterizes the human condition is the first point of attack. On the practical or ethical level, Deleuze-Spinoza recommends a two-pronged approach: first, devalue sad passions; second, carry out an analysis of the systems of relations of the parts of bodies to determine which relations are compatible. This sparks the production of a geography that moves from merely joyful passive affections, to compatible relations as the cause of joy and finally, to the Spinozan ethical imperative: become active!

2   Collaborations with Félix Guattari

In 1969, Deleuze met Félix Guattari, a practising psychoanalyst and political activist. They collaborated on three explosive and radical books of philosophy: *Capitalisme et schizophrénie*, vol. 1, *L'Anti-Oedipe* (1972), vol. 2, *Mille Plateaux* (1980) (*Capitalism and Schizophrenia*, vol. 1, *Anti-Oedipus*, 1977, vol. 2, *A Thousand Plateaus*, 1987) and *Qu'est ce que la philosophie?* (1991) (*What is Philosophy?*, 1994). In this collaboration, an assemblage was constructed: 'Since each of us was several, there was already quite a crowd', and the geography of the encounter was practised: 'We are no longer ourselves', 'We have been aided, inspired, multiplied.' *Anti-Oedipus* is less an argument against the idol of psychoanalysis than a demonstration of the relation between, on the one hand, the herd instinct and the desire to be led that motivates those who profess their faith in Oedipus or in the state; and on the other, state fascism and the fascism we all carry with us.

Deleuze and Guattari address the key question posed by Wilhelm Reich: 'How could the masses be made to desire their own repression?' They hypothesize that fascism is lying in wait wherever the judgment 'He is evil, so I am good' is made and wherever what they call *lines of escape* or deterritorialized flows of desire, have been reduced to state, family or religious hierarchies. In the first case, we recognize what Nietzsche condemned as base valuations that can end only in nihilism. In the second, we find state institutions, hierarchies committed to binary thinking and dedicated to limiting or breaking the connections that allow for the construction of the multiplicity known as the assemblage, as well as heading off encounters between assemblages.

A Thousand Plateaus operates on many planes at once. Thus it serves as an embodiment of the open whole, which Deleuze and Guattari now call the 'rhizome'. Each chapter or 'plateau' of this book can

be read independently of any other, and each is accompanied by a date, though in no particular order and not always of importance in any traditional history: the date of Freud's analysis of the Wolf-man, the date the *Reichsmark* was declared to be no longer money, the date of the destruction of the Jewish Temple, the date of vampires. These dates or events take their place in various *semiotic* systems, some of which are linguistic and some not. But they never appear in the despotic linguistics of the signifier-signified relation, wherein all aspects of life are reduced to language. For, even when Saussure's linguistics released the signified (concept) from any constant relation to the word or sound image, it did so only by elevating the signifier, insofar as the relations between signifiers always determine the value (meaning) of any signified (see SAUSSURE, F. DE).

If meaning-events are the effects of bodies, then an entirely different relation between bodies and linguistic systems has to be established. If, following Nietzsche, a thing has as many meanings as there are forces capable of seizing it, and if each force consists of a complex of other forces, then in place of the old dualism of substance and form Deleuze and Guattari assert two substance/form complexes: one of content and one of expression. These two assemblages of forces cannot be separated from one another. A distinction between form of expression (an order and organization of functions) and form of content (an order and organization of qualities) can only arise for purposes of analysis: for example, in the encounter between a nomad war machine (form of expression) and itinerant metallurgy (form of content). Nor is the encounter necessarily or even primarily linguistic – linguistics is merely one of many semiotics, and not the most important.

The role of language and the task of philosophy regarding language are also crucial to *What is Philosophy?*, the end of the experiment between Deleuze and Guattari, an end sealed by Guattari's death in 1992. In this book, the Stoic treatment of bodies and events implicit throughout *A Thousand Plateaus* re-emerges forcefully, as Deleuze and Guattari argue that the task of philosophy – as opposed to science – is the creation of concepts, the extraction of events from beings and things so as to create a plane of immanence, a plane of consistency. For philosophy does not seek an external plane of reference or truth, as science does. The distinction between bodies and events is important here, for while philosophical concepts are constituted from immanent variations of consistent events, scientific functions refer to states of affairs or mixtures in bodies. Thus, while philosophical concepts are enunciated by conceptual personae (the friend, the stammerer) that are not the philosopher, but that trace out the line of becoming that is the concept, scientific functions are enunciated by the scientific observer situated within the perspective of a particular state of affairs (the relativity traveller).

3 Minor literature and nomad arts

Given Deleuze's interest in the history of philosophy and in social and political philosophy, his careful attention to literature and the arts may be unexpected. Yet, his two books on cinema, books on Sacher-Masoch and Sade, Kafka, Proust and Francis Bacon, as well as articles and constant references to a host of literary, musical, and artistic works and persons all evidence the central role of literature and the arts to philosophical geography. Thus, there is *Le Pli: Leibniz et la baroque* (1988) (*The Fold, Leibniz and the Baroque*, 1993) celebrating the pleat, the curve, the twisting surface of science and mathematics, but also of music, architecture, the line and the word; a sensuous view of the world that lives in the work of art. Nomad arts are blocs of sensations or a 'fold'. Each is a compound of percepts and affects wrested from the subject and its states by means of the material of each art. By means of its material, words and syntax, affective writing is the becoming-multiple that deterritorializes a major language and produces minor writing, which is the composing and decomposing of saturated percepts, rather than a record of memories, fantasies or travels. Thus, everything that is written takes its place within the open whole which is the social world. Likewise, cinema is sensation conditioned by cinema's plastic mass of visual material that puts into operation the open whole as both incessant flux and instantaneous disjunction. In place of language, art gives us percepts, affects and blocs of sensation put into motion. This is not philosophy, yet it makes philosophy happen by giving the event a body, a life, a universe.

See also: ALTERITY AND IDENTITY, POSTMODERN THEORIES OF §3; SELFHOOD, POSTMODERN CRITIQUE OF

List of works

Deleuze, G. and Cresson, A. (1952) *David Hume: sa vie, son oeuvre, avec exposé de sa philosophie*, Paris: Presses Universitaires de France. (Deleuze's early account of Hume's empiricism and Hume's life.)

Deleuze, G. (1953) *Empirisme et subjectivité: essai sur la nature humaine selon Hume*, Paris: Presses Universitaires de France; trans. C.V. Boundas, *Empiricism and Subjectivity: An Essay on Hume's*

Theory of Human Nature, New York: Columbia University Press, 1991. (Approaches Hume's empiricism as a doctrine of ideas that are external to one another thus always differing from one another while qualifying and making a subject of the mind that contemplates them.)

—— (1956) 'La conception de la différence chez Bergson', *Les Études Bergsoniennes* 4: 77–112. (Differentiates Bergson's ontology of difference from Hegel and Plato by separating differences of degree from difference in nature or kind and by arguing that repetition is difference.)

—— (1962) *Nietzsche et la philosophie*, Paris: Presses Universitaires de France; trans. H. Tomlinson, *Nietzsche and Philosophy*, New York: Columbia University Press, 1983. (Reads Nietzsche as the overthrow of Platonism that affirms becoming and change and rejects Ideas as a priori norms or concepts.)

—— (1963) *La Philosophie critique de Kant: doctrines des facultés*, Paris: Presses Universitaires de France; trans. H. Tomlinson and B. Habberjam, *Kant's Critical Philosophy: The Doctrine of the Faculties*, Minneapolis, MN: University of Minnesota Press, 1984. (Rejects the Kantian faculty's regulation of the senses, thought and morality in favour of the Kantian sublime as the unregulated exercise of all the faculties.)

—— (1966) *Le Bergsonisme*, Paris: Presses Universitaires de France; trans. H. Tomlinson and B. Habberjam, *Bergsonism*, New York: Zone Books, 1988. (Argues that duration is the qualitative and heterogeneous becoming operating in all life and the virtual and creative process of unconditioned change.)

—— (1968a) *Différence et répétition*, Paris: Presses Universitaires de France; trans. P. Patton, *Difference and Repetition*, New York: Columbia University Press, 1994. (A sustained reading of the history of philosophy that defines repetition as difference and not as representation.)

—— (1968b) *Spinoza et le problème de l'expression*, Paris: Éditions de Minuit; trans. M. Joughin, *Expressionism in Philosophy: Spinoza*, New York: Zone Books, 1990. (Finds Spinoza's concept of substance to be a concept of the One as an open-ended and differentiated whole that expresses itself by means of an infinity of attributes in modes that unfold from the One.)

—— (1969) *Logique du sens*, Paris: Éditions de Minuit; trans. M. Lester and C. Stivale, ed. C.V. Boundas, *The Logic of Sense*, New York: Columbia University Press, 1990. (Revives the Stoic conception of logic which articulates the event as an effect of bodily mixtures and as the surface between bodies and language.)

—— (1970) *Spinoza: philosophie pratique*, Paris: Éditions de Minuit; trans. R. Hurley, *Spinoza: Practical Philosophy*, San Francisco, CA: City Lights Books, 1988. (Opposes Spinoza's Ethical philosophy to moral thought.)

Deleuze, G. and Guattari, F. (1972) *Capitalisme et schizophrénie*, vol.1, *L'Anti-Oedipe*, Paris: Éditions de Minuit, 2nd enlarged edn, 1980; trans. R. Hurley, M. Seem and H.R. Lane, *Capitalism and Schizophrenia*, vol. 1, *Anti-Oedipus*, New York: Viking Press, 1977, reprinted Minneapolis, MN: University of Minnesota Press, 1983. (A revolutionary reconception of desire as productive and positive social force that reconfigures the Oedipal psychoanalysis of lack as a schizoanalysis of creative flows.)

—— (1980) *Capitalisme et schzophrénie*, vol. 2, *Mille Plateaux*, Paris: Éditions de Minuit; trans. B. Massumi, *A Thousand Plateaus*, Minneapolis, MN: University of Minnesota Press, 1987. (Fifteen chapters, called plateaus, traversing traditional disciplines and analyses. Each plateau develops its own concepts to construct new thematics in place of the traditional ones.)

Deleuze, G. (1981) *Francis Bacon: logique de la sensation*, Paris: Éditions de la Différence, 2 vols; trans. D. Smith, *Francis Bacon: The Logic of Sensation*, Cambridge, MA: MIT Press, forthcoming. (A study of the work of the artist Francis Bacon as a painter who frees the figure from representation to render sensation in and of itself.)

—— (1986) *Foucault*, Paris: Éditions de Minuit; trans. S. Hand, *Foucault*, Minneapolis, MN: University of Minnesota Press, 1988. (Reads the work of Michel Foucault as a new functionalism that produces the topology of diffuse and local rather than globalized power.)

—— (1988) *Le Pli: Leibniz et le baroque*, Paris: Éditions de Minuit; trans. T. Conley, *The Fold: Leibniz and the Baroque*, Minneapolis, MN: University of Minnesota Press, 1993. (Develops the fold as an anti-extentional concept of the multiple, an anitdialectical concept of the event and an anti-Cartesian concept of the subject.)

Deleuze, G. and Guattari, F. (1991) *Qu'est-ce que la philosophie?*, Paris: Éditions de Minuit; trans. H. Tomlinson and G. Burchell, *What Is Philosophy?*, New York: Columbia University Press, 1994. (The last work co-written by Deleuze and Guattari, differenciates philosophy from science, logic and art.)

References and further reading

Bogue, R. (1989) *Deleuze and Guattari*, New York: Routledge. (An introduction to Deleuze's best-known work including *A Thousand Plateaus*.)

Boundas, C.V. (1993a) 'Introduction', in C.V. Boundas (ed.) *The Deleuze Reader*, New York: Columbia University Press. (An outline of all of Deleuze's work, including the historical texts.)

—— (ed.) (1993b) *The Thought of Gilles Deleuze*, special issue of *Journal of the British Society for Phenomenology* 24 (1). (Selected critical essays.)

Boundas, C.V. and Olkowski, D. (1994) *Gilles Deleuze and the Theatre of Philosophy*, New York: Routledge. (A collection of critical and explanatory essays covering all phases of Deleuze's work by philosophical, literary and cultural critics.)

Foucault, M. (1977) 'Theatrum Philosophicum', in *Language, Counter-Memory, Practice*, ed. D. Bouchard, Ithaca, NY: Cornell University Press. (Focuses on Deleuze's innovative thinking in *The Logic of Sense* and *Difference and Repetition*.)

Goodchild, P. (1994) *Deleuze and Guattari: An Introduction to the Politics of Desire*, London: Sage.

Hardt, M. (1993) *Gilles Deleuze, An Apprenticeship in Philosophy*, Minneapolis, MN: University of Minnesota Press. (A detailed examination of Deleuze's work on Nietzsche, Bergson and Spinoza articulating Deleuze's anti-Hegelianism and the influence of scholastic philosophy.)

L'Arc (1972) *Deleuze*, special issue of *L'Arc* 49; revised edn, 1980. (Essays on Deleuze by French scholars including Clément, Gandillac and Klossowski, and an interview with Foucault by Deleuze.)

Martin, J.-C. (1993) *Variations: la philosophie de Gilles Deleuze*, Paris: Éditions Payot; trans. C.V. Boundas, *Variations: The Philosophy of Gilles Deleuze*, Atlantic Highlands, NJ: Humanities Press, 1997. (A complex and knowledgeable treatment of multiplicity from an aesthetic point of view.)

Massumi, B. (1992) *A User's Guide to Capitalism and Schizophrenia: Deviations from Deleuze and Guattari*, Cambridge, MA: MIT Press. (A practical elaboration of the two volumes from a postmodern cultural perspective.)

Olkowski, D. (forthcoming 1998) *The Ruins of Representation*, Berkeley, CA: University of California Press. (A feminist-oriented account of Deleuze's ontology of becoming through Hume and Bergson.)

SemioText(e) (1977) '*Anti-Oedipus*', special issue of *SemioText(e)* 2 (3). (Special issue devoted to essays on *Anti-Oedipus* including several translations of the commentaries of French scholars.)

SubStance (1984) *Gilles Deleuze*, special issue of

SubStance 44/5. (Special issue devoted to essays on Deleuze, focuses especially on literary criticism.)

DOROTHEA E. OLKOWSKI

DELMEDIGO, ELIJAH (*c*.1460–93)

Throughout the treatises and translations commissioned by his many patrons in Italy, Elijah Delmedigo championed Aristotle and Ibn Rushd (Averroes). In Latin texts prepared for Pico della Mirandola, Delmedigo affirmed such cardinal Averroist notions as the absolute unity of all human minds and the role of God as the unmeditated principle of intelligibility in the universe. In the Hebrew Behinat ha-Dat *(The Examination of Religion), Delmedigo urges the superiority of a rationalistic Judaism over other religions, especially Christianity, and over the nonphilosophic, improperly philosophic and antiphilosophic versions of Judaism. Sections of this work amount to a nuanced critique of Kabbalah. Combining ardent Averroism with qualified admiration for Maimonides, Delmedigo repeatedly argued for the compatibility of Judaism with secular philosophic speculation.*

Born to a distinguished family of rabbinic scholars and intellectuals in Candia on the island of Crete, Delmedigo migrated to Italy in 1480. He spent the next ten years expounding and defending Ibn Rushd's controversial version of Aristotelian philosophy (see IBN RUSHD; AVERROISM, JEWISH). Residing mainly in Padua, Venice, Bassano and Florence, Delmedigo was commissioned by such figures as Girolamo Donato, Domenico Grimani, Antonino Pizzamano and the Neoplatonic enthusiast of Kabbalah, Giovanni PICO DELLA MIRANDOLA, to translate Hebrew versions of Ibn Rushd's texts into Latin and to write systematic accounts of the latter's views. Seeking a wider audience, Delmedigo translated at least three of his own Latin works into Hebrew: two treatises dealing with the unicity of the hylic intellect and conjunction with the 'active intellect' – *Shete she'eloth 'al ha-Nefesh* or *Shene derushim 'al Hanefesh* (Two Questions on the Soul) - and *Ma'amar 'al 'etzem ha-Galgal*, his exposition of Ibn Rushd's *De Substantia Orbis* (On the Substance of the Celestial Sphere). Slavishly literal, these Hebrew translations differ from Delmedigo's Latin originals only by the interpolation of autobiographical data and discussions of religious topics that Delmedigo considered relevant to the Jewish community.

In the late 1490s, Delmedigo returned to Crete and began writing *Behinat ha-Dat*. He faulted Christianity for its irrational dogmas and excoriated Jewish mystics for their excessively Neoplatonic metaphysics and 'idolatrous' interpretations of Jewish ritual observance. He also chided MAIMONIDES and other unspecified rationalist theologians for confounding religious faith with philosophic speculation. Framing his criticism of the revered Maimonides diplomatically, he blamed him and the others for undermining social unity with their rationalist interpretations of religion. To avoid sectarian strife, Delmedigo counselled against publication of written doctrinal interpretations of Scripture and the law. He also argued that it was imprudent to convey the mistaken impression that religious belief and practice are rationally grounded rather than prophetically instituted.

Delmedigo was nevertheless eager to establish the compatibility of Judaism and philosophy. He emphasized the congenial parallel between Talmudic logic and philosophic argumentation, explaining that just as the rabbis use a set of well-defined principles for drawing inferences from Scripture, so the philosophers use syllogisms for reaching demonstrative truths. Delmedigo was intent on mitigating conflicts within the Jewish community. He balanced his trenchant criticisms of the Kabbalah by lacing *Behinat ha-Dat* with conciliatory remarks addressed to the Jewish mystics, highlighting the accords of Kabbalah, rational belief and popular religion.

Averroists are notoriously difficult to pin down; their utterances often seem inconsistent or contradictory. Their explications of Aristotle can be read as detached scholarship or partisan advocacy. They are known for tolerating what they deem to be mistaken popular beliefs that preserve the social order. Their overriding concern sometimes seems to be to make society safe for philosophy. The elusive Delmedigo was no exception. Most of his writings are not systematic statements of his own philosophy. Rather, they are secular commentaries and polemical treatises expounding Aristotle as interpreted by Ibn Rushd, who was, in turn, often misunderstood by the likes of JOHN OF JANDUN, a Latin Averroist whose many mistakes in interpretation Delmedigo seldom failed to mention and correct. Extracting Delmedigo's own convictions regarding physics, metaphysics and political philosophy from exegetical sources of this kind is difficult. *Behinat ha-Dat* is not as direct a help as we might wish. It was motivated as much by a diplomat's eirenic 'love for the words of our Torah, for our sages, and for the people of our nation' as it was by a medieval philosopher's austere devotion to logic, reason and truth. Knowing how anxious Delmedigo was to keep the peace makes it hard to determine where his devotion to Aristotelian philosophy ends and his love for Judaism begins.

Regardless of motive, Delmedigo unequivocally declared Aristotle the supreme philosopher and Ibn Rushd his only trustworthy commentator. With equal tenacity he affirmed philosophy and Judaism to be compatible, but only 'when they are properly understood'. These philosophical commitments put him at loggerheads with most of his contemporaries. Expounding Ibn Rushd's controversial monopsychism and its corollary, impersonal and unindividuated immortality, Delmedigo affirmed two of the most notorious doctrines against which Thomas AQUINAS and other theologians had argued vehemently. Defending Ibn Rushd's understanding of God as a self-sufficient mind whose rationality constitutes the unmediated principle of intelligibility and regularity in the universe, Delmedigo staked out his position among a heroic minority. Arrayed against him were Italian Neoplatonists and Kabbalists who embraced the metaphysics of emanation. Opposed to him also were obscurantists, who ridiculed philosophy, and scholastic theologians of all creeds, who defended radically voluntaristic doctrines of God's utter transcendence, unfettered will and direct awareness of particulars.

Delmedigo's enduring contributions to philosophy are twofold: he defended the secular autonomy of philosophy, its right to follow its own course, free of theological preconditions; and, if we take him at his word, he legitimized philosophy by stressing its power to establish and maintain civil order – without which philosophy itself would be unattainable.

See also: AVERROISM; AVERROISM, JEWISH; IBN RUSHD; KABBALAH; MAIMONIDES, M.; MESSER LEON, J.; PICO DELLA MIRANDOLA, G.

List of works

Delmedigo, E. (1482) *Shete she'eloth 'al ha-Nefesh* or *Shene derushim 'al Hanefesh* (Two Questions on the Soul), MS Milan: Biblioteca Ambrosiana, 128, and MS Paris: Bibliothèque Nationale, Hebrew 968. (Delmedigo's Hebrew translations of his own Latin treatises (no longer extant), composed originally for Pico della Mirandola, the first dealing with the unicity of intellect, the second dealing with the conjunction of the human intellect with the active intellect.)

—— (1485) *Ma'amar 'al 'etzem ha-Galgal* (Commentary on *De Substantia Orbis*), MS Paris: Bibliothèque Nationale, Hebrew 968. (Delmedigo's translation of and supercommentary to Ibn Rushd's treatise.)

—— (1486) *Letter to Pico della Mirandola*, MS Paris: Bibliothèque Nationale, Latin 6508. (Delmedigo's personal letter to Pico on various personal and philosophic issues, with an important section of the purchase of Kabbalistic books and their doctrinal meaning.)

—— (1488) 'Quaestiones: De Primo Motore, De Mundi Efficientia, De Esse et Uno' ('Questions: On the Prime Mover; On the World's Efficiencies; On Being and Unity'), in John of Jandun, *Super octo libros Aristotelis de physico auditu subtilissimae quaestiones* (On the Eight Books of Physics by Aristotle), Frankfurt: Minerva, 1969. (Delmedigo's analytic discussions and paraphrases of themes in Aristotelian metaphysics and physics.)

—— (c.1480–90) *Behinat ha-Dat* (The Examination of Religion), ed. with notes by J.J. Ross, *Sefer Behinat Ha-Dat of Elijah Del-Medigo*, Tel Aviv: Chaim Rosenberg School of Jewish Studies, 1984. (Critical edition of the Hebrew original. Delmedigo's treatise on the philosophy of religion, critique of Christianity and Kabbalah, and the role of rationality in revealed traditions.)

—— (c.1480–90) *Parafrasi Della Repubblica Nella Traduzione Latina Di Elia Del Medigo* (Latin Paraphrase by Elia Del Medigo of the *Republic*), ed. A. Coviello and P.E. Fornaciari, *Delmedigo's Latin Translation of Ibn Rushd's Paraphrase and Commentary to Plato's Republic*, Florence: Leo S. Olschki Editore, 1994. (Delmedigo's Latin translation of Ibn Rushd's paraphrase and commentary to Plato's *Republic*.)

—— (c.1480–90) *In Meteorologica Aristotelis* (Epitome of Aristotle's *Meteorology*), MS Vatican 4550. (Delmedigo's Latin translation of Ibn Rushd's *Epitome* of Aristotle's *Meteorologica*.)

—— (c.1480–90) *Aristotle's Book Lambda of the Metaphysics*, MS Paris: Bibliothèque Nationale, Latin 6508. (Delmedigo's Latin translation of the introduction to Book 12 of *Mah she'ahar ha-Tev'a*, Ibn Rushd's Hebrew version of Aristotle's *Metaphysics*.)

—— (c.1480–90) *Averrois Commentatio in Metaphysica Aristotelis* (Epitome of Aristotle's *Metaphysics*), MS Paris: Bibliothèque Nationale, Latin 6508. (Delmedigo's Latin translation of Ibn Rushd's *Epitome of Mah she'ahar ha-Tev'a* (Metaphysics).)

References and further reading

Bland, K.P. (1995) 'Elijah Del Medigo, Unicity of Intellect, and Immortality of Soul', *Proceedings of the American Academy for Jewish Research* 61: 1–22. (A description of Delmedigo's literary style, attitude toward faith and reason, and treatment of Averroist psychology.)

—— (1991) 'Elijah del Medigo's Averroist response to the Kabbalahs of fifteenth-century Jewry and Pico della Mirandola', *The Journal of Jewish Thought and Philosophy* 1: 23–53. (Focuses on the often discussed relationship to Pico and on Delmedigo's diplomatic critique of Jewish mysticism; footnotes cite the modern scholarship on Delmedigo.)

Geffen, D. (1973/4) 'Insights into the Life and Thought of Elijah Medigo Based on his Published and Unpublished Works', *Proceedings of the American Academy for Jewish Research* 61/2: 69–86. (Based on an unpublished doctoral dissertation which contains an English translation of *Behinat ha-Dat*; the footnotes lead the reader deeply into Delmedigo's world.)

KALMAN BLAND

DEMARCATION PROBLEM

The problem of demarcation is to distinguish science from nonscientific disciplines that also purport to make true claims about the world. Various criteria have been proposed by philosophers of science, including that science, unlike 'non-science', (1) is empirical, (2) seeks certainty, (3) proceeds by the use of a scientific method, (4) describes the observable world, not an unobservable one, and (5) is cumulative and progressive.

Philosophers of science offer conflicting viewpoints concerning these criteria. Some reject one or more completely. For example, while many accept the idea that science is empirical, rationalists reject it, at least for fundamental principles regarding space, matter and motion. Even among empiricists differences emerge, for example between those who advocate that scientific principles must be verifiable and those who deny that this is possible, claiming that falsifiability is all that is required.

Some version of each of these five criteria – considered as goals to be achieved – may be defensible.

1 What is the problem and why is it raised?
2 'Science is empirical'
3 'Science seeks certainty'
4 'Scientists follow a scientific method'
5 'Science describes only the observable world'
6 'Science is cumulative and progressive'
7 Is a criterion of demarcation possible?

1 What is the problem and why is it raised?

'The problem of demarcation' is an expression introduced by Popper to refer to 'the problem of finding a criterion which would enable us to distinguish between the empirical sciences on the one hand, and mathematics and logic as well as "metaphysical" systems on the other' ([1934] 1959: 34). Although Popper mentions mathematics and logic, other writers focus on distinguishing science from metaphysics and pseudoscience.

Some, including Popper, raise the problem because of an intellectual desire to clarify this distinction. Logical positivists had in addition the aim of overthrowing non-scientific disciplines such as metaphysics and theology that purport to describe the physical world but, being unverifiable, are (they claimed) lacking in meaning. Others have more practical aims. In a country such as the USA, which officially attempts to separate church and state, religion is not to be taught in the public schools, but science is. So the practical question becomes what to count as science (for example, is 'creation science' appropriately named?).

2 'Science is empirical'

Metaphysics, philosophy and theology are not. What this means, however, can vary from one view to another. On one typical account, science consists of propositions (such as the law of conservation of energy) that are either directly verifiable by sensory observation, or can be inferred from such observations by the use of inductive reasoning from observed members of a class to all members, or are derivable from either of these using deduction. By contrast, the propositions of metaphysics (for example, 'Platonic universals exist') fail to satisfy these criteria. Newton, who held such an empiricist view, claimed to derive his three laws of motion and law of gravity from observed phenomena using induction and deduction (see NEWTON, I. §4). Similar views have been held by many empiricists, including J.S. Mill and the logical positivists. A significantly different empiricist view is espoused by Popper, who, following Hume, regards inductive reasoning as lacking in logical justification. For Popper, although scientific laws cannot be verified inductively, they can be falsified by observing a single negative instance; accordingly, falsifiability by observation, rather than verifiability, is what makes science empirical (see POPPER K.R. §2).

Although the vast majority of influential writers on science have held that scientific propositions are empirical, there are significant exceptions, especially as regards fundamental principles involving space, matter, and motion. Descartes believed that the most basic principles of physics (no less than those of metaphysics) are knowable a priori by the use of rational intuitions and deductions from them (see DESCARTES, R. §7). Other a priorists include Kant, who asserted that these principles are synthetic a priori (see KANT, I. §7), and Poincaré, who defended them as conventions of language (see POINCARÉ, H. §§3–4). Whewell suggested a mixed view according to which, although scientists must first arrive at propositions empirically, as their scientific ideas become clarified they realize that these propositions are necessary and knowable a priori (see WHEWELL, W.).

3 'Science seeks certainty'

In this respect it is like mathematics and unlike metaphysics, theology and astrology, which, it is alleged, can never be more than speculative. In his *Regulae ad directionem ingenii* (Rules for the Direction of the Mind) (1620–*c*.9) Descartes' second rule is that 'we must occupy ourselves only with those objects that our intellectual powers appear competent to know certainly and indubitably'. Empiricists are more divided. Newton, who rejected Descartes' idea that science should aim at indubitable propositions, recognizes in his fourth rule of scientific method that any proposition, no matter how strongly supported, is liable to exception as further phenomena become observed. Nevertheless, scientists should always aim at the highest certainty possible in an empirical endeavour, which is obtainable by 'deducing propositions from phenomena and rendering them general by induction'.

Among empiricists at the other extreme from Newton are Popper and Laudan. For Popper a high degree of certainty is not possible in science since the use of any inductive generalizations that might generate such certainty is unjustified. Nor is it desirable, since scientists should make the strongest possible and hence the least likely generalizations. For Laudan (1977) science aims at providing 'adequate' solutions to 'interesting' problems, for which questions of truth, certainty and even probability are irrelevant.

An empiricist view that lies between these extremes is taken by Carnap and other probabilists. Scientists should aim at providing empirical evidence for a theory that increases its probability without necessarily rendering it high (see Achinstein 1983 for a critique).

4 'Scientists follow a scientific method'

Practitioners of non-sciences do not. A scientific method is a set of rules scientists should follow in discovering and testing laws and theories. Whether there are such rules and if so, what forms they take, whether they are universal for all sciences or even within a science, whether they change from one period to another, are all hotly disputed questions (see SCIENTIFIC METHOD).

On one view, there are rules for testing scientific theories that hold for all science during all periods. This view was espoused by Descartes, who proposed twenty-one such rules; it was also championed by the empiricist Newton (1687), who proposed four 'Rules of Reasoning in [natural] philosophy', comprising two for inferring causes of things, and two for making inductive generalizations from observed phenomena.

The two most prominent empiricist positions committed to a universal scientific method are hypothetico-deductivism and inductivism. According to the former, the scientist confronted with data and a problem begins by proposing an hypothesis, which is not inferred deductively or inductively from the data or anything else, but is simply offered as a conjecture. From it, and possibly other assumptions, observational conclusions are generated deductively, using logic and frequently mathematics. If the conclusions are established by observation the hypothesis is tentatively accepted. If they are found to be false, the hypothesis is rejected and a new one proposed. This is Popper's view.

By contrast, inductivists require one further step, an inductive argument giving independent support to the hypothesis or theory. This involves arguing from observed instances of a law to all cases or from similar effects to similar causes. Inductivists such as Newton and Mill reject the hypothetico-deductive method on the grounds that numerous conflicting hypotheses can entail the same data; what is required is independent inductive support for one of these.

The existence of a universal scientific method has been challenged by several twentieth-century writers, particularly since the 1960s. Thomas KUHN (1962), arguing for a historical, relativistic approach, asserts that scientists at a given time work within a 'paradigm' which consists of a set of concepts, practices, standards of evaluation, rules of reasoning and methods of observation that vary considerably from one science and period to another. The paradigm sets the problems to be solved and the methods for doing so. There is no scientific method common to all paradigms.

Finally, a sociological approach to science has been advocated (see, for example, Pinch 1986), a strong version of which rejects appeal to methodological rules in explaining how scientists proceed. Theories, being underdetermined by the data (see UNDER-

DETERMINATION), are not inferred from those data by using rules. One must look instead at social factors within the scientific community that explain how a scientific theory is developed and how the group 'negotiated' to accept it (see CONSTRUCTIVISM).

5 'Science describes only the observable world'

Metaphysics, theology and even mathematics describe worlds underlying, or beyond, or independent of, what can be observed. This is a view upheld by instrumentalists and other 'antirealists' and rejected by realists. Antirealists claim that the aim of science is to 'save the phenomena' by formulating theories that will correctly predict what is observable. Some antirealists, for example, Duhem and van Fraassen, believe that an unobservable world exists, but deny that the aim of science is to describe it. For Duhem that is the aim of metaphysics and theology (see DUHEM, P.M.M. §4). Other antirealists, for example, logical positivists of the 1950s and 1960s, held a strong form of instrumentalism, according to which claims about unobservables in science are to be construed, not as speaking of real entities, but as linguistic devices in a theory for generating claims about what can be observed. For these writers both science and metaphysics introduce terms for unobservables that do not denote objects in the world. The difference between the two disciplines is that scientists but not metaphysicians tie these terms to observables in such a way as to allow observational predictions.

Realists, by contrast, claim that there is a physical world that exists independently of our minds, our observations and our theories. This world contains not only things and events scientists can observe (for example, the planets), but ones they cannot (for example, quarks). The job of the scientist is to describe both the observable and the unobservable worlds. To accept a theory involves a commitment that what it says about both is true. For the realist the distinction between science and metaphysics is not to be drawn by saying that science, but not metaphysics, describes the observable (see SCIENTIFIC REALISM AND ANTIREALISM).

6 'Science is cumulative and progressive'

Metaphysics, theology and philosophy are not. The history of philosophy, for example, is just the history of one theory after another; the more different the new theory from the old, the more it conflicts with it, the better its chance of being taking seriously. Science, by contrast, develops in an incremental, progressive way, so as to retain and build upon much of what has come before. In addition, as science advances it yields more and more truths about the world (or saves more and more phenomena); philosophy does not.

This idea, forcefully defended by logical positivists, came under strong challenge in the 1960s particularly from FEYERABEND and Kuhn. Both argued that a predecessor theory is usually not derivable from a successor. Sometimes, as Feyerabend (1993) noted, the two are not even logically compatible. Sometimes the two are 'incommensurable': they use concepts that completely depend for their meanings on different theories and that cannot be translated from one theory to the other. For Kuhn this occurs when, as in Newtonian and relativistic mechanics, the theories are parts of different paradigms (see INCOMMENSURABILITY).

7 Is a criterion of demarcation possible?

One might suppose not, in view of such controversies over what constitutes science. Indeed, even the need for a demarcation criterion has been challenged by some philosophers, especially ones who think that philosophy itself is or ought to be construed as part of science (for example Quine 1973).

Nevertheless, we do tend to distinguish science from other disciplines. Newton's mechanics is a scientific theory, but his theory of scientific method is not; it is a philosophical theory. One helpful step might involve taking science, or even a particular science such as physics, at a given historical time and saying something general about the goals of practitioners at the time, while recognizing that these may change and that not all scientists accept them. With this in mind, we might say that the previously quoted claims reflect scientific goals to be achieved at some point.

For example, in modern physics as well as other sciences, a goal is to present empirically testable ideas – even if at the moment (as with superstring theory) it is not known how to test the ideas empirically. For J.J. Thomson, who in 1897 claimed that cathode rays are charged particles not waves, it was not enough simply to postulate that this is so. He wanted to show how in principle this claim could be tested empirically by demonstrating that the rays can be electrically deflected, something that had not previously been accomplished. The goal of making hypotheses empirically testable is one generally shared by physicists but not by philosophers. Physicists can be just as speculative as metaphysicians, but they cannot be so for too long.

Another goal is to achieve certainty, at least as much as possible, by actually carrying out such tests. Although philosophers, theologians and mathematicians may also crave certainty, their route to it is a priori argumentation, not empirical testing. (For a contrary viewpoint regarding the status of philosophy of science, see Donovan *et al.* 1988) This is related to two further goals. Even if both physicists and metaphysicians postulate 'unobservable' entities, one of the aims of physics, but not metaphysics, is to eventually render them 'observable' – to detect and measure them. It was not sufficient for Thomson simply to postulate the existence of the particles (electrons), or even to describe an experimental procedure for electrically deflecting them and measuring their mass to charge ratio. He also attempted (successfully) to perform the experiment. Nor was this the end of the matter. Thomson sought to *argue* for his theory of charged particles from the results of his experiments. He did so, as Newton and Mill suggest, using both deduction and inductive generalization (see Achinstein 1991). Achieving as much certainty as possible through empirical testing requires the use of logical arguments in accordance with a 'scientific method'. Without such arguments mere 'negotiation' within a group is not enough.

Finally, physics today is much more cumulative and progressive than metaphysics or other fields of philosophy. A physicist may present completely new ideas, but in working out consequences it is desirable to make use of general principles, such as conservation laws, that are empirically established. Otherwise deductions to testable conclusions would be much rarer than they are. Even in contemporary philosophy, by contrast, few if any general principles are considered by most philosophers to be established.

Assuming these represent goals of many physicists (but not of philosophers or other 'non-scientists'), a job for philosophers of science is to provide a critical, systematic account of them. Philosophers of science may also try to determine the extent to which these goals, so clarified and systematized, can be attributed to scientists in other fields and at different times.

See also: LOGICAL POSITIVISM §5

References and further reading

* Achinstein, P. (1983) *The Nature of Explanation*, New York: Oxford University Press. (A defence of a pragmatic concept of explanation; chapters 10 and 11 discuss the concept of scientific evidence. See §3.)
* —— (1991) *Particles and Waves*, New York: Oxford University Press. (This work discusses methodological issues in nineteenth-century physics, including the discovery of the electron by J.J. Thomson. See §7.)
Carnap, R. (1962) *Logical Foundations of Probability*, Chicago, IL: University of Chicago Press. (An important and influential work that defends an a priori account of probability and an increase-in-probability definition of evidence. See §3.)
* Descartes, R. (1988) *Selected Philosophical Writings*, New York: Cambridge University Press. (See particularly the work 'Rules for the Direction of the Mind'. See §§2–4.)
* Donovan, A., Laudan, L. and Laudan, R. (eds) (1988) *Scrutinizing Science*, Dordrecht: Kluwer. (Contributors to this volume offer empirical tests for the validity of various scientific methods.)
Duhem, P. (1991) *The Aim and Structure of Physical Theory*, Princeton, NJ: Princeton University Press. (A modern classic in the philosophy of science.)
* Feyerabend, P.K. (1993) *Against Method*, London: Verso. (A controversial but always interesting attack on traditional views of rationality in science.)
Fraassen, B. van (1980) *The Scientific Image*, Oxford: Oxford University Press. (Defence of antirealism.)
Kant, I. (1786) *Metaphysical Foundations of Natural Science*, Indianapolis, IN: Bobbs-Merrill, 1970. (See particularly chapter 3 'Metaphysical Foundations of Mechanics'.)
* Kuhn, T. (1962) *The Structure of Scientific Revolutions*, Chicago, IL: University of Chicago Press. (One of the most influential works on the nature of science in the twentieth century.)
* Laudan, L. (1977) *Progress and its Problems*, Berkeley, CA: University of California Press. (Very readable defence of a problem-solving approach to science.)
Mill, J.S. (1843) *A System of Logic*, London: Longmans, 1959. (Book III of this classic contains Mill's defence of induction and his attack on the hypothetico-deductive method.)
* Newton, I. (1687) *Philosophiae Naturalis Principia Mathematica*, Berkeley, CA: University of California Press, 1966. (Book III begins with Newton's four rules of scientific method.)
* Pinch, T. (1986) *Confronting Nature: The Sociology of the Solar-Neutrino Detection*, Dordrecht: Kluwer. (A sociological approach to scientific discovery and change.)
Poincaré, H. (1902) *Science and Hypothesis*, New York: Dover, 1962. (Classic defence of a conventionalist approach to science.)
* Popper, K. (1934) *The Logic of Scientific Discovery*, London: Hutchinson, 1959. (The most famous twentieth-century defence of hypothetico-deductivism and the idea that science is falsifiable but not verifiable.)
* Quine, W.V. (1973) *The Roots of Reference*, La Salle, IL: Open Court. (The 1971 Paul Carus Lectures.)

Snyder, L. (1994) 'It's *All* Necessarily So: William Whewell on Scientific Truth', *Studies in History and Philosophy of Science* 25, 785–807. (A novel interpretation of Whewell's a priorism.)

Whewell, W. (1847) *The Philosophy of the Inductive Sciences*, New York: Johnson Reprint Corporation, 1967. (One of the great works of nineteenth-century philosophy of science.)

PETER ACHINSTEIN

DEMOCRACY

Democracy means rule by the people, as contrasted with rule by a special person or group. It is a system of decision making in which everyone who belongs to the political organism making the decision is actually or potentially involved. They all have equal power. There have been competing conceptions about what this involves. On one conception this means that everyone should participate in making the decision themselves, which should emerge from a full discussion. On another conception, it means that everyone should be able to vote between proposals or for representatives who will be entrusted with making the decision; the proposal or representative with most votes wins.

Philosophical problems connected with democracy relate both to its nature and its value. It might seem obvious that democracy has value because it promotes liberty and equality. As compared with, for example, dictatorship, everyone has equal political power and is free from control by a special individual or group. However, at least on the voting conception of democracy, it is the majority who have the control. This means that the minority may not be thought to be treated equally; and they lack liberty in the sense that they are controlled by the majority.

Another objection to democracy is that, by counting everyone's opinions as of equal value, it considers the ignorant as being as important as the knowledgeable, and so does not result in properly informed decisions. However, voting may in certain circumstances be the right way of achieving knowledge. Pooling opinions may lead to better group judgement.

These difficulties with democracy are alleviated by the model which concentrates on mutual discussion rather than people just feeding opinions into a voting mechanism. Opinions should in such circumstances be better formed; and individuals are more obviously equally respected. However, this depends upon them starting from positions of equal power and liberty; rather than being consequences of a democratic procedure, it would seem that equality and liberty are

instead prerequisites which are needed in order for it to work properly.

1 **What democracy is**
2 **The value of democracy**
3 **The paradox of democracy**
4 **Democracy and knowledge**
5 **The use of democracy**
6 **Other consequences**

1 What democracy is

Democracy means rule by the people. It is a form of decision making or government whose meaning can be made more precise by contrast with rival forms, such as dictatorship, oligarchy or monarchy. In these rival forms a single person or a select group rules. With democracy this is not so. The people themselves rule and they rule themselves. The same body is both ruler and ruled.

Philosophical accounts of democracy analyse its nature and discuss its value. The two cannot be completely separated. Any account which explains the value of democracy has to provide or presuppose an account of what it is holding to be of value. Conversely, supposedly neutral analyses of the nature of democracy are influenced by values. For example, someone who thinks that democracy is a good thing is liable to analyse it in terms of other features also thought to be good.

The concept of democracy therefore may naturally be thought of as what W.B. Gallie called an essentially contested concept. Such concepts are concepts whose analysis is unresolvable because different analysts read into it their favoured values. For example, before the reunification of Germany, both East and West Germany called themselves democracies. Yet each had very different political systems, one being a Marxist single-party state, the other having economic and political competition with several parties and contested elections. A dispute about which one was really a democracy would be irresolvable.

This account and this example presuppose that democracy is desirable, so there is a competition to lay claim to the honorific title. However, for most of the time since the invention of the concept of democracy it has not been taken to be a term of honour. A kind of democracy did exist in ancient Athens. But, this was a form of government criticized by the leading Greek thinkers of the time, Plato and Aristotle. For most of the time since this early democracy ended, democracy has neither existed nor been thought to be desirable.

Much later, with the creation of the USA, we reach a system which most people today would take to be a paradigmatic example of democracy. Unsurprisingly it was defended by its founding fathers. However, what might surprise us more today is that in one of the most famous of these defences, James Madison was careful not to use 'democracy' as the name for the system he supported. He identifies things called democracies and does not support them; the description he uses instead for the fledgling USA is 'republic' (Madison, Hamilton and Jay 1787–8).

What Madison means by a republic is 'a government in which the scheme of representation takes place', and by a democracy 'a society consisting of a small number of citizens, who assemble and administer the government in person' (Madison, Hamilton and Jay [1787–8] 1987: 126). It might be thought that the central question here is one of size. Commentators writing just before Madison, such as ROUSSEAU (§3) (1762) and MONTESQUIEU (§3) (1748), held that democracy was only possible in small states; and Madison can be taken to be marking the transition to the modern world, with large states rather than small ones; and a corresponding move from direct democracy to representative government. What is today standardly called democracy is very different from what was standardly so called in the ancient world.

However, size is not the only important distinction here. Individuals in very large modern political units can now be so linked together by modern technology that they can relate to each other much as if they all met together. On the other hand, political decisions by and for small groups are still made in the modern world. It can still be asked of these whether they should be made democratically; and, if so, which sort of democracy is appropriate. So, whatever the size of political unit, questions can arise about the importance of participation or discussion before decisions are made. It can be asked whether democracy should be seen primarily as a mechanism in which people vote for policies or representatives without assembly, participation or discussion. At one extreme (as with Joseph SCHUMPETER (§3) (1943)), we could analyse democracy as a competition for votes between professional politicians. At the other extreme, we could analyse democracy as a system in which unanimous decisions are reached after a prolonged discussion which respects the equal autonomy and participation of everyone involved. The former seems more practical, but may not uphold any (other) ideals; the latter seems impressively ideal, but may be ineffective in practice.

It has just been said that voting and representation is at least practical. However, this ignores one prominent problem. This is that the collective view which results from voting may not be related in the way we would wish to the individual views expressed in the votes. In particular this applies if there are three or more options to be arranged in order of preference and there are three or more such individual orderings (see SOCIAL CHOICE). These problems will not be discussed further here; although it should be recognized that many people (such as W.H. Riker (1982)) think that they are an insuperable objection to democratic decision making.

2 The value of democracy

Once we have an idea of democracy, the next question is why, or whether, it is of value. The Greek historians identified the original introduction of democracy with the advance of liberty and equality. Since both liberty and equality are usually thought to be of value, this would seem to be a natural answer to the question. Democracy is of value because it produces liberty and equality. With dictatorship or other forms of special leadership, a particular person or group has more power than others. By contrast, in democracy everyone is equal. Everyone has the same (political) power. So democracy is egalitarian as compared with other forms of government or decision making.

Similarly for liberty. A democracy introduced by the overthrow of a dictator increases political liberty. People have been freed from the control of the dictator. Hence democracy promotes liberty. There are several connected terms here: liberty, freedom, autonomy. However, whichever term is used, this argument seems to work. Consider autonomy. It means, literally, self-rule. Yet this is exactly what happens in democracy, as opposed to other forms of government. The people rule themselves.

However, as always, further inspection makes matters less obvious. Suppose decisions are made by majority vote and someone is in the minority. This person is outvoted and so their wants will not be put into effect. Therefore we can question whether in this (democratic) situation, this person is really autonomous. They are being made to do something which they do not want to do. Hence they are not really autonomous. Similarly for equality. Not everyone is treated equally when majority decisions are adopted, because only the views of some people (the majority) are put into effect. The minority's views are disregarded. Hence they are not treated equally. The winner takes all, and hence winners and losers are not equally treated.

If a community is divided into two parts living in mutual antipathy, this becomes even more obvious. The majority community could, by democratic vote, bear heavily down on the minority community, restricting or removing things it holds to be of fundamental value. In such circumstances the members of the minority community could hardly be said to be at liberty; nor could it be said that they were being equally treated. Hence the phrase, used by Tocqueville (1835) and taken over by J.S. Mill (1859), 'the tyranny of the majority'. The initial contrast between democracy and dictatorship has now been left behind. If democracy is really the dictatorship of the majority, then it is not so obvious that democracy promotes freedom and equality.

3 The paradox of democracy

If we examine democracy from the standpoint of the minority, as in the last section, this helps to focus the problem of its value. A democrat thinks that the majority view ought to be enacted. But in voting they also declare their own view about what ought to be enacted. When they are in a minority these diverge and they seem to be caught in a contradiction. There are two incompatible policies, A and not-A. Yet the minority democrat seems to think both that A ought to be enacted (because that is what the majority want) and also that not-A ought to be enacted (because that is their own view). Richard Wollheim (1962) called this the 'paradox of democracy'.

However, if democracy can be given a value, the paradox is resolvable. For what we then have is a simple (and familiar) conflict of values. The democrat's direct view of the matter indicates the value of the course of action for which they voted. But once it is defeated by the majority this rival course of action also possesses value. For it inherits the value of democracy. If, for example, democracy is taken to be an egalitarian procedure then adopting this rival course of action has egalitarian value.

An example: four of us in a car have to decide to go either to the beach or to the town. There is only one car and we can go to only one place. We agree to decide democratically, by vote. The vote is taken. I vote for the beach, and am outvoted by three to one. The beach is of value to me. This is shown by my vote. However, I am also a democrat. After the vote, the town also has value to me. With the town three people's views are respected; with the beach only one. If I hold that people are of equal value, then I have a reason for the car to go to the town.

4 Democracy and knowledge

In his *Republic* Plato says that 'it is not in the natural course of things for the pilot to beg the crew to take his orders' (c.380–367 BC: 489b). The implication is that if we want as a group to go to the right place, it is not sensible to assume that everyone has an equally valid opinion. Instead we should follow the lead of those who know. Hence democracy, which treats everybody's opinions equally, is inefficient as a means of determining the right thing to do (see PLATO §14).

This argument makes several presuppositions and can be resisted by contesting them. Some people can only know more than others about something if there is indeed something to be known. That is, if there is a truth about the matter independent of people's opinions. But this is precisely what might be contested when the question is what the state should do. This being a matter of value, it might be held that no independent truth, and hence no knowledge, is available. More precisely, it might be thought that a line can be drawn between areas in which knowledge is available, and which, for example, might be handled by a professional, trained civil service; and areas for which no knowledge is obtainable, and which should be left to democratic, untrained, amateur decision. Benjamin Barber (1984), for example, takes the area of politics to be one of action, not truth; and for him democracy takes over in the areas where metaphysics fails, creating its own epistemology.

It should be noticed, however, that an argument for the goodness of democratic decision making cannot simply be made on the basis of a complete scepticism about values. For if no truths about values are available, then no truths about the value of democracy are available either. Hence a valid argument cannot be made from this premise to a conclusion that it is true that democracy is of value.

Conversely, even if it is allowed that there are independent truths about value, it does not directly follow that democracy is an inappropriate way of discovering these truths. For it is quite possible that the truth about what in general the state should do is the kind of truth about which people have a roughly equal capacity. Furthermore, even if people do not have equal capacity, as long as it cannot be told which ones are superior, democracy may still be the appropriate method to use. The Platonic argument assumes that there is a truth about what should happen; that this truth is better known to some people than others; and that it is possible to tell independently of their views which these people are. All these assumptions could be resisted.

If people are of roughly equal capacity (or it cannot be told who is superior) then, as long as everyone is more likely than not to be right, voting and adopting the majority view is an efficient method to use. For the majority decision has a higher probability of being right than any individual decision, as CONDORCET (§2) was the first to show. In other words, if I have to make a sequence of decisions about the truth of something and I am in a group each of whose members gets the answer right more often than not, then I do much better systematically following the majority view of the group than my own initial views.

Even if some people clearly have better informed views than others, it still does not follow that democratic decision making is inefficient. For if it is obvious who the experts are, then people with an interest in discovering what is right will generally follow their views. In other words, the same answers will be arrived at as would happen if, as in Plato, the better informed were made dictators. Democracy will not be inferior in discovering of the truth, and will have other advantages.

On the other hand, if it is not obvious who the experts are, then it is indeed the case that the majority view may not follow expert opinion. But, if some people are dictators, it may also be the case that the people who are made dictators are not the ones who are better informed. The dangers of mistake in following majority opinion are matched by the dangers of mistake in making the wrong people the dictators. The Platonic argument only works if the experts can be recognized in advance, for example (as in Plato's *Republic*), because they are educated in a way which ensures that they will have expertise.

5 The use of democracy

Other justifications for democracy are possible. One standard device for justification, for many areas, is utilitarianism (see UTILITARIANISM). Something is justified if it promotes general happiness or utility. It can be asked of a form of government, just like anything else, whether it does tend to promote this. The answer, at least of the classical utilitarians such as BENTHAM (§6) and James MILL, is that democracy does.

This argument is expressed most simply in James Mill's short essay, *Government* (1820). He starts with an evaluative and a factual premise. The evaluative premise is utilitarianism. Actions are right in so far as they promote the general happiness. The factual premise is universal self-interest. People seek those things which promote their own interests. The problem is to find the form of government in which both of these premises can be true together, to find the form in which people seeking their own interest will nevertheless do those things which promote the general happiness. It is not difficult to show that representative democracy is the answer. Kings will promote the interest of kings, dictators of dictators, oligarchies of oligarchies. In all cases the interest promoted is that of the ruling group, not that of the people as a whole. However, if the people as a whole are put in charge, they will promote the interests of the people as a whole. Seeking their own interests,

they will produce general happiness. Hence both premises are satisfied simultaneously.

It is perhaps unsurprising that the greatest happiness of the greatest number results if the majority (the greatest number) are put in charge. However the answer does depend upon certain presuppositions. It assumes that people act in their own interests. Even if this is what they generally intend to do (which might be disputed), it does not follow from this that they are successful. For they may not know their interests. For example, it is often held that people discount the future too severely, so they prefer less important immediate interests to more important long-term interests. If this is so, then democratic decisions will lead to too short-term results, which are not even in the interests of those voting (see NEEDS AND INTERESTS; PUBLIC INTEREST).

A related point is that this model takes preferences as they are, without allowing them to be changed by the democratic process. Yet if people are ill informed about what is good for them, it would be better to operate on the preferences before counting votes. Democracy treats all votes equally. But people may not be equally informed about their interests. So the result may be that some interests are catered for better than others. Analogously, treating votes equally means that strongly held and weakly held views are considered of equal importance. Yet if the goal is to maximize utility, it may be wrong to follow the weakly held view of a majority rather than the strongly held view of a significant minority. If the utility of getting something is supposed to be roughly proportional to the strength of the desire for it, then it could be that the total of less people multiplied by a greater utility per person is higher than the total of more people multiplied by less utility per person.

6 Other consequences

The idea of utilitarianism as a mere preference-satisfying machine, in which antecedently given preferences are satisfied, has often been criticized. One alternative is to treat the values more objectively. Democracy can then be shown to be good in terms of these independently specified consequences. Such was the approach of J.S. Mill (1861) and more recent defenders such as William Nelson (1980). Democracy is justified as a form of education or development; it is taken to be a political system in which individuals are made to think for themselves and are therefore improved. Even if the decisions they make are not the best decisions, it is better for individuals if they try and take part in such decisions.

Another consequence which might justify democracy is the supposed promotion of dynamic economic activity; as opposed to the sluggish effects supposedly emanating from more centralized planning and control. Yet even if democracy does correlate with such beneficial economic circumstances, it is not clear that this by itself can be used as an argument for promoting democracy. Jon Elster (1986) identifies the questionable role of such arguments based on indirect effects. For it may be that these other effects only happen if people are attached to democracy for more direct reasons (such as thinking that it is a just form of government). If people were only to support democracy because they thought that it encouraged economic dynamism, then the democracy would not work, and so the economic dynamism would not follow either.

This relates to another familiar problem with starting from antecedent preferences and then taking democracy to be a sort of market mechanism in which these preferences are traded. If people only act through self-interest, trying to get their antecedently given preferences fulfilled, then it is not obvious why they should vote at all. For the advantages of voting will come to them if the others vote and their own vote seems to be merely a cost. At the national government level, it is exceedingly unlikely that any one vote will be decisive. So they would be better off not voting at all.

One answer to all of these problems is to dispense with the idea of democracy being a mechanism for satisfying antecedently given preferences. Instead of taking these as given, democracy should be held as a device in which people develop and discover their views about what is right. And, in thinking about what is right, they should think about what is right for the group as a whole, and not just themselves. People should therefore participate in a form of decision making in which they share their ideas, discuss together and, with luck, eventually reach general agreement.

The form of arguments people can use in such discussions is naturally constrained, as people seeking agreement should look as if they are appealing to general principles rather than merely appealing to self-interest. The condition of publicity (that is, of what can be said publicly) imposes constraints. If people think from the general point of view rather than in terms of their own individual interest, the forms of reasoning and the antecedent judgements will be different. Discussion rather than voting becomes the central feature of democracy, and it is important that people can meet and talk together before decisions are made.

These ideas promoting discussion and participation have several presuppositions. They presuppose that people will be better able to work out the truth (about what is good for the group) by working in groups rather than individually. This may be the case if they are all independently motivated by the same desire to discover the truth. It is less obviously the case if there are deep conflicts of interest (such as capital against labour; or country against town; or this world against the next). The supposition is that group discussion leads to more rationality; but in some circumstances group dynamics merely increase and inflame passion, so that people behave badly together in a way that they never would separately.

The values considered at the start of this discussion – namely, liberty and equality – now reappear; only now not as the consequence of democratic activity but as its prerequisites. For if discussion is to reach the right answer, it needs to start with roughly equal power between the discussants. Otherwise discussion will be forced in the interests of the stronger. Hence the idea that democracy needs circumstances of roughly equal wealth (held by Montesquieu and Rousseau). Hence the Marxist criticism that Western liberal democracy works on the fiction of an idealized equality when the real situation is one of greatly unequal economic power. Hence John Rawls' argument (1971) that political parties should be paid for by the state to avoid the economically powerful buying votes (see RAWLS, J. §2). Hence also the objections of feminist theorists. If men and women are antecedently in a situation of different power, then the supposed equality of democracy will only result in most of the power remaining with the men. Discussion, yes: but only if the forum is subject to powerful antecedent control and regulation. Otherwise we return to the bad old world of bargaining between antecedently given preferences from which this optimistic espousal of discussion was meant to save us.

See also: CONSTITUTIONALISM; GENERAL WILL; REPRESENTATION, POLITICAL; SOCIAL DEMOCRACY

References and further reading

* Barber, B. (1984) *Strong Democracy*, Berkeley, CA: University of California Press. (Referred to in §4.)
Copp, D., Hampton, J. and Roemer, J.E. (eds) (1993) *The Idea of Democracy*, Cambridge: Cambridge University Press. (Full collection of studies on truth, antecedent preferences and publicity.)
Dahl, R.A. (1989) *Democracy and its Critics*, New Haven, CT, and London: Yale University Press. (Presentation of criticisms and reply; useful on equality.)
* Elster, J. (1986) 'The Market and the Forum', in J. Elster and A. Hylland (eds) *Foundations of Social*

Choice Theory, Cambridge: Cambridge University Press. (Mentioned in §6.)

Estlund, D. (1989) 'The Puzzle of the Minority Democrat', *American Philosophical Quarterly* 26: 143–51. (Contains an account and full bibliography of the paradox of democracy.)

* Gallie, W.B. (1956) 'Essentially Contested Concepts', *Proceedings of the Aristotelian Society* 56: 167–98. (Discussed in §1.)

Graham, K. (1986) *The Battle of Democracy*, Brighton: Wheatsheaf. (Analyses democracy in terms of various normative grounds; good defence in terms of autonomy and also useful on Marxist theories.)

Harrison, R. (1993) *Democracy*, London: Routledge. (Historical account and analysis of value in terms of such values as equality, knowledge and autonomy.)

* Madison, J., Hamilton, A. and Jay, J. (1787–8) *The Federalist Papers*, ed. I. Kramnick, Harmondsworth: Penguin, 1987. (Paper number ten, written by Madison, is quoted in §1.)

* Mill, J. (1820) *Government*, reprinted in J. Lively and J. Rees (eds) *Utilitarian Logic and Politics*, Oxford: Oxford University Press, 1978. (Referred to in §5.)

* Mill, J.S. (1859) *On Liberty*, in *Utilitarianism/On Liberty/Considerations on Representative Government*, London: Dent, 1910. (Chapter 1 refers to the 'tyranny of the majority', mentioned in §2.)

* —— (1861) *Considerations on Representative Government*, in *Utilitarianism/On Liberty/Considerations on Representative Government*, London: Dent, 1910. (Discussed in §6.)

* Montesquieu, C.L. de S. (1748) *De l'esprit des lois* (The Spirit of the Laws), trans. A. Cohler *et al.*, Cambridge: Cambridge University Press, 1989. (The statement about size, referred to in §1, is in Book 8, chapter 16.)

* Nelson, W.N. (1980) *On Justifying Democracy*, London: Routledge. (Mentioned in §6; criticizes various supposed bases.)

Phillips, A. (1991) *Engendering Democracy*, Cambridge: Polity Press. (Feminist analysis and critique of democracy.)

* Plato (*c.*380–367 BC) *Republic*, trans. with introduction and notes by F.M. Cornford, Oxford: Oxford University Press, 1941. (Referred to in §4.)

* Rawls, J. (1971) *A Theory of Justice*, Cambridge, MA: Harvard University Press. (Section 23 is on publicity; sections 53 and 54 are on majority rule; the proposal to pay political parties, mentioned in §6, occurs on page 226.)

* Rousseau, J.-J. (1762) *Du contrat social*, ed. and trans. G.D.H. Cole in *The Social Contract and Discourses*, London: Dent, 1973. (That states should be small and fortunes equal as preconditions for democracy is claimed in Book 3, chapter 4; however, it is the first two books which have been most influential, particularly about the general will.)

* Riker, W.H. (1982) *Liberalism against Populism*, San Francisco, CA: W.H. Freeman. (Mentioned in §1.)

* Schumpeter, J.A. (1943) *Capitalism, Socialism, and Democracy*, London: Allen & Unwin. (Part IV criticizes the classical account of democracy and proposes instead that democracy should be seen as the competition between various elites bidding for votes.)

Singer, P. (1973) *Democracy and Disobedience*, Oxford: Oxford University Press. (Argues that participation in a democratic procedure places the participants under an obligation to accept its results.)

* Tocqueville, A. de (1835) *De la democratie en Amerique (Democracy in America)*, ed. J.P. Mayer and M. Lerner, London: Fontana, 1966. (Part I, chapter 15, is the section on the 'tyranny of the majority', referred to in §2.)

* Wollheim, R. (1962) 'A Paradox in the Theory of Democracy', in P. Laslett and W.G. Runciman (eds) *Philosophy, Politics and Society*, 2nd series, Oxford: Blackwell. (The article referred to in §3.)

ROSS HARRISON

DEMOCRITUS (mid 5th–4th century BC)

A co-founder with Leucippus of the theory of atomism, The Greek Philosopher Democritus developed it into a universal system, embracing physics, cosmology, epistemology, psychology and theology. He is also reported to have written on a wide range of topics, including mathematics, ethics, literary criticism and theory of language. His works are lost, except for a substantial number of quotations, mostly on ethics, whose authenticity is disputed. Our knowledge of his principal doctrines depends primarily on Aristotle's critical discussions, and secondarily on reports by historians of philosophy whose work derives from that of Aristotle and his school.

The atomists attempted to reconcile the observable data of plurality, motion and change with Parmenides' denial of the possibility of coming to be or ceasing to be. They postulated an infinite number of unchangeable primary substances, characterized by a minimum range of explanatory properties (shape, size, spatial ordering and orientation within a given arrangement). All observable bodies are aggregates of these basic substances, and what appears as generation and corruption is in fact the formation and dissolution of these aggregates. The basic substances are physically indivisible (whence the term atomon, *literally 'uncuttable') not merely in fact but in principle; (1) because (as Democritus argued) if it were theoretically possible to divide a material thing* ad infinitum, *the division would reduce the thing to nothing; and (2) because physical division presupposes that the thing divided contains gaps. Atoms are in eternal motion in empty space, the motion caused by an infinite series of prior atomic 'collisions'. (There is reason to believe, however, although the point is disputed, that atoms cannot collide, since they must always be separated by void, however small; hence impact is only apparent, and all action is at a distance.) The void is necessary for motion, but is characterized as 'what-is-not', thus violating the Eleatic principle that what-is-not cannot be.*

Democritus seems to have been the first thinker to recognize the observer-dependence of the secondary qualities. He argued from the distinction between appearance and reality to the unreliability of the senses, but it is disputed whether he embraced scepticism, or maintained that theory could make good the deficiency of the senses. He maintained a materialistic account of the mind, explaining thought and perception by the physical impact of images emitted by external objects. This theory gave rise to a naturalistic theology; he held that the gods are a special kind of images, endowed with life and intelligence, intervening in human affairs. The ethical fragments (if genuine) show that he maintained a conservative social philosophy on the basis of a form of enlightened hedonism.

1 **Life and works**
2 **Physical doctrines**
3 **Epistemology and psychology**
4 **Theology**
5 **Ethics and politics**

1 Life and works

Democritus lived from approximately the middle of the fifth century BC to well into the following century. Though he was a co-founder of atomism with LEUCIPPUS, the exact relation between the two is obscure; Aristotle and his school agree in treating Leucippus as the originator of the theory, but also in assigning its basic principles to both, while later sources treat the theory as the work of Democritus alone. He may have collaborated with Leucippus, and almost certainly developed the latter's theory into a universal system.

Very little is known about Democritus' life. He came from Abdera, on the north coast of the Aegean (also the native city of Protagoras). He describes himself as being young in the old age of Anaxagoras, that is, probably in the 430s BC, and was traditionally reported to have lived to a very great age. He is said to have visited Athens and to have had some slight acquaintance with Socrates. The list of his works preserved by the third-century AD biographer Diogenes Laertius is long and encyclopedic in scope, including a complete account of the physical universe, the *Lesser World-System* (so called to distinguish it from his predecessor Leucippus' *Great World-System*), and works on astronomy and other natural sciences, epistemology, ethics, mathematics and literature. None survives. Ancient sources preserve almost 300 purported quotations, the great majority on ethics, from two different, although overlapping, collections of ethical maxims, one by the fifth-century anthologist Stobaeus, the other from a collection, probably earlier than that of Stobaeus, traditionally known as 'The Sayings of Democrates'. The authenticity of the ethical fragments is disputed. Sextus Empiricus preserves some important quotations on epistemology, and Plutarch, Galen and others preserve a few other miscellaneous quotations. For our knowledge of the physical doctrines we are reliant on the doxographical tradition stemming ultimately from Aristotle, who discusses atomism extensively (see DOXOGRAPHY).

2 Physical doctrines

According to Aristotle, the atomists attempted to reconcile the observable data of plurality, motion and change with the Eleatic denial of the possibility of coming to be or ceasing to be. Accordingly they postulated unchangeable primary substances, and explained apparent generation and corruption as the formation and dissolution of aggregates of those substances. Since the theory had to account for an assumed infinity of phenomena, it assumed an infinite number of primary substances, while postulating the minimum range of explanatory properties, specifically shape, size, spatial ordering and orientation within a given arrangement. All observable bodies are aggregates of basic substances, which must therefore be too small to be perceived. These corpuscles are physically indivisible (*atomon*, literally 'uncuttable'), not merely in fact but in principle; Aristotle reports an (unsound) atomistic argument, which has some affinities with one of Zeno of Elea's arguments against plurality, that if (as Anaxagoras maintained) it were theoretically possible to divide a material thing *ad infinitum*, the division must reduce the thing to nothing (see ZENO OF ELEA §4; ANAXAGORAS §2). This Zenonian argument was supported by another for the same conclusion; atoms are theoretically indivisible because they contain no void. On this view, bodies split along their interstices; hence, where there are no interstices, as in an atom, no splitting is possible. (The same principle accounts for the immunity of the atoms to other kinds of change, such as reshaping, compression and expansion; all require displacement of matter within an atom, which is impossible without any gaps to receive the displaced matter.) It is tempting to connect the assumption that bodies split only along their interstices with the Principle of Sufficient Reason, which the atomists appealed to as a fundamental principle of explanation (arguing, for example, that the number of atomic shapes must be infinite, because there is no more reason for an atom to have one shape than another (Simplicius, *On Aristotle's Physics* 28.9–10), and that there must be infinitely many worlds because there is no more reason for one to have been formed here than elsewhere. Given the total uniformity of an atom, they may have thought that there could be no reason why it should split at any point, or in any direction, rather than any other. Hence, by the Principle of Sufficient Reason, it could not split at all.

Atoms are in a state of eternal motion in empty space; the motion is not the product of design, but is determined by an infinite series of prior atomic collisions (whence two of Aristotle's principle criticisms of Democritus: that he eliminated final causation and that he made all atomic motion 'unnatural', that is to say, imposed by external force). Empty space was postulated as required for motion, but was characterized as 'what-is-not', thus violating the Eleatic principle that what-is-not cannot be. We have no evidence of how the atomists met the accusation of outright self-contradiction. As well as explaining the possibility of motion, the void was postulated to account for the observed plurality of things, since the atomists followed Parmenides (fr. 8.22–5) in maintaining that there could not be many things if there were no void to separate them (see PARMENIDES §6). The theoretical role of the void in accounting for the separation of atoms from one another has an interesting implication, recorded by Philoponus (*On Aristotle's On Physics* 494.19–25, *On Aristotle's On Generation and Corruption* 158.26–159.7). Since atoms are separated from one another by the void, they can never strictly speaking come into contact with one another. For if they did, even momentarily, there would be nothing separating them from one another. But then they would be as inseparable from one another as the inseparable parts of a single atom, whose indivisibility is attributed to the lack of void within it (see above); indeed, the two former atoms

would now be parts of a single larger atom. But, the atomists held, it is impossible that two things should become one. Holding atomic fusion to be theoretically impossible, and taking it that any case of contact between atoms would be a case of fusion (since only the intervening void prevents fusion), they perhaps drew the conclusion that contact itself is theoretically impossible. Hence what appears to be impact is in fact action at an extremely short distance; rather than actually banging into one another, atoms have to be conceived as repelling one another by some sort of force transmitted through the void. Again, although no source directly attests this, the interlocking of atoms which is the fundamental principle of the formation of aggregates is not strictly speaking interlocking, since the principle of no contact between atoms forbids interlocking as much as impact. Just as impact has to be reconstructed as something like magnetic repulsion, so interlocking has to be reconstrued as quasi-magnetic attraction. If this suggestion is correct (and it is fair to point out that no ancient source other than Philoponus supports it), it is a striking fact that, whereas the post-Renaissance corpuscular philosophy which developed from Greek atomism tended to take the impossibility of action at a distance as an axiom, the original form of the theory contained the a priori thesis that all action is action at a distance, and consequently that impact, as far from giving us our most fundamental conception of physical interaction, is itself a mere appearance which disappears from the world when the description of reality is pursued with full rigour (see BLASIUS OF PARMA §4; BRUNO, G. §5).

3 Epistemology and psychology

Democritus seems to have been the first philosopher to recognize the observer-dependence of the secondary qualities. Perception of the secondary qualities reveals merely how things seem to us (and these qualities are said to be merely *nomōi*, or 'convention'), as opposed to how they really (*eteēi*) are – aggregates of unobservable corpuscles. The perception of any secondary quality is a response, not to the properties of an individual atom, but to a physical stimulus constituted by a continuous bombardment of a series of arrays of atoms. Thus visual perception, including the perception of colour, is a response to the impact on the visual organs of a continuous succession of films of atoms (*eidōla*) flowing from the surface of the perceived object. For an object to be red, for example, is thus for it to emit films of atoms of such a nature that, when those films collide with an appropriately situated perceiver, the object will look red to that perceiver.

It is therefore a necessary consequence of the atomists' account of the secondary qualities not merely that secondary qualities are among the causally significant properties of the atoms, but, more strongly, that atoms have no secondary qualities. Colour, sound, taste and smell are qualities of aggregates, not of single atoms. To ascribe one of these qualities to a subject is to describe that subject as so structured as to prompt a certain sensory response in a certain kind of perceiver; and the structure in question as described in terms of the intrinsic properties (shape and size) and relational properties (arrangement and orientation) of its constituent atoms. The persuasiveness or otherwise of the account of the secondary qualities cannot be separated from that of the whole theory of perception of which it is part, and that in turn cannot be separated from the theory of human nature, and ultimately of the natural world as a whole. As presented by the atomists, the theory is entirely speculative, since it posits as explanatory entities microscopic structures of whose existence and nature there could be no experimental confirmation. Modern developments in sciences such as neurophysiology have revised our conceptions of the structures underlying perceptual phenomena to such an extent that modern accounts would have been unrecognizable to Leucippus or Democritus; but the basic intuitions of ancient atomism – that appearances are to be explained at the level of the internal structure of the perceiver and of the perceived object, and that the ideal of science is to incorporate the description of those structures within the scope of a unified and quantitatively precise theory of the nature of matter in general – have stood the test of time.

According to some sources, Democritus used the contrast between unobservable atomic structures and the appearances which they present to us to demonstrate the unreliability of the senses. He then faced the problem of the justification of his theory, which was founded on data provided by the senses; in a famous fragment quoted by Galen the senses say to the mind, 'Wretched mind, you get your evidence from us, and yet do you overthrow us? The overthrow is a fall for you' (fr. 125). It is disputed whether Democritus drew a sceptical conclusion, or whether his position was rather that, since there can be no ground for preferring one piece of sensory information to another, the task of theory is to provide an account of how all appearances are appropriate representations of an underlying unobservable reality (that is, all appearances are true, a thesis which Aristotle attributes to him, and which was later explicitly maintained by the Epicureans; see EPICUREANISM (§6)).

Democritus' uncompromising materialism extended to his psychology. Although there is some conflict in the sources, the best evidence is that he drew no distinction between the rational soul or mind and the non-rational soul or life principle, giving a single account of both as a physical structure of spherical atoms permeating the entire body. This theory of the identity of soul and mind extended beyond identity of physical structure to identity of function; Democritus explained thought, the activity of the rational soul, by the same process as that by which he explained perception, one of the activities of the sensitive or non-rational soul. Both are produced by the impact on the soul of extremely fine, fast-moving films of atoms (*eidōla*), constantly emitted in continuous streams by the surfaces of everything around us. This theory combines a causal account of both perception and thought with a crude pictorial view of thought. The paradigm case of perception is vision; seeing something and thinking of something alike consist in picturing the thing seen or thought of, and picturing consists in having a series of actual physical pictures of the thing impinge on one's soul. While this assimilation of thought and experience has some affinities with classical EMPIRICISM, it differs in one crucial respect; whereas the basic doctrine of empiricism is that thought derives from experience, for Democritus thought is a form of experience, or, more precisely, the categories of thought and experience are insufficiently differentiated to allow one to be characterized as more fundamental than the other. Among other difficulties, this theory faces the problem of accounting for the distinction, central to Democritus' epistemology, between perception of the observable properties of atomic aggregates and thought of the unobservable structure of those aggregates. We have no knowledge of how, if at all, Democritus attempted to deal with this problem.

4 Theology

Another disputed question is whether Democritus' materialistic account of the universe left any room for the divine. According to most of the ancient sources he believed that there are gods, which are living, intelligent, material beings (of a peculiar sort), playing a significant role in human affairs. They are atomic compounds, and like all such compounds they come to be and perish. They did not create the physical world (of which they are part), nor, although they are intelligent, do they organize or control it. They are as firmly part of the natural order as any other living beings. Specifically, Democritus believed the gods to be living *eidōla*, probably of gigantic size, possessing intelligence, moral character and interest in human affairs. While some sources suggest that these *eidōla* emanate from actual divine beings, the majority of sources agree that they are themselves the only divine beings which Democritus recognized. Some modern scholars (for example, Barnes 1982) interpret this as amounting to atheism, taking Democritus to have held that the gods are nothing more than the contents of human fantasy. But for Democritus *eidōla* are not intrinsically psychological; they are not contents of subjective states, but part of the objective world, causing psychological states through their impact on physical minds. In this case his theory must explain their source and their properties, notably their being alive. Since the gods were of human form, it is plausible to suggest that their source is actual human beings, possibly giants living in the remote past. They are themselves alive in that, flowing from beings permeated with soul-atoms, they contain soul-atoms themselves. Consistently with this naturalistic theology Democritus gave a naturalistic account of the origin of religion, identifying two types of phenomena as having given rise to religious belief: first, the occurrence of *eidōla* themselves, presumably in dreams and ecstatic states; and second, celestial phenomena such as thunder, lightning and eclipses.

Democritus' theology thus contrives to incorporate some of the most characteristic features of the gods of traditional belief, notably their anthropomorphism, power, longevity (although not, crucially, immortality), personal interaction with humans and interest (for good or ill) in human affairs, within the framework of a naturalistic and materialistic theory. It is thus, despite the bold originality of its account of the divine nature, notably more conservative than some of its predecessors (especially the non-anthropomorphic monotheism normally attributed to Xenophanes) and than that of its Epicurean successor, whose main concern is to exclude the gods from all concern with human affairs (see XENOPHANES §3; EPICUREANISM §§8–9).

5 Ethics and politics

The evidence for Democritus' ethical views differs radically from that for the areas discussed above, since while the ethical doxography is meagre, our sources (see §1) preserve a large body of purported quotations on ethical topics. While the bulk of this material is probably Democritean in origin, the existing quotations represent a long process of excerpting and paraphrase, making it difficult to determine how close any particular saying is to Democritus' own words. Various features of style and content suggest that Stobaeus' collection of maxims contains a greater proportion of authentically Democritean material

than does the collection which passes under the name of 'Democrates'.

Subject to the limitations imposed by the nature of this material, we can draw some tentative conclusions about Democritus' ethical views. He was engaged with the wide-ranging contemporary debates on individual and social ethics of which we have evidence from Plato and other sources. On what Socrates presents as the fundamental question in ethics, 'How should one live?' (Plato, *Gorgias* 500c, *Republic* 352d), Democritus is the earliest thinker reported as having explicitly posited a supreme good or goal, which he called 'cheerfulness' or 'wellbeing', and which he appears to have identified with the untroubled enjoyment of life. It is reasonable to suppose that he shared the presumption of the primacy of self-interest which is common both to the Platonic SOCRATES (§6) and to his immoralist opponents, CALLICLES and THRASYMACHUS. Having identified the ultimate human interest with 'cheerfulness', the evidence of the testimonia and the fragments is that he thought that it was to be achieved by moderation, including moderation in the pursuit of pleasures, by discrimination of useful from harmful pleasures and by conformity to conventional morality. The upshot is a recommendation to a life of moderate, enlightened hedonism, which has some affinities with the life recommended by Socrates (whether in his own person or as representing ordinary enlightened views is disputed) in Plato's *Protagoras*), and, more obviously, with the Epicurean ideal of which it was the forerunner.

An interesting feature of the fragments is the frequent stress on individual conscience. Some fragments stress the pleasures of a good conscience and the torments of a bad one (frs 174, 215) while others recommend that one should be motivated by one's internal sense of shame rather than by concern for the opinion of others (frs 244, 264, 'Sayings of Democrates' 84). This theme may well reflect the interest, discernible in contemporary debates, in what later came to be known as the question of the sanctions of morality. A recurrent theme in criticisms of conventional morality was that, since the enforcement of morality rests on conventions, someone who can escape conventional sanctions, for example by doing wrong in secret, has no reason to comply with moral demands. Proponents of such a belief include ANTIPHON (fr. 44), Critias (fr. 25) (see PHYSIS AND NOMOS) and Plato, in Glaucon's tale of Gyges' ring in the *Republic* (359b–360d). A defender of conventional morality who, like Democritus and Plato, accepts the primacy of self-interest therefore faces the challenge of showing, in one way or another, that self-interest is best promoted by the observance of conventional moral precepts.

The appeal to divine sanctions, cynically described in Critias' fragment 25, represents one way of doing this, and there are some traces of the same response in Democritus. While his theory of the atomic, and hence mortal, nature of the soul admits no possibility of postmortem rewards and punishments, the theory allows for divine rewards and punishments in this life. Fragment 175 suggests a complication: the gods bestow benefits on humans, but humans bring harm on themselves through their own folly. Is the thought that the gods do not inflict punishment arbitrarily, but that humans bring it on themselves? Or is it rather that the form which divine punishments take is that of natural calamities, which humans fail to avoid through their own folly? The latter alternative would make the pangs of conscience one of the forms of divine punishment, while the former would see it as a further sanction. Either way (and the question is surely unanswerable), we have some evidence that Democritus was the earliest thinker to make the appeal to 'internal sanctions' central to his attempt to derive morality from self-interest, thus opening up a path followed by others including Bishop BUTLER (§§2–4) and John Stuart MILL (§11).

The attempt, however pursued, to ground morality in self-interest involves the rejection of the antithesis between law or convention (*nomos*) and nature (*physis*) which underlies much criticism of morality in the fifth and fourth centuries BC (see PHYSIS AND NOMOS). For Antiphon, Callicles, Thrasymachus and Glaucon, nature prompts one to seek one's own interest while law and convention seek, more or less successfully, to inhibit one from doing so. But if one's long-term interest is the attainment of a pleasant life, and if the natural consequences of wrong-doing, including ill health, insecurity and the pangs of conscience, give one an unpleasant life, while the natural consequences of right-doing give one a contrastingly pleasant life, then nature and convention point in the same direction, not in opposite directions as the critics of morality allege. (We have no evidence whether Democritus had considered the objections that conscience is a product of convention, and that exhorting people to develop their conscience assumes that it must be.) Although the texts contain no express mention of the *nomos/physis* contrast itself, several of them refer to law in such a way as to suggest rejection of the antithesis. Fragment 248 asserts that the aim of law is to benefit people, thus contradicting Glaucon's claim (Plato, *Republic* II 359c) that law constrains people contrary to their natural bent. Fragment 248 is supplemented and explained by fragment 245: laws interfere with people living as they please in order only to stop them from harming one another, to which they are prompted by envy. So law

frees people from the aggression of others, thus benefiting them by giving them the opportunity to follow the promptings of nature towards their own advantage. The strongest expression of the integration of *nomos* and *physis* is found in fragment 252: the city's being well run is the greatest good, and if it is preserved everything is preserved, while if it is destroyed everything is destroyed. That is to say, a stable community is necessary for the attainment of that wellbeing which is nature's goal for us. This quotation encapsulates the central point in the defence of *nomos* (emphasized in Protagoras' myth at (Plato, *Protagoras* 322a–323a) that law and civilization are not contrary to nature, but required for human nature to flourish, a point also central to the Epicurean account of the development of civilization.

See also: ATOMISM, ANCIENT

References and further reading

* Barnes, J. (1982) *The Presocratic Philosophers*, London: Routledge & Kegan Paul, 2nd edn. (Scholarly and argumentative; excellent bibliography; contains English translations.)

—— (1987) *Early Greek Philosophy*, Harmondsworth: Penguin, 244–88. (Fragments and testimonia of Democritus in English translation.)

* Democritus (mid 5th–4th century BC) Fragments, in H. Diels and W. Kranz (eds) *Die Fragmente der Vorsokratiker* (Fragments of the Presocratics), Berlin: Weidmann, 6th edn, 1951, vol. 2, 81–230. (The standard collection of the ancient sources, includes Greek texts with translations in German. *Antiphon*, fragment 44, can be found in vol. 2 pages 346–55 (English trans. Barnes (1982), 509–12) and *Critias* fragment 25, in vol. 2 pages 386–9; English translations of the latter two can be found in Barnes (1982: 509–12 and 451–2).)

Furley, D. (1987) *The Greek Cosmologists* vol. 1, Cambridge: Cambridge University Press, 115–68. (Deals with principles of atomism, cosmology and anthropology.)

Guthrie, W.K.C. (1962–78) *A History of Greek Philosophy*, Cambridge: Cambridge University Press 6 vols. (Volume 2, pages 386–507 offer a comprehensive survey.)

Luria, S. (1970) *Demokrit*, Leningrad: Nauka. (A fuller selection of texts than Diels and Kranz (1951), with Russian commentary.)

Makin, S. (1993) *Indifference Arguments*, Oxford: Blackwell. (Atomistic arguments using the Principle of Sufficient Reason.)

McKirahan, R.D., Jr (1994) *Philosophy Before*

Socrates, Indianapolis, IN: Hackett, 303–43. (Translation and commentary, covering both Leucippus and Democritus.)

Salem, J. (1996) *Démocrite: Grains de poussière dans un rayon de soleil* (Democritus: grains of dust in a ray of sunlight), Paris: Vrin. (Comprehensive review of ancient evidence and modern literature; original texts in footnotes.)

Taylor, C.C.W. (1967) 'Pleasure, Knowledge and Sensation in Democritus', *Phronesis* 12: 6–27. (A sceptical rejoinder to Vlastos (1945, 1946).)

Vlastos, G. (1945, 1946) 'Ethics and Physics in Democritus', *Philosophical Review* 54: 578–92 and 55: 53–64, repr. in D.J. Furley and R.E. Allen (eds) *Studies in Presocratic Philosophy*, London, Routledge, 1975, vol. 2. (Argues for connection between ethical and physical theories.)

C.C.W. TAYLOR

DEMONSTRATIVES AND INDEXICALS

Demonstratives and indexicals are words and phrases whose interpretations are dependent on features of the context in which they are used. For example, the reference of 'I' depends on conditions associated with its use: as you use it, it refers to you; as I use it, it refers to me. In contrast, what 'the inventor of bifocals' refers to does not depend on when or where or by whom it is used. Among indexicals are the words 'here', 'now', 'today', demonstrative pronouns such as 'this', reflexive, possessive and personal pronouns; and compound phrases employing indexicals, such as 'my mother'. C.S. Peirce introduced the term 'indexical' to suggest the idea of pointing (as in 'index finger').

The phenomenon of indexicality figures prominently in recent debates in philosophy. This is because indexicals allow us to express beliefs about our subjective 'place' in the world, beliefs which are the immediate antecedents of action; and some argue that such beliefs are irreducibly indexical. For example, my belief that I am about to be attacked by a bear is distinct from my belief that HD is about to be attacked by a bear, since my having the former belief explains why I act as I do (I flee), whereas my having the latter belief explains nothing unless the explanation continues 'and I believe that I am HD'. It seems impossible to describe the beliefs that prompt my action without the help of 'I'. Similarly, some have argued that indexical-free accounts of the self or of consciousness are necessarily incomplete, so that a purely objective physicalism is impossible. In a different vein, some

(such as Putnam 1975) have argued that our terms for natural substances, kinds and phenomena ('gold', 'water', 'light') are indexical in a way that entails that certain substantive scientific claims – for example, that water is H_2O – are, if true, necessarily true. Thus, reflection on indexicality has yielded some surprising (and controversial) philosophical conclusions.

1 Semantic data
2 The Kaplan–Perry theory

1 Semantic data

An indexical is context-dependent: its interpretation varies with changes in aspects of the context of use. Yet almost any expression exhibits variation in interpretation with respect to some parameter or other. For example, a contingent sentence is one which is possibly true and possibly false, so we may think of it as varying in truth-value with changes in possible worlds. But mere contingency is not a species of indexicality. Similarly, tensed verbs induce variation in interpretation with respect to the passage of time, but tense is not usually viewed by linguists and logicians as a kind of indexicality (although there is some confusion about the matter). The difference between true context dependence and mere 'parameter dependence' can be seen as follows. Consider the sentence

(1) Jones will remember what Smith said just now.

The truth or falsity of this sentence at a moment in time t depends on the truth or falsity of the present tense sentence

(2) Jones remembers what Smith said just now

at moments t' future to t. But the referent of the occurrence of 'now' in (2) must refer back to t and not to any of the future moments t'. This means that the semantic rule for 'now' cannot be simply the rule which states that at any time t, 'now' refers to t. Instead, the rule must say that a use of 'now' at a time t will refer at time t and at any other time to t. Thus, the rule for 'now' must be 'double-indexed'. In general, the semantic rules for indexicals must involve the pairing of two sorts of parameter: contextual and circumstantial. The contextual parameters (speaker, time of utterance, place of utterance, world of utterance, addressee and so on) fix the referent of an indexical, so that its interpretation is unaffected by any circumstantial parameter (possible world, moment of time) required by the presence of tense or modal elements. Hereafter, the phrase 'context-dependent' will refer to the dependence of indexicals on both context and circumstance.

Indexicals are 'referential' in that they invariably have wide scope when embedded in tensed, modal or propositional attitude constructions. For example, consider the two statements 'The mayor might not have been a Democrat' and 'That person over there, the Mayor, might not have been a Democrat'. The former statement could be interpreted to mean merely that the office of mayor might have been occupied by a non-Democrat; but the latter statement can only be interpreted to mean that a certain person (who happens to be the mayor) might not have been a Democrat. This property of indexicals is an effect of their context dependence. The referent of the indexical phrase 'that person' is fixed by the context and not by circumstances required to interpret the modal element 'might have been'.

Though the interpretation of an indexical will vary with the context, indexicals are not in general ambiguous. Your use of 'I' and mine are linked by a common meaning. The language supplies a rule – the same rule for both of us – for the use of 'I'. The rule is roughly this: 'As x uses "I" in such and such a context, "I" refers to x in all circumstances'. But this sort of meaning is not like the Fregean sense of a definite description or proper name; it is not a concept of some fixed object and it cannot be combined with the sense of a (non-indexical) predicate to yield a complete proposition (see FREGE, G. §§2–3). Some theorists believe that this fact requires the introduction into semantics of a whole new level of meaning distinct from both sense and reference. Kaplan, for example, draws a three-way distinction between the 'character' (linguistic meaning), content (roughly, sense) and referent of an indexical expression such as 'my mother' (1970). Kaplan's view may not be inevitable, however. It may be that 'I' has an 'incomplete sense', in the way that the sense of a functional expression 'the square root of x' or 'the author of x' is incomplete. If so, that would explain why the linguistic meaning of 'I' cannot be combined with a predicate to yield a complete proposition and there would be no need to postulate a kind of meaning in addition to sense and reference.

Some subscribe to the principle that for one to understand an 'object-dependent' proposition – a proposition that such and such an object has such and such a property – one must be able to identify the object in question; one must be able to say who or what it is. This principle seems to be directly contradicted by propositions involving indexicals. I can know that I am hungry or that it is raining now without having any substantive information about who I am or what time it is. Similarly, if I point to something and say 'I don't have the slightest idea what that is' I might well speak the truth! Yet these propositions are object-dependent in that they would not be available if the objects they are about did not exist. Let us mark the fact that speakers can use indexicals with total understanding without having any substantive knowledge of their referents by saying that indexicals are 'transparent'.

Some indexical sentences have the property of being true in any context of use. For example, one who says (or thinks) 'I exist' or 'I am here now' or 'I am saying (or thinking) something now' must be right. These sentences, then, are somewhat similar to logical truths. But if I say 'I exist', then what I say (that HD exists) is not a *necessary* truth, for there are possible circumstances in which I do not exist. So a sentence such as 'I exist' is contingent in one respect and yet non-contingent in another. Any theory of indexicality must explain how this is possible.

Perhaps the most puzzling aspect of indexicals is that some of them seem to be ineliminable and their ineliminability seems to have to do with the baffling distinction between subjectivity and objectivity (see CONTENT, INDEXICAL). Perry gives the following example (1979). Suppose a meeting is set for Tuesday at noon. All week you believe that the meeting will start at noon on Tuesday. At a certain point, you leave to go to the meeting. Obviously, you must have acquired some new information, a new belief, distinct from the belief that the meeting starts at noon on Tuesday, for you now act in a way you have not acted all week (that is, you leave to go to the meeting). What belief is this? It is the belief that the meeting starts *now*, or, more elaborately, the belief that the meeting starts at noon on Tuesday and it is *now* noon on Tuesday. The use of 'now' in describing your new belief seems essential, and not eliminable in favour of non-indexical designations of noon on Tuesday. Moreover, your new 'indexical belief' places you within the fabric of time in a way that the beliefs you acquire when you look at your appointment book to determine the time of the meeting do not. An observer 'outside of time' could have the belief that the meeting starts at noon on Tuesday, but not the belief that the meeting starts 'now'. In this way, your indexical belief seems linked to your subjective place in the world. Perry calls such beliefs 'self-locating' beliefs. Yet all this is quite puzzling. Is your belief that it is 'now' noon on Tuesday something that you can believe only 'now'? Certainly, you can believe truly that it is now noon on Tuesday only at noon on Tuesday. But can you not at a later time continue to hold precisely the belief you expressed earlier by saying 'It is now noon on Tuesday'? Yet if you believe at the later time exactly what you believed at the earlier, then why do you not, at the later time, do just what you did at the earlier time – namely, head off to the meeting? Similarly, I believe that I am HD. Can you not believe that too? If you believe just what I do when I believe that I am HD – that is, if you believe exactly the proposition I do, it would appear to follow that our mental states *vis-à-vis* this belief must be identical, then why do you not have any inclination, as I do, to identify yourself as HD? Let us call this 'the puzzle about indexical belief'. The puzzle has two parts: first, one argues on the basis of behavioural changes (for example, your getting up to go to the meeting) that an indexical belief (assertion, thought) is not equivalent to any non-indexical counterpart of it. Second, however, similar behavioural changes – or the lack of any – seem to show that such beliefs are 'isolated' – that they cannot be retained over time or shared by different persons: only I can know that I am HD, and that seems counterintuitive. Any adequate theory of indexicality must solve this puzzle about indexical belief.

2   The Kaplan–Perry theory

The most influential theory that has had some success explaining the semantic data about indexicals as outlined above was developed by Kaplan in a series of papers originating in the late 1960s and early 1970s. In the mid-1970s, Perry applied Kaplan's theory to explain the data about the ineliminability of indexicality and the puzzle about indexical belief – data that were first noticed and systematically studied by Castañeda (1967).

According to Kaplan–Perry theory (KPT), each indexical expression has a 'character' or linguistic meaning (Perry's term is 'role') and, given a context, a 'content' in that context. The content in a context of a (declarative) sentence containing an indexical is a 'singular proposition' – a proposition containing the very referent of the indexical as a 'constituent' rather than a sense or concept of that referent. So the content of my use of 'I am hungry now' at a time t is a proposition to the effect that HD is hungry at time t – with HD right there 'in' the proposition, in at least a metaphorical sense. Kaplan takes the character of an indexical to be a function (in the mathematical sense) that takes context into content. Contexts are treated as n-tuples $c = \langle a, t, p, w, \ldots \rangle$ with coordinates for the 'agent of the context' (to handle 'I'), the 'time of the context' (to handle 'now'), the 'place of the context', the 'world of the context' and so on (for example, there should be a coordinate for the 'day of the context' to handle 'yesterday', 'today' and 'tomorrow'). To deal with pure demonstratives such as 'this', Kaplan adds a coordinate for a 'demonstration'. This is a kind of abstract counterpart of an act of pointing. For example, the sentence 'That is mine

now' will be true at a parameter $\langle a, t, p, w, d, \ldots \rangle$ if the demonstrated object d belongs to agent a at t in place p and world w.

Kaplan distinguishes between 'contexts' and 'circumstances'. Formally, the latter are pairs $\langle t, w \rangle$ with t a time and w a possible world. Strictly, expressions are evaluated relative to parameters of the form $\langle$context, circumstance$\rangle$. So the semantic rules are double-indexed. In addition, Kaplan claims that indexicals are 'directly referential'. By this he means that an indexical refers without the aid of a Fregean sense. In this respect indexicals are like proper names. But proper names are, in Kaplan's view, unlike indexicals in that the latter possess characters whereas the former do not (see PROPER NAMES §§2–3).

By appealing to the content/character and context/circumstance distinctions, KPT can readily explain the fact that indexicals are context-dependent, referential and univocal. Moreover, the character/content distinction helps to explain the transparency of indexicals. One need only grasp the character of an indexical to use it with understanding. On occasion, its content may be hidden, as in the case of amnesiacs, who, despite their affliction, can certainly use the first person pronoun perfectly competently. KPT can also explain the special status of sentences such as 'I exist'. The character of 'I exist' always produces a true content in any context. But that content may turn out to be false in further circumstances. For example, if you now write 'I exist' in your diary, the content you express is true now. But, inevitably, that content will be false years hence in circumstances in which you no longer exist and someone then reads these words in your diary. According to KPT, 'I exist' is a logical truth, although its necessitation, 'Necessarily, I exist', and its temporal necessitation, 'It is always the case that I exist', are not. KPT thus involves a novel conception of logical truth. For it is usually assumed that the class of logical truths contains 'Necessarily, P' and 'It is always the case that P' if it contains P. Finally, KPT solves the problem of indexical belief by appealing to the notion of character. KPT holds that belief is linked to action via character, not content. If you and I have beliefs with the same content but different character we may well behave differently. But if we have beliefs with the same character and different content we may well behave in the same way. When each of us thinks 'I am about to be attacked by a bear' (same character, different content) we both run for our lives, but when I think 'I am about to be attacked by a bear' and you think 'You are about to be attacked by a bear' (same content, different character) I run for my life and you do not. Similarly, you can retain the belief that the meeting starts now but you can express it at a later time only by using words having a character distinct from that of 'The meeting starts now', and it is the difference in character that accounts for the fact that, at the later time, you do not do what you did at the earlier time. Likewise, KPT appeals to character to account for the difference between the thought that I am about to be attacked by a bear and the thought that HD is about to be attacked by a bear. The former has a certain character which the latter does not, and that makes all the difference. Similarly, consider the difference between the thought that I am HD and that HD is HD. The former is informative whereas the latter is not. Again, the difference can be traced to the fact that 'I' has a certain character which 'HD' does not.

KPT needs only the character/content and context/circumstance distinctions to account for the semantic data. But it goes further in claiming that indexicals are 'directly referential' and that indexicals give rise to 'singular propositions'. Proponents of KPT argue in several ways for the direct reference thesis. First, Kaplan argues that 'I' does not have the sense of 'the speaker' or any description such as 'the utterer' or 'the thinker'. He would argue, for example, that since 'I am not the speaker' is not contradictory, whereas 'The speaker is not the speaker' is contradictory, 'I' and 'the speaker' are not synonymous. But this argument seems equivocal. Any candidate synonym for 'I' must be context-dependent (and not just parameter-dependent). If we associate a context-dependent rule with 'the speaker' – so that it refers in any circumstance to the 'speaker of the context' – then 'I am not the speaker' is indeed contradictory. It is only by treating 'I' as context-dependent and 'the speaker' as merely parameter-dependent (as it is in one sense) that there is a discrepancy. Second, Kaplan argues in the following way. The descriptive meaning of 'now' is given by the following rule: at t, 'now' refers to t. Thus, the descriptive meaning of 'now' is 'either inapplicable or irrelevant to determining a referent with respect to a circumstance of evaluation' (1989: 500). Hence, 'now' is directly referential – its descriptive meaning does not serve as the route to its referent in a circumstance. This argument does not work either. One can take the view, as explained above, that the descriptive rule for 'now' is not the one Kaplan assumes. (So the first premise of Kaplan's argument is false.) And if we substitute the double-indexed rule for 'now' it cannot be argued that descriptive meaning (that is, the double-indexed rule) of 'now' is 'irrelevant or inapplicable' to determining its referent in a circumstance.

See also: LOGICAL AND MATHEMATICAL TERMS, GLOSSARY OF; REFERENCE §5

References and further reading

Braun, D. (1995) 'What is Character?', *Journal of Philosophical Logic* 24: 227–40. (A critical and relatively nontechnical discussion of some aspects of Kaplan's notion of character.)

* Castañeda, H.-N. (1967) 'Indicators and Quasi-Indicators', *American Philosophical Quarterly* 4: 85–100. (This is a representative example of several pioneering papers by this author exploring the behaviour of indexicals in propositional attitude constructions.)

Forbes, G. (1989) *Languages of Possibility*, Oxford: Oxford University Press. (This work includes a detailed neo-Fregean theory of indexicality. In contrast, the Kaplan–Perry theory discussed above may be described as 'anti-Fregean'.)

Kamp, H. (1971) 'Formal Properties of "Now"', *Theoria* 37: 227–73. (This paper develops a double-indexed semantics for certain tense logics with an operator representing 'now'. Kamp was the first to recognize the need for the double-index technique.)

* Kaplan, D. (1970) 'On the Logic of Demonstratives', *Journal of Philosophical Logic* 8: 81–98. (The pioneering paper in which the key distinctions between character and content and context and circumstance were first introduced.)

* —— (1989) 'Demonstratives', in *Themes from Kaplan*, ed. J. Almog, J. Perry and H.K. Wettstein, Oxford: Oxford University Press. (This is a classic meditation on the anti-Fregean aspects of the Kaplan–Perry theory.)

Perry, J. (1977) 'Frege on Demonstratives', repr. in P. Yourgrau (ed.) *Demonstratives*, Oxford: Oxford University Press, 1990. (This paper attempts to demonstrate the inability of Frege's semantics to handle indexicality and the inadequacy of Frege's own attempts to deal with the phenomenon.)

* —— (1979) 'The Problem of the Essential Indexical', *Noûs* 13: 3–21. (By means of several ingenious examples this paper uncovers and attempts to solve the problem of indexical belief.)

* Putnam, H. (1975) 'The Meaning of "Meaning"', in *Mind, Language and Reality: Philosophical Papers*, vol. 2, Cambridge: Cambridge University Press. (This paper is the main source of the view according to which our terms for natural substances, kinds and phenomena are indexical.)

Yourgrau, P. (ed.) (1990) *Demonstratives*, Oxford: Oxford University Press. (This is a collection of essays on indexicality which emphasize not only semantic issues but also metaphysical and epistemological themes.)

HARRY DEUTSCH

DENMARK, PHILOSOPHY IN

see SCANDINAVIA, PHILOSOPHY IN

DENNETT, DANIEL CLEMENT (1942–)

A student of Gilbert Ryle and a connoisseur of cognitive psychology, neuroscience and evolutionary biology, American philosopher Daniel Dennett has urged Rylean views in the philosophy of mind, especially on each title topic of his first book, Content and Consciousness *(1969). He defends a broadly instrumentalist view of propositional attitudes (such as belief and desire) and their intentional contents; like Ryle and the behaviourists, Dennett rejects the idea of beliefs and desires as causally active inner states of people. Construing them in a more purely operational or instrumental fashion, he maintains instead that belief- and desire-ascriptions are merely caculational devices.*

Dennett offers a severely deflationary account of consciousness, subjectivity and the phenomenal or qualitative character of sensory states. He maintains that those topics are conceptually posterior to that of propositional-attitude content: the qualitative features of which we are directly conscious in experience are merely the intentional contents of judgments.

1 **Propositional attitudes**
2 **Freedom of the will**
3 **Consciousness**

1 Propositional attitudes

Rejecting the idea of beliefs and desires as inner causes, Dennett maintains instead that ascriptions of belief and desire are merely calculational devices, that happen to have predictive usefulness (see RYLE, G.; BEHAVIOURISM, ANALYTIC). In interpreting other creatures, which is something we do constantly without knowing a thing about those creatures' insides, we start by trusting that they will believe what they should believe given their perceptions and desire what they should desire given their needs; then we correct empirically for observed departures from those normative ideals. Such ascriptions are often objectively true, he grants, but not in virtue of describing inner mechanisms, any more than references to centres of gravity, kinematic vectors and the Equator describe inner mechanisms.

Thus Dennett is an instrumentalist of sorts about propositional attitudes, such as belief and desire. To ascribe a 'belief' or a 'desire' is not to describe some segment of physical reality, Dennett says, but is more like performing part of a calculation. But he also protests that his own interpretation-based view does not rob his propositional-attitude concepts of their objectivity, for he understands the truth of an attitude ascription as being determined by whether someone's taking a certain interpretive stance *would in fact* achieve good predictive results. Still, for Dennett, attitude content is conceptually constructed out of purpose-relative interpretation; his objectivity does not amount to determinacy (he explicitly endorses Quine's indeterminacy thesis for content); and for him, a thing's innards (including the matter of whether it has any) are conceptually irrelevant to its having intentional states.

Dennett has always used mathematical abstractions, such as centres of gravity, to illustrate the sort of view he favours. It should be noted, however, that he has recently used this comparison to moderate his line. In an important paper, 'Real Patterns' (1991a), he emphasizes the reality of mathematical abstractions and de-emphasizes interpretation.

Dennett offers five grounds for his rejection of the common-sensical inner-cause thesis. (1) He thinks it ludicrously unlikely that any science will ever turn up any distinctive inner-causal mechanism that would be shared by all the possible subjects that had a particular belief. (2) He offers numerous objections to 'language-of-thought psychology', the most popular inner-cause theory (see LANGUAGE OF THOUGHT). (3) He compares the belief/desire interpretation of human beings to that of lower animals, chess-playing computers and even lightning rods, arguing that in their case we have no reason to think of belief- and desire-ascriptions as other than mere calculational or predictive devices, and then that we have no more reason for the case of humans to think of belief- and desire-ascriptions as other than such devices. (4) Dennett argues that the verification conditions of belief- and desire-ascriptions are basically a matter of extrapolating rationally from what subjects ought to believe and want in their circumstances, and then he boldly identifies the truth-makers of those ascriptions with these verification conditions, challenging inner-cause theorists to show why instrumentalism does not accommodate all the actual evidence. (5) He argues that in any case if a purely normative assumption (the 'rationality assumption', that people will generally believe what they ought to believe and desire what they should desire) is required for the licensing of an ascription, then the ascription cannot itself be a purely factual description of a plain state of affairs (see PROPOSITIONAL ATTITUDES).

2 Freedom of the will

In *Elbow Room* (1984) Dennett defends a common-sensical compatibilism regarding free will and determinism against attacks by metaphysicians and also against other common-sensical 'intuitions' that he takes to be confused. Here his style as well as his substance is Rylean: he does not engage serious contemporary incompatibilist arguments, but only jollies the reader into thinking that such arguments must be misguided. However, he does offer positive compatibilist accounts of practical reason, control over one's actions, deliberation and the appropriateness of holding people responsible (see FREE WILL).

3 Consciousness

Dennett's mature view of consciousness and related topics is expounded at length in *Consciousness Explained* (1991b). His main claims are that there is nothing to the human mind that is not already constituted by the brain; that the brain itself is but a bag of tricks, an only very loose improvised association of little specialists whose individual actions contribute piecemeal and somewhat haphazardly to a subject's operative psychological state; that linguistic utterances do not normally express determinate pre-existing thought contents; and that there is no single 'whole me', or self or Boss Unit or even CPU within the brain, serving as chief executive of my utterings and other actions (see CONSCIOUSNESS).

Dennett is especially concerned to deny that there is any determinate stage of information processing that is the locus of conscious mental states or events; there is no such locus at all, however physically characterized. He calls his target 'Cartesian materialism', that being the usually tacit assumption that there is a physically realized spatial or temporal turnstile in the brain, a stage where 'it all comes together' and the product of pre-processing is exhibited 'to consciousness'.

Dennett gives two arguments against Cartesian materialism. First, given his naturalism about brains and the unplanned nature of their organization, it is unlikely that nature has furnished the human brain with any central viewing-room or single monitor to do the viewing; nor is there any positive neurophysiological sign of such organs. Second, Dennett adverts to the famous 'temporal anomalies' of consciousness discovered by psychophysical research, such as color phi, the cutaneous rabbit and Libet's 'backward referral' of sensory experiences, in which, for example, the mind seems to detect a stimulus before that stimulus could possibly have been processed by the brain. Dennett argues at length that

those curious phenomena are anomalous only as long as Cartesian materialism is being assumed; jettison the assumption, and the phenomena are readily explained.

Dennett's recommended alternative to Cartesian materialism is the 'Multiple Drafts' model:

> What we actually experience is a product of many processes of interpretation – editorial processes, in effect. They take in relatively raw and one-sided representations, and yield collated, revised, enhanced representations, and they take place in the streams of activity occurring in various parts of the brain.... Once a particular 'observation' of some feature has been made, by a specialized, localized portion of the brain, the information content thus fixed does not have to be sent somewhere else to be rediscriminated by some 'master' discriminator.
>
> (1991b: 112–13)

The resulting stream of contents, subject to continual editing by many processes distributed around in the brain, is not altogether like a narrative, because of its multiplicity; at any point in time there are 'multiple drafts' of narrative fragments at various stages of editing in various places in the brain.

Dennett grants that there is something of the sort often called 'the stream of consciousness': 'Conscious human minds are more-or-less serial virtual machines implemented – inefficiently – on the parallel hardware that evolution has provided for us' (1991b: 218). They are 'Joycean' virtual machines that formulate synthesized reports of their own passing states, though the reports are almost never entirely accurate.

By way of *explaining* consciousness as advertised, Dennett offers a 'method for phenomenology', called 'heterophenomenology'. He says the method is designed to 'do justice to the most private and ineffable subjective experiences, while never abandoning the methodological scruples of science' (1991b: 72). It is to listen carefully to a subject's introspective reports, respect them as perfectly sincere, and take them as serious descriptions of the subject's 'heterophenomenological world'. That world is 'a stable, intersubjectively confirmable theoretical posit' (1991b: 81). But the cognitive scientist is to take the subject's narrative as fiction, or, less pejoratively, as a narrative that may or may not be true, just as an anthropologist takes the narratives of a primitive people. The job of the psychologist is then to discover whatever it is in the brain's great chaos of information processing that makes subjects produce the narratives that they do. To make that discovery is, in one sense, to explain the subject's consciousness.

Some readers have insisted that Dennett has simply avoided the real issues. If all the scientist need do is explain propositional sayings in terms of internal propositional states and episodes, then we know already that neither the scientist nor Dennett will find or even seek anything about phenomenal character, subjectivity, qualia, or any other feature of consciousness that makes it interesting over and above bare intentionality or aboutness *per se*. It may seem that Dennett has simply changed the subject. But he does squarely address the questions of subjectivity and phenomenal character in particular. He rejects the thesis of Thomas NAGEL and Frank Jackson that an omniscient objective science would necessarily leave the introspectible first-person aspects of sensory experiences unexplained and even unrecorded, and he treats phenomenal properties of sensations essentially as representational contents, properties ascribed truly or falsely to external objects or to parts of one's own body (see QUALIA).

List of works

Dennett, D.C. (1969) *Content and Consciousness*, Routledge & Kegan Paul. (Dennett's early views on intentionality, conscious awareness and the mind–body problem.)

—— (1978) *Brainstorms*, Montgomery, VT: Bradford Books. (Most of Dennett's classic papers, on propsositional attitudes, consciousness and personhood.)

—— (1984) *Elbow Room*, Cambridge, MA: Bradford Books/MIT Press. (Dennett on freedom of the will.)

—— (1987) *The Intentional Stance*, Cambridge, MA: Bradford Books/MIT Press. (Dennett's mature theory of intentionality and propositional attitudes.)

——(1991a) 'Real Patterns', *Journal of Philosophy* 88: 27–51. (A shift, at least of emphasis, in Dennett's theory of propositional attitudes.)

—— (1991b) *Consciousness Explained*, Boston, MA: Little, Brown. (Dennett's mature theory of consciousness and the qualitative character of experience.)

—— (1994) 'Self-Portrait', in S. Guttenplan (ed.) *A Companion to the Philosophy of Mind*, Oxford: Blackwell. (A summary of Dennett's philosophy of mind.)

—— (1995) *Darwin's Dangerous Idea*, New York: Simon & Schuster. (An interpretation of Darwin's theory of evolution by natural selection, and a drawing of philosophical morals for the general reader.)

—— (1996) *Kinds of Minds*, New York: Basic Books. (A new summary of Dennett's philosophy of mind, with some changes of emphasis and some extra attention to nonhuman animals.)

References and further reading

Dalhbom, B. (ed.) (1993) *Dennett and His Critics: Demystifying Mind*, Oxford: Blackwell. (Essays on Dennett and a collective reply. Full bibliography of Dennett's writings.)

Philosophical Topics (1994) Special journal issue 22 (1, 2). (An issue devoted to Dennett's work; essays and a collective reply.)

Stich, S.P. (1981) 'Dennett on Intentional Systems' *Philosophical Topics* 12 (1): 39–62; repr. in W.G. Lycan (ed.) *Mind and Cognition*, Oxford: Blackwell, 1990. (A very clear exposition and critique of Dennett's intentional instrumentalism.)

Symposium (1988) *The Intentional Stance, Behavioral and Brain Sciences* 11 (3): 495–546. (Dennett's own précis of the book, twenty-four brief commentaries by philosophers and various cognitive scientists, and Dennett's collective response.)

WILLIAM G. LYCAN

DENOTATION *see* DESCRIPTIONS; PROPER NAMES; REFERENCE

DENYS THE CARTHUSIAN (1402/3–71)

Denys de Leeuwis was born in the village of Rijkel, in modern Belgium. In 1421 he matriculated at the University of Cologne, where he received the Master of Arts degree in 1424. There he followed 'the way of Thomas Aquinas', whom he calls his 'patron' in his early works. Later Denys adopted 'Albertist' against 'Thomist' positions on a number of philosophical issues. After leaving the University, he entered the Carthusian monastery in Roermond, where, save for brief periods, he spent the rest of his life. He corresponded with Nicholas of Cusa and dedicated two or three works to him. Denys was a voracious reader of the ancient and medieval philosophers whose writings were available in Latin, and of scholastic theologians. Because of his extensive references to authorities, historians often call him 'eclectic'. Yet from his sources he educes his own distinctive philosophy. Like Albert the Great, Denys practised philosophy and theology by paraphrasing and analysing their histories.

Denys was one of the most prolific writers of the Middle Ages. His writings include scholastic, mystical, moral and pastoral commentaries and treatises, commentaries on each book of Scripture, over 900 sermons, and paraphrase/commentaries on works by AQUINAS. His major philosophical works are *De lumine christianae theoriae* (The Light of Christian Theory), encyclopedic commentaries on Peter Lombard's *Sentences* (see LOMBARD, P.) *compendia* of philosophy and theology that distill materials from his commentaries on the *Sentences* and summarize his own positions, a commentary on Boethius' *Consolation of Philosophy* (see BOETHIUS, A.M.S.) and commentaries on all of the writings of PSEUDO-DIONYSIUS. In Book I of *De lumine*, Denys analyses the teaching of many 'Peripatetic' and 'Platonic' philosophers on a wide range of metaphysical questions. Likewise, on each question of the *Sentences* he reports and interprets the teaching of many scholastic doctors. He discounts the arguments of 'nominalists' as more concerned with 'terms' than 'realities', returning instead to the teachings of thirteenth-century masters.

Like many fifteenth-century philosophers, Denys was preoccupied with the question of the soul's immortality. Influenced especially by Avicenna (see IBN SINA) and ALBERT THE GREAT, he maintains that the immortality of the soul can be demonstrated by reason alone (see SOUL, NATURE AND IMMORTALITY OF). In this context, he argues against Aquinas that the human mind need not have recourse to phantasms in every act of knowing and that it is capable of knowing separated substances. The mind's ability to know the essences of things without phantasms is the surest evidence of its immortality, and its natural capacity for pure abstraction is the foundation for the imageless contemplation of mystical theology.

Denys' understanding of the soul's self-subsistence and its ways of knowing affects other philosophic doctrines. He argues that the soul knows some first principles by immediate self-reference, and that the individuation of persons is not effected by matter alone, but by the whole human composite, most powerfully by its spiritual form. He disputes a 'real' distinction between essence and existence in creatures, arguing instead – in a way reminiscent of HENRY OF GHENT – for an 'intentional' distinction between them (see EXISTENCE). His noetic theory admits the possibility of a natural, philosophic beatitude, wherein the soul contemplates separated substances in the participated light of the lowest Intelligence in the hierarchy of celestial beings. In accord with these conclusions, Denys draws a sharp distinction between 'natural, philosophic wisdom' and 'supernatural, theological wisdom', which are analogically coordinated and touch at the points of God's existence, unity and attributes. True philosophical conclusions never contradict divine revelation. Here Denys'

'eclecticism' serves him well; among the philosophers he discovers those teachings most accordant with the 'analogy of faith', reconciles them among themselves, and brings them into rapport with the divinely revealed standard. Denys' departure from Thomistic conceptions was prompted by his reading of Pseudo-Dionysius, whom he considered to be the greatest authority of Christian wisdom.

Nevertheless, Denys retained many of the insights of Aristotle and Thomas Aquinas. He states that Aristotle's understanding of God as 'the pure act of being' is one of the most sublime of all philosophical teachings. He affirms that the intellectual soul is the single, substantial form of the human body, grants that human knowing ordinarily requires phantasms, and argues a 'real distinction' among the faculties of the soul. He maintains the priority of the intellect over the will in every human act, and teaches that love in the will is exactly commensurate to light in the intellect.

Denys conceived his philosophical enterprise as a remedy to attitudes common among his monastic brethren, who often scorned scholastic teaching and exalted the affections and the will in the spiritual life. Beyond that, he sought to reconcile the varying doctrines of the philosophers and the scholastic theologians by means of the higher, unified light of mystical theology.

See also: ARISTOTELIANISM, MEDIEVAL

List of works

Denys the Carthusian (1402/3–71) *Opera omnia*; ed. monks of the Carthusian Order, *Doctoris ecstatici D. Dionysii Cartusiani Opera omnia*, Montreuil/Tournai/Parkminster: Typis Cartusiae S.M. de Pratis, 1896–1935, 42 vols. (Essentially a reprinting of sixteenth-century editions, with excellent indexes of names and topics.)

—— (1440–5) *De contemplatione* (On Contemplation); in *Opera omnia* 41: 133–289. (This is Denys' major work on contemplative theory and practice; it treats the different kinds of contemplation, recites the teaching of the most notable patristic and medieval masters, and resolves disputed questions concerning the nature of mystical union.)

—— (c.1451) *De lumine christianae theoriae* (The Light of Christian Theory); in *Opera omnia* 33: 233–513. (In the first book of this work, Denys recites and analyses philosophical doctrines about the 'going out' of all things from the first principle; in the second book, based largely on Aquinas' *Summa contra gentiles*, he treats the 'return' of human creatures to God through Christian grace and perfection.)

—— (c.1464) *Commentaria in IV libros Sententiarum* (Commentaries on the Four Books of the *Sentences*); in *Opera omnia* vols 19–25. (In these massive commentaries, Denys arranges dialectically, recites and comments upon or criticizes the opinions of many scholastic thinkers on each question of Peter Lombard's *Sentences*.)

—— (c.1465) *Elementatio philosophica* (Elements of Philosophy); in *Opera omnia* 33: 21–231. (This is an epitome of the strictly philosophic matters and questions extracted from the commentaries on the *Sentences* and arranged in a proper philosophical order.)

—— (c.1465) *Elementatio theologica* (Elements of Theology); in *Opera omnia* 33: 21–231. (In this work, Denys extracts from his commentaries on the *Sentences* strictly theological matters and questions and states his own conclusions.)

—— (c.1466) *Ennarationes in V libros De consolatione philosophiae B. Severinii Boetii* (Commentary on Boethius' Consolation of Philosophy); in *Opera omnia* vol. 26. (In this work, cast in the form of a dialogue between a master and a disciple, Denys gives a 'literal' philosophic commentary on Boethius' famous text, to which he joins 'allegorical', theological readings.)

—— (1466–7) *Commentaria in libros S. Dionysii Areopagitae* (Commentaries on the Writings of Dionysius the Areopagite); in *Opera omnia* vols 15–16. (With Albert the Great, Denys was the only Latin writer to comment on each work in the Dionysian corpus, including the letters; his commentaries are line-by-line, and include articles about disputed points of interpretation.)

References and further reading

Beer, M. (1963) *Dionysius' des Kartausers Lehre vom 'desiderium naturale' des Menschen nach der Gotteschau* (Denys the Carthusian's Teaching on the Human Being's 'Natural Desire' for the Vision of God), Münchener theologische Studien II: Systematische Abteilung 28, Munich: M. Hueber. (A study of Denys' teaching on the human being's natural desire for beatitude, which involves important questions on the relations between nature and grace, philosophy and theology. On this topic, Denys criticized the teachings of Thomas Aquinas and Giles of Rome.)

Emery, K., Jr (1988) 'Twofold Wisdom and Contemplation in Denys of Ryckel (Dionysius Cartusiensis, 1402–1471)', *Journal of Medieval and Renaissance Studies*, 18: 99–134. (A study of Denys' hierarchical noetic ordering of philosophic, scholastic and mystical wisdom.)

—— (1990) 'Theology as a Science: The Teaching of Denys of Ryckel', in R. Työrinoja, A.I. Lehtinen and D. Føllesdal (eds) *Knowledge and the Sciences in Medieval Philosophy: The Proceedings of the Eighth International Congress of Medieval Philosophy (S.I.E.P.M.)*, Helsinki: Publications of Luther–Agricola Society, series B 19, 376–88. (The scientific foundation of scholastic theology is the vision of the blessed, accessible in part to transient mystical intuition.)

—— (1991) *Dionysii Cartusiensis Opera selecta 1: (Prolegomena) Bibliotheca manuscripta 1A-1B: Studia bibliographica*, Corpus Christianorum Continuatio Mediaeualis 121–1a, Turnhout: Brepols. (A study of the surviving manuscripts of Denys' writings; a newly established list of the authentic works, and studies of the transmission of spurious works.)

—— (1992a) 'Denys the Carthusian and the Doxography of Scholastic Theology', in M.D. Jordan and K. Emery, Jr (eds) *Ad litteram: Authoritative Texts and their Medieval Readers*, Notre Dame, IN: University of Notre Dame Press, 327–59. (A study of the composition and method of Denys' commentaries on the Sentences, and his evaluation of the scholastic tradition on questions concerning the divine attributes, individuation, and so on.)

—— (1992b) '*Sapientissimus Aristoteles* and *Theologicissimus Dionysius*: The Reading of Aristotle and the Understanding of Nature in Denys the Carthusian', in A. Speer and A. Zimmerman (eds) *Mensch und Natur im Mittelalter*, Miscellanea Mediaevalia 21/2, Berlin: de Gruyter, 572–606. (A study of Denys' philosophy of nature, on questions concerning issues such as the immortality of the soul, the composition of human beings, eternity of the world, emanation, and the authority of Aristotle and Pseudo-Dionysius.)

—— (1994) 'Denys the Carthusian and the Invention of Preaching Materials', *Viator* 25: 377–409. (A study of the organization of Denys' moral writings and their philosophic foundation.)

Macken, R. (1984) 'Denys the Carthusian, Commentator on Boethius's *De consolatione philosophiae*', *Analecta Cartusiana* 118: 1–70. (A study of Denys' treatment of noetic questions in the commentary.)

Maginot, N. (1968) *Der 'Actus humanus moralis' unter dem Einfluss des Heiligen Geistes nach Dionysius Carthusianus* (The 'Moral Act' Under the Influence of the Holy Spirit According to Denys the Carthusian), Münchener theologische Studien II. Systematische Abteilung 35, Munich: M. Hueber. (A study of Denys' analysis of the requirements for consciously moral action, in relation to his teaching on the gifts and influence of the Holy Spirit in human action. This is a classic topic in the tradition of neo-scholastic philosophy.)

Stoelen, A. (1957) 'Denys le Chartreux', in *Dictionnaire de spiritualité ascétique et mystique, histoire et doctrine*, Paris: Beauchesne, vol. 3: 430–49. (An excellent introduction to Denys' life, works and doctrine, with a chronology of the works and a good bibliography of older scholarship.)

Teeuwen, P. (1938) *Dionysius de Karthuizer en de philosophisch-theologische Stroomingen aan de Keulsche Universiteit* (Denys the Carthusian in the Philosophical and Theological Cross-Currents of the University of Cologne), Brussels/Nijmegen: Standaard-Boekhandel. (An important study, in Dutch, of Denys' relation to the philosophic disputes in the fifteenth-century University of Cologne.)

Wassermann, D. (1996) *Dionysius der Kartäuser: Einführung in Werk und Gedanktwelt* (Dionysius the Carthusian: An Introduction to His Work and World of Thought), Analecta Cartusiana 133, Salzburg: Institut für Anglistik and Amerikanistik. (Wassermann argues that Denys, like the Carthusians in general, followed an older, monastic pattern of learning, and he emphasizes Denys' concern for personal and social religious reform.)

KENT EMERY, JR

DEONTIC LOGIC

Deontic logic is the investigation of the logic of normative concepts, especially obligation ('ought', 'should', 'must'), permission ('may') and prohibition ('ought not', 'forbidden'). Deontic logic differs from normative legal theory and ethics in that it does not attempt to determine which principles hold, nor what obligations exist, for any given system. Rather it seeks to develop a formal language that can adequately represent the normative expressions of natural languages, and to regiment such expressions in a logical system.

The theorems of deontic logic specify relationships both among normative concepts (for example, whatever is obligatory is permissible) and between normative and non-normative concepts (for example, whatever is obligatory is possible). Contemporary research beginning with von Wright treats deontic logic as a branch of modal logic, in so far as (as was noted already by medieval logicians) the logical relations between the obligatory, permissible and forbidden to some extent parallel those between the necessary, possible and impossible (concepts treated in 'alethic' modal logic).

1 **Standard deontic logic (SDL)**
2 **Two alternatives to SDL**
3 **Combining the two approaches**

1 Standard deontic logic (SDL)

Deontic logic is the logic of normative reasoning. It is common in deontic logic to take one of the three concepts – 'obligatory', 'forbidden', 'permissible' – as primitive and to define the others in terms of the chosen one, the most popular approach defining the permissible and forbidden in terms of the obligatory. In 'standard deontic logic' (SDL) a modal operator O is added to the language of propositional logic so that if p is a sentence of the language, then so is Op, which informally expresses 'It is obligatory that p'. (Alternative approaches treat O as a predicate applied to names of act types, or as an operator on what Castañeda (1981) calls 'practitions'.) The standard definitions of 'permissible' and 'forbidden' are $Pp = {\sim}O{\sim}p$ and $Fp = O{\sim}p$, respectively.

Possible worlds semantics for SDL assumes that relative to any given normative system there is for each possible world w a non-empty set of 'deontic alternatives' for w. This set functions as the normative standard for w, so that Op is said to be true at w (relative to the given normative system) just in case p is true at each of w's deontic alternatives.

This is put more formally in terms of model structures $\langle W, R \rangle$, where W is a set of possible worlds and R a two-place relation on W. An SDL model is a model structure $\langle W, R \rangle$ plus a function I which assigns truth-values to each $\langle p, w \rangle$, for atomic sentences p and worlds w, and obeys the usual conditions for truth-functional compounds as well as the following condition for O: Op is true at w in $\langle W, R, I \rangle$ just in case p is true in $\langle W, R, I \rangle$ at all worlds w^* such that Rww^*. A sentence p is valid in SDL iff it is true at all worlds of all models.

Just as there are different systems of alethic modal logic (see MODAL LOGIC), different systems of deontic logic are determined semantically by imposing various requirements on R. Consider, for instance, a chief respect in which the parallel between alethic and deontic notions breaks down. 'If it is necessary that p, then p' is logically valid but, to our daily chagrin, 'If Op, then p' is not. This difference is reflected in SDL by *not* requiring that R be 'reflexive', that is, not requiring that w be a deontic alternative for itself (whereas an alethic modal system would require reflexivity on its alethic-accessibility relation). For SDL we require only that R is 'serial'; that the set of deontic alternatives for each world is non-empty. It is this requirement that validates $Op \supset {\sim}O{\sim}p$. SDL is characterized axiomatically by tautologies T, OT,

$Op \supset \sim O \sim p$ and $O(p \supset q) \supset (Op \supset Oq)$. Rules of proof are *modus ponens* and substitution. SDL can be extended by imposing additional constraints on R, such as 'reflexivity once removed' (which validates $O(Op \supset p)$) and 'transitivity' $(Op \supset OOp)$, among many others.

A number of so-called 'paradoxes' in SDL motivated the development of alternative systems. The most important inadequacies of SDL were revealed by thought experiments such as Chisholm's 'contrary to duty imperative' example (1974). Normative systems often specify what should happen in case certain requirements are violated, for example, that one should apologize or pay reparations or not cry (while mopping up). A set of simple rules of this type may say, for instance, that you ought to tell neither Ann nor Bert a certain secret; and yet were you to go ahead and tell either Ann or Bert then you should tell the other as well. This set obviously is consistent. How can it be represented in SDL? If a abbreviates 'You tell Ann', and b, 'You tell Bert', $O \sim a$ and $O \sim b$ together plausibly represent the primary requirements not to tell either one the secret. What about the conditionals which tell you what to do if you violate one of these rules? It is here that SDL gets into trouble.

A 'wide scope' representation $O(a \supset b)$ of the conditional 'You ought to tell Bert if you tell Ann' is a poor choice since it follows in SDL from $O \sim a$ (whereas intuitively the rules are logically independent). Moreover, there is no way to detach expression of the obligation to tell Bert, after you tell Ann: $O(a \supset b)$ and a together do not entail Ob in SDL. (The conditional $a \supset b$ may be true in all deontic alternatives and a true in the actual world, even though b is not true in all the alternatives.) A 'narrow scope' representation $a \supset Ob$ of the rule is no better since it follows from $\sim a$ (and yet the rule itself is logically independent of a). Moreover, while this option permits detachment of Ob given a by means of *modus ponens*, Ob is not consistent in SDL with $O \sim b$ (because of the validity of $Oq \supset \sim O \sim q$). So detachment generates an inconsistency that is counterintuitive, since the original rules are logically consistent with the fact that a. This may suggest rewriting the original unconditional obligations as $\sim b \supset O \sim a$ and $\sim a \supset O \sim b$. No inconsistent detachment is possible now, but the suggestion is not viable because the revised rule set would be wholly complied with if you told both Ann and Bert, whereas the rules obviously are violated in some sense if both a and b are true. Theorists seeking formal solutions to these problems proposed two types of response, corresponding broadly to refinements on the wide- and narrow-scope proposals.

2 Two alternatives to SDL

Von Wright proposed a new type of dyadic (two-place) deontic operator to represent expressions of conditional obligation. $O(q/p)$ is read informally as 'It ought to be that q given p'. Danielsson, Hansson, Lewis (1973), van Fraassen, Åqvist and others developed semantics in terms of rankings $\leqslant$ of worlds according to their relative acceptability (similar to the way in which orderings of worlds are used to interpret subjunctive conditionals). Let $\leqslant$ be a dyadic relation, on a set of worlds, which is transitive and strongly connected (that is, for any two worlds u and v in the set, either $u \leqslant v$ or $v \leqslant u$). $O(q/p)$ is true relative to $\leqslant$ iff some $p \& q$-world is ranked more highly in $\leqslant$ than any $p \& \sim q$-world. The unconditional Oq is defined as $O(q/T)$, for tautology T, so that Oq holds just in case q is true in all most acceptable worlds. The rules in the Ann/Bert example may be represented consistently as $\{O \sim a, O \sim b, O(a/b), O(b/a)\}$ and, significantly, it would be consistent to add further rules of the form $O(\sim b/a \& c)$ and $O(b/a \& c \& d)$ and so on. No member of the set is entailed by any other member, and all are independent of factual circumstances. So this language is well suited for representing the content of normative systems with rules and principles that have exceptions or are 'defeasible' like $O \sim b$ in our example (there are circumstances, such as when a is true, in which $O \sim b$ should not be used to guide action). Since typically the rules of a system or practice are used to justify actions or states of affairs, a shortcoming of this approach taken alone is that there is no means even for expressing the unconditional 'all-out' obligations that may hold in non-ideal circumstances. For instance, in circumstances in which the non-ideal a is true obviously one ought (in some sense) to tell Bert because $O(b/a)$, but this obligation is not entailed by $O(b/a)$ and a. All most acceptable a-worlds may be b-worlds, and a may be true in the actual world, but nothing follows from this because the actual world may not be a most acceptable a-world.

A second approach, developed by Montague, Chellas (1984), Thomason (1981), van Eck (1982), Feldman (1986) and others, ties the semantics of O to specific factual circumstances by interpreting O relative to both worlds *and times*. One way to do this is to index O to a time t, so that '$O_t q$' is read 'It ought at time t to be that q' and is interpreted relative to what is 'historically necessary' (or 'settled') at t in w (see TENSE AND TEMPORAL LOGIC). The set of deontic alternatives at t in w is the set of most acceptable worlds (according to a given normative system) of those that are compatible with what is settled at t in w; and $O_t q$ is true at w just in case q is true at all the deontic alternatives at t in w. So 'all-out' obligations at t are relative to what is settled at t. Let the alethic '$N_t q$' say 'q is settled at t' and be true in w just in case q is true at all worlds historically possible at t in w. At times t when neither a nor b is settled at w (as in our example), $O_t \sim a$ and $O_t \sim b$ are true. But if $N_{t^*} a$, for a later time t^*, then $O_{t^*} b$.

What about the 'rules' of the system? There is no straightforward way to formalize them on this approach, though it can be done indirectly by quantifying over time: for example, $(t)(\sim N_t a \supset O_t \sim b)$ replaces $O \sim b$, and $(t)(N_t a \supset O_t b)$ replaces $O(b/a)$. This approach works for the example and permits detachment by *modus ponens* of appropriate all-out obligation statements. The paradoxes of material implication reappear, however, so a first difficulty is distinguishing 'genuine' from spurious rules. More importantly, the formal representation of 'You should not tell Bert' as a conditional is awkward compared with the English.

3 Combining the two approaches

In any case, the elegant treatment of rules in the first approach is perfectly compatible with the second's temporal treatment of all-out obligation, and combining the two approaches also solves the main problem associated with the first. Given a ranking of worlds, all-out obligations at t are determined by restricting the ranking to worlds that are possible at t. If S expresses all and only what is 'settled' at t in w, then $O_t q$ is true at w iff $O(q/S)$ is true according to $\leqslant$. This means $O_t q$ is true at w just in case q is true in all most acceptable worlds, according to $\leqslant$, of those that are still accessible at t in w. (An agent-relative O_t can be formulated in terms of the best worlds within an agent's control.) To detach $O_t q$ from $O(q/p)$ when p does not express all that is settled at t, it is useful to express the idea that there is no r such that $N_t r$ and $\sim O(q/p \& r)$. Let $R_t(q, p)$ say as much. This enables us to reason with $O(a/b)$ even if other rules like $\sim O(a/b \& c)$ also hold. The schema $O(q/p) \& N_t p \& R_t(q, p) \supset O_t q$ can be validated in the combined semantics and a family of normative concepts defined precisely in its terms.

There is an 'all-out' (conclusive) reason for q at t (according to a certain normative system) iff $O_t q$ holds (for that normative system), while q is *prima facie* 'obligatory' at t iff there is some p such that $O(q/p)$ and $N_t p$. $O(q/p)$ is 'undercut' at t iff there is some r such that $N_t r$ and $\sim O(q/p \& r)$; and $O(q/p)$ is 'overridden' at t iff there is some r such that $N_t r$ and $O(\sim q/p \& r)$. $O(q/p)$ is 'defeated' at t iff it is either undercut or overridden. A *prima facie* reason for q based on $O(q/p)$ is defeated if $O(q/p)$ is defeated.

There is a *prima facie* conflict at t iff there are p, q, r and s such that $N_t(q \& s)$, $O(p/q)$, $O(r/s)$ and $N_t \sim (p \equiv r)$.

The combined system does not solve all of the problems that SDL encounters. In SDL and in the combined approach, Op entails Oq if p entails q. So, for instance, since h: 'You help the man who was robbed' entails r: 'The man was robbed', $O_t h$ entails $O_t r$, a counterintuitive result (hence the 'Good Samaritan paradox').

Also in the combined system, as in SDL, no all-out conflict (for example, of the form $O_t p \& O_t q$, where p and q are contraries) is consistent, but arguably there are coherent normative systems in which genuine conflicts are a possibility, and if so it is not the business of deontic logic to legislate otherwise.

So the combined system, like SDL, is arguably too 'strong' in the sense that it validates too much. It can be weakened semantically by interpreting $O(q/p)$ not in terms of $\leqslant$, but rather in terms of a 'neighbourhood' selection function f that assigns to each proposition (set of worlds) q a set of subsets of W (the set of propositions that are obligatory given q). $O(q/p)$ is true iff $q \in f(p)$. Let $R_t(q, p)$ be true iff for all r, if $N_t r$, then $q \in f(p)$ iff $q \in f(p \& r)$; and $O_t q$ is true iff there is some p such that $O(q/p)$, $N_t p$ and $R_t(q, p)$. $O_t p$ does not entail $O_t q$ even if p entails q, and $O_t p \& O_t q$ is consistent even for contraries p and q. (In general, there is an 'all-out conflict' at t iff there is a *prima facie* conflict at t, as described above, and neither $O(p/q)$ nor $O(r/s)$ is defeated at t.) There is so little logical structure here (the only rule of proof is substitution) that it is difficult to envisage complaints grounded in its excessive strength. None the less, it can be used, exactly as above, to define all of the concepts defined earlier. While the weakness of this very minimal system probably is excessive, at least for applications to many normative systems, it is an appropriate starting point for developing stronger systems, and for structuring discussion of the appropriate strength of deontic logics for particular applications.

See also: LOGICAL AND MATHEMATICAL TERMS, GLOSSARY OF

References and further reading

* Castañeda, H.-N. (1981) 'The Paradoxes of Deontic Logic: The Simplest Solution to All of Them in one Fell Swoop', in R. Hilpinen (ed.) *New Studies in Deontic Logic*, Dordrecht: Reidel, 37–85. (Develops a distinction between propositions and practitions, and uses this distinction to address the problems of SDL in a unique way.)

* Chellas, B.F. (1980) *Modal Logic*, Cambridge: Cambridge University Press, esp. 190–203, 272–7. (Discusses SDL and its extensions, the dependence of obligation on time, and conditional obligation.)

* Chisholm, R. (1974) 'Practical Reason and the Logic of Requirement', in S. Korner (ed.) *Practical Reason*, New Haven, CT: Yale University Press, 1–16. (Presents an informal account of many of the definitions in §3.)

* Eck, J. van (1982) 'A System of Temporally Relative Modal and Deontic Predicate Logic and its Philosophical Applications', *Logique et Analyse* 25: 249–90, 339–81. (Develops a temporally relative logic as in the 'second approach' with quantifiers and a subjunctive conditional, and offers alternative definitions of some of the terms defined in §3.)

* Feldman, F. (1986) *Doing the Best We Can*, Dordrecht: Reidel. (Application to an act-utilitarian ethics of a temporally relative deontic logic that uses world rankings and defines an agent-relative conception of 'settled'.)

Føllesdal, D. and Hilpinen, R. (1971) 'Deontic Logic: An Introduction', in R. Hilpinen (ed.) *Deontic Logic: Introductory and Systematic Readings*, Dordrecht: Reidel, 1–35. (Good introduction to SDL and its history.)

Humberstone, I. (1983) 'The Background of Circumstances', *Pacific Philosophical Quarterly* 64: 19–34. (Develops a time- and agent-relative all-out ought.)

* Lewis, D.K. (1973) *Counterfactuals*, Oxford: Blackwell. (Discusses the defeasibility of expressions of conditional obligation and presents logics for the dyadic operator discussed in §2.)

—— (1974) 'Semantic Analyses for Dyadic Deontic Logic', in S. Stenlund (ed.) *Logical Theory and Semantic Analysis*, Dordrecht: Reidel, 1–14. (Compares different semantics for the dyadic operator discussed in §2.)

Loewer, B. and Belzer, M. (1983) 'Dyadic Deontic Detachment', *Synthese* 54: 295–319. (Expands on the 'combined approach' discussed in §3.)

* Thomason, R. (1981) 'Deontic Logic as Founded on Tense Logic', in R. Hilpinen (ed.) *New Studies in Deontic Logic*, Dordrecht: Reidel, 165–76. (Discusses the dependence of obligation on time as in the 'second approach'.)

MARVIN BELZER

DEONTOLOGICAL ETHICS

Deontology asserts that there are several distinct duties. Certain kinds of act are intrinsically right and other kinds intrinsically wrong. The rightness or wrongness of any particular act is thus not (or not wholly) determined by the goodness or badness of its consequences. Some ways of treating people, such as killing the innocent, are ruled out, even to prevent others doing worse deeds. Many deontologies leave agents considerable scope for developing their own lives in their own way; provided they breach no duty they are free to live as they see fit.

Deontology may not have the theoretical tidiness which many philosophers crave, but has some claim to represent everyday moral thought.

Deontology (the word comes from the Greek *deon* meaning 'one must') typically holds that there are several irreducibly distinct duties, such as promise-keeping and refraining from lying (see DUTY; MORAL PLURALISM). Some deontologists, such as W.D. Ross (1930), maintain that one of these duties is a duty to do as much good as possible. Most deny that there is such a duty, while conceding that there is a limited duty of benevolence, a duty to do *something* for the less fortunate (see HELP AND BENEFICENCE). All agree, however, that there are occasions when it would be wrong for us to act in a way that would maximize the good, because we would be in breach of some (other) duty. In this respect they are opposed to act-consequentialism (see CONSEQUENTIALISM §§1, 2).

Most deontologies include two important classes of duties. First, there are duties which stem from the social and personal relationships in which we stand to particular people. Parents have duties to children, and children to parents; people have duties in virtue of their jobs and the associations to which they belong; debtors have a duty to repay their creditors, promisors to keep their promises and borrowers to return what has been lent to them (see FAMILY, ETHICS AND THE; FRIENDSHIP; PROFESSIONAL ETHICS; PROMISING; SOLIDARITY). Some of these social relationships are ones we enter voluntarily, but many are not. The second kind take the form of general prohibitions or constraints. We should not lie to, cheat, torture or murder *anyone*, even in the pursuit of good aims (see TRUTHFULNESS).

Deontology is often described as an agent-relative moral theory, in contrast to act-consequentialism, which is an agent-neutral theory. According to act-consequentialism the identity of the agent makes no difference to what their duty is on any particular occasion; that is determined solely by which of the courses of action open to them will produce the best consequences. In deontology, by contrast, a reference to the agent often plays an ineliminable role in the specification of the duty. This is especially clear in the case of duties which stem from social relationships. I have a duty to help *this* person. Why? Because he or she is *my* friend, or *my* child. I have a duty to pay *my* debts and to keep *my* promises.

Constraints also involve agent-relativity, though in a slightly different way. The duty not to murder does not take the form of enjoining us to minimize the number of murders. The rule tells me not to commit murder myself even if I could thereby prevent something worse being done, such as two murders being committed. Proponents of deontology think of this as moral integrity; their opponents refer to it disparagingly as 'keeping one's hands clean'.

Many deontologists hold that our duties, though sometimes very onerous, are quite limited in scope. Provided I am in breach of no duty, I am morally at liberty to devote quite a large part of my time and effort to pursuing my own projects in whatever way I please. This latitude leaves room for acts of super-erogation: heroic or saintly acts that clearly go beyond the call of duty, and deserve high praise (see SUPER-EROGATION).

There is a sharp division in the deontologist camp over the status of constraints. Some, such as Fried, think of them as absolute: they have no exceptions and may not be breached in any circumstances which we are likely to encounter. Others regard the fact that an act would breach a constraint as providing a weighty objection to it, but one which could be overcome if there were a sufficiently pressing duty on the other side. Conflicts between two duties which are not absolute must be settled by determining which duty is the more pressing in the circumstances.

Deontology gains much of its appeal from the fact that it seems to capture the essential outlines of our everyday moral thinking, but it is open to several objections. First, its claim that there is a plurality of distinct duties runs counter to the theoretician's search for simplicity. The deontologist will reply, of course, that a theory must do justice to the complexity of the phenomena. Second, many deontologists further defy the supposed canons of good theorizing by denying that there is any overarching explanation of why there are the duties there are; they record our conviction that there are such duties without seeking to justify them. Others, usually inspired by Kant (1785), do attempt such an explanation based on some broader precept, such as respect for persons (see KANT, I. §§9–11; RESPECT FOR PERSONS; KANTIAN ETHICS). Third, those who hold that some kinds of action, such as lying, are absolutely prohibited have to provide clear and detailed criteria for determining the boundary between lying and some supposedly less nefarious activity, such as 'being economical with the truth'. Such casuistry can appear both excessively legalistic and incompatible with the spirit of morality (see CASUISTRY). Fourth, deontology provides no procedure to settle conflicts of duty (though some might think that an advantage). Finally, from a consequentialist perspective, the notion of a constraint seems perverse. If what is wrong with murder is that it is a bad thing, how can it be rational to forbid an agent to commit one murder in order to prevent two? If deontology is to answer this challenge, it must show how it can be that one's duty does not rest (wholly) on the goodness or badness of the results of acting in that way.

See also: DOUBLE EFFECT, PRINCIPLE OF

References and further reading

Dancy, J. (1993) *Moral Reasons*, Oxford: Blackwell, chaps 10–12. (A challenging and idiosyncratic defence of a broadly deontological moral theory.)

Darwall, S. (1986) 'Agent-Centred Restrictions from the Inside Out', *Philosophical Studies* 50: 291–319. (A lucid and stimulating attempt to defend the broadly Kantian project of showing that constraints can be justified if we start with the considerations that should weigh with a person of good character.)

Davis, N. (1993) 'Contemporary Deontology', in P. Singer (ed.) *A Companion to Ethics*, Oxford: Blackwell, 205–18. (An accessible discussion of deontologists of an absolutist stripe, such as Fried.)

* Fried, C. (1978) *Right and Wrong*, Cambridge, MA: Harvard University Press. (A readable and vigorous defence of an absolutist deontology.)

* Kant, I. (1785) *Grundlegung zur Metaphysik der Sitten*, trans. with notes by H.J. Paton, *Groundwork of the Metaphysics of Morals* (originally *The Moral Law*), London: Hutchinson, 1948; repr. New York: Harper & Row, 1964. (A classic work of moral philosophy, which defends absolute constraints. It has become fashionable to deny that Kant is a deontologist, but he certainly qualifies as a member of the tradition. Difficult but rewarding.)

McNaughton, D. and Rawling, P. (1991) 'Agent-Relativity and the Doing-Happening Distinction', *Philosophical Studies* 63: 167–85. (An attempt to provide a satisfactory account of the distinction between the agent-neutral and the agent-relative using formal logic, and to address the relationship between this distinction and that between consequentialism and deontology.)

McNaughton, D. (1996) 'An Unconnected Heap of Duties?', *Philosophical Quarterly* 46 (185): 433–47.

(Argues that deontology, in the form advocated by Ross, can offer a systematic account of our distinct duties.)

Nagel, T. (1986) *The View from Nowhere*, Oxford: Oxford University Press, ch. 9. (A fascinating attempt to find a place for constraints by appeal to the importance of the personal point of view.)

* Ross, W.D. (1930) *The Right and the Good*, Oxford: Clarendon Press, ch. 2. (The finest modern systematic exposition of a moderate deontology.)

DAVID McNAUGHTON

DEPENDENT ORIGINATION

see SUFFERING, BUDDHIST VIEWS OF

ORIGINATION OF

DEPICTION

How do pictures work? How are they able to represent what they do? A picture of a goat, for example, is a flat surface covered with marks, yet it depicts a goat, chewing straw, while standing on a hillock. The puzzle of depiction is to understand how the flat marks can do this.

Language poses a similar problem. A written description of a goat will also be a collection of marks on a flat surface, which none the less represent that animal. In the case of language the solution clearly has something to do with the arbitrary way we use those marks. The word 'leg', for example, is applied to legs, but any other mark would do as well, providing we all use it in the same way. In the case of pictures, however, something different seems to be going on. There is not the same freedom in producing a picture of a goat on a hillock chewing straw – the surface must be marked in the right *way, a way we are not free to choose. So what is the right way?*

A helpful thought is that the surface must be marked so as to let us experience it in a special way. With the description, we merely need to know what the words it contains are used to stand for. With the picture, we must instead be able to see *a goat in it. However, although this does seem right, it is difficult to make clear. After all, we do not see a goat in the same way that we see a horse in a view from a window. For one thing, there is no goat there to be seen. For another, it is not even true that looking at the picture is like looking at a goat. It is partly because of the differences that, as we look at the picture, we are always aware that it is*

merely a collection of marks on a flat surface. So what is this special experience, seeing a goat in the picture? This is the question that a philosophical account of depiction must try to answer.

1 **The question posed**
2 **Resemblance and its problems**
3 **Goodman's radical alternative**
4 **Our experience of pictures**
5 **Interpreting depiction**
6 **Resemblance revisited**

1 The question posed

How do pictures represent? Like many other things, they represent in a variety of ways. Consider Picasso's *Guernica*. It pictures a certain scene – horses, mutilated people, a light bulb, an explosion. It expresses the horror of war, and exemplifies that art which is engaged with the moral and political world. In all these respects the picture may be said to represent something, but the forms of representation involved are not the same. Only one of these is distinctively pictorial, a form that may be dubbed 'depiction'. What is this form of representation?

One way to focus this question is to contrast depiction with other ways of representing. The most useful comparison is with words. Words and pictures may perform many of the same tasks, and may represent many of the same things; yet, at least at first glance, they seem fundamentally different. A description of the scene depicted in *Guernica* would differ considerably from the painting, and it is tempting to think that this reflects differences in the forms of representation involved. Perhaps exploring the contrast with linguistic representation will illuminate depiction itself.

2 Resemblance and its problems

Philosophers have offered many different accounts of the nature of depiction; indeed the variety can be bewildering. But there is one answer which, in the light of its venerable age and undeniable appeal, deserves early consideration. This is the thought that pictures represent by *looking like* what they depict. This appears to capture neatly the difference between the ways that words and pictures represent – *Guernica* looks like a scene of mayhem and destruction, whereas a description of such a scene does not. Moreover, the suggestion implies that depiction is a peculiarly visual form of representation – and that idea too has considerable initial appeal.

Unfortunately this view faces many difficulties, some very serious. It is natural to take the claim to be stating that one thing depicts another only if the two resemble each other in respect of some visible property. So understood, its two most important drawbacks are as follows.

First, resemblance makes demands on the world which depiction does not. For resemblance to hold, two things must exist – the thing resembling and the thing resembled. By contrast, depiction does not require there to be two things; one depicting, the other depicted. The picture alone suffices, since it may depict what does not exist. For example, it may depict a horse, but no horse in particular. (Horses exist, but none of those that do is depicted by the picture.) Alternatively, the picture may depict something of a type of which there are no instances, say a 53-sided regular polyhedron. In view of these facts, the resemblance account must do two things. It must find a way to accommodate depiction where there is no thing depicted; and it must explain how that depiction is related to the depiction of things that do exist. This last condition is necessary, since it is now clearly possible that the account will offer two distinct analyses of depiction.

Second, the intuition that pictures look like what they depict is undermined by the difficulty of saying *in what respect* the two resemble. A picture need not resemble what it depicts in shape – *Guernica* is flat, the scene depicted is not. Nor need the two resemble in colour – a simple line drawing is black and white, but need not depict a black-and-white scene. Nor need picture and depicted match in the materials of which they are made. In fact, for any respect which might provide the resemblance, difference is as common as similarity. It seems, then, that the resemblance view may have to surrender the intuition on which it drew. Unless it can locate the putative resemblance, the thought that there must be one, and that depiction turns upon its presence, cannot be maintained.

3 Goodman's radical alternative

The most radical reaction to these difficulties would be to abandon not merely the idea of resemblance, but also the strong contrast between depiction and linguistic representation, and the idea that the former is peculiarly visual. The key exponent of such an approach, and indeed of the criticisms of resemblance that motivate it, is Nelson GOODMAN (§2).

Goodman locates the difference between the ways in which pictures and words represent things in formal features of the representational systems in question. To do this, he develops a set of theoretical tools. Marks on surfaces are grouped as inscriptions of different characters. For example, you are currently looking at marks, each of which is an inscription of a character in the Roman alphabet. Characters are grouped so as to form symbol schemes – the Roman alphabet is one such scheme, while the first eight characters in it form another. If the characters are correlated with a field of reference, the result is a symbol system. Examples include the system for naming the eight notes in a musical octave, and, at a higher level of complexity, written English.

What is special about symbol systems that are pictorial? Goodman identifies three important features. First, such systems are 'syntactically dense'. That is, they involve infinitely many characters, and are ordered so that between any two characters lies a third. Second, they are 'semantically dense'. The field of reference of the characters is so ordered that between any two referents there is a third. Finally, they are 'relatively replete' – a relatively wide range of properties of the mark determines which character it inscribes. Roughly, this amounts to the following. Pictorial systems are ones in which, for a wide range of properties of the mark on the surface, the tiniest differences in that property affect what is represented. This is not so for linguistic systems – consider, for instance, the English names for the constellations. More generally, Goodman claims that all three features are exhibited by pictorial systems, and that they are not all exhibited by those which represent linguistically. Beyond this simple differentiation claim he is reluctant to tread.

Many of Goodman's critics have sought to attack his position by counterexample. A graph might be used to track the various properties of a colourless gas over time. With 'time elapsed' represented by distance along the x-axis and temperature along the y-axis, thickness of the plotted line might represent the density of the gas, colour might represent its radioactivity, and so on. Such a graph could be a symbol in a system that is both syntactically and semantically dense, and relatively replete. No difference in the graph is in principle too small to affect the precise state of the gas represented. Despite this, the graph would not depict anything.

It has not always been recognized that these examples prove little as they stand, save that Goodman was right not to claim to provide conditions sufficient for depiction. None the less, they may be used to make a stronger case against Goodman since they raise the question *why* it is so plausible that, in this example, the graph does not depict the gas.

One plausible answer is that this representation lacks certain features common to all depiction. For one thing, the graph does not represent the gas from any particular point of view. Pictures, by contrast, always represent what they depict from some perspective – sometimes several. Further, the graph does not represent any properties of the gas that are properties of its visual appearance. The gas has no visual appearance, and is not represented as having one. But, again, depiction is always the representation of things as having an appearance. Finally, although the graph has a comparatively complex content, it might easily not have done so. Had every one of the above features fed in some weighted manner into the representation of the temperature of the gas, the graph would still have met Goodman's conditions for belonging to a pictorial symbol system, but would have represented nothing more than temperature. Yet pictures always have comparatively detailed contents, even when relatively schematic. This, after all, is the truth of the common saying 'a picture paints a thousand words'.

The force of the example can now be made clear. It not only shows that the account is incomplete, but also indicates how seriously it is so. The graph, at least in its second form, meets Goodman's differentiation conditions without having any of the three features characteristic of depiction. An adequate theory of depiction must be a theory of a form of representation with those features, and should ideally explain why they hold. As it stands Goodman's account plainly does not meet either of these requirements. Moreover, it does not seem that it could readily be developed to meet them. For what might be added to the specification of formal features of the symbol system so as to obtain this result? It seems that the only emendations to suffice would amount to gerrymandering. Thus the only course, if these features are to be accommodated, seems to be to return from Goodman's radicalism towards views which bind depiction more closely to the visual.

4   Our experience of pictures

One such course which has very often been proposed in some form or other is an appeal to the idea that depictions are *experienced* in a special way. Suppose yourself confronted by a picture, but one you do not yet understand at all. You can see quite clearly what colour lies where on its surface. Perhaps you can even see *that* it is a picture of something or other; certainly your experience may give you good grounds to suspect this. But you cannot see what is depicted by the picture. Then, in a moment, you 'get the point'. You can see that the picture is of a horse, that the strange shaped lump that had puzzled you depicts its head, those straggly lines of colour depict its legs, and so forth. It does not seem to you that anything in your environment has altered. You still see the same patches of colour in the same locations. And yet in some sense things now look very different. You see the surface organized in a way you could not see before.

There are two experiences of the picture here, one accompanying the successful interpretation, the other preceding it. The second experience has a distinctive phenomenology, or subjective character, for anyone who enjoys it. It is a way of seeing the coloured surface, but a way somehow involving the thought of what is absent – in this case, a horse. And it is, in some sense, an integrated whole; unlike, for instance, the experience of seeing a castle while visualizing a horse.

Some, most notably Richard Wollheim (1987), have argued that every picture can in principle be experienced in two ways, parallel to those above. Moreover, they have claimed that experiences like the second hold the key to depiction. The idea is that in those experiences one's awareness of the picture's surface involves the thought of something else, and that thing is just what the picture depicts. In the standard terminology, one *sees* in the picture what is depicted. For such philosophers, the key task is to characterize this experience more fully. After all, what has been said thus far fails to distinguish 'seeing-in' from many other experiences, those forming one sort of aspect perception (SEE WITTGENSTEIN, L.).

Wollheim's own account of the experience of seeing one thing in another is as follows. It is a visual experience of a differentiated surface, and has two 'folds', or aspects. One aspect is in some way analogous to the experience of seeing the surface without seeing anything in it. The other is in some way analogous to the experience of seeing (face-to-face) whatever is seen in the surface. It is not possible to say anything illuminating about the nature of the analogies here involved; indeed to ask for such clarification would be a sign of confusion.

Of those sympathetic to this broad approach, many have thought that more than this can be said. This response is vindicated by the need to offer an account of depiction that accommodates the features mentioned in §3. For unless Wollheim can say more about seeing-in, he cannot hope to offer explanations of those features. Consider, for example, the fact that depiction is always from a point of view. It is natural for the defender of seeing-in to try to account for this by tying what is depicted to what is seen in a surface, and then by establishing that seeing something in a surface itself necessarily involves a point of view on that absent item. But what reason can there be to assert this last claim? The answer must come from the fact that one fold of seeing-in is analogous to an experience, that of seeing the absent item face-to-face, which itself necessarily involves a point of view. However, this is only the sketch for an explanation until that analogy is clarified – what features of the analogy guarantee the presence of perspective in the fold, given its presence in the analogous experience?

There have been other attempts to characterize seeing-in, but the obstacles to success are considerable. Kendall Walton, for instance, makes skilful use of an appealing idea: that seeing-in involves the visual imagination (1990). In essence, his claim is that when I see a horse in a picture, I imagine of my seeing the picture's surface, that it is my seeing a horse. The fundamental difficulty with any such view is that it is ambiguous, and that on either reading it is equally problematic. The ambiguity turns on whether or not the imagining in question involves visualizing. Visualizing has its own distinctive phenomenology. For this reason, it is plausible to claim that any experience with which it is involved will have a distinctive character informed by that phenomenology, but hard to see how that experience can form an integrated whole. On the other hand, imagining that is not visualizing lacks any distinctive phenomenology. It is therefore easy to integrate into a unified experience, but ill-suited to contributing to a distinctive character. Since seeing-in is both phenomenologically distinctive and an integrated whole, the prospects for characterizing it using the imagination are not good (see IMAGINATION).

5   Interpreting depiction

The task of characterizing seeing-in is one of the most challenging in this area. Given this, and scepticism about some of the central notions which any such characterization must deploy, there have been attempts to clarify in other ways the thought that depiction is peculiarly visual. For example, some have attempted to analyse depiction using the epistemic resources required to interpret it. The idea is that what is special about pictures, as opposed to words, is what one needs to know in order to interpret them. For language, one must know the conventions governing the words' use, conventions specific to individual words. Understanding pictures, in contrast, requires a rather different sort of knowledge. Flint Schier, for example, claims that one must know what the depicted item looks like (1986). Moreover, this is in essence *all* one needs to know to interpret pictures, provided that one has a general competence with depiction, that is, the ability to interpret any pictures at all. Since this is so, Schier speculates that a depiction of something engages our ability to recognize that thing, and that it is definitive of depiction to do so.

Schier's view has many advantages. In particular, it finally allows for accommodating and explaining the features of depiction noted in §3. Pictures engage our abilities to recognize what they depict, but those abilities are relative to points of view. I may be able to recognize you seen from the front, while being unable to do so from directly above you. So what individual pictures must engage is the ability to recognize what they depict from a particular point of view – hence the perspectival nature of depiction. Further, visual recognitional abilities are engaged in clusters, rather than singly – I recognize you because I recognize a person with such and such features standing before me. So if a picture is to engage a visual recognitional ability of mine, it will engage others at the same time. Thus there is no depicting something without depicting it as having a certain appearance, and there is no depiction which is not fairly complex in content.

Despite this, there is one form of attack to which Schier's position is vulnerable. For, as he himself admits, it is tempting to think that there is a deeper explanation for why depiction engages our recognitional capacities – that pictures do after all resemble what they depict. If this line can be made good, explanations can not only be provided for the features of §3, but for Schier's view too, along with his observations on the epistemic resources depiction requires. However, the problems facing the resemblance view were severe. Can solutions be found for them?

6   Resemblance revisited

The intuition that pictures look like what they depict was clarified above in the claim that depicting and depicted resemble in respect of some visible property. The discussion of seeing-in provides an opportunity to present the intuition another way. Depiction should be understood by characterizing our experience of it. Thus the better way to understand the intuition is as advocating a certain view of seeing-in: that it is the experience of likeness.

So understood, the view fares somewhat better with the first problem presented in §2. Resemblance may require there to be two things, one resembling, one resembled; the experience of resemblance does not. For instance, I may experience a sound I hear as resembling another, even if that other sound is one I have merely on occasion conjured in my imagination, and even if I am fully aware of this. This opens the way for a single account of depiction, whether or not there exists something depicted. In either case, the picture is experienced in a special way. It is seen in a way somehow involving the thought of the thing depicted (existing or not), and the proposal is to understand that way of seeing the picture as an experience of resemblance.

However, this still leaves the second problem

entirely untouched. In what respect is resemblance experienced? For it is no more plausible to say that a picture need be *experienced as* resembling what it depicts in shape, colour, material composition and the like than it is to say that the two must resemble in those respects.

The answer lies in a property of things that we regularly perceive, but rarely articulate. Consider the thought that in one way a circular disk seen at an oblique angle looks elliptical, yet for all that its 3–D shape is clearly unchanged. What is picked out here is a shape property of an unusual kind. For it is relative to a point – in this case, the point from which the disk is seen. In fact, it is the property of subtending a certain solid angle at that point. For convenience, call this property the 'outline shape' the disk has at that point. This is not, however, simply the shape of the object's silhouette. For if the disk is marked with concentric circles, each of those will also subtend a certain solid angle at the point, and the outline shape of the whole may be taken to include these nested sets of angles too. So understood, it is at least clear that many pictures which do not resemble what they depict in 3–D shape may do so in outline shape.

Seeing-in, then, is essentially the experience of likeness in respect of outline shape. Depiction may then be understood as that representation which works through the deliberate generation of this experience. This leaves many details to work through, and many objections to counter. None the less it is a position with great promise. For it offers a way to perform all the most pressing tasks encountered above – accommodating our intuitions about depiction, explaining various of its features, and characterizing the experience to which it gives rise.

See also: FICTIONAL ENTITIES; PHOTOGRAPHY, AESTHETICS OF

References and further reading

Gombrich, E.H. (1977) *Art and Illusion*, 5th edn, Oxford: Phaidon. (An influential and seminal work, deploying immense knowledge of art history, philosophy and psychology.)

* Goodman, N. (1969) *Languages of Art*, 2nd edn, Oxford: Oxford University Press. (Difficult, technical, but brilliant treatment of this and several other problems concerning the arts.)

* Goodman, N. and Elgin, C.Z. (1988) *Reconceptions in Philosophy*, London: Routledge. (Goodman's later thoughts on the matter – and some useful replies to criticism.)

Hopkins, R. (1995) 'Explaining Depiction', *Philosophical Review* 104 (3): 425–55. (For more on the notion of outline shape, and its relevance to depiction; and for some sense of what other ingredients a complete account of the latter requires. Moderately difficult.)

Peacocke, C. (1987) 'Depiction', *Philosophical Review* 96: 383–410. (A difficult attempt to put forward something very close to a resemblance view, and the source of the original gas example of §3.)

* Schier, F. (1986) *Deeper Into Pictures*, Cambridge: Cambridge University Press. (A fascinating full-length exploration of pictures, although sometimes moderately difficult.)

* Walton, K. (1990) *Mimesis as Make-Believe*, London: Harvard University Press. (A highly influential and readable account, rooted in a grand theory of representation.)

Wollheim, R. (1977) 'Representation: The Philosophical Contribution to Psychology' *Critical Inquiry* 3 (4): 709–23. (A useful and non-technical introduction to the range of views available – although it has its axe to grind.)

* —— (1987) *Painting As An Art*, London: Thames & Hudson. (An impressive and elegant exploration of depiction and many issues more directly related to the appreciation of pictorial art.)

R.D. HOPKINS

DERRIDA, JACQUES (1930–)

Jacques Derrida is a prolific French philosopher born in Algeria. His work can be understood in terms of his argument that it is necessary to interrogate the Western philosophical tradition from the standpoint of 'deconstruction'. As an attempt to approach that which remains unthought in this tradition, deconstruction is concerned with the category of the 'wholly other'.

Derrida has called into question the 'metaphysics of presence', a valuing of truth as self-identical immediacy which has been sustained by traditional attempts to demonstrate the ontological priority and superiority of speech over writing. Arguing that the distinction between speech and writing can be sustained only by way of a violent exclusion of otherness, Derrida has attempted to develop a radically different conception of language, one that would begin from the irreducibility of difference to identity and that would issue in a correspondingly different conception of ethical and political responsibility.

1   **Historical context and influences**
2   **Deconstruction**
3   **Early reception and subsequent clarifications**

1 Historical context and influences

To identify all of the philosophical problematics at stake in Derrida's writings, it would probably be necessary to have some familiarity with the works of Kant, Hegel, Marx, Nietzsche, Husserl, Heidegger, Levinas, Saussure, Lévi-Strauss, Austin, Foucault, Freud, Lacan, Nicolas Abraham and Maria Torok. Lacking such familiarity, readers of Derrida are often not in a position to recognize – let alone assess – the philosophical moves he makes. Ill-equipped commentators have ascribed to Derrida theses that have nothing to do with his actual philosophical concerns. Some of the confusion can be traced to the borrowing of Derrida's term 'deconstruction' by the literary critic Paul DE MAN and others for whom the term has come to refer to a style of reading texts. For Derrida, deconstruction is less a reading technique than it is a way of approaching the 'wholly other' and of attempting thereby to conjure 'an experience of the impossible'.

Derrida's work can be situated within the broad constellation of post-Hegelian efforts to consider whether a rigorous critique of the language of metaphysics can free philosophical thinking from its regularly repeated dogmatic gestures. The theme of avoiding metaphysical dogmatism is one that could be traced back to Kant and the British empiricists, and even to Descartes in certain respects. But criticizing metaphysical *dogmatism* and criticizing metaphysical *language* are not necessarily the same enterprise, and it is only in the post-Hegelian world that the project of interrogating language becomes a steady theme for Western philosophers. Defined in this way, the constellation of figures to which Derrida belongs would include members of the pragmatist and logical positivist movements as much as it would those thinkers associated with continental philosophy. But it is primarily out of the continental tradition that Derrida's own philosophical concerns have developed.

In his earliest writings, Derrida is drawn to the Husserlian phenomenological project as a rigorous attempt to develop an account of signification (see HUSSERL, E.). Noting, however, that Husserl retains the philosophical ideal of univocal language, Derrida argues that Husserl's phenomenological method remains motivated by a traditional metaphysical appeal to the value of truth as self-presence. To some extent, HEIDEGGER had already criticized Husserlian phenomenology on similar grounds. Appreciative of Heidegger's arguments but also hesitant about some of his conclusions, Derrida takes Heidegger's attempt to define a 'task for thinking' at the 'end of philosophy' to pose a number of crucial questions to which he has repeatedly returned in his own work.

In his later writings, Heidegger critiques the claim that language is something which 'belongs to man', substituting for this the attempt to show how 'man belongs to language'. Were he simply advancing a proposition thereby, Heidegger would seem to be saying that thought does not determine language; rather, language determines thought. But it would be a mistake to read Heidegger as making an empirical claim of the Whorfian variety. If the beings that comprise the world manifest themselves as such only by way of language, then language is that which opens up the world *as such* – that is, as a sphere of particular beings which can be studied empirically. Such a claim would be analogous to the Kantian thesis that the basic categories of human thought are not mere empirical concepts which we get from our observation of objects; rather, they constitute the very objectivity of the world. Kant's thesis is transcendental. For Heidegger, the fact that different languages constitute the world differently for different speakers renders problematic the Kantian appeal to universal concepts. If thinking is always limited by a finite language which it cannot master, it follows that thinking can at most raise regional problems about the ways in which it is so determined.

2 Deconstruction

It is out of his reflections on the implications of this position that Derrida comes to clarify the task of deconstruction. Derrida first proposed the French *déconstruction* as a way of translating Heidegger's use of the German word *Destruktion*, a term which appears in *Being and Time* (1927). According to Heidegger, the task of thinking time as the horizon of Being requires a *Destruktion* of the history of metaphysical concepts, especially the concept of time as developed in Aristotle, Descartes, and Kant. Heidegger does not equate *Destruktion* with obliteration. For Heidegger, the history of metaphysics consists in the tightening of a structure – what he later calls the *Gestell* – and it is his aim to 'loosen' the hold that this structure has on thinking. Considered in this way, *Destruktion* would be a freeing-up: a de-structuring. It is partly in order to capture this particular sense of the Heideggerian term that Derrida invokes the word *déconstruction*.

But Derrida takes his work of translation to be one which also transforms the Heideggerian conception of 'freeing-up', for Derrida sees Heidegger as recapitulating certain gestures of the metaphysics of presence. Derrida is especially suspicious of those places where Heidegger seems to suggest that the *Destruktion* of the history of metaphysics can bring thought back to some sort of 'original' relation to language as a poetic

'Saying' of 'the Being of beings'. For Derrida, there can be no 'original' position from which thinking begins or to which it could return.

For Derrida, the history of Western metaphysics consists in a series of repeated efforts to affirm self-presence as the paradigm of truth. At the heart of this tradition is the definition of 'man' as that being who can signal his self-presence to himself through language. Against this pretension of 'man's' unique position among beings – and in crucial respects his position here is closer to Hegel's than is usually acknowledged – Derrida argues that no thought, not even that of an 'I think', can ever be immediately present to itself (see SELFHOOD, POSTMODERN CRITIQUE OF). To understand this position, we need to see why Derrida is drawn away from the theme of language to that of writing.

In order to maintain the value of self-presence, Western philosophers have traditionally tended to ignore the degree to which thinking is dependent on language. Yet the fact of such dependence could not be dismissed entirely. Accordingly, philosophers from Plato to Rousseau to Hegel distinguish between an ideal language in which thought would be immediately transparent to itself, and a secondary language into which this original and univocal 'language of thought' could then be translated. *Spoken* words – because they exist only in the disappearing moment in which they are spoken, and because they can be heard 'in the head' of the speaker – would seem to be directly expressive of thought. By contrast, *written* words, because they can function even in the absence of their producer, would seem to be exterior to thought. Speech immediately embodies thought; writing is merely a sign of speech: such would be the founding claim of philosophy's pretension to self-presence through a forgetting of the materiality of signification. On the basis of this flimsy argument, Western philosophers writing alphabetically have insisted that their own 'phonetic' writing is more intelligible – that is, a sign of greater intelligence – than the 'non-phonetic' writing of non-Europeans – this despite the contravening fact that, as in Leibniz, the ideal of a formal language has necessarily found its exemplar in the model of non-phonetic writing.

Obviously, there are all kinds of empirical reasons why it should seem impossible to say what counts as phonetic writing and what counts as non-phonetic writing. More significantly, Derrida argues, it is impossible to make sense of the ideal of a purely expressive language. For in its dependence on iterable signifiers, all language requires that very non-expressive element which has traditionally been ascribed to non-phonetic writing. Accordingly, there is simply no basis for drawing a rigorous distinction between 'speech' and 'writing'.

In this way, Derrida purports to deconstruct the 'logocentric' or 'phonocentric' basis of the metaphysics of presence. The hierarchical privileging of speech over writing turns out to be but one of an indefinite series of hierarchical oppositions upon which traditional metaphysics founds itself. In each case, that which would function as something 'other' to the pretension to self-presence is excluded by being accorded the same 'fallen' status that non-phonetic writing is said to have. Derrida's aim is not to 'reverse' these hierarchical oppositions – as it would be if he were interested in privileging writing over speech – but to deconstruct the very logic of such exclusionary founding gestures.

On Derrida's account, then, the untenability of the speech/writing distinction makes the concept of writing just as suspect as the concept of speech. On the other hand, writing continues to function as an exemplary figure of otherness. For this reason, it is tempting to say that, much as Heidegger suggests that the task of thinking is 'to bring language as language to language', so deconstruction tries 'to bring writing as writing to writing'. To deconstruct the metaphysics of presence would be to disclose thinking *as* writing – rather than writing as a way of recording pure thoughts. Derrida stresses this point by describing 'arche-writing' – the archival character of a thought without *arkhe*, or origin – as *différance*, a term he introduces to name the impossibility of naming a 'first' or 'central' term of any sort. As a way of opening up the possibility for thinking otherwise than metaphysically, it is necessary to free up writing from its metaphysical interpretation as language intended to express a self-present 'meaning' or 'truth'.

Toward this end, Derrida has developed a number of different writing strategies. One strategy is to produce irreducibly multiple 'texts' which resist being read as unified 'books'. Derrida's *Glas* (1974; the word can be translated as 'death knell') is fragmented in this way. Its basic structure consists of two separate 'columns', one of which examines a number of issues related to Hegel's conception of a crypt, and the other of which juxtaposes to this first column a multi-faceted examination of the signature of Jean Genet as a kind of crypt that is regularly inscribed in Genet's writings. Among other things, *Glas* can be read as a deconstruction that would 'free up' the writings of Genet from the quasi-Hegelian 'summing-up' of Genet which Sartre presented in his *Saint Genet* (1952). Another strategy of Derrida's is to produce textual marks – such as *différance* – that are specifically designed to render problematic the traditional concept of a signifier. Such marks are not quite 'neologisms', since they are neither words nor signifiers, but deconstructive 'surds' which call attention to their own resistance to intelligibility.

3 Early reception and subsequent clarifications

The thematics of *différance* have given rise to a number of misunderstandings about Derrida's work, and some of his writings of the 1980s and 1990s are attempts to specify the task of deconstruction more precisely. The fact that *différance* indicates the unsayability of a 'final word' about something like 'Being' has been read by some as resonating with the language of negative theology. Derrida shows why the apparent affinity is unavoidable but warns that to equate deconstruction with negative theology would be to reaffirm the eschatological orientation of the metaphysics of presence. Instead, Derrida has argued that every experience is structured by an undeconstructible messianic promise which interrupts the presence of the here-and-now without being reducible to the prophecy of a determinate future. Perhaps the Heraclitean conception of 'becoming' comes closest to indicating what Derrida is after with his writing of *différance* – provided that we read Heraclitus' affirmation of becoming as compatible with Derrida's account of the experience of the promise.

Such a reading of Heraclitus can perhaps be found in Nietzsche's writings, the deconstructive aspects of which Derrida takes Heidegger to overlook. According to Heidegger, Nietzsche's texts represent the single thought of a single thinker at a singular moment in the history of Being. Derrida counters this suggestion by calling attention to aspects of Nietzsche's writing styles. Rather than express a meaning or truth, Nietzsche's writings introduce textual problematics meant to rule out recourse to the traditional conceptual resources of interpretation. Derrida demonstrates this, in *Éperons: les styles de Nietzsche* (1978) (*Spurs: Nietzsche's Styles*, 1979), by showing the difficulties that would arise for any interpretive decision concerning a scrap of paper on which Nietzsche has scribbled (in German) 'I have forgotten my umbrella.' At issue is not only the question of whether a text can have a single meaning, but whether it makes sense to speak of any 'thing' as having a single identity. Rather than speak of *Nietzsche*'s texts, Derrida writes of those texts that are signed with the *signature* – or, as it will turn out, signatures – of 'Nietzsche'. The problematic of the signature thereby becomes an important issue which arises in many of Derrida's texts, and the question of his 'own' signature features prominently in these considerations. Derrida is especially attentive to what he calls the 'iterability' of signatures – their ability, as marks, to function in

the absence of any determinable addressee. On Derrida's analysis, iterability (which is the condition for the possibility of a written mark's ability to function as a signifier) disrupts the concept of a fixed context that would determine a set of rules governing signification.

Although he has seemed, to some critics, merely to duplicate the writing strategies of Nietzsche, Derrida expresses some reservations about certain of Nietzsche's gestures. For example, while he notes that the term 'woman' functions in Nietzsche's writings as a trope for non-truth – and thus as an exemplary textual 'site' for deconstruction – he also calls attention to the violence of such gestures. Derrida seeks a strategy that would exploit the subversive potential of marginal subject positions without reifying the logic of marginality. In this way, deconstruction becomes a way of thinking about the political. From his earliest writings Derrida has been concerned with the relationship between justice and violence. Taking off from Heidegger's essay on the Anaximander Fragment (1946), Derrida engages Levinas and others on the question of whether or not it is possible to thematize a purely non-violent conception of justice.

What exactly a more fully developed deconstructive politics might look like is a topic that has received a great deal of attention in recent years. The fact that *différance* implies an endless deferral of what, from the standpoint of metaphysics, would be the 'meaning' or 'truth' of beings (or of Being), has led some critics to suggest that deconstruction undermines the very possibility of making ethical and political determinations. Such interpretations overlook the constant concern with justice that informs Derrida's works. Working both with and against the Kantian conception of regulative ideals, Derrida seeks to delineate a conception of justice as an *aporia* which both calls for, and is called forth by, the work of deconstruction.

Despite evidence to the contrary, Habermas, Gadamer and their followers insist that deconstruction implies an affirmation of indeterminacy and thus the complete inability to make political judgments. These critics argue for a politics based on an ideal of consensus, and they take to task philosophers such as Derrida who do not share their consensus that consensus is a goal that no one needs to be coerced to accept. By calling nearly every position substantively different from his own a 'performative contradiction', Habermas exhibits the very sort of normative violence that deconstruction questions.

Derrida has countered such criticisms by more explicitly addressing ethical and political issues. Toward this end, he has drawn on a wide variety of traditional texts, among them Aristotle and de Montesquieu on friendship; Aristotle on the difference between economics and chrematistics; Marx on commodity fetishism; Kant on international politics, and Benjamin on the messianic. A constant concern of Derrida's has been that of developing a rigorously deconstructive conception of responsibility, a theme he often develops with reference to the work of Levinas.

Derrida's contributions to social theory cannot be fully understood, I would argue, without some sense of his response to Nicolas Abraham and Maria Torok's recasting of psychoanalytic problematics along lines that connect Husserlian and Freudian conceptions of subjectivity. Abraham and Torok's reworking of such psychoanalytic concepts as incorporation, introjection, mourning and haunting, are frequently invoked in Derrida's writings. In *Spectres de Marx* (1993) (*Specters of Marx*, 1994), Derrida develops a conception of 'hauntology' which uses many of these terms to work through questions concerning the texts of Marx and the political programmes associated with Marxism. Making explicit a complex problematic of 'the spectral' in Marx's texts, Derrida juxtaposes the force of Marx's account of the spectrality involved in commodity fetishism with Marx's resistance to the concept of spectrality. By way of considering Marx's conflicted relationship with Stirner, Derrida calls for a return to a Marxist thinking that would not banish the spectral dimension which Stirner opens up. In so doing, Derrida implicitly suggests that Marx's attempt to banish Stirnerian concerns parallels the attempt of contemporary social theorists to 'conjure away' the spectre of deconstruction.

See also: DECONSTRUCTION; POSTMODERNISM; POST-STRUCTURALISM; TEL-QUEL SCHOOL

List of works

Derrida, J. (1962) 'Introduction', in E. Husserl, *L'Origine de la géometrie*, trans. J. Derrida; trans. D. Allison, *Edmund Husserl's 'Origin of Geometry': An Introduction*, Pittsburgh, PA: Duquesne University Press, 1978. (Critique of the value of univocity in Husserl's account of ideality.)

—— (1967a) *La Voix et le phénomène*, trans. D. Allison, *Speech and Phenomena and Other Essays on Husserl's Theory of Signs*, Evanston, IL: Northwestern University Press, 1973. (Argues that the indicative, or written, element of language cannot be reduced in Husserl's account of meaning.)

—— (1967b) *De la grammatologie*, trans. G. Spivak, *Of Grammatology*, Chicago, IL: University of

Chicago Press, 1974. (Shows that the history of philosophy has been governed by a privileging of speech over writing.)

—— (1967c) *L'Écriture et la différence*, trans. A. Bass, *Writing and Difference*, Chicago, IL: University of Chicago Press, 1978. (Includes the important essay, 'De l'économie restreinte à l'économie générale: un hégélianisme sans réserve' (From Restricted to General Economy: A Hegelianism Without Reserve) as well as essays on Foucault and Levinas.)

—— (1972) *Marges – de la Philosophie*, Paris: Éditions de Minuit; trans. A. Bass, *Margins of Philosophy*, Chicago, IL: University of Chicago Press, 1982. (Includes 'Le Puits et la pyramide: introduction à la sémiologie de Hegel' (The Pit and the Pyramid: Introduction to Hegel's Semiology) in which he discusses Hegel's theory of signs, and essays on Heidegger and other philosophers.)

—— (1974) *Glas*, Paris: Éditions Galilée; trans. J. Leavey and R. Rand, *Glas*, Lincoln, NE: University of Nebraska Press, 1986. (Difficult but richly textured readings of Hegel and Genet.)

—— (1978) *Éperons: les styles de Nietzsche*; trans. B. Harlow, *Spurs: Nietzsche's Styles*, Chicago, IL: University of Chicago Press, 1979. (A short, and in some ways exemplary, deconstructive reading of Nietzsche.)

—— (1987) *De l'esprit: Heidegger et la question*; trans. G. Bennington and R. Bowlby, *Of Spirit: Heidegger and the Question*, Chicago, IL: University of Chicago Press, 1989. (Examines the use of the German term *Geist* and its derivatives in Heidegger.)

—— (1992) 'Force of Law: The "Mystical Foundation of Authority"', in D. Cornell, M. Rosenfeld and D.G. Carlson (eds) *Deconstruction and the Possibility of Justice*, New York: Routledge. (Widely cited essay in which Derrida distinguishes between justice and law.)

—— (1993) *Spectres de Marx*; trans. P. Kamuf, *Specters of Marx*, Chicago, IL: University of Chicago Press, 1994. (Juxtaposes readings of *Hamlet*, Heidegger and Marx as a way of conceiving the relationship between justice, mourning, responsibility and spectrality.)

References and further reading

* Abraham, N. and Torok, M. (1994) *The Shell and the Kernel*, vol. 1, trans. and ed. N. Rand, Chicago, IL: University of Chicago Press. (An important collection of essays that have influenced Derrida's attempt to think together certain phenomenological and psychoanalytic themes.)

Cornell, D. (1992) *The Philosophy of the Limit*, New

York: Routledge. (An original interpretation of the philosophical implications of deconstruction, emphasizing its relevance to ethics and social theory.)

Gasché, R. (1994) *Inventions of Difference: On Jacques Derrida*, Cambridge, MA: Harvard University Press. (Essays which examine specific aspects of Derrida's philosophical problematics in detail.)

Harvey, I. (1986) *Derrida and the Economy of Différance*, Bloomington, IN: Indiana University Press. (A good account of the relationship between deconstruction and continental philosophy beginning with Kant.)

* Heidegger, M. (1927) *Sein und Zeit*, trans. J. Macquarrie and E. Robinson, *Being and Time*, New York: Harper & Row, 1962. (Heidegger's magnum opus, an important touchstone for all his later work.)

* —— (1946) 'Der Spruch des Anaximander', trans. D. Farrell Krell and F. Capuzzi, 'The Anaximander Fragment', in *Early Greek Thinking*, New York: Harper & Row, 1975. (Philological and theoretical reflection on the use of the Greek term *dike* (justice), in the fragment of a pre-Socratic philosopher.)

Jameson, F. (1995) 'Marx's Purloined Letter', *New Left Review* 209. (Review essay of Derrida's *Specters of Marx.*)

Kofman, S. (1984) *Lectures de Derrida*, Paris: Éditions Galilée. (Discusses a number of important themes in Derrida's writings.)

Laclau, E. (1991) *New Reflections on the Revolution of our Time*, London: Verso. (An investigation of deconstruction as articulating a logic of the political.)

Mallet, M. (ed.) (1994) *Le Passage des frontières: autour du travail de Jacques Derrida*, Paris: Éditions Galilée. (A collection of essays presented by various authors at a conference focusing on the work of Derrida.)

* Sartre, J.-P. (1952) *Saint Genet*, trans. B. Fechtman, New York: Braziller.

Spivak, G. (1993) *Outside in the Teaching Machine*, New York: Routledge. (A unique philosophical statement, but one influenced by the works of Derrida.)

ANDREW CUTROFELLO